# DICTIONARY OF HISPANIC BIOGRAPHY

# DICTIONARY
# OF HISPANIC
# BIOGRAPHY

**Joseph C. Tardiff &
L. Mpho Mabunda, Editors**

**Foreword by
Rudolfo Anaya**

Gale Research

*An ITP Information/Reference Group Company*

**Changing the Way the World Learns**

NEW YORK • LONDON • BONN • BOSTON • DETROIT
MADRID • MELBOURNE • MEXICO CITY • PARIS
SINGAPORE • TOKYO • TORONTO • WASHINGTON
ALBANY NY • BELMONT CA • CINCINNATI OH

## Staff

L. Mpho Mabunda, Joseph C. Tardiff, *Editors*
Sharon Malinowski, Shirelle Phelps, Anna J. Sheets, *Contributing Editors*
Dawn R. Barry, Ned Burels, Melissa Walsh Doig, Jeffrey Lehman, David Oblender, *Associate Editors*
Aileen Collins, Assistant Editor
Neil Schlager, *Managing Editor, Multicultural Department*

Marlene S. Hurst, *Permissions Manager*
Margaret A. Chamberlain, *Permissions Specialist*
Margaret McAvoy-Amato, *Permissions Associate*

Mary Beth Trimper, *Production Director*
Mary Kelley, Shanna Heilveil, *Production Associates*
Cynthia Baldwin, *Product Design Manager*
Pamela A. E. Galbreath, *Art Director*

♾™ This book is printed on acid-free paper that meets the minimum requirments of American National Standard for Information Sciences-
Permanence Paper for Printed Library Materials, ANSI Z39.48-1984.

Library of Congress Catalog Card Number 95-38261
A CIP record is available from the British Library

ISBN 0-8103-8302-0

Printed in the United States of America

**Library of Congress Cataloging-in-Publication Data**

Dictionary of Hispanic biography / Joseph C. Tardiff & L. Mpho
   Mabunda, editors ; Rudolfo Anaya, author of foreword.
      p. cm.
   Includes index.
   ISBN 0-8103-8302-0
      1. Spain--Biography--Dictionaries.  2. Latin America--Biography-
   -Dictionaries.  3. Hispanic Americans--Biography--Dictionaries.
   I. Tardiff, Joseph C., 1966-  .  II. Mabunda, L. Mpho, 1967-
   CT1343.D53   1995
   920.046--dc20                                          95-38261
                                                              CIP

I(T)P™  Gale Research Inc., an International Thomson Publishing Company.
          ITP logo is a trademark under license.

# Contents

# Preface

Based upon the need for a one-stop, comprehensive reference source inclusive of all Hispanic origins in both academic and public libraries, Gale presents this extensive compilation of biographical information on more than 470 notable Hispanic women and men from the 15th century to the present. A vast array of endeavors are covered, including activism, art, business, education, entertainment, journalism, politics, religion, science, and sports. While 70 percent of the entries focus on contemporary or twentieth-century individuals, approximately 30 percent of the entries center on historical figures from earlier periods. Each one- to three-page signed narrative essay includes a list of reference sources, and, wherever applicable, a list of relevant, selected works—writings, discographies, videographies, etc. *Dictionary of Hispanic Biography* also contains more than 200 photographs.

## Preparation

In the early stages of preparing this work, a six-person advisory board was assembled to assist in the selection of featured entrants. More than 700 names were considered for possible inclusion in this volume: lists were collected for review by the advisory board, whose recommendations were then incorporated into the overall scheme. Whenever possible, mailings were made to living entrants to ensure complete, accurate, and current data.

## Entry Format

The entries featured in *Dictionary of Hispanic Biography* provide in-depth biographical information on a selection of both historical and contemporary figures recognized as notable by the Hispanic community. Many of the biographies are collectively unavailable in any other single reference source. The format of each entry is designed for ease of use— by students, teachers, scholars, librarians, and the general public.

## Additional Features

A table of contents earmarks each entrant's historical period and provides a quick guide to the biographies presented in this publication. Similarly, the occupation index, nationality/ethnicity index, and subject index all provide references to other individuals, movements, organizations, key events, etc. discussed within the entries. This information will assist the reader in quickly finding information on a variety of topics.

## Acknowledgements

The editors gratefully acknowledge Rudolfo Anaya and the members of the advisory board for their expertise and collaboration; Sharon Malinowski for her generous and skillful assistance in project management; Margaret McAvoy-Amato, for her adept handling of picture permissions, and Roger Valade for his technical contributions.

## Commentary

The editors hope that you find *Dictionary of Hispanic Biography* a useful reference tool and welcome comments and suggestions on any aspects of this work. Please send comments to: The Editors, *Dictionary of Hispanic Biography,* Gale Research, Inc., 835 Penobscot Building, 645 Griswold St., Detroit, MI 48226-4094; or call toll-free at 800-357-GALE; or fax to 313-961-6741.

# Acknowledgements

The photographs and illustrations appearing in the *Dictionary of Hispanic Biography* were received from the following sources:

The Granger Collection: **pp. 65, 110, 189, 258, 305, 387, 450, 472, 681, 724, 740, 833**; Photographs by Lutfi Ozkok; **pp. 14, 17, 207, 399, 469, 480, 657**; UPI/Bettman: **pp. 38, 45, 62, 136, 161, 205, 349, 386, 45, 446, 546, 620, 718,794, 848**; UPI/Bettman Newsphotos: **pp. 47, 265, 290, 298, 321, 334, 349, 355, 382, 390, 513, 607**; AP/Wide World Photos: **pp. 13, 22, 59, 74, 81, 88, 93, 96, 104, 131, 130, 135, 156, 163, 175, 180, 183, 185, 195, 215, 218, 233, 240, 251, 263, 313, 325, 329, 337, 338, 342, 361, 362, 366, 426, 443, 445, 454, 459, 463, 476, 488, 494, 518, 525, 529, 534, 538, 541, 558, 568, 625, 631, 637, 667, 669, 675, 678, 684, 706, 745, 755, 772, 767, 787, 797, 817, 839, 846, 876, 901, 913, 955**; Mary Evans Picture Library: **pp. 5, 210, 396, 565, 697, 929**; Photographs by Jerry Bauer: **pp. 295, 352, 359, 595, 601, 627, 708, 875, 887**; Photographs by Layle Silbert: **pp. 53, 226, 643, 646, 864, 915, 963**; Arte Público Press: **pp. 11, 90, 118, 160, 173, 213, 244, 311, 335, 424, 428, 465, 503, 522, 543, 544, 596, 613, 654, 736, 759, 822, 842, 885, 904, 949**; Courtesy of Mary Rose Wilcox: **pp. 1, 482, 497, 617, 665, 940, 959**; Courtesy of Rita Esquive/U.S. Department of Transportation: **p. 314**; Courtesy of Fred McDarrah: **p. 880**; Courtesy of Gary Soto: **p. 886**; Courtesy of Jack Mitchell: **p. 844**; Courtesy of Bill Eichner: **p. 33**; Courtesy of Christina Saralegui Enterprises: **p. 826**.

# Advisory Board

# Foreword

The *Dictionary of Hispanic Biography* provides an excellent biographical history on the role of Hispanics in world events. Yes, biographies provide a history, for history is created and molded by people. The poets, musicians, actors, doctors, and scientists you will read about in this book are people who have created the broad outline of Hispanic history, both in the Old and New Worlds, and who have made an impact on their own time by the force of their personalities and accomplishments.

The people selected to represent the Hispanic world in this resource are prominent individuals in their professions. Included are achievers from the past as well as contemporaries—people whose role in our lives will be better defined because of the *Dictionary of Hispanic Biography*. Hispanics have created much of the history of the Americas, and as the Hispanic populations of this hemisphere grow, their role becomes more evident.

Broad areas of history are represented here. The first group of people you meet you are those that were born in the Iberian peninsula, the culture from which we take the term, *hispanidad,* or the contemporary label, Hispanic. Today some groups resist this label, preferring to be known by national, regional, or cultural ties. For example, some Chicanos believe the term Hispanic is a government label that does not fit their self-identity. Other groups exist in the United States, who feel the term Latino closer approximates their self-definition.

This is understandable, since new groups are constantly evolving from old roots and defining themselves with their own appellations. This, too, is part of the evolution of the cultures of the Americas. Perhaps the label Hispanic most appropriately serves us when we describe ourselves as products of the language, religion, and folklore that come from Spain. Those core elements of culture have shaped a commonality in our consciousness.

In 1492, the discovery and conquest of the Americas began. The Old World met the New World, and the meeting was defined by violence and subjugation. The religious, military, and cultural forces of the Iberian peninsula came to change the Native American world of the Americas, and, in turn, they became the reshaped communities of the Americas. The people you read about in this book are the products of that history, for their ancestors came from both of those worlds. But the history of the Americas is far more complex than the convergence of the Old and New Worlds, so you will also find Hispanics who have African, Jewish, and Islamic ancestors.

The era of conquest and exploration quickly spread the Spanish and Mediterranean influence throughout the Caribbean Islands, Mexico, and South and Central America. After the era of conquest came to an end, the rise of the future nations of the Americas began, with each state of the New World hemisphere carving out its own national identities. The people in this book represent those religions and nations, as well as Hispanic groups who settled in the United States of America long before such a nation existed on the world map.

If the Americas have come to represent such a diverse grouping, it is fair to ask what we have in common. In the shifting landscape of identifying with this nation or that, with this group or that, it is the Spanish language that continues to be the tie connecting Hispanic America. In the United States of America, an English-speaking country, Hispanic groups argue for the sustaining of the Spanish language, not only because it is the language of our ancestors, but because it binds us to the other diverse populations of the Americas.

The indigenous influence of the Americas cannot be overemphasized. As you read through these essays, you will find that some manifestation of ethnic pride has contributed to the accomplishments of virtually every person in the *Dictionary of Hispanic Biography.* The land of the *patria,* or the mother country, is very strong in our lives. We proudly claim the inheritance of our ancestors and the land they settled, whether those ancestors be from across the sea or part of the original populations. This pride is illustrated in our appreciation of the artistic and spiritual creations of the indigenous Americans and the influence they have in our lives.

Today a growing sense of a pan-Hispano, or call it pan-Latino, movement is evolving. The age of instant communication has brought us closer together. The accomplishments and problems of the Americas concern us all. Perhaps it is this communication that will provide us with a new, heightened, awareness of each other and thus initiate a new era of unity in our history. Recognition of the more universal ties that bind us abound. Yet even as we are drawn closer together, the pride in being Puerto Rican, Cuban, Mexicano, or Chicano remains. We are learning to balance this desire to understand each other and the greater unity it can create with the natural impulse to take pride in our region.

We are a complex group, and even as we speak of our common heritage, we celebrate our differences. The same communication that creates a homogenized world urges us to cling to our traditions, our cultures. Some of us born in the United States worry when our children can no longer speak Spanish, the language of our ancestors. We realize most of us cannot speak even one of the hundreds of indigenous languages that still define the variety of the Americas. And yet we feel connected as Hispanics, Latinos, or by other designations. Many of the values that connect us are illustrated in the biographies of those included in this book.

The biographies in this dictionary provide you—the reader—with an opportunity to extend your education on the role of Hispanics in the world. From the *Dictionary of Hispanic Biography* you can go to other sources, perhaps to a deeper investigation of the individuals you first meet here. It is your analysis and understanding that will provide a clearer picture of this important community. So let this book be a springboard. Here you will meet fascinating pioneers, leaders, and achievers who will stir your imagination to learn about and arrive at your own conclusions of this diverse, yet compelling people.

—*Rudolfo A. Anaya*

# Featured Entries

# Contributors

D.D. Andreassi

Sylvia P. Apodaca

Joan Axelrod-Contrada

Amanda Beresford

Maurice Bleifield

Kenneth K. Brandt

Leonard C. Bruno

Julie Catalano

Andrés Chávez

Melissa Clark

Catherine A. Clay

Kathe A. Conti

Jane Stewart Cook

Margaret DiCanio

Simon Dixon

Erika Dreifus

Julia Edgar

Bill Evans

Enrique Fernandez

Sally Foster

Ellen Dennis French

Jason Gallman

Ronie-Richele Garcia-Johnson

Marian C. Gonsior

Conner C. Gorry

Rosalva Hernandez

Jonathon J. Higuera

Carol Hopkins

Kelly King Howes

Julie Henderson Jersyk

Anne Janette Johnson

J. Sidney Jones

Cynthia R. Kasee

Janet Kieffer Kelley

Ellen Kellner

Jennifer Kramer

Karen Bober Kuhn

Marie Kusinitz

Penelope Lawbaugh

Brett A. Lealand

Benedict A. Leerburger

Jeanne M. Lesinski

Maria A. López

James McCarthy

Peg McNichol

Anna Macias Aguayo

Ann Malaspina

Denise Marecki-Arriola

Sandra Márquez

Diane Martínez

Oralia Michel

Paul B. Miller

David E. Newton

Phyllis Noah

Silvia Noro Pena

Eric Patterson

Tom Pendergast

David Petechuk

Stephanie Poythress

Lewis Pyenson

John-Michael Rivera

Carlos Roca

Margaret Rose

Shari Rudovsky

Joel Simon

David Sprinkle

Sandy J. Stieffer

Allison Carb Sussman

Joseph C. Tardiff

Diane Telgen

Christopher B. Tower

Michelle Vachon

Luis Vasquez-Ajmac

Ana Veciana-Suarez

Carol von Hatten

Denise Wiloch

Natasha Wimmer

Rodolfo A. Windhausen

Karen Withem

Lisa A. Wroble

# DICTIONARY
## OF HISPANIC
## BIOGRAPHY

# Marie Acosta-Colón
## 1949-
### Hispanic American arts advocate and administrator

Throughout her life, Marie Acosta-Colón has made a point of getting involved, be it on stage or off. Formerly active in the political theater groups Grupo Mascarones and the San Francisco Mime Troupe, Acosta-Colón has become a prominent advocate for art funding and an experienced arts administrator. She has worked extensively for the California Arts Council and is the head of the Mexican Museum in San Francisco.

Acosta-Colón was born on December 8, 1949, the second of five children in her family. Because her father was in the U.S. Navy, she lived in several states, including Hawaii, but most of her childhood was spent on the West Coast. Her father, Frank Acosta, is Native American; her mother, Beatrice, is Hispanic and a homemaker.

*Marie Acosta-Colón*

### 1968 Democratic Convention Sparked Political Activism

Acosta-Colón's political activism began during her college years when she was a political science major at Los Angeles Valley Junior College in Los Angeles, California. In the summer of 1968, she went to the Democratic National Convention in Chicago as a volunteer for presidential candidate Senator Eugene McCarthy. There she observed the violent police crackdown on anti-Vietnam war demonstrators that alerted the entire nation to the strength of the anti-war sentiment that had been building in the late 1960s. Acosta-Colón recalled that the convention—one of the most violent on record with bloody confrontations occurring between young demonstrators and Chicago police—changed her life. "The values I had grown up with were thrown into question, the beliefs in a government by the people and for the people. It was so obvious there was injustice going on. I came back [to California] and discovered that the politics of the day dictated that I had to become a more active citizen."

Her early life had not prepared her for what she saw in Chicago. "My father was in the service, and when you're in the service, you're not inclined to find other families questioning your government's practices toward other people in your own country. You pretty much believe that government is good, that government is fair and that everything is wonderful." It was then, she decided, that she was going to try and right "social, political, and economic inequities." She switched schools and attended California State University for two years, remaining active in the Chicano student movement.

Mexico, Acosta-Colón says, has always held a special place in her heart. In the summer of 1969, she traveled to Mexico City to study economics at the Universidad Nacional Autonoma de Mexico. Prior to this time, Acosta-Colón had been thinking about becoming a lawyer. Her Mexican summer altered her decision. "When I saw the discrepancy of poverty and wealth in Mexico, law didn't seem the fix." The young student was repelled by the stark differences, she says, between the "haves and the have-nots." In 1971, she returned to Mexico—she never graduated from college—and became an actress with Grupo Mascarones, a theater group which performed plays with political themes in Mexico and the United States. She remained in Mexico until 1974. Looking back, Acosta-

Colón remembers her years there fondly. "It was one of the more vibrant moments of our history. Salvador Allende was in Chile; the Vietnam War was on. It was much more compelling for me to be in Mexico where the theater I was working with was the center for international cross-fertilization of ideas and creativity. We had some of the finest theater directors from Latin America [working with us]."

Because of its limited budget and personnel, the theater group relied on its members to assist with some of the administrative tasks. In 1972, Acosta-Colón became the group's tour coordinator and company manager, responsible for publicity, sales, and booking. In retrospect, Acosta-Colón believes this early experience has given her a unique perspective for her work today. "If I'd gone through graduate school and studied for a business degree, I wouldn't have [the same awareness]. There's a whole other dimension of understanding the arts business if you've been an artist."

In the mid–1970s in the United States, many Chicano theater groups were beginning to gain notoriety. With nearly four years of stage and administrative experience to her credit, Acosta-Colón began to consider returning to America. She heard of work available with a traditional Mexican troupe and with the San Francisco Mime Troupe. She chose the mime troupe, she said in an interview with Carol Hopkins, because of her history in Mexico. "It seemed to me more could be said with an international or mixed perspective than with a culturally specific one. The mime troupe included people from different communities, and the plays were very accessible to a lot [of people]." The Tony Award-winning San Francisco Mime Troupe, known for its strong social commentary, was Acosta-Colón's "family" for eleven years.

For six years she was a performer with the only mime troupe "that talked," said Acosta-Colón. "I had a variety of roles. We weren't given a script and told, 'Mold this character.' We had to form the character ourselves." Around this time, Acosta-Colón married. In 1978, her first child, Carlos Antonio Colon, was born. She later had another son, Nicolas. Having a young child made touring extremely difficult, Acosta-Colón stated. While the actress adapted to the changes in her life, fundamental changes were going on inside the mime group as well. The loosely organized troupe realized it needed more structure and decided to separate acting and business responsibilities in order to take pressure off the performers. In 1980 Acosta-Colón became the Troupe's general manager. She served in this capacity until 1985.

## Promoted Arts in California

During this period, Acosta-Colón began serving on several arts-related panels and boards. In 1980 she was one of the founding members of the Arts Eco-

nomic Development Consortium of San Francisco. For much of the 1980s she sat on several panels for the California Arts Council. From 1982 to 1984 she was a board member of the People's Coalition in San Francisco. Since 1984, Acosta-Colón has been a member of the Association of Performing Arts Presenters' National Task Force on Presenting and Touring. She continues to serve as a site evaluator for the National Endowment for the Arts as she has since she was first appointed in 1985. Her extensive background in the arts as an administrator, activist, and advocate have made her a valued participant on many boards. Acosta-Colón commented that "a lot of arts advocacy was brewing at the same time I became an administrator."

In 1986 she left the San Francisco Mime Troupe and became project director of the Professional Management Assistance Project, where she designed a statewide technical assistance program for multicultural arts organizations in California. Her work experience continued to grow. After many years of volunteering for the California Arts Council, Acosta-Colón was hired as a special assistant to the director in 1986. While working with the council, she coordinated California Dialogue II, the 1988 statewide conference of multicultural artists. In 1989, officials from San Francisco's Mexican Museum approached Acosta-Colón about becoming the art institute's third director. After some hesitation, she accepted the position. "For me the motivating factor was that this museum represented a unique opportunity for the Latino community," she told Hopkins. "Generally art and culture in this country are all based on Western European traditions. With this museum we have an opportunity of putting into place the contributions of an ethnic-specific community, one that has made great contributions to art and culture in this country."

The museum, located in San Francisco's Marina district, has a 19-member staff which oversees about 9,000 pieces ranging from pre-Columbian to Chicano art. Because space in the building is limited, only a small portion of the museum's collection can be exhibited at any given time. One of the museum's most notable collections belonged to former U.S. vice president and famed millionaire Nelson Rockefeller. During his lifetime of collecting, he sometimes purchased all of a Mexican artist's work at once, thereby obtaining obscure samples of some of Mexico's best craftspeople. After his death, Rockefeller's daughter chose The Mexican Museum as the recipient of his large and diverse collection of folk art. Under Acosta-Colón's leadership, the museum's budget has increased three-fold from around $550,000 to $1.5 million.

Reports indicate that more and more visitors are viewing the many exhibitions held at The Mexican Museum each year. Acosta-Colón is proud of the work she is doing. She strongly believes the Latino community needs a cultural place to call its own. "If people go through a civic or cultural center of a city and ... not see something that reflects them, the sense of ownership and contribution and the sense of belonging aren't the same as for the people who take it for granted. I want the museum to be that for the communities in the United States that emanate from Latin America, Cuba, Spain, Puerto Rico, and Mexico," she declared to Hopkins. Acosta-Colón also acknowledged that the proximity of the cultural institution is also important—to be relevant, it should be located in or near the community whose art it reflects. It has been Acosta-Colón's goal one day to build a new museum in the heart of San Francisco. In 1993 her goal was about to be fulfilled; the San Francisco Redevelopment Agency awarded the museum a new location in the Yerba Buena Gardens district where the new San Francisco Museum of Modern Art, the Center for the Arts, and other museums are now located. The following year, the museum received $7.5 million from a bond issue, which will be matched by fundraising. In March 1995, world-class Mexican architect Recardo Legorreta was named design architect for the new building, which is expected to open to the public in early 1998.

Acosta-Colón has remained politically active in her community. In 1989, five artists and arts administrators gathered in her kitchen and formed the San Francisco Arts Democratic Club. When asked if she might ever run for an elected office, she noted that people often ask her that question. "I wouldn't rule it out, but I don't see it in the cards. I'm very active in San Francisco politics but very specifically with issues having to do with the arts and trying to encourage legislators to utilize and fund the arts."

Even with cutbacks in the arts nationwide, Acosta-Colón is hopeful about the future. "I think in hard times the arts is often more creative and more responsive and has more of a social conscience than when times are good." Acosta-Colón, a self-described intense worker, is still affiliated with several Bay area committees and boards. She is presently serving as an appointee on the mayor's task force on cultural affairs. In 1991, she was named Woman of the Year by California Assembly Speaker Willie Brown for his district. Even with all of her accomplishments, as she looks to the future, Acosta-Colón considers something she once left behind in the past. She contemplates returning to school to fulfill her dream of becoming a lawyer. She once believed that the law had not corrected many fundamental inequalities in society. While her perception has not changed greatly, Acosta-Colón believes that a law degree would be of great value in her continuing community efforts. She told Hopkins: "If there was anything I could wish for, it would be a fellowship so I could get a law degree. I think I need that in order to continue to contribute at a greater level. That [would give me] the educational

validity ... and flexibility I need for what I do next."

## SOURCES:

### Periodicals

*Grantmakers in the Arts* (newsletter), summer 1992, p. 9.
*Latin American Art,* fall 1990, pp. 95–98.
*San Francisco Chronicle,* May 26, 1991, p. E1.
*San Francisco Independent,* December 26, 1991, p. 3.

### Other

Acosta-Colón, Marie, telephone interview with Carol Hopkins, September 1, 1992.

—*Sketch by Carol Hopkins*

---

# Rodolfo Francis Acuña
## 1932-
### Mexican American scholar

Rodolfo Acuña is a scholar and the chairman of the Department of Chicano Studies at California State University at Northridge. He has published many books and textbooks on issues in the Latino communities of America. *Occupied America: The Chicano's Struggle Toward Liberation,* originally published in 1972, is perhaps Acuña's best-known work. Acuña has also won numerous awards, including the Liberty Hill Foundation community service award, a Ford grant, a Rockefeller Humanities fellowship, and other citations of academic merit. He has remained a controversial figure throughout his academic career, and continues to challenge American society for what he calls its "endemic racism."

### Ideas of Justice Developed in Childhood

Born in Los Angeles on May 18, 1932, to Francisco and Alicía (Elías) Acuña, young Rodolfo grew up in a strongly Catholic, Mexican American environment. Through his religion, Acuña told James McCarthy in a 1994 interview, he developed "a sense of the just and the unjust." He saw the treatment of Mexicans and other Latinos in Los Angeles as overtly unjust and saw America as a society that was riddled with inequity and systematic unfairness directed at racial minorities.

Acuña also credited his military experiences during the Korean Conflict for widening the breadth of the bigotry he perceived in society. As a 19 year-old U.S. Army volunteer, Acuña found himself for the first time among large numbers of people of all races. He cited the mix of poor whites with Latinos and blacks in the training camps as the cause of the "race riots" among the soldiers themselves. "There were many soldiers from Harland County, Kentucky," he said, "and there were a lot of bigoted people from there." As a microcosm of the country, the army exposed what Acuña saw as the fundamental racism in American life. In the army, Acuña said, racism simply found a more volatile expression.

Since the 1953 armistice came before his unit could be rotated into Korea, Acuña spent most of his enlistment in Europe. When he returned from military service, he took his first teaching job as a high school social sciences instructor. He also worked as a columnist for the *Los Angeles Herald-Examiner*. He earned his B.A. in social science in 1957, another B.A. in general studies in 1958, and an M.A. in 1962, all from California State University at Los Angeles. In 1968 Acuña completed his Ph.D. at the University of Southern California, and took a position as professor of Chicano Studies at California State University at Northridge the following year. Acuña founded the department and developed most of the curriculum. With 22 professors, the department has grown to be the largest of its kind in the country.

### Tackled Controversial Issues

In 1972, Acuña published the controversial *Occupied America*. In this study, Acuña described the American Southwest as an "internal colony" made up of lands and people formerly belonging to Mexico and retaining that country's cultural identity. Acuña further asserted that Mexican Americans continued to experience the negative consequences of Anglo exploitation and racism. Some scholars, like Victor C. Dahl in the *Western Historical Quarterly*, criticized the book as "an angry polemic . . . [which] abounds with generalizations defying either substantiation or refutation." Others like the *American Historical Review* praised Acuña for bravery in having taken on such a complex subject.

Acuña published revised editions of *Occupied America* in 1981 and 1988. Although he shifted his focus from the "internal colony" idea, his conviction that American Latinos continue to suffer from racism has not flagged. Indeed, in late 1994 Acuña told McCarthy of a work in progress to be called *Anything But Mexican*. The book examines Los Angeles, Acuña's birthplace and lifelong home, as a place that purports to be multicultural and cosmopolitan, but in fact still exhibits strong bigotry against Latinos. The book also deals with the relative "invisibility" of Latinos' problems. Events such as the 1992 Rodney King beating and the ensuing riots, Acuña asserted, have brought at least some awareness of racism to much of the United States. In contrast, the obstacles Latino communities face have gained no more—and perhaps less—attention.

Acuña acknowledged the development of a Latino middle class, which existed "in no significant numbers" when *Occupied America* was first published. He told McCarthy that "although [this development] is a good thing because now we have more voices [in government, business, etc.], it could also have bad effects, because the interests of the middle class are not always the same as [those of the] working class." Acuña also stated that he feared "a backlash" against all Latinos caused by those in the middle-class who were willing to "play the race card" but who were no longer the people who would "pay the price in the streets." For Acuña, race and class issues within the Latino community have assumed an ominous divergence. He cited other ethnic groups whose communities became more conservative as they moved into the middle and upper classes. With significant numbers of Latinos left behind in the working class, however, Acuña expressed fear that the net result of Latino advances in the last two decades will be negative for many.

In 1991 Acuña sought a tenured professorship from California State University, which was denied. Acuña felt that he had run into one of the very barriers about which he had written. He filed a lawsuit against the university, claiming that he had been denied tenure not on the basis of his scholarship, but rather because of his age, ethnicity, and political beliefs. The trial date was set for March 1995, but in late 1994, Acuña told McCarthy that he was very confident about the outcome. He also asserted that he could demonstrate that California State University "use[s] a cap" to determine the number of Latinos to be hired. Acuña added that the university has spent over two million dollars defending themselves in this case, including one million dollars in lawyer's fees. A small newspaper called *For Acuña* regularly solicits support for his cause, which has gathered much media attention. Win or lose, Acuña insisted that his case will make it easier for others to sue on the basis of discrimination in cases similar to his.

### SELECTED PUBLISHED WORKS:

*The Story of the Mexican Americans: The Men and the Land,* American Book Company, 1969.
(With Peggy Shackleton) *Cultures in Conflict: Problems of the Mexican Americans,* Charter School Books, 1970.

*A Mexican-American Chronicle,* American Book
 Company, 1971.
*Occupied America: The Chicano's Struggle Toward
 Liberation,* 1972; 2nd edition, 1981; 3rd edi-
 tion, Harper, 1987.
*Sonoran Strongman: Ignacio Pesquiera and His
 Times,* University of Arizona Press, 1974.
*A Community Under Siege: A Chronicle of Chica-
 nos East of the Los Angeles River, 1945–1975,*
 University of California, Los Angeles, Chicano
 Studies Research Center, 1984.

## SOURCES:

### Books

Gann, L. H., and Peter Duignan, *Hispanics in the
 United States,* Boulder, Westview Press, 1986.
*Hispanic Writers,* edited by Bryan Ryan, Detroit,
 Gale, 1993.

### Periodicals

*Chronicle of Higher Education,* February 23, 1994,
 p. A18.

### Other

Acuña, Rodolfo, interview with James McCarthy,
 October 28, 1994.

—*Sketch by James McCarthy*

*Isaac Albéniz*

# Isaac Albéniz
## 1860-1909
### Spanish composer and pianist

At the twilight of the nineteenth century, music
occupied a privileged position in European
culture: in no other genre or area of cultural activity
did the reaction against the tenets of the classical style
manifest itself so dramatically. Isaac Albéniz, born in
1909 in Camprodón, in the Catalan province of
Gerona in Northern Spain, was an important figure
among many composers that tried to break away from
the centralizing and internationalizing influence of
the Austrio-Germanic tradition in order to create a
national musical idiom. These composers, including
Enrique Granados and Manuel de Falla in Spain,
searched for formal ways to capture or evoke local
impressions like folk songs and dances, and have
come to be known as belonging to the Romantic
movement in Spanish and European music.

Isaac Albéniz's career as a concert pianist began
at the age of four. He went on to become an important
composer of the romantic period, with his opus
magnum being the piano suite *Iberia.* Yet he emerges
most as a romantic figure in his life's story. His
travels, experiences, and long list of successes are well
documented; and those who left testimonies of his
acquaintance are unanimous in their adoration of his
personality and charm. His life itself seems to read
like something out of romanticism, its duration not
withstanding: Albéniz died just after having composed his greatest work, *Iberia,* at the age of 48.

In the nineteenth century, popular culture like
bullfighting and flamenco already played an important role in the nation's ethos, or understanding of
itself. The popular instrument was undoubtedly the
guitar, and not the piano. Pola Baytelman, in her
catalog of Albéniz's piano works, points out that there
is no evidence of any keyboard music published in
Spain in the first part of the eighteenth century. And
so it should not be surprising that one of Albéniz's
most important innovations as a composer should
have been his discovery of flamenco guitar motifs that
he adapted for the piano.

Henri Collet, in his important biography of
Albéniz, reports that the composer often declared, "I
am a Moor," thus allying himself—at least aesthetically—more with Andalusia than with his native

Catalonia. And Gilbert Chase, in his seminal *The Music of Spain,* quotes Albéniz as having declared that the place in Spain where he felt most at home was the Alhambra in Granada. Evidently it was through Albeniz's fascination with Andalusia that he was able to import so many flamenco motifs into his piano works.

It was Albéniz's father, a customs administrator from Vitoria, who first sensed his son's musical inclination. It is reported that he began to play the piano at the age of one, and his father enthusiastically encouraged or mandated a rigorous regimen of practice on the keyboard, to the exclusion of the rudiments of literacy. Naturally it was his father who organized his first concert at the age of four. The *New Grove Dictionary of Music and Musicians* reports that the concert took place at the Teatro Romea in Barcelona, and that the young Albéniz's playing so astounded the public that some kind of trickery or sleight-of-hand was suspected.

### Left Home to Pursue Career

While still very young, Albéniz broke away from his father's tyrannical management of his career. After the family moved to Madrid in 1869, Albéniz began to read the adventure stories of Jules Vernes and this fed his already innate adventurousness. And so at or around the age of ten, Albéniz ran away from home for the first time; he climbed aboard the first train he could catch and arrived at El Escorial, where he made his way into the casino and entertained an audience with his playing. He was sent to rejoin his parents in Madrid, but took another train that led him to Avila, then Zamora and Salamanca, where he managed to organize successful concerts. This nomadic pattern of playing concerts, getting paid for them, and moving on to the next town continued in Valladolid, Palencia, Leon, Galicia, Logroño, Zaragoza, Barcelona, and Valencia.

Albéniz returned to his father's house around 1871 and began to study in earnest, taking four or five months of piano lessons; he soon grew restless and left home again in 1872. By this time he had reached the ripe age of 12, and his journeys would carry him much farther. When the mayor of Cadiz threatened to deport him back to his parental supervision in Madrid, Albéniz stowed away on a boat bound for America. He was discovered without a ticket, and offered to play piano on board to cover his expenses. Although many of the passengers recognized the child prodigy and took up a collection, not enough money was collected to cover his passage and, following maritime laws, the stowaway was left at the first port of arrival—Buenos Aires.

One can only imagine what 12-year-old Isaac Albéniz must have experienced in Buenos Aires, which in the early 1870s was not yet the cosmopolitan capital it was to become 50 years later. For the first time this romantic, nomadic lifestyle that he had scripted for himself became deadly serious: Albéniz was homeless and broke, eating whenever he could. But once again the sheer force of his talent as a performer saved him: after hearing him perform in a café, a "fellow Spaniard" helped him to organize concerts in Argentina, Uruguay, and Brazil. He also reached Puerto Rico and Cuba, where, in the greatest of ironies, he discovered his father, who had been transferred to an administrative post there. Yet when his father saw that he had money, and could continue to earn it, he let Albéniz continue on to the United States. In New York City, Albéniz had more financial difficulties, and so invented a new eye-catching gimmick: he began playing the piano facing *away* from it, with the backs of his fingers. This trick earned him enough money to visit San Francisco, and pay for his passage back to Spain, where he arrived in 1873.

Back in Europe in at the age of 14, Albéniz resolved to pursue his studies, but not before giving concerts in London, Liverpool, and Leipzig. In this last city he studied with professors at the conservatory, and returned to Spain in 1875, expressly to seek the economic patronage of the Count de Morphy, secretary to King Alfonso XII, who gave him a stipend to study at the Brussels conservatory. There he studied piano and solfege, with a brief deferral of studies to return to North America.

Back in Brussels, Albéniz fell, by all accounts, into a "dissipated" lifestyle. Collet quotes at length a letter written to him by the violinist Arbos, friend of Albéniz in Brussels, that describes a curious account wherein Albéniz forms a mysterious friendship with a South American that involved a great deal of "excess," and with whom he evidently made a suicide pact. This mysterious friend carried out alone his part of the pact, and Albéniz went on to play in the conservatory's competition and won first prize in 1878.

### Studied with Franz Liszt

Albéniz took to the road again, but with a more singular purpose in mind: to meet and study with the great Hungarian pianist Franz Liszt. While there are opposing accounts regarding the extent of Albéniz's relationship with Liszt, Albéniz's daughter quoted her father's diaries, which reported his having met and studied with Liszt on several occasions, following him from Budapest to Weimar and Rome. Liszt was delighted by his playing and especially by Albéniz's improvisation on a Hungarian dance.

Another concert tour took him back to Cuba, where he played piano concertos by Mendelssohn, and works by Chopin, Schubert, and Liszt. His repertoire during the next few years of concerts would come to include works by Bach, Handel, Haydn, and

Mozart. Meanwhile he was composing prolifically, but still within the romantic style of his contemporaries rather than in any style that could be properly called Spanish.

In 1883 Albéniz married Rosina Jordana, and gave up his Bohemian peregrinations. But 1883 was even more important for him musically, since he began studying composition with the figure who almost single-handedly launched Spain's musical renaissance at the end of the nineteenth century— Felipe Pedrell. Pedrell had visited countless churches in Spain and catalogued the music he found in their libraries. He encouraged young Spanish composers to draw on the wealth of musical resources to be found on the Iberian peninsula and its history rather then to imitate other European models of composition. Both Enrique Granados and Manuel de Falla in addition to Albéniz were inspired by Pedrell's ideas.

Before 1883 Albéniz had published mostly sonatas and salon pieces. But in the *Suite Española* there is a format that Albéniz would repeat many times: it includes a suite of pieces whose titles are the names of towns or regions in Spain, with subtitles that indicate a dance or musical form from that same town or region. Albéniz was to add pieces to *Suite Española,* over the course of his career. Some of them include: "Granada: serenata;" "Cataluña: corranda;" "Sevilla: sevillanas;" "Cádiz, canción;" "Asturias, leyenda;" "Aragón, fantasía;" "Castilla, seguidillas;" and "Cuba, capricho."

Many of these pieces were immediately popular when Albéniz performed them in concert; and some, like "Granada" and "Sevilla" were technically approachable by the amateur and made it into thousands of homes where there were pianos. Since many of these pieces borrow from the guitar for their motifs, all of them have been transcribed for the classical guitar. The Andalusian or flamenco guitar phrasing which Albéniz transcribed to the keyboard was both rhythmic—imitating the wrist flourish of the guitarist's *rasqueo,* and melodic—copying the phrases of his *punteo* or single-note solo. "Sevilla" was transcribed in Albéniz's own time by Francisco Tárrega, a contemporary guitarist and composer. It is reported that when Tárrega performed "Sevilla" on the guitar for Albéniz, the latter responded that the guitar version was exactly how he had conceived it. Today "Sevilla" is a showpiece for the classical guitar, which Frederick Noad believes to have been played as an encore more than any other work for the guitar. "Granada," "Cataluña," "Cádiz," and "Cuba," in addition to "Sevilla," have been beautifully transcribed and recorded by Manuel Barrueco, a guitarist who has also made a television commercial playing Albéniz's widely known "Asturias" in the back seat of a luxury car.

Albéniz's career as a composer in the remaining years of his life was not entirely successful. He speaks of a "Faustian pact" that he made with an English banker, Francis Money-Coutts, who wrote librettos and made Albéniz a generous financial offer to set them to music. By all accounts, these librettos were of extremely poor quality and—dealing primarily with Arthurian legend—were not at all suited to Albéniz's compositional temperament. Nevertheless Albéniz accepted the commission and spent many years composing music for bad operas. The one important exception is *Pepita Jiménez*—Albéniz had convinced Money-Coutts to at least try his hand at adopting a Spanish subject, which had successful performances in Barcelona, Prague, Brussels, and Paris.

### *Iberia*

Around the turn of the twentieth century in Paris, Albéniz came under the influence of some progressive composers, like Fauré, Bordes, Dukas, and d'Indy, who inspired Albéniz to continue his exploration of the piano as a vehicle for composition. Albéniz was to turn back to the path he had taken with *Suite Española,* with piano works that would be like impressionistic evocations. The fruition of this orientation would be the two piano suites *La Vega* and *Iberia,* the latter coming to be known as Albéniz's masterpiece.

*Iberia* includes four books of piano works published between 1906 and 1909. The works are subtitled "Impressions," and Albéniz's music can be considered a precursor to the "impressionism" of Debussy and Ravel, who were both influenced by *Iberia.* The pieces continue the pattern of *Suite Española* by creating musical evocations of places in Spain. Some of the most famous pieces are entitled "El Albaicín," after the gypsy quarter of Granada; "Triana," an area around Seville; "Almería;" and "Rondeña," after the town of Ronda in Andalusia. Though these pieces are also reminiscent of *Suite Española* in their use of popular dance rhythms (with the perennially Spanish alternating meter of 3/4 and 6/8), they are also considerably more elaborate than the earlier works. They make tremendous technical demands on the performer, and do not lend themselves to transcription as easily as the earlier works.

As Collet pointed out, *Iberia* was to be Albéniz's "swan's song." Plagued by illness for years (he possibly contracted nephritis, or Bright's disease—a kidney disorder, as a young vagabond), he moved to Cambô-les-Bains, in the French Pyrenees, where final illness set in. He died on May 18, 1909, after receiving news that he had been awarded the Grand Cross of the Legion d'honneur by the French government.

Claude Debussy, one of the most important figures in twentieth-century music, had the highest praise for *Iberia.* He wrote, "Never has music achieved such diversified, such colorful impressions: one's eyes close, as though dazzled by beholding such a wealth of imagery." Thus from Franz Liszt in the nineteenth century to Debussy in the twentieth, Albéniz evoked praise from Europe's most important musical figures. Many of the pieces from *Iberia* have been recorded on a number of occasions by perhaps the most distinguished contemporary interpreter of Albéniz, Alicia de Larrocha.

## SOURCES:

Albeniz, Isaac, *Suite Española,* transcribed for guitar by Manuel Barrueco, Miami, Belwin-Mills, 1981.

Baytelman, Pola, *Isaac Albéniz: Chronological List and Thematic Catalogue of His Piano Works,* Michigan, Harmonie Park Press, 1993.

Chase, Gilbert, *The Music of Spain,* New York, W. W. Norton, 1941.

Collet, Henri, *Albéniz et Granados,* Paris, Libraraire Plon, 1948.

Marco, Thomas, *The New Grove Dictionary of Music and Musicians,* London, Macmillan, 1980.

*The Romantic Guitar,* edited by Frederick Noad, New York, Amsco Publications, 1986.

—*Sketch by Paul B. Miller*

# José Alcalá
## 1940-
### Puerto Rican anatomist

Much of what is known about the membranes of cells that make up the lens of the human eye was discovered by José Alcalá, a Puerto Rican professor of anatomy who developed laboratory methods to study the histology of this ocular tissue. Alcalá's work helped to explain the development of cataracts, a condition in which the lens of the eye becomes cloudy. Alcalá has also helped other researchers to develop animal models of cataracts in order to study this condition.

José Ramón Alcalá was born on May 1, 1940, in Ponce, Puerto Rico. His father, José Antonio Alcalá, a civil engineer, died when his son was eight years old. His mother, Aurea Estela Ruiz, a registered nurse, remarried the following year. Alcalá's stepfather was a U.S. Army sergeant who took his new family to back to Fort Leonard Wood, Missouri, where he was stationed. After graduating from Waynesville High School, Alcalá returned to Puerto Rico to work but soon traveled back to Missouri to earn money for college. He graduated from the University of Missouri, Columbia, in 1964, the same day he married Susan E. Vesper. He received his M.S. in zoology from the University of Missouri in 1966.

For his master's thesis, Alcalá studied the uterus masculinus (remnant of the embryonic uterus) in male tree shrews. He demonstrated that the structure developed into a secondary sexual gland in conjunction with the prostate gland and the seminal vesicles. Because this structure is present in some species of tree shrews and not in others, Alcalá proposed, some species should be reclassified. For his doctoral research at the University of Illinois Medical Center in Chicago he studied the immunological characteristics of tubulin, a protein in the brain that is a component of nerve axons and dendrites.

After receiving his doctorate in 1972, Alcalá joined the faculty at Wayne State University School of Medicine in Detroit, Michigan, as assistant professor of anatomy He was promoted to full professor in 1987 and held a joint appointment as associate professor of ophthalmology from 1986 to 1988. In addition, Alcalá served as Wayne State's academic director of the post-baccalaureate program for disadvantaged students for many years. In 1990 he was named director of the gross anatomy programs of the School of Medicine. He was also supervisor of the body bequest program and a member of the anatomy board of the state of Michigan.

During the 1970s, Alcalá analyzed the structure of the fiber cell membranes of the eye's lens. He developed a technique for isolating these membranes in cows and chickens, as well as laboratory tests for studying their protein and lipid composition. He later modified this technique and used it to analyze human lens fiber plasma membranes. This research led to a better understanding of the aging of the human lens and the process of cataract formation.

Alcalá's work also contributed to an understanding of the lens fiber gap juncture, an area in which adjacent cell membranes are separated by a narrow cleft. He also explained that the difference between the physiological functioning of the lens gap and the gap junctions of other organs is due to the presence of a lipid called sphingomyelin. His later studies examined the breakdown of protein in the lens fiber plasma membranes and helped to clarify the development of cataract.

Alcalá returned to Puerto Rico in 1992 to become chair of the anatomy department at the Ponce School of Medicine, in Ponce, where he continued his studies of lens proteins. He is supervisor of the school's body donation program and a member of the state anatomy board of the Commonwealth of Puerto Rico. Alcalá is a member of the New York Academy of Sciences, the American Association of Clinical Anatomists, the Association for Research in Vision and Ophthalmology, the International Society for Eye Research, and the American Association of Anatomists.

## SELECTED PUBLISHED WORKS:

(With C. H. Conaway) "The Gross and Microscopic Anatomy of the Uterus Masculinus of Tree Shrews," *Folia Primatologica,* Volume 9, 1968, pp. 216-45.

(With J. Valentine and H. Maisel) "Human Lens Fiber Cell Plasma Membranes. I. Isolation, Polypeptide Composition and Changes Associated with Ageing," *Experimental Eye Research,* Volume 30, 1980, pp. 659-77.

(With D. Putt and H. Maisel) "Limited Proteolysis of Gap Junction Protein Is Intrinsic in Mammalian Lens Fiber-Cell Plasma Membranes," *Biochemical and Biophysical Research Communications,* Volume 147, 1987, pp. 846–53.

(With W. Harries) "Crosslinkage of MP26 Membrane Domains and Its Effect on the Limited Proteolysis of MP26," *Investigative thalmology and Visual Science* (Supplement), Volume 33, 1992, p. 866.

—*Sketch by Marc Kusinitz*

# Ciro Alegría
## 1909-1967
### Peruvian novelist and short story writer

Ciro Alegría was a founding father of modern Peruvian literature. Often identified as an Indianist (or Indigenist) writer, he addressed the concerns of the native Peruvian population in a rich, evocative prose. Alegría's talent was recognized world-wide in 1941, when *El mundo es ancho y ajeno* (*Broad and Alien is the World*) won the Pan American Union's Latin American Novel Contest. Alegría's third novel, described the struggle of a communal Indian society against a repressive landowner. Alegría also supported the Indian cause politically. As a result of his political activities with the socialist Aprista Party (APRA), he was exiled to Chile in 1934 and did not return to Peru until 1957.

Alegría was born in northern Peru, at Marcabal Grande, a small family estate near Sartimbamba, Huamachuco. His parents, José Alegría Lynch and Herminia Bazán Lynch, were of Spanish-Irish origin. Both parents encouraged Alegría in his literary and political tendencies, but it was José Alegría who provided a lasting example for his son as a champion of Indian rights. In *Joy in Exile,* Eileen Early's guide to Alegría's life and fiction, the author wrote that the Indians on the Alegría estate were treated "not as chattels—part of the estate—but as workers who should (and did) enjoy the same rights and freedoms as the non-Indian ranch hands." A literate man, Alegría's father was for a short time the editor of the Trujillo newspaper, *La Razón.* He taught his son to read at the age of four, and he kept a substantial library, where Alegría read Victor Hugo and Balzac.

Alegría's childhood was divided between Trujillo, the provincial capital, and Marcabal Grande. In Trujillo, his kindergarten teacher was César Vallejo, the legendary Peruvian poet. Although Alegría remembered little about Vallejo, his memories of the pre-secondary school year he spent working with the Indians on his father's estate remained vivid and eventually surfaced in his novels. In *Mucha suerte con harto palo,* Alegría's collected memoirs, the author writes that the experience enabled him to "deeply understand the Indian and 'chola' way of life" (translation by Natasha Wimmer).

### Political Activism Began Early

As a student, Alegría was deeply influenced by the essayist **José Carlos Mariátegui,** founder of the Peruvian Communist party. He became a staff writer for the newspaper *El Norte,* and later, an active member of the popular revolutionary APRA. Thrown in jail for his activism, Alegría was finally deported to Chile in 1934. Life was difficult for the young writer in exile. "How could he establish himself literarily in Chile, where the culture was much superior to that of Peru?" (translation by Natasha Wimmer) asked Dora Varona, Alegría's third wife, in her biography of her husband, entitled *La sombra del condor.*

*La serpiente de oro* (*The Golden Serpent*) and *Los perros hambrientos* (*The Starving Dogs*), Alegría's first two novels, proved the author's talents in Chile, but it was the success of *El mundo es ancho y ajeno* that brought him international fame. As Alberto Escobar observed in *Américas,* Alegría "confessed writing it in four months." Some reviewers have criticized the text's fragmented, episodic nature, but the general response was overwhelmingly positive. Besides winning the Latin American Novel Contest, it garnered praise from John Dos Passos; and a reviewer for the *New York Times* called it "an impressive novel in any language."

Eileen Early referred to *El mundo es ancho y ajeno* as a "folk epic." The struggle between an Indian collective and a materialistic landowner between hero Rosendo Maqui, and villain Don Alvaro, takes place in the Peruvian Andes, the region Alegría knew so well and described with such insight and affection. According to Escobar, "The author abandons romantic idealization or sentimentalizing the Indian's past, and by using concrete situations he brings the land problem within a 'cultural' context that uncovers deep national traits and offers the reader, even the foreigner, a profound picture of Peru."

After the publication of *El mundo es ancho y ajeno,* Alegría lived in the United States for eight years, teaching at Columbia University and working as a journalist. From the United States, he moved to Puerto Rico, and then to Cuba, where he married the Cuban poet Dora Varona (his first two wives were Rosalía Amézquita and Ligia Marchand). After the success of *El mundo es ancho y ajeno,* Alegría failed to produce anything as ambitious as his first three novels, and most his subsequent work consisted of collections of essays or stories edited by Varona.

Twenty-three years after he was exiled from Peru, Alegría returned to his native country, where he lived until a heart attack resulted in his death in 1967. He continues to be remembered as a man whose fiction, in Eileen Early's words, is "of a piece with his nonfiction and, indeed, with his life as journalist, novelist, politician, and professor of literature."

## SELECTED PUBLISHED WORKS:

*La serpiente de oro* (novel), Nascimiento, 1935; translation by Harriet de Onís published as *The Golden Serpent,* Farrar & Rinehart, 1943.
*Los perros hambrientos* (novel), Zig-Zag, 1940.
*El mundo es ancho y ajeno* (novel), Ercilla, 1941; translation by Onís published as *Broad and Alien Is the World,* Farrar & Rinehart, 1941.
*Novelas completas* (collected novels), Aguilar, 1959.
*Duelo de caballeros; cuentos y relatos* (short stories), Populibros Peruanos, 1963.
*Gabriela Mistral, íntima,* compiled by Dora Varona, Universo, 1968.
*Mucha suerte con harto palo: Memorias,* edited by Varona, Losada, 1976.

## SOURCES:

### Books

Alegría, Ciro, *Mucha suerte con alto palo: Memorias,* edited by Dora Varona, Losada, 1976.

Early, Eileen, *Joy in Exile,* Washington, D.C., University Press of America, 1980.
*Hispanic Writers,* edited by Bryan Ryan, Detroit, Gale Research, 1991.
*Latin American Writers,* edited by Carlos Soté, New York, Charles Scribner's Sons, 1989.
*Spanish American Authors of the Twentieth Century,* edited by Angel Flores, New York, H. W. Wilson, New York, 1992.
Varona Lima, Dora, *La sombra del condor,* Diselpesa, 1993.

### Periodicals

*Américas,* February 1963.
*New York Times Book Review,* March 30, 1941; June 22, 1941.

—*Sketch by Natasha Wimmer*

# Fernando Alegría
## 1918-
### Chilean writer and scholar

Fernando Alegría is a Chilean-born writer and poet noted for his fictionalized biographies of heroes overlooked in Chile's history. His poetry and narratives express a commitment to humanity and a passion for his native land. Through his writing Alegría serves as the voice for the social injustices suffered by the oppressed.

Alegría was born in Santiago, Chile, on September 26, 1918. His father, Santiago Alegría Toro, was a businessman. During his adolescence, the family lived in a house owned by an Italian nobleman. Here Alegría read voraciously, including the complete works of Fyodor Dostoyevsky and writings by Knut Haumsun, Panait Istrati, and Romain Rolland. His love for words and his burgeoning creativity were partly influenced by his mother, Julia Alfaro, who played old songs on the guitar, and by his godmother, the poet Horténsia Olivares. Alegría began his secondary education at the Academia de Humanidades, run by Dominican Fathers. While still a student there some of his prose writings were published in *La Nación,* Santiago's daily newspaper. He completed his studies at the Instituto Nacional, eventually leaving for the United States to study psychology.

Alegría attended Bowling Green University, shifting his focus from psychology to literature after taking a course on the life of Walt Whitman. He received his master's degree in 1941 and then headed

*Fernando Alegría*

to the University of California at Berkeley to pursue his doctorate. While at Berkeley Alegría met Carmen Letona Meléndez, a Salvadoran medical student. They married in 1943, and eventually had four children. World War II precluded the opportunity for post-doctoral European travel. Instead, the couple traveled throughout Central America and also spent time in Washington, D.C.

### Voice for the Unsung Heroes

Even during his late teenage years, Alegría possessed an awareness of heroes and historical events that were selectively withheld from Chilean national history. He focused on the forgotten, discredited, and unknown, becoming, as Juan Armando Epple stated in *Spanish American Authors: The Twentieth Century,* "a creator who approaches the historical experience in order to imagine and re-formulate it as an adventure and an ethic." Examples include *Recabarren,* the fictionalized biography of Luis Emilio Recabarren, founder of the Chilean labor movement; Alegría published this book at the age of 18. *Lautaro, joven libertador de Arauco* appeared in 1943. *Lautaro,* which weaves the tale of a Mapuche page who becomes a military leader after learning the invader's techniques, won an international writing contest prize sponsored by Farrar & Rinehart in New York, the Latin American Prize for Literature. Motivated by this prize, Alegría focused on literary history. He compiled the first part of a history of Chilean poetry

and studied Whitman's influence had on Latin American literature. With the support of a Guggenheim fellowship, Alegría wrote *Walt Whitman en hispanoamérican,* which was published in Mexico in 1954.

Accepting a faculty position at the University of California at Berkeley, Alegría focused his energies on life in California, finding similarities with his native Chile in both the terrain and the working class. Observing Spanish stevedores in San Francisco and the farm workers in the Sacramento Valley, Alegría recorded his insights in *Caballo de copas.* The manuscript remained hidden in his desk for several years until he allowed a visitor, Dr. Juan Marín, to read it. Impressed, Marín returned to Chile with the manuscript; it was published there in 1956 by Zig-Zag Publishing House. The book became a best-seller, winning two awards in Chile, the Premio Atenea and the Premio Municipal. By this time, Alegría had returned to his homeland. His work was enthusiastically read. Alegría also participated in a Conference of Chilean Writers and a conference for Latin American writers, both of which enhanced the recognition of the Latin American voice in literature.

### Allende and the Popular Unity Movement

In May of 1960, an earthquake leveled the city of Concepción in southern Chile. Moved by the devastation, Alegría wrote a poem entitled "Viva Chile M!." The poem was recorded by Roberto Parada and became quite popular. Alegría issued 500 special copies of the recording and presented them to Salvador Allende for use in his presidential campaign. Alegría also served on the campaign staff, traveling to various cities to promote Allende and the Popular Unity Movement, a type of Marxist socialism. Allende won the 1970 presidential election and assigned Alegría to the Chilean Embassy in Washington, D.C. Positive transformation began to lift Chile to new levels in social reform, but a military coup destroyed the progress when it overthrew Allende's regime in 1973. Alegría was in Santiago at the time and managed to escape the country. Since that time, he has remained in exile.

Alegría wrote a personal testament of the events of the coup that was published in 1975. *El paso de los gansos* follows his typical fictionalized narrative style. The novel's protagonist is based on a Chilean photographer named Cristián Montecino who was killed by a military patrol while watching a demonstration. Alegría has continued to champion the plight of the oppressed in subsequent works of narrative prose and poetry. Since the coup of 1973 he has added exiles to the list of those he supports, his voice resonating from personal experience.

### SELECTED PUBLISHED WORKS:

*Recabarren,* Antares, 1938.

*Ideas estéticas de la poesía moderna,* Multitud, 1939.

*Leyenda de la ciudad perdida,* Zig-Zag, 1942.

*Lautaro: joven libertador de Arauco,* Zig-Zag, 1943, fifth edition, 1965.

*Ensayo sobre cinco temas de Tomás Mann,* Funes, 1949.

*Camaleón,* Ediapsa, 1951.

*La poesía chilena: Origenes y desarollo del siglo XVI al XIX,* University of California Press, 1954.

*Walt Whitman en hispanoamérica,* Stadium, 1954.

*El poeta que se volvió gusano,* Cuadernos Americanos, 1956.

*Caballo de copas,* Zig-Zag, 1957, second edition, 1961, reprinted, Case de las Américas, 1981; translation by Carlos Lozano published as *My Horse Gonzáles,* Casa de las Américas, 1964.

*Breve historia de la novel hispanoamericana,* Stadium, 1959, second edition published as *Historia de la novela hispanoamericana,* De Andrea, 1965; published as *Nueva historia de la novel hispanoamericana,* Ediciones del Norte, 1985.

*El cataclismo,* Nascimento, 1960.

*Las noches del cazador,* Zig-Zag, 1961.

*Las fronteras del realismo: Literatura chilena del siglo XX,* Zig-Zag, 1962, second edition published as *Las literatura chilena del siglo XX,* 1967.

(Editor) *Novelistas contemporaneos hispanoamericanos,* Heath, 1964.

*Mañana los guerreros,* Zig-Zag, 1964.

*Viva Chile M!,* Editorial Universitaria, 1965.

(Editor and translator) Rene Marill, *Historia de la novela moderna,* Union Tipografica Editorial Hispano Americana, 1966.

*Genio y figura de Gabriela Mistral,* Editorial Hispano Americana, 1966.

*La novela hispanoamericana, siglo XX,* Centro Editor de America Latina, 1967.

(Translator with others) Nicanor Parra, *Poems and Antipoems,* edited by Miller Williams, New Directions, 1967.

*Los días contados,* Siglo XXI, 1968.

*Ten Pastoral Psalms* (bilingual edition; English versions by Bernardo Garcia and Matthew Zion), Kayak, 1968.

*Como un árbol rojo,* Editora Santiago, 1968.

*La maraton del palomo,* Centro Editor de America Latina, 1968.

*Los mejores cuentos de Fernando Alegría,* edited with prologue by Alfonso Calderon, Zig-Zag, 1968.

*La literatura chilena contemporánea,* Centro Editor de America Latina, 1969.

*Instructions for Undressing the Human Race/Instrucciones para desnudar a la raza humana* (bilingual edition; English version by Matthew Zion and Lennart Bruce), Kayak, 1969.

*Amerika (manifiestos de Vietnam),* Editorial Universitaria, 1970.

(With others) *Literatura y praxis en América Latina,* Monte Avila Editores, 1974.

*Retratos contemporaneos,* Harcourt, 1979.

*Coral de guerra,* Nueva Imagen, 1979.

*El paso de los gansos,* Laia, 1980.

*The Chilean Spring,* translated by Stephen Fredman, Latin American Literary Review Press, 1980.

(Contributor of poetry) Moraima de Semprún Donahue, *Figuras y contrafiguras en la poesía de Fernando Alegría,* Latin American Literary Review Press, 1981.

(Author of prologue) Pablo Neruda, *Canto general,* second edition, Biblioteca Ayacucho, 1981.

(Editor and contributor) *Chilean Writers in Exile: Eight Short Novels,* Crossing Press, 1982.

*Una especie de memoria,,* and Editorial Nueva Imagen, 1983.

*Changing Centuries: Selected Poems of Fernando Alegria* (includes selections from *Instrucciones para desnudar a la raza humana),* translated by Stephen Kessler, Latin American Literary Review Press, 1984, second edition, 1988.

*Los trapecios,* Ediciones Agua Pesada, 1985.

*The Funhouse,* translated by Kessler, Arte Publica, 1986.

(Editor with Jorge Ruffinelli) *Paradise Lost or Gained? The Literature of Hispanic Exile,* Arte Publico, 1992.

## SOURCES:

### Books

*Hispanic Writers,* edited by Bryan Ryan, Detroit, Gale Research, 1991.

*Spanish American Authors: The Twentieth Century,* edited by Angel Flores, New York, H. W. Wilson Company, 1992.

### Periodicals

*Américas,* November/December 1992, pp. 30–38, 39; May/June 1993, pp. 60–61.

　　　　　　　　　　　　*—Sketch by Lisa A. Wroble*

# Ricardo Enrique Alegría
## 1921-
**Puerto Rican anthropologist and scholar**

Prominent historian Ricardo Enrique Alegría has worked extensively in the field of anthropology . As director of the Instituto de Cultura Puertorriqueña (Institute of Puerto Rican Culture) from 1955 to 1973, he headed an extremely prestigious archaeology center.

Alegría was born April 14, 1921, in San Juan to José S. and Celeste (Gallardo) Alegría. He received his B.A. from the University of Puerto Rico in 1943. Four years later he earned an M.A. from the University of Chicago. In 1947, he also married artist Carmen Pons, with whom he eventually had two children, and returned to Puerto Rico. There he assumed an associate professorship in history at the University of Puerto Rico, Rio Piedras. A Guggenheim fellow from 1953 to 1955, Alegría opted to continue his education; he obtained a Ph.D in anthropology from Harvard University in 1955. Upon receiving his doctorate, Alegría accepted a promotion to full professor at the University of Puerto Rico, where he has worked ever since. He served as director of the Institute of Puerto Rican Culture from 1955 to 1973 and as the director of the Office of Cultural Affairs, San Juan from 1973 to 1976.

Since the 1950s, Alegría has written numerous books, beginning with a history of Indians in Puerto Rico entitled *Historia de nuestros indios* and illustrated by his wife. Among some of his other notable titles are *The Three Wishes: A Collection of Puerto Rican Folktales* for which he selected and adapted traditional folklore for publication; *Historia de Puerto Rico*, a comprehensive summary of the Puerto Rican legacy; and a couple books about the West Indies, including *Las primeras noticias sobre los indios caribes* and *Ball Courts and Ceremonial Plazas in the West Indies.*

*Ricardo Enrique Alegría*

**SELECTED PUBLISHED WORKS:**

*Historia de nuestros indios,* Seccíon de Publicaciones e Impresos, Departamento de Instruccíón, 1950.

*La fiesta de Santiago apóstol en Loíza Aldea,* Artes Graficas, 1954.

*El Instituto de Cultura Puertorriqueña: Los primeros cinco años, 1955-1960,* Instituto de Cultura Puertorriqueña, 1960.

*El tema del café en la literatura puertorriqueña,* Instituto de Cultura Puertorriqueña, 1965.

*Café,* Instituto de Cultura Puertorriqueña, 1967.

*Cuentos folkloricos de Puerto Rico,* Editorial El Ateneo, 1967.

*The Three Wishes: A Collection of Puerto Rican Folktales,* Harcourt, 1968.

*Descubrimiento, conquista y colonizacion de Puerto Rico, 1493-1599,* Colección de Estudios Puertorriqueños, 1969.

*El fuerte de San Jeronimo del Boquerón,* Instituto de Cultura Puertorriqueña, 1969.

*A History of Our Indians,* Urban Media Materials, 1970.

*Apuntes en torno a la mitología de los indios taínos de las Antillas Mayores y sus orígenes suramericanos,* Centro de Estudios Avanzados de Puerto Rico y el Caribe, Museo del Hombre Dominicano, 1978.

*El Instituto de Cultura Puertorriqueña, 1955-1973: Dieciocho años contribuyendo a fortalecer nuestra conciencia nacional,* Instituto de Cultura Puertorriqueña, 1978.

*Fort of San Jeronimo del Boquerón,* Gordon Press, 1979.

*Institute of Puerto Rican Culture,* Gordon Press, 1979.

*Utuado Ceremonial Park,* Gordon Press, 1979.

*Cristobal Colón y el tesoro de los indios taínos de La Española,* Fundación Garcia Arevalo, 1981.

*Las primeras noticias sobre los indios caribes,* Editorial Universidad de Puerto Rico, 1981.

*Ball Courts and Ceremonial Plazas in the West Indies,* Yale University Publications in Anthropology, 1983.

(With Lucas Moran Arce and others) *Historia de Puerto Rico,* Librotex, 1985.

**SOURCES:**

**Books**

*Hispanic Writers,* edited by Bryan Ryan, Gale Research, 1991.

**Periodicals**

*Book World,* August 17, 1969
*New York Times Book Review,* May 4, 1969.

**Other**

*America Online* Encyclopedia.

—*Sketch by Melissa Clark*

*Vicente Aleixandre*

# Vicente Aleixandre
## 1898-1984
**Spanish poet**

Winning the 1977 Nobel Prize for literature, Vicente Aleixandre, little known outside of his native country, was the first Spaniard in decades who was not in exile when he received the honor. Poor health kept the Surrealist poet from fleeing **Francisco Franco**'s dictatorship; it heavily influenced Aleixandre's writings and outlook on life. One of his more famous poems, *La destruccion o el amor* (*Destruction of Love*), celebrated his recovery from tuberculosis: "[This] is apparent in his eagerness to expose his senses to the exuberance of nature and go digging for sensations with an insistence charted in his enthusiastic use of repetition and enumeration," critic C. B. Morris wrote in *A Generation of Spanish Poets: 1920–1936.* "Aleixandre let his words and images stream erratically over the page as his volatile fantasy raced over the universe; too impulsive to linger in any one place, he wandered ceaselessly in *La destruccion o el amor* around the elements, from the earth, where he lay . . . , to the sea, which he celebrated . . . to the air, whose freedom entranced him so much."

Vicente Pio Marcelino Cirilo Aleixandre y Merlo was born on April 26, 1898, in Seville, Spain. His mother, Elvira Merlo Garcia de Pruneda, came from a middle-class Andalusian family. His father, Cirilo

Aleixandre Ballester, was an engineer and native of Valencia who came from a family of prosperous artisans. According to *Current Biography,* the Aleixandre-Merlo family was close-knit and offered the children—Aleixandre and his sister—security, affection, and freedom. In 1902 the family moved to Malaga on the Mediterranean coast. The sunny skies, abundant vegetation, and stunning ocean views left a lasting impression on the young boy; the mysteries of the sea feature prominently in Aleixandre's poetry.

Aleixandre's literary proclivities were stirred largely by his grandfather, who entranced him with stories and encouraged him to read. *Current Biography* noted that as a youth Aleixandre read Spanish history, the nineteenth-century realists, the dramatists of Spain's Golden Age, and the prose writers of the Generation of 1898. He read works by foreign authors Fyodor Dostoyevsky and Friedrich Schiller as well. Ironically, Aleixandre did not read poetry during his school years. When his family moved to Madrid in 1909, Aleixandre attended a secular school, completing his *bachillerato* degree in 1913. The following year, he entered law school at the University of Madrid. During the summer of 1917, he met **Damaso Alonso**, who later became president of the Royal Spanish Academy. The young men became life-long friends; it was Alonso who introduced him to poetry.

Aleixandre delved into the works of contemporary Spanish and French poets. According to *Current Biography,* Aleixandre attributed his poetic formation to the writings of Antonio Machado, **Juan Ramon Jiménez**, Paul Valéry, and the Symbolists, and James Joyce. Later, he read the German and French Romantics, English poets, and the Surrealists. In 1919 Aleixandre earned his law degree and a degree in business administration. He then taught courses in commercial law at the Central School of Commerce for two years before moving on to a position with the railroad for which his father had formerly served as an engineer. Aleixandre's first published work was an article on railroad problems. Although Aleixandre had been writing poetry privately since the age of 18, he did not initially believe he could be a published poet.

### Poetry As a Career

In 1922 Aleixandre established a friendship with Rafael Alberti who later became a Surrealist poet. At this time, Aleixandre experienced his first serious illness, infectious arthritis. Three years later he developed tuberculosis of the kidney, a malady that forced him to leave his job. Eventually, a kidney was removed, and Aleixandre was confined to his bed for long periods of time. Throughout this adversity, Aleixandre continued to write poetry. When he was 27, friends discovered his writing habit and encouraged publication. In 1926 his poetry appeared in an intellectual review. Aleixandre and his literary cohort, the Group of 1927, had arrived. "His generation was the astounding one, a concentration of genius unheard of in Spain for centuries, amazing in any country," Robert Bly wrote the *New York Times* in 1977. Allen Josephs added in the *New Republic:* "The lyric poetry of that generation [1927]—which I would not hesitate to call the finest poetry in the twentieth century—deserves more recognition in the United States than it has generally received outside the usual confines of Hispanism." Aleixandre's first book of poetry, *Ambito,* was published in 1928. At this time Aleixandre began reading the works of Sigmund Freud, which influenced his writing significantly. He commenced *La Destruccion o el amor,* in 1932 and completed it the following year, when he was also awarded the National Literary Prize of Spain.

When the Spanish Civil War erupted in 1936, many artists fled the country; but Aleixandre was forced to remain due to illness. Although most of his poetry was censored by the Franco regime, Aleixandre continued to write and to support young poets in Spain and abroad.

Well before he was awarded the Nobel Prize, Aleixandre was highly praised for his poetic genius. Morris explained: "His collected poems have about them a remarkable sense of organic growth deriving from their central theme, which is nothing less than creation itself. With the theme goes a view of the poet as visionary: in Aleixandre's own phrase, a 'timeless prophet,' who is as much concerned with bringing the past to life as with speculating on the future." Critic Kessel Schwartz emphasized the impact of Aleixandre's frequent illnesses on his poetry in *The Meaning of Existence in Contemporary Hispanic Literature:* "Sickly, alone, withdrawn, a man who fought death constantly and sought life instinctively, Aleixandre wanted a refuge from a world indifferent to his pain and found it in a dream world of the unconscious where he might escape the reality of his impotence. Aleixandre was never able nor willing to give an adequate explanation of his poetry, but he recognized it as a necessity based on subconscious desires."

### "Longing for the Light"

Some might view Aleixandre's early poetry as pessimistic. Given his frequent illnesses and the rigid control over publication exercised by the Spanish dictatorship, gloom is perhaps not surprising. But in later years Aleixandre rose above this dark outlook and eclipsed his pessimistic tendencies. Critic Lewis Hyde saw this change as a remarkable achievement and in a 1977 piece in the *New York Times,* he wrote: "Mr. Aleixandre's early poems—for almost 20 years—are filled with the kind of loneliness we usually associate with exiles. . . . He has love poems and there are poems with a sort of surrealist wit, but what runs beneath all of them is a nostalgia for a fsubdise that has been lost." The poet himself, Hyde observed, described his work as a "longing for the light" and agreed that much of his early work was written with "black light." His emergence from this darkness, Hyde declared, was dramatic and rare among this century's poets and began with *The Story of the Heart,* a book published in 1954. "Death and loss still hover over these later poems but they seem accepted now, passed over to something else," wrote Hyde. "The book affirms human fellowship, a spiritual unity, friendliness. The poems are social, the style is narrative, almost talky. Where before he had been attentive to nature and longed to join it, now nature is just the back for the lives of human beings." Aleixandre, Hyde concluded, deserved the Nobel Prize . "He is a poet of intellectual vigor, spiritual depth and tenacity. He did the work, he went far down into the soul and brought back pieces of life as a gift for the rest of us."

Aleixandre lived most of his life quietly in the countryside near Madrid with his sister. In addition to his poetry, he contributed to anthologies and wrote articles for Spanish journals. He died December 14, 1984, from kidney failure and shock following intestinal hemorrhage.

## SELECTED PUBLISHED WORKS:

*La destrucción o el amor,* Signo Madrid, 1935; second edition, 1967; translation by Stephen

Kessler of selected poems published as *Destruction or Love: A Selection From La destrucción o el amor of Vicente Aleixandre,* Santa Cruz, California, Green Horse Three, 1976.

*Mundo a solas,* Madrid, Clan, 1950; translation by Lewis Hyde and David Unger published as *World Alone/Mundo a solas* (bilingual edition), Great Barrington, Massachusetts, Penmaen Press, 1982.

*Poems* (bilingual edition), translations by Ben Belitt, Alan Brilliant, and others, Department of English, Ohio University, 1969.

*Vicente Aleixandre and Luis Cernuda: Selected Poems,* (bilingual edition), translations by Linda Lehrer and others, Providence, Rhode Island, Copper Beach Press, 1974.

*The Cave of Night: Poems* (bilingual edition), translation by Joeffrey Bartman, San Luis Obispo, California, Solo Press, 1976.

*Twenty Poems,* edited by Hyde, translations by Hyde and Robert Bly, Madison, Minnesota, Seventies Press, 1977.

*The Crackling Sun: Selected Poems of the Nobel Prize Recipient, 1977,* translated and introduced by Louis Bourne, Madrid, Sociedad General Española de la Librería, 1981.

*Poems-Poemas,* (bilingual edition) Unicorn Press, 1978.

*A Longing for the Light: Selected Poems of Vicente Aleixandre,* edited by Hyde, translations by Kessler and others, New York, Harper, 1979.

*A Bird of Paper: Poems of Vicente Aleixandre,* translated by Willis Bornstone and David Garrson, Ohio University Press, 1982.

## SOURCES:

### Books

*Contemporary Authors,* Detroit, Gale Research, Volume 85–88, 1980; Volume 114, 1984.

*Current Biography Yearbook 1978,* edited by Charles Mortz, New York, H. W. Wilson, 1978.

*Hispanic Writers,* edited by Bryan Ryan, Detroit, Gale Research, 1991.

Ley, Charles David, *Spanish Poetry Since 1939,* Washington, D.C., Catholic University of America Press, 1962.

Morris, C. B., *A Generation of Spanish Poets: 1920–1936,* Cambridge University Press, 1969.

Schwartz, Kessel, *The Meaning of Existence in Contemporary Hispanic Literature,* University of Miami Press, 1970.

### Periodicals

*New Republic,* December 24 & 31, 1977, pp. 25–27.

*New York Times,* October 7, 1977; October 30, 1977.

—*Sketch by Kathe A. Conti*

# Isabel Allende
## 1942-
### Chilean novelist, journalist, dramatist, and juvenile fiction writer

The author of several novels and a short fiction collection, as well as plays and stories for children, Isabel Allende has received international acclaim for her writing. She earned the Quality Paperback Book Club New Voice Award nomination for her debut novel, *La casa de los espíritus* (1982; *The House of the Spirits*)—which became a best seller in Spain and West Germany in the 1980s and a 1994 movie—and the *Los Angeles Times* Book Prize nomination for *De amor y de sombra* (1984; *Of Love and Shadows*). In 1988 Allende's third novel, *Eva Luna,* was voted One of the Year's Best Books by *Library Journal.*

Many of Allende's books are noted for their feminine perspective, dramatic qualities of romance and struggle, and the magic realism genre often found in Latin American literature. Her female characters survive hardships—imprisonment, starvation, the loss of loved ones—but never lose their spirit or ability to love others. Of Allende's *House of Spirits,* which has been compared to that of the Nobel prize-winning author **Gabriel García Márquez**'s *One Hundred Years of Solitude,* Lori Carlson observed in *Review:* "There is a lot of love in *The House of the Spirits.* The love-making of powerful men and naive women, worn-out married couples and anxious rebels might even conjure up the reader's personal experience. But there is another kind of love in this book with which the reader cannot identify. It is a kind that requires forgiving the person whose torturous hand has shoved your face into a bucket of excrement. A spiritual force that can overcome a world sutured with evil, to beget art. Isabel Allende . . . tells in this, her first novel, a vibrant story of struggle and survival dedicated to her mother, grandmother, and 'other extraordinary' women in a country unnamed. Given the descriptions of events and people in the book . . . Chile quickly comes to mind."

*Isabel Allende*

Allende was born on August 2, 1942, in Lima, Peru. Her parents, Tomás, a Chilean diplomat, and Francisca (Llona Barros) Allende divorced when she was three, and she traveled with her mother to Santiago, Chile, where she was raised in her grandparents' home. Allende graduated from a private high school at the age of 16; three years later in 1962, she married her first husband, Miguel Frías, an engineer. Allende also went to work for the United Nations Food and Agricultural Organization in Santiago, where she was a secretary for several years. Later, she became a journalist, editor, and advice columnist for *Paula* magazine. In addition, she worked as a television interviewer and on movie newsreels.

### Fled Chile

When her uncle, Chilean president **Salvador Allende**, was assassinated in 1973 as part of a right-wing military coup against his socialist government, Allende's life changed profoundly. Initially, she did not think that the new regime would endure, but later she came to realize that it was too dangerous to stay in Chile. As a result, Allende, her husband, and their two children fled to Venezuela. Although she had established a successful career as a journalist in Chile, Allende nevertheless had a difficult time finding work in journalism in Venezuela.

During her life in exile, Allende was inspired to write *The House of the Spirits*. The novel was adapted for the screen by the Danish writer and director Bille

August and released in the United States in 1994. Based on Allende's memories of her family and the political upheaval in her native country, the book chronicles the personal and political conflicts in the lives of successive generations of a family in an anonymous Latin American country. These events are principally communicated through the memories of the novel's three central characters: Esteban and Clara, the patriarch and matriarch of the Trueba family, and Alba, their leftist granddaughter who falls into the hands of torturers during a military coup.

*The House of Spirits* was followed by *Of Love and Shadows*, which concerns the switching at birth of two infant girls. One of the babies grows up to become the focus of a journalist's investigation, and the revelation of her assassination compels the reporter and photographer to go into exile. The *Detroit Free Press* described *Of Love and Shadows* as "a frightening, powerful work," in which Allende "proves her continued capacity for generating excellent fiction," while the Toronto *Globe and Mail* commented that "Allende has some difficulty in getting her novel started because she has to weave two stories separately, and seems to be relying initially too much on her skills as a journalist."

On a lecture tour to San Jose, California, to promote the publication of *Of Love and Shadows* in the United States, Allende met William Gordon, a lawyer, who was an admirer of her work and with whom she fell in love. Having been divorced from her first husband for about a year, she married Gordon in 1988, and has lived with him in their suburban home in Marin, California, ever since.

### Became Powerful Storyteller

Allende's next book, *Eva Luna*, focuses on the relationship between Eva—an illegitimate scriptwriter and storyteller—and Rolfe Carlé—an Austrian émigré filmmaker haunted by his father's Nazi past. The novel received positive reviews; for example, Abigail E. Lee in the *Times Literary Supplement* wrote, "Fears that Isabel Allende might be a 'one-book' writer . . . ought to be quashed by *Eva Luna*. . . . Allende moves between the personal and the political, between realism and fantasy, weaving two exotic coming-of-age stories—Eva Luna's and Rolfe Carlé's—into the turbulent coming of age of her unnamed South American country." Further, Alan Ryan of the *Washington Post Book World* asserted that *Eva Luna* is "a remarkable novel, one in which a cascade of stories tumbles out before the reader, stories vivid and passionate and human enough to engage, in their own right, all the reader's attention and sympathy."

Allende followed up this novel with *Cuentos de Eva Luna* (1991; *The Stories of Eva Luna* ), in which the heroine of *Eva Luna* relates several stories to her lover Carlé. According to Alan Ryan in *USA Today,* "These stories transport us to a complex world of sensual pleasures, vivid dreams and breathless longings. It is a world in which passions are fierce, motives are profound and deeds have inexorable consequences." Anne Whitehouse of The *Baltimore Sun* noted that "Ms. Allende possesses the ability to penetrate the hearts of Eva's characters in a few brief sentences.... These are profound, transcendent stories, which hold the mirror up to nature and in their strangeness reveal us to ourselves."

The Eva Luna stories were followed by *El plan infinito* (1993; *The Infinite Plan* ) which, in a stylistic departure for Allende, features a male hero in a North American setting. Gregory Reeves is the son of a traveling preacher and prophet who settles in the Hispanic barrio of Los Angeles after becoming ill. As the only Anglo boy in the district, Reeves is tormented by local gang members. Eventually, he finds his way out of the barrio, does a tour of duty in Vietnam, and goes on to study law at Berkeley. *The Infinite Plan* received less praise than Allende's previous books; Michiko Kakutani of the *New York Times* described the novel as a "Bildungsroman-cum-family saga that owes more to Judith Krantz than to Gabriel García Márquez," concluding that it is "disappointing and mechanical." Still, as novelist Jane Smiley pointed out in her *Boston Globe* review, "Not many [émigré authors] have even attempted writing a novel from the point of view of a native of the new country."

Allende's latest work, *Paula* (1995), is a heartrending account of the circumstances surrounding the lengthy illness and death of her daughter in 1991. Commenting on the deeply emotive effect of *Paula,* the reviewer for *Publishers Weekly* declared that "[only] a writer of Allende's passion and skill could share her tragedy with her readers and leave them exhilarated and grateful."

## SELECTED PUBLISHED WORKS:

*Civilice a su troglodita: Los impertinentes de Isabel Allende,* Santiago, Lord Cochran, 1974.
*La casa de los espíritus,* Barcelona, Plaza y Janés, 1982; translated by Magda Bogin and published as *The House of the Spirits,* New York, Knopf, 1985.
*La gorda de porcelana,* Madrid, Alfaguara, 1984.
*De amor y de sombra,* Barcelona, Plaza y Janés, 1984; translated by Margaret Sayers Peden and published as *Of Love and Shadows,* New York, Knopf, 1987.
*Eva Luna,* Barcelona, Plaza y Janés, 1987; translated by Margaret Sayers Peden and published as *Eva Luna,* New York, Knopf, 1988.
*Cuentos de Eva Luna,* Barcelona, Plaza y Janés, translated by Margaret Sayers Peden and published as *The Stories of Eva Luna,* New York, Atheneum, 1991.

*El plan infinito,* Barcelona, Plaza y Janés, translated by Margaret Sayers Peden and published as *The Infinite Plan,* New York, HarperCollins, 1993.
*Paula,* translated by Margaret Sayers Peden, HarperCollins, 1995.

## SOURCES:

### Books

*Contemporary Literary Criticism, Yearbook 1985,* Vol. 39, Detroit, Gale, 1986, pp. 27–36.
Hart, Patricia, *Narrative Magic in the Fiction of Isabel Allende,* Rutherford, NJ, Fairleigh Dickinson University Press, 1989.
*Hispanic Writers: A Selection of Sketches from Contemporary Authors,* edited by Bryan Ryan, Detroit, Gale, 1991, pp. 15–18.

### Periodicals

*Baltimore Sun,* March 3, 1991.
*Boston Globe,* May 16, 1993, pp. B39, B42.
*Chicago Tribune Bookworld,* May 19, 1985, pp. 37–38.
*Christian Science Monitor,* June 7, 1985; May 27, 1987.
*Cosmopolitan,* January 1991.
*Dallas Morning News,* February 1991, pp. 6J, 8J.
*Detroit Free Press,* June 7, 1987.
*Detroit News,* June 14, 1987.
*Globe and Mail* (Toronto), June 24, 1985; June 27, 1987.
*London Review of Books,* August 1, 1985, pp. 26–27.
*Los Angeles Times,* February 10, 1988; December 28, 1990, p. E5.
*Los Angeles Times Book Review,* June 16, 1985; May 31, 1987.
*Mother Jones,* December 1988, pp. 42–46.
*Nation,* July 20/27, 1985, pp. 52–54; March 11, 1991, pp. 314–16.
*New Statesman,* July 5, 1985, p. 29.
*Newsweek,* May 13, 1985, p. 82.
*New York,* April 11, 1994, p. 56+.
*New York Newsday,* July 23, 1993.
*New York Review of Books,* July 18, 1985, pp. 20–23.
*New York Times,* May 2, 1985; May 9, 1985, p. 23; May 20, 1987; February 4, 1988; June 25, 1993.
*New York Times Book Review,* May 12, 1985, pp. 1, 22–23; July 12, 1987; October 23, 1988; January 20, 1991.
*Observer,* June 7, 1985, p. 21.
*People,* June 10, 1985, p. 145; June 1, 1987.
*Philadelphia Inquirer,* March 3, 1991.

*Publishers Weekly,* March 1, 1985, p. 70; May 17, 1985; March 20, 1995.

*Review,* January-June, 1985, pp. 77–78.

*Spectator,* August 3, 1985.

*Time,* May 20, 1985, p. 79.

*Times* (London), July 4, 1985; July 9, 1987; March 22, 1989; March 23, 1989.

*Times Literary Supplement,* July 5, 1985; July 10, 1987; April 7–13, 1989.

*Tribune Books* (Chicago), October 9, 1988.

*U.S. News and World Report,* November 21, 1988.

*USA Today,* June 7, 1985, p. 4D; March 1, 1991.

*Village Voice,* June 4, 1985, p. 51; June 7, 1985.

*Voice Literary Supplement,* December, 1988
   Moctezum

*Washington Post Book World,* May 12, 1985, pp. 3–4; May 24, 1987; October 9, 1988.

—*Sketch by Alison Carb Sussman*

# Salvador Allende
## 1908-1973
### Chilean statesman

Salvador Allende is best remembered for his attempts to make Chile a socialist country—peaceably. Elected the country's president in 1970, Allende was determined to enact change; but some—particularly among the middle and upper classes—resisted. Less than three years after he assumed office, Allende was challenged by a military coup that brought an end to socialism in Chile—and to Allende's own life.

Salvador Allende Gossens was born in Valparaiso, Chile, July 26, 1908, to lawyer Salvador Allende Castro and Laura Gossens. According to *Current Biography,* he came from a freethinking, upper-middle-class family with an illustrious background. One grandfather, a doctor, organized medical services for the Chilean army during the War of the Pacific . The other grandfather, a radical senator, founded Chile's first secular school. Later, Allende's sister, Laura Allende de Pascal, served in the national Chamber of Deputies and was a member of the Socialist Party's central committee. Allende himself volunteered for military service at 16, after completing his secondary schooling.

Allende then studied medicine at the University of Chile, where he was president of the student medical center and vice chairman of the student federation as well as a delegate to the university council. It was at this time that Allende's radical tendencies became apparent; he read the works of political theorists Karl Marx and Vladimir Lenin and became convinced that revolution would solve Chile's social and economic problems. Activities such as participating in an occupation of the university landed him in prison twice; he was eventually expelled. Allende did return and completed his medical degree in 1932; but his actions made it difficult to find a job, and for a time he worked in a variety of lower-level, assistant medical positions.

In 1933 Allende and other leftists who did not favor Soviet Marxism founded the Socialist Party of Chile. Allende served as the party's secretary general twice; in 1937 he was elected to the Chamber of Deputies, Chile's lower house of Congress. Allende soon developed a reputation as a champion of the poor. As a legislator, he initiated more than 100 bills, most of which dealt with public health, social welfare, and women's rights.

In 1939, Allende became the minister of health, working to improve the government's social insurance program and industrial safety laws. His book, *La realidad médico-social chilena (The Medical-Social Reality in Chile )* was published by the Ministry of Health and awarded a Van Buren prize. In his book, Allende criticized capitalism for causing the poverty and sickness that plagued the lower classes. He presented programs to reform public health, housing, nutrition, and social security.

Allende's tenure as minister ended in 1942. Three years later he was elected to the Senate—the upper house of Congress—for the first time. He served a total of three eight-year terms and became vice president as well as president of the Senate. He made his first bid for the national presidency of Chile in 1951. It was unsuccessful, as were his next two attempts.

### President by a Narrow Margin

Allende had collaborated with the Chilean Communist Party to help gain votes. His greatest challenge in the first three presidential elections came from Christian Democrats. Eventually, Allende formed a party that combined the socialists, communists, middle-class radicals, dissident Christian Democrats, and others into the Unidad Popular (Popular Unity). It was through this party that Allende finally won the presidency—but by a narrow margin. Since Allende did not win a majority in the 1970 election, it was left to the Senate and Chamber of Deputies to cast the final votes and confirm Allende's victory. According to *Current Biography,* some 15,000 upper-class Chileans left the county after the election, withdrawing vast sums of money and causing a near-crisis.

In retrospect, the results were far more significant than Allende realized. "In office Allende made at least two crucial political mistakes," a 1973 *Time* article reported. "One was to forget—or at least ignore—the fact that he had entered office as a minority winner . . . even though nearly two thirds of the voters preferred other men. But he ruled as though he had the nation behind him."

Allende moved ahead with socialist reforms during his first year in office. As Alan Angell summarized in a 1972 *Current History* article: "Allende is no ideologist, no enthusiast for the latest variety of Marxist thought, no advocate of violent revolution. He is a tactician, a maker of political alliances. He is not a compromiser—for his devotion to his principles is unquestioned—but, in contrast to many in his party, he is a political realist."

Allende preferred, Angell noted, reform by parliamentary and legal methods. Allende's first major act was to nationalize the copper industry, which three large U.S. companies controlled. According to Angell, copper provided Chile with three-quarters of its export earnings at the time. When Allende nationalized the industry, the American companies demanded compensation; a battle ensued over rights and money. On this one issue, Chile united behind Allende's actions. All political parties agreed that copper should be in Chilean hands.

That first year, Allende also increased the purchasing power of the poorer class by increasing wages and freezing prices on basic goods. In addition, he instituted agrarian reforms. But the middle and upper classes resented these changes and challenges to their wealth. Chile's political situation did not help. Allende led a six-party alliance; two of the parties split, creating a new total of eight parties. It was "a tribute to his skill . . . that he . . . kept tension at a low level and has prevented several incipient crises from developing into major disputes," Angell reported.

But even Allende's skill could not handle every problem; soon costly strikes crippled Chile. In a July 1973 *Newsweek* article, Allende spoke bluntly about his country's problems: "[Chile's economic situation] is grave. We need dollars. We have massive inflation. We need food. . . . Distribution is frightful. Distances are so great. We lack infrastructure. Railroads don't work, trucks break down, the ports are inadequate. This is all economic, but I still insist the solution to the problem must be political."

Critics later argued that perhaps Allende's reforms came too quickly for an unprepared country. "The problem is that the Chilean road to socialism is at a point where, although capitalism has been partially dethroned, we don't yet have the advantages of socialism," the president himself explained to *Newsweek*.

## The Coup

By September of 1973, with political factions fighting in the Congress and strikes damaging Chile's economy, the previously non-political military overthrew Allende's democratically elected government. The coup, *Time* reported, was extraordinarily violent even by Latin American standards. Several thousand people were killed or injured. Allende, who refused to surrender inside the Presidential Palace, reportedly killed himself as the soldiers closed in. But rumors persisted that the military murdered him. Allende's peaceful socialist experiment ended in bloodshed.

The military quickly established a junta rule. "The military shut down all of Chile's airports and closed the borders to Argentina, Bolivia, and Peru," *Time* recorded. "A state of siege was imposed throughout the country, and Santiago was subject to a round-the-clock curfew." Stories circulated that soldiers bayoneted prisoners to death while pro-Allende suspects were gathered. "Although many, if not most of its future goals were unclear, the junta made unmistakable its determination to change the leftward course of Allende's foreign policy." According to *Time,* Allende mistakenly assumed that the middle and upper classes would accept his socialist agenda as long as it was effected constitutionally. "'If we have to burn half of Chile to save it from Communism, then we will do it,' threatened Roberto Thieme, leader of an extremist right-wing organization called Fatherland and Liberty," *Time* reported.

Allende's body was buried in an unmarked, seaside grave, presumably to keep his burial site from becoming a shrine. But the country never forgot him and in 1990, Allende's body was publicly reburied amid immense grief. Chilean playwright **Ariel Dorfman** attended the funeral and recorded his reaction for the *Nation:* "Now that Salvador Allende, so dead and so alive, has been returned to the earth we set aside for him all these years, we can begin to live with him and without him, in a world that needs more than ever the social justice and full participation he dreamt of for all."

None of the problems Allende tried to eradicate from Chile had disappeared. Living standards worsened, and economic, technological, and cultural autonomy eluded the country. Allende was survived by his wife, Hortensia Bussi of Valparasio, a teacher whom he married in 1939. They had three daughters: Carmen Paz, Beatriz, and Isabel.

## SOURCES:

### Books

*Current Biography Yearbook 1971,* edited by Charles Moritz, New York, H. W. Wilson, 1971.

**Periodicals**

*Current History,* February 1972, pp. 76–80.
*Nation,* October 8, 1990, pp. 384–86.
*Newsweek,* July 2, 1973, p. 29.
*Time,* September 24, 1973, pp. 35–46.

—*Sketch by Kathe A. Conti*

# Nestor Almendros
## 1930-1992
### Spanish cinematographer

Hailed as one of the world's finest cinematographers, Nestor Almendros achieved international recognition in a field that does not usually generate public acclaim. Noted for his unconventional lighting techniques, Almendros shunned the use of artificial light and filters, relying instead on available light whenever possible. The resulting luminous beauty and realism were hallmarks of his photography.

Honored for his innovative work, Almendros received an Academy Award in 1979 for cinematography on Terrance Malick's *Days of Heaven* as well as a César in 1981 for Francois Truffaut's *The Last Métro.* He also received the American Association of Film Critics award for both Eric Rohmer's *My Night at Maud's* (1969) and Truffaut's *The Wild Child* (1970). He was nominated for an Oscar for his photography on the films *Kramer vs. Kramer* (1980), *The Blue Lagoon* (1981), *Sophie's Choice* (1982), and *Places in the Heart* (1984).

### Cinema Was a Refuge in Youth

Born in Barcelona, Spain, to Hermino and Maria (Cuyas) on October 30, 1930, Almendros grew up during the upheaval of the Spanish Civil War. The family was anti-**Francisco Franco** and his father immigrated to Cuba in 1940. Almendros followed him in 1948, but spent the difficult intervening years from escaping the fascist power structure by going to movie theaters. In his autobiography, *A Man with a Camera* (1984), Almendros credits the cinema as "a temporary refuge in a world of fantasy, away from the grim reality we had to live in." He became an obsessive movie-goer and cites silent films such as Fritz Lang's *Die Niebelungen* as figuring decisively in his developing appreciation of cinema as art, not just entertainment.

Almendros entered the University of Havana in 1948, but pursued a film education first in New York and then at Rome's Centro Sperimentale in 1956. Almendros rebelled against the technical rules he was taught in Rome—an attitude that would serve him throughout his career. He explained in his autobiography that, "from this ... I developed a principle: Every time I make a film I ask myself, 'How is this kind of scene normally shot? Suppose we did the opposite?'" Unable to find film work in Italy, Almendros returned to the United States, where he made his first complete film. Called *58–59,* it dealt with a New Year's Eve scene in New York's Times Square. Notably, it was shot at night, entirely with available light.

Almendros returned to **Fidel Castro**'s Cuba in 1959, where he made his first professional films—government-sponsored, political and educational documentaries. These films were mostly shot in the countryside, and filming conditions were primitive. Covering inside walls with white paper and using mirrors to direct sunlight inside dim peasant huts, Almendros found creative solutions to lighting needs. These were innovations he would use throughout his career.

### Exile in Paris

As the revolution in Cuba gradually smothered individuality, Almendros prudently chose a third exile—going to Paris in 1962. There he was fascinated by New Wave directors Rohmer and Truffaut, but could not get film work. Discouraged, he finally met Rohmer in 1964. Present at the shooting of *Paris vu par ...* (*Paris seen by ...* ), Almendros offered his services as cameraman when the cinematographer abruptly quit. He was accepted for a one-day trial, but Rohmer and producer Barbet Schroeder were sufficiently impressed to have him finish the film. Almendros called this event "a stroke of luck that happens only once in a lifetime."

Almendros began to work with Rohmer, making educational documentaries for French television. He photographed his first feature film in 1966—Rohmer's *La Collectionneuse.* Almendros wrote in his autobiography that *La Collectionneuse* "contains in embryonic form everything I would do later on." The film went on to win a Silver Bear at the Berlin Film Festival. The success of *La Collectionneuse* established Almendros as a cinematographer, and more work followed, including *The Wild Racers* (1967) and *More* (1968). He filmed Rohmer's *My Night at Maud's* (1969) in black and white. It was shown at Cannes, was nominated for an Oscar, and is considered a classic. Impressed with his photography on this film, Truffaut asked Almendros to make *The Wild Child* in 1969. This was the beginning of Almendros's long collaboration with Truffaut.

Almendros also collaborated extensively with Eric Rohmer and Barbet Schroeder over the years. He had developed an association with American directors by the mid–1970s, filming *Goin' South* (1977), *Days of Heaven* (1978), and *Kramer vs. Kramer* (1980), among many others. Almendros directed two powerful documentaries depicting human-rights conditions in Castro's Cuba, *Improper Conduct* (1984) and *Nobody Listened* (1988). Almendros felt these stories needed to be told. Almendros died in 1992 at the age of 61, of lymphoma.

## SELECTED PUBLISHED WORKS:

*A Man with a Camera,* translated by Rachel Phillips Belash, New York, Farrar, Straus, Giroux, 1984.

## SOURCES:

### Books

Almendros, Nestor, *A Man with a Camera,* translated by Rachel Phillips Belash, New York, Farrar, Straus, Giroux, 1984.
*Current Biography Yearbook,* edited by Charles Moritz, New York, H. W. Wilson, 1989.
*Current Biography Yearbook,* edited by Judith Graham, New York, H. W. Wilson, 1992.
*Variety Obituaries, 1991–1992,* compiled by Barbara Bergeron and Chuck Bartelt, Nework, Garland, 1993.

### Periodicals

*New York Times,* March 5, 1992, p. B15.

—*Sketch by Ellen Dennis French*

# Pedro Almodóvar
## 1951-
### Spanish filmmaker

Colorful and controversial, Almodóvar is Spain's foremost contemporary filmmaker. Filmmaking is Almodóvar's passion; according to an entry in *Current Biography,* Almodóvar recalled feeling "absolutely possessed" when making a film, adding: "It's an extraordinary gift to be able to represent your own fantasies and give them life. Not just your dreams, but everything that excites you and interests you. It's a virtue that few other professions can provide you. It

*Pedro Almodóvar*

gives your life a lot of meaning." He has garnered numerous international accolades, including the best foreign film of 1988 Oscar nomination for *Mujeres al borde de un ataque de nervios* (*Women on the Verge of a Nervous Breakdown,* 1988), which also stands as the most financially successful Spanish film ever produced.

Humorous, high-kitsch, and outrageous, Almodóvar's cinematic creations exude sexuality and hedonism. Their risque edge has frequently been judged excessive, much to Almodóvar's consternation. The Motion Picture Association of America X-rated *¡Atame!* (*Tie Me Up! Tie Me Down!,* 1990), and *Pepi, Luci, Bom y otras chicas del montón* (*Pepi, Lucy, Bom and Other Girls on the Heap,* 1980)—his debut feature-length film—has never been released in the United States. To shock, however, is not his intent. "I *never* set out to shock," he informed Iain Blair in a *Chicago Tribune* interview. "It's more important for me to tell the kind of story that I like the way I like."

Almodóvar's stories focus on the present. Madrid, where he lives, has been an enduring fascination and source of inspiration. Women are central to Almodóvar's work. Accused by some critics for his portrayal of women, Almodóvar looks beyond high heels and tight skirts, arguing that women should command equal respect, whatever their attire. Typically, his women are strong and independent.

Identifying a universal thread within his work, Almodóvar told Peter Besas (*Behind the Spanish*

*Lens,* 1985), "If there's any theme common to my films it's a striving for absolute individual freedom carried to the extreme." His characters are generally amoral and apolitical, a reflection of his desire to completely break with Spain's Francoist past. "I never speak of Franco; I hardly acknowledge his existence. I start *after* Franco." He demonstrated his own political loyalty, however, while shooting *Kika* in 1993; alongside members of the cast he expressly declared his support for **Felipe González** and his Socialist Party against "intolerance."

Pedro Almodóvar was born September 25, 1951, in Calzada de Calatrava, a poor village in southwestern Spain, the third of four children. His mother, Francisca Caballero, who had cameo roles in several of his films, was the dominant household figure. Almodóvar was never close to his father, a bookkeeper. When he was eight his family moved to Caceras, an isolated town. At the age of ten, having demonstrated intellectual aptitude by teaching local villagers to read, Almodóvar was awarded a scholarship to attend a school run by Salesian priests. He was sexually abused by his Salesian teachers. At his insistence, his parents moved him to an alternative school, but the scars remained.

With his faith in the Catholic church destroyed, he turned to the cinema. "I had to build a form of anti-religion in which Hollywood actresses were saints," he explained to Karen Krizanovich in the London *Times* in 1992. His infatuation with U.S. films continues to pervade his own work, a recasting of Hollywood into his crazy Spanish mold. Almodóvar greatly admires the Spanish director **Luis Buñuel**, Billy Wilder, and Alfred Hitchcock.

At 17, eager to become "Madrid's most modern person," Almodóvar left Caceras. He worked as a street vendor, selling crafts until he secured a job at Telefónica, the state-run telephone company, in 1970. Though he found the job satisfactory, he told Iain Blair that it left him with the feeling that the telephone "was invented for liars." Blair observed that the telephone served as "a destructive symbol of a doomed relationship" in *Mujeres al borde de un ataque de nervios.*

## Makes First Film

In Madrid, Almodóvar participated in various underground artistic movements. Generating a cult following, he performed with a punk rock band called Almodóvar and McNamara, dressed in a leather mini-skirt, stockings, and platform shoes. He wrote comic strips and short fiction, including articles contributed to the magazine *La luna* under the pseudonym Patty Diphusa (*patidifusa* means "flabbergasted" in Spanish), a fictional porn star. The stories were later collected and published as *Patty Diphusa y otros textos* (*Patty Diphusa and Other Writings* ) in 1991. Almodóvar joined Los Goliardos, an avant-garde theatre group. Carmen Maura, one of his future leading ladies was also a member. He shot short films, such as *Sex Comes, Sex Goes,* in Super–8, and presented them at bars and parties.

Almodóvar's break came with *Pepi, Luci, Bom y otras chicas del montón.* Originally a photo-novel commissioned by an underground newspaper, the project evolved into a feature-length film. Shot only on weekends—because Almodóvar was still working for the telephone company—on a budget of $5,000, the film took a year and a half to make. Almodóvar obtained the financial support of José Esteban Alenda, a Madrid distributor, and converted the film to 35 millimeter. Screened at the San Sebastian film festival in 1980, *Pepi, Luci, Bom y otras chicas del montón* was a hit, particularly with younger audiences, although its sexual content was considered disgraceful by some. Almodóvar's national cult status was augmented by his second film, *Laberinto de pasiones* (*Labyrinth of Passion,* 1982), of the "pop" film genre. In stark contrast to its predecessor, it was shot in four and a half weeks on a budget of $175,000.

## International Reputation Grows

Almodóvar achieved international notoriety when his third film, *Entre tinieblas* (*Dark Habits,* 1983), which centers on an order of nuns whose motto is "Sin is our chosen path," was shown at the Miami and Venice film festivals in 1984. He attained his first significant commercial success in Spain with {*Qué he hecho yo para merecer esto?* (*What Have I done to Deserve This?,* 1985), which gained critical acclaim when it was brought to the New Directors/New Films Festival in New York in 1985. His following venture, *Matador,* confirmed his reputation.

Around 1986 Almodóvar established his own production company, El Deseo, which he manages with his producer brother, Agustín. El Deseo has produced three of five of Spain's highest earning films. Its debut release, *La ley del deseo* (*Law of Desire* ), was Almodóvar's first film concentrating on a homosexual love story. The film was an enormous success, standing as the most popular film of 1986 in Spain.

Almodóvar's international reputation was projected to star status with *Mujeres al borde de un ataque de nervios* (1988), a film inspired by American comedies from the 1950s about female loneliness. The film, an international box office smash, won more than 50 awards, including an Oscar nomination and a citation from the New York Film Critics Circle. The venture was, however, his last with Carmen Maura, who had been with him since his Los Goliardos underground days. One Almodóvar's trademarks is his retention of a loyal troupe of actors who repeatedly appear in his films. His estrangement from Maura in 1989 led to her replacement by Victoria Abril.

His subsequent film, *¡Atame!*, is probably Almodóvar's most controversial picture to date, with the exception of his first. David Leavitt in the *New York Times Magazine,* described the plot of *¡Atame!* as the "story of a mental hospital patient who kidnaps a porno- and horror-film actress in order to persuade her to fall in love with him, it begins as a hostage melodrama, then, after a series of thoroughly unpredictable turns, unfolds into a bizarre kind of love story." Perhaps a key to Almodóvar's success is his innovative and rigorous promotion of his films, which involve elaborate schemes to capture the public eye. At the gala preview of *¡Atame!* he traveled to Madrid's Cine Fuencarral in a garbage truck, flanked by four of his stars.

With *Tacones lejanos* (*High Heels,* 1991) Almodóvar won the award for the best foreign language film at the French César awards. His co-nominees were Woody Allen, Robert Altman, and James Ivory. Somewhat controversially, however, recognition was conspicuously lacking at Spain's own Goya awards, perhaps a tacit reminder of the polemic content of many of Almodóvar's films.

His films contain biographical references. "Absolutely all of my life is in my films. The way in which I do my autobiography is never direct. I am behind, in the shadow, of everything," he disclosed to Karen Krizanovich in the London *Times* in 1992, although he refrains from revealing his inner self, preferring to study others. "I am much more interested in other people's lives than I am in myself," he said.

## SELECTED PUBLISHED WORKS:

*Patty Diphusa y otros textos,* Barcelona, Editorial Anagrama, 1991; translated by Kirk Anderson as *Patty Diphusa and Other Writings,* Boston and London, Faber and Faber, 1991.

## SELECTED VIDEOGRAPHY:

*Pepi, Lucy, Bom y otras chicas del montón* (*Pepi, Lucy, Bom and Other Girls on the Heap*), 1980.
*Laberinto de pasiones* (*Labyrinth of Passion*), 1982.
*Entre tinieblas* (*Dark Habits*), 1983.
*¡Qué he hecho yo para merecer esto?* (*What Have I Done to Deserve This?*), 1984.
*Matador* (*Matador*), 1986.
*La ley del deseo* (*Law of Desire*), 1987.
*Mujeres al borde de un ataque de nervios* (*Women on the Verge of a Nervous Breakdown*), 1988.
*¡Atame!* (*Tie Me Up! Tie Me Down!*), 1990.
*Tacones lejanos* (*High Heels*), 1991.
*Kika* (*Kika*), 1993.

## SOURCES:

### Books

Besas, Peter, *Behind the Spanish Lens: Spanish Cinema Under Fascism and Democracy,* Denver, Arden Press, 1985.
*Current Biography Yearbook,* New York, H. W. Wilson, 1990.
Smith, Paul Julian, *Desire Unlimited,* London, Verso, 1994.

### Periodicals

*Chicago Tribune,* December 25, 1988, pp. 8–9.
*New Yorker,* October 5, 1992, pp. 59–60.
*New York Times Magazine,* April 22, 1990, pp. 36–42.
*Times* (London), January 4, 1992, pp. 18–19.

—*Sketch by Amanda Beresford*

# Alicia Alonso
## 1921?-
### Cuban ballerina

Alicia Alonso has been fascinating audiences with her performances for more than fifty years. The winner of the Golden Metal of the Gran Teatro Liceo de Barcelona, the Grand Prix de la Ville de Paris, the "Anna Pavlova" Prize of the Dance University of Paris, and the Cuban Women's Foundation's highest award, the "Ana Betancourt," Alonso is a classic artist of the dance. She broke cold war barriers to dance *Giselle,* and she even went on to perform the same piece when she was blind. She brought ballet to Cuba and Cubans to the ballet as she established the Ballet Nacional de Cuba and a national ballet school. She has tirelessly fought to dance and to give others the opportunity to dance. She has done all this because, as she explained in 1979 in the *Saturday Review,* "I live when I dance. I live not just for myself. When I'm on stage with my dancers, I live with them. It is life."

The ballerina was born Alicia Ernestina de la Caridad del Cobre Martinez on December 21 (the year of Alonso's birth has been variously listed as 1917, 1921, and 1922). The petite girl with black hair and eyes was raised in the city of her birth, Havana, Cuba, by her parents Antonio Martínez and Ernestina (Hoyo) Martínez. Antonio Martínez was a lieutenant in the Cuban army, and he housed his family in the privileged section of the city known as the Vedado.

Ernestina Martínez cared for her four children at home; Alicia Alonso credits her mother with encouraging her talent. She recalled in *Dance* magazine, "Mama used to put me in a room with a phonograph and a scarf. That would keep me quiet for a few hours, doing what I imagined was dancing." Alonso's parents did more than leave the girl to develop her talent alone; they provided her with dancing lessons. At the Sociedad Pro-Arte Musical in the capital, the young girl received her first dancing lessons. By age ten Alonso had her public debut when she danced in a waltz in *Sleeping Beauty.*

The best place, at that time, for a gifted dancer to learn and to begin a career was New York City. Alonso and her husband, Fernando Alonso, moved to that city soon after their marriage on February 19, 1937. While Fernando Alonso, a dancer Alicia met at the Sociedad, worked with New York's Mordkin Ballet Company, Alicia Alonso trained at the School of American Ballet with some of the best private teachers of classical ballet, including Alexandra Fedorova, Anatole Vilzak, and—later in London—Vera Volkova.

Oddly enough, Alonso did not begin to dance as she had been taught. Her first performances on stage were as a tap dancer in comedies in the late 1930s. In the musicals *Great Lady* and *Stars in Your Eyes,* the latter starring Ethel Merman and Jimmy Durante, Alonso danced as a chorine. By 1939 Alonso was chosen to join the American Ballet Caravan as a soloist and soon thereafter she signed with Ballet Theatre, or the American Ballet Theatre, as a ballet dancer. Alonso's talent was recognized, and she was given solo parts, such as that of the Bird in *Peter and the Wolf* and that of Carlotta Grisi in *Le Pas de Quatre.*

### Vision Problems Hinder Career

Alonso was well on her way to success when severe problems with her vision halted her career. The ballerina's retinas detached, and she was temporarily blinded. The three operations performed to restore her vision were very delicate, and Alonso was confined to bed for a full year. She could not turn her head, laugh, or even cry. Despite her physical problems, Alonso did not lose her passion for the ballet. She began to envision herself dancing; by this technique, she learned the movements necessary to dance *Giselle.* When the heavy bandages were removed and Alonso found that she could see, she first had to learn how to walk again. It was not long before she was dancing the very role she had rehearsed over and over again as she lay blind in bed.

At the Metropolitan Opera House in 1943, Alonso danced Giselle in place of Alicia Markova, who was ill. The ballerina's dance with Anton Dolin was lauded by the *New York Times* as "one of the most distinguished performances of the season." Alonso would become famous for her unique interpretation of *Giselle.* Her grandson, Ivan Monreal, would say of her years later that, when dancing with her in *Giselle,* he did not think of Alonso as his grandmother. He told the *Saturday Review,* "I think of her as Giselle. . . . Because she *is* Giselle."

After three years of dancing *Giselle* for Ballet Theatre with Dolin, André Eglevsky, and Igor Youskevitch, Alonso was honored with the position of principal dancer. She danced in contemporary ballets such as *Undertow, Fall River Legend, Theme and Variations, Romeo and Juliet, Aleko, Circo de España, Gala Performance, Billy the Kid, Petrouchka, Lilac Garden, Graduation Ball, Waltz Academy, On Stage!, Caprichos,* as well as in standard classics such as *Swan Lake, La fille Mal Gardée, Aurora's Wedding, Les Sylphides,* and *The Nutcracker.* Alicia Alonso's reputation as a supreme dancer was growing.

### Returns to Cuba to Form Ballet Company

In 1948 Alonso decided to return to her native Cuba to found her own ballet with her husband Fernando Alonso serving as the general director and his brother working as artistic director. The Ballet Alicia Alonso, as the company was called, provided Ballet Theatre dancers with work and inspired potential dancers and ballet enthusiasts alike throughout South America.

However, Alonso was not content with this success. Too many of Ballet Alicia Alonso's dancers were non-Cubans. Alonso wanted to give the young people of her native land the opportunity to excel as dancers. In 1950, with the proceeds from her South American tour, a subsidy from the Cuban Ministry of Education, and donations from patrons of the ballet, Alonso was able to open the Alicia Alonso Academy of Ballet in Havana. Alonso had recruited some of the world's best dancers to become instructors at her school; these instructors taught their enthusiastic students well, and soon, the ranks of Ballet Alicia Alonso were swelling with young Cuban dancers.

Alonso's dreams of bringing ballet to Cuba had come true. Her company, once consisting of more non-Cubans than Cubans, was now a showcase for Cuban talent. The company staged *Swan Lake, Don Quixote, Aurora's Wedding, Coppélia, Estampas Cubanas* and *Songoro Cosongo, La Fille Mal Gardée,* and, of course, *Giselle.*

Unfortunately, by 1956, Alonso found it necessary to disband her ballet company as well as her school. **Fulgencio Batista**'s regime, which had granted an annual subsidy to Alonso's company, had been decreasing the amount of the subsidy every year. Alonso's dancers, determined to keep dancing despite their low pay, were forced to keep other jobs as well;

they were consequently exhausted when it was time to dance. When the government promised Alonso $500 every month if she promised, in return, not to make public the problems with the unsatisfactory subsidy, Alonso refused. She decided that it would be better to shut down operations altogether, and she left the country to dance elsewhere.

## Embarks on Tour behind Iron Curtain

Alonso next worked as a guest artist with the Ballet Russe de Monte Carlo for the next three years, during which time she was honored with an invitation to dance in the Soviet Union. This highly unusual invitation demonstrated the respect Alonso had received throughout the world. No Western dancer had ever before been invited to dance behind the communist iron curtain in the Soviet Union during the Cold war. For two-and-a-half months in the winter of 1957, Alonso toured cities including Moscow, Riga, Leningrad (now St. Petersburg), and Kiev as she danced in *Giselle* and *Swan Lake*. The great ballerina danced as a guest with the Leningrad Opera Ballet and even appeared on television in Moscow. After this exciting tour, Alonso returned to the United States.

After the Cuban Revolution in 1959, the prima ballerina Alicia Alonso decided to leave the United States and return to her native country. With so many Cubans fleeing their homeland to live in America, Alonso's decision was almost unheard of; many people thought that she was making a mistake, and they told her so. Despite their concerns, Alonso was determined to become a part of the revolution that would, supposedly, bring opportunity to all. As a one-time principal dancer with Ballet Theatre in New York, the first Western ballerina ever invited to dance in the Soviet Union, the winner of *Dance* magazine's award for 1958, and the founder of the Ballet de Cuba, Alonso believed that she could make important contributions to her people now that Batista's regime was out of power.

## Provides Dance Training to Cubans

**Fidel Castro**, eager to enrich Cuba with cultural and educational organizations, provided Alonso with $200,000 to begin again. She reopened her school, and her new ballet company, the Ballet Nacional de Cuba, was given official status and guaranteed backing by the federal government. Soon, the Ballet could count more than 100 members, and a system of dance schools had been established on the island. As every child was promised a free education in Cuba, any student who was talented and serious enough could receive ballet instruction. After an audition, a child could pass to an elementary level school which emphasized training in the arts. The next stage was Cubanacán, a beautiful academy of the arts near Havana. The final stage before actually entering the

Ballet Nacional was training at Alonso's school of the Ballet Nacional de Cuba in Havana. Alonso explained the system in the *Saturday Review* in 1979: "A rural child has an equal opportunity with the city child. If there is dance talent, we will find it; if the child has a desire to dance, we will give him every chance to develop his talent." As one example of the system, *Saturday Review* reminded its readers that Jorge Esquivel, who was Cuba's premier danseur and Alonso's usual partner despite his youth, was once a "forgotten orphan."

The government's enthusiasm for Alonso's work enabled her to bring ballet to the Cuban people in other ways as well. Choreographers were encouraged to create original works for the Ballet Nacional, and the best of these works were performed along with the classics such as *Coppélia, La Fille Mal Gardée, The Nutcracker, Les Sylphides,* and again, *Giselle*. Those who stood more to gain from watching than from creating also benefitted from the government's support of the Ballet. The company traveled to perform in front of all kinds of audiences—the poor and the rich alike enjoyed the ballet in parks, schools, and even factories.

The only audience for which the company was prohibited from performing was the one in the United States. The Ballet Nacional de Cuba went instead to many countries which were, at the time, communist. The People's Republic of China, Mongolia, North Vietnam, and countries in Central and South America were treated to performances. Alonso herself traveled elsewhere as a guest artist with many companies. These included the Grands Ballets Canadiens and the Royal Danish Ballet. Alonso danced *Giselle* at Montreal's Expo 67 and received standing ovations. Although Alonso had been a star of Ballet Theatre in the United States, she was not allowed to dance there for some years. When Cold war tensions were peaking, the U.S. State Department would not allow Alonso to enter the country because of her support for the communist administration of Fidel Castro.

## Tours North America

It was not until 1971 that the Ballet Nacional de Cuba could make a North American tour. Alonso danced a piece from *Swan Lake, Oedipus the King, La Dame aux Camélias, Carmen,* and *Giselle*. After viewing Alonso's performance in Giselle, a critic from the *New York Times* reported, "In some respects the physical command is not so certain as it was years ago, but [Alonso] is now a far better dancer than she was. The nuances and grace notes that distinguish great classic dancing from the superbly accomplished are now very evident, and her musical phrasing is as individual as ever."

The fact that Alonso performed so beautifully was a testament to her great skill and talent; the dancer was almost completely blind. She had to be led onto stage—once she was there, she found her position with the aid of bright spotlights. After her performance she had to follow a voice to get off the stage. Alonso did not want people to view her performance in light of this handicap, and she insisted that the dance should be enjoyed without external considerations. Her vision was restored by Barcelona surgeons in 1972, and she was healthy enough to perform by 1975. During the latter half of the 1970s she danced as a guest performer throughout the United States, and of course, in Cuba with the Ballet Nacional.

Besides touring with the Ballet Nacional and on her own, Alonso has been involved in many other activities during the years since 1958. She has choreographed works such as *Ensayo sinfónica, The Circus, Lidia,* and *The Little Thief.* Alonso trains students and decides which should advance to the next level of the training system. She has been a member of the World Council for Peace since 1974, and she has served as vice president of the National Union of Cuban Writers and Artists. Alonso also does her share of the work that is delegated to all Cubans—she toils, along with members of the company, in the coffee fields to fulfill her agricultural duties. Alonso also spends time with her family. By 1977, she had divorced Fernando Alonso and married a writer and lawyer named Pedro Simon. Her daughter, Laura Alonso, is a soloist with the Ballet Nacional; she trains her mother every morning, correcting the veteran dancer as she were a beginnier when she misses a step.

In 1990, Alicia Alonso, at the approximate age of seventy years, gave a performance of the pas de deux from *Swan Lake,* Act II, at the American Ballet Theatre's fiftieth anniversary celebration. While it was "an excruciatingly slow and rickety performance," as Laura Jacobs wrote in the *New Leader,* it was also passionate. According to Jacobs, Alonso's "[19]40s technique of soft turn-out and sachet-like port de bras gave the ballet a glow that was missing from every performance by ABT's young beauties in their spanking new *Swan Lake* last spring." Despite her age, the beauty of Alonso's dance will never fade. Dancing is in fact what revives her. She was quoted in the *Saturday Review:* "Dance works on the total being. By that I mean the mind and the spirit as well as the purely physical parts, and I think of dance as the *total* antibiotic for healing."

**SOURCES:**

*Dance,* December, 1953; June, 1980, p. 117; November, 1981, p. 110; April, 1982, p. 118; June, 1982, pp. 74+; October, 1982, pp. 35+; January, 1983, pp. 97+; January, 1985, p. 72; August, 1987, p. 58; September, 1989, pp. 68–69; August, 1990, pp. 32+.

*New Leader,* March 5, 1990, pp. 21–22.
*New York Times,* November 3, 1943; June 21, 1971.
*Saturday Review,* January 6, 19.
*World Press Review,* April, 1982, p. 62.

—*Sketch by Ronie-Richele Garcia-Johnson*

# Dámaso Alonso
## 1898-1990
**Spanish poet and literary critic**

Dámaso Alonso was one of twentieth-century Spain's most distinguished intellectuals. After the Spanish Civil War (1936–1939), he precipitated a revival of Spanish poetry with *Hijos de la ira* (*Children of Wrath,* 1944). In this and later poetic works he eschewed Spain's prevailing neoclassicism and adopted a colloquial free verse. As a literary critic, Alonso developed an eclectic approach to texts that encompassed intuitive perceptions as well as linguistic analysis. Alonso's reappraisal of several sixteenth- and seventeenth-century poets—particularly **Luis de Góngora**—significantly modified Spanish literary history.

Alonso was born in Madrid on October 22, 1898, the son of upper middle-class parents—Dámaso Alonso y Alonso, a mining engineer, and his wife, the devoutly religious Petra Fernández de las Redondas y Díaz. Alonso was educated in private Catholic elementary and secondary schools. Under the tutelage of the renowned philologist Menéndez Pidal at the University of Madrid, Alonso devoted himself to the study of literature, linguistics, and philology, taking his doctorate in 1928.

### Poetry Published

Alonso's first book of poetry—*Poemas puros* (*Pure Poems,* 1921)—was written in an abstract, imagistic style. During this time Alonso was a member of the literary circle known as the "Generation of 1927, " which included **Federico García Lorca** and Rafael Alberti. This promulgated art for art's sake rather than the social relevance of verse. In 1926 Alonso published his translation of James Joyce's *Portrait of an Artist as a Young Man* (*El artista adolescente*).

Alonso's 1927 prose edition of Góngera's *Soledades* (*Solitudes*) did much to elucidate the Baroque poet's complex language and style. A revised version of Alonso's 1927 doctoral dissertation, *La lengua poetica de Góngora* (*The Poetic Language of Góngora*), was published in 1935 and awarded the National Prize for Literature. In 1929 Alonso married fellow writer Eulalia Galvarriato, embarking on a permanent, stable union. He held the chair of Spanish language and literature at the University of Valencia (1933–1939) and was professor of Romance linguistics at the University of Madrid (1939–1968). He also taught at other universities, including Berlin, Cambridge, Harvard, Oxford, Stanford, and Yale.

### War Inspired Poems of Protest

The atrocities of the Spanish Civil War and World War II prodded Alonso out of the austerity of *Poemas puros* to confront the more humanistic concerns of a civilization staggering out of devastation into an uncertain future. Published in 1944, *Hijos de la ira* is Alonso's most highly regarded poetic work. Elias Rivers maintained that "this book was the beginning of authentic poetry in postwar Spain.... *Hijos de la ira* extended the frontiers of poetry in Spain." Alonso discarded the cold, formalistic norm of pre-war Spanish poetry for a blatantly emotional free verse. He declared that "it is a book of protest and probing. What does it protest against? Against everything." In the famous opening poem, "Insomnia," the speaker confronts spiritual decay: "And I spend long hours asking God, asking him why / my soul is slowly rotting away, / why more than a million corpses are rotting away in / this city of Madrid, / why a billion corpses are slowly rotting away in / the world."

*Oscura notica* (*Dark Message*, 1944) elaborated on many of the themes in *Hijos de la ira*. As Andrew Debicki stated in his study *Dámaso Alonso*, *Oscura notica* dramatizes "man's search for religious and personal transcendence on the one hand, and his temptation to egotism, pettiness and destruction on the other." Alonso's other important poetic works include *Hombre y Dios* (*Man and God*, 1955), which explored the intermingling of the divine and the human, and *Gozos de la vistas* (*Joys of Sight*, 1981), a collection of poems centered on the blessings and limitations of human insight.

### Literary Analyses Drew Praise

In 1950 Alonso published his most significant critical work, *Poesía española* (*Spanish Poetry*), a quintessential study of six Spanish Golden Age poets of the sixteenth and seventeenth centuries. In this study Alonso executed close readings using methods similar to those of formalists I. A. Richards and William Empson and conducted linguistic analyses that show the influences of Charles Bally and Ferdinand de Saussure. "As an interpreter of texts," noted Helmut Hatzfeld, "Dámaso Alonso represents the most objective imaginable type of scholarly scrutiny and pedagogical ability.... He is more concerned with exact description that with explanation at all costs. But the explanations are always convincing." Alonso described his criticism as "the study of everything which individualizes a work of literature." He believed that "a work of literature exists by virtue of what is virginal in it, what is uncontaminated and unique in its mode of being."

A member of the Royal Academy of the Spanish Language since 1945, Alonso served four terms (1968–1982) as its director. In 1978 he was awarded the Miguel de Cervantes Prize, the highest honor for Spanish language writers. Over the course of his career he received honorary degrees from a number of universities including Oxford, San Marcos, and Rome. After enduring serious respiratory problems for three years, Alonso died on January 24, 1990.

## SELECTED PUBLISHED WORKS:

*Poemas puros, poemillas de la ciudad,* Madrid, Galatea, 1921.
*Soledades,* by Luis de Góngera, edited with prose version by Dámaso Alonso, Madrid, Revista de Occidente, 1927.
*La lengua poética de Góngora,* Madrid, Aguirre, 1935.
*Hijos de la ira. Diaro íntimo,* Madrid, Revista de Occidente, 1944; translated by Elias L. Rivers as *Hijos de la ira: Children of Wrath* (bilingual edition), Baltimore, John Hopkins University Press, 1970.
*Oscura noticia,* Madrid, Hispánica, 1944.
*Poesía española. Ensayo de métodos y límites estilísticos,* Madrid, Gredos, 1951.
*Hombre y Dios,* Málaga, Arroyo de los Angeles, 1955.
*Obras Completas,* ten volumes, Madrid, Gredos, 1972–93.
*Gozos de la vista,* Madrid, Espasa-Calpe, 1981.

## SOURCES:

### Books

Alonso, Dámaso, *Hijos de la ira: Children of Wrath* (bilingual edition), translated by Elias L. Rivers, Baltimore, John Hopkins University Press, 1970.
*Contemporary Literary Criticism,* Volume 14, Detroit, Gale Research, 1980, pp. 18–20.
Debicki, Andrew, *Dámaso Alonso,* New York, Twayne, 1970.

*Dictionary of Literary Biography,* Volume 108: *Twentieth-Century Spanish Poets: First Series,* edited by Michael L. Perna, Detroit, Gale Research, 1991, p. 30–41.

*Hispanic Writers,* edited by Bryan Ryan, Detroit, Gale Research, 1991.

*Modern Spanish and Portuguese Literatures,* New York, Continuum, 1988.

*World Authors 1975–1980,* edited by Vineta Colby, New York, H. W. Wilson, 1985.

## Periodicals

*New York Times,* January 27, 1990, p. 32.

## Other

"Introducción Biográfica Y Crítica" in *Hijos de la ira,* edited by Miguel J. Flys, Madrid: Clásicos Castalia, 1986.

—*Sketch by Kenneth K. Brandt*

# Maria Conchita Alonso
## 1957-
### Cuban Venezuelan actress and singer

Entertainer Maria Conchita Alonso has accomplished the formidable task of balancing a thriving career as a Hollywood film actress with success in Spanish pop music. In addition to making records and movies, she has worked as a magazine model and a television actress, and has created her own film production company. For her contributions to both the entertainment industry and to the Hispanic community, Alonso was named Hispanic Woman of the Year by the Mexican American Opportunity Foundation in 1990, and in 1992 she was named Hispanic Entertainer of the Year for the Cinco de Mayo celebration.

Alonso was born in Cuba to Jose and Conchita Alonso. The Alonso family, which includes older brothers Ricardo and Roberto (whom Alonso refers to as her "biggest fans"), emigrated to Venezuela when the actress was still a child. When she was growing up, Alonso's parents sent her to schools in France and Switzerland, and although she loved her years in Europe, she remains proud of both her Cuban blood and her Venezuelan upbringing.

Alonso's artistic calling came early. By age fourteen, she was modeling and doing television commercials. In 1971 Alonso was named "Miss Teenager of the World" and in 1975 she represented Venezuela in the "Miss World" Pageant. In an interview with the *Los Angeles Times,* she recalled her stay in London for the Miss World Pageant: "I love food. I love to eat. Because I was nervous about the contest, I ate and ate. So much so that when it came to the night of the contest, I couldn't even get into the dress I'd bought." She still walked away from the pageant as sixth runner-up. Her parents provided a balanced perspective on her success as a beauty contestant that helped Alonso in later endeavors. "They kept my feet firmly on the ground," she recalled in an interview. They helped her realize that "it's not looks, it's what is inside you, it's what you do with your life that's important."

Alonso returned to Venezuela and went on to star in ten Spanish-language television soap operas (shown throughout Latin America and the United States) while also carving a niche for herself as one of the hottest singers in Spanish pop-rock music. Although she quickly became a favorite with Hispanic audiences, she opted to expand her career and try her luck in the United States. In 1982 she moved from Caracas to Los Angeles. Her motto: "Dare to try new things." Her goal: the movies.

### Move to Hollywood Pays Off

The gamble paid off when she was cast as Robin Williams's Italian immigrant girlfriend in the film *Moscow on the Hudson.* Her "simpatica" effervescence caught the eye of Hollywood filmmakers and landed her roles in nine more films, including *Colors,* starring Robert Duvall and Sean Penn, and *Running Man,* in which Alonso played opposite Arnold Schwarzenegger. Other movies featuring Alonso were *Extreme Prejudice, Touch and Go, Blood Ties, A Fine Mess, Vampire's Kiss, Predator II,* and *McBain.* Although not box-office blockbusters, the films established her as a capable actress in both comedy and drama who could hold her own against Hollywood's top leading men.

Alonso looks to Arnold Schwarzenegger (her co-star in *Running Man*) as a type of role model, a fellow foreigner in the American film industry. She considers him "number one in the world, yet he is a foreigner. . . . And with an accent heavier than mine. And with a name more difficult to pronounce than mine!" In a more serious tone she added, "I would like to reach the place Arnold's at, or even further. . . . I don't think he'll ever be nominated for an Academy Award because the type of movies he makes are not for that. I do want to be nominated for an 'Oscar.' In this aspect, I'd like to surpass him."

Alonso has worked as a television actress as well. In 1989 she starred in the short-lived NBC-TV series *One of the Boys,* which told the experiences of a young Hispanic girl newly arrived in the United States.

When asked by this contributor if she enjoyed the experience, Alonso recalled: "We got ratings, but NBC didn't think it would be a long-running hit and they canceled it. I was happy because I don't want to do that type of television yet. Perhaps when I'm older, but for now I want to do my movies, my concert tours."

The entertainer's sparkling personality and witty repartee make her a favorite guest on the television talk-show circuit, where she is frequently asked about the difficulty of working in Hollywood as a Hispanic. She related to *Hispanic* magazine that when television host David Letterman once inquired if she minded playing Hispanic roles, Alonso replied, "Why not? That's what I am. The important thing is that they be good parts." When this contributor asked her if it was difficult for foreigners to find work in Hollywood, she pointed out, "It's difficult for any foreigner, but it's also difficult for someone from here. My best friend is an American actress and she works less than I. It's hard for anybody, but even more so for a foreigner." Alonso does not believe being a Hispanic makes the challenge more difficult: "I always try not to say 'for a Hispanic' because I don't believe being Hispanic has anything to do with the fact we don't get much work. It has to do with being a foreigner, to speak with a different accent, to have a different 'look.'" Reflecting on the particular obstacles for a woman in acting, Alonso stated, "There are fewer roles for women than for men. And there are two or three actresses who usually corner the female role in movies."

## Musical Talent Wins Grammy Nominations

As a singer and live performer, Alonso's musical career has kept pace with her film work. In 1988 she was nominated for Best Latin Pop Performance at the Grammy awards for the single "Otra Mentira Mas." This was her second Grammy nomination. In 1985, she was short-listed for Best Latin Artist for her self-titled album *Maria Conchita.* The record was certified platinum internationally and her previous four albums, including *O Ella o Yo,* went gold. Another album, *Hazme Sentir,* coproduced by Alonso and K. C. Porter, garnered gold records in several countries after the release of only two singles. Alonso looks forward to recording in English, but has turned down offers from two separate labels because the companies were interested in a type of music that is different from what she likes to do. She explained to this contributor: "I believe it is preferable to start off doing what one likes; it's more difficult to change to what you want later. So I haven't yet signed a contract. I'm waiting to do what I want and to be in a position in which the contract be a good one instead of simply being 'just a contract.' I'll keep at it until it does happen."

In 1991 Alonso signed a 52-show contract with Channel 13, the Mexican government's commercial TV channel, to star in *Picante!* (which means "spicy"), a weekly prime time variety program. The show, coproduced by Alonso, was conceived and shaped to showcase her many talents—singing, dancing, acting, comedy, and interviewing guest stars. Because it coincided with the series' debut, and because she "felt like it," she appeared in the December 1991 issue of *Playboy, Mexico* which, according to Alonso, ran a set of "sexy but not nude" photos. Alonso had rejected prior offers from *Playboy, USA* because "they show more." In addition to her television work, Alonso created her first video in 1992. The dance and fitness program was released in Spanish as *Bailalo Caliente!* and in English as *Dance it Up!*

Reflecting on the unique challenges of maintaining two careers, Alonso admitted, "I'm very dispersed. My dedication is placed in many things." She also feels she's sacrificed some of her Hispanic career by doing American movies: "Yes, I've lost some ground. My name in the Hispanic market has maintained itself, but I've lost in the sense that other artists in the Latin market, for instance singers, that's all they do. And they spend 24 hours a day, 12 months a year doing that—their record, their concert tour, their promotions. They dedicate their mind, their energy, everything exclusively towards that goal. Same thing with Hispanic soap opera actors. They do one soap here, another there. That's the only thing they do. Instead I do too many things. . . . So, of course, I've probably lost some following. . . . In my movies, in my television program, in records, in modeling, in other side businesses I have."

Managing careers on two continents and in two diverse fields requires a discipline that Alonso explained to this contributor: "Patience and perseverance, and believing in yourself." And she offered this insight: "It [is] important not to have a big ego. No Hispanic artist is likely to be valued or respected in the American market as they are valued and respected in the Hispanic market. That's why the majority of Latin stars don't do anything in the U.S. Because they can be a big star elsewhere, but be a nobody here. An artist's ego is very big and they can't take the rejection. I think you need a very tranquil ego, very controlled. You also have to be a hard worker."

## Speaking Out Brings Risks and Rewards

Both the Hispanic entertainment community and Hollywood insiders have labeled the multi-faceted artist a true fighter. Frank and outspoken, her free-spirited image tends to belie the intensity of her mission. This contributor asked Alonso if she ever fears that being vocal could bring negative repercussions to her career. As always, Alonso replied honestly: "I'd probably be very unhappy were I to shut my mouth. I never think of what could happen. If I considered the consequences, I maybe wouldn't do many things. But instead, I prefer simply to behave as I feel at that moment and forget about what could happen. And then, when things do happen, I think 'I blew it!'"

Alonso does concede that her maverick spirit has lost her some movie roles. She explained in an interview: "I find that my personality—because I am a bit rebellious, very spontaneous, very open—many producers don't see beyond that. I've had problems in getting certain roles because they don't realize that my personality can be the way it is, but as soon as I begin to act I can become whatever I want to be. It doesn't matter how I am in my daily life; what I can do as an artist is something else. When I act, I can become whatever my role requires."

Alonso's professional choices are not based on money but on personal instinct. Often one path is pitted against another. But she insists "that's the way it is and I don't want to change." She is constantly becoming involved in new projects, even in the business end of "show-business." A savvy entrepreneur, Alonso has formed a production company to develop film and television properties, in English and Spanish.

Alonso acknowledged that an important part of her success is that "I've always been 'Latina,' but with a very European mentality. My mother was an adventurer, very daring. She did not become a performer because her family wouldn't let her. My father had also been quite an adventurer and he told me to launch myself; that while one has health, energy and strength, one can conquer the world. The family's support is the most important." And what will happen the day Maria Conchita Alonso accomplishes all her goals? With her customary honesty Alonso reflected for a moment and told this contributor: "Then I'll semi-retire. There's a conflict within me. I want to work in this business because I adore my career. But I also suffer a lot. There are many lonely and sad moments. So, even though I don't think I'll completely give up my career, I will slow down in order to have a life with my man, or for whatever other reasons." Maria Conchita Alonso—beauty queen, pop-rock singer, television star, film actress, business executive—declared to this contributor that she prefers to be known "as an all-around entertainer. As someone who can do it all. An artist."

## SELECTED DISCOGRAPHY:

*Maria Conchita,* 1985.
*O Ella o Yo,* c. late 1980s.
*Hazme Sentir,* EMI Latin, c. late 1980s.
*En Vivo-Mexico,* Capitol/EMI Latin, 1992.
*Grandes Exitos,* Polygram Latino, 1993.
*De Coleccion,* Polygram Latino, 1994.

## SELECTED VIDEOGRAPHY:

*Moscow on the Hudson,* 1984.
*Fear City,* 1985.
*A Fine Mess,* 1986.
*Touch and Go,* 1986.
*Blood Ties,* 1987.
*Extreme Prejudice,* 1987.
*The Running Man,* 1987.
*Colors,* 1988.
*Vampire's Kiss,* 1988.
*Predator II,* 1990.
*McBain,* 1991.
*Teamster Boss: The Jackie Presser Story,* 1992.

## SOURCES:

### Periodicals

*Hispanic,* May 1989, pp. 14–16.
*Hispanic Business,* July 1992, p. 22.
*Los Angeles Times,* August 9, 1986.
*Time,* July 11, 1988, p. 72.

### Other

Alonso, Maria Conchita, interviews with Elena Kellner, February 1992 and May 1992.

—*Sketch by Elena Kellner*

# Linda Alvarado
## 1951-
### Hispanic American business owner

Linda Alvarado doesn't believe in following any traditional paths. As the only girl in a family of six children, she was accustomed to "hanging out with the guys." Years later, she is still doing so as president of the Denver-based general contracting firm Alvarado Construction, Inc., and part owner of the Colorado Rockies major league baseball team. In fields usually dominated by white males, Alvarado is one of only a few female executives; in addition, she has made history as the first Hispanic owner of a major league baseball team.

Born Linda G. Martinez, she grew up in Albuquerque, New Mexico. Her father worked for the Atomic Energy Commission, and her mother was a homemaker. "It was a very positive environment," Alvarado told Carol Hopkins in a telephone interview. "Even though I was the only girl, the expectation for me was no different." She credits her parents with giving her "huge doses" of confidence and self-esteem and encouraging her to excel both in the classroom and in athletics. Active in both high school and college sports, she lettered in girls' basketball, volleyball, and softball and also ran track.

### Launches Career in Construction Industry

Alvarado says she entered the construction industry "by default." After graduating from California's Pomona College, she was briefly employed at the botanical gardens, where she "overwatered and drowned all the plants." She then took a job with a California development company as a contract administrator and learned all phases of the construction business, from preparing bids to assembling a contract. When interest rates skyrocketed, her employer decided to form a construction management group to speed up the process of getting new projects under way. Alvarado was transferred to the construction group, and to her surprise, she liked it. She then went back to school and took classes in estimating, blueprint, and critical path method scheduling to expand her knowledge of the business.

In 1974, she and a partner established the Martinez Alvarado Construction Management Corporation. Within two years, she bought out her partner and soon became a general contractor. Now known as Alvarado Construction, Inc., the company boasts a list of accomplishments that includes dozens of projects such as commercial buildings, high-rise offices, a convention center, and airport hangars. "I love what I do," enthuses Alvarado. She especially enjoys following a project from concept to construction. "There is enormous satisfaction knowing that one started from ground zero and successfully completed the project, something of great permanence and beauty."

### Joins Ranks of Major League Baseball Team Owners

Outside the world of construction, Alvarado is a partner in the Colorado Rockies, a major league baseball franchise which began play in 1993. When asked why she chose to become involved in baseball, she says she wanted to show that women can get involved in nontraditional fields. "I am entering it with money that I earned as an entrepreneur," she explains. "That is important, that we [women] participate in big business." Alvarado was also drawn to baseball because she views it as one sport where Hispanics have enjoyed tremendous success. "There are so many role models in [baseball]," she says. "I think [having a Hispanic team owner] brings the sport full circle."

As Alvarado reflects on her career, she believes her greatest challenge has been changing people's attitudes. "There is a perception that you had to be 6'2", burly, and have muscles like Popeye's to be a contractor," she notes. "These are myths. [It has sometimes been a problem] finding men who would forget the myths, men who know that this is a business that requires brains, not just brawn." She admits there are still "pockets of resistance," but they are gradually disappearing.

In the future, Alvarado envisions becoming more involved with development. "Our core business will always be construction. We're just finding new applications like design-build projects or turnkey projects. We're positioning ourselves so that if the construction industry changes and financing shrinks, we're not going to be inflexible."

Alvarado is a member of several Fortune 500 corporate boards. When she has had occasion to resign from a directorship, she recommends another Hispanic or a woman to replace her. "I'm not there because I'm good," she explains. "I'm there because someone ahead of me was great."

### SOURCES:

#### Periodicals

*Minority Business Entrepreneur,* July/August, 1989.

#### Other

Additonal information for this profile was obtained by a *DHB* telephone interview with Linda Alvarado, September 15, 1992.

*—Sketch by Carol Hopkins*

# Julia Alvarez
## 19??-
### Dominican American novelist and poet

In her poetry and prose, Julia Alvarez has expressed her feelings about her immigration to the United States. She was born in New York City of Dominican parents, who returned to their native land with their newborn daughter. After her family's reimmigration to the United States when Alvarez was ten, she and her sisters struggled to find a place for themselves in their new world. Alvarez has used her dual experience

*Julia Alvarez*

as a starting point for the exploration of culture through writing. Her most notable work, *How the Garcia Girls Lost Their Accents*, fictionally discusses her life in the two countries and the hardships her family faced as immigrants. Apparently the culmination of many years of effort, the 15 stories which make up the novel offer entertaining insights for a wide variety of potential readers that includes both Hispanics and non-Hispanics.

## Background in the Dominican Republic

Reminiscing about her youth in an article in *American Scholar,* Alvarez wrote, "Although I was raised in the Dominican Republic by Dominican parents in an extended Dominican family, mine was an American childhood." Her family lived close to her mother's family. Life was somewhat communal; Alvarez and her sisters were brought up along with their cousins and supervised by her mother, maids, and many aunts. Although her own family was not as well off as some of their relatives, Alvarez did not feel inferior. Her father, a doctor who ran the nearby hospital, had met her mother while she was attending school in the United States. While such extravagances as shopping trips to America were beyond their financial means, Alvarez's family was highly influenced by American attitudes and goods. Alvarez and her sisters attended the American school, and for a special treat, ate ice cream from the American ice cream parlor. The entire extended family was ob-

sessed with America; to the children, it was a fantasy land.

As Alvarez acknowledges in her article in *American Scholar,* her family's association with the United States may have saved her father's life. The members of her mother's family were respected because of their ties with America. Alvarez's uncles had attended Ivy League colleges, and her grandfather was a cultural attaché to the United Nations. The dictator of the Dominican Republic, **Rafael Leonidas Trujillo Molina**, could not victimize a family with such strong American ties. However, when Alvarez's father secretly joined the forces attempting to oust Trujillo, the police set up surveillance of his home. It was rumored that, respected family or not, her father was soon to be apprehended. An American agent and the offer of a fellowship at a New York hospital helped the family escape the country. Describing the scene as their plane landed in the United States in *American Scholar,* Alvarez wrote, "All my childhood I had dressed like an American, eaten American foods, and befriended American children. I had gone to an American school and spent most of the day speaking and reading English. At night, my prayers were full of blond hair and blue eyes and snow. . . . All my childhood I had longed for this moment of arrival. And here I was, an American girl, coming home at last."

## American Experiences

Alvarez's homecoming was not what she had expected it to be. Although she was thrilled to be back in America, she would soon face homesickness, alienation, and prejudice. She missed her cousins, her family's large home, and the respect her family name demanded. Alvarez, her parents, and her sisters squeezed themselves and their possessions into a tiny apartment. As she related to *Brújula Compass,* the experience was like a crash: "The feeling of loss caused a radical change in me. It made me an introverted little girl." Alvarez became an avid reader, immersing herself in books and, eventually, writing.

Alvarez went on to college. She earned undergraduate and graduate degrees in literature and writing and became an English professor at Middlebury College in Vermont. She received grants from the National Endowment for the Arts and The Ingram Merrill Foundation in addition to a PEN Oakland/Josephine Miles Award for excellence in multicultural literature. She published several collections of poetry including *Homecoming*, which appeared in 1984, and by 1987 she was working on a collection of stories. When Alvarez published *How the Garcia Girls Lost Their Accents* in 1991, the novel received considerable attention. The past decade had seen a surge of ethnic novels, and *Garcia Girls* came to be known as an exemplary example of the genre.

## How the Garcia Girls Lost Their Accents

Rather than a straight narrative, *How the Garcia Girls Lost Their Accents* is a reverse-chronological order series of 15 interwoven stories chronicling four sisters and their parents. A comparison with Alvarez's article in *American Scholar* suggests that these stories are based on her own experience; like her family, the Garcia family is Dominican and displaced in America. Like Alvarez and her sisters, the Garcia girls struggle to adapt to their new environment and assimilate themselves into the American culture.

The first group of stories is dated "1989–1972." Thus, the novel's first story seems to be its ending. Entitled, "Antojos," which is Spanish for "cravings," this story is a memory of one of the sisters, Yolanda, and her return to the Dominican as an adult. Yolanda—whose story ends the novel and who acts as Alvarez's alter ego—has secretly decided to make her home there, having found life in the United States unfulfilling. When she ignores the warnings of her wealthy relatives and drives into the country for the guava fruit she has been craving, she faces disappointment. She is regarded as an American despite her native roots, and although she finds her guavas, her romantic journey is marred by her feelings as an outsider. Alvarez ends this story ambiguously—similar to the rest of the stories. The attempts of Yolanda and her sisters to lead successful lives in the United States are presented more as memory fragments than stories with definite beginnings and endings.

The next story focuses on Sofia, the youngest of the girls. At this point, however, the four girls are women, with husbands and careers. The details of Sofia's break with her father over her decision to take a lover before marriage are presented, and the events at a birthday party she prepared for her father are recounted. Sofia cannot be totally forgiven, nor can she ever return to the Dominican Republic; in the process of becoming an American girl of the 1960s, she has gone beyond the moral limits imposed by her father, who personifies life in the old world.

The third story relates some background information as it reveals a mother's perceptions of her four girls. During a family gathering, Mami tells her favorite story about each of the girls, and the reader learns that Sandi spent time in a mental institution after almost starving herself to death. The fourth story about Yolanda reveals that she too had a mental breakdown of her own after a failed relationship, and in the next story she becomes the narrator. In "The Rudy Elmenhurst Story," Yolanda's tale of her reluctance to sleep with the dashing young man she loved because of his casual approach to the matter explains her ensuing trouble with men as well as her problems

assimilating into American youth culture: "Catholic or not, I still thought it a sin for a guy to just barge in five years later with a bottle of expensive wine and assume you'd drink out of his hand. A guy who had ditched me, who had haunted my sexual awakening with a nightmare of self-doubt. For a moment as I watched him get in his car and drive away, I felt a flash of that old self-doubt."

The memories in the second section of the novel recall the years from 1960 to 1970. The girls are younger, and they are experiencing their first years as immigrants. Attempts they made to reconcile themselves to their new culture are challenged by their parents, who want their children to "mix with the 'right kind' of Americans," and the girls are threatened with having to spend time on the island, which they have come to dread. In this section, the girls save their sister from a macho cousin's imposition, a pervert exposes himself to Carla, and Yolanda sees snow for the first time and thinks it is fall-out from a nuclear bomb.

The final story in this section, "Floor Show," focuses on Sandi's perception of events as the family spends a scandalous evening with an American doctor and his drunkenly indiscreet wife in a Spanish restaurant. Sandi is shocked and upset when this woman kisses her father and later dances with the flamenco dancers that the young girl had so admired. Cautioned by her mother to behave at the important dinner, Sandi does as she is told and stays quiet until she is offered a flamenco doll by the American woman, who seems to understand her desire for it. 'Sandi was not going to miss her chance. This woman had kissed her father. This woman had ruined the act of the beautiful dancers. The way Sandi saw it, this woman owed her something." The woman gave Sandi something more than the doll; her smile "intimated the things Sandi was just beginning to learn, things that the dancers knew all about, which was why they danced with such vehemence, such passion."

In third and final section, "1960–1956," America is still a dream—the family is still on the island. The first story is divided into two parts and recalls the family's traumatic encounter with the *guardia,* or secret police, and their subsequent flight from their home. From that moment on, the tales regress to the girls' early memories of life in the huge family compound. Yolanda tells of the presents her grandmother brought the children from America and an ensuing encounter with her cousin, Sandi recalls her art lessons and the fright she had at the instructor's home, Carla remembers the mechanical bank her father brought her from F.A.O. Schwartz in New York and the maid who desperately wanted it.

Finally, Yolanda concludes the novel with one of her earliest memories—she stole a kitten from its mother and then abandoned it, even though she had been warned by a strange hunter: "To take it away would be a violation of its natural right to live." The mother cat haunted the girl until she left the island, and, as Yolanda confides in her narration, "There are still times I wake up at three o'clock in the morning and peer into the darkness. At that hour and in that loneliness, I hear her, a black furred thing lurking in the corners of my life, her magenta mouth opening, wailing over some violation that lies at the center of my art."

The praise Alvarez received for her first novel outweighed the criticism that a new novelist often encounters. The *New York Times Book Review* found that Alvarez "beautifully captured the threshold experience of the new immigrant, where the past is not yet a memory and the future remains an anxious dream." *Hispanic*'s critic wrote, "Well-crafted, although at times overly sentimental, these stories provide a glimpse into the making of another American family with a Hispanic surname." And the *Library Journal* reported, "Alvarez is a gifted, evocative storyteller of promise."

Alvarez's second novel, *In the Time of Butterflies,* was published in 1994. This work recounts the lives and tragic end of the Mirabel sisters—Patria, Minerva, and Maria Terese (Mate)—who were assassinated after visiting their imprisoned husbands during the last days of the Trujillo regime in the Dominican Republic. Each sister in turn relates her own aspect of the narrative, beginning with their childhood and gradually defining how they came to be involved in the liberation movement. Their story is framed by that of the surviving sister, Dedé, who adds her own tale of suffering to the memory of her martyred sisters. *In the Time of Butterflies* received a favorable reaction from reviewers, some of whom admired Alvarez's ability to express the wide range of emotions brought on by the revolution. For example, the reviewer for *Publishers Weekly* observed that "Alvarez captures the terrorized atmosphere of a police state, in which people live under the sword of terrible fear and atrocities cannot be acknowledged. As the sisters' energetic fervor turns to anguish, Alvarez conveys their courage and their desperation, and the full import of the tragedy." The novel was a finalist for the National Book Critics Award in 1994. Alvarez's most recent project, a collection of poems entitled *The Other Side/El Otro Lado,* was published in 1995.

## SELECTED PUBLISHED WORKS:

*Homecoming,* Grove Press, 1984.
*How the Garcia Girls Lost Their Accents,* Algonquin Books, 1991.
*In the Time of Butterflies,* Algonquin Books, 1994.
*The Other Side/El Otro Lado,* Dutton, 1995.

## SOURCES:

*American Scholar,* Winter 1987, pp. 71–85.
*Atlanta Journal,* August 11, 1991, p. A13.
*Boston Globe,* May 26, 1991, p. A13.
*Brújula Compass* (Spanish-language; translation by Ronie-Richele Garcia-Johnson), January-February 1992, p. 16.
*Hispanic,* June 1991, p. 55.
*Los Angeles Times,* June 7, 1991, p. E4.
*Library Journal,* May 1, 1991, p. 102; August, 1994, 123.
*Más* (Spanish-language; translation by Ronie-Richele Garcia-Johnson), November-December, 1991, p. 100.
*New York Times Book Review,* October 6, 1991, p. 14.
*Nuestro,* November 1984, pp. 34+; March 1985, pp. 52+; January-February 1986, pp. 32+.
*Publishers Weekly,* April 5, 1991, p. 133; July 11, 1994, p. 62.
*School Library Journal,* Septemr 1991, p. 292.
*Washington Post,* June 20, 1991, p. D11.

*—Sketch by Ronie-Richele Garcia-Johnson*

# Linda Alvarez
## 19??-
**Mexican American television newscaster**

Every weekday afternoon at four o'clock, Linda Alvarez coanchors the news on Los Angeles television station KNBC familiar to thousands of viewers throughout southern California. Originally a teacher, she broke into television as a weather reporter in Chicago and quickly moved into the newsroom. By 1992, she had won numerous awards—including six Emmys—for her broadcast skills as well as for her contributions to the community.

Alvarez seems to have inherited her determination to excel from her family. Seeking to improve their lives, her grandparents had moved from Mexico to Los Angeles when their son Ray (Alvarez's father) was just six years old. To earn a living, they made tamales and sold them from their car to workers in the city's garment district; in time, they saved enough money to open a restaurant.

Ray Alvarez was as determined to succeed as his parents. After graduating from high school, he joined the navy and worked as a mechanic during World War II in the Pacific theater. Upon his return to the United States, the new citizen worked as a mechanic in a gas station, then became the station's manager and later its owner. Around the same time, he met and married Margarita Larios, a fourth-generation Californian of Mexican and Chilean descent. The couple's daughter, Linda Alvarez, was born in her grandmother's bedroom, one mile from downtown Los Angeles.

### Close Family Bonds Nurture a Budding Talent

As a little girl, Alvarez helped her grandparents peel and tear the corn husks they used to encase their tamales, and from them she learned to work hard and take pride in her efforts. From her gregarious father she learned the value of getting along with others. And from her book-loving mother she gained an appreciation of the written word, a sense of curiosity, and the desire to travel.

Alvarez did well in the strict Catholic schools she attended as a young girl. She graduated from Venice High School at the age of sixteen and made plans to enroll in college. Although her father wanted her to be a doctor, Alvarez was unsure about her future. She thought that she shou forld understand more about the medical profession before making her decision, so she spent a year working as a receptionist in a doctor's office and earning money for college.

When Alvarez received a scholarship to attend the University of California at Los Angeles (UCLA), she decided to major in English and minor in Spanish and French. She loved to write, and because there were very few career options for women at the time, she decided to become a teacher when she graduated in 1963. She spent an additional year at UCLA earning her teaching credentials and then went to work at Venice High School. For two years, she taught English and Spanish, a job she enjoyed very much.

In her spare time after school, Alvarez taught Spanish to Peace Corps volunteers and was soon inspired to go to South America herself. In addition to teaching at the University of Carabobo in Venezuela, she set up her own English-language school.

### Wins Teaching Position at the United Nations

Upon her return to the United States, Alvarez taught English, literature, and Spanish for two years at a public school in Westchester, New York. When she heard of openings for language teachers at the United Nations, she applied but was told that instructors would be hired to teach only their native languages and that she was therefore eligible to teach English but not Spanish. Alvarez reluctantly decided to try out for a job teaching English, but just moments before she was to deliver a sample lesson to a group of students and judges, she decided to do it in Spanish instead of English, figuring she had nothing to lose. The gamble paid off; Alvarez was praised as an

exemplary teacher at the close of the auditions and was assured a job teaching Spanish.

Alvarez says that she herself learned two important lessons from that experience. The first was that she could take risks, and at several junctures in her career, she has done just that. The second lesson was even more revealing, and it has also influenced her greatly. After her audition, one of the interviewers who had expected to hear a lesson in English called Alvarez into his office and gave her a wry smile. "Do you know why you did that?" he asked, referring to her impromptu Spanish lesson. Alvarez was still too surprised at her own boldness to reply, so the interviewer answered the question himself. "You like who you are when you are speaking Spanish," he said. With that simple observation, he verbalized something that Alvarez had never consciously realized, and she has not forgotten his words.

After a "wonderful" two-year stint teaching at the United Nations, Alvarez moved on. During a period when she was teaching in Hartford, Connecticut, throughout the regular school year, she spent a summer in Mexico City teaching at the Universidad Autonoma Nacional. She then went on to work for the Department of Health, Education, and Welfare in Chicago as a director of an adult basic education program in which immigrants were taught "survival" English.

### Makes First Television Appearances in Chicago

While Alvarez was working in Chicago, one of her friends, the producer of the bilingual talk show *Nosotros* on Chicago's WTTW, noticed that she had no accent when she spoke either Spanish or English. The station offered her the chance to make public service announcements in both languages once a week, for which she was paid six dollars.

In addition to gaining media experience, Alvarez began to attract attention. Officials at Chicago's NBC-TV affiliate, WMAQ, let her know they had an opening for a weather person at their station. Although Alvarez had always enjoyed watching the news on television, she had never considered a career in the media; she certainly did not envision herself becoming the stereotypical "weather girl." But her supervisor pointed out that the weather reporting position could serve as a stepping-stone to other opportunities. She noted that Alvarez enjoyed teaching, and as a news reporter she would have the opportunity to inform and instruct thousands of people. That advice convinced Alvarez to try for the position, which she won.

But Alvarez knew that she had a lot of work to do if she wanted to become a bona fide news reporter. First, she had to excel as a weather person. Uncomfortable with the idea of giving weather reports without knowing what actually caused the conditions she was discussing, she began to study meteorology. And since she knew that she needed experience as a reporter, she asked endless questions of her colleagues and followed them around town on their assignments on her own time. Within six months, the woman whose knees had knocked during her first weather reports was hired as a reporter on a new news program at WMAQ. In another six months, Alvarez became cohost of a live, 90-minute, on-location talk show called *Chicago Camera*. She spent three and a half years on the show and in the process learned how to think on her feet, how to interview, and how to condense ideas.

Still determined to make it as a news reporter, however, Alvarez took a 50 percent pay cut to move to Los Angeles and cohost KNBC's *The Saturday Show*. Then a television station in Phoenix contacted her about an opening as a general assignment reporter, and once again she decided to take yet another pay cut to accept the position. Within six months, she was an anchor for the five o'clock news. Within another year, she was reporting for the ten o'clock broadcasts as well, and within two years, she was an anchor for weekday news broadcasts at five o'clock, six o'clock, and ten o'clock. By 1983 Alvarez had also begun to produce documentaries on issues that were yet to become talk-show standards, including AIDS, sexual abuse, and gun control. On a more personal note, it was during her seven and a half years in Phoenix that she met and married cameraman Bill Timmer.

### Wins Coveted Coanchor Spot

In August 1985, Alvarez was offered a position back in Los Angeles with KNBC-TV as a weekend coanchor. Pleased with the chance to return to her hometown as well as further her career, Alvarez accepted the offer. Before long she was coanchoring a half-hour weekday newscast at six o'clock. She held this position from September of 1986, until April of 1988, when she was promoted to an hour-long coanchor spot weekdays at four o'clock.

Alvarez's work for KNBC has been very exciting. She reported on the Mexico City earthquake from the Mexican capital in 1985, the Los Angeles earthquake in 1987, and the San Francisco Bay area earthquakes in 1989. She also covered Pope John Paul II's visit to Los Angeles and even traveled to Seoul, South Korea, to report on the 1988 Summer Olympic Games. In addition, she was the first American television journalist to interview Mexican President **Carlos Salinas de Gortari** at length at the presidential palace in Mexico City. Alvarez has also prepared a number of special programs for KNBC. One of these, a public affairs series entitled "Health Fax," won an Emmy Award in 1988.

Some of Alvarez's most satisfying pieces, however, are those she creates with the people of southern California. When she finds the opportunity to do so, she likes to report on minorities who are dedicated to helping their communities, especially young, inner-city teenagers who are working to make a difference in their neighborhoods. She is especially proud of a series of stories she did that focus on youths who have managed to "beat the odds," noting that such pieces combat stereotypes by allowing viewers to see aspects of the city's people that are usually ignored by the media.

### Reaches Out to Young Hispanic Women

Given Alvarez's commitment to cover such stories, it is not surprising that she contributes to her community during her free time as well. Despite her busy schedule, she makes a point of serving on the boards of the YMCA of Metropolitan Los Angeles, the National Conference of Christians and Jews, Big Sisters of Los Angeles, and the Neighborhood Youth Association. She also speaks quite frequently to groups of young women in junior high school and high school about her life, her career, and the importance of setting goals and seeking help from those with more experience. In her talks, Alvarez credits her family, as well as the scholarship she received to attend UCLA, for giving her a "wonderful background." As she explained to interviewer Ronie-Richele Garcia-Johnson, "I don't think of myself as a minority. I think of myself as a Hispanic woman who has learned the value of working hard from [her family] and working smart from school.... I can choose what I want to do." Alvarez hopes that by sharing her own story with young women, she can encourage them to set goals and do the work necessary to achieve them.

Alvarez's professional and personal contributions have not gone unrecognized. By 1992, she had won a total of six Emmy awards, the Ruben Salazar Media Award, several press club awards for news series and documentary reports, and certificates of commendation from Women in Communications, Women in Radio and Television, and the National Association of Hispanic Journalists, to name just a few. Alvarez has also been honored with the 1988 Silver Achievement Award for communications from the YWCA, the 1989 and 1990 John Swett Award for media excellence in education reporting from the California Teachers Association, and a 1991 award for professional achievement and community service from the Women's Council and the Mexican American Legal Defense and Educational Fund (MALDEF). In 1992, Alvarez was lauded by the Variety Boys and Girls club and named as a Golden Woman of the Year.

**SOURCES:**

Alvarez, Linda, interview with Ronie-Richele Garcia-Johnson, September 1, 1992.

— *Sketch by Ronie-Richele Garcia-Johnson*

# Luis Alvarez
## 1911-1988
### Hispanic American physicist

*Luis Alvarez*

Luis Alvarez's scientific contributions to the military during World War II included the development of a narrow beam radar system that allows airplanes to land in inclement weather. He was also involved in the Manhattan Project to develop the world's first nuclear weapons. One of Alvarez's more controversial theories involved the possibility of a massive collision of a meteorite with the earth 65 million years ago, an event that Alvarez believed may account for the disappearance of the dinosaurs. Among the many honors that Alvarez received was the 1968 Nobel Prize for physics for his development of giant bubble chambers used to detect a variety of subatomic particles.

Luis Walter Alvarez was born in San Francisco, California, on June 13, 1911. His father, Dr. Walter Clement Alvarez, was a medical researcher at the University of California at San Francisco and also maintained a private practice. Luis's mother was the former Harriet Skidmore Smythe. His grandfather Alvarez was born in Spain but ran away to Cuba, and later made a fortune in Los Angeles real estate before moving to Hawaii and then to San Francisco. Luis's mother's family, originally from Ireland, established a missionary school in Foochow, China. Alvarez's parents met while studying at the University of California at Berkeley.

Alvarez attended grammar school in San Francisco and enrolled in the city's Polytechnic High School, where he avidly studied science. When his father accepted a position at the prestigious Mayo Clinic, the family moved to Rochester, Minnesota. Alvarez reported in his autobiography *Alvarez: Adventures of a Physicist,* that his science classes at Rochester High School were "adequately taught [but] not very interesting." Dr. Alvarez noticed his son's growing interest in physics and hired one of the Mayo Clinic's machinists to give Luis private lessons on weekends. Alvarez enrolled at the University of Chicago in 1928 and planned to major in chemistry. He was especially interested in organic chemistry, but soon came to despise the mandatory chemistry laboratories. Alvarez "discovered" physics in his junior year and enrolled in a laboratory course, "Advanced Experimental Physics: Light" about which he later wrote in his autobiography: "It was love at first sight." He changed his major to physics and received his B.S. in 1932. Alvarez stayed at Chicago for his graduate work and his assigned advisor was Nobel Laureate Arthur Compton, whom Alvarez considered "the ideal graduate advisor for me" because he visited Alvarez's laboratory only once during his graduate career and "usually had no idea how I was spending my time."

Alvarez earned his bachelor's, master's, and doctoral degrees at the University of Chicago. His doctoral dissertation concerned the diffraction of light, a topic considered relatively trivial, but his other graduate work proved to be more useful. In one series of experiments, for example, he and some colleagues discovered the "east-west effect" of cosmic rays, which explained that the number of cosmic rays reaching the earth's atmosphere differed depending on the direction from which they came. The east-west effect was evidence that cosmic rays consist of some kind of positively charged particles. A few days after passing his oral examinations for the Ph.D. degree, Alvarez married Geraldine Smithwick, a senior at the University of Chicago, with whom he later had two children, Walter and Jean. Less than a month after their wedding Alvarez accepted a position at the University of California, Berkeley, where Luis became a research scientist with Nobel Prize-winning physicist Ernest O. Lawrence, and initiated an association with the University of California that was to continue for forty-two years.

Alvarez soon earned the title "prize wild idea man" from his colleagues because of his involvement in such a wide variety of research activities. Within his first year at Berkeley, he discovered the process of K-electron capture, in which some atomic nuclei decay by absorbing one of the electrons in its first orbital (part of the nuclear shell). Alvarez and a student, Jake Wiens, also developed a mercury vapor lamp mercury vapor lamp consisting of the artificial isotope mercury–198. The wavelength of the light emitted by the lamp was adopted as the official standard of length by the U.S. Bureau of Standards. In his research with Nobel Prize-winning physicist Felix Bloch, Alvarez developed a method for producing a beam of slow moving neutrons, a method that was used to determine the magnetic moment of neutrons (the extent to which they affect a magnetic field). Just after the outbreak of World War II in Europe, Alvarez discovered tritium, a radioactive isotope (a variant atom containing a different number of protons) of hydrogen.

## World War II Research Leads to Atomic Bomb

World War II interrupted Alvarez's work at Berkeley. In 1940 he began research for the military at Massachusetts Institute of Technology's (MIT's) radiation laboratory on radar (radio detecting and ranging) systems. Over the next three years, he was involved in the development of three new types of radar systems. The first made use of a very narrow radar beam to allow a ground-based controller to direct the "blind" landing of an airplane. The second system, code-named "Eagle," was a method for locating and bombing objects on the ground when they could not be seen by a pilot. The third invention became known as the microwave early-warning system, a mechanism for collecting images of aircraft movement in overcast skies.

In 1943, Alvarez left MIT to join the Manhattan Project research team working in Los Alamos, New Mexico. His primary accomplishment with the team was developing the detonating device used for the first plutonium bomb. Alvarez flew in the B–29 bomber that observed the first test of an atomic device at Alamogordo, south of Los Alamos. Three weeks later, Alvarez was aboard another B–29 following the bomber "Enola Gay" as it dropped the first atomic bomb on Hiroshima, Japan. Like most scientists associated with the Manhattan Project, Alvarez was stunned and horrified by the destructiveness of the weapon he had helped to create. Nonetheless, he never expressed any doubts or hesitation about the decision to use the bombs, since they brought a swift end to the war. Alvarez became one of a small number of scientists who felt strongly that the United States should continue its nuclear weapons development after the war and develop a fusion (hydrogen) bomb as soon as possible.

After the war, Alvarez returned to Berkeley where he had been promoted to full professor. Determining that the future of nuclear physics lay in high energy research, he focused his research on powerful particle accelerators—devices that accelerate electrons and protons to high velocity. His first project was to design and construct a linear accelerator for use with protons. Although his machine was similar in some ways to the electron accelerators that had been available for many years, the proton machine posed a number of new problems. By 1947, however, Alvarez had solved those problems and his forty foot long proton accelerator began operation.

## Particle Accelerator Research Results in Nobel Prize

Over the next decade, the science of particle physics (the study of atomic components) developed rapidly at Berkeley. An important factor in that progress was the construction of the 184-inch synchrocyclotron at the university's radiation laboratory. The synchrocyclotron was a modified circular particle accelerator capable of achieving much greater velocities than any other type of accelerator. The science of particle physics involves two fundamental problems: creation of particles to be studied in some type of accelerator and detection and identification of those particles. After 1950, Alvarez's interests shifted from the first to the second of these problems, particle detection, because of a chance meeting in 1953 with University of Michigan physicist Donald Glaser. Glaser had recently invented the bubble chamber, a device that detects particles as they pass through a container of superheated fluid. As the particles move through the liquid, they form ions that act as nuclei on which the superheated material can begin to boil, thereby forming a track of tiny bubbles that shows the path taken by the particles. In talking with Glaser, Alvarez realized that the bubble chamber could be refined and improved to track the dozens of new particles then being produced in Berkeley's giant synchrocyclotron. Among these particles were some with very short lifetimes known as resonance states.

Improving Glaser's original bubble chamber involved a number of changes. First, Alvarez decided that liquid hydrogen would be a more sensitive material to use than the diethyl ether employed by Glaser. In addition, he realized that sophisticated equipment would be needed to respond to and record the resonance states that often lasted no more than a billionth of a second. The equipment he developed included relay systems that transmitted messages at high speeds and computer programs that could sort out significant from insignificant events and then analyze the former. Finally, Alvarez aimed at constructing larger and larger bubble chambers to record a greater number of events. Over a period of about five years, Alvarez's chambers grew from a simple one inch glass tube to his most ambitious instrument, a seventy-two inch chamber that was first put into use in 1959. With these devices, Alvarez eventually discovered dozens of new elementary particles, including the unusual resonance states.

The significance of Alvarez's work with bubble chambers was recognized in 1968 when he was awarded the Nobel Prize for physics. At the awards ceremony in Stockholm, the Swedish Academy of Science's Sten von Friesen told Alvarez that, because of his work with the bubble chamber, "entirely new possibilities for research into high-energy physics present themselves. . . . Practically all the discoveries that have been made in this important field [of particle physics] have been possible only through the use of methods developed by Professor Alvarez." Alvarez attended the Nobel ceremonies with his second wife, Janet Landis, whom he married in 1958. Largely as a result of their war-related separation, Alvarez and his first wife had divorced. With Janet, Alvarez had two more children, Donald and Helen.

### Examines Dinosaurs' Demise

Advancing years failed to reduce Alvarez's curiosity on a wide range of topics. In 1965 he was in charge of a joint Egyptian-American expedition whose goal was to search for hidden chambers in the pyramid of King Kefren at Giza. The team aimed high energy muons (subatomic particles produced by cosmic rays) at the pyramid to look for regions of low density which would indicate possible chambers. However, none were found. Alvarez shared the last major scientific achievement with his son Walter, who was then a professor of geology at Berkeley. In 1980, the Alvarezes accidentally discovered a band of sedimentary rock in Italy that contained an unusually high level of the rare metal iridium. Dating techniques set the age of the layer at about 65 million years. The Alvarezes hypothesized that the iridium came from an asteroid that struck the earth, thereby sending huge volumes of smoke and dust (including the iridium) into the earth's atmosphere. They suggested that the cloud produced by the asteroid's impact covered the planet for an extended period of time, blocked out sunlight, and caused the widespread death of plant life on earth's surface. The lost of plant life in turn, they theorized, brought about the extinction of dinosaurs who fed on the plants. While the theory has found favor among many scientists and has been confirmed to some extent by additional findings, it is still the subject of debate.

Alvarez's hobbies included flying, golf, music, and inventing. He made his last flight in his Cessna 310 in 1984, almost exactly 50 years after he first learned to fly. In 1963 he assisted the Warren Commission in the investigation of President John F. Kennedy's assassination. Among his inventions were a system for color television and an electronic indoor golf-training device developed for President Eisenhower. In all, he held 22 patents for his inventions. Alvarez died of cancer in Berkeley, on September 1, 1988.

### SELECTED PUBLISHED WORKS:

*Alvarez: Adventures of a Physicist,* Basic Books, 1987.

### SOURCES:

*The Annual Obituary, 1988,* edited by Janet Podell, St. Martin's, 1988, pp. 411-13.
*Current Biography 1947,* H. W. Wilson, 1947, pp. 9–10.
*Current Biography 1988,* H. W. Wilson, 1988, p. 88.
Daintith, John, et al., *A Biographical Encyclopedia of Scientists,* Volume 1, Facts on File, 1981.
*McGraw-Hill Modern Scientists and Engineers,* Volume 1, McGraw-Hill, 1980, pp. 12–13.
*Nobel Lectures in Physics, 1963–1970,* Elsevier, 1972, pp. 291–92.
*Nobel Prize Winners,* edited by Wasson Tyler, H. W. Wilson, 1987, p. 12–14.
Weber, Robert L., *Pioneers of Science: Nol Prize Winners in Physics,* American Institute of Physics, 1980, pp. 212-14.

*—Sketch by David E. Newton*

# Angeles Alvario de Leira
## 1916-
### Spanish American marine scientist

Angeles Alvarino de Leira, known professionally as Dr. Angeles Alvarino, is a fishery research biologist and marine scientist. For more than four decades, she has made an immense contribution to knowledge about marine zooplankton, and its ecology and geographic distribution. During the course of her work, she has discovered 22 new ocean species.

Alvarino was born on October 3, 1916, in El Ferrol, Spain to Antonio Alvarino Grimaldos and Maria del Carmen Gonzales Diaz-Saavedra de Alvarino. An intelligent, curious child, Alvarino often enjoyed her physician-father's library, including his volumes on natural history. She aspired to become a physician herself, but her father discouraged such a choice. He did not want her to experience, as he had, the pain associated with patients whose suffering could not be alleviated.

Alvarino studied a wide range of courses in physical and natural sciences, social science, and humanities during her undergraduate years from 1930 to 1933 at the Lycee. After passing final examinations and completing two dissertations for baccalaureate degrees in both science and letters, she graduated summa cum laude in 1933 from the University of Santiago de Compostela, Spain.

During the next year, Alvarino's desire to study medicine persisted, but her father's viewpoint remained unchanged. Therefore, she entered the University of Madrid in 1934 to study natural sciences. Her studies were interrupted when the University was closed during the Spanish Civil War (1936–39).

In 1940 Alvarino married Sir Eugenio Leira Manso, Captain of the Spanish Royal Navy and Knight of the Royal and Military Order of Saint Hermenegild. Alvarino continued her studies at the University of Madrid and in 1941 was awarded a master's degree in natural sciences. From 1941 to 1948, she taught biology, zoology, botany, and geology at various colleges in El Ferrol.

In order to do active research, Alvarino left teaching in 1948 to become a research biologist with the Spanish Department of Sea Fisheries in Madrid. That same year, in spite of a ban against women, she began to conduct research and study oceanography at the Spanish Institute of Oceanography in Madrid. The quality of her work persuaded officials to admit her as a student researcher in 1950. During those same years, academic work at the University of Madrid led in 1951 to a doctoral certificate, for which she wrote three separate theses, in experimental psychology, chemistry, and plant ecology.

An Institute appointment in 1952 as a marine biologist-oceanographer resulted from Alvarino's success in a competitive examination. In 1953 a British Council Fellowship enabled her to work on zooplankton at the Marine Biological Laboratory in Plymouth, England. At the Plymouth lab, she met Dr. F. S. Russell, who directed her attention to chaetognaths, siphonophores, and hydromedusae, in which she has never lost interest.

In the 1950s, these animals had been so little-studied that Alvarino designed and made plankton nets, which she provided to captains of Spanish fishing vessels and research ships so they could collect zooplankton samples for her research.

## New Opportunities in the United States

A Fullbright Fellowship in 1956 enabled Alvarino to conduct research in Massachusetts at the Woods Hole Oceanographic Institut e. Impressed by her work, Mary Sears, president of the first U.S. Oceanographic Congress, recommended Alvarino to Dr. Roger Revelle, the director of the Scripps Institute of Oceanography at La Jolla, California. He offered Alvarino a position as a biologist and she accepted.

Alvarino's years of research at Scripps produced a significant body of knowledge about chaetognaths, siphonophores, and hydromedusae. Her Scripps research also contributed toward completion of work toward a doctoral degree at the University of Madrid, which awarded her a Doctor of Sciences degree in 1967, summa cum laude.

To expand her research opportunities further, Alvarino accepted a position as a fisheries biologist in 1970 with the Southwest Fisheries Science Center (SWFSC) in La Jolla, a division of the newly formed National Marine Fisheries Service. There, she continued research on predatory chaetognaths, siphonophores, and hydromedusae and their relationship to larval fish survival.

Although she officially retired in 1987, Alvarino continues her work, adding to the body of knowledge about zooplankton she has already compiled. She has shed light on how zooplankton relate to the dynamics of the oceanic environment and about which ones are "indicator species," those species associated with specific currents or concentrations of other aquatic life, including spawning fish and their eggs and larvae.

On July 23, 1993, Alvarino was awarded the Great Silver Medal of Galici a by King Juan Carlos I and Queen Sophia of Spain. She participated in numerous expeditions aboard research vessels of several countries, and was the first woman to serve as a scientist aboard a British research vessel.

Alvarino and her husband live in La Jolla. Their only child, Angeles Leira-Alvarino, is an architect and city planner. In addition to her first love, marine science, Alvarino enjoys classical music, literature, and art. She believes visual art and music in their clarity are "the best expression of the human being."

## SELECTED PUBLISHED WORKS:

"The Depth Distribution, Relative Abundance and Structure of the Population of the Chaetognatha, *Sagitta Scrippsae*," Alvarino, 1962, in the

California Current off California and Baja California," *Anales del Instituto de Ciencias del Mar y Limnologia,* Universidad Nacional Autonoma de Mexico, 1983, pp. 47–84.

*Atlantic Chaetognatha, Distribution and Essential Notes of Systematics,* Travaux Spanish Institute of Oceanography, 1969.

*Siphonophores of the Pacific; with a Revision of the World Distribution,* Bulletin Scripps Institution of Oceanography, University of California Press, 1971.

'The Relation Between the Distribution of Zooplankton Predators and Engraulis Mordax (Anchovy) Larvae," *California Cooperative Oceanic Fisheries Investigations Reports,* 1980, pp. 150–60.

"Chaetognatha, Oogenesis, Ovopostion, and Oosorption," in *Reproductive Biology of Invertebrates,* edited by K. G. and R. G. Adiyodi, Vol. I, pp. 585–610, John Wiley & Sons Ltd., 1983.

"Chaetognatha, Spermatogenesis and Sperm Function," in *Reproductive Biology of Invertebrates,* Vol. II, pp. 531–44, John Wiley & Sons Ltd., 1983.

"Abundance of Zooplankton Species, Females and Males, Eggs and Larvae of Holoplanktonic Species. Zooplankton Assemblages and Changes in Zooplankton Communities Related to *Engraulis mordax* Spawning and Survival of the Larvae," *Mem. III Encontro Brasileiro de Plancton,* 1989, pp. 63–149.

"Fertilization, Development and Parental Care in Chaetognatha," in *Reproductive Biology of Invertebrates,* edited by K. G. and R. G. Adiyody, Vol. IV, pp. 255–82, Oxford & IBH Publishing Co. PVT Ltd., 1990.

"Sexual Differentiation and Behavior in Chaetognatha. Hermaphroditi," in *Reproductive Biology of Invertebrates,* edited by K. G. and R. G. Adiyody, Vol. V, pp. 424–70, Oxford & IBH Publishing Co. PVT Ltd. 1992.

**SOURCES:**

Biographical sketch prepared from interviews with Dr. Alvarino by Susan Smith and Connie Blair of the SWFSC Public Information staff.

*—Sketch by Margaret DiCanio*

# Rudolfo Anaya
## 1937-

**Mexican American novelist, short story writer, poet, and essayist**

Rudolfo Anaya is one of the premier Mexican American writers working today. With the publication of his award-winning novel *Bless Me, Ultima* in 1972, he established himself as a distinct voice of the Chicano people, expressing a reverence for the Mexican American culture. His writing is rich in symbolism, poetry, and spiritualism as he works to make sense of the mystery of life, his cultural heritage, and those individuals who comprise the cumulative ancestry of the southwestern United States. "If I am to be a writer, it is the ancestral voices of these people who will form a part of my quest, my search," Anaya wrote in a 1986 autobiographical sketch. "They taught me that life is fragile, that there are signs given to us, signs that we must learn to interpret."

Among those most important in his quest were his parents. His father, Martín—a man whom Anaya has described as being "without pretension"—came from a family of ranchers and cattle workers; Anaya's mother, Rafaelita (Mares) was the daughter of a poor farmer. In succeeding years, Rudolfo would struggle to understand his parents' disparate heritage in both his life and writings. The union into which Anaya was born on October 30, 1937, in the small village of Pastura, New Mexico, was the second marriage for both of his parents; Rudolfo was the fifth of their seven children. Anaya recalls his mother telling him that when he was a still a baby she put him on a sheepskin on the floor, surrounded by different objects, and he crawled directly to a pencil and a piece of paper, a first step in the long journey toward becoming a writer.

When Anaya was a young child, the family moved from Pastura to Santa Rosa, New Mexico, a thriving community on the Pecos River. His family spoke Spanish at home, and his youth was filled with references to the mystery and superstitions of the Roman Catholic faith, as well as the richness of Mexican American culture. The lines between magic, legend, religion, and reality were often obscured throughout Anaya's childhood. He found a way to make sense of them—or at least point to the truths they contain—in his writing. He populated his fiction with characters such as La Grande, based on a woman who assisted his birth and who some said had powers to cure sickness, as well as the legendary La Llorona, the tortured spirit of a woman who killed her children and went insane. Through his fiction Anaya accepted the mystery of his youth. The result is a body of work with a strange and powerful sense of the unknown.

Anaya has said that as a child he felt great freedom within a close-knit community. In Santa Rosa, he played outdoors independently and happily, but when the family moved to Albuquerque in 1952, the change from rural to city life was drastic in several ways for Anaya. In the city, he discovered various cultural and ethnic differences and he became familiar with the painful experience of racism and prejudice against Chicanos. Yet in some ways, his adolescent life was typical of many teen-age boys growing up in the 1950s, focusing on girls, cars, and music.

### Childhood Tragedy Alters Life

During this period of emerging identity, Anaya received a severe injury in a swimming accident, a pivotal event which would reshape his life. While diving with some friends, he broke two vertebrae in his neck and nearly died. His convalescence was long and painful, but an experience which he has characterized as a blessing in disguise. He became determined to recover from his injury, and after a long period he did so. After his recovery, Anaya says he felt a passion for action and pleasure he might never have had, had he not so nearly lost his life. "So who is to judge whether an adversary comes to crush us or to reshape us," he wrote. Themes from this period are incorporated into his novel *Tortuga* (1979).

Anaya graduated from Albuquerque High School in 1956, and he attended the University of New Mexico in Albuquerque. There he developed an acute sense of being a Mexican American man in a predominantly white culture. His formal education had provided him with little or no understanding of the history of his culture, and he now longed for a sense of identity. To combat his feelings of isolation and alienation, Anaya went through a period of cathartic writing, much of which he has since destroyed, but which he credits with helping him to develop his own set of values. In 1963, he received his bachelor of arts degree in English, and took a teaching position in a small New Mexico town. Three years later, he married Patricia Lawless, whom he has credited with supporting his desire to become a writer, as well as being a fine editor.

While working as a teacher, Anaya tried to write a novel. Early on, he found himself struggling to find his stylistic voice: "I was still haunted by the voices of my childhood, and I had to capture the memory of those times and people," he recalled, "But I was still imitating a style and mode not indigenous to the people and setting I knew best. I was desperately seeking my natural voice, but the process by which I formed it was long and arduous." He tells of a kind of mystical experience which helped him discover his voice and the vision for his work. As he was working on his novel one night, he turned and saw an old woman dressed in black entering his room: "In the process of writing, the serious writer enters planes of vision and reality that cannot be induced with alcohol or drugs" Anaya states in his autobiography. "And in that stage of creativity, when the juices flow and the story begins to write itself, the soul of the writer seems to enter the story. The trance can only be explained as a sort of spiritual high."

### Writes Award-winning *Bless Me, Ultima*

And that was how *Bless Me, Ultima* was born. The woman who visited Anaya in his vision became Ultima, the healer who helps lead the story's hero on his journey. Through that mystical experience, Anaya found his voice; through the book itself, he found an audience. *Bless Me, Ultima* has since sold well over 400,000 copies, and has met with resounding praise. In 1982, Antonio Márquez wrote that "*Bless Me, Ultima* has inspired the largest body of criticism in contemporary Chicano literature"; further, Márquez offered praise for what he called "Anaya's imaginative mythopoesis and his careful and loving attention to the craft of fiction."

Anaya was awarded the prestigious Premio Quinto Sol national Chicano literary award for *Bless Me, Ultima,* marking an auspicious start to his long career as a writer. Anaya has since published the novels: *Heart of Aztlán* (1976); *Tortuga* (1979); *The Legend of La Llorona* (1984); *Lord of the Dawn: The Legend of Quetzalcoatl* (1987); and *Albuquerque* (1992), for which he received the PEN-West Fiction Award. In addition, he has written numerous short stories, including the 1982 collection entitled *The Silence of the Llano.* His non-fiction work includes *A Chicano in China* (1986). Additionally, he has written a children's story, *The Farolitos of Christmas: A New Mexican Christmas Story* (1987), an epic poem, *The Adventures of Juan Chicaspatas* (1985), as well as numerous essays, plays, screenplays, magazine and literary journal articles, and literary criticism. He is also an accomplished editor and translator.

For 30 years Anaya has taught English, at both the high school and university level, affording him the opportunity to write, as well as nurture and learn from young writers. He is currently professor emeritus in the English Department of the University of New Mexico, where he has worked in varying capacities since 1971. Although he has traveled extensively—throughout such countries as Mexico, Costa Rica, Panama, Puerto Rico, the Caribbean, Europe, and China—Anaya has remained rooted to the New Mexico of his youth. Today, he lives in Albuquerque with his wife, not far from his ancestral home. There he is working to complete the third and fourth books in a series begun with *Alburquerque.* He still writes daily, a habit begun decades ago, and one which keeps him steeped in his ongoing search for meaning. As he said in his autobiography: "Each of us is neither all good nor all bad, we share the human emotions. A writer is no different from the vast swarm of mankind, only in us, something is heightened, that vibration of creativity forces us to look closer into the lives of our brothers and sisters."

## SELECTED PUBLISHED WORKS:

*Bless Me, Ultima,* Tonatiuh International, 1972.
*Heart of Aztlán,* Editorial Justa, 1976.
*Tortuga,* Editorial Justa, 1979.
*The Silence of the Llano,* Tonatiuh/Quinto Sol International, 1982; *The Legend of La Llorona,* Tonatiuh/Quinto Sol International, 1984.
*The Adventures of Juan Chicaspatas,* Arte Público, 1985.
*A Chicano in China,* University of New Mexico Press, 1986.
*The Farolitos of Christmas: A New Mexican Christmas Story,* New Mexico Magazine, 1987.
*Lord of the Dawn: The Legend of Quetzalcoatl,* University of New Mexico Press, 1987.
*Alburquerque,* University of New Mexico Press, 1992.
*The Anaya Reader,* Warner, 1995.
*Zia Summer,* Warner, 1995.
*Rio Grande Fall,* Warner, 1996.

## SOURCES:

### Books

*Contemporary Authors: Autobiography Series,* Vol. 4, edited by Adele Sarkissian, Detroit, Gale Research, 1986, pp. 15–28.
*Dictionary of Literary Biography: Chicano Writers First Series,* Vol. 82, edited by Francisco A. Lomelí and Carl R. Shirley, Detroit, Gale Research, 1989, pp. 24–35.
*Hispanic Writers,* edited by Bryan Ryan, Detroit, Gale Research, 1991, pp. 24–26.

### Periodicals

*New York Times Book Review,* November 29, 1992, p. 22.
*Publishers Weekly,* June 5, 1995, p. 41.

### Other

Additional formation for this profile was obtained from a 1993 curriculum vitae provided by Rudolfo Anaya.

—*Sketch by Karen Bober Kuhn*

# Luis Ernesto Aparicio, Jr.
## 1934-
### Venezuelan professional baseball player

Luis Aparicio was the first Venezuelan to be inducted into the Baseball Hall of Fame in Cooperstown, New York. One of the greatest shortstops in the history of the major leagues in the United States, he holds records for consecutive games played, fielding, and stolen bases.

Luis Ernesto Aparicio, Jr.—known as "Little Looie"—was born April 29, 1934, in Maracaibo, Venezuela, situated in the northwest part of the country off the Gulf of Venezuela on Lake Maracaibo. Aparicio's father—Luis E. Aparicio, Sr.—was the first Venezuelan ever offered a major league baseball contract. He drove a tractor for an oil company and played baseball in the Venezuelan leagues; and although he weighed only 145 pounds, he was quick and sturdy, playing until he was 41 years old. He taught Aparicio how to field and work the baseball diamond.

Aparicio attended the public schools in Maracaibo, growing to a height of 5'9" by high school and weighing only 155 pounds. Aparicio left high school before beginning his junior year and joined an amateur baseball team in the Venezuelan capital of Caracas. He batted an astounding .350 for the Venezuelan team and helped lead them to the Latin American World Series. He then switched teams and played for the Barquisimeto Cardenales. Already he had assumed the field position of his father and the position he would play throughout his life—shortstop. In 1953, Aparicio delivered the coup de grace when he replaced his father as shortstop for the Maracaibo Gavilanes.

### Signed Major League Contract

Luman Harris spied Aparicio playing in Maracaibo and signed him to a contract with the Chicago White Sox for $6,000. Aparicio moved to the United States, excited to play in the major leagues. He started as shortstop in the minors playing with Waterloo, a White Sox farm team in 1954. He did not hit as well as he had at home, but the right-handed batter still managed an impressive .282 average over 94 games. In 1955 he moved to the Southern Association, playing with Memphis and hit a strong .273 over 150 games. Already Aparicio began to show the skills for which he would become known—he led the Southern League for stolen bases with 48, total putouts, and assists. Unfortunately, he was still learning his way around the diamond, and also led the league in errors.

*Luis Ernesto Aparicio, Jr.*

In 1956 he joined the Chicago White Sox in the American League (AL), replacing Venezuelan Chico Carrasquel as the starting shortstop, thus continuing the fine fielding by Venezuelan players that the White Sox enjoyed for many years. He also married Sonia Llorente on October 1, 1956, with whom he has five children. That same year, he earned the title of American League Rookie of the Year with his impressive playing. Not only did his fielding improve, but he batted a steady .266, stole 21 bases, and led AL shortstops in putouts, assists, and errors. He played with the White Sox for seven consecutive seasons and returned later to play for another three seasons near the end of his career. Not only was he was boyish-looking, but he was considered one of the most easy-going, friendly players on any team. In 1959 Al Lopez—then White Sox manager—told *Newsweek* that Aparicio was as good as players like Leo Durocher and Phil Rizzuto and "he could get better." He did.

## Runs and Steals

It was during his first seven years, from 1956 to 1964, that Aparicio established his presence in major league baseball and began to set the records that would win him accolades as one of the greatest shortstops of all time. For the next nine years, he led the American League in stolen bases. He reached his highest mark in 1959 with 56 stolen bases. Surely, Aparicio's base stealing helped propel the White Sox over the New York Yankees that year, who had ruled

as the American League champions since 1949. In fact, it was Aparicio who made the final out of the season that won the team the AL pennant.

Though it was the first pennant Chicago had won in 40 years, the White Sox did not win the World Series that year. They lost to the Los Angeles Dodgers four games to two. Yet, Aparicio batted .308 during the series. He became known for his base stealing, amassing 160 stolen bases from 1959 to 1961, and earning the honor as the first major leaguer since Ty Cobb to score 50 or more stolen bases in three consecutive seasons.

## Won Gold Gloves

Aparicio consistently reduced his error percentage until he was a Gold Gloves fielder. With his cannon-like arm and deadly accuracy, playing deep to gain more range, he won the Gold Gloves as the best AL shortstop every year from 1958 to 1962 and then every other year in 1964, 1966, 1968, and 1970. He led the AL shortstops in fielding for eight consecutive seasons, tying a major league record. He broke a major league record by leading the American League six straight years in assists. He also led the AL in games played in five different years. He and Chicago teammate and close friend second-baseman Nellie Fox (for whom he named one of his sons Nelson) lead the AL in double plays in 1960 with 117. In 1959, after watching Aparicio make a bare-handed catch as part of a double play, White Sox president Bill Veeck said that "Luis always makes the plays that can't be made yet he makes them almost every day.... He's the best I've ever seen." Because of this level of play, not only was he a Gold Glove winner, but he ranked as the *Sporting News* all-star team shortstop every other year from 1964 to 1972.

## Traded to Orioles

In 1963, when a new general manager came to Chicago, the White Sox traded Aparicio to the Baltimore Orioles. In 1966, Aparicio helped drive his new team to the World Series by batting .276; the Orioles beat the Dodgers in four straight games. Aparicio had two runs batted in and two doubles in the series, with four hits in 16 at bats. He continued to play well for the Orioles and was the starting shortstop each year. In 1963 he achieved the highest fielding percentage of any shortstop in a season with a .983 average, although that record has been broken since. He also led the majors that year with 40 stolen bases, though his best year was in 1964 with 57. His stellar abilities won him a place on the All-Star team as shortstop from 1958 to 1962, in 1969, and again in 1970.

In 1968 he returned to the White Sox and played there until he was traded to the Boston Red Sox in

1971, where he played until he retired after the 1973 season. His batting turned a corner with his best two seasons in the twilight of his career. In 1969 he hit .280 out of a major-league-leading 659 at bats; and in 1970 he managed a career-high .313 batting average in 146 games. After ending his major league career, Aparicio moved back home and managed several winters in Maracaibo, Venezuela, and co-owned a baseball club there. In 1984 he was inducted into the Baseball Hall of Fame in Cooperstown, New York.

During his 18-year major league baseball career, Aparicio set records for lifetime achievement that remain unchanged. He leads both the all-time list of number of games played by a shortstop with 2,581 games and the all-time shortstop leaders for assists with 8,016. He is also number one in lifetime double plays for a shortstop with 1,553. In his career, he amassed 2,677 hits, 394 doubles, and 1,335 runs. He also managed to steal 506 bases. He revived base-stealing as a common practice and proved that smaller players could generate fan excitement through base running and fielding that others gained through home runs.

## SOURCES:

### Books

*The Ballplayers: Baseball's Ultimate Biographical Reference,* edited by Mike Shatzkin, New York, William Morrow, 1990.
*The Baseball Encyclopedia,* edited by Rick Wolff, et al., New York, Macmillan, 1990.
*Biographical Dictionary of American Sports: Baseball,* edited by David L. Porter, New York, Greenwood Press, 1987.
*Hispanic-American Almanac,* edited by Nicolás Kanellos, Detroit, Gale Research, 1993.
*Total Baseball,* edited by John Thorn and Pete Palmer, New York, Warner Books, 1989.
*Who's Who in Professional Baseball,* edited by Gene Karst and Martin J. Jones, Jr., New York, Arlington House, 1973.

### Periodicals

*Newsweek,* June 29, 1959, pp. 86–87.

—*Sketch by Christopher B. Tower*

# Alfonso Arau
## 1932(?)-
### Mexican filmmaker

Alfonso Arau is a prominent member of the new generation of Latino directors, writers, and actors dedicated to altering stereotypical portrayals of Hispanics in film. In the United States, Arau is known for his role as Lieutenant Herrera in Sam Peckinpah's western, *The Wild Bunch* (1969). In his native Mexico, he is famous for directing films such as *The Barefoot Eagle* (1967), *Calzonzin Inspector* (1974), *Mojado Power* (1980), and *Chido Guan* (1984).

But the recognition Arau has received for his inspired direction of the 1993 film, *Like Water for Chocolate,* has virtually eclipsed his previous accomplishments. The film grossed $21.6 million in the United States alone during its first year. In 1994, the *New York Times* reported that *Like Water for Chocolate* had become "the highest-grossing independently produced foreign film of all time in the United States." Both the novel upon which the film was based and the screenplay were written by Arau's wife, **Laura Esquivel.** *Like Water for Chocolate* was described by *Maclean's* (1993) as "a lushly photographed family saga about the enchantments of food and unrequited love." Arau's direction in the magic realism genre earned glowing reviews. *Vogue* stated in 1993 that "magic realism is an acquired taste, but Alfonso Arau's film makes it delicious. The link between food and love has never been shown so clearly and with such gaiety." *Newsweek* (1993) called his direction "sensuous but ironic." *Maclean's* described the film as "lyrically directed." Reviewer Julie Salamon wrote in the *Wall Street Journal* (1993) that "Arau has directed in a lilting, magical style, probably the only possible approach—though not as easy to pull off as gracefully as he has."

### Evolution of a Director

Arau has successfully pursued a variety of career choices, all of which have been related to the entertainment business. The son of a dentist, Arau was born around 1932 in Mexico City, Mexico. He was a medical student when he met and fell in love with a ballerina. In order to be near her, he quit medical school and joined the ballet company, where he danced for two years. There, he became acquainted with the ballerina's brother, Sergio Corona, a fellow dancer. Arau paired up with Corona and the two became a comedy team. Billed as Corona y Arau, the duo toured Mexico and Latin America. Their biting satire made them famous. During this period, Arau was also enrolled in the drama program at the

*Alfonso Arau*

University of Mexico and began to act, both on television and in Mexican films.

In 1959 Arau left Mexico and went to **Fidel Castro**'s Cuba, where he secured his own television variety show. Called "El Show de Arau," the program ran for five years. In 1964, Arau moved to Paris and studied pantomime under Marcel Marceau's instructors, Etienne da Croux and Jacques le Coq. Arau then assembled a solo mime show and toured both Europe and Latin America. He returned to Mexico in the late 1960s, where he directed *The Barefoot Eagle,* his first film. The *New York Times* (1994) described this film as a "critical success . . . [that] became a cult film in Mexico."

### Developed Commitment to Change Stereotypes

In 1968, Sam Peckinpah went to Mexico to film his classic, *The Wild Bunch.* He cast Arau as Lieutenant Herrera, henchman of the vile General Mapache. This role marked Arau's first part in an American film. Arau continued to direct films in Mexico while also appearing in other Hollywood films, such as *Posse, Used Cars, Romancing the Stone,* and *Three Amigos.* In a 1994 interview with Guy Garcia in the *New York Times,* Arau commented on his Hollywood acting career. He stated that "*The Wild Bunch* opened a whole career for me as an actor in the United States, but at the same time I was typecast, usually as a drug dealer or bandito."

Following his 1986 appearance as El Guapo in *Three Amigos,* Arau decided to devote his energies exclusively to directing. *Like Water for Chocolate* was his sixth film, and its success guaranteed the director's bankability in Hollywood. Garcia wrote that "[it] also took a toll on his 16-year marriage." Arau and Esquivel were divorced in 1993.

The year 1994 found Arau directing his first American-produced feature film, *A Walk in the Clouds.* Released in 1995, the film starred Keanu Reeves, Aitana Sanchez-Gijon, Anthony Quinn, and Giancarlo Giannini. Arau has taken his responsibility as a Latino director seriously. He told Garcia that "Mexicans have been portrayed in a not very realistic way in Hollywood. Now, as a director, I have a chance to change that image." Toward that end, he has hired a largely Latino cast for *A Walk in the Clouds* and has made a slight but significant change in the story. The script initially established the setting as a vineyard owned by a wealthy Italian family. Arau convinced the producers to make the owners an upmen than fper-class Mexican family instead.

Arau hopes to help change traditional Hollywood stereotypes of Hispanic actors. He explained to Garcia: "Hollywood creates myths. But this new mythology is going to help a lot of Hispanic actors in the future, because people will think of better parts for them. I'm always optimistic. If you work hard and wish for things, you will get them."

### SELECTED VIDEOGRAPHY:

*The Barefoot Eagle* (director), 1967.
*The Wild Bunch* (actor), 1969.
*Scandalous John* (actor), 1971.
*Calzonzin Inspector* (director), 1974.
*Posse* (actor), 1975.
*Mojado Power* (director), 1980.
*Used Cars* (actor), 1980.
*Chido Guan* (director), 1984.
*Romancing the Stone* (actor), 1984.
*Three Amigos* (actor), 1986.
*Dynamite and Gold* (actor), 1988.
*Like Water for Chocolate* (director), 1993.
*Posse* (actor), 1993.
*A Walk in the Clouds* (director), 1995.

### SOURCES:

#### Books

*Film Directors,* seventh annual international edition, compiled and edited by Michael Singer, Beverly Hills, California, Lone Eagle, 1989.

## Periodicals

*Maclean's,* April 26, 1993, p.44.
*Newsweek,* March 15, 1993, p.74.
*New York Times,* January 30, 1994, pp. H32, H40; August 28, 1994, pp. H9, H16.
*Vogue,* April 1993, p. 212.
*Wall Street Journal,* February 25, 1993, p. A12.

—*Sketch by Ellen Dennis French*

# Jacobo Arbenz Guzmán
## 1913-1971
### Guatemalan political leader

Jacobo Arbenz Guzmán was elected as the second president of Guatemala in 1950. He was overthrown by the U.S. Central Intelligence Agency (CIA) in 1954. Arbenz was the son of a Swiss druggist, Jacobo Arbenz, who immigrated to Guatemala in 1901. His mother was a Salvadoran, Octavia Guzmán de Arbenz. He was born in Quetzaltenango, Guatemala, September 14, 1913. Arbenz graduated first in his class in 1935 at the national military academy, Excuela Politecnica, in Guatemala, where he became an instructor and director. In 1939, he married Maria Cristina Vilanova Castro, whose family in El Salvador were coffee plantation owners.

Arbenz was a military captain in 1944 under the dictatorship of Jorge Ubico y Castaneda. When Castaneda turned the government over to a military triumvirate, Arbenz resigned from the army to protest government repression. He and two other men, Jorge Toriello and Major Francisco Javier Arana, worked together in the Guatemalan Revolution of 1944 to overthrow Castaneda. In December 1944, the three men supervised the elections and voters elected the first democratic president of Guatemala, Juan Jose Arevalo Bermejo. Arbenz was appointed minister of defense under Arevalo. He was a supporter of Arevalo's social and economic reform program. After Arevalo became president, the Communist Party infiltrated the labor unions and they were reorganized as the Guatemalan Labor Party. It was in Guatemala that **Ernesto "Che" Guevara de la Serna** first learned about Karl Marx and Vladimir I. Lenin. During Arevalo's administration, around 32 attempts were made to overthrow him.

When Arevalo could not run in the next election, Arbenz was approached by the two revolutionary parties to become their candidate. Arbenz became a leading political figure of the liberal left wing and Arana was a leader of the conservative right wing faction. Arbenz and Arana were two of the most popular presidential candidates in the 1950 elections. Before the elections, a rumor surfaced that Arana was planning a coup and he was assassinated July 18, 1949. Arevalo supported Arbenz in his presidential candidacy. Arbenz won the election with more than 60 percent of the votes cast for him.

### Reforms Are Called "Marxist"

One of the biggest controversies during Arbenz's presidency was his agrarian reform legislation of 1952. The provisions of the bill stipulated that the government would take parcels of land that was not cultivated from large landowners and redistribute it. The United Fruit Company, a U.S. company, was the country's largest commercial enterprise and the battle between the company and the government began during Arevalo's administration in 1948. At that time, the company refused to follow the provisions of the Labor Codes. When Arbenz instituted the agrarian reform legislation, the government offered the company the amount it had declared as the land's value on its taxes. Outraged, the company launched an extensive public relations campaign and opponents to the reform called it "Marxist" and denounced the Arbenz administration for communist influence. Many politicians in Washington, D.C., were calling Guatemala a "Soviet satellite." John Foster Dulles, U.S. Secretary of State, called for a resolution to isolate Arbenz at an Inter-American Conference held in Caracas, Venezuela. However, Arbenz was not a communist, and although he was aware of their participation in the labor unions, he considered them no real threat to Guatemala.

### CIA Overthrows Arbenz

Arbenz decided to form a militia and when the army would not supply arms to civilians, he bought them from Czechoslovakia. The U.S. government was incensed by this action, stating that it was a move toward communism. The CIA was formed as an executive agency of the U.S. government in 1947 at the beginning of the Cold War; they were organized to analyze Soviet political plans, military power and collect intelligence. They also had the authority to conduct covert espionage activities. The CIA made plans to overthrow Arbenz beginning in 1952 by training Guatemalan exiles. At an expense of close to $20 million, an army and an air force were organized and trained to invade Guatemala in 1954. They entered the country from Nicaragua and when the Guatemalan army refused to fight them, they forced Arbenz to resign. Former Guatemalan Colonel Carlos Castillo Armas, who was in command of the invasion, replaced Arbenz with a military regime. Latin American opinion ran high against the United States for this intercession in Guatemalan politics. Arbenz left the country and lived in Switzerland, Czechoslovakia, Uruguay, and Mexico. The family moved to Cuba before returning to Mexico City in 1970; on January 27, 1971, Arbenz died of natural causes Mexico City.

## SOURCES:

*Biographical Dictionary of Latin American and Caribbean Political Leaders*, edited by Robert J. Alexander, New York, Greenwood Press, 1988, pp. 21–22.
*The Cold War*, edited by Benjamin Frankel, Detroit, Gale Research, 1982, pp. 17–18, 124–125, 134.

—*Sketch by Phyllis Noah*

# Reinaldo Arenas
## 1943-1990
### Cuban novelist, poet, and essayist

Cuban-born writer Reinaldo Arenas was a figure of international stature, yet he suffered great political persecution in his homeland because of the content of his work and his homosexuality. A recipient of several significant literary honors, including a 1982 Guggenheim Fellowship, Arenas's writings have been published in English, Italian, German, Dutch, Japanese, Polish, Portuguese, and French. In his native Cuba, however, Arenas's poetry and fiction marked him as an enemy of the state. Only one of his books, *Celestino antes del alba* (1967; translated as *Singing from the Well,* 1987), an early work about adolescence, was ever published in Cuba. In 1980, several years after being forced to endure persecution and imprisonment, Arenas was boatlifted from Cuba and settled in New York. He wrote several novels while in America, further solidifying his literary reputation. Arenas also contracted AIDS; he committed suicide in 1990.

In a discussion of the life and death of Arenas, Roberto Gonzalez Echevarría wrote in a *New York Times Book Review* that "this was a dramatic ending to a dramatic life, the final flight of someone who was always escaping—first from abandonment and neglect as a child, later from stark poverty and finally from sexual and political persecution." Arenas was born on July 16, 1943, in the rural Cuban province of Oriente. He was raised by his mother—his father

abandoned them—and a succession of other young women in impoverished conditions. His childhood pastimes reflected the bleak environment around him. As Echevarría notes, Arenas spent long hours of his childhood "running through fields shouting hymn-like poems of his own invention, listening with rapture to the stories told by his grandmother and following the soap operas the women heard on their dilapidated radio. This was Arenas's sentimental and literary education."

Arenas was 15 years old when **Fidel Castro**'s revolutionary army swept across Cuba. Although he joined Castro's army, "[A]ll along, though, Arenas remained in the margins," wrote Achy Obejas in the *Nation.* "Seeing how revolutionary justice was meted out against boys discovered to be homosexual, he hid his own sexuality," Obejas continued. "It was this experience, though, that really began to reveal for him the hypocrisy of power. While the revolution persecuted common homosexuals, it protected those with linkage to power—even flamboyant, unapologetic homosexuals."

At the age of 19 Arenas won a scholarship, moved to Havana and enrolled in the university. The following year he won another contest that involved telling the best children's story in five minutes. Shunning all the well-known stories, Arenas told one of his own tales. His performance led to a job at the National Library, where he was able to devote additional time to his writing. While working at the library, Arenas wrote *Singing from the Well,* which received second place in a 1965 literary contest. Two years later the novel was published by the National Union of Cuban Writers and Artists. Arenas also utilized the library's resources to conduct research on topics that interested him. The young writer discovered an autobiography of Friar Servando Teresa de Mier during one of these forays into the holdings of the library. Arenas identified fully with the revolutionary Mexican friar who spent his life traveling through Europe in flight from intellectual persecution. Arenas would later find himself running away in the same manner. Adopting the friar's personality for his own use, Arenas rewrote the biography as *El mundo alucinante (Hallucinations: Being an Account of the Life and Adventures of Friar Servando Teresa de Mier)* in 1969.

This work received an honorary mention from the National Union of Cuban Writers and Artists, but Cuban government authorities refused to publish it. Frustrated with Cuba's state-sponsored censorship practices, Arenas looked to foreign shores. After his first two works were published in Mexico, Arenas reputation grew, in Mexico as well as other areas of the globe. In 1969 he was honored as the best foreign novelist in France.

Despite his literary accomplishments, however, Arenas led an unhappy and secretive existence. His personal relationships were gloomy affairs that typically involved physical beatings and betrayal. In several instances, physically abusive men returned to their wives and girlfriends after turning him over to authorities to escape persecution themselves.

### Jailed as Counterrevolutionary

Arenas's homosexuality put him in disfavor with Cuban authorities, but it was his literary work that resulted in his incarceration. Many Cuban intellectuals and writers who were suspected of engaging in dissident activity in the late 1960s and early 1970s had been exiled. Those who chose to have their works published overseas were regarded as counterrevolutionaries. In 1970 Arenas and a number of other Cuban writers were sent to a sugarcane plantation for forced labor. While he was at the camp, Arenas wrote *El central* (*El Central: A Cuban Sugar Mill*), a long poem. It was secretly delivered to Spain and eventually published in 1981. Arenas then started work on his next novel, *Otra vez el mar* (*Farewell to the Sea*), which was published in 1982. The troubled life of this novel was indicative of the obstacles that were typically erected in Arenas's path. The first version of the novel disappeared in Havana in 1969, while the second version was confiscated in 1971. The manuscript was finally smuggled out of Havana in 1974.

From 1974 to 1976 Arenas was imprisoned in the same facility that held Friar Servando while he was in Cuba. "Months pass before he [was] brought to trial on a morals charge. In the meantime he [was] sexually abused, forced to live in the most degrading and unsanitary conditions, reduced to a subsistence diet that he [supplemented] by eating, among other things, sparrows that another inmate [had] taught him how to capture," noted Echevarría. Although the morals charge was eventually dropped, Arenas was not permitted to leave prison until he confessed to counterrevolutionary activities. The authorities also forced him to promise to forsake homosexual activities and write only novels that were optimistic in outlook.

In 1980 Arenas fled Cuba during the Mariel boatlift in which thousands of Cubans sailed to Florida. He published new work, revised some of his earlier works, and launched a monthly publication, *Mariel*. Arenas served on the faculty at universities in both Florida and New York and lectured at a number of universities around the globe that he had long been prevented from visiting. In 1982, only two years after he came to the United States, Arenas earned the Guggenheim Fellowship. Arenas also won a Woodrow Wilson Center Fellowship in 1987.

Arenas's *El asulto* (*The Assault*) was published in 1993, three years after his death. A furious denuncia-

tion of Fidel Castro and Post-Revolution Cuba, the book portrays a society built on betrayal and blind nationalism. "Here he takes deadly aim at Cuba's glorious 'represident,' in whose service the narrator rounds up dissidents and deviants to be juiced for patriotic irrigation," commented Jack Shreve in *Library Journal*. "People are nameless insects who aspire to 'disacquaintance' with their neighbors." *Publishers Weekly*, while critical of the structure of *The Assault*, noted that "Arenas does draw a disturbing portrait of the political extremes and superfluous nationalism of a society headed toward a point where 'every person will find joy in betraying every other person, eating every other person, and for that they will even patiently wait their turn.'"

### Autobiography of an Outcast

The single most informative document of Arenas's life, however, was his autobiography, *Antes que anuchezca* (*Before Night Falls*). Published in 1993, "it is an absorbing book," writes Echevarría, "with the fascination one finds in stories by survivors of death camps or in lives of the saints." *Before Night Falls* provides details on the author's life from his childhood to his suicide letter, a document in which he lays his many misfortunes, including his death, at Castro's feet. But while *Before Night Falls* documents the betrayals and punishments Arenas endured in Cuba, it also records his continued unhappiness in the United States. Obejas wrote that Arenas was forgotten by an exile community that grew uncomfortable with his work and that "Arenas was always caught between a desire to be free and an inability to free himself. In Cuba, he was trapped by the clash between his senses and the puritanical revolution; in the United States, between poverty and the political convenience of others; even his powerful sex drive was torn between its insistent urges (and too much love of truth to deny it) and his own antiquated notions of what it is to be homosexual." Obejas contended that "Ultimately, no matter how often he'd been screwed over by his exile brethren, Arenas was more comfortable among them than in the U.S. gay and lesbian community; he was terrified of being labeled a 'gay' writer . . . and comforted by being a 'Cuban' writer."

### SELECTED PUBLISHED WORKS:

*Celestino antes del alba,* Havana, 1967; translated by Andrew Hurley as *Singing from the Well,* Viking, 1987.

*El mundo alucinante,* Diógenes, 1969; translated by Gordon Brotherston as *Hallucinations: Being an Account of the Life and Adventures of Friar Servando Teresa de Mier,* Harper, 1971.

*Con los ojos cerrados,* Arca, 1972.

*Le palais des tres blanches mouffettes,* Editions de Seuil (Paris), 1975; first published in Spanish as *El palacio de las blanquísimas mofetas,* Monte Avila, 1980.

*El central,* Seix Barral, 1981; translated by Anthony Kerrigan as *El Central: A Cuban Sugar Mill,* Avon, 1984.

*Otra vez el mar,* Argos, 1982; translated by Andrew Hurley as *Farewell to the Sea,* Viking, 1986.

*Arturo, la estrella más brillante,* Montesinos, 1984.

*Necesidad de libertad,* Kosmos, 1985.

*Persecución: Cinco piezas de teatro experimental,* Ediciones, 1986.

*La loma del ángel,* New York, 1987; translated by Alfred MacAdam as *Graveyard of the Angels,* Avon, 1987.

*El portero,* Presses de la Renaissencse, 1988.

*El asulto,* 1990; translated by Andrew Hurley as *The Assault,* New York, Viking, 1993.

*Antes que anuchezca,* 1992; translated by Dolores M. Koch as *Before Night Falls,* New York, Viking, 1993.

## SOURCES:

### Books

*Latin American Writers,* Vol. 3, edited by Carlos A. Solé, New York, Charles Scribner's Sons, 1989 pp. 1451–56.

### Periodicals

*Library Journal,* June 15, 1994, p. 92.

*Nation,* March 21, 1994, pp. 387–389.

*New York Times Book Review,* October 24, 1993, p. 1.

*Publishers Weekly,* May 2, 1994, p. 281.

—*Sketch by D. D. Andreassi*

# José María Arguedas
## 1911-1969
### Peruvian writer and ethnologist

In his novels and short stories, José María Arguedas portrayed the Quechua people (Incan descendants) with compassionate accuracy. Quechua was Arguedas's first language, and his intimate understanding of Indian culture—delineated through a refined literary aesthetic—made him Peru's most accomplished pro-indigenous author. In *Review,* **Mario Vargas Llosa** lauded, "In his novels and short stories, José María Arguedas succeeds—the first to do so in Latin America—in replacing the abstract and subjective Indians created by the Modernists and Indigenists with real characters, that is, with concrete beings, portrayed objectively and situated both socially and historically."

Arguedas was born January 18, 1911, in the city of Andahuaylas in the Peruvian state of Apurímac. His father, Victor Manuel, was a provincial traveling judge and his mother, Dona Victoria (Altamirano), died when Arguedas was only three. Arguedas's father subsequently married Grimanesa Arangoitia, a widow with three other children who neglected her new stepson. Addressing a group of fiction writers in 1965, Arguedas described his childhood experience in his stepmother's household: "Since I was the object of as much of her scorn and rancor as the Indians, she decided that I was to live with them in the kitchen, eating and sleeping there. My bed was a wooden trough of the kind used to knead bread. . . . Resting on some sheepskins and covered with a rather dirty but very sheltering blanket, I spent the nights talking and living so well that if my stepmother had known it she would have removed me to her side." This early, benevolent bond with the Indians engendered Arguedas's outspoken pro-indigenous social values and informed his life's work.

### Developed Style of Linguistic Integration

In his first book, a collection of three stories entitled *Agua* (*Water,* 1935), Arguedas employed what would become his signature style: a hybrid language that combines Quechua idioms and syntax with Spanish. This linguistic integration, which Arguedas continued to refine throughout his career, constituted an effort to provide a balanced view of the tumultuous and fragmented intersection between two competing modes of perception, while at the same time proposing cultural unification.

From 1932 to 1937 Arguedas worked for the post office in Lima, Peru. In 1937 he received his undergraduate degree in literature from the University of San Marcos. That same year he was imprisoned for 12 months in the Lima prison El Sexto for organizing a protest against Italian fascism. He expounded on the injustice of his imprisonment in his 1962 novel *El sexto* (*The Sixth One*).

Arguedas took his doctorate in anthropology in 1948 from the University of San Marcos. He married Cilia Bustamente Vernal in 1939; they later divorced and he married Sybila Arredondo in 1966. In his professional career as an ethnologist and teacher, Arguedas was devoted to promoting the cultural heritage of the indigenous population. He translated an anthology of Quechuan folklore entitled *Canciones y cuentos del pueblo quechua* (1949) (*The Singing Mountainers: Songs and Tales of the Quechua People*). In 1953 he became the director of the Institute of Ethnological Studies for the Peruvian Museum of Culture (later serving as the director of the museum from 1964–1969). From 1959 to 1969 he was professor of regional cultures of Peru at the University of San Marcos, as well as professor of Quechua at Universidad Agraria from 1963 to 1969.

The novel *Los Ríos profundos* (*Deep Rivers*) is usually considered Arguedas's masterpiece. It focuses on the clash between the Indian and the Hispanic cultures through the plight of Ernesto, a young boy who is raised by Indians but later sent to a Catholic boarding school. Torn from the Indian's mystical communion with nature, a distraught Ernesto finds that the Hispanics adamantly dismiss all things Indian. Ernesto's tragedy is that he becomes trapped between two cultures: it is impossible for him to live in both simultaneously, and he is incapable of merging fully into either. A reviewer for the *New Yorker* commented that the novel "movingly dramatizes the differences between the worlds of the Indian and the Spaniard, and so is an essential part of the canon of the new Latin-American literature. The violation of the Indians' dignity by the harsh imposition of Spanish order is made both tangible and inevitable."

Arguedas's other novels include *Yawar fiesta* (*Blood Feast*, 1941), which explores the oppression of indigenous people and their primitive rituals. *Todas las sangres* (*All the Races*, 1964) deals with a case of sibling rivalry while encompassing larger conflicts between landowners and Indians. According to Peter Gold, Arguedas's novels "are not works of denunciation, protest or propaganda; rather they are attempts to explore the cultural and social conflicts in Peru, and to reveal the significance of Indian values within Peruvian culture and society." In honor of his literary achievements, Arguedas received the Inca Garcilaso Prize in 1968. A personal history of severe depression combined with overwork led to his death on December 2, 1969, from a self-inflicted gunshot wound.

## SELECTED PUBLISHED WORKS:

*Agua* (*Water*), Lima, 1935.
*Yawar fiesta* (*Blood Feast*), Lima, CIP, 1941; translated by Frances Barraclough, University of Texas, 1985.
*Canciones y cuentos del pueblo quechua,* Lima, Editorial Huascaran, 1949; translated by Ruth Walgreen Stephan as *The Singing Mountaineers: Songs and Tales of the Quechua People,* University of Texas Press, 1957.
*Los Ríos profundos,* Buenos Aires, Editorial Losada, 1958; translated by Frances Barraclough as *Deep Rivers,* introduction by John V. Murra, Austin: University of Texas Press, 1978.

*El sexto* (*The Sixth One*), Mejía, 1961.
*Todas las sangres* (*All the Races*), Editorial Losada, 1964.

## SOURCES:

### Books

Arguedas, José, Deep Rivers, introduction by John V. Murra, Austin: University of Texas Press, 1978.
*Contemporary Literary Criticism,* Volume 18, Detroit, Gale Research, 1981.
*Hispanic Writers,* edited by Bryan Ryan, Detroit, Gale Research, 1991.
*Latin American Writers,* Volume 3, New York, Scribner's, 1990.
*Spanish American Authors: The Twentieth Century,* New York, H. W. Wilson, 1992.

### Periodicals

*New Yorker,* October 16, 1978, pp. 194–95.

—*Sketch by Kenneth K. Brandt*

# Manlio Argueta
## 1936-
### Salvadoran novelist and poet

Manlio Argueta's novels have won him great acclaim and awards. His 1980 novel *Un día en la vida* (*One Day of Life*) received mixed critical reviews, a government ban, and continued exile from his home. The novel depicted the civil war in El Salvador that divided the country throughout the 1980s, focusing especially on special government forces—the death squads—that ruled. It won him the national prize from the Catholic University of San Salvador and became the first best-seller in Central America, despite the fact that it was banned by the Salvadoran government.

Manlio Argueta was born November 24, 1936, in San Miguel, El Salvador. Argueta has identified San Miguel as a forgotten region of the country. He characterized his native region as unaware and intolerant of literature. These attitudes led him to conceal his early love for writing. When Argueta went to the university in San Salvador, he discovered an enormous difference between the two communities. Finally, he could break his silence and openly discuss his

*Manlio Argueta*

feelings about writing and his ideas with others. The new ideas that Argueta encountered in San Salvador at the University and later at law school had a profound influence on his life and his work.

Considered one of the privileged in a country with a 76 percent illiteracy rate, Argueta joined a group of writers who were discussing how to reflect the modernization of themselves and their city in their writing. Highly active in politics and cultural organizations, Argueta also published poetry that questioned the national problems of El Salvador. Like all the other voices that spoke out against the military government that had ruled the country since 1931, Argueta and his colleagues were considered possibly dangerous to the public order, subversive, and even anarchistic.

## Begins to Publish Novels

After graduation, Argueta continued to run the Salvadoran University Press. During this time, Argueta became better known for his novels than his poetry, which he considered his main emphasis as a writer. His first novel, *El Valle de las hamacas* (*The Valley of the Hammocks*) won the National Literary Prize in El Salvador in 1968 even though it was not published until 1970. His second novel, *Caperucita an la Zona Roja* (*Red Riding Hood and the Red Zone*) won the Casa de las Americas Prize in Havana in 1977. But it was his breakthrough work, *Un día en la vida* that won him the national prize from the Catholic University

of San Salvador in 1980, becoming the first best-seller in Central America. It has been translated into German, Dutch, Turkish, Greek, and English. Though Argueta followed his 1980 success with another novel in 1986, *Cuzcatlán donde bate la mar del sur* (*Cuzcatlán: Where the Southern Sea Beats*) and a screenplay for *Cuzcatlán Stories,* neither received the same attention as his 1980 offering.

## Flees El Salvador Underfire

In 1972, Argueta fled El Salvador when the national army interceded at the university. He moved his wife and children to San José, Costa Rica where he lived off and on throughout the 1970s while trying to keep involved in activities in his home country. But life in El Salvador proved perilous for the author; he was extremely outspoken in his charges against the government and its death squads and openly supported the guerilla rebel cause. He took up permanent residence in Costa Rica in 1980 when the Salvadoran military government seized all existing copies and halted publication of his novel *One Day of Life.*

In Costa Rica, he founded and directed the Cultural Institute of El Salvador, worked in the Editorial Universitaria Centroamericana, and served as president of the Association of Central American Writers. In 1993, Argueta returned to El Salvador and took a post teaching literature at the National University and as director of the library.

## Nature of Work

Argueta's work is deeply rooted in the history of his people: from the era of colonization by the Spaniards, to the 1932 massacre when 30,000 Salvadorans were slaughtered by the national army, and to the civil war that erupted in 1980. His poems also are infused with a historical perspective, focusing on the problems of modern life and the importance of the city center to the culture and development of a people. Argueta is well known, especially abroad, for introducing the female perspective to what had been a male-dominated Central American literature. This is particularly evident in *One Day of Life,* which focuses on the plight of a peasant woman. In an interview in the *Village Voice* in 1987, he spoke of the peasant as symbolic of many of his people: "The poor in El Salvador are the majority, and they are the heirs of Mesoamerican culture, which was once so powerful. They remain on the fringes, but they are impossible to destroy. And the rulers of El Salvador are still terrified." Even before Argueta returned to his own country his books began to be published and circulated throughout El Salvador. His books, even *One Day of Life,* were being read in the schools and universities.

Argueta began work on a new novel, *Night of the Children,* after completing text accompanying photographs by Adam Kufeld in *El Salvador,* published in 1990. In a 1992 interview with Victoria Garcia Serrano, he explained that he would prefer to continue doing the cultural work he had undertaken in Costa Rica, especially making books for schools and for children.

## SELECTED PUBLISHED WORKS:

*En el costado de la luz,* Editorial Universitaria de El Salvador, 1968.

*El Valle de las hamacas,* Sudamericana, 1970.

*Caperucita en la Zona Roja,* Casa de las Américas, 1977.

*Un día en la vida,* UCA, 1980; translated by Bill Brow as *One Day of Life,* Random House, 1983.

*Cuzcatlán donde bate la mer del sur,* Guaymuras, 1986; translated by Clark Hansen as *Cuzcatlán: Where the Southern Sea Beats,* Vintage, 1987.

*Magic Dogs of the Volcanoes,* Children's Book Press, 1990.

### Other

*El Salvador,* with photographs by Adam Kufeld, New York, Norton, 1990.

## SOURCES:

### Books

Argueta, Manlio, *One Day of Life,* New York, Random House, 1983.

*Cambios estéticos y nuevos proyectos culturales en Centroamerica: Testimonios entrevistas y ensayos,* edited by Amelia Mondragon, Washington, D.C., Literal, 1994.

*Chicano Literature: A Reference Guide,* edited by Julio A. Martinez and Francisco A. Lomeli, Westport, Connecticut, Greenwood Press, 1985.

*Contemporary Authors,* Volume 131, Detroit, Gale Research, 1991.

*Contemporary Literary Criticism,* Volume 31, Detroit, Gale Research, 1985.

*Dictionary of Literary Biography,* Volume 145: *Modern Latin American Fiction Writers, Second Series,* edited by William Luis and Ann Gonzalez, Detroit, Gale Research, 1994.

*Hispanic Literature Criticism,* Volume 2, Detroit, Gale Research, 1994.

*Hispanic Writers,* edited by Bryan Ryan, Detroit, Gale Research, 1991.

### Periodicals

*New Republic,* November 21, 1983, p.46.
*New Statesman,* December 11, 1987, p.33.
*Village Voice,* September 22, 1987, p.57.
*Voice,* Number 9, 1992, p.3.

—*Sketch by Christopher B. Tower*

# Ron Arias
## 1941-
### Mexican American novelist and journalist

"Magic realism" is the term applied to a modern literary form that blends realistic style with the fantastic; Ron Arias is regarded as a master of the form. Although he has written extensively for journals and periodicals, he is most widely known for his 1975 novel, *The Road to Tamazunchale.* Critics who favor his work contend that his themes of death, redemption, hope, and humor address the human condition in a way that transcends culture and language.

Ronald Francis Arias, was born in Los Angeles, California, on November 30, 1941. His mother was Emma Lou (Estrada) Arias; his father, a career Army officer, was Armando Arias (some sources say Arias was Ron's stepfather). Because Armando Arias's career in the Army required frequent movement from one locale to another, the family decided it would be better if young Ron lived with his maternal grandmother. It was through her tutelage that he became knowledgeable about the region's rich Chicano culture. While still in high school in the 1950s, Arias realized his talents lay in writing. An adept contributor to his high school newspaper, he continued to hone his skills in this area at a variety of colleges and universities in Spain (University of Barcelona); Argentina (National University at Buenos Aires); and the United States (Oceanside Carlsbad College, the University of California, Berkeley, and the University of California, Los Angeles, where he received his B.A. and his M.A.).

In the 1960s, Arias immersed himself in social and political events that would have a significant impact on his later writing. As a recipient of an Inter-American Press Association Scholarship, Arias secured a writing position with the *Buenos Aires Herald.* In 1962 Arias authored several vanguard articles on the Neo-Nazi Movement in Argentina. The research work that he undertook for that investigative series, combined with his two-year service with the Peace Corps, served to galvanize the fledgling author's interest in social and political issues. In fact, his Peace Corps experience in Cuzco, Peru, proved to be a particularly grim one, for it was during that period that he witnessed a massacre of Peruvian peasants.

In 1967 Arias returned to California. He attended school and wrote for several newspapers and international wire services. This year was also significant for another reason: Arias' discovery of **Gabriel García Márquez**'s novel *Cien anos de soledad* (*One Hundred Years of Solitude*). Márquez was an acknowledged master of the literary genre of magic realism. In discussing the impact the novel had on him with Juan Bruce-Novoa in *Chicano Authors: Inquiry by Interview,* Arias said, "For me, García Márquez transformed, *deepened* reality in so many of its aspects—tragic, humorous, adventurous, wondrous. The work was alive, entertaining at every word."

Buoyed by his introduction to magic realism, Arias wrote several short stories over the next few years. The short story "El Mago" ("The Magician"), published in 1970, introduced a character who would haunt several of Arias's later pieces, a trickster who teaches other characters valuable lessons about their own shortsightedness. Other Arias short stories during this period included "The Interview" (1974), "The Wetback" (1975), "The Castle" (1976), and "Chinches" (1977).

Having enjoyed success with his short stories, Arias turned his attention to writing his first novel, *The Road to Tamazunchale,* which was published in 1975. This work, which was nominated for a National Book Award, established Arias as a major figure in Chicano literature. The fantastic story details the last days of an encyclopedia salesman, Fausto Tejada, and his surrealistic journey to Tamazunchale, a village that symbolizes the final resting place after death. In the course of the novel, Arias sends his protagonist skipping through a series of events wherein boundaries of past and present, reality and illusion, and life and death are blurred. Many critics found the book to be a rich and imaginative tale. Alejandro Morales, writing in the *Los Angeles Times Book Review,* praised the novel's "magical realistic imagination, its precise crisp prose, its relationship to the 'new reality' of Spanish American fiction and its compassionate treatment of death, its central theme." *The Road to Tamazunchale* did have its critics, however; Mariana Marín, commenting in *De Colores,* rejected the novel as a poor parody of Miguel de Cervantes's *Don Quixote* and found the allegory of "Fausto" to Marlowe's *Dr. Faustus* a weak one.

Ronald Arias continued to pursue his twin interests in fiction writing and journalism into the mid–1990s. He maintained his longstanding affiliation with *People* magazine as a senior editor, while also remaining involved in teaching at institutions such as San Bernadino Valley College and Crafton Hills College. He married business executive Joan Londerman in 1966; the couple has one adult son, Michael. Arias most recent work-in-progress was the largely autobiographical "journey" piece, *The Secret Man: The Search for My Real Father.* A resident of Stamford, Connecticut, Arias is also a collector of pre-Columbian artifacts.

## SELECTED PUBLISHED WORKS:

"El Mago," *El Grito,* Spring 1970, p. 51–55.

"Chicano Books a Rare Item," *El Chicano,* November 1971, p. 3, 10.

"The Barrio" and "We're Supposed to Believe We're Inferior," in *The Chicanos: Mexican American Voices,* Baltimore, Penguin, 1971.

"The Interview" and "Stoop Labor," *Revista Chicano-Riqueña,* Winter 1974, p. 2–6, 7–14.

"A House on the Island" and "The Story Machine," *Revista Chicano-Riqueña,* Autumn 1975, p. 3–8, 9–12.

*The Road to Tamazunchale,* Reno, West Coast Poetry Review, 1975.

"The Wetback," in *First Chicano Literary Contest Winners,* Irvine, University of California, 1975.

"The Castle," *Bilingual Review/Revista Bilingue,* May-August 1976, p. 176–182.

"El señor del chivo," *Journal of Ethnic Studies,* Winter 1976, p. 58–60.

"Chinches," *Latin American Literary Review,* Spring-Summer 1977, p. 180–184.

"The Interview," *Revista Chicano-Riquena,* Winter 1979, p. 1–7.

"The Boy Ate Himself," *Quarry West,* 1980, p. 23–27.

*Five Against the Sea,* New York, New American Library, 1989.

## SOURCES:

### Books

Bruce, Novoa, "Ron Arias" in his *Chicano Authors: Inquiry by Interview,* Austin, University of Texas Press, 1980, p. 235–252.

*Chicano Writers, First Series,* Vol. 82, edited by Francisco A. Lomelí and Carl R. Shirley, Detroit, Gale Research, 1989, pp. 37–44.

*Hispanic Literature Criticism,* Vol. 1, edited by Jelena Krstović, Detroit, Gale Research, 1994, pp. 91–109.

*Hispanic Writers,* edited by Bryan Ryan, Detroit, Gale Research, 1991.

### Periodicals

*American Literature,* No. 50, 1979.

*De Colores*, Vol. 3, No. 4, 1977, p. 34–38.
*Latin American Literary Review*, Spring-Summer 1976, p. 111–12.
*Los Angeles Times Book Review*, April 12, 1987.

—*Sketch by Cynthia R. Kasee*

# Oscar Arias Sánchez
## 1941-
### Costa Rican statesman

Oscar Arias Sánchez became the youngest president in the history of Costa Rica when he was elected that country's top post in May 1986 at the age of 44. The following year, Arias won the Nobel Prize in recognition of his authorship of the Guatemala Accord, a Central American peace plan. He assumed the duties of peacemaker in Central America in order to keep Costa Rica, often called the Switzerland of the hemisphere, from being pulled into a conflict between Nicaragua's Marxist Sandinista government and the United States-backed Contra rebel movement that sought to overthrow the regime. The international community embraced Arias's role as mediator because of a general recognition of his neutral stance on the conflict. While Arias had been an adamant critic of Nicaragua's Sandinista government, he had also argued vehemently against the U.S.'s funding of the Contra rebels. Arias insisted that such funding could be better spent on peaceful means of promoting democracy in Central America.

Seth Rolbein wrote in *Nobel Costa Rica* about Arias's hopes for peace. "When asked if the peace plan really could succeed, he answered grimly, 'Now, more than ever, no one wants the war to go on. The war is incompatible with the future happiness of our children. . . . There must be peace. We cannot fail.' Then, with a smile beginning to appear, he shrugged his slightly hunched shoulders. 'Todo es posible,' he concluded, eyes twinkling. All things are possible."

Arias was born on September 13, 1941, near the town of Heredia in Costa Rica's Central Plateau. His parents were Juan Rafael Arias Trejos and his wife, the former Lilian Sánchez. Arias, the oldest of three children, had asthma as a youngster, a condition that limited his participation in sports. Instead, Arias devoted his free time to books, an interest that laid the groundwork for his future schooling and political pursuits. Reading material was not difficult to obtain, for his parents' families were part of Costa Rica's young aristocracy and among the richest families of

the country. Rolbein noted that "when Arias refers to his roots he prefers to mention his grandfather, a humble ox-car driver who worked hard and slowly began to amass money, then land, and then more land. As is so often the case with hardworking, successful people, higher education for the next generation was a priority that ranked with consolidating and strengthening the coffee business."

While coffee production was the key to the family's wealth, however, it was not their only interest. Arias's father was an unsuccessful vice-presidential candidate in the 1970s on a ticket with Luis Alberto Monge, who later went on to serve as president just prior to Arias's ascension to the position. Both of Arias's grandfathers were prominent legislators as well.

### Affected by American Politics

After attending the Escuela República Argentina in Heredia and Colegio Saint Francisa in Moravia, Arias studied in Boston and Great Britain. Early on, Arias decided he wanted to be a doctor, but it was not long before he learned he had other aspirations. American politics fascinated him, and its influence had a tremendous impact on his life. Arias was in Boston at the time that John F. Kennedy ran for president; Rolbein reported that Kennedy's performance during the Kennedy-Nixon debates impressed him so much that he used ideas and phrases from Kennedy's campaign speeches later on during his own campaign. 'The torch must be passed to a new generation," Arias said during his own presidential campaign in Costa Rica 25 years after he heard those words in Boston.

After two years of schooling in Boston, Arias returned home and entered the University of Costa Rica to study law economics. He later joined the university's faculty as a professor of political science. During the mid–1960s Arias also became actively involved with the Partido de Liberación Nacional (PLN). He established a relationship with **José Figueres Ferrer**, a key member of the PLN who eventually became Arias's political mentor.

Arias graduated in 1967 and continued his education in England with a scholarship from the British government. Figueres, who was returned to the presidency in May 1970 after a 12-year absence, named Arias Costa Rica's minister of planning in 1972. During the five years that Arias held the position he established an elaborate program designed to stimulate national economic growth, technological development, and full employment. He also launched the construction of Plaza de la Cultura, a cultural park in the center of San José. Another cornerstone of his tenure was the development of a symposium where prominent leaders in various fields discussed the socioeconomic and political development of Costa

Rica. During this time Arias married Margarita Penón Góngora, a biochemist who was also educated in the United States. They eventually had two children, Silvia Eugenia and Oscar Felipe.

While Arias's responsibilities in the Costa Rican government in the 1970s were significant, he also wrote several books analyzing various aspects of Costa Rican life and history. His 1971 treatise, *Grupos de presión en Costa Rica,* an examination of pressure groups in Costa Rica, garnered him the Premio Nacional de Ensayo the following year. Other books penned by Arias include *Democracia, independencia y sociedad latinoamericana* (1977); *Los caminos para el desarrollo de Costa Rica* (1977); and *Nuevos rumbos para el desarrollo costarricense* (1980).

Arias served on the board of several universities and corporate entities during the 1970s. At the same time he continued to rise in the ranks of the PLN. He was chosen as the party's international secretary in 1975 and was elected to the position of general secretary, the PLN's top post, in 1979. This growing body of work further solidified the foundation Arias was building for a bid for the presidency. Arias worked his way up, wrote Rolbein, steadily drawing closer to the presidency. "He was not an electrifying speaker, he was not blustery, he was not innately comfortable in crowds and within the carnival of politics. In many ways he remained a shy, quite reader, best one on one. He would become known as an uncharismatic man." Yet in a few short years Arias emerged as a favorite to win the country's presidency.

Arias gave up his post of secretary general of the PLN in January 1984 to pursue nomination as the party's candidate for presidency. Since the party's popular incumbent president, Luis Alberto Monge, was prevented from running for another term because of the country's constitution, Arias was able to secure the nomination. His chief opponent in the election was Rafael Angel Calderon Fournier, a former foreign minister. Arias launched a campaign emphasizing three goals, "roofs, jobs, and peace." According to J. S. Fuerst, who interviewed Arias for *Commonweal* in 1986, Arias championed educational reforms and economic policies that rejected Communist concepts of land redistribution but called for "greater equalization of income by increasing real wages, by raising taxes on the middle and upper classes, by enhancing education, health, and housing services, and by intensifying the program of cooperatives—both consumer and producer." He promised to tackle Costa Rica's tremendous foreign debt without leaving its populace destitute.

Arias's path to the presidency proved to be a difficult one, for while he remembered John F. Kennedy's inspiring words from years earlier, he did not have Kennedy's charisma. As Rolbein wrote in *Nobel Costa Rica,* "He is a shy man, perhaps the most self-contained political leader I have ever seen. I don't get the sense he needs to press the flesh or that his juices flow with the rush of the crowd; more, he seems to be on an individual quest, perhaps looking for his place in history. Few expected him to win the presidency in 1986. . . . No one expected his combination of stubborn independence and a true statesman's vision."

On February 2, 1986, Arias was elected to a four-year term as president of Costa Rica with 52 percent of the vote. In his inaugural address Arias said: "We will keep Costa Rica out of the armed conflicts of Central America and we will endeavor through diplomatic and political means to prevent Central American brothers from killing each other."

### The Arias Plan

While his domestic economic initiatives were of great interest to citizens of Costa Rica, it was Arias's work on a regional peace plan for Central America that drew international attention. The Guatemala Accord, which Arias drafted and promoted, called for an end to armed conflicts in Nicaragua, Guatemala, and El Salvador. It also sought to introduce freedom of the press, religion, and assembly in those countries. Commonly known as the Arias Plan, the agreement was signed on August 7, 1987, by five Central American heads of state. Later that year, Arias was awarded the Nobel Peace Prize for his efforts to bring peace to Central America. The Nobel committee cited his "outstanding contribution to the possible return of stability and peace to a region long torn by strife and civil war."

In his Nobel Prize acceptance speech Arias repeatedly praised and gave credit to the other Central American presidents who agreed to the peace accord. He also addressed areas where improvement must be made. "We have said that in the name of economic growth, we are not going to renounce our dreams for a more egalitarian society. Today we are the nation with the lowest rate of unemployment in the Western hemisphere. We hope to be the first nation in Latin America which eliminates slums. We are convinced that a country free of slums will be a country free of hatred, that working for progress and liberty can also be a privilege of poor countries." Arias also urged all countries of the world to act on their desire for peace and understand that when people are free anything is possible. He accepted the award on behalf of the people of Central America: "I receive this prize as one of 27 million Central Americans. More than one hundred years of pitiless dictators, injustice, and widespread poverty precede the democratic awakenings in Central America. Either to live in violence for another country, or reach a peace overcoming the fear of liberty; this is the challenge facing my little America. Only peace can write a new history."

## Launched Arias Foundation

Arias used the Nobel Prize money to establish the Arias Foundation for Peace and Human Progress, which was designated to focus on socioeconomic issues such as the preservation of rain forests and the creation of local job opportunities. Asked by an interviewer for *Colonial Homes* about producer nations' responsibility to conserve tropical forests, Arias replied, "They must realize that their tropical forests are valuable resources that should be managed wisely so they can truly become engines for social and economic development. They also need to end subsidizing activities that destroy the forest, and instead, subsidize sustainable forests." Arias noted that Costa Rica set aside 12 percent of its land as national parkland, while another 15 percent is protected under other classifications.

Arias also pointed out that Costa Rica had pioneered important initiatives such as "debt-for-nature," a program wherein a country's national debt is adjusted in return for the implementation of environmental protection plans, national preserve buffer-zone protection, and reforestation projects. "But time is running out to protect the remaining tropical forests worldwide. We need political will, legal support, appropriate economic policies and sustainable technologies—all at the same time. It is one of the greatest challenges of our era."

## Arias Awarded Liberty Medal

In 1991 Arias shared the Philadelphia Liberty Medal with a French organization, Medecins Sans Frontieres (Doctors Without Borders). Each received a medal along with a $50,000 cash award. The Philadelphia Liberty Medal honors an individual or organization from anywhere in the world that has demonstrated leadership and vision in the pursuit of liberty of conscience or freedom from oppression, ignorance, or deprivation. The international selection committee cited the Costa Rican politician's authorship of the Guatemala Accord in honoring Arias. The Arias Plan, it was noted, had opened the way for the 1990 election in Nicaragua and the peaceful transition to a democratic government there. Due in large measure to his efforts, the commission said, all of the countries in Central America are ruled by civilian leaders chosen in competitive elections for the first time in 168 years. Arias was also commended by the committee for launching the Arias foundation and for promoting programs of conflict resolution and of development.

"We call for freedom, not just freedom of expression or the freedom of election, but freedom from want, sickness and deprivation," Arias said at the award presentation. Arias cautioned that the struggle for peace in Latin America was an ongoing one and called for an end to the use of military force everywhere. "We need a new liberation army," he said. "We need the soldier to lay down his arms and take up a plow. Each elegantly marching soldier costs our nations one hundred empty stomachs. Each tank, each warship, each fighter plane is a sad testimony to the hundreds of thousands of hungry and homeless men, women and children."

## SELECTED PUBLISHED WORKS:

*Grupos de presión en Costa Rica*, Costa Rica, 1971.

*Quién gobierna en Costa Rica? Un estudio del liderazgo formal en Costa Rica*, Editorial Universitaria, 1974.

*Democracia, independencia y sociedad latinoamericana*, CEDAL, 1977.

*Los caminos para el desarrollo de Costa Rica*, CEDAL, 1977.

*Nuevos rumbos para el desarrollo costarricense*, Editorial Universitaria, 1979.

## SOURCES:

### Books

Rolbein, Seth, *Nobel Costa Rica,* New York, St. Martin's Press, 1989.

### Periodicals

*Christian Science Monitor,* May 8, 1986, p. 14.
*Commonweal,* May 9, 1986, p. 272.
*Philadelphia Daily News,* July 5, 1991.
*Philadelphia Inquirer,* June 8, 1991, p.6A.
*Time,* October 26, 1987, p. 44.
*U.S. News & World Report,* Dec. 21, 1987, p. 40.

—*Sketch by D. D. Andreassi*

# Homero Aridjis
## 1940-
### Mexican writer

A prolific poet and writer of fiction, Homero Aridjis is also the head of a Mexican environmental group. A journalist as well, he has contributed to several North American newspapers, including the

*Homero Aridjis*

*New York Times,* the *Christian Science Monitor,* and the *Los Angeles Times.* An award-winning author, he was a recipient of the Guggenheim fellowship in 1966 and 1979, and the Premio de Novela Novedades in 1988. In *World Literature Today,* Ana María Hernández described him as "one of Mexico's great living poets."

Born April 6, 1940, in Contepec in the Mexican state of Michoacán, Homero Aridjis attended the Universidad Nacional Autónoma de Mexico, graduating in 1961. From 1957 to 1961 he founded and served as editor-in-chief of *Correspondencias.* In 1958, at the age of 18, his first book of poetry, *Musa roja,* was published. From that time, he has published regularly, and has edited books as well.

In 1964 Aridjis won his first literary award, the Xavier Villarrutia Prize. A year later he married Betty Ferber, and in 1966 he received his first Guggenheim fellowship and also became assistant editor of *Diálogos.* Aridjis published his first novel, *Perséfone,* in 1967; in 1986 his wife translated the novel and Vintage published it as *Persephone.* His literary career has included serving as a visiting professor and lecturer at the University of Indiana and New York University. He was also poet in residence at Columbia University's Translation Center.

As with many modern Latin American writers, Aridjis' style is influenced by the Mexican master poet, Octavio Paz. In 1977, following the publication of a book of poetry, *Vivir para ver,* Eliana Rivero compared qualities in Aridjis' work with that of Paz, and described him in *World Literature Today* as a "lyrical 'seer'" and his style as "terse and open." William Ferguson said of Aridjis' *Obra Poética,* "Every new reading of Aridjis's work, from the charming word games of the 1960s to the more somber tones of his latest volumes, tends to confirm Paz's not-entirely-playful characterization."

Showing versatility in genres, Aridjis wrote *Espectáculo del año dos mil,* a play in which "Aridjis's subtle sense of humor and his uncanny perception of the grotesque prevail throughout," according to Ana María Hernández in *World Literature Today.* Divided into three sections, the book first describes the beginning of the twenty-first century, where ritualistic celebration by grotesque figures is interrupted with commercials and the chaotic hawking of wares. The second part relates Aztec mythology and history, and the third, wrote Hernández, "displays Aridjis's dazzling dexterity with words and images" as the world comes to an end while the last woman and man on earth make love, reaffirming "the poets belief in the immortality of human love." His versatility shows his growth and maturation as a writer. In a 1983 review, Alberto Blasi said that the quality of Aridjis's *Construir la muerte* was a "result of a stringent reformulation of [Aridjis's] own poetics."

## Novel Favorably Reviewed

His critically acclaimed novel, *1492: The Life and Times of Juan Cabezón of Castile,* deals with a subject as yet untouched by most writers: the persecution, expulsion and the murder of Spanish Jews in the fifteenth century. The main characters, Juan Cabezón, his blind friend, Pero Meñique, and Cabezón's lost love, Isabel de la Vega, are three converted Jews, and the book is their story of survival in the horrific world of the Spanish Inquisition. Aridjis extensively researched historical sources for authenticity and applied his lyrical style to bring the period to life. According to Ana María Hernández in *World Literature Today,* Aridjis succeeded in bringing to the reader a "richness of detail in re-creating the language, the foods, the incidents of daily life in fifteenth-century Spain." In his *New York Times* review, Herbert Mitgang said the book is "really history in disguise" and that "as such, it demands close attention to separate fact from fiction . . . [and] like one of James A. Michener's informational novels, it is a palatable education about a time and place a reader might not otherwise pursue." The book, first published in Mexico in 1985 as *1492: Vida y tiempos de Juan Cabezón de Castilla,* was translated by his wife and published by Summit Books in 1991.

Aridjis, in addition to developing his creative writing talents, has also been involved in journalism. His articles have appeared in major U.S. newspapers on subjects ranging from civil rights in Mexico to environmental issues. He has been Mexico's ambassador to Switzerland and the Netherlands, and he also serves as president of a Mexican environmental group, the Group of 100. He has publicly denounced the killing of dolphins in the Mexican tuna harvests and has been criticized and received death threats as a result. Aridjis makes his home in Mexico with his wife and children.

## SELECTED PUBLISHED WORKS:

*Musa roja,* Mexico, 1958.

*Perséfone,* J. Mortiz, 1967; translated and published as *Persephone,* Vintage, 1986.

*Los espacios azules,* J. Mortiz, 1968; English-Spanish edition published as *Los espacios azules/Blue Spaces: Selected Poems of Homero Aridjis,* Seabury Press, 1974.

*Vivir para ver,* J. Mortiz, 1977.

*Espectáculo del año dos mil,* J. Mortiz, 1981.

*Exaltation of Light* (English-Spanish edition), edited and translated by Eliot Weinberger, Brockport, New York, Boa Editions, 1981.

*Construir la muerte,* J. Mortiz, 1982.

*1492, Vida y tiempos de Juan Cabezón de Castilla,* Siglo Veintiuno, 1985; translated and published as *1492: The Life and Times of Juan Cabezón of Castile,* Summit, 1991.

*Obra poética 1960–1986,* J. Mortiz, 1987.

## SOURCES:

### Books

*Exaltation Of Light,* edited and translated by Eliot Weinberger, Brockport, New York, Boa Editions, 1981.

*Hispanic Writers,* edited by Bryan Ryan, Detroit, Gale Research, 1991.

### Periodicals

*Library Journal,* May 1, 1991, p. 102.

*New York Times,* July 31, 1991, p. 16; October 7, 1991, p. 17.

*Publishers Weekly,* April 26, 1991, p. 47.

*World Literature Today,* fall 1978, pp. 599–600; summer 1983, pp. 433–34; winter 1983, p. 72; summer 1986, p. 448; summer 1988, p. 439.

—*Sketch by Sandy J. Stiefer*

# Roberto Arlt
## 1900-1942
### Argentine writer

Roberto Godofredo Christophersen Arlt was an Argentine novelist, short story writer, playwright and journalist. Most critics see him as a good narrator and innovator. A reading of his literary work draws attention to the variety of languages found in his writings. In "Arltilian" language is found the use of *lunfardo,* a language of the thieves, and the language of the *porteños* (the people of Buenos Aires). The reader also encounters vulgar language, foreign words, Castilian Spanish, scientific language, and, in some cases, lyricism. In "The Language of the Argentines," published in 1930, Arlt showed his interest in linguistics and said that language is alive and is constantly evolving by accepting new terms.

In *Cuadernos Hispanoamericanos,* Raúl Crisafio said that the work of Arlt shows the arrival of the Argentine narrative in the modern novel and marks the entry of conflicts in urban society as a theme in the novels of the Río de la Plata. On the other hand, Jean Franco stated in *Historia de la Narrativa Latinoamericana* that Arlt belongs to the formal group that the academics call Boedo and that his novels show the influence of Dostoyevsky, Gorky, and Nietzsche. He made the least traditional use of their influence. He also did not make use of the fictional forms of the time.

Many critics find autobiographical elements in much of his work. His dauther, who is a playwright herself and studied her father's work all her life, agreed. In the prologue of *Los siete locos,* (*The Seven Madmen*), Mirta Arlt said that his work is, in some ways, autobiographical. In *Los siete locos, Los lanzallamas* (*The Flamethrowers*), and *El amor brujo* (*The Love Sorcerer*), it is easy to establish a valid connection between the author and some characters.

Arlt was born in Buenos Aires, Argentina, on April 26, 1900, in the Flores Barrio. There is disagreement about Arlt's birthdate. In a biographical note for *Cuentistas argentinos* (*Argentine Storytellers*), Arlt himself gave April 7 as the date he was born, but in *El juguete rabioso* (*The Rabid Toy*), he said that he was born April 26. He died of a heart attack on July 26, 1942. His parents were Carlos Arlt, a German, and Catalina Iobstraibitzer, from Tirol, an Italian town in Trieste. They arrived in Argentina when they were already in their thirties and were never able to master the Spanish language completely. Carlos Arlt had many jobs and never excelled at any of them. Roberto Arlt had two sisters. The first died of tuberculosis at a very young age; the second, born after Roberto, called

Lila, also died of tuberculosis in 1936. He portrayed her in *El juguete rabioso* as Lila, the sister of Silvio the protagonist.

Poverty struck the Arlt family and his father had to go to the provinces to work for months at a time, but their economic situation did not improve. Arlt grew up in a very low income home. His father was tyrannical, and physically abused his children. Arlt left home when he was 16 years old, running away not only from his father's tyranny, but also in search of juvenile adventures that were later included in his novel *El juguete rabioso*. Arlt wrote the first part of this novel when he was 19 years old as an article called "Las ciencias ocultas en la ciudad de Buenos Aires" ("The Occult Sciences in the City of Buenos Aires").

He was expelled from primary school as "worthless" at the age of ten. He read widely and can be said to be self-taught. After he did his military service in Córdova, he married Carmen Antinucci, who had tuberculosis. He never forgave her for not telling him before they married. The couple stayed in Córdova for her health. His first child, Mirta was born in 1923 in this city. Another child was born in 1942 after his death, by his second wife, Elizabeth Shine.

### Published First Story as Teenager

When he was 16, Arlt published his first short story in *Revista Popular*. Arlt started writing police chronicles in the *Ultima Hora,* and published "Epístolas" in *Don Goyo,* a humor magazine. In 1927 Natalio Botana invited him to write in *Crítica.* Much later he joined *El Mundo* and wrote his *Aguasfuertes Porteñas.* Arlt spent most of his life in Buenos Aires except for a few short trips. In 1935 Arlt was sent, as a correspondent of *El Mundo,* to Spain and North Africa. On this trip he wrote his *Aguasfuertes Españolas,* published in one volume in 1936.

His first novel was *El juguete rabioso,* published in 1926. The narrator of this novel is a first-person protagonist named Silvio. Critics believe the novel possesses many biographical elements. The novel is divided into four chapters which show four different moments in the life of Silvio Astier. Arlt painted the protagonists as social beings and as individuals who worry more about their own well being than the problems of the humanity. The central theme is Silvio's apprenticeship. The author, argued Rita Gnutzmann, confronted Silvio at different times of his existence. Silvio fails in everything he undertakes.

*The Seven Madmen* was published in 1929 and *The Flamethrowers* in 1931. *The Seven Madmen* was called weird and disorientating, noted Foster in *Currents in the Contemporary Argentine Novel.* These three novels are considered a trilogy. In 1932 his last

novel, *El amor brujo,* was published. After writing this novel, he discovered the theater to which he then dedicated his life. He also published short stories. Nine of them appear in *El jorobadito,* (*The Little Hunchback*)—his favorite book—published in 1933. *El criador de Gorilas* (*The Gorila Breeder*) contains 15 of his short stories.

### The Theater and the Critics

*Prueba de amor* (*Test of Love*), and *El fabricante de fantasmas* (*The Ghost Maker*) were his first dramatic works. Raúl Castagnino said in *El Teatro de Roberto Arlt* that the play unanimously moved the newspaper critics of the time. The most prestigious columnists saw an intellectual density in the play as well as great temperamental force and a great number of concepts. A columnist for *La Nación* favorably reviewed the play saying that it stood up proudly, and gained the attention of the viewer with its ideas, fantasy and especially its emotion. Castagnino summed up the fissure that characterized the theater of Roberto Arlt. Among other elements he emphasized the simplicity of the subjects, the duality of the planes of reality and fantasy. He also lauded Arlt's constant reach for the surprise solution and the use of the theater as a catharsis.

### SELECTED PUBLISHED WORKS:

*El Juguete rabioso,* Editorial Losada, 1958; edited by R. Gnutzmann, Cátedra, 1985.
*Teatro Completo,* Editorial Schapire S.R.L., 1968.
*Los siete locos,* Losada, 1978.
*Los siete locos* [and] *Los lanzallamas,* Biblioteca Ayacucho, 1978.
*Aguasfuertes porteñas,* Hispamérica, 1986.

### SOURCES:

#### Books

*Buenos Aires y Arlt,* Insula, 1977.
*Currents in the Contemporary Argentine Novel: Arlt, Mallea, Sabato, and Cortazar,* University of Missouri Press, 1975.
*Hispanic Writers,* edited by Bryan Ryan, Detroit, Gale Research, 1993.
*Historia de la literatura hispanoamericana,* Editorial Ariel, 1981.
*Obra narrativa de Roberto Arlt,* Minor Nova, 1978.
*Roberto Arlt y la rebelión alienada,* Hispamérica, 1980.

**Periodicals**

*Cuadernos Hispanoamericanos* (edición conmorativa dedicada a Roberto Arlt), Volume 11, 1993, pp. 37–46.

—*Sketch by Sylvia P. Apodaca*

# Desi Arnaz
## 1917-1986
**Cuban American entertainer**

*Desi Arnaz*

Desi Arnaz was best known for the popular 1950s television show *I Love Lucy*, a situation comedy that he helped create along with his wife Lucille Ball, to whom he was married from 1940 to 1960. Arnaz played "Ricky Ricardo," a struggling Cuban-born bandleader whose high-spirited wife Lucy (played by Ball) was forever engaged in some sort of comedic mischief. Behind the scenes, Arnaz was known as a savvy businessman and producer and a trailblazer in the early years of television.

Although network executives were at first reluctant to cast the heavily accented Arnaz alongside an all-American redhead like Lucy, Arnaz and Ball agreed to contribute $39,000 from their salaries toward production costs of *I Love Lucy* to ensure that the series would be launched. The comedy quickly emerged as one of the most popular shows of the decade. As *Scholastic Update* noted in 1988, Arnaz's role on the show helped Americans to "accept Hispanic immigrants not just as exotic outsiders, but as Hispanic-Americans."

Desiderio Alberto Arnaz y De Acha was born on March 2, 1917, in Santiago, Cuba. His father Desiderio was mayor of Santiago and a wealthy property owner whose holdings included a cattle ranch, two dairy farms, and a villa on a small island in Santiago Bay. Desi's mother, the former Dolores de Acha, was the daughter of one of the founders of the Bacardi rum company. As a teenager, Arnaz was expected to attend college before embarking on a career in law and politics.

However, political unrest in Cuba dramatically changed the direction of Arnaz's life. In August 1933, the Arnaz home in Santiago was burned and ransacked. While Arnaz and his mother escaped to safety beforehand, his father, a newly elected congressman, was put in prison. While there, he was advised by the new chief of state, **Fulgencio Batista**, that he would be freed if he left the country. Promising to send for his wife (whom he'd later divorce) and son, Arnaz's father set out for Miami.

In June 1934, the 17-year-old Desi arrived in America and was greeted by his father, who had established an import-export company with two other refugees in Miami. To save money, father and son lived in the company warehouse and ate cans of pork-and-beans. They used baseball bats to ward off the rats that scurried through the building. After school, young Arnaz worked cleaning bird cages for a man who sold canaries on consignment in area drug stores.

During this time, Arnaz was recommended to a bandleader by a girlfriend's grandfather. Armed with a used guitar purchased for $5 from a pawn shop and a facility with the instrument—he'd used it often in Cuba to serenade the opposite sex—Arnaz persuaded his father to let him take this new $39-a-week job at the Roney Plaza Hotel. Before long Arnaz was discovered by **Xavier Cugat**, the "king" of Latin dance music. Upon graduating from high school and serving a stint in the Cugat orchestra, Arnaz debuted his own band in Miami Beach in December 1937.

The Desi Arnaz Orchestra won favorable reviews in New York and Miami and the attention of collaborators Lorenz Hart and Richard Rodgers, who asked the young orchestra leader to audition for their upcoming Broadway musical *Too Many Girls*. Arnaz landed the part of the Latin American exchange student. Soon the 23-year-old was on his way to Hollywood to appear in the film version of the musical, starring 28-year-old studio actress Lucille Ball.

## Lucy, Not Lucille

"Lucy and Desi's first scene together in the movie *Too Many Girls* required him to take one glance at her and swoon dead away in ecstasy," commented Warren G. Harris in *Lucy & Desi*. "It didn't take much acting skill; by then, they were already in love in real life." The relationship was passionate and tumultuous from the start, punctuated by clashes of temper and jealousy. Many of the disagreements centered on Arnaz's flirtatious and exhibitionist nature. Still, they came to care deeply for one another. Arnaz called her "Lucy" even though she had long called herself "Lucille." "I didn't like the name Lucille," Arnaz recalled in his autobiography. "That name had been used by other men. 'Lucy' was mine alone."

On November 30, 1940, Ball and Arnaz were married in Connecticut with a wedding ring purchased at the last minute from Woolworth's. "Eloping with Desi was the most daring thing I ever did in my life," Ball recalled, according to *Lucy & Desi*. "I never fell in love with anyone quite so fast. He was very handsome and romantic. But he also frightened me, he was so wild. I knew I shouldn't marry him, but that was one of the biggest attractions." Upon returning to California, the couple settled into a five-acre ranch in Chatsworth, just outside of Los Angeles. Mindful of the practice of naming their residence after themselves as actors Douglas Fairbanks and Mary Pickford had done, the couple decided on Desilu after eliminating such other possibilities as Arnaball, Ballarnaz, and Ludesi.

In May 1943, Arnaz received his draft notice to serve in World War II. Because of an injury, however, he saw only noncombat duty at Birmingham Hospital, 15 minutes away from Desilu. Convinced that Arnaz was being unfaithful to her, Ball filed for divorce in September of 1944. The divorce, though, was voided by a quick reconciliation.

Arnaz officially shortened his name during his stint in the service (from Desiderio Alberto Arnaz y de Acha to Desi Arnaz). When his military service concluded, he returned to Hollywood, only to find his opportunities limited by his heavy accent. Despite critical acclaim for his performance in the movie *Bataan* and gossip columnist Louella Parson's prediction that he'd be the next Rudolph Valentino, Arnaz found it difficult to secure significant parts. The new 22-piece Arnaz Orchestra, though, was getting favorable reviews, and Arnaz eventually landed a role in the movie *Cuban Pete,* in which he was touted as "The Rhumba-Rhythm King."

In 1948 Arnaz and Ball formed Desilu Productions to coordinate their various stage, screen, and radio activities. A year later, Arnaz asked Ball to marry him again—this time in an official Catholic ceremony. The ceremony was later played out again, albeit in a more fanciful manner, in an episode of *I Love Lucy*.

By 1950, Arnaz and Ball had both established themselves in the medium of radio. Arnaz first served as the bandleader for Bob Hope 's radio show, then as host of the musical quiz show *Your Tropical Trip;* Ball portrayed the scatterbrained housewife on the radio serial *My Favorite Husband*. When the CBS television network decided to turn *My Favorite Husband* into a TV series, Ball insisted that Arnaz be cast as her husband. As the show's producer as well as its leading man, Arnaz helped bring movie-quality techniques to live television and negotiated a deal whereby Desilu retained full ownership of the show.

## Fame and Fortune

Ball gave birth to the couple's first child, Lucie Desiree, on July 17, 1951, just as scriptwriters were putting the finishing touches on *I Love Lucy* for the show's October 15, 1951, premiere. The principal characters were Ricky Ricardo, a struggling Latin bandleader who'd burst into Spanish whenever he got particularly exasperated, and his wife Lucy, a wacky housewife with showbiz aspirations but no real talent. Before long, *I Love Lucy* was a smash hit, televised around the world. The show won Emmies in 1952 and 1953 for Best Situation Comedy.

"Rather than repelling audiences as CBS had feared," wrote Harris, "Desi's flamboyant Cuban-ness apparently had the opposite effect of attracting viewers." Casting Arnaz as a TV husband was "a case of awkwardness being recognized as an asset," observed a critic for the *New York Times*.

As stars of the most popular show in America, Arnaz and Ball were under constant pressure to live up to the happily married image of their TV counterparts. But while tensions in the marriage increased, the series' popularity continued to grow. More Americans watched the January 13, 1953, episode featuring the birth of "Little Ricky" than tuned into the inauguration of President Eisenhower, according to the *New York Times*. Lucille Ball gave birth to Desi, Jr., the very same day.

Arnaz attributed the success of the show mostly to his wife's performance as the daffy Lucy. Madelyn Pugh Davis, a writer for the show, said in *People* magazine in 1991: "He always knew she was the star. Never in all those years did I ever hear him say, 'Where's my part?'" Under Arnaz's direction, Desilu Productions became a media giant. In 1955 *I Love Lucy* began rebroadcasting earlier episodes —the first reruns ever shown of a current prime-time show—because so many viewers with brand-new televisions had missed the show's early years. As the *New York Times* observed, "The appeal of reusable filmed programs led eventually to a seismic shift in television production from New York to Hollywood, and made the program's creators millionaires."

In addition to *I Love Lucy*, Desilu produced such hits as *Our Miss Brooks, The Untouchables*, and *The Danny Thomas Show*. Arnaz and Ball also appeared together in movies such as *The Long, Long Trailer* and *Forever, Darling*. In 1957 Desilu bought RKO Studios, where he and Ball had met in 1940. By the mid–1950s Desilu was an empire that grossed about $15 million annually and employed 800 people.

Arnaz's personal life, however, was less healthy. Diagnosed with diverticulitis, a disease of the colon, he worked out a deal with CBS to replace *I Love Lucy* with a series of one-hour specials. Of greater importance, though, was the state of his marriage with Ball. Arnaz's well-documented drinking and womanizing took a tremendous toll on the relationship. "The more our love life deteriorated, the more we fought. . . . The more unhappy we were . . . the more I drank," Arnaz wrote in his autobiography. "The one thing I have never been able to do is work and play concurrently and in moderation, whatever that means."

On March 2, 1960, Arnaz's forty-third birthday, *I Love Lucy* was brought to a close after 179 half-hour episodes, 13 one-hour specials and nine years on the air. Ending with the usual kiss-and-make-up ending, the last show gave no inkling about the state of the marriage off-the-air. On the following day, March 3, 1960, Ball filed for a divorce, which, for the sake of the two children, was amicable. Two years later, in 1962, Arnaz pulled out of Desilu Productions, selling his stock to Ball for $3 million. Running Desilu had "ceased to be fun," he said in his autobiography. "I was happier cleaning birdcages and chasing rats."

Arnaz spent much of his time immediately after the divorce on his 45-acre horse-breeding farm in Corona, California. Still, his bond with Ball was never completely severed, and, in the fall of 1962, he was brought in as executive producer of his ex-wife's new series *The Lucy Show*.

Throughout the 1960s and 1970s, Arnaz remained active in show business. In 1967 he launched the NBC series *The Mothers-in-Law*, starring Eve Arden and Kaye Ballard. In 1976 Arnaz published his autobiography, *A Book*, which included an epilogue about Ball that stated, "I loved her very much and, in my own and perhaps peculiar way, I will always love her." Arnaz appeared on *Saturday Night Live* with Desi, Jr. to promote the book.

In 1986, after years of smoking four or five huge Cuban cigars a day, Arnaz was diagnosed with lung cancer. Ball stayed with him for several hours before he lapsed into a coma. He died in the arms of his daughter, Lucie, on December 2, 1986. He was "a good daddy, but a lonely man at times, one who chose a difficult path," she said of him in *Lucy & Desi*.

## SELECTED PUBLISHED WORKS:

*A Book,* New York, William Morrow and Company, Inc., 1976.

## SOURCES:

### Books

Harris, Warren G., *Lucy & Desi,* Thorndike, Maine, Thorndike Press, 1992.
Metz, Robert, *CBS: Reflections in a Bloodshot Eye,* Playboy Press, 1975.

### Periodicals

*Ladies Home Journal,* May, 1992, p. 86.
*New York Times,* March 1, 1953, p. 16; December 3, 1986, p. D26.
*People,* February 18, 1991.
*Scholastic Update,* May 6, 1988, p. 14.
*Video Review,* October 1991, p. 103

—*Sketch by Joan Axelrod-Contrada*

# Claudio Arrau
## 1903-1991
### Chilean pianist

Musical genius, prodigy, and boy wonder are some of the words most often used to describe Claudio Arrau. Regarded my many music critics as a master interpreter and impassioned artist, Arrau enjoyed a stellar, if sometimes unorthodox, career that spanned over 80 years. Arrau was born on February 6, 1903, in Chillan, Chile. His father died less than 12 months after he was born, but his mother, an amateur pianist, recognized and nurtured his musical genius, and became his first teacher.

Chilean legend says that Arrau could read music before he could read words. He made his formal performing debut in Chile at the age of five, playing selections composed by Mozart, Beethoven, and Chopin. It became clear long before he reached ten years of age that his talents surpassed those of the

*Claudio Arrau*

available teachers, and that his musical education would require the molding of a master mentor. In 1912 Arrau was sent to study with Martin Krause at the Stern Konservatorie in Berlin at the expense of the Chilean government.

It was through Krause that Arrau was first linked to the music of Ludwig van Beethoven in what would prove to be a profound lifelong musical and spiritual connection. Arrau's life was threaded to the composer's through a direct line of four teachers: Beethoven taught Karl Czerney, who taught Franz Liszt, who taught Krause. Once Arrau left Chile, Krause was his only teacher.

Young Arrau's introduction to the European concert scene came early. He performed before royalty and in salons, and in 1914, at the age of 11, made his formal recital debut in Berlin, marking the official start of his career as a solo pianist. In 1922 he made his London debut in a recital with Dame Nellie Melba and the violinist Branislaw Hubermann.

Life in Berlin provided Arrau with the opportunity to bathe in the richness of European culture. Arrau considered it the duty of every great artist to become not only proficient in his or her field of expertise, but also to know as much as possible about all art—painting, sculpture, literature, and theater. He collected Etruscan and pre-Columbian art and was knowledgeable about European classic literature. Arrau felt that his appreciation of the wide range of arts and culture helped inform his interpretations of the

music he played. Arrau's concert schedule, which over the course of his life took him all around the globe, enabled him to indulge in his interest in the world around him. Whether in Europe, America, Australia, South Africa, Israel, India, or Japan, the young pianist studied the local art and culture and collected artifacts.

Martin Krause died in 1918, when Arrau was in his late teens, an event that deeply shook the young musician. Arrau was further rocked in 1923–24 by a disastrous U.S. reception on his first tour there. Performing with the Boston Philharmonic and the Chicago Symphony, Arrau found that U.S. acceptance of his style and work came slowly. Mournful about the loss of his mentor and concerned about maintaining his career, Arrau experienced a period of emotional, artistic, and financial insecurity. He eventually found a psychological and spiritual mentor in Jungian analyst Dr. Hubert Abrahamsohn, with whom he remained close throughout his life.

Arrau adhered to Carl Jung's notion of the "collective unconscious" in which the psychologist posits that the same universal aspects of human experience lie dormant in all people, clothed in symbolism, waiting to be exposed, felt, and lived. Arrau willingly underwent analysis throughout his life because he believed that if he could tap into his unconscious he could set in motion powerful creativity. He remained humble within this context, acknowledging his creativity as something available to all humans, his talent a gift.

Arrau's accomplishments and the honors he received throughout his career were myriad. In 1927 he won the International Prize for Pianists in Geneva, which helped build his early reputation as a Bach pianist. This link to the composer became firmly established in 1935 when Arrau completed the entire cycle of Johann Sebastian Bach's keyboard works. After completing the cycle, though, he decided that the harpsichord was the most appropriate instrument on which to play Bach's works, and chose not to play them again. He did, however, find this cyclical approach to composers' works satisfying. For example, he played a cycle of Beethoven's works in Mexico City in 1938, and later did the same with compositions by Mozart and Schubert.

Arrau married soprano Ruth Schneider in 1940, and shortly thereafter left Germany to live in New York City. He and his wife had children after moving to the United States. Although he lived there for years, he did not become a naturalized U.S. citizen until 1979.

## Arrau's Mastery Is Acknowledged

In 1991, *New York Times* music critic Donal Henahan called Arrau's musical contributions "exemplary," noting in particular his detailed interpretations of Beethoven. "Arrau played a great deal of 19th-century music with great virtuosity and insight, but also with a well-tailored refinement that prompted critics early in his career to characterize his style as 'aristocratic,' a somewhat misleading label that stuck with him."

But Arrau was not merely a traditionalist. In fact, his musical taste and affinities varied greatly. Although primarily considered a Beethoven specialist, he also played the modern music of Schoenberg, Stravinsky, and Busoni before they achieved fame in their own right. Whatever the composition, music critics found that Arrau's playing was marked by a thoughtfulness and consideration of detail not often evident in others' work.

Arrau was also regarded by many as a man of particularly sensitive and passionate temperament. He found it difficult, and often emotionally painful, to live up to the expectations thrust upon him by the public, the artistic and financial communities, and himself. Because he was so focused on his emotional life, he was considered by some to be temperamental. He would on occasion cancel performances if he felt that his spiritual affinity to a piece was out of balance.

In addition to his musical talents, Arrau was a man of great political passion and conscience. On one occasion he performed a benefit concert that raised $190,000 in contributions for Amnesty International's campaign for the release of political prisoners around the world. In addition, he refused to play in his native Chile for years in protest against the Marxist government of **Salvadore Allende** and later that of the right-wing military dictatorship of **Augusto Pinochet**. He did return to his homeland in 1981, though, arriving to a hero's welcome. The Chilean government declared a day of national mourning when he died. A nephew reported at the time that Arrau had claimed that, while his mind and intellect belonged to Germany, his heart was still with Chile.

Although Arrau was a dedicated teacher for many years, in his later life he became disillusioned with teaching because he saw a trend in the musical world towards placing an emphasis on technique rather than the personal development of the artist. He was committed to the notion that a pianist not only had to know myriad aspects of culture to be a well-rounded artist, but also must know him or herself emotionally. Arrau felt that many of his students were unwilling to take such steps. Still, he found comfort in having chosen and adhered to his own personal path of growth and exploration.

Arrau gave up performing after his wife died in 1989. He had been scheduled to perform a recital, his first in three years, when he died in 1991 at the age of 88 after undergoing intestinal surgery. He is best remembered for his personalized interpretations of the work of some of the greatest piano masters of all time, as well as his willful artistic spirit.

## SELECTED DISCOGRAPHY:

*Les Jeux d'eau á la Villa d'Este,* 1929.
*Goldberg Variations,* 1942.
*Complete Beethoven Sonatas,* 1962–69.

## SOURCES:

### Books

*The Annual Obituary, 1991,* edited by Deborah Andrews, London, St. James Press, 1992, pp. 318–320.
*The New Grove Dictionary of Music and Musicians,* Vol. 1, edited by Stanley Sadie, London, Macmillan Publishers Limited, 1980, p. 633.
*Newsmakers, 1992: Cumulation,* edited by Louise Mooney, Detroit, Gale Research, 1992, pp. 555–56.

### Periodicals

*New York Times,* June 16, 1991.

—*Sketch by Karen Bober Kuhn*

# Juan José Arreola
## 1918-
**Mexican short story writer, editor, dramatist, and actor**

Juan José Arreola is a short story writer and editor whose uniquely satirical style has garnered significant critical notice. He was born on September 12, 1918, in the town of Ciudad Guzmán in the Jalisco state of Mexico, about 120 miles south of Guadalajara. From an early age, Arreola demonstrated a keen interest in drama, studying the theater at the College of Mexico and later in Paris, France, in 1945.

Although Arreola trained for a career as an actor and obtained acting parts in Mexico City, he found writing to be more lucrative. His first short stories appeared in the magazine *Pan,* which was published in Guadalajara in the early 1940s. He later co-edited the magazine. Arreola also started and edited another literary magazine called *Eos.*

## Eclectic Satire

Some reviewers have commented that Arreola's work typically defies definition within the context of literary genre; for lack of a better description, his work is generally characterized as satire. Arreola draws his eclectic style from the best of several different types of literary traditions. In the introduction to Arreola's *Confabulario and Other Inventions*, George D. Schade commented that "in an age when many writers take themselves so seriously as to be solemn, it is refreshing to come across an author like Arreola, who laughs gleefully and wickedly at man—and by implication, at himself—puncturing all the foolishness he indulges in and cutting through the glaze of manners society sets so much store by."

Arreola's first published book was a series of short stories written in 1949 entitled *Varia Invención* (*Various Inventions*). His second book of short stories, *Confabulario* (*Speaking Informally*)—an odd collection of modern short stories, fables, and parodies—has become his best known work and has been updated a number of times since it first appeared in 1952. It was followed by a one-act play, *La hora de todos: Juguete cómico en un acto* (*All The Time: A Comedy In One Act* ), in 1954. The play received first prize recognition in the INBA Drama Festival.

Four years later, Arreola published two more volumes of short stories. One of these, *Bestiario*, was a collection of stories that featured animals who often took on human qualities. For example, in "The Bear," Arreola writes, "Between the open hostility of the wolf, for example, and the abject submission of the monkey, who is capable of sitting down with the family to breakfast at our table, stands the cordial moderation of the bear, who dances and rides a bicycle, but who can go too far and crush us in his embrace. It is always possible to strike up a friendship with him—at a distance—if we don't have a honeycomb in our hand." Other stories worked on several levels. "The Bison," for instance, paid tribute to an endangered animal, but was also an allegory for the last fight between the white man and the native people of North America.

During the 1960s, Arreola edited or compiled several books and continued to write short stories. In 1963 he published his first novel, *La feria* (*The Fair*), which focused on the unconventional life cycle of a Mexican village. Arreola also published his first anthology of his work in 1969.

Arreola's work has often reflected "a depressing view of most human relationships," wrote Schade. "In a large number of his stories and satires he chips away at love and its illusions. . . . the impossibility of finding happiness in marriage is a recurring theme and echo in his work." In his works, he often blames women, whom he regards as treacherous and adulterous, for this state of affairs. As many authors do,

Arreola also uses his writing to search for answers to some of life's most basic questions, such the reason for human existence. In "God's Silence," which appeared in *Confabulario and Other Inventions*, Arreola asks, "Is a lost soul a little thing?" And in the end of the short story, God answers him with "I want you to see the world as I contemplate it: like a grandiose experiment."

Arreola's writing has attracted critics and fans in Latin America and the English-speaking world. Described by Schade as a "mingling of the logical and the absurd, a blend of imaginative frivolity and Orwellian grimness," Arreola's style is sometimes esoteric, full of allusions to medieval and other historical events and references to various fields of study. As Schade commented, "There is no doubt that [Arreola] has a voice of his own, an inimitable style of utterance."

## SELECTED PUBLISHED WORKS:

*Gunther Stapenhorst: Viñetas de Isidoro Ocampo,* 1946.
*Varia invención* (*Various Inventions*), Tezontle, 1949.
*Confabulario* (*Speaking Informally*), Fondo de Cultura Económica, 1952.
*Le hora de todos: Juguete cómico en un acto* (*All The Time: A Comedy in One Act*), Los Presentes, 1954.
*Confabulario y Varia invención, 1951–1955,* second edition, 1955.
*Bestiario,* Universidad Nacional Autónoma de México, 1958.
*La feria* (*The Fair*), Joaquín Mortiz, 1963.
*Confabulario and Other Inventions,* translated by George D. Schade, University of Texas Press, 1964.
*Antología de Juan José Arreola,* Oasis, 1969.
*Cuentos,* Casa de las Américas, 1969.
*Palindroma,* Joaquín Mortiz, 1971.
*Mujeres, animales, y fantasías mecánicas,* Tusquets, 1972.
*La palabra educación,* Secretaria de Educación Pública, 1973.
*Y ahora, la mujer,* Utopía, 1975.
*Inventario,* Grijalbo, 1976.
*Confabulario personal,* Bruguera, 1980.
*Estas páginas mías,* Fondo de Cultura Económica, 1985.

## SOURCES:

### Books

Arreola, Juan José, *Confabulario and Other Inventions,* translated by George D. Schade, Austin, University of Texas Press, 1964.

*Hispanic Writers,* edited by Ryan, Detroit, Gale, 1991.

**Periodicals**

*Américas,* 46, No. 4, 1994, p. 64.

—*Sketch by Catherine A. Clay*

# José Gervasio Artigas
## 1764-1850
### Uruguayan revolutionary

As military leader, national hero, and spokesman for the Uruguayan people, José Gervasio Artigas played a fundamental role in the origins of Uruguayan nationhood. Attracted early to Uruguay's struggle for independence against its Spanish and English rulers, Artigas commanded an army of Uruguayan patriots that achieved considerable success.

Uruguay—one of the smallest countries in South America—lies between the River Uruguay and the Atlantic Ocean to the east, Brazil to the north, and Argentina to the south. Thus, Uruguay serves as a buffer state between these two larger powers. The Río de la Plata—a significant element in the national struggle—forms a natural boundary between Argentina and Uruguay. For colonial powers this region was of great importance because it provided entrance to the interior shipping routes in central South America. It was the Río de la Plata region that a military junta, based in Buenos Aires, wrested from Spanish control. Artigas commanded the Uruguayan forces in this revolution.

Artigas was born in Montevideo on June 19, 1764. He was the third son of Martín José Artigas and the grandson of Juan Antonio Artigas, whose family had helped found Montevideo. These early Montevideo clans were mostly landowners and soldiers. As landed gentry the family emphasized a commitment to public service and this public spirit was instilled in young Artigas from his earliest years. As a young man choosing the direction his life would take, he looked to both paternal and maternal examples. His maternal grandfather stipulated in his will that Artigas would be financially supported if he went into the church. But the public stature of his paternal grandfather in Montevideo and his years of military command prevailed—Artigas became a soldier and a revolutionary.

### A Rough Youth

His formative years were spent on his family's cattle ranches, which made him tough, self-reliant, and a leader. He was educated by the Franciscan fathers in the San Bernardino monastery. His fellow students included others who later would be influential in Uruguay's independence movement, such as Father Dámasco Antonio Larrañaga, José Rondeau, Nicolás de Vedia, and Francisco Xavier de Viana. His studies included reading, writing, arithmetic, some Latin, and religion. This was considered an adequate education for well-to-do boys who would follow established tradition and become ranchers, merchants, or soldiers.

As a young man, Artigas engaged in some questionable activities through an occupation as a purveyor of hides and cattle products. Cattle rustling and smuggling were two of the charges leveled against him. The accusations seem not to have caused any problems in the social circles in which Artigas moved, and he certainly retained the support and affection of his family. Artigas's family, according to John Street, in *Artigas and the Emancipation of Uruguay,* called him "a great gadabout, very fond of society and paying visits as well as of dressing in fine clothes like a town-councillor or like the dandies." At any rate, the knowledge of country terrain, men, and trade routes that Artigas gained while pursuing his business activities proved very useful to him in his later revolutionary exploits.

Artigas married his cousin, Rafaela Rosalía Villagrán, in 1805. His only legitimate son, José María, was born a year after their marriage. Two daughters died within a few months of birth. His wife became increasingly distraught during these years, and began to suffer from the mental illness that plagued her the rest of her life.

Artigas's leadership skills were recognized early, not only among the gauchos (cowboys) with whom he did business, but also within his family and Montevideo society. By the time he was 30 years old, he had begun to assume the obligations of public service that were family tradition. In an ironic switch of allegiances, he became an officer in a Spanish guard that was charged with ridding the countryside of outlaws, and bringing peace and security to the Brazilian border and Uruguayan interior. In a further attempt to keep the peace, a regiment of tough gauchos was formed. Artigas joined this regiment in 1797. Because of his influence with the gauchos, he was put in charge. In 1798 he was made a captain of the Cavalry Militia. As a military man in the service of Spain, he began an honorable career in support of the Spanish government, which continued until 1810.

### Revolution and the Rise of Artigas

Relations between Montevideo and Buenos Aires had always been strained, but the "English Invasions" in 1806 and 1807 exacerbated the hostilities. Spain was losing control in the area, and British occupation of Montevideo and Buenos Aires hastened the process. The native-born people (Creoles) of the region wanted neither Spain nor England as ruler. They decided to fight and forced the British to evacuate. Although Montevideo and Buenos Aires had banded together to fight the British, the patriotic junta, based in Buenos Aires, was not recognized as the authority for the region—some even continued a Spanish allegiance. Preparations were made to move against the junta. In the area along the Río de la Plata, a counter-insurgency was forming—led by none other than José Artigas.

A man of the open spaces, Artigas was described in George Pendle's *Uruguay* as "a hawk-nosed, fair-skinned gaucho chieftain who, with a following of horsemen, had already made a name for himself by frequently raiding the southern border regions of Brazil." In 1810, Artigas offered his services to the junta, recruited troops from the gauchos and renegades of the Uruguayan interior, and attacked Las Piedras, opening the way to Montevideo. The Spanish commander, Javier Elío, saved the city from Artigas by calling on Portuguese forces from Brazil. The Brazilians responded; now Artigas and his junta troops faced both the Portuguese and the Spanish. A treaty between Montevideo and Buenos Aires in 1811 provided that the siege of Montevideo be lifted and all troops—Spanish, Portuguese, and junta—be withdrawn. Artigas, in an evacuation renowned in Uruguayan history, took his 3,000 troops—along with 13,000 men, women, and children—just over the border to Ayúi in Argentina. (This number was equal to about a quarter of the entire population of Uruguay at the time.) For months, they lived in rude shelter, exposed to the elements. Back in Montevideo, the treaty was ignored and the siege resumed.

By this time, Artigas was championed as a leader of the federalists, who favored more autonomy for the provinces and a weaker central government, as opposed to the Buenos Aires centralists, who advocated a strong central government at the expense of the provinces. Thus, Artigas came to represent those who were disillusioned with the military junta leadership. During a constitutional assembly in 1813, the Artigas delegates were rejected by the Buenos Aires junta, causing a civil war to erupt between the two factions. During that war, Artigas' forces were successful in capturing Montevideo. Artigas, as the Platine province chieftain, defeated the Portuguese and forced them from Uruguay in 1815. Street, in a description of Artigas at the height of his powers, spoke of him as looking nothing like a general: "His dress was civilian, and very simple: trousers and jacket of blue without froggings or facings, shoes and white cotton stockings; a round hat with crown, and a cloak of thick cloth. . . . His conversation is pleasant, he speaks quietly and slowly; it is not easy to take him in with long-winded arguments, since he reduces the difficulty to a few words, and, full of great experience, he possess foresight and extraordinary judgement."

But the Río de la Plata region was vast, and Artigas was unable to consolidate his forces effectively. He could not resist another invasion from Brazil in 1816. He was defeated after a four-year struggle when the Portuguese, hoping to annex portions of the Río de la Plata regions to Brazil, invaded Uruguay. After his defeat, the Río de la Plata region was officially made part of Brazil, and given the name "Cisplatine Province." Thus, Montevideo, the old Spanish colonial city, came under the domination of the Brazilian Portuguese. It was not until 1828 that a treaty created the region as an independent buffer state called República Oriental del Uruguay.

Artigas left Uruguay to live in exile in Paraguay, unable to return even when Uruguay attained independence in 1828. A change of government in that country raised fears about the old revolutionist, and in 1840, at the age of 76, he was judged to be a threat to public peace and security, he was imprisoned at San Isidro for six months. His property was seized, and he was forced to start anew upon his release. He died in Asunción on September 23, 1850. Although he favored a concept of province confederacy—rather than independence—for the Río de la Plata region, Artigas is remembered as embodying the spirit of regional pride which eventually led Uruguay to nationhood.

## SOURCES:

### Books

Fitzgibbon, Russell H., *Uruguay: Portrait of a Democracy,* New York, Russell & Russell, 1966.

*McGraw-Hill Encyclopedia of World Biography,* New York, McGraw-Hill, 1973.

Pendle, George, *Uruguay,* London, Oxford University Press, 1963.

Street, John, *Artigas and the Emancipation of Uruguay,* London, Cambridge University Press, 1959.

Wilson, Major Carlos, *The Tupamaros,* Boston, Branden Press, 1974.

*—Sketch by Jane Stewart Cook*

# Nora Astorga
## 1949(?)-1988
**Nicaraguan revolutionary and diplomat**

Nora Astorga Gadea was a chief delegate to the United States for Nicaragua. She was one of heroes of the Sandinista revolution, which overthrew the dictator Anastasio Somoza Debayle in July 1979. Astorga's father was a wealthy landowner and her grandfather was defense minister for the Somoza regime. Brought up as a socialite, her only goals as a young girl were to marry an aristocrat, participate in the social scene, and have children. Her father had different plans for Astorga. He pressed her to go to college and she enrolled at the Catholic University in Washington, D.C. She studied there from 1967 to 1969, then she returned to Nicaragua to attend law school. While Astorga was in Washington, racial tensions were high in the United States. It was during this period that Martin Luther King, Jr., was killed and for the first time she realized the class differences even in her own country.

Astorga studied law at the Universidad Centroamericana in Managua, a Jesuit-run university. It was while she was at the university that she became involved in the Frente Sandinista (FSLN) revolutionary group. The Sandinistas were named after **Augusto Cesar Sandino** who was an anti-imperialist folk hero who spoke against U.S. involvement in Central America. He was assassinated in 1934 by direct order from **Anastasio Somoza Garcia**. In 1956, Somoza Garcia was assassinated by a young poet, Rigoberto Lopez. After that the Somoza regime continued in power through his heirs, first, Luis Somoza Debayle, then, Anastasio Somoza Debayle.

Sandino spoke of spiritual insight and divine law and he sided with the masses and the poor. He was like a "Robin Hood" to the Nicaraguan people taking from the rich who supported the enemy and giving to the poor. The early Sandinista, the FSLN, was founded by Tomas Borge, Carlos Fonseca, and Silvio Mayorga in 1961. Through Fonseca's efforts, the group was named Sandinista, although the early "National Liberation Front" studied the writings of Marx, Lenin and Sandino. When Astorga joined the Sandinistas, Astorga used her social status to work undercover for the revolution, but she really wanted to go to the guerilla camp. She married another activist, Jorge Jenkins, when she was 22 and they had two children before the marriage ended five years later.

### Became Heroine for the Revolution

A Nicaraguan construction company hired Astorga as a corporate lawyer. She lived in Managua in an upper-class neighborhood and continued working undercover for the Sandinista. But it was not enough for her—she wanted to fight for the revolution in a more profound way. Through her work, she met the notorious deputy commander of Nicaragua's National Guard, General Reynaldo Perez Vega. He was nicknamed *El Perro* ("The Dog") and hated by the Nicaraguans for his brutal treatment of prisoners. Vega had an interest in Astorga and she told her compatriots about him. The Sandinistas planned a tryst between Astorga and Vega in 1978, when she lured him to her home. Sandinista revolutionaries were planted in Astorga's bedroom and when she and Vega went into the room, a struggle ensued and Vega's throat was slit. The original plan had been to capture Vega and exchange him for 59 political prisoners. After Vega was killed, Astorga fled with the Sandinista to a guerilla camp in the jungle on the Costa Rican border. She met José María Alvarado at the camp. Their relationship produced two children. Astorga also adopted a boy whose mother was killed in the revolution.

Astorga returned to Managua in 1979 after the fall of the Samoza regime. She became a heroine of the revolution and was appointed as chief special prosecutor heading a tribunal that heard charges against over 6,000 Somoza National Guardsmen. She became the deputy foreign minister in 1983. A year later, Astorga was denied the position as ambassador to the United States by the Reagan administration. Three years later, she was appointed to the United Nations as ambassador for the Nicaraguan Mission. Astorga appeared many times on television and traveled to colleges and churches throughout the United States. She spoke out against the Reagan administration and CIA involvement in aiding the contra rebels.

Astorga rented a large house in Scarsdale, New York, where she moved with her widowed mother, five children, and two teenaged nieces. In 1986, the same year she was appointed ambassador to the United Nations, Astorga became ill with cancer. She had a mastectomy and continued working at the United Nations. Two years later, she became ill again and returned to her home in Managua. She died in a Managua hospital on February 14, 1988.

**SOURCES:**

**Books**

Gilbert, Dennis, *Sandinistas: The Party and the Revolution,* New York, Basil Blackwell, 1988.
*Newsmakers: 1988 Cumulation,* edited by Peter M. Gareffa, Detroit, Gale Research, 1989.

**Periodicals**

*New York Times,* February 15, 1988, p. A18.
*New York Times Magazine,* September 28, 1986,
pp. 28–29.

—*Sketch by Phyllis Noah*

---

# Miguel Angel Asturias
## 1899-1974
### Guatemalan statesman and author

The work of Miguel Angel Asturias has long been recognized as being in the forefront of the Latin American literary movement. With the English publication of *Mulata detal* in 1967—the same year Asturias was awarded the Nobel Prize in Literature—English-speaking readers became aware of his considerable talent as well. Using ancient Mayan Indian myths and legends—many of which still influence modern-day Guatemalans—Asturias can be counted among the very few Latin American authors who have managed to penetrate the surface of Indian consciousness, incorporating nature into his novels not as mere background but as a constant and formidable presence. Dedicating his life as author, diplomat, and journalist not only to his homeland of Guatemala but to all Latin American people, Asturias combined his literary mastery and political experience to write plays, poetry, and novels that portrayed Latin America's social, ideological, and economic history.

Miguel Angel Asturias was born in Guatemala City on October 19, 1899, to Ernesto Asturias, an attorney, and Maria Rosales de Asturias, a teacher, just one year after the rise to power of the Guatemalan dictator Manuel Estrada Cabrera. The events that shaped Asturias's life and work began in 1903, when medical students in the capital staged a strike against the dictator. Apprehended, the ringleaders were sent before Asturias's father, a district judge who—in view of their age and circumstances—dismissed the case. The judge was then himself dismissed and disenfranchised by Estrada Cabrera; and the Asturias family, fearing for their lives, were sent to the small town of Salama.

The power-mad and paranoid dictator exerted a profound influence on young Asturias, who was barely four when his family began three years in exile in a place vastly different from the home he had known in the capital. At an early age, Asturias became keenly aware of political and social issues, and his experience later provided him with a model for the dominant presence in his most well-known novel, *El Senor Presidente*. It was in Salama's dirt streets and shanties as well that Asturias encountered the descendants of the Maya Indians. Two women who greatly shaped his attitude during this time—his mother and his Indian nanny Lola Reyes—transmitted the legends and folk tales that became the basic elements of many of his writings. Asturias later paid homage to those early years with his first book, *Leyendas de Guatemala* (*Legends of Guatemala*), which contains the dedication: "A mi madre que me contaba cuentos" ("To my mother who used to tell me stories").

The Asturias family returned to Guatemala City in 1906, and the former judge became a sugar and flour importer. Estrada Cabrera was not removed from office until 1920; by that time Asturias was a militant university student who saw only that military oppression had replaced the dictatorship. As one of the "Generation of 1920," as the writers and journalists who had fought to overthrow the dictatorship were called, Asturias withdrew from politics and founded the People's University, where lawyers, engineers, and doctors conducted free classes for workers and peasants. By this time, Asturias had received his law degree from the Universidad de San Carlos de Guatemala.

### A Destiny in Exile

That same year, political unrest again forced Asturias to leave Guatemala City. In *Seven Voices,* Asturias told author Rita Guibert: "I believe every man is born to a destiny, and that my destiny was to be an exile." After a brief stay in London, Asturias settled in Paris. Finding a course at the University of Paris's Sorbonne on the myths and gods of Central America, Asturias began studying under Georges Raynaud, an authority on Mayan culture and religion. Raynaud had spent 40 years translating the *Popul Vuh,* the sacred book of the Mayans, into French; Asturias proceeded to translate from the French into Spanish. For five years Asturias lived and wrote in Paris, supporting himself as a European correspondent for Central American and Mexican newspapers and later as a university lecturer. He also traveled extensively throughout Europe, spending long periods in Italy and Spain, as well as visiting Greece, Egypt, and the Holy Land. From evenings spent in cafés with such Surrealist poets as André Breton and Paul Eluard, the young author began to develop a creative spirit.

Caught up in the myths of legends of the Guatemalan Indians, Asturias wrote his first book, *Leyendas de Guatemala,* in 1930. It consisted of a series of eight narratives and an allegorical play. The subject matter and the author's poetic vision attracted favorable critical attention, especially in France, where the French Symbolist poet Paul Valéry praised the book by saying that "it should be drunk rather than read." Translated into French, German, and Italian, *Leyendas de Guatemala* was hailed as one of the most important books of the year.

In 1933, Asturias returned to Guatemala and encountered the stifling regime of Jorge Ubico, which he endured until 1944 by publishing only elegantly cynical poetry. In 1945 he joined the diplomatic service under the reformist regime of Dr. Juan Jose Arevalo. By 1946, a more liberal government ruled the country, and Asturias finally published his first novel, a *tour de force* about an unnamed dictator in an unspecified Central American country. Asturias secretly had been working on the book since 1922. *El Señor Presidente,* an expressionistic and surrealistic story of life under a ruthless dictator, was voted best foreign novel in France. In *Masterpieces of Latino Literature,* one reviewer observed: "It is chiefly for this bitter picture of a morally sick Latin American nation under dictatorship, a disease suffered by many Latin American nations, that [Asturias] is recognized as an important author. The pictures of human misery in this novel make a powerful impression even on those critics who find it aesthetically weak. *El Señor Presidente* is an example of *esperpéntica,* a mixture of satire and the grotesque." John S. Brushwood, writing in *The Spanish American Novel,* claimed that this "grotesque quality is the very essence of the novel. . . . The cultivation of the grotesque laces the novel with fear." A *New Statesman* review in 1963 described the work as "incomparably visual, its texture composed in striking and beautiful images . . . perhaps the book itself is not so much a novel or even a political novel as a vision of hell conceived in the livid and writhing tradition of Spanish painting." In this, his trademark novel, Asturias wielded with consummate artistry the techniques he had learned from his surrealist companions. Filled with local color and references to regional folklore, the book includes an eight-page vocabulary and glossary.

## Magic, Myth, and Metaphor

From 1947 to 1951 Asturias served as cultural attaché for the Guatemalan embassy in Buenos Aires. In 1949 he published *Hombres de maíz* (*Men of Maize*), a novel of magic and metaphor in which mythological dimensions are interwoven with a tale of foreign exploitation of the Indian peasant and his land. A novel-like work in six parts—seen entirely through the eyes of a Guatemalan Indian—the story deals with the crisis that traditional Indian culture experiences when faced with "modern" technology. This work of fiction is considered Asturias's most controversial novel as well as his best; it has been praised and panned by critics since its inception. Using several coded elements borrowed from Mayan mythology, Asturias linked a word—such as corn—to an animal, a color, a number, and an historical epoch,

all of which are interrelated according to their role in pre-Columbian mythology. What emerges in place of a chronological plot is an associative one, using a complex network of symbols that forms the novel's infrastructure. Brushwood wrote: "The language play, always attractive and often amusing, enhances the nonrational communication; and so does the loose structure that makes us expect more unity than we get. The novel is not a somber experience. Readers are likely to have the feeling of being pleasantly tricked."

In *Seven Voices,* Asturias told Guibert that of all his books, *Hombres de maíz* was his favorite: "When I return to it myself I find a great many native elements, vegetable elements, so that it's as if . . . a series of phantoms and myths emerged that had been shut up inside. . . . And the Spanish language of *Hombres de Maíz* doesn't always seem like Spanish, at times it seems to be the music of another tongue."

## A Voice of Social Conscience

With the publication of *Hombres de maíz,* Asturias commenced a phase of social protest. Although he did not completely relinquish the use of native myth, his next three novels comprised his "Banana Cycle" and focused on political commentary—*Viento fuerte* (*Strong Wind*) in 1950; *El Papa verde* (*The Green Pope*) in 1953; and *Los ojos de los enterrados* (*The Eyes of the Interred*) in 1960. The books attacked the North American domination of Central American economies, and critics in turn attacked the books as having more journalistic than literary merit. Less imaginative and artistic than his previous work, the trilogy represented Asturias's turn toward realism as a vehicle for social commentary. In the *New Republic,* a reviewer wrote that *Strong Wind* "is in the main a disappointing book." Michael Wood, in the *New York Review of Books,* said of *The Eyes of the Interred:* "The book is skillfully decorated with symbols and myths, all the characters are convincingly realized, in a bookish way, and the only question in my mind is why Asturias should have bothered to write it, and why we should bother to read it." Nevertheless, Asturias countered in *Seven Voices* that these books "are the marrow of my work."

In 1954 Asturias was again exiled from Guatemala for his support of the leftist government of **Jacobo Arbenz Guzman,** which succeeded Arevalo's regime and which was itself overthrown in 1951. Living in Buenos Aires during this period, Asturias contributed to various newspapers and wrote numerous plays, including an historical drama about Indian slavery in colonial Spanish America, *La Audiencia los confines.* When a change in government in Argentina prompted him to once again seek a new home, Asturias moved to Genoa, Italy. In 1963, his novel *Mulata de tal* (*The Mulatta and Mr. Fly*) was published. Here Asturias returned to the familiar ground of Indian myths. The plot centers around a peasant who sells his wife to the corn god in exchange for wealth and the love of a sensual concubine named Mulata. The moon, the sun, and the devil all figure prominently in this exotic tale that echoes a recurring theme throughout Asturias's work—the continuous clash between the Spanish Christian culture and that of the Mayans and their descendants. *Mulata*'s success and the Nobel Prize awarded to its author in 1967 prompted the English-language publication of Asturias's other works, which led to new audiences and widespread acclaim. At the time Asturias acknowledged that the Nobel had been granted to him as a representative of Latin American literature as a whole and in recognition of its important position in world literature.

### Appointed Guatemalan Ambassador to France

In 1966, Asturias received the Lenin Peace Prize from the Soviet government. His exile ended with the election in Guatemala of the leftist Julio Cesar Mendes Montenegro as president. Asturias accepted the post of Guatemalan ambassador to France, a decision that was much criticized by the Latin American leftist intelligentsia. He held that position until he retired in 1970 to devote all his time to writing.

Little is known about Asturias's personal life. In *Miguel Angel Asturias's Archaeology of Return*, author René Prieto observed that "the longest-running legend Asturias ever wrote was his own biography" and that Asturias's "many travels, frequent exiles, and profound reticence to talk about himself or keep a diary have also contributed to the dearth of written biographical information." Still, a few details emerge: his first wife was Clemencia Amado, with whom he had two sons, Rodrigo and Miguel Angel. In an uncharacteristically revealing moment, he recounted in *Seven Voices* how he met his second wife, Blanca Mora y Araujo, at the Buenos Aires home of the poet Oliverio Girondo: "She was preparing a thesis on *El señor presidente* in the Faculty of Letters of the University of Buenos Aires. . . . From that evening, from that meeting, from that spark, my new life was born. And in one of my sonnets I say, 'She who sang songs in a voice born to bathe this blind man's face, so that he opened his eyes and believed in life.' Through her I began to believe in life again, in other words I was reborn and have become a different person."

Critics have often wondered about the unusual role that female characters occupy in Asturias's work, pointing to the possible influence of his mother as one explanation. Prieto wrote: "In [his] fiction women are always portrayed as being beyond men's reach. There are no exceptions to this rule: no happy marriages, no households filled with the patter of tiny feet. Instead, the women either disappear into thin air . . . run away . . . or turn their backs on men (literally) and

refuse, or are unable, to conceive. . . . In other words, Asturias's female characters are either unattainable or sterile."

In his later years, Asturias and his wife settled in Paris in an apartment filled with antiques and modern paintings by Latin American artists as well as the complete works of Valéry, Francisco Gomez de Quevado y Villegas, **Cervantes**, Hemingway, Shakespeare, Dostoyevsky, and numerous translations of *El Señor Presidente*. He died on June 7, 1974, at the age of 74. His obituary in the *New York Times* lauded him as "the first Latin American writer to present the Indian fully and convincingly from within."

## SELECTED PUBLISHED WORKS:

*Leyendas de Guatemala,* Madrid, Oriente, 1930.
*El Señor Presidente,* Mexico, Costa-Amic, 1946; translated by F. Partridge, New York, Atheneum, 1964.
*Hombres de maíz,* Buenos Aires, Losada, 1949; translated by G. Martin, *Men of Maize,* New York, Delacorte, 1975.
*Viento fuerte,* Buenos Aires, Losada, 1950; translated by G. Rabassa, *Strong Wind,* New York, Delacorte, 1968.
*El Papa verde,* Buenos Aires, Losada, 1954; translated by G. Rabassa, *The Green Pope,* New York, Delacorte, 1971.
*Weekénd en Guatemala,* Buenos Aires, Goyanarte, 1956.
*Los ojos de los enterrados,* Buenos Aires, Losada, 1960; translated by G. Rabassa, *The Eyes of the Interred,* New York, Delacorte, 1973.
*El alhajadito,* Buenos Aires, Goyanarte, 1961.
*Mulata de tal,* Buenos Aires, Losada, 1963; translated by G. Rabassa, *Mulata,* New York, Delacorte, 1967.
*Teatro,* Buenos Aires, Losada, 1964.
*Clarivigilia primaveral,* Buenos Aires, Losada, 1965.
*Maladron,* Buenos Aires, Losada, 1969.

## SOURCES:

### Books

Brushwood, John S., *The Spanish American Novel: A Twentieth-Century Survey,* Austin, University of Texas Press, 1975.
*Contemporary Literary Criticism,* Volume 3, Detroit, Gale Research, 1975.
Guibert, Rita, *Seven Voices,* translated by Frances Partridge, New York, Alfred A. Knopf, 1973.
*Masterpieces of Latino Literature,* edited by Frank N. Magill, New York, HarperCollins, 1994.

*Miguel Angel Asturias edicion critica de las obras completas,* Paris, Klincksieck, and Mexico, Fondo de Cultura Economica, 1977.

Prieto, René, *Miguel Angel Asturias's Archaeology of Return,* New York, Cambridge University Press, 1993.

**Periodicals**

*New Republic,* February 22, 1969, pp. 24–27.
*New Statesman,* October 25, 1963, p. 578.
*New York Times,* June 10, 1974, p. 25.

—*Sketch by Julie Catalano*

*Patricio Aylwin Azócar*

# Patricio Aylwin Azócar
## 1918-
**Chilean president**

Patricio Aylwin Azócar became president of Chile in March 1990, after the country had been ruled by a repressive military regime for 17 years. A family man, he and his wife, Leonor Oyarzun, have raised five children. Of Spanish Basque and Welsh lineage, he was born in the resort suburb of Valparaiso, Chile in Vina del Mar, November 26, 1918. Politics was in his blood as evidenced as far back as his great-grandfather who initially came to Chile as British Consul; Aylwin's father was a lawyer and president of the Chilean Supreme Court.

### Elected President of the Christian Democratic Party

Following in his father's footsteps, Aylwin became a lawyer active in politics. A Christian Democrat, he was elected to the Chilean Senate in 1965. Aylwin was a staunch supporter of the first Christian Democratic president of Chile, Eduardo Frei Montalva, who reigned from 1964 to 1970, and was succeeded in an election by radical Socialist, **Salvador Allende Gossens**. The nationalization program Allende instituted caused the country to plummet into economic confusion. In 1972, Gossens imposed martial law because of protest strikes against his administration. The country reached a state of emergency.

In 1973, Aylwin was elected president of the Christian Democrats and one of his first duties was to meet with Allende to propose reforms in the ruler's programs and to remove martial law. Although Aylwin convinced Allende to add several military leaders to his cabinet—a move many people called "the white coup"—Allende did not act upon the other party proposals, leading the Christian Democrats to refuse further cooperation with him.

Allende remained steadfast in his nationalization program and after several months on September 11, 1973, a military coup led by General **Augusto Pinochet Ugarte** wrested power from Allende, who died in the struggle. Aylwin first advocated Pinochet, but quickly removed his support when he discovered that the military regime did not want to restore democracy to Chile. Pinochet remained in power for 17 years. During this time, Aylwin continued to lead the Christian Democratic party; in his law practice, he defended activists who were persecuted by Pinochet's regime.

Meanwhile Aylwin served six separate terms as leader of the Christian Democratic party. In 1987, he decided to push Pinochet into a democratic election. Confident that the people would keep the military regime in power, Pinochet agreed to give the people a choice. Aylwin's supporters—including leftist parties from the Allende government—launched a united campaign known as the Coalition of Parties for the Democracy (CPD or Concertacion).

On election day, October 5, 1988, 55 percent of the seven million voters rejected the Pinochet regime. Having gracefully lost, Pinochet called for a general election for a president and both houses of Congress for the following year. The coalition decided to only back one opponent. In February of 1989, Aylwin survived challenges from Andres Zaldivar, Gabriel Valdes and Eduardo Frei, Jr. to win the congressional nomination. In turn, Hernan Buchi, former finance minister under Pinochet, was nominated by the National Renovation party and the conservative Independent Democratic Union. Buchi was credited with reestablishing economic stability for Chile after the Allende regime. Francisco Javier Errazuriz, a food merchant, entered the race independently. The polls correctly predicted victory for Aylwin; on December 14, 1989, he was elected as the new president of Chile with 55 percent of the vote. Aylwin's brother Andres and his son-in-law Manuel Matta were both elected to the House of Deputies.

### Assumed Presidency

Aylwin was sworn in as president on March 11, 1990, in Valparaiso, where the new legislative seat of the Chilean government was planned. Attending his inauguration was Pinochet, who remained as commander-in-chief of the military though Aylwin had asked him to resign. When Aylwin returned to Santiago after his inauguration, thousands of well-wishers cheered him as he traveled the parade route to the presidential palace.

As president, one of Aylwin's first orders was the release of many of the political prisoners. He ordered an inquiry into the charges of human rights abuses and torture by the military, organizing the Truth and Reconciliation Commission to handle the investigation. During Aylwin's four-year term, Chilean economy grew at a rapid rate. He encouraged expansion of the export trade and privatization. Under his administration, the minimum wage was increased by 36 percent.

In 1993, Eduardo Frei, son of the first Christian Democratic president, Eduardo Frei Montalva, was elected president in Chile, replacing Aylwin in 1994.

### SOURCES:

**Books**

*Current Biography Yearbook: 1990,* edited by Charles Moritz, New York, Wilson, 1990, pp. 41–44.

**Periodicals**

*New Perspectives Quarterly,* Fall 1993, pp. 4–7.
*World Press,* February 1994, p. 36.

—*Sketch by Phyllis Noah*

# Emilio Azcárraga
## 1930-
**Mexican media magnate**

Emilio Azcárraga has built a vast Mexican media empire. *Business Mexico*'s Andrew Paxman wrote in 1992 that Azcárraga "is recognized by *Fortune* magazine as Latin America's richest man, with personal assets of US $2.8 billion." Much of Azcárraga's work is rooted in *Grupo Televisa, S.A.,* of which he is president.

Televisa's success—it is a multi-billion dollar operation—can be attributed to three factors. First, the strong relationship between Mexico's dominant political party El Partido Revolucionario Institucional (PRI) and the Mexican television industry has created a de facto monopoly for Televisa; the company commands a 90 percent share of the Mexican viewing audience. Second, as president of Televisa, Azcárraga has exhibited a natural flair for vertical and horizontal integration of his industries. To integrate vertically, Televisa acquired a satellite in 1992 and owns 41 production studios. To integrate horizontally, Televisa began buying other television stations around the world. These included a 25 percent share in Univision (a Spanish-language network in Miami) and a 48 percent share in Red Megavision Televisiva in Chile. The third factor that has contributed to Azcárraga's success is his ability to diversify. This includes ventures such as the ownership of professional soccer teams and Spanish-language publications.

### Born Into Powerful Family

Emilio Azcárraga Milmo, Jr.—nicknamed El Tigre or "The Tiger" for the shock of white running through his otherwise jet black hair—is the son of Emilio Azcárraga and Laura A. Milmo. Born in Mexico City in 1930, the younger Azcárraga was educated at the Culver Military Academy in Culver, Indiana. He graduated in 1948 and returned to Mexico to work alongside his father at the family-owned radio station.

The Azcárragas were a well-established Mexican family with powerful ties to Mexico's ruling elite; this included the PRI, Mexico's dominant political party since 1929. During the 1930s and 1940s, the Azcárragas established their control over Mexican radio audiences with their high-powered stations that broadcasted throughout the country. When television technology emerged in the 1950s, Azcárraga's father was ready to expand his radio communications firm to include it. The manner in which Azcárraga, Sr., received licensing permission from the government is characteristic of the relationship between the Mexican government and Televisa. According to George W. Grayson in *Prospects for Mexico,* "Mexican commercial licensing practices were reminiscent of eighteenth century British monarchical licensing in publishing; the president handed out licenses to friends and politically reliable individuals." Thus President Miguel Alemán Valdés granted Mexico's second television license to Azcárraga's father in 1951.

Azcárraga and his father presided over the new venture, which was named Televimex. When Alemán left office in 1952, he joined the Azcárraga's media business. This marriage of public and private interests formally cemented the future of the Azcárraga empire with the Mexican government. When Azcárraga assumed control of Televimex from his father, Mexico was threatened by political upheaval sparked by student riots in 1960s. This situation was particularly hazardous for Televimex because the government of President Luis Echeverria threatened to expropriate privately held commercial television stations. Televimex was allowed to remain private and acquire additional stations through a 1970 agreement that required the station to televise more cultural and pro-government programming. Three years later, Televimex purchased another commercial station called Channel Eight. The name of the new venture was Televisa.

### The Televisa Empire

Although government-owned television stations exist in Mexico— Telesecundaria is one example— Mexican viewers prefer Televisa programs. The most popular shows include *telenovelas* ("soap operas"); news programs such as *24 Horas* and *Eco;* sporting events; and movies. Televisa captured its majority share through four national networks and 169 regional stations. But it is not only popular programming that makes Televisa successful. In the words of Mexican media critic Raul Trejo Delarbre, quoted in the *Los Angeles Times,* "Imagine if ABC, CBS, and NBC were one company. That is what Televisa has been in Mexico." This virtual monopan Missioly over the Mexican television industry, coupled with the comfortable relationship with the government, has brought Televisa and Azcárraga under attack. Critics cite the 1988 presidential campaign and the 1994 Chiapas revolt as clear indicators that Televisa is broadcasting incomplete reports of events. To justify this shortcoming the former President of Televisa, Miguel Alemán, Jr., admitted to George W. Grayson in *Prospects for Mexico,* that "indecision [has] created a form of self-censorship."

Perhaps due to increased criticism or the eventual threat of competition, Azcárraga decided to diversify his holdings. This strategy allowed for decreased financial dependence on the success of Televisa 's programming and gave Azcárraga more flexibility

within international markets. As of 1994, Azcárraga—under the Televisa banner—owned ten radio stations, a cable television outfit, a dubbing studio, three record companies, three talent schools, 41 production studios, and a Mexican paging service. His influence extends to print media as well; Azcárraga bought Grupo America, a Miami based Spanish-language publisher with over 80 titles in print, and *Ovaciones,* a Mexico City newspaper. In addition, Azcárraga's portfolio boasts two professional Mexican soccer teams—Necaxa and América—and the arena in which they play, Azteca Stadium in Mexico City. In 1988, he attempted to buy two more Mexican interests—Mexicana de Cobre and Mexicana de Aviacion—but he failed on both counts.

Having consolidated control over the Mexican television market, or in the words of *Business Mexico* editor Joel Russell, having "conquered its universe of nearly 350 million Spanish speakers"—Televisa and Azcárraga began to look for opportunities outside Mexico. His first attempt to infiltrate the U.S. market, Univision Holdings, Inc., was foiled by the Federal Communications Commission (FCC) when it ruled in 1987 that non-U.S. citizens could not hold the majority shares in an American broadcasting company. Undaunted, Azcárraga acceded to the FCC's ruling and sold Univision to Hallmark Cards for $620 million. Still, Azcárraga retained his vision for an internationally powerful Televisa empire: in 1993, he bought back a 25 percent share of Univision.

Although Televisa was already broadcasting to 63 foreign countries in 1992, Azcárraga wanted more. Consequently, that year he purchased a 50 percent share in the world's first private satellite, PanAmStat. Televisa then could beam its programming worldwide and increase its earnings by permitting other global stations to lease time on the satellite. For Azcárraga, the joint-venture also proved a formidable method with which to extend his empire. He participates in several such projects with the Hearst Corporation, Rupert Murdoch's News Corporation and the Discovery Channel.

Azcárraga has also pursued interests on the cultural front, not all of which have been successful. Azcárraga's passion for sports drove him to launch a Mexican sports publication in the early 1980s called *El Estadio.* He sold it because it was losing money, but Azcárraga began another sports paper, *The National,* in the United States in 1990. This periodical failed after only two years.

Where art is concerned, Azcárraga has been more successful. Televisa controls what Mary Farquharson and Stephen Baker of *Business Week* have called "Mexico City's most important private museum El Centro Cultural de Arte Contemporaneo." Farquharson and Baker added that "Televisa is probably the biggest single promoter of art.... The TV giant boasts a collection that includes important pre-Hispanic as well as modern works." Azcárraga is recognized as one of the world's top 200 international private art collectors.

In 1989 Azcárraga bought a yacht port in Manhattan's Battery Park City called North Cove Harbor. To his dismay, there were not as many yachtsmen as Azcárraga had expected and North Cove Harbor began to lose money. Always the entrepreneur, Azcárraga devised a solution to fill his empty port. By changing the name to the New York Yacht Exchange, Azcárraga began profiting by berthing yachts looking for buyers. Making money is Azcárraga's specialty, and it would be surprising if he and his media empire were not able to find more opportunities outside their homeland.

## SOURCES:

### Books

Grayson, George W., *Prospects for Mexico,* U.S. Department of State, Washington, D.C., 1988.

### Periodicals

*Business Mexico,* September 1992, pp. 12–14; Special Edition 1994, pp. 68–69.
*Business Week,* August 21, 1989, p. 30; May 18, 1992, pp 104–06; June 1, 1992.
*Euromoney,* September 1993, p. 36.
*Forbes,* January 6, 1992, p. 44.
*Los Angeles Times,* November 10, 1991, p. 24; October 20, 1992, p. H10.
*Wall Street Journal,* December 14, 1993, p. A12.

—*Sketch by Conner C. Gorry*

# Mariano Azuela
## 1873-1952
### Mexican novelist and physician

Mariano Azuela pursued two careers through some of the most dramatic decades of Mexican history. Author of more than 20 novels as well as biographies and histories, Azuela played a significant role in the toppling of the government of **Porfirio Diaz** in 1910. Throughout the power struggle that continued for several years after the Mexican Revolution, he remained committed to the principles of its original leader, **Francisco Madero**. Although many critics now associate Azuela with the Mexican Revolution, he did not receive popular or critical success until the 1920s. He continued to work as a physician until age 65, offering his services free of charge to the poor. He remained active in various pursuits until the time of his death, and his reputation among critics has grown steadily since then.

Born January 1, 1873, in Lagos de Moreno in Jalisco, Mexico, Mariano grew up in a middle-class environment. His father, Evaristo Azuela, who had borrowed several hundred pesos from a relative to open a grocery store with his wife Paulina Gonzalez, prospered. Azuela developed an interest in reading and literature early in life, sometimes taking advantage of his father's naps to read the "prohibited books" his father had hidden in the soap boxes.

In 1887 Azuela left home and went to the seminary. Unhappy with life under the strict supervision of the monks, he left the institution two years later. Azuela, in an interview with José Pichel in 1959, said, "My passage through this institution was incidental." By 1891, he had finished his preparatory work and went on to medical school in Guadalajara. He completed his medical degree eight years later.

### Combined Love of Literature with Medical Studies

During his time as a medical student, Azuela divided his attention between his studies and his love for literature. Although he claimed to experience actual "physical suffering" upon first reading Emile Zola, Azuela nevertheless adapted elements of Zola's naturalistic style. He also discovered Balzac, in whose books he became absorbed. In the first decade of the twentieth century, Azuela served his apprenticeship as a physician and became a novelist. He married his childhood sweetheart, Carmen Rivera, in 1900, and in the years leading up to the Mexican Revolution of 1910 published two books, *Los fracasados* and *Mala yerba*. The relative calm of that decade would contrast dramatically with the next.

The Mexican Revolution changed the direction of his life. Francisco Madero, born the same year as Azuela, successfully challenged long-time dictator Diaz and won. Azuela took up the *maderista* banner in his hometown, overthrowing the local politicians and being named political boss of the city of Lagos. He did not stay in the position long, but he continued to support the revolution long after Madero himself had died at the hands of counter-revolutionaries. General **Pancho Villa** had risen as one of several leaders who tried to maintain the spirit of Madero's revolution, and for a time Azuela accompanied Villa as a military physician.

### Revolution Politicized Novels

In the meantime, Azuela's novels had taken on a revolutionary theme and voiced the injustices of

Mexican society. In 1914 he wrote *Los caciques,* following *Andres Perez, maderista,* which biographer **Luis Leal** called the "first novel of the revolution." In 1915 he published his most famous novel, *Los de abajo* (*The Underdogs*), which collected many of the tales told by General Medina to Azuela about war and revolution.

After the revolution Azuela moved to Mexico City, where he tried to establish a literary reputation along with his new medical practice. He wrote three experimental novels in an effort to attract some attention from critics, but met with only limited success. Azuela was finally recognized when a movement in the 1920s to discover vital Mexican literature pointed critics toward *Los de abajo,* which led to general interest in all his works.

Throughout his career Azuela criticized the Mexican government, but recognition from critics and readers grew and gave him financial independence and international acclaim, which perhaps shielded him from persecution faced by others with similar opinions. Translators have given English, German, Japanese, Russian, Portuguese, and Italian readers a chance to experience his characters and stories of Mexico.

Following his death due to a heart attack on February 23, 1952, many of the most illustrious of Mexico's literary and academic figures attended his funeral. Some of the many honors Azuela received include being named a member of the Seminario de Cultura Mexicana in 1942, a life member of the Colegio Nacional in 1943, and posthumous recognition by the Colegio Nacional in 1953 as an outstanding author. He is buried in the Rotunda de Hombres Ilustres, similar in prestige to England's Westminster Abbey, and the Mexico City street where he spent much of his professional career now bears his name. Azuela had five sons and five daughters.

## SELECTED PUBLISHED WORKS:

*Maria Luisa,* 1907.
*Los fracasados,* 1908.
*Mala yerba,* 1909.
*Andres Perez, maderista,* 1911.
*Sin amor,* 1912.
*Los de abajo,* 1915.
*Los caciques,* 1917.
*Las moscas,* 1918.
*Domitilo quiere ser diputado,* 1918.
*Las tribulaciones de una familia decente,* 1918.
*La Malhora,* 1923.
*El desquite,* 1925.
*La luciernaga,* 1932.
*Pedro Moreno, el insurgente,* 1933–1934.
*Precursores,* 1935.
*El camarada Pantoja,* 1937.
*San Gabriel de Valdivias, comunidad indigena,* 1938.
*Regina Landa,* 1939.
*Avanzada,* 1940.
*Nueva burguesia,* 1941.
*La marchanta,* 1944.
*La mujer domada,* 1946.
*Sendas perdidas,* 1949.
*La maldicion,* 1955.
*Esa sangre,* 1956.

## SOURCES:

### Books

Leal, Luis, *Mariano Azuela,* New York, Twayne, 1971.
Robe, Stanley, *Azuela and the Mexican Underdogs,* Berkeley, University of California Press, 1979.

—*Sketch by James McCarthy*

# Jimmy Santiago Baca
## 1952-
### Hispanic American and Mestizo poet, playwright, and novelist

An ex-convict who taught himself to read and write while in prison, Jimmy Santiago Baca is an award-winning poet. After his release, Baca won the American Book Award in 1988 for *Martín and Meditations on the South Valley,* a book of poems. Considered an extremely talented writer, Baca is also lauded as different from most "prison writers" in that his work is not solely filled with fury and desperation.

Jimmy Santiago Baca was born in 1952 in Santa Fe, New Mexico, to Damacio Baca, a Mestizo or an *Indio* of Apache and Yaqui descent. "Half of my family are Apaches, on my father's side," Baca said in an interview published in the book *This is About Vision* in 1990. "And on my mother's side everybody is Hispanic, European. . . . So I think that Mestizo means that we are deeply mixed bloods."

Jimmy Baca's father, Damacio Baca, escaped the dusty bean fields of the Estancia pueblo at 19 years of age. He married Cecilia Padilla and in a few short years, they had three children—Jimmy Baca was the youngest. Damacio soon abandoned the family except for occasional monthly visits, spending his time drinking and gambling. Of his father, Baca said in a 1993 interview in *Esquire:* "Once a month . . . I saw him in the worst condition a child could ever see a father: literally on his knees in a drunken stupor or raping or beating my mom. She would hold me in front of her so he wouldn't hit her."

### Abandoned by Parents

In his father's absence, Cecilia took up with a man named Richard Besgrove when Baca was four. One day, Cecilia and her new "husband" bought the children new clothes and boots, told them they were going for soda pop, and then left Jimmy and his brother and sister with Baca's *Indio* grandparents in Estancia. Jimmy lived with his grandparents for two years, literally crawling under the floor boards of the house to hide from their tyranny, until he and his brother were taken to the orphanage in Albuquerque.

Baca recalled life in the orphanage—Saint Anthony's—in *Esquire:* "They put me on the top floor the first night. I'm six years old. There's tons of kids, our beds divided by sheets, rain dripping from leaks in the roof. Dripping in the dark. I scream and scream." He recalled that a nun beat him senseless when he ran from the dining hall after a woman he thought was his mother. Baca did not stay in the orphanage long. He continually fled each spring and was adopted by the women of the barrio. He lengthened his stays away from the orphanage until he left for good at the age of 13 and spent the remainder of his teenage years on the streets of Albuquerque. He did odd jobs to pay for a room, a bed, cigarettes, and comic books that he could not read.

In 1973, at the age of 20, Baca was sentenced to five years in an Arizona maximum security prison on a charge of narcotics possession. He turned himself in when he learned that a "shoot-to-kill" bulletin had been issued against him. Police, vengeful over the death of a cop shot by a Marine with whom Baca was dealing drugs, broke Baca's jaw and beat his hands so severely that they were too swollen for him to even be fingerprinted. Later, he pleaded guilty and began to serve his time in prison.

### Discovered Poetry in Prison

Baca's life in prison was no better than his life on the streets. Due to his aggressive and disobedient nature, Baca earned extra time, four years of which he spent in solitary confinement. The prison officials also administered electric shock therapy to him, hoping to cure his aggression. Despite the adversity he faced in prison, Baca found a way to turn the time into something positive. He taught himself to read and write and earned his G.E.D., although not without a fight. Many of his punishments resulted from his possession of "nuisance contraband" or having too many books. Later when his request to attend G.E.D. classes was denied, Baca refused to work. This protest made Baca unpopular with the other inmates, with the guards, and with the warden.

Despite his environment, Baca found a refuge in writing poetry. A fellow inmate encouraged him to send his poems to *Mother Jones* magazine. Denise Levertov, then the poetry editor of the magazine and an award-winning poet herself, not only published Baca's poems but helped him find a publisher for his first book. *Immigrants in Our Own Land* was published in 1979. As Baca explained to the *Los Angeles Times* in an interview in 1989, "I took a wild chance.

I didn't even know how to put the stamp on the envelope and address it. . . . [In prison] I saw all these Chicanos going out to the fields and being treated like animals. I was tired of being treated like an animal. I wanted to learn how to read and write and to understand. . . . I wanted to know how to function in this world. Why was I so ignorant and deprived? . . . The only way of transcending was through language and understanding. . . . It was the language that saved [me]."

Upon his 1978 release Baca visited Virginia Love Long in North Carolina, a poet with whom he had been corresponding. Baca was still tormented by prison and his life. He stopped writing, carried a gun, used drugs. Finally, he left Long after driving her car off a mountain road. A year later in Albuquerque, Baca married Brooklyn therapist Beatrice Narcisco.

### Reunion with Mother Turned Tragic

In 1985, Baca learned his mother, Cecilia, had returned to Albuquerque and still lived with Richard Besgrove. Baca's attempts at a reunion with his mother produced a lukewarm response. She never acknowledged him as a son, but rather as a family friend. In July 1985, Besgrove shot Cecilia in the head. Three days later, Baca told doctors to turn off the respirator that kept her alive. Though Baca suffered greatly over his mother's death and lost himself for a long time in drug addiction, his poetry endured. Baca's first book *Immigrants in Our Own Land* was accepted with very positive reviews. John Addiego in *Northwest Review* called Baca's book "a howl, a growling wail . . . I think it's valuable." In the *American Book Review* in 1982, Ron Arias said that "for Baca such an obvious peek into the furnace of anger is quite rare . . . Baca frequently transcends the obvious." And Denise Levertov wrote in *Commonweal* (1980) that Baca's work "is rich in image and music, full of abundant energy and love of life even when describing the brutal and tragic."

Baca followed his first book with *Swords of Darkness* in 1981 and *What's Happening* in 1982. But it was his fourth book, *Martín and Meditations on the South Valley,* that won him great acclaim in the literary world and the coveted American Book Award from the Before Columbus Foundation in 1988. Levertov, consistently one of the strongest voices praising Baca, wrote in the book's introduction: "[Baca] draws directly upon personal and documentary material rather than on more distanced fictive constructions; he writes with unconcealed passion: detachment is not a quality he cultivates . . . what makes his work so exciting to me is the way in which it manifests both an intense lyricism and that transformative vision which perceives the mythic and archetypal significance of life-events." In the *Hudson Review* Liam Rector added that *Martín and Medita-*

*tions* was "a powerful orchestration and revision of a narrative and lyrical admixture . . . it's a page turner, almost a novel in verse . . . the skills brought to the writing are . . . heroic . . . forging a form which supersedes any discussion of the craft brought to bear."

He followed his 1988 success with another book the next year. This book, *Black Mesa Poems,* won him the Wallace Stevens Poetry Award and the National Hispanic Heritage Award. In 1992 he published a collection of autobiographical essays entitled *Working in the Dark: Reflections of a Poet in the Barrio.* Baca has served as a poet in residence at Yale and at the University of California Berkeley. He has rejected many offers to lecture and teach and has remained on his farm in Albuquerque with his wife Beatrice and his children, Antonio and Gabriel.

### Wrote Screenplay for Film

In 1993, Baca was brought up on charges of assault, disturbing the peace, and resisting arrest when he attempted to defend a friend who suffered a racial incident in Bernalillo. The same year that Baca was jailed for the Bernalillo incident, his first motion picture, *Bound by Honor,* which he co-wrote and produced, was released by Disney's Hollywood Pictures. A story of Chicano gang culture lived by three young men in East Los Angeles, the film is based on Baca's experiences. It became a hot seat for Disney executives who saw it as a controversial, hyper-violent movie. A gang fight occurred outside a movie theater in Las Vegas that was showing the film, which alarmed the producers and director Taylor Hackford. Critical reception was mixed. Vincent Canby wrote in the *New York Times* that "though it's not the epic it means to be, it is not a failure." Despite his Hollywood work, Baca continued to write and to read his poetry all over the country. In a 1993, *Esquire* article, Richard Farris Thompson of Yale said, "Baca's sophistication echoing others embodies a new Chicano America."

Baca's work has been likened to Allen Ginsberg—whom Baca read first in prison before he discovered many other poets—and Walt Whitman. Though Baca's poems speak to the experiences of people in the American Southwest, particularly the Chicano Mestizo people, his poems strike a universal chord: the quest of one individual for identity and meaning. Baca said of his writing in *This Is About Vision,* "The way the Indians say 'seeing' is how close you can come to the way things really are, the way a deer sees a rock, or the way a frog sees water; we call that 'seeing.' Every human being has that seeing in them, and someone who gets up and writes every day, all he or she is trying to do is get close to his seeing capabilities. No class is going to teach you that."

**SELECTED PUBLISHED WORKS:**

*Immigrants in Our Own Land,* Louisiana State
    University Press, 1979.
*Swords of Darkness,* Mango Publications, 1981.
*What's Happening,* Curbstone Press, 1982.
*Martin and Meditations on the South Valley,* New
    York, New Directions, 1987.
*Black Mesa Poems,* New York, New Directions,
    1989.
*Working in the Dark: Reflections of a Poet in the
    Barrio* (essays), 1992.
*Bound By Honor* (screenplay), Hollywood Pictures,
    1993.

**SOURCES:**

**Books**

*Hispanic Writers,* edited by Bryan Ryan, Detroit,
    Gale Research, 1991.
Salidvar, Ramon, *Chicano Narrative,* Madison,
    University of Wisconsin Press, 1990.
*This Is About Vision,* edited by William Balassi,
    John F. Crawford, and Annie E. Eysturoy,
    Alburquerque, University of New Mexico
    Press, 1990.

**Periodicals**

*American Book Review,* January-February 1982,
    pp. 11–12.
*Commonweal,* December 5 1980, p. 698.
*Esquire,* June 1993, pp. 48–56.
*Hudson Review,* summer 1988, pp. 393–400.
*Los Angeles Times,* February 15, 1989, p. C12.
*New York Times,* January 14, 1994, p. D16; A5,
    1993, p. C15; April 30, 1993, p. C8.
*Northwest Review,* 1983, pp. 154–55.

—*Sketch by Christopher B. Tower*

# Joan Baez
**1941-**

**Mexican American singer, songwriter, and
activist**

Singer, songwriter, and activist Joan Baez was an
important part of the fabric that made up the
1960s experience. During that decade she appeared
on the cover of *Time* magazine, sang to a crowd of

*Joan Baez*

350,000 gathered at the Lincoln Memorial for Martin
Luther King, Jr.'s "I Have a Dream" speech, toured
with legendary entertainer Bob Dylan, campaigned
against the Vietnam War, and performed at Woodstock. Despite her connection with so many of the
important events and personalities of the sixties, she
refuses to see herself as a symbol of that era. In a
*Rolling Stone* interview with Mike Sager, she maintains that she would rather be seen as an example "of
following through on your beliefs, using your talents
to do so."

Baez's beliefs and her talents have brought her
considerable fame during a 30-year career. She was
born Joan Chandos Baez on January 9, 1941, in
Staten Island, New York, to Joan Bridge Baez,
originally from Scotland, and Albert Baez, who came
to the United States from Mexico. From her parents
the singer inherited both a rich multicultural background and the nonviolent Quaker religious beliefs
that inspired her own interest in issues of peace and
justice. Her father was a physicist whose moral
concerns caused him to turn down lucrative defense
work and devote his life to academic research.
Commenting on the consequences of her father's
decision in her 1987 autobiography *And A Voice to
Sing With*, Baez notes: "We would never have all the
fine and useless things little girls want when they are
growing up. Instead we would have a father with a
clear conscience. Decency would be his legacy to us."

Because of her Hispanic roots, Baez was introduced to racial inequality at a young age. In her

autobiography, she recalls being taunted as a child because of the color of her skin and relates her experiences in junior high school where she felt isolated from both the Mexican and Anglo children. She writes: "Few Mexicans were interested in school and they were ostracized by the whites. So there I was, with a Mexican name, skin, and hair: the Anglos couldn't accept me because of all three, and the Mexicans couldn't accept me because I didn't speak Spanish." She was also considered strange because of her pacifist beliefs. While other students spoke with fear of the Soviet Union and the echoed anticommunist feelings firmly held by most adults at the time, Baez took an anti-military stance that she learned from family discussions and Quaker activities.

Baez admits that loneliness was an important factor in her desire to become a singer. Seeing music as a path to popularity, she spent a summer developing her voice and learning to play the ukulele. She soon gained a reputation as an entertainer and made her first stage appearance in a school talent show. She was also known among her peers as a talented artist who could sketch Disney characters and paint school election posters with ease. At 14 she wrote a short, self-illustrated essay entitled "What I Believe" in which she related her beliefs on many topics. The essay expresses many of the truths that would serve as a moral guide for Baez's actions throughout her life. The excerpt she includes in her autobiography ends with her musing, "I think of myself as hardly a speck. Then I see there is no use for this tiny dot to spend its small life doing things for itself. It might as well spend its tiny amount of time making the less fortunate specks in the world enjoy themselves."

### Discovers Folk Scene in Boston

A family move from California to the Boston area after her high school graduation provided the circumstances that eventually allowed Baez to help "the less fortunate specks" mentioned in her essay. Although she started classes at Boston University, intellectual pursuits were quickly superseded by her growing interest in folk music. Bolstered by the popularity of such folk musicians as Pete Seeger and the Kingston Trio, the genre had experienced a revival during the late 1950s. Coffee houses that featured local singers became popular gathering spots for college students throughout the country. At first Baez and a roommate sang duets at coffee houses in the Boston area, but Baez soon went solo. She accepted an invitation to perform two nights a week at Club Mt. Auburn 47, a Harvard Square jazz club that was hoping to add folk enthusiasts to its clientele.

In 1959 Baez had gathered enough of a following to record her first album, titled *Folksingers 'Round Harvard Square*, that she recorded with two friends. That same year she sang for a couple of weeks at the Gate of Horn, a Chicago nightclub. While there she met popular folk singer Bob Gibson, who invited her to appear with him at the first Newport Jazz Festival that August. Her three-octave soprano voice captivated the festival crowd of 13,000 and made her an instant celebrity. Although she returned to her coffee house engagements after the festival, Baez sensed the increasingly important role that music would play in her life. In *And a Voice to Sing With* she notes that after her Newport appearance she realized that "in the book of my destiny the first page had been turned, and that this book could no longer be exchanged for any other."

Turning down more lucrative deals with larger record companies, Baez chose to sign her first contract with Vanguard, a small label known for its quality classical music recordings. Her first solo album, simply titled *Joan Baez*, was released near the end of 1960. The album was made up entirely of traditional folk songs, including "All My Trials" (an often requested favorite among Baez fans) and "The House of the Rising Sun," a song previously popularized by Huddie Ledbetter (Leadbelly), a black blues singer. A song in Spanish as well as the popular Scottish ballad, "Mary Hamilton," were also included. The album was a success, reaching the number three spot on the sales charts. Near the time of the record's release, Baez moved to California.

From her new home in California, Baez often commuted to the East coast, playing colleges with other folk artists. In November 1960, she played her first solo concert to an audience of 800 in New York City. By 1963, she was playing at the Hollywood Bowl with nearly 20,000 in attendance. As her career seemed to take over her life, she began to think about the essay that she wrote as a teenager and what was truly important to her. In her autobiography she writes, "I was in a position now to do something more with my life than just sing. . . . I could reach lots and lots of people. It would be a while before this sentiment would take root and grow into something tangible, but the intent was now evident and becoming stronger by the day."

### Becomes Active in Vietnam War Protest

The Vietnam War protest became the cause to which Baez would devote an increasingly larger amount of energy as the sixties progressed. In 1964, she announced that she would stop paying the 60 percent of her federal income tax that she figured went to financing the U.S. Defense Department. The following year, she founded the Institute for the Study of Nonviolence (now called the Resource Center for Nonviolence) in Carmel Valley, California. Her political beliefs at times affected her career. In 1967, citing the singer's strong antiwar stance, the Daughters of the American Revolution (DAR) refused Baez the permission to play at their Constitution Hall in Washington, D.C. When news of the refusal received sympathetic coverage in the press, Secretary of the Interior Morris Udall gave Baez permission to play an outdoor concert at the base of the Washington Monument, where an estimated 30,000 people came to hear her sing. Several months later she was arrested and jailed for her active opposition to the Vietnam War draft. The following year she married David Harris, a leader in the draft resistance movement, and in 1969, while Harris served time in prison for avoiding the draft, gave birth to their son, Gabriel.

Baez's social activism during the sixties sometimes overshadowed the reason for her rise to fame: her voice. From the beginning of her career, reviewers had struggled to describe its quality. In two early reviews appearing in the *New York Times,* music critic Bob Shelton referred to Baez's voice first as "a soprano voice, surprisingly never trained, that has a purity, penetrating clarity and control that not a few art singers would envy," later adding that it was "as lustrous and rich as old gold." The writer of a *Time* cover story on Baez discovered in her voice "distant reminders of black women wailing in the night, of detached madrigal singers performing calmly at court, and of saddened gypsies trying to charm death into leaving their Spanish caves." In *A Voice to Sing With* Baez refers to her voice as her "greatest gift" closely followed by a "second greatest gift," that of "a desire to share that voice, and the bounties it has heaped upon me, with others."

Despite her increasing involvement in political concerns, Baez's shared her voice with others in concert appearances and on numerous albums during the 1960s. Reluctant to leave traditional melodies behind, she slowly added more contemporary music to her repertoire. Her fourth album, *Joan Baez in Concert, Part Two*, included a Bob Dylan song, "Don't Think Twice, It's All Right." She helped Dylan's career by inviting him to appear with her during her 1993 concert tour. The two singers eventually toured together with equal billing and Baez later recorded *Any Day Now*, a double-album of Dylan tunes. She further expanded the scope of her musical offerings during the decade with *Baptism*, an album of spoken and sung selections from the poetry of Arthur Rimbaud, **Federico García Lorca**, James Joyce, and others, and an album of country and western music called *David's Album*. In one of the highlights of her career, Baez appeared at what many consider to be the pinnacle of 1960s culture, the Woodstock Music Festival. The five-day event was held in 1969 in upstate New York and brought together some of the most important and influential musicians of the decade. The concert drew more than 500,000 people with its theme of "five days of peace, love, and music."

The seventies saw Baez emerge as a songwriter on her album *Blessed Are . . . ,* which featured several songs based on her experiences as a wife and mother, including "Fifteen Months" and "Gabriel and Me," a lullaby written for her son. In 1973 Baez and Harris were divorced and she decided to end her association with Vanguard. "The Night They Drove Old Dixie Down," a cut from her last Vanguard album, *Blessed Are . . . ,* became one of the most popular songs of 1972 and Baez's biggest commercial success. Continuing her political activism that same year, she and a small group of friends toured North Vietnam to witness the effects of the continuing war on the Vietnamese people. During 11 of the 13 days, Baez stayed in the capital city of Hanoi, where the United States carried out the heaviest raids of the war. On her return home, Baez edited 15 hours of tapes she had recorded during her trip and made them into her 1973 album, *Where Are You Now, My Son?,* a very personal plea for an end to the war.

Baez remained active with political and social concerns in the United States as well. The same year as her Vietnam visit, she organized a gathering of women and children who joined hands around the Congress building in Washington, D.C., to protest continued U.S. involvement in Vietnam. Some 2,500 marchers, who had to brave flood waters left in the wake of Hurricane Agnes, linked arms around Congress while simultaneous demonstrations took place in San Francisco, Palo Alto, Minneapolis, and Boise. Since 1973, Baez has served on the national advisory board of Amnesty International, a worldwide organization that works for the release of people imprisoned for their religious or political beliefs, and she was instrumental in founding the group's west coast branch. In 1979 she founded Humanitas International, for which she served as president until the organization disbanded in 1992. Based in Menlo Park, California, the Humanitas promoted human rights, disarmament, and nonviolence through seminars and other educational opportunities.

## Career Sees Resurgence

In her autobiography, Baez notes how sometime during the late 1970s she "began the painful and humiliating process of discovering, ever so slowly, that though I might be timeless in the world of music, at least in the United States I was no longer *timely.*" Her waning popularity received a boost in 1985 when she opened the U.S. portion of Live-Aid, a multi-act rock concert designed to raise funds for relief of African famine victims. In 1986 she took part in the "Conspiracy of Hope" concert tour celebrating Amnesty International's 25th anniversary.

In 1987, *And a Voice to Sing With* was reviewed in a number of major periodicals in the United States and once again brought Baez's life and music to the attention of the national media. In the book, and in the interviews that followed its publication, Baez spoke of the materialism she saw pervading society. In a *Christian Science Monitor* review Amy Duncan referred to the fact that "Baez writes a bit dispiritedly about the '80s, and decries particularly the 'me generation' mentality and what she sees as a lack of ethical and humanitarian values." In a conversation with Alvin P. Sanoff appearing in *U.S. News & World Report,* Baez contrasted the politically concerned music of her early career to the music of today, stating, "The prevailing ethos is: No negative thoughts, and everything is beautiful!" Baez continued, "You just jog, eat enough of the right yogurt, and everything is going to be all right."

Social historian Barbara Goldsmith characterized Baez's work as the story of not just one person but of an entire society. "Baez's 20-year metamorphosis from popular folk singer to 80's survivor provides an instructional tale from which one could extrapolate the changes in values in our society in the past two decades," Goldsmith wrote in the *New York Times Book Review.* Whatever changes Goldsmith detected in Baez's value system, Baez herself minimizes. As Cathleen McGuigan pointed out in *Newsweek,* "Baez's music may have gone out of style, but according to her book, she never altered her art or her politics to suit fashion." In the preface to *And A Voice to Sing With* Baez appears proud of the fact that despite what she has been through, her "social and political views have remained astoundingly steadfast." She continues: "I have been true to the principles of nonviolence, developing a stronger and stronger aversion to the ideologies of both the far right and the far left and a deeper sense of rage and sorrow over the suffering they continue to produce all over the world." Baez continues to attract public attention with both her voice and her activism. In a 1989 *New York Times* review of a Baez concert that coincided with the 30th anniversary of *Joan Baez*'s release, Stephen Holden wrote: "Her voice, though quite different in texture from the ethereal folk soprano of her first albums, remains a powerful instrument." In 1992 *Play Me Backwards* was produced on the Virgin Records label and nominated for a Grammy award; a year later a three-CD boxed set entitled *Rare, Live, & Classic*—featuring 60 tracks from the years 1958 to 1989—was released by Vanguard Records. In addition to maintaining her music, she continued to dedicate her time to causes in which she believes. In the late 1980s Baez toured Israel and the occupied territories of the Middle East seeking a peaceful end to the conflict there. Further, in 1993 Baez visited Bosnia-Herzegovina in a trip sponsored by Refugee International and the Soros Foundation in an effort to focus international attention on the suffering in the war-torn region. She has survived what she calls in her autobiography, "the ashes and silence of the 1980s," and appears firm in her dedication to do what she can

to make life easier for "the less fortunate specks in the world."

## SELECTED PUBLISHED WORKS:

*Daybreak,* Dial, 1968.
*And a Voice to Sing With,* Summit Books, 1987.

## SELECTED DISCOGRAPHY:

(With others) *Folksingers 'Round Harvard Square,* Veritas, 1959.
*Joan Baez,* Vanguard, 1960.
*Joan Baez in Concert,* Vanguard, 1962.
*Joan Baez in Concert, Part Two,* Vanguard, 1963.
*Joan Baez/5,* Vanguard, 1964.
*Joan Baez in San Francisco,* Fantasy, 1964.
*Farewell, Angelina,* Vanguard, 1965.
*Joan,* Vanguard, 1967.
*David's Album,* Vanguard, 1969.
*One Day At a Time,* Vanguard, 1969.
*Any Day Now,* c. 1970.
*Baptism,* c. 1971.
*Blessed Are . . . ,* Vanguard, 1971.
*Come From the Shadows,* A&M, 1972.
*Gracias a la vida,* A&M, 1974.
*Diamonds & Rust,* A&M, 1975.
*From Every Stage,* A&M, 1976.
*Honest Lullaby,* Portrait, 1979.
*Live Europe '83,* Ariola, 1983.
*Recently,* 1987.
*Diamonds & Rust in the Bullring,* Gold Castle, 1989.
*Speaking of Dreams,* Gold Castle, 1989.
*Play Me Backwards,* Virgin Records, 1992.
*Rare, Live & Classic,* Vanguard, 1993.

## SOURCES:

### Periodicals

*Christian Science Monitor,* September 3, 1987, p. 21.
*New York Times,* November 7, 1960; November 13, 1961; December 12, 1989, p. C24.
*New York Times Book Review,* June 21, 1987, p. 30.
*Rolling Stone,* November 5, 1987, p. 163
*Time,* June 1, 1962, p. 39; November 23, 1962, p. 54.
*U.S. News & World Report,* June 29, 1987, p. 60.

—*Sketch by Marian C. Gonsior*

# Lourdes G. Baird
## 1935-
### Ecuadorean American attorney and judge

Although Lourdes G. Baird had what she described to the *Los Angeles Times* as a "rather Spanish colonial upbringing," she was not inclined to perform as the traditional "colonial" wife and mother. Instead, after bearing three children the homemaker decided to go back to school, and she is now one of five women in the United States serving as an attorney general. While her late mother would "be very surprised" if she knew of Baird's prestigious position, Baird's colleagues are not; her work as an attorney and as a judge has been repeatedly praised.

The *Los Angeles Times* wrote of her reputation, "Baird is widely praised in legal circles for her judgment, fairness, administrative skills, her sense of humor and her ability to relate to a wide variety of individuals and groups." Baird was so well suited to a position of high authority that two Republicans—a U.S. senator and the president of the United States— nominated the Democrat for the office of U.S. Attorney for the Central District of California. She was, in fact, nominated ahead of three highly qualified Republican male candidates. Considering that this Hispanic woman began her career late in life, it is a testament to her abilities that she presides over the largest federal judicial district in the nation. With her determination and consequent success, Baird provides an inspirational example for both Hispanics and women.

Baird was born the seventh child of James C. Gillespie and Josefina Delgado on May 12, 1935, in Quito, Ecuador. The family relocated to Los Angeles when Baird was just one year old. Because her mother was a devout Catholic, Baird was educated in Catholic, all-girl schools. She told the *Los Angeles Times,* "There's something in retrospect that was great about going to an all-girls high school." Because the nuns who ran the schools provided positive role models and encouragement to the girls, the Catholic schools instilled independence in Baird's character.

Baird married businessman William T. Baird in December, 1956, after graduating from Immaculate Heart High School and spending time in secretarial school. Together the couple had three children, William Jr., Maria, and John. Baird stayed home to take care of the children for 11 years. By the time John, their youngest child, was born, Baird had decided that it was time for her to go to school.

### Education and Early Judicial Career

Baird became a part-time student at Los Angeles City College. Admitting one of her fears about going back to school, Baird recalled in the *Los Angeles Times* that she was afraid that her "Blue Chip stamps would fall out of my purse and I'd be discovered for what I was." Five years later, the homemaker had earned her associate of arts degree. With her confidence renewed, she transferred to the University of California at Los Angeles (UCLA). By 1973, Baird had received her B.A. in sociology, and was headed for law school at the same university. Although her marriage faltered—she and her husband divorced in 1975—Baird did well in law school. After graduation, she passed the California Bar exam the first time she took it. She was 41 years old.

Baird began her career in 1977, working as a prosecutor in the United States Attorney's Office. In 1983, she became a private attorney as a partner in the firm Baird, Munger & Myers. By 1986 she had become a judge in the East Los Angeles Municipal Court, maintaining that position until 1987. After an appointment by Governor George Deukmejian in 1987, Baird served as a Los Angeles Municipal Court judge. With Deukmejian's next appointment, Baird became a Los Angeles Superior Court judge in 1988. She held that office, in which she worked in the Juvenile Court until 1990.

These were not the only experiences Baird would bring to her post as U.S. Attorney; her activity in social and civic organizations complimented her career. She has been involved with the California Women Lawyers Association since 1980, and she served as the UCLA School of Law Alumni Association president from 1981 to 1984. From 1983 to 1986 Baird worked on the Ninth Circuit Court of Appeals advisory committee and as a Ninth Circuit Judicial conference lawyer representative. In 1986, she became a member of the Mexican American Bar Association, the Latino Judges Association, and the National Association of Women Judges and remains a member of these organizations.

### Nominated for U.S. Attorney Post

When a position opened for the U.S. Attorney in California's Central District, Baird's long resume was scrutinized. Special qualifications were needed to become U.S. Attorney for the largest federal district in the nation—with its seven counties and 14 million people, the district was rife with drug trafficking, money laundering, savings and loans scams, and cases of defense industry fraud. In addition, the new U.S. Attorney would also oversee more than 150 lawyers. When Republican U.S. Senator Pete Wilson nominated Baird for the position in November 1989, observers were pleasantly surprised. It was not that Baird was unqualified for the position—she was clearly an excellent judge—it was that a Republican had nominated her, and that, if she were confirmed, she would be the first U.S. attorney in many years who was a member of the party opposing the president. While Senator Wilson was praised for his decision, some remarked that the choice reflected his political savvy; the nomination would garner Hispanic, Democratic, and female supporters for the Senator, who was a gubernatorial candidate at the time. The *Los Angeles Times* endorsed Baird's nomination in an editorial in early December with the headline, "Baird for US Attorney? Of Course."

The president, and later, the senators, who were to ensure Baird's appointment to the office of U.S. Attorney, had to consider Baird's opinions as well as her reputation. A Republican turned Democrat, Baird believed the death penalty to be justifiable in certain cases. She was in favor of equal rights for women and increasing child care options for families. Baird would not tell the *Los Angeles Times,* however, her stand on abortion. She was quoted as saying, "My duty is to enforce federal law and it's not up to me to judge what I like and don't like."

After a formal background check by the FBI, it took President George Bush six months to nominate Baird for the position. When Baird heard the news of her nomination by President Bush, she was thrilled. "I'm delighted," she told the *Los Angeles Times.* "I know there are incredible challenges out there [in the district]."

The *Los Angeles Times* reviewed Baird's career and provided the opinions of several of her peers regarding her possible performance as U.S. Attorney. She was lauded by Judge Paul Boland, who had watched Baird handle more than a year's worth of child abuse cases, and by Robert Brosio, the interim U.S. Attorney. Assistant U.S. attorney William F. Fahey, head of the government fraud unit and a co-worker of Baird's in the early 1980s, remarked in the *Los Angeles Times,* "I think she'll be a great leader." Baird herself felt good about the cases she had worked on as a prosecutor for the government.

One person who did not favor Baird's nomination, Lew Gutwitz, reminded the media of a case which exemplified Baird's tough stance towards criminals. Gutwitz, a lawyer who had defended American Indian activist Leonard Peltier in 1979, thought that Baird had been "meanspirited" during the proceedings. Peltier had been imprisoned for consecutive life sentences for killing two FBI agents. He later escaped from a federal prison in Lompoc, California, insisting that he had to escape to avoid being killed by the government. When U.S. District Judge Lawrence T. Lydick did not allow Peltier's attorneys to defend the convict on the basis of the alleged government conspiracy, the attorneys attempted to circumvent the decision. Baird and her co-counsel, Robert Biniaz, objected to these activities, and their objections were sustained by the district judge. Peltier was finally convicted, and, despite Gutwitz's objections, Baird

was proud of her contribution to that outcome. The entire Peltier case was brought to new light in the early 1990s with the release of director Michael Apted's documentary film *Incident at Oglala.*

One-and-a-half months after Bush's action, Baird's nomination for the position of U.S. Attorney of the Central District of California was confirmed by the U.S. Senate. When she was sworn into office by U.S. District Judge Manuel L. Real in mid-July 1990, Baird was 55 years old. Her proud children were grown—William Jr. was working in television in Los Angeles, Maria was a mother herself and living in Berkeley, California, and John was a student at the University of California at Santa Cruz. While Baird had proven that it is possible to achieve success as a woman, a mother, and Hispanic, she also demonstrated the benefits of returning to school to find a rewarding career after raising a family.

### From Drug Issues to the Rodney King Trial

After her confirmation, Baird was eager to begin work on the many different problems that awaited her in a district notorious for its criminal activity. She would deal with cases in an area that ranged from San Luis Obispo to San Bernardino. As she told the *Los Angeles Times,* she was anxious about the drug abuse situation in the district. "Crime is rampant. My experience on the bench has indicated to me the horror of drugs—the main problem in the United States." She continued discussing the relationship of drug abuse to alcohol and substance abuse, "Drugs pervade the society. I'm not a prophet of doom, but I can't tell you how it's going to be overcome." While the new U.S. Attorney intends to fight drug abuse with tough sentencing, she also states that more treatment facilities are needed to rehabilitate drug users.

Observers also hoped that Baird would deal with another thorny issue. The mayor of Los Angeles, Tom Bradley, had been the subject of a federal grand jury investigation for some time. His relationship with a local bank was questionable, and there was some indication that he might have benefitted from insider stock knowledge. The U.S. Attorney would have to decide whether to bring federal charges against the mayor.

Dealing with such issues meant that Baird would have to restructure the U.S. Attorney's office itself. The office would be dealing with a higher percentage of cases than when Baird worked there as an assistant attorney. These cases were becoming more and more complex. Additional attorneys would have to be hired to handle the savings and loan fraud cases. Finally, the new attorneys, along with the veteran attorneys, would have to be organized to work efficiently.

In April of 1992 Baird became involved in one of the most controversial cases to surface in the 1990s. In March of 1991 a black motorist named Rodney King was stopped by several white police officers. What ensued remains controversial and hotly debated, but a videotape emerged that showed the police officers savagely beating King. What motivated the beating remains an issue that may never be resolved. The incident was investigated by both federal and state law enforcement agencies. The officers were brought to trial in the state court and eventually acquitted. The black community in Los Angeles erupted in a rage, sparking one of the worst riots in U.S. history. When the smoke cleared, 60 people were dead and more than 800 million dollars in damage had been wrought. In the wake of the acquittal, Baird headed up the continuation of the federal investigation and prosecution of the officers. Civil rights charges were leveled not only at the officers who actually beat King but at the officers who looked on but failed to interfere with his beating. Baird's prosecution and administrative skills would figure prominently in the federal case.

With a district as large and as densely populated as the Central District of California, Baird has a busy schedule. Observers cite her past achievements in predicting her future performances and successes—whether she serves justice as attorney general or moves on to a position of even more authority. In September 1992, Baird was appointed as a District Court judge in the federal court of the Central District of California. In this capacity she presides over civil and criminal cases brought in federal court.

## SOURCES:

*Detroit Free Press,* August 6, 1992, p. 3A; August 9, 1992, p. 2F.
*Los Angeles Times,* November 30, 1989, p. B1; December 4, 1989, p. B6; May 15, 1990, p. B1; May 21, 1990, p. B6; July 11, 1990, p. B6; July 19, 1990, p. B1.

—*Sketch by Ronie-Richele Garcia-Johnson*

# Joaquín Balaguer
## 1907-
### Dominican statesman

For most of his life, Joaquín Balaguer has been a public servant of the Dominican Republic. Although he has at times expressed a preference to be known as a scholar, poet, and lawyer, Balaguer is remembered as a statesman who has navigated the troubled political currents that have long affected the Dominican Republic. In 1965 *Newsweek* reported that "Balaguer is neither an orator, nor a schemer, and . . . many Dominicans consider him an honest, kindly reformer." A year later, the same publication called him "slight, ascetic . . . and sad-eyed." But while he may be an unassuming man, he is also a resilient one. Balaguer, though struck blind by glaucoma, was voted into the office of the presidency of the Dominican Republic for the sixth time in 1994 at the age of 87.

Balaguer was born on September 1, 1907, to middle-class parents, Jaoquín Balaguer Lespier and Carmen Celia Ricardo. His father, of Catalonian descent, was born in Puerto Rico; his mother was born in Puerto Plata in the Dominican Republic. *Newsweek* reported in 1966 that Balaguer was ten years old when U.S. Marines arrived to stop a revolt in the Dominican Republic. "Their eight-year occupation shaped his life as it did that of all his countrymen. When the Marines finally departed, they left the ruthless **Rafael Trujillo** in command of the army, and by 1930 Trujillo became despot for life." Though Trujillo was to have a lasting impact on Balaguer, as a young man his passion was poetry.

Balaguer published his first volume of poetry when he was 16 years old; a year later, he won a poetry award in high school. He graduated from La Escuela Normal in Santiago in 1924 with a degree in philosophy and letters. Fluent in French and English and an adept student, Balaguer would go on to pursue his interest in academic matters throughout his life, writing numerous books on literature, history, and politics.

Balaguer earned a law degree in 1929 from the University of Santo Domingo and became a state attorney in a land court. He joined the foreign service in 1932 and worked for a time in Madrid; he also continued his studies at the University of Paris, receiving his doctorate in law and political economy in 1934.

When Balaguer returned to the Dominican Republic, he went to work for the Trujillo government. In 1936 he was named Undersecretary of State of the presidency. In succeeding years, he held a variety of other positions as well, including ambassador to Columbia and Venezuela in 1940, Secretary of Education and Culture in 1949, and Secretary of Foreign Affairs in 1954. He also held the post of professor of law at the University of Santo Domingo. In 1957 Balaguer was elected vice-president of the Dominican Republic under President Hector B. Trujillo, who had been appointed ceremonial ruler of the country by his brother. When Hector Trujillo resigned in 1960, Balaguer was sworn in as chief of state.

*Joaquín Balaguer*

With the assassination of Rafael Trujillo in 1961, the political landscape of the Dominican Republic changed dramatically. *Newsweek* related how Balaguer was able to emerge from the turmoil surrounding Trujillo's assassination with his political life still intact: "Young Balaguer entered the Trujillo regime as an educator, emerged as the dictator's speech writer and ultimately became his figurehead President. Somehow, Balaguer managed to remain aloof from the brutality and corruption of the Trujillo era, and, after the dictator's assassination in 1961, he gave his political image a little shine by introducing a few mild reforms and handing out some Trujillo property to peasants. In 1962, he was exiled by a caretaker junta, and quietly retired to his sister's modest apartment in upper Manhattan."

### Short-lived Retirement

Balaguer's retirement was a brief one. Supported by the U.S. government and businesses with interests in the country, he soon returned to the Dominican Republic to become one of only four presidents in the country's history to be elected freely by its citizens. In June 1966, he was elected to his first term as president by a majority of nearly 57 percent, defeating **Juan Bosch**, who had previously held power in the country and who became Balaguer's life-long rival. According to *Newsweek,* "Amid the fanfare, [Balaguer] socked home in his mild voice a pledge to give war-weary Dominicans peace, tranquillity and a better life."

Balaguer came to power in a troubled time for the Dominican Republic. Nearly one third of the labor force was jobless, one third of the country's children had never entered school, and the country was one of the most underdeveloped in the Western Hemisphere. Balaguer backed up his austerity pledge by cutting his salary in half to $750 a month and reducing the pay of other public and government workers. In his first term, he put a ceiling on pensions, banned strikes by government industries, and promised to replace politicians entrenched in government industries with skilled technicians. By the end of his term, Balaguer had made some progress in reviving the social and economic conditions in the Dominican Republic. "Going into the 1970 election, he has the backing of most of the country's businessmen. In his three and half years in office, he has curbed inflation, balanced the budget and attracted a modest but vital flow of foreign capital," *Time* commented.

However, Balaguer's first term in office was not without controversy. He changed the Dominican constitution to allow him to run for re-election, a decision that sparked some concern among the public. Balaguer responded that "the re-election crisis reflects the deeply ingrained Dominican worry about 'continuismo'—the Latin American habit of hanging on to power," reported *Time.* "Conflicts will continue even if Jesus Christ descends to this seat. I, señores, am an instrument of destiny." Despite the controversy, he won re-election in 1970 and 1974. In 1978 he was defeated by **Antonio Guzman** but rallied to win a fourth term in 1986. He won a fifth term as the Dominican Republic's president in 1990.

Though he has served his country for most of his life, Balaguer has not been able to rid the Dominican Republic of all its problems. Writing in *America,* James Gaffney noted that in the 1994 election, a rival's campaign slogan of "he will invest in the people" referred to "the Balaguer Government's record of investing in grandiose building and 'beautification' projects, appealing to foreign-based luxury tourism, while for the poor, who constitute the nation's vast majority, social conditions and public services continue to deteriorate. . . . Even the central bank conservatively estimates that some 45 percent of Dominican families lack sufficient income for adequate nutrition. And it is notorious that 'beautification' projects regularly destroy poor but livable neighborhoods, driving their former residents into appalling slums." Mark Holston commented in 1994 in *Hispanic* that "an unemployment rate that has exceeded 30 percent in recent years and the pressures that the growing population of almost 9 million is placing on the nation's infrastructure of public services will demand immediate action."

Despite these enduring problems, Balaguer was elected to a sixth term as president in 1994 as the representative of the Partido Reformista Social Cristiano party. He remains an active politician who steadfastly professes a strong desire to see the lamentable socioeconomic conditions in the Dominican Republic addressed and resolved.

## SELECTED PUBLISHED WORKS:

*La Realidad Dominicana,* 1947; translated into English as *Dominican Reality: Biographical Sketch of a Country and a Regime,* 1949.
*Historia de la Literatura Dominica,* 1955; translated into English as *History of Dominican Literature,* 1978.

## SOURCES:

### Books

*Current Biography Yearbook 1966,* New York, H. W. Wilson Company, 1966, pp. 14–17.

### Periodicals

*America,* May 21, 1994, pp. 10–12.
*Hispanic,* May 1994, p. 12.
*Newsweek,* June 14, 1965, p. 66; June 13, 1966, p. 51.
*Time,* April 13, 1970, p. 34.

—*Sketch by Kathe A. Conti*

# Vasco Núñez de Balboa
## 1475(?)-1519
### Spanish explorer and conquistador

Vasco Núñez de Balboa was one of the many intrepid explorers who left Spain in the 1500s to discover and claim new lands for the Spanish Empire. Balboa sailed from Spain in 1501 with Rodrigo de Bastidas, but almost all that is known of his life takes place in the ten-year period between 1509 and 1519, the year of his death. It was during this time that Balboa served as governor of Darién, the first mainland colony established in the Americas, and became the first European to see the Pacific Ocean.

This signal discovery in 1513 had implications far beyond its face value. According to historian Joachim Leithäuser in *Worlds Beyond the Horizon,* "[Balboa's] discovery stands historically second only to that of Columbus, achieved twenty-one years

earlier, for it unveiled the greatest secret held by the New World and allowed mankind its first comprehensive view, beyond all previous frontiers and horizons, over all the continents and oceans of the world in their proper relationship to one another." Because hostile natives proved difficult if not impossible to colonize along the Atlantic coasts of South America, Balboa's discovery takes on added importance: it opened up the previously unknown Pacific coasts, both north and south, to Spain. "The history of the Spanish Empire really begins on the day when Balboa waded . . . into the water of the Pacific with drawn sword, waving on high the banner of Castile, and declared the ocean and all of its adjacent lands to be Spanish possessions," Leithäuser asserted.

Little is known of Balboa's early life. One source of information is **Bartolomé de las Casas**, who knew Balboa and recorded his recollections of the explorer long after the fact. It is accepted that Balboa was born in 1475, although the date "rests solely on the shaky authority of a guess at his age made by Casas long afterwards," according to Kathleen Romoli in *Balboa of Darién: Discoverer of the Pacific.* Balboa, one of four sons, was born in Jerez de los Caballeros, a town in the province of Estremadura, in Spain. His father is believed to have been Don Nuño Arias de Balboa. His mother is unnamed, but was "a lady of Badajoz," Romoli stated. She added that Balboa's parents "were patrician, Catholic, racially 'pure' and properly married—a combination not too easily come by in fifteenth-century Castile." This so-called "racial purity" was of some significance, for Balboa grew up during the Spanish Inquisition, in which Muslims, Jews, and other "pagans" were persecuted.

### Joins Bastidas on Voyage to New World

As befitted his social station, young Balboa served as a page in another household, that of Don Pedro Puertocarrero, Lord of Moguer. He was trained in the traditional art of fencing and is said to have been an excellent swordsman. Although trained all his life to be a warrior, by the time Balboa reached his late teens, there was no war to be fought. In 1492 the Moors were finally subdued and Christopher Columbus discovered what he thought was an alternate route to the Orient. In addition to the excitement for exploration sweeping Castile, the decision to join the Bastidas expedition may have been aided by Balboa's patron, Lord Moguer. Romoli noted that the House of Moguer "had a mighty maritime tradition and a special interest in the Indies. Its men had sailed with Columbus; the Admiral's favorite caravel was built in its yards." Whatever the reason, Balboa was about 25 when he volunteered to accompany Bastidas on a voyage to the New World in 1501. (Although many historians date this departure in 1500, Romoli argues that Bastidas's presence in Seville is documented as late as February 18, 1501.)

*Vasco Núñez de Balboa*

Bastidas sailed south along the coast of present-day Columbia to the Gulf of Urabá and the Isthmus of Panama. The armada put in to various bays along the way, and found that most natives wore gold ornaments and were quite hostile. The expedition happened upon the Indian village of Darién on the Isthmus in about October 1501. The natives were more friendly at this locale, and Bastidas was able to obtain some pearls, a little gold, and some native textiles and artifacts.

After leaving Darién, the ships began to leak, having become infested with broma, a tiny wood-eating worm common to the area. The small armada attempted repairs off the coast of Hispaniola (now Haiti and the Dominican Republic), since Bastidas's license did not allow him to make port there. The ships, thoroughly riddled by shipworm, eventually sank in the Gulf of Xaraguá. The explorers made their way overland to Santo Domingo, where Bastidas was promptly arrested for illegal entry. He was returned to Spain in 1502, but Balboa remained in Hispaniola.

### Stowaway Becomes Governor of Darién

As with other colonists in Hispaniola, Balboa was given some land to farm, with a five-year residency requirement. An unsuccessful farmer, Balboa sank heavily into debt. To avoid a law that prohibited debtors from leaving the island, Balboa stowed away on a departing ship by hiding in a provisions barrel. He remained in hiding until the following police ship had made its routine search and allowed the ship to proceed.

The ship Balboa has chosen was part of Alonso de Ojeda's fleet and was commanded by Martín Fernández de Enciso, a wealthy lawyer and Ojeda's partner. Ojeda and Rodrigo de Nicuesa were the two men licensed to explore the lands around the Gulf of Urabá. Ojeda had rights to explore and govern east of the gulf, and Nicuesa's rights lay to the west. When Balboa finally emerged from hiding, Enciso was furious, but was apparently persuaded it would benefit the expedition to have another able swordsman along. The group headed for San Sebastian, a settlement on the inhospitable Gulf of Urabá. When they arrived, however, the settlement was in ruins. Required by contract to establish a settlement, Enciso was at a loss as to where such a settlement should be begun. Balboa suggested Darién, which he remembered from his voyage with Bastidas. Enciso was persuaded and the settlement of Santa María la Antigua del Darién was established.

Enciso took command of Darién in Ojeda's absence and quickly established several unpopular laws, including one that proclaimed that only he could trade with the Indians for gold. Eventually the Spaniards ousted Enciso from power on the basis that neither Enciso nor Ojeda had authority in Darién, since the settlement was located within Nicuesa's territorial grant. The settlers elected Balboa and Martí de Zamudio as co-governors. Although resentful, Enciso had no support and had to abide by the decision.

In November 1510, one of Nicuesa's lieutenants arrived in Darién. Although he would have been within his rights to claim the settlement for Nicuesa, he did not do so. Instead, he chose to continue to search for Nicuesa, whom he was to meet along the coast. Meanwhile, Nicuesa's expedition was experiencing failure on a grand scale, losing seven ships and most of his 785 men to hunger and disease. When finally found, his complement had been reduced to one dinghy and a few men.

Nicuesa was delighted to learn of Darién's existence. He made plans to go there as soon as his men had recovered, and to severely punish all who had taken gold from "his" Indians. Word was sent ahead to Darién of the impending visit of the rightful governor. Alarmed, those in Darién voted to reject Nicuesa as governor. A notary duly noted the names of all the men—including Enciso—who swore this oath. When Nicuesa arrived in 1511, he was sent away in a leaky ship and he died elsewhere. Trouble continued to brew in Darién, however, and Enciso was the source. Finally, Zamudio took Enciso to court on the charge of misusing his authority. Preferring to argue his case before the king, Encase went to Spain.

Zamudio returned to Spain as well to ensure fairness in the hearing.

## Inland Expeditions Lead to Discovery

Balboa spent the next two years exploring and conquering the areas surrounding Darién. In due course, Balboa's expeditionary force came to the Indian province of Careta, which was presided over by a chief named Chima. Although Chima's army was 2,000-men strong, the Spaniards had the advantage of horses, metal weapons, and primitive guns. They also had the element of surprise, and attacked the village in the middle of the night. Many Indians were killed, and Chima, his family, and several others were taken hostage. Chima, realizing that he had been defeated, proposed a treaty to Balboa. In exchange for Balboa's aid in his ongoing battle with Ponca, another tribal chief, Chima's Caretaes would supply Darién with food and serve as guides on future expeditions. Chima also made a payment in gold and offered Balboa his daughter, whom Balboa eventually married. Romoli wrote that "Chima became Balboa's devoted friend and adherent from that time forth." Balboa's decision to accept Chima's terms was most unusual for a Spaniard at that time. The standard conquest method was violent and complete destruction of the enemy. Balboa, however, continued to turn the Indians into allies whenever possible.

Helping Chima conquer the Ponca Indians turned out to be a simple exercise in looting and burning; the tribe had fled in advance of the campaign. Chima, pleased with the results of this intimidation, next proposed that Balboa form an alliance with Chief Comogre, another powerful ruler. It was during the ceremonial visit to Comogre that Balboa first learned of the existence of the ocean on the other side of the mountains and the riches of other tribes along its coast. Comogre's son was the source of this information; he offered to guide the Spaniards on an expedition.

## Balboa Discovers the "South Seas"

Returning to Darién, Balboa received two letters. One letter, from Hispaniola, confirmed his appointment as captain-general of Darién. The other was from Zamudio in Spain. Zamudio was in hiding, as public opinion had turned against Balboa. The correspondence indicated that Enciso had convinced the king that Balboa had hoarded gold and treated his men poorly. Consequently, Balboa had been charged with treason and the king had decided to send a new governor to Darién. In an attempt to clarify matters, Balboa wrote the king a lengthy letter. He defended his treatment of his men and explained that by dealing honestly with the Indians he had learned of the whereabouts of still more gold and the existence of the great sea he expected to find and claim for Ferdinand. Toward that end, he requested weapons and 1,000 men to lead on an expedition. When months passed with no reply, Balboa decided to act.

Balboa set out on September 1, 1513, with 190 Spaniards and 800 natives. They made their way through treacherous swamps infested with crocodiles, snakes, and insects. In the jungle ahead, they came upon a Ponca village. Again the Indians had fled, but Balboa persuaded them to return and gave gifts to the chief. In return, Balboa received large amounts of gold and tribesmen who would act as guides. Maureen Ash commented in *Vasco Núñez de Balboa* that, "once Balboa and his men came to the end of their guides' territory, they found new guides. Then they rewarded the old ones and sent them home. Every conquistador after Balboa used this method."

Most historians date Balboa's discovery of the Pacific to Tuesday, September 25, 1513. It was so reported a few years after the event. Both Romoli and *The Oxford Book of Exploration,* however, suggest that the date may have actually been September 27, since the 25th fell on Sunday in 1513, and the significance of such a discovery on a Sunday would have likely been noted. Told by his guide that the sea lay just ahead, Balboa went alone to the top of a hill and was thus the first European to view it. A few more days' trek brought them to the shore. Daniel Boorstin, writing in *The Discoverers,* remarked that "Balboa, wearing his armor and carrying his unsheathed sword, waded into the surf, raised the banner of Castile, and for his Catholic sovereigns formally took possession of this Mar del Sur, the Southern Sea." The sea was so called because the point at which he discovered it was south-facing. It would be called the South Sea until 1520, when Ferdinand Magellan renamed it the Pacific.

## Treachery Leads to Trial and Execution

Returning to Darién from his profitable conquests, Balboa sent a report of his discoveries and the crown's share of the treasure to the king. While he had been away, a spy from the king had arrived in Darién. The spy, Arbolancha, was impressed with Balboa and soon returned to Spain with a favorable report. As soon as he departed, however, the new governor, Pedrarias, arrived. He brought with him Enciso, who had been elevated to the position of mayor. Balboa was arrested and brought to trial. The charges were numerous, and included allegations of theft—including a listing of goods supposedly stolen from Enciso (with a separate charge for each). He was also charged with murder for forcing Nicuesa from Darién, a departure that resulted in his death. None of the other men whose names appeared on the notarized list of rejecters of Nicuesa's governorship were prosecuted.

The trial went on for months. At last a letter arrived from King Ferdinand, who had heard Arbolancha's report. Balboa was restored to the king's good favor and given the title of *Adelantado* ("Admiral"), a rank held previously by only one other man: Christopher Columbus. Balboa was also appointed governor of the South Sea, Panama, and Coiba, although he was subject to Pedrarias's authority.

Balboa grew frustrated under Pedrarias, who refused to give Balboa permission to embark on any further expeditions. In 1515 Balboa decided to mount an expedition to the South Sea anyway. He planned to explore the coast of the South Sea and hoped to find the reported riches of Peru. An undertaking of massive proportions followed. Over the next four years, timber was cut and large amounts of shipbuilding materials, including rigging and anchors, were transported over the same treacherous route across the isthmus to the coast, where four ships were to be built. The proposed armada was reduced to two ships when it was discovered that much of the wood was already worthless because of shipworm. Setting out to sea, the ships were nearly destroyed by bad weather and an encounter with a group of whales. The vessels were forced to abort the voyage and return. Discouraged, Balboa made plans to rebuild his ships and establish a new settlement in Panama. He noted in his journal that it would be of benefit to Spain to cut a channel across the isthmus, an idea that would become a reality some 400 years later.

Balboa was ultimately betrayed by a man named Garabito, who told Pedrarias that Balboa had four large ships almost completed and that he planned to sail to Peru and set himself up as ruler there. Pedrarias lured Balboa to Acla, a village near Darién, with a message that he wished to discuss supplies for the ships. Unsuspecting, Balboa went to Acla. "There," according to Boorstin, "Pedrarias falsely accused Balboa of planning to abandon his Spanish sovereigns and set himself up as emperor of Peru. Before Balboa's supporters could consolidate their defense, Balboa and four companions were beheaded in the public square, and their bodies were thrown to the vultures." Balboa's severed head remained on a pole for several days.

Vilhjalmur Stefansson noted in *Great Adventures and Explorations* that a historian of the sixteenth century, Alonso de Ovalle, remarked that Balboa's "death was much resented, and appeared very unjust in Spain, because, indeed, the King lost one of his bravest captains, and one who would have discovered Peru with more facility, and without all those tumults which since happened. For his prudence, valor, and zeal were above the ordinary size." Instead, **Francisco Pizarro**, who arrested Balboa, conquered Peru and destroyed the glittering civilization he found there.

**SOURCES:**

**Books**

Ash, Maureen, *Vasco Nùñez de Balboa,* Chicago, Children Press, 1990.
Boorstin, Daniel J., *The Discoverers,* New York, Random House, 1983.
*Great Adventures and Explorations,* edited by Vilhjalmur Stefansson, New York, Dial Press, 1952.
Leithäuser, Joachim G., *Worlds Beyond the Horizon,* translated by Hugh Merrick, New York, Knopf, 1955.
*The Oxford Book of Exploration,* edited by Robin Hanbury-Tenison, Oxford, Oxford University Press, 1993.
Romoli, Kathleen, *Ba of Darién: Discoverer of the Pacific,* Garden City, New York: Doubleday & Co., Inc., 1953.

*—Sketch by Ellen Dennis French*

# Seve Ballesteros
## 1957-
### Spanish golfer

Seve Ballesteros has established himself as one of the foremost players on the Professional Golfers Association (PGA) tour. He has won dozens of professional tournaments including the Masters Open, the French and British Opens and many more. Through the 1980s Ballesteros consistently appeared at or near the top of professional golf's player rankings. He has an immense fan following, particularly in Europe. His sometimes flashy style and flair for making highly improbable shots have earned him the nickname "Lucky" among some fans.

### An Athletic Tradition

Severiano Ballesteros Soto was born April 9, 1957, in Pedrena, Spain. Significantly for Ballesteros, the house in which he was born overlooked the Real Club de Golf de Pedrena, whose construction King Alfonso XIII had ordered in the 1920s. Ballesteros' family had owned the house for two generations, and the family found it comfortable. Ballesteros recalls, however, that at times it seemed that he could have used just a little more space. "When we were growing up," Ballesteros told a London *Times* interviewer, "Manuel had one bedroom, Baldomero, my eldest brother, had another, and I shared with Vincente."

*Seve Ballesteros*

The two youngest boys even shared the same bed for many years, but as the youngest, Seve had to fight for his space even there. Some days his mother would come in to wake Seve up for school and find him sleeping on the floor. "When I was asleep," Ballesteros said, "[Vincente] would push me out. I got my own bed when I was ten."

Ballesteros's father, Baldomero Ballesteros, inspired some of his son's athletic ambitions. The elder Ballesteros had gained local celebrity as a five-time champion of the Regatta de Traineras, a centuries-old boat race. The three-mile race had such a rich tradition and garnered so much fan interest that Seve's father remained a hero in the eyes of the people long after his rowing days ended. Ballesteros' uncle, Ramon Sota was also an accomplished athlete. In fact, as a professional golfer, Sota paved Ballesteros' path to his profession.

Ballesteros started golfing at age seven. He showed enthusiasm from the start, but he got little respect from the adults on the Pedrena course. His only club he made from a discarded and rusty club head, which he polished, and a stick, which he carefully fashioned to fit the club head. Not surprisingly, the paying customers on the King's links did not take his presence well. "It was tough for me to begin with because I wasn't allowed on the golf course," Ballesteros told the London *Times,* "And like any child, when someone stops you from doing something, then you want it more badly." Fortunately, the proximity of his house to the course allowed him to steal onto the course at night and play the second hole. Sometimes he would simply tee off from his own backyard onto the green below.

Ballesteros also had a chance to caddy. He used the money he earned there to wager on games of golf with the other young caddies. He usually came home with more money than honest labor alone would have provided him. He got his first pair of golf shoes two years later from a club member who was going to throw them away. Only 12 years old, Ballesteros had to improvise some stuffing to make the adult-sized shoes fit, but he wore them in the caddy championship and won.

### Professional Ambitions

With dreams of becoming a professional golfer, Ballesteros did not allow obstacles to stop him. He recalls giving up drinking at the age of 14 because he knew the trouble it could get him into. One day at age 12, Ballesteros came back from school for lunch to find a bottle of wine on the table with his meal. His parents had both returned to work, so the boy served himself four generous glasses and soon forgot about lunch. "I was drunk when I got back to school," he said. "I slapped the woman teacher and I was suspended. It was revenge because she had smacked me across the hand with a ruler because I was talking in class." Ballesteros made the decision to give up drinking, but he also gave up school. "I didn't like it at all," Ballesteros said. "I only enjoyed playing with my friends and running."

In 1974 Ballesteros turned pro. The 15-year-old won the Spanish National Under 25 championship and the Vizcaya Open the same year. He repeated as Under 25 champion in 1975 before becoming the Catalonian National Champion in 1976. He also won the Dutch Open and several other professional events that year. Ballesteros began to win consistently. In 1977 he took the French Open, Braun International, UniRoyal International, Swiss Open, Japanese Open, the Dunlop Phoenix Tournament, Otago Charity Class, and the Kenya International. At 20 years old, Ballesteros entered the company of world class golfers. Yet he still qualified to play in under–25 tournaments

In 1979 Ballesteros claimed his first big tournament victory. At the British Open he battled golf legends Jack Nicklaus and Ben Crenshaw on the final day to win the event by three strokes. During that victory, Ballesteros made the shot that gave him the nickname of "Lucky." He teed off on one hole and sliced the ball. The shot left the course and landed in a parking lot. Ballesteros successfully recovered with a strong shot out of the parking lot; but for the "parking lot champion," as some reporters called him, the shot meant that he would have to prove that his victory had not been by mere chance. Golf great Hale Irwin played alongside Ballesteros on the last day of that 1979 British Open. He remarked, "You just can't hit the ball that crooked and win consistently. I have to believe it will catch up with him." Irwin's off-the-cuff comment reverberated through the golf press, angering Ballesteros, who responded with a terse, "No comment."

The next year Ballesteros won the Masters Open in Augusta, Georgia. Considered by many to be the most important tournament in the world, the Masters represents any golfer's dream. Even though Ballesteros swept the field, winning by four strokes, he could not shake his "Lucky" moniker. During one round of the tournament, his tee shot on the seventeenth hole landed on the green of the seventh hole. Between Ballesteros and the seventeenth green stood a 20-foot high scoreboard, which not only blocked the ball but also prevented Ballesteros from even seeing his target. Somehow he used a seven-iron to knock the ball over the scoreboard and right onto the green. He birdied the hole and won the tournament.

Eventually the staggering regularity of Ballesteros' victories retired the title of "parking lot champion," and Ballesteros became one of golf's best players. He also continued to inspire fan admiration with his flamboyant and improbable shots. In 1982 he won the World Match tournament in a playoff with Sandy Lyle by making a 35-foot putt. In 1983, he outgunned Ben Crenshaw and Tom Kite on the last round of the Masters and claimed his second green jacket—the traditional prize given to the Masters champion. He won two more British Open championships, one in 1984 and one in 1988. In 1989 *Maclean's* magazine published the Sony Rankings, which placed Ballesteros at the top of the golf world for the previous three years, with 14 tournament victories in 1986–1988 alone.

Ballesteros has had some open disputes with PGA tour administration. For a time Ballesteros chose not to renew his tour membership because he objected to the 15-event minimum that the Association imposed on the players. Under the complicated rules, a PGA player had to play 15 tournaments in the United States. Ballesteros, however, wanted to spend more time on the maturing European PGA tour. In the late 1980s, however, Ballesteros and the PGA resolved most of their differences, and one of the game's greatest players returned to its richest tour.

His success on the links dominated his life for years. In 1988 he married his girlfriend, Carmen Botin. A graduate of Brown University in Rhode Island, Botin came from the wealthiest family in Santander, Spain. Carmen's parents had reservations at first about the marriage, but eventually came to accept Ballesteros as a member of the family. Since their marriage, the couple has had two sons and a daughter.

The early 1990s saw Ballasteros' avalanche of victories slow. Between March 1992 and May 1994, he failed to win a single tournament. He had dropped to twenty-seventh in the tournament rankings. His back began to give him trouble, and he felt that he needed help to reduce the excess motion in his swing. He sought the counsel of Mac O'Grady, who helped Ballesteros with his swing and reduced the strain on his back. Though Ballesteros has not brought home as many trophies over the last few years, he acknowledges that with a family, just coming home can be the most important thing. Ballesteros decided to build a house for his family on the land overlooking the golf course in Pedrena. In his new house it is unlikely that anyone will spend any uncomfortable nights on the floor.

## SOURCES:

### Books

*Who's Who in Spain,* edited by John Dove, Who's Who in Italy, 1992.

### Periodicals

*Los Angeles Times,* July 10, 1983, Part 3, p. 3.
*Maclean's,* April 10, 1989, p. 54.
*New York Times,* June 9, 1988, p. D31; July 12, 1994, p. B10.

—*Sketch by James McCarthy*

# José Agustín Balseiro
## 1900-
### Puerto Rican composer and writer

José Agustín Balseiro is best known as a writer, but he is also a talented composer whose works have been performed in Carnegie Hall. He gained early recognition as a poet and novelist. As his reputation and professional stature grew, he began to focus on works of literary and music criticism, for which he is best known. He has taught Spanish language and literature at many colleges and universities in the United States and Puerto Rico. A well-traveled man, Balseiro became a kind of cultural ambassador to the world. His lectures on the arts and the role of the artist as a conduit between the Hispanic and American cultures earned him praise throughout the world, especially within the Spanish-speaking countries.

Balseiro was born in Barceloneta, Puerto Rico, on August 23, 1900, to Rafael and Dolores (Romos-Casellas) Balseiro. His marriage to Mercedes Pedreira in 1924 produced two daughters. He was educated at the University of Puerto Rico, graduating in 1921 with a Bachelor of Laws degree. In 1930 he came to the University of Illinois at Urbana to teach Romance languages. In 1933 he returned to his native country to become visiting professor of Spanish literature at the University of Puerto Rico, Rio Piedras. He returned to Urbana in 1936, where he remained for two years. The ensuing period until 1946 was spent as a U.S. representative to various international academic conferences. He then came to the University of Miami at Coral Gables, Florida, where he taught Hispanic literature for more than 20 years. He was sought after as a consultant on Hispanic literature and summer lecturer at institutions across the United States.

Balseiro's early works of poetry included *Flores de primavera* (*Flowers of Spring*), *Música cordial* (*Friendly Music*), and *Las palomas de Eros* (*The Doves of Eros*). *La copa de Anacreonte* (*The Crown of Anacreon*) is an early attempt at modernism. Novels such as *La ruta eterna* (*The Eternal Way*) and *En vela mientras el mundo duerme* (*Vigil While the World Sleeps*), both published during the early- to mid–1920s, also brought him recognition.

### Growing Reputation as a Critic

Balseiro established his reputation early on as a music and literature critic. Some of his best-known critical writings are *El vigía* (*The Watchman*), and works discussing such writers and musicians as **Miguel de Unamuno**, **Rubén Darío**, **Valle Inclán y Baroja**, and Blasco Ibáñez. His essay, *Crítica y estilo literario en Eugenio María de Hostos*, received an award from the Institute of Puerto Rican Literature in 1939. A writer for the *London Times* during the 1920s claimed that "the originality of Señor Balseiro's criticism consists in the fact that it is both Spanish and international." In the 1940s, a reviewer for the *South Atlantic Bulletin* remarked that Balseiro is more than a "Spanish-American critic examining the works of Spanish writers; rather, he is an international scholar who knows no boundaries, and whose criterion is world literature."

He was an active international lecturer and cultural ambassador throughout his career, and has spoken on such topics as the philosophies and biographies of poets, public leaders, artists, and musicians. Both through his scholarly writings and lectures, he repeatedly emphasized the connections between the Hispanic and American cultures, and set himself the goal of interpreting the spirit of each of those cultures to the other. This emphasis is apparent in his *The Americas Look at Each Other* published in 1969.

Balseiro has contributed to numerous periodicals, including *Cuadernos Americanos, Nosotros, Hispanic Review,* and *La Torre,* and has edited many Spanish publications.

During a lecture at the University of Miami in the 1950s, Balseiro was quoted by *Miami Herald* writer Sandy Flickner: "The nearer we approach our neighbors by the disinterested paths of art, literature, scholarship, and open-hearted friendship, the sooner will we demolish the prejudices that hamper the constructive development of human nature." To honor his contributions to international cultural unity, Miami University established an essay contest, called the José A. Balseiro Award, in 1967.

## SELECTED PUBLISHED WORKS:

*Flores de primavera* (*Flowers of Spring*), [San Juan], 1919.

*Las palomas de Eros* (*The Doves of Eros*), [Madrid], 1921.

*La copa de Anacreonte* (*The Crown of Anacreon*), Madrid, Editorial Mundo Latino, 1924.

*El vigía* (*The Watchman*), Madrid, Editorial Mundo Latino, Volume 1, 1925, Volume 2, 1926, Volume 3, [San Juan], 1942.

*La ruta eterna* (*The Eternal Way*), [Madrid], 1926.

*Música cordial* (*Friendly Music*), Havana, Editorial Lex, 1926.

*El Quijote de la España contemporánea: Miguel de Unamuno* (*The Quixote of Contemporary Spain*), E. Giménez, 1935.

*Blasco Ibáñez, Unamuno, Valle Inclán y Baroja, cuatro individualistas de España* (*Four Spanish Individualists*), University of North Carolina Press, 1949.

*Saudades de Puerto Rico* (*Homesickness for Puerto Rico*), Aguilar, 1957.

*Vísperas de sombras y otros poemas* (*Eves of Shadow and Other Poems*), Mexico, Ediciones de Andre, 1959.

*Seis estudios sobre Rubén Darío* (*Six Studies About Ruben Dario*), Madrid, Editorial Gredos, 1967.

*The Americas Look at Each Other,* translated by Muna Muñoz Lee, University of Miami Press, 1969.

*En vela mientras el mundo duerme* (*Vigil While the World Sleeps*), Mnemosyne Publishing, 1969.

*The Hispanic Presence in Florida,* E. A. Seeman, 1977.

## SOURCES:

### Books

*Contemporary Authors,* Volumes 81–84, edited by Frances Carol Locher, Detroit, Gale Research, 1979.

Hill, Marnesba D., and Harold B. Schleifer, *Puerto Rican Authors,* Metuchen, New Jersey, Scarecrow Press, 1974.

*Hispanic Writers,* edited by Bryan Ryan, Detroit, Gale Research, 1991.

*The Oxford Companion to Spanish Literature,* edited by Philip Ward, Oxford, Clarendon Press,

### Periodicals

*Miami Herald,* April 29, 1974.

—*Sketch by Jane Stewart Cook*

*Antonio Banderas*

# Antonio Banderas
## 1960-
**Spanish actor**

Movie star Antonio Banderas has quickly earned a reputation as one of the most versatile and sought-after actors in the 1990s film industry. Before moving to Hollywood in 1992, Banderas enjoyed significant international recognition, having appeared in more than 30 Spanish films and working with such directors as Antonio de Real, Rodolfo Kuhn, Pedro Costa, Carlos Saura, Luis Garcia Sanchez, and Juan Minon. However, the greatest contribution to Banderas's success may lie in his working relationship with renowned Spanish filmmaker **Pedro Almodovar**, with whom he made such acclaimed movies as *Women on the Verge of a Nervous Breakdown* and *Tie Me Up! Tie Me Down!.*

Banderas was born in Malaga, Spain. After acquiring a formal education, he studied theater at the School of Dramatic Art in Malaga. During this time, Banderas also honed his acting skills with an independent theater company in Malaga. In 1981 the young actor moved to Madrid and worked in both theater and television before Pedro Almodovar discovered him and cast him in *Labyrinth of Passion.* This opportunity led to several other film projects with Almodovar, including the feature films *Women on the Verge of a Nervous Breakdown* and *Tie Me Up! Tie Me Down!,* for which he earned Spain's equivalent of an Oscar nomination for best actor.

Banderas arrived in Hollywood in 1992 to make his American movie debut opposite Armand Assante in the film adaptation of *The Mambo Kings,* based on **Oscar Hijuelos**'s Pulitzer prize-winning novel entitled *The Mambo Kings Play Songs of Love.* In the film, Banderas portrays the soulful Cuban musician and composer Nestor Castillo, a role for which he had to learn how to play the trumpet.

After starring in *The Mambo Kings,* Banderas has appeared in three 1994 films: *Philadelphia,* directed by Jonathan Demme and starring and Denzel Washington; the film adaptation of **Isabel Allende**'s *House of Spirits,* directed by Bille August and starring Meryl Streep, Jeremy Irons, Glen Close, and Winona Ryder; a screen version of Anne Rice's *Interview With the Vampire,* directed by Neil Jordan and starring Tom Cruise and Brad Pitt and the romantic comedy *Miami Rhapsody,* which also featured Sarah Jessica Parker and Mia Farrow.

In 1995 Banderas was also seen in *Desperado,* director Robert Rodriguez's sequel to his first film, *El Mariachi; Four Rooms,* released by Miramax; TriStar Pictures' *Never Talk to Strangers;* and *Assassins,* directed by Richard Donner and starring Sylvester Stallone. The following year Banderas was set to star in Fernando Trueba's *Two Much,* along with female leads Melanie Griffith and Daryl Hannah.

## SELECTED VIDEOGRAPHY:

*Labyrinth of Passion,* Cinevista, 1982.

*Women on the Verge of a Nervous Breakdown,*
Orion Home Video, 1988.
*Tie Me Up! Tie Me Down!,* Columbia Trisar
Home Video, 1990.
*The Mambo Kings,* Warner Home Video, 1992.
*Philadelphia,* Tristar, 1993.
*House of Spirits,* Miramax, 1993.
*Interview with the Vampire,* Warner Brothers,
1994.
*Miami Rhapsody,* Hollywood Pictures, 1995.
*Of Love and Shadows,* Miramax, 1995.

## SOURCES:

### Periodicals

*Newsweek,* November 11, 1991, p. 46.
*World Press Review,* August 1992, p. 41.

### Other

Banderas, Antonio, biography provided by Wolf
Kasteler Public Relations, November 18, 1994.

—*Sketch by Karen Bober Kuhn*

# Romana Acosta Bañuelos
## 1925-

**Mexican American businesswoman and former
U.S. treasurer**

Romana Acosta Bañuelos began what would
become a highly successful business with an
aunt and a tortilla machine, founded a bank, and
became the treasurer of the United States. No one
would argue against the idea that Bañuelos has
achieved the American dream. Bañuelos, however, is
not one to rest on her laurels, so despite her success,
she has continued to rely on her sound business
judgement and to work on a number of challenging
projects.

Bañuelos was born on March 20, 1925, in Miami,
Arizona, a small mining town. Her parents were born
in Mexico and the family was poor. In 1933, as the
effects of the Great Depression were still being felt
throughout the country, Arizona officials told a
number of Mexican families, including the Bañuelos
family, that they had to return to Mexico. According
to the authorities, the economic situation was not
improving and since jobs were scarce, the family

would be better off in their own homeland of Mexico.
The families were informed that if they would leave,
the cost of transporting themselves and their furniture
to the border would be paid. Bañuelos told an
interviewer for *Nuestro:* "They told us we could come
back anytime we wanted to, as soon as the economy
got better. So my mother and father believed what
they were told, and we left."

The family moved to Sonora, Mexico, to work on
a small ranch that relatives owned. There, Bañuelos
rose early with her parents to tend to the wheat, corn,
potatoes, and peanuts that her father had planted. She
also helped her mother as she made the *empanadas*
("turnovers") which her mother sold to local restaurants and bakeries. Bañuelos explained to *Nuestro*
that her mother was a excellent role model as a
resourceful businesswoman: in addition to marketing
her baked goods, she decided to raise chickens. "My
mother was the type of woman that taught us how to
live in any place and work with what we have."

### Versatility Key to Bañuelos's Achievements

Perhaps this inherent versatility has allowed
Bañuelos to become the success that she is today.
Although she had married, borne two sons, and
divorced by the time she was 19 years old, she did not
hesitate to set high goals for herself and to make the
most of her life. As a young single mother, Bañuelos
packed up her children and returned to her native
country, the United States. Upon her arrival in Los
Angeles, she found a job, began to work, care for her
family, and save money. By the time she was 21 years
old, she had remarried and saved $400. With this
savings, and the help of an aunt, a tortilla machine, a
grinder, and a fan, the ambitious Bañuelos set up a
tortilla factory the heart of downtown Los Angeles. At
the end of their first day in business, in 1949, she and
her aunt had made $36.

Business gradually picked up as Bañuelos and her
aunt persuaded restaurant and store owners to buy
their tortillas. The small company they began, Ramona's Mexican Food Products, Inc., was booming by
the mid–1960s. By 1979, Ramona's employed 400
people, distributed 22 different food products, and
the company's sales had soared to $12 million
annually. While consumers were familiar with the
brand name of Ramona's—the largest independent
Mexican food processing plant in the state of California by 1990—some people confusedly referred to
Romana Bañuelos incorrectly as Ramona. The company, however, was named after an early Californian
folk heroine named Ramona, and not Bañuelos
herself.

As Bañuelos's business prospered, she began to
think of the plight of other Hispanics who were less
fortunate than herself. She is a founder and trustee of
Ramona's Mexican Food Products, Inc. Scholarship

Foundation, which assists high school graduates of Mexican American heritage in their educational goals. Bañuelos also turned her focus on those Hispanics who wanted to start their own businesses. She realized that, if Hispanics could increase their financial base, they could increase their political influence. Toward this goal of community empowerment, in 1965 Bañuelos, along with some partners, started the Pan-American National Bank. By 1969, Bañuelos had become the chairperson of the board of directors of the bank, and had received recognition from her peers in the business world. She was named the Outstanding Business Woman of the Year in November, 1969, and during that same year, Mayor Sam Yorty presented Bañuelos with a commendation award from the board of supervisors of the county of Los Angeles. Bañuelos's banking venture became another huge success for her. By 1979, according to *Nuestro*, Pan-American National Bank held deposits of $38,864,000 and assets of $41,472,000. By 1992, Bañuelos had served as chair of the bank's board of directors for three terms of office.

Bañuelos's business talent as the leader of the Pan-American National Bank ultimately led her to embark on a political career in the early 1970s. After Richard Nixon was elected president of the United States, she was asked by the Republican party if they could place her name on the list of possible candidates for the position of treasurer of the United States. Although she thought that she had no chance to win the nomination and confirmation, she decided to allow herself to be considered for the office. To her surprise, President Nixon selected Bañuelos as his candidate for U.S. treasurer and initiated the nomination process.

### Nomination to Become U.S. Treasurer Jeopardized

Before Bañuelos could truly savor the fact that she had been nominated for the position of U.S. treasurer, Ramona's Mexican Food Products, Inc. was raided by U.S. immigration agents. Instead of the usual, quiet inspection, the agents loudly stormed through the building. The raid received broad media attention and seemed to damage Bañuelos's chances of securing the appointment. President Nixon continued to support Bañuelos, who claimed that the raid had been politically motivated. Summoned before a Senate investigative committee, Bañuelos argued that the Democratic party was responsible setting in motion the chain of events that resulted in the raid. Later testimony corroborated these claims, and the Senate committee ruled that Bañuelos had been unfairly targeted to cause embarrassment for the Nixon administration.

Despite the upsetting and unfair raid, Nixon's appointment of Bañuelos was confirmed. She resigned her position at the Pan-American National Bank to go to Washington, D.C. and serve as a public official. On December 17, 1971, she took the oath of office and became the treasurer of the United States as well as the highest ranking Mexican American in the United States government during this administration. Bañuelos enjoyed her time as U.S. treasurer. "It was a beautiful experience," she told *Nuestro.* "I will always be grateful to President Nixon."

In February 1974, Bañuelos resigned as U.S. treasurer so she could devote more time to her family, businesses, and philanthropical projects. She was recognized in 1975 with a honorary doctorate of business administration from the City University of Los Angeles. In 1976, she was included in the Library of Human Resources as one of the United States's "Valuable Resources" by the American Bicentennial Research Institute for her professional and civic contributions to the country. The East Los Angeles Community Union honored her with the Board of Directors Woman Achievement Award in 1977.

In recent years, Bañuelos has divided her time between Ramona's Mexican Food Products, Inc. and the Pan-American National Bank. While she serves as the president of Ramona's, her children Carlos A. Torres, Ramona A. Bañuelos, and Martin A. Torres are involved in the day-to-day business operations of the company in various positions. Bañuelos is also currently serving as the president of the Pan-American National Bank.

### SOURCES:

*Nuestro,* June/July, 1979, pp. 34+.

—*Sketch by Ronie-Richele Garcia-Johnson*

# Maria Gertrudes Barcelo
## 1800-1852
### Mexican entrepreneur

Maria Gertrudes Barcelo, the notorious "La Tules," is one of the most colorful and fascinating legends from an era known for extravagant personalities. An aggressive entrepreneur of posh gambling palaces and an astute businesswoman, Barcelo found fame and a sizeable fortune in the male-dominated old Southwest.

Born in 1800 in the state of Sonora in northern Mexico to a privileged family, Barcelo was well educated by her parents. Shortly after Mexico won its independence from Spain in the early 1820s, Barcelo and her family moved to the village of Valencia in New Mexico. Whether her desire for independence was the result of education or of her own self-sufficiency cannot be determined, but Barcelo was ahead of her time in both the financial acumen and a feminist consciousness she displayed as a young woman. When she married at the age of 23, she refused to relinquish either her right to make contracts or the deeds to her property to her husband as custom dictated. Furthermore, Barcelo retained and used her maiden name.

### Casinos Bring Fame and Fortune

Seeking better financial opportunities, Barcelo and her husband relocated to the Santa Fe area. In 1825, she began operating a game of chance in the Ortiz Mountains, where she came to be nicknamed "La Tules." After several years, Barcelo saved enough to purchase her casino in Santa Fe. The gambling house soon became one of the most popular casinos in Santa Fe and favored by society's elite. Customers were drawn not only by the 'magnificent pier-glass mirrors" and the "brussels carpets" described by Ralph Emerson Twitchell in *Old Santa Fe,* but the by the reputed beauty and the charm of the best monte dealer in Santa Fe, the notorious "La Tules."

In 1837, new taxes, increased government centralization, and the revised Mexican constitution caused an uprising in which the governor, Albino Perez, was assassinated. General Manual Armijosuppressed the uprising and was appointed Governor of New Mexico by President Santa Anna. As Bar." Fortunately, tcelo gained fortune and fame, she advanced in Santa Fe society and soon became a great favorite in official Mexican circles. She was transformed from the infamous "La Tules" to the acclaimed Señora Dona Gertrudes Barcelo. The new governor was attracted to Barcelo and it was reputed that she not only became his mistress but was the power behind the throne.

### Gambling Empire Grows to Include Trade and Investment

Barcelo did not limit her enterprises to gambling houses, but became involved with trade and investing, as well. In 1843, she sent $10,000 to the United States to be invested in goods. During the late 1820s, traders and settlers from the United States began to relocate in the Mexican dominion. Early chronicles provide insights into the cultural clashes between the native Mexican population and the Anglo Americans who moved to the southwest. The popularity of dancing and gambling across all Mexican classes seemed incomprehensible to many straight-laced Anglos, and the infamous "La Tules" remained an enigma to many of them. A contemporary eyewitness and diarist, Susan Shelby Magoffin, described her as "a stately dame of a certain age, the possessor of a portion of that shrewd sense and fascinating manner necessary to allure the wayward, inexperienced youth to the hall of final ruin."

In 1846, Santa Fe, occupied by General Philip Kearny in response to the United States declaration of war on Mexico, established a civilian government. The Mexican-American War, fought primarily in old Mexico, ended in 1948 with the Treaty of Guadalupe Hidalgo which ceded all of New Mexico to the United States. By 1850, New Mexico joined the United States as a "free" (non-slave holding) state. During the U.S. military occupation of New Mexico, Barcelo sided with the American forces and was a popular figure among the military officers. During the occupation, Barcelo received information regarding a conspiracy from one of her servants. She relayed the information to American military and civilian authorities. In addition, she provided a substantial loan to the United States occupation forces for supplies. The loan terms required that one of the officers escort her to a military ball. Colorful and flamboyant to the end, Barcelo arranged that her own funeral be one of the most expensive and ornate in Santa Fe history. She was buried with full church honors in 1852.

Driven by ambition, but aided by beauty and skill, Barcelo advanced to the inner circles of Mexican society in Santa Fe. As a successful businesswoman catering to the pastimes of both Mexicans and Anglos, she enjoyed great, if not universal, popularity and achieved wealth and political influence. Her legacy as one of the great characters of the wild west lives on today.

**SOURCES:**

*Down the Santa Fe Trail and into Mexico: The Diary of Susan Shelby Magoff in 1846–1847,* edited by Stella Drumm, Yale University Press, 1926.
Duffus, R. L., *The Santa Fe Trail,* Tudor, 1934.
Gregg, Josiah, *Commerce of the Prairies,* University of Oklahoma Press, 1954.
*Introduction to Chicano Studies,* 2nd edition, edited by H. Russell Bernard and Duncan Livie Isauro, Macmillan, 1982.
Robinson, Cecil, *With the Ears of Strangers: The Mexican in American Literature,* University of Arizona Press, 1963.
Twitchell, Rph Emerson, *Old Santa Fe: The Story of New Mexico's Ancient Capital,* Rio Grande Press, 1963.

—*Sketch by Sally Foster*

# Pio Baroja y Nessi
## 1872-1956
### Spanish novelist

Admired by the American novelist Ernest Hemingway for his frank, unpolished style, Pio Baroja wrote widely about the moral and social ills of early twentieth-century Spanish life.

"As a physician concentrates on disease, so Baroja [who was trained as a physician] concentrates on the diseases and sores of the individual and of society," wrote Helen S. Nicholson in her monograph *The Novel of Protest and the Spanish Republic.* "To be sure, an unsavory procession of social derelicts, thieves, prostitutes, gamblers, anarchists, physical and moral degenerates marches through his pages, but these are shown as victims of a defective social order, somehow responsible for their existence."

Although generally included in The Generation of '98, a group of literary rebels who came together after Spain's defeat in 1898 in the Spanish-American War, Baroja preferred to see himself as an individualist. Nevertheless, he shared with other members of the group a personal preoccupation with the problems of thought and action posed by such negativistic philosophers as Arthur Schopenhauer and Friedrich Nietzsche

"Pio Baroja . . . is no exception to the predominently destructive spirit current among the end of the century critics," wrote John T. Reid in *Modern Spain and Liberalism: A Study in Literary Contrasts.* "Almost unanimously his commentators have agreed that one of the unchanging factors of his work, if not the main factor, is his rebellious custom of tearing down."

Critical of both the left and the right, Baroja was arrested by agents of the extreme right during the Spanish Civil War (1936–1939). He was eventually tolerated though not accepted by the regime of **Francisco Franco.** Baroja wrote more than 100 novels in his lifetime.

In 1950, Baroja said, according to *The New York Times:* "I have always been the same. In literature I have been a realist with a little romanticism, in philosophy an agnostic and in politics an individualist and liberal, which is to say unpolitical. I have not avoided my political responsibility, for I had none."

Described by some critics as an existential writer, Pio Baroja y Nessi was born December 28, 1872 in the Basque coastal city of San Sebastian. He had a close relationship with his mother, Carmen Nessi y Goni, who was part Italian. His father, a wealthy mining engineer, had an extensive library and introduced his son to such romantic and adventure novelists as Victor Hugo and Jules Verne. In school, though, Pio was only a mediocre student.

In *Youth and Egolatry,* he wrote: "I have a suspicion myself that I shall never amount to anything. Everybody who knows me has always thought the same. . . . I was cursed with an instinctive slothfulness and sluggishness which were not to be denied."

Baroja entered medical school at the University of Madrid in 1887, completing his studies in Valencia four years later. In 1893, Baroja read his doctoral thesis on *Pain, a Psychophysical Study.* The next year, his brother Dario died of tuberculosis. "Life seemed to him meaningless," Daniel M. Friedenberg wrote in *The New Republic,* "man the most disgusting thing on the planet."

In 1894, Baroja became a municipal doctor in Cestona and began writing short stories to pass the time. After a year and a half, Baroja left medicine to run his aunt's bakery in Madrid, finding a stimulating intellectual and cultural atmosphere in the nation's capital. In 1898 he traveled to Paris where he became familiar with the philosophy of Friedrich Wilhelm Nietzsche and Arthur Schopenhauer.

"In Schopenhauer . . . Baroja found a totally congenial mind," wrote Donald L. Shaw in *The Generation of 1898 in Spain.* "He learned from Schopenhauer that life was in its very nature suffering in various forms, that such suffering was proportionate to intellectual awareness, and that all action tended to intensify it."

### Outcasts and Vagabonds

Upon returning to Madrid, Baroja published, at his own expense, a 500-copy edition of his first group of short stories, *Vidas sombrias* (1900), (*Somber Lives*). He was already something of an iconoclast: 28 years old, unmarried and unwilling to pursue a professional career. The stories in *Somber Lives,* about vagrants, vagabonds and other outcasts, explored the degradations of the poor in Madrid. The collection, though, sold fewer than 100 copies. Baroja was so distressed, he took back the unsold copies and burned them. One critic, however, praised the stories, comparing them to the works of Edgar Allan Poe and Feodor Dostoevsky. *Somber Lives* also came to the attention of Martin Ruiz, later known as Azorin, who, along with Baroja, became the center of The Generation of '98.

With the support of Azorin and others, Baroja composed his first novel *La casa de Aizgorri* (1900) *The House of the Aizgorri,* the story of a decadent family whose distillery is destroyed by fire. In October of 1901 Baroja and Azorin helped found the magazine *Juventud.* When that magazine collapsed in March of 1902, Baroja moved to *El Globo,* a daily which had already serialized his second novel *Aventuras inventos y mixtifacaciones de Silvestre Paradox* (1901) *(Adventures, Inventions and Hoaxes of Silvestre Paradox)*. Writing at incredible speed, Baroja produced several of his best-known novels between 1901 and 1912, including his 1904 trilogy *La lucha por la vida (The Struggle for Life)* composed of *La busca* (*The Quest*), *Mala hierba* (*Weeds*) and *Aurora roja* (*Red Dawn*).

The trilogy follows the life of Manuel Alcazar who, like thousands of Spaniards at the time, arrives in Madrid from the countryside. Thrust into a city unable to absorb its surplus labor, Manuel sleeps on rubbish dumps, works for a ragpicker, learns the printing trade, gets drawn in by a group of gangsters and goes to jail. Finally, in the last volume, Manuel sets up a small printing establishment. But his brother, a political activist, dies, his work unfinished. Manuel is left to lead what his brother would have called a typical bourgeois existence.

Other novels of this period are set in England, France, or Italy as well as Spain, thus reflecting Baroja's travels abroad. In 1906, he traveled to England, partly to see the settings of Charles Dickens' novels, finding inspiration in the London of the disinherited and dispossessed. The result: *La ciudad de la niebla* (1909; *The City of Fog*).

In 1911, Baroja published his highly autobiographical novel *El arbol de la ciencia (The Tree of Knowledge)*, hailed by Shaw as Baroja's masterpiece. The main character of the novel, Andres Hurtado, is a physician aliented from his family and disheartened by the moral bancruptcy of the world around him. His advice to a group of young idealists: Give up the struggle and emigrate. Eating from the Tree of Knowledge only leads to misery, he believes. So, bereft of any meaningful course of action, Andres withdraws to a small rural community and kills himself.

"[Hurtado's] decision to be conquered by death rather than to be the conqueror is indicative of Baroja's virtually obsessive need to flee rather than to confront, to terminate an unbearable reality by ultimately refusing to deal with it in positive terms," wrote Beatrice P. Patt in *Pio Baroja* (Twayne's World Authors Series).

In 1909 and 1918 Baroja ran for political office as a Radical Liberal, both times unsuccessfully. In *Las horas solitarias* (1918; *Solitary Hours*), he wrote about his abortive 1918 bid for Congress, criticizing the corruption and inefficiency of the Spanish political system.

## Adventure Novels

As Baroja became increasingly convinced that contemporary society was beyond redemption, he transfered his ideal of action, heavily influenced by

Nietzsche, to the past, particularly the nineteenth century. He wrote his first two adventure novels, *Zalacain el aventuero* (1909; *Zalacain the Adventurer*) and *Las inquietudes de Shanti Andia* (1911; *The Restlessness of Shanti Andia*), with a gusto uncharacteristic of his works of deeper vision, according to Shaw. *Zalacain* was Baroja's best money-maker, Shaw added.

During the autumn of 1911, Baroja began research on one of his distant relatives, Eugenio de Aviraneta, a nineteenth-century liberal conspirator, spy and agitator. What began as a short piece eventually grew into the 22-volume series of novels, *Las memorias de un hombre de accion* (1913–1935; *Memoirs of a Man of Action*), narrated by a cast of secondary characters. Like the vagabonds of Baroja's earlier books, the adventurous Aviraneta lived outside the narrow confines of ordinary Spanish society.

"The activities of each political, social, or military group were chiefly characterized by errors, follies and vices," wrote Shaw in *The Generation of 1898 in Spain.* "There are thus plenty of knaves and fools in Baroja's picture of nineteenth-century Spain, but no heroes."

Between 1917, by which time six Aviraneta books had appeared, and 1919, when three more had been written, Baroja published several collections of essays, including *Juventud, egolatria* (1917; *Youth and Egolatry*). American journalist H. L Mencken wrote the foreword to the English-language edition. "In place of gaudy certainties [Baroja] offers disconcerting questionings; in place of a neat and well-rounded body of doctrine he puts forward a sort of generalized contra-doctrine," Mencken wrote.

Baroja's later works show an increasing preoccupation with the problems of love and sexuality. In *Solitary Hours,* he wrote: "I live in retirement not because I like solitude but because I cannot find an acceptable social life." Like the heroes of many of his novels, Baroja was a lifelong bachelor who rarely acted decisively in romantic situations and, when he did, was often disappointed.

In 1934, Baroja was elected to the prestigious Royal Spanish Academy and, characteristically, had to buy his first dress suit for the occasion. In his acceptance address, according to Patt, he described the orientation of his youth as "Believe nothing, affirm nothing." Success had done little to alter his pessimism.

Shortly before the outbreak of the Spanish Civil War in 1936, Baroja advocated a dictatorship for Spain. But he hated the military officer caste and so found himself in complete disagreement with the regime of Francisco Franco. Arrested by the Nationalist forces near Pamplona early in the Spanish Civil War, Baroja, who was about to be executed, escaped at the last minute to France. He returned to Madrid in

1940 and spent his final years writing his memoirs and a collection of poetry.

In 1954, Baroja was nominated for a Nobel Prize but failed to receive it. Longtime friend Hemingway said in 1956 that Baroja "should have received the Nobel Prize many times over," according to Patt.

In old age Baroja suffered from arteriosclerosis and frequent lapses of memory. Hemingway visited the Spaniard three weeks before his death on October 30, 1956 and attended Baroja's funeral in Madrid. In keeping with Baroja's anti-clericalism, there was no religious ceremony. Hemingway was asked to be a pallbearer but refused, saying he felt unworthy of such an honor, according to Patt.

Baroja left a body of work so large, varied and difficult to read that he's been described as "the best known, the most translated and the least read novelist of contemporary Spain," according to the *New York Times*. He wrote quickly, seldom stopping to revise. His narratives are loosely structured, his prose unadorned and functional. "Baroja's production is an outstanding example of literary overkill," wrote Patt. But others see the author's work as a stellar example of realism. Observed Friedenberg: "Baroja's novels are more like life than art."

## SELECTED PUBLISHED WORKS:

*The House of the Aizgorri* (novel; *La casa de Aizgorri*), 1900.
*The Lord of Labraz* (novel; *El mayorazgo de Labraz*, 1903.
*Red Dawn* (novel; *Aurora roja*), 1904.
*The Quest* (novel; *La busca*), 1904.
*Weeds* (novel; *Mala hierba*), 1904.
*Paradox King* (novel; *Paradox*), rey, 1906.
*Caesar or Nothing* (novel; *Cesar o nada*), 1910.
*The Tree of Knowledge* (novel; *El arbol de la ciencia*) 1911.
*The Restlessness of Shanti Andia* (novel; *Las inquietudes de Shanti Andia*, published in *The Restlessness of Shanti Andia and Other Writings*), 1911.
*The City of the Discreet* (novel; *La feria de los discretos*), 1917.
*Youth and Egolatry* (essays; *Juventud, egolatria*), 1917.

## SOURCES:

### Books

De Madariaga, Salvador, *The Genius of Spain and Other Essays on Spanish Contemporary Literature* Oxford, Oxford University Press, 1923.

*Hispanic Literature Criticism,* Jelena Krstovic, editor, Detroit, Gale, 1994.
Nicholson, Helen S., *The Novel of Protest and the Spanish Republic,* Tucson, University of Arizona, 1939.
Patt, Beatrice P., *Pio Baroja* (Twayne's World Authors Series), New York, Twayne Publishers, Inc. 1971.
Reid, John T., *Modern Spain and Liberalism: A Study in Literary Contrasts,* Stanford University, Stanford University Press, 1937.
Shaw, Donald L., *The Generation of 1898 in Spain,* New York, Barnes & Noble Books, 1975.

### Periodicals

*New Republic,* December 3, 1956, p. 419–24.
*New York Times,* October 31, 1956, p. 33; November 1, 1956, p. 39.

*—Sketch by Joan Axelrod-Contrada*

# Ray Barretto
## 1929-
### Puerto Rican American musician and bandleader

Congo player Ray Barretto's numerous performances and recordings have helped popularize salsa—a fusion of traditional Latin dance music with elements of jazz, blues, and rock—for more than three decades. In doing so, *Modern Percussionist* contributor Brooke Sheffield Comer praised Barretto for "overcom[ing] the fear of inferiority imposed on Latin musicians in America. . . . Barretto proves that it is possible to escape the Latin-musician stereotype. His prowess on percussion transcends any one idiom. His art is not defined by his culture, but by his soul and spirit."

Barretto has described the difficulty of playing congas in interviews. The conga is a physically demanding instrument, and many players have calloused and bruised hands to attest to the fact. Yet Barretto has shunned the use of drum sticks; his hands simply go numb after awhile. He prefers wooden congas over composite ones, and he absolutely abhors drum machines.

Barretto was born in New York City on April 29, 1929. When he was four years old, his father deserted the family, leaving his mother to care for him and his two siblings. Barretto took comfort in music. "I was poor, sick—I had asthma—and always deprived. Music was my only joy," Barretto recounted to Jeanne Brody of *Jazz Magazine*. His mother also enjoyed music and often listened to pieces by Latin artists, such as Machito on the radio. In the evenings, while his mother attended English language classes, Barretto listened to the radio because he was afraid to fall asleep. During these times he discovered some of the great performers of the jazz world: Duke Ellington, Count Basie, Benny Goodman, and Harry James. Little by little, Barretto learned their music and memorized their solos.

While music was a delight, school was torture for Barretto, an indifferent student. "I never studied much. . . . I could never sit still in class. I was claustrophobic," he explained to Brody. "When I was 17, I asked my mother for permission to join the army, and I quit school." Barretto's stint in the military proved to be pivotal. While stationed in Munich, he visited jazz clubs, where African American soldiers jammed with European jazz musicians. Then when a friend played a record of Dizzy Gillespie and Chano Pozo, an African Cuban percussionist, Barretto discovered jazz with a Latin influence. He told Brody that the listening to the recording "was a turning point in my life. The next day I played with a group—taping on an old banjo, I tried to imitate Chano Pozo."

Barretto befriended the European musicians. Buying himself a pair of conga drums and some elongated bass drums, he taught himself how to play. By the time he was discharged from the army he had a goal—to perform. "I had a hunger. Nothing distracted me," he informed Comer in *Modern Percussionist*. "I just knew that there were places to pay jazz and salsa in New York [City]. I wanted to be there. I had to be a part of it." Soon he was. In New York City, Barretto worked odd jobs to survive and played the congas for free, then found paid work with Latin bands. He played jam sessions in small clubs with Charlie Parker and Art Blakey, which led to more steady work with Eddie Bonemere's Latin jazz combo and José Curbelo's band. At the same time, Barretto made recordings with Red Garland, Dizzy Gillespie, Cannonball Adderly, Gene Ammons, Wes Montgomery, and Sonny Stitt. When Mong Santamaria left **Tito Puente**'s big band, Puente asked Barretto to take his place. It was Barretto's big break. "To be playing both Latin music and jazz was a marvelous experience for me," Barretto assessed in *Modern Percussionist*. "I had the best of both worlds."

After making a recording with Prestige Records, Barretto decided to quit Puente's band. He worked with Herbie Mann for several months before forming his own group in 1961. This new band featured violins and flutes, but Barretto later developed a different sound that highlighted trumpets and a

rhythm section. Through he had put together a traditional Latin dance band, Barretto's sound combined Latin music and jazz elements to create a fusion known popularly as salsa. Upon the debut of his album *Acid* in 1967, Barretto was a big name in salsa. During the 1970s and 1980s, he recorded more than 30 albums, many on the Atlantic label, and performed throughout the world, solidifying his reputation as a master of genre.

## SELECTED DISCOGRAPHY:

### Solo Recordings

*Acid,* Fania, 1967.
*Eye of the Beholder,* Atlantic, 1977.
*Can You Feel It?,* Atlantic, 1978.
*Aqui se puede,* Fania, 1987.
*Descarga Criolla* (1960s), Fantasy, 1993.
*Viva Watusi,* Polygram Latino, 1993.

### With Ray Barretto and New World Spirit

*Ancestral Messages,* Concord Picante, 1993.
*Carnival,* Fantasy, 1993.
*Taboo,* Concord Picante, 1994.

## SOURCES:

### Books

Boggs, Vernon, *Salsiology: Afro-Cuban Music and the Evolution of Salsa in New York City,* Westport, Connecticut, Greenwood, 1992.
*New Grove Dictionary of Jazz,* vol. 1, edited by Barry Kernfield, Macmillan, 1988.
Roberts, J. S., *The Latin Tinge: The Impact of Latin American Music on the United States,* New York, Oxford University, 1979.

### Periodicals

*Boston Globe,* September 16, 1990, p. B29; October 1, 1990, p. 31.
*Chicago Tribune,* September 10, 1991, section 1, p. 20.
*Crescendo International,* June 1982, p. 26.
*Denver Post,* July 4, 1993, p. E1.
*International Herald Tribune,* July 11, 1981, section W, p. 8.
*Jazz Magazine,* June 1981, pp. 44–46; September 1982, pp. 46–47; March 1984, p. 26; January 1986, p. 36.
*Modern Percussionist,* June 1985, pp. 22–25.
*Variety,* September 9, 1981, p. 82; November 17, 1985, p. 140.
*Village Voice,* March 23, 1982, pp. 68–69.

—*Sketch by J. M. Lesinski*

# Fulgencio Batista y Zaldívar
## 1901-1973
**Cuban dictator**

*Fulgencio Batista y Zaldívar*

Fulgencio Batista was the most dominant figure in Cuban politics for nearly a quarter of a century. He first came to power in 1933 as the leader of what later came to be known as the "Sergeant's Revolution"—a bloodless coup in which a group of sergeants, corporals, enlisted men, and student leaders, overthrew Carlos Manuel de Céspedes, the provisional president who succeeded the longtime dictator Gerardo Machado Morales. For the next six years, the "Strong Man of Cuba" ruled the country through various puppet presidents, and is credited with restoring social order and economic stability to the island. During his own tenure as president from 1940 to 1944, he initiated a broad range of social reforms, including the establishment of rural hospitals, minimum-wage legislation, and public works projects. He also brought Cuba into World War II on the side of the Allies, a policy that received widespread support from the United States and fostered an economic boom after the war. Following the defeat of his hand-picked successor, Batista took an eight-year respite from politics. But in 1952 he returned to orchestrate a second bloodless coup, unseating the Auténtico party government, and remained in power until 1959, when he was ousted by **Fidel Castro** and his guerilla revolutionary forces.

Fulgencio Batista y Zaldívar was born in Banes, in what was then the Santiago province on the extreme eastern end of Cuba, on January 16, 1901, 15 months after his native land became a sovereign nation, marking the end of 400 years of Spanish rule. The first-born child of Belisario Batista Palerma, a farm worker who fought as a sergeant in the Independence War, and the former Carmela Zaldívar Gonzales, Batista grew up in a small *bohio,* a thatch-roofed, earthen-floored, rural cabin. As a young boy, nicknamed "Beno," he contributed to his poor family's income by cutting sugar cane during the day, before attending a night school run by American Quakers. An avid reader despite the paucity of books available to him, young Batista was fascinated with biographies of great historical figures such as Abraham Lincoln. At the age of nine, though, he left the Quaker school to work as a tailor's apprentice. After working a variety of jobs—as a cane-field laborer, grocery clerk, bartender, railroader, and barber—the 20-year-old Batista enlisted in the National Army as a recruit in April 1921.

As a private at Camp Colombia, near Havana, Batista, while performing his army duties during the day, engaged in a rigorous program of self-improvement during his spare time in the evenings and long into the night. In an attempt to fulfill his dream of entering the legal profession, he read every law book that he could find on the base, earning the nickname "*el literato*" from a sergeant who often found his late-night study sessions in violation of the army's "lights out" regulation. But Batista lacked the prerequisite high school courses for law school and thus opted for a new profession—stenography. Having acquired shorthand and typing skills through a correspondence course based in New York, in 1923 he enrolled in San Mario College in Havana to take night classes in stenography. During his time there he also published articles in a small college magazine called *The Mercantile Educator,* protesting various social injustices. Upon finishing his first enlistment in the army that same year, Batista planned to enter the commercial field, but the poor Cuban economy hindered his efforts. He returned to the school and sat in on various classes before he was offered a position as an assistant professor of commercial grammar.

Although Batista was promoted to full professor and greatly benefitted from the educational opportunities offered by the college, he re-enlisted in the army and continued his studies at a library near his rural post. By 1928 he had worked his way up to the rank of sergeant—the highest possible rank for a non-commissioned officer—and was assigned as chief clerk and stenographer at Camp Colombia. While serving in thisSometi capacity, he was called upon to record the military trials of several political opponents of the dictator General Gerardo Machado, who was at the height of his power. Having witnessed firsthand the abuses of the ruthless dictator, Batista joined the ABC, an anti-Machado secret organization.

## Led "Sergeant's Revolution"

On August 12, 1933, the Cuban military forced Machado to resign and flee the country, and a provisional president was installed briefly, before then Secretary of State Carlos Manuel de Cespedes was appointed as president. But the new leader proved to be ineffectual in the face of the economic hardships brought on by the world-wide depression, the persistence of strikes as labor groups grew more militant, and widespread rioting in the streets. The end of his government came from "a most improbable and unexpected source," though, observed Georgetown University historian Luis E. Aguilar in *Cuba: A Short History.* On the evening of September 3, a group of sergeants, corporals, and enlisted men met to discuss their grievances concerning proposed military pay cuts and reductions. They concluded their deliberations with a list of demands to be submitted to the commanding officers. When the senior officers refused to discuss the matter and retired from the army post, the group of non-commissioned officers, under the direction of Batista, exhorted their troops to hold the post until the army command agreed to their demands. What began as a protest against military service conditions quickly evolved into a rebellion against the government when several anti-government student groups joined the soldiers' cause. Out of this "coalition of convenience," as Aguilar phrased it, a revolutionary junta emerged under the banner of the new Provisional Revolutionary Government, pledging itself to the affirmation of national sovereignty and the establishment of modern democracy.

Opposition to the new government came from a variety of sources, perhaps the most formidable being the U.S. Ambassador Sumner Welles, who believed that the coup had undermined the constitutional legality and conservative authority that he had strongly supported. However Batista, who had been promoted to the rank of colonel and made chief of staff of the army soon won over the ambassador, who said that he was "the only individual in Cuba today who represents authority." Welles informed the army chief that he had the support of Cuba's commercial and financial interests as well as that of the United States and encouraged him to create a new government. Accordingly, in January 1934 Batista withdrew army support from the provisional government of Ramón Grau San Martín and backed the conservative Carlos Mendieta, whom the United States officially recognized five days later. Order quickly returned to Cuba: the United States lowered tariffs, stabilizing the sugar industry; labor strikes, the last vestiges of the revolu-

tion, were broken up by the military, and the army took control over every division of public administration. Batista was now the most powerful man on the island.

For the next six years Colonel Batista wielded his power through a series of puppet presidents, presiding over an era of relative social tranquility that came to be known as the Pax Batistiana. In addition to increasing the size of the army from 8,000 to 20,000 men, the dictator committed the armed forces to his social agenda. For instance, in 1937 he unveiled the *misiones educativas* (educational missions), a new civic-military school system in which sergeants served as schoolmasters throughout the country. Designed to provide information concerning hygiene, agriculture, and nutrition to rural communities, more than 1,000 schools served the needs of children during the day and adults in the evening. Batista's program of "disciplined democracy" also called for the pardoning of political prisoners and even the legalization of the Communist Party, which began to exert its influence among labor unions.

## Elected President of Cuba

By the end of the decade, Cuba's newfound economic and political stability made conditions favorable for constitutional reform. With his political position firmly established, Batista oversaw the largely non-partisan writing of a progressive constitution that called for the use of referendum, universal suffrage, and free elections, as well as social provisions that included maximum hours and minimum wages, pensions, and workers' compensation. With this constitutional framework in place, Batista called for a general election in 1940 and ran for the presidency against his old rival Grau San Martín, who had returned from exile. In an election that was among the most honest in the Cuban republic's history, Batista received more than 800,000 votes to his opponent's 575,000. A year after taking office, Batista brought Cuba into World War II on the side of the Allies, following the Japanese attack on Pearl Harbor. Cuba furnished aid to the anti-submarine campaign and produced more than 4,000,000 tons of sugar made available for U.S. war purposes.

Showing his respect for the constitution he had authorized, Batista, at the conclusion of his term in 1944, dutifully saw to the election of the next president. That his hand-picked successor, Dr. Carlos Saladrigas, lost the election to Grau, underscored his commitment to the laws he had helped institute. After handing over the reins of leadership, Batista embarked on an extensive tour of Central and South America, before settling in Daytona Beach, Florida. There he wrote *Sombras de América,* a book that chronicled his political life and policies and offered his views on various problems facing Latin America.

Batista's departure from public life also brought a change in his personal affairs. In 1945 he and his first wife, Elisa Pilar Godínez Gómez, with whom he had three children, were granted a divorce in Mexico. Shortly thereafter, Batista married Marta Fernandéz Mircada; the couple later had two children.

In 1948 Batista returned to Cuba to run for the office of senator from Santa Clara province and to support his party's candidate for president, Ricardo Nuñez Fortuondo, against the choice of the outgoing Grau, Carlos Prío Socarrás. Although his party was unsuccessful in the presidential campaign, Batista succeeded in gaining the senatorial seat. Over the next two years, he worked to re-organize his Unitary Action party, which gained five seats in the 1950 election. In December of that same year he announced that he would again make a bid for the presidency in 1952, declaring that the Cuban people were tired of the "corruption" of the existing administration and were ready for a change.

### Staged a Second Coup

Three months before the elections were to be held, however, Batista took matters into his own hands and mounted his second coup in 18 years. At 2:40 a.m. on March 10, 1952, Batista's rebels seized all the capital's major army posts and gained control over the city's transportation and communication systems. The university and opposition press offices were closed and various union and Communist Party headquarters were occupied; leading activists were arrested and constitutional guarantees were suspended. In just one hour and 17 minutes, Batista was back in power. The ease at which the dictator was able to regain his authority, Aguilar contends, reflected the level to which the public had grown tired of nearly a decade of political corruption and scandal at all levels of civilian government. What is more, the widespread cynicism and indifference to politics made conditions favorable for a military takeover. The ousted government lacked the credibility to arouse public outrage, and many in the business community, welcomed the return of order, stability, and labor tranquility promised by Batista. Although the United States initially disapproved of the coup, they officially recognized the Batista government on March 27.

Having promised to hold elections in 1954, Batista again ran for president and succeeding in winning. But the major opposition parties were so dissatisfied with the political system that they withdrew their candidates. Batista's victory was hardly a cause for celebration: running unopposed he received a majority of the mere 40 percent of the electorate that voted. As dissent among opposition forces—such as those being organized by Fidel Castro—grew, a final attempt to procure a political rather than a military settlement was attempted. In 1955 a group of representatives from the moderate opposition planned to hold a series of conferences with Batista in an attempt to obtain a promise for new elections. The dictator refused, setting the stage for an armed confrontation.

### Ousted by Castro

Although student demonstrations resulted in clashes with the army and police as early as 1955, it was among the peasants of the Sierra Maestra mountains that Batista's political fortune would ultimately be decided. After two unsuccessful insurgencies, Castro and his Argentine comrade, **Ernesto "Che" Guevera**, began waging guerilla war against a few isolated outposts of the Rural Guard. For several years commanders of these posts had arbitrarily terrorized the rural communities; consequently, Castro had little trouble gathering peasant support for his revolution. As news of the guerilla successes grew, urban underground groups, such as the Civic Resistance movement, launched a campaign of terrorism in Cuba's major cities. In addition to the rebel movement, Batista's government was hampered by poor economic conditions that led to mounting popular opposition, and by political conflict within his own army. And in 1958, even the United States lost confidence in the troubled ruler and imposed an arms embargo, protesting the triumph of his designated successor in that year's rigged election.

On December 9, 1958, U.S. financier William D. Pawley, as part of a covert mission conducted by the State Department, held a three-hour conference with Batista, offering him a chance to retire unmolested in Florida with his family. But Batista refused the offer. During the last weeks of 1958, as the urban resistance and guerilla forces grew dramatically, Batista's fall was certain. On New Year's Day, at which point the rebel army numbered 50,000, he fled the country. Although a provisional president was installed in his place, Castro soon arrived in Havana to seize control of the island. Batista lived the remainder of his life in exile, dying of a heart attack in Marbella, Spain, on August 6, 1973.

### SELECTED PUBLISHED WORKS:

*Sombras de América,* [Mexico City], 1946.

### SOURCES:

### Books

Chester, Edmund A., *A Sergeant Named Batista,* New York, Holt, 1954.

*Cuba: A Short History,* edited by Leslie Bethell, New York, Cambridge, 1993.

*Current Biography Yearbook, 1952,* New York, Wilson, 1952.

**Periodicals**

*Life,* May 8, 1944, p. 21.
*Newsweek,* April 13, 1964, p. 38; August 20, 1973, p. 47.
*New York Times,* March 11, 1952, p. 13.
*Time,* April 26, 1937, p. 30; March 17, 1952, p. 36.

—*Sketch by Jason Gallman*

# Gioconda Belli
## 1948-

### Nicaraguan poet and novelist

Although not well-known in the United States, Gioconda Belli is celebrated in her native Nicaragua not only for her feminist poetry, but also for her role in the Sandinista Revolution. A key player in the "Revolution of the Poets"—a term coined in recognition of the large number of prominent poets and writers who helped engineer the overthrow of the Somoza dictatorship—Belli is considered one of Nicaragua's finest poets and one of the most accomplished in all of Latin America. Her first collection of poetry, *Sobre la grama,* originally published in 1974, earned the Marino Fiallos Gil Prize for Poetry from the Universidad Nacional Antónoma, Nicaragua's largest university. In a postscript to the 1983 edition of that collection, celebrated Nicaraguan poet Jóse Coronel Urtecho ranked Belli with "all the great women poets that have existed since Sappho." Her second collection, *Linea de fuego,* won the Casa de las Americas Prize—perhaps the most prestigious award in the Spanish-language literary world—in 1978.

In 1989 Belli published her first novel, *La mujer habitada (The Inhabited Woman),* an allegory of Latin American revolution that was translated and released in the United States in 1994. Although *Publishers Weekly* called the book "a disappointing treatment of a topic that deserves better novelistic exploration," it has been translated into six languages and was recognized in Germany as the best political novel of 1989. It has sold more than 500,000 copies.

Belli's poetry centers on progressive feminist and political lines, and many poems deal with issues of sexual and political equality. Interviewed by Kevin Baxter for the *Los Angeles Times* in 1995, Belli commented, "I think there is a tendency in feminism and in feminist literature to talk about the ordeal of the woman and the woman as victim. . . . [But] what I am trying to do is talk as a woman who is a maker of history and not just an object of history and subject of history."

Gioconda Belli was born in December 1948, in Managua, Nicaragua, and received a conservative Catholic education. The Belli family was one of Managua's oldest, wealthiest, and most prominent. Her father, a successful businessman, and her brother, Humberto Belli—who has served as Nicaragua's minister of education, were both well-known public figures.

Belli began writing poetry at the age of 21 and saw her first poems published a year later, in 1970. Her work appeared in Latin American publications such as *La Prensa Literaria, El Gallo Ilustrado,* and *Nicarauac.* Although she was an unlikely rebel, this privileged poet was an active member of the Sandinista Front and took part in arms smuggling, establishing safehouses, and other dangerous missions. According to the *Los Angeles Times,* Belli "helped plan the Christmastime commando raid on the house of Somoza supporter Chema Castillo, holding several prominent Nicaraguans hostage." They were ransomed for $1 million and the release of political prisoners.

Circumstances forced Belli to flee Nicaragua in 1975. She went into exile in Mexico, where she was tried and convicted in absentia for activities against the Somoza regime. It was after her arrival in Mexico that she wrote many of the poems that became *Linea de fuego.* Exiled for four years, Belli lived first in Mexico and then in Costa Rica. During this time she traveled extensively in South America and Europe, publicizing the human rights transgressions of the Somoza government and soliciting support for the Sandinista Front.

When the dictatorship fell in 1979, Belli returned to Nicaragua to lend her support to the new government. She developed a television station, hosted a talk show, and was an integral part of **Daniel Ortega**'s successful presidential campaign in 1984. She also served as managing director of the state-run advertising and public relations corporation. In 1986 she resigned in order to pursue writing full time.

### Revolution Defines Work

Although Belli formally withdrew from the Sandinista party in 1994, expressing her disillusionment with its lack of effect, she remains associated with it through her work. For many, the political aspects of her poetry are synonymous with the Sandinista Revolution. Belli's work has also paved the way for others. The *Los Angeles Times* stated that "the attention Belli earned through her political courage opened doors for many lesser poets and helped make feminist writing acceptable, even fashionable, in places where machismo reigns."

Belli married former National Public Radio reporter Charlie Castaldi in 1987. The couple has one adopted daughter. Belli has three other children from other relationships. She moved to Santa Monica, California, in late 1993, where she continues to write. She admits to some guilt about her prosperity. "Maybe I don't dream dreams anymore about 'the people.' I think sometimes one harms the people more than benefits them by trying to think for them," she told Baxter, "Now what I want to do is accept who I am and use my privileges, . . . my intelligence, . . . my knowledge, my education to ignite the imagination of the people. I think that's the most I can aspire to."

## SELECTED PUBLISHED WORKS:

*Sobre la grama,* Grupo BANIC, 1974, 1983.
*Linea de fuego,* H, CAH, 1978.
*Truenos y arco iris,* Nueva Nicaragua, 1982.
*Amor insurrecto,* Nueva Nicaragua, 1984; edited and translated by Marc Zimmerman in *Nicaragua in Reconstruction and at War,* MEO, 1985.
*De la costilla de Eva,* Nueva Nicaragua, 1987; translated by S.F. White and published as *From Eve's Rib,* Curbstone Press, 1989.
*1492–1992, la interminable conquista* (with D. Heinz), Mortiz/Planeta, 1990.
*La mujer habitada,* Taxalaparta, 1990; translated by Kathleen March and published as *The Inhabited Woman,* Curbstone Press, 1994.

## SOURCES:

### Books

*Open to the Sun: A Bilingual Anthology of Latin-American Women Poets,* edited by Nora Jacquez Weiser, Van Nuys, California, Perivale Press, 1979.
*Spanish American Authors: The Twentieth Century,* edited by Angel Flores, New York, H.W. Wilson Co., 1992.

### Periodicals

*Los Angeles Times,* January 15, 1995, pp. El, E4.
*Publishers Weekly,* May 30, 1994, pp. 36–37.

—*Sketch by Ellen Dennis French*

# Enrique Beltrán
## 1903-
### Mexican biologist

Enrique Beltrán was Mexico's first professionally trained biologist. He is an authority on single-celled organisms and united the different disciplines of zoology, agriculture and public health in his work. His importance derives not only from his work as a research scientist, but also from his administrative efforts in a wide variety of fields. He was largely responsible for the establishment of biology as a science in its own right in Mexico. Later in his career, Beltrán became interested in conservation and served as Mexico's first secretary of forests and game for several years. His work in the history of science led to the creation of the Mexican Society for the History of Science and Technology.

Beltrán was the grandson of a French colonel who had been sent to Mexico with the expeditionary force of Napoleon III. His father, an official in the Mexican navy who held diplomas in both civil engineering and law, was part of the group that constructed the corvette "Zaragoza," a Mexican training ship, in France. From the time of his youth, Beltrán was familiar with the literature of both France and Mexico. He formed the notion of a biological vocation from Luis Murillo's *Animales de México,* featuring chromolithographic illustrations, as well as from books by Paul Bert, Henri Milne Edwards, and Georges Cuvier.

### First Mexican Biologist

In the second decade of the twentieth century, professional biology as such did not exist in Mexico. Biologists and naturalists all held positions unrelated to their discipline. Upon graduating from secondary school, Beltrán went to the National University of Mexico, which had just been reorganized following the Mexican revolution. There, he matriculated in the Facultad de Altos Estudios, the university faculty where students could prepare for a career in science. He took basic courses with botanist Guillermo Gándara and zoologist Agustín Reza (by training as a surgeon), and he was assistant to the botanist Ezequiel Chávez. In 1921, as Chávez's assistant, eighteen-year-old Beltrán gave the first biology lectures in the faculty. (In 1902 Alfonso L. Herrera, a parasitologist, had given the first biology lectures in Mexico at the teacher's college in the capital.) Beltrán's wages were four pesos per day. Then he studied advanced biology with parasitologist Herrera and also with Carlos Reiche.

In 1923, under Herrera, Beltrán began to work on a thesis dealing with protozoansin Lake Xochimilco. Single-celled animals thereafter became the focus of Beltrán's scientific research, allowing him to move freely among specialists in zoology, agriculture, and public health. Beltrán's thesis was completed in 1925 under extreme conditions, for at the end of 1924 the government had suspended the faculty's budget and then changed its name to the more conventional Facultad de Filosofía y Letras en la Especialidad de Ciencias Naturales. Near the close of 1926, Beltrán graduated from the faculty with the diploma Profesor Académico en Ciencias Naturales. The diploma was the Mexican equivalent of a doctorate.

Having received certification as Mexico's first trained biologist, Beltrán began teaching in a succession of posts in the capital. (Mexico's system of higher education resembled that of France in its multiplicity of independent schools for advanced study and in the academic practice of holding down teaching assignments at a number of schools at once.) Beltrán directed the Marine Biological Station at Veracruz until it was suppressed in 1927; by then he had attracted the attention of administrators in both the educational and agricultural ministries, each of which funded schools of science. In 1931 he received a part-time professorship for biology at the Escuela Nacional Preparatoria. However, the Mexican political climate induced him to spend 1932 at Columbia University, where he worked as a Guggenheim fellow with the senior protozoologist Gary Nathan Calkins. His research netted him a Ph.D. there. Beltán returned to Mexico in 1933, where for the next 20 years he trained students and carried out research in a succession of posts, notably a chair in the faculty of sciences at the national capital. In 1936 he entered the Mexican National Academy of Medicine—an unusual honor for someone who was not a physician, and from 1937 to 1939 he served as the head of secondary instruction in Mexico.

### Environmental Concern

Between 1939 and 1952, Beltrán served as head of the Department of Protozoology of the Institute for Tropical Health and Disease. His output in the 1940s alone was remarkable—127 papers and 10 books. In the following year, he founded the independent Mexican Institute of Renewable Resources, and over the next decades he focused his efforts on guiding its fortunes. His organizing ability led to his appointment in 1958 as head of the new ministry of state (*subsecretaría*) of forests and game. In the 1960s, he revived a longstanding interest in history of science to organize an series of colloquia and publications leading to the creation in 1964 of the Mexican Society for the History of Science and Technology; he was the society's first president.

Enrique Beltrán occupies a unique position in twentieth-century Mexico. For the life sciences, he is the *bucinator*—the trumpeting herald—the value of whose patronage may be measured in the work of scores of talented colleagues.

### SELECTED PUBLISHED WORKS:

"*Curriculum vitae* de Enrique Beltrán," followed by "Bibliografía de Enrique Beltrán (1924–1949)" and "Veinticinco años de ciencias biológicas en México," *Revista de la Sociedad Mexicana de Historia Natural*, 10, 1949, pp. 5–26.
*Medio siglo de ciencia mexicana, 1900–1950*, Mexico, Secretaria de Educación Pública, 1952.
*Medio siglo de recuerdos de un biólogo mexicano*, Sociedad Mexicana de Historia Natural, 1977.
*Contribución de México a la biologia*, [Mexico City], 1982.
"Cómo y cuándo me interesé en la historia de la ciencia," *Quipu*, 2, No. 2, 1985, pp. 319–28.

### SOURCES:

*Homenaje al Dr. Enrique Belán*, edited by Avelino B. Villa Salas, Mexico, Academia Nacional de Ciencias Forestal, 1980.

—*Sketch by Lewis Pyenson*

---

# Jacinto Benavente
## 1866-1954
### Spanish playwright

J acinto Benavente was a popular and prolific playwright in pre-Civil War Spain. Although Benavente won the Nobel Prize in 1922, the merit of his work has been the subject of some debate. Credited with introducing European techniques and structure to contemporary Spanish theater, Benavente was also accused of lacking artistic depth and sincerity. Critic Federico de Onís, in an article for the *North American Review*, praised Benavente's "broad comprehensive interpretation of life," but modern criticism was more likely to echo Manuel Durán's negative assessment of Benavente's career in *World Literature Today*. Durán wrote, concerning Benavente's Nobel citation: "Another prize was squandered in 1922. The laurel went

*Jacinto Benavente*

that year to Jacinto Benavente, whose vast production is now mostly obsolete and was already out of phase with modern times when the medallion was conferred."

The third son of Mariano Benavente and Venancia Martínez, He was born Jacinto Benavente y Martínez in Madrid on August 12, 1866. Mariano Benavente, the playwright's father, was a celebrated pediatrician, a member of the Royal Academy of Medicine, and director of the Hospital of the Child Jesus. An adoring public immortalized the doctor with a bust erected in the Buen Retiro Park in Madrid, and Benavente himself kept his father's memory alive in the children's plays that he wrote. In Walter Starkie's seminal biography of the playwright, *Jacinto Benavente,* Benavente is quoted memorializing his father: "Only those who knew him and saw him at the pillow of a sick child can realize how a doctor can be an artist, a sage, and a saint." It was through his father that Benavente first came into contact with many of the important figures of an earlier generation. **José Echegaray**, also a playwright, as well as the first Spaniard to win the Nobel Prize, frequently consulted the doctor. Other household visitors were writer Juan Valera, politicians Bravo Murillo and Francisco Silvela, and actress María Tubau, later associated professionally with the younger Benavente.

## Puppet Theatre Led to Playwriting

As a child, Benavente was fond of putting on plays in a puppet theater. At first the plays were improvisational, but as he grew older, he began to write scripts. Even as an elderly man he remembered the name of the first drama he wrote and performed, *El gato pardo.* In childhood and adolescence, Benavente read everything he could, equally fascinated by Spanish classics and foreign literature. Cervantes was one of his early favorites, and when he had learned French and English, he was captivated by Shakespeare and Moliére, and the more contemporary Alfred de Musset. Despite his love for reading, Benavente did not enjoy his primary school studies at the Institute of San Isidro. As cited in Marcelino Peñuelas' biography, he confessed: "The only good memory I have of my school years is playing hooky."

When his father died in 1885, the 19-year-old Benavente abandoned the study of law to devote himself to the theater, at first as an actor. He had always been attracted to an acting career, as he made clear in a quote transcribed by Peñuelas: "I had never thought of being an author, but an actor, yes, it had been the great illusion of my life." The budding actor traveled through France, Germany, and Russia, and in 1890 toured Spain with actress María Tubau, later forming his own short-lived traveling company. Around this time, Benavente began submitting plays to a family friend, the director of Madrid's Teatro de la Comedia. "I had presented ten or twelve plays to Don Emilio Mario before he would accept any one of them even as a bad play," remembered the playwright, quoted by Peñuelas. "This went on for six or seven years."

In the years before his first play was performed, Benavente set about acquiring a base in journalism. He wrote early articles for *La Epoca,* and later contributed to *El Imparcial, Revista contemporánea, El arte del teatro,* and *La ilustración española,* among others. In 1899 he became the director of *La Vida Literaria,* a review which, according to Starkie, "was mainly responsible for giving a voice to the young authors of the New Movement." The first book Benavente published was a collection of poetry, *Versos* (1893), heavily influenced by Gustavo Adolfo Becquer and Ramón de Campoamor y Campoosorio, poetic idols of the late nineteenth century. Later nonthespian works by Benavente include *Cartas de mujeres* (*Letters from Women*)—sometimes credited as feminist, and *Recuerdos y olvidos: Memorias* (*Things Remembered and Forgotten: Memories*).

## Second Play Established Reputation

*El nido ajeno* (1894), Benavente's first play to reach the stage, was not a success, but the second, *Gente Conocida* (1896), established the playwright as a counterpoint to the histrionics of Echegaray's romanticism. "*Gente Conocida,*" wrote Starkie, "was the first product of a reaction against the old Spanish romantic drama with its shouting and bombast." *El nido ajeno* and *Gente conocida* belong to Benavente's first period of production, most often classified as the satiric. Some of the most popular plays of this phase included *La comida de las fieras* (1898), *Lo cursi* (1901), and *La Gobernadora* (1901). The satiric plays, wrote Onís, "were almost devoid of plot, composed of a series of pictures and scenes of the social life of the day, in which the members of the middle and upper classes of Madrid appeared before themselves as audience." Spanish society, before the Civil War of the late 1930s and long after the triumphs of the Golden Age, provided ample material for social satire. Teetering on the brink of economic collapse, the citizens of Madrid persisted in living beyond their means.

Benavente was at first honored by members of the Generation of '98, who related to his criticism of a bankrupt society. The playwright, however, as stated in *Books Abroad,* "shared neither their devotion to art nor their passionate search for the meaning of things Spanish." Benavente's peers were not '98 revolutionaries like **Ramón María del Valle-Inclán** and **Miguel de Unamuno y Jugo**, but French writers of the Théatre Libre, like Capus, Donnay, and Lavedan. Benavente himself cited as influences Shakespeare, **Lope de Vega**, Moliére, Ibsen, and George Bernard Shaw; but Peñuelas persisted, like most critics, in linking Benavente principally to the French playwrights of the late nineteenth century. The new techniques of the French movement, transferred by Benavente to the Spanish stage, included, according to Peñuelas, "simplicity of action . . . study of reality and the creation of more natural characters . . . and conciseness and swiftness of movement." "Benavente's theater is like a full-flowing river," wrote Alfredo Marquerie for *Topic,* "bearing characters and passions, themes and conflicts, as presented by life itself."

In the first years of the twentieth century, Benavente made a move away from a hard-edged analysis of society toward a broader, comedic vision. Starkie saw this shift as Benavente's attempt "to probe the hidden depths of society, to reach the fundamental causes of the great problems of life," but another factor in the change was Benavente's desire to appeal to a wider public. *Los malhechores del bien* (1905) was a success in this respect, attracting a larger and more varied audience than previous plays. "Benavente's world had grown," wrote Onís. "It was no longer the one social class, or the cosmopolitan, somewhat artificial society he had been portraying thitherto. Here were all strata of society, upper, middle, and lower, the last painted with as much vigor as the first with refinement." From this point on in his career, Benavente wrote plays of increasingly

varied description, making it difficult to set a standard system of classification.

Of the later plays (many grouped under "Miscellaneous" by Peñuelas), the most critically acclaimed was *Los intereses creados* (*The Bonds of Interest*) (1907), and the most popular was *La malquerida* (*The Passion Flower*) (1913). Both plays were translated into English by John Garret Underhill and performed in the United States. *Los intereses creados,* a departure from most of Benavente's other work, refers back to the puppet plays of his youth. It is written, in Onís' words, "in the manner of the ancient farce, the Italian commedia dell'arte," revolving around the rogue Crispín. Peñuelas credited the play with "the best virtues of Benavente's theater." More controversial is *La malquerida,* another anomaly in Benavente's production. "It is an unusual work for Benavente," wrote Onís, "a tragic drama on classic lines without real national bearing or spirit." Instantly popular in the United States, the play received mixed critical reviews.

"Few men have been so greatly honored in their lifetime, and this to the very end," wrote a reviewer for *Books Abroad.* Although Benavente was elected to the Spanish Royal Academy in 1912, most of his awards were presented to him after he had passed the pinnacle of his success, set alternatively by most critics either in 1907, with *Los intereses creados,* or in 1912, with *La malquerida.* The depreciating quality of the playwright's work, combined with his vacillating political stances (he supported the Germans in World War I), caused contemporaries like Ramón Perez de Ayala to seek a deflation of his reputation. Benavente, however, continued to produce until the end of his life, and was selected to receive the Nobel Prize in 1922. Two years later, he was awarded the Grand Cross of King Alfonso XII in his native country. Jacinto Benavente died in 1954.

## SELECTED PUBLISHED WORKS:

*Cartas de mujeres,* 1893, reprinted, Espasa Calpe, 1965.

"El nido ajeno," 1894; translated as "Another's Nest," *Nineteenth Century Spanish Plays,* 1935.

"Gente conocida," 1896.

"La gobernadora," 1901; translated as *The Governor's Wife: A Comedy in Three Acts,* R. G. Badger, 1913.

"La noche de sábado," 1903; translated as *Saturday Night: A Novel for the Stage in Five Tableaux,* R. G. Badger, 1918.

"No fumadores," 1904; translated as *No Smoking: A Farce in One Act,* Baker, 1935.

"Los malhechores del bien," 1905, Macmillan, 1933.

"El encanto de una hora," 1905; translated as *The Magic of an Hour: A Comedy in One Act,* Baker, 1935.

"Los intereses creados: Comedia de polichinelas en dos actos, tres cuadros y un prólogo," 1907; translated as *The Bonds of Interest,* Scribner's, 1921.

"La sonrisa de Gioconda," 1908; translated as *The Smile of the Mona Lisa: A Play in One Act,* R. G. Badger, 1915.

*El marido de su viuda: Comedia en un acto,* R. Velasco, 1908; translated as *His Widow's Husband: A Comedy in One Act,* Baker, 1935.

*De cerca: Comedia en un acto,* Hernando, 1909; translated as *At Close Range: A One-Act Play,* Samuel French, 1936.

*El príncipe que todo lo aprendió en los libros: Comedia en dos actos y siete cuadros,* Artes Gráficas Mateu, 1910; translated as *The Prince Who Learned Everything Out of Books: A Fairy Play in Three Acts and Five Scenes,* R. G. Badger, 1919.

"La malquerida," 1913; translated as *The Passionflower: Twenty-five Modern Plays,* 1953.

*La Verdad,* 1915; translated as *The Truth: A Play in One Act,* Baker, 1935.

*Recuerdos y olvidos (memorias),* Aguilar, 1959.

## SOURCES:

### Books

*Hispanic Writers,* edited by Bryan Ryan, Detroit, Gale, 1991.

Peñuelas, Marcelino, *Jacinto Benavente,* New York, Twayne, 1968.

Starkie, William, *Jacinto Benevente,* London, Oxford University Press, 1924.

### Periodicals

*Books Abroad,* winter 1955, pp. 41–43

*North American Review,* March 1923, pp. 357–64.

*Topic,* spring 1968, pp. 30–37.

*World Literature Today,* spring 1988, pp. 214–17.

—*Sketch by Natasha Wimmer*

# Roy P. Benavidez
## 1935-
**Hispanic American soldier**

Roy Benavidez was a Vietnam War hero and the last such soldier to be awarded the Medal of Honor, February 24, 1981. He was born Raul Perez Benavidez, May 8, 1935, on a farm in Lindenau near Cuero, Texas. His father was Salvadore Benavidez, Jr., a Texas sharecropper, and his mother was Teresa Perez, a Yaqui Indian born in Monclova, Coahuila, in northern Mexico. The Benavidez family had been in Texas since 1833 and fought for Texas in the War of Independence from Mexico. They were *vaqueros* (cowboys), originally from Mexico. His father died of tuberculosis in 1937, the same year his brother Rogelio was born, and his mother moved to Cuero to work as a domestic. She later married Pablo Chávez and they had a daughter, Lupe. Before going to public school, Benavidez was sent to school to learn English. He was very industrious as a young boy. In order to earn money to go to the movies, Benavidez began working on the streets, selling empty soda bottles, running errands, and cleaning for the local stockyard. He became a tough kid and he liked to fight. When Benavidez was seven years old, his mother became ill with tuberculosis and died. He and his brother were taken to El Campo, Texas, and lived with his uncle, Nicholas Benavidez, his wife Alexandria, their eight children, and his grandfather Salvadore.

Benavidez began working as a shoe shine boy at the bus station nearby and also worked as a translator for the local cab driver, who only spoke English. Taunted by racial slurs as a young boy, he would get into fights constantly. He fought over anything that angered him. His uncle Nicholas decided to send all the boys to a gym to train for the Golden Gloves. But Benavidez did not like to follow rules and eventually dropped out after he lost in a state championship. His uncle and grandfather were highly respected in the community and instilled high values in the young Benavidez. The family worked together, traveling to Colorado in the summer to pick sugar beets. They also worshiped together, attending mass every Sunday. Although his grandfather stressed the importance of an education, Benavidez dropped out of school at the age of 15. When he was hired to work at a local Firestone store Benavidez turned his life around. His boss reinforced the values his family had been teaching him all his life. At the age of 17, Benavidez joined the Texas National Guard and continued to work at Firestone. He went to boot camp at Fort Knox, Kentucky, and became a corporal. Because of his temper, he lost his stripes twice.

After two years in the guard, Benavidez decided to join the army. His dream was to go to Airborne training, but the army had other plans for him. Benavidez went into basic training at Fort Ord, California, and changed his name from Raul to Roy. In 1955, Benavidez was sent to Korea for 16 months. He was a member of the Buffalo Regiment of E Company, Second Battalion, Seventeenth Infantry Regiment. When he returned to the States, he was sent to Fort Chaffee, Arkansas, where he received orders to go to Germany. Benavidez first went to Augsburg, where the Eleventh Airborne Division was based. He finally had an opportunity to go to jump school, but he got into a fight and was kicked out before he even started. He was sent immediately to Berlin, where he spent the next 16 months.

### Dreams Became Reality

In the meantime, he and Hilaría "Lala" Coy, a girl from El Campo, whom he had admired for several years, began writing to each other. When he returned to the States, they began dating and in 1959, they were married in El Campo. They moved to Fort Gordon, Georgia, where Benavidez was a driver for several generals. He was assigned as a driver for General William Westmoreland, commander of the 101st Airborne. General Westmoreland was there to recruit for the Airborne. When he asked Benavidez if he had ever thought about going Airborne, Benavidez answered, "General, sir, that's all I have ever thought of. I'm due to re-up and I'd pay my own way if I had to." Two months later, he re-enlisted and his papers for Airborne were already prepared. Benavidez and his wife moved to Fort Bragg, North Carolina, where he went to jump school. He was made platoon sergeant and became a member of the 82nd Airborne.

### Wounded in Vietnam on First Tour

In 1965, Benavidez received orders to go to Vietnam. At that time, military personnel were told they were being used as "military advisers" in Vietnam. The reality of the situation in Vietnam hit Benavidez on his first combat patrol as "adviser" for a squad of South Vietnamese soldiers. A sniper shot a round at them while they were eating. It was the first time Benavidez had ever been shot at in his ten years in the army. An experienced warrant officer was with him on patrol and shot the sniper; he also taught Benavidez how to survive in the jungle. The American post, Payne Compound, was in Tam Ky, about 20 miles east of the Black Virgin mountains where the famous Ho Chi Minh trail is located. Benavidez stayed at Tam Ky until he was wounded while out on patrol in 1966. He never remembered what happened to him that day. He was dressed in Vietnamese clothes—black pajamas and sandals made out of rubber tires—and he had a Russian AK–47 at his side. At first, when the U.S. soldiers found him, they thought he was Viet Cong until they found a set of dog tags sewn into his pajamas.

Benavidez was evacuated to Brooke Army Medical Center at Fort Sam Houston in San Antonio, Texas. From the doctors' reports, Benavidez stepped on a land mine that did not explode as it should have and his spinal cord was traumatized. The doctors said that he would never walk again. The army wanted to discharge him on full disability but Benavidez wanted to stall their decision until he could walk again. He received no therapy, but he was determined to walk and began exercising at night. He worked to strengthen his shoulders and arms. He would crawl and try to stand, with excruciating pain. Many times the nurses would find him sitting on the floor after one of his "self-therapy" treatments. The other men in his ward began placing bets on whether he would fall or not. When the head of orthopedics, a colonel, came in to tell him about his discharge, Benavidez got out of bed to show the colonel the progress he had been making. The colonel insisted they were going to process his discharge anyway but Benavidez insisted even more. The men in the ward began shouting at the colonel to let him stay in the army. Benavidez told the colonel that he would personally ask General Westmoreland to put him in a hospital where he could get proper therapy. The colonel left and Benavidez never saw another senior officer and he was not discharged. After five months in the hospital, he began therapy to help him walk, despite the constant pain.

After two months of therapy, Benavidez was back on limited duty, working at a desk job for the 82nd Airborne. In July of 1966, he moved his wife back to Fort Bragg from El Campo, the same month their first daughter, Denise, was born. He lived in a fog, taking pain killers. Finally, his doctor told Benavidez he had to quit taking the drugs and advised him to begin exercising. He began running and working out in a gym, getting stronger. One of his Airborne buddies asked him to go out to watch them jump. Benavidez, although he was afraid, he forged papers and jumped three times that day. Before going to Vietnam, he had applied for Special Forces. His paperwork could not be found anywhere, so Benavidez forged another set of papers to recreate the ones that were lost. About a month later, he was sent to Special Forces training to become a Green Beret, still in pain from his injuries.

In January 1968, Benavidez was sent back to Vietnam. The Green Berets usually worked as trainers and support teams, but now they were sent into combat. Benavidez volunteered to go to the B–56 unit, which was right in the middle of the fighting. The unit was trained to gather intelligence and he was assigned to the Fifth Special Forces Military Assistance Command Vietnam Studies and Observation Group (MACV-SOG). It was also known as Special

Operations Group (SOG) or "Special Ops." During this time, Benavidez earned the nickname, Tango Mike/Mike ("The Mean Mexican").

In May, Benavidez was sent with a team to Quon Loi near the Cambodian border for a special mission. He was monitoring the radio, waiting for an assignment when a 12-man team went into the Cambodian jungle on a reconnaissance mission. They ran into the North Vietnamese Army (NVA) and were attacked with heavy force. When Benavidez heard about the men, he volunteered to go with one of the helicopter pilots, Larry McKibben, to rescue the soldiers. When McKibben could not get his helicopter down, Benavidez took a bag of medical supplies and rolled out of the chopper. He was shot in the leg immediately. He found eight wounded soldiers and signaled McKibben with green smoke to locate them. He was hit with a round of bullets in his thigh while helping the wounded to the chopper. Benavidez went back to get his old friend, Leroy Wright, who was one of the American contingents. Wright was the team leader and he was killed trying to save the other members of his team. Benavidez wanted to get Wright's body out and ensure that the North Vietnamese did not get the intelligence documents Wright was carrying. While he was dragging Wright's body to the chopper, a bullet hit Benavidez in the back. He passed out and when he came to, the chopper had crashed. Benavidez got the wounded men out of the chopper and set up a small perimeter where he administered first aid. Over 350 NVA surrounded the small group of men. A chopper came down in front of the wounded men and a Special Forces medic, ran to help the men. Under constant fire, Benavidez carried the men to the chopper. Benavidez was now suffering from shrapnel wounds around his head. Blood was streaming down his face as he loaded men into the chopper. There was one man left, Mousseau, and Benavidez went back to get him. He picked Mousseau up to carry him to the chopper when an NVA soldier slammed the butt of his rifle twice into Benavidez head. The soldier sliced his arms and his hand with a bayonet and Benavidez stabbed him with his Special Forces knife. When the last round hit Benavidez in the stomach, his intestines spilled out and, holding them in with his hands, he ran for the chopper. The next thing he remembered was being placed in a body bag. As the zipper was being closed, someone recognized his face and screamed, "Get a doc!" His jaw was broken, and he had over 37 bullet wounds. The doctor looked at Benavidez and said there was nothing he could do for him. Unable to speak, Benavidez spit at him.

Benavidez was sent to a hospital in Tokyo and then to Brooke Army Medical Center in San Antonio, where he spent a year recovering. During that time he received two purple hearts and a Distinguished Service Cross. He returned to duty and worked as a driver for General Robert Linville at Fort Riley,

Kansas for the next three years. Then, General Patrick Cassidy asked Benavidez to drive for him and he was transferred to Fort Sam Houston, Texas. He and his wife had two more children. Yvette was born in Kansas November 20, 1969, and a son, Noel, was born August 26, 1972, in Texas.

### Recommended for Medal of Honor

Lt. Colonel Ralph Drake recommended Benavidez for the Congressional Medal of Honor but he was turned down. In 1976, Benavidez retired from the army. When the local editor of the *El Campo Leader News* wrote an editorial about Benavidez, the Associated Press picked it up and newspapers around the world published it. His old buddy, O'Conner, saw it in Australia, and wrote a ten-page letter to the Department of the Army about Benavidez's heroic deeds. Although President Jimmy Carter signed the orders for his Medal of Honor, it was not until February, 1981, that he received the award from President Ronald Reagan. But the battles for Benavidez did not end. He appeared before Congress in 1983 when disability benefits to soldiers, widows, and dependent children were being cut back. Benefits were restored with his help. Benavidez now lives in El Campo with his wife and works with a non-profit organization called LifeSupport, Inc. and also tours the country lecturing.

### SELECTED PUBLISHED WORKS:

With Oscar Griffin, *The Three Wars of Roy Benavidez,* San Antonio, Texas, Corona, 1986.
With John R. Craig, *Medal of Honor: A Vietnam Warrior's Story,* Washington, D.C., Brassey's, 1995.

### SOURCES:

#### Books

Benavidez, Roy P., and John R. Craig, *Medal of Honor: A Vietnam Warrior's Story,* Washington, D.C., Brassey's, 1995.
*The Hispanic American Almanac,* edited by Nicolás Kanellos, Detroit, Gale Research, 1993.

#### Periodicals

*Reader's Digest,* April 1983, pp. 121–25.

—*Sketch by Phyllis Noah*

# Mario Benedetti
## 1920-
### Uruguayan writer

Mario Benedetti is widely recognized as one of the most popular and prolific contemporary writers in Latin America. In a literary career that has spanned nearly half a century, he has explored his evolving aesthetic and political vision in a variety of genres, publishing more than 50 works of fiction, poetry, drama, and prose. Although Benedetti had been writing extensively since the late 1940s, he, like many of his Latin American contemporaries, did not achieve international fame until the late 1960s when he published *La muerte y otras sorpresas* (*Death and Other Surprises*), a collection of short stories examining the social reality of Montevideo's middle class. Since that time he has grown to become one of Latin America's most lucid voices of protest against political repression and bourgeois apathy, as well as the imperialist policies of the United States that he believes have fostered the social and moral decline of the continent. As Bart L. Lewis stated in *Chasqui,* "Activism, productive contemplation and awareness of the need for Latin American solidarity are central features of Benedetti's essays ... while his prose fiction makes a major contribution to the luster emanating from the modern Latin American novel."

Benedetti was born September 14, 1920, in Paso de los Toros, Tacuarembo, Uruguay, the son of Brenno Benedetti and Matilde Farrugia. After attending the Colegio Alemán, he worked as an accountant in Montevideo, Uruguay, and as a journalist for the weekly periodical, *Marcha.* He also worked as a literary, film, and theater critic for *El Diario, Tribuna Popular,* and *La Mañana.* In the wake of the economic, political, and moral crisis of the late 1950s brought on by the ascension of the Uruguayan dictatorship, he travelled extensively through Europe in the mid–1960s. After the successful Cuban revolution led by **Fidel Castro**, Benedetti served as the organizer and director of a literary research center in Cuba from 1969 to 1971. Since that time he has supported himself and his wife, Luz López, through his immensely popular writing, which as Ana María Hernández described in *World Literature Today,* "reaches through all levels of society at a time when serious literature has long renounced mass appeal."

Perhaps Benedetti's best known and most critically acclaimed novel in the United States comes from the early phase of his career. First published in Uruguay in 1960 and translated into English nine years later, *The Truce* portrays the life of a middle-aged accountant who becomes attracted to a young assistant on the eve of his retirement. Written in the form of a journal, this "short, well defined" book "has something classic about it, it is the vehicle of a vision of life," observed Arthur Gold in the *New York Times Book Review.* In a similar fashion, J. A. Crow of the *Saturday Review,* found 'the stark language and probing mind" of the author characteristic of "one of the best novels to come out of Latin American in recent years."

### From Realism to Experimentalism

After operating primarily within the genre of realism during the 1940s and 1950s, focusing on the everyday life of Uruguay's urban lower class, Benedetti turned to more experimental, formal techniques in the turbulent 1960s. The title story of *La muerte y otros sorpresas,* for example, portrays a man near death who has the surreal experience of feeling "objects going away from him" as he watches the houses of Montevideo shrink into non-existence. While another story, *"A imagen y semejanza "* ("Imagery and Conformity") examines through the ridiculous and sudden death of an ant. The purpose beyond Benedetti's decision to suspend conventional narrative constraints, as a *New York Times Book Review* critic explains, is perhaps to make "an attempt to get at something beyond ... [to expose the existential] notion of death."

Concomitant with the experience of repression in his native country and his life, Benedetti's later work has featured a more militant voice of social protest, especially in his nonfiction and poetry. For instance, in *El escritor latinoamericano y la revolución posible* (*The Latin American Writer and the possible Revolution*), a collection of essays written between 1968 and 1973 that draw from his experience with the Cuban revolution, he powerfully articulates "the need for revolution in cultural, literary and political life in Latin America," according to Lewis, demonstrating "his progression from sensitized critic of his own country to narrator of crisis in fiction to voice of a continent." Likewise in *Viento del exilio* (*The Exile Wind*), one of his better known volumes of poetry, he "contemplates his continent's reality," stated Alberto Blasi in *World Literature Today.* "The rhetoric of exile is omnipresent in his lines: tragic winds, a rejection of literary traditions, the impulse to seek refuge in memoirs of everyday life in Montevideo, ironies about daily events or how well people are ignoring the exile's sufferings."

## SELECTED PUBLISHED WORKS:

### Fiction and Poetry

*Esta mañana,* Montevideo, 1949.
*El último viaje y otros cuentos,* Número, 1951.
*Quién de nosostros,* Alfa, 1953.

*Poemas de la oficina,* Número, 1956.
*Montevideanos,* Alfa, 1959.
*La tregua,* Alfa, 1960; translation by Benjamin Graham published as *The Truce,* Harper, 1969.
*Poemas del hoyporhoy,* Alfa, 1961.
*Inventario,* Alfa, 1963.
*Gracias por el fuego,* Alfa, 1965.
*Contra los puentes levadizos,* Alfa, 1966.
*Antología natural,* Alfa, 1967.
*A ras de sueňo,* Alfa, 1967.
*La muerte y otras sorpresas,* Siglo XXI, 1968.
*El cumpleaňos de Juan Angel,* Siglo XXI, 1971.
*Letras de emergencia,* Alfa, 1973.
*Poemas de otros,* Alfa, 1974.
*Cotidianas,* Siglo XXI, 1979.
*Pedro y el capitán: Pieza en cuatro partes,* Nueva Imagen, 1979.
*Poesía trunca: Poesía latinoamericana revolucinaria,* Visor, 1980.
*Viento del exilio,* Nueva Imagen, 1981.
*Antología poética,* Alianza, 1984.
*Geografías,* Nueva Imagen, 1984.
*Noción de patria: Próximo prójimo,* Visor, 1985.

### Essays and Other Writings

*Peripecia y novela,* Montevideo, 1948.
*Marcel Proust y otros ensayos,* Número, 1951.
*El país de la cola de paja,* Asir, 1960.
*Literatura uruguaya siglo XX,* Alfa, 1963.
*Letras del continente mestizo,* Arca, 1967.
*Sobre artes y oficios,* Alfa, 1968.
*Cuaderno cubano,* Arca, 1969.
*Crítig coca cómplice,* Instituto Cubano del Libro, 1971.
*Crónicas del 71,* Arca, 1972.
*El escritor latinoamericano y revolución posible,* Alfa Argentina, 1974.
*El ejercicio del criterio: Crítica literaria, 1950–1970,* Nueva Imagen, 1981.
*Escritos políticos,* Arca, 1985.

### SOURCES:

### Books

*Hispanic Writers,* edited by Bryan Ryan, Detroit, Gale Research, 1991.
*International Who's Who,* Europa, 1994/1995.

### Periodicals

*Chasqui,* February/May 1982, pp. 3–12.
*New York Times Book Review,* October 19, 1969, p. 55.
*Saturday Review,* January 10, 1970, p. 44.

*Times Literary Supplement,* September 18, 1970; August 6, 1976, p. 9.
*World Literature Today,* spring 1982, p. 310; spring 1983, p. 251; spring 1985, p. 245; winter 1988, p. 95.

—*Sketch by Jason Gallman*

# Jellybean Benitez
## 19??-
### Puerto Rican American record producer

Born John Benitez and raised in the South Bronx, Jellybean Benitez gained a reputation as an energetic disc jockey, remixer, and record producer. According to *New York Magazine*'s Dinah Prince, "He was undoubtedly one of the major forces behind the move from disco to hip-hop in the late seventies." In a career that has ranged from the dance clubs of New York to production studios around America— where he produced the recordings of artists such as Barbra Streisand and Madonna—Benitez has maintained his enthusiasm for his work.

Benitez was the son of Puerto Rican immigrants, who divorced when he was ten years old. Jellybean—a nickname given him by his younger sister—was a music fan from his earliest years. The owner of a portable battery-operated turntable, Benitez used money given him by his mother to buy records. As a youngster, Jellybean brought his record player and records to local parties, where he acted as disc jockey. As he grew older he slipped into local clubs to watch the disc jockeys work. A *New York* article noted that Benitez "became intrigued by a D.J. at the Sanctuary. 'I was mesmerized by what he was doing.... He would play a song, and they would scream.'"

In 1976 Benitez was thrown out of DeWitt Clinton High School for truancy. His career as a disc jockey continued to grow, however, and he became a fixture at several popular nightclubs. He later earned his high-school-equivalency diploma and enrolled in Bronx Community College as a psychology major.

Benitez continued to work as a D.J., commuting from Long Island to Manhattan to work clubs including Hurrah, Les Mouches, and New York New York, eventually settling at Electric Circus and Xenon. He worked as a remixer, using two turntables to manipulate songs by adding rhythms and beats, extending songs, and teasing the audience with certain riffs. Benitez's keen sense of crowd dynamics and music knowledge kept people on the dance floor. As Prince acknowledged, "His hyper brand of hustle and funk made him a major figure in the New York clubs at a time when D.J.s were becoming prime movers in establishing hits." Record companies began to reward Benitez when songs that he featured were successful. Soon these companies hired him as a in-house remixer.

In 1983, while working in New York's Funhouse club, Benitez was introduced to Madonna, a fledgling recording artist at the time. His suggestion to include the song "Holiday" on her debut album, and his demand to produce it, launched both Madonna and Benitez into stardom. The two were romantically involved for a period of time.

In 1984 Benitez landed a producing deal with EMI America records, where he worked as a producer and remixer. In recent years he has produced recordings and remixes for an eclectic group of artists including Barbara Streisand, Billy Joel, David Bowie, Talking Heads, The Pointer Sisters, and ZZ Top, among others. 1984 also marked the year that Benitez came out with the album *Wotupski?!?*, on EMI records, which featured unknown artists as well as the song "Sidewalk Talk," composed by Madonna. The song reached number one on the Billboard music charts. His follow up albums include *Just Visiting This Planet* (1987), on Chrysalis, and *Spillin' the Beans* (1993), on Atlantic; both albums contain his own songs, mixed with songs from lesser-known artists. Benitez himself sings and raps on *Spillin' the Beans*. In a discussion of the performer, Atlantic Record's Joey Carvello told *Billboard*'s Larry Flick, Jellybean "has a knack for creating great songs, as well as an eye for discovering vocalists with real star potential."

Benitez has worked closely with the film industry as well, producing movie soundtracks for Mel Brooks' *Spaceballs, The Principal, The Muppets,* and *Mi Vida Loca,* among others. His charismatic personality has made him a popular and gregarious guest at celebrity parties. Commented *New York:* "Celebrities seemed to feel not only at ease with Jellybean but also charmed by his nonchalance. He was the personification of eighties cool. [*Village Voice* gossip columnist Michael] Musto says, 'He has that street quality [be]cause he's from the Bronx, and I think a lot of people think "Oh, how cool, I'm hanging out with this cool hip-hop type of guy." Yet there is nothing intimidating about him. . . . He's very slick.'" In addition to his work with established artists, Benitez's record company, Jellybean Music Group, helps find and launch new artists, and he has both music and production companies on both the East and West coasts. Such diverse pursuits help enable Jellybean Benitez to continue to work as one of the record industry's most sought-after producers and remixers.

## SELECTED DISCOGRAPHY:

*Wotupski?!?* EMI Records, 1984.
*Just Visiting This Planet,* Chrysalis, 1987.
*Spillin' the Beans,* Atlantic, 1993.

## SOURCES:

*Billboard,* January 26, 1991, p.40.
*New York Magazine,* March 28, 1988, p.70.

—*Sketch by Melissa Clark*

# Manuel Phillip Berriozábal
## 1931-
### Hispanic American mathematician and educator

Manuel Phillip Berriozábal is an educator who has done extensive work in developing programs that help Hispanic students and other minorities to stay in school and to succeed at higher-level education. In his particular area of expertise—mathematics—Berriozábal has explored reasons why statistics indicate that minorities have greater difficulty succeeding in that discipline. In 1988 his findings were incorporated into a pilot program for freshman engineering students called "The Texas Prefreshman Engineering Program: A Model for a Statewide Precollege Intervention Program." In related work, he took part in a task force that examined the problems mathematics pose for minority students. His observations and conclusions appeared in a 1989 paper titled "Why Hasn't Mathematics Worked for Minorities?"

Berriozábal has also been active in various organizations designed to support minority education, especially in the fields of mathematics and science. He has served as co-chairman of the Mathematical Association of America's Committee on Minority Participation in Math and joined both the Society for the Advancement of Chicanos & Native Americans in Science and the Texas Association of Chicanos in Higher Education.

Berriozábal was born on July 21, 1931, in San Antonio, Texas. He is the son of Manuel Jaime Berriozábal and Emma Louise Wand. In 1975 he married Maria Antonietta Rodriguez, who has served as a government official for the city of San Antonio and has also championed the needs of Hispanic youth in her work. Professor Berriozábal began his higher

*Manuel Berriozábal*

have the ability to succeed at the college level. It also provides academic motivation and a support system to encourage these students to consider engineering and science studies. Financial and in-kind support for the program comes from various government agencies and professional organizations, colleges, and universities, local school districts, and private industry. Each year, PREP holds an eight-week summer session at host colleges and universities in Texas. At the sessions, students attend classes designed to develop abstract reasoning and problem-solving skills. They are also presented with information that helps identify career opportunities in science and engineering.

The results of Berriozábal's program have been encouraging. By 1988, more than 1,741 students—78 percent of whom were minorities—had completed at least one eight-week session. A survey indicated that of those students who attended the program, 88 percent had gone on to college or were college graduates. Of those students, 67 percent were science or engineering majors.

Berriozábal has been recognized for his accomplishments in this area of minority education. In 1989 he received a National Achievement Award in Education from *Hispanic Engineer Magazine,* and in 1991 he was a recipient of the Mathematics/Science Leadership Development and Recognition Program Award from the U. S. Department of Energy. The educator has also received awards from a wide range of other professional, educational, and corporate groups.

education at Rockhurst College and received his M.S. degree from the University of Notre Dame in 1956. He holds a Ph.D. from the University of California at Los Angeles, and he began his career in education there as an instructor; he later worked as a lecturer at the university. He became assistant professor of mathematics at Tulane University in 1962. In 1966 he took a position as associate professor at the University of New Orleans and was made professor of mathematics in 1972. From there, he moved to the University of Texas at San Antonio in 1976. Since settling in Texas, much of his work has focused on strategies and programs to increase the number of Hispanic students and other minorities receiving science and mathematics education.

Science and mathematics educators in general have been concerned that minorities are under-represented in those disciplines. Educators in the states of Texas, Arizona, and California have been leaders in developing ways to help minorities—especially Hispanics—to stay in school and to succeed in pre-college coursework. Such efforts, it is hoped, will result in an expansion of the number of minorities who not only go on to college, but successfully secure a degree.

Professor Berriozábal's program at the University of San Antonio is illustrative of the above goals. The Prefreshman Engineering Program (PREP) has been conducted at the university since 1979. PREP identifies junior high and high school students who

## SOURCES:

### Books

*Notable Hispanic American Women,* Detroit, Gale, Detroit, 1993.

### Periodicals

*Change, the Magazine of Higher Learning,* May/June 1988, pp. 61–4.

—*Sketch by Jane Stewart Cook*

# Adolfo Bioy Casares
## 1914-
### Argentine writer

Although overshadowed for much of his career by his more illustrious friend and collaborator **Jorge Luis Borges,** Adolfo Bioy Casares—also known as "Bioy" and "Bioy-Casares"; pseudonyms include

Javier Miranda and Martín Sacastru; joint pseudonyms with Jorge Luis Borges include H(onorio) Bustos Domecq, B. Lynch Davis, B. Suárez Lynch—is a prolific writer, best known for his novels and short stories. He figures prominently in the development of twentieth-century Latin American literature, particularly in the genre known as fantastic literature; some of his work has been adapted for the screen. Alberto Manguel, writing in Toronto's *Globe and Mail* in 1989, called Bioy Casares "one of the wisest interpreters of our unfathomable and bewildering existence." The writer's many awards include the prestigious Premio Miguel de Cervantes de Literatura, which he won in 1990. According to Caleb Bach, writing in *Américas,* Bioy Casares's acceptance speech for that prize exemplified "the wry humor and self-deprecating modesty for which he is famous."

Bioy Casares was born in Buenos Aires, Argentina, on September 15, 1914, the only child of upper-class parents Adolfo Bioy and Marta Casares. His father's family traced its lineage to the Béarn region of southwestern France, an area that appears in some of Bioy Casares's work. Bioy Casares's maternal relatives owned a prosperous dairy chain. His parents encouraged his literary proclivities; both transmitted a love for reading and his father facilitated the publication of Bioy Casares's first book, *Prólogo,* when the author was a teenager. For her part, Bioy Casares's mother provided the link that connected her son to Borges, asking the writer and critic **Victoria Ocampo** to recommend a mentor for the adolescent "Adolfito." Family, books, sports, and travel—to Europe, the United States, and the Middle East—were all important parts of Bioy Casares's youth. Although he recalled his parents reading to him from early childhood, Bioy Casares pinpointed 1929 in the "Chronology" he prepared for *Review* as the year when "I discover literature; I search for it avidly, where it is and where it is not, in classical, modern, Spanish, Argentine writers, in the Bible, in the *Divine Comedy,* in *Ulysses,* in tango lyrics."

He began studies at the University of Buenos Aires's School of Law in 1933, and soon transferred to the faculty of philosophy and letters before withdrawing two years later. In the "Chronology," Bioy Casares described 1934 as the year when both Silvina Ocampo (Victoria's sister and Bioy Casares's future wife—they married in 1940 and became the parents of a daughter, Marta, in 1954) and Borges encouraged him to devote himself to his writing. "Borges tells me that if I want to be a writer, I can't be a lawyer, a professor, a publisher, or a magazine editor."

He had met Borges two years earlier, at Victoria Ocampo's home. Borges was 15 years older than Bioy Casares. It was the beginning of a long relationship that ended only with Borges's death in 1986. "Life has filled me with many happiness and the friendship with Borges was one of them," Bioy Casares told Bach

in *Américas.* Their first collaboration, as Bioy Casares recalled in the "Chronology," was "a pamphlet on curdled milk," produced in connection with Bioy Casares's family dairy. Over the course of their lives their joint efforts included short stories, filmscripts, anthologies, and a short-lived journal, *Destiempo.*

### Created Another Voice With Borges

While critics have often tried to discern the individual contributions of Borges and Bioy Casares to their joint works, Bioy Casares has described the existence of a "third writer," a presence, he told Bach, "whom we had not invited who was a *burlesco,* who made one joke after another." Borges's biographer, Emir Rodriguez Monegal, quoted an interview with Ronald Christ in which Borges elaborated: "When we collaborate, we call ourselves H. Bustos Domecq. Bustos was a great-grandfather of mine and Domecq was a great-grandfather of his. Now the queer thing is that when we write, and we write mostly humorous stuff . . . when our writing is successful, then what comes out is something quite different from Bioy Casares' stuff and my stuff; even the jokes are different. So we have created between us a kind of third person; we have somehow begotten a third person that is quite unlike us."

Bustos Domecq's first major work, *Seis problemas para Don Isidro Parodi* (*Six Problems for Don Isidro Parodi*), was published in 1942, although earlier stories appeared in *Sur,* the prominent journal founded by Victoria Ocampo. The book is structured around six murder mysteries, puzzles that different visitors present to Don Isidro Parodi, a barber-turned-detective who sits in a prison cell for a crime he did not commit. When the translation appeared in 1981, Denis Lynn Heyck, writing in the *Chicago Tribune Book World,* called it "an extremely funny book. The plots are improbable and confused, as are the characters; both are vehicles for a broad-ranging parody of the detective story, Argentine politics and culture, literary culture, and narrative language itself."

Bustos Domecq reappeared in the 1967 *Crónicas de Bustos Domecq* (translated in 1976 as *Chronicles of Bustos Domecq*), which was published this time under the true names of its authors. Paul Gray, in his *Time* magazine review, called the book a "collection of mock essays about mock artists." Here the author Bustos Domecq has become the central character. He is a literary critic, "an inept critic," Gray wrote, "a figure of Chaplinesque pathos: a tastemaker totally lacking in taste, a perpetual target of the avant-garde's custard pies." Clarence Brown deemed the book "sheer nonsensical hilarity" in the *New Republic,* adding that "it is also an exercise in one of the rarest and most perilous of literary genres, deliberate self-parody." The *Atlantic*'s Phoebe-Lou Adams called

Bustos Domecq "hilariously awful and a great creation."

## Pioneer of Fantastic Literature

In 1940 Bioy Casares, Borges, and Silvina Ocampo published an *Antología de la literatura fantástica* (*Anthology of Fantastic Literature*). Bioy Casares authored the anthology's prologue, which included discussions of the genre's history and technique. Earlier that same year Bioy Casares had already turned the theory into practice, publishing *La invención de Morel* (*The Invention of Morel*), a novel that critics as well as Bioy Casares himself considered the true starting point of his literary career.

*The Invention of Morel,* for which Bioy Casares won the Premio Municipal de la Ciudad de Buenos Aires, combined elements of traditional adventure and detective stories in a new way. The central character is a narrator trapped on a remote island. This narrator falls in love with a woman, Faustine, only to discover that Faustine and her companion Morel are no more than imaginary projections formed by a machine. Borges wrote a prologue to the novel, pages that are often cited for their own bold, lucid exposition of the theory behind fantastic literature. Here Borges criticized conventional psychological and realist fiction and concluded: "In Spanish, works of reasoned imagination are infrequent and very rare. . . . *The Invention of Morel* . . . brings a new genre to our land and our language."

*The Invention of Morel,* like another oft-cited Bioy Casares novel, *Plan de evasión* (*A Plan for Escape*) is set on an island. Both books also, as Robert M. Adams noted in *Review,* "center on that favorite figure of our cultural fantasies, the mad scientist." But Bioy Casares also plunged into local urban scenes to create his settings, and his characters were not limited to scientists. Wherever the stories unfold and whoever the characters may be, the fictional works of Bioy Casares share a basic enigmatic quality. "Bioy Casares's novels and short stories are comic masterpieces whose fundamental joke is the gap that separates what his characters know from what is going on," D. P. Gallagher commented in the *Bulletin of Hispanic Studies.* "On the one hand," Gallagher wrote, "there is a vast and inscrutable universe, manipulated by arcane and deliberate mystifiers; on the other hand a little man—a Venezuelan patriot, a car mechanic, a doddering *porteño* widower—who is painfully obliged to observe and suffer it."

Especially earlier in his career, these enigmas and twists on reality resulted in complicated plot structures. "In maturing and mellowing," Rodriguez Monegal asserted in *Review,* "Bioy Casares has learned how to substitute for the most unbearable complexity of *A Plan for Escape* and the stories of *The Celestial Plot,* a fluid narrative style which is already evident in *El sueño de los héroes* [*The Dream of Heroes* ] and reaches a perfect balance in the stories of *Guirnalda con amores* [*A Garland of Love,* 1959]." Rodriguez Monegal believed that by 1975, "this balance . . . reached a perfect, unassuming mastery."

Love themes, especially stories of the quest for love, appear frequently in Bioy Casares's work. But for Bioy Casares, as Manguel remarked in his *Globe and Mail* review of *The Dream of Heroes,* "this pursuit is not an abstract occupation, a gentle musing in a smoky cafe." Rather, it is "something as breathless and muscle-wrenching as Captain Ahab's sea sport. The understanding of love, the comprehension, however dim, of the agonies and frustrations of desire, drive Bioy's men and women on storm-tossed voyages that are in turn terrifying and ridiculous, compassionate and hideously selfish."

Another aspect common to much of Bioy Casares's work is, as Margaret L. Snook pointed out in the *Latin American Literary Review,* the situation that "many of the first person narrators of Bioy Casares's fantastic fiction are writers, men whose literary interests vary from poetry to journalism. This literary background, often important in the characterization of the narrators, usually plays another vital role in the thematic development of the work. It provides the perfect opportunity for presenting theories related to creativity and writing, both recurrent themes in Bioy Casares's prose."

In 1963 Bioy Casares won Argentina's Segundo Premio Nacional de Literatura for *El lado de la sombra.* Six years later he captured the country's Primer Premio, for *El gran serafín.* The Argentine Society of Writers awarded him its Gran Premio de Honor in 1975. The 1980s witnessed his receipt of the Premio Mondello for *Historias fantásticas* and the Premio Internacional Literario IILA (Rome) for *Historias fantásticas* and *Historias de amor.* In addition to the Spanish Cervantes Prize, he has also won Mexico's Premio Alfonso Reyes.

As his eightieth birthday approached, Bioy Casares was occupying "a spotlight solely his," as Bach observed in *Américas,* still reading and writing, serving as a member of the panel that chooses the Premio Cervantes, and maintaining a rigorous travel schedule. Both autobiography, *Memorias,* as well as a collection of previously published short stories, *Selected Stories,* were published in 1994.

## SELECTED PUBLISHED WORKS:

### Books

*Prólogo,* Biblos, 1929.
(As Martín Sacastru) *17 disparos contra lo porvenir,* Tor, 1933.
*Caos,* Viau & Zona, 1934.

*La nueva tormenta; o, La vida múltiple de Juan Ruteno,* Colombo, 1935.

*La estatua casera,* Jacaranda, 1936.

*Luis Greve, muerto,* Destiempo, 1937.

*La invención de Morel,* Losada, 1940; translated by Ruth L. C. Simms in her *The Invention of Morel and Other Stories,* University of Texas Press, 1964.

(With Jorge Luis Borges, as H. Bustos Domecq) *Seis problemas para Don Isidro Parodi,* Sur, 1942; translated by Norman Thomas di Giovanni as *Six Problems for Don Isidro Parodi,* Dutton, 1981.

*El perjurio de la nieve,* Emecé, 1944; translated by Simms as *The Perjury of the Snow,* Vanishing Rotating Triangle, 1964.

*Plan de evasión,* Emecé, 1945; translated by Suzanne Jill Levine as *A Plan for Escape,* Dutton, 1975.

(With Silvina Ocampo) *Los que aman, odian,* Emecé, 1946.

(With Borges, as Bustos Domecq) *Dos fantasías memorables,* Oportet, 1946.

(With Borges, as B. Suárez Lynch) *Un modelo para la muerte,* Oportet & Haereses, 1946.

*La trama celeste,* Sur, 1948.

*Homenaje a Francisco Almeyra,* Destiempo, 1954.

*El sueño de los heroes,* Losada, 1954; translated by Diana Thorold as *The Dream of Heroes,* Quartet, 1987, and Dutton, 1988.

(With Borges) *Los orilleros; El paraíso de los creyentes,* Losada, 1955.

*Historia prodigiosa,* Obregón, 1956; enlarged edition, Emecé, 1961.

*Guirnalda con amores,* Emecé, 1959.

*El lado de la sombra,* Emecé, 1962.

*La tarde de un fauno,* Cuadernos Hispaoamericanos, 1964.

(With Borges) *Crónicas de Bustos Domecq,* Losada, 1967; translated by di Giovanni as *Chronicles of Bustos Domecq,* Dutton, 1976, and Lane, 1982.

*El gran serafín,* Emecé, 1967.

*La otra aventura,* Galerna, 1968.

*Diario de la guerra del cerdo,* Emecé, 1969; translated by Gregory Woodruff and Donald A. Yates as *Diary of the War of the Pig,* McGraw-Hill, 1972.

*Adversos milagros,* edited by Enrique Pezzoni, Monte Avila, 1969.

*Memoria sobre la pampa y los gauchos,* Sur, 1970.

(As Javier Miranda) *Breve diccionario del argentino exquisito,* Barros Merino, 1971.

*Historias de amor,* Emecé, 1972.

*Historias fantásticas,* Emecé, 1972.

*Dormir al sol,* Emecé, 1973; translated by Levine as *Asleep in the Sun,* Persea, 1978.

(With Borges) *Nuevos cuentos de Bustos Domecq,* Libería La Ciudad, 1977.

*El héroe de las mujeres,* Emecé, 1978.

*Páginas,* Celtia, 1985.

*La aventura de un fotógrafo en La Plata,* Emecé, 1985; translated by Levine as *The Adventures of a Photographer in La Plata,* Dutton, 1989.

*Obras escogidas,* two volumes, Emecé/Círculo de Lectores, 1986.

*Historias desaforadas,* Emecé, 1987.

*Una muñeca rusa,* Tusquets, 1991; translated by Levine as *A Russian Doll and Other Stories,* New Directions, 1992.

*Un campéon desparejo,* Tusquets, 1993.

*Memorias,* Tusquets, 1994.

*Selected Stories,* New Directions, 1994.

### Screenplays

(With Jorge Luis Borges and Hugh Santiago) *Invasión,* 1969.

(With Borges and Santiago) *Les Autres,* 1974.

### Other

(Editor, with Silvina Ocampo and Jorge Luis Borges) *Antología de la literatura fantástica,* Sudamericana, 1940; enlarged, 1965.

(Editor, with Ocampo and Borges) *Antología poética argentina,* Sudamericana, 1941.

"Rudyard Kipling, la litera fantástica," *Sur,* 95, August 1942, pp. 80–81.

(Editor with Borges) *Los mejores cuentos policiales,* two volumes, Emecé, 1943, 1951.

(With Borges) "El hijo de su amigo," *Número,* 19, April-June 1952, pp. 101–119.

(Editor with Borges) *Cuentos breves y extraordinarios,* Raigal, 1955; translated by Anthony Kerrigan as *Extraordinary Tales,* Herder & Herder, 1971.

(Editor with Borges) *Poesía gauchesa,* Fondo de Cultura Economica, 1955.

(With Borges) "La fiesta del Monstruo," *Marcha,* September 30, 1955, pp. 20–23.

"Un nuevo surco," *Crisis,* 9, January 1974, pp. 44–47.

"Chronology," *Review 75,* fall 1975, pp. 35–39.

## SOURCES:

### Books

*Hispanic Writers,* edited by Bryan Ryan, Detroit, Gale Research, 1991.

*Latin American Writers,* Volume 3, edited by Carlos A. Solé and Maria Isabel Abreu, New York, Charles Scribner's Sons, 1989.

*Modern Latin-American Fiction Writers,* First Series, edited by William Luis, Detroit, Gale Research, 1992.

Rodriguez Monegal, Emir, *Jorge Luis Borges: A Literary Biography*, New York, Dutton, 1978.

*Spanish American Authors: The Twentieth Century*, edited by Angel Flores, New York, H. W. Wilson, 1992.

### Periodicals

*Américas*, November/December 1993, pp. 14–19.

*Atlantic Monthly*, April 1976, p. 116; January 1979, pp. 98–99; April 1981, pp. 122–24.

*Bulletin of Hispanic Studies*, July 1975, pp. 247–66.

*Chicago Tribune Book World*, April 19, 1981, p. 3.

*Choice*, April 1993, p. 1470.

*Globe and Mail*, January 21, 1989, p. C17.

*Latin American Literary Review*, spring/summer 1979, pp. 45–51.

*Library Journal*, September 15, 1989, p. 134.

*Nation*, October 11, 1965, pp. 226–28.

*New Republic*, June 5, 1976, pp. 24–26.

*New Yorker*, February 5, 1990, pp. 116–20.

*New York Times Book Review*, November 6, 1994, p. 37.

*Publishers Weekly*, September 1, 1989, p. 74.

*Review 75*, fall 1975, pp. 34–54.

*Time*, March 29, 1976, p. 74;

*Washington Post Book World*, April 19, 1981, pp. 9–11.

—*Sketch by Erika Dreifus*

# Rubén Blades
## 1948-
### Panamanian musician, actor, screenwriter, lawyer, and political activist

One of the biggest stars in Latin American music, Rubén Blades is known for revolutionizing salsa with his own distinctive sound. His artful lyrics touch the social conscience of his audiences while working to shatter cultural stereotypes and champion the ordinary man. Having made his mark as a Grammy-winning singer and songwriter as well as actor, lawyer, and political activist, Blades has combined artistry and social awareness as few others have, attracting large followings among Anglos and Hispanics alike. During the 1980s, he emerged as one of the most intriguing figures on the international scene, a cross-cultural pioneer and a charismatic leader of the *Nueva Cancion*, or New Song movement—a mix of poetry, politics, and tropical rhythms that has left an imprint on Latin music.

Rubén Blades was born in Panama City, Panama, on July 16, 1948. He was the second of five children born to Rubén Blades Sr., a police detective, bongo player, and basketball star, and Anoland Blades, a Cuban-born bolero singer, pianist, and radio actress. He was raised by his paternal grandmother, Columbian-born Emma Bósques Laurenza, whom Blades described to Jay Cocks of *Time* as a "wonderfully crazy" woman far ahead of her time—a feminist, Rosicrucian, vegetarian yogi "who practiced levitation and instilled in me the silly notion that justice is important, and that we can all serve and be part of the solution." Blades's unconventional grandmother had a profound influence on his life, teaching him to read at age four, introducing him to modern art, and taking him to American movies to escape the oppressive heat of Panamanian summers.

By the time Blades was old enough for school, he was also becoming more aware of music. "We were a radio family," he told Betty A. Marton, author of *Rubén Blades*. "In those days, you had a lot of time your hands, so we would sit down wherever we could . . . and listen to the radio." The mix was eclectic—everything from Nat King Cole and Glenn Miller to Perez Prado, and Blades became an avid fan of Beny Móre. But it was rock and roll—particularly Frankie Lyman and the Teenagers—that provided the turning point for the young, impressionable Blades. By the time the first Beatles tune was released in Panama in 1963, the budding musician was hooked forever on this intoxicating form of self-expression. "We were just as much a part of the rock and roll movement as young people in the States," he explained to Marton in his biography. "And that was true everywhere."

Blades made his first public appearance as a vocalist with his brother Luis's band, The Saints, in 1963. But his infatuation with U.S. music and pop culture ended one year later when U.S. troops killed 21 Panamanians and injured 500 during riots triggered by the refusal of Canal Zone North Americans to allow the Panamanian flag to fly opposite the Stars and Stripes at Balboa High School. "I stopped and looked at myself and realized that I was a Panamanian, and that my eyes weren't going to turn blue," he recalled to Marton. "I realized that I had to deal with the reality of who I am."

Blades redirected his energy and enthusiasm into Latin music at the same time that his growing social consciousness was turning toward the problems of poverty and injustice in his homeland. He stopped singing in English; he also began to do more reading in history and politics. Blades became deeply concerned about and disillusioned with Panama's political future, and by age 20, he was already an astute political observer. He enrolled in the University of Panama to study law, partly at the urging of his parents, to develop a more stable career than that of a musician. He continued to perform, and his first album was with a group called Bush and the Magnificos. Hearing Blades's voice, New York producer Pancho Cristal asked him if he would be interested in replacing Cheo Feliciano, who was leaving Joe Cuba's band. Blades rejected the tempting offer in order to stay in school, but when classes were suspended due to student unrest, Blades went stateside the following year.

Arriving in New York City in 1969, with the salsa movement in full swing, Blades quickly recognized that there was a need for more depth and sophistication in the Latin music of the time. He cut a *bugalú* album with Pete Rodríguez and his combo, *De Panama a Nueva York* (*From Panama to New York*), but it never sold. When the University of Panama reopened, Blades returned to school, received his bachelor's degree in law, and went to work as an attorney for the Banco Nacional de Panamá, counseling prisoners in his spare time.

Writing his own songs and performing with local bands, Blades never lost his passion for music, and a new idea started to take shape. For the first time, Blades began to believe that he could reach more people with his political ideas as a singer-songwriter than as a lawyer. To him, music was a way for poor Hispanics to reach beyond the barrio, and he felt that salsa musicians were unaware of the impact they had on audiences. His years at the university had given him a deep understanding of political issues, and more than anything, he wanted to sing about issues that affect the heart, soul, and life of Latin Americans. In 1974, Blades quit his job and headed back to New York to begin a full-time musical career.

Blades's first job in the music business was in the mail room at Fania Records, America's leading salsa label, for $73 a week. In 1975 he became a vocalist and songwriter with the **Willie Colón** combo, and for the next five years he established himself on the *cuchifrito,* or fast food circuit of clubs in Manhattan. He toured internationally with the Fania All Stars, and collaborated with Colón on several Fania albums beginning with *Metiendo Mano* (*Butting In*) in 1975 and ending with *Canciones del Solar de los Aburridos* in 1982. Their most successful album was *Siembra* (*Planting*) in 1977, which featured several hit singles including "Pedro Navaja," at that time the largest-selling salsa single in history. Borrowing both musically and lyrically from the Brecht-Weill ballad "Mack the Knife," "Pedro Navaja" tells the story of a barrio murder. It has since become Blades's signature song.

## Found His Own Voice

Blades's first experience with a major musical controversy came in 1980, when he wrote and record-ed "Tiburon" ("Shark"), a biting parable which depicted the U.S. and Soviet superpowers as prowling, sleepless predators in their roles in Caribbean intervention. The song got Blades banned from Miami's most popular Latin radio station, which accused him of having Communist sympathies. Deeply stung by the failure of Cuban critics to understand what he was saying, and rattled by several death threats, Blades thought it best not to perform in Miami for a time.

Outside Miami, however, the controversy did nothing to dampen the burgeoning popularity of Blades and his music. Anxious to reach out to Anglo Americans and show them the social and political issues affecting the lives of Latin people, Blades was unwilling to limit his appeal to a purely Latin audience. After nearly a six-year partnership with Willie Colón, both men decided that they needed to travel in different directions. Specifically, Blades was ready to sing his own unique stories in his own unique voice, a path he had been preparing for almost from the beginning of his career. Before breaking with Colón in 1982, Blades wrote the opera *Maestra Vida,* (*Life, the Teacher*) which Fania Records issued in two parts. The opera chronicles three generations in a Latin American family representing the urban proletariat.

After forming his own band, Seis del Solar (the Tenement Six) Blades left Fania Records in 1984 and joined Elektra/Asylum, becoming the first salsa musician in years to sign with a mainstream record company and the first ever with a contract for both Spanish and English albums. His first album, *Buscando America* (*Searching for America*), sold more than 400,000 copies, was nominated for a Grammy Award, and was named one of the top ten albums of the year. Jay Cocks wrote in *Time:* "All the record's seven cuts are sung in Spanish, but if there is a better album this year in any language, its impact will have to be measured off the charts. On the Richter scale, maybe." Among the most chilling of the cuts was "El Padre Antonio y el Monaguillo Andrés" ("Father Antonio and the Altarboy Andres"), a powerful narrative inspired by the murder of Salvadoran Bishop **Oscar Arnulfo Romero** on the steps of his cathedral.

## Crossover Dreams

To the shock and dismay of millions of fans, Blades took a sabbatical from his musical career in academic year 1984–85 in order to earn a master's degree in international law at Harvard University. His thesis was on the historical differences between the concepts of law and justice. Around this time, he turned his attention to another career, this time as an actor. In the independent English-language film *Crossover Dreams,* Blades stars as Rudy Veloz, a

Latin boxer and aspiring singer who makes it big in English-speaking America. The film brought Blades critical praise and wider recognition with mainstream audiences. Blades went on to receive mostly favorable reviews in more than a dozen films, including *The Milagro Beanfield War, The Two Jakes,* and 1994's *The Color of Night.* For his performance in the made-for-cable *Dead Man Out,* Blades received an ACE award for best actor, and earned an Emmy nomination for another cable special, *The Josephine Baker Story.*

Blade's return from musical hiatus with 1985's *Escenas* was greeted with a Grammy Award. Three years later, *Antecedente* won a Grammy Award, too. Blades also released his first English-language album in 1988; entitled *Nothing But the Truth,* the work was completed with the help of collaborators Lou Reed and Elvis Costello. In 1990, Blades and his band released the live recording *Rubén Blades y Son del Solar.* Of the work, *The Daily News of Los Angeles* critic Fred Shuster reported, "The 11-piece Son del Solar is superb, handling tricky reggae rhythms side by side with polyrhythmic Latin jams. And the use of two keyboards and three trombones in place of salsa's traditional horn section is just one example of Blades's forward-looking vision."

### Launched New Political Party

Promising a new era of clean politics in Panama, Blades launched a new political party, Papa Egoro, or Mother Earth in 1991, and announced as a presidential candidate in 1993. Describing his independent party as one that would speak for those Panamanians not represented by General **Manuel Noriega** or the U.S.-backed government, Blades disclosed to Guy Garcia in *Time:* "What I propose is to create what up to this point has been a mythical place: a Latin America that respects and loves itself, is incorruptible, romantic, nationalistic and has a human perception of the needs of the world at large." Two weeks before the 1994 election, polls showed Blades running second in a field of seven candidates, but in the end he garnered only 17 percent of the votes and lost the election to Ernesto Perez Balladeres.

The subject of some criticism for his 1987 marriage to blonde, blue-eyed actress Lisa Lebenzon, Blades has often had to defend the integrity of his work and his Latin identity. Of his own "crossover dreams," Blades revealed to Jay Cocks of *Time,* "I would rather think more in terms of converging than of crossover, because if you cross over it might be lonely on the other side."

## SELECTED DISCOGRAPHY:

(With Pete Rodriguez) *De Panama a Nueva York,* c. 1969.

**With the Willie Colon Combo; on Fania Records**

*Metiendo Mano,* 1976.
*Siembra* (includes "Pedro Navaja"), 1977.
*Canciones del Solar de los Aburridos,* 1982.

### Solo LPs

*Maestra Vida,* Fania, c. 1982.
*Buscando America* (in Spanish; includes "El Padre Antonio y el Monanguillo Andres"), Elektra, 1984.
*Escenas,* Elektra, 1985.
*Nothing But the Truth,* Elektra, 1988.
*Antecedente* (in Spanish), Heritage, 1988.
*Rueben Blades Y Son Del Solar: Live!,* Elektra, 1990.
*Agua de Luna.*

## SELECTED VIDEOGRAPHY:

*Last Flight,* 1982.
*Crossover Dreams,* 1985.
*Critical Condition,* 1986.
*Fatal Beauty,* 1987.
*Homeboy,* 1988.
*The Milagro Beanfield War,* 1988.
*Dead Man Out,* 1989.
*Disorganized Crime,* 1989.
*The Josephine Baker Story,* 1990.
*The Lemon Sisters,* 1990.
*The Milagro Beanfield War,* 1990.
*Mo' Better Blues,* 1990.
*One Man's War,* 1990.
*Predator 2,* 1990.
*The Two Jakes,* 1990.
*Crazy From the Heart,* 1991.
*The Super,* 1991.
*The Color of Night,* 1994.

## SOURCES:

### Books

*Contemporary Musicians,* edited by Michael L. LaBlanc, Gale, 1990.
Marton, Betty A., *Rubén Blades,* New York, Chelsea House, 1992.

### Periodicals

*Daily News* (Los Angeles), September 12, 1986, p. L1; March 24, 1988, p. L25; April 29, 1988, p. L30; March 27, 1989, p. L20; April 13, 1990, p. L42; June 5, 1990, p. L3; August 31, 1990, p. L4; March 13, 1991, p. L18; August 19, 1991, p. L13; November 27, 1991, p. N14.
*Harper's Bazaar,* March 1994, pp. 326–329.

*New Republic,* November 1, 1993, pp. 10–11.
*New York Times,* August 19, 1994.
*People,* May 9, 1994, pp. 181–182.
*Philadelphia Inquirer,* November 29, 1993, p. A13.
*Stereo Review,* September 1993, p. 102.
*Time,* July 2, 1984, p. 82; January 29, 1990, pp. 70–72; May 23, 1994.

*—Sketch by Julie Catalano*

# Simón Bolívar
## 1783-1830
### Venezuelan revolutionary leader and statesman

*Simón Bolívar*

Revered by many South Americans as "El Libertador," Simón Bolívar led a successful 14-year revolution to relinquish Spain's colonial rule of the area that presently comprises Bolivia, Colombia, Ecuador, Peru, and Venezuela. During this conflict, he earned a reputation as a resolute commander and an exceptional military tactician, but perhaps his most enduring contribution to the South American independence movement was his political vision for the colonies he liberated. This vision consisted of an unusual combination of authoritarianism, based on Bolívar's admiration for Napoleon's conquest of Europe, and republicanism, influenced by his familiarity with Jean Jacques Rousseau's philosophy of political and social reform. Ultimately, Bolívar's lifelong ambition was to replace the Spanish colonial system in Latin America with a closely allied confederation of republics that share common political and economic goals.

Bolívar was born into a wealthy Creole family in Caracas, Venezuela, on July 24, 1783. His parents died when he was just a boy, and during the remainder of his childhood Bolívar lived unhappily with his relatives. However, he did establish a relationship of respect and close friendship with a private tutor named Simón Rodríguez. At the age of 16, Bolívar was sent to Europe to finish his education; he studied in Spain for three years, and there he married the daughter of a Spanish nobleman. He returned to Venezuela with his bride in 1802, but she died less than a year later of yellow fever. Grief-stricken, Bolívar traveled back to Europe, where he became reacquainted with Rodríguez, who now resided in Paris. There, Bolívar resumed his studies with his boyhood mentor, who introduced him to the philosophy of several rationalist thinkers, as well the more recent teachings of Montesquieu, Voltaire, and especially Rousseau, who had a profound impact on Bolívar's evolving political philosophy. During this time, Bolívar also witnessed firsthand Napoleon's martial exploits as the wily general pushed opposing armies across the European continent with relative ease, and even audaciously proclaimed himself emperor of France. While Bolívar admired Napoleon's military accomplishments, he nevertheless resented the general's betrayal of the original republican reform objectives of the French Revolution for his own personal gain.

### Sowing the Seeds of Revolution

When Bolívar returned to Caracas in 1807, he was eager to apply all that he had learned in Europe to the nascent independence movement in Venezuela. For the next three years, he was a vocal member of numerous conspiratorial gatherings that plotted the overthrow of the colonial government. By 1810 revolution was sweeping through many regions of South America; on April 19, rebel leaders deposed the colonial governor of Venezuela and expelled him from the country. Later that year, Bolívar was given the rank of colonel in the rebel militia and sent on a mission to London to secure military and financial support for the independence movement, but he failed to convince the English to become involved in the conflict. The trip was not a complete failure, however, for Bolívar succeeded in recruiting the exiled Francisco de Miranda—who had attempted to liberate Venezuela unsuccessfully in 1806—to become commander-in-chief of the Venezuelan army.

In March 1811, a national congress convened in Caracas to deliberate over Venezuela's political future; after much debate, the representatives formally declared independence from Spain on July 5 and drafted a constitution similar in many respects to that of the United States. By this time, the Spanish royalist forces had regrouped and made preparations to suppress the rebellion by seizing Puerto Cabello, a strategic port that was deemed crucial for Venezuela's success. Bolívar was ordered to defend the city, but he was betrayed by some officers who opened the fortress to the advancing Spanish army. As a result, Bolívar's troops were forced to surrender. Miranda considered the defeat at Puerto Cabello a devastating blow to the independence movement, and he entered negotiations with the Spanish to end the rebellion. After signing an armistice agreement in July 1812, Miranda attempted to leave Venezuela secretly; however, a furious Bolívar denounced him as a traitor and turned him in to the Spanish. Miranda spent the rest of his life in a Spanish prison.

### "El Libertador"

Determined to keep the independence movement alive, Bolívar retreated to Cartagena in New Granada (known today as Colombia) to gain new support for his cause. The rebel forces there acknowledged his leadership and made him commander of an expeditionary force to defend the city from advancing royalist troops. Bolívar defeated this force and then pressed his advantage by invading Venezuela. He crossed the border with his army in 1813, and although he had to battle Spanish garrisons nearly every step of the way, he eventually subdued the royalist forces and regained control of the capital. On August 6, 1813, Bolívar triumphantly entered Caracas with his troops; there, his followers proclaimed him "El Libertador," and he assumed dictatorship of the country.

Despite the success of Bolívar's campaign against the Spanish, many separatist factions in Venezuela refused to recognize the new government, and a brutal civil war ensued. Furthermore, Bolívar had to contend with a renewed threat from the Spanish, who had fortified their troops with *llaneros,* fierce horsemen of the Orinoco Valley who quickly gained a fearful reputation for their savage fighting tactics. In a desperate attempt to maintain control of Venezuela, Bolívar declared a "war to the death" on both the rival separatists and the Spanish, but in the face of such divisiveness, the general was unable to repel the marauding *llaneros.* In 1814 he was forced to abandon Caracas and again retreat from Venezuela. When Bolívar returned to New Granada, he participated in forays against both the Spanish and rival separatist factions, but because he was unable to unite the various revolutionary factions into a cohesive and formidable threat, he fled to Jamaica to avoid being captured by the Spanish. While in exile, Bolívar wrote his famous "Jamaican Letter" of September 6, 1815, in which he perceptively comments on the lamentable social and political circumstances in Latin America and confidently predicts that his countrymen will prevail in the revolution.

In the course of the next three years, the Venezuelan independence movement was plagued by military setbacks and indecisive confrontations with Spanish forces. The tide of the war shifted in favor of the rebels in 1817, however, when they captured the city of Angostura (known today as Ciudad Bolívar) deep in the heart of the Orinoco Valley. Bolívar turned this remote area into a military stronghold and spent the next two years marshaling his forces, hiring thousands of mercenaries from the recently concluded Napoleonic wars, and establishing relations with other revolutionary factions in the region. Upon joining forces with two other formidable rebel leaders, **José Antonio Páez** and **Francisco de Paula Santander**, Bolívar conceived of an ambitious campaign to delay liberating Venezuela and instead attack the Spanish viceroyalty in Bogotá, which governed all of New Granada.

### The Battle of Boyacá

Bolívar's invasion of New Granada is considered one of the boldest tactical maneuvers in military history. With a small army of approximately 2,500 men, the general marched across the Venezuelan plains during the rainy season, where the rivers had overflowed and become lakes. After the troops had successfully accomplished this feat, they were confronted with an even greater challenge—the Andes mountains. Bolívar decided to cross the mountain range at Pisba, which was commonly regarded as an impossible approach for an army. During the long and arduous trek, adverse weather and fatigue beset the troops and as many as one-third died of exposure to the elements. Despite the devastating toll of the march, Bolívar attacked the Spanish at Bogotá and took the royalist forces completely by surprise. The Spanish army never fully recovered from the audacious attack and they were routed in the pivotal Battle of Boyacá on August 7, 1819. Three days later, Bolívar assumed control of Bogotá. This military victory proved to be the turning point in the revolution.

### The Liberation of Gran Colombia

The triumphant Bolívar returned to Angostura where a newly formed national congress appointed him president and military dictator of a new republic named Gran Colombia, which encompassed the whole region of New Granada, Ecuador, and Venezuela. This proclamation was largely immaterial, however, because both Ecuador and Venezuela were still held by the Spanish. But after Bolívar's victory in New Granada his momentum was such that his troops defeated the royalist army in Venezuela with considerable ease as they pushed on toward the capital. The contest for Venezuela culminated in the Battle of Carabobo on June 24, 1821, in which Bolívar's army overwhelmed the Spanish defenders and marched triumphantly into Caracas. Bolívar had liberated his homeland once and for all from Spanish colonial rule.

Determined to capitalize on his military success, Bolívar immediately turned his attention to the liberation of Ecuador. Upon crossing the border, the general confronted the Spanish forces in the northern mountain region while dispatching one of his most talented officers, Antonio José de Sucre, to invade Ecuador from the Pacific coast. While Bolívar clashed with royalist forces in the high country, Sucre battled his way toward Quito—Ecuador's capital. After several skirmishes, Sucre decisively defeated the Spanish army at Pichincha on May 24, 1822. The two leaders then reunited at Quito a month later. During the celebration that followed Ecuador's liberation, Bolívar met Manuela Sáenz, an attractive and provocative woman who was passionately committed to the revolution. From that point on, she accompanied Bolívar on many of his marches amid the everpresent scorn from his peers that she was nothing more than a distracting courtesan.

Now that Bolívar had recovered all of the territory of Gran Colombia from the Spanish, only Peru remained occupied by the royalist forces. In fact, **José de San Martín**—the general whose reputation rivals that of Bolívar in Latin America for liberating Argentina and Chile from Spanish colonial rule—had already seized Lima, Peru's capital, and proclaimed the country's independence. The Spanish royalist army had been forced to retreat to the mountains outside the city, where they maintained a virtually unassailable position and continued to pose a considerable threat to San Martín's forces in Lima. On July 26, 1822, Bolívar and San Martín met in Guayaquil, Ecuador, to discuss how to resolve the Peru problem. The two liberators held a secret meeting and what actually transpired during that session has been a source of significant controversy ever since. The surprising result of the conference was that San Martín returned to Lima and subsequently withdrew to Argentina without explanation, leaving his army behind. This action allowed Bolívar to enter Peru unimpeded, and in September 1823, he arrived in Lima and assumed command of San Martín's vacated troops.

In the summer of 1824, Bolívar's army ascended into the mountain region outside of Lima to meet the Spanish forces in battle. The general easily defeated his adversaries in the Battle of Junín on August 4, 1824—the first major confrontation—and having sufficiently weakened the Spanish opposition, Bolívar

turned the command over to Sucre and returned to Lima. On December 9, 1824, after several minor skirmishes the royalist army lost a key battle at Ayacucho and surrendered to Sucre. The next year, Sucre del cliberated the region of Upper Peru, the last territory of the continent still held by the Spanish. The grateful new nation elected to name itself Bolivia after man who had brought independence to a significant portion of South America.

### From Liberty to Civil War

In the immediate aftermath of the revolution, Bolívar enjoyed the greatest popularity and power of his career. In 1826, he realized his lifelong dream of organizing a league of Latin American states to promote solidarity among the developing nations, and he proposed the adoption of a constitution which would ease the nascent republics gradually toward democracy. Relatively few countries participated in this summit or ratified his constitution, however, preferring instead to focus on establishing their own individual autonomy.

In this era of instability, disputes over territory and policy began to erode the fragile relations between the new nations. Not a year after Peru's liberation, Bolívar's old generals Páez and Santander—who governed Venezuela and New Granada, respectively—entered into a dispute over constitutional authority, and at length their quarrel turned into a full-blown civil war. Unable to reconcile the differences between Páez and Santander or to persuade the states to accept his plan of government, Bolívar returned from Peru and seized control of Gran Colombia in 1827, declaring himself absolute dictator. Unfortunately, the general learned just how far his popularity had plummeted since the revolution when on the night of September 25, 1828, assassins attempted to murder him at the presidential palace. He barely escaped with his life by jumping out of a high bedroom window and fleeing to safety while his lover Manuela Sáenz boldly confronted his attackers.

In the midst of this political turmoil, Venezuela and Ecuador seceded from Gran Colombia, and a disillusioned and infirm Bolívar, realizing that he could no longer bring stability to the region, resigned from the presidency in 1830. Later that year on December 17, he died of tuberculosis near the town of Santa Marta. Shortly before his death, Bolívar dejectedly reflected on the long struggle for independence from Spain and its dire consequences, observing that "America is ungovernable. Those who have served the Revolution have plowed the sea."

### SELECTED PUBLISHED WORKS:

*Selected Writings of Bolívar: Volume One, 1810–1822,* compiled by Vicente Lecuna, edited by Harold A. Bierch, translated by Lewis Bertrand, New York, Colonial Press, 1951.

SOURCES:

**Books**

*Encyclopedia of Latin America,* edited by Helen Delpar, New York, McGraw-Hill Inc., 1974.
*Historic World Leaders, Volume 4: North & South America, A-L,* edited by Anne Commire, Detroit, Gale Research, 1994.
Masur, Gerhard, *Simón Bolívar,* Albuquerque, University of New Mexico Press, 1948.
*Simón Bolívar and Spanish American Independence: 1783–1830,* edited by John J. Johnson, Princeton, New Jersey, D. Van Nostrand Company, 1968.

**Periodicals**

*National Geographic,* March 1994, pp. 38–51, 56–7, 62–5.
*The Unesco Courier,* 42, June 1989, pp. 34–5.

—*Sketch by Joseph C. Tardiff*

# María Luisa Bombal
## 1910-1980
### Chilean writer

Although María Luisa Bombal published only two novels and a number of short stories during her lifetime, she is widely considered one of the most influential Latin American writers of the early twentieth century. Writing against the grain of the machismo that dominated South American fiction through the 1930s, Bombal is commonly credited with having introduced a new, proto-feminist aesthetic to Chilean literature. Her oeuvre is especially noted for its examination of the conflicts faced by women in a South American society dominated by males. In *The Shrouded Woman,* for instance, Bombal questioned the validity of the traditional, subservient role assigned to women, with her protagonist asking, "Why, why must a woman's nature be such that a man has always to be the pivot of her life?" The winner of the 1977 prize from the Chilean Academy of Arts and Letters, Bombal—through her blending of fantasy with realism—is also thought to have had a prominent influence on several Latin American writers of the next generation, including **Jorge Luis Borges**, **Carlos Fuentes**, **Gabriel García Márquez**, and **José Donoso**.

Bombal—who was of Argentine and German parentage—was born June 8, 1910, in Viña del Mar, Chile. After completing her secondary education in Chile she entered the Sorbonne at the University of Paris, where she received a degree in philosophy and literature.

### Began Promising Career

After spending most of the 1920s in Paris, Bombal moved to Buenos Aires, where she shared an apartment with poet **Pablo Neruda** and his wife, writing her first novella at their kitchen table. First published in 1935, *La ultima niebla* (*The Final Mist*), which was later revised and published in English as *The House of Mist,* chronicles the life of Helga, a South American woman who finds pleasure only with the lover of her dreams after realizing that her husband, Daniel, is still devoted to his dead first wife. The imagery suggested by the title figures prominently in the novel. Helga finds the white mist that rolls up from the lagoon—where Daniel's first wife drowned—a symbolic reminder of her profound unhappiness. American critics for the most part, reacted favorably. Richard Sullivan of the *New York Times,* for instance, found that although "Bombal's heroine dwells far too steadily on her raptures," the "dexterous, amoral, delicate" book was pervaded by "a kind of engaging breathlessness of manner."

Three years later, Bombal published her second novella, *La amortajada,* which was later translated into English by Bombal and published as *The Shrouded Woman.* The story focuses on the reflections of a dead woman, Ana María, as she lies in state at her own funeral. Argentine novelist and art critic Marta Traba, referring to the Bombal corpus as "the literature of despair," observed in *Américas* that the novella "describes with terrifying clarity the revenge the woman protagonist achieves through her own death, watching others unseen, eavesdropping undetected. For the first time in the world of spiritual indignities to which [Ana] was subjected, she takes the offensive." In a similar vein, the *Saturday Review*'s Marjorie Brace found the novella "amazingly horrid and uncommonly dreadful."

### Involved in Shooting Incident

But after such a promising beginning to her literary career, Bombal was jailed in 1941 for shooting and seriously wounding her anticommunist lover, Eulogio Sánchez Errazuriz. Banished from Chile after his recovery, she immigrated to the United States, where a few years later she married Wall Street financier, Count Raphael de Saint-Phalle, a U.S. citizen of French background who helped her with the English translations of her books. Having worked as a screenwriter for Sonofilm in Argentina during the late 1930s (she wrote the script for *La Casa del Recuerdo*

[*The House of Memory* ], which art critic Jose Gomez-Sicre observed in *Américas* as "a milestone in the intellectual achievement of the Argentine cinema, unprecedented in the annals of Latin American films up to that time"), Bombal dreamed of seeing one of her novels on screen. Although a Hollywood studio bought the rights to *La Ultima Niebla* and had asked Bombal to write the script, the project never materialized.

After her husband's death in 1970, Bombal returned to her native Chile, where she died in her sleep a decade later, after suffering from a long-term battle with alcoholism and depression. But after Bombal's death, her English-speaking audience increased. In 1982, *New Islands and Other Stories,* a translation that included the original version of *La última niebla,* was released. With a laudatory preface by Borges, the book attracted mostly favorable attention from American critics. Finding female characters who "construct and inhabit lush, sensuous kingdoms of the imagination," the *Nation* 's James Polk asserted that although Bombal's fiction at times "trembles perilously close to the romance rack at the corner drugstore," it nevertheless "takes the daring imaginative flights we have come to expect from a later generation of Latin Americans, for whom she must rank . . . as a Founding Mother."

## SELECTED PUBLISHED WORKS:

*La última niebla,* Sur, 1935; expanded edition translated by Bombal as *The House of Mist,* Farrar, Straus, 1947.
*La amortajada,* Sur, 1938; translated by Bombal as *The Shrouded Woman,* Cassell, 1950.
*La historia de Maria Griselda,* Editorial, 1977.
*The New Islands and Other Stories,* translated by Richard and Lucia Cunningham, Farrar, Straus, 1982.

## SOURCES:

### Books

*Hispanic Writers,* edited by Bryan Ryan, Detroit, Gale Research, 1991.
*Reference Guide to Short Fiction,* edited by Noelle Watson, Detroit, St. James Press, 1994.

### Periodicals

*Américas,* February, 1981, pp. 49–51.
*Nation,* December 11, 1982, pp. 634–35.
*New York Times Book Review,* April 13, 1947; December 19, 1982.
*Saturday Review,* May 1, 1950.

*Times Literary Supplement,* December 9, 1983, p. 1372.

—*Sketch by Jason Gallman*

---

# Bobby Bonilla
## 1963-
### Hispanic American professional baseball player

Though Bobby Bonilla bounced from club to club throughout his early career, he was distinguished as the highest paid baseball player in 1992, when he signed a contract with the New York Mets for $29 million over five years, or $5.8 million annually.

Born in New York City on February 23, 1963, Bobby Bonilla grew up in the Bronx, a borough of New York City. Throughout his childhood, he lived a few blocks from Yankee Stadium; ironically he would end up playing for the rival Mets. As a youth, Bonilla started his career in baseball on the streets and the playgrounds of the Bronx. Bonilla felt he was part of a tremendous fan base for the Yankees that still exists in the Bronx—"a black and Hispanic fan base" he was quoted as saying in the *New York Times* in 1994.

Bonilla went to New York Technical College before entering the rank and file of baseball. By 1981, he signed with the Pittsburgh Pirates on the recommendation of Syd Thrift, but when the Pirates chose not to "protect" him from free agency, he left for the Chicago White Sox in 1985. Bonilla only stayed in Chicago for one year. Thrift became general manager of the Pirates and brought Bonilla back to Pittsburgh.

Bonilla really shone after his return to Pittsburgh. On July 12, 1987, he made history at the city's Three Rivers Stadium by hitting only the seventh upper deck home run in the life of the stadium. A powerful switch-hitter, Bonilla hit a .300 in 1987—his highest career batting average.

Bonilla opened 1988 leading the National League throughout the first half of the season in home runs (HR) and runs batted in (RBI). He finished the season at .274 with 24 HR and 100 RBI; however, the respectable statistics were not representative of the numbers he had recorded earlier in the season. Nonetheless, Bonilla reaped many achievements, including making the *Sporting News* National League All-Star Team and the Silver Slugger Team. He earned National League player of the month honors in April and May. He also played in the major league All-Star game that year. From 1988 to 1990, Bonilla would play in all but four games; his average of 160

*Bobby Bonilla*

games per year was an amazing feat given how aggressively Bonilla played the game.

Though his offense was stunning—Bonilla's hitting consistency helped him to displace all-star Mike Schmidt at third base—Bonilla's fielding was somewhat problematic. His unusual sideways-facing defensive stance won him both praise and criticism from sports critics. Having earned the starting position at third base, Bonilla proved unable to match Schmidt's defensive skills. In a series of lackluster performances, Bonilla logged in 32 errors during the second half of the season, which also coincided with his worst hitting slump.

In 1989, Bonilla batted .281 with 24 HR and 86 RBI, and in 1990, he batted .280 with 32 HR and 120 RBI. He kept his batting average steady in the .280 range during his career with the Pirates and averaged 35 doubles, 24 homers, and 96 RBI per year. Bonilla also managed to improve his defense enough to win the title for most double plays in 1989. Even so, he lost his infield position; in 1990, Pirates manager Jim Leyland moved Bonilla into right field. Taking Bonilla off the defensive hot seat probably contributed as much to the club's success as his renewed hitting prowess did. The Pirates won the National League East title that year, and, fueled by Bonilla's hitting, the team captured the title again in 1991.

### Landed Baseball's Highest Salary

Bonilla signed with the Mets for the 1992 season after a tumultuous year of financial angst with the

Pirates after hitting .302 with 18 HR and 100 RBIs. Open to free agency, the Mets general manager Al Harazin and manager Jeff Torborg outbid all of Major League Baseball to sign Bonilla to a five-year contract worth $29 million. Bonilla become that year's highest paid player in baseball, which in turn set the stage for the league-wide big money contracts that would follow in subsequent years, escalating until the owners decided to impose a salary cap and the players went on strike in 1994.

Bonilla was the great hope for the New York Mets. The city welcomed Bonilla, and he was honored at his alma mater in the Bronx. Bronx Borough president Fernando Ferrer even proclaimed a Bobby Bonilla Day. For his part, Bonilla contributed to his old neighborhood by running a baseball clinic at a local high school. But back at the ballpark, speculation arose as to whether Bonilla could hit under the pressure of his new, inflated pay check.

### Fell Into Hitting Slump

Despite all the hype and money, Bonilla did not produce like he had for the Pirates. He had a career-low of .249 in 1992; fans constantly booed him against which he wore ear plugs, which he only took out to call the press box to argue a ruling. Pitchers delivered an endless stream of off-speed pitches across the plate, and he only managed 19 HRs and 70 RBIs. He also lost his standing as baseball's highest paid player to former teammate Barry Bonds whom the San Francisco Giants promised to pay $43.75 million over six years.

In 1993 Mets management moved Bonilla to third base. He improved his batting average to .265 with 34 HRs and 87 RBIs before rupturing a ligament in his left shoulder in September, but his injury did not hinder his accomplishments the following season. Before the baseball strike began on August 12 1994, Bonilla led the Mets batting .294 with 20 HRs and 62 RBIs. He worked on his defense in the spring and managed to perform more impressively at third base than he had in past seasons. Bonilla continues to carve his place as one of the best players in baseball in the 1980s and 1990s.

### SOURCES:

#### Books

*The Ballplayers: Baseball's Ultimate Biographical Reference,* edited by Mike Shatzkin, New York, William Morrow, 1990.
*The Baseball Encyclopedia,* edited by Rick Wolff et al., New York, Macmillan, 1990.

**Periodicals**

*Mets Magazine,* Vol. 31, no. 1, 1992.
*New York Times,* July 20 1994; July 29 1994;
    August 3 1994; August 17 1994; August 24,
    1994, B:10.
*Sporting News Baseball Yearbook,* 1989, 1990,
    1991, 1992, 1993, 1994.

—*Sketch by Christopher B. Tower*

# Tony Bonilla
## 1936-

### Mexican American civil rights activist and attorney

*Tony Bonilla*

Civil rights activist Tony Bonilla has lived almost his entire life in the state of Texas. He has spent more than 30 years working to bring issues confronting the Hispanic community to the forefront of public debate. He works as a trial lawyer for the firm of Bonilla and Berlanga in Corpus Christi, Texas, and he also serves as the chairperson of the National Hispanic Leadership Conference, an organization he co-founded in 1983.

Born on March 2, 1936 in Calvert, Texas, Bonilla grew up in the small, rural community. In an interview with the *Dictionary of Hispanic Biography*'s James McCarthy, Bonilla described the population of 2,500 as racially divided. According to Bonilla, the "ten or 15" Hispanics living in Calvert found themselves separated from the whites who made up nearly half of the town's population. Along with the blacks, who also made up nearly 50 percent of the populace, the Hispanics literally lived on the "other side of the tracks" from the caucasians. Recalled Bonilla in his conversation with McCarthy, "There was a Main Street running through the middle of the town, and parallel to the street ran a set of railroad tracks. On one side of the street lived all the whites, and on the other side lived all the blacks. And us."

Bonilla's parents, Ruben and Maria, emigrated from Mexico unable to speak, read, or write any English. By the time Bonilla was born, his father owned a service station, and both parents encouraged their children to learn from what they saw growing up. "I saw a lot of inequity, and a lot of unlawful acts," Bonilla said. All eight Bonilla children attended college and four of the siblings, including Tony, became attorneys—each interested in civil rights and Hispanic issues.

## Professional Career in Law

After attending Del Mar College on a football scholarship, Bonilla graduated from Baylor University in 1958. Two years later he finished his law degree at the University of Houston, and later that year he became a partner at Bonilla, Read, Bonilla, and Berlanga. He served in the Texas State legislature from 1964 to 1967 and as president of the League of United Latin American Citizens (LULAC) from 1972 to 1975.

As a member of LULAC, Bonilla began approaching Hispanic issues from a legal point of view. In 1983 he cofounded a "think tank" known as the National Hispanic Leadership Conference (NHLC). As the NHLC president since the conference's infancy, Bonilla has led many efforts to improve the condition of Hispanics and other minorities in the United States and abroad. For example, through Bonilla's direction, the NHLC has set up prevention and support programs against drug abuse in Hispanic communities throughout the United States. They have also worked with communities in major drug-producing nations like Colombia, Bolivia, and Ecuador.

Often coordinating with other civil rights organizations like Operation PUSH and LULAC, Bonilla's group also strives for economic improvement. In the early to mid–1990s the NHLC helped negotiate an agreement with Miller Brewing Company and the Southland Corporation, owners of 7-Eleven convenience stores, to allow for more minority opportunities within those companies. Bonilla's group also made efforts to eliminate the under-representation of Hispanics and other minorities in the news media.

In speaking to writer James McCarthy, Bonilla stated that one of the conferences major goals was to provide "an alternative voice" to the "political mood swing" of the 1994 Congressional elections. He believed that "voices of progressives have been effectively silenced. Some are even embarrassed or scared to call themselves progressive." Calling the new conservatism the "New McCarthyism," Bonilla says his group feels the obligation to say "enough is enough."

Bonilla credits his parents for the values that have brought him and his siblings professional success. He explained what he felt to be the most important factors: "Hard work, being goal-oriented, and integrity. Those are the trademarks handed to us by our parents, and they have served us well over the years."

## SOURCES:

Bonilla, Tony, interview with James McCarthy, November 28, 1994.

—*Sketch by James McCarthy*

# Jorge Luis Borges
## 1899-1986
**Argentine short story writer and poet**

Jorge Luis Borges, called one of the great writers "of this century . . . who has long been recognized as such" by Yves Bonnefoy, was an Argentine writer and poet who has left an enduring legacy to the literature world. Borges was a significant influence on celebrated Latin American writers such as **Carlos Fuentes**, **Gabriel García Marquez**, and **Mario Vargas Llosa**. Jorge Luis Borges was born August 24, 1899, in Buenos Aires, Argentina. He died June 14, 1986, in Geneva, Switzerland, of liver cancer. The writer's father, Jorge Guillermo Borges, was English and his mother, Leonor Acevedo, was native-born. His mother's maiden name was among the oldest family names found in a local register of Portuguese descent. Borges married Elsa Astete Millan, in 1967 and they were divorced in 1970. He married Maria Kodama shortly before his death.

Borges's broad literary education sprang from his father's extensive library. A university professor of psychology and modern languages, his father kept many classical literary works on his shelves. Most books were published in English, giving Borges his earliest language exercises. He once wrote, "If I were to name the chief event in my life, I should say my father's library. In fact, I sometimes think I have never strayed outside that library." A lecturer and infrequent writer, his father had a keen interest in the metaphysical, an area of study that would leave an indelible imprint upon the young Borges and his literary work. Almost equally as indelible were the teen years Borges spent in Switzerland, where he learned French, Latin, and German. Such a foundation would allow him great flexibility and breadth as he embarked on his literary endeavors.

In 1914, at the start of World War I, Borges's family moved to Geneva. His father pursued early retirement and moved everyone from Buenos Aires. They were in Europe for seven years, spending some of that time in Spain, returning in 1921 to Argentina. In Spain, Borges began to publish some of his poetry and literary essays. Expected to be a writer, Borges understood as a youth that he would fulfill the literary destiny denied his father by circumstance. His father had begun to lose his sight early in his life, passing the hereditary condition of blindness on to his son, who contracted it while in his fifties.

Alastair Reid wrote of the acclaimed author in 1986, "I can think of no other writer whose life was so bound up with books as was Borges's. In Buenos Aires, he edited and wrote for a number of small literary magazines, and introduced many foreign writers into Spanish. He also began to translate, for which he was admirably prepared, and produced distinguished translations of James Joyce, Virginia Woolf, and William Faulkner." Reid went on to state, "His early books of poems and collections of literary essays gained him a not inconsiderable reputation as a writer."

On the advice and financial support of his father, 24-year-old Borges decided to publish his first book. Entitled *Fervor de Buenos Aires* (*Fervor of Buenos Aires*), it was his fourth or fifth manuscript, and was published in 1923 before his family departed for Europe. The volume was highly praised in a Spanish review by distinguished writer **Gomez de la Serna**. By 1926 the young author was already a well-known poet. His work was included in an anthology of Argentine poetry titled *Exposicion de la Actual Poesia Argentina* (*Showcase of Recent Argentine Poetry*).

In 1938, at age 39, Borges accepted a position located on the periphery of the city as municipal library assistant. For eight years he held the position until Argentina's dictator **Juan Perón** had him dismissed for speaking out against him. A crucial year in

Borges's life and career, 1938 is the year he suffered an accident resulting in septicemia, as well as the year he began to pen the stories that made up *Ficciones* (1944), his most famous single work."

A recipient of numerous international literary awards and honors, Borges has been considered one of the most influential writers of the twentieth century. The author weaves together the ethereal, mystical components of human existence, using language to position humanity in time and space—but never to confuse language with reality. Borges described all of his stories as verbal constructs that brought chaos into a temporary verbal order: "fictions." The paradox at the heart of his work reflects an understanding of all literary creations as fictitious. Intrinsic to this belief is the idea that language itself is not to be trusted, for while it might be able to illumine reality, it will remain only language and will never be reality.

## The Labyrinth as Theme

Borges's signature in literature is the construct known as the labyrinth. The writer's life is transmuted into images that are re-animated in his work. Reid wrote, "The library becomes the infinite library of Babel, containing all the possible books and turning into nightmares." Motifs that are hallmarks of Borges's writing can be found readily within a labyrinthine framework: the mirror representing duality, the tiger symbolizing physical reality and "being beyond language."

In *Raritan,* John T. Irwin postulates that the author "produced his three detective stories ['The Garden of the Forking Paths,' 'Death and the Compass,' and 'Ibn Hakkan al-Bokhari, Dead in His Labyrinth'] as an antithetical doubling, an interpretive reading-rewriting of the origin of the analytic detective genre, Poe's three Dupin stories ['The Murders in the Rue Morgue,' 'The Mystery of Marie Rogêt,' and 'The Purloined Letter']." Irwin focuses on the central image of the labyrinth in Borges's detective stories, and on the fact that there is a "locked-room puzzle" central to Poe's first detective story, "The Murders in the Rue Morgue." Poe's writing impacted Borges's handling of the detective story. Poe deeply impressed him, as did Oscar Wilde, whom he held in great esteem.

In a 1983 interview with Nicomedes Suárez-Aráuz in the *Massachusetts Review,* Borges discussed his discovery of the labyrinth as a youth in his father's library. A French book by Garnier included a large engraving of a building with many cracks. With his myopic vision, Borges thought that with a magnifying glass he would find a minotaur within the seemingly exitless maze. Of the experience he stated, "That labyrinth was, besides a symbol of bewilderment, a symbol of being lost in life. I believe that all of us at one time or another, have felt that we are lost, and I saw in the labyrinth the symbol of that condition."

The lost labyrinth is a particularly favored form in the author's work, especially "The Garden of the Forking Paths." Borges told Suárez-Aráuz that such a construct was something magical to him. He said that the "lost labyrinth seems to me to be something magical because a labyrinth is a place where one loses oneself, a place (in my story) which in turn is lost in time. The idea of a labyrinth which disappears, of a lost labyrinth, is twice as magical. That story is a tale which I imagined to be multiplied or forked in various directions. In that story the reader is presented with all the events leading to the execution of a crime whose intention the reader does not understand."

## Experienced Anti-Semitism

Some sources deny the author's Jewish lineage while others confirm it. Early in Borges's career, he was under suspicion of political heresy for speaking out against Argentina's dictator, Juan Perón. In effect, he merely stated disagreement with Perón's political activities. This, however, was enough to draw an attack on his origins. He was also removed from his position as president of the Society of Writers because he refused to hang Perón's portrait in his office.

An economic crisis preceded by the crash of 1929 led to governmental instability and extremist rule. By Borges's account, Perón's dictatorship brought "harsh years" to the country. With some insight into the history of Argentina's political strife, Gene H. Bell-Villada stated in *Salmagundi* that in an increasing attempt to define itself, the country turned to scapegoating various undesirable groups. Political leaders "shared anti-immigrant and anti-Semitic attitudes, and were also anti-British, a fact which, in a country long dominated by British imperialism, could appeal to the patriotic reflexes of otherwise unsympathetic Argentinians." According to Bell-Villada, citizens and leaders alike began to forcefully counter-pose a "model of Hispanic traditionalism and a nostalgic, idealized vision of Catholic Spain."

Borges was one of the first victims of Perón's nationalism. Early in his career, when questioned by a local newspaper regarding his heritage, the author denied his Jewish bloodline. Yet, several decades later, during an interview with Clark M. Zlotchew for the *American Poetry Review,* Borges confirmed his Jewish heritage. Although Borges did not indicate when this knowledge was made available to him, a good deal of his writing is influenced by Judaic thought, especially the Kabbalah (Jewish mysticism). *The Aleph and Other Stories* reflects a strong Hebrew influence.

During the last two decades of his life, Borges traveled widely to different parts of the world to lecture, giving readings and interviews. He received—from early in his career—a fair amount of coverage. Written primarily in Spanish, numerous critical and biographical studies have been published about Borges and his work. As his life unfolded, there were many published and filmed interviews. Toward the end of his life, the British Broadcasting Company (BBC) made a film documentary about him.

In the spring of 1986, Ana Cara-Walker traveled to Geneva with a small number of Borges's *milonga* poems intended for English translation. In *World Literature Today*, she wrote of the completed *milongas*, "Fashioned after the traditional, often improvised, verbal art of the countryside gaucho men and singers from the Buenos Aires outskirts, Borges's *milonga* poems sing the deeds of ordinary folk, historical events, and local heroes."

## SELECTED PUBLISHED WORKS:

*Ficciones*, edited by Anthony Kerrigan, Grove Press, 1962.
*Dreamtigers*, University of Texas Press, 1964.
*Other Inquisitions, 1937–1952*, University of Texas Press, 1964.
*A Personal Anthology*, edited by Anthony Kerrigan, Grove Press, 1967.
*The Book of Imaginary Beings*, Dutton, 1969.
*The Aleph and Other Stories*, Dutton, 1970.
*Labyrinths: Selected Stories and Other Writings*, edited by Donald Yates and James Irby, New Directions, 1972.
*Selected Poems, 1923–1967*, edited by Norman Thomas di Giovanni, Delta, 1972.
*Borges: A Reader*, edited by Emir Rodriguez Monegal and Alastair Reid, Dutton, 1981.

## SOURCES:

### Books

*Contemporary Authors, New Revision Series*, Volume 33, Detroit, Gale, 1991.
*Latin American Writers*, Volume 2, edited by Carlos A. Solé, Macmillan, 1989.

### Periodicals

*American Poetry Review*, September/October 1988, pp. 22–26.
*Antaeus*, spring 1993, pp. 11–13; spring 1994, pp. 226–41.
*Comparative Literature Studies*, fall 1983, pp. 305–16.
*Explicator*, spring 1994, pp. 175–76.

*Massachusetts Review*, autumn 1983, pp. 501–15.
*MLN*, March 1985, pp. 330–47.
*Modern Fiction Studies*, autumn 1986, pp. 469–75; summer 1990, pp. 149–66.
*New Literary History*, autumn 1989, pp. 163–73.
*North American Review*, September 1986, pp. 75–78.
*PMLA*, October 1986, pp. 778–87.
*Raritan*, spring 1991, pp. 40–57.
*Salmagundi*, spring/summer 1989, pp. 305–19.
*Studies in Short Fiction*, winter 1984, pp. 25–39.
*Symposium*, spring 1994, pp. 51–61.
*Wilson Quarterly*, winter 1986, pp. 142–47.
*World Literature Today*, winter 1988, pp. 5–9.

*—Sketch by Brett A. Lealand*

# Juan Bosch
## 1909-
### Dominican writer and statesman

Juan Gavion Bosch has had a long and productive career as a short story writer, novelist, biographer and essayist but he is also known as a statesman. Bosch served as president of the Dominican Republic for seven months in 1963 before being deposed in a military coup by forces loyal to **Rafael Leonidas Trujillo**. Bosch's subsequent attempts to return to power all proved unsuccessful. His most fruitful years as a short story writer ended in the 1960s; from that time he devoted his energies to nonfiction writing on social, historical, and political matters.

Bosch was born June 30, 1909, in La Vega and spent his early years amid the rural poverty of the Dominican Republic. His father, a stonemason, was from the Catalonian town of Tortosa; his mother came from Puerto Rico. In an autobiographical sketch published in *Spanish-American Authors*, Bosch recalled that although his family came from an artisan class, many displayed a strong interest in education and the arts. Bosch also named a teacher—musician and band leader Rafael Martinez—as a strong shaping force in his life. Bosch recalled that Martinez "was a man preoccupied with the higher destiny of the country and by the fate of people in the world." At school in La Vega and Santo Domingo, Bosch showed early signs of artistic creativity: he began to draw, sculpt, and write at nine; and by the age of 14 he had published his first short story in a newspaper.

Bosch began his adult literary career in the capital city of Santo Domingo, where he joined the

*Juan Bosch*

literary group "La Cueva." His first publication of a short story came in 1929; and in 1933 he published his first collection, *Camino real,* which contained one of his most enduring and successful stories, "La mujer." Among his general literary influences Bosch cited *Don Quixote, The Brothers Karamazov,* and *Huckleberry Finn,* but as an apprentice short story writer in search of a master, he looked to Kipling, Maupassant, and Oscar Wilde. The protagonists of Bosch's realistic short stories often exist at some outer limit of human experience—either as animals, inanimate objects, or damaged humans suffering from an illness or handicap that turns them into ironic observers. In 1936 Bosch published his first novel, *La Mañosa,* a work that Doris Sommer in *Boundary 2* has described as "semi-autobiographical." It takes place in a rural community and follows the fortunes of a petty bourgeois family overtaken by civil war. The political and social issues the novel raises are a crucial link to Bosch's other career, that of statesman and militant essayist.

**Years in Exile**

Soon after the publication of *La Mañosa,* Bosch began a period of 24 years in exile from the Trujillo dictatorship. In 1939 Bosch helped found the *Partido Revolucionario Dominicano,* consolidating his official involvement in political activism. During his years of exile Bosch lived in Cuba, Venezuela, and Costa Rica, and wrote political essays against the Trujillo regime.

At the same time he produced many short stories, which were later published in two volumes under the title *Cuentos escritos en el exilio* (1962) and *Más cuentos escritos en el exilio* (1964). Bosch's exile ended in 1961 following the assassination of Trujillo; Bosch launched a social democratic political campaign for the presidency and came to power in a landslide victory in 1962.

Bosch's brief tenure as president ended in September 1963 when he was deposed in a military coup. Bosch's supporters attempted a counter-coup in 1965, but the military intervention of the United States—ostensibly to protect the lives of Americans—stymied Bosch's restoration to power. Bosch's anger at American realpolitik prompted a series of essays and books, including *Viaje a los Antípodas* (about American intervention in Vietnam) and *Pentagonism: A Substitute For Imperialism* (1967), which strongly criticized American foreign policy.

After the mid–1960s Bosch continued to mount presidential campaigns on a socialist platform, but without success. At the same time he focused his literary endeavors on a variety of nonfiction projects. His works from this period include memoirs and broadsides from his own political life, critiques of United States policy in Latin America and the Third World—especially concerning the Dominican Republic, political biography, history, and political science.

## SELECTED PUBLISHED WORKS:

*Camino real* (short stories), 1933; Santgago, El Diario, 1937.

*La mañosa: Novela de las revoluciones* (novel), Santgago, Dominican Republic, El Diario, 1936.

*Cuentos escritos en el exilio y apuntes sobre el arte de escribir cuentos* (short stories), Santo Domingo, Libería Dominicana, 1962.

*David: Biografía de un rey,* Librería Dominicana, 1963; translation by John Marks published as *David: The Biography of a King,* New York, Hawthorn Books, 1966.

*Más cuentos escritos en el exilio* (short stories), Santo Domingo, Libería Dominicana, 1964.

*Crisis de la democracia de América en la República Dominicana,* Guadalquivir, Centro de Estudios y Documentación Sociales, 1964; translation published as *The Unfinished Experiment: Democracy in the Dominican Republic,* New York, Praeger, 1965.

*Cuentos escritos en el exilio,* Santa Domingo, Lisrería Dominicana 1964.

*El pentagonismo: Susitituto del imperialismo,* Santo Domingo, Publicaciones Ahora, 1967; translation by Helen R. Lane published as *Pentagonism: A Substitute for Imperialism,* New York, Grove, 1968.

*El oro y la pas* (novel), [Santo Domingo], 1977.
*Viaje a los Antípodas,* Santo Domingo, Alfa y
    Omega, 1978.
*Obras completas,* 1989.


## SOURCES:

### Books

*A Dictionary of Contemporary Latin American Au-
    thors,* compiled by David William Foster, Ari-
    zona State University, 1975.
*Encyclopedia of Latin America,* New York,
    McGraw Hill, 1974.
*Hispanic Writers,* edited by Bryan Ryan, Detroit,
    Gale Research, 1991.
*Spanish American Authors: The Twentieth Century,*
    edited by Angel Flores, New York, H. W.
    Wilson, 1992.

### Periodicals

*Boundary 2,* fall/winter 1982–1983, pp. 258–262.

                                    —*Sketch by Simon Dixon*

*Fernando Botero*

# Fernando Botero
## 1932-
### Colombian painter

Internationally acclaimed as one of Latin America's
foremost twentieth-century artists, Fernando Botero has produced a prolific array of highly individual-
ized paintings, sculptures, and drawings, encompassing subjects from portraits and nudes to landscapes
and bullfights. In *Fernando Botero,* Abram Lerner
stated: "Botero's unique style is instantly recognizable. Whether a bishop, an apple, or a presidential
family his subjects exist in a universe populated
exclusively by oddly exaggerated pneumatic beings.
Seemingly larger than life, at once solid and voluptu-
ous, they skirt the grotesque and establish themselves
as elements of a mordantly humorous reality."

Fernando Botero Angulo was born in Medellín,
Colombia, on April 19, 1932, to David Botero and
Flora Angulo de Botero. His father was a salesman
who traveled to remote areas on horseback. After
attending the Ateneo Antioqueño primary school,
Botero won a scholarship to the Jesuit Bolivariano
secondary school. At the age of 12, Botero was sent by
his uncle to a school for apprentice matadors, where

he stayed for two years. The corrida remained an
abiding passion for Botero and was the subject of his
1985 exhibition at the Marlborough Gallery in New
York.

Botero launched his artistic career in 1948 when
he began contributing drawings to the Sunday supplement of *El Colombiano,* Medellín's chief newspaper.
That same year Botero organized his first public
exhibition. From a tender age Botero was intrigued by
pre-Columbian art and the colonial baroque Spanish
style. His earliest paintings were influenced by the
Mexican muralists **Diego Rivera**, **David Alfaro Siqueiros**, and **Josê Clemente Orozco**; *Woman Crying*
is representative of this period. In a 1986 interview
published in *Fernando Botero: Paintings and Drawings,* Botero remarked that the poet **César Vellejo** was
"the most important influence in my life at that
time." When Botero's artistic pursuits transgressed
his Jesuit school's bounds of acceptance—with the
publication of nude drawings and an article on
Picasso and nonconformity in art—he was expelled.
Botero completed his education at the Liceo San José
in Marnilla and the Liceo de la Universidad de
Antioquia in Medellín, graduating with his baccalaureate in January 1951.

### Solo Exhibition Debut

Botero worked briefly in 1951 as a set designer
for a Spanish theater company, Compañia Lope de
Vega, before moving to Bogotá, where he encountered

broad artistic horizons. He successfully mounted his debut solo exhibition at the Galerías de Arte Foto-Estudio Leo Matiz and then moved to the Caribbean village of Tolü, where he painted the Isolina restaurant with murals. Botero returned to Bogotá and held a successful exhibition of his Tolü works. In July 1952 he won second prize for *In Front of the Sea* at Colombia's Ninth Annual Salón. The prize money enabled him to travel to Europe.

Botero arrived in Barcelona in August 1952. After touring the local art museums he traveled to Madrid, where he enrolled at the Real Academia de Bellas Artes de San Fernando and the Museo del Prado. While studying, he supplemented his income by selling copies of works by **Velásquez, Goya,** and Titían. After visiting Paris the following summer, Botero traveled to Florence, where he studied fresco techniques and attended Roberto Longhi 's lectures. His works from this period were inspired by Piero della Francesca, Paolo Uccello, Andrea del Castagno, and Giorgio de Chirico; *The Departure* is characteristic of his Florentine paintings.

In 1955 Botero returned to Bogotá and displayed a collection of his Florentine paintings at the Biblioteca Nacional; none was sold and he was forced to seek alternative employment. He tried selling car tires and then worked on magazine layouts. In 1956 he moved to Mexico City, where he was able to earn a living as a painter and developed his personal artistic style. In *Still Life with Mandolin* he first flirted with the concept of enlarging forms, which later became his trademark. In April 1957 Botero attended his debut solo exhibition in the United States at the Pan American Union in Washington, D.C. Although all his paintings were sold, critical acclaim was not forthcoming. He returned to Bogotá, winning second prize for *Counterpoint* at Colombia's Tenth Annual Salón.

### Talents Recognized

By 1958 Botero was recognized as Colombia's leading young artist. He was appointed professor at the Escuela de Bellas Artes in Bogotá. At Colombia's Eleventh Annual Salón he was awarded first prize for *Homage to Mantegna.* He held his second North American exhibition, again in Washington; it was a major success and his work was included in the Guggenheim International Award exhibition.

Botero's *Apotheosis of Ramón Hoyos,* displayed at the Salón in 1959, heralded the introduction of Pop Art in Colombia. His works at this time were reminiscent of Abstract Expressionism, the prevailing vogue in North America. In 1960 Botero moved to New York, but as a Latin American he found acceptance there difficult; the Abstract Expressionists did not conceal their dislike for his paintings. In *Fernando Botero,* Cynthia Jaffee McCabe asserted

that "Botero's paintings were unresolved" although they were "obviously the work of a talented eclectic." In November he was conferred with the Colombian section of the Guggenheim International Award for *Battle of the Arch-Devil*; however, his first New York exhibition was unsuccessful.

In July 1964 Botero was awarded first prize for *Apples* at the Bogotá Museum of Modern Art's Primer Salón Intercol de Artistas Jóvenes. He held his first major European exhibition in Baden-Baden, Germany, in January 1966; his work was warmly received by the European critics. After dividing his time between New York, Bogotá, and Paris for several years, Botero settled in the French capital.

Botero's work has been the subject of frequent exhibitions since the early 1970s. In 1976 he was honored with the Order Andrés Bello by the Venezuelan president and the Museo de Arte Contemporáneo de Caracas. He then turned his attentions to sculpture, having developed an interest in that art form as a professor at the Escuela de Bellas Artes. His sculptures belonged to the post-Rodin figurative tradition of Gaston Lachaise and Henry Moore. His first solo sculpture exhibition was held in Paris in October of 1977.

Botero's first retrospective exhibition was held in 1979 at the Hirshhorn Museum and Sculpture Garden in Washington. Another retrospective was mounted in Japan the following year. Since 1986 retrospectives have been organized in Caracas, Munich, Tokyo, Belgium, Switzerland, Berlin, and Florence. His works have been acquired by such notable museums as New York City's Museum of Modern Art and the Metropolitan Museum of Art.

Botero has been married twice: to Gloria Zea (1955–1960), and to Cecilia Zambrano (1964–1975). He has three children: Fernando, Lina, and Carlos. Another son, Pedro, who was the subject of a loving series of paintings, was killed in an automobile accident in 1974.

## SOURCES:

### Books

*Fernando Botero: Paintings and Drawings* (includes short stories by the artist and an interview conducted with Peter Stephan on May 8, 1986), Munich, Prestel-Verlag, 1992.

McCabe, Cynthia Jaffee, *Fernando Botero: Hirshhorn Museum and Sculpture Garden, Smithsonian Institution,* Washington, D.C., Smithsonian Institution, 1979.

—*Sketch by Amanda Beresford*

# Ricardo Bressani
## 1926-
### Guatemalan biochemist

Ricardo Bressani is a prominent Central American food scientist who has contributed significantly to the knowledge of human nutrition and food production. Long associated with the Institute of Nutrition of Central America and Panama (INCAP), Bressani has focused his chief efforts toward increasing the availability of high quality foods for humans. His contributions include improving production of high nutrition foods; investigating the composition and nutritional value of basic foods such as maize, sorghum rice, beans, and amaranth; studying the effects of food processing on nutritional value; evaluating food storage techniques; and analyzing the efficient biological utilization of foods.

Ricardo Bressani Castignoli was born on September 28, 1926, in Guatemala City, Guatemala, to Primina (Castignoli), a homemaker, and César Bressani, a farmer. He obtained a B.S. degree from the University of Dayton (Ohio) in 1948. In 1951 he was awarded a master's degree from Iowa State University and began directing the food analysis laboratories at INCAP. Then two years old, INCAP had assessed the nutritional status of Central America, finding widespread malnutrition and a heavy reliance by Central Americans on cereals and legume grains. This first, brief association with INCAP stimulated Bressani's interest in the serious nutrition problems of populations in Central America.

In 1952 Bressani enrolled in Purdue University in Indiana, where he was a graduate research assistant at the Biochemical Research Institute and where he obtained his Ph.D. in 1956. He then returned to Guatemala to head INCAP's agricultural and food sciences division, a position that he held for 32 years. During this time, from 1963 to 1964, he was a visiting professor in the Department of Food Science at Rutgers State University in New Jersey; and in 1967 he was a visiting lecturer in the food science and nutrition department at the Massachusetts Institute of Technology. Other positions he has held for INCAP include that of research coordinator from 1983 to 1988; research advisor in food science and agriculture from 1988 to 1992; and consultant in food science, agriculture and nutrition beginning in 1993.

### Identifies Nutritive Value of Natural Resources in Central America

Bressani conducted important studies regarding the nutritionalvalue of resources already in abundance in Central America, such as Brazil nuts, rubber tree seeds and jicara seeds, caulote, jack beans, African palm, corozo, and buckwheat. These studies resulted from his concern that these resources held food value yet would vanish from the area because populations were ignorant of their nutritional value. The grain and vegetable amaranth, for instance, cultivated by Aztec, Mayan, and Inca civilizations, was rediscovered and converted into highly nutritional flour. In addition, Bressani's research on legumes not indigenous to Central America nor normally consumed by its populations—such as the jack bean and the cowpea—spurred agricultural production of some high-yield as well as highly nutritional beans. For instance, he obtained a protein isolate from the jack bean, uncovering it as a valuable food resource. The Central American Cooperative Program for the Improvement of Food Crops (PCCMCA) honored Bressani and his staff for their outstanding work in cereal and legume research.

As early as 1956, in Bressani's Ph.D. dissertation, he expressed concern about the nutritional problems of people whose diets consisted mainly of corn and beans. He conducted research into the effects of soil fertilization with minor elements on the yield and protein value of cereals and legumes. According to his dissertation, he was convinced that "in order to produce a corn of a high nutritive value, the ratio of germ to whole grain must be increased, or else the relative quantities of proteins other than zein should be increased in the endosperm." Eight years later at Purdue, scientist Edwin T. Mertz successfully isolated the Opaque–2 gene, the chemical-nutritive qualities of which follow the postulations in Bressani's dissertation. Subsequently, such organizations as INCAP, ICTA (Guatemala), and CIMMYT (Mexico) developed a superior maize called NUTRICTA. It was ready for agricultural production in October 1983.

Bressani has made numerous other contributions to nutrition and agriculture in Central America and has published over 450 articles in scientific journals. He is married to Alicia Herman, and they have seven children. He enjoys farming, horseback riding, reading, and photography.

## SELECTED PUBLISHED WORKS:

*Maize in Human Nutrition,* F.A.O, 1992.
*Nutritional Value and Use in Human Feeding of Some Authochtonous Underexploited Crops of Middle America,* F.A.O., 1994.

## SOURCES:

Bressani, Ricardo, correspondence with Janet Kieffer Kelley, February 28, 1994.

*—Sketch by Janet Kieffer Kelley*

# Cheryl Brownstein-Santiago
## 1951-
### Hispanic American journalist

Cheryl Brownstein-Santiago is a *Los Angeles Times* news editor and associate editor of the newspaper's bilingual supplement, *Nuestro Tiempo*, which currently has a circulation of nearly 500,000. As one of the few Hispanics in the country with a long career in the newspaper business, she actively encourages her fellow journalists to hire and promote minorities in the newsroom. In her view, it is as much a matter of economics as justice, for Brownstein-Santiago insists that members of the Hispanic community want the media to reflect a more diverse view of their world.

The veteran reporter was born October 9, 1951, in New York City, the youngest of three children. Her father, Robert S. Brownstein, was the son of Jewish immigrants who arrived via Ellis Island. A World War II veteran, he was a government clerk when he met Ruth Santiago, who had left her native Puerto Rico for a similar clerical job in New York. The two eventually married, and Brownstein worked as a diamond cutter before opening his own fruit and vegetable business.

When Brownstein-Santiago was in second grade, her parents divorced, a process that included a move to Nevada and culminated in Ruth's return to Puerto Rico after an 18-year absence. While Brownstein-Santiago and her sister stayed with their maternal grandmother, Ruth and her son lived in San Juan so that she could work as an executive secretary and save enough money to start her own business.

### Successfully Copes with Culture Shock

The experience of living in a community where nearly everyone but Brownstein-Santiago and her siblings spoke Spanish came as a shock. Her teachers were perplexed; should they put the fourth-grader into a class with younger children so that she could learn the language, or should they let her absorb Spanish naturally? After a brief but unhappy stay in a second-grade class, she was finally transferred to the fourth grade. Fortunately, Brownstein-Santiago's grandmother knew enough English to act as an interpreter, and she also taught Spanish to her granddaughters. But the entire affair was very unsettling, and as Brownstein-Santiago told interviewer Peg McNichol, "I'm a very strong opponent of total immersion [in the classroom] as a result of that experience."

After two years, the family was finally reunited in San Juan. By then, two changes had occurred. One was that Puerto Rican law required two last names, the father's followed by the mother's, and as a result Cheryl and her siblings had to take the name Brownstein-Santiago. The other was that the children were well on their way to becoming completely bilingual. But in San Juan, the language tables were turned once again. Ruth Santiago, by then an executive secretary with the Puerto Rican telephone company, was able to enroll Cheryl in Commonwealth Junior High School, a private, English-language facility for the sons and daughters of American businessmen. The school was expensive (Ruth often had to work as many as three different jobs to pay the tuition) but offered a much better education than the public system.

Later, at Academia San Jose High School, Cheryl found she was much sought after as one of the few bilingual students. By the time she graduated, she had joined the chess club, learned to play the clarinet, edited the school newspaper, and worked as yearbook photographer. Ruth Santiago had remarried and opened a pharmacy in San Juan, hoping to earn enough money to send all three of her children to college.

### Leaves Puerto Rico to Attend College in Ohio

Faced with opportunities to continue her education in Puerto Rico, Spain, or the United States, Brownstein-Santiago chose Ohio University in Athens, Ohio. Her goal was to obtain a degree in commercial photography and in the process become self-sufficient, as both her grandmother and mother had in the face of numerous hardships. Seeing them triumph over difficult circumstances gave Brownstein-Santiago a great deal of inner strength and the conviction that she would always be able to support herself.

When she discovered that photography was more fun as a hobby than as a possible career, Brownstein-Santiago took stock of her choices. She wanted to switch to psychology, but it would require more than four years of school and she wanted to be independent with just a four-year degree. She then considered social work, but her counselor instead suggested journalism since she had enjoyed working on her high school newspaper. She picked newswriting and editing as a major, with a minor in psychology.

During the summer of 1972, Brownstein-Santiago combined work at her mother's pharmacy with an internship at the *San Juan Star*. One of the drugstore's customers was a teletypist who told the young woman about an opening at the San Juan bureau of United Press International (UPI). The job turned out to be "excellent experience for someone new to the profession," according to Brownstein-Santiago. Most of the work involved providing ten to 15 stories a day on the Caribbean region to UPI's radio service.

## Joins Staff of *El Miami Herald*

After graduating from college, she continued to work for UPI, but as her sister, brother, and mother left Puerto Rico one by one to settle in the United States, Brownstein-Santiago herself grew anxious to see more of the world. In 1976, she asked UPI for a transfer, and when that did not materialize, she quit and moved to Florida. Within a few months, she had secured a job as staff reporter on *El Miami Herald*, a Spanish-language newspaper for Cuban Americans. She moved up to chief assistant editor, supervising four reporters and seven translators in addition to fulfilling her own editorial duties. She also joined the National Conference of Puerto Rican Women in 1979, serving as Miami chapter parliamentarian until 1981.

Eager for the opportunity to write for an English-language newspaper, Brownstein-Santiago took a job with the *Boston Globe* editing national copy. She did not stay up north for long, however, noting that "if Boston had been in the Sunbelt, I never would have left. But I decided to get back to Miami before the second winter hit."

## Secures Reporting Job with the *Miami News*

Brownstein-Santiago returned to Florida as a staff reporter for the *Miami News*, covering spot news and national trends as well as immigration stories. Her territory was the Caribbean, her old UPI beat. She made several trips to Cuba at a time when Cuban-born American journalists were banned from that country. She covered the U.S. invasion of Grenada and presidential candidate Jesse Jackson's 1984 tour of Central America. She was also among the few reporters who witnessed **Fidel Castro**'s first public visit to a church.

Around this time, Brownstein-Santiago and some of her colleagues founded the Florida Association of Hispanic Journalists, a group whose mission is to encourage other Hispanics to consider a career in journalism. Brownstein-Santiago served as the organization's secretary in 1984 and 1985. In another attempt to reach out to young people and give back to the community, she also served as board member of the YWCA of Greater Miami from 1983 until 1985.

By the mid–1980s, Brownstein-Santiago had been promoted to editorial writer for the *Miami News;* she also did recruiting for the paper. She was active professionally in other ways as well, attending the Editors' Conference on Latin America at the Woodrow Wilson International Center for Scholars in 1984 and the Editorial Page Editors and Writers Seminar at the American Press Institute in 1987.

## Heads West to Work for the *Los Angeles Times*

But in 1988 the *Miami News* folded, and Brownstein-Santiago was forced to look elsewhere for a job. She soon landed one with the *Los Angeles Times*, joining a department that produces a monthly bilingual supplement entitled *Nuestro Tiempo*. Though her work on *Nuestro Tiempo* mostly involves editing the writing of others, Brownstein-Santiago occasionally authors editorial pieces of her own, including one on the political future of Puerto Rico. She has also learned much more about the differences within the U.S. Hispanic community.

Brownstein-Santiago remains fiercely committed to drawing more Hispanics into the field of journalism. "When I started out in this business," she noted, "there were newspaper managers who would say, 'Gee we'd like to hire Latins, but we can't find any who are qualified.' That's the reason most Hispanic groups got started, as a way of saying, 'Here are some perfectly qualified people.'" As part of this effort, Brownstein-Santiago volunteers to work on writing contests and scholarship committees and makes career-day visits to schools. She is also a member of the board of directors of the National Association of Hispanic Journalists and a member of the California Chicano News Media Association. "Being a Latina in major market new media in the U.S., I feel a strong responsibility to give back to the Latin communities that have been so supportive of me throughout my career," she explained.

When she is not busy with her editorial and civic duties, Brownstein-Santiago enjoys walking on the beach and swimming in the ocean near her condominium. A self-described "happily single" woman, she owns a cockatiel and a canary and still enjoys dabbling in photography.

**SOURCES:**

Brownstein-Santiago, Cheryl, telephone interview with Peg McNichol, September, 1992.

*—Sketch by Peg McNichol*

# Luis Buñuel
## 1900-1983
### Spanish Mexican film director and screenwriter

Described by Virginia Higginbotham in her biography as "one of the greatest directors ever to work in cinema," fanciful filmmaker Luis Buñuel ridiculed the vanity of bourgeois, or middle-class society and satirized rigid conventions by focusing on religious and moral problems. Buñuel attempted to expose the institutions of civilization as facades that hide the animal side of human nature. The anarchist strain in Buñuel's dispassionate analysis of capitalist society—which has been related to his interest in entomology—lent his work a singular personal stamp. He won many prestigious film awards, including the Palme D'Or at the Cannes Film Festival and an Academy Award.

Buñuel spent much of his directing career in exile, working in the Mexican commercial film industry and later in France. Several critics have noted that in the films upon which his international reputation rests, his Spanish heritage and his Catholic upbringing are crucial elements. Peter Harcourt commented in *Film Quarterly* that "Spanish Catholicism" in particular "must have brought home to the young Buñuel the surrealist antagonism between the ideals of the spirit and the exigencies of the flesh." Similarly, in an essay included in *The World of Luis Buñuel,* André Bazin noted that Buñuel's surrealism is "part of the rich and fortunate influence of a totally Spanish tradition. His taste is for the horrible, his sense of brutality, his tendency to delve into the utmost extremes of humanity—these are all the heritage of [Spanish painters] **Francisco Goya**, Francisco de Zurbarán, José Ribera."

The eldest of seven children, Buñuel was born on February 22, 1900, in Calanda, Spain, to Leonardo Buñuel González, a successful merchant, and María Portolés Cerezuela. Shortly after his birth the family moved to Zaragoza, where Buñuel spent a secure and comfortable childhood. His Jesuit education at the Colegio del Salvador in Zaragoza left a deep impression on Buñuel. A bright student, his spirited conduct caused frequent conflicts with school authorities, and he insisted on spending his final two years at the local public high school. At this time Buñuel was introduced to the writings of philosophers Karl Marx and Jean-Jacques Rousseau, and his reading of naturalist Charles Darwin's controversial *The Origin of Species*—which explicated his theory of evolution—confirmed his growing religious skepticism.

When Buñuel enrolled at the University of Madrid in 1917, he intended to study entomology and agronomy with a view to managing his father's estates. However, he became increasingly interested in literature and philosophy and joined a group of artists and writers in the college dormitory, the Residencia de Estudiantes. Among this group—which became known as the "Generation of '27"—were **José Ortega y Gasset**, **Salvador Dalí** and **Federico García Lorca**, who would become well known as a philosopher, artist, and writer, respectively.

In 1925 Buñuel made his first visit to Paris, where he began to write film reviews for the *Cahiers d'Art.* Viewing Fritz Lang's *Destiny* (1921) convinced Buñuel to become a filmmaker. He began as an assistant to Jean Epstein on *Mauprat* (1926) and then worked on Epstein's *The Fall of the House of Usher* (1928).

### Caused a Scandal

In 1928, Buñuel cowrote his first film with Salvador Dalí; an unsettling montage, *Un Chien Andalou* embodies the irrationality of surrealism. The public was scandalized, but the film earned the approval of Surrealist leader André Breton. Buñuel's next film, *L'Age d'or,* was released in 1930 and caused an even greater scandal. Its images of unbridled sexual passion and its unflattering depiction of the Roman Catholic church brought strong official condemnation.

For Buñuel, notoriety meant success; the film caught the attention of executives at the famed Hollywood studio, Metro-Goldwyn-Mayer. He was invited to learn studio film techniques in California. In his 1984 memoir, *My Last Breath* Buñuel described this period as an interlude of well-paid idleness in the company of Charlie Chaplin and other movie stars. This brief introduction to Hollywood was cut short by a disagreement with the studio on the terms of his employment, so Buñuel returned to Spain, where he made *Las Hurdes* (*Land Without Bread*) in 1932.

Ostensibly a documentary, *Las Hurdes* breaks with the scandal-mongering of Buñuel's first films, but he noted in an interview with José de la Colina and Tomás Pérez Turrent in *Objects of Desire: Conversations With Luis Buñuel,* that it shared "the same outlook" as its "imaginative" Surrealist predecessors. *Las Hurdes* was Buñuel's last personal film until the release of *Los Olvidados* 18 years later. However, he remained in the film industry, working for Paramount and Warner Brothers in Paris and Madrid. When the Spanish Civil War broke out he served as an attaché at the Spanish Embassy in Paris, producing films on the Spanish Civil War.

Six years later, Buñuel returned to the United States to work in Hollywood. When it became clear that **Francisco Franco** was winning the Civil War, the project was dropped and his contract was cancelled. Buñuel then began work in the film department at the Museum of Modern Art in New York City, but he resigned his position under pressure from the Catholic church following the publication of Dalí's autobiography, *The Secret Life of Salvador Dalí* in which Dali described Buñuel as an atheist.

In 1940, Buñuel returned to Hollywood, where he found work dubbing Spanish versions of propaganda films for Metro-Goldwyn-Mayer; then as World War II came to a close he made Spanish language versions of U.S. films for Warner Brothers. When Buñuel was offered an opportunity to direct his own films in Mexico, he accepted, and soon afterwards, he became a Mexican citizen.

### Resumed Solo Filmmaking

In the late 1940s, after many years of working on other people's movies, Buñuel returned to filmmaking with a series of low-budget commercial films produced by Oscar Dancigers. This work was to sustain Buñuel for more than ten years until he could secure funding for his own projects. Even so, the style of these commercial Mexican films—beginning with *Gran Casino* (1947), and including *El gran calavera* (1949), *Mi huerfanito, jefe!* (1950) and *La ilusión viaja en tranvía* (1953)—was reflective of Buñuel's authorial hand.

With 1950's *Los Olvidados*, Buñuel had full artistic control over his work; the film won him prizes for best director and the international critics prize at the Cannes Film Festival of 1951. His subsequent movie, *Subida al cielo* was a 1952 prizewinner at Cannes for the best avant-garde film. These films established him as a major film auteur, each picture extending the scope of his personal vision.

The serious literary intent of Buñuel's major work began with adaptations of the classic novels *Robinson Cross* and *Wuthering Heights*. He wrote original screenplays for many of his classic films, including *The Exterminating Angel, The Milky Way,* and *The Discreet Charm of the Bourgeoisie,* but even his adaptations betray a distinctly Buñuelian vision.

Buñuel's view of the human predicament, as *Film Quarterly'* s Harcourt has said, is that of "a man distressed by his own vision of the universe but who has also a keen eye for the multitude of self-deceptions that, for many of us, make life bearable." In 1958, Buñuel had further success when *Nazarín,* which tells the story of a young Mexican priest at odds with church authorities, won the prestigious Palme D'Or at Cannes.

### Invoked Another Furror

After 25 years in exile, Buñuel was permitted to return to Spain to direct *Viridiana* in 1961. The story of a young novice surrounded by a cast of grotesques, it once more casts the ideal of Christian charity in a skeptical light. The Spanish censors approved the screenplay, but each day after shooting Buñuel sent the rushes to Paris where, at the editing table, he turned an innocuous script into a film depicting suicide, rape, and debauchery. At Cannes *Viridiana* won the Palme D'Or and the Society of Film Writers Award, but in Spain the censors who had permitted the shoot were dismissed and the film was banned. Buñuel was able to return to Madrid for three months

the following year, but his attempts to make another film proved fruitless.

Buñuel's early surrealist strategy of shocking an audience now took the form of telling stories about the bourgeoisie in which the norms of civilized conduct were revealed to be fragile conventions. Buñuel's next film, *The Exterminating Angel,* traced the regression of a company of Mexican bourgeois from a state of high civilization to a primitive condition induced by the decline of conventional social mores and educational standards.

Buñuel followed that film with 1963's *The Diary of a Chambermaid.* Set in 1920s France, it is the story of a maid whose experiences provide an ironic commentary on the hypocrisy and absurdity of middle-class life. Its interwoven themes of fetishism, sexual crime, latent fascism, and religious devotion are set in the classically Buñuelian context of the bourgeois household.

Made three years after *The Diary of a Chambermaid,* Buñuel's blunt satire on Christian piety *Simon of the Desert*—which Brian Murphy described in a review cited in *Contemporary Literary Criticism* as "absolutely essential for a complete understanding of the man's thought and work"—remained unfinished and had to be released as a medium-length film. Less than an hour long, the movie depicts "an ascetic stand[ing] on a pillar in the desert for several decades—closer to God, farther from temptation," according to *Videohound's Golden Movie Retriever 1994.* Despite its small budget and the truncated ending, *Simon of the Desert* received the Silver Lion of St. Mark at the Venice International Film Festival. The obsessive theme of religion would be reprised in *The Milky Way.*

### Settled in Europe

In 1966 Buñuel returned to France to make *Belle de Jour.* This, Buñuel's first major box office success and a prize-winner at the Venice Film Festival, starred Catherine Deneuve. Buñuel felt his movie could only be redeemed by erasing the boundaries between the heroine's masochistic fantasies and reality. While *Belle de Jour* tempered the quality of the bizarre that Buñuel's name had always evoked, and while its large budget, highly recognizable film star lead, and high production values marked it as the work of an established film director, it nonetheless continued Buñuel's surrealist exploration of the unconscious.

*Tristana,* released in 1970 and based on the epistolary novel of **Benito Pérez Galdós**, was filmed in Toledo, Spain, and coproduced by a French, Italian, and Spanish team. In *Luis Buñuel: A Critical Biography,* J. Francisco Aranda applauded the movie Buñuel's "most Spanish film" in its "study of characteristic national situations and characters." Mexican author **Carlos Fuentes** agreed, describing *Tristana* as "Buñuel's most intimate, autobiographical, Spanish, provincial movie ... with its immediate, tangible symbols of fear, deception, mutual damnation, and ridiculous social convention."

*The Discreet Charm of the Bourgeoisie* (1972) takes the form of a series of frustrated dinner parties, with each attempt at a gathering interrupted by a different, but equally gratuitous intrusion. Of Buñuel's bourgeois victims Fuentes commented that "they are endowed with a reluctantly charming dimension: they are doomed, yet they survive." One of Buñuel's most popular films, it placed him in cinema's highest pantheon, when he won an Academy Award. At the ceremony he was toasted by some of Hollywood's finest directors including Alfred Hitchcock, Billy Wilder, William Wyler, and George Cukor.

With *The Phantom of Liberty* Buñuel explored the influence of chance on human destiny in a series of absurd episodes reminiscent of the free associations of *L'Age d'Or*. Another parody of bourgeois values, *The Phantom of Liberty* also explodes the myth of freedom offered by Marx and Engels in the Communist Manifesto, staging a series of absurd vignettes in which the spectator's expectations are repeatedly frustrated.

Buñuel's last picture, *That Obscure Object of Desire* was based on Pierre Louÿs's novel *La Femme et le pantin* and features a bourgeois gentleman describing to his fellow railway passengers his frustrated desire for a dancer. The man's tale is punctuated by terrorist attacks. After retiring from filmmaking, Buñuel returned to Mexico permanently. He died on July 29, 1983, six years after making his final movie, in Mexico City. His wife, Jeanne Rucar de Buñuel, published a memoir of her life with him entitled *Memorias de una mujer sin piano* in 1990.

## SELECTED PUBLISHED WORKS:

*L'Age d'Or & Un Chien Andalou: Films by Luis Buñuel,* translated by Marianne Alexandre, New York, Simon & Schuster, 1968.

*Three Screenplays: Viridiana, The Exterminating Angel, Simon of the Desert,* New York, Orion Press, 1969.

*Belle de Jour,* New York, Simon & Schuster, 1971.

*Tristana,* New York, Simon & Schuster, 1971.

*The Exterminating Angel, Nazarín, Los Olvidados: Three Films by Luis Buñuel,* translated by Nicholas Fry, New York, Simon & Schuster, 1972.

*My Last Breath,* translated by Abigail Israel, London, Jonathan Cape, 1984.

*Objects of Desire: Conversations With Luis Buñuel,* José de la Colina and Tomás Pérez Turrent, edited and translated by Paul Lenti, New York, Marsilio Publishers, 1992.

## SELECTED VIDEOGRAPHY:

*Un Chien Andalou,* 1928.
*L'Age D'Or,* 1930.
*Las Hurdes* (*Land Without Bread*), 1932.
*Gran Casino,* 1947.
*El gran calavera,* 1949.
*The Great Madcap,* 1949.
*Los Olvidados,* 1950.
*Mi huerfanito, jefe!,* 1950.
*Mexican Bus Ride,* 1951.
*Susana,* 1951.
*A Woman Without Love,* 1951.
*El Bruto* (*The Brute*) 1952.
*El: This Strange Passion,* 1952.
*Robinson Cross,* 1952.
*Subida al cielo,* 1952.
*La ilusión viaja en tranvía* (*The Illusion Travels by Streetcar*), 1953.
*Wuthering Heights,* 1963.
*The Criminal Life of Archibaldo de la Cruz,* 1955.
*El,* 1955.
*Nazarín,* 1958.
*Fever Mounts at El Pao,* 1959.
*Viridiana,* 1961.
*The Exterminating Angel,* 1962.
*Diary of a Chambermaid,* 1964.
*Belle de Jour,* 1966.
*Simon of the Desert,* 1966.
*The Milky Way,* 1968.
*Phantom of Liberty,* 1968.
*Tristana,* 1970.
*The Discreet Charm of the Bourgeoisie,* 1972.
*That Obscure Object of Desire,* 1977.

## SOURCES:

### Books

*Contemporary Literary Criticism,* Vol. 16, edited by Sharon R. Gunton, Detroit, Gale, 1981.

Durgnat, Raymond, *Luis Buñuel,* Berkeley, University of California Press, 1968, revised edition, 1978.

Higginbotham, Virginia, *Luis Buñuel,* Boston, Twayne, 1979.

*Hispanic Writers,* edited by Bryan Ryan, Detroit, Gale, 1991.

*Luis Buñuel: A Critical Biography,* J. Francisco Aranda, translated and edited by David Robinson, New York, Da Capo Press, 1976.

*Videohound's Golden Movie Retriever 1994,* edited by Martin Connors and Julia Furtaw, Visible Ink, 1994.

*The World of Luis Buñuel,* edited by Joan Mellen, New York, Oxford University Press, 1978.

**Periodicals**

*Film Comment,* May-June 1975, pp. 52–59.
*Film Quarterly,* Spring 1967, pp. 2–19.
*The New Yorker,* December 5, 1977, pp. 53–72.
*New York Times,* July 30, 1983.

—*Sketch by Simon Dixon*

# Álvar Núñez Cabeza de Vaca
## 1490(?)-1560
**Spanish explorer**

Álvar Núñez Cabeza de Vaca was the first European to cross the continent of North America. Landing on the Florida shore near Tampa Bay in 1527, he spent the next eight years exploring Florida, Texas, New Mexico, Arizona, and northern Mexico, covering more than 5,000 miles of country that had never before been seen by a European. His account of the journey—and the legends that emerged—played a principal role in inspiring the extensive explorations of southern and southwestern North America by **Hernando de Soto** and **Francisco Coronado**. Although the adventures of Cabeza de Vaca and his companions served as a catalyst for the chain of events that resulted in the Spanish colonization of the Southwest, his "more lasting significance," according to William T. Pilkington in the epilogue to *Cabeza de Vaca's Adventures in the Unknown Interior of America,* "has been literary and cultural not historical." Indeed, Cabeza de Vaca's journal, published in 1542 under the title *La Relacion* records the various peoples, animals, and vegetation that inhabited the continent, and has served as an unparalleled source of information for anthropologists and biologists, as well as historians. Moreover, the journal, which has been viewed by some literary scholars as a prototype for later American writing, earned Cabeza de Vaca the distinction of being the first writer of the American Southwest.

Álvar Núñez Cabeza de Vaca, who was born around 1490, grew up in the sherry wine center of Jerez de la Fontera, a southern Spanish city located just eight miles from the sea and 12 miles from the port of Cádiz. He was the eldest child of a family that boasted a rich ancestry. While his father, Francisco de Vera, was an alderman of little distinction, his paternal grandfather, who lived with the family for about eight years, was Pedro de Vera Mendoza, a first generation conquistador who led the conquest of the Canary Islands. The aspiring explorer, however, adopted the name of his mother, Doña Teresa Cabeza de Vaca, whose ancestors acquired the name in the early thirteenth century by leading a Spanish army through a mountain pass with the skull of a cow—*cabeza de vaca*. Following the tradition established by his family and his social class, the young Cabeza de Vaca embarked on a military career while still in his teens. At around the age of 21, he saw his first combat while marching in the army that King Ferdinand sent to aid Pope Julius II in 1511. On April 11, 1511, he fought against the French in the Battle of Ravenna, where 20,000 died. He then served as an ensign at Gaeta, outside Naples, before returning to Spain in 1513 to help the Duke of Medina Sidonia suppress the uprisings of the Comuneros in 1520. He also fought in later battles against the French in Navarre.

Although Cabeza de Vaca served honorably in the wars, he may have remained in obscurity had he not come in contact with Panfilo de Narvaez, who had explored the Indies in 1500, served as chief captain under **Diego de Velásquez** in the conquest of Cuba in 1510, and spent three years in a Mexican prison after leading an unsuccessful campaign against **Hernán Cortés** in 1518. Humiliated and defeated, Narvaez returned to live for several years on his plantation in Cuba. On November 17, 1526, though, the King gave him the opportunity to "discover, conquer and people" the area from Rio de las Palmas in northeast Mexico to the island of Florida. Three months later, Narvaez, who was responsible for financing his own voyage, signed on Cabeza de Vaca as his treasurer, assigning him the principal duty of collecting the King's Fifth—the requisite five percent tax on all gold and silver obtained during the expedition. In addition to the responsibility of collecting other taxes and paying officers their salaries, Cabeza de Vaca was also instructed to provide the Crown with reports on the discipline of the volunteers and the treatment of the natives—especially with regard to "the teaching of the Indians in the Holy Faith," which his writings suggest was his most important charge.

### Set Sail for the Americas

The expedition of five ships and some 600 men, set sail from San Lucar on June 17, 1527. In early August, the fleet arrived on the shores of their proposed destination of Santo Domingo, where they stayed for 45 days, collecting provisions and horses for the forthcoming journey. Tempted by the wealth of the country or tired of the stinginess of Narvaez, 140 men deserted the expedition. Those who elected to remain sailed to the Cuban port of Santiago, where Cabeza de Vaca was given command of two ships to gather more supplies in Trinidad. While he was ashore, the ships—along with 60 men and 20 horses—were destroyed by a hurricane. Having suffered such an inauspicious beginning, the expedition spent the winter in the Cuban port of Xagua, before sailing to the Florida coast, where they arrived in April.

On May 1, following a dispute with Narvaez, Cabeza de Vaca led a group of 340 men on a journey inland where they met several Native American tribes and discovered such animals as the opossum. By the time the party was ready to set sail again, though, attacks from various tribes, disease, and starvation had resulted in heavy losses; fewer than 200 men, after killing and eating their last horse, returned to continue the journey by sea. For the next several days, the small fleet struggled among the bars and shallows of the vague coast. Facing imminent starvation, they were aided by a group of natives who led them to their village and provided them with fish and water. However, while the chief was entertaining the Spaniards, the natives attacked without warning, forcing them to flee. Several days later the explorers, "so emaciated that the bones could be counted," as Cabeza de Vaca wrote in his journal, encountered a different tribe of natives, who gave them food and, after seeing the Spaniard's boat capsize, wept openly for them and agreed to take the remaining 30 men to their village. Lacking provisions and any means of transporting them, the Spaniards spent the winter on what they later discovered to be an island—present-day Galveston Island—where blizzard conditions brought about starvation, forcing some of the men to eat their dead. At winter's end, only 15 men remained. Accordingly, the survivors dubbed the place *Malhado*—the "Island of Doom."

Cabeza de Vaca and his fellow survivors spent the next year living with the natives there, the Capoques and the Han, observing and recording various aspects of their culture, including their use of incisions to heal sickness. Encouraged to practice the art of healing himself, Cabeza de Vaca adopted the method of blessing the sick by breathing upon them, reciting a prayer, and concluding with the sign of the cross. As he stated in his journal, the technique was often successful and resulted in benevolent treatment from the natives. But after falling ill, Cabeza de Vaca's status as a kindly treated medicine man was reduced to that of a harshly treated slave. Finding his life with the Capoques "unbearable," he escaped in 1530.

## Life Among the Natives

For the next six years, Cabeza de Vaca travelled throughout the surrounding coastal region, living naked and alone among the natives. He was able to survive by gathering and bartering for various materials that the natives valued—conch shells, sea-beads,

flint, and fruit from mesquite trees. "Wherever I went, the Indians treated me honorably and gave me food, because they liked my commodities," he wrote in his journal. "They were glad to see me when I came and delighted to be brought what they wanted." Despite his relative success as an itinerant merchant, Cabeza de Vaca still had to endure the "peril and privation" of a life alone in the wilderness. The reason that he stayed for so long, he wrote, was to convince Lope de Oveido, one of the other remaining survivors, to accompany him on a search for other Christians. Finally, in November of 1532, Oveido consented to ford the bay and continue the journey, but after encountering some natives along the way who threatened and beat them, Oveido turned back with some native women to the island. Cabeza de Vaca was again alone.

Shortly after his comradés departure, however, he was overtaken by a new group of natives, the Mariames, and taken to their camp on the Guadalupe River. There he came in contact with another of his fellow adventurers, Andres Dorantes, and experienced "a day of as great joy as we ever knew" before he was consigned as a slave to Dorantes' master. Six months later, in September of 1534, the two made their escape, eventually locating another surviving Spaniard, Alonso del Castillo, who was staying with a neighboring tribe, the Avares. Largely on the strength of Castillo's reputation as a powerful medicine man, the three spent an amicable eight months there, recording miraculous feats of healing. After parting from their weeping hosts, many of whom followed them to their next destination, Cabeza de Vaca and the others proceeded toward the Guadalupe Mountains, encountering various native tribes and languages along the way. While travelling in the vicinity of Carlsbad, New Mexico, they encountered a tribe that brought before Cabeza de Vaca a man who had been severely wounded by an arrowhead. With only a flint knife, the Spaniard opened his chest and removed the arrowhead that was lodged near his heart and stitched the wound with hair from a hide. The surgery proved to be a remarkable success; as Cabeza de Vaca wrote, "This cure so inflated our fame all over the region that we could control whatever the inhabitants cherished."

## Encountered Fellow Europeans

Having gained the trust—and considerable provisions—from the natives of the region, the Spaniards continued their travels through northern Mexico. In January of 1536, they came across a native who was wearing a small sword-belt buckle with a horseshoe nail stitched to it around his neck—a sign that other Europeans might be nearby. Their speculations were confirmed; around March, Cabeza de Vaca and his fellow explorers overtook a group of Spaniards and natives under the command of Diego de Alcaraz.

Instead of being a cause for celebration, though, the long expected meeting brought only disappointment. Cabeza de Vaca, objecting to Alcaraz's wish to enslave the natives, aroused the jealousy of his countryman, who in turn tried to tell the natives, through an interpreter, that as Cabeza de Vaca's superior in Spain he should be obeyed and served. But as Cabeza de Vaca wrote: "The Indians paid no attention. Conferring among themselves, they replied that the Christians lied … we healed the sick, they killed the sound … we coveted nothing but gave whatever we were given, while they robbed whomever they found and bestowed nothing on anyone." Cabeza de Vaca encouraged the natives to leave Alcaraz to rebuild their villages; however, he was summarily arrested and led into the forest by some of Alcaraz's native allies.

Meanwhile, the Alcalde Mayor, Melchor Díaz, who happened to know of the Narvaez expedition, came to their rescue, providing them with food and condemning the actions of Alcaraz. At Díaz's request, Cabeza de Vaca again summoned the natives to return to their villages and begin planting their fields, saying that it was their "Christian duty" to do so. Having heard of the healing powers of Cabeza de Vaca, the natives consented and bestowed numerous gifts upon the Spaniard whom they believed to have divine power. Cabeza de Vaca stayed in Saint Miguel for another month before travelling to Mexico City, where he prepared for his departure to Spain in April of 1537.

When he returned to Spain six months later, his primary ambition was to find a way to get back to North America, this time as first in command. But his delay in getting home to Spain, brought about by the capsizing of his intended vessel at Veracruz, precluded such an opportunity. An expedition with Hernando De Soto at the helm had already been arranged. While De Soto made every effort to sign Cabeza de Vaca on as his second in command, his experience under the incompetent Narvaez prevented him from consenting. Cabeza de Vaca, instead, was appointed by King Charles V to serve as *adelantado,* or governor, of the large South American provinces of the Rio De la Plata.

Upon his arrival in 1540, the new governor attempted to rescue the struggling colony of Asunción. Rather than take the year-long sea route through Buenos Aires, he opted for the shorter—but more perilous—land route, and proceeded to lead an expedition across 1,000 miles of unknown territory. Travelling barefoot through the supposedly impenetrable jungles, mountains, and cannibal villages, he finally reached his destination in March 1542, four months later. The next summer he embarked on an even more treacherous journey, traveling about the same distance up the Paraguay River in search of the legendary Golden City of Manoa. But, having endured a series of heavy tropical rains in the fall, he was forced to turn back after his men refused to continue.

### Returned to Spain in Chains

Upon returning to Asunción, Cabeza faced problems of a different kind. Too weak from illness to assume control of his government, he fell victim to a revolutionary plot led by some of his fellow royal officers. Having grown tired of the governor's systematic prohibition of the enslavement, rape, and looting of the natives—as well as his demand that a fine camp bed be carried through the jungle for him—the revolutionaries, composed mostly of artisans, common soldiers, and Franciscans, jailed Cabeza de Vaca, charging that he had "called himself King." The beleaguered governor, who had survived ten years battling the natives and the elements in North America, was finally overcome by his fellow Christians, who sent him to Spain in chains, in 1543. The King's Council for the Indies, however, did not bring the case to trial until 1551, at which time Cabeza de Vaca was sentenced to banishment to Africa for eight years. Largely as a result of his wife's appeals, the sentence was annulled, and he was awarded a modest pension the year before his death. Although his last years were spent in captivity, preventing him from making further expeditions, he was able to leave what was perhaps a more lasting legacy. *Comentarios,* the narrative account of his South American adventure, nearly three times the length of his North American chronicle, was published the year before he died.

### SELECTED PUBLISHED WORKS:

*La Relación,* 1542.
*Comentarios,* 1555.

### SOURCES:

#### Books

Bishop, Morris, *The Odyssey of Cabeza de Vaca,* New York, Century, 1933.
Blacker, Irwin R., and Harry M. Rosen, *The Golden Conquistadores,* Indianapolis, Bobbs-Merrill, 1960.
*Cabeza de Vaca's Adventures in the Unknown Interior of America,* translated and edited by Cyclone Covey, Albuquerque, University of New Mexico Press, 1983.
Hallenbeck, Cleve, *Álvar Núñez Cabeza de Vaca: The Journey and Route of the First European to Cross the Continent of North America, 1534–1536,* Port Washington, New York, Kennikat, 1940.

Terrel, John Upton, *Journey into Darkness,* New York, Morrow, 1962.

—*Sketch by Jason Gallman*

# José A. Cabranes
## 1940-
### Puerto Rican American judge

José A. Cabranes has the distinction of being the first Puerto Rican appointed to a federal court in the continental United States, and he has twice been a top candidate for a Supreme Court nomination. He is a pragmatic and skilled judge and legal scholar, with a reputation for being intelligent and fair. Once a registered Democrat, some legal experts and colleagues have since determined that his rulings challenge U.S. political party boundaries.

Born in Mayaguez, Puerto Rico, Cabranes is the son of teachers Manuel Cabranes and Carmen Lopez. In 1946, the family moved to to the South Bronx, New York, where the senior Cabranes became director of Melrose House, a settlement house serving newly arrived Puerto Rican migrants in a working-class neighborhood in transition. As Cabranes explained in his *Citizenship and the American Empire,* his parents left Puerto Rico to seek a better life and more opportunities for their children. Still, Cabranes's mother and father transmitted their deep love for their native land to their offspring.

Similar to the experiences of many other early immigrants, life in New York City was not easy; the Cabranes suffered cultural shock, but were able to survive and achieve success for their family. Cabranes spent his primary and secondary years in the public schools in New York City. He graduated from Columbia College with a A.B. in 1961; four years later he earned a J.D. from Yale Law School. Cabranes then studied at Cambridge under a Kellett Research Fellowship from Columbia University a Humanitarian Trust Studentship in Public International Law from the Faculty Board of Law of the University of Cambridge. In 1967 the University of Cambridge awarded him a M.Litt. in International Law. In the midst of all that studying, he married Kate Stith, a professor at Yale Law School in New Haven.

In the ensuing years, Cabranes occupied several positions teaching and practicing law. He worked as an attorney in New York City and as a special counsel to the governor of Puerto Rico. Cabranes also taught at Rutgers University Law School and spent four years as Yale University's general counsel. In 1979, Yale University Press published his book, *Citizenship and the American Empire: Notes on the Legislative History of the United States Citzenship of Puerto Ricans.* The work's objective, as Cabranes stated in the preface, was "to trace how, between the years 1900 and 1917, the Congress of the United States decided that the people of a distant colonial territory should be made American citizens."

When, in spring of 1994, U.S. president Bill Clinton was faced with selecting another Supreme Court nominee, the *New Republic* opined that Cabranes would be a more than satisfactory choice: "Cabranes combines a concern for civil liberties with a suspicion of crusading activism. . . . It would be good for the country to have a Hispanic on the court who has complicated views on race, and who argues them with intellectual force. Cabranes has reflectiveness without which no justice can help build a consensus." The *New York Times'* Mary B. W. Tabor noted that "prosecutors and defense lawyers alike describe him as intelligent and fair. They also say that the judge, known to talk to Hispanic plantiffs and defendants in Spanish, rules with compassion."

Although Cabranes earned endorsements from many Hispanic groups—the Congressional Hispanic Caucus and the Hispanic National Bar Association among them—some organizations were silent. The reserve that characterized the National Council of La Raza and the Mexican American Legal Defense and Education Fund "underscored the continuing division within the Hispanic community about whether Cabranes's views would be too conservative," according to the *Washington Post's* Ruth Marcus and Kenneth J. Cooper, "and is part of a private but intense effort . . . to prod the Clinton administration to select a more liberal nominee." Ultimately, Cabranes was not chosen.

That did not keep Cabranes from defending civil rights. Tabor quoted one speech whereupon he declared: "We all know too well that there are critical areas of civil rights in which advances are either thereatened or remain yet to be consolidated, most notably in matters involving privacy and sexual orientation. We also know that for women, victimization as a class by discriminatory laws and social practices, and a collective failure to take sexual violence seriously is a vivid and palpable reality. This reality is unacceptable, and we must take direct and affirmative measures to change it. New legal protections are needed."

Yet Cabranes decries victim mentality, as Tabor demonstrated in citing a speech the judge delivered before Hispanic law students: "We should reject, especially in our education and in our public life, the idea that we are life's victims now and forever and that our fate is to exist at the margins of our national culture, clinging to our ethnic identity as a substitute for full engagement in the broader culture."

## SELECTED PUBLISHED WORKS:

*Citizenship and the American Empire: Nostes on the Legislative History of the United States Citizenship of Puerto Ricans,* New Haven, Yale University Press, 1979.

## SOURCES:

### Periodicals

*Houston Chronicle,* April 15, 1994.
*Los Angeles Times,* April 14, 1994, p. A18; June 29, 1991, p. A18.
*New Republic,* May 23, 1994, pp. 9.
*New York Times,* May 9, 1994, pp. B5.
*Washington Post,* April 8, 1994, section A, p. 1; April 15, 1994, section A, p. 7.

### Other

Additional information from this profile was obtained from Lillian M. Olejarczyk, secretary to Judge José Cabranes.

—*Sketch by Sylvia P. Apodaca and Erika Dreifus*

# Lydia Cabrera
## 1900-1991

### Cuban ethnologist and writer

Writer Lydia Cabrera was considered by contemporaries as the premiere Cuban ethnologistand the island's matriarch of letters. Her collections of Afro-Cuban folklore, both fiction and nonfiction, were a major contribution to the anthropological study of her native land. When she died in September of 1991, Miamian Marcia Morgado wrote to the *Miami Herald:* "Her death deprived us Cubans of our cultural mother. She gave birth to the offspring from the marriage between European and African myths, legends and mores. She penetrated the previously closed world of former African slaves and deciphered for us their secrets . . . she brought to life a world populated by exquisitely sensuous and mischievous deities, wise animals, and breathing rocks."

### Writes Seminal Work on *Santeria*

Born May 20, 1900, in Havana, Cuba, Cabrera was the daughter of a prominent intellectual. She became interested in Afro-Caribbean culture when she left Cuba in 1927 to study Asian religions at L'Ecole du Louvre in Paris, France. She returned to Cuba in 1938, after publishing the first of her 23 books. This work, Cuentos Negros de Cuba, was initially issued in French in 1936, then in Spanish. Among her later writings is El Monte, her best-known book. Published in 1954, the volume is a seminal work on santeria, the hybrid of Roman Catholic and African religious practices that evolved in Caribbean countries. The **Castro** government reissued the book without her permission in 1991. She explored Cuba's African heritage in other works of fiction as well as in scholarly tomes. She also compiled a dictionary of the Afro-Cuban Yoruba language.

Cabrera lived in Cuba, writing and researching, from 1938 to 1960, when she left first to Madrid, Spain, and later to Miami, Florida. In exile, she continued her work, publishing more than a dozen books. Her home in Miami became a mecca for young exiled writers, artists, and anyone interested in the Afro-Cuban culture. For many intellectuals, she became a guiding light. "She befriended old, former slaves in Havana and Matanzas, in the fields and hills," wrote *Miami Herald* reporter Lizette Alvarez in a 1991 article. "On their porches, inside their thatched-roof huts known as *bohios,* she heard their stories and translated them into tales, fictional stories based on folklore rooted in Africa and passed down from generation to generation."

### Teaches Value of Cuba's African Roots

Various reviewers have lauded her work for being thoroughly researched firsthand and for possessing a poetic, lyrical style. In a 1991 editorial, a writer for the *Miami Herald* eulogized her: "Ms. Cabrera combined a graceful prose style with rigorous attention to the truth. With respect, humility and charm, she wrote about her country . . . its plants and animals, its folklore, its legends, its popular medicine." Ramon Mestre, a *Miami Herald* columnist, also noted: "Lydia Cabrera . . . taught me to cherish a hidden Cuba, a country that rarely appears in official histories. Enraptured by its magic, I read her work and learned to value Cuba's African roots, an essential element in their national identity that too many Cubans either scorn or ignore."

## SOURCES:

*Miami Herald,* September 21, 1991, p. 1A, 22A; October 4, 1991, p. 15A; October 5, 1991, p. 23A.

—*Sketch by Ana Veciana-Suarez*

# Guillermo Cabrera Infante
## 1929-
### Cuban writer

Guillermo Cabrera Infante, a Cuban-born writer who eventually became a British citizen, was born during a time of political revolution in his native country. His writing reflects the social conditions he observed and experienced. Cabrera was involved in the political underground that helped bring **Fidel Castro** to power in Cuba. Like other artists, writers, and intellectuals of the time, however, he quickly grew disillusioned when it became apparent that the Castro regime expected their conservative cooperation, though it had been their radical expressions that had helped bring Castro to power.

Cabrera does not write of revolution, but of the issues integral in Cuban life: poverty, equality, economics of sugar production (Cuba's chief agricultural product), and urban life. He is a writer in love with the spoken word, which he "translates" to a written form. Much of his prose contains puns, allusions, and word play, bringing humor to serious and solemn subjects.

### Born Into Political Turmoil

Cabrera was born on April 22, 1929, in Gibara, Cuba, a small city on the northern coast of the country. His father, Guillermo Cabrera, and his mother, Zoila Infante, were founders of the local branch of the Communist Party. In 1932 Cabrera's father and uncle took part in a local uprising against the dictator **Gerardo Machado**. Machado had been elected president in 1924 but after taking office he ruled as a dictator. To crush the uprising in Gibara, Machado ordered the city bombed. A year later, Machado was forced out of office and **Fulgencio Batista** took control. Because of their communist involvement, Cabrera's parents were arrested and imprisoned.

After their release from prison, Cabrera's father was blacklisted. Unable to find employment, he moved his family to Havana in 1941. The family moved to various tenement rooms in the nation's capital city, settling in room 408 of the Zuleuta, of which Cabrera writes in his autobiographical novel *La Habera par un infante difuto* (*Infante's Inferno*). Though Cabrera refers to the Zuleuta as home, it, like each location they rented in Havana, was a room with access to communal kitchens, baths, and a courtyard.

Cabrera's father was employed in Havana by the Communist Party newspaper *Hoy* (*Today*), setting type and writing articles. Though Cabrera never joined the Communist Party, he was greatly influenced by his parents' political activities. Writers, artists, and influential members of the party, including Carlos Franqui, a leader in Fidel Castro's "26th of July Movement," and editor of the newspaper *Revolución,* frequently visited the family.

Cabrera's first story—"Aguas de recuerdo" ("Waters of Memory")—was published in June 1948 by *Bohemia.* It is the tale of a woman who, after her fisherman husband and sons are lost at sea, is reduced to memories as her sole possession. The fishing village depicted in the story was reminiscent of Gibara, while the thematic center of the story—the struggle to survive in poverty—was another facet with which Cabrera had firsthand familiarity. "The story tries to show how poverty and hunger reduce people to the level of animals. The stilted, artificial prose and melodrama are totally uncharacteristic of Cabrera Infante's mature style, but they show how the adolescent author attempted to capture the style then current in Cuban and Spanish-American literature," commented Alfred J. MacAdam in an essay on Cabrera in *Latin American Writers.*

This use of autobiographical elements in his fiction emerged as a pattern in much of Cabrera's work. His early exposure to political activism can thus be seen in a number of his stories. Though Cabrera never dedicated himself to the political cause that attracted his parents, he was not shy about speaking out against social injustice. In October 1952 *Bohemia* published another of his short stories. "Resaca" ("Undertow") brought him to the attention of a wider audience. It tells the story of two men who burn a sugar cane field. Shortly after this story was published, another story—"Balada de plomo y yerro" ("Ballad of Lead and Error")—caught the attention of Batista 's censors. Cabrera was jailed, fined, and forced to leave journalism school for two years because of his use of English obscenities in the story. To earn a living, Cabrera wrote movie reviews under the pseudonym G. Caín. Cabrera was quite interested in film, and had begun his career as a scriptwriter. In 1953 he married Marta Calvo.

### Politically Ostracized

Despite the punishment from the government authorities, Cabrera continued to comment on the social and political conditions in Cuba in the underground newspaper *Revolución.* When Batista 's regime was overthrown, Cabrera became editor of *Lunes,* the weekly literary supplement to *Revolución.* Cabrera fell out of political favor, however, and was sent to Belgium as cultural attaché in 1962. While in Belgium, a collection of Cabrera's short stories entitled *Así en la paz como en la guerra: Cuentos* was translated into French, Italian, and Polish. This collection, which contained material dating as far back as the late 1940s, garnered significant European attention.

Cabrera returned to Cuba in 1965 for his mother's funeral. Embittered that she had received insufficient care during her illness, and disillusioned by the changes that had taken place in Havana, he wrote a series of vignettes that eventually became *View of Dawn in the Tropics.* The government detained him in Havana. When they finally allowed him to return to Brussels at the end of 1965, he took with him his second wife, Miríam Gomez, and his two daughters from his first marriage, which had ended in divorce.

Cabrera and his family left Brussels quickly and took up residence in Madrid, Spain. Caught in political turmoil within Spain, and denounced as a traitor in Cuba, he took his family to London in 1966. In self-exile he reworked a manuscript that became his first novel. *Tres tristes tigres* (*Three Trapped Tigers*), which examined the lives of a group of friends partaking of the nightlife of pre-Castro Havana, received nearly universal critical acclaim. The novel established Cabrera "as the punmaster of Spanish-American literature," according to *New Republic* contributor Gregory Rabassa, and won the Biblioteca Breve Prize in 1964.

In 1968 Cabrera used the forum of *Primera Plana,* an Argentinean magazine, to denounce Fidel Castro and his regime. Reaction to his diatribe was swift. Cuban authorities condemned the author, while supporters of the Castro government were no less outraged. Such political turmoil, coupled with financial difficulties, took their toll on his mental and emotional health. He wrote the *Vanishing Point* screenplay for Twentieth Century-Fox and did some translation work, but was hospitalized in 1972. His recovery was a slow one, but by the end of the 1970s he had published two collections of essays—*O,* in 1975, and *Exorcismos de esti(l)o,* in 1976.

In 1979 Cabrera published *Infante's Inferno,* his autobiographical account of coming-of-age in Havana. The work received a mixed critical reception. *New York Review of Books* critic Michael Wood charged that Cabrera's book "unrepentedly mangles language" and simply didn't work, while Enrique Fernández commented in the *Voice Literary Supplement* that Cabrera employed "an everyday Cuban voice, unaffected, untrammeled [and] authentic." *Holy Smoke*—the first book Cabrera wrote in English—was published in 1985. It is an interesting, factual account of the history of the cigar and contains an anthology of famous smoking scenes from literature and film. In 1993 Cabrera published two works—*Mea Culpa* and *Writes of Passage. Mea Culpa* features a discourse on Cuban politics, as well as reminiscences about such Cuban friends as **Reinaldo Arenas**. *Writes of Passage* is a collection of 15 short stories originally published in Spanish in 1960 when Cabrera was struggling to

define his artistic voice. Detecting the artistic immaturity of many of the stories, Peter Mathews in *The Observer* asserted that the book was "innocuous-seeming while yofferenu read it, but gaining weight and poignancy when you think it over afterwards."

## SELECTED PUBLISHED WORKS:

*Así en la paz como en la guerra: Cuentos,* Havana, Revolución, 1960.
*Vista del amanacer en el trópico,* Barcelona, Seix Barral, 1965; translated by Suzanne Jill Levine as *View of Dawn in the Tropics,* Harper, 1978.
*Tres tristes tigres,* Barcelona, Seix Barral, 1967; translated by Donald Gardner, Suzanne Jill Levine, and the author as *Three Trapped Tigers,* Harper, 1971.
*Vanishing Point,* Twentieth Century-Fox, 1970.
*O,* Barcelona, Seix Barral, 1975.
*Exorcismos del esti(l)o,* Barcelona, Seix Barral, 1976.
*La Habana para un infante difunto,* Barcelona, Seix Barral; translated by Suzanne Jill Levine and the author as *Infante's Inferno,* Harper, 1984.
*Holy Smoke,* Harper, 1985.
*Mea Culpa,* Plaza & Janes, 1993; translated into English by the author and Kenneth Hall for Farrar, Straus, & Giroux, 1995.
*Writes of Passage,* translated by John Brookesmith, Peggy Boyars, and the author, Faber & Faber, 1993.

## SOURCES:

### Books

*Hispanic Writers,* edited by Bryan Ryan, Detroit, Gale, 1991.
*Latin American Writers,* edited by Carlos A. Solé, New York, Charles Scribner's Sons, 1989.

### Periodicals

*Booklist,* September 15, 1994, p. 119.
*Hispanic,* April 1995, p. 74.
*New Republic,* July 9, 1984.
*New York Review of Books,* December 16, 1971; June 28, 1984; May 8, 1986.
*The Observer,* October 10, 1993, p. 20.
*Publishers Weekly,* January 31, 1994.
*Voice Literary Supplement,* April 18, 1968; October 12, 1984; August 29, 1986.

*—Sketch by Lisa A. Wroble*

# Alberto P. Calderón
## 1920-
### Argentine American mathematician

Alberto Calderón's revolutionary influence turned the 1950s trend toward abstract mathematics back to the study of mathematics for practical applications in physics, geometry, calculus, as well many other branches of this field. His award-winning research in the area of integral operators is an example of his impact on contemporary mathematical analysis. Widely considered as one of this century's foremost mathematicians, Dr. Calderón's career spans more than 45 years, during which he has left behind many seminal works and ideas.

Calderón was born on September 14, 1920, in Mendoza, Argentina, a town at the foot of the Andes. His father was a descendant of notable nineteenth-century politicians and military officers and was a renowned medical doctor who helped found and organize the General Central Hospital of Mendoza.

After completing his secondary education in his hometown and in Zug, Switzerland, under Dr. Save Bercovici, who encouraged Calderón's interest in mathematics, he enrolled in the School of Engineering of the National University of Buenos Aires, from which he graduated in 1947. He soon became a student of Alberto González Domínguez and of the celebrated mathematician Antoni Zygmund, who was a visiting professor in Buenos Aires in 1948. He continued his mathematical studies at the University of Chicago with a Rockefeller Foundation fellowship, and received his Ph.D. there in 1950.

Calderón began his academic teaching career as an assistant to the Chair of electric circuit theory at the University of Buenos Aires in 1948, and after graduating in the United States, continued it as a visiting associate professor at Ohio State University from 1950 to 1953. Calderón was also a member of the Institute for Advanced Study in Princeton (1954–1955) and later served as an associate professor at the Massachusetts Institute of Technology (MIT) between 1955 and 1959. He then moved to the University of Chicago, where he served as professor of mathematics from 1959 to 1968, Louis Block professor of mathematics from 1968 to 1972, and chairman of the mathematics department from 1970 to 1972.

By that time, Calderón's prestige was well established in scientific circles, and his research in collaboration with his longtime mentor Zygmund had already been dubbed "the Chicago School of Analysis," also known today as "the Calderón-Zygmund School of Analysis." Their contribution, which profoundly affected modern mathematics, included reversing a predominant trend towards abstraction and turning back to basic questions of real and complex analysis. This work, completed in tandem with Zygmund, came to be known as "Calderón-Zygmund theory."

A landmark in Calderón's scientific career was his 1958 paper titled "Uniqueness of the Cauchy Problem for Partial Differential Equations," which the American Mathematical Society has called "a real watershed in the theory of singular integral operators, taking it beyond its traditional role in the study of elliptic equations." Two years later, he used the same method to build a complete theory of hyperbolic partial differential equations.

His theory of singular operators, which is used to estimate solutions to geometrical equations, contributed to link together several different branches of mathematics. It also had practical applications in many areas, including physics and aerodynamic engineering. This theory has dominated contemporary mathematics and has made important inroads in other scientific fields, including quantum physics. Although some authors have introduced and used the notion of pseudo-differential operator, which is a sum of compositions of powers of the Laplacian with singular integral operators with kernels which are infinitely differentiable off the diagonal, the original idea and basic applications remain credited to Calderón.

Calderón's extensive work has transformed contemporary mathematical analysis. In addition to his work with singular integral operators, he also did fundamental work in interpolation theory, and was responsible, together with R. Arens, for what is considered one of the best theorems in Banach Algebras. Calderón also put forth an approach to energy estimates that has been of fundamental importance in dozens of subsequent investigations, and has provided a general model for research in this area.

### A Brief Return Home

In 1971–1972, Calderón briefly returned to his home country to serve as professor and direct mathematical doctoral dissertation studies at his alma mater, the National University of Buenos Aires. He continued to encourage mathematics students from Latin America and the United States to pursue their doctoral degrees, in many instances directly sponsoring them. Some of his pupils, in turn, have become reputed mathematicians, as, for example, Robert T. Seeley, whose extension of the Calderón-Zygmund results to singular operators on manifolds became the foundation of the now-famous Atiyah-Singer index theorem.

After his stay in Argentina, Calderón returned to MIT as a professor of mathematics, and in 1975 he became University Professor, a special position, at the University of Chicago until his retirement in 1985. Between 1989 and 1992, he was a professor emeritus, with a post retirement appointment at that same institution. In 1979 he was awarded the Bôcher prize for a paper on the Cauchy integral on Lipschitz curves. In 1989 he shared the Mathematics Prize of the Wolf Foundation of Israel with his American colleague John W. Milnor. He received innumerable other honors around the world. The American Mathematical Society honored Calderón again with the prestigious Steele Prize (fundamental research paper category) in 1989, and President George Bush, in granting him the 1991 National Medal of Science, cited "his ground-breaking work on singular integral operators leading to their application to important problems in partial differential equations."

### Author and Lecturer

As an author, Calderón has published more than 75 scientific papers on various topics, from real variables to partial differential equations and singular integrals. A number of those papers were written in collaboration with his teacher Antoni Zygmund. Calderón has lectured in major cities the world over.

A member of the American Mathematical Society for over 40 years, Dr. Calderón has served as member-at-large of its Council (1965–1967) and in several of its committees. He has also been associate editor of various important scientific publications, such as the *Duke Mathematical Journal,* the *Journal of Functional Analysis* and others.

Dr. Calderón married in 1950. With Mabel Molinelli, his first wife who died in 1985, he had two children: María Josefina, who holds a doctorate in French literature from the University of Chicago, and Pablo Alberto, also a mathematician who studied in Buenos Aires and New York. In 1989 Calderón married again. His second wife, Dr. Alexandra Bellow, is also a distinguished mathematician and a professor of mathematics at Northwestern University in Evanston, near Chicago.

### SELECTED PUBLISHED WORKS:

"Uniqueness in the Cauchy Problem for Partial Differential Equations,"*American Journal of Mathematics,* 80, 1958, pp. 16–36.
"Lecture notes on pseudo-differential operators and elliptic boundary-value problems," *Instituto Argentino de Matemáticas,* Buenos Aires, 1976.

### SOURCES:

Atiyah, M. F. and Singer, I. M., "The Index of Elliptic Operators on Compact Manifolds," *Bulletin of the American Mathematical Society,* 69, 1963, pp. 442–53.
Beals, R. W., Coifman, R. R., and Jones, P. W., "Alberto Calderón Receives National Medal of Science," *Notices of the American Mathematical Society,* 39, No. 4, April 1992.
González Domínguez, Alberto, "Dr. Alberto P. Calderón—Premio Bocher 1979," *Ciencia e Investigación,* 34, November-December 1978, Buenos Aires, pp. 221–23.

*—Sketch by Rodolfo A. Windhausen*

# Pedro Calderón de la Barca
## 1600-1681
### Spanish dramatist

Pedro Calderón de la Barca was one of Spain's most important playwrights. He inherited the position left vacant by the death of **Lope de Vega** as the country's official playwright during the seventeenth century. Although he was not as prolific as his predecessor, Calderón wrote some 120 *comedias,* 80 *auto sacramentales,* and 20 minor theatrical works. He is remembered especially for his *comedias*—three-act plays in verse dealing principally with honor and romance—which have come to be known as "cloak and sword" plays. Calderón also used the stage to champion the cause of the Roman Catholic church in its fight against the Protestant Reformation and to praise the monarchy.

Calderón was born in Madrid on January 7, 1600, the second son and third child of seven children. His father was secretary to the treasury board under King Philip II. Both parents were devout Christians who educated their children in accordance with their elite social status. By some reports Calderón's father was a harsh, tyrannical man who ran an unhappy and strained household, causing grief that would later be reflected in some of Calderón's plays. During the first years of Calderón's life the Spanish court often changed location between Madrid—the site of the royal court—and Valladolid, a city to the northeast. As a result the Calderón family frequently shuttled between theses two cities, finally settling in Madrid in 1606. Calderón suffered his first tragedy in 1610 when his mother died in childbirth—Calderón's newborn sister died soon after. Like many prominent Spaniards, he enrolled in the Jesuits' college. After finishing his studies with the Jesuits he moved on to the University of Alcalá de Henares, where he studied scholastic theology and philosophy and seemed destined for a church career.

Calderón's father died suddenly in 1615. His testament—published by Narciso Alonso Cortés in 1915—offers numerous insights into the family's dynamics. It is here that the father's despotic character is revealed (although this authoritarianism may also be considered characteristic of the epoch). The father also declared his desire for young Calderón to persevere with his studies. Rather than completing his studies in Alcalá, Calderón decided to attend the University of Salamanca, possibly because he wished to study civil law, which was not taught at Alcalá.

By 1619 Calderón had written some verse in Salamanca, and in 1620 he wrote some poetry to celebrate the canonization of St. Isidro. When he was 24 he began an active career as a soldier and may even have been present at the Siege of Breda, the battle on which his 1625 play, *El Sito de Bredo* ("The Siege of Breda") is based. Although the length of his military service is unclear, by 1630 Calderón had established a reputation as an important playwright and even Lope de Vega recognized him as his successor.

### Became Spain's Chief Playwright

Lope de Vega was the father of the Spanish National Theater and creator of the Spanish *comedia*. When Lope de Vega died in 1635 the entire city of Madrid plunged into mourning for nine days. Although Calderón assumed Lope de Vega's place as the nation's premier playwright, the two were very different. Calderón's personal life was as discreet and proper as Lope de Vega's was irreverent and frantic. Although Calderón fathered a son during the 1640s, both mother and son died during that decade. Calderón took orders for the priesthood in 1651 and lived an exemplary life from that time. He lived discreetly and quietly and occupied his mind with philosophical and religious concepts.

As court dramatist Calderón wrote his plays for presentation at the newly constructed theater in the palace of the *Buen Retiro* in Madrid. This theater had been built in 1633. Its resources far surpassed those of the public stages (known as *corrales*) and it was capable of presenting spectacular productions. The court plays thus developed a distinct baroque quality combining drama with dancing, music, and visual effects. Through the use of visual effects the world of the mundane was left behind and the audience was transported to historical and mythological settings.

Calderón is also associated with the rise of opera in Spain; he wrote his first opera, *La púrpura de la rosa* ("The Purple of the Rose") in 1660. He also wrote *zarzuelas,* plays in two acts in which the dialogue alternates between speaking and singing. The first of his *zarzuelas, El jardín de Falerina* ("The Garden of Falerina") was written in 1648.

Lope de Vega may be said to represent the creation of Spanish national drama in all its freshness and youth whereas Calderón perfected the genre he inherited, giving it more maturity and depth. Calderón created dramas with complex interlocking patterns. *El pintor de su deshonra* ("The Painter of His Own Dishonor"), written about 1645, exemplifies his mastery of this style. Dominant symbols link characters and action with the effect of illuminating the theme.

Whereas the works of Lope de Vega were spontaneous and popular, those of Calderón were the result of a superior intellect and careful academic work. Calderón worked under the strong influence of two literary trends of the time, Gongorism and Conceptism. **Góngora** was the leading poet who developed an ornate and obscure style characterized by a highly Latin syntax, mythological illusion, and rhetorical devices such as archaic words, neologisms, and hyperbole. "Conceptism" refers to the use of plays on words and highly developed subtleties. Modern critics often place both Gongorism and Conceptism under the common heading of "Baroque". As much as Calderón drew on these two styles he employed them sparingly, fearing the complexity might alienate his audience. The modern reader of Calderón's work may need an annotated edition to explain the obscure mythological and historical allusions.

### Art and Christian Symbolism in *auto sacramentales*

Although Calderón's era and court position dictated that he write many *comedias*, Calderón also developed one-act religious plays known as *auto sacramentales,* written for open-air performance on the Feast of Corpus Christi. The plays—rather than employing personal characters—used allegorical figures such as Truth and Beauty to make abstract ideas accessible. Every major city in Spain staged a new *auto sacramental* annually and competed to present the finest one. Calderón provided Madrid with two *auto sacramentales* every year from 1651 to 1681. As Calderón aged, his *auto sacramentales* dealt with more theological problems and contained increasingly elaborate scenic effects.

Two of Calderón's most famous *auto sacramentales* are *Los encantos de la culpa* ("The Charms of Guilt") and *El gran teatro del mundo* ("The Great Stage, the World"). *Los encantos de la culpa* celebrates the rational order of human character, and *El gran teatro del mundo* praises self-control and social hierarchy, assigning meaning to human existence within the context of a divine plan. The key characters are the symbolic King, the Poor Man, the Rich Man, and the Laborer. They epitomize abstract spiritual qualities such as beauty and discretion. Each character must remember that his life is lived only to prepare for the after-life, and he must not place any faith in the pursuit of pleasure.

The doctrines in these plays accurately reflected those of the Catholic church, which was then fighting the Protestant Reformation of northern Europe. The Catholic Council of Trent marked the beginning of a Counter-Reformation. The Council focused on defense against Protestantism and Catholic revitalization and lasted 18 years. Calderón, as a staunch Catholic, supported his church. The visual arts were one of the most important weapons used in this fight due to their exemplary value for the masses.

### Enhanced the *Comedias*

Calderón is best-known for his secular dramas, among them, *El médico de su honra* ("The Surgeon of His Honor") in 1635, *El alcalde de Zalamea* ("The Mayor of Zalamea") around 1640, *La hija del aire* ("The Daughter of the Air") in 1653, and his most famous, *La vida es sueño* ("Life is a Dream") in 1635. The *comedia* was so popular during its time that people missed work to attend performances. Finally, morning performances were forbidden. The *comedias,* which provided a welcome escape for people who could not travel and who lived a life of drudgery, dealt with popular themes such as exaltation of the monarchy, defense of one's honor, and praise of the Catholic church. Other conventional aspects were love affairs and the clown (*gracioso*) who provided comic relief in even the most serious dramas. But under Calderón the *comedias* took on a deeper mood, with heros who grappled with such metaphysical and theological issues as fate and free will. *La vida es sueño* treats the idea that everything in this world is an illusion and that it is impossible for human beings to differentiate between dreams and reality. It also deals with the individual's ability to ultimately conquer himself, to take control and be master of his own destiny.

Based on Spanish history and legend, *El alcalde de Zalamea* proves that common people may possess both honor and dignity and that, when required, military authority should yield to civil authority. The key concept is the idea that all people possess honor. One manifestation is *Honor calderoniano* ("Calderonian honor"). This refers to a sense of honor that places a husband in a position where he must kill his wife if she has been maligned by scandal—even if she is innocent. In *El médico de su honra* the main character states: "A stain on one's honor, sir, is washed in blood." For many years Calderón was censured for writing plays that were deemed as condoning violence, but recently critics have begun to interpret them differently. It is now believed that Calderón's honor plays were intended to condemn the honor code and its absurd cruelty rather than condone it.

Plays such as *La vida es sueño* were appreciated by the German Romantics, who elevated Calderón to the position of a great philosopher. They believed that Calderón not only *presented* life's great problems in his plays but that he *resolved* them. The Romantics were undoubtedly attracted to Calderón's tendency to deal with metaphysical abstraction and spiritualism as well as his Catholicism. Calderón's philosophical plays, although filled with obscure baroque imagery, remain appealing in contemporary times. The problems of free will, the true nature of reality, and the purpose of life continue to attract audiences to his works.

## SELECTED PUBLISHED WORKS:

*Calderon de la Barca, Obras completas, comedias,* second edition, edited by Angel Valbuena Briones, [Madrid], 1960).
*Three Mythological Plays of Calderón,* edited by Pedro León and Hohn Warden, [Toronto], 1990.
*Six Plays of Calderón de la Barca,* edited by Edwin Honig, [New York], 1993.

## SOURCES:

### Books

Halkhoree, P., *Calderón de la Barca: El Alcalde de Zalamea,* London, Grant & Cutler, 1972.
Hesse, Everett W., *Calderón de la Barca,* New York, Twayne, 1967.
Hilborn, H. W. *A Chronology of the Plays of Don Pedro Calderón de la Barca,* [Toronto], 1938.
Maraniss, E. James, *On Calderon,* Columbia, University of Missouri Press, 1978.
Trench, Richard C., *Calderón: His Life and Genius with Specimens of His Plays,* New York, Redfield, 1856.

*—Sketch by Enrique Fernández*

# Héctor Camacho
## 1962-
### Puerto Rican professional boxer

Héctor "Macho" Camacho was born in Puerto Rico in 1962. He made his way into professional boxing and reigned as world champion in two different weight divisions. His flashy style and consid-

*Héctor Camacho*

erable talent place him among the most memorable fighters in the lighter weight classes during the 1980s.

Born in Bayamon, Puerto Rico, in 1967, Camacho fought his first professional fight in September 1980. Called "an exciting stick-and-move fighter" by *Sports Illustrated,* Camacho won 40 of his first 41 professional fights, claiming the World Boxing Council (WBC) and World Boxing Organization (WBO) lightweight world championships. Although the WBO does not have the recognition of most major boxing promoters or the participation of top fighters, the WBC world championship titles carry as much clout as any accomplishment in the sport. By defeating José Luis Ramirez in a memorable bout in 1985 for the WBC lightweight title, Camacho moved to the top of his profession.

### Became Super Lightweight Champion

By 1987 Camacho could no longer make the 137-pound weight limit for the lightweight division, so he became a super lightweight. In his new division, Camacho had more difficulty finding big fights, and as he aged, he found he could no longer rely on the speed that had once characterized his fighting style. Between 1985 and 1994, Camacho fought only seven times. In 1992 *Sports Illustrated* called Camacho a "shameless runner and hugger," which refers to a fighter who avoids exchanging blows with his opponent by either holding on to the man's body or constantly moving away from him. Yet, in March 1989, Camacho defeated former World Boxing Association (WBA) lightweight champion Ray "Boom Boom" Mancini for the lightly regarded WBO super lightweight championship; and in 1992 his fight with Julio Cesar Chávez commanded worldwide attention and a personal payday of $3 million.

Camacho remains a memorable figure for many boxing fans because of the often outlandish costumes he wore into the ring. Appearing as a matador, "Puerto Rican Superman," or other variations of "The Macho Man," Camacho never settled for conventional athletic equipment. He even traded boxing trunks for a sequined gold skirt on occasion.

Camacho's personal life has often made headlines. In an interview with the *Chicago Tribune,* Camacho estimated that he has spent about $1.5 million in legal fees over the course of his career. In 1988 Camacho faced arrest on drug and assault charges, and in 1993 faced accusations—of which he was found innocent—of gun trafficking to Puerto Rico. In the same year Camacho settled out of court with a man who claimed Camacho had assaulted him. Camacho said, "A guy accused me last year [1993] of breaking his leg in a club. We had a disagreement, and it got a little too rough and nasty." According to Camacho, the two incidents in 1993 alone cost him $600,000.

Camacho has tried in recent years to downplay his "Macho Man" image now preferring simply, "Mr. Camacho." At the age of 32, Camacho insisted that it was "time to take my life out of fifth gear and down to third." Camacho has never married, but he has three children. He lives in San Juan with his longtime girlfriend Amy Torres and their two children: Macho Christian Camacho, born in 1992, and Justin Camacho, born in 1990. He also has a son from a previous relationship, Hector, who has begun his own career as a boxer. Though Camacho claimed not to miss the glamour of the "Macho Man" days, he confessed to a certain nostalgia for times when he "showed up in my Macho Man clothes ... [and] places went crazy." Camacho's professional record is 45 wins, 21 by knockout, and three losses. Camacho has also pursued ambitions in show business. Though he admitted, "I'm no Sinatra or Michael Jackson," Camacho has recorded music. He once hired well-known rock musician Martha Davis and her group the Motels as a personal voice coach.

### SOURCES:

*Chicago Tribune,* June 9, 19, Section 4, p. 3.
*Sports Illustrated,* May 23, 1988, p. 24; September 21, 1992, p. 28.

—*Sketch by James McCarthy*

# Pedro Albizu Campos
## 1891-1965
### Puerto Rican revolutionary leader

Pedro Albizu Campos, described by contemporaries and historians alike as an intelligent and eloquent revolutionary figure, was one of the leaders in the fight to create a sovereign and independent republic of Puerto Rico. His father, Don Alejandro Albizu Romero "El Vizcaino," was a Basque merchant. His mother, Juliana Campos, was a mestiza of Spanish, Indian, and African heritage. Albizu Campos's parents were not married when he was born on September 12, 1891, in the district of Mochuelo Abajo. Albizu Campos lived in Ponce, where he received his early education. He received a scholarship from the Aurora Lodge of Ponce after graduating from high school and went to college in the United States at the University of Vermont. An exceptional student, Albizu Campos received his doctorate in sciences and, in 1913, received a scholarship and a job at Harvard University. He worked as a translator, assisted students in preparing for examinations, and wrote for the *Christian Science Monitor.*

Albizu Campos joined the U.S. Army during World War I in hopes of securing an assignment to the Puerto Rican Expeditionary Forces. Instead, the military placed him in a "Negro" battalion as a private and later moved him to the "Las Casas" encampment for cadets in Massachusetts. Albizu Campos was an aide to General Cristna when the armistice was signed. At that point he received a letter from United States President Woodrow Wilson directing him to represent Harvard in Paris at a European Congress. He was put on board a U.S. warship for passage. When the ship docked at a port in the southern United States, though, Albizu Campos grew outraged at the mistreatment of black people that he witnessed. Instead of proceeding on to the congress in Paris, he walked off the ship.

Albizu Campos returned to Harvard in 1918 to study law after his discharge from the army as a first lieutenant. He mowed lawns in order to supplement his income while attending Harvard. On campus, Albizu Campos was active in two student movements to support the independence of Ireland and India. He was also the president of the Cosmopolitan Club, an organization that worked with foreign students. His involvement in these international issues continued to grow during his stay at Harvard. At one point, he organized a group of professors and students to discuss Irish independence. Albizu Campos proceeded to offer his own heartfelt appeal for the independence of Ireland.

Two Catholic priests at Harvard—Father Ryan and Father Luis —proved to be a significant influence on Albizu Campos. Theosophy and Rosicrucianism were the predominant religious practices on the islands of his birth, but he converted to Catholicism while he was at Harvard. He also met his wife, Laura Meneses, at Harvard. She was a Quechua Indian from Peru who was studying at Radcliffe. Meneses had graduated from the Universidad de San Marcos in Lima, Peru, with a doctorate in natural science. Introduced to each other through a friend, Albizu Campos insisted that she have lunch with him. She refused, but he persisted until she relented. After three consecutive days of lunching together, he proposed to her.

Albizu Campos received several offers to work in the United States. He was invited to return to the University of Vermont to study and lecture. After one of his lectures, he was offered a job traveling the United States lecturing for $200 a month with all of his expenses paid by a private company. A religious organization offered him $15,000 a year to head a Spanish American division. He was also offered a position in the Diplomatic Corp of the United States working with the Border Commission. Still another opportunity arose when a position as an assistant in the Supreme Court of the United States at $500 a week was tendered. But Albizu Campos declined all the offers. He received his degree in law and returned to Puerto Rico in 1921.

All during his time in the United States, Albizu Campos had grown more certain that his mission in life was to fight for the independence of Puerto Rico. Eager to acquire all the knowledge he could for his life's work, he had left the United States with a stunning array of academic accomplishments in a diverse number of fields of study that included philosophy, science, art, civil engineering, industrial chemicals, and law. His fiancé continued her education as well, attending the Marine Biology Laboratory of Woods Hole in Massachusetts on a scholarship.

In July 1922 Meneses went to Puerto Rico and married Albizu Campos. She returned to Harvard to complete her studies but became ill and Albizu Campos traveled to New York to take his wife back to Puerto Rico. They lived in a poor area of La Cantera in Ponce. Although he was offered a position as judge of Yauco, he declined and practiced private law working with the poor. Many of his cases involved anti-American activity. As his law practice became more renowned, he and his wife had three children, Pedro, Laura, and Rosa Emilia. They continued to live among the poor although they could have been quite wealthy. His wife stood beside him and supported his ideals. They both declined teaching positions at the university because of the political regime.

## Joins Nationalist Party

When Albizu Campos returned to Puerto Rico, he was 30 years old. He joined a political party, the Partido Union de Puerto Rico ("Puerto Rican Unity Party"). When the Union Party joined with the island Republican Party, they eliminated the fight for Puerto Rican freedom from their agenda. Albizu thus quit the Union Party and joined the Partido Nacionalista ("Nationalist Party"), which formed in 1912 because of the desire to liberate Puerto Rico. Politically, the Nationalist Party was not very effective. Albizu Campos began writing for the party's weekly newspaper, *El Nacionalista de Ponce.* Unknown at the time to many of his people, Albizu Campos soon became a voice for the cause of freedom.

In the elections of 1925, Albizu Campos was appointed vice president of the party under the president, Federico Acosta Velarde. Albizu Campos traveled throughout Latin America to get support from other countries for the freedom of Puerto Rico. His wife took the children to live in Peru with her parents while Albizu Campos used the money they had saved to journey on behalf of the Nationalist Party for the next two and a half years.

Albizu Campos received support from two of the Dominican Republic's exceptional intellectuals, Federico Henriquez Carvajal and Americo Lugo. The Dominican Republic, which had recently become independent, proved to be fertile ground for his efforts. Albizu Campos founded the Pro-Independencia Puertorriquena ("For the Independence of Puerto Rico") in the Dominican Republic and built a significant support group there. He traveled to Haiti, still occupied by Americans, where he risked his life to talk to the nationalist leaders there. The story of his visit to that country is now a part of Haitian history. He also made use of his column in *El Nacionalista de Puerto Rico,* speaking out in defense of freedom for Haiti, the Dominican Republic, and Nicaragua. He went to Cuba and spoke out against the dictatorship of General **Gerardo Machado.** He was forced to leave the country. He also traveled to Panama, Venezuela, and Mexico during his tour.

In 1929 Albizu Campos journeyed to Peru. He gathered his family and traveled back to Puerto Rico in early 1930. When they arrived in Puerto Rico, he found that the Nationalist Party had weakened while he was away. He immediately began reorganizing the party. Albizu Campos was elected president of the Nationalist Party in May 1930 at a general assembly at the Ateneo Puertorriqueno.

Unyielding in his fight for freedom, Albizu Campos instituted a policy of non-cooperation with the regime. At an assembly held on December 17, 1932, the Nationalist Party organized an Army of Liberation. The members, who were also called Cadets of the Republic, wore black shirts and white pants to represent the mourning of Puerto Rico's colonial rule. The Cuerpo de Enfermeras ("Nurses' Corps")—a female counterpart to the Army of Liberation—was organized at the same time.

Puerto Rico suffered economically during the 1930s. Destructive hurricanes had destroyed crops and a change in power had contributed to poor economic conditions on the islands. In addition, the repercussions of the Great Depression in the United States impacted Puerto Rico as well. Such conditions contributed to the emergence of Albizu Campos as one of the most powerful figures in Puerto Rico in the 1930s. He won support of the working people, intellectuals, and students. With such a broad base of support, Albizu Campos's authority continued to grow. One of his campaigns in 1933—a strike against gasoline consumers—immobilized the island. The large sugar plantation workers went to Albizu Campos and asked him to lead them in a strike. He helped them in a successful strike but he told them to get their own labor leaders. He did not want to lead them. Many of his supporters felt that he was in danger of being killed.

Albizu Campos was arrested many times during his career for his activities. He was described as an eloquent speaker and a brilliant intellectual and a man who would never compromise his values. At one point the Chief of Police, Colonel Francis Riggs, approached Albizu Campos and offered the party $150,000 while he acted as a party sympathizer. Albizu Campos considered it a bribery attempt and avoided the money. Afterwards the police restrained the Nationalist Party at all of their demonstrations. In addition, the attitude of the United States against the Nationalists grew increasingly harsh.

## Nationalists Declare War on Regime

The Nationalists declared war on the Puerto Rican regime after several members were killed by the police at a public meeting. The declaration, however, divided the party, for while some of the members wanted to use violent tactics for independence, others argued that peaceful means were preferable. A new party was organized in 1934 by the members that wanted to use legal means to fight for independence. It was named Partido Independentista Puertorriqueno ("Puerto Rican Independence Party").

Albizu Campos and his family moved to Aguas Buenas, where guards assigned to protect the revolutionary leader were on duty around-the-clock. In 1936 the police chief Riggs was assassinated by two Nationalists who were subsequently arrested and murdered at police headquarters. Albizu Campos spoke out against Riggs at the funeral for the slain Nationalist Party members. He argued that the police force had perpetuated crimes in Puerto Rico and dismissed

Riggs as a tyrant who had sanctioned cold-blooded murder by police forces.

In 1937 Albizu Campos was imprisoned by authorities. He was later transferred to a facility in Atlanta, Georgia, where he stayed until 1943. He was accused of being a Communist by some but it has been proven that his party had no links with the Communist Party. In 1950 the Nationalists were warned about a plot to assassinate its leaders. The party responded by organizing a movement called the Nationalist Rebellion of 1950. Several coups were planned for October 30 in different towns on the island.

Albizu Campos was at his home—which was also the party's main headquarters—on October 30, 1950. Police surrounded his home and fired machine guns and artillery into the house. One woman was injured in the barrage. When two other people carried her out they were arrested. The police continued to fire upon the house until November 2, when they fired tear gas into the home. Albizu Campos and Alvero Rivera Walker were the only two left in the house. By the time the conflicts across Puerto Rico had ended, more than 1,000 men and women had been arrested.

Other allegations against Albizu Campos surfaced at this time as well. Two Nationalists living in New York went to Washington D.C. on November 1 and tried to assassinate President Harry S Truman. Albizu Campos was charged with inciting the would-be assassins. He almost died in a San Juan prison because of the lack of food and ventilation in his cell. After a period of recuperation he was brought to trial. He was sentenced to 53 years in jail at the State Prison of Puerto Rico.

The Nationalist Party was declared a subversive organization by the United States but the party received support from Spanish American and European countries. Albizu Campos sent messages out of prison that he had been burned all over his body and that he was attacked day and night. The U.S. Justice Department charged that he was suffering from senile dementia praecox and declared him insane. He was pardoned on September 28, 1953, by Governor Munoz Marin. Albizu Campos refused the pardon because his comrades were not pardoned but they released him anyway. A doctor who attended the bedridden revolutionary leader after his release stated that the burns he had were caused by radiation.

In 1954 several Nationalist Party members from New York fired shots in the U.S. House of Representatives, wounding five congressmen. Reaction to the attack was swift. Albizu Campos's house was once again raided by police and he was taken to jail after being overcome by tear gas. His pardon was revoked. In 1956 he became ill with an embolism, then suffered a cerebral thrombosis. His wife, who was living in Mexico at the time, was denied a visa to visit her husband, although her children were able to see him. When he was released from the hospital, Albizu Campos was taken back to prison, although his right side remained paralyzed as a result of the stroke. In 1961 supporters from around the world held rallies in Albizu Campos's honor on the occasion of his 70th birthday. His health became worse in 1964. With imminent death approaching, he was pardoned a second time under pressure from many countries and was released from incarceration. Four months after his release, on April 21, 1965, Albizu Campos died in Hato Rey, Puerto Rico.

## SOURCES:

Ribes Tovar, Federico, *Albizu Campos: Puerto Rican Revolry,* translated by Anthony Rawlings, New York, Plus Ultra Educational Publishers, Inc., 1971.

—*Sketch by Phyllis Noah*

# Nash Candelaria
## 1928-
### Hispanic American novelist and short story writer

Although he spent much of his career as a marketing writer, publicist, and account executive for a variety of scientific corporations, Nash Candelaria is best known for a series of historical novels which explore the lives and ancestry of a Chicano family in New Mexico. Born and raised in "Anglo" California, Candelaria nonetheless felt a greater affinity for the New Mexico home of his parents and ancestors. This combination of history, ethnicity, and place is an important feature of Candelaria's fiction. Although his novels and short stories focus on Chicano life and culture, they are written in English and address a wide readership.

Candelaria was born in Los Angeles on May 7, 1928, the son of Ignacio N. Candelaria, a railway mail clerk, and Flora Rivera Candelaria. Both his parents were native New Mexicans, and his younger sister was born in Albuquerque. Candelaria's family genealogy—which informs much of his interest in New Mexican history—can be traced on his father's side to 1706 and the founding of Albuquerque. Throughout Candelaria's childhood his parents returned frequently to their extended family in New Mexico. At such

*Nash Candelaria*

times, Candelaria related to Bruce-Novoa in an interview published in *De Colores,* he found himself "between two cultures," understanding Spanish but not speaking it, yet feeling a close connection to his Chicano roots.

A bright student, Candelaria showed an early gift for writing, winning a prize for a wartime bond publicity slogan. But, at the University of California in Los Angeles, Candelaria studied chemistry. His first employment following graduation in 1948 was as a chemist in Glendale, California. After a year, Candelaria made a significant career change to combine his writing with his scientific training, taking up the first of many positions which enabled him to apply and develop his writing skills in a professional environment.

From 1952 to 1953, during the Korean conflict, Candelaria served in the U.S. Air Force, becoming a second lieutenant. While in the military he wrote his first novel and acquired the confidence to continue writing. Although Candelaria turned down an opportunity to attend the University of Iowa Writers Workshop, he took night classes to improve his writing skills and continued to work as a business writer. On November 27, 1955, Candelaria married Doranne Godwin, a fashion designer; they had two sons: David Luis, and Alex Miguel.

### Published First Novel Himself

Candelaria wrote seven novels in his spare time but failed to find a publisher. These apprentice pieces included two science fiction novels and another he described as "a pseudo-Hemingway mishmash." Convinced, despite some encouraging notices from editors, that his work would not otherwise see print, he published *Memories of the Alhambra* (1977) himself. This novel, beginning the saga of the Rafa family, received wide critical acclaim. In one review, Carlota Cárdenas de Dwyer noted that it "dramatizes the painful and apparently insoluble dilemma of the New Mexican Hispano," a point confirmed by Candelaria in the Bruce-Novoa interview. Candelaria claimed that the Rafa saga grew from a desire to "impart" to his sons "something of their Hispano-Indian background" as he began to realize "there was very much to be proud of" in Chicano history.

*Memories of the Alhambra* concerns the search by an alienated New Mexican, José Rafa, Sr., for his cultural identity. Through José's misguided pilgrimage to Mexico and Spain in search of his European past and his rejection of his mestizo origins, Candelaria explores the complex intersections of history, myth, and genealogy in Chicano culture. These issues are developed in the second novel of the Rafa family, the award-winning *Not by the Sword* (1982), which is set during the years of the Mexican War with the United States (1846 to 1848) and the third, *Inheritance of Strangers* (1985), which covers the aftermath of the war and the power struggle between Hispanos and Anglos. Candelaria continued his exploration of the links between family and history in New Mexico with *Leonor Park* (1991).

### SELECTED PUBLISHED WORKS:

*Memories of the Alhambra,* Palo Alto, Cíbola, 1977.
*Not by the Sword,* Ypsilanti, Bilingual/Editorial Bilingüe, 1982.
*The Inheritance of Strangers,* Binghampton, Bilingual/Editorial Bilingüe, 1985.
*The Day the Cisco Kid Shot John Wayne,* Tempe, Bilingual/Editorial Bilingüe, 1988.
*Leonor Park,* Tempe, Bilingual/Editorial Bilingüe, 1991.

### SOURCES:

**Books**

*Chicano Literature, a Reference Guide,* edited by Julio A. Martínez and Francisco A. Lomelí, Greenwood Press, 1985.
*Dictionary of Literary Biography,* Vol. 82: *Chicano Writers, First Series,* edited by Francisco A. Lomelí and Carl R. Shirley, Gale, 1989, pp. 68–73.
*Hispanic Writers,* Gale, 1991, pp. 114–115.

**Periodicals**

*De Colores,* 1980, pp. 102–110, 115–129,
    130–132.
*Plural,* August 1987, pp. 41–47.
*Western American Literature,* Summer 1978, p.
    191.

—*Sketch by Simon Dixon*

# Jose Canseco
## 1964-
### Cuban American professional baseball player

*Jose Canseco*

Jose Canseco is the only baseball player in history to have hit 40 home runs and stolen 40 bases in a single season. Blessed with remarkable speed to go along with his powerful six-foot-three, 240-pound frame, the former American League rookie of the year and most valuable player is widely regarded as one of the most gifted athletes in professional sports. After amassing 209 homers in his first six seasons with the Oakland A's, Canseco was hampered by injuries to his back and throwing arm that have at times lowered his output. After every set back, though, he came back to record strong numbers.

Sporting a knack for controversy, Canseco is nearly as famous for his off-the-field antics as his Herculean build and powerful swing. "A lot of people say I'm a spoiled brat," he once told *Sport* magazine's Ron Kroichick when questioned about his arrests for hand-gun possession and excessive speeding. "But I'm willing to take risks."

Jose Canseco, Jr. and his fraternal twin brother, Osvaldo ("Ozzie"), were born in Regla, a suburb of Havana, Cuba, on July 2, 1964, to Jose Canseco, Sr. and his wife, Barbara (Capaz) Canseco. A descendent of one of the Havana area's most prominent families, the elder Canseco—who has kept up the tradition of giving his sons five dollars for every home run they hit—once held a management position with a U.S. petroleum company. Following the Communist revolution in 1959, however, he lost his job and his house and was forced to support his family by giving English lessons.

In December of 1965, the Cancesos were given permission to leave Cuba and immigrated to the United States, settling with a relative who lived just outside Miami in Opa-Locka, Florida. Having arrived with less than $50 to his name, Jose Canseco, Sr. provided for his wife, daughter, and two sons by working a variety of menial jobs, before climbing his way up to a regional manager position for Amoco Oil.

As a child, Jose, Jr. was encouraged by his parents to succeed in the classroom rather than on the athletic field. "What I did in school was what mattered to my parents," he told *Sports Illustrated's* Peter Gammons. Although Canseco played soccer and basketball as a child, he did not pick up his first baseball until he was 13, and he failed to make the Coral Park High School varsity team until his senior year.

Once Canseco was given a chance to demonstrate his talent, though, the then-six-foot-three, 170-pound third baseman hit .400, drawing scholarship offers from several college coaches and the attention of Camilo Pascual, a local scout for the Oakland A's, who convinced the organization to make him a 15th-round selection in the 1982 draft.

### Begins Professional Career

Canseco began his professional career with an A's Rookie League team in Miami, hitting just .111 before being shipped to another Rookie team in Idaho, where he hit .263 over the course of 28 games. After another season of mild improvement in Class A ball—14 home runs in 285 at-bats—and more work on his hitting and fielding skills in the A's Arizona Instuctional League, Canseco began a weight training program that would transform him into one of the most powerful hitters in the game.

After taking off one month to recover from the tragedy of his mother's death in April of 1984, a psychologically stronger Canseco came back to lead his California Class A team in home runs and runs batted in. During the off-season, he intensified his efforts in the weight room, adding 30 pounds of muscle before reporting to spring training.

In what would be his last year of apprenticeship in the minor leagues, Canseco hit well over .300 and hit 36 home runs, while splitting his time between a Huntsville, Alabama Class-AA team and a Tacoma, Washington Class-AAA team. In addition to winning the *Sporting News* minor-league player of the year award, Canseco became the first player in 26 years to hit a ball out of Tacoma's Cheney Stadium.

### Joins Major League

In September of that season, Canseco received the call from the Oakland A's and made his first major league appearance, striking out as a pinch hitter in a game with the Baltimore Orioles. It would not, however, take Canseco long to make his mark: in 29 games he hit .302, with 13 RBI's and five home runs—including a mammoth blast onto the roof of the Chicago White Sox's Comiskey Park.

Billed as "The Natural" after the popular Robert Redford baseball movie, Canseco dazzled spectators with 500-foot home run blasts in spring training, raising the expectations of Oakland fans. He did not disappoint them. At midseason, he led the American League in home runs and RBIs and was selected to his first All-Star team; by season's end he had tallied 33 home runs and 117 RBIs, and he was named the American League's rookie of the year. But Canseco also struck out a rookie record 175 times.

After a solid sophomore season in which he improved his batting average nearly 20 points while maintaining his home run power, Canseco boldly predicted that he would hit 40 home runs and steal 40 bases during the 1988 season—not knowing that the extraordinary feat of strength and speed was without precedent. While Canseco's bravado drew criticism from some sportswriters, he fulfilled his promise on September 23 and finished the season with a major-league leading 42 homers and 124 RBIs, 40 stolen bases, a .307 batting average, and 120 runs scored.

The American League most valuable player and Associated Press player of the year also led his team to a league-leading 104 wins. Behind the strength of Canseco's three home runs and .313 batting average, the A's went on to sweep Boston in the championship series. Canseco's hitting streak continued with a grand slam in the first game of the World Series against the Los Angeles Dodgers, but the Dodgers, on the strength of Kirk Gibson's dramatic ninth-inning pinch-hit home run, won the game and went on to take the series.

Canseco's record-breaking numbers on the field resulted in a new $1.64 million contract—more than three-and-one-half times his 1988 salary. The league's biggest star was reprimanded, however, for his off-season behavior, which included arrests in Miami, for driving 125 miles per hour in his Jaguar, and in San Fransisco, for carrying a semiautomatic pistol in his car while on a college campus.

Canseco was also hampered by a spring-training injury to his wrist that forced him to miss the first 88 games of the season. Once his injury healed, though, it did not take him long to return to All-Star form: he homered five times in his first nine games and finished the season with 17 home runs and 65 RBIs in just 65 games, while helping the A's to win their second consecutive division title.

During the championship series, in which the A's defeated the Toronto Blue Jays in four games, Canseco blasted one of the longest home runs in league history—an estimated 540-foot shot into the fifth deck of Toronto's Skydome stadium. Canseco turned in another strong performance in the World Series, leading the A's to victory over the San Fransisco Giants with a .357 average.

The next year the A's found themselves in their third straight World Series. While battling a series of injuries that caused him to miss 31 games and dealing with the pressures that accompanied a new five-year, $23.5 million contract—the most lucrative in baseball history at that time—Canseco managed to finish the regular season among the league leaders in home runs and RBIs. Canseco performed poorly in post-season play, however, as the heavily favored A's lost the World Series to the Cincinatti Reds in just four games.

Benched by manager Tony LaRussa for failing to catch a fly ball in the second game of the series, the multi-millionaire drew criticism from fans and teammates as well for blaming his sub-par play on his ailing back. But Canseco rebounded strongly in 1991 with one of his finest seasons, recording a career-high 44 home runs, 122 RBIs, and 115 runs scored. For the first time in four years, however, the A's failed to win their division. Midway through the next season, the organization ended its ten-year relationship with the slugger, trading him to the Texas Rangers for three-time All-Star right fielder Ruben Sierra and two pitchers.

In June of 1993, Canseco suffered the most serious injury of his career, tearing a ligament in his right elbow during a one-inning relief pitching appearance. After a successful rehabilitation program—and the formal ending of his much-publicized 1988 marriage to former Miss Miami, Esther Haddad—he came back to hit 31 home runs and 90 RBIs in just 111 games during the strike-shortened 1994 season. In December of that same year, Canseco was traded once again: hoping to add right-handed power to their lineup, the Boston Red Sox sent outfielder Otis Nixon and a minor league third baseman to the Rangers in exchange for the home run specialist.

Canseco has the potential—if he stays healthy—to finish his career as one of the game's all-time leading home run hitters. Meanwhile, Canseco may one day be remembered for his something else—his charitable endeavors, including a visit to and the delivery of ten tons of toys to the children of the Guantanamo Bay Cuban refugee camp in October of 1994. Perhaps the early assessments of his character may have been premature.

## SOURCES:

### Books

*Current Biography Yearbook, 1991,* New York: Wilson, 1991.

### Periodicals

*Dallas Morning News,* December 6, 1992; June 29, 1993; October 10, 1994.
*Gentleman's Quarterly,* May 1989, pp. 224–229.
*Indianapolis Star,* December 11, 1994.
*New York Times,,* December 8, 1994, p. B8.
*San Jose Mercury News,* September 2, 1992.
*Sport,* April 1992, pp. 20–24.
*Sports Illustrated,* October 2, 1989; pp.72-79; February 11, 1991, p. 208; March 14, 1994, pp. 38–40.

*—Sketch by Jason Gallman*

*Cantinflas*

# Cantinflas
## 1911-1993
### Mexican comedian and philanthropist

The comic actor Cantinflas was one of Latin America's most popular cinematic figures. A gifted physical comedian, Cantinflas appeared in 49 films over the course of a half-century of entertaining. His long career began in 1930 as a performer in the vaudevillian *carpa,* the itinerant tent shows that toured the Mexican countryside. He was a clown, a song-and-dance man, an acrobat. Indeed, the comedi-an was widely known in Mexico before he ever appeared on screen. Always the bedraggled underdog, Cantinflas's performance trademark was a disjointed and garbled patter. *Collier's* described it in 1942 as "madcap gibberish delivered in a solemn manner and made up of double-talk, innuendos, unfinished ideas followed by equally incomplete ones, and words nonexistent or mispronounced. His long speeches are usually of this type, ad-libbed in the W.C. Fields manner, but his repartee makes sense and is sharp."

Cantinflas was born **Mario Moreno** on August 12, 1911, in Mexico City, Mexico. The sixth of 12 sons and three daughters of José and María (Guizar) Moreno, Mexico's most famous clown grew up in a poor but respectable neighborhood. Although young Mario attended good schools, beginning with Bartolomé de las Casas School, he found that the streets stirred his imagination far more than educational institutions. He won several street contests with his *valero* (a ball-and-stick toy) and was highly skilled at shooting marbles. The streets taught him the skills he would need as a *carpa* performer. He found dancing tutors in his teenage years as well, and became expert at the fox trot, the tango, and the Charleston.

At the age of 15 Cantinflas enrolled in the national agricultural school at Chapingo, but he did not complete his coursework. Nine months into the course, he ran away to Jalapa, where he joined the *carpa* as a dancer. Raoul Vilada wrote in *Americas* that Cantinflas's "childhood heroes were those U.S. film actors of the twenties who could do everything—

ride horseback, drive a car, handle a motorcycle, fly a plane, swim, deep-sea dive." He eventually learned to do all these things, and learned to bullfight as well.

Cantinflas did not achieve the instant success he had hoped for, and he returned home briefly. He soon left again, joining the Campañia Novel in Tacámbaro as a dancer, where he was compensated with a dollar a day. Not satisfied with the pay, he deserted the tent show for a time and pursued amateur boxing. He was lured back to the Campañia Novel with a raise to three dollars a day.

### Stage Fright Launches Career

The *carpa* audiences consisted of soldiers, peasants, and laborers who paid between one and three cents' admission to be entertained with drama, comedy, and acrobatics. Audiences were typically rowdy and unrestrained, and the young comedian was particularly adept at making them laugh, and handled the hecklers with ease.

While still with the Campañia Novel, he was asked to fill in for a sick announcer. Used to doing memorized pieces, he was stricken with stage fright. Vilada described the scene in *Americas:* "He found himself unable to put two sentences together. Words tumbled out, right words, wrong words; he suppressed verbs, created adjectives." The audience loved it and screamed with laughter. Vilada continues, "Someone in the audience shouted 'Cállate (shut up), Cantinflas.'" Thus, his nonsensical name was born. Moreno adopted the name and made the "language" produced by stage fright his trademark. His fame spread to the point that variations of his name were introduced into the language: "cantinflear" meant to talk voluminously but incomprehensibly, while "cantinflesque" emerged as a word used to describe disjointed speech.

In 1937 Cantinflas married Valentina Subareff, who performed in a *carpa* owned by her father. Her parents were emigreés who had been famous Russian circus performers. By 1938 Cantinflas was working for the Folies-Bergè in Mexico City for five dollars a day. He was discovered by Santiago Reachi, owner of an advertising agency. Reachi, recognizing Cantinflas's widespread popularity among the country's rank and file, cast him in a film short advertising cab-over-engine trucks. The short film proved enormously popular, and Reachi was inundated with requests by theatre owners for other films. Encouraged by this reaction to Cantinflas on film, Reachi produced two full-length films—*Ahí Está el Detalle (Here's the Point)* in 1940 and *Ni Sangre Ni Arena (Neither Blood nor Sand)* in 1941—that made box-office history in Mexico and throughout Latin America, breaking all previously-held records. Given his talent for entertaining, the *New York Times* pronounced that "Cantinflas' emergence as a top ranking screen star was as inevitable as death and taxes."

Other popular Cantinflas films followed in quick succession, including *El Gendarme Desconocido (The Unknown Cop)*, *Los Tres Mosqueteros (The Three Musketeros)*, and *Romeo y Julieta (Romeo and Juliet)*, among many others. Based on these successes, rumors of his imminent debut in an American film were rampant. While he negotiated with Columbia and MGM, he did not appear in an American film until Michael Anderson's *Around the World in Eighty Days* appeared in 1956. He gained international notice—including a Golden Globe award—for his role in that film as Passepartout, Phileas Fogg's valet. His only other American film was *Pepe* (1960), in which he had the title role.

### Mexico's Charlie Chaplin

Cantinflas was often compared to Charlie Chaplin, the famous American film comedian. Chaplin himself, after seeing *Neither Blood Nor Sand,* called Cantinflas the greatest comedian alive. In comparing Cantinflas's style to that of Chaplin, George Creel wrote in *Collier's* that, "like Chaplin, . . . [he] is a master pantomimist, using eyes, hands and legs with the same exquisite sense of timing. Many of his scenes are played without a spoken word. Like Charlie, too, he never varies his character, always playing the down-and-out cargador, or public porter, who blunders into every variety of incredible complication, only to pull out in the last reel by virtue of gay impudence and a beguiling grin."

Although many called Cantinflas Mexico's Charlie Chaplin, others drew a finer distinction. Creel argued, "Here and there . . . the Mexican comic has the edge on Chaplin, for in addition to being a magician of parts, like Chaplin, he is an athlete extraordinary, and has a voice with as many stops as an organ. According to his own modest confession, he can crack his vocal cords like a whip." The *New York Times* suggested that Cantinflas wielded "an even sharper satirical edge" than Chaplin, while *Americas* contended that "unlike Chaplin, the actor of frustration, Cantinflas is the actor of triumph. In his compensation mechanism, he pretends always to come out on top of his interlocutor, leaving him completely deflated. In everything he tries he triumphs: as a doctor, a flyer, a shoemaker."

Cantinflas's film roles soon made him a millionaire, and by the time of his death he maintained five homes, including a particularly opulent one in Mexico City, and piloted and owned his own plane. During the early 1950s, however, his name became increasingly associated with a message of social justice and philanthropy. His films began to reflect his philosophy, especially *Si Yo Fuera Disputado (If I Were a Member of Congress)* and *El Bombero Atomico (The Atomic Fireman)* Many critics felt that the quality of

Cantinflas's films began to deteriorate at this point, citing hackneyed hooks and cheap sentimentalism.

As the wealth accrued by Cantinflas increased, he became increasingly known for his attention to the poorer citizens of Mexico City. Called "a legendary soft touch" by the *New York Times,* Cantinflas was famous for dispensing up to $175,000 a year to the poor people who lined up at his door. The *New York Times* noted, "At one time he was sole support of more than 250 destitute families in a Mexico City slum called Ganjas, where he later built 64 apartment houses. He sold the units to the poor for a fraction of their worth." In addition to this personal philanthropy, Cantinflas made many benefit appearances each year in order to raise money for charity.

Cantinflas died in Mexico City on April 20, 1993, of lung cancer at the age of 81. He was survived by his only child, Mario, Jr., and three grandchildren. Fans of his work came by the tens of thousands to his three wakes to pay homage to the man who poked fun at so much of what made life difficult. Ramiro Jimenez, an actor who worked with Cantinflas, told the *New York Times,* "Mexicans feel like he was their reflection. There isn't anyone like that now."

## SOURCES:

### Books

*Current Biography,* edited by Marjorie Dent Candee, New York, H.W. Wilson, 1954; edited by Judith Graham, New York, H.W. Wilson, 1993.
*International Dictionary of Films and Filmmakers: Actors and Actresses,* 3rd edition, edited by Nicholas Thomas, Detroit, St. James Press, 1992.

### Periodicals

*Americas,* March, 1953, pp. 6–46.
*Collier's,* May 30, 1942, pp. 62–64.
*New York Times,* June 15, 1941, Section 9, p. 3; April 22, 1993, p. D6; April 23, 1993, p. A4.
*Theatre Arts,* November, 1951, pp. 46–87.

—*Sketch by Ellen Dennis French*

# Luisa Capetillo
## 1879-1922
### Puerto Rican union activist, feminist, and author

A leader in the political and labor struggles of the working class at the beginning of the twentieth century in Puerto Rico, Luisa Capetillo condemned the exploitation of workers by political parties, religion, and capitalism. She also was a tireless feminist crusader who denounced the cultural and social system that enslaved women in ignorance and forced them into marriages based not on love but on a financial arrangement between two sets of parents. And as a suffragist, she struggled to obtain universal voting rights for both men and women. Besides her notable leadership activities, Capetillo left behind many written works that are just now being rediscovered and studied by scholars who may well conclude that her name belongs among those of the other "greats" in the American women's movement.

Luisa Capetillo was born in Arecibo, Puerto Rico, on October 28, 1879. Her mother, Margarita Perón, was French, and her father, Luis Capetillo, was Spanish. Her biographers agree that while she might have had some formal schooling, she was primarily self-taught; the knowledge of French she gained from her mother, for example, enabled her to read the works of French writers. History remembers her as the first woman to wear pants in public, which could be considered symbolic of the personal freedom she expressed in her actions and writings.

### Champions the Cause of the Female Worker

Capetillo lived in a period when the industrialization of Puerto Rico had just begun; wages were low for men and lower still for women. She believed that good wages were a worker's right, that better pay would result in happier families, less domestic violence, and more educational opportunities for children. While she acknowledged that men were as oppressed as women, she was especially concerned with the plight of the female worker. Her skill was in the way she managed to relate and interweave the issues of the private world (such as the family, single motherhood, and women's rights in general) with those of the public world (such as politics, wages, and education).

As Edna Acosta-Belén observes in *The Puerto Rican Woman: Perspectives on Culture, History and Society,* during Capetillo's lifetime the women's movement was "characterized by two major trends: the petit bourgeois and the proletarian." Although

Capetillo was supportive and understanding of both groups, she definitely focused on the world from the perspective of the proletarian, or working, woman rather than her middle-class sisters. In her book *Mi opinión sobre las libertades, derechos y deberes de la mujer como compañera, madre y ser independiente*, she pointed out that affluent women were never touched by the problems that affected working women, mainly because they didn't have to take jobs outside the home to help support their families and they always hired another woman to take care of their children.

### Joins Puerto Rican Labor Movement

Capetillo's involvement in the labor movement began in 1907 when she participated in a strike in Arecibo's tobacco factories. Within a year she was an active member of the Federation of Free Workers (FLT), and in 1910 she became a reporter for the federation's newspaper. Also in 1910 she founded the newspaper *La mujer*, which addressed women's issues.

Over the next few years, Capetillo traveled extensively, journeying to New York in 1912 and contributing some articles to the newspaper *Cultura Obrera*, visiting Florida in 1913 to collaborate with some union workers, and settling in Cuba from 1914 until 1916 to lecture on how to start cooperatives. By 1918 she was back in Puerto Rico, this time organizing strikes by agricultural workers in Ceiba and Vieques. That same year Capetillo was arrested for violence, disobedience, and being insubordinate to a police officer.

### Writings Reveal the Philosophical Basis for Her Activism

A thorough examination of Capetillo's writings from her activist days provides some insight into her opinions and the ideas for which she fought all her life. In many ways she was so far ahead of her time that the society she envisioned could exist only in her imagination. *Ensayos libertarios* appeared in 1907. Dedicated to all workers, male and female, it is a compilation of articles that Capetillo originally published between 1904 and 1907. In 1910, in *La humanidad en el futuro*, she describes a utopian society in detail and from a broad perspective. She also discusses the power of the church and the state, the institution of marriage, and private and common property. In her 1911 work entitled *Mi opinión sobre las libertades, derechos y deberes de la mujer como compañera, madre y ser independiente*, she analyzes the situation of women in society, focusing on what she viewed as the oppression and slavery of women and affirming that education is the key to freedom.

Also among Capetillo's writings are several dramas. According to Angelina Morfi in *Historia crítica de un siglo de teatro puertorriqueño*, the theater provided Capetillo with an alternative way to express her ideas effectively, especially her opinions about the oppression of women and the moral codes that strangle them culturally and socially.

On April 10, 1922, Capetillo died of tuberculosis in Río Piedras at the age of 42. She was survived by her three children, Manuela, Gregorio, and Luis. As Yamila Azize declares in *Luchas de la mujer en Puerto Rico,* "The more we know the life of this woman and become familiar with her ideas and writings, we confirm the special importance of Capetillo in our history."

### SELECTED PUBLISHED WORKS:

*Ensayos libertarios,* Imprenta Unión Obrera, 1907.
*La humanidad en el futuro,* 1910.
*Mi opinión sobre las libertades, derechos y deberes de la mujer como compañera, madre y ser independiente,* Times Publishing Company, 1911.
Capetillo, Luisa, "La mujer," contained in *Voces de liberación,* Editorial Lux, 1921, pp. 4–6.

### SOURCES:

#### Books

Acosta-Belén, Edna, "Puerto Rican Women in Culture, History, and Society," in *The Puerto Rican Woman: Perspectives on Culture, History and Society,* edited by Edna Acosta-Belén, Praeger, 1986, p. 7.
Azize, Yamila, *Luchas de la mujer en Puerto Rico, 1898–1919,* Litografía Metropolitana, 1979, p. 80.
Azize, Yamila, *La mujer en la lucha,* Editorial Cultural, 1985, pp. 79–169.
López Antonetty, Evelina, *Luisa Capetillo,* Centro de Estudios Puertorriqueños (Hunter College), 1986.
Morfi, Angelina, *Historia crítica de un siglo de teatro puertorriqueño,* Instituto de Cultura Puertorriqueña, 1980, pp. 271–74.
Valle Ferrera, *Luisa Capetillo: Historia de una mujerproscrita,* Editorial Cultural, 1990.

—*Sketch by Sylvia P. Apodaca*

# Ernesto Cardenal
## 1925-
### Nicaraguan priest, poet, and political activist

A Nicaraguan priest who served as that country's minister of culture for a time, Cardenal has also produced critically acclaimed poetry and commentary. He is considered a man of deep religious and philosophical beliefs; according to David Johnson in the *National Catholic Reporter*, "Cardenal has viewed poetry as an agent of social change, not the private reflections of an outsider or recluse.... Cardenal identifies with large numbers of his people, and has accepted one of the highest moral callings of the poet: to consistently give voice to individuals who, for reasons of politics and poverty, have been silenced."

In addition to his literary contributions, Cardenal's beliefs have manifested themselves in other ways. He founded a religious commune on Solentiname, an archipelago on Lake Nicaragua near the Costa Rican border. Furthermore, Cardenal's tenure as minister of culture for the Sandinista government from 1979 to 1988 was marked by his attempts to launch a cultural revitalization and provide a renewed sense of national identity and pride.

Cardenal was born January 20, 1925, in Granada, Nicaragua, to Rodolfo and Esmeralda (Martinez) Cardenal. He attended the University of Mexico from 1944 through 1948 and continued his education in the United States at Columbia University from 1948 to 1949. Cardenal entered the political arena when he became an active member of National Union for Popular Action, a revolutionary group in Nicaragua.

Cardenal converted to Christianity in 1956 and studied for the priesthood in the Trappist Monastery at Gethsemani, Kentucky, where the Trappist poet Thomas Merton lived. Merton became an important influence on his life and his writings. Cardenal recounts his time at the monastery in *Gethsemani, Ky.*, a book of poems published in 1960. He published two other books during this time as well—*Hora O* (1960) and *Epigramas* (1961).

### Mentor Compliments Cardenal's Work

Merton displayed a tremendous respect and admiration for Cardenal's work, insights, and clarity in his introduction to Cardenal's book *Vida en el amor* (1970; *To Live is to Love*). "In a time of conflict, anxiety, war, cruelty and confusion, the reader may be surprised that this book is a hymn in praise of love, telling us that 'all beings love one another,'" Merton wrote. He went on to say that the purpose of *To Live is to Love* is to "open our eyes to what ought to be obvious but sounds incredible: that 'all beings love one another,'" that "all life is love . . . The lucid and 'Franciscan' simplicity of Father Cardenal shows us the world not as we see it, with fear and distrust in our hearts, but as it is in reality."

Merton also explained in the introduction that while he was at the monastery in Kentucky, he knew of Cardenal's poetry, but that he never realized what a great impact it would have on the lives of either man. Merton wrote: "He spoke to me about his ideas and meditations. I also knew about his simplicity, his loyalty to his vocation, and his dedication to love. But I never imagined that some day I was going to write an introduction to the simple meditations he was writing down in those days, nor that in reading them (almost ten years later) I would find in them so much clarity, profundity and maturity." Then, bestowing the highest honor on Cardenal's insights and depth, Merton said: "Ernesto Cardenal left Gethsemani because of ill health. However, today I can see that this is not the only reason: it did not make sense to continue at Gethsemani as a novice and as a student when actually he was already a teacher."

Before Cardenal wrote *To Live is to Love*, though, he completed his studies in Cuernavaca, Mexico, and LeCeja, Colombia. He was ordained in Managua in 1965. In 1979 Cardenal's philosophical views changed, shifting from Merton's brand of pacifism to one that bridged Christianity and Marxism. He became a field chaplain for the Sandinista National Liberation Front, which toppled the dictatorship of Anastasio Somoza in 1979. About that time, Cardenal was named minister of culture for the new Sandinista government. He held the post until 1988, during which time he promoted literary workshops throughout Nicaragua. Johnson writes that Cardenal had an impact on the country's people: "By giving people their voices, he created a cultural rebirth in his country, and the recreation of national identity and pride among the working class."

Throughout this time, Cardenal proved a prolific poet, writing 35 books of verse. Some of the translated work included *The Psalms of Struggle and Liberation, Flights of Victory: Songs in Celebration of the Nicaraguan Revolution*, and *Marilyn Monroe and Other Poems*. His poetry was influenced by the work of such great writers as Ezra Pound, T. S. Eliot, and William Carlos Williams, as well as several Chinese and Japanese poets.

After leaving his position in the Sandinista government, Cardenal continued to use his written work as an outlet for his thoughts. In his book *Golden UFOs: The Indian Poems*, published in 1992, Cardenal focuses "on the myths and legends of America's autochthonous inhabitants," according to Lawrence Olszewski in *Library Journal*. Less militant than his *Zero Hour*, Olszewski added that "this bilingual edition consolidates the corpus of Cardenal's Indian poetry." Pat Monaghan's review of the book in *Booklist* commented that *Golden UFOs: The Indian Poems* "is accessible, political and mystical. . . . In them, a sometimes romantic vision of savage nobility is tempered by astute observation of the ways in which politics and economics interact to the detriment of the people."

### Cosmic Canticle **Receives Praise**

In 1989 Cardenal published *Cosmic Canticle,* a "magnum opus in which he sets his communalistic social philosophy within a majestic vision of the cosmos," wrote Johnson. The book, which was translated into English by John Lyons, melds politics with verse "while speaking forthrightly about the history of exploitation in the Americas," Johnson said. The nearly 500-page poem recalls Genesis and some of the Old Testament and touches on the works of modern-day scientists and science writers, including Lewis Thomas, Carl Sagan, Stephen Hawking, Richard Feynman, and Richard Dawkins, "at times cited by name, in an attempt to justify the ways of God to Nicaragua and Latin America," according to a review in *Publishers Weekly.* Rual Nino wrote in *Booklist* that Cardenal's *Cosmic Canticle* "arrives like songs from the darkness, questioning who we are and where we came from and keeping the tradition of the long poem alive. . . . This is, then, a book of faith—faith in humanity and in a creator."

In 1994 Cardenal published *El estrecho dudoso* (*The Doubtful Strait*), a critical examination of the voyages of Christopher Columbus. The book, which uses many of Columbus's own log entries, was praised by Elizabeth Gunderson in *Booklist* as "a passionate alternative history of the Spanish encounter with Central America."

In addition to his literary work, Cardenal went on to direct Casa de los Tres Mundos, a cultural organization. He founded a Christian community on the island of Solentiname in Lake Nicaragua and took up residence there. Cardenal explained the nature of the religious services that take place on the commune in the introduction to the second volume of his book *The Gospel in Solentiname.* The people there gather each Sunday to take part in a dialogue rather than hear a sermon in the traditional manner. Cardenal explained that commentaries by the people are "usually of greater profundity than that of the Gospel itself. This is not surprising: The *Gospel* or 'Good News' (to the poor) was written for them, and by people like them. Some friends urged me not to let these commentaries be lost, but to put them together and publish them as a book. That's the reason for these volumes. I first began collecting them in my mind, insofar as I could. Later, with more common sense, we used a tape recorder."

Cardenal noted that the comments were gleaned from services that took place in a variety of settings. He made it clear that he believed the setting of such services did not need to be a conventional one. "Occasionally, we have had the Mass and the Gospel dialogue in the open air on other islands, or in a small house that we get to by rowing along a beautiful river through very tropical vegetation." Of far greater importance, he said, is the content of what is said. The true author of the book, Cardenal said, was the Spirit that inspired the commentaries.

Merton wrote in the introduction of *To Live is to Love* that Cardenal's commune was located precisely where it was needed the most—in Central America, where there are no contemplative religious orders. "The book of Father Cardenal, this hymn to life and love, gives testimony of the renewal of the Church in Latin America," Merton said. "It is, we believe, a sign of the dawn of a new day in these countries of the future. They will not only attain temporal freedom and prosperity, but will also learn to sing hymns to life and to love, thus bringing to fruition the abundant potentialities that are still dormant and hidden in that rich, volcanic soil."

## SELECTED PUBLISHED WORKS:

*Ansias lengua de la poesía nueva nicaraguense,* 1948.

*Gethsemani, Ky.,* Ediciones La Tertulia, 1960.

*Hora O,* Revista Mexicano de Literatura, 1960.

*Epigramas: Poemas,* Universidad Nacional Autónoma de Mexico, 1961.

*Oración por Marilyn Monroe, y otros poemas,* Ediciones La Tertulia, 1965; translated by Robert Pring-Mill as *Marilyn Monroe and Other Poems,* Search Press, 1975.

*Antología de Ernesto Cardenal,* Editora Santiago, 1967.

*Poemas de Ernesto Cardenal,* Casa de las Américas, 1967.

*Salmos,* Institución Gran Duque de Alba, 1967; translated by Emile G. McAnany as *The Psalms of Struggle and Liberation,* Herder & Herder, 1971.

*Mayapan,* Editorial Alemania, 1968.

*Homenaje a los indios americanos,* Universidad Nacional Autónoma de Nicaragua, 1969; translated by Carlos Altschul and Monique Altschul as *Homage to the American Indians,* Johns Hopkins University Press, 1974.

*Vida en el amor,* Lohlé, 1970; translated by Kurt Reinhardt as *To Live is to Love,* Herder & Herder, 1972.

*La hora cero y otros poemas,* Ediciones Saturno, 1971; translated by Paul W. Borgeson and Jonathan Cohen as *Zero Hour and Other Documentary Poems,* edited by Donald D. Walsh, New Directions, 1980.

*Antología: Ernesto Cardenal,* edited by Pablo Antonio Cuadra, Lohlé, 1971.

*El Evangelio en Solentiname,* Ediciones Sigueme, 1975; translated by Donald D. Walsh as *The Gospel in Solentiname,* Orbis Books, 1976.

*La santidad de la revolución,* Ediciones Sigueme, 1976.

*Poesía cubana de la revolución,* Extemporáneos, 1976.

*Vuelos de Victoria,* Visor, 1984; translated by Marc Zimmerman as *Flights of Victory: Songs in Celebration of the Nicaraguan Revolution,* Orbis Books, 1985.

*Golden UFOs: The Indian Poems,* translated by Carlos Altschul and Monique Altschul, Indiana University Press, 1992.

*Cosmic Canticle,* translated by John Lyons, Curbstone, 1993.

*The Doubtful Straight: El estrecho dudoso,* translated by John Lyons, Indiana University Press, 1994.

## SOURCES:

### Books

Cardenal, Ernesto, *The Gospel in Solentiname,* Vol. 2, New Directions, 1978.

Cardenal, Ernesto, *To Live is to Love,* New York, Herder & Herder, 1972.

*The Oxford Companion to Spanish Literature,* Oxford, 1978.

*Contemporary Authors, New Revision Series,* Volume 2, Detroit, Gale, 1981.

### Periodicals

*Booklist,* April 1, 1992, p. 1425; December 1, 1993, p. 674.

*Library Journal,* March 13, 1992, p. 91; January, 1994, p. 119.

*National Catholic Reporter,* May 27, 1994, p.28.

*Publishers Weekly,* November 6, 1993, p. 60.

—*Sketch by D. D. Andreassi*

# Blandina Cárdenas Ramírez
## 1944-
**Hispanic American educational administrator and association executive**

The recurring theme in [Blandina] Cárdenas Ramírez' professional experience," said Margaret Cerrudo in *Intercambios Femeniles,* "is her life long commitment to education, Hispanic culture, children, and the rights of individuals." Indeed, for much her life, Blandina (Bambi) Cárdenas Ramírez has been part of the vanguard for civil rights and education. Appointed to the U.S. Commission on Civil Rights, she told Cerrudo that she is "fighting for equal access laws and the development of human capital."

Born October 25, 1944, in Del Rio, Texas, Cárdenas Ramírez is the youngest of three daughters who grew up in a supportive and traditional household. As Cárdenas Ramírez described her home life to Connie Paige in *Ms.,* "My family was very traditional about the maternal role. On the other hand, that did not diminish my family's respect for women and the clear aspirations that the next generation would do something. For us there was a strong sense of responsibility to make a contribution to improve the position of Hispanics." Also recollecting a childhood memory of her father to Cerrudo in *Intercambios Femeniles,* Cárdenas Ramírez recalled her father's words: "There is nothing my daughter can't do."

Cárdenas Ramírez's father, a civil service employee, and her mother, a homemaker, as well as the local church and school, were major influences in her life. Cárdenas Ramírez followed in the footsteps of her parents as a strong proponent of bilingual and bicultural education . In fact, by the time she entered first grade, she could read both English and Spanish. Completing elementary and secondary school at the San Felipe Independent School District in Del Rio, Texas, Cárdenas Ramírez graduated at the age of 16 in 1961. She subsequently went to Texas Women's University until 1962, when she resumed her studies at the University of Texas at Austin, where she completed a B.A. in journalism and public relations in 1967. She later obtained a doctoral degree in educational leadership and administration from the University of Massachusetts in 1974.

As a student and thereafter, Cárdenas Ramírez earned many academic honors and awards. Beginning in 1962, she earned the Freshman Writer of the Year from Texas Woman's University. In 1971 she was awarded the Ford Foundation Fellowship in Educational Leadership and the Rockefeller Fellowship in Leadership and Public Policy in 1974. Cárdenas

Ramírez was also the recipient of the Chancellor's Medal from the University of Massachusetts and received an Honorary Degree from Kean College of New Jersey in 1991.

Cárdenas Ramírez has also received numerous accolades as a leader in her community and advocate of civil rights, including "El Aguila Azteca," the highest honor given to a non-citizen by the President of Mexico. She was also named Outstanding Hispanic Woman in Texas by the National Hispanic Woman Institute, won awards from the American Educational Research Association and the National Education Association, and was honored by the National Council of La Raza and the San Antonio City Council.

### Interest in Education Leads to Politics

Cárdenas Ramírez began her professional career as a teacher and educational administrator in 1967, when she started teaching migrant pre-school, third grade, and high school English at San Felipe Independent School District in Del Rio, Texas. She also developed innovative methodology for teaching disadvantaged children. In 1969, Cárdenas Ramírez continued her assistance to migrant children as assistant coordinator of the Texas Migrant Educational Center within the Southwest Educational Development Laboratory in Austin, Texas.

Moving to San Antonio, Texas, Cárdenas Ramírez began work in 1969 at the Edgewood Independent School District as special assistant to the superintendent and as director of the Career Opportunities Program. Her responsibilities as special assistant included the development of all innovative programs in the school district and fundraising. The programs, developed to serve the needs of a highly disadvantaged population, received wide national recognition, and the Career Opportunities Program, which Cárdenas Ramírez oversaw, included teacher training programs designed to enable one 125 teacher aides to become teachers.

While completing her doctoral degree from 1971 to 1974, Cárdenas Ramírez advised numerous national projects as a consultant. Exposed to civil rights issues, she consulted for the Office of Civil Rights of the U.S. Department of Health, Educational, and Welfare and the U.S. Justice Department. She also assisted the Southwest Education Development Laboratory Bilingual Children's Television project and the National Education Association.

Upon the completion of her Ed.D. from the University of Massachusetts, Cárdenas Ramírez became a Rockefeller fellow assigned to the U.S. Senate Committee on Children and Youth, chaired by then Senator Walter F. Mondale, from 1974 to 1975. As a fellow, she drafted legislation, coordinated external relations, and organized hearings. The major leadership development program of the Rockefeller Foundation also identified four minority individuals for placement on key policy making settings.

Before returning to San Antonio, Texas, Cárdenas Ramírez was hired as commissioner for the Administration for Children, Youth, and Families and chief of the Children's Bureau within the Department of Health, Education, and Welfare from 1977 to 1979. Shortly thereafter, she began working as director of training and development for the Intercultural Development Research Association in San Antonio from 1979 to 1985. There, Cárdenas Ramírez focused on improving the quality of instruction and the quality of education opportunity for all children, particularly in the state of Texas. As director, she was responsible for the development of products and strategies to assist school districts in comprehensive planning to meet state and federal regulations for developing programs in parent education and involvement, school board and administrator training, and faculty and staff training.

### Works as Civil Rights Commissioner and Education Director

One of Cárdenas Ramírez's most visible civil rights ventures came in 1980 when she was appointed to the eight-member U.S. Commission of Civil Rights. Originally appointed by then-President Jimmy Carter, she was the first Hispanic to ever serve on the commission. Established in 1957, the U.S. Commission on Civil Rights monitors the enforcement of civil rights laws by the executive and provides recommendations to the president and Congress on the need for policies and procedures to advance civil rights in the nation. As a commissioner responsible for overseeing the government's compliance with civil rights laws, Cárdenas Ramírez became a vocal opponent of President Ronald Reagan and criticized his civil rights record.

In 1983, President Reagan tried to remove her, along with two other commissioners, by appointing replacements considered more politically conservative. But Cárdenas Ramírez would not go willingly. She sued for an injunction forbidding the termination, and a federal court reinstated her position as commissioner, a role Cárdenas Ramírez still holds. Cárdenas Ramírez recalled the incident to Paige in *Ms.:* "The furor over the Civil Rights Commission has been difficult and painful, but from an individual standpoint very growth-producing. One did not imagine there would be a civil rights movement, or a Women's Movement. And suing the President of the United States and winning—and even though winning is not easy—it was a miracle of our democracy." Devoted to her work as a commissioner, Cárdenas Ramírez said to Cerrudo in *Intercambios Femeniles*, "It's my love. . . . It's what it's all about."

In 1988, Cárdenas Ramírez began working at Our Lady of the Lake University, a small private liberal arts institution in San Antonio, Texas, as vice president for Institutional Advancement. As vice president, she was responsible for the Offices of Development, Alumni Affairs, and Public Affairs. Subsequently, in 1989 Cárdenas Ramírez became director of the Office of Minorities in Higher Education at the American Council on Education in Washington, D.C.

The American Council on Education is considered the umbrella membership organization for institutions of higher education in the country. Her priority as director is increasing the participation of minorities in higher education. As director, she represents the association before Congress and the president. She also provides leadership, information, and service on minority issues to more than 50 higher education organizations which make up the Washington Higher Education Secretariat. Cárdenas Ramírez is frequently requested to make presentations on educational issues, diversity, and minority participation before a broad spectrum of audiences. Some of the notable organizations to which Cárdenas Ramírez has spoken include the New Jersey Education Association, the Center for Adolescent Schooling, and the National Conference on Black Student Retention.

In addition to speaking to organizations on educational and minority issues, Cárdenas Ramírez participates and continues to be active in major commissions, committees, and task forces on a national and international scale. She has been selected as a board member of numerous organizations, including the National Foundation for the Improvement of Education in Washington, D.C., the National Resource Center for Children in Poverty in New York and Quality Education for Minorities in Washington, D.C. Cárdenas Ramírez is also founding chairperson of the Mexican American Womenake the remaining 's National Association, in Washington, D.C.

Cárdenas Ramírez is involved in many organizations and issues, and she is regarded as a professional willing to take risks. As related to Paige in *Ms.,* "There comes a time in a person's life when you almost have no choice. You cannot shirk the responsibility. You come to understand that the things you care about have much more to do with the process of history and the development than with yourself."

**SOURCES:**

*Intercambios Femeniles,* Summer, 1989.
*Ms.,* April 1986.
*Nation,* November 12, 1983, p. 451.
*Time,* November 7, 1983, p. 68.

—*Sketch by Luis Vasquez-Ajmac*

# Manuel Cardona
## 1934-
**Spanish American physicist**

The elements germanium and silicon are the focus of Manuel Cardona's research. Those basic substances, which at ordinary temperatures conduct electricity with a potential somewhere between a metal and an insulator, are also at the very heart of the information age, used to manufacture the silicon chip of the personal computer. Cardona, employing basic experimental models and investigative tools such as optical spectroscopy, has helped to elucidate the properties of these all-important elements and thus stretch the boundaries of both semiconductor and superconductor research.

Born on September 7, 1934, in Barcelona, Spain, Manuel Cardona showed an early propensity for technology, building and repairing all sorts of electric equipment. His father, Juan Cardona, was a small business owner who barely eked out a living, and his mother, Angela Cardona, was a school teacher. Brought up during the Spanish Civil War, Cardona personally experienced the vicissitudes of that conflict: his father was arrested by **Francisco Franco**'s regime for supposed "contacts" with Freemasons.

Cardona attended a state high school in Barcelona, where he first focused on his twin loves, mathematics and physics, with the encouragement of several excellent teachers. By graduation, he had set his course on a career in science, studying physics at the University of Barcelona from 1950 to 1955, and earning his Licenciado Degree summa cum laude and winning the Spanish National Prize for the best academic record in sciences. The following year he went to do graduate work at Harvard University, researching the effects of light, magnetism, and electricity on germanium and silicon, work which led to his Doctor of Science degree from the University of Madrid in 1958. Further research on dielectric or nonconducting properties of germanium and silicon led to a Ph.D. from Harvard in 1959. That same year, he married Inge Hecht. They have three children: Michael, born in 1959, Angela born in 1961, and Steven, born in 1964.

### From Semiconductors to Superconductors

Cardona joined RCA labs in Switzerland upon graduation from Harvard, and then moved to their labs in New Jersey until 1964 when he accepted a position at Brown University as associate professor of physics. In 1966, he became a full professor and remained at Brown until 1971 when he was offered the prestigious directorship of the newly founded

Max-Planck-Institute of Solid State Research in Stuttgart, Germany, where he has remained ever since. His work during these years included not only spectroscopic analysis of germanium and silicon, but also of materials exhibiting superconductivity. Certain metals and alloys are capable of being almost perfect conductors of electricity at temperatures close to absolute zero. Cardona investigated such materials from 1962 to 1971; later research at the Max-Planck-Institute has included a return to superconductivity research, but at high temperatures. He characterizes his research methods as an attempt to extract the maximum amount of information possible from basic experiments. Simplicity is his trademark. Many of his over 800 technical papers have become classics in the field, and several of his books are standard texts. In addition to his research and administrative duties at the Max-Planck-Institute, Cardona has trained a new generation of solid state physicists as well as served as editor for several technical journals. A holder of honorary doctorates around the world, Cardona has also been recognized for his research by the 1984 Frank Isakson Prize from the American Physical Society and the 1992 Excellence in Superconductivity award of the World Congress on Superconductivity. Cardona is a naturalized U.S. citizen.

## SELECTED PUBLISHED WORKS:

*Modulation Spectroscopy,* Academic Press, 1965.
*Light Scattering in Solids,* Vols. 1–6, Springer Verlag, 1975.
"Spectroscopic Ellipsometry with Synchrotron Radiation," with others, *Review of Scientific Instruments,* July 1989, pp. 2209–12.
"Phonons in GAAS/ALAS Superlattices Grown Along the [111] Direction," with others, *Physical Review B-Condensed Matter,* March 15, 1990, pp. 5904–13.
"Temperature Dependence of Direct Transitions in Angle-Resolved Photoemission and Its Application to INSB," with others, *Physical Review B-Condensed Matter,* May 15, 1990, pp. 1068–81.
"High TC Superconductors—An Introduction and Raman Spectroscopy," with others, *Journal of the Less Common Metals,* October 15, 1990, pp. 989–93.
"Strongly Dispersive Low Frequency Raman Modes in Germanium," with others, *Solid State Communications,* May 1991, pp. 579–82.
"The Origin of Visible Luminescence from Porous Silicon—A New Interpretation," with others, *Solid State Communications,* January 1992, pp. 307–12.
"Dielectric Tensor of YBA2CU4O8—Experiment and Theory," with others, *Physical Review B-Condensed Matter,* August 1, 1993, pp. 3993–4001.

*The Physics of Semiconductors,* with Peter Y. Yu, Springer Verlag, 1994.

## SOURCES:

### Books

*American Men & Women of Science 17th Edition,* Vol. 2, R. R. Bowker, 1989.

### Other

Cardona, Manuel, interview with J. Sydney Jones conducted February 8, 1994.

—*Sketch by J. Sydney Jones*

# David Cardús
## 1922-
### Spanish American physician

A specialist in cardiology and biomathematics, David Cardús is known for his work with mathematical and computer applications for the study of physiological systems, as well as for his research on experimental exercise and respiratory physiology. Cardús married Francesca Ribas in 1951, and they have four children. He became a U.S. citizen in 1969.

Cardús was born August 6, 1922, to Jaume and Ferranda Pascual Cardús of Barcelona, Spain. He received B.A. and B.S. degrees at the University of Montpellier in France in 1942, then attended the University of Barcelona, earning an M.D., magna cum laude, in 1949. He completed his internship at Hospital Clínico, University of Barcelona, and his residency at Sanatorio del Puig d'Olena in Barcelona. In 1953 Cardús accepted a two-year French government research fellowship in cardiology in Paris. He returned to take his diploma in cardiology at the University of Barcelona, then accepted a British research fellowship at the University of Manchester's Royal Infirmary, after which he departed Europe to take up residence in the United States.

In 1957, Cardús joined the Lovelace Foundation in Albuquerque as a research associate. Three years later, he began a long association with the Institute for Rehabilitation and Research at Baylor College of Medicine in Houston, where he has served on the medical staff, as a professor in the rehabilitation and

*David Cardús*

physiology departments, as director of the biomathematics division, and as head of the exercise and cardiopulmonary laboratories. In addition, he has taught mathematical sciences and statistics at Rice University in Houston for many years and has served as a consultant to the U.S. Public Health Service in the planning of health facilities.

Active in many professional societies, Cardús was president of the International Society for Gravitational Physiology in 1993, and vice chairman of the Gordon Conference on Biomathematics in 1970. His work has been recognized with numerous awards from professional organizations both in the United States and in Spain. In the United States, he received a gold medal from the International Congress of Physical Medicine and Rehabilitation for a 1972 exhibit demonstrating the use of computers and telecommunications in rehabilitation, and first prizes from the International American Congress of Rehabilitative Medicine and the American Urological Association for other exhibits.

Cardús also earned an award for science writing from the American Congress of Physical Medicine and Rehabilitation. Honors garnered in Spain include recognition by the Generalitat de Catalunya and the Instituto Catalan de Cooperación Iberoamericana Fundación Bertran. In addition, Cardús has served as chairman of the board of the Institute for Hispanic Culture in Houston and as president of Spanish Professionals in America.

## SOURCES:

*American Men & Women of Science,* 18th edition, New York, Bowker, 199
*The Hispanic-American Almanac,* edited by Nicolás Kanellos, Detroit, Gale, 1993.

—*Sketch by Penelope Lawbaugh*

# Rod Carew
## 1945-
### Panamanian professional athlete

Rod Carew is widely recognized as one of the best hitters of his generation. During his 19 seasons with the Minnesota Twins and the California Angels, he lined, chopped, and bunted his way to 3,053 hits, winning seven batting titles and hitting .300 or better 15 consecutive seasons. Thought by many sportswriters and fans alike to have elevated the skill of hitting a baseball to an art form, Carew was named to 18 straight All-Star teams and received American League Rookie of the Year honors in 1967 and the American League Most Valuable Player award ten years later. In 1991, five years after his retirement, Carew became only the twenty-third player elected to the Baseball Hall of Fame in Cooperstown, New York, in his first year of eligibility. A national hero in both his native Panama—where he proudly retains his citizenship—and the United States, Carew has spent his retirement years running a batting school for young players in suburban Los Angeles.

The early years of the fleet-footed athlete were marred by illness and poverty. On October 1, 1945, Olga Carew went into labor and boarded a train in Gatun, Panama, hoping to reach a Gamboa clinic in time for doctors to attend to her child's delivery. The baby would not wait, however. Margaret Allen, a nurse, and Dr. Rodney Cline, a physician, both of whom happened to be on the train, delivered the woman's second son. While the excited mother asked the nurse to become the child's godmother, she honored the doctor by naming her son Rodney Cline Carew. As a young boy, Carew was frequently ill and contracted rheumatic fever at the age of 12. The weakness that accompanied the disease brought only contempt and rejection from his father. Carew's uncle, Joseph French, who was a recreation official and Little League coach in Panama, attempted to fill the void. French cultivated the boy's interest in baseball and encouraged him to develop his athletic abilities despite the illness. As Carew grew stronger, he joined the other boys in pickup games played with a broom handle and rag balls wound in tape. His outstanding play in the local Little League even won him a Ted Williams bat, a prized possession that he often carried with him—even to bed, where he dreamed of traveling to the United States and becoming a big-league baseball player.

### Sandlot Discovery Led to Tryout

When Carew was 15, his mother immigrated to New York City, where after finding a job and a place to live, she sent for her two sons. Once in New York, Rod enrolled at Manhattan's George Washington High School, but a part-time job at a grocery store to help support the family prevented him from trying out for school sports. The family's financial concerns, though, did not prevent Carew from participating in weekend sandlot games in Macombs Dam Park next to Yankee Stadium. It did not take long for him to show his skill at the plate; after a few weeks of play, a teammate's father—an unofficial scout for the Minnesota Twins—took notice of the talented kid from Panama and made a phone call to another scout. When the Twins came to town for a series with the Yankees, Carew came to Yankee Stadium for a tryout. Once inside the batting cage, the skinny 18-year-old demonstrated a hitting power that belied his six-foot, 170-pound frame. So many balls landed in the bleachers that Twins Manager Sam Mele—afraid the Yankees might offer him a higher signing bonus—halted the tryout. One month after the tryout, Carew signed with the Twins for a $5,000 bonus.

### Moved Quickly to Major League

Unlike most players who need several years in the minor leagues to develop their skills, Carew spent only three years in the farm system before Twins owner Calvin Griffith brought him up to the big league club, inserting him into the starting lineup at second base for the start of the 1967 season. Although some within the organization—including Mele—did not believe the 21-year-old from the Class-A farm team was ready for the majors, Carew silenced the skeptics by hitting .292 his first season and winning the American League Rookie of the Year award. While quickly becoming one of the game's leading hitters, Carew also dazzled fans with his speed on the base paths with a record-breaking seven steals home. In one game that same season he stole second, third, and home in a single inning—a feat performed only once before in the previous four decades.

Despite his success on the field, Carew developed a reputation in his early years as "a loner who made friends slowly and suffered slights poorly," according to *Time*. Much of this changed, however, after he was introduced to Marilynn Levy at a local nightspot. At first the white Jewish woman was not interested in the

black baseball player from Panama. As Marilynn told *Time*, "Sports? I didn't know from the Twins, and like a cocky little broad, I wasn't impressed." Despite the inauspicious beginning, the two began dating and married in October of 1970. While Carew was quickly accepted into the Levy family, he received a number of death threats and insults from Twins' followers. The two did not let racism prevent them from settling in Minneapolis, where they would have three daughters.

Although Carew won four batting titles between 1972 and 1975 and missed his fifth straight by .002 points, he did not receive the media attention granted to far lesser players. This was due in part to the fact that Carew prided himself in hitting singles rather than home runs. In 1975, Twins owner Griffith turned down Carew's request for a modest salary increase, claiming that the future Hall of Famer did not hit enough home runs to deserve the pay raise. The arbitrator sided with the Twins management and fixed Carew's salary at only $120,000—more than modest by league standards for a man of his ability. As if to prove his critics wrong, Carew hit 14 home runs the following season.

It was Carew's performance in 1977, however, that reserved him a position in the Hall of Fame and gained the respect of the national media. As Carew made his bid to become the first player in 36 years to hit .400, he appeared on the cover of *Time* as well as several sports publications and was featured in *Newsweek*. After one blazing hitting streak in late June that brought his average to .411, Carew told *Newsweek*'s Peter Bonventre that every pitch that came to the plate during that banner season "look[ed] like a basketball." When asked by Bonventre how to get Carew out, Gaylord Perry, a Hall of Fame pitcher for the Texas Rangers replied, "Greaseball, greaseball, greaseball. That's all I throw him, and he still hits them. He's the only player in baseball who consistently hits my grease. He sees the ball so well, I guess he can pick out the dry side." Although his average hovered above the mark well into the season, Carew finished at .388. But with 100 runs batted in and 100 runs scored to go with his lofty average, he was still the runaway winner of the American League's Most Valuable Player award.

Despite Carew's singular performance that season, he could not reach a contract agreement with management and was traded to the California Angels just two years later. After spending seven years in California, where he hit better than .300 five times, he was suddenly released after the 1985 season. Angered by the way Carew was treated, a Minneapolis media celebrity led an unsuccessful campaign to bring him back to Minnesota for a farewell season in 1986. No one was more disappointed than Marilynn Carew with the failed effort. "I'm still angry about it," she told the *St. Paul Pioneer Press-Dispatch*. "With the d.h. rule, Rod should still be playing. He would have done a lot for [Minnesota]." After the initial feelings of bitterness, however, her husband was ready for life on the other side of the basepaths. "Once I started coaching my daughters in softball and then started the hitting school," he said. "I found out I could get along without baseball."

### Inducted into Baseball's Hall of Fame

The transition to civilian life was made easier in 1991 when Carew was elected to the Hall of Fame in his first year of eligibility, receiving more than 90 percent of the sportswriters' votes. "He was one of the best hitters I've ever seen." Twins owner Griffith told the *St. Paul Pioneer Press-Dispatch.* "He was just a natural up there. That's all there was to it. He had a stroke that God gave him and he took advantage of it." Former manager Mele, who initially opposed Carew's promotion to the majors, shared Griffith's sentiment. "I don't know who you could compare him with . . . ," he told the *Minneapolis Star and Tribune.* "You could put him in a tunnel with the lights out and you still know he's going to hit." While many used the occasion to remember Carew's brilliance on the field, others recalled his regular travels to the Mayo Clinic to visit patients, his winning of the 1976 Roberto Clemente Award for distinguished community service, and his strong attachment to his Panamanian background. As former Twins Manager Gene Mauch stated in *Time,* "As impressed as I am with Rod Carew the hitter, Rod Carew the baseball player, I am more impressed with Rod Carew the man."

### SOURCES:

*Los Angeles Times,* January 9, 1991.
*Minneapolis Star and Tribune,* January 9, 1991.
*Newsweek,* August 11, 1969, pp. 61–62; July 11, 1977, pp. 46–47.
*St. Paul Pioneer Press-Dispatch* (Minnesota), July 20, 1987; January 9, 1991; July 22, 1991.
*Time,* July 18, 1977, pp. 52–62.

—*Sketch by Jason Gallman*

# Mariah Carey
## 1970-
### Hispanic American singer and songwriter

Mariah Carey took the pop music scene by storm with her 1990 debut album entitled *Mariah Carey.* Largely unknown prior to her album's arrival, Carey was nominated for three Grammy awards in

*Mariah Carey*

1991, winning best pop female vocalist and best new artist. All 11 songs on the album were cowritten by Carey and she produced "Vanishing," a piano and vocal track. The track "Visions of Love" reached number one on *Billboard*'s pop, black and adult-contemporary charts.

What impressed listeners and critics alike was Carey's remarkable range—it includes an amazing five octaves. Hillel Italie wrote in the *Chicago Tribune* in 1990, "This a voice that can probably shatter glass and then put it back together, that sounds as if she's taking the words and twirling them over her head like a cowboy with a lasso. David Gates of *Newsweek,* writing in 1990, was equally astounded by her voice, "all seven octaves or so of it, from purring alto to stratospheric shriek. Up in this dog-whistle register, she can scream into precise, synthesizer-like phrases. She has the good taste not to overuse this device, but how could anyone—especially a 20-year-old—resist showing off just a little."

In the first year of its release, *Mariah Carey* sold about six million copies and held *Billboard*'s number one spot for 22 consecutive weeks. At the time, Carey was the third artist in the history of the Grammy awards to be nominated in the same year for best album, best song, and best new artist. With her second album, 1991's *Emotions,* Carey proved she was a phenomenon with staying power. By 1993, *Emotions* had sold three million copies and the title track was a number one single. *Mariah Carey MTV Unplugged,* released in 1992, sold two million copies within its first year of release. Carey's fourth album, *Music Box,* released in 1993, also rose to the top ten and its ballad "Dreamlover" spent two months at number one.

Although fans have proven their devotion, critics have not been so easily won over. Aside from admiring her vocal range, various critics have described Carey's music as "banal love complaints" and "hackneyed high-school poetry." What seems to irritate some of her detractors most is that Carey rose to stardom so rapidly without having to pay her dues. Becoming a singer, however, was not as simple as getting her demo tape heard.

## Survived a Difficult Childhood

When she was three years old, Carey's parents— Alfred Roy Carey, a black, Venezuelan aeronautical engineer and Patricia Carey, an aspiring Irish American opera star—separated. Prior to the separation, the interracial couple had trouble fitting into the United States of the 1960s. Carey explained to Steve Dougherty of *People* in 1993, "They went through some very hard times before I was born. They had their dogs poisoned, their cars set on fire and blown up. It put a strain on their relationship that never quit. There was always this tension. They just fought all the time."

Separation turned into divorce in 1972 and Carey's older sister lived with her father and her older brother left home. Carey was raised by her mother who worked as a singer and free-lance voice coach. "I sort of took care of myself a lot," Carey revealed to Dougherty. "I always felt like the rug could be pulled out from me at any time. And coming from a racially mixed background, I always felt like I didn't fit [in] anywhere."

At an early age, Carey's talent was obvious. Her mother told Dougherty that "from the time Mariah was a tiny girl, she sang on true pitch; she was able to hear a sound and duplicate it exactly." While rehearsing in 1972 for her New York City Opera debut, Patricia missed her cue, but Mariah chimed right into the song. "She sang it—in Italian—at exactly the right point. She wasn't yet 3." Patricia became her daughter's personal coach, but was never a pushy stage mother, Carey recalled.

Carey told Edna Gundersen of *USA Today* that her mother did not try to pass her musical preferences onto her daughter. "She never said, 'Give it more of an operatic feel.' I respect opera like crazy, but it didn't influence me." Instead, she preferred the gospel music of Edwin Hawkins, the Clark Sisters, and Shirley Caesar; the soul music of Gladys Knight, Stevie Wonder, Al Green, and Aretha Franklin; and the jazz of Billie Holiday, and Sarah Vaughan. All was absorbed by her eager, young mind.

Though music was her constant companion, Carey says her childhood was difficult. "At the time I was growing up, things were hard with my mother not having a lot of money and moving around a lot . . . feeling different from everybody," she told Robert Johnson of *Jet* in 1994. "And that is what always made me look inside myself and have to really depend on myself and know that only I could make things happen [for me]."

Her classmates did not understand Carey's biracial heritage. "It was a very alienating thing for me," she told Lynn Norment of *Ebony* in 1994. "But lucky for me, my mother never said anything negative about my father. She never discouraged me from having a good feeling about him. She always taught me to believe in myself, to love all the things I am."

Because Carey spent much time on her own and moved often, she developed an independent attitude. Although that helped her in her singing career, it was difficult in school. Carey struggled to graduate from high school. Of her former teachers, she told *Jet* in a 1994 interview, "I don't blame them for trying to encourage me to do better scholastically because they never heard me sing. They just saw this kid that had a dream of making music and being a singer."

In 1993, Carey told *TV Guide*'s Carl Arrington her rebellious attitude developed early on. "I have always had a problem with authority. I remember one time at dinner when I was little and I started singing a little song. My father, who was very strict about manners, said, 'There's no singing at the table.' I kept singing and he said again, 'Mariah, *no* singing at the table!' Right then I marched over to the coffee table nearby and stood on top of it singing as *loud* as I could, looking right at him."

While still in high school, Mariah commuted to Manhattan to write songs with composer Ben Margulies. She often did not return to her mother's Long Island home until two in the morning. As soon as Carey graduated from Harborfields High in 1987, the 18-year-old moved to the city. A struggling singer, Carey worked as a waitress, coat checker, restaurant hostess and part-time backup singer for rhythm-and-blues singer Brenda K. Starr until the big break came.

## Dream Came True

In fairy tale fashion, Carey was "discovered" by Tommy Mottola, the president of Sony Music Entertainment, parent company of Columbia Records. Her friend and supporter, Brenda K. Starr, took Carey to a record industry party in November of 1988, where she gave Mottola her demo tape. On his way home, Mottola listened to the tape in his limousine and was so impressed, he ordered the car to return to the party, but Carey was gone. "When I heard and saw Mariah, there was absolutely no doubt she was in every way destined for stardom," Mottola told Fred Goodman of the *New York Times* in 1991.

It took about a week to find her, and when Mottola did, he signed her with Columbia Records. From there, Carey's career skyrocketed. Before her debut album's release, she appeared at a recording industry convention, did a nine-city promotional tour and sang "America the Beautiful" before the first game of the NBA championship series. When her album arrived at last, the public was primed. It is this careful planning by Columbia Records that some critics have used to discredit Carey's success. "To others, it may seem like it happened very fast," she told *TV Guide*, "but to me it seems like it took forever, since this is all I ever wanted to do from the time I was four! When other kids were singing 'Mary Had a Little Lamb,' I was singing the Rolling Stones' 'Satisfaction.'"

### From Studio to Stage

Her third album, *Mariah Carey MTV Unplugged*, recorded on Music Television (MTV) in 1992 proved Carey was more than just a studio performer. "'Unplugged' is an artists' show," Joel Gallen, the program's executive director, told *TV Guide*. "Mariah goes well with its concept. I can safely say she's the best singer we've ever had on it. She just shines." The switch for Carey was stressful. "The setup there was very raw, and I'm used to hearing more of a studio sound when I sing," Carey told *TV Guide*'s Bruce Kluger. "I'm really very hard on myself, so when I hear imperfections, I get freaked out. Still, the whole idea of 'Unplugged' is cool. It allows the artist to be an artist without having to be a video star or lip-syncing their record. You can go out there and really be true to what you do."

In June 1993, Carey married the recently divorced Mottola, who is 20 years older than Carey. As for the critics who seem to focus on every aspect of her life, from her career to her marriage, Carey dismisses them. "My whole life I've been working toward this," she told Norment. Success isn't a scale for talent, Carey said. "I don't want to be a 'big star,' but I want to be respected as an artist . . . this is my love. I want to sing for the rest of my life."

## SELECTED DISCOGRAPHY:

*Mariah Carey* (includes "Vanishing" and "Visions of Love"), Columbia, 1990.
*Emotions*, Columbia, 1991.
*Mariah Carey MTV Unplugged*, Columbia, 1992.
*Music Box* (includes "Dreamlover"), 1993.

## SOURCES:

### Books

*Current Biography Yearbook 1992*, edited by Judith Graham, Wilson, 1992, pp. 103–105.

### Periodicals

*Chicago Tribune,* August 16, 1990.
*Ebony,* March 1991, pp. 54–58; November 1993, pp. 36–37; April 1994, pp. 55–60.
*Jet,* January 24, 1994, pp. 53–57.
*Newsweek,* August 6, 1990.
*New York Times,* April 14, 1991; September 15, 1991.
*People,* December 30, 1991, p. 90; November 22, 1993, pp. 82–88.
*TV Guide,* May 16, 1992, pp. 28–30; Nov. 13, 1993, pp. 22–24.
*USA Today,* September 17, 1991.

—*Sketch by Kathe A. Conti*

# Alejo Carpentier
## 1904-1980
### Cuban poet and writer

Alejo Carpentier was a prominent Latin American novelist who was born in Cuba on December 26, 1904. Carpentier's father, Georges Carpentier, was French and his mother was Russian. Residents of Cuba for two years before he was born, Carpentier's architect father met his mother in Switzerland, where she was a medical student. Carpentier grew up in affluent circumstances. When he was in elementary school in 1912, the family traveled to Russia to receive an inheritance. After an extensive tour of Austria, Russia, and Belgium, the family stayed in Paris for a time. While there Carpentier attended the Lycee Jeanson de Sailly school and learned to speak French fluently, a complement to his understanding of Spanish, which he had learned from his friends on the streets in Cuba.

Carpentier was an avid reader—sampling the work of **Pio Baroja**, Honoré de Balzac, Gustave Flaubert, and Emile Zola, among others—and recalled his impressions of his father's library in several of his works. Carpentier began writing at the age of 15 after the family moved back to the countryside near Havana. An asthmatic condition kept him at home much of the time, so he spent much of his time playing the piano, writing, and reading. When Carpentier returned to Cuba, he attended Colegio Mimo and later Candler College. Carpentier organized concerts of modern music while in college and wrote music reviews for *El Heraldo de Cuba* and *La Discusion*. He began a study of architecture at the Universidad de la Habana, but in 1922 his father disappeared and he quit college to help support the family. By 1924, Carpentier had assumed the mantle of chief editor for *Carteles,* an avant-garde weekly magazine.

### Becomes Involved in Revolutionary Movement

Cuba was in political turmoil in the 1920s. In 1925 **Gerardo Machado y Morales** became dictator of the small Caribbean island. Carpentier became involved in a Grupo Minorista, an anti-Machado political force led by a cultural group of intellectuals. Machado became known to his opponents as "el asno con garras" ("the ass with claws") because of his violent acts against the revolutionaries. In the meantime, Carpentier helped found the radical nationalist magazine *Revista de Avance.* He signed a literary and political manifesto that spoke out for reforms in the art world, education, economic independence, and the rejection of Yankee imperialism and dictatorships. In the Revolucion del '33, the revolutionaries almost won over the dictatorship when the United States intervened in such a way that they could never come to power in Cuba.

In 1927 Carpentier's anti-Machado activities landed him in prison for seven months. While in prison, he began work on his first novel, *Ecue-Yamba-O* (*Praised be the Lord*). After he was released from jail, he was not permitted to travel abroad. Instead, Carpentier organized a series of concerts with a composer friend, Amedeo Roldan, and actively promoted Afro-Cuban and Afro-Antillian movements. Carpentier wrote scenarios and Roldan composed the music for the Afro-Cuban ballets *El milagro de Anaquille* (1927) and *La Rebambaramba* (1929). In 1928 Carpentier went to Paris and presented an Afro-Cuban burlesque entitled *Yamba-O* that featured the music of composer M. F. Gaillard. He also wrote Afro-Cuban poems and collected Afro-Cuban paintings by **Wilfredo Lam**.

A new style of writing was emerging in Latin America during this period. Previous Latin American writers had followed a more European style of writing. In 1926, however, the *criollista* novel, which emphasized portrayals of Latin American people, culture, and environment, reached a peak of popularity. Influenced by this trend, Carpentier explored the Latin American reality in his first novel. Carpentier's early work also reflected an increased interest in the culture of indigenous people in the rural areas of Latin America. In the 1930s an increasing number of novels depicted a more realistic view of the Indian people's plight and explored their oppression in the white society.

### Escapes to Paris

In 1928 Carpentier again came under the suspicion of Cuban authorities. Through the intercession of a friend, Robert Desnos, Carpentier was able to borrow papers that allowed him to flee to Paris. He spent the next 11 years in France. But while he had been forced to leave Latin American soil, he spent eight of those years reading everything he could find about Latin America and the United States. He later wrote: "I dedicated myself for years to reading everything I could find on America, from the letters of Christopher Columbus to the writers of the 18th century, going through the Inca Garcilase de la Vega. I did nothing else for years, I believe, but read American texts. America was seen as an enormous nebula that I tried to understand, because I felt vaguely that my work originated there, that it was going to be profoundly American."

When Carpentier arrived in Paris, the surrealist movement was underway in the art world and he wrote an article for *Social* about his impressions of the movement. The discovery of surrealism brought about a change in Carpentier's perception of reality in the Latin American world, although he later broke away from the surrealism school as it split into two factions. During his exile in France, Carpentier established friendships with André Breton, **Pablo Picasso**, Giorgio de Chirico, Heitor Villa-Lobos, and other well-known artists and writers of the day.

In 1933 Carpentier published his first novel, *Ecue-Yamba-O,* in Madrid. Although it was never acclaimed as a successful work, the novel was written with an element of social protest and featured an exploration of the black culture and the black identity in Cuba. In addition, it is recognized as the first important work that broke with the traditional style of writing in Cuba. His later work was called "magical realism." After his first novel was published, Carpentier returned to journalism; he did not begin another novel until 1943. That work, *El clan disperso,* a depiction of the artistic lifestyle in Cuba in the 1920s, was never completed. Instead, he took parts of this novel and used them in other novels he published much later: *El siglo de las luces* (1962) and *La consagracion de la primavera* (1978).

### Works in Music and Writing

During his stay in Paris, Carpentier worked in broadcasting in the music department of French radio and directed Foniric, a literary recording company. He continued to write articles for the Cuban magazines *Carteles* and *Social* as well. For *Social,* Carpentier wrote articles on the changing art world in Europe. He also penned a fashion column under the pseudonym "Jacqueline."

Carpentier's life changed significantly in the space of a few years. He became involved in the political anti-fascist movement. He was married in Paris, too, but his wife died from tuberculosis soon after they were married. He then married his second wife, Eva Frejaville, at a time when an increasing number of Spanish American artists and writers were relocating to Paris, which had come to be considered the mecca of the arts.

In 1939 the 35-year-old Carpentier returned to Cuba and was named editor of *Tiempo Nuevo,* a journal in Havana. Carpentier worked for Cuban radio stations and as a musicologist at Cuba's National Conservatory of Music. He divorced Frejaville in October 1939 and married Lilia Esteban Hierro, a member of a wealthy Cuban family, in 1941. After his marriage to Esteban Hierro, Carpentier dedicated every book he wrote to her. In the early 1940s a series of articles entitled "El ocaso de Europa" ("The Dusk of Europe") was published in *Carteles.* These articles came to be regarded by many critics and scholars as among his most accomplished literary work.

In 1943 Carpentier traveled to Haiti with French actor Louis Jouvet. He became fascinated with the Haitian culture and the black Haitian emperor Henri Christophe. The visit eventually inspired him to write what is considered his first important novel, *El reino de est mundo* (*The Kingdom of This World*), published in 1949. He also received a contract to write *La musica en Cuba,* a history of Cuban music, which was published in 1946.

In 1945, while working on both *El reino de est mundo* and *La musica en Cuba,* Carpentier was invited to Caracas, Venezuela, to help found an advertising agency. The Publicidad Ars agency was created with an old friend from Paris, Carlos Frias. While in Venezuela, Carpentier also became involved in teaching, journalism, and television. While in Caracas, he visited the interior of Venezuela and wrote a series of four articles entitled "Vision de America" ("Vision of America") for *El Nacional* in 1947. He traveled the next year to the Upper Orinoco and was inspired to write *Los pasos perdidos* (*The Lost Steps*), a novel that in 1953 was honored as the best foreign book of the year in France. Another novel written by Carpentier—*El siglo de las luces* (*The Century of the Lights* )—proved to be an influential one on writers such as **Gabriel García Marquez.** A best-seller, critics have long argued about the presence (or lack thereof) of commentary in the book on subjects such as the Cuban Revolution and Marxism.

Carpentier stayed in Caracas until 1959, when **Fidel Castro** came to power in Cuba. A supporter of Castro, Carpentier returned to Cuba, where he assumed the reins as head of the Editorial Nacional and taught at Havana University. In 1966 he was appointed cultural attache for European affairs for Cuba and relocated to Paris.

### 70th Birthday Honors

On the occasion of Carpentier's 70th birthday in 1974, the Cuban government declared an official celebration and gave the writer an honorary doctorate from the University of Havana. He received the Alfonso Reyes Prize in Mexico and the Cerro del Duca Prize. In 1976 Carpentier was elected as Honorary Fellow of the University of Kansas and in 1979 he received the Prix Medici. Carpentier died at his home in Paris on April 24, 1980, shortly after the publication of *Consagracion de la primavera,* the first book in a planned trilogy. Carpentier was buried in Cuba in the Necropolis de Colon.

## SELECTED PUBLISHED WORKS:

*Poemes des Antilles,* Gaillard, 1931.

*Ecue-Yamba-O!* (*Praised be the Lord*), Espana, 1933.

*Viaje a la semilla,* Ucar & Garcia, 1944.

*La musica en Cuba,* Fondo de Cultura Economica, 1946.

*El reino de este mundo,* Ibero Americana, 1949; translated by Harriet de Onis as *The Kingdom of This World,* Knopf, 1957.

*Tristan e Isolda en Tierra Firme,* Nacional, 1949.

*Los pasos perdidos,* Ibero Americana, 1953; translated by Harriet de Onis as *The Lost Steps,* Knopf, 1956, Gollancz, 1956.

*Guerra del tiempo,* General, 1958; translated by Frances Partridge as *The War of Time,* Knopf, 1979, Gollancz, 1979.

*El siglo de las luces* (*The Century of the Lights*), General, 1962; translated by John Sturrock as *Explosion in a Cathedral,* Little, Brown, 1963, Gollancz, 1963.

*El derecho de asilo,* General, 1962.

*Literatura y conciencia politica en America Latina,* Corazon, 1969.

*Papel social del novelista,* Hombre Nuevo, 1969.

*La cuidad de las columnas,* Lumen, 1970.

*Los convidados de plata,* Sandino, 1972.

*El Recurso del metodo,* Siglo XXI, 1974; translated by Frances Partridge as *Reasons of State,* Knopf, 1976, Gollancz, 1976.

*El periodista: Un cronista de su tiempo,* Granma, 1975.

*Cronicas,* 2 volumes, edited by Jose Antonio Portuondo, Arte y Literatura, 1975.

*Cuentos,* Arte y Literatura, 1977.

*Afirmacion literaria americanista,* Universidad Central, 1978.

*La consagracion de la primavera,* Siglo XXI, 1979.

*Bajo el signo de la Cibeles,* edited by Julio Rodriguez Puertolas, Nuestra Cultura, 1979.

*El adjetivo y sus arrugas,* Galerna, 1980.

*La novela latinamericana en visperas de un nuevo siglo y otros ensayos,* Siglo XXI, 1981.

## SOURCES:

Flores, Angel, *Spanish American Authors: The Twentieth Century*, New York, H. W. Wilson, 1992, pp. 168–172.

*Modern Latin-American Fiction Writers, First Series*, Volume 113 of *Dictionary of Literary Biography*, edited by William Luis, Detroit, Gale, 1992.

Shaw, Donald L., *Alejo Carpentier*, Boston, Twayne, 1985.

—*Sketch by Phyllis Noah*

*Vikki Carr*

# Vikki Carr
## 1940-
### Mexican American entertainer and singer

When President George Bush gathered with presidential predecessors Ronald Reagan, Gerald Ford, and Richard Nixon at the dedication of the Nixon library in July 1990, the event culminated in a new burst of American activity for Grammy-winner Vikki Carr. The longtime popular singing star, who had concentrated much of her activities in the Hispanic market, was selected as the featured singer at the event in front of four presidents whom she had individually entertained during their terms in the White House.

For Carr, it was like a return home to a country's welcoming arms. Her English language album for Sony Music, *Set Me Free*, had quickly become a popular seller, and she had just finished headlining at the famed Desert Inn Hotel in Las Vegas. In addition, Carr's perennial hit, "It Must Be Him," which remains a favorite on the airwaves, was featured in the top-grossing film, *Moonstruck.*

### Hails from Musical Family

Vikki Carr—originally named Florencia Bicenta de Casillas Martinez Cardona—was born in El Paso, Texas, on July 19, 1940, the eldest of seven children of construction engineer Carlos Cardona and his wife, Florence. The young girl grew up singing. Her father played the guitar at home, and at age four Florencia made her singing debut in a Christmas play. The family moved to southern California when Carr was an infant. She grew up in Rosemead, an eastern suburb of Los Angeles, attending parochial school and then Rosemead High, where she took all of the music courses she could and participated in all of their musical productions. On weekends she sang with local bands and, upon graduating in 1958, landed a vocalist spot with Pepe Callahan's Mexican-Irish Band performing at Palm Springs' Chi-Chi Club. The petite eighteen year old with a big voice called herself "Carlita." Solo engagements followed and then a long-term contract with Liberty Records in 1961. She toured Australia and returned to become featured vocalist with the Ray Anthony television series.

From then on it was a steady rise in the night club circuit: Reno, Las Vegas, Lake Tahoe, Hawaii. Her first headlining engagement was at the world-famous Coconut Grove in Los Angeles. By the 1960s she had become one of the top female vocalists in the country, guesting on virtually every major television variety show in the U.S., including shows hosted by Dean Martin, the Smothers Brothers, Carol Burnett, and Bob Hope. In the process she shortened her rather lengthy name to "Vikki Carr." In an interview with the *Saturday Evening Post*, she recalled that when she changed her name from "Carlita" to "Carr" and adopted the Americanized name "Vikki Carr," her father was hurt. But she promised him, "I'll be as well known as a Mexican American as an Anglo." She has kept her word.

Carr's first major recording success was in Australia with "He's a Rebel" and then in England with "It Must Be Him," which skyrocketed her to stardom. That song was later released in the United States, but it was another year before it became a hit in the

United States. Subsequently she signed a recording contract with Columbia Records.

## Becomes International Singing Sensation

This was followed by successful tours to England, Australia, Mexico, Venezuela, El Salvador, and Panama. Her status as an international star was confirmed in 1967 when she was invited to perform for Queen Elizabeth II at a Royal Command Performance in London. The following year she packed the London Palladium, setting a precedent for her sold-out concerts in Germany, Spain, France, England, Australia, Japan, and Holland. The previous year Carr and Danny Kaye had toured military bases in Vietnam, which provided one of the most fulfilling experiences of her career.

In 1970 the songstress was invited to a White House concert at a dinner in honor of Venezuelan president Rafael Caldera, and another performance at the inaugural of the Kennedy Music Center, in Washington, D.C. Carr became a darling of the White House, performing regularly at State dinners and at Richard Nixon's 1973 Inaugural celebration. She also performed for Presidents Ford, Reagan, and Bush during their time in the White House.

Proud of her Mexican heritage, Carr reminds her audiences that she was born "Florencia Bicenta de Casillas Martinez Cardona." (Although she calls herself "Mexican American," she is second generation American. Her father was born in Texas, her mother in California. Her grandparents are from Guadalajara, Chihuahua, and Sonora.) Carr admitted to *La Opinión* that "for business I'm very American, but my heart is totally Latin."

Since making her first appearance in Mexico in 1972, a mutual love affair developed between the two. It was also the year she recorded her first album in Spanish, *Vikki Carr, en Español*. Her sojourn into the Spanish music world would add an exciting new facet to her career. Already a favorite of American audiences, she was to become one of the most recognized voices of the Hispanic musical panorama. She has been awarded Mexico's "Visiting Entertainer of the Year," has hosted television specials on the Mexican networks and, beginning with *Vikki Carr y el amor* in 1980, has garnered gold, platinum and diamond records for her Spanish language albums.

Carr's 1992 album, *Cosas del amor*, for Sony Music, won that year's Grammy as "Best Latin Pop Album." The title song held the number one position for ten weeks on the *Billboard* charts and was named "Single of the Year" by the trade journal *Radio y música*. The album hit number one on *Billboard* charts, remaining in the top 20 for more than six months, placing number one in Puerto Rico, Costa Rica, Colombia, Venezuela, and Ecuador, going

"gold" in most of these countries, and in the United States. In March 1992, *Cosas del amor* was named "Album of the Year" in Venezuela, that country's equivalent to the "Grammy."

Carr, who resides in Beverly Hills, has been divorced twice. She told *La Opinión:* "I wasn't ready to marry the first time. Yes, I was in love, but we were both too young." She recalls that the three years following her 1974 divorce from husband/manager Dan Moss were the best, because there was no one in her life and she could dedicate herself fully to her career. In 1978 she met her second husband. "I told him, I'd like to marry you, but I won't stop singing, I was not born to be a housewife." But eventually the success of her career and the touring which kept them apart strained the marriage and the couple separated in 1991.

Carr maintains a busy schedule of domestic and international dates with her concert show and has achieved success in all areas of entertainment: theater, television, night clubs, international concert stages, and personal appearances. In 1992 she sold out two headlining engagements at Caesar's in Atlantic City and the prestigious McCallum Hall in Palm Springs, California.

## Joins Linda Rondstadt in Mariachis Revival

Having aided the resurgence of mariachis in Mexico and noting her friend **Linda Ronstadt**'s homage to this music form in the United States, Carr joined Ronstadt to perform in concerts together with mariachi groups in Los Angeles and Tucson, Arizona, including headlining at the Hollywood Bowl. *Los Angeles Times* music critic Don Heckman described Ronstadt and Carr's concert at UCLA's seventh-annual Mexican Art Series as "gifted and glossy."

In 1990 Carr made a loving return to England with a date at London's Royal Festival Hall. Sifting offers to return to the musical theater, Carr also remains open to new television and feature film scripts. In 1992 she completed an English-language television pilot entitled *Who Will Sing the Songs?* When at that time Carr was asked by *La Opinión* what she considered to be the most important aspect of her career, she answered: "My dream is the television series. It's about time that Latins have a show which treats us with the respect and dignity we deserve. Because we are not all gardeners or drug-dealers. Besides, not everyone who lives here in the United States speaks only Spanish. There's many of us who were born here and speak English."

Carr has recorded 50 best-selling records, including 17 gold albums. She was a Grammy nominee for *It Must Be Him* (1967) and *With Pen in Hand* (1969), and won Grammys for her Spanish language albums *Simplemente mujer* (1985) and *Cosas del amor*

(1992). With respect to her *Cosas del amor* Grammy win—the popular hit was a duet with Mexican songstress Ana Gabriel—Carr told *La Opinión:* "It's like winning an Oscar, because it again placed the name of Vikki Carr very strongly everywhere."

In addition to her command performances for royalty and presidents, Carr has received numerous honors. For her contributions to Chicano education, the young lady who never went to college was awarded an honorary doctorate in law by the University of San Diego. Other prestigious awards include being named "Woman of the World" by the International Orphans Fund, the 1984 "Hispanic Woman of the Year," the 1972 American Guild of Variety Artist's "Entertainer of the Year" and the *Los Angeles Times*'s highly respected "Woman of the Year" for 1970. In 1988 Carr was honored by the Nosotros group with their "Golden Eagle Award" for outstanding performer. She earned the "Career Achievement Award" of the Association of Hispanic Critics, Chicago's "Ovation Award," the YWCA "Silver Achievement Award" and was honored in 1990 by the City of Hope with the "Founder of Hope" award.

In 1968, upon hearing of the financial difficulties of Holy Cross High School in the San Antonio barrio, Carr initiated the first of a series of annual benefits that have netted more than a quarter of a million dollars for the school. In 1989 the school showed its gratitude by naming its library after her.

### Initiates Scholarship for Mexican Americans

In 1971 she established the Vikki Carr Scholarship Foundation to encourage Mexican American youths to pursue higher education. By 1992 the foundation had awarded over 175 scholarships to students who went to Yale, Harvard, Radcliffe, Stanford, and other universities around the country. Carr personally participates in the final screening and selection process. "These kids have become part of my family. I don't have any children of my own, but all of these youngsters are like my own family, and I couldn't be more proud of what they are doing," she told the *Saturday Evening Post,* adding, "A good education is the most important thing all of us Americans can do for our kids." Respected as an artist and a humanitarian, she has also done benefit performances and work for a wide range of organizations: March of Dimes, Vista, Tuberculosis Association, American Cancer Society, St. Jude Children's Research Hospital and the American Lung Association.

On the musical theater stage, the petite, five-foot, two-inch dynamo has garnered high critical acclaim for her leading roles in *The Unsinkable Molly Brown* (1968) with the John Kenley Players in Ohio and *South Pacific* (1969) at the Starlight Theater in Kansas City. In 1983 her starring performance in *I'm*

*Getting My Act Together and Taking It on the Road* was so successful it broke house records at the Westport Playhouse in St. Louis.

Enthusiastic about the prospects of doing television and feature films, the versatile star formed her own production company to pursue projects. Juggling engagements, recording sessions and charity events, the pace is frantic, but she remains cool and calm. Smart, successful, warm and engaging, Carr's energy and style are as radiant and irresistible as her voice. "God knows why He does things," she philosophized to *La Opinión.* "I lost two children, but He has given me much more, and a career to which I am married until death separates us."

## SELECTED DISCOGRAPHY:

*It Must Be Him,* 1967.
*With Pen in Hand,* 1969.
*Vikki Carr, en Español,* 1972.
*Vikki Carr y el amor,* 1980.
*Simplemente mujer,* 1985.
*From the Heart,* Pair, 1986.
*Cosas del amor,* Sony, 1992.
*It Must Be Him: The Best of Vikki Carr,* EMI, 1992.
*Greatest Hits,* Curb/CEMA, 1994.
*Hits of Today,* Columbia.

## SOURCES:

*La Opinión* (Panorama Section; translated from Spanish by Elena Kellner), April 30, 1992.
*Los Angeles Times* (Calendar Section), April 13, 1992.
*Más* (translated from Spanish by Elena Kellner), November-December 1991, p. 91.
*Saturday Evening Post,* September 1975, p. 11.

—*Sketch by Elena Kellner*

# José Carreras
## 1946-
**Spanish opera singer**

Considered one of the world's most gifted lyric tenors, José Carreras has had a meteoric career. Since his 1970 professional debut as Flavio in *Norma,* Carreras has maintained an exhausting schedule that has taken him to the world's most famous opera venues, including Milan's La Scala, both the New

*José Carreras*

York Metropolitan and City Operas, the Vienna Staatsoper, and the Salzburg Festivals. His repertoire includes leading roles from more than 40 operas. He is also a prolific recording artist with a lengthy discography and an extensive videography. Carreras's fame expanded beyond the opera world when he performed with fellow tenors **Plácido Domingo** and Luciano Pavarotti on the eves of the World Cup soccer finals in both 1990 and 1994.

Often compared to the young Giuseppe di Stefano, Carreras possesses a voice described as lyrical, naturally beautiful, and of a rich, warm timber. That voice was seriously endangered in 1987, when Carreras fell ill with leukemia. He was forced to withdraw from singing for a year while he underwent treatment for the disease. But Carreras battled back and returned to the stage in 1988 in a triumphant outdoor concert in Barcelona. This concert—and many others since—have benefited the José Carreras International Foundation Against Leukemia, which Carreras established following his recovery.

### Love of Singing Begins in Childhood

Carreras was born Josep Maria Carreras-Coll on December 5, 1946, in Barcelona, Spain. He is the youngest child of Josep Carreras-Soler, a traffic policeman, and Antonia Coll-Saigi, a hairdresser. Carreras and his wife, Mercedes, have two children, Alberto and Julia.

While Carreras did not actually decide to pursue an operatic career until he was 21, the catalysts for that choice occurred in childhood. When he was six years old, his parents took him to the theater to see Mario Lanza in the film, *The Great Caruso.* Carreras wrote in his 1991 autobiography, *Singing from the Soul,* that "it wasn't the story about Caruso that fascinated me . . . what really excited me about the film was the music—the arias and the way Mario Lanza sang them." Carreras claimed that despite the fact that he had never heard these arias previously, he "repeated them to perfection" the next day, much to the amazement of his family. From that time on, Carreras sang arias at every opportunity, eventually earning the nickname "Rigoletto" at school.

When Carreras was eight, he enrolled at the Barcelona Conservatory, where he studied music for three years. It was also at age eight that he went to see his first opera at Barcelona's Gran Teatro del Liceo. The performance was *Aida* and Carreras was entranced. He recalled its profound impact in his autobiography: "In every person's life, there are certain moments that can never fade or die. For me that night was one of those occasions. I will never forget the first time I saw singers on a stage and an orchestra." He continued, "It was the first time in my life that I'd stepped into a theatre, but the place was as familiar to me as if I had always known it. At the time, I couldn't understand my feeling. Today I can describe it this way: from the moment I crossed the threshold, I knew it was my world, I knew it was where I belonged."

Soon after that experience, Carreras gave his first public performance: singing for a National Radio benefit program. He later speculated that this performance may have led to his first Liceo invitation to sing: he was asked to portray Trujaman in de Falla's *El Retablo de Maese Pedro.* Carreras was just 11, and the performance is often cited as his debut. The young Carreras performed twice more at the Liceo in small parts, but was eventually forced to reject offers because his voice had begun to change. All decisions regarding an operatic future were postponed.

Formal voice training began in 1964, under Maestro Puig. A year later, continuing his singing lessons, Carreras enrolled at the University of Barcelona, where he studied chemistry for a time. But his first love was singing. Having begun to study voice under the tutelage of Maestro Juan Ruax in 1966, Carreras abandoned chemistry a year later.

### *Norma* Debut Marks Formal Career

In 1970, Carreras debuted in the role of Flavio in Bellini's *Norma.* His performance attracted the attention of soprano Montserrat Caballé, who requested him for the lead tenor role opposite herself in *Lucrezia Borgia.* Carreras considered this role to be his professional debut. Thanks to the Caballé's sponsorship, Carreras's career was launched. In addition to his role as Gennaro in *Lucrezia Borgia,* he appeared as Ismael in *Nabucco.* Carreras won the Verdi Singing Competition in Parma in 1971, securing his future. From that point on, he performed in opera houses all over the world, taking only about three years to achieve a prominence usually requiring a decade of work.

Carreras has performed numerous roles throughout the course of his career, including Riccardo (*Un ballo in maschera*), Don José (*Carmen*), Rodolfo (*La Bohème*), and Cavaradossi (*Tosca*). He has also worked with many conductors; his favorite was Maestro Herbert von Karajan. The two collaborated regularly from 1976 until Karajan's death. Karajan was responsible for pushing Carreras to attempt heavier roles not always suited for his voice, such as his much-criticized performance of Radames (*Aida*) at Salzburg in 1979—Carreras subsequently dropped this role from his repertoire. Carreras has not limited himself strictly to the operatic stage, nor solely to operatic material. He has sung folk songs, *zarzuela* excerpts, and even pop songs, both in concert and in the recording studio.

### Illness Halts Career

Carreras was diagnosed with acute lymphoblastic leukemia in 1987. He sought treatment for the disease at the Hutchinson Cancer Research Institute in Seattle, Washington. The treatment was grueling, and included an autologous bone marrow transplant, radiation, and chemotherapy. It was possible that even if Carreras survived, his voice might not, since radiation and chemotherapy often scar the vocal chords. Carreras never stopped hoping that he would both conquer the disease and sing again. In an interview with William Livingstone for *Stereo Review* in 1992, he credited fellow tenors Dómingo and Pavarotti for their support and also thanked his fans for helping to bolster him emotionally during that time: "The thousands of letters I received from people I didn't know touched me deeply, and were fundamental to my recovery."

His comeback concert was held, appropriately, at the Arch of Triumph in Barcelona in July 1988. That same year Carreras established his International Foundation Against Leukemia. In a 1993 interview with Serafin Garcia for the *Unesco Courier,* Carreras outlined the organization's goal. "We have some very ambitious plans and program[s]," he said. "Our main aim is to help scientific research with funding and grants. Scientists believe that the best way to fight the disease is to step up research efforts." Toward that end, Carreras has sung in several benefit concerts for the Institute.

Carreras's battle with leukemia is movingly described in his autobiography, *Singing from the Soul,* originally published in 1989. It has appeared in nine languages and sold 650,000 copies. It has received mixed reviews, called "disappointingly slight" by *Publishers Weekly* (1991) and "compelling" by *Library Journal* (1991). The title is derived from Carreras's personal theory on singing, which he explained to the *Unesco Courier:* "When you're a tenor, you must start singing in the heart, move up to the head, then let it out through the voice. . . . It is by that subtly circuitous route that the voice . . . can genuinely express the emotions of the heart while at the same time obeying the instructions of the mind."

### Performances Increase Fame

In 1990, Carreras helped raise opera to a new level of public appreciation. Billed as "The Three Tenors," Carreras, Dómingo, and Pavarotti performed in concert for the World Cup soccer finals in Rome. The idea originated with Carreras, and it was an astounding success, televised to an estimated international audience of 800 million. The *New York Times* placed the number of recordings sold at ten million, with video sales exceeding the one-million mark. The three tenors re-created the concert for the World Cup finals again in 1994, at Dodger Stadium in Los Angeles, with even greater exposure. With a live audience of more than 50,000, the concert was televised to an estimated 1.3 billion viewers.

In June of 1994, Carreras joined members of an Italian opera company in a tribute to the dead of war-torn Bosnia. In a televised concert set in the ruins of Sarajevo National Library, Zubin Mehta conducted the singers and the Sarajevo orchestra and chorus in Mozart's "Requiem Mass."

Carreras has expressed the hope that performances like these—outside traditional opera-house settings—will increase opera's popularity. In his interview with the *Unesco Courier,* he said: "Like any other form of artistic expression, music needs an audience. It can only be decoded and become accessible if it reaches the public—you can't love anything until you know it."

### SELECTED PUBLISHED WORKS:

*Singing from the Soul,* translated by John Ellis Thomas and others, Seattle, Y.C.P. Publications, 1991.

### SOURCES:

#### Books

*Concise Oxford Dictionary of Opera,* second edition, edited by Harold Rosenthal and John Warrack, London, Oxford University Press, 1979.

*International Dictionary of Opera,* Volume 1, edited by C. Steven Larue, Detroit, St. James Press, 1993.

*Metropolitan Opera Encyclopedia,* edited by David Hamilton, New York, Simon and Schuster, 1987.

*New Grove Dictionary of Opera,* Volume 1, edited by Stanley Sadie, London, Macmillan Press, 1992.

## Periodicals

*Library Journal,* April 15, 1991, p. 94.
*New York Times,* June 20, 1994, p. A4; July 14, 1994, p. C11; July 18, 1994, p. C11.
*Publishers Weekly,* April 5, 1991, p. 129.
*Stereo Review,* August 1992, p. 88.
*Unesco Courier,* February 1993, pp. 4–6.

—*Sketch by Ellen Dennis French*

*Lynda Carter*

# Lynda Carter
## 1951(?)-
**Mexican American actress**

Although many television viewers remember Lynda Carter from her years as Wonder Woman in the television series of the same name, few realize how diversely talented the actress is. Carter has starred in several movies made for television, including *Rita Hayworth: The Love Goddess* and *Daddy.* She sings in her own nightclub show and with a rock band. Further, she served as a consultant and beauty director for the cosmetics company, Maybelline, for 12 years. Carter is now spokesperson for Lens Express, Inc., and she contributes her time and money to several deserving causes.

As the actress herself told *Vanity Fair,* Lynda Carter is "a working person" from "humble beginnings." During the early 1950's, Lynda Jean Cordoba Carter was born on July 24 in Phoenix, Arizona, to a mother of Mexican descent, Jean, and a furniture-dealing father of English heritage. When the girl was just ten years old her father divorced her mother and left the family—Jean Carter raised her three children on her own. She worked nights at a factory in Phoenix, assembling parts for television sets. Lynda admired her mother; she told *People,* "She taught me more than anything to survive in a dignified, honorable, gracious way."

At 15 years of age, Carter made her acting and singing debut in a pizza parlor, and at 17, she began to make $400 a week acting in lounges in Reno and Las Vegas, Nevada. Upon graduating from high school she attended Arizona State University in Tempe; her academic career, however, was cut short when she became Miss World-U.S.A. in 1973. For some time, Carter trained for the stage with Stella Adler and Charles Conrad. It was not long before she won the role for which she would become the most famous, that of Diana Prince/Wonder Woman in the television series *Wonder Woman.*

### Garners National Fame as "Wonder Woman"

The 25-year-old, 5'9", strikingly beautiful brunette won thousands of fans when she first appeared in the 1975 pilot for the television series as the super-powered Wonder Woman. Clad in shiny red boots, a red-white-and-blue, starred-and-eagled body suit, and a gold headband and bracelet, Lynda Carter managed to battle evildoers and impress audiences at the same time. In the words of a writer for *Vanity Fair,* Carter as Wonder Woman was "a bona fide feminist superhero, albeit an amply endowed feminist superhero who wore a skimpy spangled corset." Carter starred in both *Wonder Woman,* which aired on ABC from 1976 to 1977, and *The New Adventures of Wonder Woman,* which aired on CBS from 1977 to 1979. During that time, the actress found time to appear in such shows as *The Olivia Newton-John Show, Battle of the Network Stars,* and *Circus of the Stars.* Carter also portrayed Bobbie Jo James in the 1976 motion picture *Bobbie Jo and the Outlaw* and starred in *Lightning in a Bottle* with Dee Wallace Stone, Marty Kove, and Matt McCoy in 1993.

Although her career thrived during the *Wonder Woman* years, Carter's personal life began to disintegrate. One year after her debut as Wonder Woman, Carter married an agent, Ron Samuels. Samuels directed her career and shared her $3 million annual income. The marriage, however, was an unhappy one. "It was the first thing in my life that failed," Carter told *People.* "It failed because it was based on work." Carter divorced Samuels in 1982.

When *The New Adventures of Wonder Woman* was discontinued in 1979, Carter kept herself busy with various projects. She appeared in two CBS television movies in 1980, portraying Brooke Newman in *The Last Song* and Brianne O'Neil in *Hotline.* She promoted herself with her own highly rated CBS television specials, *Lynda Carter's Special* in 1980, *Lynda Carter: Encore* in 1980, *Lynda Carter's Celebration* in 1981, *Lynda Carter: Street Life,* in 1982, and *Lynda Carter: Body and Soul* in 1984. For this last special, Carter was nominated for an Emmy Award.

### Plays Rita Hayworth in Television Movie

Carter regularly appeared on television. She starred in television movies such as *Born To Be Sold* in 1981 and *Rita Hayworth: The Love Goddess* in 1983. This latter role received a great deal of attention; some friends of **Rita Hayworth** did not want the details of the actress's life televised. Some even objected to Carter's involvement with the show. Despite these opinions, Carter was determined and excited to portray the "Love Goddess." "I really wanted the challenge," Carter told *People* magazine. "We both had Hispanic backgrounds. We were both in show business at an early age. We both sing and dance. We were both married to our managers." One friend of Hayworth's, Gloria Luchenbill, agreed in *People* that Carter should play the part: "I know both ladies, and when you look around, who else would play the part? She has that same quality of shyness and naiveté that Rita had." Carter has also starred in *Partners in Crime* and *Stillwatch,* and in 1986 she won a Golden Eagle Award for Consistent Performance in Television in Film.

An established television star, Carter has enjoyed similar success performing live. She developed her own nightclub act and took it to Las Vegas and Reno, soon after the demise of the *Wonder Woman* series. She has since taken this show to the Palladium Theatre in London, the Sporting Club in Monte Carlo, Monaco, the Hotel de la Reforma in Mexico City, and Atlantic City, New Jersey. She won a Mexican Ariel Award for International Entertainer of the Year. Carter did not limit her live performances

to large shows. For a time, she sang with the rock group, Garfin Gathering.

Carter's career extends further still. She became the beauty and fashion director of Maybelline cosmetics and served as a consultant for the company. Carter even modeled Maybelline cosmetics for magazine advertisements. Her influence on consumers dramatically affected sales figures: Within two years of Carter's arrival at the company, sales of Maybelline cosmetics tripled. The astute businesswoman even founded her own company: Lynda Carter Productions.

Although the International Bachelors Association named Carter one of the "Ten Most Exciting Women In The World," those bachelors can be sure that the actress will have nothing to do with them. In 1984 Carter married Robert Altman, an attorney from Washington, D.C. She explained her life with Altman in *People.* "My life has changed since I met Robert. I feel a sense of security with him that I've never known before. He offers advice, but only when I ask. I think, finally, I'm finding my own life." After Lynda married Altman and joined him to live in Washington, D.C., the couple had two children, a son, Jamie Clifford, and a younger daughter, Jessica. The relocation to the capital city of the United States did not end Carter's career. She starred in two television movies in 1991, *Posing* and *Daddy.*

Despite Altman's involvement and ultimate conviction of guilt in the notorious Bank of Credit and Commerce International scandal, Carter's loyalty to her husband has not waned. In fact, Carter has been his most adamant supporter. She stated in *Vanity Fair,* "To tell you the truth, I know my husband has done nothing. I know that he is a strong and brilliant guy, a loving husband, a great father, a wonderful friend, and we love each other and are going forward." According to Blaine Trump, who spoke of Carter in *Vanity Fair,* the actress's loyalty and determination typify Carter. "Lynda is the type of person who has always worked hard to get where she is. She has very solid beliefs and commitments to her family and her life, and I think that commitment has gotten her through just about every situation she has faced in life. She's not a quitter. And she's not afraid to take chances."

Despite her success and her busy schedule, Carter has not forgotten her "humble beginnings." She has eagerly contributed to many causes. She served as the American Cancer Society's national crusade chairperson from 1985 to 1986, and worked as the honorary chairperson for the Exceptional Children's Foundation from 1987 to 1988. She was a member of the United Service Organization's board of governors, the National Committee on Arts for the Handicapped, Feed the Hungry, and the Committee for Creative Nonviolence. Carter has also been very active with charitable organizations in the Washington, D.C., area. In the 1990s, she has been involved with the Susan G. Komen Foundation & Washington's Race for the Cure for breast cancer research and education and remains active with the American Red Cross. In addition, Carter has been honored with the Jill Ireland Award for Volunteerism and Unihealth's Pinnacle Award for her charitable acts. Such activity speaks for itself; the woman who once played Wonder Woman is not just another pretty face.

**SELECTED VIDEOGRAPHY:**

*Bobbie Jo and the Outlaw,* 1976.
*The Last Song,* 1980.
*Born to be Sold,* 1981.
*Hotline,* 1982.
*Rita Hayworth: The Love Goddess,* 1983.
*Partners in Crime,* c. 1986.
*Stillwatch,* c. 1986.
*Daddy,* 1991.
*Posing,* 1991.
*Lightning in a Bottle,* 1993.

**SOURCES:**

**Books**

*Contemporary Theatre, Film, and Television,* Volume 5, Detroit, Gale, 1988, pp. 49–50.

**Periodicals**

*Harper's Bazaar,* January, 1985, pp. 134+.
*Money,* January, 1980, pp. 50+.
*People,* November 7, 1983, p. 109; March 19, 1984, p. 9; October 15, 1984, p. 11; February 9, 1987, p. 7.
*Saturday Evening Post,* May-June, 1983, pp. 42+; September 2, 1991, pp. 58+.
*Teen,* September, 1982, pp. 82+.

*TV Guide,* October 24, 1981, pp. 16+.

—*Sketch by Ronie-Richele Garcia-Johnson*

# Lourdes Casal
## 1938-1981
### Cuban American writer and political activist

Writer and intellectual Lourdes Casal will be best remembered for her efforts to reconcile Cuban exiles in the United States with the revolution set off by **Fidel Castro** in their homeland in 1959. Casal became the best and most outspoken exponent of a third alternative for young Cuban American intellectuals torn between the liberalism of their American counterparts and loyalty to their conservative elders.

Casal was born in 1938 in Havana, Cuba, to middle class parents of mixed black and white ancestry who provided their highly studious and intelligent daughter with excellent educational opportunities. Casal studied for seven years at the Catholic University of Santo Tomas de Villanueva in Havana, where she originally majored in chemical engineering. Finding the practical application of science too confining, she devoted herself to the study of psychology. By 1957, together with other Catholic students, she was collaborating with Fidel Castro's 26th of July Movement in an effort to unseat the dictatorship of **Fulgencia Batista**. But the communist leanings of the triumphant revolution after 1959 forced Casal into the opposition and by 1961 she sought exile in the United States.

### Exile in the United States

Settling in New York, Casal completed her studies in psychology, receiving a master's degree in 1962 and a doctorate in 1975 from the New School for Social Research. During this same period she compiled her book *El caso Padilla: literatura y revolucion en Cuba* (1971), a series of documents exposing the deteriorating relationship between writers and revolutionary officials in Cuba, exemplified by the suppression of Cuban poet Heberto Padilla's work. *Los fundadores: Alfonso y otros cuentos*, a collection of short stories which some critics deemed autobiographical, was published in 1973.

Casal's unflinching interest in her homeland found outlet in such projects as the first and second Reuniones de Estudios Cubanos (Symposia of Cuban Studies), which lead to the founding of the Instituto de Estudios Cubanos (Institute of Cuban Studies) and to her participation in creating the *Revista Areito*. One of the aims of this magazine was to publish articles that would explore both the positive and the negative aspects of the Cuban government. This alternative position from a group of young Cuban intellectuals in exile lead to an invitation from the Havana government to visit the island nation. Only Casal accepted.

### Accepts Cuban Government's Invitation to Return

A second trip to her homeland to participate in a gathering of intellectuals at the University of Havana came shortly after her initial visit in September 1973. This time Casal returned to New York converted to the Castro revolution and *Revista Areito* became the mouthpiece for those who shared Casal's point of view. A desire to share this experience of re-encounter with Cuba led Casal to foster the creation of the Antonio Maceo Brigade, which enabled young Cuban exiles to visit Cuba, and the Circulo de Cultura Cubana, which brought together artists and intellectuals who wished to establish closer ties with Cuba. In 1978 she played an important role in the dialogue with the Castro government that made it possible for exiles to visit their families in the homeland. Casal returned to Cuba permanently in 1979, and she died in 1981 from a kidney ailment. A volume of her poetry, *Palabras juntan revolucion* (1981), was published in Havana by Casa de las Americas.

Casal wrote and published extensively in the fields of psychology and the social sciences. She was on the faculty of several colleges and universities, including Dominican College in Blauvelt, New York, Brooklyn College, and Rutgers University. She was the recipient of numerous awards, including the Cintas Fellowship from the Institute for International Education (1974–75), the Social Science Research Council grant for research in Cuba (1978), a fellowship from the Woodrow Wilson International Center for Scholars (1978–79), and a grant from the Ford Foundation Competition on the Movement of Caribbean Peoples (1977–78).

### SOURCES:

Burunat, Silvia, "Lourdes Casal," in *Biographical Dictionary of Hispanic Literature in the United States,* edited by Nicolás Kanellos, Greenwood Press, 1989, pp. 49–55.

De la Cuesta, Leonel Antonio, "Perfil biografico," in *Itinerario Ideologico: Antologia de Lourdes Casal,* edited by Maria Cristina Herrera and de la Cuta, Instituto de Estudios Cubanos (Miami, Florida), 1982, pp. 3–8.

—*Sketch by Sylvia Novo Pena*

---

# Pablo Casals
## 1876-1973
### Spanish cellist, conductor, and composer

Identified most readily for his extraordinary talents as a cellist, Pablo Casals offered many additional contributions to the international community during his nearly 97 years of life. His musical talents encompassed conducting and composition as well as performance. Casals is also remembered for his intense moral convictions and his dedication toward world peace—he was nominated for a Nobel Peace Prize in 1958.

Pablo (or, Pau—the Catalan equivalent of Pablo) Carlos Salvador Defilló de Casals was born on December 29, 1876, about 40 miles from Barcelona in the market town of Vendrell, Catalonia. He was the second of 11 children born to Carlos Casals and his wife, Pilar Defilló de Casals. Only three of the Casals children lived to adulthood; of these, Pablo was the eldest. As much as he loved his native Catalonia—especially the seaside town of San Salvador where his lifelong attachment to the ocean began—Casals' early life was not easy. "Casals' youth was not, except in romantic accounts, a carefree period of happiness and security," Robert Baldock wrote in his biography, *Pablo Casals.* "Life for the family was tough. His parents were young, poor and very largely alone: unusually, they did not have a wide network of family support."

Casals' father served as Vendrell's church organist and choir leader. On a secular level, Carlos Casals established a men's chorus and was known to perform with local musicians at fiestas and other occasions. He also taught music to private pupils. For his son, Carlos Casals served as an early instructor in piano, voice, violin, and organ. Young Casals discovered the cello relatively late: he was 11 years old.

### Left Vendrell for Barcelona Opportunities

Despite his father's own musical background, it was Casals' Puerto Rican-born mother who prevailed

*Pablo Casals*

over her doubting husband in 1888, taking their son to Barcelona, where the boy enrolled in the Escuela Municipal de Música ("Municipal School of Music"). There he studied cello, music theory, and piano. It was also in Barcelona that the then 13-year-old Casals—browsing in a small music shop with his father—discovered Bach's six unaccompanied cello suites, which Casals practiced for 12 years "before he dared play them in public," according to Ralph Thibodeau in *Commonweal*. "They are, more than any other works, his great musical and spiritual legacy." In the *New York Times*, Alden Whitman assessed the crux of the artist's imprint on the musical world: his "single-handed restoration to the repertory of Bach's cello music" and his "innovations in bowing and fingering that gave the cello a new and striking personality."

Casals soon attracted a following through a part-time job playing cello in a trio at Barcelona's Café Tost, where he earned just four pesatas each day. In 1891 more lucrative opportunities arose at another café, La Pajarera. It was there that the prominent pianist **Isaac Albéniz** journeyed to hear Casals play. An impressed Albéniz urged the teenager to accompany him to London. Casals' mother refused. Albéniz desisted, but not before giving Casals' mother a letter of introduction to Madrid's powerful arts patron, Count Guillermo de Morphy. Casals did not use that letter until after he graduated from his Barcelona school in 1893. He then began attending Madrid's Royal Conservatory of Music and, perhaps more

significantly, acquired the patronage of the Spanish royal family. This included Queen María Cristina, who gave him financial support, and the Queen's adviser, the Count de Morphy, who supervised Casals' general education and training.

After an unsuccessful attempt to further his musical education in Brussels, Belgium, Casals—accompanied by his mother and two younger brothers—arrived in Paris in 1895. Disobeying the wishes of his Madrid patrons (the Count de Morphy wanted Casals to continue to study musical composition and eventually elevate the status of Spanish music), Casals was cut off from his royal stipend. He found a low-paying job playing second cello with the unremarkable Folies Marigny orchestra, but the strain of supporting the three other family members was too much. They all returned to Spain in 1896.

Back in Barcelona, Casals was soon appointed to teach at his former school. "Teaching absorbed much of his time," Baldock wrote, "as it would throughout his life. Casals became one of the great cello teachers of the twentieth century." He also served as principal cellist in the Gran Teatro del Liceo orchestra. The following year he performed as a soloist with the Madrid Symphony Orchestra, and, having repaired his relations with his royal patrons, was awarded the Order of Carlos III. When he returned to Paris in 1899, his circumstances were considerably improved, and with the Count de Morphy's assistance, Casals established an important connection with the eminent conductor Charles Lamoureux.

### Developed International Reputation

Thereafter Casals began his international career, playing at London's Crystal Palace and before Queen Victoria, serving as soloist with the Lamoureux Orchestra in Paris, and touring Europe and the Americas. In 1904, just past his twenty-seventh birthday, Casals performed for U.S. President Theodore Roosevelt at the White House. As a cellist, Whitman wrote, "Casals was able to demonstrate what luminescent and human music could be drawn from the strings of a rather awkward instrument.... He provoked awe and applause for the profundity of his insights, the felicity of his playing, and, above all, the soaring purity of his interpretations of baroque and classical composers." His network of friendships within the musical community expanded. Casals' Trio, including the violinist Jacques Thibaud and the pianist Alfred Cortot, "is probably the most famous in musical history," according to Baldock. "It was certainly among the longest-lasting ... and the first to achieve international celebrity."

Casals had spent most of the years since the turn of the century outside Spain, but after the World War I he returned to Barcelona, entering a period of his career that he regarded, as he later told Albert E.

Kahn for a book called *Joys and Sorrows: Reflections by Pablo Casals,* "in many ways, as the most fruitful of my life." He nurtured his interest in conducting, establishing the Orquestra Pau Casals in 1919, and leading its first concert the following year. He personally financed the 88-member group until the orchestra became self-sufficient. Casals loved conducting, and over the course of his career he led orchestras throughout the world. It was the conductor's role, Whitman said, that Casals "fancied as his real métier." In his book *Casals and the Art of Interpretation,* the master's student David Blum declared: "At no time did Casals communicate his ideas about music more clearly or eloquently than when rehearsing an orchestra."

Another of Casals' achievements in Barcelona—and one that indicates Casals' manner of combining his musical talent and his civic principles—was the establishment of a Workingmen's Concert Association. For a small fee, members could attend six Orquestra Pau Casals concerts held on Sunday mornings. There, they would hear major artists, including Casals himself. "The Sunday-morning programs were not 'pops' programs," Bernard Taper asserted in his book *Cellist in Exile,* since "such condescension would have been offensive both to Casals and to his audience."

The proclamation of the Spanish Republic in 1931 ushered in a time of intense engagement for Casals, who had inherited his father's republican loyalties. Kahn recorded Casals' reflections on the moment decades later: "The first years of the Spanish Republic . . . were among the most meaningful years of my life. I am not a politician. . . . But an artist with a conscience cannot separate himself from certain political issues. Chief among those issues are justice and freedom. And it was the republican government that brought justice and freedom to Spain." Among his other activities, Casals served as president of Catalonia's music council.

Then came the Spanish Civil War. "The only weapons I have ever had," Casals told Kahn, "are my cello and my conductor's baton. And during the Civil War I used them as best I could to support the cause in which I believed—the cause of freedom and democracy." Whitman elaborated on this subject, saying that Casals "gave hundreds of benefit concerts abroad for the Republic and put a large part of his personal savings at its disposal. The government, in turn, named streets and squares for him and encouraged his exertions to bring great music to the common people."

## Opposed Franco Regime and Worked for Peace

When the Republic collapsed, Casals went into exile, vowing not to return to Spain until democracy was restored. After a short, despondent stay in Paris,

Casals settled in the southern French village of Prades, close to the Spanish border. There he worked to assist Catalans held in French concentration camps. He resumed his concert career briefly at the end of World War II, but when he saw that the Allied Powers' victory had left **Francisco Franco**'s dictatorship untouched, he declared that he would stop performing altogether.

In 1950 Casals was convinced to appear as conductor and cellist on the occasion of the bicentennial of Bach's death. Thus began a series of festivals known as the Prades Festivals, led by Casals until 1966. Casals continued his Prades affiliation even after he left France to settle in Puerto Rico in 1956. He exerted a strong influence on the musical culture of his adopted home. It was on Casals' recommendation that a conservatory was established there. Puerto Rico also became the site of the annual Festival Casals.

During the remaining years of his life Casals taught master classes in Switzerland, Italy, and the United States, perhaps most notably at the annual Marlboro Music Festivals in Vermont and at the Festival in Puerto Rico. Perhaps his most publicized performance during this time occurred when he agreed to play the cello at President John F. Kennedy's White House in 1961, despite continued U.S. recognition of the Franco regime.

It was during these later years that Casals' work as a composer became more widely known. Among his main composition achievements is his oratorio, *El pessebre* ("The Manger"), which he composed in Prades and conducted at its 1960 debut in Acapulco, Mexico. Casals envisioned the repeated performances of this work as a crusade for peace and conducted it more than 60 times. Casals is also remembered for his "Himno a las Naciones Unidas" ("Hymn of the United Nations"), a work that he first conducted in 1971.

Not unexpectedly for a man who lived nearly a century, Casals did not live a simple personal life. From 1906 to 1912, Casals was romantically involved with the Portuguese cellist Guilhermina Suggia, who came to identify herself as "Madame P. Casals-Suggia," although it is not clear that she and Casals ever officially married. In 1914 Casals married the American singer Susan Metcalfe; they separated in 1928 but did not divorce until 1957. At that time, he married a woman 60 years his junior—his student Marta Montañez—with whom he lived until his death. "The years I have shared with Martita," Casals told Kahn, "have been the happiest years of my life."

Throughout that long life, Casals never ceased to combine his music and his conscience. Whitman quoted Casals' 1962 statement: "As a man, my first obligation is toward the welfare of my fellow men. I will endeavor to meet that obligation through music, the means which God has given me, since it transcends language, politics, and national boundaries." Casals offered a more expansive explanation in his conversations with Kahn: "To see people gathered in a concert hall came to have a symbolic significance for me. When I looked into their faces, and when we shared the beauty of music, I knew that we were brothers and sisters, all members of the same family. Despite the dreadful conflicts of the intervening years and all the false barriers between nations, that knowledge has never left me. It will remain with me until the end. I long for the day when the peoples of the world will sit together, bound by happiness and love of beauty, as in one great concert hall."

Casals died on October 22, 1973, due to complications resulting from a heart attack. Puerto Rican Governor Rafael Hernandez Colón, who delivered Casals' eulogy, declared three days of official mourning. The exile from Spain was posthumously honored by the government of King Juan Carlos II in 1976, with the issuance of a postage stamp commemorating the centennial year of Casals' birth. In November of 1979, four years after Franco's death, Casals' body was returned to Catalonia.

## SOURCES:

### Books

*Baker's Biographical Dictionary of Musicians,*
    eighth edition, revised by Nicolas Slonimsky,
    New York, Schirmer, 1992.
Baldock, Robert, *Pablo Casals,* Boston, Northeastern University Press, 1992.
Blum, David. *Casals and the Art of Interpretation,*
    New York, Holmes and Meier, 1977.
Kahn, Albert E., *Joys and Sorrows: Reflections by
    Pablo Casals,* New York, Simon and Schuster,
    1970.
Taper, Bernard, *Cellist in Exile,* New York,
    McGraw-Hill, 1962.

### Periodicals

*Commonweal,* December 14, 1973, pp. 292–93.
*High Fidelity,* May 1989, p. 59.
*Newsweek,* November 5, 1973, pp. 110–11.
*New York Times,* October 23, 1973, pp. 1, 26,
    52; October 24, 1973, p. 50; October 28,
    1973; p. D17; January 2, 1991, pp. C9, C12.
*Time,* November 5, 1973, pp. 77–78; October 12,
    1992.

—*Sketch by Erika Dreifus*

# Rosario Castellanos
## 1925-1974
### Mexican writer, educator, and diplomat

Rosario Castellanos, prolific writer of poetry, fiction, and essays, and an insightful and impassioned social critic, gave Mexico one of its most eloquent twentieth-century voices for the rights of indigenous populations and the concerns of women.

The elder of two children of César Castellanos and Adriana Figueroa de Castellanos, Rosario was born in Mexico City on May 25, 1925, but passed her childhood on her parents' extensive holdings in the town of Comitán de las Flores, near the Guatemalan border in Mexico's southernmost state of Chiapas. This remote and beautiful region, ancient home of the Maya, had been largely bypassed by the effects of the Mexican Revolution. It remained during Castellanos' childhood much as it had since the time of the conquistadors, with most of the land in the hands of wealthy *ladinos* (whites) while Indians were reduced to lives of poverty, misery, and servitude.

Castellanos—ignored by her parents in favor of her younger brother—was a solitary, observant child, who early developed what would prove to be a lifelong empathy with the plight of the Indians of Chiapas. This affinity was fostered by her Indian *nana,* a Mayan woman named Rufina, who infused in the child the culture and mythology of her people. Castellanos later brought these people and their homeland vividly to life in her most important fiction.

The Castellanos family suffered severe reverses during Rosario's childhood, first through the death of the favored younger brother, Mario Benjamn, and then through the loss of their lands, which were expropriated and redistributed to the Indians during the Agrarian Reform instituted by President **Lázaro Cárdenas**. Although the effect of the reform was devastating to Castellanos' parents, she herself later saw it as a liberating event in her own life, freeing her from the restricted existence she might have expected as the protected daughter of a landed family.

When she was 17 years old, the family moved to Mexico City, where she completed high school. She then studied philosophy and literature at the Universidad Nacional Autónoma de Máxico, where she earning a master's degree in philosophy in 1950. Her thesis, *Sobre Cultura Feminina (On Feminine Culture)* is considered by some critics a seminal work of feminist thought. The years following her graduation from Universidad Nacional were remarkably productive. These years encompassed European study and travel and then an extended period in her native

Chiapas, working and writing for the Instituto Nacional Indigenista (National Indigenist Institute), for the benefit of the Indians.

### Indigenous Works Gain Critical Acclaim

Her first book of poetry, published in 1948, was favorably greeted by critics, who recognized in her an important young writer with "a new voice." In 1955 she published *Balun-Canan,* the first of the four works of fiction collectively known as her "Chiapas Cycle," completed in 1964. Her empathy with the Indian characters who are central to these works set her books apart from the run of "indigenist" writing. Displaying Indians in all the complexity of human nature rather than as the one dimensional victims seen in much indigenist literature, Castellanos explained that she tried in all her books to bring to light "the essential ambiguity of the human being . . . along with the series of contradictions that prevails in all social relationships."

A companion to the theme of the plight of the Indian in Chiapas in Castellanos' writings is the relationship between men and women. In both cases critics have discerned patterns of dominator and dominated, of oppression and submission. Castellanos believed along with Simone Weil, whose work she admired, that power debilitates those who wield it as well as those against whom it is wielded.

Heavily committed to her work, in 1958 Castellanos married philosophy professor Ricardo Guerra, who respected her literary work and encouraged her to continue writing. The couple had one son, Gabriel, born in 1961, who became a focal point of his mother's life. The marriage, however, ended in divorce in 1971.

From 1960 to 1966, Castellanos was director of the department of journalism and information at the Universidad Nacional, where she also taught Spanish American literature. Castellanos spent 1966 and 1967 in the United States teaching at the Universities of Wisconsin, Indiana, and Colorado, and later returned to the Universidad Nacional.

### Award-winning Literature

The inventory of Castellanos' accomplishments is impressive. From childhood, the writing of poetry was a habit with her, a way of exploring the pain in her life, of seeking "another way to be," even a means of survival. All her life, her writing would serve similar purposes. As an adult, the range of her writing extended to fiction, essays, and a weekly column for the Mexican newspaper *Excélsior,* which she continued until her death. She once told a friend, "I can always write, even when things are not going well, when I am depressed." The important literary influences in her life were the Chilean novelist **Gabriela Mistral**, Simone de Beauvoir, and Virginia Woolf.

Castellanos won recognition for her work during her lifetime; she was the recipient of a number of literary prizes, including the Premio Xavier Villaurrutia in 1961 for *Ciudad Real* ("Royal City"), and the Sourasky Prize for Literature in her later life. In 1967 she was named Mexico's Woman of the Year. In 1971, President Luis Echeverria appointed her Mexico's Ambassador to Israel, and there she spent the last years of her life, adding to her ambassadorial duties by teaching and writing. Castellanos' life was cut short in August of 1974, when she was electrocuted in a household accident.

Her death occasioned a further shower of praise not only for her work, but for the great love and dedication she brought to all aspects of her life. The poet Carlos Pellicer was moved by her death to speak of "her progressive ideas . . . her goodness, her moral integrity," all of which made her, he said, "an eminent example of the new Mexican woman."

### SELECTED PUBLISHED WORKS:

*Apuntes para una declaracion de fe* (*Notes for a Declaration of Faith*), América/Educación Pública, 1948.
*Sobre cultura feminina* (*On Feminine Culture*), América/Educación, 1950.
*Balun-Canan* (*The Nine Guardians*), Fondo de Cultura Económica, 1957.
*Ciudad Real* (*Royal City*), Universidad Veracruzana, 1959.
*Oficio de tinieblas* (*The Dark Service*), Mortiz, 1962.
*Los convidados de agosto* (*The Guests of August*), Era, 1964.
*Juicios sumarios* (*Summary Judgements*), Universidad Veracruzana, 1966.
*Album de familia* (*Family Album*), Mortiz, 1971.
*Mujer que sabe latin* (*Women Who Know Latin*), SEP-Setentas/ Educación Pública, 1973.
*El uso de la palabra* (*The Use of the Word*), Excélsior, 1974.

### SOURCES:

#### Books

*Another Way to Be,* translated and edited by Myralyn F. Allgood, Athens, University of Georgia Press, 1990.
Bonifaz, Oscar, *Remembering Rosario,* translated and edited by Myralyn F. Allgood, Potomac, Maryland, Scripta Humanista, 1990.

*Contemporary Women Authors of Latin America,* edited by Doris Meyer and Marguerite Fernández Olmos, Brooklyn, Brooklyn College Press, 1983.

*Homenaje a Rosario Castellanos,* edited by Maureen Ahern and Mary S. Vasquez, Valencia, Ediciones Albatros Hispanofila, 1980.

Munoz, Willie O., "Rosario Castellanos," in *Dictionary of Literary Biography,* Volume 113, Detroit, Gale, 1992.

*Women Writers of Spanish America,* edited by Diane E. Marting, New York, Greenwood, 1987.

**Periodicals**

*Nation,* June 29, 1989, pp. 891–93.
*New York Times,* August 9, 1974, p. 36.

—*Sketch by Julie Henderson Jersyk*

# Carlos Castaneda
## 1925(?)-
**Peruvian American writer and anthropologist**

Carlos Castaneda gained recognition in the late 1960s and early 1970s with his mysterious and controversial collection of "autobiographical" books revolving around his experiences as an apprentice to Yakqui Indian Don Juan Matus. *Time* book reviewer Robert Hughes commented that "no explorer has worked more lucidly at the very edge than Castaneda, describing a system of power and magic terrifyingly alien to his own culture." Carlos Castaneda's life, like his fiction, is embedded in mystery. Although immigration records show his birth date as December 25, 1925, Castaneda claims that he was born on December 25, 1931. He also claims the name Castaneda is an adopted one, whereas records reveal it as his given name. It is known, however, that he was born in the small town of Cajamarca, Peru. His father, Cesar Arana Burungaray, was a goldsmith and watchmaker. His mother, Susana Castaneda Navoa, died when he was 24 years old.

According to Castaneda, he was placed with a foster family in Los Angeles by his uncle when he became too difficult to manage. He graduated from Hollywood High School and moved to Milan, where he took courses in sculpture at the Academy of Fine Arts. Eventually he moved back to Los Angeles, where he started an anthropology course at the University of California, Los Angeles (UCLA), the school where he would obtain his B.A. (1962), M.A. (1964), and Ph.D. (1970) degrees.

In 1968 Castaneda traveled to the Southwest to study medicinal plants used by local Indians. During this time, Castaneda recalls, he met Don Juan Matus, a shaman or sorcerer. Castaneda was apparently chosen by Don Juan to become a "man of knowledge." Over a period of ten years, Castaneda served as Don Juan's apprentice. His diligent note-taking over this period of time resulted in his eight-book series about his relationship with the old shaman. In his introduction to *The Eagle's Gift,* his fourth book in the series, Castaneda wrote that he was "reporting . . . on the events that unfold in my life as a direct result of having adopted an alien set of interrelated ideas and procedures."

Castaneda's first two books, *The Teachings of Don Juan: A Yakqui Way of Knowledge* (1968) and *A Separate Reality: Further Conversations with Don Juan* (1971) introduce the enigmatic Don Juan and describe the author's experiences with a variety of hallucinogenic drugs, part of a larger effort to attain certain experiences and reach heightened levels of consciousness.

The next book in the series continued the account of the author's apprenticeship and related "grueling desert marches and arduous disciplines, apparitions and struggles in fog and bright sunlight, as well as some mind-wrenching magic tricks," according to Hughes. *Journey to Ixlan: The Lessons of Don Juan* (1972) was "An astonishing document of friendship and moral responsibility. The warrior is existential man at full stretch."

In *Journey to Ixlan,* Castaneda reported on gaining power by "seeing" rather than using the usual means of perception. Castaneda further explored these themes in *Tales of Power* (1974), *The Second Ring of Power* (1977), *The Eagle's Gift* (1981), *The Fire From Within* (1984), and *The Power of Silence: Further Lessons of Don Juan* (1987). Castaneda became a best-selling author on the strength of the series, which has been translated into 11 languages.

Since the first installment to the series, Castaneda and his books have become the subject of no small amount of debate. Critics have long argued as to whether Castaneda's books are non-fiction or fiction, with many reviewers questioning whether Don Juan Matus really exists. In the *New York Times Book Review,* Robert Bly suggested that Castaneda's books welded together the work of others, gathering the results of research and musings on spirituality and power undertaken by others and making it his own. Bly charged that Castaneda "dishes out a sample goulash with new vegetables, standing behind the counter of . . . the spiritual supermarket." He further contends that "By the second book it was clear that Castaneda was making up the conversations" with

Don Juan. Critic Richard de Mille devotes an entire book to his argument that Castaneda and his books are a hoax. In *The Don Juan Papers,* de Mille writes, "The power of Castaneda and his works is to catch some people at the borders of their world and fix them there, to hold them at the boundary between what they think they know and what they would like to believe." Yet other critics praise Castaneda and his work. Elsa First, writing in the *New York Times Book Review,* for instance, commended Castaneda for putting his readers inside the shaman's consciousness and described his work as "original and important."

## SELECTED PUBLISHED WORKS:

*The Teachings of Don Juan: A Yakqui Way of Knowledge,* University of California Press, 1968.
*A Separate Reality: Further Conversations with Don Juan,* Simon & Schuster, 1971.
*Journey to Ixlan: The Lessons of Don Juan,* Simon & Schuster, 1972.
*Tales of Power,* Simon & Schuster, 1974.
*Trilogy,* 3 vols., Simon & Schuster, 1974.
*Don Juan Quartet,* Simon & Schuster, 1975.
*The Second Ring of Power,* Simon & Schuster, 1977.
*The Eagle's Gift,* Simon & Schuster, 1981.
*The Fire From Within,* Simon & Schuster, 1984.
*The Power of Silence: Further Lessons of Don Juan,* Simon & Schuster, 1987.

## SOURCES:

### Books

*Contemporary Literary Criticism,* Volume 12, Detroit, Gale, 1980.
*The Don Juan Papers,* edited by Richard de Mille, Santa Barbara, California: Ross-Erikson, 1980.
*Hispanic Writers,* edited by Bryan Ryan, Detroit, Gale, 1991.

### Periodicals

*New York Times Book Review,* October 27, 1974, p.35; January 22, 1978, p. 7.
*Psychology Today,* December, 1977, p.42.
*Time,* March 5, 1972; November 6, 1972, p. 30.
*Washington Post,* December 18, 1987.

*—Sketch by Melissa Clark*

# Jorge G. Castañeda
## 1921-
### Mexican writer and political analyst

Author of several Spanish-language books, Jorge G. Castañeda is one the leading political analysts of modern Mexico. A graduate professor of political science since 1959 at the National Autonomous University of Mexico in Mexico City, Castañeda has also served as visiting professor of international relations at the University of California, Berkeley. Often confronting ethical dilemmas, his contributions to major periodicals from the early to mid–1990s have focused on human rights concerns, politics and the economy, and the corruption he perceives in Mexican politics.

Jorge G. Castañeda was born October 1, 1921, in Mexico, the son of Jorge Castañeda and Carmen Alvarez de la Rosa. He was educated at the National Autonomous University of Mexico, joining the Mexican Foreign Service in 1950. After, he held various Mexican diplomatic positions, including ambassador to Egypt and France. Castañeda also served as a delegate to numerous international conferences, including many sessions of the United Nations General Assembly. In 1985 he married Alicia C. de Castañeda.

An analyst of Latin American politics, Castañeda takes a liberal political position. Castañeda's work, including *Limits to Friendship,* co-authored with Robert Pastor, is considered a field classic and is used widely in university courses on Mexico-United States relations. Both *Limits to Friendship* and *Utopia Unarmed: The Latin American Left After The Cold War,* Castañeda's first book published originally in English, attempt to obscure his ideological stance. He believes that while Latin American leftists have been potent influences politically, they have failed to live up to their ideals by seizing power and making revolution.

While La Reforma began in 1859 with Mexico's struggle for clerical independence and human dignity, true reform has yet to be realized in Mexico. An air of autocratic rule lingers, with remnant memories of a time when economic progress came at a crushing price to the people. Poverty and labor provided material for **Porfirio Diaz**—one of the country's most notable dictators from 1876–1911—to direct his regime and shape policy well beyond the four decades he held power. By 1993, 270 million Latin Americans lived in poverty; citing similar statistics, some feel Mexico's government in the 1990s is parallel to the Porfirian regime of a century ago. In the early 1990s, appeared to echo the sentiments.

*Jorge G. Castañeda*

Believing that inequity in a technological age represents a political powder keg, Castañeda writes with poignance and a small amount of divine retribution in his voice. For example, while the first part of *Utopia Unarmed* is an analysis on the recent history of key leftist groups ranging from the Peruvian Shining Path to the Nicaraguan Sandinistas, the latter part addresses ways in which not just Mexico, but all of Latin America's leftist groups need to change to maintain political influence.

In speaking with *Christian Science Monitor*'s David Scott, Castañeda revealed his belief that the political pendulum is swinging back to the left. Scott reported, "In *Utopia Unarmed*, [Castañeda] argues that the dire conditions—poverty, injustice, violence—which originally spawned the left are more compelling today and make fertile political ground for another generation of leftist leaders."

Castañeda suggests Latin America's leftists should assume a more capitalist stance. Advocating a nationalism beyond Mexico, he suggests "a new longitudinal nationalism'" for Latin America. Castañeda believes, as have many before him, that governmental problems in Latin America derive from corruption in the elite infrastructure. He feels the size of government is not problematic, but instead, lack of accountability and a rigid resistance to democracy.

Castañeda clearly illustrates these points when addressing the 1994 Mexican Zapatista eruption in the *Los Angeles Times*. He wrote, "Chiapas was something of a showcase for President **Carlos Salinas de Gortari**'s much touted Solidarity anti-poverty program: more money from the Salinas government and the World Bank was funneled into Chiapas than to any other state. The problem is that the authoritarian, corrupt, oligarchical structures that have characterized Chiapas for decades were left untouched—or even were strengthened. The local authorities and the army worked with the cattle grazers in dispossessing the Indians of their communal lands. . . . The Salinas regime threw money . . . at the local problems but left the underlying causes intact."

## SELECTED PUBLISHED WORKS:

*Limits to Friendship: The United States and Mexico,* Knopf, 1988.
*Utopia Unarmed: The Latin American Left After the Cold War,* Random House, 1993.

## SOURCES:

*Los Angeles Times,* February 6, 1992, p. B7; May 20, 19. B7; January 5, 1994, p. B7.
*Christian Science Monitor,* October 20, 1993, p. 13.

*—Sketch by Brett A. Lealand*

# Ana Castillo
## 1953-
### Mexican American poet and novelist

Initially known for her elegant feminist poetry, Ana Castillo is a distinguished Chicana writer from the Chicago area. Over the years, Castillo has broadened her artistic contributions to include musical performance and prose. Her feminist message can be found in such diverse media as high school texts and an early musical theater piece.

Ana Castillo was born in Chicago, Illinois, on June 15, 1953, to Mexican American parents. Her interest in different aspects of creative experience prompted her to major in art at Northeastern Illinois University, where she received her a B.A. in art education in 1975. The heady artistic, activist and intellectual climate of the 1970s fostered her interest in writing and performing her poetry. She was an early contributor to *Revista Chicano-Riquena* (now *The Americas Review*), a literary magazine edited by

Nicolas Kanellos which captured the artistic ferment of Midwest Hispanics. Her first collection of poems, *Otro Canto*, was published as a chapbook in 1977 with a grant from the Illinois Art Council. Two years later, coinciding with her graduation from the University of Chicago with an M.A. in social sciences, she published a second collection of poems, the chapbook *The Invitation*, with a grant from the Playboy Foundation.

### Adapted Poetry to Music

In the early 1980s, Castillo's work took on musical tones. Her interest in flamenco led her to create and manage the Al-Andalus flamenco performance group from 1981 to 1982. She adapted her collection of poems in *The Invitation* for music and they were performed at the 1982 Soho Art Festival in New York City.

Castillo's elegant style and feminist thematic put her poems in great demand. Her work appeared in a variety of anthologies which include *Women Poets of the World*, published by McMillan in 1982, *The Third Women: Minority Women Writers of the U.S.*, published by Houghton-Mifflin in 1979, and a high school text, *Zero Makes Me Hungry*, published by Scott, Foresman in 1975. Her next two poetry collections were *Pajaros enganosos*, published by Cross Cultural Communications in 1983, and *Women Are Not Roses*, published by Arte Público Press in 1984.

In later years, Castillo has developed consistently as a writer of prose fiction. Already in 1984 one of her short stories was included in the anthology *Cuentos Chicanos*. In 1986 Castillo's first novel, *The Mixquihuala Letters*, was published by Bilingual Press. This novel, written in epistolary form, was widely acclaimed for its treatment of women. It received the Before Columbus Foundation Book award in 1987 and in 1988 won an award from The Women's Foundation of San Francisco, California. Castillo's latest work is the short-story collection *My Father Was a Toltec*, published by Bilingual Press. Castillo lives in Albuquerque, New Mexico, and continues to write, perform and lecture.

### SELECTED PUBLISHED WORKS:

*Otro Canto* (chapbook), 1977.
*Pajaros enganosos*, Cross Cultural Communications, 1983.
*Women Are Not Roses*, Arte Público Press, 1984.
*The Mixquihuala Letters* (novel), Bilingual Press, 1986.
*My Father Was A Toltec* (short stories), Bilingual Press.

### SOURCES:

*Archives,* Arte Público Press, Houston, Texas.

—*Sketch by Silvia Novo Pena*

# Sylvia L. Castillo
## 1951-
### Mexican American sociologist and organization founder

Sylvia L. Castillo, a clinical social worker who has been honored by the United Nations Council on Women and the California State Assembly, led efforts in the 1980s to encourage communication and support between Hispanic professional women across the country and find new ways to encourage young Hispanic females to pursue higher education and challenging careers. Castillo founded the National Network of Hispanic Women and its accompanying English-language magazine, *Intercambios*. At its height in the 1980s, the Los Angeles-based network had some 500 members, and the magazine had a circulation of 6,500 issues to students, teachers, school counselors, and professionals from all fields. The network and magazine sought to prepare Hispanic women, often first generation Americans, for leadership positions in the public and private sector.

Castillo was born on September 2, 1951, in Los Angeles, California. Her parents, Henry and Lucille Miramontes Castillo, also born in Los Angeles, were the children of Mexican immigrants. Henry was a truck driver and Lucille worked as a retail clerk in a pharmacy and, later, as a medical representative for a home health care agency. Castillo's mother was an influential presence in her life. "She was a link between the old ways and the new ways. She helped us through her experience see there were opportunities all the time. She passed on an incredible sense of confidence," Castillo told the *Rocky Mountain News*.

Before going to college, Castillo attended an all-girl parochial school, Our Lady of Loretto High School, in Los Angeles, where she graduated in 1969 after serving as the student body president in her senior year. Castillo dreamed of becoming a psychologist and, for a while, pursued that dream. "I always thought that I was going to be a psychologist and director of a community mental health center," Castillo told interviewer Ann Malaspina. She was especially interested in women's mental health issues. "If a mother feels good, then her daughters feel good.

*Sylvia L. Castillo*

If a mother has good self-esteem, her children will have good self esteem," she said.

Although both her parents held jobs, Castillo found her own way through higher education and into the professional world. She earned a B.A. in social psychology at the University of California at Santa Barbara in 1973. In 1976 she received a master's degree in social welfare administration from the University of California at Berkeley, where she was a National Institute of Mental Health fellow. After graduation, Castillo received a postgraduate clinical fellowship from the University of Southern California to study how to improve child abuse programs in several communities.

### Interest in Hispanic Women's Issues Piqued

Soon afterwards, Castillo joined her professor, Dr. Grant Miller, as part of a mental health team at California Polytechnic State University at San Luis Obispo. From 1976 to 1979, she worked as a career and mental health counselor at Cal-Poly, where she helped found the campus's first women's re-entry and career mentoring programs for minorities and women. This was followed by an administrative fellowship in 1979 from California State University at Long Beach to study the challenges faced by college presidents. She spent a year working under Dr. Gail Fullerton, the first woman president at California State University at San Jose. While researching upward mobility in higher education, Castillo began

wondering what it takes for a student to succeed. She recalled asking herself, "What does the institution have to do? Why will one Hispanic succeed and another won't?"

Also that year, she interviewed dozens of Hispanic women in higher education. Castillo discovered a common thread: despite their outward success, these women were unhappy and dissatisfied with their careers. Many were hired in the 1970s when universities, responding to student demands, hired token minorities. Now, the women were reassessing their careers and futures. "They were very isolated and didn't know their counterparts in the system," said Castillo. It was during her research that Castillo became interested in exploring the difficulties faced by Hispanic professional women. Prior to that time, studies on Hispanic success focused on the individual and his or her background, family, and education. Castillo wondered what institutions could do to encourage young Hispanics. "I was curious about why there were so few role models," she said.

She decided to start a newsletter—to be circulated to school counselors and students—allowing Hispanic women to share their experiences and providing practical information on career choices. After the newsletter began its circulation, Stanford University offered Castillo a job advising students in the placement office. "They wanted to know why students weren't making it," said Castillo. She took the job, with the stipulation that she could also publish the newsletter, and served as assistant dean of student affairs for academic advising and counseling from 1980 to 1985.

### Birth of *Intercambios* and the NNHW

The first issue of the newsletter, initially called *Intercambios Femeniles* ("Interchange of Women"), appeared in December 1980. With 14 pages per newsletter, each "issue was a resource, with a networking list, statistics, and information," said Castillo. Each issue also had a theme, such as careers in science and technology, health and the Hispanic women, and leadership. The magazine profiled successful Hispanic women, reported on the latest studies on Hispanics, and tackled topics from how to preserve cultural traditions to debating affirmative action. At first, Castillo used Stanford students to do the research, and friends and colleagues sent her information and student dissertations.

Over the years, hundreds of women contributed to *Intercambios*. Later, as the magazine, which came out four times a year, became a glossy, full-color periodical with sophisticated graphics, Castillo was assisted by executive editor and filmmaker Ruth Carranza, as well as free-lance editors and writers from around the country. But Castillo wanted to move beyond the magazine. "I wanted to develop an information clearinghouse about educational advancement, career preparation, and leadership development," she said. "I had real big dreams." She hoped to link Hispanic women across the country who could share each other's expertise. Her focus, however, always remained firm: education, careers, and leadership development for Hispanic women.

*Intercambios* planted the seeds for the National Network of Hispanic Women (NNHW), which was first called Hispanic Women in Higher Education. To gather ideas for the newsletter, Castillo, who worked without pay, organized a board of directors with a broad spectrum of perspectives, including Latina organization leaders, teachers, administrators, an entrepreneur, and a graduate student. They debated ways to improve opportunities for young Hispanic women and how to organize a national resource center. Gradually becoming an important force in itself, the NNHW filled a void for many Hispanic women, who often could not get the kind of support they needed from their families and community. "We're talking about perhaps the first generation of college-educated Hispanic women—the first generation of professional Hispanic women," Castillo told *Hispanic Business* magazine. The board recruited members from a cross section of professions, geographic regions, and ethnic backgrounds. Members included bank executives, university administrators, corporate vice presidents, scientists, small business owners, community activists, and others. The network, funded by corporations and foundations, conducted studies, served as an information resource, and provided networking and mentoring opportunities for Hispanic women of all ages. Always fighting an uphill battle to secure financial backing, Castillo eventually established an NNHW office in Los Angeles that was run by a part-time staff.

Hoping to provide new links between Hispanic women and the corporate world, Castillo organized seminars for companies interested in recruiting Hispanic women. Beginning in 1982, she set up what she called the Roundtable for Hispanic Women and worked with companies such as Pacific Bell, Sears Roebuck, Avon Products, Anheuser-Busch, and other large businesses to identify better ways to hire and promote Hispanic women. "I see our role as a network to be a broker between the talented Hispanic woman and the needs of corporate America," Castillo told *Hispanic Business*. In 1985, Castillo received a grant from Anheuser-Busch to study Hispanic women in business. She called her project the National Roundtable for Hispana Business and Corporate Leaders. Also that year, she resigned from her Stanford job to devote all her time to *Intercambios* and the NNHW.

The national network hosted the first National Roundtable in Denver, Colorado, in March 1985. The theme of the gathering, attended by 500 women, was "An Investment in America's Future." The conference focused on career preparation, mid-management career opportunities, and women entrepreneurs, with special focus groups on leadership issues. The meeting was so successful that the NNHW conducted two more National Roundtables: one in Miami in 1987, and another in Los Angeles in 1989. Meanwhile, Castillo was facing a personal crisis. In 1986, she was forced to resign her active leadership roles at *Intercambios* and the NNHW because of illness. She took a year off to regain her health. At the age of 32, Castillo felt she had been so busy that she had neglected her personal life and her health. "I felt my health had failed and I had failed," she told Malaspina.

During that year, she married Steven Castillo Long, a friend from childhood, and moved with him to the island of Maui, Hawaii. But she could not stay uninvolved. Castillo became active in the Puerto Rican community and women's groups in Hawaii. She helped start and direct the Children's Advocacy Center in Wailuku. She also worked part time as administrative coordinator for the graduate school of social work at the University of Hawaii at Manoa and in the business and marketing office at a private school, all the while keeping in touch with the NNHW. In 1988, she was selected as one of 60 women in the United States to participate in Leadership America, a year-long national training institute for women in public policy.

## Challenges for the Future

By the early 1990s, both *Intercambios* and the NNHW faced difficulties in funding and organization. As a result, the NNHW took a hiatus from activity and *Intercambios* interrupted its publishing schedule. But Castillo and others remained determined to revive these unique efforts—perhaps in slightly different forms—to promote Hispanic women in the professions. The economic uncertainties of the 1990s that have caused problems for the NNHW and *Intercambios* also now pose new challenges for Hispanic women, according to Castillo, who returned to Los Angeles in 1990. "The word 'opportunity' is going to be redefined. I think we will have limited opportunity. We barely have started to make a presence; the opportunities as they diminish will close the doors for this generation," said Castillo. "As we're affected by down-sizing, mergers, job loss, we're going to have to redefine success, otherwise it will be easy for the Hispanic woman to internalize that she's failed."

To handle these difficult times, Castillo urges Hispanic women to reassess their values and goals and to organize and communicate with each other. "The more isolated we stay as women, the less opportunity we have," she said. She would like to build a national federation of Hispanic women's groups with fund-raising abilities and the clout to have women's voices heard on issues such as education, teenage pregnancy, and health care. Along with keeping the NNHW and *Intercambios* alive, Castillo has been involved in the Commission on Hispanic Underrepresentation and Policy at California State University and the American Council on Education's Office of Women, and she has worked as an advisor on the Ford Foundation Study: the Chicana Project. Having settled in Menlo Park, California, Castillo is considering options for her own future, such as finishing her doctorate, teaching, or becoming involved in a new organization. But whatever she does, Castillo will always have her eye on her first love: ensuring that Hispanic women get the opportunities they deserve.

## SOURCES:

### Periodicals

*Hispanic Business,* July 1988, pp. 25–6.
*Hispanic USA,* May 1985, pp. 14–15.
*Intercambios,* Winter 1990; Spring 1991.
*Intercambios Femeniles,* Winter 1985; Spring 1987.
*Rocky Mountain News,* March 12, 1985, pp. 39, 42.

### Other

Castillo, Sylvia L., interview with Ann Malaspina, October 1, 1992.

—*Sketch by Ann Malaspina*

# Fidel Castro
## 1926(?)-
### Cuban statesman

Fidel Castro led the overthrow of the Cuban dictator **Fulgencio Batista** in 1959 to become the leader of the first communist nation in the Western Hemisphere. For over 35 years, he has defied international opposition, the fall of communism in Eastern Europe, and a collapsing economy to remain president of Cuba. Whether he is a romantic revolutionary or a ruthless dictator, Castro, at the height of his power in the 1960s, could "weave a spell over his masses," wrote biographer Georgie Anne Geyer in *Guerrilla Prince: The Untold Story of Fidel Castro.*

Educated by the Jesuits and trained as a lawyer, Castro is a superb orator. He has been hailed by *The New Republic* as the "magician of eloquence," and his followers have seen in his intelligent and convincing speeches a man who could lift Cuba from its Third World status. "The revolution bestowed on Cuba extraordinary gifts of social justice and equality, advances in public health and education, and an equitable distribution of the national wealth, and Fidel Castro deserves total credit for it," wrote Tad Szulc in *Fidel: A Critical Portrait.* Yet critics say Castro runs a totalitarian state where human rights are suppressed, free elections are stifled, and entrepreneurship is banned. "Fidel is merciless with those he considers traitors," noted Szulc. During Castro's reign, tens of thousands of Cubans have fled into exile in the United States. An advocate of violent revolution, Castro used guerrilla warfare and terrorism to accomplish his revolution and export it around the globe.

### Reared on a Plantation

Fidel Alejandro Castro Ruz was born in either 1926 or 1927 in Birán in the Mayarí region of Oriente Province, Cuba. His father, Angél Castro y Argiz, was a youth when he fled the poverty of Galicia in northwest Spain. According to some accounts, Angél joined a contingent of Spanish soldiers who fought in Cuba's war for independence in the 1890s. By the time Castro was born, Don Angél was a prosperous landowner in the Mayarí region, dominated by the United Fruit Company 's sugar plantations. Fidel's mother, Lina Ruz González, who came from a poor, religious family, was Angél's second wife. She was the family maid, while Angél was still married to María Louisa Argota, with whom he had two children, Pedro Emilio and Lidia. Castro's parents were married in the Catholic Church after the births of Angelita, Ramón, and Fidel. The couple had three more children, including Raúl, who would become minister of the armed forces in Castro's government.

Castro led a privileged life on the family's 10,000 acre hacienda, "Manacas." Hundreds of peasants worked the land. "I was born into a family of landowners in comfortable circumstances. . . . Everyone lavished attention on me, flattered and treated me differently," Castro is quoted in Geyer's account of his life. Castro grew up alongside peasants, which may have led to his lifelong desire to help Cuba's poorest citizens.

As a young boy, he attended the Marist brothers' La Salle school in Santiago, where he lived with his godparents. At age nine, he began his Jesuit education at the Dolores boys' school. He entered Belén College, an exclusive Jesuit high school in Havana, in 1941. Even as a child, Castro was a rebel. At Belén, he was a non-conformist with a fiery temper, according to

Geyer. Although he was bright, he was not interested in studying. He was a sports hero in school, where he ran track, pitched for the baseball team, and excelled in basketball. From his youth, Castro's hero was the Cuban martyr, **José Martí**, a nationalist killed in 1895 during Cuba's war for independence from Spain.

Castro first tasted political action when he entered law school at the University of Havana in 1946. Havana, then a prosperous tourist haven, was embroiled in a battle between two gangster groups; rival student gangs fought bitterly. Castro joined the Anti-Imperialist League. At one point, he was wounded by police during a student protest against the rise in bus fares. On November 27, 1946, he made his first speech before students at the Colón cemetery during a nationalist ceremony.

In 1949, Castro joined the failed Cayo Confites Expedition, led by Dominican writer **Juan Bosch** to overthrow **Rafael Leónidas Trujillo**, the dictator of the Dominican Republic. The expedition was called off during the trip overseas. Castro jumped ship and swam through the shark-infested waters of the Bay of Nipe holding a gun above his head. Only 21-years-old at the time, he was already becoming a legend.

### Became Interested in Politics

On October 10, 1948, Castro married Mirta Díaz-Balart, the daughter of one of Cuba's wealthiest families. Her family had ties with the Batista regime, so it came as no surprise that her brother, Rafael, later became a political enemy of Castro. Their son, Fidel Castro Díaz-Balart, or Fidelito, was born in 1949, but Castro had no job and could barely support his family. The marriage would not last, but women devoted to him and his revolution played important roles throughout his life. Celia Sánchez, for example, whom he met while hiding in the Sierras, would become a lifelong companion and devoted adviser until her death in 1980.

After receiving his law degree in September 1950, Castro worked for the law firm of Azpiazu, Castro y Rosendo in Old Havana, but he spent most of his time in politics. He had joined the Cuban People's Party (Ortodoxos) in 1947. During the early 1950s, Castro became a leader of the Ortodoxo Party, filling the shoes of Eduardo Chibás, an idol of Castro's who had committed suicide on the radio in August 1951. Castro ran for the House of Representatives on the Ortodoxo ticket in 1952, but before the elections, General Fulgencio Batista overthrew the government of President Carlos Prío Socarráson March 10 of that year. Batista had been rising in power for many years. He was Army Chief of Staff from 1934 to 1940 and president from 1940 to 1944. Castro, a sworn enemy of Batista, went into hiding and began to organize his revolution.

Castro hoped to lead a mass movement for political and social change in Cuba. At first, he did not call himself a communist; most of his followers came from the Ortodoxo Party. They were working- and middle-class Cubans, sugar cane workers, mountain farmers, intellectuals, students, and labor organizers. By 1953, an estimated 1,200 men and women called themselves "Fidelistas," pledging absolute loyalty to their leader.

### The Cuban Revolution

At dawn on July 26, 1953, Castro planted the first seeds of the Cuban Revolution. He and a small band of followers in handmade uniforms attacked the Moncada military barracks in Santiago de Cuba. The attack failed, and Castro and his followers fled into the Sierra Maestra, a remote mountain region. Castro and the others were caught and imprisoned a few days later.

At his trial in Santiago in September 1953, Castro—serving as his own lawyer—gave his famous speech, *¡La historia me absolverá!*, introducing the manifesto of his revolution. He excoriated the Batista government, calling for land reform, political and civil liberties, no new taxes, rural improvements, and profit sharing for workers and employees. Castro lost his trial. He was sentenced to 15 years in prison, where he read books and wrote to friends, describing a radical populist revolution for the poor. Meanwhile, Mirta filed for divorce—which became final in 1954—because of his involvement with Naty Revuelta, who later bore Castro a daughter, Alina Revuelta.

Fidel and his comrades, including his brother, Raúl, were released by Batista on May 15, 1955. On July 7, 1955, Castro left Cuba for exile in Mexico City. Castro named his group the 26th of July movement, or M–26–7, after the date of the Moncada attack. With his followers, Castro prepared to overthrow the Cuban government. **Ernesto "Che" Guevera**, a poor Argentinean with revolutionary ideas, and Frank País, were among his confidantes.

In June 1956, Batista's forces in Mexico City arrested Castro, but failed to discourage the young rebel. On December 2, 1956, the yacht *Granma,* carrying Castro and his group from Mexico, landed on the Oriente coast of Cuba. Unable to achieve the planned coup, Castro and his followers hid in the Sierra Maestra, fending off attacks from Batista. For two years, Castro lived in the mountains, gathering support from peasants, writing manifestos and letters, and planning his armed overthrow of the government. Meanwhile, País, until his assassination in 1957, organized rebels in the cities.

On April 9, 1958, Castro's forces called for a general strike. "Today is the day of liberation," was the announcement on radios. Batista fought back, ordering his police to kill dissidents on sight, which led to a bloodbath in the streets. The strike was a failure. Only months later, the tide had turned in Castro's favor, as Batista failed to stop the guerrillas. "In December, town after town, city after city, and army post after army post fell to Castro's rebels," wrote Geyer.

On New Year's Eve, 1959, Batista fled Cuba. On January 2, Castro began the 600-mile trip to Havana, leading a parade of tanks, armored cars, buses and army trucks. "In every city and town, he took over the army barracks and designated a July 26 supporter as mayor," wrote biographer Robert E. Quirk in *Fidel Castro*. On January 8, a helicopter brought Castro into Havana, where crowds shouted "¡Viva Fidel!," threw confetti, and waved revolutionary banners.

Castro took office as prime minister in February 1959. He held "purge" trials, executing or imprisoning his political opponents. Castro filled his government with revolutionaries and began seizing property to redistribute the nation's wealth. He lowered finance charges on new cars, fixed gas prices, reduced mortgage interest rates, and made medical care more affordable. He delayed elections and shut down newspapers critical of his government.

### The Bay of Pigs and the Cuban Missile Crisis

As a result of Castro's communist agenda, relations between the United States and Cuba soon deteriorated. On January 29, 1960, Castro appropriated three U.S. oil refineries, and then began to import crude oil from the Soviet Union. Within months, he nationalized all U.S. properties in Cuba, including sugar mills, oil refineries, and utilities. In March 1960, President Dwight D. Eisenhower authorized the training of Cuban exiles as counterrevolutionaries.

The crisis escalated further when on July 6, Eisenhower announced that the United States would not import the remainder of the 1960 Cuban sugar quota and would not buy sugar from Cuba until further notice. Castro then moved to expel U.S. businesses from Cuba. On October 18, Eisenhower recalled the U.S. ambassador to Cuba, and then prohibited the export of all commodities except medical supplies and some food to the country. "Those two formerly 'closest friends' of nations were catapulting toward becoming the closest of enemies," wrote Geyer.

Newly elected President John F. Kennedy had vowed during the 1960 elections to overthrow Castro. On January 2, 1961, Castro ordered the remaining American embassy officials to leave the country, and he mobilized troops. Diplomatic relations between the United States and Cuba ceased on January 3, 1961. Hoping to oust Castro, Kennedy launched an unsuccessful military attack on Cuba. On April 15,

Cuban exiles trained by the U.S. Central Intelligence Agency (CIA) in Guatemala flew B–26s from Nicaragua to bomb Cuban airfields. On the morning of April 17, Brigade 2506, a group of nearly 1,500 exiles, landed at the Bay of Pigs. The exiles were outmaneuvered by Castro's forces, however, and received no backup from U.S. armed forces. As a result, over 100 men died, and most of the rest were captured.

In 1962 the political brinkmanship between the two countries nearly escalated to a full-scale nuclear war during the Cuban Missile Crisis, which resulted from the Soviet Union stationing in Cuba ballistic missiles aimed at the United States. On October 22, President Kennedy issued an ultimatum that any nuclear weapon launched from Cuba would be considered a Soviet attack, and the United States would retaliate in full measure against both countries. After 13 tense days, the Soviets agreed to withdraw their weapons and Kennedy pledged that the United States would not seek to overthrow the Cuban government. For his part, Castro was upset that Kennedy and the Soviet Premier Nikita Khrushchev resolved the crisis without him. Despite Kennedy's promise not to depose the Cuban leader, evidence exists that the CIA continued trying to assassinate Castro. For example, Szulc wrote that in 1964, an employee in a Havana cafeteria slipped cyanide into a milk shake meant for Castro, but the capsule accidentally froze and broke.

In 1962, the Organization of American States (OAS) suspended Cuba's membership. Two years later, the OAS voted to end all diplomatic and trade ties with Cuba—only Mexico did not join the boycott. Increasingly isolated, Cuba sought military and economic support from the Soviet Union, while the Soviets found Cuba a convenient strategic base in Latin America. Castro was soon calling himself a Marxist-Leninist and he formed a new Cuban Communist Party (CPP), with a Central Committee, Politburo, and National Assembly of People's Power, much like the Soviet Union. He nationalized industries, transportation, communications, and most of the agriculture.

### Aftermath of the Cuban Revolution

"It was the obsession of Fidel Castro to do away with human, social, and economic underdevelopment in Cuba," wrote Szulc. Castro was determined to spare Cubans from the extreme poverty of many Latin American countries. His early agrarian reforms gave peasants land; his urban reforms reduced rents and banned the ownership of more than one dwelling. Castro ended Cuba's dependence on the United States and gave Cubans a sense of national pride and identity.

Castro believed doctors and teachers were as important as soldiers, wrote Szulc. The Cuban Revolution put an end to illiteracy; even post-graduate education was free. Castro built clinics in the country-side and hundreds of new hospitals. His revolution brought 94 percent literacy, 76-year-life expectancy, and infant mortality of only 11 per 1,000 births, reported the *U.S. World and News Report* in 1994. Castro also increased equality for the 35 percent of Cubans who are mulatto or black, wrote Geyer.

Yet Cuba was a tightly controlled one-party state. Castro took the titles of President of the Councils of State and Ministers, First Secretary of the Communist party, and Commander in Chief of the armed forces. "Fidel Castro had wanted and demanded supreme power," wrote Quirk. Power was centralized in a bureaucracy run by Castro's comrades. He allowed no national elections. Only communist and government media, like the newspaper *Granma,* were permitted, and all opposition was repressed. In the mid–1960s, 60,000 political prisoners crowded Cuba's jails.

Castro also formed the Committees for the Defense of the Revolution (CDR). The CDRs were Castro's citizens' intelligence service, with Cubans spying on Cubans to ensure that they attended political meetings and nightly "vigilance" patrols, and did not oppose the revolution. By the 1980s, 80 percent of Cubans were in the CDRs, according to the *New York Times.*

While Castro remained friends with prominent international figures such as Colombian novelist **Gabriel García Márquez**, he was criticized for human rights abuses. "During his tenure, he has imprisoned and persecuted homosexuals, political dissidents, intellectuals, artists, and even former friends. In 1970 the most prestigious Cuban novelists and poets suddenly discovered that no publishing house or magazine would publish their work—no explanation given," wrote Szulc. The 1989 execution of General Arnaldo Ochoa Sánchez, a celebrated war hero in the Sierra and Angola, was one of many former comrades targeted by Castro. Ochoa and three high-ranking officers were accused of drug-smuggling, but biographers believe Castro feared that they would betray him. After a group of dissidents, the Democratic Solidarity Party, signed a letter in 1992 calling for economic and political reform, many of the signers lost their jobs. "Here no one can go against the government," a Cuban told *U.S. World & News Report* in 1994.

Castro tried to export his revolution by supporting rebels around the globe. In the late 1970s, he had authorized the use of approximately 40,000 Cuban troops in two dozen countries, and Cuba was considered the former Soviet Union's chief military ally. Cubans fought alongside the Soviets in the 1975 Angolan Civil War. In 1978, Cuban soldiers helped Ethiopia fend off an invasion from Somalia. Cuba also aided guerrilla movements in South and Central America, including the Sandinistas in Nicaragua.

## The Mariel Boat Lift

Castro never fully suppressed opposition at home. Instead, he periodically sanctioned emigration, creating a large exile community in Miami, Florida. In 1980, Castro allowed the exodus of some 120,000 Cubans after dissidents stormed the Peruvian embassy in Havana. On April 19, 1980, Castro opened the port of Mariel, and Cuban exiles from Miami brought boats to pick up relatives in what came to be known as the Mariel Boat Lift. Soon, Castro was forcing ships to take prisoners and psychiatric patients as well, provoking a refugee crisis for the United States.

Reforms in the Soviet Union under President Mikhail Gorbachev in the mid–1980 pressured Castro to change. World leaders advised him to accept capitalism, democracy, and public debate, wrote Quirk, "Instead, he shored up his defenses. . . . He reorganized the structure of government and centralized authority in the capital. He quashed every evidence of an opposition, however innocuous."

By the 1990s, Castro's revolution was disintegrating. 'Today the patriarch sits on the edge of an abyss and gambles with his country's future," wrote *The New Republic* in 1991. Communism's collapse in Eastern Europe in 1989 and the dissolution of the Soviet Union damaged Cuba, which had relied on its preferential trading status with the communist countries. Soviet oil and grain subsidies dropped drastically. Without gas, bicycles became common in Havana. "Most citizens line up each day to receive a single loaf of bread made from Soviet-supplied grain," reported *Newsweek* in 1991. In 1992, the United States passed the Cuban Democracy Act, tightening its trade embargo because of human rights violations. Many Cubans were out of work.

While Cuba still boasted free education, housing, and health care, the nation was supported by a crumbling economy. The model health care system had begun to "seriously erode," reported the *New York Times* in October 1994. Medicine was scarce, materials for diagnostic tests had disappeared, and ambulances had no fuel. "At many hospitals, patients are told to bring their own sheets, and their visitors are sometimes asked to help mop floors," wrote reporter Tim Golden.

Castro looked to biotechnology and tourism to revive the economy, and his gradual reform to a market economy brought signs of hope. He reduced subsidies to state-run companies and encouraged investment from Spain, Mexico, France, and Canada. In interviews, Castro seemed willing to cooperate with the United States in economic relations, financial investment, and fighting crime and drug trafficking, reported *The New York Times.*

Still, Castro refused to make the only move necessary to lift the U.S. trade embargo: ending his communist dictatorship. "The missing piece there is any kind of movement forward in terms of democracy and human rights. Our position is that Fidel has to take the first step now," a U.S. Department of State official told the *New York Times* in 1994. Castro told *U.S. News & World Report* in 1994 that gradual economic reform would be tolerated, but not major political liberalization. "This country can only be ruled by the revolution," said Castro.

In August 1994, more than 30,000 Cubans fled in boats for the United States, following a riot in Havana, with protestors shouting "Down with Fidel!" Cubans "are simmering in anger and frustration," reported *U.S. News & World Report.* Castro seems to have few remaining allies. "Castro appears a lonely man—frustrated one day, triumphant the next, but lonely, and still searching for something that is impossibly elusive," wrote Szulc.

## SOURCES:

### Books

Geyer, Georgie Anne, *Guerrilla Prince: The Untold Story of Fidel Castro,* Boston, Little, Brown and Company, 1991.

Quirk, Robert E., *Fidel Castro,* New York, W. W. Norton & Company, 1993.

Szulc, Ted, *Fidel: A Critical Portrait,* New York, William Morrow and Company, 1986.

Timerman, Jacobo, *Cuba: A Journey,* New York, Alfred A. Knopf, 1990.

### Periodicals

*The New Republic,* April 22, 1991, pp. 32–8.

*Newsweek,* July 29, 1985, p. 53; November 24, 1986, pp. 1–2; September 9, 1991, p. 39.

*The New York Times,* September 26, 1994, p. A13; October 30, 1994, pp. A1, A8; November 7, 1994, pp. A1, A8; December 2, 1994, p. A18; December 5, 1994, p. A3.

*U.S. News & World Report,* September 26, 1994, pp. 55–63.

*—Sketch by Ann Malaspina*

# George Castro
## 1939-
### Mexican American physical chemist

George Castro's work in photoconductors and superconductors has led the way to new and improved electrophotographic copying machines as well as digital information storage systems. Additionally, he has worked for more than 25 years in civic activities on behalf of the Hispanic American community to ensure adequate education and employment opportunities.

Castro was born on February 23, 1939, in Los Angeles, California, the second of five children. His parents are both of Mexican descent. Castro grew up in Los Angeles, where he attended Roosevelt High School. Graduating in 1956, Castro won the Los Romanos Scholarship. Although it provided him with only a small amount of money, the scholarship was an important vote of confidence from the local Hispanic community. Castro was the first of his family ever to attend college. He went to UCLA, where he earned a B.S. in chemistry. He then became a research fellow in the chemistry department at Dartmouth College. Castro returned to Los Angeles in 1963 and married Beatrice Melendez, with whom he had attended both junior high and high schools. He finished his graduate studies at the University of California at Riverside, earning his Ph.D. in physical chemistry in 1965. For the next three years, Castro served as a postdoctoral fellow, first at the University of Pennsylvania, and then at Caltech.

### Photogeneration Research

In 1968, Castro joined the staff of IBM at its San Jose Research Lab. By 1971, he had become a project manager, and by 1973, a department manager. His early work was in photoconduction—the increased electrical conductivity of a substance when subjected to light waves. In particular, Castro discovered how organic photoconductors were generated by intrinsic charge carriers, an essential element in the technology of both electrophotographic copying machines and laser printers. His early work contributed to the understanding of the principles of the photogeneration process, which is essential to both copying and printing technology. Research teams he managed also discovered a mechanism called photochemical hole burning. By this mechanism, very high densities of digital information can be stored in solids at greater numbers than accomplished by other optical processes.

In 1975, Castro was made manager of the entire physical sciences division of the IBM San Jose

Research Lab. Under his directorship the lab has made breakthrough discoveries in superconductors, high-resolution laser techniques, and new methods for investigating magnetic materials. From 1986 to 1992, Castro worked jointly with a team from Stanford University to develop a synchrotron X-ray facility—one which utilizes the mechanism of synchronized acceleration produced in atomic particles passing through an electrically energized magnetic field. Other research he has supervised includes the construction of a photoelectron microscope for high resolution spectroscopic studies.

### Active Volunteer

Castro has consistently taken time from his busy work schedule to become involved in the education of Hispanic youth. He has taught math and science classes on a volunteer basis, served on the boards of numerous local associations and schools, and developed on-the-job training programs at IBM. Castro won the Outstanding Innovation Award from IBM in 1978, the Outstanding Hispanic Professional award from the San Jose Mexican American Chamber of Commerce in 1984, and the Hispanic in Technology National Award from the Society of Hispanic Professional Engineers in 1986; he was elected a member of the American Physical Society in 1990. He and his wife have four children.

## SELECTED PUBLISHED WORKS:

(With J. F. Henry) "Multiple-Charge Carrier Generation Processes in Anthracene," *Journal of Chemical Physics,* Volume 42, 1965, pp. 1459–1460.

"On Wannier Excitons in Anthracene," *Journal of Chemical Physics,* Volume 46, 1967, pp. 4997–4998.

"Photoconduction in Aromatic Hydrocarbons," *IBM Journal of Research and Development,* Volume 15, 1971, pp. 27–33.

(With D. Haarer) "Singlet Exciton Diffusion and Exciton Quenching in Phenanthrene Single Crystals," *Journal of Luminescence,* Volumes 12–13, 1976, pp. 233–238.

(With F. Cuellar) "Photochemical and Nonphotochemical Hole Burning in Dimethyl-s-tetrazine," *Journal of Chemical Physics,* Volume 54, 1981, pp. 217–225.

## SOURCES:

Castro, George, interview with J. Sydney Jones conducted April 12, 1994.

—*Sketch by J. Sydney Jones*

# Lauro F. Cavazos
## 1927-
### Mexican American former U.S. Secretary of Education, administrator, and educator

Lauro Cavazos has lived a life of many milestone "firsts," from being one of the first Mexican American children admitted to an all-white Texas elementary school to being the first Hispanic American in the United States history to be appointed to the presidential cabinet. The theme connecting both landmark events is education—a chief priority in Cavazos's life.

Lauro Fred Cavazos, Jr., was born on January 4, 1927, on a southern Texas ranch. His parents, Lauro Fred and Tomasa (Quintanilla) Cavazos, belonged to families who had lived in Texas prior to the state's independence from Mexico. The senior Cavazos, a cattle foreman, was the driving force behind his children's education. Cavazos's younger brother, Joe, told Jim Nesbitt of the *Dallas Time Herald* in 1988: "I think about Dad and the importance he put on education. That's the reason Larry [Lauro] is so successful. Larry lives education. I can remember Dad saying all the time, 'Get an education, get an education.' Larry took it to heart."

When Cavazos and his siblings were young, they attended a ranch school for the children of Mexican laborers. The one-room schoolhouse was cramped and inadequate, and Cavazos's father convinced local officials in Kingsville to admit his children to the town's all-Anglo school in 1935. Though bilingual, Cavazos retained memories of the difficult transition to an English-speaking school. When he became Secretary of Education, Cavazos told reporters at a press conference: "You are dealing with a young child . . . with a person who arrives at school the first day and doesn't understand what's going on, scared to death—scared to death if you can speak English, but it's double when you can't speak English."

His father's encouragement took Cavazos far from the ranch where he was born. After graduating from high school in 1945 and serving in the infantry during the last days of World War II, he planned on becoming a commercial fisherman. But his father convinced his him to take some courses at the university in Kingsville. Cavazos then transferred to Texas Technological College—now Texas Tech University—in Lubbock, where he earned a bachelor's degree in zoology in 1949 and a master's degree in zoological cytology two years later. After studying at Texas Tech, Cavazos matriculated at Iowa State University, earning a doctorate in physiology in 1954. He became an associate professor at the Medical

*Lauro F. Cavazos*

College of Virginia in 1960, and during his stay there he served on the editorial board of the *Medical College of Virginia Quarterly.*

## Embarks on Career in Educational Administration

In 1964 Cavazos moved on to the Tufts University School of Medicine in Medford, Massachusetts, where he served as a professor and chair of the anatomy department. While researching and teaching, Cavazos was also drawn to the administrative side of university life. Initially, he served as associate and acting dean of the medical school before becoming full dean in 1975. During this time, Cavazos also served on editorial boards of the *Anatomical Record* and the *Tufts Health Science Review.* When he received an offer to become the first alumnus named president of Texas Tech University and its Health Science Center in 1980, Cavazos accepted.

At Texas Tech, Cavazos oversaw the education of 24,000 students. At that time, the university was the largest in the nation run by a Hispanic American. According to *Current Biography Yearbook 1989,* Cavazos made increasing minority enrollment a personal crusade. Hispanic enrollment at Texas Tech nearly doubled to 6.3 percent of the student body, and black enrollment increased by one third to 2.4 percent. Cavazos also cut back administrative costs per student to the lowest level of any major university in Texas. For his efforts, Cavazos was named Hispan-

ic Educator of the Year by the Texas chapter of the League of United Latin American Citizens in 1983.

## Becomes Secretary of Education

Although a registered Democrat who had publicly criticized federal cutbacks in the student loan program, Cavazos was appointed Secretary of Education by the Republican President Ronald Reagan towards the end of Reagan's second term in office. When sworn in on September 20, 1988, Cavazos became the first Hispanic American appointed to the cabinet. While his predecessor, William J. Bennett, had earned a reputation for his belligerent and aggressive style of leadership, Cavazos offered a new approach. "Cavazos has brought a willingness to listen and a less combative tone than we've had in the past," Wilmer Cody, Louisiana's superintendent of education, told *Time* in 1989. A little over a year later when George Bush became president, Cavazos was reappointed to the cabinet post.

Cavazos's chief priorities upon taking office were to reduce the high school dropout rate, demand greater teacher accountability, and build higher standards in education. He also pledged to meet regularly with the National Education Association and other education groups. Further, perhaps due to his own experience as a child, Cavazos supported limited bilingual instruction for children, as well as vigilant involvement on the part of parents. "Particularly for Hispanics, there are barriers to parental participation that we must work to diminish," Cavazos was quoted as saying in the *New Perspectives Quarterly* in 1990. "A Hispanic parent who speaks little or no English, for example, may be reluctant to visit school and talk to teachers about a child's performance . . . illiteracy among parents is also a barrier to participation in their children's education."

Although Cavazos was initially praised for espousing a more cooperative style than that of Bennett, he soon became a target for heavy criticism by opponents to his educational policies. Andrew Griffin, executive officer of the Georgia Association of Educators told *Time* in 1989 that Cavazos was "all talk, no action." Pat Williams, a Democratic congressman from Montana and chairman of the House post-secondary education sub committee, added that "He believes the job can get done with Rose Garden ceremonies." Jeanne Allen, the education policy analyst at the Heritage Foundation observed that Cavazos "keeps telling us that the problems are disgraceful, but he doesn't come up with any solutions."

## Views Generate Controversy

Cavazos also came under attack for his stance on the role of minorities in education. According to *New*

*Perspectives Quarterly:* "Cavazos has generated considerable controversy by arguing that Hispanics should stop blaming others for their poor performance in school and look to their own lack of emphasis on education. Arguing that 'parental involvement and language competency are basic,' he has also argued that children who don't speak English aren't ready for public education." In addition, Cavazos emphasized the importance of parental and community involvement in education rather than increasing federal funding for schools. In a speech adapted and reprinted in *New Perspectives Quarterly,* Cavazos declared, "I have been criticized because I have continued to insist that additional funding is not the answer." He pointed out that in the 1980s, educational spending rose by $42 billion, or a 29 percent increase over inflation, and yet there was no marked improvement in reading skills, math scores, or ACT and SAT scores.

In December 1990, President Bush asked Cavazos to resign as Secretary of Education. Calling Cavazos's ouster long overdue, *Time* reported in 1990 that "although he stumped for 'choice'—a favored Bush approach that gives parents more say over which public school their children attend—Cavazos never became a bully pulpiteer like his predecessor, William Bennett. Cavazos was handicapped further by Bush's desultory leadership."

Upon his resignation, Cavazos returned to Tufts University Medical School as an adjunct professor. Among the honors that he has received during his distinguished career as an educational administrator are the Outstanding Leadership Award in Education from President Reagan in 1984; election to the Hispanic Hall of Fame in 1987; and the Medal of Honor from UCLA and the President's Medal from the City College, New York, in 1989.

## SOURCES:

### Books

*Current Biography Yearbook 1989,* edited by Charles Moritz, New York, H. W. Wilson Company, 1989, pp. 95-8.

### Periodicals

*Dallas Times Herald,* August 11, 1988.
*New Perspectives Quarterly, A Publication of the Center for the Study of Democratic Institutions,* Fall 1990, pp. 6-8.
*Time,* May 29, 1989, p. 76; December 24, 1990, p. 64.
*U.S. News & World Report,* December 5, 1988, pp. 10-11; December 24, 1990, p. 22; August 31/September 7, 1992, p. 30.

—*Sketch by Kathe A. Conti*

# Camilo José Cela
## 1916-
### Spanish novelist, short story writer, and poet

When Camilo José Cela won the Nobel Prize in Literature in 1989, he said on Spanish state radio: "I offer it to all Spanish literature. I think other Spanish and Latin American writers in Spanish could have won it as well as me." At the time, Cela was the fifth Spaniard to win the award. A reverence for his native language and a deep love for Spain in all its tormented glory are two pillars of Cela's writings. Sheila Rule of the *New York Times* described Cela as an author "given to blunt, irreverent, often profane observations on life and Spain." Others have described his writings as grotesque naturalism and *tremendismo* (a literary device which roughly translates as "enlarging the negative aspects of existence").

"Among the older writers, Cela represents the searching for a better literature from the Franco years, through the democratic experiments and into European Spain," Julio Ortega, a Hispanic studies professor at Brown University, told Rule. "At the same time, he remained very Spanish, keeping the cultural traditions of Spanish art and literature in his writing. He didn't follow a European literature, but developed his own style, and so, in his way, symbolized Spain's going through a long period of adjustment."

Although he was a supporter of General **Francisco Franco** during the Spanish Civil War, Cela was often at odds with the fascist ideology of the Spanish dictatorship during his literary career. Throughout the Franco regime, Cela's works were often subject to government censorship, in which many of his books were banned or removed from the shelves. Although the Franco regime held tight control over the Spanish people from 1939 to 1975, it ultimately failed to contain Cela's tenacious pursuit of writing.

Cela was born on May 11, 1916, to an English mother, Camila Enmanuela Trulock y Bertorini, and a Spanish father, Camilo Cela y Fernández (a custom official and part time writer) in the northwestern province of La Coruña. After the family settled permanently in Madrid in 1925, Cela's poor health bothered him until, in 1934, he entered a tuberculosis sanitarium for the first time. During his recuperation, Cela studied. "The boy read through the entire seventy-volume collection of Spanish classical authors," D. W. McPheeters noted in *Camilo José Cela,* "[thus], the future novelist acquired a grounding in the literary traditions of Spain."

Cela's early education included taking courses in medicine, philosophy, and law in Madrid. In 1935, his first poems were published in a daily Argentinean

*Camilo José Cela*

and idyllic and productive nation under Franco's absolute rule. Realistic and often grotesque, the novel centers on the squalid, brutal life of a peasant in the aftermath of the Spanish Civil War who languishes in prison after being condemned to death for the murder. According to David W. Foster in the 1990 issue of *World Literature Today,* "Cela's novel so effectively challenged the fantasies of the mythic never-never land of Franco 's image of Spain for export . . . that it inaugurated the entire tradition of anti-Franco cultural honesty which has affirmed itself with such emphasis in present-day constitutional, socialized Spain." Despite being censored in Spain, *La familia de Pascual Duarte* propelled Cela to international prominence. The work has since become, after **Miguel de Cervantes**'s *Don Quixote,* probably the most widely read novel in Spanish literature, according to the *New York Times.*

## Publishes a Masterpiece

Cela's next major novel, *La Colmena* (*The Hive*), cemented his reputation as one of the leading novelists of the twentieth century. Originally published in Buenos Aires, Argentina, in 1951, *La Colmena* was not distributed in Spain until 1963, and even then, Ugarte noted, it was "not officially banned but . . . distributed with extreme caution and lack of financial support." Like the complex configuration of a beehive, Cela's second novel knits together the lives of more than 150 characters in Madrid who experience hardship and oppression in the lean years following the Spanish Civil War. According to Ugarte, "[it] is this very collectivity and simultaneity of action that has made *The Hive* one of the most important Spanish novels of the twentieth century, for Cela was able to weave together a variety of people and situations within a city that both mirrored and contained post-civil war ennui."

In the midst of writing his two famous novels, Cela married Maria del Rosario Conde Picavea in 1944; two years later, Maria gave birth to a son named Camilo José. The remarkable success of his first two novels provided Cela with the financial means to move to the countryside of Mallorca in 1954. He also began to accept lecturing invitations abroad. Within two years, he founded a monthly literary review entitled *Papeles de Son Armadans,* which published essays that often took a markedly contradictory stance to the Franco regime on a variety of issues. In 1957, Cela was voted into the Spanish Royal Academy.

newspaper; the following year, he completed a volume of poetry which was not published until nearly ten years later. When the Spanish Civil War broke out in 1936, Cela was still a university student. He joined Franco 's Nationalist army as a private to fight against the Republicans and was wounded in battle. Discharged from the army in 1939 as a corporal, Cela returned to Madrid to study law. Before embarking on his literary career, he tried working as a bullfighter, a civil servant, a painter, and an actor. For a short time, he was a government-appointed censor for a pharmaceutical journal, an orphan's school bulletin, and a religion magazine.

## Political Consciousness Evolves

While many Spanish artists and academics fled their homeland to avoid the cultural and intellectual repression of Franco's fascist government, Cela decided to stay. As Michael Ugarte observed in *The Nation,* "Spain became a cultural wasteland for nearly a decade. Cela not only stayed in the wasteland, he was on the side of the nationalists, and immediately after the war he supported the Franco regime." He contributed articles to various Spanish periodicals and he started writing his novel *La familia de Pascual Duarte* (*The Family of Pascual Duarte*). Through his writing, Cela began to break from the fascist ideology of the Franco regime.

Published in 1942, *La familia de Pascual Duarte* challenged the fascist propaganda about Spain being

In the years that followed the publication of *La Colmena,* Cela delved deep into the deconstruction and reexamination of the novel as a literary form. The results of this foray are a string of novels generally classified by scholars as experimental, beginning with *Mrs. Caldwell habla con su hijo* (1953; *Mrs. Caldwell*

*Speaks to Her Son*). The form of this novel is unusual in that while the book amounts to little more than 200 pages, it contains 212 chapters. Cela's preoccupation with the novel form manifested itself in at least two other notable works: the first, *Vísperas, festividad y octava de San Camilo del año 1936 en Madrid* (1969), contains no paragraphs; the second, *Oficio de tinieblas 5; o, Novela de tesis escrita para ser cantada por un coro de enfermos* (1973), features no capital letters.

### Receives Honors

After Franco's death in 1975, his designated successor King Juan Carlos I authorized a return to democracy for Spain. Two years later, the king appointed Cela to a seat in the first Parliament of the fledgling democracy. In this capacity, Cela helped draft the new Spanish constitution. In 1984, Cela won Spain's national literary prize for *Mazurca para dos muertos,* a novel which takes place in the area of his birth, Galicia, and which "embeds regional mythology and superstition in a dreamlike tale of murder and transgression," Ugarte wrote in *The Nation.*

In 1989, Cela was awarded the Nobel Prize in Literature. The selection committee declared that he was being honored "for a rich and intensive prose, which with restrained compassion forms a challenging vision of man's vulnerability." Upon winning the Nobel Prize, Cela was quoted in the *New York Times* as saying: "I suppose I'll pay off a debt or two. I'll dine with some friends, and reserve myself the right to order double portions."

### SELECTED PUBLISHED WORKS:

*La familia de Pascual Duarte,* Madrid, Aldecoa, 1942; translated by John Marks as *Pascual Duarte's Family,* Eyre & Spottiswoode, 1946; translated by Anthony Kerrigan as *The Family of Pascual Duarte,* Little, Brown 1964, reprinted 1990; Spanish/English version by Herma Briffault published as *Pascual Duarte and His Family,* Las Américas Publishing, 1965.

*Pabellón de reposo,* Madrid, Alfrodisio Aguado, 1943. (First published serially in *El Español,* March 13 to August 21, 1943); Spanish/English by Herma Briffault published as *Rest Home,* Las Américas Publishing, 1961.

*Las botas de siete leguas: Viaje a la Alcarría, con los versos du su cancionero, cada uno en su debido lugar,* Revista de Occidente, 1948, reprinted, Destino, 1982; translated by Frances M. López-Morillos as *Journey to the Alcarría,* University of Wisconsin Press, 1964, reprinted, Atlantic Monthly Press, 1990.

*Caminos inciertos: La Colmena,* Buenos Aires, Emecé, 1951; published as *La Colmena,* Bar-celona, Noguer, 1955, reprinted, Madrid, Castalia, 1984; translated by I. M. Cohen and Arturo Barea as *The Hive,* Farrar, Straus, 1953, reprinted, 1990.

*Mrs. Caldwell habla con su hijo,* Destino, 1953, reprinted, 1979; translated by Jerome S. Bernstein as *Mrs. Caldwell Speaks to Her Son,* Cornell University Press, 1968.

*Vísperas, festividad y octava de San Camilo del año 1936 en Madrid,* Alfaguara, 1969, Noguer, 1981.

*Oficio de tinieblas 5; o, Novela de tesis escrita para ser cantada por un coro de enfermos,* Noguer, 1973.

*Mazurca para dos muertos,* Hanover, NH, Ediciones del Norte, 1983.

*Cristo versus Arizona,* Barcelona, Seix Barral, 1988.

### SOURCES:

#### Books

Diaz-Plaja, Guillermo, *A History of Spanish Literature,* New York University Press, 1971, pp. 341, 355–56.

*Hispanic Writers,* edited by Bryan Ryan, Detroit, Gale, 1991, pp. 129–33.

McPheeters, D.W., *Camilo José Cela,* Twayne Publishers, Inc., 1969, pp. 15–31.

#### Periodicals

*The Nation,* November 27, 1989, pp. 646–50.

*The New York Times,* October 20, 1989, p. C32.

*Time Magazine,* October 30, 1989, p. 86.

*World Literature Today-A Literary Quarterly of the University of Oklahoma,* Winter 1990, pp. 5–8.

*World Press Review,* January 1990, p. 71.

—*Sketch by Kathe A. Conti*

# Lorna Dee Cervantes
## 1954-
### Mexican American poet

Lorna Dee Cervantes has the distinction of being one of only a few Mexican American poets to have been published by a major publishing company. Her work, according to Marta Ester Sánchez in *Contemporary Chicana Poetry: A Critical Approach to an Emerging Literature,* is characterized by "two conflicting but central positions." In Cervantes's poetry, the critic finds both a "desire for an idealized, utopian world" and "a realistic perspective that sees a world fraught with social problems." The tension created between these two perspectives is a central element in understanding Cervantes's work.

Cervantes was born on August 6, 1954, in San Francisco, California, but grew up in San Jose. She began writing poetry when she was eight years old and published some of her earliest poems in her high school's newspaper. In 1974, she gave her first poetry reading at the Quinto Festival de los Teatros Chicanos in Mexico City, Mexico. The poem she read that day, "Barco de refugiados" ("Refugee Ship"), was published in *El Heraldo,* a Mexico City newspaper. The following year, several of her poems appeared in the *Revista Chicano-Riqueña,* and she began contributing verse to other periodicals as well.

By the end of the 1970s, Cervantes had gained a reputation both as a poet and as the editor and publisher of *Mango,* a small literary review. In addition to her work on the magazine, she edited chapbooks composed by other Chicanos that were published through the Centro Cultural de la Gente of San Jose and Mango Publications. Her efforts soon garnered critical attention, and in 1978 she received a National Endowment for the Arts grant. While on a poetry fellowship at the Fine Arts Work Center in Provincetown, Massachusetts, in 1979, she completed the poems that make up her 1981 collection, *Emplumada.*

### Poetry Depicts Alienation in Anglo Society

*Emplumada* is divided into three sections containing several poems. While the poetry of the first two portions deals with social conflicts, the verse in remaining third is perceived by critics as being more lyrical. Some commentators note that the alienation Cervantes feels as a Chicana in an Anglo society is evident in pieces such as "Poem for the Young White Man Who Asked Me How I, An Intelligent Well-Read Person, Could Believe in the War Between Races" and "Visions of Mexico While at a Writing Symposium in Port Townsend, Washington." Sánchez notes that in the first poem, Cervantes explains her feelings at having a "subordinate place in society as Chicana, as woman, and as poet." In the second, which deals with the theme of migration and opposing societal values, Roberta Fernández concludes in *Dictionary of Literary Biography* that Cervantes "comes to terms with herself, finding resolution for the many conflicts in her life and in her role as poet."

*Emplumada* also contains "Beneath the Shadow of the Freeway," which Fernández describes as "Cervantes's most celebrated poem." The work depicts a young Chicana who must formulate her own world view after learning about male-female relationships and life in general from an idealistic grandmother and a cynical mother. Sánchez maintains that the poem "not only confronts the question of Cervantes' existential voice as a woman and as a Chicana, but it also brings out the conflict between her two literary voices: a discursive one and a lyrical one. By juxtaposing these two poetic voices, 'Beneath the Shadow of the Freeway' combines the principal elements of Cervantes' style, thus suggesting that it also confronts the question of her literary voice."

Since publication of *Emplumada,* Cervantes has obtained a bachelor of arts degree in creative arts from San Jose State University. She has also taken graduate courses at the University of California, Santa Cruz. In addition, she gives readings from an unpublished poetry collection entitled *Bird Ave.*

### SELECTED PUBLISHED WORKS:

*Emplumada,* 1981.

### SOURCES:

*Dictionary of Literary Biography,* Volume 82: *Chicano Writers, First Series,* Gale, 1989.
Sánchez, Marta Ester, *Contemporary Chicana Ptical Approach to an Emerging Literature,* University of California Press, 1985.

—*Sketch by Marian C. Gonsior*

# Miguel de Cervantes
## 1547-1616
### Spanish novelist

Miguel de Cervantes Saavedra, a prominent Spanish writer, was the author of the novel *Don Quixote,* which is considered a masterpiece of world literature. A book that inaugurated the modern novel as a new genre, it has been translated into more than 60 languages and its central character, Don Quixote of la Mancha, has become a prominent mythic figure in Western civilization. Don Quixote's image has been popularized in films, musicals, and paintings; and his name has become synonymous with doomed idealism. His creator, known as Cervantes, lived at the end of the glorious years of the Spanish Empire and fought heroically at the decisive sea battle of Lepanto. However, throughout his life Cervantes

*Miguel de Cervantes*

## Fugitive, Soldier, Captive

The year 1570 found Cervantes in Italy, serving the Cardinal Giulio Acquaviva. The Spanish General Record Office in Simancas possesses an order of arrest—dated September 1569—issued against a certain Miguel de Cervantes for the stabbing of Antonio de Segura during a Madrid duel. It is uncertain that this Miguel de Cervantes was the same person who became a famous writer, however, if he were, Cervantes probably left Spain to avoid suffering the consequences of this action. Or perhaps he was seduced by the flourishing atmosphere of Renaissance Italy and decided to experience it personally. These years in Italy were decisive in Cervantes' intellectual formation. He completed his education by reading Italian literature and philosophy. Years later, in one of *The Exemplary Novels,* Cervantes described the amazement of a young Spaniard as he faced the exuberant cities of sixteenth-century Italy for the first time, using his own experiences as literary inspiration.

In 1570 Cervantes joined Diego de Urbina's Spanish forces at Naples. At this time the Spanish troops formed the most powerful army in Europe, feared by Spain's numerous enemies. Depending on the fragile political alliances of the European nations, the enemies of Spain changed from time to time, but common enemy all Europe faced was Turkey. Spain identified the Turk with the Moor, the traditional foe that the Catholic King and Queen, Ferdinand and Isabella, had finally expelled from the Iberian peninsula in 1492—after eight centuries of fighting. Now the Turks threatened maritime traffic in the Mediterranean with piracy. On October 7, 1571, the Spanish Armada faced the Turkish fleet in the Gulf of Lepanto, near Corinth. Cervantes was aboard the ship *La Marquesa.* Although he was ill he insisted on staying on deck during the confrontation; he fought heroically in the battle and received three wounds—two in the chest and one that maimed his left hand and rendered it useless for the rest of his life. Cervantes took pride in these wounds, and throughout his life he considered them "not ugly but beautiful, since they were inflicted at the greatest episode of history." The Christian fleet won the battle of Lepanto and earned the gratitude of the European nations threatened by the Turkish empire.

After his wounds healed Cervantes remained in Italy as a soldier and participated in other campaigns (Navarino, Tunis, and La Galeta). Perhaps in order to obtain a promotion to the position of captain, he left Italy in 1575 and returned to Spain. But off Marseille, three Turkish galleys intercepted his ship, which was forced to surrender. All the crew and passengers were taken as captives to Algiers, a center of the North African Christian slave trade. Cervantes' brother, Rodrigo, travelled on the same boat and was his companion in captivity. For five fearful years Cer-

lived on the margins of society in a continuous struggle for survival. On occasion he was subjected to all the mishaps of his picaresque character, with extended periods in captivity and ceaseless economic hardship. All this is reflected in the novel's narrative, which is sympathetic and touchingly humane.

Cervantes was born in Alcalá de Henares, a village close to Madrid, in 1547. He was the fourth of seven children born in modest family of Rodrigo de Cervantes, a barber-surgeon, and Leonor de Cortina. His birth coincided with the final years of the powerful rule of the emperor Charles V. The young Cervantes followed his family as the father, pressed by debts, made an itinerant living from town to town (Valladolid, Córdoba, Seville, Madrid). Little is known about Cervantes' education. He probably studied with the Jesuits, as suggested by some references in "*El coloquio de los perros*" ("Colloquy of Dogs"), one of *The Exemplary Novels,* a collection of 12 short stories. In 1569 the Erasmian humanist, Juan López de Hoyos, headed a municipal school in Madrid and mentioned Cervantes as "his beloved disciple." At the same time Cervantes' first poem appeared, dedicated to the death of Elizabeth of Valois, the young spouse of Philip II. Cervantes never attended university, so his vast erudition was acquired through a lifelong devotion to independent reading.

vantes lived as a prisoner in harsh conditions. Several escape attempts failed—on two occasions due to denunciation by other captives. Cervantes was under the control of Dali Mami, a cruel renegade of Greek origin. The letters of recommendations that Cervantes carried with him created the impression that he was an important person. This misconception made Dali Mami demand an exorbitant ransom, but it probably also saved Cervantes from being impaled or tortured after his escape attempts. In 1580—with the help of the Trinitarian friars, a religious order committed to the rescue of Christian captives—Cervantes' family finally managed to pay the 500 escudos ransom that secured his freedom. Years later Cervantes described the terrible experiences of the Christian captives in his plays, *Los baños de Argel* (*The Bagnios of Algiers;* lost), and *Los tratos de Argel* (*The Traffic of Algiers*), as well as in the "Story of the Captive" in *Don Quixote*.

## Writer and Civil Servant

Cervantes' years of service in Italy and his subsequent years of captivity did not win him any privileges upon his return to Spain. He was not appointed to an official position, as he may have been expecting, although he managed to be sent to Oran as a royal messenger for a brief visit in 1581. He struggled financially and tried to immigrate to the New World, but was denied official permission. During these years he wrote his first novel, *La Galatea* (1585), a conventional pastoral romance with a Neoplatonic image of love. The novel gave him some prestige but not much economic help. In 1584 he married Catalina de Salazar y Palacios, 18 years his junior. She came into the marriage with a small dowry, but little is known about their sentimental relationship. The previous year, Cervantes had fathered an illegitimate daughter with Ana Franca de Rojas, wife of the owner of a tavern that was a meeting place for writers and comedians. Cervantes did not legally recognize this daughter, Isabel de Saavedra—his only offspring—until she was 15.

During these years Cervantes tried without success to become a playwright. In Madrid, frequenting theaters had become a very popular form of entertainment, comparable to contemporary movie-going. There were several open air theaters in the city, and the appetite of Madrideans for new plays was avid. Cervantes decided to try his fortune in the affluent market of the comedies. He wrote several plays, but only two have survived from this period: *Numantia* and *The Traffic of Algiers*. The former is a tragedy that describes the heroic resistance peninsula's of the early native population against Roman invaders. The latter is noteworthy for its autobiographical elements. Cervantes' theatrical attempts were not very successful. Lope de Vega—a prolific writer who claimed the ability to write a play in one evening—was the

public's favorite and Cervantes' competition. Later, in 1615, at a bookseller's request, Cervantes collected some of his plays and published them under the title of *Ocho comedies y ocho entremeses* (*Eight Plays and Eight Interludes*).

In 1587 the Spanish fleet entered Cervantes' life again, and Cervantes was appointed commissary for the Spanish Armada. The Armada's mission was to subjugate the British fleet, which posed a continuous threat to the Spanish galleons sailing back from America. Spain's decaying economy depended heavily on the punctual arrival of the galleons with their precious cargo. Cervantes' position did not allow for a repetition of his previous heroic behavior; his duty was simply to requisition of grain from rural Andalusian communities. Not only did the Armada expedition end in a military catastrophe, but Cervantes' assignment brought him endless distress. The reluctance of municipalities and local church authorities to pay, combined with the complexity of the official financial system, placed Cervantes in a labyrinthine process. Accused of mismanagement, he was imprisoned in 1592 and 1597 in Córdoba and Seville, respectively. It was probably during his last imprisonment that he conceived the idea of writing *Don Quixote*.

Although he published *The Exemplary Novels* in 1612, Cervantes had written them during the 1590s. In the prologue, Cervantes declared himself the first person ever to write novellas (short fictitious stories in the Italian manner) in Spanish. The story "*El coloquio de los perros*" ("Colloquy of Dogs") depicts the conversation of two dogs in a nearly picaresque style. "*La española inglesa*" ("The Anglo-Spanish Lady") recounts the romantic adventure of a young girl who is kidnapped and taken to England where she keeps her Catholic faith and falls in love with the son of her captor. "*El Licenciado Vidriera*" ("The Glass Licentiate") anticipates the madman in *Don Quixote*: a scholar who becomes insane and believes that he is made out of brittle glass. His temporary insanity gives him remarkable understanding of the problems of his society. Critics have observed an Erasmian influence in this story.

## The Masterpiece: *Don Quixote*

In 1605 Cervantes published the first part of the novel that is often hailed as the masterpiece of Spanish literature: *El ingenioso hidalgo Don Quixote de la Mancha*. This novel contains within itself a synthesis of most of the genres popular at the time—the pastoral, the Byzantine novel, the picaresque novel, the chivalric romance, etc. Cervantes originally intended to mock the popular chivalric romances and the adventures stories of errant knights. He created Don Quixote, an elderly gentleman who becomes insane due to his excessive passion for reading chivalric romances. Don Quixote leaves his home, having decided to revive heroic times by reenacting knightly feats. Later, with the promise of fabulous rewards, he convinces the poor peasant, Sancho Panza, to be his squire. The novel narrates in a magisterial way the absurd adventures of knight and squire through Spain, and depicts characters who reflect their society.

The book was an immediate success and was reedited several times in subsequent years. It was translated into English as early as 1612 and appeared in French and other European languages. Seventeenth-century readers immediately popularized the burlesque image of the Don Quixote astride his skinny horse accompanied by plump Sancho on his donkey. Early readers especially appreciated the novel's comic side. But since the German Romantic movement, several other significant aspects have been noted. The subject of the perception of reality through the senses is central to *Don Quixote*. The madman's eyes deform reality to the point of making us unsure of the validity of our own perception of it. Hence Don Quixote was elevated from a comical character to a heroic figure who embodies the epistemological dilemma of the human being. The contrast between the idealistic Don Quixote and the pragmatic Sancho, and how they influence each other, has become emblematic of the dualism of human nature. Some episodes, such as the famous fight with the windmills, continue to earn universal recognition and admiration.

*Don Quixote*'s success was so extraordinary that in 1614 a certain Avellaneda attempted to write a spurious sequel. This work enraged Cervantes to the point that he decided to write the second part of *Don Quixote*, which was successfully published in 1615. This continuation is considered to be, if not superior, at least equal in quality to the first part. Part two is more reflective and possesses greater structural unity. At the conclusion, Don Quixote dies having recovered his lucidity much to the distress of a transformed Sancho who is eager to engage in more adventures. With Don Quixote's death, Cervantes ended the possibility of further adventures for his character.

Writers in Cervantes' time lost the economic rights of their work after selling it to a merchant. Cervantes' success did not grant him the economic security that best-sellers bring their authors today.

Cervantes' chief literary achievements came late in his life—he was close to 60 when the first part of *Don Quixote* was published. Death found him trying to finish what would be his last book, *Los trabajos de Persiles y Segismunda* (*The Labors of Persiles and Segismunda*). His widow published this novel after his death. Cervantes was very proud of this Byzantine-style novel. He thought that its success would exceed that of *Don Quixote*—but it did not. Cervantes

signed the dedication of the book to the Count of Lemos on April 19, 1616. He died four days later and was buried in an unmarked grave in the Trinitarians' convent in Madrid. His wife survived him by ten years, and his daughter Isabel de Saavedra died in 1662.

All Cervantes' major works have been translated into English, and *Don Quixote* is one of the few books translated into most languages. *Don Quixote*'s literary influence has been immense. Direct traces can be identified in the work of Laurence Sterne, Henry Fielding, Tobias Smollet, Fyodor Dostoyevsky, Gustave Flaubert, Pérez Galdos, and others. In addition, thinkers and philosophers have dedicated essays to the myth of Don Quixote. Twentieth-century musical productions (*The Man of La Mancha*) and movies have been inspired by *Don Quixote,* and modern artists like **Pablo Picasso** have immortalized the image of the errant knight escorted by his faithful squire.

## SELECTED PUBLISHED WORKS:

*El Ingenioso hidalgo Don Quixote de La Mancha,* 1605 (first part), 1614 (second part); translated by Samuel Putnam as *Don Quixote: A New Translation,* New York, Viking Press, 1949; translated by J. M. Cohen as *The Adventures of Don Quixote,* New York, Penguin, 1963.

*Novelas Ejemplares,* 1613; translated by C. A. Jones as *The Exemplary Novels,* New York, Penguin, 1972.

*Ocho comedies y ocho entremeses,* 1615; translated by Edwin Honig as *Interludes,* 1964.

*Los trabajos de Persiles y Segismunda,* 1617; translated by L. D. Stanley as *The Wandering of Persiles and Segismunda: A Northern History,* 1854.

## SOURCES:

### Books

Byron, William, *Cervantes: A Biography,* New York, Doubleday, 1978.

Canavaggio, Jean, *Cervantes: en busca del perfil perdido,* Madrid, Espasa-Calpe, 1992.

*Cervantes Across the Centuries,* edited by Angel Flores and M. J. Bernardete, New York: Gordian Press, 1969.

Durán, Manuel, *Cervantes,* New York, Twayne, 1974.

Juan-Arbó, Sebastián, *Cervantes: The Man and His Time,* New York, Vanguard Press, 1955.

Nav-Ledesma, Francisco, *Cervantes: The Man and the Genius,* New York, Charterhouse, 1973.

—*Sketch by Enrique Fernandez*

# Carlos Chávez
## 1899-1978
**Mexican musician and composer**

*Carlos Chávez*

Also known as Carlos Antonio de Padua Chávez y Ramírez, Carlos Chávez is considered the twentieth century's foremost Mexican musician and one of the three most important Latin American composers. He forged a unique style which blended traditional classical music with contemporary elements and the harmonies and rhythms of the traditional Indian music of Mexico.

Of mixed Spanish and Indian heritage, Chávez was born in Popotla, a suburb of Mexico City, on June 13, 1899; he was the youngest of six children born to Augustín, an inventor, and Juvencia Ramírez Chávez, a teacher. Augustín died while Carlos was still a young child, and Juvencia supported the family from her earnings as director of the Normal School for Young Women.

Chávez studied piano with his brother, Manuel, until the age of eleven or so and then became the pupil of composer Manuel M. Ponce, and then of Pedro Luis Ogazón. Chávez later credited Ogazón with introducing him to the best of classical music and developing his musical taste. He studied harmony with Juan B. Fuentes. Although he would later consider himself primarily a composer, Chávez never formally studied composition, rejecting such available instruction as imitative of nineteenth-century European music. He preferred to learn by analyzing, on his own, the work of the great masters.

Chávez began composing at an early age, and had written a symphony by the age of 16. The first public performance of his work occurred in 1921. His style, which eventually came to be described as progressive, could clearly be seen as a departure from the nineteenth-century tradition that still dominated Mexican music at that time. Although partly influenced by the European masters he had studied, he had also ventured into the realm of modern music. In addition, the influence of indigenous Mexican music was discernible in his compositions. In 1921 Chávez produced what is considered his first important work, a ballet reflecting Aztec influence, called *El fuego nuevo* (*The New Fire*), commissioned by the newly

formed Secretariat of Public Education. Indeed, the blossoming of Chávez' career parallels and reflects the changed attitude toward culture, which was one of the fruits of the Mexican Revolution of 1910.

In 1922, Chávez married Otilia Ortiz, a talented concert pianist, and the two embarked upon European travels that took them to France, Austria, and Germany. Reportedly disappointed in the state of music in Europe, Chávez turned to the new world for inspiration. He visited New York in 1923 and became interested in jazz and the relationship of electronics to music. He returned to New York in 1926 and remained there until 1928 furthering his interest in progressive music and forging important relationships—notably with Aaron Copland and Edgard Varése.

### Directed Mexican Orchestra

Returning to Mexico in 1928, Chávez became musical director of the newly formed Orquesta Sinfónica de México. During his 21-season tenure there, Chávez succeeded in building the first stable orchestra in Mexico. His repertoire included a quantity of new music, as well as traditional works, many representing Mexican or world premieres. Chávez' impressive repertoire and high standards of performance, made the orchestra, as biographer Robert L. Parker has said, "a reason to visit Mexico."

From 1928 until 1935, Chávez served as director of The Conservatorio Nacional de Música. During his years there, he completely transformed the ill-organized, tradition-bound academy, overturning the curriculum, bringing in progressive teachers, and providing new performance opportunities for the most promising students. Chávez, himself, taught the course in composition. As a part of the new political regime's efforts to breathe new life into the arts, Chávez was also asked to serve as chief of the Department of Fine Arts. In this position, he engaged in the collection, study, and performance of native music and instruments.

Chávez' biographer and critic Robert L. Parker assessed Chávez' composition during the 1930s as nationalistic—employing native subject matter, instrumentation, texts, and themes. At the same time, Parker pointed out, Chávez was moving in the direction of abstract music, experimenting with the adaptation of the music of other composers. In 1937 Chávez had his U.S. conducting debut, with the New York Philharmonic Orchestra. Critic Olin Downes said in the *New York Times* that Chávez's conducting "surpassed any achievement since that of Toscanini."

From 1936 onward, Chávez spent a great deal of his time traveling and conducting throughout the United States, South America, and Europe. The rearing of his three children—Anita, Augustín, and Juanita—fell largely to his wife, Otilia. During these years and throughout his professional life, he balanced composing, conducting, and teaching.

In 1946 Chávez was named director general of the Instituto Nacional de Bellas Artes, a new entity to which President Miguel Alemán delegated the attention of the arts and literature in Mexico. Chávez remained at this post until 1952. In 1947 he organized what became the Orquesta Sinfónica Nacional, which moved into the breach left by the disbanding of the Orquesta Sinfónica de México in 1949.

From 1958 to 1959 he held the Charles Eliot Norton Chair at Harvard University. His lectures there were published in the collection *Musical Thought.* In his later life, Chávez once more focused his attention on Mexico, becoming embroiled in political and artistic dispute by criticizing what he saw as a decline in the quality of Mexican music. He continued to compose, conduct and lecture. His last conducting appearance took place in Washington, D.C., only a few months before his death, in Mexico City, on August 2, 1978.

## SELECTED PUBLISHED WORKS:

*Toward a New Music,* New York, W. W. Norton, 1937.
*Musical Thought,* Cambridge, Harvard University Press, 1961.

## SOURCES:

### Books

*Baker's Biographical Dictionary of Musicians,* eighth edition, edited by Nicolas Slonimsky, New York, Schermer/Macmillan, 1992, pp. 320–21.
*Book of Modern Composers,* edited by David Ewen, second edition, New York, Knopf, 1956.
*New Grove Dictionary of Music and Musicians,* Volume 4, New York, Macmillan, 1980, pp. 185–88.
Newlon, Clarke, *Men Who Made Mexico,* New York, Dodd, Mead, 1973.
Parker, Robert L., *Carlos Chavez, Mexico's Modern-day Orpheus,* Boston, G. K. Hall, 1983, pp. 433–44.

### Periodicals

*American* winter 1987, pp. 433–44.
*Musical Quarterly,* October 1936, pp. 435–45.

*—Sketch by Julie Henderson Jersyk*

# César Estrada Chávez
## 1927-1993
### Mexican American labor activist

Called "one of the heroic figures of our time" by Robert Kennedy in 1968, César Chávez was a grass-roots labor organizer who rose from the ranks of California migrant workers to form and lead the National Farm Workers Association (NFWA). Now called the United Farm Workers, AFL-CIO, it was the first effective agricultural union in the United States. In 1965, Chávez led the NFWA into a strike against grape growers in Delano, California. The strike failed but a nationwide boycott of table granal, socialized Spainpes followed, successfully forcing union contracts with growers in the Imperial, Coachella, and San Joaquin valleys in 1970.

Selfless and deeply religious, Chávez worked tirelessly for years to bring farm workers into the union. "No farm worker has impacted the fields and corporate boardrooms of California agriculture like César Chávez," eulogized Roger Cardinal Mahony in the *National Catholic Reporter.* That publication's editors stated that Chávez "was unique and played a special role in U.S. Hispanic history. In the late 1960s

*César Chávez*

and early 1970s, he gave the flowering Chicano movement a visible national leader."

### Childhood Poverty Influenced Life's Work

César Estrada Chávez was born near Yuma, Arizona, on March 31, 1927. One of five children, he grew up in unrelenting poverty. The small farm on which he was born was foreclosed when he was ten, and the family joined the hordes of migrant workers who followed the harvests in California during the Great Depression. The family lived in tents or shacks in migrant labor camps. By his own estimate, Chávez attended 65 different elementary schools as a result of this nomadic existence, and attained only a seventh-grade education before leaving school to work in the fields. This childhood, combined with a concern for others learned from his mother, provided the impetus for Chávez to dedicate his life to improving the plight of the migrant worker. In 1933 Arthur Jones asserted in the *National Catholic Reporter:* "A few men and women have engraved their names in the annals of change through nonviolence, but none have experienced the grinding childhood poverty that Chávez did." Jones added that "it is likely that it was both knowing and witnessing poverty and the sheer drudgery and helplessness of the migrant life that drove him."

Chávez was first exposed to unions in 1939. He was 12 when a CIO union began organizing dried-fruit workers in San Jose, where the family was then

living. Chávez's father and uncle both joined and picketed in a strike that followed. Although the strike failed and the union disbanded, his father joined every new union that appeared. The idea of unionizing had a profound effect on Chávez, who joined the National Agricultural Workers Union at age 19.

Chávez served in the U.S. Navy during the last two years of World War II but returned to migrant work when his service ended in 1945. In 1948 he met and married Helen Fabela while working in Delano. They eventually had eight children.

### Began Organizing Activity

In 1952 Chávez began his active involvement in organizing when recruiter Fred Ross persuaded him to work for the Community Service Organization (CSO). Chávez spent the next ten years building CSO chapters, leading voter registration drives, and aiding dispossessed Mexicans and Mexican Americans on issues of immigration, welfare, and police abuse. In 1958 he was named general director of the CSO. Chávez resigned in 1962 after the organization refused to endorse his proposal to form a farm workers union. With the $1,200 that comprised his life savings, Chávez then formed the National Farm Workers Association in Delano. Chávez spent several months in the fields of the Imperial and San Joaquin valleys, convincing farm workers to join the union. These were difficult times financially for Chávez, and he was often forced to beg for food from the workers he was trying to organize. As membership grew, so did the strength of the union. With the aid of priests and lawyers, Chávez was able to pressure growers to settle individual grievances. With membership at 1,700 by 1965, the union was successful in forcing pay-raise concessions from two Delano growers. Because it was still a fledgling union, Chávez felt it would not be strong enough to undertake a strike for another three years. However, when the predominantly Filipino Agricultural Workers Organizing Committee (AWOC)—a previously inactive AFL-CIO affiliate—went on strike against Delano growers in September 1965, the NFWA was asked to join the effort. Chávez agreed. *La huelga*—"the strike"—had begun, and *La Causa*—"The Cause"—had been born.

*La Causa* signified more than just the union; it was a movement. Characterized by marches, rallies, boycotts, and a dedication to nonviolence that echoed the tactics of Gandhi and Martin Luther King, Jr., the movement also integrated the precepts of the Catholic church. According to Cardinal Mahony, "The constitution and bylaws of the . . . union were taken directly from the Catholic church's social teaching documents." Cardinal Mahony also noted: "Every major initiative by the . . . AWOC . . . began with prayer, often an outdoor mass celebrated on an irrigation ditch levee near some farm or ranch. Images of Our Lady of Guadalupe preceded every march, picket line and boycott demonstration." Catholic priests had been involved in grievance resolution from the beginning, and in 1969, California bishops formed the Ad Hoc Committee on Farm Labor to serve as a mediation panel for negotiations between the union and growers. Cardinal Mahony, then a monsignor, was appointed the California field secretary and worked alongside Chávez and the growers. As Jones wrote, "It was a very Catholic fight."

The strike that began in 1965 lasted five years. Chávez obtained the endorsement of a broad spectrum of supporters from political leaders Eugene McCarthy and Robert Kennedy, to the United Auto Workers, AFL-CIO, and to publications such as the *New Republic.* In early 1967, Chávez led a 25-day march that spanned the 300 miles from Delano to Sacramento. Originally begun by 65 farm workers, the march was joined by 10,000 supporters and made newspaper headlines.

In 1966 the NFWA merged with the AFL-CIO, becoming the United Farm Workers Organizing Committee. By 1968 the UFWOC had made several gains with major wine grape growers such as Christian Brothers' and the Gallo winery, but table grape growers were unyielding. A nationwide boycott of all table grapes (90 percent of which were grown in California) began in the spring of 1968.

Both to dramatize the boycott and to emphasize nonviolence, Chávez began the first of his well-publicized, life-threatening fasts, which lasted 25 days. In the years that followed, Chávez continued to undertake fasts as a response to violence occurring in the path of the union's struggle. In addition to drawing national attention to union boycott efforts, fasting underscored Chávez's complete dedication to *La Causa.* The *National Catholic Reporter* indicates that at the end of his first fast, Chávez told friend and ally Father Victor Salandini, "I am convinced that the truest act of courage . . . is to sacrifice ourselves in a totally nonviolent struggle for justice."

By 1970 the growers had signed union contracts. The union began to lose ground in 1973 when the contracts came up for renewal. The Teamsters moved in and snapped up "sweetheart" contracts with the larger growers. After the initial success of the table grape boycott, Chávez redirected his focus to the working conditions of the Salinas lettuce pickers. A strike and boycott followed. Primarily due to Chávez's efforts, the California Labor Relations Act was passed in 1975, guaranteeing secret ballot union elections for farm workers.

## UFW Lost Momentum

Although great strides had been made, by the early 1980s it was clear that the heyday of the UFW was over. In 1982, George Deukmejian became governor of California, signaling the end of sympathetic state government. In 1993, the *Progressive* quoted **Arturo Rodriguez**, UFW Vice-President: "We haven't had any input into the law since." Then union membership began to decline significantly.

In the late 1980s, Chávez turned his attention to the dangers of pesticide use by growers. To focus national attention on this issue, he initiated another major table grape boycott. To publicize the effort, he also undertook his most extended fast, lasting 36 days. The fast, according to *Newsweek,* "turned out celebrities from **Martin Sheen** to Jesse Jackson but it felt more like a last hurrah than a new beginning."

The decline of the UFW was due primarily to the overwhelming power of California agribusiness. Secondary reasons may be found within the union infrastructure. Frank Bardacke suggested in the *Nation,* "Within the UFW the boycott tail came to wag the farmworker dog. While it was not wrong of Chávez to seek as much support as possible, this support work, primarily the boycott, became the essential activity of the union. Ultimately, it interfered with organizing in the fields."

Chávez died in his sleep on April 23, 1993, while on union business in Arizona. An estimated 35,000 mourners were part of the funeral procession. Despite the setbacks experienced by *La Causa,* Chávez had a significant impact on countless lives. In a *New Yorker* eulogy, Peter Matthiessen wrote of Chávez: "Self sacrifice lay at the very heart of the devotion he inspired, and gave dignity and hope not only to farmworkers but to every one of the Chicano people, who saw for themselves what one brave man, indifferent to his own health and welfare, could accomplish."

## SOURCES:

### Books

*Current Biography 1969,* edited by Charles Moritz, New York, H. W. Wilson Co., 1969.
*Current Biography Yearbook,* edited by Judith Graham, New York, H. W. Wilson Co., 1993.
*Hispanic-American Almanac,* edited by Nicolás Kanellos, Detroit, Gale Research, 1993.

### Periodicals

*Christian Century,* May 12, 1993, pp. 513–14.
*Nation,* July 26-August 2, 1993, pp. 130–35.
*National Catholic Reporter,* May 7, 1993, pp. 5–7, 28.
*Newsweek,* May 3, 199f *New Yorker,* May 17, 1993, p. 82.

*Progressive,* July 1992, p. 14.

—*Sketch by Ellen Dennis French*

# Denise Chávez
## 1948-

**Hispanic American playwright and short story writer**

Y"ou don't have to go anywhere. Not down the street. Not even out of this house. There's stories, plenty of them all around." With these words the mother of a character in the title story of Denise Chávez's short story collection, *The Last of the Menu Girls*, gives advice on writing to her daughter. Chávez might have been penning these words to herself, for her short stories and plays are characterized by their focus on characters and scenes from everyday life. Chávez explains that the presence of the ordinary in her work springs from her belief that as a Chicana writer she needs to speak for those who have no one to vocalize for them. "My work as a playwright is to capture as best as I can the small gestures of the forgotten people, the old men sitting on park benches, the lonely spinsters inside their corner store," she told *Contemporary Authors.*

Daughter of Ernesto E. Chávez, an attorney, and Delfina Rede Favor Chávez, a teacher, the future dramatist was born on August 15, 1948, in Las Cruces, New Mexico. She earned a bachelor of arts degree in 1971 at New Mexico State University and in 1974 received a master's degree in fine arts from Trinity University in San Antonio, Texas. In 1984, she obtained a master's degree in arts from the University of New Mexico. While she has considered herself a full-time playwright since 1977, she has also spent much time teaching, including two years as an instructor of English at Northern New Mexico Community College, in Espanola. She has also taught at the American School in Paris, and she has served as an assistant professor of drama at the University of Houston in Texas since 1989.

### Early Writings Earn Critical Acclaim

In 1970, her writing talents received early recognition. In that year she won the New Mexico State University Best Play Award for her work, *The Wait.* During the remainder of the decade, she wrote nearly a dozen plays and saw most of these produced in Taos, Santa Fe, or Albuquerque, New Mexico. Since 1980, she has added other genres to her repertoire, including a poetry anthology, *Life Is a Two-Way Street*, and a collection of short stories, *The Last of the Menu Girls.* But she has continued to write for the theater, including *Novena narrativas*, a one-woman show, and *The Last of the Menu Girls,* a one-act adaptation of her short story of the same title. Her work has been selected in several collections, including *An Anthology of Southwestern Literature, An Anthology: The Indian Río Grande*, and *Voces: An Anthology of Nuevo Mexicano Writers.*

Chávez's work has continued to draw critical recognition. She has received grants from the New Mexico Arts Division, the National Endowment for the Arts, and the Rockefeller Foundation. In 1982, she received a creative writing fellowship from the University of New Mexico and, in 1990, a creative artist fellowship from the Cultural Arts Council of Houston, Texas. In 1986, her short story, "The Last of the Menu Girls," from the collection of the same title, received the New Mexico State University's Steele Jones Fiction Award. The stories in the volume revolve around the life of Rocío Esquibel, a 17-year-old whose job is delivering menus to hospital patients. Writing in *New York Times Book Review,* Beverly Lyon Clark noted that many of the stories revealed "Chávez's strengths in dialogue and in juxtaposing evocative scenes."

Married to photographer and sculptor Daniel Zolinsky, Chávez currently resides in Houston, Texas. Throughout her career, she has demonstrated a social conscience that has led her to serve as a teacher at Radium Springs Center for Women, a medium-security prison, and as co-director of a senior citizen workshop in creative writing and puppetry at Community Action Agency in Las Cruces, New Mexico. This social conscience is also present in her written work as a continuing theme of love, a theme that Chávez finds in the landscape of the American Southwest. She explained this concept in *Contemporary Authors:* "I write about the neighborhood handymen, the waitresses, the bag ladies, the elevator operators. They all have something in common: they know what it is to love and to be merciful. . . . My work is rooted in the Southwest, in heat and dust, and reflects a world where love is as real as the land. In this dry and seemingly harsh and empty world there is much beauty to be found. That hope of the heart is what feeds me, my characters."

### SELECTED PUBLISHED WORKS:

*Life Is a Two-Way Street* (poetry anthology), Rosetta Press, 1980.
*The Last of the Menu Girls* (stories), Arte Público, 1986.
*Face of an Angel,* Arte Público, 1990.

(With Georgic McInnis) *The Red Dress* (photographic essay with text), Arte Público, 1990.

## SOURCES:

### Books

Chávez, Denise, *The Last of the Menu Girls,* Arte Público, 1986.
*Contemporary Authors New Revisions Series,* Volume 191.

### Periodicals

*New York Times Book Review,* October 12, 1986, p. 28.

—*Sketch by Marian C. Gonsior*

*Dennis Chávez*

# Dennis Chávez
## 1888-1962
**Mexican American statesman and politician**

The first Hispanic American to be elected to the United States Senate, Democrat Dennis Chávez led a long and distinguished career in government service, first as a member of the U.S. House of Representatives and then as a senator from the state of New Mexico. Noted primarily for his long and unrelenting fight to create a federal Fair Employment Practices Commission, Chávez was also a staunch supporter of education and civil rights.

The third of eight children, Dionisio Chávez was born to David and Paz (Sanchez) Chávez on April 8, 1888. His family lived in Los Chávez, in what was then the United States Mexican Territory. The area did not become the state of New Mexico until 1912. When he was seven, the family moved to Albuquerque. At school his name was changed to Dennis. Chávez quit school in the eighth grade and went to work. For the next five years he drove a grocery wagon to help support the family. He joined the Albuquerque Engineering Department in 1905, earning a substantial increase in income. Even after Chávez left school, he spent evenings at the local public library, reading about Thomas Jefferson and politics—his passions.

Chávez worked as an interpreter for senate candidate Andrieus A. Jones during the 1916 campaign. Jones rewarded him with a clerkship in the U.S. Senate in 1918–1919. While clerking, Chávez also entered Georgetown University through a special entrance examination to study law. He earned a Bachelor of Laws degree from Georgetown in 1920, and returned to Albuquerque, where he established a successful law practice.

### Political Career Began with State Legislature

A Democrat in the tradition of his hero Thomas Jefferson, Chávez became active in local politics, winning election to the New Mexico House of Representatives. In 1930 he ran successfully for a seat in the U.S. House of Representatives, handily defeating the incumbent Republican, Albert Simms. He served as the thinly populated state's only representative. He was reelected once and then turned his sights toward the U.S. Senate. In 1934 he ran against the powerful Republican incumbent, Bronson Cutting. After a hard-fought, bitter campaign and a narrow defeat, Chávez challenged the validity of Cutting's victory, charging vote fraud. The issue reached to the Senate floor. The matter was still pending in May 1935, when Cutting was killed in an airplane crash. Chávez was appointed by New Mexico's Governor Tingley to serve in Cutting's place. Five senators expressed their disapproval by walking out of the Senate as Chávez was being sworn in. Chávez, however, was the people of New Mexico's clear choice when he was officially elected to the position in 1936, defeating a popular Republican candidate.

## Served with Distinction

New Mexico voters showed their support for Chávez by reelecting him to the Senate five times. Although his often independent stands on various issues generated controversy, Chávez was a strong supporter of President Franklin Roosevelt's New Deal programs. His service on important Congressional committees allowed him to fight for causes he believed in. Chávez was a member of the Committees on Territories and Insular Affairs, the Education and Labor, Appropriations and Indian Affairs. In the last, he protested measures affecting Navajo grazing stock and also demanded an investigation of Indian Affairs Commissioner Collier.

In 1938 Chávez co-authored the Chávez-McAdoo bill, which established a federal radio station to counter Nazi and Fascist broadcasts into South America. In a curious move the following year, he advocated U.S. recognition of Spain's fascist leader, General Francisco Franco. He usually took a liberal stance on farm issues, voting for the draft deferment of farm laborers and against reductions in farm security appropriations. He was also active in measures regarding tariffs, employment programs, and unemployment benefits.

Chávez earned the nickname "Puerto Rico's Senator" in 1942 when he initiated an investigation into the causes of social and economic conditions in Puerto Rico. His support of a Senate bill to extend public works projects in that territory and the Virgin Islands was decisive in its passage.

Chávez attracted national attention during his long fight for enactment of a federal Fair Employment Practices Commission. The bill was designed to prevent employers or labor unions doing government work from discriminating on the basis of race, creed, color, ancestry, or national origin. The bill was eventually defeated in 1946—by only an eight-vote margin.

Dennis Chávez worked tirelessly to further the interests of the state of New Mexico. He is credited for garnering significant amounts of federal funding as well as key defense installations for the state. Chávez married Imelda Espinoza in 1911. They had three children: two daughters and a son. Chávez died of a heart attack on November 18, 1962, at the age of 74.

## SOURCES:

### Books

*Current Biography, 1946,* edited by Anna Rothe, New York, H. W. Wilson, 1947.

*Current Biography, 1963,* edited by Charles Moritz, New York, H. W. Wilson, 1963.
*Hispanic-American Almanac,* edited by Nicolás Kanellos, Detroit, Gale Research, 1993.
*Mexican American Biographies, A Historical Dictionary: 1836-1987;* edited by Matt S. Meier, Westport, Connecticut, Greenwood Press, 1988.

—*Sketch by Ellen Dennis French*

# Fray Angélico Chávez
## 1910-

### Hispanic American priest, scholar, and writer

New Mexico's most prominent historian, Fray (Friar) Angélico Chávez has had a lengthy career as a writer, poet, historian, and Franciscan priest. With more than 20 books to his credit, he has also authored numerous stories and articles for Catholic magazines and various journals. His historical scholarship includes works such as *Origins of New Mexico Families in the Spanish Colonial Period* (1954), *Archives of the Archdiocese of Santa Fe* (1957), and *But Time and Chance: The Story of Padre Martínez of Taos* (1981).

Chávez published mostly poetry from the beginning of his writing career in 1939 until the early 1950s. His poetry has been favorably compared in form and technique to that of English lyric poets John Donne, William Blake, and Gerard Manley Hopkins. Writing in the *Southwest Review* in 1946, Robert Hunt suggested that "it becomes increasingly evident that this Franciscan Father is the natural offshoot and spiritual inheritor of a tradition which fostered many of the great metaphysicians—and mystics—of the past: from Donne, Cowley, Crashaw and Blake to the nineteenth century's Francis Thompson and Gerard Manley Hopkins." In addition to acclaim such as this, one of Chávez's poems, *The Virgin of Port Lligat* (1959), received praise from poet T. S. Eliot.

Baptized as Manuel Ezeguiel, Chávez is the oldest of 10 children. He was born on April 10, 1910, in Wagon Mound, New Mexico, to Fabián (a carpenter) and Nicolasa (Roybal) Chávez (a teacher). His love of English literature and New Mexico history began in childhood. Drawn to the Franciscan order because of its prominence in New Mexico's history, Chávez entered the St. Francis Seminary in Cincinnati, Ohio, in 1924. It was there that Chávez began to write. He received the name Fray Angélico when he entered the novitiate, and has written under this name—which recognizes his love for painting in its tribute to the Florentine painter Fra Angélico—ever since. Chávez graduated from Detroit's Duns Scotus College in 1933, and was ordained in Santa Fe four years later. He has the distinction of being the first native New Mexican to join the Franciscan order.

Chávez spent the next several years ministering to both the Pueblo Indians and the inhabitants of the town neighboring Peña Blanca, where he lived. His missionary work was interrupted twice, for service in the U.S. Army. Chávez served as a chaplain in the Pacific during World War II and in Germany during the Korean Conflict.

### Writings Reflect Regional Awareness

Between priestly duties and military service, Chávez continued to find time to write. He regularly published poetry as well as some historical work and short fiction between 1939 and 1957. Genaro Padilla, writing in *Pasó por Aquí* in 1989, stated that despite an "outpouring of material about the Hispano experience in New Mexico, Chávez has been largely overlooked as one of the pioneers of Chicano writing in this century." Although Chávez has been criticized for being overly occupied with Church history and for vague references to racial memory, "blood," and environment, Padilla defended Chávez's historical scholarship. He wrote, "Chávez's history is grounded in the world, even when that world is seen from a religious perspective and lyrically. Fray Angélico's Franciscan habit of mind understandably informs his interest in church-related history, but that history has been conducted with painstakingly archival research."

Perhaps Chávez's most discussed work is the highly autobiographical *My Penitente Land: Reflections on Spanish New Mexico* (1974). Kenneth Weber, in a *Journal of Ethnic Studies* review summarized it as "A difficult book to characterize, it is at the same time historical, theological, philosophical, sociological . . . and a treatise on the influence of environment on the development of personality types and religions." Of this much-discussed book, Weber further clarified: "As the subtitle accurately indicates, this is not a scholarly book . . . but rather a scholar's *Reflections* —his personal, intuitive, even mystical account of what he feels makes Spanish New Mexicans the way they are."

Both Chávez's history and short fiction demonstrate a singular regional awareness of New Mexico's past, from its Spanish heritage and attendant class concerns to the indelible presence of the Catholic church. Padilla wrote that "Chávez's writing reveals a complex interplay between the artist's fictive imagination, his moral and religious perspectives, and his historian's knowledge of the troubling realities of New Mexico's intercultural conflicts."

In a cordial parting, Chávez left the priesthood at the age of 63 to pursue writing full-time. Since then he has published several volumes of historical works and short stories, and has worked as an editor and translator. One of his books, *Missions of New Mexico, 1776*, was chosen as the state's official book for the country's bicentennial observation. Chávez has lectured at the University of New Mexico, and was honored for his substantial body of work in 1976 by New Mexico's governor.

### SELECTED PUBLISHED WORKS:

*Clothed with the Sun,* Santa Fe, Writer's Editions, 1939.

*Seraphic Days; Franciscan Thoughts and Affections on the Principal Feasts of Our Lord and Our Lady and All the Saints of the Three Orders of the Seraph of Assisi,* Detroit, Duns Scotus College, 1940.

*New Mexico Triptych; Being Three Panels and Three Accounts: 1) The Angel's New Wings; 2) The Penitente Thief; 3) Hunchback Madonna,* Paterson, NJ, St. Anthony Guild, 1940.

*Eleven Lady-Lyrics, and Other Poems,* Paterson, NJ, St. Anthony Guild, 1945.

*Our Lady of the Conquest,* Albuquerque, University of New Mexico Press, 1948.

*The Single Rose; the Rose Unica and Commentary of Fray Manuel de Santa Clara,* Santa Fe, Los Santos Bookshop, 1948.

*La Conquistadora: The Autobiography of an Ancient Statue,* Paterson, NJ, St. Anthony Guild, 1954.

*Origins of New Mexico Families in the Spanish Colonial Period. In Two Parts: The Seventeenth (1598–1693) and the Eighteenth (1693–1821) Centuries,* Santa Fe, Historical Society of New Mexico, 1954.

*Archives of the Archdiocese of Santa Fe, 1678–1900,* Washington, D.C., Academy of American Franciscan History, 1957.

*From an Altar Screen/El retablo: Tales from New Mexico,* New York, Farrar, Straus & Cudahy, 1957; republished as *When the Santos Talked: A Retablo of New Mexico Tales,* Santa Fe, Gannon, 1977.

*The Virgin of Port Lligat,* Fresno, CA, Academy Literary Guild, 1959.

*The Lady from Toledo,* Fresno, Academy Literary Guild, 1960.

*Coronado's Friars,* Washington, D.C., Academy of American Franciscan History, 1968.

*Selected Poems, With an Apologia,* Santa Fe, Press of the Territorian, 1969.

*The Song of Francis,* Flagstaff, Northland, 1973.

*My Penitente Land: Reflections on Spanish New Mexico,* Albuquerque, University of New Mexico Press, 1974.

*But Time and Chance: The Story of Padre Martínez of Taos, 1793–1867,* Santa Fe, Sunstone, 1981.

*Trés Macho–He Said,* Santa Fe, Gannon, 1985.

*The Short Stories of Fray Angélico Chávez,* edited by Genaro M. Padilla, Albuquerque, University of New Mexico Press, 1987.

## Other

*Missions of New Mexico, 1776, A Description by Fray Francisco Atanasio Domínguez With Other Contemporary Documents,* edited and translated by Chávez and E. B. Adams, Albuquerque, University of New Mexico Press, 1956.

*The Oroz Codex; or Relation of the Description of the Holy Gospel Province in New Spain and the Lives of the Founders and Other Note-Worthy Men of Said Province Composed by Fray Pedro Oroz: 1584–1586,* edited and translated by Chávez, Washington, D.C., Academy of American Franciscan History, 1972.

*The Domínguez-Escalante Journal: Their Expedition Through Colorado, Utah, Arizona, and New Mexico in 1776,* edited by Ted J. Warner, translated by Chávez, Provo, Utah, Brigham Young University Press, 1976.

## SOURCES:

### Books

*Dictionary of Literary Biography,* Vol. 82, edited by Francisco A. Lomelí and Carl R. Shirley, Detroit, Gale, 1989.

*Hispanic Writers,* edited by Bryan Ryan, Detroit, Gale, 1991.

*Mexican American Biographies,* edited by Matt S. Meier, New York, Greenwood Press, 1988.

*Pasó por Aquí,* edited by Erlinda Gonzales-Berry, Albuquerque, University of New Mexico Press, 1989.

### Periodicals

*Journal of Ethnic Studies,* Vol. 3, No. 2, 1975, pp. 119–21.

*Southwest Review,* Vol. 31, summer 1946, pp. 266–68.

—*Sketch by Ellen Dennis French*

# Linda Chávez
## 1947-
### Hispanic American government official and writer

Formerly the highest-ranking woman in the Reagan White House and a Republican candidate for U.S. Senator from Maryland, Linda Chávez has made a career out of defying expectations and refusing to be classified. Although she is proud of her Hispanic heritage, Chávez has insisted on making her own way in politics and is opposed to many "traditional" policies relating to minorities, such as racial hiring quotas, comparable worth and pay equity, and bilingual educationprograms. Although she is a conservative Republican, Chávez has not been hesitant to speak out against problems in the Reagan administration. Commenting on the covert activities of Lieutenant Colonel Oliver North, for example, Chávez told the *Christian Science Monitor* that "Ollie North is no conservative" and added that "zealots have no place in democratic governments." "It would be easier for me to be a liberal Democrat, I guess," she explained in the *Washington Post.* "People would expect that. But I guess I'm just stubborn. I do go against the grain. I do things that are not always popular. There's a tenacity there. I guess I've always thought of myself as different and sometimes I've gotten more attention for myself than I wanted."

While Chávez has been accused by many of abandoning the Hispanic community, she notes that her ethnic background has contributed to her conservative beliefs. Chávez was born in Albuquerque, New Mexico, in 1947, the daughter of Velma, an Anglo, and Rudy Chávez, a conservative Spanish American whose family has been established in the Southwest for over three hundred years. When she was nine the family moved to Denver, Colorado, where Chávez first began to notice racial discrimination. As a teenager she marched against segregation and recalls that in school she was never encouraged to excel or further her education. Motivated by her father, a World War II veteran who taught her to value her Spanish heritage without using it as an excuse, Chávez finished high school and entered college. As her mother, Velma Chávez, told the *Washington Post,* Linda's "dad would tell her screaming and yelling doesn't accomplish anything. You have to think about things, decide what's wrong and do something about it and that's it."

### Believes in Hard Work, Not Quotas

It was in college during the late 1960s that Chávez first showed indications of the conservative views she was later to espouse as a public official. At the University of Colorado, where she told *Washington Monthly*, "I made it on hard work," Chávez began tutoring Mexican American students in a remedial program; she became disenchanted, however, when she found the students were urging the administration to lower their minimum grade requirements. After receiving a B.A. in 1970, Chávez went on to graduate study in English literature at the University of California, Los Angeles. Because of her background, Chávez found herself pressured into teaching a course on Chicano writing, despite her assertions that there was not enough material by Hispanic Americans to develop an entire course. Instead of coming prepared to work, Chávez relates, her students "sort of expect-ed that this was the course they could take to come and 'rap,' in the jargon of the day," as she told *Washington Monthly*. She recalls that her students wanted to discuss their own experiences instead of doing class work: "They *lived* Chicano literature," she recalls, so "they didn't [want to] have to read books about it." Things took a turn for the worse when, as she states in *Hispanic*, "some of the students stood up and turned their backs to me. I had to lecture with a class of kids facing their backs to me—it was a disaster." When she failed her students for not completing the reading list, they retaliated by vandal-izing her home and threatening her family. Discour-aged by this experience and her treatment as a "token" Hispanic, Chávez left the university in 1972 and traveled to Washington, D.C., to join her hus-band, Christopher Gersten, whom she married in 1967.

In the mid-seventies, Chávez began working for Democratic and liberal causes in Washington, holding a series of jobs with the Democratic National Com-mittee and the National Education Association. While she wanted to learn more about specific issues, she felt the organizations failed to treat her as an individual with opinions and instead saw her only as an ethnic representative: "They were specifically looking for an Hispanic woman," she reported to *Washington Monthly*. "It was very clear to me they expected me to be the Hispanic lobbyist, to be their link to the Chicano caucus inside the NEA. I balked at that." After serving with the Department of Health, Education, and Welfare as a consultant on education, Chávez joined the staff of the American Federation of Teachers (AFT), where she was allowed to express her views. While editor of the AFT quarterly, *American Educator*, Chávez wrote a series of articles urging a return to "traditional values" in American schools. These writings soon brought her to the attention of conservatives in Washington, and in 1981 she began working as a consultant for President Ronald Rea-gan's administration.

In 1983 Chávez was asked to become a member of the U.S. Commission on Civil Rights, a non-partisan agency designed to monitor the government's progress in enforcing civil rights laws. Dissatisfied with the offer, however, Chávez held out for a position of greater power and influence and was eventually appointed staff director of the agency. Chávez immediately stirred up controversy by issuing a memo counseling the reversal of many traditional civil rights measures, such as racial hiring quotas, a practice she believes demeans people by reducing them to an ethnic category. She also authorized a study to explore the negative effects of affirmative action on minorities. In addition, Chávez hired many temporary employees and consultants "to promote work that would reflect her and the commission majority's views," as the *Washington Post* described it. Many civil rights activists criticized Chávez for what they perceived as changing the traditionally impartial agency into an instrument of the Reagan administration, but Chávez claimed she was only remedying the liberal bias of past years. As the *Washington Post* summarized, "Chávez counter[ed] that she helped redirect the agency toward its tradi-tional goal of a colorblind society.... She main-tain[ed] that her critics have been unable to separate their ideological differences from their assessments of her character and performance."

### Becomes Highest-Ranking Woman in Reagan Administration

It was her performance as the commission's director, however, that helped her become the direc-tor of the White House Office of Public Liaison in 1985, a position that made her the highest-ranking woman in the White House. Appointed because of her strong conservative background, despite her Demo-cratic affiliation, Chávez nevertheless changed to parties, becoming a Republican, and began working to promote administration policy among members of Congress and public groups. Chávez lasted only ten months in the position, however, for as she noted in *Policy Review*, "I learned while in the administration ... how little policy actually emanates from the White House, whether by design or accident. My chief reason for wanting to leave the Civil Rights Commis-sion to join the White House staff was to be able to have a greater role in influencing administration policy on a broad array of issues. What I discovered was that the White House was more involved in process than policy." Upon leaving the Office of Public Liaison in early 1986, Chávez was encouraged to seek a political office of her own.

Chávez began campaigning for the Maryland Republican nomination for senator in 1986, and she gained attention during the primaries when she gave more correct answers than any other candidate during a television quiz on current affairs. A victor in the primaries, Chávez began to prepare for a tough race against Democratic Representative Barbara Mikulski.

The contest brought the national spotlight upon Maryland, for it was only the second U.S. Senate race ever contested by two women.

Despite her success in the primaries, Chávez was at a disadvantage in a state whose voters consisted of two-thirds registered Democrats. In addition, she was drawing criticism for her conversion to the Republican party and her short term as a Maryland resident. When Chávez, married and the mother of three children, called the unmarried Mikulski a "San Francisco-style Democrat" and accused her of being "anti-male," she drew fire for her campaign tactics and was accused of mud-slinging. Her strategy backfired, and despite a successful fund-raising effort that included appearances by President Reagan, Chávez lost the election by over 20 percent of the vote.

After the long campaign, Chávez retired from public office and became president of U.S. English, a private non-profit organization lobbying to make English the official national language. In addition, Chávez has frequently appeared as a political commentator on both television and radio. She has not avoided controversy, however, for in late 1988 she resigned from U.S. English; her reasoning was that she could not work with its founder John Tanton, who, in Chávez's estimation, had demonstrated an "anti-Hispanic" and "anti-Catholic" bias. An "embarrassing question," according to Anna Maria Arias in *Hispanic,* "is how Chávez could have allowed herself to be duped by what many believe is a racist organization."

### Joins Conservative Think Tank

After leaving U.S. English, Chávez went on to become a senior fellow at the Manhattan Institute for Policy Research, a conservative think tank in Washington, D.C. Her recent duties include serving as director of the Center for the New American Community, which, according to Arias, "will study a common heritage that is threatened by multiculturalism."

One of the fruits of Chávez's work for the Institute has been *Out of the Barrio: Toward a New Politics of Hispanic Assimilation,* a 1991 book that discusses such topics as affirmative action and Hispanic involvement in all levels of politics. One of the motivations for writing the work arose out of a debate she had with Arnold Torres, the former executive director of the League of United Latin American Citizens. While Torres felt that Hispanics were largely poor and disadvantaged, Chávez had a different view. "I saw lots of opportunity," she told Arias. "I saw Hispanics rapidly moving into the middle class. I saw my generation, and particularly the generation after me, making huge strides, and yet I didn't see that reflected in the rhetoric." Some have attacked the book for using oversimplifications and generalizations. Chávez defended her book, telling Arias, "I think that to the organized Hispanic movement, what I say is not in their best interest. If you were an organization out there trying to get support from the private and public sector to help Hispanics who are poor and disadvantaged ..., my coming along and saying, 'Wait a second, we are really doing okay, we're moving into the middle class and discrimination has not been nearly as severe as it has been for blacks'— that isn't a view you want out there."

While she has frequently been criticized for her conservative views, Chávez maintains that her liberal detractors are guilty of stereotyping her; they assume that because she is Hispanic, she must hold the political views that a minority is "supposed" to espouse. Countering criticisms that she has changed her views to further her career, Chávez explained to *Washington Monthly* that her opinions have changed, in part, "from watching [the Reagan] administration. I look around, and I see things sort of working and the country working and inflation having been brought down.... So I moved on those kinds of issues ... relatively recently." She also notes that many different groups are included within the "Hispanic" designation, and that her own Spanish American background, as opposed to that of Mexican Americans or Puerto Ricans, is traditionally conservative. "I'm very proud of my heritage," she told the *Washington Post.* "I see myself as what I am. I've never run away from being Hispanic. It doesn't mean I have to endorse the whole agenda."

**SOURCES:**

*Christian Science Monitor,* December 11, 1986, p. 26.
*Fortune,* March 4, 1985, pp. 161–64, November 21, 1988, p. 188.
*Hispanic,* August, 1992, pp. 11–16.
*New Republic,* May 13, 1985, p. 11, February 24, 1986, pp. 8–10, August 3, 1987, pp. 12–13.
*New York Times,* August 31, 1986, p. A58, September 10, 1986, p. A15, October 16, 1986, p. B16.
*People,* November 3, 1986, pp. 115–16.
*Policy Review,* winter 1988, pp. 46–7.
*Savvy,* January, 1987, pp. 43–48, 75.
*Transition,* Issue 56, 1992, pp. 112–22.
*Wall Street Journal,* August 15, 1986, p. 36.
*Washington Monthly,* June 1985, pp. 34–9.
*Washington Post,* July 25, 1986, p. A1, August 15, 1986, p. A17, October 24, 1986, p. C3, p. C5, October 28, 1986, p. A15, October 29, 1986, p. A1, August 16, 1988, p. A22, October 20, 1988, p. A18.

—*Sketch by Diane Telgen*

# José Santos Chocano
## 1875-1934
### Peruvian poet and diplomat

José Santos Chocano was a literary giant of his time, once proclaimed the "Poet of America." His turbulent and colorful life began in Lima, Peru, May 14, 1875. Chocano was very proud of his heritage. His father was José Félix Chocano de Zela, an army captain of Andálusian descent, and his mother was María Aurora Gastanodi de la Vega the Basque descended daughter of a wealthy Spanish miner. In 1811 one great-grandfather, Francisco Maria de Zela, had been honored in 1811 for his early advocacy of Peruvian independence from Spain. Chocano was also a direct descendant of Don Gonzalo Fernandez de Cordoba, who was called "The Great Captain." Chocano's motto was taken from the family coat-of-arms: "*O encuentro camino o me lo abro*" ("Either I find a way or I make one").

Chocano was four years old, when Chile declared war on Peru in the War of the Pacific. For the next two years, he lived through the war hearing the cannons and witnessing death and destruction. For three more years, Chocano was forced to live like a prisoner in his own home while the Peruvian territory was occupied by Chilean soldiers. After the soldiers left, Chocano's father moved the family to a resort on the Pacific Ocean, Chorrillos—a stylish town that had been scarred by the war. Chocano began school at the Colegio Aleman and attended secondary school at the Colegio de Lima. He received a Gold Medal for his scholastic achievements and was asked to teach mathematics. His mother hoped he would become an engineer but Chocano had other ideas. Chocano began writing before the age of ten. In 1891, he was offered the chance to edit a prestigious literary journal, *El Peru Illustrado*. He was 15 at the time and before his next birthday, he enrolled at the University of San Marcos in the faculty of letters.

### Sent to Jail for First Time

Chocano became a published writer in 1891 and wrote for several journals. He left the university in 1893 rebelling against "the oppressive atmosphere." That same year, he wrote provocative verse published in a liberal weekly journal, *La Tunda,* opposing dictator General Andres Avelino Caceres and using the pseudonym "Juvenal." News of this daring reached the dictator and Chocano prepared to leave the country. But before he and a friend could escape, they were captured by police and were ordered to be shot. One of the guards admired Chocano's poetry and asked whether he might send a telegram to Chocano's family. Chocano refused, thinking the gesture was a trick. As he and his friend were being led to the sea to be shot, the police chief arrived and sent them back to police headquarters. Chocano's father arrived the next day. He had received a telegram from the guard and used his influence to save Chocano's life. Chocano was imprisoned and spent the next two years in a dungeon of the Real Felipe in Callao.

One of the Peruvian leaders of the War of the Pacific, Nicolas de Pierola, returned to Peru in 1895 to oppose the Caceres dictatorship. A bloody battle ensued and Caceres disappeared. After this victory, Chocano was released from prison and appointed private secretary to the minister of the treasury and the junta. Within a short time, Chocano was supervising the state press and publishing the poetry he had written while in prison, *Iras santas* (*Holy Wrath*), a work full of fury against his oppressors. At the same time, Chocano published a less passionate work about Chorrillos and the countryside near Lima, *En la aldea* (*In the Village*). His third book, *Azahares* (*Orange Blossoms*) was published in 1896. Chocano also started a newspaper, *Siglo XX,* and wrote several plays. In the meantime, he had married Consuelo Bermudez and had begun writing poems of love. They had three sons: Eduardo Adolfo, José Alberto, and José Santos. The marriage ended after the third son was born in 1903.

After 1898, Chocano's poetry reflected the inspiration he received from his first trip into the interior of Peru. His entrepreneurial spirit had prompted the trip when he decided to investigate the possibility of establishing a coffee plantation in the vant Biolley of Chanchamayo. Chocano traveled by train through the Andes mountains and by horseback into the jungle. He had never before seen the mountains or experienced the extreme changes in weather. Chocano was moved by the sites, the silence, and the lush tropical plants of the jungle. His impressions were reflected in his book *Selva virgen* (*Virgin Forest*) and in other poems for several years. Two of Chocano's poems, *El Derrumbe* (*The Debacle*) and *La epopeya del Morro* (*The Epic of the Morro*) were especially successful and elevated his literary standing. After he wrote *La epopeya del Morro,* his poetry was published in journals throughout Latin America.

Before the Second Panamerican Conference was held in Mexico around the turn of the twentieth century, Peruvian President Eduerdo Lopez Romana appointed Chocano special commissioner, charging him with the mission of traveling through Central America to sway other countries votes on the issue of "compulsory arbitration." Thus began a lifetime travel. Everywhere he traveled, Chocano was greeted by admirers who had read his poetry. He became friends with the Guatemalan President Estrada Cabrera. After he had persuaded three governments to vote for "compulsory arbitration," he was named Peruvian consul-general of Central America. In 1903, he helped avert war between Guatemala and El Salvador by meeting with the El Salvador dictator, General Tomas Regalado, and arranging a summit between the two dignitaries. That same year Chocano was appointed chargé d'affaires in Central America. Throughout his diplomatic years, he continued to write his poetry. Chocano's first anthology, *Los cantos del Pacifico* (*Songs of the Pacific*) was published in Paris in 1904. Because of disputes with Ecuador over the Amazon boundaries, Chocano was sent to the king of Spain as secretary of a special mission for arbitration. He left for Spain in 1905 and stayed away from his homeland for almost 17 years. Chocano published his first book in Spain in 1906 entitled *Alma América,* dedicated to King Alfonso XIII. This book and a later book *Fiat Lux!* (*Let there be Light!*) were considered two of his greatest works.

### Worked for Pancho Villa in Mexico

Chocano married his second wife, Guatemalan-born Margot Batres Jauregui in 1912. They had two children, Alberto and Maria Angelica. In 1915, Chacono became known as the "Word of the Revolution" when he stayed in Mexico with **Francisco (Pancho) Villa** and edited *Sumario del programa de la revolution mexicana* (*Summary of the Program of the Mexican Revolution, 1915*). In 1919, he returned to Guatemala to serve the dictator, his friend Estrada Cabrera. When Cabrera was overthrown in 1920, Chocano was imprisoned and sentenced to death. His wife pleaded with dignitaries throughout the Spanish-speaking world. After the intervention of 12 countries and the king of Spain, Chocano was set free. He returned to Lima in 1921 and was acclaimed throughout Peru, receiving a special "Coronation" from the president.

At the age of 49, Chocano married his third wife, 21-year-old Margarita Aguilar Machado. Shortly thereafter he quarreled with another Peruvian writer, Edwin Elmore. The bitterness culminated in a fight in which Chocano fatally shot Elmore. Chocano was sentenced to three years in prison, but was pardoned halfway through his term due to his friends efforts. Chocano then moved to Santiago, Chile, where he and his wife became the parents of a son, Jorge Santos. Although they lived in poverty, Chocano continued to write prolifically and published *Primicias de oro de Indias* (*First Fruits from the Gold of the Indies*) in 1934.

Chocano's dreams of finding riches haunted him. He became involved in ventures to seek hidden treasures. On December 13, 1934, while riding a streetcar, Chocano was stabbed to death by Manuel Bruce Badilla, who thought Chocano was trying to take treasures that belonged to him. Badilla, assailant

was later declared insane. Many of Chocano's books were published after his death, a fitting reminder of his often uttered statement: "I always compose my verse after I have lived it."

### SELECTED PUBLISHED WORKS:

*Iras santas* (*Holy Wrath*), 1895.
*En la aldea* (*In the Village*), 1895.
*El canto del siglo* (*Song of the Century*), 1901.
*El fin de Satán y otros poemas* (*The End of Satan, and Other Poems*), 1901
*Poesías completas* (*Complete Poems*), 1902.
*Los cantos del Pacifico* (*Songs of the Pacific*), 1904.
*Alma América* (*Soul of America*), 1906.
*Fiat Lux!* (*Let There Be Light*), 1908.
*Puerto Rico Lírico* (*Lyric Puerto Rico*), c. 1914.
*Sumario del programa de la revolución mexicana* (*Summary of the Program of the Mexican Revolution*), 1915.
*Idearium tropical* (*Tropical Ideas*), 1922.
*Ayacucho y los Andes* (*Ayaucho and the Andes*), 1924.
*El libro de mi proceso* (*My Trial*), 1927–28.
*Primicias de oro de Indias* (*First Fruits from the Gold of the Indies*), 1934.
*Poemas del amor doliente* (*Poems of a Suffering Love*), 1937.
*El alma de Voltaire y otras prosas* (*The Soul of Voltaire and Other Prose*), 1940.
*Memorias. Las mil y una aventuras* (*Memoirs. The Thousand and One Adventures*), 1940.
*Oro de Indias* (*The Gold of the Indies*), four volumes, 1939–41.

### SOURCES:

Rodríguez-Peralta, Phyllis, *José Santos Chocano,* New York, Twayne, n.d.

—*Sketch by Phyllis Noah*

# Antonio Cisneros
## 1942-1989
**Peruvian poet and scholar**

Antonio Cisneros has garnered an international reputation for his poetry, which often challenges and questions current and past society and its values. Critics note that his poetry appears especially distinct

*Antonio Cisneros*

in light of the conservatism of most twentieth-century verse to appear in Peru. His major poetic collections include: *Commentarios reales* (1964), for which he won the Peruvian National Poetry Prize in 1965, and *Canto ceremonial contra un oso hormiguero* (1968), for which he received the Casa de las Americas prize. *The Spider Hangs Too Far From the Ground* (1970), an English translation that contains selections from both of his most celebrated collections, gained significant attention, while another collection—*At Night the Cats* (1985)—brought together 76 of Cisneros's poems from different collections into one bilingual edition; the presentation and selection of this volume drew praise from critics as well.

## Early Achievements

Born on December 27, 1942, in Lima, Peru, Cisneros took an early interest in literature, particularly in poetry. At the age of 19 Cisneros published his first book of verse. Entitled *Destierro* (1961), it attracted little critical attention. A year later he published *David* (1962), and though both of these works have gained some acclaim since that time, they produced little recognition for their author at the time of publication. The appearance of *Commentarios* in 1964 marked Cisneros's first critical and popular success. The collection impressed critics, for it featured a spare use of language that nonetheless succeeded in creating dramatic imagery. Critics also noted Cisneros's ironic sense of humor and will-

ingness to lampoon even the most sacrosanct of Peruvian institutions, historical heroes, and cultural qualities. While critics appreciated this boldness, they perceived that Cisneros's wit served not simply to degrade his nation but to hold it up to gentle, but insistent, scrutiny. The year after its publication, *Commentarios* won the Peruvian National Poetry Prize, establishing Cisneros as a permanent poetic voice in his nation.

Cisneros followed that success with *Canto ceremonial contra un oso hormiguero,* which incorporated many of Cisneros's reflections on his international travels. After teaching at the University of Huamanga in Ayacucho, Peru, for two years, Cisneros spent three years in the late 1960s teaching at the University of Southampton in England. As a scholar, Cisneros was able to bring his ideas about culture and history to a receptive and intellectually curious body of students. The political dynamism on college campuses in the 1960s created an environment suited to Cisneros's own ideas about the deep flaws in historical and present-day culture. After three years in England, Cisneros moved to Nice, France, where he took a position at the University of Nice until 1972.

The poet returned to Peru in 1972 a more cosmopolitan man as a reslut of his European travels, and his subsequent poetic works reflected those experiences. Despite his evocation of these exotic locations in his work, his main subject of discussion within his poetry remained the cultural past and present of his own country. Some observers speculated that his academic experiences abroad perhaps heightened his sense of Peru as a country with a troubled history and an uncertain future.

Cisneros's host countries did not escape his critical eye, however. As a Latin American interested in the history of his region, Cisneros could not help but comment on Europe's historical role as a champion of the colonialism —the practice of settling and "civilizing" distant lands—that was prevalent in the nineteenth century. By living in those European countries—with their own decidedly different historical perspectives on colonialism—Cisneros came to see those countries and Peru more clearly. His time abroad gave him a sharpened perspective on the world around him as well as a keener view of his own Peruvian culture.

After studying literature at Catholic University in Lima, Cisneros took a position at the National University of San Marcos in Lima and completed work toward his Ph.D. He then journeyed abroad again, travelling to the University of Budapest in Hungary, where he spent one year as an exchange professor. After his year in Hungary, Cisneros returned to Lima to teach at the National University at San Marcos, where he continued to work as a poet and scholar.

## Continued Scholarly and Artistic Pursuits

Cisneros's first major poetic collection after returning to Peru appeared in 1978. Titled *El libro de Dios y los húngaros,* the selections again drew on his experiences in Europe. Other themes of the collection included censure of Western culture and criticism of modernism as a force that isolates humans from nature and deprives people from experiencing the full range of sensory possibilities in the world.

In 1985 Cisneros published *At Night the Cats,* an anthology of his work that combined selections for his previous titles. The bilingual text attracted renewed attention to Cisneros's work from the English-speaking world. Gloria Waldman called the book "an excellent introduction . . . for those not previously familiar" with Cisneros's poetry. Acknowledged by many critics as a representative sampling of the poet's earlier and later work, *At Night the Cats* conveyed a true picture of Cisneros' talent, according to Jack Schmitt of the *Los Angeles Times Book Review.* Schmitt praised the author's "intensely poetic imagination; his stunning images and metaphors, often surreal; his incisive irony and droll humor . . . ; his personal, confessional tone; his decorum and reserve, so typical of Peruvians, and also his passion and tenderness." In addition to his poetic anthologies, Cisneros contributed to several anthologies and wrote many scholarly essays until his death in 1989.

## SELECTED PUBLISHED WORKS:

*Destierro,* 1961.
*David,* El Timonel, 1962.
*Commentarios reales,* Ediciones de la Rama Florida and Ediciones de la Biblioteca Universitaria, 1964.
*Canto ceremonial contra un oso hormiguero,* Casa de las Americas, 1968.
*The Spider Hangs Too Far From the Ground,* Cape Goliard, 1970.
*Agua que no has de beber,* CMB Ediciones, 1971.
*Como higuera en un campo de golf,* Instituto Nacional de Cultura, 1972.
*El libro de Dios y los húngaros,* Libra–1, 1978.
*Cuatro poetas: Victor García Robles, Antonio Cisneros, Pedro Shimose, Armando Tejada Gómez,* Casa de las Americas, 1979.
*At Night the Cats,* Red Dust, 1985.
*Monologo de la casta Susana y otros poemas,* Instituto Nacional de Cultura, 1986.

## SOURCES: BOOKS

*Hispanic Writers,* edited by Bryan Ryan, Detroit, Gale, 1991.

## Periodicals

*Hispania,* September, 1987.
*Los Angeles Times Book Review,* October 27, 1985.
*Times Literary Supplement,* August 21, 1970.

    —*Sketch by James McCarthy*

# Henry Cisneros
## 1947-
### Mexican American politician

Henry Cisneros is one of the brightest political stars to emerge from the ranks of Mexican Americans, serving four terms as the first Hispanic mayor of a major United States city, his hometown of San Antonio, Texas. With his personal magnetism, intellectual ability, and political acumen, he was once called a "natural resource" by former Secretary of Health, Education and Welfare Elliot Richardson. From his simple roots in a middle-class neighborhood to his appointment as Secretary of Housing and Urban Development (HUD) under U.S. President Bill Clinton, Cisneros is best known for his attempts to help the urban poor through fair housing policy and inner-city revitalization. Although his professional accomplishments have sometimes been overshadowed by a turbulent personal life, Cisneros is credited with changing the political complexion of the nation's tenth-largest city at a time when virtually every position of power was occupied by an Anglo American.

Descended on his father's side from early Spanish settlers in the American Southwest, Henry Gabriel Cisneros was born June 11, 1947, in a San Antonio neighborhood that bordered the city's west side barrio. His father, George Cisneros, was a civilian administrator for the U.S. Army. His mother, Elvira Munguia Cisneros, was the daughter of Romulo Munguia, a Mexican printer, journalist, and intellectual who fled his native country in 1926 during the oppressive regime of Mexican dictator **Porfirio Diaz**. With his two sisters and two brothers, Cisneros was the product of a supportive extended family, motivated primarily by his mother, who envisioned a special destiny for each of her children.

Cisneros received a Catholic education, first at the Church of the Little Flower, where he skipped the third grade, and then at Central Catholic High School. He enrolled at Texas A & M University in 1964, and switched his major from aeronautical engineering to city management in his sophomore year. In 1967 Cisneros was selected to attend a student conference on U.S. Affairs at West Point, where he first learned that U.S. cities were in serious trouble. Relating what he heard to the problems in his hometown, the event was a personal and professional turning point for him. Graduating from A & M with a bachelor of arts degree in English in 1968, he went on to earn a master's in urban and regional planning. That summer, he was hired as an analyst by the San Antonio branch of President Lyndon B. Johnson's Model Cities program for urban revitalization. In 1970, one year after marrying his high school sweetheart, Mary Alice Perez, Cisneros moved to Washington, D.C. There he landed a full-time job as an administrative assistant to the executive vice president of the National League of Cities. He became a White House fellow in 1971, the year his first daughter, Theresa Angelica, was born.

From 1972 to 1974, the Cisneroses lived in Boston with the help of a $10,000 Ford Foundation grant, and Cisneros earned a master's degree in public administration from Harvard University. He worked as a teaching assistant at the Massachusetts Institute of Technology, and received a doctorate from George Washington University. Turning down a full time teaching position at MIT, Cisneros returned to the San Antonio political scene to assume a faculty position in the division of environmental studies at the University of Texas at San Antonio.

### Began Political Career

When Cisneros arrived back home, he found that the stagnant political scene in San Antonio was experiencing strong undercurrents of ethnic discontent. For two decades, the Anglo-dominated Good Government League (GGL) had run the city, and the Mexican American community believed that they had been neglected for too long by their leaders. Displaying an early talent for working within the system, Cisneros ran as a candidate of the GGL. After a whirlwind campaign, Cisneros, at age 27, was elected the youngest city councilman in the city's history in 1975, the same year his second daughter, Mercedes Christina, was born. Reelected twice, Cisneros quickly assumed the hands-on leadership that he had promised in his campaigns. In order to learn all he could about life in the city, Cisneros collected garbage with the garbage collectors, rode in police patrol cars, went to fires on fire trucks, and interviewed prisoners in jail.

During this time Cisneros strategically aligned himself with Communities Organized for Public Service (COPS), a powerful grass-roots Hispanic advocacy group founded in 1973. He later found himself at odds with this group over local water supply issues when he tried to appease both environmentalists and developers. This middle-of-the-road

stance would cause problems throughout his career. In *Señor Alcalde* ("Mr. Mayor"), John Gillies wrote: "He tried to avoid a political label, such as Democrat or Republican, because he wanted to consider the needs of all of San Antonio's groupings. . . . He formed a bridge between conservatives and liberals, which was often a no-win situation. Conservatives often criticized him for supporting government programs, and liberals accused him of being too 'big business'-oriented."

### First Hispanic Mayor

By 1980, Cisneros was ready to make his move on City Hall, announcing himself as an independent candidate for mayor in 1981. An extremely persuasive and enthusiastic speaker, his infectious energy and hopeful visions of the future united the rich old guard of San Antonio and the increasingly vocal Mexican American middle class. His campaign attracted the national media, who pegged the tall, handsome, and impeccably groomed Cisneros as the symbol of a growing Hispanic population. On April 4, 1981, Cisneros became the first Hispanic mayor of a major U.S. city—and the first Mexican American to be elected mayor of San Antonio since 1842—with 62 percent of the vote. He went on to be reelected to three more terms, including winning an unprecedented 93 percent of the vote in the 1983 election.

Cisneros's eight years as mayor ushered in a new era in local politics, one in which he shrewdly combined economic development efforts with ethnic sensibilities. His pro-development stance made him a favorite of business leaders, but he never forgot his roots. Throughout his term, he and his family lived in the same small west side house that once belonged to his grandfather. His philosophy of "trickle down economics" often alienated him from Hispanic activists who advocated more direct solutions. His diplomatic skills shone brightest, however, when getting diverse groups to work together on economic development projects. While Cisneros was mayor, $200 million was spent on the city's Hispanic west side for streets, gutters, libraries, and parks. He was the single most important force behind the city's Alamodome, a massive downtown sports and convention arena that ignited controversy among city leaders because of its cost to taxpayers. One of the political highlights of his mayoral term occurred in 1984, when he was interviewed by Democratic presidential nominee Walter Mondale as a possible vice presidential running mate. Mondale, however, chose Congresswoman Geraldine Ferraro.

In 1987, at what most observers agree was the peak of his political career, Cisneros chose to leave public life. Several factors contributed to Cisneros's decision. His son, John Paul Anthony, was born in 1987 with asplenia syndrome, a birth defect in which there is no spleen and a heart with two right atria. In addition, his daughters were rapidly approaching college age. As one of the lowest paid mayors in the country, Cisneros had supplemented his income by teaching and lecturing, but the prospects of huge medical bills and college tuition were daunting. After 15 years of public service, Cisneros quit politics to make money and spend more time with an ailing son whose doctors had given no more than six years to live and whose life would be filled with major surgeries. When John Paul reached his sixth birthday in 1993, Cisneros told Sophfronia Scott Gregory in *Time* of his son's ongoing fight for life, "Nothing in my life has prepared me for this."

Probably the biggest single factor behind his stunning announcement to leave politics, however, was his disclosure of a two-year affair with former campaign aide Linda Medlar. Political observers decreed that it would destroy Cisneros's image as a Catholic family man and signal the end of his career. Rather than subject his marriage and family to continued stress and scrutiny, Cisneros chose to leave public life and reconcile with his wife. In 1989, he founded Cisneros Asset Management Company, a national fixed-income asset management firm for tax-exempt institutions. He was still a major political player, serving as a board member of the Rockefeller Foundation, trustee of The American Assembly, chair of the National Civic League, and deputy chair of the Federal Reserve Bank of Dallas. And in spite of the scandal that forced him out of public office, Cisneros remained popular, with occasional rumors of a bid for either the governor's office or state senator.

### Appointed Secretary of HUD

On December 17, 1992—his extramarital affair long over and his once-shaky marriage back on track—Cisneros was indeed back in the political game when President-elect Bill Clinton named him secretary of Housing and Urban Development. Cisneros then sold his interests in his management company, Cisneros Benefit Group Inc., U.S. Long Distance, and Cisneros Metro Service.

Cisneros took charge of HUD in January 1993, filled with optimism and ambitious plans to do everything possible to reform the problem-plagued $28 billion department. By May, he told Thomas G. Donlan of *Barron's,* "As exciting as the opportunity is to work at HUD, there are days when I wonder whether the President really did me the honor that it is all cooked up to be." Compounding the problem was an unprecedented number of homeless in the cities, a situation that Cisneros pledged to make his number one priority. His efforts, however, were often thwarted by a slow-moving bureaucracy. He described his frustration to Jill Smolowe in *Time,* "I can't believe how gridlocked the system is . . . how

irrelevant it is to things that are happening out in the country." He renewed his attack on public-housing segregation and mortgage discrimination. "Fair housing," he told Guy Gugliotta of the *Washington Post,* "is so vital that we cannot accomplish any of the other goals without it." He even dismissed members of a local public-housing authority for allowing African American tenants to be harassed out of a Texas public-housing project. He unveiled a plan for HUD to provide $70 million in rental vouchers to help people in housing projects move into surrounding middle class and affluent suburbs, a controversial plan that brought opposition from critics and tenants alike. Author James Bovard, writing in *American Spectator,* stated: "Fair housing programs have moved far from their original goal of reconciling disparities between blacks and whites. They now amount to a project to dictate where welfare recipients live in every county, city, and cranny across the nation."

Cisneros was at the helm of HUD for just a year and a half when Linda Medlar resurfaced in July 1994 with a breach of contract lawsuit against Cisneros. She claimed that he violated a promise to financially support her until her daughter's graduation from college. Cisneros had, in fact, made payments totaling $213,000 over the four years following the end of their affair, discontinuing them when he could no longer afford them on his cabinet salary of $148,400. Medlar also produced 40 hours of taped phone conversations suggesting that Cisneros may have misrepresented the amount of payments to the Federal Bureau of Investigation during the confirmation process for his nomination to the cabinet. In March of 1995, Attorney General Janet Reno recommended a special prosecutor be appointed to investigate Cisneros. After offering to submit his resignation to President Clinton—who rejected it with a public statement that described Cisneros as "a good man and an effective public servant"—Cisneros decided to stay in his position, adding in a statement in the *San Antonio Express-News,* "I regret any mistakes that I have made but affirm once again that I have at no point violated the public's trust."

Described as high-strung, driven, and often impatient, Cisneros has maintained a rigorous jogging regimen for years, shuns red meat, coffee, and alcohol, and takes seven vitamins a day. In July 1994 his son underwent a successful operation to correct his congenital heart defect. Dedicated to saving HUD, he presented a plan in 1995 to trim the department's budget by $13 billion over five years. He told the *San Antonio Express-News:* "There are efforts under way to eliminate important national efforts which provide shelter and assistance to millions of low-income Americans. I intend to stay and fight for our nation's commitment to people who need help and to reform HUD." He continued, "This may be the last opportunity I have to be in public life . . . I just want to do everything I can to make the biggest difference I can."

Of his uncertain political future, Lynnell Burkett of the *San Antonio Express-News* noted that "something irreplaceable has been lost. Lost is the integration of character and competence in an energetic, charismatic person who desires public service. Whatever Cisneros is in the future, it is less than he might have been." Cisneros's past contributions to urban renewal and revitalization, his efforts to help the poor and disenfranchised, and his commitment to improving cities are all a matter of unchangeable record. In his 1993 book, *Interwoven Destinies*, Cisneros wrote: "The strength of the nation's economy, the contact points for international economics, the health of our democracy, and the vitality of our humanistic endeavors—all are dependent on whether America's cities work."

## SELECTED PUBLISHED WORKS:

*The Entrepreneurial City*, New York, Ballinger, 1986.
*Interwoven Destinies*, New York, W.W. Norton & Company, 1993.

## SOURCES:

### Books

Diehl, Kemper, and Jan Jarboe, *Cisneros Portrait of a New American*, San Antonio, Corona Publishing Company, 1985.
Gillies, John, *Señor Alcalde: A Biography of Henry Cisneros*, Minneapolis, Dillon Press, Inc., 1988.
Roberts, Naurice, *Henry Cisneros: Mexican-American Mayor*, Chicago, Children's Press, 1986.

### Periodicals

*American City & County*, April, 1993, p. 14.
*American Spectator*, September, 1994, pp. 26–32.
*Barron's*, May 24, 1993, p. 10; September 12, 1994, p. 30.
*Christian Century*, June 1–8, 1994, p. 569.
*Mother Jones*, March/April, 1993, pp. 11–12.
*National Review*, March 7, 1994, pp. 57–59.
*New Republic*, March 14, 1994, pp. 12–16.
*New York Times*, March 15, 1995.
*People*, May 9, 1994, p. 98.
*San Antonio Express-News*, November 29, 1994; January 6, 1995, p. 5B; February 24 , 1995, p. 19A; March 1, 1995, p. 11A; March 14, 1995, p. 6A; March 15, 1995, p. 3A; March 19, 1995, p. 1A; March 21, 1995, p. 1A, p. 4B; March 22, 1995, p. 14A; March 23, 1995, p. 2A; March 26, 1995, p. 2L; April 3, 1995, p. 2A.
*Time*, June 21, 1993, p. 17; December 6, 1993, p. 28–31.
*U.S. News & World Report*, July 5, 1993, pp. 40–41; February 21, 1994, pp. 30–31; July 18, 1994, pp. 28–29. *Washington Monthly*, July/August, 1994, p. 6.
*Washington Post*, November 4, 1993.

—*Sketch by Julie Catalano*

# Sandra Cisneros
## 1954-
### Mexican American poet, novelist, and short story writer

Sandra Cisneros is a new voice in mainstream American literature. In her poetry and fiction, Cisneros presents vivid and compelling vignettes of the lives and loves of Chicanos and Latinos from a distinctly feminine perspective. In a review of her 1991 collection of short fiction, *Woman Hollering Creek and Other Stories*, *Newsweek*'s Peter S. Prescott wrote that "her feminist, Mexican American voice is not only playful and vigorous, it's original—we haven't heard anything like it before. . . . Noisily, wittily, always compassionately, Cisneros surveys woman's condition—a condition that is both precisely Latina and general to women everywhere." A commentator for *Washington Post Book World* deemed Cisneros "a writer of power and eloquence and great lyrical beauty," while a *Mirabella* reviewer described her as "the foremost Mexican American woman writer."

The first Chicana to receive a major publishing contract, Cisneros is one of the leading writers in the field of Latino literature. The author, who sees herself as something of a pioneer, asserted to Jim Sagel of *Publishers Weekly*: "I'm trying to write the stories that haven't been written. I feel like a cartographer. I'm determined to fill a literary void." In an interview for *Authors and Artists for Young Adults* (*AAYA*) Cisneros further explained that in *Woman Hollering Creek and Other Stories* she attempted "to populate [the] book with as many different kinds of Latinos as possible so that mainstream America could see how diverse we are."

Cisneros was born in Chicago, Illinois, in 1954 to a Mexican father and a Chicana mother. The only daughter of seven children, Cisneros grew up in poverty. During her childhood she developed a fear of mice—an anxiety that was not "a female thing, but a class thing," she told Sheila Benson of the *Los Angeles Times*. "To me mice are all my poverty, the whole neighborhood I grew up in, embodied in a little skittering creature that might come to get me at any moment." Many of her early years were spent moving from place to place, with regular trips to Mexico City, Mexico, so her paternal grandmother could see her favorite son.

The frequent relocations were unsettling, she recalled in *Publishers Weekly*. "The moving back and forth, the new school, were very upsetting to me as a child. They caused me to be very introverted and shy. I do not remember making friends easily. . . . Because we moved so much and always in neighborhoods that appeared like France after World War II—empty lots and burned out buildings—I retreated inside myself." Being the only girl in her family also contributed to her shyness. Cisneros stated in her interview: "I spent a lot of time by myself by just the fact that I was the only daughter, and my brothers—once they became socialized—pretty much hung out with their own gender. They all kind of teamed up and excluded me from their games." Cisneros acknowledges, however, that one positive aspect of her shyness was that she became an astute observer of the people and things around her, a trait that would stand her in good stead in her later literary career.

Cisneros attended Catholic schools in Chicago. In *Authors and Artists for Young Adults* (AAYA) she judged her basic education "rather shabby." She added, "If I had lived up to my teachers' expectations, I'd still be working in a factory, because my report card was pretty lousy. That's because I wasn't very much interested, or I was too terrified to venture or volunteer." Not wanting to be ridiculed, she was afraid to display her creative talents because she felt the nuns dismissed the importance of the minority experience. She wrote secretly at home. Fortunately, her parents stressed education. Her mother was self-taught and saw to it that all her children had library cards; her father wanted his offspring to study hard. As Cisneros recalled in a column for *Glamour*, "My father's hands are thick and yellow, stubbed by a history of hammer and nails and twine and coils and springs. 'Use this' my father said, tapping his head, 'not this' showing us those hands."

## Finds Creative Voice

It was in high school that Cisneros first began to express her creativity publicly. At first, because of her skill in oral interpretation, she was called on to read poetry from class texts, and then in her sophomore year, "I had a teacher who was . . . a would-be writer," she told *AAYA*. "I started writing for her. I became more public through that class and she encouraged me to work on a literary magazine . . . which I did—and I became the editor eventually." After high school, Cisneros attended Loyola University. Her father supported her efforts, believing that college would be a good place for his daughter to find a husband. As Cisneros commented in *Glamour*, "In retrospect, I'm lucky my father believed daughters were meant for husbands. It meant it didn't matter if I majored in something silly like English. After all, I'd find a nice professional eventually, right?"

What Cisneros found was a profession: writing. In the late 1970s, one of her undergraduate teachers helped her enroll in the poetry section of the Iowa Writers' Workshop, a program which led to a master's degree. However, Cisneros found herself alienated from her surroundings and her classmates. As she explained in *AAYA*, "It didn't take me long to learn—after a few days being there—that nobody cared to hear what I had to say and no one listened to me even when I did speak. I became very frightened and terrified that first year." When these feelings finally surfaced, they lead Cisneros to a great insight.

During a seminar discussion of archetypal memories in Gaston Bachelard's "Poetics of Space,", her classmates spoke about the house of the imagination, using their childhood homes as examples. They described houses with attics, stairways, and cellars—dwellings that were a far cry from the miserable bungalow of Cisneros's childhood. Focusing on her early poverty made her doubt herself. Who was Sandra Cisneros compared to these children of privilege from the finest schools in the country? "They had been bred as fine hothouse flowers. I was a yellow weed among the city's cracks," she recalled in *Publishers Weekly*. Describing the cultural epiphany that changed her, she added: "It was not until this moment when I separated myself, when I considered myself truly distinct that my writing acquired a voice. I knew I was a Mexican woman, but I didn't think it had anything to do with why I felt so much imbalance in my life, whereas it had everything to do with it! My race, my gender, my class! That's when I decided I would write about something my classmates couldn't write about."

## Revelation Led to *The House on Mango Street*

This revelation enabled Cisneros to write her first book, *The House on Mango Street*, in which she described her house of imagination. "It's small and red with tight steps in front and windows so small you'd think they were holding their breath. Bricks are crumbling in places, and the front door is so swollen you have to push hard to get in. There is no front yard, only four little elms the city planted by the curb.

Out back is a small garage for the car we don't own yet." Published in 1984, *Mango Street* features a series of interlocking vignettes told by Esperanza Cordero, a young Chicana growing up in a Chicago barrio. Through Esperanza's eyes the reader obtains a glimpse of the lives of the people around her. She wants a better life for herself and, by end of the book, Esperanza has gained a measure of the power and determination to achieve it. "I have decided not to grow tame like the others who lay their necks on the threshold waiting for the ball and chain." However, Esperanza is reminded by one of the characters that leaving the barrio does not mean leaving one's identity: "When you leave you must remember to come back for the others. A circle, understand? You will always be Esperanza. You will always be Mango Street. You can't erase what you know. You can't forget who you are."

Students from junior high school through graduate school have used the book in classes ranging from Chicano studies to psychology. Stanford University has adopted the work as part of its new curriculum. Cisneros came to the attention of literary agent Susan Bergholz, who began a search for the author. Some four years elapsed before the two would actually connect. Cisneros received her master's degree from Iowa in 1978 and worked at the Latino Youth Alternative High School—an alternative school for returning drop-outs—from 1978 until 1981. She then took a job as a college recruiter/counselor for the now defunct Educational Opportunity Program at Loyola University—a program that looked to recruit disadvantaged students. She moved from Chicago to Cape Cod in 1982 and, upon receiving her first National Endowment of the Arts (NEA) fellowship that same year, she travelled to Europe. When she returned to the United States a year later, she took employment as an arts administrator in San Antonio, Texas. In the spring of 1986 she received a Dobie-Paisano fellowship. Before leaving Texas, she she finished *My Wicked, Wicked Ways*, a book of poetry, which was published in 1987. The verses show an independent woman, a wife and mother to none, who says, "I've learned two things./ To let go/ clean as a kite string./ And to never wash a man's clothes./ These are my rules." She adds, "What does a woman owe a man/ and isn't freedom what you believe in?/ Even the freedom to say no?"

For Cisneros herself, the late 1980s represented the lowest period of her life because she was unemployable in Austin and was reduced to passing out fliers in supermarkets and laundromats in a vain attempt to organize a private writing workshop. She described this period in her life to *Publishers Weekly:* "I found myself becoming suicidal. . . . I was drowning, beyond help. . . . It was frightening because it was such a calm depression." Finally, she left Texas to accept a guest lectureship at California State Univer-

sity in Chico—her first position teaching at the university level. "Except for visits to classes, or a guest stint a week or so here and there, I'd never dared apply for a university position," Cisneros explained to the editors of *Dictionary of Hispanic Biography*. "To apply at a university one had to believe one had something to share. I had no such confidence. I believe my first year of teaching at Chico [contributed to her depression] precisely because I felt, as a working class person, I had no right to be there."

She received a second NEA fellowship in fiction, funding which revitalized Cisneros both financially and spiritually. She was then awarded a semester teaching at the University of California, Berkeley and Irvine, in addition to the University of Michigan and University of New Mexico. She finally contacted Bergholz, whose Manhattan phone number she had carried in her pocket for months—a call that led to a contract with Random House and the publication of *Woman Hollering Creek*. Cisneros remarked to the editors of *Dictionary of Hispanic Biography* that "Now I make my living from my writing and teach only when I want to."

### Signed with Random House

With Random House behind her, Cisneros was thrust into the national limelight, and *Woman Hollering Creek* received wide distribution. A series of short stories about the lives and loves of Chicanas on both sides of the Texas-Mexican boarder, the tales feature strong womencharacters. For her work Cisneros received glowing reviews from various critics, being lauded as a new star on the literary horizon. A commentator for *Los Angeles Times* called the collection "stunning," while a reviewer for the *New York Times Book Review* deemed the work's protagonists "as unforgettable as a first kiss." A *Washington Post Book World* critic said the stories were "a kind of choral work in which the harmonic voices emphasize the commonality of experience."

Although some Latinos who find success feel uncomfortable becoming a "representative" of their ethnic group, Cisneros does not mind the label. She told *AAYA:* "I don't feel any sense of self-consciousness about my role as a spokesperson in the writing, because I've taken that responsibility on from the very beginning. That isn't something I'm nervous about or begrudging about. Actually, the fact that I *can* write about the things I write about. . . . I feel very honored to be able to give them a form in my writings and to be able to have this material to write about is a blessing." In her next book, Cisneros plans to explore father-daughter relationships and aspects of growing up in the middle between Mexican and Chicano cultures.

**SELECTED PUBLISHED WORKS:**

*The House on Mango Street,* Arte Público Press, 1984.
*My Wicked, Wicked Ways,* Third Woman Press, 1987.
*Woman Hollering Creek and Other Stories,* Random House, 1991.

**SOURCES:**

**Books**

*Authors and Artists for Young Adults,* Volume 9, Detroit, Gale Research, 1992.

**Periodicals**

*Glamour,* November 1990, pp. 256–57.
*Los Angeles Times,* May 7, 1991, p. F1.
*Los Angeles Times Book Review,* April 28, 1991, p. 3.
*Mirabella,* April, 1991, p. 46.
*Newsweek,* June 3, 1991, p. 60.
*New York Times Book Review,* May 26, 1991, p. 6.
*Publishers Wely,* March 29, 1991, pp. 74–5.
*Washington Post Book World,* June 9, 1991, p. 3.

—*Sketch by Andrés Chávez*

*Roberto Clemente*

# Roberto Clemente
## 1934-1972
**Puerto Rican professional baseball player**

Roberto Clemente was widely recognized as one of the most talented baseball players of his generation and perhaps the best Latin American player ever. In his 18 seasons with the Pittsburgh Pirates, he amassed more than 3,000 hits while recording a lifetime batting average of .317—the highest among all active players. An excellent fielder as well as a skilled batter, Clemente was awarded 12 Golden Glove awards for his outfield play and was named to the league's All-Star team a dozen times. In 1966, he received the National League's Most Valuable Player award. Perhaps his finest hour came in the 1971 World Series when, with a .414 average at bat and several remarkable plays in the field, he led the Pirates' victory over the heavily favored Baltimore Orioles. Considered by some veteran managers to be

the greatest all-around player of his era, Clemente was also noted for his outspoken expressions of Latin pride and his many charitable contributions. In December 1972, while spearheading Puerto Rico's efforts to aid earthquake victims in Managua, Nicaragua, Clemente died in a plane crash. Shortly after his death, a special election was held to waive the usual five-year waiting requirement and to immediately induct him into the Baseball Hall of Fame.

Born in Carolina, a suburb of San Juan, Puerto Rico, in 1934, Roberto Walker Clemente was the youngest child in a large, hard—working family. While his father was employed as a foreman on a great sugar-cane plantation, his mother ran a grocery and meat market for the workers. "My mother and father, they worked like racehorses for me," Clemente told *Sports Illustrated*'s Myron Cope. While growing up in Puerto Rico, Clemente played softball—from which he developed his patented underhand throw—rather than baseball. It was not until he was 17 that his softball coach, Roberto Marin, convinced Clemente that he had the potential to earn a lot of money playing baseball in the United States.

### Outstanding Even in Minors

A standout from the beginning, Clemente was originally signed in Puerto Rico by the Brooklyn Dodgers in 1954 for a $10,000 bonus. According to league rules at the time, any first-year player receiving more than $4,000 was required to spend at least one full season in the minors when, the following November, he would be eligible to be drafted by another club. While the Dodgers could have protected Clemente by placing him in their own club, they chose to try to hide him on their Montreal farm team, playing him sparingly in hopes that no other club would try to sign him. Despite being benched after strong performances, Clemente's talent showed through in batting and fielding practice—enough for Pirate scout Clyde Sukeforth to take Clemente from the Dodgers for the bargain price of $4,000.

While Clemente's numbers during his rookie season—a .255 batting average and only five home runs—were modest, he showed evidence of the talent that would one day land him in the Hall of Fame. After a game in which Clemente performed especially well, he was invited to appear on a post-game interview. When the announcer told Clemente that he reminded him of the great Willie Mays, Clemente, according to a *Sports Illustrated* eulogy, paused and boldly responded, "Nonetheless, I play like Roberto Clemente." Such a statement not only represented Clemente's confidence in his abilities, but it also suggested that his playing style was, in fact, truly unique. Clemente's uncanny ability to hit pitches several inches outside the strike zone, for instance, frustrated pitchers like no other batter in the league. As former Giants' pitcher Juan Marichal once stated in *Time,* "He can hit any pitch. I don't mean only strikes. He can hit a ball off his ankles or off his ear." When asked if he knew of any effective way to pitch to such a batter, former Dodger great Sandy Koufax said in the same article, "Sure, roll the ball."

Clemente's fielding skills were just as distinctive. Early in his career he acquired a reputation for having the strongest, most accurate throwing arm of any outfielder in the league. While he attributed the accuracy to his training as a high school javelin thrower, he credited the strength to his mother—who, as Clemente told *Time,* "could throw a ball from second base to home with something on it." While noted for his ability to throw runners out at home plate from as far as 420 feet, Clemente also dazzled fans with his acrobatic catches. Some of Clemente's patented home run-saving, wall-crashing grabs continue to rank among the greatest catches of all time.

For all of Clemente's skills, though, he received at least as much media attention for his innumerable illnesses and injuries. Nicknamed "Mr. Aches and Pains," Clemente endured slipped discs, bone chips, blood clots, and malaria, while also complaining of headaches, cramps, insomnia, and a nervous stomach. Although these various conditions often kept Clemente out of the lineup, many believed that the worse he said he felt, the better he played. After once scoring all the way from first on a single to beat the Dodgers, Clemente, according to a *Sports Illustrated* profile by C. R. Ways, said "I had a sore foot. I wanted to rest

it." His critics often labeled him a hypochondriac, but when questioned about the physical existence of his ailments, Clemente often responded, "If a Latin player is sick, they say it is all in his head."

Clemente, who comprehended practically no English when he entered the league in 1954, was often misunderstood by the American press. He often complained that his status as a Latin player prevented him from receiving the recognition granted to a Willie Mays or a Hank Aaron. Calling attention to his own three batting titles, Clemente repeatedly declared, "For me, I am the best ballplayer in the world," provoking indignation among players and the media. But, as Cope explained, viewing Clemente as a braggart was a misunderstanding; for in Spanish, the expression "For me, I am best," is meant only as a common statement of self-respect.

After several brilliant seasons, in which Clemente was among the league leaders in hitting and won Golden Glove Awards for his fielding, he was finally named the National League's Most Valuable player—after hitting .317, blasting 29 homers, and driving in 119 runs during the 1966 season. It was Clemente's performance in the 1971 World Series, however, that stands as perhaps his crowning achievement. After telling reporters at the outset of the Series, "Nobody does anything better in baseball than me," Clemente went out and proved it, hitting a remarkable .414 and controlling the game with a sparkling fielding display. Finally silencing his critics with his performance, Clemente viewed the Series' Most Valuable Player Award as a victory for all Latin players. "Now they [the writers] know they can't be sarcastic about Latins," he stated after the Series, according to *Newsweek.*

## Committed to Philanthropy

Clemente's commitment to Latin America, though, extended far beyond his baseball career. In addition to donating the money he received from making endorsements in Spanish countries to charities, Clemente dreamed of opening, upon his retirement, a Puerto Rico sports camp open only to the very poor, who could attend free of charge. It was his goal that "every single child from poverty [could] learn to play sports and someday maybe make some success as I did," according to Roger Kahn's *Sports Illustrated* profile. To that end, Clemente—shortly after recording his 3,000th hit in his last game—took an amateur Puerto Rican baseball team to play a series of games in Nicaragua. While travelling in the country, he met a hospitalized child without legs and asked him why he had no artificial limbs. When the boy said that he could not afford the $800 legs, Clemente responded, "When I go back to Puerto Rico I will raise the money," according to Kahn.

Five weeks later, after Managua was ravaged by an earthquake, Clemente organized a relief campaign, appearing on television and radio to ask for money, food, and medical supplies. While helping to load supplies—despite his aching back—Clemente learned that Nicaraguan soldiers were stealing supplies and selling them to earthquake victims. Aware of his fame throughout Latin America, he quickly boarded a plane: "If I go to Nicaragua, the stealing will stop," he said, according to Kahn. "They would not dare steal from Roberto Clemente." Shortly after takeoff from San Juan on December 31, 1972, the cargo plane, loaded with some 26 tons of food and $150,000 in relief money, developed engine problems and crashed into heavy seas about one mile off the coast. Clemente, three crew members, and another passenger were killed.

While his life ended at 38, Clemente left a rich legacy: at a cost of more than $13 million, the utopian sports camp he had envisioned was constructed and named the Roberto Clemente Sports City Complex in his honor. Clemente's wife, Vera, has routinely spent six days week at the 600-acre facility, where one of Clemente's sons, Roberto, serves as a director. After holding a special election to induct Clemente into the Hall of Fame, baseball bestowed him another honor: creating the Roberto Clemente Award, which is given annually to the major league player who makes the greatest contribution to community service. Clemente, as *Newsweek*'s Peter Bonventre observed, "died as he would have wished to—still trying to give too much."

## SOURCES:

### Books

Gerber, Irving, *Roberto Clemente: The Pride of Puerto Rico*, Brooklyn, Book-Lab, 1978.
Musick, Phil, *Who Was Roberto?: A Biography of Roberto Clemente*, Garden City, New York, Doubleday, 1974.

### Periodicals

*Life*, May 24, 1968, pp. 70–71.
*Los Angeles Times*, December 25, 1992.
*Newsweek*, January 15, 1973, p. 75.
*New York Times Magazine*, April 9, 1972, pp. 38–40.
*Sporting News*, December 28, 1992.
*Sports Illustrated*, March 7, 1966, pp. 30–40; January 15, 1973, p. 11August 30, 1976, pp. 32–36, 72.
*Time*, May 26, 1967, p. 56; January 15, 1973, pp. 42–43.

—*Sketch by Jason Gallman*

# Judith Ortiz Cofer
## 1952-
### Puerto Rican educator, poet, and novelist

We lived in Puerto Rico until my brother was born in 1954," wrote poet, essayist, and fiction writer Judith Ortiz Cofer. "Soon after, because of economic pressures on our growing family, my father joined the United States Navy. He was assigned to duty on a ship in Brooklyn Yard ... that was to be his home base in the States until his retirement more than twenty years later." In these brief sentences from an essay published in *Georgia Review* and included as part of her *Silent Dancing: A Partial Remembrance of a Puerto Rican Childhood*, the reader is introduced to the dual reality that makes up Cofer's literary universe. Her work focuses on the effect on Puerto Rican Americans of living in a world split between the island culture of their homeland and the teeming tenement life of the United States.

Although Cofer was born on February 24, 1952, in Hormigueros, Puerto Rico, the daughter of J. M. and Fanny Morot Cofer, she was brought to the United States when quite young. The family's official residence was in Paterson, New Jersey, but whenever her father's Navy job took him to sea, Cofer and her mother and brother stayed in Puerto Rico with her maternal family. As a child Cofer spoke only Spanish at first, and later was introduced to the English language, a process she found difficult, but rewarding.

### Begins Career as English Teacher

She eventually earned a bachelor of arts degree in English from Augusta College in 1974 and a master of arts in English from Florida Atlantic University in 1977. Since receiving her advanced degree, Cofer has served as an English instructor at several institutions, including the University of Miami, the University of Georgia, and the Georgia Center for Continuing Education. Since 1992, she has worked as an associate professor of English and Creative Writing at the University of Georgia. In addition, Cofer has held visiting writer positions at such institutions as the University of Michigan, the Arizona University System, and the University of Minnesota (Duluth), to name a few. "It was a challenge, not only to learn English," she notes in *Contemporary Authors*, "but to master it enough to teach it and—the ultimate goal—to write poetry in it."

Cofer's first books of poetry were three chapbooks—*Latin Women Pray, The Native Dancer*, and published *Among the Ancestors*—published in the early 1980s. Three more volumes of poetry followed in the same decade: *Peregrina* in 1986 and *Terms of*

*Survival* and *Reaching for the Mainland* in 1987. Branching out from poetry by the end of the decade, Cofer saw the release of her novel, *The Line of the Sun*, in 1989, and a volume of poetry and personal essays, *Silent Dancing,* in 1990. In the early to mid–1990s, Cofer published two more books: a collection of prose and poetry entitled *The Latin Deli* (1993) and a compilation of short stories entitled *An Island Like You: Stories of the Barrio* (1995). Among the honors she has received for her work are a 1989 National Endowment for the Arts fellowship in poetry and the 1990 Pushcart Prize for Nonfiction. Cofer was also awarded the O. Henry Prize in the short story in 1994, and earned the Anisfield-Wolf Award in Race Relations for *The Latin Deli* that same year.

Cofer's first novel, *The Line of the Sun,* was lauded by various critics for its poetic qualities. In the *New York Times Book Review,* for example, Roberto Márquez described Cofer as "a prose writer of evocatively lyrical authority." In the *Los Angeles Times Book Review* Sonja Bolle also referred to the beauty of many of the novel's passages. The book is narrated by Marisol Santa Luz Vivente who tells the story of three generations of her family. The first part of the book describes the origins of the Vivente clan in the Puerto Rican village of Salud and introduces the reader to the culture and landscape of the island. The second part of the novel is set in Paterson, New Jersey, where Marisol strives to find an equilibrium between the clashing values of her Puerto Rican ancestors and those of her new American home.

### Work Delves into Dual Culturalism

The same conflict appears in the autobiographical essays and poems that make up Cofer's *Silent Dancing.* The title is derived from the author's memories of a silent home movie filmed at a New Year's Eve party when her parents were young, which ends with a silent conga line of revelers. As each of the dancers comes into view she comments on how each has responded to the cultural differences in their lives. She writes of her fascination with the short clip in the book's title essay: "The five-minute movie ends with people dancing in a circle—the creative filmmaker must have set it up, so that all of them could file past him. It is both comical and sad to watch silent dancing."

In *Contemporary Authors* Cofer explained her use of autobiographical elements in her poetry. Her words seem equally applicable to her more recent works of fiction and autobiography. "My family is one of the main topics of my poetry," she notes. "In tracing their lives, I discover more about mine. The place of birth itself becomes a metaphor for the things we all must leave behind; the assimilation of a new culture is the coming into maturity by accepting the terms necessary for survival. My poetry is a study of

this process of change, cultural assimilation, and transformation."

### SELECTED PUBLISHED WORKS:

*Peregrina,* Riverstone Press, 1986.
*Reaching for the Mainland,* Tempe, AZ, Bilingual Press, 1987.
*Terms of Survival,* Arte Público, 1987
*The Line of the Sun,* University of Georgia Press, 1989.
*Silent Dancing: A Partial Remembrance of a Puerto Rican Childhood,* Arte Público, 1990.
*The Latin Deli,* University of Georgia Press, 1993.
*An Island Like You: Stories of the Barrio,* New York, Orchard Books, 1995.

### SOURCES:

**Books**

*Contemporary Authors New Revision Series,* Volume 32, Gale, 1991.

**Periodicals**

*Georgia Review,* Spring/Summer 1990, pp. 51–9.
*Los Angeles Times Book Review,* August 6, 1989, p. 6.
*New York Times Book Rew,* September 24, 1989, pp. 46–7.
*Women's Review of Books,* December 1990, p. 9.

—*Sketch by Marian C. Gonsior*

# Margarita Colmenares
## 1957-
### Mexican American environmental engineer

Margarita Colmenares was the first Hispanic engineer to be selected for a White House fellowship, and she was also the first woman to be elected national president of the Society of Hispanic Professional Engineers (SHPE). Employed by Chevron USA since 1981, and presently an air-quality specialist in its office for environmental affairs , she has in her short career established herself as a national leader in the fields of both education and engineering.

Margarita Hortensia Colmenares was born in Sacramento, California, on July 20, 1957, the eldest of five children. Her parents, Luis S. Colmenares and Hortensia O. Colmenares, had emigrated from Oaxaca, Mexico, and her childhood world was bicultural and bilingual. Her parents believed strongly in the importance of a good education and sacrificed to send their children to private Catholic schools. In high school, Colmenares founded an organization for Mexican American students in her all-girls school. She began her college career at California State University in Sacramento studying business, but she realized in her freshman year that engineering was the field she really wanted to pursue. She returned to junior college for more chemistry, physics, and calculus courses, and she also accepted a part-time engineering job with the California Department of Water Resources. Funded by five different scholarships, she entered Stanford University and graduated with a B.S. in civil engineering in 1981.

### Joined Chevron Corporation

Between her junior and senior years at Stanford, Colmenares entered the Chevron Corporation's Co-Op Education Program, and after graduation she joined that company as a field construction engineer. By 1982 she had founded the San Francisco chapter of SHPE. After serving Chevron as a recruiting coordinator, she took on a field construction position whose duties led her to Colorado, Utah, Idaho, and Nevada. Her upward path at Chevron continued as she became a foreign trade representative in 1983 and subsequently won promotion to compliance specialist. It was in this position that she first became involved with environmental issues . In 1986, she was the lead engineer for an $18 million environmental cleanup project at the Chevron refinery in El Segundo, near Los Angeles. Following this experience with environmental engineering , Colmenares was promoted in 1989 to air-quality specialist at the El Segundo plant.

In that same year, she was elected to be SHPE's first woman president. As president of this national society, Colmenares achieved a platform from which she could address many of the issues facing the engineering community in general and Hispanics in particular. Her agenda was based on the importance of education, and she stressed to the society's members that they should seek election to positions that could have an impact on education, engineering, or policy making. Following her term as society president, she applied for a White House fellowship and was chosen as one of the 16 members of the class of 1991–1992. Colmenares became the first Hispanic engineer selected since the program was established in 1964. As part of this program, she chose to work at the Department of Education and became special

assistant to David T. Kearns, the department's deputy secretary.

Colmenares has received many honors and awards during her career. In 1989 she was named Outstanding Hispanic Woman of the Year by *Hispanic* magazine, as well as Hispanic Role Model of the Year by SHPE. That same year she also received *Hispanic Engineer* magazine's Community Service Award. In 1990 and 1992, *Hispanic Business* magazine named her one of the 100 most influential Hispanics in the United States, and in 1991 she was the youngest recipient ever to receive the California Community College League's Outstanding Alumni Award. Her career was also profiled on the Public Broadcasting Service (PBS) series "Choice for Youth."

Colmenares plans to continue her education, possibly in the area of public policy, and she would like to continue working for the betterment of the educational system in the United States. One of her many avocations is an interest in Mexican folk dance and during college she taught, directed, and performed with the Stanford Ballet Folklorico.

## SOURCES:

### Books

*Notable Hispanic American Women,* edited by Diane Telgen and Jim Kamp, Detroit, Gale Research, 1993, pp. 104–07.

### Periodicals

*Hispanic Engineer* (conference issue), 1989, pp. 43–46.

—*Sketch by Leonard C. Bruno*

# Jesús Colón
## 1901-1974
**Puerto Rican American writer**

Jesus Colón communicated with equal ease in English and Spanish. His bilingual abilities also helped him organize activities for causes such as labor reform and the Puerto Rican independence movement. Colón's 1961 collection of newspaper sketches, entitled *A Puerto Rican in New York,* served as inspiration for later Hispanic writers who came to be called Nuyoricans. He also fostered Spanish writing by publishing new works through his own small press, Editorial Hispanica.

Of African descent, Colón was born in Cayey, Puerto Rico, in 1901. He arrived in the United States as a stowaway when he was just a teenager in 1918, along with a wave of other hopeful, mostly working-class immigrants eager to try their luck on northern shores. New York City was a popular destination for many of these people, as Juan Flores explained in his 1982 foreword to Colon's *A Puerto Rican in New York,* because the city was one of the major centers for cigar manufacturing.

While lacking in formal education, Colón had been nurtured in an atmosphere that respected literacy. Even cigar rollers, the *tabaqueros,* would nominate readers called *lectores,* who would recite aloud the news of the day or read from books for audiences at factories. This practice was part of how local folk kept each other informed, a civic effort which continued stateside.

Menial jobs were a necessity for Colón, sustaining him through his career as a newspaperman. He put in time at dishwashing, clerical work at a post office, and longshoreman's duties on the docks. As early as the 1920s he wrote as a New York correspondent for Puerto Rican papers such as *Justicia* and *Unión Obrera.* He also contributed to a weekly publication known as *Liberación,* which began as a protest vehicle against the Francisco Franco regime in Spain during the 1940s. *Liberación* addressed other topics of nationality and independence in Latin American countries, and Colón provided analysis of the political situation of expatriate Puerto Ricans and their relationships with the Puerto Rican independence movement. He was also a newsman for New York area socialist papers like *The Daily Worker, The Worker,* and *Mainstream,* but he found time to write more literary pieces as well. Bernardo Vega, a colleague in New York, published his own weekly called *Gráfico,* which took on Colón as a contributor. *El Machete Criollo* and *El Nuevo Mundo* also printed his poems and anecdotal writings. Loosely autobiographical sketches with characters symbolic of the dilemmas experienced by Puerto Rican immigrants served as the basis for Colón's main body of work, the book he first finished in 1959.

Friends and neighbors drew Colón into activism, especially during the 1950s. As plans for Puerto Rican development displaced more people, the flow of incoming migrants found themselves labeled as part of the "Puerto Rican problem," and McCarthyism only exacerbated the tensions. The Nationalist Party and other Hispanic groups came under pressure for their activities, but Colón never renounced his connections with the Communist Party. Instead, he ran for local office as a communist in both 1952 and

1969. While he did not gain the attention of the mass media in his first race, he did appear on television during the 1969 debates after announcing his candidacy for the position of city controller. The *New York Times* excerpted the television interview with Colón, and quoted him as supporting a platform of more equitable taxation to finance city services. Although he was unsuccessful in both bids for election, he remained active throughout his life in various political, civic, and cultural organizations. He held offices in the International Workers, Order and the American Labor Party, and participated in strikes and other forms of orchestrated protest.

Colón's most ambitious effort was launching his own company, Hispanic Publishers, which was also known as Editorial Hispánica. In addition to books on history and politics, this small press produced literary material, such as the debut work of José Luis González. Along the way Colón translated works from English into Spanish, including poetry. He was also listed as co-author of a book by Kenneth B. Hoyt on vocational education, which was published by the U.S. Department of Health, Education, and Welfare after Colon's death in 1974.

The literary output of Colón, his contemporaries, and other Hispanic writers who followed them drew from a folk tradition of oral communication and bicultural adjustment. Colón especially addressed issues of race and class, since as an immigrant of color he suffered discrimination on many fronts. However, such titles in his collection of stories as "How to Rent an Apartment When You Don't Have Any Money" and "The Origin of Latin American Dances (according to the Madison Avenue Boys)" demonstrate that he could face difficulties with humor and dignity while keeping a foot on each coastline.

## SELECTED PUBLISHED WORKS:

*A Puerto Rican in New York, and Other Sketches,* Mainstream Publishers, 1961, second edition, International Publishers, 1982.

(Translator and author) With Kenneth B. Hoyt, *Fundamentos basicos de career education,* U.S. Government Printing Office, Department of Health, Education, and Welfare, Office of Education, 1979.

## SOURCES:

### Books

*Hispanic Writers,* edited by Bryan Ryan, Detroit, Gale Research, 1991.

*Hispanic-American Almanac,* edited by Nicolas Kanellos, Detroit, Gale Research, 1993.

**Periodicals**

*New York Times,* October 27, 1969, p. 48.

—*Sketch by Jennifer Kramer*

# Willie Colón
## 1950-

**Puerto Rican American bandleader**

Willie Colón has earned considerable fame as a salsa musician and bandleader. He has played with nearly all the greats of the form, and for many years worked with **Rubén Blades**. Many credit Colón with bringing an urban feel to the Afro-Cuban sound, giving it what music critic Enrique Fernández called "an attitude." Like Blades, Colón uses his music to address issues of concern, especially Latin American ones. While he is foremost an entertainer, Colón has also campaigned for political candidates, raised money for drug prevention programs, and worked for environmental groups. In 1994 he ran unsuccessfully for the Democratic nomination for New York's 17th Congressional district.

## Musical Success

Willie Colón was born on April 28, 1950, in the Bronx, New York. He has lived most of his life among whites, Puerto Ricans, blacks, Cubans, and other ethnic groups. Growing up in this ethnically diverse environment, Colón absorbed cultural and musical influences which have shaped his career and music. Called by Fernández "a total New York musician," Colón brings to his music the cosmopolitan feel of the city of his birth.

His interest in music began early, and at age 16, Colón released his first album. Although he dropped out of high school, Colón's canniness about urban life has informed his music from the very beginning. As one of his supporters in the 1994 election said, "When one has spent much of life on the streets, one knows much more." Colón's street smarts and musical talent made *El malo,* released in 1967, an enduring favorite among salsa fans, and Colón became one of the music genre's rising stars.

Colón started working with Rubén Blades when, as Colón said, a "confluence of ideas and ideals" between the two men brought them together. The two musicians recorded several albums, including *Siembra* in 1978 which sold three million copies around the world. Colón has recorded ten gold albums (an album is designated "gold" when sales exceed 500,000 copies). He has also received ten Grammy nominations.

Although in recent years Colón and Blades have parted musically, the two men continue to share both political and musical common ground. Like Blades, Colón finds more appreciative listeners outside the United States. In fact, Fernández said that "in Latin America [Colón's] stature is downright mythic." *The Hispanic-American Almanac* names Colón and Blades as two of the musicians responsible for 'strengthening" the "style and instrumentation" of various latin music forms, like the *rumba-guaguancó* and *son,* made popular by **Tito Puente**, Machito, and Tito Rodriguez in the 1950s. Colón helped bring those sounds together into the modern musical form known as salsa. Blades and Colón also played dramatic roles in expressing the Latin American and Caribbean *barrio* experience in music which could not be imagined without them.

## Political Ambitions

In 1992, Congressional redistricting made the northern Bronx and southern Westchester County areas of New York into a district almost equally populated by blacks, hispanics, and whites. Taking advantage of the new demographics, Colón decided to run for Congress, hoping that his celebrity would outweigh his inexperience in the minds of the voters. A neophyte in the world of campaigning, Colón says he feared that someone would yell "Willie, where's your trombone?" as he rose to make his campaign speeches, but he later told the *New York Times* that his supporters "were urging me on" to enter politics. He found significant support for his crossover attempt into the political world, although Representative Eliot Engel eventually defeated him for the nomination.

Despite losing the nomination, Colón seems likely to try again in the future. His involvement in politics has not ended his musical career, of course, and Colón continues to produce, write and perform.

**SELECTED DISCOGRAPHY:**

*El malo,* 1967.
*Cos nuestra,* 1972.
*The Good, the Bad, the Ugly,* 1975.
*Ciembra,* 1978.
*Tiempo pa matar,* 1984.

**SOURCES:**

**Books**

*The Hispanic-American Almanac,* edited by Nicolás Kanellos, Detroit, Gale, 1993, pp. 615–16.

**Periodicals**

*New York Times,* June 25, 1994, p. A25; September 10, 1994, p. A21; September 11, 1994, p. C1; September 14, 1994, p. B5; September 19, 1994, p. B2.
*Village Voice,* January 31, 1989, p. 78.

—*Sketch by James McCarthy*

# Angel Cordero
## 1942-
### Puerto Rican jockey

*Angel Cordero*

One of the most successful jockeys in horse racing, Angel Cordero has amassed over 7,000 trips to the winner's circle in his 31-year career. He has ridden to victory three times in the Kentucky Derby, and was inducted into the Thoroughbred Racing Hall of Fame in 1988.

Angel Tomás Cordero, Jr., was born in Puerto Rico, where both his father and grandfather were jockeys-turned-trainers. Originally Cordero had planned to become a dentist, in accord with his mother's wishes; but he followed his paternal career path and began riding when he was 17. Cordero went to New York in 1962 at age 20—determined to become a jockey—but trainers did not trust him with their horses. Still unemployed after a few months he returned to his homeland to work on his English skills and his riding technique. In 1964 he settled in the United States once more.

Cordero's break finally came, and he began to get regular mounts. "I couldn't stand losing," he told the *New York Times* 's Steven Crist. Although this statement was directed toward his betting experiences, it applies to his racing as well. Cordero developed a talent for handling horses, earning a reputation for getting his mounts out front and keeping them there—even if the horse was tired or had been rated as unable to go longer distances. Cordero explained to Crist: "It's an inner thing, knowing a horse, having a feel for him. It's what being a horseman is about."

### Exhibited Strong Desire to Win

Cordero's desire to win is strong, although, as he admitted to Crist, "Sometimes I push too hard." Aggressiveness has led to the victory, but has also provoked trouble and unpopularity. Fines and suspensions have been levelled against him. Cordero has been accused of reckless riding for actions such as inserting his horse where there is no room and intimidating other jockeys with his on-track positioning. Although trainers have asked Cordero to ride their horses and have been delighted with his wins, they have also resented the tactics he employs when riding opposing horses.

Along with his skill in handling horses, Cordero also developed a unique style of celebrating his wins, a style that has both amused and antagonized horse-racing fans. He has been described as jaunty, noisy, and flamboyant. He has been considered cocky for twirling his whip, vaulting from the horse, and tossing the whip to a groom. Cordero has often been unpopular with the fans—not only for his flamboyance and daring riding strategies—but also for 1978 accusations of race-fixing. In that instance, Cordero's name was mentioned along with seven other New York jockeys; he repeatedly denied having taken part in any such schemes. Although no official charges were ever brought against him, many fans continued to believe he was guilty. They showed their disapproval at the track each time Cordero's name appeared.

In 1982 Cordero found himself in the winner's circle many times as he worked to win more races and earn more money than rival jockey Laffit Pincay, Jr.; to do so would win him the Eclipse Award as the country's outstanding jockey. Cordero earned over $9 million, setting a record for jockey earnings in a season.

Every jockey assumes risks. At Belmont Park in August 1983, Cordero was in the lead and riding the rail. Another horse moved up and veered into Dr. Johnson, Cordero's mount. The two horses and jockeys fell, with Cordero and Dr. Johnson flying over the rail and hedge. Dr. Johnson landed with a foot on the back of the 40-year-old, 113-pound Cordero. "I . . . tried to get up, but couldn't," Cordero told the *New York Times'* s Ira Berkow. Cordero was taken to a hospital for treatment. Three days later he was racing again. But after an accident at the Aqueduct on January 12, 1992, in which Cordero sustained injuries to his ribs, intestine, and kidneys, and was almost killed, the 50-year-old jockey accepted his doctors' advice and announced his retirement.

Following in the steps of his father and grandfather, Cordero became a trainer, something he had always wanted do. His first race in this new position occurred in the spring of 1992 at Belmont Park. Cordero told *Sports Illustrated:* "I was just praying, saying, 'I don't care if you don't win. Just don't finish last. Don't embarrass me.'" His horse finished fifth. Victory finally came to trainer Cordero in July 1994, with Holy Mountain winning the $75,000 Grade III Lexington Stakes.

## SOURCES:

### Periodicals

*New York Times,* July 18, 1994, p. 7.
*New York Times Biographical Service,* December 1982, pp. 1579–82; August 1983, pp. 920–21.
*Sporting News,* August 22, 1988, p. 46.
*Sports Illustrated,* May 18, 1992, pp. 13–14; June 1, 1992, pp. 75.

—*Sketch by Sandy J. Stiefer*

# Francisco Vásquez de Coronado
## 1510-1554
### Spanish explorer

Francisco Vásquez de Coronado, a Spanish explorer selected to lead an expedition in search of the legendary Seven Cities of Cíbola, was the first European to explore Arizona and New Mexico. His findings opened the southwestern region of North America to colonization. From the moment the first Spanish conquerors set foot in New Spain, they had heard rumors of gold and wealth among distant native tribes. When **Hernán Cortés** discovered the riches of **Montezuma** and his Aztec people in 1519, the race began to claim other territories and their fortunes in the name of Spain.

In 1536 and 1539 sightings of seven Zuni Indian villages that featured buildings made of gold and decorated in turquoise were reported by Spanish explorers and a group of missionaries, respectively. The report by the explorers had been particularly exciting to the government of Spain. A group of four explorers had made their way home bringing tales of wealth at a settlement believed to be the legendary Cíbola. These men—**Álvar Núñez Cabeza de Vaca**, Dorantes, **Bernal Díaz del Castillo**, and the slave Estevnico—had been part of the 1533 expedition to explore Florida, but had been enslaved for several years by natives after a shipwreck off the coast of Texas. The men prepared a report for Antonio de Mendoza, the Spanish colonial administrator, that included a map of the regions they had visited or traveled through. Their report was corroborated by Marcus de Niza, a missionary. Marcus recounted glorious stories of the riches he had seen at Cíbola, Chichilticalli, and other locales. He reported that these locations were only a moderate march north of Mexico City and accessible through lands of greenery and beauty.

Assuming these were the legendary seven cities, an expedition was organized in 1539 with the 28-year-old governor Coronado at the helm. Though they found the Cities of Cíbola, they found no gold. While searching for gold in other settlements, they extended the domain of New Spain north into Arizona, across New Mexico, and northeast into the prairies of present-day Kansas. Smaller groups branched from the main expedition, making separate trips in search of the golden cities. These groups are credited with discovering the Grand Canyon and exploring the Rio Grande valley. Coronado and the main expedition were among the first Europeans to see buffalo and to reach the Palo Duro Canyon in Texas.

### New Wealth in the New World

Coronado was born in Salamanca, Spain, around 1510. A younger son of the aristocrat Vásquez, and therefore not entitled to the family fortune, Coronado sailed to New Spain in the entourage of Antonio de Mendoza, the viceroy of Mexico, in the year 1535. According to Herbert E. Bolton in *Coronado: Knight of Pueblo and Plains,* "Coronado rose rapidly, for he was attractive and popular, and, more to the point, he enjoyed the viceroy's favor. We may assume that he was handsome . . . [his] prestige was vastly enhanced when, within two years after his arrival, he married

Doña Beatríz, daughter and heiress of wealthy Alonso de Estrada, deceased treasurer of New Spain."

Estrada was rumored to have been an illegitimate son of King Ferdinand. Whether this story was true or false, Estrada was credited as having a blood connection to Spanish royalty. Señora Estrada gave the young couple half of a large and prosperous ranch located south of Mexico City as a wedding gift. Coronado's marriage to Beatríz thus provided him with both wealth and a stronger connection to nobility.

In 1537, the same year as his marriage, Coronado was sent to squelch an uprising in the mining district of New Spain, just outside Mexico City. He successfully completed this duty. As reward Mendoza appointed him to the city council of Mexico, a position Coronado would hold until his death.

When the state of affairs in the province of New Galicia required stabilization after a period of cruel and corrupt rule, the viceroy sent Coronado to assume the governorship. This role had previously been filled by Nuño de Guzmán, a conquistador who had searched for the Amazons as well as the Seven Cities of Gold a decade earlier. In 1538 Coronado left Mexico City with his wife and their daughter for Compostela, the capital city of New Galicia. "Thus were heavy responsibilities put on the shoulders of a youth of twenty-eight. Coronado now occupied the key position with reference to the development of the Northwestern frontier," wrote Bolton.

In the meantime, far across the ocean, Mendoza weighed the statements of the four explorers who had returned to Spain. He decided to send an expeditionary force after the treasure of the Seven Cities of Cíbola with the slave Estevnico serving as guide. Seeing Marcus de Niza's interest in such an expedition, the viceroy included him in the plans, for the missionaries were known for their stamina and were used to working and living among the natives of the frontier.

Coronado was aware of plans for the expedition but assumed his role was simply to assist in whatever way possible in his capacity as governor of New Galicia. Many expected leadership of the expedition to fall to Cortés, so when Coronado was named commander by Mendoza instead, the honor was a significant one.

The viceroy's approach to the claim of the unmarked territory was to send two forces, one by land and another by sea. Paul Horgan explained the approach in *Conquistadors in North American History:* "The main one of these was the land force commanded by General Vásquez de Coronado, which would be guided to Cíbola by Marcus de Niza. The other was a sea force under the command of Captain Hernando de Alarcón, consisting of a ship and a sloop, which was to go north by sea and keep abreast of the land march, if contact could be maintained."

Late in February 1540, Coronado, arrayed in gleaming armor crowned by a helmet gilded with gold, set out from Compostela. In his command was an army of 300 Spanish soldiers, 32 infantry, four friars, a surgeon, hundreds of other workers, and huge numbers of sheep, cattle, horses, mules, and hogs—animals never before seen in the region. It took the expedition a month to reach the frontier on the outskirts of Culiacán. Coronado, anxious to reach the unknown territories, grew irritated with the slow pace of the caravan. He placed Captain Tristan de Arellano in charge of the main body and took a small party that included Marcus and Estevnico ahead with him. They took minimum rations with them because the friar's reports indicated that living off the land would be fairly easy.

They soon learned the harsher truth as they scratched their way northward over rough land. Mountain passes that had been described by Marcus as easily passible proved to be extremely hazardous. When the men finally reached Chichilticalli, which according to Marcus' report should have been a settlement, they found only a hut with a collapsed roof. Coronado and his companions grew increasingly suspicious of the missionary.

A small party from the group ventured to the settlement of nearby natives with the hopes of bartering food for the hungry explorers. The natives were hostile, however, and the slave Estevnico was killed in the conflict. Coronado's men fought off their attackers, but Coronado was hard-pressed to convince his troops from harming the increasingly unpopular friar. The main column caught up and the entire entourage continued to press northward. As provisions ran dangerously low, Coronado sent a group, led by Melchior Díaz, toward the sea to meet up with the ships and return with provisions. The rest of the group camped while they waited for the party to return.

Díaz and his men returned after a time with letters that Alcarón had buried at the base of a tree. These letters explained that Alcarón had sailed as far as he could into what is now the Gulf of California and waited for contact from Coronado's expedition. When no word came they set course for home. Coronado left a group of men at the camp site, which he named Corazones. Though many chose to stay and settle there, many others pressed on with visions of wealth and gold at the end of their journey. Again Coronado headed north, taking a smaller party ahead while the main force followed more slowly behind.

On June 23 Coronado and his force entered a desert. The climate took its toll, killing both horses and men, while provisions dwindled away. A scouting party reported green grasses and cool rivers ahead.

Messengers from Cíbola arrived as well, assuring Coronado that their settlement was two days' march ahead. Coronado suspected the messengers were scouting an attack and made preparations to withstand an attack sometime that evening. During the night the natives did attack, but they retreated when they found their enemy was not taken by surprise.

When the group reached the valley that contained Cíbola, they ate berries and vegetation that grew there while the missionaries went ahead with officers to read the "Requirement of 1513," which claimed the land in the name of the King of Spain. A brief battle ensued after which the men gained entry to the village. Since the lodgings were made of mud, not gold, the men searched from room to room looking for gold. They found no gold but did discover supplies of food, of which they were in desperate need. It was clear upon examination of the village that the missionary's story had once again proven false. Coronado sent the friar back to Mexico City with several disillusioned men.

Coronado learned from Zuni Indians in the settlement that it had indeed been one of a group of seven. He traveled to each village, but had no success in finding gold. Villagers suggested that Quivira might be the location he sought. A slave at one of the settlements who once lived in Quivira agreed to lead the expedition there.

To be certain the golden cities did not exist west of Cíbola, Coronado appointed Captain Pedro de Tovar and Cárdenas, his right-hand man, to lead a small party northwest. The group traveled as far as the Grand Canyon before turning back. After learning the results of this secondary expedition, Coronado selected a moderate army of men and set off with the slave, called the Turk, as their guide. The guide proved untrustworthy, however, and Coronado found that the Turk had intended to leave the expedition hopelessly lost in a strange land.

Coronado selected a group of about 30 men to accompany him as he continued his search for Quivira in a northeasterly direction. They departed in early summer 1541, while the rest of the group waited for their return. In autumn 1541 Coronado and his expedition returned empty-handed. Since winter was fast approaching, they busied themselves preparing to camp there until the snows subsided. Two days after Christmas in 1541, while exercising his horse, Coronado fell from his seat and suffered a severe blow to the head. According to Horgan, "He was carried to his quarters where for days he lay close to death. How could he have fallen? They found that his saddle girth, long neglected and rotting, had broken. When slowly he began to recover it seemed that his confidence was gone." When the army received word that the native peoples were rebelling, Coronado fell ill again.

In April 1452 the army marched westward toward Cíbola. On good days Coronado rode a horse, on bad days he was carried in a litter. Upon reaching New Galicia in 1542, Coronado was accused of brutal acts against the natives. The charges were eventually dismissed. In 1545 a royal inquiry held in the city of Mexico reported Coronado was a "changed man" due to the fall from his horse. Though granted honor for his accomplishments before and during the expedition, Coronado remained an invalid until his death on September 22, 1554, at the age of 44. His body was laid to rest under the altar of the Dominican church in the city of Mexico.

## SOURCES:

### Books

Bolton, Herbert E., *Coronado: Knight of Pueblos and Plains,* Albuquerque, University of New Mexico Press, 1949.

Castañeda, Pedro, *The Journey of Coronado,* Williams-Barker Co., 1904, reprinted 1966, University Microfilms, Inc.

Hgan, Paul, *Conquistadors in North American History,* New York, Farrar, Straus and Co., 1963.

*—Sketch by Lisa A. Wroble*

# Lucha Corpi
## 1945-
### Mexican American poet, novelist, and educator

Although born and raised in Mexico and not a resident of the United States until nearly 20, Lucha Corpi has identified herself with the Chicano community. She has contributed her poems to Chicano journals and has seen her work included in an important anthology of Chicano literature, *Chicanos: Antología histórica y literaria.* Critic Barbara Brinson Curiel finds the focus of Corpi's work in the plight of women in modern culture. In Curiel's *Dictionary of Literary Biography* essay she writes that two of Corpi's most important "concerns are women cornered by the circumstances of their lives and a notion that fate is inescapable."

Corpi was born on April 13, 1945, to Miguel Angel Corpi and Victoria C. de Corpi, in Jáltipan, in the state of Veracruz, Mexico. She received her bachelor of arts from the University of California,

*Lucha Corpi*

foreign Spanish conquerors and, therefore, allowed herself to be violated, Corpi's poetry speaks of a woman fated to be an unwilling accomplice. In *Contemporary Chicana Poetry: A Critical Approach to an Emerging Literature,* Marta Ester Sánchez explains: "Corpi's Marina does not actively resist the rape. Rather, the reader must presuppose a reluctant Marina who felt she had no other choice but to submit, as men would force sex upon her in spite of her objections."

Curiel comments on Corpi's sensitive treatment of the historical figure of Marina. "Corpi portrays Marina," she notes, "as an individual rather than as a sorceress who through her evil caused the downfall of her people. She sees her as a victim caught between an old world and a new world, a woman who had journeyed from one culture and society to another and yet who had no home." Curiel maintains that "Marina reflects the experiences of many women from many cultures through time. Through her, Corpi reinterprets the historical circumstances which have fostered the devaluation of all Mexican women." The critic finds "The Marina Poems" deal with themes expressed in "Tres mujeres," an early story by Corpi.

Corpi is primarily known as a poet but has also written award-winning short fiction and novels. Her work has appeared in numerous anthologies, including *Chicanos: Antología histórica y literaria,* published in Mexico in 1980, and *A Decade of Hispanic Literature: An Anniversary Anthology,* published in 1983. Corpi's longer works include a novel, *Delia's Song,* which deals with a female character who leaves her family to study in California, and *Eulogy for a Brown Angel,* a 1992 feminist mystery novel featuring civil-rights activist Gloria Damasco, who discovers the body of boy killed during a 1970 Chicano demonstration in Los Angeles.

Corpi has received several awards for her writing, including a National Endowment for the Arts creative writing fellowship in 1979; first place in the *Palabra Nueva* literary competition for her short story, "Los cristos del alma," in 1983; and first place in the Chicano Literary Contest held at the University of California, Irvine, in 1984.

Berkeley, in 1975, and a master of arts in comparative literature from San Francisco State University in 1979. Since 1973, Corpi has taught English as a Second Language through the Oakland (California) Public School system. She has also worked as an instructor at Vista Junior College and served on the board of Aztlán Cultural, a Chicano organization for the arts.

In *Dictionary of Literary Biography,* Curiel maintains that Corpi's most important contribution to Chicano literature is a series of four poems called "The Marina Poems," which first appeared in the anthology *The Other Voice: Twentieth-Century Women's Poetry in Translation,* published by Norton in 1976 and subsequently included in Corpi's *Palabras de mediodia/Noon Words,* a bilingual edition published by *Fuego de Aztlán* in 1980. These poems are meditations on Doña Marina (also known as Malintzín Tenepal and *La Malinche*), the Indian woman who served as translator to **Hernán Cortés** during his conquest of Mexico.

These poems include Corpi's personal vision of the woman she chooses to call Marina, her Spanish name, rather than the derisive name, *La Malinche,* with which she is usually referred. Since the woman aided the man who conquered her country, the name *La Malinche* has become synonymous with traitor in the Hispanic culture. While contemporary male Mexican writers, such as **Carlos Fuentes** and **Octavio Paz,** see Marina as a woman who was fascinated by the

**SOURCES:**

*Dictionary of Literary Biography,* Volume 82: *Chicano Writers,* Gale, 1989.

Sánchez, Marta Ester, *Contemporary Chicana Poetry: A Critical Approach to anmerging Literature,* University of California Press, 1985.

*—Sketch by Marian C. Gonsior*

# Julio Cortázar
## 1914-1984
### Argentine writer and translator

Also known as Julio Denís, literary innovator Julio Cortázar played a key role in the growth of twentieth-century Spanish-American literature. Together with fellow writers such as **Jorge Luis Borges**, **Gabriel García Marquez**, and **Carlos Fuentes**, Cortázar helped bring Latin American literature and politics to international prominence. Author of the short story that inspired Michelangelo Antonioni's 1966 film *Blow-Up,* Cortázar was also well-known for his 1963 novel *Rayuela* (*Hopscotch*). With its elaborate structure, which required the reader to skip back and forth between chapters, *Hopscotch* evoked comparisons to the works of Marcel Proust and James Joyce. "Although not 'easy' reading," wrote Evelyn Picon Garfield, author of *Julio Cortázar, Hopscotch* "is a rewarding and unique adventure."

Cortázar was a constant experimenter and a member of the literary avant-garde. His works probed the connections between the real and the surreal, the ordinary and the extraordinary, the individual and the state. Although Cortázar advocated socialism and supported the Cuban and Nicaraguan revolutions, he also upheld the need for individual freedom.

Strongly influenced by the works of the French surrealists, Cortázar experimented with literary form to challenge the reader's view of everyday reality. He countered conventional adult logic with a child-like sense of wonder, professing a life-long affinity with J. M. Barrie's character Peter Pan. "I am still very much a boy and am adolescent in many ways," he told Garfield in an interview. "In my life relationships, in my feelings, there is an adolescent element that prevails in me. In that sense I think I am never going to get old."

Cortázar viewed writing as a game of sorts —"a contest with words," according to Terry J. Peavler, author of *Julio Cortázar.* From the 1950s on, according to Peavler, Cortázar turned out a dizzying array of work: more than 80 short stories, five novels, two books of poetry, two plays, and numerous essays, prose poems, and travelogues. Critiques of his work abound. A 1985 bibliography on Cortázar, for instance, contained more than 2,600 entries of primary and secondary sources, underscoring the importance of the writer and his work.

Julio Cortázar was born August 26, 1914, in Brussels, Belgium, the son of Argentine citizens, Maria Scott and Julio Cortázar, abroad on business. When Julio was four, his family returned to Argentina and settled in Banfield, a suburb of Buenos Aires. "I

don't have happy memories from my childhood," Cortázar recalled in *The Final Island: The Fiction of Julio Cortázar.* "Too many chores, an excessive sensitivity, a frequent sadness, asthma, broken arms, first desperate loves (my story 'The Poisons' is very autobiographical)."

Young Julio read voraciously, and was particularly fond of the works of Edgar Allan Poe. He wrote his first novel at the age of nine but never tried to get it published. After attending school in Buenos Aires, Cortázar was certified in 1935 as a secondary and preparatory school teacher. He then attended the University of Buenos Aires but left after a year to help with the financial situation at home. Cortázar's father had left home when Julio was a small child.

Cortázar taught high school in two towns in the province of Buenos Aires. In 1938 he published *Prescencia* (*Presence*), a collection of poems, under the pseudonym Julio Denís. In 1944 he was hired to teach French literature, including surrealism, at the University of Cuyo. After being arrested for participating in a demonstration against president-to-be **Juan Domingo Peron**, Cortázar resigned his position and returned to Buenos Aires, where he became the manager of a publishing association. In 1946 his first short story, "Casa tomada" ("House Taken Over") was published in the journal *Anales de Buenos Aires,* edited by Jorge Luis Borges.

Cortázar began his studies in public translating, a field combining languages and law, at this time. The combination of work and school was so exhausting that Cortázar suffered from stress-related ailments, including nausea, that would later provide inspiration for some of his classic stories.

In 1949, Cortázar published "Los reyes" ("The Kings"), a dramatic poem based on the classical legend of the half bull/half human Minotaur and the Athenian king. Cortázar reversed the outcome of the story, making the Minotaur the hero. Peavler noted that Cortázar explained that "the Minotaur is the poet—the being who is different from others, a free spirit, who therefore has been locked up, because he's a threat to the established order."

Although "The Kings" was greeted with indifference, Cortázar's first collection of short stories, entitled *Bestiario* (*Bestiary*), went over well. Nevertheless, Cortázar left Argentina to take advantage of a government scholarship to study in Paris. In 1952 he began work as a translator for UNESCO, a job he continued throughout his life. The following year he established permanent residency in Paris. In 1953 he married Aurora Bernandez, who he later collaborated with in the translation of the prose works of Edgar Allan Poe.

## Move to France

Although Cortázar maintained a keen interest in Argentina, he spent most of his adult life in France. In 1981 he became a French citizen, but he never renounced his citizenship in Argentina. "There is a very French Cortázar and another who is profoundly Argentinian," Cortázar explained to Garfield. He considered himself an international writer whose works explored the human, rather than the regional, condition. "In some ways writing is like an exorcism, a rejection of invading creatures," he wrote in *Ultimo Round* (*Last Round*), one of his collections of miscellaneous works.

Cortázar's short stories, in particular, are filled with examples of invading creatures: a tiger roams through the house of a middle-class family; a narrator vomits rabbits; a dead character is more alive than the living. Rather than using supernatural forces to fuel reader fears, Cortázar, according to *Final Island*'s Alazraki, used "the fantastic" to expose "overly naive forms of realism." Some critics dismissed Cortázar's innovations as mere gimmickry. In a review in the *New Yorker,* however, John Updike defended a volume of Cortázar's stories, writing that while "he cannot get started without a gimmick . . . once the trick is established . . . Cortázar pushes beyond it with surprising powers of realistic development."

*Final del juego* (*End of the Game* ), Cortázar's second collection of short stories, was published in 1956. It included "Blow-Up" as well as a longer short story, "The Pursuer." Wrote Alazraki in *The Final Island:* "With the long story 'The Pursuer,' [Cortázar] begins to unloose the stylistic perfection with which his stories are knitted." The author, according to Peavler, believed that "the novel wins by points, while the short story must win by a knockout." In 1960 Cortázar published *Los Premios* (*The Winners*), his first novel. *The Winners* concerned a group of Argentines on a cruise. In the novel, the passengers are denied access to the ship's stern and must decide whether or not to challenge the authorities. "*The Winners* is significant in that it continues Cortázar's criticism of what he perceived to be the Argentines' blind acceptance of authority and of rigid class divisions," wrote Peavler in *Julio Cortázar.*

In 1962 Cortázar published *Historias de cronopios y de famas* (later published as *Cronopios and Famas*), a collection of miscellaneous fables and flights of fancy which, a critic for *The Atlantic* wrote, "served rather as an exercise book for *Hopscotch.*" The "Instruction Manual" section of *Cronopios and Famas* was inspired by a conversation Cortázar had with his wife about a staircase. In "The Instruction Manual" Cortázar described in precise detail such everyday occurrences as crying, singing, climbing stairs, and combing hair. About crying, he wrote: "a general contraction of the face and a spasmodic sound

accompanied by tears and mucus." "Cronopios" and "famas" are two types of people he created: the cronopias are the playful innovators, the famas the respectable traditionalists.

## The Book as a Hopscotch Board

In 1963 Cortázar published *Hopscotch,* an experimental novel that included a "Table of Instructions" informing the reader to read the first 56 chapters before leapfrogging to Chapter 73 and hopscotching all around. The main character in this elaborate design is Horacio Oliveira, an Argentinian expatriate adrift in Paris. Oliveira surrounds himself with a small circle of friends, including his female companion La Maga (The Magician) who, although more intuitive and straightforward than the other members of the group, is perceived by herself and others as intellectually inferior. After La Maga's son dies unattended while the adults are discussing the meaning of life, Oliveira journeys to Buenos Aires, either to look for La Maga or his own identity, before stopping off at a one-room circus and an insane asylum. Interspersed with this quest for identity is a plot about reconstructing the novel as an art form.

*Hopscotch* met with mixed reviews. While *The New Republic* hailed it as "a spiraling, convulsive, exploding universe of a novel . . . the most powerful encyclopedia of emotions and visions to emerge from the postwar generation of international writers," the *New York Review of Books* called it "monumentally boring." In 1967, one year after being published in English in the United States, *Hopscotch* won the National Book Award. Published during an era of student protests in the United States, France, Mexico, and elsewhere, *Hopscotch,* according to Peavler, "reflects the dissatisfaction of the time, and the search, no matter how futile, for something better."

Cortázar conceived his next novel, *62 modela para armar* (*62: A Model Kit*), as a sequel to *Hopscotch.* This experimental work required that readers assemble their own novel. Cortázar found *62: A Model Kit* his hardest novel to write because of the rigors of its precise instructions. "When I finished it, I was more than content," Cortázar told Garfield, "I was relieved."

*Libro de Manuel* (*A Manual for Manuel*), Cortázar's next novel, reflected the author's political coming of age, according to Garfield. Cortázar interspersed the narrative of *A Manual for Manuel* with reprints of news clips, merging story with history, and donated proceeds from the book to two Argentinian organizations that aided families of political prisoners. The novel, however, presented an ambivalent view of political protest. The main character, Andres Fava, an Argentinian exile in Paris, attends meetings of a group of revolutionaries in exile called the Screwery but is less committed than the others.

Finally, as the police close in on the group, Andres finds his cause: compiling a scrapbook of clippings for Manuel, the young son of two Screwery members.

Cortázar, like Andres, refused to sacrifice his personal and creative freedom to a revolutionary cause. He did not completely ignore political events, however. Although Cortázar supported the Cuban revolution, he, like other prominent Latin American intellectuals, signed a letter in 1971 protesting the imprisonment of Cuban poet **Heberto Padilla** for writing poetry deemed counterrevolutionary. In the 1970s Cortázar frequently took part in the Thursday demonstrations outside the Argentine Embassy in Paris. These demonstrations were held to protest the Argentine government's involvement in the disappearance of thousands of Argentineans.

The Nicaraguan revolution of 1979 gave Cortázar new hope for a socialism that encouraged, rather than squelched, creative freedom. He believed that fine literature, itself, was revolutionary. In *Julio Cortázar,* Peavler wrote: "Julio Cortázar thus sought, as he himself declared, to be a **Che Guevara** of literature." Some of Cortázar's experiments in form were so revolutionary they defied categorization. *La vuelta al dia en ochenta mundos* (*Around the Day in Eighty Worlds* ), *Ultimo round* (*Final round*), and *Un tal Lucas* (*A Certain Lucas*) were particularly daring collections of miscellaneous short stories, essays, poems, photographs, and vignettes.

In 1983 the government of Nicaragua awarded Cortázar the Ruben Dario Order of cultural independence "for his intellectual position in agreement with the yearnings for freedom of Latin American peoples and his profound identification with the Sandinista popular revolution." Also in 1983, Cortázar made his final trip to New York to address the United Nations Commission on International Humanitarian Issues.

Cortázar wrote *Nicaragua tan violentamente dulce* (*Nicaragua, So Violently Sweet*) with his companion Carol Dunlop shortly before her death in 1982 of leukemia. After Dunlop's death, Cortázar's own health declined. He died on February 12, 1984, of leukemia and heart disease in Saint Lazare hospital in Paris at the age of 69.

## SELECTED PUBLISHED WORKS:

*End of the Game and Other Stories,* translated by Paul Blackburn, Pantheon Books, 1963, 1967.
*Los premios* (*The Winners*), translated by Elaine Kerrigan, Pantheon, 1965.
*Rayuela* (*Hopscotch*), translated by Gregory Rabassa, Pantheon Books, 1966.
*Blow-up and Other Stories,* translated by Paul Blackburn, Collier, 1968.

*Historias de cronopios y de famas* (*Cronopios and Famas*), translated by Paul Blackburn, Pantheon, 1969.
*62 modelo para armar* (*62: A Model Kit*), translated by Gregory Rabassa, Avon, 1972.
*Libro de Manuel* (*A Manual for Manuel*), translated by Gregory Rabassa, Pantheon, 1978.
*Nicaragua tan violentamente dulce* (*Nicaragua, So Violently Sweet*), 1983.

## SOURCES:

### Books

Del Castillo, Ana Hernández, *Keats, Poe, and the Shaping of Cortázar's Mythopoesis,* Amsterdam, John Benjamins B.V., 1981.
*The Final Island: The Fiction of Julio Cortázar,* edited by Jaime Alazraki and Ivar Ivask, Norman, OK: University of Oklahoma Press, 1976, 1978.
Garfield, Evelyn Picon, *Julio Cortázar,* New York, Ungar, 1975.
*Hispanic Writers,* edited by Bryan Ryan, Detroit, Gale, 1991.
King, Sarah E., *The Magical and the Monstrous: Two Faces of the Child-Figure in the Fiction of Julio Cortázar and Jose Donoso,* New York, Garland, 1992.
Peavler, Terry J., *Julio Cortázar,* Boston, Twayne, 1990.

### Periodicals

*Atlantic,* June, 1969; October, 1973.
*Nation,* September 18, 1967.
*New Republic,* April 23, 1966; October 21, 1978.
*New York Times,* February 13, 1984.
*New Yorker,* February 25, 1974.
*Time,* April 29, 1966; June 13, 1969; October 1, 1973.

—*Sketch by Joan Axelrod-Contrada*

# Hernándo Cortés
## 1485-1547
### Spanish explorer and conquistador

The Spanish adventurer Hernándo Cortés conquered the Aztec Empire and founded colonial Mexico in the early sixteenth century, paving the way for Spain's domination of the Americas for three centuries. In his quest for power and gold, Cortés destroyed an advanced civilization. He built new cities on the ashes of the Aztec temples, transplanted European culture and the Catholic religion, sent conquistadors south and west, and accumulated great personal wealth and power. "The conquest and destruction of the Aztec empire, which Cortés achieved in the thirty-one months after leaving Cuba, ranked with the great military feats of the ages," wrote William Weber Johnson in *Cortés.* To attain that end, he massacred and enslaved tens of thousands of Indians.

Little in Cortés's youth suggested that the sickly child—not expected to survive infancy—would become one of Spain's great conquistadors. Cortés was born in 1485, in Medellín, a city in Estremadura, the only child of Catalina Pizarro Altimarano de Cortés and Martín Cortés de Monroy, a retired captain in the Spanish infantry.

When he was 14, Cortés was sent to Salamanca to study law at the university. He stayed only two years, and returned home without a degree. In 1504 Cortés sailed with trader Alonso Quintero for the West Indies. Cortés landed at Santo Domingo on the island of Hispaniola (now the Dominican Republic and Haiti). He was granted land with a few Indians and was appointed notary for the town council of Azúa and notary public for the village of Azúa. For the next few years, Cortés farmed, mined, gambled, and enjoyed himself, according to Richard Lee Marks in *Cortés.* He also became friendly with **Diego Velázquez de Cuéllar**, who received permission from Spain to invade Cuba and serve as governor of the island.

In 1511 Cortés accompanied Velázquez on his conquest of Cuba, then settled in Cuba, after receiving a land grant to farm and mine. While in Cuba, Cortés married Catalina Xuárez, the daughter of a respected Spanish family.

In 1518 Velázquez ordered Cortés to lead an expedition to the Mexico's Yucatán Peninsula, which was thought to contain great riches in gold as well as unfriendly Indians. Spaniards had landed on the shores earlier, but the Indians had driven them away. Suspecting Cortés was too ambitious and might threaten his authority, Velázquez rescinded his order, but Cortés mortgaged his estate, borrowed money, and set sail from Cuba secretly in February 1519.

## The Yucatán Peninsula

Ruthless, fearless, and ambitious, Cortés combined skillful diplomacy with brute force and superior armaments. Cortés was also a devout Catholic who would justify his invasion by converting the Indians to Christianity. Bolstering his religious zeal was the Spaniards' shocking discovery that the Aztecs held mass human sacrifices as part of their religious ceremonies. Yet he was also motivated by the promise of wealth and power. "His adventures would make him wealthy, the dream of every conquistador. To obtain gold was the goal," wrote "Ramón Eduardo Ruiz in *Triumphs and Tragedy: A History of the Mexican People.*

Cortés's 11 ships stocked with supplies, horses, small cannon, and some 600 soldiers, landed first on the island of Cozumel, where the Spaniards met little resistance from the Indians. In March, Cortés sailed to the mouth of the Tabasco river, where he was met by unfriendly Tabascan Indians. The Spaniards and Indians fought, but Cortés won their loyalty by promising to free them from Aztec rule. Marina, or Malinche, an Indian slave, given to Cortés by the Tabascans, would become important to the conquest. She translated for Cortés and became his mistress. Marina later gave birth to Cortés's son, Martín, one of the first mestizos, those of mixed Indian and Spanish blood who would populate modern Mexico.

The Aztecs built great cities, a highly organized military and government, and a successful economy, dependent on taxes from the subjugated Indian tribes. Other Indians paid tribute to the Aztecs in corn, chili, copper, gold, jade and turquoise, and quetzal feathers. The Aztec princes lived like royalty, served by slaves, while some of the Indian tribes grew rebellious. Since 1502, the Aztec Empire had been ruled by a powerful monarch, Moctezuma II, or **Montezuma**, who lived in Tenochtitlán, now Mexico City, 210 miles from the coast. Some Indians, including perhaps Moctezuma, believed Cortés was Quetzalcóatl, the great Aztec god, and, initially, looked upon the Spaniards as their saviours. On Good Friday, April 21, 1519, Moctezuma's ambassadors arrived on the coast to meet the Spaniards, bearing gifts of "shields, helmets, leather back and breast armor, embossed plates and ornaments of pure gold," wrote Beatrice Berler in *The Conquest of Mexico: A Modern Rendering of 'William H. Prescott's'' History.* Cortés presented the Aztecs with shirts, beads, and an armchair for Moctezuma. The Spaniards displayed their weapons and held a Catholic service on the beach.

They soon learned that Moctezuma forbade them to journey to Tenochtitlan, requesting instead that they return home. In fact, Cortés did not have permission from Spain to conquer the Aztecs, only to explore the coast. Even so, he decided to stake a claim in Mexico. He founded a town near where the Spanish had camped, calling it Villa Rica de la Vera Cruz ("The Rich Town of the True Cross"), the modern Veracruz. In doing so, he defied Velázquez. Cortés wrote a letter to Charles V explaining what he had done. When Velázquez heard of his action, he was furious and sent an army under Pánfilo de Narváez to Mexico to capture Cortés.

## Fall of the Aztec Empire

By the time Narváez arrived in Mexico, Cortés, with 400 soldiers and several hundred Indian warriors, had begun his famous march through the mountains of Mexico to find Moctezuma. "That journey of 83 days and more than 400 miles, a landmark feat of perseverance and arms, opened the way to a cultural amalgamation that produced modern Mexico, part Indian, part Hispanic," reported S. Jeffrey K. Wilkerson in *National Geographic*. Cortés chose a route that would allow him to enlist the help of thousands of rebellious Indians. They soon reached Tlaxcala, inhabited by fierce warriors who despised the Aztecs. The Tlaxcalans joined the Spaniards and became their strongest allies, providing them with men and supplies. In Cholula, a major commercial center, Cortés at first found friends, but soon discovered a plot, instigated by Moctezuma, to ambush the Spaniards. Cortés ordered his soldiers to make an example of the Cholulans. Cortés claimed to have slaughtered 3,000 Indians before continuing the march.

On November 8, 1519, Cortés entered Tenochtitlán leading 7,000 troops. Moctezuma greeted them and appearing friendly, he invited Cortés to stay in a palace. When Cortés heard two Spaniards had been killed by Indians in Veracruz, he took Moctezuma prisoner. The Aztec emperor voluntarily walked to the Spaniards' palace, surrendering his rule to Cortés. For six months, Cortés governed Tenochtitlán.

When Cortés learned that Narváez had landed in Veracruz, he left for the coast, determined to defend his authority. A battle took place and Cortés took Narváez prisoner, then enlisted nearly all of his men. While he was away, the Aztecs attacked the Spanish in Tenochtitlán, resulting in a bloodbath on both sides. Realizing his men were in trouble, Cortés asked Moctezuma to allow the Spaniards to leave the city, but the Aztec king was unexpectedly killed. He "requested to be taken out on to the flat roof of the fortress, where he would speak to the leaders of the people and make them stop fighting . . . a stone from one of their slings struck him on the head so severely that he died three days later," wrote Cortés in his *Five Letters,* a chronicle of his life from 1519 to 1526.

On June 30, 1520, the famous Noche Triste, the Spaniards tried to flee. In the ensuing battle, nearly 900 Spaniards and over 1,200 Tlaxcalans were killed, and much of their gold, silver, horses, and weapons were lost. "When it was all over, legend has it, Cortés sat under a huge cypress and wept," wrote Ruiz in *Triumphs and Tragedy*. But his luck quickly changed. Assisted by Spanish troops from Cuba, Haiti, and Jamaica, Cortés gained territory across Mexico and, finally, won Tenochtitlán—then ruled by Moctezuma's successor Cuauhtemoc—in the summer of 1521. "Yet the Aztecs never surrendered; to occupy their city, Cortés had to ravage it. No temple, palace, or idol survived," wrote Ruiz.

On the ruins of Tenochtitlán, Cortés built the new city, Mexico. Cortés established a colonial government and sought to extend his territory. The Spanish took over Michoacán, west of Tenochtitlán, and arrived at the Pacific, where they began building ships. On October 15, 1522, Charles V appointed Cortés governor and captain-general of New Spain, ending the power struggle between Cortés and Velázquez.

## Honduras Expedition

Once he was securely in power, Cortés sought to expand New Spain. He sent Pedro de Alvarado south to conquer Guatemala, inhabited by the Mayans. Cristóbal de Olid, one of Cortés's best soldiers, was sent to Honduras, also a Mayan region. But in 1524, Olid, influenced by Velázquez, declared his independence from Cortés.

Determined to regain his authority, Cortés set out for Honduras with a force of soldiers, including the Aztec ruler, Cuauhtemoc, who was brutally killed by the Spaniards during journey. For two years, he travelled through jungles and swamps, many of his soldiers dying from diseases and Cortés himself suffering a head wound. When he arrived at the Spanish settlement, he discovered his officer Francisco de las Casas had already arrived to hang Olid. By the time he returned to Mexico City in May 1526, the Spaniards were quarreling and reporting back to Spain their dissatisfaction with Cortés. Cortés decided to return to Spain and defend himself to Charles V.

## Returned to Spain

Cortés made a triumphant return to Spain in 1528. He brought Indians, exotic animals such as albatrosses and armadillos, Indian handicrafts, and 20,000 pesos of fine gold. Cortés wore a pouch with five emeralds, which he gave to his new wife Juana de Zúñiga, an aristocrat whom he married in Spain after the death of Catalina in Mexico. At the Imperial Court in Toledo, Charles V bestowed many honors on Cortés, making him captain-general of New Spain and Marquis of the Valley of Oaxaca. He did not, however, restore Cortés to governor of New Spain, foreshadowing Cortés gradual loss of power in Mexico.

In 1535, Charles V made Mexico a kingdom of Spain and appointed a viceroy, Don Antonio de Mendoza, who outranked Cortés, placing New Spain under Madrid's control. Realizing he was no longer preeminent, Cortés turned to further exploration, hoping to gain new land and treasures. He tried unsuccessfully to find a strait linking the Pacific with the Gulf of Mexico. In May 1535, Cortés landed in La

Paz, Baja, California, calling it Santa Cruz and claiming it for Spain. With little left to challenge him in New Spain, Cortés returned to Spain in 1540 with his sons Martín and Luis. In 1541, he joined a Spanish expedition against the Algiers pirates, but was injured in a shipwreck, losing the five Mexican emeralds. Cortés fell ill with stomach problems and died at Castilleja de la Cuesta on December 2, 1547, at the age of 63. He asked to be buried in Mexico. His remains are now in Mexico City at the Hospital de Jesús, founded by Cortés in 1524.

Cortés changed the course of Mexican history, yet his achievements were tarnished by the Spaniards' wholesale destruction of Indian lives and culture. "Their success, which laid the foundations of colonial Mexico, cost the native dearly. Yet out of the exploitation of Indians by Spaniards, there emerged a new people, the Mexicans, and with them a distinct way of life," wrote Ruíz. Modern Mexico looks back at the great conquistador with mixed emotions. "By the time Mexico threw off Spanish rule, three centuries after the conquest, there was widespread hatred of Cortés and a thirst for vengeance," according to William Weber Johnson. The Mexican artist **Diego Rivera** painted two unflattering portraits of Cortés in his 1951 "Colonial Domination" mural on the National Palace in Mexico City. Johnson wrote, "Cortés's fame swung ... between grandeur and humiliation in his lifetime. More than four centuries after his death the pendulum continues to swing."

## SOURCES:

### Books

Berler, Beatrice, *The Conquest of Mexico: A Modern Rendering of William H. Prescott's History,* San Antonio, Texas, Corona, 1988.

Castillo, Bernal Díaz del, *The Discovery and Conquest of Mexico,* New York, Farrar, Straus and Cudahy, 1956.

Cortés, Hernando, *Hernando Cortés: Five Letters,* translated by J. Bayard Morris, New York, W. W. Norton, 1991.

Gómera, López de, *Cortés: The Life of the Conquerer by His Secretary Francisco López de Gómera,* translated and edited by Lesley Byrd Simpson, Berkeley, University of California Press, 1964.

Johnson, William Weber, *Cortés: Conquering the New World,* New York, Paragon House Publishers, 1975, 1987.

Kanellos, Nicolás, *The Hispanic Almanac: From Columbus to Corporate America,* Detroit, Gale Research, 1994.

Marks, Richard Lee, *Cortés: The Great Adventurer and The Fate of Aztec Mexico,* New York, Alfred A. Knopf, 1993.

Ruiz, Ramón Eduardo, *Triumphs and Tragedy: A History of the Mexican People,* New York, W. Norton & Company, 1992.

### Periodicals

*National Geographic,* October 1984, pp. 420–59.

—*Sketch by Ann Malaspina*

# Ramon C. Cortines
## 1932-
### Hispanic American educator

During a time of great economic and social difficulties for the nation's educational system, Ramon C. Cortines distinguished himself as an individual who could tackle seemingly insurmountable problems of bankruptcy, substandard curricula, and high dropout rates. He was offered public offices more than once, and eventually took a position with the Clinton administration before accepting a chancellorship in New York, a city plagued with financial and political difficulties.

Cortines was born in Texas on July 22, 1932. While little is widely known about his parents, his father was reportedly a master chef who cultivated his son's taste in fine food. Higher education began for Cortines after a stint in the U.S. Army. His first responsibilities were military related, as a recruit trainer. Cortines earned a B.A. from Pasadena College in 1956. Masters degrees were awarded to him from the same institution, in school administration (1964) and adult learning (1966).

For two years, Cortines was the director of student activities at South Hills High School in Covina, California. In 1972 he secured his first superintendent position in Pasadena. This was a difficult time, since shortly after Cortines's promotion, a court order was issued to desegregate the local school system. The local school board was intent on fighting the order, and the lack of cooperation offered by Cortines cost him his job in 1978. City elections brought Cortines back into Pasadena local politics the next year, when Cortines was duly returned to his superintendency, which he sustained until 1984.

That year the San Jose school district was declared bankrupt. Within two years, Cortines negoti-

*Ramon C. Cortines*

ated settlements that revived the embattled system. His impressive performance led to an appointment in a comparable San Francisco post. As superintendent there, he established a fundraising record of $5 million each year. Cortines attracted corporate sponsors by involving them directly in the experiences of the school system. His "Adopt a School" program invited them to play "principal for a day" and solicited thank-you notes from the schoolchildren themselves. The more than 100 schools in his district began to develop positive trends in many areas. The dropout rate was nearly cut in half, according to the *Christian Science Monitor.* Absenteeism and suspensions were also reduced. Cortines also displayed his commitment to a solid curricular base with innovative second-language acquisition programs, and by instituting Saturday programs and college preparatory classwork.

### Presidential Material

In 1992 Cortines became a member of U.S. president Clinton's transition team. Cortines played a role in the interagency and intergovernmental task force that year. During 1993 he held an assistant secretary position within the U.S. Department of Education. Cortines rose to the challenge when offered the position of chancellor of the board of education of the City of New York. From the time he was instated, Cortines faced controversies over appointments, budgeting, multicultural curriculum planning, educational standards, and a host of other difficulties faced by many school systems. He expressed an intent to decentralize the system and increase parent and student involvement with methods he first tried in California.

During his chancellorship, Cortines has tried to be moderate on such issues as the promotion of alternative lifestyles and sex education. His approach to decentralization endorses a slow transfer of responsibilities to local school districts in the boroughs of New York City, while keeping certain functions under direct control of the city in order to maintain accountability. He has not expressed approval of experimental teaching methods, but instead champions the "Three Rs," or "readin', writin', and arithmetic."

Cortines's management style is personal, which he has maintained by remaining in direct contact with employees and parents and by dropping in on schools unannounced to check up on developments. In an interview with Mary Harbaugh in *Instructor's 3Rs,* "To make change stick, you've got to involve people who are going to do the changing. It's that simple." He has admitted more than once to being short-tempered, but attributes it to a high level of commitment that he expects others to match at all times. he otherwise workaholic chancellor enjoys running in his spare time, and has no wife or children.

### SELECTED PUBLISHED WORKS:

"Superintendents: Don't Dread Technology," *Electronic Learning,* November-December 1991, pp. 6–7.
"The Chancellor's Response," *New York Times,* August 22, 1994, p. A12.

### SOURCES:

*Christian Science Monitor,* June 17, 1991, p. 12.
*Hispanic Business,* February 1994, p. 18.
*Instructor's 3Rs,* Fall 1987 special issue, pp. 38–39.
*New York Times,* September 5, 1993, p. 14.
*Washington Post,* December 11, 1992, p. A25.

—*Sketch by Jennifer Kramer*

# Martha P. Cotera
## 1938-
**Mexican American civil rights activist, historian, and educator**

Though the media labeled her a radical during the famous Crystal City walk-out in December of 1969, Martha Cotera knew she was partaking in the most American of democratic experiments. Cotera remembers those days as "great fun." She and her husband, architect Juan Estanislao Cotera, helped to orchestrate what amounted to a massive walk-out by students protesting their exclusion by an Anglo minority that governed Crystal City, which is located near San Antonio, Texas. Cotera, 54, says the town was 95 percent Mexican American at the time. The walk-out began with a group of school cheerleaders who had been denied access to academic courses and extracurricular activities. "It was part of a history of walk-outs that happened in relation to the civil rights movement in the 1960s." Cotera noted in an interview with Julia Edgar. "My husband and I helped to sign up tutors to do a teach-in, and we went ourselves. It was the beginning of inclusion of Mexican Americans in Texas politics. It was to show people it was possible to take control of their lives at a local level." Crystal City, still a farming community, now has a Chicana school superintendent and Hispanics in high-ranking governmental posts.

Cotera was born January 17, 1938, in Nuevo Casa Grande, Chihuahua, Mexico. In 1946, she immigrated to the United States with her mother, Altagracias Castanos, and settled in El Paso, Texas. Her sister, Velia Luna, still resides there. Cotera earned a bachelor of arts degree in English, with a minor in history, at Texas Western College (now the University of Texas at El Paso) and a master's degree in education at Antioch College in Yellow Springs, Ohio. She has also begun graduate work in history at the University of Texas in Austin.

In the late 1950s, Cotera worked as a librarian in El Paso and Austin. In 1964, she became director of documents and information at the Texas State Library in Austin, a position she held until she became director of the Southwest Educational Development Laboratory in 1968. In 1970, Cotera and her husband went to Mercedes, Texas, with the Antioch College Graduate School of Education to help found Jacinto Trevino College, which eventually split off to become Juarez-Lincoln University. The purpose of the college, which is now defunct, was to prepare teachers for bilingual education programs. Cotera and her husband were faculty members until 1975. In 1974, one year after she helped found the Texas Women's Political Caucus, Cotera founded the non-profit Chicana Research and Learning Center in Austin.

### Founds Chicana Research and Learning Center

The Center, of which she serves as executive director and education coordinator, is an umbrella organization that assists in funding projects and obtaining grants for them, particularly for minority women. The Center is also an information and research center. Cotera's 28-year-old daughter Maria Eugenia, for example, received assistance for a documentary film project she and other students made about Raza Unida and the Crystal City walkout.

Out of the turbulence of the walk-out and ensuing events was born Raza Unida, a "third political party" which fielded Mexican American candidates for nearly a decade, drawing its strength from Latinos who felt discriminated against because of their heritage. Cotera herself ran for a seat on the state board of education in the Winter Garden area of Texas in 1972, and the party fielded candidates for governor and lieutenant governor of Texas. Raza Unida has remained a grassroots organization, dedicated to politicizing Hispanics and improving Hispanic-Anglo relations in Texas. Members have worked to diversify local law enforcement in Austin, whose police department is now headed by a woman. Raza also sponsors voting drives at low-income housing projects and has been instrumental in building a Mexican American cultural center in Austin for dance, art and drama.

While she lived in Crystal City, Cotera headed the Crystal City Memorial Library and her husband served as urban renewal director of the town. She published the *Educator's Guide to Chicano Resources* as a board member of the Committee for Rural Democracy. Crystal City gave Cotera and her husband, whom she married in 1963, a taste of the power imbalance they were about to experience first-hand. Her radicalization began when they moved to Austin, the capital of Texas. "We, like a lot of Hispanics, are aware of a lot of discrimination. We experienced that when we came to Austin. That radicalized us. There was a lot of police brutality, and we were very concerned because we were starting a family. We just felt that if you wanted things to be good, you had to work for it," she said during her interview.

Cotera is a writer as well. She has written extensively on the role of women in Hispanic culture, publishing *Chicanas in Politics and Public Life* in 1975 and *Dona Doormat No Esta Aqui: An Assertiveness and Communications Skills Manual for Hispanic Women* in 1984. She has contributed essays addressing the problems of Hispanic women to various books and professional journals, including *The Women Say/The Men Say: Women's Liberation and Men's Consciousness, El Caracol,* and *Twice a Minority:*

*Mexican American Women.* Cotera's writings are directed to middle-class and educated Hispanic women, because they are less likely, ironically, to immerse themselves in community or grassroots politics. "What I wanted to do with Hispanic women was to have them feel comfortable with their position as leaders and activists in the Hispanic community and the mainstream community, for them not to believe and accept the stereotypes of Hispanic women as passive women," she explained. "The grassroots women have no hang-ups. The college-educated women bought into the stereotypes."

Cotera believes that women who are politically aware generally are feminists, but she has drawn a distinction between Anglo and minority feminists, sometimes to the chagrin of other women who would like to present an image of unity to the world. Today, she says, Latina feminists have less contact with Anglo feminists than in the 1970s, partly because the emphasis of the contemporary women's movement is rights, not liberation. Also, as Cotera stressed in her interview, there is a strain of racism among white women who would prefer to consider minority counterparts as "clients." "They don't need us at all. . . . It's not the women at fault as much as our educational system, which has never educated people about diversity and never educated people to accept diversity. These people have grown up with blinders on, so it's hard for them to see us as real people and contributing people and strong people."

Cotera's writings on education include the *Handbook on Educational Strategies and Resources for Sex-Cultural Relevant Classroom Practices and Materials,* published by the United States Department of Health, Education and Welfare, Women's Educational Equity Program, in 1980, and the *Parent Education Training Program* for the Texas Association of School Boards in 1989. With her training and background in research and resource development, Cotera began working as a special staff consultant in 1975 with the Benson Latin American Collection at the University of Texas, an important archives of Mexican American historical material. In that role, Cotera helps build the collection, traveling to places rich in Mexican American lore and "snooping around," as she explained in her interview. "We run across things all the time: civil rights material, turn of the century material. We discovered a collection on bilingual education and Cuban culture in Key West. A lot of our focus is in Texas. Texas has a long history of archival material, because the first Spanish exploration was in the 1560s, 30 years or so before Roanoke. That's our first Hispanic entrance to the United States."

### Opens Publishing Company

Cotera's daughter, a graduate student at the University of Texas, shares her love of history. The two are busy compiling an encyclopedia on outstanding Hispanic women from pre-Columbian times. They now have compiled over 1,000 entries on women from Mexico, South America, and Spain. When it is finished, they will call it *Mujeres Celebre.* Cotera, who also has a 20-year-old son, Juan Javier, started a company called Information Systems Development in 1975 that publishes, among other things, the *Austin Hispanic Directory.* The bilingual guide includes local civic, individual, and business information. The company, she noted, "is as successful as I want to make it. We gross about $150,000 [annually], but it's a real fun company. I do what I like to do, which is to publish the *Austin Hispanic Directory* and other minority and women data bases. I publish things nobody else wants to publish." ISD, which has been featured on the cover of *Texas Business* magazine, also published the *Publisher's List for Adult Chicano Materials, Chicana Feminist: Essays,* and *Diosa y Hembra: History and Heritage of the Chicana in the United States.*

In 1980, Cotera co-founded the Mexican American Business and Professional Women in Austin, again to politicize women and help young Latinas get the help they needed. "We just wanted to get in and see the mayor, so we gave ourselves a real establishment name," Cotera joked. The MABPWA began a district-wide Stay in School campaign in 1981 in which members acted as mentors to junior high school students in eight public schools.

Cotera, who also teaches American history at Austin Community College, is a member of several professional and political organizations. For the past 25 years, she has conducted workshops and training sessions on subjects ranging from sexual equality to information access for low-income populations, for various community and national groups. She was named Outstanding Woman of Austin in 1975 by the *Austin American Statesman* and Outstanding Citizen of Mexican American Descent in 1975 by the International Good Neighbor Council. Cotera is also an honorary member of the Alpha Theta Phi and Sigma Delta Phi fraternities.

Cotera and her husband, although busy, are still politically active in their community, working on voter registration drives and campaigning for or against local bond issues. "Both my husband and I are very much interested in the democratic process, in the sense that there are a lot of positive things about the U.S. political process," she concluded in her interview. "We're very interested in making it work and getting people involved in it, as long as people are willing to participate."

### SOURCES:

Cotera, Martha P., telephone interview with Julia Edgar, September 26, 1992.

*—Sketch by Julia Edgar*

# Alfredo Cristiani
## 1947-
### Salvadoran statesman

Alfredo Cristiani was the first freely elected president to replace another freely elected president in El Salvador's history. Cristiani tried to negotiate with leftist rebels in effort to an end the long civil war in El Salvador. Cristiani succeeded in arranging a cease-fire in 1992.

Alfredo "Freddy" Cristiani was born November 22, 1947, in San Salvador, El Salvador. His family was wealthy and controlled coffee, pharmaceutical, and cotton businesses. Cristiani attended the American School in San Salvador. He traveled to Washington, D.C., for his college education, receiving a degree in business administration from Georgetown University in 1968. After college, he married Margarita Llach, a member of one of the 14 families who once ruled El Salvador.

His resume as a presidential candidate was eclectic because as a younger man, he had interests other than politics. He was the leader of a motorcycle gang called the Bad Guys, with whom he won a national motocross title. He also won a national squash championship and played on a Salvadoran basketball team.

By 1980, he headed up the Coffee Producer's Association. During an incident in which Cristiani and several other businessmen were held hostage for two weeks at the Ministry of Economics building, Cristiani discovered a proclivity for leadership. He negotiated the release of the hostages.

Cristiani joined the Nationalist Republican Alliance (Arena) in 1984. Arena was a paramilitary group founded by Roberto d'Aubuisson and was believed to be responsible for sometimes lethal attacks on leftist Salvadorans. Because of these links to "death squads," d'Aubuisson stepped aside as Arena's leader, appointing Cristiani as his replacement in 1984. Though Cristiani worked to moderate Arena's "death squad" reputation and attracted many young, middle-class business people to the organization, he was criticized as a front for d'Aubuisson and his changes as merely cosmetic.

### Won Election

Cristiani rose to greater political fame in 1988 when Arena scored a decisive victory over then-President **José Duarte**'s Christian Democrats and won a majority in the legislature. Cristiani won a seat in the legislature and was soon positioned by his party as a presidential candidate running against the Christian Democrat Fidel Chávez Mena. Cristiani purposefully distanced himself from his party's affiliations with death squads and promised the Salvadoran people moderate solutions to the nation's problems. Promising solutions to land reform and other issues, Cristiani counteracted the opposition's comparison of Arena to Nazi Germany and Cristiani as an "El Salvadoran Hitler." Many worried that Cristiani was still simply a front man for d'Aubuisson and the extreme rightist death squads. Cristiani maintained that d'Aubuisson's death-squad reputation was unfounded, but also stated that d'Aubuisson would have no post in his cabinet if he were elected. Despite an Farabundo Marti National Liberation Front (FMLN) boycott of the election and election-day violence, Cristiani won by 54 percent.

In his inaugural address Cristiani promised to work for peace, which he did. By August 1989, he joined four other Central American leaders in signing an agreement for his government to work for peace with the FMLN resistance. But the peace initiative was short-lived and in November, the FMLN launched a major assault on the capital. In response, Cristiani imposed a curfew, suspended civil liberties, and strengthened the police force. Then Cristiani launched his own assault on the FMLN, ordering government gunships and aircraft to bomb FMLN-controlled neighborhoods in San Salvador and rejecting FMLN pleas for Red Cross relief workers and supplies. Nine days later, Cristiani had retaken the capital. He had the support of other countries, including the United States, until six Jesuit priests, their cook, and the cook's daughter were shot and killed in what appeared to be a government-sponsored slaying. Cristiani denied any government role in the murders.

### Won Peace

Cristiani managed to win the peace he promised. His perseverance was tested in November 1991, when it seemed as if the FMLN had launched another offensive on the anniversary of the 1989 attack. Cristiani was ready to pull his government from peace talks, but he remained, and peace became a reality. A comprehensive agreement was designed on December 31, 1991; a cease-fire began on February 1, 1992. The FMLN violated the accord throughout 1992, but Cristiani persisted. Disarmament began and on December 15, 1992, the conflict officially ended after 13 years of fighting, 80,000 deaths, 550,000 homeless, and 500,000 refugees. Cristiani's term ended in 1994 and he was succeeded by former running mate Dr. Armando Calderon Sol.

## SOURCES:

### Books

*Current Biography Yearbook,* edited by Charles Moritz, New York, H. W. Wilson, 1990.

*International Who's Who,* 58th edition, London, Europa Publications, 1994.

*South America, Central America, and the Caribbean,* fifth edition, Kent, U.K., Europa Publications, 1995.

Whitfield, Teresa, *Paying the Price,* Philadelphia, Temple University Press, 1994.

### Periodicals

*New York Times,* March 12, 1989.

—*Sketch by Christopher B. Tower*

# Celia Cruz
## 1929(?)-
**Cuban singer**

Celia Cruz is the undisputed queen of salsa. After more than 40 years of performing professionally, she continues to intrigue Hispanics and non-Hispanics alike around the world with the rhythms of her Cuban homeland. A remarkable performer and person, she loves her fans as much as she loves her music. As she said in *Más,* "Music is what gave me the courage to fight and get out of poverty and touch the universe. . . . The only important thing is music." Celia Cruz has indeed brightened the world with her songs, and in doing so she has realized her dreams. She commented in the *New York Times,* "When people hear me sing, I want them to be happy, happy, happy. I don't want them thinking about when there's not any money, or when there's fighting at home. My message is always *felicidad*—happiness."

Celia Cruz will not divulge the year of her birth. The attempts of some biographers to uncover that date have failed, and they can only estimate that she was born around 1929. It is well known, however, that Cruz's birthday is October 21, and that she was born in Havana, Cuba, to Simon and Catalina (Alfonso) Cruz. Although Simon and Catalina Cruz had only four children of their own (Celia was the second eldest), 14 children, including nieces, nephews, and cousins, occupied the Cruz home in a poor part of Havana, the Santa Saurez *barrio,* or neighborhood.

As a young girl, Celia Cruz loved music. She was responsible for putting the children who lived in her home to sleep with lullabyes; the songs she sang not only kept the children awake, they lured neighbors to the house. It was apparent at that time that Celia was gifted with a beautiful voice. With her aunt, she listened to the radio and went to ballrooms. She made friends with Cuban musicians. Instead of aspiring to become a singer, however, Cruz prepared herself for a career as a teacher. "I wanted to be a mother, a teacher, and a housewife," Cruz recalled in the *New York Times.* Cruz's father encouraged her to become a teacher; he wanted the young woman to have a respectable job. Celia Cruz graduated from the República de Mexico public school in Havana, and went on to the Escuela Normal para Maestros.

Fortunately for salsa fans, Cruz never became a teacher of literature. Despite her father's wishes, she left school and did not return after her singing career began to take off in the late 1940s. Cruz was initially encouraged to become a professional singer while she was still in school, following her victory in a talent show called "La Hora de Té," which aired on the García Serra radio network in 1947. Cruz sang the tango "Nostalgia" in bolero tempo and, in addition to winning a cake, she became a local hit. She appeared in amateur shows and was soon sought after as a paid entertainer. One of her first jobs was to sing on the Radio Progreso Cubana for one week; she also sang on Radio Unión for some months. Cruz sang, at first, because she needed money to buy food and school books. Later, however, a teacher told her that she should forget teaching and concentrate on singing. Cruz remembered the teacher's words in the *New York Times:* "You're going to sing because you'll earn more money in a day than I will in a month."

At this point Cruz became serious about her musical career. Already noted for her pregón singing (a vocal style which evolved from the calls, chants, and cries of street vendors) and the songs "Manicero" and "El Pregón del Pescador," Cruz enrolled at the Conservatory of Music to study voice and theory. With her own good behavior, as well as her mother's help, Cruz persuaded her father once and for all that a career as a singer would not disgrace her or the family. As a student, she worked hard, and whenever she traveled to performances, a female relative accompanied her as a chaperone. After three years at the conservatory, Cruz was equipped with the skills necessary to succeed as a musician; her baggage also included the whole-hearted support of her family.

### Opens Career with Las Mulatas de Fuego

At first, Cruz sang with the dancing troupe Las Mulatas de Fuego, and kept the audience entertained while the dancers changed costumes. She also sang with the orchestra of Gloria Matancera. In 1949, she was hired to sing Yoruba songs at a radio station. Finally, in August of 1950, Cruz was chosen to replace Myrta Silva, the lead singer of La Sonora Matancera, Cuba's most popular orchestra. Although fans listening to Radio Progreso wrote angry letters about the replacement, they were soon won over to Cruz's style, and Cruz became a star. In early 1951, she began to release recordings such as "Cao Cao Mani Picao/Mata Siguaraya," "Yerboro," "Burundanga," and "Me Voy al Pinar del Rio."

For 15 years, or Cruz's golden era, as it is called, Cruz sang with La Sonora Matancera. Headliners at Havana's world-famous Tropicana nightclub and casino, the group became popular enough to work on television and in movies as well as on radio. The orchestra appeared in five movies (*Una Gallega en Habana, Olé Cuba, Rincón Criollo, Piel Canela,* and *Amorcito Corazón*) and toured the United States and Central and South America. La Sonora Matancera's fame and frequent tours served the individuals in the group well; when **Fidel Castro** took power after the 1959 revolution, they were able to escape Cuba by pretending that they were going on another tour, and they were welcomed abroad. From 1960 to late 1961, La Sonora Matancera entertained audiences in Mexico. Then, the orchestra packed up its act to enter the United States.

Although the singer would come to love the United States, Cruz could never forget her homeland. She continues to remember it in song, but she cannot return to Cuba. Castro, angered by the singer's defection, would not even allow her to visit the country when her mother was sick, or when her father died. If Celia Cruz continues to be unhappy about her expatriation, she seems to have accepted the situation, and Hispanics have certainly shown their appreciation of her work in the United States. "If I die now," the singer stated in the *New York Times* in 1985, "I want to be buried here."

As the *New York Times* remembered, Cruz's "early years in the United States were less than memorable; young Latinos were more interested in rock-and-roll than in music from the old country." Cruz had to work very hard to earn her fame in the United States. One good thing, however, did occur during those early years in America. On July 14, 1962, Cruz married Pedro Knight, the first trumpeter of La Sonora Matancera; she had known him for over 14 years. Knight has served as Cruz's protector, manager, and musical director ever since. He has helped her make important decisions and has provided enthusiastic support; he gave her the golden "Salsa" engraved earrings she still wears. In 1987, Louis Ramirez, an arranger of songs for Cruz, explained Knight's role in Cruz's professional life in the *New York Times.* "When discord arises on how best to sing or play a part, everyone turns to Pedro. Pedro presides quietly in a corner, with his arms crossed.

After he hears us argue back and forth, he says 'si' or 'no.'"

Although Cruz did not sell many records during the 1960s, her production was prolific. She signed with Seeco records, and recorded 20 albums of La Sonora Matancera songs in just one year. These albums included *Con Amor, La Reina del Ritmo Cubano, Grand Exitos de Celia Cruz, La Incomparable Celia, Mexico qué Grande Eres, Homenaje a los Santos, Sabor y Ritmo de Pueblos, Homenaje a Yemaya de Celia Cruz, Celia Cruz Interpreta El Yerbero y La Sopa en Botella, La Tierna, Conmovedora, Bamboleadora,* and her most popular Seeco album, *Canciónes Premiadas.* After signing with Tico Records in 1966, the woman who would later be crowned the "Queen of Salsa" recorded 13 more albums, toured South America and the United States, and, just as importantly, began to work with **Tito Puente,** a man who would come to be known as the "King of Latin Swing."

Puente recalled in the *New York Times,* "I was listening to the radio in Cuba the first time I heard Celia's voice. I couldn't believe the voice. It was so powerful and energetic. I swore it was a man, I'd never heard a woman sing like that." Cruz recorded eight of her 13 Tico albums with Puente, including *Cuba y Puerto Rico Son, El Quimbo Quimbunbia, Alma con Alma,* and *Algo Especial Para Recordar.* Cruz and Puente performed more than 500 times together before 1987, and countless times after.

### Interest in Salsa Grows among Young Hispanics

It was not until the early 1970s that Cruz, the woman whom the *New York Times* would call "salsa's most celebrated singer," began to be appreciated by young Hispanics. She was chosen to play the role of Gracia Divina in the opera *Hommy* at Carnegie Hall in early 1973. Her remarkable voice and boundless energy captured the audience, which was just beginning to enjoy the new music called "salsa." Just as Cruz is not a limited performer, salsa is not a limited music: the word salsa can be used variously to describe guaracha, rhumba, merengue, and guaguanco rhythms. As *Time* magazine put it, salsa "is a catchall term that became current in the early '70's. . . . Instrumentation features piano brass, percussion (like the congas or the timbales). . . . The rhythm is often complex and layered, but at root there is a steady beat." *Time* also noted that "real salsa, old-country music [is] preserved in the persons of Cruz and Puente."

Older fans who remembered their lives in Cuba were thrilled to hear the music of their youth as Celia Cruz sang to the salsa beat, and younger fans were genuinely enthusiastic about Cruz's fast-paced scatting. No one could help being impressed by Cruz's costume. She was and is a flamboyant dresser. Her usual costume involves feathers, sequins, or lace, and yards and yards of brightly colored fabric. Legend has it that Cruz never wears a costume twice, that each of her costumes costs more than the amount needed to produce one of her albums, and that some of her costumes have taken up a whole stage. Cruz herself acknowledges that some of her costumes prohibited other singers from comfortably moving around the stage. The exotic, outrageously flashy costumes Cruz wears reflect the energy she radiates as she performs.

Listening to her music is not enough; to experience Cruz, one must be able to watch her as she illuminates the stage and fascinates her audience. She loves to sing powerfully and with a great deal of volume, and because of this she usually sings to large audiences in structures that can withstand the amplification. Celia Cruz is always animated and completely engaged in her performances. As a reviewer for the *New York Times* wrote, Cruz "leaps, dances, flaunts, flirts, and teases to the gyrating beat of salsa." Although Cruz has her serious, passionate moments, she is never predictable; one never knows when she will break into improvisation or joke with the audience and the band. Seemingly tireless, the singer has been known to perform at her explosive pace for more than three hours.

After Cruz's contract with Tico Records expired, she took advantage of the opportunity to work with Johnny Pacheco, a long-time admirer of Cruz. Pacheco was a rumba band leader and a flutist of the charanga style. For Vaya Records, they revised Cruz's Sonora Matancera pieces to produce *Celia and Johnny,* which was released in 1974. This record, not surprisingly, went gold as Hispanics throughout the United States snatched it up. *Tremendo Cache* and *Recordando El Ayer,* Cruz's next collaborative albums, met with similar success, as did other albums she recorded on the Vaya label. Another album she recorded in 1974, with conga player **Ray Barretto**, won a Grammy Award.

Cruz's popularity among Hispanics began to grow. Fans throughout the world went wild when she performed. During the 1970s, she sang in concert with Johnny Pacheco in the United States, and with Tito Puente and members of the Fania All-Stars, throughout Africa and France. The *New York Daily News* named her the best female vocalist in 1977 and 1979, and *Billboard* did the same in 1978; in polls conducted by *Latin N.Y.,* the singer was similarly honored annually from 1975 to 1982.

In 1982, Cruz was reunited with La Sonora Matancera, and the group released exciting new songs on their album, *Feliz Encuentro.* Later that year, Cruz was the honored performer in a concert in Madison Square Garden. 20,000 people there, as well as television viewers throughout the world, watched and danced as she sang with those who had contributed to her career over the years: La Sonora Matancera, Tito Puente, Cheo Feliciano, Johnny Pacheco, Pete Rodríguez, and **Willie Colón**. Cruz was presented with a gold record (along with Ray Baretto and Adalberto Santiago) for their album, *Tremendo Trio,* by Fania Records in 1983.

## Remains a Busy Performer

During the latter half of the 1980s, Cruz was as busy as ever. She met the demands of salsa fans, recorded albums, and gave concerts. In 1985, she sang with various groups and lit up the stage with music based on Yoruba religious chants which once praised West African deities. In 1986, Cruz was given an Ellis Island Medal of Honor, also known as the Mayor's Liberty Award, by the National Ethnic Coalition of Organizations. In 1987, Vaya Records released Cruz's 53rd album, a collaboration with Willie Colón entitled *The Winners.* She performed in New York's Annual Salsa Festival at Madison Square Garden, and also won a fourth Grammy nomination, a New York Music Award for Best Latin Artist, and an Obie, or Off-Broadway award, that year.

Among her many notable concerts was a 1988 tribute to Frank Grillo, or Machito, a musician who was essential to the development of Afro-Cuban jazz, and who had worked with Cruz for years. According to the *New York Times,* Cruz's performance was as dazzling as usual. Her "voice, piercing and intense, ripped through the glittery band arrangements; as an improviser, Miss Cruz phrases as if she were a drummer." Cruz gave a concert in Harlem on October 21, 1989, along with the Cuban jazz star Mario Bauza (and Machito's brother-in-law), Tito Puente, Chico O'Farill, Marco Rizo, Max Roach, and Henry Threadgill. The *New York Times* reported, "Mr. Bauza's band played one of his modernist compositions and Miss Cruz, who was celebrating her birthday, sang a set of her tunes, shouting out phrases with the authority of a trumpeter; she's one of the world's great singers, and she proved it again." Cruz ended the decade by earning another Grammy Award. In the Latin category, she won the Best Tropical Performance for *Ritmo En El Corazon,* the album she recorded with Ray Barretto.

From Manhattan to Miami, salsa is a huge element of Hispanic youth culture. Popular singers such as **Gloria Estefan**, who says she was inspired by Cruz, base their songs on a salsa beat. Cruz explained the lure of salsa in *Time* magazine in 1988: "We've never had to attract these kids. They come by themselves. Rock is a strong influence on them, but they still want to know about their roots. The Cuban rhythms are so contagious that they end up making room for both kinds of music in their lives." According to *Time,* "young Cuban Americans have gathered to see the reigning Reina de la Salsa, Celia Cruz, who was entertaining their parents and their parents' parents in the smoky dens and fancy nightclubs of pre-Castro Cuba long before they were born." While Celia Cruz has changed with the times, some aspects of her performances have maintained themselves despite her age. She is still tireless, she continues to dress in fantastic gowns, and she will always enthrall those who see her.

Although Celia Cruz has been exciting audiences since the late 1940s with her inexhaustible energy and her unique voice and has recorded more than 70 albums, she refuses to retire or even slow down. Cruz, who is over 70 years of age, was quoted as saying in the *New York Times,* "I have no choice, really, but to put in as much time and energy as I do. I have a lot more to do." Cruz, however, does wonder what things will be like after she can no longer sing, and wishes that more women would sing salsa. "Someday, I have to die," she mused in the *New York Times.* "I want people to say, 'Celia Cruz has died, but here is someone who can take over.'"

*Sor Juana Inés de la Cruz*

## SOURCES:

*Boston Globe,* March 20, 1988, p. 48.
*Chicago Tribune,* October 2, 1988, Section 13, p. 14.
*Los Angeles Times,* June 17, 1991, p. 2F.
*Más* (Spanish-language; translated by Ronie-Richele Garcia-Johnson), November 1991, p. 77.
*New York Times,* November, 1985; August 30, 1987, Section 2, p. 14; July 1, 1988, p. 22C; July 4, 1988, p. 16A; October 29, 1989, Section 1, p. 62.
*Nuestro,* May 1980, p. 60.
*Rolling Stone,* September 21, 1989, p. 55.
*Time,* July 11, 1988, pp. 50–2.
*Variety,* November 27, 1985, p. 140; October 5, 1989, p. 69; November 5, 1990, p. 90.
*Vogue,* June 1984, p. 70.

—*Sketch by Ronie-Richele Garcia-Johnson*

# Sor Juana Inés de la Cruz
## 1651(?)-1695
### Mexican poet and nun

Described as witty, brilliant, an intellectual prodigy, and the "Tenth Muse," Sor Juana Inés de la Cruz was one of the greatest lyric poets and writers in colonial Mexico. Most sources agree she was born in a farm house on November 12, 1651, in San Miguel Nepantla, Mexico, to Pedro Manuel de Asbaje y Vargas Machuca and Isabel Ramírez de Santillana. As a result of Cruz's intellect, she quickly came to be regarded as a precocious child. She learned to read when she was three years old by obtaining instruction from her older sister's teacher. She also studied a wide variety of other subjects including astronomy, painting, and mathematics. When she was eight, she wrote a *loa,* or brief dramatic poem, in honor of the festival of the Blessed Sacrament. The talent she displayed in this early work was noted by those who read it.

At the age of nine, Cruz began to study Latin in Mexico City. She conquered that language in only 20 short lessons. At one point in her early life, she begged her parents to dress her as a boy so that she might study at the university. As a female in colonial Mexico, however, her only options were to enter the church or to marry, not to become a scholar.

Cruz eventually came to the attention of the Viceroy of Mexico. She spent three years at the palace of the Marqueses de Mancera in Mexico City as a mistress to the wife of the viceroy. Cruz was popular at court, where her intelligence impressed the Viceroy and his guests.

Apparently, Cruz decided to enter the Convent of the Carmelitos Descalzas at San Jose on July 14, 1667, at the age of 15. It was when she became a novice at this convent that she took the name Juana Inés de la Cruz. A few months later on November 18,

1667, she abandoned the convent to recover from an "illness and dejection," apparently the result of her difficulty in adjusting to the requirements of a religious life, according to Julio Leguizamón in *Historia de la Literatura Hispanoamericana*. A year later, the viceroy arranged to have Cruz examined by some 40 professors from the university in Mexico City. She was asked questions in a number of subjects including theology, scripture, philosophy, mathematics, history, poetry, and other humanities. The professors declared her to be a genius.

### Entered Convent

When Cruz resolved to forsake marriage, the only option that remained was to enter the convent and take religious vows. She entered the convent at San Jerónimo on February 24, 1669, so that she could devote her life to her studies. She spent most of the rest of her life studying the sciences, writing, and collecting a library of some 4,000 volumes. Jean Franco, though, commented in *A Literary History of Spain: Spanish American Literature Since Independence* that "her entry into the convent did not bring her complete tranquility. Throughout her life, the demands of an unquiet intellect led her to try and express her conflicts in every kind of writing," from poetry and drama to religious polemics and prose writings. While at the convent, Cruz often was visited by the viceroy or members of his court as well as by other members of the church or political leaders. Beatrice Gilman Proske remarked in *Spanish-American Literature in Translation* that "her cell in Mexico city became the center of the capital's intellectual life."

Cruz's poetry is most often recognized as her chief claim to fame. She wrote in a wide range of forms and subjects. While she penned many spiritual poems, she also wrote poems of love, humor, anger, and other emotions. Other works exhibit a feminist point of view. Cruz also did not hesitate to question her own beliefs or argue the qualities of reason and irrationality within the same piece. Often, the contradictions she examined involved the emotion of love. "Liras" was considered to be one of her most famous romantic poems. Among her other romantic works were "Romancero de la ausencia," "Rendondillas en que describe rationalmente los efectos irracionales del amor," and "Romance en que expresa los efectos del amor divino."

Critics of Cruz's work have suggested that she brushed the edges of the same style used by **Don Luis de Gongora**, a baroque Spanish poet. Baroque poetry or literature tends to be very complex and often uses bizarre, obscure meanings and expressions or exaggerated devices to express an intentional ambiguity. Regarded as one of Cruz's most ambitious poems, "El Sueño" ("The Dream"), also known as "Primero Sueño" ("First Dream"), was often described as an imitation of Gongora's style of writing. Franco commented that "she lacks the Spanish poet's sensuality and plasticity. Hers is an intellectual approach. In the poem's description of the soul enveloped in sleep, the poet is more concerned with sleep as a physical phenomenon than with the irrational dream world of which it is the threshold." However, Enrique Anderson-Imbert asserted in *Spanish-American Literature: A History* that the poem "best represents not only Sor Juana, but her entire epoch." The poem was also thought to be somewhat autobiographical and descriptive of Cruz's search for knowledge.

Cruz also used many references to other races of people in Mexico in her poetry. Anderson-Imbert wrote that "Sor Juana, with the open curiosity of the baroque, poetizes the Negro and uses him to give color and rhythm to her poetry." Cruz also excelled at writing sonnets; two of her better known examples of this poetic form are "Retrato" and "Detente sombra de mi bien esquivo."

### Collaborated to Write Plays

Although Cruz was best known for her poems, she also wrote a number of plays. Many of her *loas* actually were used to introduce plays, and at least one play was written jointly with her confessor, the priest Juan de Guevara. The second act of *Amor es más laberinto* (*Love is a Labyrinth*) was written by Guevara. She also wrote comedies such as *Los empeños de una casa* (*The Obligations of a Home*).

*Divino Narciso* (*Divine Narcissus*), which is perhaps her best-known play, was written by Cruz in about 1680 at the request of the wife of her former employer, the viceroy. In it, Cruz compared the religious beliefs of the native people with those of the Catholic church. Anderson-Imbert cited the play's "value as a spectacle, its lyrical songs, the rigor of its intellectual construction, the intertwining of Biblical and Greco-Latin themes, the originality in the handling of poetic ideas and intuitions, and the vigorous parallelism of Indian and Christian rites" as reasons why it should be regarded as "one of the better mysteries in all Castilian literature."

### Church Intervention

Cruz also wrote prose, mostly in the form of letters and critiques of the work of other writers. On one occasion representatives of the Catholic church, unhappy with her fame, rebuked her by criticizing one of these prose works. In 1690 she wrote a letter in which she commented on a sermon by Jesuit priest Antonio de Vieyra that discussed the difference in views held by St. Augustine and St. Thomas. The bishop of Puebla, who objected to the education of women, decided that the letter should be published under the heading of *Carta athenogórica* (*Athenagoric Letter*) with an introduction directed at Cruz. The introduction—titled *Filotea de la Cruz*—suggested that Cruz needed to do a better job of directing her efforts toward the study of religion.

Cruz responded to the reprimand with *Respuesta a Sor Filotea de la Cruz* (*Reply to Sor Filotea de la Cruz*) in 1691. This essay became one of her most famous and admired pieces of writing. Anderson-Imbert noted in *Spanish-American Literature: A History:* "Here she tells of her early desire for learning, her insatiable intellectual curiosity, the disadvantages of being a woman, her efforts to free herself of the impertinences, prejudices, incomprehension, and stupidities with which people trammel their betters." Cruz noted in her spirited defense of her scholarly interests that "since the first ray of reason struck me, the inclination to letters has been so vehement and powerful that neither the reprimands of others (of which I have had many) nor my own reflections (of which I have made not a few) have sufficed to dissuade me from following this natural impulse that God placed in me." She contended that she was powerless to leave this desire to learn, for even in the convent she "brought this addiction to study, my greatest enemy, that I cannot determine whether the Heavens gave me as a natural gift or as a punishment, for to extinguish or hinder it by the duties that Religion demands, would make me explode like gunpowder."

Despite her valiant argument to be allowed the right to continue her studies without interference from the Catholic church, she gave up her fight two years later in 1693 to devote herself exclusively to the religious duties prescribed by the church. She sold all her books and gave the money to the poor, then gave up all contact with the world outside the convent walls. She died on April 17, 1695, while caring for other sisters during an epidemic.

## SELECTED PUBLISHED WORKS:

*El Divino Narciso* (*Divine Narcissus*), 1680.
*Los empeños de una casa* (*The Obligations of a Home*), 1683.
*Amor es más laberinto* (*Love is a Labyrinth*), 1689.
*Inundación castálida,* 1689.
*Carta athenogórica* (*Athenagoric Letter*), 1690
*Respuesta a Sor Filotea de la Cruz* (*Reply to Sor Filotea de la Cruz*), 1691.
*Segundo volumen de las obras de Soror Juana Inés de la Cruz,* 1692.

## SOURCES:

### Books

Anderson-Imbert, Enrique, *Spanish-American Literature: A History,* Detroit, Wayne State University Press, 1969, pp. 85–105, 146–47.
Briggs, Donald C., and Marvin Alisky, *Historical Dictionary of Mexico,* Metuchen, New Jersey: Scarecrow Press, 1981.
Franco, Jean, *A Literary History of Spain: Spanish American Literature Since Independence,* London, Ernest Benn Limited, 1973, pp. 1–15.
Harss, Luis, and Barbara Dohmann, *Into the Mainstream: Conversations with Latin-American Writers,* New York, Harper and Row, 1967.
Leguizamón, Julio A., *Historia De La Literatura Hispanoamericana,* Buenos Aires, Editoriales Reunidas, 1945.
Martin, Michael Rheta, and Gabriel H. Lovett, *Encyclopedia of Latin-American History,* Indianapolis, Bobbs-Merrill, 1968, p. 110.
*An Outline History Of Spanish American Literature,* edited by E. Herman Hespelt, New York, F. S. Crofts, 1941, pp. 1–21.
*Spanish-Americrature in Translation,* Volume 1, edited by Willis Knapp Jones, New York, Ungar, 1966.

—*Sketch by Catherine A. Clay*

# Cuauhtemoc
## 1495-1525
### Aztec emperor

Also known as Cuatemo, Cuauhtemoc, the last emperor of the Aztec empire, was the principal leader of the opposition against **Hernan Cortes**, the Spanish conquistador who invaded and conquered Mexico in the early sixteenth century. A critic from the outset of Montezuma II 's policy of appeasement to the Spaniards, Cuauhtemoc was largely responsible for organizing the resistance to the Spaniards during Montezuma's imprisonment and, according to some accounts, he may have even been responsible for throwing the stone that led to the famous emperor's death. Elected emperor in 1520 following the death of his cousin, Cuitlahuac, Cuauhtemoc had the unenviable task of recruiting allies among tribes who were formerly under the Aztec umbrella, but who either feared Cortes or hated the Aztecs for their past tyrannical rule. Noted for his bravery in combat,

Cuauhtemoc repeatedly refused to surrender the capital city of Tenochtitlan—or what is now Mexico City—despite seemingly insurmountable odds. Instead, he led his exhausted and half-starved men in numerous counterattacks that prolonged the war. Despite his later support for Cortes and his assistance in pacifying outlying rebel tribes, Cuauhtemoc was imprisoned, tortured, and hanged by the Spaniards.

Cuauhtemoc was born in Tenochtitlan in 1495, the son of Ahuitzotl, the emperor who preceded Montezuma. As a member of the noble class, he attended the temple school, the *calmeac,* where he was subjected to its strict ascetic lifestyle, the regular drawing of his own blood as penance, and the deliberate hardening of the body against the cold. He also learned the songs of the gods and other religious texts, performed manual labor in the temple, and acquired knowledge of Aztec numerology and mythology. At about the age of 12, Cuauhtemoc attended the "house of young men," where he learned to become a warrior, gaining skill in the use of the obsidian-bladed Aztec war club. Some accounts have suggested that evidence of his courage was visible even during his adolescent years. Cora Walker, in her book *Cuatemo: The Last of the Aztec Emperors,* noted that when Cuauhtemoc was just 15 he scaled the fortified wall of the Lascalans, an enemy tribe, successfully gaining information of an imminent attack and gaining the favor of then-emperor Montezuma. Six years later, Cuauhtemoc was promoted to the equivalent of General in Command of the Army of Iztapalapan, in what is now the state of Guerrero.

### Perceived Cortes's Challenge

Following the arrival of Cortes and his fellow conquistadors in 1519, Cuauhtemoc—though still in his mid-twenties—had the wisdom to perceive the invasion's true objectives. Although Montezuma may have entertained the thought the Cortes was the reincarnation of the Aztec god Quetzalcoatl, the simpler, stronger, and less theological Cuauhtemoc, as historian Hugh Thomas has contended in his book *Conquest: Montezuma, Cortes, and the Fall of Old Mexico,* had little doubt that the Spaniards were anything other than modern day "political terrorists." Further Cuauhtemoc viewed Montezuma's deification of Cortes and his entourage as "an excuse for procrastination about what to do."

Having served for some time as military leader in Iztapalapa and in an administrative or political capacity in Tlatelolco, Cuauhtemoc began organizing an underground resistance to the Spaniards. As one who remained out of prison, Cuauhtemoc was most likely among the few who maintained communication with Montezuma after he was taken captive by Cortes in early 1520. Moreover, Cuauhtemoc is believed to have been one of the chief architects in the building of

a new Mexican army, a project that began as early as March of 1520—despite the fact that traditional war season had passed and the entire military chain of command had been disrupted by Montezuma's imprisonment. Cuauhtemoc is also credited with sending messengers to tributary monarchs to ask for military support in Tenochtitlan for the purpose of expelling the intruders.

The growing tension between the conquistadors and the Mexicans peaked in late April, near the Christian celebration of Easter, and during the Aztec festival held in honor of the god Huitzilopochtli at Toxcatl. In the midst of the ritual dances that were performed by some 400 men—dressed in feathered costumes and armed with war clubs and shields, and witnessed by several thousand Aztec citizens—Tonatiuh Alvarado led a group of Spaniards and their Indian allies in a surprise attack that resulted in the murder of most of the dancers and thousands of unarmed bystanders. From this point forward, Montezuma, forced by Alvarado to order the Aztec people to stop their counterattack, never recovered his authority as emperor.

News of the massacre quickly reached Cuauhtemoc in Iztapalapan, and after learning that his brother, Cuitlahuac—the army commander at the time—had been imprisoned, he immediately journeyed by canoe to Tenochtitlan to lead the resistance. In the midst of heavy fighting in late June, Montezuma—at Cortes's request went to the rooftop of his palace prison in an attempt to end the fighting. But before he could speak, he was hit by a stone that may have been thrown by Cuauhtemoc, who according to sources cited by Thomas, demanded, "What is that which is being said by that scoundrel of a Montezuma, whore of the Spaniards? Does he think that he can call to us, with his woman-like soul, to fight for the empire for which he has abandoned out of fright. . . . We do not want to obey him because already he is no longer our monarch, and, indeed, we must give him the punishment of a wicked man."

### Became Emperor

Upon the fallen emperor's death three days later, Cuitlahuac was elected emperor, but he soon died of smallpox. Cuauhtemoc was chosen by the council of electors to succeed him. Only in his mid-twenties, the young military leader had impressed his elders with his bravery and battlefield strategy. But no amount of courage or education could have prepared him for the battles he would face with the unconventional tactics of Cortes and his band. During the months that followed, the new emperor attempted to gain support from tribes that were formerly under Aztec rule, promising tribute remission to numerous old subject cities. But the resentment of the empire and the fear of Cortes remained strong. Nevertheless, that winter

Cuauhtemoc began stockpiling Tenochtitlan with warriors and weaponry in preparation for an offensive. But Cortes cut off supplies to the city by destroying canoes and occupying the causeways and launched an attack that made his final victory seem certain by the end of June of 1521. Two sons of Montezuma, in fact, led a group of nobles to begin negotiations with the Spaniards, but Cuauhtemoc apparently had them executed.

Under the direction of their courageous commander-in-chief, the Aztecs showed remarkable resilience. "Remember the bold hearts of the Mexica-Chichimeca, our ancestors, who, though few in number, dared to enter this land and to conquer it," exhorted Cuauhtemoc in a speech to his chief followers, quoted by Thomas. "O Mexica, do not be dismayed or be cowardly. On the contrary, strengthen your chests and your hearts." Although their obsidian-edged weapons and arrows were not originally designed to kill, but to wound a victim in prefsubtion for sacrifice, the Aztecs were able to slow the Spanish and allied advances throughout the first month of the siege. While there are no existing historical records mentioning Cuauhtemoc's direct participation in the fighting, he is believed to have played an important diplomatic role in gaining support for his army. For instance, he negotiated a deal with the ex-subject city of Tlatelolco, enlisting their military support in exchange for management of the empire. Despite the inevitable prospect of complete defeat, the Mexican refused to surrender, inducing Cortes to massacre thousands on his way to the new stronghold in Tlatelolco. Cortes sent one of his men to Cuauhtemoc to persuade him to capitulate; the emperor promptly sent the messenger to be sacrificed and ordered a counterattack. Everything in his military and religious training prevented him from submitting, but in August—after most of his men had stopped fighting—the emperor finally surrendered. At least 100,000 Aztecs had been killed, according to Thomas's estimates.

Although Cortes promised to treat the defeated Cuauhtemoc and his people with kindness—in spite of the emperor's own wish to be executed—the conquistadors, and especially their Indian allies, failed to adhere to their pledges. Despite offering 15,000 troops to Cortes to aid his attempts to pacify the outlying provinces, the defeated emperor remained in jail for four years and was reportedly tortured before he was eventually hanged in 1525, charged with involvement in a rebellion. According to the account of his first wife, Xuchimatzatzin (later named "Maria"), he left an infant son, known as "Diego de Mendoza Austria y Monteczuma," whom Cortes granted *encomienda*, taking over care of the child in 1527.

## SOURCES:

Thomas, Hugh, *Conquest: Montezuma, Cortes, and the Fall of Old Mexico,* New York, Simon & Schuster, 1993.
Walker, Cora, *Cuatemo: Last of the Aztec Emperors,* New York, Dayton, 1934.

—*Sketch by Jason Gallman*

# Xavier Cugat
## 1900-1990
### Spanish American musician, bandleader, and caricaturist

Xavier Cugat was a violinist and bandleader who became known as the "King of Rumba" during the American musical era of big bands and movie musicals. Born Francisco de Asis Cugat Mingall de Bur y Deulofeo on January 1, 1900, in Gerona, Spain, Cugat came to believe that his birth date was a good omen, for it coincided with the date that his father was released from prison. Cugat's father, Juan Cugat de Bur, believed strongly in democracy and often spoke out against King Alfonso III of Spain and various other government officials. When Cugat was four years old, his father was given an ultimatum to leave Spain or be executed for his treasonous speeches. As a result, he closed his electric supply shop in Gerona, packed up his family, and boarded a ship bound for Mexico. When the ship stopped in Havana, Cuba, the elder Cugat was offered a job installing modern light fixtures in a factory. He decided to settle his family in Cuba rather than continue on to Mexico. Cugat's mother ensured that the family stayed together under one roof. "My mother made home the most comforting place I could ever be," Cugat wrote in his autobiography, *Rumba is my Life.*

One year, in honor of the Fiesta de Reyes, the owner of a small guitar and violin store across the street from the Cugat home gave young Xavier Cugat a miniature violin. Within four months, the young Cugat was playing simple pieces for the customers of a local candy store. Impressed by his son's aptitude with the instrument, Cugat's father enrolled him in the Centro de Dependientes and later the Peyrellade School of Music. A child prodigy, by the age of seven Cugat often practiced nine hours a day. Cugat ended his formal education, except for lessons in basic skills taught by his mother and aunt, after the fifth grade.

*Xavier Cugat*

## A Professional At Age Nine

At the age of nine, Cugat got his first professional job playing the violin at the El Teatro Payret, a motion picture theater in Havana. He was 12 years old when he auditioned for the Teatro Nacional Symphonic Orchestra; he was immediately made the first chair violinist. One year later, he played with the Metropolitan Opera Company during their tour in Cuba. That event gave Cugat the opportunity to meet opera singer Enrico Caruso, who helped Cugat arrange for his first concert at Carnegie Hall in New York City at the age of 15. The critics, however, were not kind to the young violinist.

While in New York, Cugat studied with Henry Schradieck. He then went on to Berlin to study at the Conservatory of Music under Willy Hess. He spent a year there before beginning his first European tour. In 1925 Cugat returned to Carnegie Hall, but he was criticized by reviewers once more. He decided to play more popular music with Vincent Lopez's big band at the Casa Lopez. Within a year, Cugat moved to Los Angeles, where he played at the Los Angeles Philharmonic Auditorium. American critics remained unimpressed with Cugat's performance. Stung by his inability to sway his critics, Cugat left classical music forever.

As a child, one of Cugat's only activities outside of the realm of music had been his practice of drawing caricatures of people. When he decided to leave classical music, Cugat went to work as a caricaturist for the *Los Angeles Times*. While the job lasted for less than a year, it resulted in an encounter with Mexican-born Carmen Castillo, an actress, singer, and dancer. In 1929 she became his first of five wives. Cugat's career as a caricaturist proved to be a short one—and he always regarded his drawing as little more than a hobby—but by 1948 he had drawn some 35,000 caricatures. Many of these works were eventually hung in Grauman's Chinese Theater or the Waldorf-Astoria Hotel, or published in a number of national magazines.

Cugat left the *Los Angeles Times,* though, as he became involved in film. Actor/director Charlie Chaplin, who had heard Cugat play the violin at the Los Angeles Philharmonic, determined that the musician would be an ideal choice to play a spirited violin solo in a new comedy film with sound. The Chaplin film became the first of many films for Cugat. In 1928 Cugat invested $35,000 in a Spanish musical film, only to learn after filming had been completed that Latin American movie theaters were not equipped to handle sound. About the same time, Warner Brothers signed Cugat to do a musical short film called *Cugat and His Gigolos.* This was the first film in which the musician actually appeared.

## The King of Rumba

Cugat formed his own Latin American dance band in 1928. The group first played at Montmartre, then at Jack Dempsey's hotel in Ensenada, Mexico, before being hired as a relief band at the Coconut Grove in Los Angeles. In 1933 he and his band were offered the opportunity to open the new Starlight Roof room at the Waldorf-Astoria Hotel in New York City. Cugat's group remained the featured band at the hotel for the next 16 years. Cugat's salary at the Waldorf-Astoria at the beginning of his relationship with the hotel was $500 a week; by the end of his tenure there he was earning $7,000 a week.

The social whirl that accompanied Cugat's increasing success contributed to problems in his marriage, however. When his manager suggested replacing his wife as the lead vocalist for the band with Lina Romay, Castillo returned to California. Soon after his move back to New York, Cugat starred in a variety of radio programs. The first of these was *Dinner at the Waldorf.* That program was followed by *Let's Dance* in 1934 and 1935, the *RCA Magic Key* program in 1936, *Xavier Cugat's Rumba Review* in 1941 and 1942, and the *Camel Caravan* in 1942 to 1943. He spent winters touring the United States playing at a wide variety of popular hotels and lounges. He also did broadcasts from army and navy bases around the country.

In the early 1940s the American Society of Composers, Authors and Publishers became embroiled in a financial dispute with the radio networks about playing Society members' music on the air. As a result, the radio networks could only air music that was not controlled by the Society. Most Latin music was outside that group's domain, which allowed the radio networks to air the new sound. As a result, the rumba and other Latin music were brought into the mainstream and became the most popular music of that day. In 1945 Cugat and his od energy as I rchestra performed a concert at the Hollywood Bowl that broke all previous attendance records. He had to put on another show a few days later to satisfy all those fans who were unable to attend the first. A second concert in 1947 also sold out.

Along with directing the band, Cugat composed and recorded hundreds of songs for RCA and Victor Records. His more popular songs included "Chiquita Banana," "Rumba Rhapsody," "Kasmiri Love Song," "Rain in Spain," "Babalu," "My Shawl," "Rendezvous in Rio," "Brazil," "Walter Winchell Rumba," "Is It Taboo," and "I'll Never Love Again." Cugat, who said his quest in life was "for the three things all Spaniards desire . . . salud, dinero y amor ("health, wealth, and love")," said in his autobiography that he "would rather play 'Chiquita Banana' and have my swimming pool than play Bach and starve."

## Cugat's Film Career

While Cugat's musical efforts proved tremendously successful in the 1930s and 1940s, this success was due at least in part to his involvement in films. Cugat appeared in a number of short films, including *Luxury Liner* and *Let's Go Latin,* in the early 1930s. The latter film was actually more of a demonstration of how to perform the rumba. Cugat later boasted that it was this film that created the widespread interest in the Cuban dance.

After signing a contract with Metro-Goldwyn-Mayer in the early 1940s, Cugat appeared in several full-length feature films in which he always played himself. It was during the filming of *You Were Never Lovelier* in 1942 that star Fred Astaire first called Cugat by the name "Coogie." It was a name that was used often by Cugat's friends throughout the rest of his life. Critics contended that *You Were Never Lovelier* was a Hollywood effort to amuse South Americans. But Alfred Charles Richard, Jr., commented in *Censorship and Hollywood's Hispanic Image* that it was Cugat's orchestra rather than performances by non-Hispanic actors and actresses that did the most to "bridge the gap between the Americas." Other films featuring Cugat from this period included *Neptune's Daughter, Bathing Beauty, Weekend at the Waldorf, On an Island With You,* and *Holiday in Mexico.*

It was on the set of *Holiday in Mexico* that Cugat first saw Lorraine Allen, a Chicago-born actress who played a housemaid in the film. Cugat was so enamored with the young actress that he asked her to lunch at the commissary every day after that until the film was completed. He married her in 1948, but later divorced her to marry Brooklyn-born Abbe Lane, the singer who travelled with his orchestra during the 1950s. His fourth wife was Cuban Rita Montaner. Spanish guitarist and singer Charo Baeza, also known simply as Charo, was Cugat's fifth wife. He often appeared with Charo on television talk shows during the 1960s and 1970s.

Cugat's career frequently interfered with his personal relationships. The *Washington Post* noted that Cugat was somewhat philosophical about his marriages. "If I had it to do all over, I'd marry the same ones. We always divorced for our careers. You cannot play the violin in Philadelphia when your wife is in Rome making a movie with Marcello Mastroianni."

In addition to his film and music interests, Cugat invested in a number of businesses that also promoted his orchestra. Companies as diverse as Cugat's Nugats, which made a fruit and nut candy; Cugat's Tumblers, a producer of rum drinks; Cugat's Dream of Love, a perfume company; and Cugat's sunglasses all advertised Cugat's band. He also wrote several books about his life, including *I, Cugat, My Wives,* and *Rumba is my Life.* Cugat retired from show business in the late 1970s and returned to Spain. He died in Barcelona at the age of 90 on October 27, 1990.

## SOURCES:

### Books

Claghorn, Charles Eugene, *Biographical Dictionary of American Music,* West Nyack, NY: Parker Publishing, 1973.

Cugat, Xavier, *Rumba is my Life,* New York, Didier Publishers, 1948.

*Current Biography Yearbook 1991,* edited by Charles Moritz, New York, H.W. Wilson, 1991.

McNeil, Alex, *Total Television: A Comprehensive Guide to Programming From 1948 to the Present,* New York, Penguin Books, 1991.

Richard, Alfred Charles, Jr., *Censorship And Hollywood's Hispanic Image,* Westport, CT: Greenwood Press, 1993.

### Periodicals

*New York Times* October 28, 1990, Sec. 1, p. 38.

*Washington Post,* October 28, 1990, B7.

—*Sketch by Catherine A. Clay*

# Salvador Dalí
## 1904-1989
### Spanish artist, filmmaker, and writer

Famous for his paintings of hallucinatory, disturbingly incongruous dreamscapes, Salvador Dalí combined technical mastery with enormous imaginative power to create some of the most memorable images of the twentieth century. Dalí also produced drawings, prints, sculptures, ready-made pieces, jewelry, films, and a great deal of autobiographical writing, much of which, like his artwork, was calculated to shock and disturb—and to advance his name in the international art world. A master of self-advertisement and outrageous eccentricity, his clowning at gallery openings and art world functions kept his name in the press and his work in the public eye.

Dalí was born in Figueres (formerly Figueras) near Barcelona to Salvador Dalí y Cusi, a notary, and Felipa Domenech on May 11, 1904. From 1914 to 1918 Dalí studied at a Marxist school. Dalí later recalled his childhood as violently high-spirited and self—conscious, and he claimed it as an important source of ideas for his paintings. A precocious talent, Dalí began his art studies in Figueres, painting in Impressionist and Pointillist styles. However, by the time of his admission to the San Fernando Academy of Fine Arts in Madrid in 1921, Dalí had already moved on to a new aesthetic, taking on the "metaphysical" style of the Italian painter Giorgio de Chirico. It was in Madrid that Dalí met his future Surrealist collaborator **Luis Buñuel** and the poet **Federico García Lorca**, who were to become Dalí's closest friends.

In 1924 Dalí was suspended from the Academy on suspicion of inciting his fellow students to revolt. That same year he served a short prison term for his political activities. His subsequent return to the Academy was brief—in 1926 he was expelled permanently for refusing to take an examination. His excuse was that he already knew more than his examiners. He had already had his first one-man show in Barcelona, and his artistic reputation was growing. Generally associated with the artistic upheavals of Modernism, Dalí nonetheless rejected the work of such modernists as Cézanne and Matisse, looking back instead to Ernest Meissonier and the pre-Ra-

*Salvador Dalí*

phaelites as models and to the meticulous technique of academic art.

### Met the Surrealists and Gala

In the 1920s Paris was the world center for avant-garde art, and Dalí followed his compatriots **Pablo Picasso**, **Joan Miró**, and Luis Buñuel to the French capital. Over a period of just three days in 1928, Dalí and Buñel cowrote a film that would bring them immediate notoriety: *Un Chien Andalou* (1929). Designed to elicit strong reactions of distaste and shock thereby subverting the typical story-telling tendencies of cinema, it succeeded admirably— audiences were duly horrified. Dalí's future involvement with film was scant, but his penchant for causing public outcry at art events was thoroughly cultivated. Though he had little input on Buñuel's *L'Age d'Or* (1931), Dalí's name was included in the credits. Dalí profited from the film's negative publicity: the scandalous effect of *L'Age d'Or* eclipsed even that of *Un Chien Andalou*. The film's premiere was sabotaged by members of the Anti-Jewish League and the Patriotic League, who threw ink at the screen and destroyed the Surrealist paintings on display in the theater lobby. After additional protests the film was banned and all prints were seized.

In the same year Dalí began his association with the Surrealist group, led by André Breton and including Paul Eluard, Max Ernst, Buñuel, and Louis Aragon. His first Paris exhibition, at the Galérie Goemans in November of 1929 was a great success, marking his arrival in the Paris art world and the beginning of his life as a public figure. In the exhibition catalog the Surrealist leader Breton hailed Dalí as "a true menace." Through his association with Eluard and Breton, Dalí was introduced to a woman who would become the single greatest influence on his life: Gala. A Russian émigré, Gala was Eluard's wife and had been Breton's mistress, but she soon became Dalí's lover, and eventually, his wife, muse, banker, model, business manager, and keeper. Gala was Dalí's constant companion for the next 50 years.

In November of 1933 Dalí had his first one-man show at Julien Levy Gallery in New York City. The show included one of his most famous paintings, *The Persistence of Memory,* which depicts soft, drooping watches in a coastal landscape. In 1935 Julien Levy published Dalí's essay "The Conquest of the Irrational," an important exposition of Dalí's "paranoiac-critical method" that marked a fundamental stage in his artistic development. For Dalí, this "method," which he described in the essay as an "interpretative-critical association of delirious phenomena," sought to reveal truths about human experience by recognizing, laying bare, and depicting the unconscious conditions that underlie and determine conscious experience.

Dalí's reputation grew steadily, and Gala's influence on his fortunes increased; she secured the patronage and interest of a group of wealthy aristocrats and such high society figures as Coco Chanel, Elsa Schiaparelli and couturiere Jeanne Lanvin. In 1933, at Gala's behest, a group of 12 patrons, headed by Prince Faucigny-Lucinge, formed the Zodiac Group, each member undertaking to provide Dalí with one month's financial support in return for art work. This support, and Dalí's association with European aristocracy, continued until his exile to the United States. Although officially expelled from the Surrealist group in 1934, Dalí maintained contact with the Surrealists for another five years. So strong were the links between the painter and the movement that even Dalí's exile to the United States and his later support of Spain's notorious dictator **Francisco Franco** did little to weaken the public's association of Dalí with this group, whose earliest intention had been to join the Communist Party.

As his fame grew and his popularity began to rival that of Hollywood movie actors such as his friend Harpo Marx, Dalí began to incorporate exhibitionist acts into the art exhibition event. In 1935, at

the Museum of Modern Art, Dalí gave a sober and informative slide lecture on the Surrealists and discussed the automatist basis for his work. Explaining the dream-symbolism of his paintings, Dalí described himself as "the first to be surprised and often terrified by the extravagant images that I see appear with fatality on my canvas." In 1936 at the International Surrealist Exhibition in London, Dalí was less restrained and more memorable, appearing in a diving suit. Such behavior paid off, for in December of the same year he appeared on the cover of *Time* magazine.

## Exiled in the United States

The international character of Dalí's career was significantly influenced by political events in Europe. Dalí spent the years of the Spanish Civil War with Gala in Paris and London, his position initially ambivalent but increasingly opportunistic. He gradually shifted towards the Falangists as Franco's forces began to wrest control of the country. The Civil War destroyed the world of Dalí's youth; much of Figueres and Cadaqués were destroyed and scores of villagers and fishermen were killed. Dalí's college friend, poet Federico Garcia Lorca was executed by a Falangist firing squad, and Dalí's sister Ann Marie was imprisoned and tortured by the Spanish Republicans. Dalí focused on his work and stayed away from the struggle.

In March and April of 1939 Dalí had another show at Julien Levy Gallery, and he was invited to represent Spain at the New York World's Fair. Dalí's exhibit, which featured, as a reinvention of the mermaid, a woman with the head of a fish, caused an uproar. Dalí's response, published as "The Declaration of the Independence of the Imagination and the Rights of Man to His Own Madness" was an important statement of artistic intent from this period.

Dalí and Gala's return to Europe was brief; they arrived in Arcachon, France, shortly before the German invasion and soon—their passage paid with a loan from Pablo Picasso—they fled back to the United States via Portugal. Dalí remained in the United States for the next eight years, dividing his time between a studio in Pebble Beach, California, and the St. Regis Hotel in New York City.

In 1941 an important retrospective exhibition of Dalí's work, featuring 50 paintings, was held at the Museum of Modern Art. The exhibition, which traveled to eight more U.S. cities, helped consolidate Dalí's reputation in that country, even though an *Art Digest* reviewer inquired, "Is Dalí Crazy?" and compared his work to Ringling's circus acts. Such questions continued to mitigate Dalí's popularity, as his technical prowess and his inventiveness did battle with his capacity to appall. English novelist George Orwell—who had served as a private in the Spanish

Civil War on the Republican side—commented famously in 1944 that Dalí's paintings were "diseased and disgusting and any investigation ought to start out from that fact."

During his exile Dalí's creative and commercial interests continued expanding; he published his autobiography, *The Secret Life of Salvador Dalí* (1942), wrote the novel *Hidden Faces* (1944), executed a series of designs for a ballet and produced advertisements for *Vogue*. He collaborated with film director Alfred Hitchcock on the latter's *Spellbound* (1945), providing the designs for a dream sequence. A brief period of work with Walt Disney followed, but the production was canceled for commercial reasons.

Dalí and Gala returned to Spain in 1948, and settled at Port Lligat, where they rebuilt and extended their fisherman's cottage. There Dalí produced a series of large paintings with religious subjects, including *The Madonna of Port Lligat* (1950), *Christ of Saint John of the Cross* (1951), *Crucifixion (Corpus Hypercubus)* (1954), and *The Last Supper* (1955). Settled once more in Catalonia, Dalí maintained a high profile in the art world, delivering a lecture at the Sorbonne with the title "Phenomenological Aspects of the Paranoiac-Critical Method" (1955) and publishing the treatise *Dalí on Modern Art: The Cuckolds of Antiquated Modern Art* (1956). Dalí's relatively conservative religious paintings of this period coincided with a personal rapprochement with the Catholic church, resulting in an audience in 1955, with Pope Pius XII, to whom Dalí submitted *The Madonna of Port Lligat* for approval. In 1958, following the death of Gala's first husband Paul Eluard, Dalí and Gala were married in Girona in a Catholic ceremony.

### Influenced a New Generation

The 1960s brought Dalí a new generation of admirers. He received Spain's highest honor, the Grand Cross of Isabella the Catholic, but he also found himself—like the rock stars who cultivated his friendship—the celebrated symbol of eccentric nonconformity. As Dalí's old circle of aristocratic patrons passed away, they were replaced by a cottage industry of publications and reproductions overseen by Gala. Dalí's flamboyant style was taken up by television and the print media, and in the art world his commercialism and outrageous exhibitionist performances—the diving suit of 1936, a rhinoceros performance piece in the Paris zoo of 1955—were now seen as far ahead of their time. In 1965 an important retrospective was held at the Gallery of Modern Art in New York, featuring 370 works. Orwell's 1943 question arose again in *Art News* in December 1965. G. R. Swenson's article asked, "Is Dalí Disgusting?" This time, however, the answer was, yes, "admirably." While he continued to paint in the 1960s and 1970s, the importance of being Dalí began to eclipse the

canvases, and the autobiographical writings, *Diary of a Genius* (1965) and *Dalí by Dalí* (1970) took on even greater significance.

The recognition of Dalí's importance to twentieth-century art began taking on more concrete form in the 1970s as Dalí grew older and assessments of his work became increasingly monumental and officially sanctioned. In 1971, A. Reynolds Morse opened the Salvador Dalí Museum in Cleveland, Ohio, and Dalí's own museum, the Teatro Museo Dalí was inaugurated in Figueres in 1974. In 1979 Dalí was elected to France's Beaux Arts Academy, and the following year a major retrospective was held at the Centre Georges Pompidou in Paris.

When Gala died in 1982, Dalí was grief-stricken. After many years of Gala's fierce protection, he was suddenly alone, and he declined into depression. Dalí's final years were beset with periods of physical infirmity, exacerbated when he suffered severe burns in a fire at his home in Pujol in 1984. After this point he led a reclusive life in Figueres, appearing only occasionally to denounce the fraudulent sale of spurious Dalí lithographs or to campaign to make Barcelona the site of the 1992 Olympic Games. Dalí died of heart failure on January 23, 1989. He is buried in the Teatro Museo Salvador Dalí in Figueres.

### SELECTED PUBLISHED WORKS:

*The Secret Life of Salvador Dalí,* New York, Dial, 1942.
*Hidden Faces,* New York, Dial, 1944.
*Dalí on Modern Art: The Cuckolds of Antiquated Modern Art,* New York, Dial, 1957.
*Diary of a Genius,* New York, Doubleday, 1965.
*Dalí by Dalí,* New York, Harry N. Abrams, 1970.

### SOURCES:

#### Books

Ades, Dawn, *Dalí,* London, Thames and Hudson, 1982.
Descharnes, Robert, *Salvador Dalí,* New York, Harry N. Abrams, Inc., 1993.
Etherington-Smith, Meredith, *The Persistence of Memory,* New York, Random House, 1992.
Salvador Dalí Foundation, Inc., *Dalí,* Boston, Bullfinch Press, 1991.
Soby, James Thrall, *Salvador Dalí,* New York, Museum of Modern Art, 1968.

#### Periodicals

*Art Digest,* February 1, 1935, p. 10, August, 1939, p. 9, May 1, 1941, p. 3.

*Art in America,* March 1989, pp. 21–22, April 1989, p. 288, October 1991, pp. 57–59.

*Art News,* December 1965, pp. 50, 65–67, April 1989, p. 69.

*New York Times,* January 24, 1989, pp. A1, D23.

*The Studio,* September 1939, pp. 108–113.

—*Sketch by Simon Dixon*

# Roque Dalton
## 1935-1975
### Salvadoran poet and political leader

A poet of considerable reputation, Roque Dalton cut an interesting figure on the national stage of El Salvador. He helped found the El Salvadoran People's Revolutionary Army, known by its Spanish acronym, ERP. A devoted member of the Communist Party, he had strong connections to the working classes of Latin America, particularly the poor of his own nation. He mingled with the elite of Spanish America's literary pantheon during the 1960s and 1970s, but always longed to return to the struggle for political freedom in his own country. A splinter group of his own organization captured him in 1975, and after a farcical trial, in which they accused him of working for both the U.S Central Intelligence Agency (CIA) and the Soviet Union, Dalton died at the hands of an executioner.

In the introduction to *Roque Dalton: Clandestine Poems,* Margaret Randall reports that Dalton described his mother as "a poor, hard-working Salvadoran" in an introduction one of his volumes of poetry. He was not close to his father, with whom he never lived. Yet, his father acknowledged Dalton and provided financial support for him and his mother. He also made sure that the young boy had the money to get a good education at Jesuit institutions. Dalton went to universities in Mexico and Chile, gaining a more cosmopolitan and well-informed view of the world.

Dalton aligned himself with his country's Communist Party at a young age. His "working class commitment" to the well-being of ordinary Salvadorans inspired him to devote much of his life to the political goals of his party. In Randall's words, Dalton joined those in his country who took "a history of struggle in hand and [said] 'We're going to do something about all this.'"

## Uniting Art With Politics

Dalton established the University Literary Circle at the University of El Salvador. Artists of that country had long held a safe silence in the face of governmental repression. Dalton inspired young artists to use their talents to be the voice of the oppressed to comprise a unique expression of the people's experience.

In 1972 Dalton helped found the ERP, but the government strongly disapproved of its activities. It rounded up ERP leaders and supporters; some even faced execution. Randall described her first meeting with Dalton in Mexico City in 1964: "Roque arrived on the scene fresh from a jail break." Dalton boasted of his escape from a "CIA firing squad" thanks to a timely earthquake that brought the prison walls down.

Dalton left El Salvador for a time, but continued writing poetry. During his career he also wrote personal diaries and political essays. Randall said that "his political essays were—and are—important to those of his generation and to others. His polemic on the *foco* theory—a military tactic whereby insurrections are launched and maintained from a center of strategic import—of armed struggle . . . was a reference point for what concerned many at that time."

During the last few years of his life, Dalton travelled in the Communist world, living for a while in Vietnam. He returned to El Salvador, but openly publishing poetry would have put his life in jeopardy. Dalton invented five separate pseudonyms to give him adequate anonymity; each represented a different aspect of his artistic vision. In May of 1975, members of the ERP captured, tortured, and executed Dalton amid improbable charges of spying for the CIA, the Soviet Union, and even Cuba.

### SELECTED PUBLISHED WORKS:

*Miguel Marmol,* 1974.

*Pobrecita poeta que era yo (Poor Little Poet, I Was),* 1976.

*Poesia* (poetry), 1980

*Poesia Escogida* (poetry), 1983.

*Roque Dalton: Clandestine Poems,* introduction by Margaret Randall, Solidarity Publications, San Francisco, CA, 1983.

### SOURCES:

*Mirrors of War: Literature and in El Salvador,* Gabriela Yanes, Manuel Sorto, et al., editors, Zed Books Ltd., 1985.

*Roque Dalton: Clandestine Poems,* introduction by Margaret Randall, Solidarity Publications, San Francisco, CA, 1983.

—*Sketch by James McCarthy*

# Rubén Darío
## 1867-1916
### Nicaraguan poet

One of the greatest Hispanic poets of his generation, Rubén Darío was at the helm of the Modernist movement. The critic Jean Franco in *An Introduction to Spanish-American Literature* declared that "his innovations permanently enriched Spanish poetry." Darío supported his poetry as a journalist and a diplomat, and therefore spent much of his life outside his native Nicaragua. His poetic success was mirrored by personal tragedy: the death of his first wife shortly after their marriage, his addictions to alcohol and morphine, and his suffering from ill health and depression. Pivotal to his insecurity was a crisis of faith.

Born Félix Rubén García y Sarmiento on January 18, 1867, in Metapa (later Cuidad Darío), Nicaragua, his parents, Manuel García and Rosa Sarmiento, separated before his birth. Darío was raised by his great aunt and uncle in León. A child prodigy, Darío learned to read when he was three years old. He enrolled at Jacoba Tellería's kindergarten in 1870, using the name Ramírez. He proceeded to a public school in 1874, where his teacher, Felipe Ibarra, encouraged him to write his first verses. In 1877, Darío received a private education, but was forced to leave after fighting with his cousin, whose father paid Darío's school fees. Between 1878 and 1880 he attended a Jesuit school, where Padre Valenzuela, a poet, kindled his poetic career.

The 13-year-old Darío quickly developed a reputation as the 'boy poet," when his first poem, "Una lágrmia," appeared in *El Termómetro* on June 26. 1880. In his teens, Darío's poetry generated ripples in the literary arena, and he became a regular contributor to the journal *El Ensayo.* In 1881 he studied at the Instituto de Occidente, where he forged individualistic religious and political ideas. He taught Spanish grammar at a friend's school, which fortuitously prevented him from being apprehended as a vagrant after he quit the Instituto. After leaving school he traveled to Managua hoping to receive financial support from the government to study in Europe. He was offered a stipend on the condition that he enroll at a Nicaraguan school. Rejecting this offer, he departed for El Salvador, where he received a warm welcome from President Rafael Zaldívar.

In El Salvador Darío was introduced to contemporary European literature, particularly French works, by Francisco Gavidia, whose literary circle was experimenting with the French Modernists' ideas in Spanish verse. Darío especially admired Victor Hugo, Théophile Gautier, and Paul Verlaine. He returned to Nicaragua in 1883 and obtained a position working for President Adán Cárdenas on the plan for a Central American Union. His first published book, *Epístolas y poemas (Epistles and Poems)* appeared in 1885. Darío was offered a position at Nicaragua's National Library in Managua, where he familiarized himself further with literary works. In 1886 he cofounded the newspaper *El Imparcial.*

With a modest grant from President Cárdenas and assignments from *El Mercardo, El Diario Nicaragüense,* and *El Imparcial,* Darío moved to Chile in June of 1886, where he remained for the next three years. Darío first encountered sophisticated European culture during his stay in Chile. He expanded his journalistic repertoire, contributing regularly to the Chilean publication *La Epoca.* He also developed an important friendship with Pedro Balmaceda Toro, the Chilean president's son, which helped him make influential contacts. In 1887 he earned first prize for his *Canto épico a las glorias de Chile* in a competition sponsored by Pedro Nolasco Préndez. Around this time Darío moved to Valparaíso to work as a customs inspector.

1888 was a pivotal year for Darío for it witnessed the publication of *Azul* ("Azure," 1888), which established his literary status in Santiago. The collection of poems and verse contained experimental and innovative verse forms, the kernel of Modernism, marking a departure from Darío's more traditional *Abrojos* ("Thistles," 1887) and *Rimas* ("Rhymes," 1887).

Darío returned to Central America in 1889, following news of his father's death. He journeyed to El Salvador in June and was greeted by President Menéndez. There he founded *La Unión.* Later that year, on June 21, Darío married Rafaela Contreras; during the wedding reception news of Menéndez's assassination was received which prompted Darío's retreat to Guatemala. With financial support from Guatemala's president, Lisandro Barrillas, Darío launched the newspaper *El Correo de la Tarde.* The enlarged second edition of *Azul* appeared in 1890, reflecting Darío's reinforcement of the Modernist trend. In 1891 Darío traveled to Costa Rica with his family; his son, Rubén Darío Contreras, was born on November 11.

Darío contributed to Francisco Gavidia's *La Prensa Libre,* before serving as a correspondent on *El Heraldo* in 1892. Several months later he departed for Guatemala, where he learned that he had been nominated the Nicaraguan representative to the Quadricentennial Celebrations in Spain marking the discovery of America. Darío departed for Madrid later that year, also on assignment as a foreign correspondent for *La Nación,* Latin America's most prestigious newspaper. Darío returned to Nicaragua via Cuba and Colombia. In Colombia he met Colombia's renowned poet, Rafael Núñez, who organized Darío's diplomatic appointment in Buenos Aires.

Darío's first wife, Rafaela died on January 26 1893. Shortly after her death, on March 8, Darío married Rosario Emelina Murillo; their son was born six weeks later. In April, Darío was nominated Colombian Consul to Buenos Aires. Before taking up this position he traveled to New York City and Paris. He arrived in Buenos Aires in August. His consular obligations were minimal, enabling him to devote much of his time to his literary calling. He became the leader of a group of poets and cofounded *Revista de América* with Ricardo Jaimes Freyre. The consulate post was abolished in 1894, and Darío made a living as a journalist. Suffering from the alcoholism and depression that haunted him throughout his life, Darío rested on the island of Martín García during the fall of 1895. In 1896 he became secretary to Carlos Carlés, the director of postal services in Buenos Aires. During his residency in Argentina he wrote a collection of short stories in the magic and horror genre. He continued working for *La Nación*.

Modernism emerged with Darío at the helm following the publication of *Prosas profanas* ("Profane Prose") in 1896. Darío's time in Buenos Aires was productive, it included the publication of *Los raros* ("The Eccentrics," 1896), a collection of essays on contemporary writers such as Edgar Allan Poe, Verlaine, Huysmans and Leconte de Lisle.

Darío spent most of his remaining years in Europe. In 1898 he returned to Spain as a reporter for *La Nación*, assigned to the coverage of the effects of the Spanish-American War; his articles are compiled in *España contemporánea* ("Contemporary Spain," 1901). Shortly after his arrival in Spain he met Francisca Sánchez, who remained his partner until his death.

Darío's poetry was highly acclaimed in Spain; in fact, his time there heralded another productive literary era with the publication of *Cantos de vida y esperanza* ("Songs of Life and Hope," 1905) and *El canto errante* ("The Wandering Song," 1907). He reported on the Paris Exposition in 1900 for *La Nación*. When he visited Italy he was granted an audience with Pope Leo XIII. His critical observations from his Italian and French travels are collected in *Peregrinaciones* ("Pilgrimages," 1901). Later that year Francisca gave birth to a daughter Carmen, who died the following year. Darío then traveled to London, Brussels, Dunkirk, and Paris; the stories based on these journeys are collected in *La caravana pasa* ("The Caravan Passes On," 1902).

In 1902 Darío was named Consul of Nicaragua to Paris, a position he retained until 1907. Rubén Darío Sánchez was born, although he died several years later in 1905. Darío spent the next few years traveling throughout Europe and parts of North

Africa: Morocco, Germany, Hungary, Austria, Italy, England and Belgium. His travels are chronicled in *Tierras solares* ("The Lands of Our Ancestral Home," 1904). *Cantos de vida y esperanza* ("Songs of Life and Hope"), widely considered to be Darío's greatest work, was published in 1905. Through fear he turned to religion, but was plagued with uncertainty and doubt; solace evaded him.

Darío attended the 1906 Pan-American Conference in Rio de Janeiro in July and August as secretary of the Nicaraguan delegation. He returned to Europe, and spent time recuperating from alcoholism on the Spanish island of Mallorca in the Mediterranean. On October 2, 1907, Rubén Darío Sánchez, his second son by Francisca was born. Later that year he returned to Nicaragua, endeavoring to obtain a divorce from Rosario and to seek employment in the diplomatic field. He failed in his first objective but became Nicaragua's Minister to Spain and consul in Paris. He returned to Europe. In 1910 he was named Nicaraguan representative to Mexico's centenary independence celebrations. Nicaragua's President José Madriz was overthrown while Darío was journeying to Mexico and Darío's diplomatic career terminated.

Towards the end of his life Darío was sick and his literary output diminished. In financial straits he accepted the editorship of *Mundial*, a Spanish magazine in Paris, on a poor salary. The publication was a success, and Darío toured with the magazine around Europe and to Latin America. During his latter years he scribed several autobiographies, which first appeared in various issues of *La Nación*. He compiled *Canto a la Argentina y otros poemas* in Barcelona.

In 1914, following the outbreak of World War I, Darío embarked on a world peace tour to New York City and Guatemala giving lectures and poetry readings. The deterioration in health necessitated his final move to León in Nicaragua. After two unsuccessful operations Darío died on February 6, 1916, from atrophic cirrhosis of the liver.

## SELECTED PUBLISHED WORKS:

*Epístolas y poemas* (Epistles and Poems), 1885; reprinted as *Primeras notas* (First Notes), Tipografía Nacional, 1888.

*Azul* (poetry and short prose; title means "Blue"), [Chile], 1888, reprinted, Espasa-Calpe, Madrid, 1984.

*Los raros* (literary biography and critical essays; title means "The Rare Ones"), 1893, reprinted, Universidad Autónoma Metropolitana, Mexico, 1985.

*Prosas profanas* (title means "Profane Prose"), 1896, reprinted, introduction and notes by Ignacio M. Zuleta, Castalia, Madrid, 1983.

*Castelar*, B. R. Serra, Madrid, 1899.

*España contemporánea* (title means "Contemporary Spain"), Garnier, Paris, 1901, reprinted, Lumen, 1987.

*Cantos de vida y esperanza, Los cisnes, y otros poemas* (title means "Songs of Life and Hope, The Swans, and Other Poems"), [Madrid], 1905, reprinted, Nacional, Mexico, 1957.

*El canto errante* (poetry; title means "The Wandering Song"), M. Perez Villavicencio, Madrid, 1907, reprinted, Espasa-Calpe, 1965.

*El viaje a Nicaragua; e, Intermezzo tropical* (travel writings), Biblioteca "Ateneo", Madrid, 1909, reprinted, Ministerio de Cultura, 1982.

*Poema del otoño y otros poemas* (title means "Poem of Autumn and Other Poems"), Biblioteca "Ateneo", 1910, Espasa-Calpe, 1973.

*Muy antiguo y muy moderno* (poetry; title means "Very Old and Very Modern"), Biblioteca Corona, Madrid, 1915.

*El mundo de los sueños: Prosas póstumas* (title means "The World of Dreams: Posthumous Prose"), Librería de la viuda de Pueyo, Madrid, 1917.

*Sol del domingo* (title means "Sunday Sun"), Sucesores de Hernando, Madrid, 1917.

*Alfonso XIII y sus primeras notas* (addresses, essays, lectures and biographical text; title means "Alfonso XIII and His Principal Notes"), R. Darío Sánchez, Madrid, 1921.

*Baladas y canciones* (title means "Ballads and Songs"), prologue by Andrés González-Blanco, Biblioteca Rubén Darío Hijo, Madrid, 1923.

*Sonetos* (title means "Sonnets"), Biblioteca Rubén Darío, Madrid, 1929.

*En busca del alba* (poetry; title means "In Search of Dawn"), Arístides Quillet, Buenos Aires, 1941.

*Brumas y luces* (poetry; title means "Fogs and Lights"), Ediciones Argentinas "S.I.A.," 1943.

*Wakonda: Poemas,* Guillermo Kraft, Buenos Aires, 1944.

*"El ruiseñor azul": Poemas inéditos y poemas olvidados* (title means "The Blue Nightingale: Unpublished and forgotten Poems"), prologue by Alberto Ghiraldo, Talleres Gráficos Casa Nacional del Niño, c. 1945.

*Quince poesías* (title means "Fifteen Poems"), illustrated by Mallol Suazo, Argos, Barcelona, 1946.

*Cerebros y corazones* (biographical sketches; title means "Minds and Hearts"), Nova, Buenos Aires, 1948.

*La amargura de la Patagonia* (novella; title means "The Grief of Patagonia"), Nova, Buenos Aires, 1950.

*El manto de Ñangasasú* (novella; title means "The Cloak of Ñangasasú"), S.A.C.D.I.C., 1958.

*El sapo de oro* (novella; title means "The Golden Toad"), G. Kraft, Buenos Aires, 1962.

**In English**

*Obras completas* (title means "Complete Works"), 22 volumes, edited by author's son, Rubén Darío Sánchez, illustrations by Enrique Ochoa, Mundo Latino, Madrid, 1919.

*Obras poéticas completas* (title means "Complete Poetic Works"), twenty-one volumes, edited by Ghiraldo and González-Blanco, [Madrid], 1923–29, new edition edited by A. Méndez Plancarte, [Madrid], 1952.

*Cuentos completos* (title means "Complete Stories"), edited with notes by Ernesto Mejía Sánchez, preliminary study by Raimundo Lida, Fondo de Cultura Económica, Mexico, 1950, reprinted, 1983.

*Poesías completas* (title means "Complete Poems"), two volumes, edited by Alfonso Méndez Plancarte,1952, revised edition edited by Antonio Oliver Belmás, 1967.

## SOURCES:

### Books

Anderson Imbert, Enrique, in *Latin American Writers,* edited by Carlos A. Solé, translated from the Spanish by Peter Latson, Volume 1, Charles Scribner's Sons, New York, 1989, pp. 397–412.

Davis, Harold E., *Latin American Leaders,* Cooper Square Publishers, Inc., New York, 1968, pp. 134–40.

Ellis, Keith, *Critical Approaches to Rubén Darío,* University of Toronto Press, 1974, pp. 170.

Franco, Jean, *An Introduction to Spanish-American Literature,* Cambridge University Press, 1969, pp. 138–49.

Franco, Jean, *A Literary History of Spain: Spanish-American Literature Since Independence,* Ernest Benn Ltd., London and New York, 1973, pp. 111–20.

*Hispanic Writers: A Collection of Sketches From Contemporary Authors,* edited by Bryan Ryan, Gale Research Inc., Detroit, 1991, pp. 152–54.

### Periodicals

*The Dial,* June 14, 1917, pp. 509–11.

—*Sketch by Amanda Beresford*

# Angela de Hoyos
## 1945(?)-
### Mexican American poet

Whether her audience consists of highly educated Chicanos, recent immigrants from Mexico, middle-class, mainstream Americans, or academics of many countries, Angela de Hoyos enthralls listeners with her poetry. As a voice for those who, until recently, have not been heard, she speaks of inequality, injustice, and oppression. She writes of alienation and the problems of assimilation. She encourages solidarity and empowerment. Finally, she instills hope with her words and phrases. Angela de Hoyos, however, is more than a poet of her people. She is an internationally known and respected writer who has made outstanding contributions to international and national literature.

Ironically, two traumatic moments of de Hoyos's childhood contributed to her success as a poet: a horrible accident and a difficult transition. The first occurred in the Mexican state of Coahuila, where she was born on January 23, 1945 (some sources say 1940). The three-year-old de Hoyos was severely burned by a gas heater; she suffered wounds on her neck and chest, and the smoke she had inhaled made her very ill. During the long, painful periods she spent in bed, de Hoyos began to create rhymes and verses in her head, and as she did, she began to develop her poetic talent. De Hoyos's mother encouraged such wordplay—an artistic woman, she often read poetry to the girl. After the accident, de Hoyos's father left his dry cleaning business and moved the family to San Antonio, Texas. There, she attended local schools and academies. The move to Texas would prove to be another stimulus to de Hoyos's poetic instinct; in the United States, the girl would come to see the prejudice and inequality of which she would later passionately write.

De Hoyos's poetry was first published in her high school newspaper. Her work was well-received, and by her early twenties, some of the poems that were published by literary journals won international acclaim. As she seemed to have a bright future as a poet, de Hoyos wanted to enrich herself with knowledge. She did not, however, attend a four-year university program. Partially because of her health and partially because she preferred to follow her own curriculum, she did not choose a specific degree plan at any one school. Instead, she chose her own course of study in fine arts and writing. She attended classes at the University of Texas at San Antonio, San Antonio College, the Witte Museum, and the San Antonio Art Institute. De Hoyos also began to socialize with some of the leaders of the growing Chicano movement in the San Antonio area, Juan E. Cárdenas and Mía and Ceilio García-Camarillo. She was asked to give readings of her poetry at Chicano gatherings throughout the Southwestern United States, such as the Festival Floricanto III, Canto al Pueblo, and Sol y Sangre. As de Hoyos educated herself, she gave readings of her poetry and continued to write. Between 1969 and 1975, she had established her reputation; she had also written enough poems to form at least two collections of her work.

The first collection, *Arise, Chicano: and Other Poems,* was published in 1975 after de Hoyos's mentor, translator, and friend, Dr. Mireya Robles, encouraged the poet to make the poems she had written in 1969 available to the public. The influence of the Chicano movement is apparent in the four politically charged poems about Chicanos of the collection; these poems promote the idea that Chicanos should empower themselves to overcome oppression. The poem "Arise Chicano" reflects the feelings of one Hispanic woman as well as the mood of a generation of Mexican Americans.

### Depicts Anglo Oppression of Chicanos in Poetry

The title poem of *Arise Chicano: and Other Poems,* "Arise Chicano," provides a thematic summary of the collection as a whole. In the poem, Anglos dominate the world of the Chicano, who is consequently disgraced and degraded. Migrant workers live from "hand to mouth" and work "under the shrewd heel of exploit;" their children "go smileless to a cold bed." The migrant workers are enslaved by Anglos and locked into poverty. If they have maintained they integrity by working hard, they have lost their dignity by allowing themselves to be underpaid for exhausting and sometimes humiliating work. Accordingly, the Chicanos themselves bear some responsibility for their plight. They will have to look to themselves for salvation—"You must be your own messiah," the poet writes.

Another poem in the collection, "The Final Laugh," explores racial discrimination as it encourages Chicanos to overcome oppression. In this poem, the narrator discusses the notion that the color of Chicanos will prevent them from ever achieving equality. Whites possess power, and those whose parents are not white, or bland and "mail-order," can expect to experience hardship. Even though the Chicano may take pride in her heritage, dignity will not be enough to dispense with a tradition of ignorant prejudice. The Chicano has two choices. She may be "content with the left-overs of a greedy establishment," or rebel, and find her own place in the world. "The Final Laugh" is an internationally known and respected poem. Published separately before the other poems in the collection, it received the 1972 Diploma de Benemerenza, which is the second prize of the Italian Academia Leonardo Da Vinci.

The poem "Brindis: For the Barrio" advocates militant social protest and calls for solidarity. An answer to "La cena miserable," a poem by the great Peruvian **César Vallejo**, "Brindis" is about hope. If man must suffer today, surely tomorrow victory over oppression will come. Working together, Chicanos may hope to find their way out of poverty and alienation. The awkwardness and unfairness of that alienation is portrayed in the poem, "Gracias, Meester!" in which a young man agonizes over his poor English as well as his accent.

### Displays Growth in Work and Concern for Chicanos

The poems in de Hoyos's second book, *Chicano Poems for the Barrio,* were also published in 1975. This collection, which discusses cultural conservation within the barrio, or Chicano neighborhood, demonstrates the increasing maturity of the poet as well as a growing concern for the plight of her people. No longer content to merely advocate a socio-economic "uprising," de Hoyos rebels herself, within the text. Instead of peppering her English with a few Spanish words, as she did in *Arise, Chicano: and Other Poems,* she uses English as a frame to display Spanish terms and phrases; Spanish words are the substance of the poems, giving them their color and meaning. De Hoyos's use of language is symbolic as well as realistic: just as Spanish is woven into an English text, Chicanos are embedded in an Anglo world. The use of Spanish in everyday life as well as in any piece of literature written by a Chicano necessarily preserves the Chicano culture. De Hoyos is obviously aware of the significance of Spanish in her poems; as she liberally and skillfully writes with Spanish words, she breaks away from the English-dominated literature of the United States.

Another of de Hoyos's literary acts of rebellion is also historical. It is found in the poem "Hermano" ("Brother"). In "Hermano," de Hoyos uses the well-known incident during Texas's battle for independence from Mexico, the fight for El Alamo, to remind her readers that before Texas belonged to the United States it belonged to Mexicans, and that before the Mexicans occupied the territory the land belonged to Native Americans. Anglos therefore have no right to tell Mexicans to "go back where you came from." De Hoyos's clever revision of history, or better, correction of history, was remarkably fresh at the time she wrote "Hermano"; the idea that Columbus did not "discover" America, and that the history books read by the children of the United States contained misleading and biased information was not widespread. The substance, then, as well as the language of

de Hoyos's poems, are compelling and, to the literature of the United States, rebellious.

De Hoyos urges Chicanos to do what they can to assert themselves. In "It's the Squeaky Wheel/That Gets The Oil," she reviews the Chicano situation. Chicanos have the power to change that situation, and when they use that power, and make "progress," they will be able to incorporate themselves into society in the United States. They too will be able to enjoy economic prosperity and political influence.

### Works to Preserve Chicano Culture in America

Although de Hoyos encourages assimilation, she fears that an entire culture may be lost in the process. Some Chicanos seem too eager to ignore their roots in order to emulate Northern Americans. De Hoyos wrote in "Small Comfort": "En tierra de gringo/vamos poco a poco/sepultando todo," or, "In the gringo's land, we go little by little, burying everything." Assimilation and incorporation do not require the loss of culture, especially when those of the culture appreciate its unique beauty. Other poems in de Hoyos's second collection, such as "Para una ronda agridulce" ("For a Bittersweet Round"), and "Blues in the Barrio" present the reader with this beauty. The Chicano culture that is contained within the boundaries of the barrio is precious. The poet demonstrates this as she promotes the idea that, while incorporation is important, Chicano idioms, customs, values, traditions, and foods must not be forgotten.

Once again, de Hoyos has done more than advocate. She has actively preserved a piece of her culture. As she writes, she freezes what seems to be fleeting, as well as the process of a culture's passing, in her own words. De Hoyos's poems have captured some images (such as one of a mother rolling out tortillas) that Hispanics and non-Hispanics alike may appreciate. It must be remembered, however, that de Hoyos is not a Mexican poet. She is a Chicano poet. The metaphor of the barrio serves the poet well, for just as the barrio is a Chicano space within the Anglo world, the culture de Hoyos describes in *Chicano Poems for the Barrio* is alienated, and out of place, and because of this, it is a culture in transition.

De Hoyos's next collection of poetry, *Selecciones,* was published in Mexico in 1976; it was republished with a bilingual title in 1979, *Selected Poemas Selecciones.* The poems from this collection, which all focus on life and death, were written between 1965 and 1973. Notable among them are "Mi dolor hecho canción, mi canción hecho dolor," in which the narrator struggles against the peaceful urge to die and go back to the "womb of earth/from where I came," and "One Ordinary Morning," in which the inevitability of death is explored. The introspective poems in *Selecciones* are pessimistic: everyone, regardless of race or social standing, dies, and most people do not get the chance to truly live freely. In "This Fitting Farewell" the poet suggests that, while artists and poets may attempt to overcome the problems of living in such a world, they can do no more than "laugh/in the face of pain," as they create perfect worlds that are imaginary.

*Woman, Woman,* de Hoyos's fourth collection, was published in 1986 by Arte Público. Poems such as "Ex Marks the Spot" and "Fairy-Tale: Cuento de Hadas" speak of experiences with which many women are familiar—the betrayal of lovers. Two other poems, "Two Poems: Inebrieties" and "Mona Lisa: Marguerite" combine Spanish and English cleverly. In the former poem, de Hoyos presents part of the poem in Spanish and part in English to relate the feelings of falling in love from the perspectives of both Hispanic and Anglo women. The poet distinguished the latter poem by writing the beginning of each stanza in English and finishing it in Spanish.

De Hoyos's work has been well-received by critics. She has won numerous prizes and awards for her poetry. Among the most prestigious are the Honorable Mention from Avalon World Arts Academy, U.S.A. (1965), the Diploma Di Benemerenza from the Centro Studi E Scambi Internazionale, Italy, (1967, 1968), a Second Prize in the International Poetry Competition, (1974), the Diploma Di Benemerenza, Accademia L. Da Vinci, Italy, (1969, 1970), and the Distinguished Service Citation, magna cum laude, from the World Poetry Society Inter-Continental, India, (1970, 1971). Her work has been included in textbooks and anthologies such as *Chicano Perspectives in Literature: A Critical and Annotated Bibliography* and *Latin American Women Writers: Yesterday and Today.* Finally, she has contributed to various journals and other publications throughout the world such as *Poema Conviadado, Quaderni Di Poesia, Ediciones Cosmos, Esparavel, El Aguila, Poetry Dial, Modern Poetry in Translation, Poet Monthly, Masters of Modern Poetry,* and *La Voz del Bronx.*

Angela de Hoyos continues to contribute to causes which concern Hispanics and women as well as the international and national literary scene. Her her fifth collection, entitled *Dedicatorias,* is dedicated to those who have influenced de Hoyos and her work: Rodolfo Anaya, Rolando Hinojosa-Smith, Willie Velasquez, and others. A sixth collection, *Gata Poems,* is a relatively humorous book, encouraging readers to laugh at themselves. Although she is an internationally recognized poet, one might have to travel to Texas to hear de Hoyos read her poetry. She usually confines her activities to the San Antonio area for reasons of health.

Although de Hoyos is considered to be one of the most important Chicana poets, and while she is known around the world by those who study literature, the inevitable critical books that follow the

success of any writer have yet to appear. The critical works regarding de Hoyos that are found in literary journals are, however, generally enthusiastic about the poet's future. De Hoyos's diverse audience has much to anticipate.

## SELECTED PUBLISHED WORKS:

*Arise, Chicano: and Other Poems,* 1975.
*Chicano Poems for the Barrio,* 1975.
*Selecciones,* [Mexico], 1976; bilingual edition published as *Selected Poemas Selecciones,* 1979.
*Woman, Woman,* Arte Público, 1986.
*Dedicatorias.*
*Gata Poems.*

## SOURCES:

### Books

*Contemporary Authors,* Volume 131, Detroit, Gale Research, 1991.
*Dictionary of Literary Biography,* Volume 82: *Chicano Writers, First Series,* Detroit, Gale Research, 1989.

*—Sketch by Ronie-Richele Garcia-Johnson*

# Angustias de la Guerra Ord
## 1815-1890
### Mexican American historian

Angustias de la Guerra Ord was born into a world in transition. de la Guerra Ord watched firsthand as her native California moved from Spanish-Mexican rule to U.S. statehood. Her account of those transitional years, Occurrences in Hispanic California, is an important documentary record and a gripping story of betrayal and political intrigue, seen through the eyes of one who knew the major actors in the drama personally. The editor of the English language edition of the work commented in the foreword: "The narrative . . . adds considerably to our knowledge and understanding of California history for the Spanish-Mexican period."

In 1846, the year de la Guerra Ord's narrative ends, California had a population of about 12,000 people—excluding native Americans—and for years the governments of England, France, Spain, Mexico, the United States, and even Russia had been manipulating people and events in the hope of taking possession of this vast territory. De la Guerra Ord dictated her recollections of these events to Thomas Savage of the Bancroft Library in Berkeley, California, in 1878. The 156-page manuscript, which was entitled *Ocurrencias en California,* became part of the library's Hubert Howe Bancroft Collection, and was translated into English and published by the Academy of American Franciscan History in 1956 under the title *Occurrences in Hispanic California.* In the foreword to the English edition, the editor noted that "the *Ocurrencias* does much to fill out the fragmentary story we have of these complicated years" of prestatehood. Her story is told through "the elaboration and interpretation of important events of the times, the description of familiar persons, and the listings with brief comment in most cases of unfamiliar figures, by one whose background and experiences enabled her to speak authoritatively."

## A Prestigious Spanish Family

De la Guerra Ord was born in San Diego, California, on June 11, 1815, into one of California's most prestigious Spanish families. Her father, Jose de la Guerra y Noriega—called "El Capitan" by all Californians—had to obtain royal permission to marry her mother, Maria Antonia Carrillo, who was of noble blood. Forty days after de la Guerra Ord's birth, her family moved to Santa Barbara, California, where her father took command of the Presidio. Her life soon became entangled with the political events of the time.

In 1833, de la Guerra Ord married Manuel Jimeno Casarin and moved to Monterey, which was then the capital of California. During the course of his career Jimeno Casarin served as secretary of state, senior member of the Assembly and on a few occasions acting governor. Jimeno Casarin's position enabled his wife to witness the political unrest that followed the California Departmental Assembly's declaration of independence, and to report such news in her recollections. She detailed the alliance between native Californians and "a force of foreign riflemen" from the United States. This alliance eventually pushed the Mexican rulers out of the territory. De la Guerra Ord also spoke at length of the secularization of the missions implemented by Governor Alvarado upon orders from Mexico, which proved highly controversial. She strongly denies that the missionaries executed grand scale cattle slaughters to retain their hides. She emphasizes that if it were true, she would have known through her father—the well-respected "El Capitan" would have been informed—and through her two brothers-in-law, who were missionaries.

Power struggles, personal conflicts and armed rebellions continued to permeate California's daily life throughout the period of Mexican rule, which finally ended in 1846 when California fell under U.S. military rule. De la Guerra Ord noted in her memoirs that "the conquest of California did not bother the Californians, least of all the women. It must be confessed that California was on the road to most complete ruin. On one hand the Indians were out of hand, committing robberies and other crimes on the ranches, with little or nothing being done to curb their depredations. On the other hand were the differences between the people of the north and of the south, and between both against Mexicans and other bands. But the worst cancer of all was the plundering which was carried on generally. There had been such looting of the resources of the government, that the treasury chest was 'scuttled.' General [Jose] Castro maintained a corps of officers sufficient for an army of 3,000 men. . . . Of these officers, few offered their services when the hour came to defend the country against the [American] invasion. The greater part performed no more service than the figurehead of a ship."

## California Statehood Lessens Hispanic Families' Power

With the appropriation of California by the United States, the Mexican families' political influence began to dwindle. In the latter part of the nineteenth century, feuds between newly arrived Americans and established Spanish and Mexican families even led to bloodshed. The de la Guerras were among the few families that managed to keep their social identity and to retain some political influence. De la Guerra Ord's brother, Pablo, was a delegate at the state's first constitutional convention in 1849. Popular with both Americans and Hispanics, he served in the state Senate throughout the 1850s, and became California's lieutenant governor in 1860. De la Guerra Ord's prominence also persisted under American rule.

De la Guerra Ord's husband died of cholera in 1853 during a visit to Mexico. She had borne him 11 children, one of whom, Porfirio, would serve as captain of the California volunteers during the U.S. Civil War. Three years after her husband's death she married James L. Ord—a surgeon with the U.S. Army whose father was the son of King George IV of England and Maria Fitzherbert—and moved back to Santa Barbara. De la Guerra Ord and her husband visited Washington, D.C., and Mexico in 1871, and had the opportunity to meet U.S. President Ulysses S. Grant at the White House and Mexican President Benito Juarez at the castle of Chapultepec. In 1875, de la Guerra Ord obtained the dissolution of her marriage with Ord. After her father's death, she involved herself in a legal battle over his estate. She died on June 21, 1890, and was buried, at her request, in the Santa Barbara Mission's cemetery with the words "I wish to rest with those I loved so well" written in Spanish on her tombstone. The de la Guerras' family home, which remained in the family until 1943, now constitutes one of Santa Barbara's architectural landmarks.

## SELECTED PUBLISHED WORKS:

*Occurrences in Hispanic California,* Academy of American Franciscan History, 1956.

## SOURCES:

### Books

de la Guerra Ord, Angustias, *Occurrences in Hispanic California,* Academy of American Franciscan History, 1956.
Thompson, Joseph A., *El Gran Capitan,* 1961.
Tompkins, Walker A., *Santa Barbara History Makers,* 1983.

### Periodicals

*Santa Barbara Daily News,* May 20, 1922.
*Santa Barbara News-Press,* December 2, 1956, p. B14.

—*Sketch by Michelle Vachon*

# Oscar de la Renta
## 1932-
### Dominican American fashion designer

Known for ornate designs inspired by exotic themes and cultures, Oscar de la Renta is as an international fashion designer. His dramatic creations—based on fashions of the *belle époque,* abstract art prints, and flamboyant flamenco dresses—command attention with their bold yet controlled use of color and unabashedly feminine style. Presiding over Oscar de la Renta Ltd. in New York City, the elegant and charismatic designer is as well known in social, celebrity, and charity circles as he is in the fashion world. A devoted patron of the arts, de la Renta serves on the boards of the Metropolitan Opera and Carnegie Hall. He is also on the board of directors for the Americas Society and the Spanish Institute.

The Oscar de la Renta name rests primarily on opulent women's clothing. Throughout de la Renta's

career he has worked with simple silhouettes and complicated ornamentation to produce the romantic eveningwear for which he is most famous, like his "portrait" dresses of rustling taffeta and ruffled décolletés. De la Renta's fashions have been described as magical, flashy, gorgeous, dreamy, and flirty. By 1967, his clothes had become a parody of those worn by the self-styled counterculture—hot pants worn under a silk mini-dress, coats made of bandanna-print denim, caftans in chiffon, psychedelic sari silks, and crushed velvet. By the early 1970s, de la Renta's day clothes had become more casual while maintaining his traditional close-fitting waist and deep V-neckline. During this time, de la Renta also began working with gypsy themes, creating both day and evening ensembles with full skirts, aprons, fringed shawls, boleros, and peasant blouses.

De la Renta was born in Santo Domingo, Dominican Republic, on July 22, 1932, to Oscar and Maria Antonia deFiallo de la Renta. He grew up surrounded by women—six sisters and a fiercely protective mother. He told June Ducas in *Woman's Journal:* "My mother was very loving and sometimes very strict. I was often frustrated because I wasn't allowed to play in the street like other boys." Although his father hoped that this only son would take over the family's insurance business, de la Renta knew from an early age that "all I wanted was to become a painter, but that was not considered a proper career for a man."

After completing his studies in 1950 at the Escuela Normal, de la Renta enrolled at Santo Domingo's National School of Art, where he had a one-man show of paintings when he was only 17. At 18, he left the Dominican Republic to study painting at the San Fernando Art School in Madrid, where he soon discovered his aptitude for fashion and began sketching for fashion magazines. It was in Madrid that his distinctive sketches caught the attention of Mrs. John Lodge, the U.S. ambassador's wife. She immediately commissioned him to design a gown for her daughter's society debut, and the dress and its wearer appeared on the cover of *Life* magazine. This soon led to an apprenticeship with Spain's most revered couturier, Cristobál Balenciaga, and later to a job as couture assistant to Antonio Castillo at Lanvin in Paris.

### Moved to New York City

It was not long before the young designer set his sights on New York City as the clearest path to fame and fortune. After meeting Elizabeth Arden at a dinner party in 1963, de la Renta was offered a job as her top in-house designer. In 1965 he left Arden to buy into the Seventh Avenue ready-to-wear firm of Jane Derby, Inc., with partners Ben and Gerald Shaw. After Derby's death a year later, the label was changed to carry the Oscar de la Renta signature, and in 1967 de la Renta won his first Coty American Fashion Critic's Award. The privately owned New York-based company has since expanded into Europe, the Orient, and North and South America, and includes not only ready-to-wear but a large number of licenses: swimwear, scarves, umbrellas, costume jewelry, shoes, and tableware, among others. De la Renta became a U.S. citizen five years after the company assumed his name.

One third of de la Renta's business consists of fragrances. He launched his first signature scent, "Oscar," in 1977, and it continues to be one of the top five fragrances sold in the United States. A men's fragrance, "Pour Lui," followed. In 1992, de la Renta introduced a third fragrance—"Volupté"—in a 24-day, 22-city tour that illustrated the designer's combination of charm and business savvy. During the "Volupté" launch, de la Renta told M. Alexandra Nelson of the *Miami Herald* of an early entrepreneurial memory: "When I was a boy growing up in the Dominican Republic, we had a big yard. I have six sisters, and we each had a plot. All of them grew flowers, but I was growing vegetables that I wanted to sell to my mother. I grew spinach and corn. This upset my sister. She thought it spoiled the total look. But I always believed in free enterprise."

De La Renta's early foray into gardening, however mercenary, evolved into to a lifelong fascination with landscape design. A 200-acre estate in Connecticut is what de la Renta calls his "emotional home," where he can indulge his passion for nature and a love of plants, flowers, color, and design. He learned to garden by trial and error, studying nursery catalogues and planting guides. After initially consulting with the great landscape artist Russell Page, de la Renta became his own designer. Formal gardens of flowers and herbs, hedges, shrub borders, and trees surround the estate's greenhouses, stables, pool, and outdoor sculptures. At his Dominican Republic house and working fruit plantation, Casa de Madera ("House of Wood")—where de la Renta spends six weeks of every year—the inner courtyard is a green jungle of fish-tail palms, tropical flowers, and ferns. Nearly all the furniture is made from the island's indigenous mahogany in de la Renta's own workshop—de la Renta promised the Dominican government that for every tree chopped down he would replant ten.

### Entered the House of Balmain

When the House of Balmain presented its spring collection to the fashion world in February of 1993, it was attempting to revive its sagging fortunes and prestige after the 1982 death of designer Pierre Balmain and the challenges posed by ready-to-wear. De la Renta's selection as main designer heralded the first time that an American had led a French couture business, and de la Renta defied critics and jealous colleagues who said the enterprise would fail. Writing in *Time*, Martha Duffy stated that de la Renta's talent "lies in translating the traditional into the distinctly contemporary. He emphasizes wearable clothes, however luxurious they may be. If Balmain wants to catch up to the 1990s without leaping into the 21st century, the house made a very shrewd choice." Proclaiming him a perfect fit for the Balmain aesthetic, Duffy noted his "peerless eye for fabric, detail and nuance."

De la Renta's first wife, former French *Vogue* editor Francoise de Langlade, was credited by many for his entrée into the social circles that provided him with important business connections. One year after she died of cancer in 1983, de la Renta adopted a son, Moisés Oscar. The two were united through a home close to Casa de Madera that de la Renta founded, where 22 orphans live and approximately 350 more children receive basic education, food, and recreation while their mothers are at work. De la Renta married his second wife, Annette Engelhard Reed, heiress to the Engelhard metals fortune, in 1989.

### Honored by His Homeland

In 1988, de la Renta received the prestigious Jack Dempsey Award for his humanitarian efforts. In 1990, he was honored with a Lifetime Achievement Award by the Council of Fashion Designers of America. Equally important to him is the recognition given him by the Dominican Republic, where de la Renta serves as a kind of "ambassador by default," according to *Vogue*. The country has honored its best-known native son with the order al Merito de Juan Pablo Duarte and the order of Cristobal Colon.

## SOURCES:

### Books

*Earl Blackwell's Celebrity Register 1990*, Detroit, Gale, 1990.
Milbank, Caroline Rennolds, *Couture: The Great Designers*, New York, Stewart, Tabori & Chang, Inc., 1985.

### Periodicals

*House and Garden*, April 1992, pp. 94–102.
*Miami Herald*, April 29, 1992, p. 3E;
*Time*, February 8, 1993, p 68–70.
*Vogue*, April 1992, pp. 436–42, 516–519.
*Woman's Journal*, June 1992.

*—Sketch by Julie Catalano*

# Abelardo Barrientos Delgado
## 1931-
### Mexican American poet, educator, and activist

Abelardo Barrientos Delgado is among the best-known Mexican American poets and oral performers to emerge during the decade of the 1960s. Delgado—who was born November 27, 1931, in La Boquilla de Conchos in Chihuahua, Mexico—is the son of cattle rancher Vicente Delgado and Guadalupe Barrientos. In 1944, Delgado—who is often called "Lalo" by his friends—and his mother immigrated to El Paso, Texas, where he lived until 1969. He attended elementary school in Mexico and Bowie High School in El Paso. He was vice president of Bowie's National Honor Society chapter and was considered an excellent student despite early problems understanding English.

After high school, Delgado worked in a variety of construction and restaurant jobs before he married Dolores Estrada on October 11, 1953. Their union produced eight children. In 1955, Delgado became the special activities and employment director at Our Lady's Youth Center. He continued to work at the center until 1964. It was during this period that he began attending the University of Texas at El Paso on a part-time basis. He earned his bachelor's degree in secondary education there in 1962. He also completed a year of postgraduate work in El Paso and two years at the University of Utah in Salt Lake City.

Delgado has taught and lectured at many colleges and universities throughout the country. Since the mid–1980s, he has held positions at Aims Community College in Fort Lupton, Colorado and St. Thomas Seminary and Metro State College in Denver. In addition to teaching, Delgado has worked for a variety of social service programs, including those concerning youth or migrant labor.

### Writing a Life-Long Passion

Writing and poetry have been a part of Delgado's life since his elementary school years. Because many publishers have not always viewed minority publishing as a lucrative business, many Mexican Americans have tapped into their tradition of oral story-telling to reach their audiences. Delgado was among those poets during the 1960s who found an outlet for his work by holding public readings before students and workers. Since much of his writing deals with the condition of Mexican Americans and their struggle for political, economic, and educational equality, the oral performances of his work inspired his audiences to take action. In addition to public performances, Delgado established his own publishing company, called Barrio Press.

Perhaps Delgado's best known work is his first book, *Chicano: Twenty-five Pieces of a Chicano Mind,* which he self-published in 1969. Written in both Spanish and English, the book advocates equality for Mexican Americans and condemns white America for its injustices and lack of respect for Mexican American culture. Delgado defines words and concepts originating in the Mexican American culture, such as *machismo* and *chicanismo,* and he examines what it is like to live and work in Mexican American neighborhoods, or *barrios.*

Throughout the next 20 years, Delgado travelled widely performing his poems and publishing a number of books of poetry, including *The Chicano Movement: Some Not Too Objective Observations, Bajo el sol de Aztlán: Veinticinco soles de Abelardo* (*Under the Sun of Aztlán: Twenty-Five Suns of Abelardo*), *It's Cold: 52 Cold Thought-Poems of Abelardo,* and *Reflexiones: Sixteen Reflections of Abelardo.* In 1982, Delgado published his first short novel, *Letters to Louise.* That book was awarded the Premio Quinto Sol (Fifth Sun Award), a national award created and presented by the Tonatiuh-Quinto Sol Internationalpublishing house. The award carries a $1,000 prize and a publishing contract.

Delgado has also been awarded the *El Paseño* Newspaper Prize for Poetry in 1988, the Denver City Mayor's Award for the Arts in 1988, and the Interracial Books for Children Prize for Short Stories in 1972. He is widely recognized in the Mexican American community for his activist role in the Chicano Movement and for founding several social service organizations to help improve the conditions of other Mexican Americans. In addition, Delgado is an authority on Caló, which is a dialect of Spanish-English spoken in barrios.

### SELECTED PUBLISHED WORKS:

*Chicano: Twenty-five Pieces of a Chicano Mind,* Barrio, 1969.
*The Chicano Movement: Some Not Too Objective Observations,* Colorado Migrant Council, 1971.
*Mortal Sin Kit,* Idaho Migrant Council, 1973.
*Bajo el sol de Aztlán: Veinticinco soles de Abelardo,* Barrio, 1973.
*It's Cold: Fifty-two Cold-Thought Poems of Abelardo,* Barrio, 1974.
*A Thermos Bottle Full of Self-Pity: Twenty-five Bottles of Abelardo,* Barrio, 1975.
*Reflexiones: Sixteen Reflections of Abelardo,* Barrio, 1976.
*Under the Skirt of Lady Justice: Forty-three Skirts of Abelardo,* Barrio, 1978.

*Here Lies Lalo: Twenty-five Deaths of Abelardo,*
    Barrio, 1979.
*Siete de Abelardo,* Barrio, 1979.
*Totoncaxihuitl, A Laxative: Twenty-five Laxatives
    of Abelardo,* Barrio, 1981.
*Letters to Louise,* Tonatiuh-Quinto Sol Interna-
    tional, 1982.
*Unos perros con metralla,* Barrio, 1982.

### SOURCES:

*The Hispanic-American Almanac,* edited by Nico-
    lás Kanellos, Detroit, Gale, 1993, pp.
    421–431, 448.
*Hispanic Writers,* edited by Bryan Ryan, Detroit,
    Gale, 1991, pp. 155–156.
Meier, Matt S., *Mexican American Biographies,*
    New York, Greenwood, 1988, pp. 69–70.
Meier, Matt S., and Feliano Rivera, *Dictionary of
    Mexican American History,* Westport, Green-
    wood, 1981, p. 118.

—*Sketch by Catherine A. Clay*

*Hernando de Soto*

# Hernando de Soto
## 1500(?)-1542
**Spanish explorer**

Credited as the discoverer of the Mississippi
River, Hernando de Soto (sometimes cited as
**Fernando de Soto**), was also the first European to
explore the southeastern half of what was to become
the United States. As a young man he helped lead the
conquest of Nicaragua and later accompanied Francisco Pizarro in the conquest of the Incas. De Soto
later served as governor of Cuba and as royal deputy
of Florida.

De Soto was born into a noble—but impoverished—family sometime around 1500. Scholars disagree about the location of his birth place, but it is
likely that he was born in Spain's mountainous
Estremadusa region. Wealthy nobleman, Don Pedro
Arias de Ávila, known as Pedrarias, became de Soto's
patron. Theodore Maynard, author of *De Soto and the
Conquistadores,* stated that Pedrarius "paid for [de
Soto's] education at the University of Salamanca,
[and later] provided his equipment and passage to the
New World, and obtained for him the commission of
a captain of dragoons." De Soto's education surely
prepared him for a career as Conquistador; as John C.

Abbott explained in his *Ferdinand de Soto: The
Discoverer of the Mississippi:* "Literary culture was
not then in high repute; but it was deemed a matter of
very great moment that a nobleman of Spain should
excel in horsemanship, in fencing, and in wielding
every weapon of attack or defence."

While de Soto was attending the university,
Pedrarias was appointed governor in Panama. In the
patron's absence a romance developed between young
de Soto and Pedrarias's daughter, Isabella. Pedrarias
considered de Soto a poor employee and unworthy of
his daughter. According to Abbott, Pedrarias offered
de Soto the captaincy and free passage to Panama in
order to separate the young couple; thus, de Soto
sailed for the New World at the age of 19.

In Panama de Soto participated in campaigns to
subdue the natives and became known for his skill as
a soldier and horseman. Pedrarias had a reputation
for cruelty and jealousy, as evidenced by his treatment and his eventual death sentence for the explorer,
**Vasco Núñez de Balboa**, but de Soto was a loyal
employee and received ample compensation in gold
and slaves. In 1523, following Pedrarias's orders, de
Soto went to Nicaragua, serving as a lieutenant to
Hernández de Córdoba during their subjugation of
the region. Eventually de Soto broke from the ambitious and authoritarian Pedrarias and forged ahead
with a previously-arranged business partnership with
**Hernán Ponce de León** in the slave trade. De Soto
had become a wealthy man.

## Conquered the Incas

In 1530 de Soto joined **Francisco Pizarro**'s expedition to Peru, pursuing the conquest of the Incas. De Soto was promised an appointment as lieutenant-governor in Peru and was second in command to Pizarro. With an army of 200 men, de Soto set sail in December. Challenged by hostile natives, famine, and the wilderness, many of the men—including de Soto—become disenchanted with Pizarro's talk of riches. De Soto's partner and fellow member of the expedition, **Ponce de León**, returned to Panama. De Soto chose to remain, dealing with the expedition's challenges, Pizarro and his brothers, and rival partner Diego de Almagro; the other men's behavior and military choices increasingly angered de Soto.

In 1532, de Soto become the first European to meet the Inca emperor, Atahualpa. According to Maynard's *De Soto and the Conquistadores,* de Soto was initially unable to elicit much response from the emperor during their encounter in Caxamarca. But realizing the emperor was interested, de Soto put on a dazzling display of horsemanship. He impressed Atahualpa, but he also frightened some of the Peruvian soldiers; Atahualpa later ordered those who had shown fear to be killed.

The Spaniards captured Atahualpa, conquered the city, and demanded a ransom of gold and silver. De Soto's share consisted of 180 pounds of gold and 360 pounds of silver, enough to assure him wealth and power in Spain. After the ransom was collected, Pizarro planned to kill Atahualpa, de Soto was against this plan. Pizarro sent de Soto away on business and then had Atahualpa killed. De Soto was infuriated both by Pizarro's act of murder and the treachery he had used to accomplish the deed; this seriously undermined what was left of their troubled collaboration.

A year after the taking of Caxamarca, the Spaniards marched on the Incan capital of Cuzco, where de Soto became lieutenant governor and, according to historians, fathered a number of children by an Indian mistress. In 1534 de Soto returned to Spain, likely spurred by the constant arguments between Pizarro and Almagro.

In Spain, de Soto received a hero's welcome. Pedrarius had died while de Soto was in Peru and could no longer prevent de Soto's marriage to his daughter. De Soto married Isabella de Bobadilla in 1536. Abbott, in his book on de Soto, reported that after two years of living an extravagant lifestyle, de Soto found his vast fortune was rapidly disappearing. In addition, de Soto had become restless. He asked the Spanish court for permission to commerce new explorations. In 1537 King Charles appointed him governor of Cuba and *adelentado* ("royal deputy") of Florida—as-yet unconquered territory in North America. The king ordered de Soto to "conquer,

pacify, and populate" the area. De Soto spent one year in Cuba establishing his rule and planning the Florida expedition. He sailed for Florida in November of 1538, leaving Isabella to serve as Cuba's governor in his absence.

## Explored Florida

De Soto and his 700 men arrived in Florida in May of 1539. Similar attempts had already been made by Ponce de León and Pánfilo de Narváez. De Soto's expedition was attacked by hostile Indians almost immediately, as Sylvia Whitman explained in *Hernando de Soto and the Explorers of the American South,* "[De Soto's] expedition benefitted from the geographical data [previous expeditions] had gathered, but it also harvested the ill will they had sown among Native Americans."

De Soto searched for Florida's rumored riches. The Spaniards discovered the lone survivor of the Narváez expedition, Juan Órtiz, who had been living with the natives for almost ten years; he joined the expedition as an interpreter. Órtiz tried to convince de Soto that no gold was to be found in Florida, but since Órtiz's knowledge of the country was limited, de Soto was unconvinced. He had heard rumors throughout Cuba, South America, and Spain, favorably comparing the rest of North America with Mexican and Aztecian wealth.

De Soto's expedition faced Indian attacks, swamps, rough terrain, and food scarcities, searches for food in the quest for gold. Villages were either deserted or full of natives anxious to ensure peace. The Spaniards habitually captured Indians as slaves, and held village chiefs hostage while a ransom of slaves was supplied and to expedite travel through hostile territory. The natives falsely directed the Spaniards farther north to be rid of them.

## Found Cutifachiqui Pearls

In 1540 the Spaniards were told of a chieftess at Cutifachiqui, in present-day South Carolina. This location was to be the only place they found objects of worth: de Soto took 350 pounds of pearls there. But many were worthless because the natives had used fire to open the shells, discoloring the innards or had pierced the pearls with fire-heated tools to string them for necklaces. The natives attached no value to the pearls, viewing them simply as ornamental beads. Members of the expedition implored de Soto to establish a colony at Cutifachiqui, because of its beauty and of wealth, but de Soto sought still better territory and was driven by the lure of more treasure.

De Soto's trust of the Indian chief Tuscaloosa proved disastrous to the Spaniards, who were attacked in a carefully planned skirmish at the Indian fort of Mabilla. The Spaniards lost many men and de

Soto himself was injured in the ensuing fight. The Spaniards managed to overcome the surprise attack, killed thousands of Indians, and burned the fort. Although they were victorious in battle, the Spaniards had lost everything their native porters had carried: extra arms, tools, medical supplies, food, clothing, bedding, and the pearls from Cutifachiqui. After this disastrous episode, de Soto's men were thoroughly discouraged, and de Soto "developed a fortitude that became appalling, bleak, inhuman," Maynard maintained in *De Soto and the Conquistadores.*

### Discovered the Mississippi River

One month after the Mabilla attack, de Soto gave the order to head north, rather than south to the sea, where his men planned to sail back to Cuba. Maynard credited de Soto's "capacity for command" as the reason his men did not desert. They marched in rags and were attacked again, this time, by natives at Chicaca. It was a bedraggled group that discovered the Mississippi River, which they named Rio del Espiritu Santo in May of 1541.

After a fruitless journey west and south, the group returned to the Mississippi. Only 300 of the original 700 expedition members remained. Lost, de Soto sent scouts looking for the sea; he planed to build ships and go back to Cuba for supplies. But when his scout returned having found the terrain impossible to travel, de Soto lost all hope. Weakened and disillusioned, de Soto was worn down by privation and fever. De Soto died on May 21, 1542, nearly one year after having discovered the Mississippi. On his deathbed, de Soto appointed Luis de Moscoso to assume leadership of the expedition. The Spaniards tried to conceal de Soto's death. They thought that if local Indians knew de Soto had died they would attack; de Soto had maintained peace by proclaiming himself the Child of the Sun, or a god from heaven. The Spaniards weighted de Soto's body with sand and sank it in the water of the Mississippi. Isabella died a few days after receiving the news of her husband's death.

Some scholars have discredited de Soto's discovery of the Mississippi, crediting Pineda, who found the river's mouth. Still de Soto is remembered as a brave explorer and as a leader who shared his companions deprivations and ruled by example.

### SOURCES:

Abbott, John S. C., *Ferdinand de Soto: The Discoverer of the Mississippi,* New York, Dodd & Mead, 1873.
Kathleen, Jan, and Thompson Gleiter, *Hernando de Soto,* Milwaukee, Raintree Publishers, 1989.
Maynard, Theodore, *De Soto and the Conquistadores,* New York, Longmans, Green and Co., 1930.
*Narratives of the Career of Hernando de Soto,* Vol. II, edited by Edward Gaylord Bourne, New York, Allerton Book Company, 1904.
*The Great Explorers,* Piers Pennington, New York, Facts on File, 1979.
Syme, Ronald, *De Soto: Finder of the Mississippi,* New York, William Morrow, 1957.
Whitman, Sylvia, *Hernando de Soto and the Explorers of the American South,* New York, Chelsea House Publishers, 1991.
Zadra, Dan, *De Soto: Explorer of the Southeast,* Mankato, MN, Creative Education, 1988.

—*Sketch by Sandy J. Stiefer*

# Henry F. Diaz
## 1948-
### Hispanic American meteorologist

A distinguished atmospheric scientist, Henry F. Diaz has written extensively on climatic variability and global and regional climate analysis. He has also co-edited a book on the phenomenon of El niño, a periodic warming of Pacific ocean currents that has the potential to affect weather conditions worldwide.

Born in Santiago de Cuba on July 15, 1948, Diaz is the son of Francisco Diaz, an attorney of Spanish and French descent, and Maria Vias. He became interested in geography and tropical weather after moving to Havana in 1959. During the early 1960s, Diaz emigrated to the United States, attending high school in Miami and later college at Florida State University in Tallahassee. After earning an undergraduate degree in meteorology, he matriculated at the University of Miami and received a master's degree in atmospheric science in 1974.

### Began Work with NOAA

Following graduation, Diaz found employment as a meteorologist with the National Oceanic and Atmospheric Administration (NOAA) in Washington, D.C. A year later, he moved with his wife, Marla Cremin, and his son to Asheville, North Carolina, where he had accepted a position in the Climate Analysis Division of NOAA's National Climatic Data Center. In 1980, intrigued by the phenomenon of climatic variability, Diaz enrolled at the University of

Colorado in Boulder on a NOAA scholarship. He received his doctorate in geography with a specialization in climatology five years later.

During his 20-year career with NOAA, Diaz has published numerous articles, atlases, and technical reports on climatic fluctuation; he is best known, however, for his 1992 study *El Niño: Historical and Paleoclimatic Aspects of the Southern Oscillation.* Diaz presently works for NOAA in Boulder and has received several awards for his work. His professional associations include membership as a fellow in the Cooperative Institute for Research in Environmental Sciences (CIRES) of the University of Colorado, where he also is adjunct associate professor in the Department of Geography. An avid outdoorsman, Diaz has been honored as a visiting scientist by the Scripps Institution of Oceanography (summer 1982), the University of Massachusetts (1988–89), and the Swiss Federal Institute of Technology in Zurich.

## SELECTED PUBLISHED WORKS:

"Some Characteristics of Wet and Dry Regimes in the Contiguous United States: Implications for Climate Change Detection Efforts," in *Greenhouse-Gas-Induced Climatic Change,* edited by M. E. Schlesinger, Elsevier, 1991, pp. 269–96.
*El Niño: Historical and Paleoclimatic Aspects of the Southern Oscillation,* Cambridge University Press, 1992.
"Documenting Natural Climatic Variations: How Different Is the Climate of the 20th Century from that of Previous Centuries?," in *Climate Variability on Decade to Century Time Scale,* National Academy of Sciences, 1994.

—*Sketch by Margaret DiCanio*

# Porfirio Diáz
## 1830-1915
### Mexican general and president

José de la Cruz Porfirio Diáz, who served as Mexico's president for more than three decades, maintained one of the longest dictatorships in world history. His autocratic tenure from 1876–1911 has earned the historical label "Porfiriato." Diáz was dedicated to modernizing and industrializing his country, but the emphasis he placed on economic progress over social reform and justice led to his ultimate downfall.

*Porfirio Diáz*

Diáz was born in Oaxaca, Mexico in 1830, and belonged to a middle-class, urban family of Spanish and Indian descent. His father was an innkeeper and veterinarian who died when young Diáz was only three years old. Mestizos, the Diáz's were descendants of both Spanish and Indian bloodlines.

Diáz's mother hoped her son would enter the priesthood and sent him to study in a seminary. Diáz saw other possibilities for his future; he commenced law studies under **Benito Juárez** at Oaxaca's Institute of Arts and Sciences. His education at this time had decidedly liberal overtones. Diáz emerged from legal training committed to reducing the overwhelming power that the army, the Catholic church, and wealthy landowners maintained over the Mexican populace.

### Rose to Power

Nineteenth-century Mexico still bore the scars of its colonial past, with a poorly developed economy, a history of civil wars, and a territory vastly reduced by cessions to foreign powers. War with the United States from 1846 to 1848 was one of Mexico's devastating experiences. "La Reforma," a revolution that took place from 1855–1859 pitted anticlerical liberals against proclerical conservatives. The succeeding fight to preserve liberal reforms took the shape of the "Three Years' War," a civil struggle that attracted intervention by British, French, and Spanish troops. Diáz supported the liberal cause as a guerilla officer and was appointed a brigadier general in 1861, the year the conflict ended.

Another challenge soon arose in what is known as the French Intervention of 1862 to 1867. During this time, the France's Emperor Napoleon III sought to place Austrian Archduke Maximillian on the throne of Mexico. Ultimately, France withdrew its troops under pressure from the United States. Juárez, now the liberal president of Mexico, ordered Maximillian shot. Juárez's victory was due largely to the energetic support of regional *caudillos,* including Díaz, whose military contributions during this period included the successful defense of Puebla in 1862; the siege of Oaxaca; command of 20,000 troops; and the capture of Mexico City.

Entertaining presidential ambitions, Díaz ran for the office opposite Juárez in 1867. Unsuccessful, the returned to his native province the following year and focused on sugarcane production on his new farm, La Noria, bestowed him by Oaxaca's citizens. He pursued the presidency once again in 1871, and once again Juárez emerged victorious.

Refusing to accept this defeat, Díaz attempted to overthrow Juárez. The president responded quickly to Díaz's rebellion; Díaz's brother Felix was killed in the ensuing violence. Although Díaz abandoned this fight, he resumed his quest for power once Juárez died, overthrowing the president's successor, Sebastián Lerdo de Tejada, in 1876. "In the name of the Reform and democracy," Thomas Benjamin and Marcial Octavio-Meléndez asserted in the *Hispanic American Historical Review,* "Díaz became the dictator of Mexico."

## The Porfiriato

Díaz was elected president eight times between 1876 and 1911. Having initially won support on a "no-reelection" platform, he did relinquish power when his first term expired, entrusting his ally, General Manuel González, with the country's leadership from 1880 to 1884. For those four years, Díaz served as governor of Oaxaca.

The widower Díaz also entered his second marriage during this period, wedding wealthy Carmen Romero Rubio in a union sometimes referred to as the "aristocratization of Porfirio Díaz." The new Señora Díaz was a highly respected woman who facilitated her mestizo husband's entry into elite creole society. One no-incidental side effect of Díaz's marriage to this devout Catholic was a smoothing of relations between the church and the government.

In 1884, Díaz—having watched the country sink into bankruptcy under González's tenure—returned to the presidency. Benjamin and Octavio-Meléndez, in characterizing his government over the next decades stated: "Díaz gave Mexico a measure of political stability and economic growth. Although he respected the formalities of the Reform's Constitution of 1857, its democratic and anticlerical provisions were not observed. The regime awarded generous concessions to foreign entrepreneurs and enacted reforms aimed at establishing a rational and capitalistic economic environment."

The economic measures resulted in significant development for Mexico. Benjamin and Octavio-Meléndez noted, "As a result, foreign capital built a network of railroads, revitalized mining, expanded and modernized the textile industry, and transformed commercial agriculture." Particularly under the leadership of finance minister José Ives Limantour, Mexico underwent considerable modernization.

As far as the political situation was concerned, Benjamin and Octavio-Meléndez explained that "Díaz's personal monopolization of power occurred at the expense of institutional development and respect for law." The Porfiriato was an increasingly rigid system, with officeholders entrenched in power and little bureaucratic turnover.

Many scholars have noted that whatever progress the country experienced under the Porfiriato was counterbalanced by the tolls it exacted from poorer segments of Mexican society. "For too many people," declared Benjamin and Octavio-Meléndez, "modernization meant an increase in the cost of living and declining rural and urban wages." The Cientificos—wealthy creoles at the heart of Díaz's regime—were avidly pro-European and sought to relegate Mexico's Indian and mixed citizens to eternal inferiority. More than 85 percent of the population was illiterate. Many people were demoralized by their deplorable and seemingly unchangeable living conditions.

During the early years of the twentieth century, Mexico suffered "an economic recession, increasing labor unrest, and a succession crisis" according to Benjamin and Octavio-Meléndez. **Francisco Madero** was the beneficiary of the simmering resentment against Díaz. When the aged president realized the threat Madero posed to his power, he jailed his challenger. Madero escaped and initiated an insurrection. Díaz found himself without support, especially once his weak military forces succumbed.

On May 25, 1911, Díaz resigned. He fled the country, settling in France, where he died a poor man on July 2, 1915. His family was not permitted to return to Díaz's remains to his native country. Instead, an urn containing Mexican soil was placed at his grave in Paris.

## Unsettled Historical Verdict

The historical record on the Porfiriato is vast and complex. During Díaz's own time, such works tended to be laudatory. But historical interpretations change.

Not every scholar, for example, still agrees with the idea the Diáz truly advanced modernization in Mexico. In their 1984 article, Benjamin and Octavio-Meléndez concluded: "A new consensus ... is emerging that stresses the importance of the Porfirian inheritance to what Mexico became. While some still point to the age of Diáz in justifying the Mexican Revolution, more are citing the lessons of the age of Diáz to justify a real break with the past."

Diáz's rule left an undeniable imprint on Mexico's national memory. The country remains scattered with grand edifices and railroads dating from his era. Diáz's legacy is so controversial that when new history textbooks portrayed him in a fairly benevolent manner in 1992, Secretary of Public Education **Ernesto Zedillo Ponce de Leon** ordered the remarks removed. But in 1994, one of Mexico's most popular historians, Enrique Krauze, collaborated with the Nobel prize-winning poet **Octavio Paz** to arrange that an extended series on Diáz's life and times be televised. The programs were generally considered as positive.

## SOURCES:

### Books

*Historic World Leaders,* Vol. 4, edited by Anne Commire, Detroit, Gale, 1994.
Kinder, Hermann, and Werner Hilgemann, *Anchor Atlas of World History,* Vol. II, translated by Ernest A. Menze, New York, Anchor, 1978.

### Periodicals

*The Americas,* October 1993, pp. 207–232.
*Aztlán,* Fall 1983, pp. 289–306.
*Business History Review,* Autumn 1987, pp. 387–416.
*Hispanic American HistorReview,* May 1984, pp. 323–364.
*New York Times,* July 16, 1994.

—*Sketch by Brett A. Lealand and Erika Dreifus*

# Patricia Diaz Dennis
## 1946-
### Mexican American lawyer and government official

Patricia Diaz Dennis was enthusiastic about her appointment as assistant secretary of state for human rights and humanitarian affairs. "You have few opportunities to leave a legacy and change

people's lives for the better besides raising healthy and sane children," Diaz Dennis told Luis Vasquez-Ajmac. "This job is one where you can't do enough," she continued. "I couldn't say no to the appointment."

Diaz Dennis's response to a new challenge was not surprising, for she has taken on many challenges in her life. She decided to pursue a career in law instead of teaching school. After building an impressive reputation in labor law, she again changed career plans at the age of 40 by becoming President Ronald Reagan's appointee as a commissioner for the Federal Communications Commission (FCC). Although she maintained a heavy work schedule, Diaz-Dennis made spending time with her three children and her husband, Michael John Dennis, a priority.

Born October 2, 1946, in Santa Rita, a small town outside Silver City, New Mexico, Diaz Dennis is the oldest of five children. Her father, Porfirio Diaz, and her mother, Mary Romero Diaz, were close, loving parents. Porfirio Diaz was a sergeant in the army; his job required that the family travel and relocate frequently. Diaz Dennis spent several years in Japan as a teenager and lived in Santiago, Chile, where she graduated from high school. Living in foreign countries exposed Diaz Dennis to different cultures and environments. She explained to Vasquez-Ajmac, "When you're an American living abroad, you're automatically in a different social grouping even if you're not in the same economic status as the social group." As a result of her travels, Diaz Dennis believes that her world view changed dramatically.

### First in Her Family to Attend College

With the encouragement of her parents, Diaz Dennis became the first in her Mexican American family to go to college. Concerned about their daughter leaving home and adjusting to the United States, Diaz Dennis's parents thought it best that she be near relatives and attend the San Francisco College for Women, a Catholic school. After several semesters at that institution, she transferred to the University of North Carolina-Chapel Hill. The young woman returned to California to marry Michael Dennis after her junior year. She completed an A.B. degree in English literature at the University of California-Los Angles (UCLA) in 1970 and received the Fouragere honors at graduation.

Meeting Michael Dennis was a turning point in Diaz Dennis's life. She credits her husband, who is also a lawyer, as the one giving her the support and initiative to practice law. She recalled in 1989 in *Executive Female,* "I had been applying to graduate school for an advance degree in English literature when he suggested I apply to law school instead. He figured that since I won all the arguments at home I should put that skill to good use."

## Became a Lawyer

Diaz Dennis was admitted to Loyola University School of Law in Los Angeles and began to attend school there. She served as the executive editor of the *Loyola Law Review* and was on the dean's list when she earned her J.D. in 1973. That same year, Diaz Dennis passed the California State Bar Exam. Later, she was admitted to practice before the District of Columbia Court of Appeals, and the Supreme Court of the United States.

Diaz Dennis worked at Paul, Hastings, Janofsky & Walker in Los Angeles while she was still a law student at Loyola. This job sparked Diaz Dennis's love for labor law. She told *Executive Female,* "I found I really enjoyed reconciling conflicts. There are legitimate concerns on both sides of the bargaining table—management and employee—and a labor lawyer has to reconcile them." Diaz Dennis returned to the prestigious labor law firm after graduation to become not only the first female lawyer, but also the firm's first Hispanic lawyer. It was here that she built her solid background in labor law.

When Diaz Dennis gave birth to her first child , she discovered that the long hours required by a major law firm were, as she said in *Executive Female,* "incompatible with good parenting." Though she frequently nursed her child at work while maintaining her regular heavy caseload, she opted to leave the law firm of Paul, Hastings, Janofsky & Walker in 1976 for more predictable hours at Pacific Lighting Corporation.

As a lawyer at Pacific Lighting Corporation, a holding company for a California utility that also had an agricultural subsidiary, Diaz Dennis represented management in labor negotiations with the United Farm Workers. That position, as explained in *Broadcasting,* "could be 'emotionally difficult' because union members, some of whom spoke only Spanish, questioned whether she [Dias Dennis] wasn't on the wrong side of the bargaining table." Dias Dennis remarked in that same article, "I guess those are the sorts of experiences that toughen you."

## Traveled to Hollywood to Join ABC-TV Management

In 1978, Diaz Dennis was recruited to represent management in labor issues at ABC-TV in Hollywood, California. The change was comforting, she commented in *Executive Female,* because unlike the unaccommodating structure for women with growing families at the Pacific Lighting Corporation, ABC's structure was very conducive to balancing work and family.

After one year at ABC, Diaz Dennis was promoted to assistant general attorney. She said of her experience at ABC in *Executive Female,* "I really enjoyed my job at ABC. There's a special aura about broadcasting and I had some great cases." The magazine noted, "One of her [Dias Dennis's] more unusual cases involved negotiations with a group of inmates at Folsom Prison who had been used as extras in an ABC movie and were demanding more than Screen Actors Guild's minimum."

During her tenure at ABC, Diaz Dennis accepted a presidential appointment to the National Labor Relations Board (NLRB), an independent agency that prevents and remedies unfair labor practices. After extensive interviews, President Reagan nominated her to the NLRB and the Senate confirmed her; she moved to Washington, D.C., with her family and became the second female board member and the first Latina in the agency's history.

Diaz Dennis's nomination came, in fact, as a surprise to her since no one in Washington paved the way for her. Her connection, she told Vasquez-Ajmac, was "literally through a friend of a friend of a friend who knew someone in the White House personnel office." In *Broadcasting,* Diaz Dennis was quoted as saying, "It really is a testament to democracy. The fact that someone like me was able to walk into the White House and then take on such an important public responsibility is a testament to how wonderful our country is. In no other country could someone like me have achieved this kind of job."

Perhaps because Dias Dennis had a reputation for fairness and was an expert in labor law, her nomination to the NLRB did not upset unions, even though she had represented management in all her years of practice. "I believe unions didn't oppose me," remarked Diaz Dennis in *Executive Female,* "because I had established a reputation for fairness. That is really the quality to bring to decision-making. Because if people know that you gave them a fair shot, they will ultimately give you grudging respect."

## Nominated by President Reagan to Head FCC

Diaz Dennis worked at the NLRB for three years before making a major career move in 1986 at the age of 40. Nominated by President Reagan to replace former FCC Commissioner Henry Rivera, Diaz Dennis became the second female and second Hispanic commissioner in the 55-year history of the FCC. "I was leaving the familiar and secure to start all over again in an incredibly complex industry," related Diaz Dennis in *US West.* "Communications issues are not readily understandable. They take study. The FCC's responsibility is tremendous—shaping a vision of what we want telephony to become over the next 20 years and then setting the right path for implementation."

Though Diaz Dennis was a self-proclaimed "rookie" when she started at the FCC, she emerged as an independent-minded, hard working, and thoughtful commissioner. As an FCC Commissioner, Diaz Dennis deliberated such issues as regulation of "Indecent Broadcasts"; policy regarding racial, ethnic, and gender preferences in license assignments; Open Network Architecture (ONA) proceedings; the development of the telephone system as it interrelates to small business and other common carrier issues, while remaining a strong defender of the First Amendment.

According to Diaz Dennis, one of her greatest accomplishments at the FCC involved implementing minority preferences for broadcast licenses, an issue eventually upheld by the Supreme Court. Deeming it an important issue because minorities today hold only two percent of all broadcasting licenses in the United States, she told Vasquez-Ajmac, "One of the cornerstones of the Communications Act of 1934 is diversity of programming and viewpoint. One way to ensure diversity of programming and viewpoint is to ensure diversity of ownership."

After Diaz Dennis's three-year term with the FCC expired in June 1989, she resumed private practice as partner and chair of the communications section of the law firm of Jones, Day, Reavis & Pogue in Washington, D.C. Diaz Dennis went on to serve as vice president of government affairs for U.S. Sprint's Washington office and its parent company, United Telecommunication, Inc., now called Sprint Corporation, in March 1991. There, she represented Sprint before the FCC, Congress, and other federal agencies.

### Appointed Assistant Secretary of State

Diaz Dennis was appointed assistant secretary of state for human rights and humanitarian affairs by President George Bush and was confirmed by the Senate. She viewed the appointment as a "rare opportunity to make a difference, to do some good for people, to save lives." She told Vasquez-Ajmac, "There are so many parts of the world where human rights are not being observed.... Someone who brings passion and commitment to the job will make a difference."

To many people, Diaz Dennis is that someone with passion and commitment. As a career woman, she is known to make decisions thoughtfully, competently, and fairly; she is also a devoted wife and the mother of three children. As an active member of the National Network of Hispanic Women, she cares deeply about the Hispanic community's problems. "It is my responsibility," she told *Executive Female*, "to be involved because any time one of us is successful, it means more of us can make it." Diaz Dennis "spends much of her spare time," according to *US West*, "advising young Hispanics that getting an education ... being as 'good as you can be' are keys

to taking advantage of challenges." Most importantly, she explained to Vasquez-Ajmac, "You have to have one person in your life who says you're special. Those of us who are successful," she concluded, "are obligated to extend our hands to those who come after us."

## SOURCES:

### Periodicals

*Broadcasting,* March 9, 1987, p. 87; September 25, 1989, p. 34.
*Business Radio,* October 1987, pp. 16–27.
*Communications Week,* June 1, 1987, pp. 8, 33; March 4, 1991.
*Communiqué,* April 1987, pp. 14–20.
*Executive Female,* January/February 1989, pp. 35–36, 67–68.
*Hispanic Business,* December 1987, pp. 44, 47; May 1991, p. 6; August 1991, p. 44.
*Hispanic Review of Business,* April 1987, pp. 10–15.
*Michigan Chronicle Pontiac Education,* June 4, 1991.
*National Journal,* March 2, 1991, p. 529.
*Phone Plus,* February 1989, pp. 19–26.
*Rural Telecommunications,* spring 1987, pp. 50–53; fall 1987, pp. 42–44; spring 1989, pp. 10–13.
*US West,* spring 1987, pp. 29–30.

### Other

Diaz Dennis, Patricia, taped interview with Luis Vasquez-Ajmac, July 23, 1992, MAYA Corporation of America, Washington, D.C.

—*Sketch by Luis Vasquez-Ajmac*

# Remedios Diaz-Oliver
## 1938-
### Hispanic American entrepreneur

Remedios Diaz-Oliver has struggled against revolution, jail, exile, and poverty, not to mention gender and ethnic barriers, to become president and CEO of one southern Florida's top companies. After founding American International Container, a supplier of glass and plastic bottles, from a trailer on January 10, 1976, her work enabled the new company to take in $800,000 in sales its first year. By 1990,

*Remedios Diaz-Oliver*

or anger that sets her apart. This value was instilled in her by her mother, who brought from her native Spain an austere work ethic. "The only way you can succeed in life is by working hard, she taught me," Diaz-Oliver related. "I graduated from high school one year before everyone else. I had to get a special government permit to do it. I think I wanted to succeed!" Chosen valedictorian of her high school class, Diaz-Oliver went on to earn a Master's in Business Administration from Havana Business University and a Ph.D. in Education from the University of Havana. She had already begun a diplomatic career, was fluent in English, French, and Italian, and had planned to begin her career as a full-time educator, when circumstances obliged her to abandon her home. She believes that she would have been equally successful had she been able to stay on the island despite her admission that being a female executive may have been more difficult in Latin America.

### Started New Life in Miami

However, being a penniless Hispanic woman refugee in Miami, a sleepy provincial town in 1961, also suggested its share of difficulties. Trained first and foremost as an educator, Diaz-Oliver had no time to become certified to teach in the United States or to wait for the new school terms to begin, so urgent was the need to support her infant daughter. This led her into the job market where she accepted the first employment opportunity she could find. She took a position with Emmer Glass, which sold containers, in the accounting department, working five-and-a-half days a week for $55. The need for a Spanish-speaking employee to communicate with potential clients arriving from Cuba and other parts of Latin America motivated Diaz-Oliver to familiarize herself with the business. She began to take the company's catalogues and technical books home with her to study. Within a year she was in charge of the newly formed "International Division." She was placed in charge of exporting containers for a company that had never exported before. She handled sales in Central America, and within six years under her control the International Division had earned the company a number-one ranking among companies exporting containers to that area, as reported by the U.S. Department of Commerce. In 1968 she was the first woman to earn the "E" Award—Excellence in Export—given by President Lyndon Johnson.

As head of the International Division she rapidly acquired a market that at that time had been almost exclusively controlled by exporting container companies from France and Italy. Under Diaz-Oliver's guidance, the United States for the first time made an inroad in that area. However, her rapid road to success did not remain unimpeded by difficulties or negative encounters. Being not only Hispanic but a woman as well meant encountering double-barreled

according to the *Miami Herald,* Diaz-Oliver's company grossed $68 million, with revenues of $90 million in 1991. The company was listed 33rd on *South Florida Business Journal*'s list of top privately owned companies. In 1992, Diaz-Oliver left American International to found a family-run competitor, All American Containers.

When Diaz-Oliver was born on August 22, 1938, her Galician father was a hotel owner in Cuba who also distributed hotel supplies throughout the island. He took his daughter along with him on his various business trips to the United States and Spain, exposing her to an international perspective at an early age. Her father knew Cuban dictator **Fidel Castro** in the early days of the revolution, but the family eventually lost everything. Diaz-Oliver recalled an encounter with Castro in early 1960 in which he spoke to her, remembering her as the daughter of a former friend. "'Nenita (which my father used to call me) how are you?,' he said. I looked at him and I said, 'Surprised that you didn't keep your promises!' He didn't throw me in jail right then and there probably because I was pregnant, but I was in jail a year later," she related. Diaz-Oliver was jailed for a short time for protesting against government imposed mail inspections; upon her release she emigrated with her husband, Fausto, and her daughter of only a few months, Rosa, to the United States on May 11, 1961.

Such an experience would understandably produce feelings of anger and betrayal in the victim, yet it is Diaz-Oliver's refusal to be sidetracked by adversity stereotypes. Diaz-Oliver reacted with her own typical aplomb. "I was contacted on one occasion by a gentleman when I was already vice president of the company," she related. "He asked to speak to the boss, and when I told him that *I* was the boss, he said, 'Come on, let me speak to the boss. You must be the secretary.' He then said, 'My God! I will never do business with a woman and I will never do business with a Cuban!' I said, 'Don't worry; I'll transfer your call to someone who is not a woman and who is not a Cuban!' He got into some trouble about a year later with an inventory problem and he called. . . . He said, 'I don't think I have any choice. Do you have such and such an item?' The next day the containers were delivered to his door and we saved him a lot of money. A year later I received an invitation for his son's wedding. He was marrying a Cuban girl!" Diaz-Oliver's handling of the situation and her refusal to react to the customer's insults "not only saved a client," she pointed out, "but we turned out to be friends! He recommended me to a lot of people because he saw I had a sense of humor and that I could take the heat. You can't get anything accomplished with anger."

### Founded Container Company

By 1976, Diaz-Oliver and her husband had founded American International Container with Frank H. Wheaton, Jr., one of the most respected names in U.S. glass manufacturing. Her reputation in and around southern Florida had spread so widely that the support given her by the community buoyed the fledgling corporation to almost instant success. Seeming to have an instinctual understanding of how a cyclical economy like Miami's operates, she realized the potential for stability that a container supplier could have. With her husband and two children she founded All American Container in 1991, which distributes packaging products and materials, including plastic and glass bottles and containers, to companies including Coca-Cola, Pepsi, McCormick, and Kraft. She has sales offices in Panama City, Panama; San Jose, Costa Rica; Caracas, Venezuela; Guayaquil, Ecuador; and Santiago, Chile; as well as European locations including London and Sydney, Australia.

Over the years Diaz-Oliver has been able to respond to changing markets with an acumen that has allowed her to thrive through various recessions. In the eighties, when much of Latin America was in economic crisis, she shifted much of her market concentration back to the United States, especially Texas and the Carolinas. As much of Latin America is prospering in the nineties, she has begun to re-expand those markets. She also enjoys the opportunity for family involvement provided by her company. "The whole family works together," she noted, including her daughter, son, and husband.

Diaz-Oliver attributes her success to the community that supported her and makes many attempts to give something back. In addition to her executive responsibilities, she has also been very active in the Greater Miami Chamber of Commerce, Latin Chamber of Commerce, and the City of Miami and has worked towards increased tourism and investment in the greater Miami area. She has received accolades from Presidents Lyndon Johnson, Ronald Reagan, and George Bush, the State of Florida, the City of Miami, and Metropolitan Dade County and was named Entrepreneur of the Year by the Latin Chamber of Commerce in 1987 and Woman of the Year by the U.S. Hispanic Chamber of Commerce. She was also named Outstanding Woman of the Year in 1983 and 1984 by the Association of Critics of Radio and Television and Woman of the Year in 1984 by Latin Business and Professional Women. Numerous other organizations, including the American Red Cross, the American Cancer Society, and the United Way, benefit from her volunteerism. One of her greatest passions of the last few years has been to support education, especially at the University of Miami's Jackson Memorial Hospital. Education is the one quality that she values above all others, and that she insists is irreplaceable.

When asked what qualities she hopes her grandchildren will have inherited from her, she does not say "thrift" or "industriousness," as one might expect from a business owner, but rather "patriotism, and a sense of ethics and family values toward every person they meet."

### SOURCES:

### Periodicals

*Intercambios Femeniles,* spring 1987, p. 14.
*Miami Herald,* January 11, 1988.
*South Florida Business Journal,* September 23, 1991, p. 10.

### Other

Diaz-Oliver, Remedios, telephone interview with Paul Miller, July 30, 1992.

—*Sketch by Paul Miller*

# Fabián Dobles
## 1918-
### Costa Rican novelist, poet, and short story writer

One of Central America's preeminent literary figures, Fabián Dobles's work includes poetry, novels, and short stories. He was born in San Antonio de Belén in Costa Rica in 1918. His work has been translated into several languages, including German and Russian.

Dobles is a writer with distinct Marxist ideological inclinations. A prevalent theme in his work, described by Enrique Anderson Imbert in *Spanish American Literature: A History,* is the portrayal of the "painful reality of injustices and social miseries."

This focus emerges in his novel *Ese que llaman pueblo* (*This Thing Called People*), first published in 1942, in which Dobles relates the story of a young peasant and his hardships. When the peasant borrows some money in order to get married he is burdened with crippling interest rates. Again, Dobles clearly sympathizes and identifies himself with the poor in *El sitio de las abras,* which deals with the inequitable distribution of land.

Dobles has been formally acknowledged as one of Costa Rica's finest contemporary novelists and poets. He is the recipient of several major awards. In 1945 the Premio Centroamericano was bestowed upon him for his poetry collection *Verdad del agua y del viento.* He was awarded the Premios Nacionales Aquileo J. Echeverría from the Costa Rica Ministerio de Cultura in 1967, and the Premio Nacional de la Cultura Magón (Costa Rica's National Prize for Literature) from the Costa Rica Ministerio de Cultura in 1968.

## SELECTED PUBLISHED WORKS:

*Ese que llaman pueblo* (novel), Letras Nacionales, San José, Costa Rica, 1942, 5th edition, Editorial Costa Rica, San José, 1982.

*Aguas turbias* (novel), Trejos Hermanos, San José, 1943, reprinted, Editorial Costa Rica, 1983.

*Una burbuja en el limbo* (novel), L'Atelier, San José, 1946, 4th edition, Editorial Costa Rica, 1978.

*La rescoldera,* L'Atelier, 1947.

*El sitio de las abras* (novel), originally published in 1950, 2nd edition, Editorial Costa Rica, 1970, 6th edition, 1976.

*Historias de Tata Mundo* (short stories), Trejos Hermanos, 1955, 2nd edition published under same title with *El maijú, y otras historias de Tata Mundo,* Editorial Costa Rica, 1966, 8th edition, 1979.

*El maijú, y otras historias de Tata Mundo* (short stories), Trejos Hermanos, 1957.

*El violín y la chatarra* (short stories), P. Presbere, 1960.

*Los leños vivientes* (novel), [San José], 1962, 2nd edition, Editorial Costa Rica, 1979.

(With Mario Picado) *Yerbamar* (poetry), Impr. Tormo, San José, 1965.

*En el San Juan hay tiburón* (novel), L'Atelier, 1967.

*Cuentos de Fabián Dobles* (short stories), Universitaria Centroamericana, San José, 1971.

Also the author of *Cuentos escogidos de Fabián Dobles,* 1982; *La pesadilla y otros cuentos,* 1984.

## SOURCES:

*A Dictionary of Contemporary Latin American Authors,* edited by David William Foster, Center for Latin American Studies, Arizona State University, 1975.

*Hispanic Writers,* edited by Bryan Ryan, Detroit, Gale, 1991.

Imbert, Enrique Anderson, *Spanish-American Literature: A History,* translated by John V. Falconieri, Detroit, Wayne State University Press, 1963.

*The Oxford Companion to Spanish Literature,* edited by Philip Ward, Oxford, Clarendon Press, 1978.

—*Sketch by Amanda Beresford*

# Plácido Domingo
## 1941-
### Spanish opera singer and conductor

Plácido Domingo has long been established as one of the world's preeminent tenor opera singers. Entering the mid–1990s, Domingo remained a vital and successful artist who has charted a career of extraordinary breadth—the opera star sang his 108th role in 1994. His work, according to Martha Duffy of *Time Magazine,* "ranges from lyric opera to darkest Wagner. He is the better actor and the finer musician, a good pianist, a conductor who is growing in stature, the new artistic director of the Washington Opera—in all, an opera superstar."

*Plácido Domingo*

Domingo rose to stardom on his singing and acting ability. Critics have long pointed to his stage presence, typically commanding and unforgettable, as a key factor in his rise to the top of the opera world. In a review of the Metropolitan Opera's 1994 production of *Otello,* which starred Domingo, critic Paul Griffiths of the *New Yorker* noted that "When the character exhibits power ... Mr. Domingo shows not only the charisma but the fragility, the nervousness, the insecurity ... when he exhibits affection for Desdemona, the warmth and gentleness are cut with worry, perhaps self-doubt." His performance, Griffiths states, is superb. "Just once in the terrifying monologue ... [he] takes the opportunity of low-lying and quiet music to leave aside the demands of heroic brilliance and appear vocally naked." Domingo's performance, Griffiths continues, was "bleak, grim, and heavily baritonal, revealing the raw grain of the wood, without the polish. The purpose of the evening was to honor Mr. Domingo on the silver anniversary of his first appearance with the company, and honor him it did, as much as he honored it."

### Musical Heritage

Born on January 21, 1941, in Madrid, Spain, Domingo was raised in a musical family. His parents, Plácido Domingo and Pepita (Embil) Domingo, were professional singers who specialized in the "zarzuela" —comic Spanish operettas with spoken dialogue. His mother was known as the "Queen of the Zarzuela" in the early 1940s and many operettas were composed for her. When he was around nine years old, Domingo's family moved to Mexico and eventually created their own Mexico City operetta company, which featured nearly 80 members. He learned to play the piano as a youngster and studied at the National Conservatory of Music in Mexico City. He made his first musical appearance in a comedy in which he sang as a baritone until he was advised to try singing as a tenor. Domingo talked to Howard Klein of the *New York Times* about the switch in 1968. "I used to force a lot. I was not at all secure on high notes. But I worked, and little by little I began to dominate the sound instead of vice versa. Now I have a good high C, but if I have to sacrifice a long, high note in order to give more importance to a middle section of an aria, I don't hesitate because in singing I try to mean every word of the text."

After his official operatic debut in 1961 and performances in Texas in 1962, Domingo joined the Israel National Opera Company. During his two and a half years in Tel Aviv, he played 11 roles and sang in 280 performances, including two operas in Hebrew. In an interview with Herbert Kupferberg of *High Fidelity* in 1968, he recalled, "It was a fantastic experience for a young singer and there were many of us there. I remember a 'Don Giovanni' we gave in Italian in Tel Aviv. There was a British conductor, a Japanese Zerlina, a Greek Donna Anna, an Italian Don Giovanni and my wife, Marta Ornelas, was Donna Elvira." A lyric soprano, Ornelas married Domingo before the move to Israel and the couple eventually had three sons, José, Plácido, and Alvaro Maurizio. In 1965 the tenor returned to the United States and joined the New York City Opera. Three years later he made his debut with the famous Metropolitan Opera Company.

"The debut was eminently successful," critic Allen Hughes of the *New York Times* declared. "Mr. Domingo's voice sounded fresh and clear and seemed to have more luster in the Metropolitan than in the New York State Theater." Harriet Johnson of the *New York Post* agreed. "Gifted with one of the most beautiful voices to be heard anywhere today, he sings very well, technically and artistically. He doesn't shout. He colors his voice by the emotions he conveys and he conveys many." Domingo's debut at the Met still drew comment 25 years later. "The 1968–69 season was an important one for Met history," Walter Price reported in 1993 for *Opera News.* "the emergence of two new tenors, Plácido Domingo and Luciano Pavarotti ... put a unique stamp on the season. ... Though it was easy to predict solid careers for both, few at the time would have envisioned superstardom—and superrivalry—on such a scale."

Buoyed by his sensational performances with the Metropolitan Opera, Domingo was soon entrenched as one of the opera kingdom's brightest lights. Domingo's repertory over the years has included the works of

Giuseppe Verdi, Richard Wagner, Wolfgang Amadeus Mozart, and Giacomo Puccini. But while the singer has made numerous recordings over the years, his career has not been confined solely to performing opera. He has appeared in opera films and conducted opera from the orchestra pit.

### Domingo as Conductor

Although Domingo first made his reputation as an opera singer, his interest in conducting dated back to the earliest years of career. Domingo occasionally conducted his parents' zarzuela company, and in 1972 he conducted an album with Sherrill Milnes. David Stearns of *Opera News* wrote in 1986 that "even back then, he says, he saw conducting as a way to prolong his professional career in music beyond the life of his voice." But Domingo certainly didn't wait for his voice to fail. He conducted his first complete opera—*Die Fledermanus*—for Angel-EMI in November 1986. Conducting added a new dimension to his career, Domingo explained to Stearns. "To conduct is actually a bit dangerous, because you have a lot of perspiration, lots of physical exercise, and you could catch cold. I've learned to control myself. I try to keep my singing performances before the conducting performance, so I can sing today and conduct tomorrow. . . . Conducting takes a lot of physical energy."

Musicians, accustomed to seeing Domingo on stage, found his direction in the orchestra pit commendable. Contrabassoonist Toni Lipton of the Metropolitan Opera Orchestra explained to Stearns that "he's a masterful musician. With Domingo we try especially hard, because we love him. I can't wait to see him in a couple of years. I can't believe that a man as bright as he won't get better and better." Principal trumpeter Melvyn Broiles added that Domingo was a joy to work with. "It's almost a pleasant humility. He wouldn't know how to be a phony. He's sincere and honest."

In addition to his operatic performances, Domingo has branched out into other entertainment fields as well. He has dabbled in popular music and television and even performed in feature films such as *Carmen, La Traviata,* and *Otello.* Fans and critics alike have wondered if this full schedule might eventually take a toll on his voice. "His secret is that he saves his voice for the stage," *Life* reported. "Able to memorize his scores—he knows 90 operas, 30 of them well enough to perform on a moment's notice—by studying the music at the piano, he doesn't have to use his voice to practice." Domingo added his observations. "The problem is that you live with your instrument. Anything and everything affects the throat." The day of a performance, he doesn't talk and may even spend the day in a quiet retreat with his wife.

Domingo explained to Jane Scovell of *Opera News* that his intense schedule makes him happy. "I have done it this way all of my life, and from the beginning people have said, 'Oh, Plácido, this is too much, too much. Nobody knows more than I what is my stamina, what I can do and what I cannot do." The voice, he said, is a strange instrument that sometimes works better the more he uses it. "I don't work as much as people think. It's the combination of things that makes my schedule very demanding. I know many colleagues who sing more than I do, by far, but everything I do is so visible."

Indeed, even Domingo's work outside the theater drew attention. Scovell noted: "Long after the headlines about the [September 1985] Mexican earthquake had been replaced . . . Domingo continued his all-out efforts for the relief program. He's still at it. In the aftermath of the tragedy . . . he searched for his relatives, some of whom died. Because he is a known and beloved public figure, his anguish, which reflected Mexico's, became our anguish." His efforts in Mexico City served as clear evidence that Domingo had not forgotten his roots. In 1994, due to his association with the Los Angeles Music Center, a "zarzuela grande," *El Gato Montés* (*The Wild Cat*) was performed. Donna Perlmutter of *Opera News* wrote "[It] could hardly be more appropriate to Los Angeles, a city whose name and population attest to its Hispanic heritage." As a child, Domingo had performed this operetta with his parent's company. "Any quibbles with the merit of this undertaking," Perlmutter continued, "would perhaps be mitigated by evidence that the local Hispanic community had indeed found its way to the city's chandeliered emporium, home of haute culture."

While Domingo's varied interests and robust schedule made him one of the opera world's most visible figures, it was probably his alliance with two other renowned tenors, Luciano Pavarotti and **José Carreras**, that did the most to increase the general public's awareness of his talent. In 1990 the three tenors recorded a live concert at the World Cup Soccer competition in Rome. As Martha Duffy commented, "The concept was already grandiose, but its success outstripped the wildest expectations of those involved. About 800 million people worldwide saw the television broadcasts. The record turned into by far the best-selling classical album of all time." The three tenors repeated their performance at the 1994 World Cup in Los Angeles to more acclaim. Jamie James, in a 1994 article for *Stereo Review,* noted that the excitement surrounding those performances "has prompted record executives and other music-industry professionals to dream of a new golden age of classical music."

### SELECTED PUBLISHED WORKS:

*My First Forty Years,* Knopf, New York, 1983.

## SELECTED DISCOGRAPHY:

*Romantic Arias,* RCA, 1969.
*Domingo Conducts Milnes! Milnes Conducts Domingo!,* RCA, 1972.
*Carmen,* London, 1975.
*Carmen* (soundtrack), RCA, 1984.
*Otello,* RCA, 1978.
*Perhaps Love,* CBS, 1981.
*Tangos,* Pansera/DG, 1981.
(With Andrew Lloyd Weber) *Requiem,* Angel, 1985.
*Nights at the Opera,* CBS, 1986.
*Be My Love . . . An Album of Love,* Angel, 1991.
(With The London Symphony Orchestra) *The Broadway I Love,* Atlantic, 1991.
(With Paloma San Basilio) *Por Fin Juntos,* Capitol/EMI Latin, 1991.
*Canta Para Todos,* Capitol/EMI Latin, 1991; reissued, Polygram Latino, 1993.
(With Luciano Pavarotti and Jose Cerreras) *Domingo, Pavarotti, Carreras in Concert With Mehta,* Mobile Fidelity, 1993.
*De Mi Alma Latina,* Angel, 1994.
*Granada: The Greatest Hists of Placido Domingo,* Deutsche Grammophon, 1994.

## SOURCES:

### Books

*Contemporary Musicians,* Vol. 1, edited by Michael L. LaBlanc, Detroit, Gale, 1989.
*Current Biography 1972,* New York, H.W. Wilson, 1972, pp. 109–111.

### Periodicals

*Life,* October 1989, p. 73.
*New Yorker,* April 11, 1994, pp. 92–93.
*New York Post,* October 3, 1968, p. 80.
*New York Times,* September 30, 1968; November 3, 1968, p. 19.
*Opera News,* December 6, 1986, pp. 24–26; September 1993, pp. 8–9.
*Stereo Review,* July 1994, pp. 73–75.
*Time Magazine,* July 18, 1994, pp. 52–54.

—*Sketch by Kathe A. Conti*

# José Donoso
## 1924-
### Chilean writer

José Donoso is among Chile's most celebrated writers. He began his literary career in 1955 with a collection of short stories, *Veraneo y otros cuentos* (*Summertime and Other Stories*), which was chosen for Santiago's Municipal Literary Prize that year. Donoso's first novel, *Coronacion* (1957), initially secured his position in the pantheon of Latin American literary "Boom" writers of the 1960s and 1970s. His international reputation was confirmed with the 1970 publication of his monumental novel, *El Obsceno pájaro de la noche* (*The Obscene Bird of Night*).

Called a "grotesque masterpiece" by Ricardo Gutiérrez Mouat in the *Review of Contemporary Fiction* in 1992, *The Obscene Bird of Night* is a hallucinatory, mutating narrative with bizarre characters and settings that took Donoso eight years to complete. Robert Coover, writing in the *New York Times Book Review* in 1973, noted that "*The Obscene Bird of Night* is a dense and energetic book, full of terrible risk-taking, populated with legendary saints and witches, mad old crones and a whole estate-full of freaks and monsters, and narrated by a disturbed deaf-mute, many times disguised. The story line is like a great puzzle." Critics have agreed that the work is both unprecedented and unique.

Some of the influences on Donoso's writing can be traced to his youth. He was born October 5, 1924, to José (a doctor) and Alicia Yáñez Donoso, in Santiago, Chile. The eldest of three sons, Donoso grew up in a middle-class family. The home was dominated by women: his Nana, a servant who raised the children, a grandmother who slowly succumbed to madness, and great-aunts in their dotage. Images of the aged recur in Donoso's work, often inspired by the elderly caretakers of his childhood. A chain of illnesses in his youth also exerted a significant impact on Donoso's writing and eventually set the stage for *The Obscene Bird of Night*.

### Pain Forged a Literary Voice

The concept of voice is very important to Donoso. He described his theory of literary voice and its importance in an article he wrote for *Review of Contemporary Fiction* in 1992. There he asserted that "the voice chosen, adopted, found, forged, contrived, manufactured, is the very essence of literature . . . since the quest for a distinct literary voice . . . lies at the center of a writer's endeavor: it is his most important creation, the most radiant at the same time as the most misty of all his metaphors. . . . The voice adopted is the most powerful of all the writer's artifices."

Never robust as a child, Donoso did not grow stronger as he entered adolescence. To avoid the required sports at school, he successfully feigned stomach pains. The fictional malady was diagnosed as the start of an ulcer. Donoso considered this bit of fakery to be the first effective "voice" of his own making. Unfortunately, the pretended ulcer assumed larger proportions in his future.

After idealistic ventures working variously as a shepherd and dockhand, Donoso entered the Instituto Pedagógico of the University of Chile in 1947. He studied literature there for two years. He was awarded a scholarship to Princeton University, where he earned his B.A. in 1951. Upon his return to Chile the following year, Donoso began to write in earnest; but every time he attempted to write, he was seized with stomach pains located in the same place as the pretended ones. A few years later a duodenal ulcer was diagnosed—this time it was real. The pain continued to both spark and inhibit Donoso's creativity for years.

In 1955 Donoso's first collection of short stories was published—but only after guaranteed sales of 100 copies. He and his friends were forced to sell the book on Santiago street corners. A second book, *Dos cuentos* (*Two Short Stories*, 1956), as well as *Coronación,* were sold in a similar fashion. Originally published in 1957, and translated as *Coronation, Coronación* did not begin to garner critical acclaim until a few years later. In 1962 it received the William Faulkner Foundation Prize. A third short story collection, *Charleston and Other Stories,* met with little success.

But Donoso had begun to write his magnum opus, *The Obscene Bird of Night.* Originally entitled *The Last Azcoitía,* it was a seemingly endless mass of loosely connected sketches. Meanwhile, the ulcer pains grew so severe that Donoso was forced to leave his job as a journalist for *Ercilla,* a Chilean weekly magazine. He married Maria del Pilar Serrano, a Bolivian painter and translator, in 1961 and continued to work on his manuscript. In 1964 Donoso and his wife attended a writers' conference in Mexico. At the invitation of writer **Carlos Fuentes**, the Donosos moved into a house on Fuentes's property. It was during this time that Donoso wrote his next two novels, *El lugar sin limites* (*Hell Has No Limits*) and *Este Domingo* (*This Sunday*), both published in 1966. These two novels are considered by many critics to mark the beginning of Donoso's departure from social realism, which had been characterized in his earlier work by primarily urban settings and realistic story lines. The new novels were distinguished by themes of self-disintegration and madness—both hallmarks of *The Obscene Bird.* In fact, *Hell Has No Limits* sprang

directly from Donoso's other ongoing manuscript. Donoso excised a very small part of the original and created the new novel from it.

## Rewrite Triggered by Medical Emergency

Donoso soon accepted a two-year teaching position at the University of Iowa. In 1967 the Donosos moved to Majorca, Spain, where their daughter, Maria, was born. Donoso continued to work on *The Obscene Bird* despite the recurrent ulcer pain. In 1969 he was invited to teach in Ft. Collins, Colorado. A week after his arrival, the ulcer hemorrhaged, requiring immediate surgery. Donoso credited this operation and its aftermath as the turning point in the writing of *The Obscene Bird.* Given painkilling morphine—to which he was allergic—Donoso experienced a temporary hallucinatory descent into madness, followed by a lengthy period of paranoia. He returned to Mallorca, but soon moved his family to Barcelona. From his experiences, he acquired the voice that enabled him to rewrite his novel completely in eight months.

## The "Boom"

Living in Barcelona in a community of exiled Latin American writers, Donoso was in the midst of the literary boom at its peak. Cultural changes in Latin America had propelled a surge in literature, and European and American markets had opened. Marta Mestrovic stated in *Publishers Weekly* in 1992 that Donoso "attributes the initiation of 'the Boom' to the efforts of Spanish publisher Carlos Barral . . . whose firm, Seix Barral, first published many of these Latin American writers."

Donoso's next book was—in yet another stylistic departure—a book about the "Boom" itself. Published in 1972, *The Boom in Spanish-American Literature* is a straightforward assessment with commentary on many noted Latin American writers, including Fuentes and **Mario Vargas Llosa**.

## Pinochet Coup Changed Focus

Chile sank into political crisis when the **Agusto Pinochet** coup brought the country under military dictatorship in 1973. These events changed the course of Donoso's writing. In an interview with *Publishers Weekly* in 1992, Donoso said: "Since the Pinochet coup I have been writing political novels. It has invaded my emotion and my subconscious." In 1978 Donoso published *A House in the Country,* a fictionalized account of the political situation in Chile. "I accept all the political interpretations given that book," Donoso told *Publishers Weekly.*

Donoso's next novel was *The Garden Next Door,* published in 1981. It tells the story of a Chilean writer who has reached middle age without having achieved the status of his "Boom" era peers. His attempt to write a masterpiece social novel ends in failure, and he disappears from the novel. A change of narrators at the end reveals that the story has actually been told by the protagonist's wife. The backdrop of the novel is, again, the political upheaval of dictatorship.

Donoso returned to Chile in 1981 and was welcomed back. Since then he has written several novellas, a play, and the 1986 novel, *Curfew*. **Fernando Alegría** assested in the *Review of Contemporary Fiction* in 1992, "For years José Donoso has beaten the path of metaphor to express his way of feeling and understanding Chile, a path both difficult and dangerous." *Curfew* boldly confronts the harsh nightmare of the Pinochet regime, and Alegría continued: 'Perhaps the most important thing is not so much to remember the facts ... but to examine objectively what those crimes have done to the character of the Chilean people as they deal with the crisis. It is in this connection that Donoso abandons his typical metaphoric strategy and confronts the collapse of Chilean society in images and portraits bound to cause a stir ... among his compatriots." *Curfew* was not well-received in Chile. Mestrovic suggested that its poor reception was "probably because its criticism of Chilean society was too close to home."

Donoso has received several honors including the Chile-Italia prize for journalism (1960) for his work with the Chilean national magazine, *Ercilla*. He has also been awarded the Mondello Prize (Italy, 1989), the National Prize for literature (Chile, 1990), and the Roger Caillois Prize (France, 1991). Donoso has taught at Princeton University, Dartmouth College, the Catholic University of Chile and the University of Chile. He has also begun to instruct a new generation of Chilean writers through several workshops he has organized in Santiago.

## SELECTED PUBLISHED WORKS:

*Veraneo y otros cuentos,* Santiago, Universitaria, 1955.

*Dos cuentos,* Santiago, Guardia Vieja, 1956.

*Coronación,* Santiago, Nascimento, 1957; translated by Jocasta Goodwin as *Coronation,* New York, Knopf, 1965.

*El charleston,* Santiago, Nascimento, 1960; translated by Andrée Conrad as *Charleston and Other Stories,* Boston, David R. Godine, 1977.

*El lugar sin límites,* Mexico City, Joaquin Mortiz, 1966; translated by Suzanne Jill Levine as *Hell Has No Limits,* in *Triple Cross,* New York, Dutton, 1972.

*Este domingo,* Santiago, Zig-Zag, 1966; translated by Lorraine O'Grady Freeman as *This Sunday,* New York, Knopf, 1967.

*El obsceno pájaro de la noche,* Barcelona, Seix Barral, 1970; translated by Hardie St. Martin and Leonard Mades as *The Obscene Bird of Night,* New York, Knopf, 1973.

*Cuentos,* Barcelona, Seix Barral, 1971.

*Historia personal del "boom",* Barcelona, Anagrama, 1972; translated by Gregory Kolovakos as *The Boom in Spanish-American Literature,* New York, Columbia University Press, 1977.

*Tres novelitas burguesas,* Barcelona, Seix Barral, 1973; translated by Conrad as *Sacred Families: Three Novellas,* New York, Knopf, 1977.

*Casa de campo,* Barcelona, Seix Barral, 1978; translated by Levine and David Pritchard as *A House in the Country,* New York, Knopf, 1984.

*La misteriosa desaparición de la Marquesita de Loria,* Barcelona, Seix Barral, 1980.

*El jardín de al lado,* Barcelona, Seix Barral, 1981; translated by St. Martin as *The Garden Next Door,* New York, Grove Press, 1992.

*Poemas de un novelista,* Santiago, Ganymedes, 1981.

*Cuatro para Delfina,* Barcelona, Seix Barral, 1982.

*Sueños de mala muerte,* Santiago, Nascimento, 1985.

*La desesperanza,* Barcelona, Seix Barral, 1986; translated by Alfred MacAdam as *Curfew,* New York, Weidenfeld & Nicolson, 1988.

*Taratuta,* Madrid, Mondadori, 1990; translated by Gregory Rabassa as *Taratuta and Still Life With Pipe,* New York, Norton, 1992.

## SOURCES:

### Books

*Contemporary Authors,* Volume 81–84, edited by Frances C. Locher, Detroit, Gale Research, 1979.

*Dictionary of Literary Biography,* Volume 113, edited by William Luis, Detroit, Gale Research, 1992.

*Latin American Writers,* Volume 3, edited by Carlos A. Solé, New York, Charles Scribner's Sons, 1989.

### Periodicals

*New York Times Book Review,* June 17, 1973.

*PMLA,* January 1991, pp. 60–69.

*Publishers Weekly,* November 30, 1992, pp. 30–31; December 1992, p.42.

*Review of Contemporary Fiction,* summer 1992, pp. 7–10, 18–31, 77–79.

*—Sketch by Ellen Dennis French*

# Ariel Dorfman
## 1942-
### Chilean Argentine writer, poet, and playwright

Writer Ariel Dorfman is a political activist best known for his outspoken opposition to the Augusto Pinochet regime in Chile. Revolution, repression, and exile have been the defining aspects of his life and writing. Born May 6, 1942, in Buenos Aires, Argentina, to a family well-acquainted with the horrors of war and the pain of exile, his Jewish grandparents fled the pograms of Eastern Europe.

At two years of his age, Dorfman experienced the first of many moves spurred by politics. His father, Adolfo, an economist, engineer, and government advisor, left Argentina for a position with the United Nations in New York City accompanied by his wife Fanny (Zelicovich), a Spanish literature teacher, and their young son. Ten years later, Dorfman's family returned to South America, choosing Chile as their new residence. The country became home to Dorfman, and he completed his education there. In 1966, he married Maria Angelica Malinarich, an English teacher and social worker. He became a Chilean citizen in 1967.

Though much of his youth was shaped by upheaval, writing and other creative expressions remained constant. By Dorfman's own account, he began artistically expressing himself through painting. By the age of seven he began writing children's fiction. Later, in adulthood, Dorfman worked as an activist, journalist, and writer. He published his first novel, entitled *Moros en la costa* ("The Coast is Not Clear in Chile") and a variety of nonfiction essays. In 1972, in collaboration with Armand Mattelart, he wrote *Para leer al Pato Donald* ("How to Read Donald Duck: Imperialist Ideology in the Disney Comic") which examined how the popular cartoon characters subtly transmit capitalist ideology to Latin American audiences.

Early on, Dorfman actively protested against political oppression in Chile and paid the price of his beliefs with lifelong exile. When Chile's democratically-elected *Salvador Allende* and his Marxist government were overthrown in a coup by *Augusto Pinochet* in 1973, the author found himself in opposition to those in power. Following Allende's death, thousands of intellectuals, writers, clergymen, and politicians were expelled from Chile—including Dorfman. He settled in France with his family, working for the Chilean resistance movement in Paris and teaching Spanish American literature at the Sorbonne. For two years following the coup, Dorfman was so distraught he could not write. "During the first years after the

*Ariel Dorfman*

coup, I think I was unable to write because the pain overwhelmed me and also because I felt that the language in which I had written during the revolution was partly responsible for the failure of that revolution," he explained to in a *Contemporary Authors* interview.

## Reflected Horrors of Dictatorship

The first work he attempted after his long writer's block was a selection of poems on torture, murder, and abductions entitled *Missing,* published in English in 1982. The poetry focused on the desaparecidos—people the Chilean government termed subversive who were taken from their homes by the secret police, never to be seen or heard from again. "I discovered a way in which I could become a meeting ground of the living and the dead—a way to give voice to the missing, which was also a metaphor for the whole country and what had been irretrievably lost," Dorfman explained to Leslie Bennetts of the *New York Times.* "All of my poems are ways of giving voices to those who have disappeared and those who are left behind; I am a bridge between them. Words become a way of returning to your county—a cemetery, but also a resurrection ground."

Dorfman left France and worked as a chief research scholar at the University of Amsterdam from 1976 to 1980, when he accepted a Woodrow Wilson fellowship in Washington, D.C. His return to the United States was marked by a resumption of novel writing; his second major work of fiction, *Viudas* ("Widows"), was published in 1981, translated into English in 1983, and adapted for the stage in 1988. *Viudas* was applauded for both its political relevance and its intense portrayal of the agony and stress that the disappearances put on the families of the missing. In 1983, *La última canción de Manuel Sendero* ("The Last Song of Manuel Sendero") was published. The novel centers around unborn fetuses who organize a revolt and refuse to be born until the existing generations correct their mistakes. This novel was also praised for its complexity and for its blending of artistic and political concerns.

In 1983, after ten years of exile, Dorfman was offered the opportunity to temporarily go back to Chile. He divided time between Santiago and teaching as a visiting professor at Duke University. Though he was allowed to return to Chile, the author did not still his voice or beliefs, writing articles and editorials for international publications. In a bizarre twist to the stories of the missing, Dorfman was pronounced murdered in Chile in 1986 though he was alive and well in North Carolina. "The news came at the end of one of the most depressing weeks in my country's history," Dorfman recalled in an article in *The Nation* in 1986. "After the failed attempt on his life, on September 7, Augusto Pinochet, our dictator for the past 13 years, went wild. This was the pretext he had been waiting for to crush an opposition that had been mounting a campaign of protracted civil disobedience against him. He declared a state of siege, shut down six magazines and a couple of news agencies, raided shanty-towns, expelled foreign priests. His secret policemen picked up a number of prominent dissidents." And for a short time it was believed, through journalistic error, that Dorfman was one of the casualties.

"Once again the county was being destroyed, and I was far away. The horror was compounded by its familiarity: it was as if we were all caught up, one more time, in the endless repetition of the 1973 coup. The terror was widespread." In addition, Dorfman had to deal with the mistaken reports of his own death, which brought the horrors even closer to home. "As a child, I always wanted to survive my own death," he wrote in *The Nation*. "I desired no more than a couple of hours. It would be fun, I thought, to witness how people reacted." Reality, however, was anything but a child's game. "Besides the pain to one's family and friends, the feverish calls all around the world, what is hard to dismiss is the sensation that in some odd way you may, indeed, have died." Though he uncovered the reporting error that led to the erroneous report, Dorfman could not help but wonder if the Chilean government was sending him a message to stay in complete exile.

Dorfman noted in his *The Nation* piece: "I have learned that in order to live under a dictatorship, you must tame your imagination. Signs of violence and foreboding are everywhere, and if you do not want to be paralyzed by fear, you must learn to shut those signs out," he wrote. "Ever since the coup that terminated democracy in Chile" he continued, "I have been living on borrowed time—trying either to escape that death or to ignore it. My exile 13 years ago was a way of avoiding it; my return to Chile at the end of last year, while Pinochet was still in power, was a way of making believe it would not touch me."

Dorfman continued to live, write, and protest. In the late 1980s, he published another book of poetry and completed *Mascara* in 1988—the least politically obvious of his works. The thriller was an attempt to branch out into new areas of his writing, to escape the influence of the Pinochet dictatorship.

In 1990, Dorfman released a translated collection of short stories entitled *My House Is on Fire. The Nation*'s Michael Ugarte reviewed the narrations about the children of dictatorship. "The collection is typical of Dorfman . . . in its humane yet critical treatment not only of children but of those who encircle them: parents, other relatives, even authorities," Ugarte wrote. "As Dorfman shows us, to be a child is to be riddled with fears of all types, and in a police state the terror increases tenfold. . . . Dorfman deals earnestly with the mentality and the contradictions that lead to compliance, treating these characters with sympathy and critical understanding." Dorfman is interested in how people relate and communicate, Ugarte claimed. "The object of Dorfman's political search is a language that is open but never arbitrary or without motive, dialogical but never vacuously pluralistic. Dorfman is interested in relations."

Dorfman brought his voice to the stage for a second time when his play, *Death & The Maiden* debuted on Broadway in 1992—the first time for an Hispanic playwright. Though it opened to mixed reviews and the Hispanic community complained that all the stars were Anglo-Americans, it was quite an achievement for a man driven from his home. Roman Polanski directed a movie version of *Death & the Maiden* in 1995.

## SELECTED PUBLISHED WORKS:

### Novels

*Moros en la costa* (*The Coast Is Not Clear in Chile*), Sudamericana 1973, translation by George R. Shivers published as *Hard Rain*, Readers International, 1990.
*Viudas*, Siglo XXI, 1981, translation by Stephen Kessler published as *Widows*, Pantheon Books, 1983.

*La última canción de Manuel Sendero,* Siglo XXI,
1983, translation by Ariel Dorfman and
George R. Shivers published as *The Last Song
of Manuel Sendero,* Viking, 1987.
*Mascara,* Viking, 1988.

## Other

*Imaginación y violencia en América* (essays; title
means
"Imagination and Violence in Latin America"),
Universitaria, 1970.
(With Armand Mattelart) *Para leer al Pato Don-
ald,* Siglo Vientiuno Argentina, 1972, transla-
tion by David Kunzle published as *How to
Read Donald Duck: Imperialist Ideology in the
Disney Comic,* International General, 1975,
2nd edition, 1984.
*Ensayos quemados en Chile: Inocencia y neocolo-
nialismo* (essays; title means "Essays Burnt in
Chile: Innocence and Neocolonialism"), Edi-
ciones de la Flor, 1974.
*Culture et resistance au Chile* (essays; title means
"Culture and Resistance in Chile"), Institut
d'Action Culturelle, 1978.
*Cría ojos* (short stories), Nueva Imagen, 1979,
translation by Ariel Dorfman and George R.
Shivers published as *My House Is on Fire,*
Viking, 1990.
*Pruebas al canto* (poems; title means "Soft Evi-
dence"), Nueva Imagen, 1980.
*Reader's nuestro que estás en la tierra: Ensayos
sobre el imperialismo cutural* (essays; title
means "Our Readers That Art on Earth")
Nueva Imagen, 1980, translation by Clark
Hansen published as *The Empire's Old
Clothes: What the Lone Ranger, Barbar, and
Other Innocent Heroes Do to Our Minds,* Pan-
theon, 1983.
*Missing* (poetry), translation by Edie Grossman,
Amnesty International British Section, 1982.
*Hacia liberación del lector latinoamericano* (es-
says), Ediciones del Norte, 1984.
*Dorando la píldora* (stories; title means "The
Medicine Goes Down"), Ediciones del Ornitor-
rinco, 1985.
*Pastel de choclo* (poetry), Sinfronteras, 1986, trans-
lation by Arial Dorfman and Grossman pub-
lished as *Last Waltz in Santiago and Other
Poems of Exile and Disappearance,* Penguin,
1988.
*Missing Continents,* Pantheon, c. 1991.

## SOURCES:

### Books

*Contemporary Authors,* edited by Susan M. Trosky, Detroit, Gale, 1990.

*Hispanic Writers,* edited by Bryan Ryan, Detroit,
Detroit, 1991.

### Periodicals

*The Nation,* October 18, 1986, pp. 370–374, February 190, pp. 245–246.
*New York Times,* February 17, 1987; April 14,
1988; October 8, 1988.

—*Sketch by Kathe A. Conti*

# José Napoleón Duarte
## 1926-1990
### Salvadoran statesman

José Napoleón Duarte was appointed as the president of civil war-torn El Salvador in 1980 and
served until 1982, when he was removed from office.
He was elected president by the Salvadoran people in
1984. Duarte attempted but failed to settle the civil
war. He served as president through 1989 during one
of the roughest, most tragic times in El Salvador's
history.

José Napoleón Duarte (Fuentes) was the second
of three sons born to José Jesús Duarte in San
Salvador, El Salvador, in 1926. Before marriage,
Duarte's mother worked both as a seamstress and as a
servant. His father, who came from poverty, became
the owner of a successful candy manufacturing business after working for years as a tailor. Duarte spent
the majority of his youth in the Boy Scouts and
remained true to its precepts throughout his life.

He graduated from the Liceo Salvadoreño, a
Catholic school, and in 1944 left for the United
States. There he attended Notre Dame University.
Duarte did not know any English, but he succeeded at
Notre Dame by working non-stop on his studies and
odd jobs.

Shortly after El Salvador entered the United
Nations, Duarte returned to his homeland in 1948
having earned a degree in civil engineering. He
married Ines Duran, with whom he had six children.
Until 1964, Duarte worked in partnership with his
father, who owned a successful construction firm. He
also taught engineering and volunteered his time to
the Boy Scouts and the Red Cross.

In 1960, Duarte became one of the founding
members of the Christian Democrat Party (PDC)
with whom he served as general secretary until 1964.
A large majority elected him mayor of San Salvador

*José Napoleón Duarte*

in 1964. He served three consecutive terms and focused his attention on community development. As a mayor, he was "a booster, a back-slapper, a businessman with a conscience. . . . He made himself immensely popular by forming neighborhood self-help groups, by installing the city's first modern street lighting, and by making the rich pay up decades of back sewer and water taxes on their hilltop mansions," according to a 1981 *New Yorker* article. He became president of the PDC in 1972.

Duarte entered the El Salvadoran presidential race as a candidate of the National Opposition Union (UNO), an alliance of the PDC; the National Revolutionary Movement (MNR); and the Nationalist Democratic Union (UDN). When it looked as if Duarte would win by a wide margin, the government intervened, creating a news blackout and altering the vote totals, and Duarte was declared a loser.

The fraudulent election angered Duarte's supporters to the point that those in the military launched a coup d'etat on March 25, 1972, and attempted to overthrow the government. Duarte had no prior knowledge of the intentions of his supporters, and so he belatedly lent his support to the rebellion. However, it was to no avail. 200 people lost their lives in the coup, and it was quelled. Duarte attempted to find asylum in the Venezuelan Embassy, but soldiers broke into the embassy, arrested and tortured him, breaking his cheekbones and nose. Before he could be court martialed and executed,

Duarte won his freedom through the efforts of the Venezuelan government, the Vatican, the president of Notre Dame University, and others. He lived in exile in Venezuela until 1979, resting, creating oil paintings of peasant life, and working as an engineer.

Duarte returned to El Salvador in 1980 and joined the Third Junta, a group that had sprung from the 1979 coup and the civil war that raged through the country. With the backing of the U.S. military and the Salvadoran army, Duarte was appointed president of El Salvador in 1980. Duarte seemed hopeful for reelection in 1982. In the *New Yorker* in 1981, he said that "I have a second chance. The situation is very different [than in 1972]. I have more enemies and much of the world is against me. But I think we [Duarte and the PDC party] will succeed." But Duarte's optimism was short-lived, and he was removed from office in 1982.

## Won Second Presidential Term

In May of 1984, Duarte was elected president of El Salvador by a 54-percent popular vote over his opponent, the incumbent Robert D'Aubuisson. He was inaugurated on June 1, 1984. Duarte attempted to end the civil war with the left-wing FDR/FMLN, despite obstacles stemming from the military and the right-wing business community. Still, Duarte made progress in 1984 toward improving human rights in El Salvador, such as convicting members of the military for murders for the first time in the country's history, and decreasing death squad activity.

On September 29, 1985, guerilla rebels kidnapped Duarte's daughter. Duarte negotiated a truce on October 24. 22 FMLN prisoners and 100 guerillas were given safe passage out of the country for the release of his daughter and 23 village mayors who were also held hostage.

## Lost Support of the People

In 1986, the United States poured $1 million in aid each day into El Salvador. The United States mounted a campaign of propaganda films, mariachi bands, and provocative dancers to increase the population's support for the government against the rebels. Despite the best efforts of the United States to support the government, the situation in El Salvador went from bad to worse. Problems arising out of the 1986 earthquake and a severe drought further eroded Duarte's popularity. Labor unrest and disputes over taxes furthered discontent.

Duarte attempted to resume the talks with the rebels in 1987 but failed. His own party, the PDC, was beset by bickering and split into two parties. Other dilemmas, including a corruption scandal involving Duarte's son and the return of the death squads, contributed to the erosion of his popularity.

Increasingly, civil unrest intensified, further weakening Duarte's public influence. By the end of his term in 1989, his administration was completely powerless.

In 1988, Duarte was diagnosed with cancer. After exploratory surgery on June 7, 1988, at Walter Reed Army Medical Center in Washington, DC, doctors claimed Duarte only had months to live. He died in 1990.

**SOURCES:**

**Books**

*Current Biography Yearbook,* edited by Charles Moritz, New York, H.W. Wilson Co., 1981.
*The Dictionary of Contemporary Politics of Central America and the Caribbean,* edited by Phil Gunson and Greg Chamberlain, New York, Simon and Schuster, 1991.
Webre, Stephen, *José Napoleón Duarte and the Christian Democratic Party in Salvadoran Politics, 1960–1972,* Baton Rouge, Louisiana State University Press, 1979.

**Periodicals**

*Newsweek,* March 16, 1981, p.37.
*New Yorker,* June 22, 1981, p.41+.
*New York Times Magazine,* September 2, 1984, p.14.

—*Sketch by Christopher B. Tower*

# Roberto Durán
## 1951-

**Panamanian boxer**

Roberto Carlos Durán is a four-time winner of world championship boxing titles—one each of the lightweight, welterweight, junior middleweight, and middleweight titles. He was born June 16, 1951, in Chorillo, Panama, a rundown barrio at the mouth of the Panama Canal across from Fort Amador. His parents, Clara Esther Samaniego and Margarito Durán, were of Indian and Spanish blood. His mother had nine children. Durán's father, who was a Mexican national left when he was a young boy and he did not see him again until he became a champion boxer. His mother moved the children to Guarare, a town 150 miles from Panama City and returned to Chorillo a few years later. Because of their extreme poverty, his mother gave him to friends and relatives to feed when she could not provide for him. When Durán was in the third grade, he hit a boy and was thrown out of school. He was 13 at the time and never returned to school. At the age of 14 he roamed the streets, shining shoes, painting, and selling newspapers to help his family. Durán would swim two miles across the canal with a sack, steal mangoes and then sell them. He was also a natural entertainer and he would sing, dance, and play drums on the streets to get tips. He would lead gang raids over the border into the Canal Zone at night. Always close to his family, when Durán became wealthy from his boxing, he bought his mother a house in Panama.

Durán would go to a local gym with his brother Domingo who was boxing there. When Domingo quit boxing, trainer Nestor Quinones encouraged Durán to stay. Durán was 14 at the time. He turned pro at the age of 16. Quinones stayed with him throughout his career. Out of his first 16 amateur fights, Durán won 13. After he became a professional boxer, Carlos Eleta, a wealthy sportsman and former tennis champion, bought his contract for $300 from Alfredo Vasquez. Eleta owned Air Panama, various sports teams, thoroughbred horses, TV and radio stations. He first met Durán when he was only ten years old; he caught Durán stealing coconuts from his estate. Eleta took the young Durán into his huge home and gave him some money. Eventually Durán became so close to Eleta, he called him "Papa."

Eleta convinced one of the best ring tacticians in American boxing, Ray Arcel, to come out of retirement to train Durán. Arcel had been retired from boxing since 1956. Durán had been a right-handed boxer until Arcel taught him to use both hands. Arcel worked with Durán on a part-time basis, and Eleta hired Freddie Brown, a trainer for 12 world champions, to work with him every day. In 1971, Durán married Felicidad and they had four children, Dalia, Jovani, Irichelle, and Roberto, Jr. He won his first title in 1972, when he became the world lightweight champion in a fight against Ken Buchanan. Durán defended his title 11 times and out of his first 71 professional fights, he won 70. Durán's nickname was *manos de piedra* (hands of stone) because of the way he fought.

In 1975, the controversial Don King became Durán's promoter. The only fighter who beat him as a lightweight in a non-title fight was Esteban DeJesus. Durán was sick during the fight. He fought DeJesus twice after that and both times dropped him in the first round with a left hook. In January of 1978, Durán and DeJesus fought again. This time Durán's trainers urged him to fight for several rounds before dropping DeJesus. He did what they suggested and in the twelfth round, Durán knocked DeJesus out. That was Durán's last fight as a lightweight.

Durán was famous in Panama and by 1975, he bought a $150,000 home in the same neighborhood as Aristides Royo, then president of Panama. He had cars, real estate, and money in the bank—a long way from the poverty he had known only a few years before. But he never forgot his old neighborhood in Chorillo. He hired people from Chorillo to work for him and he would return to his old neighborhood frequently. Every Sunday, he would go to Farfan Beach in Chorillo where he and his wife would set out tables of food and drinks and invite anyone who wanted to picnic with them. They would play dominoes and listen to salsa music on the beach.

Durán liked to eat and battled with his weight. Freddie Brown kept a watchful eye on what the fighter ate to keep him in the lightweight division and worked with him constantly to keep his weight down. But Durán had a penchant for food and it was a battle for Brown to keep him at 135 pounds—the lightweight division's top weight. At times, Durán would gain up to 30 pounds. Durán was also known for his fiery temperament. He gave up his lightweight title on February 1, 1978, and began welterweight bouts, where he could make more money than in lightweight fights. With Brown and Arcel, Durán sharpened his skills throughout the years. Durán went up against one of the greatest welterweight fighters of the century, Sugar Ray Leonard, in what was considered "the prizefight of the decade." In June 1980, Durán battled with Leonard and won the World Boxing Council's (WBC) welterweight champion title.

### Walked Out of Ring

Durán returned to Panama a national hero and the parties began. His weight shot up from 147 to 185 pounds, and he was out of control; when the next fight with Leonard was scheduled, the real battle began. Brown worked hard to get his weight down and Durán had to train in a rubber corset. He took a diuretic before the weigh-in and then gorged himself on steaks and juice. On November 25, 1980, in a rematch with Leonard at the Superdome in New Orleans, Durán walked out of the ring in the eighth round before the fight was over, yelling, *"No más . . . no peleo más"* *("No more, I don't box anymore"). That fight was labeled the "No más" fight by journalists throughout the country.* There were many speculations as to why he abruptly quit, but Durán said that he was ill and severe stomach cramps caused him to walk out of the ring. He was not in shape to face Leonard after the months of overindulging. Durán was paid $3 million for the fight; millions of dollars were lost on the fight and many people were angry. Brown walked out over a disagreement with Eleta, and Arcel retired.

Durán was disgraced when he returned to Panama. People harassed him and his family, calling Durán names. They stayed locked in their house for

months. He gained weight and Eleta, with the help of the Panamanian ruler, General Omar Torrijos Herrera, took Durán to Coiba, a penal island off the coast of Panama, to train him. Durán was isolated from outside influences and the lifestyle he enjoyed. He soon was ready to fight again. At his comeback fight with Wilfred Benitiz, Durán did not win but he fought hard for 15 rounds and regained his honor. In 1982, Eleta and Durán split after 14 years. He asked an old friend, Luis Spada, to become his manager. King dropped him and Durán asked Bob Arum to promote him. Durán wanted to fight junior middleweight champion, Davey Moore.

### Won Middleweight Title

In 1983, Durán fought in the junior middleweight division and became the new world champion after defeating Moore at Madison Square Garden. He was on top again. After losing a round of bouts, including a 15-round loss to Marvelous Marvin Hagler, Durán was unable to get a championship bout until 1989. He trained for two months in Miami for the big fight. After 22 years of fighting, at the age of 37, Durán won the WBC middleweight title in a fight with middleweight champion Iran Barkley.

Durán was the first Latin fighter to have held four championship titles in four weight divisions, and the only boxer to defeat Sugar Ray Leonard. Durán wanted to fight Leonard again, and finally had his chance in December 1989. He fought Leonard in the outdoor arena at the Mirage Hotel in Las Vegas. Leonard won by judges' decisions over Durán. It was Leonard's last fight. Durán continued to fight and in 1991, he beat super middleweight champion, Tony Biglen. He wanted another chance at Iran Barkley.

At the age of 43, Durán was considered the "old man" in the arena. He fought 32-year-old Vinny Pazienza for the international Boxing Council's (IBC) super middleweight title in 1995 and lost. They fought for 12 rounds and Pazienza won by unanimous decision. Durán did not make it an easy win for Pazienza—he knocked Pazienza down in the fifth round. Pazienza was also cut over his right eye later in the round and it bled for the remainder of the fight. Pazienza later commented that he thought it would have been an easier win than it was. Durán proclaimed himself the real winner and earned $619,000 for the fight. Pazienza wanted Durán to retire after the fight but Durán just grinned at the suggestion.

### SOURCES:

#### Books

*The Hispanic-American Almanac,* edited by Nicolas Kanellos, Detroit, Gale Research, 1993.

**Periodicals**

*New York,* June 23, 1980, pp. 26, 28, 31–33; December 15, 1980, pp. 32–33, 36, 38, 40–41.

*New York Times,* June 15, 1994, Section 1, p. 36; June 26, 1994, p. B14; November 29, 1994, p. B21; January 16, 1995, p. C7.

*Sports Illustrated,* June 16, 1980, pp. 30–42; February 8, 1982, pp. 22, 24–27; November 83, pp. 78–79; March 6, 1989, pp. 18–19; December 18, 1989, pp. 24–25; October 12, 1992, p. 78.

—*Sketch by Phyllis Noah*

# María Elena Durazo
## 1954(?)-
### Mexican American labor leader

As the first woman, let alone Hispanic woman, to head a major union in the city of Los Angeles, María Elena Durazo is more than a leader: she is a groundbreaker. Her election as president of the Hotel and Restaurant Employees Local 11, a union with a 70 percent Hispanic membership, proves that Hispanics are capable of gaining greater respect and authority. As she told *Hispanic Business,* Durazo understands how her position has affected Hispanics in the community. "I think my election is absolutely a turning point for Hispanics. . . . It would signal a new confidence in being able to decide their own future. . . . They don't have to be second-class citizens anymore."

Even before Durazo was elected president of the union, she proved that Hispanic women could excel at roles traditionally held by non-Hispanics and men. The daughter of migrant workers from northern Mexico, Durazo knew firsthand the hardships that many underpaid people face. As her parents traveled from town to town to work in the fields, the children of the Durazo family accompanied them. Durazo and her brothers and sisters slept in the back of her father's pickup truck. There was never enough money to pay for everything; despite the long hours her parents put in, they could not make enough to get out of the situation. It was Durazo's childhood that inspired her to fight for the rights of immigrants and other people forced to live as her family had.

### Vows to Work for Immigrants

As a young woman, Durazo was influenced by the Chicano movement of the 1970s. Determined to educate herself and assist other Chicanos to empower themselves, she worked her way through the Los Angeles People's College of Law. As she studied, she began to utilize her knowledge and skill to advocate for immigrants who had no idea of how to protect themselves. She believed in what she was doing, and worked without pay, even though she was a single mother and had a son, Mario, to support.

It was not until 1979, when the International Ladies Garment Workers Union hired her as an organizer, that Durazo began to work professionally, fighting for the rightsof those who worked in the factories of the designer-label manufacturers. She made house calls and worked in the office of that union until she was hired to work as a law clerk for Abe Levy, a labor lawyer. Levy represented Local 11, and he helped her get a job with the union over which she would later preside.

At the time, the Hotel and Restaurant Employees union was not supportive of the majority of its members. As some of its leaders were retired members, or non-minorities unfamiliar with the actual membership of the union, many disagreements occurred. One of these arguments centered on what was considered a fundamental aspect of union membership—understanding what transpired at the meetings. Although 70 percent of the union's members were Hispanic, and many of those Hispanics spoke only Spanish, the union leaders refused to run bilingual meetings. They argued that the members should learn to speak and read English instead.

Due to unsympathetic policies such as this one, the union leaders were extremely unpopular with Hispanic members. The local's membership dropped by 50 percent, or more than 12,000 members, and it failed to protect its remaining members as vehemently as other locals had across the United States. The union leader, Andrew (Scotty) Allan, had been presiding over the union for 23 years when Durazo decided that enough was enough. She was sure that the union could do a better job of representing its members, and that it could even recruit the thousands of unrepresented workers in the Los Angeles area.

### Becomes Union Leader, Members' Advocate

Although Durazo had been working as an organizer and arbitrator for the union for only three years, its members already looked to her for leadership. She began to persuade them that if they used the power their numbers created and voted together they could transform the union into an organization that worked for them. "I had complete faith that there were enough workers here with the talent and the motivation to make the change," Durazo explained in the *Los Angeles Times.* By 1987, Durazo had garnered enough support from the union's members to present them with a slate of candidates to challenge Allan.

As the elections took place, however, both parties charged election irregularities. The international union seized control of the local and placed it in a trusteeship. Miguel Contreras was sent in as administrator. After weeding out many union staffers, Contreras hired Durazo as a staff director to help him return the union to its proper function. Together, the pair turned the union around.

First, they hired immigrants and other representative members as union officials. They then began to conduct union meetings in Spanish as well as English, and encouraged Hispanic members to delve into contract negotiations. By encouraging members to wear union buttons at work, to recruit new union members, and to demonstrate, Contreras and Durazo helped members to feel that they had more clout. Employers sensed this new confidence, and when new contract negotiations began, union members gained their biggest wage increase in 20 years. Existing employees were promised the benefits of seniority as well as opportunities for promotions, and illegal aliens were protected from unnecessarily hard labor. The salaries of maids would increase $1.50 more per hour over three years, and waiters would receive a raise of $.80 per hour. Finally, the local union was representing its members, and members were representing themselves.

In 1989, Durazo once again put herself and a 15-person slate up for the union's elected offices. Despite the efforts of a former friend, Javier Rodriguez, who challenged her and charged that she was merely a front for the international union and received unfair assistance for her campaign from it, Durazo was successful. She was elected president of the union, and her 15-person slate of candidates won as well. The 85 percent of union members who voted for Durazo were pleased, and despite their positions as employers, hotel and restaurant owners in the community were not unhappy with the results. Irving Baldwin, the president of the Hotel-Restaurant Employers' Council of Southern California, told *Hispanic Business,* "We can expect [Durazo's] union to be more aggressive now, but I think she's definitely business oriented. . . . We look with concern at what she's doing, but I have no reason to cut her. She listens and she's realistic." Apparently, other business leaders feel the same way about Durazo. They know she intends to represent the needs of the local's members, and they also know that she understands that businesses need to be profitable in order to offer employment at all.

### Foresees Bright Future for Hispanic Union Workers

Durazo works ten to 12 hours a day, six days a week, planning, working, and coordinating demonstrators. She has been arrested, along with other union members, and charged with trespassing during demonstrations. While her primary objective is to keep the union functional, she believes that there is a great amount of potential for growth. She figures that 90 percent of the present restaurant and hotel workers in the Los Angeles area are unrepresented, and that many new restaurants and hotels will be built in the future. Since many illegal aliens have been given amnesty by the U.S. government, and since more immigrants, or their children, are expected to enter the work force as service workers, the union may have many more Hispanics to represent. Durazo, however, knows that before any major recruiting takes place, her staff will have to be organized, and the local membership itself will need some restructuring.

While presiding over an organization with 13,000 members, a staff of 35, and an annual budget of $2.5 million has its difficulties, Durazo has made progress herself. "I'm learning that there are times when decisions have to be made that don't necessarily seem like the best decisions at first, but there are lots of ramifications—legal and financial—that have to be taken into consideration," she remarked in *Hispanic Business.* The leader, who was just 36 years of age when she was elected in 1989, has been gaining popularity within the union as well as in the Los Angeles community at large. She inspires and encourages Hispanics and non-Hispanics alike to stand up and be heard. One union member declared in the *Los Angeles Times,* "Many of us come from countries where the powerful always have their way. María Elena has made us realize that united we can take control and run things the way we want. Now we can speak up when there is an injustice. María Elena has instilled this in us."

Also, since Durazo has been working for the union, she has found some personal success apart from her career. She married Miguel Contreras, the international union representative who controlled the local for two years and who has since left the local union. While some members were suspicious of the marriage, the enthusiasm Durazo shares with Contreras for defending Hispanics is obvious. She commented in *Hispanic Business,* "We see our union work as a cause—not a job."

In addition to empowering rank-and-file members of a union, and making the lives of busboys, waiters, cooks, and maids more livable, Durazo has enabled thousands of Hispanics in the Los Angeles area to dream about their futures. Knowing that her concern for them is genuine, and that they, too, can make the contributions that she has made makes all the difference for people who once went without representation. Durazo, the woman who fights for the rights of Hispanics in the United States, who actively supports action against the U.S. policy in Central America, and who even struggles in the battle for nuclear disarmament, is a working role model for Hispanics as well as evidence that a once-standard situation is in a state of transformation. As Jesus Jimenez, an international representative for the United Furniture Workers of America, noted in the *Los Angeles Times,* Durazo's presidency represents "the kind of change that is needed."

## SOURCES:

### Periodicals

*Hispanic Business,* May 1990, pp. 36–40.
*Los Angeles Times,* May 6, 1989, Section 1, p. 1.

—*Sketch by Ronie-Richele Garcia-Johnson*

# José Echegaray
## 1832(?)-1916
### Spanish playwright

The career of José María Waldo Echegaray y Eizaguirre spanned academia, politics, and dramaturgy. Originally a mathematics and hydraulics professor, he moved into politics around 1868 and occupied various ministerial posts, notably as the minister of finance. During his political career he founded the Bank of Spain. Echegaray is best remembered, however, as the greatest Spanish dramatist of his generation; J. Hunter Peak in *Social Drama in Nineteenth-Century Spain,* described him as "the monarch of the Spanish stage in the last quarter of the nineteenth century." In 1904 he was the first Spaniard to be honored with the Nobel Prize for literature, which he shared with the French poet Frédéric Mistral.

Echegaray was born around 1832 (sources vary between 1832 and 1835) in Madrid in Spain. His father, of Basque descent, taught Greek at the local school in Murcia. Echegaray received his formative education at his father's school. In 1847 he enrolled at the University of Madrid where he majored in mathematics. In 1853 he received a diploma in civil engineering.

Echegaray's early career intentions lay in the teaching profession. He began his career as a mathematics teacher in the provinces and later returned to Madrid to take up the position of professor of hydraulics at the Central School of Civil Engineering. As a teacher and the author of several mathematical papers, Echegaray earned a considerable reputation in the academic field.

### Political Career

Echegaray entered the political realm, as a Liberal, after the Spanish Revolution of 1868. Before 1868 he had been closely associated with prominent Liberals, particularly through his articles on economics and his belief in free trade. As a politician he gained a reputation as an eloquent spokesman. He held several posts in the revolutionary government, including the minister of finance and the colonies. In 1873 he was briefly exiled to France following a conflict with the Republican Party. He returned to Spain in 1874 as a

*José Echegaray*

member of the Ministry of Conciliation, but his position was short-lived; the Restoration of 1874 excluded him from public life.

Echegaray returned to politics in 1880 attending the *Cortes* (Spanish parliament) as a Progressive Republican until 1881, when the dissolution of his party caused him to retire again. He reentered politics for the last time to serve under the transient Liberal Administrations of 1905 and 1906. His final political foray caught the public eye when he chose his own portrait to appear on the new Spanish bank notes.

### The Dramatist

Echegaray was an enormously popular and successful playwright whose comedies and melodramas commanded the Spanish stage for three decades from 1875. He was elected to the Royal Spanish Academy in 1894 and was awarded the Nobel Prize for literature in 1904. He started writing on the premise, as stated in the London *Times* in 1916, that any person who "knows a little grammar, has some imagination, and a tolerable ear for music," can write poetry.

Echegaray began writing plays in 1874, following the temporary cessation of his political career. His dramatic career was launched when Matilde Diez, a popular contemporary actress, agreed to perform *El libro talonario* (*Tit for Tat*) in 1874. Appearing under the pseudonym Jorge Hayaseca y Eizaguirre the play was greatly acclaimed. The strong Spanish flavor of Echegaray's work generally precluded its popularity outside Spain, although *El gran Galeoto* (*The Great Galeoto,* 1881), considered one of his finest plays, was produced in English in 1908 under the title *The World and His Wife.*

Echegaray's plays adopt the romantic style of the nineteenth century, combined with elements of social awareness that marked the twentieth century. E. A. Peers in *A History of the Romantic Movement in Spain,* wrote of Echegaray's plays: "In his late, as well as in his early dramas, we find the same characteristic affection for sensation and horror, his breathless melodramatic movements, his grandoise language, his sweeping rhetoric, his picturesqueness and color, his hurricane stage effects, his frequent use of coincidence and his grotesque improbabilities. The conventional comes as easily to him as the sensational and he indulges freely in both." However, critics were not unanimous in their praise, some regarded Echegaray's dramas too melodramatic or too contrived. Echegaray died in Madrid in 1916.

## SELECTED PUBLISHED WORKS:

## Plays

(Under pseudonym Jorge Hayaseca y Eizairre) *El libro talonario,* [Spain], 1874.

*La esposa del vengador* (title means "The Wife of the Avenger"), Madrid, José Rodríguez, 1875.

*En el puño de la espada,* [Madrid], 1877.

*O locura ó santidad* (title means "Folly or Saintliness"), Madrid, Imprento de J. M. Ducazcal, 1877; translation by Ruth Lansing published as *Madman or Saint,* Boston, R. G. Badger, 1912.

*El gladiator de Ravena,* Madrid, T. Fortanet, 1877.

*Como empieza y come acaba,* Madrid, T. Fortanet, 1877.

*Ni la paciencia de Job,* Madrid, José Rodríguez, 1879.

*Mar sin orillas,* Madrid, José Rodríguez, 1880.

*La muerte en los labios,* Madrid, José Rodríguez, 1880.

*El gran galeoto,* [Spain], 1881; translation by Hannah Lynch published as *The Great Galeoto,* New York, Doubleday, 1914.

*Haroldo el Normado,* Madrid, José Rodríguez, 1881.

*Conflicto entre dos deberes,* Madrid, Cosme Rodríguez, 1883.

*Correr en pos de un ideal,* Madrid, Cosme Rodríguez, 1883.

*En el pilar y en la cruz,* Madrid, Cosme Rodríguez, 1883.

*Un milagro en Egipto,* Madrid, Cosme Rodríguez, 1883.

*La peste de Otranto,* Madrid, José Rodríguez, 1884.

*Piensa mal . . . ¡y acertarás,* [Spain], 1884.

*Obras dramáticas escogidas* (contains *La esposa del vengador, En el puño de la espada, O locura ó santidad, En el seno de la muerte, La muerte en los labios,* and *El gran galeoto*), 12 volumes, Madrid, Imprento de Tello, 1884–1905.

*Mancha que limpia,* [Spain], 1885.

*Vida alegre y muerte triste,* Madrid, José Rodríguez, 1885.

*Dos fanatismos,* Madrid, José Rodríguez, 1887.

*Manantial que no se aga,* Madrid, José Rodríguez, 1889.

*Los rigidos,* Madrid, José Rodríguez, 1889.

*Siempre en ridículo,* [Spain], 1890; translation by T. Walter Gilkyson published as *Always Ridiculous,* Boston, R. G. Badger, 1916.

*Un crítico incipíente,* Madrid, José Rodríguez, 1891.

*Irene de Otranto,* music by Emilio Serrano, Madrid, José Rodríguez, 1891.

*El hijo de Don Juan,* [Spain], 1892; translation by James Graham published as *The Son of Don Juan,* Boston, Roberts Brothers, 1895.

*Mariana,* [Spain], 1892.

*A la orilla del mar,* [Spain], 1893.

*El estigma,* Madrid, E. Odriózola, 1896.

*El prólogo de un drama,* Madrid, E. Odriózola, 1896.

*El poder de la impotencia,* Madrid, José Rodríguez, 1897.

*La duda,* [Spain], 1898.

*El loco dios* (title means "The Insane Gods"), [Spain], 1900; translation published as *The Madman Divine,* 1908.

*Sic vos non vobis,* Madrid, R. Velasco, 1905.

*A fuerza de arrastrarse,* [Spain], 1905.

*Silencio de muerte,* Madrid, R. Velasco, 1906.

*El preferido y los cenicientos,* [Spain], 1908.

*Tierra baja,* Madrid, R. Velasco, 1909.

*El primer acto de un drama* (continuation of *El prólogo de un drama*), Madrid, R. Velasco, 1914.

*La rencorosa,* Madrid, R. Velasco, 1915.

*Lo sublime en lo vulgar,* Madrid, R. Velasco, 1918.

*Teatro escogido* (contains *El libro talonario, La última noche, En el puño de la espada, O locura ó santidad, En el seno de la muerte, La muerte en los labios, El gran galeoto, Piensa mal . . . ¡y acertarás, De mala raza, Sic vos non vobis, Mancha que limpia, La duda,* and *A fuerza de arrastrarse*), Madrid, Aguilar, 1955.

## Other

*Teoría matemática de la luz,* Madrid, Imprenta de la Viua de Agualo, 1871.

*Disertaciones matemáticas sobre la cuadratura del círcula, el médo de Wantzel, y la división de la circunferencia en partes iguales* (mathematics), Madrid, Impreno de la Viuda é Hijo de D. E. Aguado, 1887.

*Algunas reflexiones generales sobre la crítica y el arte literario,* [Spain], 1894.

*Discursos leídos ante la Real Academia Española* (lectures), Madrid, Imprenta de los Hijos de J. A. Carcia, 1894.

*Discurso leído en la Universidad central en la solemne inauguración del curso académico de 1905 á 1906* (mathematical physics), Madrid, Colonial, 1905.

*Cuentos* (short stories), [Spain], 1912.

*Recuredos* (autobiography), three volumes, Madrid, Ruiz Hermanos, 1917.

## SOURCES:

### Books

*Hispanic Writers: A Collection of Sketches from Contemporary Authors,* edited by Bryan Ryan, Gale Research, Detroit, 1991, pp. 174–176.

Peak, J. Hunter, *Social Drama in Nineteenth-Century Spain,* Chapel Hill, University of North Carolina Press, 1964, pp. 71–80.

Peers, E. Allison, *A History of the Romantic Movement in Spain,* Volume 2, Cambridge University Press, 1940, pp. 348–51.

### Periodicals

*Times* (London), September 16, 1916, p. 10.

—*Sketch by Amanda Beresford*

# Esteban Echeverría
## 1805-1851
**Argentine poet and political activist**

Esteban Echeverría was a noted romantic poet who was also a leader in the struggle for democratic reforms within the political system in Argentina. His poetry is considered a forerunner in the literary development in Argentina. Echeverría introduced the romantic literary movement, popular in Europe, to Argentina.

José Esteban Antonino Echeverría was born in Buenos Aires, Argentina, on September 2, 1805. His father, who died when Estaban was young, was Spanish, and his mother was an Argentine. The family lived in the rough part of the city. In 1822 he attended the local university and studied philosophy for one year. When he was 20 years old, he went to Paris to continue his education. It was in Paris where he was inspired by reading Shakespeare, Schiller, Goethe, and Byron.

### Introduced Romantic Era to Argentina

When Echeverría returned to Argentina he became so depressed over the government repression that he withdrew into himself and he wrote poetry. His first book, *Elvira, o la Novia de la Plata* ("Elvira, or the Bride of the Plata"), was published in 1832 and it is considered the first romantic work created in Argentina. However, it went unnoticed until much later. *Los consuelos* (*Consolations*) was published in 1834. This book received more attention than *Elvira* but not enough for Echeverría. He was disappointed with his poetry's reception and moved to Mercedes, a small town near the Rio Negro. There he led the simple life of a countryman. It was in Rio Negro that he was inspired to write a poem that was considered significant. It was not until he published the book *Las rimas* (1837) that included the epic poem in verse, *La cautiva* ("The Captive Woman"), that literary intellectuals took notice. He used the indigenous culture, history, the *criollo* landscape and tradition in *La cautiva,* which inspired other writers to explore Argentine culture and reject Spanish influence. Before Echeverría introduced French Romanticism to Argentina, the intellectuals had lived in the Age of Reason, which was humanitarian and rationalistic.

### Organizes the Association of May

Echeverría became involved in a movement to promote democracy and in 1838 helped found the Asociación de Mayo (Association of May). At the first meeting he organized, Echeverría read his *Palabras*

*Simbolicas de la Fe de la Joven Generacion* ("Words Symbolic of the Faith of the Younger Generation"). This became part of the Association's credo. Their goal was to promote romantic ideas by organizing political liberalism and writing literature based on national concerns. He wrote their philosophy, which was published in the book *Dogma socialista.* Because of their involvement in the Association, Echeverría and many of the members were forced to leave Argentina by the dictator Juan Manuel de Rosas (1839–1851). Echeverría moved to Montevideo, Uruguay, where he wrote one of his best-known short stories, "El matadero" ("The Slaughter House"). In this highly acclaimed story, he symbolically attacks the dictator, Rosas, and his supporters for their brutal treatment of the Argentine people. It was a story describing how a brutal and savage people become desensitized to the bloody nature of their work.

Echeverría became ill and died January 19, 1851, in Uruguay, one year before Rosas fell from power and just two years before the new Argentine constitution was drafted. Some of the former members of the Asociación de Mayowrote the Constitution and several became ministers and members of parliament. Two of the members, **Bartolomé Mitre** and **Domingo Sarmiento**, later became presidents of the new republic. Echevierría's group of young men were credited with laying the foundation of the national political organization of their country. Many of them became noted writers of Spanish American literature. In the *Dogma,* he wrote, "Only those doctrines will be progressive for us that, with the future in view, endeavor to give impetus to the gradual development of class equality and that are always in the vanguard of human advancement. We shall seek enlightenment from European ideas, but with certain conditions. The world of our intellectual life will be at the same time national and humanitarian; we shall always have one eye on the progress of nations and the other on the heart of our society."

## SELECTED PUBLISHED WORKS:

*Elvira, o la novia del Plata,* 1832.
*Los consuelos,* 1834.
*Las rimas,* 1837.
*Dogma socialista de la Asociación de Mayo, pre-cedido de una ojeada retrospectiva sobre el movimiento intelectual en el Plata desde el ano 37* (essay), 1846.
*Obras completas de D. Esteban Echeverría* (in-cludes short story "El Matadero"), five volumes, 1870–74.
*El Matadero* ("The Slaughter House"), 1959.
*Páginas autobiográficas* (autobiography), 1962.

## SOURCES:

### Books

*Nineteenth-Century Literature Criticism,* edited by Janet Mullane, Detroit, Gale Research, 1988.

### Periodicals

*Américas,* April 1952, pp. 21–23, 46.

—*Sketch by Phyllis Noah*

# Jaime Escalante
## 1930-
### Bolivian American educator

With his trademark corduroy cap and cardigan, and flamboyant classroom style, Jaime Escalante is the nation's most celebrated high school math teacher, taking unruly, low achieving math students at an East Los Angeles high school and turning them into models of academic excellence for the rest of the country. Already a highly respected Bolivian math and physics teacher when he immigrated to the United States in 1964, Escalante's devotion to and unshakable faith in his students soon became legendary in his new home as well. Escalante is best known as the subject of the 1988 hit movie *Stand and Deliver,* based on his phenomenal success with under-privileged Hispanic students at Garfield High School. In a little more than ten years, he guided more than 500 inner-city students successfully through the Advanced Placement calculus exams, tests so difficult that fewer than two percent of American students even attempt them. Equally important as the subjects he teaches, however, is Escalante's singular brand of philosophy and discipline that he uses to motivate his students. "I do not teach only math," he told David Hill in *Education Week.* "I also teach discipline and responsibility and morality."

Born Jaime Alfonso Escalante Gutierrez on December 31, 1930, in La Paz, Bolivia, Escalante was one of four children born to Zenobio and Sara Escalante. His parents were poorly paid teachers who worked in a small Aymara Indian village called Achacachi. As a child, Escalante spent much of his time creating games for himself, or taking walks with his maternal grandfather, a retired teacher who played spelling games with him. His father was volatile, often abusive, and Escalante's mother left the family home abruptly in 1939, taking three of her four children with her. Nine-year-old Jaime was later reunited with them in La Paz. At 14, he was sent to San Calixto, a prestigious Jesuit high school, where he became enthralled by physics, thanks mainly to a teacher from France, Father Descottes. Often exasperating to his teachers because of his quick, irreverent wit and talent for creative mischief, Escalante was nevertheless a good student with a special fascination for math and engineering. But without money, Escalante put aside his dream of engineering school and worked at odd jobs before joining the army for a brief stint during the Bolivian rebellion in 1949. Following that, while he was studying at Normal Superior, he was offered a teaching job at San Calixto. After his mornings at his alma mater, he taught at National Bolivar in the afternoons, and a late class at the Commercial High School. Escalante became a minor legend as the teacher who was working at three different schools before he had even graduated. On November 25, 1954, he married Fabiola Tapia Cochabamba, and his son Jaime, Jr., was born the following year. His second son Fernando was born in 1969.

## Moved to the United States

On his arrival in the United States in 1963, Escalante joined the ranks of immigrants who were readily absorbed by the U.S. job market, usually at the low end of the scale of education and experience. For a 33-year-old physics teacher with almost no English skills, however, Escalante found far less opportunity than he expected. Without an American college degree, he could not teach. So for the next 11 years, one of the most prominent Bolivian teachers of his generation held jobs as a busboy, a fry cook, and an electronics factory technician while earning a degree in mathematics from Cal State.

In 1974 Escalante was hired as a basic mathematics teacher at Garfield High School in East Los Angeles, a troubled inner-city school where the student body—98 percent Latino—was deemed unteachable at best and dangerous at worst. The dropout rate was astronomical. Pregnancy, drugs, and gang activity regularly interfered with learning. Academically, it could not get much lower. When Escalante began his job there, the Western Association of Schools and Colleges had threatened to revoke the school's accreditation. But he soon discovered that his students, like the ones he had known in Bolivia, relished a challenge if it was properly presented. He taught lessons in the language of sports and small business. Students filled out time cards each day, clocked out when they left, and learned fractions by figuring out how much—at a penny an hour—Escalante owed them for showing up.

## Employed Innovative Teaching Methods

But more important than what he taught was how he taught. Escalante used eccentric teaching methods, alternately scaring, amusing, and captivating his students. He developed a new language—Escalantese—to communicate difficult math concepts in simple ways: "Secret agent" was the minus sign inside the parenthesis; "give and go" was the breaking down of an absolute value; and "in love" was factoring by grouping. He made them sign learning contracts. Escalante yelled in his thick Bolivian accent and paced across the classroom, pronouncing students *burros* when they failed to grasp a concept, or *hyatolas* when they did not work at their maximum. To a student who was absent because of the Chinese New Year, David Hill reported in *Education Week,* Escalante proclaimed, "The problem in this school is that there are too many holidays! I don't take off Cinco de Mayo!" Not all his students liked him, but no one could ignore him. Jay Mathews, in *Time,* wrote: "When the father of a truant algebra student failed to return his calls, [Escalante] rang the man at 5 a.m. 'I wanted to catch you before you went off to work,' he said sweetly to the sputtering parent. The student returned to class."

Escalante's methods paid off, and he proved beyond a doubt that poor Hispanic students were just as capable of excelling at difficult subjects as were the most privileged Anglo students. By 1987, Garfield had an almost unbelievable record: only three other public schools in the nation were producing more advanced-placement calculus students than they were. By 1991, 570 students at the school took advanced placement examinations in 14 different subject areas.

## Subject of Motion Picture

The 1988 film *Stand and Deliver,* which starred Edward James Olmos as the unorthodox Escalante, told the dramatic and poignant story of how Escalante overcame cheating accusations leveled against his calculus students when their high test scores on the advanced placement tests made them suspect. It made the colorful Escalante an instant celebrity outside of the academic world. Visitors, eager to get a firsthand look at Escalante in action, streamed in and out of his classroom. Escalante enjoyed the attention, but felt the movie was important not because of him, but because of the way it shattered stereotypes about Hispanic students. He wrote in *The Jaime Escalante Math Program:* "First, no one expected severely disadvantaged barrio students to achieve academic excellence. The movie also revealed that some educators hold the false and racist idea that Hispanic students . . . shy away from courses that require hard work. . . . I am happy to say that our program has proved that logic to be faulty." In 1989, the film swept the Independent Sprit Awards with best film, best screenplay, best supporting actress (Roseanna de Soto ), best supporting actor (Lou Diamond Phillips), best director (Ramon Menendez), best actor, and best feature. The awards are given by the largest association of independent filmmakers in the United States.

The media attention brought Escalante much-needed financial support from foundations, as well as the controversy that often accompanies fame. At Garfield, he was not known for his diplomacy, and these characteristics were magnified in the spotlight. Jay Mathews wrote in *Escalante: The Best Teacher in America:* "All great successes produce jealousy and suspicion. Escalante's temper and distaste for compromise hurt feelings. His influence and the media stardom he achieved after 1982 brought resentment." The outspoken Escalante did not hesitate to criticize teachers who did not measure up to his high standards, a trait that caused a few clashes over the years. "Now I keep my mouth shut," he told Hill in *Education Week.* "I'm not gonna be the one to create a problem."

Fed up with what he called the ingratitude of some of his colleagues and frustrated by parents who, he said in *Education Week,* did not value academic achievement, Escalante left the school that had benefited so much from his expertise. His one-time protege, Benjamin Jimenez, succeeded him. Despite the rancor that surrounded his departure, Garfield math department chairman Stu Adler admitted to Hill in *Education Week,* that "losing Jaime Escalante was a heavy blow to our program. . . . Our students really do miss their mathematics teacher." Escalante, in turn, has fond memories of his Garfield students. He keeps a large scrapbook in his office with photographs of each advanced placement calculus class he taught at the school, accompanied by a printout of the students' test scores.

In 1991 Escalante was hired by Hiram Johnson High School in Sacramento, California. The school, one of the district's lowest achieving schools, has a student body of 2,300 in a truly multicultural mix: 28 percent Asian, 20 percent African American, 19 percent Hispanic, 32 percent white, one percent American Indian. Nearly half of the students come from families dependent on some form of welfare. The school had a high dropout rate, and gang violence had resulted in two serious on-campus shootings. Escalante called the school his "second home" in *Education Week,* insisting that he would repeat the success he had at Garfield: "The whole picture's gonna change. It's gonna be much better than Garfield."

At Johnson, some teachers were initially wary of Escalante, and the resultant media attention caused some discordance. But Johnson principal Donald Giusti defended Escalante's classroom perks—an air-conditioned classroom, private telephone, personal photocopy machine, all funded by grants—by telling David Hill in *Education Week* that whatever Escalante receives that the others do not, such as a new

position on the pay scale, is "the reality of the business." Giusti admitted that "there was some animosity. But most of us look at him as just another teacher who happened to be taking over a class that we desperately needed a teacher for."

Although his focus remains on teaching, his fundraising abilities have brought large foundation grants for programs such as the Saturday and summer program for students and teachers he established in 1983 at East Los Angeles College. The program, funded in part by the National Science Foundation, provides accelerated instruction to more than 600 junior and senior high school students each year and helps train other teachers in Escalante's methods. In the fall of 1993, Escalante received a three-year, $363,000 National Science Foundation (NSF) grant to expand the summer and after school program at Johnson High School.

Escalante continues to stay in the national spotlight, most visibly in his collaboration with the Foundation for Advancements in Science and Education (FASE), based in Los Angeles. He and his FASE colleagues produce "Futures with Jaime Escalante," a Peabody Award -winning Public Broadcasting Service (PBS) math and science video series that illustrates how math is applied in real life in such diverse fields as fashion, design, architecture, and space exploration. Reviewing the series in *Electronic Learning,* Hilary Cowan wrote that Escalante "prances and dances his way through each tape, inspiring students to stay involved in the learning process. A consummate teacher and salesman, Escalante provides the backbone for fast-paced episodes that inched on-location scenes and interviews as well as thousands of superb graphic images."

In 1989, Escalante spoke to 300 members of Dade's Future Educators of America chapter in Florida, telling them to have the "*ganas* " (desire) to work hard. "Hard work is the future," he said in his speech, reported by Tananarive Due in the *Miami Herald.* "And the future belongs to you. If you have *ganas,* you have the commitment." Of teaching, Escalante wrote in *The Jaime Escalante Math Program:* "When students of any race, ethnicity, or economic status are expected to work hard, they will usually rise to the occasion . . . and do the work. If we expect kids to be losers they will be losers; if we expect them to be winners they will be winners."

## SOURCES:

### Books

Mathews, Jay, *Escalante: The Best Teacher in America,* New York, Henry Holt, 1988.

## Periodicals

*Education Week,* March 30, 1994, pp. 20–22.
*Electronic Learning,* January 1993, p. 36.
*FASE Update* (Foundation for Advancements in
    Science and Education), winter 1994, p. 1.
*Miami Herald,* November 16, 1989, p. 16; June
    15, 1991, p. 16A; June 19, 1991, p. 12A;
    February 27, 1993, p. 3B.
*Newsweek,* July 20, 1992, pp. 58–59.
*Winds of Change: American Indian Education &
    Opportunity,* (Boulder), winter 1992.

## Other

*Futures,* PBS Video, Alexandria, Virginia, 1992.
*The Jaime Escalante Math Program,* (original arti-
    cle in *Journal of Negro Education,* Bureau of
    Educational Research, Howard University,
    summer 1990), National Education Association
    reprint, July, 1990.

—*Sketch by Julie Catalano*

*Paul Espinosa*

# Paul Espinosa
## 1950-

### Hispanic American filmmaker and producer

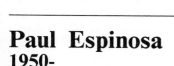

Paul Espinosa has written, produced, and directed numerous critically acclaimed films and documentaries for public television. He has spent most of his professional career in California, where he has addressed issues of concern to the Latin American community as well as anthropological issues regarding the U.S.-Mexico border. Espinosa told James McCarthy in a recent interview that he intended to continue to make films that deal with the "contact and conflict . . . between Mexicans and Americans in the border zone."

Born on August 8, 1950, in Alamosa, Colorado, Espinosa moved with his parents, Theodore and Rosemarie, and his four brothers and sisters to Albuquerque, New Mexico, where Espinosa spent most of his childhood. After his high school graduation, he traveled east to Brown University in Rhode Island, where he earned his B.A. in anthropology in 1972. He went on to Stanford University in California for his M.A., which he finished in 1976. He secured his Ph.D. in anthropology from Stanford in 1982. His doctorate studies specialized in the cultural analysis of television communication.

While still working on his Ph.D., Espinosa became the director of Hispanic Affairs at KPBS-TV in San Diego. Married in 1981 to Marta Sanchez, Espinosa began to make films for the Public Broadcasting System in 1983. That year he produced and wrote *The Trail North,* a program about a family traveling to the United States from Mexico. The next year he produced *Ballad of an Unsung Hero,* an examination of pioneering Hispanic television announcer Pedro Gonzalez. In 1986 he produced and wrote *The Lemon Grove Incident,* a film about school desegregation. Two years later he produced and wrote *In the Shadow of the Law,* which depicted the flight of four families of illegal immigrants to the United States. Espinosa's work continued in this vein with his next project, which was released in 1990. Produced, directed, and written by Espinosa, *Uneasy Neighbors* concerned increasing tensions between migrant workers and wealthy homeowners in San Diego.

Espinosa noted in his interview with McCarthy that he feels that the challenge of his job lies in making his anthropological scholarship accessible to a television viewership—most of whom would never pick up a book of anthropology. His fascination with "cross-cultural anthropology" inspired him to develop ways to explain those issues within the limitations of a television production. He achieves this by "looking for personal stories" among cultural phenomenon. By using the story of an individual, Espinosa can make his films "emotional and engaging" to a broad range of people.

Espinosa produced *The Hunt for Pancho Villa* as part of the *American Experience* series in 1990. Villa's appeal as a character and a figure of legend helped Espinosa convey the story of the general's conflict with American forces. Espinosa has produced several other films as well, including . . . *and the earth did not swallow him,* a 1994 film about a Mexican American boy.

Espinosa has won many awards and received numerous grants over the years in recognition of his work. Funding sources have included the Corporation for Public Broadcasting, the National Endowment for the Humanities, American Playhouse, and many other sources. He received an Emmy nomination for News and Documentary Achievement for *In the Shadow of the Law* and a Golden Mike Award. Espinosa has also been the recipient of top documentary awards from several film festivals, and his films have won recognition from many organizations, including the California Teacher's Organization, the American Civil Liberties Union, and the American Bar Association.

Although Espinosa has been a successful presenter of Mexican life in America, he recognizes that in the "regular, everyday media" the representation of Hispanics has far to go. A staunch defender of public broadcasting and a critic of conservatives who have voiced a desire to cut public broadcasting funding, Espinosa pointed to public television as a medium that is much more welcoming of presentations of Hispanics. On network television, he told McCarthy, "Hispanics are very, very marginalized. They are under-represented and when they are represented it's usually in a very stereotyped way." He conceded that during his career, some Hispanic actors such as **Andy Garcia**, **Jimmy Smits**, and **Edward James Olmos** have successfully established themselves in the entertainment mainstream, but he also pointed to a statistic which he says shows that representation of Hispanics on network television has actually decreased since the 1950s. "Back then it was 3 percent, but now it's only 1 percent," he said, "despite the fact that Hispanics make up a much larger segment of the population."

## SOURCES:

Espinosa, Paul, interview with James McCarthy, January 17, 1995.

—*Sketch by James McCarthy*

# Laura Esquivel
## 1950-
### Mexican novelist and screenwriter

Laura Esquivel is a Mexican novelist and television screenwriter whose written work has garnered kind words from both critics and the general public. Her 1980s screenplay, *Chido One, El Tacos de Oro,* was nominated for Mexico's Ariel award—the equivalent of an Oscar—for best screenplay by the Mexican Academy of Motion Pictures. In 1992 the movie version of Esquivel's *Like Water for Chocolate* won ten Ariel awards, including one for Esquivel's screenplay, which was based on her first novel of the same name. The novel proved to be a bestseller in both Mexico and the United States. The art film, which garnered prizes outside of Mexico as well, was directed and produced by Esquivel's husband, **Alfonso Arau**, who is also Mexican.

Laura Esquivel was born in Mexico in 1950. Her career has been fueled, in part, by her interest in teaching and writing for children. After taking a course in education and specializing in children's theater she and a group of friends established a school as part of the public education system to teach youngsters about literature and theater. In 1979 and 1980 she wrote children's programs for a local television station. During the early 1980s, she taught art to children in workshops at an interdisciplinary center she founded.

In 1983 Esquivel developed an interest in writing screenplays. She took a course taught by Alfonso Arau, her future husband, and then made her cinematic debut with the screenplay she wrote for *Chido One, El Tacos de Oro* (*The Cool One, Tacos of Gold*), which was released in 1985. During the late 1980s she began work on her novel *Like Water for Chocolate.* Published in 1989, the book was penned in a Latin American style that used magical realism but also featured a feminist outlook. When the book was translated into English in 1990 it became a bestseller in the United States and its author was profiled in *People* and *The New York Times.* She subsequently wrote the script for the movie version of the novel.

### Questioned Rural Mexican Women's Traditional Roles

The movie and novel were widely reviewed and raised interesting questions about the traditional role of women in rural Mexico. Much of the action in the book and movie takes place in the kitchen—a place still reserved for women in Mexican society. The heroine Tita, forbidden by her mother from marrying her beloved, is relegated to a domestic life that

*Laura Esquivel*

includes cooking for the man she loves, a man who married Tita's sister only to be closer to Tita. As Howard Kissel noted in the *Daily News,* "Since Tita cooks for the whole family, she blends her resentments and passions into the food."

The critical reception to the *Like Water for Chocolate* novel was a mixed one. On a negative note, *Village Voice* reviewer Georgia Brown wrote, "Esquivel isn't much of a stylist; her prose is flat, literal, and explicit, explaining perhaps why the book was Mexico's 1990 No. 1 bestseller." The judgment of other reviewers, however, was more favorable. The *Times Literary Supplement,* for instance, called it "two books for the price of one: a cookery book and a love story, with a distinctive Hispanic flavour."

The film version of the novel, while not universally hailed, was generally popular with film reviewers. As David Denby wrote in *New York,* "The lovely Mexican fantasy *Like Water for Chocolate,* based on Laura Esquivel's celebrated novel, has been spreading its charm for some time. . . . Nothing in this golden dream of cooking and sex completely makes sense, but everything in it shines. . . . In this female-centered world, the men are seen for their erotic possibilities, and cooking becomes the magic and mystery of life."

During the early 1990s, Esquivel wrote a script for a children's film and the cinematic adaptation for a novel by the author Antonio Velasco Pina. In addition, Esquivel studied television writing, participated in literary seminars and writers conferences in

Mexico, and traveled to the United States to promote her first novel.

## SELECTED PUBLISHED WORKS:

*Like Water for Chocolate,* New York, Doubleday, 1992.

## SOURCES:

*Americas,* July/August 1993, pp. 60–61.
*Booklist,* September 15, 1992, p. 122.
*Daily News,* February 17, 1993.
*Library Journal,* September 1, 1992, p. 213; February 15, 1993, p. 224; March 15, 1993, pp. 47, 50.
*Los Angeles Times,* November 1, 1992, p. 6.
*Newsweek,* March 15, 1993.
*New York,* April 5, 1993.
*New York Observer,* November 8, 1993.
*New York Post,* February 17, 1993.
*Publishers Weekly,* August 24, 1992, p. 61.
*Time,* April 5, 1993.
*Times Literary Supplement,* April 16, 1993, p. 22.
*Village Voice,* February 23, 1993.

*—Sketch by Alison Carb Sussman*

# Rita Esquivel
## 1932-
### Mexican American educational administrator

Rita Esquivel can claim many "firsts" in her life. As a youth, she was the first on either side of her family in the United States to graduate from high school. In 1963 she was the first Hispanic to teach at the elementary schools in the Santa Monica-Malibu Unified School District in California. She became the first female assistant superintendent at the district and is currently the first female director of the Adult Education Center, also a part of the Santa Monica-Malibu Unified School District. Esquivel worked for the U.S. Department of Education from 1989 to 1992 and was the first Chicana ever to head the Office of Bilingual Education and Minority Language Affairs (OBEMLA).

Like her mother, Esquivel was born in San Antonio, Texas. She is the oldest daughter, born November 4, 1932, to Juan and Juanita Esquivel, who are of Mexican descent. Her father, a self-employed

*Rita Esquivel*

car radiator repairman, and her mother, a home-maker, were the biggest influences in her life when growing up. It is they who assumed she would go to college. The second biggest influence in Esquivel's formative years were her high school teachers, Catholic nuns. Throughout her school days, she attended private schools for girls and women in San Antonio and saw the sisters as paradigms of female success. They were women with doctorate degrees, acting as principals and college presidents. Attending private girls' schools also allowed Esquivel to take on leadership roles and to be elected to various offices, positions that might otherwise go to boys. For these reasons, Esquivel remains an advocate of all women's schools.

### Reluctantly Pursued Teaching Career

Teaching was not Esquivel's first career choice. When Esquivel graduated from high school, she wanted to become an attorney. But "in 1949 Mexican girls didn't go to law school," she remarked in an interview with Luis Vasquez-Ajmac. Taking her father's advice, she pursued a B.A. in social work at Our Lady of the Lake University in San Antonio and graduated in 1953. After searching for a job in her area of study and not finding one, Esquivel took her first elementary teaching position in 1955 while teaching swimming lessons at the local pool in San Antonio. In great need of teachers, the personnel director of San Antonio's Edgewood School District

offered Esquivel a job. Desperate for work at that time, she accepted the offer. Esquivel recalled, "I was literally soaking wet in my swimsuit as I signed the contract in the superintendent's office."

Her first year in teaching did not go as smoothly as she anticipated. After one month, she was ready to resign. "Kids were jumping out the window," Esquivel told Vasquez-Ajmac, and she was exasperated. Refusing her resignation, the school principal brought in a supervisor from the Central Office who taught her how to teach and helped her through the first year of a long, industrious career in education. In 1963 Esquivel left San Antonio to work in California's Santa Monica-Malibu Unified School District where she has remained for more than 30 years in various schools and positions. First hired as the only Hispanic elementary teacher at the John Muir Elementary School, she moved on to teach secondary education at the Lincoln Junior High School from 1965 to 1971 as a Spanish-language teacher and school counselor. She later became a school principal in 1973 at the Will Rogers Elementary School. Esquivel found the Santa Monica-Malibu Unified School District a very positive experience and nurturing environment with room for professional growth. After becoming the principal of the Will Rogers Elementary School in 1973, she worked her way up to coordinator of community relations from 1973 to 1976 and to supervisor for state and federal projects for five years thereafter. In 1981, Esquivel became the first woman assistant superintendent of education and later assistant to the superintendent from 1987 to 1989.

### Named OBEMLA Director by President Bush

The next three years were to become Esquivel's most significant professionally. In 1989 she moved to Washington, D.C., chosen by President George Bush as the first Chicano appointee to the Office of Bilingual Education and Minority Language Affairs (OBEMLA) in the United States Department of Education. Her responsibilities there involved managing a budget of $225 million, for discretionary funds. It was her duty to direct English as a Second Language (ESL) and bilingual education programs for the nation. In so doing, Esquivel identified model projects to fund and produced models for other schools to replicate. She also became deeply involved in research, and headed two major evaluation centers and 16 multifunctional centers across the nation. As director of OBEMLA, Esquivel also assisted the secretary of education in setting policy for children with limited English proficiency and worked with other assistant secretaries in the education of non-English-speaking children.

Esquivel is very proud of her three years as OBEMLA director. "I feel I've done something meaningful and that I have instituted change," she commented in the *National Hispanic Reporter.* Esquivel believes that she bridged the ill feeling between the U.S. Department of Education and the community in the field during her tenure, helped build relationships with professional associations, and took positive steps in regard to the Academic Excellence Program, a plan that enables OBEMLA to publicize excellent work accomplished by school districts. Esquivel is equally pleased that she helped expand the development of bilingual education programs and further developed the fellowship program to include almost 500 participants, including institutions like Harvard University. Esquivel also played a major role in establishing a research symposium for practitioners in the educational field and set policy on a national level. "That," Esquivel explained to Vasquez-Ajmac, "is the greatest thing I've done in my profession."

Thoroughly enjoying her experience in Washington, Esquivel stayed with OBEMLA longer than her 18-month appointment. Esquivel was drawn to the city's vitality, the challenge of her job, seeing the capital at night and driving through Rock Creek Parkway to work. But after three years in Washington, she felt she had served her party and country well and wished to return to the basis of what education is about—people. Esquivel resumed her career with the Santa Monica-Malibu Unified School District as the first female director of the Adult Education Center in May of 1992. As director, Esquivel took on a new direction and role, a change from educating children. "I am now into mentoring and fostering adults so that they can go upward and onward," Esquivel noted. She has also taught doctoral students at the University of Southern California and is further influencing adults and teachers to enter the administrative ranks. Simply encouraging an individual to believe that he or she can achieve success is important in Esquivel's mind. Reflecting back on her early days as an elementary teacher at the San Antonio Independent School District, she recalled what an impact mentoring had on her and how that support helped her to obtain a master's degree in education at Our Lady of the Lake University in July 1960.

### Promotes Parenting Classes for Immigrants

What is immediately notable about Rita Esquivel when speaking to her about education is her enthusiasm for it. After more than 40 years as an educator, school administrator, and policy maker, she can still find challenges. One of Esquivel's major goals at the Adult Education Center is to change the focus of the program while maintaining the ESL programs for adults. She wants to provide parenting classes for Hispanic parents at the school and provide a model for every school to adopt. Esquivel believes that offering parenting classes will teach Hispanic parents how the U.S. educational system functions as well as enable them to assist their kids at home and to feel

comfortable in a school setting. Her most ambitious goal is to make the Adult Education Center in Santa Monica a showcase for the entire nation by the mid–1990s. In addition to offering parenting classes at the Adult Education Center, Esquivel also directed the General Equivalency Diploma (GED) program.

While working to improve the educational system in the United States, Esquivel has been awarded numerous honors. In 1991 Esquivel was selected as one of the 100 most influential Hispanics in America by *Hispanic Business* magazine and was chosen a NABE Honoree by the National Association for Bilingual Education. She also received the American Council on the Teaching of Foreign Languages' President's Award in 1990 and was presented the Hispanic Woman of the Year award from the Mexican-American Opportunities Foundation in 1989. Esquivel also received a Doctor of Letters, *honoris causam,* by Our Lady of the Lake University in May 1991. Although Esquivel has accomplished a great deal in the field of education on a local and national level, she still sees room for improvement. She would like to see bilingual education expanded to help the growing number of immigrants adjust to a new educational system and democratic society. More importantly, Esquivel would like to reiterate to people fearful of bilingual education that its primary purpose in the United States is to teach children English and enable them to experience the world in more than one language. As she noted in *Hispanic National Reporter,* "Changing people's minds about bilingual education will always be a challenge."

### SOURCES:

**Periodicals**

*National Hispanic Reporter,* June 1992, p. 1.

**Other**

Esquivel, Rita, interview with Luis Vasquez-Ajmac, July 16, 1992.

*—Sketch by Luis Vasquez-Ajmac*

# Gloria Estefan
## 1958-
### Cuban American singer and songwriter

From Hispanic roots to the pop music mainstream, Gloria Estefan and the Miami Sound Machine are the embodiment of the American dream come true. The Miami Sound Machine was originally a Cuban American quartet that performed popular music with decidedly Latin influences. The band grew from being a sensation in Spanish-speaking countries to international best-seller status, due to the talent and hard work of Estefan and the sound business sense of her husband, Emilio, a onetime member of the band and later its manager.

Estefan was born Gloria Fajardo in Cuba in 1958; as a toddler she fled Cuba with her family when Communist dictator **Fidel Castro** rose to power. Her father, José Manuel Fajardo, had been a Cuban soldier and bodyguard of President **Fulgencio Batista**. After coming to the United States, Fajardo was recruited into the 2506 Brigade, a Central Intelligence Agency-funded band of Cuban refugees that was involved in the unsuccessful 1961 Bay of Pigs invasion. After President John F. Kennedy negotiated the release of the captured soldiers, Fajardo rejoined his family. He eventually joined the U.S. Army and served for two years in Vietnam.

As a child Estefan liked to write poetry, and though she took classical guitar lessons, she found them tedious. She had no inkling that she would some day become a popular music star, but music played a very important role for her as a teenager. After her father's return from Vietnam, he was diagnosed as having multiple sclerosis, possibly as a result of having been exposed to the herbicide Agent Orange while serving in the army. Estefan's mother, who had been a teacher in Cuba, worked to support the family during the day and attended school at night. Young Gloria was left to take care of her father and younger sister. She had little social life, and because she felt the weight of such responsibilities she turned to music as a release. "When my father was ill, music was my escape," Estefan told *Washington Post* reporter Richard Harrington. "I would lock myself up in my room for hours and just sing. I wouldn't cry—I refused to cry. . . . Music was the only way I had to just let go, so I sang for fun and for emotional catharsis."

### Joined Future Husband's Band

In 1975 Gloria met keyboardist Emilio Estefan, a sales manager for the rum dealer Bacardi, who also led a band called the Miami Latin Boys. The band played popular Latin music, but because there was no lead singer, the quartet members took turns singing. A mutual friend asked Emilio to advise Gloria and some friends about organizing a band for a special event. Emilio heard Gloria sing, and when he met her again at a wedding at which the Miami Latin Boys were entertaining, he asked her to sit in with the band. A few weeks later Emilio asked Gloria to perform as lead singer with the band, and she accepted. At first Gloria sang only on weekends, because she was still attending the University of Miami. A year and a half after Gloria joined the group, by then renamed the

Miami Sound Machine, the band recorded its first album for a local label. *Renacer* was a collection of disco pop and original ballads sung in Spanish.

Although Estefan was somewhat plump and very shy when she joined the band, she slimmed down with a rigorous exercise program and worked to overcome her natural reticence. After several months on a professional level, Emilio and Gloria's professional relationship turned personal, and on September 1, 1978, they were married. Their son Nayib was born two years later, about the time that Emilio quit his job at Bacardi to work full time with the band, then made up of bassist Marcos Avila, drummer Kiki Garcia, keyboardist, arranger, and saxophonist Raul Murciano, keyboardist Emilio, and soprano Gloria.

By 1980 the group had signed a contract with Discos CBS International, the Miami-based Hispanic division of CBS Records. Between 1981 and 1983 the Miami Sound Machine recorded four Spanish-language albums made up of ballads, disco, pop, and sambas. The Miami Sound Machine first met with success in Spanish-speaking countries. The group had dozens of hit songs around the world—particularly in Venezuela, Peru, Panama, and Honduras—but enjoyed little recognition in the United States.

### Success in North America with First English Songs

The Miami Sound Machine's first North American hit was from the band's first English album, *Eyes of Innocence.* The disco single "Dr. Beat" went to the top of the European dance charts. The song's popularity prompted CBS to move the group to Epic, a parent label, and inspired group members to write songs in English, first with a couple of numbers on the otherwise Spanish-language record *Conga.* The rousing dance number "Conga" itself became the first single to crack *Billboard*'s pop, dance, black, and Latin charts simultaneously. Estefan reminisced to Jesse Nash of the *New York Tribune,* "I'll never forget when we first did 'Conga.' A producer told us that the song was too Latin for the Americans and too American for the Latins. 'Well, thank you,' I said, 'because that's exactly what we are!'" Estefan and the group, the membership of which has changed over the years, pride themselves on the combination of Latin rhythms, rhythm and blues, and mainstream pop that makes up their hybrid sound.

In 1985 the album *Primitive Love*, the band's first recording entirely in English, set off a string of hit singles. "Bad Boys" and "Words Get In the Way" made their way onto Billboard's Top 10 pop chart. Behind the scenes was the work of the trio known as the "Three Jerks"—producer-drummer Joe Galdo and his partners Rafael Vigil and Lawrence Dermer—who wrote, arranged, and performed the majority of the music on *Primitive Love* and the follow-up album, *Let It Loose*.

As a band, the Miami Sound Machine developed a split personality. In the studio the "Three Jerks" and session players made records, and for concerts the road band, which included Garcia and Avila, performed. Estefan was the common denominator. Extensive tours, concerts in 40,000-seat stadiums, and music videos on MTV and VH-1 made the Miami Sound Machine a leading American band. Estefan gradually became the star attraction, and the act came to be billed as Gloria Estefan and the Miami Sound Machine or sometimes simply Gloria Estefan. Some commentators on the popular music scene called Estefan a demure, Hispanic version of Madonna.

After the *Let It Loose* album, Galdo and friends quit working with the Miami Sound Machine, so the band was on its own creatively. Early in its evolution, the band's biggest hits were rousing dance numbers, but by the end of the 1980s it was Estefan's ballads that engendered its success. "Ballads are basically what I'm about," Estefan confessed to Dean Johnson of the *Boston Herald*. "I just feel you can express yourself more completely and eloquently in a ballad. It's easier to identify with someone else and form a closer bond with the audience." From the *Let It Loose* album the singles "Rhythm Is Gonna Get You," "Betcha Say That," and "1-2-3" made it to *Billboard*'s Top 10 list, but it was the ballad "Anything for You" that topped the charts.

Despite the group's popularity with English-speaking listeners, the Estefans have not forgotten their roots. There are always Spanish-language projects in the works, and the title of their 1989 album *Cuts Both Ways* attests to their intention to live up to their international reputation. Estefan contributed to *Cuts Both Ways* in more capacities than as just the lead singer. She was involved in its planning and production, composed some of the music, and wrote lyrics to most of the songs. The rollicking salsa finale "*Oye Mi Canto*" ("Hear My Song") rivaled "Conga" for its appeal.

### Fractured Spine in Traffic Accident

Emilio Estefan relinquished his position as keyboardist with the Miami Sound Machine after the birth of son Nayib. He then devoted his considerable energy and managerial talent to promoting the band and the other enterprises that were to eventually make the Estefans producers of their own and others' records. While Estefan toured with the band, her husband ensured that Nayib would have at least one parent at home. A close family, the Estefans would arrange to meet as often as possible during tours. While traveling together on March 20, 1990, the band's bus was involved in an accident with a tractor trailer on snowy Interstate 380 near the Pocono Mountains of Pennsylvania. While Nayib suffered a fractured shoulder and Emilio received minor head and hand injuries, Gloria suffered a broken vertebra in her back. In a four-hour operation several days later, surgeons realigned Estefan's spine and implanted steel rods to buttress the fracture. With a prognosis for complete recovery doubtful, Estefan retired to her home on Star Island, near Miami, to begin her long recovery.

Thanks to extensive physical therapy, intense determination, and the support of her family and fans, Gloria Estefan made what many consider a miraculous comeback. She marked her return to performing with an appearance on television's American Music Awards in January of 1991, and beginning in March, she launched a year-long tour to tout her comeback album *Into the Light*. According to *People*, her "long, sometimes uncertain recovery" gave the singer-songwriter "a renewed feeling about life," as she told writer Steve Dougherty. "It's very hard to stress me out now. It's hard to get me in an uproar about anything because most things have little significance compared with what I almost lost." She added that "so many people got behind me and gave me a reason to want to come back fast and made me feel strong. Knowing how caring people can be, how much they gave me—that has changed me forever."

## SELECTED DISCOGRAPHY:

*Eyes of Innocence*, Discos CBS, 1984.
*Primitive Love*, Epic, 1985.
*Let It Loose*, Epic, 1987.
*Cuts Both Ways*, Epic, 1989.
*Into the Light*, Epic, 1991.
*Greatest Hits*, Epic, 1992.
*Mi Tierra*, Epic, 1993.
*Christmas Through Your Eyes*, Sony/Epic, 1993.
*Hold Me, Thrill Me, Kiss Me*, Epic, 1994.

## SOURCES:

*Boston Herald*, March 7, 1990; March 14, 1990.
*Detroit Free Press*, August 1, 1988.
*Los Angeles Daily News*, September 12, 1989.
*Los Angeles Herald Examiner*, January 29, 1989.
*Miami Herald*, September 30, 1988; May 7, 1989; July 9, 1989; May 27, 1990.
*New York Post*, July 25, 1988; February 28, 1990; March 21, 1990; March 22, 1990; March 23, 1990.
*New York Tribune*, September 14, 1988; December 13, 1989.
*People*, October 27, 1986; February 18, 1991.
*Rolling Stone*, June 14, 1990.
*Washington Post*, July 17, 1988.

—*Sketch by Jeanne M. Lesinski*

# Clarissa Pinkola Estés
## 1943-
### Hispanic American writer and Jungian analyst

In her first book, Clarissa Pinkola Estés tells stories with the warmth and compassion of a mother to her child at bedtime. And like that mother, Estés hopes lessons will be learned. Her message in *Women Who Run With the Wolves: Myths and Stories of the Wild Woman Archetype* is clear: women must trust their powerful and often neglected instincts. *Women Who Run With the Wolves* achieved a great deal of acclaim, appearing on the *New York Times* best-seller list only five weeks after it was officially published by Ballantine Books in the summer of 1992. "In fact, its success could even be termed a 'sensation' or even a full-fledged phenomenon," according to her publicist, Malka Margolies, in a press release. Estés is also a Jungian analyst and an artist-in-residence for the state of Colorado.

Estés was born in January of 1943 to Cepción Ixtiz and E. M. Reyés, who were *mestizos*— Mexicans of Spanish and Indian decent. She was adopted by Maria Hornyak and Joszef Pinkola, immigrant Hungarians living in the United States. Estés was raised in Michigan near the Indiana state line. There she was surrounded by woodlands, orchards, farmland, and the Great Lakes. Her community was filled with people of different Eastern European cultures, as well as Mexicans, Puerto Ricans, African Americans, and families from the backwoods of Tennessee and Kentucky. While growing up, however, Estés "carried in her blood" the mestizo stories, according to a *San Francisco Chronicle* article. She told the *Chronicle* that after World War II her foster father brought his four widowed sisters from Eastern Europe to America. These women, Estés recalled, treated her as though she "was the future, and they tried to pour everything they knew" into her. That folklore along with a love of nature—especially wolves—became an integral part of her life.

She began to better understand herself when she was in her thirties and found her original family, who "not only embraced me but recognized my poetic spirit and told me all the stories that I already knew," she stated in the *San Francisco Chronicle*. "But receiving them orally is different from finding them through dreams and the inner imagination." Estés also told the *Chronicle* that when she was young she thought it was tragic that she was torn from her family. But as an adult she saw it as a miracle: "People who are twice born as adoptees, especially if they are adopted into another culture, have the special ability to bridge those groups."

In the 1960s Estés migrated west toward the Continental Divide and lived amidst Jewish, Irish, Greek, Italian, African American, and Alsatian "strangers who became kindred spirits and friends," Estés said in *Women Who Run With the Wolves*. In 1976 she graduated with a bachelor of arts degree in psychotherapeutics from Loretto Heights College in Denver, Colorado. Five years later she earned her doctorate in philosophy in ethno-clinical (multicultural) psychology from the Union Institute in Cincinnati, Ohio. Ethno-clinical psychology is the study of both clinical psychology and ethnology, the latter emphasizing the study of the psychology of groups, particularly tribes. In 1984 Estés was awarded her postdoctoral diploma in analytical psychology from the Inter-Regional Society of Jungian Analysts in Zurich, Switzerland. This post-doctorate diploma certified Estés as a Jungian analyst.

### Jungian Theory Informs Storyteller's Work

Estés, who is married and the mother of three daughters, practices analysis in Colorado and Wyoming. She has served as the executive director of the C. G. Jung Psychoanalytic Institute in Denver, Colorado. A senior Jungian analyst, Estés is a specialist in cross-cultural mythology. In the early 1900s, Carl Jung used storytelling for studying archetypal patterns as an opening to the unconscious. Estés uses Jung's work as a springboard into writing a new psychology for women.

Estés won a grant and apprenticeship from the Rocky Mountain Women's Institute at Denver University for work on the manuscript *Las brujas* (*The Old Healers*). She explained in *Women Who Run With the Wolves,* "My life experience as a *cantadora-mesemondo*, poet, and artist informs my work with analysands equally." Estés went on to describe what she does in her consulting room to help women return to their wildish nature: "I place substantial emphasis on clinical and developmental psychology, and I use the simplest and most accessible ingredient for healing—stories." She added that she also follows the patient's dream material, which contains many plots and stories. "The analysand's physical sensations and body memories are also stories which can be read and rendered into consciousness," she asserted.

Estés teaches a form of powerful interactive trancing that is proximate to Jung's theory of active imagination. This produces stories which further the client's psychic journey. "We contact the wildish Self through specific questions and through examining fairy tales, folktales, legends, and mythos. Most times we are able, over time, to find the guiding myth or fairy tale that contains all the instruction a woman needs for her drama. It is like a play with stage instructions, characterizations, and props," Estés maintained in *Women Who Run With the Wolves.*

As a *cantadora* (keeper of old stories) in the Hispanic tradition, Estés is an artist-in-residence for the state of Colorado. Her work is funded by the National Endowment for the Arts. *La invitada* ("a guest" or "the empty chair"), Estés explained in *Women Who Run With the Wolves,* "is always present at storytelling. Sometimes during a telling the soul of one or more of the audience comes and sits there for it has a need. Although I may have a whole evening of material prepared, I often change it to mend or play with the spirit that comes to the empty chair. The guest always speaks to the needs of all."

An award-winning writer, Estés has created best-selling audio tapes in the Jungian storyteller series, including *The Creative Fire,* on incubation and creativity; *The Wild Woman Archetype,* on the instinctual nature of women; and *In the House of the Riddle Mother.* Her poetry has been published in *Exquisite Corpse, Los mochis, The International Signal, Fennel Stalk, Icon, Palabras,* and *Muse.* Her conversations with Dr. James Hillman, poet Robert Bly, and artist Nicole Hollander were published by *Bloomsbury Review.*

### Draws on Archetypes to Help Women

She earned the most acclaim, however, with *Women Who Run With the Wolves,* a book based on 20 years of researching, writing, and collecting countless stories from diverse ethnic groups. In the first few pages of *Women Who Run With the Wolves,* Estés explains her inspiration for the work: "Traditional psychology is often spare or entirely silent about deeper issues important to women; the archetypal, the intuitive, the sexual and cyclical, the ages of women, a woman's way, a woman's knowing, her creative fire. This is what has motivated my work on the Wild Woman archetype for the better part of two decades." A *Library Journal* contributor observed that the book, written in a "clear, richly evocative style," was a "perceptive study of women's deep nature."

In *Women Who Run With the Wolves* Estés remembered that growing up in the northern woodlands she always felt close to wolves. She states, "Healthy wolves and healthy women share certain psychic characteristics: keen sensing, playful spirit, and a heightened capacity for devotion. Wolves and women are relational by nature, inquiring, possessed of great endurance and strength. They are deeply intuitive, intensely concerned with their young, their mate, and their pack. They are experienced at adapting to constantly changing circumstances, they are fiercely stalwart and very brave. So that is where the concept of the wild woman archetype crystallized for me, in the study of wolves." A review in *Publishers Weekly* noted that this comparison "defines the archetype of the wild woman, a female in touch with

her primitive side and able to rely on gut feelings to make change."

Estés' stories are designed to teach women to trust their instincts. The story "La loba" in *Women Who Run With the Wolves* teaches the transformative function of the psyche; "Bluebird" talks about wounds that will not heal; and "Skeleton Woman" gives the reader a glimpse of the mystical power of relationship and how dead feelings can be revived. Together the stories advocate "wolf rules for life: eat, rest, rove in between; render loyalty; love the children; cavil in moonlight; tune your ears; attend to the bones; make love; howl often."

Estés tells her readers that the wild woman "passed through" her spirit twice: once by her birth into a "passionate Mexican-Spanish bloodline," and later through "adoption by a family of fiery Hungarians." In an interview with her publisher she asserted that she comes from "a long line of storytellers. I've spent many hours seated at the feet of old Hungarian and Latina women who storytell in plain voices. For them, story is a medicine which strengthens and arights the individual and community. From them I learned that story greases and hoists the pulleys, shows us the way out, down, in and around, cuts for us fine, wide doors in previously blank walls—doors that lead us to our own knowing as wildish women."

Estés' work delves into the healing power of the female psyche. She avoids, however, denigrating men, saying in a *USA Today* article that she is "tired of divisiveness." In *Women Who Run With the Wolves,* Estés shows how the "wild woman archetype" is damaged by a stifling culture that discounts what is feminine. By using stories and myths from Inuit, Asian, European, Mexican, and Greek traditions, Estés shows her readers how they can reclaim their soul life. She claims that women who study the meaning of the stories can find inner-power of self-determination and creativity that will lead to power and freedom. Through the tales she explores the female power in sex, love, money, marriage, birthing, death, and transformation.

The first in a proposed trilogy, *Women Who Run With the Wolves* is scheduled to be followed by *The Dangerous Old Woman and the Power of Age* and *The Mother-Daughter-Sister Relationship.* She ends her first book with the following message: "I hope you will go out and let stories happen to you, and that you will work them, water them with your blood and tears and your laughter till they bloom, till you yourself burst into bloom. Then you will see what medicine they make, and where and when to apply them. That is the work. The only work."

## SELECTED PUBLISHED WORKS:

*Women Who Run With the Wolves,* Ballentine, 1992.

*The Gift of Story: A Wise Tale About What Is Enough*, Ballentine, 1994.

**SOURCES:**

*Library Journal,* June 15, 1992.
*Publishers Weekly,* May 1, 1992.
*San Francisco Chronicle,* August 2, 1992.
*USA Today,* August 13, 1992.

—*Sketch by D. D. Andreassi*

# Sandra María Esteves
## 1948-
### Hispanic American poet

Sandra María Esteves is a poet affiliated with the Nuyorican group of writers. Her work reflects the conflicts of living between two languages and two cultures, as well as the problems of surviving as an Hispanic woman in a world dominated by Anglo males. She has been compared to Julia de Burgos, a poet from a previous generation of émigrés whose double burden as a woman and as a Puerto Rican living in New York led to her untimely death.

The child of immigrants, Esteves was born in the Bronx, New York, on May 10, 1948. Her mother, a garment factory worker from the Dominican Republic, and her father, a sailor from Puerto Rico, separated when Esteves was very young; at age six the child was sent to a Catholic boarding school. The seven years she spent at Holy Rosary Academy left an indelible mark on the poet's psyche. Subjected to the strictures of Irish-based American Catholicism, she was not permitted to speak Spanish at the Academy, where she remained during the week. Weekends, she returned to the Puerto Rican world of her family, specifically the home of her paternal aunt, who cared for the girl so that her mother could go to work. Esteves's early experiences formed an awareness of living in two cultures which would later be manifested both in the themes and in the bilingualism of her early poetry.

### Ethnicity and Poetry

After graduating from high school in 1966 and attempting to study art at the Pratt Institute, Esteves went to Puerto Rico, where she intended to remain. She returned to New York after a few months, however, now fully conscious of her ethnicity and proud of it. Esteves was soon participating in various protest movements of the 1970s and expressing her new awareness through poetry. After Nuyorican poet Jesus Papoleto Melendez introduced her to the world of young Hispanic artists, she became one of a group of young Nuyorican poets that included Tato Laviera and Miguel Algarin. She also became part of "El Grupo," a collective of Nuyorican socialist poets, performers, and musicians committed to taking the message of protest throughout the eastern United States. Her work as a painter followed a similar course through her contact with the Taller Boricua art collective.

In 1978 Esteves received her bachelor's degree in fine art from the Pratt Institute. In 1980 her first collection of poetry, *Yerba buena,* was published by Greenfield Review Press and selected as the Best Small Press Publication for 1981. At this time Esteves began to write almost exclusively in English to express her experiences as an urban Hispanic woman living in the United States. The following decade was one of intense creativity and cultural involvement for Esteves. Among her many accomplishments were her participation in the Cultural Council Foundation of the CETA Artistic Project (1978–80) and her appointment as executive artistic director of the African Caribbean Poetry Theater. Two other collections of Esteves's poetry have been published, *Tropical Rains* (1984), and *Bluestown Mockingbird Mambo* (1990). Esteves resides in New York City and is the mother of three daughters.

**SELECTED PUBLISHED WORKS:**

*Yerba buena,* Greenfield Review Press, 1980.
*Tropical Rains,* 1984.
*Bluestown Mockingbird Mambo,* 1990.

**SOURCES:**

Gordils, Yanis, "Sandra María Esteves," *Biographical Dictionary of Hispanic Literature in the United States,* edited by Nicolas Kanellos, Greenwood Press, 1989, pp. 85–94.

**Other**

Archives, Arte Público Press, Houston, Texas.

—*Sketch by Silvia Novo Pena*

# Emilio Estevez
## 1962-
### Hispanic American actor, director, and screenwriter

The eldest son of actor **Martin Sheen**, Emilio Estevez is famous in his own right for his acting in many films since 1982, including *Repo Man* (1984), *The Breakfast Club* (1985), and *Young Guns* (1988). He has also directed films and has written screenplays. Estevez chose his father's original Spanish surname in a conscious decision to avoid the inevitable comparisons. In a 1985 interview with Thomas Wiener of *American Film,* he explained that constant references to his father are bothersome. "It's a sore subject," he said. "Talking about him, period, is a sore subject. I mean, I'm not ashamed of him in any way. But a lot of times, for the most part, it's not Emilio Estevez on the street, it's Martin Sheen's son, and I think the more that I disassociate myself, the more the public sees Emilio Estevez without that identification following him."

When directors and producers in Hollywood did make the connection between Estevez and Sheen, it was a problem as well. "I don't think it's helped me get any jobs; I know that for a fact," he told Wiener. "I think in some ways it has hurt me because they have expected . . . let's see Martin Sheen now." He acknowledged that the decision to use Estevez was made early on. "I did a play with him [Martin Sheen] down at the Burt Reynolds Dinner Theatre, *Mister Roberts,* when I was seventeen, and I changed the name to Estevez for the program. I saw it in print on the program, and I said, 'This looks better.' It looks better in print, and it is also the dividing line."

At the time of the 1985 *American Film* interview, Estevez had appeared in four films: *Tex* (1982), *Nightmares* in (1983), *The Outsiders* in (1984), and *Repo Man* (1985). At the time, *Repo Man* was just becoming a cult film among teenagers and college students. Soon after the interview with Wiener, Estevez no longer needed to worry about disappearing into his father's shadow. The American audience not only recognized his name but wanted to see more of it. Regardless of how being Martin Sheen's son may have hampered his self-esteem in the early years of his career, Estevez has benefited from the legacy of his father's talent and expertise and from his mother's fortitude.

### An Acting Family

On May 12, 1962, in New York City, Estevez was born to Martin Sheen and Janet Estevez. Sheen,

*Emilio Estevez*

originally named Ramon Estevez, was a stage actor when his first son was born. Estevez's grandfather was an emigrant from Spain who worked as a drill-press operator at National Cash Register. In an early studio biography, according to *Hispanic* in 1994, Estevez described his family as close. "My mother is very strong and pragmatic. She grounded me. My dad taught me to trust myself and to always search for the truth in whatever I was doing."

Estevez went to public school in Malibu, California, and appeared in several school plays. For a time, high school sports were his forte. When he realized that professional sports were beyond his grasp, he turned to acting with a career in mind. "I knew I had an ability to perform from an early age, to really excel at it," Estevez stated in his studio biography. "So I began taking acting seriously and started auditioning." Even at this age, writing intrigued him as well. He told Wiener about his first try at writing and producing. "I had written a play when I was in high school about the Vietnam War, and had it produced. And when I graduated from high school, I wrote a screenplay that I never let anyone see, about a boy searching for his father, and I canned it right away. It was terrible. I think that if I wasn't an actor that I'd be a journalist, something to do with writing."

On the day he graduated from Santa Monica High School, Estevez was cast in an afternoon television special called *Seventeen Going on Nowhere.* Other television dramas followed. Estevez broke into movies with the film *Tex* in 1982. Based on an adaptation of the S. E. Hinton novel, the movie starred Matt Dillon. The following year Estevez had a small role in another Hinton-based movie, *The Outsiders.* Many other young actors, including Ralph Macchio, Patrick Swayze, and Tom Cruise got their start in this film. These young men were called the "Brat Pack" of Hollywood.

During the filming of *The Outsiders,* Estevez read the rest of Hinton's novels and was intrigued with another work entitled *That Was Then . . . This Is Now.* "As soon as I read the book I said to Hinton these are incredible characters, and if anyone is to make one of your books, it should be this one," Estevez explained to Wiener. "She had been approached by ABC for one of those after-school specials. But she didn't want to do it. She saw a much bigger scope for it." With only one film under his belt, Estevez optioned the book from Hinton and wrote a screenplay on it, updating it from the 1960s to the present. The author even suggested Estevez play the lead. Before his screenplay was produced, Estevez shot to stardom on the backs of two wildly opposite films: *Repo Man* and *The Breakfast Club.*

## From Punk Rocker to Jock

"This quirky film," Wiener wrote about *Repo Man* released in 1984, "featured Estevez as a wide-eyed punker taking in the bizarre world of Los Angeles car reposssessors . . . [and was a] flop in its initial theatrical release, [but it] found a second life on videocassette and was then miraculously revived in theaters like New York's Eighth Street Playhouse, where it ran for months." Before filming *Repo Man,* Estevez said he did not understand the punk movement. "I think I feared that whole movement, because it was so dark. And then I get this script for *Repo Man,* and the lead character is this punk. [T]he script was just hysterical," Estevez told *American Film.*

In his next film, *The Breakfast Club* released in 1985, Estevez played a high school jock. Both films appealed to the public. The range of roles, served him well. That same year, another film starring Estevez, *St. Elmo's Fire,* was released. This time he played a character his own age. Also in 1985, *That Was Then, This Is Now,* for which Estevez wrote the screenplay, was also released. "I think *That Was Then* was my swan song to high school films," he told Wiener. Estevez is described in the film as giving a genuine portrayal of an alienated teenager struggling to understand the world around him. From then on, the actor starred in a variety of films and played numerous characters. He was in Stephen King's *Maximum*

*Overdrive* in 1986 and wrote and directed *Wisdom* in the same year. Estevez was, at 23, the youngest person ever to write, direct, and star in a major motion picture.

Several action/adventure movies followed, including *Stakeout* in 1987, *Young Guns* in 1988 and its sequel two years later. Estevez has continued writing and directing. He wrote and directed the comedy *Men At Work* in 1990 in which he co-starred with brother **Charlie Sheen.** Working with his brother was a memorable experience. "As kids, we used to make 8mm films together that he would shoot and I would act in," Estevez said. "One day on the set of *Young Guns,* we were doing a scene sitting across the table from one another. I had to stop the scene and say to Charlie, 'Can you believe this? We're working together.' It's been a real treat for both of us."

According to *Hispanic,* Estevez has been involved in two paternity suits and has two children out of wedlock. In 1992, Estevez married renowned pop singer Paula Abdul. They were divorced two years later. Some members of the public might still associate his name with his father's, but there is no doubt that Emilio Estevez stands on his own.

## SELECTED VIDEOGRAPHY:

*In the Custody of Strangers,* 1982.
*Tex,* 1982.
*Nightmares,* 1983.
*The Outsiders,* 1983.
*Repo Man,* 1984.
*The Breakfast Club,* 1985.
*That Was Then . . . This Is Now,* 1985.
*St. Elmos Fire,* 1985.
*Maximum Overdrive,* 1986.
*Stakeout,* 1987.
*Wisdom,* 1987.
*Never on Tuesday,* 1988.
*Young Guns,* 1988.
*Nightbreaker,* 1989.
*Men At Work,* 1990.
*Young Guns II,* 1990.
*Freejack,* 1992.
*The Mighty Ducks,* 1992.
*Another Stakeout,* 1993.
*National Lampoon's Loaded Weapon I,* 1993.

## SOURCES:

*American Film,* March 1985, pp. 42–42, 58.
*Hispanic,* May 1994, pp. 14–18.

—*Sketch by Kathe A. Conti*

# René Geronimo Favaloro
## 1923-
### Argentine surgeon

One of the pioneers of bypass heart surgery, in which a vein from the patient's leg is substituted for a damaged artery at the heart, René Geronimo Favaloro also established one of Latin America's leading medical teaching facilities, the Institute of Cardiology and Cardiovascular Surgery in Buenos Aires, Argentina.

Favaloro was born in La Plata, Argentina, to Ida Y. Raffaelli, a dressmaker, and Juan B. Favaloro, a carpenter. He attended the National College and Medical School at the University of La Plata, receiving his M.D. in 1949. His internship, residency and first staff position were at the Instituto General San Martin in La Plata, and he took a postgraduate course at Rawson Hospital in Buenos Aires. After 12 years practicing medicine in the remote Pampas of Argentina, he visited the Cleveland Clinic in 1961, curious about the latest techniques in myocardial revascularization (increasing a restricted blood supply to the heart). The *Cleveland Plain Dealer* recounted a story that the visiting professional—tall, dark, handsome and quite imposing but speaking little English— walked into a doctor's office at the Clinic and said softly, "I want to work here."

### Helps Pioneer Coronary Bypass Surgery

Attempts at revascularization began before World War II with little success. Donald R. Effler, head of the thoracic and cardiovascular department at the Clinic, said in his introduction to Favaloro's book, *Surgical Treatment of Coronary Arteriosclerosis,* that he believed the primary reason for this lack of success was inadequate diagnosis; treatments were largely based on clinical assumptions. In 1957, Dr. F. Mason Sones, Jr., of the Cleveland Clinic was searching for a simple diagnostic tool to accurately identify coronary arterial disease. He developed angiography, in which dye is inserted via catheter into the arteries, exposing on X-rays the exact location of blockages. The technique also enabled much finer diagnostic evaluations, allowing the individual needs of each patient to be identified, a relatively accurate prognosis predicted, and the appropriate therapy undertak-

en. The tool became the major determinant in selecting candidates for bypass surgery.

When Favaloro joined the thoracic and cardiovascular team at the Clinic as an observer 1962, revascularization was still tenuous. Two techniques were being used: the pericardial patch graft, in which the wall of a blocked artery is opened and "patched" with part of a leg vein in an attempt to increase the size of the artery; and the mammary artery implant, in which one end of the mammary artery in the chest is inserted into the wall of the left ventricle, supplying the ventricle with blood to be pumped into the vessels. Favaloro's observations went far beyond the operating room, however. He plunged into all the documentation he could find on revascularization. In his now famous 1967 bypass operation, he inserted one end of the saphenous vein, removed from the patient's leg, into the aorta, the large artery above the heart. The other end he inserted into an artery below the obstruction, fully restoring the blood flow.

Although the first to perform a full bypass at the Clinic, Favaloro was not the first to use the procedure. David Sabiston, Jr., of Duke University in North Carolina unsuccessfully performed the first known human bypass in 1962. The first successful bypass was by H. Edward Garrett in 1964. Both operations were used in emergency situations. Neither doctor considered or developed the procedure as a standard treatment, nor did they publish documentation on the procedure for almost ten years.

Favaloro approached the procedure from an entirely different perspective. His research convinced him the procedure would be effective in treating certain types of heart disease. He planned his first bypass, fully intending to adopt it as a standard procedure for appropriate candidates, and published a paper on it in 1968. The *New York Times* quoted Lawrence H. Cohn, chair of the Cardiac Surgery Committee of the American College of Cardiology as saying, "Favaloro was the first to recognize the importance of this technique and develop it."

Over the years, the coronary bypass has been refined and improved. Some critics declare it "overused," causing many patients to pay for unnecessary surgery. However, the procedure lasts longer than more recent treatments, such as angioplasty (inserting a tiny balloon into the restricted artery via catheter and inflating the balloon to compress plaque against the artery wall), and remains the most important treatment for coronary arteriosclerosis.

By 1970, Favaloro and the cardiovascular team at the Clinic had performed more than 1,000 bypass operations, of which almost a quarter were multiple bypasses, with the death rate an astonishingly low 4.2 percent. In 1971, at the height of his surgical career, Favaloro left the Clinic, returned to Buenos Aires, and established the Favaloro Foundation to teach bypass surgery. In 1992, after 20 years of dedication and hard work, Favaloro's lifelong dream was fulfilled with the completion of his ten-story, $55 million Institute of Cardiology and Cardiovascular Surgery, one of the finest medical teaching institutes in Latin America. By then, his programs had trained more than 300 heart surgeons, half of whom are Latin American, and his team had performed thousands of by-pass operations.

Favaloro is married to Maria A. Delgado. He is a member of the Medical Society of La Plata and the Societe Internationale de Chirurgie. He was elected a fellow of the American College of Surgeons in 1967, which also made him an honorary fellow in 1990. He has also served in the Army of the Republic of Argentina as a lieutenant.

Considered a hero by both his medical colleagues and the people of his nation—who frequently suggest him as a presidential candidate—the surgeon who, contrary to the norms of society, turned his back on fame and fortune both at the beginning and the height of his career, described himself in an interview with the *Cleveland Plain Dealer* as "still a simple, country doctor."

## SELECTED PUBLISHED WORKS:

*Surgical Treatment of Coronary Arteriosclerosis,* Williams & Wilkins, 1970.
*Do You Know San Martin?,* [Buenos Aires], 1986.
*The Challenging Dream of Heart Surgery: From the Pampas to Cleveland,* Little, Brown, 1994.

## SOURCES:

*Cleveland Clinic Foundation Fellow,* Volume 1, number 4, 1983, pp. 1, 4.
*Cleveland Clinic Newsletter,* October, 1967, p. 1; July, 1971, p. 3.
*Cleveland Plain Dealer,* September 11, 1987; November 8, 1992.
*New York Times,* August 18, 1992.

—*Sketch by David Petechuk*

# José Feliciano
## 1945-
### Puerto Rican singer and guitarist

José Feliciano, a self-taught guitar virtuoso who "puts his heart on his sleeve for a ballad," as a *Rolling Stone* reviewer noted, has entertained Latin American and U.S. audiences for three decades. He also achieved American mainstream success with the album *Feliciano!* (1968)—"a classic make-out album" according to *The Rolling Stone Record Guide* —and its hit single, "Light My Fire."

Feliciano was born on September 10, 1945, in Puerto Rico, the second of twelve children. He grew up in poverty in Manhattan's Lower East Side, where his father worked as a longshoreman. "Money was a problem, so was discrimination against me and my family," Feliciano told Matt Messina of the *New York Sunday News* in 1969. Because of congenital glaucoma, Feliciano was blind at birth, but that did not stop him from becoming an accomplished musician. By the age of six, Feliciano had taught himself to play the concertina by listening to records. By his teens, he had mastered the acoustic 12-string guitar. When he was 16, Feliciano, whose influences included Ray Charles and Sam Cooke, started playing folk, flamenco, and pop guitar music for spare change at Greenwich Village coffee shops.

Feliciano dropped out of high school at 17 to perform full-time, playing his first professional show at the Retort Coffee House in Detroit in 1963. In the summer of that year, Feliciano played at Gerde's Folk City in New York, where Robert Shelton of the *New York Times* recommended people go "to witness the birth of a star.... Instrumentally, he seems to know no bounds." An RCA Victor representative went to Gerde's to watch another artist, but instead signed Feliciano to an exclusive contract.

Feliciano's first album was *The Voice and Guitar of José Feliciano* in 1964. While this first release made no impact on the popular music charts, it did receive airplay. For the first few years, RCA producers attempted to create a suitable marketing angle for Feliciano, but none fit his style. "They wanted me to do a rock album, then a country and western album. It was all wrong," Feliciano told Bob Micklin of *Newsday* in 1969. RCA had more success in promoting Feliciano's Puerto Rican heritage to Latin American audiences; in 1966 Feliciano played to an audience of 100,000 in Buenos Aires, Argentina.

In 1968 Feliciano achieved mainstream success. On the album *Feliciano!,* he covered The Doors' 1967 hit "Light My Fire" with what *Rock Movers and Shakers* described as a "slowed-down, sparse acoustic-

*José Feliciano*

with-woodwind arrangement and soul-infected vocal." "Light My Fire" became the third most popular single in the United States, and *Feliciano!*, which covered other hits, reached number two on the album charts. "I always wanted to be a star," Feliciano told *Newsweek.* "I used to listen to the radio and say, 'That's where I want to be.'"

Because of his success, Feliciano was invited to sing the national anthem before the fifth game of the 1968 World Series, but his highly stylized performance touched off a national furor among anthem purists. RCA Victor rushed a release of the performance; the record reached number 50 on U.S. singles charts. In December 1968, Feliciano performed before 100,000 people at the Miami Pop Festival in Hallendale, Florida, the first major East Coast music festival. The next spring, Feliciano won Grammy awards for Best New Artist of 1968 and Best Contemporary Male Pop Vocal Performance for "Light My Fire."

But 1968 marked the peak of Feliciano's U.S. popularity. Subsequent releases have not enjoyed the same success. His only minor hits in America since the 1960s were the theme song for the television show *Chico and the Man* and the Christmas staple "Feliz Navidad (I Wanna Wish You a Merry Christmas)". After leaving RCA in the mid–1970s, Feliciano recorded for several labels, including Motown, with little U.S. success. In 1982 Feliciano married Susan Omillion, with whom he has had two children; he had

previously been married to Hilda Perez, the manager of one of the cafes he had frequented at the beginning of his career.

While his popularity in the United States has faded over the years, Feliciano has remained enormously popular with international and American Latino audiences. Feliciano has earned 40 international gold and platinum records and won Grammy awards for best Latin pop performance in 1983, 1986, 1989, and 1990. "I want to sell more records than **Julio Iglesias**," Feliciano told *Billboard* in 1984. Yet despite the success of his distinctive style, his relationships with record producers were often turbulent. "I want to record it my way, so I'm always struggling," Feliciano said.

While reviewers praise Feliciano's virtuosity on instruments—he can also play bass, banjo, organ, bongo drums, mandolin, harmonica, piano, harpsichord, and several Latin instruments—his vocal capabilities have not always impressed critics. *Time* wrote in 1968 that "his high, quavery tenor, though obviously brimming with feeling, was merely good," and Stephen Holden noted for *Rolling Stone* that Feliciano's rock songs "are embarrassingly stiff."

## SELECTED DISCOGRAPHY

*The Voice and Guitar of José Feliciano*, RCA, 1964.
*Feliciano!*, RCA, 1968.
*Feliciano/10 to 23*, RCA, 1969.
*Souled*, RCA, 1969.
*Fireworks*, RCA, 1970.
*José Feliciano*, RCA, 1971.
*Sweet Soul Music*, Private Stock, 1976.
*José Feliciano*, Motown, 1981.
*Escenas de Amor*, Motown Latino, 1983.
*Me Enamore*, Profono, 1983.
*Te Amaré*, RCA International, 1986.
*Nina*, Capitol/EMI Latin, 1990.
*Latin Street '92*, Capitol/EMI Latin, 1992.

## SOURCES:

### Books

*Contemporary Musicians,* edited by Julia M. Rubiner, Detroit, Gale, 1994.
*Current Biography Yearbook,* edited by Charles Moritz, New York, H. W. Wilson, 1970.
*Rock Movers and Shakers,* edited by Dafydd Rees and Luke Crampton, Santa Barbara, Calif., ABC-CLIO, 1991.
*The Rolling Stone Record Guide,* edited by Dave Marsh with John Swenson, New York, Random House/Rolling Stone Press, 1979.

**Periodicals**

*Billboard,* January 7, 1984,. 41.
*Newsweek,* September 23, 1968, p. 109.
*Time,* September 27, 1968, p. 78.

—*Sketch by Eric Patterson*

# María Félix
## 1914-
**Mexican actress**

*María Félix*

"People always praised my beauty and intelligence, but I'm just a woman with a man's heart," Mexico's greatest actress María Félix told *Vanity Fair* in 1990. Félix has made nearly 50 films, aided by a magnetic allure that was noted by leaders of her native country and the many reporters who interviewed her during her career. She married five times, and her beauty was canonized by artists such as painter **Diego Rivera**. Although American critics were more likely to pan her performances, she received numerous awards, including the Ariele Award for best actress, which she accepted three times for separate film performances in 1945, 1947, and 1950. In 1989, the president of Mexico presented her with the first Mexico City Prize, for a lifetime of distinguished achievement.

Even when she had to rely on translators, Félix was eminently quotable. After a *Cue* interviewer noted in 1956 that she had been married three times, she quipped, "I'm just getting started." Her husbands included Mexican film star Jorge Negrette, who died after just one year of marriage, and singer/composer Agustín Lara.

María Félix was born in Alamos, a town in the northern region of Sonora, on April 8, 1914. Always adventurous, Félix boasted that she rode horses bareback and could leap from one galloping horse to another. She moved with her family to Guadalajara, and as a teenager she married her first husband, a cosmetics salesman, and gave birth to her only child, a son.

Félix left her husband in the early 1940s and began a liaison with a Mexican film director who groomed her for stardom. She established herself with her first film, *El Peñón de las Ánimas* ("Rock of Souls"), made in 1942 when she was 28 years old. Félix's only rival in Mexican cinema was actress Delores del Rio, who was considered more elegant than Félix.

But it was Félix who met with the greatest box office success, and in most of her films she portrayed notorious women, including the Roman empress Messalina, a cabaret singer, the tragic heroine Camille, the madame of a brothel, and a soldier. Her popularity extended to Europe, and she made films in Spain, Italy, and France.

Félix was once asked why she never made an American film, and she dismissed the question. "In Mexico I am a goddess. What do I have to gain from Hollywood?" she asked. She also decried Hollywood's tendency to stereotype. Said to be a shrewd businesswoman, she maintained a large estate outside of Mexico City, kept an apartment in Paris, and made frequent trips to the United States, where she could walk and shop in New York City with relative anonymity.

In a 1990 *Vanity Fair* interview, Félix shared her philosophy of life. "I never drank a drop of alcohol or took drugs, and believe me, it's difficult to endure success without their help. My two rules are, one, never take yourself too seriously—avoid compliments like poison—and two, accept rigid discipline . . . especially, in doing difficult, unpleasant things."

Félix also was known for the exotic company she kept. She enjoyed friendships with Rivera and his wife **Frida Kahlo**, **Che Guevara**, **Eva Perón**, and **Fidel Castro**. Mexican author **Carlos Fuentes** immortalized Félix in his 1982 play, *Orchids in the Moonlight*. His depiction was unflattering enough to draw Félix's ire, so much so that in a 1990 interview she would not refer to Fuentes by name. He, however, paid her a compliment when he told *Vanity Fair,* "María has a mythic quality, and she's a great national symbol ... only a myth can inspire imitation. But of course no one can successfully impersonate a goddess.... I find her beautiful, funny, amusing."

Félix was honored in 1982 by Nosotros, a Los Angeles-based theater group, with the Golden Eagle Life Achievement Award. Her acceptance of the recognition drew a standing ovation from the audience at the Beverly Hills Hotel ballroom.

## SOURCES:

### Books

*International Dictionary of Films and Filmmakers: Actors and Actresses,* Detroit, St. James Press, 1992, pp. 333–35.

### Periodicals

*Cue,* June 9, 1956, p. 13.
*Vanity Fair,* November 1990, pp. 207–12.
*Variety,* June 14, 1982, p. 2.

—*Sketch by Karen Withem*

# Freddy Fender
## 1937-

### Mexican American singer and musician

From humble beginnings in the Texas Rio Grande Valley to solid commercial success as a member of the Texas Tornados supergroup, the long path of Freddy Fender's career has been marked by dramatic turns of fortune. After initial success as a singer in 1959, his career was derailed by a 1960 drug arrest and a three-year stint in prison. After his release he returned to performing but labored in obscurity until 1975, when he made a successful comeback with the song "Before the Next Teardrop Falls," which garnered both a Grammy and a Country Music Association Award. Fender then maintained a steady, successful recording career and even broke into acting. He rejuvenated a faltering career in 1989 by joining fellow musicians Flaco Jimenez, Doug Sahm, and Augie Meyers to form the Texas Tornados. Their zesty blend of Tex-Mex ballads and rock and roll

proved popular not only in the United States, but in the Netherlands and Australia as well. Fender and his wife, Evangelina Muñiz, with whom he has had three children, live in Texas.

Freddy Fender was born Baldemar Garza Huerta on June 4, 1937, to Serapio and Margarita Huerta in San Benito, Texas. His parents, who were migrant workers, worked their way to the northern United States when young Baldemar was about ten years old, traveling up through Indiana, Ohio, and Michigan and returning through the cotton fields of Arkansas. As a child who quickly developed a fondness for music, he somehow always managed to keep a guitar in his possession. He dropped out of high school at the age of 16 and joined the Marine Corps, serving as a private from 1954 to 1956.

After his discharge, he decided to pursue a career in music and adopted the name Freddy Fender, which he felt would have greater appeal to "gringo" audiences. Playing local venues, he quickly became popular. He recorded a series of records in Spanish that were hits locally on both sides of the Rio Grande. In 1957 Fender was the first rhythm and blues/rock and roll singer to receive airplay in both Mexico and Latin America. 1959 signaled a newfound, wider popularity when he recorded the two Texas rockabilly hits, "Holy One" and "Wasted Days and Wasted Nights." With this success, Fender became known as "El Bebop Kid" and the "Mexican Elvis." He followed up in 1960 with the hit song "Crazy, Crazy Baby."

### Arrest Jeopardizes Career

Fender's career, in full swing, ground to a halt in May 1960 when he was arrested in Baton Rouge, Louisiana, for possession of marijuana. He was sent to Angola State Prison for three years. After his release in 1963, he spent the next five years playing and singing small engagements in New Orleans. Record deals were not forthcoming. Returning to San Benito in 1969, Fender relegated music to a part-time endeavor. He worked as a mechanic and played music on weekends. He also took his GED exam and in 1973–74 studied sociology at Corpus Christi's Del Mar Junior College.

A 1974 encounter with producer Huey Meaux allowed Fender to record "Before the Next Teardrop Falls," a shift to country music. A local hit at first, it soon went national and became a pop crossover gold record in 1975. Fender released his first album—which also went gold—the same year. Almost 20 years after his debut, national acclaim was finally his. In 1976 he received a Country Music Association Award for Single of the Year and a Grammy for Best Male Country Vocal Performance.

Armed with a voice that *Stereo Review* called a "natural wonder," Fender maintained his popularity among fans for the next several years, although critics such as Chet Flippo, writing in the *Rolling Stone Record Guide,* dismissed him as "an overworked goose that strained to lay golden eggs." He had a number of Top Ten hits, including "You'll Lose a Good Thing" (1976) and "I'm Leaving It All Up to You" (1978). Fender recorded 11 albums for the ABC label before switching to Starflite, a label distributed by Epic, in 1979. Fender became interested in acting and was cast as **Pancho Villa** in *She Came to the Valley* in 1980. He also appeared in *The Milagro Beanfield War* (1987), *La Pastorela* (1991), and *Always Roses* (1991).

### Texas Tornados Are Born

The 1980s marked another downturn in Fender's career. *Country Music* commented that "Fender recorded a lot of forgettable junk after his big hits of the 70's." He recorded his last solo album in 1981, and several years followed where the artist was without a label. Looking for a solo contract with Warner Brothers, Fender played a showcase in 1989 on a program with Doug Sahm and Augie Meyers. Warner Brothers expressed interest in signing the musicians as a group, so the Texas Tornados were born. Fender admitted to *People* in 1991 that "I had doubts. . . . I felt we were past our prime. . . . But I had big bills to pay."

The Tornados have put Fender back on top. Led by Fender's vocals, which *Country Music* described as "searing" and "dripping with . . . Texas blues flavor," the Tornados "collectively have done more to popularize the [Tex-Mex] sound around the world than anyone else," according to *Texas Monthly Stereo Review* described the Tornados as "not so much a group as a consortium of Tex-Mex musicians who have come to the realization that there's strength in numbers. Already they've enjoyed more commercial success under the group umbrella than any of them have known outside it in many years." The Tornados released three albums on the Reprise label in the early 1990s: *Texas Tornados* (1991), *Zone of Our Own* (1992), and *Hangin' On By a Thread* (1993).

### SELECTED DISCOGRAPHY

*Before the Next Teardrop Falls,* Dot, 1974.
*Are You Ready for Freddy,* Dot, 1975.
*Rock 'n' Country,* ABC, 1976.
*If You're Ever in Texas,* Dot, 1976.
*If You Don't Love Me,* Dot, 1977.
*Swamp Gold,* ABC, 1978.
*Texas Balladeer,* Starflite, 1979.

### With the Texas Tornados

*Texas Tornados,* Reprise, 1991.
*Zone of Our Own,* Reprise, 1992.

*Hangin' On By a Thread,* Reprise, 1993.

## SOURCES:

### Books

*Contemporary Musicians,* Volume 8, edited by Julia M. Rubiner, Detroit, Gale, 1933.
*The Encyclopedia of Folk, Country & Western Music,* 2nd edition, edited by Irwin Stambler and Grelun Landon, New York, St. Martin's Press, 1983.
*The New Country Music Encyclopedia,* edited by Tad Richards and Melvin B. Shestak, New York, Simon & Schuster, 1993.
*The New Grove Dictionary of American Music,* Volume 2, edited by H. Wiley Hitchcock and Stanley Sadie, London, Macmillan Press, 1986.
*The New Rolling Stone Record Guide,* edited by Dave Marsh and John Swenson, New York, Random House/Rolling Stone, 1983.

### Periodicals

*Audio,* April, 1991, p. 114.
*Country Music,* March/April 1992; March/April 1993, p. 16.
*New York Times,* September 30, 1990, p. G16
*People,* December 2, 1991, pp. 155–156.
*Stereo Review,* March 1993, p. 75.
*Texas Monthly,* October 1992, pp. 138, 216.

—*Sketch by Ellen Dennis French*

# Gigi Fernández
## 1964-
### Puerto Rican professional tennis player

Born in 1964 in San Juan, Puerto Rico, Gigi Fernández was first introduced to tennis on her eighth birthday, when she received lessons as a gift from her parents. That present has led to a stellar career in tennis that already includes accomplishments such as an Olympic gold medal, a world doubles championship, a doubles crown at Wimbledon, and a championship at the French Open. A strong server and volleyer, Fernández reached the number-one ranking in the world in doubles in 1991.

Almost as soon as Fernández first picked up a tennis racket, she found that the game came naturally to her. She was ranked number one in Puerto Rico as

*Gigi Fernández*

a junior player despite the fact that she did not practice a lot. It was not until she arrived at South Carolina's Clemson University as a scholarship student that she began to work hard at her game. During her freshman year, Fernández made the finals in the NCAA singles championship, which fueled her decision to turn professional in 1985. That same year, Fernández was recognized by *Tennis* magazine as a "player to watch" for achieving a singles ranking of twenty-third in the world. Six years later, with a singles victory in Albuquerque, a semifinal finish in Eastbourne, and a quarterfinal finish at the U.S. Open—her best finish at a Grand Slam event—Fernández was ranked seventeenth in the world, her highest singles ranking to date.

Despite her success as a singles player, many observe that her strong serve and volley game are actually better suited to doubles playing. She has garnered six Grand Slam women's doubles titles to date, including the U.S. Open in 1988, 1990, and 1992, the French Open in 1991 and 1992, and the Wimbledon championships in 1992. In 1991, she and her partner were ranked number one in doubles tennis. At Barcelona in 1992, Fernández and partner **Mary Joe Fernández** (who is no relation) captured the doubles title, making Gigi the first Puerto Rican ever to win an Olympic gold medal.

## Chance Meeting with Martina Navratilova

Fernández credits an encounter with tennis great Martina Navratilova as giving her focus as a profes-sional tennis player. The two first met at a players' party at Wimbledon when Navratilova approached Fernández, then an unknown on the tour, and asked if she had received a note Navratilova had sent in which she praised the young woman's performance against Navratilova's doubles partner, Pam Shriver. Fernández had not yet seen the note but was shocked that the best player in the world had taken the time to write to her. When she later read what Navratilova had written, she was even more surprised, for Navratilova had gone on to state that if Fernández worked hard and was disciplined, she had the potential to be among the game's best players.

"It was thrilling to me," Fernández later recalled in the *New York Times.* "I was ranked about 150 in the world and I weighed about 170 pounds. I had lost about 14 matches in a row in the first round and I was eating in frustration, porking out on ice cream and chocolate chip cookies—anything I could get my hands on. But when I read the note, I decided to change my diet and habits. I went home for a week and thought about what kind of tennis player I wanted to be."

Although Fernández said she took Navratilova's words to heart—the two even played doubles together for a time—she still intends to have as well-rounded a life as possible while maintaining her competitive edge. Her interests outside tennis include skiing, board-sailing, and modeling. She is also a promotional spokesperson for Avia clothing and footwear and Yonex racquets, and she frequently endorses products native to Puerto Rico.

While tennis is not considered a major sport in Puerto Rico, Fernández has nevertheless captured her countrymen's admiration with her winning ways. She came under some criticism, however, for her decision to compete for the United States in the Federation Cup and Olympic tournaments. This choice, which she said in *Más* was "the most difficult of her life," was based solely on professional reasons. "Representing Puerto Rico I would have lost in the first round," she explained. The comments of her detractors are "like criticizing Raúl Julia for going to work in Hollywood or Justino Díaz for singing at the Metropolitan Opera of New York."

Her success has nevertheless made her an object of pride on her home island. Also, as the first female Puerto Rican athlete to turn professional, she has paved the way for a new generation of female athletes on her island home. "In a way, it's kind of neat," she remarked in *Hispanic* magazine, "because it's opening a door for female athletes in Puerto Rico. Before, it was taboo for a female to make a living out of a sport. Girls are supposed to get married and have kids, so now maybe this opens the door."

## SOURCES:

*Hispanic,* July, 1988.
*Más* (translated from Spanish by Diane Telgen),
  November 1992, p. 53.
*New York Times,* February, 1985, pp. 180–181.

—*Sketch by Rosalva Hernandez*

# Joseph A. Fernandez
## 1935-

**Puerto Rican American educator**

Joseph "Joe" Fernandez became chancellor of New York City's schools in 1990, about four decades after he had dropped out of high school in that same system. Fernandez arrived at the job from Florida, where he had promoted the policy of school-based management. In New York, he planned to transfer control of the schools from central bureaucrats to the administrators, teachers, and parents. Although the New York City Board of Education decided not to renew his contract in 1994, Fernandez is still remembered for his efforts.

### Harlem Dropout

Joseph A. Fernandez was born December 13, 1935, to Angela and Joseph Fernandez, Sr., in a New York City apartment building. There was no one to look after the infant's sister; the young mother could not leave, even to have a baby. Angela had met her husband on the voyage from their native Puerto Rico. The elder Fernandez worked as a construction laborer, but without much education , he found it difficult to provide a comfortable life for his family.

For a man so devoted to improving education, Fernandez once looked at his own education with amazing nonchalance. He grew up on West 126th Street, and he recalled days when going to school did not even cross his mind. He told a *New York* magazine reporter about those times: "My day consisted of getting up in the morning, saying good-bye to my parents, telling them I was going to school, getting on the subway, meeting by Columbus Circle with a group of guys and gals, and going down to 42nd Street. We didn't even bother to check in at school." School administrators asked him to leave Bishop Dubois High School after the tenth grade. The situation did not improve at his next school—Manhattan's High School of Commerce. Fernandez socialized with a crowd for whom petty robbery, fighting, drugs, and trips to jail were common. By the age of 17, Fernandez had left school altogether.

### Building a Future

Fernandez joined the Air Force, despite his parents' objections. He went to Japan and Korea and served as a radio technician. He returned to New York City in 1956 and married Lily Pons, his high school sweetheart. During his enlistment he had completed his high school equivalency diploma and was eligible to take advantage of the G.I. Bill—a government program that funded tuition for military service people and veterans. Fernandez enrolled in Columbia University.

Fernandez and his wife left New York for Miami when a doctor advised that living in a warmer climate might benefit their sickly son. Fernandez finished college at the University of Miami, and in 1963 he took a job teaching math in the Coral Park school system. He earned a master's degree and won promotion after promotion: assistant principal, principal, director of community services. In 1985 he became the vice superintendent of the Dade County schools and received his Ph.D. from Nova University.

In 1987 Fernandez was named superintendent of the Dade County schools —the country's fourth-largest school system and began his reforms. He transferred a principal when he visited a school unannounced and found it dirty and poorly maintained. He removed other principals and instituted Saturday classes. Fernandez developed innovative ways to raise money, including soliciting businesses vigorously.

Chief among his goals was the desire to bring school-based managementto Dade County. Fernandez experimented with localizing control in 33 of the district's 267 schools. He developed a group of parents, teachers, and administrators in each institution who were given virtually total control. Although some in the district saw this policy as a success, others noted that the teachers' union seemed to dominate the parents and administrators.

### Returned to New York City As Chancellor

Fernandez left South Florida in 1990 to direct of the New York City school system. With nearly one million students, New York's school system represented the largest and one of the most troubled school systems in the United States. According to an October 1990 issue of *U.S. News and World Report,* Fernandez's arrival inspired cautious optimism. Although appreciative of the chancellor's enthusiasm, reporter Thomas Toch warned: "By moving so aggressively to transform the city's school system, Fernandez runs the risk of losing important allies and alienating the rank-and-file educators who ultimately must carry out his reforms." In 1994, that prediction appeared to have been realized. The New York City Board of Education decided not to renew Fernandez's contract. In *Education Digest,* Raymond Domanico wrote that although the chancellor's ideas had gained the support of New York's intellectuals, they had failed in the "temple of passive resistance"—the school system. Domanico added that Fernandez's "failure to develop a cadre of field generals and groups who supported his ideas, and were willing to put themselves on the line to see them to fruition, was a sure-fire prescription for disaster." Fernandez returned to Florida and now heads School Improvement Services in Winter Park.

## SOURCES:

### Periodicals

*Education Digest,* March 7, 1994, p. 17.
*New York,* January 22, 1990, p. 41.
*U.S. News and World Report,* October 1, 1990, p. 76.

—*Sketch by James McCarthy*

*Manuel Jose Fernandez*

# Manny Fernandez
## 1946-
### Hispanic American professional football player and business executive

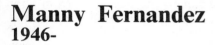

Manny Fernandez anchored the front line of the Miami Dolphins famous "No-Name Defense" of the early 1970s, helping to lead his team to back-to-back Super Bowl victories and the only undefeated, untied season in National Football League (NFL) history. Although standing six feet two inches tall and weighing only 250 pounds—a relatively small size for a down lineman of his era—Fernandez, largely through his quickness and aggressiveness, came to be regarded as one of the more talented defensive linemen of his era. In addition to being a five-time All-American Football Conference second team selection and a six-time most valuable defensive lineman, Fernandez started in three straight Super Bowls and was named to the United Press International and *Miami Herald* all-time greatest Super Bowl All-Star Team. Although a knee injury prematurely ended his football career, he has remained closely tied to the game, serving as the NFL alumni chairman of the board, while also working as an executive for a title insurance company.

Manuel Jose Fernandez was born July 3, 1946, in Oakland, California, the son of Manuel and Dolores Fernandez. After graduating from high school in 1964, he enrolled at Chabot University—a junior college located in Hayward, California—where he studied and played football for two years before transferring to the University of Utah, where he was a standout on the gridiron for the remainder of his college career.

### Drafted by the Miami Dolphins

In their first two years of play in the fledgling American Football League (AFL), the Miami Dolphins lacked a defense strong enough to move out of the Western Division cellar. Although the offense, behind the accurate arm of quarterback Bob Griese, showed signs of great potential, the defensive unit struggled, especially against the run, giving up an average of 153 yards per game during the 1967 season—the most of any team in either the American or National league. In an effort to solidify the front line, the Dolphins recruited Fernandez to play defensive tackle, signing him as a free agent in 1968. In his first season as a pro, Number 75 made an immediate impact as a big-play artist, providing the Dolphins with a pass-rush for perhaps the first time in their young history, as they moved into the middle of the Eastern Division with a record of five wins and eight losses. At the conclusion of the season Fernandez was named the team's most valuable defensive lineman, an honor he would win every year that he was healthy.

The following season, however, the Dolphins slipped back into last place in the division, and the organization lured Don Shula, who would later become the NFL's all-time most-winning coach, from the Baltimore Colts to replace head coach George Wilson. The Dolphins also added five rookies to the starting defensive lineup, to go along with a nucleus of veterans that included middle linebacker Nick Buoniconti, defensive back Dick Anderson, and Fernandez. With Shula at the helm, the defense was transformed from a mediocre unit to the league's best, allowing an average of just over 16 points a game—the lowest of any team in the newly-formed American Football Conference (AFC). More important, the Dolphins moved up to second place in the Eastern Division, finishing with a record of 10–4. And for the first time, the Dolphins made it to the playoffs, where they lost to the Oakland Raiders.

### Played in First Super Bowl

The next season saw the Dolphins take another major step in their dramatic turnaround. After finishing the season with a division leading mark of 10–3–1, they went on to attain their first playoff victory, defeating the Kansas City Chiefs and earning a spot in the AFC championship game against the Baltimore Colts. From his spot in the middle of the defensive unit, Fernandez contributed a solid performance, providing strong support against the run and constant pressure on Colts' Hall-of-Fame quarterback Johnny Unitas. At game's end, the vaunted Baltimore offense, held to only 93 yards rushing, had failed to cross the goal line. The Dolphins, in only their sixth year of existence, were Super Bowl bound. Their opponent, the Dallas Cowboys, proved to be too much for the AFC champions, however, behind the passing attack led by Roger Staubach and the powerful running of Duane Thomas; the Cowboy offense dominated Fernandez and the rest of the Miami defense, winning Super Bowl VI 24–3.

### "No-Name Defense"

In 1972 the Miami Dolphins turned in what has widely been recognized as the finest single-season performance in NFL history. With a balanced offense led by Griese and running backs Larry Csonka and Mercury Morris, and the stingiest defense in the NFL, the Dolphins finished the regular season with a perfect 14–0 record. Despite holding opponents to less than two touchdowns a game, the Miami defense was comprised of a cast of virtually anonymous players and came to be known as the "No-Name Defense." While not offering a cast of marquee players, the defense worked as a collective unit, with each member responsible for a specific job. As middle linebacker Nick Buoniconti—the unit's only "name"—explained to *Sports Illustrated*'s Tex Maule:

"We don't have any superstars playing defense. It's a crashing cliché to say this, but it's true. Since we don't have the great individuals, we do it on teamwork. We come up with the big plays." Fernandez's role in the defensive scheme, while not one that enabled him to often make headlines, was of paramount importance. As the nose tackle on the Fifty-three—one of the Dolphins principal defensive formations, consisting of three down linemen, two ends, and three linebackers—Fernandez's primary responsibility was to maintain his ground and occupy blockers so that others might make the tackle. "He plays under tremendous pressure and does a fine job," Miami Defensive Line Coach Mike Scarry told *Sports Illustrated*'s Maule. He's always got two people blocking him—a guard and the center—and lot of times a back stays in to pick him up if he splits the double block. That means he doesn't get in on the quarterback very often, but we don't expect him to. What he does is bust in there and force things to happen."

After defeating the Cleveland Browns and the Pittsburgh Steelers in the playoffs, the Dolphins again found themselves playing for the Super Bowl ring, this time against the Washington Redskins and the passing attack of Billy Kilmer and a rushing game headed by Larry Brown. The No-Name Defense and Number 75—as he was known to most fans—were up to the challenge. While the Redskins were limited to only a touchdown—and even that came as a result of an error in the kicking game—the free agent from Utah enjoyed perhaps his finest hour as a professional. "Fernandez played the biggest part in the Dolphins' line victory . . . ," concluded *Sports Illustrated*'s Maule. "He is not overpowering, but he is strong and quick and indefatigable, too." Shula also applauded Fernandez and his colleagues on the front line: "We wanted to whip them up front, which takes away the run. There's no doubt we won there." Perhaps the most convincing words of praise, came from Redskins' offensive guard John Wilbur, who lined up directly opposite Fernandez most of the afternoon. "They're like swarming bees," he stated in *Sports Illustrated*. "You think you've blocked them well, and you only get two, three, four yards before they're all over you." When asked about the Dolphins' 14–7 victory, Fernandez himself simply replied, "I think we outplayed them, outexecuted them."

Almost a month after turning in a performance that earned him a spot on the UPI and *Miami Herald* all-time greatest Super Bowl All-Star Team, Fernandez married Marcia Lee Schoonover, with whom he later had three children: Christina, Diane, and James Gabriel. A year later he was wearing his second Super Bowl ring, following the Dolphins' 24–7 domination of the Minnesota Vikings. Again Fernandez and the rest of the No-Names controlled the line of scrimmage, holding star Viking running back Chuck Foreman to just 32 yards rushing. Having won two of the last three Super Bowls, the Dolphins drew comparisons with the Green Bay Packers of the Vince Lomabardi era, who also won consecutive titles. Marv Fleming, who played on both teams, however, stated that Shula's Dolphins were "the greatest team ever."

While Fernandez was at the peak of his career, he suffered a knee injury early in the 1974 season that forced him to spend most of his final playing days on the sidelines. With his retirement from the game in 1977, came the opportunity to devote more time to his business career. Having gained valuable experience operating a mobile home sales business—one that had become a casualty of the energy crisis of the 1970s—while still playing football, he became the vice president of a real estate development company shortly after retiring. He later moving on to work in the loan office of a mortgage company until 1986. Since that time, he has been employed in the insurance industry, where he has served as the vice president of Ticor Title Insurance. An avid hunter and Nation Rifle Association member, Fernandez has spent much of his spare time serving the needs of his fellow retired professional football players, from his post as chairman of the NFL Alumni Board of Directors, to which he was appointed in 1989.

## SOURCES:

### Books

*The Sports Encyclopedia: Pro Football,* sixth edition, edited by David S. Neft and Richard M. Cohen, New York, St. Martin's Press, 1988.
*Who's Who in Football,* edited by Ronald L. Mendell and Timothy B. Phares, New Rochelle, New York, Arlington House, 1974.

### Periodicals

*Life,* January 14, 1972, pp. 32–33.
*New York Times,* January 15, 1973, pp. 1, 37; November 28, 1973, p. 53; January 14, 1974, pp. 1, 33.
*Sports Illustrated,* January 10, 1972, pp. 15–17; November 27, 197 pp. 28–31; January 8, 1973, pp. 14–17; January 22, 1973, pp. 17–21; October 13, 1975, pp. 72–73.

*—Sketch by Jason Gallman*

# Mary Joe Fernández
## 1971-
### Dominican professional tennis player

A well-known name on the women's professional tennis circuit, Mary Joe Fernández has been playing professionally since the age of 14. It has only been since 1990, when she started playing the women's circuit full-time, that Fernández has begun to make a serious bid to become the world's top-ranked female player. Probably her brightest moment in tennis was when she and doubles partner **Gigi Fernández** of Puerto Rico captured the gold medal for the United States at the 1992 Olympics in Barcelona, defeating Spain's own Arantxa Sánchez Vicario and Conchita Martínez with **King Juan Carlos** looking on. She also won a bronze medal in singles and reached three Grand Slam finals.

Born in 1971 in the Dominican Republic to José and Silvia Fernández, Mary Joe moved with her family back to Miami when she was six months old. At age three she began to play tennis. Her sister Silvia recounted to the *New York Times* that when her father took her to play tennis, Mary Joe would often tag along. To keep Mary Joe occupied, José bought her a racquet so she could bounce tennis balls off of a wall. Two years later, Fernández started taking lessons from a professional tennis player.

### Won Succession of Youth Tournaments

Fernández showed talent for the game very early on. At age ten, she won the United States Tennis Association Nationals for players 12 and under. At 11, she won the Orange Bowl singles title for players 12 and under, and proceeded to win the title again at age 14 for 16-and-under, and at age 14 for 18-and-under players. She also won the United States Tennis Association championship for 16-and-under players and the U.S. Clay Court Championship for her age in 1984. She played in her first professional tournament when she was 13, participating as an amateur. She beat her first round opponent, 33-year-old Pam Teeguarden, but lost the following match. That same year, she defeated the world's tenth-ranked player, Bonnie Gadusek, reaching the quarters of the Lipton tournament. She is also the youngest player to win a match at the U.S. Open.

As a 14-year-old freshman at Carrollton School of the Sacred Heart, Mary Joe began to feel pressure to turn pro and play the professional circuit full-time. Despite financial considerations, she resisted and became a straight-A student at Carrollton. "I just decided that if I was going to go to school, I was going to do it right," she told *Sports Illustrated* in 1991.

*Mary Joe Fernández*

"And I wasn't ready to sacrifice being with my friends." Fernández did, however, enter four Grand Slam tournaments and various other tournaments over the next three-and-a-half years, working them in around her high school classes. "If Mary Joe doesn't want to study, we make her study," her father José told *Sports Illustrated.* "If she doesn't want to play tennis, we don't make Mary Joe play."

Many credit that balanced approach with preventing her from burning out on the game too soon or pushing her body too early as some of her contemporaries such as Tracy Austin and Andrea Jaeger have done. But she did gain valuable experience in the few Grand Slam events in which she competed. In her very first Wimbledon match as a 14-year-old, she faced her idol, Chris Evert Lloyd, losing in straight sets. She also missed her high school graduation because she was competing in the semi-finals of the French Open.

### Experienced Highs and Lows During Professional Debut

The year 1990, Fernández's first as full-time participant on the pro tour, proved both encouraging and discouraging. She won 40 of 50 singles matches and two tournaments, including her first ever professional tournament championship in the Tokyo Indoors. With endorsements, her earnings topped $1 million that year. However, Mary Joe received several injuries during the year. In March of 1990, she tore a

hamstring in a Virginia Slims match against rival Gabriela Sabatini; two months later her back went out during a third-round match in the German Open; prior to Wimbledon, a severe knee sprain prevented her from competing in that tournament; finally, after losing in the final of the Australian Open to Steffi Graf, she returned home with tendinitis in her right shoulder. Many speculated and Fernández herself acknowledged that some of the injuries may have resulted from her lack of a consistent conditioning program. Her coaches often encouraged her to build her upper body strength. Since her injuries, she has begun a conditioning regimen using a strength coach.

The conditioning has paid off: Fernández, consistently ranked among the top seven women players in the world, reached as high as fourth in late 1990 through early 1991. One of the roadblocks she has had to overcome to maintain her competitiveness with the top women has been mental toughness. "[Steffi] Graf and [Monica] Seles go into tournaments expecting to win," former coach Tim Gullickson told *Sports Illustrated.* "Mary Joe hopes she'll win. . . . When she does, I think she's still a little bit surprised."

With Olympic gold and bronze medals under her belt, Fernández is still moving toward her goal: becoming the top female player in the world. In 1992, she reached the semifinals in the singles at the U.S. Open before losing to eventual champion Seles. Observers say she has had more success in doubles, winning eight tournaments with various partners, including the 1991 Australian Open with Patti Fendwick, the Lipton with Zina Garrison, and the Toyko Nichirei twice with Pam Shriver and Robin White, respectively. In 1991, at age 17, she became the thirty-third woman to earn more than $1 million; her career earnings top $2.1 million.

### SOURCES:

*Los Angeles Times,* June 25, 1986, Section II, p. 1.
*New York Times,* September 21, 1984.
*Sports Illurated,* February 11, 1991, pp. 76–79.
*World Tennis,* February, 1991, pp. 25–26.

*—Sketch by Jonathan J. Higuera*

# Ricardo R. Fernández
## 1940-
**Puerto Rican American educator and administrator**

After years of research and counseling in the areas of bilingual and multicultural education, Ricardo R. Fernández assumed the presidency of City University of New York's Lehman College, a public college in the Bronx. Fernández was born on December 11, 1940 to Ricardo F. and Margarita Marchese Fernández in the city of Santurce, Puerto Rico, where they lived for the next 20 years.

By 1962, the young Fernández had relocated to Milwaukee, Wisconsin, and earned a bachelor's degree in philosophy, followed by a master's in Spanish literature in 1965, both from Marquette University. On August 7, 1965, he married Patricia M. Kleczka, an attorney. He served as an assistant professor of Spanish at Marquette after earning a master's degree in Romance languages at Princeton University in 1967, but returned to Princeton for a Ph.D. in that specialty over the next three years.

Fernández's 20-year association with the University of Wisconsin took the form of various posts associated with community studies, educational equity, outreach to Spanish speakers, and desegregation policies. Throughout his career, Fernández has focused specifically on the dropout phenomenon in terms of its effects on Hispanic and other non-English speakers. Research awards have enabled him to study the drop-out patterns in five cities, minority employment in the University of Wisconsin system, the vocational needs of migrant workers, and desegregation in Chicago. He also has found time to consult with various businesses and public sector entities throughout the United States. Additionally, his civic commitments range from New York City's Lower East Side Tenement Museum to the Environmental Education Center at the Bronx Zoo.

In 1990 Fernández accepted the post of president at the City University of New York's Lehman College. His long association with the University of Wisconsin ended as he moved to the Bronx with his wife and his two youngest children. In his first convocation address at Lehman College, he underscored his commitment to multicultural endeavors and open communications. He praised the newly established link with a sister campus in Chiyoda, Japan and the exchange program instituted with it. The following year, the Riverdale Jewish Community Council recognized Fernández for his outreach efforts with their Interfaith Brotherhood Award. During Lehman College's twenty-fifth anniversary festivities in 1993, Fer-

*Ricardo R. Fernández*

nández praised the college's namesake, former New York governor and state senator, Herbert Lehman, for his lifetime of open-mindedness and egalitarian spirit. Support for that kind of philosophy, Fernández has often pointed out, must be manifested in a larger program of literacy training and vocational skills improvement, which a public college owes its immediate community.

A prolific writer, Fernández has collaborated on a variety of books, monographs, book chapters, research reports, and articles. More recent efforts have included the book *Reducing the Risk* (1989), and a chapter co-written with Adrian Chan in a book published in the University of Wisconsin System Institute on Race and Ethnicity's Ethnicity and Public Policy Series. He also has participated in a range of conferences, panels, and debates across the country. He has taken editorial positions at the *Latino Studies Journal* (1990- ), *Hispanic Journal of Behavioral Sciences* (1988- ), and with the *Journal of Contemporary Puerto Rican Thought* (1974–76). One of his more groundbreaking efforts was the 1989 publication of his research findings for ASPIRA, the Hispanic advocacy group. This culmination of a three-year study was the first comparison of drop-out rates among Mexican, Cuban, Puerto Rican, and Central American students in the United States.

The National Puerto Rican Coalition honored him with a Lifetime Achievement Award by 1990, but Fernández has given no indication of slowing down.

His vision of the role of higher education emphasizes preparing students and members of the surrounding area for a changing world. He has rejected the medieval, Victorian, and European models of university life for a more interactive paradigm. To this end, he has continued to research ways of increasing minority and female participation in faculty and administration. As Lehman College's president, Fernández also has announced plans to restore the main library and build a computer center, as well as to pursue additional funding for scholarships and faculty development.

Even during his tenure at Lehman College as president and professor of Romance languages, Fernández has remained active in other areas. He was granted the Promesa Community Service Award in 1992 and attended the Institute for Educational Management at Harvard that same year. In 1994 the Society of Indian Academics in America honored him with an award saluting his "Contribution to the Cause of Cultural Diversity in Education."

## SELECTED PUBLISHED WORKS:

With W. Hawley, R. Crain, C. Rossell, M. Smylie, J. Schofield, R. Tomkins, W. Trent, and M. Zlotnick, *Strategies for Effective Desegregation,* Lexington Books, D. C. Heath, 1983.

*Five Cities High School Dropout Study: Characteristics of Hispanic High School Students,* ASPIRA Association, Inc., Institute for Policy Research, Washington, D.C., October, 1989.

With G. Wehlage, R. Rutter, G. Smith, and N. Lesko, *Reducing the Risk: Schools as Communities of Support,* Philadelphia, Falmer Press, 1989.

## SOURCES:

### Books

*The Hispanic-American Almanac,* edited by Nicolás Kanellos, Detroit, Gale Research, 1993.

### Other

Fernandez papers, Office of College Relations, Lehman College, CUNY, Bronx, New York.

—*Sketch by Jennifer Kramer*

# Tony Fernández
## 1962-
### Dominican professional baseball player

Shortstop Tony Fernández has set major league records for both fielding and hitting. A four-time Golden Glove Award winner, a career batting average of almost .300, and an All-Star in 1986, 1987, and 1989, he is one of the highest-rated shortstops in major league baseball history.

Born Octavio Antonio Fernández y Castro in San Pedro de Macorís, Dominican Republic in 1962, Fernández grew up in the neighborhood of the Tetelo Vargas stadium. It is easy to understand the influence of baseball since he could no doubt hear the sound of the crowds from where his house was situated outside the ballpark fence. In fact, in a *Sports Illustrated* article Steve Wulf mentioned that Pirates catcher Tony Peña once hit a home run against one of the walls of the Fernández home.

The Caribbean has a rich history of baseball, and Fernández, like many Caribbean boys, spent countless hours playing the game, even skipping school to do so. Fernández told *Sports Illustrated,* "[My mother] would hit me, especially if I missed Sunday school to play baseball." When Fernández wasn't playing baseball, he was at the ballpark working on the grounds or in the clubhouse, and watching the techniques of "real" players.

Fernández excelled at baseball as a teen and already showed promise at shortstop when restaurant owner Evilio Oliva recommended him to Detroit Tigers scout Orlando Peña. When nothing came of that, Oliva contacted Toronto Blue Jays scout Epy Guerrero. While Guerrero recognized the 15-year-old's talent, he thought Fernández appeared to be somewhat slow. *Sports Illustrated'*s Wulf said Guerrero helped the family to arrange and pay for an operation on the promising shortstop's right knee; a chipped bone had made it painful for him to run. Guerrero signed Fernández to the Toronto Blue Jays in 1983.

### Called to the Big League

Fernández did very well on the Toronto farm team and was called to the big league during the 1984 season. Wulf wrote, "His ascent was so swift that he presented the Jays with a major problem: What do they do with [Alfredo] Griffin *and* Fernández?" Griffin was traded to the Oakland A's after the season was over. In 1986 Fernández won the Golden Glove Award, leading American League shortstops in fielding percentage, and he had a record 200-hit season.

*Tony Fernández*

Toronto infielder Garth Iorg told *Sports Illustrated,* "[Fernández] makes the spectacular commonplace." Wulf noted, "You need only see him over the course of a few games to know how graceful and quick and imaginative he is." Fernández's solid and record-setting statistics appeared to come easily to a man who as a child was been described as a skinny, knock-kneed boy with a head so large it was out of proportion to the rest of his body, and which earned him the nickname *Cabeza,* or "head."

Versatility has been key in Fernández's success. A switch-hitter, his career average numbers are almost the same whether he bats left or right. He has played third base, been designated hitter, and he has excelled at shortstop, earning the Golden Glove Award in four straight years, from 1986 to 1989, for defensive fielding. Playing for the Blue Jays in 1990, Fernández led the American League in triples with a total of 17.

Like many athletes, Fernández has played with injuries. As Neil MacCarl reported in *The Sporting News,* "He has always toughed things out, battling back from a fractured right elbow and a gimpy left knee during the 1987 season and a fractured cheekbone in the first week of the 1989 season." Fernández also played with a sore thumb for two years, experiencing a tough 1991 season; he had surgery to repair a torn ligament in the thumb in 1992.

Fernández's highs have often been tied to his lows; for example, earlier in the 1989 game in which Fernández was hit in the face, he hit his first grand slam. He then spent 21 days on the disabled list recovering from surgery to repair the fracture near his right ear. When he returned, he hit 11 home runs—a career high—but in August of that year, Fernández experienced a slump, hitting .199, far below the .299 career average with which he had entered the season.

The early–1990s were transitional for Fernández. 1992 found Fernández playing for the San Diego Padres, where as leadoff hitter he became known as one of the "Four Tops." Fernández, Tony Gwynn, Gary Sheffield, and Fred McGriff were all hitting above .300, and in a June *Sports Illustrated* issue, Peter King called them the "most fearsome first foursome" in the league.

But after the 1992 season Fernández was traded to the New York Mets, where it was hoped that he, along with Barry Bonds, Sid Fernández, and Al Harazin would give the team a big boost. However, Tony Fernández experienced a slump in which he hit only .225 in 48 games.

In June of 1992 Fernández returned to the Blue Jays and his batting average jumped to .306. In 1993 he helped lead the Blue Jays to the world championship but was not re-signed in 1994 because of salary demands. Fernández, represented by the Davimos Group, was seeking a three-year, $8 million-plus contract, which the Blue Jays rejected.

Fernández then hired agent Bruce Weinstein, who could not find a team who could afford Fernández, even with his lifetime .285 average; he was, quite simply, one of the highest-rated fielders among shortstops in major league history and had contributed greatly to the 1993 world championships. In March of 1994, Fernández was signed by the Cincinnati Reds for $500,000. He played second base and shortstop. In the 104 games played, he held third base position 93 times; he doubled 18 times, tripled six, hit eight home runs, and his season batting average was .279.

A Pentecostal Christian, Fernández can often be found reading his Bible in the locker room. He also devotes off-season time at home to missionary work, as well as working with the youth of Santo Domingo—where he lives with his family—who aspire to baseball greatness.

## SOURCES:

### Books

*The Ballplayers,* edited by Mike Shatzkin, New York, Arbor House Morrow, 1990.
*The Baseball Encyclopedia: The Comprehensive and Definitive Record of Major League Baseball,* 9th ed., edited by Rick Wolff, New York, MacMillan, 1993.

Oleksak, Michael M. and Mary Adams Oleksak, *Béisbol: Latin Americans and the Grand Old Game,* Masters, 1991.

*Total Baseball,* 2nd ed., edited by Pete Palmer and John Thorn, New York, Warner, 1991.

**Periodicals**

*Baseball,* 1995, pp. 171, 184.

*Maclean's,* April 6, 1987, pp. 38–40.

*Sports Illustrated,* February 9, 1987 pp. 138–140; June 15, 1992 pp. 36–38; March 7, 1994 pp. 88; April 25, 1994, pp. 69.

*The Village Voice,* April 27, 1993, pp. 166.

—*Sketch by Sandy J. Stiefer*

*José Ferrer*

# José Ferrer
## 1912-1992
### Puerto Rican actor and director

José Ferrer had a long and distinguished career as an actor and director. Renowned for his versatility, Ferrer played serious and comic roles on both stage and screen. In addition to substantial theater and film work, he performed in operas and ballets and appeared in numerous television movies and series. Despite his great success in film and television, Ferrer's first love remained live theater; in later years he served as president of the Players Club and spoke out against the impact of film and television on drama. Ferrer also directed and produced plays and films. He received many professional awards and honors, including two Tony awards, an Academy Award, and the National Medal of Arts.

José Vicente Ferrer de Otero y Cintrón was born in Santurce, Puerto Rico on January 8, 1912. Both Ferrer's parents came from patrician families in Spain; his father was a successful lawyer and his mother's family were plantation owners. Ferrer moved with his family to New York when he was six. After passing Princeton University's entrance examination at a precocious 14, he spent a year in Switzerland before beginning his studies in architecture in 1928. Already an accomplished musician, Ferrer's acting career began in the Triangle Club, Princeton's drama society, where James Stewart and Joshua Logan were among his contemporaries. Graduating in 1934, Ferrer made his Broadway debut in 1935 with a one-line part in *A Slight Case of Murder.* In 1938 he married actress Uta Hagen; they had a daughter, Leticia.

Ferrer's first major Broadway role came in 1940 with the lead in *Charley's Aunt.* The play's great success established Ferrer as a rising star. Demonstrating both versatility and stamina, he followed *Charley's Aunt* with *Let's Face It,* taking over from Danny Kaye, and then played Iago in Shakespeare's *Othello* (1942) opposite Paul Robeson, in a run that broke records for the number of consecutive performances of a Shakespeare play. Ferrer's Iago was described by one critic as "a character creation of the first magnitude" and another commented on "the sheer malevolence that Ferrer gave to the part."

In 1947 Stanley Frank of the *Saturday Evening Post* hailed Ferrer as "Broadway's New Matinee Idol," calling him "probably the best, and certainly the most versatile, actor on the American stage." Flushed with the success of his Broadway *Cyrano de Bergerac,* of which he was both title character and producer, Ferrer nonetheless acknowledged he "may have to go to Hollywood someday, for eating money. God forbid." Indeed, the overwhelming popularity of the play—Frank called it a "genuine financial gusher"—paved the way for Ferrer's second major career, that of movie star.

**Made His Screen Debut**

Ferrer's first Hollywood film, *Joan of Arc* (1948), met with generous critical praise; he was nominated for an Academy Award for his role of the Dauphin, playing opposite Ingrid Bergman. In the same year, following his divorce from Uta Hagen, Ferrer married Phyllis Hill. He played in Otto Preminger's *Whirlpool* (1949) and the following year opposite Cary Grant in *Crisis* (1950), before achieving his first major screen success with the film version of *Cyrano de Bergerac* (1950). A *New York Times* reviewer noted the "eloquence and grace" of Ferrer's film performance, adding that its "style . . . is in the theatrical tradition of gesture and eloquence. He speaks the poetry of Rostand with richness and clarity such as only a few other actors have managed on the screen." Ferrer's performance won him the Academy Award for best actor for 1950.

Despite this screen triumph, Ferrer next returned to the stage, establishing a demanding pattern of alternating film and theater work that would continue throughout his career. Ferrer directed and played opposite Gloria Swanson in *Twentieth Century* at the American National Theater and Academy. In 1952 he received a Tony Award for directing three plays, *Stalag 17, The Shrike,* and *The Fourposter,* and a second Tony Award for acting the role of Jim Downs in *The Shrike. New York Times* drama critic Brooks Atkinson, noting Ferrer's busy schedule, described him as "the most terrifying man of action in our theater" and wrote admiringly of his stamina and "the virtuosity of his accomplishments." Ferrer also received his third Academy Award nomination for his role as Toulouse-Lautrec in John Huston's *Moulin Rouge* (1952). Following his divorce from Phyllis Hill, Ferrer married singer Rosemary Clooney in 1953. They had five children.

The fulsome praise that greeted Ferrer's every production eventually proved finite. When he took on the title role in *Richard III* late in 1953 a *New Yorker* reviewer called him a "darkly gifted artist" and noted his penchant for "portrayals of the misshapen, the aberrant, and the damned." Shortly afterward, the energetic display of versatility, noted in *Theater Arts* with the admiring title "4 Parts in 8 Weeks," now struck reviewer Richard Hayes in the *Commonweal* as "coarse and unreflective" and he added that "no performer of our time has enjoyed such critical favor, or abused it so tastelessly." This critical turnaround was addressed by Ferrer's philosophical observation in a 1987 interview that "you do the best you can and then you take the praise—which is often excessive— or the criticism—which is also often excessive."

## Began to Direct Films

After the success of *Moulin Rouge,* Ferrer's film career continued to shine, albeit with less brilliance; although he starred less often, he had important parts in a series of major releases, including the role of Mister Davison in *Miss Sadie Thompson* (1953) and Navy lawyer Barney Greenwald in *The Caine Mutiny* (1954). In the late 1950s Ferrer added film direction

to the range of his accomplishments, directing himself in the film version of *The Shrike* (1955), *I Accuse!* (1957) in which he played the role of Dreyfus, and *The High Cost of Loving* (1958).

Ferrer had a minor, but significant, role in David Lean's *Lawrence of Arabia* (1962), in which he played opposite Peter O'Toole as a Turkish governor. In 1987 he told interviewer Michael Buckley that he would like to be remembered for this role, adding, "I don't think I can get any purer than that. I don't think I can attempt to accomplish more—while, at the same time, doing less." Following *Lawrence of Arabia,* he revived his Oscar-winning character Cyrano in Abel Gance's *Cyrano et d' Artagnan* (1963). In the 1960s and 1970s, as the Hollywood studios began to feel the increasing force of television, Ferrer continued to find a variety of small film roles, including Stanley Kramer's *Ship of Fools* (1965), George Stevens' *The Greatest Story Ever Told* (1965), the star-studded *The Voyage of the Damned* (1976), and *The Fifth Musketeer* (1979). His work took him around the world to shoots in Spain, Greece, South Africa, and Colombia. Ferrer also made an important return to Broadway in 1966–1967 with *The Man of La Mancha.* In 1967 his marriage to Rosemary Clooney ended in divorce. He married his fourth wife, Stella Magee.

## Turned Reluctantly to Television

As the major successes of his first films eluded him, Ferrer lent his prestige as a classical actor to a series of modest film and television projects where his cameo presence lent lustre to otherwise dull material. Beginning in the 1970s Ferrer began to work increasingly in television, appearing in such TV movies as *The Marcus-Nelson Murders* (1973) (the pilot for the series *Kojak*), *Gideon's Trumpet* (1980), and **Evita Perón** (1981). His film roles, while no longer as illustrious as *Cyrano de Bergerac* or *Moulin Rouge,* continued to show Ferrer's versatility and craftsmanship, and included Billy Wilder's *Fedora* (1978), Woody Allen's *A Midsummer Night's Sex Comedy* (1982), and David Lynch's *Dune* (1984).

In a notable interview with *U.S. News & World Report* in 1979, Ferrer was outspoken in defense of the theater, especially playwrights. Making a distinction between the art of stage acting, which he said "has ceased to exist," and the commerce of movies and television, he noted that actors work in movies and television "to pay your bills, and you act in the theater to save your soul—to remind yourself of why you became an actor in the first place." Through television, he added, "we have been blunted to the finer nuances of entertainment."

Toward the end of his career, Ferrer acknowledged that his film career had "been dominated by *Cyrano de Bergerac* and *Moulin Rouge.* I have learned to live with the situation, but I regret the form my career has taken." Despite his animosity toward television, Ferrer made occasional appearances on the comedy series *Newhart*, about which he admitted, "I absolutely adore doing it!" In addition to his presidency of the Players Club and his work with the Actors Fund, Ferrer continued to act and direct well into his seventies, appearing in England in 1990 and directing theater in New York and Los Angeles. At the time of his death he had been preparing a Broadway role in *Conversations with My Father*. Ferrer died on January 26, 1992.

## SELECTED VIDEOGRAPHY

*Joan of Arc*, 1948.
*Whirlpool*, 1949.
*Crisis*, 1950.
*Cyrano de Bergerac*, 1950.
*Anything Can Happen*, 1951.
*Moulin Rouge*, 1952.
*Article Fifty-five*, 1952.
*Miss Sadie Thompson*, 1953.
*The Caine Mutiny*, 1954.
*Deep in My Heart*, 1954.
*The High Cost of Living*, 1958.
*Forbid Them Not*, 1961.
*Lawrence of Arabia*, 1962.
*Nine Hours to Rama*, 1962.
*Progress for Freedom*, 1962.
*Verspätung in Marienborn*, 1963.
*Cyrano et d'Artagnan*, 1963.
*The Greatest Story Ever Told*, 1965.
*Ship of Fools*, 1965.
*Enter Laughing*, 1966.
*Le Avventure e gli amori di Miguel Cervantes*, 1968.
*The Little Drummer Boy*, 1969.
*The Aquarians*, 1970.
*Cross Current (The Cable Car Murders)*, 1971.
*Banyon*, 1971.
*El clan de los immorales*, 1973.
*The Marcus-Nelson Murders*, 1973.
*E' Lollipop*, 1975.
*Paco*, 1975.
*The Missing Are Deadly*, 1975.
*The Art of Crime*, 1975.
*The Sentinel*, 1976.
*The Big Bus*, 1976.
*Voyage of the Damned*, 1976.
*Zoltan ... Hound of Dracula*, 1977.
*Who Has Seen the Win?*, 1977.
*Crash*, 1977.
*Exo-Man*, 1977.
*The Swarm*, 1978.
*The Amazing Captain Nemo*, 1978.
*Fedora*, 1978.
*The Private Files of J. Edgar Hoover*, 1978.
*The Fifth Muskateer*, 1979.
*Natural Enemies*, 1979.

*The Big Brawl*, 1980.
*Gideon's Trumpet*, 1980.
*Pleasure Palace*, 1980.
*The Murder That Wouldn't Die*, 1980.
*Evita Peron*, 1981.
*Berlin Tunnel 21*, 1981.
*A Midsummer Night's Sex Comedy*, 1982.
*Blood Tie*, 1982.
*The Being*, 1983.
*This Girl for Hire*, 1983.
*To Be Or Not To Be*, 1983.
*Blood Feud*, 1983.
*The Evil That Men Do*, 1984.
*Dune*, 1984.
*George Washington*, 1984.
*Samson and Delilah*, 1984.
*Christopher Columbus*, 1985.
*Seduced*, 1985.
*Hitler's SS: Portrait in Evil*, 1985.
*Bloody Birthday*, 1986.
*The Violins Came With the Americans*, 1986.
*Strange Interlude*, 1988.
*Hired to Kill*, 1989.
*Old Explorers*, 1990.
*The Horror of It All*, 1991.
*A Life of Sin*, 1992.

## SOURCES:

### Books

*International Dictionary of Films and Filmmakers*, Volume 3: *Actors and Actresses*, second edition, Detroit, St. James Press, 1992.
Shipman, David, *The Great Movie Stars: The International Years*, London, Angus and Robertson, 1972, pp. 168–170.

### Periodicals

*Commonweal*, January 15, 1954, pp. 378–79.
*Films in Review*, February 1987, pp. 66–75; March 1987, pp. 130–45.
*Harper's*, February 1951, pp. 102–3.
*Newsweek*, July 25, 1960, pp. 98.
*New Yorker*, December 19, 1953, pp. 76–78.
*New York Times*, November 17, 1950, January 27, 1952, February 11, 1953, November 26, 1953, January 27, 1992.
*Saturday Evening Post*, March 8, 1947, p. 28.
*Theater Arts*, January 1954, p. 32.
*U.S. News and World Report*, October 29, 1979, p. 67.
*Variety*, February 3, 1992, p.93.

*—Sketch by Simon Dixon*

# Angel Flores
## 1900-1992
### Puerto Rican writer, scholar, and translator

Angel Flores spent his life teaching and translating Spanish literature and promoting the acceptance of Hispanic writers in America. He also wrote books concerning history and literature.

Flores was born October 2, 1900, in Barceloneta, Puerto Rico. His father, Nepomuceno Flores was a businessman, and his mother Paula (Rodríguez) was a teacher. He studied literature and Spanish in America, first at New York University, where he graduated with a bachelor's degree in 1923. From there, he studied at Lafayette College, earning a master's degree in 1925. He completed his doctorate at Cornell University in 1947. In 1936, he married writer Kate Mann Berger, with whom he had three children: Ralph, Juan, and Barbara.

Flores taught Spanish at Union College in Schenectady, New York, while working on his master's degree in 1924–1925. He continued his teaching career at Rutgers University in New Brunswick, New Jersey, where he added the teaching of Spanish literature to his language class load until 1929. For two years—1929 to 1930—he worked as editor of *Alhambra,* a literary magazine. He was a Spanish instructor at Cornell University from 1930–1933, until he assumed an editorial position with *Literary World* in 1934, where he continued to work until 1945.

While he put the finishing touches on his Ph.D., he joined the faculty of Queens College of the City University of New York in Flushing, first as an assistant professor until 1947, and then as an associate professor until the college made him a full professor of romance languages and comparative literature in 1952. He continued to teach as a faculty member at Queens College until his retirement in 1970. The college conferred upon him the title of professor emeritus in that year.

Flores was first to translate T. S. Eliot's *The Wasteland* into Spanish. In the 1940s he started Dragon Press at Cornell University. Flores was active for the Loyalist cause during the Spanish Civil War. He was good friends with famous author Federico Garcia Lorca.

Flores spent his life championing the cause of Spanish literature and working for its acceptance by the Anglo-American literary world. In an introduction to *Great Spanish Stories* in 1956, he outlined some of his views on the place of works by Spanish and Hispanic authors in the world of literature: "At the outbreak of the Civil War (1935), Spanish fiction was sharply divided between 'proletarian,' or more broadly, socially-conscious writers ... and the highly dehumanized art-for-art's-sake exponents. ... During the Civil War the sharp lines of demarcation separating social from esoteric art became untenable, for at the crucial hour even the most recalcitrant art-for-art's-sakists found themselves in the trenches or in the barracks editing books and newspapers for the soldiers."

Though he taught for most of his life at Queens College, Flores worked in other capacities as well. He served as visiting professor at the University of Wisconsin, as a professor at the Graduate Center of the City University of New York, and as a member of the Pan American Union's Division of Intellectual Cooperation. Flores died on January 3, 1992, in Guadalajara, Mexico. He was 91 years old.

## SELECTED PUBLISHED WORKS:

*Spanish Literature in English Translation,* New York, H .W. Wilson, 1926.
*Lope de Vega: Monster of Nature,* Brentano's, 1930, reprinted, Kennikat, 1969.
(With M. J. Benardete) *Cervantes Across the Centuries: A Quadricentennial Volume,* Dryden, 1947, reprinted, Gordian, 1969.
*Masterpieces of the Spanish Golden Age,* New York, Rinehart, 1957.
*The Medieval Age,* New York, Dell, 1963.
*The Literature of Spanish America,* five volumes, Las Américas, 1966–69.
*Ibsen: Four Essays,* Haskell Booksellers, 1970.
(With Helene M. Anderson) *Masterpieces of Spanish American Literature,* two volumes, New York, Macmillan, 1972.
*A Bibliography of Spanish-American Writers, 1609–1974,* Gordian, 1975.
*A Kajika Bibliography, 1908–1976,* Gordian, 1976.
*The Problem of "The Judgement": Eleven Approaches to Kafka's Story,* Gordian, 1977.

## SOURCES:

### Books

*Great Spanish Stories,* edited by Angel Flores, New York, Modern Library, 1956.
*Hispanic Writers,* edited by Bryan Ryan, Detroit, Gale Research, 1991.

### Periodicals

*New York Times Book Review,* May 3, 1987, pp. 38–9.

*Publisher's Weekly,* February 10, 1992, p. 13.

—Sketch by Christopher B. Tower

*Archbishop Patrick F. Flores*

# Patrick Flores
## 1929-
### Mexican American religious leader

Patrick Flores was born in 1929 to a large Mexican American family. He entered the priesthood and began a remarkable career that eventually brought him into the hierarchy of the Catholic Church in America, becoming a bishop in the 1970s. Flores has always involved himself vigorously in his community, taking part in activities as diverse as married-couple retreats and a "Kiss-a-Pig" contest in San Antonio. He has travelled the world in various pursuits, often representing the American Catholic Church. He lives in San Antonio, Texas.

### Seventh Son

Patricio Flores, Sr., and his wife Trinidad Fernández de Flores lived in Ganado, Texas, when Mrs. Flores gave birth to the seventh of her nine children, Patrick, on July 26, 1929. Patrick Flores attended Ganado Elementary School, and later another school before graduating from Kirwin High School in Galveston, Texas. His Catholic background pointed him toward religion and Flores eventually decided to study for the priesthood. He entered St. Mary's Seminary in 1949. After leaving that institution in La Porte, Texas, he went to the seminary of the same name in Houston, where he completed the requirements for entry into the priesthood.

### Ordination and Activities

Bishop Wendellin Nold ordained Flores as a Catholic priest on May 26, 1956, in St. Mary's Cathedral in Galveston, Texas. He soon celebrated his first mass as an ordained priest in the Guardian Angel Parish in Pasadena, but took his first position in the Diocese of Houston. He served at the Holy Name Parish, then the Guardian Angel Parish, and finally the St. Joseph's-St. Stephen's Parish. He worked in Houston as a pastor and assistant pastor until 1970. During that time he acted as the director of the Christian Family Movement and the Bishop's Committee for the Spanish Speaking.

Pope John Paul VI made Flores the auxiliary to the archbishop of San Antonio in May of 1970, and later that year he became a bishop himself. As the first Mexican American to reach that level in the Catholic Church, Flores felt an obligation to represent the community from which he had come. In 1972, he and others brought to fruition plans for a Mexican American Cultural Center in San Antonio. At present, he retains his title as honorary chairman. He also played a part in the successful creation of the National Foundation of Mexican American Vocations and the National Hispanic Scholarship Fund. In 1978, Flores became the bishop of the Diocese of El Paso, Texas, but he only served there for a year. In 1979 he left El Paso to answer the church's request that he become the archbishop of San Antonio, in which capacity he continues to serve.

### Achievements and Interests

Throughout his career as a clergyman Flores has tried to help people. In 1976, for example, he helped establish the "Telethon Navideno" (Nativity Telethon). His personal biographical materials describe the purpose of that event as "to help the needy of San Antonio and surrounding areas in extreme emergencies." It raises money to pay utility bills for families unable to have their heat or power restored, or help people with sudden medical emergencies with costs they have trouble paying. Flores also supports the San Antonio Battered Women's Shelter with an annual benefit breakfast. He cooks, serves food, and occasionally entertains diners by singing.

Flores has participated in the annual "Kiss-a-Pig" contest, which benefits the American Diabetes Foundation. Flores joined others in trying to raise funds to fight diabetes. The winner claims the dubious prize of being allowed to kiss a live pig. He has also made efforts to create a support group for parents of death row inmates. He wants to help those without the financial means or transportation to be able to visit their sons on a monthly basis.

He has been recognized by many groups for his work. The San Antonio Council of Churches gave him their Distinguished Churchman Award in 1995. He has received honorary doctorates from several universities, and has won the American Jewish Committee's Human Relations Award.

## SOURCES:

### Books

McMurtrey, Larry. *The Mariachi Bishop,* 1987.

### Other

Biographical materials from the office of the Most Reverend Patrick Flores.

—*Sketch by James McCarthy*

# Ricardo Flores Magón
## 1873-1922
### Mexican revolutionary and writer

Ricardo Flores Magón was noted for his intellectual leadership in the Mexican Revolution of 1910 and as co-publisher of *La Regeneración,* an opposition newspaper in the early 1900s. He was born in San Antonio Eloxochitlán, in the Tiotitlan district of the State of Oaxaca in southern Mexico on September 16, 1874. Ironically, his birthday was the same day as Mexican Independence day. His father was Teodoro Flores, a Zapotec Indian, and his mother was Margarita Magón, a *mestiza*—half Spanish and half Indian. His father was a Liberal and a Lt. Colonel for the Mexican Army during the French invasion. They were a very poor family, but his father taught his libertarian ideas to Flores Magón at a very early age. He had three brothers, Ricardo, Jesús, and Enrique.

Flores Magón received his primary and secondary education in Mexico City and attended the Escuela Nacional Prepatoria (National Preparatory School). As a student, Flores Magón participated in protest marches against **Porfirio Díaz**, dictator of Mexico. He was jailed for five months for sedition. He graduated and enrolled in the Escuela Nacional de Jurisprudencia (National School of Law) in 1893. He worked for the newspaper *El Demócrata* as a proofreader while he was in law school and barely escaped arrest when police arrested the entire staff of the paper. Flores Magón went into hiding for three months. During this time, his father died and he and his brothers helped support their ill mother while they continued their studies. He received his law degree in 1895 and passed the Mexican bar. He practiced law for a short time and continued his studies, but in 1898, because of his political activities, Flores Magón was expelled from school. In 1900, he and his brother Jesús, founded the newspaper, *La Regeneración,* where he attacked the rule of Díaz in numerous articles. Flores Magón also wrote for other well-known opposition periodicals, including *Excelsior, La República Mexicana,* and *El Hijo del Ahuizote.* He joined the Liberal Party, in 1900 and his name became well-known as a rebel against the dictatorship of Díaz.

Flores Magón was imprisoned several times for his opposition to the government. In 1901 he and Jesús were put in the dungeons of Belen prison in Mexico City for 12 months. Jesús left the movement to practice law and Flores Magón, his brother Enrique, and Santiago de la Hoz took over an anti-Díaz newspaper, *El Hijo del Ahuizote.* The staff was arrested and they were sentenced to four months in prison. When they were released from prison in 1903, Flores Magón and his brother Enrique immigrated to the United States. They went to San Antonio, Texas, where they began publishing *La Regeneración* again, smuggling the newspaper across the border for the opposition. Several activists from Mexico joined the brothers and worked with them in their struggle to fight the Mexican dictatorial government. Antonio Villarreal, Librado Rivera, the brothers Juan and Manuel Sarabia, Lázaro Gutiérrez de Lara, Praxedis Guerrero, and Antonio de Pío Araujo, joined the Flores Magón brothers in the United States. They were forced to move several times because of their activities and lived in St. Louis, Missouri.

### Self-Declared Anarchist

In numerous articles, Flores Magón urged the working people of Mexico to emancipate themselves from the tyrannical dictatorship of Díaz. He encouraged them to revolt and overthrow the government. Flores Magón became an anarchist in 1900 but he did not openly admit it until 1910. He believed that anarchy was the only solution to overthrow the dictatorship. He studied famous European revolutionaries such as Malatesta, Peter Kropotkin, Bakunin, and Jean Grave. A large anarchist movement of workers' organizations began in Mexico in 1863 when Plotino C. Rhodakanaty —a philosophy professor— founded the movement. Díaz had been suppressing labor unions and robbing communal land from peasants in Mexico for many years, claiming they had no proof of ownership. When a group of peasants resisted in Vera Cruz, they were murdered and their land was taken. More than 20,000 people had lived on the land previously and one family became the new property owners. Throughout the country, Díaz robbed the peasants and turned the land over to one or two families. In many areas, the peasants then became slaves working for the new landowners. In 1908, the Yaquis Indians' land was taken and the Indians were sold for $95 each. A mass suicide was committed by the Indians, who would rather die than become slaves. About 50 families became the landowners in Mexico and almost a million peasants were homeless. Flores Magón revived the anarchist movement and relentlessly spoke out against Díaz and his dictatorship.

Flores Magón wrote about the injustices, the slavery, and the horrible working conditions in Mexico. The new Liberal Party helped organize labor strikes throughout Mexico. The government banned any article written by Flores Magón before he was forced into exile in the United States. When the group moved to St. Louis, they formed the Junta Organizadora del Partido Liberal (PLM), in September 1905 with Flores Magón as president. The first goal of the group was to institute a propaganda campaign and to that end, *La Regeneración* was sent to couriers near the border to smuggle into Mexico. The PLM published a manifesto of reforms to be distributed by their couriers. The manifesto was written by Juan Sarabia with Flores Magón's assistance. Many reforms were proposed, including assurance of all basic civil liberties, a one-term presidency, improvement in educational facilities, land reforms, abolition of child labor, a guaranteed minimum wage, Mexican citizenship as a prerequisite for property ownership, and many other social and economic reforms.

The second goal of the Junta was to overthrow the dictatorship by armed resistance. Although there were many small raids in various locations in Mexico, because of a lack of equipment and funds, very little was accomplished. When U.S. authorities began harassing Flores Magón and raided the office of the organization, he, his brother Enrique, and Sarabia were arrested. They fled to Canada. When they were released on bail, they went to Los Angeles, California, to hide. They began publishing *Revolución* to replace *La Regeneración*. In September 1907, they were arrested and while in prison wrote a manifesto to the American people defining their ideals and the persecution by the U.S. authorities. For three years, from 1907 to 1910, Flores Magón remained in prison. Three Junta members—Flores Magón, Villarreal, and Rivera—were convicted of violating of neutrality laws and sent to Florence penitentiary in Arizona.

### Revolution in Earnest

When they were released in August 1910, they returned to Los Angeles where they immediately set up a fund drive to sell subscriptions to *La Regeneración*. They also changed their motto from "Reform, Liberty, and Justice" to "Land and Liberty." While they were in prison, an election was held in Mexico under the control of Díaz; **Francisco I. Madero**, a member of the Anti-Reelectionist Party, ran for president. Díaz won the election and after Madero accused the dictator of "rigging the elections," he had to flee the country. Madero declared that revolution was the only way to bring democracy to Mexico. In a deceitful attempt to gain supporters while Flores Magón was in prison, Madero proclaimed that the Maderists and the PLM had joined forces. He wanted to be declared "provisional president" after the revolutionaries took over the country.

On November 20, 1910, the revolution began under Madero's leadership. The movement was slow until the PLM's armed forces began participating in December. The PLM forces were active while Madero signed a peace treaty with Díaz in May 1911. Madero thought the revolution was over and began a move to suppress the Liberals. The PLM continued to fight and many were arrested. Land was expropriated for the next few years as the peasants began taking back the land. By October, Madero was placed as president. Flores Magón and his group worked harder than ever to obtain funds for the revolution. The Junta decided to open a campaign in Baja California, a rugged peninsula on the coast. They invited their followers to colonize. Because funds were lacking, the settlers would have to pay for their own costs to go to Baja. This attempt at anarchism by Flores Magón failed.

Subscriptions to *La Regeneración* rose to 27,000 and they had the funds needed to purchase arms and recruit armies for the revolution. Meanwhile, **Emiliano Zapata**, a famous revolutionary, fought against Madero. There were many revolutionary factors in Mexico, including the Zapatistas, the Orozquistas, the Maderistas, and the Magonistas (Magón's group)— each named for its primary leader. The U.S. government was investigating the PLM's activities and in June of 1912, they arrested Flores Magón, his brother Enrique, Librado Rivera, and Anselmo Figueroa, indicting them on violation of neutrality laws. Also arrested were Caryl Ap Rhys Pryce and Richard Ferris.

After Flores Magón was released from prison in 1914, he immediately began efforts to continue the battles of the revolution. While he was in prison, General Victoriano Huerta assassinated Madero and declared himself ruler. Venustiano Carranza, governor of Coahuila, ousted Huerta and with the help of Zapata and **Pancho Villa**, became the next dictator. Both Zapata and Villa turned against Carranza when he convinced a workers' organization, the Casa del Obrero Mundial (Workers' Hall) to sign a pact to form "Red Battalions" to crush the revolutionaries. Flores Magón spoke out against the workers who associated with Carranza. In 1914, Flores Magón and Enrique were arrested for attacking Carranza's regime. Carranza became president of Mexico in 1916 with the workers help and then closed down the workers' organization with threats of the death penalty to anyone who resisted him. Flores Magón wrote a lengthy article to the workers denouncing Carranza and condemning workers who joined him. He was arrested in 1916 and jailed for a year. Flores became ill with diabetes and respiratory complaints.

In 1918, Flores Magón and Rivera were arrested for alleged violation of a newly instituted Espionage Law for a manifesto he had addressed to the Anarchists of the World. He was sentenced to 20 years imprisonment and was eventually sent to Leavenworth prison in Kansas. In November 1942, Flores Magón died in his cell. Librado Rivera said he thought Flores Magón was strangled. He saw large bruises on his throat, but prison officials forced Rivera to say that he died from a heart attack. The true cause of his death is unconfirmed. Flores Magón was admired by his countrymen and on May 1, 1945, his remains were interred at the Rotunda of Illustrious Men in Mexico City. Just before his death, he wrote: "Farewell, O comrades, I scorn life as a slave! I begged no tyrant for my life, though sweet it was; Though chained, I go unconquered to my grave, Dying for my own birth-right—and the world's."

## SELECTED PUBLISHED WORKS:

(With Jesús Magón) *Batalla a la Dictadura,* Mexico, Empresas Editoriales, 1948.
*Land and Liberty: Anarchist Influences in the Mexican Revolution,* edited by David Poole, Montreal, Black Rose Books, Cienfuegos Press, 1977.
*Ricardo Flores Magón: Vida y Obra,* ten volumes, Mexico City, Grupo Cultural Ricardo Flores Magón, 1923–1925.

## SOURCES:

### Books

Blaisdell, Lowell L., *The Desert Revolution, Baja California, 1911,* Madison, University of Wisconsin Press, 1962.
*Encyclopedia of Latin America,* edited by Helen Delpar, New York, McGraw-Hill, 1974.
Flores Magón, Ricardo, *Land and Liberty: Anarchist Influences in the Mexican Revolution,* edited by David Poole, Montreal, Black Rose Books, Cienfuegos Press, 1977.
*Mexican Polical Biographies, 1884–1935,* edited by Roderic A. Camp, Austin, University of Texas Press, 1991.

—*Sketch by Phyllis Noah*

# María Irene Fornés
## 1930-
### Cuban American playwright

Although she is not well known by casual theatergoers, María Irene Fornés is often ranked among the most original contemporary writers and producers of plays. She has been dubbed the "Picasso of theatre" by *Hispanic* magazine, and has earned six Obie Awards, presented for the year's best Off-Broadway shows. Her list of achievements is all the more impressive when one considers that she did not begin to write until she was 30 years old.

Fornés was born in Havana, Cuba, on May 14, 1930, to Carlos Luis and Carmen Hismenia (Collado) Fornés. Although he had worked for the government at one time, Carlos Fornés was what *Hispanic* described as an "intellectual rebel." Descended from a family of educators, Fornés's father read a great deal. He made sure that his daughters could do so as well, and taught them at home. While María Fornés attended Escuela Publica No. 12 in Havana from the third to the sixth grade, her intellectual growth was a result of her father's caring instruction.

After the death of her husband, Carmen Fornés packed up her family of six daughters and left Cuba for New York. María Fornés was just 15, and she could not speak English. She found her first job as a worker in a ribbon factory, where she kept military decorations in their proper positions on an assembly line. Two weeks was enough of that job. Fornés learned to speak English, and she found work as a translator. Even this, however, would not suit Fornés. Eventually working as a doll maker to support herself, Fornés began to paint seriously. She became a naturalized citizen of the United States in 1951, and some years later she left the country to paint in Europe. After three years Fornés returned to New York in 1957; she worked there as a textile designer until

1960. Although Fornés's works went unacclaimed, the ten years she painted were well spent—her painting contributed to the structures of the award-winning plays she would later write.

## Painting Paves Way for Later Writing

In an interview for *Contemporary Authors* (*CA*), Fornés explained how her concept of dramatic structure was linked to her experience as a painter: "Hans Hofmann always talked about push-and-pull ... the dynamics created between colors when you place one color very close to another or anywhere else in the canvas. ... The color and shape of the form would create this tension ... that had a very strong impact on my play writing, because I compose my plays guided not by story line but more by energies that take place within each scene, and also the energies that take place between one scene and the scene that follows." While she was painting, however, Fornés had no idea that one type of art would lead to another. She only knew that she had difficulty disciplining herself to paint. "I thought that it was normal for a young person to prefer being in coffee houses to working at home," she recalled in the interview.

In retrospect, Fornés understood her trouble. She told *CA*, "I think the reason I was having a hard time painting was that it wasn't the form of art that was best suited for me." Fornés discovered her calling around 1960. Legend has it that in an effort to help her roommate, the now famous philosopher and critic, Susan Sontag, break her writer's block she began to write a play. *Hispanic* even asserted that for this play Fornés borrowed "her words from a cookbook." Whatever precipitated her first attempt to write, Fornés acknowledges that the urge to write consumed her, and she spent 19 days working on her first play. As she explained to Rachel Koenign and Kathleen Betsko in *Interviews with Contemporary Women Playwrights,* "I loved [writing] it, it was such a thrill. I started writing late; I was around thirty. I had never thought I would write; as I said, I was an aspiring painter. But once I started writing it was so pleasurable that I couldn't stop."

Fornés's first published play, *La Viuda,* or *The Widow,* appeared in 1961 in *Cuatro Autores Cubanos;* she subsequently received a John Hay Whitney Foundation fellowship in 1961, and a Centro Mexicano de Escritores fellowship in 1962. Fornés's inspiration and enthusiasm soared. She had seen Zero Mostel perform in *Ulysses,* and unconsciously she imagined him as a character in what became her first produced play, *There! You Died.* "It wasn't that I saw the play [*Ulysses*] and thought, I'm going to write plays," Fornés insisted in *CA*. She had intended to write a play about a power struggle between a man and a computer, but she realized that the computer would be better replaced by a person, a Zero Mostel-like

character. In the play, two male lovers battle as father and son, teacher and pupil, in a seemingly endless tango, until Leopold murders Isidore in a bullfight. *There! You Died* (or *Tango Palace*) finally appeared in 1963 and was a success. Fornés's career as a serious playwright had begun.

Her next important play, *Promenade,* first shown in April of 1965 Off-Off-Broadway, was also a hit. A comedy about two escaped prisoners, 105 and 106, who return to prison after they experience the outside world, *Promenade* strongly criticizes a society in which those with the most money and the most power are the most cruel. A critic for the *New York Times* remarked, "One definition of *Promenade* might be that it is a protest musical for people too sophisticated to protest." Fornés won an Obie, or Off-Broadway theatre award, for distinguished play writing in 1965 for *The Successful Life of 3* and *Promenade.* Another play which Fornés produced in 1965 was *The Office,* which previewed on Broadway but which never officially opened. Also in 1965, Fornés received an award from the University of Minnesota.

Fornés was very active from 1966 to 1970. She received a Yale University fellowship in 1967–68, a Cintas Foundation fellowship in 1967, and a Boston University-Tanglewood fellowship in 1968. She produced her play *A Vietnamese Wedding* in 1967 and 1969 Off-Broadway as a protest to American involvement in the Vietnam War. The play, which was first performed during Angry Arts Week, utilized members of the audience to demonstrate the universal elements of a Vietnamese tradition. *The Annunciation* was produced with *The Successful Life of 3,* in 1967 Off-Off-Broadway. *Dr. Kheal* appeared in the spring of 1968 Off-Off-Broadway in the United States and in London in 1969. One of Fornés's most frequently produced plays, it portrays a single character, Dr. Kheal, as he gives eccentric lectures on ancient intellectual questions. *The Red Burning Light: or Mission XQ,* was also written to protest the Vietnam War. It was first produced in Zurich, Switzerland, in 1968 for the Open Theatre European Tour, and then at La Mama Experimental Theatre Off-Off Broadway in the spring of 1969. *Molly's Dream,* which demonstrates cinema's influence on people's expectations, was produced Off-Off-Broadway in 1968. In the play legendary movie-star characters interact with a saloon waitress, Molly, in her daydreams; while Molly is caught in her dreams a man who could have fulfilled her longing comes into the saloon and then departs before she can awake to find him. All of these plays, including *Tango Palace* and *Promenade,* were published in a book entitled *Promenade and Other Plays* by Winter House in 1971. Fornés won a Rockefeller Foundation grant that same year.

## Founds New York Theatre Strategy

In 1972, Fornés founded the New York Theatre Strategy with a few other playwrights. Serving as the group's president from 1973 to 1978, and in other offices until 1980 when the group dissolved, Fornés hoped to help make opportunities available for playwrights whose works would not otherwise be produced. The New York Theatre Strategy's efforts have contributed to the production of countless experimental productions. From 1972 to 1973 Fornés also found a second way to assist playwrights like herself: she became a teacher with Theatre for the New City in New York City.

In 1972, Fornés received a Guggenheim fellowship as well as a Creative Artist Public Service grant. Her next play, *The Curse of the Langston House,* was first produced in Cincinnati in late 1972. It was followed by *Aurora,* which appeared Off-Off-Broadway in 1974. Fornés won a grant from the National Endowment for the Arts this same year, and in 1975, she received another Creative Arts Public Service grant. *Cap-a-Pie,* written in Spanish and with music by José Raúl Bernardo, was produced in May of 1975 at INTAR (International Arts Relations), the native Spanish theatre of New York. *Washing* appeared Off-Off-Broadway in late 1976. Also in 1976, Fornés received a grant from the New York State Council on the Arts. In 1977, *Lolita in the Garden,* also written in Spanish, was first shown at INTAR. *Fefu and Her Friends,* one of Fornés's most successful plays, was produced Off-Off-Broadway at New York Theatre Strategy in 1977.

According to a reviewer in *Performing Arts Journal,* "one could say that *Fefu* and the plays that followed it ... have paved the way for a new language of dramatic realism, and a way of directing it." The critic continued, "Fornés brings a much needed intimacy to drama, and her economy of approach suggests another vision of theatricality, more stylized for its lack of exhibitionism." Many critics recognized these traits in *Fefu and Her Friends.* About a gathering of eight friends in the New England home of Fefu in 1935, this play symbolically discusses feminism and a host of other interrelated issues. *Fefu and Her Friends* is noted for its originality; for the second act, the audience is asked to travel to four different rooms to view four different scenes. This enables the audience to share an intimate, personal space with the characters and get to know them up close as they ponder alone in bed or review a lost lesbian love affair. Fornés won an Obie for *Fefu and Her Friends* in 1977.

Fornés went on to write and produce *In Service* at the Claremont, California, Padua Hills Festival in 1978. *Eyes on the Harem* was her next project. Produced in 1979 Off-Off-Broadway at INTAR, this play exploits feminist themes in legends from the Turkish Ottoman empire. A critic for the *New York Times* wrote that while it was "farfetched" at times, the play was "hardly ever ponderous." The critic noted that there was a "deliberate fragmentation of

chronology and tone," and that "some of the sketches" were "very funny." Critics enjoyed the "Meet Me in St. Louis" scene which, according to a reviewer for the *New Yorker,* was "indelible." For this play, Fornés won another Obie Award for distinguished direction.

During the early 1980s, Fornés continued her rapid pace; she wrote (or adapted) and produced plays prolifically. In 1980, Fornés produced *Evelyn Brown (A Diary)* Off-Off-Broadway. She next adapted two plays, *Blood Wedding,* by Spain's leading 20th-century poet and playwright, **Federico García Lorca**, and the surreal *Life Is Dream,* a famous play written during Spain's Golden Age by the great Pedro Calderon de la Barca, in 1980 and 1981 respectively. Both were produced at INTAR. *A Visit* and *The Danube,* both Fornés's own works, were produced for the Padua Hills Festival in California and later Off-Off-Broadway. The former, which appeared in 1981, was a musical comedy which, according to the *New York Times,* juxtaposed "lascivious behavior and ornate dialogue." Its main character is a young girl who flits about the home of a family in Lansing, Michigan, in 1910, and allows herself to be seduced by various men and women. The latter play, *The Danube,* was produced in 1982, 1983, and 1984; in it, Paul and Eve fail to communicate with each other and thus destroy their relationship. Frequent backdrop changes and foreign language tapes contribute to the idea that men and women speak different languages. To top off 1982, Fornés won another Obie Award for sustained achievement.

*Mud,* which is about another, more violent love triangle, was produced in 1983, for the Padua Hills Festival in California. As with every play Fornés wrote for this festival, *Mud* was designed for its set. It was performed outdoors, and it ended near sunset—freezes were used to end scenes instead of blackouts, and the fading light made the costumed characters look drab. Fornés liked these effects and kept them even when the play was produced in New York. *Sarita* tells the story of a young girl so obsessed with a man that she kills him and ends up in a mental institution; it was produced at INTAR in 1984. *No Time* was produced at the Padua Hills Festival in 1984. Fornés's hard work during these years paid off: in 1984, Fornés received an Obie Award for *The Danube, Mud,* and *Sarita,* and won grants from the Rockefeller Foundation and the National Endowment for the Arts.

In 1985, Fornés received the prestigious American Academy and Institute of Arts and Letters Award in Literature. Fornés's play *The Conduct of Life,* a story about a Latin American man who is forced to perform violent acts as a government torturer and who acts just as violently within his own home, was produced Off-Off-Broadway, and it received an Obie for best new play. She then adapted and translated

Virgilio Pinera's *Cold Air,* and it was produced at INTAR; for her translation she won a Playwrights U.S.A. Award. *Mud, The Danube, Sarita,* and *The Conduct of Life* were published in *María Irene Fornés: Plays* in 1986 by PAJ Publications. The book's preface was written by Fornés's former roommate, Susan Sontag.

In March of 1986, *A Matter of Faith* appeared Off-Off-Broadway, and *Lovers and Keepers,* actually three one-act musicals, was produced in April at INTAR. This latter play featured music by the famous Latin-jazz musicians Tito Puente and Fernando Rivas. Fornés's next project was an adaptation from Anton Chekhov's story "Drowning." She produced this adaptation, also entitled *Drowning,* as a one-act play with six other one-act plays by other authors in 1986 under the title *Orchards. Art* was produced Off-Off-Broadway in 1986, and *The Mothers* was produced at the Padua Hills Festival that same year. *Abingdon Square,* a shocking play about a 15-year-old girl who, married to an older man, seeks a real love, was produced by Fornés Off-Broadway in 1987; it won her yet another Obie. Also in 1987, Fornés adapted Chekhov's "Uncle Vanya" for a play of the same name and produced the play Off Broadway. In 1989, the playwright wrote *Hunger,* a play set in a warehouse that explores an imaginary future of socio-economic collapse and its human consequences; it was first produced Off-Off-Broadway by En Garde Productions. *And What of the Night,* a show which included *Hunger, Springtime, Lust,* and *Charlie* (previously entitled *The Mothers*), was produced in Milwaukee, Wisconsin, in 1989.

### Works with Novice Playwrights

Fornés told *CA* that, although there is "a rich Spanish tradition of classic theater . . . there hasn't been a strong modern Hispanic theater—by that I mean since the turn of the century." According to Fornés, the "Hispanic American doesn't have a model yet." She believes that it is "very important to try to work with Hispanic playwrights at a level where they are just beginning to write, so that they don't dismiss possibilities of ways of writing that would be very original to them but ways they would not see models for in the active American or English or German theater." Fornés does more than advocate such instruction; she is an active teacher of young Hispanic writers. She has continually instructed students at the Padua Hills Festival in California and at INTAR; in 1988, she taught a workshop at Manhattanville College in Purchase, New York.

A leader as well as a playwright, Fornés has made an invaluable contribution to the arts. Her plays are remarkable for their exciting and unusual forms, their striking contents, and their memorable characters. Besides writing and producing plays, Fornés is an instructor of young playwrights. She has assisted countless authors as they struggle to find their own voices, or even a theater in which to produce their plays. Finally, Fornés is a champion of Hispanics and women; she writes to inspire and acknowledge both groups, and serves as an extraordinary role model for them.

As a critic for the *Chicago Tribune* wrote, Fornés is "one of the art form's most cherished secrets. Ask playgoers about her, and they are apt to answer with a blank look. Mention Fornés to those who work in the theater, and their faces light up." Many critics assert that Fornés is one of the best playwrights the United States has to offer, and that her work will one day be widely known and respected. Whether or not the public appreciates her work, Fornés enjoys the process of creation. As she told *CA,* "I find more pleasure in the creating part of [my work], and I think that's the reason why I am always willing to keep experimenting and inventing things."

## SELECTED PUBLISHED WORKS:

*Promenade and Other Plays* (includes "Tango Palace," "The Successful Life of 3," "Promenade," "A Vietnamese Wedding," "Dr. Kheal," "The Red Burning Light: or Mission XQ3," and "Molly's Dream"), Winter House, 1971, reprinted, PAJ Publications, 1987.

*Maria Irene Fornes: Plays* (includes "Mud," "The Danube," "Sarita," and "The Conduct of Life"), preface by Susan Sontag, PAJ Publications, 1986.

*Lovers and Keepers,* Theatre Communications Group, 1987.

*Fefu & Her Friends,* PAJ Publications, 1990.

## SOURCES:

### Books

Betsko, Kathleen, and Rachel Koenig, *Interviews with Contemporary Women Playwrights,* Beech Tree Books, 1987, pp. 154–67.

*Contemporary Authors New Revision Series,* Volume 28, Gale, 1990.

*Contemporary Literary Criticism,* Volume 61, Gale, 1990.

*Contemporary Theatre, Film, and Television,* Volume 1, Gale, 1984.

*Dictionary of Literary Biography,* Volume 7: *Twentieth-Century American Dramatists,* Gale, 1981.

Fornés, María Irene, *Lovers and Keepers,* Theatre Communications Group, 1987.

Fornés, María Irene, *María Irene Fornés: Plays,* PAJ Publications, 1986.

Fornés, María Irene, *Promenade and Other Plays,* Winter House, 1971.

Marranca, Bonnie, and Guatam Dasgupta, *American Playwrights: A Critical Survey,* Volume 1, Drama Books Specialists, 1981.

**Periodicals**

*Chicago,* April, 1990, p. 89.

*Chicago Tribune,* June 14, 1969; February 8, 1988, Section 5, p. 3; February 9, 1988, Section 2, p. 10; May 27, 1988, Section 5, p. 4.

*Hispanic,* July, 1988, pp. 44–46.

*Los Angeles Times,* August 2, 1989, Section 6, p. 7.

*Nation,* April 6, 1985, p. 412; April 23, 1988, p. 580.

*Newsweek,* January 25, 1982, p. 73.

*New Yorker,* May 7, 1979, p. 131; January 4, 1988, p. 59.

*New York Times,* April 17, 1968; June 5, 1969; February 22, 1972; January 14, 1978; January 22, 1978; April 25, 1979; December 30, 1981; October 25, 1983; March 13, 1984; March 20, 1985; April 17, 1986; April 23, 1986; October 17, 1989, p. A16, December 15, 1987, p. C21.

*Performing Arts Journal,* Number 1, 1984.

—Sketch by Ronie-Richele Garcia-Johnson

*Francisco Franco*

# Francisco Franco
## 1892-1975
**Spanish dictator**

Francisco Franco Bahamonde was born December 4, 1892, to a dry-land sailor and his wife in El Ferrol, Spain. Franco rose from a middle-class background and the malaise of post-colonial Spanish society to be a powerful general and eventually the ruler of Spain for nearly 40 years, from 1936 until his death in 1975. Even as World War II brought down nations and leaders far stronger than Franco, and the Cold War put two giants into globe-shaking conflict, Franco held tight to power. Sheelagh Ellwood called Franco "the most enigmatic of this century's dictators," and more than one biographer has found an explanation for his remarkable longevity elusive. Ellwood grants one undeniable fact, however: "that Francisco Franco was a man determined to leave his mark on his country." None of his various biographers can deny that he succeeded in doing that.

### Youth in Galicia

Franco grew up in El Ferrol in the Spanish northwest near Portugal. His father, Nicolás Franco Salgado-Araujo, worked as an administrator in the Spanish Navy, as had five generations of his family before him. As a navy administrator, the elder Franco, though of a family of some local prestige, remained a second-class "sailor" because his work did not actually take him to sea. His mother, Pilar Bahamonde y Pardo de Andrade, also came from a family of some limited prestige, tracing their lineage to a fifteenth-century nobleman. In Franco's day, however, the family rested firmly in the middle class, and as the second of four children, Franco looked to his studies as a way to social mobility. His mother encouraged his modest achievements in school, but his father paid little attention to his children generally, and Franco never seemed to have developed a very warm relationship with him.

Franco's childhood coincided with the great wars Spain fought in the 1890s for her colonial possessions in the Pacific and the Americas. Although in many ways Galicia took little part in the cultural and economic mainstream of Spanish life, war brought the town prominence. On the Atlantic coast at a time of large naval mobilizations, El Ferrol served as the base for about one-third of the Spanish Navy, and a disproportionate number of that navy's sailors came from the otherwise isolated region of Galicia. Although the colonial wars happened when Franco was too young to understand their importance, he later saw them as a regrettable and terrible thing to be prevented in the future. Spain, which had suffered a gradual loss of prestige since the height of the empire in the sixteenth century, lost the last of her colonial territories—ceding the Phillipines and Puerto Rico to the United States and granting Cuba its independence. This inspired a "regeneration" movement in the country that repudiated the idea that Spain should simply accept its relative weakening and demanded that Spain be reinvigorated in the new century. In 1962 Franco wrote that "the obsession with public finance prevented Spain from realizing that she was being left behind in everything. . . . What was inadmissible was the political status quo . . . which presided over the complete collapse of our Empire." Many Spaniards shared those feelings, which Franco rode to power.

In 1907, Franco met with disappointment. The "obsession with public finance" of which he would later write led the government to close the Naval Academy, ending Franco's dream of becoming a true sailor. Instead he turned to the Army, where he joined the Infantry Academy in Toledo. He graduated in 1910, 251st in a class of 312. Since Spain was no longer fighting any wars, Franco drew an assignment in his hometown. As a second lieutenant, he received a modest salary, but with the uniform came at least a modicum of prestige. In 1911 Franco left El Ferrol to fight in Morocco, where hostilities with Spain had begun again.

## A Tumultuous Military Career

Franco spent a total of 11 years—from 1912 to 1926—serving in the Moroccan conflict. Many of the attitudes that would one day characterize his rule probably developed from his African experience: a distrust of politicians and an instinct for self-preservation, even as a leader. Indeed, Alan Lloyd credits Franco's willingness to save his own skin, when other officers might consider such actions undignified, for part of his military success: "By the end of 1915, only seven out of forty-two officers . . . remained unwounded. Franco was among them. Survival had assured him, at little more than twenty, the rank of captain."

The next year Franco did sustain a serious wound to the stomach. He had to return to Spain and spent months recovering. Instead of taking his injury in stride, he used it as evidence of his deserving a promotion, which he received. Francisco Franco became the army's youngest major when he was 24 years old.

Franco's military success continued at a remarkable pace through his entire service in Morocco. By 1923, Franco had risen to the rank of Lieutenant Colonel and commanded the entire Spanish Foreign Legion. In that same year he also married Carmen Polo of Oveido, where he had served briefly after his injury in 1916. As Franco moved up in rank, he became obliged to spend more time on the Iberian peninsula. Nevertheless, he came to play a crucial role in extracting Spain from the Moroccan conflict with dignity. Franco ignored a retreat order and defeated the enemy forces south of Ceuta. Although Spain could not claim total victory in the conflict, Franco had helped to insure that it could leave the conflict as a conqueror, rather than a nation trying to get out of a costly, long, and increasingly pointless war. Franco became a brigadier general. Ellwood points out that at 33, Franco was "the youngest general in Europe."

## Became a Spanish Power

The late 1920s saw Spanish politics shifting unsteadily in several directions. Although the monarchy had quickly reclaimed its power after the first Spanish Republic—declared in 1873 and dissolved in 1874—republicanism again enchanted many Spaniards. Franco's brother Ramon led one of the anti-monarchy, pro-democracy groups, going so far as to fly an aborted bombing mission over the king's palace. Francisco Franco, however, took every opportunity to reassert his loyalty to the throne, often trying to convince his brother to abandon his revolutionary ideas. The first round of elections held on April 5, 1931, showed support for Monarchist candidates, but many alleged widespread fraud and voter intimidation, particularly in rural areas. The second round of voting showed overwhelming support for Republican candidates, and though the people had clearly shown their preference, Franco considered military action to prevent the newly elected Republicans from taking power. With no other support in the military, Franco decided against action but condemned the "lack of moral fiber" among the other Monarchist military leaders. King Alphonso abdicated on April 14, 1931, and the Second Spanish Republic was born.

This revolution affected Franco even more directly because the leaders of Spain's new republic immediately closed down the Military Academy at Saragossa, where Franco had been serving as the director since 1929. Despite this development and his fervent Monarchism, Franco made a public peace with the new leaders of Spain, though remaining defiant within the law: "At the same time, he made it clear that he was no Republican, for he insisted on applying military regulations to the letter and would not hoist the new Republican flag until he had received the order in writing. This was a carefully calculated gesture of protest, designed to make a point without incurring penalty."

Franco suffered the humiliation of a relatively insignificant command assignment on the Balaeric Islands, but returned to prominence in 1934 as the general who would crush the Asturian Miners Revolution. As much as Franco despised the Republicans, he loathed the Communistic Workers' Groups even more. As a reward for this service, Franco became the commander-in-chief of the Army of Africa. For the old *Africanista,* the job was perfect. Yet he did not stay long in Morocco because new Minister of War Robles asked Franco in 1935 to become the chief of the Central General Staff. Franco thought of refusing the assignment, but eventually the prestige of that office outweighed his love for Morocco. According to Ellwood, this promotion made Franco "by position and by reputation, not only the country's most important military figure, but also an increasingly significant political figure."

In 1936—with Spain divided into Nationalists and Republicans— Franco, in command of the Army of Africa, held the power to determine victory for one side or the other. On July 19, Franco landed at the port of Tetuan, giving the Rebellion against the Republic new vigor. On September 29, rebel leaders nominated Franco as the new Spanish head of state and military supreme commander. After three years of fighting, the leaders of the Republic surrendered in 1939.

### Ruled Spain

Franco became *caudillo,* or absolute dictator, and unlike those he had accused of lacking "moral fiber," Franco tolerated little dissent. According to Ellwood, he placed a premium on "uniformity and conformity" rather than "plurality and diversity." He saw himself as the savior of the nation and therefore would suffer no one to stop him. He used military tribunals to try any manner of offense, and observers suspect that hundreds or thousands of political captives and other prisoners were executed between 1939 and 1943. Franco also used bureaucratic tools to harass the general public into loyalty. By requiring written authorizations for work or food purchases, ultimate authority rested in those issuing the cards, who, of course, owed loyalty to Franco. This system did not reward hard work or merit and fell into widespread corruption.

Franco came to power at a time when Europe's second Great War had just begun, and though Franco proclaimed his neutrality, his sympathies clearly lay with the Axis. Yet Franco never entered the war. Franco cannily watched the tide of the war shift toward the Allied powers and made some motions of reconciliation to them. In the end, however, the United Nations condemned Spain for its wartime behavior and called for a withdrawal of all ambassadors from Madrid in 1946.

In 1947 Franco promulgated the Law of Succession, which made Spain a monarchy again and gave Franco the power to name the new monarch at his leisure. Although Spain had become a pariah nation, Franco had become still more powerful. Perhaps because of its moral isolation, Spain had no leader but Franco. The Cold War divided wartime allies, and Franco's position again improved. As a strategically crucial piece in the global puzzle, Spain attracted diplomatic attention. The United States reestablished normal diplomatic relations in 1950 and in 1953, President Dwight D. Eisenhower made an offer of military and economic assistance in exchange for the right to build military bases in Spain. Franco also benefited from the recognition of the Vatican the same year.

In 1956 Franco peaceably allowed Moroccan independence in response to growing nationalism, the French repudiation of claims in Morocco, and a rising tide of colonial independence worldwide. By now Franco had projected himself as an enemy of communism and tried to tie Spain's impoverished condition to the juggernaut of post-war American capitalism. Though he did not allow any opposition to his rule, Franco did oversee a gradual improvement in living conditions for most Spaniards. He also engineered eventual entry into the United Nations in 1955 and preferential trade status entry into the European economic community in 1970. In 1966, the Organic Law of the State passed with an overwhelming majority, creating a head of state with whom Franco would share some executive power.

In 1969 Franco designated Don Juan Carlos de Borbon the prince of Spain. In 1975, after suffering a heart attack, Franco died, making Juan Carlos the new king of Spain and its head of state.

**SOURCES:**

Coles, S.F.A., *Franco of Spain,* London, Neville Spearman, 1955.

Crozier, Brian, *Franco: A Biographical History,* London, Eyre and Spottiswoode, 1967.

Ellwood, Sheelagh, *Franco,* London, Longman Group, 1994.

Lloyd, Alan, *Franco,* London, Longman Group, 1970.

—*Sketch by James McCarthy*

# Carlos Fuentes
## 1928-
### Mexican writer

Carlos Fuentes is widely considered to be Mexico's foremost contemporary novelist and one of the world's most important writers. He is usually associated with the "El boom" of the 1960s, a period in which several Latin American writers such as **Gabriel García Márquez** and **Julio Cortazar** rose to international prominence. According to the assessment of Chilean novelist **José Donoso**, writing in his autobiographical account *The Boom in Spanish American Literature*, Fuentes was "the first active and conscious agent of the internationalization of the Spanish American novel."

Throughout his extensive corpus, Fuentes draws extensively from Aztec culture, the history of the Spanish conquistadors, and the failed ideals of the Mexican Revolution, in an attempt to construct a viable national identity for modern Mexico. Like most writers of the "boom" era, Fuentes is also known for his technical experimentation. Some of his most favorably received works, such as *La región más transparente* (1958; translated in 1982 as *Where the Air Is Clear*), *La muerte de Artemio Cruz* (1962; translated in 1964 as *The Death of Artemio Cruz*) and *Terra nostra* (1975; translated in 1976), are noted for their nonlinear chronological development, multiple narrative perspectives, and montage-like scene construction. Fuentes—a former diplomat who was once denied entrance into the United States for his controversial leftist political views—has also received considerable attention for his numerous nonfiction publications covering various aspects of Mexican culture and politics.

### Mexican Roots, International Childhood

Fuentes was born in Mexico City on November 11, 1928, one of the two children of Rafael Fuentes Boettiger, a prominent diplomat, and the former Berta Macías Rivas. His father's career enabled Fuentes to live in various capitals as a child, including Washington, D.C., where he learned to speak English at the age of four. Fuentes was a popular student in a Washington public school—until the Mexican government expropriated foreign-oil holdings in the late 1930s. "I became a leper in my school," Fuentes stated in a *Paris Review* interview. "Nobody would talk to me ... because there were screaming headlines everyday talking about Mexican communists stealing 'our' oil wells. So I became a Mexican chauvinist as a reaction." Fuentes recalled attending a film in 1939 and jumping up in his seat when an

*Carlos Fuentes*

Alamo scene appeared. Fuentes yelled, "Death to the gringos! Viva Mexico!"

With his father's encouragement, Fuentes began writing at an early age, publishing his first short story in a magazine when he was 13. He attended secondary school in Chile at the prestigious Grange School in Santiago. Back in Mexico, he enrolled in the Colegio Mexico, where he was once suspended for a month for attempting to celebrate the birthday of **Benito Juarez**—the former Indian president of Mexico and one of the country's symbols of liberalism. The rigidity of the Catholic school, however, enhanced Fuente's writing. "The school made me into a writer because it taught me about sin, that everything you did was sinful," he said in the *Paris Review*. "So many things could be sins and therefore become so pleasurable that they set me to writing."

After completing his secondary education in 1946, Fuentes studied law at Mexico's Colegio Frances Morelos primarily because his parents, as he told *Paris Review*, "said I would die of hunger if I tried to live off my writing in Mexico." After receiving his bachelor of laws degree in 1948, Fuentes began postgraduate study at the National University of Mexico law school, where he taught himself French by reading Balzac's novels with a dictionary. He then went to Geneva for a year to study at the Institut des Hautes Études Internationales before completing his dissertation, which he published privately in 1951. While in Geneva, Fuentes also served as a member and then secretary to the International Labor Organization; secretary of the Mexican delegation to the International Law Commission of the United Nations; and cultural attaché to the Mexican Embassy. When he returned to Mexico, he worked at the University of Mexico's cultural department and the Foreign Affairs Ministry department of cultural relations. While establishing the literary review *Revista Mexicana de Literature* and editing three other periodicals, he also wrote his first book of short stories, *Los dias enmascarados* (*Masked Days*), which was published in 1954. Two years later, he was awarded a fellowship from the Centro Mexicano de Escritores, enabling him to finish his first novel.

### A Novelist, Not a Lawyer

"I might have become a corporate lawyer," Fuentes told *Paris Review*, "but I wrote *Where the Air Is Clear* instead." Set in 1951, but connected with Mexico's revolutionary past through a series of flashbacks and cinematic techniques, the novel chronicles the life of Federico Robles, a former revolutionary who has risen from humble origins to become a millionaire through a series of unethical financial practices, including credit fraud. Although the novel's Marxist overtones and its critique of Mexico's spiritual decadence provoked controversy upon its publication in 1958, most reviewers reacted favorably. What distinguished the novel, wrote Saul Maloff in the *Saturday Review,* was Fuentes's "ability to manage firmly and sensitively—always as an artist, never as an ideologist—the kind of packed and turbulent social scene that is so often the undoing of the 'political' novelist." Likewise, Anthony West stated in The *New Yorker* that "in a succession of brilliant, imaginative penetrations, Senor Fuentes uncovers the burdens of memory and of present feeling carried by each of [his characters]."

After writing a second novel, *The Good Conscience,* which received less critical attention than his first, Fuentes gained international recognition for *The Death of Artemio Cruz* in 1962. This novel, perhaps his best known, continues his examination of the decay of revolutionary ideals in modern Mexico through its title character, a tycoon who has attained wealth and position through ruthless means. Relying on a series of flashbacks, the narrative shifts between Cruz's thoughts on his deathbed, his participation in the Revolution, and his career trajectory. Such a technique, as several critics have suggested, enabled Fuentes to contrast revolutionary ideals with the corruption of modern society. Although some reviewers found the novel's fragmented style problematic, most praised the novel for both its ambitious thematic statement and technical innovation. "To attempt to synthesize in one man's existence the life of a whole nation for half a century is as difficult as it is ambitious," observed Walter M. Langford in The

*Mexican Novel Comes of Age.* "That Carlos Fuentes brings it off with patent success is a measure of his novelistic breadth and depth." Praising the "changing narrative viewpoint," John S. Brushwood observed in *Mexico in Its Novel: A Nation's Search for Identity:* "I doubt that there is anywhere in fiction a character whose wholeness is more apparent than in the case of Artemio Cruz."

Five years later, Fuentes received his first major literary award, the 1967 Premio Biblioteca Breve of the Barcelona publishing house Seix Barral, for one of his most controversial novels, *A Change of Skin.* The novel, which follows the existential conflicts of its four central characters, was officially banned in Spain because it was considered pornographic and communistic. Although many reviewers were highly critical of its graphic sexual material, most agreed with R. J. Coleman of the *Saturday Review,* who deemed the novel "bursting in energy, capacious in content, gripping in evocation, and humanitarian in its universal tolerances."

In 1969, Fuentes returned to Mexico after four years of self-imposed exile. That same year he divorced his wife of ten years, Rita Macedo, a movie actress with whom he had one daughter, Cecilia. While writing several articles on Latin American politics and culture and other nonfiction publications, including the book *El mundo de Jose Luis Cuevas*—a study of the renowned Mexican artist, Fuentes continued to produce fictional works. In 1975, he published one of his most expansive and ambitious works, *Terra nostra,* which was awarded the Romulo Gallegos Prize in Venezuela. The novel presents a circular model of history by incorporating scenes from the twenty-first century into a narrative tracing the development of Mexican culture from the Spanish conquest to modern times. Although *Newsweek*'s Peter S. Prescott found the 800-page novel "unreadable," *Village Voice* contributor Jonah Raskin praised Fuentes for his ability to "plunge readers into the hidden recesses of his characters' minds and at the same time allow language to pile up around their heads in thick drifts, until they feel lost in a blizzard of words that enable them to see, to feel, in a revolutionary way."

That same year Fuentes was appointed Mexican ambassador to France, where he served for two years. Although his commitments as a diplomat prevented him from writing, Fuentes found the experience beneficial to his craft. "I didn't know how to write before and I guess I learned by being a bureaucrat," he told *Paris Review.* "You have so much mental time on your hands when you are a bureaucrat: you have time to think and to learn how to write in your head." Shortly after leaving his post to return to writing full-time, Fuentes published several novels, including *Hydra Head* (1979), an examination of the nature of power in contemporary Mexico, and *Distant Relations* (1981), a metaphysical ghost story exploring the nature of writing. With the 1985 publication of *The Old Gringo,* Fuentes became the first Mexican to appear on the *New York Times* best-seller list. The novel, which focuses on Mexican American relations, won several awards, including the Cervantes Prize from Spain.

While continuing to write critically acclaimed novels such as *The Orange Tree* (1994)—a series of novellas focusing on the life of Cortes, which adds a new dimension to his exploration of Mexican history—Fuentes has also served as a lecturer or visiting professor at institutions throughout the world, including the University of Paris, the University of Mexico, Harvard University, and Columbia University. The recipient of numerous honorary degrees, Fuentes has lived in New Jersey for several years with his second wife, Sylvia Lemus, with whom he has a son, Carlos Rafael, and a daughter, Natasha.

## SELECTED PUBLISHED WORKS:

### Novels

*La región más transparente,* Fondo de Cultura Económica, 1958; translation by Sam Hileman published as *Where the Air Is Clear,* Ivan Obolensky, 1960.

*Las buenas consciencias,* Fondo de Cultura Económica, 1959; translation published as *The Good Conscience,* Ivan Obolensky, 1961.

*La muerte de Artemio Cruz,* Fondo de Cultura Económica, 1962; translation by Hileman published as *The Death of Artemio Cruz,* Farrar, Straus, 1964.

*Aura,* Era, 1962; translation by Lysander Kemp, New York, Farrar, Straus, 1965.

*Zona sagrada,* Siglo XXI, 1967; translation by Suzanne Jill Levine published as *Holy Place,* New York, Dutton, 1972.

*Cambio de piel,* Mortiz, 1967; translation by Hileman published as *A Change of Skin,* New York, Farrar, Straus, 1968.

*Cumpleaños,* Mortiz, 1969; translation published as "Birthday" in *Holy Place & Birthday: Two Novellas,* New York, Farrar, Straus, 1991.

*Terra Nostra,* Seix Barral, 1975; translation by Levine, New York, Farrar, Straus, 1976.

*La cabeza de hidra,* Mortiz, 1978; translation by Margaret Sayers Peden published as *Hydra Head,* New York, Farrar, Straus, 1978.

*Una familia lejana,* Era, 1980; translation by Peden published as *Distant Relations,* New York, Farrar, Straus, 1982.

*El gringo viejo,* Fondo de Cultura Económica, 1985; translation by Peden and Fuentes published as *The Old Gringo,* New York, Farrar, Straus, 1985.

*Christopher Unborn,* translation by Cristóbel Nonato, New York, Farrar, Straus, 1989.

*Agua Quemada,* Mondadori, 1993.

*El Naranjo,* Santillana, 1993.

*The Orange Tree,* translation by Alfred MacAdam, New York, Farrar, Straus, 1994.

### Short Stories

*Los días enmascarados,* Los Presentes, 1954.

*Cantar de ciegos,* Mortiz, 1964.

*Dos cuentos mexicanos,* Instituto de Cultura Hispánica de Sao Paulo, Universidade de Sao Paulo, 1969.

*Poemas de amor: Cuentos del alma,* Madrid, Imp. E. Cruces, 1971.

*Chac Mool y otros curentos,* Salvat, 1973.

*Agua quemada,* Fondo de Cultura Económica, 1981; translation by Peden published as *Burnt Water,* New York, Farrar, Straus, 1980.

*Constancia and Other Stories for Virgins,* New York, Farrar, Straus, 1989.

### Nonfiction

*The Argument of Latin America: Words for North Americans,* Radical Education Project, 1963.

*Paris: La revolución de mayo,* Era, 1968.

*La nueva novela hispanoamericana,* Mortiz, 1969.

*Casa con dos puertas,* Mortiz, 1970.

*Tiempo mexicano,* Mortiz, 1971.

*Cervantes; o, La crítica de la lectura,* Mortiz, 1976; translation published as *Don Quixote; or, The Critique of Reading,* Institute of Latin American Studies, University of Texas at Austin, 1976.

*On Human Rights: A Speech,* Dallas, Somesuch Press, 1984.

*Latin America: At War With the Past,* CBC Enterprises, 1985.

*Myself With Others: Selected Essays,* New York, Farrar, Straus, 1988.

## SOURCES:

### Books

*Authors in the News,* Volume 2, Detroit, Gale, 1976.

Brushwood, John S., *Mexico in Its Novel: A Nation's Search for Identity,* University of Texas Press, 1966.

*Contemporary Literary Criticism,* Gale, Volume 3, 1975, Volume 8, 1978, Volume 19, 1979, Volume 13, 1980, Volume 22, 1982, Volume 41, 1987.

*Current Biography Yearbook 1972,* edited by Marjorie Dent Candee, New York, Wilson, 1972.

Donoso, Jose, *The Boom in Spanish American Literature: A Personal History,* New York, Columbia University Press, 1977.

Guzman, Daniel de, *Carlos Fuentes,* New York, Twayne, 1972.

*Hispanic Writers,* edited by Bryan Ryan, Detroit, Gale, 1991.

Langford, Walter M., *The Mexican Novel Comes of Age,* Diana, 1975.

**Periodicals**

*Nation,* June 1, 1964.

*New Yorker,* March 4, 1961; January 26, 1981; February 24, 1986.

*New York Review of Books,* June 11, 1964.

*New York Times Book Review,* November 7, 1976; October 19, 1980; October 27, 1985; August 20, 1989.

*Paris Review,* winter 1981.

*Saturday Review,* October 30, 1976.

*Times Literary Supplement,* June 10, 1994.

—*Sketch by Jason Gallman*

*Alberto Fujimori*

# Alberto Fujimori
## 1938-
### Peruvian politician

Alberto Fujimori was elected president of Peru in 1990. After two years of democratic rule he organized an *autogolpe* (self-coup), which abolished the constitution, the Congress, and the Supreme Court. Assuming absolute power, Fujimori nevertheless assured the press that his government was a true democracy.

Fujimori was born in the Peruvian capital of Lima on July 28, 1938. He is the son of two Japanese immigrants, Naochi and Matsue Fujimori. In 1974, Fujimori married an engineer, Susana Higuchi, who earned the popular sobriquet of "Señora Susana." The Fujimoris are the parents of four children: Keiko Sofía, Hiro Alberto, Sachi Marcela, and Kenji Gerardo.

During his elementary school years, Fujimori attended both the Colegio de Nuestra Señora de la Merced (Our Lady of Mercy), a private school, and a public school. He finished his secondary studies at Gran Unidad Escolar of Alfonso Ugarte (Great Unity School). He graduated at the top of his class and earned the award of *excelencia* ("excellence"). Fujimori then entered the National Agricultural University (UNA) and became an agricultural engineer. He did post-graduate work in France, then continued his studies in the United States, where he earned a master's degree in mathematics from the University of Wisconsin in 1969. He became dean of the faculty of sciences at the UNA and served in that post until 1989, when he was elected the institution's president. He also served as president of the Chancellors Assembly of the Peruvian Universities for two years.

Fujimori joined other professionals in founding the Cambio Movement 90. In November of 1989, he registered the group in the National Jury of Elections as the Movimiento Político Independiente Cambio 90 (Independent Political Change Movement 90), and was its candidate in the presidential elections.

### The Opposition

Fujimori had no major political experience before he became a candidate for the Peruvian presidency. His campaign emphasized promises to eliminate violence, the Shining Path guerilla group's activities and corruption. His chief opponent was **Mario Vargas Llosa**—the prominent Peruvian writer—a conservative candidate who promulgated neo-liberal policies: free market, balanced budget, and private enterprise. Shortly after he was elected, Fujimori embraced a neo-liberal economic system as advocated by his opponent.

As president, Fujimori eliminated the Shining Path by incarcerating its leader, Abimael Guzmán.

But B. J. Kowalski of the *World Press Review* quoted Professor Ponciano del Pino, who disagreed with the idea that the Shining Path—known as Sendero Luminoso in Spanish—had been defeated. Poncino del Pino cautioned: "As Peruvians, we should not deceive ourselves . . . into believing that Sendero Luminoso has been defeated."

Among Fujimori's adversaries is his wife, Susana Higuchi. She has accused the wife of the president's brother of having profited from the sale of clothes donated by Japan. She has also charged her husband and some of his ministers with corruption, broken campaign promises, and authoritarianism. Higuchi announced that she was running for the presidency in 1995. Fujimori fired her as First Lady and restricted her to quarters on one side of the palace, and accused her of being unstable. As soon as his wife declared her presidential candidacy, Fujimori arranged for the passage of a law prohibiting any of the president's family members from seeking the presidency or criticizing the president. This law became known as the Susana Law. Violeta Bermudez, a Peruvian feminist, told Lloyd Grove of the *Washington Post* that Señora Higuchi is a symbol of the abuse of women, rich or poor. Señora Higuchi left the Palace with three of the Fujimori sons and announced that she was building a ticket for the 1995 election under the name of "Harmony 21st Century."

### Accomplishments and Human Rights

Decreased inflation, a growing economy (in 1993 and 1994), simplified import tariffs, and foreign investments have also characterized the Fujimori administration. In November 1993 Fujimori won an important constitutional referendum. Still, complaints of human rights violations remain. Fujimori has been accused by an Army general, Roberto Robles, of running a death squad with General Montecinos as his key adviser.

## SOURCES:

### Books

*The Shining Path of Perú,* edited by David Scott Palmer, New York, St. Martin's Press, 1992.
Vargas Llosa, Alvaro, *The Madness of Things Peruvian,* New Brunswick, New Jersey, Transaction, 1994.

### Periodicals

*Economist,* February 19, 1994, pp. 43–44; May 7, 1994, p. 48.
*National Catholic Reporter,* April, 24, 1992.
*National Review,* November 1993, pp. 78–79.
*NPQ,* fall 1993, p. 10–12.
*Washington Post,* December 8, 1993, Section 8, p. 28; September, 8 1994, Section C, p. 1.
*World Press Review,* December 1993, p. 32.

### Other

Embassy of Perú, "Biografía del señor Alberto Fujimori presidente-electo del Perú," December, 6, 1994.

*—Sketch by Sylvia Apodaca*

# Ernesto Galarza
## 1905-1984
### Mexican union leader and writer

Ernesto Galarza, sometimes known as Ernest Galarza, fought against the exploitation of American and Mexican farm workers. He especially opposed the poor wages and the foul living conditions in worker camps. He was also the author of an autobiography, many books of poems and fiction, an autobiography, books of juvenile fiction, and books of nonfiction prose about a wide range of issues relevant to Hispanics.

Ernesto Galarza was born in 1905 in the Sierra Madre mountains in western Mexico. His father, also Ernesto, was a merchant and his mother, Henriqueta, a homemaker. He lived in a small Indian village known as Jalcocotán, Nayarit. He later wrote of his home in his autobiography, *Barrio Boy:* "I showed up in an adobe cottage with a thatched roof at one end of the only street of Jalcocotán . . . Jalco for short. Like many other small villages in the wild, majestic mountains of the Sierra Madre, my pueblo was a hideaway."

Galarza lived in Jalco until he was six years old, when his mother and two uncles joined a migration of hundreds of thousands fleeing the Mexican Revolution, hoping to find work in America. Galarza's uncles found work in Sacramento, California on the railroads. Galarza attended school there, quickly adapting to and mastering the English language. In fact, he began his career as a union leader at the age of eight, when he was asked to a strike committee as the only Mexican worker with an understanding of English.

His mother's and uncle's deaths while in high school left him without an immediate family and without money. He worked odd jobs to stay in school. He proved himself such a perspicacious student that he won a scholarship to Occidental College, from which he earned a bachelor's degree in 1927. Shortly after graduation, in 1928, Galarza married school-teacher Mae Taylor, with whom he had two daughters. He continued his education after his marriage, earning his Master's from Stanford in 1929 and later a Ph.D. with honors from Columbia University in 1944.

## Accepted Position with Pan-American Union

He probably would have received the Ph.D. sooner if it had not been for his interest in helping his people. In 1936, he moved to Washington, D.C. to work for the Pan American Union (PAU). The PAU grew from the Commercial Bureau of the American Republics founded in 1890 to bring benefits to the people of North, Central, and South America. Galarza worked for the PAU for 11 years, first as an education specialist and then as director of the Division of Labor and Social Information. It was in this position that Galarza began to fight for workers' rights, particularly Mexican workers. He wrote and spoke out for improvements in Latin American labor conditions and treatment, for better education of Latin American laborers, and related political issues. In 1941, he wrote a two-volume book published by the PAU called *Labor Trends and Social Welfare in Latin America.* In 1947, he resigned his position maintaining that the PAU was not only ineffectual in stopping the exploitation of Mexican agricultural workers by U.S. businesses but abided it as well.

## Led Struggle of Farm Labor Union

After leaving the PAU, Galarza returned to his home in the Sacramento Valley and fought the *bracero* system. The braceros, or Mexican workers— also known as migrant or interim workers—were contracted by corporations for farming and other manual labor. They were "a highly mobile task force" according to the Assistant Secretary of Agriculture as quoted by Galarza in his 1977 book *Farm Workers and Agri-business in California, 1947–1960.* In the same book Galarza quoted the American Farm Bureau Federation as declaring that "Mexican workers [braceros] unaccompanied by wives and families . . . can fill our seasonal peaks and return home . . . without creating difficult social problems." From 1942 through 1960 the bracero population numbered 2,000,000 in California alone. They were housed in camps of deplorable conditions. The braceros were originally intended as supplemental workers, but they replaced the domestic laborers when money-conscious business owners discovered that the braceros would work for lower wages. The domestic work force—without a union to protect it—lost jobs to the braceros, who were also non-unionized and expendable.

To combat the exploitation of these braceros and the domestic workers, Galarza joined the National

Farm Labor Union in its infancy (for which he served as Vice President) and later the National Agricultural Workers Union (for which he served as Secretary). With these organizations, Galarza attempted to unionize the Mexican braceros and the American labor force. He was continually opposed by the agricultural corporations that profited from the bracero system. In 1947, Galarza and the union organized a group of workers for the DiGiorgio Fruit Corporation and convinced them to strike. DiGiorgio, an agri-behemoth of the time, enlisted the aid of the U.S. Congress to end the strike and started litigation procedures against Galarza for libel. Galarza did not admit defeat. He continued the fight. He organized workers to strike for their rights again in 1951. Later, he described these struggles in his books, such as *Spiders in the House and Workers in the Field*.

### Fought Life-long Battle for Workers' Rights

Galarza continued to fight for workers' rights throughout his life. As a writer, he published reports like *Strangers in Our Fields* that depicted the abominable, squalid living conditions and food shortages of the braceros. Finally, his 1964 exposé *Merchants of Labor* forced the hands of the government. New immigration laws put an end to the bracero system, which in turn led to the rise of the United Farmworkers.

Galarza retired from active union work in the late sixties and devoted himself to community service, such as teaching elementary school. Throughout the 1970s, he continued to speak out for workers' rights as a conference leader and frequent guest lecturer at universities across the country. He served at Notre Dame University as an associate research professor in sociology. As a distinguished visiting professor at San Jose State University, he taught in the Mexican Graduate Studies program.

After retiring from the labor unions he also began to concentrate more earnestly on his writing. One of his most well-known books was his autobiography *Barrio Boy*, published in 1971. In the book *Chicano Narrative*, Ramón Saldívar called it a "real American story" and John Womack referred to it in the *New York Review of Books* as "a long and vivid memoir of his childhood, . . . one of the unheralded wonders of modern America." After *Barrio Boy*, he returned to nonfiction with *Farm Workers and Agri-business in California, 1947–1960* in 1977. He published several books for young people throughout the 1970s. His last book, *Kodachromes in Rhyme*, came out in 1982.

Galarza died on June 22, 1984, survived by his wife and two daughters. In his obituary in the *New York Times*, José Villa, a professor at San Jose State University said, "He was our pre-eminent Chicano scholar and organizer. He was an inspiration."

## SELECTED PUBLISHED WORKS:

*Thirty Poems*, Jamaica Estates, Yearlong School, 1935.
*La Industria Eléctrica en México*, Fondo de Cultura Económica, 1941.
*Labor Trends and Social Welfare in Latin America*, PAU, 1941.
*Strangers in Our Fields*, Joint United States-Mexico Trade Union Committee, 1956.
*Merchants of Labor: The Mexican Bracero Story; An Account of the Managed Loftin, Migration of Mexican Farm Workers in California, 1942–1960*, McNally, 1964.
*Spiders in the House and Workers in the Field*, Univeristy of Notre Dame Press, 1970.
*Barrio Boy*, Univeristy of Notre Dame Press, 1971.
*Farm Workers and Agri-Business in California 1947–1960*, Univeristy of Notre Dame Press, 1977.
*The Tragedy at Chualar*, McNally & Loftin, 1977.
*Kodachromes in Rhyme* (poems), Univeristy of Notre Dame Press, 1982.

### Children's Works

*Zoo-Risa: Rimas y Fotografías de Ernesto Galarza*, McNally & Loftin, 1968.
*Aquí y Allá en California*, Almadén, 1971.
*Poemas Párvulos* (poems), Almadén, 1971.
*Rimas Tontas*, Almadén, 1971.
*La Historia Verdadera de Una Botella de Leche*, Almadén, 1972.
*Más Poemas Párvulos* (poems) Almadén, 1972.
*Poemas pe-que pe-que pe-que-ñitos: Very, Very Short Nature Poems*, Almadén, 1972.
*Un Poco de México*, Almadén, 1972.
*Chogorrom*, Almadén, 1973.
*Todo Mundo lee*, Almadén, 1973.

## SOURCES:

### Books

Galarza, Ernesto, *Barrio Boy*, University of Notre Dame Press, 1971.
Galarza, Ernesto, *Farm Workers and Agri-business in California, 1947–1960*, University of Notre Dame Press, 1977.
*Hispanic Writers*, edited by Bryan Ryan, Detroit, Gale Research, 1991.
*Mexican American Biographies: A Historical Dictionary 1836–1987*, edited by Matt S. Meier, Greenwood Press, 1988.
Moore, Joan, and Harry Pachon, *Mexican Americans*, Prentice-Hall, 1976.

Rivera, Feliciano, *Mexican American Sourcebook,* Educational Consulting Association, 1970.

Saldivar, Ramón, *Chicano Narrative: The Dialectics of Difference,* University of Wisconsin Press, 1990.

**Periodicals**

*New York Review of Books,* August 31, 1972, pp. 12–18.

*New York Times,* June 24, 1984.

—*Sketch by Christopher B. Tower*

*Eduardo Galeano*

# Eduardo Galeano
## 1940-
### Uruguayan journalist, historian, and political activist

Eduardo Galeano is one of Uruguay's most celebrated writers and political activists. His often polemical works passionately evoke outrage and scorn for the centuries of exploitation and imperialism in Latin America by Europe and the United States. Not surprisingly, Galeano's opus has generated a significant amount of controversy. Caleb Bach observed in *Américas:* "Although respected for his hard-nosed scholarship, sharp eye for detail, and majestic style, Galeano has been assailed for his strident tone and impassioned subjectivity." Nevertheless, he also has a large number of supporters, including Chilean novelist **Isabel Allende,** who is quoted in *Town & Country* as saying that Galeano "has more firsthand knowledge of Latin America than anybody in the world. And he is a great storyteller, a very great storyteller, with a new language—one that goes straight into our minds and hearts at the same time. He is a poet: strange, brave, subversive."

Eduardo Hughes Galeano was born on September 3, 1940, in Montevideo, Uruguay, to Eduardo Hughes and Ester Galeano. He attended school until the age of 13, when he quit because he felt that he could learn more on the streets of Montevideo than through a formal education. During his teens, Galeano worked as a messenger for factories and offices to earn pocket money. He also drew caricatures and political cartoons which appeared in *El Sol,* a socialist weekly newspaper, and he began writing essays about the arts and labor movement as early as 1954. By his early twenties, Galeano had assumed the editorship of *Marcha,* a weekly political magazine, and the directorship of *Epoca,* a daily periodical.

## Written Work Reveals Political Views

At the age of 22, Galeano published his first novel, *Los días siguientes* (1962); two years later, he published the first of many political studies entitled *China 1964: Crónica de un desafío.* Galeano's role as a political agitator reached its apex in 1971 when he published *Las venas abiertas de América Latina* (*The Open Veins of Latin America: Five Centuries of the Pillage of a Continent*). According to Juana Ponce de Léon in *Town & Country,* this controversial, forthright work presents "a scorching indictment of the powers responsible for Latin America's poverty, devastation and violence."

In 1973 a military coup in Uruguay forced Galeano—whose leftist political views had become well known in his homeland—to flee to Argentina. Settling in Buenos Aires, he founded a radical monthly periodical entitled *Crisis* and served as its director from 1973 through 1976. During these years in exile, Galeano wrote the novel *La canción de nosotros,* for which he was awarded the Premio Casa de las Américas in 1975. He won this prize again in 1978 for the book *Días y noches de amor y de guerra* (*Days and Nights of Love and War*). In 1976 Galeano's literary career was again interrupted when a military coup in Argentina forced him to flee to Spain. For the next 12 years, he lived in Calella de la Costa, near Barcelona, until he was able to return to Uruguay in 1984.

## Compiles Unorthodox History

During his exile in Spain, Galeano was inspired to write a history of the exploitation of Latin America by Europe and the United States. He began the monumental task of researching this project in the enormous Spanish libraries which had collected volumes of information on the plundered continent's colonial era. Galeano told Bach in *Américas* that "[exile] gave me the time, even a measure of objectivity that can only come from looking at familiar things from a distance. Sure, often it was boring work, drudgery, hard on the backside, and yet just as one person can inexplicably shine in a crowd, so too even the dullest of books can yield some nugget or magical turn or phrase that in miniature captures the essence of larger forces at work."

Galeano's painstaking historical research led to his epic trilogy entitled *Memoria del fuego* (1982–86; *Memory of Fire*). In this trilogy, the author employed a unique literary device by which he composed seemingly mundane or trivial vignettes that ultimately serve to frame larger, well-known historical events in an often ironic, or even sardonic, context. About this approach, Galeano remarked to Bach that "[it] occurred to me that history could talk about itself. 'Story windows' or spaces open to time could help the reader relate to events as if they were happening now. That's why I wrote it in the present tense." The first volume in the trilogy, *Los nacimientos* (1982; *Genesis)*, provides chronological anecdotes from the first two centuries of Spanish rule in the New World. The second volume, *Las caras y las máscaras* (1984; *Faces and Masks*), covers events from the eighteenth and nineteenth centuries. The third volume, *El siglo del viento* (1986; *Century of the Wind*), centers on the numerous power struggles in the Americas during the twentieth century. Reviewers hailed *Memoria del fuego* as a seminal analysis of the history of the Western Hemisphere; Jay Parini, writing in the *New York Times*, praised the trilogy is "a vast and visionary epic, [in which] images from centuries of life in the Americas were combined to form a shimmering mosaic of history and political commentary." In 1989 Galeano received the American Book Award for *Memoria del fuego*.

In the years since the tremendous success of *Memoria del fuego*, Galeano has continued to produce works which candidly examine the political and social conditions—past and present—in Latin America. *Nosotros decimos no: Crónicas (1963-1988)*, originally published in 1988 and updated and translated into English in 1991, is a collection of 35 articles, essays, and speeches written by Galeano, coupled with conversations with Pelé, **Juan Perón,** and **Che Guevara.** This collection resumes where the chronology of *Memoria del fuego* ends, providing a historical account of the years from 1961 to the early 1990s and featuring Galeano's trademark blunt opinions on a wide range of subjects, including his myriad criticisms of U.S. meddling in Latin American affairs. The reviewer for *Library Journal* asserted that *Nosotros decimos no* "brings to an American audience forceful, serious journalism about the current fate of Latin America."

This work was followed by *El libro de los abrazos* (*The Book of Embraces*), first published in 1989 and translated into English in 1991. Considered by critics to be a much more personal work that most of Galeano's previous efforts, *The Book of Embraces* contains a broad mixture of political commentary, social philosophy, autobiographical reminiscences, and even some of Galeano's drawings. Commenting on the author's moving depiction of people and events in this work, Parini declared that "Mr. Galeano has confected an ingenious blend of image and text that moves from autobiographical vignettes to philosophical musings, from reporting to storytelling."

## SELECTED PUBLISHED WORKS:

*Los días siguientes*, Alfa, 1962.
*China 1964: Crónica de un desafío*, Jorge Alvarez, 1964.
*Los fantasmas del día del léon, y otros relatos*, Arca, 1967.
*Guatemala: Clave de Latinoamérica*, Ediciones de la Banda Oriental, 1967; translated by Cedric Belfrage as *Guatemala: Occupied Country*, Monthly Review Press, 1969.
*Reportajes: Tierras de Latinoamérica, otros puntos cardinales, y algo más*, Ediciones Tauro, 1967.
*Siete imágenes de Bolivia*, Fondo Editorial Salvador de la Plaza, 1971.
*Las venas abiertas de América Latina*, Universidad Nacional de la República, 1971; 2nd edition, 1972, translated by Cedric Belfrage as *The Open Veins of Latin America: Five Centuries of the Pillage of a Continent*, Monthly Review Press, 1973.
*Crónicas latinoaméricanas*, Editorial Girón, 1972.
*Vagamundo*, Ediciones de Crisis, 1973.
*La canción de nosotros*, Editorial Sudamericana, 1975.
*Días y noches de amor y de guerra*, Editorial Laia, 1978; translated by Judith Brister as *Days and Nights of Love and War*, Monthly Review Press, 1983.
*Los nacimientos*, Siglo XXI, 1982; translated by Cedric Belfrage as *Memory of Fire: Genesis*, Pantheon, 1985.
*La piedra arde*, Lóguez Ediciones, 1983.
*Las caras y las máscaras*, Siglo XXI, 1984; translated by Cedric Belfrage as *Memory of Fire: Faces and Masks*, Pantheon, 1987.
*Contraseña*, Ediciones del Sol, 1985.

*El siglo del viento,* Siglo XXI, 1986; translated by Cedric Belfrage as *Memory of Fire: Century of the Wind,* Pantheon, 1988.

*Aventuras de los jóvenes dioses,* Kapelusz, 1986.

*El libro de los abrazos,* Siglo XXI, 1989; translated by Cedric Belfrage with Mark Schafer as *The Book of Embraces,* Norton, 1991.

*Nosotros decimos no: Crónicas (1963–1988),* Siglo XXI, 1989; translated by Mark Fried and others as *We Say No: Chronicles 1963–1991,* Norton, 1992.

## SOURCES:

### Books

*Hispanic Writers,* edited by Bryan Ryan, Detroit, Gale, 1991.

### Periodicals

*Américas,* 44, No. 5, 1992, pp. 16–21.
*Harper's Magazine,* February 1990, pp. 19–23.
*Library Journal,* May 15, 1992, p. 105.
*New York Times,* April 21, 1991, Section 7, p. 14.
*Publishers Weekly,* July 13, 1990, p. 30; February 1, 1991, p. 76; March 8, 1991, p. 59; June 8, 1992, p. 45.
*Town & Country,* May, 1992, pp. 105–134.
*Washington Post Book World,* July 7, 1991, p. 7.

—*Sketch by Catherine A. Clay*

# Rómulo Gallegos
## 1884-1969
### Venezuelan novelist and politician

Rómulo Gallegos was the most celebrated Venezuelan literary figure of his generation—a *Times Literary Supplement* critic deemed him "one of the great masters of the Spanish tongue." Gallegos's *Doña Bárbara,* published in 1929, remains a classic in Latin American literature. As an intellectual Gallegos was a leading proponent of spiritual, social, and political freedom, and racial integration. In the political field, Gallegos distinguished himself by serving as the first democratically elected president of Venezuela.

Rómulo Ángel del Monte Carmelo Gallegos Freire was born in Caracas on August 2, 1884, to

*Rómulo Gallegos*

Rómulo Gallegos Osíe and Rita Freire Guruceaga. He was educated at the Seminario Metropolitano from the age of ten until his mother's death in March 1896. His father then sent him to the Colegio Sucre, where he published his first article, "Una hoja periodística de vida bravísima," in the school magazine. He graduated in 1902 and then began law studies at Caracas's Central University. In 1903 he co-founded El Arco Iris, with his friend S. F. Bermúdez; there they published articles on literature, politics, and entertainment. Gallegos withdrew from his legal training in 1905.

In November of 1905, Gallegos started working for the railroad system, while simultaneously continuing his literary pursuits. In 1909 he helped create the literary review *La Alborada,* which sponsored debates on themes of social protest; Gallegos contributed numerous essays on educational issues. Censorship pressures led to the magazine's termination and the subsequent strengthening of Gallegos's social conscience. He continued writing for the famed journal *El Cojo Ilustrado* until its collapse in 1915.

In 1912 Gallegos embarked on a teaching career, becoming the director of the Colegio Federal de Varones of Barcelona (Venezuela). His influence in the academic arena was immense. Not only was he a fervent advocate of education and modernization, but several of his pupils later became civilian leaders. He soon transferred to Caracas, where he assumed the assistant directorship of the Liceo de Caracas. On

April 15, 1912, he married Teotiste Arocha, with whom he had two children: Alexis and Sonia.

The year 1913 witnessed the publication of Gallegos's first book, *Los Aventureros,* a collection of short stories. His debut novel, *Reinaldo Solar* (also known as *El último Solar*), was published in 1920; it portrays the intellectual world of Gallegos's youth, while an underlying theme criticizes Venezuelan corruption. From 1922 to 1930 he served as director and professor of philosophy at the Liceo Andrés Bello. Gallegos's second novel, *La trepadora,* was published in 1925. It adopts a political and moral stance and urges social and racial integration, important threads in most of his novels.

Gallegos's ensuing novel, *Doña Bárbara,* is often considered his masterpiece. Set in the vast domain of the Venezuelan plains, it tells the epic story of Doña Bárbara—a symbol of barbarianism—and her conflicts with neighboring rancher Santos Luzardo, who symbolizes civilization. In *The Spanish American Novel: A Twentieth Century Survey,* John Brushwood hailed *Doña Bárbara* as "a standard reference point in Latin American literature." *Doña Bárbara* was critically acclaimed; Gallegos was honored by the Asociación del Mejor Libro del Mes in Madrid, Spain. Venezuela's incumbent dictator, Juan Vincente Gómez, felt threatened by the novel's reformist content; he sought to suppress Gallegos' ideology by nominating him Senator for the El Apure region. Unable to condone the Gomez regime, Gallegos never attended a Senate session. In 1931, he went into voluntary exile. Gallegos spent the following five years in Spain and the United States, where he wrote and published *Cantaclaro* and *Canaima,* both highly praised novels that draw on the Venezuelan landscape and people for their inspiration.

After Gomez's death in 1935 Gallegos returned to Venezuela and became increasingly active in politics. In 1936 he was named the minister of education under President Eleazar López Contreras, but resigned after six weeks due to opposition against his reforms. He participated in Organización Venezolana, the core of which later became Acción Democrática. In 1937 he was elected to the Congress of Deputies where he was the main opposition spokesman to the López Contreras government. That same year he published *Pobre negro,* the story of black rebel Pedro Miguel Candelas. Here Gallegos portrayed slavery and the fight of the mulattoes. In 1939 Gallegos was elected to the Council of Naiguate. By 1942 he was a presidential candidate.

Gallegos was elected President of Venezuela in 1947. He became Venezuela's first democratically elected leader after taking the oath of office on February 15, 1948. His presidency was short-lived; in November 1948 he was deposed by a right-wing coup. After a brief period of imprisonment he was exiled with his family, spending time in Cuba, the United States, Mexico, and France. Gallegos returned to Caracas in 1958, following the overthrow of Marcos Pérez Jiménez. He assumed the role of a senior statesman. Gallegos received innumerable honors. He was granted an honorary doctorate from Columbia University in 1948—he later relinquished it because he did not wish to hold the same honor granted to Guatemalan dictator Colonel Castillo Armas. From Venezuela he was awarded the National Literature Prize and was proclaimed Illustrious Son of Caracas. In 1960 Gallegos was nominated for the Nobel Prize in literature. He also served as chairman of the Inter-American Commission of Human Rights. Gallegos died in Caracas on April 4, 1969.

## SELECTED PUBLISHED WORKS:

### Novels

*El último Solar,* originally published in 1920, published as *Reinaldo Solar* (Venezuela), 1930.

*La trepadora,* Caracas, Venezuela, Tipografía Mercantil, 1925.

*Doña Bárbara, Araluce,* Araluce, 1929; translation by Robert Malloy, J. Cape and H. Smith, 1931.

*Cantaclaro,* Araluce, 1934, reprinted, Madrid, Espasa-Calpe, 1982.

*Canaima,* Araluce, 1935; translated with notes by Jaime Tello, Venezuela, Caracas, North American Association of 1984.

*Pobre negro,* Caracas, Elite, 1937.

*El forastero,* Elite, 1942; published as *La primera versión de El forastero,* Caracas, Equinoccio, 1980.

*Sobre la misma tieura,* Elite, 1943, reprinted, Espasa-Calpe, 1981.

*La brizna de paja en el viento,* Havana, Selecta, 1952.

### Other

*Los aventureros* (stories), 1913.

*El milagro del año* (play), first produced c. 1914.

*Programa político y discursos del candidato popular, Rómulo Gallegos,* Elite, 1941, reprinted, Comisión Centenario del Natalicio de Rómulo Gallegos, 1985.

*La rebelión, y otros quentos* (stories), Caracas, del Maestro, 1946, reprinted, Espasa-Calpe, 1981.

*Obras completas* (complete works), Havana, Lex, 1949.

*Una posición en la vida,* Mexico, Humanismo, 1954.

*La doncella (drama) y El último patriota (cuentos)* (play and stories), Mexico, Montobar, 1957.

*Obras selectas* (selected works), Madrid, EDIME, 1959.

*Sus mejores cuentos* (stories), Organización Continental de los Festivales del Libro, c. 1959.

*Antología de Rómulo Gallegos,* edited with introduction by Pedro Díaz Seijas, Mexico, B. Costa-Amic, 1966.

*Centos venezplanos* (stories), Buenos Aires, Espasa-Canley Kramealpe Argentina, 1966.

*Tierra bajo los pies,* Alianza, 1971.

*Cuentos* (stories), Havana, Arte y Literatura, 1973.

*Vida y literatura,* Embajada de Venezuela, 1977.

*Cuentos completos* (complete stories), Caracas, Monte Avila, 1981.

*Apreciación de Andrés Eloy Blanco: Con apédice de textos del poeta,* Los Teques, Venezuela, Gobierno del Estado Miranda, 1985.

*Rómulo Gallegos, la "segura immortalidad,"* Caracas, Centauro, 1985.

*Pensamiento y acción política de Rómulo Gallegos,* introduction by Marco Tulio Bruni Celli, [Caracas], c. 1985.

*Rómulo Gallegos, multivisión,* Ediciones de la Presidencia de la República, Comisión Ejecutiva Nacional para la Celebración del Centenario del Natalicio de Rómulo Gallegos, 1986.

## SOURCES:

### Books

*Biographical Dictionary of Latin American and Caribbean Political Leaders,* edited by Robert J. Alexander, Westport, Connecticut, Greenwood Press, 1988.

Brushwood, John S., *The Spanish American Novel: A Twentieth Century Survey,* Austin and London, University of Texas Press, 1975.

Flores, Angel, *Spanish American Authors: The Twentieth Century,* New York, H. W. Wilson Company, 1992.

Franco, Jean, *A Literary History of Spain: Spanish Literature since Independence,* London and New York, Ernest Benn, 1973.

*Hispanic Writers: A Selection of Sketches from Contemporary Authors,* edited by Bryan Ryan, Detroit, Gale Research, 1991.

*Latin American Writers,* Volume 2, edited by Carlos A. Sole, New York, Scribners, 1989.

### Periodicals

*Times Literary Supplement,* February 10, 1961, p. 88.

—*Sketch by Amanda Beresford*

# Griselda Gambaro
## 1928-
**Argentine playwright, novelist, and short story writer**

Griselda Gambaro grew up as a member of a poor, working-class family in Buenos Aires, Argentina, and went on to become a world-renowned dramatist and author. She was born on July 28, 1928, to a sailor and a postal employee. Her parents were first-generation Argentines and her grandparents were of Italian descent. Gambaro learned about theater, drama, and literature on her own, without the benefit of extensive schooling.

In *Interviews with Contemporary Women Playwrights,* Gambaro recalled her early love of books: "There were no books [in our family]. I am the youngest of five, and have four brothers. There weren't any books because there were family needs that were more primary." When asked how, in growing up without books, she discovered literature and her desire to write, Gambaro answered, "I always had a deep love of the written word, even in early childhood. Once I started going to school, I discovered the public library in my barrio. Then I learned a lot by chance. I didn't see much theater, but I read plays by O'Neill, Chekhov, Pirandello." Evelyn Garfield, author of *Women's Voices from Latin America,* asked her how she developed her affinity for writing plays. "I simply have a dramatic intuition. You see, I completed five years of secondary education ['el bachillerato'] and then worked for two years for a publisher and later in business and accounting until I got married and my husband emancipated me."

Her first forays into writing were not successful. "When I was twenty-four I published a book of stories that I don't want to remember," she explained in *Interviews* in 1984. "It was so immature, so full of the sort of imperfections that mar many first books. And then when I was thirty-four, I published again, three short novels collected in one volume entitled *Madrigal en Ciudad.* This manuscript won a prize, El Fondo National de las Artes, which consisted of publication, in 1964. The prize I won for this book enabled me to enter the theater easily, comfortably."

Garfield commented that Gambaro's work often focused on interpersonal relationships. "The image of mankind prevails in its more grotesque dimensions. Individual relationships and situations among friends, family, and acquaintances, as well as those that involve paternalistic societal and state institutions, reflect vividly and unabashedly man's inhumanity towards his fellow man. Under the guise of protectionism, the oppressor's insidious authoritarianism relies on the oppressed's passivity in order to isolate him and deprive him of his identity and liberty. For the most part, Gambaro's characters are either victimizers or the victimized."

## Gambaro's Study of Passivity

Passivity is the central theme of Gambaro's early works; the writer acknowledges that she herself has struggled with its unhealthy aspects. "One often has a single theme, and I probably have mine, the problem of passivity. It must be due to personal reasons; I am a very cowardly woman," she admitted to Garfield. "Very cowardly in every way. I'm not brave; I find it difficult to be brave. I am very preoccupied with passivity and the non-assumption of individual responsibility. In society it is that way and, also, in my plays. Perhaps I have altered that view somewhat now. It is less bitter only on the human level but not on the political one, or the social one." But while Gambaro's self-examination was a critical one, some critics and readers have found her work to be incisive and perceptive examinations of the search for dignity in an often forbidding world.

In 1964 Gambaro published *El desatino,* a collection of short stories that won the Emecé Publishers Prize for that year and garnered the attention of literary critics. During the 1960s Gambaro also wrote four plays that brought her international recognition: *Las paredes, Los siameses, El campo,* and *El desatino* —a play based on the title story of her short story collection. These plays examined normal interpersonal relationships—often featuring family members— that warp into relationships between tormentor and victim. Garbaro's plays broke with the constraints of realistic drama in several respects: they were not clearly set in a time or a place and the action that took place was often illogical and frightening. In *Las paredes,* for example, an unnamed Youth is held in a room for questioning by an Official and a Custodian. He never learns why he is being held and his captors do not seem to care—their goal is to destroy his will through psychological torture. In the end, after his tormentors are gone and the door is left open, the Youth, his psyche badly damaged, is unable to leave the room.

The playwright was admired and praised by some commentators, but her work was also scorned by others. Gambaro's unique approach and troubling themes were compared disparagingly to the theaters of cruelty or absurdity. Some critics suggested that her work was unrealistic, un-Argentine, or irrelevant to Argentine struggles. "I have remained rather isolated, even in Argentina," Gambaro told Garfield. "When my theater emerged in the midst of the Realistic School, I was attacked for my view of reality. Around 1965, I was opposed to the traditional 'realism' in drama and still believe that each of us has his own

voice. . . . But the public has trouble accepting me. I'm not a popular author, although, strangely enough, Argentina is a country steeped in the grotesque, in grotesque theater."

In the 1970s, as the Argentine government became more dictatorial, the playwright's work became a visible expression of her social concern. Her play *Información para extranjeros* was an experimental one that depended on dividing the audience into small groups and leading them through various rooms and hallways where scenes of torture and terrorism were played out. A novel, *Ganarse la muerte* appeared around the same time and captured the stark life of an Argentine woman. The dictatorship in power took notice of her work. "There were raids, the army paid us 'visits' during which they looked at all the material in the house," Gambaro recalled in *Interviews.* "As any material was considered subversive—Marx, Freud—a big burning of books resulted. Everyone who owned books burned them." Fearful of the Argentine government, the playwright destroyed the manuscript for her experimental play *Información para extranjeros* and was only able to reconstruct it years later because it had been published in Italy.

In 1977, when the government banned *Ganarse la muerte,* Gambaro, her husband, and two daughters became voluntary exiles in Europe, where they lived for three years. The move to Europe expanded her feminine consciousness. "I wrote that banned novel, *Ganarse La Muerte.* The main character was a woman," she told Betsko and Koenig in *Interviews.* I didn't think she reflected the state of women; I thought she reflected Argentina. But the novel was published in France . . . and they invited me to France. I had the opportunity to meet the feminists of France, and I began reading about the specific problems related to women. I started to realize things which, before that time, I had only felt in an instinctive way."

Gambaro's next novel, a metaphor for herself in exile, also featured a woman as the main character. *Dios no nos quiere contentos* related the experiences of a trapeze artist named the Ecuyére, who is repeatedly abused and abandoned by the circus where she works. Yet she seeks out the circus over and over to keep performing. David Foster commented in a 1980 review for *World Literature Today* that "the texture of Gambaro's narrative is ostensibly chaotic, trivializing and absurd. Not only are there inexplicable jumps and parentheses, but the omniscient narrator speaks a jumble of disingenuous folk sayings. . . . The result is a novel that is exceedingly difficult to read." Foster goes on, however, to admit that the novel is also a "truly original work of fiction."

## After Exile

In the early 1980s, the dictatorship lost power in Argentina and Gambaro and her family returned home. After the Falklands War, the government collapsed and democracy returned. The affect on the Argentine artist community was marked. "The difference is the lack of terror," Gambaro said in *Interviews.* "We lived not only with terror, but with censorship and fear. It was a time of extreme risk, where the game was to survive—nothing else. And now, well, one feels that one can talk, that one can communicate with others." Recipient of a Guggenheim fellowship in 1982, Gambaro was able, for the first time in her career, to make a living as an author and playwright.

*Theater Journal* observed in 1992 that while Gambaro's work was "widely known and respected throughout Latin America for her powerful and innovative dramaturgy, translated and produced in Europe and Scandinavia," it has registered on the consciousness of the American drama community only gradually. In the early 1990s, however, American performances of Gambaro's plays became more frequent.

Gambaro's *Penas sin importancia,* which was completed in the early 1990s, was different from her previous dramas. Adam Versényi reported in *Theater Review* that the play marked a significant change in thematic tone for Gambaro. "Rather than the political implications of state power, [the play] concentrates upon personal emotions. This is the softest, gentlest play that Gambaro has written. . . . In *Penas sin importancia* we see an accomplished playwright experimenting with new forms . . . like Argentina itself, Gambaro seems to be in transition. Since the fall of the military junta and the return to democracy the Argentinian context altered substantially, and in the midst of her nation's current economic and political crisis, Griselda Gambaro's dramaturgy is also changing. I expect that she will astonish us once again."

## SELECTED PUBLISHED WORKS:

*Cuentos* (short stories), Américalee, 1953.
*Madrigal en ciudad* (short stories), Goyanate, 1963.
*El desatino* (short stories; title means "The Blunder"), Emecé, 1965.
*El desatino* (two-act play; based on her short story of the same title), Centro de Experimentación Audiovisual del Instituto Torcuatro Di Tella, 1965.
*El campo* (two-act play), Insurrexit, 1967, translation by William I. Oliver published as *The Camp* in *Voices of Change in the Spanish American Theater,* University of Texas Press, 1971.
*Un felicidad con menos pena* (novel; title means "Happiness With Less Sorrow"), Sudamericana, 1968.

*Nada que ver con otra historia* (novel; title means "Nothing to Do With Another Story"), Noé, 1972.
*La cola mágica* (children's stories), De La Flor, 1975.
*Ganarse la muerte* (novel; title means "To Earn Death"), De la Flor, 1976.
*Conversaciones con chicos: Sobre la sociedad, los padres, los afectos, la cultura*(nonfiction), Timerman, 1977,
*Dios no nos quiere contentos* (novel; title means "God Does Not Want Us to Be Happy"), Lumen, 1979.
*Teatro: Las paredes* [and] *El desatino* [and] *Los siameses* (plays) Argonauta, 1979.
*Lo impenetrable,* Torres Agüero, 1984.
*Teatro* (plays; contains "Real envido," "La malasangre," "Del sol naciente," "Dar la vuelta," "Información para extranjeros," "Puesta en claro," "Sucede lo que pasa," "Viaje de invierno," Sólo un aspecto," "La gracia," "El miedo," "Decir sí," "Antígona furiosa," and several others), three volumes, De la Flor, 1984–89.
*The Impenetrable Madam X,* translation by Evelyn P. Garfield published in Latin American Literature & Culture Series, Wayne State University Press, 1991.

## SOURCES:

### Books

Betsko, Kathleen, and Rachel Koenig, *Interviews with Contemporary Women Playwrights,* New York, Beech Tree Books, 1987, pp. 184–99.
Garfield, Evelyn Picon, *Women's Voices from Latin America,* Detroit, Wayne State University Press, pp. 55–71.
*Hispanic Writers,* edited by Bryan Ryan, Detroit, Gale, pp. 202–05.

### Periodicals

*Theater Journal,* January 1992, pp. 519–21.
*World Literature Today,* Summer 1980, pp. 407–08.

—*Sketch by Kathe A. Conti*

# Andy Garcia
## 1956-
### Cuban American actor and director

*Andy Garcia*

Andy Garcia has established himself as one of Hollywood's leading actors. He has starred in a number of popular films in the late 1980s and 1990s, including *The Untouchables* (1987), *Stand and Deliver* (1988), *The Godfather, Part 3* (1990), *Internal Affairs* (1990), and *Jennifer 8* (1992). Garcia has lived in the U.S. since he was a child, but his choice of film projects in the mid-1990s is indicative of his strong interest in his Latin American roots. He has signed on to serve as producer of a documentary on Cuban mambo artist Israel (Cachao) Lopez, and he is slated to star as the early twentieth-century Spanish poet **Federico García Lorca** in a film biography.

Garcia was born in 1956 in Havana, Cuba, where his father was a lawyer and land owner. He also operated a successful produce business. Two years after Garcia was born, Cuba became embroiled in revolution, and in January 1959 **Fidel Castro** assumed power in that country. Garcia's father lost his property as a result of Castro's confiscation of land from private owners. In 1961 the U.S. government backed an invasion of Cuba by anti-Castro forces. That invasion effort failed and caused many Cuban residents to flee to Spain or the U.S. for safety. In the midst of this political turmoil, when Garcia was five years old, he and his family moved to Miami, Florida. In an interview with Jaime Diamond in *The New York Times,* Garcia remarked that "[we] were not immigrants. We were in political exile in Miami."

Once in Miami, Garcia was suddenly forced to learn the English language. The actor noted in his interview with Diamond that "[when] you struggle with a foreign language, you're surrounded by people who don't know what you're saying, and you don't know what they're saying. So you are in isolation. That probably has a definite impact on your point of view." He attended high school in Miami, where he played basketball for a time. After contracting mononucleosis, which he believed dulled his athletic edge, he discovered acting. He went on to study acting at Florida International University and performed in regional theater productions until 1978.

### Moved To Hollywood

Like many other struggling actors who dream of stardom, Garcia was attracted to Hollywood, the hub of the movie industry. In 1978 he moved to what he referred to in Diamond's interview as "a hooker community" in Hollywood. He worked as a waiter to earn a living while he auditioned for parts. In 1980 he secured a role with an improvisational group at the Comedy Store in Los Angeles. It was there that a casting agent for the television series *Hill Street Blues* spotted him. That discovery enabled him to land a role as a gang member in the pilot episode of the show in 1981. That same year, Garcia married Maria Victoria, a Cuban American, with whom he has had three children.

In 1983 Garcia made his film debut in *Blue Skies Again,* a movie about baseball. That was followed in 1984 with *The Mean Season,* while in 1985 Garcia appeared in *Eight Million Ways To Die.* His big break came in 1987 when he landed a significant role in the blockbuster film *The Untouchables,* which starred Kevin Costner. Garcia, who played a cop turned government agent in the film, received his first critical acclaim for acting. The next year, he appeared in *Blood Money: The Story of Clinton and Nadine,* an original Home Box Office telefilm. He also appeared in *American Roulette,* a spy thriller, and *Stand and Deliver.*

### Breaking the Stereotype

Critics have long charged that Hollywood films often place Hispanic Americans into stereotypical roles. According to the National Hispanic Media Coalition Chairwoman Esther Renteria in The *Washington Post:* "We represent one character out of every fifty roles on television. And the roles tend to typecast Latinos as gang members, drug addicts, drug pushers, maids, gardeners and long-suffering mamas. We are two times more likely to be a stereotype than a white character, and three times more likely than a black." Breaking through this stereotype, *Stand and Deliver* was one of the first Hispanic-controlled films to achieve success in the American mainstream, The film, which starred **Edward James Olmos**, told the true story of **Jaime Escalante**, a Bolivian mathematics teacher living in Los Angeles who helped Chicano high school students learn calculus. Hispanics not only appeared in the film, but also controlled the script writing, directing and financing for the film, a unique state of affairs for Hollywood. Garcia's role in the film, while a relatively small one, was his first in a film that explored the cultural identity and struggles of people of his heritage.

In 1989 Garcia made two more films, *The Sixth Family* and *Black Rain,* in which he co-starred with Michael Douglas. In 1990 Garcia's portrayal of Vincent Mancini in *The Godfather, Part 3* garnered him widespread critical appreciation and recognition. He received an Academy Award nomination for Best Supporting Actor, as well as a Golden Globe Best Supporting Actor nomination and the Nosotros Best Actor Award. That same year, Garcia co-wrote the script for and appeared in *Internal Affairs* opposite Richard Gere. The National Association of Theater Owners, in recognition of his roles in those two 1990 films, awarded him their Star of the Year prize. He also was awarded the Harvard University Foundation Award for his outstanding contributions to American performing arts and intercultural relations.

### Established as Star

Garcia's handsome physical appearance has garnered many comments from interviewers and critics alike. Diamond noted in The *New York Times* that "with his magnetic eyes and his high-voltage smile, Mr. Garcia belongs to that group of men women swoon over. Even his face, with its prominent widow's peak, is a valentine." David Quinlan, writing in *Quinlan's Illustrated Registry of Film Stars,* described the actor as "dark, low-browed, large-eyed, smooth . . . His face can look honest or untrustworthy at the lowering of a lid or opening of an eye." But it is not just Garcia's looks that makes him appealing to directors. He has been described as intellectually bright and quick to display a sophisticated sense of humor.

Throughout the 1990s, Garcia has solidified his reputation as one of America's leading actors. In 1992 he co-starred with Dustin Hoffman and Geena Davis in *Hero.* He also appeared in *Jennifer 8* as a policeman who protects a blind witness. It was in that film that Garcia achieved leading man status and, as Diamond wrote, "his name appears for the first time above the title—Hollywood semiotics for 'He's No

Longer a Second Banana.'" In 1994 Garcia starred with Meg Ryan in the drama *When a Man Loves a Woman* and made his directorial debut with the film *Cachao . . . Como Su Ritmo No Hay Dos* (*Cachao . . . Like His Rhythm There Is No Other* ). The movie, a documentary about Israel "Cachao" Lopez, a Cuban composer of the mambo and bass player, received high praise from critics worldwide. Garcia also produced an album based on that film that was nominated for a Grammy award.

## SELECTED VIDEOGRAPHY:

*Blue Skies Again,* 1983.
*A Night in Heaven,* 1983.
*Eight Million Ways to Die,* 1985.
*Mean Season,* 1985.
*The Untouchables,* 1987.
*American Roulette,* 1988.
*Blood Money: The Story of Clinton and Nadine,* 1988.
*Stand and Deliver,* 1988.
*Black Rain,* 1989.
*The Godfather, Part 3,* 1990.
*Internal Affairs,* 1990.
*A Show of Force,* 1990.
*Dead Again,* 1991.
*Hero,* 1992.
*Jennifer 8,* 1992.
*When a Man Loves a Woman,* 1994.
*Cachao . . . Como Su Ritmo No Hay Dos,* 1994.

## SOURCES:

### Books

*The Hispanic-American Almanac,* edited by Nicolás Kanellos, Detroit, Gale, 1993, pp. 543–94.
Quinlan, David, *Quinlan's Illustrated Registry Of Film Stars,* New York, Henry Holt, 1991, p. 178.

### Periodicals

*New York Times,* November 22, 1992, section 2, p. 13.
*Washington Post,* January 4, 1991, p. D6; August 23, 1991, p. C7; September 1, 1991, p. G1.

*—Sketch by Catherine A. Clay*

# Frances Garcia
## 1938-
### Mexican American politician

Frances Josephine Garcia still remembers the racial discrimination her family experienced when she was a child. They were not allowed to eat in certain restaurants, and when they went to the movies, they had to sit in the balcony. These immigrants from Mexico were not even able to enjoy malteds inside the drug store—they were expected to drink them outside. "Times," however, "are changing," said Garcia during an interview with Ronie-Richele Garcia-Johnson. Garcia, who has served two terms as the mayor of Hutchinson, Kansas, has been a part of this change. Hutchinson's population of 41,000 people is just 2 percent Hispanic—clearly, her political success has had more to do with her confidence, her qualifications, and her dedication to her community than with her ethnicity.

Frances Garcia's parents were born in Mexico; seeking better lives, their families immigrated to the United States and settled in Hutchinson, Kansas. While neither Garcia's mother or father graduated from high school, they were hard workers and believed in education. Her father, Joe G. Calvillo, who found a job in manufacturing during the war, became a naturalized citizen and educated himself. He was a voracious reader, and he loved math. He told his daughter, who was born on June 4, 1938, in Hutchinson, "You can do anything you want to with hard work and common sense," but advised her to "never expect anything to be given to you."

Garcia's mother, Micaela (Chavez) Calvillo, who was raised to be a good wife and mother, understood the value of education as well as the meaning of community. As Garcia recalled in the *Hutchinson News,* her mother continually assisted those who came from the nearby train tracks. "My mother was always feeding someone who got off the train.... [She] would always sit them down on the porch and give them a meal." Micaela Calvillo did not hesitate to invite travelers in for Thanksgiving dinner. While Micky instilled her daughter with the traditional values she had learned from her own mother, she earned her United States citizenship and encouraged Garcia to seek education and a good life.

After Garcia graduated from Hutchinson High School in 1956, she attended a junior college near her home. Garcia could not decide whether she wanted to study business or become a teacher (she had received a Business Certificate from Salt City Business College in 1954), so she earned an Associate bachelor's degree in liberal arts from Hutchinson Community College

in 1958. During this time in school, she dated the man who was to become her husband, John T. Garcia. The couple were married on August 27, 1960. Today, they have two sons, John Jr. and Geoffrey.

While her husband worked as a farm machine operator, Garcia stayed at home to raise her children. In 1966 she went to work at the Wells Department Store Credit Office as a credit officer. By 1968, she had left that job to become a clerk/typist at the Reno County Clerk's Office. Then, in 1972, Garcia became a savings consultant and Loan Secretary. She earned a Savings and Loan Training for Savings Consultant certificate the next year. Garcia worked as a consultant until 1981, when she suffered back problems which necessitated surgery. In 1983, she became a volunteer outreach worker and interpreter with the Hutchinson Methodist Ministry; she served in this position until 1990.

### Launches Political Career

It was not until the mid-1980s that Garcia, who had two grandchildren by that time, became seriously involved in Hutchinson politics. A friend of hers, Tony Flores, encouraged her to run for one of the three seats available on the city council. According to Garcia, she thought she might "give it a try." Her family was generally supportive of her decision to run for the council. During an interview with Garcia-Johnson, Garcia laughed when she recalled the advice of her youngest son. When he asked her, "Mother, do you know that your life will never be your own?" she knew he was right, but she also knew that the question was motivated from his own self-interest as well. Her sons, who had been blessed with a wonderfully caring mother, were beginning to realize that they would have to share her with the entire town if she won the election. That, however, was fine with Garcia. She knew that she had some valuable contributions to make to her community.

When Garcia first made the commitment to run for city council, she did not know how to run a campaign. Harkening back to her father's advice about "hard work and common sense," she utilized both. It made sense to her to reach out to the people of Hutchinson, and the best way to do that was to walk the streets of the town, going door to door and introducing herself. It was a lot of work, but Garcia was determined to allow voters to get to know her before election day. She explained in *Vista,* "I worked hard and I didn't promise anything except to try to do a good job and create a good, healthy living environment for Hutchinson."

Garcia's father was correct—she could do anything with hard work and common sense. In the interview with Garcia-Johnson, Garcia spoke of the moment when she was told just how effective her door-to-door canvassing tactic had been. "Mrs. Garcia," began the official who had called her to his office, "Has the newspaper contacted you?" Garcia shook her head, "No." "Well," continued the official, "you better have a seat. You are the top vote getter—you could be the next mayor." Garcia, who had been unknown before her campaign, was one of six candidates and had not expected to do very well in this first election. The news that she might very well become mayor of her home town left her shocked. Her supporters and her family were elated.

Garcia was featured in the *Hutchinson News* on that Tuesday, March 26, 1985, when she was named the top vote getter. The newspaper explained why the elected council person with the most votes would probably become the mayor: "Traditionally commissioners choose the top vote-getter as mayor, although it is not mandatory. . . ." Garcia's stands on campaign issues were also emphasized in the newspaper. She was concerned about employment, commerce, crime, and the city's growth, and she insisted that she could be a fair representative in Hutchinson. "Comments from people tell me the city as a whole is not being represented. I think I can represent all the people. People need to know you're there ready to listen any time." Garcia also mentioned the Hispanics in the community who made up just two percent of the population. "Maybe they (Hispanics) could relate a little better to the commission if I were elected."

**Wins Mayoral Race**

Garcia was still surprised when she won a spot on the city council and the mayor's seat. When she took office in April, 1985, she became the first Hispanic woman mayor in the Midwest. Hispanics throughout the country were proud of Garcia. Her parents felt honored. Her husband and sons were thrilled. Garcia continued to earn the praise of those who knew her as she began to work.

Garcia served as Hutchinson's mayor from April 1985 to April 1986 and continued as a city commissioner for the next three years. At the Midwest Voter's Registration Conference in 1987, she presented a workshop on "Women's Involvement." She also spoke during the Topeka, Kansas Hispanic Heritage Week held in 1985. Garcia told Garcia-Johnson that, as mayor, she enjoyed working with the people of Hutchinson, her fellow commissioners, and the town's chamber of commerce.

In 1988, Garcia decided to run for the Kansas Senate. Explaining this decision in a campaign leaflet, she wrote, "the issues regarding the quality of our education, and availability of health care services, our environment and our ability to help small businesses grow, are simply too critical to sit back and not at least try to make a difference." She emphasized the need for quality education, economic development, environmental protection, and accessible health care

in Kansas as she campaigned. Garcia's approach to the problems facing the state of Kansas was best summed up by a statement she wrote for this piece of campaign literature: "For our people to fulfill their capacities by their own hard work and determination, we must provide them with the best educational training and retraining opportunities possible. I believe the citizens of Kansas are ready for bold leadership in the areas of education, economic development, health care and environmental protection if it will lead to real progress." Once again, Garcia promised to give the average person the opportunity to voice her or his own concerns.

Despite the backing of Reno County and many supporters, Frances Garcia did not win the election. She did, however, win a good proportion of votes, especially considering that she ran against a well-known businessman who was seeking a second term as a state senator for the 34th Senatorial District. Garcia did win her bid for re-election to the city council. Once again, from April 1989 to April, 1990, she led the city as its mayor. In 1992, she was still a Hutchinson City Commissioner. Former City Manager George Pyle explained the reason for Garcia's success as a mayor and commissioner when he spoke to the *Hutchinson News* in mid-1990. "She listens, she sympathizes, she empathizes," he said of the leader. "I do remember how impressed I was with her ability to stand up in front of a group and communicate." Garcia herself confirmed her willingness to learn about and from the people of Hutchinson. "My phone is always open to anybody," she told the *News*.

While occupying a seat as a city commissioner is in itself a full-time commitment, Garcia serves her community in other ways. She has been a vice-president of the Kansas Art Commission as well as a member of such groups as the American Business Women Association, the Hutchinson Symphony Board, and the Committee for the National League of Cities. In the past, Garcia has been an active member of numerous community advisory boards and has also served as the president and vice president of the Kansas League of Municipalities—she is the second person from Hutchinson to have ever done so.

**Balances Career and Family**

As busy as she is, Garcia always finds time to spend with her family. Her husband is understanding and supportive of her work. While the couple often meet each other as they are coming and going through the door of their home, John occasionally travels with Frances to her various meetings in Kansas and throughout the United States. Frances Garcia also enjoys spending time with her parents, who have always encouraged her to excel, her sons, who have been as proudly supportive of her efforts as their father, and her six grandchildren.

Garcia has won many awards of recognition for her efforts. Among the most notable was that from the League of United Latin American Citizens, which awarded Garcia with a plaque and certificate of recognition at the 1985 1st Annual Mayors Ball held in Denver, Colorado. Garcia was also honored at LULAC's 1986 Women's Symposium. The Kansas Advisory on Hispanic Affairs presented her with a Certificate of Recognition in 1987, and the American GI Forum State Convention praised her with an Outstanding Award the next year. In 1989, she was awarded a certificate of recognition for her work with the Hutchinson Leadership Program. Finally, Garcia was chosen as one of 47 "outstanding" representatives of Kansas Hispanics and profiled in the book, *El Camino Real: The King's Highway,* by the Kansas Advisory Committee on Hispanic Affairs in 1990. According to the *Hutchinson News,* the book "chronicles the stories of Hispanic heroes who have led the way for others" and was to be distributed to schools and libraries throughout Kansas.

"Only in the United States," remarked Frances Garcia during her interview with Garcia-Johnson, "could the daughter of a migrant from Mexico be the mayor of the city." While the environment in which she was raised contributed to this Hispanic woman's political success, most of the credit for her accomplishments belongs to Garcia and her supportive family. "It has been an honor and a learning experience," the leader says of her time as mayor and city commissioner, "and I hope that I have opened the door for young people and especially women."

## SOURCES:

### Periodicals

*Hutchinson News,* March 26, 1985; July 22, 1990, p. 45, 48.
*Vista,* July 5, 1986.

### Other

Garcia, Frances, telephone interview with Ronie-Richele Garcia-Johnson, August, 1992.

—*Sketch by Ronie-Richele Garcia-Johnson*

# Jerry Garcia
## 1942-1995

**Spanish American guitarist, songwriter, and singer**

The rock and roll industry has seen its share of bands and singers. What is remarkable about the Grateful Dead in particular is that the band has been performing since the 1960s and its following is bigger and more visible than ever before. At the head of this long-lived group was singer and guitarist Jerry Garcia. The band has become a benchmark in music history. According to *Rolling Stone,* the Grateful Dead was ranked 29th among the 40 highest-paid entertainers in 1989, with an estimated annual income of $12.5 million. "[A]fter decades of touring with a consistency and success unmatched by any other band, the Grateful Dead have a relationship with the Deadheads—the fans who follow the band with a near-religious fervor—that is unique in the history of rock and roll," Fred Goodman wrote in *Rolling Stone* in 1989. "On the eve of the release of their 22nd album, *Built to Last,* the Grateful Dead stand as an American dynasty like no other."

Heading that dynasty, Garcia was as much a product as a shaper of his time. On August 1, 1942, in San Francisco, Jerome John Garcia was born to a family of music lovers. His father, Joe Garcia, was a ballroom jazz musician and bartender who came to California from Spain in the 1920s. His mother, Ruth Garcia, was a Swedish-Irish nurse whose family immigrated to San Francisco during the gold rush. In a 1991 interview with James Henke of *Rolling Stone,* Garcia talked about his father. "He played woodwinds, clarinet mainly. He was a jazz musician. He had a big band—like a 40-piece orchestra—in the 1930s. The whole deal, with strings, harpist, vocalist. I remember him playing me to sleep at night. I just barely remember the sound of it. But I'm named after Jerome Kern, that's how seriously the bug bit my father."

When he was just five years old, Garcia lost his father in an accident. "He was fishing in one of those rivers in California, like the American River," Garcia recalled in the interview with Henke. "We were on vacation, and I was there on the shore. I actually watched him go under. It was horrible. I was just a little kid, and I didn't really understand what was going on, but then, of course, my life changed. It was one of those things that afflicted my childhood. I had all my bad luck back then, when I was young and could deal with it." The other childhood trauma was the loss of a finger on his right hand. "[T]hat happened when I was five too. My brother Tiff and I were chopping wood. And I would pick up the pieces of wood, take my hand away, pick up another piece, and *boom!* It was an accident." The shock, however, came when the bandages were removed and young Garcia realized his finger was truly gone. "But after that, it was okay, because as a kid, if you have a few little things that make you different, it's a good score. So I got a lot of mileage out of having a missing finger when I was a kid."

After his father's death, he lived for a time with his grandparents and then returned to live with his mother, who took over her husband's bar. Located next to the Sailor's Union of the Pacific, the bar was frequented by sailors who traveled around the world. "They went out and sailed to the Far East and the Persian Gulf, the Philippines and all that, and they would come and hang out in the bar all day long and talk to me when I was a kid. It was great fun for me," he told Henke. One sailor, an old sea captain, he remembers distinctly: "he'd tell me these incredible stories. And that was one of the reasons I couldn't stay in school. School was a little too boring. And these guys also gave me a glimpse into a larger universe that seemed so attractive and fun, and you know, *crazy.*"

Ironically, Garcia's first foray into music was boring as well. He took piano lessons for eight years and hated them. "I took lessons on the piano *forever*—my mom made me," he said to Anthony DeCurtis of *Rolling Stone* in 1993. "None of it sank in. I never did learn how to sight-read for the piano—I bluffed my way through. I was attracted to music very early on, but it never occurred to me it was something to do—in the sense that when I grow up I'm going to be a musician." And then Garcia's older brother started tuning in to early rock and roll and rhythm and blues. "When I was 15, I fell madly in love with rock and roll. Chuck Berry was happening big, Elvis Presley—not so much Elvis Presley, but I really liked Gene Vincent, you know, the *other* rock guys, the guys that played guitar good: Eddie Cochran, Buddy Holly, Bo Diddley." At that time, the electric guitar was a new phenomenon and as soon as he heard it, Garcia was hooked. He asked his mother for one for his birthday and started on the road he still travels. "I was just beside myself with joy. I started banging away on it without having the slightest idea of *anything.* I didn't know how to tune it up. . . . I never took any lessons. I don't even think there was anybody teaching around the Bay area. I mean electric guitar was like from *Mars,* you know. You didn't *see* 'em even."

## The Birth of a Band

Lessons or no lessons, Garcia learned his way around the instrument and immersed himself in the radical music of the day. "Rock and roll wasn't cool, but I *loved* rock and roll," he explained to DeCurtis about his formative years. "I used to have these fantasies about 'I want rock and roll to be like *respectable* music.' I wanted it to be like *art. . . .* I wanted to do something that fit in with the art institute, that kind of self-conscious art—'art' as opposed to 'popular culture.'" Independent and strong-willed, Garcia took to spending time with a rowdy group of San Francisco teenagers. At 17, he joined the U.S. Army and was stationed in San Francisco. Garcia, with idle time on his hands, practiced acoustic guitar in the barracks, learned

songs over the radio by ear, and copied finger positions from books.

After nine months, he left the army and took to living in his car, playing music, and absorbing the "scene" of San Francisco in the early 1960s. At about that time, he went to the Art Institute in San Francisco to study painting. "I wasn't playing guitar so much—I'd picked up the five-string banjo in the army," he told Bill Barich of *New Yorker* in 1993. "I listened to records, slowed them down with a finger, and learned the tunings note by note. By then I was getting pretty serious about music—especially about bluegrass." He and a friend toured numerous bluegrass festivals in the Midwest and absorbed the unique sound of the music. Although he made a little money giving lessons, he often lived in his car in a vacant lot in East Palo Alto, California. He began to meet other young musicians, like folk guitarist Bob Weir and blues-harmonica player and organist Ron McKernan. They formed the Mother McCree's Uptown Jug Champions in 1964. Once the Beatles invaded the United States, Garcia's band reformed as an electric blues band, the Warlocks, in 1965.

At the same time, radical events were taking place in San Francisco. Ken Kesey, who was taking part in government-sponsored LSD tests, began throwing parties called the Acid Tests. It was at these energetic happenings that the Warlocks developed the sound that became known as psychedelic rock. "What the Acid Test really was was formlessness," Garcia explained to *Rolling Stone's* Goodman in 1989. "It's like the study of chaos. It may be that you have to destroy forms or ignore them in order to see other levels of organization. For me, that's what the Acid Test was—that's what it was a metaphor for. If you go into a situation with nothing planned, sometimes wonderful stuff happens. LSD was certainly an important part of that for me." Late in 1965 the band changed its name after Garcia picked "grateful dead" at random from a dictionary. Essentially ignoring the definition included, the band members chose to interpret the new phrase as signifying "cyclical change." In 1966 the band members moved into a house in San Francisco to live communally and performed at well-known music halls. In addition, the Grateful Dead also performed free concerts at Golden Gate Park to contrast the business attitudes that were beginning to pervade rock and roll and threaten their anarchist, hippie lifestyle.

Their first album, *The Grateful Dead,* was released by Warner Brothers in 1967. The band's early experience with a large studio corporation and extensive touring was not a happy one. "Their first four albums had not sold well, leaving them in debt to their label, Warner Brothers," Barich of *New Yorker* reported. "But they recouped with two straight hits in 1970, *Workingman's Dead,* and *American Beauty,* which were both primarily acoustic and were distinguished by the richness of the songs and the band's clean, crisp playing." The Grateful Dead used their success to leave the label, buy a small house, and begin handling their own business affairs. Barich continued, "In 1972, they tipped off their fans to their new free-form operation by inserting an apparently harmless message in the liner notes of a live album recorded on tour in Europe. 'DEAD FREAKS UNITE!' the message read. 'Who are you? Where are you? How are you? Send us your name and address and we'll keep you informed.' With one gesture, the Dead eliminated the barriers between themselves and their audience, and established a direct flow of communication." At last count, Barich noted, there were 90,000 Deadheads —as their fans are known— on the U.S. mailing list and 20,000 on the European one.

### The Golden Years

Members of the Grateful Dead, Garcia included, have survived the turbulent 1960s, the wrath of critics and fans alike—when albums and concerts did not hold up to expectations—drug abuse, the death of some band members, and several decades of changing musical tastes. Yet Garcia's band was still going strong in what he termed their "golden years," the 1990s.

Remarking on the appeal of the Grateful Dead to succeeding generations, Garcia commented to Henke in the 1991 *Rolling Stone* interview that "here we are, we're getting into our fifties, and where are these people who keep coming to our shows coming from? What do they find so fascinating about these middle-aged bastards playing basically the same thing we've always played? I mean, what do seventeen-year-olds find fascinating about this? I can't believe it's just because they're interested in picking up on the 1960s, which they missed. Come on, hey, the 1960s were fun, but shit, it's fun being young, you know; nobody really misses out on that. So what is it about the 1990s in America? There must be a dearth of fun out there in America. Or adventure. Maybe that's it, maybe we're just one of the last adventures in America."

When speaking with Barich of *New Yorker*, Garcia offered another angle from which to understand the band's success: "He thinks that the band affords its followers 'a tear in reality'—a brief vacation from the mundane," Barich wrote. "The Dead design their shows and their music to be ambiguous and open-ended ... they intend an evening to be both reactive and interactive. A Deadhead gets to join in on an experiment that may or may not be going anywhere in particular, and such an opportunity is rare in American life." In addition to the limitless possibilities of their music, the Grateful Dead also offer a spiritual release for both band members and fans. Garcia explained to Henke in 1991: "I thought

that maybe this idea of transforming principle has something to do with it. Because when we are on stage, what we really want . . . [is] to be transformed from ordinary players into extraordinary ones, like forces of a larger consciousness. And the audience wants to be transformed from whatever ordinary reality they may be in to something a little wider, something that enlarges them. So maybe it's that notion of transformation, a seat-of-the-pants shamanism, that is something to do with why the Grateful Dead keep pulling them in. Maybe that's what keeps the audience coming back and what keeps fascinating us, too."

Success has come at a price, however. In July 1986, Garcia went into a diabetic coma for a day. He has struggled with drugs, cigarettes, and weight problems as well. In the early 1990s, the guitarist had trimmed down and began following a better diet and healthier lifestyle. He branched into the clothing business with a line of ties based on his drawings— even though Garcia never wears a tie. When asked by Peter Watrous of *Musician* in 1981 what the point of music was, Garcia said: "You need music. I don't know why, it's probably one of those Joe Campbell questions, why we need ritual. We need magic, and bliss, and power, myth and celebration in our lives, and music is a good way to encapsulate a lot of it."

From the creative mind of a San Francisco child who hated school and homework grew one of the most influential bands in decades. Despite his abhorrence of school, Garcia was a scholarly man and perhaps that has been an intrinsic part of his appeal. "I owe a lot of who I am and what I've been and what I've done to the beatniks of the 1950s and to the poetry and art and music that I've come in contact with," he said to Henke in 1991. "I feel like I'm part of a continuous line of a certain thing in American culture, of a root."

### SELECTED DISCOGRAPHY

#### With the Grateful Dead

*Grateful Dead,* Warner, 1967.
*Anthem of the Sun,* Warner, 1968.
*Aoxomoxoa,* Warner, 1969.
*American Beauty,* Warner, 1970.
*Live Dead,* Warner, 1970.
*Workingman's Dead,* Warner, 1970.
*The Grateful Dead,* Warner, 1971.
*Europe '72,* Warner, 1972.
*Wake of the Flood,* Grateful Dead Records, 1973.
*From Mars Hotel,* Grateful Dead Records, 1974.
*Blues for Allah,* Grateful Dead Records, 1975.
*Steal Your Face,* Grateful Dead Records, 1976.
*Terrapin Station,* Arista, 1977.
*Shakedown Street,* Arista, 1978.
*Go to Heaven,* Arista, 1980.
*Dead Set,* Arista, 1981.

*Reckoning,* Arista, 1986.
*The Dead Zone: The Grateful Dead CD Collection,*
    1987.
*In the Dark,* Arista, 1987.
*Built to Last,* Arista, 1989.
*Without a Net,* Arista, 1990.

## Solo Recordings

*Cats Under the Stars,* Arista, 1988.
*Run for the Roses,* Arista, 1988.
*Jerry Garcia Band,* Arista, 1991.

## SOURCES:

### Books

*Current Biography 1990,* H.W. Wilson Co., New
    York, 1990, pp. 264–267.

### Periodicals

*Musician,* October 1981, p. 60.
*New Yorker,* October 11, 1993, pp. 96–102.
*People,* July 25, 1994, p. 48.
*Rolling Stone,* November 30, 1989, pp. 66–118;
    October 31, 1991, pp. 34–108; January 21,
    1993, p. 20; September 2, 1993, pp. 42–76.

—*Sketch by Kathe A. Conti*

# Federico García Lorca
## 1898-1936
### Spanish poet and playwright

Federico García Lorca left a deep imprint on
twentieth-century literature, for both his poetry
and his dramatic works. A member of the group that
contributed to a renaissance of Spanish poetry between World War I and the Spanish Civil War—a
literary generation that included **Jorge Guillén,** Pedro
Salinas, Rafael Albertí, and Gerardo Diego—Lorca
was a major figure whose work has been translated
into more than two dozen languages. He was "a
consummate artist," Allen Josephs wrote in the *New
York Times Book Review,* "whose genius in the
theater, music, art and poetry rather defies description or comparison." Lorca's execution at the hands
of Falangist rebels at the age of 38 cut short a life of
immense talent and achievement, and engendered an
image of the martyred artist that survives to this day.

Lorca was born on June 5, 1898, in the Andalusian valley town of Fuentevaqueros, near Granada in
southern Spain. He was the first-born son of Federico
García Rodriguez, a wealthy landowner, and Vicenta
Lorca García. Lorca's father had been married once
before, and it was as a 37-year-old widower that he
had married Vicenta, the town's young schoolteacher.
In the traditionally conservative and Catholic village,
Lorca's father was known for his kindness, generosity,
and business acumen. Doña Vicenta, for her part,
provided her son's first music lessons and introduced
him to the alphabet. "From her," Carl W. Cobb
asserted in *Federico García Lorca,* "[Lorca] felt he
had received his intelligence and his artistic inclinations; from his father, his passionate nature." Lorca's
earliest years were pleasant; Reed Anderson, in his
study *Federico García Lorca,* quoted a 1928 interview
in which Lorca recalled: "My childhood consisted of
learning reading and music with my mother and being
a rich and overbearing child in a small village."

The idyllic setting shifted in 1909, when Lorca's
family moved to Granada, where the children's
educational opportunities were greater. Lorca and his
younger brother, Francisco, were sent to a nonreli-
gious *colegio.* From an early age, it was Francisco who
outshone his brother in the classroom. Lorca, nevertheless, entered the University of Granada in 1914.
He was officially enrolled in a combined program of
philosophy, letters, and law. He promptly failed three
classes, including one literature course. Lorca placated his parents by earning a law degree.

### Beyond Granada: The Move to Madrid

But his university career was significant for other
reasons. Among the faculty he encountered the pro-
gressivist reformers Fernando de los Ríos and Martín
Domínguez Berrueta, both of whom exerted important influences on his development. By the time he
transferred to the University of Madrid in 1919,
Lorca had already published his first book, a travel-
ogue inspired by his observations during excursions
led by Berrueta. The book—entitled *Impresiones y
paisajes* (*Impressions and Landscapes*)—was published because of financing provided by Lorca's
father.

De los Ríos introduced Lorca to several major
writers, such as **Juan Ramón Jiménez,** during this
period, and facilitated the young man's admission to
Madrid's Residencia de Estudiantes. Lorca's study
habits hardly improved living in this vibrant dormitory, but the setting proved formative. Privately sponsored and modeled on the residential colleges of elite
British universities, the "Resi" was Lorca's home for
ten years, and was the setting in which he became
acquainted with other young talents such as **Luis
Buñuel** and **Salvador Dalí.**

Lorca's charisma and gifts impressed all his new friends. "When I met him for the first time," Anderson quoted Guillén as saying, "he astonished me, and I've never recovered from that astonishment." Howard T. Young, in his *Victorious Expression,* further explained that "Lorca's personality gave the impression of a man for whom song was the equivalent of life and silence the ultimate terror. Possessing overwhelming vitality, spirited imagination, a disconcerting smile, and no mean musical ability, he charmed everyone he met by his intense ingenuity and his gift of turning all that he touched into poetry." Lorca's versatility translated into engagements in acting, directing, set and costume design, piano and guitar performance, drawing and painting, and, of course, writing: essays, plays, and poetry. His penchant for reading his works aloud, coupled with his love for performance, entranced audiences from his student days to his later international tours.

The atmosphere surrounding Lorca and the company he kept in Madrid undoubtedly contributed to his artistic formation during these years. In an introduction to a book of critical essays on Lorca's work, Manuel Duran described the period and its challenges: "Cubism, Surrealism, and the experimental styles of the Twenties enriched the Symbolism that, since [Nicaraguan poet] **Ruben Darío**, had renewed Spanish poetry. The task was to assimilate these movements without destroying the Spanish tradition, or rather to assimilate them in a way that would allow this tradition to make itself felt again, to acquire a new vitality."

### Lorca, The Prolific Poet

Lorca was notoriously careless with his manuscripts and publications, but in 1921 he managed to produce the *Libro de poemas.* Duran saw these early poems as "mostly connected with adolescent longings and disappointment." According to William Berrien, writing in *World Literature Today,* the collection made clear that "although [Lorca] knew and had assimilated the ultra-modern tendencies flourishing in France and Spain at that time," he was at heart "an essentially Spanish poet." G. Grant MacCurdy, author of another Lorca study, found that the *Libro de poemas* "clearly lacks the aesthetic and technical virtuosity of [Lorca's] later work," but nevertheless "reflects themes which are seen throughout Lorca's work, especially his preoccupation with the experience and expression of life in the most fundamental sense of biological vitality. The poems are instructive, both for their own merit and because the young author's world view is apparent in poems which are often more accessible than some later works with extremely subtle and complex symbolism."

Lorca's creative development was also influenced by the composer Manuel de Falla. Together, the two men re-examined the old gypsy *cante jondo,* or deep song. Lorca helped his friend organize a 1922 festival celebrating the *cante jondo,* and wrote poems for the event that eventually became the collection entitled *Poema del cante jondo.* Here Lorca issued what Young called "a naked lament raised against the indifference of the world. It was in these songs that Lorca first felt the dark roots of art that dominate most of his poetry. He became the troubadour of Andalusia and elevated its folklore to the level of sophisticated poetry."

The Andalusian gypsy influence appeared also in the work *Romancero gitano* (*Gypsy Ballads*), first published in 1928. This collection became one of Lorca's best-known works. Berrien claimed that "it is safe to affirm that in Spain and in Latin America the *Romancero gitano* had been read and imitated by more poets than any other single collection of poems published in the last decades." With this book, wrote **Francisco García Lorca** in a preface to a collection of his elder brother's work, the poet "returned to the epic tradition of the *romance* and enriched the form with vivid new interpretations." According to Cobb, the principal theme of the *Gypsy Ballads* "is the omnipresence of the sexual instincts, not love but mere physical passion, passion normal and prohibited, passion repressed and incestuous." Such tumultuous elements lead, Cobb wrote, to aggression and to death: "In summary, the *Gypsy Ballads* is a book which reveals [Lorca's] unsurpassed imagination in transmuting the materials of Andalusian popular tradition into an expression of his own tragic outlook on life."

"Not the least of [Lorca's] contributions to the literature of his land," Berrien stated, "was fresh and chastened interpretation of the Andalusian theme. . . . He proved in poetry that the real Andalusia could be a source of profound and noble beauties and was something more than the land of garish warmth of color, of facile humor, of conventional picturesqueness." As much as he loved his Andalusian home, Lorca resented those who saw him solely as a regional writer, and continued to harbor considerable ambivalence toward his Andalusian-inspired works.

Though already extremely popular as a poet, and blessed with a large circle of friends, Lorca suffered from depression. Observers point to the year 1929 as a particularly rocky period of his life. Lorca's increasing anguish over his homosexuality, a painful romantic rupture with the young sculptor Emilio Aladrén, and the deterioration of his once-intense friendship with Dalí all contributed to Lorca's misery during this time. Biographers have also speculated that Lorca may have interpreted a cinematic collaboration between Buñuel and Dalí—a strange film that appeared in Paris called *Un Chien andalou* (*An Andalusian Dog*)—as a work intended to ridicule him.

At this point, Lorca decided a change of scenery was in order. During the summer of 1929 he moved to New York, ostensibly to study English at Columbia University. Although the Spanish-speaking community welcomed him, Lorca remained haunted and despairing. "He spent most of his time alone," MacCurdy wrote, "walking the streets, the bridges, and spending countless hours in the speakeasies and nightclubs of Harlem." It was with African Americans, whom he regarded as fellow outcasts, that Lorca felt the deepest bond in New York.

Despite his continued unhappiness, Lorca wrote prolifically during his United States sojourn, producing the poems that were published posthumously as the *Poeta en Nueva York* collection. The spirit behind this work may best be described in Lorca's own words, which Cobb cited. Introducing his New York poems at a Buenos Aires reading, Lorca stated: "I bring you a bitter and living poetry to lash your eyes open. . . . I want to wrestle with you, disturb you, belabor you, to fight you to a fall or be struck down in turn." Francisco García Lorca later elaborated: "These poems reveal the shock and anguish [Lorca] experienced as he, the representative of a traditional culture, was confronted with the seeming chaos of a new industrial civilization. If one thing distinguished *Poeta en Nueva York* from all his earlier books, it is the total absence of irony and humour: nourished by the 'bitter root,' these poems speak tragically and grotesquely on a prevailing desolation."

The book's ten sections contain, in Cobb's view, "some of the most turgid, despairing, rebellious, and ironically difficult poetry in Spanish literature." With titles such as "The King of Harlem", "Dance of Death", "Landscape of the Vomiting Multitudes", and "Nocturne of the Void", the poems form what Cobb deemed "a painful, tormented, prophetic book, worthy of being included among the finest examples of the alienation of spirit in modern man." As far as the poet's technique was concerned, *Commonweal* critic Jack Patterson found that Lorca had "turned away from the nature lyrics and gypsy ballads that had brought him prominence, to record the impact of a dizzying megalopolis. His horror, disgust and pain demanded a new style, and he began to write a kind of surrealistic verse, whose kaleidoscopic, broken images mirrored his own whirling emotions."

### Time for the Theater

Lorca returned to Spain during the summer of 1930 following a successful lecture tour in Cuba. Once in Spain, Lorca channeled his artistic energies toward another of his cultural loves: the theater. He did so despite a bad experience in that area a number of years before. One of his poems had been turned into a play, *El maléfico de la mariposa,* back in 1920; the derision it received from its Madrid audience on opening night scarred Lorca. He avoided future theatrical endeavors for a considerable period thereafter. But eventually, as Berrien explained, "the poet who in childhood had gathered together brothers and classmates to give popular plays in his home, and who had later been a leading spirit in dramatics at the Residencia de Estudiantes, could hardly do otherwise than turn playwright." In 1927 Lorca's reconstruction of a nineteenth-century Granadine historical episode, *Mariana Pineda,* was successfully staged in Barcelona thanks to the efforts of the celebrated Spanish actress, Margarita Xirgu. This considerably more successful dramatic presentation further encouraged Lorca to pursue his theatrical interests upon his return to his homeland in 1930.

Armed with a play called *El Público (The Public)* that was nearly complete, Lorca tested its contents with friends, who were shocked at the play's bizarre and controversial content. A surrealistic drama, *El Público* dealt with themes of homosexuality, deception, and the power of death over love. Lorca's friends convinced him to set the play aside. The poet was determined, however, to further explore the possibilities of the stage.

"The most important single moment in Lorca's career as a dramatist," Anderson asserted, "came in November of 1931 when he announced to his close friends an idea that he had conceived for the founding of an itinerant theatre company that would carry the great works of the classical Spanish theatre to the provincial capital cities of Spain, and into the villages of the isolated countryside." With financial support from the republican government—Lorca's friend de los Ríos was the new education minister—Lorca and his student troupe, *La Barraca* ("The Hut"), presented works by Cervantes, Lope de Vega, Calderón de la Barca, and others.

Lorca learned a great deal as La Barraca's artistic director, and he wrote several plays over the next number of years. The best-known of these plays may be three works commonly grouped together as the "rural trilogy": *Bodas de sangre, Yerma,* and *La casa de Bernarda Alba.* Cobb deemed the first of these, *Bodas de Sangre (Blood Wedding),* as "Lorca's most enduringly popular drama, both in the Hispanic countries and internationally." The play tells the story of a couple that wishes deeply to be together, although committed to other people. *Bodas de Sangre* is a work in which, Cobb said, "the interplay of the poetic and the realistic, the sincere and the ironic, the lucid and the enigmatic indicates that Lorca had not yet come to terms with himself or with his culture."

*Yerma,* which premiered in December 1934, is named after the principal character in the play, a young woman who wants desperately to become a mother. The word *yerma* means "barren" in Spanish, and, indeed, Yerma—whose husband is unable to give her children—lives a starved, unfulfilled existence. Lorca completed *La casa de Bernarda Alba* (*The House of Bernarda Alba* ) in 1936, and read the work aloud to his friends shortly before his death, but did not live to see it produced.

Anderson argued that "the foundation of Lorca's effort to revolutionize the theater of his day" rested on "his conviction that great drama had been and always would be poetic drama." He cited Lorca's statement that "The theatre is one of the most expressive and useful vehicles for the edification of a country's people, and a barometer that marks the country's greatness or decline." Viewed in its entirety, Cobb wrote, Lorca's drama resembled much of European drama in its choice of material: "the importance of the instincts; primitive drives, usually specifically sexual; overwhelming civilized reason; the problems of man's isolation; and death as enigma and finality."

The Argentine actress Lola Membrives and her husband Juan Reforzo were especially enchanted by *Bodas de sangre*. They invited Lorca to Buenos Aires to see their production late in 1933. Thus began Lorca's last trip to the Americas. He remained in Argentina for several months, with a short break in February of 1934 to visit Uruguay. He delivered lectures, saw stage productions of other plays he had written, and cultivated relationships with luminaries of the literary community such as the Chilean poet **Pablo Neruda.**

When his bullfighter friend Ignacio Sánchez Mejías was killed in the ring during August of 1934, Lorca plummeted into a profound sadness. He told friends that in the bullfighter's demise he had seen a foreshadowing of his own impending death. Josephs observed that "even in the most death-conscious country in Western tradition—where, as Lorca once pointed out, death is the national spectacle—his obsession with the subject was remarkable." The elegy Lorca wrote in Sánchez's honor received immense praise. Duran called it Lorca's "best sustained effort as a poet . . . a brilliantly orchestrated piece, rich in bold images, where death and destruction are condemned and accepted at the same time."

The Spanish Civil War broke out in 1936, splitting the country into leftist and rightist camps. In Madrid, Lorca disregarded the pleas of his friends and decided to return to his parents' home in Granada, a rebel Conservative stronghold. Lorca did not envision himself as a political figure; although he had publicly criticized the Conservatives and joined in the populist fervor of the Republic, he had never joined the Communist Party. His return to Granada proved fatal, though, and his life ended sadly. Well-known as a liberal artist and suspected of being a homosexual, Lorca was hunted down, captured, and imprisoned for a short time. He was executed on August 19, 1936; his body was thrown into an unmarked mass grave.

"Lorca saw too clearly, was too catholic and popular," Aratari reflected almost twenty years after the writer's death, "to survive in a deadlocked situation created by prejudiced parties struggling for power and bent on separating good from good." For many years following his death, Lorca was viewed as a taboo subject in Spain. It was not until the 1950s that his work become readily available again. Critical discussion and research, however, remained limited until the death of the Spanish dictator **Francisco Franco** in 1975.

## SELECTED PUBLISHED WORKS:

*Impresiones y paisajes,* Traveset, 1918; translated by Lawrence H. Klibbe as *Impressions and Landscapes,* University Press of America, 1987.

*Libro de poemas,* Maroto, 1921.

*Canciones,* Litoral/Imprenta Sur, 1927; translated by Lorca and Philip Cummings as *Songs,* Duquesne University Press, 1976.

*Mariana Pineda,* Farsa, 1928; Aris and Phillips, 1987.

*Primer romancero gitano,* Revista de Occidente, 1928; republished as *Romancero gitano,* Revista de Occidente, 1929; translated by Langston Hughes as *Gypsy Ballads,* Beloit College, 1951.

*Poema del cante jondo,* Ulises/Iberoamericana, 1931; translated by Carlos Bauer as *Poem of the Deep Song,* City Lights, 1987.

*Oda a Walt Whitman,* Alcancía, 1933; translated by Bauer in his *Ode to Walt Whitman and Other Poems,* City Lights, 1988.

*Llanto por Ignacio Sánchez Mejías,* Cruz & Raya/Arbol, 1935; translated by A.L. Lloyd as *Lament for the Death of a Bullfighter,* Heinemann, 1937; Oxford University Press, 1937.

*Bodas de sangre,* Cruz & Raya/Arbol, 1936; translated by Richard L. O'Connell and James Graham-Luján as *Blood Wedding* in *Three Tragedies of Federico García Lorca,* New Directions, 1947; London, Falcon, 1948.

*Poeta en Nueva York,* Séneca, 1940, translated by Rolfe Humphries in his *The Poet in New York and Other Poems of Federico García Lorca,* Norton, 1940.

*Selected Poems of Federico García Lorca,* edited by Francisco García Lorca and Donald M. Allen, New Directions, 1955.

*Conferencias y charlas,* Consejo Nacional de Cultura, 1961.

*Casidas,* Arte y Bibliofilia, 1969.

*Prosa,* Alianza, 1969.

*Selected Letters,* edited and translated by David Gershator, New Directions, 1983.

## SOURCES:

### Books

Anderson, Andrew A., "Federico García Lorca," in *Twentieth-Century Spanish Poets,* first series, edited by Michael L. Perna, Volume 108 of *Dictionary of Literary Biography,* Detroit, Gale, 1991.

Anderson, Reed, *Federico García Lorca,* London, Macmillan Press, 1984.

Barea, Arturo, *Lorca: The Poet and His People,* translated by Ilsa Barea, New York, Harcourt/Brace, 1949.

Campbell, Roy, *Lorca: An Appreciation of His Poetry,* New Haven, Yale University Press, 1952.

Cobb, Carl W., *Federico García Lorca,* New York, Twayne, 1967.

Gibson, Ian, *Assassination of Federico García Lorca,* Harmondsworth, Middlesex, England, Penguin Books, 1983.

———, *Federico García Lorca: A Life,* New York, Pantheon Books, 1989.

*Hispanic Writers,* edited by Bryan Ryan, Detroit, Gale, 1991.

Klein, Dennis A., *Blood Wedding, Yerma, and The House of Bernarda Alba: García Lorca's Tragic Trilogy,* Boston, Twayne, 1991.

Lima, Robert, *The Theatre of García Lorca,* New York, Las Americas Publishing, 1963.

*Lorca: A Collection of Critical Essays,* edited by Manuel Duran, Englewood Cliffs, NJ: Prentice-Hall, 1962.

MacCurdy, G. Grant, *Federico García Lorca: Life, Work, and Criticism,* Fredericton, New Brunswick, Canada, York Press, 1986.

Young, Howard T., *The Victorious Expression: A Study of Four Contemporary Spanish Poets,* Madison, University of Wisconsin Press, 1964.

### Periodicals

*Commonweal,* August 12, 1955, pp. 472–75; September 2, 1955, pp. 548–49; October 21, 1955; pp. 67–68.

*New York Times Book Review,* October 8, 1989, pp. 1, 40–41.

*World Literature Today,* Spring 1989, pp. 188–89.

—*Sketch by Erika Dreifus*

# Gabriel García Márquez
## 1928-
**Colombian novelist, short story writer, journalist, and political activist**

Gabriel García Márquez has been internationally recognized as one of the greatest fiction writers of the twentieth century. He—along with writers such as **Julio Cortazar** and **Jorge Luis Borges**—was an essential force in establishing the vitality of Latin American fiction throughout the literary world. García Márquez rose to international prominence in the 1960s, a remarkable decade of achievement in Latin American letters commonly referred to as "El boom." Although García Márquez wrote several significant short stories and novellas during the 1940s and 1950s, he did not gain widespread recognition until 1967, when he published *Cien años de soledad* (*One Hundred Years of Solitude*). This mythic story of the founding and decline of the fictional Colombian coastal town of Macondo has sold millions of copies in at least 25 languages and stands as the "greatest revelation in the Spanish Language since the *Don Quixote* of **Miguel de Cervantes**," contended Chilean poet **Pablo Neruda** in *Time.* While such colossal critical and popular success on the basis of a single work could have proven ultimately crippling to a lesser writer, García Márquez has "gradually confirmed his position as a rare storyteller richly endowed with a material, from imagination and experience, which seems inexhaustible," according to the Swedish Academy, which awarded him the 1982 Nobel Prize in Literature.

García Márquez was born on March 6, 1928, the first child of Gabriel Eligio Garcia, a telegraph operator, and Luisa Santiaga Marquez, the daughter of a retired colonel. Having married against the wishes of Luisa's parents, the couple allowed Gabriel, the first of their sixteen children, to live with his maternal grandparents in Aracataca, a small town located in the Caribbean coastal region of Colombia that became the model for the town of Macondo depicted in *One Hundred Years of Solitude.* His grandparents, both of whom regaled the boy with their storytelling abilities, had a significant impact on him. His grandfather, García Márquez said in a *New York Times Book Review* interview with Marlise Simons, "told endless stories of the civil war of his youth"; he also "took me to the circus and the cinema and was my umbilical cord with history and reality." Likewise, his grandmother was "always telling fables, family legends and organizing our life according to the messages she received in her dreams." She was "the source of the magical, superstitious and supernatural view of reality." At the age of seven, however,

García Márquez's idyllic childhood came to an abrupt end with the death of his grandfather. He left Aracataca to live with his parents in Bogotá, the nation's capital city, which was located in the Andean central region.

### Early Literary Endeavors

During his teenage years, García Márquez developed an interest in becoming a writer after reading such works as Franz Kafka's "Metamorphosis", a story that enabled him to see the power of imaginative literature and, later, served as a model for his own early attempts at fiction. In the tradition of many Latin American writers, though, he first planned to study law. He subsequently enrolled at the Universidad Nacional de Colombia in 1947. His interest in literature and journalism, however, soon overwhelmed other pursuits. The same year that he entered the university, he published his first story in *El Espectador.*

In 1948 the university caught fire during the violent riots that followed the assassination of Jorge Eliecer Gaitan, an event that triggered nearly two decades of rural violence in which over 200,000 people were killed by various Liberal and Conservative forces. After the university was closed, he transferred to the Universidad de Cartagena, where he contributed many journalistic pieces to *El Universal* between 1948 and 1949. The following year he met Ramon Vinyes, a Catalon republican with a passion for books who introduced him to writers such as Virginia Woolf and William Faulkner. García Márquez abandoned his legal studies forever and returned to the Caribbean region, settling in the town of Barranquilla. During his two-year stay there, he worked for the local paper *El heraldo.* He wrote a regular column under the pseudonym "Septimus" that featured an eclectic blend of short stories, notes for a projected novel, and essays that often commented on economic and social issues.

García Márquez's training in Barranquilla prepared him for a position as a regular correspondent with *El Espectador,* a larger paper published in Bogotá. He served as the paper's film critic, a position that fostered a life-long interest in film that eventually led him to a teaching position at a film school in the 1980s. He also served as an investigative reporter for the paper, an experience that further sharpened his interest in political issues.

The young journalist's controversial leftist political views prompted a period of self-imposed exile in Europe during the mid-1950s. Based primarily in Paris, he worked as an international correspondent for *El Espectador* and *El Independiente.* After Colombian authorities shut down the latter paper, he was left without a source of income. García Márquez continued to write fiction, though, and completed *El coronel no tiene quien le escriba* (*No One Writes to the Colonel*) by 1957.

Although he lived for a time in a state of poverty, García Márquez viewed his time in Paris as one that furnished him with experience valuable to his writing career. "The most important thing [it] gave me was a perspective on Latin America," he told Simons. "It taught me the difference between Latin America and Europe and among the Latin American countries themselves through the Latins I met there." Towards the end of 1957, he left Europe after being asked by his friend Plinio Apuleyo Mendoza to help edit the weekly *Momento* in Caracas, Venezuela. The following year he returned to Colombia to marry the daughter of a Barranquilla pharmacist once nicknamed "the sacred crocodile" for her exotic Egyptian looks, Mercedes Barcha Pardo, whom he had known since their early teens.

Shortly after the marriage, García Márquez and Mendoza resigned their positions at *Momento* to protest the paper's editorial stance, which criticized the popular demonstrations against the visit of then U.S. vice-president Richard Nixon. The two journalists traveled to Cuba, a country undergoing tremendous changes following the success of **Fidel Castro**'s revolution. They went to work for the regime's news organization, Prensa Latina, establishing branch offices in Bogotá and, later, New York.

In 1961 García Márquez resigned his position with the organization in the midst of internal conflicts in Cuba and was again left without stable employment. Unlike earlier periods of economic hardship, though, he now had a family to support—one that had expanded with the birth of his first son, Rodrigo. Although the family intended to return to Colombia, they instead settled in Mexico City, where a second son, Gonzalo, was born in 1962. During his first three years in Mexico, García Márquez wrote screenplays, edited two magazines, and worked for an advertising agency to support his family and his writing. While he had already published several books by this time, including critically acclaimed novellas such as *La hojarasca* (*Leaf Storm*), *El coronel no tiene quien le escriba* (*No One Writes to the Colonel*), *La mala hor* (*Luis Perez*), and short story collections such as *Los funerales de la Mama Grande* (*Big Mama's Funeral*), his fiction at this point still did not sustain a full-time writing career.

### Writes *One Hundred Years of Solitude*

While walking on the road between Mexico City and Acapulco one day in 1965, García Márquez had a vision of the novel that would bring him international fame. As he told Simons, "*One Hundred Years of Solitude* travelled in bits and pieces through my head for 17 years. In the end I was able to talk the book. I walked around with its fragments until they burst.

Then I sat down and it took me 18 months to write." When he came out of his study with the manuscript his hand, his wife greeted him with $10,000 worth of bills. As events unfolded, however, it became clear that they would be able to pay off those debts fairly quickly.

In 1967 the novel was published in Buenos Aires, "provoking a literary earthquake throughout Latin America. The critics recognized the book as a masterpiece of the art of fiction and the public endorsed this opinion, systematically exhausting new editions, which, at one point, appeared at the astounding rate of one a week. Overnight, García Márquez became almost as famous as a great soccer player or an eminent singer of boleros," recounted Chilean novelist **Mario Vargas Llosa** in *Gabriel García Márquez: Modern Critical Views. National Observer* reviewer William Kennedy wrote that *"One Hundred Years of Solitude* is the first piece of literature since the Book of Genesis that should be required reading for the entire human race."

Drawing heavily on García Márquez's childhood memories of Aracataca, the novel originated in the stories and fables of his grandparents—often cited by the author as his greatest literary influence. His eccentric grandmother, who often awakened her grandson in the middle of the night to tell him stories and repeatedly chatted with ghosts who came to visit her, proved to be the primary source for his development of magical realism—a technique that Donald J. Greiner, in a Nobel tribute, defined as an "exuberant sighting of the marvelous in the real—*lo real maravillos*—of the inevitable union of the surreal and the street, of the freedom of fantasy in the confines of the mundane." His grandfather provided the author with a model of solitude that served as the inspiration for the fictional character José Arcadio Buendia, who founded the town of Macondo in an attempt to escape the ghost of the man he had murdered.

*One Hundred Years of Solitude* chronicles the lives of several generations of the Buendia family and the rise and fall of Macondo, a fictional setting that critics have often compared favorably to William Faulkner's Yoknapatawpha County. Like his American literary forefather, García Márquez created through his tale of complex family relationships and generational conflicts a forum to examine a variety of sweeping cultural, historical, and political themes. This quality led Vargas Llosa to conclude that García Márquez's *tour-de-force* is a "'total' novel in the tradition of those insanely ambitious creations which aspire to compete with reality on an equal basis, confronting it with an image and qualitatively matching it in vitality, vastness and complexity." Yet, Vargas Llosa adds, the novel is, as its immense international success testifies, "one of the rare instances among major, contemporary literary works that can be read, understood, and enjoyed by all."

After the unprecedented success of *One Hundred Years of Solitude*, García Márquez was able to devote himself fully to writing. His long-awaited next novel, *El otono del patriarca* (*The Autumn of the Patriarch*) did not appear until 1975. The novel was thought by several reviewers, including *Newsweek*'s Walter Clemons, to be something of a letdown: "After the narrative vivacity and intricate characterization of the earlier book, [*The Autumn of the Patriarch*] seems both oversumptuous and underpopulated." Most critics, however, applauded the author's effort, and it has taken a prominent place in the García Márquez canon. Viewed by many to be a further examination of the solitude experienced by his earlier characters, the novel examines the isolation of a political tyrant who has ruled for so long that no one can remember any other ruler. "In this fabulous, dream-like account of the reign of a nameless dictator of a fantastic Caribbean realm, solitude is linked with the possession of absolute power," explains the *National Review*'s Ronald De Feo. The novel drew praise not only for the powerful thematic statements contained therein, but also for the literary form in which those statements were expressed. John Sturrock of the *Times Literary Supplement,* for instance, observed that the novel "is sophisticated and its language is luxuriant to a degree. Style and subject are at odds because García Márquez is committed to showing that our first freedom—and one which all too many Latin American countries have lost—is of the full resources of our language."

García Márquez postponed the publication of his next novel in order to voice his protest of despotic terrorism in Latin America. He pledged not to publish any fiction until the regime of Chilean dictator General **Augusto Pinochet** was either disbanded or overthrown. Obviously, the author's strong political views, evident in his work since his early journalistic days, had not dissipated with time.

It was not until 1982, then, that García Márquez's next work, *Cronica de una muerte anunciada* (*Chronicle of a Death Foretold*), appeared in print. The plot of the widely praised novella centered around the historical narrative of a young woman whose husband discovers, on the night of their wedding, that she is not a virgin and returns her to her family. Angered by what they find to be an affront to the family's honor, the woman's brothers construct a plot to kill their brother-in-law, informing everyone in the town, save the victim himself, of their intentions. Told from the perspective of a former citizen who has returned to reconstruct the events that he himself witnessed, the novella has been interpreted as a commentary on "eye-witness" accounts that provide the bases for journalism and, in a larger perspective, history itself. García Márquez's narrative technique—in which he presented information filtered through second and third-hand sources, thus exposing the distortions and contradictions often contained in "objective" reports—drew heavily from his own journalism experience. The narrative device received widespread praise. Bill Buford of the *Times Literary Supplement* found that by employing a journalistic angle in telling his story, García Márquez "has written an unusual and original work: a simple narrative so charged with irony that it has the authority of a political fable." John Blades of the *Chicago Tribune Book World,* expressing a similar assessment, suggested that it was "by far the author's most absorbing work to date."

## Awarded 1982 Nobel Prize in Literature

In 1982 García Márquez was awarded the Nobel Prize in Literature. In bestowing the prestigious award, the Swedish academy described him as a writer "who combines the copious, almost overwhelming narrative talent with the master of the conscious, disciplined and widely read artist of language." They also praised him for being "strongly committed politically on the side of the poor and the weak against domestic oppression and foreign economic exploitation." In accepting the award, García Márquez—whose political involvement with controversial figures such as Castro and the former Panamanian leader General Omar Torrijos has at times overshadowed his fiction—took care to place his fiction within the reality of Latin American politics. "Why is the originality so readily granted us in literature so mistrustfully denied us in our difficult attempts at social change? Why think that the social justice sought by progressive Europeans for their own countries cannot also be a goal for Latin America, with different methods for dissimilar conditions?"

After winning the Nobel Prize, García Márquez continued to strengthen his reputation as a major writer of the twentieth century, adding significant works to his canon through the 1980s and into the 1990s. Among his works of this period, *El amor en los tiempos del colera* (*Love in the Time of Cholera*), the winner of the 1988 *Los Angeles Times* Book Prize for fiction, received perhaps the most favorable critical reception. American novelist Thomas Pynchon stated in *The New York Times Book Review* that while "it would be presumptuous to speak of moving 'beyond' *One Hundred Years of Solitude*," the story of an aging couple's love—based in part on recollections of his parents' marriage—reveals a movement "into deeper awareness of the ways in which 'nobody teaches life anything.'" Likewise, *New York Times* critic Michiko Kakutani asserted that the novel "has revealed how the extraordinary is contained in the ordinary, how a couple of forgotten, even commonplace lives can encompass the heights and depths of grand passion."

In 1989 García Márquez published *El general en su laberinto* (*The General in His Labyrinth*), a novel that imagined the last months of **Simón Bolivar,** a historical figure who achieved independence for the Spanish colonies in the northern half of South America but failed to realize his larger ambition of uniting all of the colonies. While García Márquez addressed the familiar themes of solitude that pervade his corpus, he succeeded in "reversing the narrative premise" of his early work by placing the fiction within a historical frame, remarked Michael Bell in *Gabriel García Márquez: Solitude and Solidarity.* García Márquez continued this trend in his later fiction, turning away from "flamboyant and overt fantasy for something altogether more realistic and authentic," wrote novelist William Boyd in *The New York Times Book Review* in his assessment of *Strange Pilgrims,* a 1993 collection of stories that the critic found to be "a fascinating and memorable addition to the canon." Such work has served to solidify the international recognition of Gabriel García Márquez as one of Latin America's leading literary and political voices.

## SELECTED PUBLISHED WORKS:

*La hojarasca,* Ediciones Sipa, 1955

*El coronel no tiene quien le escriba,* Aguirre Editor, 1961.

*La mala hora,* Talleres de Gráficas, 1961; translated by Gregory Rabassa as *In Evil Hour,* Harper, 1979.

*Los funerales de la Mamá Grande,* Editorial Universidad Veracruzana, 1962.

*Cien años de soledad,* Editorial Sudamericana, 1967; translated by Gregory Rabassa as *One Hundred Years of Solitude,* Harper, 1970.

*Isabel viendo llover en Macondo,* Editorial Estuario, 1967.

*No One Writes to the Colonel and Other Stories* (includes "No One Writes to the Colonel" and stories from *Los funerales de la Mamá Grande*), translated by J. S. Bernstein, Harper, 1968.

*La increíble y triste historia de la cándida Eréndira y su abuela desalmada,* Barral Editores, 1972.

*El negro que hizo esprar a los ángeles,* Ediciones Alfil, 1972.

*Ojos de perro azul: Nueve cuentos desconocidos,* Equisditorial, 1972.

*Leaf Storm and Other Stories* (includes *La hojarasca* and *Isabel viendo llover en Macando*), translated by Gregory Rabassa, Harper, 1972.

*El otoño del patriarca,* Plaza & Janés Editores, 1975; translated by Gregory Rabassa as *The Autumn of the Patriarch,* Harper, 1976.

*Todos los cuentos de Gabriel García Márquez: 1947–1972,* Plaza & Janés, 1975.

*Crónica de una muerte anunciada,* La Oveja Negra, 1981; translated by Gregory Rabassa as *Chronicle of a Death Foretold,* J. Cape, 1982, Knopf, 1983.

*Viva Sandino,* Editorial Nueva Nicaragua, 1982.

*Collected Stories,* translated by Gregory Rabassa and J. S. Bernstein, Harper, 1984.

*El amor en los tiempos del cólera,* La Oveja Negra, 1985; translated by Edith Grossman as *Love in the Time of Cholera,* Knopf, 1988.

*El cataclismo de Dámocles,* Editorial Universitaria Centroamericana, 1986.

*El general en su laberinto,* Madrid, 1989, translation by Edith Grossman published as *The General in His Labyrinth,* Knopf, 1990.

*Doce cuentos peregrinos,* Mondadori, 1992; translated by Edith Grossman as *Strange Pilgrims,* Knopf, 1993.

*Del amor y otros demonios,* Mondadori, 1994.

## SOURCES:

### Books

*Authors & Artists for Young Adults,* Volume 3, Detroit, Gale, 1990.

Bell, Michael, *Gabriel García Márquez: Solitude and Solidarity,* New York, St. Martin's, 1993.

*Contemporary Literary Criticism,* Detroit, Gale, Volume 2, 1974; Volume 3, 1975; Volume 8, 1978; Volume 10, 1979; Volume 15, 1980; Volume 27, 1984; Volume 47, 1988; Volume 55, 1989.

*Dictionary of Literary Biography Yearbook: 1982,* Detroit, Gale, 1983.

*Gabriel García Márquez: Modern Critical Views,* edited by Harold Bloom, New York, Chelsea House, 1989.

*Hispanic Writers,* edited by Bryan Ryan, Detroit, Gale, 1991.

Janes, Regina, *Gabriel García Márquez: Revolutions in Wonderland,* London, University of Missouri Press, 1981.

### Periodicals

*Chicago Tribune Book World,* November 11, 1979.

*National Observer,* April 20, 1970.

*National Review,* May 27, 1977.

*Newsweek,* November 8, 1976.

*New York Times Book Review,* December 5, 1982, pp. 7, 60–1; April 10, 1988, pp. 1, 48–9; November 7, 1993, p. 9.

*Time,* March 16, 1970.

*Times Literary Supplement,* April 15, 1977; September 10, 1982.

*—Sketch by Jason Gallman*

# Carlos Gardel
## 1890-1935
### French Argentine composer

Singer and songwriter Carlos Gardel was born Charles Romuald Gárdes on December 11, 1890, at Saint Joseph de la Grave hospital in Toulouse, France, to a French woman named Berthe Gárdes; his father, Paul Lasserre was married to someone else. Hoping to avoid the stigma of illegitimacy, Gárdes emigrated to Argentina—where she could say she was a widow—with her two-year-old son. They boarded the *S.S. Don Pedro,* a steamer in Bordeaux, and arrived in Buenos Aires March 11, 1893. Gárdes found immediate work as an ironing woman. She changed their names to the Spanish translations, thus Charles became Carlos; later he changed Gárdes to Gardel, but his friends called him *el francesito,* or "Frenchie."

Buenos Aires was booming with immigrants around the turn of the twentieth century. While his mother worked, Señora Rosa de Franchini took care of Gardel until he was school age. Even when he was very young, Gardel demonstrated a love for music, and he always wanted to be a singer. At age seven, he would sit outside his door and sing while a crowd of people gathered around him. Described as "mischievous" and "a clown" when he was young, the bright child was enrolled in the Colegio Pio IX, a special school for training artists and craftsmen, in 1901. He began singing in the school choir. Gardel finished his schooling at the Colegio San Estanislao at the age of 14.

Upon graduation, Gardel tried working at several jobs but never settled down with any one profession. Traveling throughout Argentina, he worked variously for a jeweler, as a cardboard maker, and in a print shop as an apprentice linotypist. He frequently went to the opera, and he would hang around the theaters. Gardel became an extra on stage at the theater playing in crowd scenes and various bit parts. He would entertain people on the street imitating Caruso or Titta Ruffo, a famous baritone at the time.

In his late teens, Gardel began entertaining at private parties. He became well-known at the Mercado de Abasto—Buenos Aires' principal market district—where he would sing and play guitar at an Italian restaurant, the Cafe O'Rondeman. In his free time, Gardel would hang out at cafes and bars at night with his friends and amuse the public. People were amazed at his singing ability, and Gardel became the *barrio,* or district singer at Abasto. He also played at conservative *comites,* or political meetings. Gardel earned several more nicknames during this era,

*Carlos Gardel*

including *el zorzal* (the thrush) and *el Morocho,* which has no translation but infers his fame at Abasto.

Another barrio singer, Jose "Pepe" Razzano, heard about Gardel and set up a *tenida,* or singing competition with him in the Abasto. By the end of the evening, the singers were singing together instead of competing, and they became friends. In the tradition of the *tenida,* Gardel then had to compete with Razzano at his barrio, the Cafe del Pelado in the Balvanera Sur district. Because the cafe was not large enough to hold the people who went to watch the two singers, they sang at a private home nearby. Enrique Falbi, the owner of the house, suggested that they form a duo and begin touring.

At first Razzano did not want to tour, so a third singer, Francisco Martino, wanted to go. In 1912, Gardel and Martino traveled 200 miles on the first tour, and when they returned to Buenos Aires, Razzano was ready to join them. Another experienced musician, Saul "Viper" Salinas, wanted to join them in a quartet and arranged a tour. The group sang the popular creole folk songs of the day. Around this time Gárdes changed his name to Gardel. In the meantime, the Casa Tagini asked Gardel to make some records on the Columbia label—14 songs were recorded on seven two-sided discs and released in March of 1913.

The quartet began their tour, but faced with no money from a failed performance, they fled their hotel without paying the bill in Zarate. When they arrived in San Pedro, the town was very receptive and opened their doors to the singers. Salinas left and the three singers, Gardel, Martino, and Razzano continued without him. When Martino became ill, Gardel and Razzano were down to two.

They returned to Buenos Aires, but soon after were singing together again at a private room at the Armenonville, a fashionable upper-class cabaret, when the owner heard them and he offered to pay them 70 pesos a night to perform in his club—more money than they ever made for one performance. A smash, the set led to an offer to perform at the *Teatro Naciónal* in Calle Corrientes for a season of plays. On January 8, 1914, they performed in the theater for the *fin de fiesta,* or end of the show.

### Birth of the Tango

The Gardel-Razzano Duo became the leading creole singers of the day. They made their first recording together in April of 1917, on the Nacional-Odeon label. Around 1918, Gardel began composing a new type of popular song based on the tango. "*Mi Noche Triste*" ("My Sad Night") became an instant hit. A record was released in January of 1918, and thousands of copies were sold. In 1920, Gardel met Isabel del Valle and fell in love. Although they never married, the affair lasted well into the 1930s. Meanwhile, the duo toured extensively in South America and abroad; though he and Razzano remained lifelong friends, Gardel began performing solo in the mid-1920s.

In 1933, Gardel signed a contract with Paramount Pictures to do two films, where he directed and composed the music. Gardel was very successful in the movie business; the theme song for the first movie *Cuesta Abajo* (*Downward Slope*) became one of his most popular songs. In 1935, a South American tour was planned to promote Gardel's movies. The night before leaving Bogotá, Columbia, Gardel broadcast from Radio La Vox de la Victor. The next day, June 24, 1935, Gardel's plane taxied for take-off at Olaya Herrera Airport in Medellín. Before the plane had left the ground, it swerved and hit another plane waiting for clearance. The planes exploded, and Gardel, with 14 others, perished.

Gardel's tomb and monument is in Buenos Aires at the Chacarita Cemetery, where people continue to visit. As testament to his popularity, in 1985, on the fiftieth anniversary of his death, commemorative services were held.

### SOURCES:

Collier Simon, *The Life, Music & Times of Carlos Gardel,* University of Pittsburgh Press, 1986.

*—Sketch by Phyllis Noah*

# Antonio Gaudí y Coronet
## 1852-1926
### Spanish architect

Architect Antonio Gaudí y Coronet blended the movements known as Art Nouveau and Neo-Gothic. Gaudí himself considered architecture to be living sculpture and sought to create what he termed "Mediterranean Gothic." Taking the classic elements of Greek architecture, the engineering characteristic of Gothic cathedrals, and the decorative nature motifs of the Romantic movement, he worked to adapt architecture to the Mediterranean climate. In their biography *Antoni Gaudí,* James Johnson Sweeney and Josep Lluís Sert described Gaudí as "the architect who perhaps more than any other in the nineteenth century recognized the lost structural principles of the Gothic, who recovered and restressed them for the architecture of today and tomorrow, and at the same time brought back an interest in the associational and imaginative factors of architectural expression."

Gaudí's designs integrated sculptural elements, perhaps because he often used three-dimensional models rather than relying only upon two-dimensional drawings. He is remembered for using ornate ironwork, curved and warped surfaces, textured tiles and building materials, and mosaics. Perhaps Gaudí's greatest achievement was the development of the "slanted" column to replace the flying buttresses used in Gothic and Romanesque cathedrals. His columns leaned on a slight angle and branched at the top to further support the ceiling stresses of the tall and open buildings. He studied the angles and curves of natural structures—such as trees—to find solutions for stress support problems that had impeded architects for centuries.

Using the helicoids, hyperbolas, and parabolas he noted in nature, Gaudí experimented on scale models, performing calculations to engineer columns, vaults, and arches that allowed a taller ceiling height with a more open floor area. Joan Bassegoda, a Catalan professor, summarized Gaudí's genius in *Time:* "Instead of the geometry of rectangles and circles, he took his structures from nature, studying what forms allow trees and humans to grow and stay upright."

## Catalan Heritage

Gaudí was born in Reus, Catalonia on June 25, 1852. His mother, Rosa Serra Gaudí, was a Reus native. His father, Francisco—originally from a farming family in Riudoms—worked as a coppersmith in Reus. The youngest of five children—two of whom had died at young ages—Gaudí was a frail and sickly child. To strengthen his health he spent a great deal of

*Antonio Gaudí y Coronet*

time at his grandparents' farm in Riudoms. Perhaps it was during this stay that he began to develop the keen awareness of nature that influenced his architectural designs.

He attended secondary school in Reus, at the local *Instituto.* Even as an adolescent he showed an interest in architecture and design. In 1867 he and two friends, Eduard Toda and José Ribera, drew up plans and a proposal for the restoration of the abandoned monastery of Poblet. César Martinell, in *Gaudí: His Life, His Theories, His Work,* described the fascination the ruins held for youth and its lifelong influence on his vocation. "The crumbling vaults and arches revealed in skeletal form the mechanics of architectural structure which he had never seen so explicitly in well-preserved buildings."

In 1873 Gaudí left Reus for Barcelona, enrolling in the Provincial School of Architecture. Although his enthusiasm for architecture never faltered, his motivation for his studies did. His attendance—and therefore his success—in his classes was erratic. To supplement the meager financial assistance his family was able to offer, Gaudí worked as a draftsman for a number of Barcelona architects, including Don Francisco de Paula del Villar, Joan Martorell, and José Fontseré Mestre. Although this preoccupation removed him from the inner circle of student friendships, he greatly benefitted from the professional experience. He was able not only to apply what he learned while at the School of Architecture, but also to produce one project that enabled him to pass a class.

During the 1874–75 school year Gaudí was employed by Fontseré, a master builder who was constructing the Ciudadela Park. An assistant had begun the calculation of a water depository, and Gaudí was entrusted with continuing it. Gaudí did not agree with the method chosen by the assistant. Although Gaudí devised another solution, Fontseré was concerned about his lack of experience. Fontseré asked his friend, Juan Torras, a professor at the School of Architecture, to review the calculations. Torras—who taught resistance materials—was intrigued and asked wanted to know who had derived the calculations.

Finding out that Gaudí was responsible, Torras enrolled him in resistance materials. Gaudí rarely attended class, but Torras found such merit in the depository project solution that he allowed Gaudí to pass the class after taking a cursory exam. Gaudí completed his studies and took his comprehensive exam in 1877; he received the title of architect in Madrid in March 1878.

## Stylistic Development

Gaudí's first commission as an architect was for the design of a decorative lamppost for the City of Barcelona to be used in the Plaza Real and the Plaza de San Sebastián. He attacked the project meticulously. He presented the municipal board with sketches, a watercolor rendering, and a detailed study that included a budget, suggested placement of the fixtures, and details on their construction. The lamppost design consisted of an ornate candelabra with gold-gilded details surrounded by four lamps. Although he was not fully compensated for his work, "his professional dignity insisted that the first of his projects to be put on public view, small as it was, should be executed with the greatest possible perfection without regard for expenditure of effort or for personal profit," according to Martinell in his book on Gaudí.

Gaudí used ironwork in future commissions, including the Casa Vicens (1878–80), a house in the village of Gracia near Barcelona. The design included symbols and motifs from nature that were popular at the time due to the Romantic Revivalist movement. More impressive than the ironwork was Gaudí's use of materials for the exterior. Unplastered brick was patterned with brightly colored ceramic tile, in a style reminiscent of Arabian architecture. Gaudí used the same mix of decorative building materials and ironwork in El Capricho (1883–85), a house in Comillas in northern Spain. With these two houses Gaudí elevated his architectural designs with his creative use of color and texture. Even at this early stage he was incorporating the elements of art—form, color and texture—with architectural design.

In 1882, Gaudí received his initial commission from Count Eusebi Güell, a textile manufacturer and leader in Catalonian industrial development. Güell became the architect's close friend and lifelong patron. At this time Count Güell requested stables on the family estate and a Barcelona town house. The facade of the Palacio Güell is dominated by what became Gaudí's trademark; two wide, parabolic arches with ornate ironwork gates filling the entrances. With the stables, the 30-year-old architect declared his structural independence. He used an elaborate vaulting system sectioned off with arches formed by mushroom columns. The horses descended into the stables using a spiral ramp, which allowed an open, flowing space at the ground level.

## Church of the Sagrada Familia

Gaudí was granted a major commission November 3, 1883. He worked intermittently on the Church of the Sagrada Familia from that time until his death in 1926. Most of Gaudí's other projects during those years served as investigations in solving problems he experienced in completing the Sagrada Familia. The church had originally been commissioned to Francisco de Paula del Villar, for whom Gaudí had worked while a student. Villar was also a teacher at the School of Architecture and the diocesan architect. The cornerstone for the church was laid in 1882. Villar resigned one year later.

Villar had designed the church in the revivalist style fashionable at the time. Gaudí redesigned the elements of the church, completing the crypts as Villar had designed them. Work progressed slowly but steadily during the course of 43 years. Neo-Gothic, Moorish, and primitive African influences are evident in the design. The arches, columns, mosaic decoration on the finials of the spires, and ornamental nature-motif decorations parallel other projects Gaudí worked on between 1883 and 1908.

In the Episcopal Palace at Astorga (1887–1894), Gaudí developed a symmetrical design stressing open interior space. Each floor's rooms surround a vertical central open space. For the College of Santa Teresa de Jesús in Barcelona (1889–94) Gaudí exhibited exterior walls of patterned rubble, brick, and terra cotta. High, narrow parabolic arches of plaster on brick piers create are an exercise in structural precision. Two secular projects, the Case Batlló (1905–07) and the Casa Milá Apartment House (1905–07), exhibited free-form windows, curving balconies, and warped surfaces.

In 1908, Gaudí began to use models for designing elements in the Church of the Sagrada Familia and relied less frequently on design drawings. He performed exact calculations to determine loads and stresses on the "tilted" columns he was developing for the church, and used models with weighted wires to verify his calculations. The columns slanted slightly and branched at the top, like trees. Sweeney and Sert explained Gaudí's theory in their biography of him: "Each branch of the 'tree-column' is directed towards the center of gravity of the section of the vault that it is supposed to carry. Each of these sections of the vaults is reinforced by steel rods, their shapes are hyperboloids and hyperbolic paraboloids."

From 1908 until his death, Gaudí concentrated only on the Sagrada Familia, with the exception of Parc Güell, a 38-acre exercise in landscape architecture with a surrealist-fantasy appeal, which he began in 1900 and in which his slanted column came to fruition. To adapt this barren hill into an intricate system of roads and footpaths, Gaudí studied the topography and struggled to retain the landscape's original structure. The result was an enormous network of curving retaining walls.

Many sections of the roads were built as overpasses supported with massive tilted columns to prevent destruction of the natural landscape. Materials were selected to blend in with the natural elements, rough stone or warped surfaces built of brick, and decorated with tile and broken-glass mosaics. Covered areas provided shelter from the sun and rain and an open-air theater faced the slope of a hill where spectators sat. The theater stage doubled as the roof of the marketplace.

Elaborating on the tilted columns used in the Parc Güell, Gaudí was able to achieve a height of 325 yards in the nave of the Sagrada Familia. As Gaudí aged he became more and more absorbed in his votive church, describing to all who visited his studio how the finished church would appear. Although he fell sick in 1911, Gaudí continued working. But funds for the church were seriously diminished. Gaudí began to help his friend Josep Dalmases, grandson of the original promoter, in soliciting funds for the project's completion.

More than 40 years after having embarked in the Sagrada Familia project, Gaudí was hit by a trolley car while crossing the street. He lingered for three days before dying on June 10, 1926. Gaudí was buried in the crypt of the Sagrada Familia, close to where he had magnificently toiled for so long.

## SOURCES:

### Books

Martinell, César, *Gaudí: His Life, His Theories, His Work,* translated by Judith Rohrer, Cambridge, MIT, 1975.
Solà-Morales, Ignasi de, *Gaudí,* New York, Rizzoli, 1983.
Sweeney, James Johnson and Josep Lluís Sert, *Antoni Gaudí,* New York, Praeger, 1960.

### Periodicals

*Time,* January 28, 1991, p. 92.

—*Sketch by Lisa A. Wroble*

# Alberto Ginastera
## 1916-1983
### Argentine composer

Reportedly, as a five-year-old boy, Alberto Evaristo Ginastera attempted to play the Argentine national anthem on his toy flute. When the instrument's limited range stymied him, the child burst into tears of frustration. So began the musical career of Argentina's foremost twentieth-century composer, one who left a legacy of operas, ballets and many kinds of instrumental and vocal music.

Born in Buenos Aires on April 11, 1916, Ginastera was a third-generation Argentine, of Spanish and Italian descent. His parents, Alberto and Luisa (Bossi) Ginastera, were not themselves musically trained, but their son began piano lessons when he was seven years old. Ginastera entered the Williams Conservatory in Buenos Aires in 1928 and studied there until 1935. He then continued his musical training at the National Conservatory of Argentina, from which he graduated at the age of 22 in 1938. Throughout the 1930s Ginastera worked intensively on his musical compositions. He earned special honors at the National Conservatory for a composition inspired by Psalm 150. But Ginastera later destroyed this piece, along with many of his early works, declaring that he wanted to be remembered only for his very *best* compositions.

During the next decades Ginastera became increasingly well known, first in his native country and later in an international context. In 1940 he was awarded the National Prize of Argentina for the ballet *Panambí,* and the following year he received the National Grand Prize for the Arts from Argentina's Ministry of Culture and Education. He began teaching musical composition; his first posts were at the National Conservatory and at the National Military Academy in Buenos Aires. These early years of his career were also marked by his first marriage, in 1941, to Mercedes de Toro. They had two children, Alejandro and Georgina.

*Alberto Ginastera*

Despite his talents and contributions, Ginastera did not find life in Argentina easy. He was an outspoken man with strong political views and he criticized Argentine military governments for what he saw as restrictions on free speech and artistic expression. Twice the Government dismissed him from his teaching positions. After the first dismissal in 1945, Ginastera—having been awarded a Guggenheim fellowship—traveled to the United States, where he resided 1946–1947. During the summer of 1946 Ginastera studied with the eminent composer Aaron Copland at the Berkshire Music Theater in Tanglewood, Massachusetts.

Upon his return, Ginastera worked assiduously to advance music in Argentina. In 1948 he organized the Argentine section of the International Society of Composers and Musicians. 1948 was also the year he became Founding Director of the Conservatory of Music and Scenic Arts in La Plata, the first of three conservatories established due to his efforts. The third such school, the Center for Advanced Musical Studies in Buenos Aires, is now considered Latin America's premier site for the study of musical composition.

## Aspects of His Compositions

Ginastera's compositions rely on traditional forms, percussion instruments, and strong rhythms, such as those associated with Argentine folk music. One school of musical thought divides Ginastera's work into two phases. The first period, lasting until about 1960, is viewed as markedly nationalistic. It produced piano solo compositions, string quartets, string duos, songs for the voice and piano, orchestral works, and ballets, such as *Estancia,* the 1941 ballet Lincoln Kirstein commissioned Ginastera to create, and work that included scenes from Argentine country life.

The later period yielded cantatas, operas, and concertos, works that some critics have seen as more sophisticated. One such creation is the opera *Bomarzo,* which premiered in Washington in 1967. Marked by dissonance and provocative scenes of violence and sexuality, the opera was banned in Ginastera's native country. Ginastera responded by forbidding any performances of his compositions in Argentina until the ban was lifted—which happened in 1972.

Not everyone agrees with the two-phase vision of Ginastera's work. According to Malena Kuss, writing in *Alberto Ginastera: A Complete Catalogue,* "It is more accurate to view the fifty-four opus-numbered works that represent his total oeuvre [1937–1983] as an uninterrupted search for synthesis between the sounds that carry the stamp of his culture and the twentieth century techniques he learned to master with consummate virtuosity." In any case, Ginastera's talents and achievements were immense, recognized in many countries throughout the composer's life with honorary degrees, association memberships, and festivals of his music.

Ginastera died in Geneva on June 25, 1983. He and his second wife—the cellist Aurora Natola, for whom he wrote a cello sonata and the *Second Cello Concerto*—had lived in Switzerland since their marriage in 1971. Ginastera left an unfinished work at the time of his death: he had completed seven of the eight movements for *Popul Vuh,* a work Kuss deemed was "conceived on a monumental scale" a symphonic fresco based on the creation of the world according to the Mayas and an apotheosis of that elusive pre-Columbian past that nourished his musical imagination intermittently since the earliest ballet."

## SOURCES:

### Books

*Alberto Ginastera: A Complete Catalogue,* revised edition, London and New York, Boosey and Hawkes, 1986.
*Annual Obituary 1983,* edited by Elizabeth Devine, Chicago, St. James Press, 1984.
*Baker's Biographical Dictionary of Musicians,* eighth edition, revised by Nicolas Slonimsky, New York, Schirmer, 1992.
*Dictionary of Contemporary Music,* edited by John Vinton, New York, Dutton, 1974.

*New Grove Dictionary of Music and Musicians,*
　Volume 7, edited by Stanley Sadie, London,
　Macmillan, 1980.
Storni, Eduardo, *Ginastera,* Madrid, Espasa-Calpe,
　1983.
Urtubey, Pola Suárez, *Alberto Ginastera,* Buenos
　Aires, Ediciones Culturales Argentinas, 1967.

　　　　　　　　　—*Sketch by Erika Dreifus*

# Luis de Góngora y Argote
## 1561-1627
**Spanish poet**

*Luis de Góngora y Argote*

Luis de Góngora y Argote is a central figure of the Spanish Golden Age of Literature. Few writers have been both so controversial and so influential. The convoluted Baroque style of Góngora's poetry was mercilessly denigrated by Quevedo, **Lope de Vega**, and other contemporaries. Traces of Góngora's style, however, can be discerned in their own writing. Two of Góngora's major poetic works, "Las Soledades" ("The Solitudes") and "La Fábula de Polifemo y Galatea" ("Fable of Polyphemus and Galatea"), opened a new dimension in Spanish Literature. The Latinized language employed by Góngora in these works was rich, while the syntax was complex. Allusions to myths and legends were abundant as well. Study of these characteristics required profusely annotated editions and commentaries even in the seventeenth century.

During his lifetime, Góngora witnessed the gradual decline of Habsburg Spain, as the powerful Philip II was succeeded by the incompetent Philip III (1598) and Philip IV (1621). The latter two kings left power in the hands of corrupt and inept favorites, while the imperial economy decayed in spite of the gold imported every year from the New World through the port of Seville. As a participant in activities of the royal court and one who depended on the patronage of the nobility, Góngora had an unobstructed view of the political and social intrigue and decadence of the period. However, he also belonged to an era of flourishing literary achievements. Góngora's enemies and admirers were among the most gifted writers in Spanish literary history. While **Miguel de Cervantes** praised the young Góngora in his poem "Canto de Calíope" ("Song of Calliope" ), other colleagues were not so kind. Lope de Vega, and especially Quevedo, ruthlessly attacked him and his work. Much of this vilification of Góngora was aimed at the poet more than his work. Such attacks were regarded as a part of life in the royal court, where writers engaged in literary rivalries for the patronage of the powerful.

The fourth child of an illustrious and prosperous family, Luis de Góngora was born in 1561 in Córdoba, Spain, at the peak of the Spanish Empire under the rule of Philip II. His father was a judge with a reputation for being a cultivated man. Góngora benefited from his father's well-furnished library, a rare commodity in those times. He studied in the local Jesuit school and received the best possible education for the times, an advantage shared by many brilliant writers of the period.

While details of Góngora's childhood are few, an injury that he suffered during this period has been the subject of considerable speculation over the years. A head injury incurred while playing proved to be a serious one. The doctors brought in to treat him feared he would die, but at the last minute somebody brought a relic from Saint Alvaro to his bed. According to the tale, the relic miraculously cured him. Some of his biographers have attributed Góngora's obscure poetic style to this childhood head injury, although their views of the merit of his work colored their opinions on whether the incident was a fortuitous one.

Góngora's family was very interested in their son's education. They sent him to the University of Salamanca to study canon law. By this time, the economic situation of the family had deteriorated. Góngora's maternal uncle, Francisco de Góngora, prebend of the Cathedral of Córdoba, made his nephew his protégé, conveying several ecclesiastic benefices to him and supplying him with money to pursue his studies. In order to accept these benefices Góngora had to take minor orders. This patronage may explain why Góngora always used his maternal family name instead of his paternal one (Argote), as was the Spanish tradition.

Góngora's four years of study in Salamanca from 1576 to 1580 were not academically successful ones. He immersed himself in light-hearted student life in detriment to his studies. He developed a gambling habit that stayed with him for the rest of his life. Still, these years were decisive in his formation as a poet. His ingenio ("acuteness") did not go unnoticed, and he began to develop a reputation as an ingenious writer of short poems. Biographers believe that he probably wrote some of his sonnets of Petrarchan influence during these years.

In 1580 Góngora left Salamanca without a degree in canon law. Once again, his uncle interceded on his behalf and provided young Góngora with church responsibilities. In order to fulfill his new duties in the cathedral of Córdoba, Góngora took minor orders up to the position of deacon, although he had no intention of entering the priesthood.

### Enemies and Intrigues

During his years back in Córdoba, Góngora continued to write poetry. His efforts became increasingly successful. In 1580 he had his first poem published in Gómez Tapia's translation of Camoen's "Os Lusiadas" ("The Lusiads"). In 1584 one of his sonnets served as a preface to Juan Rufo 's "La Austriada" ("The Austriad"), an epic that celebrated the Habsburg dynasty. His minor compositions, usually imitations of folk genres such as the romances and *letrillas,* were written in this first stage of his career. These celebrated poems were included in 1605 in Pedro de Espinosas's *Flores de Poetas Ilustres* (*Flowers of Illustrious Poets*).

In 1587 the new bishop of the Cathedral of Córdoba accused Góngora of not fulfilling the duties attached to his position in the cathedral. Góngora had reportedly been seen attending bullfights and talking excessively during the choir services, among other ungodly activities. Góngora refuted these accusations in a humorous way, and flatly denied a charge that he had written profane verses. The accusations did not seem to have any further consequences.

In 1590 Góngora embarked on the first of several trips through Spain that he was obligated to take because of his position in the church. In 1593, on a trip to Salamanca, Góngora met Lope de Vega, whom he immediately disliked. In 1603 he went to Valladolid, where the court had moved temporarily. There he met several famous writers, among them Cervantes and Quevedo. The latter figure became Góngora's mortal enemy for the rest of his life.

### Góngora's Poetic Revolution

1611 was a banner year in Góngora's life. He resigned his prebend at the cathedral—offering it to his nephew—and retired to live in his country home, La Huerta de San Marcos. Here he wrote his two major works: *The Solitudes* and *Polyphemus and Galatea.* These two major compositions were without precedent in Spanish Literature, although some critics contend that traits of these works can be found in his earlier, shorter compositions. *The Solitudes* did not have a traditional plot. Instead, the work presented a resentful lover who lands in an Arcadian country after a shipwreck. This survivor meets some shepherds, joins a local wedding, then arrives on an island. Although Góngora had planned to write four parts, he actually only composed two. This decision may have been influenced by the abrupt attacks that the poem attracted, noticeably Quevedo's parody "Aguja de navegar culto, con la receta de hacer 'Soledades' en un día" ("The Compass for Navigating Learnedly, with the Recipe for Concocting 'Solitudes' in One Day").

Góngora's other major composition, *Polyphemus and Galatea,* was based on the myth of the Cyclops Polyphemus, a popular fable of the time. Influenced by Ovid's *Metamorphosis,* the poem detailed the well-known affair of the lovers Acis and the sea nymph Galatea, and the subsequent violence meted out by the one-eyed Cyclops Polyphemus. The monstrous and jealous Polyphemus butchers the handsome Acis, who is finally metamorphosed into a river.

Góngora's innovative treatment of the language made these poems both controversial and influential. This completely new poetic language came to be known as Gongorismo. This new language featured a highly complex syntax influenced by Latin, a Latinized vocabulary, rich imagery, and a wealth of mythological allusions. Góngora's contemporaries' attitude toward these two major poetic works and their revolutionary poetic language was not unanimous. Most criticism was directed at the innovative Latinized vocabulary and the complexity and obscurity of the poems, and Góngora was accused of being bombastic and pretentious. Quevedo and Lope de Vega were among the most famous antagonists. Juan de Jauregui wrote "Antidote Against the Solitudes" in 1613 and was one of his most hostile critics. Despite such ridicule, many poets and theorists supported Góngora's polemical work, as the many commentaries written on the poems at the time testify.

In 1617, with the help of his benefactors in the court, Góngora managed to obtain a position as Chaplain of Honor to Philip III. The appointment—an honorary position with little economic reward—

required that he be ordained a priest. His life in the court was closely tied to his benefactors, though, and as they lost the favor of the king his position in the court was threatened. During all his life Góngora went through economic hardship, and his spending and gambling habits did not help his situation. The poet's economic situation deteriorated further in the early 1620s. His implacable literary enemy Quevedo bought Góngora's house in an auction in 1625, then further humiliated the man by evicting him. Góngora's final years were marked by sickness and debt. He suffered an apoplectic stroke that destroyed part of his memory and left him paralyzed. In the last year of his life Góngora returned to Córdoba, where he died in 1627. Even his nephew, Luis de Saavedra, who Góngora had protected before, forgot his ailing uncle. Upon Góngora's death de Saavedra inherited his unpublished manuscripts. His nephew never published them, however, so most of Góngora's prose works were lost.

The *Solitudes* and *Polyphemus and Galatea,* while the subject of countless debates in the seventeen century, remained influential for a time. In the same century Sor Juana Inés de la Cruz wrote "First Dream" in accordance with Góngora's style. During the eighteenth and nineteenth century, however, Góngora's work was disregarded as affected and in poor taste. Only in the late nineteenth century, when Paul Verlaine and the French symbolist movement found certain ties between their poetry and that of Góngora, did his work return to prominence. The Nicaraguan poet and Nobel Prize winner **Ruben Darío**, founder of Modernism, discovered Góngora during his stay in Paris and praised him in his prologue to *Cantos de Vida y Esperanza* (*Songs of Life and Hope*) in 1905.

The "Generation of 1927" —a literary group that took its name from the 300th anniversary of Góngora's death—championed his work as well. Poets of this generation, including such renowned figures as **Federico Gárcia Lorca**, rehabilitated Góngora's memory. Another member of this generational group, **Dámaso Alonso**, a poet and literary critic who became the president of the Spanish Academy, emerged as one of his most important scholars. Over the last number of years Góngora's poems have been re-edited several times and a vast amount of scholarship has been dedicated to his poetry. The major works of Góngora have been translated into English, in some cases with extensive commentaries that help the modern reader approach the rich complexity of Góngora's poetry.

## SELECTED PUBLISHED WORKS:

*Obras completas de Don Luis de Góngora y Argote,* edited by Juan Millé y Giménez and Isabel Millé y Giménez, Aguilar, 1967.

*"The Solitudes" of Don Luis de Góngora,* translated by Gilbert F. Cunningham, edited by Alexander Parker, John Hopkins Press, 1968.
*Polyphemus and Galatea: A Study in the Interpretation of a Baroque Poem,* translated by Gilbert F. Cunningham, edited by Alexander Parker, University of Texas Press, 1977.
*The Fable of Polyphemus and Galatea: A Bilingual Version with a Critical Analysis,* Volume 75 of American University Studies, translated by Miroslav John Hanak, Peter Lang, 1988.

## SOURCES:

Alonso, Dámaso, *Góngora y el Polifemo,* Madrid: Gredos, 1961.
Alonso, Dámaso, and Eulalia Galvarriato de Alonso, *Para la biogafía de Góngora: documentos desconocidos,* Madrid: Gredos, 1962.
Artigas y Fernando, Miguel, *Don Luis de Góngora y Argote: biografía y estudio crítico,* Madrid: Real Academia Española, 1925.
Comás, Antonio, and Juan Regla, *Góngora: su tiempo y su obra,* Barcelona: Teide, 1960.
Foster, David William, and Virgina Ramos Foster, *Luis de Góngora,* New York: Twayne, 1973.

*—Sketch by Enrique Fernández*

# Felipe González
## 1942-
### Spanish prime minister

Felipe González has been Spain's socialist prime minister since 1982. That election victory established Spain's first leftist government since the Spanish Civil War. After his election to a fourth successive term in 1993, the Spanish newspaper *El Mundo* heralded González as "one of those politicians who come once in the lifetime of a nation." Charles Bremer of The *London Times* asserted that "Both friends and foes agree that the socialist party's survival [in the 1993 elections] ... was due to the grace and staying power of the Andalusian charmer who has run Spain for the last eleven years." González has endured as Spain's most popular politician despite accusations of corruption in the Socialist Party of which he is a member and an economic slump in the early 1990s. González has enjoyed a solid international reputation and ranks as one of Europe's senior statesmen.

*Felipe González*

The 'Felipe factor' has been fundamental to the electoral success of the Spanish Socialist Worker Party (PSOE) in recent years. González is widely regarded as the man who was able to make socialism electable in Spain. He adopted a moderate political strategy that appealed to a broad spectrum of the population. An exponent of pragmatic socialism, González expressed his dedication to the establishment of democracy. González's early political activity, however, was undertaken in clandestine fashion, for under the authoritarian rule of the dictator **Francisco Franco**—who ruled Spain for 36 years until 1975—democracy did not exist and the PSOE was regarded as an illegal organization.

Felipe González Márquez was born on March 5, 1942, in Seville, Andalusia, one of four children. His father was a cowherder who eventually built a small dairy of his own. There were no books in the González household, where González's affectionate and warm mother was an important influence on her children. Educated by Roman Catholic priests, the young Felipe was not a studious pupil. Eventually, he was expelled from school in his final year because of a girlfriend. He suffered from asthma as a child, which he claims conditioned him to exist on five hours of sleep a night, but was also a middle- and long-distance runner. His early political allegiance lay hesitantly between left-wing Catholicism and socialism.

González's political activist roots can be traced back to his student days at Seville University, where he studied law, specializing in labor relations. He joined the Socialist Youth and met Alfonso Guerra, who later became his deputy prime minister; the two forged a lasting personal and political friendship. Guerra's ability and loyalty proved important to González's creation of a cohesive administrative unit in his future government. In 1964, while still at the university, González joined the PSOE. Together with Guerra he convened with various left-wing militants in the cellars of the archbishop's palace, under the guise of attending workers' lectures. The archbishop consented to their presence as the Catholic Church began to distance itself from the Franco regime.

After graduating from Seville University in 1965, González won a scholarship to Loauvian University in Belgium but left, dispirited with the lifestyle. He told Susan Crosland of The *Sunday Times Magazine* that he "couldn't stand that leaden low sky. And I did not like the programmed drunkenness that starts at six thirty on Friday evenings when everybody goes home." After a period of military service he returned to Seville and practiced as a lawyer with Guerra. Concerned with the plight of ordinary working class people, González in 1966 opened the first legal advice office in Seville. There he offered legal advice and assistance to workers involved in industrial disputes. He devoted all his spare time to politics, traveling around Spain contacting various members of the illegal Socialist Party. Though he operated in secret under the code name "Isidoro" he was often trailed by the secret police.

Between 1965 and 1970, González was a member of the Seville Provincial Committee and the National PSOE Committee. He rapidly ascended the party ladder, becoming a member of the Executive Committee in 1970. In 1974, at the PSOE's last congress in exile in Paris, the 32-year-old González was elected secretary general. Following Franco's death in 1975 and tentative moves by King **Juan Carlos** towards democratization and liberalization, the PSOE was finally legalized in 1977. In June 1977 the first democratic general elections since 1936 were held and González was elected deputy for Madrid.

González was never a Marxist. He refused to stand for re-election to the post of secretary general at his party's 28th congress in May 1979. He objected to the party's self-described Marxist ideology; the PSOE acquiesced and the Marxist definition was discarded. This action was integral to the PSOE's broad appeal in future general elections. González professed that he had no prime ministerial aspirations at this juncture, and declared in *Time* that "I know it is politically bad to say this. I have said it before and I will say it again, I never had any personal ambition to be Prime Minister at any time."

Spain's fragile democracy nearly ended on February 23, 1981, in an attempted coup headed by Colonel Antonio Tejero. Spain's parliamentary chambers were stormed and González was among a number of leading politicians who were held hostage at gunpoint. González recalled his thoughts at that time to Susan Crosland in an interview for The *Sunday Times Magazine.* "For twenty years we worked to regain freedom, and at last obtained democracy. Now we had lost it. Everyone would have to start all over again. I had this terrible feeling of tiredness." King Juan Carlos personally intervened, however, with a public declaration of his opposition to the conspirators, and the coup failed.

### González Named Prime Minister

On October 28, 1982, González led the PSOE to electoral victory, capturing 46 percent of the vote, a parliamentary majority. González was elected president of the government on December 1, 1982. His election victory countered criticism that people perceived him as too young, naive, and inexperienced to govern. The election of a socialist government epitomized the dramatic transformation of Spain's political landscape. In the formative years of González's government there was still an air of uncertainty as to whether democracy could survive; Spain had to pass González's own litmus test of democracy—"hearing a knock on the door in the morning and knowing it's only the postman"—as The *New York Times* noted. Repeated electoral successes, albeit with fewer seats, in 1986, 1989, and 1993 illustrated that González and the PSOE had political durability.

González's personal socialist ideology has been called into question. He has adamantly and passionately declared himself a socialist and a democrat. However, some observers have questioned his socialist credentials, charging that Gonzalez has never been that concerned with issues such as redistributing wealth in Spain. Before the 1982 elections, in fact, a reporter for The *New York Times* asked him if he intended, once in power, to strip the rich of their wealth. He answered, "No, we want to get rid of the poor." The *Economist* contended in 1991 that, "Once unblushing red, Mr. Gonzalez's socialism has paled to a whiter shade of pink." Others feel that Gonzalez's socialist manifesto has simply become more flexible and point to his statements that he does not adhere to political philosophies that do not work. This increasingly conservative brand of socialism, sometimes termed *Felipismo,* has been criticized by left-wingers and union leaders. When asked what characteristics still identified him as a socialist, he told The *Financial Times* that "my rejection, my repugnance of the fact that a person's health can be subject to the rule of the market place. If you can afford the product, buy it. You can't? Well, you are finished. If someone without money needs a kidney transplant our duty is to give them the opportunity."

Gonzalez presided over a flourishing economy in the 1980s. A committed and enthusiastic European, Gonzalez brought Spain into the European Economic Community, contributing to the end of Spain's isolationism. He has introduced reforms that have helped to support and endorse democracy and modernization in Spain. However, Spain in the 1990s has been plagued by endemic unemployment—22 percent in 1993—and suffered with the rest of Europe under that continent's protracted recession.

González is married to Maria del Carmen Romero López, who was a secondary school teacher in Andalusia. She later entered the sphere of politics and became a PSOE member of parliament. They have three children: Pablo, David, and Maria. Richard Wigg of The *Times* noted that Gonzalez's early commitment to socialism has caused him to reflect with some regret that he had little time to enjoy life, resulting in a paucity of "inner biography."

### SOURCES:

*Economist,* May 4, 1991, pp. 47–8.
*Financial Times,* December 17, 1990, p. 36; October 11, 1993, p. 32.
*New York Times,* October 30, 1982, p. 1, 4.
*Sunday Times Magazine,* February 10, 1985, pp. 20–3.
*Time,* June 9, 1980, pp. 30–1.
*Times* (London), October 27, 1983, p. 8; September 21, 1988, p. 7; June 8, 1993, p. 7.
*Washington Post,* January 31, 1993, p. 20, 23.

*—Sketch by Amanda Beresford*

# Henry B. Gonzalez
## 1916-
### Mexican American statesman

Veteran U.S. Congressman Henry B. Gonzalez is credited with having paved the way for other Hispanics to succeed in politics. The first Mexican American to be elected to the Texas State Senate in modern times, Gonzalez has represented the state's 20th district in Washington, D.C., for more than 30 years. He has received numerous honors, including the National Alliance to End Homelessness Award, the Texas Civic Leadership Award, the 1992 National Rural Housing Legislator of the Year, and the 1994

Profile in Courage Award from the John F. Kennedy Foundation.

Enrique Barbosa Gonzalez was born in San Antonio, Texas, on May 3, 1916. His parents—Leonides and Genoveva (Barbosa) Gonzalez—had fled from Mexico and the revolution there in 1911. Gonzalez's father had served as the mayor of Mapimi in the northern Mexican state of Durango; in San Antonio, he became managing editor of the Spanish language daily newspaper, *La Prensa.* One of six siblings, Gonzalez was impressed with the importance of education at a young age. He studied at San Antonio Junior College and the University of Texas at Austin and earned a law degree from St. Mary's University School of Law in 1943. By that time he had married Bertha Cuellar; they became the parents of eight children. During World War II, Gonzalez served as a censor in military and naval intelligence. In 1943 he became an assistant juvenile probation officer, and by 1946 he was chief juvenile probation officer for San Antonio, where he was responsible for getting the deficient juvenile system changed. Gonzalez resigned the position in 1946 after he was told he could not hire a black staff member.

Before entering politics, Gonzalez served as executive secretary for the Pan American Progressive Association; ran a Spanish-English translation service; wrote for bicultural publications; became a director for the International Ladies Garment Workers Union; and worked with the Housing Authority for the City of San Antonio.

In 1950 Gonzalez mounted an ultimately unsuccessful bid to serve on the Texas State Legislature. Three years later, however, he succeeded in winning a seat on the San Antonio City Council. In his newfound political station, Gonzalez aimed to counter the prejudice against Mexican Americans he had experienced since childhood by working to desegregate city facilities.

Gonzalez became a state senator in 1956, the first of Mexican descent in the history of the Senate. The man who had experienced discrimination when he was young now faced it in the senate where he was referred to as "that Mexican." Gonzalez spent five years in the Texas Senate where, biographer Eugene Rodriguez observed, he left an indelible impression for having "[opened] the minds of thousands of Texans who impulsively believed in segregation." In May 1957, Gonzalez and Senator Abraham "Chick" Kazen of Laredo made national headlines when they set a state record for a 36-hour filibuster that killed all but one of the ten segregation bills. Rodriguez declared, "Gonzalez's uncompromising stand on segregation lifted him into a position of state-wide prominence."

## Won Congressional Seat

With the urging of his supporters, Gonzalez ran an unsuccessful race for the Texas governorship in 1958. When U.S. Congressman Paul Kilday vacated his House of Representatives seat to accept a military court appointment in 1960, Gonzalez decided to campaign for the empty position. Rodriguez wrote: "Gonzalez was the best known politician in San Antonio. His fame as an orator, a champion of the people, and a dedicated public official was established." With endorsements from Governor Price Daniel, the Texas House delegation, Senator Ralph Yarborough, President John F. Kennedy, and Vice President Lyndon B. Johnson, Gonzalez won. Thus began a career of over thirty years in the House of Representatives.

In Congress, Gonzalez has pursued his interests in banking, insurance, urban renewal, and housing and consumer affairs. In a 1964 interview with Rodriguez, Gonzalez declared that one of his primary objectives as an officeholder was to vote on every issue so that the public would always know his position.

In his emphasis on information and knowledge, Gonzalez has disseminated newsletters and written articles for various periodicals. In *Harper's Magazine,* Christopher Hitchens described observing a House "session" only to discover Gonzalez speaking to an empty room. Known for his after-hours speeches, Gonzalez has used the tactic for years to speak directly to U.S. citizens watching the C-SPAN cable network; it also has allowed his speeches to be recorded in the Congressional Record. Hitchens wrote that on that particular day he visited—during President Ronald Reagan's term—Gonzalez "was warning his country, if none of his peers, of the impending calamity of the savings and loan business."

In 1989 Gonzalez became chairman of the U.S. House Banking, Finance, and Urban Affairs Committee, where he conducted hearings on the savings and loan fiasco and was instrumental in developing the subsequent bailout bill with its lending and accounting regulations. He also focused on the commercial banking industry, warning of the need for better regulation.

The outspoken Congressman has not always found support among his peers. "Loose cannon," "crackpot," and "eccentric" are terms Hitchens used to describe some peer appraisals. Gonzalez's call for the impeachment of President George Bush in 1991 for the U.S.'s role in the Persian Gulf War with Iraq drew little support. Similarly, Gonzalez had called for the impeachment of Ronald Reagan on two separate occasions: in 1983 for the invasion of Grenada, and in 1987 for the Iran/Contra affair. Although he was not supported in his impeachment efforts, he was praised for his honest investigation of the savings and loan problems and the Keating Five. Hitchens quoted Wisconsin Republican Toby Roth in *Harper's Magazine* as saying that Gonzalez "has the stick-to-itiveness of an English bulldog. He's a genuine old-fashioned public servant."

## SOURCES:

### Books

*Current Biography Yearbook 1993,* edited by Judith Graham, New York, H. W. Wilson, pp. 214–17.

Rodriguez, Jr., Eugene, *Henry B. Gonzalez: A Political Profile,* New York, Arno Press, 1976.

### Periodicals

*Forbes,* April 12, 1993, pp. 138.
*Fortune,* August 9, 1993.
*Harper's Magazine,* October 1992, pp. 84–96.
*Mother Jones,* July-August 1991, pp. 12–13.
*Time,* May 13, 1957, pp. 27; January 21, 1991, pp. 57.

—*Sketch by Sandy J. Stiefer*

# Manuel González Prada
## 1844(?)-1918
### Peruvian essayist and poet

Manuel González Prada was a preeminent essayist and poet whose radical and revolutionary thought persists in Peru to the present day. In *Makers of Democracy in Latin America,* 1968, Harold Davis asserted that "For years González Prada was the Peruvian conscience." González Prada's ideological stance shifted from a staunch condemnation of the ruling oligarchy of Peru: the aristocracy, the Catholic Church and the military, to a vehement espousal of anarchism and outright revolution led by the working classes. He was a powerful voice; of his literary skills Enrique Anderson Imbert, in *Spanish American Literature,* 1963, praised, "There is not, in these years, either in Spain or America, a prose as sharp and incisive as that of González Prada."

Manuel González Prada was born on January 5, 1844 (some sources say January 6 or 1848), the third son of Francisco González de Prada and Josefa Alvárez de Ulloa, in Lima, Peru. His family was wealthy and aristocratic, tracing its noble roots to the

courts of Charles V, Philip II and Philip III. González Prada's father served as Minister to Bolivia until a revolution drove the family into exile to Chile.

González Prada received his early education at the Colegio Inglés in Valparíso, Chile, where he learned English and German. When his family returned to Lima, he enrolled at the Seminary of Santo Toribo until 1861, when he entered the Colegio de San Carlos; there he engendered an interest in science. His desire to study engineering in Belgium was quashed by his mother; against his will, he attended San Marcos University as a law student, where he immersed himself in literature. After a year he left university to manage the family estate in Cañete, south of Lima, where he devoted himself to scientific pursuits and writing.

### A Polemic Essayist and Political Thinker

During the War of the Pacific with Chile from 1879 to 1883 González Prada was an officer in the reserves. Chile's occupation of Lima exposed Peru's deep social and economic wounds, and aroused González Prada's abiding concern for his country. He instigated and led a Peruvian intellectual revival, condemning Peru's ruling oligarchy, deeming them detached and out of touch with the people. In particular González Prada identified the urgent necessity of Indian integration as a precursor to a truly proper Peruvian nation. The faults Gonzalez Prada perceived in Peruvian society inspired him to write propagandist essays, collected in *Págines Libres,* published in 1894. Despite his fervent speeches and essays he was a shy and private man.

In 1885 he became president of the Círculo Literario, a group of liberal writers, whose objectives were the regeneration and democratization of Peru; their slogan was "Propaganda and Attack." He announced that his duty was "to show the people the horror of their debasement and misery, a good autopsy was never made without dissecting the body, and no society can be thoroughly known without taking the flesh off the skeleton" (cited by Jean Franco in *An Introduction to Spanish-American Literature,* 1969). The Círculo Literario subscribed to the positivist philosophy; Gonzalez Prada adhered to the conviction that science was the liberating force, particularly of the Indian cause. In a speech made in 1888 Gonzalez Prada declared his belief in scientific progress, "that a single century of industrial application has brought more good to Humanity than entire millenia of Theology and Metaphysics" (cited by Jean Franco, 1969). In 1891, together with members of the Círculo Literario, Gonzalez Prada founded La Unión Nacional, one of the first political parties in Peru.

Gonzalez Prada suddenly abandoned La Unión Nacional, spending the following seven years in Europe, c. 1892 to 1898 (sources vary: 1887–94,

1885–91). France was his wife's native country—he married Adrienne Verneuil on September 11, 1887—and the birthplace of their son, Alfredo. He attended lectures at the Collége de France and had contact with radical thinkers, such as Renan, and movements of the Old World. His return to Peru marked a move into anarchist sympathies. His European influences materialize in his essays in *Horas de lucha*, 1908, which preach for the reform of Peruvian society from within through revolution and damn the ruling oligarchy. In one of his essays in *Nuestra indios*, he claimed: "To the Indian one should not preach humility and resignation but pride and rebellion. What has he gained by three or four hundred years of conformity and patience?" When the outlets of his published writings, such as the newspapers, were closed, his anarchist philosophies and his bitterness deepened.

As a celebrated but lesser-known poet, González Prada's work was characterized by an individualistic and innovative style of verse, which utilized French and German metrical forms. Much of González Prada's poetry was escapist; the poet wrote in *Minúscular*, 1900, "Since it is best to be resigned, let us be resigned in prose, for in verse, we fight for the lily and the rose" (cited by Jean Franco, 1969). However, not all of González Prada's poetry was free of political comment. Many critics consider *Baladas Indias* to be among his most original contributions. Here the poet reminisced on the plight of the Indians: "Why do some starve and others eat well?" (cited by Jean Franco, 1969). In the poetry of his later years González Prada reveals his frustrations and nihilism; Jean Franco, in *A Literary History of Spain*, 1973, judged this to be his best work—the meaninglessness of existence combined with elements of optimism.

Towards the end of his life González Prada organized working-class movements and contributed articles to *Los Parias,* founded in 1905. In 1912 he became the director of the National Library (some sources say 1914) until his death on July 22 1918; he briefly resigned the post when President Guillermo Billingshurst was overthrown, resuming the position when a new constitutional president was appointed. His office and home provided meeting places for intellectuals, including future leaders Victor Raúl Haya de la Torre, the founder of A.P.R.A. (Alianza Popular Revolucionaria Americana), and José Carlos Mariátegui, the founder of the Peruvian Communist Party.

## SELECTED PUBLISHED WORKS:

*Páginas libres,* (essays and speeches), Tipografís de P. Dupont, 1894, abridged edition, Tipografía librería de A. Quiroz Perea, 1934, corrected definitive edition, Editorial P.T.C.M., 1946, reprinted in two volumes, Ediciones Páginas Libres, 1960.

*Los partidos y la Unión nacional, conferencia del señot Manuel G. Prada, Lima,21 de agosto de 1898,* Imprenta Grau (Callao, Peru), 1899.

*Minúsculas,* (poems), Ediciones de Cien Ejemplares, Lima, Peru, 1901, 3rd edition, Librería e Imprenta "El Inca", Lima, 1928, 4th edition, Adoración, 1986.

*Manuel G. Prada: El catolicismo y la mujer; Tirada: Three Thousand ejemplares,* Asociació de Propaganda Liberal, 1904.

*Horas de lucha,* (title means "Hours of struggle"), Tipografía "El progreso literario", Lima, 1908, 3rd edition, Callao, Peru, 1935, reprinted, Editorial Universo, 1972.

*Manuel G. Prada: Exóticas,* Tipografía de "El Lucero," 1911, reprinted, Tipografía de Louis Bellenand et Fils, Paris, 1933.

*Bajo el oprobio,* Tipografía de L. Bellenand et Fils, 1933, reprinted, Imprenta Editores Tipo-offset, 1979.

*Manuel G. Prada: Baladas peruanas,* (poems), with prologue by Luis Alberto Sánchez, Prensas de la Editorial Ercilla, 1935, reprinted, Bendezú, 1969.

*Manuel G. Prada: Anarquía,* Ediciones Ercilla, 1936, 4th edition published as *Anarquía,* Editorial P.T.C.M., 1948.

*Manuel G. Prada: Grafitos,* edited by son, Alfredo González Prada, Tipografía de L. Bellenand et Fils, 1937.

*Manuel G. Prada: Nuevas páginas libres,* Ediciones Ercilla, 1937.

*Manuel G. Prada: Libertarias,* Tipografía de L. Belland et Fils, 1938.

*Manuel G. Prada: Baladas,* edited by A. González Prada, Tipografía de L. Bellenand et Fils, 1939.

*M. González Prada: Propaganda y ataque,* Ediciones Imán, Buenos Aires, 1939.

*Manuel González Prada: Antologís poética,* edited by Carlos González Prada, Editorial Cultura, 1940.

*González Prada: Pensamientos,* selection and prologue by Campio Carpio, Arco Iris, 1941.

*M. González Prada: Prosa menuda,* Ediciones Imán, 1941.

*González Prada,* selection and prologue by Andrés Henestrosa, Secretaría de Educación Pública, 1943.

*El tonel de Diógenes, sequido de Fragmentaria y Memoranda,* Edición Tezontle, Mexico, 1945.

*Florilegio: Poesía, ensayo, critica,* [Lima], 1948.

*Ensayos escogidos,* selection and prologue by Augusto Salazar Bondy, Patronato del Libro Peruano, 1956, 3rd revised and enlarged edition, Editorial Universo, 1970.

*Sus mejores páginas,* Editora Paracas, c. 1962.

*Figuras y figurones: Manuel Pardo, Pierola, Romaña, José Pardo,* Bendezú, 1969.

*Poemas desconocidos,* selection by Elsa Villanueva de Puccinelli, Ediciones de la Clépsidra, 1973.

*Letrillas,* Editorial Milla Batres, 1975.

*Pensamiento político de González Prada,* (selections), Instituto Nacional de Cultura, 1975.

*Antología: Páginas libertarias,* Ediciones peisa, 1976.

*Manuel González Prada,* Ministerio de Cultura, Juventud y Deportes, Departmento de Publicaciones, 1977.

*Ortometria: Apuntes para una ritmica,* Universidad Nacional Mayor de San Marcos, Dirección Universitaria de Biblioteca y Publicaciones, 1977.

*Nuestros indios,* Universidad Autónoma de México, 1978.

*Sobre el militarismo; antología; Bajo el oprobio,* (selections), Editorial Horizonte, 1978.

*Cantos del otro siglo,* Universidad Nacional Mayor de San Marcos, Dirección Universitaria de Biblioteca y Publicaciones, 1979.

*Textos,* (selections), SEP-UNAM, 1982.

*Obras,* (collected works), Ediciones Copé, Departmento de Relaciones Públicas de PETRO-PERU, 1985.

## SOURCES:

### Books

Alexander, Robert J., editor, *Biographical Dictionary of Latin American and Caribbean Political Leaders,* Greenwood Press Inc., Westport, Connecticut, 1988, pp. 192–3.

Anderson Imbert, Enrique, *Spanish-American Literature: A History,* translated by John V. Falconieri, Wayne State University Press, Detroit, 1963, pp. 220–222.

Davis, Harold Eugene, *Latin American Social Thought: The History of Its Development Since Independence, With Selected Readings,* University Press of Washington, D.C., Second American Edition, 1966, pp. 195–208.

Davis, Harold Eugene, *Makers of Democracy in Latin America,* Cooper Square Publishers, Inc., New York, 1986, pp. 80–84.

Delpar, Helen, editor, *Encyclopedia of Latin America,* McGraw-Hill Book Company, New York, 1974, pp. 256–7.

Franco, Jean, *An Introduction to Spanish-American Literature,* Cambridge University Press, 1969.

Franco, Jean, *A Literary History of Spain: Spanish Literature Since Independence,* Ernest Benn Ltd., London and New York, 1973, pp. 94–7.

Klein, Leonard S., editor, *Latin American Literature in the Twentieth Century,* Oldcastle Books Ltd., London, 1988, pp. 212–3.

Ryan, Bryan, editor, *Hispanic Writers: A Selection of Sketches from Contemporary Authors,* Gale Research Inc., Detroit and London, 1991, pp. 236–7.

—*Sketch by Amanda Beresford*

# Francisco Goya
## 1746-1828
### Spanish painter

The importance of Francisco de Goya y Lucientes in the history of Spanish art cannot be overestimated. Goya's work towers over the eighteenth and nineteenth centuries, like the giant in his painting "El Coloso" ("The Colossus"). His paintings, drawings, engravings, and other graphic work, both in terms of technique and subject matter, leave the polite social decor of the eighteenth century far behind, while anticipating many of the aesthetic and philosophical concerns of nineteenth- and twentieth-century art.

Perhaps the most intriguing aspect of Goya's life is its duality. Goya was at once a very successful public painter and "Pintor de Cámara" ("Royal Painter"); at the same time he was a privately tormented individual, suffering a series of misfortunes, including a sickness that left him deaf. Even his privileged situation of royal favor could not secure his position in a Spain ravaged by war and murderous politics. He exiled himself to France, and died in Bordeaux at the age of 82.

Goya was born in Fuendetodos, in the Spanish province of Aragon, on March 30, 1746. His father, José, was a gilder from Zaragoza, and his mother, Gracia Lucientes, belonged to the lower Spanish nobility. In his book on Goya, Antonina Vallentin points out that Goya would later reclaim this genealogical link to the nobility adding the "de" before the name Goya.

Romantic legends about a poor, illiterate peasant whose genius erupted inexplicably have obscured the true facts of Goya's childhood. His father acquired a post as master gilder in Zaragoza in 1760, and this permitted Goya a solid education under the Scolopian Fathers—one of Goya's later paintings, "The Last Communion of St. Joseph of Calasanz," acknowledges his debt to the Scolopians. Goya received some fundamental training in art and learned the rudiments of reading and writing. Perhaps most important, he befriended Martín Zapater, with whom he shared a correspondence for 25 years.

*Francisco Goya*

Goya studied in the workshop of José Luján, who had received his artistic formation in Italy. His teaching emphasized reproducing Italian masterpieces. Goya complained about having wasted his time copying Italian art, but the practice provided him with a drawing mastery that would be valuable to him later. While still under Luján, Goya enrolled in a school of drawing founded by Juan Ramírez and further honed his skills as a draftsman. By studying sculptures that Ramírez had brought from Italy, Goya acquired a familiarity with the corporal form that would serve him well when he painted the early "Christ on the Cross" and the later "La Maja Desnuda" ("The Magi Unclothed").

In 1763, at the age of 17, Goya visited Madrid for the first time. Though once again the fanciful myth speaks of a turbulent young man who fled Zaragoza after having committed some mysterious crime of passion, the truth is probably that Goya went to the capital to try his luck as a young painter. Goya was probably eager to join the circle of younger painters that was forming around the Venetian master Giambattista Tiépolo and the German painter Anton Raphael Mengs.

In Madrid Goya entered a canvas in a competition, which received no prize or honorable mention. Two years later he tried a second time. Again, not a single vote was given in recognition of Goya's entry. Undaunted by this resounding failure, Goya continued to paint. Some of his work has survived from that

earliest period, paintings from the church of Fuendetodos from around 1762.

After the initial failures in Madrid, Goya visited Italy, where, according to Pierre Gassier and Juliet Wilson in *Vida y Obra de Francisco Goya,* he probably stayed for one year. He entered a canvas in another competition in Parma, and while he still was not victorious, he received six votes and an honorable mention from the jury. Critical praise from one of the most important academy in Italy must have had an extraordinary impact on the confidence of a young painter who had already experienced several disappointments. Perhaps inspired by this turn of events, Goya cut short his stay in Italy, and was back in Zaragoza by June of 1771.

### First Commissions

On October 21, 1771, Goya was offered his first important commission: to paint the basilica of Pilar, in Zaragoza. The fresco, called *Adoración del Nombre de Dios* ("Adoration of God's Name") represents a celestial scene of angels looking upward at the word "Jehova" written in Hebrew. Gassier and Wilson describe the technique as "typically baroque." In essence, the work launched Goya's career. He soon become well known in the province of Aragon, decorating churches and monasteries.

In 1773 Goya married Josefa Bayeu, the sister of Francisco and Ramon Bayeu, two Aragonese painters who had integrated themselves successfully into the Madrid art establishment. By 1774, Mengs, at the Bayeus' request, had summoned Goya to Madrid to paint in the service of King Charles III of Spain. The following year Goya was contracted to paint tapestry "cartoons" depicting courtly and popular scenes. Intended as decorations for the many royal palaces and retreats, they were called cartoons because the original medium was cardboard or "carton." The paintings served as models for woven renderings of the scenes depicted. Goya was able to rapidly adapt to the new medium.

Some of Goya's important tapestry cartoons painted between 1775 and 1886 include the "The Parasol," "The Straw Manakin," and "The Wedding." In the final cartoons painted in the mid-1880s, Goya pushed the medium to its limit, creating works that no longer seemed like mere decoration, and whose rendering in tapestry seemed unlikely. These include "The Snowstorm," "The Wounded Mason," and "The Prairie of San Isidro." However, Goya had begun complaining in his letters to his friend Zapater about his tapestry obligations. In fact the Royal Tapestry Factory had taken official measures to force Goya to continue producing the cartoons.

In less than 20 years Goya painted 63 tapestry cartoons. Their commission brought Goya wealth and success. In 1785 he was named director of the Academy of San Fernando, and finally, in 1789, personal painter to King Charles IV. Goya had triumphed. He received commissions to paint the portraits of the most illustrious personages in Madrid, like the Duke and Duchess of Osuna, the Marquesa de Pontejos, and the Countess-Duchess de Benavente, among others. Having reached the height of upward mobility, Goya's career seemed to have reached its limit. Then Goya became so severely ill in 1792 that it seemed he would never see the nineteenth century.

### Sickness and *Los Caprichos*

While already in Andalusia for reasons of health, Goya fell seriously ill in Cádiz. The nature of the illness has been widely disputed, but given the symptoms and the air of secrecy surrounding it, syphilis seems the most likely diagnosis. For ten days Goya was close to death, but the danger passed. He was left, however, with a continuous ringing in his ears and would remain deaf for the rest of his life.

During his convalescence from 1792 to 1793, Goya was able to entirely redefine himself as an artist. The 46-year-old inaugurated an agenda for art that would survive intact well into the twentieth century. This applied not only to color and line but also to subject matter. Rather than the quest for the Italian notion of beauty, which had dominated Europe for centuries, Goya introduced war, cruelty, and madness to art.

Yet as Ortega y Gassett points out in *Papeles sobre Velázquez y Goya,* the artist had been primed for an intellectual assessment of his work since he had been introduced to the milieu of the royal court in Madrid. As Goya was painting the portraits of the Spanish nobility, surely he would surely listen and speak to them—men and women of the Spanish enlightenment, preoccupied with ideas that originated with the French philosophers Denis Diderot, Voltaire, and especially Jean-Jacques Rousseau.

Goya, who had probably led a rather rustic existence up to that point, was suddenly confronted with intellectuals for whom life was filtered through a faculty of philosophical reflection. Horrified by his misfortunes but freed from the burden of tapestry commissions that had stagnated his expression, Goya was able to forge a style that was his own. Convalescing in San Lucar in the company of the Duchess of Alba, Goya painted a series of portraits and kept a notebook of drawings that document the evolution of his style.

Perhaps nothing reveals Goya's temperament of the 1790s better than two self-portraits from around 1796. Unlike the earlier self-portraits, these two reveal a man with stern eyes, a tightly closed mouth, and unruly hair, strangely reminiscent, as Gassier has

noted in *The Drawings of Goya* of another great contemporary of Goya who was also deaf—the great composer Ludwig van Beethoven.

Goya may have painted his famous "La maja desnuda" ("The Magi Unclothed") during his stay at San Lucar. The painting was deemed scandalous at the time because nudes had been prohibited in Spain by the Inquisition and were punishable by up to one year in prison. Goya also began a new project that would mark another radical technical and thematic departure consisting of a series of caricature engravings that expressed, sometimes cruelly, the excesses of Spanish society.

These engravings were called *Los caprichos* ("The Fancies") and their satiric nature was daring enough that Goya had to wait until the political climate was propitious to publish them. A February 6, 1799 advertisement for *El Diario de Madrid* describes the pieces as "a collection of prints, dealing with capricious affairs, invented and engraved by Francisco de Goya."

In the *Caprichos* Goya mainly targeted the pretensions of the Madrid bourgeoisie and nobility, whose favorite pastime was imitating the dress and diversions of the working classes. The subjects of Goya's satire included young and old women and the clergy. Much in *Los caprichos* goes beyond satire, entering the realm of the grotesque. Many of the engravings represent witches, monstrously distorted human bodies, and anthropomorphic beasts out of some hellish world.

Perhaps the most famous *Capricho* is number 43, entitled "El sueño de la razón produce monstruos," or the "sleep of reason produces monsters." "Sueño" also translates as "dream." Thus, the play on the word "sueño" amounts to an interesting commentary on the Age of Reason.

### Artist as Historian

Goya inaugurated the nineteenth century with one of his most important paintings, "The Royal Family of Charles IV." With prodigious technique, he composed the painting from a series of individual sketches of the family members. The ensemble, portrayed with a stunning combination of colors and light and shadow play, includes a self-portrait of Goya to the left of the canvas, in a silent but unmistakable homage to one of his acknowledged masters, **Diego Velázquez.**

Perhaps even more extraordinary than the maturity of Goya's technique is the Royal Family itself: King Carlos IV, who was far more occupied with hunting than ruling; his wife María Luisa, of whom Napoleon would say that her face must seen to be believed; and the heir apparent, Fernando VII. Goya captures with ruthless honesty all the decadence and buffoonery of the Bourbon dynasty, in what Carlos Rojas has called a grotesque tragedy in his *El Valle de los Caídos.* Shortly after the painting was completed, the political situation in Spain came to a head.

Goya was in Madrid when The Spanish War of Independence erupted. Witness to the uprising and some of the executions, Goya created two paintings to represent the bloodshed. "The Third of May, 1808" depicts a squadron of faceless French soldiers that Hugh Thomas, in *Goya: The Third of May, 1808,* likened to a relentless killing machine firing on a man whose arms are outstretched in what seems like a Christ-like pose. Another man who has already been shot, lies sprawled on the ground in a pool of blood. Thomas identified a new technique in painting; Goya applied the red paint with a spoon rather than a brush. He published another series of graphic engravings called *The Disaster of the War.* The painter was recording history.

### The Black Paintings

In 1819 Goya bought a modest country house where he planned to spend his retirement. Falling gravely ill once again, Goya immortalized his doctor Arrieta in a painting that depicts the old painter agonizing under the care of the doctor. Though Goya was still painting commissioned portraits and was still a very public figure, he painted 14 of his most immortal works on the walls of his house for no one's eyes but his own. The series became known as *The Black Paintings* and included "Saturn Devouring his Children," "The Pilgrimage to San Isidro," and "The Dog." Goya, who publicly advocated reason and fought against popular superstition, represented on the walls of his own home the very figures of madness, demons, and nihilism.

After the Spanish War of Independence and the restoration of Fernando VII, perhaps the cruelest and most repressive of all Spanish kings, many Spanish artists and intellectuals were forced into exile. Goya's position as the most important artist permitted him to stay, however. Yet when Fernando reinstated the Inquisition, Goya too, at age 77 moved to Bordeaux, France.

Once in France, Goya visited Paris briefly in 1824. Goya returned to Bordeaux, where there was a small community of Spanish exiles, including one of the most important literary figures of the period, Nicolás Fernández de Moratín, of whom Goya painted a portrait in 1824. Goya's learning in France translated into artistic innovation. There he discovered the engraving technique of the lithograph, and instead of the laborious process then practiced, Goya added a rapid, portable technique.

Goya painted his last great portrait, "The Milkwoman of Bordeaux," partially paralyzed and going blind. Yet a certain peace seems to have returned to his spirit, judging by the tranquil beauty of tones and expression in this painting. Goya took ill once again in 1828, and died on the April 16 of that year. Buried in Bordeaux, his remains were transferred to Madrid in 1901, and were buried in the chapel of the church of San Antonio de la Florida, whose cupola was he had painted in 1798.

### SOURCES:

Boudaille, Georges, *Goya,* Nouvelles Editions Françaises, 1979.

Gassier, Pierre, *The Drawings of Goya,* Harper & Row, 1975.

Gassier, Pierre, and Juliet Wilson, *Vida y Obra de Francisco Goya,* Editorial Juventud, S.A., 1974.

*Goya in Perspective,* edited by Fred Licht, Prentice Hall, 1973.

Gudiol, José, *Goya,* Harry N. Abrams, Inc.

Helman, Edith, *Trasmundo de Goya,* Alianza Editorial, 1963.

Licht, Fred, *Goya: The Origins of the Modern Temper in Art,* Harper & Row, 1979.

Malraux, André, *Saturn: An Essay on Goya,* Phaidon, 1957.

Ortega Y Gasset, José, *Papeles sobre Velázquez y Goya,* Alianza Editorial, 1950.

Pérez Sanchez, Alfonso E., and Eleanor A. Sayre, *Goya and the Spirit of Enlightenment,* Little, Brown and Company, 1989.

Rojas, Carlos, *El Valle de los Caídos,* Ediciones Destino, 1978.

Thomas, Hugh, *Goya: The Third of May, 1808,* Penguin, 1972.

Vallentin, Antonina, *Goya,* Editions Albin Michel, 1951.

—*Sketch by Paul Miller*

# Juan Goytisolo
## 1931-
**Spanish writer**

Often considered one of the best Spanish novelists living in the late twentieth century, Juan Goytisolo is the prolific author of novels, short story collections, travel narratives, essays, and memoirs. Goytisolo's vehement opposition and criticism of General **Francisco Franco**'s regime forced him to

*Juan Goytisolo*

move to France, where he lived in exile until Franco's death.

Goytisolo's novels often deal with the dichotomy of the tragic, painful real world, and the fairy tale dimension to which his characters frequently escape. Goytisolo concentrates on the suffering of the Spanish people; the poverty in the rural areas; the crude, harsh world of government housing; the homeless; the disintegration of the world—and how characters managed to escape.

Juan Goytisolo Gay was born January 5, 1931 in Barcelona, Spain, the city where his parents had also been born—his surname suggests that his family's roots lie in the Basque region of Spain, although his father's family were colonial Cuban sugar-plantation owners. The maternal side of his family was Catalonian; as a child, Goytisolo spoke Castilian. During the Spanish Civil War (1936–39), Goytisolo and his family lived in a small village in the Republican Zone of Catalonia.

At the age of five, Goytisolo suffered a profound loss: his mother was killed in a bombing raid ordered by Franco on March 17, 1938. She had left the house that day to shop and to visit her parents and her sister Consuelo. Goytisolo wrote that he did not ever learn exactly what happened to his mother. He grew up feeling alienated from a country embroiled in a war that killed his mother and a regime that did not tolerate his emerging bisexuality. His lifelong sorrow was also exacerbated by estrangement from his father,

who also disapproved of his son's homosexual leanings.

## Signs of Literary Talent

Goytisolo's early literary talents did not surprise anyone; his maternal uncle and both of brothers—the poet José and Luis, a novelist—were writers. Goytisolo composed his first novel, a story of Joan of Arc, at age 11. A few years later, Goytisolo wrote a cowboy novel. Although he never published these early novels, he was highly aware of his abilities. His passion for writing emerged more vigorously after he finished his *Bachillerato,* or high school/junior college at a Jesuit school. He continued his education by studying law, first at the University of Barcelona and then at the University of Madrid.

In 1951, while studying in Barcelona, Goytisolo founded the "Turia" literary group, which included novelist Ana Maria Matute. It was during this year that Goytisolo wrote his first short stories: "El ladron" ("The Thief") and "El perro asirio" ("The Assyrian Dog"). The next year he began his award-winning career by winning the Joven Literatura ("Young Literature") Prize for his story "El mundo de los espejos" ("The World of Mirrors"), which was censored and not published at that time.

## Reacted to Civil War

With "The World of Mirrors," Goytisolo began to experience the negative reactions engendered not only by his anti-Fascist political beliefs but also by what critic John W. Butt in the *Times Literary Supplement* called the "frantic machismo" predominant in Spain at the time. From these early years, Goytisolo developed a literary voice that derived from the inhuman, impotent, and cynical fallout from the Civil War.

In 1954, Goytisolo published his first novel, *Juegos de manos,* later translated into English as *The Young Assassins.* This first novel won Goytisolo instant validity and acclaim in the literary world. Some critics compared his work to Jack Kerouac's and marked him as a member of Spain's restless generation.

*Juegos de manos* tells the story of a group of young students and their plot to murder a politician. The students ultimately turn their attentions inward and kill the very student selected to commit the original murder. Kessel Schwartz, in *Juan Goytisolo,* found that the novelist described "beautifully the process of growing up, of adolescent hate, love, and rebellion, of what he terms 'the terrible generation of our time.'" Despite such praise, the book, written in 1952, was not published for two years because of its perceived "leftist" and "pro-revolutionary" overtones. Eventually the Ministry for Information and

Tourism approved the book for publication, and Goytisolo's literary career accelerated.

Goytisolo wrote four novels during the next four years. His second novel, *Duelo en el paraíso,* was translated into English in 1958 as *Children of Chaos.* When it was published in Spain in 1955, it won the Index of Arts and Letters prize and took third place in the *Planeta* prize. *El circo* ("The Circus") appeared in 1957; *La resaca* ("The Undertow") in 1958; and *Fiestas,* also in 1958.

### Sought Exile in France

Goytisolo lived in Barcelona for a few years after the publication of his first novel. He continued writing and spending time with friends who shared his political views. He often visited farmers and peasants to speak to them about revolution. But soon it seemed dangerous for Goytisolo to continue residing in Spain. His brother Luis was arrested, and the news media began slandering Juan for his "anti-Spanish" activities in France.

In 1957, Goytisolo left for France, where he worked for Gallimard Publishing. There he met and fell in love with Monique Lange, whom he eventually married. With the exception of 1965, when he worked as a journalist in Cuba, Goytisolo remained in France until Franco died in 1975, then returned to Spain.

Of all Goytisolo's novels, the books comprising the *Mendiola* trilogy are perhaps his best. The trilogy consists of *Señas de identidad* (*Marks of Identity*), *Reivinidicación del conde don Julián* (*Count Julian*), and *Juan sin tierra* (*Juan the Landless*). Of the three titles, *Count Julian* is considered by many to be Goytisolo's master work, utilizing a variety of techniques borrowed from Genet, **Pablo Picasso**, and James Joyce, among others. It is an explosive tale of retribution against a cruel and hypocritical Spain as told by Julian, an outcast living in Africa.

Goytisolo wrote several more books after the trilogy, including novels, works of short fiction, travel narratives, and two memoirs: *Coto vedado* (*Forbidden Territory: The Memoirs of Juan Goytisolo*) and *En los reinos de tafia* ("In the Realms of Moorish Kings").

Goytisolo is recognized for a career of clear vision and depth, but he defies classification by critics. His political views and narrative style shifted equally. An experimentalist and innovator with language and form, Goytisolo has managed to write books of great universal truth and compelling characterization. As Abigail Lee Six wrote in her work of Goytisolo criticism: "Goytisolo is practicing what his fiction preaches, for he will not be fitted in to any orderly categories, but remains a free and fluid combination—a Spaniard but also a Parisian and a Moroccan; a writer and a critic; a traditionalist and an iconoclast."

## SELECTED PUBLISHED WORKS:

*Juegos de manos,* Destino, 1954; published as *The Young Assassins,* translated by John Rust, Knopf, 1959.

*Duelo en el paraiso,* Planeta, 1955; published as *Children of Chaos,* translated by Christine Brooke-Rose, Macgibbon and Kee, 1958.

*El circo* ("The Circus"), Destino, 1957.

*Fiestas,* Emecé, 1958; published as *Fiestas,* translated by Herbert Weinstock, Knopf, 1960.

*La resaca,* ("The Undertow"), Club del Libro Español, 1958.

*La isla,* Seix Barral, 1961; published as *Island of Women,* translated by Jose Yglesias, Knopf, 1962.

*Señas de identidad,* J. Moritz, 1966; published as *Marks of Identity,* translated by Gregory Rabassa, Grove, 1969.

*Reivindicación del Conde don Julián,* J. Moritz, 1970; published as *Count Julian,* translated by Helen R. Lane, Viking, 1974.

*Juan sin tierra,* Seix Barral, 1975; published as *Juan the Landless,* translated by Helen R. Lane, Viking, 1977.

*Makbara,* Seix Barral, 1980; published as *Makbara,* translated by Helen R. Lane, Seaver Books, 1981.

*Paisajes despues de la batalla,* Montesinos, 1982; published as *Landscapes After the Battle,* translated by Helen R. Lane, Seaver Books, 1987.

### Short Fiction

*Vivir acqui* ("To Live Here") Sur, 1960.

*Fin de fiesta: Tentativas de interpretación de una historia amorosa,* Seix Barral, 1962, published as *The Party's Over: Four Attempts to Define a Love Story,* translated by Yglesias Weidenfeld & Nicoloson, 1966.

### Travel Narratives

*Campos de Nijar,* Seix Barral, 1960; published as *The Countryside of Nijar,* Alembic Press, 1987.

*Pueblo en marcha: Instantaneas de un viaje a Cuba* ("People on the March: Snapshots of a Trip to Cuba"), Libreria Española, 1963.

*Cronicas sarracinas* ("Saracen Chronicles"), Iberica, 1982.

### Other

*Problemas de la novela* ("Problems of the Novel"), Seix, Barral, 1959.

*Las mismas palabras,* Seix Barral, 1963.

*Plume d'hier:* Espagne d'aujourd'hui, Editeurs Francais Reunis, 1965.

*El furgon de cola* ("The Caboose"), Ruedo Iberico, 1967.

*Spanien und die Spanien,* M. Bucher, 1969.

*Obras completas* ("Complete Works"), Aguilar, 1977.

*Coto vedado,* Seix Barral, 1985; published as *Forbidden Territory: The Memoirs of Juan Goytisolo,* North Point Press, 1989.

*En los reinos de taifa,* Seix Barral, 1986.

*Contracorrientes,* Montesinos, 1985.

*Space in Motion* (essays), Lumen Books, 1987.

*Quarantine,* translated by Peter Bush, Normal, IL, Dalkey Archive Press, 1994.

## SOURCES:

### Books

*Contemporary Literary Criticism,* vol. 23, edited by Sharon R. Gunton and Jean C. Stine, Detroit, Gale, 1983.

*Forbidden Territory: The Memoirs of Juan Goytisolo, 1931–1956,* translated by Peter Bush, San Francisco, North Point Press, 1989.

Goytisolo, Juan, *Marks of Identity,* translated by Gregory Rabassa, New York, Grove Press, 1969.

Goytisolo, Juan, *Quarantine,* translated by Peter Bush, Normal, IL, Dalkey Archive Press, 1994.

*Hispanic Writers,* edited by Bryan Ryan, Detroit, Gale, 1991.

Schwartz, Kessel, *Juan Goytisolo,* New York, Twayne, 1970.

Six, Abigial Lee, *Juan Goytisolo: The Case for Chaos,* New Haven, Yale University Press, 1990.

### Periodicals

*Hispania,* December, 1971, pp. 960–66.

*The Nation,* March 1, 1975, pp. 250–52.

*The New York Times Book Review,* January 22, 1967; February 12, 1987, p. 12.

*The Times Literary Supplement,* May 31, 1985; September 9, 1988; November 17, 1989.

—*Sketch by Christopher B. Tower*

# Maria Grever
## 1894-1951
### Mexican composer and songwriter

Maria Grever, a pioneer in the field of twentieth-century popular music, was the first Mexican woman to become a successful composer. Her romantic songs and ballads, like "Jurame" and "What a Difference a Day Makes," achieved widespread popularity beginning in the 1920s among audiences in Spain, South America, Mexico, and the United States. Although a few of her songs remain international favorites today, Grever has been accorded scarcely a footnote in the pages of music history. She is not even mentioned in most listings and encyclopedias of composers. Yet many of her songs, estimated to number in the hundreds, live on, kept alive by recording stars like **Placido Domingo** and Aretha Franklin.

Grever was born to a Spanish father and Mexican mother on September 14, 1894, in Mexico City. Her maiden name was Maria de la Portilla. She spent much of her childhood in Spain and travelled widely in Europe with her family. At the age of 12, she returned to Mexico. According to a *New York Times* article, Grever composed her first piece of music—a Christmas carol—when she was four years old. Grever settled in New York after marrying Leo A. Grever, an American oil company executive, who was best man in her sister's wedding. She was wed to Grever four days after her sister's nuptials.

She studied piano, violin, and voice, although one account of her life suggests that she learned to read music only in her later years. In fact, most of her songs were written in one key. Grever was said to have the gift of perfect pitch. A 1919 review of one of her first New York City concerts in the *New York Times* mentions that Grever, a soprano, performed opera in Madrid early in her career.

Grever was an extraordinarily versatile musician. She frequently wrote both the melodies and lyrics of her pieces and then performed the pieces in live concerts. During her career, which peaked in the 1930s and 1940s, she wrote film scores and lyrics for Broadway shows, and organized concerts combining theatre, music, dance, and song. She was also a voice teacher. But Grever's strongest legacy is her songs. Often based on the folk rhythms and styles of Latin American music, particularly Mexican or Spanish tangos, the lyrics are lushly romantic, full of feeling, and easy to recall. Her message is always direct. For example, her song "Yo No Se" ("I Know Not") begins with the stanza: "When at night my thoughts are winging / To you, my dear, / Then your voice, an old song singing, / I seem to hear; / You are kneeling by me, blending, / Though far away, / Your voice with mine ascending, / In a song of love's first day."

Grever often worked with American lyricists, who translated the songs from Spanish to English to make them accessible to audiences in the United States. In fact, Grever collaborated with three of the leading songwriters of her day—Stanley Adams, Irving Caesar, and Raymond Leveen.

### Eighteen-Year Old's First Hit Became Million-Seller

Her first published song, "A una Ola" ("To a Wave"), appeared when she was 18 and sold some three million copies, according to a biography on a 1956 retrospective album of Grever's work. Grever published "Besame" ("Kiss Me") in 1921, and in 1926, Grever's Spanish tango "Jurame" ("Promise, Love") found a large audience. Grever's first major hit was "What a Difference a Day Makes," or "Cuando Vuelva a Tu Lado," written in 1934. That song is one of Grever's longest-lasting hits; it is included on many currently available recordings by artists as diverse as Chet Baker, Ray Conniff, Dinah Washington, and Bobby Darin.

The same year Ella Fitzgerald sang "A-Tisket A-Tasket" and Cole Porter won over the nation with "My Heart Belongs to Daddy," Grever scored one of her biggest sensations, a nonsensical tune entitled "Ti-Pi-Tin." One account of Grever's music claims that "Ti-Pi-Tin," written in 1938, broke with her usual style, and her publisher rejected it. But bandleader Horace Heidt and his orchestra, performing on NBC radio, took the song to the air and contributed to its eventual hit status.

Grever's songs, broadcast frequently on the radio during her time, include "Lamento Gitano," "Lero, Lero from Brazil," "Magic Is the Moonlight," "Make Love with a Guitar," "My First, My Last, My Only," "Rosebud," "Thanks for the Kiss," "My Margarita," "Andalucia," "Cancionera," and many more. Estimates of her musical output range from 200 to 500 songs, depending on the source.

One of the reasons Grever's songs became well-known was that leading performers of her era adopted them in their repertoires. Singers like Enrico Caruso, Lawrence Tibbett, Tito Schipa, Nino Martina, and Jessica Dragonette helped popularize Grever's work. Along with other albums which included Grever's tunes, the 1956 album "The Bobby Hackett Horn," a Columbia label, adapted "What a Difference a Day Makes," and the 1959 Columbia Classic album "Happy Session," performed by Benny Goodman and his orchestra, featured "Cuando Vuelva a Tu Lado."

Grever also wrote film scores, including the music for the 1944 movie "Bathing Beauty," featuring her song "Magic Is the Moonlight," or "Te Quiero Dijiste." In 1941, "Viva O'Brien," a musical with music by Grever and lyrics by Leveen, had 20 performances on a New York stage. Some of the show's songs were entitled "El Matador Terrifico," "Mood of the Moment," "Broken Hearted Romeo," and "Wrap Me in Your Serape."

### Enjoyed International Acclaim

Grever apparently enjoyed performing before live audiences and organizing concerts of her work by other musicians. In 1919, one of her earliest New York recitals of Spanish, Italian, and French music, at the Princess Theatre, received positive reviews from critics. During the height of her fame, she made concert tours in Latin America and Europe. In New York, Grever's music was heard live in many of the city's concert halls. In 1927, she organized a concert at the Little Theatre, which featured an Argentine cabaret, song dramas complete with costumes, scenery, dialogue, and dancing, and a short play, "The Gypsy." The evening opened with performances by a jazz orchestra. One of her first successful New York concerts took place in 1928 at the Pythian Temple before an audience that included the ambassadors of Spain, Mexico, Cuba, and Argentina.

The *New York Times* reviewed a 1939 concert at the Guild Theatre, in which Grever presented popular songs and a miniature opera, entitled "El Cantarito." She performed a few songs, but was assisted by dozens of other singers and musicians, including a large chorus, dance troupe and orchestra. The *Times* critic praised her "innate gift of spontaneous melody," and commented that, while some of Grever's music is not to be taken too seriously, "her more earnest endeavors were sincere and effective."

In the late 1930s, she was threatened with blindness as a result of an eye infection. In 1942, Grever hosted a benefit for the Spanish-American Association for the Blind, with headquarters in New York City. She served as mistress of ceremonies for a program which included musical performances by students at the New York Institute for the Education of the Blind. The funds raised were to benefit the blind in Spanish-speaking countries.

At the time of her death at the age of 57, on December 15, 1951, following a lengthy illness, she was living in the Wellington Hotel on Manhattan's Seventh Avenue. She was survived by her husband and two children, son Charles Grever, a New York music publisher, and daughter Carmen Livingston of Chicago, according to her obituary in the *New York Times*. Following her death, she was honored by a musicale at the Biltmore Hotel by the Union of Women of the Americas. She was named "Woman of the Americas," 1952, by the UWA before her death.

Grever was a member of the prestigious American Society of Composers, Authors, and Publishers.

In 1956, RCA released a retrospective album, "Songs of Maria Grever," with 12 songs performed by Argentine singer Libertad Lamarque, accompanied by the orchestras of Chucho Zarzosa and Mario Ruiz Armengol. Along with her more famous songs, the album featured "Volvere" ("I Will Return"), "Eso Es Mentira" ("That Is a Lie"), and "Asi" ("Thus"). The album jacket, written by Bill Zeitung, argues that Grever never enjoyed widespread name recognition, despite the fact that her songs achieved "an immensely deserved run of popularity." Her music "is on every hand," wrote Zeitung. "Yet the name is familiar to only a few."

## SOURCES:

### Books

Lewine, Richard, and Alfred Simon, *Songs of the Theatre,* Wilson, 1984, p. 828.

Mattfeld, Julius, *Variety Music Cavalcade 1620–1961,* Prentice-Hall, pp. 420, 493, 521–26, 551.

Spaeth, Sigmund, *A History of Popular Music in America,* Random House, 1962, pp. 516–17.

### Periodicals

*New York Times,* December 15, 1919, p. 15; February 14, 1927, p. 14; February 27, 1928, p. 16; March 6, 1939, p. 11; December 16, 1951, p. 90; May 5, 1952, p. 18.

*Variety,* July 31, 1940.

### Other

Music research collections, New York Public Libry for the Performing Arts at Lincoln Center.

"Songs of Maria Grever," RCA record album, 1956.

*—Sketch by Ann Malaspina*

# Che Guevara
## 1928-1967
**Argentine revolutionary**

Ernesto "Che" Guevara was an internationally famous Marxist revolutionary, considered by many to be the primary intellectual force behind the Cuban revolution led by **Fidel Castro** in the 1950s. As Castro's one-time second-in-command, Guevara held prominent positions within the Cuban regime and is credited with formulating and implementing plans for the nationalization of Cuban industry and agriculture. A widely renowned theoretician of guerrilla warfare, he outlined military strategies outlined in his influential training manual *Guerrilla Warfare* that has been used by the U.S. military and figured prominently in revolutionary causes.

Guevara's absolute political positions and controversial military practices provoked widespread criticism, particularly in the United States, during his life and after his death in 1967. But his supporters have continued to view him as a courageous revolutionary who never wavered from his commitment to fight oppression throughout the world. French philosopher Jean-Paul Sartre, for instance, called Guevara "the most complete man of his age," and Castro held him up as a martyr to be viewed as an example for Cuba's children, exhorting the Cuban people with the refrain, "Let them be like Che!"

Ernesto Guevara de la Serna was born in Rosario, eastern Argentina, on June 14, 1928, the eldest child of Ernesto Guevara Lynch, a part-Irish civil engineer, and his wife, Celia de la Serna. Although the future revolutionary grew up in an upper-middle class household, his parents refused to follow the restrictive social codes and conservative politics often associated with the Latin American bourgeoisie. Ricardo Rojo, a friend of the family, stated in his biography *My Friend Che,* that the free-thinking Guevaras' displayed "a passion for justice, a hatred of fascism, a love for literature, and a prejudice against money and the ways of making it."

Like his parents, Guevara—who was nicknamed "Che," the Argentine equivalent of "Hey, you"—stood out among his peers, showing a broad range of interests and unconventional values. Not only did he share his mother's love for the works of the Chilean Communist poet **Pablo Neruda,** but he earned a reputation as a first-rate swimmer and rugby player—in spite of a severe asthmatic condition that would affect him throughout his life.

While the other boys of his social group spent most of their money on the latest fashions, Che was content to wear worn-out trousers and an old nylon shirt. He neither smoked nor drank, preferring an herbal tea made from Paraguayan holly leaves to alcohol. Although Che's political views were not formed until much later, he joined the Partido Unión Democrática at the age of 14, and fought in street fights against *peronistas*—supporters of the Argentine dictator **Juan Perón.**

At the age of 19, after graduating from high school with honors, Guevara entered the medical school at the University of Buenos Aires, with the goal of finding a cure for the cancer that had taken the life of his grandmother and would later infect his mother. But in 1952, he interrupted his studies to accompany a friend, Alberto Granados, on a 3,000 mile motorcycle tour through Chile, Peru, Ecuador, Colombia, and Venezuela. The pair supported themselves by working as truck drivers, porters, doctors, and dishwashers.

For Guevara the most influential experience of the trip was his work as a nurse at a leper colony in San Pablo on the Amazon, where, as Andrew Sinclair stated in his book *Che Guevara,* he "saw that the highest kinds of human solidarity and loyalty were formed among lonely and desperate men." Although Guevara returned to medical school to complete his degree in 1953, with a thesis on allergies, his firsthand observation of poverty, hunger, and disease had given him a new focus: instead of attempting to make a great contribution to medical science, he would devote his life to helping the poor, who lacked the means to benefit from the medical technology that was already available.

In order to escape military service in Perón's army, Guevara left Argentina for Bolivia, where he witnessed firsthand a large-scale program of social reform in progress. Although he was not yet a Marxist and showed little interest in politics, he joined a group of leftist Argentine students in supporting the new revolutionary government of Jacobo Arbenz in Guatemala.

When the country was invaded in 1954 by the troops of Castillo Armas —who were covertly trained by the U.S. Central Intelligence Agency (CIA)—and the Guatemalan government failed to arm the people, Guevara, for the first time, joined the resistance. He moved from one small group of revolutionaries to another in an unsuccessful attempt to mount a campaign to take over Guatemala City. Angered by the CIA's attempts to protect North American financial interests in Guatemala, Guevara, after a two-month stay in the Argentine Embassy, left for Mexico, where he began reading the complete works of Karl Marx and Vladimir Ilich Lenin, as well as a variety of other leftist theorists.

## Met Fidel Castro

Guevara's period of intensive study and growing radicalism prepared him for his meeting in the summer of 1955 with Fidel Castro, who had been jailed and exiled from Cuba after leading a failed coup against the dictator, **Fulgencio Batista.** On the night of their first meeting, Guevara joined Castro and his brother Raúl in the planning of the Cuban revolution. In December of 1956, the threesome, along with some 80 poorly equipped and trained men, invaded the south coast of Cuba's Oriente Province. Shortly after their arrival, however, they were surrounded by Batista's troops, who killed all but 12 of the revolutionaries.

In his *Reminiscences of the Cuban Revolutionary War,* Guevara described the ill-fated invasion as "both ridiculous and tragic," but he also found that the experience clarified his mission: "This was perhaps the first time I was faced with the dilemma of choosing between my dedication to medicine and my duty as a revolutionary soldier. At my feet were a pack full of medicines and a cartridge box; together, they were too heavy to carry. I chose the cartridge box, leaving behind the medicine pack." Guevara's full commitment to the revolution also brought about the end of his marriage to Hilda Gadea, a member of the Peruvian revolutionary movement who, ironically, first introduced him to Castro.

The survivors among the guerrilla force regrouped in the Sierra Maestra Mountains in Cuba, where Guevara—who eventually attained the rank of major, second only to Castro—led them in a rigid military program during the day, while fashioning the ideology behind the social revolution at night. Guevara also read to the insurgents from works of revolutionary literature and political philosophy. As support from peasant sympathizers grew, Guevara was able to set up a weapons plant, a bakery, a shoe shop, a rebel radio station, and a network of schools.

Largely on the strength of Guevara's guerrilla warfare strategy of immobilizing the enemy force by killing the first few men in a line of marching troops, the rebel forces swept through Camagüey and Las Villas provinces, before gaining control over the Cuban government after a decisive victory at the battle of Santa Clara. As he would later write in his book *Guerrilla Warfare,* published in 1960, the success of the revolution "proved the people's ability to free themselves from an oppressive government through guerrilla warfare."

## Theoretician of the Cuban Regime

The first few months of the new Castro regime saw Guevara play an important background role: "Just as he was the theoretician of the war, so he was the theoretician of the administration," observed Sinclair. While Castro, as the *jefe maximo,* bargained for the political deals that would enable the fledgling government to survive, his subordinate concentrated his efforts on constructing the theoretical model for the Communist state.

After visiting several neutral countries in an attempt to negotiate commercial treaties, Guevara was appointed to his first formal position as head of the industrial department of the National Institute of Agrarian Reform (INRA). The INRA was an agency established to carry out Cuba's agrarian reform law nationalizing all of the country's plantations, large farms, and major properties, in May of 1959. From this post, Guevara attempted to free Cuba from its dependence on foreign trade by encouraging farmers to diversify their crops, instead of relying solely on revenues from sugar—which were subject to the political whims of foreign markets.

In November of that same year, Guevara was named to the top economic position in the country, president of the National Bank of Cuba, despite having no formal training in economics and a strong hatred for money. For Guevara, the value of a given product or service was defined by its moral and social worth rather than by supply and demand. Likewise, one's work was to be conceived in terms of "social duty" and "human pleasure" rather than as a commodity to be sold to the highest bidder.

In addition to making the difficult "value" judgments that accompanied such theories, Guevara negotiated a commercial treaty with the Soviet Union in February 1960, enabling Cuba to receive oil, machinery, and other essential products in exchange for sugar. In June of 1960 Guevara authorized the seizure of American and British oil refineries, arguing that their refusal to process Russian oil was a violation of Cuban law.

As relations between the United States and Cuba grew increasingly hostile, Guevara retained his radical stance, blaming American subsidization of Cuban sugar for inhibiting Cuba's industrial development and insisting that the agrarian revolution demanded the acquisition of land first. Such policies led to the US boycott of Cuban goods, requiring Guevara to negotiate further treaties with the Soviet Union that called for the building of 100 industrial plants in Cuba.

Following the reorganization of the Cuban government on February 24, 1961, Guevara was given the responsibility of heading the newly formed Ministry of Industry, which took over control of agencies formerly under the auspices of the INRA. Shifting his emphasis from agrarian reform to the industrial development of Cuba's cities, Guevara constructed a four-year plan designed to bring Cuba's industrial technology up to the level of the Communist bloc nations.

While Guevara's critics found this new point of emphasis problematic, his supporters found the shift a logical extension of his political philosophy, arguing that the bourgeoisie, concentrated in the cities, had now replaced the land owners as the enemies of the revolution. Sinclair, for instance, concluded that "The interaction between Che's ideology and public policy was almost a marriage of minds."

Although Guevara was noted for his staunchly anti-American speeches denouncing "Yankee imperialism,"—especially after the failed invasion by American troops and anti-Castro exiles at the Bay of Pigs in

April, 1961 in which Guevara was wounded—he led the Cuban delegation to President John F. Kennedy's August, 1961 conference establishing the Alliance for Progress program of economic aid to Latin America. Adopting a relatively moderate position, he offered proposals for a peaceful coexistence between the Alliance for Progress reforms and the Cuban revolution, and after the conference, he visited Argentina and Brazil, reportedly for the purpose of gaining Latin American support for reopening trade relations with the United States.

Brazilian president, Jânio da Silva Quadros bestowed Guevara with his country's highest medal, the Grand Cross of the Cruzeirodo Sul, for his role in building economic and cultural relations throughout Latin America. In August of 1962, however, Guevara went to the Soviet Union to ask for increased armaments and technical specialists to prepare for perceived threats of "imperialist aggression."

The buildup of Soviet arms and the extension of the Soviet's sphere of influence into the Western Hemisphere, led President Kennedy to blockade Cuban shipping on October 22, 1962. During the Cuban Missile Crisis, Guevara was reported to have said that any act of aggression by the United States would result in the firing of nuclear missiles on American cities.

Meanwhile, Guevara's economic reforms in Cuba were being undermined by shortages in raw materials, poor harvests, and mediocre worker output. Guevara, however, identified a deeper cause. "We did not owe all our planning mistakes to our decisions," he stated in a speech quoted by Sinclair. "We owed them to the action of imperialism, which forced upon us a process of acceleration far beyond the best that the party was capable of doing."

While Guevara claimed that the reforms had achieved some success, the Russians and Eastern Europeans who were supporting the Cuban economy found their own economies also lagging. As Sinclair suggested, they exerted pressure on Castro to "put his house in order" by returning to the policy of exchanging sugar for Russian goods and credit, and implementing material incentives in industry—compromises that Guevara vehemently opposed. Also frustrated with the Russian policy of non-aggression toward the United States following the Missile Crisis, a more radical Guevara, in a speech to the General Assembly of the United Nations in December, 1964, quoted by Sinclair, argued that "peaceful coexistence does not include coexistence between the exploiters and the exploited, the oppressor and the oppressed."

Preferring to further the revolutionary cause through guerrilla warfare rather than continue to struggle with the inefficiency and complexity of the Cuban bureaucracy, Guevara left Cuba to rejuvenate the dying revolutionary effort in Bolivia. Writing in his farewell letter to Castro, he said that he had to fulfill "the most sacred of duties; to fight against imperialism wherever it may be."

## Murdered in Bolivia

The success of the revolution in Cuba, however, would not be repeated in Bolivia. Friction between the Cuban and Bolivian segments of the guerrilla forces, lack of peasant support, and the failure of parallel uprisings in Peru and other Latin American countries were some of the factors that led to Guevara's defeat. What is more, Guevara refused to compromise with the Bolivian Communist Party and lost their support.

After 18 months of fighting against the Bolivian military and U.S. Army Rangers trained specifically for guerrilla combat, Guevara was wounded in a battle at Quebrada del Yuro, and was reportedly murdered in a prison near Vallegrande, a large village in southeastern Bolivia. The Bolivian government, however, claimed that the legendary revolutionary was killed in battle. Guevara was survived by his second wife, Aleida March, a former schoolteacher who served as his secretary, and a daughter from his first marriage.

While Guevara was widely respected and loved by his admirers and feared by his enemies during his life, his role as a martyr is perhaps his most powerful legacy. As Hans Koningsberger concludes in his book *The Future of Che Guevara*, "For Latin Americans, Che gave a face to the rocky and impersonal theories of socialism, Marxism, and social revolution. Che, a dead prophet, is a more powerful unifying force for them than any living man, any national of one country on their continent, could ever be."

## SELECTED PUBLISHED WORKS:

*Complete Bolivian Diaries of Che Guevara and Other Captured Documents,* Stein and Day, 1969.
*Guerilla Warfare,* Monthly Review, 1961.
*Reminiscences of the Cuban Revolutionary War,* Monthly Review, 1968.
*Vencerémos! [his] Speeches and Writings,* edited by John Gerassi, Macmillan, 1968.

## SOURCES:

### Books

*Current Biography Yearbook, 1963,* edited by Charles Moritz, Wilson, pp. 166–169.
Koningsberger, Hans, *The Future of Che Guevara,* Garden City, Doubleday, 1971.

Rojo, Ricardo, *My Friend Che,* translated by Julian Casart, Dial, 1968.
Sauvage, Léo, *Che Guevara: The Failure of a Revolutionary,* Prentice-Hall, 1973.

### Periodicals

*New York Times,* November 27, 1959, pp. 10, September 3, 1962, pp. 2.
*Time,* August 8, 1960, pp. 36.

—*Sketch by Jason Gallman*

# Jorge Guillén
## 1893-1984
### Spanish poet

Jorge Guillén grew up in Old Castile, Spain, and became a prominent writer during the 1920s. A highly regarded poet, he was also associated with the Generation of 1927, a literary group whose members supported the short-lived Spanish Republic and participated in the poetic renaissance of Spain. Driven from Spain by **Francisco Franco**'s rise to power in 1936, Guillén spent most of the rest of his life in the United States as a university scholar. He compiled a massive body of critically-acclaimed work in his lifetime. In *Jorge Guillén,* biographer Grant MacCurdy called Guillén "a sculptor of finely wrought verse who avoided fashionable extremism in favor of a poetry that exhibited permanence in both form and thematic content."

## Early Life of Education and Opportunity

Born on January 18, 1893, Guillén had parents who were able to give him every opportunity for a thoroughly cosmopolitan education. His father, Julio Guillén Saenz, was a businessman with interests in literature and politics. In addition to his full-time business pursuits, the elder Guillén sat on the administrative board of the newspaper *El Norte de Castilla,* which was highly regarded for its literary quality.

Guillén went to school, completing his studies at the Institute of Valladolid in 1909. His father provided him with the funds to continue his education in Switzerland at the Maison Perreyve in Fribourg. After finishing his secondary schooling abroad, he returned to Spain to attend the famed Residencia de Estudiantes. While there, Guillén likely was exposed to some of the great poetic and artistic minds of the day. Poets such as **Juan Ramon Jimenez** and Antonio Machado

—who had begun to concern themselves with questions of national identity prompted by the final loss of Spanish empire in 1898—roamed the halls in which Guillén studied. In 1913 Guillén moved on to Granada and received a licentiate in letters. He continued to travel and settled in Germany until 1917, when he accepted an appointment as a lecturer at the Sorbonne in Paris.

In the introduction to one of his collections, Guillén wrote, "I was twenty-five when I began writing. Why had I never written before that? Because I never dared." In contrast to many poets who develop their poetic voice after years of revision and growth, Guillén began his career late and didn't publish a volume of poetry until he was 35 years old. Some biographers date Guillén's earliest poems at 1918, for while he taught at the Sorbonne, many of his poems appeared in various journals. Some of these early poems served as the foundation for Guillén's 1928 work *Cantico,* the first edition of which contained only 75 poems.

While in Paris Guillén married a French woman named Germaine Cahen in 1921. The next year brought good news with the birth of their daughter, Theresa, but in 1923, the poet's mother, Esperanza Alvarez Guerra, died in Old Castile. He left France that same year and returned to Madrid.

Until 1924 Guillén studied at the University of Madrid, compiling his dissertation on **Luis de Góngora.** The university awarded him a doctorate in letters, recognition that enabled him to seek a professorship. Germaine had a second child, Claudio, as Guillén studied for the rigorous examinations given to candidates for professorships in Spanish language and literature. Guillén passed the examinations in 1925.

In 1926 Guillén began his long professorial career at the University of Murcia. There he published what would eventually become the heart of his body of work. Although it contained only 75 poems when it appeared in 1928, *Cantico* made an impression on readers because it shamelessly celebrated life in the face of the post-war nihilism found in much European art of the period.

In 1927 a number of young artists gathered in Seville to pay tribute to Luis de Góngora, about whom Guillén had written his doctoral dissertation. Although not massively influenced by Gongora, the poets—who would come to be known as the Generation of 1927 —saw him in a favorable light as a "kindred spirit in the pursuit of pure poetry," as MacCurdy noted. This gathering, which Guillén attended, also included **Dámaso Alonso**, Rafael Alberti, **Federico García Lorca**, and other luminaries who comprised what many critics call a "golden age" of Spanish poetry. MacCurdy wrote that this movement, which began with Becquer and expanded with Macha-

do and Jimenez, found "a culmination in the bright young men who met to honor Gongora in December of 1927."

Guillén lectured at Oxford University, then returned to Spain to take a professorship at the University of Seville. He traveled briefly to lecture in Romania in 1934, but it was in 1936 that his life underwent dramatic change. An expanded version of *Cantico* containing 125 poems was published, but the start of the Spanish Civil War quickly overwhelmed the impact of the volume's release. The Generation of 1927, many of whom were outspoken supporters of the Spanish Republic, fled into exile or were thrown into prison. García Lorca was executed at the hands of fascist troops, while Guillén himself spent time in Pamplona behind bars as a political prisoner.

Not as directly involved in politics as some of his friends, Guillén avoided execution and remained in Spain for another two years. Civil war continued, but by the time Guillén left Spain for the United States in 1938, the Spanish Republic had very little chance of surviving. The next year, Francisco Franco asserted his dictatorship, cruelly punishing those who had supported the Republic during the conflict.

A world traveler for most of his life, Guillén adapted to his new surroundings easily. He accepted a position at Wellesley University in Massachusetts in 1940 and remained at that institution for 17 years. In 1945 he published the third edition of *Cantico,* this time attaching the subtitle *Fe de vida* (*Testimony of Life*). The third edition contained 270 poems. In 1950, the fourth and final edition of *Cantico: Fe de vida* brought together 334 of his poems. In the latter part of the 1950s Guillén published *Maremagnum* (*Sea of Confusion*), the first volume of his *Clamor* series. Between publication of the third and fourth editions of *Cantico,* though, his wife Germaine died, inspiring the work *. . . Que vanndal a dar en la mar* ( *. . . We Will End at the Sea*), the second volume of *Clamor,* published in 1960.

Throughout the 1950s Guillén taught at several universities in the United States and Mexico, including Harvard University and the College of Mexico City. Recognition of his poetry grew throughout the literary world. He received the Award of Merit of the American Academy of Arts and Letters in 1955, the Poetry Prize of the City of Florence in 1957, and the Etna-Taormina Poetry Prize in Sicily in 1959.

Guillén married an Italian woman named Irene Mochi Sismondi in 1961. He completed the *Clamor* series in 1963 with *A la altura de las circunstancias* (*To Rise to the Occasion*). In 1968 he compiled the work *Aire nuestro* (*Our Air*), a volume that brought together *Cantico, Clamor,* and *Homenaje,* another Guillén title. Several U.S. universities held symposiums devoted exclusively to his work; one at the

University of Oklahoma celebrated the poet's 75th birthday.

Upon Franco's death in 1975, Guillén returned to Spain and lived in Malaga. In his last years the poet receive accolades of all kinds, including the Miguel de Cervantes Prize of the Spanish Royal Academy in 1976. His last collection, *Final*, appeared shortly before his death in 1984.

## SELECTED PUBLISHED WORKS:

*Cantico,* 1928; revised edition, 1936; 3d revised edition, 1945; 4th revised edition, 1950.
*The Poetry of Jorge Guillén,* translated by Frances Avery Pleak, Princeton University Press, 1942.
*Maremagnum* (*Sea of Confusion*), Volume one of *Clamor: Tiempo de historia,* 1957.
*Que van dar a la mar* (*We Will End at the Sea*), Volume two of *Clamor: Tiempo de historia,* 1960.
*A la altura de las circunstancias* (*To Rise to the Occasion*), Volume three of *Clamor: Tiempo de historia,* 1963.
*Homenaje: Reunion de vidas,* 1967.
*Aire Nuestro,* 1968.
*Y otros poemas,* 1973.
*Final,* 1981.

## SOURCES:

### Books

*Hispanic Writers,* edited by Bryan Ryan, Detroit, Gale, 1993.
MacCurdy, G. Grant, *Jorge Guillén,* Twayne Publishing, 1982.

—*Sketch by James McCarthy*

# Ricardo Güiraldes
## 1886-1927
**Argentine writer**

Best-remembered for *Don Segundo Sombra,* the novel for which he won Argentina's Gran Premio Nacional de Literatura, Ricardo Güiraldes was one of the most famous Argentine novelists of the early twentieth century. *Don Segundo* has become a classic work.

Ricardo Guillermo Güiraldes was born near Buenos Aires on February 13, 1886. His father, Manuel Güiraldes, was a wealthy landowner and young Güiraldes grew up on the family ranch, "La Porteña." He received an excellent education and traveled extensively—he embarked on his first trip abroad at the age of two and learned to speak fluent French and German as a child. He studied architecture and law in college. In 1910 he began a two-year world tour, spending considerable time in Europe. He read European literature avidly, and possessed a keen interest in the avant garde style of contemporary French authors.

### Began Publishing

In 1913, Güiraldes married Adelina de Carril. Two years later, at the age of 29, he published his first book, *El cencerro de cristal* ("The Glass Cowbell"). This volume of poetry was not well received at the time; its own avant garde style was not yet popular in Argentina. The same year—1915—Güiraldes also published *Cuentos de muerte y de sangre* ("Tales of Death and Blood"), a short story collection reflecting more traditional Argentine themes of ranch and country life.

It was in the stories "Al rescoldo" ("Embers") and "La estancia vieja" ("The Old Ranch") that Güiraldes's most famous character, Don Segundo Sombra, first appeared. In fact, Güiraldes developed several characters in more than one of his works. Members of the Galván family—a family which has been likened to Güiraldes's own—have appeared in *Xaimaca* ("Jamaica"), *Raucho: Momentos de una juventud contemporánea* ("Raucho: Moments In The Life of a Contemporary Youth"), and *Don Segundo Sombra.*

In 1917 Güiraldes published *Raucho: Momentos de una juventud contemporánea,* a tale of a young Argentine man leading the life of a contemporary, wealthy young man. Raucho's story begins on the family ranch, where Güiraldes vividly evokes the ranch atmosphere The restless Raucho moves to Buenos Aires, and then travels to Europe, much as Güiraldes and other upper-class Argentines had done. But after destroying his health with drugs and alcohol, Raucho returns to the ranch and realizes that it is the country life on his native soil that gives him peace.

### Developed Writing Style

According to Jefferson Rea Spell in *Contemporary Spanish-American Fiction,* writing was for Güiraldes "merely a diversion . . . as he was wealthy, and his literary work is very limited in extent, [but] it is of a very superior type." Although Güiraldes may not have had to worry about earning a living, he was deeply engaged in the use of language and the writing craft. He continued to publish poetry after his first book, but his interests shifted to prose and his work consisted of short stories and novels.

Although Güiraldes's career was short, he had developed his talent and craft and incorporated the influences of diverse masters. He was quite cosmopolitan, having spent much time away from the family ranch. Although several of his stories reflected his knowledge of European ways, his most artistic works stemmed from his native background. His stories, "Máscaras" ("Masks"), "Ferroviaria" ("A Train Trip"), and "Sexto" ("The Sixth"), were styled to appeal particularly to an Argentine audience.

Güiraldes's stories were products of their time. He emphasized poetics; action and characterization were secondary. Spell declared: "Güiraldes . . . with all of his excellent qualities as a writer . . . is not the truly great novelist that some enthusiastic critics would have us believe. His novels . . . are limited in scope, rather one-sided. For, while his style is poetic, while his sharp-toned pictures of certain strata of Argentine society remain with one long after his books are read, he is sadly lacking in two essentials of a great novelist: he gives no evidence of ability to develop character or to weave a plot that is much beyond that of the picaresque novel."

### Published Final Work

*Don Segundo Sombra* epitomizes Güiraldes's picturesque tendencies. The story focuses on an Argentine boy, the illegitimate son of a wealthy ranch owner who lives with two maiden aunts. The boy aspires to a more adventurous life than the one provided by his aunts and his school environment. He has seen and admired Don Segundo, a *gaucho*, or cowboy. The boy runs away from home, and Don Segundo becomes his guardian, teaching him the practical skills of a gaucho as well as his personal philosophy on life.

When the boy is finally acknowledged as the wealthy ranch owner's son he inherits a large estate. The boy is appointed a more formal guardian and begins a new lifestyle, learning to become a cultured young man. Although Don Segundo initially remains with him, he eventually leaves to return to his gaucho existence, feeling the young man no longer needs him.

Güiraldes has been highly praised for *Don Segundo Sombra's* poetic style. The work noted for its rich evocations of the pampas and the gaucho ways and for its use of authentic rustic dialogue. Güiraldes created an artistic work that combined the poetic traditional Argentine novel with a blend of European literary influence.

Güiraldes's life was also devoted to activities outside of his own writing. Together with Pablo Rojas Paz and another friend and author in his own right,

Jorge Luis Borges, Güiraldes founded Proa, a publishing house, in Buenos Aires. He also found time for political activities, serving as a Congressman and as the mayor of Buenos Aires.

Güiraldes died of Hodgkin's disease on October 8, 1927, in Paris, where he had spent much time during his life. Three of Guiraldes's works were published posthumously: *Poemas solitarios* ("Poems of Solitude"), *Poemas místicos* ("Mystic Poems"), and *Seis Relatos* ("Six Stories"). While the contents of the books of poetry had not been published before, five stories in *Seis Relatos* had been previously published. His works have been reprinted, translated, and published in the United States, the Netherlands and Spain, and his work was also included in many anthologies.

## SELECTED PUBLISHED WORKS:

*El cencerro de cristal,* 1915, reprinted Losada, Buenos Aires, 1952.

*Cuentos de muerte y de sangre,* 1915; reprinted Losada, 1958.

*Raucho: Momentos de una juventud contemporánea,* 1917; Centro Editor de América Latina, Buenos Aires, 1968.

*Rosaura,* 1922; reprinted Sudamericana, Buenos Aires, 1960.

*Xaimaca,* 1923; reprinted Losada, 1967.

*Don Segundo Sombra,* Proa, 1926; reprinted Losada, 1940; reprinted G. Kraft, Buenos Aires, 1960; translated, published as *Don Segundo Sombra: Shadows on the Pampas,* Farrar & Rinehart, 1935; abridged, edited, published under original title by Holt, 1945.

*Poemas místico,* 1928; reprinted 1969.

*Poemas solitarios,* Colón 1928; reprinted 1970.

## SOURCES:

### Books

*Cyclopedia of World Authors,* edited by Frank N. Magill, New York, Harper & Row, 1958.

*Hispanic Writers,* edited by Bryan Ryan, Detroit, Gale, 1991.

Spell, Jefferson Rea, *Contemporary Spanish-American Fiction,* Chapel Hill, The University of North Carolina Press, 1944.

—*Sketch by Sandy J. Stiefer*

# Ana Sol Gutiérrez
## 1942-

**Salvadoran American aeronautical engineer and public servant**

Ana Sol Gutiérrez is a woman of many accomplishments. She is the first elected Hispanic member on a board of education in Maryland and the first Hispanic of Salvadoran descent ever elected to public office in the history of the United States. "The time has come simply because there is a critical mass of immigrant or ethnic minority students," she said to Amy Goldstein of the *Washington Post*. She has attained her position and the support of the people in Montgomery County, Maryland, because of her dynamism, assertiveness in community affairs, and commitment to education.

Gutiérrez was born Anna Emma Sol in Santa Ana, El Salvador, on January 11, 1942, the daughter of Ana Pérez, a homemaker, and Jorge Sol-Castellanos, El Salvador's first finance minister, director of the World Bank and the International Monetary Fund, and an economist for the Organization of American States. Divorced from Fernando Gutiérrez, she is the mother of three sons: Fernando, Alejandro (Alex), and Rodrigo.

A resident of Montgomery County since she was five years old, Gutiérrez attended various local schools, including Chevy Chase Senior High School. She then studied liberal arts and chemistry at the University of Geneva in Switzerland before graduating from Pennsylvania State University with a bachelor of science degree and later from American University with a master of science in management and computer sciences.

At the time Gutiérrez began her career in aeronautical engineering, her work didn't fit the traditional role mode expected for a women. Mercedes Olivera observed in *Vista*, "A woman as an astronaut, aerospace engineer or electrician was a rare sight three decades ago, rarer still if she had a Spanish surname." When asked by contributor Sylvia P. Apodaca if her parents had some influence in her career, Gutiérrez declared: "Absolutely! My father was especially supportive and a strong role model to achieve to my fullest potential both professionally and individually."

After completing her education, Gutiérrez moved to Bolivia and then Venezuela. In Bolivia, she taught as a professor of mathematics and computer sciences at the Universidad Mayor de San Andrés, and in Venezuela she taught undergraduate- and graduate-level courses in systems engineering and computer systems. Also in Venezuela, Gutiérrez served as a manager at INTEVEP, the Venezuelan Petroleum Research Institute, where, in 1976, she developed a computer-based technical information system to support the company's research and development laboratory activities. In addition to her teaching and managerial responsibilities, Gutiérrez worked as an international management consultant in Venezuela, Bolivia, and Peru.

After returning to the United States, Gutiérrez continued to work in the aerospace field. Until mid-1992 she was a systems engineer for Loral Aerosys in Seabrook, Maryland. As a senior consultant engineer for Computer Sciences Corporation (CSC) since 1992, she is an operations manager of the FAA (Federal Aviation Administration) Advance Automation System Program. In this position, Gutiérrez is responsible for managing two departments, Product Assurance and Configuration Management. She also serves as senior consultant on Total Quality Management (TQM) to other CSC corporate centers and has worked on programs for the National Aeronautics and Space Administration (NASA) and the Goddard Space Flight Center in Greenbelt, Maryland.

Gutiérrez's many civic activities primarily focus on education. She has long been active in the Montgomery County PTA and other community-based organizations, including the education committee of the League of United Latin American Citizens (LULAC), and the National Council of La Raza. She is also a member of Senator Barbara A. Mikulski's academic review board, the National Coalition of Education Activists, the Hispanic Education Issues Committee of Montgomery College, and the National Science Foundation Advisory Committee for the Minority Education Project. In her view, education is a very important issue for everybody, but it is especially important for Hispanics. Schools are "the instruments for not just the individual to succeed, but for us as a community to succeed," Gutiérrez told *Washington Post* reporter Retha Hill.

Gutiérrez is currently pursuing her Ph.D. in engineering at George Washington University. Her future plans include serving out her term on the Montgomery County Board of Education while continuing to work as a senior consulting engineer.

## SOURCES:

### Periodicals

*Vista,* October 5, 1991, p. 20.
*Washington Post,* November 3, 1990, p. B5; May 9, 1991, section MDM, p. 1.

### Other

Gutiérrez, Ana Sol, telephone interview with Sylvia P. Apodaca conducted on August 22, 1992.

—*Sketch by Sylvia P. Apodaca*

# Antonio Guzmán Blanco
## 1829-1899
### Venezuelan dictator

Antonio Guzmán Blanco, a dictator who dominated Venezuela for 25 years, came out of the *caudillo* tradition. *Caudillo* is the Spanish word for chief, leader, head of state. In Venezuela, as in many other South American countries, the *caudillo* phenomenon arose during the wars of independence fought against Spain during the early-to-middle years of the nineteenth century. In the economic and civil disorder that characterized Venezuela after its liberation from Spanish rule, strong leadership was called for in order to hold the country together. This leadership most often took a dictatorial form. Abuse of power often ensues in such arrangements, but Guzmán Blanco's tenure, which ended in a coup d'etat, was generally regarded to be a benevolent one marked by government reform.

Officially, Guzmán Blanco's elected terms of office were from 1870 to 1877, 1879 to 1884, and 1886 to 1888. But prior to 1870—and in the interim periods between his terms—Guzmán Blanco's power and influence were so great that those holding the title of President did so in name only. More educated, clever, and forceful than his predecessors **José Antonio Páez**, José Monagas, and Juan Falcón, he was better able to control the political and military unrest that plagued Venezuela after the revolution. As a strong leader, he was known for his ability to control and exploit both the military and the commercial-bureaucratic elite. Good administration, an influx of foreign money, and relative peace and prosperity were hallmarks of his rule. He effected moderate reforms in education and separation of church and state powers. Although he associated himself with the country's Liberal Party, his was a charismatic and personal regime. He amassed great personal wealth through his control of Venezuela's finances and economy, and subverted constitutional reform, which he had promised the people of his country.

Guzmán Blanco, who called himself the "Civilizer" and "Illustrious American," was showered with honors during his rule. Statues of him were erected in Caracas, La Guaira, and other cities. States were named after him. Gold medals were struck with his name and accomplishments, and a special emblem called the Sun of April was awarded him by the congress to commemorate his military victory over the conservative forces on April 27, 1870. When power was finally wrested from his grasp in 1888, he settled in Europe. Guzmán Blanco never returned to Venezuela.

Guzmán Blanco was the son of Antonio Leocadio Guzmán, a Liberal politician and minister of the interior under Venezuelan president José Páez. His mother was Carlota Blanco, a relative of the Venezuelan hero and liberator **Simón Bolívar**. The young boy was exposed early to his father's radical politics. In 1847 his father was sentenced to death for conspiring against the government. It is said that the boy and his mother personally pleaded with then-President José Monagas to spare his life. Monagas commuted the sentence and sent Guzmán into exile; remarkably, he later brought him back to serve in his cabinet. While Leocadio Guzmán had ambitions to succeed Monagas as president, his ambitions were not fulfilled.

Guzmán Blanco attended Central University in Caracas, where he received a law degree. He entered foreign service, and was posted abroad to the New York Consulate and the Embassy in Washington, D.C. He returned to Venezuela in the 1850s and joined the Liberal Party. When a leading Liberal candidate, Juan Falcón, was exiled in 1859, Guzmán Blanco went with him. This turned out to be a wise political decision and paved the way for his eventual rise to power.

Guzmán Blanco recognized that a military career would help him attain political success. He transferred from a civilian post in Falcón's provisional government to a military post in the army. There, his strategic abilities earned him the rank of commandant, and later, general. Meanwhile, the war between conservative and liberal political factions over who would rule Venezuela finally ended after five years with the ratification of the Treaty of Coche. Guzmán Blanco was directly involved in the negotiation and terms of the treaty. Even though he was criticized by his opponents for personally profiting from the financial deals struck to end the war, this episode served to advance him politically. Personal advancement soon emerged as an essential aspect of his political governance.

### Rise to Presidential Power

In 1863 Falcón was elected provisional president, while Guzmán Blanco assumed the position of vice president. Falcón assumed power over a country that, after 50 years of revolution and political instability, was in a weakened condition both economically and politically. Under the Falcón government, Guzmán Blanco played an important role in the rebuilding of the country. He consolidated its political structure, developed its communications and transportation systems, and strengthened its agriculture and commerce. During this time, Falcón was president in name only—Guzmán Blanco was really the one in command. Not only did he succeed in putting the country on a firmer financial footing, he also made himself enormously wealthy. Guzmán Blanco's success was due to several accomplishments: he obtained foreign loans to shore up Venezuela's economy, he instituted constitutional reform based on the precepts of the Federal Party, and he proved himself an able and decisive administrator.

Guzmán Blanco had often talked of Venezuela's need to secure foreign loans. In July 1863 he was made secretary of the treasury. He left for Europe a month later with authority to negotiate those loans. His government had given him the power not only to negotiate and mortgage any natural resources he felt necessary, but also to dispense the loan monies in any way he saw fit. He was in complete control of the country's purse strings. In London he successfully negotiated a loan of a million-and-a-half pounds, only to meet with opposition in Venezuela when he sought congressional approval. Many in the public and in the government believed the main reason for the loan was to further his personal gain. Despite such misgivings, the loan was approved by a large majority in 1864.

This assembly also wrote the federal constitution that year. This constitution divided Venezuela into federal autonomous states, provided for universal suffrage, abolished the death penalty, and provided for free speech and freedom of the press. While the legislation addressed a number of concerns, it also set the stage for a clash between the country's need for strong central control and local and class loyalties. This situation proved to be a major problem for Guzmán Blanco throughout his political career.

While Guzmán Blanco was out of the country, Falcón's weaknesses as president and his long absences from the capital reversed civil progress made since the end of the war. When Guzmán Blanco returned, Falcón willingly turned presidential duties over to him. For more than a year, from November 1864 to May 1866, he was unofficially the head of government.

Guzmán Blanco used his authority effectively. By exercising control over local chiefs and placing his support behind the federal legislatures, he established order in the country. He regulated finances by reducing unauthorized expenditures, requiring detailed reports from government agencies on income and disbursements, and decreeing that public servants and the army be paid on time instead of months late. He reorganized the postal system, established a better accountability system for the federal budget, and created a bank whose purpose was to finance a central railroad through Venezuela.

As Falcón's presidential power continue to weaken, Guzmán Blanco declared his intention to seek the position in the coming election. A coalition of conservatives and disaffected liberals who sought to advance the candidacy of a former president, José Monagas, forced Guzmán Blanco to flee the country under threat of death. He assembled an army of supporters and fought his way back to Caracas, the nation's capital, on April 27, 1870. On July 20, he took office as president, making formal the office he had in reality held since 1864. His powers were absolute and his word was law, a state of affairs of which he was swift to make his enemies aware. A leader who possessed military aptitude as well as superior political and administrative abilities, Guzmán Blanco began his long tenure as the official leader of his country.

### Years of Power and Progress

Pressing economic problems occupied Guzmán Blanco throughout his first term. Venezuela's credit was ruined by war and continuous military expense. He formed a credit commission to stabilize the treasury and issued guaranteed government bonds to pay creditors. At the same time, he shored up the country's failing agricultural system and began a massive construction program to rebuild Venezuela's major cities, the country's infrastructure, and its communication systems. Turning his attention to Caracas, he constructed a new capital building, university, theater, museum, and numerous palaces for government officials. He also established a department of statistics that eventually became the country's national census bureau. He was re-elected to a second term in 1873 by an overwhelming popular vote. When the results of the election were clear, Guzmán Blanco immediately left the capital to inspect his ongoing construction projects and receive the adulation of his people. As first designate to the presidency, General Francisco Linares Alcántara was left in charge.

In 1874 Guzmán Blanco was forced to put down an insurrection in the state of Coro. This victory strengthened his rule over the states and the country in general, and further solidified his prestige. The revolt, however, was indicative of continual rumblings in the country about his abuses of power and unwillingness to grant certain civil rights.

In 1877 Guzmán Blanco's first designate, Alcántara, was elected president. Guzmán Blanco had declared for Alcántara, perhaps theorizing that he would still have control of Venezuela behind the scenes. Soon after Alcántara took office, however, accusations about Guzmán Blanco's conduct in office proliferated. He left for Europe with Alcántara's blessing and served as minister plenipotentiary to Germany, France, Italy, the Vatican, Spain, and Switzerland.

Guzmán Blanco's departure to Europe did nothing to quell the tide of criticism of his performance as president, however. Several parties were particularly accusatory. Conservatives, upon whom Guzmán Blanco had extracted revenge after their wars of opposition; local *caudillos*, who were shorn of their power when he brought peace and order to the countryside; and liberals eager to bring about a genuinely representative government for Venezuela all vilified Guzmán Blanco. Even so, his supporters clamored for his return, and Alcántara's loyalty to Guzmán Blanco kept criticism in the background.

Circumstances changed dramatically when Alcántara died in November 1878. Guzmán Blanco's opponents, who had gained a majority in congress, voted to annul the honors given him and directed that all statues of Guzmán Blanco in the capital be smashed. These actions provoked an armed reaction from his supporters against the interim government, and Guzmán Blanco was recalled from Europe in 1879 to resume interim presidential powers. He was well received on his return, and all statues were restored to their previous places of honor.

Upon returning to Venezuela, Guzmán Blanco modified Venezuela's constitution by, as stated in George Wise's *Caudillo, A Portrait of Antonio Guzmán Blanco,* "substitution of the political rights of the Swiss Confederacy for the public rights of the United States of North America, which have until now served us as a model, without the good success achieved by the latter." Constitutional reform was eventually voted in by the congress, with the result that power became more centralized and civil rights more abridged.

Guzmán Blanco's rule during this period was marked by a dramatic surge in railroad construction in the country. Venezuela's economy was an anemic one, but public debt bonds were selling at a good price and private capital was fostering industrial growth. A plague of locusts ruined the country's fruit crop and coffee export prices were dropping, but the arrival in Caracas in June 1883 of the first train on the new railroad brought cheers. Guzmán Blanco made a trip out of the capital to celebrate the end of his five-year reign. His egotism is evident in a speech given at Villa de Cura and recorded in Wise's *Caudillo:* "For my successor there are only two choices: the way of Guzmán Blanco who, finding nothing, had to create everything . . . ; or the way of Alcántara who, having everything, lost everything through his personal plans and rapacious ambitions and his disloyal behavior. There will be two horizons open to the elected: one which will blazon the dishonor and shame of Alcántara and another of glory through the gratitude and love of the people, which is that of Guzmán Blanco."

General Joaquin Crespo was elected as Venezuela's new president in 1884. Guzmán Blanco's preference for Crespo was a deciding factor in his election.

He then left for Europe as envoy and minister to Britain, Belgium, Spain, Italy, and the Vatican, leaving Venezuela in Crespo's hands. As in the past under a puppet president, there was much criticism of Guzmán Blanco's political practices among his opposition and the general public. Civil violence broke out and the country's fragile economy suffered as a result. Pointing to Venezuela's tenuous state, Guzmán Blanco's supporters argued that only he had the power to restore order in the country. In 1886 the Venezuelan congress voted unanimously to return Guzmán Blanco to the presidency.

This final reign, however, was a troubled one. Opposition to Guzmán Blanco was significant, and a movement grew to form a new party to accommodate and consolidate that opposition. The president suppressed that idea by jailing those involved, a development that further strengthened the resolve of his enemies. Several attempts were made to assassinate Guzmán Blanco—one at the Guzmán Blanco Theater, one in the baths of a private home, and another at the funeral of the president's aunt. Concerned for his safety, Guzmán Blanco informed his party he would not offer himself for re-election. Before leaving office, though, he issued contracts for a series of public works projects and distributed huge sums of money to his political allies. Turning over the presidency to General Hermógenes López, Guzmán Blanco left Venezuela for the last time. From his new home in Europe, he placed his support behind Dr. Rojas Paúl, who was elected president in 1888. Guzmán Blanco died in 1899, a little more than a decade after leaving Venezuelan politics.

## SOURCES:

### Books

Lombardi, John V., *Venezuela, The Search for Order, The Dream of Progress,* New York, Oxford University Press, 1982.

Marsland, William D., and Amy L. Marsland, *Venezuela Through Its History,* New York, Crowell, 1954.

Moron, Guillermo, *A History of Venezuela,* edited and translated by John Street, London, George Allen & Unwin Ltd., 1964.

Wise, George, *Caudillo, A Portrait of Antonio Guzmán Blanco,* Westport, CT, Greenwood Press, 1951.

*—Sketch by Jane Stewart Cook*

# Rita Hayworth
## 1918-1987
### Hispanic American actress

Whether illuminating the screen with a song and dance or beaming from a magazine photo, Rita Hayworth was an unforgettable sight. Capitalizing on her inherited beauty and talent to become a legendary motion picture star, Hayworth captured the hearts of countless American servicemen during the 1940s. At her peak, she epitomized American beauty, and her career produced several memorable moments: dance routines with Fred Astaire in *You'll Never Get Rich* (1941); a glamorous photo in *Life* magazine; a scandalous striptease in *Gilda* (1946); and mature sophistication in *The Lady From Shanghai* (1949). While Hayworth's death in 1987 saddened America, it alerted the nation to the plight of those threatened by Alzheimer's disease, the illness that slowly killed her.

Born Margarita Carmen Cansino to Eduardo and Volga Haworth Cansino on October 17, 1918, in New York City, Rita Hayworth was no stranger to show business. Her father, a headliner on vaudeville, was descended from a line of famous Spanish dancers, and her mother, a Ziegfeld showgirl, came from a family of English actors. When the girl was nine years old, the family moved to Los Angeles, California, where the motion picture industry was rapidly growing. There, Eduardo taught dancing and directed dance scenes for various studios. She began her education at the Carthay School and later spent her first and only year of high school at Hamilton High. Throughout her school years, she continued family tradition by taking acting and dancing lessons.

At eleven, the girl found her first acting role in a school play, and by 1932, she had made her professional debut. She appeared in a stage prologue for the movie *Back Street* at Carthay Circle Theater. At this point, Eduardo Cansino decided that his attractive twelve-year-old daughter was ready for work. The perfect dance partner, she was introduced as Eduardo's wife when they danced at the Foreign Club in Tijuana, Mexico, for a year and a half, and then later on a gambling boat off California's coast. The "Dancing Cansinos" performed twenty times per week.

*Rita Hayworth*

### Makes Film Debut in *Dante's Inferno*

Rita Cansino, as she was called during this time, received her first big break when she was noticed dancing with her father in Agua Caliente, Mexico. Winfield R. Sheehan of the Fox Film Corporation hired the young woman, then sixteen, for a role in a movie starring Spencer Tracy entitled *Dante's Inferno* (1935). Though the film was not successful, Rita Cansino was given a year-long contract with Fox. During this year she held minor, ethnic roles in the motion pictures *Charlie Chan in Egypt* (1935), *Under the Pampas Moon* (1935), *Paddy O'Day* (1935), and *Human Cargo* (1936), in which she played Egyptian, Argentine, Irish, and Russian dancers respectively. When her contract expired and was not renewed, the actress spent a year playing Mexican and Indian girls; she earned $100 for each role.

When Rita Cansino was 18, she married Edward C. Judson, a car salesman, oil man, and businessman who became her manager. According to the *New York Times,* Judson "transformed" the actress "from a raven-haired Latin to an auburn-haired cosmopolitan" by altering Rita's hairline and eyebrows with electrolysis and changing her professional name. Rita Cansino took her mother's maiden name, added a "y" to ensure its proper pronunciation, and became Rita Hayworth. Magazines and newspapers captured the image of the new Rita, who won the favor of Harry Cohn and a seven-year contract with his Columbia Pictures.

After fourteen low-budget movies, Hayworth was finally given a leading role. She was hired by Howard W. Hawks to portray an unfaithful wife in *Only Angels Have Wings* (1939), which starred Cary Grant. Good reviews of her performance attracted attention: she was borrowed from Columbia by Warner Brothers Pictures for the film *Strawberry Blonde* (1941) with James Cagney, and in that same year, she made *Blood and Sand* (1941) with Fox. Hayworth began to shine. According to *Time,* "something magical happened when the cameras began to roll"; the woman who was "shy" and "unassuming" offstage "warmed the set." The *New York Times* wrote that Hayworth "rapidly developed into one of Hollywood's most glamorous stars."

Hayworth achieved celebrity status when she starred as Fred Astaire's dance partner in *You'll Never Get Rich* (1941) for Columbia. She appeared on the cover of *Time* and was dubbed "The Great American Love Goddess" by Winthrop Sargent in *Life.* In 1942, she made three hit movies: *My Gal Sal, Tales of Manhattan* and *You Were Never Lovelier,* with Fred Astaire. As her career skyrocketed, however, Hayworth's marriage failed; she divorced Edward Judson that same year.

**Marries Orson Welles**

During the early forties, Hayworth's personal life improved and she established her professional allure. She married Orson Welles, the famous actor, director, and screenwriter, in 1943; they had a daughter, Rebecca, two years later. Hayworth was earning more than $6,000 a week as Columbia's leading actress. After she starred in *Cover Girl* (1944) with Gene Kelly, *Life* presented a seductive photograph of the actress wearing black lace which, according to the *New York Times,* "became famous around the world as an American serviceman's pinup." The *Times* also noted that, in what was "intended . . . as the ultimate compliment, the picture was even pasted to a test atomic bomb that was dropped on Bikini atoll in 1946."

Hayworth's fame continued to grow after she made *Tonight and Every Night* (1945) and *Gilda* (1946). Of these films, critics contend that *Gilda* is the most memorable. A scene in which Hayworth sang "Put the Blame on Mame" and stripped off her long, black gloves scandalized conservative viewers. It was testimony to her popularity that her 1947 film, *Down to Earth,* was included in a twentieth-century time capsule despite the fact that the film itself received some bad reviews.

Hayworth did not mind the attention she garnered. "I like having my picture taken and being a glamorous person," she was quoted as saying in the *New York Times.* "Sometimes when I find myself getting impatient, I just remember the times I cried my eyes out because nobody wanted to take my picture at the Trocadero." Hayworth's daughter Yasmin Aga Khan confirmed this in *People:* "Mother was very good with her fans, very giving and patient."

While Hayworth starred as a sophisticated short-haired blonde in *The Lady From Shanghai* (1948) with her husband Orson Welles—who also directed the movie—she was in the process of divorcing him. She was later quoted in *People* as saying, "I just can't take his genius anymore," and in *Time,* she noted, "I'm tired of being a 25-percent wife." After making *The Loves of Carmen* (1948), she married Prince Aly Kahn, with whom she had been having an affair, in 1949. This was an off-screen scandal, for Hayworth was already pregnant with their daughter, the Princess Yasmin Aga Kahn. Although she was quoted in *Time* as saying, "The world was magical when you were with him," this marriage did not last as long as her second; the couple divorced in 1953.

Hayworth's career began to wane. After making the movies *Affair in Trinidad* (1952), *Salome* (1953), and *Miss Sadie Thompson* (1953), she once again entered a marriage (1953–1955) that would prove to be unsuccessful as well as destructive. This fourth husband, the singer Dick Haymes, "beat her and tried to capitalize on her fame in an attempt to revive his own failing career," said Barbara Leaming, a Hayworth biographer, in *People.* While Hayworth came out of her temporary retirement after her divorce to make *Fire Down Below* (1957), which met with some positive reviews, she had only a supporting role in the film *Pal Joey* (1957). Failing to maintain her glamour, this movie was Hayworth's final appearance as a contracted actress.

At this point in the actress's life, Hayworth's personal life seemed to parallel her professional career. She married producer James Hill in 1958 and divorced him in 1961. *People* reported that Hill had wanted Rita to continue to make movies instead of "play golf, paint, tell jokes and have a home." After the failure of this fifth and final marriage, it was apparent that Hayworth did not have good luck with the men in her life. While Hayworth was quoted in *People* as saying, "Most men fell in love with *Gilda* but they woke up with me," biographer Barbara Leaming asserted that these "doomed" relationships were due to Hayworth's abusive father, Eduardo Cansino. Leaming told *People,* "Eduardo raped her [Hayworth] in the afternoons and danced with her at night." In her biography of Hayworth, *If This Was*

*Happiness,* Leaming elaborates on this revelation, which she says was given to her by Orson Welles.

### Develops Alzheimer's Disease

While critics agreed that Hayworth gave one of her best performances as a traitorous American in *They Came to Cordura* (1959), they also noted that her trademark beauty was fading. As a free-lance actress, Hayworth found fewer roles. *The Story on Page One* (1960), *The Poppy Is Also a Flower* (1967), and *The Wrath of God* (1972) were some of her last films. Hayworth's 1971 attempt to perform on stage was aborted; the actress could not remember her lines.

Biographers, relatives, and friends now believe that the first stages of Alzheimer's disease were responsible for Hayworth's memory lapses, alcoholism, lack of coordination, and poor eyesight during the last three decades of her life. Although Alzheimer's, a disease which was relatively unknown at the time, was not diagnosed as the source of Hayworth's problems, it was obvious that Hayworth was ill. In 1981 she was legally declared unable to care for herself. Her daughter, Princess Yasmin Aga Kahn provided shelter, care, and love for her mother, and sought to enlighten the public to the symptoms of the obscure neurological disease by helping to organize Alzheimer's Disease International and serving as its president.

Hayworth's mind slowly began to deteriorate. When she died in her New York apartment on May 14, 1987, she did not even know her own family. Nevertheless, the "All-American Love Goddess," as *Time* called her, was not forgotten by her fans. The *New York Times* reported at the time of her death that President Ronald Reagan, a former actor, stated: "Rita Hayworth was one of our country's most beloved stars. Glamorous and talented, she gave us many wonderful moments . . . and delighted audiences from the time she was a young girl. [First Lady] Nancy and I are saddened by Rita's death. She was a friend whom we will miss."

## SELECTED VIDEOGRAPHY

*Hit the Saddle,* 1937.
*Trouble in Texas,* 1937.
*Renegade Ranger/Scarlet River,* 1938.
*Only Angels Have Wings,* 1939.
*Angels Over Broadway,* 1940.
*The Lady in Question,* 1940.
*Music in My Heart,* 1940.
*Susan and God,* 1940.
*Blood and Sand,* 1941.
*Strawberry Blonde,* 1941.
*You'll Never Get Rich,* 1941.
*My Gal Sal,* 1942.
*Tales of Manhattan,* 1942.
*You Were Never Lovelier,* 1942.

*Cover Girl,* 1944.
*Tonight and Every Night,* 1945.
*Gilda,* 1946.
*Down to Earth,* 1947.
*The Lady From Shanghai,* 1948.
*The Loves of Carmen,* 1948.
*Affair in Trinidad,* 1952.
*Miss Sadie Thompson,* 1953.
*Salome,* 1953.
*Fire Down Below,* 1957.
*Pal Joey,* 1957.
*Separate Tables,* 1958.
*They Came to Cordura,* 1959.
*The Story on Page One,* 1960.
*Circus World,* 1964.
*The Love Goddess,* 1965.
*The Poppy Is Also a Flower,* 1967.
*Road to Salina,* 1968.
*The Wrath of God,* 1972.

## SOURCES:

### Books

Leaming, Barbara, *If This Was Happiness,* Viking, 1989.

### Periodicals

*American Film,* July, 1986, pp. 69–72.
*Good Housekeeping,* August, 1983, pp. 118–27; September, 1983, pp. 74–82.
*Harper's Bazaar,* November, 1989, pp. 156–59.
*Ladies' Home Journal,* January, 1983, pp. 84–89.
*Ms.,* January, 1991, pp. 35–38.
*New York Times,* May 16, 1987.
*People,* November 7, 1983, pp. 112–17; June 1, 1987, pp. 72–79; November 13, 1989, pp. 129–32.
*Time,* May 25, 1987, p. 76.
*Variety,* May 20, 1987, pp. 4–6.

—*Sketch by Ronie-Richele Garcia-Johnson*

# Antonia Hernández
## 1948-
### Mexican American civil rights lawyer

As president and general counsel for the Mexican American Legal Defense and Educational Fund (MALDEF), a Latino civil rights organization, Antonia Hernández has become a highly visible advocate for the nation's large and growing Latino community. Her opinions and advice on how a given issue will affect U.S. Hispanics/Latinos have often been featured in newspaper editorial pages, national magazines, television talk shows, and numerous other media outlets. Immigrant rights, employment discrimination, educational inequities, U.S. Census figures, redistricting, voting and language rights, are among her regular topics of concern.

### Leader in Civil Rights Activism

Hernández began working for MALDEF in 1981 as a staff attorney in its Washington, D.C., office. Two years later she became employment litigation director in the Los Angeles office. During those years she sought greater opportunities for Hispanics in federal employment and promoted affirmative action in private and public sector jobs. It was also a period when MALDEF initiated several lawsuits to get employers to compensate bilingual workers whose second language capabilities were part of their job. In 1985, Hernández became president and general counsel of MALDEF, succeeding Joaquin Avila. "Every person who heads [MALDEF] gives it his or her flavor," Hernández told *Hispanic.* "My flavor has been taking the helm of an organization and helping it into institutional maturity."

Her tenure with MALDEF has been marked by controversy. In 1987, an executive committee of the MALDEF Board of Directors abruptly terminated her, citing questionable administrative and leadership abilities. Hours later they appointed former New Mexico Governor Toney Anaya to the post and gave him a $100,000 salary—$40,000 more than Hernández had been making. But Hernández refused to be dismissed, maintaining that only the full board had the power to fire her. A state judge from Texas agreed, requiring that the full board determine her status. They voted 18 to 14 to retain her.

Since then, she has gone on to become an organizational mainstay and MALDEF's most visible spokesperson. A public interest lawyer since graduating from the University of California at Los Angeles (UCLA) Law School in 1974, her advocacy is informed by her personal experiences of growing up as an immigrant in East Los Angeles, California. For example, her experiences as a child learning English by the "sink or swim" method has made her an effective advocate of bilingual education. "I made it. But just because I made it cannot be used as an example that it works," she told the *Los Angeles Daily Journal.* "I say 'Don't look at me, look at all those who didn't make it.' Because you're not judged by whether you made it, whether the minority made it. You're judged by whether the majority makes it." Because of her work, she told *Hispanic,* her children "will have the opportunities I had to fight for. As a

consequence, they'll have a bigger responsibility to give to their community."

Born on May 30, 1948, in the Mexican state of Coahuila in the town of Torreón, Hernández came to the United States with her family when she was eight. They settled in Los Angeles. Her father, Manuel, was a gardener and laborer. Her mother, Nicolasa Hernández, was a homemaker raising her six children but she also took on odd jobs whenever possible. As the oldest child, Antonia was often called upon to help raise her younger siblings and to do unconventional tasks for young women of that time period such as car maintenance. "In my time, women didn't have the freedom that women have today," her mother told *Parents,* "but I wanted my daughters to have that, to learn, to travel, to work, to do whatever they wanted to do." While the Hernández family was not rich in material possessions, they provided a nurturing environment, says the younger Hernández. "I grew up in a very happy environment but a very poor environment," she told *Parents.*

Hernández credits her early upbringing in Mexico as instilling pride in her Mexican roots. "When I came to the United States, I was very proud of who I was. I was a Mexican. I had an identity. I had been taught a history, a culture of centuries of rich civilization so I had none of the psychoses of people who don't know who they are," she told the *Los Angeles Daily Journal.* Her belief in the extended family can be seen in her daily life. She, her husband, and their three children now live in Pasadena, near her mother and her sisters.

All of her brothers and sisters have earned college degrees and several are teachers. "My parents instilled in us the belief that serving the public interest was a very noble thing to do," Hernández told *Parents.* Hernández was on her way toward earning a postgraduate degree in education when she decided she could be more useful to her community with a law degree. She had already received her bachelor's degree and a teaching certificate from the UCLA in 1971. She was working in a counseling program, she told *Parents,* when she "realized that we couldn't help the kids or teachers unless we did something about the laws that were holding them back."

Although her professors encouraged her to attend Harvard or Stanford, she chose UCLA so she could remain near her family. "I was the oldest in our family, and my parents were sacrificing everything they could to help me with school," she explained to *Parents.* "They were looking forward to me graduating and working as a teacher so I could help them with the rest of the kids. So my feeling was that if I were to ask them to sacrifice three more years, moving away would be too drastic."

Although not a straight-A student in law school, her professors recall her as bright and articulate. "She had the ability to get her point across without alienating other people and people respected her for that," recalled one professor in the *Los Angeles Daily Journal.* Hernández acknowledges her priority wasn't top grades but the organizations and issues she cared about. During law school, she served on the admissions committee and several Chicano student organizations. "I wasn't out there to make the law firm roster," she told the *Los Angeles Daily Journal.* "I knew I was going to be [in] public interest [law]. . . . To me, to be a really good lawyer, you have to be a well-rounded person."

### A Lawyer on Her Own Terms

After receiving her juris doctorate, she became an attorney for the East Los Angeles Center for Law and Justice, where she handled criminal and civil cases, often involving police brutality. After a year there, she became directing attorney of the Lincoln Heights office for the Legal Aid Foundation, where she directed a staff of six attorneys and took part in case litigation and fought for bills in the state legislature.

By then she had already married Michael Stern, an attorney she met while a law clerk for California Legal Rural Assistance in 1973. Two years later Stern came to Los Angeles as the deputy public defender in the federal Public Defender's Office. An old friendship turned to courtship and they were married in 1977. Stern practices with a private law firm.

In 1978, Hernández was offered a job as staff counsel to the United States Senate Judiciary Committee, which was chaired by Senator Ted Kennedy. After initially declining, Hernández took the position, with a little prodding from her husband. "I was very happy doing poverty law and being near my family," Hernández told *Parents.* "They called me back because they thought it was the salary, and so they raised it. I didn't want to explain what the problem was so I said yes. As a professional woman you just don't say 'My mother said I shouldn't do this.'" Her husband took a more pragmatic view, telling *Parents:* "We didn't have children; we had very little furniture and few responsibilities. I figured I'd get a job."

### Political Experience Shaped Career

Overcoming her reluctance to leave her hometown, Hernández gained valuable experience in the nation's capital. At the Senate Judiciary Committee, she drafted bills and briefed committee members, specializing in immigration and human-rights work. She even took a brief leave of absence to coordinate Kennedy's Southwest campaign during his unsuccessful bid for the Democratic presidential nomination. "In that degree I played the Hispanic role," she told the *Los Angeles Daily Journal.* "But on other issues, I was just another staff member who had to do the work that had to be done."

Soon after the Democrats lost control of the Senate in 1980, Hernández was out of work. Within days, MALDEF asked her to join their Washington, D.C., staff. Her progress at MALDEF was steady, working as associate counsel, director of the employment litigation program, executive vice president, and deputy general counsel before moving into the top slot. One of her brightest moments was her role in defeating the Simpson-Mazzoli immigration bill, which would have required Latinos to carry identification cards. Immigrant rights has been one area that Hernández has been especially effective in pushing the federal government to recognize. Throughout her tenure at MALDEF, the organization has created historic changes through court litigation for the U.S. Hispanic community, including the creation of single member election districts and favorable public school equity court decisions in Texas, and successful challenges to district boundaries in Los Angeles County.

Hernández says her time in Washington, D.C. has given her a broader understanding of the diversity within the U.S. Latino community. "Living on the East Coast has helped me transcend the regional aspect of the organization by mixing with Puerto Ricans, Cubans and other groups," she told *Hispanic.* She has sought to increase the cooperation among civil rights organizations across racial and ethnic lines. "If we allow ourselves to be sucked into believing we should fight over crumbs, we will." Her resolve on that issue was tested in late 1990 when the Leadership Conference on Civil Rights failed to support the repeal of employer sanctions found in the 1986 Immigration Reform and Control Act. Citing the government's own General Accounting Office study showing that the provisions led to increased discrimination against Hispanic-looking job applicants, Hernández threatened to pull MALDEF out of the coalition, which was gearing up for an intense lobbying campaign for what would later become the 1992 Civil Rights bill. In the end, the National Association for the Advancement of Colored People (NAACP) voted to support the repeal.

As much as her performance is measured by court decisions, she understands the human element of her work. "A court victory is important but just the beginning of the process. It must translate into empowerment. It is the people that have the power to give life to those court victories," she told *La Paloma.* However, despite her professional success, she acknowledges that the 1980s were not the best of times for the U.S. Hispanic community. "The 1980s was not the decade of the Hispanic," she told *Hispanic.* "Madison Avenue put up the expectation and said we failed. The 1990s is a threshold decade. We need to move. Otherwise, we'll develop into a community with a small middle class and a large poverty class."

Antonia says family comes first despite her high-powered job. She describes her children as "my greatest accomplishment." Balancing the needs of her family with a career has been a continual struggle, but one she has become adept at. She's often gone from home for long stretches of time, testifying before Congress or addressing other national organizations. "I try to balance my life and it has worked," she told *Hispanic.* "But I have little time to myself and very few good friends." She acknowledges that having a husband who was familiar with her culture through his work with farmworkers and able to speak Spanish has helped. Although of Jewish descent, Stern has embraced his wife's strong cultural ties. "I don't want him to feel uncomfortable because he's living our way," Hernández told *Parents.* "But he's very accommodating. I don't know if I could be as accommodating if it was the reverse."

Her community involvement includes serving on the boards of California Tomorrow, Quality Education for Minorities Network, California Leadership, Latino Museum of History, Art, and Culture, and Los Angeles 2000. And, after the 1992 riots in Los Angeles, Hernández began recruiting others into community service. Appointed by Mayor Tom Bradley to the Rebuild L.A. commission to spearhead revitalization efforts in the beleaguered city, Hernández has been adamant in calling for immigrants and Latinos to be involved in the rebuilding process.

## SOURCES:

*Hispanic,* December 1990, pp. 17–18.
*Hispanic Business,* February, 1992, p. 10.
*Intercambios Femeniles,* spring 1988.
*La Paloma,* December 1991.
*Los Angeles Daily Journal,* September 3, 1985, p. 1.
*Los Angeles Times,* August 5, 1985, section II, p. 1.
*New York Times,* March 2, 1987, p. A15.
*Parents,* March 1985, pp. 96–100, 170–174.

—*Sketch by Jonathan J. Higuera*

# Enrique Hernández
## 1951-
**Puerto Rican physician and educator**

Physician Enrique Hernández has a special interest in gynecologic oncology and has written or co-written over 70 articles for medical journals. He also co-authored *Manual of Gynecologic Oncology* with N. B. Rosenshein, M.D., and co-edited *Clinical Gynecologic Pathology.* He has been the recipient of many awards, including the Bristol Award for outstanding academic achievements and human qualities from the Puerto Rico Medical Association, and the resident teaching award in 1989 and 1990 from the Medical College of Pennsylvania, where he serves as professor and director of the Division of Gynecologic Oncology. In 1994 Hernández received the Council on Resident Education in Obstetrics and Gynecology National Award for Excellence in Teaching at the Medical College of Pennsylvania. He has also received funding awards for several research studies involving cancer of the female reproductive system.

Born October 25, 1951, in Vega Baja, Puerto Rico, to Nathathiel Hernández and Ana Lopez, Hernández entered the University of Puerto Rico in 1969 to study biology; while there, he also played varsity judo. He married Marta Jimenez in 1971. Hernández taught high school biology for one semester in 1973 at Academia Santa Mónica. He earned a Bachelor of Science, graduating Magna Cum Laude that year. When the teaching position ended in June, he worked for a month as a laboratory assistant in the biology department of the University of Puerto Rico. Hernández pursued his medical degree at the University of Puerto Rico, and during that time he also worked as a clinical clerk at the Adjuntas Health Center and the Carolina Health Center, both in Puerto Rico. He received his medical degree in 1977.

Hernández came to the United States to intern in obstetrics and gynecology at the Johns Hopkins University School of Medicine, where he served as assistant resident for two years. Already a member of the Medical Corps of the U.S. Army Reserve, he was promoted to first lieutenant in 1977, captain in 1980, major in 1987, and lieutenant colonel in 1990. In 1980, Hernández also became chief resident in obstetrics and gynecology at the Johns Hopkins Hospital. He began his formal medical teaching in 1981 when he became an instructor at the Johns Hopkins University School of Medicine. He was also a fellow in gynecologic oncology at Johns Hopkins, and a fellow of the American Cancer Society. He served on active staff at Johns Hopkins Hospital in the department of Gynecology and Obstetrics from 1981 to 1983. For a year, Hernández was assistant professor of gynecology and obstetrics at Johns Hopkins University School of Medicine.

Hernández moved to Hawaii in 1983, where he served for three years as chief of the gynecologic oncology and gynecologic pathology service at Tripler Army Medical Center in Honolulu. Concurrently, he was also training officer in the department of obstetrics and gynecology at Tripler. Hernández instructed at the College of Osteopathic Medicine of the Pacific from 1985 to 1986, and was a fellow of the American College of Obstetricians and Gynecologists. Hernández's skill as a teacher earned him the outstanding staff teacher award from Tripler Army Medical Center in 1986. He was also a fellow of the American College of Surgeons.

## Becomes Director

In 1987 Hernández returned to the mainland, becoming director of the division of gynecologic oncology at the Medical College of Pennsylvania, a position he still held in 1995. He was appointed associate professor of obstetrics and gynecology. Hernández became a full professor in 1989, receiving tenure in 1993.

In addition to his teaching, Hernández has published many papers, including "The Practice of Obstetrics in the Early Times" in *Buhiti,* which he wrote in 1977 while he was in medical school. His articles focus on cancer of the female reproductive tract and have been published in many medical journals, including *American Journal of Obstetrics and Gynecology, Southern Medical Journal, Journal of Surgical Oncology, Military Medicine,* and *Journal of the American Medical Association.* He has also given numerous presentations and has been the recipient of many awards and honors, including the Council on Resident Education in Obstetrics and Gynecology National Award for Excellence in Teaching at the Medical College of Pennsylvania in 1994. He was also named a "top doctor" by *Philadelphia Magazine* in 1991 and 1994. During the late 1980s, Hernández pursued activities in St. Anthony Church of Kailua, where he was Hispanic Catholic apostolate and director of the Hispanic choir; he also participated in cultural events of the Puerto Rican Heritage Society of Hawaii. Together with his sons, he was active in the Boy Scouts as a Tiger Cubs leader. When he finds time, Hernández enjoys running at distances from five kilometers to 26.2 miles.

## SOURCES:

### Books

*Hispanic-American Almanac,* edited by Nicolás Kanellos, Detroit, Gale Research, 1993.

### Other

Additional information for this profile was obtained from *Curriculum Vitae* materials provided by Enrique Hernández, M.D., 1995.

—*Sketch by Sandy J. Stiefer*

# Maria Latigo Hernandez
## 1893?-1986
### Mexican American community leader and civil rights activist

Maria Latigo Hernandez is best known for her life-long efforts to achieve justice, equality, and educational opportunity for Hispanic Americans. Her work with organizations such as Orden Caballeros de America, La Liga por Defensa Escobar, and La Raza Unida Party virtually chronicles the Mexican American civil rights movement in Texas. She documented her social philosophy in her book, *Mexico y los cuatro poderes que dirigen al pueblo.*

Hernandez was born at the end of the nineteenth century in Mexico. Because of the political unrest in that country following the Great Revolution of 1910, her parents sought safety in the United States, bringing Hernandez and her five siblings to Texas. They settled in Hebbronville. In 1915, she met and married Pedro Hernandez, who was an extremely influential part of her career as an activist. In 1918 the young couple moved to San Antonio, where they opened a grocery store and bakery. At this time, the Hispanic community had already developed many societies for burial services and health assistance. The Hernandez family set out to make a special study of the civic-oriented groups, such as Los Hijos de Texas and La Orden Hijos de America.

Pedro Hernandez described their reasons for exploring the ideals of these new organizations in *A War of Words:* "Born in the mind of my wife and I was the idea of organizing a civic group to awaken more and more the civic consciousness of our own . . . toward the end increasing the number of voters in the elections, and thereby making good use of civic rights. We shall take to power those responsible elements of our community." In 1924, Maria and Pedro Hernandez joined La Orden Hijos de America.

## Provided Medical Services for Community

While both Pedro and Maria continued their roles as civil rights leaders and advocates for better quality education, in the 1920s Maria Hernandez began to care for her ill and aging father. She worked for her father's physician, who was impressed with her natural abilities and encouraged Hernandez to further her medical training. "She entered training as a midwife. She served in that capacity for years serving people who couldn't afford medical care," recalled her son, Pedro, in an article in the *San Antonio Express-News.*

During this time, a compatriot of Maria and Pedro, Alonso Perales, was also establishing a new organization in south Texas. In 1927, Perales formed the Liga de Ciudadanos Latino Americanos from chapters of other established groups. With an expanding membership, Perales changed the name of the organization to League of United Latin American Citizens (LULAC) two years later.

The local La Orden chapter in San Antonio refused to join the LULAC organization. Both Maria and Pedro Hernandez, members of the original group, disagreed with the LULAC goals and strategies. "They didn't have what I mostly was interested in, fraternal and civic activity for both sexes. Other groups exclude their women, form auxiliary women's groups. To my view, the sexes are different but equal in their rights," explained Pedro Hernandez in *A War of Words.* Both Pedro and Maria promoted a well-developed feminist viewpoint at a time when American women had only recently been granted the right to vote. There was also disagreement with the implications involved in changing the organization name from the Spanish language to the English language. Furthermore, the emphasis on voting, political accountability of leaders, and a "Pan Americanism" vision as set forth by Pedro and Maria Hernandez did not fit with the precepts set by the LULAC.

## Advocated Bilingual Education

By restricting many of her speeches and articles to the Spanish language, Maria Hernandez contrasted with the assimilationists who advocated the almost exclusive use of English to increase acceptance of Hispanics in American society. Assimilationists felt that the increased acceptance of English-speading Hispanics would expand their civil rights. By her dogged insistence on using the Spanish language and maintaining Hispanic cultural awareness, Hernandez became a pioneer in the applications of bilingualism in education today.

In 1929, Maria and Pedro Hernandez founded a new organization, the Orden Caballeros de America, which focused on civic and civil rights. "From that date to [the 1970s], they have participated in the most important events of Chicano history in Texas," stated Martha Cotera in *Profile on the Mexican American Woman.* Maria Hernandez was in the forefront of expanding educational opportunities for Hispanic children. In 1934, Hernandez formed La Liga Por Defensa Escolar en San Antonio. Its purpose was to challenge the deplorable conditions in the schools for Mexican children: the outrageous teacher to student ratio of 1/130, lack of heat, and uninhabitable facilities. Marches and rallies were used to gain public awareness and to force the State Board of Education to receive a list of complaints.

One event illustrating Hernandez's oratory skills, ability to inspire, and commitment to education occurred at a rally sponsored by Liga por Defensa Escolar and LULUC at Lanier High School. The demonstration was attended by the superintendent of public schools, L.L. Woods. Among the featured speakers, Hernandez was the only one who addressed the crowd of 5000 in Spanish. A dynamic orator, she inspired parents to rise to her call against injustice. As quoted in *A War of Words,* Hernandez then addressed the superintendent and challenged him: "[The students are] not at fault for being born with black eyes and brown hair and not with blue eyes. We are all supported by the stripes and stars of the flag. I want you to take this gesture of this community as a protest and disgust over the terrible conditions." In response to the crowd of parents and community leaders who applauded Hernandez's statements, the superintendent promised to return to Austin and work to improve the classroom conditions.

## Hosted Radio and Television Shows

Using her skills as a great communicator, Hernandez embarked on another career beginning in the 1930s. She was the host of one of the first Spanish-speaking radio programs in San Antonio. Her afternoon program, "La Voz de las Americas," was aired daily on KABC-radio. It began as a half-hour program but was soon expanded to one hour. Later, in the 1960s, Hernandez ventured into another media, television. She hosted a weekly television program called "La Hora de la Mujer" on station KWEX.

In 1939, Hernandez was appointed goodwill ambassador to Mexico by several San Antonio organizations. She met with President **Lasaro Cardenes** and his wife. As a gesture of his country's esteem, President Cardenes presented Hernandez with an Aztec calendar design engraved on a large silver platter. This tribute was publicly displayed in San Antonio.

As the United States entered World War II, Hernandez vigorously supported the war effort. With two sons in military service, she sold war bonds, raised funds, and wrote articles for Spanish-language newspapers. A supporter of Franklin Delano Roosevelt, she campaigned for him in the Hispanic community.

In 1945, Hernandez wrote a book entitled, *Mexico y los cuatro poderes que dirigen al pueblo.* In the work, she discussed the importance of family and political action. She emphasized the importance of home life as the foundation of society and the basis of the formation of individual character. While society tests everyone's character and citizenship, Hernandez noted, it also reflects on the quality of the community's leaders. She expressed no tolerance for those leaders who have used a community agenda for personal aggrandizement, stating in the book that by acting politically, citizens will increase the awareness of social problems. She declared in *Mexico y los cuatro poderes que dirigen al pueblo* that political activism is a moral responsibility to one's family, one's community, and one's country.

### Campaigned with Husband for La Raza Unida Party

Both Hernandez and her husband, Pedro, served among the vanguard of the Mexican civil rights movement for more than 50 years. Long after they had reached "retirement age," both continued their political and social involvement in the Chicano movement of the late 1960s and 1970s through the political party, La Raza Unida Party (RUP). The RUP was formed by 300 Mexican-Americans in Crystal City, Texas in 1970 as a political party. Other organizations had also used the name "La Raza Unida" ("The People United"). The RUP of 1970 was founded to organize unregistered Mexican Americans into an independent voting bloc. It was hoped that the party would be able to elect candidates in areas or districts where Mexican Americans voters formed a majority. Furthermore, La Raza Unida Party would be an effective voice representing Mexican American issues in elections where they did not have a voting majority and act as a balance of power between major political parties.

While the RUP was initially denied ballot access, it was able to help elect its first officeholder through the skillful organization of a write-in campaign. Other RUP candidates won victories in municipal, school district, and nonpartisan elections. As the party became increasingly established, RUP was able to win majorities on the Crystal City and San Juan city councils in southern Texas. Hernandez first became involved with RUP when she was the featured speaker at a statewide conference in 1970. Both Pedro and Maria were active and strong supporters in the development of this separate party. In 1972, the two activists traveled throughout southern and central Texas at their own expense to campaign on behalf of the RUP gubernatorial candidate, Ramsey Munoz, and Martha Cotera, the RUP State Board of Education candidate.

After the death of her husband in 1980, Hernandez continued to live at the ten-acre ranch in southwest Bexar County that she and Pedro had purchased in 1955. She always acknowledged the importance of her husband as a positive force in her life. Their lifetime of partnership and work was a union of the heart, mind, and soul. At the time of her own death in 1986, she was survived by one son and four daughters, 19 grandchildren, 23 great-grandchildren and eight great-great-grandchildren.

Hernandez's life was dedicated to her family, her community, and her country. Whether nursing her father, campaigning for political candidates, selling war bonds, or championing educational opportunities for Hispanic children, her life's work stressed the importance of family and the power of citizen advocacy. In assessing her contribution to the Mexican American community, Hernandez related in Cotera's book, "I feel my husband and I have worked very hard since 1924 for the betterment of our people. I feel we have not accomplished very much because of our limited resources. But when a person dedicates all his life to the movement, that in itself is worth more than money."

### SOURCES:

**Books**

Cotera, Martha, *Profile of the Mexican American Woman,* National Educational Laboratory Publishers, 1976.

Hammerback, John C., Richard J. Jensen, and Jose Angel Gutierrez, *A War of Words: Chicano Protest in the 1960s and 1970s,* Greenwood Press, 1985.

Hernandez, Maria L., *Mexico y los cuatro poderes que dirigen al pueblo,* Imprinta Munguia de San Antonio, 1945.

Lewels, Franciso Jr., *The Uses of the Media by the Chicano Movement: A Study in Minority Access,* Praeger Press, 1974.

Munoz, Carlos, *Youth, Identity, Power,* Verso, 1989.

Perales, Alonso, *Are We Good Neighbors?,* Artes Graficas, 1948.

Pinon, Fernando, *Of Myths and Realities: Dynamics of Ethnic Polics,* Vantage Press, 1978.

**Periodicals**

*San Antonio Express-News,* January 11, 1986.

—*Sketch by Sally Foster*

# Carolina Herrera
## 1939-
### Venezuelan fashion designer

When she introduced her first collection in 1981, Venezuelan socialite Carolina Herrera stunned high society and stirred the fashion industry with her innovative creations. The deep necklines and

*Carolina Herrera*

exaggerated sleeves featured in her collection reminded audiences of traditional beauty while promoting a contemporary elegance. The renowned designer Bill Blass recognized her talent. "I think she has tremendous potential," he was quoted as saying of Herrera in *People*. "She is going to be a force in the fashion world." Since that time, Herrera has invigorated fashion design and dressed some of the world's most famous women. A recipient of the 1987 MODA Award for Top Hispanic Designer, she has secured her place among the world's most heralded fashion designers.

Herrera's success as a designer has much to do with her upbringing as a member of fashionable society. Born in Caracas, Venezuela, in 1939, to Guillermo Pacanins, an officer in the Venezuelan Air Force and, later, a governor of Caracas, Maria Carolina Josefina Pacanins y Nino was raised by people who enjoyed hosting parties in their glamorous homes and reveled in wearing the latest fashions. As a young girl, she designed garments for her dolls, and as a young woman, she designed for herself and for her friends. As *People* noted, she was "very sad" because she was not allowed to dress "like a vamp" in red as a child. Her grandmother introduced the stylish thirteen-year-old to the famous couturier Cristobal Balenciaga at a fashion show in Paris; at her first ball she wore a white gown from the House of Lavin.

When the elegant young woman married Reinaldo Herrera, her childhood friend and the eldest son of Mimi Herrera, in 1969, she found even more incentive to dress glamorously. Her mother-in-law was a wealthy art patron as well as the owner of "La Vega," an enormous house built in 1590 in Caracas. Herrera suited herself to her classically luxurious surroundings. She first made the Best Dressed List in 1971, and has been a perennial listee since. She won a spot in the Fashion Hall of Fame in 1981.

### Diversion Becomes a Career

As Herrera told an interviewer with *Hispanic,* she began her professional career as a designer because her children were grown and she "wanted to try something new." She felt capable of designing successfully. When Armando de Armas, a Venezuelan publishing magnate, provided the financial backing Herrera needed for a venture into the business world of fashion, she "changed from being a mother with nothing to do but arrange flowers and parties to being a professional who works twelve hours a day at the office," she told *Newsweek*. While Herrera was optimistic about her chances for success, some of her societal peers and members of the fashion industry supposed that Herrera's designs would not merit a second glance.

Ellin Saltzman, the fashion director for Saks Fifth Avenue, recalled in *People* that she had her own doubts about Herrera when she first heard of her 1981 collection. She had assumed that Herrera was "another socialite designing a fly-by-night collection no one will ever buy or wear." Herrera, however, proved that she was not an amateur. Herrera's work, which utilized layers, diverse fabrics, and various lengths, was received with enthusiastic praise. The skeptical fashion director from Saks Fifth Avenue found Herrera's collection to be "sensational," as she remarked in *People,* and experts with authority agreed. According to *People,* Herrera was dubbed "Our Lady of the Sleeves" by *Women's Wear Daily* because of the "exaggerated shoulders" on her fanciful evening gowns. While features such as fairy-tale sleeves and plunging necklines attracted attention, the industry respected the classic taste and superb tailoring of Herrera's work. The fashion world was buzzing—Herrera's collection promised to inspire other designers as well as incite new trends.

### Popularity Spawns Success

By the end of 1982, Herrera's creations were widely acclaimed. Royal personalities, such as Princess Elizabeth of Yugoslavia, Spain's Duchess of Feria, and Countess Consuelo Crespi, were wearing Herrera's designs. Other public figures, the First Lady Nancy Reagan and the well-known actress Kathleen Turner among them, were donning Herrera gowns. Reagan and Turner sported the same silver-blue, one-shouldered gown of coupe de velours, which was paired with a marvelous maribou feather cape. Garments such as these, and other, sleek, striped, silver and gold gowns, captured the fancies of many women and made Herrera a star designer.

It is Herrera's understanding of the socialite's lifestyle and her extraordinary talent, along with her social contacts, that attract some of the world's most famous celebrities to her clothing. As Ivana Trump, ex-wife of the wealthy Donald Trump, explained in a *Newsweek* article, Herrera's designs catch the fancies of people like herself because she "is in society, she travels and goes to the same restaurants and parties as the women who buy her clothes." Ellin Saltzman, the fashion director at Saks Fifth Avenue, noted in the same article that Herrera contributed "dressy lunch and evening clothes that women couldn't find anywhere else" to the market. The fine quality and unique design of Herrera's works make her originals highly desirable. There is a great demand for her clothing despite exclusive prices. A luncheon suit might cost anywhere between $1,500 to $3,800. Pajamas of silk made especially for lounging at the pool were tagged at $1,200 in 1982. Herrera's exquisite gowns were priced at $2,100 to $4,000 in the same year.

## Designs Garner Accolades

During the 1980s, Herrera continued to establish herself as a respected designer. As she understood the desire for slim clothing, she produced dresses and outfits that were less exaggerated than those she had previously designed; she contributed to the trends of the mid-eighties with her own adaptations of the sleek style. In 1986, Jacqueline Kennedy Onassis, a Herrera client who as the First Lady set the standard for American fashion in the 1960s, asked Herrera to create a wedding dress for her daughter Caroline Kennedy. Finally, Herrera won the MODA Award as the Top Hispanic Designer in 1987 from Hispanic Designers, Inc., an award which had been previously won by the prestigious designers Adolfo and Oscar de La Renta.

1988 was the year that Carolina Herrera introduced her own perfume. "Carolina Herrera," as it is called, has been enthusiastically received by consumers. According to *Hispanic,* this perfume is her "most accessible and perhaps personal product." The perfume's odor of jasmine and tuberose is reminiscent of Herrera's happy childhood—a jasmine vine in the family's garden scented the girl's bedroom—and denotes her success as an adult. Herrera has been wearing this original mixture for years, and it permeates the atmosphere of her New York office.

While by late 1989 Herrera had been designing leather goods, eyewear, and furs for Revillon, and developed a less expensive line of clothing which she named "CH," her most exclusive apparel was featured along with those of the likes of designer Bill Blass in the media's fashion reports. Her collection for the fall of 1989 exemplified the reason for her fame: her creations were fun yet functional, elegant yet bold. Herrera was among those designers who utilized animal prints in their collections for the season. Herrera's particular adaptation of the theme was daring: she mixed the prints with crimson sequins and velvet. *Hispanic* displayed a "leopard print wool challis dress with a black persian velvet jacket lined with the same leopard spots" which could make "the switch from daytime into night" that was unusually stunning and versatile.

## Collections Showcase Unique Designs

The *New York Times* reported on Herrera's 1989 fall show at the Plaza and emphasized other aspects of the collection: shorts that were "styled with a ripply fullness that makes them almost impossible to differentiate from skirts," "graphic black and white cotton pique suits" with combinations of hearts and stripes, dresses and jackets in pastel shades which were "harbingers of a new suit look to come," and "trouser outfits" with pants "either wide or narrow." Especially striking was Herrera's "upwardly mobile version" of the motorcycle jacket; in pink, chartreuse, or orange satin and with rhinestones instead of nailheads, these jackets contributed to "fun" outfits. Herrera's various evening gowns were characteristically beautiful, whether they were long and black, reminiscent of Fabergé eggs, or white with crystal beading. Herrera's diverse designs are testimony to her ideas. She told *Hispanic,* "Nowadays, everything [in fashion] is accepted. . . . There's a craziness going around the world." Despite this "craziness," Herrera acknowledges that odd designs are not as marketable as designs that take the needs of the buyer into account. In the same interview, she quipped, "Nobody wants to look like a costume. . . . The thing to do is to have a sensational simple dress."

Herrera continues to produce versatile, elegantly designed clothing. The *New York Times,* discussing her fall fashion show at the Plaza in 1991, noted that she had highlighted red plaids for daytime, and lamé, wool crepe, and "bold checks" for night. She utilized opaque tights in mustard and red for daytime, and feathers, silver sequins, and rhinestones with her evening wear. According to the *Times,* the "basic Herrera look is slick and uncomplicated, expressed in lamé jumpsuits and jersey dresses," yet her designs were not "shy and retiring." The *Times* observed that Herrera offered women the choice to wear a suit or a dress "in the same fabric," slim long gowns, or puffy short ones. "Clearly she is thinking about the different figures and needs of her followers."

Herrera's life is very busy. She has, however, managed to balance her roles as a designer and businesswoman, as a wife, a mother to four daughters and grandmother to three grandsons, as well as homes in New York and Caracas and an active social schedule. Although she believes that it is imperative that a designer observe and involve herself in social activity, she commented in *Newsweek,* "I never go to lunch anymore. It interrupts my day and it's boring." While it is obvious that Herrera is very serious about her work, she insists that she loves it. "The more I do the more I like it," she told *Hispanic.*

Herrera has earned her place as a distinguished fashion designer, and she is prepared to continue to dress women beautifully, refresh the world of fashion, and introduce exciting new products. As she confessed in an interview in *Hispanic,* "I am never satisfied. I'm a perfectionist. When I see the show is ready and the collection is out and they're quite nice, I still say, 'I could do much better.'"

## SOURCES:

### Periodicals

*Americas,* September-October, 1990, p. 30.
*Architectural Digest,* April, 1987, p. 128; September, 1988, p. 178.
*Boston Globe,* September 15, 1988, p. 65.
*Harper's Bazaar,* August, 1986, p. 152; September, 1989, p. 380.
*Hispanic,* March, 1989, pp. 28–30; October, 1989, pp. 36–37.
*Newsweek,* June 30, 1986, pp. 56–57.
*New York Times,* October 31, 1989, p. B8; April 9, 1991, p. B8.
*Nuestro,* October, 1985, p. 60.
*People,* May 3, 1982, p. 122
*Vogue,* March, 1987, p. 342; June, 1990, p. 2704; January, 1991, p. 132.

—*Sketch by Ronie-Richele Garcia-Johnson*

# Oscar J. Hijuelos
## 1951-
### Cuban American novelist

Oscar Hijuelos is the first Hispanic American novelist to win the Pulitzer Prize for fiction for his 1989 novel *The Mambo Kings Play Songs of Love.* Born in New York City on August 24, 1951, he is the son of José Hijuelos, a hotel worker, and Magdalena Torrens, a homemaker. Both of his parents had

Oscar J. Hijuelos

immigrated to the United States from Cuba. Hijuelos attended public schools in New York before entering City College of New York. He received his bachelor of arts degree in 1975 and a masters degree in English and writing in 1976 from City College. One of his instructors in the creative writing program was Donald Barthelme.

After leaving the university, Hijuelos secured a position as an advertising media traffic manager at Transportation Display, Inc., from 1977 to 1984. During this period, he devoted a significant amount of his free time to writing, penning a number of short stories. Some of the stories were eventually published in the *Best of Pushcart Press III* anthology in 1978. One of his first professional works, "Columbus Discovering America," received an outstanding writer citation from Pushcart Press in 1978. The exposure from this award led to an Oscar Cintas fiction writing grant and, in 1980, a Breadloaf Writers Conference scholarship. Hijuelos also received grants from the Creative Artists Programs Service in 1982 and the Ingram Merrill Foundation in 1983.

### Embarks on Career as Novelist

Hijuelos's first novel examines the life of a Cuban immigrant family in America during the 1940s. Published in 1983, *Our House in the Last World* provided Hijuelos with a outlet to examine his feelings about his Cuban heritage. Critics praised the novel as a warm and vibrant depiction of the family's experiences in America and noted that the work reflected a departure from other Cuban writers who often focused on the political struggles in Cuba or life in exile. In 1985 Hijuelos received a creative writing fellowship from the National Endowment for the Arts, largely on the strength of the acclaim for *Our House in the Last World.*

In 1989, Hijuelos published his second novel, *The Mambo Kings Play Songs of Love.* Described by Thomas Mallon in The *New York Times* as "a propulsive ballad of Cuban-American fraternal machismo," this novel concerned the lives of two brothers, Cesar and Nestor Castillo, who move from Havana to New York at the beginning of the 1950s. The two men form an orchestra, write the music that brings them the title of Mambo Kings, and appear with **Desi Arnaz** on the hugely successful *I Love Lucy* television show. The *New York Times* remarked that "the novel paints a portrait of the brothers, their families, their fellow musicians and lovers, and it also brings to life the sights and sounds of an era in music and unsung moment in American life."

*The Mambo Kings Play Songs of Love* garnered significant praise from reviewers. Bob Shacochis of The *Washington Post Book World* described the novel as "exhilarating and exuberant and passion-rocked," while Michiko Kakutani of The *New York Times* found it to be "street-smart and lyrical, impassioned and reflective." The novel was nominated for a National Book Critics Circle Award in 1989, as well as the National Book Award from the National Book Foundation. One year later, the work earned Hijuelos the Pulitzer Prize for fiction.

While critics lauded the novel, Hijuelos's depiction of several real people in his narrative resulted in a highly publicized lawsuit. Gloria Parker, who was the leader of Glorious Gloria Parker and Her All-Girl Rumba Orchestra, brought a $15 million libel suit against Hijuelos and his publisher, alleging that her reputation had been ruined by the novel. The lawsuit was regarded as an important test case because it involved a work of fiction rather than non-fiction. In 1991, a federal district court in New York dismissed the case, arguing that it was unlikely that the average reader would think the novel defamed Parker.

### Third Novel Brings Mixed Reviews

In 1993 Hijuelos published his third novel, *The Fourteen Sisters of Emilio Montez O'Brien.* Mallon described the book as "the author's paean to femininity, an exuberant history of a Pennsylvania household so vital with food and music and decoration as to be, literally, magnetic." While all fourteen daughters alluded to in the title are characterized, Emilio, the youngest of the children and the lone boy, is the central character. In an interview with The *New York Times,* Hijuelos said that he wanted *The Fourteen Sisters of Emilio Montez O'Brien* "to portray a world in which women were very powerful. I took the idea of machismo and pushed it, getting inside the skin of the characters. . . . I wanted to look behind the basic images of women."

The reviews of Hijuelos's third book were mixed. Mallon suggested that by stuffing the novel with so many characters, "Mr. Hijuelos is inevitably reduced to overly vivid shorthand characterizations. He usually relies on a single trait to keep each sister distinct." Yet the reviewer concedes that as a whole, the book was "not only satisfying but brave" and remarked that the author "gets it all right and he serves it up with surpassing joy." In addition, Kakutani stated that "Mr. Hijuelos moves confidently from one character's story to the next, leaping ahead in time to foreshadow the future, then jumping backward in time to show us the seeds of hope and despair. . . . Indeed, one finishes [it] reluctantly, the way one finishes a long letter from a beloved family member, eager for all the news not to end."

While writing is obviously a large part of his life, Hijuelos has a wide range of other interests. He is a collector of old maps, turn-of-the-century books, and graphics. He also draws pen-and-ink style sketches and enjoys jazz music.

## SELECTED PUBLISHED WORKS:

*Our House in the Last World,* Persea Books, 1983.
*The Mambo Kings Play Songs of Love,* Farrar, Straus and Giroux, 1989.
*The Fourteen Sisters of Emilio Montez O'Brien,* Farrar, Straus and Giroux, 1993.

## SOURCES:

### Books

*Hispanic-American Almanac,* edited by Nicolás Kanellos, Detroit, Gale, 1993, pp. 440–42, 450–51.
*Hispanic Writers,* edited by Bryan Ryan, Detroit, Gale, 1991, pp. 255–56.

### Periodicals

*New York Times,* April 13, 1990, p. A17; July 19, 1991, p. B7; March 2, 1993, p. C17; March 7, 1993.
*Washington Post,* July 20, 1991, p. C3.

*—Sketch by Catherine A. Clay*

# Maria Hinojosa
## 1961-
### Mexican American radio reporter

*Maria de Lourdes Hinojosa*

Perhaps because she has always recognized the powerful beauty of her cultural inheritance, Maria Hinojosa has made a point of making it accessible to others. She has captured the opportunity to celebrate Mexican and Mexican American culture as she works, writes, and creates, and she is determined to make the most of that opportunity. With her radio reports and shows, her artwork, and her social and organizational activities, Hinojosa continues to contribute to the cohesiveness of a booming New York City community.

The fourth child of Raul and Berta (Ojeda) Hinojosa, Maria de Lourdes Hinojosa was born on July 2, 1961, in Mexico City. When she was 18 months old, the Hinojosa family moved to the United States, where her father, a medical research doctor, studied and worked. After spending some time in New England, the family settled in Chicago. According to the reporter, instead of forgetting about their roots, the elder Hinojosas maintained strong ties with their family in Mexico; each summer, the family took a car trip to a different part of the country. Those exciting trips to her native land instilled a love of Mexican culture in Hinojosa and gave her a profound sense of pride in her heritage. "I was very, very proud to be a part of this huge country," she explained during an interview with Ronie-Richele Garcia-Johnson.

While the trips Hinojosa took to Mexico made her aware of her cultural roots, they also opened her eyes to socioeconomic inequity. She noticed that the poverty she had witnessed in Mexico was present in areas of Chicago, and she began to become politically active. When she went to a private school for the first time, at the University of Chicago High School, she created the organization Students for a Better Environment. It was important to her that the students there realize that not everyone lived the privileged life that they enjoyed, and that they should be thankful.

At that point in her life, however, Hinojosa had no idea that she would pursue a career as a socially committed radio reporter. She wanted to be an actress. She applied to Barnard, a women's college at Columbia University in New York City, and was accepted. Hinojosa was enthusiastic about school and New York, but she became increasingly frustrated as an aspiring actress. As she was just five feet tall and couldn't be described as looking either Mexican or white, there didn't seem to be a place for her in theatre. While her failure as an actress was disap-

pointing, it allowed Hinojosa to get involved in radio when friends suggested that she try it.

It was just by chance that Hinojosa heard about an opening for a Latino show on Columbia's 24-hour student radio station, WCKR-FM. She started out with the radio show *Nueva cancion y demas.* As producer and host of this program, Hinojosa spent three hours each week on the air playing alternative Latin American music, announcing the news and discussing Latin American issues in a talk show format. While she continued to produce *Nueva cancion y demas* Hinojosa went on to become the program director of WCKR. While serving in this demanding position, she maintained excellent grades and majored in both Latin American studies and political economy.

### Joins National Public Radio

In 1985, when Maria Hinojosa graduated magna cum laude from Barnard, she wasn't quite sure what she should do. She applied for an internship with the National Public Radio and was given a position as a production assistant in the Washington, D.C., office. For the *Weekend Edition-Saturday* show, Hinojosa produced mini-documentaries and news stories. Her next position, which she accepted in late 1986, was associate producer of *Enfoque nacional,* National Public Radio's weekly Spanish language national news program, at KPBS in San Diego, California. Hinojosa lived in Tijuana, Mexico, during her time in this position. In 1986, for her work on "Immigration and Detention," she won a Silver Cindy Award.

By 1987, however, Hinojosa was ready for a change. She returned to New York to become a producer with CBS News. For CBS, she produced the network radio broadcasts *The Osgood File, Where We Stand, with Walter Cronkite, Newsbreak, Today in Business, First Line Report,* and *Newsmark.* January of 1988 found Hinojosa working as a researcher/producer on live segments of *CBS This Morning.* In August of 1988, Hinojosa returned to National Public Radio as a free-lance reporter/producer in Washington, D.C. She worked as a contract reporter for NPR's *Latin File* and programs such as *All Things Considered, Morning Edition, Weekend Edition, Crossroads, Latino,* and *Horizons* documentary series, and *Soundprint of American Public Radio.* Hinojosa won a 1989 Corporation for Public Broadcasting Silver Award for the piece "Day of the Dead."

Hinojosa returned to New York City in January, 1990, to work general assignments as a staff member of WNYC Radio. In August of that year, she began to work as a general assignment reporter for NPR's New York Bureau. By September, Hinojosa was ready to take on another challenge. She began to host her own live call-in public affairs prime-time television talk show, *New York Hotline,* which aired on WNYC Television. She was the first Latino to host a prime-time public affairs news television show in New York.

Hinojosa has quite a bit of television experience. She hosted a national broadcast called "Beyond the Browning of America," which was produced in conjunction with the Center for Puerto Rican Studies and aired on public television stations throughout the United States. Another program, "Crosswalks," aired on the municipal cable system and featured the Democratic National Convention. Finally, Hinojosa has moderated and hosted the public access television show *Latinos in accion.*

Hinojosa did not go unrecognized for the outstanding work she produced in the early 1990s. In 1990, she won an International Radio Festival of New York Silver Award for "Drug Family," and a fellowship from the New York Foundation for the Arts for work in radio. In 1991, for "Crews," a piece about members of youth gangs, she won the Unity Award from Lincoln University, a Top Story and First Place Radio Awards from the National Association of Hispanic Journalists, and a First Place from the New York Newswomen's Club. Also in 1991, she earned a First Place Award from the Associated Press for her coverage of Nelson Mandela's visit to New York City on WNYC. Her 1992 distinctions include a Kappa Tau Alpha Award for Excellence in Journalism from New York University, a Latino Coalition for Fair Media Award for Outstanding Service in Journalism,

and a first place, radio, from the National Association of Hispanic Journalists for "Body Bags."

## Dedicated to Community Involvement

In late 1992, Hinojosa was working for NPR as a New York Bureau Staff Reporter. Her beats as a general assignment reporter included latino and multicultural affairs, race relations, youth issues, and labor and politics. She also hosted the show she had begun in 1980, *Nueva cancion y demas,* for WCKR-FM. She is a member of the boards of the Northstar Fund, the Committee for Hispanic Children, and Families 10th Year Anniversary Program. Hinojosa is a frequent guest lecturer at Princeton University, Haverford College, the Ohio Statewide Hispanic Conference, Mujeres Latinas en Accion/Chicago, and the City University of New York.

Known in New York for her artistic talent as well as for her radio personality, Hinojosa has been building altars in celebration of the Day of the Dead, a traditional Mexican holiday, since 1988. One of these, dedicated to undocumented immigrants, is especially moving. It features paper bags, which are symbolic for those bags carried by the people who cross the border into the United States, as well as tiny skeletons. Hinojosa has also highlighted the plight of those victimized by the AIDS virus in her altars. One of Hinojosa's altars was installed in the Bronx Museum of Art. Hinojosa told Garcia-Johnson that, in addition to enjoying the actual construction of each altar, she considers their creation and presentation as a way of establishing a Mexican American cultural presence in New York City and as a method of reaching out to the Mexican American community in the city. She wants the city to realize that Mexican Americans are a social and cultural force in the city and she wants the Mexican Americans themselves to revel in their cultural heritage.

Hinojosa seems to thrive on her schedule. While she spends a great deal of her day working, she always manages to find time for her friends and for her husband, Gérman Perez, whom she married on July 20, 1991. Perez, who was born in the Dominican Republic, is a painter of large-scale acrylic works and shares Hinojosa's devotion to Hispanic American culture and her love of New York City.

The influx of Mexicans and Dominicans into New York during the 1980s and their growing cultural influence has contributed to the Pan-American community which enthralled Hinojosa during her first years in the city. She finds the cultural transformation taking place in the city exciting. That transformation is part of the reason why Hinojosa enjoys her job as a reporter. She told Garcia-Johnson that she loves "being on the street" and allowing "those [Hispanic] voices to be heard." Radio reporting to Hinojosa is "a part of my life." Hinojosa intends to continue enjoying her "dream job" in New York—she is not interested in administrative work in radio. She is collaborating on a video production about Latinos in the United States called "The U.S. Mambo: One Step Forward, Two Steps Back." Finally, she is determined to finish a book she has started about the Crews, or Latino gangs, she has been studying.

Hinojosa's remarkable contributions to Mexican and Pan-American culture in New York City are becoming increasingly important as that community grows and as people throughout the United States become aware of the influence of Hispanics in the country. Young Hispanics, especially, will benefit from the appreciation of the historical and actual culture in transformation that Hinojosa promotes. With her determined effort to celebrate the culture that she loves, Hinojosa has not only achieved personal success, she has given voice to the concerns of a community.

## SOURCES:

Hinojosa, Maria, telephone interview with Ronie-Richele Garcia-Johnson, August, 1992.

—*Sketch by Ronie-Richele Garcia-Johnson*

# Rolando Hinojosa
## 1929-
### Hispanic American author and educator

Rolando Hinojosa is best known as the creator of the fictitious village of Klail City, a town set in mythic Belten County, Texas, which Hinojosa invented to explore the lives of the Chicano people. He has produced a series of interconnected novels called *The Klail City Death Trip* series—all set in the community of that little town—using an intriguing variety of literary styles, including poetry, letters, interviews, and first-person narratives. Awarded the prestigious Casa de las Américas novel prize in 1976 for *Klail City,* the judges praised the novel for its "richness of imagery, the sensitive creation of dialogues, the collage-like structure based on a pattern of converging individual destinies, the masterful control of the temporal element and its testimonial value."

In commenting on Hinojosa's vibrant community and the triumphs and disappointments of the characters that walk its streets, Charles Tatum wrote in a review for *World Literature Today* that "[we]

become progressively more familiar with both their tribulations and joys through the simple technique of repetition. Characters are introduced, disappear for pages at a time and reappear in different forms: as narrators, as part of another character's memories or gossip, as a casual reference in a conversation." Of the hundreds of characters that appear in Hinojosa's work, only four reappear consistently. This technique, Tatum declares, is a deliberate decision on the part of the author. "The relative lack of characterization corresponds to the creation of a collective protagonist made up of many fictitious creations. As individuals, the vast majority lack dimension, but together they form an intricately related community of emotions, values and traditions."

### Spanish Upbringing

Rolando Hinojosa-Smith was born on January 21, 1929, in Mercedes, Texas, to Manual Guzman and Carrie Effie Smith Hinojosa. His father, a farmer, came from a family that settled in the upper part of the Lower Rio Grande Valley around the 1740s. His mother, a homemaker and teacher, arrived in the valley as a child and was bilingual like her husband. Explaining his family roots to Juan Bruce-Novoa in *Chicano Authors, Inquiry by Interview,* Hinojosa said, "My father—like so many other Chicanos—was in the Mexican Revolution. He was in and out of Mexico for a long time while my mother kept home and family together on the American side. My mother had been a teacher as had her mother before her; of the five children in our family, four of us went into teaching and we're still in the profession." As a young child, Hinojosa spoke only Spanish; he still prefers that language in writing his novels. "My early life, indeed up to seventeen when I enlisted, my daily life was really lived, for the most part, in Spanish. This comes out in my writing and it's no state secret. I speak both languages with equal fluency. . . . although I prefer to write fiction in Spanish."

Hinojosa's first educational experience consisted of a neighborhood school run by a Mexican national. In *Inquiry,* he recalled those early days: "We were all there, some fifty to sixty of us reciting aloud, working on penmanship, arithmetic, and somehow, reading. I can still remember the cover of the third year reader: *Poco a poco* (*Little by Little*) . . . I read everything that came my way and, being a sickly child for some two to three years there, I could read all day if I wanted to and I did." He particularly enjoyed "pulps"—translations of American and French novels and short stories. "Reading was something everyone did in our family and, according to my family, I taught myself to read. That's probably true." He only vaguely recalls his first attempts at writing in high school. Although his teachers praised his early efforts, Hinojosa was dissatisfied with his work. "They were written in English, of course. Most of what followed was also in English and all of it bad, sloppy, and stilted."

Later, when Hinojosa joined the army and attended university, he was able to indulge his appetite for reading. "The Army was a good place for reading and every library post was well stocked," he told *Inquiry*. "At the University of Texas it was the same thing: I worked in the reserve room and this was like choosing a rabbit to guard the lettuce patch. The reserve reading room was full of books on history, biographies, the classics in translation, and M.A. and Ph.D. theses, horrendous stuff like that." Hinojosa earned his bachelor's degree in Mexican and Hispanic American literature and nineteenth-century Peninsular from the University of Texas at Austin in 1953. He went on in higher education to earn a master's from the New Mexico Highlands University in 1963 and a doctorate in 1969 from the University of Illinois.

When asked by Bruce-Novoa whether formal education helped or hindered his development as a writer, Hinojosa noted, "[formal] education, in my case, has been an advantage: I tend to be wary of excesses in language or direction. Literature has too many good examples to draw from and so many bad ones to avoid that it is just a matter of following one and avoiding the other. Didacticism, totalitarian themes, boxed-in theses, and set propositions are intolerable and inexcusable for the serious writer of fiction and nonfiction, or of criticism for that matter."

### Klail City Death Trip

Hinojosa began his writing career with the publication of his first novel, *Estampas del valle y otras obras* (*Sketches of the Valley and Other Works*) in 1972. A set of loosely connected sketches, narratives, monologues, and dialogues that compose a picture of Chicano life in Klail City, this work was the first in the author's *Klail City Death Trip* series. It also introduced readers to Jehu Malacara and his cousin Rafa Buenrostro, two characters who reappear in subsequent novels. The novel not only brought him broad recognition, but it won Hinojosa his first literary award: the Quinto Sol Literary Award for best novel in 1972. Bruce-Novoa called the award the "most prestigious literary prize in the field of Chicano letters at that time."

Hinojosa continued to explore the Chicano experience in *Klail City y sus alrededores* (*Klail City*), a 1976 novel that garnered him the Premio Casa de las Américas award for best novel of the year. On the strength of these first two books, Hinojosa had established himself as an celebrated literary figure. Bruce-Novoa described the author's appeal: "His style—precise, clean, with not a word of excess; his ironic and subtle humor, so well within the Hispanic tradition; his undeniably popular and regional

themes, incarnating universal verities while portraying faithfully his South Texas neighbors; and a persistent, welcome understatement—all blend to make Hinojosa's work unmistakable, and a joy to read."

Hinojosa's third and fourth novels—*Korean Love Songs from Klail City Death Trip* (1978) a novel set in verse, and *Claros varones de Belken* (1981; *Fair Gentlemen of Belken County*)—continued the Klail City saga. The author followed his two characters, Jehu and Rafa, as they serve in the Korean War, attend the University of Texas at Austin, and begin careers as high school teachers in Klail City. The Klail City Death Trip series finally concluded after six novels. In 1985 Hinojosa branched out into another genre by a detective thriller entitled *Partners In Crime*. The 1990 novel *Los Amigos de Becky* (*Becky and Her Friends*) marked another effort on the part of the author to relate the history of the Lower Rio Grande valley through his fiction.

### From Klail City to Yoknapatawpha County

Mark Busby, in an essay for *MELUS* published in 1984, compared Hinojosa's style to that of William Faulkner, the Chicano writer's favorite author. "Stylistically, Faulkner and Hinojosa shun using traditional plot structures and concentrate on fragmentary chapters to build tapestries that are ultimately nearly seamless," Busby wrote. "Finally, both writers concentrate on the theme of human endurance." Like the acclaimed Faulkner, who based so much of his enduring fiction in the mythic Yoknapatawpha County, Mississippi, Hinojosa found the setting of his novels, Klail City, to be of utmost importance to the integrity of his work. Busby quotes Hinojosa as saying, "For the writer—this writer—a sense of place was not a matter of importance; it became essential. . . . Place is merely that until it is populated, and once populated the histories of the place and its people begin."

Though on the surface, his novels may seem fragmented and scattered, there is a definite unity to his work, as Hinojosa explained in *The Texas Literary Tradition*. "My stories are not held together by the *peripeteia,* or the plot, as much as by what the people who populate the stories say and *how* they say it; how they look at the world out and the world in; and the works, then, become studies of perceptions and values and decisions reached by them because of those perceptions and values which in turn were fashioned and forged by the place and its history."

Busby concluded that, while Hinojosa's fiction is unlikely to reach the same heights of critical regard that Faulkner's work is held in, the Chicano author has produced a significant body of literary work. "What I do want to indicate is that Rolando Hinojosa is a serious writer, a writer who is conscious of his craft, and one who consciously draws from a distinguished literary tradition ... he has effectively merged some of Faulkner's techniques with his own experience as a Mexican-American who grew up in Texas' Rio Grande valley. Within him is a deep sense of the spirit of the place, the importance of its people's lives.... Hinojosa is especially good at rendering the Mexican-American's ability to endure. These are, to be sure, great American themes, and Hinojosa's work shows every sign of long life."

## SELECTED PUBLISHED WORKS:

*Estampas del valle y otras obras* (*Sketches of the Valley and Other Works*), Quinto Sol, 1972, bilingual edition, 1980; revised English edition published as *The Valley*, Bilingual Press, 1983.
*Klail City y sus alrededores*, Casa de las Américas, 1976; Justa Publications, 1977; translated by Hinojosa as *Klail City*, Arte Publico Press, 1987.
*Korean Love Songs from Klail City Death Trip*, Justa Publications, 1978.
*Claros varones de Belken*, Justa Publication, 1981; translated as *Fair Gentlemen of Belken County*, Bilingual Press, 1987.
*Mi querido Rafa*, Arte Publico Press, 1981; translated by Hinojosa as *Dear Rafe*, 1985.
*Rites and Witnesses*, Arte Publico Press, 1982.
*Partners in Crime*, Arte Publico Press, 1985.
*Los amigos de Becky* (*Becky and Her Friends*), Arte Publico Press, 1990.
*The Useless Servants*, Arte Publico Press, 1993.

## SOURCES:

### Books

Bruce-Novoa, Juan, *Chicano Authors: Inquiry by Interview*, Austin, University of Texas Press, 1980, pp. 49–65.
*Hispanic Writers*, edited by Bryan Ryan, Detroit, Gale, pp. 256–58.
*The Texas Literary Tradition*, University of Texas Press, 1983, p. 122.

### Periodicals

*MELUS*, Winter 1984, pp. 103–109.
*World Literature Today*, Summer 1977.

—*Sketch by Kathe A. Conti*

# Eugenio María de Hostos
## 1839-1903
### Puerto Rican patriot, educator, and writer

A progressive educator and prolific writer, Eugenio María de Hostos—also known as Eugenio María Hostos—was also a committed Puerto Rican patriot whose lifelong dream and campaign for the liberation and unification of a Federated Antillean Republic was never realized. Hostos's stated objective was to "teach the continent to think." Toward that end, he promoted the advancement of education. His accomplishments in education had a significant and lasting impact in Santo Domingo, where he established the country's first normal school for teachers, and in Chile, where he taught at two universities. His educational and political campaigns were supported by his writing. Remarkably diverse, in both topic and type, Hostos's works ranged from philosophical criticism and constitutional law to short stories and plays for his children.

### Fervor for Independence

Eugenio María de Hostos y Bonilla was born in Rio Canas, Mayagüez, Puerto Rico, on January 11, 1839. His schooling began in San Juan, but at the age of 13 he was sent to Spain, where he attended high school in Bilbao. At 18, he entered the Central University of Madrid's Law School, where he earned his Juris Doctor in 1860. While in college, Hostos published several articles urging the liberation of the Spanish-American colonies, marking the beginning of a life-long devotion to the cause.

Pedro Henríquez-Ureña explained Hostos's desire in *Obras:* "From early youth he dreamed of the independence of his native island, Puerto Rico; not as a tiny nation by itself by itself, but as a member of a confederacy of the Antilles, together with Cuba and Santo Domingo. Since both Cuba and Puerto Rico were still under the rule of Spain, he gave much of his time during more than 30 years (1868–1899) to the cause of their liberation."

Hostos was active in militant Spanish republican politics in the 1850s and 1860s, convinced that a republican government in Spain would result in promised liberation for the colonies of the Spanish West Indies. But when Emelio Castelar, Spain's first republican president, refused to liberate the islands, Hostos denounced him, and was, subsequently, banished from the country in 1869. He emigrated to the United States, working with the Cuban Revolutionary Junta of pro-independence Cuban exiles in New York City. He was also the editor of their newspaper, *La revolución.*

*Eugenio María de Hostos*

In 1870, Hostos embarked on a tour of South America in an effort to generate backing and publicity for Cuban and Puerto Rican independence, and to promote the expansion and modernization of education. During the early 1870s, he taught at the University of Santiago in Chile. He also wrote numerous newspaper articles during this time, became a widely respected voice throughout Central America.

### Supported Educational Reforms

In 1875, Hostos went to the Dominican Republic. From there he traveled to Venezuela, where he promoted education and married the daughter of a Cuban emigré. In 1880, he was invited to Santo Domingo, where he spent the next nine years. At the time, the educational systems in the Spanish American colonies were exceptionally backward. Within this environment, Hostos organized Santo Domingo's public school system along modern lines, serving as inspector general of public instruction.

Hostos also founded and served as dean of the Santo Domingo Normal School. A school for teachers, it was the first of its kind in the Dominican Republic. Henríquez-Ureña's *Obras* noted that the institution's effects were far-reaching, stating that Hostos gave the school "a curriculum of which science was the nucleus and establish(ed) pedagogical methods that were in advance of his time. The influence of his school was enormous; it changed the intellectual atmosphere."

Hostos's *Social Ethics* was published in 1888. He was expelled from Santo Domingo the same year by the regressive dictator Ulises Heureaux. From Santo Domingo, Hostos went to Chile, where he served two years as headmaster of the Miguel Luis Amunátegui secondary school. In 1890, the University of Chile in Santiago granted him a professorship, and he taught international law there until 1898.

### Continued Struggling for Independence

When Cuba received independence from Spain as a result of the Spanish Civil War in 1898, Hostos traveled to the United States to urge their recognition of Puerto Rico's sovereignty. Instead, the United States occupied and annexed the island. Henríquez-Ureña observed that Hostos "never recovered from the blow of this disaster." In 1898, Hostos organized the fleeting League of Puerto Rican Patriots to protest and resist United States domination. According to Henríquez-Ureña, "Hostos went to Washington in 1899 as a member of the delegation to ask President McKinley for the freedom of Puerto Rico. His disappointment was, naturally, very keen."

Hostos left Puerto Rico in 1899, feeling that he could not continue to live in his native land under foreign dominion. Utterly disillusioned, he returned to Santiago, where he spent his last years reorganizing the educational system there. Hostos died in Santo Domingo on August 11, 1903 at the age of 64, convinced that his political efforts on behalf of Puerto Rican independence and an Antillean confederation had been useless.

### Reflected Diverse Concerns

Throughout his career, Hostos wrote prodigiously. At the age of 24, Hostos had published his first novel, *La peregrinación de Bayoá* ("The Pilgrimage of Bayoán"), an allegorical tale revolving around a tragic figure's travels throughout the Caribbean and Spain. His collected works, published in 20 volumes as *Obras completas* in 1938, contain lectures, poetry, short stories, letters, diaries, a novel, criticism, essays, plays, and nonfiction. This collection has been translated and was published in 1979 as *The Complete Works of Eugenio María de Hostos.*

Written under several variations of his name, including E.M. de Hostos, Eugenio M. de Hostos, and Eugenio María Hostos, his work explores a wide variety of subjects, from a critical essay of Shakespeare's *Hamlet* to a textbook of lectures on constitutional law—*Lecciones de derecho constitucional*—and *Tratado de sociología* ("Treatise on Sociology"), a major work on sociology. Both are considered seminal works by experts in their respective fields.

Hostos's ground-breaking teaching methods are represented in part by *La enseñanza científica de la mujer* ("Teaching Women Scientifically"). His progressive positions on educational opportunity—particularly regarding the inclusion of women—were delineated in the brilliant address, "To the Masters of the Normal School." Hostos's most important work is generally agreed to be *Moral Social* ("Social Ethics"). Planned as a text for Hostos's students in Santo Domingo, it is representative of his best ethical thought.

Hostos's pedagogical and literary accomplishments were acknowledged during his lifetime. Although his political dreams remained unfulfilled, his devotion to his country inspired awe. Margot Arce de Vázquez wrote in tribute in 1950: "Eugenio María de Hostos was a patriot, and also a symbol of the moral meaning of our homeland. Its most prominent virtues were incarnate in him, and in bringing them together he enriched them with his spiritual action. . . . The sentiment of the homeland was always the basis on which his acts were founded, acts that are, truly, love along with good intentions."

## SELECTED PUBLISHED WORKS:

*La peregrinación de Bayoán,* 1863, revised and annotated, edited by Julio C. López, University of Puerto Rico Press, 1988.

*Hamlet,* originally published separately, 1873, published with a critical essay on *Romeo and Juliet,* Edil, 1972.

*Lecciones de derecho constitucional,* 1887, Santo Domingo, Publicaciones ONAP, 1982.

*Moral Social,* Santo Domingo, Imprenta de Garcia Hermanos, 1888, reprinted, Barcelona, Vosgos, 1974.

*Geografía evolutiva,* 1895, reprinted, Santo Domingo, Talleres Tipográficos "La Nación", 1932.

*Tratado de sociología,* Madrid, Imprenta de Bailly-Bailliere e Hijos, 1904, reprinted, Buenos Aires, El Ateneo, 1942.

*Meditando,* Paris, Ediciones Literarias y Artísticas, 1909.

*Obras completas,* 20 volumes, Havana, Cultural, 1939, reprinted, Editorial de la Universidad de Puerto Rico, 1988, translation published as *The Complete Works of Eugenio María de Hostos,* Gordon Press, 1979.

*Páginas dominicanas,* originally published in *Hostos en Santo Domingo,* (Dominican Republic), c. 1939, portions selected by E. Rodríguez Demorizi published separately, Librería Dominicana, 1963.

*Antología,* selected by son, Eugenio Carlos de Hostos, Madrid, Litografía y Encuadernación, 1952.

*Páginas escogidas,* Buenos Aires: A. Estrada, 1952.

*Obras,* compiled by Pedro Henríquez-Ureña, Havana, Casa de las Américas, 1976.

*Eugenio María de Hostos: Sociólogo y maestro,* Antillana, 1981.

*Hostos: Ensayos inéditos* (unpublished essays), Edil, 1987.

*América, la lucha por la libertad,* Mexico, Siglo Vientiuno, reprinted Ediciones Compromiso, 1988.

## SOURCES:

*An Outline History of Spanish American Literature,* 3rd edition, edited by John E. Englekirk, New York, Appleton-Century-Crofts, 1965.

*Borinquen: An Anthology of Puerto Rican Literature,* edited by María Teresa Babín and Stan Steiner, New York, Alfred A. Knopf, 1974.

*Contemporary Authors,* Detroit, Gale, vol. 123, edited by Hal May and Susan M. Trosky, 1988; vol. 131, edited by Susan M. Trosky, 1991.

*Literary Currents in Hispanic America,* by Pedro Henríquez-Ureña, Cambridge, MA: Harvard University Press, 1945.

*The Literary History of Spanish America,* by Alfred Coester, New York, Macmillan, 1916.

*Spanish-American Literature,* by Jean Franco, Cambridge, Cambridge University Press, 1969.

*Twentieth-Century Literary Criticism,* vol. 24, edited by Dennis Poupard, Detroit, Gale, 1987.

*—Sketch by Ellen Dennis French*

# Dolores Huerta
## 1930-
### Hispanic American labor leader and social activist

Cofounder and first vice president of the United Farm Workers union, Dolores Huerta is the most prominent Chicana labor leader in the United States. For more than thirty years she has dedicated her life to the struggle for justice, dignity, and a decent standard of living for one of the country's most exploited groups, the women and men who toil in the fields. The recipient of countless community service, labor, Hispanic, and women's awards and the subject of many newspaper articles, as well as *corridos* (ballads) and murals, Huerta serves as a singular role model for Mexican American women living in the post World War II era. Although Huerta is widely acclaimed and celebrated, her early history, family life, transformation from volunteer to labor activist, and career are barely known.

Dolores Fernández Huerta was the second child and only daughter born to Juan and Alicia (Chávez) Fernández on April 10, 1930, in the small mining town of Dawson in northern New Mexico. On her mother's side of the family, Huerta is a third-generation New Mexican. Like her mother, Huerta's father was born in Dawson but to a Mexican immigrant family. The young couple's marriage was troubled, and when Huerta was a toddler her parents divorced. Her mother moved her three children—Juan, Dolores, and Marshal—first to Las Vegas, New Mexico, and then to Stockton, California, where she had relatives.

### Raised Primarily by Mother

As a single parent during the Depression in California, Alicia Chávez Fernández experienced a difficult time supporting her young family. Describing her mother in an interview with this author, Huerta noted, "She was a very genteel woman, very quiet but very hard working," as well as very "energetic, motivated, and ambitious." To make ends meet, her mother worked at a cannery at night and as a waitress during the day. For child care, Alicia Fernández depended on her widowed father, Herculano Chávez, who had followed her to Stockton. In the same interview, Dolores Huerta recalled his importance: "My grandfather kind of raised us. . . . He was really our father. . . . My grandfather's influence was really the male influence in my family." The gregarious Huerta enjoyed a close relationship with her grandfather Chávez in a happy childhood with attentive supervision, respect for one's elders, Mexican *corridos,* and rosary recitations. Considering herself to be a dutiful but playful child, she remembered in the interview, "My grandfather used to call me seven tongues . . . because I always talked so much." Verbal skills would serve her well in later life.

The family's economic fortunes improved during the war years. Alicia Chavez ran a restaurant and then purchased a hotel in Stockton with her second husband, James Richards, with whom she had another daughter. Particularly during the summers, Dolores Huerta and her brothers helped run these establishments located on the fringes of skid row, catering to working-class and farm-worker clientele. Huerta relished the experience and believed she learned to appreciate all different types of people, as she conveyed in the interview. "The ethnic community where we lived was all mixed. It was Japanese, Chinese. The only Jewish families that lived in Stockton were there in our neighborhood. . . . There was the Filipino pool hall . . . , the Mexican drug stores, the Mexican bakeries were there." While Huerta was exposed to a vibrant community life, her relationship with her stepfather was strained, and eventually her mother's marriage ended in divorce.

In the early 1950s, Alicia Chavez Richards married her third husband, Juan Silva. This happy union produced another daughter, Elen Silva, and endured until her mother's death. Huerta spoke admiringly of her mother's entrepreneurial and personal spirit and her expectations for her children. Again she reminisced, "My mother was always pushing me to get involved in all these youth activities. . . . We took violin lessons. I took piano lessons. I took dancing lessons. I belonged to the church choir. . . . I belonged to the church youth organization. And I was a very active Girl Scout from the time I was eight to the time I was eighteen." Mother and daughter shared a caring relationship extending into Huerta's adult years.

Although Huerta's primary family influences derived from her mother and grandfather, she did not lose contact with her father. His work history and activities inspired her. Like most people in Dawson, Juan Fernández worked in the coal mines. To supplement his wages, he also joined the migrant labor force, traveling to Colorado, Nebraska, and Wyoming for the beet harvests. Indignant over inferior working conditions, frequent accidents, and low wages, Fernández also became interested in labor issues. Leaving Dawson after the dissolution of his marriage, he continued his labor activism becoming secretary-treasurer of the CIO local at the Terrero Camp of the American Metals Company in Las Vegas. Using his predominately Hispanic local union as a base, he won election to the New Mexico state legislature in 1938, representing San Miguel County. He worked with other sympathetic members to promote a labor program, including the proposal of New Mexico's "Little Wagner Act" and a wages-and-hours bill. Yet due to his independent demeanor and his outspoken temperament, he lasted only one term in the state house.

After her parents' divorce, Huerta had only sporadic contact with her father, but as a sickly eleven-year-old she spent a summer traveling around New Mexico with him while he made a living as a pots-and-pans sales representative. In her adult years she had more contact with her father, particularly after he settled in Stockton, where he lived in a labor camp for a time, worked in the asparagus fields, held other odd jobs, and returned to school for a college degree. Huerta remained proud of her father's union activism, political achievements, and educational accomplishments. Remembering her father she revealed in the interview, "He was always supportive of my labor organizing," but she added he was less approving of her personal lifestyle. Their relationship remained aloof and distant until the end of his life.

As a youngster growing up in Stockton and especially after her mother's improved economic circumstances and remarriage, Huerta experienced a more middle-class upbringing. She attended Lafayette grammar school, Jackson Junior High, and graduated from Stockton High School. A former high school classmate recalled in an article in the *Stockton Record,* "When we were in school, she was very popular and outspoken. She was already an organizer, but I didn't think she'd get so serious and work for such a cause." Unlike most Hispanic women of her generation, the outgoing Huerta continued her education at Stockton College, interrupting her studies temporarily with her first marriage to Ralph Head. After her divorce, and with financial and emotional help from her mother in raising two daughters, Celeste and Lori, she returned to college and received an A.A. degree in education.

Huerta held a variety of jobs in Stockton before, during, and after her brief marriage. Before her marriage she managed a small neighborhood grocery store that her mother had purchased but which eventually went bankrupt. Then she obtained a job at the Naval Supply Base as the secretary to the commander in charge of public works. During and after her first divorce, she worked in the sheriff's office in records and identifications. Dissatisfied with this employment option, she resumed her education, pursuing a teaching career and obtaining a provisional teaching credential. An interview published in *Regeneración* in 1971 revealed her subsequent frustrations with this profession: "I realized one day that as a teacher I couldn't do anything for the kids who came to school barefoot and hungry."

### Influenced by Postwar Activism

A part of her consciousness grew out of a new wave of civic activism that swept through Mexican American communities after World War II. The postwar organization that would eventually alter her life course was the Community Service Organization (CSO), a Mexican American self-help association that was founded in Los Angeles—it was instrumental in electing Edward Roybal, the first Hispanic member of the Los Angeles City Council in the twentieth century—and then spread throughout California and the Southwest.

Huerta's transformation to social and labor activism occurred gradually. Initially suspicious of the CSO and its chief organizer, Fred Ross, when he came to Stockton in the mid-1950s, Huerta reported to *Regeneración,* "I was told he was a communist, so I went to the FBI and had him checked out. . . . See how middle class I was. In fact, at the time, I was a registered Republican, the party of Abraham Lincoln." Her misgivings allayed, Huerta soon became very active. Changing her party affiliation, she participated in the civic and educational programs of the CSO, registering people to vote, organizing citizenship classes, pressing local government for barrio improvements. As a result of her skills, she was hired to lobby in Sacramento for CSO legislative initiatives, such as the ultimately successful old-age pensions for non-citizens.

During the course of these activities she met and married her second husband, Ventura Huerta, who was also involved in community affairs. This relationship produced five children: Fidel, Emilio, Vincent, Alicia, and Angela. The marriage deteriorated, however, because of incompatible temperaments, but also because of disagreements over Dolores Huerta's juggling of domestic matters, child care, and her interest in civic activism. Huerta summed up the contention in an article that appeared in *The Progressive.* "I knew I wasn't comfortable in a wife's role, but I wasn't clearly facing the issue. I hedged, I made excuses, I didn't come out and tell my husband that I cared more about helping other people than cleaning our house and doing my hair." During trial separations (that eventually ended in divorce), Huerta's mother again provided her with important emotional and financial support as well as backing her CSO career, contributing baby sitting, housing, and household expenses. Speaking with this interviewer more than twenty years after her mother's early death from cancer in 1962, Huerta disclosed the depth of her loss. "When she died, it took me years to get over it. In fact, I still don't think I'm over it. . . ."

### Cofounded United Farm Workers Union with César Chávez

At the same time that Dolores Huerta was struggling to balance a failing marriage, family, and work with a commitment to social concerns in the late 1950s, she became drawn to the conditions of farm workers. She organized a northern California community interest group, the Agricultural Workers Association (AWA). It later gained the support of the AFL-CIO's Agricultural Workers Organizing Committee (AWOC), for which Huerta served as secretary-treasurer. During these years she also met **César Chávez,** a CSO organizer who shared her interests in farm labor. The two cooperated to bring rural labor issues to the attention of the CSO. Huerta and Chavez made a joint decision that if the CSO would not sponsor their farm-worker organizing effort, they would both leave the organization. Frustrated with the CSO's unresponsiveness, first Chávez and later Huerta left the CSO to devote their time to organizing field workers and thus to change the course of agricultural and labor history in California with the founding of the Farm Workers Association (FWA), the precursor to the UFW, in Delano in 1962.

The full extent of the Chávez-Huerta close collaboration has only recently been documented with the availability of correspondence between the two and others. Writing to his CSO mentor, Fred Ross, in 1962, Chávez communicated, "Dolores was here [Delano] for one and a half days. I filled her in on all the plans and asked her to join the parade. . . . While here we did some work on the list of towns to work in throughout the valley. . . . Also she, Helen [Chávez's wife], and I [decided] on the name of the group. 'National Farm Workers Assn.'"

From the founding of the union, Huerta has held decision-making posts and maintained a highly visible profile. As second in command to Chávez, she has exerted a direct influence on shaping and guiding the fortunes of the UFW. In the 1965 Delano strike, she devised strategy and led workers on picket lines. She was the union's first contract negotiator, founding the department and directing it in the early years. In these and other positions Huerta fought criticism based both on gender and ethnic stereotyping. Reacting to Huerta's uncompromising and forceful style, one grower exclaimed in a 1976 story in *The Progressive,* "Dolores Huerta is crazy. She is a violent woman, where women, especially Mexican women, are usually peaceful and calm." Such attacks highlighted the extent of her challenge to the political, social, and economic power of California agribusiness, as well as to patriarchy.

Another major responsibility for Huerta was the directorship of the table grape boycott in New York City and later her assignment as the East Coast boycott coordinator in 1968 and 1969. Her critical leadership there, the primary distribution point for grapes, contributed to the success of the national boycott effort in mobilizing unions, political activists, Hispanic associations, community organizations, religious supporters, peace groups, student protestors, and concerned consumers. In New York Huerta also became aware of the potency of the emerging feminist movement through her contacts with Gloria Steinem. As a result of this influence, Huerta began to incorporate a feminist critique into her human rights philosophy. As reported in Ronald Taylor's book on the union, Huerta explained her approach: "The whole thrust of our boycott is to get as many supporters as you can." After five years, the growing power of this grassroots coalition across the nation finally forced Coachella and Delano grape producers to negotiate the historic contracts of 1970.

Huerta's organizing expertise and inspiration were felt again when she returned to New York to administer the lettuce, grape, and Gallo wine boycotts of the 1970s. The concerted pressure of the renewed cross-class and cross-cultural cooperation in New York City and in other major cities across the U.S. resulted in the passage of the Agricultural Labor Relations Act (ALRA) in 1975, the first law to recognize the collective bargaining rights of farm workers in California.

In the midst of boycott duties and a heavy traveling and speaking schedule, Huerta began a third relationship with Richard Chávez, César's brother. This liaison produced Juanita, María Elena, Ricardo, and Camilla, bringing the total number of her children to 11. Huerta alluded in her interview to the sacrifices her position placed on all her children as a result of her frequent absences: "I don't feel proud of the suffering that my kids went through. I feel very bad and guilty about it, but by the same token I know that they learned a lot in the process."

During the late 1970s, Huerta directed the political arm of the UFW, as she carried the union's battle to protect the new farm labor law into the legislative arena in Sacramento. In the 1980s she was involved in another ambitious UFW project, the founding of Radio Campesina, the union's radio station, KUFW. Her schedule continued to accommodate speaking engagements, fund raising, publicizing the renewed grape boycott of the 1980s, and testifying before state and congressional committees on a wide range of issues, including pesticides, health problems of field workers, Hispanic political issues, and immigration policy.

### Severly Injured During Peaceful Demonstration

At great personal cost Huerta has committed her energies to the UFW as an outspoken leader, executive board member, administrator, lobbyist, contract negotiator, picket captain, and lecturer. In addition she has also been arrested more than 20 times and suffered a life-threatening injury in a 1988 peaceful demonstration against the policies of then presidential candidate George Bush, who was campaigning in San Francisco. Rushed to the hospital after a clubbing by baton-swinging police officers, Huerta underwent emergency surgery in which her spleen was removed. She remained hospitalized to recover from the operation and four broken ribs. According to a 1991 report in the *Los Angeles Times,* the incident caused the police department to change its rules regarding crowd control and police discipline; another result was a record financial settlement to Huerta as a consequence of the personal assault.

Recovering from this medical setback, Huerta gradually resumed her work for the farm workers in the 1990s, a period of time when conservative political forces seemed triumphant, awareness of the farm workers' cause had dimmed, and the union itself went through a difficult process of internal reassessment and restructuring. Still Huerta asserted that the UFW legacy remains strong for the Hispanic community and beyond. Towards the end of her interview with this contributor, she affirmed, "I think we brought to the world, the United States anyway, the whole idea of boycotting as a nonviolent tactic. I think we showed the world that nonviolence can work to make social change. . . . I think we have laid a pattern of how farm workers are eventually going to get out of their bondage. It may not happen right now in our foreseeable future, but the pattern is there and farm workers are going to make it."

## SOURCES:

### Books

Day, Mark, *Forty Acres: Cesar Chavez and the Farm Workers,* Praeger, 1971.

Dunne, John Gregory, *Delano: The Story of the California Grape Strike,* Farrar, 1976.

Levy, Jacques, *Cesar Chavez: Autobiography of La Causa,* Norton, 1975.

London, Joan, and Henry Anderson, *So Shall Ye Reap,* Thomas Crowell, 1970.

Majka, Linda C., and Theo J. Majka, *Farm Workers, Agribusiness, and the State,* Temple University Press, 1982.

Matthiessen, Peter, *Sal Si Puedes: Cesar Chavez and the New American Revolution,* Random House, 1969.

Meister, Dick, and Anne Loftis, *A Long Time Coming, The Struggle to Unionize America's Farm Workers,* Macmillan, 1977.

*The New Mexico Blue Book, State Official Register, 1939-1940,* Optic Publishing Company, 1941.

Taylor, Ronald B., *Chavez and the Farm Workers,* Beacon Press, 1975.

### Periodicals

Baer, Barbara L., "Stopping Traffic: One Woman's Cause," *The Progressive,* September, 1975, pp. 38-40.

Baer, Barbara L., and Glenna Matthews, "'You Find a Way': The Women of the Boycott," *Nation* February 23, 1974, pp. 232-38.

*Bakersfield Californian,* January 25, 1991, p. A1-2.

Carranza, Ruth, "From the Fields into the History Books," *Intercambios Femeniles,* winter, 1989, pp. 11-12.

Coburn, Judith, "Dolores Huerta: La Pasionaria of the Farmworkers," *Ms.,* November, 1976, pp. 11-16.

"Dolores Huerta Talks About Republicans, Cesar, Children, and Her Home Town," *Regeneración,* Volume 2, number 4, 1975, pp. 20-24.

"Labor Heroines: Dolores Huerta," *Union W.A.G.E.,* July-August, 1974, p. 6.

*Los Angeles Times,* January 25, 1991, p. A3; February 14, p. E5.

Murphy, Jean, "Unsung Heroine of La Causa," *Regeneración,* Volume 1, number 11, 1971, p. 20.

Rose, Margaret, "'From the Fields to the Picket Line: Huelga Women and the Boycott,' 1965-1975," *Labor History,* summer, 1990, pp. 271-293.

Rose, Margaret, "Traditional and Nontraditional Patterns of Female Activism in the United Farm Workers of America, 1962 to 1980," *Frontiers,* Volume 11, number 1, 1990, pp. 26-92.

*Santa Fe New Mexican,* November 10, 1938.

*Stockton Record,* March 2, 1986.

"A Woman's Place Is . . . on the Picket Line!," *El Malcriado,* July 1, 1970, pp. 16-18.

### Other

Huerta, Dolores, interviews with Margaret Rose, March 16, 1984, February 4, 1985, February 8, 1985, February 12, 1985, February 19, 1985, (La Paz) Keene, California, and February 26, 1985, Bakersfield, California.

Rose, Margaret Eleanor, "Women in the United Farm Workers: A Study of Chicana and Mexicana Participation in a Labor Union, 1950 to 1980" (dissertation), University of California, Los Angeles, 1983.

*—Sketch by Margaret Rose*

# Vicente Huidobro
## 1893-1948
### Chilean poet, novelist, editor, and critic

Poet Vicente Huidobro was known both as a leading twentieth-century Latin American author and as a contentious, controversial figure. "Born into a patrician South American family" in Santiago, Chile, in 1893, "Vicente Garcia Huidobro Fernandez, heir to the title Marqués de Casa Real, was earmarked for a life of leisure," René de Costa noted in his biography *Vicente Huidobro, The Careers of a Poet.* "For a number of reasons, Huidobro broke out of this comfortable, albeit confining mould, and used his privileged position in a rather unorthodox way: to foment change."

Huidobro challenged authority and the status quo from the early days of his youth. His first literary work, written as a student at Colegio San Ignacio, an exclusive Jesuit school, reflected an early talent for generating controversy. In 1914 the school published a collection of his writings. The first essay, an autobiographical sketch, did not meet with the Jesuits' approval. De Costa reprinted the offending text. "I was born the 10th of January, 1893. An old woman, part witch and quite wise, predicted that I would be a thief or a great man. Which of these options should I take? To be a thief is unquestionably very artistic. Crime must have its delightful compensations. To be a great man? That depends. If I am to be a great poet, a man of letters; yes. But to be a great Congressman, Senator, or a Cabinet member, that seems to me most unaesthetic." Another paragraph in the essay was a blistering account of his disillusioning experiences under the tutelage of the Jesuit priests. Not surprisingly, the edition was banned and burned. The controversy surrounding this early essay proved to be a foreshadowing of things to come.

Huidobro married Manuela Portas Bello in 1912, a period in which Huidobro immersed himself in various literary activities. He founded the literary review *Azul* in 1913, the first of many literary journals—including *Nord Sud* (1916), *Creación* (1921), *Ombligo* (1934), and *Total* (1936)—that he founded or co-founded. Huidobro's first books of poetry, largely symbolist in tone, were published in Chile in 1911 and 1913. After completing his studies of Hispanic modernism in Chile, Huidobro moved to Europe in 1916 to study cubism and dadaism. He settled in France and, in 1918, began publishing with the cubists. During this period, Hays noted, Huidobro was arranging poems in pictorial shapes in the manner of Guillaume Apollinaire. By 1921 an exhibit of his poems was displayed in a picture gallery. Huidobro visited Madrid, Spain, as well.

Eventually Huidobro launched his own view of the creationism movement. Hays commented that Huidobro "says his theories were formulated as early as 1916. They emphasize the conscious creation of new images. 'The poet creates the world that ought to exist outside of the one that does exist . . . the poet is concerned with expressing only the inexpressible.'" Hays interpreted Huidobro's poetry as a musical pattern of images, an international language unique unto itself. While Huidobro insisted that he was the inventor of creationism—a self-assessment that some scholars agree with—others argue that although Huidobro was part of the literary style, he was not its inventor.

## European Politics

Politics were as essential to Huidobro's life as writing. De Costa described the effects of Huidobro's attack on the British Empire when he defended the Irish bid for independence in 1925. "For this he is reportedly kidnapped. Back in Chile in 1925, he is beaten and his house is bombed as he makes a yellow-press bid for the Presidency, accusing the establishment of all sorts of crimes against the nation. A decade later, we find him in Madrid, championing the Republican cause during the Spanish Civil War. And, with the outbreak of the Second World War . . . he is a War Correspondent with the Allies."

In addition to his deep involvement in political matters, Huidobro acquired a reputation as one who often questioned the established notions of what was acceptable in the world of literature. "Amid stunning successes in Paris and Madrid there are bitter polemics," de Costa wrote, "culminating in 1925 with *Manifestes,* an attack on Breton's Surrealism. In fact, at one time or another Huidobro seems to have quarreled with every major writer of his generation." Despite the rhetoric and frayed tempers, some contemporaries admired Huidobro's work. De Costa noted that **Pablo Neruda** once said that "I consider Huidobro to be one of the classic poets of our language. . . . While most of his prose is flawed by his person, his prankish personalism, his poetry is a mirror in which are reflected images of pure delight along with the game of his personal struggle. It seems to me that Huidobro was consumed by his own game and his own flame. In spite of the fact that his poetic intelligence is the master key to his brilliance, he had such a predilection to forge himself a legend that in the end consumed him, masking his work and burying him. Fortunately, his poetry will rescue his remembrance, a remembrance that will continue to grow and spread."

Others were not so generous. A comment made in 1942 by Arturo Torres Ríoseco, noted *Kentucky Romance Quarterly,* led many to disregard Huidobro's poetry: "In speaking of Spanish-American poetry, one cannot avoid mentioning Vicente Huidobro, poetically a third-rate talent, but at the same time a writer who has achieved wide notoriety for his literary manifestoes. . . . He gave expression to poetical theories which attracted wide attention, but his creative work was not able to maintain his reputation."

While Huidobro's work has been the subject of much debate, most reviewers concede that he was a talented writer. Merlin H. Forster, writing in *Kentucky Romance Quarterly,* detailed his impressions of Huidobro's longest and most complex poem: *Altazor, o viaje en paracaidas* (*Altazor: A Voyage in a Parachute*). Published in Madrid in 1931, the poem consists of seven cantos of varying lengths. "The image of a fall through space implied in the full title of the poem is used constantly in the development of its main theme: a fall from coherence to incoherence, from life to death, from verbal question to inarticulate wail." The poem is, Forster noted, a complex interweaving of different thematic threads. "To begin with, the entire poem might be easily taken as indeed Silva Castro and others have done, as an unstructured and overly complicated mass with no esthetic value.

... *Altazor* as a work of art rises far above that negative assessment. The poem is long, and at times overly diffuse, but its rich thematic texture and its intricate formal structure create their own unity and strength. Verbal patterning is complex and at times ostentatious, but with some few exceptions, these unusual sequences are organic to thematic or structural development." For Forster, Huidobro's poem created an emotional link between author and reader. "...I see *Altazor* in all its consciously brilliant verbosity and symphonic structure as a moving expression of the anguished artist-man coming to grips with the ultimate and insoluble problems of his existence."

Critic H.R. Hays, writing in *12 Spanish American Poets,* also found Huidobro's writings important in the development of Latin American literature. "Huidobro is active as well as a novelist and playwright. His work is extremely literary, elegant in design, and remarkable for humorous verbal legerdemain. Conservative critics disparage its value. They cannot forgive him for the picture poems, his disregard for punctuation, and his fantastic imagery. He is important, however, as a pioneer of the vanguardist movement in both French and Spanish literature and his poetry has undeniable charm."

Vicente Huidobro died of a stroke, complicated by shrapnel wounds from the war, in 1948. His work consisted of 15 volumes of poetry, six novels, two plays, five volumes of essays, and numerous articles. "The only constant element in Huidobro's complicated life [was the] change and the ferocity with which he defended the integrality of his thinking as it evolved," de Costa wrote. "He was a tireless theorist, one who not only enjoyed explaining his point of view, but endeavored to persuade everyone to think just like himself. The problem of course is that the goals and purposes of his work changed so often that even the most ardent disciple would have difficulty keeping the faith."

## SELECTED PUBLISHED WORKS:

*Altazor, o el viaje en paracaidas* (*Altazor: A Voyage in a Parachute*), Compania Iberoamericana de Publicaciones, 1931, 1981; translated by Eliot Weinberger, Graywolf, 1988.
*Relativity of Spring: Thirteen Poems,* Sand Dollar, 1976.
*The Selected Poetry of Vicente Huidobro,* New Directions, 1981.

## SOURCES:

### Books

*Contemporary Authors,* Volume 131, Detroit, Gale, 1991.
de Costa, René, *Vicente Huidobro, The Careers of a Poet,* Oxford, Claredon Press, 1984.
*12 Spanish American Poets,* edited by H.R. Hays, Boston, Beacon Press, 1943, 1972.

### Periodicals

*Kentucky Romance Quarterly,* XVII, no. 4, 1970, pp. 297–307.

—*Sketch by Kathe A. Conti*

# Jorge Icaza
## 1906-1979
### Ecuadorean writer and educator

Jorge Icaza is remembered especially for realistic and socially scathing novels that dealt with the unjust treatment of Ecuadorean Indians and *mestizos.* With his first novel, *Huasipungo,* Icaza established himself as a member of the Generation 30, a group of socially-conscious Ecuadorean writers that included José de Ia Cuadra, Demetrio Aguilera Malta, Enrique Gil Gilbert, Joaquín Gallegos Lara, and Alfredo Pareja Diezcanseco.

His debut novel was perhaps Icaza's most popular and critically acclaimed. Kessel Schwartz noted in *A New History of Spanish American Fiction,* "*Huasipungo,* which to this day has not lost its tremendous impact and whose truth has not appreciably changed, is probably the most direct indictment and most famous Spanish American novel of social justice involving the Indian ever written."

Icaza was born on July 10, 1906, in Quito, Ecuador, to José Icaza Manso, a landed farmer, and Carmen Coronel. After her husband's early death Icaza Manso's widow married a Liberal party politician. To escape persecution for their political stance, the family moved to a relative's country estate, where many of the servants where Indians.

At first Icaza aspired to a medical career. After graduating from the Instituto Nacional Mejía in 1924, he attended the Central University of Quito until his mother and stepfather died in the mid-1920s. Icaza then began to study drama at the Conservatorio Nacional. He soon joined the Compañia Dramática National, where he worked as an actor, stage manager, and playwright. With *La comedia sin nombre* and *Por el viejo* Icaza gained a reputation as a promising dramatist. In 1929 Icaza formed the theatrical troupe Compañia Dramática Marina Moncayo, featuring the famous actress Marina Moncayo, whom Icaza married in 1936. But when the troupe mounted Icaza's adaptation of *The Dictator* by French playwright Jules Romains, the Ecuadorean government banned the production, and Icaza's employers fired him.

To make a living, Icaza turned to writing. In 1933 he published a collection of short stories, *Barro de la sierra,* in which he presented the themes of social oppression that he developed throughout his oeuvre. The following year his most famous work, the novel *Huasipungo,* appeared despite its publisher's misgivings. Icaza shocked readers not only with his subject matter, but with the vulgar language he employed to tell his tale. *Huasipungo* was later translated into several languages, including Russian and Chinese.

In his survey of Latin American fiction, *Spanish American Authors of the Twentieth Century,* Angel Flores described the novel: "*Huasipungo* is a vigorous testimony of denunciation/accusation of the tragedy of the Indian people. It neither resorts to stock figures and traits nor to unusual characters; rather, its underlying thesis is that the degradation of the Indians is not a result of their innate depravity but of the conditions imposed on them by cruel masters."

Icaza's second novel, *En las calles,* was published in 1935; the book won first prize in a national contest. By 1944, Icaza had found a position with the Ecuadorean Cultural Council, where he was employed for almost two decades. He continued to write, producing four novels, including *Huairapamushcas* and *El chulla Romero y Flores,* as well as a collection of short stories called *Viejos cuentos.* In these works, Icaza sustained his indictment of the wealthy and confronted the dilemma of the middle-class mestizo searching for his own identity.

According to Manuel Corrales Pascual, writing in *Latin American Writers,* Icaza's work developed gradually: "The narrative work of Jorge Icaza, seen as a whole and in its historical milieu, resembles a pilgrimage in search of the proper invocation of theme and tone, of language and the world." Pascual maintained that while Icaza has often been viewed solely in an Indianist context, he was truly a champion of the mestizo, a person of mixed white and Indian ancestry. Mestizos comprise the majority of Ecuadoreans. In his writings, Icaza also experimented with language, retreating from literary Spanish to syntax that reflected natural speech patterns.

In 1959 Icaza became the director of the national library, where he worked until 1973, when he entered diplomatic service as ambassador to the Soviet Union, Poland, and East Germany. In the three-volume fictionalized autobiography *Atrapados,* Icaza described many of his political, cultural, and literary activities. During his later years, he lectured at universities in South America, China, the Soviet Union, and the United States. Icaza left an unfinished novel upon his death on May 16, 1979.

## SELECTED PUBLISHED WORKS:

*Barro de la sierra,* Quito, Labor, 1993.

*Huasipungo,* Quito, Talleres Gráficos Nacionales, 1935, 9th edition, 1973, translation by Bernard M. Dulsey published as *The Villagers,* Carbondale, IL, Southern Illinois University Press, 1973.

*En las calles* ("In the Streets"), Talleres Gráficos Nacionales, 1935.

*Cholos,* Quito, Editorial Sindicato de Escritores y Artistas, 1937.

*Media vida deslumbrados,* Quito, Editorial Quito, 1942.

*Huairapamushcas,* Editorial Casa de la Cultura Ecuatoriana, 1948, published as *Hijos del viento* ("Children of the Wind"), Plaza y Janés, 1973.

*El chulla Romero y Flores,* Editorial Casa de la Cultura Ecuatoriana, 1958.

*Viejos cuentos* ("Old Stories"), Editorial Casa de la Cultura Ecuatoriana, 1960.

*Obras escogidas,* edited by F. Ferrándiz Alborz, Mexico City, Aguilar, 1961.

*Atrapados,* vol. 1: *El juramento* ("The Oath"), vol. 2: *En la ficción* ("In Fiction"), vol. 3: *En la realidad* ("In Reality"), Buenos Aires, Losada, 1972.

## SOURCES:

### Books

*Contemporary Authors,* vol. 85–88, vol. 89–92, edited by Frances Carol Locher, Detroit, Gale, 1980.

*Cyclopedia of World Authors,* edited by Frank N. Magill, New York, Harper, 1958.

Flores, Angel, *Spanish American Authors of the Twentieth Century,* New York, Wilson, 1992.

*Hispanic Writers,* edited by Bryan Ryan, Detroit, Gale, 1991.

*Latin American Writers,* vol. 3, edited by Carlos A. Solé, New York, Scribners, 1989.

Schwartz, Kessel, *A New History of Spanish American Fiction,* vol. 2, Coral Gables, University of Miami, 1971.

### Periodicals

*Hispania,* 1961, pp. 99–102.

*Inter-American Quarterly,* vol. 2, 1940, pp. 37–38; November 1942, pp. 33–35, 52.

—*Sketch by J.M. Lesinski*

# Julio Iglesias
## 1943-
### Spanish singer and songwriter

Julio Iglesias is one of the most popular entertainers in the world. A tremendously successful recording artist and concert performer, the Spanish singer has enjoyed a career that dates back to the late 1960s. In a review of one of Iglesias's 1991 New York concerts, *New York Times* writer Stephen Holden observed that Iglesias "personifies, like no other pop star, the suave international playboy who is confident and worldly yet sensitive and charmingly self-effacing." He sings in six languages and has sold more than 100 million records, a feat which has earned him a Guinness Book of World Records listing and a Diamond Disc award. Winner of a Grammy Award in 1987, Iglesias has also received a Vermeil Medal from the City of Paris.

The singer was born in Madrid, Spain, on September 23, 1943, to Julio Iglesias Puga, a physician, and Maria del Rosario de la Cueva Iglesias. As a young man, Iglesias attended England's Cambridge University, where he studied law. He then joined the Real Madrid soccer team, playing goalkeeper. Swimming, cycling, and sailing, all activities that he first practiced as a young man, remain among his recreational interests.

In the mid-1960s, Iglesias was involved in a near-fatal automobile crash that left him temporarily paralyzed. Determined to regain his previous physical health, he refused to use a wheelchair and swam hours every day for physical therapy. During his extended convalescence he studied the guitar and began to write songs.

Iglesias captured national attention in 1968 when he won first prize at Spain's Benidoerm Festival for "La vida sigue igual." At the 1970 Eurovision Festival Iglesias represented his native country with "Güendoline." Two years later, he won the Eurovision Song Contest. In 1978 he signed a contract with CBS Records International.

But while the singer's career was blossoming, events in his personal life buffeted him during the 1970s and early 1980s. As *Newsweek's* Jim Miller once remarked, "Despite his comfortable origins and charmed career, Julio comes across as a man unlucky in life and love." Iglesias's 1971 marriage to Isabel Preisler—a union that produced three children Chaveli, Enrique, and Julio José—ended eight years later. In 1981 Iglesias's father was kidnapped by Basque terrorists; ultimately, he was released unharmed. In 1984 Iglesias was accused of having infringed on another writer's song. After years of legal

*Julio Iglesias*

arguments, a New York federal district court judge finally dismissed the complaint in 1991.

Reporters describe Iglesias's life as a frenetic, nomadic one: "Julio follows the sun," Holly G. Miller wrote in the *Saturday Evening Post.* The singer maintains residences in several countries, but *Time* magazine's Gerald Clarke commented that Iglesias's "real home is a Mystère-Falcon 20, which jets him from gig to gig."

### Pursued United States Market

During the 1980s, guided by CBS Records International, the William Morris Agency, the Los Angeles publicity firm of Rogers and Cowan, and his own staff, Iglesias made a concerted effort to increase his popularity in the United States. For while Iglesias had been a Miami resident since 1978 and had already become a star in America's Latin community, the broader United States market posed a greater challenge, both in terms of concert tour performances and album sales. "This country normally doesn't open the doors to any music which is not Saxon," Iglesias told *Newsweek,* "but maybe I'll be lucky." He elaborated in *Time:* "I want to make a bridge between Latin music and American music that others can cross afterward. In the music business the U.S. is tops. A No. 1 song here goes all over the world. I have taken a risk in coming here, and I have put my challenge in front of everyone."

The bid proved to be a fruitful one. Iglesias was greeted by sell-out concert crowds, huge record sales, and massive media attention. In 1984 his first album featuring English lyrics, *1100 Bel Air Place,* sold one million copies in the first five days following its release. The album included collaborations with a number of other noted recording artists, a strategy that paid significant dividends. Both "To All the Girls I've Loved Before," a duet with country singer Willie Nelson, and "All of You," a song that Iglesias sang with Diana Ross, were hit singles. *1100 Bel Air Place* also highlighted such artists as Stan Getz, The Beach Boys, and the Pointer Sisters. Subsequent record releases by Iglesias have continued this practice of collaboration with other popular English-singing performers.

### Aspects of His Appeal

After the 1994 release of Iglesias's album "Crazy," *New York Times* critic Holden noted that "Whatever Mr. Iglesias sings, he communicates variations of the same sentiment: I may be the ultimate cosmopolitan smoothie . . . but my heart is lonely unto breaking." *Newsweek*'s Miller characterized Iglesias's appeal this way: "Using every technique of the modern recording studio and his own diaphanous voice, he has taken the Mediterranean pop ballad and raised it to a spectacular new pitch of melodramatic grandeur." "What Iglesias has done, more than any other performer," Clarke commented in *Time,* "is bring back to popular music the romantic style of the '40s and '50s." *Billboard*'s Diane Patrick, reviewing an Iglesias concert in 1991, declared: "Iglesias sings well, he sings songs, in many languages, about feelings, and he has charm and grace. That is the very simple 'secret' of his popularity."

But other factors have contributed to Iglesias's success. Many of his associates over the years have cited the Spaniard's tenacity, perfectionism, and hard work, noting his long hours and thorough involvement in all aspects of his records' production.

Iglesias's multilingualism—he sings in Spanish, French, Italian, Portuguese, German, and English—is another of his distinguishing characteristics. His *Calor* was released in 1992 as a Spanish-language album with tracks recorded in several languages, tailored to appeal to audiences in different countries. Marco Bissi, a vice-president for Sony Music International, told *Billboard* that Iglesias's multilingual abilities allowed the company to market the album more effectively and added: "What's fantastic is that Julio was able to give the same emotion to a song, whether it was done in Spanish, Italian, or French. That is very difficult to do." In that same article Iglesias acknowledged that multilingual recordings are challenging. "It's so complicated to go into the studio to do an album and then to do it in different languages. There's so much doubt, and you discuss and discuss and in the end you are so tired."

Iglesias has his own thoughts about his work and style. He told the *Saturday Evening Post* that "I'm not a musician, but I have the instinct of a musician. . . . You don't need to play piano like Rubinstein to write a wonderful melody, and you don't have to know everything about music to express yourself musically. I don't. If you have both traits, maybe you are a genius. I'm not." Genius or not, Iglesias is passionate about music. "I love recording," he told Lynn Van Matre of the *Chicago Tribune*. "I wake up in the morning, I do my exercises, I have lunch and I go to the studio. The only thing exciting to me is when I am in the studio recording."

## SELECTED DISCOGRAPHY

*Como el álamo al camino,* Alhambra, 1972.
*Julio Iglesias,* Alhambra, 1972.
*Soy,* Alhambra, 1973.
*A México,* Alhambra, 1975.
*El Amor,* Alhambra, 1975.
*América,* Alhambra, 1976.
*A mis 33 años,* Alhambra, 1977.
*Emociones,* Alhambra, 1978.
*Hoy,* CBS, 1980.
*De niña a mujer,* CBS, 1981.
*El disco de oro,* CBS, 1981.
*Momentos,* CBS, 1982.
*Julio,* CBS, 1983.
*1100 Bel Air Place,* CBS, 1984.
*Libra,* 1985.
*Un hombre solo,* 1987.
*Non Stop,* 1988.
*Et l'Amour créa la Femme,* 1989.
*Raices,* 1989.
*Starry Night,* 1990.
*Calor,* Sony, 1992.
*Crazy,* 1994.

## SOURCES:

### Books

*Entre el cielo y el infierno,* Barcelona, Planeta, 1981.
Daly, Marsha, *Julio Iglesias,* New York, St. Martin's Press, 1986.

### Periodicals

*Billboard,* February 23, 1991, p. 87; July 27, 1991, p. 28; June 27, 1992, p. 17.
*Chicago Tribune,* February 26, 1984, sect. 13, pp. 22–3.
*Newsweek,* July 11, 1983, p. 69.

*New York Times,* June 13, 1991, p. C14; June 3, 1994, p. C3; June 19, 1994, sect. 2, p. 25.
*Saturday Evening Post,* December, 1985, pp. 44–7, 103, 110.
*Time,* September 10, 1984, p. 60.

—*Sketch by Erika Dreifus*

# Miguel Induráin
## 1964-
### Spanish bicycle racer

Miguel Induráin is a Basque-native Spanish bicycle racer who captured his fifth straight Tour de France win in 1995. Induráin was born in Navarre, Spain, in 1964. His name is pronounced "een-doo-rine." Induráin spent seven years of his early cycling career as a support rider for Pedro Delgado, a Spaniard and winner of the Tour de France.

Many have claimed that Induráin is a mystery. Delgado, who later became Induráin's *domestique* on the Banesto team, emphasized in *Sports Illustrated* in 1992 that "I was his roommate for years. And even I don't know him." Induráin maintained a distance from reporters during his four-year reign of the Tour de France, winning consecutively from 1991–1994, and tying the record of four consecutive wins held by France's Jacques Anquetil. If Induráin wins in 1995, he will hold the record for consecutive wins of the Tour. He shared clichéd answers with reporters, and the only glimpses into his personal life that he offered were his love of his Mercedes sedan and his "steering clear" of the Basque separatist cause.

In 1992, Induráin beat 197 other riders to win the Tour de France. Induráin proved that he could excel in the time trials of the race, a one-on-one competition between the racer and the clock. Induráin made some reporters think he was playing mind games when he claimed "I could have gone faster" after beating the current holder for a 65-kilometer time trial by three minutes. And then he proved his boast by breaking all time trial records held since 1903, averaging 52.35 kilometers an hour. He also excelled at climbing, especially for a biker who stands 6' 2" tall and weighs (as of 1994) 172 pounds.

In 1993, Induráin repeated his winning ways, easily dominating the others in the race. But before the 1993 Tour, he married his longtime sweetheart, Marisa, and moved into a new house in Pamplona, a mile from his previous lodgings in his parents' farm

*Miguel Induráin*

**SOURCES:**

*New York Times,* July 20, 1994; July 25, 1994.
*Outside,* July 1994, p. 52.
*Sports Illustrated,* August 3, 1992, pp. 64–65; August 2, 19, p. 53, August 1, 1994, pp. 39–43.
*Washington Post,* July 25, 1994, pp. C1, C44.

—*Sketch by Christopher B. Tower*

*Post* as stating, "[Induráin's] never really accomplished any great individual physical exploits, other than a lot of winning races. For that reason, I don't think he deserves to be considered among the true greats of the sport." Induráin responded "I respect all opinions but I cannot accept Guimard's. After all, what have the French racers managed to do in recent years?" Induráin told reporters he has plans to pursue records and titles before he retires, like breaking the world record for per-hour speed.

house. He has been characterized as a simple man of minimal needs by journalists, who have managed to get him to admit that he foregoes "discos, restaurants, and cafes so he can crash in his bed by 10 p.m."

On July 20, 1994, Induráin held a seven-minute, 21-second lead over second place Richard Virenque of France despite losing 35 seconds. As of July 25, he had won again by five minutes and 39 seconds over then second place Pyotr Ugrumov. This marked Induráin's best of the four Tour wins. Induráin won by a 3:36 margin 1991, by 4:35 in 1992, and 4:59 in 1993. Induráin finished the tour of 3,978 kilometers (2,474 miles) in 103 hours 38 seconds at an average speed of 38.3 kph (24 mph). He won by defeating riders much lighter than he, riders who should have been able to match or surpass his mountain speeds, but they could not. Only 117 riders out of 189 finished the 1994 Tour de France.

Induráin managed to complete his 1994 race, free of illness and exhaustion. The Spaniard was reluctant to discuss his life despite his championship. He was seen by *New York Times* reporters in 1994 as "a man of no outward flash. Sporting no earrings or gold chains, he wears only a wedding band on his right hand, European-style, and a plastic, inexpensive-looking watch." Induráin claimed to be "reserved." "I feel a need to protect my private life," he told reporters.

Despite his championship status, Induráin has received stringent criticism. Cyril Guimard, one of France's top coaches, was quoted in the *Washington*

# Pedro Infante
## 1917-1956
### Mexican actor

A Mexican superstar of the screen whose name is known throughout Mexico nearly 40 years after his death, Pedro Infante was more a distinct individual than a dramatic artist, often portraying himself in films as an open-minded, honest type. His best roles were a city laborer or a rural Mexican cowboy. He played roles that required both sentimentality and tenderness, but never surrendered his male image. Unlike other popular male actors, among them Pedro Armendariz and Jorge Negrete, Infante did not keep apart from his audience when acting but deliberately interacted with viewers, often by staring right into the camera or winking and laughing while singing. He was such a big star that screenplays were written around him.

Infante's funeral in 1956 drew thousands of people, among them popular stars of Mexican movies, and mariachi bands. Despite his death he is still a celebrity: his movies appear every week on Mexican television, his records sell well, and roughly 10,000 people showed up to honor the twenty-fifth anniversary of his death.

When he was alive, Infante received several awards for his work—the Mexican Ariele Award s in 1955 and 1956, and Best Actor at the Berlin Festival

*Pedro Infante*

in 1957 for his title role in the film *Tizoc.* Of his acting, Hedy Clark observed, in *Theatre Arts,* "We did see him on the screen and were charmed by his acting, his sentimental tenor and his dark-haired handsomeness."

Infante was born Pedro Infante Cruz, in Mazatlan, Mexico, in November or December of 1917. He quit school after the fourth grade and worked running errands and doing carpentry. In 1939 he began singing *rancheras* on Radio Station XEB in Mexico City. In 1942 he made his first film appearance as an extra.

### Gained Fame From Movie Role

In 1947 his role as the poverty stricken but noble Pepe el Toro in the Mexican box-office hit *Nosotros los pobres* (*We the Poor*) made Infante famous. Audiences liked this film so much that the director Ismael Rodriguez made a sequel to it, *Ustedes los ricos* (*You the Rich*), in 1948. In *Mexican Cinema: Reflections of a Society 1896–1980,* author Carl J. Mora called *Nosotros los pobres* "a melodrama of the urban poor" that "combined in a disconcerting way elements of musical comedy, melodrama, and stark, brutal realism" to draw on viewers emotions as they watched the misadventures of Pepe.

Infante played multiple parts in several movies. His theatrical abilities shone in films about male friendships, including *Dos tipos de cuidado* (*Two Wild and Crazy Guys*), *A toda máquina* (*Full Speed Ahead*),

and *¿Qué te ha dado esa mujer?* (*What Did That Woman Give You?*). In the film, *Dos tipos,* Infante underscored the importance of male friendships, comparing betrayal by a woman and a man. "When a woman betrays us, well, we forgive her—because finally she's a woman. But, when we're betrayed by the man we think is our best friend—ay, Chihuahua—that really hurts." In another movie, *Dicen que soy mujeriego,* (*They Say I'm a Womanizer*)—the title of which suggests a macho attitude toward women and refers to the actor's real-life behavior—Infante implied it was more masculine to suffer than to be the cause of someone else's suffering.

In his personal life Infante was romantically involved with at least three women. He wed María Luisa León (whom he credited with having made him an actor) but later divorced her, though their divorce was not legally acknowledged in the courts in Mexico. He had two children with Lupita Torrentera and lived with Irma Dorantes.

When he was not acting, Infante was a commercial pilot—believing God had made him so. Fellow pilots described him as "crazy," particularly since he had been involved in several near-fatal crashes. He finally died in a crash in Mérida on April 15, 1956. He had appeared in more than 50 films during his career.

### SELECTED VIDEOGRAPHY

*La feria de las flores,* 1942.
*Jesusita en Chihuahua,* 1942.
*La rázon de la culpa,* 1942.
*Arriba las mujeres,* 1943.
*Cuando habla el corazón,* 1943.
*El ametralladora,* 1943.
*Mexicanos al grito de guerra,* 1943.
*Viva mi desgracia,* 1943.
*Escándalo de estrellas,* 1944.
*Cuandolloran los valientes,* 1945.
*Si me han de matar manaña,* 1946.
*Los tres Garcia,* 1946.
*Vuelen los Garcia,* 1946.
*La barca de oro,* 1947.
*Soy charro de Rancho Grande,* 1947.
*Nosotros los pobres,* 1947.
*Cartas marcadas,* 1947.
*Los tres huastecos,* 1948.
*Angelitos negros,* 1948.
*Ustedes los ricos,* 1948.
*Dicen que soy mujeriego,* 1948.
*El seminarista,* 1949.
*La mujer que yo perdí,* 1949.
*La oveja negra,* 1949.
*No desearás la mujer de tu hijo,* 1949.
*Sobre las olas,* 1950.
*También de dolor se canta,* 1950.
*Islas Marias,* 1950.
*El gavilán pollero,* 1950.

*Las mujers de mi general,* 1950.
*Necesito dinero,* 1951.
*A toda máquina,* 1951.
*Qué te ha dado esa mujer?,* 1951.
*Ahi viene Martin Corona,* 1951.
*El enarmorado,* 1951.
*Un rincón cerca del cielo,* 1952.
*Ahora soy rico,* 1952.
*Por ellas aunque mal paguen,* 1952.
*Los hijos de Maria Morales,* 1952.
*Dos tipos de cuidado,* 1952.
*Ansiedad,* 1952.
*Pepe El Toro,* 1952.
*Reportaje,* 1953.
*Guitana tenias que ser,* 1953.
*Cuidado con el ser,* 1954.
*Cuidado con el amor,* 1954.
*El mil amores,* 1954.
*Escuela de vagabundos,* 1954.
*La vida no vale nada,* 1954.
*Pueblo, canto, y esperanza,* 1954.
*Los Gavilanes,* 1954.
*Escuela de música,* 1955.
*La tercera palabra,* 1955.
*El inocente,* 1955.
*Pablo y Carolina,* 1955.
*Tizoc,* 1956.
*Escuela de rateros,* 1956.

## SOURCES:

### Books

Blanco, Jorge Ayala, *La aventura del cine mexicano,* Mexico, 1979.
Blanco, Jorge Ayala, *La busqueda del cine mexicano,* Mexico City, 1986.
Blanco, Jorge Ayala, *La condicion del cine mexicano,* Mexico City, 1986.
*International Dictionary of Films and Filmmakers,* Volume 3: *Actors and Actresses,* edited by Nicolas Thomas, Detroit, St. James Press, 1992.
Mora, Carl J., *Mexican Cinema: Reflections of a Society 1896–1980,* Berkeley, University of California Press, 1982.
Riera, Emilio Garcia, *Historia documental del cine mexicano,* Vols. 2–6, Mexico, 1970–74.

### Periodicals

*Dicine,* October 1987.
*El universal,* July 29, 1953.
*Theatre Arts,* May 1956, pp. 15–16.

*—Sketch by Alison Carb Sussman*

# Amparo Iturbi
## 1899-1969
### Spanish concert pianist

The younger sister of one of the world's most famous, brilliant, and flamboyant pianists, Amparo Iturbi had a hard act to follow most of her life. A polished, well-known, and gifted pianist in her own right, Iturbi nevertheless spent most of her musical career in the shadow of her celebrated brother, José. Despite world tours, hundreds of concerts, record albums, widespread critical and popular acclaim, and performances on radio, in movies and on television, little information exists on Iturbi in comparison to José. Although they were extremely close, and José considered her one of the top women musicians in the world, he was fond of repeating one of his favorite quips, quoted in *Time:* "I am my sister's worst enemy."

Iturbi's life and career were inexorably entwined with her brother's from her birth in Valencia, Spain, on March 12, 1899. Her mother was Maria Theresa Baguena Iturbi and her father was a pianomaker and tuner. By the time she was three, she had developed an unusual musical talent for singing, but seven-year-old José's prowess at the piano was already well established throughout the neighborhood. When she was six, José was already earning a living as an accompanist at a singing academy. For Iturbi, the piano soon won out over her dreams to become an opera singer, and she studied diligently under her first teacher, Maria Jordan, and later, José. Although she occasionally bristled in later life when being referred to as her brother's pupil, she recalled idolizing José in her youth. In 1937, she told a reporter for the *New York Times,* "When we were small I used to follow him around everywhere. Everything he did, I did. That is why I play with the same technique he uses. My hands are like his."

When José left for the Paris Conservatory at 15, Iturbi wanted to follow him, but her brother rejected the idea. Many years later, he told *Time* the reason for his refusal: "It's all work. One gets nothing but exhaustion. And [for her] it's not necessary." At 14, Iturbi gave her first piano recital at the Valencia Conservatory of Music, then another in Barcelona under the tutelage of Eduardo Chavarri. In the audience was the renown Spanish composer, Enrique Granados, who so delighted in her performance that he invited her to play for his pupils at his Academia Granados. Following the recital, Granados performed some of his own compositions for the young girl. At the peak of her career, Iturbi was considered one of the foremost interpreters of Granados's music (particularly his difficult *Goyescas*), an accomplishment some critics believe was inspired by this early experience. A 1957 review in the *New York Times* was typical of those received for her performance of the Granados piece: "It took real courage to present in its entirety so demanding a suite, and the results could be greeted with admiration."

## Makes Concert Debut in Paris

At 18, Iturbi arrived in Paris and gave her first concert six years later in 1924. The performance met with such success that she was soon in demand all over Europe, giving solo concerts in France, Holland, Belgium, Italy, England, and Spain. She lived in Paris until 1937, when she and her mother moved to the United States. Reunited with her brother, who achieved celebrity as the most famous Spanish pianist during the period immediately prior to World War II, Iturbi was enthusiastically received in the United States. She made her New York debut at Lewisohn Stadium on July 7, 1937, appearing with José before an audience of 12,000. They performed 18th-century Austrian composer Wolfgang Amadeus Mozart's concerto for two pianos in E flat, a work that Mozart allegedly wrote for himself and his sister. The evening, according to many commentators, was an unqualified success. Iturbi performed two encores for the cheering crowd, and critic Noel Straus wrote in the *New York Times:* "Her attainments so closely rival [José's] that there was little to choose between them. Her tone, feeling for phrase and nuance, and even her approach to her work were strikingly akin to those of her brother."

Iturbi did not fare as well in her December 24 concert with the Philharmonic Orchestra that same year. Called in as a last-minute replacement for ailing Brazilian pianist Guiomar Novaes, Iturbi attempted the solo part in 19th-century German composer Ludwig van Beethoven's Fourth Piano Concerto. Recalling her triumphant debut at Lewisohn, Straus wrote in the *New York Times:* "[The musical selections at her debut] were more congenial to her talents than the Beethoven concerto, which made far greater demands on her powers as interpreter. Possibly no woman should ever attempt this particular creation of the Bonn master, for in spite of its restrained character, it is completely masculine in essence."

Occasional mixed reviews aside—many of them contrasting her more delicate style with that of her more dazzling brother—Iturbi was immensely popular during a performing career that spanned four decades. She played in nearly every state in the union, with major orchestras under the baton of John Barbirolli, Otto Klemperer, Ignace Strasfogel, Eugene Ormandie, Alexander Smallens, Frederic Stock, and many others. During World War II, she played hundreds of concerts for the United States Army and Navy, and in 1944 alone she performed 304 concerts

in seven months, covering 57,000 miles over the African front. Although she told *Time* in 1948 that concertizing "is a crazy life," she had lined up a 30-concert tour for that fall. In one season she crossed and recrossed the Atlantic three times for concert tours in England and Europe. Various critics praised her impeccable technique and musical phrasing. After one solo concert in New York in 1944, a writer for the *New York Times* stated that Iturbi "again showed her remarkable talent and extraordinary similarity to her brother as an artist. . . . Miss Iturbi's technique is comprehensive and sure, notable for its fleetness, distinctness and ease. She received an ovation at the end of the Fantasia and played three encores . . . with dash and brilliance."

## Performs with Brother José Iturbi

Audiences turned out in droves to see the Iturbis play as a team. Of their program at Carnegie Hall in 1938, a commentator for the *New York Times* said, "Miss Iturbi's methods of applying color and nuance, her attacks and her tone resembled those of her brother, and the result was balance and cohesiveness of the two instruments. Mr. Iturbi was perhaps the dominant personality in the concerted works, but his sister held up her share with poise and assurance." Some commentators believe that such reviews appropriately described the siblings' offstage relationship as well. Iturbi—poised, gracious, and somewhat shy—was a distinct counterpoint to the more outspoken, charming José who loved the limelight. In her autobiography *September Child,* Jean Dalrymple—who later became the duo's personal manager and publicist—described Iturbi as "slim and beautiful, like a Spanish painting." José, in addition to receiving more press for his performing abilities, often made headlines for his opinions regarding women's unsuitability for musical careers, describing the feminine gender in the *New York Times* as "temperamentally limited, making it impossible for them to attain the same standards as male musicians." Despite such statements, Iturbi never publicly refuted her brother.

In 1940 Iturbi's life was shaken with the death of her mother. More tragedy followed with the suicide of her niece Maria, José's only child, in 1946. The incident occurred after years of hearings in which José petitioned the court to grant him full custody of his two granddaughters. According to a report in the *New York Times,* he asserted that his daughter was "not the proper person" to have charge of the children. Following this saga, 28-year-old Maria shot herself in her father's Beverly Hills. Iturbi and her daughter Amparin had also moved to the city and lived nearby. In the same year, however, Iturbi began to share briefly in her brother's more extensive movie career, appearing in the Metro-Goldwyn-Mayer film, *Holiday in Mexico.* She later had a role in MGM's *That Midnight Kiss* in 1949. Iturbi and José also recorded numerous albums together for RCA Victor and Angel Records, although she described the recording process in *Time* as "the ultimate torture of our century."

In later years, Iturbi turned to teaching full-time. Dalrymple, in an interview with Julie Catalano, said that Iturbi "didn't care about wandering around and going places to make a small amount of money. She preferred to stay in Beverly Hills where she had a beautiful home and lots of very fine pupils." Among her students was pianist, composer, and teacher Bruce Sutherland. Iturbi's final concert was in Los Angeles on October 2, 1968. She made her last concert appearance in New York in November of that year. On Christmas Day, however, she was hospitalized at Cedars of Lebanon Hospital in Los Angeles with a brain tumor. She died in her home on April 22, 1969, at age 70. One of her last visitors was Spanish guitarist **Andres Segovia**, who played at her bedside. On November 14, 1971, her brother performed a memorial concert in her honor in Los Angeles. José died of a heart attack at age 84 on June 29, 1980. In 1986, Marion Seabury, José's longtime secretary, established the Iturbi Foundation in Beverly Hills, a nonprofit organization which helps young professionals in all artistic fields.

## SOURCES:

### Books

Dalrymple, Jean, *September Child,* Dodd, 1963.
O'Connell, Charles, *The Other Side of the Record,* Knopf, 1947.

### Periodicals

*Newsweek,* May 5, 1969, p. 78.
*New York Times,* January 23, 1936, p. 25; May 2, 1937, section XI, p. 10; July 8, 1937, p. 21; September 19, 1937, section XI, p. 12; December 24, 1937, p. 21; February 6, 1938, section X, p. 7; February 8, 1938, p. 16; May 8, 1939, p. 20; January 3, 1940, p. 21; April 18, 1946, p. 29; July 24, 1944, p. 18; April 23, 1969, p. 47; June 29, 1980, p. 20.
*Time,* July 5, 1948, p. 46; May 2, 1969, p. 80.

### Other

Dalrymple, Jean, interview with Julie Catalano, August 18, 1992.
Seabury, Marion, correspondence with Julie Catalano, September 18, 1992.

—*Sketch by Julie Catalano*

# Agustín de Iturbide
## 1783-1824
**Mexican politician**

Iturbide was proclaimed the Emperor of Mexico in 1822 following his country's declaration of independence in 1821. Although Iturbide gained Mexico her independence he is not greatly admired, Mexico preferring to honor the revolutionaries Hidalgo, Morelos and Guerrero. Jan Bezant explained in *A Concise History of Mexico,* "First he fought against his fellow Creoles; then he betrayed Spain. Turncoats and renegades have never been loved by the people." Historian William Spence Robertson, writing in *Rise of the Spanish-American Republics,* asserted that as a military officer he "won an unsurpassed reputation for cruelty and bravery."

Agustín Cosme Damian Iturbide, of noble descent, was born to José Joaquin de Iturbide, a prosperous landowner, and María Joseta Arámburu, in the city of Valladolid, in Michoacá, Mexico, on September 27, 1783. Iturbide was not a diligent student and acquired only a rudimentary education from the Valladolid seminary; his papers show evidence of illiteracy. At an early age, Iturbide demonstrated an interest in military affairs. Records at Simancas establish that he joined the infantry regiment of Valladolid on October 16, 1797. His appointment was confirmed by royal order on July 6, 1798. As a young man, Iturbide spent much of his time assisting his father with the management of the family's haciendas. In 1805 he married María Huarte.

When the revolution for independence, led by Miguel Hidalgo y Costilla, began in 1810, Iturbide traveled to Mexico City, denouncing the insurgents and joining—as an officer—with the royal Spanish troops. He gained distinction under Colonel Trujillo at the Battle of Las Cruces. In June, 1812, he captured the insurgent leader Albino García. He earned a notorious reputation, particularly for his execution of insurgent priests without a trial. By September, 1815, Viceroy Calleja rewarded Colonel Iturbide for his achievements by appointing him commander of a military district composed of Guanajuanto and Michoacàn. However, because of financial improprieties and the discontent that Iturbide's leadership generated, Calleja was forced to recall him in April, 1816, and he retired to his haciendas.

In November, 1820, Iturbide was reinstated and charged with suppressing the remaining followers of independence. The reasons for his appointment are unclear; Bezant suggested that he may have been considered the best royalist officer available. However, Iturbide had transferred his loyalty to the

*Agustín de Iturbide*

movement of independence. Without informing the viceroy, Iturbide entered into negotiations with the insurgent leader, Vincente Guerrero, and together they conceived the Plan of Iguala on February 24, 1821. The Plan of Iguala contained a declaration of independence from Spain under a monarchy. This plan enjoyed widespread Mexican support, but was condemned by Viceroy Apodaca, who declared Iturbide an outlaw. In August the last Spanish viceroy, Juan O'Donojú, alarmed at the Iturbidista revolution, held discussions with Iturbide in Córdoba. Iturbide demanded that Mexico be recognized as a sovereign and independent nation and O'Donojú acquiesced. On September 27, 1821, under the Treaty of Córdoba, Mexican independence was secured.

In Mexico Iturbide was hailed as the father of his country. In Spain the government declared that O'Donojú had not been authorized to grant Mexican independence. Nevertheless, on May 18 1822, Iturbide was proclaimed Emperor Agustín I, which was ratified by congress on May 20. Iturbide's eldest son, Agustín, was named his successor and entitled Prince Imperial. On July 22, Iiturbide was ostentatiously crowned emperor in a cathedral in Mexico City.

Iturbide became increasingly disliked; he was extravagant and despotic and his autocratic rule was resisted. A rebellion led by Antonio López de Santa Anna forced him to abdicate on March 19, 1823. On May 11 Iturbide and his family set sail for Italy, where they remained for several months. In December they traveled to London where Iturbide received the misguided advice to return to Mexico. Unaware that on April 28, 1824 congress had denounced him a traitor, he set off for Mexico on May 11 accompanied by his family. According to William Spence Robertson in *The Rise of the Spanish-American Republics,* he declared that "my sole object is to contribute by my voice and by my pen to the support of the liberty and independence of Mexico."

His ship arrived on July 12, 1824, near Soto la Marina in Tamaulipas. He was detained and executed in Padilla on July 19, 1824. His last words, as reported in the *Times* (London), November 27, 1824 were, "Mexicans, at the very moment of dying I recommend to you to love your country and to observe our holy religion—these will conduct you to glory. . . . I die with honor, and not as a traitor. That stain will not rest upon my sons and their descendants. I am no traitor. Be subordinate and obedient to your chiefs in executing what they and God may command. I do not say this in vanity for I am far from being vain. I pardon all my enemies with all my heart."

## SOURCES:

### Books

Bazant, Jan, *A Consise History of Mexico: From Hidalgo to Cárdenas 1805–1940,* London, Cambridge University Press, 1977.

*Biographical Dictionary of Latin American and Caribbean Political Leaders,* edited by Robert V. Alexander, Westport, Connecticut, Greenwood Press, 1988.

*Encyclopedia of Latin America,* edited by Helen Delpar, New York, McGraw-Hill, 1974.

Robertson, William Spence, *Rise of the Spanish-American Republics,* New York and London, D. Appleton and Company, 1921.

### Periodicals

*Times* (London), November 27, 1824, p. 2.

—*Sketch by Amanda Beresford*

# Juan Ramón Jiménez
## 1881-1958
**Spanish poet**

Juan Ramón Jiménez, a prolific poet who associated with some of the most renowned artists of his time, did most of his writing in an era of Spanish self-doubt. He gained an enviable international reputation over the years, and was awarded the Nobel Prize for Literature in 1957. Credited by Critic Paul Olson as the poet responsible for "the modern renaissance of the Spanish lyric," Jiménez has come to be regarded as one of the finest of Spain's literary figures.

### Andalusian Childhood

Born in Moguer in the province of Huelva on December 23, 1881, Jiménez grew up in traditional Andalusian surroundings. A rural and hilly region, Moguer attracted Jiménez's father, Victor Jiménez y Jiménez, from northern Spain with the possibility of agricultural prosperity. A wine merchant, the elder Jiménez provided a comfortable life for his four children, of whom Juan Ramon was the youngest. Jiménez's mother, Purifacacion Mantecon y Lopez Parejo, spent her whole life in Andalusia. From the poet's various writings, critic Donald Fogelquist surmised that "she was a very good mother, although probably more indulgent toward her youngest child than was beneficial for him."

The rural comfort of Jiménez's youth provided him with opportunities to appreciate nature in a way that perhaps contributed to his sensibilities as a poet, although he would later express dissatisfaction at the lack of cultural opportunities in his hometown. He left Moguer after about four years of elementary school to attend Jesuit school elsewhere in the region. Though he felt constrained by the discipline of the religious school, he did well in his studies. Jiménez left to study painting in Seville in 1897, but this period also marked his development into an avid student of poetry. A frequent reader of the Romantic poets, especially Becquer and Rosalia de Castro, Jiménez eventually gave up painting in favor of writing. He briefly studied law, but his lack of interest in the coursework caused him to fail one of his first classes. He returned to Moguer and continued to write despite a bout of ill health.

*Juan Ramón Jiménez*

In 1898 Spain lost wars for its colonies in Cuba, Puerto Rico, and the Phillipines. The Spanish Empire had truly ended, but while some mourned the loss of Spain's former glory, others saw an opportunity in the turn of events. In June 1898, a new magazine appeared in Madrid called *Vida Nueva* (*New Life*). It spoke for many young Spaniards who felt that Spain needed to re-examine its old ways of doing things. Fond of the philosophy the publication espoused, Jiménez submitted some poetry to its editors. The magazine's founders, Francisco Villaespesa and **Ruben Dario**, read Jiménez's poetry and invited him to join them in Madrid. Jiménez set out for the city in 1900.

Although his first stay in Madrid lasted only three months, Jiménez befriended some of the most significant names in Spanish letters of the twentieth century, including Salvador Rueda and **Ramon del Valle-Inclan**, as well as Villaespesa and Dario. He also published two volumes of poetry, *Almas de violeta* and *Ninfeas,* which received modest critical praise.

Shortly after Jiménez's return to Moguer, his father died of a sudden illness. Jiménez had been very close to his father; his death upset him terribly. He developed a fear of his own death and in 1901 had to go to a French sanatorium to recover. Jiménez filled his days with reading during this time of convalescence, and his condition gradually improved. He also wrote *Rimas* while under a doctor's care. Though it exhibited some of the sentimentality of his earlier works, Fogelquist noted that "some of the verbiage and superficiality of the earlier poems was lost."

Jiménez left France and returned to Madrid, where he was supervised by Doctor Simarra. In 1903 he moved to the doctor's house, where he lived for two more years, publishing two more books and a literary review called *Helios*. During this time he befriended Antonio Machado and Manuel Machado, both well-known writers.

In 1905 Jiménez returned to Moguer, where he lived for seven years, devoting most of his time to writing poetry. Nine new volumes emerged from his relative isolation. His *Baladas de primavera* reflected his poetic eye for the natural settings of his hometown; they celebrated nature in a way that contrasted with the elegies that followed several years later. In those volumes, the poet detailed his dissatisfaction with erotic love and made harsh criticisms of conventional social patterns.

In 1910 Jiménez refused an offer of membership to the Royal Spanish Academy, the highest honor given by Spain to literary figures. Although his celebrity as a poet had grown steadily since 1900, Jiménez remained in isolation. Melancholy themes continued to pervade much of his work. He wrote *La soledad sonora* (*The Sonorous Solitude*) and *Poemas magicos y dolientes* (*Magic and Sorrowful Poems*) along with two other volumes before going back to Madrid in 1912.

### Increasing Celebrity

Situated at the very heart of Spanish letters and intellectualism, the Residencia de Estudiantes attracted students, teachers, and others to its halls to live. This center of philosophical discussion, cultural events, and scholarly publications of high quality enticed Jiménez back to the capital. There he often met with leading Spanish thinkers such as philosopher Miguel de Unamuno y Jugo. He also became acquainted with Zenobia Aymar after his return to Madrid. Aymar had an American grandfather and had gotten much of her education in the United States. Jiménez married her in New York City in 1916. Later that year he published *Diario de un poeta recien casado* (*Diary of a Newly Married Poet*).

The publication in 1914 of Jiménez's extraordinary prose work *Platero y yo* (*Platero and I*) brought him remarkable fame. He returned from his wedding trip in the United States to settle down with his new wife in Madrid. For the next 20 years, Jiménez continued to write. He published four new volumes of poetry and many prose pieces of various lengths. He grew increasingly outspoken in his political support for the Spanish Republic, which had been declared in the late 1920s. In 1936 he began to compile *Cancion*, a volume of his complete works.

The Spanish Civil War interrupted the project. Jiménez accepted a position as a cultural attache to Washington, D.C., representing the Spanish Republic in the early stages of the fighting. The government of Manual Azana collapsed about one month later, a development that prompted Jiménez to take his wife and live in Puerto Rico. His friendship with Dario had already given him some knowledge and interest in the western hemisphere, but Jiménez could not have known in 1936 that he would spend the rest of his life there.

Among Spanish-American writers and scholars Jiménez enjoyed almost unrivalled prestige. Travelling from Puerto Rico to Cuba, Jiménez spoke to eager admirers. He also wrote widely in prose and verse. According to Fogelquist, "there was probably not a single Spanish-American periodical or newspaper of consequence . . . which did not publish poems, aphorisms, essays, letters by Jiménez." Fogelquist noted that this period was also marked by a "surge of enthusiasm and creativity" among young Cuban writers who were "stimulated by the presence of Juan Ramon Jiménez."

Jiménez traveled to the United States again in 1939. Though relatively obscure in many areas of America, he lectured at the University of Miami and continued to write. His *Romances de Coral Gables* was published at this time. In 1942 he moved to Washington, D.C., and worked for the State Department as a coordinator of a program that broadcasted materials in support of the Allied war effort to Latin America. The poet also found himself increasingly comfortable in American society, and he established contacts with writers and thinkers in much the same manner that he had in Madrid. He sometimes met with Ezra Pound, and he often gave Spanish lessons to U.S. vice president Henry Wallace.

Jiménez continued to write, though less prolifically. In 1951, he toured Argentina and Uruguay, giving lectures on poetry. As bouts of bad health increased in frequency and seriousness, Jiménez moved to the warmer climate of Puerto Rico, where he lectured at the university in San Juan. In 1956 the Nobel Prize Committee in Stockholm informed Jiménez that he would be receiving the Nobel Prize for literature. Only two days later, his wife Zenobia died of cancer. Fogelquist commented in his study of the poet that without Zenobia "life [for Jiménez] . . . was empty and purposeless." After publication of his *Tercera antologia poetica* (*Third Poetic Anthology*) in

1957, Jiménez's health worsened again. He died in 1958 and was buried next to Zenobia in Moguer.

## SELECTED PUBLISHED WORKS:

### Published in Madrid unless otherwise noted

*Almas de violeta,* 1900.
*Ninfeas,* 1900.
*Rimas,* 1902, reprinted, Tauraus, 1981.
*Arias tristes,* 1903, reprinted, Tauraus, 1981.
*Jardines lejanos,* 1904, reprinted, Tauraus, 1982.
*Jardines galantes,* 1904.
*Jardines misticos,* 1904.
*Jardines dolientes,* 1904.
*Pastorales,* 1911, reprinted, Tauraus, 1982.
*Olvidanzas I: Las hojas verdes 1906,* 1909, reprinted, Aguilar, 1968.
*Elegias puras,* 1908, reprinted, Losada, 1964.
*Elegias intermedias,* 1909.
*Elegais lamentables,* 1910.
*Baladas de primavera,* 1910.
*Poemas magicos y dolientes,* 1911, reprinted, Losada, 1965.
*Melancolia,* 1912, reprinted, Taurus, 1981.
*Laberinto,* 1913, reprinted, Taurus, 1982..
*Platero y yo,* 1914, reprinted as *Platero y you, elgía andaluza,* Losada, 1940, translation by William and Mary Roberts published as *Platero and I: An Andalusian Elegy,* P.C. Duchenes, 1956, reprinted, Paragon House, 1986.
*Sonetos espirituales,* Calleja, 1917, reprinted, Taurus, 1982.
*Diario de un poeta recien casado,* 1916, reprinted, Taurus, 1982, published as *Diario de poeta y mar,* Aguado, 1955, 3rd edition, Losada, 1972.
*Poesias escogidas,* Hispanic Society of America, 1917.
*Eternidades,* 1918, new edition, Taurus, 1982.
*Piedra y cielo,* 1919, reprinted, Taurus, 1982.
*Segunda antologia poetica,* [Madrid-Barcelona], 1922, published as *Segunda antología poética 1898–1918,* Espasa-Calpe, 1956, reprinted, 1976.
*Belleza,* 1923, reprinted, Taurus, 1981.
*Unidad,* 1925.
*Presente,* 1933.
*Cancion,* 1936.
*Espanoles de tres mundos,* 1942.
*Voces de mi copla,* Editorial Sylo, 1945, reprinted, Molinas de Agua, c. 1980.
*La estacion total,* [Buenos Aires], 1946.
*Romances de Coral Gables,* Editorial Stylo, 1948, reprinted as *La Florida en Juan Ramón Jiménez,* edited by Ana Rosa Nuñez, 1968.
*Diario de poeta y mar,* 1948.
*Animal de fondo,* [Buenos Aires], 1949.

*Tercera antologia poetica,* Editorial Biblioteca Nueva, 1957, reprinted, 1971.
*Libros de poesia,* Aguilar, 1957.
*Cartas,* 1962.

## SOURCES:

Fogelquist, Donald F., *Juan Ramón Jiménez,* Boston, Twayne, 1976.
Olson, Paul R., *Circle of Paradox: Time and Essence in the Poetry of Juan Ramon Jiménez,* Baltimore, Johns Hopkins Press, 1967.

*—Sketch by James McCarthy*

# Juan Carlos
## 1938-
### Spanish monarch

Juan Carlos I ascended the Spanish throne in 1975, following the death of the dictator **Francisco Franco.** The king has played a fundamental and definitive role in guiding Spain away from an authoritarian regime to a democratic constitutional monarchy. Because of this peaceful transition to democratic stability and "his own personal qualities," noted the *Times* in 1986, "Juan Carlos has achieved a wide popular following, so that the Socialists, who form the present government, and even the Communists, two parties which were long hostile to the monarchy, have fully accepted him as King."

Juan Carlos has described himself as the devoted servant of the Spanish people. He has greater powers than most European royalty, and is theoretically able to choose the country's prime minister, subject to the approval of the Spanish Parliament. Although he provides counsel if requested, he generally does not intervene in Spain's political affairs. The one exception to this stance was displayed during an attempted military coup in 1981. Juan Carlos's conduct during that episode transformed him from an inconsequential figure in the national consciousness to one of significant power and popularity.

Juan Carlos Alfonso Victor María de Borbón y Borbón was born in Rome, Italy, on January 5, 1938, to Juan de Borbón y Battenberg, the Count of Barcelona, and Maria de las Mercedes de Borbón y Orleans, the exiled heirs to the Spanish throne. Spain had been proclaimed a republic in 1931 and Juan Carlos's grandfather, Alfonso de Borbon y Habsbur-

*Juan Carlos I*

completed his education at Madrid University in 1960 and 1961, studying law, political science, and philosophy.

Franco officially designated Juan Carlos as his successor in 1969. On July 22, 1969, Juan Carlos swore an oath of allegiance to Franco and the Movimiento Nacional. He gained a limited amount of practical political experience serving in various ministries, although most of his assignments were ceremonial. He maintained a degree of silence and discretion regarding his ideological stance. As *Newsweek* noted in 1975, "Juan Carlos's discretion makes it difficult to know his precise positions on political issues. Right-wingers suspect he is too liberal; his father complains that he 'thinks like a Fascist.'" Others dismissed him as the *idiota perdido* ("lost fool"). *Time* commented that his life, it seemed, "consisted of cutting ribbons, reviewing parades and hovering discreetly in the background at state functions." During Franco's last years, however, Juan Carlos covertly contacted a number of intellectuals, journalists, and left-wing politicians, some of whom were smuggled into his private residence at the Zarzuela Palace. Juan Carlos would soon confound all his critics.

## Overseeing Spain's Peaceful Transition to Democracy

Juan Carlos assumed the Spanish throne on November 22, 1975, succeeding Franco at his death. He was unsure if the Spanish people would accept him; Spain was a country devoid of any royal sentiment. He inherited a position as absolute ruler in an authoritarian regime that had been occupied by the same dictator for 36 years. At his investiture speech he pronounced that a "new phase in Spanish history begins, which we must undertake together in peace, hard work and prosperity," according to the *Times*. "the institution which I personify unites all Spaniards and I invite you now to serve Spain." His address to the nation alluded to future democratization and proclaimed that a "free and modern society requires the participation of all in the decision-making process," noted the *New York Times*.

Initial democratic changes were circumscribed by the Francoist constitution, however, and Juan Carlos did not wish to alienate the extreme right. At first he made restrained political modifications, appointing Adolfo Suárez, a former general secretary of the Movimiento Nacional, as prime minister in 1976. Suárez, though, shared the king's democratic principles and introduced sweeping reforms, commencing with the Law on Political Reform. In 1977 outlawed political parties were legalized. The right to strike was recognized, trade unions were legalized, and the Movimiento Nacional was abolished. In June 1977 the first free democratic elections were held since 1936. Believing that the survival of the Spanish crown

go-Lorena, led the royal family into exile. He abdicated in 1941 in favor of his son, Juan de Borbón y Battenberg. The Count of Barcelona did not renounce his claim to the Spanish throne and formally recognized his son, Juan Carlos, as king until 1977.

In 1942 the Bourbon family moved to Lausanne, Switzerland. In 1946 they relocated in Estoril, Portugal, to be closer to their homeland. In March 1947 Franco declared Spain a monarchy under the Law of Succession; Franco would choose his own monarchical successor. He told the Count of Barcelona that for the restoration of the Bourbon monarchy to occur, Juan Carlos would have to be educated in Spain. The dictator hoped to inculcate his own ideology on the young man. Juan Carlos thus visited Spain for the first time in November 1948.

Juan Carlos was educated privately in Madrid and San Sebastián, surrounded by an elite group of students. He passed his school examinations, the *bachillerato,* in 1954. At the insistence of Franco, Juan Carlos studied at the top military academies belonging to the three branches of the armed forces, a course of study of which his father disapproved. In 1955 he enrolled at the General Military Academy in Saragossa. He then attended the Naval Military School at Marín in 1957 before moving on in 1958 to the General Academy of the Air Force at San Javier. At the three military establishments he earned the respect and knowledge essential to his future position as commander-in-chief of Spain's armed forces. He lay as a constitutional monarchy, the constitution was redrawn in 1978 and endorsed in a referendum of universal suffrage on December 6 of that year.

### Juan Carlos Defies Military

The defining moment of Juan Carlos's tenure as king took place on February 23, 1981, the day he saved Spain's fragile democracy from a coup d'etat. Commented Richard Wigg in The *Times:* "King Juan Carlos's conduct during those twenty hours, forged an awareness among millions of ordinary Spaniards that this Bourbon monarch had irrevocably tied the survival of his throne to the survival of Spanish democracy."

The attempted coup began when the forces of a group of senior right-wing generals and the Civil Guard, led by Lieutenant-Colonel Antonio Tejero Molina, stormed the parliamentary chamber, held leading politicians hostage, and imposed martial law. Juan Carlos personally contacted leading military figures on the telephone and declared his opposition to the coup. He appeared on national television and told the conspirators that "action against a constitutional government . . . would be regarded by the king as a direct attack upon the crown," according to José Luis de Vilallonga in *The King: A Life of King Carlos of Spain.* The coup failed and democracy prevailed as a direct result of Juan Carlos's intervention; many Spaniards felt that he had finally become king in his own right. "'After that, the King is god,' says a leading Spanish magazine publisher," according to The *Times.*

### A Modern Monarch

*Newsweek* reported that Juan Carlos once confided to a close friend "If . . . I become King, I'll be the best king anyone has ever seen." Most observers concur that he has set himself above ideologies and partisan politics. As he told José Luis de Vilallonga, he listens to "everyone: the Left, the Right, the unions, the employers, the communists." He believes that as a modern monarch he should not interfere with people's lives. *Time* noted that "Juan Carlos is a man of few pretensions, most comfortable outside the formal confines of his office." Such preferences set him aside from some other European royal families who surround themselves with protocol. He has no formal court in Madrid and has distanced himself from the old aristocracy of Spain. On ascending the throne he chose to stay at Zarzuela; he does not live in a magnificent, opulent palace. He acknowledges the importance of maintaining ties within the community. He often meets with old with friends from university and holds as many as a hundred audiences a week.

In his ambassadorial role Juan Carlos attends numerous international functions. He regards his royal status as an important factor in his country's relationship with many foreign powers, particularly the Arabian countries. He has encouraged special relations with Latin America, emphasizing cultural similarities and the unifying bond of the Spanish language. Although he is not an intellectual, his interest in innovations, the academic world, and democracy have been acknowledged. A number of honorary doctorates have been conferred upon him from prestigious academic institutions, including Harvard, Oxford, Cambridge, and Bologna.

"If I wasn't King, I feel sure I would be a sailor," Juan Carlos told José Luis de Vilallonga in an interview for *The King;* he is a passionate yachtsman and avid sportsman. Other pastimes include skiing, photography, and reading science fiction. Juan Carlos was married to Sofia de Grecia de y Hannover on May 14, 1962. The Queen, like her husband, enjoys sailing; she was a reserve member of the Greek sailing team in the 1960 Olympics. They have three children, Elena, Christina, and Felipe, the Prince of Asturias. Felipe, as the male heir, will succeed his father to the Spanish throne. His daughter Elena was married on March 18, 1995, in Seville in a nationally televised ceremony that according to the *Detroit Free Press,* "captivated her country."

## SOURCES:

### Books

Vilallonga, José Luis de, *The King: A Life of King Juan Carlos of Spain,* translated by Anthea Bell, London, Weidenfeld and Nicolson, 1994.

### Periodicals

*Detroit Free Press,* March 19, 1995, p. F10.
*Newsweek,* November 3, 1975, p. 10; February 16, 1981, pp. 8–11; March 9, 1981, pp. 8–10.
*New York Times,* October 31, 1975, p. 1, 11; November 23, 1975, p. l, 3.
*Sunday Times Magazine* (London), September 8, 1991, pp. 18–24.
*Time,* February 16, 1981, pp. 18–19.
*Times* (London), November 21, 1985, p. 12; April 21, 1986, p. 27.

### Other

*The Royal Household,* Spanish Ministry of Foreign Affairs, Diplomatic Information Office, December 1993.

*—Sketch by Amanda Beresford*

# Benito Júarez
## 1806-1872
### Mexican revolutionary and politician

Benito Júarez, arguably the most revered of all Mexico's presidents, was a fullblooded Zapotec Indian who overcame early obstacles to acquire an education and pursue a distinguished legal and political career. A dedicated public servant wedded to liberal ideals, Júarez never used political office for personal gain. He is remembered today as a model of integrity and selfless patriotism.

Pablo Benito Júarez was born on March 21, 1806, to Marcelino Júarez and Brigida Garcia, who lived in a small village in the state of Oaxaca. His family—like most Indians of the region—was poor, and made a living by farming and tending small flocks of sheep. Both parents died when Júarez was barely three. The boy and his older sisters were then cared for by paternal grandparents. After his grandparents' deaths Júarez was reared in the home of an uncle, where he made himself useful by tending the family sheep. The uncle took an interest in his young nephew's education, teaching him to read and sending him to a local school. He hoped Júarez would study for ordination to the priesthood, one of the few avenues to advancement open to the poor at the time.

Júarez's life was irrevocably altered one day when one of the sheep in his charge was stolen. Fearful of his uncle's wrath, the 12-year-old fled to the city of Oaxaca. He found temporary refuge in the home of Don Antonio Mazza, where his older sister was employed as a cook. Soon afterward, he found a benefactor in the person of Don Antonio Salanueva, a bookbinder, who offered him an education in exchange for his labor.

In 1821, Júarez entered the seminary in seeming fulfillment of his uncle's hopes. But it became apparent that the priesthood was not his vocation. He delayed ordination by persuading Don Antonio Salanueva to allow him to pursue a course of study in the arts, and then escaped altogether in 1829 by entering the newly established, secular Institute of Arts and Sciences. In contrast to the conservatism of the seminary, the institute's atmosphere was distinctly liberal, and Júarez thrived there. He studied jurisprudence and physics, and by 1831 he had begun both to practice law and to teach physics. He was elected an alderman in the city of Oaxaca that same year.

### Early Political Career

Politically, Júarez was drawn to the liberal philosophy which held that the powers of the privi-leged classes—composed primarily of wealthy land owners, the military, and the clergy—needed to be curbed. Power should be returned to the people.

Júarez's law clients were drawn from Oaxaca's poor. One 1834 case impressed him profoundly: he was asked to defend the inhabitants of a village called Loricha against the extortion practiced by their curate. The case Júarez constructed failed due to the curate's exercise of political influence. In the end, Júarez—as well as a number of the complainants—was jailed for a time. The experience fostered Júarez's growing conviction that the powers of the privileged classes must be curtailed, and caused him to ally himself more closely with reform-minded liberals. However, the episode also had a cautionary effect, leading him to retire to private life for a time. He spent the next several years quietly practicing law and accepting a succession of minor political appointments until, in 1841, he was appointed a judge—a position in which he enjoyed some prestige and served with distinction.

In 1843, Júarez married Margarita Mazza, daughter of the man in whose home he had found refuge as a child. The marriage solidified Júarez's social status, for the Mazza family was highly respectable. The union proved to be a long, fruitful and happy one, sustaining Júarez emotionally to the end of his life.

In 1845 Júarez was elected to the state legislature, and in 1846 to the national Congress, where he soon tired of the constant debate over ways of raising money. Upon his return to Oaxaca in 1847, he was appointed provisional governor and was elected to a term in that office in his own right the following year. He served as governor for five years, setting an example of sound management unparalleled in the country at that time, and thus attracting national attention. Hallmarks of his administration were public spirit, fairness, honesty, and thrift.

Many crucial benefits resulted from Júarez's sound policies. They included improved educational opportunities, especially for the poor and for women; improved communications resulting from new roads and ports; and perhaps most important of all, conciliation between classes, which Júarez effected by carefully balancing traditional clerical privileges and the impetus for reform. Through his tact he was able to foster cooperation between church and state, which in turn facilitated many of his civic projects, including the opening of a road to the Pacific. When he retired from office the state—whose resources had been exhausted when he arrived—was solvent.

### Years of Turmoil

In 1852, Júarez completed his term as governor and returned to the Institute of Arts and Sciences as director. He also resumed his law practice. The following year, he suffered the consequences of an earlier decision: in 1847, former President Antonio López de Santa Anna, fleeing the capital in the wake of defeat by United States troops, had applied for asylum in Oaxaca. Júarez had refused the request. Once returned to the presidency in 1853, Santa Anna lost no time in seeking revenge. Júarez was arrested, carried to Veracruz, and held there without explanation. After a period of imprisonment, he was exiled to Havana. From there he made his way to the United States. He settled in New Orleans, where a group of liberal Mexican exiles made their temporary home.

In New Orleans, Júarez found employment as a cigarmaker. He lived on his earnings and on what money his wife—who had opened a shop in Oaxaca in his absence—was able to send. He joined forces with the expatriate supporters of the liberal revolutionaries Juan Alvarez and Ignacio Comonfort, bitter opponents of the despotic Santa Anna regime. Under Alvarez's leadership, the Plan of Ayutla—calling for the overthrow of Santa Anna and the creation of a new constitution which would reflect liberal ideas—was issued in Mexico in 1854. Facing overwhelming support for the plan and bowing to military defeat, Santa Anna capitulated. Alvarez became president of Mexico. Júarez returned from exile and served as minister of justice in Alvarez's cabinet. In his new position, he issued the Ley Júarez (Law of Júarez), which abolished the rights of the military and the clergy to be tried in their own courts for violations of law. Two years later, Júarez became chief justice of the Mexican Supreme Court, a position which carried with it the office of the vice presidency of the nation. Under President Ignacio Comonfort, who succeeded Alvarez, the *Ley Lerdo*—which proscribed institutions (including the church) from owning surplus lands—was passed. The intention was to distribute land more equitably and to raise revenue for the bankrupt government. But, few Mexican citizens had the means to purchase land, and the law had the unforseen consequence of concentrating the auctioned lands among a few wealthy ranchers and speculators, who exploited workers in a way that the church had not. In the end the landless peasants suffered more.

### Presidency and the Empire

The crowning act of the reform-minded regime was the Constitution of 1857. The constitution abolished slavery, compulsory military service, and titles of nobility. It provided for universal male suffrage and included a bill of rights to guarantee personal freedoms. The constitution was so bitterly contested that civil war resulted. Comonfort was forced into exile and his place as president was usurped by the conservative Felix Zuloaga. Júarez, asserting his constitutional right to succeed Comonfort, escaped

the capital and established set up a rival government at Veracruz. During the three-year struggle that followed, Júarez used customs receipts to secure weapons and wage war against the Zuloaga regime. He also passed reform laws that resulted in complete separation of church and state. Marriage became a civil contract; freedom of worship was established; and Church lands were nationalized without compensation, this last measure aimed at curtailing the use of church wealth to support the conservative cause. By 1860, military victory favored the liberal forces, and in 1861, Júarez returned to Mexico City. In March of that year he was elected president once more.

Júarez inherited a bankrupt and divided nation. In an attempt to restore fiscal stability, he temporarily suspended repayment of staggering foreign debts. This action alarmed the governments of France, Spain, and England, all of whom had substantial investments in Mexico. In a joint effort the three countries landed troops in Veracruz in early 1862. But the French emperor, Napoleon III, conceived a separate plan to conquer Mexico and rule the country through a puppet emperor. England and Spain withdrew from the venture when they realized the extent of Napoleon's ambition, and the French forces proceeded to march toward Mexico City independently. At Puebla, they were repulsed by the Mexican army under the command of General Ignacio Zaragoza in a defeat so decisive that the date gave its name to a new Mexican holiday, the Cinco de Mayo (Fifth of May). Napoleon sent massive reinforcements. With the aid of these troops, the French eventually rallied. They succeeded in taking Mexico City in June, 1863. The Júarez government retired from the capital, and Júarez himself withdrew to the still-unconquered northern provinces. Supported by loyal troops, he asserted his position as president and governed from the modest black coach in which he travelled.

The following year, Napoleon III installed the Austrian Archduke Maximilian as emperor of Mexico. Maximilian had been duped into believing that the Mexican people would welcome his rule. The disastrous empire lasted barely three years. In 1867, facing continued resistance by Júarez loyalists and pressure from the United States, Napoleon withdrew the French troops. Maximilian himself was soon arrested, tried by court martial, and executed.

### Victory

Júarez, whose term had officially expired in 1865, returned to the capital following Maximilian's death. Campaigning on a platform of liberal reform, he was elected to a third term as president in October, 1867, defeating his principal rival, the popular General **Porfirio Díaz.** Mexico then entered the period known as the "Restored Republic." After ten years of war, Júarez worked to restore stability and solvency.

He drastically reduced the size of the military—thus reducing expenditures and military influence—and he established a rural national police force to secure the highways for travel and trade. Under Júarez's guidance, an ambitious plan for economic recovery was planned and successfully implemented. Industry and agriculture were revitalized and foreign investment encouraged. The construction of a railroad linking Mexico City with Mexico's principal port of Veracruz was begun. Educational reform was also a priority.

Júarez's attempts at liberal reform were hampered by opposition from conservatives; by growing factionalism among liberals; and by continuing Indian unrest. In 1871, Júarez prevailed in a hotly contested three-way presidential election in which the choice fell to congress in the absence of a clear winner. Defeated rival Porfirio Díaz contested the outcome and mounted an unsuccessful revolt. Júarez spent much of the following year in attempts at conciliation as differences increased among rival liberal factions in addition to opposition from traditional quarters. His efforts were cut short by his sudden death from a heart attack on July 18, 1872.

In a society heavily influenced by a class system, Júarez was remarkable for having transcended the liability of having been born poor and Indian, as well as that of being a civilian in a political system whose leaders were almost invariably drawn from among military figures. He was buried in the Pantheon, Mexico's cemetery for heroes.

## SOURCES:

*Cambridge Encyclopedia of Latin America and the Caribbean,* edited by Simon Collier, Thomas E. Skidmore and Harold Blakemore, New York, Cambridge University Press, 1992.
Hammett, Brian, *Júarez,* London, Longman, 1994.
Miller, Robert Ryal, *Mexico: A History,* Norman, University of Oklahoma Press, 1985.
Newlon, Clarke, *The Men Who Made Mexico,* New York, Dodd, Mead, 1973.
Roeder, Ralph, *Júarez and His Mexico,* Volume 1, New York, Greenwood Press, 1968.

—*Sketch by Julie Henderson Jersyk*

# Raúl Juliá
## 1940-1994
**Puerto Rican actor**

Raúl Juliá was an internationally renowned stage and film actor credited with transcending the cultural stereotypes often associated with Latin actors. One of Puerto Rico's most famous actors, he first rose to prominence as a Shakespearian performer, appearing in the New York Shakespeare Festival's *Macbeth* in 1966 and later starring in such plays as *The Taming of the Shrew,* opposite Meryl Streep, in 1978. Between 1971 and 1982, Juliá received four Tony nominations for his performances in *The Two Gentlemen of Verona, Where's Charley, Threepenny Opera,* and *Nine.* During the later stages of his nearly 30-year acting career, he spent much of his time before the camera rather than a live audience, giving perhaps his most memorable performance in the two *Addams Family* movies in the early 1990s. Juliá also received praise for his more politically charged roles, such as his portrayal of a Marxist political prisoner in *The Kiss of the Spider Woman* in 1985, and a rain forest activist in the Home Box Office (HBO) film *The Burning Season* in 1994. Juliá's social consciousness was also evident in his passionate attempt to lead the fight against world hunger through the international organization Hunger Project.

Raúl Rafael Carlos Juliá y Acelay was born in San Juan, Puerto Rico, on March 9, 1940. He was the eldest of four children born to Raúl Juliá—a prosperous restaurateur who reportedly introduced pizza to Puerto Rico, and his wife, Olga Acelay. As a first-grade student in a suburban Catholic school run by American nuns, Juliá made his acting debut as a devil in a class play. The experience enabled the shy child to display—perhaps for the first time—the creativity within himself. "It was a marvelous experience in which I entered and let go of myself," he told *Newsday*'s Allan Wallach. Juliá cultivated his interest in theater by performing at parties and in school productions; however, after graduating from San Ignacio de Loyola High School, he followed the advice of his parents and began studying law at the University of Puerto Rico. Unable to abandon acting, Juliá spent much of his time performing in various amateur productions and soon relinquished his aspirations for a legal career.

### Moved to New York

During an appearance in a variety show at a San Juan nightclub, Juliá caught the attention of a vacationing American stage actor, Orson Bean, who invited the him to New York City to study acting with

*Raúl Juliá*

and teaching Spanish, Papp once helped by hiring him as house manager for a new production at the Public Theater.

After notable performances in such plays as *Titus Andronicus* and *The Ox Cart,* Juliá made his Broadway debut as the servant Chan in Jack Gelber 's 1968 production of *The Cuban Thing.* The drama focused on Fidel Castro's revolution from the perspective of an upper-class family that gradually accepts Castro's ideas. Although the play was a failure, it provided Juliá with exposure to other directors and producers, leading to prominent roles, such as Jesus in *Conerico Was Here to Stay.* In November 1970 Juliá received some of his best reviews with his portrayal of Paco Montoya, a fugitive Latin revolutionary in Mel Arrighi's *The Castro Complex.* Finding praise for the actor's "attractive stage personality" and "attractive stage presence," *Cue*'s Marilyn Stasio, for instance, suggested that Juliá had "a future in better plays."

Papp provided just that opportunity a year later, asking Juliá to play the unfaithful, irritable Proteus in the new musical version of Shakespeare's romantic comedy *The Two Gentlemen of Verona.* Largely on the strength of Juliá's Tony award-nominated performance, the play was so popular that it was moved from a Central Park theater to Broadway. While portraying Proteus at the St. James Theatre, Juliá demonstrated the full range of his talents by also playing the obsequious courtier Osric in a New York Shakespeare Festival production of *Hamlet* alongside such notable actors as Stacy Keach and James Earl Jones. "It never occurred to me that Osric could have so much grace, passion, and venom," said Clive Barnes in his *New York Times* review.

In 1974, after several more critically acclaimed performances in Papp's Shakespeare productions, Juliá starred as the Oxford undergraduate Charley Wykeham in the Frank Loesser-George Abbott musical *Where's Charley?.* In winning his second Tony nomination, Juliá received high praise from such critics as Tom Donnelly of the *Washington Post,* who noted his unique ability to "get the audience in the palm of his hand." Two years later Juliá won his third Tony nomination in six years—this time for his sinister portrayal of Mack the Knife in the Bernolt Brecht-Kurt Weill classic, *Threepenny Opera.* The rest of the decade saw Juliá receive rave reviews for his performances in Chekhov's *The Cherry Orchard,* the Broadway hit *Dracula, The Taming of the Shrew,* and *Othello.* During the 1980s, Juliá continued to expand the range of his acting talents, playing the role of a British literary agent—complete with upper-class English speech—in the Broadway production of Peter Hall's *Betrayal.* Two years later he was again recognized with a Tony nomination for his portrayal of the middle-aged film director Guido Contini in *Nine,* the winner of the Tony award for best musical.

the famous acting coach and artistic director of the American Place Theatre, Wynn Handman. Juliá altered his plans to pursue an acting career in Europe and went to New York in 1964, shortly after completing the work for his bachelor's degree. A few weeks after his arrival, he made his New York debut, portraying Astolfo in a Spanish-language production of Calderon's *Life Is a Dream.* Offered a position with the Phoebe Brand's Theater in the Street, Juliá soon began performing English and Spanish plays in ghetto neighborhoods. Although he was once showered with eggs and bottles during a performance of Chekhov's one-act play *The Proposal,* Juliá found that the openness of the unique stage environment enabled him to generate the type of strong audience response essential to the theater experience. "I want to feel an audience, not forget it," he once told Guy Flatley of the *New York Times.*

In 1966 Broadway producer Joseph Papp gave Juliá his first major break, hiring him to play Macduff in the New York Shakespeare Festival's Mobile Unit production of *Macbeth.* Through his long association with Papp, Juliá landed several major Shakespearian and classical roles that had seldom before been performed by Puerto Rican actors. "[Papp] saw actors for what they had to offer, no matter what their background was," Juliá stated in the Los Angeles *Daily News.* "He wouldn't see you as an ethnic group or as a stereotype. He saw you as an actor." While Juliá was struggling to support himself between performances by selling *Life* magazine subscriptions

## Film Roles and Philanthropy

Although Juliá preferred the audience connection that the stage provided, he spent a large portion of his last years in film. After breaking into the medium in the early 1970s with minor roles in *The Organization Man* and *Panic in Needle Park,* Juliá continued with more prominent parts in such films as *The Escape Artist, One From the Heart,* and *The Eyes of Laura Mars* in the 1980s.

In 1985, Julia played a major role in the film adaptation of noted author **Manuel Puig**'s *Kiss of the Spiderwoman.* The story revolves around two prison cellmates, one a revolutionary played by Julia and the other, a homosexual ostensibly imprisoned because of his sexuality, played by William Hurt. Described in *Videohound's Golden Retriver 1994* as "literate, haunting, powerful," the film received a pleathora of accolades, including Academy Award nominations for best adapted screenplay and for Hector Babenco, best director.

Perhaps Julia's most famous role was as the off-beat patriarch Gomez Addams in *The Addams Family* (1991) and its sequel, *Addams Family Values* (1993). Juliá also played opposite Mel Gibson in *Tequila Sunrise,* Harrison Ford in *Presumed Innocent,* and Clint Eastwood in *The Rookie,* while also appearing as a regular on the children's show *Sesame Street.* While taking on such roles was quite a change for the Shakespearian actor, it only served to demonstrate the actor's willingness to venture to try something new. "If I see a role that I'm sure I can play, what's the challenge?" he once remarked in the Los Angeles *Daily News.*

While maintaining his reputation as one of the hardest working actors in the industry, Juliá also found time to take an active role in various philanthropic activities. Often described as an "actor with a conscience," he devoted much of his offstage energy during his last 15 years to the Hunger Project, an international organization whose goal is to eradicate hunger by the year 2000. "When I found out in 1977 that we have the technology to end hunger on the planet, I had to get involved," he explained in the *Los Angeles Times.* Juliá was also active in the Hispanic Organization of Latin Actors (HOLA), which works to develop theater in the Spanish language.

Two years after his critically acclaimed starring performance in the Broadway musical *Man of La Mancha,* Juliá suffered a massive stroke that resulted in a coma and his death eight days later, on October 24, 1994, at North Shore University Hospital in Long Island. Survived by his second wife, dancer Merel Poloway, and their two young sons, Raúl Sigmund and Benjamin, Juliá was buried in Puerto Rico, after two days of national mourning. Juliá was, according to longtime fan Providencia Rivera's statement in The *San Juan Star,* "a universal man who could reach everyone, beyond ideology and social classes." Or as Handman, his first acting teacher in New York, stated in the *Daily News,* "He was a natural who made people feel better about life when they saw him perform."

## SELECTED VIDEOGRAPHY

*Stiletto,* 1969.
*The Organization,* 1971.
*Death Scream,* 1975.
*Panic at Needle Park,* 1975.
*Gumball Rally,* 1976.
*Eyes of Laura Mars,* 1978.
*Escape Artist,* 1982.
*One From the Heart,* 1982.
*The Tempest,* 1982.
*Overdrawn at Memory Bank,* 1983.
*Strong Medicine,* 1984.
*Compromising Positions,* 1985.
*Kiss of the Spider Woman,* 1985.
*Morning After,* 1986.
*The Alamo: Thirteen Days to Glory,* 1987.
*Florida Straits,* 1987.
*Trading Hearts,* 1987.
*Moon Over Parador,* 1988.
*The Penitent,* 1988.
*Onassis,* 1988.
*Tango Bar,* 1988.
*Tequilla Sunrise,* 1988.
*Mack the Knife,* 1989.
*Romero,* 1989.
*Frankenstein Unbound,* 1990.
*Havana,* 1990.
*Presumed Innocent,* 1990.
*The Rookie,* 1990.
*The Addams Family,* 1991.
*A Life of Sin,* 1992.
*Addams Family Values,* 1993.
*Streetfighter,* 1994.

## SOURCES:

### Books

*Current Biography Yearbook, 1982,* edited by Charles Mortiz, New York, Wilson, 1982.
*Videohound's Golden Movie Retriever 1994,* edited by Martin Connors and Julia Furtaw, Detroit, Visible Ink, 1994.

### Periodicals

*Boston Herald,* March 6, 1992; October 25, 1994.
*Cue,* November 28, 1970.
*Los Angeles Daily News,* September 15, 1994.
*Los Angeles Times,* October 25, 1994.
*Newsday,* October 29, 1978.

*New York Daily News,* October 25, 1994.

*New Yorker,* August 20, 1979.

*New York Times,* December 26, 1971; July 10, 1977; January 20, 1980.

*San Juan Star,* May 17, 1992; October 27, 1994; October 28, 1994.

*Washington Post,* January 19, 1975; February 9, 1992.

—*Sketch by Jason Gallman*

# Frida Kahlo
## 1907-1954
### Mexican artist

Frida Kahlo was a painter whose work fascinated prominent and diverse artists around the world. The wife of world-renowned Mexican muralist **Diego Rivera**, Kahlo forged a place in the art world that was completely her own. Her dramatic work consisted primarily of self-portraits, although she did capture her family and friends on canvas on occasion. Some critics contend that Kahlo's paintings were reflections of her personal history, her relationship with Diego Rivera, her damaged physical condition, her philosophy of nature and life, and her individual and mythological worldview. Although Kahlo never had formal training in art, she developed into an artist who fascinated a wide range of fellow artists, including Soviet filmmaker Sergei Eisenstein, painter **Pablo Picasso,** and novelist André Breton. In addition to these literary and artistic luminaries, her circle included political figures such as Leon Trotsky and the Rockefeller family.

Frida Kahlo lived between 1907 and 1954 in a time of incredible worldwide movements and changes. The Mexican Revolution occurred just three years after she was born, a development that triggered dramatic social and economic change in Mexico. A new sense of nationalism surged throughout Mexico as the people rejected dictator **Porfirio Diaz** and his policies, and a renaissance of cultural renewal glorifying Mexico's native roots took place. The Mexican muralist tradition grew out of these changes and proved to be an important and enduring method of expressing national pride. Kahlo was an active participant in the social, economic, and political landscape that characterized her life.

Frida Kahlo was born Magdalena Carmen Frieda Kahlo y Calderón on July 6, 1907, in her parents' house in Coyoacán, Mexico, a suburb of Mexico City. In about 1935 she dropped the "e" in her first name. Her father, one of Mexico's foremost photographers, was the son of Hungarian Jews from the German town of Baden-Baden who emigrated to Mexico. Guillermo Kahlo married her mother, Matilde Calderón, a Mexican of Indian and Spanish ancestry. The family home, called the *Casa Azul* ("*Blue House*"), was built by Guillermo Kahlo a few years before

*Frida Kahlo*

Frida's birth. She was born, raised, lived, and died in her family's home.

Kahlo's father had a profound influence on her life. Her mother was a meticulous housekeeper and devout Catholic whose conventional patterns of thought created some distance between her and her daughters. Kahlo's father, on the other hand, recognized and encouraged her intellectual independence and curiosity.

At the age of seven, Kahlo was afflicted with polio, a disease that left her right foot turned outward and stunted the growth of her entire right leg. Her father nursed her back to health and subsequently encouraged her to play various active sports not typical for a Mexican girl at that time. Kahlo's bout with polio held her back in school, so in 1922, when she entered the National Preparatory School, she falsified her age. Some historians have speculated that she chose 1910 as her birth date to coincide with the year the Mexican Revolution started. Kahlo was adamant in her commitment to the ideals of revolution. She expressed her bond to the Mexican people in her art, in her dress, her behavior, and the decorations of her home.

During her days at the National Preparatory School, Kahlo became known as something of a prankster and was a highly visible presence. She often wore elaborate indigenous jewelry and colorful native clothing, and was fond of piling her hair high upon her head and decorating it brightly with ribbons and bows in the fashion that the natives of Oaxaca, Mexico, favored. Kahlo regarded every occasion as a cause for rejoicing, and celebrated birthdays, baptisms, and all the popular holidays with great enthusiasm.

### Involved in Serious Traffic Accident

It was at the National Preparatory School that she first met Diego Rivera, an artist whose work she admired. Her attraction to the painter was considerable, and one story from that period of her life alleged that she declared to her school friends her ambition to have a child by Diego Rivera. In 1925, however, Kahlo was involved in a tragic accident that dramatically changed her life. Traveling home from school on a bus, the vehicle collided with a trolley car, driving a piece of iron into her pelvis and back. Kahlo struggled with the effects of this accident and the pain it caused for the rest of her life. She underwent as many as 35 operations over the course of her life, most of them on her spine and her polio-deformed right foot. It was during Kahlo's convalescence from the bus accident that she began painting. Kahlo was required to spend long periods of time flat on her back in bed, so her mother bought her a special easel that she could use despite her physical limitations. She began to express her explosive feelings through painting.

Kahlo never returned to school after her release from the hospital. Instead, she concentrated on her painting. About this time, she met the Italian-born American photographer Tina Modotti. It was through her friendship with Modotti that Kahlo was introduced to an exciting new sphere of art and leftist politics. Diego Rivera was a member of this circle, and he and Kahlo soon became involved. Kahlo joined the Young Communist League, an organization that Rivera founded and led. The 22-year-old Kahlo married the 42-year-old Rivera in a civil ceremony in 1929.

### Kahlo's Turbulent Marriage with Rivera

The marriage proved to be a tumultuous one. Kahlo lamented that she suffered through two accidents in her life: one was the trolley car incident, the other her marriage to Rivera. Both had extramarital affairs, and several of Kahlo's relationships were with other women. Kahlo and Rivera separated for a long time, divorced, and eventually remarried. All during their stormy association, however, they served as the hub of an international intellectual circle. Their political activism continued, unaffected by the state of their marriage, as both Kahlo and Rivera used their artistic talents to express their social and political views.

In 1938 André Benton visited her in Mexico and remarked that she was a surrealist. Kahlo disagreed, arguing that she painted her reality. She did, however, travel to Europe and New York to show her work in surrealist exhibitions. Later, she firmly rejected the surrealist label, contending that her work dissolved the distinctions between reality and fantasy. In the 1940s Kahlo taught art students at her husband's urging. Her students became known as Los Fridos. Although her students spent a great deal of time with her at her home, in her studio, and out in the streets, they never saw her paint. She painted alone, a practice that led some critics and friends to describe her painting process as a form of therapy.

Kahlo's marriage to Rivera was but one of the difficulties she grappled with during her adulthood. She suffered numerous miscarriages that caused her great grief. In addition, the injuries suffered in the bus accident continued to hound her, relegating her to her bed for months at a time and keeping her in a state of almost constant pain. Finally, in 1953, her right leg was amputated due to gangrene.

Throughout all of these difficulties, Kahlo continued to paint. She became addicted to the medicine prescribed for pain, though, and her later paintings reflect this. Critics note a lack of definition and clarity in her later work, as well as an unsteady hand and heavy paint. Despite her failing body, Kahlo endeavored to maintain the old ways of gaiety, excitement, and drama. Her last public appearance was at a demonstration protesting C.I.A. intervention in the overthrow of leftist President **Jacobo Arbenz** of Guatemala. She died seven days later on July 13, 1954, at the age of 47.

During the early 1980s Kahlo came to be regarded as a pioneer in feminism and a cultural patriot. As Hayden Herrera noted in *Frida Kahlo: The Paintings,* Kahlo became a symbol of perseverance and strength for women. Unintimidated by the fame and ferocious artistic drive of her husband, she charted her own artistic course and created work of enduring power and significance. In 1984 the Mexican government recognized Kahlo's work as important to the country's national heritage. The governmented noted its unquestioned aesthetic value and unanimous recognition within the national artistic community.

### SOURCES:

*Frida Kahlo Masterpieces,* New York, W.W. Norton & Company, 1994.

Grimberg, Salomon, *Lola Alvarez Bravo, The Frida Kahlo Photographs,* New York, Distributed Art Publishers, 1991.

Herrera, Hayden, *Frida Kahlo: The Paintings,* New York, HarperCollins, 1991.

———, *Frida: A Biography of Frida Kahlo,* New York, HarperCollins, 1991.

Rivera, Guadalupe, and Marie-Pierre Colle, *Frida's Fiestas, Recipes and Reminiscences of Life with Frida Kahlo,* New York, Clarkson Potter/Publishers, 1994.

Tibol, Raquel, *Frida Kahlo: An Open Life,* translated by Elinor Randall, Albuquerque, NM: University of New Mexico Press, 1993.

Zamora, Martha, *Frida Kahlo: The Brush of Anguish,* translated by Marilyn S. Smith, San Francisco, Chronicle Books, 1990.

—*Sketch by María A. López*

*Nicolás Kanellos*

# Nicolás Kanellos
## 1945-
**Puerto Rican American writer and publisher**

Nicolás Kanellos has written and published prolifically on many subjects, but as the founder and director of Arte Público Press in Houston, Texas, he oversees operations at one of the foremost publishers of Hispanic American scholarship and literature. A full tenured professor at the University of Houston, Kanellos has received some acclaim as a scholar, and in 1994 President Bill Clinton named him to the National Council on the Humanities.

Kanellos was born January 31, 1945, in New York City to a Puerto Rican mother, Inés de Choudens García, and a Greek father, Charles Kanellos. He attended Fairleigh Dickinson University, where he graduated in May 1966 with a B.A. in Spanish. From there he moved on to the University of Texas in Austin, where in 1968 he completed a Master's Degree in Romance Languages and in 1974 a Ph.D. in Spanish and Portuguese. He also attended the University of Lisbon in Portugal and Universidad Autónoma de México, where he studied Mexican literature, history, and culture.

### Founded Arte Público Press

From a strong academic background, Kanellos taught Hispanic literature at Indiana University Northwest from 1973 until 1979. In 1980 he accepted a professorship at the University of Houston. Kanellos founded Arte Público Press in 1979, which produces over 30 titles of Hispanic literature and culture. Arte Público also publishes *The Americas Review,* a periodical formerly known as *Revista Chicano-Riqueña,* one of the oldest and most respected magazines of U.S. Hispanic literature and art. The magazine has won two Citations of Achievement from the Coordinating Council of Literary Magazines and the General Electric Literary Award. Kanellos's periodical also provides source material for educational curriculum from elementary to post-secondary schools around the country.

As an author, Kanellos has written five books on Hispanic issues, including *Two Centuries of Hispanic Theatre in the Southwest* and *Mexican American Theater: Legacy and Reality.* A scholar of Hispanic theater, Kanellos has contributed some of the most widely read work in the field. His scholarly writing also includes contributions to journals like *Hispania, Latin American Theater Review, Vista,* and *Journal of Popular Culture.* He is also an editorial board member of five different academic journals, including *Latin American Theater Review.*

Kanellos has received many honors for his work including the American Library Association's Award for Best Reference Work of 1993 for *The Hispanic-American Almanac: A Reference Work on Hispanics in the United States.* Chief among his other awards are Outstanding Editor from the Coordinating Council of Literary Magazines in 1979; the Hispanic Heritage

Award for Literature presented by Ronald Reagan in 1988; a commendation for high standards of academic achievement by the Governor of Texas in 1989; the Texas Institute of Letters's recognizing his *A History of Hispanic Theater in the United States: Origins to 1940* the Book Making the Most Significant Contribution to Knowledge in 1991; and being named by *Hispanic Business* one of the 100 Most Influential Hispanics in the United States in 1989 and 1993.

As a Hispanic publisher, Kanellos believes he has a responsibility to use his position to bring Hispanic life and Hispanic writers more attention. He describes his feelings about his work as those of a "missionary who has to convert people to their own religion and identity." He feels that Hispanic culture represents a crucial piece of the diverse puzzle of American culture, and he rejects the notion of America as a "purely white, Anglo-Saxon" nation.

## SELECTED PUBLISHED WORKS:

(Editor) *Los Tejanos: A Texas-Mexican Anthology,* Houston, Arte Público, 1980.

(Editor) *A Decade of Hispanic Literature: An Anniversary Anthology,* Houston, Arte Público, 1982.

(Editor) *Mexican American Theater: Then and Now,* Houston, Arte Público, 1983.

(Editor) *Hispanic Theater in the United States,* Houston, Arte Público, 1984.

*Two Centuries of Hispanic Theater in the Southwest,* Houston, Arte Público, 1985.

*Mexican American Theater: Legacy and Reality,* Pittsburgh, PA, Latin American Literary Review Press, 1987.

(Editor) *Biographical Dictionary of Hispanic Literature in the United States: The Literature of Puerto Ricans, Puerto Rican Americans, Cuban Americans, and Other Hispanic Writers,* Westport, CT, Greenwood Press, 1989.

(Editor with Jorge A. Huerta) *Nuevos Pasos: Chicano and Puerto Rican Drama,* Houston, Arte Público, 1989.

*A History of Hispanic Theater in the United States,* Austin, University of Texas Press, 1990.

(Editor) *Hispanic-American Almanac: A Reference Work on Hispanics in the United States,* Detroit, Gale, 1993.

## SOURCES:

### Books

*Hispanic Writers,* edited by Bryan Ryan, Detroit, Gale, 1991.

### Other

Kanellos, Nicolás, autobiographical materials from Arte Público.

—*Sketch by James McCarthy*

# Louise Año Nuevo Kerr
## 1938-
### Hispanic American educator and administrator

While other high-school teachers ignored Louise Año Nuevo Kerr, a typing instructor helped her fill out a scholarship application that forever changed the young girl's life. "I was always grateful for that, and I've always seen the irony," Kerr told interviewer D. D. Andreassi. She won the four-year *salsipuedes* ("get out if you can") scholarship, which allowed her to attend college and eventually pursue a career as a history professor and dean. Even though her professional life has revolved around universities, Kerr stated that she is not "just an ivory tower scholar. I see the university as needing to contribute in the larger world and to know what is going on out there."

Kerr was born December 24, 1938, in Denver, Colorado to Roseana Bertha Lopez and Bonifacio Benjamin Año Nuevo. Her mother was Mexican American and her father was a native Filipino. The oldest of four children, Kerr grew up in California where her family worked on farms. "We were all migrants for a while," she said in her interview. Her father eventually became a sedentary farm worker and a sharecropper in California.

### Traumatic Incident with Immigration Officers

Kerr vividly remembered a traumatic incident that occurred when she was working in a field at the age of thirteen. At the time, in the mid-1950s, there were a lot of Mexican farm workers and "often times they were not documented," Kerr said in the interview. "Immigration people came to the field doing roundups, and they stopped me and it was a terrifying experience, because you had to prove you were a citizen. . . . It was important in that day and time not to have an accent. They asked me where I was born, and I said 'St. Anthony's Hospital in Denver.' It was telling in my view of the unfair treatment of Mexicans. The idea of the oppression was for me unfair and it raised a lot of anger, because it was governmentally imposed. It was very significant in my life and maybe I've never come to grips with it."

Her life took a turn for the better when Kerr, the first person in her family to graduate from high school, won a scholarship and began attending the University of California. She graduated with a bachelor of arts degree in sociology in 1960. Six years later she earned a master's degree in history. She married Howard H. Kerr on October 4, 1963, and they had two children, Catherine and Sarah. The family moved to Illinois when Howard was offered a teaching position at the University of Chicago. "I had always assumed that what you aspired for was not to work," Kerr told this interviewer. "I was happily enjoying being home with my kids." One day in 1970, however, she was listening to the radio and was surprised to find a Spanish station. She learned there were 250,000 Hispanics living in Chicago. "I arranged to take a course to find out more about it," she recalled in the interview.

A short time later she was offered an assistant teaching post at the University of Illinois, a job she held through 1972. Kerr became a member of the Organization of American Historians in 1973 and later chaired the group's membership committee from 1982 to 1984. She also became a member of the American Historical Association in 1973. Meanwhile, she finished her course work and earned her Ph.D. in history in 1976 from the University of Illinois.

After completing her Ph.D., Kerr's employment opportunities included a teaching position and fellowship presented to her simultaneously from Loyola University. Luckily she was able to accept the teaching position and take a leave of absence to work on the fellowship. As a teacher she led classes focusing on United States history and the role of Hispanics in the United States. Kerr was active in many organizations, including the Illinois Humanities Council, which she was a member of from 1973 to 1982, serving as vice-chair the last two years. She was also a member of the National Council on the Humanities from 1980 to 1987.

In 1980 Kerr received a National Research Council Ford Foundation Fellowship. About the same time she was offered the position of assistant dean in the college of arts and science at Loyola. She told this interviewer that one of the reasons she took the offer was because her daughter, Catherine, was starting college and it was an opportune time to make extra money. She soon became associate dean at Loyola and continued teaching until 1988. Kerr went on to become the associate vice-chancellor of academic affairs at the University of Illinois at Chicago.

Kerr has not limited herself to academic activities. In 1986 she joined the Committee on the Status of Women and in 1989 she became involved with the Committee on Decent and Unbiased Campaign Tactics (CONDUCT). Regarding CONDUCT, Kerr told this interviewer that "its exclusive purpose is to make sure that campaigns remain on a high plain. That's been a very important organization in Chicago, especially since the election of [Chicago Mayor] Harold Washington." Her civic involvement has included work with the Salvation Army in Chicago and 4-H clubs. "In a larger professional sense, I've always seen myself as an active participant in the civic community and the community at large," Kerr related.

She has strived to maintain her work as a historian by contributing to various books and periodicals. She served as editor of *Mid-America: An Historical Review* in 1981, and in 1984 her work appeared in both *Illinois History* and *Ethnic Chicago*. Kerr has served on the editorial boards of scholarly journals, including the *Journal of American Ethnic History, Aztlan: International Journal of Chicano Studies,* and the *Journal of National Public History*. In addition, Kerr has had articles published in *Mexican-Americans in Multi-Culturalism in the United States* and *Chicanas in the Urban Mid-West: Crossing Borders*. When asked about her writing, Kerr noted that she has always considered herself a historian: "I've never given up my work in history and have in fact continued recently to publish."

Kerr's achievements have been acknowledged with several accolades including the Congressional Hispanic Caucus Humanities Award in 1979, the Illinois Humanities Council Public Humanities Award in 1984, the Mexican American Business and Professional Woman Pioneer Award in 1979, and the Young Women's Christian Association (YWCA) Metropolitan Chicago Leadership Award in Education.

In 1992, Kerr attended a Harvard University course for creative academic leadership. "I'm in the process of rethinking where I want to go next, whether I want to remain an administrator or go back to the classroom," Kerr said. She asserted that her goal is to "open opportunities to others or at least to help. Particularly to young people to help them find many options for themselves and to do the same for myself and perhaps in that respect to be a role model." Kerr maintained that she wants to raise the hopes and expectations of young people "in a way that mine had been raised for me by my family, by those who did support me and, I suppose, by myself."

## SOURCES:

Kerr, Louise Año Nuevo, interview with D. D. Andreassi, October 6, 1992.

*—Sketch by D. D. Andreassi*

# Wilfredo Lam
## 1902-1982
### Cuban painter

*Wilfredo Lam*

Wilfredo Lam incorporated several cultures as well as art movements into his paintings. The product of a rich and diverse heritage, Lam became in his lifetime the most internationally known artist to emerge from his native country of Cuba. The catalog for an exhibition at the University of Notre Dame Art Gallery in 1961 described the artist's work: "A savage elegance is possibly the characteristic which strikes us most forcibly in Wilfredo Lam's latest work. But beneath this elegance is a suggestion of tension, of dread, of unfamiliar forces at work. His art is nocturnal art; but a night art in full daylight with all the cruelty of a tropical sun and all the dark mystery of the lush jungle it propagates. This mystery and tropicality have marked Lam's work from the outset . . . but the interior poetry of Lam's painting has its roots in a heritage for which he either has a wise and profound regard, or is unable to shake off."

Lam was born in Sagua la Grande, Cuba, in December 1902, and named Wilfredo Oscar de la Conception Lam y Castilla Mazzola. According to the exhibit catalog, Lam's mother was of mixed African, Indian, and European background. His father—a businessman from Canton—was Chinese and had settled in Cuba. His father's name, Lam Yam, supposedly meant "the man from the wild cape, watching the blue sky."

Julia Herzberg describes Lam's heritage and early childhood in her essay in *Wilfredo Lam and His Contemporaries 1938-1952.* The village of his birth, Sagua la Grande, was in a sugar farming province. His father, Herzberg reported, practiced ancestor worship in transcribing the writings of Confucius and Lao Tse. "His mother, Ana, was predominately Congolese and inherited her traditional Afro-Cuban beliefs from her mother, who had been brought to Cuba as a slave from the Congo and set free when she married a Cuban." Lam grew up in a Chinese neighborhood that bordered the area where many Afro-Cubans lived. "Although the artist was exposed to his father's teaching and practices, it was his mother's cultural and religious beliefs that were central to his formation." During his formative years, Lam was surrounded by people speaking African dialects and practicing

traditional religions combined with Catholicism. A key person in Lam's youth, according to Herzberg, was his godmother and spiritual guide, Mantonica Wilson. "She was a priestess of Changó, the Yoruba thunder god (of the Santería religion) . . . [and] she brought Lam under the guidance of Changó," Herzberg wrote. His godmother gave him an amulet that Lam carried with him throughout his life.

James Johnson Sweeney, in the Notre Dame Art Gallery's catalog, said that Lam began his art studies at the Academy of San Alejandro in Havana where he worked for two years. Then, in 1924, he traveled to Madrid, Spain, and continued his education at the Free Academy. He also worked under Fernando Alvarez di Sotomayor, the director of the Prado Museum. "He found the relatively academic atmosphere in Madrid little inspiring," Sweeney recorded. "Still, with frequent trips to Cuba and back, he remained in Spain until the end of the Spanish Civil War." Though Lam was not prone to making political statements in his art, he was not adverse to joining a cause. In Lowery Stokes Sims' essay in *Wilfredo Lam,* the artist's involvement in the Spanish Civil War is detailed. "Lam had been a committed Republican since he joined the party in 1932. He put his artistic talent in the service of the Republican cause by producing propaganda posters, and he was drafted to fight in the defense of Madrid in 1936, when the Civil War broke out." In late 1937, or early 1938, Lam was hospitalized in Barcelona for either an illness or war-related injury. While recovering he met two people who would be influential in his life: Helena Holzer and Manuel Hugué. Holzer, a German research associate in neurobiology, became his partner for 12 years. Hugué, a Catalan artist known as Manolo, gave Lam letter of introduction to **Pablo Picasso** in Paris. The letter would introduce Lam to a new way of approaching his art and change his life forever.

### Paris and the Cubists

From 1924 to 1929, Lam had dedicated his art to the school of realism. "Around 1934, he briefly [experimented] with biomorphic imagery and with a type of Surrealist narrative ... between 1924 and 1936, Lam launched into a prolific production of still lives, interiors, landscapes, cityscapes, and portraits in which form is simplified, at times into separate window-like segments," Sims noted. This tendency peaked around 1935–1936 when another shift occurred in the artist's work. In 1936, Lam saw his first Picasso exhibit in Madrid. Sims quoted his response as "not only a revelation but ... a shock." The impact of the famous Cubist on Lam was both political and artistic-Picasso was a strong and visible supporter of the Republican cause in the Spanish Civil War. Lam was forced to flee to Paris in the spring of 1938 when the war ended and the Republican side lost.

Sims noted that even prior to meeting Picasso in Paris, Lam's work showed an adaptation of Cubism as well as a connection to his multicultural heritage. "We can therefore conclude that the works begun in Paris in the spring of 1938 ... show a much more 'Africanized' character. His figures are now defined with strong angular outlines that clearly articulate the planes of the body parts—breasts, collarbones, and shoulder blades are often summarized in a zig-zag motion, approximating the formal synthesis of human anatomy seen in African art styles such as that of the Dogon of Mali." The first meeting of Picasso and Lam went well and generated the myth that the famous Cubist had an incredible influence on Lam's art. But the critics disagree that Picasso "formed" Lam's unique style. "Picasso merely served as [a] catalyst to Lam's search for a personal interpretation of modernist syntax," Sims claimed. "As a descendant of peoples who were displaced in the diaspora and discouraged—officially—from following the practices of their forefathers if they aspired to access to the mainstream. Lam, along with others of his generation, found encouragement in the embrace of their despised cultures by European artists and intellectuals."

Sims argued that the more renown major contribution of Picasso and André Breton was lending authenticity to the style of "primitive" modern art. "Lam was never a tribal artist; he had come to a modernist style in much the same way as any artist of his generation. Lam's distinctive achievement is the fusion of Cubist and Surrealist stylistic strategies with referents from Santería, a traditional African-based religion with which he was intimately acquainted as an 'insider.'" Although Lam has been called both a Cubist and a Surrealist, his art is a movement of its own, as unique and individual as the artist who created it. Lam's stay in Paris was interrupted by World War II and the German invasion of Paris. In 1940 he traveled to Bordeaux and then Marseilles, where he finally escaped on a boat that traveled through the Virgin Islands and the Dominican Republic before returning Lam to his native Cuba.

### Returned Home

Sims quoted Lam's reaction to returning home after leaving the international artistic scene in Paris. "Because I had left everything behind in Paris, I told myself I was at point zero." Sims wrote that in his fortieth year, Lam was poised to finally come into his own artistically and create the best works of his career. Herzberg's essay focused on the ten-year period Lam spent in Havana from 1941 to 1952. "Lam never forgot the stories about the chicherekú, the long-toothed gnomes who lived in his back yard, or the guije, the spirits who lived in the river next to his house. When he returned to Havana in mid-1941, he was again reminded of the sounds of the Afro-Cuban drums and the sights of the ceremonial dances and street corners strewn with grains of corn and dead cocks adorned with strands of beads. Lam's years in Havana during World War II were a time of redefinition."

Sweeney recorded this change as well. "Back on his native soil once more Lam was able to make full use of the artistic experience he had acquired in Paris. But the subject matter became more Antillean than previously—more haunted and savage. And at the same time the domination of his forms by Picasso's diminished." Herzberg related a conversation Lam had regarding these years in Cuba. "Lam said that his return to Havana was like going back to his early beginnings and that the only way he could deal with them was to find a way to integrate in his art the transculturation that had occurred in Cuba among the aboriginals, Spaniards, Africans, Chinese, French, pirates, and others that formed the Caribbean peoples." In 1944, Alejo Carpentier said of Lam's work that it seemed to reveal everything that is magical, imponderable, and mysterious in the Cuban world.

By this point, Lam's work was more well known in Paris and New York than his native country. Though, in time, his art would become admired in Cuba as the most famous art the country had produced. "Critical thinking privileges Lam as a progenitor of an aesthetic that occupies a singular place globally in the art of his time. Lam, who trained in the western academic tradition and mastered the modernist idioms of Surrealism and Cubism, created a personal symbology to express the Afro-Cuban heritage," Herzberg wrote. "Lam is considered a paradigm for having given a voice to Afro-Cubans, and by extension Pan-Americans of African descent, who had peripheral in the discourse of art history."

Lam, who died in 1982, spent most of his years after Havana living in Paris. Sims, in another essay, stated that Lam was a master for our time. "Lam was one of few individuals who actually could bridge the Parisian and the New York art worlds, which became increasingly estranged from each other as the 1950s progressed. Until his death, Lam continued to move back and forth between continents and philosophies with an openness that was unparalleled, while the marketing strategies of the art world stressed sharply defined national distinctions." Lam was survived by his wife, Lou Laurin-Lam, and three sons, Eskil Soren, Obeni and Ian Erik Timour. Cuba honored its famous son with the creation of the Wilfredo Lam Center, which opened in December of 1993. His works are displayed in museums and galleries around the world, from a 1992 exhibit at the Queen Sofia National Museum in Madrid to the Studio Museum in Harlem in 1993.

## SOURCES:

### Books

*Wilfredo Lam,* University of Notre Dame Art Gallery, 1961.
*Wilfredo Lam and His Contemporaries 1938–1952,* New York, Studio Museum in Harlem and Harry N. Abrams, 1992.

### Periodicals

*Art in America,* Annual Guide 1993, p. 30; October 1994, pp. 43–44.
*New York Times Biographical Service,* 1982, p. 1207.
*World Press Review,* December 1992, p. 54.

—*Sketch by Kathe A. Conti*

# Bartolomé de las Casas
## 1474-1566
**Spanish missionary and writer**

Of the numerous autobiographical and historical documentation of the Spanish conquest of America, Bartolomé de las Casas's writings pose as some of the most notable and controversial works of the sixteenth century. Las Casas's manuscripts document the first 74 years of the Spanish discovery and conquest of the New World. His works are viewed by scholars as some of the best documentation of the sixteenth century; however, the most distinguishing aspect of las Casas' writings was his unorthodox arguments against the Spanish monarch's ideologies towards the inhabitants of the New World.

In his writings and until his death in 1566, las Casas fought against the Spanish monarch's decree, which enforced the enslavement of the Indians of the New World. Las Casas's work for the rights of these Indians helped reform the laws and philosophies of both his Dominican colleagues and the monarchs of the sixteenth century. As scholar Francis Augustus Macnutt argues in *Bartolomé de las Casas: His Life, His Apostolate, and His Writings,* "Born in an age of both civil and religious despotism, his voice was incessantly raised in vindication of the inherent and inalienable right of every human being to the enjoyment of liberty. He was preeminently a man of action to whom nothing human was foreign, and whose gift of universal sympathy co-existed with an uncommon practical ability to devise corrective reforms that commanded the attention and won the approval of the foremost statesman and moralists of his time."

Though no official record exists, scholars believe that las Casas was born in Seville in 1474 in the month of August. His father, Pedro de las Casas, was a native of Tarifa and from Segovian ancestry. His mother died young and there was little mention of her in his memoirs. Las Casas spent most of his childhood in Seville with his father and three sisters. Las Casas's father and three uncles, Francisco, Gabriel, and Diego de Penalosa, traveled with Christopher Columbus on his second voyage to the New World in 1493. At the request of his father, las Casas was enrolled in the cathedral school in the Colegio de San Miguel to study to become a priest.

In 1502, las Casas traveled with his father on the expedition to the Indies with commander Nicolás de Ovando. Though debated by many scholars, las Casas's manuscripts note that he was hired as a *tonsure* because of his knowledge of Latin, which he acquired during his studies at Seville. He aspired to the position of *doctrinero*—a well-paid position of the

*Bartolomé de las Casas*

priesthood that spread the gospel of Christianity in the Indies. Las Casas arrived in Santo Domingo in 1502 on the April 15. Upon his arrival in the New World, las Casas lived as all the other settlers and conquistadors lived in the region of Hispaniola. Although there is no mention of inhumane treatment in any documents about las Casas while in Hispaniola, las Casas and his father did participate in various campaigns against the Indians in Santo Domingo. They also held various *encomiendas* —a piece of land or small village whose Indians were awarded to a Spanish colonist—given to them by Columbus upon their arrival. Under this law, the colonists of the New World had the right to enslave the Indians and force them to work in agricultural fields or gold mines.

### Protector of the Indians

In 1513, las Casas traveled with Pánfilo de Narváez on the Spanish conquest of Cuba, where he again was awarded an *encomienda* by Governor Diego Veláquez and became a successful farmer. While in Cuba, las Casas witnessed the horrible massacre of the Indians at the hands of the Spaniards at Caonão in 1514. Las Casas's manuscripts note that witnessing the destructive actions of the Spaniards during the Indian massacre affected his soul tremendously. This pivotal scene in las Casas's life led him to a lifelong crusade to help the Indians and fight the *encomienda.* Las Casas's first action for reform in the New World was in 1514 during the Feast of the

Assumption at Espítu Santo. Las Casas passionately sermonized that the Spanish rule in the Indies was unjust and tyrannical because it went against the moral and sacred foundations of a Christian people.

Scholars also believe it was in Cuba when las Casas sketched a "community scheme" which he hoped would replace the *encomienda* system. Las Casas's "community scheme" intended on settling the Indians in villages of their own, grouped around a central Spanish town, in which they would obtain profits from their work. Historian George Sanderline notes in *Witness: Writings of Bartolomé de Las Casas* that "in 1516, Las Casas rewrote the plan [community scheme] in 'court style' and it became the basis for the instructions of an Investigative Commission of Jeronymite friars sent to govern Hispaniola." Thereafter, las Casas was appointed as the Protector of the Indians and accompanied the Jeronymites to Hispaniola in 1516–1517. However, las Casas's work would again be dismissed by the colonists and his "community scheme" was never enacted. Furthermore, the Jeronymites committee yielded to the pressure of the colonists and the *encomienda* system remained in the New World.

After failing to end the *encomienda* system in both Venezuela and Puerto Rico, las Casas entered the Dominican novitiate in Santo Domingo and was professed a Dominican in 1523. As a Dominican, las Casas was sent to found the Dominican monastery at Puerto de Plata, on the north Coast of Hispaniola. In Hispanola he would began to write his most celebrated work, *Historia de las Indias* (*History of the Indies*). Las Casas began to write this book in 1527 and did not finish until 1561. The first part of the book, *Apologética Historia* (*Apologetic History*) was completed in 1559. In this work, las Casas described Indian customs, social and political organizations, and religious practices. Viewed by many as a philosophical treatise, las Casas brilliantly used Aristotelian philosophies to argue that the Indian cultures of the New World were equal to the European Christian cultures. *Historia de las Indias* vividly chronicles the Spanish conquest from 1492–1520 and is valued one of the best literary and historical narratives of the sixteenth century. Renowned scholar Henry Raup Wagner wrote in *The Life and Writings of Bartolomé de las Casas,* "The Historia [History] remains the most valuable single account of the discovery of the New World and the early Spanish period on the islands and Tierre Firme. Casas was not only an eyewitness of much that he told, and a friend of many chief actors, but a most painstaking historian besides; he used and preserved for us masses of documentary material, the most priceless being the diary of Columbus' first voyage."

Las Casas returned to Spain in 1540 and continued to write controversial works about the cruelties inflicted on the Indians by the colonists in the New

World. In Spain, he wrote the first version of the *Brevíssima relación de la destruición de las Indias* (*Very Brief Account of the Destruction of the Indies*) and had the opportunity to read it in the Spanish court. In this treatise, las Casas vividly describes the destruction of the Indians as well as various details of Spanish cruelty in the New World. Furthermore, he argued for specific reforms and the immediate removal of the encomienda system. Because of las Casas's work, as well as the monarch's worries that neofeudalism would develop in the New World under the *encomienda* system, Charles V created *Las Leyes de Indias* (New Laws of the Indies) on November 20, 1542. Under these new laws Indians would no longer be enslaved in the New World and *encomiendas* would no longer be awarded to the colonists.

On July 10, 1544, las Casas left Spain and for Chiapa in order to take his new post as the bishopric. Upon his arrival, he enacted the new laws and ordered all Spaniards with Indians to free them immediately. Las Casas's actions in the reform of the encomienda system made him the most hated man in Mexico. Furthermore, as a result of the enactment of the new laws both Peru and Nicaragua were in flames from a Spanish revolt. Realizing that the new laws had divided his people, in 1545 Charles V revoked the laws which abolish the *encomienda*. In 1546, las Casas returned to Spain in order to change the monarch's mind. However, because of his unpopularity in Spain he was accused of treason for his brief essay entitled *Confesionario* (*Confessions*), in which he continued his attack against the Spaniards' actions in the New World and argued that the Spaniards' claim on the new world was unlawful.

In 1550, las Casas had the opportunity to defend himself in the "great debate" with Juan Gines de Sepúlveda, the emperor's chronicler and Renaissance humanist. In this debate, las Casas defended the Indians by arguing that the Indians of the New World were an intellectual culture and should be given the opportunity to be free Christians. This debate would be a major factor in the reformation of the policies of the Council of the Indies as well as a major contributor to the ending of the old practices of conquest in the New World.

Because of the instability of the new laws in the New World, las Casas continued to write controversial manifestos while in Seville. Las Casas revised his most his most controversial treatise *Brevíssima relación de la destruición de las Indias* in 1552 (*The Very Brief Account of the Destruction of the Indies*). The revised *Brevíssima relación* focused on the debate with Sepúlveda and also contained a controversial "census" of how many Indians were destroyed by the Spaniards in the New World. The treatise was later translated into six languages and given wide circulation by the enemies of Spain. This work infuriated the Spaniards because it helped spread "Leyenda Negra"

(Black Legend) of Spanish cruelty in the New World throughout Europe.

Las Casas tirelessly fought for the rights of the Indians until his death on July 18, 1566, in the monastery of Atocha in Madrid. Las Casas's works have remained some of the most bitterly argued pieces in Spanish history; they have been seen by scholars throughout history as both revolutionary and destructive to the Spanish culture. Despite these and among other controversial interpretations of las Casas's works and life, scholars contend that his work as the Protector of the Indians helped reform both the philosophies and laws of the Spaniards in the New World during the sixteenth century.

## SELECTED PUBLISHED WORKS:

*Historia de las Indias,* three volumes, edicion de Agustín Millares Carlo, Buenos Aires and Mexico: Fondo de Cultura Económica, 1951.
*Obras escogidas de Fray Bartolomé de las Casas,* five volumes, edited by Juan Pérez, Madrid, Biblioteca de la Autores Españoles, 1957.
*Devastation of the Indies: A Brief Account,* Johns Hopkins, 1992.

## SOURCES:

### Books

*Bartolomé de las Casas In History: Toward an Understanding of the Man and His Work,* edited by Juan Friede and Benjamin Keen, Illinois, Northern Illinois University Press, 1971.
Hanke, Lewis, *Bartolomé de las Casas: An interpretation of His Life and writings,* Netherlands, The Hague, 1951.
Hanke, Lewis, *All Mankind Is One: A Study of the Disputation Between Bartolomé de Las Casas and Juan Ginés de Sepúlveda in 1550 on the Intellectual and Religious Capicity of the American Indians,* DeKalb,, Northern Illinois University Press, 1974.
Macnutt, Francis Augustus, *Bartolomé de las Casas: His Life, His Apostolate, and His Writings,* New York, G. P. Putnum and Sons, 1909.
Wagner, Henry Raup, *The Writings of Bartolomé de las Casas,* Albuquerque, University of New Mexico Press, 1967.
*Witness: Writings of Bartolomé de las Casas,* edited by George Sanderline, New York, Orbis Books, 1971.

# Luis Leal
## 1907-
### Mexican American literary critic and scholar

Luis Leal is a prominent scholar of Latin American and Chicano literature. He has published numerous books—ranging from focused critical studies of individual writers to comprehensive anthologies, bibliographies, and histories—and has written more than 200 journal articles for both United States and Latin American audiences. His professional affiliations include the Modern Language Association of America, the American Association of Teachers of Spanish and Portuguese, the Instituto Internacional de Literatura Iberoamericana, and the Asociación de Escritores Mexicanos. He is also the recipient of an Aztec Eagle award (1991).

Born in Linares, Nuevo Leon, Mexico, on September 17, 1907, Leal is a naturalized United States citizen. He married Gladys Clemens in 1936. They are the parents of two sons: Antonio and Luis Alonso. Leal earned his bachelor's degree from Northwestern University in 1940. His studies continued at the University of Chicago, where he received a master's degree in 1941 and a doctorate nine years later. His graduate education was interrupted by World War II, when Leal spent two years in the Pacific theater. Leal taught at the University of Chicago for several years, serving as an assistant professor of Spanish from 1948 to 1952. Over the following decades he held posts at the University of Mississippi, Emory University, the University of Illinois at Urbana-Champaign, and the University of California, Santa Barbara, where he served as acting director of the Center for Chicano studies.

### Earns Praise For Scholarly Contributions

Reviewers have often commended Leal's additions to previously neglected subjects. When Leal's history of the short story, *Historia del cuento hispanoamericano,* first appeared, C. W. Butler declared in *Hispania* that the book was "a fine scholarly contribution to a field in which such a reference work has long been needed." In a similar vein, Leal's short story anthology, *Cuentistas Hispanoamericanos del siglo veinte,* earned the praise of the *Modern Language Journal*'s reviewer, Jorge R. Ayora, who asserted that the book "was very much needed" and that "one should be grateful that a specialist in the short story of the stature of Luis Leal has undertaken the task." Leal's contributions in this regard have transcended general reference works and anthologies. *World Literature Today*'s reviewer T. O. Taylor found that Leal's 1983 book on the Mexican writer **Juan Rulfo** "excels

precisely in areas where clarity and additional information are needed."

Clarity and comprehensiveness are oft-cited qualities in discussions of Leal's scholarship. Discussing Leal's work on the Mexican writer **Mariano Azuela** in the *Modern Language Review,* D. L. Shaw called *Mariano Azuela, vida y obra* "the only reasonably accessible full-length study of the creator of the Novel of the Mexican Revolution." When an English-language version appeared in 1971, *Choice* found that "nothing in English compares with Leal's comprehensiveness" and recommended that the book "should be a part of every college library." Djelal Kadir elaborated in the *Modern Language Journal:* "The portrayal of Mariano Azuela has a human completeness to it; we are presented not only with the inventions of a novelist but also with the man, his apprenticeship, professional and literary . . . as well as being exposed to the atmosphere and human context in which Azuela lived and labored."

*Juan Rulfo* earned similar praise. Taylor deemed it "a compact yet thorough introduction . . . useful for both the specialist and the general reader." *Choice* noted that Leal's plot summaries, "concise and well written, as well as fascinating enough to induce the uninitiated to delve into Rulfo's works," were also "skillfully combined" with other historical and critical material "to afford a rounded picture of Rulfo's work and Rulfo the man in literary, historical, and social context." Even Leal's larger-scale projects are characterized by clarity and completeness. Alberto J. Carlos, writing in *Hispania,* called Leal's *Panorama de la literatura mexicana actual* "a remarkably concise and penetrating study" that was "without a doubt the comprehensive critical survey of 20th-century Mexican literature. "Leal's style and scope have enabled him to communicate with a wide audience. As Lon Pearson wrote in a *Modern Language Journal* review of Leal's *Breve Historia de la literatura hispanoamericana* that the book, "written in clear and precise Spanish," was "not only an excellent history for literature survey courses," but it could also be "a great aid to the graduate student or teacher who wants a concise and objective text for review purposes."

In 1978 Leal was honored by a conference and a book of essays, *Homenaje a Luis Leal: Estudios sobre literatura hispanoamericana,* edited by Donald W. Bleznick and Juan O. Valencia. In 1988 Salvador Güereña and Raquel Quiroz González edited the book *Luis Leal: A Bibliography with Interpretive and Critical Essays.* Since 1980 he has been a distinguished lecturer at the University of California, Santa Barbara, which has established the "Luis Leal Endowed Chair in Chicano Studies," the first in the nation dedicated to this subject. In his ninth decade of life, he has continued to write and publish.

## SELECTED PUBLISHED WORKS:

*México: Civilizaciones y culturas,* Houghton, 1955, revised edition, 1971.

*Breve historia del cuento mexicano,* Ediciones de Andrea, 1956.

(Editor) *Antología del cuento mexicano,* Ediciones de Andrea, 1957.

*Bibliografía del cuento mexicano,* Ediciones de Andrea, 1958.

(With Edmundo Valadés) *La revolución y las letras: Dos estudios sobre la novela y el cuento de la revolución mexicana,* Departamento de Literatura, Instituto Nacional de Bellas Artes, 1960.

(Editor with Carlos Castillo) *Miguel de Cervantes Saavedra, La ilustre fregona,* Heath, 1960.

*Mariano Azuela: Vida y obra* ("Mariano Azuela: Life and Work"), Ediciones de Andrea, 1961.

(Editor) *El cuento veracruzano: Antología,* Universidad Veracruzana, 1966.

*Historia del cuento hispanoamericano,* Ediciones de Andrea, 1966, 2nd edition, 1971.

(Editor) *El cuento mexicano de los orígenes al modernismo,* Editorial Universitaria de Buenos Aires, 1966.

*El cuento hispanoamericano,* Centro Editor de América Latina, 1967.

*Mariano Azuela,* Centro Editor de América Latina, 1967.

*Panorama de la literatura mexicana actual,* Unión Panamericana, 1968.

(With Joseph H. Silverman) *Siglo veinte,* Holt, 1968.

(Editor) Juan Rulfo, *Pedro Páramo,* Appleton, 1970.

(With Frank Dauster) *Literatura de Hispanoamérica,* Harcourt, 1970.

*Breve historia de la literatura hispanoamericana,* Knopf, 1971.

*Mariano Azuela,* Twayne, 1971.

(Editor) *Cuentistas hispanoamericanos del siglo veinte,* Random House, 1972.

(Editor) *Mariano Azuela: Páginas escogidas,* Universidad Nacional Autónoma de México, 1973.

*Cuentos de la revolución,* Universidad Nacional Autónoma de México, 1977.

(Co-author) *A Decade of Chicano Literature, 1970–1979: Critical Essays and Bibliography,* Editorial La Causa, 1982.

*Juan Rulfo,* Twayne, 1983.

*Aztlán y México: Perfiles literarios e históricos,* Editorial Bilingüe, 1985.

(With Roberto G. Trujillo) *Literatura chicana,* Floricanto Press, 1985.

*Cuento hispanoamericano contemporaneo,* Premía, 1988.

## SOURCES:

### Books

*Hispanic-American Almanac,* edited by Nicolás Kanellos, Detroit, Gale, 1993.

*Hispanic Writers,* edited by Bryan Ryan, Detroit, Gale, 1991.

*Homenaje a Luis Leal: Estudios sobre literatura hispanoamericana,* edited by Donald W. Bleznick and Juan O. Valencia, Madrid, Insula, 1978.

### Periodicals

*Choice,* June, 1971, p. 555; September, 1972, p. 821; January, 1984, p. 710;

*Hispania,* September, 1967, pp. 610–11; September, 1968, pp. 598–99; September, 1970, pp. 583–84; March, 1973, pp. 190–91.

*Modern Language Journal,* December, 1972, p. 526; January, 1974, pp. 77–8; March, 1974, p. 134.

*Modern Language Review,* April, 1973, pp. 431–32.

*World Literature Today,* Winter, 1985, p. 65.

—*Sketch by Erika Dreifus*

---

# Ernesto Lecuona
## 1896-1963
### Cuban pianist and composer

The songs of Ernesto Lecuona, the Cuban pianist and composer, helped to popularize the music of the Caribbean in concert halls and juke boxes around the globe. Describing him in 1946 as "Cuba's Light Music King," William A. Taylor wrote in the *Musical Courier:* "Six or seven of his major works are purely 'serious,' but most of his published compositions are sung, whistled, hummed and danced to." At the time of his death in 1963, the *New York Times* observed, "Mr. Lecuona's songs are a part of Latin-American culture" and "continue to be perenially in demand."

A talented pianist, Lecuona gave his first New York piano recital when he was in his early twenties. "Mr. Lecuona has been described as the George Gershwin of Cuba and, like Gershwin, he was an outstanding performer," according to the *New York Times.* He was also a skilled conductor, who toured and conducted the Havana Casino Orchestra and the Orquesta Lecuona. Whether he was penning film

*Ernesto Lecuona*

scores or conducting orchestras, Lecuona brought the rhythms of his island birthplace to his music. He was the man "who introduced the rumba and conga rhythms to this continent (and) is thus responsible for there being so much Latin dancing and music around here," wrote Patrick Tyson for *King Features Syndicate.*

### A Musical Prodigy

Lecuona was born to a middle-class family in Guanabocoa, Cuba, on August 7, 1896. His father was a newspaperman in Havana. Although his parents were not musical, his sisters Ernestina and Elisa, and brother Luis, became pianists, while his brother, Teodor, played the violin. Two other brothers were also musicians. Lecuona made his piano debut in Havana at the age of five. He studied music theory with the Spanish composer Joaquin Nin, father of the writer Anais Nin. When he was 11 years old, he published his first song, "Cuba y América," a two-step performed by Cuban military bands. As a teenager, he organized orchestras to perform in silent movie houses and ballrooms in Havana. In 1913, he graduated as a teacher of singing and piano from the National Conservatory in Havana.

In 1917, Lecuona gave his first New York piano recital and made his first Victor recordings. In the following years, he toured Spain, Colombia, and Venezuela. He would go on to publish four albums of his piano work. "Mr. Lecuona was a pianist who

never practiced—except when he felt in the mood for playing," wrote a *New York Times* contributor. After a U.S. tour, he returned to New York in 1922 for an eight-week appearance at the Capitol Theatre. He participated in some of the first live radio broadcasts by Samual (Roxy) Rothafel. In 1930, he toured Europe and presented a concert of Cuban music at the Salle Pleyel in Paris. Along with his own work, he played light pieces by late nineteenth- and early twentieth-century Cuban composers.

### Top Hit Songs in the 1930s

Lecuona composed and published over 400 songs for dance bands, orchestras, musicals, films and the radio. As a young man, he studied composition with Maurice Ravel in Paris. His song "Siboney" was a top hit in 1929, and "Andalucia" and "Malagueña" led the music charts in 1930. For the popular "Malagueña," he used traditional folkdance tunes from the Spanish province of Malaga. Among his other famous tunes were "Say Si Si," "Always in My Heart," "Jungle Drums," "Aquella tarde," "Canto Carabili," "Como arrullo de palmas," "Dame tus dos rosas," "El crisantemo," "María la O," and "Mariposa." His principal publisher was the Edward B. Marks Music Corporation.

Lecuona was musical director of the MGM film *Under Cuban Skies* (1930), and composed the score for *Carnival in Costa Rica* (1947). He also wrote the scores of more than 30 musical productions, including *Maria La O, Rosa la China,* and *El Cafetal.* As a conductor, he led the Orquesta de la Habana in the late 1930's, as well as the Havana Casino Orchestra. His dance band, Lecuona's Cuban Boys, toured the United States, Latin America, and Europe.

In October 1943, he held a successful concert in Carnegie Hall, featuring "Siboney" and other well-known compositions, and the premier of his "Rapsodia Negra" ("Black Rhapsody"). Insisting on authentic sound, he brought Afro-Cuban musicians and their native instruments from Cuba for the performances, while playing one of the piano parts himself. "In the triple role of batonist-composer-pianist, Mr. Lecuona ranged over wide tracts of Latin-American rhythms and motifs, woven into compact lyric and symphonic form. As featured premier, Black Rhapsody proved Lecuona's grasp of native idiom and his flair for heaving rhythmic sequences," reported an unidentified New York newspaper, collected by the NBC Music Research Files at the New York Public Library.

A meticulous perfectionist, Lecuona composed his scores at a card table, without using a piano. "His completed manuscripts are as clean-cut and legible as a copper plate, an act he explains by stressing the regularity of his life," wrote Taylor in the *Musical Courier.* He composed in spurts, then rested for a few months. On January 6, 1929, he wrote four hit songs,

"Blue Night," "Siboney," "Say Si Si," and "Two Hearts That Pass in the Night," reported Taylor.

A heavy-set, melancholic figure with famously dark eyes, Lecuona lived in New York and Havana, moving easily between the two cultures. In 1943, Cuban President **Fulgencio Batista** named him cultural attaché to the Cuban Embassy in the United States. After **Fidel Castro** came to power in 1959, Lecuona left Cuba to live in the United States, Spain, and the Canary Islands. He never married, but he was a popular host who invited friends to play music in his home in Jackson Heights, Queens, though he would escape on solitary walks when the company got to be too much. "Besides liking to play the piano, and collecting wood and stone sculpture of the Aztecs, Mayas, the ancient Peruvian Incas, his greatest delight is brewing strong, black Cuban coffee," reported Taylor. Lecuona died of a heart attack, while recovering from a lung ailment, in Santa Cruz de Tenerife in the Canary Islands, on November 29, 1963.

## SOURCES:

### Books

Lax, Roger, and Smith, Frederick, *The Great Song Thesaurus,* second Edition, New York, Oxford University Press, 1989, pp. 55, 56, 202, 313.
*The New Grove Dictionary of Music and Musicians,* Volume 10, edited by Stanley Sadie, London, Macmillan Publishers, 1980, p. 595.

### Periodicals

*Musical Courier,* October 15, 1946, p. 9.
*New York Times,* December 1, 1963, p. 84.

### Other

NBC Music Research Files, collected by the New York Public Library.
Works by Patrick Tyson for King Features Syndicate, 1946.

*—Sketch by Ann Malaspina*

# John Leguizamo
## 1965-
### Colombian American actor, writer, and comedian

John Leguizamo, a Colombian-born actor, has appeared in several films, plays, and television programs. He has also written, produced, directed, and starred in two solo shows: *Spic-o-rama* and *Mambo Mouth.* These shows, as with much of Leguizamo's work, won him both praise and stringent criticism.

John Leguizamo was born on July 22, 1965, in Bogotá, Colombia. His salesman father, Alberto, and his mother Luz, left Leguizamo and his younger brother Sergio with grandparents and moved to Queens, New York. A year later, once the Leguizamos had found a place to live and jobs—Albert worked as a waiter and Luz worked in a factory—they sent for the two boys. While Leguizamo was growing up, his parents fought when they were not working; and although they divorced when Leguizamo was 13, this home life had a profound effect upon him. "I became this crazy maniac, always causing trouble," he told Joe Treen in a 1991 *People* interview.

Though this "crazy maniac" was the foundation for the talented actor, comedian, and writer Leguizamo became, as a youngster he was labeled a troublemaker. Shortly after his parents divorced, Leguizamo and a friend took over the public-address system on one of the New York City subway trains and delivered a joking monologue "as your new subway deejays." The police did not find the situation nearly as funny as Leguizamo and his friend or the other passengers. Consequently, Leguizamo was returned to Colombia at the age of 14 to live with relatives.

### Discovers Acting

A year later, he returned to New York City and found that his reputation as a troublemaker had not dwindled. The public school system recommended that Leguizamo attend a Youth Counseling League run by the city. One teacher recognized Leguizamo's talents and urged him to channel his energies into acting rather than trouble. Leguizamo listened and randomly selected a performing arts school from the yellow pages. In 1983, he began to study acting. Leguizamo's mother told *People* in 1991: "[Leguizamo] said he wanted to be a veterinarian. But he would lock himself in the bathroom and practice his voices for hours."

## Begins Acting Career

After studying drama at New York University, Leguizamo landed a small role on *Miami Vice.* Shortly thereafter, he was cast as a Hispanic soldier in the movie *Casualties of War.* "I grew up a lot there [in the role]," Leguizamo told Treen in 1991. "From Sean [Penn] I learned that acting is real and you can let it go as big as you want."

Leguizamo's first solo show, *Mambo Mouth,* began as an off-Broadway show, moving from the SubPlot Theatre, to the American Place Theatre, to the Orpheum. It landed on HBO in 1991 after Leguizamo's appearances in the movies *Regarding Henry, Hangin' With the Homeboys,* and *Die Hard II.* Leguizamo delivered cutting satirical performances ranging from a transvestite prostitute to a Hispanic businessman who patterns himself after Japanese businessmen. Leguizamo used this character, called "The Crossover King," to satirize the Hispanics desire for assimilation. He donned thick glasses and lectured an imaginary audience about how they can be "Latino-free."

Although Leguizamo's work has been criticized for being "politically incorrect," he has remained undaunted. He told Treen in 1991, "Some Latins wonder why I'm not doing these Bill Cosby-type doctors. My show's not about creating new images. It's about taking old images and twisting them inside out and saying all these horrible things about our feelings of inferiority and racism that we feel inside and have heard growing up. For me, it is an exorcism."

Many Hispanics have disagreed, condemning Leguizamo for furthering negative and sexist stereotypes. *Village Voice* columnist Coco Fusco accused Leguizamo of "refried machismo" and "woman bashing." She wrote of *Mambo Mouth,* "A pit formed in my stomach as I witnessed how his cracks drew so many cackles, and as far as I know, not one peep of protest from the female sector.... Would the chauvinism still be funny if it rolled off a white boy's tongue?" Leguizamo responded to Guy Garcia in 1991, "Latin culture is very subliminal. There's still a lot of self-hate. It's underneath this mat and rug hidden in the basement, and it's the beast that wants to come out and chop our heads off. I'm letting out a lot of monsters."

Despite critical dissent, *Mambo Mouth* won an Obie and an Outer Critics Circle Award in 1991. Leguizamo moved on to create *Spic-o-Rama* in 1992, which he first performed at the Goodman Theatre in Chicago and later at the Westside Theatre in New York City. *Spic-o-Rama* received rave reviews and made its way to HBO. Leguizamo then worked on the film *Super Mario Brothers* and landed his own TV show on the Fox network in 1995 called *House of Buggin'.* He also appeared in *Carlito's Way.* Leguizamo summed up his goals as a creative artist to Treen in 1991: "I want to contribute Latin culture to American culture, to show our sensibilities and our passions."

## SELECTED VIDEOGRAPHY:

*Casualties of War,* Columbia 1989.
*Die Hard 2: Die Harder,* 1990.
*Street Hunter,* 1991.
*Hangin' With the Homeboys,* 1991.
*Regarding Henry,* 1991.
*Whispers in the Dark,* 1992.
*Super Mario Brothers,* 1993.
*Carlito's Way,* 1994.

## SOURCES:

### Books

*Contemporary Theatre, Film, and Television,* Volume 11, edited by Emily J. McMurray, Detroit, Gale, 1994.
Reyes, Luis, and Peter Rubie, *Hispanics in Hollywood: An Encyclopedia of Film and TV,* New York, Garland, 1994.

### Periodicals

*Newsweek,* December 14, 1992, p.87.
*People,* November 11, 1991, pp.148–9.
*Time,* October 28, 1991, p.85.
*Village Voice,* April 9, 1991, p.24.
*Vogue,* April 1993, pp. 242, 250, 258.

—*Sketch by Christopher B. Tower*

# Tania Leon
## 1943-
### Cuban composer, conductor, and music director

A multi-faceted musician, Tania Leon is an international figure in the music world. She has carved a niche for herself in contemporary music as a composer, conductor, and music director, in the process receiving numerous commissions and awards.

The daughter of Oscar Leon Mederos and Dora Ferran, Leon was born in Havana, Cuba, on May 14, 1943. Leon studied piano, violin, and music theory, earning multiple bachelors degrees and a masters degree in music from a Cuban university. From 1964 to 1967 she performed as a piano soloist in Cuba and acted as music director for a television station in Havana.

While in the United States, Leon met Arthur Mitchell in the 1969, who offered her the music directorship of his new dance troupe, the Dance Theatre of Harlem. Leon accepted his offer and held the post until 1980. When the Dance Theatre performed at the Festival of Two Worlds in Spoleto, Italy in 1971, Leon was unexpectedly given the opportunity to conduct the Juilliard Orchestra, which was accompanying the troupe. "I was encouraged by Arthur Mitchell and Gian-Carlo Menotti to work with the orchestra," reminisced Leon to Anne Lundy in the *Black Perspective in Music*. "They encouraged me to do that, and I had never done it in my life. It was my very first time, but I picked up the baton, and I conducted the performance."

Back in the United States, Leon began to study conducting formally with Lasslo Halass, one of the founders of the New York City Opera. Encouraged, she enrolled at the Julliard School of Music to study with Vincent LaSilva and later attended New York University, where she earned a masters degree in composition in 1975. Three years later, Leon studied at the Berkshire Music Center at Tanglewood with many guest conductors, among them the renowned Leonard Bernstein and Seiji Ozawa.

Leon took over conducting responsibilities with the Dance Theatre, and soon she was immersed in composing for the troupe as well. With Mitchell, she composed her first commission for the troupe—*Tones*—in 1970. The ballets *The Beloved, Dougla,* and *Spiritual Suite* quickly followed. *Dougla,* in particular, met with success, becoming a regular part of the repertoire of European dance companies.

Leon remained active as a conductor. At the invitation of Lukas Foss, she founded the Brooklyn Philharmonic Community Concert Series in 1977. She also served as the music director-conductor of the 1978 Broadway production of *The Wiz* and the "Dance in America" series for public television. In 1979 she directed Robert Wilson 's *Death, Destruction, and Detroit* and several years later composed and directed the music for his *Maggie Magalita and The Golden Window.* After leaving her position with the Dance Theatre, Leon appeared as a guest conductor at venues in the United States and Puerto Rico. Leon saw this as a pioneering time for her, and she faced problems "like any pioneer would," she told *Ebony.* "It's not common for a woman of my skin color to conduct serious music, so I have to know the score inside out, or work twice as hard as male conductors."

### Finds Musical Voice

In the mid-1980s, Leon began to express her diverse musical background in her compositions. In *Carabal,* a piece for orchestra, Leon employed rhythms and improvisation from Cuban jazz, in a far-ranging blend of tonal colors and rhythmic patterns. Explaining that the Carabali are Africans who fought off slave traders to become known as an indomitable people, Leon described in *Peer-Southern Concert Music* the piece named *Carabali* as "a symbol of a spirit that cannot be broken." Leon added, "I have tried to convey such an image by creating a body of sounds propelled by a persistent rhythmic language."

Leon's compositions garnered praise and soon earned her recognition as a new voice in the music world. In 1985 she was awarded a residency at the Lincoln Center Institute in New York City and won the Dean Dixon conducting award. She also joined the composition faculty of the Brooklyn College Conservatory, where she was made full professor in 1994.

In the 1990s, Leon hit her stride, with a steady stream of residencies, guest conducting appearances, and commissions for new pieces. She won grants from the National Endowment for the Arts, the Copland Fund, and the American Academy of Arts and Letters, which allowed for recordings to be made of her works, including *Indigena, Paisanos Semos!,* and *Batéy.* She has been invited to appear as a guest conductor/composer at Harvard University, Yale University, the Cleveland Institute, the Ravinia Festival in Chicago, the Bellagio Center in Italy, and elsewhere.

In 1993 Leon accepted a three-year appointment as Revson Composer Fellow for the New York Philharmonic to advise conductor Kurt Masur about contemporary music. She also acted as artistic director for the concert series on Latin American music sponsored by the American Composers Orchestra. For her opera *Scourge of Hyacinths,* based on a play by Nobel Prize-winning dramatist Wole Soyinka of Nigeria, Leon won the BMW Prize for Best Composition at the 1994 Munich Biennale for New Music Theater.

Leon does not like to be categorized by race or gender, preferring to be judged by her musical accomplishments. "My chosen purpose in life is to be a musician, a composer, a conductor," she told Lundy. "This is the way I am making my contribution to mankind."

### SOURCES:

#### Books

*Bakers Biographical Dictionary of Musicians,* 8th edition, edited by Nicolas Slonimsky, Schirmer, 1992.

Cohen, Aaron I., *International Encyclopedia of Women Composers,* Volume 1, 2nd edition, Books & Music, 1987.

*Hispanic-American Almanac,* edited by Nicolas Kanellos, Detroit, Gale, 1993.

Southern, Eileen, *Biographical Dictionary of Afro-American and African Musicians,* Westport, Conn., Greenwood Press, 1982.

**Periodicals**

*Black Perspective in Music,* fall 1988, pp. 213–25.

*Ear,* 1986–1987, p. 16.

*Ebony,* February, 1989, pp. 54–62.

*New York Times,* December 10, 1991, p. C19.

*Notes: Quarterly Journal of the Music Library Association,* 1988, pp. 581–82.

*Peer-Southern Concert Music,* fall 1992, pp. 1–2; winter 1994–1995, p. 4.

*San Francisco Chronicle,* October 10, 1994, p. E3.

*Symphony,* 1988, p. 27.

—*Sketch by J. M. Lesinski*

*José Lezama Lima*

# José Lezama Lima
## 1910(?)-1976
### Cuban poet and novelist

José Lezama Lima, often referred to as a "Proust of the Caribbean," was one of Cuba's foremost poets. He was a renowned conversationalist and a charismatic literary force. Gordon Brotherston, writing for the *Times Literary Supplement* in 1975, declared that Lezama Lima was "a point of reference outstanding and original in every sense." Lezama Lima devoted his life to literature, immersing himself in a literary world divorced from the harsh and violent reality of Cuba's dictatorships. "As against the limitations of an unjust society, he saw art as a sphere of liberty and the poet as the 'engenderer of images'," observed Jean Franco in *A Literary History of Spain* in 1973. Lezama Lima's work has been considered inaccessible and bewildering. Edmund White reviewed *Paradiso,* Lezama Lima's controversial masterpiece, for the *New York Times Book Review* in 1974 and asserted, "Depending on your taste or tolerance for elaborate diction, you will find Lezama's style either intoxicating or repellent."

José Lezama Lima was born on December 19, 1910 (some sources place the year at 1912), in Cuba to a bourgeois, Creole family. His father was an army colonel who died suddenly of influenza when Lezama Lima was eight. His death profoundly influenced Lezama Lima, engendering a deep sense of absence and loss that permeated much of his literary work. In accordance with his mother's desires, Lezama Lima studied law, theology, and history at the Universidad de la Habana. He practiced law at a private firm from 1938 to 1940 and worked as a bureaucrat, but his literary vocation always remained of paramount importance.

Lezama Lima's writing career was launched during his student days at the Universidad de La Habana. At the age of 21 he wrote *Muerte de Narciso* (*Death of Narcissus*), a volume of poetry. Lezama Lima also founded a succession of influential literary reviews. The first, *Verbum,* was established in 1937 and served as a forum for transcendentalist poetry. It was followed by *Espuela de Plata* (1939–1941), *Nadie Parecía* (1942–1944) and *Orígenes* (1944–1956). *Orígenes* endowed Cuban poetry with a fresh impetus; with Lezama Lima's leadership, it served as the nucleus for a group of writers, artists, musicians, and philosophers who dominated Cuba's contemporary intellectual life.

### After the Revolution and *Fsubdiso*

Lezama Lima supported the Cuban Revolution of 1959 and was subsequently honored by **Fidel Castro**'s regime. In 1960 he was named director of the literature and publications department of the National Council of Culture. He was also elected one of six vice-presidents of the National Union of Cuban Writers and Artists in 1961. Despite his recognition, Lezama Lima was not held in high favor by the Castro regime: his poetry was criticized for its escapism and he was unjustly associated with the beliefs of the Batista regime. Afflicted with asthma since childhood, Lezama Lima was prevented from traveling, except for rare visits to Mexico and Jamaica. Restricted from exile, Lezama Lima instead journeyed into "his own imaginative universe," observed a critic for the *Times Literary Supplement* in 1974. Like other Hispanic poets of his generation, Lezama Lima was inspired by the Spanish Golden Age poet **Luis de Góngora** (1561–1627). A *Times Literary Supplement* reviewer declared in 1970 that Lezama Lima had "no difficulty in talking of Góngora as if he were a contemporary, in dealing with Góngora's beliefs as if they were his own."

In 1966 Lezama Lima received international acclaim with the publication of *Paradiso*, his monumental and polemic novel. Deemed controversial by many reviewers for its explicit homosexual and heterosexual encounters, and for its highly elaborate language, it was scorned and praised. *Paradiso* is Lezama Lima's semi-autobiographical evocation of José Cemí, his childhood and maturation, and his formation as a poet. Typical of the novel's admirers, Peter Moscoso-Gongora in a 1994 essay in the *Nation* deemed that *Paradiso* "triumphs as a work of pure aestheticism, of absolute digression and linguistic tour de force, in which, as with Góngora, everything is subsumed—sometimes soundly abused—in favor of the word."

Lezama Lima spent much of his life living with his mother in Havana until her death in 1964. In 1965 he married María Luisa Bautista, who rejuvenated his literary work and roused him from a state of depression. In his later years, Lezama Lima was plagued by asthma and circulatory problems; he died on August 9, 1976.

## SELECTED PUBLISHED WORKS:

*La fi jeza*, Orígenes, 1949.
*Analecta del reloj* (essays), Orígenes, 1953.
*El padre Gazteluen la poesía*, Orígenes, 1955.
*La expresión americana* (lectures), Ministero de Educadión, 1957.
*Tratados en la Habana*, Universidad Central de Las Villas, 1958.
*Dador* (poems), [Havana], 1960.
*Antología de la poesía cubana*, Consejo Nacional de Cultura, 1965.
*Orbita de Lezama Lima*, Unión Nacional de Escritores y Artistas, 1966.
*Paradiso* (novel), Unión Nacional de Escritores y Artistas, 1966; translation by Gregory Rabassa published under same title, Farrar, Straus, 1974.

*Lezama Lima* (anthology), J. Alvarez, 1968.
*Los grandes todos*, ARCA, 1969.
*Posible imagen de José Lezama Lima* (poems), Libres de Sinera, 1969.
*Esferaimagen*, Tusquets Editor, 1970.
*La cantidad hechizada* (essays), UNEAC, 1970.
*Poesía completa* (poems), Instituto de Libro, 1970.
*Las eras imaginarias*, Editorial Fundamentos, 1971.
*Algunos tratados en La Habana*, Editorial Anagrama, 1971.
*Introducción a los vasos órficos*, Barral Editores, 1971.
*Coloquio con Juan Ramón Jiménez*, Estudios Gráficos de CBA, 1973.
*Obras Completas*, two volumes, Aguilar, 1975–77.
*Cangrejos y golondrinas*, Editorial Calicanto, 1977.
*Oppiano Licario*, Ediciones Era, 1977.
*Fragmentos a su imán*, Editorial Arte y Literatura, 1977.
*Cartas (1939–1976): José Lezama Lima*, compiled and edited by Eloísa Lezama Lima, Orígenes, 1979.
*El reino de la imagen*, Biblioteca Ayacucho, 1981.
*Imagen y posibilidad*, Editorial Letras Cubanas, 1981.
*Juego de las decapitaciones*, Montesinos, 1982.
*Cuentos* (short stories), Editorial Letras Cubanas, 1987.

## SOURCES:

### Books

Flores, Angel, *Spanish American Authors: The Twentieth Century,* edited by Angel Flores, New York, H. W. Wilson Company, 1992, pp. 477–80.
Franco, Jean, *A Literary History of Spain: Spanish Literature since Independence,* London, Ernest Benn, 1973, pp. 232–34.
*Hispanic Writers: A Selection of Sketches from Contemporary Authors,* edited by Bryan Ryan, Detroit, Gale Research, 1991, pp. 280–81.
*Latin American Writers,* Volume 3, edited by Carlos A. Solé, New York, Charles Scribner's Sons, 1989, pp. 1125–30.

### Periodicals

*Nation,* May 11, 1974, pp. 600–01.
*New York Times,* August 10, 1976, p. 32.
*New York Times Book Review,* April 21, 1974, pp. 27–8.
*Times* (London), August 12, 1976, p. 14.
*Times Literary Supplement,* 1970, p. 1514; 1974, p. 1062; 1975, p. 925.

—*Sketch by Amanda Beresford*

# Aliza Lifshitz
## 19??-
### Mexican American physician and reporter

Aliza Lifshitz served as the president of the 1,300-member California Hispanic American Medical Association from 1991 to 1995. One of the first Latina physicians to become involved in the struggle against AIDS, she devotes about one third of her Los Angeles practice to the care of people diagnosed with the HIV virus. Many of her patients are undocumented workers, so-called illegal aliens. "They come here seeking the American dream," she observed. "Most of them are very young. And now they are alone, frightened and devastated by this dreaded disease." In a public service ad taken out by the American Medical Association, Lifshitz stated that "the first principle of medical ethics is to offer compassion and respect for human dignity. For me, this pledge includes the illegal alien dying of AIDS. . . . It is so easy to stereotype these people simply as 'illegals with AIDS.' But I want people to know they are human, too. That they have a mother or a father or a child who will miss them when they are gone." As part of her work she participates on AIDS committees for both the California Medical Association and the Los Angeles Medical Association, as well as other state and private organizations.

A private-practice physician specializing in internal medicine, clinical pharmacology, and endocrinology, Aliza Lifshitz likens herself to an old fashioned doctor. She has worked with community-based organizations to offer low-cost treatment to indigents, and she works with patients who can not afford payment. Her "old fashioned" style has made her popular. Some of her patients travel great distances to see her and bring small tokens of their appreciation. As she explained in an interview with Diana Martínez, "I really like my patients, and sometimes some of the patients that I see will either knit something, or make something I can hang on the wall or they bring some cookies that they prepared or some fruit. . . . I guess that's old fashioned too, but I love it." She says communicating and giving time to her patients is very important to her. She explained, "Recently, I had a new woman patient, and I did her medical history and her physical examination, as I do with all my patients. As I was examining her, I was explaining what I was doing and describing the laboratory tests I would be asking for. As I was finishing up, I asked her what she did for a living. When she told me she was a neurologist, I almost died. I apologized for explaining things the way I did. And she said, 'Oh no, I loved it,' and later wrote me a letter that said it was nice to see

*Aliza Lifshitz*

that there were still some old fashioned doctors around. I felt very complimented by her letter."

Lifshitz was born in Mexico City to Jewish Mexican parents. Her father, in addition to being an engineer, graduated from the Music Conservatory in Mexico as a classical pianist. Her mother, a painter, would occasionally work with him. Her parents enrolled Lifshitz in the American elementary school in Mexico City to expose their daughter to culturally diverse children and to learn English. She attended Mexico City's Jewish High School before studying at the Catholic Universidad LaSalle. After graduating with honors, she opted for a medical career. As she explained to Martínez, "I wanted to do something that was creative and would help people. . . . I've always seen medicine as an art that is based on a science. The greatest majority of the healing that we do is actually through listening to the patient and communicating with them." She enrolled at the Universidad Nacional Autonoma de México, graduating cum laude in 1976. She completed her medical training and residency in the United States attending Tulane University and the University of California at San Diego.

### Followed Example Set by Parents

Lifshitz's patients have often referred to her as compassionate. She attributes this trait to her parents. She told Martínez, "Both my parents were dedicated to helping people. My mother had more time to practice it. It was one of those things I always admired about her. She was always there for people, and I thought 'Wow if I could ever be like that!' My mother had a tremendously big heart for people. I remember her taking care of everything from a limping dog on the street to making sure she bought food for people who she saw needed it. That's what my mother was all about."

Known for communicating with her patients one-on-one, Lifshitz also deals with the media in the same manner. As she told Martínez, "I can reach so many more people and get so much more information out through the media. With one written article or one television health report, I'm able to reach more people than I would be able to reach in an entire year with my practice." Lifshitz believes the Latino community, in particular, needs more information on the HIV virus and other health concerns. In an interview published in *Unidos* magazine, she said "In 20 to 30 years, AIDS will be primarily a minority disease. It is evident the gay community has been more effectively reached regarding AIDS education and awareness." Echoing these sentiments, Lifshitz told Martínez, "There is so much information out there for someone who speaks English. In very many instances it has been said, and it continues to be said, that Hispanics are not interested in preventive health. But many times it's simply because Hispanics don't have access to that information. Once data are made available to them, they are very interested."

Lifshitz is currently the health reporter for the Spanish-language Univision, a television network, and local television in Los Angeles. In addition to reporting, she has produced prime-time specials on various health-related topics. She is also a charter and board member of the National Association of Physician Broadcasters, editor-in-chief of *Hispanic Physician*, and medical columnist for *L.A. Opinion*, Los Angeles's Spanish-language daily newspaper. Recalling the beginning of her media career, which began in 1986 on KSCI-TV in Southern California with a live 30-minute call-in program, she told Martínez: "I received hundreds of calls and would spend my weekends answering mail. That's when I saw the wealth a program like that was for our community." She added, "I enjoy everything I do. I enjoy contact with my patients, so when you like something so much it's not difficult to do it. It's what keeps me going. I feel that I'm very privileged that I have been able to accomplish a lot and I am able to do what I'm doing. Sometimes I'm tired but I'm always excited about my work."

## Advocate of Universal Basic Health Care System

Lifshitz is very concerned with the state of health care in the United States. She explained to Martínez some of her principal concerns. Like many health care professionals, she sees a need for universal basic health care. "We have more working poor without insurance, we have more elderly retired with health care needs. We have less people carried through government aid." She continued, "And there has been a lot of cost shifting to insurance companies to cover for uncompensated care. We have overloaded hospitals and they are closing their emergency rooms. We need to be able to provide basic health care for everyone, in a country that is supposed to be a developed country. If we are going to rate how civilized a country is according to how they treat their poor, I think we're becoming more and more uncivilized."

Additionally, Lifshitz is concerned about issues regarding women's health. In an interview for the Spanish-language publication *Vanidades* she said, "I believe that things are changing. However, I think that as a woman, one still has to work twice as hard to receive recognition for your merits. But I believe that women who come after us will have a slightly easier road than we have now." She postulates that as women attain greater recognition in the health field, more attention will be paid to women's medical issues. In an interview with *Hispanic* magazine, Lifshitz noted, "The impact that women have had on health care beyond nursing has not been recognized. People don't realize that there are some really interesting and great women in health care. Most research projects in the past have focused on men; the medical world needs to focus more on women."

When asked what drives her, Lifshitz concluded: "I would basically like in some way to leave this world a little bit better than what I found it." She has received community recognition awards, including the University of Southern California Los Amigos De La Humanidad of the School of Social Work's "Distinguished Contributor to Social Welfare," in 1992; Multicultural Area Health Education Center's "Physician of the Year," in 1991; Comision Femenil's "Women Making History Award," in 1991; and Comision Femenil's "Women in the Health Sciences Award," 1991.

## SOURCES:

### Periodicals

*Hispanic,* October 1991, p. 15.
*Unidos,* April 1992, pp. 16–18.
*Vanidades* (Spanish-language; translation by Diana Martínez), August, 1992, pp. 100–01.

### Other

Lifshitz, Aliza, interview with Diana Martínez, 1992.

*—Sketch by Diana Martínez*

# Enrique Lihn
## 1929-1988
### Chilean poet and novelist

*Enrique Lihn*

Enrique Lihn was one of the best-known Chilean poets of the twentieth century. His work built on the legacy of Surrealism in South America, but his poetic voice was unique and defiantly unclassifiable. He called himself an anti-poet, but he rejected even such anti-definition. "The counter-culture aspect of anti-poetry leaves me cold; also, for me, culture is a myth and a reality of which I would not dare to unburden myself," he wrote in "Curriculum Vitae," published in *Review.* Dedicated to exploring the complexities of life and language, Lihn has earned the respect of a discerning public. Mary Crow, a frequent translator of Lihn's poems, called him "one of Latin America's most celebrated contemporary poets," in an article for the *American Poetry Review. The Dark Room and Other Poems,* an anthology in English translation published in the United States in 1978, brings the poet closer to American audiences.

Lihn was born in Santiago, Chile, on September 3, 1929. He was the son of Enrique Lihn Döll and María Carrasco, but he grew up with his maternal grandmother, who initiated him into a mystical understanding of the universe. "I was her favorite grandson," Lihn told Pedro Lastra in *Conversaciones con Enrique Lihn,* "and a kind of metaphysical confidant of her concerns and anxieties" (translation by Natasha Wimmer). It was Lihn's uncle, artist Gustavo Carrasco, who encouraged the boy to pursue a career in painting and drawing, arranging his nephew's admission to the Escuela de Bellas Artes in Santiago. Lihn enjoyed the freedom of the art school, but he took his studies lightly. "I made a show of superficial ability," he wrote in "Curriculum," "and of a dedication to drawing that excluded or postponed academic discipline."

## Writing Displaces Painting

It was at this time that Lihn began writing, experimenting in the medium that would soon displace painting as his chosen mode of expression. He wrote art reviews and poetry, influenced by **Vicente Huidobro, Neruda**'s *Residencias,* and **Gabriela Mistral**'s *Tala* and *Lagar.* His true predecessor, however, was **Nicanor Parra**, the original anti-poet and author of *Poemas y Anti-Poemas.* Together with other writers, they created *Quebrantahuesos,* a kind of newspaper-mural in the vein of Surrealist collages. Lihn lauded Parra in "Curriculum" for a "democratization of poetic diction, and ... the breaking with certain currents—neo-romanticism, for example—and with

the artificial barriers of genre," but at the same time, notes the differences between his work and that of the older poet. "In contrast to Parra's ... my poetry postulates, instead of discontinuity, the coherence (delirious, in the best of cases) of a continuous discourse." It was characteristic of Lihn to balk at group classification.

Lihn's first collection of poetry, *Nada se escurre,* was published in 1949, when he was only 20 years old. By his death in 1988, he had completed 14 works of poetry, one collection of short stories, and five novels, proving himself a prolific writer. The themes he touched upon cover a wide spectrum: Ricardo Gutier-rez-Mouat, writing for the *American Poetry Review,* cited "death and childhood, [and] the poet's role in the upheavals of history [and] love" as some of Lihn's recurring concerns. The complexities of love haunt *La pieza oscura (The Dark Room),* and social and political tensions inhabit *El Paseo Ahumada (Ahumada Mall).* The constant in Lihn's poetic code, however, was his distrust of language itself, and his constant questioning of poetic discourse. F. A. Butler, in *Books Abroad,* agreed with Chilean poet Rojas that Lihn's poems "may well be called poems of contradiction, poems that are the documents of a conflict, the self-destruction of poetry by its creation."

Lihn married Yvette Mingram in 1957; they divorced in 1960. His only child was a daughter, Andrea. The poet spent most of his working life alternating between positions as university professor or editor of literary journals, both in Chile and abroad. His travels began with a fellowship from UNESCO in 1965, and a first visit to Europe impressed Lihn greatly. Paris, especially, lived up to its reputation as artistic inspiration to generations of Latin American writers and artists. Ten years later, Lihn was equally overwhelmed by New York City. On his first trip to the United States, the writer gave readings of his poetry at several universities; and on his second trip, in 1976, he lectured as a visiting professor at the University of California, Irvine. Upon receiving a fellowship from the Guggenheim Foundation in 1977, Lihn was pleased to realize he could continue to travel as he liked. "I am a sedentary person who likes to travel working, an occasional poet," he wrote in "Curriculum."

Lihn examined life; he was also destined to examine his own death. Diagnosed with cancer, the poet completed his last collection of poems, *Diario de muerte,* in the months before his death. W. Nick Hill, for *World Literature Today,* called the poems "unflinching." Truly, Lihn carried his commitment to a treacherous language further than most poets who trust in language's integrity. Gutierrez-Mouat phrased it another way: "The perennial outsider, Lihn nevertheless left a courageous record of the poet's métier in contemporary Chile."

## SELECTED PUBLISHED WORKS:

*Nada se escurre,* 1949.
*La pieza oscura,* Santiago, Ediciones Renovación, 1955.
*Poesía de paso,* Havana, Casa las Américas, 1966.
*Batman en Chile; o, El ocaso de un ídolo; o, Solo contra el desierto rojo* (novel), Buenos Aires, Ediciones de la Flor, 1973.
*La orquesta de cristal* (novel), Buenos Aires, Sudamericana, 1976.
*París, situación irregular,* Santiago, Ediciones Aconcagua, 1977.
*El Paseo Ahumada,* Santiago, Ediciones Minga, 1983.
*Al bello aparecer de este lucero,* Hanover, New Hampshire, Ediciones del Norte, 1983.
*Diario de muerte,* Santiago, Editorial Universitaria, 1989.

## SOURCES:

### Books

*Contemporary Spanish American Poets: A Bibliography of Primary and Secondary Sources,* compiled by Jacobo Sefamí, New York, Greenwood Press, 1992.

*Hispanic Writers,* edited by Bryan Ryan, Detroit, Gale, 1991.
Lastra, Pedro, *Conversaciones con Enrique Lihn,* Xalapa, Mexico, Universidad Veracruzana, 1980.
*Spanish American Authors of the Twentieth Century,* edited by Angel Flores, New York, H. W. Wilson, 1992.

### Periodicals

*American Poetry Review,* September-October 1989, p. 19; July-August 1991, p. 23.
*Books Abroad,* winter 1971, p. 90.
*Camp de l'Arpa,* Volume 55–56, 1978, p. 67–69.
*Review,* Volume 23, 1978, p. 6–14.
*World Literature Today,* winter 1985, p. 60; winter 1991, p. 89.

—*Sketch by Natasha Wimmer*

# José Arcadia Limón
## 1908-1972
### Mexican American dancer and choreographer

José Arcadia Limón is remembered as a pioneer of modern dance and choreography. He was born January 12, 1908, in Culiacan, Sinaloa, Mexico, and lived in Cananea, Sonora, until he was six years old. Limón's father, Florencio Limón, was French and Spanish; and his mother, Francisca Traslavina, was Indian and Spanish. His father was the director of the State Music Academy and traveled extensively with the military band in Mexico.

In 1913, three years after the Mexican Revolution of 1910 erupted, the revolutionists attacked the Federalists in Cananea. Limón and his family hid in their cellar for three days while artillery fire zoomed overhead. The family moved to Nogalas, a border town across from Arizona, and by 1915 they moved to Tucson, Arizona, where Limón's father worked as musical conductor for the Union Pacific Railroad orchestra and band. For Limón, moving to the United States was a frightening experience—the seven-year-old boy had heard horror stories about the treatment of Mexicans in the states. The transition was facilitated by Tucson's convent schools; the Catholic child found stability in his religion.

Limón's family were cultured people who spoke Castilian but they were very poor. They moved to Los Angeles where Limón attended Abraham Lincoln High School. As a student he belonged to the Atheni-

*José Arcadia Limón*

an Society and was very active in the arts—painting, literature, and music. It was in high school that Limón first became interested in dance, learning technique and dance history. When he graduated from high school in 1926, he wanted to become a painter; his father insisted that he go to college and earn a degree, so Limón enrolled at the University of California.

Soon after Limón began college, his mother died in childbirth. Limón quit college to work in a factory and help support the seven children at home. He had loved his mother very much and, in his grief, he blamed his father for her death—a doctor had warned them not to have any more children. For two years, Limón's only respite was time spent with his artist friends. New York City was considered the heart of the art world and Limón and his friends dreamed of going there. Two friends soon moved to New York and a year later Limón arranged to travel there himself. He decided to go first to San Francisco and find a job on a steamship line to the East Coast through the Panama Canal. With less than $50 in his pocket, Limón left Los Angeles.

## Hitchhiked to New York City

Since the steamship lines wanted only experienced workers, Limón began selling newspapers on the street corner. A friend of one of his school teachers hired him to wash dishes at her nursery school and gave him a place to stay. Limón saved

about $27 and decided to hitchhike across the country. He arrived in New York City in October of 1928, after a ten-day journey. He enrolled in art school and worked in the evenings, posing for artists at the Pratt Institute. Limón was six feet tall, slender, and muscular. He liked to run and swim but never participated in sports. After six months of art school, he realized he did not want to become a painter.

## Introduced to Modern Dance

Depressed, Limón spent his days visiting movie houses and walking the streets. In the evenings, he would run up and down Riverside Drive near his home. A career in dance had not yet occurred to him until he saw a 1929 performance at the Knickerbocker Theater by German Expressionist dancer Harald Kreutzberg. In an interview with Barbara Pollack in *Dance Is a Moment: A Portrait of José Limón in Words and Pictures,* Limón said: "When the curtain rose, I nearly died. The dancers were really supreme. It was the moment of my rebirth. They were so overwhelming. 'My God.' I said to the girl who was with me, 'Where has this been all my life?' This is what I've always wanted to do. I did not know it." Such was Limón's introduction to Kreutzberg and modern dance.

Awed, Limón sought out the new dance form's primary artists in New York, Doris Humphrey and Charles Weidman. He became obsessed with the dance. In 1932, after three years of study, Limón participated in the first appearance of modern dance on Broadway with the Humphrey-Weidman Company in the play *Americana.* Modern dance became popular and Limón began teaching with Weidman at colleges in New York and Philadelphia. He also appeared on Broadway and in night clubs with Letitia Ide.

Bennington College in Vermont began the first summer school for modern dance in 1934, and Limón taught there during the summer for many years. In 1935, Limón began composing his own dance production and two years later he choreographed his first group dance, *Danza de la Muerte,* a satire on dictators. Limón received a fellowship to the Bennington School of Dance in 1937. He went on road tours twice a year. His career was interrupted in 1943 when he was drafted into the U.S. Army. Most of his three years in the Army, Limón was assigned to Special Services and performed in camp shows. He also choreographed a Lynn Riggs poem, *We Speak For Ourselves,* using soldiers in the production.

## Formed Dance Company

After Limón was discharged from the army in 1945, he formed a small dance company and began working with Doris Humphrey again. Critics have considered *The Moor's Pavane* (1949), based on *Othello,* as one of his most important productions of his career. Other notable works include *La Malinche* (1949); *The Exile* (1950); *The Traitor* (1954); *Emperor Jones* (1956); *There Is a Time* (1956); *Missa Brevis* (1958); and *A Choreographic Offering* (1964). In 1950, Limón received an award from *Dance Magazine* for outstanding achievement in modern dance choreography. He performed in Mexico several times from 1950 to 1951 and was invited to settle in his native country, but he decided to return to New York. In 1954 Limón's company was invited by the State Department to travel abroad. He was sent to three South American countries to perform and lecture. He offered young dancers from Mexico and South America scholarships to his dance school as long as the students could support themselves in New York. In 1957 he was sent to Europe for a tour with the American National Theater and Academy. His tours abroad earned Limón the Capezio Award in 1964.

Limón's creative process required much time and concentration. Before he composed *There Is a Time,* a dance for a passage from the Book of Ecclesiastes, Limón thought about it for a year and a half. Limón also composed while he was working with dancers. He taught modern dance throughout the United States at schools and universities including Bennington College, the Dance Players' Studio, Connecticut College for Women, Mills College, the University of California, Sarah Lawrence College, the University of Pittsburgh, Katherine Dunham School, Temple University, the University of Pittsburgh, and the Juilliard School. His last appearance as a dancer took place in 1969; he continued to compose dances until his death in 1972. Two of his last works—*Orfeo* and *Carlota*—were performed about a month before his death. He died on December 2, 1972, after a brief illness at Hunterdon Medical Center in Flemington, New Jersey, near his residence in Stockton, California. His wife, Pauline, had died the previous year. They met the first day Limón entered the Humphrey-Weidman School, where Pauline had worked as a receptionist, and married in 1941. Over the years, Limón's wife had supervised the business and costuming for the dance company.

Upon Limón's death, Clive Barnes wrote in the *New York Times:* "As a man he was austere, grave and kindly. There was a courtliness to his every gesture, and he moved through the world like a prince. As a dancer he was an eagle. As a choreographer he was extremely gifted and fluent. He was never a particularly innovative artist, but possessed an innate understanding of that fusion of dance, drama and music that is the core of his work. He has left half a dozen ballets, at least, that should find a permanent place in the American repertory."

## SOURCES:

### Books

Pollack, Barbara, and Charles Humphrey Woodford, *Dance Is a Moment: A Portrait of José Limón in Words and Pictures,* Pennington, N.J., Princeton Book Company, 1993.

### Periodicals

*New York Times,* December 3, 1972, pp. 1, 86.

—*Sketch by Phyllis Noah*

# Nancy Lopez
## 1957-
### Hispanic American professional golfer

Since becoming a professional golfer in 1978, Nancy Lopez has consistently ranked among the top women on the circuit. She is one of only five women in the sport to have earned more than $1 million in her career. In addition, she has won over 40 tournament victories and was the youngest woman ever to be named to the Ladies Professional Golf Association (LPGA) Hall of Fame.

Born January 6, 1957, in Torrance, California, Lopez first became a golf enthusiast as a child when her parents, Domingo and Marina Lopez, took up the game for her mother's health. By the age of 11, she was a better golfer than either of her parents. Her father became convinced that Nancy was champion material and began to groom her for tournament play. The family scrimped on its own needs to finance her golfing. The family's dedication seemed justified by her performance on the golf course. At the age of 12, she won the first of three state women's tournaments. While still in high school, she finished second in the Women's Open. In 1972 and 1974, she won the U.S. Girls Junior title. And as a student at the University of Tulsa, she won the intercollegiate title before dropping out of school to turn professional.

### Record-Breaking First Year

During her first year on the professional circuit, Lopez broke several standing records. She began the year by winning the Bent Tree Classic at Sarasota, Florida, in February, then went on to win a record five tournaments in succession, including the prestigious LPGA title. (Lopez has since won her second

*Nancy Lopez*

and third LPGA titles as well as a Nabisco Dinah Shore title.) By August of 1978 she had surpassed the highest earnings record, $150,000, set by Judy Rankin in 1976. Lopez went on to earn more than $200,000 by the end of the year. She also endorsed or made commercials for various golf products.

Since her initial appearance on the pro circuit, Lopez has always been ranked at the very top of her sport. In 1979, she won 8 of the 19 tournaments she entered, a feat Bruce Newman of *Sports Illustrated* called "one of the most dominating sports performances in half a century." Lopez had her best year in 1985, when she earned more money—over $400,000—than any other player on the circuit. She won five tournaments and set a record scoring average of 70.73. In 1987 Lopez was named to the LPGA Hall of Fame, "which has the most difficult requirements for entry of any sports Hall of Fame in the nation," as Gordon S. White, Jr., noted in the *New York Times.* Thirty tournament victories, two of them major titles, are needed for Hall of Fame inclusion. Also in 1987, she authored a book, *Nancy Lopez's the Complete Golfer.*

Through it all, Lopez has managed to balance the demands of a sports career with those of a wife and mother. In fact, she told Joseph Durso of the *New York Times:* "I like being a wife and mother more than I like professional golf." She and her husband, baseball player Ray Knight, share the necessary domestic duties between them. "We complement

each other," Knight told Durso. "We help each other with the chores." And Knight occasionally caddies for his wife. Because of their respective status in golf and baseball, Lopez and Knight are "probably the most prominent married couple in sports," according to Durso. They are also among the happiest. Lopez told Jaime Diaz in *Sports Illustrated:* "I'm so happy with my life, that now when I play, there is no pressure. It's just all fun, and when it's fun, you perform better."

## SOURCES:

### Periodicals

*Hispanic,* June, 1989, pp. 15–16.
*New York Times,* March 31, 1985; May 19, 1988.
*People,* April 25, 1983.
*Sports Illustrated,* August 5, 1985; August 4, 1986; February 9, 1987; May 29, 1989, p. 65.

—*Sketch by Denise Wiloch*

# José Ignacio López de Arriortua
## 1941-
### Spanish automotive executive

José Ignacio López is a controversial figure in the contemporary U.S. automotive industry. He burst upon the insular and conservative automotive community in May of 1992, and immediately became a fixture in both local Detroit and national media. As vice president of worldwide purchasing for General Motors (GM), he transformed the dispirited employees of GM's purchasing department, long considered a corporate ghetto, into zealous "warriors" who descended on suppliers in cost-cutting teams. But after less than one year with General Motors, he turned down an offer of the company's presidency and moved to Germany, where he took a highly placed position with Volkswagen (VW). Very shortly thereafter, both he and Volkswagen were embroiled in industrial espionage accusations as General Motors accused him of stealing sensitive documents and turning them over to Volkswagen.

### Early Career

José Ignatio López de Arriortua was born January 18, 1941, in Amorebieta, a poor Basque region of

Spain. He studied at Bilbao University, receiving a Ph.D. in production engineering and plant control in 1966. He worked in Spain in relative obscurity for over 20 years, first for Westinghouse and Firestone, then as director of industrial organization at General Motors España's auto plant in Saragossa.

In 1986 López was appointed director of materials management in Saragossa, and in 1987 he was transferred to Rüsselheim, Germany, and placed in charge of production and purchasing. A year later he was promoted to executive director of central purchasing for GM-Europe.

It was while at GM-Europe that López's name became well known to industry watchers. The division had been foundering for some time; in 1986 alone GM-Europe's losses totaled $340 million. López eliminated a layer of middlemen involved in materials purchasing, and shook up GM-Europe's cozy relationships with a few German supplier cartels. Prior to López's arrival, more than 70 percent of the division's components were purchased from one group of German suppliers. López wasted no time in doing away with that arrangement. He immediately contracted with Spanish, Belgian, and Turkish suppliers who offered far better prices. The division's suppliers suddenly found themselves having to compete with previously uninvolved firms across Europe.

But López had more in mind than merely instituting free-market competition among his suppliers. He intended that GM should become an integral part of the component manufacturing process. López instituted a process known as Program for Improvement and Cost Optimization of Suppliers (PICOS) in which his suppliers were required to participate. Under PICOS, a team of GM management and technical consultants would enter a supplier's facility and scrutinize every aspect of a particular component's design and manufacture. In many cases they were able to make almost incredible improvements in productivity, cost, and delivery lead times. As an incentive to undergo the grueling process, López rewarded participating suppliers with contracts valid for the lifetime of the car model as long as they continued to improve their processes and pass the savings on the General Motors.

With this hold on their suppliers, GM-Europe went from being an economic basket-case to the most profitable arm of General Motors. All of this was accomplished under the watchful eye of Jack Smith, who was destined to become CEO of General Motors. When Smith assumed the supreme position, one of his first actions was to bring López to Detroit.

## López Moves to Detroit

The General Motors establishment never quite knew what to make of López. He was a fruit-and-nuts vegetarian, began his 15-hour working days at five or six in the morning, forbade such substances as coffee or sugar at his staff meetings. López, who was called "Inaki" by his allies, behaved as if he were on a religious crusade. One of the first things he did upon his arrival was distribute a copy of a pamphlet called "Feeding the Warrior Spirit," which advocated a strict, Spartan diet devoid of sugar, potatoes, and white flour. Overweight bodies, he declared, led to overweight minds. López insisted that there was "a direct correlation between nutrition and professional efficiency, between health and the warrior spirit."

His reference to his staffers as "warriors" with all its lunatic-fringe connotations was initially the cause of considerable amusement among observers. But despite his peculiarities, López quickly established himself as a person to be taken seriously. He transformed General Motors' purchasing department to a focal point in GM's turnaround and rebirth. For the first time, people were actually trying to get into the department, when only months before they could not wait to get out. López's staff had been ripe for a messiah; they loved being "warriors" and they were willing to follow "Inaki" anywhere he chose to lead. In one well-publicized move, López switched his watch from his right to his left wrist and exhorted his managers to do the same, with the stated goal of making them uncomfortable until GM's North American profits revived. Soon not only they, but every executive at GM and some corporate wives were wearing their watches on the wrong wrist.

General Motors' suppliers had an entirely different reaction. Within the vendor community, "Inaki" earned another nickname: "The Grand Inquisitor." According to one industry observer, "GM's own suppliers ... viewed López's arrival as one more plague visited upon them by their most important and most difficult client." López had pledged to save billions in vendor costs, and he had demonstrated the ability to do just that. The suppliers knew from whose pockets those savings would come, and they were understandably apprehensive.

López's tactics with suppliers were draconian. He would seek bids from many applicants and choose several finalists, based on price and service. Then he would name targets far lower than any of the bids and demand that the finalists match them. All contracts were up for revision. On at least one occasion, he sought new bids for one component two times in three weeks, and was accused of providing a supplier's blueprints to a competitor in the hope of getting the same part at a lower price.

He also brought his PICOS system into the American industry. A 200-member PICOS team, led in part by Spaniards who had worked for him at GM-Europe, traveled to supplier facilities across the country on five-day visits that often transformed the supplier's manufacturing processes. These visits frequently made real improvements in productivity and cost control. But they also caused uproar and hostility among many manufacturers who had enjoyed long-term relationships with General Motors, and who now talked of López's "reign of terror."

The reaction of labor, as represented by the United Auto Workers (UAW), was no warmer. Although López's purchasing department had jurisdiction only over GM's suppliers, most of those were union shops. Also, it seemed only a matter of time before his methods were turned on GM's own manufacturing process, which was hardly a model of efficiency. The UAW feared massive layoffs as a result of López's seemingly inevitable attention, and he did little to allay their fears when he spoke of encouraging suppliers to manufacture components inside GM plants to make use of "surplus" UAW workers.

All these reactions were irrelevant to General Motors' top management, since López's cost-cutting tactics bore remarkable fruit. By February 1993, López and his "warriors" had cut GM's purchasing expenditures by an estimated $7 billion. "Inaki's" departmental restructuring was beginning to look like an industry-wide revolution. In addition to his PICOS teams, whose emphasis was on improving supplier manufacturing processes, he instituted almost 500 "Creativity Teams," whose purpose was the elimination of unnecessary and redundant parts and components. One such team learned that General Motors purchased 25 different types of cigarette lighters, but only required five. They immediately eliminated the purchasing of the unneeded 20 components, at a savings of $1.7 million.

At this time, in early 1993, López began advertising an idea for a completely new manufacturing process, which he called "Plateau Six." This concept called for suppliers to actually assemble their components onto the vehicles on the assembly line, and if successful would result in a vehicle which required only ten man-hours to complete. GM's engineers were skeptical at first, but worked out a way that it could actually be done.

This planned move from purchasing to manufacturing, though predictable, made López new enemies in the GM establishment. He was moving into areas that other executives considered already-occupied territory. Less than a year earlier, few outside the automotive industry had ever heard of the charismatic Spaniard. Now the clannish Detroit establishment began to move from bewilderment to alarm. But none of that altered the facts: López had shown the way to reverse the ailing giant's decline. And Jack Smith, the new CEO who was still consolidating his power base, could claim López as his very own. In Smith, López

had an ally so powerful that he could afford to ignore his rivals.

### The Move to Volkswagen

Others outside the Detroit establishment had also been watching. Ferdinand Piëch, CEO of Volkswagen, was head of a company in even greater need of a miracle than GM had been. He was deeply impressed by José López. It was suspected that Piëch and his people had been quietly raiding General Motors for talent for quite some time. In late 1992, according to some, VW had contacted between 40 and 50 of GM's international staff with offers of higher pay and better benefits. Few accepted the offers, but they did inspire a personal call from Smith to Piëch with a demand to "lay off my people." Little did Smith know that Piëch was aiming for the most visible and valuable of his people—López himself. The offer Piëch made to López set off one of the most bizarre episodes in American automotive history.

By March 1993 rumors began to fly that Volkswagen had offered José López an enormous amount of money to leave Detroit and perform the same services for Volkswagen that he had for General Motors. López was coy about responding to these rumors. It was further rumored that López wanted more than just money. López had two dreams. First, he wanted to see his "Plateau Six" concept in action. This would require the construction of an entirely new assembly plant. General Motors, still burdened with excess plant capacity, was in no position to construct such a plant even if López could prove its value, which he certainly could not until the plant was constructed. Second, López wanted the plant built in his home province of Amorebieta, a poor Basque region of Spain. This would not be a particularly good location for an auto plant from the automaker's point of view, but López had never forgotten his home, and he wanted to be the provider of the local prosperity such a plant would certainly bring.

General Motors had no intention of building such a plant any time soon. Piëch, however, promised to do so if only López would come work at Volkswagen as the company's top purchasing executive. Reportedly, he also offered a $20-million salary over the next five years. Volkswagen was in an even worse position to build the promised factory than GM was. But Piëch was, by this time, desperate to have access to López's cost-cutting genius. Whether he was really planning to keep his promise will probably never be known.

López officially resigned from General Motors on March 10. Smith was inundated with pleas from GM staffers to do something, anything, to keep López. Under pressure, and seeing his prize cost-cutter snatched away from him, Smith offered López the number-two spot at General Motors: executive vice president and president of North American Operations. Despite apparently having a signed contract with Volkswagen, López agreed on March 13. The following Monday, March 15, the GM Board of Directors ratified the promotion, and a press conference was scheduled for that afternoon to make the announcement. News had been leaked well in advance, and the assembled reporters expected to see Smith and López on the platform together.

Instead, Smith appeared alone, white-faced and furious. "Today I intended to announce that Inaki López was staying with General Motors and would be given added responsibilities," he said. "Unfortunately, a short time ago, Mr. López sent me a letter saying he was not going to accept the position and is leaving General Motors. It is not clear to me what his intentions are or where he is at this time." Where López was, was at Detroit Metro Airport getting ready to board a plane for Germany. Exactly what happened to change his mind has never been entirely clear. But that was not the end of the story, as far as General Motors was concerned.

Immediately after López arrived at Volkswagen, the effort to recruit GM employees increased dramatically, this time with López's help. According to Lou Hughes, head of GM-Europe, López had personally called 29 people with job offers within two weeks of his resignation. Several did in fact resign from General Motors and follow López. GM finally resorted to obtaining an injunction against López and VW in the German courts to stop the raiding.

But the worst was yet to come. Less than a week before López's resignation, he had attended key international strategy meetings held at GM's Adam Opel headquarters in Rüsselheim and at Opel's Dudenhofen test track where he had seen all Opel's latest prototypes. Nothing was hidden, and López came into possession of sensitive documents concerning both those prototypes and GM's long-range international strategy. After his resignation, those documents could not be found. On March 22, GM demanded that López affirm in writing that he had not left GM with confidential documents. López provided that assurance. Unconvinced, GM complained to the German government and demanded an investigation. In late June, the district attorney's office for the city of Darmstadt raided an apartment building near Wiesbaden. At what had been the home of a friend of López, they found what they later described as "four large boxes of documents that should not have been there." GM-Europe later verified that many of the papers found were from among the missing documents. As of this writing, both López and Volkswagen continue to deny any wrongdoing and the investigation continues. But although López remains with Volkswagen at the moment, it is impossible to tell for how long; also, all plans for Inaki's dream of a Spanish Basque auto plant seem to be gone.

## SOURCES:

### Books

Keller, Maryanne, *Collision: GM, Toyota, Volkswagen, and the Race to Own the Twenty-first Century,* Doubleday, 1994.
*Newsmakers 1993,* Detroit, Gale Research, 1993.

### Periodicals

*Business Week,* August 31, 1992, p. 29; March 29, 1993, p. 28; April 19, 1993, p. 31; July 26, 1993, pp. 32–34; August 9, 1993, p. 29; May 9, 1994, p. 42.
*Newsweek,* March 29 1993, p. 42
*New York Times,* July 26, 1993, pp. D1–2.

*—Sketch by Joel Simon*

# José López Portillo
## 1920-
### Mexican politician and writer

José López Portillo's expansive career has embraced politics, academia, law, and literature. He was the president of Mexico from 1976 to 1982; his tenure of office fluctuated between extremes of success and failure. López Portillo's political fortunes were largely dictated by the Mexican oil boom, the world oil crisis and his detrimental handling of the situation. In 1979 David Butler of *Newsweek* heralded him as "a consumate politician"; López Portillo (also known as Lapis Partial) had effectively engineered the liberal reforms of 1977 and was presiding over increased oil discoveries. However, by 1982 Mexico was embroiled in a financial crisis: inflation, devaluation of the peso and the flight of money abroad. López Portillo will be remembered for his bewildering response to this economic breakdown: the nationalization of Mexico's private banks.

José López Portillo y Pancheco was born on June 16, 1920, in Mexico City into a distinguished upper-middle-class family that traces its history back 400 years to a Navarre village in Spain. His grandfather, **José López Portillo y Rojas**, was secretary of foreign relations under Victoriano Huerta and the state governor of Jalisco, while his father, José López Portillo y Weber, was a renowned historian.

López Portillo attended state schools in the Federal District, completing his preparatory studies at the National Preparatory School in 1937. Significantly, one of his school friends was Luis Echeverría, who preceded him in the Mexican presidency. They studied law together between 1942 and 1945 at the University of Santiago in Chile on political science scholarships from the Chilean government. López Portillo received a second law degree from the National School of Law, UNAM in 1946.

López Portillo began his career as a lawyer and an academic; according to Alan Riding in *Distant Neighbors: A Portrait of the Mexicans,* 1986, he "showed little passion or ambition for politics . . . his political career was almost accidental." From 1947 to 1958 he was Professor of Law at UNAM, teaching classes in law, political theory and public administration. He was also a practicing lawyer, specializing in the legal theory of the state and civil rights.

In 1959 López Portillo accepted a job as an adviser to the Ministry of National Patrimony to act as a legal and technical consultant to reform several articles of the constitution. Under Díaz Ordaz he became director general of legal affairs in the Ministry of the Presidency, rising to the position of under secretary of the presidency. Echeverría named him to a succession of posts including head of the state electricity monopoly in 1972 and minister of finance in 1973. His selection for presidency was unexpected due to his lack of political experience. This led some observers to conjecture that he was chosen so that Echeverría could maintain a degree of political influences after leaving the presidential office. Until his selection as the presidential candidate for the Institutional Revolutionary Party, the PRI, López Portillo had never run for elected office.

### Presidential Years

On December 1, 1976, after winning 68 percent of the electoral vote, López Portillo was sworn in as Mexico's sixtieth president. At his inaugural address he called for unity and austerity to combat the country's economic and social problems. He devised a program with the International Monetary Fund to appease foreign creditors; this resulted in a decline in living standards. To diffuse the disaffection caused by this program, and through a genuine desire, he instituted significant liberalizing reforms. In 1977 protest marches were legalized and congress approved a political reform that facilitated the registration of new parties, including the Communist Party. In *Distant Neighbors* Alan Riding asserted that "It was a skillful performance for a man not thought to be a politician." These reforms also reflected López Portil-

lo's tolerant attitude and his genuine commitment to civil and political liberty.

Between 1977 and 1981 the Mexican economy experienced a boom period. The combination of oil wealth, following significant discoveries in 1978, and expanded foreign borrowing, generated considerable financial resources for the Mexican government and contributed to eight percent growth rates until 1981. With apparent success on the domestic front López Portillo turned his attention to foreign affairs. Some analysts have contended that he launched a grandiose foreign policy, beyond the real scope of Mexico's capability, simply because he wished to enhance his own image. He clashed with the Carter administration over Nicaragua after the 1979 revolution, providing the Sandinista regime with financial and technical assistance. He later conflicted with Reagan over Cuba, El Salvador and again, Nicaragua.

However, as explicated by George Philip in *The Presidency in Mexican Politics,* the economy was both unbalanced and fragile: in 1981 the Mexican economy ingested $45 billion of foreign exchange, approximately ten times the value of Mexico's exports in 1976. This economic situation was not sustainable. The slump in world oil prices triggered a financial crisis. If López Portillo had cut oil prices and reduced the public deficit the crisis would not have been so profound. However, he was not an economist and relied upon a multitude of economic advisers of various ideological persuasions. As a compromiser he endeavored to accommodate them all but succeeded only in a lack of decisiveness and economic cohesiveness. He did not respond to the ailing economy. Fears of inflation and devaluation prompted the private sector to export capital. López Portillo publicly avowed to defend the peso "like a dog," only to devalue it a couple of days later. This caused a total loss of confidence and money flooded out of the country. The payment of foreign debts was suspended. On September 1, 1982, López Portillo stunned Mexican bankers by announcing the nationalization of Mexico's private banks. He accused the private banks of encouraging the flight of capital from the country, famously declaring, according to the *Economist,* "They have looted us. They will not loot us again." A dispirited, but conspicuously wealthy man left the presidential office, describing himself as "devalued" analogous to the devaluation of the peso. He declared that all he wanted to do was "grow my beard, paint and write."

### A Fascination with Indian Culture

Although López Portillo will be remembered as the Mexican president who nationalized the banks, he has had flourishing interests outside the realm of politics. Quetzalcóatl, the mythical pre-Hispanic white god known as the Plumed Serpent was the subject of one his two lyrical philosophical novels. In

*Quetzalcóatl* López Portillo expounds the story of Quetzalcóatl, a bearded white man, who preaches the revocation of the old gods and blood sacrifice for a new religion imbued with love. He is initially worshipped but when he is rejected in favor of the old rituals, he departs, a legend.

His second novel, *Don Q,* is, "a constant disquisition about metaphysics, aesthetics, theology, ethics and lesser ponderous matters . . . as a blend of ideas from Western and native philosophies," reported Luis Leal in *Journal of Inter-American Review of Bibliography,* continuing, "this is a book that provokes thought, and although its contents are weighty, the witty style makes its reading a pleasure."

López Portillo expressed an affinity and a concern with Mexico's native population; according to Alan Riding in *Distant Neighbors,* he once declared: "What would Mexico be were it not for what you signify and represent. . . . It is painful to see how, as one climbs higher into the sierra, our Indian groups are to be found, where they have fled injustice and slavery. . . . If any cause is evident in the country it is the Indian cause." Politically, López Portillo did make some attempts to improve the Indian situation with programs for fresh drinking water, health clinics and an emphasis on bilingual education.

His personal interest and passion inspired him to write a four volume book, *Dinamica Politica de México,* which recounts the Indian past and its legacy that fused with the culture and institutions of the colonial world and modern Mexico. López Portillo fervently believes that to understand Mexico's modern political system it is fundamentally important to look at it in a historical context and understand Mexico's past, López Portillo's son José explained to Amanda Beresford in an interview.

López Portillo's captivation with Mexican history also materializes in his private paintings. They fall into two categories firstly, his symbolic, conceptual and philosophical interpretation of Mexico's past and secondly, paintings based on his personal life experiences: his political campaigns, his own life cycle and his time in government. These paintings have been hung at a small, joint exhibition with his daughter in Mexico.

López Portillo has been married twice, first to Maria del Careen, by whom he has three children: José Radon, Careen Betrays, Pauline; and second to Alexandra, a former Yugoslavian, by whom he has two children: Navila and Alejandro.

## SELECTED PUBLISHED WORKS:

*Quetzalcóatl,* [Mexico], 1965; translated by Eliot Weinburger and Diana Goodrich, England, James Clarke, c. 1977.
*Don Q,* New York, Seabury Press, 1976.

*Ellos Vienen: la conquista de Mexico,* Mexico, Fernanandez Editóris, c. 1987; translated by Beatrice Berler as *They Are Coming: The Conquest of Mexico,* University of North Texas Press, 1992.
*Mís Tiempos* (autobiography), Mexico, Fernandez Editoris, 1988.
*Dinamica Politica de Mexico,* four volumes, Mexico, Editoris Planeta Groupo, 1993-.

## SOURCES:

### Books

Camp, Roderic Ai, *Mexican Political Biographies,* University of Arizona Press, 1982.
Philip, George, *The Presidency in Mexican Politics,* London, Macmillan Academic and Professional, 1992.
Riding, Alan, *Distant Neighbors: A Portrait of the Mexicans,* Random House, New York, 1986.

### Periodicals

*Economist,* September 4, 1982, p. 80.
*Journal of Inter-American Review of Bibliography,* Volume 8, No. 4, 1978.
*Library Journal,* March 15, 1992, p. 126.
*Listener,* February 17, 1977, p. 221.
*Newsweek,* October 1, 1979, pp. 24–25.
*New York Times,* December 2, 1976, pp. 1, 3.
*Observer* (London), March 6, 1977, p. 25.

### Other

Interview with López Portillo's son, José Radon Lapis Partial, by Amanda Beresford on November 19, 1994.

—*Sketch by Amanda Beresford*

# Frank A. Lorenzo
## 1940-
### Spanish American business executive

Frank A. Lorenzo was founder of Texas International Airlines and he was credited with developing the company into the largest carrier airline company in the United States. He was born Francisco Anthony Lorenzo, May 19, 1940, in New York City. His parents were Olegario and Ana Lorenzo, Spanish

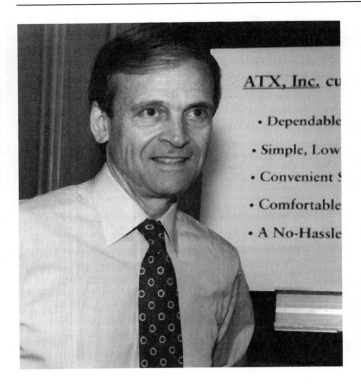

*Frank A. Lorenzo*

immigrants. They lived in Queens near La Guardia Airport and operated a New York beauty parlor. Lorenzo worked his way through college at Columbia University where he received his B.S. degree in 1961. He went to Harvard University and received his master's degree in business administration in 1963. After college, Lorenzo worked at TWA as a financial analyst until 1965, when he went to work for Eastern Airlines as a manager and financial analyst. On October 14, 1972, Lorenzo married Sharon Neill Murray and they had four children.

In 1966, Lorenzo founded Lorenzo, Carney & Co., an airline consulting firm, with Robert J. Carney, a friend from Harvard. They formed a new company in 1969, Jet Capital Corporation, and after they each invested $25,000, they offered public stocks and raised $1.4 million. When Chase Manhattan Bank asked the partners to save a failing airline, Texas International Airlines (TXI), they were paid $15,000 a month to analyze the airline's financial problems. In 1972, Lorenzo proposed to take over TXI. His company invested $1.15 million and National Aviation Corporation invested $350,000. The creditors extended and reissued the debts for the balance of a $35 million recapitalization plan Lorenzo presented. Lorenzo became president and chief executive officer with 26 percent of the profits and 59 percent of the voting power. Carney and Donald C. Burr, who worked for National Aviation Corporation, became executive officers in the company.

Lorenzo began cutting employees and in 1974, he ordered the union, the Airline Employees Association, to cut back up to 30 percent of the employees to work on a part time basis. A strike ensued, grounding the airlines for four months, and the other unions walked off the job. The major airlines paid members who were shut down because of a strike under the Mutual Aid Pack. Mutual Aid Pact funds were paid to TXI in the amount of $10 million, which was more than the airline would have earned if it were flying. The union finally yielded and the strike ended.

During this time the federal government regulated the airlines and Lorenzo requested permission to lower some fares for TXI by as much as half. In 1977, a one-year trial period of the lower rates was granted to TXI. Soon other major airlines requested lower rates. In the meantime, Lorenzo bought stock in National Airlines in an attempt to take over the airlines. Pan Am bought National and Lorenzo made a profit of $40 million. When Congress deregulated the airlines in 1978, most of the airline executives objected but Lorenzo took advantage of the situation and by 1980, he founded the first non-union airline in the country, New York Air. Airline union leaders were upset with Lorenzo's moves to keep them out of New York Air. Lorenzo wanted business from the established Eastern Airlines shuttle service from Boston to Washington. He founded a corporation, Texas Air Corporation, that served as the parent company of both TXI and New York Air.

Lorenzo planned a hostile takeover of Continental Airlines, which was having financial problems. He bought stocks in the airline and Continental fought with Lorenzo to keep him from taking over. Continental's chief executive, Alvin L. Feldman, committed suicide at his Los Angeles office by shooting himself in the head. Now, Lorenzo expanded his airline business with the purchase of Continental and he began attacking the unions. First, he went after the machinists union, the International Association of Machinists and Aerospace Workers (IAM), and then the Air Line Pilots Association (ALPA). The machinists went on strike and then the pilots went to the picket line. In an unprecedented move, Lorenzo declared bankruptcy and then he was able to get rid of the unions legally at the airline. He offered employees half of the union pay and twice the hours. This time, there was no Mutual Aid Pact, which had been removed since the airline deregulations, and Lorenzo was losing money. But Lorenzo held out and employees began going back to work. Strike breakers were harassed and threatened by union pilots who would not break the picket lines. Continental had 12,000 employees who conceded and now worked for half their wages. He was in a position to offer lower rates and in order to compete, the other major airlines asked employees to take cuts. In the end, Lorenzo came out a winner with Texas Air stock going up. He raised $1 billion and bought out People's Express, owned by his former partner Don Burr. He also bought Frontier Airlines and several other small airlines. Continental tripled in size by 1986.

Continental now had another problem. Employees were dissatisfied and began leaving the airline for better jobs. Lorenzo hired an independent consulting firm, the Hay Group, to survey the employees about their jobs at Continental. They discovered that overall the employee morale at Continental was the worst they had ever surveyed. But Lorenzo thought that most of his 32,000 employees liked working at Continental. When Texas Air stock reached an all-time high of $50 a share, Lorenzo sold his shares and made over $7 million. He sold the stock to his own company, Jet Capital. Lorenzo was still in control with or without the stocks. His next big move was to take over Eastern Airlines, the country's third largest airline. In 1986, Lorenzo had control of Eastern and now Texas Air had almost 50,000 employees. Lorenzo had put together the largest airline company in the United States. His next move was to cut labor costs. Joe Leonard was the new president of Eastern just before it was sold to Lorenzo. He began a shake-up to cut costs. He laid off over 1,500 people and about 500 of those were machinists. Hundreds of managers were let go, flights were cut back and a maintenance contract was given to an engine manufacturer which eliminated around 300 machinists jobs. Even with all his work in reducing costs to the airlines, Leonard was demoted when Lorenzo took over as chairman of the company.

Lorenzo used similar management tactics he had used at Continental. The two unions were angry with Lorenzo and pulled together in a battle with him. Lorenzo's management team began firing machinists, especially union leaders. More demands were put on pilots, breaking Federal Aviation Authority (FAA) safety regulations. Eastern pushed the pilots and instituted a new policy of terminating pilots for absenteeism. They also instituted a new termination policy with machinists who were absent or tardy after three days, retroactive for two years. Eastern management hit the flight attendants hardest with almost 600 being threatened with dismissal over the new absentee policy. In two years, 840 union machinists were fired. Employees were intimidated as stringent rules were laid down. By September of 1987, almost 4,000 Eastern employees were without jobs and many employees left to find new jobs, including over 100 pilots. Then Eastern cut back another 3,500 jobs. The machinists' contract was up for renewal in 1987 and Eastern management presented a 60-page proposal to change the contracts. Management wanted to separate the machinists from the baggage handlers and other service jobs which were in the same union.

After months of unsettled negotiations, Eastern was prepared for a strike. Lorenzo made preparations with a contract with Orion Air to train nonunion pilots on Eastern planes in case the pilots walked out. He also arranged for Continental to provide services in case of a strike. Lorenzo was armed and ready with strike contingency plans. He had even looked into bankruptcy for Eastern. Lorenzo created numerous spin-off companies at this time to provide services to the airline that would eliminate Eastern employees. He created Protective Services Corporation to employ security guards and Airport Ground Services Corporation to employ baggage handlers. He also sold pieces of Eastern to Continental including their System One Direct Access (SODA) computer reservations system for a $100 million note and then turned around and leased the system to Eastern for about $10 million a month. Continental also purchased 11 airport gates at Newark for an $11 million note, which were appraised at twice that much by an outside consulting firm. Continental bought six A–300 jets from Eastern for $162 million that they turned around and sold at a $7 million cash profit. In all the sales and spin-off companies, Lorenzo either depleted Eastern's resources or took jobs from the unions.

In an unusual move, the unions began trying to buy Eastern from Texas Air. The pilots union actually started the move to purchase the airline right after Lorenzo took over. A battle ensued between Lorenzo and the unions. Charlie Bryan, who represented the machinists union, wanted to stall. Lorenzo wanted a showdown because he thought he could win if the machinists went on strike. Walter Wallace, who was on the mediation board, wanted to bring the two sides together. On March 4, 1989, after 17 months of negotiations, machinists went on strike with the support of the flight attendants and pilots. Ninety percent of the airline's flight operations were closed down. Eastern was losing about $5 million a day and several options were proposed to the board of directors including bankruptcy, selling more assets, etc. The board met and decided to file a Chapter 11 bankruptcy. On March 9, five days after the strike began, Eastern filed bankruptcy. But it was not as easy for Lorenzo this time as it was when he placed Continental into bankruptcy. By now, Congress had amended loopholes that Lorenzo used in his favor such as canceling the union contracts. This time he had to prove to the courts that in order to save the company the new wage structure was necessary and he had to negotiate with the unions.

Then Lorenzo decided to sell Eastern. After heated and lengthy negotiations, Peter Ueberroth, former baseball commissioner, appeared to be the likely buyer. Then, Lorenzo called off the sale. The bankruptcy judge, Burton R. Lifland, in New York said it was his decision, not Lorenzo's, whether Eastern should be sold. The judge approved the sale of Eastern's shuttle service to Donald Trump. Finally, in April 1990, Judge Lifland removed Lorenzo from

Eastern and appointed Martin Shugrue as trustee of the courts to run the airline. From the time that Lorenzo had bought Eastern in 1986, the airline had dropped from third largest airline to ninth largest airline. Lorenzo resigned as chairman of Continental Airlines, August 7, 1990, when he made an agreement with Scandinavian Airlines System to sell his stock in the airlines to them. Eastern never recovered, liquidated its assets and closed down January 18, 1991.

## SOURCES:

### Books

Bernstein, Aaron, *Grounded: Frank Lorenzo and the Destruction of Eastern Airlines,* New York, Simon and Schuster, 1990.
*The Hispanic American Almanac,* edited by Nicolas Kanellos, Detroit, Gale Research, 1993.

### Periodicals

*Facts on File, World News Digest,* March 10, 1989, p. 158G3; June 2, 1989, p. 401D1; April 27, 1990, 303A3; August 17, 1990, p. 604E2; January 24, 1991, p. 48E1.

*—Sketch by Phyllis Noah*

# Ignacio Lozano, Jr.
## 1927-
### Hispanic American publisher

Born in 1927 Ignacio Lozano has distinguished himself as an editor and publisher. Working primarily for the southern California newspaper *La Opinion,* Lozano has succeeded professionally and involved himself deeply in the community of which he has been part. He sits on the board of directors of several major companies including the Bank of America and the Walt Disney Company. He served during the 1970s in the United States diplomatic corps, and has won many awards. He lives in Los Angeles.

### Catholic Schooling

The son of Ignacio and Alicia Lozano, Ignacio, Jr., was born on January 15, 1927 in San Antonio, Texas. His parents sent him to the St. Anthony School in San Antonio, and he attended Central Catholic High School. When he left high school in 1943, he went to the University of Notre Dame in South Bend, Indiana. During college he studied to prepare himself for a career in journalism, taking a B.A. in that subject in 1947, before moving to southern California.

His lifelong employment at *La Opinion* began the same year. He worked first as an assistant publisher on the newspaper. He would stay in that position for six years. During that time he married Marta Navarro. Eventually the couple would have four children: Leticia, Jose, Monica, and Francisco.

He became publisher and editor of the paper in 1953 and remained at that post until 1976. That year the president of the United States nominated him as the ambassador to El Salvador. His nomination met with approval, and he served there until 1977. He returned to his former job at *La Opinion.* After another decade of hard work, Lozano become the editor-in-chief of that paper in 1986. He retains that title presently.

### Involvement and Awards

A member of the California Press Association, Lozano has involved himself both in charitable work and business. He currently serves as the head of the Tomas Rivera Center, the Santa Anita Foundation, the South Coast Reperatory, and the Youth Opportunities Foundation. As a trustee of his alma mater, the University of Notre Dame, Lozano has shown concern with education and young people. He has served as a board member for the Boy Scouts of America, the chairman of the El Pueblo de los Angeles State Historic Park Commission, and the director of the Los Angeles Metropolitan YMCA.

Many organizations have honored him for his contributions. The American Lung Association gave him their Award for Outstanding Service in 1986. The Dominican Republic awarded him the Silver Cross of the Order of Christopher Columbus in the same year. The University of Notre Dame and Pepperdine University have conferred honorary degrees on Lozano.

He is currently active on the Council of American Ambassadors and the Council on Foreign Relations. He sits on the board of directors of several major companies, and he received the U.S. Small Business Administration's Lifetime Achievement Award in May of 1991. Among other awards, Lozano won the National Hispanic Employee Association's Outstanding Board Member Award in 1995. He lives in the Los Angeles are

## SOURCES:

Personal biographical material from the office of Ignacio E. Lozano, Jr.

*—Sketch by James McCarthy*

# Wendy Lucero-Schayes
## 1963-
### Hispanic American Olympic athlete and broadcaster

I n over ten years of competitive diving, Wendy Lucero-Schayes has had a distinguished career that includes participation in the 1988 Olympic Games. A member of the U.S. Diving National Team for eight consecutive years, Lucero-Schayes is the winner of nine national titles, three U.S. Olympic Festival titles, and several medals in international competition, including a silver at the 1991 World Championships. Her accomplishments are not limited to athletics, however; she has also begun a career in television broadcasting, appearing on national networks as a sports commentator and hosting a local talk show in her hometown of Denver. Her ability to develop her athletic talents, providing herself with opportunities to travel the world and get an education, has made Lucero-Schayes an example for those who would also succeed through hard work and determination.

Wendy Lucero-Schayes was born on June 26, 1963, in Denver, Colorado, to Shirley and Don Lucero. The son of Spanish immigrants, Lucero-Schayes's father worked as an electrician; he was able to work steadily because employers thought he was Italian, not Hispanic. Her mother, of Irish extraction, maintained the household, raising Lucero-Schayes and her sister and brother. The family was active and athletic; Lucero-Schayes began swimming and dancing at an early age, and she picked up gymnastics, tennis, and diving while tagging along to her older sister's lessons. She became competitive in each of her endeavors; sports provided an opportunity for a tomboy to excel, in contrast to school, where she felt teachers frowned upon her because of her energetic nature.

Her sister provided an additional motivation to excel, for the two often ended up competing in the same age group at meets. Their two-year age difference doomed her to being second best, Lucero-Schayes revealed in a personal interview. "For me to compete with my sister—well, she's my older sister, she's always going to win because she's two years older." Always being the runner-up "kept me in a 'trying to achieve' mode," she explained. "I would always strive to be the best I could be because I wanted to grasp what my sister was attaining—but I wanted it now, even though I was two years younger." When Lucero-Schayes began to close the gap between them, her sister moved on to other activities; but the young athlete still felt driven to excel.

*Wendy Lucero-Schayes*

### Ice Skating Star Inspires Olympic Dream

Part of Lucero-Schayes's ambition was to fulfill a dream she had harbored since she was nine: to compete in the Olympic Games. At first, she thought she would compete in gymnastics, but she realized her late start in the sport would limit how far she could go. Then, she related in her interview, "I fell in love with ice skating. After I saw Dorothy Hamill in 1976 win the Olympic gold, that really inspired me. I knew I wasn't going to be an Olympic gymnast; so I thought 'Well, I'll make it in ice skating.'" Besides providing her an outlet for athletic endeavors, figure skating gave Lucero-Schayes a chance to express herself artistically. "I did enjoy it because of the aesthetic ability" the sport required, she explained. "Being able to dance to the music and perform, and be creative that way—I just fell in love with that aspect."

After competing for four years, however, she came to the conclusion that she would not attain her Olympic dream through ice skating. Not only did she come late to the sport, which left her at a disadvantage in the exacting school figures portion of competitions, but her family lacked the financial resources needed to be successful in national competition. "As far as getting into the Ice Capades, I probably could have done that," Lucero-Schayes recalled, "but I wanted to get a college education, and ice skating wouldn't have done that." In the early 1980s, at the time she was thinking about continuing her education, a series of federal laws and court decisions had mandated that universities give women equal access to athletic scholarships. By competing in a varsity sport, Lucero-Schayes would be able to take advantage of the full-ride scholarships being made available to female athletes.

While in high school Lucero-Schayes returned to diving, which she had tried for a time as a preteen. Her gymnastics training served her well, and she quickly became very competitive on the springboard events. She placed fourth in her state's championships as a sophomore, and came in second as a senior. By the time she finished high school, she was competing in the Junior Olympic Championships, where she placed sixth in the three-meter event, and the Phillips 66 National Diving Championships, where in both the indoor and outdoor competitions she finished in the top twenty on the one-meter springboard. Her success led her to be named 1981's Hispanic Athlete of the Year, citation as an Academic All-American, and also resulted in a scholarship offer from the University of Nebraska.

Lucero-Schayes was looking forward to the challenges of college; although she had encountered problems with teachers as a very young student, her competitive nature soon emerged and she was earning top grades by the time she entered high school. In addition, her parents had instilled in her the value of an education; because neither of them had been to college, they wanted their children to have the advantages higher education could give them. "My parents were great role models to me, my mother was *the* highest role model that I had," Lucero-Schayes stated in her interview. "I had other role models, the sports role models like the Dorothy Hamills and the Peggy Flemings and the Olga Korbuts. But my mother was always the one I respected and that I thought of as the most wonderful; and I had a dad that was very supportive and tried to give his kids whatever he could with the limitations that he had. They were successful enough with what they had done, but they wanted me to be as self-confident as I could be, because they knew the outside world wasn't going to give that to me."

### College Scholarship Spurs Athletic Career

While attending the University of Nebraska Lucero-Schayes had the difficult task of balancing her classes with a demanding schedule of training and competition. She had to work particularly hard to master the three-meter springboard, a new event for her. "I was born and raised in a climate that really was for winter sports," the athlete explained in her interview. "I was really lucky they had some high school pools, but they only had the lowest springboard [one-meter] available to me and that's what you dove in high school anyway. So I really didn't learn the Olympic springboard event [three-meter] until col-

lege, which is a very late date to start out. I've been trying to play catch-up ever since." After two years she transferred to Southern Illinois University, seeking a more compatible coach and better opportunities to compete nationally. The move proved quite successful; she won the 1985 NCAA championship on the one-meter event and earned her first national titles, placing first at the 1984 and 1985 Phillips 66 Outdoor Championships. During these years she was also named an Academic All-American for her performance in the classroom.

Lucero-Schayes had goals outside of athletics, however, and worked hard to achieve those as well. To complement her education—she earned a B.S. in television sales and management in 1986—with hands-on experience, she sought opportunities to work in broadcasting and television production. "As I was training for the Olympic Games in 1988 and the few years before that, I would try to be a production assistant for golf tournaments, horse tournaments, Monday Night Football—anything I could do," she related in her interview. She worked as a freelance sportscaster for NBC, ABC, and ESPN—including a stint as a commentator for the 1991 World Championships—and hosted a talk show, "Focus Colorado," in her hometown of Denver. She particularly enjoyed that experience, she revealed, "because then I could get involved with people that have helped shape not only the state, but eventually the U.S. and what we think."

Training and competing in preparation for the 1988 Olympic Trials was her immediate focus coming out of college, however, and Lucero-Schayes was making great progress. Although she felt she had the potential to dive well on the ten-meter platform, she relinquished the opportunity to learn the event in order to focus on what would be her best shot to make the Olympic team, the three-meter springboard. Her rigorous training for the Olympic event began paying off; in 1987 she won her first three-meter diving titles, at the U.S. Olympic Festival and the American Cup II; she was also attending more international meets, winning bronze in one-meter events at the McDonald's International and at a competition between the U.S. and the Soviet Union.

### Mother's Illness Interrupts Olympic Training

But during the time Lucero-Schayes was making great strides toward her Olympic goal, two separate incidents hindered her training: her mother, who had been a constant source of encouragement throughout her career, was diagnosed with an advanced form of breast cancer; meanwhile, her coach was undermining her self-confidence. Although she had won the HTH Classic early in 1988, in three subsequent competitions she placed no better than fourth—and she needed to finish second at the trials to make the

Olympic team. She related her difficulties in her interview: "I had people in my life that basically didn't believe in me; I had a coach, a top Olympic coach who told me, 'I'm sorry, but you remind me of me and you'll never make it.' I didn't stay with that person and I ended up realizing that I wanted to prove him wrong."

Lucero-Schayes switched coaches and continued training for the trials; her previous coach's lack of faith only deepened her determination. Another motivating factor was her mother, who had completed chemotherapy for her cancer and would be able to attend the Olympic trials. Lucero-Schayes cites this meet as her most memorable, for the recovery of her mother and her presence at the meet allowed her to enjoy the competition. She turned in one of the best performances of her career and finished second, just eighty-one hundredths of a point ahead of the next diver. She had made the Olympic team, vindicating herself in the face of her former coach's doubt. "To try to believe in myself and surpass what other people think was a big step for me, and I ended up competing and winning, overcoming his top people that he thought *would* succeed."

Lucero-Schayes competed at the 1988 Olympics in Seoul, Korea, finishing sixth. Although she didn't win a medal, she recalls the trip fondly for other reasons: "One of my favorite incidents was with the Russian coach—her name was Tatiana—she gave me a wonderful gift," the athlete remembered in her interview. "We had been creating a nice friendship throughout my couple years of seeing her in international competitions, and I really liked her. After the Olympic games were over, she ended up giving me this wonderful china bowl. And that friendship and that bond—I'll never forget that. I think that is one of the neatest things that could have ever happened, because you cross boundaries through sports that you could not do with anything else."

### Employs Tale of Success to Motivate Others

After competing in the Olympics, Lucero-Schayes continued her work in communications, increasing her involvement in public speaking. She has participated in conferences and charity events, and has visited schools. Although she enjoys her work in television, she gets a special reward from speaking to people in person. "I end up being able to touch people's lives that way," she said in her interview, "and I think it's more important because people really need to see you face-on—to talk to you and be able to touch you. The experience may be a short span of time but enough to give them one positive thought that maybe will change their lives for the better." Lucero-Schayes has served as a spokesperson for the American Cancer Society, and often appears as a motivational speaker, periodically in front of Hispanic organizations. "The success I've had in sports overcoming those people who didn't think that I could [succeed] has made me like myself better and find out, 'Yeah, I am capable and I'm not going to let them determine what I can do.' Hopefully I can share that with others."

Public appearances also introduced the diver to her husband, professional basketball player Dan Schayes. The two were appearing at a benefit for a charity promoting organ donation; he gave her a note, joking "I will share my organs with you anytime," and she gave him her number. They began dating, and two years later, in late 1991, they married. The couple often trains together; but more important is the support they provide as each undergoes the strains of competition. "I had dated athletic guys before, but not elite athletes, and it makes a big difference," Lucero-Schayes revealed to Michelle Kaufman of the *Detroit Free Press*. "Danny understands what it feels like to be under pressure, to win and to lose."

The pressure was certainly on Lucero-Schayes going into the Olympic year of 1992. She had continued to improve her diving, winning Olympic Festival titles in 1989 and 1990, and capturing one-meter and three-meter championships those same years. She followed those performances with her best year ever in 1991: she took both springboard events in the indoor championships, placed first in the one-meter and second in the three-meter outdoors, and garnered silver medals at the Sixth World Championship and Alamo International competitions. For her efforts she was voted the U.S. Female Diving Athlete of the Year in both 1990 and 1991. Although a severe parasitic intestinal infection prevented her from competing in late 1991 and hampering her training time going into 1992, Lucero-Schayes was still considered a likely Olympian and a medal contender for Barcelona. These expectations were harder on her than the physical difficulties of training, she commented in her interview. "It's definitely more mental than it is physical, because as much as I have trained, my body now knows [what to do]; it's letting the mind relax and do what I have trained it to do for years. It is more of a mindset, whether or not I feel I'm capable of getting out there and performing to the best of my ability and overcoming the stress and the pressure. But I think this is good," she explained, "because in a way if you're not learning or growing or achieving in that aspect then it's not fun to do it."

Lucero-Schayes finished third in the 1992 Olympic trials, one place short of making the team. Although competing in a second Olympics, in the country of her ancestors, would have been "a dream come true," the athlete still finds much to be satisfied within her career. "Diving has been wonderful to me; not only did it pay for a college education, but I was able to travel around the world, nothing that my parents were ever financially capable of doing. Not only did it expand my horizons and make me understand what the world is all about," she added, it gave her the opportunity to experience "camaraderie, getting to create friendships with [athletes from] other countries." At the end of the 1992 season, she was still investigating the possibility of combining competitive diving with lecturing and various opportunities in broadcasting. In the long term, Lucero-Schayes and her husband plan to return to Denver, where she will continue her career in communications. Now that she has made her mark in the world of athletics, she wants to inspire others on a broader scale. "I always felt that communications—whether radio and television, or through newspapers and journalism—it's going to shape our world, it is the up-and-coming future. I really believe that instead of being on the other side just watching it happen, I want to be involved with helping in a positive way."

## SOURCES:

### Periodicals

*Atlanta Constitution,* July 28, 1989, p. F3; August 2, 1990, p. F7.
*Detroit Free Press,* April 14, 1992, p. D1.

### Other

Lucero-Schayes, Wendy, interview with Diane Telgen conducted April 15, 1992, Ann Arbor, MI.

—*Sketch by Diane Telgen*

# Leopoldo Lugones y Argüello
## 1874-1938
### Argentine poet, writer, and historian

Lugones was one of the most influential figures in Argentine twentieth-century literature, esteemed by most critics to be the greatest Modernist poet of his era. Manuel Belloni in *Américas,* January 1969, hailed Lugones as "the first Argentine writer; that is the first intellectual totally dedicated to letters, the first home des lettres who as such heralded a step forward in Argentine culture." However, the changes in Lugones's political and literary tenets determined that he and his work were highly polemic. Extolled as an innovator and "an extraordinary verbal gymnast" (Enrique Anderson Imbert in *Spanish American Liter-*

*ature,* 1963), he was also condemned for imitating his avant-garde contemporaries. Dorothy McMahon, writing in *Modern Philogy,* attributed Lugones's philosophical vacillations to his search for his roots, "He was seeking a set of values to which he could cling, a force that would give him a longed-for stability."

Leopoldo Lugones y Argüello was born in Villa de Santa María del Río Seco in the province of Córdoba on June 13, 1874, the eldest of four children. Lugones's origins were inherently important to him and his poetry was often nostalgic; "He was always a mountain man. His native countryside marked the face of his soul", asserted Manuel Belloni in *Américas.* At the age of nine Lugones's family moved to the provincial capital, Córdoba, leaving him with a sense of dislocation from his beloved birthplace. He attended a Catholic secondary school in Córdoba, but his rebellious nature ensured that he did not finish his formal education. He also rejected the Catholic Church. Dorothy McMahon in *Modern Philogy* explained that "As a result of this break with the teachings of his early childhood, Lugones was left with the problem of attempting to fill the void left by his displaced beliefs, and, from this time on, his whole emotive and intellectual energy was directed toward seeking a set of beliefs to sustain him."

1896 Lugones, a young anarchist, was drawn to Buenos Aires, where gained employment in the Post Office and Telegraph Service, while pursuing his literary and journalistic vocation. In late 1896 he married Juana González, with whom he had a child, Leopoldo. In Buenos Aires he was befriended by various poets, including Rubén Darío, who foretold: "Time will teach you many things. Among them the fact that ideas evolve and colors change," according to Merlin Foster in *Latin American Writers.* Lugones became an adherent to socialism, writing for militant journals, such as *La Vanguardia (The Avantgarde)* and *La Montaña (The Mountain),* which he also co-founded. His first volume of poetry *Las montaña del oro,* part of his modernist phase, was published in 1897.

Although primarily self-taught, Lugones was a notable force in the field of education, who energetically sought to implement reforms. He joined the National Department of Secondary and Normal Education, as an inspector in 1901, rising to Inspector General of Education in 1904 (some sources say 1902). During this time he published several articles on educational issues, such as *La reforma educacional (Educational Reform)* in 1903. Around 1903 he served a brief tenure as Professor of Literature at the Colegio Nacional of Buenos Aires. He spent time in various European countries during 1906 studying educational systems on behalf of the Argentine government. 1906 also witnessed the publication of *Las fuerzas extrañas* ("Strange Forces"), one of the original works of Hispanic science fiction; the compilation of short stories reflects Lugones's fascination with the occult and the inexplicable. Lugones resigned from the Ministry of Education in 1907 and became an independent journalist.

In 1909 he wrote *Lunario sentimental* ("Sentimental Lunar Poems"), regarded by many critics to be his literary masterpiece, and cited as an influence by Jorge Luis Borges and the Martinfierrista group. Utilizing the moon as its central motif, the poems reflect Lugones's disdain for humanity and rejection of the rational for the irrational. His following collection of poetry *Odas seculares* ("Secular Odes," 1911), a eulogy of the Argentine countryside, signals an artistic shift towards Lugones's utilization of national subjects and imagery. In 1911, while serving as Secretary of the Samiento Centenary Commission, Lugones wrote *Historia de Samiento* ("History of Samiento"), at the specific request of the National Council of Education.

Between 1911 and 1914 Lugones spent time in Paris and London, establishing close relations with European writers. In Paris he founded the literary and cultural journal *La Revue Sud-Américaine,* which served as a forum for Latin American ideas. With the onset of the First World War Lugones returned to Argentina and joined the editorial staff of *La Nación.* In 1915 he was appointed liberarian at the National Council of Education, a post he held until his death. From 1915 to 1916 he was Professor of Aesthetics at the University of La Plata, and entered his Hellenic literary phase.

Around 1916, as Darío had predicted, Lugones's socialist convictions began to waiver in favor of support for the Anglo-Franco European democracies. His literary output from this period mirrors his newly held convictions, for example, *Mi beligerancia* ("My Belligerence," 1917). During the 1920's Lugones' political and artistic tenets shifted again; artistically his work adopted a more simplistic form, while politically he moved closer to traditional Argentine values. His personal ideologies transgressed yet further to the reactionary right; discouraged with postwar developments in Argentina and Europe he began to denounce liberalism.

In 1924 Lugones was invited by the Peruvian government to the centenary observance of the Battle of Ayacucho, where he delivered his controversial "Hour of the Sword" speech, in which he expressed his support for a stronger military. His belief in the need for a powerful army is captured in his poetic works, such as *La patria fuerte* ("A Strong Homeland"), 1930. His ideology was endorsed by his actions; he colluded in the coup d' état that overthrew Hipólito Irigoyen on September 6, 1930 and imposed General José Uriburu.

In 1926 Lugones's literary achievements were rewarded with the National Prize for Literature.

However, his later years were marked by neuroticism and depression. He was alienated from his friends and colleagues for his espousal of fascism and never found the solace he yearned for. His work "was the outpouring and the searching of a tortured and bewildered soul which never acheived that inner tranquility it sought so fervently," concluded Dorothy McMahon in *Modern Philogy.* On February 19, 1938 he committed suicide by ingesting cyanide, leaving no explanation, in Isla del Tigre, outside Buenos Aires.

## SELECTED PUBLISHED WORKS:

*El imperio jesuítico,* (essays), Compañia Sudamericana de Billetes de Banco, 1904, reprinted with introduction by Roy Bartholomew, Editorial de Belgrano, 1981.

*La querra gaucha,* (novel: title means "The Gaucho War"), 1905, 10th edition, corrected and annotated by son, Leopodo Lugones, Ediciones Centurión, 1962.

*Los crepúsculos del jardín,* (poetry: title means "The Evening Shadows of the Garden"), 1905, reprinted, Editorial Babel, 1926, reprinted with prologue and notes by Ana María Amar Sánchez, Centro Editor de América Latina, 1980.

*Las fuerzas extrañas,* (short stories and an essay: title means "Strange Forces"), 1906, 4th edition, with preliminary notes by son Leopoldo Lugones, Huemul, 1966.

*Lunario sentimental,* (poetry: title means "Sentimental Lunar Poems"), 1909, 3rd edition, Ediciones Centurión, 1961.

*Odas seculares,* (poetry: title means "Secular Odes"), 1910, new corrected edition, Editorial Babel, 1923.

*Prometeo,* Talleres de Otero y Co., 1910.

*Historia de Samiento,* (history), Otero and Co., 1911, revised edition, Editorial Babel, 1931, reprinted, Editorial Universitaria de Buenos Aires, 1960.

*El ejército de la Iliada,* Otero and Co., 1915.

*Elogio de Ameghino,* Otero and Co., 1915.

*El payador,* Otero Impresores, 1916, reprinted with sketches by Alberto Güiraldes, Ediciones Centurión, 1961, published as *El payador: Antología de poesía y prosa,* prologue by Jorge Luis Borges, notes by Guillermo Ara, Biblioteca Ayacucho, Caracas, 1979.

*El libro de los paisajes,* (poetry), Otero y García, 1917.

*Mi beligerancia,* Otero y García, 1917.

*Las industrias de Atenas,* Talleres Gráficos "Atlántida," 1919.

*Selecció,* (selected poetry), M. García, Montevideo, Uruguay, 1919.

*La torre de Casandra,* Talleres Gráficos "Atlántida," 1919.

*Las horas doradas,* (poetry), Editorial Babel, 1922.

*Cuentos fatales,* (short stories), Editorial Babel, 1924, 2nd edition, with preliminary notes by son, Leopoldo Lugones, Huemul, 1967.

*Estudios helénicos,* four volumes, Editorial Babel, 1924.

*Romancero,* (poetry), 1924, 2nd edition, Editorial Babel, 1925.

*Filosofícula,* (poetry), Editorial Babel, 1924.

*La organización de la paz,* La Editora Argentina, 1925.

*El ángel de la sombra,* (novel: title means "The Angel of the Shadow"), M. Gleizer, 1926.

*Nuevos estudios helénicos,* Biblioterca Argentina de Buenas Ediciones Literarias, 1928.

*Poemas solariegos,* (poetry: title means "Ancestral Poems"), Biblioteca Argentina de Buenas Ediciones Literarias. 1928.

*La patria fuerte,* (essays), Taller Gráfico de L. Bernard, 1930.

*La grande Argentina,* Editorial Babel, 1930, reprinted with prologue by son, Leopoldo Lugones, Huemul, 1962.

*El estado equitative: Ensayo sobre la realidad Argentina,* La Editora Argentina, 1932.

*Roca,* prologue by Octavio R. Armadeo, "Coni," 1938, published as *Historia de Roca,* introduction by Tomás Alva Negri, Editorial de Belgrano, 1980.

*Romancero del Río Seco,* (poetry), sketches by Alberto Güiraldes, Las Pransas de Francisco A. Colombo, 1928.

*Antología poética,* (poetry), selected with an introduction by Carlos Obligado, Espasa-Calpe, Argentina, 1941.

*Obras poéticas completas,* (poetry), prologue by Pedro Miguel Obligado, Agiular, Madrid, 1948.

*Antología de la prosa,* selected with commentary by son, Leopoldo Lugones, Ediciones Centurión, 1949.

*Obras en prosa,* selected with prologue by son, Leopoldo Lugones, Aguilar, 1962.

*Leopoldo Lugones: Selección de poesía y prosa,* selected and edited by son, Leopoldo Lugones, Ediciones Culturales Argentinas, 1962.

*Las primeras letras de Leopoldo Lugones,* preliminary notes by son, Leopoldo Lugones, Ediciones Centurión, 1963.

*La estatua de sal,* (short stories), selected with a prologue by Borges, Ediciones Siruela, Madrid, 1985.

## SOURCES:

### Books

Anderson Imbert, Enrique, *Spanish-American Literature: A History,* translated by John V. Falconieri, Wayne State University Press, Detroit, 1963, p. 272.

Forster, Merlin H., *Latin American Writers,* edited by Carlos A. Solé, Volume 2, Charles Scribner's Sons, New York, 1989, pp. 493–502.

Klein, Leonard S., (editor), *Latin American Literature in the Twentieth Century,* Oldcastle Books, Harpenden, England, 1988, pp. 24–6.

Martin, Percy Alvin, (editor), *Who's Who in Latin America,* Stanford University Press, 1935, pp. 224–25.

Ryan, Bryan, (editor), *Hispanic Writers: A Selection of Sketches from Contemporary Authors,* Gale Research Inc., Detroit and London, 1991, pp. 288–90.

### Periodicals

*Americas,* Vol. 21, No. 1, January 1969, pp. 15–20.

*Inter-American Review of Bibliography,* Vol. 25, April-June 1975, pp. 134–49.

*Modern Philology,* February 1954, pp. 196–203.

—*Sketch by Amanda Beresford*

# Antonio Maceo
## 1845-1897
**Cuban revolutionary**

*Antonio Maceo*

Known as the "Bronze Titan," Antonio Maceo was one of the most feared and powerful fighters for Cuba's independence during the Ten Years War (1868–1878). He acquired a reputation equal to those of other Hispanic freedom fighters, such as **Che Guevara.** Maceo was a staunch anti-imperialist and spokesman for Cuban equality.

José Antonio de la Caridad Maceo y Grajales was born June 14, 1845, in Majaguabo, San Luis, Oriente, Cuba. Better known as Antonio Maceo, he was a mulatto, the son of a free black man—Marcos Maceo—and a light brown-skinned woman—Mariana Grajales y Cuello. Marcos Maceo was a Venezuelan who observed the fight for independence from the loyalist side, watching **Simon Bolivar** work to liberate all of South and Central America from the Spaniards. After fleeing to Cuba, Marcos Maceo opened a commercial-agricultural business and married Mariana Grajales, a widow, in a common-law marriage. Antonio was their first child, although Mariana already had four sons from her first marriage.

Maceo received some schooling but was educated primarily at home and on the streets. He worked in his father's business beginning at age 16, and he travelled throughout eastern Cuba, learning its terrain and mastering equestrian skills, which aided him later in life. He married Maria Magdalena Cabrales y Fernandez on February 16, 1866. Later that year, they had a daughter, Maria de la Caridad Maceo.

### Fought for Cuban Independence

As a young man, Maceo grew increasingly interested in politics. As a laborer, he developed a hatred of slavery and of the Spanish economic domination of the Cuban people. Despite his father's service as loyalist, Maceo joined a circle of revolutionaries in the Masonic Lodge of Santiago de Cuba in 1864. When Marcos Maceo learned of his son's politics, he fully endorsed the involvement. During Maceo's first night of fighting in the village of Ti-Arriba in October of 1868, he earned such respect that the revolutionaries immediately made him a sergeant in their army. To avoid reprisals by the Spanish, the entire Maceo family abandoned their home and joined the rebels, living in camps scattered throughout the countryside.

Maceo proved himself to be one of the greatest fighters in guerilla warfare history and earned the sobriquet of "Bronze Titan." Commanding a unit of Cuban rebels in January of 1869, he so harassed the Spanish rear guard that he was promoted to commander. Later that same month, for his effective guerilla assaults, he earned the rank of lieutenant colonel. But Maceo did not spend all his time fighting. He also established hospitals, workshops, living quarters, and food stores in *palenques,* the abandoned shelters built by fugitive slaves deep in the forests and mountains.

When rebel leaders Luis Marcano and Donato Marmol were killed in 1870, General Máximo Gómez became Maceo's commanding officer. Under Gomez's command, Maceo evolved into an even more threateningly powerful guerilla warrior. Maceo and Gómez became the central military figures in the struggle for Cuba's independence. Now in command of the third battalion (187 men), Maceo often fought against forces with superior numbers, using surprise, quickness, and confusion to triumph. Maceo acquired the rank of full colonel in 1872 after winning a battle against 1,000 Spaniards with his 187 men. A few months later, Maceo temporarily replaced Gómez as general in command of the Oriente province. Maceo served as general for only a short time before he was replaced by General Calixto Garcia. Then Maceo became a brigadier general in charge of the Second Division of the First Corps of the Liberating Army. During this command, Maceo had many decisive victories that won him the personal attention of President Cespedes of the revolutionary government. Maceo's auspicious victories helped weaken the Spanish invasion from western Cuba and secured the liberating army's eastern Cuban position enough for it to begin its invasion of western Cuba in 1874. Gómez led the invasion with Maceo as his immediate subordinate.

### Western Cuba Invasion

Maceo won a decisive victory when he led the 200-strong rebel cavalry and 50 infantry against the 2,000-soldier Spanish contingent. The Spanish added another 4,000 men to the battle, but still they retreated as Maceo's troops pursued them. According to Colonel Manuel Sanguilly: "General Maceo, like a colossus, was seen seizing the soldiers nearest him by the collars and belts and propelling them against the Spanish positions like projectiles." The Spanish suffered 1,037 in casualties, and the Cubans lost 174. Maceo, as he had been many times before, was critically wounded in the battle, but recovered in time to witness the death of his brother, Miguel, a few months later.

The Spanish rejoiced at the death of any Maceo family member, but wished most ardently for Antonio Maceo's death. Another decree for his death was issued after his brother's demise. Maceo also met with opposition from his rebel peers. The conservative government feared the rise of the black man to dominance as had already occurred in Haiti and Santo Domingo. They feared that if Maceo continued to gain power and influence the black population of Cuba might rally behind him and overtake the white Cubans. To sabotage this possibility, the rebel government began publically slandering Maceo. The government succeeded in fomenting disloyalty by racial prejudice. In the wake of troops defecting from Maceo's leadership, Maceo was moved from the western front back to Oriente to fill the position of Calixto Garcia, who had been captured. The western invasion soon faded because of false fears that Cuba would become a "second Haiti," and the Cubans lost the ground they won in the west, the more economically important section of the island, that Spain continued to control.

With Maceo's support, Gómez violated orders and continued his assault westward, successfully invading Las Villas and crossing the *trocha,* the Spanish line against the Cubans. The slander campaign against Maceo continued, especially after he sided with Gomez. In response, Maceo told his officers and soldiers that there were no black and white soldiers in the revolution nor would one race dominate another in the new republic.

### Refused to Accept Peace with Spanish

While the Cuban Republic met with Spanish General Martinez Campos at Zanjon, Camaguey, Maceo continued fighting the Spanish. And when most of the rebel generals laid down their arms and complied with what came to be known as *Pacto del Zanjón* (Treaty of Zanjón), Maceo continued fighting in Oriente. He continued his struggle into 1878, until he was asked to surrender and comply with the treaty. Maceo announced that he did not agree with the treaty, that it did not free the Cuban people from the Spanish, and that it did not abolish the slavery of Cuban (black) people.

Maceo continued to seek independence and was the last to hold out against ending the Ten Years' War. In March of 1878, 1,500 rebel officers and soldiers whole-heartedly endorsed Maceo's opposition to the Treaty of Zanjon. The "Protest at Baragua," as it became known, renewed the hopes of the Cuban masses, black and white, as Maceo led the last effort to attain the revolution's goals: independence from Spain and the abolition of slavery. Maceo led the rebels' intensified military campaigns against the Spanish. Neither the Spanish government nor the rebels who capitulated to Spain understood how to defeat Maceo or convince him to abide by the treaty. Finally, the government devised a way to order Maceo to leave the country on a special mission under the pretext that the forces he led would not surrender in his absence. On May 10, 1878, Maceo left Cuba, the rebels who served with him surrendered, and the war was over.

Although the war had ended, Maceo continued for many years to garner support for the revolution in other countries such as Haiti, Jamaica, and the United States. Eventually he took up residence in Costa Rica and joined **Jóse Martí** in leading the Cuban Revolutionary Party in 1893. Maceo returned to Cuba in 1895 to begin work on a new revolution. He commenced a series of battles with Spanish general Valeriano Weyler. Weyler hoped to trick Maceo into relenting or crossing into Spanish territory. He did, and Maceo was killed.

### SOURCES:

**Books**

Adams, Jerome, *Liberators & Patriots of Latin America,* Jefferson, North Carolina, Mcfarland Inc., 1991.

*Encyclopedia of Latin America,* edited by Helen Delpar, New York, McGraw-Hill, 1974.

Foner, Philip, *Antonio Maceo,* New York, Monthly Review Press, 1977.

*South America, Central America, the Caribbean,* edited by Francis Lambert, Kent, England, Europa Publications, 1995.

**Periodicals**

*New York Times,* January 8, 1897; February 9, 1897; February 19, 1897.

—*Sketch by Christopher B. Tower*

# Gerardo Machado y Machado
## 1871-1939
### Cuban statesman

Gerardo Machado y Machado, Cuba's fifth President, was born on September 29, 1871 in Camajuan in the County's Santa Clara district. He came to power in 1924 after a successful military career. Although he remained in power until the 1933 revolution, Machado resorted to dictatorial means to support his failing authority in the final years of his presidency. Many Cubans see the revolution against Machado as the beginning of the revolution that in years to come would bring the Communists to power in that country.

From the beginning of his adult life, Machado had many opportunities to shape an independent Cuba. The wars fought among Americans, Spaniards, and Cubans between 1895 and 1898 left the U.S. triumphant, Spain humiliated, and Cuba politically independent, if still in the shadow of its enormous neighbor to the north. Machado fought through the entire war, winning some distinction for bravery. Coming from a family of relative privilege, Machado entered the military as an officer, rising to Brigadier General by the age of 27. After Cuban independence—won primarily by three years of struggle by rebellious Cubans and solidified by U.S. intervention—Machado returned to his home province to embark on what Louis Perez, in his book *Cuba: Between Reform and Revolution,* called "an undistinguished career in politics." Machado joined the Liberal party, which supported economic development and diversification and eventually came to be associated with Americanism. He always remained active in the party and held several offices in the Republic's early years, including inspector general of the army, secretary of *gobernacion,* and mayor of his hometown of Santa Clara. Early on, military success outshone his modest political stature.

## Rose to Prominence

Independent Cuba faced increasing problems through the first two decades of the twentieth century. Socially, Afro-Cubans and white Cubans were not equal. Illiteracy and poverty, though high among whites, soared even higher among black Cubans. Class issues also vexed the new government. The Creole bourgeoisie found itself still overpowered by Spanish wealth and competing with growing foreign investment, especially by very large U.S. capitalist concerns. In the chaos of a new political system, many Cuban public officials turned to corruption. Perez estimated that until about 1920 corruption consumed $8 million annually. Armed uprisings intensified, as did U.S. intervention to maintain stability.

When Machado became the leader of the Liberal party in 1920, he recognized the importance of balancing popularity among the masses with acceptability to the U.S. government. Under the Platt Amendment of 1901, Congress had the power to intervene in Cuban affairs. This angered many Cubans, who did not believe repeated U.S. insistence that it had no territorial designs on Cuba. Machado spoke strongly against the Platt Amendment while advocating U.S.-style economic development. By 1924, the Zaya government had become so weak and divided that its Conservative party seemed destined to face defeat in the presidential elections. The Liberal party's candidate was almost certain to become the new president.

Colonel Carlos Mendieta opposed Machado for the liberal nomination. Mendieta had broad public popularity, which Machado—a politician of little renown—did not. Mendieta strongly advocated reform, but lacked political savvy. Machado, on the other hand, advocated many of the same principles but also campaigned confidently, cultivating important friendships in Cuba and abroad. Luis Aguilar, in his book *Cuba 1933,* wrote that "it is an accepted fact of Cuban history that Machado had the backing of Henry W. Catlin, president of Electric Bond and Share Company, and of powerful Spanish interests." Though loved by the masses, Mendieta lost the nomination, but he refused to challenge party bosses by appealing to his supporters to show their anger. Instead, Machado accepted the nomination. He used the slogan "Water, roads and schools," and reinforced his populist message when his opponent's campaign published a picture of its candidate on horseback. The Liberals responded with a photograph of Machado in a crowd and the slogan *Con el pueblo y a pie* ("With the people and on foot").

Machado won the election, which Aguilar described as "basically honest." Machado's "era of regeneration" began with his promise to hold another honest election four years later and "never to seek re-election." Machado became popular as a president who balanced economic development and stable foreign relations with the often conflicting impulses of Cuban pride and nationalism. He also appealed to Congress to pass his public works bill. This plan included the construction of a "Central Highway" more than 700 miles long, the building of a Capitol, and projects to beautify Havana.

Machado also took steps to control the all-important sugar industry. In 1920, sugar accounted for 92 percent of Cuba's exports. Fluctuations in sugar prices could take Cuba's economy to extremes. Overproduction often resulted from the near complete *laissez-faire* policy which the government applied to the industry, but Machado took steps to regulate production and diversify the agricultural base. Machado's call to "assure our political independence through economic independence" met with strong support. He further advocated popular programs to eliminate corruption, build technical schools, and rehabilitate Havana's prostitutes.

The kind of popularity that inspired the popular slogan "God in Heaven, and Machado in Cuba" does not always last. One telling anecdote revealed that as Machado visited a certain town, he asked the mayor for the time. The mayor replied, "The time you wish, my General." By 1925, even the leader of the Conservative opposition party publicly stated that "true opposition" to Machado would be "unpatriotic." Machado possessed overwhelming power. In August of 1925, *El Dia* published a cartoon critical of President Machado—later that month, its editor died at the hands of an assassin. The era of good feelings in Cuba started to recede as Machado assumed increasingly dictatorial tendencies.

By the mid-1920s, sugar prices began to drop. From a high of 22.5 cents per pound in May 1920, the commodity hit 4.2 cents in 1924 and 2.5 cents in 1928. Sugar's declining value created many economic and social problems: greater unemployment, salary cuts, renewed tensions among the classes, and generalized anxiety. Against this backdrop, Machado ran for re-election in 1928, breaking his earlier vow. Perez stated that Machado secured the nomination of all parties through "a combination of intimidation, coercion, and bribery." As the sole candidate, Machado won another six-year term.

The world economy plunged into depression in 1930, making Machado's situation still more desperate. Government power abuses increased, but opposition became more brazen, often attacking members of Machado's government. Machado responded with brutality. According to Perez, "Jails filled with government opponents, and they were the fortunate ones. More often, suspects were executed summarily at the site of capture." Conservatives called for U.S. intervention to depose Machado and prevent a popular rebellion.

By 1933, U.S. President Franklin Delano Roosevelt saw the situation as a crisis and dispatched U.S. Secretary of State Sumner Welles to Cuba to mediate a compromise. The United States began to urge Machado to step down, but Machado refused. By August, a bus drivers' strike turned violent and caused sympathetic workers to paralyze the country with a general strike. On August 7, police killed and injured many demonstrators, and the strike became a revolution. Members of Machado's party began to defect. The parties drafted a measure requiring Machado's early resignation. On August 12, the army—fearing U.S. intervention—turned on Machado, who left the country for the Bahamas that same day. Machado died in Miami Beach, Florida, on March 29, 1939.

## SOURCES:

Aguilar, Luis, *Cuba 1933: Prologue to a Revolution,* Ithaca and London, Cornell University, 1972.

Carrillo, Justo, *Cuba 1933: Students, Yankees, and Soldiers,* New Brunswick, New Jersey, Transaction Publishers, 1994.

Pérez, Louis A., Jr., *Cuba,* New York and Oxford, Oxford University Press, 1988.

Ruiz, Ramon, *Cuba: The Making of a Revolution,* City University of Massachusetts Press, 1968.

—*Sketch by James McCarthy*

# Salvador de Madariaga
## 1886-1978
### Spanish writer and diplomat

Madariaga was a formidable intellectual and one of Europe's premier twentieth-century liberal figures. A leading liberal—sometimes quixotically so—he wrote in his autobiography *Morning without Noon: Memoirs:* "For me liberty is a primary need of the spirit of man." He was **Francisco Franco's** anathema, described by the general's official biographer as "Franco's enemy number one," according to Paul Preston in *Salvador de Madariaga and the Quest for Liberty in Spain.* Despite his pursuit of liberty he never voted nor did he belong to a political party.

A gifted writer, Madariaga authored more than 60 books; his literary genres included novels, politics and history. He wrote in Spanish, French, English, and German. His liberal tenets earned him many honors, including the Charlemagne Prize in 1973 and nomination for the Nobel Peace Prize in both 1937 and 1952.

Salvador de Madariaga y Rojo was born July 23, 1886, one of 11 children, to Colonel José and Ascensión (Rojo) de Madariaga in La Coruña, Spain. Despite his literary inclinations, he studied engineering in France to comply with his father's wishes. He attended the Collège Chaptel, graduating in 1906, and studied at the Ecole Polytechnique from 1906 to 1908. He completed his studies at the Ecole Nationale Supérieure des Mines, graduating in 1911.

The experience of living abroad cultivated Madariaga's love for history and his international outlook. Preston quotes him in 1987: "It was then that I began to see Spain from the outside, a perspective which completes the view from within. Moreover, I was starting to acquire an international, or to be more exact, a human and worldwide, stance even with regard to events in Spain."

In 1911 Madariaga embarked on a career in engineering with the railway company Ferro Carriles Del Norte. Professionally an engineer, his true passion lay with literature; he maintained his literary contacts, contributing literary and political articles to publications in Madrid. His literary activities brought him into contact with the "los hombres de 1914" group, led by **José Ortega y Gasset.**

Madariaga married Constance Helen Margaret Archibald, a Scottish economic historian whom he had met in Paris, on October 10, 1912. After she died in 1970, he married Emilie Szekely Rauman on November 18, 1970. He had two daughters from his first marriage: Nieves and Isabel.

In 1916 Madariaga moved to London, working as a journalist for the *Times* news department of the Foreign Office. After World War I, he was compelled, for financial reasons, to return to Madrid and resume his engineering career, although he continued to contribute to the *Times Literary Supplement* and the *Manchester Guardian.*

In 1921, Madariaga's uncle procured him a post at the League of Nations transit conference in Barcelona. In August of 1921 he was permanently sequestered to the press section of the League Secretariat in Geneva, Switzerland. In 1922 he joined the disarmament section of the League, rising to departmental head, where he remained until 1927.

Madariaga continued a parallel career in journalism, writing for *El sol* in Madrid, under the pseudonym Sancho Quijano. He wrote in his memoirs that during his final year in the secretariat he experienced "books springing unannounced, unprepared, unthought-of, out of my mind, like volcanic eruptions," such as *The Sacred Giraffe.* He resigned from the League in 1927.

### The Reluctant Academic

Madariaga was offered the Alfonso XIII Chair of Spanish Studies at Oxford, England, following his recommendation from Henry Thomas of the British Museum. Upon accepting the post, the university bestowed him with a Master of Arts degree. The frugal lifestyle at Exeter College did not suit him; he fled from his university accommodation to the comforts of the Randolf Hotel with the comment, in *Morning Without Noon: Memoirs,* "My own chief impression was Tibet." He found that he was equally ill-suited to teaching, declaring in his memoirs that teaching was "one of my anti-vocations, for I frankly detest it." At Oxford he wrote *Disarmament* (1929).

### Ambassador, Diplomat, and Minister

In the fall of 1930 Madariaga embarked on a sabbatical lecture tour of the United States, Mexico, and Cuba. Upon his arrival in Havana on May 1, he learned from the newspapers that King Alfonso had resigned and that he himself had been appointed the Republican ambassador to Washington by the new Republican government; he had never been consulted and had never professed his political preferences. Dumbfounded, Madariaga decided to accept the appointment.

Although officially he served for seven months as the ambassador to Washington, in reality Madariaga stayed for only seven weeks. Of his ambassadorship in Washington he wrote, "My chief problem in Washington was to defend my stock of sherries and whiskies." (The U.S. was in its prohibition period.) His commission was interrupted by the appointment of Lerroux as the minister of foreign affairs who needed his expertise at the League of Nations in Geneva. Madariaga was seconded to Geneva and soon reappointed as the ambassador in Paris, although he was mostly resident in Geneva. Madariaga's moral and intellectual stance frequently conflicted with his role as Spain's representative, drawing criticism from Spain. Preston wrote that Spain's foreign minister, Luis de Zulueta remarked, "Madariaga forgets at times that he represents our country in the League of Nations and instead he acts like an intellectual."

At the League Madariaga was a prominent opponent of the 1931 Japanese invasion of Manchuria, interpreting it as an affront to the League itself.

He also played a prominent role in the disarmament conference and South American conflicts. He was also conscious of the League's inadequacies, particularly the domination of the richer and stronger nations. In the spring of 1934 he briefly served as the minister of education and then as the minister of justice. He left the government in 1934 (some sources say 1936) to pursue his vocation as a free-lance writer and occasional "free-lance politician."

After leaving the government he wrote *Anarquía y jerarquía*, which developed the concept of "organic democracy." To his disgust, the Francoists adopted its philosophies in a mutated state and hailed him as a precursor to the right wing regime. At the League of Nations he become the chairman of the Committee of Five, which endeavored to halt Italian offensives in Ethiopia.

### Liberal Exile of the Spanish Civil War

Following the outbreak of the Civil War on July 18, 1936, Madariaga traveled as a voluntary exile first to Geneva and then to London. He refused to support the Republicans, citing their ineffectual management of Spain's economic problems; he rejected Franco's totalitarianism. He was a leading proponent for international humanitarian intervention to halt the Civil War.

After the war Madariaga played an invaluable role representing and uniting Spanish exiles. His neutrality during the war made him a credible figure to most exiles. He strongly abhorred the Francoist regime. Madariaga then published *Victors Beware*. Of this work, Preston wrote, "In it, the dominant themes of the rest of his political life came together: European unity and the re-establishment of democracy in Spain." Franco stood in the way of these goals. Madariaga supported the restoration of the monarchy under **Juan Carlos** as a means of attaining these objectives.

As a prominent liberal figure, Madariaga claimed many prestigious posts in other arenas. He worked as a broadcaster to Latin America for the British Broadcasting Corporation. He was one of the founders of the Collège d'Europe, and also served as its president. He was dynamic member of UNESCO, though he later resigned in objection to Spain's admission.

Madariaga was named president of the Cultural Committee of the first Congress of Europe at the Hague, a post he retained until 1964. He utilized his station to ensure that leading members of the Spanish opposition, such as Gil Robles, a monarchist, and Prieto, a socialist, were brought to international venues. At the Spanish Federal Council of the European Movement he also included the Catalans and the Basques. He succeeded in uniting all factions of Spanish politics, except the fascists and the communists.

Madariaga played a fundamental role in the creation of a liberal option to **Franco** in Spanish politics. He was designated the first president of Liberal International, serving as the organization's honorary president from 1947 to 1952. In May of 1960, as president of Liberal International, Madariaga founded an assembly which united Spain's antifascist politicians and was supported by the Asociación Española de Cooperación Europa, headed by Gil Robles.

At the Fourth Congress of the European Movement in Munich in 1962, Spain's political situation headed the agenda. The Congress worried the Spanish authorities, particularly as the meeting coincided with a period of discontent, and Franco declared martial law. Madariaga also tried utilizing his international prestige in the League of Nations to create concern for Spain's political affairs. His actions of international liberalism were acknowledged with the Charlemagne Prize for his contribution to European unity. Madariaga returned to Spain in May of 1976, following Franco's death, and reclaimed his seat as a member of the Spanish Royal Academy. He died on December 14, 1978, in Locarno, Switzerland.

## SELECTED PUBLISHED WORKS:

### Biography and History

*Quatre Espagnols a Londres,* Plon, 1928.
*Spain,* New York, Scribner, 1930.
*Christopher Columbus* (first in "New World" trilogy), Hodder & Stoughton, 1939.
*Hernán Cortés* (second in "New World" trilogy), Macmillan, 1941.
*Spain,* two volumes (first volume based on previous book of same title), J. Cape, 1942.
*Cuadro histórico de las Indias,* Buenos Aires, Editorial Sudamericana, Volume 1: *El auge del Imperio Español en América,* 1945; translation published as *The Rise of the Spanish-American Empire,* Macmillan, 1947; Volume 2: *El ocaso del Imperio Español en América,* 1945; translation published as *The Fall of the Spanish-American Empire,* Hollis & Carter, 1947.
*Bolívar* (third in "New World" trilogy), two volumes, Mexico, Editorial Hermes, 1951; translation by author published in abridged edition with same title, Hollis & Carter, 1951.
*De Colón a Bolívar,* Barcelona, Editorial y Distribuidora Hispano Americana, 1956.
*El ciclo hispánico,* two volumes, Buenos Aires, Editorial Sudamericana, 1958.
*Spain: A Modern History,* Praeger, 1958.
*Españoles de mi tiempo,* Editorial Planeta, 1974.

*Memorias, 1921–1936: Amanecer sin mediodía,* Espasa-Calpe, 1974.

## Politics

*La guerra desade Londres,* Tortosa, Editorial Monclús, 1918.

*Disarmament,* New York, Coward, 1929.

*Discursos internacionales,* Madrid, M. Aguilar, 1934.

*Anarquía o jerarquía,* Madrid, M. Aguilar, 1935; translation by author published as *Anarchy or Hierarchy,* Allen & Unwin, 1937.

*Theory and Practice in International Relations,* Swarthmore College, University of Pennsylvania Press, 1937.

*The World's Design,* Allen & Unwin, 1938.

*¡Ojo, vencedores!,* Buenos Aires, Editorial Sudamericana, 1945; translation by author published as *Victors, Beware,* J. Cape, 1946.

*De l'Angoisse a la liberte,* Paris, Calmann-Levy, 1954; translation of second part published as *Democracy Versus Liberty,* England, Pall Mall Press, 1958.

*Rettet die Freiheit!* (selected articles originally published in *Neue Zuercher Zeitung,* 1948–57), Bern, Francke, 1958.

*¡General, márchese usted!* (collection of lectures broadcast for the Spanish Service of Radiodiffusion Francaise, 1954–57), Ediciones Ibérica, 1959.

*The Blowing Up of the Parthenon; or, How to Lose the Cold War,* Praeger, 1960.

*Latin America Between the Eagle and the Bear,* Praeger, 1962.

*Weltpolitisches Kaleidoskop* (second collection of articles originally published in *Neue Zuercher Zeitung*), Zurich, Frez & Wasth Verlag, 1965.

## Essays

*Shelley and Calderón, and Other Essays on English and Spanish Poetry,* Constable, 1920.

*The Genius of Spain, and Other Essays on Spanish Contemporary Literature,* Clarendon Press, 1923.

*Arceval y los ingleses,* Madrid, Espasa-Calpe, 1925.

*Guía del lector del "Quijote,"* Madrid, Espasa-Calpe, 1926; translation by author as *Don Quixote: An Introductory Essay in Psychology,* Wales, Gregynog Press, 1934.

*Englishmen, Frenchmen, Spaniards: An Essay in Comparative Psychology,* Oxford University Press, 1928.

*Americans,* Oxford University Press, 1930.

*On Hamlet,* Hollis & Carter, 1948.

*Bosquejo de Europa,* Editorial Hermes, 1951; translation by author published as *Portrait of Europe,* Hollis & Carter, 1952.

*Essays with a Purpose,* Hollis & Carter, 1954.

*Presente y porvenir de Hispanoamérica, y otros ensayos,* Buenos Aires, Editorial Sudamericana, 1959.

*De Galdós a Lorca,* Buenos Aires, Editorial Sudamericana, 1960.

*El Quijote de Cervantes,* Buenos Aires, Editorial Sudamericana, 1962.

*Retrato de un hombre de pie,* E.D.H.A.S.A., 1965; translation by author published as *Portrait of a Man Standing,* University of Alabama Press, 1968.

*Memorias de un federalista,* Buenos Aires, Editorial Sudamericana, 1967.

*Mujeres españolas,* Espasa-Calpe, 1972.

*Obras escogidas: Ensayos,* Buenos Aires, Editorial Sudamericana, 1972.

*Mi respuesta: Artículos publicados en la revista Ibérica (1954–1974),* Espasa-Calpe, 1982.

## Novels

*The Sacred Giraffe: Being the Second Volume of the Posthumous Works of Julio Arceval* (satire), Hopkinson, 1925.

*Sir Bob* (juvenile), Harcourt, 1930.

*El enemigo de Dios,* Madrid, M. Aguilar, 1926.

*Ramo de errores,* Editorial Hermes, 1952.

*La camarada Ana,* Editorial Hermes, 1954.

*Sanco Panco,* Mexico, Latino-Americana, 1963.

## Poetry

*Romances de ciego,* Madrid, Publicaciones, 1922.

*La fuente serena,* Editorial Cervantes, 1927.

*Elegía en la muerte de Unamuno,* Oxford University Press, 1937.

*Elegía en la muerte de Federico García Lorca,* Oxford University Press, 1938.

*The Home of Man* (18 sonnets), privately printed, 1938.

*Rosa de cieno y ceniza,* Buenos Aires, Editorial Sudamericana, 1942.

*El sol, la luna y las estrellas: Romances a Beatriz,* Barcelona, Editorial Juventud, 1954.

*La que huele a tomillo y romero,* Buenos Aires, Editorial Sudamericana, 1959.

*Poppy* (bilingual Spanish and English edition), Lugano, Imprenta Bernasconia, 1965.

*Obra poética,* Barcelona, Plaza y Janés, 1977.

## Plays

*Elysian Fields,* Allen & Unwin, 1937.

*El toisón de oro, y tres obras más: La muerte de Carmen, Don Carlos y Mío Cid* (the first a lyrical fantasy; the following three dramatic poems), Buenos Aires, Editorial Sudamericana, 1940.

*Don Juan y la Don-Juania* (one-act verse play), Buenos Aires, Editorial Sudamericana, 1950.

*Los tres estudiantes de Salamana,* Buenos Aires, Editorial Sudamericana, 1962.

*La Mappe-monde et le Pape-monde* (three-act verse play), Buenos Aires, Editorial Sudamericana, 1966.

*La cruz y la bandera [y] Las tres carabelas* (romances), Buenos Aires, Editorial Sudamericana, 1966.

*Nuamance* (opera), libretto by Henri Barraud, Boosey & Hawkes, 1970.

*Diálogos famos: Campos eliseos—Adán y Eva,* Buenos Aires, Editorial Sudamericana, 1970.

## SOURCES:

### Books

*Hispanic Writers,* edited by Bryan Ryan, Detroit, Gale Research, 1991.

Judy, Robert Dale, *Time: Now!,* Denton, Texas, RDJ Associates, 1992.

*Liber Amicorum: Salvador de Madariaga. Recueil d'études et de témoignages édité à l'occasion de son quatre-vingtième anniversaire,* edited by H. Brugmans and R. Martinez Nadal, Bruges, Tempelhof, De Tempel, 1968.

de Madariaga, Salvador, *Morning Without Noon: Memoirs,* Saxon House, 1973.

Preston, Paul, *Salvador de Madariaga and the Quest for Liberty in Spain,* Oxford, Oxford University Press, 1987.

### Periodicals

*Times* (London), December 15, 1978, p. 6.

—*Sketch by Amanda Beresford*

# Francisco Madero
## 1873-1913
### Mexican revolutionary and statesman

Known as the father of the Mexican Revolution, Francisco Madero became the first freely elected president of Mexico after the defeat of a dictatorship that had subjected Mexico and its people at the turn of the twentieth century. Though killed in a coup, Madero worked to achieve freedom and better lives for the Mexican people. His assassination made him a martyr.

Francisco Indalecio Madero was born October 30, 1873, at Parras, Coahuila, Mexico. He was the first of 15 children born to Francisco Madero, Sr., and Mercedes Gonzalez (Trevino) de Madero. The senior Madero was a businessman who had amassed a small fortune through mining and cattle raising. Mercedes was from a very large and wealthy Monterrey family, the youngest of 16 children. As a child, Madero was small and sickly. Because of his physical limitations, he was inclined to be more contemplative than active.

Madero received his primary education in the small town of Parras from local residents who served as surrogate instructors, and studied reading, writing, and music. At the age of 12, Madero enrolled in the Jesuit College of San Juan in Satillo, the capital of Coahuila. He briefly entertained the notion of joining the clergy, but abandoned this idea after less than a year at St. Mary's College in a suburb of Baltimore, Maryland.

After a short time back home, Madero left for France, where he remained from 1887 through 1892. He enrolled first at the Lyćee of Versailles and then at the School of Advanced Commercial Studies in Paris. There he studied accounting, manufacturing, political economy, finance, and civil law. Madero enjoyed his time in France immensely, owing to what he claimed to be a Latin affinity for the French.

Madero underwent a transformation in France after discovering the Spiritist writings of Allen Kardec. His studies of Kardec led Madero to Asian religions, like the Hindu faith and the *Bhagavad Gita.* The influences of these religions and beliefs would shape Madero's life in the years that followed.

### Improved Working Conditions

In 1893, Madero entered the family business. He worked agricultural properties using modern machinery. During this time he became acquainted with the plight of the rural peoples, particularly the Mestizo Indians of the south and central sections of Mexico. Madero worked as hard to improve the lives of his workers as he did to improve the yield of crops in the semi-arid fields. In one instance—despite a drought and inflated food prices—Madero organized a public dining room for those without the means to buy food. He also established and funded a hospital in San Pedro for the field workers.

Madero spent his days in philanthropic pursuits and attending to his business. He discovered the virtues of homeopathic medicine, which he claimed saved his mother's life from typhoid in 1901. This prompted Madero to redirect his life. He stopped smoking and drinking alcohol, vehemently advocating temperance. He also became a vegetarian. Part of turning his life around included his January 26, 1903, marriage to his great love, Sara Perez, daughter of a landowner. Shortly thereafter, Madero decided to enter politics.

In 1906, Madero represented the Center for Psychological Studies at San Pedro de las Colonias before the First National Spiritist Congress in Mexico City. This experience solidified the studies that had begun in Paris. Madero began thinking of Spiritist ways in which he could aid his people. At that time, Madero wrote that there was a "great political struggle which is being prepared for the not too distant future." Madero realized that something must be done about the **Porfirio Díaz** dictatorship that dominated the nation.

Porfirio Díaz had controlled Mexico since he took power during an 1876 military coup. Díaz kept wages low and crushed the workers' attempts to form labor unions. Díaz perpetuated indentured servitude—even feudalism—in rural areas of Mexico. Indians lost their lands to the rich landowners. Díaz controlled elections by refusing to allow any effective opposition to challenge him, and removed his enemies by imprisonment or murder. Madero was determined to end this government.

In 1905, Madero and his friends formed the Benito Júarez Democratic Club in San Pedro. Madero and his Democratic Club fought the candidacy of Frumencio Fuentes in the Coahuila gubernatorial elections of 1905. When Madero's opposition caused the state authorities to issue a warrant for his arrest, he fled the country with his wife, briefly seeking asylum in the United States.

Back at home in San Pedro, Madero continued to advocate the cause of democracy. Although many of his colleagues called for violent action against the Porfirian dictatorship, Madero sought peaceful action. In 1906, he refused to participate in an uprising, claiming that he considered it "a crime to stain the country with blood in the interest of his personal ambitions." Though he opposed violence, Madero worked diligently to attack "the ruling despotism" with his democratic movement. He searched for others who were dissatisfied with the government.

## Fueled Revolutionary Fervor with Book

Madero began writing *The Presidential Succession in 1910* (published in 1909) after a 1908 interview with Díaz incensed the Mexican people. Madero worked so indefatigably on his book that he suffered from eyestrain in late 1908; he had to remain in darkened rooms to recover. Madero's purpose in writing the book was to contribute to the successful creation and operation of an independent democratic party opposing Díaz. Though criticized as having "scant literary merit," Madero's book grappled with the political issues of the times and added to the

public awakening that precipitated the Mexican Revolution.

Madero rose to political prominence after the failure of General Reyes's candidacy opposing Díaz. In 1909, Madero embarked on his own national political campaign. He distributed his book and used his newspaper *El Democrata* —and personal contacts to win supporters. In June, Madero began a tour of Mexico, promoting the ideas in his book and openly opposing Díaz's reelection through his National Anti-reelectionist Party. Madero spoke to large, cheering crowds throughout the country. He published another booklet in March of 1910, hoping to gain further support for his party. *El partido nacional Antireeleccionista y la proxima lucha electoral* (*The National Anti-Reelectionist Party and the Next Electoral Struggle*) advocated Madero's plans to establish democratic practices.

Madero met with Díaz in April of 1910, and was surprised by Díaz's frailty and his ignorance of the Anti-Reelectionist movement. After the meeting, Madero said: "Porfirio is not an imposing chief. Nevertheless, it will be necessary to start a revolution to overthrow him. But who will crush it afterwards?" Madero continued to tour the country and became a symbol for the people who had recently become politically aware. Through Madero's efforts, the Mexican people prepared to begin their social revolution. But Díaz did not intend to allow Madero to continue unimpeded.

On June 3, 1910, Madero was arrested on the pretext of assisting a fugitive. Once the fugitive was found, Madero remained in prison, charged with fomenting a rebellion and insulting authorities. Arresting Madero backfired on Díaz. Although his opponent was off the streets, popular opinion supported Madero. Many considered him a victim of government persecution. The elections proceeded while Madero and 5,000 of his followers were in prison. Díaz's reelectionists won. On July 19—after the elections, Madero and many others were released from prison on the condition that they remained in the city. When Madero heard rumors that he would be rearrested, he escaped to the United States. Although Madero denied any intention of organizing a revolution, his self-imposed exile was perceived by many as the first step in the Mexican Revolution.

Despite the early denials, Madero began to call for the Mexican people of Mexico to revolt from his haven in San Antonio, Texas. He proclaimed that November 20, 1910, should be the Revolution's first day. He asked the Mexican people to "throw the usurpers from power, recover your rights as free men and remember that our ancestors left us a heritage of glory which we are not able to stain. Be as they were: invincible in war, magnanimous in victory." According to historian Stanley Ross: "[Madero] became a symbol for the discontented. He came to symbolize the deep desire for a change—a social economic, as well as political change." Despite Madero's rallying cry, attempts at revolution in 1910 were quashed, and Madero himself remained in the United States unable to muster a substantial military force.

But the idea of revolution had not died. Revolutionaries in Chihuahua attacked the federalists there along the Mexican Northwestern Railroad. Madero was rejuvenated by the news of the unrest in Chihuahua. On February 14, 1910, Madero returned to Mexico and eventually joined the revolutionary forces at Chihuahua (Guadalupe). Madero's forces encountered some setbacks in their progress to overthrow Díaz, such as a loss at Casas Grandes, but Madero eschewed defeatist sentiments. Madero was determined to capture Ciudad Júarez for its provisional capital, in memory of the city's namesake. Porfirio Díaz's forces were concentrated around Chihuahua City; the revolutionaries managed to take many of the towns in the state with little opposition. Díaz scrambled to maintain control by suspending the citizens' rights and replacing unpopular governors throughout Mexico.

Despite attempts at negotiations, the positions of Madero and of Díaz were intractable. On May 8, 1911, Madero and his troops attacked Ciudad Júarez. The revolutionaries succeeded in taking the city. This defeat led to the downfall of the Díaz regime. The Treaty of Ciudad Júarezbecame a reality on May 22, 1911. The treaty called for Díaz's resignation. Madero was eager to end the bloodshed that the Revolution had wrought. He hoped to install a favorable democracy in Mexico. But Mexico was not ready for a democratic government. On May 24, crowds filled the streets of Mexico City crying for Díaz's resignation. The next day—after some fatal civil unrest—Díaz resigned and fled the country. A few days later, Madero travelled to Mexico City and was welcomed by a jubilant crowd of at least a 1,000,000 admirers.

## Became President of Mexico

Insurrections—such as those led by **Emiliano Zapata**—continued in the wake of Díaz's resignation and the appointment of an interim president. Still democratic progress continued. Madero agreed to take Pino Súarez as his electoral running mate. The elections, according to historian John Ross, "were the cleanest, most enthusiastic, and most democratic elections in Mexican history. On November 2, 1911, Madero and Pino Súarez were declared elected as the first president and vice-president of the newly free, democratic Mexico.

Madero embarked on his oft-dreamed of course of action: to provide a government that would represent and unite all Mexicans. But he was short-sighted and forgave those who had rebelled against him. He retained members of the old regime, and he placed too much faith in the federal army. Madero's cabinet was divided and failed to produce effective policies. Still, Madero pursued his reformist goals. He sold public lands, worked to improve irrigation of dry lands, and lent money to *ejidos* (communal farms) for the peasant Indians. He instituted a Department of Labor within the government. He implemented new education programs and fed 5,800 students each day under his student dining room policy. Damaged railroads were repaired, and a road inspector was appointed to improve the neglected road system.

## Became Revolutionary Martyr

Despite all these good works, Madero's government did not perform quickly enough to pacify the people, and his administration was beset by many rebellions. Each rebellion was quelled in turn. Although the government remained stable, the repeated rebel efforts demonstrated that Madero was unpopular and possibly incompetent. Though Madero's government had stopped the revolts, 1913 brought a new uprising. By February, the Madero government faced a large rebel force and calls for Madero's resignation. This began a period known as the Ten Tragic Days of 1913. Fighting raged throughout Mexico City. The U.S. Ambassador, siding with the rebels indicated that if Madero did not resign there would be international (as in U.S.) intervention to oust him from the presidency. Still Madero refused to resign.

On February 18, military forces led by General Victoriano Huerta occupied the National Palace and arrested Madero, Suarez, and other members of the government. Huerta declared that he had overthrown the government. He forced Madero to sign a resignation proclamation at gunpoint. On February 21, told that they were being transferred to the penitentiary, Madero and Súarez were shot to death by one of Huerta's majors. Madero thus became the first Mexican president ever to be assassinated.

In death more than in life, Madero became a symbol and martyr of the Revolution. Although his detractors criticized him brutally, Madero was a sincere idealist. His accomplishments were overlooked in the revolutionary furor. He had improved labor conditions, agricultural practices, and education. In a eulogy, one of Madero's colleagues said: "Madero the apostle is simply magnificent, enormous, indisputable, and sublime. Guide of the popular conscience which he awakened from the lethargy of thirty years, he deserves gratitude." And Pino Súarez predicted it best: "Like all apostles ... they hated him unto death and glorified him unto immortality."

## SOURCES:

### Books

*Biographical Dictionary of Latin America and Caribbean Political Leaders,* edited by Robert J. Alexander, New York, Greenwood Press, 1988.

*Cambridge Encyclopedia of Latin America,* edited by Simon Collier, Thomas Skidmore, and Harold Blakemore, City Cambridge University Press, 1992.

Cumberland, Charles Curtis, *Mexican Revolution: Genesis Under Madero,* Austin, University of Texas Press, 1952.

*Encyclopedia of Latin America,* edited by Helen Delpar, New York, McGraw Hill, 1974.

Meyers, William K., *Forge of Progress: Crucible of Revolt,* Albuquerque, University of New Mexico Press, 1994.

Ross, John, *Francisco I. Madero,* New York, Columbia University Press, 1955.

### Periodicals

*Americas,* January 1986, pp. 311–31.

—*Sketch by Christopher B. Tower*

*Diego Maradona*

banned by the FIFA, international soccer's ruling body. Maradona was thrown out of the competition; many doubt that he will ever compete again in the international soccer world.

### A Star Rises in Argentina

Diego Armando Maradona was born on October 30, 1960, in Lanus, Argentina. His family was poor, and as the fifth son, Diego looked to soccer for his identity. The game of soccer is a tremendously popular one throughout much of the world, and many of its players in Latin America first learned to play the sport in poor regions. From the age of seven, when he received a soccer ball as a gift from his cousin, Maradona played the game with unbridled enthusiasm. His family moved to Barrio Fiorito on the outskirts of Buenos Aires when Maradona was still very young. There he played soccer with other poor South American boys, honing his game. Even in that highly competitive soccer culture Maradona excelled. He became a professional player with the Argentinos Juniors in 1973.

Maradona, a prolific and flamboyant goal scorer, quickly emerged as a favorite of the Argentine fans. Celebrities such as Evita Peron turned out to see Maradona in his first year with Argentinos. Even at age 13, his prodigious ability and colorful manner put Maradona in the spotlight.

In 1978 Argentina hosted the World Cup, the preeminent international soccer event which takes

# Diego Maradona
## 1960-

### Argentine soccer player

Diego Maradona emerged as the leading player in world soccer in the 1980s. A highly skilled and competitive athlete, Maradona has come to be regarded by many fans and sports journalists as the greatest player in soccer. Maradona's behavior and legal entanglements away from the soccer field, however, have tarnished many of his athletic accomplishments.

Maradona played in his first international soccer match at age 16; not even the famous Brazilian soccer player Pele began his career at such an early age. The flashy Argentinean played in three consecutive World Cup Finals (winning one in 1986), and led his team to the prestigious Italian league championship on two occasions. Maradona's irresponsible behavior over the years constantly interfered with his career, though. Fines for unruly behavior, suspensions, lawsuits, and repeated arrests for drug possession ultimately took their toll. Yet Maradona still managed to lead the Argentine team through the first rounds of the 1994 World Cup, only to test positive for five substances place every four years. Some feared that General Jorge Videla, who had come to power in 1976 with the backing of the Argentine military, would try to squeeze political gain out of the competition. While the soccer world worried about Videla, Maradona had to accept the disappointment of exclusion from the national team by Coach Cesar Luis Menotti. After a year of international play, Maradona felt that he was ready for this unique opportunity to win a World Cup in front of the adoring Argentine throngs. Menotti disagreed, contending that Maradona lacked experience. With Maradona on the sidelines, Mario Kempes led Argentina to its first World Cup championship in 1978.

The following year Maradona led the Argentina team to the World Youth Championship in Tokyo. Accepted as a permanent and crucial member of the national side, Maradona's career soared. He became South America's greatest player and Argentina's highest scorer. His exploits gained the attention of Pele, who had become an elder statesman of South American soccer by that time. He warned Maradona to "accept the applause but don't live only for it." As relevant as those words would perhaps one day become, the years between the 1978 and 1982 World Cups allowed Maradona little time for such reflection.

### "Maradona is Soccer"

After Maradona's success in the World Youth Championships, the Boca Juniors club bought his contract from Argentinos Juniors for a phenomenal $1.5 million in transfer fees alone in 1979. Two years later, Boca Juniors won the Argentine soccer championship, a feat that prompted the newspaper _El Grafico_ to exclaim, "Maradona is soccer." Praise was not in short supply from the media or from members of the international soccer establishment, who had watched Maradona's game mature.

The European soccer leagues soon beckoned. Although South American players and national teams were often as talented as those fielded in Europe, professional leagues in Europe clearly exceeded their South American counterparts in prestige and player salaries. Maradona's move to the Barcelona club in Spain proved his stature as an international soccer star of the first order. Barcelona spent a record $5 million for Maradona's contract.

Clearly Maradona felt some pressure to produce victories and championships, given the generous terms of his employment. Before he settled in with his new Spanish club, however, Maradona headed home to train with the Argentine national team for the 1982 World Cup to be held in his new home, Spain.

Many observers felt that Argentina's continental rival, Brazil, had the strongest team in the field. Speculation grew that the 1982 World Cup could turn into a battle between Maradona and Zico, Brazil's finest player. But Maradona, the new "golden boy" of soccer, found that such stature had its disadvantages. Double-teamed, triple-teamed and, he felt, very roughly treated by opponents throughout the tournament, Maradona became frustrated and made sure the public knew it. He lashed out at the press as well, expressing his anger at their "misguided" attentions. Maradona even earned himself expulsion from a first-round game. Although his on-field contributions in Spain were still considerable, he failed to emerge as a leader who could galvanize the defending champions to repeat their 1978 performance. The Italian team ultimately upset both Argentina and Brazil on its way to the crown. Maradona's World Cup experience was again a bitter one.

Late in 1982 Maradona was stricken with hepatitis, an illness that sidelined him for three months. In 1983 a rough tackle broke Maradona's left ankle in a game. The injury again limited Maradona's playing time and ability to lead his Barcelona club. By 1984 Maradona decided to leave Spain and compete instead in the tremendously competitive Italian league. Napoli football club president Corrado Ferlaino paid a record $8 million for the rights to the boy from Lanus.

Maradona's status as a sports celebrity reached even greater heights in Napoli. When Maradona attended his first practice on July 5, 1984, at Napoli's San Paolo Stadium, 60,000 fans packed the stadium. As the season unfolded, Maradona's success on the soccer field blunted the impact of his frequent visits to "undesirable places" in Naples and his lackadaisical approach to training. This bravado actually endeared him to many fans. His ability to do all the wrong things and still perform on the field gave him an air of nonchalant resilience to which people responded with cheers and adulation.

### Wins World Cup

The 1986 World Cup in Mexico City soon arrived. The world soccer community anticipated great things from the Argentine captain, and Maradona met all expectations. Argentina's coach Carlos Bilardo described his team as "Maradona and ten to be named." Coach Bilardo then forced his great player to train hard and give up the excesses of his partying lifestyle. Maradona started the 1986 World Cup in the best condition of his career.

Led by Maradona, Argentina manhandled its first opponents. They then defeated England in a controversial match that featured a disputed goal by Maradona. The Argentine captain was credited with a goal that he scored by using his hand, a serious rules infraction. After the game, a press member asked Maradona how the ball made its way into the net, and he responded that the "hand of God" had intervened.

Argentina played Belgium in the semifinals. Maradona scored two goals, and his team moved to the finals to face West Germany. The West German team utilized a "shadowing" technique similar to one employed by the Italians four years earlier in an effort to neutralize Maradona. Lothar Matthaus trailed Maradona all over the field and kept Maradona from victimizing West Germany as he had every other team in the tournament. Still, Argentina took a two-goal lead with no contribution from Maradona, and with twenty minutes remaining, Argentina looked certain to claim its second World Championship.

In eight minutes of play, however, the West Germans scored two goals to tie the match, and their morale soared. Two minutes later, with about seven minutes left until overtime, Maradona finally slipped his defender and made a brilliant pass to teammate Jorge Burruchaga, who scored a goal that the West German team was unable to match. With its second championship in three World Cup tournaments, Argentina had become the capital of international soccer.

After the 1986 World Cup Maradona set his sights on an Italian League championship with his Napoli club. The following year, he succeeded, although his relationship with the club ownership grew shaky. 1987 also saw the birth of his first daughter, Djalmita, and his first paternity suit, brought by a woman named Cristiana Sinagra. Maradona eventually yielded and agreed to pay child support. Such bad publicity began to accumulate. Napoli won the continent-wide UEFA Cup in 1989 and another Italian League title in 1990, but many Italian fans had come to see Maradona in a less flattering way.

In 1990 Italy hosted the World Cup, and Maradona again led Argentina. The Italian crowds showered him with a mixture of cheers and jeers. Although fans in Naples still loved him, fans in other venues had different feelings. The defending champions lost the opening game to Cameroon, a huge upset, but they still managed to make it past the first round. Argentina defeated Italy in the semi-finals and moved on to face West Germany once again. The short-handed Argentinean squad—five players had been disqualified from playing—succumbed to the West German squad 1–0 on a penalty kick.

### A Troubled Celebrity

Since 1990, Maradona's soccer exploits have gathered far less attention than his personal problems. In February 1990 police alleged that Maradona had tried to make illegal drug purchases; a month later Maradona tested positive for cocaine and was suspended from soccer for 15 months. In April Napoli sued Maradona's marketing firm for damage to the team incurred because of Maradona's "negative image". Later that month Maradona was arrested in Argentina on drug possession charges, and in June he was indicted on a cocaine charge in Naples. Another paternity suit was leveled against the soccer player that year as well.

Maradona served his suspension and moved to the Seville club in Spain in 1992, where he played well. He fought with management, however, and soon left for Argentina. Maradona dropped out of public view for a while. When he returned he was 40 pounds lighter and observers speculated that he had stopped his drug use. Maradona voiced his desire to lead Argentina in the 1994 World Cup held in the United States.

Argentina's team faced elimination from the tournament in the qualification rounds held in the two years previous to the tournament, but Argentina coach Alfio Basile still believed in Maradona's skills and asked him to join the team. In the playoff game to determine the last of the 24 teams to meet in the 1994 Cup, Maradona led Argentina to victory over Australia.

Indeed, in his first two games in the United States Maradona led the team to two impressive victories. Argentine optimism soared and fans began to dream of a third championship. But Maradona was caught with what one doctor described as "a cocktail of drugs" in his system. He tested positive for five substances banned by the FIFA. Maradona was thrown out of the World Cup, and Argentina lost in the round of 16.

## SOURCES:

### Books

*Soccer! The Game and The World Cup,* edited by Charles Miers and Elio Trifari, New York, Rizzoli International Publishing, 1994.

### Periodicals

*Sports Illustrated,* June 10, 1991, p. 14; July 11, 1994, p. 10.
*Time,* May 6, 1991, p. 73.

—*Sketch by James McCarthy*

# José Carlos Mariátegui
## 1894-1930
### Peruvian socialist, journalist, and organizer

José Carlos Mariátegui rose to prominence at the beginning of the 20th century as a leading Socialist thinker and organizer. Considered one of the most insightful analysts of his time, Mariátegui provided penetrating political insights as a journalist and helped found the Peruvian Socialist Party.

José Carlos Mariátegui was born in 1894 in Moquequa, in southern Peru. As a child, he suffered a knee injury that left him with a permanent limp. His mother, Maria Amalia LaChira Ballejosde Mariátegui, was a devout Catholic. She taught and encouraged his religious life, which he never abandoned even after he embraced socialist ideals. Mariátegui never knew his father—secretary to the First Congress of Peru, Dr. Francisco Javier Mariátegui de Telleria — who left the family when Mariátegui was very young. The disappearance of his father afflicted his poor, lower middle-class family. His mother supported them all with work as a seamstress.

A frail young man, who often complained of fevers and pains, Mariátegui persevered. He began his early school studies in Huacho and continued them in Lima. But at the age of 15, Mariátegui had to abandon his studies to help support his family. In 1909, he found a job close to his interests, as a proofreader for *La Prensa,* a newspaper in Lima. In 1915, he organized the Circulo de Periodistas, his first political venture.

### Radical Voice for Change

Mariátegui left *La Prensa* after tiring of its conservative bent and worked at *El Tiempo* from 1915 until 1918. Mariátegui changed at the new journal. With the greater pay and prestige of *El Tiempo,* Mariátegui became part of the middle class. He also changed his writing, producing more radical pieces. He started a column called "*Voces*" in which he took shots at the government and other members of the ruling class.

A developing socialist, he also wrote for *Nuestra Epoca* and *La Razon,* both of which he had a hand in creating. He wrote in favor of reform at the university and for organized labor. *La Razon* played a key role in the workers' and students' strikes of 1919. His opinions did not win favor with Peruvians, and in 1919, President Augusto B. Leguía sent him to Europe by naming Mariátegui the "Peruvian Agent of News, Propaganda, and Publicity" in Italy. Leguía, who did not appreciate Mariátegui's criticisms of his government, offered the young journalist the post as an alternative to imprisonment.

Mariátegui blossomed and discovered his true voice as a Marxist during his four years in Europe. His marriage to Anna Chiape in Florence produced a son. Mariátegui studied the Italian, French, and German languages while traveling extensively. He returned to Peru in 1923, fully motivated by a stronger grounding in Socialist theory.

### Spearheaded Socialist Movement in Peru

Mariátegui returned to Peru intending to start a leftist publication to promote socialism. Upon his return in 1923, Victor Raul Haya de la Torre invited him to speak at the Gonzalez Prada People's University—named for a leftist revolutionary who had been deported from Peru. Haya was forced out of Peru for his activities, but before he left, he named Mariátegui his successor editor of Haya's journal *Claridad.*

Mariátegui wanted to unite both the workers and the intellectuals against the government. His goals were temporarily delayed in 1924 when he had a cancerous leg amputated, which confined him to a wheelchair for the remainder of his short life. Mariátegui persisted despite this adversity and worked even harder than before to attain his goals. In 1925, he published his first book, *La Escena Contemporanea,* a collection of essays.

The next year he fulfilled his wish to start a publication devoted to leftist, socialist politics. The literary magazine *Amauta* debuted in September of 1926, publishing writing by many prominent intellectuals throughout the Americas. Mariátegui continued to edit the magazine until he died in 1930. *Amauta* reached a wide audience in Peru and abroad. At first it was not political in its ideology. Though Mariátegui was cagey about his intentions at first, he felt that *Amauta* would further the revolution in Peru by developing an analysis of Peru's problems from a global point of view. By polarizing the intellectuals of Peru, Mariátegui hoped to unify them again for the cause of Socialism.

Through these years, the Leguía regime closely observed Mariátegui, closed down his journals several times, arrested him once, and seized his papers. Consequently, Mariátegui prudently conducted his political work out of the public eye and never disclosed his political leanings publicly. In response to threats of exile the *Unesco Courier* reported that he wrote, "I prefer exile to resigning myself to silence."

*Amauta* opened new doors for Mariátegui, and later proved to be the name by which he would most often be called: "master." It jump-started the nation's political climate and critically influenced Peru's intelligentsia. In 1928, with his brother Julio Cesar, he opened the Minerva publishing house and bookstore.

Mariátegui launched another publication—a newspaper called *Labor* —in 1928, which paved the way for the formation of the General Confederation of Peruvuian Workers (CGTP). He worked tirelessly throughout these years, pioneering the cause of the avant—garde, such as the writing of James Joyce or the work of the surrealist painters. He also explored the parallels between Freudianism and Marxism.

Later in 1928, Mariátegui published his highly acclaimed *Siete Ensayos de Interpretacion de la Realdid Peruana* (*Seven Interpretive Essays on Peruvian Reality*). It was the first socialist interpretation of the Peruvian past. Though the seven essays—all previously published—were neither historically accurate nor even realistic, they achieved Mariátegui's purpose: to propagate the socialist ideal. The first three essays dealt with the economy with two of those focusing on the Peruvian Indians and their land. These were followed by essays on education, religion, and the political administration of Peru with one organizing thoughts on regionalism and another—the most militant of the seven—concentrating on literature.

The essays were not warmly received, but later were shown to be both brilliant and original. One local writer referred to the book as a set of "affectionate commentaries" while other newspapers and journals completely ignored the book. The seven essays laid the groundwork for his next major undertaking, the *Defensa del Marxismo,* published as installments in *Amauta* in 1927. In this work, Mariátegui married his ideas—both Marxist and non-Marxist—into one ideology, especially responding to charges of a departure from so-called "orthodox Marxism."

It was Mariátegui's collection of seven essays which inspired the creation of the Socialist Party of Peru in 1928 by the author and, ironically, seven colleagues. Ideologically, Mariátegui argued for a political party that represented workers, peasants, and the middle class which he believed better suited Peruvian reality. He wrote a paper that said as much and promoted Marxist/socialist ideas rather than communist ones. The paper was delivered at the first meeting of the Latin American Communist Parties held in Buenos Aires in 1929 and was castigated for lacking a sense of international, orthodox Communist dogma. Mariátegui was denounced as a romantic, nationalistic populist, and these opinions endured long after he died. Unable to reason with the members of the party, Mariátegui resigned his post as secretary general and named his replacement.

Mariátegui made plans to leave for Buenos Aires because the authoritarian government and the continual police raids jeopardized his safe residence in Peru. Unfortunately, before he could leave, he fell very ill with a staphylococcus infection. He died on April 16, 1930 at 8:50 a.m. On April 17, at 4 p.m., all the trolleys and motor cars stopped for five minutes in his honor. As a result of his death and the loss of his leadership, the Socialist party split into the Socialist and Communist parties of Peru.

Eventually, Mariátegui was recognized by historians as an important and instrumental voice for his time. The Chinese later touted his precepts in international discussions of politics. And his ideas regarding the need for fundamental change were revived in 1968 to guide the revolution led by General Juan Velasco Alvarado. Through closer study, Mariátegui became revered as a beacon of Marxist thought and action not just in Peru but in all of South America.

## SELECTED PUBLISHED WORKS:

*La Escena Contemporanea,* 1925.
*Siete Ensayos de Interpretacion de la Realdid Peruana,* 1928, 1971.

## SOURCES:

### Books

*Biographical Dictionary of Latin American and Caribbean Political Leaders,* edited by Robert J. Alexander, New York, Greenwood Press, 1988.
*Cambridge Encyclopedia of Latin America,* second edition, edited by Simon Collier, Thomas E. Skidmore, Cambridge, Cambridge Press, 1992.
Chavarria, Jesus, *José Carlos Mariátegui and the Rise of Modern Peru 1890–1930,* Albuquerque, University of New Mexico Press, 1979.
*Encyclopedia of Latin America,* edited by Helen Delpar, McGraw-Hill, New York, 1974.
*Marxism in Latin America,* edited by Luis E. Aguilar, New York, Alfred A. Knopf, 1968.

### Periodicals

*Americas,* July 1987, pp. 108–09.
*Christian Century,* October 14, 1987, pp. 885–887.
*Unesco Courier,* December 1994, p. 48.

—*Sketch by Christopher B. Tower*

# Cheech Marin
## 1946-
### Mexican American comedian, actor, and director

*Cheech Marin*

Cheech Marin is best known for being half of the comedy team Cheech and Chong. Marin and his partner Tommy Chong have enjoyed enormous success in the entertainment industry, from earning a Grammy award for their comedy album *Los Cochinos* in 1973 to starring in the multi-million dollar box office hit *Cheech and Chong's Up In Smoke* (1979).

Richard Anthony Marin was born on July 13, 1946, in Central Los Angeles to Oscar, a police officer, and Elsa Meza Marin. He was later nicknamed "Cheech" after a Mexican snack of deep-fried pork skins called *chicharron*. His parents raised Marin and his three brothers and sisters in the San Fernando Valley. He earned a straight 4.0 grade point average throughout his school years, and he worked as a janitor and a dishwasher to put himself through college. Marin received a B.A. in English from California State University, Northridge.

Fleeing to Canada to avoid being drafted in the Vietnam War in the late 1960s, Marin met Tommy Chong and joined City Works, an improvisational comedy and musical group in Vancouver, British Columbia. The comedy duo of Cheech and Chong gradually grew out of their performances with City Works. After City Works disbanded in 1970, the two comedians took their act on the road, performing in clubs and concert halls throughout the United States and Canada. At first they performed as a rock band, but after successfully interspersing their music with comedy routines, they eventually left the music behind and stuck with the comedy.

### Wins Grammy Award

During the 1970s, Cheech and Chong were among the first entertainers to introduce of a new brand of comedy that spoofed hippies and marijuana smokers. Though their humor often ran to coarse and scatological extremes, the duo became extremely popular. After signing with Warner Brothers, Cheech and Chong made a series of comedy records that were all smash hits: *Cheech and Chong,* released in 1971, went gold; their next album, *Big Bambu,* was voted the number one comedy record of 1972; and *Los Cochinos* won a Grammy award for Best Comedy Record in 1973. This third album rose to number two on the record charts over a span of 29 weeks and brought Cheech and Chong's humor to its widest audience yet. Other albums released by Cheech and Chong include *Wedding Album, Sleeping Beauty, Let's Make A Dope Deal, Greatest Hits,* and *Get Out of My Room.*

### Embarks on Successful Movie Career

The success of their comedy albums launched Cheech and Chong into an movie career beginning in 1979 with *Cheech and Chong's Up In Smoke.* In this film, Cheech and Chong play a buffoonish pair of "burn-outs" whose misadventures lampoon sex, drugs, and rock & roll. *Up In Smoke* was a box-office hit, yielding over $100 million and becoming the highest grossing film of the year. Considered by many to be the duo's best film, *Up In Smoke* has achieved the status of a cult favorite.

The team followed the success of their first film with a sequel entitled *Cheech and Chong's Next Movie* in 1980. Featuring the same lead characters from *Up In Smoke,* this movie tracks the pair as they experience goofy adventures in a massage parlor, a welfare office, a nightclub, and a flying saucer. *Cheech and Chong's Next Movie* fared reasonably well at the box office, but it did not match the success of their first film. The comedy team made several more movies in subsequent years, including *Cheech and Chong's Nice Dreams* (1981), *Things Are Tough All Over* (1982), *Cheech and Chong: Still Smokin', Yellowbeard* (1983), and *Cheech and Chong's The Corsican Brothers* (1984).

Cheech and Chong went their separate ways after playing a pair of bumbling burglars in Martin Scorsese's *After Hours* in 1985. In the years following the break up, Marin has appeared in such films as *Echo Park* (1986), *Ghostbusters II, Rude Awakening, Troop Beverly Hills* (all in 1990), and as the voice of Stump in *Fern Gully: the Last Rainforest* (1993). He has also made appearances in various television programs, including *The Tracey Ullman Show* in 1987 and *The Golden Palace* in 1992, and the TNT movie *The Cisco Kid* in 1994.

Perhaps Marin's most successful venture in the post-Cheech and Chong period was the production of *Born in East L.A.* in 1987. This film—which Marin wrote, directed, produced, and starred in—is considered the second commercial Chicano film to be released in the United States, after **Gregory Nava**'s *El Norte* in 1983. *Born in East L.A.* satirizes the controversial issue of immigration in the United States by focusing on a Mexican American who cannot speak Spanish and who knows little about his Mexican heritage who is mistakenly deported to Mexico. The film traces the hero's misadventures in Mexico until the defining moment occurs when he crosses the U.S. border with hundreds of illegal immigrants as Neil Diamond's song "Coming to America" swells in the background.

Although reviewers generally censured *Born in East L.A.*, the movie proved to be a winner at the box office. Further, it won an important film festival award in Havana, Cuba, in 1988. Despite criticism of the film's production values, many commentators have pointed out that the true significance of *Born in East L.A.* lies in its adept use of humor and satire to highlight important social issues common to the Hispanic American community.

## SELECTED DISCOGRAPHY:

*Cheech and Chong*, Warner Brothers, 1971.
*Big Bambu*, Warner Brothers, 1972.
*Los Cochinos*, Warner Brothers, 1973.

## SELECTED VIDEOGRAPHY:

*Cheech and Chong's Up In Smoke*, Lou Adler, Lou Lombardo, 1979.
*Cheech and Chong's Next Movie*, Universal, 1980.
*Cheech and Chong's Nice Dreams*, Columbia, 1981.
*Things Are Tough All Over*, Columbia, 1982.
*Cheech and Chong: Still Smokin'*, Paramount, 1983.
*Yellowbeard*, Carter De Haven, 1984.
*Cheech and Chong's, The Corsican Brothers*, Orion Pictures, 1984.
*Born in East L.A.*, Universal, 1987.

## SOURCES:

*Contemporary Theatre, Film, and Television,* Vol. 2, edited by Linda S. Hubbard and Owen O'Donnell, Detroit, Gale, 1989.
*Handbook of Hispanic Cultures in the U.S.: Literature and Art,* edited by Francisco Lomelí, Houston, Arte Público Press, 1993.
*Hispanic-American Almanac,* edited by Nicolás Kanellos, Detroit, Gale, 1993.
*International Motion Picture Almanac 1994,* edited by Barry Monush, New York, Quigley Publishing, 1994.
O'Neil, Thomas, *The Grammys: For the Record,* New York, Penguin, 1993.
Quinlan, David, *Quinlan's Illustrated Directory of Film Comedy Actors,* New York, Henry Holt, 1992.
Reyes, Luis and Peter Rubie, *Hispanics in Hollywood: an Encyclopedia of Film and TV,* New York, Garland, 1994.
*Video Hound's Golden Movie Retriever 1994,* edited by Martin Conners and Julia Furtaw, Detroit, Visible Ink, Gale, 1994.

*—Sketch by Christopher B. Tower*

# René Marqués
## 1919-1979
**Puerto Rican writer**

An influential voice in the Hispanic literary world, Marqués was the foremost Puerto Rican writer of his generation. Marqués achieved his greatest acclaim as a dramatist; he was renowned for his innovations and enthusiasm, which contributed to the revival of the Puerto Rican theater. The recipient of numerous and prestigious literary honors, his plays enjoyed an international audience.

A fundamental and ubiquitous theme in Marqués' work is the search for Puerto Rican identity and the synonymous political and cultural subjugation of Puerto Rico by its powerful American neighbor. Eleanor Martin wrote in *René Marqués* that "Marqués' work is a mirror of his time; it is particularly a reflection of United States intervention in Puerto Rico's economy, culture, and politics since the turn of the century." Marqués saw his literary vocation as an instrument for creating a greater awareness of his country's maladies through which, he believed, he could incite people into action.

René Marqués was born on October 4, 1919, in Arecibo, Puerto Rico, to Juan Marzués and Pura (Garcia) Marqués. His formative years were spent in Arecibo and on his grandparents' haciendas of San Isidro, near Lares, and Carrizales, near Hatillo. He was brought up in an intellectual environment and surrounded by influential relatives, particularly Dr. Francisco Maria Susoni and Doña Padrina Padilla de Sanz, who imbued him with a love for Puerto Rico and a yearning for its independence. His literary aspirations were enhanced through reading books acquired from his maternal grandmother's library, while regular visits to the cinema and theater with his mother kindled his dramatic inclinations.

Despite his early absorption in the arts, Marqués earned a degree in agronomy from the Colegio de Agricultura y Artes Mecánicas (College of Agriculture and Mechanical Arts) in Mayagüez in 1942, following the family tradition of farming. In the same year he married Serena Valesco, with whom he had three children—Raùl Ferando, Brunhilda María, and René Francisco. (He and Valesco divorced in 1957.) In 1944 his first significant work, a volume of poetry called *Peregrinación,* was published. He obtained employment as an agronomist for the Puerto Rican government, but decided to pursue his literary interests.

### Marqués' Literary Career Begins

In 1946 Marqués traveled to Spain with his family, where he embarked on courses in literature and classical and contemporary Spanish theater at the University of Madrid. During this year abroad he wrote two plays: *El hombre y sus sueños* (*Man and His Dreams*) and *El sol y los MacDonald* (*The Sun and the MacDonalds*). Marqués also debuted as an essayist, penning a series of articles entitled "Crónicas de España"("Chronicles from Spain") that covered various aspects of Spanish literature for the Puerto Rican daily newspaper *El mundo.*

Marqués returned to Puerto Rico in 1947. He briefly served as a manager in Velasco Alonso, Inc., a department store, in Arecibo. Adhering to his artistic vocation, he created and directed a small theater group called Pro Arte de Arecibo. He also produced literary criticism and reviews for the journals *Asomante* and *El mundo.* His essays were well received; in 1947 the Institute of Puerto Rican Literature awarded him a journalism prize for an article on Franciso Arrivi's drama *María Soledad.* In 1948 Marqués moved to San Juan, where he worked as a writer on *El Diario de Puerto Rico.* During the same year his play *El hombre y sus sueños* was published in Asomante.

In 1949 Marqués accepted a fellowship, awarded to him the preceding year, from the Rockefeller Foundation. He traveled to New York, where he studied drama at Columbia University and enrolled in additional courses at Erwin Piscator's Dramatic Workshop. In the United States Marqués also visited a number of experimental theaters at Yale University, the Catholic University in Washington, D.C., and the Cleveland and Karami Playhouses in Cleveland. At Columbia University he wrote the English-language play *Palm Sunday* as an assignment for Dr. Theodore Apstein. *Palm Sunday* focused on the slaughter of 21 Puerto Ricans at a nationalist demonstration on Palm Sunday in 1937 by the colonial police force. In the play, Marqués is highly critical of the domination of Puerto Rico, a prevailing theme in his work. Political and cultural suppression and protest were central subjects of Puerto Rican literature during this period. A member of a group of writers known as the Generation of the Forties that often examined such issues, Marqués and his work enshrined the philosophies of the group and their belief in the pen as a means to liberation.

### Marqués' Contribution to Puerto Rican Drama

In 1950 Marqués returned to San Juan, where he became actively involved in writing and various theatrical ventures. He was employed as writer for the División de Educación de la Comunidad (Division of Community Education in the Department of Public Education), rising to the position of Director of the Editorial Division, where he remained until 1969. His play *El sol y los MacDonald* premiered at the University of Puerto Rico, and in 1951 Marqués became secretary of the board of the Ateno Puertorriqueño (Experimental Theater of the Atheneum) with his friend José M. Lacomba. The theater served as a platform for Puerto Rican culture and continued as the theater division of the atheneum. In 1954 a controversy over the staging of his play *La carreta* (*The Oxcart*) led the group to move to the Tapia Theater; with a larger stage and commensurate audience Marqués achieved greater success.

The 1950s proved a prolific and industrious era for Marqués. In 1951 he wrote *La carreta,* his most popular drama. *La carreta* is the tale of a peasant family's migration to San Juan and then to the slums of New York in search of a better life; their endeavors fail and they return to their land. The play reflected Marqués' deep concern for the effects of "Operation Bootstrap," a government program that he felt failed to consider indigenous needs and caused the widespread abandonment of the Puerto Rican countryside. *La carreta* premiered in New York in December 1953 and two months later in San Juan. It became the first contemporary Puerto Rican play to be staged in Europe when it premiered at the National Theater María Guerrero in Madrid.

During this period, Marqués wrote several other major works that explored the suppression of Puerto

Rican culture and endorsed political autonomy, notably *Juan Bobo y la Dama de Occidente* (*Juan Bobo and the Lady of the Occident*), *Otro día nuestro* (*Another Day of Ours*), and *La muerte no entrará en palacio* (*Death Shall Not Enter the Palace*). The political content of the latter has prevented it from being produced, although it is regarded by some critics to be his best dramatic work. The play draws on the historical political events surrounding Governor Muñoz Marin's signing of the Commonwealth Agreement, though in Marqués' drama the fictional character is assassinated before he signs the document and the liberation forces triumph.

Marqués returned to New York in 1957 and accepted the Guggenheim Scholarship he was accorded in 1954. There he composed his semi-autobiographical first novel *La vispera del hombre* (*The Eve of Manhood*). In this novel he "traced the pattern of Americanization that meant 'progress' to some, but to Marqués signalled the loss of Puerto Rican values and the sense of Puerto Rican identity," related Eleanor Martin in *René Marqués*. In 1962 the novel won the Iberian-American prize from the William Faulkner Foundation.

Marqués visited Mexico City in 1958 as an official member of the Puerto Rican delegation to the First Interamerican Biennial of Painting. Upon returning to Puerto Rico he worked for the government radio station. He was honored with the prestigious Ateneo awards for four different works, including the short story "La sala" ("The Living Room"); and his play *Un niño azul para esa sombra* (*A Blue Child for That Shadow*).

In 1959 Marqués co-founded the Club del Libro de Puerto Rico (Book Club of Puerto Rico) with Eliezer Curet Cuevas. His drama *Carnaval afuera, carnaval adentro* (*Carnival Outside, Carnival Inside*), written in 1962, was greeted by controversy; it was a tale that depicted grim and chaotic lives. The play gained honorable mention in a Casa de las Américas literary contest, but Marqués was prevented from entering the United States to attend the premiere. In 1969 Marqués became a professor of literature at the Universidad de Puerto Rico, a position he retained until his retirement in 1976. Marqués retired to the house he had built on the Cubuy River, where he remained until his death on March 22, 1979. Just three days before he died he was conferred with a diploma of honor from the Institute of Puerto Rican Culture in recognition of his contribution to Puerto Rican culture.

## SELECTED PUBLISHED WORKS:

*Peregrinación*, Arecibo, 1944.

*La carreta*, Asomante, 1951–52; Editorial Cultural, 1961, fifth edition, 1969; translated by Charles Pilditch and published as *The Oxcart*, Scribner, 1969.

*Juan Bobo y la dama de occidente: Pantomima puertorriqueña para un ballet occidental*, (*Juan Bobo and the Lady of the Occident*), Los Presentes, 1956, second edition, Antillana, Rio Piedras, 1971.

*La Vispera del hombre*, (*The Eve of Manhood*), Club del Libro de Puerto Rico, 1959, Editorial Cultural, 1981.

*La casa sin reloj*, (*The House Without a Clock*), Universidad Veracruzana, 1962.

*Mariana; o, el alba*, (*Mariana or, The Dawn*), Rumbos, 1966.

*Ensayos, 1953–1966*, Antillana, 1966; translated by Barbara B. Aponte and published as *The Docile Puerto Rican: Essays*, Temple University Press, 1976.

*Sacrificio en el Monte Moriah*, (*Sacrifice on Mount Moriah*) Antillana, 1969.

*Un nino azul para esa sombra*, (*A Blue Child for That Shadow*), Editorial Cultural, 1970.

*La muerte no entrara en palacio*, (*Death Shall Not Enter the Palace*), Editorial Cultural, 1970.

*El sol y los MacDonald*, (*The Sun and the MacDonalds*), Editorial Cultural, 1971.

*Carnaval afuera, carnaval adentro*, (*Carnival Outside, Carnival Inside*), Antillana, 1971.

*Ese mosaico fresco sobre aquel mosaico antiquo*, Editorial Cultural, 1975.

*Immersos en el silencio*, (*People Immersed in Silence*), Antillana, 1976.

## SOURCES:

### Books

Flores, Angel, *Spanish American Authors: The Twentieth Century*, New York, H.W. Wilson, 1992, pp. 509–13.

*Hispanic Writers*, Detroit, Gale, 1991, pp. 301–2.

*Latin American Writers*, Volume 3, New York, Charles Scribner's Sons, 1989, pp. 1237–45.

Martin, Eleanor J., *René Marqués*, Boston, Twayne, 1979, p. 168.

### Periodicals

*New York Times*, March 25, 1979, p. 34.

—*Sketch by Amanda Beresford*

# José Martí
## 1853-1895
**Cuban poet and revolutionary**

José Martí, known alternately as the father of Cuban independence and the father of the modernist poetry movement, was a brilliant essayist, poet, thinker, and motivator. He published an extensive body of work covering various themes, including the independence struggle against Spain, the conditions of Cuban jails, the state of affairs in Guatemala, and children's stories. However, Martí was probably best known for his essays and oratory, which became the blueprint for Cuba's successful insurgency against Spanish colonialism in the late 1800s. This last contribution made Martí Cuba's most revered figure and won him international acclaim as a political strategist.

José Julian Martí y Pérez was born on January 28, 1853, in Havana, Cuba, just three years after his father had immigrated to the Caribbean island from Spain. His father, Don Mariano Martí y Navarro, had worked for the Royal Artillery Corps before he came to Cuba and married José's mother, Leonore Pérez. The Martí household was not always economically stable, and as a young boy Martí would work with his father when possible to help provide for his mother and five sisters. Yet Martí's passion was always politics, and Cuba in the 1800s provided him ample circumstances to fuel that passion.

At school in Havana, the Instituto de Segunda Ensenanza de la Havana, Martí got his first taste of Cuban politics from his mentor, Rafael Maria de Mendive. During this period, the Spanish were exerting furtive control over their Caribbean colony, which was divided along separatist and colonialist lines. Those advocating continued colonialism were part of the ruling class and did not want their position threatened. On the other side were the lower classes and intellectuals, who favored separatism. This desire for independence was political, economic, and cultural. According to Louis A. Pérez in *Cuba between Reform and Revolution,* there was a "growing awareness of the contradictions of empire, real and potential, and the deepening conflict between interests Spanish and interests Cuban. The needs of an oligarchy based on land and dependent on free trade did not always coincide with the needs of a metropolis." Martí, his mentor, and other students at the Instituto were part of this growing awareness. Unfortunately for Martí, his first taste of politics was short-lived.

### Exiled to Spain

Martí began writing political poems at a young age and had his first piece published in 1869, at age

*José Martí*

sixteen, in *La Patria Libre* ("The Free Fatherland"). The poem, entitled "Abdala," told the story of a patriot who dies while defending his country. Infused with nationalism, a heretofore foreign concept, "Abdala" marked Martí as a young, outspoken separatist. That same year, Martí and a classmate, Fermin Valdés Dominguez, faced trial after they were searched and captured with separatist writings. At the outset of the trial Martí announced that Cuba had a right to self-determination, sovereignty, and independence from Spain. The judge sentenced him to six years in prison. After serving one year doing hard labor, Martí's parents successfully lobbied for their son to be exiled to Spain.

Shortly after Martí arrived in Spain in January 1871, he enrolled in the University of Zaragoza, from where he received simultaneous bachelor's degrees in philosophy and law in 1874. During this period, Martí also published an excerpt from what would be his first book, *El presidio politico en Cuba* ("Political Prison in Cuba"). This testimony was the first glimpse of Martí's brilliance and dedication regarding the independence of Cuba. In Martí's *Our America: Writings on Latin America and the Struggle for Independence, El presidio politico en Cuba* is reprinted in its entirety. A short passage illustrates his talent and conviction: "A lively and resounding watchword rang in your ears and was etched upon your minds: National Integrity! And the hall of the people resounded with a single voice: Integrity! Integrity! O, your dream is not so beautiful or so heroic, for you are undoubtedly dreaming. Look, look at this painting I am going to paint for you, and if you do not shudder with fright at the wrongs you have committed, and, struck with horror, damn this face of national integrity which I am showing you, I will turn away my eyes in shame from this Spain without a heart."

In 1875 Martí left Spain for Mexico, where he was reunited with his family. By this time, Martí had established himself as an intellectual voice in the fight for Cuban independence. He developed this voice further in Mexico while both writing for the liberal publication *Revista Universal* ("Universal Magazine") and participating in Mexico City's literary salons. Martí's ascension to the top of Mexican intellectual society was truncated, however, when the liberal government of Sebastian Lerdo de Tejada was overthrown by strongman **Porfirio Diaz.** Heeding the hostile tone directed at intellectuals by the new regime, Martí set off for Guatemala in 1877.

He returned to Havana briefly to witness a fledgling independence insurgency (the Ten Years War, 1868–1878, also known as the First War of Independence), which motivated Martí to redouble his efforts to spearhead a revolutionary movement from abroad. Martí left Havana for Guatemala by way of Mexico City. While in Mexico he married Carmen Zayas Bazan, another Cuban exile. Initially, Guatemalan society was receptive to Martí. This was especially evident among the lower classes. Martí began championing populist causes such as the abolition of slavery and equal representation for the masses. Clearly, the ruling Guatemalan oligarchy did not care for this eloquent and inspiring Cuban exile, and in late 1878 he was forced to leave the country.

Although Martí would eventually settle in New York after his deportation from Guatemala, he could not resist the temptation to return to Cuba in 1878. In this year, the separatists had agreed to a peace treaty with the colonialists called the Peace of Zanjón. This brought an end to the Ten Years War, which had given Martí impetus in 1877. However, the Peace of Zanjón had hardly changed the oligarchic status quo in Cuba, and Martí's protests against the narrow gains for the masses got him deported again. Martí arrived in New York in 1881 after traveling through Europe. He spent the next 14 years consolidating the Cuban independence movement from his United States base, publishing essays on the future of the Americas, and detailing the doctrine that would ultimately form the Partido Revolucionario Cubano ("Cuban Revolutionary Party")—the political organ that brought freedom to Cuba.

Between 1881 and 1895, Martí wrote extensively on the conditions of Latin America, the role it should play in hemispheric affairs, and the paternalistic dangers inherent in courtship by the United States. His writings during this time were journalistic in nature; he contributed regularly to the *New York Sun, La Opinion Nacional* ("The National Opinion") in Caracas, and *La Nacion* ("The Nation") in Buenos Aires. Martí penned some of his most important modernist poems during this time, and his well-received collections *Ismaelillo* (1882) and *Plain Verses* (1891) marked his recognition as one of the world's leading poets.

Martí's mission to secure Cuban independence became more urgent after he came in contact with the exile community in New York. Although the exiles generally agreed that the Spanish should be ousted from Cuba, they had neither a cohesive plan nor an effective leader. From his base in New York, Martí formulated that plan and became the leader that witnessed Cuba's entry into the successful Second War of Independence. He gained the financial, ideological, and military support he needed to affect a triumphant insurgency through his stunning oratory and populist agenda.

## Founded Cuban Revolutionary Party

In January 1890, Martí and another exile, Rafael Serra, founded La Liga ("The League") in New York City. The League embodied all the fundamental aspirations Martí had for the independence movement. First, its ranks were made up of poor, landless, Negro exiles, and Martí believed that the revolution had to be led by the underclass. Second, the League had a nationalist flavor, which was one of Martí's primary ideals: to create a Cuban national identity. From the League, Martí created a popular base from which he would spread his independence movement. The League sponsored classes, workshops, and lectures designed to educate the exiles about the fundamentals of the Cuban independence struggle and to increase membership.

In Tampa, Florida, one year after the League was formed, Martí came into his own as the father of Cuban independence after delivering two extremely popular speeches to the exile community there. Martí found in the Florida exiles a stronger drive and organization for the movement than in New York. Thus, in November of that year, Martí drafted what were called the Tampa Resolutions—effectively the blueprint for the insurgency which began three years later. The Resolutions had four main points. First, they required that all existing groups of exiles unite. Second, they proposed that the fight for Cuban independence be waged with the goal of installing a popular government chosen by the people. Third, they stated that the purpose of the emerging revolutionary party was to represent a wide range of popular thought and that the republic would be built according to the needs of the majority, not the narrow minority. And last, the Resolutions declared that the revolutionary party would respect all mandates and sovereignty of existing exile organizations.

In Martí's own words, as quoted by Philip S. Foner in his introduction to *Our America,* the revolutionary groups had to unite "for the respect and assistance of the world's republics; and for the creation of a just and frank republic—unified in territory, laws, work, and cordiality, built by all for the benefit of all." The exiles took Martí's words to heart. Although it was a difficult task to appeal to all the fractious interests of so many groups, Martí was able to build a viable coalition, and on January 5, 1892, El Partido Revolucionario Cubano ("The Cuban Revolutionary Party") was formed. Two factors in particular permitted this coalition: Martí's consistent condemnation of racism (one-third of the total Cuban population was of African descent) and his warnings about United States imperialism.

Martí's revolutionary thought and organizational skills developed immeasurably during this period. He outlined an economic plan for an independent Cuba—a key component of which was abandoning its dependence on a single export, which had bound Cuba's economy to fluctuations in world sugar prices. Further, he discussed fundamental land reform and redistribution of wealth. He outlined his philosophy in a statement reproduced by Pérez in *Cuba between Reform and Reformation:* "Exclusive wealth is unjust. A nation with small landowners is rich. A country with a few rich men is not rich—only the country where everyone possesses a little of the wealth is rich. In political economy and good government, distribution is the source of prosperity." Martí also lectured vehemently on the dangers of substituting American economic imperialism for Spanish political colonialism. With these thoughts captivating his mind, Martí returned to New York to duplicate the success he experienced in Tampa.

On April 10, 1892, the first forum of the New York Council of the Cuban Revolutionary Party convened. The union of all pre-existing Cuban exile organizations served as an impressive informational and financial force. By the time the New York Council met, there were several pro-independence exile newspapers being published, including *Patria* ("Fatherland") and *La Revista de Cayo Hueso* ("Key West Magazine"). Also, the exiles had been donating to the Cuban Revolutionary Party regularly, so by early 1894 it was financially ready to launch the insurgency. Martí had assembled a formidable team to lead the effort. Máximo Gomez, a military hero from the Ten Years War, was chosen as military chief of the armed forces, and **Antonio Maceo,** also a hero from that war, was appointed to a top position in the revolutionary ranks. Both men were great admirers of Martí, despite their differences of tactical opinion during the Ten Years War. Additionally, Martí had secured a cadre of fighters in Cuba which was preparing to take up arms when the Revolutionary Party landed.

In December 1894, Martí alerted committed exiles in Costa Rica, Florida, and the Dominican Republic that the Cuban Revolutionary Party was poised to mount its offensive. The party contracted three boats to take the fighters from Florida to Cuba, stopping in Costa Rica and the Dominican Republic en route. Unfortunately for the rebels, all three boats were intercepted and detained by U.S. authorities on January 10, 1895. Martí was undaunted by this setback and immediately called for a reunion between the leading exile figures and the revolutionaries in Cuba. They agreed that forces in Cuba would start the offensive on February 24, 1895, while Martí arranged for another boat to transport the ranks of exiles. According to plan, the Second War of Independence began on that day near Santiago de Cuba.

Two months later, on April 1, 1895, Martí and five revolutionaries set out from Santo Domingo, Dominican Republic, for Cuba. After the revolutionaries were abandoned by their original crew on April 2, Martí paid a German captain to take them as passengers. On April 10, they set to sea a few miles from the Cuban shore. The insurgents rowed to land under the cloak of night and landed on Cuban soil on April 11. When the revolutionaries united with the other fighters on the island, the war was fully underway. Since the beginning of the war, the Cuban people had been taking up arms in the name of Cuban independence and José Martí. Sadly, the man who had conceived, created, and directed the Second War for Independence, the struggle that finally granted Cuba's freedom from Spain, died on the battlefield on May 19, 1895, in Dos Rios, Oriente Province. But his work had not been in vain—that September the corps of revolutionaries met in Puerto Principe to set up a provisional government under a new constitution for a free and democratic Cuba.

## SELECTED PUBLISHED WORKS:

*Presidio Politico en Cuba* ("Political Prison in Cuba"), Ramon Ramirez, 1871.

*Ismaelillo* ("Little Ismael"), Farrar, Straus, & Giroux, 1882.

*Edad de Oro* ("Golden Age"), privately published, 1889.

*Versos Sencillos* ("Plain Verses"), Farrar, Straus, & Giroux, 1891.

*Obras Completas* ("Complete Works"), Editorial Nacional de Cuba, 1963.

## SOURCES:

Adams, Jerome R., *Liberators and Patriots of Latin America,* North Carolina, McFarland, 1991.

*Cambridge Encyclopedia of Latin America and the Caribbean,* edited by Simon Collier, Thomas E. Skidmore, and Harold Blakemore, London, Cambridge University Press, 1993.

Martí, José, *Our America: Writings on Latin America and the Struggle for Independence,* New York, Monthly Review Press, 1977.

Pérez, Louis A. Jr., *Cuba between Reform and Revolution,* New York, Oxford University Press, 1988.

————, *Cuba and the United States: Ties of Singular Intimacy,* University of Georgia Press, 1990.

Skoug, Kenneth, N., "The United States and Cuba," in *Cuba Reader,* New York, Grove Press, 1989.

Suchlicki, Jaime, *Historical Dictionary of Cuba,* New Jersey, Scarecrow Press, 1988.

—*Sketch by Conner C. Gorry*

*A Martínez*

# A Martínez
## 1949-
### Mexican American actor

An actor whose work has been recognized with several nominations and awards, including an Emmy in 1990, Adolpho Martínez has won acclaim and many fans for his work in the daytime drama *Santa Barbara,* prime time series *L.A. Law,* the stage musical *Zoot Suit,* and numerous films including his role as the romantic interest of Meryl Streep in *She-Devil.* He became successful playing ethnic villains in the 1970s and early 1980s, but with the help of his stint in the role of Cruz Castillo, a sensitive policeman on the soap opera, he has carved out an identity as a leading man. He exhibits no bravado when discussing his success in a diverse array of roles. "I've had a career many people would trade for," he told a *Drama-Logue* interviewer in 1992. "Yet through it all there has been this sense of just squeaking through many critical passages. It never goes away."

The oldest of six children, Martínez was born and raised in Los Angeles. He was the third Adolpho Martínez, his grandfather and father having shared the name. So as a child he was nicknamed "Little A" and "Model A." He kept the nickname in his professional life, spelling it with no period. Martínez played semi-professional baseball and rock-and-roll before settling into his career as an actor. He played rhythm guitar and sang, fronting the Makahas, a surf band named after a Hawaiian beach. He studied theater at UCLA before dropping out to perform in small venues in Los Angeles.

### Acting Career Accelerates

In 1972, Martínez accepted a role as a Native American in *The Cowboys,* a film starring John Wayne—a childhood idol of his; he recalls feeling intimidated by the actor. Additional film roles followed in the next decade: *Once Upon a Scoundrel, The Take, Joe Panther, Players, Walking the Edge,* and *Beyond the Limit.* In 1978, Martínez won critical acclaim for his work in *Zoot Suit,* the Luis Valdez play about 1940s-era racism against Chicanos that premiered in Los Angeles.

Martínez was less than enthused, though, when he was offered the role of police officer Cruz Castillo in *Santa Barbara* in 1984. He preferred film to television, but he was growing weary of playing stereotypical Mexican villains. His decision to accept the role the fourth time it was offered brought Martínez a huge following of fans and the opportunity to build a unique character. Castillo, considered by viewers to be sexy yet sensitive, romanced and ultimately married an Anglo-American woman.

In 1989, Martínez's work was recognized with an IMAGEN award and the next year he received an Emmy award. The daytime drama is shown in 40 countries, and in Europe his character is so popular that he was mobbed in the Louvre and had to leave the museum. "I felt totally embarrassed in the presence of all this great art," he told *Us Magazine* in 1990.

The actor performed on the soap opera throughout its run from 1984 to 1992, when he began a two-year stint on the critically acclaimed nighttime series, *L.A. Law.* He portrayed an attorney and again his character was given a romantic storyline. In 1990, Martínez further rejected stereotypes when he portrayed Meryl Streep's butler-turned-lover in the feature film *She-Devil,* which also starred Roseanne Barr. In 1992, Martínez played the legendary California bandit Tiburcio Vásquez in Valdez's play *Bandido!* His most recent work includes the romantic lead in *Deconstructing Sarah,* a 1994 film for cable television's USA Network. Martínez starred opposite Ally Sheedy in New World Entertainment's *One Night Stand,* a film that marked the directorial debut of actress Talia Shire. The actor returned to musical expression in 1994 with the release of *Fragrance Thorn,* a collection of original songs.

Martínez speaks with gratitude of the male Latin stars of the past, as well as his contemporaries, who have broken ground for him and other Mexican American performers, mentioning in particular the contributions of Anthony Quinn and Ricardo Montalban. In a 1994 *Los Angeles Times* profile he states: "It's really important to the Latino community, acting and otherwise, that the development of stars occurs. Then it's viable from a business point of view for our stories to be told. That's the way this game works." Martínez lives in Los Angeles with his wife and two children.

## SELECTED VIDEOGRAPHY

*The Cowboys,* 1972.
*Once Upon a Scoundrel,* 1973.
*Starbird and Sweet William,* 1973.
*Joe Panther,* 1976.
*Powwow Highway,* 1989.
*She-Devil,* 1989.
*The Hunt for the Night Stalker,* 1991.
*Deconstructing Sarah,* 1994.
*One Night Stand,* 1994.

## SOURCES:

### Books

*Drama-Logue,* November 19–25, 1992, p. 5.
*Los Angeles Times,* June 5, 1994, p. 4.
*Us Magazine,* January 22, 1990, p. 45.

*—Sketch by Karen Withem*

# Bob Martinez
## 1934-
### Spanish American businessman, politician, and government official

Bob Martinez served as the governor of Florida from 1987 to 1991, then moved to Washington to direct the Office of National Drug Control Policy under U.S. president George Bush. A former Democrat who began his career as a classroom teacher, Martinez became active in Republican national politics and was named a co-chairman of George Bush's successful campaign for president in 1988. In January 1993 Martinez left office to found a marketing and consulting firm for businesses in the United States and Latin America.

Martinez was born on December 15, 1934, in Tampa, Florida, to Ida and Sarafin Martinez. All four of his grandparents emigrated to Tampa from Spain at the turn of the century to work in the cigar factory industry. Martinez grew up as an only child in a close-knit extended family. He was particularly close to his maternal grandmother, Isabel Carreno. "She was a great cook and I was her favorite grandchild," recalled Martinez in an interview with contributor Ann Malaspina. The family lived in the mostly Hispanic neighborhood of West Tampa.

Carreno cared for Martinez while both his parents worked. It was from her that Martinez learned Spanish. His father was a waiter at a Tampa restaurant, while his mother worked as a seamstress in a sporting goods garment factory. "My family wanted to prove they could achieve," Martinez told Malaspina. His parents taught him that hard work would eventually pay off. "You had to prove yourself and work hard, never complain, and just move forward," he said.

Martinez met his future wife, Mary Jane Marino, while he was a student at Jefferson High School in Tampa. Because their names began with the same letter, "I sat behind her in every class we had together," Martinez recalled. They began dating during their senior year. The couple was married in 1954, during Martinez's sophomore year at the University of Tampa. He graduated in 1957 with a B.S. in social science. Martinez and his wife had two children who have provided them with three grandchildren.

A "tall, lean jogger," according to the *New York Times,* Martinez played basketball and baseball in high school. His best sport, however, was baseball, a sport he played at the American Legion level. On Sundays, during college, he played with a semi-pro baseball team in Tampa. In recognition of his athletic accomplishments, Martinez was made a member of the University of Tampa Sports Hall of Fame.

### First Taste of Politics

Martinez taught in the Hillsborough County Public Schools from 1957 to 1962, and from 1964 to 1966, but decided to change careers. He returned to school to earn an M.A. in labor and industrial relations at the University of Illinois in 1964. He represented a unionized group of restaurant owners, then served as executive director of the Hillsborough County Classroom Teachers Association from 1966 to 1975. It was in his capacity as the teachers' union representative that Martinez got his first taste of politics. "I lobbied in Tallahassee and in Washington for teachers," recalled Martinez to Malaspina.

In 1975 Martinez left the teachers union and opened a family restaurant, Cafe Sevilla Restaurant, in the neighborhood in which he grew up. But while operation of the restaurant was time-consuming, Martinez remained active in public life. A month after he opened the restaurant, Florida Governor Reuben Askew asked him to serve on the state water commission board; he became vice-chairman of the Southwest Florida Water Management District.

In late 1978 Martinez ran for mayor of Tampa at the urging of a close friend. After consulting with his wife, they agreed to campaign for the non-partisan office. In 1979 Martinez became the first Tampa mayor with a Spanish surname, no small achievement in a city with a small Hispanic population. "I ran my campaign on job creation, relocating industry and commerce to Tampa, improving the arts, and bringing in new convention business," recalled Martinez to Malaspina. To revitalize Tampa's downtown, Martinez worked to develop road, water, and sewer systems while also pursuing other capital projects. Martinez remarked that during his two terms as mayor, from 1979 to 1986, Tampa became nationally recognized as a trendsetter among small cities.

In 1983 Martinez attended an Oval Office ceremony at the White House, at which time he changed his party affiliation to Republican. He became acquainted with President Ronald Reagan, Vice President George Bush, and his son Jeb Bush. As the 1980s unfolded Martinez emerged as a prominent force in national Republican Party politics. He was chosen to speak at the Republican National Conventions in both 1984 and 1988. In 1989 he served as co-chairman of the presidential U.S. delegation to El Salvador to monitor the national elections. He also sat on the White House Task Force for a Drug Free America and the Presidential Advisory Commission on Intergovernmental Relations.

### Governor of Florida

In 1987 Martinez became the first Catholic—and the only person with an Hispanic surname—to win Florida's highest political office. Several major issues—rapid growth, environmental problems, and crime—confronted the new governor.

"You have to provide a lot of protection for natural resources, which are a natural and an economic asset. Our state depends on natural resources for tourism," Martinez told Malaspina. To confront this issue, he helped establish Preservation 2000, a program that allowed the state to purchase and protect land from development, an initiative that won him recognition as Conservationist of the Year from the National Park & Conservation Association. In addition, Florida became the first state to pass solid waste legislation. Other decisions received less praise, however. His imposition of new taxes on services such as advertising, lawyer's fees, and real estate transactions proved unpopular. He later rescinded the tax.

Known as a "hard-line anti-drug warrior," according to *Time* magazine, Martinez doubled the number of prison beds in the state and worked to strengthen the court system. "He briefly called out the National Guard to crack down on smugglers and rammed through the legislature a law mandating the death penalty for drug kingpins," reported *Time*. As Martinez recalled to Malaspina: "We just didn't have enough prisons. As more people committed crimes, were arrested, tried and convicted, they had to have somewhere to go. I'd rather have done something else." He also increased anti-drug education in schools and lobbied for drug testing in the workplace.

Martinez's strong conservative stands often found the national spotlight. In 1989 he made an unsuccessful bid to limit abortions in Florida. He also turned down a grant for a new health clinic for a Miami high school because it intended to provide birth-control information. In 1990 Martinez asked the state prosecutor to bring obscenity and racketeering charges against the musical group 2 Live Crew for their rap-music album *As Nasty As They Wanna Be*. Martinez lost his 1990 campaign for a second term to former Senator Lawton Chiles, a popular Democrat.

### Anti-Drug Leader

In 1991 President Bush asked Martinez to serve as the director of the federal Office of National Drug Control Policy following the resignation of William J. Bennett, the nation's first "drug czar." During his Senate confirmation hearing, Democrats assailed him for his emphasis on law enforcement and prison expansion over drug treatment and crime prevention programs in Florida. Despite such criticisms, however, the Senate confirmed him by a wide margin in March 1991.

As the nation's drug czar, Martinez worked to strengthen and expand drug education for young people. When he took office, he told the *New York Times* that he had a "tremendous amount of interest in education and prevention" and wanted to "open up a very good dialogue with the treatment providers so that we can work together." Education was just one component of his strategy, though. "We wanted to go after the kingpins, the big organizations. And we wanted to work with employers to have drug-free workplaces. Drug abuse is a never-ending story, and too many of the stories are tragic," he told Malaspina. He negotiated with Peru, Bolivia, Mexico, Colombia, and the Bahamas to implement initiatives designed to stop drugs at the source.

Teenage drug use dropped and drug-fighting budgets rose during Martinez's tenure, according to *U.S. News & World Report.* He was criticized, though, for staff upheavals and disorganization in his office. In 1990 *Time* noted his "reputation for imperious leadership," while a *Miami Herald* editorial charged that Martinez "has talents, but persuasiveness is not high among them." In a *New York Times* interview, Martinez defended his record and described himself as "an implementer," a person who "likes to operate, to execute and to monitor what is to be done."

Like many politicians, Martinez faced charges of ethics violations. In his position as drug czar, Martinez acknowledged that he improperly used White House stationery to solicit refunds owed to his unsuccessful 1990 re-election campaign. He also made more than $63,000 available for the Bush-Quayle re-election effort in Florida. Critics claimed that he had violated federal campaign finance laws. Martinez proclaimed his innocence, and a Department of Justice investigation concluded that he had no criminal intent to flout the law. Ultimately, he was cleared of all charges. Martinez left office with the Bush Administration in January 1993.

In May 1993 Martinez joined his son, Alan, to run Bob Martinez & Company, Inc., a Tampa-based marketing, consulting, and public affairs firm. He has traveled frequently and has worked as a weekly columnist and political commentator for an ABC affiliate in Tampa. He has indicated no desire to re-enter politics. Upon reflection, Martinez told Malaspina, "I was in politics for 27 years. I enjoyed every minute of it."

## SOURCES:

### Periodicals

*Mother Jones,* July-August 1991, pp. 42–3.
*The New Republic,* November 12, 1990, pp. 17–19.
*The New York Times,* February 27, 1991, p. A15; March 22, 1991, p. A15; April 15, 1991, p. A10; January 10, 1992, p. 14; May 3, 1992, p. 21.
*Newsweek,* August 10, 1987, p. 54.
*Time,* March 12, 1990, p. 25; December 3, 1990, page 48.
*U.S. News & World Report,* February 10, 1992, p. 33.

### Other

Martinez, Bob, interview with Ann Malaspina, December 13, 1994.

*—Sketch by Ann Malaspina*

# Vilma Socorro Martinez
## 1943-
### Mexican American attorney and public speaker

Vilma Socorro Martinez is a nationally known and respected attorney and lecturer who has been committed to the cause of civil rights her entire life. She decided long before law school that this would be the focus of her career and her life. "I didn't think my parents were treated fairly and I don't think I was treated fairly," said Martinez in a telephone interview with Carol von Hatten.

Martinez was born in San Antonio, Texas, the daughter of Salvador and Maria Pina Martinez. During high school she served as an officer in the National Honor Society and planned to continue her education. But her counselor tried to dissuade her from going to college, advising her that avocational school would be more appropriate for a Mexican American. That was not the first time the young student had encountered prejudicial thinking. She recalled in an interview with the *Los Angeles Daily Journal* that some well-meaning teachers referred to her as Spanish, presuming that calling her Mexican might hurt her feelings. Martinez, however, rejected her counselor's advice and attended the University of Texas in Austin. To help finance her education, Martinez worked at the university. One of her jobs was in the biochemistry lab. There, a professor took an interest in her and encouraged her to leave Texas and pursue graduate education at an Eastern liberal university. She did follow that advice and after obtaining her degree in Austin, she enrolled in law school at Columbia University in New York City.

*Vilma Martinez*

Recalling her early days and prejudice against Mexican Americans, Martinez acknowledged in her interview: "I was bitter. I remember ranting to my mother, who told me, 'If you're going to let them destroy you like that you will be the only one hurt and no one will listen to what you have to say.'" Determined to make people listen to what she had to say, Martinez, fresh from law school in 1967, took a position with the Legal Defense and Education Fund of the National Association for the Advancement of Colored People (NAACP). Her clients were minorities and poor people living in New York City and the South. One of her most noted cases during her years with the NAACP was *Griggs v. Duke Power*. In this case, Martinez won a ruling establishing that it is a violation of Title VII of the U.S. Civil Rights Act for a company to require a high school diploma and intelligence tests because of their disproportionate impact on minority job applicants.

## Becomes President of MALDEF

In 1970, Martinez joined the New York State Division of Human Rights as an equal employment opportunity counselor. She helped draft and implement new regulations and administrative procedures on employment rights. The following year she joined the prestigious New York law firm of Cahill, Gordon & Reindel and worked as a labor lawyer. While at Cahill, Gordon & Reindel, Martinez and Notre Dame Law School graduate Grace Olivarez became the first

women to join the board of the Mexican American Legal Defense and Education Fund (MALDEF). In 1973, at the age of 29, Martinez was appointed general counsel and president of MALDEF. During her presidency, she advocated diversification of the organization. "You can accomplish only so much if you join hands only with those from your own background," Martinez stated in her interview.

One of her major accomplishments during her years with MALDEF was her tireless work expanding the U.S. Voting Rights Act to include protection of Mexican Americans. The original act, passed in 1965, applied only to blacks and Puerto Ricans. Typical violations of the U.S. Voting Rights Act had included polling places that suddenly ran out of ballots when Mexican Americans tried to vote, and ads that ran on Spanish language stations warning Mexican Americans that they would be fined or arrested if they voted. Her endeavor met some opposition from Clarence Mitchell, head of the NAACP Washington office, who argued that expanding the U.S. Voting Rights Act would dilute voting rights enforcement for blacks. However, Martinez skillfully enlisted the help of a coalition of groups to aid this important case. Supporting her effort to expand voter protection were organized labor, the Congressional Black Caucus, and Japanese Americans. Congress responded to her efforts and in 1975 extended voting protection to Mexican Americans. That victory came on the heels of a ruling the previous year in which MALDEF secured a guarantee of bilingual education for non-English speaking children attending public schools.

Another one of Martinez's important MALDEF achievements was her ground-breaking work on the *Plyler v. Doe* case which challenged a Texas law denying free public school education to undocumented children—children of illegal aliens. Before this 1982 legal decision, public school tuition of $1,000 was required for each undocumented child. As Martinez declared in her interview: "This put school out of reach for many of these children, basically our children—American children who had lived here for years but who weren't citizens. Without that educational opportunity those kids wouldn't have a chance." *Plyler v. Doe* set a precedent in extending rights to undocumented aliens.

However, Martinez believes her greatest executive accomplishment at MALDEF was to institutionalize the organization. "I was able to create a mechanism for MALDEF to exist through fund-raising, recruiting, and learning to juggle resources so it could continue to grow year in and year out," Martinez told her interviewer. When she arrived at MALDEF in 1973, the organization had no endowments and Martinez spent many restless nights worrying about how to meet the payroll. But she was determined to build MALDEF into an organization that would continue to be capable of furthering the cause of

Mexican Americans. When she left MALDEF in 1982, the organization had been transformed into a force that operated with a $4.9 million annual budget and a staff of 23 attorneys working nationwide.

## Joins Los Angeles Law Firm

"Personally and professionally it was time to move on," said Martinez in her interview. But she was uncertain what to do next. She considered running for elective office or teaching at the college level. Eventually she decided to join the Los Angeles law firm of Munger, Tolles & Olson. Becoming a partner in the large law firm would give her real independence in her career, she concluded. However, it was a move that required some thought for Martinez. During her years at MALDEF she frequently had been questioned during lectures at law schools by students worried about "selling out" to corporate institutions. That was not an issue in her move from MALDEF, Martinez decided. "People should be free to grow up and be whatever type of lawyer they want to be." At Munger, Tolles & Olson, she litigates labor disputes, including wrongful termination, employment discrimination and insurance bad-faith cases.

As a result of her extensive and successful work on behalf of civil rights, she is a sought-after speaker and has addressed groups at the University of California (All-University Faculty Conference), Yale University, Rice University, University of Notre Dame, and her alma mater, the University of Texas. She has also lectured at a number of law schools, including the law schools affiliated with Harvard University, Yale University, Stanford University, and the University of Michigan. She was a guest speaker at the Ditchley Foundation in Oxfordshire, England. She also has addressed the National Association of Hispanic Journalists and the California Newspaper Publishers Association.

Throughout her career, Martinez has been extraordinarily active in community, legal, educational, and public service projects. Many of those positions have enabled her to continue her lifelong efforts to expand opportunities for minorities. Martinez has generously given her time and expertise to serve as a board member or officer for a wide array of institutions and corporations. She is chair of the UCLA Board of Visitors and is a co-founder of its Achievement Council. The council, formed after she discovered low eligibility rates of Mexican Americans in the University of California system, seeks to increase the number of minority students attending college. She is active with Claremont College's Tomas Rivera Center, a Hispanic think tank. Continuing her 17-year campaign in the voter rights area, she serves as vice chair of the Southwest Voter Registration and Education Program. She has been a member of the board of Anheuser-Busch since 1983, and in 1984 she became

vice chairman of the board of the Edward W. Hazen Foundation in Los Angeles. In 1990, she joined the board of the Sanwa Bank of California and is a member of its Community Reinvestment Committee. She also serves on the board of People for the American Way, which she joined in 1991. Martinez is a member of the advisory board of the Asian Pacific Women's Network, the Loyola Law School's Institute for Latin American Legal Studies, and the Asian Pacific American Legal Center of Southern California. Martinez is also a member of the Council of Foreign Relations and Columbia University's Law School Board of Visitors.

Martinez served from 1975 to 1981 as an unpaid consultant to the U.S. Census Bureau, chairing a panel that persuaded the bureau to add a question on the census form asking if a person is of Hispanic origin. As a result, the heritage of Hispanics now is included in the official count of the American population; states include such information in their demographics studies; and the information has led in part to the redrawing of some electoral districts. During the Carter Administration, Martinez served as a member of the advisory board on ambassadorial appointments. In 1976, she was appointed by Governor Jerry Brown to the California Board of Regents, serving 14 years including a two-year term as chairman.

Martinez's service and achievements have not gone unnoticed or unappreciated. She has earned a number of awards, including the Jefferson Award in 1976 for public service from the American Institute; a medal of excellence from Columbia University's Law School, in 1978, and again in 1992 as a major figure in civil rights; a distinguished alumnus award from the University of Texas, 1988; and the Valerie Kantor Award for Extraordinary Achievement in 1982 for her work with MALDEF. In the early 1990s, Martinez returned to MALDEF, this time as a member of its board of directors.

Despite her busy schedule, Martinez is not solely occupied with her career and public service. She and her husband of more than two decades, Stuart Singer, also an attorney, keep busy raising their two sons, Carlos and Ricardo Singer.

## SOURCES:

### Periodicals

*Los Angeles Daily Journal,* January 6, 1992.

### Other

Martinez, Vilma, telephone interview with Carol von Hatten, September 19, 1992.

*—Sketch by Carol von Hatten*

# Antonio Martorell
## 1939-
### Puerto Rican artist

Antonio Martorell has gained an international reputation as an illustrator and designer; he has also used his talents to develop arts education in Puerto Rico. His multifaceted career includes designing political posters and children's books, as well as collaborating on performance art pieces and set designs. Art critics have noted that Martorell's work displays not only the influence of his teacher Lorenzo Homar, but also **Rufino Tamayo,** with whom Homar had been apprenticed.

While little information is available in the English language on Martorell's background, important personal themes often arise in his work. For example, several of the installations collected in his 1993 one-man show, *La Casa de Todos Nosotros,* which was exhibited at the National Building Museum in Washington, D.C., and El Museo del Barrio in New York City, reflected the theme of eviction, which Martorell had experienced as a child. Also among the constructions were "Casa Singer," which dwells upon the sewing machine and dressmaker's paraphernalia used to earn money, and "Kamikaze House," which featured four-poster bed frames adorned with mosquito nets and giant bugs. *La Casa de Todos Nosotros* received favorable reviews in the U.S. from publications like *Interior Design* and *Artforum.*

Martorell was born on April 18, 1939, in Santurce, Puerto Rico. By the time he was twenty-two, his artistic talent had been recognized, and he was rewarded with a trip to Madrid, Spain, to study for a year under Julio Martin. Upon his return to Puerto Rico in 1962, Martorell became a graphic arts apprentice to Lorenzo Homar. Homar was instrumental in forming the Graphic Arts Workshop within the Institute of Puerto Rican Culture in San Juan, after receiving government funds to improve education among Puerto Ricans. As a student of the Graphic Arts Workshop, Martorell received instruction in many forms of theatrical and graphic design and production.

In 1968 Martorell followed the example of his mentor and founded a group known as the Alacran Graphic Arts Workshop. That same year, his illustrations for the children's book *ABC de Puerto Rico* by Isabel Friere de Matos and Ruben del Rosario earned first prize from the American Institute of Art.

During the 1970s, Martorell increased his reputation as an artist, participating in many gallery and university expositions throughout the Caribbean and Latin America. He also displayed his work around the world, traveling to such countries as the U.S., Canada, France, Germany, Italy, Poland, Yugoslavia and New Zealand. Martorell has also taken part in many themed exhibits during his career, including the First and Second Biennials of Latin American Graphics, the First Salon of Spanish-American Art in Madrid, and the Fourth Biennial of Engraving in Tokyo, Japan.

While Martorell's work often displays a trademark theme of incisive political satire, he has also been known to produce moody and highly personal studies of family life and local color. In addition, some of his work shows an influence of pop culture or mass media, particularly the series of monotypes entitled *Homenaje a Hitchcock* and the xilograph entitled *Oracion por Marilyn Monroe.* Martorell's design materials range from paper to textiles. For example, an exhibit entitled *Paper Dolls* presents an assortment of different female body types as toy-like cutouts, to bizarre effect.

A number of universities, libraries, museums, and businesses in America, Cuba, Puerto Rico, Colombia and Venezuela have collected Martorell's artistic creations. Further, his designs are on display in the United States at the Metropolitan Museum of Art in New York, the Library of Congress in Washington, the Chase Manhattan Bank, and Princeton University.

## SOURCES:

### Books

*The Art Heritage of Puerto Rico,* New York, Metropolitan Museum of Art, 1973.

Bloch, Peter, *Painting and Sculpture of the Puerto Ricans,* New York, Plus Ultra, 1978.

*Glimpses de Premier Maldonado,* New York, Vantage Press, 1978.

*La Gran Enciclopedia de Puerto Rico: Tomo 8, Artes Plasticas,* edited by Vicente Baez, San Juan, PR, Puerto Rico en la Mano y La Gran Enciclopedia de Puerto Rico, Inc., 1977.

*La Tierra Prometida,* poema de Clemente Soto Velez, San Juan, PR, Instituto de Cultura Puertorriqueña, 1979.

*The Rainbow-Colored Horse,* New York, Frederick Warne Co., 1978.

### Periodicals

*Artforum,* April 1993, p. 100.

*Interior Design,* September 1993, p. 53.

*Interracial Books for Children,* 4, Nos. 1 & 2, Spring 1972.

*New York Times,* January 2, 1993, p. 8; July 29, 1993, pp. B5, C4.

*San Juan Star* (Puerto Rico), May 14, 1972, pp. 6–7.

**Other**

*Art in America Guide to Galleries, Museums, Artists,* New York, 1994–95.
*Exposicion del Album de Familia de Antonio Martorell,* catalogue, Sala de Exposiciones del Convento de Santo Domingo, 1974–78.
*Homar,* exhibition catalogue, NJ, Newark Public Library, 1994.

                                    *—Sketch by Jennifer Kramer*

*Jorge Mas Canosa*

# Jorge Mas Canosa
## 1939-
### Cuban American entrepreneur

Following the triumph of the Cuban Revolution in 1959, a mass exodus of Cubans to the United States took place: Jorge Mas Canosa was among them. As an exiled entrepreneur, Mas Canosa was so successful that, according to Linda Robinson of *U.S. News & World Report,* he would eventually be "worth [an] estimated $9 million." Mas Canosa, now a U.S. citizen and dedicated to the anti-Castro movement in Miami, was described by Irving Louis Horowitz in the *New Leader* as "a prominent businessman [and] the single most powerful force within the big exile community."

Mas Canosa is not only powerful in Miami but in Washington, DC, as well: he has served on a presidential advisory board since 1985, helped draft national legislation, and started his own Public Affairs Committee (PAC) called Free Cuba. Mas Canosa is most notably the founder and chairman of the Cuban American National Foundation (CANF), a tax-exempt, Miami-based organization begun in 1980.

Mas Canosa was born on September 21, 1939, to Ramos Mas and Carmen Canosa in Santiago de Cuba. He attended Presbyterian Junior College in Maxton, North Carolina, and studied law in Cuba at the University of Oriente. Mas Canosa was prone to popular dissent, and in the 1950s, he was arrested for condemning the military dictator **Fulgencio Batista** on the radio. Before coming to the United States—a move that was forced upon him "when the undemocratic nature of the nascent Castro government became clear [and] he resumed his political activism," as Mas Canosa told Conner Gorry in a letter—he married

Irma Santos, with whom he had three sons: Jorge Jr., Juan Carlos, and José Ramos.

Mas Canosa's first days in the United States were spent doing menial jobs: washing dishes, selling shoes, and delivering milk. In 1961, he found his calling: Mas Canosa signed up with Brigade 2506, the cadre of exiles trained by the Central Intelligence Agency (CIA) for the Bay of Pigs invasion. Although Mas Canosa did not actually fight, he continued to work for the CIA, broadcasting to Cuba through Radio Swan. Yet, while Mas Canosa was pursuing anti-Castro activities, he was also building a financial empire.

For ten years, Mas Canosa was a partner at Iglesias y Torres, a subcontractor of telephone services. In 1969, he bought the business and anglicized the name to Church & Tower, Inc. He also became chairman of Mastec, Inc., an engineering contracting firm, and Neff Machinery, which distributes construction equipment. As Mas Canosa continued to prosper during Miami's construction boom, he forged ties with Republican candidates running for state and local office; ties which include such notables as former U.S. president George Bush's son, Jeb Bush, and Republican Senator Paula Hawkins.

Political partisanship became a passion for Mas Canosa, and according to Cathy Booth of *Time,* between 1982 and 1992, "Mas [Canosa was] the biggest Hispanic [campaign] contributor nationwide." Yet, since Mas Canosa founded the Cuban American

National Foundation, which boasts more than 200,000 members, his main political aspiration has been to promote political change in Cuba.

To this end, CANF and Mas Canosa lobbied for the creation of Radio Martí —a station that has been broadcasting daily into Cuba since 1985. Since that year, Mas Canosa has headed the presidential advisory boards for that program and its sister program, TV Martí, which began broadcasting in 1990. CANF also successfully lobbied for legislation which limits the amount of family remittances to Cuba.

In 1992 CANF helped draft the Cuban Democracy Act, tightening the U.S. embargo of Cuba. Finally, in 1994, during the Cuban refugee crisis, Mas Canosa participated in top-secret negotiations with President Clinton and the White House.

In addition to being chairman of CANF, Mas Canosa has been the director of the Latin Builders Association since 1984, and the Hispanic American Builders Association since 1989. He is also a member of the United Way, the Industrial Association of Dade County, and the Latin Chamber of Commerce. Throughout his career, Mas Canosa has persevered with his vision for Cuba after **Fidel Castro**. As Malcolm S. Forbes, Jr., commented in *Forbes,* "These men [of CANF] have no intention of leaving their country's post-Castro future to chance. They are drafting a constitution." CANF has also enlisted the help of an investment firm and economist Arthur Laffer to design Cuba's future economic policy.

From a sociopolitical standpoint Mas Canosa has played an active role, founding three separate projects: Misión Martí, La Voz de La Fundación ("The Foundation's Voice"), and Project Exodus. The first is an intensive education program for those who wish to work in Cuba after Fidel Castro's regime. La Voz de La Fundación is the name given to promotion efforts of CANF's Miami radio station throughout Dade County. The last, Project Exodus, allows Cubans who join CANF to immigrate to the United States through third countries.

Although Mas Canosa has denied that he wants to be President of Cuba, he told Cathy Booth of *Time:* "I am not going to give up my right to run for president." He has positioned himself well enough to be able to make that statement. He has fought vehemently on issues regarding U.S. policy towards Cuba, been active on Capitol Hill since the Reagan Administration on those issues, and has been recognized by both domestic and international decision-makers as the principal voice of the anti-Castro movement.

## SOURCES:

### Periodicals

*Business Week,* August 21, 1989.

*Cuba Update,* summer 1993, pp. 9–13.
*Economist,* January 30, 1993, pp. 27–28.
*Forbes,* September 17, 1990, pp. 19–20.
*Nation,* July 30, 1989, pp. 14–18.
*New Leader,* March 19, 1990, pp. 9–11.
*Time,* October 26, 1992.
*U.S. News & World Report,* June, 24, 1992.

### Other

Mas Canosa, Jorge, letter to Conner C. Gorry, November 30, 1994.

—*Sketch by Conner C. Gorry*

# Eduardo Mata
## 1942-1995
### Mexican conductor and composer

Eduardo Mata was a highly-regarded conductor who served as the long-time leader of the Dallas Symphony Orchestra. A student of classical music from an early age, by the age of 17 Mata was a protege of the Mexican composer and conductor **Carlos Chavez.** He took full advantage of the rigorous teachings of his analytical and business-like mentor. His career began in earnest when he received an appointment as music director of the Guadalajara Symphony Orchestra when he was 22 years old. Two years later he assumed leadership of the University Philharmonic at the National University of Mexico.

Mata composed several works in the 1960s— symphonies, suites for ballet, chamber music, and vocal pieces—though he concentrated on conducting in his later career. His recording output was prolific, and included work on such labels as RCA, Pro Arte, Telarc, Dorian, and Vox. One of his last recordings was a series of Latin American works with the Simón Bolívar Symphony Orchestra of Caracas, Venezuela, of which he was associated as artistic advisor and guest conductor. But while he enjoyed conducting orchestras throughout Latin America, Mata also appeared with leading orchestras across Europe and the United States. His first engagement in the United States was with the Phoenix Symphony—he later became its music director—and some of his most celebrated performances took place in America and Europe. He joined the Dallas Symphony Orchestra as music director in 1977 and served behind the podium there for 16 years.

*Eduardo Mata*

## Mata's Early Musical Education

Mata was born in Mexico City on September 5, 1942. He was the son of Ana Maria de Mata. His formal musical education began in 1954, when he studied composition with Rodolfo Halffter at the National Conservatory of Mexico City. In 1960 he was chosen to participate in a composers' workshop under the tutelage of Carlos Chavez, who remained a major influence on the conductor throughout Mata's career. In 1964 Mata journeyed to the United States for a summer of study at Tanglewood. There he studied conducting under Max Rudolf, Gunther Schuller, and Erich Leindorf, but Mata never lost his pride in his Mexican musical schooling. As he told Allen Hughes in the *New York Times,* "[Tanglewood was] the only study I ever did in the United States. The rest was all in Mexico."

Mata's study of music left him little time for what he called "personal things." Throughout his life, he placed his music first. He attributed this dedication to Chavez' teachings and Chavez' insistence on the primacy in life that one's art should assume. Over the years, however, a villa in Tepoztlan, south of Mexico City, and an interest in fine cuisine helped provide relaxation for the well-traveled conductor.

Mata thought of himself as a self-taught conductor. He concentrated on composing in his early years. Among his best known works from 1961 through 1967—the primary period in which he composed—are his three symphonies and the ballet music *Débora.*

After 1967 he set aside composition in order to concentrate on conducting and recording, although he expressed an interest in someday returning to composing. In 1968 he married Carmen Cirici Ventallo, a record producer and painter.

Mata's first musical appointment was that of conductor for the Mexican Ballet Company in 1963. This was followed the next year by his work with the Guadalajara Symphony Orchestra and, from 1966 to 1975, the Orquesta Filarmonica at the National University of Mexico. In addition to his duties in Mexico during this time, he also assumed the positions of conductor and musical advisor for the Phoenix Symphony Orchestra in Arizona. Mata soon became an international musical figure. His work with the Dallas Symphony brought him worldwide attention. He also formed a professional attachment to the London Symphony, and he presided as guest conductor for other renowned orchestras in Pittsburgh, Boston, Cleveland, Chicago, and Detroit. In addition, he served as artistic director of various musical festivals, notably the San Salvador Festival and the Casals Festival. In 1983 he was named artistic advisor for the National Opera of Mexico City; he made his conducting debut with opera in 1990 at the Chicago Lyric Opera in a production of *Carmen.*

One of Mata's most well-known engagements was his stint as conductor of a series of *Mostly Mozart* concerts that began in 1975 at Lincoln Center in New York. These concerts proved pivotal in establishing Mata's reputation with American audiences. Interviewed in 1980 by Allen Hughes of the *New York Times,* Mata remarked that "I enjoy conducting Mozart probably more than anything else in the world, but I like to conduct many kinds of music, and I have not considered myself a Mozart specialist." Indeed, his recording and conducting repertoire included the works of Maurice Ravel, Ludwig van Beethoven, and Béla Bartók, though the *New York Times* contended that "Mata was at his most eloquent in music by Silvestre Revueltas, **Alberto Ginastera,** Heitor Villa-Lobos, and other Latin American composers."

## Mata's Years in Dallas

Under Mata's direction, the Dallas Symphony achieved world-class stature, was given a recording contract with RCA, toured Europe in 1985, and performed at Carnegie Hall. Mata was also instrumental in the campaign to build the Morton H. Meyerson Symphony Center in Dallas. Designed by the acclaimed architect I. M. Pei, the $108 million (originally estimated at $50 million) concert facility opened in 1989 as the new home to the Dallas Symphony. The acoustics of its 2,062-seat Eugene McDermott Concert Hall were designed to rival the Musikvereinsaal in Vienna and the Concertgebouw in

Amsterdam. Donal Henahan of the *New York Times* attended the Center's formal opening—at which Mata conducted a "bone-rattling finale" of Mahler's Symphony No. 2 in C Minor—and offered these observations: "It is too soon to say with confidence that the gamble has paid off as handsomely as comparison with those revered models would demand. . . . But after listening to a wide variety of music in three concerts over the weekend, one listener could happily conclude that Dallas has not lost its shirt on this one."

In 1993, after 16 years as conductor of the Dallas Symphony, he was named conductor emeritus. Mata's prolific musical career was cut tragically short at the age of 52, when the plane he was piloting crashed near Mexico City on January 4, 1995. The news was greeted with sadness in the classical music community and in Mexico. Mata, who had been the recipient of many awards from his native country over the years, including the Hispanic Heritage award, the Mozart Medal, and the prestigious Sourasky Prize, was regarded as one of Mexico's finest maestros. He was survived by a son, Roberto, and a daughter, Pilar.

## SOURCES:

### Books

*Baker's Biographical Dictionary of Musicians,* New York, Schirmer Books, 1992.
*The New Grove Dictionary of American Music,* edited by H. Wiley Hitchcock and Stanley Sadie, London, Macmillan, 1986, p. 192.

### Periodicals

*Detroit Free Press,* January 5, 1995.
*New York Times,* August 1, 1980; September 12, 1989, pp. C15, C22; January 5, 1995, p. B10.

—*Sketch by Jane Stewart Cook*

# Roberto Matta
## 1911-
### Chilean artist

R oberto Matta was one of the most prominent Latin American painters of the 1940s; his surrealist technique has made an enduring impact on American art. Matta, who arrived in New York prior to the outbreak of World War II, was influential in the work of Jackson Pollock, Robert Motherwell, and Arshile Gorky, as well as the development of abstract expressionism. Though born in Chile, Roberto Antonio Sebastian Matta Echaurren, has spent little of his adult life in that country, aside from brief visits. A self-proclaimed "citizen of the world," Matta has lived in Chile, France, Italy, Mexico, England, Spain, and the United States. During periods of political turmoil in Chile, such as the rise of the **Pinochet** dictatorship in that country, Matta has insisted on being described as Cuban rather than Chilean.

Trained as an architect, Matta left Chile in 1932 to work with Le Corbusier in Paris. He soon realized his true desire was art and after making the acquaintance of several poets and painters of the surrealist movement, Matta began to paint. His work came to be known for its jewel-bright, shimmering colors and swirling forms that create a sense of weightlessness and existence without boundary or spacial dimension. Putting to use his training as an architect, he often maneuvered and manipulated forms in space in an original manner.

After a visit to Mexico with Motherwell, Matta became interested in Aztec and Mayan art as well as Pre-Columbian astrological calendars. His work adopted even brighter hues, especially yellow and green, and revealed a personal mythology that often featured machine-like creations. Matta's art during this period was often described as "atomic age" and "space age." Indeed, Matta's style has a significantly individual quality. Matta's drawing teacher was Hernán Gazmuri, who had worked with Fernand Léger, a cubist French painter, in the style of European modernism. But the influence of other artists on his style is less evident than his influence on the style of others, especially Gorky. Matta has not been afraid to explore other cultures, their forms of expression, and their philosophies, all of which are absorbed into his own conceptions. Remarked Edward Lucie-Smith in *Latin American Art of the 20th Century:* "Matta's cultural polymorphism matches the actual polymorphism typical of much of his work. It was a characteristic that by the end of the 1950s was to become typical of twentieth-century Latin American art in general, and in this sense Matta can be thought of as a true precursor."

### Early Background in Architecture

Matta was born in Santiago, Chile, on November 11, 1911. His parents, Don Roberto Matta Echaurren and Mercedes Yanez, were of Basque, French, and Spanish ancestry. Born into an orthodox upper-class family, he was educated at home until the age of nine. When he was old enough to attend secondary school, he was sent to the College of the Sacred Heart in Santiago, where the Jesuits continued his education. Though he displayed an interest in art from an early age, his parents insisted that he attend architectural school. He studied architecture at the National University of Chile and received his degree in 1931.

Matta's original artistic style developed in part through classes he was required to take as part of his study of architecture. Designs for class projects displayed biomorphic and fantastic shapes that foreshadowed his later work. Jean Arp developed biomorphism in Europe, a style built around lifelike forms such as eggs, leaves, insects and birds. "Matta seems to have arrived at a kind of elementary biomorphism on his own while still a student," commented Barbara Mujica in *Américas.*

After graduating, Matta found employment as an interior designer in Santiago, the field in which his brother Sergio was employed. It proved to be a profession for which Matta had little aptitude. During this time, Matta met Lillian Lorca de Tagle, whose interest in art encouraged Matta to pursue his talent. An old feud between their families prevented the young couple from developing their friendship into anything more. Matta consigned his early works, which exhibit an abstract geometric style, to Lillian when he left the country. These works were exhibited in 1991 and have been studied by scholars interested in Matta's entire canon and the artistic philosophy contained therein. A portrait he painted in 1933 entitled *Lillian Lorca de Tagle,* for instance, reflects the influence of cubism. *Américas* contributor Rodolfo A. Windhausen, who spoke with Lillian Lorca about the artist's paintings, wrote that "those youthful creations show Matta to have been a painter of great talent even before he left Chile for Europe and fame in the 1930s."

### A Period of Rebellion

Matta eventually rebelled against both his family and his strict Catholic education. Whether frustrated that his romance with Lillian could not evolve or concerned about the political and economic instability of the country, he left Chile for Paris in 1932. He found a job working as an assistant to Le Corbusier, the functionalist architect whose concepts revolutionized modern architecture. During trips to Spain, Matta met the poets **Federico García Lorca,** Rafael Alberti, and **Gabriela Mistal.** Study of their literature and the writings of other legendary poets rekindled his desire to paint. As he sought to express the emotion and vision behind this literature that absorbed his thoughts, his interest in architecture waned. In 1935 he ceased employment with Le Corbusier and immersed himself in art. One of his first canvases even bears a title in the mode of surrealism. *The Morphology of Desire* was later described as "transparent vapors of rich color."

In 1936 **Lorca** introduced Matta to **Salvador Dalí,** the man who introduced Matta to the leader of the surrealist movement, André Breton. Matta was entirely captivated by surrealism and its emphasis on the unconscious and "automatic painting." Breton in turn was captivated by Matta. Operating the Gradiva Gallery in the rue Seine, Breton purchased two of Matta's innovative paintings and continued to encourage the young artist. According to Windhausen, "Breton stated that each painting by Matta was 'a revel at which anything can happen, a pearl transforming itself into a snowball.'" A one-man show of his works, sponsored by Lorca, brought Matta immediate acclaim.

In 1940, as the political mood in Europe grew menacing, Matta made his way to New York. He was one of the first of the surrealist group to make his home there in the 1940s. To the members of the American avant-garde, which was struggling through pangs of birth, Matta brought contact with the European ideas of modernism. His demonstration that imagery could be developed through a controlled use of accident gave artists such as Pollock and Motherwell the push they needed to release their energies into the *process,* rather than the *theory,* of creating. Abstract expressionism developed as a result.

Matta's travels to Mexico with Motherwell proved to be a pivotal event in his artistic development. While in Mexico, he discovered the beautiful yet destructive force of volcanos, and began to experiment with volcanic forms in his work. He also became interested in Pre-Columbian culture, particularly that of the Aztec and Mayan peoples. Their astrological calendars stimulated his imagination into making up a hierarchy of fantastic beings. His paintings in the 1940s often portrayed melting, pulsating, colorful worlds populated by dehumanized, robot-like figures. Critics contend that paintings from this period—such as *The Earth Is a Man* (1942) and *Wound Interrogation* (1948)—juxtapose the promise of birth with the horror of demise. Barbara Mujica commented in *Américas* that "the paintings of this group constitute a condemnation of modern technology, which in Matta's view had dehumanized life."

### Leaves the Surrealist Fold

Matta resettled in Paris in 1948 after dropping out of favor with the leaders of the surrealist movement. From 1950 to 1953 he lived in Italy and worked on pieces that reflected his reaction to the horrors of the war and the poverty he observed during a visit to Sicily. These paintings feature abstracted, victimized creatures floating in a cruel, irrational universe and carry titles such as *Do Not Think of Fleeing.*

Matta's paintings were selling at high prices when he received a commission to paint a mural for the UNESCO building in Paris in 1954. After completing the mural, he returned to Chile for a one-man show at the Galerie de Lima. His artwork was then displayed at the National Museum of Fine Arts in Santiago. During this visit, Matta was hailed as a national hero. He traveled to Peru, finally coming to terms with his Latin American heritage and his fellow native artists.

Matta returned to Italy and began to work on his first sculptured figures. The surrealists readmitted him to their circle in 1959, but by this time the movement had lost its momentum. Matta continued to explore other theories and philosophies of art and culture. During the 1960s, his work showed the influence of pop art and a fascination with the comic strip.

### Family and Heritage

An energetic and expressive artist, Matta has led a similarly turbulent personal life. He has been married four times. His first wife, Ann, later became the wife of Marcel Duchamp. He has twin sons from this first marriage. His second wife, Patricia, divorced him in 1949, and became the wife of Pierre Matisse, who had been Matta's agent during the mid-1940s. With his third wife, Italian actress Angiola Fernada, he had one son, Iago. After their divorce in 1954 he married Malitte Pope, with whom he had a daughter, Federica. He is now a citizen of France.

Though Matta denounced his heritage at one point in his life and career, his artistic expression maintained a measure of the Latin American experience. His fascination with Aztec and Maya art proved important to his changing artistic vision. His work advanced international modernism, and linked twentieth-century Latin American art with the essence of surrealism.

### SOURCES:

#### Books

Ades, Dawn, *Art in Latin America: The Modern Era, 1820–1980,* New York, Yale University Press, 1989, pp. 233–34.
Arnason, H. H., *History of Modern Art,* Englewood Cliffs, NJ: Prentice-Hall, 1982, p. 521.
Castedo, Leopoldo, *A History of Latin American Art and Architecture,* New York, Frederick A. Praeger, 1969, pp. 244–47.
Chase, Gilbert, *Contemporary Art in Latin America,* New York, The Free Press, 1970, pp. 120–25.
*Current Biography,* New York, H. W. Wilson Co., pp. 358–60.
Gaunt, William, *The Surrealists,* New York, G. P. Putnam's Sons, 1972, pp. 41–46; 253.
Lucie-Smith, Edward, *Latin American Art of the 20th Century,* London, Thames and Hudson, 1993, pp. 88–94.
Waldenberg, Patrick, *Surrealism,* Toronto, Oxford University Press, 1965, pp. 38–53.
*World Artists 1950–1980,* New York, H. W. Wilson Co., 1984, pp. 553–56.

#### Periodicals

*Américas,* March-April 1992, pp. 26–39
*Smithsonian,* August 1992, p. 121.

*—Sketch by Lisa A. Wroble*

# Rachel McLish
## 1958-
### Hispanic American bodybuilder and actress

Rachel Livia Elizondo McLish, the woman credited with bringing glamour to women's bodybuilding, first gained fame when she won first place in the 1980 U.S. Women's Bodybuilding Championship. Other titles include Ms. Olympia in 1980 and 1982 and the World Championship in 1982. McLish left bodybuilding competition when the use of steroids became a factor, prompting her to crusade against steroid use and drug abuse in general. Although she has since turned her attention to acting, writing, and the fashion world, McLish remains dedicated to promoting physical fitness, especially among women.

Born in Harlingen, Texas, to Rafael and Rachel Elisondo, McLish's interest in fitness was first sparked simultaneously by the study of ballet and her father's weight-lifting hobby. Even as a child, she was fascinated with the strength and the grace of the human form. These two diverse activities set the foundation that would later enable her to encourage women to appreciate feminine muscularity as a new physical ideal. During her high-school years, she won a spot on the cheerleading team and found herself forced to choose between cheering and ballet. She opted for cheerleading. The immediate gratification of popularity and a full social schedule overshadowed her childhood dream of becoming a professional dancer. By the time she enrolled at Pan American University in Texas, she regretted giving up dance and feared that, at age seventeen, she was too old to pursue it again. McLish missed the physically active lifestyle she had known all her life and decided to pursue her other love—working with weights. At the time, weight-training wasn't very popular with the general public and exercise clubs were scarce. McLish eventually found a spa called the "Shape Center" and fell in love with the atmosphere. Unfortunately, as an

*Rachel McLish*

impoverished college student putting herself through school, she couldn't afford the membership dues. Instead, McLish applied for and was offered a job at the spa. She started by teaching exercise classes and eventually became a manager.

### Becomes First Female Body Building Champion

In 1978, McLish earned a degree in health and physical education and formed a partnership to build the "Sport Palace," the first and largest health club facility in south Texas. The club was so successful, it eventually expanded to Corpus Christi and Brownsville, Texas. In 1980 McLish read about the first U.S. Women's Body Building Championship being held in Atlantic City. She was interested for two reasons: to promote her fitness centers but, more important, if she could win the first title, she could serve as a positive "feminine" example of a bodybuilder. She entered and walked away with the title.

As the first female bodybuilding champion, Rachel McLish was hailed as a new female role model. She appeared on magazine covers and television programs worldwide. She became a sought-after personality and traveled extensively to lecture on physiology, diet and beauty under the title of the World's First Female Body Building Champion. Her dedication and effort paid off. She won the Ms. Olympia title in 1980 and 1982 and the 1982 World Championship. When the emphasis in body-building shifted in the mid-1980s from muscle tone to massive muscular development, however, McLish decided to stop competing. While she wasn't winning bodybuilding titles, McLish wasn't idle, either. She accepted a part in the documentary *Pumping Iron II: The Women.* McLish also starred in the CBS prime-time television special *Women of the 21st Century,* a documentary exploring a woman's commitment to a physical lifestyle. She made her feature film debut in 1992 in *Aces: Iron Eagle III* opposite Academy Award-winner Louis Gossett, Jr. McLish continues to pursue a career in films, but is very selective about the roles she chooses, refusing any that she feels are demeaning to women.

### Enters Fashion World

In 1985 McLish became spokesperson for the Health and Tennis Corporation of America. Her continuing dedication to fitness and nutrition also prompted her to write two books, *Flex Appeal* and *Perfect Parts. Flex Appeal* addresses all aspects of health and fitness, including psychological conditioning, dietary responsibility, nutrition and sports medicine. *Perfect Parts* is a fitness guide on spot reducing. In 1990, McLish and K-Mart department stores joined forces to create a line of bodywear that would offer comfort, fit and fashion for active women. The collection, "Rachel McLish for The Body Company," made its debut in K-Mart's 2,200 stores on January 1, 1990. As with every other aspect of her professional life, McLish took a hands-on approach and was actively involved with the project from its conception. In a 1992 interview with Elena Kellner, McLish commented: "It's not like I'm just a spokesperson. And I feel really lucky that my mother was a seamstress and she taught me how to sew at a very early age. So when I had my first meeting in New York with the manufacturers, the pattern-makers, the fit models and all the people involved in making a line of clothing, they were pleasantly shocked in that I knew exactly how to construct a garment." She proudly added that in 1991 her line of bodywear accounted for 28% of the total sales of sporstswear in the United States.

McLish was briefly married in the early 1980s to John McLish, her sweetheart at Pan Am University in Texas. They had no children. In 1990 she wed Ron Samuels, a successful Los Angeles artists' manager and film producer who, in an interview with the *Dallas Morning News,* described his wife as a settling force: "She has an inner strength and spirituality that is very uplifting and strengthens me. She has tremendous self-esteem without any sense of arrogance."

Through her campaign against steroid abuse and unique image as a "feminine bodybuilder," Rachel McLish has become a role model for many women and has helped make weight-training and body shaping one of the fastest growing women's exercise activities. In an interview in the *Los Angeles Times,* McLish expressed her thoughts: "The point of physical fitness is not narcissism or egotism. It's well-being. Most people have no idea what it's like to feel good all over. All the time. People unfortunately take drugs to do it part of the time. But the ultimate rush is the feeling you can get from intelligent exercise. It's addictive. In the best way."

## SOURCES:

### Periodicals

*Dallas Morning News,* October 1, 1989.
*Hispanic,* September, 1992, pp. 50–54.
*Hispanic Business,* July 1992, p. 24.
*Los Angeles Times,* June 26, 1987.

### Other

McLish, Rachel, interview with Elena Kellner, April 1992.

*—Sketch by Elena Kellner*

# Margarita B. Melville
## 1929-
### Mexican American scholar and activist

Scholar and activist Margarita Melville has devoted her life to the struggle for social justice, both by personally intervening to improve the conditions of the oppressed and by voicing their plight through her scholarly works. Her long history of activism began during her years as a teacher in Guatemala, and expanded to include resistance to the Vietnam War and support for the rights of Mexican Americans. Much of her writing in support of these issues has been done in conjunction with her husband, Thomas Melville.

Margarita Bradford Melville was born on August 19, 1929, in Irapuato, Guanajuato, Mexico. She was one of five children in a family of mixed United States/Mexican ancestry and, by virtue of her birth, has experienced the phenomenon of living in two worlds. Melville's paternal grandfather, a U.S. citizen, went to Mexico to work on the construction of the national railroad system (Ferrocarriles Nacionales de Mexico) and married into a Mexican family. After spending her early childhood in her provincial Mexican town, Melville was sent to Loreto Academy in El Paso, Texas, for her high school education. Most Mexican families in the late 1940s saw no reason to provide higher education for their daughters, assuming that women would devote their lives to serving their families.

Yet Melville, like other Hispanic women of her generation who felt the challenge of improving the world around her and of going beyond the family circle to assist the less fortunate, sought another alternative. This and her desire for further education prompted her to join a religious order, and in 1949 in St. Louis, Missouri, she took her vows as a Maryknoll sister and became a Catholic nun. Historically in Latin America, the only alternative to marriage or family concerns open to young women of good families was to become a nun. Melville's choice in entering Maryknoll was fortunate, for this American congregation of missionary nuns and priests was active the world over in the struggle for social justice.

### Serves as Missionary in Guatemala

Melville left the convent to attend Mary Rogers College in Ossining, New York, where she received a bachelor of education degree in 1954. That same year, she was sent by her order to teach in Guatemala. Guatemala was a cultural shock for the young nun. Poverty was rampant, and 95 percent of the arable land was held by two percent of the population. The wealthy landowners considered any attempt to alter this state of affairs subversive, since the landless peasantry provided cheap labor for their labor-intensive coffee and cotton plantations. During her thirteen years in Guatemala, Melville taught at all levels of a Catholic girls school. One of her accomplishments was establishing a model school where her students could do practice teaching.

Outside of the classroom, with student volunteers, Melville traveled to the countryside to teach the people to read and write. She directed a group of university volunteers in health and literacy programs, from which the Cursillos de Capacitacion Social were born. The Cursillos were workshops geared toward empowering the peasantry, informing of their rights and developing the leadership and community interaction skills that would enable them to change an unjust system. Such social activism by Catholic men and women was encouraged by the spirit of the Second Vatican Council (1961–63), which proposed that the Church had a place in this world. Despite the fact that the changes that Melville and others like her were attempting to accomplish in Guatemala were grounded in accepted religious teachings, they were declared subversive. In 1967, at the request of the Guatemalan government, the United States embassy, and the bishop of the capital city, Melville, along with others, was asked to leave the country.

## Imprisoned for Protesting U.S. Policies

Back in the United States Margarita married Thomas Melville, a former priest who was part of the Guatemala struggle. One of the couple's pressing concerns was to make the American public aware of the presence of U.S. troops in Guatemala. Melville compared the situation to U.S. involvement in Vietnam, for in both cases she thought that troops placed abroad as "advisors" were in fact supporting a repressive campaign against the peasantry. Having joined the growing anti-war movement, the Melvilles participated in the burning of Selective Service records in the Baltimore, Maryland suburb of Catonsville. They were arrested as a result of this action and became part of a group known by the time of their court trial as the Catonsville Nine. Margarita was one of two women in the group and the only Hispanic. Her testimony in court was utilized in the writing of the drama, *The Catonsville Nine,* later adapted for film. Margarita was sentenced to a year in federal prison and her husband to two years. While serving her sentence—which was reduced to nine months for good behavior—in a West Virginia facility, Margarita and her husband completed a joint thesis for their M.A. degrees in Latin American studies from the American University in Washington, D.C. This work, *Guatemala: The Politics of Land Ownership,* was published in 1971. The previous year, a joint autobiography of the Melvilles, stressing their social justice activism, was published by Knopf under the title *Whose Heaven, Whose Earth?*

After their release from prison, the Melvilles decided to pursue doctorates in anthropology at the American University. In 1973, research for their joint dissertation took them to Chile for two years to study the social organization of the Mapuche Indians during the government of Salvador Allende. It was during this period that their two children were born. After the military coup that overthrew Allende's socialist government, the Melvilles were asked to teach at the Catholic University in Temuco, Chile, to fill in some of the many gaps left by their Chilean colleagues who were either forced into exile, kidnapped, or killed by agents of the Augusto Pinochet dictatorship.

After receiving her doctorate in 1976, Melville accepted a position at the University of Houston as assistant professor of anthropology. There, Melville turned her attention to the concerns of women and Chicanos. In 1977 she served as member of the Houston executive committee for the International Women's Year Commission. She helped organize activities for Chicanas and joined the board of directors of the Centro para Immigrantes, a non-profit organization which provided legal services to immigrants seeking to legalize their status or, in many cases, fight deportation. She served as chair of this organization from 1982–83, during the peak years of the exodus of people from Central America who were fleeing civil war in El Salvador and Guatemala. Her interest in this issue is revealed in her contribution to David Haines' 1985 collection *Refugees in the United States.*

## Studies Mexican American Issues

Melville's engagement in Mexican American issues has deepened over the years. She is the editor of two important studies, *Reflections of the Mexican Experience in Texas* (1979), and *Twice a Minority: Mexican-American Women* (1980), and led the University of Houston's Mexican American Studies Program in 1978–79. The author of numerous scholarly articles on Mexican American issues, Melville also served on the editorial board of *Aztlan,* an international journal of Chicano studies, between 1981 and 1985 and was a member of the board of directors of the National Chicano Research Network between 1980 and 1982. In 1986 Melville left the University of Houston to become associate professor at the University of California at Berkeley, where she serves as Coordinator for Chicano studies and, since 1988, has held the position of Associate Dean for the Graduate Division.

Regardless of her involvement in Mexican American affairs, Melville's preoccupation with Guatemala continues. Although she has never returned to that Central American nation she continues to speak for the oppressed in the region. In the early 1990s, Melville spent time in Guatemalan refugee camps in the Mexican states of Chiapas and Campeche as part of her research for a book. After interviewing the children in these camps, she discovered that the policies of scorched earth—the destruction of villages and fields—are in operation for the purpose of suppressing any efforts towards a viable way of life by the peasants. Melville has reported some of her findings in articles appearing in *Children: Guatemala's Human Resource for the Future,* edited by M. Howard, and in scholarly journals.

Melville supports Hispanic women's issues through her participation in the group Mujeres Activas en Letras y Cambio Social (Women Active in Literature and Social Change), a California-based organization that supports young Hispanic women who want to pursue higher education and retain their community and ethnic ties. Melville was named 1992 Scholar by the National Association of Chicano Studies for her significant contributions to scholarly research and writing in the area. Melville resides in Berkeley, California with her husband, Dr. Thomas Melville, and their two children.

## SOURCES:

Melville, Margarita B., interview with Silvia Novo Pena, 1992.

—*Sketch by Silvia Novo Pena*

# Rigoberta Menchú
## 1959-
### Guatemalan activist

Rigoberta Menchú, a Quiché Indian, was awarded the Nobel Peace Prize in 1992 for her courageous efforts to win social justice for the Guatemalan Indians. As a leader of the Guatemalan peasant movement, she began working in the 1970s to gain land rights, fair wages, and political equality for the Indians.

Rigoberta Menchú Tum was born in 1959 to a poor family in the village of Chimel, near San Miguel de Uspantán, the capital of the northwest province of El Quiché. In her 1983 autobiography, *I, Rigoberta Menchú: An Indian Woman in Guatemala,* she recounted the harsh life of her highland Indian family. Menchú's parents were leaders in their remote mountain village. Her father, Vicente Menchú, was an uneducated farmer, who became a revolutionary hero. Her mother, whose surname was Tum, had been abandoned as a child. Menchú was one of nine siblings who helped the family grow maize, beans, and potatoes on a small plot of land. They lived—without electricity or plumbing—in a house of cane sticks, with a roof made from palm tree leaves. The village women wove mats, cloth, and blouses, while the men worked in the fields.

Menchú's family spent part of each year on south coastal plantations, or *fincas,* picking coffee beans and cotton for subsistence wages and living in unsanitary open shacks. At the age of eight, Menchú, who had no formal education, was picking 35 pounds of coffee a day. Two of her brothers died on the plantations, one from pesticide poisoning and the other—only two years old—from malnutrition.

At age 12, Menchú began working as a maid for a wealthy family in Guatemala City. The mistreatment she experienced led her to comprehend the low status of Indians in her country. Soon after, her father was imprisoned for his efforts to save land from seizure by large landowners. He was jailed again in 1977, this time as a political prisoner.

Ever since 1954, when a series of military governments began battling the leftist rebels and the highland Indians, living conditions for the Guatemalan people worsened. In the 1970s, Guatemala's Indians—who comprised 60 percent of the population—suffered the indignities of forced relocation, forced military participation, and murder. The conflict left more than 100,000 dead, 40,000 missing, and one million displaced, according to *The Los Angeles Times.* Civilian rule returned in 1986, but tensions continued between the Indians and the government.

*Rigoberta Menchú*

Menchú's father left home in 1977 to hide in the mountains and organize the Indians. He helped found the Peasant Unity Committee (PUC), an agrarian trade union which his daughter would later lead. As a young adult, Menchú learned Spanish to communicate with other Indian groups and the Spanish-speaking mixed-blood minority, the *Ladinos,* who led the government. Like her father, she began traveling across Guatemala to unite the 22 Indian groups, each with its distinct language and culture, against exploitation.

Menchú's family suffered for its activism. In 1979, her 16-year-old brother, Petrocinio, was kidnapped, tortured, and killed by soldiers. In January 1980, Menchú's father and his comrades occupied the Spanish Embassy in Guatemala City to protest human rights violations. Police set fire to the building, and 22 demonstrators burned to death, including Vicente Menchú. Just months later, Menchú's mother was kidnapped, raped, and murdered by the army. Two of her sisters joined the guerrillas.

Fearing for her life, Menchú went into hiding and then fled to Mexico. "I'd never imagined that one day those criminals would force me to abandon my country," she wrote in her autobiography. In exile, she undertook an international crusade for indigenous peoples, joining the United Nations Working Group on Indigenous Populations and the International Indian Treaty Council.

### The Nobel Peace Prize

Menchú was awarded the Nobel Peace Prize in 1992. "Today, Rigoberta Menchú stands out as a vivid symbol of peace and reconciliation across ethnic, cultural, and social dividing lines, in her own country, on the American continent and in the world," stated the Nobel Committee. Although some Guatemalan officials criticized the award, President José Serrano Elías asked that Menchú use the prize's "influence and moral authority" to seek peace in Guatemala, reported *The New York Times.*

In accepting the prize, Menchú pledged to continue her efforts, stating, "Today we must fight for a better world, without poverty, without racism, with peace. . . . I consider this prize not as an award to me personally, but rather as one of the greatest conquests in the struggle for peace, for human rights and for the rights of the indigenous people who . . . have been the victims of genocides, repression and discrimination." She promised to use the $973,000 prize to establish a human rights foundation honoring her father.

Even in exile, she frequently returned to Guatemala, as the prestigious prize granted her new stature as peasant leader. She also continued her international efforts. In 1993, she visited Thailand to meet Burmese refugees and show her support for Daw Aung San Suu Kyi, a Nobel Peace Prize laureate detained by the Burmese military since 1989. Also in 1993, she toured the United States. In Los Angeles, she asked the government to grant temporary protected status to Guatemalan exiles; on Long Island, she told a gathering of Central American refugees that they must be committed to peace, according to reports in *The Los Angeles Times* and *The New York Times.*

### SELECTED PUBLISHED WORKS:

*Me Llamo Rigoberta Menchú Y Asi Me Nació La Concienca,* Barcelona, Editorial Argos Vergara, S.A., 1983; translated as *I, Rigoberta Menchú: An Indian Woman in Guatemala,* New York and London, Verso, New Left Books, 1984.

### SOURCES:

*Los Angeles Times,* October 17, 1992, pp. A1, A12; May 7, 1993, p. B3.
*New York Times,* October 17, 1992, pp. A1, A5; October 19, 1992, p. A7; December 11, 1992, p. A14; June 10, 1993, p. A10; September 15, 1993, p. A15; May 8, 1994, p. 34.
*Time,* October 26, 1992, p. 61.

*—Sketch by Ann Malaspina*

# Miguel Méndez
## 1930-
### Mexican American novelist, short story writer, poet, and educator

Miguel Méndez is widely recognized as a leading voice in contemporary Chicano literature. Although a large portion of his work has yet to be translated into English, he has earned widespread critical praise for his richly poetic narrative portrayal of the people who inhabit the vast borderland region where Mexico and the American Southwest merge.

Méndez, a longtime bricklayer with only a sixth-grade education, established his literary reputation with the publication of his first novel, *Peregrinos de Aztlan,* in 1974, and has since gone on to publish several novels, short stories, and poems. With the emergence of the field of Chicano literature in the United States, a few of his major works have been translated into English, promising to expand his growing audience. While adding to his diverse literary output, Méndez has taught Spanish, Mexican, and Chicano literature at the University of Arizona, where he received an Honorary Doctor of Humanities in 1984.

Miguel Méndez Morales was born in Bisbee, Arizona, just five miles from Mexico, on June 15, 1930. He spent most of his early years in a nearby government-owned farming community in Sonora, Mexico, where his father, Francisco Méndez Cárdenas, who had first gone to Arizona as a miner, supported his wife, María Morales, and their five children as a farm worker.

Taught to read by his mother, Méndez attended an elementary school where, as he later recalled in a videotaped interview at the University of California at Santa Barbara, "the teachers were just as poor and needy as the community we lived in . . . they would hide their hunger behind their books." At the age of 15, Méndez left school and his family to find employment along the Arizona-Sonora border, finding work as a fruit and vegetable picker before eventually settling in Tucson, Arizona in April 1946, where he became a bricklayer.

Despite the rigors of heavy construction work in the 115-degree heat, Méndez began writing seriously during this time, completing his first novel by the age of 18. Although he was unable to find a publisher for his work, Méndez continued to further his craft, writing numerous short stories over the next 15 years. With the advent of the Chicano movement in the 1960s, Méndez finally received his first break.

*Miguel M. Méndez*

Having found that many of the themes he had been pursuing during his long nights of writing were consistent with the movement's philosophy, Méndez submitted "Tata Casehua," an allegorical short story focusing on the trials of the Yaqui Indians of Northwest Mexico, to the Chicano literary journal, *El Grito,* which published the manuscript in 1968.

As interest in his powerful work grew, Méndez was asked to lecture at several universities and literary organizations. And in 1970 he was offered a teaching position at Pima Community College in Arizona, which enabled him to leave construction and devote more energy to his first novel, *Peregrinos de Aztlan.*

Set in modern-day Aztlan, the novel, which has been favorably compared to the work of Mexican novelist **Carlos Fuentes,** examines the lives of various individuals—prostitutes, drug addicts, poets, hippies, and politicians—who inhabit the two-thousand-mile border region, through the memories of Loreto Madonado, a former revolutionary who once rode with **Pancho Villa** but now survives by washing tourists' cars in Tijuana.

The narratives of these desolate border characters are woven together in what the *Oakland Tribune's* Abby Wine, in her review of the English translation *Pilgrims in Aztlan,* described as "an unflinching stream of consciousness." In her assessment, the novel "has provided and continues to provide a map,

a framework for the multifaceted, developing Chicano literary tradition."

Méndez has pursued similar themes from various formal perspectives. *Los criaderos humanos y Sahuaros* ("Prolific Humans and Sahuaros"), for instance, is an epic poem that focuses on the "humiliated ones" of the desert who are persecuted by the white race. Although the experimental work received little critical attention, Méndez stated in an interview in *La Palabra* that it will someday be regarded as his most significant work.

In addition to four short collections, Méndez has published a second novel, *El sueño de Santa Maria de las Piedras* ("The Dream of Santa Maria of the Stones"), which chronicles the material rise and moral decline of the city of Santa Maria de las Piedras through the stories of a group of old men. Finding "elements of expansive exaggeration and eccentricity" reminiscent of the Nobel-prize winning Colombian novelist **Gabriel García Márquez,** Cecil Robinson has concluded in his book *No Short Journeys: The Interplay of Cultures in the History and Literature of the Borderlands,* that the novel is "a mixture of realism and fantasy, history and fable. . . . In a certain sense, the town's history is the history of Mexico in microcosm."

## SELECTED PUBLISHED WORKS:

*Peregrinos de Aztlan,* Editorial Peregrinos, 1974, translated as *Pilgrims in Aztlan,* Bilingual Press, 1993.

*Los criaderas y Sahuaros,* Editorial Peregrinos, 1975.

*Cuentos para niños traviesos/Stories for Mischievous Children,* translated by Eva Price, Justa, 1979.

*Tata Casehua y otros cuentos* ("Tata Casehua and Other Stories"), Justa, 1980.

*De la vida y del folclore de la frontera* ("From Life and Folklore along the Border"), Mexican American Studies and Research Center, University of Arizona, 1986.

*El sueño de Santa Maria de las Piedras,* Universidad de Guadalajara, 1986.

*Cuentos y ensayso para reir y aprender* ("Stories and Essays for Laughing and Learning"), Miguel Méndez, 1988.

## SOURCES:

### Books

*Chicano Authors: Inquiry by Interview,* Austin, University of Texas Press, 1980.

*Dictionary of Literary Biography,* Volume 82, *Chicano Writers,* edited by Francisco A. Lomelí and Carl R. Shirley, Detroit, Gale, 1989.

*Hispanic Writers,* edited by Bryan Ryan, Detroit, Gale, 1991.

Robinson, Cecil, *No Short Journeys: The Interplay of Cultures in the History and Literature of the Borderlands,* Tucson, University of Arizona Press, 1992.

**Periodicals**

*Cuadernos Americanos,* July-August 1980, pp. 23–33.

*La Palabra,* spring-fall 1981.

*Oakland Tribune* (CA), May 23, 1993.

**Other**

Méndez, Miguel, interview with Rodriguez del Pino, Center for Chicano Studies, University of California, Santa Barbara, 1976.

—*Sketch by Jason Gallman*

*Lydia Mendoza*

# Lydia Mendoza
## 1916-
### Mexican American singer and musician

Singer and musician Lydia Mendoza was the first interpreter of rural popular Tejano and border music to acquire star status through her many recordings. As such she has made this music known beyond the borders of her region and throughout Latin America.

Mendoza was born in Houston, Texas, in 1916 to Leonor Zamaripa Reyna and Francisco Mendoza Espinosa, both from the northern Mexican state of Nuevo Leon. Until 1927, when the Mendozas settled permanently in Texas, the family traveled back and forth to Monterrey, Mexico, following Leonor, who worked for the Ferrocarriles Nacionales de Mexico as a mechanic. Mendoza's parents were lovers of music. Her father had a collection of opera records which included performances by Enrico Caruso; while in Monterrey, he often took his children to the theater to see traveling artists and zarzuela companies. Mendoza's mother, in turn, was an accomplished guitar player and singer.

From the time she was four years old, Mendoza remembers wanting to learn the guitar and even constructed her own instrument with rubber bands. In time, she mastered the guitar and mandolin, and became proficient with the violin. Although the Mendoza adults had always played and sung for their own enjoyment, when her father was forced to leave his job with the railroad for health reasons, music became their mainstay. The family of eight traveled the border towns performing at barber shops, restaurants, and street corners. The older children—Lydia was the second child—played some of the instruments as part of the accompaniment to their parents' voices. Their first big break came in 1928 when they recorded 20 songs for the Okeh Record Company in San Antonio for $140. Mendoza's father named their group the Cuarteto Carta Blanca after the Monterrey brewery where he once worked. Shortly afterwards they traveled to Michigan as migrant workers, experiencing for a brief period the hardships of this way of life. Soon, however, the family was spared the backbreaking field work; singing in Mexican restaurants and in local parties in Pontiac, as well as a job her father providentially found at a Ford Motor Company plant, supported the Mendoza brood.

The Great Depression of 1929 brought the Mendozas back to Texas. They eventually settled in San Antonio. By 1933 Lydia was well-known in South Texas because of her frequent participation in radio contests. In 1934, she was asked to record as a soloist for New York City-based Blue Bird Records. Her recording of the song "Mal hombre" became an instant hit and she was asked to sign a contract with Blue Bird. In 1935 she married Juan Alvarado, a shoemaker by trade who she had met three years earlier. At first her husband, pressured by his family, was reluctant to let his wife perform, particularly after they had a daughter, but the big record sales and royalties convinced him otherwise. Now Alvarado, as the driver, joined the Mendozas in touring the Southwest, doing variety shows which included comedy skits, dancing, and singing. Lydia became known as "La alondra de la frontera" ("The Lark of the Border"), beloved by the common people, especially the working men, and known in Latin America through her records.

With the coming of World War II, the rationing of gasoline sent Lydia into retirement, with occasional performances for local *fiestas.* For a while she sang at a club in spite of a storm of criticism from family and friends who argued that clubs were no place for a decent woman. In 1947 the Mendozas were back on the road performing under the name of Grupo Variedad. The group was formed by Lydia, brothers Andrew and Manuel, and sisters Maria and Juanita. As before the war, they did variety shows, sometimes making stops in three different towns in one night. Maria's marriage and the death of her mother in 1952 brought about the disintegration of the group. From then on, Lydia always performed solo. She toured the Southwest continually and Mexico for six months. She recorded under the Azteca, Ideal, Falcon, and Columbia labels. In 1961 Lydia's first husband died—the couple had three daughters—and in 1964 she married another shoemaker, Fred Martinez.

With the growing interest in ethnic roots beginning with the 1960s, Lydia Mendoza was recognized as a repository of traditional Mexican and Mexican American popular music. In 1971 she performed at the Smithsonian Festival of American Folklife at the World's Fair in Montreal. In 1977 she participated and performed in the Library of Congress Ethnic Recordings in America Conference. In 1984 she received the National Heritage Award and in 1985 she was welcomed into the Tejano Music Hall of Fame and the Texas Women's Hall of Fame. Mendoza presently resides in Houston, Texas.

## SOURCES:

Mendoza, Lydia, interviews with Chris Strachwitz.

—*Sketch by Silvia Novo Pena*

# Joan Miró
## 1893-1983
### Spanish artist

Joan Miró was one of the greatest creative talents in modern art, having helped develop the surrealist style popular from the 1920s. A true virtuoso, he constantly strove to develop his talents and to seek innovative ways to express himself in visual form. He became known for his use of vibrant color—namely red, blue, black, green, and yellow—and for his development of a symbol-based language used consistently in his work from the 1930s forward.

In his paintings he used various materials for the support or backing, including canvas, paper, wood, metal, cement, copper, masonite, cardboard, and sandpaper. He achieved an element of texture in his paintings by "preparing" the surface—scraping it to raise the fibers or create wrinkles. Works created after 1937 often include a collage of objects, such as a towel, to add a sculptural dimension to his paintings.

Miró devoted himself during various periods of his career to creating in a variety of media, including paint, pencil, tar, and even blackberry jam. He also incorporated his unique style and methods of artistic expression to ceramics, tapestry, sculpture, graphic work (including stencils, etchings, lithographs, and woodcuts), and theatrical scenery and costume creation. During these excursions into other media, he worked closely with noted craftsmen, demonstrating sincere respect for their skills and mastery.

### Early Life

Miró was born in Spain on April 20, 1893, in Montroig, near Barcelona, in the Catalan province. He was named after his paternal grandfather, a blacksmith in the province of Tarragona. His father, Miquel Miró i Adzerias, left the city of Cornudella for Barcelona to pursue jewelry and watch-making. Miró's mother was Dolors Ferrà, the daughter of a cabinet maker in Palma, in the province of Majorca. Joan Miró spent time in both the Tarragona and Majorca provinces during his childhood. His Catalan heritage was of overwhelming importance in his artistic development. Though he lived for periods in other locations, most notably Paris, he returned often to the environment of his childhood.

The countryside of Tarragona influenced Miró's early works. The fields and farmhouse of his youth became frequent subjects of his paintings. As Rosa Maria Malet described in *Joan Miró,* he believed the force of the earth rose through the body from the feet. "The foot which is in contact with the earth and the

*Joan Miró*

eye which contemplates all its grandeur are the two almost obsessive images that have appeared consistently throughout Miró's work, which is so very closely bound to the Tarragona countryside." In contrast, the seascape of Majorca also influenced Miró, mostly his later works. Of particular prevalence were the white sand beaches, the vivid blue of the sea, and the light of the sky.

Existing first drawings date from 1901, when Miró was eight years old. Typical objects, all very realistic, included a vase of flowers, a turtle, an umbrella. As his interest in art grew, his interest in his studies diminished. His parents enrolled him at the Commercial School in Barcelona so he would acquire skills for steady employment. Since thrift and hard work were virtues Catalonians held dear, the "indolent" life of an artist was hard for his parents to condone.

Miró did enroll in drawing classes at the art school known as the *Llotja* during the time he attended the Commercial School. Two teachers there, Modest Urgell and Josep Pascó, made lasting impressions on the diligent student. Malet described their influence on the young artist: "It was from Modest Urgell, however, that he caught the taste for empty spaces, for the line of the horizon that defines sky and earth, and for the constant presence of the stars." Josep Pascó taught Miró to appreciate the energy of pure colors. He also persuaded him to experiment and gave him rigorous training in draftsmanship.

Miró's father felt that what his son learned at the art school might be of use in the jewelry business. The young Miró did design two brooches while in Pascó's class in 1909. One was a peacock, the other a serpent. Both exemplified the sinuous lines of the Art Nouveau style popular at the time. After finishing his studies at the Commercial School, Miró took a job as an apprentice accountant. He became ill when he was 17, in part due to his inability to adapt to the demands of the position. He convalesced in Montroig and while there decided to pursue his art.

## Pursuing a Dream

After recovering and returning to Barcelona in 1915, Miró enrolled in Francesc Galí's School of Art. Galí recognized Miró's gift for color and strove to develop a sense of form in the young artist. To help Miró through his struggles in reproducing form, Galí blindfolded him, placed objects into his hands, and then requested him to draw what he had been holding. This awakened the sense of touch in the young artist and may have contributed to Miró's pursuit of texture in his paintings. While at the Academy Galí, Miró painted *The Peasant* in 1915, the first of his catalogued works. It showed the influence of his long stays in Montroig, as well as the thick brushwork and distorted forms that were influenced by fauvism and characteristic of his early work.

Miró left the academy to concentrate on painting on his own. His work showed a considerable influence of the expressionists, particularly Paul Cézanne and Vincent Van Gogh. He painted a series of landscapes, the farmhouse he grew up in featured in many. Between 1917 and 1918 he painted a series of portraits, working on the human form, which he had trouble representing while a student. The style in these portraits indicated fauvist and cubist influences. The lines and brush strokes were thick, and perspectives, such as a table top, were slightly distorted. Feet were rendered disproportionately large, a motif that was repeated throughout his career and that might be due in part to his belief that through the feet one could feel the energy of the earth.

By the end of 1918 Miró had a considerable body of work. An art dealer, José Dalmau, arranged for a one-man show in Barcelona which was a local success. In 1919 Miró made his first trip to Paris. He met **Pablo Picasso,** visited the Louvre, and had his first real encounter with avant-garde art. Dadaism—a reaction against societal restrictions and acceptable expression—was popular at the time, though it would not influence his own work for several years.

Miró returned to Barcelona without having painted while in Paris. Prior to his visit, he had achieved a balance between form and color in his paintings. After reflecting on the Parisian experience, he began to add different degrees of realism to his paintings. In 1921 he began to paint *The Farmhouse.* The subject of the painting was his childhood home in Montroig. Though the canvas was roughly 4-by–4.5 feet, it had the impact of a mural in its complexity and detail. For Miró each element was as important as every other. He studied every detail, even bringing grass from Montroig in his suitcase when he returned to Paris in 1922, where he finished the painting.

### Seeds of Surrealism Bloom

During this stay in Paris, between 1922 and 1924, Miró's interest in realism rose. He spent time with poets, writers, and other artists living on rue Blomet, where he had his studio. The group, known as the "Blomet group, " included André Masson, Michel Leiris, Georges Limbour, Robert Desnos, and Antonin Artaud. As enthusiasm for dadaism faded, the seeds of surrealism had already been sown. The artists experimented in blending realism with fantasy. For Miró this meant painting the emotional vision of reality. Instead of transcribing what he had seen, he painted its essence—the impact of what he had seen as he remembered it once back in his studio on rue Blomet. Inspired by the poets he kept company with, Miró sought to bring his painting to a lyrical and poetic level. The real and the imaginary co-existed in his paintings of this period. Stylization dominated. To express the living essence of inanimate objects, such as a tree, he gave them human attributes, such as an eye or an ear. Human characters were reduced to fundamental attributes, such as a mouth, a beard, or a mustache. Forms were rendered schematically, through either geometric shapes or single lines.

The surrealist movement tried to find resolution between the states of reality and dream. At first it was a strictly literary movement, characterized by "free-flow" or automatic writing. Whatever came to mind, no matter how distorted, was recorded on paper. The equivalent for painting was at first this same expression. Pictures from the subconscious were painted as they arose. Frequently, dream images were the result. Unlike the other surrealists, Miró did not paint dreams, nor did he paint under the influence of drugs, alcohol, or hypnosis. According to Malet, "Miró sought inspiration by concentrating on the forms produced by the cracks in a wall, damp stains, or the movement of clouds. All these observations, carefully noted in his sketch-book, were used as starting points for his compositions." Miró's style was always exceptionally personal. Though he was integrated into the surrealist group he in no way became a follower of its dictates. Using the principles that spoke to his emotions, he continually developed his own style, moving with it ever forward.

Between 1925 and 1927, his paintings featured monochromatic color schemes, dominated by the background color, usually blue, gray, or brown. He used other colors sparingly, usually to accent a detail. This created an atmosphere of dreaming for the viewer. To this style he added words or phrases toward the later part of this period. These works were called "poem-pictures," because the words themselves fit into the composition as another form or element.

Miró now spent his winters in Paris and his summers in Montroig. Treading the earth that gave him his energy and inspiration, he painted landscapes once again. The dream atmosphere disappeared, and was replaced by a horizon line defining the earth and sky. *Person Throwing a Stone at a Bird* (1926) included many characteristics typical of this period. The composition was divided by horizontal blocks of color, green above and black and yellow below the horizon line. The figure had only one enormous foot. Patches of color helped define the rock, the bird, and the single eye. Miró's work had begun to evolve into forms and symbols he would use consistently, yet in unique ways, for the rest of his career. For example, the bird was defined by a straight line connecting the head and a half-moon tail, with a curve intersecting the straight line to form wings.

In the late 1920s Duchamp organized another one-man show for Miró in Paris. Its success resulted in Miró's wider recognition and sale of his works. In 1928 he was able to afford a trip to Holland, where he visited the important museums and became captivated with the Dutch masters of the seventeenth century, such as Jan Steen. He reinterpreted these works in his series called *Dutch Interiors.* He followed these works with *Imaginary Portraits,* continuing the experiments of reinterpreting works of the masters of earlier periods.

On October 12, 1929, Miró married Pilar Juncosa in Palma. They settled in Paris on the rue François Mouthon, where he used a spare room as a studio. The couple often traveled to Montroig and Barcelona. Their daughter, Maria Dolors, was born in Barcelona on July 17, 1931.

### Diversifying and Experimenting

Also in 1931, Miró ventured into theater, designing scenery and costumes for the ballet *Jeux d'enfants.* The dancer and choreographer Léonide Massine had seen a recent exhibit of Miró's work and immediately contacted the artist. For the design of the costumes, Miró took into account the movements of the dancers. He used simple shapes and color for fundamental impact. Miró's first association with the theater had come in 1926, when he collaborated with Max Ernst on the Russian ballet's production of *Romeo and Juliet.* Miró would not have contact with the theatrical world again until the late 1970s and early 1980s.

The 1930s was a restless decade for Miró. In the years prior to the Spanish Civil War, which began in

1936, his figures were distorted, tormented in appearance, with faces displaying dagger-like teeth. His brushwork was bold, savage, and angry. Miró experimented with different materials and techniques during this period. He tore images from magazines and newspapers, composing collages on cardboard. Sometimes he added objects such as sandpaper or shells. He also painted with a variety of materials, adding sand to his paint for texture, or using egg tempera on both copper and masonite.

He took his family to Paris to live in October 1936. His restlessness began to extend beyond the easel. As James Thrall Soby recounted in *Joan Miró,* the artist wanted to reach as far as possible with his artistic expression. "In 1938 Miró had declared: 'I would like to try sculpture, pottery, engraving, and to have a printing press, to try to go further than easel painting which in my opinion sets itself a narrow aim.'" August 1939 brought Miró to a small village on the coast of Normandy called Varengeville. Always a man sensitive to scenery, Miró was inspired by the wild, stormy skies of this locale. The stars enjoyed increasing importance in the compositions he created while under the skies of Normandy, which included several series: *Varengeville I, Varengeville II,* and *Constellations.* With the advance of German troops, Miró left Normandy and settled his family once again in Barcelona. He continued to experiment with forms, adding to his repertory of signs and figures. He explored the limits of every paint media available, building upon his already abundant output.

By the close of World War II, Miró's merit was recognized internationally. In 1947 he received the commission to paint a mural for an American restaurant in Cincinnati, Ohio. He rented a studio in New York and spent eight months in the United States creating the piece. This was a tremendous accomplishment for Miró and a turning point in his career for several reasons. The first was the monumental scale of the painting—7-by-32 feet. The second was that he left his studio and his native soil, which offered him his energy and inspiration, and succeeded in performing according to his usual high standards. Large-scale commissions were offered to Miró with increasing frequency, including commissions for ceramic murals, sculptures, and tapestries.

When he returned to Barcelona, he was stimulated by his success in the States. He composed numerous paintings and also worked with craftsmen in sculpture, ceramics, graphic arts, and tapestry. Though he learned to cast his own sculptures from molds, etch his own plates, and fire his own ceramics, he often worked in collaboration with a craftsman who executed the pieces according to Miró's design.

He still pushed the craft and method to the limits of creative expression. For example, in 1955 he worked in collaboration with Josep Llorens Artigas, a ceramicist, and his son, on two murals for the UNESCO building in Paris. The mural tiles were painted with enamel glaze and fired—twice—because neither Miró nor Artigas were satisfied with the initial firing results. In 1958 Miró was awarded the Grand Prix of the Guggenheim Foundation for these ceramics.

By 1970 Miró's work was known worldwide. Exhibitions of his work took place in rapid progression in major cities of Europe, Asia, and North and South America. In 1975 Miró declared his devotion to his native country with the gift of the Miró Foundation to the city of Barcelona. The building, which houses his works and the exhibitions of other artists, was designed by Josep Lluis Sert, a great friend of Miró's. One exhibition room was dedicated to the exhibition of works by young artists who had not had the opportunity to display their works in public. The philosophy of the foundation reflected Miró's devotion to allowing twentieth-century art to live a life made up of research and discovery, expressed in a positive and novel manner. Miró died in 1983 at the age of 90.

**SOURCES:**

Arnason, H. H., *History of Modern Art,* New Jersey, Prentice-Hall, 1982.

Malet, Rosa Maria, *Joan Miró,* New York, Rizzoli International, 1983.

Soby, James Thrall, *Joan Miró,* New York, Arno Press, 1980.

Sweeney, James Johnson, *Joan Miró,* New York, Must, 1941.

Waldberg, Patrick, *Surrealism,* London, Thames and Hudson, 1978.

*—Sketch by Lisa A. Wroble*

# Gabriela Mistral
## 1889-1957
### Chilean poet, teacher, and diplomat

Gabriela Mistral was an exceptional character in twentieth-century world history who made significant contributions to the fields of education, literature, and government. She taught in schools throughout her native Chile while at the same time molding her writing talents. Her literary gift, especially in the realm of poetry, earned her the prestigious Nobel Prize in literature in 1945. Mistral also spent time as a governmental official, serving as Chilean consul in cities throughout the world and Chile's representative to several international organizations. In all respects her status transcended her native country's boundaries. Author Sidonia Carmen Rosenbaum called her "the spiritual mentor of the Spanish American world in a degree rarely equaled before by any man and never by a woman" in *Modern Women Poets of Spanish America*. After her death, Waldo Frank wrote an appreciation in *The Nation* in which he praised her work and called her an "ambassadress of the Hispanic spirit."

Mistral was born on April 7, 1889, in the province of Coquimbo in Vicuña, a small town located deep in northern Chile's Elqui Valley. Her Chilean parents—both of whom were teachers—had Basque and Indian roots. Her father, Jerónimo Godoy Villanueva, was also a "pallador," a musical performer who composed songs for festivals and sang with other village musicians. Mistral's father left the family when his young daughter was just three years old. She was then raised in Vicuña and nearby Montegrande by her mother, Petronila Alcayaga, and by her mother's daughter from an earlier marriage. Mistral's early years were marked by a particularly ugly episode in which she was falsely accused of theft, soundly scolded by her blind schoolteacher, and stoned by classmates.

In 1901 the family moved to La Serena, where Mistral eventually applied for admission to the local normal school. Denied the opportunity to enroll because of concerns about her socialist views, fifteen-year-old Mistral took a position as a primary school teacher's assistant in a remote town situated in the Andean mountains. During this time she made frequent visits to her paternal grandmother, Isabel Villanueva, who fostered her knowledge of the Bible. Mistral also started to write poetry, spurred in part by her discovery of some of her father's creations.

Mistral began to teach secondary school in La Cantera in 1906, and by 1909 she took on administrative responsibilities as well. In 1908 she first used the pen name Gabriela Mistral—a name she adopted permanently in 1914—and contributed to the literary magazine *Penumbras*. At the age of 18 she fell in love with a railroad employee, Romelio Ureta. Her life was fundamentally changed when Ureta committed suicide in 1909 after his involvement in embezzlement was discovered. Critics of her work contend that the sensations of loss and despair that permeated so much of her verse can be traced to this sad event in her life.

In 1910 Mistral assumed teaching responsibilities at Barrancas, another rural school. The next year she became professor of hygiene at a secondary school in Traiguen. This post was followed by work as an inspector general and a stint as a professor of history at Antofagasta. In 1912 she began six years' service as inspector and Professor of Castilian in the Liceo de Los Andes.

At the age of 21 Mistral met Pedro Aguirre Cerda, a man who appreciated her poetic talents. Cerda, who later became president of Chile, was a pivotal figure in ensuring that her poetry reached an audience. In 1914 she wrote "Los sonetos de la muerte" ("Sonnets to Death"), for which she won Santiago's municipal Juegos Florales contest. Mistral's body of poetry grew, but she never neglected her teaching career. From 1918 to 1922 she worked in three different schools. She ultimately reached the position of principal in a girls' school in the nation's capital. Margot Arce de Vazquez, author of *Gabriela Mistral: The Poet and Her Work*, asserted that Mistral truly loved to teach: "teaching was a calling to which she gave all her enthusiasm, freedom, and a creative spirit that abhorred routine. A large proportion of her literary work, both prose and poetry, had an educational purpose; it was intended for the classroom and was written with a view to awakening and forming within the child a moral and religious conscience and an aesthetic sensitivity. In the classroom she was a severe taskmaster, exacting hard work and strict discipline."

## Engaged in Life Outside Chile

By the early 1920s Mistral's poetry had been published in a variety of magazines and literary journals. Her most well-known work, *Desolación,* was published during this time as well. The acclaim associated with her literary work, coupled with her correspondence with a wide range of other writers and artists, made her a well-known figure on several continents. It was her reputation as a serious educator, though, that was perhaps most responsible for her early travels. Her first journey outside Chile took place in 1922, when the President of Mexico asked her to assist in that country's education reform effort, a project under the direction of Education Minister **José Vasconcelos.** While in Mexico in 1923, Mistral published a collection of essays, *Lecturas para mujeres*. After two years in Mexico, Mistral traveled to Europe and the United States, where she was received by President Calvin Coolidge at the White House.

"Latin lands still hold to the older custom of believing that artists and intellectuals bring honor to the state and should, therefore, be awarded state honors," Mildred Adams observed in the *New York Times Book Review*. When Mistral returned to Chile, she was appointed that country's representative to the Institute for Intellectual Cooperation, a part of the League of Nations. Eventually she became secretary of that organization. She also was appointed an executive member of the Institute of Educational Cinematography in Rome. In 1927 the Chilean Teachers' Association sent her as its delegate to the Congress of Educators at Locarno. The following year she represented both Chile and Ecuador at the International University Federation in Madrid.

Mistral returned to the United States, where she lectured at Middlebury and Barnard Colleges. As she journeyed back to Chile in 1931, she traveled throughout Central America and the Caribbean. In Havana she presented lectures on **José Martí,** but in other countries her visit provided her hosts with the opportunity to recognize her body of work. She was honored by universities in Guatemala and El Salvador, and was awarded the Golden Orchid, Panama's national literary prize.

This international recognition reflected an important aspect of Mistral's life: her pan-Americanism. "For [Mistral], national differences did not exist where America was concerned," Arce de Vazquez declared. "Her wish was for one great unit extending from Mexico to Patagonia, with one common citizenship." These convictions permeated her poetry, as Arce de Vazquez commented: "Her love and praise of American lands, memories of her Elqui valley, of Mexico's Indians, and of the sweet landscape of tropical islands, and her concern for the historical fate of these peoples form [an] insistent leit-motif." Although, as Rosenbaum asserted in 1945, Mistral's "main concern is, and always has been, Latin America," Mistral hoped for harmony and union between all of North and South America. She expressed such sentiments in "Pan American Manifesto", a prose poem written for the first Pan American Day in 1931 and reprinted in *Américas* shortly after her death.

In 1932 Mistral assumed the position of Chilean consul. Three years later the Chilean Congress named her the country's sole "life consul." Mistral was permitted to work in whatever setting she chose. Her earliest postings were in Guatemala and France. In 1933 she moved to Madrid, but was forced to leave two years later when the contents of a letter containing some critical personal opinions were made public. Any lingering damage from this incident was repaired when Mistral attended a 1937 meeting with Spanish writers in Paris. The group included José Bergamín, Joaquín Xirau, Carlos Rivas, and Victoria Kent.

The onset of the Spanish Civil War, coupled with the first rumblings of World War II, led Mistral to return to the Western Hemisphere. As she journeyed back to South America she was once again feted, receiving honors in Argentina, Uruguay, and Brazil. She served as consul in Veracruz before taking up residence in Brazil.

After a brief stay in the city of Niteroi, Mistral moved to Petropolis, Brazil, where she lost another of her loved ones. It was there that her seventeen-year-old nephew died in 1943. Juan Miguel Godoy, called "Yin Yin," had been adopted by Mistral as an infant shortly after his own mother's death. According to the Petropolis police, the young man had committed suicide. Mistral refused to accept this explanation, blaming the death on a racist gang. This loss was especially painful not only because Mistral was so devoted to the teenager, but also because his death occurred shortly after she learned of the double suicide of her friend Stephan Zweig and his wife.

After World War II ended, Mistral served as a delegate to the United Nations, although she ultimately resigned from that organization's Subcommittee on the Status of Women because she felt that the group was too militant. She actively promoted UNICEF and established a consulate in Los Angeles. She relocated in 1953 to Roslyn Harbor on Long Island to live at the home of her friend, Doris Dana.

### *Desolation* Marked Major New Voice

In 1945 Mistral was notified that she had won the 1945 Nobel Prize for literature. Mistral was the first Latin American writer to receive this award, although she was the third Spanish-speaking writer to be so honored, after **José Echegaray** and **Jacinto Benavente.** Mistral traveled to Stockholm to receive the prize. She then traveled to Paris where she stayed as a guest of the French government.

At the time she was given this international honor, Mistral was best known in literary circles for her poetry, although only three volumes had been widely distributed: *Desolación* (*Desolation*) in 1922; *Ternura* (*Tenderness*) in 1924; and *Tala* (*Felling*) in 1938. Mistral the poet was admired, Adams asserted in the *Nation,* for "the quality of her song, her compassionate insight, the expression she gives to the deepest emotions that move the human heart." Arce de Vazquez argued that Mistral's poetry "stands as a reaction to the Modernism of the Nicaraguan poet **Rubén Darió** . . . a poetry without ornate form, without linguistic virtuosity, without evocations of gallant or aristocratic eras; it is the poetry of a rustic soul, as primitive and strong as the earth. . . . By comparison with Hispanic-American literature generally, which on so many occasions has been an imitator of European models, [Mistral's] poetry possesses the merit of consummate originality, of a voice of its own, authentic and consciously realized." Critics also pointed to a strong Biblical presence in Mistral's work.

*Desolación,* published in 1922, is regarded by many critics and readers to be Mistral's best book. The book's publication history is noteworthy, for it was printed not in South America, but in New York City, by Columbia University's Instituto de las Españas. Columbia University's Dr. Federico de Onís had given a lecture on Mistral at the Instituto. "The audience was mostly made up of teachers," he recalled in the *New York Times Book Review,* "and they were immediately enthusiastic. Here was one of their own, a teacher, who was also a fine poet. They wanted to know where they could get her poems, and all I could give them was a handful of clippings. I told them that if they wanted a volume, enough of them would have to subscribe to copies to pay for the printing." Published in Spanish, the book did not immediately capture critical attention in New York, but it circulated throughout South America, Spain, and France.

Suffering and sadness are key elements in the work. Such characteristics are not surprising in light of Mistral's own observations about herself, revealed in correspondence such as the following, which Rosenbaum noted was written when she was 16 years old: "There is something in my being which engenders bitterness; there is a secret hand which filters gall into my heart, even though happiness surrounds me." Death is a central theme of *Desolation* and is presented in graphic terms. As Arce de Vazquez further explained, "The title *Desolation* is from the first poem of the section "Nature" ("Naturaleza") and is thus titled because it describes a desolate landscape of mist and fog, a true mental landscape, the projection of a psychological state, which dominates the book and gives the keynote and emphasis to its leading poems." Rosenbaum explored Mistral's use of "verbs of violence" in the book to convey tragedy or sadness. "Her vocabulary—which, in general, is not uncommonly rich or varied—acquires . . . an extraordinary force and intensity, mainly through the repetitious, constant use of certain words suggestive of bodily suffering or pain: of burning, of piercing, of ending, of cutting, of cleaving, of bleeding."

*Desolación* commented on the emotion of love as well. According to Rosenbaum, Mistral's book views love "as a religion—as something almost tragically serious; something one enters into everlastingly—not 'until death do us part,' but on to eternity . . . [Love's] purpose is not to appease desire, to satisfy carnal appetites, but soberly to give thought to the richest, the most precious, the most sacred heritage of woman: maternity." Other reviewers cited the subject of motherhood as one of the themes most evident in Mistral's work. As the *New York Times Book Review* related, "One Chilean critic thinks that her best claim to enduring fame lies in her making articulate and moving the tragedy of the childless woman."

Mistral's devotion to children was made even more clear in *Ternura,* a volume that included all of her poetry for children, including works that had been previously published. Critics found *Ternura* to demonstrate more hopefulness and sentimentality than Mistral's previous work. As Arce de Vazquez commented: "All the poems sing to the pleasure of motherhood, the miracle of having a child, the charm of little animals, the loving understanding between the earth and its creatures. After the tremendous passionate, sensual energy of *Desolation,* this second work reveals to us the powerful vitality, the hunger for happiness . . . the other poles of the poet's spirit."

*Tala,* Mistral's third major book, was published in 1938 by the prominent Argentinean writer and critic **Victoria Ocampo.** Disturbed by South America's lack of response to the plight of victims of the Spanish Civil War, Mistral donated the proceeds from *Tala* to Basque orphans.

Essays penned by Mistral also garnered praise from reviewers. She published numerous articles during the course of her life, many of them in leading Spanish-language periodicals. These pieces reflected a direct and passionate style and the author's wide range of interests. In discussing Mistral's work, Waldo Frank commended her "muscular swift prose," which he considered "almost as remarkable as her verse."

Mistral's literary output in her later years displayed an increased sense of maturity and peace. Such qualities, critics noted, were particularly evident in *Lagar* (*Wine Press*), published in 1954.

Mistral was awarded innumerable honors in addition to the Nobel Prize. Honorary doctorates were showered on her from around the world. In 1950 she won the Serra Prize of the Academy of American Franciscan History. The following year Chile awarded her its National Prize for literature. Recognition of her contributions to the worlds of literature and education resulted in other, more unusual, gestures of gratitude as well. Concerned about her health at a time when she was residing in the United States, the President of Mexico once offered her a large parcel of land on which she could build a home.

Mistral battled health problems much of her life, although she possessed an imposing physical presence. Frank recalled in *The Nation* that "She was very tall, and she walked—before her health began to fail—more like a man than a woman, more like an Indian than a European, more like a great rhythmic animal than like a groping human being. Her dress—always black, grey and loose; always ungainly—announced her complete obliviousness to style, except her own."

Mistral finally succumbed to cancer in Long Island's Hampstead General Hospital on January 10, 1957, at the age of 67. Chilean President Carlos Ibañez declared three days of national mourning and Mistral's remains were returned to Chile. She is still honored in many countries by the schools and libraries that bear her name.

## SELECTED PUBLISHED WORKS:

*Desolación* (*Desolation*), Instituto de las Españas, 1922; 2nd edition augmented by Mistral, additional prologue by Pedro Prado, Nascimento, 1923; Bello, 1979.

*Lecturas para mujeres,* Secretaria de Educación, 1923; 4th edition, Porrúa, 1967.

*Ternura (Tenderness),* Saturnino Calleja, 1924; 8th edition, 1965.

*Tala (Felling),* Sur, 1938; reprinted with introduction by Alfonso Calderón, Bello, 1979.

*Pequeña antología,* Escuela Nacional de Artes Gráficas, 1950.

*Poemas de las madres,* Pacifico, 1950.

*Lagar (Wine Press),* Pacifico, 1954.

*Obras selectas,* Pacifico, 1954.

*Los mejores versos,* Nuestra América, 1957.

*Canto a San Francisco,* El Eco Franciscano, 1957.

*Producción de Gabriela Mistral de 1912 a 1918,* edited by Silva Castro, Anales de la Universidad de Chile, 1957.

*Selected Poems of Gabriela Mistral,* translated by Langston Hughes, Indiana University Press, 1957.

## SOURCES:

### Books

Arce de Vazquez, Margot, *Gabriela Mistral: The Poet and Her Work,* translated by Helene Masslo Anderson, New York, New York University Press, 1964.

Castleman, William J., *Beauty and the Mission of the Teacher: The Life of Gabriela Mistral of Chile,* Smithtown, NY: Exposition Press, 1982.

*Current Biography 1946,* edited by Anna Rothe, New York, H.W. Wilson, 1947.

*Hispanic Writers,* edited by Bryan Ryan, Detroit, Gale, 1991.

*Latin American Writers,* Volume II, edited by Carlos A. Solé and Maria Isabel Abreu, New York, Charles Scribner's Sons, 1989.

Robsenbaum, Sidonia Carmen, *Modern Women Poets of Spanish America,* New York, Hispanic Institute, 1945.

*Twentieth-Century Literary Criticism,* Volume 2, edited by Dedria Bryfonski and Sharon K. Hall, Detroit, Gale, 1979.

### Periodicals

*Américas,* March, 1957, pp. 26–28.

*CLA Journal,* September, 1993, pp. 94–103.

*Commonweal,* November 30, 1945, pp. 156–57;

*Nation,* December 29, 1945, pp. 739–40; January 26, 1957, p. 84.

*New York Times,* January 11, 1957, p. 23.

*New York Times Book Review,* December 9, 1945, p. 3; January 27, 1957, p. 2.

*Publishers Weekly,* November 24, 1945.

*Time,* November 26, 1945, p. 40.

—*Sketch by Erika Dreifus*

# Bartolomé Mitre
## 1821-1906
### Argentine historian and statesman

Bartolomé Mitre was the first president of the Argentine Republic. "Mitre was a nation-builder rather than a nationalist," according to John Lynch of London's Institute of Latin American Studies. Mitre believed that studying history contributed to an individual's sense of national identity. As a young man, he fought to force Juan Manuel de Rosas from Argentina. As a military commander, president, and investigator of history, Mitre was an advocate of the people of Argentina and of the nation itself.

Born in Buenos Aires in 1821, Mitre fled the persecution of General Rosas with his family in 1931, taking up residence in Montevideo, Uruguay. Mitre grew up in the Uruguayan capital. He studied in military school and, when not practicing for war, explored his literary talents by writing poetry. After his schooling, he served in the armies of General **Fructuoso Rivera.**

### Fought For Independence Against Rosas

In 1842, he married Delfina de Vedia, whom he outlived by 23 years. Though just married, Mitre had little time for marital bliss. Rosas and his armies attacked Montevideo in 1843, and Mitre became a lieutenant colonel of the artillery force. He helped defend the city alongside his friend, Guiseppe Garibaldi, who would later return to Italy to become a famous revolutionary in the nationalist movement of his own country.

Mitre left Montevideo in 1846, hoping to join an army forming in the Corrientes province of Argentina to fight Rosas. But the army dissolved before Mitre could join, and instead of returning to Uruguay or remaining in Argentina—where he was wanted by Rosas—he wandered throughout the region in Bolivia, Peru, and Chile. In 1851, he gave up his wandering to join General Justo José de Urquiza's army with other Argentine exiles, such as **Domingo Faustino Sarmiento.** Mitre aided Urquiza in his war against Rosas, which culminated in the Battle of Caseros that began February 3, 1852, and drove Rosas from Argentina.

After the fall of the Rosas regime, the political spectrum opened up, and Mitre entered it. He moved to Buenos Aires, and like many liberal intellectuals, espoused a very anti-Urquiza line because, though Urquiza had led the forces that ousted Rosas, Urquiza did not replace the former dictator. Thereafter, Mitre and Urquiza became enemies.

## Struggled for Control of Government

The Paraguayan historian O'Leary clearly defined the struggle between Urquiza and Mitre: "Two men personify the two tendencies in the new act of the great tragedy of Argentinian life: Urquiza and Mitre. Mitre was the localist spirit of Buenos Aires. Urquiza represented provincial longings. . . . Mitre was the colonial monopoly, which fought to perpetuate its dominion. Urquiza was the reaction . . . the 'barbarism' which aspired to create a nation putting all Argentinians on the same plane. Mitre was the 'civilization' of the frock coats, beneath whose stuffed shirts throbbed a most reactionary egoism, an egoism capable of compromising the national integrity to satisfy its appetites."

Mitre and all of Buenos Aires refused to participate in Urquiza's plan for an Agentine Confederation and Buenos Aires subsequently declared its independence. Mitre became minister of the interior of the provincial government and later minister of war to aid in the city's defense against Urquiza's 1853 blockade. By 1857, Mitre had risen to the height of the political community of Buenos Aires. Mitre advocated nationalism, based on Buenos Aires' reunification with the rest of Argentina on terms favorable to Buenos Aires, unlike the autonomists, who advocated permanent separation from Argentina.

In 1857, the U.S. Minister Yaney entered into mediation between Mitre and Urquiza, but failed to obtain an agreement, as Mitre stuck to the position that Urquiza completely retire from public life for at least six years, the length of a presidential term. Though Mitre's and Urquiza's governments operated under an 1855 peace and commerce treaty, neither one honored the agreement. Urquiza's congress imposed heavy dues on goods bound up-river from Buenos Aires, and Mitre's government retaliated with stiff tariffs on the Confederation's goods. The trade war escalated to open warfare in 1859.

In 1859, when Urquiza attacked Buenos Aires, Mitre led the fight against him. Though Buenos Aires fell to Urquiza's forces, the nationalists won concessions in the pact of San José de Flores, following the Battle of Cepeda in October of 1859. Buenos Aires joined the Argentine Confederation, and the people elected Mitre governor of Buenos Aires in May of 1860. But this was only a temporary post, for Mitre hoped to regroup and still win control of the government. Mitre's group wanted to rule the Confederation rather than be ruled by it.

## Became First President

The pact between the Confederation and Buenos Aires crumbled in 1861, and Mitre once again led his people against Urquiza and his army, this time successfully. Mitre and his armies beat Urquiza at the Battle of Pavón in September of 1861, thus forcing Urquiza from both the battle field and the political arena. With his main opponent defeated, Mitre won the election held by the new federal congress, and in 1862, became the first president of the undivided, newly dubbed Argentine Republic. After ten years of civil war and struggle, Argentina was united under one government for the first time since the fall of the Rosas dictatorship.

Mitre implemented liberal programs unheard of during the harsh Rosas years. He set up new railroad systems for construction, notably the Cordoba-Rosario railway, to further economic prosperity. He worked to abolish the somewhat feudal system of *caudillo* rule in Argentina's interior. He opened the country to foreign trade and immigrants who began to arrive by the thousands. Mitre helped to modernize Argentina, and the country's merchants began to process and export agricultural products through better shipyards and port systems. But still there were many things with which he and his cabinet struggled to make a reality, one of which was a country-wide telegraph and postal communication system.

## Led Armies in Fsubguayan War

In 1865, Mitre's political and economic improvements were impeded by the War of the Triple Alliance. Argentina, along with Brazil and Uruguay, launched an effort to defeat Paraguayan dictator Francisco Solano López, who had drawn Argentina into the war by marching his troops through Argentina to reach Brazil. Mitre commanded the allied land forces (the Brazilians commanded the sea fleet) until early 1868 when he was forced to return to Argentina after his vice president died. The war continued without Mitre until 1870 when Solano López and his forces were routed; López was killed. The War of the Triple Alliance was a costly one for the allies, who lost an estimated 100,000 soldiers during the five year conflict. But the allies managed to cripple Paraguay, reducing its male population to one-tenth of its former size. The war is regarded by many historians as the bloodiest war in modern Latin American history.

After three years at war, Mitre returned to Argentina in 1868 in time for his term to end. Though Mitre had fought valiantly for the republic, twice having to abandon his armies to suppress revolts in other parts of Argentina, he did not win re-election to the presidency. His defeat was partially due to a cholera epidemic that swept Buenos Aires in 1868, cutting the city's population by half and weakening Mitre's Porteños party in their bid to win him the popular vote. Mitre was succeeded by his former comrade Sarmiento, a provincial candidate, native of San Juan, and son of a muleteer. Mitre ran again for president in 1874 but lost to Nicolás Avellaneda.

Mitre's followers, fomented to action by the former president's defeat and their suspicions of fraud, launched a rebellion against Arellaneda, led by Mitre. The government vanquished the revolt, captured and imprisoned Mitre, and sentenced him to death. Avellaneda opposed Mitre's execution and the subsequent lesser sentence of exile. In 1880, when the issue of federalization prompted the citizens of Buenos Aires to revolt, Mitre negotiated a truce, even though he sympathized with the citizens' cause.

Mitre negotiated a settlement between the Argentine government and those dissatisfied with it by forming and leading his own opposition group, the Unión Cívica (Civic Union) in 1890. When more radical members of the group incited another revolt while Mitre was in Europe, he split from his own group and formed a new one—the National Civic Union—which from then on supported the government in power. By 1901, when Mitre turned 80, he was lauded as one of the most distinguished, oldest Argentine patriots. His eightieth birthday won him praise from many dignitaries throughout the world.

Mitre pursued goals other than political ones throughout his life. He built a reputation for himself as a resolute journalist, writer, orator, and historian. In 1870, he founded *La Nación,* one of Latin America's greatest newspapers. Throughout his life he wrote poetry, novels, essays, and many translations. He died on January 19, 1906, in Buenos Aires.

**SOURCES:**

**Books**

*Biographical Dictionary of Latin America and Caribbean Political Leaders,* edited by Robert J. Alexander, New York, Greenwood Press, 1988.
*Cambridge Encyclopedia of Latin America,* edited by Simon Collier, Thomas Skidmore and Harold Blakemore, Cambridge University Press, 1992.
*Encyclopedia of Latin America,* edited by Helen Delpar, New York, McGraw Hill, 1974.
Kirkpatrick, F. A., *A History of the Argentine Republic,* Cambridge, University Press, 1931.
Rojas, Ricardo, *San Martín: Knight of the Andes,* translated by Herschel Brickell and Carlos Videla, New York, Cooper Square Publications, 1967.
*South American Dictators: During the First Century of Independence,* edited by A. Curtis Wilgus, New York, Russell and Russell, 1963.
Whitaker, Arthur, *Argentina,* Englewood Cliffs, New Jersey, Prentice-Hall, 1965.

**Periodicals**

*Americas,* July 1984, pp. 81–98.
*Journal of Latin American Studies,* May 1985, p. 263.
*New York Times,* January 20, 1906.

—*Sketch by Christopher B. Tower*

# Nicholasa Mohr
## 1935-
### Puerto Rican American writer and illustrator

As an impoverished young girl, Nicholasa Mohr used her imagination to temporarily escape her often shocking surroundings. As an adult, she uses this same creativity to relate her feelings as a woman and a Puerto Rican American, to present the reality of a people and to express her artistic talent. Once an aspiring fine arts painter and printmaker, Mohr became a writer and illustrator of her own books and received immediate acclaim. While her realistic novels and stories have won many awards and have garnered her a following among readers, Mohr has found satisfaction in being able to utilize her many talents and assist people she cares about at the same time. She explained in her *Something about the Author Autobiography Series* (*SAAS*) essay, "As a writer I have used my abilities as a creative artist to strengthen my skills and at the same time in small measure have ventured to establish a voice for my ethnic American community and our children."

Mohr was born on November 1, 1935, to Pedro and Nicholasa (Rivera) Golpe. Her parents migrated from Puerto Rico during the Great Depression to a barrio in Manhattan with their four children; Mohr was the last of three children later born in New York City and the only girl. Before long, the family moved to the Bronx. When she was just eight years old, Mohr's father died. Often ill herself, Mohr's mother struggled to ensure that her family stayed together, and she constantly encouraged her children to develop their talents and work hard themselves. As the author related in her *SAAS* essay, it was her mother who gave Mohr paper, a pencil, and some crayons—and with them, Mohr learned that "by making pictures and writing letters I could create my own world ... like 'magic.'" In the same essay, Mohr remembered her mother telling her, "*Mi hijita* [My little daughter], you are special with these God-given talents. Someday you must study so that you can become an important artist ... make an important contribution to the world and really be somebody."

### Imagination and Talent Offer Escape from Reality

Although her mother died before Mohr began high school, her mother's influence did not. "My mother's strength and independence served as a strong role model for me," the author stated in her *SAAS* essay. "As I look back, she was the first feminist I knew." Mohr had to be strong herself, and she continued to excel in school despite a lack of emotional support from her guardian aunt. Mohr's artwork in school, she believes, allowed her to partially escape the bigotry other Puerto Rican children had to endure. The gifted child was respected. Her abilities gave her confidence and the hope that she would overcome poverty and prejudice. "I used my imagination and was able to create something interesting and pleasing where previously there had been a sense of despair," she said in *SAAS*. Also, as Mohr developed her writing, drawing, and painting skills, she garnered the experience that would allow her to portray the situations and characters that later appeared in her books.

Mohr was determined to become an artist. When it was time for her to attend high school, she was mortified by her guidance counselor's insistence that she, as a Puerto Rican girl, did not need a solid academic education. The counselor wanted to send Mohr to a school to learn how to sew. Nevertheless, Mohr managed to find a school with a department in fashion illustration, and she was able to practice drawing. Upon graduation from high school, Mohr enrolled in the Arts Students' League in New York City, and attended from 1953 to 1956. She attended school while working to support herself as a waitress, a clerical factory worker, and a translator.

Although she had saved enough money to study art in Europe, Mohr decided to travel to Mexico City. There, at the Taller de Gráfica Popular, she studied the works of Jose Clemente Orozco, the murals of **Diego Rivera,** and the paintings of Rivera's wife, Frida Kahlo. The colors, figures, and methods that these artists used to express their feelings about their cultures greatly influenced Mohr. "In a profound way their work spoke to me and my experiences as a Puerto Rican woman born in New York," she wrote in *SAAS*. "The impact was to shape and form the direction of all my future work."

Mohr returned to the United States, and began to study at the New School for Social Research in New York City. It was there that she met the man who would become her husband, Irwin Mohr; he was working on a doctorate in clinical psychology. She married the native New Yorker on October 5, 1957, and they soon had a son, David. Mohr continued studying fine art at the Brooklyn Museum Art School, from 1959 to 1966, and then she began to study printmaking and silkscreening at the Pratt Center for Contemporary Printmaking from 1966 to 1969.

A second son, Jason, was born to the Mohrs in 1970, and, with the help of a grant for the artist's work, the couple moved to a home in the suburb of Teaneck, New Jersey. There, Mohr worked in her huge art studio. According to Mohr's quote in *SAAS* her prints are not "just ... literal scenes of social injustices, ... or aesthetically abstract ... [they are] filled with bold figures, faces, and various symbols of the city ... numbers, letters, words, and phrases ... a kind of graffiti." Her bold innovations brought Mohr some measure of notoriety in the New York art scene. Mohr was also an art teacher. In 1967, she had become an art instructor in art schools in New York and New Jersey, and from 1971 to 1973, she worked as an art instructor at the Art Center of Northern New Jersey. From 1973 to 1974, she was also an artist-in-residence with the New York City public schools.

As a successful artist with her own one-woman exhibitions and an art agent, Mohr had never considered writing when she was asked by a publisher to write about her life as a Puerto Rican American. Mohr thought she might try when she had time, and she wrote 50 pages of vignettes. Although the publisher liked the piece, she did not want to publish it. Mohr remembers this well in her interview with Paul Janeczko: "I think what she expected was something much more sensational, the sort of stereotypical ghetto person. So I told her that much to my embarrassment I had never stolen anything, taken hard drugs, been raped or mugged. So I guess she thought my life was uneventful."

Mohr put away her pen and continued to work as an artist until Harper and Row Publishers asked her to do a cover for one of their books. Instead, Mohr brought them her vignettes. Ellen Rudin, an editor for the company, was enthusiastic, and she encouraged Mohr to develop what she had written: Mohr was given a contract. She spent time writing at the MacDowell Colony in New Hampshire, and finished her first book, *Nilda,* which appeared in 1973. Mohr recalled in her interview with Janeczko that she "fell very much in love with writing" although she was "a little bit nervous." While it was difficult for her to make the transition from being primarily an artist to a writer, she recalled in the same interview that she "found that I could do certain things in writing and there was a crying need for what I had to say as a Puerto Rican, as someone living here, and as a woman." She found that she "could draw a picture with words, and it was extremely stimulating and eye-opening to realize what one could do with words."

### First Book Impresses Readers and Critics

While Mohr found herself intrigued with writing, readers were fascinated with what Mohr wrote. They were touched and enlightened as they read *Nilda*, the autobiographical story of a poor Puerto Rican girl living in New York's Spanish Harlem. While the story is set during the time of World War II, emphasis is given to the situation at home. Puerto Ricans, already American citizens, were called "spics" and animals by the very people who were supposed to guide, uphold, and assist their youth. Teachers, social workers, nurses, and even policemen referred to Puerto Ricans as "you people" in the book, and the young girl's peers behave just as cruelly. Particularly effective are two scenes, one in which a very poor girl is taunted for her lack of a real suitcase at camp, and another in which a girl who has just given birth to a baby is denied entrance to her home by her own embarrassed mother. One young girl found this episode to be almost overwhelming. She said in *Newsweek,* "When I found out Petra was pregnant, I had to put down the book, get myself a glass of milk, turn up the heat and cuddle up in my quilt." The book was powerful in other ways too; according to the Mohr, it would demonstrate how one could escape reality through imagination. "Once there [in her imagination], she [Nilda], would also find relief from an environment she, in fact, is powerless to change in any other way," wrote the author in *SAAS.*

*Nilda* was a great success. Critics praised the story's fresh characters, content and style, as well as the cover and eight illustrations Mohr had provided. One critic, Donald B. Gibson, lauded the work in *Children's Literature:* "There is no pity here, for the author is too much aware of the humanity of her characters and of the other implications of pity to be in any way condescending." He wrote that *Nilda* was "what I would call a significant book, a touchstone by which others may be judged." Mohr was given the Outstanding Book Award in Juvenile Fiction from the *New York Times* in 1973. She received the Jane Addams Children's Book Award from the Jane Addams Peace Association, also for *Nilda,* in 1974. She won another MacDowell Colony writing fellowship, this one for the summer of 1974. Finally, the Society of Illustrators presented Mohr with a citation of merit for *Nilda*'s book jacket design. The book eventually made *School Library Journal*'s "Best of the Best 1966–1978" list in 1979.

After her experience with *Nilda,* Mohr felt that she had to write more. Her next book, a collection of short stories complete with a book jacket of her own creation, was published in 1975. The twelve stories and the novella in *El Bronx Remembered* are set in post-war New York, and deal with once-delicate subjects frankly. One story, for example, features a doomed marriage between a pregnant teenager and an aging homosexual. Another story is about a lonely, dying old Jewish man who is befriended by a Puerto Rican family. Other stories deal with racism, religion, as well as sexuality and death. All of the stories, spiced with Spanish words, are realistic. "If there is any message at all in these stories, any underlying theme," wrote a critic in the *New York Times Book Review,* "it is that life goes on."

For *El Bronx Remembered,* Mohr was awarded the Outstanding Book Award in Teenage Fiction from the *New York Times* in 1975, and she received the Best Book Award from *School Library Journal* that same year. *El Bronx Remembered* also was a National Book Award finalist for the "most distinguished book in children's literature" in 1976. Finally, Bantam Books chose to publish Mohr's books in paperback form. Mohr realized that she could combine her love of art with her talent for writing, and reach more people, by writing books. She enjoyed her work, and she had been very successful. She made the decision to continue writing, and did so as a writer-in-residence at the MacDowell Colony.

### Continues to Write for Adults and Children

Her next self-illustrated book, *In Nueva York,* was very similar to *El Bronx Remembered.* First published in 1977, *In Nueva York*'s related short stories featured mature subjects. In one story, a woman who searches for her son finds that he is a dwarf. In another, a homosexual woman marries a homosexual man. Both "The Robbery" and "Coming to Terms" deal with the violent death of a teenage thief shot by a store owner and its consequences. "Mohr creates a remarkably vivid tapestry of community life as well as of individual characters," wrote one critic in the *Bulletin of the Center for Children's Books.* She continued, "Tough, candid, and perceptive, the book has memorable characters, resilient and responsive, in a sharply-eyed milieu." Mohr was given the Best Book Award from the *School Library Journal* and the Best Book Award in Young Adult literature from the American Library Association. The book was selected as one of the ten "Paperbacks: New and Noteworthy" books by the *New York Times* in January of 1980. It won the distinction of being named a Notable Trade Book in the Field of Social Studies by the joint committee of the National Council for the Social Studies and the Children's Book Council.

Mohr's third self-illustrated book, *Felita*, which was published in 1979, also won this last award, in 1980. A novel for younger children, *Felita* related the story of a Puerto Rican girl whose parents decide to move to a better part of town. Felita missed her old friends, and the neighbors would not let their children befriend her. Discouraged by discrimination and harassment, Felita's family returned to their old neighborhood, and Felita was forced to readjust. *Felita*, well-received by critics, won an American Book Award from the Before Columbus Foundation in 1981.

From 1977 to 1980, Mohr attempted to contribute to her community through more than her writing and artwork. She was a lecturer in Puerto Rican studies in 1977 at the State University of New York at Stony Brook, and a visiting lecturer in creative writing for various groups, including the University of Illinois Educational Alliance Program in Chicago, the Cedar Rapids, Iowa, community schools, a writers-in-residence seminar at the University of Wisconsin at Oshkosh, and the Bridgeport Connecticut public schools from 1977 to 1978. Mohr served as the head creative writer and co-producer of the television series, *Aqui y Ahora* (*Here and Now*), and as a member of the council of the New Jersey State Council on the Arts. She was a member of the board of trustees as well as a consultant for the Young Filmmakers Foundation, and a consultant on bilingual media training for Young Filmmakers Video Arts.

When Mohr's husband died and her sons went to college, the author moved to a small townhouse in Brooklyn in 1980. In 1981, Mohr's brother Vincent, to whom she was very close, also died. Mohr did not publish another book until 1985. *Rituals of Survival: A Woman's Portfolio*, a collection of short stories and a novella written for adults, was published by Arte Público Press. For this work, Mohr was presented a Legislative Resolution from the State of New York, commending her for her "valuable contributions to the world of literature."

By 1986, Mohr had written another children's book, *Going Home*, a sequel to *Felita*. In *Going Home*, Felita takes a trip to Puerto Rico with her family, and is sad to leave by the end of the summer despite the problems she had encountered with the children there at the beginning of her vacation. This book garnered a warm reception. A critic for the *School Library Journal* commented, "Felita is a vivid, memorable character, well realized and well developed. It is a pleasure to welcome her back."

Mohr has a broad list of writing and teaching experience. She has had selections of her work published in *Family in Harmony and Conflict*, edited by Peter Reinke. Her short stories have appeared in *Children's Digest*, *Scholastic Magazine*, and *Nuestro*. She is a member of the board of contributing editors of *Nuestro*, and is a member of both the Authors Guild and the Authors League of America. She is the author, with Ray Blanco, of the screenplay, "The Artist," and she has contributed to textbooks and anthologies such as *The Ethnic American Woman: Problems, Protests, Lifestyles*, which was edited by Edith Blicksilver. Finally, she wrote a piece for the radio entitled, "Inside the Monster," for the Latino Writers Symposium. Also, from 1988 to 1990, Mohr was a distinguished visiting professor at Queens College in New York City.

Mohr, who has been awarded an honorary doctorate from the State University of New York at Albany, is currently working on another novel and a screenplay. In her writing, Mohr strives to challenge readers of all ages to view the world with open eyes, to encourage them to alter their perception, and to entertain them. Mohr, who escaped reality as a child through her imagination, today uses her creative talents to try to change reality through her readers.

## SELECTED PUBLISHED WORKS:

*Nilda: A Novel*, Harper, 1973, 2nd ed., Arte Público, 1986.
*El Bronx Remembered: A Novella and Stories*, Harper, 1975, 2nd edition, Arte Público, 1986.
*In Nueva York*, Dial, 1977.
*Felita*, Dial, 1979.
*Rituals of Survival: A Woman's Portfolio*, Arte Público, 1985.
*Going Home*, Dial, 1986.

## SOURCES:

### Books

*Authors & Artists for Young Adults*, Volume 8, Gale, 1992.
*Contemporary Literary Criticism*, Volume 12, Gale, 1980.
Mohr, Nicholasa, interview with Paul Janeczko, *From Writers to Students: The Pleasures and Pains of Writing*, edited by M. Jerry Weiss, International Reading Association, 1979, pp. 75–78.
Sadker, Myra Pollack, and David Miller Sadker, *Now upon a Time: A Contemporary View of Children's Literature*, Harper, 1977, pp. 210–30.
*Something about the Author Autobiography Series*, Volume 8, Gale, 1989, pp. 185–94.

### Periodicals

*Best Sellers*, December, 1975, p. 266.

*Bulletin of the Center for Children's Books,* June, 1976, p. 161; July-August, 1977, p. 178; May, 1986, p. 178.

*Children's Literature,* Volume 3, 1974, pp. 230–34.

*English Journal,* February, 1978, p. 100.

*Essence,* May, 1980, p. 25.

*Horn Book,* February, 1976, p. 57; February, 1980, p. 56; September-October, 1986, pp. 591.

*Interracial Bulletin of Books for Children,* November 4, 1976, p. 15.

*The Lion and the Unicorn,* fall, 1978, pp. 6–15.

*Newsweek,* March 4, 1974, p. 83.

*New York Times,* January 20, 1980.

*New York Times Book Review,* November 4, 1973, pp. 27–28; November 10, 1974; November 16, 1975; May 22, 1977.

*Publishers Weekly,* July 25, 1986, p. 190.

*School Library Journal,* April, 1977, p. 79; August, 1986, p. 105.

*Vista,* May 14, 1989, p. 3.

—*Sketch by Ronie-Richele Garcia-Johnson*

*Gloria Molina*

# Gloria Molina
## 1948-
### Mexican American politican

Gloria Molina's political career has been a series of firsts: the first Chicana elected to the California State Assembly, the first Chicana elected to the Los Angeles City Council (and only the third Chicano elected in this century), and the first woman ever elected to the L.A. County Board of Supervisor, the most powerful local government in the country. She is also the first Latino since 1875 to serve on the Board of Supervisors and the first Latina to be the co-chair of the campaign committee of the Democratic presidential nominee. Molina has built her political career by grassroots campaigning and by resisting being "one of the boys" with other politicians. In a characteristic statement, reported by the *New York Times* the day after her election to the L.A. County Board of Supervisors, Molina said, "I can't go into the Board of Supervisors and start acting like them. I did not get elected to meet their needs. I got elected to meet the needs of the people of the first district."

In an interview with *Hispanic,* Molina characterized the politicians she has known as "people who don't serve the community, who don't resolve problems, people who expect to be respected by virtue of their positions, but call them to the table and they don't get involved in partnerships with their constituents. And meanwhile the people are suffering." It was statements like these which led *Hispanic* magazine in a July, 1991, cover story to describe Molina as "the confrontational fighter, the outsider who asks tough questions, speaks her mind against dirty politicians, and demands answers with an insistence that makes enemies feel attacked by a pit bull that won't let go." These attitudes have given Molina great popularity with the public. A 1991 national survey of Latinos conducted by L.A.'s Spanish language newspaper *La opinión* and Univision, a Spanish-language television network, found that Molina is the most admired Latino leader in the nation.

Molina's legendary tenacity is the result of her life experiences. The oldest of Leonardo and Concepcion Molina's ten children, Gloria Molina was born May 31, 1948, in a suburb of Los Angeles, California. Her parents had migrated from Mexico a year earlier. After attending high school in Pico Rivera, a suburb of Los Angeles, she enrolled in Rio Hondo College to study design. In 1967, when she was 19, Molina's father had an accident and she took a full-time job as a legal assistant to support her family. She continued her education by going to school at night, graduating from East Los Angeles College in 1968, and attended California State University, Los Angeles until 1970. In 1971, she became a job counselor for the East Los Angeles Community Union (TELACU), an economic development corporation.

Although involved in the Chicano movement in the 1960s, it was in the 1970s that Molina's deep involvement in community affairs blossomed. She was active in the Latin American Law Enforcement Association and was a boardmember of United Way of Los Angeles. In 1973 a group of Chicana activists organized the Comision Femenil de Los Angeles, an organization dedicated to meeting the needs of the women of the Chicano/Latino community, with Gloria Molina as the founding president. During her presidency, the Comision developed many badly needed social programs for Chicanas in the Los Angeles area. Molina was the national president of the Comision Feminil from 1974 to 1976. Molina was also a founding member of Hispanic American Democrats, the National Association of Latino Elected and Appointed Officials (NALEO), and Centro De Niños, an organization that helps children.

### Takes First Position in Politics

In 1974, Molina took the first step in her professional political career by becoming the administrative assistant to California State Assemblyman Art Torres. Three years later, President Jimmy Carter appointed her director for region nine of Intergovernmental and Congressional Affairs in the Department of Health and Human Services. In 1980, Molina returned to California to become chief deputy to the speaker of the California Assembly, Willie Brown. When the 1982 election season began, she made the fateful decision to run for the state assembly.

Gloria Molina's 1982 assembly race contained all the elements that make her the politician she is. The local Chicano politicians informed Molina that she didn't have the qualifications to run for assembly, emphasizing that the community wasn't ready to elect a woman and the funding and endorsements would go to another candidate. Angered, Molina decided to buck the establishment but admitted she had fears. "I was shaking in my boots," she told *Hispanic* magazine in 1991, "but I had to tell them, 'I will have all those things,' otherwise I would have folded. I had reservations about a good deal of it but I wasn't going to let them deny me the opportunity." Molina put together the kind of aggressive, grassroots campaign that has become her trademark. Her opponent had more money and more endorsements but in the end, it was Gloria Molina who had more votes and became the first Chicana ever elected to the California state assembly.

Molina's two terms in the assembly established her reputation as a political maverick. Molina told this story to the *San Antonio Light* newspaper: "When I went to the Assembly [in 1982], one man said to me 'Oh, I'm so glad we have you, we need someone like you to work on bilingual education and child care.' I said, 'I want to work on insurance and taxation

issues.'" Although a liberal Democrat, Molina once supported a bill to add work requirements for welfare because she thought it a sensible way to help people get jobs. She defied her former boss, Assembly Speaker Willie Brown, the second most powerful politician in California, by refusing to cut deals. It made it more difficult for Molina to get her bills passed, but as *Ms.* magazine reported, she feels, "Anytime you take a position, you run the risk of offending another legislator. You have to take risks." Nonetheless, Molina was able to have two laws passed of special concern to her district. One prevents discrimination against immigrants in auto insurance and the other requires notification if a neighborhood is to be sprayed for agricultural pests. Molina's work has been recognized with numerous awards, including Woman of the Year in 1983 from the Mexican American Opportunity Foundation and in 1984 from *Ms.* magazine. In 1983, she was named Hispanic of the Year by *Caminos* magazine and Democrat of the Year by the Los Angeles County Democratic Central Committee.

In 1986, California Governor George Deukmejian selected a site in East Los Angeles, a predominantly Chicano area, to build a new prison. Outraged residents appealed to their political leaders for help to stop the prison from being built and Molina responded. Governor Deukmejian was determined to see the prison built before he left office but he badly underestimated the depth of feeling against the prison in the East L.A. community and the skill of political leaders like Gloria Molina. A series of political and legal maneuvers stopped the construction plans. Although there were other politicians, lawyers, and community organizations involved, Molina's leadership convinced many voters that she was a politician who would not betray the interests of the community. Molina would continue fighting against the prison even after she left the assembly.

### Elected to Latino City Council

In 1987, the City of Los Angeles and the Mexican American Legal Defense and Education Fund (MALDEF) reached a settlement on a gerrymandering suit which called for the creation of a new Latino City Council seat and a special municipal election to fill the seat. Molina decided to run for the seat and once again she was opposed by a candidate of the local political establishment, along with two lesser known candidates. Molina, and her political consultant planned what the *Washington Post* called "a letter-perfect special election campaign." With four people running, most political observers expected a runoff. Molina won with 57 percent of the vote.

This victory marked a change in Molina's thinking about her future. As she told a reporter for the *San Antonio Light* in 1988, "I used to be a fatalist. Even when I was elected in 1982, I didn't think of going any farther. Now I am goal-oriented."

## Works for Better Response to Citizens' Needs

One of her goals as a city councilwoman was to make the city departments more responsive to the citizens. When people in her district complained about trash pickups, she followed trash trucks and street sweepers around the district. She confronted drug dealers on the streets and donated $75,000 from her office budget to create MASH-LA (More Advocates for Safe Homes) in an attempt to organize people to clean their own neighborhoods and take back the streets from the gangs and drug dealers. She also worked to develop public/private partnerships to increase affordable housing, improve traffic flow and increase open space in the central city. As she had when she was in the assembly, Molina continued to fight the building of a state prison in East L.A. Dr. Rudolfo Acuña, a columnist for the *L.A. Herald Examiner,* describes this scene from a 1988 hearing by the state Department of Corrections: "Attention, however, quickly shifted to Councilwoman Gloria Molina. . . . She combatively addressed the English-speaking panel members in Spanish. Translated, she said, 'This community, which already houses 75 percent of the county's inmates, does not deserve another lockup in its midst. . . . [The proposed site is located] in a community that houses 870,000 people within a five-mile radius.'" Acuña noted, "Significantly, the 'No Prison in East L.A.' movement has given [Molina] a forum to showcase alternatives to the 'Let's make a deal' politics of the Latino male establishment." The struggle against the prison would continue for four more years before the Chicanos in the state legislature would effectively kill the bill to build a prison in East L.A.

In a case that went all the way to the U.S. Supreme Court, MALDEF successfully sued the Los Angeles County Board of Supervisors for gerrymandering and forced the creation of a Latino district and a special election to fill it. The five-member Board of Supervisors has an annual budget of over $10 billion and represents nearly 10 million people. It is the most powerful locally elected governmental body in the United States. Molina decided to run for the seat and was opposed by the man who gave her her first job in politics, Art Torres. Molina won a hotly contested race and assumed office March 8, 1991, becoming the first woman ever elected to the Board of Supervisors and the first Latino since 1875 to serve as Supervisor. Molina's election changed the Board of Supervisors in more than one way. She broke the monopoly that white males have had on the job, she changed the political composition from conservative to liberal, and the county bureaucracy discovered that there was a supervisor who would unmercifully grill them if they came to board meetings unprepared to explain

their actions or how the taxpayer's money was being spent. The other Supervisors are not above Molina's criticism. In a widely reported debate over the distribution of bleach kits and condoms to drug users, a move advocated by public health officials to slow the spread of AIDS, Molina interrupted a conservative Supervisor speaking against the measure to accuse him of talking "absolute nonsense." On a different occasion, when an oil company was granted a drilling project in her district but had not bothered to inform the citizens affected by it, an angry Molina confronted the officials in a public hearing. As the *Washington Post* reported, she said, "You have demonstrated disrespect for this community. Turn around and look at them. Be respectful to this community."

Molina's abilities caught the eye of the national Democratic leadership and in July, 1992, Democratic presidential candidate Bill Clinton appointed her co-chair of the National Campaign. In a press release, Clinton said, "I'm grateful that Supervisor Molina has accepted the position. Her experience and commitment to grassroots organizing brings added energy to this campaign."

## SOURCES:

### Books

Meier, Matt S., *Mexican-American Biographies: A Historical Dictionary, 1836–1987,* Greenwood Press, 1988, pp. 142–43.

### Periodicals

*Hispanic,* July, 1991, pp. 13–15.
*Ms.,* January, 1985, pp. 80, 114.
*Los Angeles Herald Examiner,* August 5, 1988, p. A10.
*New York Times,* February 17, 1991, p. A17.
*San Antonio Light,* May 1, 1987, p. B8.
*Vista,* February 4, 1992, p. 10.
*Washington Post,* April 14, 1987, p. A4; June 17, 1991 p. A5.

### Other

Press release, Clinton/Gore presidential campaign, July 28, 1992.

—*Sketch by Andrés Chávez*

# Mario Molina
## 1943-
### Mexican American chemist

Mario Molina is an important figure in the development of a scientific understanding of our atmosphere. Molina earned national prominence by theorizing, with fellow chemist F. Sherwood Rowland, that chlorofluorocarbons (CFCs) deplete the Earth's ozone layer. In his years as a researcher at the Jet Propulsion Lab at CalTech and a professor at the Massachusetts Institute of Technology (MIT), Molina has continued his investigations into the effects of chemicals on the atmosphere.

Mario José Molina was born in Mexico City on March 19, 1943. His father was Roberto Molina-Pasquel; his mother, Leonor Henriquez. Following his early schooling in Mexico, he graduated from the Universidad Nacional Autónoma de México in 1965 with a degree in chemical engineering. Immediately upon graduation, Molina went to West Germany to continue his studies at the University of Freiburg, acquiring the equivalent of his master's degree in polymerization kinetics in 1967. Molina then returned to Mexico to accept a position as assistant professor in the chemical engineering department at his alma mater, the Universidad Nacional Autónoma de México.

In 1968, Molina left Mexico to further his studies in physical chemistry at the University of California at Berkeley. He received his Ph.D. in 1972 and became a postdoctoral associate that same year. His primary area of postdoctoral work was the chemical laser measurements of vibrational energy distributions during certain chemical reactions. The following year, 1973, was a turning point in Molina's life. In addition to marrying a fellow chemist, the former Luisa Y. Tan (the couple have one son, Felipe), Molina left Berkeley to continue his postdoctoral work with physical chemist, Professor F. Sherwood Rowland, at the University of California at Irvine.

### Conducts Landmark Investigation into the Dangers of Chlorofluorocarbons

Both Molina and Rowland shared a common interest in the effects of chemicals on the atmosphere. And both were well aware that every year millions of tons of industrial pollutants were bilged into the atmosphere. Also, there were questions about emissions of nitrogen compounds from supersonic aircraft. What impact did these various chemical discharges have on the envelope of air that surrounds the Earth? Molina and Rowland decided to conduct experiments to determine what happens to chemical pollutants that reach both the atmosphere directly above us but also at stratospheric levels, some ten to twenty-five miles above the Earth. Both men knew that within the stratosphere, a thin, diffuse layer of ozone gas encircles the planet which acts as a filter screening out much of the sun's most damaging ultraviolet radiation. Without this ozone shield, life could not survive in its present incarnation.

The two scientists concentrated their research on the impact of a specific group of chemicals called chlorofluorocarbons, which are widely used in such industrial and consumer products as aerosol spray cans, pressurized containers, etc. They found that when CFCs are subjected to massive ultraviolet radiation they break down into their constituent chemicals: chlorine, fluorine, and carbon. It was the impact of chlorine on ozone that alarmed them. They found that each chlorine atom could destroy as many as 100,000 ozone molecules before becoming inactive. With the rapid production of CFCs for commercial and industrial use—millions of tons annually—Molina and Rowland were alarmed that the impact of CFCs on the delicate ozone layer within the stratosphere could be life-threatening.

Mario Molina published the results of his and Rowland's research in *Nature* magazine in 1974. Their findings had startling results. Molina was invited to testify before the House of Representatives's Subcommittee on Public Health and Environment. Suddenly CFCs were a popular topic of conversation. Manufacturers began searching for alternative propellant gases for their products.

Over the next several years, Molina refined his work and, with Rowland, published additional data on CFCs and the destruction of the ozone layer in such publications as *Journal of Physical Chemistry, Geophysical Research Letter* and in a detailed piece entitled "The Ozone Question" in *Science*. In 1976, Mario Molina was named to the National Science Foundation's Oversight Committee on Fluorocarbon Technology Assessment.

In 1982, Molina became a member of the technical staff at the Jet Propulsion Laboratory at CalTech; two years later he was named senior research scientist, a position he held for an additional five years. In 1989, Mario Molina left the West coast to accept the dual position of professor of atmospheric chemistry at MIT's department of Earth, atmosphere and planetary sciences, and professor in the department of chemistry. In 1990, he was one of ten environmental scientists awarded grants of $150,000 from the Pew Charitable Trusts Scholars Program in Conservation and the Environment. In 1993, he was selected to be the first holder of a chair at MIT established by the Martin Foundation, Inc., "to support research and education activities related to the studies of the environment."

Molina has published more than fifty scientific papers, the majority dealing with his work on the ozone layer and the chemistry of the atmosphere. In 1992 Molina and his wife, Luisa, wrote a monograph entitled "Stratospheric Ozone" published in the book *The Science of Global Change: The Impact of Human Activities on the Environment* published by the American Chemical Society.

His later work has also focused on the atmosphere-biosphere interface which Molina believes is "critical to understanding global climate change processes." He is the recipient of more than a dozen awards including the 1987 American Chemical Society Esselen Award, the 1988 American Association for the Advancement of Science Newcomb-Cleveland Prize, the 1989 NASA Medal for Exceptional Scientific Advancement, and the 1989 United Nations Environmental Programme Global 500 Award.

## SELECTED PUBLISHED WORKS:

(With F. Sherwood Rowland) "Stratospheric Sink for Chlorofluormethanes-Chlorine Atom Catalyzed Destruction of Ozone," *Nature,* Volume 249, number 810, 1974.

(With Rowland) "The Ozone Question," *Science,* Volume 190, number 1038, 1974.

"The Antarctic Ozone Hole," *Oceanus,* Volume 31, number 47, 1990.

*—Sketch by Benedict A. Leerburger*

# Ricardo Montalbán
## 1920-
### Mexican American actor and activist

Ricardo Montalbán has become one of the most widely recognized Hispanic actors as a result of his long career on television and in the movies. He made his acting debut on Broadway in 1940, then returned to his native Mexico for several years and became a movie star. He used this experience to land a wide variety of roles in Hollywood films. In the 1980s, he gained exposure as the star of the successful television series *Fantasy Island* and as the villain in the hit movie *Star Trek II: The Wrath of Khan.* Montalbán also founded Nosotros, an organization dedicated to helping Hispanic actors and actresses gain recognition in the entertainment industry.

Montalbán was born on November 25, 1920, in Mexico City. His parents were Jenaro and Ricarda Montalbán, who had immigrated to Mexico from Spain before he was born. When Montalbán was very young, his family moved again to Torreón in Coahuila, Mexico, where his father managed a dry goods store. In 1936, at the age of fifteen, Montalbán moved to Los Angeles to attend Fairfax High School, where he took part in several school plays and became interested in acting. In 1940, he decided to go to New York City, where he succeeded in getting a part in *Her Cardboard Lover* with Tallulah Bankhead.

Montalbán returned to Mexico in 1941, despite his success on Broadway. However, he was able to use his Broadway experience to become a star in his home country. His first movie was *He's a Latin From Staten Island,* made in 1941. He followed that film with roles in *Cinco Fueron Escogidos, El verdugo de Sevilla,* and *La Razon de la Culpa* in 1942. In 1943, he starred in *La Fuga, Santa,* and *Fantasia Ranchera.* In all, he made more than two dozen movies while he was in Mexico, including *Cadetes de la Naval, La Hora de la Verda, Nosotros,* and *Pepita Jimenez.* It was his role in 1943's *La Casa de la Zorro,* however, that brought him to the attention of Hollywood. In that film, he played the son of a bawdry house owner who learns in the end that money and women cannot buy him the happiness he seeks. In 1944, he married Georgiana Young. The couple eventually had four children: Mark, Victor, Laura, and Anita.

### Signs Contract with MGM

With his dark good looks and ability to act, sing, and dance, Montalbán came to the attention of Metro-Goldwyn-Mayer (MGM) in 1946. He signed a ten-year contract with the movie studio and appeared in his first Hollywood film, *Fiesta,* with Esther Williams in 1947. Montalbán played Williams's twin brother, a sensitive man who wants to become a composer rather than a bullfighter like his father. But his twin sister is ready to be the matador in the family, and steps into the ring when her brother fails to appear. Montalbán's character then saves his sister, becomes a hero, and is allowed to pursue his dream.

He appeared in two other movies with Esther Williams. He loses her hand to Peter Lawford in *On an Island with You,* but he finally gets to marry her in *Neptune's Daughter,* their third movie together. *Neptune's Daughter* was a significant film in the view of Hispanics, because it marked the first time a Latin actor was allowed to pursue and achieve a romantic relationship with an Anglo woman in the movies.

Being under contract to MGM meant that Montalbán could only play roles his studio bosses deemed appropriate for him. His Mexican accent and Latin appearance often were viewed negatively by studio management, so he was frequently cast as the hero's friend rather than in the lead role. For example, in *The Kissing Bandit,* Frank Sinatra played the lead role while Montalbán danced with Cyd Charisse. In *Battleground*, Montalbán played the role of George Murphy's buddy and ends up dying because he tries to save his friend's life. He also played Murphy's friend in *Border Incident*.

In 1950, Montalbán starred with June Allyson in *Right Cross*. In that film, he played a fighter who distrusts all gringos until Allyson convinces him that she loves him for who he is—a poor Mexican fighter. In his second film co-starring with Allyson, *Two Weeks with Love*, he played the stereotypical Latin lover working in a Catskills resort visited by Allyson's character and her family one summer.

Montalbán was frequently cast as the Latin lover during the 1950s. Some examples include his leading roles in *Call Me Mister* in 1951, *My Man and I* in 1952, *Latin Lovers*, and *Sombrero* in 1953. Occasionally, he also played the hero in films that had a distinct Latin theme. In *Mark of the Renegade*, released in 1951, he played a Mexican government agent sent to California to prevent an Anglo from establishing his own empire outside of Mexico's control. Montalbán's character engages in a sword duel with the man to save California.

In 1955, Montalbán played the role of victim in the suspense film *A Life in the Balance*. In that movie, his character is accused of murdering a woman who lived in the same building. However, it is actually the character played by Lee Marvin who has killed the woman. This movie was unusual for the era, in that most of the players were Hispanics rather than Anglos.

### Expands Roles

While he portrayed Hispanic characters in many of his roles, Montalbán also played characters of different ethnic or national backgrounds during the 1950s and 1960s. In *Across the Wide Missouri*, for example, he played Ironshirt, a Native American who objects to the intrusion of a beaver trapper, played by Clark Gable, and the trapper's wife. The wife is killed by the Indians. Montalbán also appeared as Japanese warlord Nakamura in *Sayonara* in 1957, as a French duke in *Love Is a Ball* in 1963, and as an Italian lover in *Sweet Charity* in 1968. He even played a priest, Father Clementi, in the 1956 movie *The Singing Nun*, with Debbie Reynolds.

Although television became popular with the U.S. public in the early 1950s, it was not until 1955 that Montalbán made his first appearance in the new medium, on *Climax!: The Mojave Kid* for Capitol Broadcasting Company (CBC). He also appeared in numerous segments of *The Loretta Young Show*, which appeared on the National Broadcasting Company (NBC). From the 1950s through the 1970s, Montalbán made guest appearances on a variety of popular series, including *Bonanza*, *The Wild Wild West*, *Mission Impossible*, *The Virginian*, *The Carol Burnett Show*, *Columbo*, *Police Story*, and *Star Trek*. In fact, it was his appearance on *Star Trek*'s "Space Seed" episode in 1967 that led to his role as the villain in the movie *Star Trek II: The Wrath of Khan* in 1982.

In addition to his guest appearances, Montalbán also starred in three television series. He became best known for his role as Mr. Rourke on *Fantasy Island*, which aired from 1978 through 1984. He also appeared regularly on *McNaughton's Daughter*, which aired for only one season in 1978. From 1985 through 1987, Montalbán played the role of Zachary Powers on *The Colbys*, which was a spinoff series from the successful drama *Dynasty*. Also during the 1980s, Montalbán became a spokesman for the Chrysler Corporation pitching the Cordoba model.

### Founds Hispanic Actors Organization

While Hollywood did use Hispanic actors in movies during the 1940s, 1950s, and 1960s, they were still not accepted into the mainstream of movie-making. That meant that few Hispanic actors and actresses won critical acclaim for their work, let alone actual awards. Montalbán was no exception. It was not until he played an Indian chief in *How the West Was Won, Part II*, that he finally received an Emmy Award for Outstanding Single Performance by a Supporting Actor in a Comedy or Drama Series in 1979. He also won a Golden Aztec Award in 1988 from the Mexican American Opportunity Foundation.

The civil rights movement of the 1960s also brought attention to the disparities between Anglos and Hispanics. In 1969, Montalbán founded a small organization for Hispanic actors and actresses called Nosotros. The main goal of the group was to promote equal opportunities for Hispanic American actors and actresses. The group also sought to improve the image of Hispanics in the movies and on television. As part of this effort, Nosotros sponsored the Golden Eagle Awards to recognize outstanding performances by Hispanics.

Over his thirty-year career, Montalbán had succeeded in finding steady employment, which was a rarity for many actors in Hollywood. But with his new, more visible role as an activist pushing for equal rights for Hispanics, Montalbán discovered that work was more difficult to find. He has continued to appear on television and in several movies, including *Escape from the Planet of the Apes* in 1971, *The Train Robbers* in 1974, *Won Ton Ton, the Dog Who Saved Hollywood* in 1975, *Joe Panther* in 1976, *Cannonball Run II* in 1983, and *The Naked Gun: From the Files of Police Squad* in 1988.

## SELECTED VIDEOGRAPHY:

*Nosotros,* 1944.
*On an Island With You,* 1948.
*Battleground,* 1949.
*Neptune's Daughter,* 1949.
*Two Weeks With Love,* 1950.
*Across the Wide Missouri,* 1951.
*Latin Lovers,* 1953.
*Sayonara,* 1957.
*Cheyenne Autumn,* 1964.
*Pirate Warrior,* 1964.
*Alice Through the Looking Glass,* 1966.
*Madame X,* 1966.
*The Singing Nun,* 1966.
*Blue,* 1968.
*Iron Cowboy,* 1968.
*Black Water,* 1969.
*Sweet Charity,* 1969.
*Escape From the Planet of the Apes,* 1971.
*Ride to Glory,* 1971.
*Conquest of the Planet of the Apes,* 1972.
*Fireball Forward,* 1972.
*Train Robbers,* 1973.
*Fantasy,* 1976.
*Joe Panther,* 1976.
*Return to Fantasy Island,* 1977.
*Mission to Glory,* 1980.
*Star Trek II: The Wrath of Khan,* 1982.
*Cannonball Run II,* 1984.
*The Naked Gun: From the Files of Police Squad,*
    1988.

## SOURCES:

Bronner, Edwin, *The Encyclopedia of the Ameri-
can Theatre 1900–1975,* New York, A. S.
Barnes, 1980, p. 418.
*The Great American Movie Book,* edited by Paul
Michael, Englewood Cliffs, NJ, Prentice-Hall,
1980.
Halliwell, Leslie, *The Filmgoer's Companion,* New
York, Hill and Wang, 1967, p. 534.
*The Hispanic-American Almanac,* edited by Nico-
lás Kanellos, Detroit, Gale, 1993.
Inman, David, *The TV Encyclopedia,* New York,
Perigee Books, 1991, pp. 587–88.
McNeil, Alex, *Total Television,* New York, Pen-
guin Books, 1991.
Meier, Matt S., and Feliciano Rivera, *Dictionary
of Mexican American History,* New York,
Greenwood Press, 1981, pp. 237, 259–60.
Meier, Matt S., *Mexican American Biographies,*
New York, Greenwood Press, 1988, pp.
143–44.
*Movie Greats,* edited by Paul Michael, New York,
Garland Books, 1969, pp. 136–37.
Quinlan, David, *Quinlan's Illustrated Registry of
Film Stars,* New York, Holt, 1991, pp.
327–28.
Richard, Alfred Chars, Jr., *Censorship and Holly-
wood's Hispanic Image,* Westport, CT, Green-
wood Press, 1993.

—*Sketch by Catherine A. Clay*

# Montezuma II
## 1466-1520
### Aztec emperor

Montezuma was the ninth Aztec emperor of
Mexico. His famous confrontation with the
Spanish conquistador **Hernándo Cortés** led to the
eventual colonization of Mexico and the erosion of
the Aztec civilization during the early sixteenth
century. Montezuma, who served as *Ueitlatoani,* or
"Great Speaker," from 1502 until shortly before his
death in 1520, presided over an empire that had
reached its greatest extent, stretching to what is now
Honduras and Nicaragua.

Noted for his courage as a warrior and his piety
as a high priest, Montezuma led several military
campaigns against neighboring tribes for the purpose
of exacting tribute for the capital city of Tenochtitlan
and acquiring victims for sacrifices to the god,
Huitzilopochtli. The religious zeal that made him a
powerful civilian and military leader, however, also
brought about his demise. Believing that Cortés'
arrival was the fulfillment of Aztec prophesy, Montezuma welcomed him into the palace as the god
Quetzalcoatl and allowed himself to be taken captive.
His submission angered the Aztec people, some of
whom threw stones and arrows at their leader when
he tried to speak to them after six months of captivity.
The injuries he suffered, according to Spanish accounts, resulted in his death three days later. However, some Aztec sources suggest that he was strangled
by the Spaniards.

Montezuma II was born into one of the leading
families of Tenochtitlan, near what is now Mexico
City, in 1468. When the young prince turned three,
his father, Axayatacl, a lord noted for his battlefield
courage and irreproachable character, was named
emperor, succeeding Montezuma I, who had ruled
since 1440. As the child of a noble family, Montezuma attended the *calmeac,* the temple school where he
was subjected to its strict ascetic lifestyle and instructed in songs of the gods and other religious texts.

*Montezuma II*

Despite his parentage, Montezuma was subjected to the same rigorous training program as the other young boys. Living on a diet of two tortillas and a cup of water a day, he was made to sleep on the bare stone floor of the temple buildings, while performing such dangerous duties as gathering the calcined bodies of scorpions and other stinging insects that were used to make the black paint worn by priests during rituals of sacrifice.

After a year or two of training as an astronomer, or priest, in which he was taught to read the painted books of magic, Montezuma was sent to a military school, where he engaged in exercises designed to develop strength, agility, and stoicism. At the age of 12, following another stint in the temple school, Montezuma entered the "house of young men," where he learned to become a warrior, gaining proficiency in battlefield techniques such as how to handle the Aztec war club, edged with obsidian blades.

Two years later, Montezuma's father died, and his uncle, Tizoc, was named Great Speaker. Now old enough to participate in raids into border towns, Montezuma distinguished himself by capturing three prisoners in single-handed combat, a feat that enabled him to achieve the special rank of *tequihua,* or "master of cuts." Following the conventions of the Aztec religion, Montezuma tied one of his prisoners to a stone, slashing him with an obsidian-bladed club until he collapsed. At that point Montezuma offered up the victim's heart to the gods—confirming the honor of the young prince.

Despite his prowess as a warrior, Montezuma spent most of the next two years in the temple, learning to become a sacrificial priest and taking up the study of magic and religion as painted in the temple books. On some occasions, though, Tizoc ordered him to lead expeditions aimed at subduing local rebellions on the outskirts of the empire.

By the time Montezuma reached the age of 20 and had served for three years as a sacrificial priest, he was given a more prominent position in military affairs. When Tizoc died in 1486, his younger brother Ahuitzotl took over as Great Speaker and ushered in a new era of Aztec conquest. Montezuma, who from his reading in the temple had become obsessed with the idea that he was fated to reestablish the ancient empire of the Toltecs, shared his uncle's ambition and participated in several campaigns that extended the Aztec empire. With the completion of the great temple in 1487, Ahuitzotl reportedly sacrificed some 20,000—nearly two complete Mixtec tribes—to the gods. While many rejoiced at such a large offering, sure to be looked upon favorably by the gods, the great sacrifice alienated many tribes and incited fear that they too would be subject to such extermination, at the whim of such a powerful ruler.

### Became Ninth Emperor of the Aztecs

While still in his early twenties, Montezuma married Tezalco, a beautiful young woman of the ruling class, whom poets had described as the "gliding jewel" of the palace. Earning recognition for both his prowess as a warrior and his learning, Montezuma quickly rose through the ranks of the Aztec military. Shortly after he turned 30, he was chosen to become Army commander-in-chief, a position that gave him overall control of the army and the responsibility of bringing new towns into subjection and punishing those who rebelled against the empire. Having attained this higher social rank, Montezuma was entitled to take another wife, and he chose the princess Acatlan, who was noted for her gentleness. While Montezuma would later, as was appropriate to Aztec social conventions, have many more wives and father numerous children—estimates range from 19 to 150—Tezalco and Acatlan were the only ones who had the honor of being "married on the mat," a distinction that set them apart in the household.

In 1502 Ahuitzotl died unexpectedly, and Montezuma, at the age of 41, was chosen to succeed him as emperor. Following the example set by his uncle, Montezuma's tenure was marked by two primary objectives: keeping the conquered tribes in order and providing more captives for sacrifice. As a military leader, Montezuma conquered at least as many cities as his celebrated predecessor, bringing territory into the empire from the fertile coastal region near what is now Veracruz. His defeat of the Soconusco also provided the realm with an ample supply of green quetzal feathers. From the Aztec theological perspective, the thousands of hearts that had been offered to the gods during Ahuitzotl's reign had enabled the Aztec empire to expand and were required to prevent disaster to the tribe.

The zealous new leader, eager to demonstrate a piety that approached his uncle's, once delivered 12,000 captives up to the war god after defeating a rebel province from Oaxaca. While attempting to keep the military affairs of the empire in order, Montezuma also expanded trade in Mexico by providing for the open sale of cocoa beans in the markets of Tenochtitlan for the first time in several generations.

### The Arrival of Cortés

The years leading up to Cortés' arrival on the Mexican coast were marked by several events that, from Montezuma's perspective as a former high priest familiar with the sacred calendars, appeared portentous. The year 1506, for instance, marked the end of an Aztec "bundle" of 52 years, a point at which the Aztec world was possibly fated to end. Despite the ominous presence of a drought, an eclipse, earthquakes, and other signs, the Aztec world, at least for the time being, did not come to an end. The new bundle of years, instead, brought auspicious signs for the Aztecs: the alliance between the rebel provinces Tlaxcala and Uexotzinco was broken, enabling Montezuma to defeat the former in battle and negotiate a peaceful settlement with the latter. But after the first few victories of the new era, a terrible disaster followed. While in the mountainous headwaters of the Atoyac river, a Mexican army was overtaken by a severe storm that drowned 1,800 men—a sign of disfavor from the gods.

In the spring of 1518, a common laborer came before Montezuma with the ominous news that a "range of mountains" appeared to be floating just off the eastern coast. After putting the man in prison to keep him under watch, Montezuma ordered one of his chief advisors to investigate the matter. The peasant's report was confirmed: two large towers were indeed spotted moving backward and forward. What is more, they were inhabited by people with white skin and long beards. Believing the visitors to be not strangers but people long dead returning to their own land, Montezuma ordered a close watch of the coast and prepared to greet them with food and gifts. Upon their arrival, however, the Spaniards, after offering hard biscuits and beads to the Aztec emissaries who met them, left the coast, promising to return at a later date.

A year later, the Spaniards returned. Again a party of Aztec noblemen was sent to bestow gifts of food and gold. The Spaniards' leader, Cortés, a small but forceful man, received them with courtesy. Accompanying the Spanish leader was a beautiful 18-year-old girl named Ce Malinalli, whom he had first met during his three-week stay in the Mayan city of Potonchan. She was invaluable to Cortés because she spoke Chontal Maya, which enabled her to communicate with Geronimo de Aguilar, a Spaniard who had acquired the Mayan language after being shipwrecked in 1511. Through these two key individuals, a conversation between Cortés and the Aztecs was possible, and a meeting with Montezuma was arranged.

### Cortés Enters Tenochtitlan

According to most historical accounts, Montezuma believed that Cortés was the Aztec god Quetzalcoatl, who was returning to fulfill prophecy and bring about the final destruction of the Aztec people. Several affinities with the Aztec myth may have led him to this conclusion. In addition to arriving at the conclusion of the 52-year period, Cortés, consistent with the Quetzalcoatl myth, came from the east, was dressed in black, and—most important—had white skin and a beard. Nevertheless, it is unknown "whether the myth of Quetzalcoatl, or Texcatlopoca, or any other deity, did or did not exercise a decisive influence over Montezuma's actions," argued Hugh Thomas in his book *Conquest: Montezuma, Cortés, and the Fall of Mexico*. "But he was exceptionally superstitious, even for a Mexican. He certainly seems, at the very least to have toyed with the idea of identifying Cortés with a lost lord who vanished into the east."

In November of 1519, after several days of resting and seeing the sights of Tenochtitlan with Montezuma's attendants, Cortés finally came before the Aztec emperor. Through Malinalli, now known as "Marina," and Aguilar, Cortés gave a speech on the virtues of Christianity and the evils of the Aztec gods, who in Cortés' opinion were devils. Montezuma listened patiently to his words and offered to send tribute to the great king beyond the waters. The Spaniards wished to visit one of the great temples, and after consultation with the priests, Montezuma consented and led them to the Great Temple honoring the two principal Aztec gods, Tlaloc and Huitzilopochtli. Upon witnessing the skulls of tens of thousands of men offered up to the gods and the monstrous obsidian idols, the Spaniards withdrew from the temple and requested that a place be cleared for a Christian cross to be erected. Although Cortés reportedly wished to have the idol destroyed, one of his priests wisely persuaded him to wait.

### Held Captive by Cortés

As tensions resulting from this conflict over religion mounted, Montezuma became less sure in his belief that Cortés was the incarnation of the god

Quetzalcoatl. Likewise, the Spaniards, after witnessing the capability of Aztec destruction, began to lose confidence in the friendly demeanor of their hosts. These mutual feelings of enmity were exacerbated by a report from Veracruz that a group of four Spaniards who had been invited to meet with an Aztec nobleman were attacked, leading to a bitter fight and the death of at least eight Spaniards. Fearing that the Spanish settlement in Veracruz might be destroyed and the line of communication with the sea be cut off, Cortés came up with a desperate plan: take the emperor captive in the hope that, just as European peasants would submit if their king were seized, the Aztecs would refrain from a violent attack on the Spaniards.

Accusing Montezuma of planning the attack at Veracruz, some of Cortés' leading military officials threatened to kill the emperor unless he agreed to be taken as a prisoner to the Palace of Axayacatl. Although he denied having any role in the attack, Montezuma agreed ultimately to accompany Cortés, asking only that he be allowed to take some of his family with him. As Montezuma was being led across town to his place of captivity, several men asked him if they should attack the Spaniards, but Montezuma insisted that he was only going to spend a few days with the Spaniards out of friendship. Despite being held prisoner, Montezuma continued to rule over his empire for several weeks, managing to persuade his people to not launch a major attack on the Spaniards.

In late April, near the Christian celebration of Easter, the Aztecs held a traditional festival in honor of the god *Huitzilopochtli*. At least 400 dancers, dressed in their feathered costumes and armed with war clubs and shields, and several thousand Aztecs participated. Presumably threatened by the concentration of so many warriors, Tonatiuh Alvarado, one of Cortés' leading men, launched a surprise attack, leading his fellow Spaniards and their Indian allies, the Tlaxcalans, in the massacre of most of the dancers and several of the unarmed bystanders.

The fighting soon spread to the streets surrounding the temple and a general call for war was made by the Aztecs, who mounted a fierce counterattack. Returning to the palace where Montezuma was held captive, the wounded Alvarado placed a knife in the emperor's chest and demanded that he order his men to call off the battle. Although many Aztecs continued fighting, they could not find a leader to organize their efforts. That, however, did not prevent their outrage against Montezuma, who never recovered his authority after this display of what most Aztecs considered to be cowardice.

Upon Cortés' return to the capital city, having defeated a much larger, better equipped force at Cempoalla, the fighting resumed. In late June in 1520, Montezuma was asked by Cortés to go again to the rooftop to speak to his people. After first refusing, the emperor consented to make an appeal to the Aztecs to stop the fighting. Before he could speak, he was hit by a stone. Some sources suggest that the Aztec captains openly defied Montezuma's authority. **Cuauhtemoc,** who would later become the last Aztec emperor, shouted: "We do not want to obey him because already he is no longer our monarch and, indeed, we must give him the punishment which we give to a wicked man," according to Smith.

A shower of stones followed, hitting the Emperor three times. According to Spanish sources, the Spaniards attempted to treat Montezuma's wounds. But either he refused treatment or simply wished to live no longer—possibly, as some sources suggest, so the Aztecs would be free to elect a new ruler. On the morning of June 30, as the fighting continued, Montezuma died. Denied the traditional ceremonies of an emperor's funeral, Montezuma's body was dishonorably burned at Copulco.

## SOURCES:

Burland, C. A., *Montezuma: Lord of the Aztecs,* New York, G.P. Putnam's Sons, 1973.

Thomas, Hugh, *Conquest: Montezuma, Cortés, and the Fall of Old Mexico,* New York, Simon & Schuster, 1993.

*—Sketch by Jason Gallman*

# Carlos García Montoya
## 1903-1993
### Spanish American guitarist

During a career that spanned four decades, flamenco guitarist Carlos Montoya performed for audiences worldwide, made dozens of recordings, and composed a concerto for solo guitar and orchestra. In the process, Montoya almost singlehandedly brought the flamenco guitar from the position of accompanist to center stage as a solo instrument. "Few guitarists have done as much to make people around the world aware of flamenco music," intoned Maurice Summerfield in *The Classical Guitar.*

On December 13, 1903, Carlos García Montoya was born in Madrid to Juan García, who sold mules for a living, and his wife Emilia Montoya. After his father died when Carlos was only two years old, the boy was raised by his mother, an amateur flamenco

*Carlos Montoya*

guitarist. At age eight, young Carlos began guitar lessons with his mother, and he later studied with a local barber-guitar teacher, Pepe el Barbero. Through his mother and her brother Ramón Montoya Salazar, who was a famous flamenco guitarist, the young Montoya was immersed in the dazzling sounds of flamenco. After Montoya surpassed his teacher in skill, he never studied formally again. In his autobiography, *The Gypsy in My Soul,* colleague José Greco described Montoya as being "a little rough, a little wild, a friendly fellow but unpolished . . . a string combination of sophistication and primitivism" during the years they performed together.

Flamenco guitar was in Montoya's blood. His four grandparents were Gypsies, an ethnic group that arrived in Spain from northern India in the fifteenth century and was forced by royal decree to settle in Andalusia, a province in southern Spain. During the next two hundred years, the Spanish gypsies incorporated qualities of Arab, Christian, Jewish, and Spanish folk music into their own music. In so doing, they created modern flamenco, a highly improvisatory type of music, greatly dependent upon a practioners creativity, that includes audiences' clapping and calls, dancers' toe tapping and castanet clacking, as well as singers' voices.

Despite his lack of formal instruction, Montoya was accomplished enough by age 14 to play with troupes headed by such well known performers as La Camisona, La Macarrona, Antonio de Bilbao, and

Juan el Estampio. In the evenings, while playing in bars and restaurants—the typical venue for flamenco music—Montoya learned as much as he could from fellow performers about the special Gypsy rhythms and chord patterns upon which flamenco guitarists base their improvisations. Performing paid little, so during the day he worked as a postal clerk and later at a courthouse.

As required by law, Montoya joined the army in 1924 for a three-year stint; he was stationed in Morocco, where he played his guitar whenever he was not on duty. Upon completion of his military service, Montoya settled in Madrid. There he resumed playing in cafes. In 1928, the young guitarist attracted the attention of Antônia Mercé, a famous flamenco dancer who performed under the stage name "La Argentina." Mercé hired Montoya to play with her troupe on its tour of Europe. Later Montoya teamed up with well known dancer Vicente Escudero, and in 1933, he toured the United States and the Far East with a troupe led by La Teresina. While in Japan, Montoya was offered and subsequently declined a teaching position at a university; instead, he allowed the Japanese to make a motion picture of him for instructional purposes.

Five years later, Montoya worked with flamenco dancer "La Argentinita"—also known as Encarnación López—whose troupe toured South America and the United States. While on a tour of the United States, Montoya had the good fortune to run into Sallie MacLean, a flamenco dancer from the United States known as "La Trianita"; the two had previously met in Paris at the home of MacLean's dance teacher. Hitting it off, the couple was married on May 4, 1940, and settled in Manhattan. Montoya eventually became a U.S. citizen; the evening of his naturalization, Montoya performed for U.S. president Harry Truman.

## Embarked on Solo Career

Shortly after La Argentinita's death in 1945, Montoya decided to venture out on his own. It was a move that he had been contemplating for some time. His uncle, Ramón Montoya Salazar, had already begun performing solo guitar concerts. In the role of an accompanist, flamenco guitarists traditionally were not allowed many opportunities to dazzle audiences. Following his uncle's lead, Montoya dispensed with singers and dancers and changed his typical venue from cafe-bar to a concert stage lit with pink lights, where he sat on a stool before a microphone.

In his solo performances, Montoya learned to produce a variety of percussive sounds, such as heel clacks and tambourine rattles—sounds that dancers would make in a troupe. One *New York Times* reviewer marvelled at Montoya's technique, saying of him, "The soloist was especially skillful in the suggestion of such picturesque noises as tambourines, the stamping of heels in a dance, the clatter of castanets, snapping fingers, and even the snare drums of a military band." Another listener once described hearing the sounds of an advancing army, weeping and wailing, and a religious procession. Commentators have also remarked upon the amazing manual dexterity that literally allowed Montoya to become a one-man flamenco troupe. His guitars, custom made by well known flamenco guitar maker Arcangel Fernández of Madrid, sported metal plates designed to prevent damage from the guitarist's vigorous tapping.

Expecting languid Spanish folk songs, North American audiences were not immediately receptive to Montoya's rhythmically charged playing. Montoya recalled to *The Reporter*'s Nat Hentoff, "At that time the first reaction to flamenco in most Americans I met was to ask what it was." Yet before long, with his gracious rapport and virtuoso playing, Montoya attracted sellout crowds. He thrived under the spotlight; audiences energized him. "He has to reach out to people, and that's when he starts to be creative," Sallie Montoya, the guitarist's wife, once told Janet Weiner of *International Musician*. "He's hooked on audiences. To Carlos, his music doesn't really exist except when he's playing it for people." In fact, according to his wife, Montoya would often practice silently, moving his fingers above the strings.

Montoya spent most of his life on tour in North and South America, Europe, and the Far East. He often performed at small venues—universities and colleges—as well as concert halls and invariably attracted large crowds. Acting as the guitarist's translator and interpreter, Sallie Montoya often accompanied her husband on concert tours. Throughout his long career, Montoya embroidered his concerts around only 60 themes. Yet he declared that he never played a piece the same way twice. Proud of his heritage, Montoya maintained that while non-Gypsies might learn to play in the flamenco style, only a true Gypsy could play flamenco from the heart. As he told Weiner, "You make the guitar mirror your feelings. Other than that, one cannot be said to really 'learn flamenco.'"

### Composed a Flamenco Concerto

To help preserve this art form, Montoya, who had never learned to read music, collaborated with others to notate some of his flamenco themes and give instructions on how each should be played. In the 1940s, José Iturbi was the first to encourage Montoya to create a piece for guitar and orchestra, but it was not until the 1960s that Montoya approached the effort seriously. With the help of Julio Esteban and Estela Bringuer, Montoya composed *Suite Flamenca* for solo guitar with orchestra accompaniment. The concerto consists of four parts, with solos and lengthy cadenzas for the guitar that allow the guitarist to improvise. Montoya first performed *Suite Flamenca* with the St. Louis Symphony Orchestra in January of 1966, and later recorded it on the United Artists label. Creating the flamenco concerto was one of Montoya's most memorable events of his career.

During his lifetime, Montoya made many recordings with a number of companies, among them Paramount and RCA. His albums include *Flamenco Fire, Adventures in Flamenco, Aires Flamenco, Flamenco Holiday, Recital de Guitare Espagnole, Flamenco Direct,* and *Malagueña*. Montoya especially appreciated recording for their ability to safeguard Gypsy heritage. Nonetheless, Montoya expanded the scope of his music in the 1970s to include non-flamenco elements, including folk, blues, jazz, and country. This evolution presaged the development of "new flamenco" groups, such as Ketama and Pata Negra, which combined salsa with flamenco. Though some flamencologists decried Montoya's musical fusions, audiences packed the halls.

In 1989, at age 85, Montoya toured the United States for the last time, bidding farewell to his myriad fans. He died of heart failure on March 3, 1993, in Wainscott, New York. Montoya was survived by his wife and two sons, Carlos, Jr., and Allan.

## SOURCES:

### Books

*The Annual Obituary 1993,* edited by Louise Mooney Collins and Lorna Mpho Mabunda, Detroit, St. James Press, 1993.
*Current Biography Yearbook,* New York, Wilson, 1993.
Greco, José, *The Gypsy in My Soul: The Autobiography of José Greco,* Garden City, Doubleday, 1977.
Gregory, Hugh, *1000 Great Guitarists,* San Francisco, GPI Books, 1994.
*Newsmakers: 1993 Cumulative,* edited by Louise Mooney, Detroit, Gale, 1994.
Prohen, D. E., *Lives and Legends of Flamenco: A Biographical History,* Madrid, Society of Spanish Studies, 1988.
Summerfield, Maurice J., *The Classical Guitar: It's Evolution, Players and Personalities Since 1800,* Newcastle-upon-Tyne, Ashley Mark Publishing, 1992.

### Periodicals

*Guardian,* April 5, 1993, section 2, p. 12.
*International Musician,* November, 1981, pp. 6, 15.

*Los Angeles Times,* October 16, 1989, p. F6;
   March 6, 1993, p. A24.
*New York Times,* March 5, 1993, p. A20.
*New Yorker,* June 3, 1950, p. 20.
*The Reporter,* January 8, 1959, pp. 44–46.
*Time,* March 15, 1993, p. 23.
*Washington Post,* March 6, 1993, p. C4.

—*Sketch by J. M. Lesinski*

# José Montoya
## 1932-
### Hispanic American artist, poet, and educator

José Montoya, an artist and poet, was a pioneer of the Chicano cultural movement. He is a founder of the Royal Chicano Air Force, a Sacramento-based artist collective known for its political posters and murals and community art projects. Montoya is also a leading Mexican American poet; his 1972 poem "El Louie" excited new interest in Chicano poetry. Montoya is "a literary rebel" and "one of the true legends of the *movimiento,*" wrote Ray González in *The Nation.*

An art professor at Sacramento State University since the early 1970s, Montoya has sought to encourage generations of young Chicanos to explore their cultural identity through creativity. He draws inspiration from life in the barrio, mixing an urgent call for political action with personal artistic expression. His message has always been for Chicanos to stay true to their history and culture. "But you can't be producing Chicano art if you stop being Chicana/Chicano. Chicano art was born out of struggle—the struggle goes on!" wrote Montoya in the catalog for *Chicano Art: Resistance and Affirmation, 1965–1985,* an exhibit organized by UCLA's Wight Art Gallery in 1990.

Montoya is a third-generation Mexican American. His Mexican ancestors received a federal land grant to settle in the mountains of New Mexico during the nineteenth century. He was born during a prolonged drought on a ranch outside of Albuquerque on May 28, 1932. One of nine children, Montoya was one of seven who survived. Soon after his birth, his father, Malaquías Montoya, was sent to prison in Leavenworth, Kansas, for making corn liquor during Prohibition. The boy grew up in the company of his great-grandmother and great aunts. "I have vivid memories about hardships, but I was also endowed with a lot of affection and a lot of love," recalled Montoya in an interview with contributor Ann Malaspina.

Montoya's mother, Lucia (Saiz), exposed him to art at an early age. While his father was gone, she helped support the family by painting the window frames and arches of home interiors with decorative motifs and borders. "I was enthralled at how she mixed her own colors. We used to go on excursions to look for materials and colors, tapping various levels of arroyo creeks for the yellow ocher colors," he recalled. She would grind and mix the tail of the horsefly with egg yolk to make paint. He was also fascinated by the storytelling tradition that thrived in the village.

After Montoya's father returned, the family moved to Albuquerque in 1938. Montoya began school in the barrio of Martíneztown. He did not adjust well to city life, so his parents sent him back to live with his grandparents in the mountains for a time. In 1941 Montoya's father signed up with a farm labor contractor to work in California. The family followed, taking the long trip by car and train. They were turned away from Bakersfield, California, because they were Mexican American. The family moved on to the Sierra Vista Ranches near Delano. His parents cooked for the single men, and Montoya, at age nine, worked in the fields. "Pulling grapes off the vines doesn't require you to be an adult," he said. "It was easy to exploit children."

He attended school sporadically, skipping a year when he was 13, while he worked and cared for younger siblings. "We were traveling around with three or four families who pooled their resources to move from place to place, looking for work," he recalled to Malaspina. He returned to New Mexico to finish the eighth grade. The family followed, then moved back to California, where his parents and two older sisters worked in the Oakland shipyards during World War II. In 1950 his parents separated and his father returned to New Mexico.

### A Mentor Encourages His Writing and Art

Montoya's mother decided the family should settle down. "My mother gave me the choice to quit school or go to work. She would do whatever was necessary for me to finish school. I decided to stay in school and work after school and weekends to help the family," he said. They moved to Fowler, near Fresno. His mother took public assistance so that Montoya and his younger sister could stay in school. His English teacher at Fowler High School, Adrian Sanford, became an important mentor who urged him to pursue his writing and art. He praised an essay Montoya wrote about his father's humiliating experience of being cleaned of lice in prison. "He was the first one to tell me I had a facility with words that I should do something with," he recalled to Malaspina. In 1951 Montoya became the first member of his family to graduate from high school.

But Montoya also liked to hang out on the streets of Fresno with "guys from the neighborhood," he recalled. They imitated the Chicano *pachucos* ("gangs") of the World War II period in their hairstyles and clothing. Montoya would later celebrate the *pachucos* in his art and poetry. Montoya called them "the first Chicano freedom-fighters of the Chicano movement," in *Pachuco Art: A Historical Update*. After Montoya was arrested for fighting a second time, a judge asked him to choose between the Marine Corps and six months in road camps. The Marine Corps rejected Montoya, though, because he had a tattoo of a cross that identified him as a *pachuco* gang member. He changed the cross into an anchor, and the Navy accepted him. He served on a minesweeper from 1951 to 1955 during the Korean War. He read books in his spare time and grew particularly fond of the work of John Steinbeck.

After the war, Montoya married his first wife, Mary Prieto; they eventually had six children. The newlyweds moved to San Diego, where he worked for a window company. He also attended night school at San Diego City College under the GI Bill, a program wherein the United States government paid for the college education of military veterans. He earned an associate of arts degree in 1956. In 1957 Montoya received an art scholarship to the California College of Arts and Crafts in Oakland, where he earned a bachelors degree in fine arts. He decided to stay an extra year to get teaching credentials in 1962. His teaching career began at Wheatland High School in Wheatland, California, in 1963. He also joined in efforts to unionize local farm workers.

The Chicano movement began in the 1960s on several fronts. Farm workers in California and Texas, students on college campuses, the land grant owners of New Mexico, and the working class families of the Southwest and Midwest all contributed to the growth of the movement. The word "Chicano" derived, in part, from "Mexicano," a derisive term for unskilled Mexican workers. Earl Shorris in *Latinos* wrote that Mexican American activists call themselves Chicanos "as an act of defiance and a badge of honor." Chicano art, which often took the form of murals and posters, was a crucial piece of the movement, which peaked in the late 1960s and early 1970s. Many artists grouped together to create community-based and public art during this period.

In 1959 Montoya and other Chicano students exhibited their art during a conference sponsored by the Mexican American Political Association. "We realized we'd be involved in changing things for the Chicano people," he recalled to Malaspina. Montoya then joined with Esteban Villa, Malaquías Montoya, Manuel Hernández, and other activists to form the Mexican American Liberation Art Front (MALAF). In 1969, as the Chicano movement surged in popularity, Montoya was offered a fellowship to Sacramento State University. He earned a master of fine arts degree in 1971 and began to teach in the school's department of art education; by 1981 Montoya was a full professor at Sacramento State.

## The Royal Chicano Air Force

In 1970 and 1971, Montoya and Villa joined with students at Sacramento State to organize the Rebel Chicano Art Front, which became a well-known collective of Chicano artists. "The idea was to use art as an organizing tool for the movement," explained Montoya to Malaspina. The motto of the group was *La locura lo cura* ("Craziness is its own cure") and the members often used humor to reach out to the community. After people noticed the acronym was identical to the Royal Canadian Air Force, the group renamed itself the Royal Chicano Air Force. "People began to make us into an air force. They donated flying machines. Someone gave us an old army jeep," recalled Montoya to Malaspina. The artists even dressed the part. "We would boycott Safeway in jeeps, looking like World War II bomber pilots."

The RCAF "sprang from and celebrates Chicano barrio life and the farms and factories where Chicanos work," wrote Maya Valverde in *Artweek* in 1991. In her review of an RCAF poster art retrospective at the Galeria de la Raza in San Francisco, Valverde asserted that "Art-as-activism is the raison d'etre for the Royal Chicano Air Force," and credited the RCAF with defining Chicano art as a genre. The themes of RCAF poster art "mix the modern with traditional Chicano/Mexicano cultures, and link past and present," observed Valverde. "There are posters for the migrant workers, the United Farmworkers Union, the cannery workers . . . and many other community struggles that sought out the RCAF posters to announce their cause."

The RCAF formed a community arts program called "Art in the Barrio" in Sacramento, and offered art classes to Chicano children, high school students, and senior citizens. The program also sponsored poster-making and mural projects. Classes were held at the Centro de Artistes Chicanos, a cultural center founded in 1972 by Montoya and others that was also used as the site for numerous poetry and theater projects. "Art is actually a very necessary means to pass on, continue the culture, to keep it vibrant and alive, and use to do political organizing," noted Montoya in his interview with Malaspina.

As an artist, Montoya was influenced by the Mexican engraver José Guadalupe Posado and muralists **Diego Rivera, José Clemente Orozco,** and **David Alfara Siqueiros.** Montoya's work appeared in one of the first national exhibitions of Chicano art in 1973 at Trinity University in San Antonio. He was named to the National Task Force on Hispanic Arts, formed by the National Endowment for the Arts in November

1977. His paintings and graphic art projects have been widely exhibited.

Montoya's most memorable art includes his 1977 *Pachuco Series,* a depiction of the tough urban Chicano of the 1940s and 1950s. Michael Ennis, writing in *Texas Monthly,* described Montoya's work as a "deft black and white paean to this colorful subculture. In one brush-and-ink drawing, Montoya depicts the characteristic long shoulder-padded coat in a few vertical strokes, the face in a few uncannily evocative horizontal movements."

### His First Poems Are Published

Although Montoya had been an avid reader and writer since his youth, he was not published until 1969, when nine of his poems appeared in *El Espejo,* a Chicano anthology. Among the poems published was one of Montoya's favorites, "La jefita" ("Little Woman Chief"), a work about his mother. The poem mixed fond sentiment with the harsh reality of his mother's hardworking life as an itinerant farm worker.

Like his art, Montoya's poetry combined political messages, cultural awareness, and personal insight. He used the powerful *caló* vernacular, mixing Spanish and English slang, to explore Chicano themes. "I got in trouble using that way of writing with professors who insisted I should write in Spanish or English," recalled Montoya in his interview with Malaspina. His influences include Walt Whitman, William Faulkner, William Carlos Williams, the American Beat Poets, and French symbolists. Although he admired Steinbeck, he felt that his depictions of farm workers were not always accurate. "The way he portrayed Mexicans in California (in *Tortilla Flat*) made me very mad. I knew these people and I knew they didn't behave like that."

Most of Montoya's writing was published in pamphlets, chapbooks, and small-press collections. In 1972 Montoya published his first book, *El sol y los de abajo and Other R.C.A.F. Poems.* The title poem—"The Sun and the Underdogs"—attempts to describe the Chicano world view. "It includes the recognition that we have a legitimate claim to this continent," explained Montoya to Malaspina. His widely anthologized poem "El Louie" discusses a man named Louie Rodríguez, with whom Montoya grew up. He was a hero in Korea, came home, got involved in drugs, and finally died as a result. One of the best-known of Chicano poems, it is considered by some critics to be a classic portrayal of a *pachuco.* In recognition of his work Montoya received several honors, including a Writer's Fellowship from California State University and a National Endowment for the Arts Writing Fellowship. In 1982 he married his second wife, Juanita Jue, and had three children with her.

Montoya's second book, *Information: 20 Years of Joda,* appeared in 1992. Reviewing the book for *The Nation,* Ray González wrote: "Coming from one of the true legends of the movimiento, Montoya's selected poems will create vicious arguments, along with laughter, dismay and whoops of joy because many people never expected him to get this far." The book collected poems from 1969 to 1989 and included "El Louie," "Eslipping and Esliding," "Until They Leave Us A Loan," and "Arroz Is Arroz Is Arroz." Gonzalez contended that "[Montoya's] poetry, twenty-five years after the marches, boycotts and brown berets, still cries out against the social injustice that binds his people." Montoya continues to live in Sacramento and teach at Sacramento State. In the mid-1990s he continued work on a new book entitled *How I Came to America.*

## SELECTED PUBLISHED WORKS:

*El sol y los de abajo and Other R.C.A.F. Poems,* Pocho-Che, 1972.
*Pachuco Art: A Historical Update,* Royal Chicano Air Force, 1977.
*Thoughts on la Cultura, the Media, Con Safos and Survival,* Galeria de la Raza/Studio 24, 1979.
*Information: Twenty Years of Joda,* Chusma House, 1992.

## SOURCES:

### Books

*Chicano Art: Resistance and Affirmation, 1965–1985,* Los Angeles, Wight Art Gallery, University of California, 1991.
*Dictionary of Literary Biography: Chicano Writers,* second series, edited by Francisco A. Lomelí and Carl R. Shirley, Detroit, Gale, 1992, pp. 177–82.
*The Latin American Spirit: Art and Artists in the United States, 1920–1970,* New York, Bronx Museum of the Arts and Harry N. Abrams, Inc., 1988.
*Mexican American Biographies: A Historical Dictionary, 1836–1987,* edited by Matt S. Meier, New York, Greenwood Press, 1988, pp. 144–45.
Shorris, Earl, *Latinos: A Biography of the People,* New York, W. W. Norton & Company, 1992.

### Periodicals

*Art in America,* June 1992, pp. 85–90.
*Artweek,* February 28, 1991, p. 15.
*The Nation,* January 31, 1994, pp. 131–33.
*Texas Monthly,* July 1993, pp. 52–7.

**Other**

Montoya, José, interview with Ann Malaspina, December 23, 1994.

—*Sketch by Ann Malaspina*

# Richard Montoya
## 1960-
### Mexican American actor and comedian

Richard Montoya is an actor and comedian who cofounded the comedy troupe Culture Clash. Group members explore serious issues through humorous sketches they write and then perform. The group has generated some controversy even as it has captured audiences with its biting social and political commentary. The members of Culture Clash have been compared to the Marx Brothers, and have appeared in several films together, including the feature film *Hero,* starring Dustin Hoffman.

Montoya was born in Sacramento, California, in 1960. He remarked in an interview that his original aim when he co-founded the troupe in 1984 was to entertain Latinos, but Culture Clash has garnered a broad enough audience to sustain a show of the same name for the Fox Television Network. The success of the show, in turn, caused the group's stage work to be more technically sophisticated. Montoya told *Drama-Logue,* "We pride ourselves that we push the limits to what we believe Chicano theater has not done in the past, and we really have fused theater with audio and visuals—the sound that you hear, the lights, it's a whole experience that we push to its boundaries."

The group, which originally had six members, began in the San Francisco area and performed in small theaters in California before launching a successful television series and a film career. The group also made an independent short film that debuted at the Sundance Film Festival. *Columbus on Trial,* released in 1993, addresses the debate surrounding explorer Christopher Columbus and his so-called "discovery" of America, which was followed by the plundering of indigenous peoples who had settled in the western region of the United States.

Stage shows produced and performed by Culture Clash include *The Mission* and *A Bowl of Beings.* The latter show was performed at the Los Angeles Theatre Center and televised as a PBS special. For this, Culture Clash received the Golden Eagle Award in 1992 from Nosotros, a Los Angeles-based theater company. Following the 1992 Los Angeles riots, the comics wrote and performed *SOS-Comedy for These Urgent Times,* which was performed at the Japan-America Cultural Center.

The troupe performed in the films *Falling Down,* which starred Michael Douglas and Robert Duvall, the teen comedy *Encino Man,* and *Hero,* starring Hoffman and Geena Davis. They also performed in the 1993 film, *Mi Vida Loca.* Culture Clash also put their talents to use as writers of the comedy screenplay, *Gomez, Gomez and Gomez,* the story of three bumbling detectives hired by a museum to find and recover a stolen Mexican Indian headdress. Like all of their work, the story lampoons the different levels of society. Culture Clash was negotiating a production deal for the film in 1994.

By 1994, the troupe had three members: Montoya, Ric Salinas, and Herbert Siguenza. A fourth founding member—and the only woman—Marga Gomez, who had left to pursue a solo career, rejoined Culture Clash for its stage show "Carpa Clash." *Carpa* means tent in Spanish, and the show was inspired by tent shows—the Mexican equivalent of the vaudeville acts of the 1930s, 1940s, and 1950s. The comedy troupe followed the tradition of combining news-telling with social commentary in the show, drawing especially on current political trends.

Montoya described the show as "complex storytelling" with "well-informed" material. He remarked in *Drama-Logue:* "There's a number of storylines in 'Carpa Clash,' but mainly it's how we got together—why it is we do what we do, what holds us back, what pushes us forward, what galvanizes us, and what sends us out in different ways. What we're seeing is that we are uniquely American. Culture Clash is an American comedy group."

**SOURCES:**

*Drama-Logue,* December 2–8, 1993, p. 6.
*Hollywood News,* April 28, 1994, p. 4.
*Variety,* April 28, 1994, pp. 3, 33.

—*Sketch by Karen Withem*

# Manuel Montt
## 1809-1880
### Chilean president

Manuel Montt, who served as president of Chile from 1851 to 1861, was a controversial figure. Though he instituted important reforms to the Chilean economy and educational system, the intense opposition he engendered led to two civil wars and the formation of distinct political parties. His later success as a diplomat helped him to be viewed more positively by historians.

Montt was born in 1809 to a well-connected but poor family. He was educated at the Instituto Nacional, and he became its deputy rector in 1832 and its rector in 1835. At the time, the university had begun to emphasize the fields of literature and philology. "The educational system quickly responded to these new impulses," Isaac Joslin Cox wrote in the 1935 book *Argentina, Brazil, and Chile since Independence.* Montt and his contemporaries, educated during this time of expansion in teaching, passed on the legacy. "The National Institute, under the rectorship of Manuel Montt and Antonio Varas, trained men both for secondary teaching and for political careers," Cox noted. The study of science was also encouraged.

Montt entered politics as a senior official in the Ministry of the Interior. Later he became Minister of the Interior and External Relations from 1840 to 1841, serving in the posts again from 1845 to 1846. He was Minister of Education from 1841 to 1845. Montt grew to be considered as a likely candidate for the presidential succession at the end of Manuel Bulnes's term as president. The Liberal party in Congress was strongly opposed to the selection of Montt, however, and formed the radical Sociedad de la Igualdad ("Society of Equality") in response. The party objected to Montt because of his conservative views and achievements. In fact, the objections to Montt eventually resulted in two civil wars. "Montt, though of a comparatively poor country family, was a thorough supporter of the existing conditions, and as the designated candidate for the presidency, let no chances interfere with his prospects," Cox explained.

Prior to the election, the government suppressed the Sociedad de la Igualdad, which in turn resorted to an armed revolt. "Making use of its extraordinary powers, the government declared a state of siege, stopped opposition papers, and exiled leaders," Cox described. "This repression served to spread the mischief rather than to stop it." In April 1851, a mutiny broke out in Santiago and 100 lives were lost. The opposition was not beaten yet, however. A second revolt broke out in La Serena, where 3,500 men were led by General José María de la Cruz.

### Takes Office during Civil War

Thus, as Montt took office on September 18, 1851, in a win supported by the Bulnes government, Chile was in the midst of a civil war. Troops loyal to the outgoing president soon quelled the insurrection, but Montt nonetheless instigated sweeping emergency powers. During his ten-year term as president, he was an active yet conservative leader. He was determined to improve Chile's economy by stimulating private

enterprise, which would in turn enhance national development.

Several of his presidential accomplishments included the near-completion of the Santiago-Valparaiso railroad as well as the first stage of the publicly financed railroad leading south from Santiago. He also presided over installation of the country's first electric telegraph lines, the first use of gas lighting on city streets, and a reorganization of the postal service. Montt's government also established the Caja de Crédito Hipotecario ("Land Mortgage Bank") in 1856 to stimulate more productive agriculture. As a holdover from Montt's days as a rector, the government also expanded and improved the country's educational system. Toward the end of his tenure, however, his presidency was plagued with economic recession and political tension.

Because Montt was not on the best of terms with the Archbishop of Santiago, some of his party felt alienated and formed their own Conservative party, which then joined forces with the Liberals in an opposition alliance called the Liberal-Conservative fusion. By December 1858, the opposition had become so vocal that Montt declared a state of siege and imprisoned leading members of the group. In 1859, revolts broke out in several cities, one of which, in the north, took some time to suppress.

After retiring as president in 1861, Montt held several other high government positions, including President of the Supreme Court, senator, and Councillor of State. In 1864, he represented Chile at the American Congress in Lima, Peru. "Led by Manuel Montt of Chile, the congress protested against the Chincha occupation [Spanish-held islands off of Peru], and in October and again in December negotiated with the chief of the Spanish forces for their return to Peru and for the restoration of friendly relations between Lima and Madrid," Robert N. Burr noted in *By Reason or Force.* "Montt of Chile convincingly argued for a voluntary arrangement, emphasizing the merits of unrestricted national sovereignty." The ensuing Treaty of Union and Defensive Alliance and Treaty on the Conservation of Peace, signed at the conference, provided a testament to Montt's diplomatic skills.

William F. Sater, in *Chile and the War of the Pacific,* noted that Montt remained politically active late in his life. For example, he and Antonio Varas again joined forces to create the Montt Varistas party. "A secular version of the Conservatives, they sought to retain the Portalian state without having to pay homage to the Catholic Church," Sater wrote. "Over the years, however, the lines distinguishing the National party from its contemporaries had blurred; instead of advocating firm political ideals, it had degenerated into an epicene clique."

Despite his diplomatic successes, Montt was still not favored by everyone. Sater noted that Varas was "aware that his involvement with Montt had made him one of the most despised men in Chile." The years preceding Montt's death in 1880 were relatively tranquil, however. The intense political rivalries he had engendered during his time in office were eventually forgotten, and even some of his strongest opponents came to appreciate his energy and vision.

## SOURCES:

### Books

*Argentina, Brazil, and Chile since Independence,* edited by A. Curtis Wilgus, Washington, DC, George Washington University Press, 1935, pp. 311–313.

Burr, Robert N., *By Reason or Force: Chile and the Balancing of Power in South America, 1830–1905,* Los Angeles, University of California Press, 1967, pp. 92–96.

*Encyclopedia of Latin America,* edited by Helen Delpar, New York, McGraw-Hill, 1974, pp. 387–388.

Sater, William F., *Chile and the War of the Pacific,* Lincoln, University of Nebraska Press, 1986, pp. 181–183.

—*Sketch by Kathe A. Conti*

# Pat Mora
## 1942-
### Mexican American poet and educator

While Pat Mora has earned distinction as both a poet and an educator, she is best known for the cause that requires all of her talents: cultural appreciation and conservation. Mora has been essential to the movement to understand and uphold Mexican American culture. As a poet, she explores the theme of identity, especially that of woman and her connection with the earth. As an educator, she has promoted cultural exploration by others. Mora, who has led many to ponder their own cultural backgrounds, has worked variously as an instructor, an assistant to administrators, and a museum director; she has also given poetry readings and presentations, served on various committees, written, and performed as a wife and mother simultaneously. She provides an excellent model for young Hispanics who

are just beginning to understand the past and are about to experience promising futures.

Mora was born January 19, 1942, to Raul Antonio and Estella (Delgado) Mora. She grew up in the town of her birth, El Paso, Texas, where her father was a practicing optician. Mora's mother, Estella, stayed home to care for her children. As many young minorities do, Mora eschewed family customs. The knowledge that some mainstream Americans thought that Mexican Americans were inferior fed her preference to look and feel "American." The young Mora would speak Spanish at home to her grandmother and her aunt, but she would try to ignore her ethnicity in school, and would cringe when her father played Mexican music on the radio. She would not realize that assimilation meant a loss of cultural identity until later.

Shortly after receiving a bachelor's degree from Texas Western College in 1963, Mora married William H. Burnside. With Burnside, she had three children, William, Elizabeth, and Cecilia. Mora began to teach at a school in the El Paso Independent School District, where she stayed until 1966. By 1967, Mora had earned her master's degree from the University of Texas at El Paso, and from 1971 to 1978 she taught English and Communications part-time at El Paso Community College. Changing to a part-time lecturer in 1979, Mora remained in this position until 1981, the same year that she and her first husband divorced. It was also during 1981 that she became the assistant to the vice president of academic affairs.

### Discovers Value of Mexican Heritage

Living near the Mexican border and surrounded by Mexican American relatives and friends, Mora could not fight the influence of Mexican culture. She finally began to appreciate her birthright for the gift that it was. As she explained in the *Christian Science Monitor,* she is now devoted to her culture. "I revel in a certain Mexican passion not for life or about life, but *in* life, a certain intensity in the daily living of it, a certain abandon in such music, in the hugs, sometimes in the anger."

Mora's intense concern for her culture needed an outlet; she began to express her feelings in writing. She related her desire to write in *Contemporary Authors.* "For a variety of complex reasons, anthologized American literature does not reflect the ethnic diversity of the United States. I write, in part, because Hispanic perspectives need to be part of our literary heritage; I want to be part of that validation process. I also write because I am fascinated by the pleasure and power of words." Mora believes that Hispanic writers need to make their mark on American literature, and that Hispanic culture can be preserved by and in literature.

Despite the stress that inevitably accompanies a divorce and a change in career, Mora managed to establish a reputation in literary circles during the early 1980s. She contributed to *Revista Chicano-Riquena: Kikiriki/Children's Literature Anthology,* which was published by Arte Público Press in 1981 under the editorship of Sylvia Cavazos Pena. Shortly thereafter, Mora's career as a writer and advocate of cultural appreciation began to take off. From 1983 to 1984, she hosted the radio show, *Voices: The Mexican-American in Perspective,* on KTEP, a National Public Radio affiliate. She received her first important literary award for her creative writing in 1983, when she was recognized by the National Association for Chicano Studies.

## Gains Fame as Writer

Mora's next award came from New America: Women Artists and Writers of the Southwest, for her poetry, in 1984. She found time to serve on the board of her local YWCA, and did so until 1988. 1984 was a year of professional and personal triumph for Mora. In addition to the New America award, she was honored with the Harvey L. Johnson Book Award from the Southwest Council of Latin American Studies. Her first poetry collection, *Chants,* was published by the Arte Público Press of the University of Houston in 1986. Soon after, she married Vernon Lee Scarborough, an archaeologist who studies the Maya of Central America.

In 1986, Mora once again contributed to a children's literature anthology edited by Pena, *Tun-Ta-Ca-Tun.* That same year, she also received a Kellogg National Fellowship. With this aid, she began to study international and national issues of cultural conservation. Mora's work made her an invaluable source of information—she was asked to become a consultant to the W. K. Kellogg Foundation on U.S.-Mexican youth exchanges, and to serve on the advisory committee for the Kellogg National Fellowship program. She served as a member of the Texas Commission on the Arts's Literary Advisory Panel from 1987 to 1988, and as a poetry judge for the Texas Institute of Letters in 1988. Also in 1988, Arte Público released *Borders,* Mora's second collection of poetry. Both *Chants* and *Borders* won Southwest Book Awards from the Border Regional Library Association. Mora was named to the El Paso Herald-Post Writer's 1988 Hall of Fame.

While Mora was gaining fame as a writer, she continued to distinguish herself as an educator at the University of Texas at El Paso. She won a Leader in Education Award from El Paso Women's Employment and Education, Inc., in 1987. Later that year she was recognized with the Chicano/Hispanic Faculty and Professional Staff Association Award for her outstanding contribution to the advancement of Hispanics at the University of Texas at El Paso. Finally, in 1988 Mora became the director of the University Museum as well as the assistant to the University's president.

## Continues Efforts to Conserve Heritage

In September, 1989, Mora gave up her life in El Paso to move to Ohio where Mora admitted that she began to crave the sound of the Spanish language in an article she wrote for the *Christian Science Monitor:* "When I hear a phrase in Spanish in a Cincinnati restaurant, my head turns quickly. I listen, silently wishing to be part of that other conversation—if only for a few moments, to feel Spanish in my mouth."

Mora did, however, begin to appreciate her new Midwestern environment. She enjoyed the lush greenery and the cold snow in the winter. She also began to recognize the differences between her new home in the Midwest and her old home in the desert. She wrote in the *Monitor,* "No forest conceals the shacks on the other side of the Rio Grande. . . . I miss that clear view of the difference between my comfortable life as a U.S. citizen and the lives of my fellow human beings who also speak Spanish. . . ." Instead of losing her affiliation for and loyalty to her culture, Mora was able to view it from a fresh perspective.

The decade of the 1990s has presented many more opportunities for Mora to contribute to cultural conservation. She has already made a great start: her third collection of poetry, *Communion,* was published by Arte Público Press in 1991. And by 1992, her illuminating work had been included in many anthologies and textbooks: *Woman of Her Word: Hispanic Women Write, The Norton Introduction to Literature, Sisters of the Earth* (Vintage), *American Mosaic* (Houghton Mifflin), *New Worlds of Literature* (Norton), *Literature: Reading, Reacting, Writing* (Holt), *Mexican American Literature* (HBJ), *Adventures in Reading* (HBJ), *Face to Face* (Scott, Foresman), and *Hispanics in the United States* (Bilingual Review Press). Mora, who is a member of the Poetry Society of America, the Academy of American Poets, and the Texas Institute of Letters, has also contributed articles and stories to periodicals, including *Hispanics in the United States: An Anthology of Creative Literature, New America: Women Artists and Writers of the Southwest, Kalliope: A Journal of Women's Art,* and *Calyx.* Mora's poems and stories have been translated into Spanish, Italian, and Bengali.

In 1991 Mora published *Communion,* her third collection of poetry to date. While this volume is similar to *Chants* and *Borders* in theme, critics contend that it is more universal in both content and scope. Mora's collection of personal essays entitled *Nepantla: Essays from the Land in the Middle* was published in 1993 by the University of New Mexico Press. She has also written several children's books, including *Tomás and the Library Lady* (1989), *A*

*Birthday Basket for Tia* (1992), *Pablo's Tree* (1993), and *Agua, Agua, Agua* (1994).

As a successful Hispanic writer, and a writer who writes about and for Hispanics, Mora is an exemplary role model for the young people of an increasingly multicultural America. Mora is aware of the influence she may have on minority youths. While she noted in *Horn Book* that some young minorities are "proud of their cultural roots," she acknowledges that advertisements "convince us that our cars, clothes, and even our families aren't good enough," and that "being beautiful is being thin, blond, and rich, rich, rich." Mora hopes to counter the influence of a post-literate, consumption-oriented and often prejudiced society. She wrote of her battle against destructive and misleading conceptions and values in *Horn Book:* "I write to try to correct these images of worth. I take pride in being a Hispanic writer. I will continue to write and to struggle to say what no other writer can say in quite the same way."

## SELECTED PUBLISHED WORKS:

*Chants* (poems), Arte Público, 1984.
*Borders* (poems), Arte Público, 1986.
*Tomás and the Library Lady,* 1989.
*Communion* (poetry), Arte Público, 1991.
*A Birthday Basket for Tia* (children's book) Macmillan Child Group, 1992.
*Nepantla: Essays from the Land in the Middle,* University of New Mexico Press, 1993.
*Pablo's Tree* (children's book), Good Year Books, 1994.
*Agua, Agua, Agua* (children's book), Good Year Books, 1994.
*The Desert Is My Mother–el Desierto Es Mi Madre,* Arte Público, 1994.
*Listen to the Desert–Que Dice el Desierto?,* Clarion Books, 1994.

## SOURCES:

### Books

*Contemporary Authors,* Volume 129, Gale, 1990.

### Periodicals

*Christian Science Monitor,* July 18, 1990, pp. 16–17.
*English Journal,* September, 1990, pp. 40.
*Horn Book,* July-August, 1990, pp. 436–37.
*Nation Catholic Reporter,* May 10, 1991, p. 24.
*Nuestro,* March, 1985, p. 51.

—*Sketch by Ronie-Richele Garcia-Johnson*

# Cherríe Moraga
## 1952-
### Hispanic American writer

Frank and undaunted, Cherríe Moraga has managed to express feelings that many Hispanic women share. Although she could "pass" for a white woman, and did not experience the pain of prejudice that some Hispanics face, Moraga had to cope with another type of discrimination: homophobia. As a lesbian, Moraga began to understand what her darker mother had always felt, and this realization, coupled with her passion for writing, incited Moraga to textually communicate the feelings that generations of minorities, regardless of specific race, gender, or sexual orientation, have experienced. The results of Moraga's hard work—a book of poems, collections of writings by other minorities and feminists, and several plays—have startled readers and made American literary history; in addition to encouraging women and minorities, especially Hispanics and Chicanas, to seriously consider their cultural and sexual situations, she has assisted other culturally cognizant writers to revise the norm in contemporary literature. Moraga was as a central figure in feminist, lesbian, Chicana, and American literature during the decade of the 1980s.

Moraga was born on September 25, 1952, in Whittier, California. As the product of a mixed-race marriage, she was influenced by two cultures. Her father's family was from Missouri and Canada, and her mother's family was from California, Arizona, and Sonora, Mexico. Moraga's family moved to live near her mother's relatives in San Gabriel, California, when she was nine years old. Like Moraga, Southern California is the product of Mexican and Anglo influence. Moraga was surrounded by the Spanish language, and a mixture of Spanish and English, as well as English; she experienced Mexican customs at home, and American traditions in school.

Moraga was a good student; she intended to become a teacher. In college, however, when Moraga began to study writing, her aspirations began to change. The people who wrote fascinated her as much as writing itself; she began to develop a love for art and artists. Despite this new interest in art and writing, Moraga was determined to finish school and become a teacher. When she earned her bachelor of arts from a small private college in Hollywood in 1974, she became one of the few people in her family to hold a degree.

### Reveals Sexual Preference

Following graduation, Moraga began to teach. Her first job was as an instructor of English at a private, Los Angeles high school. Moraga might have kept teaching if she had not enrolled in a writing class through the Los Angeles Women's Building. This class stimulated her artistic instincts, and she became more and more enthusiastic about her writing. At the same time she began to blossom as a writer, Moraga "came out" as a lesbian. As she no longer had anything to hide from herself or others, Moraga was finally able to express herself freely; some of her first works were lesbian love poems.

Although Moraga was happy with her personal revelation and progress as a writer, she soon found that not everyone would be willing to accept her textual expression of her sexuality. Some of the first challenges she received as an open lesbian were from members of her inspirational writing group. These members argued that, in her writing, Moraga should not refer to her lover as "she." A reading audience, they said, expected loving, sexual relationships to be heterosexual—homosexual intimations would be unsettling. Instead of persuading Moraga to write a lie, however, the reading group incited Moraga to write specifically as a lesbian, and about homosexual issues. Moraga decided to commit herself to writing what she wanted to write—her readers would just have to change their expectations.

Moraga's commitment to at least try to become a serious writer conflicted with her job as a teacher. She had taught for two years when she left the profession and Southern California for San Francisco in 1977. In San Francisco, she could avoid the influence of her family, and immerse herself in a community known for its liberal attitude as well as its artistic atmosphere. Moraga promised herself that, if she did not excel as a writer after a year of total devotion to the art, she would return to teaching.

The year in San Francisco proved to be rewarding and fruitful. As Moraga supported herself with odd jobs and unemployment, she read and wrote. Finally, she had the time to explore the world of lesbian literature. Books such as Radclyffe Hall's 1928 *The Well of Loneliness* and the works of Djuna Barnes inspired and enlightened Moraga. She also found time to talk with other aspiring artists, lesbians, and feminists in cafés. This diverse community of women supported Moraga's endeavor to write. Her poetry began to mature.

### Begins Writing Career

By the time Moraga's year was up, she had written enough outstanding poems to read in front of an audience. With the Los Angeles poet Eloise Klein Healy, she read to a packed coffeehouse. Moraga realized that she was more than a writer—she was a good writer; she had something valid to say, and she knew how to say it. She also found that, as she had hoped, audiences would appreciate the contents of her poems as much as her poetic voice. Moraga's success after this first year assured her that she should continue to write.

At this point in her career, Moraga began to think and write more about being, specifically, a lesbian of color. She was not just a lesbian, she was a Chicana lesbian. Instead of just being discriminated against for being a woman, or of Mexican American descent, she could experience prejudice for her sexual orientation as well. This sort of bias could come from anyone, even other women, feminists, and lesbians. One poet, Judy Grahn, wrote of being a lesbian of color. Her poems spoke to Moraga; they expressed something that she had been trying to pinpoint herself, and they did so simply and elegantly. Determined to meet this inspirational poet, Moraga arranged a meeting. At this meeting, Grahn gave Moraga a piece of advice which she still follows. Yvonne Yarbro-Bejarano, writing in the *Dictionary of Literary Biography,* quoted Grahn as saying, "do what nobody else can do, which is to write exactly from your own voice, the voices you heard growing up." Grahn's advice, as well as her political orientation, gave Moraga a new direction.

By the time Moraga was ready to begin her thesis for her master's degree in feminist writing at San Francisco State University, she was also ready to tackle the issue of being a feminist and/or lesbian of color. She did so by agreeing to work with Gloria Anzaldúa as she collected writings of women of color for a book. The women included essays, poems, letters and conversations that discussed feminism and lesbianism from the perspectives of women of color in the book; they even added a foreword by the well-known writer, Toni Cade Bambara. The result of this collaboration not only fulfilled Moraga's thesis requirement, but also made her a recognizable figure in the feminist world and stimulated the minds of women of color.

### Writings Recognized and Honored

Moraga received her master's degree in 1980, and *This Bridge Called My Back: Writings by Radical Women of Color* was published the next year. This "groundbreaking collection of Third World feminist theory," as Barbara Smith called it in the *New England Review,* was "solidly based in personal recollection and self-revelation." A critic for *Ms.* magazine commented, "*The Bridge* marks a commitment of women of color to their *own* feminism—a movement based not on separatism but on coalition . . ." *This Bridge Called My Back* was republished in 1983, and it won the 1986 Before Columbus Foundation American Book Award. A revised, bilingual edition of the book was published as *Esta puente, mi espalda: Voces de mujeres tercermundistas en los Estados Unidos* in 1988.

Moraga included a preface, two poems and one essay in the book she edited. The essay, entitled, "La Güera," deals with the writer's anxiety over being a lesbian as well as a minority, her guilt for not understanding the prejudice her mother faced, and, most importantly, her anger that such bias would occur at all in the free society the United States claims to be. "It wasn't until I acknowledged and confronted my own lesbianism in the flesh, that my heartfelt identification with and empathy for my mother's oppression—due to being poor, uneducated, and Chicana—was realized," writes Moraga in "La Güera." "My lesbianism is the avenue through which I have learned the most about silence and oppression, and it continues to be the most tactile reminder to me that we are not free human beings." "In this country," she continued," lesbianism is a poverty—as is being brown, as is being a woman, as is being just plain poor."

The anger, frustration, and the knowledge that change must be instigated by the oppressed themselves that are found in Moraga's essay also appear in her poems in *This Bridge*. In "For the Color of My Mother," which Moraga had written during her first year in San Francisco, the poet speaks of the anguish that her mother had never expressed, and by doing so gave her mother a voice. She wrote: "I am a white girl gone brown to the blood color/of my mother/speaking for her . . . " In "The Welder," Moraga expresses her belief in solidarity and empowerment. "I am a welder./Not an alchemist./I am interested in the blend of common elements to make/ a common thing. . . . I am the welder./ I understand the capacity of heat' to change the shape of things. . . . I am the welder./I am taking the power into my own hands." Moraga not only advocates action in her poems, she is politically active herself.

In 1981, while attempting to find a publisher for her thesis, Moraga went to Boston and then to New York. The feminist scene in these cities was exciting at the time, and Moraga found many feminists and Hispanics (especially Puerto Ricans) who shared her ideas. It was not long before she became politically involved in her new communities. She spent time with local activists, joined an organization which sought to end sexual violence, and cofounded the Kitchen Table/Women of Color Press, which would allow still more feminists and women of color to express themselves textually.

When Moraga edited one of the group's first published books, *Cuentos: Stories by Latinas*, with Alma Gómez and Mariana Romo-Carmona, she once again broke ground for Hispanic feminists and lesbians. Like *This Bridge, Cuentos* was a revolutionary anthology: it was the first collection of writings by feminist Latinas. Also, once again, Moraga included some of her own work in an anthology. The two stories in *Cuentos*, "Sin luz," and "Pesadilla" deal with sexuality, racism, homophobia, and the attempts of women to cope with all three.

In "Sin luz," which means "without light," a young girl married to an old man has trouble feeling anything, physically or emotionally. Although she never feels fulfilled with her marriage, the girl becomes pregnant. The loss of her baby at seven months thus has various symbolic implications: Can a child be created without love, or light? Is a homosexual union, which cannot produce a child, different from a union which is neither loving nor fruitful? Moraga's other story, "Pesadilla," or nightmare, describes a fictional lesbian relationship. In it, Cecilia, a Chicana, and Deborah, a black woman, attempt to love each other and live together despite the interruptions of the pervasive outside world. The symbolic violation which occurs when a man breaks into their apartment and paints homophobic slurs on the walls penetrates the souls of the women and almost spoils the love between them.

Moraga's next project was to collect some of the work that she had produced herself since just before she left Southern California. The result of this effort was *Loving in the War Years*: (Lo que nunca pasó por sus labios). As Raymund Paredes in the *Rocky Mountain Review* wrote, the pieces in this collection are "notable for their passion and intelligence." Included in *Loving* is the poem, "For the Color of My Mother," and the essay, "A Long Line of Vendidas." This latter piece, written while Moraga was in New York, discusses Chicana sexuality in light of the Chicana's cultural heritage. According to Moraga, Chicanas were always taught to think of the needs of their men before their own; Chicana's must understand their particular situation, and free themselves from this sexual and cultural oppression. Once again, Moraga had given American literature another first. As Yarbro-Bejarano noted, *Loving in the War Years* was the first published book of writing by an avowed Chicana lesbian.

## Presents Lesbian Themes in Plays

Moraga's desire to express her feelings and ideas about being a minority as well as a lesbian intensified. She began to work on a play. *Giving Up the Ghost* was read in mid-1984 at a feminist theater in Minneapolis, and later that year Moraga took her play to INTAR, the Hispanic-American Arts Center in New York City. At INTAR, the playwright-residency program directed by the renowned Off-Broadway playwright María Irene Fornes, Moraga began to develop the specific skills needed to produce a good play and started working on other plays and musicals.

Moraga's experience at INTAR contributed to her success as a playwright. *Giving Up the Ghost: Teatro in Two Acts* was published by West End Press in 1986, and has been produced twice, in 1987 in San

Francisco and in Seattle. Moraga has written two other plays that have not been published, *La extranjera,* which she wrote in 1985, and *Shadow of a Man,* which she wrote in 1988. Another of Moraga's plays, *Heroes and Saints,* was produced in Los Angeles in 1989.

*Giving Up the Ghost* is Moraga's most celebrated play. In this work, Amalia and Marisa share a homosexual relationship after Marisa is raped and Amalia's male lover dies. The play is set in an East Los Angeles barrio, and has an English script peppered with Spanish; it seems to accurately reflect the Chicana culture the audience expects. The homosexual relationship, however, as well as Moraga's symbolic treatment of it, makes the play remarkable. Raymund A. Paredes, in the *Rocky Mountain Review,* succinctly describes this underlying symbolism. He writes, "*Giving Up the Ghost* represents the most radical element of contemporary Chicana writing. Moraga portrays heterosexual love as inherently abusive, an act of violent penetration which in the context of the excessively masculine culture of Mexican Americans becomes more brutal still." Despite the negative aspects of the culture, explains Paredes, Moraga "clings to her ethnic identity fiercely, demanding in her work that the culture transform itself in behalf of women's rights of self-determination."

In 1986, Moraga returned to teaching. This time, however, she instructed students in the art of writing instead of in English. At the Chicano Studies Department at the University of California at Berkeley, Moraga could finally combine her initial desire to teach, her passion for writing, and her study of Chicana culture. She could also live in the intellectually stimulating San Francisco Bay area. Although she is teaching, Moraga continues to write: in 1993, she published *The Last Generation: Poetry and Prose* and in 1994 her *Heroes & Saints & Other Plays* was published. Moraga continues to develop her knowledge of theater, and to stage some of the plays she has written. Finally, Moraga maintains her determination to speak out against various kinds of oppression while upholding the Chicano culture she has both chided and cherished.

## SELECTED PUBLISHED WORKS:

(Editor with Gloria Anzaldúa, and contributor)
*This Bridge Called Me Back: Writings by Radical Women of Color,* Pesephone Press, 1981, revised bilingual edition (edited with Ana Castillo) published as *Esta puente, mi espalda: Voces de mujeres tercermundistas en los Estados Unidos,* Spanish translation by Castillo and Norma Alarcón, ISM Press, 1988.

*Loving in the War Years: Lo que nunca pasó por sus labios* (poetry and essays; subtitle means "What Never Passed Her Lips"), South End Press, 1983.

(Editor with Alma Gómez and Mariana Romo-Carmona) *Cuentos: Stories by Latinas,* Kitchen Table/Women of Color Press, 1983.

*The Last Generation: Poetry and Prose,* South End Press, 1993.

*Giving Up the Ghost: Teatro in Two Acts* (two-act play), West End Press, 1986.

*Heros & Saints & Other Plays,* West End Press, 1994.

## SOURCES:

### Books

*Dictionary of Literary Biography,* Volume 82: *Chicano Writers,* First Series, Gale, 1989.

Moraga, Cherríe, and Gloria Anzaldúa, editors, *This Bridge Called My Back: Writings by Radical Women of Color,* Persephone Press, 1981, revised bilingual edition (edited with Ana Castillo) published as *Esta puente, mi espalda: Voces de mujeres tercermundistas en los Estados Unidos,* Spanish translation by Castillo and Norma Alarcón, ISM Press, 1988.

### Periodicals

*Essence,* January, 1982, p. 17.
*Mother Jones,* January-February, 1991, p. 15.
*Ms.,* March, 1992, p. 39.
*New England Review,* summer, 1983, pp. 586–87.
*Rocky Mountain Review of Language and Literature,* Volume 41, number 1–2, 1987, pp. 125–28.

—*Sketch by Ronie-Richele Garcia-Johnson*

# Alejandro Morales
## 1944-
### Hispanic American novelist

Alejandro Morales is considered one of the leading Chicano novelists in the United States. Although his first novels were in Spanish, most have been translated into English. He is noted for epic histories that weave facts around fictional characters. Raised in a barrio—a Chicano neighborhood—Morales's novels delve into the life of the Chicano, both past and present.

Morales was born October 14, 1944, in Montebello, California's Simons barrio. His parents, Delfino

Morales Martinez and Juana Contreras Ramiriz, were immigrants from Guanajuato, Mexico; he was the youngest of five children. When Morales was a child, the family moved to the barrios of east Los Angeles where he received his elementary and secondary education in public schools.

In the 1960s, Morales was active in that decade's growing sociopolitical movement. He married H. Rohde Teaze on December 16, 1967, and received his B.A. from California State College in Los Angeles four years later. Morales received a Ford Foundation fellowship in 1972 and he moved to New Brunswick, New Jersey to study Spanish and literature at Rutgers University, where he received his M.A. in 1973.

Morales received an ITT International fellowship in 1973 and received his Ph.D. from Rutgers in 1975. He then became associate professor of the Department of Spanish and Portuguese at the University of California at Irvine. In 1987 Morales became full professor of Latin American and Chicano literature.

In 1975 Morales's first novel, *Caras viejas y vino nuevo*—translated as *Old Faces and New Wine*—was a finalist in a contest sponsored by Mexican Press. In the novel, the author draws on his barrio experience to present his characters in a macho, male-dominated society. The novel's main protagonists are two teen-age boys, Mateo and Julian; the primary issues are the generational differences among Chicanos and life in the barrio. Morales's chronicle of daily life depicts both positive and negative aspects of the barrio.

His second novel, *La verdad sin voz—Death of an Anglo*—was first published in 1979. The book was based upon an event that actually occurred in Mathis, Texas. An Anglo physician, Dr. Michael Logan, helps Chicanos in a Texas barrio. Idealistic and a leftist sympathizer, Logan is killed by another Anglo, barrio policeman Pistola Gorda. The novel is divided into three sections and is narrated by a university professor who is also the victim of racism, Professor Morenito.

In 1982, Morales published his third novel, *Reto en el paraíso,* in which he portrays two families: a wealthy influential Chicano family and an Irish family that becomes rich and powerful by stealing land from the Chicano family in California. It covers more than 100 years of Mexican American history.

*Reto en el paraíso* explores the historical background of the Spanish-Mexican land grant, the impact of the gold rush, and the effect of the Land Law of 1851 on the original Spanish settlers. In the 19th century, the United States was governed by a belief in "Manifest Destiny"—that the fate of the young country was to continue to expand its territories. This novel examines the impact of that belief, moving into the 20th century with the descendants of the Chicano family left landless after 1851. Mythic tales, violence, racial discrimination, insanity, and psychology are interwoven throughout the story, which appears as a factual account by its main narrator, Dennis Berreyesa Coronel.

Morales combines factual historical events with fictionalized characters to produce most of his epic novels. In *The Brick People,* for example, he portrays Chicano employees of the Anglo-owned Simons Brick Factory, incorporating the lives of two families, Chicano and Anglo. *The Rag Doll Plagues* features a Spanish-Mexican doctor who battles the plague in three locations and three different time periods: in old Mexico, in modern Southern California, and in a future setting where Mexico and California have merged into one country.

Drawing on his own experiences, Morales combines autobiography with dedicated and fastidious research when constructing his novels. He builds his complex plots from his personal perspectives and experiences within the Chicano culture he represents. Morales is a member of the Yale Project of Chicano Writers, the Association of Mexican American Educators, the Modern Language Association of America, and the National Association of Chicano Studies.

## SELECTED PUBLISHED WORKS:

*Caras viejas y vino nuevo*, Mexico, Joaquin Moritz, 1975, translated by Max Martinez as *Old Faces and New Wine*, San Diego, Maize Press, 1981.

*La verdad sin voz*, Joaquin Mortiz, 1979, translated by Judith Ginsberg as *Death of an Anglo*, Tempe, Arizona, Bilingual Press, 1988.

*Reto en el paraíso*, Ypsilanti, Michigan, Bilingual Press/Bilingue, 1982.

*El proyecto del Codigo penal; Sus grandes lineamientos, sus detales: Coleccion de articulos publicados en el diario "La Industria,"* Trujillo, Dominican Republic, Tip. Olaya, 1985.

*The Brick People*, Arte Publico, 1988.

*The Rag Doll Plagues*, Arte Publico, 1992.

## SOURCES:

### Books

*Contemporary Authors*, Volume 131, edited by Susan M. Trosky, Detroit, Gale, 1991.

*Dictionary of Literary Biography*, Volume 82: *Chicano Writers*, edited by Francisco A. Lomelí and Carl R. Shirley, Detroit, Gale, 1989.

*Hispanic Writers*, edited by Bryan Ryan, Detroit, 1991.

*The Hispanic-American Almanac: A Reference Work on Hispanics in the United States*, edited by Nicolás Kanellos, Detroit, Gale, 1993.

**Periodicals**

*Library Journal,* January 1992, p. 180.

—*Sketch by Phyllis Noah*

# Arturo Morales Carrion
## 1913-1989
### Pureto Rican historian and government official

Arturo Morales Carrión was appointed deputy assistant secretary of state under President John F. Kennedy in 1961. Morales was distinguished as the first Puerto Rican to be appointed to such a prominent position. He was a historian, author of many books, and a principal figure in Puerto Rican history. He was born in Havana, Cuba, November 16, 1913, to Arturo and Agripina (Carrión) Morales.

Although Cuban-born, Morales is considered Puerto Rican. He earned his B.A. degree from the University of Puerto Rico in 1935. Morales went to the University of Texas in 1936 where he earned his M.A. degree and then returned to the University of Puerto Rico as an instructor in history. In 1944, he became an assistant professor of history and in 1946, chairman of the history department. From 1946 until 1952, he was director of history research center and Latin American seminar at Columbia University where he received his Ph.D. in 1950.

### Becomes Involved in Politics

In 1948, Morales married Inés Arandes Rexach and they had two sons, Arturo and Edgardo, and a daughter, Inés. Morales was chairman of the history department at the University of Puerto Rico before going into politics. In 1953, he was in charge of external affairs and undersecretary of the State Department in Puerto Rico before joining the Kennedy administration. Morales was also involved with George Washington University's Center for International Studies and a member of the U.S. delegation in inter-American conferences from 1954 to 1963. The group reported the danger of communist involvement in the politics of Latin America. The report presented by the group in 1961 stated that a key problem was "to divorce the inevitable and necessary Latin American social transformation from connection with, and prevent its capture by, overseas Communist power politics."

Puerto Rico was called the "poorhouse of the Caribbean." One of the main issues on the island was the "status" of Puerto Rico. As a commonwealth of the United States, the island became divided into several factions; those who wanted a revised commonwealth status, those who wanted independence, and those who wanted statehood. Morales was a Democrat, the pro-autonomy party on the island. He wrote many books on the history of Puerto Rico, mostly in Spanish, except for *Puerto Rico: a Political and Cultural History* (1983), which was in English. In the *New Republic,* Robert Pastor described Morales's perception of Puerto Rican problems: "His [Morales] most valuable contribution is to recognize and describe the parallel behavior of North Americans and Puerto Ricans."

Morales also published numerous articles, speeches and addresses. One of the last articles he wrote was an introduction for Jack Delano in his book *Puerto Rico Mio: Four Decades of Change* (1990), a photographic look at Puerto Rico. The pictures in the book were taken over a 40-year period. Morales described the changes in Puerto Rico over the 40-year span but also noticed the constancy of his homeland. "We can also make out a thread of continuity, for no matter how much he changes, the Puerto Rican does not lose his sense of family," he wrote. He described the historic changes in the social, economic, and political dynamics associated with the Third World. Agriculture controlled Puerto Rico's main economy until World War II when **Luis Munoz Marin** encouraged U.S. investment in economic development on the island. A U.S. Naval Base and factories were built, and in 1968, the island had the highest per capita income in Latin America.

Morales received many awards, including the **Eugenio Maria de Hostos** award from the state of New York (1962) and two awards from the Institute of Puerto Rican Literature (1968, 1972). After Kennedy was assassinated in 1963, Morales became the special advisor to the secretary general of the Organization of American States. He served in that position until 1969 and then became the director of the history research center and Latin American seminar from 1970 to 1973, when he served as president at the University of Puerto Rico. Morales also served as executive director of Puerto Rico Endowment for the Humanities.

Morales was considered a distinguished Puerto Rican with insights into the problems between the island of Puerto Rico and the United States. On June 28, 1989, Morales died of cancer at his home in San Juan. Upon his death, Rafael Hernandez Colon, the governor of Puerto Rico, issued this statement: "This is a great loss for Puerto Rico. Arturo Morales Carrión is one of the principal figures in our history. He was a dedicated public servant, distinguishing himself in his work in Puerto Rico's Department of State and later in the State Department of the United States."

## SELECTED PUBLISHED WORKS:

### With Antonio Rivera

*La ensenanza de la historia en Puerto Rico,* [Mexico], 1953.

*Historia del pueblo de Puerto Rico, desde sus origenes hasta el siglo XVIII,* Departamento de Instruccion Publica, 1968.

*Ojeada al proceso historico y otros ensayos,* Cordillera, 1971.

*Puerto Rico and the Non-Hispanic Caribbean: A Study in the Decline of Spanish Exclusivism,* second edition, University of Puerto Rico Press, 1971.

*Albores historicos del capitalismo en Puerto Rico,* second edition, University of Puerto Rico Press, 1972.

*Auge y decadencia de la trata negrera en Puerto Rico, 1820–1860,* Centro de Estudios Avanzados de Puerto Rico y el Caribe, Instituto de Cultura Puertorriquena, 1978.

### With others

*Centenario de la abolicion de la esclavitud,* University of Puerto Rico Press, 1978.

*Testimonios del una gestion universitaria,* University of Puerto Rico Press, 1978.

*Puerto Rico: A Political and Cultural History,* New York, Norton, 1983.

## SOURCES:

### Books

*Contemporary Authors: A Bio-Bibliographical Guide to Current Writers in Fiction,* Detroit, Gale Research, Volume 129, 1990; Volume 131, 1991.

Delano, Jack, *Puerto Rico Mio: Four Decades of Change,* Washington, D.C., Smithsonian Institute Press, 1990.

*The Hispanic-American Almanac: A Reference Work on Hispanics in the United States,* edited by Nicolas Kanellos, Detroit, Gale Research, 1993.

### Periodicals

*New Republic,* November 12, 1984, pp. 38–43; June 30, 1989.

—*Sketch by Phyllis Noah*

# Francisco Morazán
## 1792-1842
### Honduran politician

Francisco Morazán came of age just as Spain began to relinquish its possessions in the New World. Morazán was one of Latin America's great nineteenth-century liberals, a man whose principles cost him his life. Like Simón Bolívar, Morazán envisioned the old Spanish territory as a stable and free nation that would transcend petty traditional and tribal boundaries. Like Bolívar, he saw his dream come briefly to fruition and then recede into oblivion.

As president of the Central American Federation, Morazán abolished the church, created public education, and asserted human rights. Yet in some ways he failed among the people whom he was trying to liberate. Democratic institutions overwhelmed a population that did not know how to behave in a democracy. Liberal concepts of property and freedom frightened those who clung to the old ways. When Central America restructed itself into five nations, Morazán lost favor. During a failed attempt to reassert the Federation, Morazán was captured. He was executed in Costa Rica in 1842.

### Farm Life

Morazán's father, Eusebio, was the son of a Frenchman, who had migrated from Corsica to the West Indies—where Eusebio was born—and finally to Honduras. The family made its living through agriculture, and when Eusebio and his wife, Guadalupe Quesada Morazán welcomed a son on October 16, 1792, the parents hoped that one day Francisco would become a successful farmer.

Morazán grew up in Tegucigalpa, working with his parents. In his biography of Morazán, Robert Chamberlain noted that Morazán had very little formal education, but managed to acquaint himself with some of the most esoteric and progressive ideas of his time. Chamberlain wrote that "Morazán's high attainments were the results of talent, intelligence, and driving energy. He hungered for knowledge." Born during the French Revolution with a half-French heritage, Morazán was impressed by that tumultuous political event. In *Makers of Democracy in Latin America,* Harold Davis wrote that during his limited schooling, Morazán "absorbed the liberal ideas of the French revolutionary philosophy and liberal reform."

### The Political World

Mexico gained its independence from Spain in 1821. Morazán was 29 years old, and the event affected him profoundly. With Mexico free from its colonial master, the nations on the narrow isthmus between Mexico and South America—Central America—shortly gained their freedom. Two years later, leaders of the new nations created the Central American Federation. But unity soon dissolved into bickering. Davis listed three primary "lines of conflict" among Central American decision makers: jealousy of member nations against Guatemala's preeminent role; a rift between Guatemala and El Salvador over the separation of Church and State; and the fears of moneyed Creoles and the established clergy that the liberal ideas of people like Morazán would take away their comfortable station.

In this contentious atmosphere Morazán entered the political scene. In 1824 he became the secretary general of Honduras on the appointment of the chief of the Honduran state. Chamberlain noted that after Morazán rose to the Honduran presidency, he "served with distinction."

Morazán's management of the sub-state of Honduras prepared him for a larger role. Meanwhile, Jóse Arce won election to the Central American Presidency. Arce positioned himself as a moderate, opposed to the conservative forces that wanted to attach Central America to Mexico. On the other hand, Arce promised to prevent the tide of liberalism from rising too high. Herrera—Morazán's political benefactor and Honduras's most prominent liberal—became Arce's political target. Arce enlisted Honduran Vice-Chief Milla to put military pressure on liberals in Comayagua in 1827. Meanwhile, Herrera nominated Morazán to understate a mission to enter the city secretly and raise opposition forces. Morazán failed, and Milla's troops captured him.

### Rise to Power

At this dire hour, Morazán's fortunes improved. He escaped from Milla and raised a small liberal army. On November 11, 1827, he met Arce's federal troops at La Trinidad and won. Morazán returned to Comayagua and assumed executive control of Honduras.

Morazán's daring escape and victory over Arce had increased his popularity, but the conservative forces grew stronger without Arce's restraining influence. Though in Honduras Morazán successfully established a liberal administration, throughout the rest of the Federation, Arce's absence, according to Davis, brought "reactionary forces to the fore."

Morazán's July 6, 1828, victory over Arce's forces at El Gualcho virtually ended the confrontation. Morazán's charisma and battle prowess helped him to assume leadership of the military forces in Honduras and then in El Salvador. Arce had retreated to Guatemala, where the conservatives braced for their confrontation with Morazán. Negotiations between the two sides failed, and conflict started anew.

This time the winner would claim all of Central America. The entrenched conservative forces held Morazán at bay. Eventually, Morazán and his men broke the defenders, and marched into Guatemala City on April 12, 1829. The federal government collapsed; the conservatives had lost. Morazán took Arce prisoner, and began establishing a liberal federal government.

### Problems of Governing

Morazán became the acting head of state, and he tried to restore peace throughout all the Central American nations. He placed a liberal in the Guatemalan presidency, and he convened a liberal congress on June 22, 1829. Jóse Francisco Barrundia became the government's leader, and Morazán assumed control as the general-in-chief of the Central American Federal Army.

Morazán influenced all the powerful liberals in Central America, and led efforts to liberalize the government. Davis recounted some of Morazán's early reforms: "Usury laws were abolished; the Archbishop of Guatemala was exiled . . . religious toleration and freedom of speech were established [and] . . . several states adopted the jury system." Conservative dissension grew. Costa Rica seceded briefly. King Ferdinand VII, who had never recognized Central American independence, became the darling of the Federation's conservatives, who hoped that he would intervene on their behalf. A conservative military rebellion arose in eastern Honduras in 1830, but Morazán crushed it.

Problems in almost every Central American state hung ominously over Morazán's election to the presidency. On September 14, 1830, he spoke prophetically at his inauguration about the needs of the unstable nation: "The Federal system can only be sustained through the intimate and close union of the states among themselves and with the Federal Government." Still, conservative forces rose up in El Salvador, which seceded from the Union until Morazán's troops reassested control in March of 1832. Chamberlain noted that "smaller states began demanding more power." Morazán's government moved its capital to El Salvador to try to win some popularity in that nation, but the unhappiness continued.

Morazán's decision to borrow funds to keep the nation afloat proved unpopular, and only the death of José del Valle, who won the next election, allowed Morazán to continue as president. Meanwhile, a new enemy emerged in Guatemala. Rafael Carrera had the support of conservatives, the church, and Indians. Davis suggested that Indian support came not so much from disagreement with liberal principles, but from manipulation by others: "Unrest among the Indians ... provided one of the bases upon which demagogic caudillos could rise to power."

Divisions among the liberals appeared at an inopportune moment. Carrera's forces drove government troops out of Guatemala City. Morazán led a counterattack, with partial success. Politically he had fallen far. Fortunately for him, however, the conservatives became afraid of Carrera and offered Morazán their support if he would declare himself the dictator of the country. Morazán refused. Insisting that he would stick to his ideals, Morazán declared: "Though I have enemies to fight on all sides and might be defeated, I will go down with honor."

Chaos ensued. By the spring of 1838, the federal government's best advice to the states was to "act in their own best interests." With Carrera still in the field and Morazán so weakened, Central America had virtually no government. In 1839 conservatives chose Carrera and worked to defeat Morazán. By the 1840 conclusion of hostilities, Morazán's unified nation—his reason for fighting—had vanished comletely. Morazán left for exile in Peru. He returned in 1842 to try again to establish the Union. The Costa Rican farmers on whom he had depended allowed him to be captured by his enemies. He was executed on September 11, 1842.

Carrera abolished Morazán's liberal reforms and asserted a dictatorship that lasted two decades, and set the stage for political chaos in Central America. Chamberlain called Morazán "one of the great Americans who stand as symbols of high and worthy ideals." Davis added: "With the death of Francisco Morazán ... died the best hope that a strong and united nation would arise in [Central America]. ... With Morazán, too, died the best hope of early liberal democracy in that region." John Stephens, a U.S. diplomat in Central America at the time, wrote that the people "have cast from their shores the best man of Central America."

## SOURCES:

Chamberlain, Robert, *Francisco Morazan, Champion of Central American Federation,* Coral Gables, Florida, University of Miami Press, 1950.

Davis, Harold E., *Makers of Democracy in Latin America,* New York, H. W. Wilson, 1945.

Stephens, John L., *Incidetral America, Memoirs of John L. Stephens, U.S. Diplomat,* [New York], 1841.

—*Sketch by James McCarthy*

# Jose Maria Morelos
## 1765-1815
### Mexican priest and revolutionary leader

Jose Maria Morelos is regarded as one of Mexico's leading historical figures, an advocate of independence from Spain whose forces controlled significant areas of the country for a time. Born in 1765 in Valladolid (now called Morelia) in Mexico, Morelos was forced by the death of his father to support his family from adolescence. He became a mule train driver, then a priest, and in the wake of the Indian uprisings of 1810–1811, a military leader. He led troops in the field for several years and established control over large regions of Mexico, though he was never able to topple the Spanish government. Morelos' belief in independence and his support for a liberal constitution that would establish certain legal rights fueled his revolutionary activities. Morales is today viewed as a martyr in the cause for independence and one of Mexico's greatest heroes.

### From North to South

Morelos' parents were Juana Pavon Morelos and Manuel Morelos. Though they were listed on his birth records as *espanoles,* they were probably not of exclusively Spanish lineage. Manuel Morelos was a highly-regarded carpenter in the village, his wife, Juana Pavon, had received an unusually extensive education for a woman of that era. Biographer Wilbert Timmons called her "the greatest single influence on him [Morelos] in his early years." Morelos also had one younger brother and one younger sister.

In 1779 Morelos' father died, and his family decided to send the boy south to live with his uncle, Felipe Morelos. The owner of his own hacienda, he used Morelos first as a laborer and then as a mule train driver to deliver goods from Acapulco on the Pacific Coast to Mexico City. Morelos endured harsh conditions on these hard trails, but was able to support his family in Valladolid with this regular income. This stint also gave him the opportunity to learn the terrain of the region in great detail, knowledge that would prove significant in later years.

### From Trail to Classroom

In 1790 Morelos decided to begin studying for the priesthood. His mother knew that if Morelos decided to enter the priesthood, he stood to inherit almost 3,000 pesos from his great-grandfather, who had established an inheritance that could only be released provided a complicated set of conditions were met. One of these conditions required that a descendant embark on a course of study to join the clergy. Morelos returned to Valladolid, claimed the inheritance, and began his studies at San Nicolas College. Father Miguel Hidalgo served as the rector of the college for the first two years of Morelos' studies. Some historians have speculated that Hidalgo's radical political beliefs, brought to life in the 1810 uprisings, left an impression on the young student, who joined the revolution after Hidalgo's fall.

In 1791 Jose Carnero presented a legal claim on the inheritance that Morelos had earlier collected. While his mother resolved to fight for her son's birthright, Morelos simply continued with his education. In 1792 he moved on to Seminario Tridentio in Valladolid so that he could study Latin. In 1795 he finished his bachelor's degree at the Royal and Pontifical University of Mexico. He began his ecclesiastical career in the town of Uruapan in 1796 and was eventually named a professor of grammar and rhetoric. In 1797 the Catholic Church ordained him as a priest and assigned him to the parish of Tamacuaro de la Aguacana in Churumuco. Although his assignment to such an inhospitable climate did not please him, Morelos accepted what many considered a terrible assignment with happiness. His mother and sister accompanied him to Churumuco.

His mother became ill and Morelos decided to send her back to the cooler climate of Valladolid. She did not survive the trip, however, and in 1799 Morelos requested a reassignment to a more temperate location. Plagued by malaria, he wanted to prevent his own health from deteriorating. The church instead reassigned him to Caracuaro, a village located only thirty miles from Churumuco.

Morelos became frustrated at his new assignment. The Catholic Church, he felt, saved its positions of power and prestige for Spaniards. Even if his parents truly had come of only Spanish lineage, he, as a *creole*—someone born in Spanish America of Spanish heritage—could never hope to advance in the church hierarchy beyond a certain point. For a *mestizo,* a person of mixed blood, promotion was even more elusive.

### Grito de Dolores

After ten years at Caracuaro, Morelos heard news of an enormous event. His former teacher Father Miguel Hidalgo had started an uprising among the native population of Dolores. The *grito de Dolores* inspired Morelos to action. He went to Hidalgo to ask for a position as a chaplain in the new army, but Hidalgo sent him instead to recruit men in the south of Mexico.

Hidalgo's group ultimately proved fundamentally flawed. While the band had fury and purpose, it lacked control. *Creoles, mestizos,* and pure natives had overlapping, if not identical interests, but Hidalgo's men made no distinction between Spaniards and creoles, often slaughtering both indiscriminately. Thus divided, the two revolution-minded groups failed to produce a successful change in the government. Hidalgo was executed by a firing squad in July 1811.

Morelos learned from Hidalgo's mistakes. He organized his recruits in a more thoughtful manner, trained them more thoroughly, and, perhaps most importantly, brought all non-Spaniards under the same battle flag. He fought fiercely against the forces of General Felix Maria Calleja, who called Morelos "a second Mohammed" in recognition of his military skills.

Repelling Calleja's two-month siege at Cuaulta buoyed the revolution. Morelos took the city of Oaxaca and moved on to Acapulco. It took him seven months to claim the city, a period of time that allowed Calleja to reorganize and re-equip his forces. Morelos travelled from Acapulco to Chilipancingo, where a covert Congress met to declare Mexican independence from Spain.

Many of the soldiers of Morelos' patriotic army believed that they were defending Mexico from the threat of French domination. Napoleon Bonapart had removed King Ferdinand VII from the Spanish throne and seemed to be angling for control of Spain's colonies. Although they acknowledged the risk of alienating many of their soldiers, members of the Congress decided nevertheless to declare Mexico a sovereign nation on November 6, 1813.

Morelos then decided to make an assault on his hometown of Valladolid, envisioning the city as the revolutionary capital. Royalist troops, however, surprised him with an attack from the rear. Morelos tried to rally, but royalists captured an order that was to be delivered to Morelos' troops directing them to wear black face paint to distinguish them from their enemies. Armed with this information, the royalist troops disguised themselves and infiltrated Morelos' lines. As the royalist forced attacked, Morelos' revolutionary fighters were thrown into disarray and the campaign came to an undignified end.

Morelos' troops were forced to run for their lives. Many of his senior officers died in the fighting; the survivors fled into the southwestern area of the country. When Ferdinand returned to the Spanish throne in March 1814, Morelos' revolution lost all its momentum.

Despite these setbacks, Morelos continued his struggle to create a constitution that would outline the government of the rebel congress. The rebel leaders drew up a constitution and decided to ride for Mexico's east coast in hopes of receiving help from sympathizers in the United States. Calleja's forces intercepted the band and captured Morelos. They took him back to Mexico City, where a perfunctory trial sealed his fate. Even his assigned lawyer said he believed his client to be guilty. Although Morelos insisted that he had not committed treason because his independence movement had occurred during a time in which no king sat on the throne, the court sentenced him to death. Taken out of Mexico City for fear of public demonstrations against his execution, Morelos died in front of a firing squad on December 22, 1815, at San Cristobal.

In 1823 another revolution brought independence to Mexico. The new congress brought Morelos' remains to a place of high honor in Mexico City. Later, when the government decided to declare a monument to revolutionary heroes at the Paseo de la Reforma, admirers expressed a desire to move his remains again. Most historians, however, believe that friends of Morelos had already moved them to a grave whose location remains unknown to this day.

Morelos' hometown of Valladolid changed its name to Morelia in 1828 in recognition of the efforts of the revolutionary leader. In 1862 the government took a portion of what had formerly been known as the state of Mexico and created the state of Morelos.

## SOURCES:

Timmons, Wilbert, *Morelos: Priest, Soldier, Statesman of Mexico,* El Paso, Texas Western Press, 1970.

Worcester, Donald, *Makers of Latin America,* New York, E. P. Dutton, 1966.

Young, Bob, and Jan Young, *Liberators of Latin America,* New York, Lothrop, Lee & Shepard Co., 1970.

—*Sketch by Jim McCarthy*

# Rita Moreno
## 1931-
### Puerto Rican actress, singer, and dancer

A remarkably versatile performer, Rita Moreno has received all four of show business's top awards. For her acting in *West Side Story,* Moreno won an Oscar in 1962. A Grammy followed her vocal performance on the *Electric Company Album* for

children in 1972. Her role as Googie Gómez in *The Ritz* (1975) on Broadway won her a Tony. And finally, Moreno has been awarded two Emmys: one for guest appearances on *The Muppet Show* in 1977, and another for an episode of *The Rockford Files* in 1978. Although impressive, this long list of prestigious awards merely suggests the variety of Moreno's excellent performances, and it cannot convey the determination with which she has worked to become a respected actress.

Moreno, a woman who has illuminated the screen and charged the stage since she was a teenager, had to fight to win roles that merited talent. Too often, the need to earn a living as an actress forced her to take parts which were stereotypical and sometimes even debasing; for quite some time she was cast as either a "Latin Spitfire" or an "Indian Princess." Moreno struggled to exorcise these images, especially after the media referred to her as "Rita the Cheetah" because of her roles and her personal life. When Moreno finally received the recognition she deserved after winning an Oscar for her portrayal of Anita in *West Side Story,* she became one of the few Hispanics to "cross over" into stardom and become internationally famous. She commented in an interview for *Hispanic* magazine, "I have crossed over, but never, not for one minute, have I forgotten where I came from, or who I am. I have always been very proud to carry the badge of honor as a Hispanic." While Moreno has utilized her Hispanic identity to her advantage to portray characters such as that of Anita, she has also managed to poke fun at stereotypes on stage and screen with her wit and talent, as she did as Googie Gómez in *The Ritz.*

Moreno, or Rosa Dolores Alverio, was born to Paco Alverio and Rosa María Marcano Alverio in the small town of Humacao, Puerto Rico, on December 11, 1931. Moreno's parents divorced soon after her birth, and her mother left her with relatives while she went to New York to work as a seamstress. When Moreno was five years old, her mother returned for her, and, along with other members of the family, they found a home in a Manhattan tenement. It was at this point in Moreno's life that she began to take dancing lessons. Paco Cansino, an uncle of the legendary actress and dancer Rita Hayworth, was a very effective dance teacher: the young Moreno soon began to dance professionally.

Moreno, who attended New York Public School 132, soon found herself performing in the children's theater at Macy's Department Store and entertaining at weddings and bar mitzvahs. By the time she was thirteen, Moreno had exchanged the life of a schoolgirl for that of an actress. As "Rita Cosio," she had her first role on Broadway as Angelina in Harry Kleiner's *Skydrift.* Later, she performed in nightclubs in New York, Boston, Las Vegas, and New York, and dubbed in the Spanish for Elizabeth Taylor, Margaret

O'Brien, and Peggy Ann Garner in their movies. Moreno's first film, *So Young, So Bad* (1950), led to a meeting with Louis B. Mayer, who contracted her with Metro-Goldwyn-Mayer (MGM).

### Gains Recognition with Stereotypical Roles

Under the name Rosita Moreno (her stepfather's surname), and later, Rita Moreno, the actress garnered minor roles in some twenty-five movies. The most notable of these included *The Toast of New Orleans* (1950) and *Pagan Love Song* (1950), with Esther Williams. Freelancing after she lost her contract with MGM, Moreno found only stereotypical, ethnic roles. With the exception of her part as Zelda Zanders in *Singin' in the Rain* (1952), Moreno portrayed Latin vamps in *The Fabulous Senorita* (1952), *The Ring* (1952), *Cattle Town* (1952), *Latin Lovers* (1953), and *Jivaro* (1954). She was hired to play an Arab in *El Alamein* (1953), and an American Indian in both *Fort Vengeance* (1953) and *The Yellow Tomahawk* (1954).

Although Moreno became a recognizable actress after these movies, the "Latin Spitfire" roles created a troublesome and unfair image for her. She became known as "Rita the Cheetah"; her highly publicized relationships with Marlon Brando, the famous actor, and Geordie Hormel of the Hormel meat family, exacerbated this image. Disheartened with these roles which, she later told a *New York Times* contributor, she "played . . . the same way, barefoot, with my nostrils flaring," the physically petite actress attempted to return to the stage. She lost a part in *Camino Real* because the playwright, the renowned Tennessee Williams, did not think her voice was suitable.

It seemed as if Moreno's career had taken a turn for the better when she was featured on the cover of *Life* magazine. She immediately signed a contract with Twentieth Century-Fox, singing in *Garden of Evil* (1954), and doing a Marilyn Monroe takeoff in *The Lieutenant Wore Skirts* (1955). Once again, however, she was given stereotypical roles which failed to challenge the serious actress. The casting was difficult for Moreno emotionally as well as professionally. As she recalled in the *New York Times,* she spent six and a half years in therapy "trying to get my ethnic problems untangled." Moreno was not the only one who was disappointed with her acting opportunities. After her performance in *Untamed* (1955), a writer for the *New York Post* voiced the frustration of Moreno and her fans: "Will the powers in Twentieth Century-Fox wait patiently until Miss Moreno loses half of her youth, vitality and beauty before they get around to giving her a romantic break?"

In *Seven Cities of Gold* (1955), Moreno was still not treated as a serious actress; she did not find a truly satisfying role until she was given a part as a Burmese slave girl in the hit musical *The King and I* (1956). As

Tuptim in the Rogers and Hammerstein film adaptation, she sang "We Kiss in a Shadow" and "I Have Dreamed" with Carlos Rivas. Moreno also narrated "The Small House of Uncle Thomas," which was choreographed by Jerome Robbins, for the film.

### Wins Academy Award for *West Side Story*

Despite these professional successes, Moreno found the latter half of the 1950s to be less rewarding; she made few movies from 1956 to 1960. In 1956, she won a role in *The Vagabond King,* followed by *The Deerslayer* in 1957, and after her contract with Twentieth Century-Fox expired she appeared in *This Rebel Breed* (1960). Once again, Moreno sought to return to the stage; she performed in Arthur Miller's *A View from the Bridge* in theaters in Seattle, Washington and La Jolla, California. Although she was well-received during this summer theater tour, Moreno could no longer cope with the frustration she had been experiencing—she attempted suicide with sleeping pills. When she woke in the hospital, however, she realized that she wanted to live. She recovered beautifully, and went on to star in the movie for which she is most famous, *West Side Story* (1961).

Moreno had been asked by Jerome Robbins a year after her performance in *The King and I* to try out for the role as Maria in the original theater production of *West Side Story,* but Moreno, busy as well as intimidated, did not. By the time the movie version of the play was being made, Moreno's face had matured, and she was better suited to the character of Anita, the more experienced friend of Maria, who was ultimately portrayed by Natalie Wood. As Anita, Moreno illuminated the screen with her singing and dancing. Especially memorable is the scene in which Moreno sang "America," a facetious piece in which life in America is satirized. *West Side Story* was an instant success. It won ten Academy Awards, one of which was Moreno's Oscar for best supporting actress.

During the ten years from 1961 to 1971, Moreno found that she could not rest on her laurels. While she played Rosa Zacharias in Tennessee Williams' *Summer and Smoke* (1961), and a camp follower in *Cry of Battle* (1963), she did not find these parts entirely rewarding; seeking better roles, she left Hollywood for London. There, in 1964, she portrayed Ilona Ritter in Hal Prince's *She Loves Me.* Forced to return to the United States because of British performance laws, Moreno made her way to Broadway once again. This time she won the role of Iris Parodus Brustein in Lorraine Hansberry's *The Sign in Sidney Brustein's Window,* a play which ran for 101 performances. Marlon Brando, the man whom Moreno had dated on and off for eight years, assisted Moreno as she renewed her movie career with her portrayal of a drug addict in *The Night of the Following Day* (1969). This led to appearances in various movies; she found roles in *Marlowe* (1969), *Popi* (1969), a comedy focused on East Harlem, and *Carnal Knowledge* (1971), in which she played a prostitute visited by Jack Nicholson. And in 1970 she returned to the theater to portray Sharon Falconer in *Gantry* on Broadway, and replaced Linda Lavin in *Last of the Red Hot Lovers,* by Neil Simon, in New York.

### Marries and Launches Television Career

It was during these ten years that Moreno met and married Dr. Leonard Gordon, a cardiologist and internist at Mount Sinai Hospital in New York. When they were introduced near the end of 1964, Gordon asked Moreno to attend a New Year's party with him. When she accepted, Moreno instructed Gordon to pick her up at the Henry Miller Theater, but as Gordon later told a *Hispanic* contributor, he "couldn't figure out the sense of it." "Why would this attractive young lady be going to the theater on New Year's Eve? Was she going on a date with some other guy and then planning to dump him and go out with me?" Gordon, still perplexed, waited and waited for Moreno to leave the theater long after the audience exited, while an angry Moreno waited inside her dressing room, thinking she had been stood up. It was not until Gordon checked the marquee to see if he was at the right theater and saw Moreno's name in lights that he realized his date was *the* Rita Moreno. Moreno and Gordon finally went on their date, and they were eventually married in June of 1965. A *Hispanic* contributor explained, "On the surface it might seem that a Hispanic actress and a Jewish doctor are an unlikely combination, but ... their successful partnership in all things ... is based on the wide range of interests they have in common." The happily married couple celebrated their twenty-fifth anniversary in 1990.

Moreno took a break from both theater and film to perform for television in 1971. When the Children's Television Workshop, which produces the popular educational series for pre-school children, *Sesame Street,* asked Moreno to star in *The Electric Company,* a television series for older children, she was enthusiastic. "I jumped at the chance," she told a *New York Times* writer. "I love doing that show. It's just like vaudeville, except that we play to four million kids every day. I get to do some zany characters—and not a Latin in the bunch." As Pandore, a bratty blond girl, and Otto, a movie director, she encouraged children to develop reading skills. Moreno's performance was delightful, and in 1972 her participation, with Bill Cosby and others, in the soundtrack recording of *The Electric Company,* won her a Grammy award for the best recording for children.

### Laughs at Stereotypes in *The Ritz*

This success did not develop into any other television ventures, though. Moreno's next role was that of the Shoplifter in the play *Detective Story,* which ran in Philadelphia in 1973. She then portrayed Staff Nurse Norton in *The National Health,* first in New Haven, Connecticut, from 1973 to 1974, and then in the Circle in the Square, New York City, in 1974. It was around this time that Moreno displayed the character that would eventually win her the Tony Award to playwright Terrence McNally at a party. Singing "Everything's Coming up Roses" with her mother's Spanish accent and the mannerisms she had developed during the filming of *West Side Story,* she was hilarious. McNally later invited Moreno to attend his new play, *The Tubs,* at the Yale Repertory Theater, and she was shocked to see the character she had created singing on stage. McNally asked her to portray this character, which he named Googie Gómez, when the play, renamed *The Ritz,* came to Broadway in 1975, and she accepted.

Moreno was a hit. While the *New York Times* noted that her performance as the Puerto Rican singer was "variously hailed as 'pure beauty,' 'wonderfully atrocious' and 'a comic earthquake,'" a writer for the *White Plains Reporter Dispatch,* quoted in *Current Biography Yearbook,* said it best: "In fractured English, she [Moreno] creates a portrait of tattered glory. . . . Hot, cold, tempestuous, wiggling, seething, cursing, . . . so that she tears the house down every time she opens her mouth or does a bump and grind, she is showing a new generation of theatergoers what stars are all about." *The Ritz* ran for 400 performances, and it was no surprise when Moreno received the Antoinette Perry, or "Tony," Award, for best supporting actress.

Although some in the audience worried that the performance would offend Hispanics, Moreno was not among them. She felt that the character she and McNally had created made fun of the stereotypical roles she had always been cast to play. Saying that she had not received any "feedback flak from her own people," Moreno told a *New York Times* writer, "The Spanish people who come backstage say they love what I'm doing. Of course, some *Latins* might take offense, but I don't want to meet them. I don't want to talk to anyone who doesn't have a sense of humor about themselves. . . . I have had to learn to laugh at myself—otherwise there would be lines of sorrow from my forehead to my toes."

Moreno's next appearance was in the motion picture version of *The Ritz*. While this performance was not as appreciated as the one on Broadway, many believed this was the fault of the director, Richard Lester. Later, however, guest appearances on *The Muppet Show* in 1977 won her an Emmy for outstanding continuing or single performance by a supporting actress in variety or music. She won another Emmy for outstanding lead actress for a single appearance in a drama or comedy series in 1978 for her appearance in "The Paper Palace" episode of the series *The Rockford Files.* Moreno went on to portray a Jewish mother in *The Boss's Son* (1979), and to develop a nightclub act which she has since performed in Chicago, New York City, Lake Tahoe, Toronto, Atlantic City, and on various cruise ships. Her next motion picture role did not come until 1980, when she played an Italian American mistress in *Happy Birthday, Gemini.* And in 1981, Moreno was given the opportunity to star with Alan Alda and Carol Burnett in the motion picture comedy *The Four Seasons.*

In 1982 Moreno found herself on television once again. She appeared as a secretary named Violet Newstead in ABC's *Nine to Five.* This situation comedy, based on Jane Fonda's movie of the same name, promoted the rights of working women. While it did relatively well from 1982 to 1983, its ratings fell after a time-slot change, and it was taken off the air. Despite the failure of the series, Moreno was nominated for an Emmy. Moreno's next career move was to return to the stage. With James Coco and Sally Struthers, she appeared in *Wally's Cafe* on Broadway for twelve performances in June of 1981. In 1985, she was again starring with Struthers, this time as the slobby Olive Madison in a revision of Neil Simon's comedy, *The Odd Couple,* on Broadway. The play, which was originally written for two male principals, was not well received despite its talented cast.

Since then, Moreno has been involved in a variety of activities. Although she loves to spend time with her family in their homes in Pacific Palisades, California, and Manhattan, Moreno also finds ways to spend time with Leonard Gorman and Fernanda Luisa professionally. She has appeared several times with her daughter, Fernanda, in theaters around the nation in *Steel Magnolias* and *The Taming of the Shrew.* She was a member of the board of directors of Third World Cinema and the Alvin Ailey Dance Company, and she was included on the theater panel of the National Foundation of the Arts. With her husband Gordon as her manager and partner, she is committed to the Hispanic community. She remarked in *Hispanic:* "Lenny and I are very involved in trying to make the Hispanic community understand that education is everything."

While Moreno is aware of the responsibility she has as a Hispanic role model, she is, as she explained in *Hispanic,* an actress with career aspirations. It is to Moreno's credit that she attempts to combine her love of acting with her desire to assist the Hispanic community. She told another *Hispanic* interviewer, "When I was a young starlet, I wanted to be an all-American girl. . . . But when I grew up and developed a sense of self-esteem as a Hispanic, I learned how essential it was to cling to one's own heritage, for only

in that way can we truly understand our ancestors, our culture, and ultimately understand ourselves."

## SELECTED DISCOGRAPHY:

*Pagan Love Song,* 1950.
*So Young, So Bad,* 1950.
*The Toast of New Orleans,* 1950.
*Cattle Town,* 1952.
*The Fabulous Senorita,* 1952.
*The Ring,* 1952.
*Singing in the Rain,* 1952.
*El Alamein,* 1953.
*Fort Vengence,* 1953.
*Latin Lovers,* 1953.
*Garden of Evil,* 1954.
*Jivaro,* 1954.
*The Yellow Tomahawk,* 1954.
*The Lieutenant Wore Skirts,* 1955.
*Seven Cities of Gold,* 1955.
*Untamed,* 1955.
*The King and I,* 1956.
*The Vagabond King,* 1956.
*The Deerslayer,* 1957.
*The Rebel Breed,* 1960.
*Summer and Smoke,* 1961.
*West Side Story,* 1961.
*Cry of Battle,* 1963.
*She Loves Me,* 1964.
*Marlowe,* 1969.
*The Night of the Following Day,* 1969.
*Popi,* 1969.
*Carnal Knowledge,* 1971.
*The Ritz,* 1976.
*Anatomy of Seduction,* 1979.
*The Boss' Son,* 1979.
*Happy Birthday, Gemini,* 1980.
*The Four Seasons,* 1981.
*Portrait of a Showgirl,* 1982.
*Age Isn't Everything,* 1991.

## SOURCES:

### Books

*Current Biography Yearbook,* H. W. Wilson, 1985.

### Periodicals

*Boston Globe,* September 5, 1986, p. 62; September 8, 1986, p. 26.
*Chicago Tribune,* May 3, 1988, section 5, p. 3; November 15, 1988, section 5, p. 8.
*Cosmopolitan,* August 1981, p. 14.
*Harper's Bazaar,* May, 1981, pp. 160–61; September, 1981, pp. 309–11.
*Hispanic,* October, 1989, pp. 30–33; December, 1989, p. 40; September, 1990, p. 56.

*Los Angeles Times,* November 17, 1988, section 6, p. 1.

*Ms.,* January-February, 1991, pp. 93–95.

*Newsweek,* May 25, 1981, p. 74.

*New Yorker,* June 22, 1981, p. 86; June 24, 1985, p. 78.

*New York Post,* March 13, 1955.

*New York Times,* March, 1975.

*Nuestro,* October, 1981, pp. 44–46; March, 1986, pp. 16–25.

*People,* May 3, 1982, pp. 105–07.

*TV Guide,* January 15, 1983, pp. 26–29.

*Variety,* February 26, 1986, p. 60.

*Washington Post,* March 19, 1990, p. C5.

—*Sketch by Ronie-Richele Garcia-Johnson*

# Anthony Munoz
## 1958-

### Hispanic American professional football player

Anthony Munoz, who played for the Cincinnati Bengals for more than a decade, was one of the finest offensive linemen in the history of the National Football League. Munoz appeared in two Super Bowls and ten Pro Bowls over the course of his career. In 1991 he was named the American Football Conference's Offensive Lineman of the Year, and for several years he held the title of the NFL's Strongest Man. Munoz is also known as a man who has devoted a significant amount of time and effort to various charities. He has been a visible spokesman for anti-drug campaigns, cystic fibrosis research, and other causes. After retiring from football, he joined the Fox Television Network as a sportscaster.

Born in San Bernadino, California, on August 19, 1958, Munoz grew up in Ontario, California, near Los Angeles. His mother Esther raised Munoz and her other four children herself because Munoz's father left the family when Munoz was still a young child. His mother supported her children by working at a farm, where she packed eggs into cartons. Looking back on his childhood in *Sports Illustrated,* Munoz said that "I don't even know if I was poor. We were provided for, but we didn't have any extras. We didn't have a car, but we had relatives who drove. I got everywhere I wanted to go." His wife DeDe, though, commented that "Anthony downplays it, but there was a lot of pain there, a lot of hard times. I really admire Anthony's mother. Somehow she made it all work."

For most of Munoz's childhood, baseball was his first sports love. A large and talented child, his abilities were in much demand. As Jim Semon, a mentor and baseball coach to Munoz, noted, "He was on so many teams that when they had to play each other, they would fight over him." By high school, however, Munoz had grown so large that he felt a certain obligation to play football.

Recruited by various universities for football, baseball, and basketball, Munoz settled on the University of Southern California, where he played football and baseball. At 6'6" and 280 pounds Munoz didn't resemble the typical lean college baseball player. "I was the biggest third baseman in captivity," he once told Bob Oates of the *Los Angeles Times.* He credits his experiences in other sports for at least a portion of his football success: "In basketball, I was staggering around at 260 pounds trying to guard 180 pounders. That made me work hard on my quickness . . . I really doubt if I'd be the football player I am if I hadn't liked basketball and baseball so much that I pushed myself to excel."

### Pro Bowler

Munoz joined the Cincinnati Bengals in 1980. He had experienced knee trouble in college, a factor that at one time concerned Paul Brown, the general manager of the Bengals. But Munoz's performance in the Rose Bowl against Ohio State University put Brown's mind at ease. He told *Sports Illustrated* that as he watched Munoz's final college game, he and his sons "sat there and laughed out loud. The guy was so big and so good it was a joke."

Superlatives were often used to describe Munoz's professional football career. Although an offensive lineman typically doesn't get the attention of a quarterback or a running back, Munoz had many devoted fans. His peers in the league appreciated his talents as well. Munoz's teammate in Cincinnati, quarterback Boomer Esiason, told the *Atlanta Constitution* that Munoz was "the greatest football player I've ever seen." The *Washington Post* called him possibly "the best offensive tackle in the history of pro football."

After retiring in 1991, Munoz became even more involved in the charity work he had pursued since the beginning of his career. A long-time participant in a wide range of community projects, his retirement provided him with more time to contribute to more than a dozen charitable organizations including Athletes in Action, United Appeal, Cystic Fibrosis, and the Salvation Army. He also has made frequent journeys to Mexico on missionary trips. Munoz and his wife DeDe and their two children continued to live in Cincinnati after his retirement from football.

**SOURCES:**

*Atlanta Constitution,* January 19, 1989, p. F4.
*Los Angeles Times,* January 19, 1989, section 3, p. 1.
*New York Times,* December 21, 1989, p. D23.
*Sports Illustrated,* September 10, 1990, p. 79–82.
*Washington Post,* January 18, 1989, p. C1.

—*Sketch by James McCarthy*

# Luis Muñoz Marín
## 1898-1980
### Puerto Rican politician and writer

Statesman and writer Luis Muñoz Marín played a crucial role in the development of modern Puerto Rico. During his twenty-five year tenure as the country's first elected governor, Muñoz Marín lead Puerto Rico to become a self-governing commonwealth of the United States in 1952. He also initiated a country-wide development program known as Operation Bootstrap, which improved economic and social conditions in the lesser developed areas of Puerto Rico. In his biography of Muñoz Marín, *Poet in the Fortress,* Thomas Aitken, Jr., described the Puerto Rican leader as a combination of opposites: "Poetry and politics, toughness and tenderheartedness, idealism and practicality, the colossal energy of the doer and the contemplative nature of the thinker." For his many accomplishments on behalf of his homeland, Muñoz Marín is known as "the father of modern Puerto Rico."

Puerto Rico, an island in the Caribbean Sea, was discovered by Christopher Columbus and later claimed for Spain by Ponce de Leon in the sixteenth century. For centuries the islanders desired independence from colonial rule, and in 1897 Luis Muñoz Rivera, an important member of the Puerto Rican Autonomist party and soon-to-be father of Luis Muñoz Marín, negotiated it. The island's independence was short-lived, however, for during the Spanish-American War (1898), Puerto Rico came under the control of the United States.

On February 18, 1898, in San Juan, Puerto Rico, Amalia Marín de Muñoz Rivera gave birth to her only son, Luis Muñoz Marín. Immersed in politics, the young boy grew up in New York and Washington, D.C., where his father was the Resident Commissioner for Puerto Rico, a position in which he represented Puerto Rican interests to the United States Congress. Muñoz Marín attended the Georgetown Preparatory School in Washington and studied law at Georgetown University until his father's death in 1916. Muñoz Marín then relocated to New York City, where he embarked on a writing career, contributing to such newspapers as the *Baltimore Sun, New York Herald Tribune,* and *La Democracia,* the Puerto Rican paper founded by Muñoz Rivera. His pieces also appeared in the periodicals *New Republic, Nation,* and *American Mercury,* among others. In addition to his work as a freelance journalist and translator into Spanish of works by American poets Walt Whitman and Carl Sandburg, in 1917 Muñoz Marín published two volumes of poetry: *Borrones* and *Madre Haraposa.*

It was not long before Muñoz Marín became involved in Latin American affairs. From 1916 to 1918 he worked as secretary to the Puerto Rican representative to the U.S. Congress, the position formerly held by his father. During Muñoz Marín's tenure as secretary, the Jones Act, for which Muñoz Rivera had long fought, gave American citizenship, a Bill of Rights, and a popularly elected, bicameral legislature to Puerto Ricans. Yet the island was still administered by a governor appointed by the U.S. government.

In 1919 Muñoz Marín married Muna Lee, an American poet, with whom he had two children—son Luis and daughter Munita. The couple would separate in 1940 and divorce several years later.

Muñoz Marín joined Santiago Iglesias's Puerto Rican Socialist Party in 1920, but he left it four years later in a dispute over the question of independence for Puerto Rico. Santiago sought complete independence for the island, while Muñoz Marín believed a limited association with the United States would best serve Puerto Rican interests. After working for the unsuccessful presidential campaign of Robert La Follette in 1924, Muñoz Marín returned to Puerto Rico, where he acted as the publisher and editor of the politically motivated newspaper *La Democracia.* Muñoz Marín quickly demonstrated where his sympathies lay: with the *jíbaros,* the farmer peasants of the hill country. American-owned sugar and tobacco companies ran plantations that drained dry Puerto Rican agriculture, leaving the islanders impoverished. To make matters worse, in 1928 a major hurricane devastated Puerto Ricans' one cash crop—coffee. Muñoz Marín believed it was his duty to change this state of affairs.

### Wins Senatorial Race

In 1932, voters elected Muñoz Marín to the Puerto Rican legislature, where as a senator he led the Puerto Rican Liberal Party. Like most of the world in this era, Puerto Rico was mired in a serious economic depression. Muñoz Marín succeeded in convincing the administration of American President Franklin Delano Roosevelt to send millions of dollars to

Puerto Rico, through his New Deal plan to resurrect the American economy. Muñoz Marín also used his political clout to remove the unpopular American-appointed Governor Gore from office, and to enforce a long-neglected land law to dissolve the large sugar plantations that practically enslaved the rural populace. Land that had been held in large tracts by sugar plantation owners was purchased by the government and parcelled out to Puerto Rican peasant farmers.

Eventually Muñoz Marín came to believe that the Liberal Party would not adequately fight for the interests of the *jíbaros* so he struck out on his own. During 1938, he organized the Popular Democratic Party. Muñoz Marín spoke out against independence for Puerto Rico, an issue that pre-occupied the liberals to the exclusion of other issues. In contrast, the new party championed social and economic improvements, relegating the question of independence to secondary status. On the Popular Democratic Party platform were such goals as rural electrification, enforcement of the law to break up sugar plantations, other regulations on businesses, a minimum wage, and incentives to attract new industries to the island. Running for the Senate, Muñoz Marín was a personable campaigner, giving speeches in two-thirds of the voting districts and sending recorded messages to those communities he could not visit himself. Not only did Muñoz Marín have to campaign with a new identity, he had to combat the widespread practice of selling votes.

Despite voter corruption, Muñoz Marín won a resounding victory in the 1940 election, and the Popular party narrowly gained control of the Senate, though it was unable to win a majority of seats in the House. Nevertheless, the election marked the beginning of a twenty-five year period of control by the Popular party. Muñoz Marín, who was soon elected President of the Senate, teamed up with the newly appointed governor, Rexford Tugwell, to legislate needed reforms. A massive building campaign was begun to provide an alternative to urban slums. A development corporation gave incentives, such as tax relief and labor advice, to industries willing to move their operations to Puerto Rico. A state-run utility company provided rural electrification, and the Land Authority purchased land and redistributed it among the peasant farmers, who farmed it cooperatively. These reforms brought Muñoz Marín unparalleled popularity.

The Popular Party won by a landslide the majority of seats in both the House and Senate in the 1944 election. Muñoz Marín continued to push for reforms. Believing that industrialization would raise the standard of living and slow the explosive rate of population growth on the island, he championed the Industrial Incentives Act of 1947. Under this legislation, the government financed the construction of an infrastructure (roads, education, transportation and communications systems) that could attract foreign investors. Industries previously owned by the government were sold to private entrepreneurs. On the personal front, when his divorce from Muna Lee became final in 1947, Muñoz Marín married Inés Maria Mendosa, a school teacher. They would have two daughters: Viviana and Victoria.

## Wins Governorship

When Puerto Ricans earned the right to elect their own governor in 1948, they chose their longtime champion—Muñoz Marín. Under his leadership, the Puerto Rico Industrial Development Corporation came to life. This entity was charged with the development plan that became known as "Operation Bootstrap," a loose translation of Muñoz Marín's campaign slogan "Jalda Arriba!"—Spanish for "Up the Hill." Through this plan, the Puerto Rican government again offered tax breaks and other incentives to foreign industries willing to move to the island. By 1952 nearly two hundred plants were opened, providing employment for thousands of Puerto Ricans. Yet some critics decried the low minimum wage that was used to attract foreign investors, maintaining that the factory system unfairly tied Puerto Ricans to the U.S. economy. The Puerto Rican government also financed the construction of a luxury hotel in San Juan, which was later sold to private interests. Soon more hotels sprang up along the beaches. To the astonishment of many Puerto Ricans, their island could attract millions of tourist dollars.

## Leads Country to Commonwealth Status

With some progress being made on economic and social issues, Muñoz Marín turned to the issue of Puerto Rican autonomy. In July 1950 the U.S. Congress authorized the Puerto Rican Legislature to write its own constitution and to ratify it by popular vote. Muñoz Marín, believing that Puerto Rico could not effectively meet the demands placed on American states by the U.S. federal government, crusaded for status as a commonwealth of the United States. In 1951 a large majority—seventy-six percent—of voters cast their votes in favor of Puerto Rico's becoming a Free Associated State. A constitutional convention drafted a new constitution that gave the islanders great autonomy on local issues. It was ratified in 1952.

During the fifties and sixties, voters returned Muñoz Marín to office again and again as Puerto Rico became the richest state in the Caribbean. Many of the formerly poverty-stricken *jíbaros* became industrial workers, part of the new middle class. Housing projects provided accommodations for this industrial population. The number of hospitals increased, with gains in the quality of health care, as shown by the decreasing infant mortality rate. The number of schools and students attending them grew dramatically to provide the literate workers of the future. Nevertheless, problems remained. The population continued to grow dramatically, and unemployment stubbornly topped ten percent. During the forties, twenty thousand Puerto Ricans had emigrated to the United States mainland annually. The fifties saw some fifty thousand islanders leave each year, most destined for New York City, where some six hundred thousand congregated in Spanish-speaking ghettos.

For his decades of dedicated service to the people of Puerto Rico, Muñoz Marín was awarded the Presidential Medal of Freedom in 1963. The following year, he declined the nomination for a fifth term as governor. Instead he opted to run for the Senate and was elected a senator-at-large, leaving his protégé, Roberto Sánchez Vilella, to take charge. Three years later, Puerto Rican voters again affirmed their choice of status for the island when they chose to remain a commonwealth of the United States. The next year, when the Popular Party lost control of the Legislature, signaled the end of the era in which Muñoz Marín had dominated Puerto Rican political life.

Looking forward to traveling and writing, Muñoz Marín retired from politics in 1970. However, when pro-statehood arguments began surfacing again, Muñoz Marín jumped back into the fray to defend his longtime position on Puerto Rico's status. In 1979 ill health forced the former governor to give up his independent campaign against statehood. After suffering a series of heart attacks, the father of modern Puerto Rico died on April 30, 1980 in San Juan.

## SELECTED PUBLISHED WORKS:

*Luis Muñoz Marín: Pensamiento político, económico, social y cultural, según expresado en los discursos oficiales,* Corporación de Servicios Bibliotecarios (Río Piedras), 1973.
*Mensajes al Pueblo Puertorriqueño Pronunciados ante las Cameras Legislativas, 1949–1964,* Inter American University Press, 1980. *Memorias: Autobiografía pública, 1898–1940,* Universidad Interamericana de Puerto Rico, 1982.
*Historia del Partido Popular Democrático,* El Batey (San Juan, Puerto Rico), 1984.
*Celebracíon del octogésimo octavo aniversario del natalicio de Don Luis Muñoz Marín,* Departamento de Instrucción Pública, Estado Libre Asociado de Puerto Rico, 1986.

## SOURCES:

### Books

Aitken, Thomas, Jr., *Poet in the Fortress; The Story of Luis Muñoz Marín,* New York, New American Library, 1964.

Anderson, Robert W., *Party Politics in Puerto Rico,* Stanford, Stanford University Press, 1965.
*Biographical Dictionary of Latin American and Caribbean Political Leaders,* edited by Robert J. Alexander, Westport, Greenwood Press, 1988.
*Hispanic Writers,* edited by Bryan Ryan, Detroit, Gale, 1991.
Lewis, Gordon K., *Puerto Rico: Freedom and Power in the Caribbean,* New York, Monthly Review Press, 1963.
Lopez, Adalberto, and James Petras, *Puerto Rico and the Puerto Ricans,* New York, Schenkman, 1974.
Norris, Marianna, *Father and Son for Freedom: The Story of Puerto Rico's Luis Muñoz Rivera and Luis Muñoz Marín,* New York, Dodd, Mead, 1968.
Tugwell, Rexford G. *The Art of Politics, as Practised by Three Great Americans: Franklin Delano Roosevelt, Luis Muñoz Marín, and Fiorello H. La Guardia,* Garden City, Doubleday, 1958.

### Periodicals

*Newsweek,* May 12, 1980, p. 111.
*Time,* May 12, 1980, p. 68.

*—Sketch by J. M. Lesinski*

# Alvaro Mutis
## 1923-
### Colombian writer

Alvaro Mutis is a poet and novelist who has spent most of his life outside his native Colombia. Jean McNeil asserted in the *Times Literary Supplement* that "Mutis is at heart a philosophical writer, one for whom narrative is a function of ideas." His work, which occupies a niche beyond the parameters of reality, reflects his residential state of flux, his internationalism, and his antipathy towards the violence in Colombia which has caused him to ponder the futility of life in many of his works. Mutis has

*Alvaro Mutis*

declared that he has never been politically active, and that his concerns are historically rooted in the fall of Constantinople in 1453. He is also a self-proclaimed ardent monarchist. He was awarded the El Aquila Azteca in 1989.

Alvaro Mutis was born on August 25, 1923 in Bogotá. He spent much of his early childhood in Brussels, Belgium, where he received his formative education. When visiting Colombia during his vacations, he stayed on his family's coffee and cane plantation, located at the confluence of the Cocora and the Coello rivers. Of his home region he wrote, "Everything I have written is destined to perpetuate, to celebrate, to record that corner of the warm land from which comes the very substance of my dreams, my nostalgias, my ideas. There is not one line of my work that does not refer, in a secret and subterranean or an explicit and obvious form, to that boundless world that that corner of Tolima is for me."

Mutis' debut publication, *La balanza* (*The Balance*), a joint publication with Carlos Patiño, appeared in 1948. A collection of poems that signalled a new trend in Colombian poetry, *La balanza* was inadvertantly burned during the violent uprising that followed the assassination of the liberal leader Jorge Eliécer Gaitán. During the 1940s and 1950s, Mutis belonged to a group of experimental Colombian poets, who were collectively known as "Mito." Mutis' work conveys the strong influence of the violent environment in Colombia between 1947 and 1957, which is illustrated for example, in his second compi-

lation of poems, *Los elementos del desastre* (*The Elements of the Disaster*), published in 1953 in Buenos Aires.

In 1956, Mutis moved to Mexico, where he still resides. The poetry written since his move contains the imprint of an exile. Indeed, travel has been a constant feature of his life, adding flavor to his poetry and enabling him to develop and retain literary and artistic associations on an international level. Soon after his arrival in Mexico, Mutis published several books: *Reseña de los hospitales de ultramar* (1958) and *Diario de Lecumberri* (1959), which received favorable critical reviews from celebrated writers, including **Octavio Paz.**

It was not, however, until the publication of *Summa de Maqroll el Gaviero* and *La mansión de Araucaima* in 1973, that Mutis achieved international acclaim. He followed up this success with *Caravansary* (1982), *Los emisarios* (1984) and *Crónica Regia y Alabanza del Reino* (1985); the latter collection of poetry he dedicated to King Philip II and his family. Mutis resurrects Maqroll el Gaviero in *Tribulaciones y empresas de Maqroll el Gaviero*, a trilogy of novellas: *La nieve del Almirante* (1986), *Ilona llega con la lluvia* (1987) and *Un bel morir* (1989). The trilogy is rich in language and adventure, Mutis' signatory marks.

## SELECTED PUBLISHED WORKS:

*Los elementos del desastre,* Editorial Losada, 1953.
*Diario de Lecumberri,* Universidad Veracruana, 1960.
*Los trabajos perdidos,* Mexico, Era, 1965.
*La mansión de Araucaíma; relato gótico de tierra caliente,* Buenos Aires, Editorial Sudamericana, 1973.
*Summa de Maqroll el Gaviero (Poesía 1947–1970),* Barral Editories, 1973.
*Caravansary,* Fondo de Cultura Económica, 1981.
*Puesía y Prosa,* Bogotá, Innstituto Colombiano de Culturo, 1982.
*Summa de Maqroll el Gaviero,* Bogotá, Oveja Negra, 1982.
*Los emisarios,* Fondo de Cultura Económica, 1984.
*Obra literaria,* Nueva Biblioteca Colomviana de Cultura, 1985.
*Historia natural de las cosas,* Fondo de Cultura Económica, 1985.
*Crónica regia; y, Alabanza del reino,* Ediciones Cátedra, 1985.
*Sesenta cuerpos,* Medellín, Colombia, Comité de Publicaciones, 1985.
*La nieve del almirante,* Alianza, 1986.
*Un homenaje y siete nocturnos,* Mexico, Equilibrista, 1986.
*Ilona llega con la lluvia,* Bogotá, Editorial Oveja Negra, 1987.

*La muerte de estratega*, Fondo de Cultura Económica, 1988.

## SOURCES:

### Books

*Hispanic Writers: A Selection of Sketches from Contemporary Authors,* edited by Bryan Ryan, Detroit, Gale Research, 1991.

*Spanish American Authors: The Twentieth Century,* edited by Angel Flores, New York, H. W. Wilson, 1992.

### Periodicals

*Times Literary Supplement,* June 11, 1993, p 23.
*World Literature Today,* Volume 60, 1986, p. 608.

—*Sketch by Amanda Beresford*

*José Celestino Mutis*

# José Celestino Mutis
## 1732-1808
### Spanish botanist, physician, and priest

Spanish-born botanist José Celestino Mutis gained renown in Spain and South America as a scientist and teacher; he was also a physician and priest. He served as royal physician to Ferdinand VI before going to the New World to pursue his interest in botany. A disciple of Swedish botanist Carolus Linnaeus (Carl von Linné), he headed one of three royal botanical expeditions in South America, ordered by Carlos III. Mutis's area of study was New Granada; he was responsible for the discovery and classification of thousands of plants in South America.

José Celestino Bruno Mutis y Bosio was born April 6, 1732, in Cádiz, Spain to Julián Mutis and Gregoria Bosio. Mutis attended the University of Seville, studying philosophy and grammar, and earned a Bachelor's degree in 1753. Mutis then studied medicine in Madrid, earning his medical degree in 1755. He also studied theology and became a priest. He was appointed royal physician in the household of Ferdinand VI at the age of 25. Mutis had a fascination with botany and studied when his medical duties allowed him the time.

### Studies Botany in South America

On September 7, 1760, Mutis left Madrid for New Grenada (now Colombia), where he was to serve as physician to the new viceroy, Pedro Mesía de la Cerda. Mutis had sought the appointment, as he wished to continue his botanical study and was intrigued with the unknown flora of the New World. They landed at Cartagena, where they stayed for some time. Mutis' medical duties kept him busy, and as in Spain, he studied plants and collected specimens when he could. In addition to serving as physician to the viceroy, his appointment in New Grenada was for the purpose of botanical study and adding to the royal collection in Spain; he was also interested in finding uses for new plants as well as those already known. He corresponded regularly with Linnaeus, and sent him specimens and drawings. He wished to start a botanical garden, but when he sought royal financing for his project he was turned down due to lack of funds. Mutis continued his studies and made several excursions into the interior to discover new plant life.

In 1766 he went to Pamplona, Spain, to teach medicine and botany and to further his scientific studies. He made reforms in the teaching of medicine, and was also responsible for the modernization of mining. Mutis was formally appointed first botanist and astronomer in 1782 by a new viceroy, Archbishop Antonio Caballero y Góngora. Mutis established the Botanical Expedition of New Granada in 1783 and built a botanical garden in Mariquita, but later moved it to Bogotá when headquarters were established there. He assembled vast amounts of taxonomy information regarding the plants of South America and created a botanical library for which he is renowned. He had a staff of artists and scientists to assist him in his botanical and zoological studies. His written papers numbered in the hundreds and he also wrote a massive, unpublished book, *Flora de Bogotá o de Nueva Granada,* which contained over 6,000 illustrations. Although his work was vast, it remained mostly unknown outside of Spain and South America. Europe became acquainted with his work when the German scientist Friedrich Alexander Humboldt and French botanist Aimé Bonpland published their book, *Equinoctial Plants* and dedicated it to Mutis, the "Patriarch of Botany in the New World." It was not until the mid-twentieth century that 51 volumes of Mutis's own book were published jointly by the governments of Spain and Colombia. Mutis's diary from the expedition in New Granada was published in 1957.

Mutis is credited with the development of many scholars in South America, having taught medicine, botany, astronomy, geology, zoology, and biology. It is said that some of his students later became leaders in the country's revolution in the 1800s.

## SOURCES:

### Books

Goodman, Edward J., *The Explorers of South America,* New York, Macmillan, 1972.

Gredilla, Federico A., *Biografia De Jose Celestino Mutis,* Bogotá, Colombia, Academia Colombiana De Historia/Plaza & Janes, 1982.

Miller, Robert Ryal, *For Science and National Glory,* Norman, University of Oklahoma Press, 1968.

### Periodicals

*Hispanic American Historical Review,* February 1989, pp. 163–164.

*—Sketch by Sandy J. Stiefer*

# Gregory Nava
## 1949-
### Hispanic American screen writer and director

Gregory Nava is a screen writer and director who, along with his wife and co-writer Anna Thomas, was nominated for an Academy Award for Best Original Screenplay for his 1984 film *El Norte*. Critics hailed the movie, which Nava also directed, for its innovative departure from stereotypical Hispanic roles and themes. In addition, reviewers applauded *El Norte* for its moving depiction of the striking contrast between the oppressive poverty of Mexico and the ostentatious wealth of the neighboring United States.

Nava was born in 1949, but little more information is available about his parents, early life, or education. He attended the University of California in Los Angeles, where he studied filmmaking. At the age of 28, Nava wrote *The Confessions of Amans* with Thomas, and then directed the movie. Released in 1977, it details a tragic love affair during the medieval period. Nava's second movie as co-author and director was *The End of August,* released in 1982.

With the 1984 release of *El Norte*—his third film—Nava was lavished with praise by the film critics and audiences alike. *El Norte* tells the story of a young brother and sister from Guatemala who flee that country after their father is killed. The two children travel through poverty-stricken areas of Mexico before finally reaching the United States. Although they enter the country illegally through a tunnel that crosses the border in southern California, the sister manages to find a job as a maid in San Diego, while her brother finds work as a waiter. Gradually, the siblings overcome their homesickness and learn to accept their new American lifestyles.

Despite pressure from the studio to cast Anglo actors in the lead roles in *El Norte,* Nava insisted on using Hispanics in all of the major roles. As a result, the film conveys a stark authenticity which complements the intertwined themes of the reality of squalid poverty versus the artificiality of a wealthy consumer-oriented society. Reviewers generally praised Nava's directorial vision in shooting *El Norte,* arguing that his cinematography often produced brilliant visual poetry and enhanced the poignancy of the film's suspenseful moments. The fact that the film was made on a limited budget—much smaller than the average Hollywood film budget—added to Nava's reputation for innovation. In 1985, *El Norte* was nominated for an Academy Award for Best Original Screenplay, but it did not win.

Nava's next film, *A Time of Destiny,* met with less enthusiasm from reviewers and audiences upon its release in 1988. As before, Nava co-authored the script with his wife and directed the movie. The film centers on the daughter of Italian American immigrants who decides to marry against her father's wishes. Although she elopes, the father manages to convince her to return home on her wedding night. When her new husband gives chase, the resulting car accident has tragic consequences. Undaunted by the lackluster reception of *A Time of Destiny,* Nava has turned to other film projects. His most recent screenplay, *Mi Familia, My Family,* is scheduled to be completed in 1995.

## SOURCES:

### Books

*Film Writers Guide,* edited by Susan Avallone, Los Angeles, Lone Eagle, 1991, p. 213.
*Hispanic-American Almanac,* edited by Nicolás Kanellos, Detroit, Gale, 1993, pp. 543–94.
*Hispanic Writers,* edited by Bryan Ryan, Detroit, Gale, 1991, pp. 327–28.

### Other

International Creative Management, Inc., correspondence with Catherine A. Clay, February 27, 1995.

*—Sketch by Catherine A. Clay*

# Julian Nava
## 1927-
### Mexican American educator, author, and ambassador

Julian Nava is a leading educator and respected author whose interest in Latin American history and efforts to improve American education led U.S. president Jimmy Carter to name him the United

States Ambassador to Mexico in 1979. Nava was the first Mexican American ever to serve in that position. He held the post until 1981. Once advised by a high school counselor in East Los Angeles to seek training in automobile body repair work, Nava instead pursued a career in academia, and eventually became a tenured university professor of history. Nava also immersed himself in community and public affairs, and once served as president of the Los Angeles School Board.

Nava was born in the Los Angeles barrio neighborhood of Boyle Heights on June 19, 1927. His immigrant parents, Julian Nava and Ruth Flores Nava, had fled their native country during the Mexican Revolution. As a child, Nava attended public schools and spent his summers picking fruit with his family and other Mexican American workers.

Nava went on to serve in the United States Navy Air Corps in 1945 and 1946. He took advantage of the GI Bill, a government program that paid for the cost of veterans' college education, to earn an associate degree in 1949 from East Los Angeles Community College. Nava continued his studies at California's Pomona College, which conferred his BA degree in 1951. As a graduate student at Harvard University, Nava received financial support from the John Hay Whitney Foundation and the Bravo Fund. He earned his doctorate in 1955.

Nava's teaching career began in 1953 at the United States Cultural Center in Caracas, Venezuela, where he taught English language and U.S. history courses. From 1955 to 1957, he was a lecturer at the University of Puerto Rico. He then returned to California, where he was appointed an associate professor of history at San Fernando Valley State College. Nava also served as co-director of the National Defense Education Act Institute in History at that institution. In 1962 he traveled to Spain as a Fulbright exchange professor. That same year, Nava married Patricia Lucas. The couple went on to have twin daughters and a son. In the meantime, Nava's academic career flourished. He lectured at the Universidad Vallodolid and, again supported by Fulbright funds, conducted research in Seville's Archives of the Indies. Since 1967 he has been on the faculty of the California State University at Northridge.

### Public Service Leads to Presidential Appointment

During the course of his career, Nava has served in numerous leadership positions in the academic community. He founded the Great Lakes Colleges Association Center in Bogotá, Colombia, and has served on the Governing Board of the California State Colleges's Inter-American Institute. He has also devoted much of his time to public service. Nava chaired the founding committee for the city's historical preservation in 1961–62. In 1967 he was elected to the Los Angeles School Board and eventually became its president. He has also served on the board of directors for Los Angeles's World Affairs Council. Much of his work in the public sector has involved the support of causes of interest to Hispanics. He has served on advisory committees for the Mexican Legal Defense and Education Fund, Bilingual Children's Television, and La Raza Television.

When President Jimmy Carter appointed Nava Ambassador to Mexico in 1979, the scholar became the first Mexican American ever to hold that position. Nava served as ambassador until 1981. His contributions and achievements have also been recognized by Pomona College, which awarded him an honorary doctorate in 1980, and by Whittier College, which conferred one on him a year later.

Nava's research interests include Latin American social and cultural history and the influence of the Hispanic American people on U.S. history. His published works range from history textbooks to scholarly articles in education journals. Nava has argued that the two subjects—education and history—are closely linked. In a 1987 speech entitled "Teaching and Learning for the 21st Century" that was published in *Social Education,* Nava argued that educators must "find more ways to help young people benefit from and enjoy the rich cultural diversity of America. Schools can go far toward this goal. . . . Minority groups have made valuable contributions to our society. In the social studies for the next century, it is our task to make this clearer than in the past."

### SELECTED PUBLISHED WORKS:

*Mexican Americans: Past, Present and Future,* American Book Co., 1969.
*Mexican-Americans: A Brief Look at Their History,* Anti-Defamation League of B'nai B'rith, 1970.
*The Mexican American in American History,* edited by Nava, American Book Co., 1973.
*A General History of California,* with Bob Barger, Benziger, 1976.
*California: Five Centuries of Cultural Contrasts,* with Bob Barger, Glencoe Press, 1979.
Also author of children's educational series "Bilingual Stories of Today," Aardvark Media, 1973.

### SOURCES:

### Books

*Hispanic Writers,* edited by Bryan Ryan, Detroit, Gale, 1991.

*Hispanic-American Almanac,* edited by Nicolás Kanellos, Detroit, Gale, 1993.

*National Directory of Latin Americanists,* 3rd edition, edited by Inge Maria Harman, Washington, D.C., Library of Congress, 1985.

**Periodicals**

*Social Education,* March 1988, pp. 215–16.

—*Sketch by Erika Dreifus*

*Pablo Neruda*

# Pablo Neruda
## 1904-1973
### Chilean poet and political activist

Pablo Neruda, the winner of the 1971 Nobel Prize for literature, is considered by many readers and critics to be the foremost poet of the Latin American world in the twentieth century. His poetry, which often taps into the deepest, most elementary aspects of nature and existence, has been tremendously influential. Neruda was also a passionate participant in politics. Many of his poetic works commented on political themes and issues. In addition, he was a visible and vocal supporter of communist causes. He thus traveled extensively in the communist world of the Cold War.

### Motherless Childhood

Neftali Ricardo Reyes Basoalto—the child who would grow up to be Pablo Neruda—was born to Dona Rosa Basoalto on July 12, 1904, in Parral, Chile. A month later Neruda's mother died of tuberculosis, a sickness that had plagued her for years. This early event had a significant impact on Neruda's life and poetry. In his memoirs, Neruda remarked that his mother died "before I could have a memory of her, before I knew it was she my eyes gazed upon." Two poems written in Neruda's adolescence and published in *El rio invisible* reflect the feeling of absence and lost opportunity that the poet felt toward his mother. In "Moon" Neruda wrote: "She died. And I was born / And so I bear / an unseen river in my veins."

After his mother's death, Neruda went to live with his paternal grandfather, Jose Angel Reyes Hermosilla. His father, Jose del Carmen, worked as a conductor on a ballast train. Neruda later described the ballast train workers in his memoirs as men from "the fields, from the suburbs, from jails . . . huge, muscular laborers." As a child, Neruda saw his father frequently, but his grandfather and grandmother did most of the work of raising the child.

Neruda also recorded in his journals how he took advantage of his occasional trips on the ballast trains as his father's companion. When they reached Boroa, a place Neruda called "the savage heart of the frontier," Neruda would often slip away from his father and explore the unknown jungle wilderness. "There, nature made me euphoric." He became fascinated with the creatures of the jungle, uncovering beetles with shells strong enough to stand on without crushing, birds of untold colors, and other plants and animals. An intense love of the elemental forces of the natural world would one day inform much of his poetry.

Neruda began school in Temuco at age six. In his memoirs, Neruda told the story of writing love letters on behalf of a childhood friend. The object of the other boy's affection suspected Neruda to be the true author and confronted him. When he confessed that he had indeed written the letters, the young girl forgot about the other boy and turned her attentions to Neruda. Neruda called the letters "my first literary achievement."

### The Birth of "Pablo Neruda"

Neruda's interest in books and literature never waned, although his father voiced displeasure with his devotion to literature. Poetry, his father felt, only distracted the boy from learning a legitimate profession. On some occasions Neruda's father even burned poems that he found around the house. In the meantime, Neruda prepared to send poems off to magazines in hopes of having them published. He decided to change his name to blunt some of his father's anger at his activities. The name Pablo Neruda was chosen simply because he liked how it sounded. Neruda waited 35 years before he legally changed his name.

Neruda finished school and entered the university in Santiago. At the time Neruda entered college, French reigned as the international language of prestige and high culture. Neruda pursued study of French because it would enable him to read the works of Baudelaire and Rimbaud in their original language. Thus Neruda settled on French as a means of bringing a career and his love of literature together.

Neruda completed four years of university study but never received a degree, in part because of the uninhibited lifestyle he led. Yet his college years provided him with his first meaningful contact with the world of politics. The political movements on college campuses in those days combined with the literary world of the university to give Neruda a blueprint for his entire career. In a 1973 letter published in his memoirs, Neruda described his feelings about his time spent at the university in Santiago: "my memories linger tenderly on the old university school where I knew friendship, love, the meaning of popular struggle; in other words, my apprenticeship in consciousness and life."

### Early Publications and Travel in Asia

In 1923 Neruda published *Crepusculario*. A year later, he published *Viente poemas de amor y una cancion desesperada* (*Twenty Poems of Love and a Disdaining Song*). The collection contained many poems of love and desire and made him famous in Latin America. After leaving the university he began work on a larger project. This volume, entitled *Residencia en la tierra* (*Residence on Earth*), was not published until 1933, after his return from Asia.

In 1927 Neruda accepted a position as an honorary consul in Rangoon, Burma. Neruda commented in his memoirs that "a literary prize at school, some popularity my new books enjoyed, and my notorious cape had given me a small aura of respectability beyond artistic circles." Neruda tried unsuccessfully to parlay that clout into a diplomatic assignment to Europe. After many frustrating months, an influential friend accompanied Neruda to the foreign ministry, where the minister rattled off a list of cities that had diplomatic openings. Neruda said he "only managed to catch one name, which I had never heard or read before: Rangoon." Without knowing where or

what manner of place it might be, Neruda asked for the assignment and set out for Rangoon, the capital of Burma.

From Rangoon, Neruda took other positions as honorary consul in Colombo, Ceylon (now Sri Lanka), Batavia in Java, and Singapore. His various experiences in Asia probably inspired some of the experimental poetry of *Residencia en la tierra,* but Neruda often experienced isolation and loneliness among the people of those countries. In 1932 he returned to Chile, and shortly thereafter he received an assignment to go to Buenos Aires. While in Chile, he took the opportunity to publish *Residencia,* which he had completed during his travels, and another book called *El hondero entusiasta.*

After two years in Buenos Aires, Neruda received his long-desired assignment to Europe. Neruda first went to Barcelona, but the general consul already stationed there discovered that Neruda's mathematical skills were nearly nonexistent. Neruda recalled that the general consul finally told him to go to Madrid, a haven for artists.

In Madrid, Neruda found himself surrounded by intellectuals of all kinds. Miguel Hernandez, Serrano Plaja, Jose Caballero, **Valle-Inclan,** and others became members of Neruda's social circle. Neruda's reputation grew during this period. He was soon known around the world as one of the most prominent figures of a vibrant new artistic movement.

Spain's contentious politics, however, intervened and ended the artistic associations of the group. Siding with the Republicans against **Francisco Franco,** Neruda and his friends were threatened on more than one occasion. The celebrated poet **Federico García Lorca,** a friend of Neruda's, was one member of the circle who did not survive the political turbulence. He was assassinated by a fascist squad and buried in an unmarked grave. Franco and his allies eventually triumphed in their bid for control of the country, a development that prompted Neruda to leave Spain for Chile in 1937.

Neruda wrote a book called *Espana en el corazon* (*Spain at Heart*) about his experiences in Spain. Published in the desperate hours of the losing war with Franco, the book inspired the defenders of the revolution. Neruda later recalled that Republican soldiers sacrificed space in their sacks that would normally go to food and clothing to carry copies of the book. As the soldiers fled to France, they were repeatedly bombed by Franco's forces. Victims of these attacks, he said, fell across the length of the highway, their copies of *Spain at Heart* falling to the ground with them. An original copy of this book remains one of the rarest treasures of modern printing.

## Political Career in Chile

Upon his return to Chile, Neruda began his career as a political activist. When he returned to his home country, he openly joined in Communist Party activities, in part because of the changing political landscape of his homeland. Chile of the late 1930s had seen fascism rise as a political force. Neruda wrote in his memoirs about towns whose streets lay under "forests of flags bearing the swastika."

Neruda served as the editor of an anti-Nazi magazine and found other ways of registering his opposition to fascism as well. In 1940, Neruda went to Mexico again to work for his government. Again he found himself associated with artists and intellectuals, many of whom had come to Mexico to escape the Nazi juggernaut in Europe. He stayed in Mexico until 1943. On his way home to Chile he visited the ancient Incan city of Macchu Picchu. As he wandered through the old city, Neruda envisioned a history of America rich in glories but hidden from plain sight. His identity as a Latin American crystallized around the evidence of that ancient, pre-colombian civilization: "I felt Chilean, Peruvian, American. On those difficult heights, among those glorious, scattered ruins, I had found the principles of faith I needed to continue my poetry," he remarked in his memoirs. His epic poem *Alturas de Macchu Picchu,* first published in 1943, reflected this new awareness.

After officially joining the Communist Party in 1945, Neruda became a senator. He helped Communist Party candidate Gonzalez Videla win election to the presidency, but was bitterly disappointed with his former ally's transformation while in office. Neruda berated Videla and his performance, referring to him in his memoirs as a "vile, bloodthirsty vampire." As a result of his political agitation against the increasingly right-wing president, Neruda found it dangerous to remain in Chile.

Neruda used false documents to escape to Europe, narrowly eluding Chilean authorities. Enlisting the help of **Pablo Picasso,** Neruda made his way through France and eventually visited the Soviet Union, the heart of communism. He saw much that impressed him in his journey through that country, including the great Russian love of poetry.

### Return to Chile

Neruda returned to Chile two years later, and from that time until 1971, Neruda wrote prolifically and continued to work for the Communist Party. In 1971 he again accepted a position as a diplomat and went to France to serve as the Chilean ambassador to Paris. That same year, the Swedish Academy awarded Neruda the Nobel Prize for literature in recognition of the merit of his immense body of work.

Neruda resigned from his ambassador position in 1973 because of failing health. Neruda died in Santiago on September 23, 1973. His last months were unhappy ones, for he was witness to the crumbling of President **Salvador Allende**'s government and the rise of the dictatorial regime of General **Augusto Pinochet,** who officially took power in 1974. Neruda's funeral, which was attended by many mourners, became not only a memorial to the poet but also a demonstration against the forces which he himself had battled most of his life.

## SELECTED PUBLISHED WORKS:

*Viente poemas de amor y una cancion desespera- da,* 1924; published as *Twenty Poems of Love and a Disdaining Song,* 1970.

*Residencia en la tierra,* 1933, 1935; published as *Residence on Earth,* 1946.

*Espana en el corazon* (*Spain at Heart*), 1937.

*Alturas de Macchu Picchu,* 1943; published as *Heights of Macchu Picchu,* 1967.

*Canto General* (*General Canto*), 1950.

*Las uvas y el viento* (*The Grapes and the Wind*), 1954.

*Memoirs,* Farrar, Straus and Giroux, 1977.

## SOURCES:

Santi, Enrico, *Pablo Neruda: The Poetics of Prophecy,* Ithaca, NY: Cornell University Press, 1982.

Teitelboim, Volodia, *Neruda: An Intimate Biography,* translated by Beverly DeLong-Tonelli, Austin, TX: University of Texas Press, 1991.

*—Sketch by James McCarthy*

# Josephina Niggli
## 1910-
### Mexican American writer

Novelist and playwright Josephina Niggli is best known for eschewing popular stereotypes to capture the true flavor of northern Mexican culture, particularly in her novel *Mexican Village.* In his study of Chicano literature as published in *MELUS,* Raymond A. Paredes declared, "*Mexican*

*Village* stands as a major transitional work in the development of Chicano fiction. . . . Niggli's greatest achievement was to delineate an important aspect of Mexican American experience and to create a distinctive ambience for its presentation."

Niggli started writing early, encouraged by her parents and teachers. An only child, Niggli was born to Frederick Ferdinand and Goldie Morgan, a cement plant manager and a concert violinist, respectively, on July 13, 1910, in Monterrey, Mexico. The Mexican Revolution, which erupted the year of Josephina's birth, drove the family to San Antonio, Texas, in 1913, in search of safety. "Little Niggli", as Josephina was nicknamed, was home-schooled until her teenage years, when she attended Main Avenue High School in San Antonio.

At age 15, Niggli enrolled in San Antonio's Incarnate Word College. While there, she won second place in a short story contest held by *Ladies' Home Journal.* Niggli went on to publish other pieces in magazines such as *Mexican Life* and *Collier's.* For local radio station KTSA, she wrote radio plays that proved to be quite popular. In 1928, Niggli's father paid to have a collection of her poems published under the title *Mexican Silhouettes;* shortly after publication, the chapbook won the National Catholic College Poetry Contest.

### Joined Theatrical Troupe

After earning her bachelor of arts degree in 1931, Niggli studied playwriting with Coates Gwynne, director of the San Antonio Little Theatre. Gwynne quickly recognized Niggli's talent and encouraged her to continue her education. Four years later, Niggli entered the University of North Carolina at Chapel Hill, where she began her fruitful association with the Carolina Playmakers. Displaying her versatility, she wrote, directed, designed costumes, and acted in the folk-oriented plays that were the company's specialty. During her years at Chapel Hill, Niggli wrote some of her best plays, including *Tooth or Shave, The Cry of Dolores, The Red Velvet Goat, Azteca, Sunday Costs Five Pesos, Soldadera,* and *The Singing Valley,*—all written from 1935 to 1936.

Niggli's plays ranged from lighthearted, folkloric comedies to serious historical dramas. For example, the farcical *Tooth or Shave* portrayed two married couples who disagree about appearances, while *Soldadera* depicted the efforts of women soldiers during the Mexican Revolution. *The Singing Valley,* which served as the thesis for Niggli's master of arts degree, revolved around a father who brings his U.S.-reared children to Mexico, the land of his birth.

During the middle and late 1930s, Niggli won two fellowships in dramaturgy from the Rockefeller Foundation. She also worked at the Theatre of the National University of Mexico under playwriter Rodolfo Usigli. In 1938, Niggli lived in New York City on a fellowship of the Bureau of New Plays, allowing her to attend many theatrical productions as she honed her own craft. After returning to Chapel Hill the following year, she worked as a script editor for the Carolina Playmakers radio division.

The next decade found Niggli creating several more plays, among them *The Ring of General Macías,* about a Mexican family fighting revolutionary forces in its homeland, and *Miracle at Blaise,* dealing with a Hispanic American woman's participation in the French Resistance during World War II. While teaching English and drama at the University of North Carolina, Niggli made time—in the mornings before classes and on weekends—to work on her novel *Mexican Village.*

### First Novel Won Acclaim

In 1945, *Mexican Village* received the Mayflower Cup Award for "best book of the year by a North Carolinian." The work was translated into several languages, and in 1953, a movie based on the novel was developed; Niggli worked on the screenplay of the film version, which was called *Sombrero.* Commenting more than 30 years later on Niggli's novel, Raymond Paredes remarked in *MELUS:* "In its sensitive evocation of rural life, its emotionalism, and affectionate portrayal of exotic experiences and personalities, the book culminated the romantic tradition in Mexican American writing. But *Mexican Village* also pointed forward to an emerging school of realism, confronting such issues as racism, the oppression of women, and the failure of the Mexican Revolution."

Niggli's next novel was published two years after the first. Critically and popularly well received, *Step Down Elder Brother* intertwined a love story with commentary on the rise of the middle class in Monterrey, Mexico. Niggli considered the new work to be more important than *Mexican Village* because of its social content.

Winning another fellowship in 1950 allowed Niggli to visit the Abbey Theatre in Dublin, Ireland, where she studied performances. Four years later she repeated the process at the Old Vic School in Bristol, England. In 1956, Niggli accepted a professorship at Western Carolina University. She taught English and drama for one year before being named department head, a post she held until her retirement in 1975.

### SELECTED PUBLISHED WORKS:

*Mexican Silhouettes,* Hidalgo, Nuevo Léon, Mexico, privately printed, 1928; revised edition, San Antonio, Silhouette Press, 1931.

*Mexican Folk Plays,* Chapel Hill, University of North Carolina Press, 1938.

*Mexican Village,* Chapel Hill, University of North Carolina Press, 1945.

*Pointers on Playwriting,* Boston, The Writer, 1946.

*Step Down, Elder Brother,* New York, Rinehart, 1947.

*A Miracle for Mexico,* Greenwich, New York Graphic Society, 1964.

*New Pointers on Playwriting,* Boston, The Writer, 1967.

## SOURCES:

### Books

*Contemporary Authors-Permanent Series,* volume 2, Detroit, Gale, 1978.

*Dictionary of Literary Biography Yearbook: 1980,* edited by Karen L. Rood, Jean W. Ross, and Richard Ziegfeld, Detroit, Gale, 1981.

*Hispanic Writers,* edited by Bryan Ryan, Detroit, Gale, 1991.

Spearman, Walter, *The Carolina Playmakers: The First Fifty Years,* Chapel Hill, University of North Carolina Press, 1970.

### Periodicals

*MELUS,* summer 1978, pp. 71–110.

*Yale Review,* spring 1948, p. 576.

—*Sketch by J. M. Lesinski*

# Luis Nogales
## 1943-

### Hispanic American businessman

Luis Nogales has become known as one of the most accomplished Hispanic businessmen in the United States. After obtaining a law degree from Stanford University in 1969, some of Nogales's endeavors in the business world have included acting as vice-president of United Press International (UPI) —the second-largest news agency in the world—and as president of Univisión—one of the largest Spanish-language television broadcasting companies in the U.S. Nogales has also served as chairman or as a member of various business and community boards throughout the world.

*Luis Nogales*

Before achieving success in the business world, Nogales had to overcome his modest existence as a young migrant worker in California. As Linda Lopez explained in *Low Rider: La Raza Report,* "One would never think that a farm worker could reach such a high prestige and honor. Today, Luis Nogales is a prime example that goals can be accomplished if one believes in oneself." Gregory Gordon and Ronald E. Cohen confirmed this observation in *Down to the Wire: UPI's Fight for Survival:* "Nogales never had shied from hardship, challenge or confrontation. His had been an extraordinary rise, from migrant fruit picker to the top echelons of the world's second-largest news agency."

Nogales was born October 17, 1943, to Forencia Guerrero Nogales and Alejandro C. Nogales on the side of a road in Madera, California. His early years were spent picking in the fields with his family in Calexico, California. From the beginning, Nogales realized that the life of a migrant Hispanic in California would keep him poverty-stricken. As he explained in an interview with Lopez, "No matter how hard you worked, you were always poor." With the help of his parents, Nogales achieved his dreams of leaving the fields and the hard life of a migrant worker.

Nogales's parents knew that the only way their children would be able to leave the picking fields would be by obtaining an education. Nogales described their persistence in an interview with Janet Morey and Wendy Dunn in *Famous Mexican Ameri-*

cans. "My mother was determined and wanted her children to improve their opportunities. My father had a fourth grade education, but he had a love of learning." Morey and Dunn further explained that Nogales's "father bought books on literature, history, and philosophy in both Spanish and English."

### Pursues Higher Education

After many years of hard work in the fields and in school, Nogales was awarded a scholarship to San Diego State University. While at the university during the 1960s Nogales began his long career as a community activist and founded a Mexican American student group. When he graduated from San Diego State with high marks in political science, he continued to follow his dream and attended Stanford University Law School. Nogales chose Stanford to obtain his law degree mainly because, as Morey and Dunn noted, "his family picked fruit in the area."

While at Stanford, Nogales continued to fight for the rights of his people by founding Movimiento Estudiantil Chicano de Aztlan (MECHA). Through his efforts as spokesperson and minority activist, enrollment of Hispanics at Stanford increased. As a result, "the freshman class at Stanford is now about 10 percent Hispanic, compared to only 10 students when he was attending the university in 1966," Lopez explained. Because of the respect he had gained from the school administration as well as the Chicanos on campus, Nogales was hired by Stanford as assistant to the president after he received his degree in 1969. In this role, Nogales continued to help the Chicanos on campus and to make Stanford a more diverse university.

Nogales spent the next few years as a White House Fellow in Washington, D.C. The work he performed and the experience he gained in this position later proved invaluable to Nogales in his business career. As Nogales explained to Dunn and Morey, "Being there you actually see how it is in the capital for international politics. Major international and national decisions are made every day." As a White House Fellow, Nogales had the opportunity to travel to the Soviet Union, Pakistan, Bulgaria, Poland, and East Germany; he was also part of one of the first American groups to visit Communist China in 1973.

### Launches Career as Media Executive

Upon returning from China, Nogales entered the media field and continued to serve the community. From 1973 to 1980, he served as the vice president for Golden West Broadcasters, on the board of the Levi-Strauss clothing company, and on the board of the Mexican American Legal Defense and Educational Fund (MALDEF). His tireless work during these years, both for the community and as a businessman, prepared him for his next position as the executive vice-president of UPI in 1983. UPI was the second-largest news agency in the world, and a primary component of its business involved gathering and selling news reports to newspapers and television stations throughout the world. Nogales resigned from UPI in 1985 and became the president of Univisión in 1987.

After resigning from Univisión in 1988, Nogales continued to work in the community and in the business world. He remained active on the executive boards of Lucky Stores, Bank of California, and Southern California Edison Company. He also continued his relationship with Stanford University and became a member of the board of trustees in 1988. A devoted family man, "He hopes that one day his own daughters . . . will surpass even his own success in their own ways," according to Morey and Dunn.

### SOURCES:

**Books**

Gordon, Gregory, and Ronald E. Cohen, *Down to the Wire: UPI's Fight for Survival,* New York, McGraw-Hill, 1990.
Morey, Janet, and Wendy Dunn, *Famous Mexican Americans,* New York, Cobblehill Books, 1989.

**Periodicals**

*Hispanic Business,* June 1982, p. 8; January 1983, p. 23; November 1983, p. 10.
*Low Rider: La Raza Report,* November 1991, pp. 102–03.

—*Sketch by John-Michael Rivera*

# Manuel Antonio Noriega
## 1936-
### Deposed Panamanian military ruler

Manuel Antonio Noriega is the former Panamanian military leader who commanded the Panamanian Defense Forces (PDF) from 1983 until his surrender on January 3, 1990. This surrender followed a full-scale invasion by the United States military, ordered by U.S. president George Bush's administration to bring Noriega to trial on charges of drug-trafficking. Noriega's longtime relationship with

*Manuel Noriega*

the United States, however, is one filled with complexity and contradiction. Once noted for his skillful work as an intelligence officer with close ties to the Central Intelligence Agency (CIA), Noriega received praise for his support of pro-democracy activities in Central America from the late 1960s to the mid 1980s. He is more widely recognized, though, as a convicted international criminal known to have amassed large profits from narcotics activities and to have sanctioned various cruelties on his climb to power. Nevertheless, as John Dinges concluded in his seminal biography *Our Man in Panama,* "the scale of murder and repression in Panama under Noriega was far from the killing, torture, and disappearances carried out during much of the same period in [other Latin American countries] with considerably less U.S. official condemnation." Noriega continues to deny the charges brought against him, claiming that he has been vilified by the U.S. government for political reasons. As he argued from his Miami prison cell, in an interview with film director Oliver Stone reprinted in *The Nation* magazine, "after twenty-four years of friendship suddenly I become a devil. They needed to create a devil in order to get rid of the devil."

Although Noriega rose to power largely through his ability to gather copious amounts of information on others, the details of his own early life are incomplete. He was born in the seedy Terraplen section of Panama City on February 11, 1936. His father, Ricaurte Noriega, was an accountant; his mother, Maria Moreno, supported herself as a cook

and a laundress. It is not certain whether the two ever were married; by the time Noriega had turned five they had left him to be reared by an aunt known as Mama Luisa. Born poor and a Creole—what the Panamanian classify as persons with a mixture of black, Indian, and Spanish blood—Noriega came from humble origins. As a small boy selling newspapers, he relied on his wit—and later a small pistol—to defend himself on Terraplen's sordid streets.

As a schoolteacher, Mama Luisa was able to show Noriega that books could help him rise above the poverty of the neighborhood; Noriega excelled at one of Panama's finest high schools, the National Institute. Sometime during his years there, Noriega went to live with his half-brother, Luis Carlos, an active organizer for the Socialist party who encouraged young Manuel's intellectual growth and introduced him to politics. Possibly seeing in Noriega the potential for a bright political future, Demetrio Porras—the leader of the Socialist party—gave him a monthly stipend of $15, which enabled him to stay in school and graduate near the top of his class. Noriega had planned to attend medical school and become a psychiatrist, but he was denied admission—something he attributed to his status as a poor mulatto—and was forced to take classes in medical laboratory technology instead. While struggling to pay for his courses by taking blood samples at a hospital, Noriega encountered a former National Institute classmate who encouraged him to pursue a military career. With the help of his half-brother, Noriega received a scholarship to attend Peru's Chorrillos Military Academy, where he began studying military history in 1958.

Upon his return to Panama in 1962, Noriega enlisted with the National Guard as a common soldier and soon secured a commission as a second lieutenant. Assigned to Colón, Panama's second largest city, he served under Captain Omar Torrijos. The two, according to Dinges, "quickly recognized each other as beacons of intelligence and idealism above a sea of mediocrity." Noriega's first job, however, was to oversee the patrol cars of the traffic police, who exercised the responsibility of bribing traffic offenders and regulating bars, whorehouses, and gambling houses. Despite being reprimanded by Torrijos on charges of excessive drinking and rape while serving in this position, Noriega was reassigned to a more distinguished post, as chief of the National Guard's North Zone on the Costa Rican border. While in the province of Chiriquí, he was charged with stopping the political momentum of the populist leader Arnulfo Arias, a two-time president preparing to run for another term. Noriega's men arrested dozens of "Arnulfistas," including several prominent teachers, lawyers, and farmers, who subsequently made accusations of torture and rape. Amid these charges—and the protest marches that followed—Noriega was required to take a jungle operations course at the U.S. Army School of the Americas in the Canal Zone, where he again failed to meet Torrijos's expectations.

## Begins to Show Promise

In 1966, Noriega finally began to show signs of promise in both his professional and personal life: he received his first full-time assignment as an intelligence officer; he was promoted to first lieutenant; and he met his future wife, Felicidad Sieiro, a high school teacher with whom he would have three daughters. In intelligence, Noriega at last found a vocation that suited his abilities: he "possessed the uncanny ability to absorb information, size up the options available to an adversary, place himself in the other person's shoes and astutely anticipate probable courses of action," argued Dinges. Under Major Boris Martinez's firm leadership, Noriega was given the responsibility of infiltrating and disbanding the socialist-oriented unions that the United Fruit Company's twelve thousand banana workers had organized. Some U.S. Army Intelligence reports suggest that Noriega was working as a double agent at this time, sharing his information on the potential "leftist threat" of the banana workers with the U.S.

Noriega, along with Torrijos and Martinez, vaulted into the limelight of Panamanian politics in 1968 when Arias, backed by the populist support of farmers and the middle class, succeeded in his bid for a third presidential term. Four days after his election, Arias tried to gain control of the National Guard, removing most its top leadership by retirement or reassignment to foreign posts. For instance, Torrijos, who with Noriega's help had tried earlier to squelch the Arnulfistas, was appointed as a military attaché to El Salvador. Angered by the threat of seeing the National Guard fall under Arias's control, Torrijos led a bloodless military coup, forcing Arias to seek refuge in Miami just eleven days after taking office. Noriega's role in the takeover was crucial: under Martinez's command he helped to secure Arias's power bases in the city of David and Chiriquí Province, and later, when the Arnulfistas began organizing groups of guerrilla resistance, he was assigned the task of tracking them down. By 1969 Noriega had succeeded in crushing the rebellion. Torrijos's authority was soon challenged, however, by Lieutenant Colonel Ramiro Silvera and Lieutenant Colonel Amado Sanjur, who took over the National Guard headquarters while Torrijos was on a brief vacation. Noriega was instrumental in stopping the coup, skillfully organizing several officers loyal to Torrijos and insuring his safe return to the David garrison. Once the coup had dissolved, Torrijos and Noriega led supporters in a caravan to Panama City, where they were greeted by tens of thousands of well-wishers.

Noriega's loyalty to Torrijos did not go unrewarded; he was soon promoted to lieutenant colonel and was put in charge of G2, the National Guard's newly expanded intelligence operation. As a member of Norrijos's inner circle, Noriega was given additional responsibility in forming international policy. In the mid-1970s, for instance, he began traveling to Europe and the Middle East to orchestrate weapons purchases for the National Guard. His role in international affairs also led him to an official liaison relationship with U.S. intelligence agencies such as the CIA, which paid him for sharing information. As Dinges contended, though, "little distinguished the payments, which have been estimated at more than $100,000 in some cases, from an outright bribe for Noriega's cooperation." Despite such reports, Noriega did provide valuable services for the Nixon administration, playing a crucial behind-the-scenes role in negotiating the release of two U.S. freighter crews from Havana, Cuba, in the early 1970s. Noriega also played a fundamental role in Nicaragua, funnelling arms from the National Guard's surplus stocks and organizing covert arms shipments from Cuba—via Panama and Miami—to the Sandinistas in their successful bid to overthrow the U.S.-backed dictatorship of Anastasio Somoza.

## Seeks Complete Control of Panama

With Torrijos's death in 1981, Noriega was given virtually free reign to pursue his own ambitions. While smuggling weapons to the Colombian guerilla group M–19, he was introduced to members of the nascent Colombian cocaine cartel and soon shifted his interests from guns to drugs. After gaining experience in drug trafficking in the early 1970s and spending the rest of the decade rehabilitating his image by projecting himself as an antidrug enforcer, Noriega had come full circle. His drug deals with the cartel, as Dinges argued, "were a profitable sideline that occupied little of his time." His larger objective was no less than to obtain complete control of Panama. He took a significant step towards that goal in 1983, when he succeeded General Ruben Dario Paredes as commander in chief of the National Guard. While promoting himself to general, he consolidated the military into the Panamanian Defense Forces (PDF).

As the leader of the PDF, Noriega quickly became the most feared man in Panama, exercising the authority to establish and remove political rulers as he saw fit. In 1985, Hugo Spadafora—a romantic revolutionary who was highly critical of Noriega's drug trafficking and other illicit practices—was murdered, reportedly by the PDF. While Noriega's connection has not been proved, "once Noriega found out about the killing he actively participated in covering it up," argued Dinges. In an attempt to quell public outrage over what appeared to be a blatant assassination and to prevent a thorough investigation,

Noriega pressured President Nicolas Ardito Barletta into resigning. These two events—amid the imminent Panamanian takeover of the Panama Canal, in accord with the treaty negotiated by Torrijos and U.S. president Jimmy Carter in 1977—figured prominently in U.S. president Ronald Reagan's administration's investigation into Noriega's affairs. As further evidence concerning Noriega's drug involvement and sale of restricted U.S. technology and information was discovered, the U.S. began to take a more active role. The investigation culminated on February 5, 1988, when federal grand juries in Tampa and Miami, Florida, returned two separate indictments against Noriega on drug-trafficking charges.

On October 3, 1989, Major Moises Giroldi led a U.S. supported coup against Noriega, but was repelled by the general's Battalion 2000, a specialized force trained—ironically—by the U.S. military. In response to a "pattern of aggression"—one that included the killing of a Marine and the brutalization of a Navy lieutenant and his wife—George Bush's administration ordered a full-scale invasion of Panama in an attempt to capture Noriega and bring him to trial. On December 20, under the name "Operation Just Cause," an estimated 22,500 troops, as well as "an armada of tanks, armored personnel carriers, airborne gunships, helicopters, jet fighters and six F–117A Stealth attack fighters," according to a June 25, 1990, *Newsweek* report, were implemented in an attempt to dismantle the PDF and apprehend Noriega, who had escaped the grasp of a special-forces team just four hours before the invasion. After four days of fighting—and an estimated 220 U.S. and 425 PDF casualties—the elusive Noriega finally surrendered to the Vatican Embassy in Panama City. Convicted on charges of cocaine trafficking, racketeering, and money laundering two years later, he was sentenced to 40 years in a Miami prison, and was ordered to pay $44 million to the Panamanian government.

## SOURCES:

### Books

Dinges, John, *Our Man in Panama,* New York, Random House, 1990.

### Periodicals

*Miami Herald,* July 10, 1993, p. A2.
*Nation,* January 24, 1994, pp. 80–90.
*Newsweek,* January 1, 1990, pp. 15–22; June 25, 1990, pp. 28–31.
*New Yorker,* September 23, 1991, pp. 23–24.
*Time,* May 22, 1989, pp. 40–44.

—*Sketch by Jason Gallman*

# Antonia Novello
## 1944-
### Puerto Rican physcian

When C. Everett Koop announced in late 1989 that he would retire from the post of United States Surgeon General, speculation about who his predecessor would be was particularly lively. During his eight-year tenure, Dr. Koop played an unusually prominent role in American public life, elevating the previously soft-spoken voice of the Surgeon General to a forceful, opinionated one that people paid attention to. Koop gained national prominence and respect by speaking out on controversial issues, sometimes colliding openly with the views of the administrations of presidents Ronald Reagan and George Bush on such topics as sex education and the use of condoms to prevent the spread of AIDS.

When Dr. Antonia Novello, the deputy director of the National Institute of Child Health and Human Development at the National Institutes of Health (NIH), was chosen for the Surgeon General post, many observers noted that following in the illustrious footsteps of Dr. Koop would not be easy. The first woman and the first Hispanic to hold the position, Dr. Novello brought with her a reputation for hard work and dedication, but her ability to fight for her convictions was unproven. Both Novello and administration officials admitted that questions about her views on abortion—she opposes it—had been a part of the selection process. This so-called "litmus test," allegedly applied to candidates for this and other high-level health care appointments, was a subject of widespread controversy. But Novello claimed, as reported in the *Washington Post* several months after she was sworn in, "I'm for the people who deserve help . . . how I vote is not relevant. I think that as a woman, as a Hispanic, as a member of a minority . . . I bring a lot of sensitivity to the job." Voicing a concern that echoed in other quarters, California Democratic Representative Henry Waxman told the *Post,* "I hope she's a fighter, because it's a bad time for infant mortality, for AIDS, for the homeless, for the uninsured, and this administration hasn't shown much interest in these problems . . . she can do a lot."

Novello was born in Fajardo, Puerto Rico, on August 23, 1944. She and her brother were raised by their mother, a school teacher, after their parents' divorce. Novello suffered from a painful congenital colon condition until she was 18 years old, when it was finally corrected. She has said that one of the reasons she became a doctor was to help others who were suffering as she had. Novello received both her B.S. and M.D. degrees from the University of Puerto

Rico, where she was—as described by her teacher Dr. Ivan Pelegrina in the *Detroit Free Press*—"one of our brightest students." Ana Flores Coello appears to have been a major motivating force in her daughter's life at this stage; Novello told *Glamour:* "I wasn't allowed to work until I graduated from medical school because my mother felt that once I earned money I might be sidetracked by material rewards before I got to my real work."

### Develops Early Interest in Pediatric Care

Novello did get to her "real work," beginning with an internship and residency in pediatrics from 1970 through 1973 at the University of Michigan (UM) Medical Center in Ann Arbor. She served as a fellow in pediatric nephrology at UM in 1973 and 1974, and she remembered this "first job" in *Glamour* as germinal in her eventual decision to enter government work; she "learned how many people slip through the cracks." Monitoring the progress of patients waiting for kidney transplants, Novello was dismayed at the number who could not be helped. Those cases in which she, personally, was powerless to help were especially affecting: "You become a true caring physician when you're able to share the pain."

In 1971 Novello was the first woman to receive the UM Pediatrics Department's Intern of the Year award. Her classmate Dr. Samuel Sefton, who is now a neonatologist in Kalamazoo, Michigan, told the *Detroit Free Press,* "It was difficult for women to be accepted [in the medical field] then, and I always was impressed with the way she handled situations." Barbara Lanese, head nurse (then and now) of the UM perinatal unit, concurred with Sefton: "[Antonia] was a resident when female physicians weren't as readily accepted as they are today. . . . She was a wonderful physician, and she was warm, friendly and well-respected. She was able to break the tension just by the kind of person she is."

In 1974 Novello joined the staff of Georgetown University Hospital in Washington, D.C., as a pediatric nephrology fellow. She served as a project officer at the NIH's National Institute of Arthritis, Metabolism and Digestive Diseases in 1978 and 1979, a staff physician at NIH from 1979 through 1980, and the executive secretary in the Division of Research Grants at NIH from 1981 through 1986. She earned a master's degree in public health from Johns Hopkins University in 1982.

From 1986 until her appointment as Surgeon General, Novello served as deputy director of the National Institute of Child Health and Human Development, where she nurtured a special interest in children with AIDS. Concurrently, Novello was a clinical professor of pediatrics at Georgetown University Hospital. Her colleague there, pediatric department chairman Dr. Owen Rennert, told the *New York*

*Times* that Novello "is tremendously concerned about the medical and social problems of children and she has a way of drawing others into that concern." In 1982 and 1983 Novello was a Congressional fellow on the staff of the Labor and Human Resources Committee chaired by Senator Orrin Hatch, a Republican from Utah. As reported in the *Washington Post,* Hatch later commented that she had "given good advice on several bills . . . including legislation on organ transplants and cigarette warning labels."

### Accepts Appointment to Surgeon General Post

Novello's appointment to the post of Surgeon General came at a time of controversy and hostility between some scientists involved in public health issues and the Bush administration. Several candidates for top jobs at such organizations as the NIH, the Center for Disease Control, and the Health Care Financing Administration had withdrawn their names from consideration, complaining that their interviews had included questions about their views on abortion and on the use of fetal tissue in research (another controversial practice opposed by the Bush White House). Dr. Burton Lee, the President's personal physician, might have been a contender for Surgeon General, but took himself out of the running because his views on abortion did not coincide with Bush's. In so doing, he echoed the administration's contention that it is important and appropriate that the appointee defend Bush's positions with conviction.

During Novello's two-hour interview, she was able to convince administration officials that her view on abortion was the approved one. Some observers speculated that Novello's reputation for cooperative, dedicated and essentially low-key work made her a particularly desirable choice after the outspoken reign of Dr. Koop. Yet Novello claimed at a press conference covered in the *Washington Post* that "as long as the data can be trusted and is not just hearsay, I'll say it like it is. . . . I was never told I have to keep a low profile. I really intend to be like Dr. Koop when the data is there."

As head of the 5,700 commissioned officers of the Public Health Service, Novello promised to focus her energies on AIDS-infected children, smoking (she opposes particularly the glamorous portrayal of smoking in advertisements) and such women's health issues as breast cancer and heterosexual AIDS. Other areas of concern for Novello include teenage drinking, drinking and driving, and finding ways to diminish the stigma of mental illness.

### Strives for Better Health Care

The Surgeon General's is an essentially public role, and Novello—who receives several hundred invitations to speak per month—spends much of her time on the road, promoting the cause of better health. She talks with Louis Sullivan, Secretary of Health and Human Services, three or four times a week and meets with him monthly. Sullivan, with whom Novello has pledged to work closely, described her (as quoted in the *Detroit Free Press*) as "a very commanding woman who has a tremendous ability to reach out to communities." To what extent and to what ends she will put that ability to use is a subject of concern for some, like the Congressional official (a Democrat) quoted in the *Washington Post* who said, "Toni Novello is a nice, talented, hard-working woman. But she has never stood up and shouted for the programs she directs. . . . If she wants to play anything like the role Koop did, she is going to have to learn to speak up."

Novello's own perception of the potential power and impact of her new job became more sharply defined, she told the *Washington Post,* when she visited her birthplace, Puerto Rico, shortly after becoming Surgeon General: "When I got off the plane, kids from my mother's school lined both sides of the road handing me flowers. . . . I went to the VA hospital to speak. When the veterans saw my gold braid [she is a Vice Admiral in the Public Health Service] they all stood and saluted. . . . I realized that for these people, for women, I have to be good as a doctor, I have to be good as a Surgeon General, I have to be everything."

Since her appointment to the Surgeon General post in 1989, Novello has addressed and attempted to solve many of the problems which concern her, including teenage drinking. In late 1991, she met with some of the largest beer and wine companies in the United States and asked them to stop aiming their advertising at children and teenagers. "The ads have youth believing that instead of getting up early, exercising, going to school, playing a sport or learning to be a team player, all they have to do to fit is learn to drink the right alcohol," remarked Novello during a press conference covered in the *New York Times.* The marketers of beer and wine do not see their ads as being aimed at children, and will not voluntarily back down—there may be laws in the future requiring them to include warnings in their advertisements.

In addition to her attempts to lessen teenage drinking problems, Novello has also aspired to provide better health care for children, women, and minorities. As she stated in a *Hispanic* interview shortly after her appointment: "I hope that being the first woman and minority Surgeon General since the post came into being—and the visibility the post confers—enables me to reach many individuals with my message of empowerment for women, children, and minorities."

## SOURCES:

*Detroit Free Press,* October 30, 1990.

*Glamour,* August, 1990.

*Hispanic,* January/February, 1990, p. 20; October, 1991, p. 15.

*Newsweek,* October 30, 1989.

*New York Times,* October 18, 1989, section A, p. 20; November 2, 1989; June 27, 1991, section D, p. 20; November 5, 1991, section A, p. 16; November 6, 1991, section A, p. 25.

*Parade,* November 11, 1990.

*People,* December 17, 1990.

*Washington Post,* October 18, 1989; October 24, 1989; May 8, 1990.

*—Sketch by Kelly King Howes*

# Adriana C. Ocampo
## 1955-
### Argentine American geologist

Adriana C. Ocampo has worked since high school for the National Aeronautics and Space Administration (NASA). Now a planetary geologist, she is involved in NASA's ambitious mission to Jupiter, Project Galileo, and in the Mars Observer venture. "Space exploration holds the secret to the evolution of our planet and the origin of life on earth," she told Michelle Vachon in a telephone interview. "It is part of the future of human beings. We need to study asteroids and comets, and we need to go to the Moon and Mars to try to establish a colony."

"Her love of stars and planets goes back to childhood," recalled Ocampo's mother, Teresa Uria Ocampo, in an interview with Vachon. "Instead of playing with dolls like other little girls, Adriana was making astronauts out of them, using my kitchen appliances to build spacecraft." Born on January 5, 1955, in Barranquilla, Columbia, Ocampo grew up in Buenos Aires, Argentina, where her family had moved when she was only a few months old. The year she turned fifteen, the Ocampos immigrated to the United States and settled in Pasadena, California. During her junior year in high school, she jumped at the opportunity to take a summer job at the Jet Propulsion Laboratory, the NASA facility in Pasadena. At the end of the summer, this became a part-time position that Ocampo kept during her studies in aerospace engineering at Pasadena City College and in geology at California State University in Los Angeles (CSULA). When she received her bachelor's degree in geology from CSULA, Ocampo had already been working at the prestigious laboratory for ten years. The transition from part-time to full-time employee seemed only natural—she joined the Jet Propulsion Laboratory staff in 1983.

### Researches Distant Planets

Her tasks on the Jupiter and Mars probing missions will keep her busy for years to come. On project Galileo, Ocampo serves as science coordinator for the near-infrared mapping spectrometer, one of the four remote-sensing instruments mounted on the spacecraft to analyze the planet's atmosphere. She

*Adriana C. Ocampo*

holds a similar position on the Mars Observer project—experiment representative for the thermal emission spectrometer. During the Viking mission to Mars, she produced a photo atlas of Mars's moon that, to date, is the only atlas of this moon in existence.

Ocampo is a member of the Chicxulub Consortium, an organization regrouping American, Canadian and Mexican representatives for the study of a crater in the Yucatan Peninsula in Mexico. Scientists think that this crater might have been formed by a meteorite believed to have caused the extinction of dinosaurs sixty-five million years ago. Its fall is presumed to have created clouds of dust and gasses in the Earth's atmosphere that produced acid rain and diminished the dinosaurs' food supply.

Ocampo's membership involvement with the Chicxulub Consortium is just one aspect of her international work in space resarch. A few years ago, she came up with the idea of an international gathering for North and South American scientists to share information on space exploration. "I made phone calls," she explained in an interview with Vachon, and as a result the Space Conference of the

Americas took place in Costa Rica in 1990 and in Chili in 1993. Ocampo has given workshops on planetary sciences in Mexico, Costa Rica, and Columbia as part of her involvement with the Planetary Society and the United Nations. A member of the Society of Hispanic Professional Engineers , she has served as national secretary for one term and national vice president for two terms. She presides over the society's international affairs committee, and is a member of the space committee.

In 1989, Ocampo married archeologist Kevin O. Pope, whose company conducts remote-sensing geological and ecological research. In the future, "I still would like to be an astronaut as a mission specialist," she admitted in her interview. Although her application was previously rejected, she is not giving up. "I also want to start a research foundation for the exchange of information on science and technology on a good-will basis. Together we could improve the standard of living in the Americas."

## SOURCES:

### Periodicals

*Hispanic Engineer,* Fall, 1987, pp. 22–24; Fall, 1989, p. 24.

### Other

Ocampo, Adriana C., telephone interview with Michelle Vachon, May 5, 1992.

Ocampo, Teresa Uria, telephone interview with Michelle Vachon, April 27, 1992.

Pope, Ken O., telephone interview with Michelle Vachon, April 27, 1992.

—*Sketch by Michelle Vachon*


# Victoria Ocampo
## 1890-1979
### Argentine writer and editor

"Victoria accomplished more in the area of culture than any other woman in her country's history—perhaps in the history of Latin America. . . . In her own country she is a legend," Doris Meyer declared in *Victoria Ocampo: Against the Wind and the Tide.* Renowned for her literary talents and tremendous beauty, Argentina's "Queen of Letters" was the founder and director of women's rights and the author of influential essays and criticism. Ocampo's literary achievements were formally acknowledged in 1977 when she was the first woman to be received into Argentine Academy of Letters. According to Meyer in *Spanish American Women Writers,* in Ocampo's acceptance speech to her male audience she typically alluded to women's equality, "The world is adapting to a new reality, one that can no longer be denied, one that will benefit you as much as it will us women."

The eldest of six daughters, Ramona Victoria Epifanía Rufina Ocampo was born in Buenos Aires on April 7 1890. Her parents—Manuel Silvio Cecilio Ocampo Regueria, a respected architectural engineer, and Ramona Máxima Aguirre—belonged to a wealthy, aristocratic family that included cattle barons and governors. An appreciation of Ocampo's childhood is important, Meyer asserted, because Ocampo wrote more about her youth than her adult life; she often stated that writing about her childhood was a form of self-exploration and understanding. Her childhood memories were fond ones, but they were coupled with an intense desire for freedom—freedom as a girl and later as a woman—from the restraints imposed by her society and culture.

### Freedom, Non-Conformity, and an Artistic Vocation

In accordance with her social status, Ocampo was educated privately at home. Under the watchful eye of her *dueña* ("chaperon"), Ocampo studied literature, music, religion, basic mathematics, and modern languages. She acquired perfect French and English by receiving instruction from native speakers. Ocampo later remarked that her foreign language abilities endowed her with a source of freedom. As a child she was drawn to the arts, developing a hunger for knowledge and information.

At the family home in San Isidro, Ocampo became a voracious reader. Through literature she discovered another form of freedom—she would cloak herself in the fantasy worlds of Jules Verne and Sherlock Holmes. Ocampo also developed deep theatrical aspirations, kindled by Marguerite Moreno, an actress who taught the young Ocampo French diction. In *Against the Wind and the Tide,* Meyer cited a 1908 letter in which Ocampo declared: "I was born to act. I have the theater in my blood. I am a great artist and without the theater I can have no joy or peace. It's my vocation." Despite Ocampo's rebellious nature, she yielded to her parents, who maintained that the theater was not a place for a young woman of Ocampo's standing. Seeking another more acceptable outlet for her artistic vocation, Ocampo turned to writing. One of her earliest literary endeavors was the production of a household magazine with her sister, Angélica.

During her childhood, Ocampo took two grand European tours with her family. Her experiences in France proved formative; part of her, she maintained, always belonged to France. Indeed, when Ronald Christ interviewed her for *Review* in 1972, he was struck by her Frenchness. During her foreign travels she also engendered an affection for England. While in Paris during the second tour, her parents allowed her to observe university lectures. She attended the Sorbonne and the Collége de France, where she studied English, ancient Greek literature, the origins of Romanticism, the history of the Orient, and the works of Dante and Nietzsche.

On November 8, 1912, she married "Monaco" Luis Bernardo de Estrada, hoping to escape from the restrictions of her family life. They were ill-matched; he wanted her to act the conventional wife, yet she was anything but that. Within a year the marriage was virtually over, and eventually the couple obtained a legal separation in 1922. Ocampo embraced her writing. She harbored an intense desire to write and a fascination with words. As she told Ronald Christ: "To me words are essential not because they sound well, but because they incarnate something."

Her first essays were published in the early 1920s in *La Nación*. It was a monumental feat for a young woman working in a profession usually reserved for men. Her avant-garde behavior generated controversy during this period. Breaking from the mores of aristocratic Argentine culture, Ocampo drove her Packard around Buenos Aires without a chauffeur, smoked in public, and lived alone in her own apartment. Ocampo also conducted a clandestine affair in the 1920s and early 1930s, and never revealed her lover's name. In many ways Ocampo was ahead of her time. She developed important friendships with eminent literary figures: **José Ortega y Gasset,** Count Hermann Keyserling and Rabindranath Tagore. She traveled to Europe again on several occasions, and also to New York—on a Guggenheim fellowship.

### Sur

Ocampo is remembered for the literary review, *Sur,* and for its sister publishing house. She was inextricably bound to these institutions for 40 years. Receiving encouragement and advice from Ortega and U.S. writer, Waldo Frank, Ocampo founded *Sur* in 1931: She was also its director and financial patron. Her vast wealth enabled *Sur* to survive. The *raison d'être* behind the review was "to build bridges between continents." As Ocampo explained to Christ, "My father was an engineer and built bridges. . . . I think I did the same kind of job but with different materials." *Sur* served as a forum for the best Latin American, North American, and European writers. Through *Sur,* Ocampo introduced numerous distinguished writers to Latin America: Virginia Woolf, D. H. Lawrence, James Joyce, Carl Jung, T. S. Eliot, Aldous Huxley, William Faulkner, Albert Camus, Jean-Paul Sartre, Graham Greene, and Simone de Beauvoir. Ocampo also published the future Latin American literary giants: **Jorge Luis Borges, Gabriel García Márquez, Mario Vargas Llosa, Guillermo Cabrera Infante, Carlos Fuentes** and **Gabriela Mistral.** As Mark Falcoff asserted in the *New Criterion,* the review "opened whole new horizons to two generations of Latin American writers." He continued: "*Sur* can rightly claim to have played a role in nurturing the new Latin American novel."

Although *Sur* was published just after the military coup of 1930, its contents were not tainted by political censorship. In part this was related to the journal's internationalism. The publication also survived because Ocampo consistently and vehemently declared that she—and *Sur*—were apolitical. However, Ocampo stood firmly in the anti-fascist camp and *Sur*'s contributors were overwhelmingly liberal. Under the Perón dictatorship, *Sur*'s contributors were harassed and Ocampo was labelled a dissenting intellectual. After the bomb plot of April 15, 1953, Ocampo was interrogated and imprisoned at Buen Pastor Prison for 26 days without being informed of the reasons for her detention. She was released after international figures including Mistral and India's Prime Minister, Jawaharlal Nehru, intervened. Ocampo maintained that her incarceration simply infused her writings with a new urgency.

### A Prominent Voice for Women's Rights

Ocampo was a committed feminist. She told Christ that she was "a feminist one hundred percent; and not just for myself, but for all the women in the world, beginning with the Argentine." In March of 1936, Ocampo, María Rosa Oliver, and Susana Larguía organized the Argentine Women's Union. Their initial objective was to halt a reform bill that proposed removing married women's civil rights. The Union raised awareness through meetings and the dissemination of information. In August Ocampo delivered a radio address entitled "Woman and Her Expression," demanding equal educational opportunities for women. The reform bill was defeated. The Union continued to operate, resolved to obtain universal suffrage for women. Ocampo resigned from the Union after two years, objecting to its politicization.

### The Author

As a writer Ocampo authored essays, novels, and an autobiography. In *Spanish American Women Authors,* Meyer noted the intensely personal nature of Ocampo's work: "Everything Ocampo wrote was directly related to her experience, to the point that one could say that her entire work was part of an autobiographical experience." Ocampo's monumental work, *Testimonios,* was published between 1935 and 1977 and consists of ten volumes of essays, criticism, and personal experiences. Ocampo revealed to Christ that *"Testimonios* is something that mixes life and reading . . . what I read and what I live . . . I can't separate them." She always believed that she would be read posthumously. Indeed, her autobiography, *Autobiografía,* was only published after her death—Ocampo considered the contents too intensely private to disclose during her lifetime and often threatened to destroy the work.

Always an active champion of the arts, Ocampo continued to support and promote writers through "Fondo"—the Commission of Letters of the National Foundation for the Arts in Argentina—well into her old age. Ocampo received numerous awards for her achievements. She was awarded doctorates from Harvard in the United States and the University of Visva-Bharati in India. She was an Official of the French Legion of Honor, Commander of the Most Excellent Order of the British Empire, and a recipient of the Italian Order of Merit. She died in San Isidro on January 27, 1979.

## SELECTED PUBLISHED WORKS:

*De Francesca a Beatrice: A través de La Divina Comedia* (title means "From Francesca to Beatrice: Across The Divine Comedy"), Madrid, Revista de Occidente, 1924, 1928, Sur, 1963.

*Testimonios* (memoirs, personal essays, and criticism), ten volumes, c. 1935–1975.

*Supremacía del alma y de la sangre,* Sur, 1935.

*La mujer y su expresión* (title means "Woman and Her Expression"), Sur, 1936.

Domingos en Hyde Park, (title means "Sundays in Hyde Park"), Sur, 1936.

*Viaje olvidado,* Sur, 1937.

*Emily Bronte (Terra incognita),* Sur, 1938.

*Virginia Woolf: Orlando y cia* (title means "Virginia Woolf: Orlando and Company"), Sur, 1938.

*San Isidro: Con un poema de Silvina Ocampo y 68 fotos de Gustav Thorlichen* (title means "San Isidro: With a Poem by Silvina Ocampo and 68 Photographs by Gustav Thorlichen"), Sur, 1941.

*338171 T. E. (Lawrence de Arabia)* (biography of T. E. Lawrence), Sur, 1942; enlarged and published as *338171 T. E. (Lawrence of Arabia),* New York, Dutton, 1963.

*Henry V y Laurence Olivier, con les principles pasajes de la obra* (title means "Henry V and Laurence Olivier, with Principal Passages from the Work"), Sur, 1947.

*Lawrence de Arabia, y otros ensayos* (title means "Lawrence of Arabia, and Other Essays"), Aguilar, 1951.

*Habla el algarrobo,* Sur, 1959.

(Author of prologue) Ricardo Güiraldes, *Rosaura,* Sudamericana, 1960.

*Tagore en las barrancas de San Isidro,* Isidro, Sur, 1961.

*Victoria Ocampo,* (contains anthology of works by Ocampo), edited by Fryda Schultz, Ediciones Culturales Argentinas, 1963.

*La belle y sus enamorados* (title means "Beauty and Her Lovers"), Sur, 1964.

(Contributor) *Victoria Ocampo: Against the Wind and the Tide* (includes fifteen essays by Ocampo), edited by Doris Meyer Braziller, 1980.

## SOURCES:

### Books

*Hispanic Writers: A Selection of Sketches from Contemporary Authors,* edited by Bryan Ryan, Detroit, Gale Research, 1991.

Meyer, Doris, *Victoria Ocampo: Against the Wind and the Tide,* Austin, University Texas Press, 1979.

*Spanish American Women Writers,* edited by Diane E. Marting, Westport, Connecticut, Greenwood, 1990.

### Periodicals

*New Criterion,* October 1988, pp. 27–37.

*Review,* winter 1972, pp. 5–13.

*Time,* April 8, 1946, p. 20; February 12, 1979, p. 72.

*—Sketch by Amanda Beresford*

# Ellen Ochoa
## 1958-
### Mexican American astronaut

When Ellen Ochoa became the first female Hispanic astronaut in July, 1990, she decided that being a role model for young girls and Hispanics would be one of her top priorities. She would show them that if they study hard and reach far enough the possibilities are endless. Ochoa is among the selected few who will explore the mysteries of outer space, and

*Ellen Ochoa*

like other astronauts who have ventured into space, her work is destined to influence scientists for generations. Before Ochoa turned thirty-three, she had also left a mark on the science world by developing special techniques in optical processing; she holds three patents in the field.

Immediately after the National Aeronautics Space Administration selected Ochoa to become an astronaut, she began speaking to groups, especially young girls and Hispanics, advocating the importance of education. She emphasized her Hispanic heritage, hoping they would see a part of themselves in her. "It may encourage them to do something like someone who is similar to them," Ochoa explained to D. D. Andreassi in a telephone interview. Otherwise, she said, her gender and heritage have no influence on her work. "When I'm at work, I don't consider myself any different from any other astronaut," related Ochoa. "I consider myself one of the astronauts in the office.

Ochoa was born May 10, 1958, in Los Angeles to Rosanne (Deardorff) and Joseph Ochoa, who was born in California and was of Mexican descent. Ochoa, whose parents were divorced when she was in junior high school, grew up with her mother, three brothers and one sister in La Mesa, California, in a close-knit family of high achievers. When her brother, Tyler Ochoa, a lawyer in Palo Alto, California, heard his thirty-one-year-old sister was selected by NASA, he told a *Houston Post* interviewer that she worked incredibly hard to be chosen among thousands of other applicants. "She's always been very diligent

about studying and working for what she wanted to do," remarked Tyler. He described his sister as calm, rational and thoughtful, all qualities that would be useful to her as an astronaut.

### Education Values Instilled

Ochoa's mother instilled the value of education in her at an early age. "From my mother we were all encouraged to do whatever we wanted to do," Ochoa told Andreassi. "She placed a high premium on going to college." Rosanne, a living example of her own advice, took college courses for twenty-three years, according to the *Houston Post*. The studying finally paid off when Rosanne finished a triple major in business, biology, and journalism, a field that Ochoa considered, but later decided against in favor of physics.

Ochoa was just as dedicated to school work. She did exceptionally well in math and science, but easily mastered all of her other courses as well. When Ochoa was thirteen years old she won the San Diego County spelling bee; and in junior high school she was named outstanding seventh and eighth grade girl—from then on she consistently went to the head of her class. Ochoa was valedictorian at Grossmont High School in La Mesa, and achieved the same honor at San Diego State University where she earned a bachelor of science degree in physics. "I try to work hard for whatever I try to do," she commented in her interview with Andreassi. "That's what I tried to do in school and that's what I'm trying to do now on my job."

Ochoa went on to Stanford University where she earned a masters degree and a doctorate in electrical engineering. She was the recipient of the Stanford engineering fellowship and IBM predoctoral fellowship. Ochoa told a *Hispanic* magazine interviewer that she demonstrates the value of education. "If you stay in school, you have the potential to achieve what you want in the future," she maintained. "Education increases career options and gives you a chance for a wide variety of jobs." This is often a theme of her speeches to school children; Ochoa stresses the importance of children studying math and science to increase their worth in the job market.

During all of her scholastic achievements, Ochoa kept active with her music. In high school, she became an accomplished flutist. She captured the top musician recognition at Grossmont High School and she was the student soloist winner at the Stanford Symphony Orchestra in 1983. Ochoa considered playing the flute for a career, but opted for something more stable. "I like to eat," she pointed out to Andreassi, adding that she personally knows musicians who have a hard time paying bills. When she was out of school, Ochoa expressed her love for the instrument during many hours of playing in her spare time. "I still play a lot whenever I can on the side," she continued, "so it's something that you can do as a hobby as well."

### Research Projects Lead to Patents

Ochoa took on another hobby when her older brother got his private pilot's license. She decided to follow his lead, and in 1988, two years before she would become an astronaut, she got her pilot's license for small engine planes. "I wanted to be an astronaut and I thought I should learn more about aviation," she told Andreassi. Ironically, after she became an astronaut she found that she would have little time to fly, or for her other hobbies—playing volleyball and bicycling.

During the course of her career, Ochoa has always kept busy with research projects. From 1985 through 1988 she was a research engineer in the Imaging Technology Branch at Sandia National Laboratories in Livermore, California. While scientists, artists, and inventors struggle their lifetimes to patent their ideas, Ochoa was not even thirty-three years old when she held three patents in optical processing. She developed a process that implements optics for image processing that is normally done by computer. For instance, one method she devised removes noise from an image through an optical system rather than using a standard digital computer to do the work.

While research always interested Ochoa, she observed to Andreassi that she had a difficult time trying to decide what career to pursue. Even in college she was unsure. In fact, while Ochoa was an undergraduate she changed her major five times, from music to business to journalism to computer science, before deciding on physics, according to the *Houston Post.* It was while she was a graduate student at Stanford, when friends applied to NASA, that she realized she had the qualifications to be an astronaut.

Ochoa would not have been able to consider this career before 1978, the year that NASA graduated the first six women ever selected to the program. She told a *Houston Post* interviewer that when women were accepted into the program a milestone had been reached and a lot of people were influenced. "We realized, 'Oh, it's really open to real people, not just an elite group of test pilots,'" she recalled. Little did the twenty-year-old college student know in 1978 that twelve years later she would be blazing new trails by becoming NASA's first female Hispanic astronaut.

### Earns Spot at NASA

It was a combination of Ochoa's many qualifications and persistence that won her a spot at NASA. She first applied to the program in 1985, and in 1987 she was named one of the top 100 finalists. Ochoa graduated in the astronaut class of 1990, which included eighteen men and five women, according to

the *Houston Post.* That year Ochoa reached another turning point in her life by marrying Coe Fulmer Miles of Molalla, Oregon.

Just as she had done in school, Ochoa made a name for herself at NASA, beginning in 1988 as a researcher, and later as chief of the Intelligent Systems Technology Branch at the National Aeronautics and Space Administration/Ames Research Center at Moffet Field Naval Air Station in Mountain View, California. Her progression through the ranks was rapid. Ochoa began as a researcher, and she was soon supervising almost 40 scientists before her selection as an astronaut. "She was assertive," remembers her deputy Nancy Sliwa, quoted in the *Houston Post.* "She defended (her) branch needs within NASA." Ochoa's accomplishments were acknowledged in 1989 when she was awarded the Hispanic Engineer National Achievement Award for most promising engineer in government. A year later she was given the pride award by the National Hispanic Quincentennial Commission in Washington.

Ochoa plans to put her expertise to test in space. In late 1992 her title was missions specialist civilian and she was preparing to go on her first flight, ATLAS 2 (Atmospheric Laboratory for Applications and Science). The shuttle mission, scheduled for take-off in March of 1993, plans to utilize a set of instruments to measure chemical composition, temperature, and pressure of the earth's atmosphere. The astronauts will set out to measure solar radiation and how it varies across different wavelengths. "What the scientists are hoping to do is measure what effect and variability the sun would have on the earth's atmosphere and determine values for concentration of chemical species in the atmosphere," explained Ochoa to Andreassi.

### Prepares for Space Flight

Ochoa faces tremendous challenges as she follows in the footsteps of Sally Ride, the first female the United States sent on a space flight. During the ten-day ATLAS 2 mission, Ochoa will be one of two scientists on board the shuttle. She was chosen to play a key role by deploying instruments into space that will enable scientists to look at the sun's corona. Ochoa will be one of two astronauts operating the deployment arm under stressful conditions, because there will be limited chances to achieve proposed tasks during the short mission.

Ochoa revealed to Andreassi that while she is excited about reaching her goal of flying in space, she is also aware there will be a lot to learn before the ATLAS 2 take-off. "But there's nothing else I'd rather be doing," she said. Ochoa also stated that she is not worried about an accident in space, even as she recalled the Challenger shuttle disaster in January of 1986. All seven Challenger crew members, including teacher Christi McAuliffe, died when the shuttle exploded shortly after take-off as friends and family watched horrified from the ground. "I'm sure on flight day I'll think about a lot of different things, but we train for a lot of different things," Ochoa commented in her interview, adding that every precaution will have been taken to make the mission as safe as possible. Ochoa did point out, however, that there are always some unknown elements and that risks are part of the equation that everyone who becomes involved with a space flight understands.

After she achieves her short term goal of flying in space, Ochoa told Andreassi that she hopes to continue her work as an astronaut for "quite a number of years and beyond that I'll have to wait and see what I will do." She plans to continue making public speeches, to explain her responsibilities as an astronaut, and most of all to maintain her duties as a role model. She related to Andreassi that her emphasis will be with school children, because they are at an impressionable age and are most easily influenced. "I think that's where I can make a difference." And she always remembers that her achievements are noticed especially by Hispanic groups. "A lot of those kids have come up to me and said, 'Wow, it's inspiring to see that you made it, because it shows what I can do.'" "Anything I can do along those lines is important for those people and for the country in having an educated work force." She already made an impact on youngsters shortly after she became an astronaut. According to the *Houston Post,* Ochoa gave a speech at a San Francisco Bay Area Catholic school when a Hispanic youngster, who was among a group of students who surrounded her, said: "'I'm glad you came. You've inspired us.'"

## SOURCES:

### Periodicals

*Hispanic,* May, 1990, p. 19.
*Houston Post,* July 17, 1990, p. A9; July 22, 1990, p. A9; July 23, 1990, p. A9.

### Other

Ochoa, Ellen, telephone interview with D. D. Andreassi, August, 1992.

*—Sketch by D. D. Andreassi*

# Severo Ochoa
## 1905-1993
### Spanish biochemist

Spanish-born biochemist Severo Ochoa has spent his life engaged in research into the workings of the human body. In the 1950s, he was one of the first scientists to synthesize the newly discovered ribonucleic acid (RNA) in the laboratory. This feat marked the first time that scientists managed to combine molecules together in a chain outside a living organism, knowledge that would later prove to be an essential step in enabling scientists to create life in a test tube. For this work, Ochoa received the Nobel Prize in 1959. In addition to his laboratory work, Ochoa, who was trained as a physician in Spain, taught biochemistry and pharmacology to many generations of New York University medical students.

Severo Ochoa was born on September 24, 1905, in Luarca, a small town in the north of Spain. Named after his father, a lawyer, Ochoa was the youngest son in the family. He lived in this mountain town until the age of seven, when his parents decided to move to Malaga, Spain. The move gave young Severo access to a private school education that prepared him for entrance into Malaga College, which is comparable to an American high school. By this time, Ochoa knew that he eventually would enter a career in the sciences; the only question in his mind was in which field he would specialize. Because Ochoa found mathematics at Malaga College very taxing, he decided against pursuing an engineering career, in which such skills would be essential. Instead, he planned to enter biology. After Ochoa received his B.A. from Malaga in 1921, he spent a year studying the prerequisite courses for medical school—physics, chemistry, biology, and geology. In 1923 he matriculated at the University of Madrid's Medical School.

### Acquires a Medical Education

At Madrid, Ochoa had dreams of studying under the Spanish neurohistologist Santiago Ramon y Cajal, but these were quickly dashed when he discovered that the 70-year-old histology professor had retired from teaching, although he still ran a laboratory in Madrid. Ochoa hesitated to approach Cajal even at the lab, however, because he thought the older man would be too busy to be bothered by an unimportant student. Nonetheless, by the end of his second year in medical school, Ochoa had confirmed his desire to do biological research and jumped at one of his professor's offers of a job in a nearby laboratory.

The Medical School itself housed no research facilities, but Ochoa's physiology teacher ran a small

*Severo Ochoa*

research laboratory under the aegis of the Council for Scientific Research a short distance away. Working with a classmate, Ochoa first mastered the relatively routine laboratory task of isolating creatinine—a white, crystalline compound—from urine. From there he moved to the more demanding task of studying the function and metabolism of creatine, a nitrogenous substance, in muscle. The summer after his fourth year of medical school he spent in a Glasgow laboratory, continuing work on this problem. Ochoa received his medical degree in 1929.

In an attempt to further his scientific education, Ochoa applied for a postdoctoral fellowship working under Otto Meyerhof at the Kaiser-Wilhelm Institute in a suburb of Berlin. Although the Council for Scientific Research had offered him a fellowship to pursue these studies, Ochoa turned down their offer of support because he could afford to pay his own way. He felt the money should be given to someone more needy than himself. Ochoa enjoyed his work under Meyerhof, remaining in Germany for a year.

On July 8, 1931, he married Carmen Garcia Cobian, a daughter of a Spanish lawyer and businessman, and moved with his newlywed wife to England, where he had a fellowship from the University of Madrid to study at London's National Institute for Medical Research. In England Ochoa met Sir Henry Hallett Dale, who would later win the 1936 Nobel Prize in medicine for his discovery of the chemical transmission of nerve impulses. During his first year

at the Institute, Ochoa studied the enzyme glyoxalase, and the following year he started working directly under Dale, investigating how the adrenal glands affect the chemistry of muscular contraction. In 1933 he returned to his alma mater, the University of Madrid, where he was appointed a lecturer in physiology and biochemistry.

### Spanish Civil War Forces Him to Flee Native Country

Within two years, Ochoa accepted a new position. One of the heads of the Department of Medicine was planning to start an Institute for Medical Research with sections on biochemistry, physiology, microbiology, and experimental medicine. The institute would be partially supported by the University of Madrid, which offered it space in one its new medical school buildings, and partially supported by wealthy patrons, who planned to provide a substantial budget for equipment, salaries, and supplies. The director of the new institute offered the young Ochoa the directorship of the section on physiology, which he accepted, and provided him with a staff of three. However, a few months after Ochoa began work, civil war broke out in Spain. In order to continue his work, Ochoa decided to leave the country in September of 1936. He and his wife immigrated to Germany, hardly a stable country itself in late 1936.

When Ochoa arrived, he found that his mentor Meyerhof, who was Jewish, was under considerable political and personal pressure. The German scientist had not allowed this to interfere with his work, though Ochoa did find to his surprise that the type of research Meyerhof conducted had changed dramatically in the six years since he had seen him last. As he wrote of the laboratory in a retrospective piece for the *Annual Review of Biochemistry:* "When I left it in 1930 it was basically a physiology laboratory; one could see muscles twitching everywhere. In 1936 it was a biochemistry laboratory. Glycolysis and fermentation in muscle or yeast extracts or partial reactions of these processes catalyzed by purified enzymes, were the main subjects of study." Meyerhof's change in research emphasis influenced Ochoa's own work, even though he studied in the laboratory for less than a year before Meyerhof fled to France.

Before Meyerhof left, however, he ensured that his protege was not stranded, arranging for Ochoa to receive a six-month fellowship at the Marine Biological Laboratory in Plymouth, England. Although this fellowship lasted only half a year, Ochoa enjoyed his time there, not the least because his wife Carmen started working with him in the laboratory. Their collaboration later led to the publication of a joint paper in *Nature*. At the end of six months, though, Ochoa had to move on, and friends at the lab found him a post as a research assistant at Oxford University. Two years later, when England entered the war, Oxford's Biochemistry Department shifted all its efforts to war research in which Ochoa, an alien, could not take part. So in 1940 the Ochoas picked up stakes again, this time to cross the Atlantic to work in the laboratory of Carl Ferdinand Cori and Gerty T. Cori in St. Louis. Part of the Washington University School of Medicine, the Cori lab was renowned for its cutting edge research on enzymes and work with intermediary metabolism of carbohydrates. This work involved studying the biochemical reactions in which carbohydrates produce energy for cellular operations. Ochoa worked there for a year before New York University persuaded him to move east to take a job as a research associate in medicine at the Bellevue Psychiatric Hospital, where he would for the first time have graduate and postdoctoral students working beneath him.

## Appointed Chair of NYU's Pharmacology Department

In 1945, Ochoa was promoted to assistant professor of biochemistry at the medical school. Two years later, when the pharmacology chair retired, Ochoa was offered the opportunity to succeed him and, lured by the promise of new laboratory space, he accepted. He remained chairperson for nine years, taking a sabbatical in 1949 to serve as a visiting professor at the University of California. His administrative work did not deter him from pursuing his research interests in biochemistry, however. In the early 1950s, he isolated one of the chemical compounds necessary for photosynthesis to occur, triphosphopyridine nucleotide, known as TPN. Ochoa continued his interest in intermediary metabolism, expanding the work of Hans Adolf Krebs, who posited the idea of a cycle through which food is metabolized into adenosine triphosphate, or ATP, the molecule that provides energy to the cell. The Spanish scientist discovered that one molecule of glucose, when burned with oxygen, produced 36 ATP molecules. When the chairman of the biochemistry department resigned in 1954, Ochoa accepted this opportunity to return to the department full-time as chair and full professor.

Once more ensconced in biochemistry research, Ochoa turned his attentions to a new field: the rapidly growing area of deoxyribonucleic acid (DNA) research. Earlier in his career, enzymes had been the hot new molecules for biochemists to study; now, after the critical work of James Watson and Francis Crick, in 1953, nucleic acids were fascinating scientists in the field. Ochoa was no exception. Drawing on his earlier work with enzymes, Ochoa began investigating which enzymes played roles in the creation of nucleic acids in the body. Although most enzymes assist in breaking down materials, Ochoa knew that he was looking for an enzyme that helped combine nucleotides into the long chains that were nucleic acids. Once he isolated these molecules, he hoped, he would be able to synthesize RNA and DNA in the lab. In 1955, he found a bacterial enzyme in sewage that appeared to play just such a role. When he added this enzyme to a solution of nucleotides, he discovered that the solution became viscous, like jelly, indicating that RNA had indeed formed in the dish. The following year, Arthur Kornberg, who had studied with Ochoa in 1946, applied these methods to synthesize DNA.

## Wins Nobel for Synthesis of RNA

In 1959, five years after he assumed the directorship of the biochemistry department, Ochoa shared the Nobel Prize for Physiology or Medicine with Kornberg, for their work in discovering the enzymes that help produce nucleic acids. While Ochoa was particularly delighted to share the prize with his old colleague, by this time he was no stranger to academic plaudits. The holder of several honorary degrees from both American and foreign universities, including Oxford, Ochoa had also been the recipient of the Carl Neuberg Medal in biochemistry in 1951 and the Charles Leopold Mayer Prize in 1955. Ochoa served as chairperson of NYU's biochemistry department for 20 years, until the summer of 1974, just before his seventieth birthday. When he retired from this post, he rejected the department's offer to make him an emeritus professor, preferring to remain on staff as a full professor. But even that could not keep Ochoa sufficiently occupied. In 1974, he joined the Roche Institute of Molecular Biology in New Jersey.

In 1985 he returned to his native Spain as a professor of biology at the University Autonoma in Madrid to continue his lifelong fascination with biochemical research. At the age of 75 Ochoa wrote a retrospective of his life, which he titled "Pursuit of a Hobby." In the introduction to this piece, he explained his choice of title: At a party given in the forties in honor of two Nobel laureate chemists Ochoa listed his hobby in the guest register as biochemistry, although he was at the time professor of pharmacology at New York University. Sir Henry Dale, one of the party's honorees, joked, "now that he is a pharmacologist, he has biochemistry as a hobby." Ochoa concluded this tale with the statement, "In my life biochemistry has been my only and real hobby."

## SOURCES:

*Current Biography,* edited by Charles Moritz, H. W. Wilson, 1962.
*Nobel Prize Winners,* H. W. Wilson, 1987.

*—Sketch by Shari Rudavsky*

# Bernardo O'Higgins
## 1778-1842
### Chilean independence movement leader

Born in 1778, Bernardo O'Higgins grew up in the New World, though his father had come from Ireland via Spain to become Viceroy of Peru. Educated in Spain and England, O'Higgins developed a great appreciation for the liberal and democratic institutions of early nineteenth-century England and sought to bring them to his home country. He organized a military and political movement, which brought independence to Chile and made him its supreme director. Though he later resigned and fled the country, O'Higgins still stands as a significant figure in the liberation of South American nations from colonial rule.

Probably born on August 20, 1778, Bernardo O'Higgins was the son of Ambrosio O'Higgins (who called himself simply "Higgins"), and Isabel Riquelme. Ambrosio O'Higgins grew up in Ireland and took advantage of the good will of the Spanish toward the Irish. The elder O'Higgins made his way through the Spanish colonial system by hard work in loyal service to the crown. In 1796 he received the title of Marquis of Vallenar and Osorno and Viceroy of Peru. O'Higgins' mother grew up in a middle class family. Her son Bernardo did not meet his father until he was ten years old, but Ambrosio O'Higgins never failed to provide financially for mother and son.

### Exposed to Democratic Ideas

Though not directly involved with his son's life, Ambrosio O'Higgins always sought information about young Bernardo's progress. The father lamented the lack of educational opportunities for O'Higgins in what still was a frontier colony, so he offered the boy a chance to attend school in more civilized environs. O'Higgins attended high school in Lima, Peru and then sailed for Spain in 1794. After a short time in Spain, he left for England. There he became enamored of democracy and its ideals. Free speech impressed him as one of the great blessings bestowed by the new form of government that had recently taken hold in the United States and France. Being in Europe also brought O'Higgins a keen awareness of his identity as a Chilean. He became increasingly patriotic, but lamented the absence of the freedoms in his native country. His time in England—though not always happy—seems to have exerted a strong impact on his political beliefs throughout.

Returning briefly to Spain, O'Higgins became deeply depressed when he received word that his father was disappointed with his son's apparent inability to pursue a career. O'Higgins, unable to imagine what he had done to incur his father's ire, wrote a letter in reply, saying that he had always considered his father to be most generous and would try to be a more ambitious son. His father died before the letter arrived, but O'Higgins stood to receive a significant inheritance from his father's estate and, more importantly, his last name. In 1802, he secured financing for his journey with his coming inheritance and returned to South America.

The inheritance, though disappointing in its amount of wealth, left him with one of his father's haciendas—Canteras—in the frontier town of Los Angeles. O'Higgins took the property and prospered, growing crops and raising cattle. Biographer Jay Kinsbruner called this time "the most satisfying interlude of his life," as the rural lifestyle and comforts of being the head of a modestly wealthy household suited him. He brought his mother and sister to live with him. Together they became fixtures at the *tertulias*, social gatherings where friends exchanged opinions on many subjects.

Events in Spain began to cause fundamental changes in its possessions in 1808. Though Carlos IV abdicated the crown so that his son Ferdinand could ascend, Emperor Napoleon Bonaparte intervened, forcing Carlos to reclaim his throne so that he could turn it over to Napoleon's own brother. This foreign monarch raised the Spanish populace to near rebellion, although France had an overwhelming military advantage.

For O'Higgins and his independence-minded compatriots, the usurping king represented a golden opportunity. They could display their loyalty to the crown while simultaneously working for Chilean independence. Eventually O'Higgins and his comrades established a *junta* which replaced the colonial governor. Although the new power sought little more than greater representation for Creoles in the government, its birthday, September 18, 1810, has come to be accepted as the first day of Chilean independence.

In 1813 O'Higgins and his allies faced Spanish anger over Chile's drive to sovereignty. Although ostensibly loyal to King Ferdinand, Chile's new Congress simply did not consider itself subject to Spanish rule. The Viceroy Abascal of Peru took exception and sent troops to Chile to reassert control. O'Higgins met Abascal's men with the militia of La Laja, refusing to back down when ordered to do so by colonial general Pareja. Military conflict with Royalist forces became inevitable.

When the *junta* named him General-in-Chief of the military effort to preserve Chile's independence, O'Higgins hesitated. He recognized his own lack of military training and doubted his ability to lead the campaign. Yet he accepted the post, and the war dragged on indecisively for more than a year.

O'Higgins' assessment of his abilities proved accurate; his troops often fell days behind in their marches, and his strategies produced few victories. In the end O'Higgins settled for a tense peace negotiated by Great Britain. For his part O'Higgins accepted the rank of Brigadier General and the sovereignty of Ferdinand.

Some internal fighting broke out over the terms of the treaty, but when the Viceroy of Peru rejected the treaty and invaded again, Chilean factions unified. The conflict became rather one-sided, ending in the Battle of Rancagua. There O'Higgins and his men suffered a gallant but total defeat. The Peruvians not only won the battle, but they also began to inflict punishment on the Chilean defenders and the Chilean populace at large. Though beaten badly, O'Higgins rose to the status of hero for simply standing up to outside forces. Memories of the battle would inspire the re-conquest of the country in the years to come.

### Re-Conquest and Rise to Power

O'Higgins escaped to Argentina, where he faced the daily problem of subsistence for himself and his family. He also needed to plan his return to Chile. He met **Jose San Martin,** a skilled military strategist. Together, they planned the re-conquest that returned O'Higgins to Chile and made San Martin Governor of Chile in 1817. Shortly thereafter, O'Higgins became the Supreme Director of Chile, relieving him once and for all of his military obligations. He represented Free Chile and the independence movement sweeping the continent; many saw him as a natural choice for the position.

Opinions changed as O'Higgins became increasingly prone to behavior that caused Chilean political figure Carrera to say, "One cannot arrive at greater stupidity than that of the general [O'Higgins]." O'Higgins often went beyond the limits of practical reason. He established tribunals at which all citizens had to prove their patriotism. Those failing did not qualify to work for the government, but retained their other rights. O'Higgins also interfered in affairs of the church, making many suspicious and distrustful of his rule.

He also had to contend with stubborn Royalist forces within the country. **Simon Bolivar** had predicted in 1815 that Chile would have the most enduring freedom of any nation in South America, but until 1818 that assessment remained in serious doubt. The Battle of Maipo, however, eliminated most of the remaining royalist forces, and Chile's independence moved onto more stable ground.

O'Higgins' rule continued for several years. During this time Chile adopted first a provisional and then a permanent constitution in 1822. O'Higgins had succeeded in establishing a government where there had been none, brought law and order to a country in a turbulent region, and increased international recognition of the new nation. Yet he also became essentially a benevolent dictator. He often failed to distinguish between rule of law and rule of what he thought to be right.

Under intense pressure, O'Higgins resigned in 1822 and fled to Peru, where he lived in exile until his death in 1842. Although he often made plans to return, O'Higgins never saw Chile again.

### SOURCES:

Clissold, Stephen, *Bernardo O'Higgins and the Independence of Chile,* New York, Praeger Publishing, 1969.
Kinsbruner, Jay, *Bernardo O'Higgins,* New York, Twayne Publishing, 1968.

*—Sketch by James McCarthy*

# Francisco Manuel Oller
## 1833-1917
**Puerto Rican artist**

Francisco Manuel Oller y Cestero was a major Puerto Rican artist, whose portraits of governors and slaves and landscapes of sugar plantations and peasant shacks celebrate both the island's natural beauty and its social strife. A friend to the great French artists of the late nineteenth century, he took part in the French avant-garde movements of Realism and Impressionism. "Francisco Oller was the only Latin American painter to have participated in the development of Impressionism," wrote Haydée Venegas in *Francisco Oller: Realist-Impressionist,* the catalogue of a 1983 Oller retrospective at the Ponce Art Museum in Puerto Rico.

Although he lived for many years in France and Spain, Oller always returned to Puerto Rico. "Francisco Oller was the first painter to ponder deeply on the meaning of Puerto Rico," wrote Venegas. His paintings of island life convey a strong, but not uncritical, passion for his native land. Oller's work was a "profoundly moving perspective on the virtues and defects of the Puerto Rico of his era," wrote Carlos Romero-Barceló in *Francisco-Oller: Realist-Impressionist.* Oller was inducted into the Order of King Charles III of Spain, and exhibited in Spain,

France, Vienna, and Cuba, but much of his art was lost after his death.

### Early Years

Oller was born in San Juan on June 17, 1833, the third of four children of Cayetano Juan Oller y Fromesta and María del Carmen Cestero Dávila. At age 11, he began art lessons with Juan Cleto Noa, a painter who ran an art academy in San Juan. Recognizing Oller's talent, Puerto Rico's governor, General Juan Prim, offered to send him to Rome in 1848, but his mother felt he was too young. Oller was also a gifted musician and sang with the Puerto Rican Philharmonic Society as a teenager.

From 1851 to 1853, Oller studied at the Royal Academy of Fine Arts of San Fernando in Madrid, under Federico Madrazo y Kuntz, director of the Prado Museum, and became familiar with Spanish art. On his return to Puerto Rico in 1853, he began a successful career as a portraitist, winning the Silver Medal at the Fair of San Juan in 1854 and 1855.

### Acquainted with Major Artists

In 1858, Oller travelled to Paris, staying for seven years. While working as a sexton and a baritone in an opera company, he studied under Thomas Couture and the Realist artist Gustave Courbet, and mingled with artists and intellectuals in the cafes. He knew Camille Pissarro, Antoine Guillemet, Claude Monet, Pierre Renoir, Paul Cézanne, and other artists who were later known as the Impressionists. "All of these artists helped to mold Oller's method and style of painting," wrote Edward J. Sullivan in *Arts Magazine.* He also enrolled in the Academie Suisse and was admitted to the official Salon. During this period, he painted "El estudiante" ("The Student"), using Emile Zola as model, according to Peter Bloch in *Painting and Sculpture of the Puerto Ricans.* The painting has hung in the Louvre and the Metropolitan Museum of Art.

In 1865, Oller returned to Puerto Rico, an island struggling for identity under Spanish rule. "There he used his brush, as he himself put it, 'to lash out at evil and extol the good,'" wrote Marimar Benítez in *Américas.* In 1868, Oller married Isabel Tinajero. They had two daughters, Georgina and Mercedes. Oller was part of the privileged Creole class, but he was also a nationalist and a liberal, sharply critical of colonialism and slavery. As a Realist, Oller felt art had a social, political and religious mission to contribute to society, wrote Albert Boime in *Francisco Oller: A Realist-Impressionist.*

Oller sailed back Paris in 1873, where he painted "Orillas del Sana" ("Banks of the Seine"). In 1877, he moved to Madrid, producing his famous "Autorretrato" ("Self-Portrait") in 1880, influenced by Spanish painters such as **Diego Rodríguez Velázquez.** Oller held a successful exhibit of 72 paintings at the Palace of La Correspondenciz de Espana in 1883. After a stay in Puerto Rico, he returned to Paris in 1895, embarking on his Neo-Impressionist phase, as shown in two important paintings, "Paisaje francés I y II" ("French Landscapes I and II"), 1895–1896. These natural scenes "capture the rich atmosphere and coloring of Neo-Impressionism," wrote Benítez.

In 1868, Oller founded the first of many art schools, the free Academy of Drawing and Painting in San Juan. Known for his interest in geometry and perspective, he wrote a popular book on perspective and drawing. Oller was "a born teacher," wrote Taylor. Yet his fame never translated into great wealth. "The number of private art patrons was small" in Puerto Rico, notes Bloch.

In his later years, Oller could not pay for art supplies with his small teacher's stipend. "Apparently unable to buy materials, he was reduced to painting on any surface that came to hand: stray pieces of panel, the lids of cigar and match-boxes, *yaguas* and even tambourines and smoker's pipes," wrote Dr. René Taylor in *Francisco Oller: A Realist-Impressionist.* He died on May 17, 1917, at the Municipal Hospital in San Juan.

After his death, many of his paintings deteriorated in Puerto Rico's tropical climate. In the early 1980s, the Ponce Art Museum launched a conservation effort to retrieve and restore his work for "Francisco Oller: A Realist-Impressionist," a retrospective commemorating the 150th anniversary of his birth. The exhibit of 73 paintings travelled around the United States, providing a new look at Oller and his contributions to the history of art and the art of Puerto Rico.

### SOURCES:

#### Books

Bloch, Peter, *Painting and Sculpture of the Puerto Ricans,* New York, Plus Ultra, 1978.
*Francisco Oller: A Realist-Impressionist,* edited by Marimar Benítez, Puerto Rico, Ponce Art Museum, 1983.

#### Periodicals

*Américas,* July/August 1985, pp. 36–43.
*Artnews,* April 1988, pp. 186–187.
*Arts Magazine,* May 1984, pp. 120–124.

—*Sketch by Ann Malaspina*

# Edward James Olmos
## 1947-
### Mexican American actor, director, and producer

Edward James Olmos rose out of the poverty of east Los Angeles to become a well-known actor and promoter of the belief that if he could get out of the ghetto, anybody could. Olmos has shared this belief with teenagers across the country and has played roles in a variety of movies with similar messages. *Hispanic* called Olmos "the hometown hero, Hollywood homeboy, and East L.A. celluloid *padrino*-turned-Chicano-political activist, who, against all odds, moved out the Eastside barrio and became a movie star."

As a child, acting was not what young Olmos saw as his ticket out of the barrio; it was baseball. Born on February 24, 1947, to Pedro Olmos, an immigrant from Mexico, and the former Eleanor Huizar, an American of Mexican descent, Olmos came from a long line of activists. As he explained to Guy D. Garcia of *Time,* his maternal grandparents were "'major' Mexican revolutionaries—journalists who owned the leading radical newspaper in Mexico City before moving to Los Angeles."

Olmos grew up in the Boyle Heights section of east Los Angeles, a neighborhood where Hispanics, Native Americans, Koreans, Chinese, Mexicans, and Russians lived. He told Garcia it was a fantastic environment to grow up in. "Inside this world, everyone was the same," the actor told Tom Seligson of *Parade.* "We were all poor. And the only way to survive it was through a constant struggle of trying to be better today than you were yesterday. So that's what I tried to do—first with baseball, then with music and drama."

Baseball, he explained to Seligson, was the main character-building activity of his youth. "It taught me self-discipline, determination, perseverance, and patience—all of which have been key ingredients to what I have done since." Playing baseball not only kept him from getting involved with gangs, but he also became the Golden State batting champion.

When he was 15, Olmos turned from batting to music. He recalled the switch with Seligson: "I think I felt that music could offer me bigger dreams. I wanted to sing and dance, but I really couldn't sing." He worked at it, however, like he had baseball, until he was proficient enough at singing and playing the piano to form a combo called Pacific Ocean. In the mid-1960s, the band played regularly at a Sunset Strip nightclub, where he met the woman who would become his first wife.

*Edward James Olmos*

One night Kaija Keel, daughter of actor Howard Keel, came to the club. Olmos, a long-haired Chicano rocker, and Keel, the daughter of a famous actor, had a difficult time persuading their families their relationship would last. "I was *Guess Who's Coming to Dinner* before the movie ever appeared," Olmos told Garcia. The couple was married in 1971; despite parental worries, their relationship lasted into the early 1990s and bore sons Mico and Bodie.

Olmos next made the transition from singing to acting. He studied during the day at East Los Angeles City College to earn an associate's degree in sociology while playing with the combo at night. He took a drama course with the intention of overcoming his fear of public speaking and found, to his surprise, that he enjoyed acting. "I started acting to learn how to become a better singer," he told Garcia. "Then the whole thing switched on me. I discovered that the spoken word is easier to project than the sung word." Though he decided to become an actor, Olmos did not meet with instant success. To support his family, he delivered antique furniture in addition to his acting and music gigs.

### Lands Role in *Zoot Suit*

Olmos's first big break on stage came with the musical drama *Zoot Suit,* Luis Valdez's play based on the 1942 Los Angeles Sleepy Lagoon case. Olmos auditioned for the part of El Pachuco, which Garcia described as "the strutting, posing, super-macho narrator and mordant conscience" of the play. "I spoke in *caló,* street jive from the streets of East L.A.—a mix of Spanish, English and Gypsy," Olmos explained to Garcia. "They asked me if I could dance, and I hit a perfect set of splits, turning the brim of my hat as I came up." For his performance in the play, which opened in 1978, he received a Los Angeles Critics Circle Award, and when it moved to Broadway in 1979, he was nominated for a Tony Award. Despite the lukewarm reception of the film version of *Zoot Suit,* which was released in 1982, Olmos had made his mark.

Throughout his first major theatrical experience, Olmos felt a sense of responsibility about his role. "I was bringing to life the first real Latin character and Latin culture seen on the American stage," he told Seligson in *Parade.* "The closest we'd come was *West Side Story,* and that was as real as the Polynesians in *South Pacific.*" Other acting roles for Olmos began pouring in, and he appeared in *Wolfen* in 1981 and in 1982's *Blade Runner.*

Olmos's next significant role was in the PBS special *The Ballad of Gregorio Cortez,* a story of the Mexican cowhand who was the object of one of the biggest manhunts in Texas history. In collaboration with director Robert M. Young, Olmos helped film and promote this movie. The film was most unique in the fact that the character of Cortez spoke Spanish throughout the movie, with no subtitles provided to the audience. "I wanted to put non-Spanish speaking viewers in the same predicament as the law-abiding citizens of that community," Olmos explained. "I wanted the audience to be in the shoes of Gregorio Cortez." The actor considered this film to be one of the most important of his career; after its television debut, Olmos spent another five years promoting it and getting it distributed to libraries, schools, and boys and girls clubs.

### Fame Grows on *Miami Vice*

Olmos's next significant role was as Lieutenant Martin Castillo on NBC's popular show, *Miami Vice.* The actor played Castillo as a terse cop dealing with painful memories from his past. "People started to understand that this was a man who suffered. A man who has been wounded," Olmos said. In 1985, the actor earned an Emmy for best supporting actor and the following year won a Golden Globe Award.

The television role brought Olmos fortune and fame and allowed him to accept the kind of roles he most wanted to play. The role he is perhaps most proud of is that of **Jaime Escalante,** a Bolivian-born computer scientist who dedicated himself to teaching math to Garfield High School students in the barrio— Olmos's former home. The movie, *Stand and Deliver,* focused on Escalante's amazing ability to motivate underprivileged Hispanic students who, under his tutelage, achieved amazingly high scores on 1982's college placement calculus test.

Olmos threw himself into the part, observing Escalante in and out of class for hours. In a review of *Stand and Deliver,* which was released in 1988, *New York Newsday*'s Lynn Darling noted that Olmos gave "a tremendous performance as Escalante, bullying, sermonizing, demanding, humoring the students into doing the mind-boggling amount of work involved." Olmos received an Academy Award nomination for best actor for his outstanding performance. In 1989, he appeared in *Triumph of Spirit,* followed by *Talent for the Game,* a 1991 film directed by Olmos's long-time friend Robert M. Young. The two men formed their own production company, YOY Productions.

In 1992, *American Me* was released, a film that was one of Olmos's most ambitious projects. Coproducing it with Young and Sean Daniel, he also directed and starred in this portrayal of crime and violence in the United States. Olmos plays Santana who, as a barrio gang member, eventually ends up in Folsom State Prison where his Mexican Mafia reaches beyond the prison wall to control drugs, gambling, extortion and prostitution.

"*American Me* shows the fearsome logic that makes ethnic gangs the inevitable social structures that arise with the breakdown of values and opportunity," Jack Kroll noted in *Newsweek.* "This film is not for one race, one subculture, one age range," Olmos explained to Kroll. "Gangs teach a distorted discipline, a distorted familial bonding, a distorted sense of pride and power. I made this movie to allow all society to take a journey into an uncharted land that they would never have the opportunity to go into." As he did with *Stand and Deliver* and *The Ballad of Gregorio Cortez,* Olmos attended special screenings of the movie held for teenagers and community leaders around the country.

Following the Los Angeles riots of April 1992, Olmos backed his activism with action and assisted in the clean-up effort of the city. He became a member of the Rebuild LA Committee and worked in inner-city neighborhoods to help restore them.

In the early 1990s, Olmos and Keel were divorced, and he married actress Lorraine Bracco. Since 1972 he has spent a significant amount of time working with young audiences in schools, correctional institutions, and elsewhere. In 1992 Olmos received Eastman Kodak's Second Century Award for his ongoing support of young filmmakers. "I'm a kid's worst nightmare," he told Kroll. "And also a kid's best hope. I come from a dysfunctional family, I'm a minority, I have no natural talent, but I did it. If I can do it, anybody can do it. I take away all the excuses."

**SELECTED VIDEOGRAPHY:**

*Aloha, Bobby and Rose,* 1974.
*Wolfen,* 1981.
*Zoot Suit,* 1981.
*Blade Runner,* 1982.
*Virus,* 1982.
*The Ballad of Gregorio Cortez,* 1983.
*Miami Vice 2: The Prodigal Son,* 1985.
*Saving Grace,* 1986.
*Stand and Deliver,* 1988.
*Triumph of the Spirit,* 1989.
*Talent for the Game,* 1991.
*American Me,* 1992.
*Mi Familia,* 1995.

**SOURCES:**

*Hispanic,* October 1993, pp. 14–22.
*Newsweek,* March 30, 1992, pp. 66–67.
*New York Newsday,* March 18, 1988.
*New York Times,* March 18, 1988.
*Parade,* March 17, 1991.
*Time,* July 11, 1988, pp. 54–60.

—*Sketch by Kathe A. Conti*

*Juan Carlos Onetti*

# Juan Carlos Onetti
## 1909-1994

**Uruguayan novelist, short story writer, and journalist**

Juan Carlos Onetti, one of Uruguay's most outstanding and prolific writers, is considered a father of the modern Latin American novel. He broke away from the traditional regional novel to explore the anguish and alienation of modern man, adrift in an anonymous society. *Publisher's Weekly* described Onetti as "one of this century's great Latin American writers."

Despite his stature in Latin America and Spain, where he lived from 1975 until his death in 1994, Onetti is not well-known among English-speaking readers, perhaps because of his difficult prose and the nightmarish world that he often portrayed in his fiction. "Complexity and ambiguity are the major characteristics of Onetti's novels," wrote M. Ian Adams in *Three Authors of Alienation: Bombal, Onetti, Carpentier.* James Polk, writing in *The New York Times Book Review,* described Onetti's work as "intense and highly idiosyncratic."

Onetti was born in Montevideo, Uruguay, on July 1, 1909. His father, Carlos Onetti, was a customs employee. His mother, Honoria Borges de Onetti, was from Brazil. Although he was an avid reader, Onetti did not finish high school. Instead, he accepted a variety of menial jobs, including soccer ticket vendor, doorman, waiter, and tire salesman, and wrote fiction in his spare time.

In 1930 Onetti moved to Buenos Aires. He married his cousin, María Amalia Onetti, the same year. (Their son Jorge eventually became a prominent Uruguayan novelist in his own right.) Onetti published his first story, "Avenida de Mayo-Diagonal-Avenida de Mayo", in the journal *Prensa* in 1933. Returning to Montevideo in 1934, Onetti divorced his first wife and married her sister, María Julia Onetti. While in Montevideo he continued to write short stories and began a successful career in journalism. He edited and contributed to the progressive magazine *Marcha* from 1939 to 1941. He used his weekly column in the magazine to urge Uruguayan writers to explore new avenues of language and narrative technique. He left *Marcha* in 1941 to join the Reuters news agency. Stationed in Montevideo and Buenos Aires, where he served as bureau chief, Onetti stayed with Reuters for 13 years. He also edited the Argentine magazine *Vea y Lea* during his stay in that country. He married Elizabeth María

Pekelharing in 1945, his third marriage. The couple had a daughter in 1951. He returned to Montevideo in 1954 to manage an advertising and publishing firm. That same year he married a fourth time, wedding the violinist Dorotea Muhr. In 1957 he was appointed director of municipal libraries in Montevideo. Onetti contributed literary articles for *Acción,* the Montevideo political newspaper of the day, as well.

### Onetti's Novels

In 1939 Onetti published his first short novel, *El pozo* (*The Pit*), a book that won him a small following in Montevideo. The novella "marks a turning point in the style and technique of Latin American narrative," noted Verani in *Latin American Writers.* Onetti experimented with time and space in the novel, using a narrator who, isolated in his room, creates an imaginative reality to give meaning to his grim life.

Onetti's first major novel, *Tierra de nadie* (*No Man's Land*) appeared in 1941, followed by *Para esta noche* (*For Tonight*) in 1943. *La vida breve* (*A Brief Life*), published in 1950, is considered by some critics to be Onetti's finest work. John S. Brushwood, author of *The Spanish American Novel,* wrote that it "sets a standard for the novel of alienation." The book is an examination of the mind of a character named Brausen whose life has fallen apart after a failed marriage. He is "tyrannized by his own conception of life as reality sandwiched between two walls of nothingness," according to Brushwood.

Onetti's existentialism has been compared to that of Samuel Beckett and Jean-Paul Sartre, while critics contend that Onetti's influences include writers such as Louis-Ferdinand Céline, Roberto Arlt, John Dos Passos, and William Faulkner. Onetti's protagonists are tormented by doubt, pessimism, and loneliness. "He isn't a person; he is, like all the inhabitants of this strip of the river, a determined intensity of life molding itself in the form of his own mania, his own idiocy," Onetti wrote of one of his characters in *Juntacadáveres* (*The Body Snatcher*), a 1976 novel.

Utilizing a device reminiscent of Faulkner's use of the imaginary Yoknapatawpha County, Onetti located many stories in the fictional town of Santa María, a bleak setting infused by the urban blight of Montevideo and Buenos Aires. Characters in his fiction often lived in grim tenements, spoke in street vernacular, and struggled with the corruption of human existence in modern cities. "This no man's land deserves the name not because nobody can hold it, but because nobody wants it," wrote Brushwood of *Tierra de nadie* (*No Man's Land*).

Critics point to other common elements in Onetti's complex works. Often surrealistic and tinged with black humor, Onetti's writing frequently addresses social and political issues. "His serpentine lyricism tempered by whiplash irony, Onetti is an elegist of the 20th century, its neuroses, sexual repression, mafias, anti-Semitism, office time-clocks and terminal lives," observed *Publishers Weekly* in 1991.

Fame came late to Onetti. His career was "marked by frustration and disappointment," noted Colchie in *A Hammock Beneath the Mangoes.* Onetti was a middle-aged man before his books were released widely. While he received the National Literature Prize in Uruguay in 1962 and the William Faulkner Certificate of Merit in 1963 for *El astillero,* widespread recognition of his work remained elusive.

In 1974 Onetti served as a judge on a panel for a *Marcha* literary contest. The panel awarded a prize to a story considered subversive by Uruguay's military dictatorship. Imprisoned for more than three months for his role as a judge in the contest, Onetti was released and fled to Madrid, where he settled permanently in 1975. There, new editions and translations of his early works were published. Onetti published two major novels late in life: *Dejemos hablar al viento* (*Let's Allow the Wind to Speak*) published in 1979, and *Cuando entonces* (*When Then*), released in 1987.

In 1980 Onetti received the Miguel de Cervantes Prize, Spain's highest literary award. The Latin-American PEN Club nominated him for the Nobel Prize in literature as well, and Uruguay awarded the prestigious José Enrique Rodo Prize to Onetti in 1991. Recognition of his work has not been as visible in the United States. "Perhaps—let's hope—Onetti will one day soon be as widely appreciated in this country as, say, García Marquez or Vargas Llosa . . . ," wrote Brad Hooper in *Booklist* in 1991. Critic Polk concurred, remarking in *The New York Times Book Review* that Onetti, who died of a heart attack in Madrid in 1994, was "probably the least known giant among modern Latin American writers."

### SELECTED PUBLISHED WORKS:

*El pozo* (*The Pit*), Signo, 1939.
*Tierra de nadie* (*No Man's Land*), Losada, 1941.
*Para esta noche* (*For Tonight*), Poseidón, 1943.
*La vida breve,* Sudamericana, 1950; translated by Hortense Carpentier and published as *A Brief Life,* Grossman, 1976; Serpent's Tail, 1994.
*Un sueño realizado y otros cuentos,* Número, 1951.
*Los adioses,* Sur, 1954; English translation published as *Goodbyes and Stories,* University of Texas Press, 1990.
*La cara de la desgracia,* Alfa, 1960.
*El astillero,* General Fabril, 1961; translated by Rachel Caffyn and published as *The Shipyard,* Scribners, 1968; Serpent's Tail, 1993.

*Juntacadáveres,* Alfa, 1964; translated by Alfred MacAdam and published as *Body Snatcher,* Pantheon Books, 1991.

*Cuentos completos,* Centro Editor de América Latina, 1967.

*La novia robada y otros cuentos,* Centro Editor de América Latina, 1968.

*Obras completas,* edited by Rodríguez Monegal, Aguilar, 1970.

*Tan triste como ella y otros cuentos,* Lumen, 1976.

*Dejemos hablar al viento* (*Let's Allow the Wind to Speak*), Bruguera Alfaguara, 1979.

*Presencia y otros cuentos,* Almarabu, 1986.

*Cuando entonces* (*When Then*), Mondadori, 1987.

## SOURCES:

### Books

Adams, M. Ian, *Three Authors of Alienation: Bombal, Onetti, Carpentier,* Austin, University of Texas Press, 1975.

*The Borzoi Anthology of Latin American Literature,* volume II, edited by Emir Rodríguez Monegal, New York, Alfred A. Knopf, 1993, pp. 536–539.

Brushwood, John S., *The Spanish American Novel,* Austin, TX: University of Texas Press, 1975.

*Cassell's Encyclopedia of World Literature,* volume III, edited by S.H. Steinberg, New York, William Morrow, 1973, pp. 261–262.

*Dictionary of Literary Biography: Modern Latin-American Fiction Writers: First Series,* edited by William Luis, Detroit, Gale, 1992.

*Encyclopedia of World Literature in the 20th Century,* volume 3, edited by Leonard S. Klein, New York, Frederick Ungar Publishing, 1983, pp. 435–436.

*A Hammock Beneath the Mangoes: Stories from Latin America,* edited by Thomas Colchie, New York, Penguin Books USA, 1992.

*Latin American Writers,* volume III, edited by Carlos A. Solé, New York, Charles Scribner's Sons, 1989.

*The Oxford Companion to Spanish Literature,* edited by Philip Ward, Oxford, Clarendon Press, 1978.

### Periodicals

*Booklist,* May 1, 1991.

*Kirkus Reviews,* March 15, 1991, p. 353.

*Library Journal,* May 1, 1991, p. 109.

*New York Times Book Review,* August 11, 1991, p. 6.

*Publishers Weekly,* March 29, 1991, p. 76; May 31, 1993, p. 47.

—*Sketch by Ann Malaspina*

# Manuel Ceferino Oribe
## 1792-1857
### Uruguayan independence leader

**B**orn in 1792, Manuel Oribe was instrumental in determining the fate of his native Uruguay after the independence movement swept South America. He founded one of the most important Uruguayan political parties of the nineteenth century and served as president of Uruguay. Although historians debate Oribe's politics—some call him a conservative and others a liberal—none deny his impact. He took part in some way in almost all the major battles for Uruguayan independence, and even after his retirement his enemies battled with his political legacy.

Oribe's father, Francisco Oribe, served as a captain in the Royal Artillery. Historians say very little about the elder Oribe's feelings toward the independence movement that his son supported from its very beginning in 1811. Manuel Oribe was born August 26, 1792 to Francisco and Maria Francisca Viana Oribe in Montevideo. As a leading family in the largest city in Uruguay, the Oribes took on the role of opinion leaders. When the fight for independence started in 1811, Manuel Oribe supported it.

After the achievement of independence, the struggle to define Uruguay's nationhood began. Opinions and coalitions came and went, and Oribe went into military service. He first served under Jose Rondeau, the Uruguayan patriot, and initially refused to follow General **Jose Artigas,** whose forces went to battle against those of Buenos Aires.

### Changing Allegiances

Oribe eventually joined Artigas, and fought against the forces from Buenos Aires. In 1817, however, the Portuguese occupied Montevideo, and Oribe joined the Buenos Aires forces he had once opposed. He remained there for several years during the occupation of his birthplace, but the occupying armies began to show signs of dissolution. Portugal and Brazil had agreed to a joint occupation, but tensions had developed between the armies.

Uruguayans within the Portuguese army took advantage of the lack of solidarity to plot the liberation of the city. Oribe joined the Portuguese army to be among them in 1821. Not until three years later, however, did the Portuguese leave. Even after their departure, Uruguay's various factions contended fiercely for control. Oribe went to Buenos Aires in 1824 to join countryman Juan Antonio Lavalleja, who planned his own liberation of the country.

Lavalleja called his close associates the Thirty-three, and Oribe counted himself among the most prominent. Yet once independence returned to Uruguay and a president, **Fructuoso Rivera,** had been named, Oribe opposed Lavalleja's continued challenges. Oribe backed Rivera's legitimate claim and Rivera rewarded him with the position of Minister of War and Navy, which Oribe assumed in 1833.

Rivera also promised Oribe his endorsement for the presidency when Rivera's term ended and Oribe took office in March of 1835. Almost immediately, he began to strengthen the central government at the expense of governments in the countryside. Rivera had left the presidency, but he retained the loyalty of many country dwellers. His political power frightened Oribe.

The new president tried to tighten his control over the rural areas. He also tried to humiliate Rivera by making public statements of the first president's financial malfeasance while in office. Rivera responded by ordering his supporters to revolt. The ensuing conflict gave birth to two political parties: Blanco, the white party, which stood for little more than law and order and Oribe's rule, and the Colorado, or red party, which can be said to have represented little more than opposition to Oribe specifically and central control generally.

Oribe resigned in 1838 and fled to Buenos Aires. Though he retained the title of presidency in name, he commanded Argentine troops, not Uruguayan ones, against Rivera in the early 1840s. His renewed power inspired him to try to retake all of his native country, but after nearly nine years of siege on Montevideo, he gave up his claim to the legitimacy of his Blanco government headquartered in Restauración.

Oribe left politics in 1851, but the Colorado party still feared his influence. Escaping Colorado persecution, Oribe fled to Europe in 1853. He returned to Uruguay in 1855 and made a final abortive run at retaking the nation. He died on November 12, 1857 of natural causes.

**SOURCES:**

*Biographical Dictionary of Latin American and Caribbean Political Leaders,* edited by Robert Alexander, Westport, Connecticut, Greenwood Press, 1988.

*Diccionario Uruguayo de biografías, 1810–1840,* edited by Jose Fernandez, Saldaña, Montevideo, Editorial Amerindia, 1945.
*Encyclopedia of Latin America,* edited by Helen Delpar, New York, McGraw-Hill, 1974.
Fitzgibbon, Russell, *Uruguay: Portrait of a Democracy,* New Brunswick, New Jersey, Rutgers University Press, 1954.
Willis, Jean L., *Historial Dictionary of Uruguay,* Metuchen, New Jersey, Scarecrow Press, 1974.

—*Sketch by James McCarthy*

# José Clemente Orozco
## 1883-1949
**Mexican artist**

J osé Clemente Orozco is considered by many art experts to be one of the most important artists of the twentieth century. A popular artist, he did most of his work as murals, painting the culture and history of Mexico and eventually of the entire North American continent. He painted scenes of war, unjust governments, loss of liberty, and desperation. His work influenced the North American avant-garde movement of the 1930s and profoundly affected what became Abstract Expressionism. In an article in 1949, Justino Fernandez called Orozco "the first great creative genius in American art, the first one to appear since America became America; with full awareness, like Cortés he burned his ships behind him to find out whether he could get along on his own."

José Clemente Orozco was born November 23, 1883 to Ireneo Orozco and Rosa Flores, both middle-class descendants of Spanish settlers, in Zapotlan el Grande—later renamed Ciudad Guzman—in Jalisco, Mexico. Orozco's family moved to Guadalajara in 1886 but settled in Mexico City in 1888.

### Early Tragedy Changed Direction

Orozco discovered art at an early age, passing the workshop of José Guadalupe Posada every day on his way to school. Posada mass-produced broadsheets and chapbooks for public consumption, but in his simple, linear illustrations of Mexican life, caricatures, and satirical cartoons, Orozco began to observe what art could and should be. Orozco worked with Posada as a young boy and the artist instructed him.

During these early school years, sometime before 1897, Orozco suffered a tragic loss. An accidental

*José Clemente Orozco*

gunpowder explosion deprived him of his left hand and most of his wrist. The accident also made him deaf in one ear and caused partial blindness. Other tragedies added to Orozco's dilemma and forced him to make what—at the time—was a painful decision, but later made him famous. After preparatory studies, Orozco spent, as he claimed, "a delightful three years in the country," studying at the School of Agriculture in San Jacinto. He earned a degree as an expert agriculturalist from the National Agricultural School of Mexico. He went on to study mathematics and architectural drawing at the National University of Mexico, but tragedy struck again: Orozco's father died. Crippled and without financial support from his family, Orozco was forced to make a difficult decision about his future. He took a job as an architectural draftsman for Carlos Herrera to pay his way through college. But as hard as he tried, the practical roads of agriculture, mathematics, and architecture were not for him. In his autobiography, he wrote that "my obsession with painting led me to drop my preparatory studies and return to the Academy [National Academy of Fine Arts where he was a student off and on for six years, from 1908 to 1914] ... this time with a sure knowledge of my vocation." Orozco decided to be an artist, and worked at his art when he was not enrolled in classes.

By 1910, Orozco's first artistic recognition came when some of his drawings won a place in the National Academy of Fine Arts exhibition commemorating the Centenary of Mexican Independence.

The next year, Orozco participated in an art student strike at the Academy. He also began doing cartoons for radical newspapers, like *El Imparcial* and *El Hijo del Ahuizote.* He officially began his art career in 1912, when he opened his first studio in Mexico City and began to do paintings of the local people who frequented the brothels and bars in his neighborhood. Orozco painted with blacks, the colors he claimed were "exiled from the Impressionist palette" and were reminiscent of "the pestilent shadows of closed rooms." Orozco did not turn sympathetic eyes on the people of these watercolors. He rendered the figures of prostitutes and pimps as dolls, faces like masks. These early figures would return in his later work however. Notably, one of the prostitutes from this period appeared in the foreground of the mural *Catharsis* in the Palacio de Bellas Artes.

In 1915, he moved to Orizaba in Veracruz and created cartoons and illustrations for the Carrancist newspaper *La Vanguardia.* There he met **David Alfaro Siqueiros,** along with **Diego Rivera.** Together they would make up the "Big Three" Mexican Muralists. Orozco was not painting murals yet. But at this time, Orozco was developing the vocabulary that would inform his life's work: "In the world of politics, it was ... war without quarter ... farce, drama barbarity. Buffoons and dwarfs trailing along after the gentlemen of noose and dagger.... A parade of stretchers with wounded in bloody rags, and all at once the savage pealing of bells and a thunder of rifle fire ... *La Cucaracha* accompanied by firing."

Orozco made his first trip to the United States in 1917. Upon entering the States, U.S. Customs officials confiscated many of his paintings on grounds of indecency. He remained in the United States for two years despite the problems he experienced at the border. Although he visited New York City, he spent the majority of the two years living and working on his art in California, supporting himself painting the faces of dolls and working as a sign painter.

Upon returning to Mexico in 1919, Orozco would soon find a great amount of work for which he became famous: murals. But first he faced more difficulties. Barely making ends meet doing caricatures, his one attempt to be taken seriously as an artist—a one-man show held in Mexico City—was either ignored or unappreciated. Even more damaging was further action by U.S. Customs that condemned and destroyed the work he had exhibited at the Customs House in El Paso, Texas. Despite these problems, he built a studio in Coyoacan.

### Began Mural Career

Orozco began his mural painting career in 1923 at the National Preparatory School in Mexico City. Siqueiros and Diego Rivera were also doing murals at the school. The year 1923 was one of firsts for Orozco.

Not only did he start his first mural work, but on his forty-first birthday he married Margarita Valladores with whom he would have three children: Clemente, Alfredo, and Lucrecia. In the same year, Orozco also helped found the Union of Revolutionary Painters, Sculptors, and Engravers. In 1924, he was temporarily forced to halt work on his murals at the school because of student unrest. He worked on staff at the radical newspaper *El Machete.*

Orozco did not finish the Preparatory School murals until 1926. Meanwhile, he completed a mural called "Omniciencia" ("Omniscience") in Casa de los Azulejos (House of Tiles) in Mexico City and held an individual exhibition in Paris at the Bernheim-Jeune Gallery, both in 1925. Orozco created 19 separate murals at the Preparatory School that spanned three floors and 490 square meters. In 1926, as he completed his first set of murals, he finished another, *Social Revolution,* at the Escuela Industrial in Orizaba, Veracruz.

His work began to receive international attention when D. H. Lawrence wrote about it in his novel *The Plumed Serpent* (1926). Lawrence's character Kate reacted to the murals in the Preparatory School in the novel. The book refers to "gross caricatures" in Orozco's mural "Social Justice." Though the painting depicts the poor as parodies, Orozco shed a fundamental human sympathy upon them. Yet he did so without a political agenda, for he never joined a political party, nor did he ever participate in any way in the Mexican Revolution, which for him was "the gayest and most diverting of carnivals." Orozco wrote notes in 1923 that responded to many of the reactions to his work including the one years later by Lawrence's character. He divided the "artistic atmosphere" of Mexico of the time into a movement to revive the archeological styles of Mexican Indians of the past and the movement to continue the work of the Impressionists. Neither interested Orozco, and he felt that the use of a word like "caricatures" to describe his work indicated that his work "was completely misunderstood by the people who were unaware of the new tendency represented by the works exhibited." Later in the notes he added that "the real work of art, like a cloud or tree, has nothing to do with morality or immorality, with good or evil, with wisdom or ignorance, or with vice or virtue. . . . A painting should not be a commentary but the fact itself; not a reflection but light itself; not an interpretation but the thing interpreted."

Orozco returned to America in 1927, traveling to New York City, where he entered a group exhibition at the Art Center in 1928. In a letter he referred to the show as "a total, absolute, and definite failure . . . the gallery is bad, just amateurs and beginners, the room dark, the director an imbecile, complete chaos." Nevertheless, this time he stayed in the States until 1934. In October 1928, he held a show of his drawings entitled *Mexico in Revolution* at the Marie Sterner Gallery. It was also during this time that Orozco saw exhibits of the work of many European artists who influenced him, particularly **Goya**, from whom Orozco further advanced his ideas of parody and satire.

Another major influence on Orozco during this period was "The Ashram"—named for Ghandi's Wardha lodging—Alma Reed's New York literary and cultural salon, active from 1927 to 1930, and her 57th Street Delphic Studios. Believing him to be a genius, Reed worked for Orozco as agent, dealer, patron, and later biographer. Reed and her world had a profound effect on Orozco. He felt very indebted to her and her colleague, Eva Sikelianos, whose Greek roots contributed to Orozco's selection of subject matter for his first American mural in 1930, "The Prometheus," at Pomona College in California.

Orozco was working in lithographs when the stock market crash caused the Great Depression in 1929. The "crash" had a profound effect on Orozco. In the eyes of the "desperate angry men," he saw the same tragedies that afflicted his home country. His art work began to reflect these sympathies. Over the next three years, Orozco showed a variety of work in the United States, in New York City, Philadelphia, and Los Angeles, and in cities in other countries, such as Vienna and Paris. He showed oil paintings, lithographs, and drawings, and earned commissions to do murals. From 1930–1931, a show of his work toured the major museums in the United States. In 1932 his work toured of Europe for three months.

## Completed Dartmouth Murals

With the exception of three months in Europe, Orozco spent 1932 through 1934 at Dartmouth College in Hanover, New Hampshire, creating one of the mural cycles for which he is best known. For two years, he worked on murals at Dartmouth's Baker Library. He also served temporarily on the fine arts faculty while at the college. At the college, he completed a mural cycle covering 277 square meters, or 3,000 square feet. These paintings were the most important paintings of the North American period of Orozco's career.

The murals depicted Orozco's interpretation of the evolution of civilization in America. His brush work loosened and became bolder in this work, a technique that Orozco continued in his Guadalajara murals. Orozco wrote in his autobiography, "The American continental races are now becoming aware of their own personality as it emerges from the two cultural currents, the indigenous and the European. The great American myth of Quetzalcoatl is a living one, embracing both elements and pointing clearly by its prophetic nature, to the responsibility shared equally by the two Americas of creating here an authentic American civilization." From Quetzalcoatl the murals continue, depicting the arrival of the Spaniards in the New World, the history of the Catholic church in Colonial times, and the ruin of the Industrial age, culminating in a portrait of Christ destroying his own cross.

After a show in Chicago, Orozco returned to Mexico City to create a mural in the Palacio de Bellas Artes, which he called "Catharsis." He journeyed to New York City again in 1935 as a delegate to the Congress of American Artists. Governor Evarado Topete of Jalisco, invited Orozco to live and work in Guadalajara. There over the next three years, he created murals for the Assembly Hall of the university, the Government Palace, and at the Hospicio Cabanas, a deconsecrated church that was formerly the city orphanage. In Guadalajara, Orozco created murals quite unlike those of his contemporaries, Siqueiros and Rivera. Instead of celebrating the struggle for freedom and dignity, Orozco focused on a "stark reality of human existence," Desmond Rochfort wrote in the catalogue for the Orozco show at the Oxford, England, Museum of Modern Art in 1980. According to Rochfort, "Orozco believed passionately in the sanctity of freedom but when he looked around him, in spite of the progress of the 20th century, he saw oppression and slavery." Orozco himself wrote of the criticisms of these Guadalajara murals in his autobiography, "Those who say I am an anarchist do not know me. I am a partisan with absolute freedom of thought, a real free thinker; neither a dogmatist nor an anarchist; neither an enemy of hierarchies nor a partisan of unyielding affirmations."

Orozco spent the first five months of 1940 creating murals at the Gabino Ortiz Library in Jiquilpan. He then travelled to New York City to complete his six-panel mural "The Dive Bomber and the Tank" in the Museum of Modern Art. The New York mural recalled "Catharsis" in terms of scale, but otherwise was a departure from Orozco's previous work. Here he began to seriously question his previous work and began utilizing more poetic abstractions of reality and specially charged conventional imagery. It was of this period that Orozco wrote that "a painting is a poem and nothing else." He would continue to paint in this vein until his death.

Throughout the 1940s, Orozco remained primarily in Mexico, completing murals throughout the country, most of which were in Mexico City. In 1946, he received the National Prize from Mexico's President Camacho for his murals in the nave of the Church of the Hospital of Jesus. This search for new forms of expression led him to smaller work. In addition to murals, he began doing engravings, easel paintings, and drawings, many of which were portraits. He wrote autobiographical articles which were published in *Excelsior* in 1942. Throughout the decade, he had many shows at El Colegio Nacional, of which he was a founding member.

In Orozco's last year, he painted one of his most famous and enduring murals, called "Juarez, the Church and the Imperialists." It featured a large portrait of **Benito Juarez**—leader of the reform movement of 1861 and twice president of Mexico—at the Sala de Reforma, Chapultepec Castle in Mexico City. The *Washington Post* praised Orozco highly for his work and criticized Rivera's work as "static and poster-like" compared to Orozco's "design and idea."

Orozco continued painting murals and other work up until his death on September 7, 1949; he left unfinished an open air mural in the Miguel Aleman housing complex in Mexico City. His funeral was held at the Palacio de Bellas Artes, where his work had hung many times.

## SOURCES:

### Books

Hopkins, Jon H., *Orozco*, Flagstaff, Northern Arizona University Publications, 1967.

Reed, Alma, *José Clemente Orozco 1883–1949*, San Antonio, Marion Koolger Art Institute, 1959.

Rochfort, Desmond, *Mexican Muralists*, New York, Universe, 1989.

### Periodicals

*Américas*, July 1994, p. 60.

*ARTnews*, summer 1994, pp. 187–88.

*College Art Journal*, winter 1949–1950, pp. 142–47; fall 1959, pp. 40–53.

*Southern Humanities Review*, summer 1990, pp. 297–99.

*Studio International*, November 1987, pp. 30–41.

*Time*, October 15, 1990, pp. 80–82.

*Washington Post*, August 29, 1948.

*—Sketch by Christopher B. Tower*

# Daniel Ortega
## 1945-
### Nicaraguan freedom-fighter and statesman

Working with the Sandinista Liberation Front, Daniel Ortega struggled to free his Nicaraguan people from the dictatorship of Luis Somoza Debayle (Tachito Somoza III). Once the Somoza government fell, Ortega was elected president of

Nicaragua in 1984 and served until 1990 throughout years of bloody conflict between the Sandinistas and the contra rebels.

Daniel Ortega Savedra was born November 11, 1945, in La Libertad, Chontales, Nicaragua, a small mining community east of the capital of Managua. Both of Ortega's parents, Don Daniel Ortega and Lidia Savedra Ortega, grew up in poverty and thus vehemently opposed the tyranny of Somoza. Don Daniel worked as an accountant for a local mining company. When La Libertad's mining operations closed down, the Ortegas had no income. Ortega's older brother and sister died when the family could not afford medical care. In order to survive, the Ortegas moved to Juigalpa, a town closer to Managua. Don Daniel began an import-export business and Lidia opened a bakery. They had more children: Humberto, Camilo, and Germana.

Ortega was educated intermittently in private or Catholic schools, but was forced to leave when his parents could not pay tuition bills. He received most of his education at home where his parents tried to counteract the American influences on Nicaragua prevalent after the U.S. occupation from 1909–1933. As a young boy, Ortega was inspired by the stories of former Sandinista leader **Augusto Cesar Sandino** (after whom the Sandinistas were named), who had fought for the Nicaraguan people until he was murdered in 1934 and General Anastasio Somoza seized control of the country in a military coup. Ortega decided to follow in Sandino's footsteps and return the wealth of Nicaragua to Nicaraguans. But Ortega had an uphill battle against what became a Somoza dynasty with Luis Somoza succeeding Anastasio in 1956 and Anastasio Somoza Debayle, Tachito Somoza III, following in 1967.

Of his choice to fight the Somozas, Ortega said: "I was about 14 years old, and I was from a poor family. I could have been a priest, but I chose the career of a revolutionary instead. Religious people could say they were carrying out the word of Christ, but they were really more dedicated to educating the rich. But it was my religious background that led me to choose an option in favor of change, in favor of the poor."

### Fights for Freedom

Ortega started to study law at the Universidad Centro-Americana but left to join the underground anti-Somoza guerilla army, the Frente Sandinista de Liberacpiion Nacional (FSLN) in 1963. The goals of the FSLN were to overthrow the Somoza regime, to reduce or end the economic colonization of Nicaragua by the United States, and to create a government of the people—peasants and laborers—dedicated to eradicating poverty and exploitation of the Nicaraguan people. Ortega was put in charge of the FSLN

student movement. Inspired by the writings of the Cuban revolutionary, **Che Guevara,** Ortega participated in the FSLN's first urban strikes, such as taking over a Managuan radio station, robbing the Bank of America, and fomenting the first legal labor strike in many years. Ortega's involvement in the FSLN made him a government target. In 1963, he was arrested and severely beaten for his revolutionary connections. These arrests and beatings became a repeated occurrence in Ortega's life. Despite these hardships, Ortega continued his fight for freedom from Somoza.

### Imprisoned by Somozan Government

Ortega began to lead more and more urban assaults. In January of 1967, he led a robbery on the San Sebastian bank to acquire funds for FSLN actions. Two days later, in a rally of 60,000 people supporting a non-Somoza candidate in supposedly "free" election, over 100 people were massacred in a national guard assault. A few months later, Tachito Somoza III was sworn into office, and the FSLN became more determined than ever to oust the Somozas. After the FSLN's first political assassination in late 1967, Ortega and other FSLN militants were arrested and imprisoned. Ortega was brutally tortured and nearly starved to death for seven years. He was kept in a cell with 150 prisoners and one toilet, repeatedly beaten, and often placed in isolation. Ortega developed the ability to lead quietly and to endure. He led hunger strikes and other actions from prison. The revolution continued outside the prison walls, and though the FSLN's supporters— such as national church organizations—won release for many FSLN prisoners, Ortega remained. Eventually, in 1974, Archbishop Obando y Bravo won the release of 14 prisoners, including Ortega. Bravo flew with the prisoners to Cuba as per the agreement with Somoza.

Ortega stayed in Cuba for many months, recovering from his years of imprisonment and receiving military training from **Fidel Castro**'s best guerilla warriors. A few months later, he secretly returned to Nicaragua and rejoined the FSLN. It was in Cuba that Ortega met Rosario Murillo, who later became his partner in the FSLN and his wife. Back in Nicaragua, the people were living under martial law, Somoza's army was burning mountain towns and herding peasants into resettlement camps. Also, the FSLN had become embroiled in internal conflict during Ortega's imprisonment. Two factions or tendencies within the FSLN leaned toward a Marxist doctrine, a proletariat organization. Ortega and his brothers concentrated more on rural guerilla warfare and less on ideology. Although the United States pressured Somoza to end his martial law policy because of flagrant human rights violations, Somoza won renewed U.S. aid after a military campaign led by Ortega failed to provoke country-wide insurrection.

The FSLN cause won a huge boost when journalist Pedro Joaquin Chamorro was assassinated in 1978. Chamorro had exposed an annual $12 million exploitation of the Nicaraguan people through a plasma donor business. Alhough the donors received some money for their blood, the plasma sold for ten times more those sums, with the extra money filling government coffers. After Chamorro was gunned down in the street for exposing the scam in *La Prensa,* 100,000 Nicaraguans joined in a funeral march in the streets of Managua. The "blood merchant" incident did more than inflame the passions of the Nicaraguan people, it brought international attention to the Somoza regime, condemned for being a brutal dictatorship around the world.

The Chamorro assassination finally sparked country-wide revolt. First, the Monimbo Indians fought back when the National Guard tear-gassed them for holding a mass for Chamorro. This started a series of events: government walkouts, business opposition to Somoza's government, and student strikes. Still, the United States did not come to the FSLN's aid, and instead praised Somoza for his improved human rights situation. Meanwhile, Ortega unified the various factions of the FSLN and launched a major offensive against Somoza in June of 1979. This final offensive signalled the end for the Somoza regime. The Organization of American States (OAS) rejected a U.S. proposal to intervene and restore order in Nicaragua. In fact, the OAS stopped all arms shipments to Somoza's forces and called for Somoza to step down in favor of a transitional government *(junta)* until free elections could be held. Somoza worked to destroy as much of Nicaragua as he could before the *junta* took over. He bombed industrial areas, hospitals, schools, and residential areas; he slaughtered millions of cattle; he crippled the government in debt and bad credit; and he skipped the country after looting government coffers.

### Deposes Somoza

In July of 1979, the *junta* took control of Nicaragua after Somoza fled. The people inherited a war-torn, ravaged, half-obliterated country with no money and bad debts. In September, Ortega went abroad to seek economic assistance for Nicaragua. The United States contributed $75 million out of the $580 million that Ortega raised from the countries of the world.

Ortega and the *junta* government tried to implement reforms. They instituted economic reforms to wean themselves off money borrowed from other nations. In an effort to show support for human rights reforms, the *junta* abolished the death penalty levied against the formerly U.S.-financed Somozan guardsmen. Now called contras—or contra rebels, short for counter-revolutionaries—the rebels propelled the country into a devastating civil war. Funded by President Ronald Reagan and the United States, the contras carried on the work of Somoza, obliterating the facilities like hospitals and schools. Meanwhile, Somoza was assassinated in Paraguay where he had fled after a brief stay in Florida.

Ortega worked feverishly to ameliorate the situation in Nicaragua. He and his wife worked for reforms together, creating a literacy program in addition to health care, labor, and social security programs. In 1982, Ortega appeared before the United Nations and appealed for an end to the U.S. backing of the contra rebels. In that speech Ortega said: "We have not come here to level accusations but to demand an end, once and for all, to the policy of aggression, threats, interventions, covert operations, and invasions of our homeland and the region and to make it clear that the unfairly distributed resources of humanity on this planet do not give the right to act against weak and small peoples." The United States answered Ortega by invading Grenada, sending Nicaragua an ominous message.

### Wins Presidential Election

In 1984, Ortega tried to placate the United States by endorsing a peace plan issued in the Kissinger Commission Report, but Reagan rejected Ortega's overtures. One month later, Ortega announced at the United Nations that his sources had informed him the United States was planning an invasion of Nicaragua to disrupt the upcoming elections there. The elections proceeded as planned without U.S. interference and Ortega won the presidency with two-thirds of the vote. He took office in January of 1985. Despite a CIA propaganda war against the new government in Nicaragua, a new National Assembly was elected and a new Constitution drafted. Still, the United States persisted in trying to destroy the new, democratic Nicaragua. In May of 1985, in violation of international law, the United States declared an economic embargo against Nicaragua. (In 1986, Reagan barely railroaded through Congress a $100 million aid package to the contra rebels.) By 1987, 50,000 U.S. troops were stationed in Honduras in so-called annual troop "exercises". In 1986, a U.S. pilot was caught delivering guns to the contras in violation of the 1982 Boland Agreement. The ensuing scandal became known as "Iran-Contragate."

Still, people continued to die in the struggle between contras and Sandinistas. By 1990, Ortega reported that 60,000 people had been killed thus far in the civil war despite a U.S. count of half that number. And Ortega continued to battle the U.S. embargo that threatened to destroy Nicaragua. By 1988, Ortega had made peace, declared a cease-fire, and offered amnesty to returning contras. Though diminished, the contra attacks continued killing, murdering an American nun in 1990. The U.S. opposition to Ortega's government continued as well. President Bush called Ortega "an unwanted animal at a garden party." Ortega entered into a reelection campaign hopeful but lost to Violeta Chamorro, the widow of the martyred journalist. Ortega lost to Chamorro by 13 percentage points. Two days later, 200,000 Nicaraguans filled the streets of Managua to pay tribute to Ortega; the United States changed its attitude toward Nicaragua as well. President Bush signed a $300 million aid package for the country shortly after the elections.

After the election, Ortega continued to lead the Sandinistas. In 1990, he helped negotiate an agreement between the Chamorro administration and striking workers. Ortega again sided against Chamorro in her bid to remove Ortega's brother from his post as commander of the Nicaraguan military in 1993. Ortega criticized Chamorro by declaring publicly that "you are not the owner of Nicaragua."

Still, the work in Nicaragua was not done. Ortega appeared in Washington, D.C., in 1994 to beg aid for his country as a representative of the World Bank's Consultative Group. Ortega warned that countries should "pay up or else Nicaragua will return to civil war, a civil war that will destabilize Central America once again," according to David Hirschmann's assessment of Ortega's message in the *National Review*. Hirschmann also quoted Antonio Lacayo, President Chamorro's son-in-law and the head of the Nicaraguan delegation to put Nicaragua's government transition into perspective: "The Sandinistas [under Ortega] were a closed, repressive regime. We now have [Chamorro] a closed, benevolent regime."

In May of 1994, Ortega won reelection as the leader of the FSLN, which had splintered into factions again; but Ortega still regained his seat on the party's governing body, the National Directorate, as secretary general. Despite opposition to his ideals, Ortega has won a place in the hearts of the Nicaraguan people as one of the heroes of the revolution that ousted the fascist dictatorship of Somoza and instituted democracy.

## SOURCES:

### Books

Beverly, John, and Marc Zimmerman, *Literature and Politics in the Central American Revolutions,* Austin, University of Texas Press, 1990.
*Biographical Dictionary of Latin American and Caribbean Political Leaders,* edited by Robert J. Alexander, Westport, Connecticut, Greenwood Press, 1988.
Kinzer, Stephen, *Blood Brothers: Life and War in Nicaragua,* New York, Putnam, 1991.
Miranda, Roger, and William Ratliff, *The Civil War in Nicaragua: Inside the Sandinistas,* New Brunswick, Transaction Publishers, 1993.
Ortega, James D., *Daniel Ortega,* New York, Chelsea House, 1991.
*Political Parties of the Americas,* edited by Charles D. Ameringer, Westport, Connecticut, Greenwood Press, 1992.

### Periodicals

*Current Biography Yearbook,* edited by Charles Moritz, New York, H. W. Wilson, 1984.
*Facts on File,* September 16, 1993; June 9, 1994, p. 419.
*National Review,* April 27, 1992, pp. 24–26.

*—Sketch by Christopher B. Tower*

# Katherine D. Ortega
## 1934-
### Hispanic American banker

Katherine Davalos Ortega came to national prominence in the fall of 1983 when President Ronald Reagan nominated her for the position of Treasurer of the United States. Her nomination was confirmed by the Senate and she served as Treasurer for six years. Her role as U.S. Treasurer was preceded by a series of no less admirable achievements, including being the first woman bank president in California and guiding an Alamogordo, New Mexico, financial institution to a point where it could claim $20 million in assets. In her acceptance speech following her appointment as Treasurer, Ortega is quoted in the *New York Times* as referring to her Hispanic background as a source of pride and inspiration. "I am the product of a heritage," Ortega commented, "that teaches strong family devotion, a commitment to earning a livelihood by hard work, patience, determination and perseverance."

Ortega was the ninth child of Donaciano Ortega, a blacksmith and cafe owner, and Catarina Davalos Ortega of Tularosa, New Mexico, where she was born on July 16, 1934. Her paternal grandparents had brought their family to New Mexico from Texas in the late 1880s. Ortega grew up in Tularosa, a tiny village of less than three thousand inhabitants, nestled in the shadow of the Sacramento Mountains not far from the Alamogordo atomic bomb testing site. It was here

*Katherine D. Ortega*

that Ortega learned Spanish—her first language—and, then, English. During her early years, she excelled at mathematics and was so skilled with numbers that she was allowed, even as a ten-year-old youngster, to use the cash register at her family's restaurant business. As she got older she found special pleasure and a high measure of success in her mathematics and accounting classes at school. In her last year of high school, she worked at the Otero County State Bank in Alamogordo.

### Experienced Job-Related Discrimination

After graduation from high school, Ortega took a two-and-a-half year break in her education and obtained a position at a bank where she worked in order to earn money for college. She eventually entered Eastern New Mexico State University at Portales where she majored in business and economics and graduated with honors in 1957. Ortega explained what happened after her college graduation in an interview with Marian Christy of the *Boston Globe:* "When I graduated from college, I planned to teach typing and shorthand at the high-school level. I was told by the chairman of the business school that I need not apply in the eastern part of New Mexico, where such a job was open, because of my Hispanic background. My immediate reaction was: 'That's it. I won't teach.'"

Disgusted with the discrimination that would keep her from following her chosen career path,

Ortega quickly decided to create her own career opportunity. She and one of her sisters, who was a certified public accountant, started an accounting firm in Alamogordo. During the 1960s and 1970s she held several different positions in accounting in New Mexico and later in California, where she moved in 1967. From 1969 to 1972, she was a tax supervisor at the firm of Peat, Marwick, Mitchell & Co. in Los Angeles, and from 1972 to 1975, she served as vice-president and cashier at the Pan American National Bank, also in that city. In 1975, she became the first woman president of a California bank when she accepted the position of director and president of the Santa Ana State Bank.

In 1979, Ortega moved back to New Mexico to help run the family accounting business, which eventually became the Otero Savings & Loan Association. She served as consultant to the firm from 1979 to 1982. Ortega also became a California certified public accountant in 1979. About this same time, Ortega intensified her involvement in politics, although according to a *New York Times* contributor, she once declared, "I have often said that I was born a Republican." At first, her political work was on the local and state level, with the party calling on her to play a liaison role with Hispanic and women's organizations. She was also active in the campaigns of Pete V. Domenici, a Republican senator from New Mexico; he later returned the favor when, as chairman of the Senate Budget Committee, he suggested Ortega to then-President Reagan when he needed someone to fill the treasury position.

### Nominated Treasurer of United States

Ortega received her first taste of national recognition from the Republicans in April of 1982 when Reagan selected her to be part of a ten-member Presidential Advisory Committee on Small and Minority Business Ownership. Eight months later, Reagan appointed her a commissioner on the Copyright Royalty Tribunal. This five-member panel is the federal agency that determines what royalty fees cable companies throughout the nation pay for use of copyrighted material. The tribunal, which was created in 1978, also establishes royalties paid by jukebox operators to the musicians whose music they provide. In September of 1983, Ortega learned that she would be nominated to be U.S. Treasurer and she received Senate confirmation several weeks later.

Ortega was officially nominated as Treasurer of the United States on September 12, 1983, in a ceremony marking the beginning of Hispanic Week celebrations in the nation's capital. According to the *New York Times,* in President Reagan's nominating remarks he claimed that Ortega was "symbolic of the values the Hispanic community represents" and added that "nothing is a better influence on America than the strength and decency of the Hispanic family." On October 3, 1983, Reagan again praised his appointee as she was sworn in to her post by Treasury Secretary Donald T. Regan in the Rose Garden of the White House. In *New York Times* coverage of the event the President is reported as saying, "It's important that key positions within an Administration be filled by people who reflect the goals and ideals for which the people voted. . . . And this is certainly true today." During the ceremony Ortega signed special forms that were used to add her signature to plates from which U.S. currency would be printed during her tenure, an estimated 5.5 billion bills in the first year.

The position of U.S. Treasurer has in recent years nearly always gone to a politically prominent woman. Romana Acosta Bañuelos, appointed by President Nixon in 1974, was the first Hispanic woman to serve in this capacity; Ortega was the second. Although the post is deemed to be for the most part ceremonial, the U.S. Treasurer supervises the Bureau of Engraving and Printing, the United States Mint, and the United States Savings Bond Division. Some of Ortega's duties included maintaining an account of government spending, handling claims for lost, stolen or counterfeit Government checks, and burning unusable U.S. currency. When Ortega took office, she was responsible for handling the nation's $220 million budget and overseeing 5,000 employees. In 1985, Ortega was given the added responsibility of promoting the sale of U.S. Liberty Coins, three gold and silver commemorative coins designed to raise $40 million to help pay for the restoration of the Statue of Liberty.

In 1984, Ortega flew more than 60,000 miles to speak at Hispanic and Republican events. Her most important speaking engagement came in August of that year when she flew to Dallas, Texas, to deliver the keynote address at the Republican National Convention. That this important convention role was given to a comparatively new member of the Reagan Administration surprised a lot of long-time convention observers who had expected to see Elizabeth Dole, a member of the Reagan Cabinet, or Nancy Kassebaum, a senator from Kansas, fill the bill. Ortega was undaunted by the assignment and gave a stirring speech later reprinted in *Vital Speeches of the Day*. In the address, she referred to her Hispanic heritage several times and—to the joy of Spanish-speaking delegates—even included several Spanish phrases in the text. "To those millions of Democrats abandoned by their national leadership . . . ," she declared, "we Republicans here in Dallas say: we welcome you to our home. Nuestra casa es su casa. Our home is your home."

Ortega's high-profile image at the convention served to remind those feminist groups who had complained about a lack of female appointments during Reagan's administration that he had indeed filled many positions with qualified women. Ortega mentioned in a *New York Times* article that one of her goals was "to get the message out. . . . There is a perception that Ronald Reagan has not named women to his Administration. When I'm out there, I talk about all the subcabinet appointments. I want to set the record straight." Ortega credited her father for inspiring her quest for success in the male-dominated worlds of banking and politics. She noted in the *New York Times:* "My father taught me we were as good as anybody else, that we could accomplish anything we wanted. . . . He encouraged all three of his daughters to make a living for themselves so we would never have to be dependent on anybody."

Ortega served as Treasurer of the United States until 1989. Since that time she has been for the most part self-employed. After completing her work at the Treasury, she has served as an alternative representative to the United Nations and is on the board of directors of several major corporations, including the Ralston Purina Company, the food and animal feed firm, and the Kroger Company, the grocery chain, both of which appointed Ortega to their boards in 1992. She is also on the advisory boards of Leadership America and the National Park Service and a member of Executive Women in Government and the American Association of Women Accountants. On February 17, 1989, she was married to Lloyd J. Derrickson. Her leisure activities include travel, reading and golf.

Ortega's distinguished career has brought her many awards and honors. In 1977, Eastern New Mexico University presented her with its Outstanding Alumni of the Year Award. She has also received several honorary degrees, including honorary doctor of law degrees from her alma mater, Eastern New Mexico University, in 1984, and from Kean College of New Jersey, in 1985, and an honorary doctor of social science from Villanova University in Pennsylvania in 1988. Other awards Ortega has received include the California Businesswoman's Achievement Award and the Outstanding Woman of the Year Award from the Damas de Comercio.

Ortega is quite willing to serve as an example to other Hispanics who find themselves facing the obstacle of racial bigotry. "I think of myself as a role model for my people . . . ," she told a *Boston Globe* contributor. "I hope they see me and say: 'Hey, there's hope. We can accomplish.' I think people can look at me and see what I've accomplished and pursue careers for themselves. Everyone encounters obstacles. I tell people if one road is closed, take another. I'm a stubborn person."

**SOURCES:**

*Atlanta Constitution*, May 13, 1986, p. B1.

*Boston Globe,* November 24, 1985, p. B25.

*Ms.,* August, 1984, p. 22.

*New York Times,* September 13, 1983, p. B14; October 4, 1983, p. A19

*Vital Speeches of the Day,* September 15, 1984, pp. 712–13.

—*Sketch by Marian C. Gonsior*

# José Ortega y Gasset
## 1883-1955
### Spanish philosopher

José Ortega y Gasset was one of Spain's premier philosophers; Albert Camus in a statement cited by Ignacio L. Götz in *José Ortega y Gasset: Proceedings of the Espectador Universal International Interdisciplinary Conference,* declared that the Spaniard was "perhaps the greatest European writer after Nietzche." Ortega y Gasset was a gifted academic and orator who played a central role in Spanish culture. A critic in the *London Times* averred: "His teaching as a whole must be acknowledged to possess a value to our time which is both aposite and rare." Ortega y Gasset authored major philosophical works, often dealing with contemporary issues, such as *La rebelión de las masas* (*The Revolt of the Masses,* 1930). A master of the Spanish language, he was also a celebrated journalist, whose influential articles contributed to the rebirth of the Spanish Republic in 1931.

Ortega y Gasset was born in Madrid on May 9, 1883, to José Ortega y Munilla and María Dolores Gasset Chinchilla. His family was afflluent. His father, a liberal journalist, was the editor of *La Iberia, La Patria, El Debate, El Parliamento, El Conservador,* and El Imparcial's literary supplement *Los lunes del Imparcial.* Ortega y Munilla was also involved in politics, notably as the deputy in the *Cortes* (Spanish parliament) for Padrón (Galicia).

Ortega y Gasset learned to read and write alongside his older brother Eduardo, under the tutelage of Manuel Martínez in 1887. At the age of seven he demonstrated a precocious level of intelligence when he memorized the first chapter of Cervantes' *Don Quijote* in three hours. Between 1891 and 1897 Ortega y Gasset attended the Jesuit Colegio de Miraflores del Palo, near Málaga; records reveal that he was an outstanding student. He continued his education at the Internado de Deusto in Bilbao until enrolling at the University of Madrid in 1898. Ortega y Gasset earned his *licenciatura en filosofía y letras* (M.A.) in 1902, and his doctorate in philosophy and letters in 1904.

Upon graduating, Ortega y Gasset was uncertain about his future career. His first article was published in *El Imparcial* on March 14, 1904. However, he declined to follow the familial tradition in journalism and proceeded with postgraduate studies in philosophy in Germany. Between April and November 1905, he studied at Leipzig and then transferred to Berlin, in order to attend the lectures of the philosopher Georg Simmel. He published *Descartes y el método transcendental* upon his return from Berlin to justify the financial award he had been accorded from the Spanish government. From late 1906 to 1907, he studied under neo-Kantians Hermann Cohen and Paul Natorp at Marburg. His education in Germany influenced him profoundly. In his study *The Historical Thought of Ortega y Gasset,* Christian Ceplecha cited the philosopher's declaration concerning Marburg. "In this city I passed from the twilight of my youth; to it I owe at least half my hopes and almost all my discipline." Throughout his postgraduate period he contributed to *El Imparcial* and *Faro,* a weekly publication for young adults.

### Teaching and Writing

After returning from Germany, Ortega y Gasset entered the teaching profession. He cofounded the Escuela Superior del Magisterio in June 1908, where he served as professor of psychology, logic, and ethics. He actively supported the Socialists, addressing their meetings until his opinions began to diverge from theirs around 1910. Ortega y Gasset married Rosa Spottorno y Topete on April 7, 1910. They had three children: Miguel Germán, José, and Soledad. On November 25, 1910, Ortega y Gasset was awarded the Chair of Metaphysics of the Faculty of Philosophy and Letters at his alma mater. He assumed the post in 1912, after a final period of study in Marburg.

The following year Ortega y Gasset cofounded the *Liga de educación política* (League for Political Education). He believed that Spain was floundering due to a lack of science and sought to remedy this through the establishment of an elite intellectual leadership. However, the League proved ineffetual and was disbanded in 1915. In 1914, Ortega y Gasset's first book, *Meditaciones del Quijote* (*Meditations on Don Quixote*), was published. Inspired by the works of the Spanish philosopher, **Miguel de Unamuno y Jugo,** it laid the foundations of his philosophy. Ortega y Gasset maintained his parallel career in journalism, publishing in *El Imparcial* and the magazine *Europa.* In 1915 he founded the influential review *España,* but left when it started favoring the political left. After his departure from *España,* Ortega y Gasset founded and became the sole contributor to

*El Espectador,* which remained in circulation until 1934.

In 1917 Ortega y Gasset published an article entitled "Bajo el arco en ruina" ("Beneath the Ruined Arch") in *El Imparcial,* criticizing the military junta and the monarchy. He was dismissed and consequently co-founded *El Sol*—one of the most influential newspapers in Spainsh history—with Nicolás María Urgoiti. Many of his articles from *El Sol* were later collected and published as *La redención de las provincias* (*The Redemption of the Provinces,* 1931).

During the 1920s, under the Primo de Rivera dictatorship, Ortega y Gasset was politically less vocal. He concentrated on his writing, producing major works such as *La dehumanización del arte e ideas de la novela* (*The Dehumanization of Art: Ideas on the Novel,* 1925). In 1923 he founded *Revista de Occidente,* one of Europe's leading intellectual journals before the Spanish Civil War. In addition to publishing top Spanish writers—such as Espina, Jarnés, Marañón, and Marichalar—Ortega y Gasset sought to bring the work of renowned European thinkers, like Hegel, Simmel, and Freud to his readers. The journal spawned the Revista publishing house. Ortega y Gasset also helped establish the influential Espasa-Calpe publishing house.

In 1929 Ortega y Gasset briefly resigned his Chair at the University of Madrid in opposition to Primo de Rivera's government. He continued to deliver his lectures at a rented hall, the Sala Rex; his lectures proved so popular he moved to a larger site—the Teatro Infanta Beatrix.

### Political Engagement

With the demise of the Primo de Rivera dictatorship, Ortega y Gasset became increasingly active in politics. He vigorously supported the Spanish Republic; through his powerful journalism he was an instrumental factor in the downfall of King Alfonso XIII. On February 10, 1931, Ortega y Gasset, Marañón, and Pérez de Ayala produced a manifesto in *El Sol* calling for intellectuals to defend the Republic. They cofounded *La Agrupación al servicio de la república* (Group at the Service of the Republic), which, among other things, advocated the separation of the church and the state. In the general election of April 10, the Republicans won an ovewhelming majority. Four days later, the king left Spain. Ortega y Gasset left *El Sol* and created *Cristol* and *Luz.* At this time he entered the *Cortes,* representing the province of León and Jaén. However, he soon began to disagree with the Republicans and resigned from his seat. Disenchanted with the new Republic, he left politics in the fall of 1932.

He fled Spain in September in 1936 after the July outbreak of the Civil War, aided by his brother Eduardo, a socialist representative of the Madrid City Council. Gravely ill with gallstones, he underwent surgery in Paris, and went to Holland to convalesce. In public he commented little on the Civil War. His views became anti-Republican; during the war his sympathies rested with the Nationalists. When the war concluded on April 1, 1939, Ortega y Gasset was content with the Nationalist victory.

With the onset of World War II, Ortega y Gasset—still unwell—moved first to Portugal and then to Argentina. In early 1941, he accepted the position of professor of psychology at Peru's University of San Marcos. The next year he returned to Portugal to lecture at the University of Lisbon. He returned to Madrid in 1945, but was forbidden from resuming his Chair at the University. Increasingly dispirited with the regime of Francisco Honco, he eschewed politics and devoted himself to philosophy and history. He cofounded the Instituto de Humanidades with Julián Marías in 1948, although a lack of government support doomed the project to failure two years later.

His last few years saw his international reputation grow. In 1949 Ortega y Gasset was invited to a celebration of the bicentenary of Goethe's birth in Aspen, Colorado. He gained international recognition for his contributions as a writer and a philosopher when he was named to the Bavarian Academy of Fine Arts in 1949. Two years later he gave lectures in Munich and was conferred honorary doctorates from the universities of Glasgow and Marburg. He traveled in 1954 to the United Kingdom and addressed the British Institute of Management in Torquay. He remained an active traveler, journeying despite illness through Italy, Germany, and Switzerland in 1955. Ortega y Gasset died on October 18, 1955 in Madrid, from stomach cancer.

### SELECTED PUBLISHED WORKS:

*Meditaciones del Quijote,* Madrid, Residencia de Estudiantes, 1914.

*El Espectador,* Volumes 1 and 2, Madrid, Renacimiento, 1916, 1917, Volume 3, Madrid, Calpe, 1921, Volumes 4–8, Madrid, Revista de Occidente, 1925–34.

*Personas, obras, cosas,* Madrid, Renacimiento, 1916; published as *Mocedades,* Madrid, Revista de Occidente, 1973.

*España invertebrada,* Madrid, Calpe, c. 1921.

*El tema de nuestro tiempo,* Madrid, Calpe, 1923; translation published as *The Modern Theme,* New York, Harper, 1931.

*La deshumanización del arte e ideas de la novela,* Madrid, Revista de Occidente, 1925; translation published as *The Dehumanization of Art: Ideas on the Novel,* Princeton University Press, 1948.

*La rebelión de la masas,* Madrid, Revista de Occidente, 1930; translation published as *The Revolt of the Masses,* 1932.

*La misión de la universidad,* Madrid, Revista de Occidente, 1930; translation published as *Mission of the University,* Norton, 1946.

*La redención de las provincias y de la decencia nacional,* Madrid, Revista de Occidente, 1931.

*Rectificatión de República,* Madrid, Revista de Occidente, 1931.

*Obras,* Madrid, Espasa-Calpe, 1932.

*Pidiendo un Goethe desde dentro,* Madrid, Revista de Occidente, 1932.

*Notas,* Madrid, Espasa-Calpe, 1938.

*Ensimismamiento y alteración* [and] *Meditación de la técnia,* Espasa-Calpe Argentina, 1939.

*Ideas y creencias,* Espasa-Calpe Argentina, 1940.

*El libro de las misiones,* Espasa-Calpe Argentina, 1940.

*Historia como sistema* [and] *Concordia y libertad,* Madrid, Revista de Occidente, 1941.

*Castilla y sus castillos,* Madrid, Afrodisio Aguado, 1942.

*Teoría de Andalucía,* Madrid, Revista de Occidente, 1942.

*Man and Crisis,* Madrid, Revista de Occidente, 1942.

*Two Prologues,* Madrid, Revista de Occidente, 1944.

*Obras completas,* Madrid, Revista de Occidente, Volumes 1 and 2, 1946, Volumes 3–6, 1947, Volume 7, 1961, Volumes 8 and 9, 1962, Volumes 10 and 11, 1969; Volume 12, 1983.

*Sobre la aventura ya caza,* Madrid, Afrodisio Aguado, 1949.

*Papeles sobre Velázquez y Goya,* Madrid, Revista de Occidente, 1950.

*Estudios sobre el amor,* Madrid, Aguilar, 1950.

*El hombre y la gente,* Madrid, Revista de Occidente, 1957; translation published as *Man and People,* Norton, 1963.

*Meditación de un pueblo joven,* Madrid, Revista de Occidente, 1958.

*La idea de principio en Leibniz y la evolución de la teoría deductiva,* Madrid, Revista de Occidente, 1958; translation published as *The Idea of Principle in Leibniz and the Evolution of Deductive Theory,* Norton, 1971.

*Prólogo para alemanes,* Madrid, Taurus, 1958.

*Idea del teatro,* Madrid, Revista de Occidente, 1958.

*Kant, Hegel, Dilthey,* Madrid, Revista de Occidente, 1958.

*¿Qué es filosofia?,* Madrid, Revista de Occidente, 1958.

*Apuntes sobre el pensamiento: su teurgia y su demiurgia,* Madrid, Revista de Occidente, 1959.

*Una interpretacióne la historia universal,* Madrid, Revista de Occidente, 1960.

*Meditación de Europa,* Madrid, Revista de Occidente, 1960.

*Vives-Goethe,* Madrid, Revista de Occidente, 1961.

*Pasado y porvenir para el hombre actual,* Madrid, Revista de Occidente, 1962.

*Misión del bibliotecario (y otros escritos afines),* Madrid, Revista de Occidente, 1962.

*Unas lecciónes de metafisica,* Alianza, 1966.

*Origen la filosofia,* Madrid, Revista de Occidente, 1967.

*Sobre la razón histórica,* Madrid, Revista de Occidente, 1979; translation published as *Historical Reason,* Norton, 1984.

*Investigaciónes psicológicas,* Revista de Occidente en Aianza, 1982; translation published as *Psychological Investigations,* Norton, 1987.

*¿Qué es conocimiento?,* Revista de Occidente en Alianza, 1984.


## SOURCES:

### Books

Ceplecha, Christian, *The Historical Thought of José Ortega y Gasset,* Washington, D.C., Catholic University of America Press, 1958.

Dobson, Andrew, *An Introduction to the Politics and Philosophy of José Ortega y Gasset,* Cambridge University Press, 1989.

*Hispanic Writers,* edited by Bryan Ryan, Detroit, Gale Research, 1991.

*José Ortega y Gasset: Proceedings of the Espectador Universal International Interdisciplinary Conference,* edited by Nora de Marval-McNair, Westport, Connecticut, Greenwood Press, 1987.

### Periodicals

*Times* (London), October 19, 1955, p. 11.

—*Sketch by Amanda Beresford*

# José Emilio Pacheco
## 1939-
### Mexican poet

José Emilio Pacheco is a leading Mexican poet. In addition to his impressive poetic output, he has produced a novel, short stories, criticism, and essays. His third collection of poetry, *No me preguntes cómo pasa el tiempo (poemas, 1964–1968),* published in 1969, won the National Poetry Prize. He has been a member of the prestigious Colegio Nacional since 1985.

### Early Life

José Emilio Pacheco was born in Mexico City on June 30, 1939, when, as he recalled for *Spanish-American Authors,* "**Lazaro Cardenas** was president, when the first Republican exiles from Spain were coming into the country, and only two months before the start of World War II." Pacheco's father had participated in the Mexican Revolution of 1910, but broke from the postrevolutionary regimes due to political differences.

In *Spanish American Authors,* Pacheco credited his grandparents—Emilia Abreu and Emilio Berny—with instilling in him the love of letters that led to his literary vocation. His grandmother recounted the legends and history of his country to him and his grandfather taught him to read.

Pacheco was born at a time when poetry flourished in Mexico. The stability of the last three decades of the nineteenth century and the years of the dictatorship of Porfirio Díaz, had allowed for the establishment of literary societies which were fertile ground for the exchange of ideas and provided the foundation for the rich and varied literary output of the early twentieth century. Pacheco himself studied at the Preparatoria of José Enrique Moreno de Tagle. Moreno de Tagle was also the mentor of such distinguished writers as **Carlos Fuentes** and Jaime Garcia Terrés. "To [Moreno de Tagle]," Pacheco declared in *Spanish-American Authority,* "I owe the discovery of **Octavio Paz, Jorge Luis Borges,** Martín Luis Guzmán, and many others, as well as the idea that the first duty of a writer is to express himself in the best prose and the best verse possible."

*José Emilio Pacheco*

Pacheco enrolled in the Universidad Nacional Autónoma de México in 1957 and remained there until 1964. He departed without a formal degree, but he had gained a sound grasp of Mexican and Spanish literature. During his university years, Pacheco worked for a number of literary reviews, serving as coordinator for the publication of the work of young writers for the magazine *Estaciones;* as a collaborator on *México en la Cultura,* a literary review notable for its cultural plurality; and as editorial secretary of *Revista de la Universidad de México,* known for its promotion of innovative ideas. He was chief editor of the magazine *Siempre* from 1962 until 1971. Pacheco scrupulously avoided abusing his editorial positions to advance his own work, appearing instead in publications such as *Revista Mexicana de Literatura, Cuadernos del Viento,* and *Pajaro Cascabel.*

### Diversified Career

Pacheco is best known, particularly in the United States, as a poet. Since the 1963 publication of his first book of poetry, *Los elementos de la noche,* he has continued to publish poetry collections every three or four years. His poems have also been included in a number of anthologies. In addition, Pacheco has followed the Mexican tradition of working in multiple media. He has written an important novel, *Morirás lejos,* which deals with the Nazi Holocaust, and a short novel, *Las batallas en el desierto,* an elegiac work inspired by his childhood home, which was destroyed in the earthquake of 1985. Pacheco has also produced numerous short stories. He received the National Journalism Prize in 1980 for his newspaper column "Inventario." His work as a translator includes *How It Is* by Samuel Beckett; *Epistola: In Carcere et Vinculis* by Oscar Wilde; *A Streetcar Named Desire* by Tennessee Williams; and *Old Times* by Harold Pinter. He has also written screenplays and edited several anthologies.

Pacheco has taught in universities in Canada, England, and the United States; in recent years, he has spent the fall semester at the University of Maryland. A recipient of grants from the Centro Mexicano de Escritores and the Guggenheim Foundation, Pacheco has been awarded with honorary doctorates from the Universities of Sinaloa and Chihuahua. In addition to the National Poetry Prize, he has received the Magda Donato and Xavier Villaurrutia prizes. He is based in Mexico City and is married to Cristina Pacheco; the couple have two daughters.

### The Poetry

Pacheco's generation of poets, according to critic Adriana Garcia, writing in *Mexican Literature: A History,* was molded by the urban center of Mexico City. Garcia noted that their sociopolitical poetry results from concerns about pollution, the stagnation of governmental bureaucracy, and the growing poverty of a swelling population. The attack by official forces on a student demonstration in 1968, remembered as the "Night of Tlatelolco" and followed by a period of political repression, resulted in a tone of pessimism in much of the writing of the time. Significantly, they represent the first generation to grow up in the "age of the atom."

Pacheco's poetry, almost universally well-received, has been the subject of much critical examination. He is generally regarded as a highly literate, even "bookish" poet. Merlin H. Forster, in his essay "Four Contemporary Mexican Poets," found that Pacheco's poetry "tends toward brevity and an economy of language . . . introspective and metaphysical." A reviewer in the *Times Literary Supplement* described it as "the poetry of sparseness, of a painful facing of the tragic in human existence." Although "pessimism" is a word that frequently appeals in discussions of Pacheco's work, a number of critics have also seen threads of celebration. Octavio Paz, whose own work has been an important influence on Pacheco, has noted in Pacheco's writing an "affirmation of life and poetry through nature."

In *Hispania,* Michael J. Doudoroff outlined some major elements of Pacheco's poetry as "the corrosive nature of time, the primary symbols of sea, sand, dust, and sun, an almost unremitting melancholy, elegiac tone interrupted by an occasional touch of humor." Pacheco's themes include the "radical solitude of the individual, [and] the disappearance of people and experience into a nebulous past." Forster added that "Pacheco is troubled by the cyclic flow of time and the impossibility of recapturing prior experience . . . the poet probes deep beneath the surface, often in unconventional forms and with brilliant images, in order to reach the essential meanings of life and experience."

Doudoroff, like most critics, has viewed Pacheco's poetry as falling into two periods. The earlier, embodied in his first two collections, aligns him with the "symbolist-surrealist" tradition. The second, which begins with the collection *No me preguntes cómo pasa el tiempo* (*Don't Ask Me How the Time Passes*), published in 1969, marks a shift from the surrealist and an expansion of his subject matter. Each of Pacheco's later collections contains a section of poems whose subjects are animals. These "bestiaries," or fables, provide the poet with a playful means of commentary on mankind and provide a vehicle for the humor which also creeps into his later work. In the later collections, the poet also develops more fully some of the characteristic features of his work. One of the most interesting of these is embodied in what Pacheco has called "*aproximaciones,*" his word for translations of the works of others which, says Doudoroff, "range from extreme precision to a degree of freedom admitting substantial rewriting," A selection of these is generally included in the volumes of poetry. Pacheco, according to Doudoroff, regards this work as a valid literary form in its own right. Garcia explained that Pacheco "incorporat[es] these translations into his own creative world because he does not believe that anyone writes poetry but that poetry is made by everyone." This practice contributes to the highly "intertextual" nature of Pacheco's work, which Doudoroff finds to be "one of the central characteristics of this ultraliterate poet. . . . The words of other poets pass freely through and speak for him. This openness and generosity counterbalances the other tones of irony and dismay and helps produce Pacheco's unique quality."

For Pacheco, who eschews interviews, the reader is central to the poem. According to Doudoroff, Pacheco believes that "the act of reading is the vital completion of the literary creation." In "Una defensa de anonimato," ("A Defense of Anonymity") the poet, as Doudoroff pointed out, interviews himself on his own terms and at the same time mounts a powerful attack on biographical criticism. "How shall I explain to you . . . that my ambition is to be read," it says, "not 'famous,' / that it is the text that matters, not its author, / that I am leery of the literary circus." The piece can also be read as a defense of poetry itself, a theme which appears increasingly in Pacheco's later work: "every day / there is more and more interest in poets, / and less and less in poetry." And later: "I keep thinking / that poetry is something different: / a form of love that exists only in silence, / a secret pact between two people, / almost always two strangers." Doudoroff concluded that Pacheco's "poetry arises from and bears witness at the trial of mankind in the Age of the Atom ... the poem may be one of the few things left to the powerless."

## SELECTED PUBLISHED WORKS:

### Poetry

*Los elementos de la noche,* Mexico, UNAM, 1963.
*El reposo del fuego,* Mexico, Fondo de Cultura Economica, 1966.
*No me preguntes como pasa el tiempo,* Mexico, Joaquin Moritz, 1969.
*Iras y no volveras,* Mexico, Fondo de Cultura Economica, 1973.
*Islas a la deriva,* Mexico, Siglo XXI, 1976.
*Desde entonces,* Mexico, Era, 1980.
*Los trabajos del mar,* Madrid, Catedra, 1983.
*Miro la tierra,* Mexico, Era, 1986.

### Fiction

*El viento distante,* Mexico, Era, 1963.
*Moriras lejos,* Mexico, Joaquin Moritz, 1967.
*El principio del placer,* Mexico, Joaquin Moritz, 1972.
*Las batallas en el desierto,* Mexico, Era, 1987.

## SOURCES:

### Books

*Hispanic Literature Criticism,* Volume 2, edited by Jelena Krstovíc, Detroit, Gale Research, 1994.
*Mexican Literature: A History,* edited by David William Foster, Austin, University of Texas Press, 1994.
Peden, Margaret Sayers, *Out of the Volcano: Portraits of Contemporary Mexican Artists,* Washington, D.C., Smithsonian Institute Press, 1991.
*Spanish American Authors: The Twentieth Century,* edited by Angel Flores, New York, Wilson, 1992.
*Tradition and Renewal: Essays on Twentieth-Century Latin American Literature and Culture,* edited by Merlin H. Forster, Urbana, University of Illinois Press, 1975.

### Periodicals

*Hispania,* May 1989, pp. 264–276.
*Times Literary Supplement,* June 18, 1970, p. 654.

—*Sketch by Julie Henderson Jersyk*

# Heberto Padilla
## 1932-
### Cuban poet

Heberto Padilla—a poet, journalist, and publisher—is probably best known for the incident in post-revolutionary Cuba that bears his name. The Padilla Case, as it came to be known, witnessed Padilla's imprisonment in 1971 and his subsequent ostracization from Cuban cultural life. A prolific writer who has lived in exile in the United States since 1980, Padilla embodies the dashed artistic hopes of intellectuals living under the specter of socialism.

Padilla was born on January 20, 1932, in Puerta de Golpe in Cuba's western province of Pinar del Río. His father, Francisco Padilla, was a lawyer; his mother, Dolores Lorenzo, was a homemaker. Padilla attended the University of Havana from 1952 to 1956. That year marked his departure from the university and his marriage to Berta Hernández, with whom he had three children: Giselle, María, and Carlitos. In 1957, Padilla left Cuba to work in Miami as a radio commentator. One year later, he moved to New York City and taught foreign languages at the Berlitz school.

When **Fidel Castro**'s guerilla movement ousted dictator **Fulgencio Batista** in 1959, Padilla returned to his homeland hoping to help forge a new intellectual revolution to compliment the ideological revolution. According to Cuban scholar **Lourdes Casal** in "Cultural Policy and Writers in Cuba," this time was a "honeymoon period in which many writers who had been living abroad during the fifties returned to Cuba. There were many signs of effervescence and vitality." Padilla epitomized this newfound energy; after returning to Havana he began to work for the state-sponsored newspaper *Revolución*, specifically for the paper's literary supplement, *Lunes de Revolución*. Padilla also served as a foreign correspondent for the Cuban news agency Prensa Latina and the government newspaper, *Granma*, from 1959 until 1968. His duties took him to New York City, London, Moscow, and Prague.

*Heberto Padilla*

This first decade of communist rule was filled with uncertainty as Castro's government grappled for coherent domestic policies. These included official cultural policies. Although the government had been tolerant of artistic freedom in the past, the years 1967 and 1968 witnessed a shift toward restrictiveness. Padilla's writings and criticism placed him at the center of this shift.

Anti-intellectual rumblings within the Cuban government regarding artists' thematic and contextual representations of Cuban reality began as early as 1961. At that time, artists—specifically intellectuals contributing to *Lunes de Revolución* —were accused of undermining the ideology of the revolution through their critical observations. The debate climaxed when Castro addressed a meeting of bureaucrats and artists and defined Cuban cultural policy. His fundamental point was that artists were free to express their views as long as they did not disparage the revolution. Castro declared, in Carmelo Mesa-Lago's *Cuba in the 1970s,* "Inside the Revolution everything; against it nothing." However, in the newly formed communist society, being "against the revolution" took many forms, including implicating high government officials in wrongdoing, criticizing existing government policies, and fostering elitism.

The fervor with which the Cuban government sought to instill obedience in its artists challenged many intellectuals, including Padilla. His particular clash with government officials began in 1967 when

he published a criticism of cultural bureaucrat Lisandro Otero's *Pasión de Urbino.* Padilla not only rebuffed Otero, but praised one of Otero's greatest rivals, **Guillermo Cabrera Infante,** who served as co-editor of *Lunes de Revolución* with Padilla. The results of this public debate were twofold. First, Padilla's praise for Cabrera Infante was politically and socially fatal. Since Cabrera Infante was considered an enemy of the Cuban revolution and living in exile, Padilla was guilty by association. Second, the Cuban government began a vigilant campaign to maintain revolutionary commitment among community artists.

The control that the government exercised over artistic expression became all too clear to Padilla in 1968 after he was awarded the Julián del Casal Poetry Prize from the Cuban Union of Writers and Artists (UNEAC) for a controversial work entitled "Fuera del juego." Contradicting the international panel of judges, the UNEAC bureacrats did not agree with the decision. Their recalcitrance was most likely a reaction to government insistence on revolutionary obedience—something from which Padilla's work strayed. Ultimately, "Fuera del juego" was published and Padilla was awarded the prize. However, a governmental disclaimer was included at the beginning of the work, which, according to Maurice Zeitlin in *Revolutionary Politics and the Cuban Working Class,* "denoted [the poems] as counterrevolutionary."

### Government Suppresses Artistic Expression

After the controversy of "Fuera del Juego" and the increased thematic demands placed on artists by the Castro regime, Padilla accused "the Castro government of suppressing controversial literature while championing mediocre work that toed the party line." This observation by Edwin McDowell in *The New York Times Book Review* was borne out through new regulations, requirements, and categories of acceptable literature as authorized by the Cuban Union of Writers and Artists. For example, the panel of judges for annual awards was restricted to Cubans, thereby ensuring government control over the proceedings. After 1968, revolutionary works called Testimonies (a literary genre which demanded that the work describe Latin American society) became the favored literary form among the government and literary critics. Padilla continued to follow his own artistic inclinations, however, and refused to comply with the new constraints. Consequently, he lost his job with *Prensa Latina* and *Granma* and fell into relative obscurity when the government refused to publish his work. Official regulation of artistic output continued into the late 1960s and climaxed on March 20, 1971, when Padilla was imprisoned after publicly reading from his latest work "Provocaciones." The events that led to his arrest focused on the role of the artist in political society.

The "new offensive on the cultural front" as Casal described it, landed Padilla in solitary confinement in a Cuban jail for over a month. Although he was arrested, no charges were leveled against him. This injustice sparked an outcry from international literary figures. The loose consortium of writers—including Jean-Paul Sartre, **Gabriel Garcia Marquez, Carlos Fuentes, Octavio Paz,** and others—sent a letter to Castro lambasting his repressive measures aimed at artists and writers. Padilla was eventually released from jail, but not until he had written what John Spicer Nichols calls in *The Cuban Reader* "a long, abject confession of his errors against the Revolution." This confession was coupled with a similarly apologetic declaration to the Cuban Congress on Education and Culture. Again international authors wrote to Castro, deeming Padilla's confession invalid due to the methods used to obtain it—torture. Both the Cuban government and Padilla denied this allegation.

### Immigrates to the United States

From 1971 to 1980, Padilla worked as a translator, but only after he served several months of hard labor in an agricultural camp. Although he did not publish any new work in Cuba during this period, he did continue to write. In 1980, after author Bernard Malamud (then president of the PEN American Center) and U.S. Senator Edward Kennedy intervened on his behalf, Padilla was exiled to the United States. Upon his arrival, Padilla became a fellow at New York University's New York Institute of the Humanities. He retained this distinction until 1983. Padilla found artistic freedom in the United States and published three notable works: *Legacies: Selected Poems* (1982), *Heroes Are Grazing in My Garden* (1984), and *Self-Portrait of the Other* (1990). Along with his second wife, Belkis Cuza Malé—with whom he had a son, Ernesto—Padilla began publishing *Linden Lane,* his own literary magazine, and became a contributor to *El Nuevo Herald,* the Spanish-language newspaper published by the *Miami Herald.* He has remained active in cultural and intellectual affairs, serving as the Executive Director of the Center for Hemispheric Affairs Institute for Contemporary Studies (1986–87) and participating in the literary summit Writing in Our Hemisphere: South and North (1994).

### SELECTED PUBLISHED WORKS:

*El justo tiempo humano,* Havana, Cuban Union of Writers and Artists, 1962.

*Fuera del juego,* Havana, Cuban Union of Writers and Artists, 1969.

*Sent Off the Field: A Selection from the Poetry of Heberto Padilla,* translation and introduction by J. M. Cohen, Deutsch, 1972.

*Provocaciones,* Madrid, La Gota de Agua, 1973.

*Poesía y política: Poemas escogidos de Heberto Padilla/Poetry and Politics: Selected Poems of Heberto Padilla,* translation by Frank Calzón, Madrid, Playor, 1974.

*El hombre junto al mar,* Barral, 1981; published in bilingual edition with translation by Alastair Reid and Andrew Hurley as *Legacies: Selected Poems,* New York, Farrar, Straus & Giroux, 1982.

*En mi jardín pastan los héroes,* Argos Veraga, 1981; translation by Andrew Hurley published as *Heroes Are Grazing in My Garden,* New York, Farrar, Straus & Giroux, 1984.

*Autorretrato del otro: La mala memoria,* Madrid, Plaza y Janés, 1988; translation by Alexander Coleman published as *Self-Portrait of the Other,* New York, Farrar, Straus & Giroux, 1990.

*A Fountain, A House of Stone,* New York, Farrar, Straus & Giroux, 1991.

### SOURCES:

#### Books

Casal, Lourdes, *El Caso Padilla,* Miami, Ediciones Universal, 1974.

———, "Cultural Policy and Writers in Cuba," in *The Cuban Reader: The Making of a Revolutionary Society,* New York, Grove Press, 1989, pp. 487–97.

*Hispanic Writers,* edited by Brian Ryan, Detroit, Gale, 1991, pp. 355–57.

Levinson, Sandra, "Talking About Cuban Culture: A Reporter's Notebook" in *The Cuban Reader: The Making of a Revolutionary Society,* New York, Grove Press, 1989, pp. 506–13.

Mesa-Lago, Carmelo, *Cuba in the 1970s,* Albuquerque, University of New Mexico Press, 1974, pp. 97–98.

Suchlicki, Jaime, *Historical Dictionary of Cuba,* Scarecrow Press, Inc., 1988, pp. 205–06.

Zeitlin, Maurice, *Revolutionary Politics and the Cuban Working Class,* New York, Harper & Row, 1970, p. xlv.

#### Periodicals

*Miami Herald,* October 13, 1994, p. 1G.

*New York Review of Books,* July 18, 1985, p. 34.

*New York Times Book Review,* April 11, 1982, p. 15.

*Time,* September 24, 1984, p. 53.

—*Sketch by Conner C. Gorry*

# José Antonio Páez
## 1790-1873
**Venezuelan revolutionary leader and statesman**

José Antonio Páez was a charismatic cavalry leader who became the first president of an independent Venezuela in 1831. The so-called "Lion of the Apure River," Páez led the Venezuelans under General **Simón Bolívar** to victory against Spain. Páez then broke away from Bolívar, freeing Venezuela from Bolívar's Republic of Gran Colombia. While Bolívar played a leading role in the liberation of Latin America as a whole, Páez, according to Harry Bernstein, author of *Venezuela & Colombia,* "became the primary figure in the liberation of Venezuela." As president—or the power behind presidents—in Venezuela from 1831 to 1846, Páez oversaw a period of relative political stability and economic prosperity. Páez also ruled as dictator from 1861 to 1863.

Páez was born June 13, 1790, near Aricagua, at the edge of the Venezuelan plains. He was the seventh son of Juan Victorio Páez and Maria Violante Herrera. His father worked as a clerk in the royal tobacco monopoly in Guanare. Venezuela was still a viceroyalty of Spain and young José Antonio received only a rudimentary education. As an adult, however, he studied the classics, took up the violincello, and wrote an autobiography hailed for its frank and earthy voice.

At the age of 17, Páez left home unexpectedly after encountering a group of bandits. Apparently in self-defense, Páez, who had been on his way home from performing an errand, shot and killed one of the men. Terrified that he would be charged with murder, Páez fled into the vast Venezuelan plains and became a peon on a cattle ranch.

### Cowboy of the Venezuelan Plains

Forced into a life of near servitude by his foreman, Manuel, Páez rode wild horses bareback from 3:00 a.m. until nightfall. In *Venezuela Through Its History,* wrote William D. and Amy L. Marsland: "He became a *llanero,* a strong, hardy, fierce, lusty, and unpredictable creature who measured a man by his ability to outwit a bull." Eventually Páez met the owner of the ranch and was promoted to selling cattle in a nearby town. Páez married Dominga Ortiz, a serious girl from a good family, but abandoned her in 1820. He later lived with Barbara Nieves, a beauty fond of dancing. In *José Antonio Páez,* R. B. Cunninghame Graham wrote: "What is certain is that Páez took neither his wife nor mistress with him in his long exile, and in his bulky memoirs hardly mentions them." When war broke out in 1810, Páez joined a

regiment of patriot cavalry and began his rise to power. By 1817, he was Bolívar's chief lieutenant.

"Toward his men he felt an almost paternal tenderness and pride," the Marslands wrote. "They in turn adored him, and referred to him as 'Uncle'. . . . Their respect was mingled, too, with a breath of superstititous awe, for Páez was an epileptic and frequently under the stress of excitement, rode into battle with reckless audacity, foaming at the mouth." Páez knew the land and rivers of the region well enough to take the Spanish forces by surprise. During one of his most acclaimed moments, he plunged into the water and attacked the Spanish with knives to force them off their ships. In 1821 Páez helped win the crucial Battle of Carabobo.

After the revolution, Páez became a provincial governor in Bolívar's Republic of Gran Colombia, which consisted of Venezuela, Ecuador and Colombia. But a movement was growing that advocated an independent Venezuela, with supporters arguing that one federation could not adequately represent the social and economic needs of the three different areas. Páez began championing independence. "For a while he [Páez] kept his aim secret because he wanted no fight with Bolívar (who, in turn, wanted no fight with Páez)," Bernstein wrote.

Then, at a public meeting in Caracas on November 7, 1826, Páez declared Venezuela a sovereign state without actually counting the votes for or against secession. "Thus 'democratically' Páez made Venezuela a sovereign state," the Marslands noted. Bolívar restored the union temporarily but Venezuela broke away permanently in 1830, declaring itself a democratic republic with limited suffrage.

As chief executive of the new sovereign state, Páez set about restoring order, winning the cooperation of the legendary bandit Dionisio Cisneros. "Cisneros did not submit to the authority of the state . . . ," wrote John V. Lombardi in *Venezuela: The Search for Order, the Dream of Progress,* "but instead subordinated himself to the greater personal power and charisma of Páez, the national caudillo. . . . Páez made the government legitimate, not the other way around."

### Era of the Caudillo

With the old royal regime ended but new republican institutions yet to form, Venezuela turned to Páez. In his book *Caudillism and Militarism in Venezuela, 1810–1910,* Robert L. Gilmore described Páez as the "archetype of the caudillo." Observed Gilmore: "The presidency of Venezuela became for the most part but a euphemism for extra-legal personal authority vested in a more of less charismatic leader."

Supported by the "Conservative Oligarchy" of Caracas merchants, Páez and his government built new roads and schools, modernized the tax system, permitted limited freedom of the press, established foreign credit, checked the power of the military and established civilian administration. "The Conservative oligarchy was a misnomer," observed the Marslands. "Though its members demonstrated the usual reluctance of the rich to change, their administration was more liberal in many respects than any government Venezuela had until 1935."

Yet problems remained. "There was still a vast amount to do for the country," Bernstein wrote. "Roads were lacking; most parishes did not have the schools they were promised; and a great economic gap existed between the capital and the countryside and among the different classes." As regional dissatisfaction grew, so, too, did Liberal opposition to the Conservative party. General José Tadeo Monagas, the candidate Páez supported in 1846, turned against him. In 1848, Páez called out his cavalry but received only a scant response. Observed Lombardi: "The name of José Antonio Páez no longer represented a vital, dynamic leader to the young llaneros who had only the tales of their fathers to introduce him to the General." Páez was defeated by Monagas's forces, imprisoned, and driven into exile.

In 1850 the 60-year-old Páez arrived in the United States and was publicly welcomed by officials in New York City. Páez returned to Venezuela in 1861 as dictator to lead the Conservatives in the Federal War. But the political dynamics had changed. "Forced, partly by his age and partly by his long absence from the country, to place his trust in others," Cunninghame Graham wrote, "he fell unfortunately under the influence of one Rojas, an arbitrary man and a reactionary, whose evil counsels pushed Páez into actions that destroyed his prestige."

Defeated by the Liberals and their agenda of federalism over centralism, Páez went into exile for the last time. Back in New York, he began writing his autobiography. Then—at the age of 78—Páez set out for Argentina as a commission agent for a cattle company. The government of Argentina made Páez an honorary Brigadier General, thus allowing him to collect benefits in his old age. Peru followed suit with a generous pension.

Páez spent the next two years in Argentina, reminiscing with other exiles about the revolution. An outbreak of yellow fever forced Páez back to New York where he was greeted by his son Ramon. The elder Páez died in New York City on May 7, 1873, at the age of 83. His body was eventually returned to Venezuela and buried under a simple slab of marble.

Páez's status as a Venezuelan hero has faded over the years. According to Lombardi, Páez "continued his fight for pre-eminence for too long." Yet as the Marslands observed: "The amazing thing about José Antonio Páez was not that he abused his power occasionally, but that he sometimes employed it wisely."

## SOURCES:

Beals, Carleton, *Eagles of the Andes: South American Struggles for Independence,* Philadelphia, Chilton Books, 1963.

Bernstein, Harry, *Venezuela & Colombia,* Englewood Cliffs, New Jersey, Prentice-Hall, 1965.

Dawson, Thomas C., *The South American Republics,* New York, G. P. Putnam's Sons, 1904.

Gilmore, Robert L., *Caudillism and Militarism in Venezuela, 1810–1910,* Athens, Ohio University Press, 1964.

Graham, R. B. Cunninghame, *José Antonio Páez,* Philadelphia, Macrae Smith Company Publishers, 1929.

Lombardi, John V., *Venezuela: The Search for Order, the Dream of Progress,* New York, Oxford University Press, 1982.

Marsland, William D., and Amy L. Marsland, *Venezuela Through Its History,* New York, Thomas Y. Crowell Company, 1954.

*—Sketch by Joan Axelrod-Contrada*

# Luis Palés Matos
## 1898-1959
### Puerto Rican poet and novelist

Luis Palés Matos is considered the most prominent and most widely read Puerto Rican poet. Meshing the sounds and rhythms of Africa and the black Caribbean, Palés Matos developed a genre of Latin American literature that became known as Afro-Antillian poetry. The son of the poet Vicente Palés Anés, Luis Palés Matos was born March 20, 1898 in Guayama, Puerto Rico. Palés Matos was born into a literary household. His father and his brothers, Vicente and Gustavo Palés Matos, were all celebrated as poets laureate of Puerto Rico during Palés Matos' lifetime. His mother's side of the family was also literate and well-educated.

Palés Matos read voraciously as a child, devouring books. He became fascinated with other countries, but at some point his childhood home had a profound effect on his work. Guayama was a small village with a black majority population. This early life in the village inspired the poetry that he would write all his life. Ironically, Palés Matos' father died while giving a poetry reading. Nevertheless, Palés Matos pursued his own literary career undaunted by this tragedy. At the age of 17, he left school to recoup financial losses that he acquired publishing his own volume of poetry called *Azaleas* in 1915. Though he was not wary of reading or writing poetry, he became hesitant about publishing his poetry. In his early years, he promised many volumes of poetry but often failed to deliver. The poems sometimes surfaced in magazines or during readings, but never as separate books of collected works.

Palés Matos developed a style with his early poems that was reminiscent of Edgar Allan Poe. This was a dark, atmospheric, gloomy period that eventually gave way to just the opposite; pure, dreamlike poems of white space and distance. Federico de Onís referred to these poems as "trasnochado parnasianismo" or "trasnochar." This term has no direct English translation, but loosely, it means "to stay awake all night watching."

In the 1920s, Palés Matos lived in San Juan, where he worked as a journalist and began contributing to magazines, such as *El Pueblo,* edited by F. Sárraga Figuero. With the writer J. T. de Diego Padró, Palés Matos created a new writing aesthetic early in his career. This form, known as "*Diepalismo*" (a combination of their names), utilized onomatopoeia and an increased musicality and flow of language in the poems. The first of these poems was published in *El Imparcial* in 1921 and was called "Orquestación Deipálica." These early experiments with language gave rise to Palés Matos' more mature style for which he is best known.

### Found Voice in A Mixture of Cultures

Palés Matos began to turn away from both Poe styled poems and dream-like poems in his thirties. Instead, he focused his attentions on what would be the hallmark of his career; he began to celebrate themes relevant to African peoples, using Afro-Caribbean rhythms and language in his poems. This mixture of African, Spanish, and uniquely Caribbean techniques and culture became known as the Antillean or African-Antillean style. For Palés Matos, and many other authors like **Nicolás Guillén,** this style was simple and possessed a poetic, religious, and spiritual, yet modern, strength that worked in contrast to complex, apathetic, or existential styles popular with many of the writers of Palés Matos' era.

Palés Matos mixed Antillean and African words in poems filled with neologisms and rhythms that moved like African dances. Unfortunately, in translation the rhythms became completely lost and one can only understand Palés Matos' experimentation with

the musicality of language in the original Spanish text. Palés Matos concentrated on meshing black social experiences with what he perceived as the imposition of U.S. values and culture on the people of Puerto Rico. His first Antillean poem was "Pueblo Negro" published in 1925. He published his book *Tuntún de pasa y grifería: Poemas Afroantillanos* in 1937, which furthered his work in African themes.

Palés Matos explained his own themes in a book by G. R. Coulthard published in 1962: "The Negro lives physically and spiritually within us all, and his characteristics, filtered down through the mulatto, influence in a very apparent way every manifestation of the life of our people." He furthered this idea in his verse "Mulata-Antilla": "In you, now, mulatto girl of the Antilles, I enfold myself in the warm Caribbean sea. Slow sensual water of molasses . . . And now in you, mulatto girl of the Antilles, I sail the sea of my islands." In the poem many consider his master work, "La plena de menéalo" ("The Dance of Shake It"), he characterizes Puerto Rico as a seductive mulatta who sweats rum as she dances erotically just out of the reach of the personification of the United States, Uncle Sam.

Palés Matos found a release from the strictures of Western intellectualism with the primitive stylings of the African and Antillean cultures. Many critics were displeased with his continual imposition of African themes on Puerto Rican settings and subject matter. Nevertheless, Palés Matos' "Africanization" captured a facet of Caribbean life that addressed the great effect the Negro has had on the Spanish-Caribbean cultures of Puerto Rico and all of the West Indies.

O. R. Dathone commented on Palés Matos in *Dark Ancestor: The Literature of the Black Man in the Caribbean:* "Palés Matos, in the final analysis, used Afro-New World themes to make important statements about relationships in the Black world. If at times he seems rude or frankly offensive in his expressions, he still remains one of the forerunners of Afro-New World Black poetry in Spanish." Also, Ricardo Gullón summed up Palés Matos contribution to literature in an article in *La Torre* in 1960: "Luis Palés Matos's place in the history of Puerto Rican poetry is clear. He is the most important poet of Puerto Rico, the one who has best expressed the special qualities of his land, its own passionately Puerto Rican self."

### SELECTED PUBLISHED WORKS:

### Books

*Tuntún de pasa y grifería: Poemas afroantillanos,* Biblioteca de Autores Puertorriqueños, 1950.

*Poesía, 1915–1916,* Ediciones de la Universidad de Puerto Rico, 1957, fourth revised edition, 1971.

*Luis Palés Matos: Vida y obra, bibliografía, antologia,* compiled by Federico de Onís, Universidad Central de las Villas, 1959.

*Luis Palés Matos (1898–1959): Vida y obra, bibliografía, antología, poesías inéditas,* compiled by Federico de Onís, Ediciones Atenco Puertorriqueños, 1960.

*Poesía completa y prosa selecta,* edited by Margot Arce de Vázquez, Biblioteca Ayacucho, 1978.

*Obras (1914–1959),* two volumes, edited by Margot Arce de Vázquez, Editorial de la Universidad de Puerto Rico, 1984.

## Poems

*Azaleas,* 1915.
*Pueblo Negro,* 1925.

## SOURCES:

### Books

*Caribbean Literature: An Anthology,* edited by G. R. Coulthard, University of London Press, 1966.

*Caribbean Writers: A Bio-Bibliographical-Critical Encyclopedia,* edited by Donald E. Herdeck, Washington, D.C., Three Continents Press, 1979.

Coulthard, G. R., *Race and Colour in Caribbean Literature,* London, Oxford University Press, 1962.

Dathone, O. R., *Dark Ancestor: The Literature of the Black Man in the Caribbean,* Baton Rouge, Lousiana State University Press, 1981.

*Hispanic-American Almanac,* edited by Nicolas Kanellos, Detroit, Gale Research, 1993.

*Hispanic Writers,* edited by Bryan Ryan, Detroit, Gale Research, 1991.

*Nine Latin American Poets,* translated by Rachel Beon, New York, Cypress Books, 1968.

### Periodicals

*La torre,* January-June 1960.

—*Sketch by Christopher B. Tower*

# Antonia Pantoja
## 1922-
### Puerto Rican activist and educator

An educator who has never been content with merely standing in front of a class and imparting her vast knowledge, Antonia Pantoja is the founder of many organizations dedicated to serving the Puerto Rican community and promoting community relations. A union organizer and activist as well as a teacher, Pantoja has been a pioneer and leader among Puerto Ricans by motivating them politically and intellectually. Her "dare to dream" message is the impetus behind every project with which she becomes involved.

Born in Puerta de Tierra, San Juan, Puerto Rico, in 1922, Pantoja benefitted from her parents' desire to give her a good education and also from their involvement in workers' rights. She was sent to live in Barrio Obrero ("the workers' neighborhood") with her grandfather, a cigar maker and union organizer at the America Tobacco Company. In *Portraits of the Puerto Rican Experience,* Pantoja described Barrio Obrero as "a poor slum, it had an internal social order, and people were conscious of their rights and of the need for education." In the late 1920s, Pantoja witnessed her family's strong conviction and fight for the cigar workers' rights—one of the first successful strikes in Puerto Rican history. She discovered firsthand the importance of the workers' movement, a belief she would carry with her through her life's work. In *Portraits of the Puerto Rican Experience,* Pantoja remembered her childhood in Puerto Rico as a time in which she "learned the relation between struggle and progress."

Pantoja graduated from the University of Puerto Rico, earning her Normal Diploma—a two-year education program—and began work as a teacher in the rural mountain area between the towns of San Lorenzo and Las Piedras. While the job was rewarding, the pay was very low. Pantoja sought alternatives to helping her family obtain an improved economic life, and she decided to go to America.

### Move to America Prompts Awareness of Worker Inequalities

In 1944, with World War II in progress, Pantoja journeyed with her grandfather and younger brother to Old San Juan. At the docks she boarded the SS *Florida* and, amid enemy submarines that were scattered throughout the water, completed a dangerous ten-day ocean-liner journey across the Atlantic. She finally landed in New Orleans and boarded a train for her final destination, New York City. There, weakened from her long journey—she suffered from asthma—she began work as a welder in a factory that built radios for submarines. She lived in a small apartment in the Bronx and labored in the factory from seven a.m. to ten p.m.—long hours that threatened her health further. At one point she was so tired that her welding tool fell from her hand and burned her, causing her foreman to label her accident-prone.

Leaving the radio factory, Pantoja found a job at another factory, making children's bedroom lamps. It was during this period that she realized the oppression of the Puerto Ricans in the city. Puerto Ricans were discriminated against and paid sub-minimum wages, mainly because of their lack of knowledge and political power. With the memories of her grandfather's fight against the tobacco company still vivid in her mind, and with an inherent sense of leadership, Pantoja organized her coworkers, informed them of their rights, and taught them about unions. "As a teacher in Puerto Rico, I knew the value of education," she stated in an interview published in *A Guide to Celebrate Puerto Rican Heritage and Culture.* "Once you acquire some knowledge, the doors to opportunity are open for you."

After organizing its workers, Pantoja left the factory and became acquainted with a new circle of friends: a group of artists and performers from a theatrical troupe. Leaving the Bronx, Pantoja moved to New York City's East Village. She soon adapted their bohemian lifestyle and would stay up until dawn discussing politics with her new friends. "I separated completely from my people," she remarked in *A Guide to Celebrate Puerto Rican Heritage and Culture.* "I discovered New York from the life of artists, painters, dancers and ballerinas. I was very happy with my friends ... However, I missed my people and decided to return to a job that would bring me closer to them."

Pantoja found a job working with the 110th Street Community Center, and during evenings, she took courses at Hunter College. Trying to balance her schedule of work and school was very difficult. Through extensive library research, she was able to learn of and obtain a scholarship. With it, she could continue her college education full time and do volunteer work for the Puerto Rican community. "This was the turn around of my life," she says in *A Guide to Celebrate Puerto Rican Heritage and Culture.*

### Volunteers Time for Puerto Rican Community

Pantoja earned her bachelor's degree from Hunter College in pre-social work and received a fellowship to attend Columbia University's School of Social Work. While at Columbia, she and other Puerto Rican students formed a group whose goal was to explain why so many of their people suffered from poverty and rejection in New York. Group members volunteered their time in Puerto Rican neighborhoods—cleaning, painting, seeking donations, and getting people to vote. In this project, Pantoja had started what would be the mission of her work.

In 1953, Pantoja worked as a director of a pilot project on Puerto Ricans with the Associated Charities in Connecticut. It was her job to collect data on problems facing Puerto Ricans in Bridgeport, Connecticut, and report her findings and recommendations to the mayor's committee. That same year, Pantoja and friends organized the Hispanic Young Adult Association (HYAA) with a membership of mostly second-generation Puerto Rican college students concerned about their community. Since the organization was of and for Puerto Ricans, the name was changed to the Puerto Rican Association for Community Affairs (PRACA). Its goal was to provide services to children and families, and to train the community's leaders to become influential within the power structure.

While working on her master's degree at Columbia University's School of Social Work, Pantoja was involved in a student practice at the Hudson Guild in New York City during the mid-1950s. The Guild's goal was to improve the community and develop positive relations between Irish, Jewish, Greek, and Italian residents and the African Americans and Puerto Ricans. Pantoja's special student project was to establish a housing clinic and a neighborhood committee.

Pantoja earned her master's degree in 1954 and was appointed supervisor of the adult division for the Union Settlement. She was responsible for direct supervision of staff members, development of leadership skills, and program direction at the summer camp. Later in her career, Pantoja was chosen as director of the Community Relations Division for the City of New York's Commission of Intergroup Relations. Her activities involved the establishment of objectives, programs, and budgets, as well as the supervision of staff who were assigned to respond to tense situations in the city. Pantoja strived to reduce racial conflict and enhance intercultural and interracial relations. "Everyone has the ability to grow and to succeed if they try," she remarked in *A Guide to Celebrate Puerto Rican Heritage and Culture.*

### Community Work Leads to Creation of Aspira

In 1958, Pantoja and a group of young professionals organized the Puerto Rican Forum, Inc., an agency for business and career development dedicated to creating Puerto Rican institutions in New York City. The largest and oldest Puerto Rican community social service agency, the Puerto Rican Forum led to the development of the Aspira Club of New York—an educational agency, and Pantoja's dream.

The Aspira (meaning "strive" or "aspire" in Spanish) Club promoted higher education for Puerto Ricans. Founded in 1961, its goal was to provide inspiration and guidance to Puerto Rican youths continuing their education in the professional, technical, or artistic fields. It also provided a vehicle to encourage self-confidence and identity among Puerto Ricans. Aspira Clubs have been formed in many high schools throughout New York, conducting workshops and conferences for both educators and youth. Between 1961 and 1968, Pantoja devoted almost all of her time to Aspira.

While Aspira was devoted to the intellectual needs of Puerto Ricans in New York, work yet needed to be done in the communities. Shortly after the founding of Aspira, the Puerto Rican Community Development Project was formed. Its goal was to promote a sense of identity among Puerto Ricans and help them develop community strength. The leading figure in this movement was also Pantoja.

By July of 1967, Pantoja was working as an assistant professor at Columbia's School of Social Work. She taught a course in community organization and supervised students working directly in the neighborhoods on community issues. In addition to her university duties, Pantoja continued her work in Puerto Rican organizations. She was selected as a delegate-at-large for the 1967 Constitutional Convention of New York State, serving for four months. As a member of the Bundy Panel, she fought for the decentralization of the New York City public school system. Pantoja was also a part-time lecturer. She spoke at the New School of Social Research, Center for New York Affairs.

Due to her asthma, Pantoja returned to Puerto Rico in 1968, where she taught at the University of Puerto Rico's School of Social Work. She also developed Aspira Clubs while in Puerto Rico, and acted as a consultant on private and public projects. She returned to the United States in 1970.

### Establishes Universidad Boricua

That same year Pantoja wrote a proposal and secured funds to establish the Universidad Boricua and Puerto Rican Research and Resource Center in Washington, D.C. Its purpose was to develop an informational base of resources and art objects about Puerto Ricans. With the resource center as a base, she developed the theoretical foundation for a university that would serve Puerto Ricans in the United States and provide innovative, bilingual, career-oriented programs for professionals, technicians, and workers—a foundation that would also be her doctoral thesis.

Through grants, the university was realized. In 1973, Pantoja became the Chancellor of the Universi-

dad Boricua—the university's first president. The Universidad Boricua is the only bilingual institution of higher learning that was established and controlled by Puerto Rican academicians.

Pantoja's asthma worsened, and she was advised by her doctor to move to a different climate. Relocating from Washington, D.C., to San Diego, California, Pantoja took a position as associate professor at San Diego State University, teaching social policy and community development. However, battles with the college bureaucracy led her to depart from the university. She and fellow educator Wilhelmina Perry founded the Graduate School for Community Development in San Diego, of which Pantoja was president. Serving communities and neighborhoods nationwide, its main objective was to teach people to develop institutions in society, change them, or create new ones.

In the mid-1980s Pantoja returned to Puerto Rico and participated in the development of Producir, Inc., with the collaboration of Perry. The company promotes Puerto Rican self-sufficiency through a community-based organization that creates jobs for the local economy. In 1989, Pantoja was honored by being asked to return to her alma mater, Hunter College, and deliver the keynote speech at the Bella Abzug Conference. She addressed the "erasing of the footsteps" of Puerto Rican woman in their struggle to achieve social and economic justice. In the early 1990s Pantoja received the John W. Gardner Leadership Award from Independent Sector, the national association of nonprofit organizations, as well as the Hispanic Heritage Award for leadership.

## SOURCES:

### Books

Fitzpatrick, Joseph, *Puerto Rican Americans,* Prentice-Hall, 1973.
Maldonado, Adal, *Portraits of the Puerto Rican Experience,* IPRUS, 1984.

### Periodicals

*Centro,* winter, 1989–90, pp. 48–52.

### Other

*A Guide to Celebrate Puerto Rican Heritage and Culture* (manual), Hunter College, November 1991, pp. 12–25.

*—Sketch by Stephanie Poythress*

# Américo Paredes
## 1915-
### Mexican American folklorist, educator, and writer

*Américo Paredes*

Américo Paredes is a folklore scholar known for his collections and translations of the folklore and ballads of Mexico and the Mexican American border region. His celebrated 1958 book, *With His Pistol in His Hand: A Border Ballad and Its Hero,* described the legend of Gregorio Cortez, a Mexican American ranch hand who shot a Texas sheriff and then became a hero as he eluded capture. Paredes heard the story, which ended tragically, sung as a ballad in small towns along the Rio Grande. "Borders and ballads seem to go together, and their heroes are all cast in the same mold," he wrote.

Paredes is "renowned as an ethnographer, literary critic and social historian," according to Ramón Saldívar in the foreword to Paredes's fiction collection *The Hammon and the Beans and Other Stories* (1994). Similarly, Richard M. Dorson described him as "the outstanding scholar of border folklore" in the introduction to Paredes's *Folktales of Mexico* (1970): "He is the thorough folklorist, equally at home in the field, the library, and the archives," Dorson wrote. "No one is more uniquely qualified to present the folktales of Mexico." Paredes developed Chicano and folklore studies at the University of Texas at Austin, where he was professor of English and anthropology for over 30 years. A prolific writer, he was editor of the *Journal of American Folklore* from 1969 to 1973.

Paredes was born to Justo and Clotilde Paredes in Brownsville, Texas, on September 3, 1915. He was raised between two worlds—a phrase which became the title of his 1990 book of poetry—on the Texas-Mexican border with its rich mixture of languages and cultures. In *Folktales of Mexico,* Paredes wrote that he spent childhood summers in northern Mexico, listening to storytellers. Aspiring to be a poet and fiction writer, he studied at Brownsville Junior College from 1934 to 1936, then worked as a journalist at the *Brownsville Herald* and Pan American Airways. He traveled to Japan with the U.S. Army in 1944 and 1945. As political editor for *Stars and Stripes,* he covered part of the post-World War II war crimes trials in Japan, according to notes in *The Hammon and the Beans.*

### Develops Folklore and Chicano Studies

Paredes had a long and distinguished academic career. In 1951, he received his bachelor's degree in English and philosophy, summa cum laude, from the University of Texas at Austin. He earned a master's in 1953 and his doctorate in 1956, both in English (folklore) and Spanish. He then taught at the university, rising to professor of English in 1965 and professor of anthropology in 1966, and serving on the folklore program faculty. He was later named the Ashbel Smith Professor of English and Anthropology and the Anderson Centennial Professor. After retirement, Paredes became Professor Emeritus of English and Anthropology.

In 1957, Paredes organized the Folklore Archives at the university and served as archivist. He founded the university's Mexican American Studies Program in 1972, and directed the Center for Intercultural Studies in Folklore and Oral History. Beyond the university, Paredes, who published frequently in professional journals, was president of the Texas Folklore Society in 1961–1962, and vice-president of the American Folklore Society in 1964–1965. He was also active in civil rights, bicultural education, and ethnic minority affairs for Texas and the university.

A dedicated field researcher, Paredes traveled the Lower Rio Grande border, collecting *corridos* (Mexican American ballads) and folktales from farmers, ranchers, folksingers, and others. Many of his tapes are housed in the Folklore Library at the University of Texas at Austin. His doctoral thesis, "With a Pistol in His Hand"—which was made into a public television film—is considered a classic study of the border ballad. "It illuminates the folk psychology of the

Mexican border folk," according to *The Centennial Index: One Hundred Years of the Journal of American Folklore.* "It also indicates how folklore sources can contribute to historical knowledge."

## Collecting Songs, Celebrating a People

In *Folktales of Mexico,* Paredes wrote that folklore in Mexico and the United States is a blend of "imported, indigenous and American-historical traditions," molded by a combination of "colonization, the westward movement, Negro slavery, immigration, regionalism, the rhetoric of democracy, and the technology of the mass media." Animal folktales, like "The Ram in the Chile Patch" and "Pérez the Mouse," are among the stories he collected for the book. "Folktales of wonder and adventure still are told in Mexican villages and towns with all the old embellishments," he observed.

Paredes's 1976 book, *A Texas-Mexican Cancionero: Folksongs of the Lower Border,* was "among the first folksong volumes to emphasize Mexican rather than Spanish heritage," John O. West noted in *Mexican-American Folklore.* Paredes collected the words and music of 66 folksongs from the Texas-Mexican border, and added his own historical information and interpretation of each one. "The total reveals a scholar with an impressive command of border folksong," West claimed. In addition, the book was deemed appropriate for both scholars and general readers.

Paredes was not only a scholar, but a cultural advocate who cared deeply about the history and people of his region. In the dedication to *"With His Pistol in His Hand,"* Paredes wrote: "To the memory of my father, who rode a raid or two with Catarino Garza; and to all those old men who sat around on summer nights, in the days when there was a chaparral, smoking their cornhusk cigarettes and talking in low, gentle voices about violent things; while I listened."

Paredes was still working hard in his seventies. *Folkore and Culture of the Texas-American Border* appeared in 1992. His efforts at fiction and poetry came to fruition with the publication of a novel, *George Washington Gómez* (1990), and a poetry collection, *Between Two Worlds* (1991). "These imaginary works address the predicaments of contemporary Chicano/a cultural politics, identity formation, and social transformation," Saldívar stated. Paredes's short-story collection, *The Hammon and the Beans,* published in 1994 but mostly written in the 1930s and 1940s, vividly describes the Brownsville of his youth, where Mexican Americans struggled against poverty, prejudice, and loss of cultural identity.

Paredes married Consuelo Silva in 1939. After the marriage ended, he wed Amelia Sidzu Nagamine in 1948. Paredes dedicated some of his many books to his four children, Julia, Américo, Jr., Alan, and Vicente. In 1989, Paredes was honored by the National Endowment for the Humanities with the Charles Frankel Prize for his lifelong contributions to the humanities. The government of Mexico in 1990 awarded him the Order of the Aztec Eagle, the highest award to non-citizens for preserving Mexican culture.

## SELECTED PUBLISHED WORKS:

*"With His Pistol in His Hand:" A Border Ballad and Its Hero,* Austin, University of Texas Press, 1958.

*Folk Music of Mexico,* with Joseph Castle, Chicago, M. M. Cole, 1966.

*Mexican-American Authors,* New York, Houghton Mifflin, 1972.

*Toward New Perspectives in Folklore,* with Richard Bauman, Austin, University of Texas Press, 1972.

*A Texas-Mexican Cancionero: Folksongs of the Lower Border,* University of Illinois Press, 1976.

*Between Two Worlds,* Houston, Arte Público Press, 1990.

*George Washington Gómez,* Houston, Arte Público Press, 1990.

*The Hammon and the Beans and Other Stories,* Houston, Arte Público Press, 1994.

### Editor

(And translator) *Folktales of Mexico,* University of Chicago Press, 1970.

*The Urban Experience and Folk Tradition,* with Ellen J. Stekert, Austin, University of Texas Press, 1971.

## SOURCES:

### Books

*The Centennial Index: One Hundred Years of the Journal of American Folkore,* edited by Bruce Jackson, Michael Taft, and Harvey S. Axelrod, Washington, DC, American Folklore Society, 1988.

*Hispanic Writers,* edited by Bryan Ryan, Detroit, Gale, 1991.

West, John O., *Mexican-American Folklore,* Little Rock, August House, 1988.

### Periodicals

*Journal of American Folklore,* January-March 1972, pp. 84–6; July-September 1976, pp. 857–58.

**Other**

"Curriculum Vitae," Américo Paredes.

—*Sketch by Ann Malaspina*

# Nicanor Parra
## 1914-
### Chilean poet, scientist, and educator

The world of physics and mathematics—characterized by precise formulae and rational equations—is hardly the place one expects to find a prolific poet. Yet this is the domain of Nicanor Parra. The scientifically trained writer has produced work that is often stark, shocking, and sarcastic—a postmodern style of deconstructed poetry that has earned him the label "antipoet."

Nicanor Parra was born on September 5, 1914, to Nicanor P. (a teacher) and Clara S. Parra, in Chillán, Chile. Early on, Parra demonstrated great skill in math and science. He chose to focus on the so-called "hard sciences," planning an education that eventually included the University of Chile, Brown University, and Oxford University. He received a degree in math and physics from the University of Chile in Santiago. His college teaching career also began there in 1948. Ever since that time, he has taught courses in engineering and theoretical physics.

Although Parra earned an international reputation for his work in theoretical physics—garnering visiting professorships at Louisiana State University, New York University, Columbia University and Yale—he became better known for his poetry. He began writing "antipoems" for public consumption in the 1930s, receiving his first formal award in 1937, when his *Cancionero sin nombre* won him the Premio municipal de poesía from the city of Santiago.

Throughout the 1940s and 1950s, Parra honed his writing craft, finding a ready audience in readers who rejected the flowery and often naïve school of poetry then led by **Pablo Neruda.** Neruda's work represented more traditional Spanish-language poetry, addressing the human condition in its most abstract ideals but failing to speak to the common folk. Parra's antipoetry filled this void by relying on folk characters—many profane, most mundane, but all as real as the people in the streets of Santiago.

During the 1960s, Parra's writing and his manner of presenting poetry fell just short of confrontation; both techniques were clearly meant to challenge orthodoxy in the style of the Beat Poets who enjoyed popularity throughout the Americas and Europe. Parra's habit of reading his verse and then disclaiming them has unnerved many audiences, just as his dislocated writing style and his intentional flaunting of poetic conventions has often alienated literary critics.

A favorite cultural icon of the antipoets was the 1920s construction worker-turned-prophet Domingo Zarate Vega. Parra used Zarate Vega as the narrator of his 1977 *Sermones y prédicas del Cristo de Elqui.* Zarate Vega, in his role as narrator, doubles as the Trickster, mocking the self-conscious manner of worship that places all emphasis on ritual and symbol, missing the humanistic message of Christianity. The perception of sacrilege in *Sermones y prédicas del Cristo de Elqui* has made it Parra's most controversial work.

The same irreverence he shows towards form and delivery has carried over to his dealings with the press regarding his personal life and influences. He has refused to complete interviews to which he has agreed, revealing little about his artistic philosophy or writing techniques. Similarly, little is known about his family, save that Parra married Anna Troncoso in 1948 (they later divorced), and that he married Inga Palmen some years after. The couple has seven children.

Alienation from the popular media and literary critics notwithstanding, Parra has won numerous prestigious writing awards. Among these, perhaps the most honorific were Premio Nacional de Literatura from his homeland in 1969 and a 1972 Guggenheim fellowship. However, Parra cares more for the acclaim of his readers, a cross-section of society who find his characters realistic, funny, sometimes vulgar, but eminently human. They see themselves, their neighbors, their heroes, and their enemies in the voices that grace Nicanor Parra's poetry.

## SELECTED PUBLISHED WORKS:

*Cancionero sin nombre,* Nascimento, 1937.
*Poemas y antipoemas,* Nascimento, 1954.
*Discursos* (with Pablo Neruda), Nascimento, 1962.
*Versos de salon,* Nascimento, 1962.
*La cueca larga y otros poemas,* edited by Margarita Aguirre, Editorial Universitaria de Buenos Aires, 1964.
*Poesía soviética rusa,* Editorial Progreso, 1965.
*Canciones rusas,* Editorial Universitaria, 1967.
*Poemas,* Casa de las Américas, 1969.
*Poesía rusa contemporánea,* Ediciones Nueva Universidad, Universidad Católica de Chile, 1971.
*Los Profesores,* New York, Antiediciones Villa Miseria, 1971.

*Antipoemas: Antología (1944–1969),* Seix Barral, 1972.

*Artefactos/Nicanor Parra,* Ediciones Nueva Universidad, Universidad Católica de Chile, 1972.

*Emergency Poems* (originally published as *Obra Gruesa*) New Directions, 1972.

*Sermones y prédicas del Cristo de Elqui,* Universidad del Chile Estudios Humanísticos, 1977.

*Nuevos sermones y prédicas del Cristo de Elqui,* Ganymedes, 1979.

*Poema y antipoema a Eduardo Frei,* Editorial América del Sur, 1982.

*Coplas de Navidad,* Ediciones del Camaleón, 1983.

*Poesía política,* Bruguera, 1983.

*Antipoems: New and Selected,* edited by David Unger, New Directions, 1985.

*Nicanor Parra: Biografía emotiva,* Ediciones Rumbos, 1988.

## SOURCES:

*Contemporary Authors,* vol. 85–88, edited by Frances Carol Locher, Detroit, Gale, 1980.

*Contemporary Authors, New Revision Series,* vol. 32, edited by James G. Lesniak, Detroit, Gale, 1991.

*Hispanic Writers,* edited by Bryan Ryan, Detroit, Gale, 1991.

*Oxford Companion to Spanish Literature,* edited by Philip Ward, Oxford, Clarendon Press, 1978.

*Spanish-American Literature: A History,* edited by Enrique Anert and translated by John V. Falconieri, Detroit, Wayne State University Press, 1963.

—*Sketch by Cynthia R. Kasee*

*Octavio Paz*

# Octavio Paz
## 1914-
### Mexican poet, essayist, and diplomat

Octavio Paz is widely regarded as the greatest living poet of the Spanish language and one of the most important Mexican intellectuals of the twentieth century. In recognition of a body of work that includes more than 30 volumes of poetry and over 40 major prose works on topics ranging from Mexican culture to literary theory and Eastern philosophy, he was awarded the Nobel Prize for literature in 1990—the first Mexican to receive the honor. Paz has utilized numerous styles and explored myriad themes in his writings, almost all of which have been greeted with critical acclaim. He also founded and edited several journals that provide forums for literature and debate on political issues. Paz's many contributions to the literary world were cogently summarized by Mexican novelist **Carlos Fuentes,** who stated in the poetry journal *Kosmos* that "I know of no other living writer who has so powerfully expressed the existence of a plurality of times, a plurality of possibilities for harmony and truth, outside the limited range of inherited dogmas.... I know of no other contemporary writer who has given so much of his individual expression to a poetical form that transcends him in order to establish the common voice of the hidden fraternity of civilizations."

While Paz's writing reflects his appreciation of a variety of cultures, he takes care to emphasize his Mexican roots. "When I started to write poetry, the first thing I did was learn my craft from the Spanish classics," he explained in a *New Yorker* interview. "I then read the great Latin Americans who came before me. Then suddenly, I discovered the Indian past through modernity.... And then I found out that I was not complete—that I needed to assimilate the great lessons of modern literature. Whitman showed me enormous areas of reality that traditional Spanish poetry ignored as being not poetical. From Eliot, Pound, and William Carlos Williams I came to understand formal experimentation. But, despite all this, I am not a foreign writer, I am a Mexican poet."

Paz was born on March 31, 1914, in Mexico City amid the violence and chaos of the Mexican Revolution. He was raised by his religious mother, Josefina Lozano, the daughter of Spanish immigrants. She was helped by a well-educated aunt and by Paz's paternal grandfather, a novelist and soldier who supported the dictator **Porfirio Diaz.** His father was Octavio Paz, a noted journalist and lawyer who once defended the peasant revolutionary **Emiliano Zapata** and helped initiate agrarian reform after the revolution. As a result of his political involvement, he spent little time at home. Despite the political activities of his father, however, Paz was sheltered from the violence of the revolution by his mother and the French Marist fathers who educated him. He was exposed, instead, to a Mixcoac house library filled with works containing the thoughts of classical authors, philosophers, Spanish writers, and Mexican modernists such as Amado Nervo. While completing his secondary education in Mexico City, Paz was introduced to the avant-garde magazine *Contemporaneos,* a periodical that included the work of modern Spanish poets such as Gerardo Diego and Antonio Machado.

At the age of 17, Paz published his first poem and founded *Barandal,* his first literary review. He enrolled at the National Autonomous University of Mexico in 1932. Paz completed *Luna silvestre,* his first book of poems, the following year. In 1937 Paz terminated his formal university studies. Seeking to invest his poetic reflections with tangible social action, he traveled to Yukatan, where he helped to set up a school in a poor rural area near Merida. This experience furnished him with the material for *Entre la piedra y la flor,* a long political poem that was described by biographer Jason Wilson as an attempt "to show the asphyxiating relationship that tied workers to the impersonal, abstract, capitalistic economy."

Paz's growing interest in left-wing political causes guided his travels for the next several years. In 1937, for instance, he left Mexico with his new wife, Elena Garro, for a year-long stint in Spain to participate in the second Congress of the International Association of Writers. This conference had been organized by the Alliance of Intellectuals in Defence of Culture, a group of 86 writers from 26 countries. It was in this group that Paz learned "the meaning of fraternity," according to an interview with Rita Guibert in *Seven Voices.* Upon his return to Mexico via Paris, he demonstrated his resistance to fascism by writing political articles for the left-wing *El Poplar,* giving speeches, and founding the literary periodical *Taller.*

### Begins Self-Exile from Mexico

Caught in the midst of political rivalry in Mexico and dismayed by the 1940 Hitler-Stalin pact, Paz began to question his political idealism and left for the United States in 1943 on a two-year Guggenheim fellowship. He traveled throughout the country "slowly working out his identity as a Mexican poet in the shadow of the European war, dissatisfied with a political revolution as a means of changing man and society," according to Wilson. While shaping his own poetic identity—a process influenced by his exposure to the formal experimentation of modernist American poets such as Wallace Stevens and William Carlos Williams—Paz was able to view his native land from a new perspective. He identified himself with the marginalized *pachucos* of Los Angeles and came to recognize his post-Revolution Mexican ethnicity within the larger context of modern alienation. This experience, Wilson remarked, "clarified his Mexican roots in ways that would have been impossible had he stayed on in Mexico."

After completing his fellowship, Paz was appointed cultural attaché for the Mexican embassy in Paris. In France he met the French surrealist poet André Breton—the artist who had perhaps the greatest influence on Paz's poetry. As Paz articulated in *Las peras del olmo,* surrealism became his "desperate attempt to find a way out," a way to come to terms with the problems of writing poetry in a godless world of existential alienation. Under Breton's tutelage, Paz developed the voice that would appear in some of his most important early volumes of poetry. *¿Aguila o sol?* (*Eagle or Sun?*), published in 1951, was indicative of Paz's early interest in surrealism. It examined the past, present, and future of Mexico through a series of visionary prose poems that relied on the surrealist technique of linking often unrelated images to emphasize revelatory moments of perception or to break down barriers between polar opposites such as dream and reality or life and death.

### Establishes International Reputation with *The Labyrinth of Solitude*

During his years in Paris, Paz composed *El laberinto de la soledad* (*The Labyrinth of Solitude*), one of his most widely read prose works. Interpreted by critics as an autobiography, an objective study of Mexican history and psychology, a work of existential philosophy, and a tourist's guide, the "most vivid meanings," according to Wilson, "emerge as the work of a poet exploring the absence of a meaningful life, a defense of poetry and its values." Pete Hamill, writing in *Esquire,* asserted that the book "explained the Mexican character and identity both to the world and to other Mexicans." The work has also been viewed as a seminal analysis on United States-Mexican relations. More than 40 years after it was first published, *The New Yorker* called *The Labyrinth of Solitude* "the most influential book on the differing characters of these neighboring countries."

After living abroad for 11 years, Paz returned to Mexico and wrote two of his most impressive books, *El arco y la lyra* (1956, *The Bow and the Lyre*) and *Piedra del sol* (1957, *Sun Stone*). *The Bow and the Lyre,* according to Jaime Alazraki's *World Literature Today* review, attempted to resolve the existential paradox of language: "How does language, which has separated man from the world, become a bridge between man and the world? The answer is of course through poetry, and *The Bow and the Lyre* is a meditation on the powers of poetry in the pursuit of that magical reunion." *Sun Stone,* which was written as a single circular sentence of 584 lines—a number based on the circular Aztec calendar, "can be viewed as an important precursor of the innovative work of Carlos Fuentes, **Gabriel Garcia Marquez, Julio Cortazar,** and other writers of the celebrated 'El boom' of the 1960s," suggested Sven Birkets in *The New Republic.* "Sunstone is, like so many of Paz's longer poems, a lyrically discursive exploration of time and memory, of erotic love, of art and writing, of myth and mysticism."

After another stop in Paris in the early 1960s, the 48-year-old Paz was appointed to the post of Mexican ambassador to India. During his six-year stay, he became an avid student of Eastern philosophy, evidence of which can be seen in his major poetic work of the period, *Landera este (1962–1968).* Known in English as *Eastern Slope (1962–1968),* this work was an experimental collection of meditations on love, reading, and poetry. "When I was ambassador to India," Paz stated in an interview with *New Perspectives Quarterly* editor Nathan Gardels, "I came to learn that all the great thinkers of the Oriental tradition came from India. . . . What the Indians tried to do many centuries ago was to construct a critique of reality. They believed that reality was nothingness. The real—Brahma, Nirvana—was beyond apparent reality. I have long felt that the West needed to make a similar critique of time."

## Resigns from Government Service

Paz's career as a diplomat ended abruptly in 1968, when he resigned his Indian post in protest against the Mexican government-supported massacre of 340 student demonstrators in the Plaza de Tres Culturas, Tlatelolco, before the opening of the Olympic Games in Mexico City. *Posdata* (published in English as *The Other Mexico: Critique of the Pyramid*)—a postscript to *The Labyrinth of Solitude* that was issued in 1970—specified the reasons for his resignation and offered an analysis of the communication problems that led to the massacre. While Paz's argumentative tone angered critics of various political persuasions, the book was a best-seller and was reprinted in 14 editions by the end of the 1970s.

Paz traveled extensively throughout the remainder of the decade, accepting teaching appointments at the University of Texas, Pittsburgh University, Cambridge, and Harvard. In addition to maintaining his usual prolific writing pace, he also founded *Vuelta,* a well-respected literary magazine devoted to introducing European thought and writing to Latin American intellectuals.

One of Paz's more experimental works, *El mono gramático* (1974, *The Monkey Grammarian*), also emerged from this period. It received considerable attention from critics interested in its linguistic subject matter. "This exceedingly curious book," Keith Botsford commented in *The New York Times Book Review,* "is an extended meditation on the nature of language. . . . [Paz] ponders the paradox by which words cancel out words, images destroy images, sex creates and annihilates, and the very variety of nature defeats its own identification. . . . Written in the evening of a long and brilliant poetic career, it is an old man's book. It looks back to the erotic; it contemplates the death of forms and language; it offers the wisdom of one about to drop out of time."

## Awarded Nobel Prize in Literature

Paz continued to write extensively in the 1980s and into the 1990s. He also revised and edited various collections of his life's work. Over the course of his career Paz had received numerous national and international awards, including the Miguel de Cervantes Prize from Spain in 1982 and the Wilhelm Heinse Medal from Germany in 1984. In 1990 he was honored with a Nobel Prize in Literature. Paz's selection by the Swedish Academy of Letters for his work's "sensuous intelligence and humanistic integrity" was thought by many to be overdue. Peruvian novelist **Mario Vargas Llosa** praised the selection of Paz for the award: "I admire him a lot. I think it's very well deserved. He's a great poet and a great essayist. He's also defended freedom and democracy, which is important and very unusual for Latin American intellectuals."

## SELECTED PUBLISHED WORKS:

### Poetry

*Luna silvestre,* Fábula, 1933.
*¡No pasaran!,* Simbad, 1936.
*Raíz del hombre,* Simbad, 1937.
*Bajo tu clara sombra y otros poemas sobre España,* Españolas, 1937, revised edition, Tierra Nueva, 1941.
*Entre la piedra y la flor,* Nueva Voz, 1938.
*Libertad bajo palabra,* Tezontle, 1949.
*¿Aguila o sol?* Tezontle, 1951, 2nd edition, 1973; translated by Eliot Weinberger as *Aguila o*

*sol/Eagle or Sun?* (bilingual edition), October House, 1970, revised translation by Weinberger published under same title, New Directions, 1976.

*Semillas para un himno,* Tezontle, 1954.

*Piedra de sol,* Tezontle, 1957; translated by Muriel Rukeyser as *Sun Stone/Peidra de sol* (bilingual edition), New Directions, 1963; translated by Peter Miller as *Sun-Stone,* Toronto, Contact, 1963; translated by Donald Gardner as *Sun Stone,* New York, Cosmos, 1969.

*La estación violenta,* Fondo de Cultura Económica, 1958, reprinted 1978.

*Agua y viento,* Ediciones Mito, 1959.

*Libertad bajo palabra: obra poetica, 1935–1958,* Fondo de Cultura Económica, 1960, revised edition, 1968.

*Salamandra (1958–1961),* J. Mortiz, 1962, 3rd edition, 1975.

*Selected Poems of Octavio Paz* (bilingual edition), translated by Muriel Rukeyser, Indiana University Press, 1963.

*Viento entero,* Caxton, 1965.

*Blanco,* J. Mortiz, 1967, 2nd edition, 1972; translated by Muriel Rukeyser as *Blanco,* The Press, 1974.

*Disco visuales,* Era, 1968.

*Ladera este (1962–1968),* J. Mortiz, 1969, 3rd edition, 1975.

*La centena (Poemas: 1935–1968),* Seix Barral, 1969, 2nd edition, 1972.

*Topoemas,* Era, 1971.

*Vuelta,* El Mendrugo, 1971.

*Poemas (1935–1975),* Seix Barral, 1979.

*Octavio Paz: Poemas recientes,* Institución Cutural de Cantabria de la Diputación Provincial de Santander, 1981.

*Selected Poems,* edited by Eliot Weinberger, translated by G. Aroul and others, New Directions, 1984.

*Cuatro chopos/The Four Poplars* (bilingual edition), translated by Eliot Weinberger, Center for Edition Works, 1985.

*The Collected Poems, 1957–1987: Bilingual Edition,* New Editions, 1987.

## Prose

*El laberinto de la soledad,* Cuadernos Americanos, 1950, revised edition, Fondo de Cultura Económica, 1959, reprinted, 1980; translated by Lysander Kemp as *The Labyrinth of Solitude: Life and Thought in Mexico,* Grove, 1961.

*El arco y la lira: El poema; La revelación poética; Poesía e historia,* Fondo de Cultura Económica, 1956, 2nd edition, 1967, 3rd edition, 1972; translated by Ruth L. C. Simms as *The Bow and the Lyre: The Poem, Poetic Revelation, and Poetry and History,* University of Texas Press, 1973, reprinted, 1977, 2nd edition, McGraw-Hill, 1975.

*Las peras del olmo,* Universidad Nacional Autónoma de México, 1957, revised edition, Seix Barral, 1971, 3rd edition, 1978.

*Los signos en rotación,* Sur, 1965.

*Puertas al campo,* Universidad Nacional Autónoma de México, 1966.

*Corriente alterna,* Siglo Veintiuno Editores, 1967, reprinted, 1980; translated by Helen R. Lane as *Alternating Current,* Viking, 1973.

*Conjunciones y Disjunciones,* J. Mortiz, 1969, 2nd edition, 1978; translated by Helen R. Lane as *Conjunctions and Disjunctions,* Viking, 1974.

*México: La última década,* Institute of Latin American Studies, University of Texas, 1969.

*Posdata,* Siglo Veintiuno, 1970; translated by Lysander Kemp as *The Other Mexico: Critique of the Pyramid,* Grove, 1972.

*Los signos en rotacion y otros ensayos,* edited and with a prologue by Carlos Fuentes, Alianza, 1971.

*Traducción: Literatura y literalidad,* Tusquets, 1971.

*El signo y el garabato,* J. Mortiz, 1973.

*La búsqueda del comienzo: Escritos sobre el surrealismo,* Fundamentos, 1974, 2nd edition, 1980.

*El mono gramático,* Seix Barral, 1974; translated by Helen R. Lane and as *The Monkey Grammarian,* Seaver, 1981.

*Los hijos del limo: Del romanticismo a la vanguadia,* Seix Barral, 1974; translated by Rachel Phillips as *Children of the Mire: Modern Poetry from Romanticism to the Avant-Garde,* Harvard University Press, 1974.

*The Siren and the Seashell, and Other Essays on Poets and Poetry,* translated by Lysander Kemp and Margaret Sayers Peden, University of Texas Press, 1976.

*El ogro filantrópico: Historia y politica, 1971–1978,* J. Mortiz, 1979.

*In/mediaciones,* Seix Barral, 1979.

*Sor Juana Ines de la Cruz; o, Las trampas de la fe,* Seix Barral, 1982; translated by Margaret Sayers Peden as *Sor Juana; or, The Traps of Faith,* Harvard University Press, 1988.

*Sombras de obras: Arte y literatura,* Seix Barral, 1983.

*Tiempo nublado,* Seix Barral, 1984; translated by Helen R. Lane as *On Earth, Four or Five Worlds: Reflections on Contemporary History,* Harcourt, 1985.

*Arbol adento,* Seix Barral, 1987; published as *A Tree Within,* New Directions, 1988.

*Convergences: Essays on Art and Literature,* translated by Helen R. Lane, Harcourt, 1987.

## SOURCES:

### Books

*Contemporary Literary Criticism,* Gale, Volume 3, 1975; Volume 4, 1975; Volume 6, 1976; Volume 10, 1979; Volume 19, 1981; Volume 51, 1989.

*Hispanic Writers,* edited by Bryan Ryan, Detroit, Gale, 1991.

Wilson, Jason, *Octavio Paz,* Twayne, 1986.

### Periodicals

*America,* January 26, 1991, pp. 61–3.
*Esquire,* March, 1991, pp. 46–8.
*Kosmos,* 5–6, Autumn-Winter, 1980.
*New Perspective Quarterly,* Winter, 1991, pp. 36–41; Spring 1992, pp. 4–9.
*New Republic,* March 14, 1988, pp. 36–9.
*New Yorker,* December 27, 1993, pp. 57–8.
*New York Times Book Review,* December 27, 1981, p. 8.
*Washington Post,* October 12, 1990, pp. A4-A5.
*World Literature Today,* Autumn, 1982, pp. 607–12.

—*Sketch by Jason Gallman*

# Cesar Pelli
## 1926-

### Argentine American architect and educator

Acclaimed by the American Institute of Architects (AIA) in 1991 as one of the ten most influential living American architects, Cesar Pelli has designed some of the most remarkable buildings—ranging from high-rise office towers to private homes—in the late 20th century. Chief among his award-winning achievements are the San Bernardino City Hall in San Bernardino, California; the Pacific Design Center, Phases I and II in Los Angeles, California; the United States Embassy in Tokyo, Japan; and the World Financial Center and Winter Garden at Battery Park, New York, which has been hailed as one of the ten best works of American architecture designed since 1980.

Though Pelli trained as a modern architect in the 1950s and was influenced by Eero Saarinen, he remains unclassifiable. His structures have been praised by Douglas Davis in a 1986 *Newsweek* article as "lyrical, technically sophisticated buildings that are neither 'modern' nor 'postmodern.' Each attempts to please on many levels at once, captivating clients and public but frustrating critics."

Pelli was born on October 12, 1926, in Tucumán, Argentina. He studied architecture at the University of Tucumán, earning his Bachelor's of Architecture in 1949. After graduating, Pelli married fellow student Diana Balmori, who has become an accomplished landscape and urban designer and who founded the firm Balmori Associates. For the next two years Pelli served as director of design at OFEMPE, a government organization sponsoring and building subsidized housing in Tucumán. In 1952, an Institute of International Education scholarship led Pelli to the University of Illinois School of Architecture in Champagne-Urbana, where he earned a Master's degree in Architecture in 1954.

### Influenced by Saarinen

For the next ten years, Pelli worked as a designer with the firm of Eero Saarinen & Associates in Bloomfield Hills, Michigan, and Hamden, Connecticut. With Saarinen—whom Pelli credits as one of his greatest influences along with Le Corbusier—he served as project designer for the TWA Terminal Building at JFK Airport, New York, and the Morse and Stiles Colleges at Yale University. Though he had briefly returned to Argentina to teach architectural design at his alma mater, Universidad Nacional de Tucumán in 1960, Pelli became a U.S. citizen in 1964.

The same year, Pelli took the position of director and vice president of design with Daniel, Mann, Johnson, & Mendenhall (DMJM) in Los Angeles. In 1968, he served as partner for design at Gruen Associates in Los Angeles and for two of his eight years with Gruen, Pelli was a visiting professor at the University of California. During this period, Pelli designed several award-winning projects, including the San Bernardino City Hall, the Commons of Columbus in Indiana, the Pacific Design Center, and the U.S. Embassy in Tokyo.

### Founds Own Architectural Firm

In 1977 Pelli moved to Connecticut to become the Dean of the School of Architecture at Yale University. That same year, he founded Cesar Pelli & Associates in New Haven with his wife Diana and Fred W. Clarke. Since the firm's inception, Pelli has designed each of its projects, although he actively solicits input from the more than 60 architects and designers who are employed in his studio. In 1984, he resigned his post at Yale, devoting full attention to his firm, but continues to lecture on architecture.

One of the jewels in Pelli's crown of large-scale design is the World Financial Center and Winter

Garden at Battery Park City in Manhattan. Begun in 1991, this project features four office towers, ranging in height from 34 to 51 stories; the Winter Garden; and a 3.5 acre landscaped public plaza. Other gems in Pelli's portfolio include the expansion and renovation of the Museum of Modern Art in New York City; the North Carolina Blumenthal Performing Arts Center in Charlotte; the Arnoff Center for the Arts in Cincinnati; the Francis Lehman Loeb Art Center at Vassar College; Herring Hall at Rice University; and the Boyer Center for Molecular Medicine at Yale University. Commenting on Pelli's design of Carnegie Hall Tower, Douglas Davis has pointed out in *Newsweek*, that "[despite] the vast discrepancy in their sizes, the new skyscraper and the earthbound . . . hall seem of a piece. Over and again, Pelli's buildings defer—despite their ingenuity—to their sites and to their context. His architecture is unfailingly humane and courtly."

This observation corresponds with Pelli's own philosophy, which he articulated in the August 1988 issue of *Architectural Digest:* "We should not judge a building by how beautiful it is in isolation, but instead by how much better or worse that particular place . . . has become by its addition. If the city has not gained by the addition, we should seriously question the design and the building itself, no matter how beautiful and theoretically correct it may be." Other noteworthy buildings designed by Cesar Pelli & Associates include the Norwest Center, Minneapolis, Minnesota; Nations Bank Corporate Center and Founders Hall in Charlotte; the Mathematics Building and Lecture Hall at the Institute for Advanced Study in Princeton; North Terminal at Washington National Airport; and the Physics and Astronomy Building at University of Washington/Seattle.

### Selected to Design Malaysian Twin Towers

In 1994 construction began on twin office towers in Kuala Lumpur, Malaysia, to be completed in 1996. Cesar Pelli & Associates will serve as design consultant to the architect-of-record, Kuala Lumpur City Centre (KLCC) Berhad Architectural Division, as well as a host of other U.S., Canadian, and Malaysian firms on an architectural project which will ultimately surpass the Sears Tower in Chicago as the world's tallest building. The office towers are the first phase of a multi-billion dollar development project situated on a 97-acre site in Kuala Lumpur City Centre. Petronas, Malaysia's national oil and gas company that owns 51 percent of KLCC, will occupy the towers.

In his distinguished career as an architect, Pelli has been the recipient of numerous awards from such institutions as the American Academy of Arts and Letters, the American Institute of Architects, the National Academy of Design, and the International Academy of Architecture. He has been awarded the 1995 AIA Gold Medal and the Charles Bulfinch Award; in addition, he is the only architect to have received a Connecticut State Arts Award and is among one of the few American architects to receive First Class licensure in Japan. Several honorary degrees have been bestowed upon Pelli, including an honorary doctorate from the Pratt Institute in New York City.

Perhaps Pelli's greatest reward, however, is to explore one of his completed structures; as he stated in his 1988 *Architectural Digest* essay, "[there] is nothing quite so pleasurable for me as to visit my buildings when they're finished and occupied. It is like being part of a miracle taking place. Months and even years of caring and dreaming become a reality."

## SELECTED PUBLISHED WORKS:

"Conversation: Cesar Pelli on Architectural Technology," *Architectural Record,* August 1979.

*Yale Seminars in Architecture,* editor, New Haven, Connecticut, 1979–1980.

"Skyscrapers," *Perspecta* (New Haven), January 1982.

"Architectural Form and the Tradition of Building," *Via* (Philadelphia), November 1984.

"Pieces of the City," *Architectural Digest,* August 1988.

*Cesar Pelli: Buildings and Projects 1965–1990,* New York, 1990.

"Four Buildings Responsive to Their Critical Surroundings," *Architecture + Urbanism* (Tokyo), January 1993.

Contributor to periodicals and scholarly journals, including *A + U, Architectural and Engineering News, Architectural Design, Architectural Digest, Baumeister, Controspazio, Designers West, Japan Architect, The Journal of the University of Pennsylvania School of Architecture, Progressive Architecture, San Francisco Bay Architects' Review, The Yale Architectural Journal,* and *Young Architects Forum.*

## SOURCES:

### Books

*Contemporary Architects,* 3rd edition, edited by Muriel Emanuel, New York, St. James Press, 1994, pp. 738–41.

*The Encyclopedia of American Architecture,* 2nd edition, edited by Robert T. Packard, New York, McGraw-Hill, 1995, pp. 475–79.

### Periodicals

*Architectural Digest,* August 1988, pp. 29–32, 36; July 1990, pp. 124–27, 178; August 1991, pp. 178–79.

*Architectural Record,* August 1991, pp. 100–07.
*Civil Engineering,* July 1994, pp. 63–65.
*Newsweek,* August 4, 1986, p. 61.

**Other**

Additional information for this profile was obtained from biographical materials acquired from Cesar Pelli & Associates Inc. Architects, 1995.

—*Sketch by Christopher B. Tower*

# Elizabeth Peña
## 1959-
### Cuban American actress

*Elizabeth Peña*

Her performances in movies such as *Down and Out in Beverly Hills, La Bamba,* and *Jacob's Ladder* and in the television shows *I Married Dora* and *Shannon's Deal* have won Elizabeth Peña respect and recognition. While she has always been perceived as sexy, directors are realizing that she is also extraordinarily versatile: Peña has been hilarious in some roles and serious and somber in others. Hard work and determination, combined with a gift for acting and a striking face, have made Peña a sought-after actress.

The first daughter of actor, writer, and director Mario Peña and producer Estella Marguerita Toirac Peña, Peña was named after the city in which she was born on September 23, 1959: Elizabeth, New Jersey. It was in this city that the family lived while Mario studied drama at Columbia University. Despite their affection for the city and the United States, the young family went back to Cuba four months after Peña's birth. The Cuban Revolution was new and promising, and they wanted to rejoin their families during what seemed to be an exciting time.

Unfortunately, Mario was imprisoned when he returned home; he had written a poem which the government considered to be "antisystem." When he was able to talk himself out of prison, he found that he had no choice but to flee the country and return to the United States. Estella Marguerita, Peña, and her younger sister, Tania, were not allowed to follow him and leave Cuba until 1968, when Peña was nine years old. Even as they were ready to board their plane, the officials harassed the family; their papers were in English, and no one was willing to acknowledge their authority. Finally, one official waved them through the red tape. Although, as Peña recalled in a *People* interview with Tim Allis and Nancy Matsumoto, the plane's "motors were running," Peña, her mother, and her sister, made their flight.

### Family Reunited in United States

When the family was reunited and settled in New York, the elder Peñas' careers began to take off. Mario founded New York City's Latin American Theater Ensemble with Estella, and they both became respected figures in New York's theater scene. Elizabeth owes her love of acting as well as her determination to succeed as an actor to her parents. She told an *Interview* contributor in 1987, "My father and mother are the biggest influences in my life. They've been able to survive as actors in the theater in New York and have instilled that same sense of survival in me." While she was inspired by her parents, Peña also remembers that her mother did not want her to become an actress. When she was accepted to New York's renowned School of Performing Arts, Peña recalled in her *People* interview, her mother fell to her knees as she wailed, "If you become an actress, you'll kill me." Peña retorted, "Well, you better start arranging your funeral." Aside from graduating from the School of the Performing Arts, Peña also studied acting with Curt Dempster at the Ensemble Studio Theater and Endre Hules at La Mama ETC. In addition to acting, she studied clowning with Mark Stolzenberg and speech and voice with Lynn Masters. Despite her initial dismay, Estella soon began to support her daughter's efforts to become an actress.

Peña's mother was not the only one to be persuaded by her daughter's determination to utilize her gift for acting. Peña aggressively pursued roles in motion pictures and on stage. In 1979 she played Aurelita in the movie *El Super,* and in 1980 she landed a part in *Times Square.* Her next role was that of Rita in the movie *They All Laughed,* which she followed with a number of stage appearances in New York. Included among these many roles were the parts of Jesse in *Dog Lady,* Maria in *Bring on the Night,* Cynthia in *Shattered Image,* Teresa in *La Morena,* Juliet in *Romeo and Juliet,* Beba in *Night of the Assassins,* and Teresa in *Italian-American Reconciliation.* By 1984, Peña had landed another movie role, that of Liz (Rubén Blades's girlfriend) in *Crossover Dreams.*

### Acting Career Launched

At this point in her career, Peña felt she was ready to take on Hollywood. She moved to the famous town and began to search for roles. The casting director for *Down and Out in Beverly Hills* (1986), a movie starring Richard Dreyfuss and Bette Midler, found himself deluged with photos and messages from Peña. Although she had just arrived in Hollywood and had no agent, Peña was determined to get the part, and determined to do it by herself. By the time she was given a screen test, Peña was almost broke. She gave the test her best, and the casting director was impressed. He cast Peña in her first high-profile role as the Salvadoran maid, Carmen. Peña's sexy as well as funny performance in *Down and Out in Beverly Hills* received favorable attention, and she was soon an actress in demand.

This success made 1987 a very busy year for Peña. She won a role in another hit movie, *La Bamba*; she portrayed the abused yet loyal wife, Rosie, of Richie Valens's elder brother. Later that year, Peña earned a role in a television situation-comedy about a man who marries his Central American maid so she won't be deported, *I Married Dora.* While Jeff Jarvis, writing in *People,* asserted that the show should receive a grade of "D", he also acknowledged Peña's talent. "Only one small asset rescues this sludge-brained idea from an instant F: Elizabeth Peña's charm." Still in 1987, Peña excelled in another movie, Steven Spielberg's *Batteries Not Included.*

Although she took a break from acting after she married William Stephan Kibler on July 2, 1988, Peña stayed busy. In 1988, she accepted a number of awards, including the Hispanic Women's Council Woman of the Year Award, the New York Image Award, the U.S. Congress Congressional Award, and the Nosotros Golden Eagle Award. Peña's career picked up pace again in 1990, with what a *Newsweek* contributor calls a "warm and gritty" performance as Jezzie, the girlfriend of Jacob Singer (Tim Robbins) in the eerie movie *Jacob's Ladder.* That same year, she was cast as a client/secretary of a heartbroken lawyer in the television show *Shannon's Deal.* Tom Shales, writing in the *Washington Post* and quoted in *People,* maintained that Peña's "so assertive and gutsy.... Maybe the show should be about *her.*"

The *Post*'s critic had a point. While Peña has brightened many productions, including the television shows *Hill Street Blues, TJ Hooker, Cagney and Lacey, As the World Turns, Tough Cookies* and *Saturday Night Live,* the made-for-television movies *Drug Wars: The Camarena Story* and *Found Money,* and the movies *Blue Steel* and *Fat Chance,* she has yet to find a role in which she is the star. She is not discouraged, however. "I like who I am," she tells Allis and Matsumoto. "I don't have a problem with it; I think everybody else does. That's part of *their* growing up." She went on to add: "I've never thought of [being Hispanic] as an obstacle. I think it's good. There are certainly enough five-foot-seven blonds."

## SELECTED VIDEOGRAPHY:

*El Super,* 1979.
*Times Square,* 1980.
*They All Laughed,* 1981.
*Thief,* 1981.
*Crossover Dreams,* 1985.
*Down and Out in Beverly Hills,* 1986.
*La Bamba,* 1987.
*Vibes,* 1988.
*Blue Steel,* 1990.
*Jacob's Ladder,* 1990.
*The Waterdance,* 1991.

## SOURCES:

### Books

*Contemporary Theater, Film and Television,* Volume 5, Gale, 1988.

### Periodicals

*Interview,* April, 1987, p. 34.
*Más,* fall, 1990, p. 14.
*Newsweek,* November 12, 1990, pp. 77–78.
*New York,* February 3, 1986, pp. 82–83; April 16, 1990, pp. 97–98.
*People,* September 30, 1985, p. 10; October 19, 1987, p. 15; May 13, 1991, pp. 107–108.

—*Sketch by Ronie-Richele Garcia-Johnson*

# Federico Peña
## 1947-
### Hispanic American politician and attorney

Federico Peña is a noted Hispanic American public official who served two terms in the Colorado General Assembly and two as mayor of Denver, Colorado. In 1992 he became U.S. Secretary of Transportation under U.S. president Bill Clinton. In this capacity, he has been responsible for several notable and controversial rulings and decisions.

Peña was part of the "new generation" of socially-conscious Democrats who joined the administrative branch of the Federal Government after President Clinton's election. As with so many other politicians beginning to make their mark nationally, he felt that his role was not merely to keep the system going, but to influence its direction and power in a manner that reflected his personal ideology.

In a March 1993 speech quoted in *Nation's Cities Weekly,* two months after joining Clinton's cabinet, Peña said: "My responsibility as the new secretary of transportation is a very simple one; to bring a new perspective to transportation that says that transportation investments are more than simply building bridges and viaducts and building highways—it's trying to bring in the concerns of the environment as we balance our transportation programs. It is also investing in high technology like high-speed rail, as other nations are doing."

Born on March 15, 1947, to Gustavo Peña and Lucia Farias, in Laredo, Texas, and raised in Brownsville, Federico Fabian Peña was the third of six children, the final three being triplets. The Peña family was stoutly middle-class: Gustavo was a broker for a Texas cotton manufacturer, and both parents taught their children their own hard-won values of respectfulness, loyalty, and perseverance. The Peña children were expected to achieve, and they did. All completed college; two became lawyers, two became teachers, and one a comptroller.

Federico attended St. Joseph's Academy, a local Catholic high school, from which he graduated with honors in 1965. After graduation, he entered the University of Texas at Austin. This was a highly charged time to be a college student in the United States. College campuses across the country were heavily politicized by radical faculty and student organizations, and Austin was no exception. This period of Peña's life seems to have set the pattern for his lifelong political leanings. While studying for his degree, Peña joined demonstrations against the Vietnam war and campaigned for liberal candidates for

*Federico Peña*

state offices. He graduated in 1969 and promptly enrolled in the University of Texas School of Law.

In 1972, the year he received his Juris Doctor, Peña moved to Denver, Colorado, where his brother Alfredo was already practicing law. From 1972 to 1974, he worked as a staff lawyer for the Mexican-American Legal Defense and Educational Fund, where he litigated police brutality and voting rights issues. He later became a legal adviser for the Chicano Education Project, where for four years he worked for bilingual education in the public schools and better school funding in Hispanic neighborhoods. In 1973, the brothers Alfredo and Federico opened their own law office.

### Begins Political Career

In 1978 the 31-year-old Peña successfully ran for a seat in the Colorado General Assembly. He held the position for two terms, during which he served on the House judiciary, legal services, rules, and finance committees. During his first term he was named outstanding House Democratic freshman by the Colorado social action committee.

Peña ran for mayor of Denver in 1983. He was thought to have little chance: his opponent was a 14-year incumbent, and Hispanics made up just 18 percent of Denver's population. An early poll gave him only three percent of registered voters. But the sitting Mayor, William McNichols Jr., had a scandal-ridden administration and was locked in a seething controversy over the way the Mayor's office had responded to a paralyzing snowstorm. Peña ran a positive campaign and put together a coalition of advocacy groups and intellectuals who campaigned him into office by a narrow victory.

Peña's first term was tempestuous. Unaccustomed to public office, he found it difficult to adjust to public criticism. He proposed an ambitious policy of new construction and public investment. One proposal was a new convention center at Denver's Union Station, but it was ultimately defeated by vigorous opposition and a major downturn in the city's economy.

By the end of his first term, Peña's popularity in the polls was extremely low; at one point his Republican opponent in the 1987 campaign led by 22 percentage points and received the endorsement of both of Denver's major newspapers. It was only after waging an extremely negative publicity campaign that Peña, with his strong base of support in the black and Hispanic communities, was able to eke out a victory by a two-percent margin.

Ironically, Peña became the target of a recall campaign shortly after the election over the same issue that had ruined his predecessor. While he was vacationing in Mexico in December 1987, Denver was immobilized by a blizzard. The city failed to clear the snow in many areas; parts of Denver were still unsafe for travel as late as February. Peña was a natural target for the rage of citizens' groups with whom he was already unpopular. The recall petition fell 2,000 signatures short of forcing a new election.

During his second term, Peña's public works program began to make progress. He tirelessly promoted the idea of constructing a new airport as a way of making Denver into a major regional center of trade. The new airport met with much opposition from groups who complained that it was unneeded and—at a projected cost of $1.7 billion—too expensive. Denver's existing airport, Stapleton, was a major hub for United Airlines, which opposed the idea on the grounds that a new airport would bring additional expense and unwanted competition. Stapleton, critics argued, was underutilized at the time, and a new airport was simply unnecessary.

But Peña had his way, and construction on Denver International Airport began on 53 square miles of prairie 20 miles out of town. At the same time, Peña's renewed efforts for a new convention center found success. He also fought for and won a public bond issue which raised $330 million for various infrastructure repairs and new public works. Here he showed his interest in low-pollution transportation issues, promoting the use of deoxygenated fuels in city motor vehicles.

Buoyed by his successes and an improvement in the general economy, Peña's popularity improved. However, he did not seek a third term, citing a desire to spend more time with his family. In May of 1988, he married Ellen Hart, a world-class distance runner and fellow attorney whom he had met four years earlier. They eventually had two daughters, Nelia Joan and Cristina Lucila.

After leaving office, he founded the financial management firm Peña Investment Advisors, which became known for hiring top-notch Hispanic legal talent and was also involved in a legal consultancy. He also served on a Colorado state panel that drew up a long-term statewide transportation plan with emphasis on mass transit and bicycles.

### Appointed Secretary of Transportation

In 1992, after Clinton won the presidential election, Peña joined his "transition team" for transportation issues, and was later nominated to be Clinton's Secretary of Transportation. Clinton was reportedly impressed by Peña's success with the Denver International Airport and his suitably liberal theories of transportation policy had become well-known. Clinton had also promised an ethnically diverse cabinet and Peña was by this time one of the most prominent Hispanic Democrats in the country.

At Peña's confirmation hearing, he won boosters in the airline industry and critics in the automotive industry by opposing airline reregulation and advocating policies that would boost domestic airlines in the global marketplace, while favoring higher fuel economy regulations, stricter automotive safety standards, and mass transit. He was confirmed without serious opposition, endorsed even by some former critics who applauded his conviction even though they had opposed him on specific issues.

Peña was one of the most visible and often-reported secretaries of transportation in the history of the office. He was involved in several high-profile aviation issues, including foreign investment in USAir, formal complaints against Japan and Australia for restrictions on U.S. air carriers and advocacy of tax and loan guarantees for the major airlines. He also promoted air safety issues such as an investigation into Boeing 757 wing turbulence. At the same time, Peña earned the unending enmity of the automotive industry by pushing a piece of legislation called the Intermodal Surface Transportation Efficiency Act, which encourages long-range municipal plans for alternate modes of transportation such as mass transit, bicycling, and walking.

In 1994, Peña overrode the recommendations of his own department's engineers and issued a finding that General Motors' C/K-model pickup trucks—which had been built in great numbers over some 15 years with side-mounted fuel tanks—constituted a safety hazard in side collisions and should be recalled. General Motors fought the finding with all the resources at its disposal, including a personal lawsuit against Peña. The other two U.S. automakers—Ford and Chysler—publicly backed GM.

The highly charged issue was brought to an end by a settlement in which the Department of Transportation dropped its finding that the trucks were defective, and GM agreed to pay some $51 million, matched by $27 million from the National Highway Traffic Safety Administration, for a program of research and investment in unrelated automotive safety issues, including fire safety, public education, and drug and alcohol-related driving issues.

Peña was also kept in the news by the continued efforts to open Denver International Airport. Peña's name was tied to the airport, and although he had nothing substantial to do with its construction, its technical problems—as well as its vast expense—became a source of nationwide amusement and skepticism. The airport eventually opened in early 1995, more than a year behind schedule and billions of dollars over budget. Many critcs concede, however, that the facility is state-of-the-art.

## SOURCES:

### Books

Meier, Matt. S., *Mexican-American Biographies: A Historical Dictionary, 1836–1987,* Westport, Connecticut, Greenwood Press, 1988.

### Periodicals

*Automotive News,* December 5, 1994.
*Nation's Cities Weekly,* January 4, 1993 p. 1.
*Newsweek,* August 22, 1994, p. 38.
*New York Times,* December 5, 1994, p. A16.
*Wall Street Journal,* February 11, 1993, p. A7.

—*Sketch by Joel Simon*

# Rosie Perez
## 19??-

**Puerto Rican American actress, dancer, and choreographer**

Rosie Perez, whose closest revelation of her age has been "under 25,"—in 1992—claims to be having a hard time sleeping these days—her career is not moving fast enough for her. In just a few short

*Rosie Perez*

years, she went from being a science student to becoming one of the most sought-after pop music choreographers in the industry and a rising actress. "I'm very happy with the way things are going for me right now," she relates in an interview with Frank Spotnitz for *Entertainment Weekly,* "but I still feel like they're going to slow. I want it all."

Rosa Mary Perez was born at Greenpoint Hospital in Brooklyn, New York, daughter of Ismael Serrano and Lydia Perez. Raised in Brooklyn's mostly Puerto Rican Bushwick district, Perez is one of ten brothers and sisters who grew up watching their parents dance "salsa" on weekends and holidays. Her mother was a singer in Puerto Rico, and music always filled the house. In her *Entertainment Weekly* interview, Perez reminisced: "Growing up with nine brothers and sisters was an early lesson in assertiveness training. In a family like that, you have to compete for attention."

A good student who excelled in science, Perez moved to Los Angeles at the age of 18 to attend college, where she studied marine biology as a biochemistry major. It was while dancing at a trendy Los Angeles latin club that she was first invited to dance on the television show *Soul Train.* After doing a couple of shows, Perez quit, but while she was there she met Louis Silas, Jr., senior vice president of black music at MCA Records. Silas asked if she wanted to be in a recording group, and although Perez declined, she kept in touch with him.

## Launches Choreography Career with Bobby Brown

One day Silas asked if she would choreograph one of his artists who was coming out with his third solo album. Silas wanted him to have a younger appeal and asked Perez to find some dancers who could dance "hip-hop" with him. Perez at first refused because she had no experience, but after hearing the music decided to go ahead. The artist's name was Bobby Brown and the project was a success.

After seeing Brown on the television program *Soul Train,* a new Motown recording group, the Boys, asked Perez to choreograph their show. With the double successes of Bobby Brown and The Boys, offers poured in. She and her partners, Heart & Soul, found themselves busy creating the stage and/or video choreographies for many artists, including Diana Ross and rappers Al. B. Sure, LL Cool J, Heavy D & the Boyz, and for such record labels as Motown, Polygram, and Capitol. The next step was the small screen, with Perez choreographing the Fox television program *In Living Color.* When a *GQ* contributor asked her to define her dancing style, Perez (who considers herself a better choreographer than a dancer) replied, "Clearness. Quickness. Difficult combinations. I'll never do a move for a four count—usually just a two and move on. That's what earns me respect with the club people." She then laughingly adds: "Here's my dancer's arrogance. I haven't seen anybody who can articulate hip-hop the way I do, in such a lean, crisp way, and still be authentic. There are a lot who try and do it, and it comes off very corny. I still got the flavor."

## Takes on Acting in *Do the Right Thing*

In her official "biography," Perez tells how her movie career was launched. "While I was choreographing The Boys, I was dancing at the Funky Reggae Club in Los Angeles. Spike Lee was having his birthday party there and the band EU was performing. The band asked me to dance on stage; afterwards Spike introduced himself to me. His partner, Monty Ross, gave me their phone number and asked me to call. When I told them that I was returning to Brooklyn in a couple of days, they started screaming and Spike said, 'This is fate.' I didn't know what he meant by that, because he never mentioned the possibility of a movie until a month later. When I told him I had to return for the new school semester in Los Angeles, he offered me the role of Tina in *Do the Right Thing.* Instead of finishing that semester, I decided to do the movie, and it changed my life."

In an interview with *Newsweek,* Perez described her movie debut experience as possibly the best and worst thing that happened to her. There was a nude scene involving an ice cube that, she has said, made her feel like she was "raped" by the camera. When Hispanic groups criticized her for promoting a stereo-type, Perez defended the film—"I was not portraying something that's not really out there"—but informed her agent she didn't want to play any "Tinas" in the future.

## Film Career Rapidly Progresses

By contrast, her role as Woody Harrelson's feisty girlfriend in the basketball-themed film *White Men Can't Jump,* was originally written for a white woman who'd gone to an Ivy League school. But writer/director Ron Shelton was so impressed by the instant chemistry between Perez and Harrelson that he hired her and, without making major changes to the script, the role was transformed from that of a Barnard graduate to a former Brooklyn disco queen. "It's time for us to break down the barriers," Perez maintained in a *USA Today* interview. "If it's a good role, it shouldn't matter what color you are."

In quick succession, Perez's acting credits went on to include the films *Untamed Heart* and *Night on Earth.* Television appearances include *21 Jump Street, Criminal Justice,* and a recurring role in the CBS series *WIOU.* With a successful acting career well under way, Perez concluded in a *Preview* interview: "Minorities can play regular roles too. And being a minority you have a responsibility to help other minorities along the way."

## SELECTED VIDEOGRAPHY:

*Do the Right Thing,* 1989.
*Criminal Justice,* 1990.
*Night on Earth,* 1991.
*White Men Can't Jump,* 1992.
*Untamed Heart,* 1993.

## SOURCES:

### Periodicals

*Entertainment Weekly,* April 3, 1992, p. 11.
*GQ,* August, 1992, pp. 49–58.
*Newsweek,* May 4, 1992, pp. 64–65.
*Preview,* April, 1992, p. 25.
*Rolling Stone,* May 14, 1992.

### Other

Biography of Perez, provided by Baker-Winokur-Ryder Public Relations.

*—Sketch by Elena Kellner*

# Javier Pérez de Cuéllar
## 1920-
### Peruvian diplomat

Javier Pérez de Cuéllar is a career diplomat who has spent most of his life living outside his native Peru. He was born January 19, 1920, in Lima, into a family descended from Spanish nobility. Pérez de Cuéllar's father, a prosperous businessman, died when the future diplomat was four. He studied at Roman Catholic schools and law at the Catholic University in Lima. While still a student in 1940, Pérez de Cuéllar was employed as a clerk in the Ministry of Foreign Relations. After receiving his law degree in 1943, he remained with the ministry. It was the beginning of a long career in service to his country.

### Career in Diplomatic Service

After joining the Peruvian diplomatic service in 1944, Pérez de Cuéllar was made first secretary of the Embassy in Paris. Two years later he was a member of Peru's delegation to the first session of the United Nations General Assembly. He went on to work in Peruvian embassies around the world, including those in Great Britain, Bolivia, and Brazil. He was promoted to ambassador in 1962 and served as director of various offices while concurrently working as a professor of diplomatic law at the Academia Diplomática del Peru and then as a professor of international relations at the Academia de Guerra Aérea del Peru. He wrote a manual on international law and a book that focuses on the issue of recognizing nations and governments from a diplomatic perspective. Both of Pérez de Cuéllar's books have been used as textbooks at the Academia Diplomática.

From 1964 to 1966, he was Peru's ambassador to Switzerland. Later he was the country's first ambassador to both Moscow and Poland. In 1971, Pérez de Cuéllar was appointed to the United Nations as Peru's permanent representative. During his tenure, he was involved in several difficult diplomatic relations problems. During the Cyprus crisis of 1974, Pérez de Cuéllar managed to convince the opposing factions—the Greek and Turkish leaders—to talk about their differences. The diplomat considered it one of his major achievements. In 1977, he became ambassador to Venezuela. There he remained for two years before returning to the United Nations in time to be involved in volatile issues developing between Afghanistan and Pakistan in April 1981. In October of the same year, Pérez de Cuéllar voluntarily retired from active service to his government. His career might have ended there had not a deadlock developed

*Javier Pérez de Cuéllar*

in the United Nations over who was to succeed Secretary General Kurt Waldheim.

### Became Secretary General

After much political infighting and squabbling among U.N. delegates and their countries, Pérez de Cuéllar was elected to the post of Secretary General. He was the least controversial choice at the time— "the candidate with the fewest strikes against him," Bernard D. Nossiter wrote in the *New York Times* in December 1981. As a Latin American, Pérez de Cuéllar was considered a representative of the third world who simultaneously had a Western cultural orientation.

When he was sworn into office on January 1, 1982, Pérez de Cuéllar headed a staff of 15,000 and earned a salary of $158,340 with a $22,500 hospitality allowance. In his first address to the General Assembly he said the difference in wealth between rich and poor nations was a betrayal of human rights and promised to promote the independence and integrity of the international civil service. While some critics complained that Pérez de Cuéllar was likely to maintain the status quo at the U.N. and little else, others praised him. An associate, quoted in the *Guardian Weekly,* said he was "an honorable, decent, dignified man, not strong, not terribly bright." It was pointed out that the post of Secretary General was ambiguous at best and Pérez de Cuéllar was stepping into a job that had been poorly defined by U.N.

regulations as well as past Secretary Generals' actions. "I didn't seek this job," he said at the time. "And it's important that everybody knows I won't seek another term, so that I can be independent enough to win the trust of the members and still speak out in defense of the Charter when I think this will be useful."

In early 1982, the *Christian Science Monitor* quoted Pérez de Cuéllar as well: "I am fully aware of the fact that I am not some kind of president of the world and that the U.N. is at the service of its member states. Some of those who clamor for moral leadership are the first to shout, 'Don't meddle in my affairs' when the U.N. objects to some of their own misdeeds." In April of the same year, Pérez de Cuéllar faced his first significant crisis as Secretary General: the Falkland Islands War between Great Britain and Argentina. Although his attempts at a peaceful resolution failed and war broke out, he was praised for leaving no stone unturned in trying to resolve the conflict without bloodshed. "The failure was not the result of his bumbling," Jeane J. Kirkpatrick stated. "He deserves credit for the effort if not the result. We can be proud . . . of the Secretary General." Also early in his tenure, Pérez de Cuéllar was praised for appointing women to key U.N. posts but criticized for dismissing the director of the Human Rights Division.

"I am a third-world man," he told the *New York Times* in July 1982. "But first of all I am a representative of 157 countries. I have to act in a way so that I am not only the representative of the third world." Contrary to his initial speech, Pérez de Cuéllar did serve a second five-year term as Secretary General until 1992. In 1990, Morton Kondracke reviewed his time in office for the *New Republic*. "Widely disparaged or given up for dead, the United Nations is suddenly alive again and doing useful work," Kondracke reported. "Last year it fielded an army of 8,000 soldiers, policemen, and civilians to get South Africa out of Namibia and Cuban troops out of Angola. . . . This year it monitored elections in Nicaragua, disarmed the contras, and commenced negotiations between the government and Communist rebels in El Salvador."

Kondracke described Pérez de Cuéllar as "cautious and undramatic, yet skillful and persistent. . . . By not giving up when the going was rough, by working at problems that seemed insoluble, by winning the confidence of people who trusted almost nobody else, by being in the right place when the dawn broke, and by knowing what to do afterward, Pérez de Cuéllar already is widely considered by most U.N.-watchers to be the second-most-effective secretary general ever (after Dag Hammarskjöld)." Senator Daniel Patrick Moynihan agreed with Kondracke's assessment. "Pérez de Cuéllar took an organization that had almost self-destructed and become irrelevant, and found a role for it that no one expected.

He's turned out to be the first secretary general of the post-cold war era."

One crowning achievement of his career was accepting the Nobel Peace Prize in 1988 on behalf of the U.N. peacekeeping forces. "Pérez de Cuéllar could have been Jesus Christ and five years ago he couldn't have accomplished anything," Joseph Fromm of the International Institute for Strategic Studies told Kondracke. "Now there's a shared interest in defusing conflict, and to his credit he has taken advantage of the opportunity with extraordinary skill." Pérez de Cuéllar did not seek a third term in office, Kondracke claimed, because he was ailing, had suffered a heart attack and undergone bypass surgery. "With a new era dawning when the U.N. might really become the world's peacemaking agency and problem-solving forum, it would seem to be time for a vigorous young person to take charge. On the other hand, if such a person cannot be agreed upon, the world body could do far worse than to make do a little longer with probably the best secretary general it's ever had."

In a 1992 article for *Time*, Bonnie Angelo noted that Pérez de Cuéllar's praise as a peacemaker was well deserved, "but his stewardship of the U.N. was flawed. He resented and resisted suggestions for change, taking them as personal criticisms. His most serious shortcoming during his decade in office was his unwillingness to bring the U.N. bureaucracy under control." His countrymen, however, saw Pérez de Cuéllar as a hero. In the 1994 Peruvian elections, he was touted as a possible candidate. The *Economist* reviewed his status in Peru in 1994. "His face, partially paralyzed, seems earnest and pained, never joyful. Even his closest allies admit he is a terrible speaker. And, a diplomat by profession, he has lived 50 years abroad. Yet suddenly he is being hailed as the man for Peru. Few people have had such a career: some Peruvians think of him as the former 'president of the world.'"

Pérez de Cuéllar speaks Spanish, English, and French. He is a member of numerous organizations, including the Sección Peruana de la Comisión Internacional de Juristas, the Instituto Interamericano de Estudios Jurídicos Internacionales, and the Sociedad Peruana de Derecho Internacional. During his long career, he has received awards and decorations from many countries including Peru, Argentina, Bolivia, Mexico, El Salvador, Italy, France, Japan, and West Germany. In 1975 he married the former Marcela Temple of Lima. He has a son and daughter from a previous marriage.

## SOURCES:

### Books

*Current Biography Yearbook 1982*, New York, H. W. Wilson Co., 1982.

**Periodicals**

*Christian Science Monitor,* January 11, 1982.
*Economist,* June 25, 1994, pp. 42–43.
*Guardian Weekly,* December 20, 1981.
*New Republic,* August 13, 1990, pp. 20–23.
*New York Times,* December 21, 1981; July 5, 1982.
*Time,* February 3, 1992, pp. 28–30.

　　　　　　　　　　　　*—Sketch by Kathe A. Conti*

# Adolfo Pérez Esquivel
## 1931-
### Argentine sculptor and human rights activist

Adolfo Pérez Esquivel is a sculptor known for his dedication to improving the social and economic conditions of the poor in Argentina. He was born in Buenos Aires, Argentina, November 26, 1931, the son of a coffee sales agent who immigrated to Argentina from Spain. He was young when his mother died. His father was away on business much of the time so Pérez Esquivel boarded at Roman Catholic schools. He was very religious and read many philosophical and religious books when he was young. Pérez Esquivel was inspired by the teachings of Mahatma Gandhi throughout his life. He also showed talent in the arts and continued his studies in art after his primary schooling.

Pérez Esquivel graduated from the National School of Fine Arts of Buenos Aires and La Plata in 1956. Within a few months of graduation, he married a musician, pianist, and composer, Amanda Pérez. They had three sons. He became a very successful sculptor and taught art and architecture in Argentina. His work became well known and he was awarded many prizes including the distinguished Premio La Nacion de Escultura. During Pérez Esquivel's youth, the unstable political and social atmosphere in Argentina was agitated by the dictatorial rule of **Juan Perón.** The year before Pérez Esquivel graduated from art school, a military coup seized control of the government and Perón was exiled to Spain. Many of Perón's supporters (Perónists) used violent tactics against the military *junta.*

### Active in Improving Economic Conditions

Because of his deep religious convictions, Pérez Esquivel felt an obligation to improve the conditions of the poor in Argentina. In the late 1960s the country was deteriorating and he began meeting with other intellectuals and religious groups to discuss ways to improve conditions using non-violent tactics. At a conference in Montevideo, Uruguay, in 1968, various community groups and the church met to discuss and study ways to accomplish this goal. Pérez Esquivel decided to protest the violent tactics used by the different factions and went on a hunger strike that lasted for almost two months in 1970.

At the next conference of the church and concerned citizens, Pérez Esquivel helped organize *Servicio Paz y Justicia (Service for Peace and Justice)* composed of Catholic activists who worked with the poor. He also organized a craft project in urban communities to assist the poor to become more self-sufficient. He joined a prayer group and he published *Paz y Justicia (Peace and Justice)*, a monthly magazine. In 1974 Pérez Esquivel was named general coordinator of the Service for Peace and Justice and he quit his teaching job to work full-time for the organization. He traveled throughout South America to encourage social change through non-violence. He was jailed in Brazil in 1975, and again the next year in Ecuador. He was arrested for "publicly accusing the governments of those nations of failing to respond to the needs of their people and for attributing crime and violence to poverty," according to *Nobel Prize Winners* (1987).

In 1973, Juan Perón was invited back to Argentina and was again elected president. The year after the election, he died and his wife Isabel Perón took over the presidency. After two chaotic years of economic and social disaster, the military removed her and Argentina was again ruled by a military *junta.* When Perónist guerrillas opposed the takeover, a vigilante group was formed by the conservative supporters of the military coup and an estimated 10,000 to 20,000 people disappeared—-either executed or put into prison without any charges or trials and no official records of the arrests.

Pérez Esquivel devoted much of his time to fight these injustices. He helped found two more organizations to look into the disappearances: the Permanent Assembly for Human Rights and the Ecumenical Movement for Human Rights. In 1977, Perez Esquivel was arrested and tortured for "subversive activities" and spent the next 13 months in prison. He was never charged and he never went to trial. Amnesty International adopted him as a prisoner of conscience. The Carter administration appealed to the Argentine government for his release. In May of 1978, he was released from jail and confined to his home for 14 months. In 1980, he resumed his previous activities, working for the Service for Peace and Justice. Pérez Esquivel was little known even in his own country—he preferred working behind the scenes.

## Awarded Nobel Peace Prize

In 1980, Pérez Esquivel was awarded the Nobel Peace Prize. He was awarded approximately $212,000, most of which he donated to help the needy in South America. Pérez Esquivel was chosen from 57 other individuals and 14 organizations who were also nominated for the prize. The citation issued by the Norwegian Nobel Committee when announcing his prize, was quoted in the *New York Times*. It stated: "Pérez Esquivel is among those Argentines who have shone a light in the darkness. He champions a solution of Argentina's grievous problems that dispenses with the use of violence, and is the spokesman of a revival of respect of human rights."

## SOURCES:

### Books

*Nobel Prize Winners,* edited by Tyler Wasson, New York, H.W. Wilson Company, 1987.

### Periodicals

*New York Times,* October 14, 1980, pp. 1, A14.

—*Sketch by Phyllis Noah*

# Benito Pérez Galdós
## 1843-1920
**Spanish novelist**

Benito Pérez Galdós wrote prolifically as a novelist and dramatist for several decades, earning great critical respect and a large readership. Many critics credit Galdós with having an enormous influence on Spanish-speaking novelists of the twentieth century. Galdós portrayed the diverse aspects of nineteenth-century Spain with detail and attention. His work moved Spanish scholar Salvador de Madariaga to state in *The Genius of Spain and Other Essays on Spanish Contemporary Literature* that "Galdós undoubtedly deserves to rank with the great novelists of the century." He also worked very successfully as a publisher for many years and won election to public office several times.

Galdós was born on May 10, 1843, in the Grand Canary Islands, a Spanish territory located off the coast of Africa. He grew up in the small town of Las Palmas, the last of ten children born to Dona Maria de los Dolores Galdós. Galdós' father, Sebastian Pérez, came to the Canary Islands to serve as a lieutenant colonel in the army, but his wife clearly influenced Galdós more in nature and appearance. Biographer Walter Pattison noted in *Benito Pérez Galdós* that "there are ways in which his mother's [Basque] heritage shows up in Benito: his Basque physique, his stubborn will, and his adherence to a well-ordered routine."

During his childhood, Galdós showed an affinity for music. He learned to play the piano and studied opera. His school work did not interest him as much, but his grades remained moderately high through his completion of secondary school in 1862. His mother exerted her considerable influence and convinced Galdós to leave the islands for Madrid to study law. He agreed and headed for Spain and the modern world.

## Life on the Mainland

In his first year of law school in 1863, Galdós studied a preliminary curriculum that he found moderately interesting. He grew weary of the law classes in subsequent years, however, and he simply stopped going to class. But while his enthusiasm for law school waned considerably, he spent much of his time in a literary and artistic club called the Atheneum, which he later called his "literary cradle." There he got his first exposure to high intellectual discourse on subjects ranging from the possible union of Spain and Portugal to the debate between idealism and realism. He also joined student movements against Queen Isabel II and was witness to many of the events of the failed revolution against the monarchy in 1866. His experiences during this time likely marked the birth of his anti-monarchy sentiments.

During his years as a student, Galdós also began to write for progressive journals that advocated the abolition of the monarchy and the remaking of contemporary Spain. He published his first work in 1865 in *La Nacion,* and over the next four years he contributed over 130 pieces of literary criticism, political commentary, and personal profiles of various famous figures. In 1867 he wrote *La Sombra* (*The Apparition*), but it did not appear in print until 1871, when the newspaper *El Debate* printed it in serial form. He also tried his hand as a dramatist, but none of his plays made it to the stage.

## Successful Novelist

Galdós became the editor of *El Debate* in 1871, but he quit two years later. His first novel to be published in book form—*Le fontana de oro*—had shown him where his literary strengths lay. In 1873 Galdós embarked on an ambitious literary project. Galdós started to write books at an amazing pace, grouping them under the banner of "Episodes nacionales" ("National Episodes"). By 1875 Galdós had written his first series of "Episodes," ten volumes that concerned the history of Spain from 1805 to 1812. Although these stories related historical events, the "Episodes" also reflected Galdós' own beliefs about the need for an appropriately paced change of course in Spanish politics and government.

Galdós's works proved popular and soon he was financially independent. During the composition of the second series of "Episodes," completed in 1879, Galdós decided to use his financial good fortune to turn his attention to contemporary themes. His modern stories, however, were not as successful as his historical ones. Confronted with debts that his brother Domingo had accrued prior to his death in 1870, Galdós's fiscal situation deteriorated alarmingly.

While Galdós had established a business partnership with Miguel Camara in 1874 that had been quite successful, his expenses began to overwhelm that considerable income. He had built an expensive house on the sea near Santander, taken care of his sisters, and paid off his brother's debts. He also had the added expense of a daughter, Maria, born in 1891. Finally, he was fond of traveling, and had journeyed throughout Europe. These financial pressures combined to compel him to begin the third series of "National Episodes," although he had vowed in the epilogue of the second series to never write a historical novel again.

Although Galdós non-historical works were not particularly successful on a commercial basis, reviewers commended them. In 1876 he wrote *Dona Perfecta,* widely thought to be an exaggerated, but reflective portrait of his domineering mother. He also wrote the multi-volume works *Gloria* and *La Familia de Leon Roch.* These books, like *Marianela,* reflected Galdós' belief in the detrimental effects the powerful Catholic Church had on Spain. While not anti-religious, Galdós believed in freedom of religion and the separation of church and state.

Successful dramatic stage productions of a couple of Galdós' plays took place during this period as well. His play *Realidad* appeared on the stage in 1892. It was followed in 1894 by *La de San Quintin,* which proved tremendously popular. Undeterred by a previous loss, he also won election to the Royal Spanish Academy in 1889.

Galdós returned to his "National Episodes" in April 1898; by October 1900 he had completed ten more volumes. Sales from the third series did not solve his financial problems, but in 1901 he wrote *Electra,* a play that proved fantastically popular. Performed in Spain and all over Spanish America, revenue from the play brought him most of the way out of debt. In 1902 he felt compelled to once again write another series of "Episodes." Five years later, however, he had only completed six of the planned ten volumes.

## Declining Health

Galdós' health declined in the first decade of the new century. A hemiplegic stroke suffered in 1905 marked the beginning of this slide. Many scholars contend that Galdós' lifelong tendency to become indignant with criticism of his work grew as his health deteriorated. He lashed out at critics who did not favor him and grew angry in 1905 when **José Echegaray** received the Nobel Prize for literature instead of himself. His anti-clerical beliefs and the wide appeal of his works made him popular with the common people, however, and when he lost the Nobel Prize again in 1912, his fans went so far as to collect money to compensate him for his loss.

Galdós had served in congress from 1886 to 1890, but his financial situation had taken him away from the world of politics. As his physical condition worsened, however, Galdós focused more of his attention on politics and devoted less time to his writing. In 1907 he went to congress as a Republican representative of Madrid, saying he would fight against "clerical barbarism" and work to establish a more solid scientific foundation for Spanish education. Despite his failing health, including a gradually worsening blindness, Galdós put a remarkable amount of vigor into his political career. He used fiery speeches to condemn the monarchy and their tyrannical church, saying once that in contrast to the hell of which the clergy preached, "the real hell is the friar, and . . . this visible and tangible hell must be extinguished in Spain forever."

Shortly after 1910, Galdós had gone completely blind and his mental powers had declined. He won the seat of the representative of Grand Canary in 1914, but isolated himself from friends—including the future prime minister—in the process. He published only one novel and one play in his last decade, but he got a measure of tribute from the literary world and the Spanish public at large, who called him "the grandfather." He was honored with a statue in Retiro Park in 1919 and various literary awards from Spain and other countries. When he died in 1920 Galdós returned to the front page of Spanish newspapers. More than 30,000 mourners traveled to City Hall in Madrid to honor his memory.

## SELECTED PUBLISHED WORKS:

*Doña Perfecta,* 1876, reprinted, Hernando, 1969.
*Gloria,* two volumes, 1876–77, published as *Gloria: Novela de costumbres,* Century, 1927.
*Marianela,* 1878, corrected Spanish edition edited by Nicholson B. Adams, Ginn, 1951.

*La familia de León Roch,* (*The Family of Leon Roch*), three volumes, 1878–79, published as *Leon Roch: A Romance,* W.S. Gottsberger, 1888, reprinted, Fertig, 1974.

### Novelas Espanoles Contemporaneas Series

*La desheredada,* 1881.
*El amigo Manso,* (*Friend Manso*), 1882.
*Tormento,* 1884, translated by J.M. Cohen and published as *Torment,* Farrar, Straus, 1953.
*La Incógnito,* La Guirnalda, 1889.

### Episodios Nacionales First Series

*Trafalgar,* 1873, Oxford University Press, 1941.
*Zaragoza,* 1874, translated by Minna Caroline Smith and published as *Saragossa: A Story of Spanish Valor,* Little, Brown, 1899.
*Cádiz,* 1874.

### Episodios Nacionales Second Series

*El equipaje del rey José,* 1875.
*El Grande Oriente,* 1876.
*El terror de 1824* (*The Terror of 1824*), 1877.
*Los apostólicos,* 1879.
*Un faccioso mas y algunos frailes menos,* 1879.

### Episodios Nacionales Third Series

*Zumalacárregui,* 1898.
*Luchana,* 1899, reprinted, Alianza/Hernando, 1976.
*Vergara,* 1899, reprinted, Alianza, 1978.
*Bodas reales* (*Royal Wedding*), 1900, reprinted, Alianza, 1978.

### Episodios Nacionales Fourth Series

*Las tormentas del 48* (*The Storms of '48*), Tello, 1902, reprinted, Alianza/Hernando, 1978.
*La revolución de julio,* 1903.
*Prim,* Perlado, Páez, 1906, reprinted, Alianza, 1980.

### Episodios Nacionales Final Series

*España sin rey* (*Spain Without a King*), Perlado, Páez, 1908.
*Amadeo I,* Perlado, Páez, 1910.
*Cánovas,* Perlado, Páez, reprinted, Alianza, 1980.

### Plays

*Doña Perfecta: Drama en cuatro actos,* 1896.
*Electra: Drama en cinco actos,* 1901.
*Mariucha: Comedia en cinco actos,* 1903.

## SOURCES:

### Books

Berkowitz, H. Chonon, *Pérez Galdós, Spanish Liberal Crusader,* Madison, University of Wisconsin Press, 1948.
*Hispanic Writers,* edited by Bryan Ryan, Detroit, Gale, 1991.
Pattison, Walter, *Benito Pérez Galdós,* New York, Twayne, 1975.

—*Sketch by James McCarthy*

---

# Eva Perón
## 1919-1952
### Argentine reform leader

Born in poverty and obscurity, Eva María Ibarguren rose from her humble origins to become the First Lady of Argentina. Her supporters elevated her to saint-like status both before and after her death, while others attempted to tarnish her reputation with tales of young Eva being raised in a brothel. Somewhere between these two extremes lies the story of a remarkable woman who left a lasting impression on her country and the world. Many rumors circulated at the time of Perón's rise to power, leaving behind a mass of conflicting tales which biographers have attempted to clarify over the years.

Biographers agree that Perón's beginnings were unassuming. She was born on May 7, 1919, the illegitimate child of Juana Ibarguren and Juan Duarte. Though her older siblings had their father's surname, Eva was denied it. Later, she used Duarte as her last name anyway. Joseph A. Page described her parents in *Perón: A Biography:* "Descended from Basque immigrants, Juana Ibarguren had never been able to escape her lower-class background . . . her relationship with Juan Duarte gave her a recognized, but not respected position on the fringe of local society." Perón's mother worked as a servant on Duarte's ranch. "The infant's father, Juan Duarte, had political contacts enabling him to enjoy the social status of an *estanciero,* even though he merely rented his ranch from its owner. Thus he could indulge in the perfectly acceptable social luxury of maintaining two families." His "legitimate" family lived in a town away from the ranch.

In 1926, when Perón's father died in an automobile accident, her mother and siblings went to the funeral. Page described the experience that undoubt-

*Eva Perón*

edly made a lasting impression on the young girl. "Duarte's wife refused to permit the six visitors to enter the mortuary where the body lay. They had to remain outside, peering in, until the mayor, Duarte's brother-in-law, took pity on them and decided they could make a quick pass by the flower-bedecked corpse." They were allowed to join in the funeral procession only as far as the cemetery gate. Descriptions of the confrontation between the two families ranged from "tense" to "violent" exchanges. Regardless, Eva's origins made her a social outcast.

After the funeral, it was a struggle for the fatherless family to survive. One daughter worked in the post office, and the only son, Juan, worked in a grocery store. The eldest daughter, Blanca, studied to become a teacher, while Eva, also called Evita, and her other sister went to elementary school. At this time, "Juana began to cook meals for various bachelor military men and professionals," according to Page. "This led to the canard, palpably false yet persistent component of the Evita myth, that Juana ran a bordello." Soon, Blanca married a lawyer, while the other older sister married an army major. A respectable marriage was a way out of poverty, but a path Evita chose not to follow at this point.

Instead, at the tender age of 15, she sought her fortune in the movies and radio. In *Eva Perón: The Myths of a Woman,* J. M. Taylor described Buenos Aires as a place where the dreams of many Argentine teenagers living in the countryside were fulfilled:

"Under adverse conditions, with the theatre in a crisis of competition with the increasingly popular cinema, the thin, dark child from the provinces found her way about one of the world's largest cities stalking her dream of a career as an actress. . . . For ten years, a time when her frailty and occasional hunger worried better known members of the theatre world, her hunt was grim and silent, and its trophies tiny. But amongst them, by the time she was twenty, were radio parts. To a young actress at the time, these held the promise of a growing audience, burgeoning popularity, and, finally, with luck, a contract in national cinema."

Eva's biggest break came in 1943, when she signed a contract for the title roles of a new radio series called "Heroines of History." "At twenty-four, the skinny, dark, little provincial was heard by the nation as a radiant, blonde Elizabeth I, as Catherine the Great, as Alexandra of Russia, as Carlotta of Mexico, as Sarah Bernhardt," Taylor noted. Her rise from obscurity to a nationally known actress became cause for criticism later, as Page recounted: "Evita 's detractors have reiterated that during this period she advanced her career by engaging in a series of meretricious relationships with men in positions to help her. (Rabid Evita-haters, exemplified by author **Jorge Luis Borges,** to this day insist that she was a 'common prostitute.') This is a portrayal that emerged from malicious gossip spread by political opponents after she became First Lady." Page noted that young Perón was ambitious, restless, and insecure, but not the disreputable character described by her critics.

## Art Imitates Life

During the heyday of her radio and movie careers, Evita met **Juan Perón,** a colonel in the military regime ruling Argentina. "When the dashing Perón at forty-nine met and formed a liaison with this actress half his age, his influential backing immediately made itself felt in moulding his protégé's career," Taylor reported. Page noted that neither seemed too concerned with public opinion: "Given what is known about their personalities, Evita probably took the initiative in rapidly cementing the relationship. She found new quarters for them . . . although for the sake of appearances the couple rented adjoining apartments."

At this same time, Perón obtained the best movie role of her career, in *Circus Cavalcade,* which featured several well-known Argentine stars. During the filming of this movie, Evita bleached her hair blonde and left it that way. Her blonde hair later became a trademark of her image as First Lady. She also, as Page remarked, became involved in Juan Perón's interests: "She sat in on meetings Perón held in the apartment with military and civilian associates. The colonel must have approved of her presence." Most biographers agree that until Perón's appearance in her life, Evita showed little interest in politics.

The man who wrote her roles for the popular "Heroines in History," Muñoz Azpiri, became director of propaganda in the state Subsecretariat of Information. Three times a week, Taylor noted, his show, "Toward a Better Future," provided the public with views on Eva Duarte: "Here is the voice of a woman of the people—she herself of the anonymous masses—in whose voice has been revealed day by day the nature ... of this saving revolution." Taylor quoted Eva as saying on this show: "I am a woman like you, mothers, wives, sweethearts, sisters. . . . From me came the son who is in the barracks ... or the worker who is creating a new Argentina in the land, sea, and air." She also joined a radio employee union and became head of the Asociacion Radial Argentina. Soon, Evita left her acting career and embraced the politics of her country with open arms.

Meanwhile, the military disapproved of Juan Perón's close association with Eva María. Page noted that many of Perón's fellow officers were shocked by his open relationship with an actress: "They felt Perón was setting a bad example for the army. If the colonel's personal style and direct way of speaking distinguished him as a breath of fresh air ... his flaunting of Evita went a bit too far. It was in response to criticism by his army colleagues that Perón made his classic riposte: 'They reproach me for going with an actress. What do they want me to do? Go with an actor?'" At the height of Juan and Evita's popularity, in October 1945, things began to collapse. Juan Perón was forced to renounce three government offices he had taken over—secretary of labor, minister of war, and vice-president. Shortly following this, Evita was fired from her radio job. Taylor recorded that the lovers fled, searching for a refuge in the islands near Buenos Aires. But the police caught them on October 12 and returned them. Then, with Evita abandoned in the city, Juan Perón was exiled to Martin Garcia Island.

While Juan Perón wrote her long letters, Evita was pulled from a taxi and beaten by a gang in Buenos Aires. In the meantime, workers rallied around their exiled leader in "a completely spontaneous worker's protest forming itself into the most powerful demonstration of its kind yet known in the history of Argentina," Taylor wrote. Workers, in their shirtsleeves, descended on the capital on October 17, scaring the business suit-clad inhabitants of Buenos Aires. "The numbers and appearance of these crowds in shirtsleeves appalled many," Taylor continued, "who were glimpsing for the first time another Argentina, a brown-skinned mass." The workers were called *descamisados* ("shirtless ones"), and they became the lifelong champions of Juan and Evita. She never forgot her debt to them, as the workers refused to disband until Perón appeared before them.

Within five days of his return from his brief exile, Perón married Evita and together they began his campaign for the presidency. "For the first time in the history of the nation, a wife had accompanied a presidential candidate on his campaign tours," Taylor noted. Azpiri, the radio writer, became speechwriter to both. Perón was elected in early 1946, making Eva the First Lady of Argentina.

## The Presidency and Its Pitfalls

Evita Perón immediately established herself as a force to be reckoned with in the government, and thus laid the foundations of discord over her role. While some chose to see her as the champion of workers' and women's rights, others criticized her for being too influential in a government to which she was not elected. Her first task was to aid the laborers of Argentina. In July 1946 she was named First Worker of Argentina, and she became Queen of Labour in November of the same year. She began meeting with labor delegations and established an office where she could meet the poor and hear their complaints.

According to Taylor, the wives of Argentine presidents were traditionally offered the presidency of the exclusive charity Sociedad de Beneficiencia, but Evita was not tenured an invitation. "The Executive Power took control over the aristocratic organization in September 1946, and Eva Perón established an office in the building her enemies had vacated," Taylor recorded. Her new foundation raised substantial amounts of money and became her most lasting legacy. Eva Perón also formed and headed the Women's Suffrage Association and created feminist civic centers, although her feminism was somewhat tailored to the Perón party interests.

Perhaps it was during her days in radio that Evita learned how important modern media were for reaching the people. According to Taylor, in January 1947 she bought the newspaper *Democracia,* which became a powerful tool in spreading the message of Juan Perón and praising his industrious wife. Always, in her speeches and radio addresses, she insisted Perón and she were partners. "Neither Eva nor Juan Perón ever lessened the stress they placed on Eva's identity as intermediary, as the 'bridge of love' between Perón and his people," Page wrote. After her death, Perón summed up his wife's relationship to him, as quoted by Page in his biography: "Eva Perón is an instrument of my creation. I prepared her so that she would do what she did. I needed her in the sector of social work within my leadership. And her work was extraordinary. . . . As a politician I am barely an amateur. The area in which I am professional is in leadership. A leader must imitate nature, or God. If God came down every day to solve men's problems, we would already have lost our respect for him and there would be no lack of some fool who would want to replace him. For that reason, God works through Providence. That was the role which Eva filled: that of Providence."

During her brief life with Perón, Evita also emphasized the duality of their relationship. She represented the people of Argentina to Perón, as Page recalled, "But she had been born *descamisda,* and while Perón remained forever unique, Eva's identity was collective: she did not only champion the humble; Eva was her people." Whether or not she was a "creation" of her husband and behind-the-scenes speechwriters, Eva's special ability to rouse public support cannot be discounted. "Even before Perón's election, Eva began to deliver speeches, at first on her husband's behalf, but very soon on her own," Page noted, claiming that hers was "one of the most effective rhetorical styles ever known in South America."

In 1949, the women of Argentina were granted the right to vote and Eva Perón became leader of the Perónist Women's Party. Party members became deputies and senators, and one became the world's first female congressional president. Evita was firmly entrenched in politics, with her own agendas and branch of supporters. The Eva Perón Foundation built schools throughout the country. The majority of the foundation's budget came from two days' wages subtracted annually from all workers and employees, in addition to money from other ministries' budgets. The finances of the foundation came under heavy criticism, another aspect of the myth of Evita.

The height of her popularity occurred at the time her health was at its most precarious. In mid-August 1951, the working class of Argentina wanted Eva to run for vice-president while her husband ran for another term as president. Taylor recorded one of the campaign slogans: "Perón Keeps His Word, Evita Dignifies It." Unbeknownst to most of her adoring public, Eva was seriously ill with cancer. The military, also, was highly opposed to a woman as vice-president and thus possibly their commander-in-chief. It is not entirely clear why she declined the nomination, whether it was due to her illness, or because it was not in Perón's best interests, or due to the military's disapproval. Whatever her reason, the nomination was offered amid much fanfare and public support, only to be declined. In declining she said she hoped "that it will be said of me, when they write the marvelous chapter that history will surely dedicate to Perón, that there was at his side a woman who dedicated herself to bring the president the hopes of the people, and that the people lovingly called the woman 'Evita.'"

In the fall of 1951, Evita's autobiography, *La razon de mi vida* ("My Mission in Life") was published. "The Perónist propaganda machine immediately hailed the book as a masterpiece. Critics extolled its literary merits," Page reported. "Copies of the book flowed from the printing presses. It became a required text in the schools." Page summed up the book as adulation of Juan Perón in its most extreme form, accompanied by Eva's autobiographical insights, sentiment, resentment, feminism, anti-feminism, sense, and nonsense. At the time of her book's appearance, she had been in bed for several weeks because of her weakened condition. She was operated on twice in the late fall of 1951, and though she made a few public appearances, Evita had to run business from her bed. In May 1952, on her birthday, she appeared briefly to wave at the crowds that had gathered, but she was unable to stand alone, according to Taylor. It was on this day she was designated "Spiritual Chief of the Nation." She even began her second book, *Mi mensaje* ("My Message"), which was never completed.

When she died on July 26, 1952, Evita went from being First Lady of Argentina to a martyr and heroine of her people. The public outpouring of grief was astonishing. "With the procession that accompanied the body to its funeral chapel in the Ministry of Labour and Welfare, Eva's posthumous odyssey began," Taylor wrote. "It perhaps ended only in 1975, after twenty-three years, first of public display, later of secret transport, plots and burials and finally exhumation and return to Argentina. A monumental procession carried her to the first of many places of temporary rest. It also marked the first phase of a grandiose funeral and subsequent massive morning, which was to be the focus of some of the bitterest criticism produced by the opposition." In death, as in life, controversy surrounded Eva Perón. Some people to this day insist she is not buried in Argentina.

Her obituary in the *New York Times* stated that Eva, though not an elected official, would receive all the honors of a president. Official activity was suspended for two days, and thirty days were allotted for official mourning. "As General Perón's most faithful and trusted collaborator, Señora Perón not only maintained but increased the tremendous power she had acquired in state affairs," the obituary reported. "Her influence did not abate during the course of her illness and she dictated appointments from her sickbed." The newspaper also remarked that the biggest problem left by Evita's premature death was the future of her foundation, which at the time was rumored to have at its disposal $150 million.

## SOURCES:

### Books

Page, Joseph A., *Perón: A Biography,* New York, Random House, 1983.

Taylor, J. M., *Eva Perón: The Myths of a Woman,* The University of Chicago Press, 1979.

**Periodicals**

*New York Times,* July 27, 1952, pp. 1, 56.

—*Sketch by Kathe A. Conti*

# Juan Domingo Perón
## 1895-1974
### Argentine politician, military leader, teacher, and writer

*Juan D. Perón*

Argentine President Juan Domingo Perón came to power in 1946 with the help of labor and the underprivileged masses. Although elected to the office twice by an overwhelming popular vote, Perón was viewed as a dictator until he was forced from office in 1955. He returned to power in 1973, when he was elected for the third time as president.

Perón was born October 8, 1895, in Lobos, in the province of Buenos Aires, Argentina. He was the son of Mario Tomás Perón, owner of a small ranch who also studied medicine, was a laborer, and served as a bailiff for a time. Perón's grandfather, Tomás Liberato Perón, was a physician, an Argentine senator, president of the National Council of Hygiene, an army surgeon, and probably the first Argentine to develop a rabies vaccine. Perón's mother was Juana Sosa Toledo, a farm girl of Spanish and Indian descent living near Lobos. Although some writers have speculated that Perón was an illegitimate child, it cannot be firmly established since his birth certificate has disappeared. It is well known, however, that Perón had a brother, Mario Tomás Perón, who was born in 1891 to the same parents.

In *Perón: A Biography,* Joseph A. Page described Perón's first years in Lobos as "stable and happy." Perón had the "usual childhood traumas," and once fell into a well, but his mother pulled him out. Page explained, "More typical were pranks, such as frightening a servant with the skull of Juan Moreira, a legendary outlaw." When Perón was about four years old, his father decided to leave Lobos for the more spacious Patagonia countryside and a small ranch called Chank Aike near the city of Río Gallegos. In 1900, his sons and wife joined him there. In 1904, however, the family moved again to a ranch in Chubut.

That same year, Perón and his older brother were sent to Buenos Aires to begin their formal schooling, first at Colegio Internacional at Olivos, then at Colegio International Politécnico. According to Page, Perón remembered, "At ten, my way of thinking was not as a child, but almost as a man. In Buenos Aires I managed alone, and the skirts of my mother or grandmother did not attract me as they did other kids my age. I endeavored to be a man and proceeded on that basis. It is logical that, being 2,000 kilometers from home, I would have many chances to prove myself." While in school, Perón enjoyed boxing, skiing, and fencing.

Although Perón originally planned to follow in his grandfather's footsteps and study medicine, he had a change of heart at the age of 15 and enrolled in the National Military Academy on March 11, 1911. On December 13, 1913, he was commissioned at the rank of second lieutenant in the army. When he graduated on December 31, 1915, he was promoted to first lieutenant and was assigned to the war arsenals in Buenos Aires as an instructor. In 1920, he was transferred to the Campo de Mayo garrison, where he began teaching non-commissioned officers. By 1924, he was promoted to the rank of captain. On March 26, 1926, Perón was moved to the war academy. Shortly after that assignment, Perón met Aurelia Tizón, the daughter of Cipriano Tizón, and began courting her. On January 5, 1929, the two were married. Later that same month, Perón was reassigned to the army's general staff.

### First Revolutionary Experience

Throughout Argentina's early history, the country was ruled by the elite upper class, despite many efforts to unify the various economic classes. The middle class, particularly, was excluded from the political arena until they formed their own political party, known as the Radical Union, in the last part of the nineteenth century. In 1912, they won their first victory with the election of Hipólito Yrigoyen. Yrigoyen was re-elected to office several times, and his last victory at the age of 76 began a period of political chaos in Argentina. Among other things, Yrigoyen played political favorites with military promotions and other personnel issues. Finally, in 1930, a military coup ousted the president and placed General José Uriburu into power.

Perón initially supported Uriburu's cause, but switched his allegiance to General Agustín Justo shortly before the coup, because he believed Uriburu was too disorganized to succeed. However, Perón did participate in the revolt. Following the coup, Perón was assigned as the private secretary to the new minister of war, but within a month he was removed from office as a result of his earlier abandonment of Uriburu. But since he had at first supported the new president, he was made a professor of military history at the war academy.

He used his time at the academy to publish several books on military history, including *El frente oriental de la guerra mundial en 1914* ("The Eastern Front in the World War in 1914"), *Apuntes de historia militar* ("Notes on Military History"), and *La guerra ruso-japonesa* ("The Russo-Japanese War"). Because of his early life in and fascination with Patagonia, he also wrote *Toponomia patagónica de etimología araucana* ("Patagonian Place Names of Araucanian Origin").

By the end of 1931, he was promoted to the rank of major. In addition to his teaching and writing at the academy, Perón also served as an adjutant to the chief of the general staff as well as an aid-de-camp to the minister of war during this period. In 1936, Perón was made the military attaché to the Argentine embassy in Santiago, Chile. Among his other duties, he established a network of spies to report on the activities of Chile's government and military. At the end of that year, he was promoted to the rank of lieutenant colonel. When he returned to Argentina in 1938, his wife Aurelia died of uterine cancer. They had no children.

With war in Europe threatening, Perón was assigned in 1939 as military attaché to Italy to analyze the situation. He spent most of his time there with an Italian division training for mountain warfare. He returned to Argentina at the end of 1940 and was assigned to an army school for mountain warfare in the Andes Mountains at Mendoza. On December 31, 1941, Perón was promoted to full colonel and assigned as commanding officer to a detachment of mountain troops. In March 1942, he became the inspectorate of mountain troops in Buenos Aires.

### "Infamous" Decade Leads To Revolution

During the decade preceding 1943, Argentines lost faith in democracy and party politics. The economy, battered by depression, continued to favor the wealthy. The general population was further enraged when the government moved to tie their economy closer to that of Great Britain through contracts for beef purchases. In addition to the internal problems, World War II had begun and divided the country between those who supported Germany and those who wanted to remain neutral. Finally, people recognized that Argentine president Ramón Castillo had corrupted the provincial election system.

By 1943 Perón—who was skilled at obtaining compromises and bringing people together—had formed a secret military lodge called the Grupo de Oficiales Unidos ("Group of United Officers"), or GOU, at Campo de Mayo. The group attracted members who were dissatisfied with the fraud in the political system, the loss of prestige of the army, and the continual pressure to join the Axis powers during the war. On June 4, 1943, the GOU masterminded a military coup, supposedly to save the constitution and restore law and order. At the time, Perón said, "We have done nothing more than our duty as Argentines, and we declare that we shall continue in this so as to oppose all that is not for the good of the country and the well-being of the people."

Perón had no intention at that time of becoming president, however. In fact, Perón went on record stating that "in revolution men impose their will from the second row, and not from the first, where they invariably fail and are removed." Following the coup, Perón was named interim minister of war and the head of the National Labor Department, positions from which he could impose his will "from the second row." In 1944, Perón was made vice-president and permanent minister of war. These positions made Perón the most powerful member of the military establishment.

### Evita Brings the Support of Labor

On January 15, 1944, an earthquake leveled the town of San Juan, killing more than 10,000 people. Perón took charge of the relief effort. On January 22, he organized a benefit at Luna Park in Buenos Aires to help the victims. It was there that Perón first met **Eva María Ibarguren Duarte,** a 24-year-old film actress and radio personality. Evita ("Little Eva"), as she was fondly called, became his mistress within a few days and married Perón on October 21, 1945. She often provided Perón with advice, particularly about labor issues, and helped him gain support among the working class.

During 1944 and 1945, Perón was able to establish clinics, unions, and pensions for Argentine workers, called *descamisados* ("shirtless ones"). He often ignored government policies in the process, which resulted in a growing legion of enemies as well as supporters. In late 1945, the military began to fear Perón was planning a government takeover. As a result, Perón was forced to resign as secretary of labor and minister of war. He was then arrested and exiled. The *descamisados,* fearful of losing all they had gained, held a rally on October 17, 1945, in the Plaza de Mayo to demand Perón's return. Their efforts were successful, and in November 1945 Perón announced his candidacy for president.

In February 1946, Perón was elected president of Argentina by an overwhelming popular vote. He then issued a five-year economic plan for the country, established a foreign trade organization to oversee Argentina's agricultural exports, and nationalized several critical, foreign-controlled industries, including the British-owned railroads and other utilities. He also established his own political party, the Perónist Party, and financed a number of large public works projects.

In 1947, Perón succeeded in paying off the entire balance of foreign debt and declared economic independence from foreign governments. He also encouraged legislation that reaffirmed the right of women to vote. Both hourly wages and the standard of living increased for all Argentines during Perón's first six years in office. He named his wife, Evita, to head the National Labor Department, which further consolidated his power and added to his support among the working classes.

By 1949, however, the country again faced an economic crisis, as prices for exported agricultural products dropped sharply while the prices of imported goods rose. The economic instability allowed Perón to institute a number of controls that resulted in a further consolidation of his power. Finally, in late 1949, he canceled the Constitution of 1853 and wrote his own Constitution, which allowed him to run for the presidency for a second six-year term as well as to restrict and even eliminate many individual liberties.

### Setbacks Plague Second Term

Perón won re-election in 1951, but his second term was filled with problems, beginning with the death of his popular wife from cancer in 1952. Without Evita by his side, Perón began to lose support among the *descamisados.* In 1954, Perón legalized prostitution and divorce, and placed Catho-

lic schools under the direction of the government. As a result, he lost the support of the Vatican, which excommunicated both the president and his cabinet. Corruption within the government and favoritism with military appointments finally led to the "Liberating Revolution" in 1955.

Perón was forced to flee Argentina on a Paraguayan gunboat on September 19, 1955, following a military revolt. He finally made his way to Colón, Panama, in mid-December 1955. Two days before Christmas, he met María Estela Martínez, a dancer going by the name Isabel, at a party at the Hotel Washington. Isabel was living with him by the middle of January 1956, and in 1961 Perón married her.

The United States government had watched Perón for many years and opposed his totalitarian regime and Fascist ideas. As a result, the United States put pressure on the government of Panama to expel Perón. The exiled dictator then went to Venezuela, which also expelled him after a short time. The Dominican Republic was his next stop before he made his way to Spain, where Fascist dictator **Francisco Franco** welcomed Perón in 1960.

The Perónist Party remained active in Argentina during the dictator's absence, however. From Spain, Perón encouraged his followers to block the military rulers' activities. Finally, in 1971, military leader General Alejandro Lanusse declared that constitutional elections would resume by 1973. In the March 1973 elections, the Perónists voted Hector Cámpora, an avid Perónista, into the office of president and gained a majority in the legislature. Perón was allowed to return home in June. Cámpora soon renounced the presidency, and in October a special election was held to elect Perón for a third term as president of Argentina. His wife Isabel Perón was elected vice-president.

Economic problems as well as rebel violence again plagued the aging Perón during his first months in office. Finally, on July 1, 1974, Perón died of a heart attack, leaving Isabel in charge of the government. Under Isabel's leadership, the country found itself overwhelmed by economic woes and violence. Finally, in March 1976, the military removed Isabel from office.

Perón's influence and success during his years in power continued to influence Argentine politics long after his death. The Perónist Party survived and again won the presidency in 1989. Perón's presence also remained strong in the many streets, buildings, and places named for him or his second wife.

### SOURCES:

Alexander, Robert J., *Juan Domingo Perón: A History,* Boulder, Colorado, Westview Press, 1979.

Crassweller, Robert D., *Perón and the Enigmas of Argentina,* New York, Norton, 1987.

Foster, Dereck H. N., *The Argentines: How They Live and Work,* New York, Praeger, 1972.

Goodwin, Paul B., "Juan Domingo Perón," *Historic World Leaders,* volume 5, edited by Anne Commire, Detroit, Gale Research Inc., 1994.

Owen, Frank, *Perón: His Rise and Fall,* London, Cresset Press, 1957.

Page, Joseph A., *Perón: A Biography,* New York, Random House, 1983.

*Perón Expounds His Doctrine,* New York, AMS Press, 1973.

—*Sketch by Catherine A. Clay*

*Pablo Picasso*

# Pablo Ruiz Picasso
## 1881-1973
**Spanish artist**

Universally acknowledge as the most extraordinary, compelling, and controversial artist of the twentieth century, Pablo Picasso was the undisputed vanguard of the modern art movement. He lived most of his life in exile in France, where he rose to widespread acclaim in the 1940s. Through his exploration of monochromatic color, Cubism , papires collé (paper collage), Surrealism, and other art forms, Picasso established an enormous legacy of artistic adventurism. His body of work is so vast, so varied, and so unique that it staggers the observer and defies classification. In a 1991 *Vanity Fair* article by Martin Filler, Picasso's friend and biographer John Richardson observed, "Almost every artist of any interest who's worked in the last fifty years [is] indebted to Picasso . . . whether he's reacting against him knowingly or is unwittingly influenced by him. Picasso sowed the seeds whose fruits we are continuing to reap."

### Artistic Gifts Flower in Childhood

Pablo Picasso was born October 25, 1881 in Málaga, in the Spanish province of Andalusia. His full name was registered in the lengthy Malagueño tradition: Pablo Diego José Francisco de Paula Juan Nepomuceno María de los Remedios Crispin Crispiano Santísima Trinidad Ruiz y Picasso. The eldest and only son of María Picasso y Lopez and Don José Ruiz Blasco, he was idolized by the many women who dominated the household: his mother, grandmother, several aunts, and a succession of maids. Don José had several vocations, none of which paid well. He taught drawing, served as the curator of the Málaga municipal museum, and dabbled in painting himself. He had more desire than talent, however, and his efforts were restricted to meticulous still lifes and depictions of pigeons, which he also raised. Thanks to Don José's more successful brothers, the family never experienced actual poverty, but they were never prosperous.

Despite Don José's painterly ambitions and reported minor talent in other relatives, it was a surprise to discover Pablo's very significant ability at a young age. Establishing a career that would essentially span his entire lifetime, Picasso often claimed he drew even before he learned to speak. Whether or not this is true, Picasso did spend most of his time as a child engaged in drawing. He also claimed never to have drawn like a child, but this cannot be proven. Nothing has survived prior to the age of nine or so, and Richardson states in his book, *A Life of Picasso, Vol. I* (1991), "Tempting as it is to see the germ of great art in Picasso's juvenilia, they are . . . what one would expect from a reasonably gifted child." The genius would become apparent a few years later. Little is known of Picasso's education, although it is reported that he was remarkably backward in comparison to other children his age. Biographer Arianna Stassinopolous Huffington speculates that he may have been dyslexic.

When Picasso was ten, financial considerations forced the Ruiz family to move from Málaga. Don

José secured a position as professor of drawing at the Instituto da Guarda in Corunna. Pablo was enrolled there as well and began to formally study drawing. Two events occurred in 1895 which are considered significant in Picasso's development. In January, his youngest sister died of diptheria. Symbols of her illness would appear in future paintings, and the incident triggered a lifelong horror of death and an aversion to illness.

The second incident is called pivotal and looms large in the Picasso legend: Don José transferred to the School of Fine Arts in Barcelona, where Picasso was subsequently enrolled. He was 14. By the next year, bored with school, he audaciously decided to exhibit some large "salon style" paintings. First Communion was shown at Barcelona's Third Municipal Exposition of Fine Arts. It did not sell, but did generate a commission for two altarpieces for a local convent. Science and Charity was the second painting exhibited. It won an honorable mention at the Madrid General Fine Arts Exhibition of 1897. It fared better at the Provincial Exhibition in Málaga the same year, winning a gold medal.

### Abandons Formal Disciplines for Modern Style

Success at these exhibitions convinced Don José that his son needed the challenge art school in Madrid could provide, and in the fall he was sent to the Royal Academy of San Fernando. His work was uninspired and he did not stay long. Richardson suggests, "A likely explanation is a sudden conscious urge to become a modern artist. . . . [H]e . . . set about adapting his work to the latest fad, modernism: the blend of art nouveau, symbolism and Jugendstil favored by the younger graphic artists in Madrid and Barcelona." Thus as the century was about to turn, Picasso began to explore the modern art movement that was to define his oeuvre. As the work bearing his signature began to change, so too did his signature: from "P. Ruiz" to "P.R. Picasso". By 1901 he would simply sign "Picasso."

Picasso went to Paris for the first time in 1900. He divided the next three years between Paris and Spain. Having met Pedro Manach, an expatriate Catalonian art dealer on his first trip to Paris, he was able to sell several paintings and did well financially during that time.

### Blue and Rose Period Works Are Rejected

Picasso's famous Blue period, so named for the monochromatic use of the color for its subjects, spanned from 1901 to 1904. Another key to this period is its subject matter. Biographer Pierre Cabanne attributes it in part to the suicide of his friend Carlos Casagemas. He writes in his book, *Pablo Picasso: His Life and Times* (1977): " . . . a new

malaise of bitterness and wrath now drove his work toward a tragic expressionism. The obsession with Casagemas's . . . suicide colored the entire Blue period. . . ." The blue paintings were not well-received by the public, which still preferred naturalistic subjects. His work dated 1901 and earlier, however, continued to sell.

In 1904 Picasso returned to Paris for good, settling into a studio in the Bateau-Lavoir in Montmartre. He soon took up with a woman named Fernande Olivier and his Rose period commenced about the beginning of 1905. Cabanne comments, "The Blue Period had been revolt and despair; the Rose Period was solitude and melancholy." Now populated by saltimbanques, harlequins, and jesters, Picasso's work was still unpopular, but he refused to compromise. He was rewarded in 1905 when he was "discovered" by Gertrude Stein, who became a close friend and collector.

### Primitivism Leads to Cubism

Picasso had begun appropriating the primitivism that now pervaded his work as early as 1901, when he began experimenting with geometric line and form. In 1906 he met fellow artist Georges Braque. Together they would explore African art, Cubism and paper collage techniques. In 1907 Picasso painted his avant-garde manifesto, *Les Damoiselles d'Avignon*, a brutally violent masterpiece universally unappreciated by those who viewed it. The exception was Daniel-Henry Kahweiler, a gallery owner who wanted to buy it. But *Les Damoiselles* remained rolled up in his studio for the next 15 years. Kahweiler, however, became Picasso's principal dealer until 1918, when Paul Rosenberg took over.

Picasso had begun analytic constructions that sometimes were identifiable only by the title. Cabanne writes, "As 1910 progressed, there appeared . . . a kind of internal explosion of the picture, as if, once completed, a violent punch had destroyed the positioning of the masses. . . ." Examples of this "cracked mirror" style are *Portrait of Wilhelm Uhed* and *Guitar Player*. In the spring of 1912, Éva Gouel replaced Fernande and Cubism exploded, with Picasso in the forefront. Although many at the time attributed its birth to Picasso, it was Andfe Derain who properly invented Cubism. Picasso and Braque, however, gave it life and fully developed the style. Although Cubism was ridiculed by the public, the number of Picasso collectors continued to grow.

### Cubism Gives Way to Surrealism

Éva died in December, 1915, of tuberculosis. The same year, Picasso met the writer Jean Cocteau, who would become his good friend. At Cocteau's instigation, he made his first foray into theatre, doing set and costumes for *Parade,* performed by the Ballets Russes. In 1918 Picasso married one of the Russian dancers with the troupe, Olga Khoklova. Their son Paul (Pablo), Picasso's only legitimate child, was born in early 1921. Picasso continued to do theatre work throughout this time, and his painting began to depart from Cubism, turning toward classicism. 1923 marked a turning point, as Picasso again broke new ground, this time with Surrealism. Pierre Daix asserts Picasso's leadership of this movement in his book, *Picasso: Life and Art* (1987). He writes, "Just as Picasso was a Cubist before—and beyond—the movement which claimed the title, he was a Surrealist before any of the angry young people who gave themselves that name." He participated in the first Surrealist exhibition in December, 1924. This was something he had not done with Cubism; he had shown only at Kahnweiler's.

Meanwhile, Picasso's marriage was breaking up, and a new brutality began to appear in his work, a reflection of his suffering. Olga, who had figured prominently in his work, disappeared from it in 1923. She was replaced by Picasso's fascination with American socialite Sara Murphy, although it is doubtful there was any affair.

## Women and War Are Sources of Key Paintings

In 1927 Picasso met Marie-Thérèse Walter and began a clandestine affair with her. The bond inspired a proliferation of art, but no one knew the model's identity. Picasso pursued Surrealism in paper collage, oil, lithographs, engravings, and sculpture. The relationship with Marie-Thérèse produced a child, Maya, in 1935, as well as divorce proceedings against Olga. These matters were eventually dropped, and although separated, the Picassos remained married until Olga's death in 1955. In 1936 he met photographer Dora Marr. He began an affair with her even as he continued to see Marie-Thérèse.

In the early thirties, both the Nazis and Fascists were gaining power. On April 26, 1937 German planes bombed and strafed Guernica, a small Basque town in Spain. The Nazi slaughter, abetted by Franco, shocked the world in general and Picasso in particular. The incident produced Picasso's anguished *Guernica* for the Spanish Pavilion of the Paris World's Fair. *Guernica* embodied the horror and crime of the attack and Picasso's deep pain at what was happening to his country. It remains the key masterpiece in his oeuvre. Cabanne writes that "Dora was not much consolation to him at this time, their feeling for each other having turned quite superficial. . . . Dora . . . was . . . the scapegoat of his own emotional trials." She would inspire his series of giant women as well as the convulsed; *Weeping Woman* exemplifies this period.

The next few years brought Picasso multiple shows throughout the world, several books about him, and the occupation of France. His fame and popularity were at their zenith during the forties. During the occupation he rarely ventured out of his studio, and he was occasionally harassed by the Germans. In 1943 Picasso met the artist Francois Gilot, who would replace Dora Maar. He was 62.

## Autobiographical Classicism Governs Last Years

Cabanne sums up the final chapters of Picasso's life. He writes, "From August 1944, in the very first days of France's liberation from the Nazi grip . . . he invented a second classicism: autobiographical classicism. . . . [His] final thirty years were to be a dizzying, breakneck race toward creation. That alone. And totally that." He did not blaze any new stylistic trails. He simply worked as if each day might be his last opportunity to create. He produced at a rate amazing for a young man. But Picasso was in his sixties, and he feared that the uselessness of old age (he compared it to a shipwreck) and death would arrive all too soon.

Subjects during the occupation years often had themes central to the times. Picasso had preserved Paris in landscapes when the city was under threat of destruction. He painted still lifes showing food or empty pots when food was scarce. The weeping women and the appearance of skulls in his work expressed his fears about the war. The Gilot affair remained under wraps at first, but Francois immediately appeared in Picasso's painting, as had her predecessors. Picasso joined the Communist Party in 1944, and in 1946 Francois moved in. Within the next three years, Picasso's youngest children were born: Claude in 1947 and Paloma in 1949.

A series of peace efforts ushered in the 1950s. Picasso had participated in the Warsaw Congress of Intellectuals for Peace in 1948 and the next year his "dove" painting (actually a white pigeon) was used for a poster celebrating the Paris Peace Congress. The Communist Party awarded him the Lenin Peace Prize in 1950, and he designed another dove poster for the Second Congress of Peace, which was awarded the Pennell Memorial Medal from the Philadelphia Academy of Fine Arts.

In 1953 Francois, tired of being "enslaved" to Picasso, left him. That same year he met Jacqueline Rogue (the "Madame Z" of the portraits), whom he would marry in 1961. UNESCO asked Picasso in 1957 to design a mural for its building in Paris. *The Fall of Icarus* was installed in September, 1958.

Picasso continued to create until the end of his life. One notable exception was in late 1965, when he secretly had ulcer surgery, necessitating a lengthy convalescence. Picasso died April 8, 1973 at the age of 91 of a heart attack brought by pulmonary edema. His estate yielded a phenomenal inventory of remaining works: over 35,000 pieces of art. The catalog included paintings, drawings, sculpture, ceramics, prints and woodcuts.

Arianna Stassinopolous Huffington puts the tremendous Picasso heritage into perspective in her 1988 book, *Picasso: Creator and Destroyer.* She writes, "The legacy of his art has to be seen in conjunction with the legacy of our time. He brought to fullest expression the shattered vision of a century that perhaps could be understood in no other terms; and he brought to painting the vision of disintegration that Shoenberg and Bartok brought to music, Kakfa and Beckett to literature. He took to its ultimate conclusion the negative vision of the modernist world—so much that followed has been footnotes to Picasso."

**SOURCES:**

**Books**

Cabanne, Pierre, *Pablo Picasso: His Life and Times,* Trans. Harold J. Salemson. New York: William Morrow and Co., Inc., 1977.

Daix, Pierre, *Picasso: Life and Art,* Trans. Olivia Emmet. New York: IconEditions, an imprint of HarperCollins Publishers, 1987.

Richardson, John, *A Life of Picasso, Vol. I, 1881–1906.* New York: Random House, 1991.

Stassinopolous Huffington, Arianna, *Picasso: Creator and Destroyer.* New York: Simon & Schuster, 1988.

**Periodicals**

*ARTnews,* May 1994, pp. 138–147.
*Insight on the News,* July 25, 1994, p. 26.
*Vanity Fair,* February 1991, pp. 127–153.

—*Sketch by Ellen Dennis French*

# Paloma Picasso
## 1949-
### Spanish fashion designer

As the daughter of one of the twentieth century's most influential artists, Paloma Picasso hesitated to enter the world of design. She did not want to be compared to her father, nor did she relish the

*Paloma Picasso*

unavoidable notoriety his name would provide. Once she began to show the jewelry she created for Zolotas of Greece in 1971, however, critics were genuinely impressed. The success of the pieces she produced for Tiffany & Company encouraged Picasso to design and market items ranging from fashion accessories to china. These items, including eyewear, cosmetics, and leather goods, may be identified by their bold shapes and brilliant colors, and are sold and appreciated throughout the world. Picasso's face is just as easily recognized. Posing in glossy magazine advertisements with her perfume, Paloma Picasso, the designer is, according to *Hispanic,* "her own best model." While Pablo Picasso transformed aesthetic standards in the fine arts, his trend-setting daughter has independently introduced fresh perspectives in fashion design.

Born April 19, 1949, Paloma Picasso has always been surrounded by art and artists. **Pablo Picasso,** the Spanish painter who was instrumental in the development of cubism, and Françoise Gilot, the French painter, named their daughter after the "paloma," or dove, that Picasso had created for the posters announcing an International Peace Conference in Paris, France.

As a teenager developing her own tastes and styles, Paloma Picasso was reluctant to pursue artistic goals. "In the beginning, I tried not to think that I would have to do anything artistic," she related in *Hispanic.* "From the time I was fourteen, I stopped drawing completely. . . . I thought, 'I don't want to become a painter like my father,' but I didn't know what else I wanted to become." Picasso's urge to create soon surpassed her hesitation; she began to study jewelry design and fabrication while still in her teens.

## Personal and Business Partnership with Lopez-Cambil

After the elder Picasso died, Paloma Picasso lost interest in designing. "I had given up designing when my father died in 1973," she recounted to the *New York Times.* "I didn't feel like doing anything. I just looked at all the paintings, and there was the sense of being overwhelmed." Picasso's father had left no will, and his illegitimate children, Paloma, her brother Claude, and her half-sister Maya, brought suit for their share of the estate, which was valued at $250 million. When Paloma Picasso finally won her share of the inheritance, which was estimated to be close to $90 million, she chose some of her father's works. As the French government had also received a huge sum and a collection of works as taxes from the estate, Picasso consented to assist it in the creation of the Musée Picasso in Paris.

Although Picasso had temporarily given up designing, she began another artistic endeavor. She starred in a motion picture that won the Prix de l'Age d'Or, 1974's *Immoral Tales* (*Contes Immorreaux*). Directed by Walerian Borowczyk, the movie was praised by critics, and Picasso's performance as a Hungarian countess with eccentric sexual desires was met with enthusiasm. The *New York Times* reported, "Paloma Picasso, the late Pablo's daughter . . . has a magnificent figure and a face as beautiful as her father's drawings from his classical period." While Picasso has not since pursued acting, she has often expressed her hope to portray the designer Coco Chanel in a motion picture.

Picasso met the Argentine playwright and director Rafael Lopez-Cambil (known by his pen name, Rafael Lopez-Sanchez) after her father's death. When she began to work again, it was for Lopez-Cambil; Picasso designed the sets for some of his productions. The relationship between Picasso and Lopez-Cambil became personal, and the couple married in 1978.

The wedding was an event. Wearing a red, black, and white Yves St. Laurent original for the ceremony, and a heart-shaped, red, Karl Lagerfeld gown for the disco reception, Picasso once again excited the fashion world. The *New York Times* stated that during these years, Paloma Picasso had become "something of a muse to Paris couturiers," and especially to the designers of her wedding gowns. The petite woman had once again impressed the design world.

## Association with Tiffany & Company

In 1980, John Loring, senior vice-president of Tiffany & Company, asked Picasso to create jewelry for the company. "When Tiffany's asked me about doing jewelry, I was thrilled," Picasso told the *New York Times.* She had always wanted to design for an American store. "I went into all the great jewelry shops of Paris. They are so grand, the salespeople seem to look down on you. As a customer you feel threatened. Tiffany is a great place because all kinds of people come in, just like Woolworth's." The company was equally enthusiastic about Picasso, whose pieces are priced from just over $100 to $500,000. Loring spoke of her in *Hispanic,* "Paloma has taken the gaudiness out of jewelry but kept the glitter," and Henry B. Platt, Tiffany's president, proudly exclaimed in *Newsweek* that "for the first time, people can hold a Picasso in their hands and try it on."

Brilliant gems framed in blocks of gold, large stones or metal pendants on simple cords, and gold or silver "hugs and kisses" ("X's" and "O's") are characteristic of Picasso's work. Unusual combinations of pearls, vibrant semi-precious stones, and metals are also prominent. Although her creations portend a new aesthetic for jewelry, Picasso, commented *Newsweek,* "rejects fine-art pretensions." The designer told the magazine, "This [jewelry] is something people can wear, rather than hanging it on the wall or putting it on the table. I like things to be used." In the *New York Times,* Picasso remarked that while "jewelry should be jewelry, something that you wear," it "is more permanent, less superficial than fashion." Picasso continues to design fabulous jewelry for Tiffany & Company. Her tenth anniversary collection, which was presented in 1990, was described in *Mirabella* magazine as "having the raw power of just-cut stones and just-mined minerals. Her gems are deep pools of color hung on thick veins of gold."

## Collaborated with Husband on Fragrance Development

In 1984 the plan to reinforce the Paloma Picasso image began with her fragrance, "Paloma Picasso." It seemed natural for her and her husband to come up with Paloma's own designer scent; Picasso's grandfather, Emile Gilot, was a chemist and perfume manufacturer.

With his experience in the theater, Lopez-Cambil carefully developed the fragrance project. He came up with a particular image for Paloma, which culminated in one of the most well known advertisements in the world—photographed by Richard Avedon—whereby Paloma Picasso the person was inextricably linked to Paloma Picasso the brand. As a couple and a team, this particular partnership had the advantage of a brilliant artistic director and a gifted designer.

Paloma, who habitually clothed herself in red, black, and gold, stated in *Vogue* that the perfume resembles herself: "What you see is what you get. I wanted my fragrance to be like that too." She made a similar remark in the *New York Post* when she announced that her perfume, which is priced at over $150.00 an ounce, is a "fragrance for a strong woman like myself." Paloma extended her fragrance collection and produced her signature lipstick, Mon Rouge, which escalated to her hallmark color, also know as Paloma Red.

### Expanded Paloma Image

The continual success of Paloma and Rafael's ventures encouraged them to broaden their creative horizons even further. In 1987 Rafael expanded the Paloma Picasso image by creating a New York City-based company, Lopez-Cambil Ltd., to produce and distribute Paloma Picasso accessories—handbags, belts, umbrellas, and small leather goods—to be imported from Italy. This collection, labeled as Couture accessories, gained international notoriety for its flawless quality and impeccable design, which fueled the creation of their relatively less-expensive line, entitled "By Paloma Picasso." Both casual and elegant, this collection allows Picasso to reach a larger audience, with a comprehensive range of contemporary, affordable accessories, which constitutes a fast-growing part of the company.

In 1992 the men's fragrance Minotaure was launched with great success. Picasso designed the bottle and packaging, while Lopez-Cambil developed the concept, the name, and the cologne's first advertising campaign.

In addition to Paloma Picasso boutiques in Japan and Hong Kong, Picasso's accessories are available throughout the United States, Europe, and the Far East. Paloma Picasso creations in Europe also include cosmetics and fragrances for L'Oreal in France, sunglasses and optical frames for a German company, hosiery for Grupo Synkro in Mexico, and bed ensembles, towels, bathrobes, and dressing gowns for KBC in Germany. As in the United States, home design has become a new era of creation for Paloma Picasso, with collections of bone china, crystal, silver, and tiles for Villeroy & Boch and fabrics and wall coverings for Motif.

### SOURCES:

#### Books

*Newsmakers,* Volume 1, Detroit, Gale Research, 1991, pp. 89–92.

#### Periodicals

*Harper's Bazaar,* December 1989, pp. 144–50; January 1991, pp. 123–26.
*Hispanic,* October 1988, p. 36; December 1988, pp. 28–33; May 1991, pp. 20–26.
*House and Garden,* November 1990, pp. 236–76.
*House Beautiful,* February 1989, pp. 103–104.
*Mirabella,* November 1990; December 1990.
*Newsweek,* October 20, 1980, p. 69.
*New York Post,* March 26, 1984.
*New York Times,* March 11, 1976; June 9, 1980, p. B16; April 22, 1990, p. S38.
*New York Times Magazine,* April 22, 1990, p. 38.
*Vogue,* April 1981, pp. 229–31; December 1985, pp. 318–31; January 1990, pp. 190–97.
*Working Woman,* October 1990, pp. 140–45.

#### Other

Additional information for this profile was provided by a Lez-Cambil Ltd. biography of Paloma Picasso, 1995.

*—Sketch by Ronie-Richele Garcia-Johnson*

# Miguel Piñero
## 1946-1988
### Puerto Rican playwright and poet

Miguel Piñero's career as a playwright began in New York's Ossining Correctional Facility (Sing Sing), where he was serving a sentence for armed robbery. Upon his release, his play about the brutal treatment of a child sex offender by his fellow inmates, *Short Eyes* (1974) met with strong critical acclaim. Although Piñero's reputation rests heavily on *Short Eyes,* it marked only the beginning of an important career in the theater and in television drama. For many Puerto Rican dramatists and poets, Piñero's success was groundbreaking, and he became an influential model.

Piñero was born in Gurabo, Puerto Rico to Miguel Angel Piñero and Adelina Gomez. He was brought to New York City as a child and was raised on New York's Lower East Side. Piñero's prison experience began at age 13 when he was sentenced to three years for shoplifting and other crimes. By 16 he was using drugs and committing more crimes to support his habit, and at 24 he was sent to Sing Sing prison. It was there that Piñero took part in a prison theater workshop run by Clay Stevenson, and began to write and act.

## Camillo Produces *Short Eyes*

A pivotal moment in Piñero's career was his meeting with director Marvin Felix Camillo, who agreed to stage *Short Eyes* at New York's Riverside Church theater. Camillo soon became a mentor to Piñero and an advocate for his dramatic work. Piñero and Camillo, along with a group of former prisoners, formed an acting troupe, The Family. This group, with the addition of a few professional actors, became the cast of *Short Eyes*. When the play was first produced in January of 1974, many critics stressed its artistic merits and praised Piñero's skill as a playwright. Mel Gussow, writing in the *New York Times,* called Piñero "an original writer for the theater" and Arthur Sainer of the *Village Voice* noted the play's "moral intelligence." *Newsweek*'s Jack Kroll said the play needed "no apology—it isn't occupational therapy and it isn't a freak show; it's an authentic, powerful theatrical piece." Despite Piñero's request to not compare him to French prison dramatist Jean Genêt, many critics did just that.

The success of *Short Eyes* caught the attention of producer Joseph Papp, who transferred it to the prestigious Vivian Beaumont Theatre at Lincoln Center. Papp was to become another champion of Piñero's work and an influential advisor. Piñero's position in the Puerto Rican literary community was further consolidated when he co-edited *NuYorican Poets: An Anthology of Puerto Rican Words and Feelings* (1975) with Miguel Algarin and with the publication of *La Bodega Sold Dreams* (1980) a volume of poetry. After *Short Eyes,* his dramatic work, most notably *The Sun Always Shines for the Cool* (1976) and *Eulogy for a Small-Time Thief* (1977) continued to explore the lives of pimps, prostitutes and drug dealers in blighted urban neighborhoods. No longer in jail, his characters, as critic Richard Eder noted, were still "equally confined" by their cruel circumstances. Joseph Papp's advice to "do something different" led Piñero to write what has been called his best play, *Midnight Moon at the Greasy Spoon* (1981). Here Piñero focused on the plight of two old American bigots who want to be independent but see themselves as increasingly obsolete in modern American society and fear exile to an institution for the elderly.

The success of Piñero's dramatic work in New York opened other doors; *Short Eyes* was made into a motion picture, his plays were produced in Los Angeles, and he found work as both actor and writer on such television drama shows as *Kojak, Baretta,* and *Miami Vice.* In the early 1980s Piñero taught creative writing at Rutgers University, and in 1982 he received a Guggenheim fellowship for writing. At the time of his death at the age of 41 from cirrhosis of the liver, Piñero was working on a new play for the Public Theater, *Every Form of Refuge Has Its Price.* In an obituary notice in the *New York Times* Joseph Papp described Piñero as "an extraordinarily original talent," and "a mentor and a hero" for other Puerto Rican dramatic artists.

## SELECTED PUBLISHED WORKS:

*Short Eyes,* New York, Hill and Wang, 1975.
*La Bodega Sold Dreams,* Houston, Arte Público Press, 1980.
*The Sun Always Shines for the Cool; Midnight Moon at the Greasy Spoon; Eulogy for a Small Time Thief,* Houston, Arte Público Press, 1984.
*Outrageous One Act Plays,* Houston, Arte Público Press, 1986.

## SOURCES:

### Books

*Biographical Dictionary of Hispanic Literature in the United States,* edited by Nicolás Kanellos, Westport, Connecticut, Greenwood Press, 1989.
*Contemporary Literary Criticism,* Volume 4, Detroit, Gale Research, 1974.
*Hispanic Almanac,* Detroit, Visible Ink Press, 1994, p. 490.
*The Hispanic-American Almanac,* edited by Nicolás Kanellos, Detroit, Gale Research, 1993.
*Hispanic Writers,* edited by Bryan Ryan, Detroit, Gale Research, 1991.

### Periodicals

*Los Angeles Times,* June 21, 1982, pp. 1, 5.
*New York Times,* January 8, 1974, p. 24; March 21, 1974, Section 2, p. 1; May 24, 1974, p. 21; November 28, 1977, p. 41; June 18, 1988, p. 32.
*Revista Chicano-Riqueña,* fall 1974, pp. 55–57.
*Village Voice,* April 15–21, 1981, p. 63.

—*Sketch by Simon Dixon*

# Augusto Pinochet
## 1915-
### Chilean military leader

General Augusto Pinochet led a four-man military *junta* in a bloody coup on September 11, 1973, that resulted in the death of Marxist President **Salvador Allende** and the end of nearly 150 years of democratic rule in Chile. As the president of the victorious *junta,* Pinochet immediately moved to rid the country of all vestiges of liberal opposition, arresting approximately 180,000 individuals—many of whom were subjected to torture—during the first year of his dictatorship, according to Amnesty International and other human rights commissions. Although the *junta* had planned to rotate the presidency among its members, Pinochet assumed full power as chief of state in June 1974, relegating the rest of his colleagues to a subordinate role. He retained absolute control of Chile until 1989, when he was ousted in free elections that were required under the very constitution that he had himself helped to write. Pinochet has been widely condemned for his numerous human rights violations. But he has also been credited with instituting free-market policies that have benefitted the country's economy. As Pedro del Fiero observed in the *New York Times,* the military strong man is viewed with great ambivalence by the Chilean people: "To some people, Pinochet is a monster who represents the worst of our society. But to others he's the person who has brought economic stability and order to our country." Both revered and despised in Chile, Pinochet has continued to serve as the country's military leader.

Augusto Pinochet Ugarte was born on November 25, 1915, in Valparaiso, Chile. Although his father, Augusto, a customs officer, hoped that the boy would someday become a doctor, his mother, Avelina, encouraged him to pursue his childhood dream of a military career. Because of his small stature, however, Pinochet was rejected twice by the National Military Academy before he was accepted, at the age of 18, for the four-year officers' training course at the Escuela Militar in Santiago. Regarded by his peers as an average student, Pinochet, according to the observations of Pamela Constable and Arturo Valenzuela in their book, *A Nation of Enemies,* "compensated by exhibiting unusual devotion to duty and a flair for spit-and-polish drills." Graduating in 1936 with the rank of *alférez,* or second lieutenant, Pinochet entered infantry school, where he cultivated the ideals that he believed guided his military career: patriotism, public service, and respect for authority. And he came to view his chosen vocation in terms of self-sacrifice for the good of his country: the "first duty" of a soldier, he later wrote in his book *Politica, politqueria y demagogia,* "is to renounce life and material possessions as the fatherland demands."

Early in his military career, Pinochet, like most of his fellow officers, did not take an interest in the intense political debates that dominated civilian society; he was more concerned with the study of logistics and strategy. But in 1939, after being sent on a relief mission to Concepcion following a disastrous earthquake, he came to regard the Socialist militiamen he encountered there as "two-bit thieves."

Rather than follow the military custom of marrying into a military family, Pinochet courted and married Lucia Hiriart Rodriguez, the daughter of a Radical senator and future interior minister, with whom he later had two sons and three daughters. In 1942, while serving as an instructor at the Escuela Militar, he was promoted to the rank of *teniente,* or first lieutenant. Four years later, he advanced to captain. Following the outlaw of the Communist Party in 1948, Pinochet was given command over a Pisagua concentration camp, where 400 party activists had been banished. While at this post, Pinochet was also ordered to disband the communist unions that were planning a strike in the Schwager coal mines. He would later describe communism as "not just another party," but a "system that turned everything upside down, without leaving any belief or faith."

In 1949 he returned to Santiago to attend the War Academy, where after completing his own program of study, he served as a professor, teaching geography and artillery courses while writing extensively—he eventually published several books on geopolitical strategy and a standard high school text on the geography of Chile. During his tenure with the War Academy, Pinochet was also exposed to the new anticommunist doctrine that was emerging throughout Latin American military institutions, following the development of the United States and NATO policy of "containment" adopted during the Cold War. Continuing to rise in the military ranks, Pinochet, as a major, entered the University of Chile law school in 1955. But an assignment to Ecuador to help oversee a military training project took precedence over his studies. After a brief stint in Washington, D.C., as a military attaché to the Chilean Embassy, he was sent to the northern deserts of Antofagasta, where he was appointed regimental commander. In 1964, he returned to the War Academy, serving as an assistant director and professor.

As Pinochet continued to advance in the military during the late 1960s—attaining the rank of brigadier general in 1968—he remained largely indifferent to politics. "His ideological orientation was an enigma," a younger cousin said in an interview with Sergio Marras, quoted by Constable and Valenzuela. "If he had any, he had not demonstrated it publicly." But in 1970, the reforms of Christian Democratic President Eduardo Frei Montalva were met with dissatisfaction by a Chilean population that had elected him six years earlier. Dr. Salvador Allende, who promised to bring socialism to Chile, was thus voted into office with a 36 percent plurality, becoming the hemisphere's first freely elected Marxist president. Pinochet, who was stationed in Iquique at the time, recalled in his memoirs that the election results brought Chile towards the "grave path" of communism. "My career is at an end," he later wrote in *The Decisive Day.* "As a soldier sworn to protect the fatherland, I felt inhibited from acting, because the instigator of chaos was the very government ... to which I owed allegiance."

In public, Pinochet appeared to accept the new government. Allende appointed him commanding general of the Santiago army garrison, a position in which Pinochet received his first public attention. Rioting between pro- and anti-Allende groups during December of 1971 forced the president to declare a state of emergency, leading Pinochet to institute a curfew, order more than 100 arrests, and temporarily close a right-wing newspaper. Promising to support the elected government with military force if necessary, Pinochet proclaimed that "coups do not occur in Chile." According to Constable and Valenzuela, General Carlos Prats, who later served as minister of the interior, "was so convinced of Pinochet's loyalty that he asked him to develop contingency plans in case of an antigovernment uprising."

### Military *Junta* Overthrows Allende

But behind this facade, Pinochet—who had been plotting to remove Allende from power since as early as mid-1972—was quietly organizing military opposition. On September 5, only a few weeks after he had been appointed commander-in-chief, Pinochet held a secret meeting with the other members of the *junta*—air force chief General Gustavo Leigh, Admiral Jose Toribio Merino of the navy, and national police chief General Cesar Mendoza. Six days later, just as navy units were taking control of the port of Valparaiso, Pinochet surrounded the presidential palace in Santiago and gave Allende the choice to surrender or face attack. After Allende refused to yield, the palace was shelled by tanks; when Pinochet's infantrymen entered later that afternoon, Allende was dead. According to the *junta*, the Marxist leader had taken his life to avoid surrender; but others, including Allende's widow, have maintained that he we was killed by Pinochet's troops. Although Allende supporters continued their resistance for some time, the military *junta* had taken control of Chile by the end of the day—but at the cost of 1,500 lives, according to Inter-American Commission of Human Rights statistics cited in Genero Arriagada's *Pinochet: The Politics of Power*.

Once in control, the *junta* imposed a 24-hour curfew and threatened to shoot any violators on sight. Two days later, they named Pinochet president, an office that was to rotate among each of the four members. Although the majority of officers and troops backed the coup, a few senior officers were known as Allende sympathizers. Afraid that units under such "progressive" control might disobey orders, the *junta* declared a "state of internal war," in which anyone who failed to follow orders risked being demoted, arrested, or executed—as was the case with

at least a few high-ranking officials. Among the many instruments of internal propaganda employed by the *junta*, perhaps the most elaborate was its claim to have discovered a conspiracy led by Allende and the left to assassinate senior military officials and various opposition leaders. According to most historians, evidence of such a plot, known as "Plan Z" by the Chilean military, was largely fabricated. But the sense of urgency and danger effected by the search for participants in the fictitious plot were very real. The White Book, which detailed the alleged plot, was later found to have been prepared with the help of the U.S. Central Intelligence Agency (CIA) for the purpose of justifying the coup. In Chile, the pursuit of information regarding Plan Z led to the beating and torture in hundreds of barracks and police stations.

Pinochet removed his extra-military opposition in a more direct fashion, simply exiling or executing some 14,000 leftist exiles from Cuba. He also threatened any "mentally deranged" Chileans who failed to accept the legitimacy of the new government by declaring: "I am not a murderer, but if people insist on fighting, we will act as we do in time of war." Although only 107 members of the armed forces and police were killed during the first two years of the *junta*'s rule, according to a *Que Pasa* report, Pinochet attempted to create the impression that the Marxist threat was much greater. The Superior Academy of National Security was established in 1974 to train officers in anticommunist ideology and strategy. As Colonel Eugenio Covarrubias explained in *Cosas* more than a decade later, students were taught that "subversion can act behind the kindness of a lady ... or the innocence of a child." According to Constable and Valenzuela, "Riot police with clubs and water cannons became a familiar presence in daily life, and the midnight rap on the door became a symbol of dread to hundreds of thousands of Chileans." Further, a new constitution authored by the *junta* suspended civil rights, outlawed all Marxist political parties, imposed strict codes of censorship, and purged the universities.

Although the members of the *junta* functioned as equals for a while—even holding ceremonies in rooms wide enough so that all four members could enter abreast—Pinochet persuaded his colleagues to sign Decree Law 527 on June 17, 1974, making him the chief executive. Pinochet claimed that the measure would add efficiency and coherence to the government. Through a series of deft political and legal maneuvers, Pinochet employed the privileges of his double title as army commander and *junta* president to acquire the authority to issue decrees that his colleagues had no power to veto. By December Pinochet had pressured them to give him the title President of the Republic. The man who had once stated in *Ercilla* that he had "no aspiration but to serve [his] country" now had absolute authority in Chile.

Human rights violations notwithstanding, the Pinochet regime received praise for introducing changes that brought prosperity and stability to the Chilean economy during the mid- and late–1970s. Having taken measures to desocialize the economy, largely by following the monetary policy theories of University of Chicago economist Milton Friedman, Pinochet and his team of economists, known as the Chicago Boys, eliminated the country's fiscal deficit and ushered in average annual growth rates of 6.5 percent by 1979, according to Joseph Ramos's calculations in his book *Neoconservative Economics in the Southern Cone of Latin America, 1973–1983.* Inflation had also dropped 65 percent by 1977; the number of public employees was significantly reduced, the tax system was streamlined, and 30 to 40 percent of the land that had been expropriated by the socialist government was returned to private hands.

The economic boom initially resulted in widespread support from Chile's middle class and the United States, which had officially recognized the Chilean *junta* from the outset. But the "economic miracle" was largely offset by criticism of the administration's repression of civil rights. After a 96–14 vote by the United Nations in December of 1977 that condemned Chile for human rights abuses, Pinochet—who fervently denied such charges—called for a national referendum on his rule in an effort to prove his critics wrong. On January 4, 1978, Chile supported Pinochet, with a reported 75 percent voting to "reaffirm the legitimacy of the government." According to many historians, however, the results of the plebiscite had been tallied by the interior ministry—blank ballots has been recorded as "yes" votes for the dictator. In August 1980 the Pinochet regime announced that another plebiscite would take place: this time the Chilean electorate would have the power to accept or reject a new constitution. Although the constitution had been nearly seven years in the making, the public had only 30 days to review the document before the vote. Further, Chile was placed under a state of emergency, which meant that the government had the power to arrest or exile anyone; the opposition had no access to television and only limited access to newspapers. The constitution was easily approved, but "by any objective standard of analysis," Arriagada argued, "the 1980 plebiscite was a fraud that lacked the minimum qualifications of validity."

### Chile Votes "No" to Pinochet

The new constitution called for Pinochet, the military *junta*'s candidate, to serve for another eight years. After that period, his name would be submitted to a national referendum. Although Pinochet's free-market policies from 1980 to 1988 were largely responsible for holding down inflation and generating an acceptable level of economic growth—with the exception of a recessionary period between 1983 and 1986—the opposition party organized a successful campaign to remove him from office. With the help of more that $2 million dollars from the U.S. Congress to finance opinion polls, media consultants, and a parallel vote count, the machinery required for a relatively fair election was established. On October 5, 1989, 55 percent of the Chilean electorate voted to remove Pinochet from office. He remained in office until free elections installed a new president, the Christian Democrat **Patricio Alwyn,** on March 11, 1990. Although Pinochet abdicated his title as president, he retained the influential post of army commander. Believed to be the oldest military leader in the world, Pinochet has, according to an October 1994 report by the *New York Times,* vowed to remain in office until 1997, when he is required by law to give up his command.

### SELECTED PUBLISHED WORKS:

*El dia decisivo: 11 septiembre 1973,* Andres Bello, 1979.
*Politica, politiqueria y demagogia,* Renacimiento, 1983.

### SOURCES:

#### Books

Arreagada, Genaro, *Pinochet: The Politics of Power,* translated by Nancy Morris, Boston, Unwin Hyman, 1988.
Constable, Pamela, and Arturo Valenzuela, *A Nation of Enemies: Chile Under Pinochet,* New York, Norton, 1991.
*Current Biography Yearbook, 1974,* edited by Charles Moritz, New York, Wilson, 1974.

#### Periodicals

*Harper's,* December 1989, pp. 72–76.
*New Republic,* December 18, 1989, pp. 20–23.
*Newsweek,* December 18, 1989, p. 40.
*New York Times,* September 15, 1973, p. 13; October 16, 1994, p. A9.

—*Sketch by Jason Gallman*

# Francisco Pizarro
## 1477(?)-1541
### Spanish explorer and conquistador

Francisco Pizarro, like **Hernán Cortés,** was one of the greatest Spanish military leaders and conquerors—better known as a *conquistador,* a word that refers to a daring, ruthless adventurer. Pizarro, accompanied by **Vasco Núñez de Balboa,** discovered the Pacific Ocean in 1510. Later, after years of searching for the Inca Empire, Pizarro found and conquered what is now Peru. He established the capital city of Lima and ruled the Inca Indians from 1533 to 1541.

Francisco Pizarro was born in Trujillo in the Extremadura region of west-central Spain, probably in 1477, though some sources list his birth date as anywhere from 1471 to 1478. His mother was Francisca Gonzales, the daughter of a laborer. His father was Don Gonzalo Pizarro "the Tall," a nobleman and an officer in the Spanish army. Though he lived with his mother—who was not married to his father—he was welcome in his grandfather's house in the town square. Illegitimacy was not a disreputable social class in Pizarro's time. In his youth, he worked as a herder of swine—also a reputable labor—belonging to his father; he was never taught to read.

### Sailed for the New World

Although Pizarro may have served with his father in military campaigns in Italy, he grew tired of his home life environs in Spain and hungered for new experiences and adventures. In about 1500, he left for Seville, which at that time was the center from which most of the Spanish colonial expeditions were launched. He became employed with Nicolás de Ovando, who succeeded Christopher Columbus as governor of Hispaniola (later Haiti and the Dominican Republic). Pizarro sailed to the West Indies with Ovando's fleet in 1502 and fought in the bloody defeat of the Taino Indians of Hispaniola.

From 1509 to 1510, Pizarro assisted Alonzo de Ojeda in his expedition to the Caribbean coast of South America (later Colombia). He took part in establishing the settlement of Antigua at Santa Maria de la Antigua at Panama's Gulf of Uraba. In 1513, Pizarro joined Vasco Núñez de Balboa, exploring the isthmus of Panama, and—along with other Europeans—discovered the Pacific Ocean. It was during this excursion that he first learned of a magnificently rich, native kingdom farther to the south. Natives called this kingdom "Birú," a name that was later changed to Peru. "Birú" was the home of the Inca Empire. The promise of gold lured Pizarro, but several years passed before he undertook an expedition to find this kingdom.

One problem facing the conquistadors of the New World was the lag time between events, such as discovering the Pacific Ocean, and the time it took for such news to reach Spain. Thus, despite the fact that Balboa led the group, including Pizarro, who found a new ocean that no one knew existed, King Ferdinand of Spain appointed Pedro Arias de Avila, or Pedrarias, as governor of Darien, the port from which Balboa had launched his historic expedition to the Pacific. Once Ferdinand learned of Balboa's accomplishments, he appointed the explorer assistant governor to Pedrarias. Balboa founded his own town of Acla, on the north coast of South America. Pedrarias grew jealous of Balboa's power and influence. In 1518, Pedrarias enlisted the aid of his supporters to remove Balboa on falsified charges of treason. One of these supporters was Pizarro, who arrested Balboa on behalf of Pedrarias. The governor then had Balboa and four of his followers executed in Acla.

### Launched Expeditions to Find Inca Empire

Balboa's execution in 1519 eased Pizarro's rise to greatness. He was appointed mayor of Panama City and received grants of property which increased his wealth and influence. He could have retired as a rich man, but Pizarro wanted more adventure, danger, and fortunes. In his forties, a well-respected, deliberate, calm, tall, well-built, and quite handsome man, Pizarro embarked on a series of journeys that ravaged his health and appearance repeatedly.

During this time in Panama, he explored the Pearl Islands off Panama's Pacific Coast. In 1522, Pascual de Andagoya returned from the south with accounts of an advanced Indian civilization farther down the coast. The Spaniards believed these Indians to be subjects of the great powers of the Orient and feared that attempting to conquer their empire meant risking the reprisal of China and many of the Central Asian countries. However risky, this threat did not hinder Pizarro.

After Balboa's death, Pizarro was finally in a position to launch an expedition to these lands. He signed an agreement with Diego de Almagro and Hernando de Luque to venture to the legendary land of "Birú." Using money Luque provided, Pizarro sailed forth in 1524 from the Pacific Coast of what later became Colombia. He sailed to Cabo Corrientes and up the San Juan River to Colombia's Gulf of Buenaventura until the loss of two-thirds of his 80-man crew to disease and Indian attacks forced him to return. He had more trouble though. Only 13 of his remaining men chose to join him; the others felt he was a fanatic, a "slaughterer." He set forth with these men with whom he became shipwrecked for many months. After learning of this expedition, Spanish authorities forbade Pizarro from launching any others.

Despite the prohibition of his superiors, Pizarro and Almagro, lured by the promise of great wealth, persevered. In 1526, they set for the south again and reached the Gulf of Guayaquil on the southern coast of what later became Ecuador. Pizarro and his men landed at the Inca community of Tumbes. For the first time, Pizarro saw with his own eyes the evidence of this advanced civilization and the wealth of its gold and jewels.

Tumbes did not adequately represent the breadth and grandeur of the Inca Empire. Pizarro discovered the Inca Indians at the peak of their civilization. At this time, the Inca Empire stretched 2,500 miles along the west coast of South America. The Inca nation was centered in the Andes mountains and included nearly 7,000,000 people. The roots of the Inca Empire stretched back to 2000 B.C. and its advanced state of existence in the sixteenth century can be traced to 400 A.D. when the Incas began building towns, working metals, and making beautiful pottery. The Inca Kingdom that Pizarro discovered was rich in religion, with great temples and priests who used magic to cure the sick. The Incas were also rich in the arts, with mass-produced pottery, hand-tooled ornaments and weapons, and architecturally designed walls with unmortared blocks so well set that a knife could not penetrate between them. It was rich in agriculture, with irrigation systems and carefully controlled surplus crops, rich in transportation and communication, with a vast system of roads and a message-relay service, like modern-day postal services, and rich in government, with an Emperor who ruled with the aid of a complex network of administrators and governors.

### Undertook Conquest of Inca Empire

Pizarro sent his chief mariner, Bartolomé Ruiz, down the coast on a reconnaissance mission. Ruiz confirmed that there were more and greater Incan cities farther south. Armed with the evidence of the vastness of the Inca Empire, Pizarro returned to Spain in 1528 to gain the support for a large-scale campaign of exploration and conquest. He presented the reaping of his Incan harvests to King Charles I of Spain (also Charles V, the Holy Roman Emperor), who succeeded Ferdinand and Isabelle as ruler of Spain. In Toledo, he gave King Charles gold and jewels from Peru, captured Inca Indians, several llamas (never seen before in Europe), a wild camel of the Andes, and samples of a silk-like cloth. Pizarro's timing was perfect. **Cortés** was visiting the court at the time, having just conquered the Aztecs in Mexico. Inspired by Cortés' success, King Charles sponsored Pizarro's plans, designating him captain-general and governor of New Castile, the name given to the unexplored region of what later became Peru.

In 1530, Pizarro and Almagro returned to Panama with Pizarro's half-brothers Gonzalo, Hernando, Juan, and Martín Pizarro. In January of 1531, Pizarro and a crew of 180 men and 27 horses sailed from Panama. They landed at San Mateo Bay (later in Ecuador) and conquered Tumbes without opposition, though many of the Inca Indians were weak or dead from the smallpox epidemic inadvertently delivered by the Spaniards. Soon, **Hernando de Soto** and Sebastian de Benalcazar joined Pizarro and his crew at Tumbes. Pizarro's force met with no resistance as it marched toward the interior of the Inca Empire along the Royal Inca Road, eastward toward the Andes and Piura Valley. He continued unopposed through the Sechura Desert, the high passes of Western Cordillera, and the central plateau region of the Andes.

Unbeknownst to Pizarro, Inca Emperor Atahualpa had decided to allow Pizarro free passage into the interior of the realm, where the Emperor felt the Spaniards could be more easily contained. Atahualpa had recently defeated (not killed) his half-brother Huascar in a civil war and had thus removed the only adversary to his rule. The Emperor also mistakenly acted under the presumption that the Spaniards were the legendary white gods, prophesied to arrive shortly after the death of Atahualpa's father. Thus, he felt that allowing the white men to reach the center of the Inca kingdom was fulfilling the will of the gods. Pizarro entered the city of Cajamarca, which was deserted. Atahualpa had encamped 80,000 of his men nearby. Pizarro's band of 160 were completely surrounded and outnumbered. Pizarro knew that if he hoped to prevail he need a brazen plan.

First, Pizarro sent his half-brother Hernando as an emissary to Atahualpa and the Inca Indians. Hernando presented Atahualpa with a Bible and demanded that the Inca leader swear fealty to Christianity and King Charles. Interpreting the words of the translator literally, the Emperor held the Bible to his ear expecting it to speak to him and teach him of Christ. Because the Inca civilization had no system of writing—they used strings to record numerical data—the book made no sense to Atahualpa. When the book remained silent, teaching him nothing, Atahualpa threw it to the ground. Hernando and the Spaniards left in disgust, misunderstanding Atahualpa's gesture, believing the Emperor had insulted their faith. When Atahualpa visited Pizarro with a retinue of followers hoping to make amends, Pizarro distracted the Emperor and ordered a surprise attack, including a charge of horses and a firing of the cannons.

The Inca people were unprepared for the attack. They grew so terrified that they amassed in mounds of bodies, suffocating one another. Such mass confusion allowed Pizarro's men to cut them with their razor-sharp swords. Pizarro massacred 6,000 or 7,000 Inca Indians and left thousands more limbless. In the melee, Pizarro took Atahualpa prisoner. The Spaniards, though less than 200 strong, suffered little to no casualties.

### Tricked Atahualpa

Atahualpa bargained with Pizarro, offering to fill the room (22 by 17 feet) where he was held captive with gold piled to a height of nine feet (plus filling two other rooms with silver), if released. Pizarro agreed and Atahualpa's subjects began to transport gold to Cajamarca from all over the empire in the following months. The Inca people gathered 1,325 pounds of gold, much of which had been fashioned into religious or artistic works. The Spaniards melted the entire lot into gold bars, despite any item's shape, size, or significance. Twentieth-century value for that much gold would be upwards of $100 million.

Despite Pizarro's pledge, he refused to release Atahualpa once the gold had been delivered. From captivity, Atahualpa ordered his followers to slay his half-brother Huascar before he could betray the Inca people by forming an alliance with the Spaniards. In a makeshift court of law, Pizarro tried Atahualpa for his "crimes," and after finding him guilty of murder and conspiracy against the Spanish, he condemned him to execution. De Soto and Hernando Pizarro objected to Pizarro's verdict to no avail. As a further cruelty, Pizarro sentenced Atahualpa to be burned, but after forcing the emperor to accept Christianity while tied to a stake awaiting the funeral pyre, he had him strangled to death instead. According to records, Atahualpa cursed Pizarro and all his descendants just before he was killed.

Pizarro led his forces with reinforcements brought by Almagro to the capital at Cuzco on November 15, 1533. Pizarro expropriated the city's gold and enslaved its people by setting up Huascar's brother Manco as a puppet ruler over all of Peru. On January 10, 1535, Pizarro established a city he named La Ciudad de Los Reyes (City of Kings; or, in some translations, City of the Magi) at the mouth of the Rímac River. This city later became Lima, Peru, considered one of the oldest capital cities in South America.

The level of development that the Inca Empire had reached aided Pizarro in his ability to conquer them swiftly and efficiently. The Inca road system of more than 2,000 miles allowed Pizarro and his troops quick and easy access to all parts of the Inca Empire. Though the roads were not designed for wheeled transport (since the Incas had no wheels), they were well engineered, sometimes terraced along hills, supplemented by tunnels, or linked by suspension bridges.

Pizarro managed a sweeping conquest of the Inca Empire—for which in his later years King Charles named him a marquis—but he was forced to fight internal battles among his own people. Though Pizarro was a great *conquistador,* he was neither well-schooled nor experienced at administration of government. The toll of the years of battle and adventure weighed heavily on him, and he did not take an active role in governing his new lands. The enslaved Inca Indians were forced to toil ceaselessly, men were tortured for the location of treasure, and women were raped. Pizarro did not maintain the carefully balanced Inca system of irrigation or food storage to protect the people from famine.

Pedro de Alvarado had planned to conquer Ecuador, but Pizarro persuaded him to leave. Pizarro had given his long-time partner Diego de Almagro southern lands to conquer. But when Almagro returned to Lima to help Pizarro put down an Inca revolt led by Manco in 1537, he attempted to wrest power of Lima from Pizarro. Hernando Pizarro led troops against Almagro in the Battle of Las Salinas in April of 1538. Once captured, Francisco Pizarro ordered Almagro executed. Hernando himself was responsible for executing 120 of Almagro's men.

Feeling invulnerable after defeating Almagro, Pizarro split his forces. He sent his brother Gonzalo on an expedition deep into the Andes to find the source of the Amazon River along with Francisco de Orellana. Hernando returned to Spain in 1539, where he was imprisoned for the killing of Almagro and his men; he remained in prison until 1561. Pizarro then returned to Peru. He tended his house and orchard, and wore old-fashioned clothes decorated with the cross of a knight of Santiago. He played with his four children born of Inca mothers, drank good wine, ate good food, and enjoyed life. Meanwhile, unbeknownst to Pizarro, the Almagrists formed a faction to oppose him, led by Diego's son Francisco Almagro and Panamá, a Native American woman. On June 26, 1541, the Almagrists, with a force of 20, broke into Pizarro's home while he entertained guests at dinner. He defended himself and killed one Almagrist before he was brought down by multiple lance and sword wounds.

The place where Pizarro died lies under a marble floor in the Peruvian presidential palace. In 1977, Hugo Ludeña, an archeologist, found Pizarro's coffin in an alcove of the palace that had been bricked off. A lead box was found that contained Pizarro's head. It was inscribed: "Here is the head of the Marquis don Francisco Pizarro, who discovered and won the kingdoms of Peru and brought them under the royal Crown of Castile."

The extraordinary wealth amassed by Francisco Pizarro sparked the explorations and conquests undertaken by Hernando de Soto, **Francisco Vasquez** de Coronado, and Sebastian de Benalcazar. In Peru, after his death, he left the legacies of *mestizo*—mixed Indian and Spanish blood—and the establishment of Catholicism that eventually supplanted the Inca religions.

## SOURCES:

### Books

*Concise Columbia Electronic Encyclopedia,* New York, Columbia University Press, 1994.
*Documents and Narratives Concerning the Discovery and Conquest of Latin America,* New York, Cortes Society, Kraus Reprint, 1969.
*Explorers and Discoverers of the World,* edited by Daniel B. Baker, Detroit, Gale Research, 1993.
Hemming, John, *The Conquest of the Incas,* London, Macmillan, 1970.
*The History of the Conquest of Peru,* two volumes, edited by William H. Prescott, Philadelphia, Lippincott, 1874.
*Who Was Who in World Exploration,* edited by Carl Waldman and Alan Wexler, New York, Facts on File. 1992.

### Periodicals

*National Geographic,* February 1992, pp. 90–121.

# Mary Helen Ponce
## 1938-
### Hispanic American writer and scholar

Writer Mary Helen Ponce married soon after she graduated from high school; she chose to stay home and care for her four children until her youngest son entered kindergarten. At that time, to the benefit of her readers and students, Ponce decided to educate herself and to write about her culture. While her work embraces this culture, she has not hesitated to fictionally discuss its more problematic aspects in her collection of short stories, *Taking Control,* and her novel, *The Wedding.*

Ponce was born January 24, 1938, to Tranquilino Ponce and Vincenta (Solis) Ponce in Pacoima, California. While, in a telephone interview with Ronie-Richele Garcia-Johnson, Ponce acknowledged that Pacoima was a bit like Taconos, the fictional town in

*The Wedding,* she emphasized that *The Wedding* is not autobiographical; Ponce did not grow up as Blanca of her novel did. Pacoima was, for Ponce, a good town, with "many nice families." Ponce also credits her parents, who had a "terrific sense of humor," and her very intelligent sisters, who served as role models for the young girl during her "very happy childhood."

As she told Garcia-Johnson, Ponce realized that "learning" was her "happiness," and, because of this, she was determined to educate herself when her youngest son was old enough to enter school in 1974. After earning her bachelor's degree from California State University in 1978, Ponce went on to receive a master's degree from the same university in 1980. Ponce studied from 1982 to 1984 at the University of California at Los Angeles, where she was the recipient of the History Department's Danforth Fellowship, and worked toward her Ph.D. at the University of New Mexico in 1988. Ponce then served as an instructor of Chicano studies from 1982 until 1987 at UCLA; she was an adjunct professor from 1987 to 1988. Ponce also taught at California State University of Northridge, and she was a member of the adjunct faculty at the University of New Mexico in the Women Studies Program from 1988 to 1992. In addition to studying women and Mexican American culture, Ponce has served on organizations which focus on the same subjects, including the Mexican American National Women's Association, the National Association of Chicano Studies, the Western Association of Women Historians, and Mujeres Activas en Letras y Ciencias Sociales.

Although studying, teaching, participating in various organizational activities, and caring for a family keep Ponce busy, she has managed to find time to write. She has contributed stories to magazines throughout the Southwestern United States and Mexico; during the early to mid-1980s, *Nuestro* magazine published several of her stories. In 1987, Ponce had written enough good stories to publish her first collection, *Taking Control,* and by 1989, she had finished her first novel, *The Wedding.* Ponce's *Taking Control* has been warmly received, and women have especially enjoyed *The Wedding.*

As the book's title suggests, the nine stories in *Taking Control* are about Hispanic women who do or do not take control of their lives. One of the most striking stories of this collection is "La Josie." La Josie inadvertently frightens a young, divorced mother when, every weekend, she pounds on her door to escape her abusive husband. The narrator of the story can not believe it when, the morning after every fight, La Josie once again appears to be in love with Pete, her husband. The narrator has her own problems with men; her second husband expects her to wash his jeans in hot water so they will fit him more tightly and then runs off with a seventeen-year-old girl. Upon seeing La Josie some years later, the narrator recounts, "Yesterday I saw la Josie ... and I saw myself."

While another story, "The Painkillers," deals with the suffering of a mistreated woman and her passive response, it presents a healthy relationship as a contrast. Mary Lou Lopez is sure that her husband will leave her after she fails to give birth to a boy and has a hysterectomy; after she undergoes the same procedure, Crista knows that although her family will be disappointed, the love of her husband is secure and reassuring. Crista, along with the assertive Ave in "The Campout" and Concha, the woman who decides to take control of her life in "El Marxista," are exemplary of Ponce's strong Hispanic female characters.

### Explores Problems of Assimilated Mexican Americans

More than presenting problems specific to women, some of the stories in *Taking Control,* such as "The Campout," "The New Affirmative Action Officer," and "The Permanent" deal with a Mexican American dilemma: How can the Mexican American live comfortably in American society while maintaining respect for her culture? How should educated or assimilated Mexican Americans react to criticism of those who persist in speaking Spanish and continue to work in the fields? How should those Mexican Americans who have "made it" in America treat those who have not?

The last story in the collection, "The Permanent," seems to answer these questions. After becoming angry and embarrassed at the sight of Mexican Americans who can not speak English and who dressed like Mexicans, and after pretending not to understand Spanish herself, an elderly Mexican American woman finds herself defending them. She realizes that she was wrong to feel anger and embarrassment: "Her anger was spent. But she felt guilty. Very guilty." She thinks, "I will no longer impose my value system on other Mexicanos. I will not think of them as different, as them, but as us. And, I will be of some help." In addition to presenting more assimilated Mexican Americans with a solution, the author of "The Permanent" seems to have created a guideline for herself: with her writing, Ponce is being "of some help."

Not everyone, however, would agree that Ponce positively contributes to Mexican American literature. **Alejandro Morales**, an instructor of Chicano literature at the University of California of Irvine discussed Ponce's first novel, *The Wedding*, in the *Los Angeles Times.* According to Morales, the book presents a "vision" which is "grotesque satire, naturalistic caricature that tends to bolster already damaging stereotypes of Mexican Americans and Ameri-

cans." "'The Wedding,'" wrote Morales, "is not an uncommon story. It has been told too often. Ponce's version is sadly naive, contradictory and insulting. Her story ignores the positive contributions of Chicano blue-collar workers, takes away their dignity, pride, and history. 'The Wedding' is best left unread."

In her interview with Garcia-Johnson, Ponce answered such criticism, insisting that *The Wedding*, which was originally a longer work, is first and foremost a "love story." She also stated that she would not apologize for her work because "it's honest." While many people cannot understand how Blanca could love Cricket, Ponce reminds readers that, during the 1950s, there were not many expectations for women. Blanca had no hope of educating herself, and she had no choice but to marry. Growing up in the environment he did, Cricket never had a chance either. The couple, according to the author, "didn't know any different."

### Realistically Portrays Hope and Tradition in *The Wedding*

Ponce wanted to write a realistic story about a love like Blanca's, the love of family, of tradition, independence, and of hope, which are, according to Ponce, timeless. She also wanted to write about a wedding. When Ponce was growing up near Hollywood during the late 1940s and early 1950s, a young woman's dream was to wear a colonial-style dress, like Scarlett O'Hara in *Gone with the Wind,* at her wedding, and there were many weddings during those years.

*The Wedding*'s plot centers on the preparation for a wedding and the wedding itself; as the story progresses, the reader is introduced to the bride-to-be, Blanca, the groom-to-be, Sammy-the-Cricket, and their friends and family. Instead of attempting to educate herself and work her way out of poverty, Blanca drops out of school to seek a husband. She is attracted to Sammy-the-Cricket not because he is intelligent, or because he is kind to her, but because he fights well and is a gang leader. Getting married is more important to Blanca than marriage itself; she dreams of having a wedding that will make her family proud and impress the people of her small town.

The choice of cushions, wedding dresses, flowers, bridesmaids, and even the groom are described in great detail. The wedding itself, rather than the marriage, is important to Blanca; she does not consider canceling the wedding when she realizes that Cricket will always be cheap, because to cancel the wedding would disappoint her family. While it is true that a wedding is one of the most important events in a person's life (if a person decides to marry), the symbolic significance of the union is lost in the process of planning Blanca's wedding. Although the morning of her wedding, Blanca is "transformed and excited," this fictional character can not escape reality. The moment before she walks down the aisle, Blanca's "armpits" are "damp with sweat" and "beads of perspiration" are "on her upper lip."

A perspiring, weeping bride, a groom destined for jail—the ending of *The Wedding* demonstrates that if the event was truly the "best wedding in the barrio" as Blanca wanted it to be, that is all it was. By using the pivotal social event in a young person's life, the event that unifies the sexes, as a vehicle, Ponce has presented what she seems to loathe the most: male ignorance and disrespect for females, and female ignorance and passivity. If there is any social commentary in *The Wedding*, perhaps it is a feminist one.

Many readers may not understand why Ponce chose to represent "her people" as she did. In contrast, Ponce's character Ave from "The Campout" in *Taking Control* offers an alternative view of Mexican American barrio culture. When asked by her husband and her white friends why she destroyed a sketch of poor, clam-digging Mexican children on the beach, she told them that she did not want to romanticize her subjects. "David, what you and Bitsey and Biff call beauty, art is not. Not really. It's the reality. I mean you think it's graceful, artistic . . . I mean all those words is romanticizing, distorting the reality, making suffering look noble, artistic. . . ." If Ponce's works can enable families to understand the devastation misogynic and masochistic attitudes cause, then the novel is well worth reading even if it is not written in the style of more popular Hispanic works.

Ponce told Garcia-Johnson that, since 1990, there has been a "terrific conflict" between her work as a writer and her scholarly work: she loves to write as well as study history and literature. Consequently, since the publication of *The Wedding*, Ponce has continued to write as well as teach. As of 1992, Ponce was teaching at the University of California at Santa Barbara in the Chicano Studies Department as a member of the adjunct faculty; she was also working on her dissertation.

## SELECTED PUBLISHED WORK:

*Taking Control* (short stories), Arte Público Press, 1987.
*The Wedding* (novel), Arte Público Press, 1989.
*Hoyt Street: An Autobiography,* University of New Mexico Press, 1993.

## SOURCES:

### Books

Ponce, Mary Helen, *Taking Control,* Arte Público Press, 1987.

Ponce, *The Wedding,* Arte Público Press, 1989.

### Periodicals

*Los Angeles Times,* November 19, 1989, p. 10.
*Nuestro,* December, 1983, p. 44; March, 1985, p. 54; April, 1985, p. 43; June-July, 1985, p. 50.

### Other

Ponce, Mary Helen, interview with Ronie-Richele Garcia-Johnson, August 10, 1992.

—*Sketch by Ronie-Richele Garcia-Johnson*

# Juan Ponce de Leon
## 1460-1521
### Spanish explorer

Many casual students of history remember Juan Ponce de Leon as the explorer who came to the New World looking for the fabled fountain of youth. He failed, of course, in that search, but he had a distinguished and extremely prosperous career in colonizing the Caribbean. Sailing with Christopher Columbus on his second voyage, Ponce de Leon quickly rose to prominence in the Spanish drive for colonies in the western hemisphere. Not only did he become the first person to claim part of mainland North America for Spain, but he also conquered Puerto Rico and governed it for several years. During his career, he became one of the wealthiest men in the new territories of Spanish America.

### From Poverty into Service

Although some scholars put Ponce de Leon's birthdate at 1474, most agree that he was born in Santervas in Tierra de Campos, Spain, in 1460. Each side of his family had once held great power and prestige in Aragon, and the union of the Ponces with the Leons had only increased their influence. Yet by the time Ponce de Leon was born, all of the former family glory had vanished. Although Ponce de Leon had one or two highly placed distant relatives, he found himself destitute and was unable to pursue a military career.

When he presented himself to Don Pedro Nunez de Guzman, Ponce de Leon had very little understanding of military skills. Don Pedro, acceding to the boy's spirit and the reputation of his family, accepted Ponce de Leon as a page, allowing him to be trained

*Juan Ponce de Leon*

in his spare hours. Ponce de Leon's teacher became so impressed with his progress that he asked Don Pedro to let the boy become a full-time squire, or knight in training. He quickly moved through the ranks of Don Pedro's private army, starting as a common soldier, despite his aristocratic blood. Eventually he outdid the other young soldiers and became Don Pedro's personal squire.

When the houses of Castile and Aragon entered a civil war, Ponce de Leon followed Don Pedro into battle. Although no one recorded what exact gallantry he performed, Ponce de Leon impressed King Ferdinand so much at the Battle of Toro that he received his knighthood on the battlefield. Ponce de Leon instantly became a captain in Don Pedro's private army and, shortly after the civil strife, went with Don Pedro in the final campaign against the Moors in Spain. In her book *Juan Ponce de Leon,* biographer Nina Brown Baker quoted sources at the time saying that he "displayed daring and enterprise against the Moors." Aside from that mention, however, his ten years of struggle against the Moors remain mostly undocumented.

In 1492 Christopher Columbus shook Europe with news of his western passage to India, which turned out to be the New World. Occupying territories the Moors had abandoned quickly bored the ambitious Ponce de Leon, and when Don Pedro came to him with the idea that he follow Columbus on his second voyage, to be made in 1493, he quickly joined the long list of volunteers for service in the colonizing fleet. The King selected Ponce de Leon to gather and lead a group of sixty soldiers, with whom he set sail on September 25.

## To the New World

Columbus had left forty men in Haiti after his first voyage, and in his haste to see their progress he passed several of the islands on which he had planned to resupply, eventually forcing him to stop and look for water on an unknown island. Ponce de Leon was the first to set foot on Puerto Rico; the impression it left made certain that he would one day return. For the moment, however, Ponce de Leon faced the disappointment of the rest of the expedition on reaching Haiti. Columbus' men, who had been given the task of establishing a permanent settlement, had begun searching for gold as soon as the admiral's ship left their sight. No buildings or infrastructure stood where Columbus expected an inviting, functioning Spanish town. The natives told Columbus how his men had forced them to pan for gold, had tortured and even killed those who could not find any, and had treated them with such inhumanity that they had no choice but to band together and kill the Spaniards.

Ponce de Leon labored among a group overpopulated by aristocratic wealth-seekers and underpopulated by craftsmen or people willing to work for the long-term goal of establishing permanent settlements. Hostility among the Spaniards began, and the once-friendly natives recoiled from the poor treatment they received from the Europeans. Columbus proved to be a rather ineffective leader on land, and when he sailed back to Spain in 1496, he feared that the bitter returning colonists would mutiny and kill him. He chose Ponce de Leon to lead the group of soldiers who would protect him during the journey.

Ponce de Leon did not return to Haiti until 1502. On that journey he met the woman he would soon marry, the widow Inez de la Torre. Haiti had changed since Ponce de Leon lived in a grass hut there in the 1490s, but still the conditions could not compare to the luxury Dona Inez had known. Ponce de Leon always looked to the future for justification of the hardships of the present, and his new wife supported him.

For the natives, both the present and the future rapidly began to unravel as Spanish civilization took root. Ponce de Leon himself led expeditions into the unknown territories to bring back slaves to replace those who had been worked to death by their masters. Despite Queen Isabella's decree that the natives be Christianized, the rulers of the colonies opted instead to keep them in their native state, thus denying them the rights of a Christian. For about two years, from 1502 to 1504, Ponce de Leon fought the Higuey tribe in eastern Hispaniola until they finally submitted.

Governor Ovando of Hispaniola rewarded Ponce de Leon by giving him control of the area he had conquered. Ponce de Leon wanted to run his territories in a sustainable way, but in order to do that, he believed that he had to have better relations with the natives than other Spanish lords had. Baker asserted that Ponce de Leon "ruled mildly and kindly." Ponce de Leon had the vision to forget about dreams of gold and start developing crops which could be sold on European markets for high prices. Baker also credited Ponce de Leon for learning from native methods of agriculture instead of merely imposing his own ideas.

### On to a Richer Port

Ponce de Leon had found happiness and prosperity in Haiti, but one day in 1508 a man paddled 55 miles from Puerto Rico to meet with the chief of the white men. He came and offered "yellow pebbles," which he had heard that white men loved, in exchange for a string of bells. Ponce de Leon happily made the trade, and began to consider exploring Puerto Rico. After some deliberation he set sail for the island with the visiting native and a small company of soldiers. He befriended Chief Guaybana of the island and tried to use trade rather than conquest as a means of getting gold for Spain.

Governor Ovando saw things differently, however. He had no interest in talk of trade or friendship between Spaniards and the natives. He ordered Ponce de Leon to make another expedition, but Ponce de Leon convinced him that their visits should remain peaceful for the moment. Although the larger company of men Ponce de Leon took on his second mission treated their hosts with insolence, the trip passed with no serious hostility. When Ponce de Leon returned, however, Ovando had been replaced as governor by Don Diego Columbus, Christopher's son. Columbus began immediate action to take Puerto Rico by force.

Ponce de Leon had left his wife and child on the island, and he began to fear for their lives. He joined the attacking army as a foot soldier because Columbus had deliberately left him off the list of officers who would lead the group. Back in Spain, Ovando lobbied the King to put Ponce de Leon in charge of the new colony, and so he did. Ponce de Leon could not stop the war which Spanish aggression had started, and he led the Spaniards in a bloody battle against Chief Guaybana's brother for two years before Puerto Rico finally came under his total control.

Ponce de Leon ruled Puerto Rico as governor until 1512, when the King reinstated the men who had initially led the attack on the island. Although his plantations continued to make him rich, Ponce de Leon wanted glory as well. When he began to hear rumors of a "fountain of youth" somewhere in the Caribbean, he thought that it would be the perfect way to get back in the public eye.

Ponce de Leon sailed through the Bahamas to Florida, which he thought to be an island. His party planted the Spanish flag where they landed, the first to do so on mainland North America. Florida treated him roughly, however. His rapport with other native groups in the Caribbean had made him friends, while these natives wanted nothing to do with him. He found no significant stores of treasure, and of course he found no fountain, if he had ever believed in it to begin with. He returned to Puerto Rico disappointed, not knowing the magnitude of his discovery.

Though reinstated as governor of Puerto Rico in 1514, Ponce de Leon continued to think of establishing a permanent settlement in Florida. He sailed there again in 1521, and when he landed at Charlotte Harbor, the natives attacked in force. Ponce de Leon himself took an arrow in the leg, and his men panicked. The next in command sounded the retreat, and the Spaniards sailed for Cuba. Several days later, Ponce de Leon died from the poison on the arrow's tip.

### SOURCES:

Baker, Nina Brown, *Juan Ponce de Leon,* New York, Knopf, 1966.

Floyd, Troy S., *The Columbus Dynasty in the Caribbean, 1492–1526,* University of New Mexico Press, 1973.

McAlister, Lyle N., *Spain and Portugal in the New World, 1492–1700,* Minneapolis, University of Minnesota Press, 1984.

—*Sketch by James McCarthy*

# Elena Poniatowska
## 1932(?)-
**Mexican novelist, journalist, and essayist**

Elena Poniatowska has gained recognition as one of Mexico's top journalists and novelists. Her work has ranged from controversial exposés about the covert actions of the Mexican government to best-selling novels. Beth E. Jorgensen, writing in *Spanish American Women Writers,* identified a common theme connecting Poniatowska's various works: "That common thread is the profound commitment to interpreting contemporary Mexican society, with special attention to the silenced voices and the marginalized lives that constitute the majority experience in the vast human landscape of her country."

Poniatowska was born in Paris, France, on May 19, 1932 or 1933. Her father, Yvan E. Poniatowski, was a descendent of the last king of Poland, Stanislos Augusto Poniatowsky, and Prince Josef Ciolek Poniatowsky, Marshal of France. Her mother was a Mexican nationalist, Paula Amor Iturbe, living in Paris. Poniatowska began her education in Paris, but after World War II began, her mother took her and her sister to the south of France while her father fought the Germans. They lived with her paternal grandparents, who were exiled from Poland. They moved from there to Mexico to live with her mother's family when Poniatowska was eight years old. She had never spoken Spanish before moving to Mexico, where she learned from the servants in their home. She attended a British high school, where she learned to speak English, and the Liceo Franco Mexicano in Mexico City. Poniatowska then moved to Torresdale, Pennsylvania, and finished high school at the Convent of the Sacred Heart's Eden Hall. She received a scholarship and attended Manhattanville College.

Poniatowska married Guillermo Haro Barraza, an astronomer, and they had three children, Emmanuel, Felipe, and Paula. He was a member of the Colegio Nacional, director of the Department of Astrophysics at UNAM, and head of the Instituto de Astrofisica, Optica y Electronica (INAOE). Haro won the Lomonosow Prize in 1987, the year before his death. Poniatowska was a founder of the Cineteca Nacional—the Mexican Film Library—and of the Siglo XXI publishing house. She also published a newspaper, *La Jornada,* and has written for many magazines and periodicals, including reviews for *Plural* and *Vuelta.*

Poniatowska returned to Mexico in 1954 and began working as a journalist for the newspaper *Excelsior.* Her first assignments were to interview artists, musicians, and writers. Her first work was also published in 1954, a short novel entitled *Lilus Kikus.* In 1955, she began working for *Novedades,* where she continued to work as a journalist while writing her novels. Poniatowska has been hailed as a heroine of oppressed peoples for the views she has expressed in her novels, as well as in interviews about the cultural, political, and social aspects of the Mexican community. It was not until 1969 that she began her greatest and most prolific writing period, which lasted almost twenty years. She also became a Mexican citizen in 1969. For her novel *Hasta no verte Jesús mío,* published in 1969, Poniatowska interviewed a poor, uneducated woman from the slums of Mexico City whom she met in a public washroom. The novel is not a chronicle of the woman's life, but Poniatowska created a character based upon the woman and others in a similar plight.

### Writes Story of Student Massacre

On October 2, 1968, a student movement met for a peaceful protest at the Plaza de Tlatelolco in Mexico City. Mexican troops came to the protest, however, and killed hundreds of unarmed people. Nothing was published about the massacre in the Mexican press at the time. Poniatowska interviewed hundreds of people and published the first book that documents the tragedy, *La noche de Tlatelolco,* in 1971. Her brother, Jan, was killed at Tlatelolco, and the book is dedicated to him. Poniatowska delved into documents, police records, government speeches, and policies comparing the massacre to the Spanish conquest of Mexico. In 1970, two years after the student massacre, Mexico wanted to award her the Villaurrutia Prize, but she refused to accept it. Instead, she denounced government repression, and in many later situations she continued to expose news that the government had suppressed from the media.

Poniatowska has lectured throughout the United States, Mexico, Europe, and Australia. Her work has been translated into numerous languages. She became renowned for her extraordinary interviewing techniques. Poniatowska has also received many awards, including an honorary degree from the Universidad de Sinaloa, the prize of Turismo Frances, the Mazatlan Award, the award of the Club de Periodistas, the Manuel Buendia Journalism Prize, and the radio UNAM prize for *Palabras cruzadas,* published in 1961—a collection of her interviews with Hispanic society figures of the 1950s, including **Fidel Castro**, Francois Mauriac, **Luis Buñuel**, and **Lazaro Cárdenas**. She was the first woman to receive the Premio Nacional de Periodismo in 1979.

Poniatowska has supported grassroots women's groups, and many of her novels explore the oppressed woman and the perceived traditional roles of women in society. In her 1979 novel *De noche vienes,* Poniatowska wrote several short stories with women protagonists and examined the issue of double standards for the sexes. In one story, she reversed traditional roles so that the heroine of the story, Esmeralda, is a nurse who juggles a career and five husbands. Poniatowska's semi-autobiographical novel *La "Flor de Lis"* (1988) is about a woman, Mariana, who was born in France and moved to Mexico. Mariana's father was French and her mother was Mexican. Poniatowska describes Mariana's family as aristocratic and appears to weave her own heritage into Mariana's story. The story deals with social classes and cultures and the discovery of her own identity. Utilizing her skill as a journalist, Poniatowska has often intertwined nonfiction and fiction styles of writing to create her novels.

Poniatowska wrote another short story that exemplifies the female role in society for *Américas* magazine in 1991, entitled "The Message." The story is a narrative of a young girl waiting on the front step of the home of the man she loves. He is not home, and she waits and waits. "You know, since I was a child I have sat down like this to wait; I was always docile because I was waiting for you. I was waiting for you. I know that all women wait. They wait for future life, for all those images forged in solitude, for all that forest that moves towards them, for all that immense promise that is a man."

## SELECTED PUBLISHED WORKS:

*Lilus Kikus*, Los Presentes, 1954.
*Melés y Teleo*, Revista Panoramas, 1956.
*Palabras cruzadas*, Era, 1961.
*Todo empezó el domingo*, Fondo de Cultura Economica, 1963.
*Los cuentos de Lilus Kikus*, Universidad Veracruzana, 1967.
*México visto a oho de pájaro*, Colibri, SEP, 1968.
*Hasta no verte Jesús mío*, Era, 1969.
*La noche de Tlatelolco*, Era, 1971, translation by Helen Lane published as *Massacre in Mexico*, Viking, 1975.
*Querido Diego, te abraza Quiela*, Era, 1978, translation by Katherine Silver published as *Dear Diego*, Pantheon, 1979.
*De noche vienes*, Grijalbo, 1979.
*Gaby Brimmer* (with Brimmer), Grijalbo, 1979.
*La vendedora de nubes*, Colibri, SEP, 1979.
*El león no es como lo pintan*, Colibri, 1979.
*Fuerte es el silencio*, Era, 1980.
*La casa en la tierra* (with Mariana Yampolsky), INI-Fonapas, 1980.
*Ay vida, no me mereces!*, Mortiz, 1985.
*La raíz y el camino* (with Yampolsky), Fondo de Cultura Economica, 1985.
*Estancias del olvido* (with Yampolsky), INI-Centro Hidalguense de Investigaciones Historicas, 1986.
*Tlacotalpan* (with Yampolsky), Mexico City, 1987.
*Hablando en plata* (with David Maawad), Centro Hidalguense de Investigaciones Historicas, 1987.
*México sin retoque* (with Hector Garcia), UNAM, 1987.
*La "Flor de Lis"*, Era, 1988.
*Nada, nadie: Las voces del temblor*, Era, 1988.
*Juchitán de las mujeres* (with Graciela Iturbide), Toledo, 1989.
*Compañeras de México*, University of California Art Gallery, 1990.

## SOURCES:

### Books

*Dictionary of Literary Biography, Volume 113: Modern Latin-American Fiction Writers*, edited by William Luis, Detroit, Gale, 1992.

Flores, Angel, *Spanish American Authors: The Twentieth Century*, New York, Wilson, 1992.
*Spanish American Women Writers: A Bio-Bibliographical Source Book*, edited by Diane E. Marting, New York, Greenwood Press, 1990.

### Periodicals

*Américas*, 1991, p. 56.

*—Sketch by Phyllis Noah*

# Diego Portales
## 1793-1837
### Chilean independence leader

Diego Portales was a major figure in the early national period of Chilean history. In *Makers of Democracy*, Harold Davis noted that while the conservatives and pro-fascist elements in Chile during the 1930's looked back to Portales as the founding father of a stable, prosperous, and independent Chile, socialists and other liberals used his example to assert that Chile needed more liberal reform. Portales, they said, had simply established a system which intrinsically prevented justice. Davis declared that "the real Portales was neither of these extremes."

### A Comfortable Childhood

On June 16, 1793, Maria Encarnacion Fernandez de Palazuelos Portales gave birth to a son, Diego José Victor Portales. Maria's husband, José Santiago Portales, worked as the superintendent of the Casa Moneda, the mint at Santiago de Chile where the family lived. Some historians have estimated that Portales had nearly two dozen siblings. Fortunately, the family had inherited a certain amount of wealth and prestige, and even with many of mouths to feed they managed to live comfortably.

The young Portales took little interest in books. Despite his father's objections, he remained in school only long enough to attend the Colegio de San Carlos in Santiago. Harold Davis asserted that Portale's failure to pursue university studies later caused him a "certain feeling of inferiority in the presence of other Chilean leaders of superior education and social position." His father did convince him to enter a law program, but Portales soon dropped out to enter the business world.

He passed the exam that qualified him to be a worker at the mint his father managed, but left shortly to join official monopolies as an *estanquero*. In his biography of Portales, Jay Kinsbruner noted that Portales had a natural talent for business. By the time **Bernardo O'Higgins** had successfully fought for Chilean independence in 1818, Portales had already achieved considerable success. Portales did not take an active role in the revolutionary struggle though Davis suggested that he was sympathetic toward O'Higgins and the independence movement. Still Portales remained concerned with business and his own domestic life.

When his wife died in 1821, Portales suffered greatly. He left for Peru and started a business venture with Manuel Cea. During his time there, he wrote to his father that only God could give him any solace from his grief. God had chosen to take his wife from him and he would honor the "celibacy that God has desired to present me," as he told his father in 1821. In the same letter, he insisted that "women do not exist for my shattered heart. I prefer God." Portales put his grief behind him the next year and began a serious romantic liaison. His business venture with Cea had declined, and at times his father had to send money to cover the company's debts.

## Political Life

Since 1818 factional strife had produced an unpredictable and unstable political situation in Chile. O'Higgins had removed the burden of Spanish rule, but despite his benevolent intentions, his ineptitude as a ruler led to discontent. Portales returned to Chile in 1823 and helped to organize the Pelucones, or "Big Wigs." This conservative group supported independence but despised most of the manifestations of democracy. Kinsbruner has flatly asserted that Portales simply "was not a democrat."

In his book on Chilean capitalism, Brian Loveman suggested that Portales entered politics for revenge. During his joint venture with Cea, Portales had entered a contract to import tobacco on behalf of the state. The contract was expensive, the government failed to control contraband competition, and the venture failed. No one is certain why Portales joined the political fray, but, as Loveman wrote, "Whatever the motivation, Portales' solution for political disorder, imposed in cooperation with conservative interests . . . emphasized restoration of legitimacy, law and order, and fiscal integrity." Loveman further noted that Portales' coming "autocratic republic" inspired awe in some and fear in others.

By the late 1820s, Chilean politics had become a near-vacuum. Seven presidents in two years fueled Portales' revolution. Ordinary Chileans—whose country had not known stability since 1818—longed for a reliable power locus. Portales plied his substantial connections, convincing General Freire that the time would soon be auspicious for establishing a new government. By 1829 Freire had become the supreme director under the Pact of Ochagavia. Historians have said that Portales buoyed the junta that supported him.

Kinsbruner stated that from 1829 to 1837, Portales became the "most prominent personality in Chile." Yet he refused to assume the Presidency. He preferred instead to walk behind the figurehead and make the important decisions. Although scholars disagree about whether Portales physically composed the Chilean Constitution in 1833, most concur that the principles articulated there came chiefly from him. He did not have many friends, but historians have agreed that his honesty, integrity, and sternness earned him admirers.

The Chilean people elected Joaquin Prieto as president, the first of three conservatives who each ruled Chile for a decade. Portales eventually left the national government and went to the town of Valparaiso. Davis described the port town as "one of the most lawless in the continent" before Portales' administration, but four months later "peace and order" prevailed. Portales also established the important Naval School at Valparaiso. He believed that his public career had ended.

Portales' party had defeated General Freire in the elections of 1832, but by 1835 Freire had reorganized. President Prieto summoned Portales to the aid of his country. Named minister of the interior, war, and foreign relations, Portales tried to rally the people against Freire's attack. Although the general was supported by Bolivian dictator Andrés de Santa Cruz, Freire failed to topple Prieto's government. Portales captured Freire.

Angry at Santa Cruz for supporting Freire, Portales prepared to dislodge him from power. Loveman wrote that Portales became "bent upon war" with Peru. After a naval altercation in which two Peruvian ships fell into Chilean hands, Santa Cruz agreed to relinquish the ships, but refused to apologize for a diplomatic affair that had embarassed Portales and Chile. Envisioning imminent war, Portales assumed broad emergency powers, executing some for crimes such as "disturb[ing] public order" and being "disrespectful toward the government."

Public opinion turned against Portales for initiating what Loveman called a "regime of terror." Troops which previously had served loyally grew angry. During June of 1837, Portales stood reviewing troops. Colonel José Antonio Vidaurre led a mutiny and captured Portales. The troops marched on to Santiago, bringing Portales along in shackles. They had little hope of success and decided to execute Portales before loyal troops could liberate him.

Chile successfully eliminated Santa Cruz from Bolivia despite Portales' death. The government had in fact gained a martyr, tying the assassins to Santa

Cruz. Military victory produced a national feeling of confidence, and Chile's identity solidified.

Although Chile hardly developed democratic institutions during the 19th century, one cannot ignore its success at establishing enduring institutions of any kind when most of the rest of the continent roiled in political chaos. For this Portales must take a position of the credit—or the blame.

## SOURCES:

Davis, Harold, *Makers of Democracy in Latin America,* New York, H. W. Wilson, 1945.

Loveman, Brian, *Chile: The Legacy of Hispanic Capitalism,* Oxford University Press, 1979.

Kinsbruner, J., *Diego Portales: Interpretive Essays on the Man and Times,* Hague, Martinus Nijhoff, 1967.

—*Sketch by James McCarthy*

# Estela Portillo Trambley
## 1936-
### Mexican American writer

Estela Portillo Trambley is noted for being the first Chicana to publish a short story collection and the first to write a musical comedy. Like many Chicano writers, she draws on her ethnic background for the themes that dominate her literary creations, but instead of condemning the demoralizing forces present in the poor Chicano neighborhoods she has known, she finds the *barrio* to be a source of joy and spiritual awakening for its inhabitants. She explained her position to Juan Bruce-Novoa in *Chicano Authors: Inquiry by Interview:* "When I was a child, poverty was a common suffering for everybody around me. A common suffering is a richness in itself."

Portillo Trambley was born on January 16, 1936, in El Paso, Texas, and has spent most of her life living and working in the same city. She holds both Bachelor of Arts and Master of Arts degrees in English from the University of Texas at El Paso, and followed a career in education before deciding to seriously apply herself to writing. She worked as a high school English teacher in El Paso from 1957 to 1964. She has also served as chairperson of the English department of the El Paso Technical Institute and, since 1979, has worked in the Department of Special Services of the El Paso public school system.

Her flair for the dramatic arts won Portillo Trambley a position as resident dramatist at El Paso Community College, and as such she produced and directed the college's dramatic productions and served as a drama instructor. Concurrently with her work as a dramatist, she hosted a talk show, *Estela Sez,* for one year on Radio KIZZ and wrote and hosted a cultural program, *Cumbres,* for KROD-TV in El Paso. Her experience with television writing made her realize that she wished to pursue writing as a full-time career. A year after making this decision, in 1971, her first play, *The Day of the Swallows,* was published. The following year she won the prestigious Quinto Sol Award, a literary award presented by Quinto Sol Publications.

### Blends Tradition and History in Writings

Since then, Portillo Trambley has contributed a varied and important body of work to the world of Chicano literature. Her historic collection of short stories, *Rain of Scorpions and Other Writings,* appeared in 1975, and her musical comedy, *Sun Images,* was first produced in 1976. Subsequently, she has seen *The Day of the Swallows* appear in *Contemporary Chicano Theatre,* edited by Roberto Garza, in 1976, and her play, *Puente Negro,* published in the anthology *Sor Juana and Other Plays,* in 1983. She is also the author of numerous unpublished plays and of the novel, *Trini,* published by Bilingual Press in 1986.

Drawing from her Hispanic background and its nearly mythic traditions of *machismo* and female subservience, Portillo Trambley's work often focuses on the plight of women in a male-dominated society. In *Rain of Scorpions and Other Writings,* for example, she speaks of a world where "it had been decreed long ago by man-made laws that living things were not equal. It had been decreed that women should be possessions, slaves, pawns in the hands of men with ways of beasts. It had been decreed that women were to be walloped effigies to burn upon the altars of men." A similar feminist content is found in what is considered her best play, *The Day of the Swallows,* which ends with the suicide of its desperate protagonist Josefa, who fears revelation of her lesbianism.

Although her work contains feminist sympathies, Portillo Trambley is steadfast in her desire to keep her writing from being political. She told Bruce-Novoa: "Political literature, no matter how clever it might be, tends to make stereotypes of the evil exploiter and the poor, innocent victim. That is not life. The exploiter is a human being too. He might be violent and selfish and greedy and mean, but down deep, despite having mutated into a Machiavellian oddity, he is still human. Once you take this away from your character in literature, you've taken away his life. Political literature assassinates characters."

## SELECTED PUBLISHED WORK:

*The Day of the Swallows* (play), El Espejo Quinto Sol, 1971.

*Impressions* (haiku poems), El Espejo Quinto Sol, 1971.

(Editor) *Chicanas en literatura y Arte,* Quinto Sol, 1974.

*Rain of Scorpions and Other Writings* (short stories), Tonatiuh International, 1976.

*Sor Juana and Other Plays,* Bilingual Press, 1983.

*Trini,* Bilingual Press, 1986.

## SOURCES:

Bruce-Novoa, Juan, *Chicano Authors: Inquiry by Interview,* University of Texas Press, 1980.

Tramblay, Portillo, *Rain of Scorpions and Other Writings,* Tonatiuh International, 1976.

*—Sketch by Marian C. Gonsior*

# Manuel Prado y Ugarteche
## 1889-1967
### Peruvian banker and statesman

Manuel Prado y Ugarteche was twice president of Peru, from 1939 to 1945 and from 1956 to 1962. He was born in Lima to an aristocratic family involved in politics and banking. His father, General Mariano Ignacio Prado, was also elected president of Peru in 1876. Prado studied in Peru and France, earning degrees in both science and engineering. He taught science and mathematics at the University of San Marcos. Military coups were very common in Peru and some 22 presidents were deposed by *golpes de estado* (coup d'etats). At the beginning of the republic in the early 1800s, the military was separated into groups of men who followed a particular leader (*caudillo*) who would become president after a coup d'etat. Ramón Castilla, one of the country's most honored *caudillos* (1845–1851 and 1855–1862) unified the army. There were revolts within the army and by 1870, leaders in Peru decided the military was not needed to run the government. After Manuel Pardo was elected as the first civilian president of Peru in 1872, many civilians were appointed to government posts. For the next 19 years, a constitutional government ruled Peru. During that time, the military was reunited and trained by the French military. A more professional army ensued that was discouraged from being active in politics. An alliance was reached between the military and the civilian government.

On February 4, 1914, Prado participated in the overthrow of President Guillermo Billinghurst. This was the first coup since 1895. Colonel Óscar R. Benavides became president and he promoted Prado to lieutenant. José Pardo y Barreda was elected president in 1915. The military intervened again in 1919 and Augusto Leguía became dictator until 1930. During his *oncenio* (11-year reign), Leguía attempted to become a permanent dictator and tried to destroy the political power of the oligarchy and the military. Prado was forced into exile by Leguía because of his association with the *Partido Civil* (Civil Party; or, the *Civilistas*), founded by Manuel Pardo in the 1800s. Leguía disposed of the *Civilistas* and several political parties and had himself re-elected twice, in 1924 and 1929. A revolt ensued in 1930 with the help of the military and general elections were held in 1931. Eight new political parties were organized. The most influential party, the *Alianza Popular Revolucionaria Americana* (American Popular Revolutionary Alliance; APRA) was formed by a student movement at San Marcos University. When Sanchez Cerro was elected president in 1931, the *Apristas*—as members of the APRA were known—were banned and forced to go underground. The *Aprista* labor leader, Luis Negreiro Vega was assassinated and many *Apristas* were jailed or exiled. After President Cerro was assassinated (possibly by an *Aprista*), Congress appointed General Benavides (promoted from colonel) to finish serving Cerro's term as president. Benavides also banned the *Apristas.*

### Became President of Peru

Prado was appointed finance minister and premier by Benavides and in 1934 he was appointed president of the Central Reserve Bank of Peru. With the support of Benavides, Prado was elected president of Peru in 1939. He won 77 percent of the votes, although his opposing candidate was also from a conservative aristocratic family. Prado allowed the Communist Party to operate legally and they were permitted to form the *Confederación de Trabajadores del Peru* (Confederation of Workers of Peru; CTP). During his first term as president, Prado improved relations with the *Apristas,* but the ban was not lifted until a few days before he left office. During Prado's term as president, Peru won a war with Ecuador in the Battle of Zarumilla and the economy improved greatly.

Prado, who was being pressured into instituting free elections, denied several political parties from electing candidates for the presidency in 1945. However, he did allow the newly formed *Frente Democrático Nacional* (Democratic National Front; FDN) to elect a candidate. After José Luis Bustamante y Rivero—the FDN candidate—was elected president, the economic situation in Peru began to deteriorate. Leftists in APRA began a rebellion against Bustamante with the help of the navy and General Manuel Odria and ousted him in October 1948. Odria became the new dictator of Peru and reigned for the next eight years. During his dictatorship, Odria banned APRA, the *Apristas* were persecuted, and many of their leaders went into exile until December 1955.

In 1955, the editor of *La Prensa*, Pedro Beltran, formerly the Peruvian ambassador to the United States, began a campaign against the Odria regime. Odria arrested Beltran, his employees, and other aristocratic opponents to his regime. He committed several major blunders and was forced to abandon the idea of staying in power. Prado lived in Paris during Odria's reign and in 1956, he went to the United States for surgery. While he was in the hospital, several of his supporters, known as *Pradistas,* sent representatives to the United States to convince Prado to return to Peru and run for the presidency again. Odria sent two of Prado's nephews to dissuade him from returning to Peru. The *Pradistas* convinced Prado that his country needed him. He returned to Peru two months before the elections, after the creation of the *Movimiento Demócrata Pradista* (Pradist Democrat Movement; MDP). Prado was admired for his accomplishments during his first term as president and he had many supporters. His only opposition that caused a real threat to the election was Fernando Belaunde Terry, an architect-educator who had very little experience in the political arena. Belaunde was the candidate for the *Frente Nacional de Juventudes Democráticas* (National Front of Democratic Youth), an ideological leftist party. Belaunde was unable to get the support of APRA and just before the elections, when Odria denied him candidacy, he held a mass demonstration in Lima near the presidential palace. Belaunde issued an ultimatum to the government and Odria conceded to allow him to run. He became very popular because of his opposition to Odria and received 36.8 percent of the votes. However, three other candidates from minor parties withdrew from the race and pledged their support to Prado one month before the elections. Prado was elected president again in 1956 with 45.1 percent of the votes.

After the elections in 1956, Belaunde organized the *Acción Popular* (AP) to launch his campaign for the 1962 elections. AP became well organized and it was recognized as the most important progressive party in Peru. In the 1962 elections, an unprecedented number of candidates ran for the presidency. Three candidates from minor parties of the far left were

represented, Odria returned from the United States to run, and the *Partido Demócrata Cristiano* (Christian Democrat Party) elected a candidate. The Pradist party pledged their support to APRA's old leader, Victor Raul Haya de la Torre. The seventh candidate, AP's Belaunde, received strong support throughout Peru. All of the parties, except the MDP and APRA, accused Prado's government of electoral fraud. AP leaders charged the MDP and APRA with issuing fraudulent voter's registration cards—to children, the deceased, foreigners, and illiterates. After an investigation, the National Election Jury announced that there "might have been abuses committed in the registration of persons."

Belaunde was outraged with their findings. He had previously threatened that if free elections were not held, there would be a revolution. Although the elections were held on June 10, the results were not published until July 17. Haya received 557,047 votes to Belaunde's 544,180, but because Haya only received 32.98 percent of the votes, he could not become president. Peruvian law states that a candidate must receive 33.3 percent of the vote to win. According to the constitution, it was the duty of Congress to elect a president if a candidate did not receive enough of the votes. Congress was not convening until July 28 and Prado was determined to maintain the constitution. He called a meeting with the three candidates and asked for negotiations but Belaunde refused to cooperate. The armed forces intervened by vetoing Haya's candidacy. Belaunde, who claimed to be backed by military officers, went to AP's headquarters in Arequipa on July 13 where his followers were preparing for a rebellion.

### Overthrown by Military *Junta*

On July 13, Belaunde gave Prado's administration a final ultimatum that the elections be annulled because of fraud and to appoint a Court of Honor to elect the president. He advised a military coup to take over if his demands were not met. Prado's entire cabinet resigned on July 16 but he refused to accept their resignations, except for one navy leader, Vice-Admiral Guillermo Tirado Lamb. On July 17, the National Election Jury received a letter from the Joint Command of the armed forces insisting that the elections be canceled. The Jury's president responded with a statement that the armed forces could not intervene in the election process. On July 18, a military coup of commando units and tanks surrounded the presidential palace and Prado was taken prisoner. He was held on a navy ship for ten days until his term expired on July 28. Prado went into exile in Paris and returned to Peru shortly before his death in 1967.

## SOURCES:

*Biographical Dictionary of Latin American and Caribbean Political Leaders,* edited by Robert J. Alexander, Westport, Connecticut, Greenwood Press, 1988.

*Encyclopedia of Latin America,* edited by Helen Delpar, New York, McGraw-Hill, 1974.

Payne, Arnold, *The Peruvian Coup d'etat of 1962: The Overthrow of Manuel Prado,* Washington, D.C., Institute for the Comparative Study of Political Systems, a Division of Operations and Policy Research Inc., 1968.

—*Sketch by Phyllis Noah*

# Dolores Prida
## 1943-
### Cuban American playwright

Dolores Prida is one of the most important Hispanic playwrights in the United States. Armed with a fine sense of satire and a good sense of humor, she writes plays that bring to the stage the problems of racism, social injustice, feminism and the search for identity by Hispanics torn between two cultures.

Born in Caibarien, Cuba, on September 5, 1943, Dolores Prida came to the United States with her family as part of the wave of exiles who fled **Fidel Castro**'s pro-communist government. Settling in New York, she attended Hunter College from 1965 to 1969, majoring in Spanish American literature. During her first fifteen years in the United States, Prida worked in different capacities for publishing houses and periodicals as editor and journalist. These jobs included: managing editor of the Spanish-language New York daily newspaper *El tiempo;* New York correspondent for *Vision,* the Latin American magazine, from 1977 to 1980; and executive senior editor of *Nuestro* magazine, a national English-language magazine for Hispanics. Linked to the *Revista areito,* the publication of young Cuban intellectuals who sought a new understanding with the Havana government, Prida traveled to Cuba in 1978 and 1979 to participate in a dialogue that eventually allowed visitation of the island nation by exiles who had relatives there. Although Prida's work never touched upon the area of Cuban politics, her involvement in this project have lead to death threats on the part of the more militant anti-Castro exiles and created a climate that has made it impossible for her works to be presented in parts of New Jersey and Southern Florida.

Prida made her debut as a playwright in 1977 with her bilingual musical comedy *Beautiful Señoritas,* produced by Duo Theater in New York. The work's call for the liberation of Hispanic women from the dual repression of males and the Catholic Church has made it a favorite. In 1980, it was presented as a special performance at the National Organization for Women convention in San Antonio. In 1981, Prida's *Coser y cantar* premiered at the Duo Theater. Its two characters, She, the English speaker, and Ella, her Spanish counterpart—the two sides of an uprooted Latin woman—argue throughout the one-act play, exposing the problems of living in two worlds. *Coser y cantar* has been performed repeatedly since its debut, while as a radio play it has been broadcast throughout the United States. Prida's first collection of plays, *Beautiful Señoritas and Other Plays,* was published in 1991 by Arte Público Press of Houston, Texas.

In addition to her work as a playwright and journalist, Prida has also taught a play-writing workshop at Hostos Community College and written scripts for documentary films. She has received a variety of recognitions, among them a Doctor of Humane Letters from Mt. Holyoke College in 1989, the Cintas Fellowship Award for Literature in 1976, and the Creative Artistic Public Service Award for Play-writing in 1979–1980. Prida continues to work in New York City where she is active in the theater.

## SOURCES:

### Books

Escarpenter, Jose, and Linda S. Glaze, "Dolores Prida," in *Biographical Dictionary of Hispanic Literature in the United States,* edited by Nicolas Kanellos, Greenwood Press, 1989, pp. 244–49.

Weiss, Judith, "The Theaterworks of Dolores Prida," in Dolores Prida's *Beautiful Senoritas and Other Plays,* Arte Público Press, 1991, pp. 9–16.

### Other

Archives, Arte Público Press, Houston, Texas.

—*Sketch by Silvia Novo Pena*

# Tito Puente
## 1923-
### Hispanic American musician

Tito Puente is internationally recognized for his seminal contributions to Latin music as a bandleader, composer, arranger, and percussionist. Known as "El Rey," or The King of Mambo, he has recorded an unprecedented 100 albums, published more than 400 compositions, and won four Grammy awards. "In a day when pop singers fake their way to the top and when for many artists, success is the child of hype, Puente is one of only a handful of musicians who deserve the title 'legendary,'" Mark Holston stated in *Américas.*

Credited with introducing the timbal—a double tom-tom played with sticks—and the vibraphone to Afro-Cuban music, Puente also plays the trap drums, the conga drums, the claves, the piano, and occasionally, the saxophone and the clarinet. While Puente is perhaps best known for his all-time best-selling 1958 mambo album *Dance Mania,* his eclectic sound has continued to transcend cultural and generational boundaries. As a testament to his popularity with a younger audience, Puente has recorded with rocker **Carlos Santana** and has performed regularly at college concerts throughout the country. He has also appeared in several films, received a Star on the Hollywood Walk of Fame, and performed on television's *The David Letterman Show.*

### Early Musical Leanings

Ernest Anthony Puente, Jr., was born on April 20, 1923, in the Spanish Harlem section of New York City. Shortly before his birth, Puente's parents had left their native Puerto Rico to settle in the East Side of Harlem known as "El Barrio" for its large Hispanic population. While his father, Ernest Anthony Puente, Sr., worked as a foreman in a razor blade factory, his mother, Ercilia Puente, was the first to notice her eldest son's musical talent, enrolling him in 25-cent piano lessons when he was seven. As a child Puente also attended a dancing school and played baseball before seriously injuring his ankle in a bicycle accident. Although Puente received his first formal musical training in the piano, he always took an interest in percussion. Wanting to emulate his idol, drummer Gene Krupa, Puente began studying drums and percussion around the age of ten. "I was always banging on boxes, on the window sill," he once admitted in an interview with the *New York Post*'s Edmond Newton. Also a member of a schoolboy quartet, Puente grew up listening to a variety of music, including Latin artists such as Miguelito

*Tito Puente*

Valdes and jazz musicians Stan Kenton and Duke Ellington.

While still in his early teens, Puente began playing weekend gigs near his home. "My father used to take me to the dances," he told *Down Beat*'s Larry Birnbaum. "At midnight I was already falling asleep." By the age of 15, Puente had dropped out of high school to take a winter job with a Miami Beach band, where he played Americanized rhumbas and a variety of Latin-American rhythms, including tangos, waltzes, and paso dobles. When he returned to Manhattan, Puente was hired to play drums with the orchestras of Noro Morales and José Curbelo, the latter of whom would later become Manhattan's first mambo king. Puente's first big break came when the United States entered World War II; after the regular drummer of the famous Machito Afro-Cubans was drafted into military service, Puente was given the opportunity to demonstrate his talents. "For perhaps the first time in Latin music," Holston wrote, "the *timbales* were brought to the front the bandstand." Puente, showing early signs of his trademark showmanship, also revitalized the band by playing the drums standing, instead of from the conventional sitting position.

Puente's tour with the band came to a temporary halt when he too received his call from the military; for the next three years Puente served on a U.S. Navy aircraft carrier in the South Pacific. His military stint, however, provided several positive experiences. Not only did he have a chance to learn the saxophone—which he taught himself to play while on the ship—but he had the opportunity to further his education through the G. I. Bill. In what he has cited as one of the best decisions of his life, Puente enrolled in New York's Juilliard School of Music, where he studied composition, orchestration, and conducting. Many of the compositions and arrangements he wrote during this period were played by Machito and the other leading Latin band leaders of the day.

### Becoming the King of Mambo

Following his continued work as a sideman with Machito and Curbelo, Puente formed his own band, The Picadilly Boys, in 1948. A regular at New York's famed Palladium, Puente—along with Perez Prado and Tito Rodriguez—helped popularize the new dance music from Cuba called the mambo, a fast, staccato Afro-Cuban form that Puente defined in the *New York Post* as "a particular rift that's repeated several times." Mambo, along with cha-cha, guaguanco, merengue, and other Latin styles, were later known collectively as "salsa," but Puente has rejected the commercialized term, arguing that what he plays is music, not sauce. With early hits with Tico Records such as *Ran Kan, Abaniquito, El Yoyo,* and *Picadillo,* Puente "electrified dancers across America and . . . catapulted into the front rank of Latin bandleaders," according to Birnbaum. By the mid-1950s Puente had succeeded in gaining both a large Hispanic and Anglo following. In a 1956 poll conducted by the New York daily *La Prensa,* Puente was voted "King of Latin Music," beating out his competitors Prado and Rodriguez. Two years later, RCA released *Dance Mania,* which became a perennial international best-seller.

While continuing his reign as the "King of Mambo," Puente also began playing in New York jazz clubs such as Birdland and The Royal Roost, recording albums with trumpet player Doc Severinson like *Puente Goes Jazz* and *Night Beat* that attempted "to find a marriage between Latin music and jazz," Puente told Birnbaum. "I was trying to play jazz but not lose the Latin-American authenticity." Puente unexpectedly entered another genre of music in 1970, when California rocker Carlos Santana converted one of Puente's old songs, "Oye, Como Va," into a Top–40 hit. Seven years later the two teamed up for a memorable Manhattan concert. As Pablo Guzman described in *Village Voice,* "Puente conducted his fifteen-piece orchestra with snaps of his head and sweeps of his hands while playing timbales; at one point, when he signalled with his trademark stick over the head gesture, the entire brass section, spread in a row along his left, rose as one and played counter to itself. Folks went wild."

In 1979 Puente won his first Grammy award with a tribute album to Beny Moré, *Homenaje a Beny.*

That same year he established a personal scholarship fund at Juilliard to recognize Latin percussionists in the United States. The Tito Puente Scholarship fund "gives a young Latin percussionist an incentive to learn how to read music, so that when you go into a recording studio, you know what you're doing," as Puente explained to Birnbaum. "It's not only what you learn in the streets—you've really got to go and study." Puente has continued to strengthen his commitment to the future of Latin music by performing regularly at colleges and universities across the country. "The new generation of Central and South American students want representation on campus," Puente told *Down Beat*'s Fred Bouchard.

### Work in the 1980s and Beyond

During the 1980s, Puente concentrated his efforts on blending the best of Latin and jazz music into his unique style. "Sometimes jazz can be boring, but I give it a new twist," he explained to Bouchard. "Latin music can be boring, too, because it's only tonic and dominant. [You take an] exciting progressive melodic line, then combine it with exciting rhythms . . . that's the marriage we're after. You gotta know about jazz to play these things." Two more Grammy awards during the decade—and a fourth in 1990—confirmed that Puente was still at the top of his performance. His compositions, too, have evolved over the years. According to Bouchard, Puente has written "more sharply" and "conceiv[ed] more hiply" in the early 1990s than in his previous work.

While continuing to produce solid albums, including a record 100th in 1992, Puente has become more visible to a mainstream audience. In addition to performing at the White House since the administration of President Jimmy Carter—who introduced him as "The Goodwill Ambassador of Latin American Music"—Puente has made several appearances on *The Bill Cosby Show* and *The David Letterman Show.* He has even appeared in the movie *The Mambo Kings,* an adaptation of **Oscar Hijuelos'** Pulitzer Prize-winning novel, and has been honored with a star on the Hollywood Walk of Fame. Although in his 70s by the early 1990s, Puente—who with his wife, the former Margie Asencion, has three children—maintained a busy touring schedule that took him to Russia, Japan, and Puerto Rico. But in January of 1994, he told Vionette Negretti of the *San Juan Star* that he planned to reduce his pace: "There's a lot of young people out there who need to develop their talents and old-timers like me have to give them space."

### SELECTED DISCOGRAPHY:

*Dance Mania,* RCA, 1958.
*Puente Now!,* GNP Crescendo, 1960.
*El Rey Bravo,* Tico, 1962.

(With Santos Colon) *The Legend,* Tico, 1977.
*Tito Puente and His Latin Ensemble on Broadway,* Concord Picante, 1983.
*Un Poco Loco,* Concord Picante, 1987.
(With Phil Woods) *Salsa Meets Jazz,* Concord Picante, 1988.
(With Sheila E and Pete Escovedo) *Latina Familia,* Jazzyvisions, 1989.
*Goza Mi Timbal,* Concord Picante, 1990.

## SOURCES:

### Books

*Guinness Encyclopedia of Popular Music,* Volume 3, edited by Colin Larkin, New York, Guinness, 1992.

### Periodicals

*Américas,* Vol. 42, no. 6, 1990/1991, pp. 56–57.
*Boston Herald,* January 29, 1993.
*Down Beat,* January 1984, pp. 27–29, 61; May 1991, pp. 20–21.
*Los Angeles Times,* February 22, 1992.
*New York Post,* May 18, 1974, p. 15.
*San Juan Star,* January 13, 1994.
*Seattle Times,* December 4, 1992.
*Village Voice,* March 14, 1977, p. 39.

—*Sketch by Jason Gallman*

# Manuel Puig
## 1932-1990
### Argentine novelist

Manuel Puig was associated with the "boom" of Spanish American literature that included such well-known twentieth-century figures as **Carlos Fuentes**, **Octavio Paz**, and **Mario Vargas Llosa.** Puig's work reflected concerns with Argentine and other societies. His characters faced myriad conflicts: social, political, religious, and sexual. Puig treated these struggles in a bold, innovative way. As Barbara Mujica wrote in *Américas* shortly after Puig's death: "Manuel Puig made a major contribution to Latin American fiction by breaking down barriers. He dealt with subjects—homosexuality, machismo, pressures on children, female sexuality—that were previously taboo. He exposed the loneliness and alienation of modern men and women. He depicted homosexuals

*Manuel Puig*

and others who live on the margins of society with humor and tenderness." Mujica also remembered Puig as "a kind, gentle, compassionate man and a good friend."

Puig was born on December 28, 1932, in General Villegas on the Argentine pampas. His hometown was rural and poor, but Puig's family was a well-off and respected one. His father, Baldomero, was a wine merchant, and his mother, born Maria Elena Delledonne, trained as a chemist. "I hated my town," Puig told Mujica in another *Américas* article. "There was an authoritarian, repressive atmosphere, and I saw everything in terms of a second-rate cowboy picture, a B Western. The townspeople were the villains, not the heroes. . . . I thought that once I got out of Villegas, everything would be MGM, everything would be Technicolor."

To escape the emptiness of life in General Villegas, Puig immersed himself from an early age in movies, becoming an habitue of the town's sole theater and developing an extensive familiarity with Hollywood productions of the 1930s and 1940s. "I haven't had great literary influences in my life," Puig asserted in an interview with Jorgelina Corbatta, published in the *Review of Contemporary Fiction.* "Instead, that space has been occupied by cinematographic influences."

In 1946, Puig made a more drastic escape, leaving General Villegas—which had no secondary school—to attend boarding school in Buenos Aires.

"But in Buenos Aires," he recalled for Mujica, "there was even more authoritarianism." He developed interests in literature and psychology, but enrolled in the University of Buenos Aires School of Architecture in 1950. He later transferred to the School of Philosophy.

### Travelled and Began Writing

Puig left Argentina in 1955 to study at Rome's Centro Sperimentale di Cinematografia, where he had been awarded a scholarship. Although he gained valuable experience as an apprentice for the Cinecittà film studio, it was not an altogether fulfilling time for him. Puig spent the next few years in various European cities, including London, Paris, and Stockholm. To support himself he worked as a language teacher and translator, an assistant film director, and a dishwasher. Puig returned to Buenos Aires in 1960 and worked in the film industry as an assistant director. In 1961, he was back in Rome, where he translated film subtitles. From 1963 to 1967 he lived in New York, seeking to become better acquainted with the Broadway scene while supporting himself as a clerk for Air France.

During the early years of his adult life Puig's writing mainly took the form of unsuccessful film scripts. "Friends of his, who were far enough outside his problem to have some perspective on it, saw why his screenplays were failing," Norman Lavers wrote in his book *Pop Culture into Art: The Novels of Manuel Puig.* "They counseled him to write in his native language and to write about things he knew, something particular that he had experienced." Years later, Puig reflected on his compulsion to create novels, telling Corbatta: "I write novels because there is something I don't understand in reality. What I do is locate that special problem in a character and then try to understand it."

By 1965, Puig had completed his first novel, but censorship and other problems kept *La traición de Rita Hayworth* from being published for another three years. The book did not initially receive a warm reception in Argentina, but the English version, *Betrayed by Rita Hayworth,* which appeared in 1971, was greeted more enthusiastically. Writing in the *New York Times Book Review,* Alexander Coleman called it "a masterpiece," "a triumph," and "a screamingly funny book." *Betrayed by Rita Hayworth* is a largely autobiographical work, albeit one with a healthy dose of social criticism. Set in an Argentine town modelled on General Villegas, the novel focuses on a character named Toto who, like Puig, was born in 1932 and finds solace throughout his childhood at the movies.

His next book, *Boquitas pintadas,* was translated as *Heartbreak Tango.* Mark Jay Mirsky, writing in the *Washington Post Book World,* deemed it a "more careful novel" than *Betrayed by Rita Hayworth,* and

reported being "dazzled" by the experience of reading it: "What do his novels in their patient accretion of middle-class and lower-middle-class trivia cry out from under their heavy load of realistic detail but magic, give us magic, the cheapest matinee idol will do, only touch our lives with romance, an hour of it, two, on the radio, in the cinema, give us better dreams than our lives do or we die." D. P. Gallagher reviewed the book for the *New York Times* and proclaimed that "What [Jorge Luis] Borges has done for the detective story, Puig has done for the sentimental popular novel." Calling the book "compelling, moving, instructive and very funny," Gallagher explained that the provincial town in which *Heartbreak Tango* takes place—again modelled on Puig's birthplace—is peopled by inhabitants who "are in a sense typical characters of popular romances. They identify with such magazines as *Feminine World* and *Elegant Paris,* with the tangos and the commercials, the radio-novels and the movies." With his first two novels, Puig established himself as a writer meriting attention. As early as 1973, Gallagher, in an epilogue to his book *Modern Latin American Literature,* called Puig "the most encouraging recent arrival on the Latin American literary scene."

Puig's third novel was published in Spanish in 1973, with the English title *The Buenos Aires Affair.* Although it was subtitled "Novela policial" ("detective story"), *The Buenos Aires Affair* is more of a psychological study than a typical detective novel, focusing on two main characters: art critic Leo Druscovich and sculptor Gladys D'Onofrio. The *New York Times Book Review'*s Robert Alter called it "a sustained bravura performance by a writer keenly conscious of how both the novel as a literary form and the kinds of people who are its best subjects have been caught up in the cliches of popular culture, especially in its Hollywood versions."

### Publishes *Kiss of the Spider Woman*

With **Juan Péron**'s return to power in 1973, Puig left Argentina, hoping his exile would not last long. He went to Mexico, where he wrote *El Beso de la mujer araña* (translated as *Kiss of the Spider Woman*). Jonathan Tittler, in his book *Manuel Puig,* called *Kiss of the Spider Woman* "Puig's most generally successful novel because it is, far and away, his most powerful." The story centers on the interactions between two men sharing a prison cell in Buenos Aires. Molina is a homosexual serving an eight-year sentence for soliciting young boys. Valentin is a revolutionary Marxist student being detained indefinitely. Puig's frank treatment of homosexuality—he included footnotes on the subject within the text—is often cited as one of his major contributions. "I thought that was needed," Puig told the *Washington Post*'s Desson Howe. "In 1973, when I started to write [*Spider Woman*], especially in Spanish countries, there was not much information about homosexuality." Adapted for the screen in a major 1985 production, *Kiss of the Spider Woman* gained Puig international renown. The movie was made by Brazilian filmmaker Hector Babenco, and starred William Hurt as Molina and **Raúl Julia** as Valentin.

After two years in Mexico, Puig moved to New York City, where he wrote *Eternal Curse upon the Reader of These Pages.* He wrote the book in English and set its action in New York. Like much of Puig's work, this novel depends on verbal exchange and language to sustain it. "Except for five letters, a will and a job application, which serve as a documentary denouement, the entire novel is a dialogue between an amnesiac and a dropout," declared Allen Jacobs in the *New York Times Book Review.* In an interview with Kathleen Wheaton published in the *Paris Review,* Puig explained his reliance on spoken language and his tendency to avoid omniscient narrative: "I believe in characters as vehicles of exposition. Their voices are full of hidden clues and I like to listen to them. That's why I work so much with dialogue. . . . Mine is not the classic third-person voice." Reviews of this novel were mixed. *Newsweek's* Ray Sawhill said that "Intelligent as 'Eternal Curse' is, it has little of Puig's magic," while Gilbert Sorrentino went a step further in the *Washington Post Book World,* calling the book "a structural failure."

Continuing his nomadic path, Puig moved in 1981 to Rio de Janeiro, where he was based for the next eight years. He continued to write throughout the decade, attracting more and more attention—his work was translated into two dozen languages—especially after Babenco's film was released.

Puig received numerous awards for his writing. For example, the prominent French newspaper *Le Monde* called *La traición de Rita Hayworth* one of the best foreign novels for 1968–69. Puig was also awarded the best-script prize at the 1974 San Sebastian Festival for his screen adaptation of *Boquitas pintadas.* Four years later the San Sebastian jury awarded him a prize for his adaptation of "El lugar sin límites," **José Donoso**'s novel. For *Kiss of the Spider Woman* Puig won the American Library Association's Notable Book Award in 1979. He was honored six years later by *Plays and Players* for "Kiss of the Spider Woman," the play adaptation of the novel. In 1987 the University of Aberdeen awarded him an honorary doctorate.

Awards notwithstanding, Puig's relationship with critics in the popular press was not always harmonious. He told the *Washington Post*'s Howe: "I'm always rescued by the academic world. It's in colleges that my work is discussed in the right light." Puig himself taught creative writing at New York's City College and Columbia University. Just a month before his death, Puig accepted an invitation to visit the University of Oklahoma as a special guest for a forthcoming conference on Writers of the French-Speaking and Hispanic World. He died at the age of 57 on July 22, 1990. His death was caused by cardiac arrest following a routine gallbladder operation in Cuernavaca, Mexico, his home since 1989.

## SELECTED PUBLISHED WORKS:

*La traición de Rita Hayworth,* Sudamericana, 1968, reprinted, Casa de las Américas, 1983, translation by Suzanne Jill Levine published as *Betrayed by Rita Hayworth,* Dutton, 1971, reprinted, 1987.

*Boquitas pintadas,* Sudamericana, 1969, translation by Suzanne Jill Levine published as *Heartbreak Tango: A Serial,* Dutton, 1973.

*The Buenos Aires Affair: Novela policial,* Sudamericana, 1973, translation by Suzanne Jill Levine published as *The Buenos Aires Affair: A Detective Novel,* Dutton, 1976.

*El beso de la mujer araña,* Seix-Barral, 1976, translation by Thomas Colchie published as *The Kiss of the Spider Woman,* Knopf, 1979.

*Pubis angelical,* Seix Barral, 1979, translation by Elena Brunet, Vintage, 1986.

"El beso de la mujer araña" (play; adapted from his novel), first produced in Spain, 1981, translation by Allan Baker titled "Kiss of the Spider Woman," first produced in London at the Bush Theatre, 1985, produced in Los Angeles at the Cast Theatre, 1987.

*Eternal Curse upon the Reader of These Pages,* Random House, 1982, Spanish translation by the author published as *Maldición eterna a quien lea estas páginas,* Seix Barral, 1982.

*Sangre de amor correspondido,* Seix Barral, 1982, translation by Jan L. Grayson published as *Blood of Requited Love,* Vintage, 1984.

*Bajo un manto de estrellas: Pieza en dos actos* [and] *El beso de la mujer araña: Adaptación escénica realizada por el autor,* Seix Barral, 1983.

*Under a Mantle of Stars: A Play in Two Acts,* translation by Ronald Christ, Lumen Books, 1985 (produced in the original Spanish as *Bajo un manto de estrellas*).

(Contributor) G. W. Woodyard and Marion P. Holt, editors, *Drama Contemporary: Latin America,* PAJ Publications, 1987.

*Mystery of the Rose Bouquet* (play; produced at the Bush Theatre, 1987, produced in Los Angeles, California, at Mark Taper Forum, November 16, 1989), translation by Baker, Faber, 1988 (produced in the original Spanish as *Misterio del ramo de rosas*).

*Cae la noche tropical,* Seix Barral, 1988, translation by Levine published as *Tropical Night Falling,* Simon and Schuster, 1991.

## SOURCES:

### Books

Bacarisse, Pamela, *The Necessary Dream: A Study of the Novels of Manuel Puig,* Cardiff, University of Wales Press, 1988.

*Contemporary Authors, New Revision Series,* Volume 32, edited by James G. Lesniak, Detroit, Gale, 1991.

*Contemporary Literary Criticism,* Volume 28, edited by Jean C. Stine, Detroit, Gale, 1984.

*Contemporary Literary Criticism Yearbook 1990,* Volume 65, edited by Roger Matuz, Detroit, Gale, 1991.

*Current Biography Yearbook 1988,* edited by Charles Moritz, New York, Wilson, 1989.

*Current Biography Yearbook 1990,* edited by Charles Moritz, New York, Wilson, 1991.

*Dictionary of Literary Biography, Volume 113: Modern Latin-American Fiction Writers,* edited by William Luis, Detroit, Gale, 1992.

Gallagher, D. P., *Modern Latin American Literature,* New York and London, Oxford University Press, 1973.

Kerr, Lucille, *Suspended Fictions: Reading Novels by Manuel Puig,* Urbana and Chicago, University of Illinois Press, 1987.

*Latin American Writers,* Volume III, edited by Carlos A. Solé and Maria Isabel Abreu, New York, Scribner, 1989.

Lavers, Norman, *Pop Culture into Art: The Novels of Manuel Puig,* Columbia, University of Missouri Press, 1988.

Mac Adam, Alfred J., *Modern Latin America Narratives: The Dreams of Reason,* Chicago and London, University of Chicago Press, 1977.

Tittler, Jonathan, *Manuel Puig,* New York, Twayne, 1993.

### Periodicals

*Américas,* May 1980, p. 48; May-June 1986, pp. 2–7; September-October 1990, pp. 62–63; March-April 1992, p. 60.

*Commonweal,* June 24, 1977, pp. 412–14.

*New York Times,* August 5, 1985, p. C11.

*New York Times Book Review,* September 26, 1971, p. 3; December 16, 1973, pp. 14, 16; September 5, 1976, p. 4; July 4, 1982; pp. 9, 12; September 23, 1984, pp. 11–12; December 28, 1986, p. 9; November 10, 1991, p. 9.

*New Yorker,* May 25, 1992, pp. 84–88.

*Newsweek,* October 25, 1971, pp. 120–21; June 28, 1982, pp. 74–76.

*Paris Review,* Winter II, 1989, pp. 129–47.

*Publishers Weekly,* August 23, 1991, p. 47.

*Review of Contemporary Fiction,* Fall 1991.

*Washington Post,* November 16, 1985, pp. 1, 9.

*Washington Post Book World,* November 25, 1973, p. 1; April 22, 1979, pp. 1, 5; August 1, 1982, pp. 1–2.

*World Literature Today,* Autumn 1991.

—*Sketch by Erika Dreifus*

# Anthony Quinn
## 1915-
### Mexican American actor

Anthony Quinn is widely recognized as one of the hardest working and most talented actors of his generation. Described by the *Connecticut Post*'s Joe Meyers as "one of the few performers of his age who continue to *act* rather than reprise his most famous roles or simply turn into a caricature of himself," Quinn has appeared in more than 325 films in a career that has spanned nearly six decades. Known for making the most of whatever role he was assigned, Quinn was invariably typecast as an Indian, a Latin villain, or a Mexican bandit during the early stages of his career. But after his highly acclaimed stage portrayal of Stanley Kowalski in Tennessee Williams' *A Streetcar Named Desire* in 1950, he was given the opportunity to play more favorable roles, such as the older brother of the revolutionary Emiliano Zapata in *Viva Zapata!* (1952) and the artist Paul Gauguin in *Lust for Life* (1956), winning the Best Supporting Oscar for both performances. Perhaps his most memorable, if not his most critically acclaimed, film was *Zorba the Greek* (1964), in which he starred in the title role as a rough, arrogant peasant. Quinn is one of the few actors whose resume includes work with directors ranging from Elia Kazan to Spike Lee. Some of his other notable films include *Wild is the Wind* (1957), *The Guns of Navarone* (1961), and *Lawrence of Arabia* (1962).

Anthony Rudolph Oaxaca Quinn was born April 21, 1915 in Chihuahua, Mexico amid the violence of the Mexican revolution led by **Pancho Villa**. After his father, Frank Quinn, an Irishman, left to fight in the war, his mother, Manuella (Oaxaca) Quinn, a Mexican of Aztec ancestry, took her two children and walked 400 miles to El Paso, smuggling them across the border in a wagon under a pile of coal. When Quinn was four, the family reunited in Los Angeles. There his father found employment as a movie cameraman at the Selig studio, putting his son before the cameras at an early age to play the part of a young Tarzan in a jungle film. When Quinn was nine, his father was killed in an automobile accident, and he did whatever he could to help support the family, finding work as a carpenter, shoe shiner, and window washer. While attending public school in Los Angeles, a 12-year-old Quinn developed an interest in art, winning an award for a clay bust of Abraham Lincoln. While in his teens, Quinn also found time to start his own orchestra, play the saxophone, and preach in controversial evangelist Aimee Semple McPherson's temple.

During his junior year in high school, Quinn won a prize—for architectural design—and was asked to study with the legendary architect, Frank Lloyd Wright. Impressed with his student's creativity, Wright encouraged Quinn to enroll in some acting classes to improve his speaking ability. Barred from acting in school plays because of a speech impediment, Quinn had the defect surgically corrected at age 18, and agreed to pay for the operation in installments over the next five years. During the early 1930s, while doing a stint with the Federal Theatre Project, Quinn also supported himself by working as a cement mixer, a sparring partner for heavyweight boxing champion Primo Carnera, a ditch digger, a taxi driver, and a mattress factory foreman.

### Receives First Role

In 1936, Quinn finally received his first real acting assignment, in a Los Angeles production of Mae West's play *Clean Beds*. That same year, he made his debut on the Hollywood screen, winning a bit part in *Parole* on the strength of his haggard appearance—the very real effect of Quinn's hard life. While he soon acquired several more bit parts, he grew frustrated with Hollywood and left for Arizona and Colorado, finding work on ranches and in restaurants as a dishwasher. But after stopping in a small town just across the Mexican border, Quinn came across an advertisement for Indians to play in Cecil B. DeMille's Western *The Plainsman* and quickly took the next freight to Los Angeles. When asked, Quinn told DeMille he was a Blackfoot Indian, made up some gibberish he passed off as the "language," and lied further when he claimed proficiency on horseback.

Quinn not only won the part, but the following year he married the boss's adopted daughter, Katherine, with whom he would have five children before their divorce in 1965. Under contract with Paramount, Quinn continued his long apprenticeship, playing minor rolls in such films as *The Road to Morocco* (1942), *Guadalcanal Diary* (1943), and *Back to Bataan* (1945)—usually as a villainous character of one of the more than 25 different nationalities he has portrayed during his career. But as Quinn told

Meyers, he was dissatisfied with the roles he was receiving: "I didn't mind playing Indians, but a lot of the other parts made me unhappy. I was frequently the leading man's friend or a gangster. I didn't feel I was getting anywhere."

Hoping to find better roles on the stage, Quinn travelled to New York, where in 1947 he made his Broadway debut in *The Gentleman from Athens,* playing a Greek American congressman. Although the play ran for only a week, he gained experience that would prove valuable in his next role: replacing Marlon Brando in *A Streetcar Named Desire.* During the play's two-year tour, Quinn received several positive reviews.

Having gained invaluable experience on the stage, Quinn returned to Hollywood, where he was given the opportunity to play opposite Marlon Brando in Elia Kazan's *Viva Zapata!* (1952). As revolutionary Emiliano Zapata's discontented older brother Eufemio, Quinn had at last found the appropriate role for his broad, unaffected style of acting, and he gave an Oscar-winning performance. Just four years later, after a stint in Italy in which he gave a memorable performance as the carnival strongman in Fredrico Fellini 's 1954 Oscar-winning *La Strada,* he was again honored by the Academy for best supporting actor— this time for his portrayal of artist Paul Gauguin, opposite Kirk Douglas's Vincent van Gogh in *Lust for Life* (1956). Despite his success, though, Quinn was dissatisfied with Hollywood's emphasis on plot rather than the characteristically European focus on the soul. "I'm still frustrated—even with the Oscars," Quinn stated in a 1957 *Newsweek* interview. "They scare the hell out of me because I might begin to believe in them."

Quinn returned to the stage in the late 1950s, starring opposite Laurence Olivier in *Becket.* Sharing the stage with the actor whom Quinn considered the world's best was at first intimidating; late in the run, however, he proved that he was up to the challenge, switching roles with Olivier—much to the delight of critics who had already given both stars rave reviews. Having elevated his acting skills to a new level, Quinn went back to movies full-time in the early 1960s. He took the lead role in a low-budget art film, *Zorba the Greek,* in 1964. Largely on the strength of Quinn's portrayal of the virile peasant, the movie became an international success and was nominated for several Academy Awards, including best actor.

### Accepts Challenging Roles

Although Quinn has spent the last 30 years as one of the busiest actors in Hollywood, he has yet to find, in the view of most critics, a starring role equal to "Zorba." He has been willing, however, to take on a number of small parts in movies that have not—like many of his 1930s productions—been well received.

Quinn's decision to accept roles in such forgettable films as the 1990's *Ghosts Can't Do It* can perhaps be attributed to Quinn's long-held philosophy on acting. "I've a theory about making pictures," Quinn stated in *Newsweek.* "Anybody can make beauty out of beauty. But to make beauty out of nothing is a challenge. I do the inferior pictures because of what the parts demand."

While Quinn has had the opportunity to play a number of colorful characters, his life, said friend Cindy Adams in the *New York Post,* "beats anything he has ever played on screen." In 1993, shortly after surviving a quadruple bypass, the 78-year-old Quinn fathered his eleventh child. The mother was not his second wife Iolanda Addolori, with whom Quinn has had three sons since their marriage in 1965. His notorious affairs notwithstanding, Quinn has continued to further all aspects of his career as an artist. Not only has he appeared in such critically acclaimed films as Spike Lee's *Jungle Fever,* but he has written a well-received autobiography and earned a reputation as an accomplished painter and sculptor. As Adams observed, "Whatever fires that fueled him to two Academy Awards, six nominations, a presidential medal, and walls full of other citations burn still." Still working even as he approached his 80s, Quinn appeared in Alfonso Arau's 1995 film *A Walk in the Clouds.*

## SELECTED PUBLISHED WORKS:

*The Original Sin,* [New York], 1972.

## SELECTED VIDEOGRAPHY:

*Parole,* 1936.
*Night Waitress,* 1936.
*Swing High, Swing Low,* 1937.
*The Last Train from Madrid,* 1937.
*Daughters of Shanghai,* 1937.
*Dangerous to Know,* 1938.
*Hunted Man,* 1938.
*King of Alcatraz,* 1938.
*Union Pacific,* 1939.
*Television Spy,* 1939.
*Emergency Squad,* 1940.
*Parole Fixer,* 1940.
*City for Conquest,* 1940.
*Blood and Sand,* 1941.
*They Died with Their Boots On,* 1941.
*Larceny, Inc.,* 1942.
*The Ox-Bow Incident,* 1942.
*Guadalcanal Diary,* 1943.
*China Sky,* 1944.
*Ladies of Washington,* 1944.
*Where Do We Go from Here?,* 1945.
*Back to Bataan,* 1945.
*Sinbad the Sailor,* 1947.

*Black Gold*, 1947.
*The Brave Bulls*, 1951.
*Mask of the Avenger*, 1951.
*Viva Zapata!*, 1952.
*The World in His Arms*, 1952.
*City Beneath the Sea*, 1953.
*Ride Vaquero!*, 1953.
*Blowing Wind*, 1953.
*Cavalleria Rusticana*, 1953.
*La strada*, 1954.
*Attila, Flagello di dio*, 1954.
*The Magnificent Matador*, 1955.
*Seven Cities of Gold*, 1955.
*Lust for Life*, 1956.
*The Wild Party*, 1956.
*The Ride Back*, 1957.
*The Hunchback of Notre Dame*, 1957.
*Wild Is the Wind*, 1957.
*Hot Spell*, 1958.
*The Black Orchid*, 1959.
*Warlock*, 1959.
*The Last Train from Gun Hill*, 1959.
*Heller in Pink Tights*, 1960.
*The Guns of Navarone*, 1961.
*Barabbas*, 1962.
*Lawrence of Arabia*, 1962.
*Behold a Pale Horse*, 1964.
*Zorba the Greek*, 1964.
*The Lost Command*, 1966.
*The Rover*, 1967.
*Guns for San Sebastian*, 1968.
*The Shoes of the Fisherman*, 1968.
*The Magus*, 1968.
*A Dream of Kings*, 1969.
*R.P.M.*, 1970.
*Flap (The Last Warrior)*, 1970.
*King: A Filmed Record . . . Montgomery to Memphis*, 1970.
*Arroza*, 1971.
*Across 110th Street*, 1972.
*The Voice of La Raza*, 1972.
*Deaf Smith and Johnny Ears*, 1973.
*The Don Is Dead*, 1973.
*The Destructors*, 1974.
*L'eredità Ferramonti*, 1976.
*Bluff*, 1976.
*The Inheritance*, 1976.
*The Message*, 1976.
*Tigers Don't Cry*, 1976.
*Jesus of Nazareth*, 1977.
*African Rage*, 1978.
*The Greek Tycoon*, 1978.
*Caravans*, 1978.
*The Children of Sanchez*, 1978.
*The Passage*, 1979.
*High Risk*, 1981.
*Lion of the Desert*, 1981.
*The Con Artists*, 1981.
*The Salamander*, 1981.

*Regina*, 1983.
*Valentina*, 1983.
*Ingrid*, 1984.
*The Last Days of Pompeii*, 1984.
*Isola del tesoro*, 1986.
*Onassis: The Richest Man in the World*, 1988.
*A Man of Passion*, 1989.
*Actor*, 1989.
*Revenge*, 1989.
*The Old Man and the Sea*, 1990.
*Ghosts Can't Do It*, 1990.
*Star for Two*, 1990.
*Only the Lonely*, 1991.
*Jungle Fever*, 1991.
*Mobsters*, 1991.
*Last Action Hero*, 1993.
*A Walk in the Clouds*, 1995.

## SOURCES:

### Books

*Current Biography Yearbook 1957*, edited by Marjorie Dent Candee, New York, H. W. Wilson, 1958.
*International Dictionary of Films and Filmmakers*, Volume 3, edited by Nicholas Thomas, Detroit, St. James Press, 1990.

### Periodicals

*Connecticut Post* (Bridgeport), May 22, 1994.
*Films and Filming*, February 1970.
*Las Vegas Review Journal*, September 8, 1993.
*Newsweek*, May 6, 1957, pp. 112–113.
*New York Post*, August 19, 1993.
*Premiere*, September 1992, pp. 43–45.
*Virginian-Pilot* (Norfolk), March 24, 1990.

*—Sketch by Jason Gallman*

# John Quiñones
## 1952-
### Hispanic American broadcast journalist

John Manuel Quiñones is a highly visible, Emmy award-winning network correspondent for ABC-TV and a member of the National Hispanic Journalists Association. Joining the television network in 1982, his investigations of issues involving Hispanic Americans prompted the network to name him as a correspondent to their popular *PrimeTime Live* news show in 1991.

Quiñones was born on May 23, 1952 in San Antonio, Texas to Bruno and María Quiñones. Quiñones attended St. Mary's University in San Antonio, where he received his B.A. in speech communications when he was 22 years old. Five years later he would graduate from the Columbia School of Journalism with a master of science degree. His career in broadcasting began while he was still in college; in 1973 Quiñones began a stint with KTSA-Radio as a reporter and announcer in San Antonio. After leaving St. Mary's University, Quiñones became a news editor at KTRH-Radio in Houston, Texas. Until 1978, a year before graduating from Columbia, he also served as an anchor/reporter for KPRC-TV.

By 1979 Quiñones was already garnering awards for his work at a CBS-TV affiliate in Chicago. For the local news, he covered a range of stories with national and international repercussions, as well as those of neighborhood interest. The reporter began his career-long string of stories regarding Hispanics with a 1980 document of the flight of illegal aliens across the Mexican-U.S. border. This series was honored with two local Emmy Awards. Quiñones stayed on top of breaking international news with his coverage of the Cuban boat lift of 1980 and the plight of Haitian boat people in 1982.

In 1982, ABC's network news division brought Quiñones on as a general assignment correspondent. He operated out of Miami, which allowed him to more easily cover stories other journalists found elusive. He was, for instance, one of a handful of U.S. correspondents who got a chance to report on the U.S. invasion of Panama during December 1989, while based in Panama City. Quiñones had prepared for the coup, having covered developments in Panama during 1988. In more than 50 reports filed from the capital city, the correspondent followed the events resulting from unsuccessful attempts to dislodge **Manuel Noriega** from his political bargaining position as the country's de facto leader. Other reports from Central and Latin America included analyses of the ongoing El Salvadoran civil conflict and various political and economic scandals that plagued Argentina during the 1980s.

### PrimeTime Live

After successfully covering such breaking news events as the Challenger Space Shuttle disaster in 1986, the U.S.S. Iowa shipboard explosion, and the execution of convicted murderer Ted Bundy, Quiñones proved himself capable of handling social issues in documentary form. After studying the gun control debates in Florida for *World News Tonight With Peter Jennings,* he won his first national Emmy in 1990 for "Burning Questions—The Poisoning of America," broadcast on ABC as a news special in 1988. In recognition of his service to the network, Quiñones was rewarded with a high-profile correspondent's assignment to ABC's weekly newsmagazine, *PrimeTime Live* in 1991.

Quiñones continued to cast an even wider international net for his stories in the next few seasons. He investigated the endangerment of the ancient Penan Indian nation in Sarawak, Malaysia. A similar story about the Yanomamo Indians of Venezuela, called "Window in the Past," garnered another national Emmy in 1990. He conducted hidden-camera interviews regarding a black market in adopted babies in Peru. He also investigated the Filipino trade in prostitution, and the involvement of U.S. military forces stretching back 40 years. Quiñones smuggled hidden cameras into Tibet in order to expose the oppressed state of affairs under Chinese rule for another Emmy-winning piece.

The correspondent's interest in Latino issues continued. He followed the throwaway children of Bogotá, Columbia, into the sewers beneath the city. Later that same season, Guatemala's homeless children were the focus of another exposé of cruel treatment of children at the hands of state officials. The study in Bogotá, a report named "To Save the Children," was honored with a citation from the Robert F. Kennedy Journalism Awards panel, a Gabriel award, and a World Hunger Media award. For his bulletin on the exploitative work situation of Haitian youngsters in the canefields of the Dominican Republic, Quiñones was further honored with the Overseas Press Club's Eric & Amy Burger Award for best reporting from abroad. He also received an RFK Journalism award and yet another Emmy in 1992.

### SOURCES:

*New York Times,* April 29, 1992, p. B5.

**Other**

Additional information obtained from ABC Television Network Group, 1995.

—*Sketch by Jennifer Kramer*

# Leroy V. Quintana
## 1944-
### Mexican American poet

Through his poetry, Leroy V. Quintana—strongly influenced by the traditional Hispanic folktales he heard as a child—often evokes a sense of yearning for the unity and cohesiveness of an earlier era. Quintana has used poetry to bring to life his two main areas of interest: Vietnam and New Mexico. In a *Nation* review of one of Quintana's books of poetry, Ray Gonzalez wrote: "*The History of Home* is a scrapbook of profiles created by someone who was raised in an isolated yet rich community of the fifties, painfully capturing a period of Chicano history few poets write about."

Although Quintana's work addresses such broad issues as social change, the Vietnam War, discrimination, and assimilation, his focus on the individual reveals a keen interest in psychology. A licensed marriage, family, and child counselor, Quintana explained in *Contemporary Authors,* "My foray into psychology . . . has helped me tremendously in my writing," but he also added, "In many ways I'm still basically a small-town New Mexico boy carrying on the oral tradition."

Quintana was born June 10, 1944, in Albuquerque, New Mexico, and lived with his grandparents in northern New Mexico during his early years. "I remember grandmother making candy on the old firewood-burning stove and telling us all the old *cuentos* ["stories"] deep and long into the night, and grandfather telling me the tales of walking to Wyoming and sheepherding as a kid," Quintana recalled in *Dictionary of Literary Biography.* As a child, Quintana enjoyed stories of all kinds—from movies to stanzas in the back of the catechism to comic books by the hundreds. From third grade on, he spent most of the time with his mother and stepfather, alternating summers between his parents and grandparents. He graduated from Albuquerque High School in 1962 and spent two years working with his stepfather as a roofer.

After studying for a few years at the University of New Mexico, Quintana enlisted in the army and spent one year (1967–1968) in Vietnam. Upon his return, he re-enrolled at the University of New Mexico and began writing about his war experiences. He became editor of the school's literary magazine and graduated with a B.A. in English in 1969. That same year, Quintana married Yolanda Holguin, a registered nurse; they would eventually have three children.

## Publishes First Book of Poetry

Upon graduating from college, Quintana worked as an alcoholism counselor at St. Joseph's Hospital in Albuquerque. Then he went back to school and received his M.A. in English from New Mexico State University in 1974. His first book of poetry, *Hijo del Pueblo: New Mexico Poems,* was published in an edition of 500 copies by Puerto del Sol Press in 1976. Many of the poems in *Hijo del Pueblo* are told from the perspective of a young boy and deal with the effect of the outside Anglo world on traditional small-town life in the Southwest. In "Sterling, Colorado," for example, Quintana writes: "On Saturdays we would go into town / after picking potatoes all week / and the Anglos would laugh at us / and call us dirty Mexicans."

Quintana worked as an English instructor, first at El Paso Community College, then at the University of New Mexico. He also spent a year in the early 1980s as a feature and sports writer for the *Albuquerque Tribune.* His second book, *Sangre,* was published in 1981 and received two awards the following year: the American Book Award for poetry from the Before Columbus Foundation and the El Paso Border Regional Library Association Award.

In 1982 Quintana moved to Silver Springs, New Mexico, to study under psychiatrist Humberto Quintana. He earned his M.A. in counseling from Western New Mexico University in 1984 and moved to San Diego, California, where he became a counselor for the National City Family Clinic. During this time, he continued to write, as he explained in an interview for *Bilingual Review:* "I suppose that at the base I'm a writer who is a counselor more than a counselor who writes." His poetry was featured in the anthology *Five Poets of Aztlan,* published in 1985.

In 1990, Quintana went on to become an assistant professor at San Diego Mesa College and published *Interrogations,* a collection of poems about the Vietnam War. Quintana's next book of poetry, *The History of Home,* was published in 1993, and again he won an American Book Award. The title of each short poem in *The History of Home* is taken from a person who lived in Quintana's hometown, and while the characters Quintana sketches grow up amidst poverty and hardship, they are also able to find joy. For example, a group of boys discovers that, with a little help from a nickel and a coat hanger, they can play pinball all afternoon. Further, in another poem that recounts simple pleasures, the narrator relates experience of a little boy: "One of the few sure things left / was Arturo coming back to school from lunch / every day with red chile stains / on both corners of his mouth."

## SELECTED PUBLISHED WORKS:

*Hijo del Pueblo: New Mexico Poems,* Puerto Del Sol Press, 1976.

*Sangre,* Prima Agua Press, 1981.

*The Reason People Don't Like Mexicans,* Bilingual Review/Press, 1984.

*Interrogations,* Viet Nam Generation and Burning Cities Press, 1990.

*The History of Home,* Bilingual Press, 1993.

## SOURCES:

### Books

*Contemporary Authors,* Vol. 131, Detroit, Gale, 1991.

*Dictionary of Literary Biography,* Vol. 82, Detroit, Gale, 1989.

*Hispanics in the United States: An Anthology of Creative Literature,* edited by Gary D. Keller and Francisco Jimenez, Binghamton, NY, Bilingual Press, 1980.

*Hispanic Writers,* edited by Bryan Ryan, Detroit, Gale, 1991.

### Periodicals

*Bilingual Review,* 12, 1987, pp. 218–29.

*Nation,* June 7, 1993, pp. 772–74.

—*Sketch by Joan Axelrod-Contrada*

*José Quintero*

# José Quintero
## 1924-

**Panamanian theater director, producer, and writer**

José Quintero came to prominence as an especially sensitive interpreter of the plays of Eugene O'Neill. He began his directing career at the off-Broadway theater Circle in the Square in New York City, staging a wide variety of plays by such renowned dramatists as **Federico Garcia Lorca**, Jean Genêt, Tennessee Williams, and Thornton Wilder. He was nominated for a Tony award in 1957 for *Long Day's Journey Into Night* and won the Tony as Best Director for *A Moon for the Misbegotten* in 1973. He received a "Unique Contributions to the Theatre Award" from the Drama League in 1987.

Quintero was born October 15, 1924, to Carlos and Consuelo (Palmorala) Quintero in Panama City, Panama. He traced his passion for theater to his Catholic upbringing; as a child he served as an acolyte

and was entranced by the dramatic power and sensuous appeal of ecclesiastical ceremony. In an interview with Gilbert Millstein in *Theatre Arts,* Quintero recalled discovering that "the imagination was more real than the factual world. . . . One could, for example, give life to wooden statues. Just by the fact of *believing,* one endowed them with life. That is why it is so easy for me to believe a tree in the theater is a real tree, though it is made of cardboard."

At 17 Quintero's father sent him to the University of Southern California to study medicine, but after two fruitless years he transferred to Los Angeles City College, where, in an English class, he met a group of young actors who introduced him to the theater. Quintero had found his vocation. This group, with Quintero and Theodore Mann at their head, later moved, after a short period in Woodstock, to Greenwich Village in New York City. In February 1951, as the Loft Players, they re-opened an arena theater on Sheridan Square and named it Circle in the Square. This was to be Quintero's artistic home for the next 12 years.

### Revives O'Neill

The 1956 production was a great success, leading *New York Times* theater critic Brooks Atkinson to describe Quintero as "a versatile conductor" and a "remarkably gifted artist" who knew "how to orchestrate a performance." Atkinson also noted Quintero's "extraordinarily perceptive" direction; and in a later

*New York Times* review, this time for a production of Thornton Wilder's *Our Town* in 1959, he described Quintero as an "artistic genius" whose staging was "flawless." Quintero's faithful adherence to O'Neill's work convinced Carlotta Monterey that he was the right director for her late husband's plays, and additional productions followed, most notably *Long Day's Journey Into Night* (1956) and *A Moon for the Misbegotten* (1973).

In the early 1960s, as a result of differences with his partner Ted Mann, Quintero left Circle in the Square and began to direct independently. The emotional effect of this break was traumatic for Quintero, and this, combined with an unsuccessful foray into motion pictures with *The Roman Spring of Mrs. Stone* (1961) led to a struggle with alcoholism. Quintero's memoir, *If You Don't Dance, They Beat You*, which traces his career from its beginnings to 1974, was partly written, said Mel Gussow in the *New York Times* "as an act of therapy."

In the early 1970s Quintero made a brilliant comeback with O'Neill's *A Moon for the Misbegotten*. Critic Clive Barnes noted in the *New York Times* that Quintero had directed "unerringly.... He never exaggerates, falsifies; indeed, he never cheats on the playwright's scoring." Quintero's long association with the work of the great American playwright was consolidated in 1985 with an important and acclaimed revival of *The Iceman Cometh,* and in 1988 with a reprise of *Long Day's Journey Into Night*.

In February 1983 Quintero was named professor of theater arts and artistic director of the Springold Theater at Brandeis University. In this new capacity as head of a graduate program in directing, Quintero said that he wanted to "erase the barriers between educational theater and professional theater." Quintero continued to direct throughout the 1980s, in New York City and abroad.

## SELECTED PUBLISHED WORKS:

*If You Don't Dance, They Beat You*, Boston, Little, Brown, and Company, 1974.

## SOURCES:

### Books

*Contemporary Theatre, Film, and Television,* Volume 8, Detroit, Gale Research, 1991.

### Periodicals

*Américas,* September 1955.

*New York Times,* May 9, 1956, p. 38; May 20, 1956, Section 2, p. 1; April 5, 1959, Section 2, p. 1; December 31, 1973, p. 22; January 28, 1974, p. 34; April 22, 1974, p. 46; February 18, 1983, p. C2.
*Theatre Arts,* April 1957, pp. 27–29, 88; May 1960, pp. 10–12.

—*Sketch by Simon Dixon*

# Jacinto Quirarte
## 1931-
### Mexican American educator and scholar

Born in 1931, Jacinto Quirarte is one of the most prominent Mexican American university administrators in the United States. As a scholar, Quirarte has focused primarily on pre-Colombian and Chicano art and has earned a reputation among the top experts in those areas. As an administrator, Quirarte has served several universities and was involved in the founding of the University of Texas at San Antonio during the early 1970s.

### Northern Arizona Refuge

Quirarte's father, Francisco, left Mexico in 1929. Two decades of civil violence had made Mexico a dangerous place; the United States, while unfamiliar, provided safety. Francisco Quirarte arrived in Jerome, Arizona, and took a job working in that town's primary industry, mining. By trade, Quirarte had been a cowboy in Mexico, but when he met Frutuosa Jimenez in 1930, the two decided to marry and remain in Jerome.

In 1931 Francisco and Frutuosa Quirarte had their first of six children. Jacinto was born on August 17 of that year. In an interview with *Dictionary of Hispanic Biography*'s James McCarthy, Quirarte recounted some of his the earliest memories of life in Jerome. "About half the population was Mexican," he said. "It was like a little suburb of Mexico." Quirarte's immersion in the Spanish language and Mexican culture shielded him from mainstream U.S. culture. He first heard the English language at school. Asked if he had found it strange to speak one language in school and another everywhere else, Quirarte replied: "No, not really because most of the people in the town were either Mexican or what you call 'ethnic whites.' Almost everybody spoke another language at home, so at school everyone communicated in English."

From the beginning of his academic career, Quirarte loved school. He told McCarthy about the times in elementary school when he won math drills and knowledge contests in class. His father recognized the Quirarte's abilities and wanted his son to have a wider range of opportunities than the small town could provide. Working in the mines would not satisfy the boy. Even worse, the local industry was not likely to survive more than a few more years. The elder Quirarte decided to move the family to San Francisco.

There Quirarte entered a world larger and more diverse than anything he had known. He told McCarthy that it was after moving to San Francisco that "I came from a bad neighborhood." In Jerome, he said, "we were all in it together. Everyone was poor, and nobody really thought about it." In San Francisco, Quirarte's father took a job as a warehouseman, and after a time, the family settled in a more affluent neighborhood.

Quirarte's academic success continued in high school. After graduation, he was offered a scholarship from the University of California at Berkeley. He refused. "That's how small my world was," he told McCarthy, "I couldn't even think of going across the [San Francisco] Bay to Berkeley for school." Instead he went to San Francisco State College (now University), where he joined the Reserve Officers Training Corps (ROTC) in 1951. After graduating in 1954, Quirarte served for three years in the U.S. Air Force as a flight officer and bombardier on a B–36.

After leaving the military Quirarte returned to San Francisco State and earned his master's degree in art and art history. He had an opportunity to study at the National University in Mexico City, where he received his Ph.D. in 1964. In Mexico City, Quirarte became acquainted with world-class scholars. "When I was in Mexico City, I worked with some of the incredible greats in my field," Quirarte said, "They were coming to the end of their careers, but I didn't know that."

Quirarte taught at the Colegio Americano in Mexico City and served as a professor of art history and a dean at the University of the Americas from 1962 to 1964. After teaching for two years in Venezuela, Quirarte received a significant career boost. He served as an interim replacement for the prominent Yale University scholar George Kubler, and as Quirarte told McCarthy, "after that the offers rolled in."

### To Texas

Quirarte accepted a professorship in art history at the University of Texas's flagship school in Austin in 1967. In the early 1970's he became involved with the founding of the University of Texas at San Antonio. There he continued to teach art history. He

also assumed the post of dean of the College of Fine and Applied Arts. Quirarte found the position an opportunity to make important changes in the lives of students and the community. Yet scholarship remained his true vocation. "Adminstration was a challenge," Quirarte told McCarthy, "But once we named the chairs of the departments, developed the curriculum, and established the university, it became routine." In 1979 Quirarte became Director of University of Texas-San Antonio's Research Center of the Arts, a position he held into the 1990s. Currently he is San Antonio's most senior faculty member.

Married to Sara Bel Farmer since 1954, Quirarte is the father of one daughter. He continues to live in San Antonio, where the university he helped found now has an enrollment of 18,000 and a second campus. Quirarte takes pride in his role in making the school a "beacon to Latin America" and an enhancement to life in San Antonio.

### SOURCES:

**Books**

*Hispanic Writers,* edited by Bryan Ryan, Detroit, Gale Research, 1993.

**Other**

Quirarte, Jacinto, interview with James McCarthy, April 27, 1995.

—*Sketch by James McCarthy*

# Horacio Quiroga
## 1878-1937
**Uruguayan writer**

Horacio Quiroga was acclaimed as a master of the short story, but scholars have had difficulty separating his work from the dramatic, unusual events of his life. From depictions of the jungle in which he lived for many years to the premature deaths among many of his characters, Quiroga infused his tales with the violence and unconventionality of his lifestyle. Some critics equated him with the U.S. writer, Edgar Allan Poe, finding similar style and themes in the work of both men.

## A Violent Beginning

Quiroga was born on December 31, 1878, in Salto, Uruguay. His father Prudencio—who served as an Argentinian vice-consul in Uruguay—died of shotgun wounds resulting from a hunting accident before young Horacio could even walk. This tragedy set an unfortunate tone for Quiroga's future. Quiroga's Uruguayan mother, Juana Petrona Forteza, relocated the family briefly in Argentina, but returned to Salto in 1883. Quiroga attended elementary school there, and in 1891, the family moved to the capital city, Montevideo. His mother remarried that same year. Quiroga enjoyed having a paternal figure around and became very close to his stepfather. But this happy relationship did not last. Quiroga's stepfather suffered a stroke a few years after the marriage and was left nearly helpless. He grew frustrated and miserable. In 1896 he killed himself with a gun; the 17-year old Quiroga was the one who discovered the body.

As a youth Quiroga found an important outlet in literature. By his teens he had already begun writing; in 1901 he published *Los arrecifes de coral* (*Coral Reefs*). The book contained prose and poetry in a modernist style he would soon reject. Quiroga also established relationships with people in the literary world. But tragedy struck again when Quiroga accidentally killed one of his closest companions and literary peers with a handgun in 1902. Although the courts cleared him of guilt, Quiroga's own grief and regret led him to flee to Buenos Aires to live with his sister.

Quiroga sought adventure. A visit to Paris—the mecca for young artists at that time—had not satisfied him. In 1903 he went to the Misiones province in northern Argentina. There Quiroga found vast unsettled jungles. Although he had embarked on the trip with the writer **Leopold Lugones** in order to study Jesuit ruins, he found instead a place where he wanted to build a life.

With money inherited from his father, Quiroga bought land in the Chaco Territory in 1904. He cleared the land, constructed a house and tried to raise cotton. In *Latin American Writers,* George D. Schade detailed what drew Quiroga to the inhospitable country: "The broad expanse of the Paraná River, the tropical forest, the exotic animals." Quiroga tried to make his small plantation financially self-sustaining with both the cotton and an orange liqueur developed from the fruit on his trees. Schade wrote, "While all of these experimental endaevors were financial failures, they provided him with excellent material for his collection of short stories."

During his time in the jungle, Quiroga did not abandon his writing. In 1904 he published the book *El crimen del otro* (*Crimes of Others*) and in 1905 *Los perseguidos* (*The Pursued*). In another essay, Schade noted that although critics have often dismissed the significance of some of Quiroga's early works, Quiroga's 1907 story, "The Feather Pillow," represents what may be Quiroga's first truly successful gothic story. As in many of his works, Quiroga explored madness as a source of deep horror. In his literary engagement one might discern an attempt to understand the despairing madness of both his stepfather and Quiroga himself after the accident that had killed his friend.

From 1906 to 1911 Quiroga taught at a Normal School in Buenos Aires. Among his students was Ana María Cirés. The two became romantically involved and married in 1909. Quiroga decided to return permanently to his wilderness ranch. Two years later Ana María nearly died giving birth to their daughter, Eglé. When Ana María became pregnant again, she refused to deliver the child in the jungle without a doctor and travelled to Buenos Aires to have their son Dario.

In *Latin American Writers,* Schade noted that although Quiroga and his wife loved each other they found it difficult to live together peaceably. Ana María was especially annoyed by Quiroga's desire to raise their children "as young animals," as Schade phrased it, "in what [Quiroga] thought was nature's way." The tension became palpable. Life in the jungle began to drive Ana María to despair. She had never enjoyed wilderness life or shared her husband's thirst for adventure. In 1915 she deliberately poisoned herself. She lingered in agony for several days before she died. For Quiroga, who had already seen much death and horror, his wife's suicide continued the grim chain of personal loss.

## The Despondent Widower

Quiroga found himself responsible for the care of his two children. After his initial rage directed toward his wife for committing suicide he became despondent. He left the jungle for Buenos Aires, where he entrusted his children to the care of his mother-in-law. Some critics have suggested that tragedy fueled Quiroga's writing at its most brilliant moments. Schade asserted that "the next ten years [after his wife's suicide] were the most productive of his career, wherein he published his best books." His 1917 collection *Cuentos de amor, de locura y de muerte* (*Stories of Love, Madness and Death*) stands as one of his outstanding career achievements. Schade has also pointed out that the collection's title characterizes Quiroga's entire body of work.

The year 1917 also saw Quiroga gain a position in the Uruguayan consulate in Buenos Aires. He lived comfortably and received much admiration. He began to take an interest in the cinema and wrote a column of film criticism for the magazine *Atlantida*. Quiroga's popularity also skyrocketed after the release of his

1918 book, *Cuentos de la selva* (*South American Jungle Tales*). Schade praised the work as "permeated with tenderness and humor and filled with whimsy."

The routine of a regular job drove him to desire a return to his jungle ranch. He made the move in 1925. The following year Quiroga published the critically acclaimed *Los desterrados* (*The Exiles*). As his writing career moved forward, his personal life also seemed to be moving in a positive direction when he met Ana María Palacio. Although he was nearly 30 years older than her, Quiroga fell in love. Ana María's parents did not appreciate the advances of an eccentric older man and sent their daughter away.

Heartbreak inspired Quiroga's return to Buenos Aires. His fame grew; the magazine *Babel* devoted an entire issue to him, calling Quiroga "the finest short story writer in the Spanish language." María Elena Bravo, a 20-year-old acquaintance of Quiroga's daughter, met the famous writer and found him attractive. The two married in 1927, but the marriage had few happy moments. Although María Elena gave birth to a daughter in 1928, the baby's arrival seemed only to add to the new mother's dissatisfaction with her marriage and life in the jungle.

### Divorce and Illness

The Uruguayan government had posted Quiroga to a less urban consulate in San Ignacio, and Quiroga had enjoyed his steady salary along with the access to the wilderness he loved. But the consulate closed in the early 1930s, putting Quiroga into financial difficulty. He wrote *Más allá* (*The Great Beyond*) in 1935. Schade characterized Quiroga's final literary effort as a "letdown" after his earlier successes.

Quiroga's health began to decline. Asthma and neurasthenia—a mental disorder characterized by fatigue and anxiety—compounded the misery of prostate cancer. His wife took their child and returned to the city. Quiroga could not remain in the jungle when he was so ill and reluctantly returned to Buenos Aires. When his cancer defied treatment, Quiroga ingested cyanide poison on February 18, 1937, and died. His friends raised funds to bury Quiroga in his Salto birthplace.

### SELECTED PUBLISHED WORKS:

*Los arrecifes de coral* (*Coral Reefs*), [Montevideo], 1901.
*El crimen del otro* (*Another's Crime*), [Buenos Aires], 1904.
*Los perseguidos* (*The Pursued*), [Buenos Aires], 1905.
*Cuentos de amor, de locura y de muerte* (*Stories of Love, Madness, and Death*), [Buenos Aires], 1917.
*Cuentos de la selva para los niños* (*South American Jungle Tales*), [Buenos Aires], 1918.
*Los desterrados* (*The Exiles*), [Buenos Aires], 1926.
*Mas alla* (*The Great Beyond*), 1935.

### SOURCES:

*Hispanic Writers,* edited by Bryan Ryan, Detroit, Gale Research, 1991.
*Latin American Writers,* edited by Carlos-Solé, New York, Charles Scribner's Sons, 1989.
*The Decapitated Chicken and Other Stories by Horacio Quiroga,* with an introduction by George Schade, Austin University of Texas Press, 1976.

*—Sketch by James McCarthy*

# Diana Ramírez de Arellano
## 1919-
**Puerto Rican poet, literary scholar, and educator**

Named poet laureate of Puerto Rico in 1958, Diana Ramírez de Arellano is a poet of intense imagery. Since the publication of her first collection *Yo soy Ariel* ("I Am Ariel") in 1947, Ramírez de Arellano has received numerous awards for her work, including special citations from the governments of Bolivia and Ecuador, as well as various groups in Puerto Rico. Her verse is rooted in the scenes and culture of her childhood in Puerto Rico; for example, in this piece from *Arbol en vísperas* ("Tree at Vespers"), the poet extols the Jobo tree native to the island: "Not the poplar or the laurel do I exalt here/ nor the fir nor the spruce or the aspen or the juniper/ planted in Castille's rugose palm/ or in the fertile shores of another triumph/ by my friend's magic hand/ Nor do I sing her Alfonsa-Lark's resin bearing pines/ in distant Cuellar's forests/ Nor even don Antonio's centenary elm-tree/ in Soria's unblemished hillsides/ do I invoke though I possess a little bit of it./ Love summons here, common to none, a tree unknown,/ throbbing, trembling." The passion of the poem mirrors a passion for Puerto Rico.

Born June 3, 1919, in New York City, Ramírez de Arellano moved to Ponce, Puerto Rico, with her parents, Enrique Ramírez Brau and María Teresa Rechani Ramírez de Arellano, and attended primary and secondary schools there. Her father was a noted poet and journalist, and her great-grandfather was the prominent journalist and historian Salvador Brau. She gives both of these forebears, who demonstrated how the written word could be used as an artist's palette, credit for her talents. She has also acknowledged the role of her mother in developing her work, which frequently examines various female figures in the Spanish-speaking world.

The poet has had a diverse education. She received her bachelor's degree from the University of Puerto Rico in 1941; she then attended Columbia University's teacher's college and got her master of arts degree in 1946. For the next six years she worked as an instructor of Spanish at the University of North Carolina and at Rutgers University while simultaneously working on a Ph.D. from the University of Madrid. After receiving her Ph.D. in 1952, she became an assistant professor at Rutgers; six years later she moved to the City College of the City University of New York, where she would teach until her retirement as professor emeritus in 1984. 1958 was also the year she was named poet laureate and earned first prize in literature from the Institute of Puerto Rican Literature, a citation from Club Cívico de Damas, and diploma de honor from Ateneo Puertorriqueño de San Juan, all for her volume of poetry, *Angeles de ceniza* ("Angels of Ashes"). She won the Institute of Literature's first prize again in 1961, this time for a volume of criticism on contemporary Spanish-language poetry.

### Poetry Examines Universal Themes

In her numerous poetical works Ramírez de Arellano examines literary themes of love, life, hope, memory, and exile and return to one's homeland. According to the *Diccionario de literatura puertorriqueña,* her style is based in the tradition of other Latin American poets and shares the post-modernistic sensibilities of modern Spanish masters such as Miguel de Unamuno. In addition, works such as her 1955 poem *Albatros sobre el alma* ("Albatross over the Soul") have been cited as building on the symbolism of the English poet Samuel Taylor Coleridge. Her critical work has also been praised for combining her poetic imagination with a clarity of expression.

A member of several international and national teaching and writing associations, including PEN International, the poet frequently lectures and makes appearances at colleges and literary organizations; she also has served as a consultant to arts councils in the United States and Canada, including the Ford Foundation. Ramírez de Arellano, who has remained single throughout her life, is now retired from teaching and divides her time between New York, Puerto Rico, and Spain. She currently serves as president of the Josefina Romo Arregui Memorial Foundation, an organization dedicated to the memory of the late Spanish poet who served as Ramírez de Arellano's mentor.

### SELECTED PUBLISHED WORK:

*Yo soy Ariel* (poems), Casa Unida de Publicaciones, 1947.
*Los Ramírez de Arellano de Lope de Vega,* Consejo Superior de Investigaciones Cientificas, 1954.

*Albatros sobre el alma* (poems), Colección de Poesía para Bibliofilos, 1955.

*Angeles de ceniza* (poems), Colección de Poesía para Bibliofilos, 1958.

*Un vuelo casi humano* (poems), Colección de Poesía para Bibliofilos, 1960.

*Caminos de la creación poética en Pedro Salinas,* Biblioteca Aristarco de Erudición y Crítica, 1961.

*Poesía contemporánea en lengua española,* Biblioteca Aristarco de Erudición y Crítica, 1961.

*La cultura en el panorama puertorriqueño de Nueva York,* El Ateneo, 1964.

*Privilegio* (poems), Colección Ateneo de Poetas Hispáncios, 1965.

*Del señalado oficio de la muerte,* Ateneo de Puertorriqueño de Nueva York, 1974.

*El himno deseado,* Editorial Romo, 1979.

*Arbol en vísperas,* Torremozas, 1987.

## SOURCES:

### Books

*Hispanic Writers,* Gale, 1991, pp. 393–94.

Ramírez de Arellano, Diana, *Arbol en vísperas/Tree at Vespers* (bilingual edition), Ediciones Torremozas, 1987.

Rivera de Alvarez, Josefina, *Diccionario de literatura puertorriqueña,* 2nd edition, Instituto de Cultura Puertorriqueña, 1974, pp. 1285–87.

### Periodicals

*Bulletin of Hispanic Studies* (Liverpool University), Volume 35, number 2, 1958.

*Modern Language Notes,* February, 1959.

—*Sketch by Bill Evans*

*Santiago Ramón y Cajal*

# Santiago Ramón y Cajal
## 1852-1934
### Spanish neurohistologist

The anatomical research of the Spanish neurohistologist Santiago Ramón y Cajal is central to the modern understanding of the nervous system. By adopting and improving the nervous-tissue staining process developed by the Italian scientist Camillo Golgi, Ramón y Cajal established that individual nerve cells, or neurons, are the basic structural unit of the nervous system. He also made important discoveries relating to the transmission of nerve impulses and the cellular structures of the brain. For his work in histology, the branch of anatomy concerned with minute tissue structures and processes, Ramón y Cajal shared with Golgi the 1906 Nobel Prize for Physiology or Medicine.

Ramón y Cajal was born on May 1, 1852, in the remote country village of Petilla de Aragon, Spain. He was the son of Justo Ramón y Casasús, a poor and self-educated barber-surgeon, and Antonia Cajal. The family subsequently moved to the university city of Zaragoza, where against considerable odds Ramón y Cajal's father earned a medical degree and became a professor of anatomy. As a young man, Ramón y Cajal was rebellious and independent-minded. He preferred drawing to studying, and although this passion for drawing would ultimately serve him well, it was vigorously opposed by his iron-willed father, who had determined that his son should become a doctor. As a disciplinary measure, his father apprenticed him to a barber and later to a shoemaker. During these apprenticeships, Ramón y Cajal also studied anatomy with his father—investigations that partially relied on bone specimens taken from a local churchyard.

When he was sixteen years old, Ramón y Cajal began medical studies at the University of Zaragoza, earning a degree in medicine in 1873. He then joined the army medical service and served as an infantry surgeon in Cuba for one year. He contracted malaria, however, which led to his discharge, and he returned to Spain. In 1879, still convalescent, he passed his examinations at Zaragoza and Madrid for his doctorate in medicine.

Ramón y Cajal was almost exclusively interested in anatomical research, and he embarked on an academic career. Beginning in 1879, Ramón y Cajal turned himself into a skilled histologist, initially working with an old, abandoned microscope he had found at the University of Zaragoza. He studied various anatomical tissues and began to publish articles on cell biology—complete with beautifully rendered ink drawings. His work was not immediately recognized in other countries, but the increasing prestige of his posts attests to his success in Spain. From 1879 to 1883, he directed the anatomical museum at the University of Zaragoza. In 1883, he assumed a professorship of descriptive anatomy at the University of Valencia, and in 1887 he became professor of histology at the University of Barcelona. In 1892, Ramón y Cajal assumed the chair of histology and pathologic anatomy at the University of Madrid, a post he retained until 1922.

## Research Provides Evidence for Neuron Theory

Ramón y Cajal eventually turned to the most complex tissues, those of the nervous system. His research method now drew on Camillo Golgi's method of staining tissue samples to reveal their minute components. Under Golgi's method, a potassium dichromate-silver nitrate solution stained the nerve cells and fibers black, while the neuroglia, or supporting tissues, remained much lighter. By refining this staining technique and applying it to embryonic tissue samples, Ramón y Cajal was able to isolate the neuron as the basic component of the nervous system; he also differentiated the neuron from the ordinary cells of the body. His work supported the neuron theory, which held that the nervous system consists of a network of discrete nerve fibers that end in terminal "buttons," that never actually touch the surrounding nerve cells. Up until that time, the majority of scientists were "reticularists," who held that the nervous system formed a continuous and interconnected system. Golgi was among these, and the rivalry between the two scientists was intense. Ramón y Cajal published fierce and relentless attacks both on this theory and on the scientists who held it.

Based on his studies, Ramón y Cajal became convinced that the conduction of nerve impulses occurs in one direction only—a postulate since formalized as the law of dynamic polarization. He also conducted important research on the tissues of the inner ear and the eye, as well as the tissues of the grey matter of the brain, establishing a cellular basis for the localization of different functions within the brain.

This research has formed the physiological basis for the understanding of human psychology, intelligence, and memory.

Ramón y Cajal was a prolific writer and he published many articles, textbooks, and research monographs. In 1896, he established a journal of microbiology and published his *Manual de Anatomia Pathologica General* ("Manual of General Pathologic Anatomy"). His major neurohistological work, *Textura del Systema Nervioso del Hombre y de los Vertebrados* ("Texture of the Nervous System of Man and Vertebrates"), was published from 1899 to 1904. These publications were generally printed in Spanish, often at his own expense, and they were largely ignored by the international scientific community.

His struggle for due recognition of the importance of his work came to an end in 1906, when he shared the Nobel Prize in Physiology or Medicine with his rival Golgi for their work on the structure of the nervous system. In an apparent effort to emphasize what the two scientists had in common, rather than their area of disagreement, they were described by the prize committee as "the principal representatives and standard-bearers of the modern science of neurology." But the tension between them over the reticular doctrine was still evident on the awards platform.

## Later Research and Writing

In the same year he received the prize, Ramón y Cajal turned to the problem of the degeneration of tissue in the nervous system and the regeneration of nerve fibers that had been severed. The result of these studies, the two-volume *Estudios Sobre la Degeneracion y Regeneracion del Sistema Nervioso* ("Studies on the Degeneration and Regeneration of the Nervous System"), was published in 1913 and 1914. In 1913, Ramón y Cajal also developed a gold-based method of staining neuroglia; he was able to use this to classify cell types in these tissues. This research provided the basis for the medical treatment of tumors and pathological tissues in the nervous system. A tireless researcher, Ramón y Cajal also studied the eyes and vision processes of insects.

Ramón y Cajal, a patriot, was always sensitive to the international and scientific reputation of Spain and the Spanish language—issues that had a significant impact on the dissemination of his research. It was thus fitting that in 1920 King Alfonso XIII commissioned the construction of the Instituto Cajal, which secured Madrid's position as an international histological research center. Ramón y Cajal worked at this institute named in his honor from 1922 until his death.

In addition to sharing the Nobel Prize, Ramón y Cajal received numerous awards and honors, including the Fauvelle Prize of the Society of Biology in Paris in 1896; the Rubio Prize in 1897; the Moscow Prize in 1900; the Martinez y Molina Prize in 1902; the Helmholtz Gold Medal of the Royal Academy of Berlin in 1905; and the Echegaray Medal in 1922. He also received honorary degrees from various foreign universities and held memberships in scientific societies worldwide. The Spanish government bestowed an impressive series of posthumous honors on him, including the republication of his works.

Ramón y Cajal married Silveria Fananas Garcia in 1880. They had three daughters and three sons. In addition to drawing, his hobbies included chess and photography, which he pursued as single-mindedly as his research. In a merging of his work and recreational interests, Ramón y Cajal developed his own photographic process for the reproduction of his delicate histological drawings.

Between 1901 and 1917, Ramón y Cajal published the installments of his autobiographical *Recuerdos de mi Vida* ("Recollections of My Life"). His other published works include the anecdotal *Charlas de Cafe* ("Conversations at the Cafe") and *El Mundo Visto a los Ochenta Anos* ("The World as Seen at Eighty"). Ramón y Cajal died in Madrid on October 18, 1934.

## SELECTED PUBLISHED WORKS:

*Manual de Anatomia Pathologica General* (title means "Manual of General Pathologic Anatomy"), Moya (Madrid), 1896.
*Textura del Systema Nervioso del Hombre y de los Vertebrados* (title means "Texture of the Nervous System of Man and Vertebrates"), Moya (Madrid), 1899–1904.
*Estudios Sobre la Degeneracion y Regeneracion del Sistema Nervioso*, 1913–14, translated by Raoul M. Day as *Degeneration and Regeneration of the Nervous System*, Oxford University Press (London), 1928.
*Recollections of My Life*, two volumes, 1937, Massachusetts Institute of Technology (Cambridge, MA), 1966.

## SOURCES:

### Books

Cannon, Dorothy F., *Explorer of the Human Brain: The Life of Santiago Ramón y Cajal*, H. Schuman, 1949.
Gillespie, Charles, editor, *Dictionary of Scientific Biography*, Scribner's, 1975, pp. 273–76.
Shepherd, Gordon M., *Foundations of the Neuron Doctrine*, Oxford University Press, 1992.

Wasson, Tyler, editor, *Nobel Prize Winners*, H. W. Wilson, 1987, pp. 852–55.

### Periodicals

Knudtson, Peter, "Painter of Neurons," *Science*, September 1985, pp. 66–72.

*—Sketch by David Sprinkle*

# John Rechy
## 1934-
## Mexican American writer

John Rechy made a name for himself in the literary world in 1963 with the publication of *City of Night*, a novel that candidly and compassionately depicted the sexual journey of a homosexual male prostitute in urban America. While the novel became a bestseller and was translated into at least eight languages, its early reviews were mixed. Although contemporary critics objected to the novel's controversial subject matter, it is now considered a modern classic and is often taught in modern literature courses.

Among Rechy's eight other published works, *The Sexual Outlaw: A Documentary*, a manifesto for gay rights, is perhaps his best known. While Rechy has gained notoriety for his controversial subject matter, he has been widely praised for his artistic merit as well, winning the Longview Foundation fiction prize in 1961, a National Endowment for the Arts grant in 1976, and a *Los Angeles Times Book Award* nomination in 1984. Rechy has supplemented his writing career by teaching creative writing and literature courses at such institutions as the University of Southern California and the University of California at Los Angeles.

John Francisco Rechy was born in 1934, in El Paso, Texas, the youngest of five children born to Roberto Rechy, a Scottish composer-conductor, and his Mexican wife, Guadalupe Flores. Raised during the Great Depression, he recalled to *Newsday*'s Gregg Barrios, "There was so much poverty and hunger in El Paso and Juarez that we didn't consider ourselves poor, because we ate and had a home." A sensitive and lonely child, Rechy worked as a professional child actor, once receiving rave reviews for his portrayal of Jesus as a little boy. His writing career began early: by the age of 17 he had written an historical novel called *Time on Wings*. Always an excellent student, Rechy earned his B.A. at Texas Western College. Shortly after graduating, he enlisted in the U.S. Army and planned to attend graduate classes at Columbia University immediately following his discharge.

Rechy's dream was to study with Pearl Buck, but after submitting his unpublished novel, *Pablo!*, he was rejected. "I arrived in New York with only $20," Rechy described in his unpublished autobiography, excerpted in *Newsday.* "There I met a merchant marine. He buys me hamburgers and tells me I can make quick money on Times Square—'hustling.' A new word has opened a new world to me. Instead of Columbia, I went to Times Square."

While embarking on this new career, Rechy also continued to write, attending creative writing classes at the New School for Social Research. Encouraged by a friend to turn his letters describing his Times Square experiences into fiction, Rechy began publishing short stories in the *Evergreen Review.* One story, 1961's "The Fabulous Wedding of Miss Destiny," was awarded the Longview Foundation fiction prize.

### Writes *City of Night*

In 1963 Rechy collected several of his short stories depicting the life of a Chicano hustler and wrote *City of Night*, which Grove Press published in 1963. After reading the book, novelist, and playwright James Baldwin declared Rechy "the most arresting young writer I've read in a very long time." A book that most likely would not have been accepted by the mainstream press just a few years earlier, *City of Night*, shocked many in the literary world with its graphic portrayal of what *New York Times Book Review*'s Peter Buitenhuis termed the "half-submerged world of homosexuality, the community of hustlers, lesbians, queens, and other[s] that live on the fringes and in the center of urban societies of America." Buitenhuis went on to call Rechy "an inept writer with a number of mannerisms that should have been suppressed by his editor."

But Rechy—who described such mainstream literary reviews as "notoriously homophobic," in an interview with *Dictionary of Literary Biography Yearbook*'s Jean W. Ross—felt that the formal achievements of the book were largely overlooked because its protagonist was a male prostitute. The *Saturday Review*'s Granville Hicks, however, had words of praise for the novel's writing style, which he found, though at times "tiresomely exclamatory . . . usually controlled and quietly forceful." Furthermore, he believed Rechy to be "more than a good reporter, for he has touched his materials with the imagination and the craft of a writer."

The fame that *City of Night* brought Rechy, proved to be something of a mixed blessing. "I was immediately categorized. I wasn't just a homosexual writer; some critics in the literary establishment insisted I was a hustler who wrote books, he told Barrios. "To them I was never a writer who just happened to write about hustling." The content of Rechy's second novel, *Numbers,* invited similar negative critical response after its publication in 1967.

Continuing with the sexual exploits of the first book's unnamed narrator—now called Johnny Rio—*Numbers,* according to Rechy, was intended to be a contemporary horror story about dying. After publishing two more novels that were not widely circulated, Rechy was forced to confront the death of his mother in 1970. In order to escape the reality of the grief he experienced, he turned to LSD, cocaine, and heroin. The death was especially painful for Rechy because he had bought his mother, whom he described as the greatest love of his life, a large new home with the money from his first book and had even moved back to El Paso from the Caribbean to live with her during her last years. With the help of friends who referred him to a psychiatrist, Rechy began to improve his mental health by turning to bodybuilding. "The doctor told me a very funny thing. He said he knew of people destroyed by narcissism, but he had never thought one could be saved by it," he told Barrios.

Once again translating personal experience into fiction, Rechy wrote *The Fourth Angel*, a novel that focused on a teenager who could not cope with his mother's death. Although he was able to find a new publisher, the book was virtually ignored after its 1972 publication and Rechy—ten years after the immense success of *City of Night*—was forced to return to hustling the same Los Angeles streets to make a living. His return to the streets, however, provided him with the material to write his most controversial book, *The Sexual Outlaw: A Documentary,* a graphic account of three days and nights of anonymous sex in the homosexual underground of Los Angeles. While some reviewers objected to the events presented, most agreed with *Booklist,* who found the documentary "a compelling and important one, written with the authority from research and experience described in previous novels."

Shortly after *The Sexual Outlaw*'s publication in 1977, Rechy was again back in the limelight—this time as an outspoken advocate for gay rights. While he had long kept his own sexual identity from the public view, he told *People*'s Eleanor Hoover that he made "a conscious decision not to hold back" after his latest book's release. Although some bookstores refused to carry it, Rechy's sixth work sold out in its first printing and Dell, a mainstream press, came out with a second edition for the mass market. Having found an audience once again, Rechy emerged as a militant spokesman for the gay community. Responding to what he found to be a growing climate of "heterosexual fascism," he began lecturing at universities such as Yale, advocating the "public sex" revolution and condemning the persecution of homosexuals. As Rechy stated in *The Sexual Outlaw,* "Homosexuality is not a victimless crime—the homosexual is the victim, the cop the criminal."

In his next novel, *Rushes,* Rechy moved his locale to a sadomasochistic leather gay bar and orgy room where lawyers and hairdressers alike clothed their effeminacy by playing the more "macho" roles of cowboys, motorcyclists, and construction workers. Soon after its publication in 1979, however, AIDS emerged as a threat to the world he was describing. According to Rechy, the disease has forced the homosexual community to discover their enormous capacity for courage. "Whenever I think of the thugs who call us sissies, it doubly enrages me," he told Barrios. "Right now our people are showing more courage than anyone else. We're literally living with death."

In his last two novels, Rechy has moved away from his long-held focus on the homosexual underground. 1983's *Bodies and Souls,* for instance, chronicles the lives of three runaways who have come to Los Angeles to find meaning in their existence. After receiving some of his best reviews since *City of Night,* Rechy was nominated for the 1984 *Los Angeles Times* Book Award for best body of work. Rechy's 1988 novel, *Marilyn's Daughter,* which the *San Fransisco Chronicle* called "a marvel of literary engineering," focuses on the life of Normalyn Morgan—who believes she may be Marilyn Monroe's daughter by Robert Kennedy—and her travels to Los Angeles to find the identity of her mother. In this confrontation with one of the great symbols of U.S. culture, Rechy, according to *Transcript*'s John Farrell, attempted a "truly innovative approach to narrative and a serious exploration into the origin of legends and their power over truth."

While continuing to work on his autobiography and other projects, Rechy has taught creative writing courses at various colleges and universities, including the same novel-writing workshop at Columbia where he was once rejected as a student. As Rechy told Ross, "it is a triumph to be asked to teach a course you've been 'rejected' for.... I feel similarly about the negative criticism of my work. The initial shrieks about it don't matter; the works themselves will last."

## SELECTED PUBLISHED WORKS:

*City of Night,* New York, Grove, 1963.
*Numbers,* New York, Grove, 1967.
*This Day's Death,* New York, Grove, 1969.
*The Vampires,* New York, Grove, 1971.
*The Fourth Angel,* New York, Viking, 1973.
*The Sexual Outlaw: A Documentary,* New York, Grove, 1977.
*Rushes,* New York, Grove, 1979.
*Marilyn's Daughter,* New York, Carrol & Graff, 1988.
*The Miraculous Day of Amalia Gomez,* Boston, Little, Brown, 1992.

## SOURCES:

### Books

*Contemporary Authors Autobiography Series,* Volume 4, Detroit, Gale, 1986.
*Contemporary Literary Criticism,* Detroit, Gale, Volume 1, 1973, Volume 7, 1977, Volume 14, 1980, Volume 18, 1981.
*Dictionary of Literary Biography Yearbook: 1982,* Detroit, Gale, 1983.
*Gay and Lesbian Literature,* Detroit, St. James Press, 1994.
*Hispanic Writers,* Detroit, Gale, 1991.

### Periodicals

*Booklist,* June 15, 1977, p. 1540.
*Los Angeles Times,* September 7, 1988.
*New Republic,* September 14, 1963, pp. 21–23.
*Newsday,* September 10, 1988.
*New York Times Book Review,* June 30, 1963; January 14, 1968; April 3, 1977; July 10, 1983.
*People,* May 22, 1978, pp. 61–62.
*San Antonio Light,* March 22, 1992.
*San Fransisco Chronicle,* August 7, 1988.
*Saturday Review,* June 8, 1963.
*Times Literary Supplement* (London), September 11, 1970.
*Transcript,* November 28, 1988.
*Village Voice,* August 22, 1977; October 3, 1977; March 39, 1980.

—*Sketch by Jason Gallman*

# Hermelinda Renteria
## 1960-
### Mexican American engineer

A construction engineer with the Pacific Gas and Electric Company, Hermelinda Renteria spends her life in a hard hat and construction boots overseeing million-dollar projects in California. In her capacity as contracts and technical services supervisor at the San Francisco Bay Power Plant, she puts construction packages together, assigns contracts, and supervises the work until completion. However, Renteria had to fight to get a field job and faced repeated battles to escape the office positions traditionally reserved for women engineers. "It's up to you to decide what you want to do with your career," she stressed in an interview with Michelle Vachon, "and don't let anyone tell you otherwise." Renteria regards community service as a duty for a successful career person. "We can't just sit back and enjoy our money and comfort. We need to help others share this good life—it's only fair." Her involvement ranges from sitting on both the business advisory board of San Francisco's Human Rights Commission and the board of directors of the San Francisco Girl Scouts, as well as to serving as chapter vice president/special programs of the Latina Women's Network.

Renteria was born on June 8, 1960, in Llamas Zacatecas, Mexico. In 1963, her family moved to Chico, California, and in 1966 to Watsonville, California, where she grew up with her sister and two brothers. "Our parents were farm workers and had to go wherever they could find work," she explained in the interview with Vachon. "We lived in shared housings in labor camps." When Renteria and her sister reached high school age, her father insisted on sending them to a private Catholic school. "Anything we needed for education, our parents would provide, no matter what." After high school, Renteria chose to pursue university studies in Guadalajara, Mexico. "I wanted to know more about my cultural heritage," she said. The experience was difficult at first. "I've always been a tomboy and at my Catholic high school, we had been told that we girls could do anything we wanted career-wise. Suddenly, I was at the Universidad Autonoma de Guadalajara in a class composed of three women, and 120 male students with old-fashioned views on women. They did not make life easy for the three of us." Renteria became active in student organizations, such as the Women's Affairs Committee of the Student Affairs Council. To spoof the Miss University pageant, she launched a "King Ugly" contest on the campus. This caused a stir among her teachers who were used to unobtrusive engineering students. But in 1983, the three women were among the 52 students in her class who graduated with baccalaureates in science.

Renteria found her first engineering position with the Jalisco State Department of Public Works in Guadalajara. "I'm often asked whether being Hispanic creates difficulties in my field," she stated in her interview with Vachon. "My answer is that being Hispanic is no problem; being a woman is." Although she held the title of engineering aide, Renteria nevertheless received flowers and was treated to lunch on Secretary's Day. In 1984, she returned to California. "I came back to help my parents on the farm and supervise their 170 employees. They had just come

out of retirement to save their old strawberry farm that the new owner, a relative, had let deteriorate." When the crisis subsided, Renteria took positions related to engineering—engineering aide for the City of Ventura, California, draftperson for the County of Ventura's Road Maintenance Department, and draftperson for Gerald Graebe & Associates in Salinas, California. "I had to prove that my degree and my field experience were valid. I was willing to accept any offer to gain credibility," she recalled in her interview. Then she met Joseph McGowan, a vice president with the multinational firm Granite Construction, who recommended her for a position with Pacific Gas and Electric Company (PG&E). So in 1984, Renteria joined the utility company's staff of 26,000.

### Ascends Through Ranks of PG&E

She first served as field engineer; to her displeasure, this amounted to desk work. After a few months on the job, she met with her supervisor, Tom Allen, and expressed her strong desire to work in the field. With his support, she was soon put in charge of a million-dollar construction project. "It makes such a difference when a supervisor stands by his employees," she remembered in her interview with Vachon. "Occasionally, contractors tried to go over my head. But my supervisor would tell them that he trusted my decisions. It really built up my confidence." Renteria progressed within the company; she served as field engineer at the Diablo Canyon Nuclear Power Plant in San Luis Obispo, California, then she trained in project management in San Francisco, and later she was assigned to contracts administration. One of her projects consisted of remodelling a PG&E building in San Francisco, which meant keeping the edifice's outer shell while rebuilding the inside in its entirety. On a subsequent assignment, Renteria remodelled the computer floor of the company's billing department. "We had to work at night so we wouldn't interrupt the department's activities," she remembered in her interview. "The company was nervous about this—if anything went wrong, it could have been disastrous." Renteria received the PG&E's 1988 Performance Recognition Award for the project.

Her next post was assistant to the construction superintendent for the Diablo Canyon Power Plant in San Francisco. Afterwards, she joined the marketing department and attended to the company's special clients—the U.S. Army, universities, and the school district. Finally in 1992, Renteria became contracts and technical services supervisor for the San Francisco Bay Power Plant, a position she truly enjoys. It requires dealing with outside contractors and insuring that the work be executed according to PG&E's specifications.

Renteria draws upon her own experience in the work force when she gives talks in elementary and high schools. "I tell schoolgirls that if they are interested in working on site, they have to be careful when they accept office duties, whether or not they are of a technical nature," she emphasized in her interview with Vachon. "It can be very difficult for a woman to switch back after she has been identified with desk duties for a period of time." Her work with young people extends to being involved with the educational programs of the League of Latin American Citizens (LULAC), as well as to serving as chapter president of LULAC's National Education Service Centers from 1989 to 1992.

### Serves as a Role Model for Hispanic Girls

Renteria's commitment to young people prompted her to accept an appointment to the board of directors of the San Francisco Bay Area Girl Scouts. "The organization was looking for role models to inspire Hispanic girls. I was so impressed by the board's achievements that I couldn't refuse," she explained to Vachon. "There are more than 23,000 girl scouts in the San Francisco area, and the organization's activities—pregnant teen programs, conferences on multicultural relations—really focus on the issues they face today." Renteria was also appointed to the business advisory board of the San Francisco Human Rights Commission due to her work on behalf of minority businesses. "Our goal is to insure that women-owned and minority businesses get their fair share of city contracts." In the Hispanic community, she served as vice president in charge of special projects for the San Francisco Latina Women's Network. One of her undertakings was a seminar for women contemplating the second part of their lives. "We wanted to help women in their thirties and forties decide what they will do with the rest of their lives," she said in her interview. "I met many women who planned to completely change direction. It made me think about my own life."

Renteria has played an important role locally as well as nationally in the Society of Hispanic Professional Engineers (SHPE). She was San Francisco's chapter president for four terms between 1988 and 1993, and national secretary from 1989 to 1991. According to an article in the society's publication *Hispanic Engineer,* "Renteria's positive attitude and gregarious nature, along with her dedication to hard work, ensured her development as a leader." In 1988, she received an award from SHPE and the Asociacion Mexicana de Ingenieros Mecanicos y Electricistas (Mexican Association of Mechanical and Electrical Engineers) for her contribution in organizing the Third International Conference on Engineering and Technology, which took place in Juarez, Mexico. In 1991, Renteria was recognized by SHPE for her "Outstanding Leadership and Dedication." She also belongs to the American Society of Civil Engineers and the Society of Women Engineers. A member of the PG&E Employees Association, her participation earned her the company's Community Service Award in both 1989 and 1990.

In another arena, Renteria has been a Big Sister in the youth-support organization Big Brothers/Big Sisters of America since 1987, and has guided the same "little sister" for years. "I was used to dealing with my brother who is sixteen years younger than me," she confided in her interview. "So I asked to support a girl of his age, and it has worked well. I have seen them grow up. The three of us have gone on numerous outings together." Renteria also takes part in various mentor programs. So far she has followed three students from high school to college and has encouraged them to enter graduate school. "I really believe in education. It's a stepping stone to everything in life, especially today since the simplest job requires technical training. I have seen what happens to students who drop out of school. Education opens doors, creates possibilities. You don't have to complete college right away—attend for a few years and complete later if you have to. But do it."

In 1989, the Anti-Defamation League of B'nai B'rith awarded Renteria the "Woman on the Move" Certificate of Honor for her service to the community. The following year, her work with the Mission Girls' Services Program at the Young Women's Christian Association (YWCA) of San Francisco/Marin/San Mateo earned her a Certificate of Merit "for dedication and commitment to the YWCA Mission—the empowerment of women and girls and the elimination of racism." And in 1991, the Skyline College of San Bruno, California, presented Renteria with a Certificate of Appreciation for "encouraging the education of young women and nurturing their interest in science and mathematics."

Renteria admits that she is constantly looking for challenges. She plans to pursue her studies either in engineering or in education—she would like to teach one day. She also sees marriage in her future. But "I wouldn't give up my career or my activities. I think that you can have it all—a happy marriage and family life, a successful career and community involvement—and I intend to prove it!"

### SOURCES:

### Periodicals

*Hispanic Engineer,* fall, 1989, pp. 24–25.
*Newsline* (Lawrence Livermore Laboratories newsletter, Livermore, CA), September 14, 1990, p. 2.
*Society of Hispanic Professional Engineers* (newsletter), September/October, 1990, p. 8; November/December, 1990, p. 3.

*Vanidades,* August 7, 1990, p. 100.

**Other**

Renteria, Hermelinda, interview with Michelle Vachon conducted on May 9, 1992.

—*Sketch by Michelle Vachon*

# Armando Reverón
## 1889-1954
### Venezuelan painter

Armando Reverón was one of Venezuela's greatest impressionist painters, a man whose life was clouded by bouts of intensifying madness that led to his eventual incarceration. Reverón was a prolific and eccentric artist, renowned for his original landscapes that depicted the tropics by reducing the level of color and allowing the brilliance of tropical light to predominate. Many of his works are reminiscent of those of Claude Monet, the French Impressionist, Odilon Redon, the French mystic, and the German Expressionists.

Reverón was born in Caracas in 1889, the only child of eminent Creole parents. He was brought up by the Valencia foster family. During his childhood he contracted typhoid and suffered lifelong results of the illness. He was introduced to the art world by his maternal uncle, Ricardo Montilla, who had studied in New York. Under Montilla's guidance Reverón demonstrated his artistic talents from a young age.

In 1908, at the age of 15, Reverón enrolled at the Academy of Fine Arts in Caracas. He was briefly expelled for his involvement in a strike over the nature of the curriculum and the scholarship system, but he was soon reinstated. In 1911 he graduated from the Academy with distinction. Later that year he traveled to Spain—on a grant from the city of Caracas—to study in Barcelona under the Spanish painter Rafael Monasterios. Reverón then embarked on a course at the Academy of San Fernando in Madrid, where he remained until 1913. The following year he visited Paris before returning to Caracas in 1915.

Back in Venezuela he joined the Circle of Fine Arts, a group of young Impressionist painters. Reverón was influenced by the Russian painter, Nicolas Ferdinandov, and the painters Samys Mützner and Emilio Boggio. In 1919 Ferdinandov arranged an exhibition of Reverón's and Monasterios's work at the Academy of Fine Arts. Ferdinandov also encouraged Reverón to build a house in the coastal village of Macuto, near La Guaria. Reverón heeded his advice and retreated there in 1920. He lived in virtual isolation, surrounded by his monkeys, hand-made paper and grass dummies, and cats. He made his own brushes and 'canvases', frequently composing the latter from unprimed burlap, wrapping papers and magazine covers. Consequently, many of his pictures are in fragile condition.

Reverón lived eccentrically; a reporter for *Newsweek* recounted a journalist's meeting with the artist: "Before starting to work, Reverón prepares the atmosphere . . . he rubs his arms with a rough cloth until he draws blood. Then he goes out to 'warm up his sight,' driving it to ecstasy in the colors of the landscape in the sunlight. . . . Sometimes he binds his limbs with rope so that reflex movements will not jar his hand. Suddenly he will put his brushes down, hand a special small brush to one of his monkeys, and have it paint on one of the small easels he has made for them. He commands them as if they were his pupils, tells and shows them what to do."

Suffering the debilitating effects of schizophrenia, Reverón deteriorated from 1943 and was regularly hospitalized. Critics agree that much of his finest work was completed during this period, as he became increasingly absorbed into his work. In 1953 he was committed to the Sanitoria San Jorge in Caracas, where he died the following year.

Critics have identified four distinct phases in Reverón's art. First is his early Hispanophile phase that was influenced by his studies in Caracas, Madrid, and Barcelona. Second is a blue impressionist period, of which *La cuera* ("The Cave", 1919), is a famous example. Third is a white period—around 1924 to 1936—during which Reverón created near monochrome white works. These are represented by many landscapes and depictions of Caribbean beaches, such as *El arbol* (1931). In the final stage, after 1937, Reverón created predominantly sepia compositions, particularly of figures; the scene of a woman seated by the sea is a recurrent theme.

Reverón's work was exhibited in Paris at the Galerie Katia Granoff in 1933. He was awarded first prize from the Official Salon of Venezuela in 1940. During his lifetime his work was exhibited at two further significant exhibitions: at Taller Libre de Arte in Caracas in 1949 and at the Venezuelan-American Center in 1950. Reverón has since been the subject of several retrospective exhibitions: at the Caracas Museo de Bellas Artes in 1954, and at the Museum of Contemporary Art in Boston in 1956. In 1979 the Caracas Museo de Bellas Artes held a commemorative exhibition, marking the 25th anniversary of his death.

## SOURCES:

### Books

*Art in Latin America: The Modern Era,
1820–1980,* by Dawn Ales, New Haven, Yale
University Press, 1989.
*Encyclopedia of Latin America,* edited by Helen
Delpar, New York, McGraw-Hill, 1974.

### Periodicals

*Art News,* September, 1956, p. 16.
*Newsweek,* January 23, 1956, pp. 37–38.

—*Sketch by Amanda Beresford*

# Alfonso Reyes
## 1889-1959
### Mexican writer and diplomat

Alfonso Reyes was one of Mexico's pre-eminent men of letters. Exhibiting a Renaissance-like versatility, he made significant contributions to twentieth-century Hispanic culture through essays, poetry, literary scholarship, education, and international diplomacy—political as well as intellectual. Reyes's forte was the essay, in which he displayed an eloquent synthesis of scholarly erudition and lyrical fluency. As Anderson-Imbert lauded in *Spanish-American Literature: A History,* "his prose is beaten gold."

Reyes's most highly regarded work was *Visión de Anáhuac* (1917), an evocative essay about the initial encounter between the Spanish conquistadors and the Aztec civilization. Reyes served as a diplomat in Spain and France, and later became an ambassador to Argentina and Brazil. Reyes was also highly influential through his work as Mexico's intellectual ambassador to the world. He strove to establish a cultural continuity among Mexico, Western Europe, and the rest of Latin America. Federico de Onís hailed Reyes as "the most achieved example in any literature of the international citizen of the world of classic and modern letters."

Born on May 17, 1889, in Monterrey, Nuevo León, Mexico, Reyes was the ninth of 12 children born to General Bernardo Reyes and Aurelia Ochoa. In 1905 Reyes enrolled in the Escuela Nacional Preparatoria in Mexico City and later attended the Escuela Nacional de Altos Estudios. During this time Reyes became a member of the group of intellectuals known as the "Centennial Generation " (a title which signified a century of Mexican independence).

This group, which included Pedro Henríquez Ureña and Antonio Caso, studied and discussed classical Greek and Roman literature, the Spanish Golden Age, and Modern European literatures. They were also dedicated to promoting their own sense of Mexican cultural identity. In 1909 they established a center for young intellectuals, the "Ateneo de la Juventud " ("Antheneum of Youth"), an institution that was instrumental in bringing about the Mexican Renaissance.

In 1911 Reyes published his first collection of essays entitled *Cuestiones estéticas* ("Aesthetic Questions"). Characteristic of Reyes's diverse interests, it included critical essays on Greek drama, Baroque poet **Luis de Góngora**, Johann Wolfgang von Goethe, and George Bernard Shaw. Reyes married Manela Mota in 1911, and a year later Alfonso, their only child, was born. In 1913 Reyes earned his law degree from the University of Mexico. Over the course of his literary career he garnered honorary degrees from several universities including ones in the United States, Mexico, and Cuba.

### Moves to Europe

Reyes's father authored works of military history and various practical military manuals. Interested in the arts, General Reyes fostered his son's literary interests at an early age. As Governor of Nuevo León, he was known for his progressive and enlightened leadership. But on February 9, 1913, General Reyes was killed when counterrevolutionaries stormed the National Palace. In a poem commemorating his father, entitled "+9 de febrero de 1913" Reyes wrote, "if I have continued to live since that day, / it is because I carry you with me, where you are inviolable."

In despair, Reyes chose self-exile through an appointment as second secretary of the Mexican Legation in France. With World War I and the German invasion of Paris in 1914, Reyes moved to Madrid, where he immersed himself in the literary community and wrote prolifically. The time Reyes spent in Madrid from 1914 to 1924 was the crucial stage in his intellectual development. Reyes moved comfortably into Spain's most rarified literary circles.

Reyes became closely acquainted with such notables as writer **Miguel de Unamuno**, poets **Juan Ramón Jiménez** and Antonio Machado, and philologist Menéndez Pidal. Reyes also became associated with the Residencia de Estudiantes ("Student Residence"), one of Spain's major cultural institutions. He wrote a weekly cultural page for the respected newspaper *El sol.*

Along with other literary-cultural and journalistic pieces, Reyes's *El sol* writings would be collected in the five–volume *Simpatías y diferencias* ("Sympathies and Differences," 1921–26). Reyes published *El suicida* in 1917, a collection of philosophical essays that examine both the affirmation and denial of life, freedom, and love. In that same year he published *Cartones de Madrid* ("Madrid Sketches"), a collection of instantaneous, impressionistic essays about Reyes's newfound Madrid and its inhabitants.

## Writes *Visión de Anáhuac*

**Octavio Paz** called *Visión de Anáhuac* (1917) "a great fresco in prose." The essay can be described as a prose poem, an imaginative, historical re-creation of the Old World colliding with the New World. Here Reyes depicts the historic encounter between **Hernán Cortés** and **Moctezuma** in "Anáhuacan," the Aztec name for the Valley of Mexico where their capital, Tenochtitlán, was located.

The epigraph reads, "Traveler, you have come to the most transparent region of the air." A pictorial purity envelopes the reader, as Reyes melds his language with the landscape: "Ours, Anáhuac's, is something better and more stimulating. At least for those who prefer clear-headedness and alertness of will at all times. The more fitting representation of our nature is to be found in the regions of the central highlands. There the sparse and stylized vegetation, the harmonious landscape, the atmosphere so intensely clear that color is drowned in it, the general harmony of design making up for it, the transparence of the air, which brings everything out in singular relief." In *Alfonso Reyes and Spain,* Barbara Bockus Aponte comments that "the purpose of Reyes's essay is not historical; his is a fundamentally aesthetic evocation of Mexican history . . . the pre-Columbian fragment of Mexico's 'national soul,' which he is seeking to define is reduced to an aesthetic nostalgia, a love for beauty."

In *Visión de Anáhuac* Reyes displays his signature talents as an essayist, which are, as Anderson Imbert noted in *Spanish-American Literature: A History* "to express himself in miniatures; not to lean too much on actual things; to subjectivize everything, whether it be through his sensibilities or through his imagination; to intermingle life and culture; to address himself to a sympathetic reader who possesses the same qualities that the writer possesses, and to converse with him; to watch each word."

In 1920 Reyes resumed his diplomatic career as secretary of the Mexican Legation in Spain. He published *Ifigenia cruel* ("Cruel Iphigenia") in 1924, a poetic drama that recreated the Greek myth of Iphigenia in a Latin American setting. Later that year, Reyes moved to Paris to become Mexico's minister to France. He continued his diplomatic career as ambassador to Argentina (1927, 1936–37) and to Brazil (1930–36, 1938–39). Inspired by Brazilian culture, Reyes wrote a collection of poems entitled *Romances de Río de Janeiro* ("Songs of Rio de Janeiro," 1933).

## Returns to Mexico

Reyes returned permanently to Mexico City in 1939. There he initiated the formation of a private institutional haven for exiled foreign scholars, which under Reyes's directorship became known as El Colegio de México. Published in 1944, *El deslinde* ("The Demarcation") is considered Reyes's most important work of literary criticism. In this systematic study he attempts to distinguish the characteristics of literary works through a comparison to other disciplines such as history, religion, and mathematics. In 1945 Reyes helped establish El Colegio Nacional, a center offering public lectures by leading Mexican scholars in various fields. He also taught at the Universidad Nacional and the Universidad de Morelia, Michoacán.

Colleagues dubbed Reyes the "Universal Mexican," and he called himself a "specialist in universals." He wrote and lectured on various subjects from Greek culture to Russian film director Serge Eisenstein. As Walter Bara observed, "From Aristotle to Zola, from Chaucer to Chaplin, the literary experience of Reyes is so broad that it defies comparison with the personal culture of any living writer." However, Reyes's dedication to varied cosmopolitan interests disturbed many Mexican intellectuals. Some thought he was too detached from his own Mexicanism and dismissive of Mexican culture.

In *Parnetalia* ("Parentage," 1959), Reyes defended his universalism, "As for me, I do not wish to be weighed down with any limited tradition. The universal heritage is mine by right of love and of zeal for study and work, the only authentic rewards to which I aspire." A congenital synthesizer, Reyes was interested in cultural confluences and the establishment of a panhispano-americanism that encompassed Classical and European traditions. In "Posición de América" ("Position of America," 1942), Reyes states that his concept of cultural synthesis does not "reduce the function of the American mind to the mere organizing of compendiums of European culture. Above all, we would not have recourse only to the European tradition, but to the entire human heritage. . . . Lastly, in this synthesis we do not envision a compendium or resumé just as hydrogen and oxygen on combining in the form of water do not produce a mere sum of the parts but a new substance, possessing, as does any true synthesis, new powers and qualities." Buttressed by the intellectual heritage of the Old World and fueled by the opportunities of the New World, Reyes envisioned an American culture with utopian potential.

In 1945 Reyes was awarded the National Prize in Literature, and from 1957 to 1959 he served as the director of the Mexican Academy of Languages. Near the end of his life Reyes wrote, "for my part, I do not distinguish between my life and my writings. Did not Goethe say, 'All my works are fragments of a general confession?'" On December 27, 1959 Reyes died of a heart attack. Maintained by his family, Reyes's library, "La Capilla Alfonsina" ("Alfonso's Chapel"), has become a government sponsored museum and center for literary studies.

## SELECTED PUBLISHED WORKS:

*Cuestiones estéticas,* P. Ollendorff, Paris, 1911.
*Cartones de Madrid,* Cultura, Mexico, 1917.
*El Suicida,* 1917, reprinted as *El suicida: Libro de ensayos,* Tezontle, 1954.
*Simpatías y diferencias,* 5 vols., Talleres Tipográficos del Suc. de E Teodora, 1921–26.
*Ifigenia cruel,* 1924, reprinted, Nuevo Mundo, 1961.
*La experiencia literaria,* Editorial Losada, 1942.
*El deslinde: Prolegómenos a la teoría literaria,* [Mexico], 1944.
*The Position of America and Other Essays,* foreword by Federico de Onís, ed. and translated by Harriet de Onís, New York: Knopf, 1950.
*Obras completas,* 15 vols., Fondo de Cultura Económica, 1959.
*Mexico in a Nutshell and Other Essays,* introduction by Arturo Torres-Rioseco, translated by Charles Ramsdell, Berkeley: California University Press, 1964.

## SOURCES:

Anderson-Imbert, Enrique, *Spanish-American Literature: A History,* translated by John V. Falconieri, Detroit: Wayne State University Press, 1963.
Aponte, Barbara B., *Alfonso Reyes and Spain,* Austin: Texas University Press, 1972.
*Critical Survey of Poetry: Foreign Language Series,* vol. 4, ed. Frank N. Magill, Englewood Cliffs: Salem, 1984, pp. 1317–23.
*Hispanic Writers,* ed. Bryan Ryan, Detroit: Gale, 1993, pp. 396–98.
*Latin American Writers,* ed. Carlos A. Solé, "Alfonso Reyes" by James Willis Robb, New York: Scribner, 1989 pp. 693–702.
Reyes, Alfonso, *The Position of America and Other Essays,* forward by Federico de Onís, New York: Knopf, 1950. v-xii.
*Spanish American Authors: The Twentieth Century,* ed. Angel Flores New York: Wilson, 1992, 43-7.
Stabb, Martin S., *In Quest of Identity: Patterns in the Spanish American Essay of Ideas, 1860–1960,* North Carolina University Press, 1967.
*Twentieth-Century Literary Criticism,* Vol. 33, Detroit: Gale, 1989, pp. 725–30.

—*Sketch by Kenneth Brandt*

# Julio Ramón Ribeyro
## 1929-
**Peruvian writer**

Julio Ramón Ribeyro, a novelist and playwright who has also written short stories and essays, is one of Peru's most talented authors. Ribeyro established his literary reputation after the publication of his writings in the 1950s, but it also has been dwarfed by the reputation of his compatriot, the fiction writer **Mario Vargas Llosa.** Like Llosa, Ribeyro's works have been widely published and translated, and he is one of the few leading Peruvian fiction authors to continue writing in the 1980s and 1990s.

Ribeyro's fiction often deals with alienation, particularly of people with lower and middle incomes, as well as injustice and exploitation. The author writes insightfully about urban and rural people living on the fringes of society and reveals their daily lives in a detailed, personal way rather than generally or rhetorically. Ribeyro also has been described as having the talent to make known the shades of difference and rhythms of language, as well as complicated psychological sets of circumstances.

Ribeyro was born on August 31, 1929, to a middle-class family in Lima, Peru. His father wanted him to have a normal, economically stable life; instead, Ribeyro chose a writing career. Like many modern Latin American authors, Ribeyro has lived outside the nation of his birth for much of his life. After graduating from Catholic University he left Lima and went to Europe in order to study and work. The 1950s and 1960s found him writing and living in Munich, Germany and Paris, France. He made his home in Paris, working in the Peruvian Embassy and as a translator. Since 1960 he has worked for the France-Presse Agency and UNESCO.

### Wrote About Peru's Urban Proletariat

His first and best known collection of short stories, *Los gallinazos sin plumas* ("Buzzards without

Feathers"), published in 1955, was one of the first story collections in his country to depict the daily economic and emotional problems of the mass proletariat and bourgeoisie in the city of Lima after World War II. The characters in these urban stories are day workers, servants, and beggars. The title story deals specifically with the daily experiences of two little boys whose grandfather keeps a pig he is trying to fatten and sends his charges to look for food for it—and for themselves—in the local garbage dump. The tragedy lies in how the grandfather, his humanity eradicated by his wretched surroundings, treats his grandchildren in contrast to the pig.

Ribeyro's second book, *Cuentos de circumstancias* ("Stories of Circumstances") printed in 1958, blends real-life events with unexplained ones. In his book *The Modern Short Story in Peru,* Earl M. Aldrich, Jr. described Ribeyro's stories as "fine, imaginative tales.... Some of the selections are hauntingly serious in tone, reflecting the influence of Kafka; in others, high good humor dominates. In all ... Ribeyro uses highly imaginative settings and events to provide a unique interpretation of ordinary human experience."

Ribeyro's other short story collections, *Tres historias sublevantes* ("Three Stories of Revolt"), 1964, and *Las Botellas y los hombres* ("Bottles and Men"), 1964, deal with similar subjects and protagonists as those in his first book, only generally in a different locale. *Tres historias sublevantes* tells of Peruvians living along the coast, the Andes mountains, and the Amazon jungle region.

### Novels Focused on Corruption in Peru

Ribeyro also published three novels—*Cronica de San Gabriel* ("Chronicle of San Gabriel Ranch") in 1960; *Los geniecillos dominicales* ("The Sunday Rascals"), in 1965; and *Cambio de guardia* ("Change of Guard") in 1976. His first novel, *Cronica de San Gabriel,* which was awarded the national prize for the novel in Lima, depicts the corruption in the lives of the formerly powerful and wealthy land barons in the sierra. His second, *Los geniecillos dominicales,* which won first prize in a contest sponsored by *Expreso* in 1963, tells of disillusioned university students searching for new values in a Peru with a history of military dictatorships. *Cambio de guardia* lets readers view Peruvian politics through the eyes of several protagonists during a coup d'etat, illuminating the covert machinations that accompany this sort of change.

Ribeyro's most significant plays are *Vida y pasion de Santiago el pajarero* ("The Life and Passion of Santiago, the Birdman"), 1958-1959; *El ultimo cliente* ("The Last Client"), 1966, and *Atusparia,* 1981. The first play, his best known, criticizes the government using an 18th-century backdrop. The second satirizes life in modern Lima. The third

dramatizes an actual rebellion in the Andes in the 1880s. Infante's other plays include *El sotano* ("The Basement"), 1959; *Fin de semana* ("Weekend"), 1961; and *Los caracoles* ("The Snails"), 1964.

## SELECTED PUBLISHED WORKS:

### Plays

*El sotano* ("The Basement"), 1959.
*Fin de semana* ("Weekend"), 1961.
*Los caracoles* ("The Snails"), 1964.
*Vida y pasion de Santiago el pajarero* ("The Life and Passion of Santiago, the Birdman"; also known as "Santiago, the Bird Dealer"), 1958-1959.
*Teatro* ("Theater") 1975.
*Atusparia,* 1981.

### Other

*Los gallinazos sin plumas* ("Buzzards without Feathers"), 1955.
*Cuentos de circumstancias,* 1958.
*Cronica de San Gabriel* ("Chronicle of San Gabriel Ranch"), 1960.
*Los geniecillos dominicales* ("The Sunday Rascals"), 1965.
*Tres historias sublevantes* ("Three Stories of Revolt"), 1964.
*La palabra del mundo* ("The Word of a Deaf-Mute"), 1972, 3 vols.
*La juventad en la otra ribera* ("Youth on the Other Shore"), 1973.
*Dos soledades,* 1974.
*La caza sutil: Ensayos y articulos de critica literaria* ("The Subtle Hunt"), 1976.
*Prosas apatridas* ("Narrative without a Nation"), 1975.
*Cambio de guardia* ("Change of Guard"), 1976.
*Solo para fumadores* ("For Smokers Only"), 1987.
*Dichos de Luder* ("Luder's Sayings"), 1989.

## SOURCES:

Aldrich, Earl M., Jr., *Modern Short Story in Peru,* University of Wisconsin Press, 1966, pp. 143, 146–149, 154.
*Encyclopedia of World Literature in the 20th Century,* Vol. 4, Continuum, 1984, 1989, p. 37.
Foster, William, editor, *Handbook of Latin American Literature,* second edition, Garland Publishing, 1992, pp. 525, 528, 531, 532, 535, 536, 538, 539, 540, 543.
*Spanish American Authors: The Twentieth Century,* H.W. Wilson Company, 1992, pp. 730–733.

*—Sketch by Alison Carb Sussman*

# Rita Ricardo-Campbell
## 1920-
### Hispanic American economist, government official, and writer

Rita Ricardo-Campbell launched her career in the 1940s by becoming the first woman to teach economics at Harvard University in Cambridge, Massachusetts. In 1968, she was the first woman to be appointed senior fellow at Stanford University's Hoover Institution in Stanford, California. A few years later, she joined the board of directors of the Watkins-Johnson Company and the Gillette Company, the only woman director of these two *Fortune* 500 organizations. And in the 1980s, she served as the only woman member of the President's Economic Policy Advisory Board. "I have been lucky," said Ricardo-Campbell in an interview with contributor Michelle Vachon. "I had the energy to pursue a career and raise my family. Most importantly, I could always count on the support of my husband."

A descendant of 19th-century economist David Ricardo, Ricardo-Campbell was born on March 16, 1920, in Boston, Massachusetts. She first attended Simmons College in Boston, which she described to *Hispanic Business* as "a very interesting college—all women—whose motto was "to prepare women for work, marriage, and family."" In 1941, she obtained her B.S. in library sciences, then quickly secured a scholarship and enrolled at Harvard University. During World War II "opportunities for women were much greater than at other times," Ricardo-Campbell told *Hispanic Business*. "I was there at the right time." She took her master's degree in 1945 and her Ph.D. in economics the following year. Upon receiving her doctorate, Ricardo-Campbell was promoted to university instructor—she had been working at the university since 1942, first as fellowship and research assistant and afterwards as teaching fellow and tutor.

In 1946, she married Wesley Glenn Campbell, who also taught economics at Harvard University. "I decided to hyphenate my name because I didn't want to lose my Sephardic roots," she mentioned to *Intercambios Femeniles*. In 1948, she joined Tufts University in Medford, Massachusetts, as an assistant professor. Three years later, Ricardo-Campbell and her husband moved to Washington, D.C., where her husband had been offered a position. She served as economist for the Wage Stabilization Board in 1951 and for the U.S. House of Representatives' Ways and Means Committee in 1953; she worked as a consulting economist from 1956 until 1960, when her family moved to California and her husband assumed the directorship of the Hoover Institution at Stanford

*Rita Ricardo-Campbell*

University. Ricardo-Campbell taught at San Jose State University in San Jose, California, for one year and joined the Hoover Institution in 1961. She held the positions of archivist and research fellow until she was named senior fellow in 1968.

"As a senior fellow here at the Hoover Institution, I can research whatever appeals to me," she explained to *Intercambios Femeniles*. Interested in public policy, economics and the politics of health care, in 1976 Ricardo-Campbell wrote the book *Social Security: Promise and Reality*, which is still considered the primary source of information on the social security system. In 1982, she published *The Economics and Politics of Health*, and in 1988 *Issues in Contemporary Retirement* (coedited with Edward Lazear of the Hoover Institution). Her next book is to be on the hostile takeover attempt against the Gillette Company.

### Joins the President's Economic Policy Advisory Board

Ricardo-Campbell has been repeatedly asked to serve as advisor on public policy. From 1967 through 1975, she held the post of California commissioner for the Western Interstate Commission for Higher Education and took on its chairmanship for one term in 1970. She served as a member of the President's Economic Policy Advisory Board from 1981 through 1989, as a member of the National Council on the Humanities from 1982 through 1988, and was elected member of the President's Committee on the National Medal of Science in 1988. Two years later, she chaired, in New York City, a chief-executive roundtable on health care costs containment, and spoke at the World Congress on Health Economics in Zurich. She is also a member of SRI International's advisory council and a director of the Mont Pelerin Society.

Ricardo-Campbell sits on the board of directors of Watkins-Johnson Company, the Samaritan Medical Center Management Group and the Gillette Company. "I was invited to these boards because of my understanding of economics and finance," she said to this contributor. "Surprisingly, these appointments have established my status in the business community in ways that I had never achieved while I was a president's economic advisor. Executives immediately accept me on a different level because I'm a director of *Fortune*–500 companies."

In a 1988 interview with the *Hoover Institution Newsletter,* Ricardo-Campbell predicted that the United States would be struggling until the turn of the century with the economic impact of social security, the cost of medical care, services requested by an aging population, the growth of entitlements and world trade competition. "I would add the U.S. deficit to this list of domestic issues," she remarked in her interview. "Internationally, I find these so-called ethnic cleansings that have been carried out in Eastern Europe, these so-called 'wars of conscience' extremely disturbing. This idea of ethnic groups claiming the right to live apart and by themselves spells trouble all over the world. I'm also deeply disturbed by the existence of a Russian army without leadership, and I don't see any decline necessarily in the numbers of people who are starving. These global issues will have to be addressed in the coming years."

Ricardo-Campbell, who is the mother of three daughters, expects to see women in the United States rise to higher levels in business. "Women will solidify whatever gains they have made and will increase them," she stated in her interview. "I think that it's an upward trend." Ricardo-Campbell, a grandmother, lives with her husband in Los Altos Hills, California.

## SOURCES:

### Periodicals

*Atlanta Journal/Atlanta Constitution,* July 5, 1987, p. C1.
*Hispanic Business,* March 1988, pp. 33–34.
*Hoover Institution Newsletter,* winter 1988–1989, p. 3.
*Intercambios Femeniles,* spring 1987, pp. 10–11.
*Science,* September 16, 1988, p. 1516.
*U.S. News & World Report,* July 27, 1981, p. 35.

### Other

Ricardo-Campbell, Rita, interview with Michelle Vachon, July 15, 1992.

—*Sketch by Michelle Vachon*

# Chita Rivera
## 1933-
### Puerto Rican actress and dancer

Although the general public would be most likely to recognize Chita Rivera as Anita from the musical *West Side Story* and as Rosie from *Bye Bye Birdie,* theatergoers and those in the business know that Rivera has the ability to make or break a musical. The woman of Puerto Rican descent has been illuminating theaters with her energetic, explosive dancing, her powerful voice, and her comic gestures as well as her serious expressions since she graduated from high school. In addition to headlining in numerous musicals, she has starred in movies and appeared on television. Although she has already inspired a new generation of actresses, Rivera is as radiant as ever.

The third child of Pedro Julio Figueroa and Katherine del Rivero, Dolores Conchita Figuero del Rivero was born on January 23, 1933, in Washington D.C. Her father, Pedro, a Puerto Rican musician who played the clarinet and the saxophone in the U.S. Navy Band, died when she was only seven years old. To provide for her family, Katherine del Rivero, who was of Puerto Rican and Scots-Irish descent, found a job as a government clerk. The widowed mother, however, did more than put food on the table; she enrolled the young Rivera in singing, piano, and ballet lessons.

Rivera was most enthusiastic about ballet. She performed in shows her brother Julio arranged in the basement of their home, and she demonstrated so much promise in class that her instructor, Doris Jones, encouraged her to audition for a scholarship to Balanchine's School of American Ballet. Dolores won the scholarship in 1950. In order to attend the school, that was located in New York City, she went to live with her uncle's family in the Bronx.

### Debut in *Call Me Madam* Leads to Numerous Performances

The young dancer graduated from Taft High School in 1951, and the very next year landed her first professional job as a dancer. She had accompanied a friend from the School of American Ballet to an audition for *Call Me Madam,* which was to be choreographed by Jerome Robbins, and she won a part instead of her friend. Dolores, or Conchita del Rivero, as she called herself, had been touring the country with the musical for almost a year when she decided to return to New York; she had accepted an offer to replace Onna White in *Guys and Dolls* as a principal dancer.

Conchita was on her way to becoming a sought-after performer. After her Broadway debut in *Guys in Dolls,* she found herself in the chorus of *Can-Can* in 1953, and then on television's *Imogene Coca Show* in 1954. Friends involved with the production of *Can-Can* persuaded the young woman to change her name. After three days of referring to herself as Chita O'Hara, she finally settled on Chita Rivera. It was Chita who became a singer, actress, and dancer, and joined *Shoestring Revue,* which was produced Off-Broadway, in 1955. The revue received some good reviews, and Rivera was given special attention. It was not long before she was cast as Fifi, a French prostitute in *Seventh Heaven* on Broadway. That same year, she was chosen to tour with the Oldsmobile Industrial Show.

In 1956, Chita captured the role of Rita Romano in *Mr. Wonderful,* a musical produced for Sammy Davis, Jr., on Broadway. She began to appear as a guest on variety shows at this point in her career, including such programs as *The Garry Moore Show, The Ed Sullivan Show, The Arthur Godfrey Show, The Sid Ceasar Show, The Dinah Shore Show,* and *The London Palladium Show.* Rivera's performances that year led to one of her best parts ever—that of Anita in *West Side Story.*

### Wins Acclaim with Role in *West Side Story*

A major musical conceived by Jerome Robbins, *West Side Story* is William Shakespeare's *Romeo and Juliet* in a contemporary setting; a young couple falls in love despite their dissimilar and antagonistic backgrounds, and their love is tragically ended. In *West Side Story* Romeo is Tony, a "white, American" gang member, while Juliet is Maria, the Puerto Rican sister of a rival gang member. The nurse who helps Juliet marry Romeo is transformed into Maria's brother's girlfriend, Anita. Cast as the fiery Anita, Rivera sang "A Boy Like That" and "I Have a Love," as well as the song that has become a musical classic, "America."

*West Side Story* and Chita were instant hits in 1957. The musical ran for 732 performances, and besides an offer of marriage, Chita garnered a Tony nomination. Although Chita did not win a Tony, she married Anthony Mordente, one of the dancers in *West Side Story.* When Chita became pregnant with their daughter, Lisa Angela Mordente, she left the production of the musical. After the birth of the baby, who grew up to become an actress herself, the acting couple resumed their roles when *West Side Story* found its way to London in 1958.

After the musical closed in England in 1959, Moreno starred in another hit musical on Broadway and in London. In *Bye Bye Birdie,* which ran from 1960 to 1961, Chita portrayed Rosie Grant and performed along with Dick Van Dyke. In the musical, Rosie, a secretary who wants save her advertising agency employer, hatches a contest that allows one girl to kiss a rock star, Birdie, goodbye as he leaves for military service. As she enthralled the audience with her clever acting, Rivera sang "Spanish Rose," "How to Kill a Man," and "Shriners' Ballet"; her dynamic presentation earned her another Tony nomination. She then went on to play Athena Constantine in *Zenda,* a short-lived play in California in 1963, and to act in a television show benefit with the immensely popular British rock group the Beatles in 1964 in England. Her next appearance was as Anyanka, the gypsy princess, in *Bajour* in 1964. That performance won her a third Tony nomination, a citation from Best Plays, and an invitation to become the official hostess of the "World's Fair and Summer Festival Season" in New York City.

### Develops Solo Cabaret Act

By this time, Chita Rivera was a celebrated stage star; she decided to venture out on her own. With the help of her friends Fred Ebb and John Kander, a lyricist and composer that Chita would team up with throughout her career, she developed a cabaret act. In 1966, she traveled throughout the United States and Canada with this act. However, even though the cabaret was well received, she decided to return to the stage. She went on to perform as Jenny in *The Threepenny Opera,* as Linda Low in *Flower Drum Song,* as Charity in the national tour of *Sweet Charity,* as Nickie, Charity's roommate, in the motion picture version of *Sweet Charity,* and as Christopher Columbus's mistress in the flop *1491.*

The early 1970s found the actress on tour once again, appearing in *Jaques Brel Is Alive and Well and Living in Paris,* as well as performing in standing productions like *Born Yesterday, Milliken Breakfast Show, The Rose Tattoo,* and *Sondheim: A Musical Tribute.* In 1974, she performed in the serious play *Father's Day* in Chicago; Oliver Hailey, the author of the play, had asked her to play the part of the divorcée. Next, she starred with Hal Linden as she portrayed Katherine in *Kiss Me Kate,* which toured cities in the United States. In 1975, she took her cabaret act on the road once again. "Chita Plus Two" stirred audiences at the Grand Finale nightclub in New York and at Studio One in Los Angeles. After the conclusion of her tour, Rivera played Velma Kelly in *Chicago* in New York City; for that performance with Gwen Vernon and Jerry Ohrbach she earned a fourth Tony nomination. Although the musical was extremely successful and ran for more performances than even *West Side Story,* Rivera left the production to begin another tour with her cabaret act. She spent the latter part of the 1970s and the first year of the 1980s traveling throughout the United States, Canada, and Europe. For her act she was given an award for the best variety performance in 1980 by the National Academy of Concert and Cabaret Arts.

During the early 1980s Rivera continued to perform on stage and screen. In 1981 she starred in two musicals. One, *Hey Look Me Over,* received little attention. The other, *Bring Back Birdie,* the sequel to *Bye Bye Birdie,* was not received well; however, Rivera received her fifth Tony nomination for her dancing as Rosie in "A Man Worth Fighting For" and "Well, I'm Not." Rivera then appeared on television, on the PBS special *Broadway Plays Washington: Kennedy Center Tonight* in 1982, and in *Night of 100 Stars* that same year. In 1983 she portrayed the Queen in magician Doug Henning's *Merlin;* while the musical was unsuccessful, Rivera won another Tony nomination for her performance. From 1983 to 1984, she shined in the musical *Pippin,* which was produced for the cable television network Showtime.

### Costars on Stage with Liza Minnelli

In the mid-1980's Rivera performed in two outstanding musicals and finally won a Tony Award. The first of these musicals, *The Rink,* was created specifically for Rivera by her friends Ebb and Kander. Rivera played Anna, a woman faced with closing a skating rink left to her by her husband. Starring the famous singer Liza Minnelli (as Anna's daughter Angel) along with Rivera, the musical tells the story of a strained mother/daughter relationship. Rivera and Minnelli had been friends since 1975, when Minnelli replaced Gwen Verdon for five weeks during the run of *Chicago.* Minnelli was quoted in *People* as saying of Rivera, "She's a force, and she thinks I'm a force. It's like two grounding poles, and there's this electrical thing that goes VROOM." Rivera said of Minnelli in the same article, "I look at Liza, and I see my Lisa." Partly because Rivera had just lost her mother, as Minnelli had lost her own mother, *Wizard of Oz* star Judy Garland, and partly because Minnelli had been inspired to become an actress in musicals after seeing Rivera perform in *Bye Bye Birdie,* the two performers sang and danced with more than their usual passion.

*The Rink* received some so-so reviews, but critics raved about Rivera. Richard Corliss commented on her performance in *Time* magazine: "Packing 30 years of Broadway savvy into the frame of a vivacious teen-ager, the 51-year-old entertainer could by now sell a song to the deaf; she commands the audience like a lion tamer with a whip snap in her walk; and, by the forces of magnetism and sheer will, she eats costars for breakfast." While one critic from *New York* magazine was less enthusiastic, he acknowledged Rivera's talent: "Miss Rivera's performances are knowing and efficiently executed. . . . [She] is an able singer, authoritative dancer, and clear enunciator, with an emotional range that has gradations as well as extremes, and a projection of gags with a certain zing—more vibration than punch—that is idiosyncratic and winning." The judges for the Antoinette Perry Awards recognized Rivera's achievements by awarding her a Tony as outstanding actress in the musical.

After releasing 1984's *The Rink,* an album recorded with Minnelli and the rest of the singers from the musical, and appearing in *Night of 100 Stars II* and in a televised coverage of *Macy's Thanksgiving Day Parade,* Rivera moved on to *Jerry's Girls,* a revue produced in New York City beginning in 1985, the year Rivera was inducted into the Television Academy Hall of Fame. Once again, Rivera was lauded. A critic for *New York* magazine commented, "the ageless Chita Rivera does some rousing things vocally and pedally." Unfortunately, Rivera suffered an accident that left her unable to finish the musical's run, and members of the chorus had to fill in for her. In April of 1986 suffered another accident: as Rivera make a U-turn in New York City, her car collided with a taxi. Doctors predicted that she would fully recover in three to six months. Rivera had to work very hard to overcome the compound fractures in her left leg—although she was more than fifty years of age, she bounced back from her injuries.

In the late 1980s Rivera mixed television roles with theater performances, appearing in *The Mayflower Madam* and *Can-Can* on stage, and *Celebrating Gershwin* and *Broadway Sings: The Music of Jule Styne,* among other shows, on television. By 1992, although she was almost sixty years of age, starred in *Kiss of the Spider Woman,* a musical written by the team of Kander and Ebb collaborated. Based on the novel written by the late **Manuel Puig,** *Spider Woman* deals with the dilemmas of those involved in revolutionary movements, and while it speaks to the world, it is especially pertinent to situations in some Latin American countries. In the book and the play (which Puig helped develop), two prisoners share a cell; one of them describes the movie musicals he has seen. In the play, these movie-musical scenes are acted out. Rivera, who portrayed a beautiful symbol of death, was challenged as she played such a complex character.

Rivera is worth watching in any vehicle in which she may be performing in the future. A high kick, a vivacious nod, and a soaring voice packed with emotion—all of these elements have combined in her to create an acting force who will long be remembered by those who have seen or heard her.

**SOURCES:**

**Books**

*Contemporary Theatre, Film, and Television,* Volume 8, Gale, 1990.

**Periodicals**

*Atlanta Journal/Atlanta Constitution,* March 13, 1988, sec. J, p. 2, sec. PM, p. 8.
*Boston Globe,* March 13, 1988. sec. PAR, p. 13; June 19, 1988, sec. A, p. 1; July 22, 1989, p. 6.
*Chicago Tribune,* April 8, 1986, sec. 1, p. 4; February 7, 1988, sec. 13, p. 14; February 10, 1988, sec. 2, p. 11.
*Dance Magazine,* May, 1984, pp. 146.
*Globe and Mail,* (Toronto), February 1, 1992, p. C3.
*Horizon,* October, 1984, p. 56.
*Los Angeles Times,* December 4, 1988, sec. C, p. 5; December 15, 1988, sec. VI, p. 1.
*Ms.,* December, 1984, p. 34.
*New York,* February 20, 1984, pp. 86–87; January 13, 1986, p. 50.
*New York Times,* November 26, 1989, sec. 1, p. 71.
*People,* March 5, 1984, pp. 61–64.
*Time,* February 7, 1983, p. 63; February 20, 1984, p. 84; April 21, 1986, p. 72.
*Variety,* June 5, 1985, p. 54; December 25, 1985, p. 62; June 4, 1986, p. 47; February 17, 1988, p. 180.

—*Sketch by Ronie-Richele Garcia-Johnson*

# Diego Rivera
## 1886-1957
### Mexican painter

Born in Guanajuato, Mexico, Diego Rivera combined his artistic sensibilities with a strong sense of justice to bring visual art to the Mexican people. During his nation's long revolution, Rivera both engaged in the struggle and worked to give ordinary Mexicans a graphic sense of their history and future potential. He spent several years in Europe and

*Diego Rivera*

experimented with many styles of painting, including **Pablo Picasso**'s cubism. But Rivera turned eventually to wall murals, an art form which he is often credited with having revived. His work inspired Mexicans and foreigners alike. Rivera's controversial Communist inclinations often alienated him from the upper classes, but working people admired him as an artist who actually belonged to them.

### Childhood in Guanajuato

On December 8, 1886, Maria Rivera gave birth to twin boys, Carlos and Diego. Carlos, like her three previous children, did not survive infancy, but Diego thrived. Named for his father, young Rivera was a child of great energy and curiosity. His love for the visual inspired him even as a toddler to draw on walls, tables, or whatever surface was available. Although Rivera's mother resented having to clean up after her son, his father—free from cleaning duties—indulged the boy. He gave him a room of his own and covered the walls with blackboards to encourage drawing. Rivera's father worked as a city councilor, and often represented the interests of local peasants before the government. He taught his enthusiastic son to read at an early age. Rivera possessed a strong curiosity about many things, especially machines: The Museo Anahuacalli in Mexico holds drawings of locomotives made by Rivera as early as three years of age.

Early in Rivera's youth, his family moved to Mexico City. Señor Rivera had lost favor among the moneyed classes of Guanajuato by editing and writing *El Democrata*, a weekly paper that advocated liberal causes such as land reform and civil rights for peasants. The younger Rivera spent the first few months in the capital ill and unable to draw, but when he recovered he began to make pictures of soldiers that he cut out of cardboard. He made so many soldiers that he could stage entire battles. A friend of his father's had once served as Mexico's Minister of War, and when Señor Rivera invited him to the house to see his son's work, the General cleared a path for Rivera to enter military school.

Rivera recoiled from the school's discipline, and he soon dropped out. His mother then tried to push him toward an ecclesiastical career, and he impressed several of his teachers at the Liceo Católico Hispano-Mexicano with his intelligence. His personal mentor, Padre Enrique, had submitted a special request to be the boy's teacher. But when Rivera openly called the story of the virgin birth of Jesus a lie, the Father asked the boy's family to take him out of school.

Rivera found a more suitable academic home in the San Carlos Academy of Fine Arts. The Academy's youngest student, Rivera won several prizes for his paintings and drawings. By the time he reached his thirteenth birthday in 1899, San Carlos awarded him a scholarship. Although he performed well in school, Rivera came to question many of the values the school taught. For example, he wondered why the school focused more attention on mundane—rather than spiritual—objects? And why did the school ignore altogether folk art, with which the streets of the capital teemed? Rivera led a protest along these lines, and in 1902, once again, school directors asked him not to return.

## A Budding Artist

For the next several years, Rivera drew and painted natural landscapes that he saw as he traveled across Mexico. Although he believed in a native art, he wondered if Europe could offer him an artistic training that he had not been able to find in Mexico. He spoke to his father, who petitioned his political friends for an art stipend for his son to travel abroad. Just at that time, a miner's strike broke out in Jalapa, one of the first open acts of rebellion against **President Porfirio Diaz.** Rivera—arrested during the riots—received word that his stipend had been granted and escaped the turmoil by going to Spain.

He traveled throughout Spain, Portugal, England, and France. He met a wide range of artists, but all the while he searched for his own style. He managed to have some paintings accepted by Paris galleries. Governor Dehesa, who had provided the travel stipend, invited him back to Mexico City for Diaz's centennial celebration. The president's wife bought six of Rivera's paintings. Shortly thereafter,

**Francisco Madero** began the revolution to overthrow Diaz, and Rivera vowed to join the revolutionary cause. Rivera rode for five months with **General Emiliano Zapata** in his southern campaigns against Diaz's troops, but when Diaz issued a warrant for Rivera's arrest, Governor Dehesa helped the artist escape to Europe once again.

Back in Paris, Rivera enjoyed a relatively favorable reputation. He had his first one-man show in 1914 in the Weill Gallery, but fortune eluded him. World War I began. Madero had come to power and been assassinated, and Rivera soon found himself nearly penniless. Wartime blackouts limited his ability to paint. He lived with a woman—Angelina Beloff—and when she became pregnant in 1917, Rivera despaired. The artist Pablo Picasso occasionally provided financial assistance, but Rivera's infant son weakened and died the following winter. Rivera longed to return to Mexico.

## Wall Painter

Rivera became inspired by the idea of painting Mexican history on the walls of the nation's cities. He traveled to Italy to study fresco and mural painting techniques of the fifteenth-century masters before returning to Mexico in 1920. The Minister of Education gave him space and support for his mural painting plan, and Rivera began to paint at a feverish pace. Some loved the murals and some hated them, but the work provoked such a public reaction that "Diego Rivera" became a famous name. The paintings depicted scenes of Meso-American civilization, contemporary peasants struggling with their work, familiar scenes of Mexican festivals, or the cruelty of the rich. In many ways, they stood as history for the illiterate. His murals in the Ministry of Education's courtyard brought him international attention as the initiator of the most important mural movement since the Italian Renaissance.

Married in 1922 to Guadalupe Marin, Rivera took his fame in stride, never abandoning his work. Although he did not remain faithful to his wife, the marriage lasted five years and produced two children: Guadalupe and Ruth. Rivera's art proved more of a success, and he supplemented his meager government stipend by selling canvas paintings to United States collectors. He spent two years as a member of the Communist party, but was asked to leave when his attendance record at party meetings declined. He later visited the Soviet Union as an honored guest, but when he criticized Soviet art, he was asked—once again—to leave.

Rivera married **Frida Kahlo** in 1929. She had admired his paintings since he began working for the Ministry of Education. She also had artistic ambitions and Communist leanings. Together they enjoyed some happy years, when Mexico's political situation seemed to be improving and stabilizing and Rivera's career was soaring. Rivera returned to the San Carlos Academy of Art as its new director, but his radical plan to reorganize its curriculum ensured another expulsion.

Rivera traveled throughout America during the early thirties, painting a mural in San Francisco's Stock Exchange and showing his work at New York's Museum of Modern Art. He went to Detroit, Michigan, where he painted scenes of industry and toil. Factory owners and the members of the upper classes criticized him, but factory engineers and workers loved the mural and stood as volunteer guards to prevent vandalism.

His celebrity in America attracted the attention of New York business tycoon Nelson D. Rockefeller, Jr., and resulted in one of the most controversial and publicized episodes of Rivera's career. Industrialist Edsel Ford had sponsored Rivera's Detroit mural, and Rockefeller likewise wished to patronize the arts. In early 1933, Rockefeller asked Picasso, Henri Matisse, and Rivera to submit works so that he could choose the artist for his own mural, a work which would face the RCA Building in downtown New York City. All three men refused to send material, but Rockefeller chose Rivera anyway. He asked the Mexican painter to create a mural on a particular theme: "Man at the Crossroads Looking with Hope and High Vision to the Choosing of a New and Better Future."

Rivera began in March. Crowds gathered every day to watch. The gatherings became so large that Rockefeller began issuing tickets. The mural itself contained many images. A globe, a telescope, and a microscope represented science's potential; scenes of war, the idle rich, and abuse of the poor by police showed the darker side of human nature. Rivera also painted scenes of unity and happiness, in which he included an image of Soviet leader Lenin. In her book *Diego Rivera: Artist of the people*, Anne Neimark wrote that while many people disliked that choice, Rockefeller "sent [Rivera] a note saying, 'Everybody is most enthusiastic about the work which you are doing.'" The millionaire's tolerance ended when U.S. newspapers started to criticize him for sponsoring "Communist" art. Rockefeller formally asked Rivera to remove Lenin's likeness, but the artist refused, saying that he would be happy to add a scene of Abraham Lincoln and other American heroes. On May 9, Rockefeller's representatives arrived at the mural and politely but firmly insisted that Rivera stop his work. Artists and intellectuals around the country supported Rivera side, but Rockefeller dismantled the mural and destroyed it the following year. Although he lost the battle to keep the mural on the wall, Rivera acquired many friends who supported his artistic freedom and loathed Rockefeller's attempt to limit it.

## Marriage Troubles and War

Rivera's marriage endured much turbulence, mutual infidelity, ill health, and extensive traveling. In 1939 he and Kahlo divorced, but they remarried the following year. World War II had begun, and Rivera had successfully lobbied the Mexican government to allow Soviet exile Leon Trotsky to come to Mexico and live in a house Kahlo owned. Although Rivera lost favor among Communists for his support of the disgraced Trotsky, he may have won some allies by his opposition to Nazism. Rivera learned that a ship that had been servicing Nazi submarines in the Atlantic had landed in Mexico. He informed the proper authorities. Acting on Rivera's tip, U.S. and Mexican military authorities began to search for the vessel, but its crew quickly took it to sea and scuttled it. U.S. President Franklin Delano Roosevelt gave Rivera a citation of merit.

After the war ended, Rivera painted the walls of Mexico City's National Palace with scenes of the Golden Age of the Aztecs. In contrast to the Mexico of Rivera's own day, Aztec Mexico enjoyed a higher level of civilization than almost any other place in the world. Mexicans — particularly peasants — knew very little about ancient Mexico. Rivera hoped to provide a visual rendering of history so that even the most uneducated peasant could understand this heritage. The murals depicted ornate Aztec pyramids, elaborate and colorful clothing, and people participating in native rituals. Rivera wanted to help people see that Mexico had been a great nation before the Spanish ever appeared and to instill confidence in the native ability of his country to rise to greatness again.

Rivera's Aztec murals gave viewers a sense of history, but the artist wanted more. His fame had given him enough money to invest in pre-Conquest artifacts, and he had built an impressive collection. He helped to design and construct a stone building reminiscent of the Aztec pyramids to house his sculptures, masks, and other pre-Conquest artifacts.

Frida Kahlo died in 1954, and Rivera became noticably less energetic. By now a hero among the Mexican people and a legend in contemporary art, Rivera celebrated his seventieth birthday surrounded by admirers. But in 1957 a disabling blood clot developed in his right arm, leaving him unable to paint. He had married Emma Hurtado in 1955, but his thoughts turned mostly to Kahlo. His health worsened, and he died on November 27, 1957. Thousands attended his cremation ceremony, and the Mexican government decreed that his ashes be placed at the *Rotunda de los Hombres Ilustres*, alongside other Mexican heroes in Mexico City. Neimark called Rivera "an evangelist-in-paint" for justice, whose use of walls—rather than canvases—allowed him to "make public his deepest concerns for the rights of human beings."

**SOURCES:**

*Diego Rivera: Artist of the People,* by Anne Neimark, New York, HarperCollins, 1992.
*Encyclopedia of World Art,* New York, McGraw-Hill Company, 1966.

—*Sketch by Jim McCarthy*

# Fructuoso Rivera
## 1784(?)-1854
### Uruguayan revolutionary and statesman

José Fructuoso Rivera was one of the central figures of the early national period in Uruguayan history. His patriotic engagements began in 1811, when he joined the revolts against Spanish rule that ultimately evolved into a full-fledged independence movement. In 1830 Rivera became the first elected president of the new Oriental Republic of Uruguay.

Rivera's exact birthdate remains a mystery, but sources estimate that it occurred during 1784. He was born in Pasandu, now part of Uruguay, to a ranching family. In 1811 he joined the patriot forces in their revolt against Spanish control, quickly earning the rank of captain. He soon became a follower of independence-seeker **José Gervasio Artigas.** As one of Artigas's officers, Rivera was credited for achieving an important victory at Guayabos and continued his revolutionary activities resisting a Portuguese invasion from 1816–1820.

In his book *Artigas and the Emancipation of Uruguay,* John Street wrote about Rivera in considerable detail, and cited the account of a priest who met the young man in 1815, following the Guayabos triumph: "He appeared to me about twenty-five years old, good looking, round faced, with large and modest eyes, very attentive, and expressing himself with courtesy. His dress was simple: riding boots in the English style, trousers and jacket of fine blue cloth, round hat, with no other mark of rank but the sabre and sash of crimson silk, and his aide wore the same dress. In everything these officers maintain complete equality." Rivera earned a reputation for a colorful personality, machismo, and popularity, as well as for some eccentricities.

When Artigas's power declined and he left his homeland for what turned into decades of exile, Rivera evaluated his own situation and reached a decision. In March of 1820 he allied himself with the enemy Brazilians. In exchange for his allegiance to the Portuguese King, Rivera was retained as a colonel, leading a regiment of soldiers—the Union Regiment of Dragoons—from his own land. The Brazilian leadership was pleased with its apparently loyal new recruit. Rivera was soon promoted to the rank of brigadier general and then to commander of all forces stationed in the Uruguayan countryside. Some critics might interpret Rivera's shift as disloyalty to his original superiors and ideals, but Street indicated that Rivera was actually displaying an important natural political shrewdness. Rivera, Street argued, "had not allowed himself to be suborned, but was bending before superior force in order to spring upright again when the time came to lead his compatriots to freedom and the formation of a new nation."

### Uruguay Gains Independence

This interpretation seems plausible in the context of what happened on April 29, 1825, when Rivera allowed himself and his men to be "surprised" by Juan Antonio Lavalleja, another of Artigas's protégés. Lavalleja had become the leader of an independence-seeking contingent centered around a group of patriots known as the "Immortal Thirty-Three." Rivera and Lavalleja conversed briefly before announcing that Rivera had joined in the fight *against* the Brazilians. Rivera's support was important to Lavalleja. As Street noted, Rivera was then "at the height of his powers and popularity among the [Uruguayans]. He was their only consistently successful soldier." His adherence to Lavalleja's cause brought not only "the prestige of Artigas's best lieutenant, but also the good will of a large number of cowboys and their bosses and of many waverers." Rivera was a key player in the military victories—such as those at Rincón and Sarandí—that eventually led to the treaty creating a new, independent República Oriental del Uruguay in August, 1828. Rivera returned from his battles, Street wrote, "sure of a place among the leaders of the country, since many people believed that he was the only leader who had been able to inflict real damage on Brazil."

Although Rivera appears to have been a very savvy military man, he demonstrated substantially less efficiency as a statesman. Elected President of the newly formed country in October of 1830, he served a full term. But his administration was problematic. History has faulted him on several counts: mismanaging the financial system; excluding Lavalleja from the power echelons; failing to deal with the factionalism of pro-Brazilian and pro-Argentinian elements in Uruguay; and virtually ignoring the poor relations between those cosmopolitan Uruguayans based in the country's capital and the more rural populace in the countryside. In *Uruguay: Portrait of a Democracy,* Russell H. Fitzgibbon described government under President Rivera as follows: "The sequence was simple: Rivera controlled the army; the army dominated congress; congress elected the president." Not surprisingly, this system had its critics. One such man was Lavalleja, whose opposition weakened Rivera's administration and led to the inauguration of a new president, **General Manuel Oribe,** in 1835. Rivera next assumed the post of commander of the armed forces. He soon rebelled against his new status, subordinate to Oribe, and left the job. The government's explanation for this development was that Rivera had been too extravagant with official monies.

### Civil War Breaks Out

Far from fading quietly into the background, Rivera organized a challenge to Oribe's administration, which resulted in a civil war. In 1838 Rivera gained control of the capital city, Montevideo, and briefly assumed the presidency once more. Oribe fled to Buenos Aires. With the support and encouragement of the Argentinian leader **Juan Manuel de Rosas** —a man Fitzgibbon called "the *enfant terrible* of Platine politics for many years and the chief cause— or excuse—for British and French intervention in the affairs of that area"—Oribe launched his own assault. The subsequent invasion and fighting was known as Uruguay's "*Guerra Grande*" (Great War). President Rivera returned to the battlefield. Although Rivera retained control of the capital city, Oribe's group swept through rural areas and began a siege of Montevideo that lasted from 1843–52. Rivera garnered support from the considerable European immigrant community in Montevideo: the Spanish, the French, and the Italians. One such pro-Rivera fighter was an Italian who went on to greater fame in his own country: Giuseppe Garibaldi. Still, Oribe successfully established a parallel government in 1847 and Rivera finally left the country, seeking refuge in Brazil.

The Rivera/Oribe struggle was especially significant in the context of its lasting effects on Uruguay's political culture. Most notable were the bands of supporters that coalesced around the two leaders. Raúl Jacob and Martin Weinstein have explained the origins of these groups in *Uruguay: A Country Study:* "Oribe's forces, supported by merchants, landowners, and the high clergy, became known as Blancos in reference to the white (*blanco*) hatbands they wore to distinguish their own men from the enemy on the field of battle. Rivera's forces, representing more liberal urban elements, were distinguished by red (*colorado*) hatbands and thus were designated Colorados." (The hatbands were first worn at the Battle of Carpintería, on September 19, 1836.)

From the original Blancos and Colorados were born the two parties that came to dominate Uruguayan politics in the nineteenth and twentieth centuries. Oribe's heirs clustered around the *Partido Nacional* (National Party) which, according to Jacob and Weinstein, "stood for order and conservatism and

declared itself protector of the faith." Inheritors of the Rivera tradition evolved into the *Partido Colorado* (Colorado Party) "which defended itself as the defender of Uruguayan sovereignty and as the champion of the common man and liberalism." The lasting power of these groups is impressive. Fitzgibbon declared: "In few other countries indeed in Latin America have political parties shown the longevity and tenacity of organization that these majority Uruguayan parties have exhibited."

But Fitzgibbon also argued that the lengthy state of turmoil "left a miserable bequest to Uruguay. Education and public works went virtually unsupported for long years. The legacy included predominance of military leaders—the dismal Latin American *caudillismo* —internal strife and hatreds, governmental weakness." Rivera was, however, an important player in the struggle first to attain and then to preserve Uruguayan independence. Near the end of his life, he was invited to return from exile and to serve in a provisional triumvirate that was to govern Uruguay. He began the journey back to Montevideo, but died *en route*, on January 13, 1854.

### SOURCES:

*Artigas and the Emancipation of Uruguay,* by John Street, Cambridge, England, Cambridge University Press, 1959.

*Cambridge Encyclopedia of Latin America and the Caribbean,* Second Edition, edited by Simon Collier, Thomas E. Skidmore, and Harold Blakemore, Cambridge, Cambridge University Press, 1992.

*Cambridge History of Latin America,* Volume III, edited by Leslie Bethell, Cambridge, Cambridge University Press, 1985.

*El General Fructuoso Rivera: Recopilación de Antecedentes Relativos a Su Vida,* by Carlos H. Freire, Montevideo, n.p., 1971.

*Encyclopedia of Latin America,* edited by Helen Delpar, New York, McGraw-Hill, 1974.

*Encyclopedia of Latin-American History,* by Michael Rheta Martin and Gabriel H. Lovett, Indianapolis and New York, Bobbs-Merrill, 1968.

*Fructuoso Rivera,* by Alfredo Lepro, Montevideo, Uruguay, Editorial Ceibo, 1945.

*Fructuoso Rivera,* by Telmo Manacorda, Madrid, Espasa-Calpe, 1933.

*Historical Dictionary of the Spanish Empire, 1402–1975,* edited by James S. Olson, Westport, Connecticut, Greenwood Press, 1992.

*McGraw-Hill Encyclopedia of World Biography,* Volume 9, New York, McGraw-Hill, 1973.

*Registro Rivera,* directed by Angel H. Vidal, Montevideo, Archivo General de la Nación, 1941.

*Un Caudillo: El General Fructuoso Rivera,* by José G. Antuña, Madrid, Spain, Instituto de Cultura Hispánica, 1948.

*Uruguay,* by George Pendle, Third Edition, Westport, Connecticut: Greenwood Press, 1985.

*Uruguay: A Country Study,* edited by Rex A. Hudson and Sandra W. Meditz, Washington, Federal Research Division/Library of Congress, 1992.

*Uruguay: Portrait of a Democracy,* by Russell H. Fitzgibbon, New Brunswick, New Jersey, Rutgers University Press, 1954.

*Wographical Series: Uruguay,* vol. 102, by Henry Finch, Oxford, England, Clio Press, 1989.

—*Sketch by Erika Dreifus*

*Geraldo Rivera*

# Geraldo Rivera
## 1943-
### Puerto Rican talk show host and journalist

Controversial television journalist Geraldo Rivera, host of the daytime talk show *Geraldo,* has gained a reputation as the king of tabloid television. Despite his reputation, however, Rivera has enjoyed a long, and often distinguished career. Some of his many roles have included advocacy lawyer, public speaker, charitable foundation board member, and investigative reporter.

On July 3 (some sources say July 4), 1943, Gerald Michael Riviera was born to Allen and Lillian (Friedman) Rivera. In later years, the transformed "Geraldo" questioned his mother about her misspelling of their surname on his birth certificate. Although she claimed a poor sense of spelling, Rivera asserted in his autobiography *Exposing Myself* that he believed she was attempting to deflect future discrimination from her children. Such discrimination was very real in Brooklyn, where the Riveras then lived, and the mixed marriage of Cruz, a Puerto Rican man, and Lillian, a Jewish woman, drew its share of criticism.

### From Long Island to Alphabet City

In their desire to shield their children from discrimination, the Riveras (who sometimes used the misspelled surname) moved to West Babylon, Long Island. There, young Rivera grew up in ethnic confusion. Raised in the Jewish faith of his mother, he physically resembled his father's family, many of whom still lived in Puerto Rico. To complicate matters further, his neighbors, schoolmates, and

friends were for the most part white Protestants. His desire to fit in caused him to lead a double life—an ethnic pastiche at home, and a 1950s suburban teen at school.

Even though the Riveras felt that they had to downplay their identity in West Babylon, it was a surprisingly open community. However, a blatant act of anti-Semitism at their temple in the 1950s jarred young Geraldo into a sense of what minorities in less-accepting communities faced every day. It would be the first of several instances that helped him form a deep pride in both of his heritages and at the same time alerted him that he might become a "lightening rod" for the close-minded.

As he grew up, Rivera developed career plans and concentrated on where to attend college, while ignoring the growing specter of the Vietnam War. After serving two years in the Merchant Marine, he attended New York City's Community College of Applied Arts and Sciences and the State University of New York Maritime College. Believing he needed to see what life outside New York was like, Rivera spent some summers in Puerto Rico, and eventually transferred to the University of Arizona. He earned his B.A. there in 1965. While studying in Arizona, he became aware of the reality of the war's escalation and the probability of being drafted. A friend suggested that he marry his girlfriend, thereby gaining a deferment.

Rivera married Linda Coblentz in Scottsdale, but they soon moved on to Huntington Beach, California.

Jobs were hard to come by, and Rivera often suspected that his ethnic background was the reason why so few doors opened. Many times he wondered whether he should return to calling himself Gerry Rivers, as he had done at Arizona. His new father-in-law was concerned about the couple's financial prospects, so he encouraged Rivera to attend law school. Soon the couple moved back to New York City so that Rivera could matriculate at the Brooklyn Law School. He received his J.D. in 1969 and was admitted to the New York State Bar in 1970.

Just as Rivera's career was taking off, his marriage was falling apart. In his autobiography, he admitted that this problem was due to his infidelities, a compulsion that would also cost him two subsequent marriages. Ultimately, Linda moved out of their inner-city apartment in the tough Lower East Side neighborhood called "Alphabet City." It was here that Gerry Rivers finally became Geraldo Rivera, immersing himself in his Hispanic heritage and in social advocacy. While accompanying a Hispanic pride group called the Young Lords in their "occupation" of the First Spanish United Methodist Church, he committed himself to the cause of "poverty law," eventually serving as their attorney. While in law school, he had clerked for the Harlem Assertion of Rights and Community Action for Legal Services center. Now in practice, he extended this advocacy-based service. Though he defended poor clients, he still felt he was not making any real, lasting change for them.

### Becomes a Television Journalist

The early 1970s was a time when federal jobs were opening up to underrepresented groups. During this period, Rivera gained the opportunity to become a television journalist. He had been considering a career change when the Federal Communications Commission started its initiative to get more minorities into broadcasting. As a bilingual social advocate, Rivera seemed like the ideal candidate when he applied for the position of newscaster for WABC-TV in New York City. He attended a crash course in graduate journalism at Columbia University at ABC's urging.

In broadcast news, it is common for the new face on a team to be assigned fluff pieces, usually social events or human interest stories. Assuming this was part of moving up the ladder, Rivera accepted the assignments, but longed for the day when he could cover hard news. It was a chance encounter with a suicidal heroin addict, while Rivera was going to work one day in 1970, that catapulted him into the slot of "investigative reporter." He arranged for a news crew to film the desperate pleas of the addict's brother, and within days the piece was expanded into a series, "Drug Crisis in East Harlem." The series earned him

the 1971 New York State Associated Press Broadcasters Association Award; he added to this early success, by winning the Broadcaster of the Year for 1971, 1972, and 1974.

As Rivera's fame grew, he was increasingly identified as a Hispanic role model. Nevertheless, detractors charged that he was culturally as well as ethnically Jewish, and that his emphasis on his Hispanic heritage was merely a vehicle to obtain an affirmative action job. To shore up their criticism, they pointed to Rivera's frequent name changes, his early attempts to downplay his Latino roots, and his suburban years in Long Island. They even viewed his inner-city apartment and association with the Young Lords as evidence that he was trying to become something he was not. Rivera met such criticism with commitment to minority stories, excellence in broadcasting, and the intellectual higher ground of silence, although privately the rumors irked him.

Rivera remarried in 1971, this time to Edith Bucket Vonnegut (daughter of novelist Kurt Vonnegut). "Edie," as she preferred to be called, was an artist and designer, and as the child of a famous parent she was used to the very public life that was just then buffeting Rivera. Their marriage lasted several years, but eventually succumbed to Rivera's infidelity. Despite the problems in his personal life, Rivera was about to produce the expose that would launch him into the national spotlight.

The state mental institutions of 1972 were filthy, dangerous warehouses. At the Willowbrook State School for the Mentally Retarded on Staten Island, Rivera's investigative team found mentally impaired children living in conditions unsanctioned since the reform movement of the last century. Acting on a tip from a former employee, the news crew made an unannounced visit, gaining access in a possibly illegal manner. The resulting taped report—"Willowbrook: A Report on How It Is and Why It Doesn't Have to Be That Way"—sickened America and initiated an institutional reform movement. Rivera himself gained national exposure and a promotion to national network television.

Rivera became the host of the nationally broadcast late night program *Good Night, America*. The show featured a mixture of exposé and celebrity watch, which put Rivera's face before a wider audience but did not satisfy his journalist's hunger for hard news. After all, he was the man who had produced such exposés as "The Littlest Junkie," "Migrants: Dirt Cheap," and "Marching Home, Again." As a result, *Good Night, America* became a forum for Rivera's personal opinions on controversial subjects such as the legalization of marijuana and prostitution. His tendency to editorialize had gotten him into trouble at WABC, when he publicly announced his commitment to Senator George McGovern's failed 1972 presidential campaign.

In 1978, Rivera began a seven-year stint as a special correspondent for the ABC news magazine *20/20*. Although he was back on track with "legitimate" journalists, he continued to interject his personal viewpoint into his stories. It was the sort of thing that unnerved seasoned TV journalists, but it made Rivera widely popular with audiences, who saw him as a reporter who cared about the people and issues in his stories. The downfall of Rivera at ABC was a matter of some speculation, but the spark that started it was generally acknowledged to be a story about Marilyn Monroe's supposed romantic involvement with Senator Robert Kennedy (who was then Attorney General of the United States) at the time of her death. Rivera contended that the man in power at *20/20*, Roone Arledge, killed the story due to his friendship with the Kennedys. Arledge countered that it was just the latest in a long line of stories bordering on sensationalism that Rivera had tried to bully *20/20* into airing.

### Reigning King of Tabloid TV

By 1985, Rivera had begun carving out a niche for himself in the field of syndicated documentaries. His hallmark documentary was 1985's live broadcast of *The Opening of Al Capone's Vault*. Even though the sensational build-up over two hours resulted in an anti-climax when the vault yielded little more than old glass bottles, it received the largest audience ever for a recorded live broadcast. The high ratings propelled Rivera into several other like documentaries, including *American Vice: The Doping of America*, *Murder: Live from Death Row*, and *Devil Worship: Exposing Satan's Underground*. Although some of these productions resulted in lawsuits—Rivera's camera crews filmed arrests live, ignoring the rights of innocent people who would later be released with charges dropped—his fame grew exponentially. In fact, he began to regard lawsuits, bad press, and physical confrontation as enhancements for his public image.

Rivera's tumultuous career throughout the 1970s and 1980s was matched by an equally rocky home life. After his 1976 divorce from Edie, Rivera married Sherryl Raymond, a TV producer. This marriage resulted in a son, Gabriel Miguel, though Rivera admitted that he did not properly appreciate the joys of fatherhood during the early years of his son's life. The marriage ended in 1987, the same year Rivera's signature television show was launched.

The craze of tabloid television—syndicated hour-long talk shows that take a peeping tom's look at various sensational subjects—started innocently enough. The forerunner of these shows was Phil Donahue's local program in Dayton, Ohio, in the 1960s. Donahue himself went on to host a national talk show, and in his wake followed Oprah Winfrey, Sally Jessy Raphael, Jerry Springer, and many others. However, no one's name would come to characterize this form of entertainment more than Geraldo Rivera's. His constant striving for more unusual guests and topics earned him a reputation among journalists and critics that was less than complimentary. However, Rivera reveled in the infamy, even burlesquing his own image by playing himself on television dramas. Such self-deprecating humor made him a good-natured, easy target.

Still, Rivera was very serious about his show. He was accused of inciting guests to boost ratings, but he also became the unwitting victim of guests-gone-berserk. Perhaps the most famous of these incidents was the fist fight which broke out during a show about teenage white supremacists. African American activist Roy Innis was called a racial slur by a White Aryan Resistance Youth Group member, and the resulting fracas saw a chair hurled over the front of the stage, which struck Rivera and broke his nose.

No matter how controversial the *Geraldo* show became, Rivera remained imminently popular with the public. He won ten Emmy Awards, more than 150 other broadcast journalism citations, and received three honorary doctorates. In addition, Rivera's family life appeared to stabilize after his 1987 marriage to TV producer C. C. Dyer. The couple tried to have children, undergoing several surgeries and experiencing two miscarriages. To their joy, they finally had a daughter, Caitlin, in 1993. Mother and daughter have frequently appeared in the audience during tapings of *Geraldo*, and Rivera often holds his daughter in his arms during commercial break lead-ins.

Sometimes applauded, sometimes criticized, Geraldo Rivera undoubtedly became a force to be reckoned with in U.S. television. His early triumphs have often been overlooked by those who decry his more recent exploits. On the jacket of his autobiography, Rivera cited a former NBC News president who said "Geraldo Rivera should be arrested for exposing himself." To counter the remark, Rivera titled his 1991 book *Exposing Myself.* True to its title, the book provides a highly personal and sometimes shocking portrait of the complex and controversial television personality.

### SELECTED PUBLISHED WORKS:

*Willowbrook: A Report on How It Is and Why It Doesn't Have to Be That Way,* Random House, 1972.

*Miguel Robles—So Far,* with Edith Vonnegut Rivera, Harcourt, 1973.

*Puerto Rico: Island of Contrasts,* Parents Magazine Press, 1973.

*A Special Kind of Courage: Profiles of Young Americans,* Simon and Schuster, 1976.
*Exposing Myself,* Bantam, 1991.


## SOURCES:

*Biography Almanac,* edited by Annie M. Brewer, Detroit, Gale, 1981.
*Current Biography Yearbook, 1975,* edited by Charles Moritz, H. W. Wilson, 1975.
*Hispanic Writers,* edited by Bryan Ryan, Detroit, Gale, 1991.
*Les Brown's Encyclopedia of Television,* 3rd edition, Detroit, Gale, 1992.

—*Sketch by Cynthia R. Kasee*


# Tomás Rivera
## 1935-1984

### Mexican American educator, scholar and writer

Tomás Rivera overcame extreme obstacles to become a prominent academic. The son of migrant agricultural laborers, Rivera was subjected to an interrupted and dislocated early education. Nevertheless, Rivera became a highly respected scholar and university administrator. He also acquired an impressive readership for his creative stories and character sketches. As the first Mexican American to serve as chancellor in the University of California system, Rivera set a high standard for academic professionalism and personal achievement.


### On the Road

Rivera was born on December 22, 1934 in Crystal City, Texas, the place where his parents, Florencio Rivera and Josefa Hernandez, had met and married four years earlier. The family resided in Texas, but traveled—as far north as Michigan and Minnesota—to work the fields. Rivera told a 1980 interviewer that his "earliest recollections are of living on different farms where we worked in Minnesota." Before he went to public school, Rivera attended barrio schools and learned to read and write Spanish. Rivera once described those schools as "pay-as-you-go." "You paid five cents every day," he said, "and if you didn't go you didn't pay."

Rivera began to learn English around the age of nine, but explained that "it wasn't until the fifth grade that I really could understand everything." For Rivera the capacity to understand English fully came as a revelation: "I still remember the day clearly, like a breakthrough . . . at the end of the class I had understood everything. I wasn't even aware that she had been talking in English. It was a great sensation!" Through high school, Rivera arranged his academics around the agricultural calendar: "We would leave around April 15, and return around November 1. . . .In the fall I'd finish the year before and start the next at the same time."


### From Fields to The Academy

When he entered Southwest Texas Junior College in 1956, Rivera had to curtail his farm labor because the college did not allow late registration. The next year he left agricultural work altogether. He transferred to Southwest Texas State College (now called Southwest Texas State University), and commenced the academic career that he pursued his entire life.

Rivera graduated in 1958 with a B.A. in English. He began teaching elementary school and married Concepcion Garza. While teaching in several Texas public school systems, Rivera pursued a master's degree at Southwest Texas State. In 1964 he earned his master's degree in education, and the following year he returned to Southwest Texas Junior College to teach English, French, and Spanish. He soon left Texas for the University of Oklahoma, where he pursued a Ph.D. simultaneously with another Master's degree. With these credentials Rivera returned to Texas to teach at Sam Houston University, where he taught as an associate professor until 1971.

Rivera then accepted a professorship in Spanish at the University of Texas at San Antonio, where he was named associate dean of the College of Multidisciplinary Studies in 1973 and vice-chancellor for administration three years later. Following his administrative proclivities, Rivera accepted a post as executive vice-president at the University of Texas at El Paso. In the *Dictionary of Literary Biography,* Luis Leal asserted that Rivera made these career choices because "he discovered that he could benefit the Chicano people more as a university administrator than as a professor."

In 1979 the University of Califoria at Riverside offered Rivera the office of Chancellor. After Rivera's death, Rolando Hinojosa-Smith wrote that his career had been exceptional by any standards: "it's a fact and undeniable [that Rivera had become the first Hispanic University of California chancellor] . . . But look at these facts: Tomás Rivera won his Ph.D. from the University of Oklahoma in 1969, and he was named Chancellor less than ten years later. Now *that* was an accomplishment." This statement was published in an issue of *Revista Chicano-Riqueña* dedicated to Rivera's memory. Rivera published two books along with numerous short stories and poems in periodicals and collections. His most noted book "*. . . y no se lo trago la tierra*" ("*. . . and the Earth Did Not Part*") won the Premio Quinto Sol in 1971, and has had two separate English translations. Rivera died in 1984. He is survived by his wife and three children.

## SELECTED PUBLISHED WORKS:

"*. . . y no se lo trago la tierra*"/"*. . . and the Earth did not Part,*" English translation by Herminio Ríos C., Berkeley, Quinto Sol, 1971, translated by Rolando Hinojosa-Smith as *This Migrant Earth,* Houston, Arte Publico, 1985.

## SOURCES:

### Books

*Chicano Authors: Inquiry by Interview,* Juan Bruce-Novoa, University of Texas Press, 1980.
*Dictionary of Literary Biography,* Vol. 82, Chicano Writers: First Series, edited by Francisco A. Lomeli and Carl R. Shirley, Detroit, Gale, 1989.
*Hispanic Writers,* edited by Bryan Ryan, Detroit, Gale, 1991.

### Periodicals

*Revista Chicano-Riqña,* Fall-Winter, 1985.
*Always and Other Poems,* Sisterdale, TX, Sisterhood, 1973.

—*Sketch by James McCarthy*

# Augusto José Antonio Roa Bastos
## 1917-
### Paraguayan writer

Paraguayan writer Augusto Roa Bastos is considered Paraguay's leading writer and an important contributor to modern Latin American fiction. Mexican writer **Carlos Fuentes,** in the *New York Times Book Review,* called his 1974 book, *I, the Supreme,* "one of the milestones of the Latin American novel."

Roa Bastos used the myths and legends of his country to create his own symbolic world, wrote Jean Franco in an essay in *Modern Latin American Literature.* "He allows us, if we are human enough, to imagine the oppressed in the center of history and not forever on its shores," observed Chilean writer **Ariel Dorfman** in an 1988 essay.

In his novels and short stories, Roa Bastos explored the repressive and violent history of colonial Latin America, using the techniques of magic realism and an experimental language and structure. He spent much of his life in exile, and he viewed his troubled country critically and with bitterness. "He is indignant over the exploitation of the weak, furious over the backwardness of the people," wrote Hugo Rodríguez Alcalá in an essay in *Modern Latin American Literature.*

### Early Short Stories and Poetry

Roa Bastos was born in Asunción, Paraguay, on June 13, 1917, and grew up in the provincial city of Iturbe, where his father was a clerk on a sugar plantation. As a boy, he spoke Spanish and Guaraní, the popular language of Paraguay, which he would later use in his writing. With his mother's encouragement, he began writing short stories as a young teenager. In the Asunción library of his maternal uncle, Bishop Hermenegildo Roa, he read Spanish literature. He was sent to military school in Asunción and, at 14, he volunteered to fight in the Chaco War against Bolivia.

Roa Bastos wrote an early novel *Fulgencio Miranda,* which won a prize but was never published. As a young man, he tried writing poetry, publishing *El ruiseñor de la aurora, y otros poemas* ("The Nightingale of Dawn") in 1942. In the 1940s, Roa Bastos worked as a journalist, chronicling the lives of exploited tea plantation workers in northern Paraguay for the Asunción newspaper, *El País.* He later became the newspaper's editor-in-chief.

In 1944, he received a grant from the British Council and worked for the BBC in London during the German bombing in World War II. "Because the nature of war is infernal violence, its effect on me was to intensify an already profound abhorrence of anything that might resemble that experience in the future. For me war had no romantic attraction," he told Javier M. González in a 1985 interview.

### A Writer in Exile

Roa Bastos's life changed drastically in 1947, during Paraguay's bloody civil uprising against the repressive dictatorship of General Higinio Moríñgo. After Moríñgo shut down *El País,* Roa Bastos fled to Buenos Aires, where he lived in exile for nearly 30 years. In Argentina, Roa Bastos wrote fiction and screenplays, including the successful 1969 film, *Hijo de hombre*. His first short story collection, *El trueno entre las hojas*, ("Thunder in the Leaves," 1953), is a pessimistic look at Paraguayan society, with stories such as "The Excavation", about political prisoners who escaped, then were executed. "It is easy to assert that these stories, with their emphasis on violence, on social injustice, and on the particular circumstances of the Paraguayan experience, anticipate the themes, language, and techniques of Roa's first published novel, *Son of Man,*" wrote David William Foster in *Augusto Roa Bastos*.

The award-winning *Hijo de hombre* ("Son of Man," 1959) explores Paraguay's tragic history, from Colonial times through the Chaco War in the mid-30s, using myths and legends to focus, especially, on the plight of the Indian. "It is filled with the difficult certainty of redemption, but that redemption cannot be abstracted from the implacable portrayal of the horrors that have befallen Paraguay during most of its history," wrote Ariel Dorfman in 1988. As in other writings, Roa Bastos intersperses the Guaraní language and Christian allegory. Dorfman continued, "Because the author does not lie about his ravaged land, because the violence is relentless and death apparently unending, the slow creation of hope is all the more powerful."

Riding the wave of interest in Latin American fiction, Roa Bastos won a fellowship from the John Simon Guggenheim Memorial Foundation in 1970. His second novel, *Yo, el supremo* ("I, the Supreme," 1974) considered his masterpiece, is a fictionalized account of the last days of the dictatorship of José Gaspar Rodríguez de Francia, El Supremo, who ruled Paraguay from 1814 until his death in 1840. "The result is a richly textured, brilliant book-an impressive portrait, not only of El Supremo, but of a whole colonial society in the throes of learning how to swim, or how best to drown, in the seas of national independence," wrote Carlos Fuentes in the *New York Times Book Review*.

The novel has no plot or identifiable narrator; it is a collection of myths, conversations, letters, historical documents, and other fragments. "*I, The Supreme One* is a masterful study of a sincere madman, who brought order and "prosperity' to his country at the cost of everything else. In Roa Bastos he found a worthy 'biographer,'" wrote Martin Seymour-Smith in *The New Guide to Modern World Literature*. Fuentes observed, "This is Mr. Roa Bastos's dialogue with himself through history and through a monstrous historical figure whom he has to imagine and understand if he is ever to imagine and understand himself and his people."

In the interview with González, Roa Bastos described his 1993 novel *El Fiscal* ("The Prosecutor") as the third in a trilogy with *Hijo de hombre* and *Yo, el Supremo*, which together create a "great frieze of Paraguayan life and the human condition in a specific historical circumstance." In *Vigilia del Almirante* ("The Vigil of the Admiral," 1992) Roa Bastos continued "his exploration of the realm of historical revisionism with a timely reconstruction of Christopher Columbus' voyage of discovery in 1492 and affirms Roa Bastos' place in the Latin American literary canon," wrote MaGill in 1994.

Roa Bastos left Argentina because of the military dictatorship in the mid-1970s, and took a job as an associate professor of Guaraní and Spanish American studies at the University of Toulouse in France. After visiting Paraguay in the 1970s, the government there officially expelled him in 1982. No longer a Paraguayan citizen, he was offered Spanish citizenship as an exiled Latin American writer, according to David William Foster, a Spanish professor at Arizona State University who has written extensively about Roa Bastos. Roa Bastos received Spain's Premio Cervantes in 1989. He returned to visit Paraguay in 1989 after the overthrow of President **Alfredo Stroessner**'s regime and was present for a stage production of *Yo, el supremo* in the early 1990s, Foster explained.

After an early marriage, which produced a son, ended, Roa Bastos lived for many years with a woman named Amelia Houssais in Argentina. He later married a Paraguayan anthropologist in France and they had at least two children, according to Foster.

## SELECTED PUBLISHED WORKS:

*El ruiseñor de la aurora, y otros poemas,* Asunción, Nacional, 1942.

*El trueno entre las hojas,* Buenos Aires, Losada, 1953.

*Hijo de hombre,* Buenos Aires, Losada, 1960. *Son of Man,* translated by Rachel Caffyn, London, Gollanz, 1965.

*El Naranjal ardiente: Nocturno paraguayo,* 1947–1949, Asunción, Diálogo/Cuadernos de la Piririta, 1960.

*El baldío,* Buenos Aires, Losada, 1966.

*Los pies sobre el agua,* Buenos Aires, América Latina, 1967.

*Madera quemada,* Santiago, Chile, Universitaria, 1967.

*Moriencia,* Caracas, Monte Avila, 1969.

*El génesis de los Apapokura-Guaraní,* Asunción, Alcor, 1971.

*Cuerpo presente y otros textos,* Buenos Aires, América Latina, 1972.

*Yo, el supremo,* Buenos Aires, Siglo XXI, 1974. *I, the Supreme,* translated by Helen Lane, New York, Vintage, 1986.

*El pollito de fuego,* Buenos Aires, Flor, 1974.

*Los juegos,* 2 volumes, Buenos Aires, Flor, 1979, 1981.

*Lucha hasta el alba,* Asunción, Arte Nuevo, 1979.

*Antología personal,* Mexico City, Nueva Imagen, 1980.

*Rafael Barrett,* Stockholm, Estudios Latinoamericanos, 1981.

*Contar un cuento,* Buenos Aires, Kapelusz, 1984.

*Escritos politicos,* Buenos Aires, Estudios de Literatura Latinamericana, 1984.

*Carta abierta a mi pueblo,* Buenos Aires, Frente Paraguayo, 1986.

*El tiranosaurio del Paraguay da sus ultimas boqueadas,* Buenos Aires, Frente Paraguayo, 1986.

*Semana del autor: Augusto Roa Bastos,* by Roa Bastos and others, Madrid, ICI Cultura Hispánica, 1986.

*On Modern Latin American Fiction,* edited by John King, Noonday Press, 1989.

*Vigilia del Almirante,* Madrid, Alfaguara, 1992.

*El fiscal,* Buenos Aires, Sudamericana, 1993.

## SOURCES:

### Books

Foster, David William, *Augusto Roa Bastos,* Boston, Twayne Publishers, 1978.

*Dictionary of Literary Biography, Vol. 113,* edited by William Luis, Detroit, Gale, 1992.

*Hispanic Literature Criticism,* Vol. 2, edited by Jelena Krstovic, Detroit, Gale, 1994.

*Hispanic Writers,* edited by Bryan Ryan, Detroit, Gale, 1991.

*Latin American Writers,* Vol. II, edited by Carlos A. Solé and Maria Isabel Abreu, New York, Charles Scribner's Sons, 1989.

Magill, Frank N., *Masterpieces of Latino Literature,* New York, Salem Press, 1994.

*Modern Latin American Literature,* Vol. II, edited by David William Foster and Virginia Ramos Foster, New York, Frederick Ungar Publishing Co., 1975.

Seymour-Smith, Martin, *The New Guide to Modern World Literature,* New York, The Macmillan Press, 1985.

### Periodicals

*New York Times Book Review,* April 6, 1986, pp. 1, 32–34.

### Other

David William Foster, interview with contributor Ann Malaspina, April 5, 1995.

*—Sketch by Ann Malaspina*

# Jose Enrique Rodo
## 1872-1917
### Uruguayan philosopher and essayist

Jose Enrique Rodo was recognized as a philosopher and literary critic of modernism in South America. He was considered a hero to the youth of Uruguay for his idealism and spirituality. Rodo was born in Montevideo, Uruguay in 1872. He was from a good family and he received an education in Montevideo. Rodo helped found the periodical *Revista Nacional de Literatura y Ciencias Sociales* in 1895. He taught Western literature at the Montevideo University in 1898 and he was director of the National Library in 1890. Rodo was a moderate man and a liberal. Twice he was a member of parliament, and he was the editor of a newspaper. He lived a puritanical lifestyle and withdrew from society in many ways. Rodo never married, and it was believed that he never fell in love. He wore thick glasses and spent his time in libraries. He was a loner, living within himself and sharing himself only as a profound writer. He was described as tall and thin and that he maintained an inner peacefulness throughout his life. Rodo was a seeker of truth and beauty. In all his writings, he never spoke of anything that was off-color or negative.

Rodo's philosophy was idealistic and unrealistic, but it touched the hearts of many who read his works. In 1897, his first two essays were published, *El que vendra* ("He Who Will Come") and *La Novela Nueva* ("The New World"). Rodo was a literary critic and urged writers to conform with the present realism and artistic expressions from the heart. Rodo brought a new expression into his essays using poetic prose to relay his criticisms. His literary criticisms were philosophically poetic. In 1899, Rodo published a critical analysis of the Nicaraguan poet Rubin Dario. It was considered his finest work in literary criticism. He became known as a one of the greatest philosophers in South America. He believed that true harmony was in a balance of Judaic Christianity and Hellenic paganism. Rodo caused much controversy in his philosophical thoughts. After his first novel, *Ariel,* was published in 1900, two schools of thought arose, Arielist and anti-Arielist. Rodo's philosophical impact on Latin American continued to be discussed throughout the twentieth century. He was a *modernista* and popularized French thought in South America. Rodo believed that Paris was the heart of modern culture.

Rodo's book, *Ariel*, made him famous overnight with its success. He was only 29 years old when he wrote *Ariel.* Rodo has been praised for his work, and he has been attacked for it also. Literary critics wrote numerous essays about his work, especially *Ariel.* He wrote the book right after the Spanish-American War.

It was a time when Latin Americans looked at the United States as too materialistic and mediocre in many ways. Rodo expressed these sentiments in *Ariel.* Although he wrote of his admiration of the United States, he also wrote about his disdains. He described the United States as vulgar and spiritually deformed. He took symbolism from Shakespeare's *The Tempest* and incorporated it into Ariel. In Rodo's book, Ariel represented Latin American spiritual values and Caliban represented North American utilitarian democracy. In *Ariel,* an old wise teacher who was referred to as Prospero after Shakespeare's magician in *The Tempest,* sits before his students and sagely gives his last lecture to them. Rodo addresses his first chapter to the youth of America.

During that era in South America, the principle of Positivism was dominant, and Rodo's philosophy leaned toward these principles. He was inspired by the principles of Greek and Christian ideals. He also injected "ideal optimism" into his philosophy. Before he published *Ariel,* Rodo was concerned about how the book would be accepted. A newspaper, *El Dia,* announced the publication of the book and described Rodo's work as a study on the dangerous influence the United States had on Latin America. Rodo had the newspaper issue a second announcement stating that the statements about the United States were only an illustration of the main essay.

Rodo's book, *Ariel,* was published in Spanish nine times before he died. In 1906, he published a series of letters in a book, *Liberalismo y Jacobinismo.* He was inspired by the suppression and removal of all images of the Crucified Christ by the Charity Commissioners from all the hospitals in Uruguay. Rodo was critical of the commissioners' actions because of his opposition to Jacobinism—defined as a dogmatic mental attitude. He also published *Los Motivos de Proteo* ("The Motives of Proteus") in 1909 and *El mirado de Prospero* in 1913. In *The Motives of Proteus,* Rodo profoundly expounds on renewing the spirit and the art of living. He defines "actual causes" as the "key to many enigmas of our destiny." Rodo believed that nothing happened without order. He wrote that all impressions and images leave an imprint into a person's unconscious or senses. He also wrote that every idea or act would help determine "the course of your life, the synthetic sense of your movements, the physiognomical form of your personality. The hidden little tooth that gnaws in the depths of your soul, the drop of water that falls rhythmically in its dark cavern, the silkworms that weave their finest threads there—they take no leave, they never cease; and their cooperative activities every minute kill you, remodel you, destroy you, create you ... death whose sum is death, resurrections whose persistence is life." Rodo lived as he taught, a seeker of truth, and he developed an inner spiritual peace and serenity. His fame never seemed to affect him, and he was indifferent to acclaim. Rodo exemplified his philosophies throughout his life, and his hope was that from the pain of World War I, new ideals of life and new endeavors in art would emerge. He foresaw troubled times ahead, and he thought the greatest task of the nineteenth century would be the attainment of spiritual tolerance.

In *The Motives of Proteus,* Rodo wrote: "To renew oneself is to live ... and, therefore, is not our personal transformation, in a way, a constant and infallible law of time? What does it matter if desire and the will remain fixed to one goal, when time passes and carries us away? Time is the supreme innovator. ..." Rodo concluded the book by stating that he would continue to search for truths, and that he would continue to share these "new truths" with his readers. After World War I, in 1916, Rodo was finally able to travel to Europe to visit Paris, the "center of culture" that he admired so much. Rodo arrived in Lisbon, but he had no interest in visiting Portugal. He went through Spain into Italy to visit Rome and then went to Palermo, Sicily, where he became ill with abdominal typhus. On May 10, 1917, Rodo died at the age of 45. He never made it to France.

As Mario Benedetti concluded in *Genio y figura de Jose Enrique Rodo,* "Rodo was not ahead of his time, nor did he try to be. Although he penetrated the twentieth century, he visited it as a tourist, but with the curiosity and the capacity of wonder of an intelligent tourist. His true place, his true temporal ground was the nineteenth century, and he belonged to it with all his soul ... His intellectual attitude was always marked by honesty, and his dignity as a writer was not a metaphor but a fact ... "

## SELECTED PUBLISHED WORKS:

### Books

*Ariel,* Montevideo, Dornaleche & Reyes, 1900.
*Liberalismo y Jacobinismo,* Montevideo, El Siglo Ilustrado, 1906.
*Motives de Proteo,* Montevideo, J.M. Serrano & Co., 1909.
*El Mirador de Prospero,* Montevideo, J.M. Serrano & Co., 1913.

## SOURCES:

### Books

Mario Benedetti, *Genio y figura de Jose Enrique Rodo,* Buenos Aires, Editorial Universitaria de Buenos Aires, 1966.

Crawford, William Rex, *A Century of Latin-American Thought,* Cambridge, Harvard University Press, 1961.

*Encyclopedia of Latin America,* edited by Helen Delpar, New York, McGraw-Hill Book Company, 1974.

Franco, Jean, *The Modern Culture of Latin America: Society and the Artist,* New York, Frederick A. Praeger, 1967.

*Modern Latin American Literature,* Vol. II, M-Z, Second Printing, compiled and edited by David William Foster and Virginia Ramos Foster, New York, Frederick Ungar Publishing Co., 1979.

Rodo, Jose Enrique, *Ariel,* Introduction by Gordon Brotherston, Great Britain, Cambridge University Press, 1967.

Rodo, Jose Enrique, *Ariel,* translated by Margaret Sayers Peden, Foreward by James W. Symington, Prologue by Carlos Fuentes, Austin, University of Texas Press, 1988.

Rodo, Jose Enrique, *The Motives of Proteus,* translated by Angel Flores, Introduction by Havelock Ellis, New York, Brentano's Inc., 1928.

Torres-Rioseco, *Aspects of Spanish-American Literature,* Seattle, University of Washington Press, 1963.

Torres-Rioseco, *New World Literature: Tradiation and Revolt in America,* Berkeley and Los Angeles, University of California Press, 1949.

—*Sketch by Phyllis Noah*

# Arturo S. Rodriguez
## 1949-
### Hispanic American union leader and activist

The second president of the United Farm Workers of America (UFW), Arturo Rodriguez follows in the footsteps of the renowned union activist **Cesar Chavez,** who founded the UFW and served as its president until his death in 1993. Becoming involved with the UFW as a college activist, Rodriguez rose through the ranks of the organization until he was named president in 1993. Assuming the mantle of leadership for the UFW, which has experienced a prolonged period of decline, he has before him the difficult task of regaining the union's hard-won influence of the 1960s and 1970s.

Arturo Salvador Rodriguez, III, was born on June 23, 1949, in San Antonio, Texas, to Arturo S. Rodriguez, II, a sheet metal worker, and Felice Rodriguez, a school teacher. He was educated at local Catholic grade schools and at La Salle High School, from which he graduated in 1967. Rodriguez studied sociology at St. Mary's University and earned a B.A. in 1971. While a student at St. Mary's in the late 1960s, Rodriguez participated in the famous national grape boycott, demonstrating against the purchase of the fruit at various supermarkets and produce terminals. This highly publicized boycott ultimately led to significant concessions on the part of the grape growers in 1970.

After completing his undergraduate degree at St. Mary's, Rodriguez matriculated at University of Michigan, where he earned an M.A. social work in 1973. During this time, he helped organize boycott support for the UFW in Michigan. Rodriguez also participated in a publicly funded anti-poverty program called United Migrants for Opportunity, which provided much-need assistance for field workers in Blissfield, Michigan. While the United Migrants for Opportunity made an immediate difference in providing relief for the Blissfield migrant workers, this experience convinced Rodriguez that truly momentous gains could only be won through the creation of a strong union with tough collective bargaining power.

### Begins Working Full-Time with UFW

After graduating from the University of Michigan in 1973, Rodriguez accepted a full-time position with the Detroit branch of the UFW. Working under Richard Chavez—Cesar's brother—he helped organize UFW boycotts and union activities throughout Michigan. That same year, Rodriguez met Cesar Chavez personally for the first time; he also met Cesar's daughter, Linda, who also worked as a UFW boycott organizer, and the two were married seven months later. The couple has three children: Olivia, Julia, and Arturo.

In 1975 Rodriguez left Michigan for California to help coordinate the lobbying effort for the passage of the California Agricultural Labor Relations Act, a UFW-sponsored migrant worker rights package. He quickly earned a reputation as a top UFW organizer, becoming involved in numerous key union activities. In 1975 Rodriguez helped coordinate union representation elections in the Salinas Valley, and he spearheaded the UFW campaign at the Molera Packaging Co., where artichoke workers who were previously represented by the Teamsters Union unanimously selected the UFW. When legislators refused to fund the Agricultural Labor Relations Board (ALRB) in 1976, Rodriguez devoted much of his time lobbing for the passage of Proposition 14, a UFW-led initiative to restore funding for the agency. Although Proposition 14 failed to pass, lawmakers bowed to union pressure and voted some funds for the ALRB. One year later, the law supporting the ALRB was fully restored.

After the successful reinstatement of ALRB funding, Rodriguez turned his attention to organizing UFW boycotts in California and Michigan. In 1978 he became the chief instructor at a UFW school in La Paz, California, which was established by Cesar Chavez to train union organizers. In 1980 Rodriguez established a UFW-sponsored service center in Santa Paula, California, where farm workers could resolve disputes involving labor and education issues. Enhancing his reputation as a premier organizer, Rodriguez was handpicked to work on the presidential campaigns of both Jerry Brown in 1976 and Edward Kennedy in 1980.

### Becomes National Executive Board Member

In 1981 Rodriguez was elected to the UFW National Executive Board, and he served as a board member until 1989. During the early 1980s, he ran the UFW division responsible for union organizing and contract negotiating with the California wine grape, table grape, and tree fruit industries. He also worked with Cesar Chavez on a UFW study to determine the potential ramifications of a 1984 table grape boycott on grape workers and consumers. In 1986 Rodriguez managed grape boycott activities in the mid-Atlantic region.

Throughout the late 1980s and early 1990s, Rodriguez coordinated grape boycott activities in California, where farm workers found themselves losing ground in many labor disputes with the growers. This crisis peaked in 1992 when grape workers in Coachella and San Joaquin Valleys walked off their jobs to protest eight years without a pay increase, along with poor working conditions and other grievances. To support the protesting workers, the UFW mounted an enormous walkout demonstration involving thousands of farm workers at dozens of vineyards. This measure ultimately forced the grape growers to implement a pay raise throughout the industry.

At the time of Cesar Chavez's death in 1993, the UFW had lost much of its momentum in labor relations and had suffered from a dwindling member base. That same year, Rodriguez was elected president of the union and given the difficult task of initiating the rebuilding process. Adopting a new slogan, "Every Worker An Organizer," the UFW mounted several aggressive organizing drives that have won key representation elections. In an address to a crowd of UFW supporters who participated in a 1994 march from Delano to Sacramento, California's capital, Rodriguez articulated the essence of union's reorganization: "This pilgrimage is about recommitment and penance. Penance because all of us let Cesar carry the responsibility for organizing the union on his shoulders. Now the burden for fulfilling Cesar's dreams and our own rests squarely on each of us."

## SOURCES:

### Periodicals

*Biography Today,* September 1993, p. 40.
*California AFL-CIO News,* April 9, 1994. pp. 1, 4; April 22, 1994, pp. 1, 4; April 29, 1994, pp. 1, 4.
*The Nation,* July 26/August 2, 1993, pp. 130–35.
*The Press Democrat,* September 11, 1994, pp. G1, G9.

### Other

Rodriguez, Arturo S., biographical sketch provided by the United Farm Workers of America.

—*Sketch by Sandy J. Stiefer*

# Chi Chi Rodríguez
## 1935-
### Puerto Rican professional golfer

Chi Chi Rodríguez is one of the preeminent figures in modern golf. Earning more than $1 million during his career on the senior tour, Rodríguez had eight victories, including the Denver Open and the Texas Open. After leaving the regular tour, Rodríguez joined the senior tour in 1985, where he outearned his regular tour years in less than half the time. Rodríguez has made distinguished contributions to numerous charities and started the Chi Chi Rodríguez Youth Foundation, which raises money and gives guidance to troubled young people. He has received many awards, including the 1982 Father of the Year and the Salvation Army Gold Crest Award.

Born in Puerto Rico in 1935, Chi Chi was the fifth of six children of Juan Rodríguez, Sr. Separated from his wife when his future-golfer son was only seven, Rodríguez washed dishes and worked on farms to feed his family. In the town of Rio Piedras, the young Rodríguez developed rickets and tropical sprue, making him thin-boned and sensitive to pain. Although he survived the potentially fatal disease, the effects would remain with him throughout his life. As he told *Sports Illustrated,* "if I get hit in the arm . . . it hurts me three times more than someone else."

*Chi Chi Rodríguez*

Though he grew up poor, he saw his father as a heroic figure and recalls fights among his siblings to decide who could make their father feel comfortable when he came home from his 16-hour workdays. Although his father never made more than $18 a week, Rodríguez credits him for instilling the work ethic that made his golf career possible.

### Sports as an Escape

Although quite thin, Rodríguez had athletic prowess. Baseball attracted him first. In fact, his nickname comes from a player named Chi Chi Flores, whom Rodríguez idolized for his determination. Rodríguez pitched semi-professionally with Orlando Cepeda, Juan Pizarro, and the legendary **Roberto Clemente,** who was practically his neighbor. Rodríguez recalled that Clemente became a success in more ways than one. "Roberto died caring for people less fortunate than himself," Rodríguez told *Gulfshore Life* magazine, "which is the way I'd like to die. If I could be half the man Roberto Clemente was, I'd be a giant among men."

At age seven, about the time his mother left the family, Rodríguez began caddying and spotting balls at the Berwind Country Club near his home. It gave him a chance to earn a little money; Rodríguez says he earned about 25 cents per day. More importantly, it exposed a whole world of possibilities to him. In an interview with *Golf* magazine, he describes how he and his friends would play around the entrance to the

Country Club and dream of untold wealth: "Several other kids and I would sit in it and watch the fancy convertibles drive through the gate. There I was, without shoes, telling friends that someday I'd own a car like that. They all laughed, of course. But I knew it would come true."

Simple survival taught him skills that Rodríguez feels made him a better golfer. Bats, often carrying rabies, would make their way into the shack in which he and his family lived. He and his brothers had to try to kill the bats with broomsticks. Rodríguez says that he got so good at it that he never missed. He made his own golf clubs from tree limbs and balls from tin cans, and he and his playmates would simply dig holes in the ground. By the time he ever played a round of real golf, he could already hit a tin can at 100 yards.

### Turns Professional

After joining the U.S. Army for several years Rodríguez returned to Puerto Rico, where he got a job as an assistant pro at the Dorado Beach Country Club. Making friends like Nelson Rockefeller while working at the club, Rodríguez got sponsorship to join the 1960 pro tour. Although consistently winning money, Rodríguez did not score his first tournament victory until the 1963 Denver Open. The following year he won the Lucky International Open and the Western Open and came in ninth on the overall money winner's list.

From the mid-1960s to 1985 he won only five more tournaments, his tour winnings averaging only about $40,000 per year. His income from golf exhibitions, however, often far exceeded that. A charismatic personality and entertaining speaker, Rodríguez attained a celebrity that golfers of comparable regular tour achievement hardly ever do. His speaking style and the intensity of his memories made him a real attraction. He often told stories of his father, including a memorable one in which someone ran to the Rodríguez home to tell Chi Chi's father that his son had broken the club record for 18 holes. His father, who knew nothing of golf and never saw his son play in a tournament, answered that his son had better fix it because he had no money to pay for a new one.

With stars like Jack Nicklaus and Tom Watson reaching retirement age, the PGA Senior Tour started to attract attention in the 1980s. Rodríguez turned 50 in 1985, and his transition from the regular tour to the senior tour brought him nothing but success: His eight regular-tour victories in 25 years seemed paltry next to the 22 victories in the first decade of his senior career. Rodríguez's winnings as a senior more than quintupled his regular tour prize money. In 1987 alone, when he finished first in winnings on the Senior Tour, he won seven tournaments.

The Senior Tour gave Rodríguez new vigor in his golf career, and it also allowed him the freedom to pursue the charitable causes that mean so much to him. While his lifetime contract with Toyota Motor Corporation and his speaking and golfing engagements continued to keep him financially secure, they also gave him the chance to fund the Chi Chi Rodríguez Youth Foundation. At the entrance to the Glen Oaks Golf Course, where the Foundation is based, Rodríguez has inscribed: "Glen Oaks is not the greatest golf course in the world; the Foundation's concept is not written by the smartest man in the world. But the labor of love that takes place on this land, free of fear or prejudice, allows growth and equality to flourish." Rodríguez bought the course—located in Clearwater, Florida—so that local young people referred by school officials would have the opportunity to develop job skills and self esteem. At the Foundation, Rodríguez hires people to tutor, train, counsel, and encourage kids with a variety of problems. The Foundation also teaches golf and groundskeeping.

Rodríguez sees the Youth Foundation as a way of treating the kids with respect in a way that they have never experienced. He developed the idea in the late 1970s when he visited a juvenile detention center. He saw young people with all the disadvantages he faced, but none of the luck. "Seeing those kids trapped like animals inside cells just broke my heart," he said in an interview with *Pursuits*. "I knew that I could have been one of them; I just never got caught."

Rodríguez admits that his philanthropy makes him feel good about himself. *Pursuits* quoted him as saying, "I feel like Superman when I'm here [at Glen Oaks]." Others have shared a high estimation of Rodríguez as a humanitarian as well; he has received numerous awards around the United States in recognition of his generosity. In 1982 he won the Father of the Year Award for his work with his Foundation children; in 1992 the PGA inducted him into the World Golf Hall of Fame. Rodríguez continues to play on the Senior Tour and does endorsements for several companies. He lives in Florida with his wife, Iwalami. The couple have a daughter, Donnette, born in 1962.

## SOURCES:

### Periodicals

*Golf,* May 1980, p. 57.
*Golf Digest,* February 1986, p. 119.
*Gulfshore Life,* April 1993, p. 15.
*Pursuits,* fall 1988, p. 12.
*Sports Illustrated,* November 23, 1987, p. 3

### Other

Additional biographical information provided by Eddie Elias Enterprises, Akron, Ohio.

*—Sketch by Carlos Roca*

# Gloria Rodriguez
## 1948-
### Hispanic American family advocate and activist

Teaching parents how to raise their children was a philosophy unheard of in 1973, and yet Gloria Rodriguez took that idea and turned it into a lifelong mission to provide low-income Hispanic mothers in Texas with basic parenting skills. As founder, executive director, and CEO of Avance—a Spanish word meaning "advance"—Rodriguez has helped thousands of minority women break the cycle of poverty, ignorance, and abuse through classes and programs designed to develop healthy relationships with their children, and to assist the women in taking control of their own lives through increased independence and enhanced self-esteem. As a result of years of dedication and steady fundraising efforts, Avance is regarded as a unique and phenomenal national success story among social service organizations. Considered a national model by the federal government, Avance is one of ten national family literacy models cited in the Barbara Bush Foundation for Family Literacy book, First Teachers. As Rodriguez told the *West Side Sun* in 1991, "My greatest accomplishment is that we have kept the mission alive against all odds. . . . After 18 years Avance is still expanding and in the national forefront."

Rodriguez grew up in the predominantly Hispanic and economically disadvantaged West Side of San Antonio, Texas, where she was born on July 9, 1948. Her father, Julian Garza, died when she was two, leaving her mother, Lucy Villegas Salazar, to raise eight children alone. Because the family had only $96 a month to live on, Rodriguez and her sisters often sold their mother's homemade earrings at restaurants and drive-ins. At age nine she got a job cleaning a neighbor's house, and, when she entered Kennedy High School, she worked as a department store salesclerk. Rodriguez excelled in school and became a popular cheerleader and beauty queen who graduated in 1967 with a solid academic record.

Upon graduation, Rodriguez was undecided about her future. She wanted to be a teacher but had resigned herself to a secretarial position and applied for a clerical job at City Hall. "But my life was changed," she told the *San Antonio Light,* "when I got a letter from Our Lady of the Lake University saying I was one of 30 students selected for Project Teacher Excellence." The federally funded pilot program had been designed to give disadvantaged students an opportunity to study bilingual education in exchange for their returning to the community to teach. Rodriguez had competed against 300 applicants for one of the coveted spots. She almost lost her chance, she recalled in the *Light,* when her high school principal declined to give her a recommendation, stating that she was not "college material." Rodriguez persuaded the committee to give her a chance and set out to prove the principal wrong.

"I knew college would be difficult," Rodriguez told the *West Side Sun.* "Other college students were better prepared academically and could express themselves better in the English language." Rodriguez credits her grandfather, who came to live with the family after her father died, with fostering in her a profound spiritual awareness that helped her through troubling times at college and has remained an important facet of her everyday life. "The first two years of college," she told the *West Side Sun,* "I went daily to the chapel to pray. I vowed that if I did well, I would use my training to help others."

### Discovered Link Between Education and Parenting

Rodriguez completed her bachelor of arts degree in 1970 and received her master of education degree in 1973. She was hired by the Northside School District in San Antonio as its first bilingual teacher in 1970 and given a class of 35 first graders labeled "problem learners." She was warned by school administrators not to expect much success. Rodriguez wrote in the *San Diego Union:* "Initially I thought they had a 'language problem' and assumed they simply needed a bilingual teacher. But, I found, they were as deficient in Spanish as they were in English." Rodriguez drew on her own experiences in a family that was poor and yet managed to instill respect, independence, and determination in Rodriguez and her siblings. She knew that some children blossomed even in poverty, while others were crushed by it.

"It was like a light bulb went on: It all starts with the family," Rodriguez told the *Dallas Morning News.* "Children from a strong family had a better chance at surviving. Parents must be in the front line of preparing kids for success." From that point on, Rodriguez focused on the concept of parent education. Returning to college, she enrolled in a research class and began surveying the mothers of the children in her class. She discovered that even though the mothers valued education, they did not see themselves as educators and expected the schools to begin the process of education.

"Education begins at home and the first and most important teachers are the parents," Rodriguez told the *Express News.* "I was in the wrong place. I realized that parents needed assistance in this very important area." Coincidentally, two doctoral students from Cornell University had submitted a proposal to the Zale Foundation in Dallas to fund the first Avance in that city, and the company wanted to replicate the program in San Antonio after the program's highly successful first year. Rodriguez interviewed for the job, and was hired as its first—and only—director. The organization's first site was in the Mirasol Housing Projects, a few blocks from where Rodriguez was raised.

### Launched Avance in San Antonio

Avance's beginnings were humble, to say the least. Rodriguez and three assistants went door to door in the projects to see who wanted to get off welfare and become better parents at the same time. A handful of skeptical women signed up, almost all high school dropouts and single mothers living on public assistance. Because the field was so new, Rodriguez and her associates designed the program from scratch, loosely modeling it after Houston's Parent Child Development Center, which had closed from a lack of funds. As Rodriguez studied factors contributing to child abuse and neglect, she found deep rooted problems. Isolation, depression, stress, hopelessness, and helplessness were recurring themes among the mothers. She discovered that the traditional image of a loving, close-knit, Hispanic family was often clouded by overwhelming economic and social conditions. "All of us have the potential to be warm, caring, and nurturing parents," Rodriguez told *Vista* magazine. "But environmental conditions are often adverse to growth . . . parents are under a great deal of stress, channeling all their energy into basic survival. Sometimes they take it out on their children."

Avance's nine-month program gives mothers and their preschool children a support system many have never known. Weekly three-hour sessions are geared to the mental, physical, and social health of the family in a clean, relaxed, safe, and friendly environment. While children play in supervised groups according to age, mothers construct simple toys and picture books to stimulate their child's learning environment and attend classes in child development, discipline techniques, problem-solving skills, nutrition, childhood diseases, and safety procedures. With their children, they take field trips, plant gardens, build friendships, and learn to communicate. Followup visits at home are videotaped, so mothers can watch themselves interacting with their children. "This is a prevention program," Rodriguez told *Vista.* "Before the 1970s, all treatment went to the child. But you can't separate the child from the environment, so you start with the family."

The Dallas Avance program folded after several years, but Rodriguez was determined that the San Antonio program would not meet the same fate. With grants from the City of San Antonio, the United Way, the Carnegie Corporation of New York, the Mailman Foundation, and other private and government sources along the way, Avance grew. In 1989, Avance received a $5 million grant from the Federal Head Start Bureau of the Administration for Children, Youth, and Families, allowing the agency to begin intensive prenatal services and continue them through the child's first five years.

### Expanded Avance Programs

In 1988, Rodriguez launched the groundbreaking Fatherhood Project, a program for Hispanic fathers, many of whom had been initially wary, indifferent, and occasionally hostile toward their wives' involvement with Avance. Rodriguez's goal with the pilot project was identical to the women's programs: Get the men involved in their children's education and in the process motivate them to pursue their own education and job skill training. Additional Avance programs include literacy training and job placement services for parents.

Rodriguez supervises a staff of 120 (many of them Avance graduates) and operates on a $2.7 million annual budget with six sites in San Antonio and one in Houston. Avance has attracted national attention from organizations hoping to duplicate its success. Visiting dignitaries include former first lady Barbara Bush, Great Britain's Prince Charles, former Texas governor Ann Richards, the Reverend Jesse Jackson, and Mexico's first lady Cecilia Occelli de Salinas, who plans to use Avance as a model for a program in Mexico. Expansion into the *colonias* of the Lower Rio Grande Valley in Texas began in 1992 and future programs are planned for Dallas, El Paso, and Puerto Rico.

In 1979, Rodriguez received her second masters degree from the University of Texas at San Antonio, and her Ph.D. in early childhood education from the University of Texas at Austin in 1991. From 1979 to 1982, she was project director for Project C.A.N. (Child Abuse and Neglect), a national demonstration research project. In 1988 Rodriguez was selected by *Hispanic* magazine as one of the 100 Most Influential National Hispanic Leaders. In 1990, she received the first Attitude award, presented by the Lifetime Cable Network show *Attitudes* for changing public attitudes toward family service. She has served as a charter board member of the National Family Resource Coalition, and as a consultant to the Harvard Family Research Project, Georgetown University, and the Yale Bush Center.

As an advocate for children, Rodriguez has participated in the White House Conference on Families, and presented testimony at several congressional hearings. She serves on the Council of Governors Policy Advisors and the Carnegie Corporation of New York Task Force in Early Childhood Education. She is a frequent contributor to the *San Antonio Light* and *Hispanic Link News Service,* and is on the advisory boards of *La Familia de Hoy* magazine, the Council of Families in America, and Parent Action.

Rodriguez married engineer Salvador C. Rodriguez, Jr., on June 17, 1972, and has three children: Salvador Julian, Steven Rene, and Gloria Vanessa.

Rodriguez never forgot her vow to God to use her training to help others, and her responsibility to her ethnic roots: "Some don't believe child abuse exists in the Hispanic community because traditionally we have close family units," she told the *Express-News.* "But that's a fallacy. Child abuse is everywhere—it knows no ethnic or economic barriers." Her faith in God and dedication to Avance's mission guide her in her goal to reach as many impoverished children as possible. She writes in the *San Antonio Light:* "We cannot afford to lose one child or one family to poverty and lack of education. . . . When one child gets hurt, eventually all children can get hurt. When one child hurts, we are all vulnerable."

## SOURCES:

*Business Week,* February 20, 1989, p. 151.
*Dallas Morning News,* February 16, 1992, p. 41A.
*Express-News* (San Antonio), September 4, 1982, p. 1C; April 10, 1983, p. 6E; October 25, 1989; March 27, 1990, p. 11B; March 28, 1990, p. 13A; April 13, 1991, p. 1D; March 22, 1992, p. 1A.
*Fort Worth Star Telegram,* August 25, 1991.
*New York Times,* January 1, 1988, p. 16; January 25, 1988, p. 22; March 8, 1988, p. 8Y.
*Our Kids* (San Antonio), July, 1990, p. 28.
*San Antonio Light,* September 3, 1982, p. B3; January 13, 1988, p. B5; May 22, 1988, p. K1; October 2, 1988; October 24, 1988, p. F2; May 9, 1989, p. B2; May 14, 1989, p. F1; June 11, 1989, p. F1; June 12, 1989, p. E5; September 20, 1989; October 25, 1989; June 6, 1990; June 12, 1990; October 28, 1990; April 11, 1991, p. A1; January 18, 1992, p. A1; January 20, 1992, p. D1; March 8, 1992, p. A1; April 19, 1992; May 10, 1992; July 19, 1992, p. E1; September 3, 1992.
*San Diego Union,* November 26, 1989, p. C8.

*San Juan Star* (Puerto Rico), August 1, 1992.

*Vista,* May 20, 1990, p. 16.

*West Side Sun* (San Antonio), August 30, 1979, p. 38; October 5, 1989; May 16, 1991.

—*Sketch by Julie Catalano*

# Luis Rodriguez
## 1954-
### Mexican American writer and publisher

Luis Javier Rodriguez escaped his youth as a barrio gang member. Instead of meeting a quick and violent end, he grew up to be a spokesman for urban poor on both sides of the Mexican border. In the pages of national magazines, his commentary and poems have followed such tragedies as the Los Angeles riots that erupted in the wake of the Rodney King case verdict. His fictionalized, book-length account of *la vida loca,* or the "crazy life" of gang battles and crimes, won various awards including a fellowship.

Rodriguez is considered to have been born in El Paso, Texas. However, he describes his family in *Always Running* as having been on the move from Mexico to California before and after his birthday, July 9, 1954. Maria Estela (born Jimenez) Rodriguez and Alfonso Rodriguez-Perez settled their family in Watts. However, local job opportunities just could not compare to the financial rewards offered by petty criminals. By the time he was twelve years old, the boy Luis was already enmeshed by the gang lifestyle.

### Introduced to Crips and Bloods

Rodriguez was active during the time the Crips and Bloods developed their quickly infamous rivalry. South Central Los Angeles was the territory, and the common ways to die included drug overdoses, police raids, gang assassinations, and car crashes. By the time he turned 18, Rodriguez had seen enough of his friends die in one or another of these ways. He realized that before he met the same fate, he would have to stop running and make a stable life for himself. He had already been writing in a diary for a few years, a sign of his budding talent. Yet when he reformed himself, Rodriguez first chose employment in heavy industry.

It was as a steel mill worker that he met the girl who would become his first wife, 19-year-old named Camila. Rodriguez recalled in *Always Running* that

*Luis Rodriguez*

his wife had been an A-level student at her high school, yet could not find a job without first enrolling in remedial classes. Things were difficult for the newlywed couple, when both were still in their early twenties. They bore a son, Ramiro, around 1975 and their daughter, Andrea, two years later. However, their marriage ended soon after.

Meanwhile Rodriguez was introduced to a writing career. He benefited from a special educational opportunity, the Summer Program for Minority Journalists, which granted him a certificate in 1980. Various magazines and newspapers accepted his poems and essays, from the *Hungry Mind Review* and *Guadalupe Review* to the *Nation* and the *Los Angeles Times.* He moved to Chicago and started his own publishing concern, the Tia Chucha Press. As the director of Tia Chucha Press, he published a volume of his work called *Poems Across the Pavement* in 1989.

### Reaches Out to Son

Rodriguez was settled down with his third wife, Maria Trinidad Cardenas, and a toddler named Ruben Joaquin, when first son Ramiro was sent to live with the new family. It was 1991, and Rodriguez had just received the PEN Oakland/Josephine Miles Award for excellence in poetry in honor of his second volume, *The Concrete River.* However, the reunion of father and son was uneasy. While Rodriguez's first wife had resisted the encroaching gangs in her own barrio, and Rodriguez managed to wrest himself from *la vida loca,* their son was finding himself in the middle of turf wars wherever he went.

When Rodriguez saw what was happening, he launched a campaign to keep his son from repeating his own youthful mistakes. He tried to keep Ramiro, who was gifted but disruptive, in school. He told the youngster about the Mexican *Pachucos* and the *Cholos,* both forerunners of modern urban Latino gangs in the United States. He tried to impress upon the boy that Latino men who kill each other only manage to kill themselves, by doing away with their own kind.

Finally, Rodriguez was inspired to return to that diary he had begun as a teenager, and finish it as *Always Running.* It was finally dedicated, upon publication, to the 25 companions Rodriguez had lost in his youth to gang warfare. The book went on to be excerpted in a 1993 issue of the *Los Angeles Times,* and was also chosen by the New York Public Library as one of its recommended 1994 books for teens. It won the Carl Sandburg Award for Non-Fiction Book of 1993, the Chicago Sun-Times First Prose Book Award in 1994, and earned its author an Illinois Arts Council Prose Fellowship as well.

## SOURCES:

### Books

Rodriguez, Luis J., *Always Running: la vida loca, gang days in L. A.,* Willimantic, Connecticut, Curbstone Press, 1993.

### Periodicals

*Los Angeles Times,* June 21, 1992, p. M1.
*U.S. News and World Report,* August 1, 1994, p. 31.
*Utne Reader,* July/August 1994, p. 58.

—*Sketch by Jennifer Kramer*

# Paul Rodríguez
## 1955-
### Mexican American comedian, actor, and director

Paul Rodríguez's career as a stand-up comic began as a fluke and blossomed into a multi-faceted life in entertainment, which has encompassed acting for the large and small screens, film directing, and producing for television. He has starred in three series for CBS and numerous films including *D.C. Cab* and *Born in East L.A.* He made his feature film directorial debut with *A Million to Juan,* released in 1994. Rodríguez has also participated in many charitable shows, including the well-known *Comic Relief* and numerous benefits for organizations such as the National Hispanic Scholarship Fund.

Born January 19, 1955, in Mazatlan, Mexico, the youngest of five children, Rodríguez came to the United States at the age of three with his parents and siblings. The family settled in East Los Angeles; his parents took factory jobs until an injury suffered by his father forced the family to become migrant farm workers. Since his childhood, Rodríguez has experienced much racism: from the time his family was refused service at a Crystal, Texas, hamburger stand to a more recent episode in South Pasadena, California. By now a successful film and television actor, he purchased a home in an upscale South Pasadena neighborhood. The local welcoming committee approached him as he did yard work and asked him if he was the "caretaker." Rodríguez credits his sense of humor with helping him to not dwell on people's prejudice. "If I wasn't a comedian, I'd probably be in jail now," he told *Drama-Logue* in 1986.

Rodríguez dropped out of high school and spent much of his teenage years on the streets. After four years of service in the U.S. Air Force, he moved to Long Beach, where he received the equivalent of a high school diploma and used the G.I. Bill to study at Long Beach City College, obtaining his Associate Arts degree. He entered California State University at Long Beach, where he planned to prepare for a career as a lawyer, but an elective theater class changed his future. Rodríguez's drama instructor enjoyed his lampooning of his classmates, when he stage crewed a student production of Tennessee Williams's *The Glass Menagerie.* The instructor, Murray Becker, took him to the Comedy Store's amateur night in Los Angeles, where Rodríguez was offered a job working the door and the chance to perform frequently.

Rodríguez honed his talent as a stand-up comedian throughout his twenties, performing at local clubs and college campuses throughout the country. He ultimately performed as the opening act for concerts. Television producer Norman Lear became a fan, when Rodríguez did a warm-up act for the live audience of Lear's show, *Gloria.* This led Lear to develop Rodríguez's own sitcom, *a.k.a. Pablo,* which was controversial because some members of the Latino community felt the fictional Mexican American family perpetuated stereotypes. The show was short-lived, but Rodríguez regrouped, strengthened relationships with his friends and family, and went on to star in two more television series, *Trial and Error* and *Grand Slam.*

Rodríguez made his film acting debut in 1983, in the comedy *D.C. Cab.* He also co-starred in *Miracles, The Whoopie Boys,* and *Quicksilver.* His most critically acclaimed work for motion pictures film work can be seen in *Born in East L.A.* and *Made in America,* a film co-starring Whoopi Goldberg and Ted Danson.

A decade after his film acting debut, Rodríguez had another "first"—he directed his first film. *A Million to Juan* was a comedy-drama in which he also starred, along with **Edward James Olmos** and **Cheech Marin.** The story is a contemporary adaptation of Mark Twain's "The Million-Pound Bank Note"; Rodríguez described it to the *Long Beach Press-Telegram* as "the only Latino movie that you'll see that's made in America that has no gangs, drugs or cursing in it." Rodríguez stated that he planned to direct additional films in the future. In 1994 he also produced *Loco Slam,* a comedy special for HBO television that gave Latino comedians the opportunity to showcase their talent in front of a broad American audience.

Rodríguez, who has one son, takes seriously his opportunity to serve as a positive role model for Latino youths whose response to their difficult lives is crime. He visited Adobe Mountain, Arizona, a detention center for criminals determined by the courts to be too hard-core for juvenile hall but too young for prison, and was disturbed by what he saw. After performing for the boys, he led a discussion on what they had experienced and missed in their often troubled home lives. The comedian said he feels his generation is partly responsible for the waywardness of many youth living in the 1990s. "We glorified drugs," he lamented to the *Press-Telegram.*

Although he doesn't consider himself a spokesperson, Rodríguez cares about giving something back to the community. In addition to his work for *Comic Relief,* he serves on the board of Education First, hosts the *National Leukemia Telethon,* and has used his talents to support Hurricane Relief, Project Literacy, and other organizations.

## SOURCES:

### Books

*Hispanic-American Almanac,* edited by Nicolás Kanellos, Detroit, Gale, 1993.

### Periodicals

*Dram-Logue,* August 14–20, 1986, p. 14.
*Long Beach Press-Telegram,* March 11, 1994, pp. 3–4.

—*Sketch by Karen Withem*

# Richard Rodriguez
## 1944-
### Mexican American writer

Richard Rodriguez made a name for himself in the literary world and gained media attention unprecedented for a Mexican American writer with the 1981 publication of his autobiography, *Hunger of Memory: The Education of Richard Rodriguez.* While the book garnered widespread praise for its honest and sensitive treatment of the author's educational experiences, it received more notice for its passionate attacks of bilingual education and the affirmative action programs that helped to fund his career as a student. Angering supporters of these fundamental programs of the liberal establishment, Rodriguez's controversial message found a welcome audience in conservative circles. With the publication of his second book, *Days of Obligation: An Argument with My Mexican Father,* Rodriguez—who works as a journalist and essayist for the PBS–sponsored *Mac-Neil-Lehrer NewsHour* while continuing to write—proved to many critics that the literary quality of his writing transcended his political message. "That Richard Rodriguez is a masterful writer, there is no dispute," contended the *Miami Herald*'s Alfonso Chardy. "Everyone agrees on that point, even Rodriguez's harshest critics."

Born July 31, 1944, in San Francisco, Rodriguez was the third of four children born to working-class Mexican immigrants. While raising the family in Sacramento, his father, Leopoldo Rodriguez, worked as a dental technician while his mother, Victoria Moran Rodriguez, stayed at home with the children and worked part-time as a typist. "They were nobody's victims," Rodriguez stated in *Hunger of Memory.* "Optimism and ambition led them to a house many blocks from the Mexican south side of town. We lived among *gringos* and only a block from the biggest, whitest houses."

### Learns English, Gains Confidence

For the first five years of his life, Rodriguez spoke only Spanish, knowing just enough English to run errands for his mother at stores a block away from his home. The familiar sounds of Spanish were soon invaded with the strange words of the English language when young Richard's parents enrolled him in the local Catholic school. Frustrated by six months of silence and little progress, three Irish nuns from the school visited the Rodriguezes and insisted that Richard practice his English at home. His parents were obedient to the "Church's authority," Rodriguez recalled in *Hunger of Memory.* "They agreed to give up the language that had revealed and accentuated our family's closeness. The moment after the visitors left, the change was observed. '*Ahora*, speak to us *en ingles*,' my father and mother united to tell us." With the acquisition of a new language came the acceptance of a new identity: "At last, seven years old, I came to believe what had been technically true since my birth: I was an American citizen."

Rodriguez's newfound confidence in English proved to be the catalyst for a highly successful record of classroom performance. By the time he reached high school, he had read hundreds of books and could mention sophisticated writers such as Dante and Descartes in his term papers. Having taken full advantage of a strong Catholic education, Rodriguez was awarded a scholarship—the first of many—to Stanford University, where he pursued his love of reading and majored in English. After receiving his bachelor's degree in 1967, he continued his studies at Columbia University, where he earned a master's degree in philosophy two years later. Then he entered the Ph.D. program in English at the University of California, Berkeley. In 1974, he was awarded a Fulbright fellowship that enabled him to travel to the Warburg Institute in London, where he worked for a year on a dissertation focusing on Renaissance literature.

### Rejects Affirmative Action

When Rodriguez returned to Berkeley, a promising future as an academic awaited him: recruiters from the nation's finest colleges and universities were inquiring about the talented scholar with the Hispanic surname. The offers from Ivy League schools troubled Rodriguez, however, since he had already developed a reputation as an outspoken critic of affirmative action, publishing essays and delivering speeches condemning the policies that had helped to make him a "scholarship boy." As he saw graduate school colleagues—who possessed similar talents but lacked minority classification—fail to receive job offers, he searched for a way to protest the very hiring policies that promised him such success. "I wanted to teach; I wanted to read; I wanted this life," he stated in *Hunger of Memory*. "But I had to protest. How? Disqualify myself from the profession as long as affirmative action continued? Romantic exile? But I had to. Yes. I found the horizon again. It was calm." Rodriguez further explained the rationale behind his decision to *People*'s Toni Chiu: "There seemed to be nothing that I couldn't have. Yet I knew that I was not the most talented in the department. I knew that white colleagues, as talented as I, were not getting jobs. So I wrote all the schools and asked to be removed from consideration."

Rodriguez hoped to fill the void left by his retreat from academics with a full-time writing career. A fellowship from the National Endowment for the Humanities in 1976 helped to fund the early stages of

*Hunger of Memory*. But the money soon ran out, and Rodriguez was forced to take a variety of jobs—including janitorial work and free-lance writing—to support himself during the six-year period it took to complete the autobiography. Upon the book's publication in 1981, reviews appeared in approximately fifty periodicals—including the *New York Times Book Review*, which placed its article on the front page—arguably the most for any Mexican American author. The book was further recognized with the Christopher Award the following year.

### Autobiography Stirs Controversy

*Hunger of Memory*, as Rodriguez contended in the book's prologue, is primarily "a book about language," which he called the "great subject" of his life. Identifying himself with Shakespeare's Caliban, Rodriguez discussed how he had "stolen" the language of *los gringos*, learning to speak the "public" language of English at the expense of the "private" Spanish of his home. It was this discussion of the fundamental role language plays in education and his concomitant views of bilingual education that generated the most critical attention—and the most fervent disagreement. Paul Zweig of the *New York Times Book Review* summarized the author's controversial viewpoint: "Advocates of bilingual education are wrong, he insists, in supposing that the values of home life are embodied in language, not persons. If students at school can learn their home language, it is claimed they will be less disoriented and better able to attend to the business of schooling. But the business of schooling is to take children out of the home and thrust upon them a new set of demands. Education, to work, must change children . . . it must teach them a new voice, less charged with intimate feelings than the old language, less comfortable, but appropriate to the impersonal world in which self-respect, success, money, culture, are won."

Rodriguez's rejection of bilingual education was denounced by Mexican and Chicano nationalists, who have maintained that he betrayed his ethnic identity while choosing to speak to a white audience. "People have accused me of losing my heritage," Rodriguez confirmed in a *People* interview. "That assumes heritage is this little suitcase I carry with me, with tortillas and a little Mexican cowboy suit inside, and then one day I lost it at a Greyhound depot. The fact is, culture survives whether you want it to or not." Antonio C. Marquez, a notable professor of Chicano literature, suggested in *Arizona Quarterly* that arguments over the book's political message should not overshadow its aesthetic achievements: "There is a level of artistry in *Hunger of Memory* that should not be shunned simply because Rodriguez does not meet the Procrustean bed of 'cultural awareness' or any other ideology. I contend that its ultimate value lies in its literary qualities and the uniqueness of its autobiographical form." Reviews from other prominent periodicals underscored this point. The *New Yorker*, for instance, praised Rodriguez as "a writer of unusual grace and clarity," while Zweig commended him for being "uncannily sensitive to the nuances of language learning, the childhood drama of voices, intonations."

Rodriguez's much-awaited second book, *Days of Obligation: An Argument with My Mexican Father*, did not appear until a decade later. As the title suggests, this book—more so than the first—focused on his identification with Mexican culture. "The first book was my confrontation with the United States and my Americanization. The new book is my confrontation with Mexico," Rodriguez told the *Miami Herald*. While *Days of Obligation* perhaps revealed a greater receptiveness to his Mexican roots, Rodriguez vehemently denied that it was intended to be a repudiation of his controversial positions on affirmative action and bilingual education. *Newsweek*'s Malcolm Jones, Jr., contended that "It is not so much a recantation of its predecessor as it is a more personal, less didactic rethinking of the same issues. Rodriguez still believes in the 'dreadful metaphor' of the melting pot, but he has become more sensitive to the loss of cultural identity that comes with assimilation."

Continuing in the autobiographical mode, Rodriguez "takes the confessional voice of *Hunger of Memory* one step further, proclaiming himself a practicing homosexual and a Catholic who still believes in original sin," observed *The Nation*'s Victor Perera. Rodriguez expressed his despair over the AIDS crisis, writing poignantly about friends he lost; however, the book's greatest contribution, in the view of most critics, centered again around his opinions on the conflicting cultures that form his identity. Perera went so far as to compare Rodriguez's book to 1990 Nobel laureate **Octavio Paz**'s 1950s masterwork on U.S.-Mexican relations, *The Labyrinth of Solitude*. Perera stated that the younger author "[upends] its fundamental premise of the North's economic and cultural domination over the South," positing instead that Mexico "is poised to overcome her tired, fast-declining neighbor to the north." Such a message, however, has not generated the same level of media attention as its predecessor. This, as Jones contended, "is a point in its favor. There is more here to chew on. Rodriguez has grown from being a man who demands our attention to a man who warrants it."

## SELECTED PUBLISHED WORKS:

### Books

*Days of Obligation: An Argument with My Mexican Father*, New York, Viking, 1992.
*Hunger of Memory: The Education of Richard Rodriguez*, Boston, Godine, 1981.

### Other

"A Minority Scholar Speaks Out," *Forum*, November, 1982, pp. 2–5.
"California Christmas Carols," *California*, December 1983, p. 99.
"The Head of Joaquin Murrieta," *Nuestro*, November 1985, pp. 30–36.
"The Mexicans Among Us," *Reader's Digest*, March 1986, pp. 171–176.
"Mexico's Children," *American Scholar*, Spring 1986, pp. 161–167.

## SOURCES:

### Books

*Contemporary Authors*, Vol. 110, edited by Hal May, Detroit, Gale, 1984.
*Dictionary of Literary Biography*, Vol. 82, edited by Francisco A. Lomelí, Detroit, Gale, 1989.
*Hispanic Writers*, edited by Bryan Ryan, Detroit, Gale, 1991.

### Periodicals

*Arizona Quarterly*, Summer 1984, pp. 130–41.
*Miami Herald*, November 21, 1992.
*Nation*, January 18, 1993, pp. 63–5.
*Newsweek*, December 14, 1992, pp. 80–1.
*New York Times Book Review*, February 1982, pp. 1, 26.
*People*, August 16, 1982, pp. 75–9.
*Time*, January 25, 1993, pp. 69–70.

—*Sketch by Jason Gallman*

# Robert Rodriguez
## 1969(?)-
### Mexican American filmmaker

When he was 24, a Mexican American film student from Texas named Robert Rodriguez outwitted Hollywood's experts and received almost instant recognition for making his first Western-style film, *El Mariachi*, for a mere $7,000. Young, intelligent, self-reliant, and financially inventive, Rodriguez has joined the ranks of other young filmmakers whom major studios are recruiting.

Audiences at both the Toronto and Sundance film festivals voted Rodriguez's Spanish-language movie—which he directed, co-produced, and edited, initially for the Mexican home-video market—as their favorite. It has been distributed with English subtitles in the United States by Columbia Pictures, which signed Rodriguez. An action-adventure story, *El Mariachi* features a traveling mariachi musician who arrives in a Mexican village at the same time as a narcotics dealer who is looking to settle some unfinished business with the village's drug lord. Since each carries a guitar case, their identities are confused and the musician finds himself being chased by the drug lord's assassins.

In his *New Yorker* review, Terrence Rafferty wrote: "Rodriguez, cannily, doesn't try to persuade us that he's turning base metal into gold. He's smart enough to recognize that in a shoot-'em-up genre piece like this one we don't actually need anything grander or pricier than lead, and he pumps the movie full of it. . . . [He] establishes a delirious pace—pausing only infrequently to attend to unavoidable narrative business—and keeps the bullets flying and the corpses crumpling for a brisk, and appropriately terse, eighty-two minutes. . . . He's no visual wizard—his fast cutting isn't always coherent, and he's much too fond of wide-angle lenses—but as a pop storyteller he's sly and often witty; he knows how to fulfill the audience's most fundamental narrative expectations."

## Made Home Movies as Youngster

Rodriguez—one of ten children of a nurse and a sales manager in the cookware business—raised almost half the money for his movie by volunteering to participate in a research-hospital study involving cholesterol-reducing drugs that was being conducted in Austin, Texas, his hometown. The young filmmaker, who also wrote the script for *El Mariachi*, has been making home movies since he was 12 years old, when he used the camera his father carried to make sales presentations.

One of these films—a brief comedy called *Bedhead*—was told from his nine-year-old sister's perspective and starred all of his siblings. *Bedhead* received awards at 14 festivals, including the Melbourne International Film Festival. As a youngster Rodriguez made movie "flip books" and went with his brothers and sisters to see Alfred Hitchcock and Marx Brothers film revivals, because his mother didn't have enough money to take them to newly released movies.

While studying film at the University of Texas in Austin, Rodriguez decided to make a film in Mexico. Using himself as his film crew and amateur actors who worked for free, Rodriguez constructed the screenplay for *El Mariachi* around what was available to him during the 14 days he spent shooting the film in Acuna, Mexico. As a result he used a hotel, two bars, a school bus, a motorcycle, a pit bull, and a

turtle as the elements in his story. He shot everything with a borrowed camera in one take per scene on 16mm film and then edited on videotape. Because the camera was noisy and not synchronized he was forced to record a separate audio track of the dialogue.

## Offered Deal by Columbia Pictures

His plan simply was to shoot three *Mariachi* films for the Mexican video market, financing each sequel with money earned from the previous movie. The video company he had in mind reneged on its promise to release the film, so Rodriguez dropped off a reel of his short films and a trailer for *El Mariachi* at the International Creative Management agency. Soon after, they asked to see the whole movie and accepted him as a client.

A short time later, Columbia Pictures offered him a two-picture deal that includes an *El Mariachi* sequel entitled *Desperado*. The new film, released in 1995, starred Antonio Banderas in the role of the mariachi. Picking up where the first movie ended, Banderas was out for revenge against the drug lord who killed his girlfriend.

## SOURCES:

*Daily News,* February 26, 1993; February 28, 1993, p. 5.
*Face,* May, 1993, p. 130.
*Los Angeles Times,* May 31, 1992, pp. 18, 34.
*New York Native,* March 15, 1993, p. 25.
*New York Post,* February 26, 1993.
*New York Observer,* March 29, 1993.
*New York Times,* January 28, 1993, pp. C15, C19; February 21, 1993, Sec. 2, p. 21; February 26, 1993.
*New Yorker,* February 22, 1993, pp. 169–170.
*Newsday,* February 25, 1993, pp. 52, 81.
*Time,* March 8, 1993, p. 66.
*Village Voice,* October 6, 1992; March 2, pp. 50, 52; March 9, 1993, p. 67.
*Women's Wear Daily,* February 23, 1993, p. 4.

—*Sketch by Alison Carb Sussman*

# Ricardo Rojas
## 1882-1957
### Argentine historian and critic

Ricardo Rojas was a well-respected, prolific Argentine writer and educator. Rojas, a liberal, was a strong voice for Argentine nationalism throughout his life. His greatest historical work was *El Santo de la Espada* ("The Saint of the Sword") a biography of the renowned Argentine liberator José de San Martín.

Born September 16, 1882, in Tucumán, Argentina, Rojas was the son of a mixed marriage: his mother was an Indian and his father was Spanish. Later in life Rojas was proud to have earned the sobriquet "the Indian Rojas." The family left Tucumán shortly after his birth, and Rojas grew up in Santiago del Estero, which Rojas considered the last province of the Incan Empire. His father, Don Absalón, was governor of the province.

Rojas received his secondary education in Santiago del Estero and chose to study law in Buenos Aires. But he grew dissatisfied with the law and soon began a career as a journalist, referring to himself as a "perpetual unenrolled student." The city and its urban life opened Rojas's eyes and mind. His rural-born mindset was in stark contrast to the attitudes in the capital city at the turn of the century. Buenos Aires was a city of intensity, burgeoning with vital new ideas, grandeur, and optimism. Rojas—dazzled but critical—embarked on a mission to explore and examine the national identity.

He began writing in ways that promoted subjects of a Hispanic American nature and focused on a sense of national spiritual identity. Rojas validated the indigenous cultural heritage of Argentines but did not discount Spain's contribution. He tackled the pessimism of other writers first with a condemnation of **Domingo F. Sarmiento,** who had castigated the synthesis of Indian and Spanish cultures in Argentina.

Rojas began this dialectic with his 1903 poems, *La victoria del hombre*. He continued to write about these issues in story form in 1907 with *El país de la selva* ("The Jungle Country"), and again in the essays collected in *Cosmópolis* in 1908. Rojas strongly opposed the contemptuous attitudes of many Argentinians—especially the Buenos Aires urbanites—who opposed transculturation. Rojas also supported the immigrants who flooded into Argentina, adding to the country's culture.

Rojas was respected as a voice of the people and the nation. In 1927, the University of Buenos Aires awarded him an honorary doctorate. Many other Argentine and foreign universities followed. The attention was due in large part to two of Rojas's publications. His four-volume work *La literatura argentina* (*Argentine Literature* 1917–1922), a comprehensive collection of poetry, drama, biography, essay, and history, spoke with sensitivity of Argentina's Spanish and Native American past. In addition, his book *El Cristo invisible* ("The Invisible Christ") illustrated Rojas's religious and mystical knowledge.

After receiving his honorary doctorate, Rojas served as president of the University of Buenos Aires, dean of the School of Philosophy and Letters, chair of the department of Spanish literature, and later, chair of the department of Argentine literature—this last his own creation. Despite a heavy teaching load, he continued to write prolifically as well.

Eventually, Rojas's politics worked against him. He criticized the government, its supposedly free electoral process, and its supposed democratic ideals. First he was imprisoned. In the early 1940s, he was banished to the southernmost tip of Argentina by President Agustin P. Justo. During these years Rojas wrote his two great biographical works: *El santo de la espada* ("*Saint of the Sword*," 1933) about San Martín and *El profeta de la pampa* ("*Prophet of the Pampa*," 1945) about Sarmiento. These works extolled heroic values; a revival of past ideas in which he hoped to inspire a stronger nation independent of colonialism; materialism; and depersonalization.

Rojas was "an incorruptible interpreter of Argentine reality" according to Antonio Pagés Larraya. Although he felt morally and physically ostracized from his own country during the last decade of his life, he continued to speak for the ideals of independence. He died on July 29, 1957.

## SELECTED PUBLISHED WORKS:

### Poetry

*La victoria del hombre*, Buenos Aires, 1903.
*Las lises del blasón*, Buenos Aires, 1911.
*Canciones*, Buenos Aires, 1920.
*Oda latina*, Buenos Aires, 1954.

### Plays

*Elelín*, Buenos Aires, 1929.
*La casa colonial*, Buenos Aires, 1938.
*Ollantay*, Buenos Aires, 1939.
*La salamanca*, Buenos Aires, 1943.

### Other

*El país de la selva* (short stories), Paris, 1907.
*El alma española*, Valencia, 1908.
*Cartas de Europa*, Barcelona, 1908.
*Cosmópolis*, Paris, 1908.
*Le restauración nacionalista*, Buenos Aires, 1909.

*Blasón de plata,* Buenos Aires, 1912.

*La argentinidad,* Buenos Aires, 1916.

*La literatura argentina* 4 vols. Buenos Aires, 1917–1922.

*Los arqueitipos,* Buenos Aires, 1922.

*Eurindia,* Buenos Aires, 1924.

*El Cristo invisible,* Buenos Aires, 1927; translated as *The Invisible Christ* by Webster E. Browning, New York, 1931.

*Las provincias,* Buenos Aires, 1927.

*Silabario de la decoración americana,* Buenos Aires, 1930.

*El radicalismo de mañana,* Buenos Aires, 1932.

*El santo de la espada: Vida de San Martín,* Buenos Aires, 1933; translated as *San Martín, Knight of the Andes,* New York, Cooper Square, 1967.

*Cervantes,* Buenos Aires, 1935.

*Retablo español,* Buenos Aires, 1938.

*Archipélago: Tierra del Fuego,* Buenos Aires, 1942.

*El profeta de la pampa: Vida de Sarmiento,* Buenos Aires, 1945.

*Un titan de los Andes,* Buenos Aires, 1949.

*Ensayo de crítica histórica sobre episodios de la vida internacional argentina,* Buenos Aires, 1951.

## Collected Works

*Obras de Ricardo Rojas,* 29 vols., 1923–1930.

*Obras completas de Ricardo Rojas,* 30 vols. Buenos Aires, 1947–1953.

## SOURCES:

### Books

*Argentina,* by Arthur Whitaker, Englewood Cliffs, NJ, Prentice-Hall, 1965.

*In Quest of Identity,* by Martin Stabb, Chapel Hill, NC, 1967.

*Latin American Writers,* vol. 2, edited Carlos A. Sole, New York, Charles Scribner's Sons, 1989.

### Periodicals

*Hispanic American Historical Review,* 1963, pp. 1–13.

*New York Times,* July 31, 1957.

—*Sketch by Christopher B. Tower*

# Cesar Romero
## 1907-1994
### Cuban American actor and dancer

Born to entertain, Cesar Romero grew up in New York City and started his career as a dancer on Broadway. He soon moved from stage to screen. During his career he appeared in more than 40 motion pictures, usually cast as the suave Latin lothario. The self-dubbed "Latin from Manhattan" eventually made it to the small screen as well, playing the memorable role of "The Joker" in the television series *Batman.* Never married, Romero moved among the elite of Hollywood's social scene for decades, remaining active until shortly before his death in 1994.

### Youth in New York

Romero was born on February 15, 1907, in Manhattan. His father, Cesar Julio Romero, exported machinery, and his mother, Maria Mantilla, had a modestly successful career as a singer. His grandfather was the Cuban revolutionary **Jose Marti**. According to *Variety,* Romero once called Marti "the liberator of Cuba," stating that "The Cuban War of Independence was planned in my grandfather's house." Both of his parents had immigrated to the United States from Cuba, and from the beginning Romero's professional inclinations led him away from the machinery business. In a 1965 interview quoted in the *Los Angeles Times,* Romero said that he always wanted to be in his mother's business rather than his father's: "If his business had succeeded, I'd be exporting nuts, bolts, and sugar machinery right now. What an awful thought!" From a very early age, Romero knew that his talents lay elsewhere.

Romero began his career as a dancer, appearing first in the 1927 Broadway production *Lady Do.* Romero started to get stage roles after producer Brock Pemberton spotted him in the Manhattan nightclub known as the Montmartre. Romero described that period of his life as one of elegance, but not money. His good looks, combined with his impeccable taste in fashion, made him a welcome gate-crasher at the social functions of the Broadway power brokers. This gave him much-needed exposure to the show business elite, like Pemberton.

Pemberton first cast Romero in a comedy production called *Strictly Dishonorable.* As Count Di Ruvo, Romero stepped in to replace the actor originally playing the role. From there, Romero appeared in several plays during the late 1920s and early 1930s, including the very successful *Dinner at Eight,* which opened in 1932 and ran for 300 performances. Over

*Cesar Romero*

those years, Romero went from supporting to starring roles, prompting him to consider a move into cinema.

## On to Hollywood

Romero impressed Metro-Goldwyn Mayer (MGM) executives at a screen test in 1934, and they cast him that same year as Jorgensen in *The Thin Man.* His success with the film earned him a three-year contract with Universal Pictures, during which time he starred opposite actresses Margaret Sullavan and Carole Lombard. In 1937, Romero co-starred with Shirley Temple in the film *Wee Willie Winkie* and made quite a splash in his role as Koda-Khan. MGM offered him a fourteen-year contract for motion pictures, which he accepted.

Although Romero had great success in getting roles and recognition, he also faced the typecasting many Hispanic actors experience even now. Many contemporary Latinos in show business complain that the only roles available portray them as thugs, drug dealers, or pimps, but in the 1930s—the age of Rudolph Valentino—Latin actors inevitably played the role of the debonair lover. In a 1984 interview, quoted in *Variety,* Romero discussed typecasting in the 1930s: "When I started in motion pictures in 1934, they said I was going to be the next Valentino. I was never a leading man and very seldom did I do a picture where I got the girl. But I was saddled with the label because I had a Latin name," he recalled. Although he never reached the celebrity of Valentino,

neither did Romero manage to escape the former's shadow. Romero portrayed "The Cisco Kid" in the series of the same name in the late 1930s, and 1940 brought *The Gay Caballero.* Many observers now see these roles as examples of ones in which producers and directors would typecast Hispanics regardless of their individual character as artists.

Romero joined the war effort in 1943, signing up for the U.S. Coast Guard. As an enlisted man, the famous actor accepted an ignominious role in serving his country. As he explained at the time as quoted in *Variety:* "I'm satisfied to go in at the bottom—that's the best way to learn what things are all about." While serving in the Pacific theater, Romero used his fame to rally workers at home and soldiers abroad to continue their efforts. Although he started at "the bottom," he did not stay there. By the time he returned to Hollywood in 1946, Romero had risen to the highest possible non-commissioned officer rank of chief boatswain's mate, equivalent to an army master sergeant.

Romero continued his string of successful light comedies through the late 1940s and 1950s. Appearing in movies such as *The Little Princess, Tales of Manhattan,* and *Carnival in Costa Rica,* Romero worked with many of the most celebrated actresses of the day, like Ginger Rogers. During this time he also appeared in several musicals.

In the 1950s his contract with MGM expired, but he had no trouble finding work in films, including the classic *Around the World in 80 Days,* and increasingly on the small screen. His transition to television proved to be as smooth as his earlier one to film. He appeared frequently on the enormously popular variety shows of the day—Milton Berle, Martha Raye, Dinah Shore, Betty Hutton, Red Skelton, and Jimmy Stewart all welcomed Romero on their programs. He guest-starred on *Passport to Danger* and in the late 1950s took the role that became his identity in the eyes of a generation.

## The Joker Slows Down

As Batman's arch-enemy, "The Joker," Romero donned white face paint and a green wig in the popular 1950s and 1960s series. Some film critics regret that baby boomers have no other image of Romero to balance against the cackling super-villain, but other observers suggest that Romero simply knew how to change with the times. Romero himself started to slow down in the 1960s, giving up professional dancing. After a rare dance appearance in the 1960s, Romero lamented in the *Los Angeles Times,* "Out of shape, oh, brother! I was wearing corn plasters above and below my toes and taping my ankles twice."

He appeared in his last film, *Now You See Him, Now You Don't,* in 1972, the same year he briefly bought and managed a restaurant in Los Angeles called Cappucino. After that, Romero did most of his work on the dinner theater circuit, including productions like *My Three Angels* and *The Max Factor*.

In 1984 Romero received an award for 50 years in the film industry at the Hollywood International Celebrity Award Banquet, followed in the same year by the Nosotros Golden Eagle for success as a Hispanic in show business. In 1991 he received the Imagen Hispanic Media Award for Lifetime Achievement, and in 1992 the Beverly Hills Chamber of Commerce gave him the Will Rogers Memorial Award.

Throughout his life, Romero remained a devoted bachelor, believing in 1984 that—even at age 77—a family would never fit into his busy schedule. Though single, he lived with members of his extended family, including his parents for many years, and later his nieces and nephews.

His peers in the film industry admired him for his upbeat personality and youthful spirit. According to the *Los Angeles Times,* Romero once joked, "I can't date women my own age anymore—I hate going to cemeteries." In 1965, an arts editor for the *New York Times* said, "Mr. Romero seems to have access to the same anti-age potion as [actor] Cary Grant." Romero continued to work for several charities, serving Thanksgiving dinner to the homeless less than two months before his death. He died on January 1, 1994, from complications related to pneumonia and bronchitis.

## SELECTED VIDEOGRAPHY:

*The Thin Man,* 1934.
*Show Them No Mercy,* 1935.
*Metropolitan,* 1935.
*Love before Breakfast,* 1936.
*Wee Willie Winkie,* 1937.
*Happy Landing,* 1938.
*My Lucky Star,* 1938.
*The Return of the Cisco Kid,* 1939.
*The Gay Caballero,* 1940.
*Captain from Castille,* 1947.
*Carnival in Costa Rica,* 1947.
*Deep Waters,* 1948.
*That Lady in Ermine,* 1948.
*Happy Go Lovely,* 1951.
*Lost Continent,* 1951.
*Prisoners of the Casbah,* 1953.
*The Americano,* 1955.
*Around the World in 80 Days,* 1956.
*Oceans 11,* 1960.
*The Castilian,* 1963.
*Sergeant Deadhead,* 1964.
*Marriage on the Rocks,* 1965.
*Now You See Him, Now You Don't,* 1972.

## SOURCES:

*Los Angeles Times,* January 3, 1994, p. A3.
*Variety,* January 10, 1994, p. 68.

—*Sketch by James McCarthy*

# José Rubén Romero
## 1890-1952
### Mexican novelist, poet, and diplomat

Famous for his internationally acclaimed novel, *La vida inútil de Pito Pérez* ("The Futile Life of Pito Pérez," 1938), Romero was also a prominent Mexican diplomat, who represented his country in Spain, Brazil, and Cuba.

José Rubén Romero was born on September 25, 1890 in Cotija de la Paz, in the state of Michoacán, to Melesio Romero and Refugio González. His father, a descendent of one of the original families in his native village, was a store owner and an administrator. In 1898 the Romero family moved to Mexico City, where they resided for seven years. Romero attended Pedro Barona's elementary school, where he showed an interest in nineteenth century Spanish and French literature. He began scribbling his own verses and was awarded with a signed copy of Amado Nervo's *Misticas* for his efforts.

Romero's family moved again when Romero's father was appointed District Prefect for Ario de Rosales. At the age of 14, Romero founded and contributed to the weekly magazine *Iris*. His father was dismissed and moved his family to Pátzcuaro (some sources say Tacácambaro), where Romero published his first prose, *De invierno* ("Of Winter"). Shortly after, the Romero family relocated to Sahuayo, where Romero procured his first job at the age of 17, as an administrator in the revenue office. His poetry was published in several of the state's newspapers, including *El Constitucional*. In 1908, his first collection of poems, *Fantásias* ("Fantasies") was published.

Romero's father was transferred to Santa Clara del Cobre; a move that proved to be of profound significance to Romero. It was there that he met his future wife, Mariana García, and Pito Pérez, the subject of his most successful novel. Romero was employed by General Salvador Escalante, Subprefect of Santa Clara and soon rose to the position of Chief of Staff. In 1911 Romero participated in the Madero Revolution, siding with the rebels in opposition to the dictator **Porfírio Díaz**. In the 1912 elections under the revolutionary government, he campaigned on behalf on Dr. Miguel Silva, who was elected State Governor of Michoacán; Romero was designated his private secretary and moved to the state capital Morelia.

In the counterrevolution of 1913, led by Victoriano Huerta, President Francisco I. Madero was assassinated. Romero was forced to seek refuge in Mexico City, and then in Morelia, where he avoided execution only through the expeditious intervention of his father and influential friends. In the ensuing years Romero withdrew to a quieter life in Tacámbaro, managing a small retail store. In 1917 he married Mariana García. In the same year he was compelled to flee Morelia, when the revolutionaries, under José Inés Chávez García devastated Tacámbaro. The move proved fortuitous; Romero was appointed Private Secretary to Pascual Ortiz Rubio, the governor of Michoacán. He also began teaching at the old Colegio de San Nicolás, where he remained until 1919 when he was nominated as the Permanent Representative of the Government of Michoacán to the Federal Executive Commission in Mexico City. In Mexico City he began contributing to the daily newspaper *El Universal*. In 1920 Álvaro Obregón was elected president, and he recruited Romero to the Department of Communications. The following year Romero became Director of the Office of Publicity in the Department of Foreign Relations.

Romero's friend Ortiz Rubio was elected President of Mexico in 1930, auguring the start of Romero's diplomatic career. Romero was appointed Consul General to Barcelona in Spain, where nostalgic reminiscences of his native land inspired him to write his first novel, *Apuntes de un Lugareño* ("Notes of a Villager," 1932). Of his feelings, he wrote, "My absence from my country developed into an insatiable longing to memorialize it, and I found a way of embodying my memories by writing down and describing what I carried within me of my land, my province, my childhood spent in an old country house, and my youth as a nomad in the villages and fields of my beloved Michoacán." The success of this novel prompted him to focus his attention on fiction. He returned to Mexico in 1934, becoming Director General of the Registro Civil. Romero was reappointed Consul General to Barcelona under President **Lázaro Cárdenas**, serving from 1935 to 1937. There he published *Mi caballo, mi perro y mi rifle* ("My Horse, My dog, and My Rifle," 1937), a portrayal of the Mexican Revolution. Although Romero supported the revolutionaries, this novel reveals his disillusionment; his protagonist, Julián Osorio, criticizes the revolutionary leaders for their greed and lack of real empathy with the poor.

In 1937 Romero was appointed Ambassador to Brazil. There he wrote his masterpiece, *La vida inútil de Pito Pérez* ("The Futile Life of Pito Pérez," 1938), a picaresque chronicle of the life of the real Pito Pérez, Jesús Pérez Gaona. As testimony of its popularity, it endured as a best-seller in Mexico for 25 years. Romero returned from Brazil in 1939 and was named Ambassador to Cuba, where he remained until 1945.

In July of 1950 Romero was awarded a chair in the Academia Mexicana de la Lengua (Mexican Academy of Language) in recognition of his contribution to Mexican literature. He helped establish a committee for the language academics of the Spanish-speaking world, serving as Vice President and Treasurer until his death in Mexico City on July 4, 1952, of a heart attack.

## SELECTED PUBLISHED WORKS:

### Novels

*Apuntes de un lugareño*, A. Núñez, 1932, translation by John Mitchell and Ruth M. De Aguilar published as *Notes of a Villager: A Mexican Poet's Youth and Revolution*, Plover Press, 1988.

*El pueblo inocente*, Imprenta Mundial, 1934.

*Desbandada*, 1934, A. Núñez, 1936.

*Mi caballo, mi perro y mi rifle*, A. Núñez, 1936.

*La vida inútil de Pito Pérez*, México Nuevo, 1938, translation by William O. Cord published as *The Futile Life of Pito Pérez*, Prentice-Hall, 1966.

*Anticipación de la muerte*, J. R. Romero, 1939.

*Una vez fui rico*, Imprenta Aldina, 1942.

*Rosenda*, Porrúa, 1946.

### Other

*Sentimental* (poems), Talleres Gráficos de Herrero Hermanos, 1919.

*Semblanza de una mujer*, J. R. Romero, 1941.

*Rostros*, Imprenta Aldina, 1942.

*Algunas cosillas de Pito Pé que se me quedaron en el tinero* (aphorisms), viñ de Oscar Frías, 1945.

*Como leemos el "Quijote"* (essay), 1945.

*Obras completas*, prologue by Antonio Castro Leal, Oasis, 1957.

*Cuentos y poesías inéditos* (stories and poems), edited by Cord, Ediciones de Andrea, 1963.

(With others) *Cervantes y Don Quijote*, Secretaria de Educación Pública, 1972.

*Alvaro Obregón*, Cultura, 1976.

## SOURCES:

### Books

Franco, Jean, *An Introduction to Spanish-American Literature*, Cambridge, Cambridge University Press, 1969.

*Hispanic Writers: A Selection of Sketches from Contemporary Authors,* edited by Bryan Ryan, Detroit, Gale, 1991.

*Latin American Literature in the Twentieth Century,* edited by Leonard S. Klein, Herpenden, England, Oldcastle Books, 1988.

*Latin American Writers,* Volume 3, edited by Carlos A. Solé, New York, Charles Scribner's Sons, 1989.

*Spanish American Authors: The Twentieth Century,* edited by Angel Flores, New York, The H. W. Wilson Company, 1992.

**Periodicals**

*Modern Language Journal,* No. 7, November 1953, pp. 3–338.

*New York Times,* July 6, 1952, p. 49.

*Time,* February 17, 1967, p. 58.

—*Sketch by Amanda Beresford*

*Juan Carlos Romero*

# Juan Carlos Romero
## 1937-

### Argentine American physiologist

Juan Carlos Romero is a renowned authority on the physiology of the kidney. In the past 30 years, he has issued more than 175 research papers on the functioning of the kidney. As director of the Hypertension Research Laboratories at the Mayo Clinic since 1982, he has been a prolific investigator into the relationship of the kidney to the development of hypertension, or high blood pressure. Although the human kidney is usually considered to be primarily a vital organ of excretion, with its million or so microscopic nephrons filtering wastes out of the bloodstream, it also helps maintain the appropriate balance of water and mineral salts in the body. In addition, it has been found to play a key role in the incidence of hypertension. Under certain conditions, the kidney secretes the enzyme renin, which reacts in the blood with a protein secreted by the liver to form angiotensin, a vasoconstrictor that causes the smooth muscles of small blood vessels to contract, resulting in an elevation blood pressure.

Romero has done considerable research on the renin-angiotensin system. He has also explored the effects of the atrial natriuretic peptide, produced by the atria of the heart when the blood pressure and volume of blood entering the atria are too high; this natriuretic peptide then stimulates the kidneys to excrete more salt and water into the urine, resulting in a lowering of the volume of blood and of the blood pressure.

Among other areas of Romero's expertise are: renal prostaglandin; renal synthesis of nitric oxide; responses of isolated glomeruli; and evaluation of renal function with fast cine computerized tomophy. In connection with the latter investigation, in 1991 he received the *Cum Laude* Research Award from the American Society of Computed Body Tomography for the best scientific work on cross-sectional imaging.

### Early Years

Romero born on September 15, 1937 in Mendosa, Argentina, the son of Juan Romero and Graciela (Vizcaya). He attended San Jose College in his native city and graduated with a B.S. in 1955. The next year, he was admitted to the University of Cuyo School of Medicine, Mendoza. While there, he was awarded a scholarship for being one of the two best qualified students. He took time out for military service in the Argentine Army in 1958, and rose to the rank of sergeant. He married Silvia Divinetz in 1963 with whom he eventually had two children, Patricia and Gabriela.

Romero began his career in scientific investigation when he became a research assistant in the Institute of Pathological Physiology in 1962. He then returned to medical education, receiving his M.D. in

1964. Then he continued his research efforts as a Fellow at the Onsefo Nacional de Investigaciones Cientificas, also in Mendoza, in 1966.

Romero has been honored with the competitive award of Fellow in the Eli Lilly in 1967; he came to the United States and continued with his research at the University of Michigan. There, he rose to the position of research associate in the Hypertension Section of the Department of Internal Medicine. In 1973, he left for the Mayo Foundation, Rochester, Minnesota, and has remained there ever since, becoming professor of physiology at the Mayo Medical School, and Director of the Hypertension Research Laboratories.

Romero was elected to Sigma Xi, and received a competitive award as Established Investigator of the American Heart Association, 1976 to 1981. He also won the Teacher of the Year Award of the Mayo School of Medicine in 1981. In 1991, he was elected by the Council for High Blood Pressure Research to give the Lewis K. Dahl Memorial Lecture in the American Heart Association's 464th Scientific cession. He has been a key member and chairman of numerous groups specializing in hypertension. Through the years, Romero has also been associated with 20 different scientific journals. Since 1984, he has been awarded grants from National Institute of Health totaling more than $3 million for research and training programs dealing with kidney function and hypertension. He is now a U.S. citizen.

## SELECTED PUBLISHED WORKS:

*Hypertension Physiopathology and Treatment,* edited by J. Genest, E. Koiw, D. Kuchel, New York, McGraw-Hill, 1977.
*Renal Function Tests: Clinical Laboratory Procedures and Diagnosis,* edited by C. Duarte, Boston, Little Brown, 1979.

## SOURCES:

*American Journal of Physiology,* 1986.
*Hypertension,* Volume 23, 1994.
*Physiologist,* Volume 24, 1981.

—*Sketch by Maurice Bleifeld*

# Oscar Romero
## 1917-1980
**Salvadoran Roman Catholic archbishop**

Oscar Arnulfo Romero y Galdamez was a conservative man of the church who was drawn into a violent political conflict in a country divided by turmoil and class struggle. He became an outspoken advocate of non-violence and a voice for the *campasinos,* or peasants of El Salvador during a time of political upheaval. His own violent and untimely death brought international attention to the brutal oppression and human rights violations being carried out by the military government in El Salvador during the 1970s.

Oscar Arnulfo Romero y Galdamez was born on August 15, 1917, in Ciudad Barrios, in the department of San Miguel. He was the second of eight children born to Santos Romero and Guadalupe de Jesus Galdamez. The family lived near the town plaza in a small home that also served as the telegraph office for the town. Romero's father worked as a telegrapher and postmaster, and the children helped by delivering letters and telegrams in town.

Romero was a serious and studious child. He attended the public schools, which offered classes only as far as grade three. After that, his parents sent him to study with a private teacher until he was nearly twelve years old. His father then apprenticed him to work with a carpenter.

In 1930, Romero left his small village to begin his training in the nearby seminary in San Miguel. In 1937, he continued with his theological studies in the national seminary in San Salvador, which was run by Jesuits. Later that year, Romero was sent to the Gregorian University in Rome, where he completed his studies and received his licentiate degree in theology. On April 4, 1942, he was ordained a priest, at the age of 24.

He returned home to his family in El Salvador around Christmas in 1943, and celebrated his first mass in Ciudad Barrios on January 11, 1944. Romero worked in the town of Anamoros for a few months before he was called to San Miguel to serve as the secretary of the diocese, a post he held for 23 years. While in San Miguel, he was responsible for many activities. He was the pastor of the cathedral parish, chaplin of a small church in San Francisco, the secretary to the bishop, rector of the seminary, and editor of the diocesan newspaper. He also organized catechism classes, visited prison inmates, and headed organizations that distributed food to the poor. He believed that religion, more than pious thought, should deal with daily living.

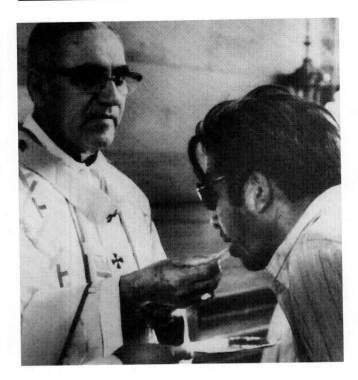

*Oscar Romero*

After almost 25 years as a priest, Romero received the title of monsignor on April 4, 1967. Several months later he was named as secretary-general of the national bishops' conference, a post that required that he move to San Salvador. Three years later he was asked to be the auxiliary bishop to Archbishop Luis Chavez y Gonzalez. On June 21, 1970, his ordination to bishop was celebrated by the bishops of El Salvador, President Fidel Sanchez Hernandez, other civil and church dignitaries, many friends, family members, and people from San Miguel. His friend, the Jesuit priest Rutilio Grande, organized much of the ceremony and acted as master of ceremonies.

### Defender of the Oppressed

Romero was appointed archbishop of El Salvador on February 22, 1977, after Archbishop Chavez retired. The country at the time was in the midst of an increasingly tumultuous struggle over land reform. The archbishop under Chavez supported the peasants' rights to organize in a country where unions were not recognized by the government. Members of the aristocracy and ruling class were pleased with the choice of Romero because of his reputation as a conservative man who usually deferred to the authority of government and church officials.

Romero's appointment came two days after General Carlos Humberto Romero succeeded President Arturo Armando Molina in a fraudulent elec-

tion. The new archbishop initially denounced the "politicization" of priests and members of the clergy, but soon was forced to change his views when tension and violence in the country began to escalate. After the election, those in opposition to the new administration staged strikes and demonstrations. Between 40,000 and 60,000 protesters gathered in Plaza Libertad to demand honest election results. After three days, troops with armored cars ordered the crowd to disperse. Soldiers then opened fire on the demonstrators who remained. After the riots, the government admitted to only eight deaths, but other estimates were as high as 300 deaths.

On March 5, the bishops of El Salvador met to discuss their response to the situation. They composed a statement condemning the murders and the campaign of intimidation being conducted by the government. With some hesitancy, Romero agreed to read the prepared statement on March 13, at the morning mass in the cathedral. His reservations quickly changed to resolve when tragedy struck on March 12. The Jesuit priest Rutilio Grande was assassinated along with two of his parishioners while they were driving to the village of El Paisnal to offer an evening mass. The next morning at the 8:00 a.m. mass in the cathedral, Romero read the bishops' statement. Monday morning, the archbishop held funeral services in the cathedral for the three slain victims. The crowds of mourners that attended overflowed into the plaza and the streets.

In response to the killings, the archbishop announced that the church would boycott official government events until a thorough investigation into the deaths was conducted. In protest, he closed the Catholic schools for three days and ruled that no Sunday services, other than a single mass, would be held in the cathedral for the service to hear their outrage expressed by Romero. He condemned the violence and called for a peaceful resolve to the current strife in the country.

Romero continued to believe that he could negotiate with the administration. However, little was done on the part of the government to answer the archbishop's demands; the terror and injustices continued. The Salvadoran people looked to the archbishop to be their spokesperson. As he became increasingly aware of the atrocities against his people, Romero became more openly direct in his vocalization against the persecution. He used his Sunday services, which were broadcast nationally on the radio, to denounce the human rights violations. As the editor of the archdiocesan newspaper, *Orientacion,* he wrote weekly editorials about the current situation and listed the names of those who had disappeared. Romero became widely respected and admired by the people of the archdiocese that he served, as he evolved from a conservative, acquiescent servant of the church to an outspoken champion of the poor.

Opponents of the church accused Romero and other priests of being involved in subversive, even communist activities. Outrages continued as priests and lay people were arrested, tortured, murdered, or expelled from the country. In May 1977, the military attacked Aguilares and occupied the church for weeks, killing many parishioners. In June, a radical right-wing group threatened to target all Jesuits in El Salvador if they did not leave the country within 30 days. In July, Romero refused to attend the inauguration of the new president because he had not yet received a satisfactory response to the murder of Father Grande.

By 1978, Romero was beginning to receive international recognition and support for his role in defending human rights. On February 14, he received an honorary doctorate from Georgetown University. In November, he was nominated for the Nobel Peace Prize by the British Parliament. He did not win the prize, but the nomination and the surrounding publicity served to enlighten the world to the crisis in El Salvador.

Despite death threats, the archbishop continued to criticize the repressive regime. His followers were inspired by his courage as he demanded the liberation of the impoverished masses and the restoration of social order in the country. James R. Brockman quoted from Romeo's sermons in his book *Romero: A Life.* In one of his last homilies, Romero implored the soldiers to put down their arms and pleaded again with the government, "In the name of God, and in the name of this suffering people, whose laments rise to heaven each day more tumultuous, I beg you, I beseech you, I order you in the name of God: Stop the repression!"

Archbishop Romero was assassinated on March 24, 1980, while celebrating mass in the chapel of the Divine Providence cancer hospital in San Salvador. Several weeks before his death, Romero, sensing his impending demise, spoke these prophetic words in an interview, "I have often been threatened with death . . . as a Christian, I do not believe in death without resurrection. If I am killed, I shall arise again in the Salvadoran people. . . . Let my blood be a seed of freedom and a sign that hope will soon be reality. Let my death, if it is accepted by God, be for my people's liberation and as a witness of hope in the future."

## SOURCES:

Brockman, James R., *Romero: A Life,* New York, Orbis Books, 1989.
*Contemporary Heroes and Heroines,* edited by Ray B. Browne, Detroit, Gale Research, 1990.
*Facts on File Encyclopedia of the Twentieth Century,* edited by John Drexel, New York, Facts on File, 1991.
Gunson, Phil, and Greg Chamberlain, *Dictionary of Contemporary Politics of Central America and the Caribbean,* New York, Simon and Schuster, 1991.

—*Sketch by Denise Marecki-Arriola*

# Linda Ronstadt
## 1946-
### Mexican American singer

Few performers in any medium have proven more daring than Linda Ronstadt, a singer who has made her mark in such varied styles as rock, country, operetta, and mariachi. In the 1970s Ronstadt churned out a veritable stream of pop hits and heartrending ballads that delighted country and rock fans alike. Just when she seemed pegged as a pop idol, however, she turned her talents to opera—in *The Pirates of Penzance* and *La Bohème*—and to torch songs accompanied by the Nelson Riddle Orchestra. Almost every Ronstadt experiment has met with critical acclaim, fan approval, and hefty record sales. *Newsweek* contributor Margo Jefferson attributed this success to Ronstadt's voice, which she describes as having "the richness and cutting edge of a muted trumpet." Jefferson concluded, "In a field where success is often based on no more than quick-study ventriloquism, Linda Ronstadt stands out. She is no fad's prisoner; her compelling voice wears no disguises." *Time* reporter Jay Cocks called Ronstadt "gutsy," "unorthodox," and "a challenger of creeds."

As the singer tells it, she developed a habit of rebellion early in life and stuck to it with singlemind-ed determination. Ronstadt was born and raised in Tucson, Arizona, the daughter of a hardware store owner who loved to sing and play Mexican music—she later made an album of his favorite songs. Ronstadt enjoyed harmonizing with her sister and two brothers—she was proud when she was allowed to take the soprano notes. At the age of six she decided she wanted to be a singer, and she promptly lost all interest in formal schooling. Aaron Latham, a class-mate at Tucson's Catalina High School, wrote in *Rolling Stone* that by her teens Ronstadt "was already a larger-than-life figure with an even larger voice. She didn't surprise anyone by becoming a singer. Not that anyone expected her fame to grow to the dimensions of that voice. But the voice itself was no secret."

Ronstadt attended the University of Arizona briefly, dropping out at 18 to join her musician boyfriend, Bob Kimmel, in Los Angeles. With Kimmel and guitar player Kenny Edwards, Ronstadt formed a group called the Stone Poneys, a folk-rock ensemble reminiscent of the Mamas and the Papas and the Lovin' Spoonful. The Stone Poneys signed a contract with Capitol Records in 1964 and released a single, "Some of Shelley's Blues," in early 1965. Their only hit as a group came in 1967, when "Different Drum," a cut from their second album, made the charts. By that time, intense touring, drug abuse, and a series of disappointing concert appearances as openers for the Doors caused the Stone Poneys to disband. Ronstadt told *Rolling Stone* that her band was "rejected by the hippest element in New York as lame. We broke up right after that. We couldn't bear to look at each other."

### Embarked on Solo Career

Ronstadt fulfilled her Capitol recording contract as a solo performer, turning out some of the first albums to fuse country and rock styles. On *Hand Sown . . . Home Grown* (1969) and *Silk Purse* (1970), Ronstadt teamed with Nashville studio musicians for an ebullient, if jangly, country sound. The latter album produced her first solo hit, the sorrowful "Long, Long Time." In retrospect, Ronstadt has called her debut period the "bleak years." She was plagued by the stresses of constant touring, difficult romantic entanglements, cocaine use, and critical indifference—and to make matters worse, she suffered from stage fright and had little rapport with her audiences. "I felt like a submarine with depth charges going off all around me," she told *Time.* Ronstadt eluded failure by moving to Asylum Records in 1973 and by engaging Peter Asher as her producer and manager. Asher collaborated with her on her first bestselling albums, *Don't Cry Now* and the platinum *Heart Like a Wheel.*

*Heart Like a Wheel* was the first in a succession of million-selling albums for Ronstadt. By the mid-1970s, with hits such as "When Will I Be Loved?," "Desperado," "You're No Good," "Blue Bayou," and "Poor, Poor Pitiful Me," the singer had established herself as rock's most popular female star. Stephen Holden described Ronstadt's rock style in a *Vogue* magazine profile. Her singing, according to Holden, combined "a tearful country wail with a full-out rock declamation. But, at the same time, her purity of melodic line is strongly rooted in folk. A *Time* contributor elaborated: "She sings, oh Lord, with a rowdy spin of styles—country, rhythm and blues, rock, reggae, torchy ballad—fused by a rare and rambling voice that calls up visions of loss, then jiggles the glands of possibility. The gutty voice drives, lilts, licks slyly at decency, riffs off Ella [Fitzgerald], transmogrifies Dolly Parton, all the while

wailing with the guitars, strong and solid as God's garage floor. A man listens and thinks 'Oh my, yes,' and a woman thinks, perhaps, 'Ah, well.'"

A leap from rock to operetta is monumental; few voices could make it successfully. In 1981 Ronstadt astonished the critics and her fans by trilling the demanding soprano part of Mabel in a Broadway production of *The Pirates of Penzance.* Her performance led *Newsweek* correspondent Barbara Graustark to comment, "Those wet, marmot eyes turn audiences on like a light bulb, and when her smoky voice soars above the staff in a duet with a flute, she sends shivers down the spine." Ronstadt's appearance as Mimi in *La Bohème* off-Broadway in 1984 was received with less enthusiasm by the critics, but the singer herself expressed no regrets about her move away from rock. "When I perform rock 'n' roll," she told *Newsweek,* "it varies between antagonistic posturing and to-the-bones vulnerability. I wanted to allow another facet of my personality to emerge. . . . I've gained confidence in knowing that now . . . I can handle myself in three dimensions, and even if never use my upper extension except in the bathtub, I've gained vocal finish."

That "vocal finish" was applied to yet another Ronstadt experiment—two albums of vintage torch songs, *What's New?* and *Lush Life,* featuring the Nelson Riddle Orchestra. Jay Cocks called *What's New?* a "simple, almost reverent, rendering of nine great songs that time has not touched. . . . No one in contemporary rock or pop can sound more enamored, or winsome, or heartbroken, in a love song than Linda Ronstadt. Singing the tunes on *What's New,* or even just talking about them, she still sounds like a woman in love." Holden wrote, "One of the charms of Ronstadt's torch singing is her almost girlish awe in the face of the songs' pent-up emotions. Instead of trying to re-create another era's erotic climate, she pays homage to it with lovely evenhanded line readings offered in a spirit of wistful nostalgia." Holden added that *What's New* "revitalized Ronstadt's recording career by selling over two million copies, and, coincidentally, defined for her generation the spirit of a new "eighties pop romanticism.'" Ronstadt also earned several prestigious awards for her 1986 album *Trio,* a joint country music venture with Dolly Parton and Emmylou Harris.

### Recorded Album Reflecting Mexican Heritage

More recent Ronstadt projects have departed even further from the pop-rock vein. In 1987 the singer released *Canciones de mi padre,* an album of *mariachi* songs that her father used to sing. "When we were little, we spoke Spanish at home, but the schools pounded it out of us pretty early," she told James Brady in *Parade.* "There was an antibilingual attitude then. So my Spanish is very rudimentary—child's

Spanish, really." *Newsweek* critic David Gates calls the work "Ronstadt's best record to date," noting that "its flawless production is the only concession to Top 40 sensibilities. And Ronstadt ... has found a voice that embodies not merely passion and heartache, but a womanly wit as well." In 1991 Ronstadt starred in *La Pastorela*, an updated version of a traditional Mexican holiday play, aired on PBS's *Great Performances*. "I loved the idea of doing a work particular to Mexico," she told Edna Gunderson in *TV Guide*. "*La Pastorela* is not found in Cuba or Venezuela. People tend to lump Hispanic cultures together. They think Ricky Ricardo would have been happy dancing the tango in a mariachi band."

While Ronstadt will not rule out recording more rock, she seems far more fascinated by other forms and other, more remote, historical periods. Gates finds the raven haired artist "the most adventurous figure in American popular music," concluding that, at the very least, Ronstadt is "commendable in her refusal to bore herself."

## SELECTED DISCOGRAPHY

### With the Stone Poneys

*Evergreen,* Capitol, 1967.
*Evergreen, Volume II,* Capitol, 1967.
*Linda Ronstadt, the Stone Poneys, and Friends, Volume III,* Capitol, 1968.
*The Stone Poneys Featuring Linda Ronstadt,* Capitol, 1976.

### Solo LPs

*Hand Sown ... Home Grown,* Capitol, 1969.
*Silk Purse,* Capitol, 1970.
*Linda Ronstadt,* Capitol, 1972.
*Don't Cry Now,* Asylum, 1973.
*Different Drum,* Asylum, 1974.
*Heart Like a Wheel,* Capitol, 1974.
*Prisoner in Disguise,* Asylum, 1975.
*Hasten Down the Wind,* Asylum, 1976.
*Linda Ronstadt's Greatest Hits,* Asylum, 1976.
*Simple Dreams,* Asylum, 1977.
*Blue Bayou,* Asylum, 1977.
*Retrospective,* Capitol, 1977.
*Living in the U.S.A.,* Asylum, 1978.
*Mad Love,* Asylum, 1980.
*Linda Ronstadt's Greatest Hits, Volume II,* Asylum, 1980.
*Get Closer,* Asylum, 1982.
*What's New,* Asylum, 1983.
(With Nelson Riddle as conductor/arranger) *Lush Life,* Asylum, 1984.
*For Sentimental Reasons,* Asylum, 1986.
*Prime of Life,* Asylum, 1986.
*Rockfile,* Capitol, 1986.

*'Round Midnight: The Nelson Riddle Sessions,* Asylum, 1987.
*Canciones de mi padre,* Asylum, 1987.
*Cry Like a Rainstorm, Howl Like the Wind,* Elektra, 1989.
*Mas Canciones,* Elektra, 1991.
*Frenesi,* Elektra, 1992.
*Winter Light,* Elektra, 1993.

### With Dolly Parton and Emmylou Harris

*Trio,* Warner Bros., 1986.

## SOURCES:

### Books

*The Illustrated Encyclopedia of Country Music,* Harmony Books, 1977.
Stambler, Irwin, *The Encyclopedia of Pop, Rock, and Soul,* St. Martin's, 1974.

### Periodicals

*Down Beat,* July 1985.
*Esquire,* October, 1985.
*Newsweek,* October 20, 1975; April 23, 1979; August 11, 1980; December 10, 1984; February 29, 1988.
*Parade,* December 22, 1991, p. 22.
*People,* October 24, 1977; April 30, 1979.
*Rolling Stone,* December 2, 1976; March 27, 1977; October 19, 1978; November 2, 1978; August 18, 1983.
*Saturday Review,* December 1984.
*Time,* February 28, 1977; March 22, 1982; September 26, 1983.
*TV Guide,* December 21, 1991.
*Vogue,* November, 1984.
*Washington Post Magazine,* October 9, 1977.

—*Sketch by Anne Janette Johnson*

# Juan Manuel de Rosas
## 1793-1877
### Argentine dictator

Juan Manuel de Rosas, the most powerful leader in Argentina in the early 19th century, controlled the Argentine Confederation from 1829 to 1852. He ended Indian raids on Buenos Aires and marshalled country-wide support for his Federalist party. Though many honored Rosas as a national hero, many others condemned him as vicious, cruel, and dictatorial in his pursuit and control of the nation's government. Many of these historians admit, however, that Rosas's atrocities are more attributable to the time period than to Rosas himself.

Juan Manuel de Rosas, or Rozas, was born March 30, 1793 to a prominent Spanish family of landholders who had emmigrated from Chile. Rosas's mother wielded the power in the Rosas household. Doña Agustina was the insuperable matriarch of the family and of the region. Once when Juan Lavalle temporarily commanded the Argentine army, Doña Agustina prevented him and his army from taking the Rosas horses, first by padlocking the stable doors and later by having all the horses killed. Her son Juan Manuel inherited this strong will and determination.

Rosas exhibited traits similar to his mother's during his school years. However, this stubbornness caused a rift between Rosas and his family. Juan Manuel was sent home from school at one point during his primary years for not doing the bidding of his instructors and for refusing to follow school policies. Doña Agustina was infuriated. She locked the young boy in a room and withheld all but bread and water until he complied. Juan Manuel proved implacable. A day later the Rosases found a note from the boy reading "I leave all that which is not mine." The boy had left behind his clothes and walked, completely naked, to the home of his cousins.

This incident changed the young Rosas. He left his family. He no longer spelled his name with a "z" but substituted an "s." He gave up school and immersed himself in the life of the city. He entered into an apprenticeship and soon earned his own *estancia* ("ranch") from his Anchorenas kinsmen becoming an *estanciero* ("large ranch owner") himself. At 18, he married Doña Maria de la Encarcacion Escurra. Having achieved success through property, he continued his studies. Rosas learned to write and do arithmetic under the tutelage of Manuel Vicente Maza, who was one of his trusted advisors in later years.

Rosas began to mount his campaign to win command of the Buenos Aires province in 1820, when he was given military leadership of his district. Soon he had amassed quite a following of willing soldiers. With such support, Rosas eventually eliminated all opposition in the areas outside the city of Buenos Aires. Once he cut off the city's food supplies, he managed to drive the army out. Rosas routed Lavalle's Unitarist army and took control of Buenos Aires.

## Becomes Governor of Buenos Aires

In 1829 Rosas became governor of the province of Buenos Aires. Though Rosas's term was only supposed to last three years, he set himself up in a dictatorship that lasted until 1852. He authored the term "Argentine Confederation" for his government, which he believed sounded less like an organization and more like despotism.

Rosas instituted an education policy that included a dress code, using the color red as the emblem for his Federalist party and outlawing the use of blue, the color of the opposing Unitarist party. Rosas centralized his support and weakened the powers of other leaders within the province; one who was once defeated remained Rosas's prisoner for seven years. Because of Rosas's authoritarian domination of the province, many Unitarists fled the country, forming a stronger opposition to Rosas's regime.

Though Rosas technically left his gubernatorial post at the end of his "term" in 1832, his wife Doña Encarnacion continued to run the country surreptitiously, with newly-elected Juan Ramon Balcarce as acting figurehead governor. Meanwhile, Rosas led a military campaign south against the Indians entrenched there. Rosas pushed back the Indian frontier and explored a little-known region of the province. Back in Buenos Aires, Balcarce became so unpopular that he was forced to resign. Rosas's former tutor Maza took over after Viamont, Balcarce's successor, resigned. Rosas was elected to a five year term in 1835 and was consistently reelected until 1852.

Beginning in 1835, Rosas entered the renaissance of his career. He built a grand home at Palermo and entertained famous people there, such as Charles Darwin, who visited during his voyage of the *Beagle*. In the journal account of his voyage (*The Voyage of the Beagle*, 1909), Darwin wrote of his first encounter with Rosas in 1833: "the encampment of General Rosas was close to the river. . . . The soldiers were nearly all cavalry; and I should think such a villainous, banditti-like army was never before collected together. . . . General Rosas . . . is a man of an extraordinary character, and has a most predominant influence in the country, which it seems he will use to his prosperity and advancement." Darwin continues, citing an example of how one of Rosas's banditos killed a man for speaking disloyally of the general, but Darwin excuses Rosas, claiming that the murder was the act of the man rather than the will of Rosas.

Tragedy struck shortly after the Rosas family settled in Palmero. Rosas's wife died in 1838, leaving him with a daughter, Manuelita. During this time Rosas applied himself to running his government, often eating one meal a day and spending all afternoon at his desk. Rosas decried inefficiency, and in matters of public administration, he was inflexible. Adept at rooting out waste and unnecessary measures, Rosas streamlined the governmental workings of Argentina. Rosas kept an eye on everything in his administration, paying attention to every detail, no matter how minute.

Rosas maintained control through terrorism and by keeping a strong and loyal military force. Toward this end, Rosas formed a secret society known as the People's Society. This organization rooted out those disloyal to Rosas. It tortured people into obedience or killed them as examples to others. The society was also known as the *Mazorca* because its members clung together like kernels on an ear of corn, though many preferred to refer to it as *mas horca* ("more gallows"). Historians are quick to point out that Rosas terrorized his populace no more or less than his predecessors, and suggest that such terrorism as a control measure was a common practice among leaders of the times and not due to any particular cruelty on Rosas's part. Some argue that terrorism was an essential element of governing in those times. Terror was used because it was the language of the masses: they understood it. Rosas wielded the power of terror expertly. In one case, Rosas destroyed a former ally, Estanislao Lopez, to better secure his position.

Though Rosas ruled Argentina with an iron hand, conflicts from outside the country weakened his power and drew his attention away from internal matters. In 1837, Rosas warred with Santa Cruz, dictator of Bolivia. Though Rosas won the war, the conflict cost him much in time, attention, and human resources. In 1838 Louis Philippe of France, aided by Lavalle's Unitarists, instituted a French blockade of Buenos Aires and of the Parana for alleged insults made to the French vice-consul. The action was precipitated by the insults as well as Rosas's policy of compulsory military conscription for the French living in Argentina. The blockade jeopardized life in Buenos Aires. With the customs duties on imports cut off, public revenue was significantly reduced. Rosas scaled back the country's costs. He closed schools, reduced salaries, and issued paper money.

### Launches Reign of Terror

A revolt to the south of the city added to Rosas's troubles, but he managed to dispatch each of these conflicts by 1842. He entered into the Mackau Agreement with the French, suppressed the civil strife in the south, and settled problems in Uruguay. José Fructuoso Rivera, then President of Uruguay, had given asylum to Lavalle and his Unitarists. Rosas backed **Manuel Ceferino Oribe,** Rivera's opponent, who massacred all the Unitarists in Rosas's name and even managed to finally kill Lavalle. Though Rosas triumphed in every case, the mounting number of conspiracies and attacks against him and his government resulted in his decision to institute a reign of terror in Buenos Aires. Rosas's *Mazorca* became more savage than ever before. Daily the tormentors and assassins of the *Mazorca,* with Rosas's authorization,

flogged people, burned homes, and cut the throats of known or suspected conspirators. The color codes were strictly enforced. All those loyal to the Rosas government were forced to wear their scarlet badges in public. Likewise, anything blue—even beards in a "U" shape (for Unitarist) — was rigorously banned. Those owning blue items—even bowls or crocks—or displaying any Unitarist imagery were butchered or imprisoned. The *Mazorca* patrolled the coasts and killed those attempting to flee the country. According to the reports of contemporary eyewitnesses, the streets ran with blood.

In 1843, aided by Oribe, Rosas laid siege to Montevideo, Uruguay and Paraguay. This action lasted nine years. Despite the fact that Uruguay and Paraguay had declared themselves independent republics, Rosas's war upon them revealed his desire to incorporate them under Argentine control. The Uruguay campaign drained Rosas's resources, and in 1845 he was dealt what would prove to be a crippling blow when Britain and France blockaded all ports of the Argentine Confederation and aided Uruguay. Without revenues from customs duties, Rosas's treasury was crippled. Rosas persisted in his war for control of Uruguay for the next seven years, despite the depleted treasury and international pressures. In 1851, a loyal military leader and governor under his command, Justo José de Urquiza, rose against Rosas and attacked his stronghold in Buenos Aires. Rosas met the challenge, but his resources were stretched too thin and his troops were defeated. In the guise of a marine, Rosas begged passage on a British steamer headed for England, maintaining to the captain that with his property confiscated he had "not a sixpence." Once Rosas fled, Urquiza assumed control of Argentina.

Rosas brought his daughter Manuelita-initially also disguised as a sailor-with him to England. Rosas lived for the nex 25 years first in a hotel and later at a small farm near Southampton. He spent his days learning to speak English and maintaining an Argentine style farm. Urquiza funded Rosas's stay in exile first from the Argentine treasury and later from his own accounts. He died of pneumonia on March 13, 1877 at the age of 84.

## SOURCES:

### Books

*Biographical Dictionary of Latin American and Caribbean Political Leaders,* edited by Robert J. Alexander, Westport, CT, Greenwood Press, 1988.

Darwin, Charles, *The Voyage of the Beagle,* New York, Collier, 1909.

Kirkpatrick, F.A., *A History of the Argentine Republic,* Cambridge, Cambridge University Press, 1931.

*South American Dictators: During the First Century of Independence,* edited by A. Curtis Wilgus, New York, Russell and Russell, 1963.

**Periodicals**

*Journal of Latin America Studies,* February 1993, pp. 188–190.

*The New York Daily Times,* October 30, 1851, April 1, 1852, April 23, 1852, May 3, 1852.

—*Sketch by Christopher B. Tower*

# Ileana Ros-Lehtinen
## 1952-

### Cuban American legislator

Being first has become something that Ileana Ros-Lehtinen does quite well. In 1982, she became the first Cuban-born female to be elected to the Florida state legislature. Seven years later, after a successful career as a state legislator, she won a special election held on August 29, 1989, to fill the seat left vacant by the death of long-time Miami political powerhouse Claude D. Pepper. A few days after her victory, Ros-Lehtinen was sworn in as the first Cuban American, as well as the first Hispanic woman, ever elected to the U.S. Congress. "As the first Cuban-American elected to Congress," *Boston Globe* commentator Chris Black noted, "she also will be likely to become one of the most visible, most quoted Cuban-born politicians in the nation."

Ros-Lehtinen (pronounced ross-LAY-teh-nin), who is known as Lily to her family and friends, was born July 15, 1952, in the Cuban capital city of Havana, to Enrique Emilio Ros, a certified public accountant, and Amanda Adato Ros. In 1960, she and her family—including her parents and a brother—fled to Miami from Cuba, a year after political leader **Fidel Castro**'s revolution rocked that tiny island nation. Almost immediately, Ros-Lehtinen's parents became involved with other recent refugees in plotting the downfall of the Castro regime. But after the failure of an invasion attempt by anti-Castro forces at Cuba's Bay of Pigs in 1961, the possibility of returning to Cuba became more and more remote, and Ros vowed to raise his children as loyal Americans. His wife recalled in a *Boston Globe* article how strongly her husband felt about his decision: "He said you

cannot educate two kids without a flag and a country. This is going to be their country, and they have to love it."

Ros-Lehtinen earned her associate of arts degree from Miami-Dade County Community College in 1972 and her bachelor of arts degree in English from Miami's Florida International University in 1975. Eleven years later she completed requirements for a master of science in educational leadership from the same institution. Since then, she has continued her studies as a doctoral candidate in educational administration at the University of Miami. Before embarking on her political career, Ros-Lehtinen worked as a teacher and was principal for ten years at Eastern Academy, a school she founded. Her love of politics came as a legacy from her father who had concentrated so much of his life on the hope of restoring democracy to his native land. He is said to have been the chief architect of her political career and was at her side when she announced her victory in her U.S. Congressional race.

### Launched Political Career as State Representative

Ros-Lehtinen's first elected office was in the Florida state legislature, where she served as a representative from 1982 to 1986 and as a state senator from 1986 to 1989. While in the state legislature she met her future husband, Dexter Lehtinen, who was also at the time a member of that legislative body. Although early in her career Ros-Lehtinen showed a tendency to focus on issues of a global nature rather than on those affecting her constituents in a personal way, Black wrote in the *Boston Globe* that Ros-Lehtinen eventually became "a politician of the opposite extreme, a pragmatic legislator focused almost exclusively on the most parochial of issues. One Miami political reporter now describes her as 'a pothole kind of legislator,' much more concerned with the specific needs of individuals and businesses in her district than broader changes in public policy."

When Ros-Lehtinen resigned her seat in the state senate shortly before the August 3, 1989, primary, it appeared—much to the dismay of the Miami area's non-Hispanic voters—that the race to fill Florida's 18th congressional district seat might be a head-to-head battle between two Cuban American women. Early favorites included Ros-Lehtinen on the Republican side and Miami City Commissioner Rosario Kennedy for the Democrats. However, the opponent who emerged from the primary was Gerald F. Richman, an attorney, a former president of the Florida Bar Association, and a Jew. The Ros-Lehtinen-Richman campaign was marked by deep cultural and racial tensions and came to be one of the most ethnically divided congressional races in Florida's history. A highlight of an otherwise brutal contest came from President George Bush who not only gave

Ros-Lehtinen his personal endorsement, but made a special trip to Miami to deliver a speech on her behalf.

Most of the controversy surrounding the campaign grew out of a response to Republican party chair Lee Atwater's announcement that since the district was 50 percent Hispanic, electing a Cuban American to the seat was of utmost importance. Richman, the Democratic candidate, was quoted in a *Time* article as having countered Atwater's claim with the assertion, "This is an American seat." Cuban American and other Hispanic voters were deeply offended by Richman's reply and the implication it carried that Hispanics are not truly Americans. Spanish-speaking radio stations in the Miami area assured their listeners that a vote for Richman would be the equivalent of voting for Castro. Another source of division during the campaign came from the National Republican Congressional Committee (NRCC) which, according to reports in *National Review,* attempted to run Ros-Lehtinen's campaign from Washington. William McGurn explained the problem with a quote from a Republican insider: "The NRCC treated this district like a colony.... Their attitude was that they knew Florida's 18th better than the people who live here."

**Won Turbulent Race for U.S. Congressional Seat**

Triumphing over the bitterness of the campaign, Ros-Lehtinen emerged victorious from the race, capturing 53 percent of the vote. Post-election analysis showed that voters largely seemed to cast their ballot based on their ethnic heritage: 96 percent of blacks and 88 percent of non-Hispanic whites voted for Democratic candidate Richman; while 90 percent of Hispanics, who voted in record numbers, voted for Ros-Lehtinen. In her victory speech, the new congresswoman maintained that she would work to heal the wounds caused by the campaign. "It's been a terrible divisive campaign," she told the *New York Times.* "But now it's time for healing. I know that there are a lot of people out there who feel alienated." Ros-Lehtinen's win was also seen as a victory for the Republican party because the seat she had captured had belonged to the Democrats for 26 years. When Ros-Lehtinen's seat came up for election in 1990, she received 60 percent of the vote and a decisive mandate to continue her political career.

During her tenure, Ros-Lehtinen has been a member of the Foreign Affairs committee and has served on its subcommittee on Human Rights and International Organizations as well as its subcommittee on Western Hemisphere affairs. She has also been involved with the subcommittee on Employment and Housing, where she is the ranking minority member. In an article focusing on Hispanic political candidates, which appeared in *Hispanic,* Anna Maria Arias

described Ros-Lehtinen's stand on issues important to voters in her district. According to Arias, Ros-Lehtinen supports bilingual education, is "in favor of a seven-day waiting period for the purchasing of guns, and voted for a bill that would improve veterans' benefits." Ros-Lehtinen is also vehemently anti-abortion, except to save a woman's life, favors a constitutional amendment to ban flag burning, and advocates the death penalty for convicted organizers of drug rings.

True to her ethnic roots, Ros-Lehtinen remains a staunch adversary of Castro and an equally outspoken champion of a free Cuba. In 1990, she expressed her strong opposition to South-African leader Nelson Mandela's visit to Florida during his eight-city tour of the United States, a trip that engendered a virtual hero's welcome for him in the other states to which he traveled. While there seemed to be a near unanimous outpouring of praise for Mandela and his efforts to end apartheid (racial segregation) in his native country, Ros-Lehtinen felt she could not honor a man who had not only publicly embraced such advocates of violent revolution as the Palestine Liberation Organization's Yasser Arafat and Libya's Muammar Gaddafi, but who also was on record as a strong supporter of Castro. She pointed out that Cuban Americans longing for a return to democracy in their country of origin could not forget that members of Mandela's African National Congress had received military training on Cuban soil.

**Voiced Opposition to 1991 Pan American Games**

Ros-Lehtinen again spoke out against Castro when she condemned participation in the Pan American Games, an Olympics-like international sports competition, held in Cuba during the first two weeks of August in 1991. She argued that Castro's bid to have the Games in his country was merely a ploy to bolster Cuba's ailing economy and to provide ready propaganda supporting his regime. In a *Christian Science Monitor* article on the topic, the congresswoman wrote: "Castro has his circus for now, but despite the fanfare of the Pan American Games, he is an anachronism in a world that values democracy and freedom. It will not be long till he follows the path of the dinosaurs into extinction. Cuba's economic crisis is so desperate that Castro would shave his own beard if that would give him the American dollars which he holds so dear."

The ethnic pride Ros-Lehtinen inherited from her father remains strong in the politician, and perhaps because of this, she is very conscious of her position as a role model for Hispanics. She also values the achievements made by other Hispanic women, and when presented with a special award from *Hispanic* magazine in 1992, she praised their successes. "[The Hispanic woman] is an accomplished writer, or a computer programmer, or an attorney, or a doctor, as well as a loving wife and mother." She also believes that Hispanic women will continue to make contributions in the future. "Now, more than ever," she wrote in *Vista*, "we Hispanic women must re-energize and refocus our efforts to realize the vast potential that lies within our grasp."

## SOURCES:

*Boston Globe*, August 31, 1989, p. 3.
*Christian Science Monitor*, August 9, 1991, p. 18.
*Hispanic*, September 1990, p. S5; October 1990, p. 26; August 1992, p. 28.
*Ladies' Home Journal*, November 1991, p. 182.
*National Catholic Reporter*, April 19, 1991, p. 1.
*National Review*, November 24, 1989, p. 39.
*New York Times*, August 31, 1989, p. A16.
*Time*, September 11, 1989, p. 31.
*Vista*, February 4, 1992, pp. 6, 22.
*Washington Post*, July 30, 1989, p. A4; August 17, 1989, p. A4.

—*Sketch by Marian C. Gonsior*

# Edward Roybal
## 1916-
### Mexican American statesman

Born on February 10, 1916, Edward Roybal spent 30 years in the U.S. House of Representatives, and in that time he set many precedents. One of few Latino members of Congress during the 1960s, Roybal overcame what he saw as the prejudice that existed even on the floor of Congress to become a powerful member of several important House committees. He took as his particular legislative interests health and education. Specifically he sponsored a movement to create national centers for research into aging and ways of prolonging life. He retired from public life in 1992.

In her biography of Roybal, Janet Morey recounts a small event in Roybal's childhood that came to have a tremendous impact on his future. A jeweler came to the Roybal household with a watch for Baudilio, Edward's father. As the jeweler handed over the repaired timepiece, the young boy got a good look at his clothes. The man wore a suit and tie, and Edward's father, a railroad worker, did not even own such clothes. Roybal asked his mother, Eloisa Tafoya

Roybal, if he, too, could wear a tie, and his mother responded, "That man is wearing a tie because he got an education and became a professional man. And you, if you want to wear a tie all the time, you have to be a professional person, and for that you have to go to school."

### The Jeweler's Tie

Roybal knew that he wanted to be a professional, though he might not even have known what that word meant at the time. As he grew up in Albuquerque, New Mexico, the oldest of eight children, he watched his father return from ten hour days at work. Though the family did not suffer poverty, Roybal prepared himself for an education, so that he would have more opportunities than his father.

He also wanted to be able to wear a tie. His mother gave him one, and he always wore it. Naturally the other children teased him, sometimes provoking him to fights. Yet Roybal insists that he was only standing up for himself and for something that he really wanted to do. "No one was going to take that tie away from me!" Roybal recalled.

The family moved to Los Angeles after a railroad strike, and after struggling to be allowed to take college preparatory classes in high school, Roybal did well. He graduated from high school in the midst of the Great Depression, however, and had to earn some money to help his family. He landed a job with the Civilian Conservation Corps. The government designed the CCC to give jobs to the needy and to do any number of public service projects. Roybal sent $25 of his $30 weekly salary home to his parents, and he learned about fair competition. The CCC, Roybal said, "made it possible for us to compete and do the best we possibly could in all our endeavors."

After the CCC Roybal went to the University of California, Los Angeles and studied business administration. After graduation he worked as an accountant for 20th Century Fox. One day in the studio, Tuberculosis Association members came to encourage studio employees to have a TB test. Roybal's life took a change of course.

He volunteered for two years in the fight against TB, eventually making it his full-time job. He became one of the leaders of the Los Angeles County Tuberculosis and Health Association. He took to the road encouraging people to be tested, and eventually he starred in a TB test promotional film that ran before Spanish language movies in theaters all over the country.

### Elected to Los Angeles City Council

After one unsuccessful run, Roybal won election to the Los Angeles City Council in 1949. He had made it to an office that no other Latino had yet occupied in the 20th century. He served four terms on the City Council, overcoming the beliefs of the other members that he was not their equal.

In 1962, he won election to California's 25th District seat in the House of Representatives. He recalled that even in Congress he faced discrimination. He once told a *Los Angeles Times* reporter that "there was discrimination when I came here [to Washington]. There were instances in which invitations were extended but not to the congressman from California."

Roybal prevailed and gained acceptance. He worked over the years on his gerontology centers, a national health plan, the nation's first bilingual education bill and others. He served on numerous committees including the powerful House Appropriations Committee. He took special pride in his work on health and education. "I would like to be remembered as an advocate of good nursing, good health, and good education," Roybal once remarked.

Edward Roybal is married to Lucille Roybal. They have three children: Lucille, Lilian, and Edward, Jr. In 1992 when Roybal retired from Congress, his daughter Lucille Roybal-Allard won election to a district neighboring Roybal's. Had Roybal chosen to remain in Congress, they might have become the first father-daughter combination ever to serve there simultaneously.

## SOURCES:

### Books

Morey, Janet and Wendy Dunn, *Famous Mexican Americans,* New York, Penguin Books, 1989.

*Mexican American Biographies: A Historical Dictionary, 1836–1987,* edited by Matt S. Meier, Westport, CT, Greenwood Press, 1988.

### Periodicals

*Los Angeles Times,* July 27, 1987, Section A, page 8, December 30, 1992, Section A, page 3.

—*Sketch by James McCarthy*

# Lucille Roybal-Allard
## 1941-
### Mexican American legislator

Lucille Roybal-Allard is the first woman of Mexican American ancestry to be elected to the U.S. Congress. She became the 33rd Congressional District's representative in November 1992. The oldest daughter of a political family, Roybal-Allard's father is the highly esteemed California Congressman **Edward Roybal**. After 30 years of Congressional service, Ed Roybal, often called the dean of California Latino legislators, retired in 1992. Congresswoman Roybal-Allard, a Democrat, previously served in the California State Assembly, representing the 56th District from 1987 to 1992. There she served on a number of influential committees, including the Assembly Rules committee and the very powerful Ways and Means committee, which oversees the distribution of public monies. She was also the chair of the Ways and Means subcommittee on Health and Human Services.

Her political style, described as quiet and conciliatory, has contributed to her many legislative victories. She won passage of what some have hailed as landmark environmental legislation, as well as new laws in the areas of domestic violence and sexual harassment. Roybal-Allard is especially proud of her work to empower local communities. As she related in an interview with Diana Martínez: "People often don't know how their lives are impacted by what's going on in Sacramento or Washington, D.C. People can take control of their lives. They can be involved in the political process and make a difference."

Roybal-Allard was born and raised in the Boyle Heights section of Los Angeles, California, a predominately Mexican American area. She attended Saint Mary's Catholic School before she earned her B.A. from California State University, Los Angeles, in 1961. She has warm memories of working on her father's campaign; he was a great example to her, but Roybal-Allard is quick to give equal credit to her mother. "My mom has been a tremendous role model," she revealed to Martínez. "She's really the one who has helped to support and spearhead my father's career. She used to run his headquarters, which used to be our home when we were kids because they couldn't afford a headquarters. So she has always been there, helping him get elected, walking precincts, registering voters, doing all the things that needed to be done. At the same time, she'd be at his side whenever she needed to be at public events. She's worked very hard and is greatly responsible for his success, because it really does take a partnership. In politics it takes the cooperation of your family; otherwise it's almost impossible to succeed."

In an interview with the *Civic Center News Source,* Roybal-Allard says she remembers working on her father's political campaigns as early as age seven. "We used to fold and stuff and lick stamps. When I got a little bit older they used to call us 'bird dogs,' and we would do voter registration. So I was a bird dog for a few years."

There was a downside to political involvement as well. As Roybal-Allard explained to the *Civic Center News Source,* "I think for me the main part of it was the lack of privacy and lack of personal identity. When my sister and I would go to a dance where people might not know who we were, we used to decide on a different last name so we could just be anonymous and have fun. . . . I remember as a freshman in college in a political science class I raised my hand to answer a question and after I finished the professor said 'Well, now we know what you're father thinks,' and went on to the next student."

Experiences such as these led Roybal-Allard to the conclusion that she did not want to be a politician. She continued to be involved in her father's campaigns and those of other Latino politicians but chose a career of community and advocacy work for herself. As Roybal-Allard explained to Martínez, her decision to work in community service was a direct result of her upbringing. "When I think you have a role model like both my father and my mother who have really dedicated their lives to the community and have taught human values and understand the value of people, it really has an impact on one's life." She served as the executive director of the National Association of Hispanic CPAs, in Washington, D.C., was the assistant director of the Alcoholism Council of East Los Angeles, and worked as a planning associate for United Way. She enjoyed community work, but as time went on she became more and more frustrated by the barriers created by political policy makers. In 1987 a combination of political opportunity and personal circumstances changed Roybal-Allard's mind about running for office.

### Decided to Pursue Political Career

The 1987 election of Assemblywoman **Gloria Molina** to the newly created seat on the Los Angeles City Council left Molina's assembly position vacant. Roybal-Allard knew Molina through their mutual community activities and she had worked on the assemblywoman's campaign. Molina asked Roybal-Allard to consider running for the vacant assembly position. Her personal situation and the request of her friend led to her decision to run. As she explained to *Hispanic,* "The timing was just right for me. My children were grown and my husband's job called for a lot of travel." Roybal-Allard's second husband,

Edward Allard III, has his own consulting firm whose clients are mostly on the East Coast. Roybal-Allard told Martínez that she received no pressure from her father to run. "I'm sure that his involvement in politics ultimately was one of the reasons . . . that I wound up getting involved in politics. But, he has always been one that believed that we needed to be independent and make decisions on our own, and if we need guidance he will be there." Once she decided to run for California's State Assembly, she received help from both her father and Gloria Molina. She easily defeated nine other candidates and won with 60 percent of the vote.

As a newly elected Assemblywoman, one of Roybal-Allard's first tasks was to continue the fight against building a prison in East L.A. A tremendous challenge for a new politician considering that her principal foe was the Governor of the State of California. In 1986, California Governor George Deukmejian proposed a site near a heavily Mexican American residential area as the location for a State prison. Deukmejian tried to steamroll the opposition to get the prison built but had his plans flattened instead. For seven years Roybal-Allard, along with Gloria Molina and other local Latino politicians, worked with grassroots organizations, professional groups, and church leaders to prevent the prison from being built. As an expression of her philosophy of local empowerment, Roybal-Allard assisted community women in organizing "The Mothers of East L.A." which was implacable in its opposition to the prison. A series of legal maneuvers halted construction of the prison but did not kill it. Deukmejian left office in 1990, but the struggle against the prison continued until September 1992 when Governor Pete Wilson signed a bill, amended by Roybal-Allard, which eliminated the funds for the construction of the East L.A. prison. This victory, coming as Roybal-Allard left the California Assembly for the U.S. Congress, gave her cause to reflect on her own feelings and what the political struggle meant to her community. As she stated in a press release, "I started my assembly career when the East Los Angles prison bill was approved, and it feels great to be leaving the assembly on this victory note. . . . This is a victory for the entire community. For seven years our community has marched against the prison, we have fought in the courts and in [California capital] Sacramento—this fight has empowered us. This community was once viewed as powerless. However, the Mothers of East Los Angeles and other community groups have served notice to the state's powerbrokers that ignoring the desires of the East Los Angeles community will no longer be accepted."

The prison was not the only struggle Roybal-Allard waged to improve the quality of life in her district. She fought against a toxic waste incinerator, again aided by the highly respected grass roots organization, Mothers of East Los Angeles. As a result of that struggle Roybal-Allard authored a bill which entitles every community in California to an environmental impact report before a toxic incinerator is built or expanded, a protection that was often omitted prior to her efforts. This bill, along with her strong voting record on the environment, earned her the Sierra Club's California Environmental Achievement Award.

### Took Action on Women's Issues

Roybal-Allard has also authored a series of laws that place her in the forefront of women's issues. Included is a requirement that the courts take into consideration an individual's history of domestic violence in child custody cases. She has also worked for legislation requiring colleges to provide information and referrals for treatment to rape victims and enacted two laws that strengthen the legal position of sexual assault victims by redefining the meaning of "consent." Another of her bills requires the California State Bar to take disciplinary action against attorneys who engage in sexual misconduct with their clients. This is the first such law adopted by any state in the country.

For her legislative efforts, Roybal-Allard has received a number of prestigious awards and commendations, including honors from the Los Angeles Commission on Assaults Against Women, the Asian Business Association, and the Latin American Professional Women's Association. Roybal-Allard was also honored in 1992 by the Mexican American Women's National Association (MANA) in Washington, D.C. She was presented with the "Las Primaras" Award for "her pioneering efforts in creating a better future for the community through the political process."

Ironically, when Roybal-Allard was first elected to the California Assembly many thought her to be too demure to be effective. But as she explained to *Hispanic* her conciliatory style is long-range effective, "People may be your enemies today on one issue, but they may be your allies tomorrow on another issue. So I've learned to work well with groups on both sides of the aisle, even with those who I oppose bitterly on particular issues." Her track record on political effectiveness to date has been impressive. A number of community members, and political observers, have speculated that when the senior Roybal left Congress in 1992, his daughter followed in his steps, continuing the Roybal legacy of effective representation.

### SOURCES:

### Periodicals

*Civic Center News Source,* January 13, 1992, pp. 1, 8, 12.

*Hispanic,* March 9, 1992, p. 20.

### Other

News release from the office of Lucille Roybal-Allard, September 16, 1992.
Roybal-Allard, Lucille, interview with Diana Martínez, September 2, 1992.

—*Sketch by Diana Martínez*

---

# Juan Rulfo
## 1918-1986
### Mexican writer

Mexican writer Juan Rulfo earned the reputation of a masterful novelist and short story writer for a small body of work that includes *El llano en llamas y otros cuentos* (*The Burning Plain and Other Stories*) and the novel *Pedro Páramo*. In these works, Rulfo combined natural Mexican language, non-linear plots, and elements of the historic and fantastic with a tragic world view. In doing so, he created fiction of enduring quality that presaged the novels of magic realism that proliferated in the later half of the twentieth century.

Rulfo was born on May 16, 1918 near Sayula in the state of Jalisco. He grew up in what was then San Gabriel, a village 300 miles northwest of Mexico City. In 1925, Rulfo's father, **Juan Nepomuceno Perez Rulfo,** was assassinated during the Cristeros Revolt that followed the Mexican Revolution. His mother, Maria Vizaino Arias, died of a heart attack two years later, orphaning Rulfo and his brothers. Rulfo lived for awhile with his grandmother, who had been entrusted with the village priest's library. Instead of religious books, however, the library contained adventure stories, which Rulfo devoured. The locals also fed Rulfo's hunger for story by spinning tales of warfare and the supernatural.

Eventually Rulfo was sent to an orphanage in Guadalajara, where he lived for several years. After finishing grade school, Rulfo studied accounting and in 1933, at age 15, he moved to Mexico City to continue his studies. Supporting himself with odd jobs, Rulfo lived tenuously while at the university, where he studied accounting, literature, and law. In 1935, when his uncle no longer wanted to pay for his courses, Rulfo joined the staff of the Mexican Immigration Department, a position he would hold for ten years. There he met coworker and short story writer

Efrén Herández, who taught him the rudiments of writing fiction.

## Finds Creative Voice

According to Luis Harss and Barbara Dohmann, authors of *Into the Mainstream: Conversations with Latin-American Writers,* Rulfo "is a man who does not quite know how he came to literature—a somewhat late vocation with him—except that one day he simply woke up in it." In 1940, Rulfo wrote a novel about life in Mexico City, which he subsequently destroyed because, as he told Harss and Dohmann, "It was a conventional sort of book, very high strung, but at bottom no more than an attempt to express certain solitary feelings. . . . I was trying to find a way out of the solitude I'd been living in, not only in Mexico City but for many years, since my days in the orphanage."

Rulfo realized that he wanted to use a simpler, more natural writing style, one that utilized the cadences of spoken language. "Practicing ways to free myself of all that rhetoric and bombast, I started cutting down, working with simpler characters." In "La Vida no es Muy Seria en sus Cosas" ("Life Is Not To Be Taken Too Seriously"), which appeared in the Guadalajaran magazine *Pan* in 1942, Rulfo wrote of the taciturn country people of Jalisco and the dry, hot, desolate lowland he knew so well from his childhood.

When Rulfo's short stories appeared in magazines in the mid-1940s and early 1950s, both the short story and novel as genres were in a process of transformation in Latin America. The Mexican Revolution and subsequent uprisings during the first three decades of the twentieth century shaped what is known as "literature of the revolution." Armed conflict and social upheavals are the subject matter for such works, which were written not for the elite but the average person. The authors of these wartime chronicles were revolutionaries themselves and wrote hastily, in unpolished prose, to make their political experiences and points quickly available. Nonfiction and fiction often merged irretrievably. Against this background, Rulfo strived to create fiction of supreme aesthetic quality, with political content relegated to the status of by-product.

During World War II, Rulfo and others in the Immigration Department interned prisoners from German ships that were impounded in local waters. Dissatisfied, Rulfo hired on with the Goodrich Rubber Company, where he worked in the sales division from 1947 to 1954. During the next five years, Rulfo wrote and published short stories in Mexican magazines. In 1952 he won a fellowship from the Centro Mexicano de Escritores. With more time to write, Rulfo collected his previously published stories, added several new ones, and submitted them to a publisher. When they appeared in 1953 as *El llano en* *llamas y otros cuentos* (*The Burning Plain and Other Stories*), they met with instant critical success. Rulfo was considered at once the last of the short story writers of the Mexican Revolution and an innovator in Latin American fiction.

In the 15 stories that make up *El llano en llamas y otros cuentos,* Rulfo deals with the hopes, fears, and despair of rural Mexicans. The stories take place amidst a murky atmosphere where characters reveal themselves through dialogue, and through action of both the realistic and the fantastic sort. Such themes as the communion of man and nature, the conflict between fathers and sons, and the nature of reality emerge. Strong passions, which often lead to murder, also figure prominently in the stories. In fact, death is an overarching theme of Rulfo's work as a whole.

## Produces Masterpiece

With the financial support of Rockefeller grants, Rulfo wrote his novel *Pedro Páramo* during 1953 and 1954. Yet the novel's true gestation took place over a much longer period. Rulfo thought of the plot ten years earlier, but he did not then know how to deal with the novel's structure. The solution occurred to him during a visit to San Gabriel. "It was my going back to the town where I had lived 30 years earlier, and I found it abandoned. It is a town I had known, of about seven to eight thousand inhabitants. When I arrived there were only 150 persons there. . . . The doors were locked up. The people had left," Rulfo recounted in *Juan Rulfo: Autobiografía armada.* From this perspective on death and decay, Rulfo decided to bring the town of San Gabriel back to life as the ghost town of Comala in *Pedro Páramo.*

At first, the plot of *Pedro Páramo* revolves around the activities of Juan Preciados, who, narrating in first person, describes his visit to Comala, where he is to reconcile with his father, Pedro Páramo, the local despot. When Preciados discovers that his father is dead, he tries to reconstruct Paramo's life from gossip. Then Preciados discovers that he is dead himself, and the reader is left to piece together the story of Paramo from the murmurs of ghosts.

*Pedro Páramo* did not initially receive good reviews because critics saw it as a disintegration of the narrative form. The novel employs several points of view—first and third—and the plot is non-linear, leaping and lurching backward, forward, and sideways without obvious transition. Instead, Rulfo integrated the novel's 66 fragments using repeated images, such as water, in a poetic fashion. Some scholars suggested that Rulfo was influenced by the works of William Faulkner, though Rulfo indicated in an interview with Carlos Landeros of *Diorama de la Cultura* that he had not read Faulkner's works until after critics mentioned the similarities. Later, many critics began to study *Pedro Páramo* more thoroughly, coming to realize the high quality of the work and calling it a fine example of the new novel—one that combined authentic subject matter and experimental language.

After the publication of his novel, Rulfo worked for the Mexican government on a development project and then, in 1958, took over the library archives at the Sociedad Mexicana de Geografía y Estadística in Mexico City. A year later he moved his family—Rulfo had married in 1948—to Guadalajara, where he was in charge of publicity for Televicentro, the state-run television station.

At this time he wrote *El gallero* (The Cockfighter), a novel that was not published but was later scripted by **Carlos Fuentes** and **Gabriel García Marquez** for the movie *El gallo de oro* (The Golden Rooster), which was released in 1964. Interested in his heritage, Rulfo edited history books and indulged in his hobby, photography, selling some photos to magazines.

Back in the capital city in 1962, Rulfo worked for the Instituto Nacional Indigenista, a government agency that helped to integrate Native Americans into Mexican society. As well as editing the institute magazine, Rulfo worked in the field, surveying problems, proposing solutions, and implementing the necessary reform measures. The 1960s saw Rulfo's reputation soar as his short stories and *Pedro Páramo* were translated into many languages and garnered critical praise.

In 1970 Rulfo won the Premio Nacional de Letras from the Mexican government, and a decade later he was inducted into the Academia Mexicana de la Lengua. However, Rulfo's demanding work schedule left little time for literary activity. For some years Rulfo worked on a second novel, *La cordillera* (*The Packtrain*), which was to trace the history of a Mexican family from the sixteenth century to the twentieth century. It and any other short stories remained unpublished when the author died of a heart attack in 1986.

## SELECTED PUBLISHED WORKS:

*El llano en llamas y otros cuentos,* Fondo de Cultura Economica, 1953, translation by George D. Schade published as *The Burning Plain and Other Stories,* University of Texas Press, 1967, 2nd Spanish edition, corrected and enlarged, Fondo de Cultura Economica, 1970.

*Pedro Páramo* (novel), Fondo de Cultura Economica, 1955, translation by Lysander Kemp published as *Pedro Paramo: A Novel of Mexico,* Grove, 1959.

*Antologia personal,* Nueva Imagen, 1978.

*El gallo de oro y otros textos para cine,* Ediciones Era, 1980.

*Toda la Obra,* edited by Carlos Montemayor, University of Pittsburgh Press, 1991.

## SOURCES:

### Books

Anderson-Imbert, Enrique, *Spanish-American Literature: A History,* Volume II: 1910–1961, 2nd edition, revised and updated by Elaine Malley, Wayne State University Press, 1969.

Brushwood, John, *Mexico in Its Novel,* Austin, University of Texas Press, 1966.

*Contemporary Literary Criticism,* volume 8, Gale, 1978.

*Tradition and Renewal: Essays on Twentieth-Century Latin American Literature and Culture,* edited by Merlin H. Forster, University of Illinois Press, 1975.

Harss, Luis, and Barbara Dohmann, *Into the Mainstream: Conversations with Latin-American Writers,* New York, Harper, 1967.

Lal, Luis, *Juan Rulfo,* Boston, Twayne, 1983.

*Juan Rulfo: Autobiografia armada,* edited by Reina Roffe, Buenos Aires, Ediciones Corregidor, 1973.

Rulfo, Juan, *The Burning Plain and Other Stories,* translation by George D. Schade, University of Texas Press, 1967.

Schwartz, Kessel, *A New History of Spanish-American Fictions,* Volume II, University of Miami Press, 1971.

### Periodicals

*Chicago Tribune,* October 2, 1994, section 14, p. 3.

*Diorama de la Cultura* (Mexico City), March 6, 1966, p. 1.

*Guardian,* May 31, 1994, section 2, p. 10.

*New Mexico Quarterly,* 1968, pp. 84–101.

—*Sketch by J.M. Lesinski*

# S

## Gabriela Sabatini
### 1970-
**Argentine professional tennis player**

As her homeland recovered from its loss in the Falkland Islands War and began to recognize the repercussions of having lived under a dictatorship, young tennis star Gabriela Sabatini brightened life on and off the courts. Her first coach, Patricio Apey, interviewed by Bruce Newman of *Sports Illustrated* in 1988, explained her appeal to her countrymen: "Suddenly in the middle of all the depression and bad news, when everything seemed to be wrong in Argentina, there comes this little angel who makes only good news. I think that is what made her an idol." Sabatini entered the professional tennis circuit at the age of 14 and received international attention after she beat three of the top ten tennis players in the world at the 1985 Family Circle Magazine Cup tournament at Hilton Head, South Carolina. Shortly after that remarkable achievement, she became the youngest semi-finalist in the French Open's history before losing to Chris Evert.

*Gabriela Sabatini*

Sabatini was born on May 16, 1970, in Buenos Aires, Argentina, to Osvaldo and Beatriz Sabatini. Her father was a director of General Motors' Argentine operations until 1986, when he decided to concentrate solely on managing his daughter's career. According to *Current Biography Yearbook,* Sabatini picked up her first tennis racket when she was six years old. The next year, her parents arranged for lessons at the local tennis club for both Sabatini and her brother. "Tennis was like a toy to me," she recalled in a *New York Times* interview with Robin Finn in 1992. "Instead of having dolls, I was playing tennis." At the age of ten, she was the ranked first in her country in the girls' twelve-and-under division. After a year of junior high school, she moved to Key Biscayne, Florida, to continue training with Apey. After her impressive showing at the 1985 French Open, Sabatini was ranked seventeenth in the world.

Despite—or because of—her success, several of her advisers worried that Sabatini was trying to accomplish too much too quickly. Dick Dell, an agent who had signed her with ProServ just after she turned 14, described his concerns to *Sports Illustrated's* Newman: "I am for anything that would give her an outlet outside tennis. Instead of being in school every

day with girls her own age, she was thrown into an adult world." Newman reported that Sabatini did not take correspondence courses or continue her schooling after moving to the United States. In addition, she did not speak English her first three years in Florida, and her natural shyness often was interpreted as aloofness. Virginia Slims tennis tournament official Tim Tinling told Newman that Sabatini's style appealed to him. "I think that aloofness is part of her charisma. There's a great arrogance about Sabatini, and it all shows in the carriage of her head. She looks almost goddesslike. Taken together, her beauty and her arrogance form a contradiction. And I don't think one should try to solve a contradiction in a beautiful woman. One has simply to accept her as she is."

### Changed Coaches and Styles

According to *Current Biography,* Sabatini was determined to beat the older, more experienced players. Coach Apey described her rigorous routine to Dudley Doust of the *Sunday Times* (London) in 1985: "Once we were working six hours on her backhand down the line. When we stopped at six in the evening, she came up to me and said, 'Patricio, I can't get it, let's go on.'" They continued to practice the shot for several hours. Her competition schedule matched her training: she played 20 out of 27 weeks on four continents and earned enough wins to be named *Tennis* magazine's rookie-of-the-year. Over the next several years, she continued to progress in the sport until she was ranked fifth in the world in 1988. This final leap into the top ranks occurred, in part, because she changed coaches and playing styles.

In 1987, Sabatini hired Angel Gimenez, a former Davis Cup player from Spain, to improve her conditioning and stamina. Newman reported in 1988 that her new training included running up to an hour a day and increasing her practice time on court in order to offset her problem of tiring too easily during matches. In 1988 all of her hard work paid off. Steffi Graf, a German tennis player, had long been Sabatini's rival; in 11 matches she had never beaten Graf. At the final match of the 1988 Virginia Slims tournament in Boca Raton, Florida, Sabatini upset Graf by winning the final two sets. "A lot of the [preceding] matches [against Graf] I was leading and didn't win," Sabatini said to *Sports Illustrated*'s Newman. "I said it won't happen today. When I was tired, I hit the ball harder. I felt that this was the time." Several weeks later she beat Graf at another tournament, though she did not win the tournament. Nonetheless, the powerful girl on the court had been replaced by a woman whose endurance and variety of strokes had taken her to the top.

Despite setbacks in 1988—she lost both the U.S. Open and the Summer Olympics finals to Graf— Sabatini earned $1 million for the year. She continued strongly in 1989, winning tournaments and more money, but she was unable to capture the major titles. Fans and foes alike began to wonder if the Argentine tennis player could ever be number one. "Technically, I have everything," Sabatini told Robin Finn of the *New York Times*. "Mentally, I know I have to be very good, and I'm getting there."

With her upsetting failure at the 1990 French Open, Sabatini decided to switch coaches again. This time she hired Carlos Kirmayr, a former top-ranked Brazilian. "Something wasn't working," Dell told Alexander Wolff of *Sports Illustrated*. "And her relationship with Angel Gimenez was getting stale." Dell suggested Kirmayr because "if he could make [Sabatini] smarter, she would be 15 or 20 percent better. She had all the shots. She just didn't know how to play points." She stopped working with weights— which had added bulk when she needed speed—and, as Wolff reported, she began seeing a sports psychologist.

The problem, as Kirmayr saw it, was that Sabatini spent too much time thinking about tennis. "It had reached a point where she was thinking about her job all the time," Kirmayr told Alison Muscatine of the *Washington Post* in 1991. "It is impossible to act and work like a professional when you live your job twenty-four hours a day." Sabatini pursued other interests, such as photography, French, and sightseeing. In addition, she ended her doubles partnership with Graf. "Gabriela was not benefiting from that relationship," Kirmayr explained to Muscatine. "Steffi was mentally stronger. I didn't think that was a good thing for [Sabatini]."

## Won First Grand Slam Title

Wolff described the tournament in which Sabatini earned her first Grand Slam title, the 1990 U.S. Open: "Sabatini has always hit broad, baroque ground strokes, even as everything about her—facile hands and a physique a male athlete would envy— suggested she could prosper as a serve-and-volleyer. It is this surfeit of athleticism that her new coach, Carlos Kirmayr, has tapped." In her semifinal match against **Mary Joe Fernandez,** Sabatini rallied. "Relying on a steadily more adventurous net game, she salvaged the first set and brought herself to match point in the third with a diving backhand volley winner." Wolff quoted Sabatini's remark after this win: "I think I'm ready to beat Steffi." That is exactly what she did. The public no longer had to wonder if Sabatini could do it: her victory in the finals earned her the number one ranking in the world.

Another young star, Monica Seles, soon presented a challenge to Sabatini's newfound success at the Virginia Slims Championships. *Sports Illustrated*'s Sally Jenkins reported that Sabatini's new training made her a lyrical shot-maker who had a deft touch at the net. "Sabatini was generally written off as being incapable of challenging Graf's supremacy. Since then, though, she has come closer then either Seles or Graf to possessing a complete game, and has even become a lively presence on the court, often buoying herself with deep grunts and air jabs. The second serve is Sabatini's one remaining weakness." Sabatini lost the championship match to Seles in an historic five-set final lasting nearly four hours.

By April of 1991, Sabatini's career earnings reached $4 million—the fifth highest total on the women's tour, according to *Current Biography*. Like other tennis players, Sabatini endorsed various products—but she was the first to have a perfume named after her. *Time* reported in 1991 that "Both [Sabatini and Seles] make millions from lucrative endorsement deals, and both will use the occasion of next week's U.S. Open to push unlikely products. Sabatini is serving up 'a flowery, exotic' perfume that bears her name and sells for a mere $50 per 1/4 oz." Though Sabatini won five tournaments in early 1992, she was bothered by tendinitis and a tentative attitude, according to *Current Biography*. Her successes came less frequently.

In 1994, Jenkins wrote about the once-promising star who had not won a tournament in two years. "But what seemed merely a slump became a full-blown crisis at the French Open last week when she could not even win a match. Sabatini, ranked No. 8 in the world, was upset in the first round by No. 108, Silvia Farina of Italy. The loss marked only the second time in Sabatini's 10-year career that she failed to advance [beyond the first round] in a Grand Slam event." She left the court as frustrated as her fans. "People keep asking me [if I'm sick or burned out]," Sabatini told Jenkins. "They want to know if I'm tired, do I need time off? No, I doubt the solution is a vacation."

Jenkins reported that the main problem with Sabatini's game is her ineffective serve. "Her first serve is rarely a weapon, and her second, a topspin whimper, has become a liability in the era of bangers and powerful big rackets." Although her coach, Dennis Ralston, advised her to take a six-month sabbatical before he was replaced by Kirmayr in his second time around as Sabatini's coach, she is determined to work through her problems on the court. "I love this sport," she told Jenkins. "I'm happy to be out there. I like to keep trying and I like to work hard. I just don't like to lose."

## SOURCES:

### Books

*Current Biography Yearbook 1992,* New York, H. W. Wilson Co., 1992.

### Periodicals

*New York Times,* November 2, 1989; April 13, 1992.
*Sports Illustrated,* May 2, 1988, pp. 52–6; September 17, 1990, pp. 23–9; November 26, 1990, pp. 42–7; June 6, 1994, p. 60.
*Sunday Times* (London), June 30, 1985.
*Time,* August 26, 1991, p. 65.
*Washington Post,* July 6, 1991.

—*Sketch by Kathe A. Conti*

# Ernesto Sábato
## 1911-
### Argentine novelist

Ernesto Sábato's influence on Latin American literature has been profound; his three novels: *El túnel* ("*The Tunnel,*" 1948), *Sobre héroes y tumbas* ("*On Heroes and Tombs,*" 1961) and *Abaddón, el Exterminador* ("*Abaddón, the Exterminator,*" 1974) rank among the most critically acclaimed in the Hispanic world. His work both mirrors twentieth-century Argentine history and explores questions surrounding the identity of man and his existence. A critic of Argentine totalitarianism and a leading moral figure, Sábato was awarded the Jerusalem Prize in 1989 for his contribution to literature and human rights.

Sábato, the second youngest of 11 brothers, was born on June 24, 1911 in Rojas, a village 160 miles from Buenos Aires. His parents, Francisco Sábato, a mill owner, and Juana Ferrari, belonged to a bourgeois family of Italian origin. Sábato received his elementary education in Rojas, and at a young age began reading Spencer, Reclus, Zola, and Darwin. At the age of 12 Sábato moved to La Plata, the provincial capital, to study at the Colegio Nacional. He remained there until 1928. The dislocation from his family deeply affected Sábato; recalling his feelings in *Salmagundi,* he explained: "My childhood was a sad one—a time of anguish and nightmare, exacerbations and introversion . . . ." Away from home he found solace in science, describing the introduction of a geometric theorum as "a portentious revelation!" continuing, "Without being aware of it, I began to discover the charms of the platonic universe—a perfect order of ideal objects, eternal and untrammeled. That miracle dominated a good part of my existence."

Between 1929 and 1936 Sábato studied at the Universidad Nacional de La Plata. Despite possessing strong literary and artistic inclinations, he majored in science and mathematics. At the university he was politically active, initially with the Anarchist group and later with the Communists. As General Secretary of the Communist Youth Movement, Sábato attended the Communist Student Congress in Brussels in the early 1930s. At the conference he became disillusioned following revelations of Stalin's regime of terror, and he rejected Communism. He abandoned the Congress and fled to Paris, where he once again turned to the ordered world of mathematics. Back in Argentina he married Matilde Kusminsky-Richter, with whom he later had two sons, Jorge Federico and Mario. In 1937 he was awarded a doctorate in physics from the Instituto de Física in La Plata.

In 1938 Sábato traveled to France on a scholarship from the Argentine Association for the Progress of Science to study atomic radiation at the Curie Laboratory in Paris. Through Ernesto Bonasso he encountered the surrealists, who gathered at the Café du Dôme in Montparnasse. Later he told Marie-Lise Gazarian Gautier in *Interviews with Latin American Writers* that his dual existence made him feel, "like a good housewife who is a prostitute at night." He became disenchanted with science, and started writing his first novel *La fuente muda* ("The Mute Fountain"). He later burned this book, as he did with several later works: He was always his own harshest critic. With the outbreak of World War II Sábato left Europe and continued his research at the Massachusetts Institute of Technology in 1939.

### Return to Argentina

He returned to Argentina in 1940 and began contributing to *Teseo,* a literary magazine; *La Nación,* one of Argentina's leading newspapers; and **Victoria Ocampo**'s *Sur.* His articles brought him into the literary circle Grupo Sur, where he encountered **Jorge Luis Borges** and others. At the same time, he pursued his scientific vocation and was appointed Professor of Theoretical Physics at the Universidad Nacional de La Plata and at the Instituto del Profesorado Secundario in Buenos Aires. He retained this post until his opposition to the **Perón** dictatorship necessitated his resignation in 1945. Some examples of his anti-Perón stance are collected in *Claves políticas* ("Political Clues") and *El caso Sábato* ("Sábato's Case").

In 1943 Sábato moved with his family to a ranch in Córdoba, where they lived primitively, lacking electricity and running water. He taught weekly classes at the Astronomical Observatory in Córdoba. Increasingly, Sábato turned away from science and moved toward literature, although he found the transition "painfully complicated". He compiled his debut volume of essays entitled *Uno y el universo,* ("One and the Universe") in 1945. The book won the Buenos Aires Municipal Prose Prize. Sábato returned to Buenos Aires in 1946—as a writer.

In 1947 Sábato accepted an executive post with UNESCO in Paris. But he resigned after two months because of the bureaucratic nature of the work, pressure from the Perón dictatorship and his growing commitment to *El túnel. El túnel,* published in 1948, brought Sábato international prestige. The novel—regarded by many as the classic Latin American existentialist novel—was praised by literary luminaries such as Thomas Mann, Graham Greene, and Albert Camus.

In 1955 he became editor of *Mundo Argentino,* a Buenos Aires newspaper, but was forced to resign because of his criticism of the Pedro Eugenio Aramburu regime and his opposition to press censorship.

Outspoken agaiorphannst totalitarianism, Sábato was imprisoned briefly. Unlike many of his contemporaries, he elected to remain in Argentina. In 1958 he accepted the post of Director of Cultural Relations in the Ministry of Foreign Relations and Culture, but resigned the post the following year because of his dissatisfaction with the Frondizi regime.

In 1961 *Sobre héroes y tumbas* was published. This novel is widely believed to be his greatest work. In *Commonweal,* Ronald Christ described the novel as "a great testimonial to its author and its nation's literature." Following the book's successful launch Sábato spent much of 1962 on a lecture tour of Europe, Puerto Rico, and the United States.

His third novel, *Abaddón el exterminador,* about the nightmare of dictatorship, appeared in 1974. While writing the book he determined that it would be his last; as he later explained to Greg Price in *Latin America: The Writer's Journey:* "In the works I've published I've said all I have to say on life and death, anxiety and hope, alienation and the sense or senselessness of existence." In 1977 the book won the Prix du Meilleur Livre Etranger, France's highest literary honor.

### After the Novels

In December of 1983 Argentine President Raúl Alfonsín established the National Commission on Disappeared Persons. Sábato was asked to chair the commission as the person "whose moral standing as Argentina's greatest living writer was without equal," according to Eduardo Rabossi in the *London Review of Books.* The Commission produced a report, known as "El informe Sábato" ("The Sabato Report") which serves as an indictment against the horrors suffered under dictatorship in Argentina.

With the degeneration of his eyesight, Sábato has devoted his time to painting. In 1989 his paintings were hung at an exhibition at the Centre Georges Pompidou in Paris. He still searches for the meaning of life. Commenting on his own existence Sábato told Angel Flores in *Twentieth Century Authors:* "I must say in all sincerity and seriousness that I am very unhappy with myself, with who I am, what I write, my mentality and my type of sensibility.... If I were born again I'd like to be an obscure bureaucrat or an obscure fireman or a simple hairdresser or something like that."

Sábato has been accorded many literary honors, including the Grand Prize of Honor from the Argentine Writers Society; the Premio Consagración Nacional (Argentina); the Chevalier des Artes et des Lettres (France); the Gran Cruz al Mérito Civil (Spain); and Chevalier de la Legion D'Honneur (France). He also has been awarded the Premio Cervantes de Literatura from the Real Academia

Española de la Lengua; the Gabriela Mistral Prize from Organization of American States; the Miguel de Cervantes Prize from the Spanish Ministry of Culture; the Commandeur de la Legion d'Honneur (France); and the Jerusalem Prize.

## SELECTED PUBLISHED WORKS:

### Novels

*El túnel*, Sur, 1948, translation by Harriet de Onís published as *The Outsider*, Knopf, 1950, translation by Margaret Sayers Peden published as *The Tunnel*, Ballantine, 1988.

*Sobre héroes y tumbas*, Fabril, 1961, translation by Helen Lane published as *On Heroes and Tombs*, David Godine, 1981.

*Abaddón, el Exterminador*, Sudamericana, 1974, translation by Andrew Hurley published as *The Angel of Darkness*, Cape, 1993.

### Essays

*Uno y el universo* (title means "One and the Universe"), Sudamericana, 1945.

*Hombres y engranajes* (title means "Men and Gears"), Emecé, 1951, reprinted, 1985.

*Heterodoxia* (title means "Heterodoxy"), Emecé, 1953.

*El otro rostro del peronismo: Carta abierta a Mario Amadeo* (title means "The Other Face of Peronism: Open Letter to Mario Amadeo"), López, 1956.

*El caso Sábato: Torturas y libertad de prensa - Carta abierta al Gral. Aramburu* (title means "Sábato's Case: Torture and Freedom of the Press - Open Letter to General Aramburu"), privately printed, 1956.

*Tango: Discusión y clave* (title means "Tango: Discussion and Key"), Losada, 1963.

*El escritor y sus fantasmas* (title means "The Writer and His Ghosts"), Aguilar, 1963.

*Tres aproximaciones a la literatura de nuestro tiempo: Robbe-Grillet, Borges, Sartre* (title means "Approaches to the Literature of Our Time . . ."), Universitaria, Chile, 1968.

*La convulsión política y social de nuestro tiempo* (title means "The Political and Social Upheaval of Our Time"), Edicom, 1969.

*Ernesto Sábato: Claves políticas* (title means "Ernesto Sábato: Political Clues"), Alonso, 1971.

*La cultura en la encrucijada nacional* (title means "Culture in the National Crossroads"), Ediciones de Crisis, 1973.

(With Jorge Luis Borges) *Diálogos* (title means "Dialogues"), Emecé, 1976.

*Apologías y rechazos* (title means "Apologies and Rejections"), Seix Barral, 1979.

*La robotización del hombre y otras páginas de ficción y reflexión* (title means "The Robotization of Man and Other Pages of Fiction and Reflection"), Centro Editorial del América Latina, 1981.

## SOURCES:

### Books

*Ernesto Sábato*, by Harley Dean Oberhelman, Twayne Publishing, 1970.

*Interviews with Latin American Writers*, by Marie-Lise Gazarian Gautier, Dalkey Archive Press, 1989.

*Latin America: The Writer's Journey*, by Greg Price, Hamish Hamilton, 1990.

*Latin American Writers*, Volume 3, edited by Carlos A. Solé, New York, Charles Scribner's Sons, 1989.

*Spanish American Authors: The Twentieth Century*, edited by Angel Flores, New York, H. W. Wilson Company, 1992.

### Periodicals

*Commonweal*, June 18, 1982, pp. 374–6.
*London Review of Books*, January 27, 1994, p. 27.
*Salmagundi*, Spring/Summer 1989, pp. 269–278.
*Times Literary Supplement*, 1982, p. 875.

—*Sketch by Amanda Beresford*

---

# Floyd Salas
## 1931-
### Spanish American novelist

An accomplished novelist, Floyd Salas incorporates his emotions and beliefs into his art so that they reflect his "emotional state at the time." As a boxer and boxing coach, Salas believes in physical strength as a source of writing power. Several of his novels have received very high critical acclaim. An extremely outspoken man, Salas's willingness to express his opinion publicly has garnered attention for his work. In addition to his writing, Salas draws and sculpts, taking inspiration from family, acquaintances, and even from beloved pets, having once written a beautiful elegy when his dog passed away.

Anita Sanchez Salas gave birth to her son Floyd on January 24, 1931, in Walsenberg, Colorado.

Floyd's father, Edward, traced his lineage in the United States back to the seventeenth century, when his ancestors came to Florida from Spain. Anita Salas's family also came from Spain, but in the sixteenth century as part of the pioneering group that traveled with the Spanish explorer Juan de Onate through New Mexico and southern Colorado. Salas spoke of his family background during an interview with Gerald Haslam for *MELUS*: "My mother's family were supposedly aristocratic Dons, while my father's father was a simple farmer. . . . Yet, it is my father who claimed I was an artist as a very little boy and who encouraged this talent before I even went to school."

Almost completely Spanish in lineage, Floyd Salas quickly points out how he challenges the expectations of some people. "They meet me and learn my [last] name, and they immediately think that I'm Mexican," he told *DHB*. "People always associate Spanish with the Oppressor," Salas continued, "but then I turn it around on them because I'm part Navajo Indian."

The Salas family moved to California when Floyd was eight years old, going from the East Bay near San Francisco to northern California near the Shasta Dam. With hardly a chance to get settled beyond being the "new kid"—he attended six high schools in four years—Salas always found himself in conflict with schoolmates. "I had to scrap my way up the pecking order every time we'd move," Salas was quoted as noting in a *Dictionary of Literary Biography* essay.

But if Salas often fought with "outsiders," those close to him have had a tremendous influence on his life. Salas attributes everything from his sense of moral purpose and responsibility as well as his compassion to his parents and siblings. He told *MELUS*'s Haslam that "My oldest brother, Eddy . . . was the greatest influence upon me as a writer. He had my father's intellect and my mother's soul and refined them and shared them with me."

Though Salas credits Eddy Salas as having had the largest impact on his writing, their brother Albert, who became an amateur boxing champion and later turned professional, strongly affected Floyd in other ways. As Salas remarked in a *MELUS* interview, Albert "had a great influence upon me, some good, some bad. In order to be loyal to him . . . I had to be faithful to his outlaw values, which came from a life I didn't live." Albert recognized the boxing talent in his younger brother, who would eventually become a skilled fighter in his own right. In the meantime, Floyd was arrested five times in a 15-month period, from the ages of 13 and a half to 15, for what he called "juvenile mischief."

Eventually, Salas put his skills to good use and won the first boxing scholarship ever awarded by the University of California at Berkeley in 1956. Years later, according to a 1980 press release, one fan described the bantamweight Salas as having "the boxing skill of Sugar Ray Leonard and the power of Roberto Duran, two world champions." As mentioned in the same press release, Salas would go on to produce three national champions as a trainer by instilling his philosophy that "the fighter of the greatest character and the purest soul becomes the greatest boxer."

"Boxing gives me power as a writer," Salas, informed *DHB*'s Jim McCarthy. Similarly, Salas told a *MELUS* interviewer that "in writing as fighting, I feel the same exhilaration during the peak of the battle, while I'm typing along inspired or when I'm unloading with both hands, slugging it out in a corner, and when it's over, I love my foe like a brother, and I love my book and everyone in it just as much."

Salas had come through difficulties, including his brother Albert's suicide, but as his collegiate academic career started, his writing began to come more readily. He started writing short stories while at Berkeley, and in 1958, he won a Rockefeller Foundation scholarship to attend El Centro de Escritores, a writing school in Mexico City.

Salas eventually returned to the United States, completing his undergraduate degree at San Francisco State University in 1963; in 1965 he took his master's degree there as well. A creative writing teacher at San Francisco State beginning in 1966, Salas played a major role in the student uprisings at the institution. One story that emerged from his involvement pitted Salas against author Saul Bellow. Bellow, a Nobel Prize-winning writer, had declared that "the university should be a haven from vulgarity for writers." Salas stood up to disagree and strong words and personal insults followed. According to Bellow scholar Mark Harris, Bellow used the incident in a later work entitled *Mr. Sammler's Planet.*

Ten days later, Salas and the students of San Francisco State launched a major sit-in demanding ten new minority faculty members, a Chicano Studies department, a black studies department, and the changing of admissions standards to allow more minority students to be admitted. The university eventually met many of the demands. Salas told McCarthy that "lots of the things that [people] take for granted at universities now, that's what we were fighting for back then."

## Explicit Description of Penitentiary Life

In 1967 Salas published *Tattoo the Wicked Cross,* a novel about a adolescent who goes to jail for being a street-brawler and emerges as a vengeful killer. Critical opinions of the novel varied widely. For example, *The Saturday Review* called *Tatoo* "one of the best and certainly one of the most important first novels published in the last ten years." *Time,* however, had grave reservations about *Tattoo's* graphic depiction of prison life, a quality that other critics found to be one of the book's great strengths.

Salas hastened to explain that *Tattoo the Wicked Cross* does not tell the story of a young Floyd Salas. Although he spent 30 days in juvenile hall and 120 in a county jail for spitting on a taxi driver, Salas has never even seen the type of prison farm in which he set his story. Nonetheless, he credited his experiences as a source of inspiration. "I listened to everything I heard in jail, I used what I heard," Salas was quoted as saying in a short biographical summary he provided to *DHB.* He further commented that his jail stint, though an artistic inspiration, taught him "to avoid prison at all costs."

Salas stayed well clear of prison, but he left San Francisco State in 1967. Over the next few years, translations of *Tattoo* appeared in Spanish and French. In 1970, Salas published *What Now My Love,* the story of three hippies who flee to Mexico after a bloody encounter with police during a drug raid. Although some members of the drug subculture condemned Salas's portrayal of them and their lifestyle, his account came directly from his own encounters. A veteran of the Haight-Ashbury district's "Summer of Love," Salas stated in biographical materials he presented to *DHB* that "I made the world's pot scenes, following the hippy trail from San Francisco to Marakesh."

Salas reflected on those events again when writing 1978's *Lay My Body on the Line.* In that book he detailed the student struggles in the San Francisco Bay area during the 1960s. The main character, a Spanish American with a background of family tragedy, again tempts the reader to associate him with the author. Salas, however, carefully distances himself from the character by pointing up the hero's moments of delusion and paranoia. Still, Salas once told a *Masterpieces of Latino Literature* interviewer that, in fact, "you never knew if you were being watched or not. I treated everything and everybody with skepticism and figured then that I would be safe."

The mixed reviews of *Lay My Body on the Line* did not prevent Salas's reputation from growing. His works, both prose and poetry, began appearing in collections throughout the 1970s, including *Forgotten Pages of American Literature, Chicano Voices,* and *Many Californias: Literature From the Golden State.* In a statement given to *DHB,* Salas expressed his artistic vision: "Being a poet and a novelist, I have two views of the creative writing process, but they are related. Substance is primary, style is secondary. There is only one thing that will make a work of writing live, and this is spirit." As a testament to that ethic, the spirited *Tattoo the Wicked Cross* won inclusion in the 1994 Harper Collins anthology *Masterpieces of Latino Literature,* nearly 30 years after the novel's original publication. The editors remarked that the book "set [Salas] apart from other Latino and Chicano writers of the time."

## Educational Career and Recognition

In 1973 Salas became the California statewide coordinator for poetry in the schools, working through San Francisco State University. Four years later he moved across the bay to Berkeley in order to teach creative writing at the University of California, where he had been an assistant boxing coach since 1975. There he was twice awarded the James P. Lynch Memorial Fellowship for Outstanding Teachers. In 1977 he also received a National Endowment of the Arts grant to write *Lay My Body on the Line.* In 1979 he accepted a position teaching novel writing at Foothill College in the Los Altos Hills, California, where he continued to teach through 1994.

Extending his teaching beyond the realm of traditional academia, Salas taught a poetry writing seminar at San Quentin prison from 1984 to 1991, and he has also tutored at Folsom and Vacaville prisons. He was so successful with these sojourns that the local Public Broadcasting Television affiliate, KQED-TV, produced a feature on those classes.

In an interview with Gerald Haslam of *MELUS,* Salas maintained that "boxing and writing have been intertwined throughout my life. Both require the same basic traits of character: dedication, durability, and courage, as well as the need to be spiritually pure and humble." In 1992 Salas published a memoir entitled *Buffalo Nickel.* The book details Salas's experiences and reflections. In a 1992 review, the *Los Angeles Times* called it "one of the most remarkable memoirs of the decade."

Following divorce from his first wife of 22 years in 1970, Salas has remarried twice and has two children. He lives near the University of California in Berkeley, though he stopped coaching boxing in 1991. Salas continues his forays into writing and remains involved in the Oakland, California affiliate—founded by Salas in 1989—of the International Association of Poets, Playwrights, Editors, Essayists and Novelists (PEN), which he has described in materials he supplied to *DHB* as "the only multicultural chapter" of the esteemed organization.

## SELECTED PUBLISHED WORKS:

*Tattoo the Wicked Cross,* Grove Press, 1967.
*What Now My Love,* Grove Press, 1971.
*Lay My Body on the Line,* Y'Bird Press, 1978.
*Buffalo Nickel* (autobiography), Arte Publico Press, 1992.

*State of Emergency,* Arte Publico Press, 1995.

## SOURCES:

### Books

*Chicano Writers, First Series,* Vol. 82, edited by Francisco Lomelí and Carl Shirley, Detroit, Gale, 1989.
*Hispanic Writers,* edited by Brian Ryan, Detroit, Gale, 1991.
*Masterpieces of Latino Literature,* edited by Frank Magill, HarperCollins, 1994.

### Periodicals

*Los Angeles Times,* October 11, 1992, Book Review, p. 1.
*MELUS,* Spring 1994, pp. 97–109.

### Other

Additional information for this profile was obtained from biographical materials provided by Floyd Salas as well as a *DHB* interview with Salas in February of 1995.

—*Sketch by James McCarthy and Lorna Mabunda*

*Rubén Salazar*

# Rubén Salazar
## 1928(?)-1970
### Hispanic American journalist

People who knew Rubén Salazar remember him as a warm and peaceful man, with tremendous skill as a writer. Those who did not know him remember him primarily because of the way he died. As a television reporter and *Los Angeles Times* columnist, Salazar often took risks, and incurred the enmity of those he criticized. Some observers have suggested that his criticism of the Los Angeles Police Department made him a special target during the 1970 riots in that city. Since Salazar's death on August 29, 1970, his name has become a rallying cry for Latinos against police brutality. Salazar became a martyr, as immortalized in the well-known "victim corrido" by Lalo Guerrêro, "El 29 de Agosto."

As a child, Salazar attended the solidly middle-class Lamar School, in El Paso, Texas. After graduating from Texas Western University in 1954, he went to work for the El Paso *Herald-Post.* There he worked

with Earl Shorris and the newspaper's boss, E. M. Pooley. In his book *Latinos,* Shorris characterized Pooley as "crabby and opinionated," but credited him for his concern for Mexican Americans and the Latino community. Pooley loved Salazar's writing style, and appreciated his inclination to find hard-hitting stories. Salazar's career received a boost when Pooley authorized him to pose as a vagrant and go to jail.

### Making News, Friends, and Enemies

The expose that Salazar produced from his incarceration shook the community with its revelations of poor sanitation and cruel treatment. With this journalistic success, Salazar left for California. In 1959 he began working for the *Los Angeles Times.* The paper sent him to Vietnam to cover the war there. His courage led to good stories, but on at least one occasion he very nearly lost his life in a Viet Cong attack. Salazar also went to Mexico City, where he witnessed a military slaughter of student protestors. He became the *Times'* Mexican bureau chief.

Salazar wanted to do more than be a beat reporter. He convinced the newspaper to allow him to write a column that would serve as a mouthpiece for the sizable East Los Angeles Latino community. He began writing with his same unfettered style, sometimes angering some readers. His criticism of the Los Angeles Police made a lasting impression on that group; the *Times* has even noted that Salazar angered

Mexican Americans by claiming that the city's original inhabitants had mostly been blacks, Indians, and poor Mexicans, not the children of Spanish conquistadors. Salazar continued to write for the *Times* after he moved to television. His job at KMEX-TV in Los Angeles gave him a new visibility. It also disturbed some Los Angelenos, like the County Sheriff who accused Salazar of "stirring up the Mexicans."

### Tragic Death

On August 29, 1970, an anti-war demonstration in East Los Angeles turned violent. Salazar was covering the story, but as the situation turned ugly, he paused at the Silver Dollar Bar to seek refuge from the gunfire outside. Los Angeles Police deputies soon entered the bar, and fired tear gas at the patrons. One officer fired a canister which hit Salazar in the head and killed him instantly. Although the officers emerged without charges of wrongdoing in Salazar's death, some believe that police may have targeted him as an "accidental" victim in revenge for his constant attacks on police integrity.

Salazar had a wife and three children. While his body lay in state, mourners came from all over the barrio and around Los Angeles. Tributes were especially profound from Hispanic leaders like Congressman Ed Roybal, who said, "Rubén Salazar's burden passes on to each one of us ... and we must continue to peacefully pursue his goals of social reform with steadfast determination." Shorris noted that "[Salazar] was not the first Latino reporter or even the first Latino columnist, but he was the best and the bravest."

### SOURCES:

#### Books

*Hispanic-American Almanac,* edited by Nicolás Kanellos, Detroit, Gale, 1993.
*Latinos, A Biography of the People,* by Earl Shorris, New York, Avon Books, 1992.

#### Periodicals

*Los Angeles Times,* August 31, 1970, Part 1, p. 15; September 1, 1970, Part 1, p. 3; August 29, 1990, Section B, p. 6.

—*Sketch by James McCarthy*

# Luis Omar Salinas
## 1937-
**Mexican American poet, editor, and interpreter**

Luis Omar Salinas is an award-winning poet, whose surrealistic verse often evokes a dark preoccupation with the brutal or tragic aspects of life. As Salinas explained in a interview with James McCarthy, "death and resignation to one's fate" rank as major concerns for him in writing. Despite his fascination with the circumstances surrounding unpleasant events, Salinas asserted that he also counts hard work and the ability to overcome life's difficulties as themes of equal weight.

Born in Robstown, Texas, on June 27, 1937, Salinas was orphaned at age four. Oralia and Alfredo Salinas, his aunt and uncle, adopted him, and Salinas has considered them his parents ever since. As a child, he lived for a few years in Mexico and Texas, before his father decided to settle the family in the central valley of California. As he grew up, Salinas developed an interest in literature. He was no stranger to work during his formative years, helping his father in his clothing business through much of his childhood and working as a field laborer in the summers. After finishing high school, he enrolled in Bakersfield Junior College, earning an associate's degree in 1958. He then matriculated at Fresno State University, where he pursued his interest in literature.

Salinas remained at Fresno State University for several years, first as a student and later as a creative writing instructor for poetry. All through his college career, he supported himself by working as a farm laborer and by selling shoes for his father. In 1972, Salinas left Fresno State and returned to help his father in the family business.

Salinas described the 1970s and 1980s to McCarthy as "a hard-working time for me." Although he was deeply involved in the family business, he also managed to work as an interpreter, and to write and publish a significant amount of work. His literary output during these years included two books of his own poetry, *Crazy Gypsy: Poems,* 1970, and *I Go Dreaming Serenades,* 1979; contributing poems to an anthology of Hispanic poets entitled *Entrance: Four Chicano Poets; Leonard Adame, Luis Omar Salinas, Gary Soto, Ernesto Trejo,* 1975; and acting as co-editor of another major anthology called *From the Barrio: A Chicano Anthology,* 1973. In addition, Salinas's poetry also appeared in numerous literary magazines and collections.

In the 1980s, Salinas began to receive critical recognition and was awarded several prizes. In 1980, he won the Stanley Kunitz Poetry Prize and the Earl

Lyon Award for his collection *Afternoon of the Unreal.* He also published several more books of original verse, including *Prelude to Darkness* (1981), *Darkness under the Trees: Walking behind the Spanish* (1982), and *The Sadness of Days: Selected and New Poems* (1987). In 1990 his collection *Follower of Dusk* won the Flume Prize.

Salinas defended his literary use of surrealism and unreality, maintaining that "sometimes life is harsh, and the poet has to find a way to escape." Yet Salinas claimed that he does not hope simply for escapism. When his poetic voices flee to other worlds to find their expression, Salinas explained that they are really talking directly about the real world. "For me that other world is just as valid as the real one," he told McCarthy, "because it's usually true to the feelings of the speaker, and true to the [meaning of] the poem."

Salinas stated that he finds his literary career gratifying, particularly when he can bring his poetry to an individual. He explained that his audience seems to enjoy his poetry much more when he reads it aloud, so he considers his poetry readings especially fulfilling. Salinas said he also takes special pride in being able to introduce young students to his work.

For Salinas, literary success has brought personal happiness where it has brought others misery. "Literary talent presents lots of traps," he told McCarthy, "like alcohol, depression, suicide." Salinas, by contrast, feels "lucky to survive in publishing and be happy. The sense of adventure you find in creativity is seriously challenged by the business world sometimes," he admitted. Nevertheless, Salinas acknowledged that he continues to find happiness in the fact that "every now and then I get a poem that is good and they want to publish it." In early 1995, Salinas was working on *Sometimes Mysteriously,* a compilation of poems he had been writing since 1990.

## SELECTED PUBLISHED WORKS:

*Crazy Gypsy: Poems,* Origenes Publications, 1970.
*I Go Dreaming Serenades,* Mango, 1979.
*Afternoon of the Unreal,* Abramás Publications, 1980.
*Prelude to Darkness,* Mango, 1981.
*Darkness under the Trees: Walking behind the Spanish,* Chicano Studies Library Publications, University of California, as for 1982.
*The Sadness of Days: Selected and New Poems,* Arté Publico, 1987.
*Follower of Dusk,* 1990.

## SOURCES:

### Books

*Hispanic Writers,* edited by Bryan Ryan, Detroit, Gale, 1994.

### Other

Salinas, Luis, interview with James McCarthy, January 24, 1995.

—*Sketch by James McCarthy*

# Carlos Salinas de Gortari
## 1948-
### Mexican president

Carlos Salinas, Mexico's President from 1988 to 1994, has been widely recognized for his attempts to propel his country's economy into the First World by stimulating free trade and reducing the size of the Mexican bureaucracy. He is perhaps best known in the United States for his prominent role in negotiating the North American Free Tree Agreement (NAFTA), which has promised to relax trade barriers between Mexico and the United States. A Harvard-trained economist, he first rose to international prominence as the budget minister under his predecessor, President Miguel de la Madrid, serving as the chief architect of the administration's stringent economic measures aimed at bringing stability to the Mexican economy.

Despite being the first Institutional Revolutionary Party (PRI) presidential nominee to receive less than two-thirds of the vote and having entered office amid cries of election fraud, Salinas quickly gained popularity through his broad economic and social reform programs. His controversial technocratic economic policies, which included a reduction of the government work force, the devaluing of the peso, and a reduction in agricultural subsidies, also drew criticism for failing to benefit most Mexicans. However, his cost-effective social programs, reductions in election fraud, and free-trade policies were, for the most part, favorably received.

Carlos Salinas de Gortari was born on April 3, 1948 in Mexico City to Raúl Salinas Lozano—a Harvard-educated economist who has served as a cabinet official, diplomat, and Nuevo León state senator—and Margarita de Gortari Carvajal, an economist who cofounded the Mexican Association of Women Economists. He spent most of his childhood in the Salinas ancestral home, located near the lower Rio Grande in Agualeguas, Nuevo León, where, as his stated in Matt Moffett's *Wall Street Journal* profile, "the air was always full of very serious discussions about the world." Prominent business leaders, such as Henry Ford II, and politicians, such as General

*Carlos Salinas de Gortari*

Lázaro Cárdenas—the father of Cuauhtémoc Cárdenas, Salinas's future political challenger—often joined in the family debates. At the age of 18, Salinas entered the National Autonomous University of Mexico, where he majored in economics, worked for a state senator, and, perhaps most important, became a favorite student of Miguel de la Madrid, a law professor who would later become president. In 1969, after submitting a senior thesis, "Agriculture, Industrialization, and Unemployment," which won critical acclaim in an economics competition, Salinas received his Bachelor's degree and remained at the university as an assistant professor of statistics. The following year, he took time off from his duties there to win a silver medal in horseback riding at the Pan American Games in Calí, Colombia.

### Obtains First Government Post

In 1971, Salinas was appointed to his first government post: assistant director of public finance under the minister of finance, one of his father's friends. As he started his climb up the bureaucratic ranks, Salinas continued his education, receiving a Master's degree in public administration from Harvard University in 1971. After completing a second Master's degree in political economy two years later, Salinas returned to Mexico to conduct research for his doctoral thesis, "Production and Political Participation in the Mexican Countryside," spending several months in the stone house of a peasant farmer in the village of Tetla. "My time in the country taught me the vitality of the Mexican people," Salinas told Moffett. "My time in government would teach me the way an excessively big state can smother that vitality."

In 1978, the same year that he received his Doctorate in political economy and government from Harvard, Salinas was named Assistant Director of financial planning. A year later, he was appointed Director General of economic and social policy, receiving his eighth promotion in as many years. As the top aide to de la Madrid, then the planning and budget minister, Salinas was able to fill executive and legislative positions with individuals who would later support his economic reforms. Moreover, he was able to strengthen his alliance with de la Madrid, who served as his political mentor. When the former professor made the decision to seek the PRI presidential nomination in 1982, he enlisted the services of his prize student to direct the campaign.

Salinas, who has been nicknamed the "Atomic Ant" for his volatile personality and five-foot five-inch, 135-pound stature, ran an aggressive campaign, publishing a scathing newspaper article accusing his conservative opponents of fascism. He so ardently defended his candidate's economic policies that he once nearly initiated a brawl. Largely through Salinas's efforts, de la Madrid received the nomination and won the election handily, subsequently promoting his campaign director to budget minister. Salinas would now have the opportunity to put the theoretical models of his academic research into practice. But the economic conditions he inherited were among the worst since the Great Depression. During the mid-1970s, the discovery of massive oil deposits had enabled the Mexican government to obtain extensive loans from international bankers who were confident that ever-increasing petroleum prices would be enough to secure such loans. However, with the collapse of petroleum prices and the Mexico City earthquake of 1986, the Mexican economy took a sharp downward turn.

Salinas, as the chief orchestrator of de la Madrid's austerity program, attempted to compensate for declining oil revenues by reducing the size and cost of government; firing thousands of government employees, privatizing hundreds of state-run businesses, and cutting crop subsidies to farmers while lowering the value of the peso in an effort to boost exports. Although these measures led to a significant increase in non-oil exports and foreign reserves, hundreds of thousands of Mexicans lost their jobs, and those who did not saw their wages outstripped by an annual inflation rate of greater than 100 percent.

The resulting widespread discontent among the electorate—combined with internal party conflicts—resulted in one of the most serious threats to the PRI since its founding. Although Salinas was considered a dark-horse candidate in the early stages of the nomination process—he was opposed by labor unions and 93 percent of the Mexican populace, according to one newspaper poll—he was able to gather enough support from party reformers and the international business community to win de la Madrid's favor. Promising to continue with his unpopular economic strategy of cutting subsidies, privatizing, and encouraging competition, Salinas faced a strong challenge from his principal rival—the populist candidate Cuauhtémoc Cárdenas, the founder of the Authentic Party of the Mexican Revolution and the son of one of the most popular Mexican presidents in history. Salinas, along with his wife, the former Yolanda Cecilia Occelli González, also drew criticism during the campaign for sending their three children to a Japanese school in Mexico City.

### Becomes President

While many believed that the strength of Mexico's one-party system was eroding, few realized the extent to which the PRI would be threatened. But on the historic July 6 election, the shift in Mexican politics became apparent: Salinas won, but with only a reported 50.4 percent of the vote—the lowest ever for a PRI candidate. In past elections, the PRI had invariably received 70 to 75 percent of the vote. What is more, Salinas's victory was tainted by widespread reports of the election fraud that had long been a hallmark of Mexican elections. As Miguel Ángel Centeno stated in his book *Democracy Within Reason*, "While the final results will always be disputed, it is possible that Cárdenas won the election by a narrow margin. Certainly Salinas did not obtain a majority, and the decision to limit this figure to 50.4 percent . . . indicated that the electoral alchemists were aware of the limits to credulity of both national and international credulity."

Once in office, though, Salinas—who prominent political columnist Juan José Hinajosa shortly after the election characterized in the *Latin American Weekly Report* as "the weakest president since the [1930s]"—became one of the most popular presidents in decades. According to the results of a *Los Angeles Times* survey, more than 60 percent of the population approved of his performance at the time of the 1991 mid-term election. This shift in the electorate reflected the dramatic turnaround of several economic factors: inflation had declined from 159 percent in 1987 to 12 percent in 1992, the peso had stabilized in value, and external debt had been trimmed more than $15 billion. Salinas also received praise, toward the end of his term, for being one of the principal negotiators of NAFTA, which was meant to give Mexican producers greater access to US markets.

While perhaps best known for his economic reforms, Salinas was also applauded for his attempts to add what Martin C. Needler labelled in *Contemporary Review*, a "human face" to his stringent fiscal policies. In addition to restoring civil rights to the Church by overturning some of the anticlerical clauses of the 1917 constitution, Salinas unveiled a new multi-billion-dollar social welfare program known as the National Solidarity Program, or PRONOSOL, during his administration. The product of his dissertation research, the program was established to channel federal funds to social projects—credits for farmers and other workers, free food and medical care, and funding for public works—that have been developed by local organizations. "Not only has the programme been hugely popular," commented Martin C. Needler in *Contemporary Review,* "but it has been extremely cost-effective in that funds are not wasted in top-heavy bureaucratic structures or siphoned off by intermediaries."

While Salinas's broad ranging reform package received favorable reviews in the early 1990s, his critics have argued that it has done little to improve the standard of living for average Mexicans. Two years into his administration, according to statistics cited by Centeno, more than 70 percent of Mexico's populace failed to earn enough money to purchase food needed to meet basic nutritional requirements, and one-third lacked access to health care. Since the foreign debt and peso crises that occurred shortly after he left office in December of 1994, many of the economic reforms he so fervently championed have been viewed as a failure. Despite the precarious state of the Mexican economy, Salinas left office on at least one positive note. The election of his successor, **Ernesto Zedillo,** was considered by a number of international officials to be free of the systematic fraud that has marred several previous elections.

### SOURCES:

#### Books

Centeno, Miguel Ángel, *Democracy Within Reason: Technocratic Revolution in Mexico,* University Park, PA, Pennsylvania State University Press, 1994.
*Current Biography Yearbook 1989,* edited by Charles Moritz, Wilson, 1989.

#### Periodicals

*Business Week,* January 24, 1994, p. 54.
*Contemporary Review,* November, 1988, pp. 241–242; July, 1993, pp. 23–27.
*Los Angeles Times,* October 22, 1991.
*Maclean's,* February 7, 1994, pp. 36–37.

*Newsweek,* March 7, 1994, pp. 42–43.

*Time,* March 20, 1995, pp. 56–57.

*U.S. News & World Report,* April 4, 1994, pp. 28–30.

*Wall Street Journal,* August 31, 1988, pp. 1, 14.

—*Sketch by Jason Gallman*

# Carol A. Sanchez

## 1961-

### Mexican American industrial engineer

Carol A. Sanchez's accomplishments at Hughes Aircraft Company have earned her the Superior Performance Award, Hughes's highest recognition to be conferred upon an individual, and the 1990 National Hispanic Engineer Achievement Award for the Most Promising Engineer. She serves as senior industrial engineer at Hughes's Missile Systems Group in Tucson, Arizona. "My work consists of offering production support to the team of experts who build missiles," she explained to this contributor in a 1992 interview. "The tasks include analyzing and developing manufacturing machinery and equipment, methods and standards, and evaluating and establishing simplified production process and motion patterns for greater output and less fatigue for the workers." Sanchez admits that she did not plan to make a career in engineering. "All I knew was that I wanted to attend the University of Arizona and do something with computers. I didn't know anything about engineering."

Sanchez was born in Tucson, Arizona, on April 24, 1961, the third child of a family of four children and a third generation Mexican American. Her parents regarded education as crucial. "You had to be sick and dying to be excused from school," she recalled in her interview. Her fondest memories of elementary school are the field trips her class took to the museum. "I loved to learn about the role American Indians and Hispanics played in our history." In high school, she shunned science and mathematics and concentrated on typing and shorthand classes. But she became interested in computer sciences at a career information fair organized by her school. "This was the early seventies and computers were up and coming. The sheer novelty of it fascinated me." So when the time came to choose a field of study, she thought of computers but without anything more specific. "I virtually came to engineering by process of elimination," she confessed. "Upon entering the University of Arizona, I had the choice to take on liberal arts, business, or engineering. The first two fields of study did not appeal to me, and the engineering courses seemed interesting. So, I took engineering." In 1984, Sanchez graduated with a B.S. in systems engineering. The following year, she joined Hughes Aircraft.

## Stresses the Importance of Communication

Sanchez is assigned to the company's Advanced Medium Range Air to Air Missile Program (AMRAAM). The project incorporates the latest digital technology and micro-miniaturized solid-state electronics to improve air-to-air capability of U.S. fighter aircraft. Sanchez provides industrial engineering support to the program. She is also on the Continuous Measurable Improvement (CMI) team for improved productivity and on the CMI tool system team. "Besides handling equipment and material, engineering means dealing with people," she stressed in her interview. "Communication, both verbal and written, might be the most important skill in an engineering career. You must learn to work with people from different cultures and backgrounds, and to respect the workers who build a unit according to your specifications as much as the managers who use your report to make a decision."

This is one tip Sanchez gives students in her lectures. She regularly visits elementary and high schools, takes part in the pre-engineering workshops held every year at the University of Arizona, and speaks at the annual Youth Convention of the League of United Latin American Citizens (LULAC). "My message is simple," said Sanchez in her interview. "I tell students to focus on education, to develop people skills and to take advantage of internship programs to acquire experience in the workplace." Sanchez is cochairperson of the Education Committee for Hughes Hispanic Employees Association (HHEA). With the help of two HHEA members, and in cooperation with the Tucson Professional Women's Network, she has launched a mentor program to support Hispanic students at Tucson's Cholla High School.

Sanchez belongs to the Society of Hispanic Professional Engineers. In 1990, she was recognized by *Professional* magazine as one of the top 20 minority engineers in the country. In 1991, the corporation AT&T selected her as a role model to be featured in an exhibit honoring Hispanic achievers. Besides getting Hughes's prestigious Superior Award in 1987, she received two of the company's High Performance Team Awards in 1989.

Sanchez has taken part in Hughes's career development program offered to employees with a promising future with the company. She plans to earn a master's degree in business administration or in a technical field and later join Hughes's management staff. In October of 1992 she married Michael W.

Conrad, an industrial engineer at Hughes Aircraft Company.

## SOURCES:

### Periodicals

*Hispanic Engineer* (conference issue), 1990, p. 60.
*Engineering Horizons* (women's edition), 1991–1992, p. 109.
*Professional,* winter 1990, p. 27.

### Other

Sanchez, Carol A., interview with Michelle Vachon, conducted on May 8, 1992.

—*Sketch by Michelle Vachon*

# David A. Sanchez
## 1933-

### Hispanic American mathematician

David A. Sanchez is a mathematics scholar with international teaching experience whose recent positions have led him into science administration and academic research program development. Through his study of calculus during his early career, Sanchez developed a particular interest in using ordinary differential equations to create mathematical models for the study of population growth and competing populations. More recently, he has been actively interested in minority participation in academics, and as the vice chancellor for academic affairs of the Texas A & M University System, he provides leadership and coordination to a system of seven universities with an enrollment of more than 75,000 students.

David Alan Sanchez was born in San Francisco, California, on January 13, 1933, to Cecilio and Concepcion Sanchez. After obtaining his bachelor of science degree in mathematics from the University of New Mexico in 1955, Sanchez entered the U.S. Marine Corps in 1956. In 1959 he left the Corps as a lieutenant to attend the University of Michigan, where he earned his M.S. in 1960 and his Ph.D. in 1964. During those graduate school years, he also worked as a research assistant in the Radar Laboratory of the university's Institute of Science and Technology, where he worked on signal processing and battlefield simulations for U.S. Army applications. In 1963 he accepted an instructor's position at the University of Chicago; he remained there until 1965 when he became a visiting professor for a year at Manchester University in Manchester, England. In 1966 he returned to the United States, becoming an assistant professor at the University of California at Los Angeles. In 1970 he took another year as visiting assistant professor, this time at Brown University in Providence, Rhode Island, and then returned to UCLA as associate professor. After spending a school year during 1973 and 1974 as visiting associate professor at the University of Wisconsin's Mathematics Research Center, Sanchez became a full professor at UCLA in 1976. In 1977 he returned to his alma mater, accepting a professorship at the University of New Mexico. He remained there until 1986, serving as chair of the department of mathematics and statistics from 1983 to 1986. He took time during 1982 to teach at the University of Wales in Aberystwyth.

### Developed Interest in Biomathematics

During this period, Sanchez developed an interest in biomathematics—math that can be applied to the study of biology. He began using mathematical models to study population growth and competing populations. In his study on an ordinary game bird, the sand hill crane, for instance, Sanchez used a mathematical model to predict the effect of an external force that reduces a population, in this case by hunting. He wanted to formulate a simple mathematical equation that could predict the point at which the crane population would face extinction because it was being hunted at a rate faster than it could reproduce and grow. In this and other research studies, Sanchez constructed mathematical models that have implications for the study of human populations.

In 1986, Sanchez made a career switch and accepted a position as vice president and provost at Lehigh University in Bethlehem, Pennsylvania. After four years of administrative experience there, he became the assistant director for mathematical and physical sciences for the National Science Foundation in Washington, D.C. In 1992 he changed from administering science funds to helping to run a federal laboratory, joining the Los Alamos National Laboratory in New Mexico as deputy associate director for research and education. On November 1, 1993, he became vice chancellor for academic affairs for the Texas A & M University System. This large state system employs more than 19,000 people and has operations in each of the 254 counties in Texas. In a *Texas A & M Fortnightly* article, university chancellor William Mobley said that Sanchez's extensive experience with academic and research program development both at the university and at the federal level made him capable of providing the long-range academic planning and linkages needed by its vast university system.

Sanchez is a member of the American Mathematical Society, the Mathematical Association of America, the Society of Industrial and Applied Mathematics, and the Society for the Advancement of Chicanos and Native Americans in Science. A specialist in differential equations, he has published more than 50 articles in professional and technical journals and also is the author of three books on mathematics. He has served on several boards of governors, directors, advisory boards, and policy committees. Always interested in minority participation in academics, he served on the American Mathematical Society's Committee on Opportunities in Mathematics for Disadvantaged Groups, and the Committee on Minority Participation in Mathematics for the Mathematics Association of America.

Sanchez married Joan Patricia Thomas in 1957, and they have two children, Bruce and Christina. Besides mathematics and administration, Sanchez enjoys fishing, bridge, and fiction writing and has published articles in *Flyfishing News* and *The Steamboat Whistle*.

## SELECTED PUBLISHED WORKS:

### Books

*Ordinary Differential Equations and Stability Theory: An Introduction,* W. H. Freeman and Co., 1968.

(With William D. Lakin) *Topics in Ordinary Differential Equations: A Potpourri,* Prindle, Weber & Schmidt, 1970.

(With R. C. Allen and W. T. Kyner) *Differential Equations: An Introduction,* second edition, Addison-Wesley, 1988.

## SOURCES:

### Periodicals

*Texas A & M Fortnightly,* September 27, 1993.

### Other

Sanchez, David A., interview with Donna Olendorf, April 20, 1994.

—*Sketch by Leonard C. Bruno*

# Luis Rafael Sánchez
## 1936-
### Puerto Rican dramatist, novelist and critic

Luis Rafael Sánchez is one of Puerto Rico's foremost literary figures; he is a radio and stage actor, a playwright, a critic, and a novelist. He achieved international acclaim with his novel, *La guaracha del macho Camacho,* ("*Macho Camacho's Beat,*"), which was described by **Gabriel García Márquez** as, "one of the best books I've read in recent years . . . an excellent demonstration of what can be done with a popular voice . . . of great artistic value." Sanchez's plays have frequented the Experimental Theater of the Puerto Rican Ateno and festivals organized by the Puerto Rican Institute of Culture.

Sánchez acknowledges the influence of Tennessee Williams, **Federico García Lorca,** Bertolt Brecht, Eugene Ionesco, and René Marqués. His literary output reflects his commitment to issues facing lesser developed countries and, like Marqués, his opposition to Puerto Rico's subjugation by the United States. Revealing the the inspiration behind his work, Sánchez told Marie-Lise Gazarian Gautier: "I write because I would like to leave an imprint behind of what it was like to be a Puerto Rican in our day and age, particularly in light of all the problems we have because of our ties with the United States." His essays and literary criticism predominately focus on Puerto Rican cultural issues and Puerto Rico's political circumstances. Sánchez's plays, novels, and short stories, though often containing political undercurrents, are highly regarded for their aesthetic qualities and rhythmic language.

Sánchez was born on November 17, 1936, in the coastal town of Humancao in Puerto Rico. A member of a working class family, he attended the local elementary and secondary schools. As an adolescent he first realized his literary aspirations. They were generated by "the desire to reorder my outlook on reality and with that desire came the need to write," he explained to Gazarian Gautier. He continued his education at the University of Puerto Rico, where he majored in theater studies. Sánchez was awarded a fellowship from the university, which enabled him to attend courses in theater and creative writing at Columbia University in New York.

After graduation he began teaching theater studies at his alma mater's experimental high school. He returned to the United States, supported by the University of Puerto Rico, to study Spanish literature at New York University, where he was awarded a Master of Arts in 1963. Back in Puerto Rico he taught

Spanish at the University of Puerto Rico. He briefly returned to Colombia University, although he never completed his studies there.

Sánchez was accorded recognition early in his literary career. His debut play, *La espera* ("The Waiting", 1960), written for an assignment as an undergraduate, earned an honorable mention from the Puerto Rican Ateno in 1958. The play premiered in 1959. He was awarded a prize for his subsequent work, a children's play "Cuento de Cucarachita Viudita" (1959), which remains unpublished.

In 1960 Sánchez's first major play, *La farsa del amor compradito* ("The Farce of Purchased Love"), appeared; an erotic farce, its rich language imparts Sánchez's regard for the Spanish writer **Valle Inclán**. Throughout the 1960s Sánchez continued to write and stage plays such as: *Los ángeles se han fatigado* ("The Angels Are Exhausted," 1960), *La hiel nuestra de cada día* ("Our Daily Bitterness," 1962) and *La pasión según Antígona Pérez* ("Passion According to Antígona Pérez," 1968). He also published a collection of short stories, *En cuerpo de camisa* (1966); they employ a baroque language which is the signature of many of his later works.

Sánchez received his doctorate from the University of Madrid in 1973. Since his return from Spain, he has been a Professor of Literature at the University of Puerto Rico at Río Piedras. He found international fame with his novel *Macho Camacho's Beat* (1980), the English translation of the highly successful *La guaracha del Macho Camacho*. The book was first published in Buenos Aires in 1976, and established him as a leading Latin American writer. Described as "a thoroughly Latin American novel" by Robert Houston in *The Nation*, the story revolves around Macho Camacho's beat, the latest hit song, whose sound resonates around the island. The novel combines popular speech with elements of Spanish baroque to create a distinctive rhythmic literary prose.

The success of *Macho Camacho's Beat* changed Sánchez's life. In 1979 he was awarded a grant from the Guggenheim Foundation, and in 1983 he was a guest scholar at the Woodrow Wilson Center in Washington. He received a grant from the Deutscher Akademischer Austrauschdienst-Berliner Künstler Programm and spent 1985 as a guest writer in Berlin. He was a visiting professor at the City College of New York in 1988 and at Johns Hopkins University in Baltimore in 1989.

## SELECTED PUBLISHED WORKS:

### Plays

*Los ángeles se han fatigo* and *Farsa del amor compradito,* Ediciones Lugar, San Juan, 1960.

. . . *O casi el alma: Auto da fé en tres actos,* (Almost the soul: Auto da fé in Three Acts; first produced in San Juan at Teatro Tapia, April 23, 1964), Ediciones Rumbos, Barcelona, 1966, published as *Casi el alma: Auto da fé en tres actos,* Editorial Cultural, Río Piedras, Puerto Rico, 1974.

*La pasión según Antígona Pérez,* (two-act; first produced in San Juan at the eleventh theater festival of the Institute of Puerto Rican Culture, May 30, 1968; produced as "The Passion of Antígona Pérez" in New York at Cathedral Church of St. John the Divine, 1972), Ediciones Lugar, Hato Rey, Puerto Rico, 1968.

*La hiel nuestra de cada día,* ("Our Everyday Bile"), Editorial Cultural, 1976.

*Teatro de Luis Rafael Sánchez,* ("Plays of Luis Rafael Sánchez"), Editorial Antillana, 1976.

*Quintupules,* ("Quintuplets;" two-act; first produced in San Juan at the Centro de Bellas Artes de Puerto Rico, October 3, 1984), Ediciones del Norte, 1985.

### Other

*En cuerpo de camisa: Cuentos* (short stories), Ediciones Lugar, 1966, fourth augmented edition, Editorial Cultural, 1984.

*La guaracha del Macho Camacho* (novel), Ediciones de la Flor, Buenos Aires, 1976, translation by Gregory Rabassa published as *Macho Camacho's Beat,* Pantheon, 1980.

*Fabulación e ideología en la cuentística de Emilio S. Belavel* (non-fiction), Instituto de Cultura Puertorriqueña, San Juan, 1979.

(Contributor) Rose S. Minc (editor), *Literature and Popular Culture in the Hispanic World: A Symposium,* Ediciones Hispanoamericanas, 1982.

*La importancia de llamarse Daniel Santos,* Ediciones del Norte, 1988.

## SOURCES:

### Books

*Spanish American Authors: The Twentieth Century,* edited by Ángel Flores, New York, The H.W. Wilson Company, 1992.

*A Dictionary of Contemporary Latin American Authors,* edited by David William Foster, Center for Latin American Studies, Arizona State University, 1975.

Gazarian Gautier, Marie-Lise, *Interviews with Latin American Writers,* Elmwood Park, IL, The Dalkey Archive Press, 1989.

*Hispanic Writers: A Selection of Sketches from Contemporary Authors,* edited Ryan, Detroit, Gale, 1991.

**Periodicals**

*The Nation,* May 23, 1981, p. 642.

—*Sketch by Amanda Beresford*

---

# Ricardo Sanchez
## 1941-

### Mexican American poet and educator

Born in 1941, Ricardo Sanchez has taken an unorthodox route to be among the ranks of scholars and artists. A high-school dropout (or "push-out," as he says) Sanchez never confused his disdain for educational institutions for apathy toward learning. From his relatively disadvantaged youth, Sanchez has become a teacher and a poet who has visited and lectured at many college campuses and other places. An accomplished writer in both Spanish and English, Sanchez has defied those like some of his elementary school teachers who told him that if he wanted to be a writer, he was "barking up the wrong tree."

Sanchez rejects the label "Hispanic." He feels more comfortable with "Chicano" because, as he told James McCarthy, "Hispanic denies the other things that I am." Quick to point out that he is "mestizo," Sanchez says, "there were no Native Americans in Spain." Born on March 29, 1941, to Pedro Lucero Sanchez and his wife Adelina Gallegos, Sanchez experienced blatant racial stereotyping in his youth which eventually helped him solidify his identity. He told McCarthy that in elementary school certain teachers seemed to "take pride in insulting us, calling us 'dirty Mexicans.'" Interested in poetry from the beginning, Sanchez says that his teachers directly discouraged him from pursuing his ambitions as an author. "They told us that Mexicans could never be poets," he said, "that we could only work with our hands."

Sanchez's disillusionment with school led him to leave without graduating because of the failure of his schools to nurture his ambitions. Sanchez later spent two separate periods in state prisons, once in Texas and once in California, but eventually earning his Grade Equivalence Diploma, he pursued his lifelong desire to study literature. He received a Ford Foundation fellowship for three years, and with no bachelor's degree, he completed a Ph.D. in American Studies in 1974 from Union Graduate School.

Degree in hand, he became poet-in-residence, funded by the National Endowment of the Arts, at El Paso Community College in 1975. In the 1970s he published *Canto y grito mi liberacion (y lloro mis desmadrados)* (1973), *HechizoSpells* (1976), and *Milhaus Blues and Gritos Nortenos* (1978). He left El Paso and went to Utah State University as an assistant professor in 1977 until 1981. During that time the Chicano Student Association of Utah State University named him as an Outstanding Faculty Member.

In the 1980s Sanchez continued to write and publish. He also owned a bookstore for several years and established himself as a free-lance writer for several newspapers. He continued his pursuit of Chicano issues as well, founding and working in organizations like Chicano Light and Power (1974–1976), and he became a trustee of the San Antonio Library in the mid 1980s.

Since 1991 Sanchez has worked at Washington State University as an Associate Professor, jointly appointed to the American Studies and English Departments. He sees literary and artistic education as "fundamental" to the success of equipping children for life. "Through art, we look at ourselves spiritually," he told McCarthy. "We are not just machines," Sanchez continued, "we need art in our existence." He feels that through teaching, he helps students to develop a sense of self based on their cultural identity, regardless of what culture it is.

Married since 1964 to Maria Teresa Silva, Sanchez enjoys a family life in which music and art play an integral part. He has imparted the value of those things to his three children. He fears, however, that too often children do not get that kind of spiritual nourishment at home. "A lot of kids are really losing it," he said, "and if we don't give them a means to develop a sense of self, their growth will fail."

Sanchez believes in the value of the identity of the individual, which has carried him through difficulties that others could not surmount. Rejecting the limitations imposed by society, Sanchez believes in justice, but not equality. "There is no such animal [as equality]," he said, "we are not entitled to anything, but we have to work with what we have." For Sanchez, "the most fascinating nature of all is human nature" and that "through art, we can see ourselves and we can become human."

## SELECTED PUBLISHED WORKS:

*Amsterdam cantos y poemas pistos,* 1983.
*Canto y grito mi liberacion (y lloro mis desmadrados),* 1973.
*Eagle Visioned/Feathered Adobes: Manito sojourns and pachuco ramblings,* 1989.

*HechizoSpells,* 1976.
*Milhaus Blues and Gritos Nortenos,* 1978.
*Selected Poems,* 1985.
*American Journeys (Jornadas Americanas),* Rob
   Lewis Publishing, 1995.

## SOURCES:

Sanchez, Ricardo, from an interview with James
   McCarthy, January 18, 1995.

—*Sketch by James McCarthy*

# Augusto César (Calderón) de Sandino
## 1895-1934

### Nicaraguan rebel and political philosopher

Augusto Sandino was born on May 18, 1895 in Niquinohomo, Nicaragua to a poor Indian girl named Maragarita Calderón and a moderately wealthy land owner named Don Gregorio Sandino. He grew up to be a fierce proponent of Latin American nationalism, and many people still revere him for refusing to surrender to U.S. Marines in their 1926 intervention in Nicaragua. His ability to elude U.S. and pro-government forces for six more years until the U.S. withdrawal has made him an enduring figure of inspiration to those who see Latin American nationalism as a valid political idea. The Sandinistas—who successfully overthrew the Somoza ruling family in Nicaragua in 1979—bear his name and revere him as a great military, political, and spiritual leader. He was assassinated in 1934 by the Nicaraguan National Guard.

### Early Days in Nicaraguan Lowlands

Born in 1895, Sandino grew up in a town of nearly 1000 people. His father, Don Gregorio Sandino, stood to inherit a considerable, but not massive, fortune. His mother, Margarita Calderón, had her child before she turned 18. According to Sandino, his father had turned 25 the year Calderón, a worker in his fields, gave him an illegitimate son. Sandino wrote that "I opened my eyes in misery and was brought up in misery." Until his early adolescence, Sandino survived without the benefit of his father's recognition or financial support. His mother worked picking coffee beans, during which time Sandino recalled

often staying at home by himself, even as a young child. As he got older he began to join his mother in the fields: "from the time I could walk I did so on the coffee plantation, helping my mother . . . in order to earn a few centavos." Sandino described his own childhood as "true sorrow" and even remembered occasions when he stole food to keep his mother from starving.

Sandino began to develop his concepts of justice and injustice at an early age. A chance meeting with his half-brother Sócrates—who lived in his father's luxurious house—showed him how well some lived and how poorly others lived, despite their hard work. At the age of nine, Sandino cared for his mother in the midst of a miscarriage. This was brought on by rough treatment from the soldiers who had thrown Margarita Calderón and her son in jail for receiving advance pay from one plantation and then accepting a better paying job at another. Sandino remarked how this moment in his life changed his thinking: "I lay down beside her on that bloody floor and thought of a thousand atrocious . . . acts of revenge. . . . Why does God love Sócrates more than he loves me? It's only us poor people who are getting screwed!"

After parting with his mother, Sandino struggled to survive. One day he met his father on the road. Sandino demanded to know if the man believed him to be his son. When he said yes, the boy asked why, then, did he favor Sócrates and do nothing for him. Don Sandino decided to bring the boy into his home, and Augusto Calderón became Augusto César Sandino, living the life he had envied after his encounter with Sócrates. He began his education, but later admitted that he was a "very bad student," concerned more with playing war and taunting the police. He did learn enough, however, to become a considerable help to his father in business and, in fact, opened his own enterprise dealing in grains. He conducted business with people in Managua and Grenada, Nicaragua, and developed a reputation as an honest businessman.

### Period of Travel and Turmoil

During this period he fell in love with his cousin Mercedes during an extended visit to Costa Rica in 1919. By 1921, Sandino planned to marry, but only a month before the ceremony another dramatic change in Sandino's life pre-empted matrimony. Sandino described how a man named Dagoberto heard rumors that his sister, "a widow, appeared to be involved with me [Sandino] in an amorous relationship." Unfortunately, the rumors persisted until Dagoberto and some friends found themselves seated in front of Sandino at church. During the mass they began to insult Sandino, who sat so passively that Dagoberto became infuriated. Dagoberto turned around and punched Sandino in the head. His patience exhausted,

Sandino "in a spontaneous and thoughtless act", shot Dagoberto at the high point of the Sunday mass.

Dagoberto only suffered an injury to the leg, but the scandal drove Sandino out of town to La Ceiba, Honduras. He worked in the Montecristo sugar plantation as a warehouseman and a mechanic. After an incident in which Sandino chased a man who stole gasoline from the Montecristo stores, he again decided to leave the country and went to Guatemala.

From Guatemala Sandino traveled to many places, working for many different kinds of companies. He took jobs with several American firms, and got his first exposure to what he came to see as American oppression of Latin America. In Tampico, Mexico in 1923, Sandino found high wages in the oil industry, an overwhelming American presence, and a growing political stability after ten years of civil war in that country. Still, many workers supported new labor movements in Mexico-including the Industrial Workers of the World, an anarchist group that eventually gave way in the 1920s to Mexican Communist groups. Sandino probably first encountered Communism in an organized form here, as well as American opposition to it.

While in Mexico Sandino also experienced his first encounter with Latin American nationalism. According to Neill Macaulay "Mexican nationalism . . . gloried in Mexico's Indian heritage." Sandino also had predominantly—though not purely—Indian roots, and he eventually developed this pride in his Indian heritage into an association with a "broad nationality embracing all Americans of Iberian and Indian descent." This nationalism crossed international lines, but remained consistent within Latin American culture, which Sandino came to contrast with North American civilization, particularly the United States.

### Violent Political Career

Though his American employers found him "in every way a most satisfactory employee," Sandino returned to Nicaragua after three years in Mexico and took work as a paymaster in a gold mine. There he began to implore the workers to demand better pay and conditions. He contrasted his experiences in Mexico—where legislation had improved the workers' lot—to what he saw in Nicaragua. Many workers liked what they heard, and Sandino developed a small following. He parlayed that following and his meager savings into an armed group of 29 men in October of 1926. Though his attack on a government garrison in Jícaro failed, Sandino managed to retain some followers, and he applied to the Constitutionalist government for men and war materiel. This new government distrusted Sandino, due particularly to his advocacy of workers' uprisings against the rich.

Eventually Sandino joined General Moncada at Prinzapolca, where the General initially ordered Sandino to surrender all the weapons he had captured as well as the ones that his soldiers carried themselves. Only coaxing from Doctor Arturo Vaca and Doctor Onofre Sandoval made Moncada grudgingly recant, allowing Sandino's men to carry their firearms. Sandino marched with Moncada and developed a stronger following, eventually establishing a 100 man outfit perched on Mount Yucapuca, near San Rafael del Norte. Sandino, now a General, found himself with a growing army and decided to attack a government position in Jinotega. After a successful invasion of the town, his troops fell to plunder. Discipline vanished and Sandino called for a retreat to San Rafael to re-establish order. Shortly thereafter, Sandino occupied Jinotega a second time, and eventually received the war equipment he had earlier requested from Moncada.

On May 4, 1927 Moncada met American diplomat Henry Stimson, who offered liberal elements control of six "departments" of Nicaragua if they would cease hostilities and accept the results of a US-monitored election. Moncada met with Sandino, who suspected from the beginning that Moncada wanted nothing more than to make a deal with the Americans. Sandino would be Governor of Jinotega, get $10 a day for each day he had already served in the Constitutionalist army, and all the mules he had used for military purposes. Sandino found the decision tormenting: "So I spent three days on El Común Hill, downcast, sorrowful, without knowing what attitude to take, whether to surrender the arms or defend the country, which was crying for commiseration from her sons." Sandino met with Moncada, who told him all the other Generals had decided to give up the fight. Sandino reacted to this disappointment by saying that he, too, would stop fighting. But the moment Moncada dismissed him back to his troops, Sandino began to formulate plans not to surrender, but to re-establish his command and march on San Rafael del Norte.

### Eluding U.S. Military Forces

Sandino decided to struggle regardless of the eventual cost. By risking his life for his nation, Sandino lived the principle which he described in a letter to his wife Blanca in October of 1927: "I prefer to lose your love and die in battle than to . . . survive in . . . oppression. I place above all loves the love of my country." Despite U.S. Marine Captain Hatfield's repeated offers of clemency if Sandino accepted surrender, the General refused. On July 13, 1927, Hatfield publicly declared Sandino an outlaw and warned any who aided him that they put themselves at risk. Sandino refuted Hatfield's charges that he lived outside the law as a bandit, explaining that he and his army survived on materials captured from the U.S. Marines and the benevolence of the Nicaraguan people. He even compared himself to George Washington, whose example he accused the American people of forgetting.

In drawing the parallel between himself and Washington, Sandino claimed that the "consciences (of the American people) had been hardened by material riches" and therefore they had forgotten that Washington struggled only for the same liberty Sandino fought for in Nicaragua. Sandino blamed the acquisition of material wealth for the loss of moral principle. In December of 1926, Sandino's statement of his political ideas closed with the words, "Property is theft!" As wealth made a country insensitive to the rights of the oppressed, personal wealth made an individual careless about the condition of liberty in his or her nation; Sandino refused offers of comfort and power from the Marines and from his own Constitutional government on several occasions.

Sandino's battles with the U.S. Marines continued for several years. He used guerilla tactics against a foe who overwhelmed him in size, training, and equipment, often ambushing the rear of an advancing army. Sandino wrote of an ambush in November of 1927 in which U.S. Marines, by Sandino's count, lost 600 men to his 30. He also recalled the recovery of a note wired to the mother of Marine Captain Bruce which read, "By the first of January we will have cut off the head of the bandit Sandino."

His forces withstood a long siege and bombing at El Chipote before having to retreat. Sandino came to see retreating from a position as less important than "maintaining our armed plan against the invaders." He wisely perceived that "it is much easier for Yankees to overcome a conventional force than Sandino and his columns." This is the same difficulty British troops had once had with American colonists.

In 1928 Moncada became President in the U.S.-supervised elections. Sandino refused to recognize the validity of the election, and continued gaining political strength in his own right. Earlier in the year, the Sixth World Congress of the Comintern in Moscow had gone on record in support of his struggle, while in the United States support for Marine operations began to flag. By December 6, the U.S. Marines fought their last battle in Nicaragua, although some officers remained to guide the new Nicaraguan National Guard. Sandino's forces continued to gain strength and enemies. Moncada encouraged "volunteers" to attack Sandino's positions, although the following year the United States asked Moncada to disband those units. By 1930, detention camps specifically for those suspected of helping Sandino or his partisans appeared. from June 6 to August 29, 1930, the Sandinista forces endured 14 battles in the northern and central areas, including one in which Sandino suffered a leg wound. Yet more recruits came to embrace his cause and his attacks increased in number and strength. In December, 1930, some National Guard troops mutinied against their commanders, perhaps out of sympathy for Sandino's cause. On January 2, 1931, Senator Borah of Idaho called for an immediate removal of all U.S. personnel from the country, reflecting dissolution of public support for President Herbert Hoover 's Nicaragua policy.

Sandino's forces also focused their attacks on U.S. business interests and in 1931 took over the headquarters of logging companies in Logtown and Luisana, as well installations of the United Fruit Company. In 1932, new Nicaraguan President Sacasa asked U.S. President Franklin Roosevelt not to withdraw U.S. troops. More and more Nicaraguan government troops deserted, however, and the situation became very sticky for the American leader. On December 24, 1932, Sandino declared his desire to negotiate a peace, and on January 1, 1933, Roosevelt recalled all U.S. Marines from the country.

After long negotiations with President Sacasa, Sandino won amnesty for all Sandinistas and sympathizers, and formed the Autonomist Party in May 1933. On June 2, his wife Blanca died giving birth to his daughter Blanca Segovia. Throughout that summer Sandino's forces found themselves under attack from the National Guard, with whom they had a truce. Negotiations continued for a peaceful end to the conflict.

On February 21, 1934 Sandino accepted President Somoza's invitation to dinner. After dinner, National Guard troops detained Sandino's car, which also carried his father, Minister Salvatierra, and Generals Estrada and Umanzor. The soldiers executed Sandino and his Generals, having already killed Sócrates Sandino earlier in the day. Although Somoza accepted the guilt for Sandino's assassination, the Nicaraguan National Congress declared an amnesty for any crimes committed between February 16, 1933 and August 25, 1934, leaving Somoza in no danger of prosecution. Somoza's family ruled Nicaragua until 1979 when they were overthrown by a rebel group calling themselves Sandinistas.

## SOURCES:

*Sandino in the Streets,* edited by Wayne Bragg, Indiana University Press, 1991.

*Sandino,* edited by Robert Conrad and Sergio Ramirez, Princeton University Press, 1990.

*Sandino's Communism: Spiritual Politics for the 21st Century,* by Donald Hodges, University of Texas Press, 1992.

*The Last Night of General Augusto Sandino,* by Domingo Ibarra-Grijalva, (translated by Gloria Bonitz), 3.

*The Sandino Affair,* by Neill Macaulay, Duke University Press, 1985.

—*Sketch by James McCarthy*

# José Francisco de San Martín
## 1778-1850
### Argentine revolutionary and statesman

José Francisco de San Martín was an Argentine national hero who retired from public life at the height of his powers. In terms of service to his country, he has often been compared to America's George Washington. The disciplined, humane professional soldier was known for his calm dignity and strength of character in securing Argentina's independence from Spain. In that he differed markedly from his fiery contemporary, **Simón Bolívar,** the Venezuelan revolutionary who also fought for independence from Spain. San Martín was also a compatriot of **José Artigas**, whose name became synonymous with Uruguay's struggle for freedom from Spanish and English domination.

A soldier in the service of the Spanish Army at a very young age, San Martín acquired, by the time he was in his early thirties, the military skills and experience needed for his role in the liberation of Argentina. His crossing of the treacherous Andes Mountains from Argentina to Chile with an army of 5,000 has been compared to Hannibal's crossing of the Alps. This military achievement opened the way to enter Peru (Spain's power center) and crush the Spanish hold on South America.

Although he was praised and revered for his military exploits, San Martín was also loved for the legacy of schools and libraries that he established for the people of Argentina. Unfortunately, San Martín's decision not to become involved in his country's internal politics after emancipation caused him to be ostracized and ridiculed. At a time when some of South America's revolutionary heroes were prone to cover themselves with glory and let personal ambition override the general good, San Martín stood out as one whose patriotism was grounded in his ethical character. Disillusioned by Bolívar's actions and those of other military and political leaders of the independence movement, he resigned his command as Peruvian protector and left South America for exile in Europe, where he remained until his death in 1850.

## Established Roots in South America

San Martín was born in the pueblo of Yapeyú in Argentina on February 25, 1778. His parents were Juan de San Martín and Jerónima Matorras, both of whom were born in Spain. His father was an officer in the Spanish Army at the time of his marriage, which was performed by proxy due to the dictates of an immediate military assignment in Buenos Aires, Argentina. San Martín's mother was a daughter of Castilian nobility. After their marriage, Juan de San Martín was made governor of the Misiones province, where the couple made their home. José was the baby of the family. He had one sister, María Helena, and three brothers—Juan Fermín, Manuel Tadeo, and Justo Rufino. All the boys were to follow their father into a military career. San Martín married Remedios de Escalada in Buenos Aires on September 12, 1812. Their only child, a daughter named Mercedes, was born August 24, 1816. His wife died in Buenos Aires on August 12, 1823.

Yapeyú was a humble Indian settlement along the Uruguay River in the Argentine province of Misiones. It was founded in 1626 by the Jesuits. This mission town was connected by its geography to Buenos Aires, which was the administrative capital of the district. In 1767, the Jesuits were banished by the government and all Jesuit property was turned over to civil authority. This action was caused in part by warring among the Portuguese in Brazil, the Spanish along the Río de la Plata, and revolutionaries on the Argentinean border.

It was in the midst of this turmoil that the young San Martín grew up, while his father served both as civil administrator of Misiones and military protector against Peruvian aggression. In 1781, the San Martín family left Yapeyú for Buenos Aires, which had now become the capitories, *En cuerpo de camisa* al of the Río de la Plata region. When he was seven the family left Argentina for Spain. None but José was to return to South America. His brothers remained behind to fight for the Spanish king, while José returned to Argentina to fight on the side of those who sought freedom from Spanish domination.

## Young San Martín in Spain

San Martín continued his early education at the Madrid Nobles' Seminary, which was founded by Philip V. There he became known for his exceptional memory, his concentration, and his good judgment. He had some talent for the arts, but was never to excel as a speaker or writer. His favorite subjects were the objective sciences. His schooling was to last only through elementary age; he entered the Peninsular Army as a cadet when he was only 11. This was partly due to his parents' need for economic assistance and partly due to his desire to follow in the footsteps of his father and brothers. San Martín became a member of the Murcia Regiment on July 9, 1789, which he marked as the beginning of his military career.

He was to serve in the Spanish Army for 20 years, but he was just 13 when he fought his first battle against the French at Orán. Spain's shifting allegiances with her neighboring countries also caused him to see action against England and Portugal—France having become an ally by that time. Later, during Napoleon Bonaparte's invasion of Spain in 1808, San Martín played a heroic part in the emperor's defeat. By 1811 he was given command of the Regiment of Dragoons of Sagunto, which was the last post he held in the Spanish Army. The following year would mark a drastic change of direction in his life.

As a young man, San Martín spent time in the south of Spain—in Andalucía, Málaga, and Seville. But it was Cádiz, the port from which many Spaniards left for America, that he frequented the most. It was there he heard the news of revolutionary unrest in Buenos Aires. Based on this, and the influence of other revolutionary ideas swirling around Europe, he renounced his allegiance to Spain and returned to South America. For someone with San Martín's background and years of Spanish fidelity, this decision was an excruciating one to make. However, he had begun to question the principles by which the Spanish Empire was guided, and in this he was not alone.

In Cádiz, there existed an underground group of native-born South Americans whose purpose was to further the cause of independence. This group had connections with a larger "lodge" based in London and headed by Francisco Miranda, famed for his part in the French Revolution. Miranda's group was part of a larger European organization, which had as its purpose the support and promulgation of liberation principles. San Martín's first step back to the land of his birth was to join the Cádiz lodge. Then on September 14, 1811, he left Cádiz for London. From there, with a group of fellow revolutionaries, he left for Buenos Aires, arriving on March 9, 1812, after a sea voyage of 50 days. Among the revolutionaries who accompanied him were three who would command armies or fight under San Martín in South America—**Bernardo O'Higgins,** Carlos de Alvear, and Matías Zapiola.

### Success in Battle

The atmosphere in Buenos Aires and other South American cities was one greatly affected by the wars of liberation going on in Europe at that time. The "colonial revolt" in the United States was also watched with great interest and sympathy by the Spanish-American bourgeoisie. In 1806, the Argentines had beaten back a British invasion by themselves, which also added to the revolutionary fever. The South American natives sent to Spain by their families for education and military careers, like San Martín, had learned lessons in liberation that would later be put to use against the Spanish Empire. The weakening of Spain by Napoleon's invasion in 1808 set the stage for a move against Spanish domination in South America.

By 1810, popular juntas were organized in Caracas, Venezuela, and Buenos Aires. On May 25 of that year, the Argentine junta forced the resignation of Don Baltasar Hildalgo de Cisneros, the last Spanish viceroy. A concerted effort toward revolution had begun. It was to the leaders of the juntas that San Martín and his group reported. Several revolutionary leaders sought his advice—in acknowledgement of his rank of lieutenant colonel and his military achievements—although some viewed San Martín with suspicion throughout his career because they could not reconcile his loyalty to the revolutionary cause with his years as a Spanish military officer. San Martín recommended that the junta strengthen the government to maintain civil order and organize an army to move against the enemy. He was chosen to command that army. By December 1812, he had recruited and trained a regiment of 300 native Misiones (the region where he was born). These soldiers went on to make a strong showing in many battles; more than 19 generals and 200 officers were promoted from under San Martín's leadership during the course of the revolution.

The years from 1812 to 1816 were spent clearing the Spanish out of Argentina. After Argentine independence was declared on July 9, 1816, the government felt able to aid Chile in its struggle for independence. San Martín was made commander of the Argentine forces in 1817 and was eager to put his plan for the liberation of Chile and Peru into action. He faced a number of difficulties, however, because government supplies and troops were slow in coming. Ricardo Rojas, in his book *San Martín, Knight of the Andes,* quoted San Martín as saying: "The army called of the Andes had for a foundation only 180 men of Battalion No. 11, without the least training and very badly disciplined. Eight months before undertaking the expedition to Chile the government sent Battalion No. 7, with 450 men and 220 mounted grenadiers; the rest of the army was recruited in Mendoza." The recruitment called for all of San Martín's ingenuity and resourcefulness. The sparsely populated area, the poverty of the province governments, and internal politics all conspired against him. Coming to his aid was the supreme director in Buenos Aires, Juan Martín de Pueyrredón, who sent money, arms, and men. Finally, San Martín had readied 4,000 troops, 1,200 auxiliary militia, and the necessary supplies to clothe, feed, and arm them.

The Andes mountain range, the second-highest in the world, separates Argentina from Chile on its western border. Peaks reach from 11,000 to 13,000 feet in the middle ranges and soar to almost 24,000 feet in isolated areas. San Martín's plan was to send a northern division and a southern division ahead into Chile to secure towns at opposite ends, while at the same time the main body of his army would come through the passes of Uspallata and Los Patos, confusing and dividing the royalist forces. The northern and southern divisions left for Chile in early January 1817 and had accomplished their mission by early February, thus realizing a large part of San Martín's strategy. The main part of the campaign split into two and moved simultaneously. A division of 800 men crossed the Andes through the Uspallata Road. Four days later, the main body of the army, under Generals Soler and O'Higgins and supervised by San Martín, followed a parallel course by way of Los Patos. It took 18 days for all his troops to cross the Andes and concentrate in Chile. San Martín gave this account in Ricardo Levene's *History of Argentina:* "The soldiers of the army with supplies for almost a month, with armament, munitions of war, and baggage have marched a hundred leagues along a road which crossed craggy peaks, defiles, folds, and deep, narrow chasms—a road intersected by four mountain ridges, where the ruggedness of the terrain competes with the harshness of the atmosphere." Thus, he led his troops through the most dangerous and difficult part of the Andes campaign.

Two major battles were fought in Chile—at Chacabuco and Maipú. The victory at Chacabuco on February 12, 1817, held great political and military significance. It demonstrated the revolutionary forces' offensive might to the Spanish; it secured a base of operations on the Pacific from which to fight; and it confined the Spanish forces in Peru, leaving them vulnerable to the oncoming army. For these reasons, the battle of Chacabuco marked the beginning of the Spain's retreat in South America. Maipú, on April 5, capped the victory at Chacabuco. From Maipú, San Martín's revolutionary forces marched into Peru, intending to join with Simón Bolívar to win independence for Peru and Bolivia—the next major step toward liberation of all South America.

### Retirement to Private Life

Ironically, the occasion of San Martín's greatest triumph was to mark the beginning of his withdrawal from service to his country. Bolívar's lack of cooperation and a dispute with San Martín over how best to end the war against Spain caused San Martín to cede the field to Bolívar. Disillusioned by dissension among military and political leadership of the independence movement, he resigned as protector of Peru on September 22, 1822. In *A History of Argentina,* he is quoted from a speech to the Congress of the newly liberated country: "My promise to the countries for which I have fought is fulfilled: to secure their independence, and to leave them to select their own

governments. The presence of a fortunate soldier, however disinterested he may be, is dangerous to newly established states." Thus San Martín revealed his moral philosophy—that the military man and the political man should not be one and the same, for such a situation placed personal ambition and power above the welfare of the state.

The Congress attempted to honor his service with the title of "America's First Soldier of Liberty," a yearly pension of 12,000 pesos, and an appointment as commander-in-chief of the land and sea forces in Peru. However, San Martín refused these honors. He left Peru and went back to Buenos Aires, and in February of 1824 he sailed from there to Europe. He was to spend the rest of his life in self-imposed exile in Grand Bourg, France, where he died on August 17, 1850, at the age of 72.

### SOURCES:

Alexander, Robert J., *An Introduction to Argentina,* New York, Praeger, 1969.

Koebel, W. H., *Argentina, Past and Present,* London, Black, 1914.

Levene, Ricardo, *A History of Argentina,* translated and edited by William Spence Robertson, New York, Russell, 1963.

Rojas, Ricardo, *San Martín, Knight of the Andes,* translated by Herschel Brickell and Carlos Videla, New York, Cooper Square, 1967.

Weddell, Alexander Wilbourne, *Introduction to Argentina,* New York, Greystone Press, 1939.

Whitaker, Arthur P., *The United States and Argentina,* Cambridge, Massachusetts, Harvard University Press, 1954.

—*Sketch by Jane Stewart Cook*

# Antonio López de Santa Anna
## 1794-1876
### Mexican general and statesman

Also known as Antonio López de Santa Anna Perez de Labron, Antonio López de Santa Anna, military hero and five-time Mexican president, played such a central role in his country's history that the years of the mid-nineteenth century in Mexico have been called the "Age of Santa Anna." As a general he was an ingenious tactician: brave, resourceful, and inspiring. As president, he was a defender of the traditional powers of the church, the military, and the landowners.

Santa Anna was born in 1794 in Jalapa, Mexico, and grew up in the nearby coastal city of Veracruz. His parents, Antonio Lafey de Santa Anna and Manuela Perez de Labron, were both of Spanish descent. Little is known of Santa Anna's childhood. His formal education was limited, and he appears to have been an uninterested student. He left school at an early age, and when he showed no interest in the mercantile vocation his father chose for him—longing instead for a military career—his father reluctantly facilitated an appointment in the Army of New Spain, the military arm of Spanish rule in Mexico.

At that time, the business of the Army of New Spain consisted largely of squelching Indian uprisings, and that is how the early years of Santa Anna's military career—first in an infantry unit, and then in the cavalry—were spent. From the outset, Santa Anna demonstrated great skill and courage as a soldier, and by 1821, he had achieved the rank of lieutenant colonel.

### Liberator of Mexico

Initially, Santa Anna's loyalty to Spanish rule was unquestioning. But when the rebel leaders Vicente Guerrero and **Agustin de Iturbide** announced their plans to fight for Mexico's independence in 1821, Santa Anna—possibly partially influenced by their offer of the rank of full colonel—joined them. Leading a rebel army, he set out to liberate Veracruz. Finding the city secured against him, he proceeded to conquer Alvarado and Cordoba. Several months later, when the Spanish military commander at Veracruz made a strategic retreat to the offshore island of San Juan de Ulua, Santa Anna returned to that city in triumph. The Treaty of Cordoba, which gave Mexico her independence from Spain, was signed on August 24, 1821, and Santa Anna was duly recognized as one of the liberators of his country.

In the chaotic conditions that followed independence, Iturbide seized power and had himself declared Emperor of Mexico. Santa Anna initially supported this move, believing that charismatic leadership was needed. Iturbide reciprocated, promoting Santa Anna to brigadier general and appointing him military commander of Jalapa and Veracruz. However, as Iturbide's methods grew more repressive, relations between the two cooled. Finally Iturbide, wary of Santa Anna's personal ambition, stripped him of his command and attempted to reassign him to a remote frontier posting. This act hardened Santa Anna's resolve against Iturbide. From his stronghold at Veracruz, Santa Anna announced his plan to oppose the empire. He declared Mexico a republic in December of 1822. With the support of insurgent leaders Guerrero, Guadalupe Victoria, and Nicolas Bravo, Santa Anna succeeded in overthrowing the Iturbide regime. He played no role in the formulation of the Constitution of 1824, which emerged from the negotiations following the overthrow of Iturbide. The new constitution divided Mexico into 19 states and four territories and provided for a balance between state and national government. Guadalupe Victoria was elected Mexico's first president.

Throughout his career, Santa Anna preferred the challenges of military encounter to the diplomatic and administrative chores of government. Following the overthrow of Iturbide, he traveled to the Yucatan to quell a revolt. He then retired temporarily to his newly-purchased estate outside of Veracruz, Manga de Clavo, where he settled with his new wife, the 14-year-old Ines Garcia. At Manga de Clavo, Santa Anna devoted himself to improving the estate and to his hobby of raising fighting cocks. The habit of retiring to the privacy of family life at Manga de Clavo between forays into political and military affairs became a pattern over the next 20 years. Visitors to the *hacienda* described Santa Anna as soft-spoken, courteous, and hospitable, an image much at odds with his public persona. His wife, Doña Ines, remained for the most part at the hacienda. The couple eventually had five children.

Guerrero became Mexico's second president. When he was narrowly defeated for re-election and decided to fight for his position, Santa Anna emerged from retirement to aid him. Santa Anna—whose military skill and personal magnetism were such that he always had the ability to raise an army at short notice—repelled the troops sent against him by Guerrero's rival, Manuel G. Pedraza, and returned Guerrero to office. His reward was appointment as governor and commandant general of Veracruz.

In 1829, Spain made a last attempt to reconquer Mexico, landing a formidable army at Tampico. Santa Anna singlehandedly raised an army and rushed to the republic's defense. The Spanish forces were superior in numbers, equipment, and training, and Santa Anna's initial attacks were parried. However, with fierce persistence, he fought the Spaniards all summer, keeping them bottled up in Tampico. In September, the Spanish commander—his ranks ravaged by yellow fever—formally recognized the independence of Mexico and was allowed to withdraw his troops to Cuba. Santa Anna was hailed as a hero and was proclaimed the Conqueror of Tampico. At about this time, he began referring to himself as the "Napoleon of the West."

### President of Mexico

Once again, Santa Anna withdrew to Manga de Clavo, but the republic continued to face problems. The vice president, General Anastasio Bustamante, led a successful uprising against President Guerrero, and become Mexico's third president. The Bustamante administration evolved into a harsh dictatorship which gave rise to revolt. In anticipation of Santa Anna's opposition, Bustamante sent troops to Veracruz, but Santa Anna fought his way past them and advanced on the capital. With Santa Anna's army looming, Bustamante capitulated. He went into exile in December of 1832, clearing the way for the nearly unanimous election of Santa Anna as president three months later.

With his characteristic lack of interest in the day-to-day affairs of government, Santa Anna departed for a military campaign, leaving his liberal vice president, Valentin Gomez Farias, in charge. Gomez Farias began implementing policies to eliminate special privileges traditionally accorded to wealthy landowners, the church, and the military. When complaints from these influential groups reached the conservative Santa Anna, he repudiated Gomez Farias and changed tactics. Santa Anna decided that Mexico needed strong personal leadership, and seized absolute power. He dissolved the congress, suspended the programs of the exiled Gomez Farias, and instituted policies aimed toward the establishment of a strong central government and protection of the privileged classes. He replaced the Constitution of 1824 with one of his own. The new constitution further strengthened the central government, relegating the states to the position of mere military departments under the president's control.

Santa Anna's repressive policies led inevitably to rebellion. In May of 1835, Santa Anna quelled an uprising in Zacatecas, accepting the title "savior" upon his return to the capital. But a more serious situation was developing. For some years, Mexico had encouraged the settlement of the northern province of Texas by North Americans as well as Mexicans. By 1830, former United States citizens outnumbered Mexicans in Texas by three to one, and conflicts began to develop between the two groups. Anglo settlers, under the leadership of Stephen F. Austin, began to demand a measure of political autonomy. The Mexican government was unwilling to make concessions and attempted to enforce control by abolishing slavery, closing the border to further colonization from the United States, and restricting trade. Santa Anna's centralization policies caused further unrest in Texas, where by 1835 opinion was divided between those who hoped for a return to the reforms of 1824 and those who wanted independence.

When Santa Anna ordered troops into Texas in that year, they faced armed resistance and were driven out by a party of volunteers led by Austin. Shortly afterward, the rebels declared Texas to be a republic. Santa Anna responded personally to the crisis, marching an army of 6,000 men north in the winter of 1835–36. In February, accompanied by half of his army, he clashed with 180 Texans who had taken up a defensive position in an abandoned Franciscan mission known as the Alamo. After a prolonged siege, Santa Anna attacked the mission with a policy of "no quarter," winning the battle and killing all the Alamo's occupants. This action earned him the undying enmity of Texans.

Santa Anna continued his victorious progression through Texas until—just six weeks after the Alamo—events changed dramatically. An army under the command of General Sam Houston dealt Santa Anna's forces a stunning blow with a surprise attack at the San Jacinto River. The Mexican Army suffered devastating losses and Santa Anna was taken prisoner. In May, Santa Anna signed two treaties with the Texans. One guaranteed that Mexican troops would be permanently withdrawn. The other—not made public at the time—specified that Santa Anna would work for Mexican recognition of the Republic of Texas in exchange for safe transport back to Veracruz. Santa Anna's activities in Texas were deeply unpopular in Mexico; indeed, the episode was the most serious setback of his career. Upon his release, he resigned as president and retired to Manga de Clavo in disgrace. Bustamante, who succeeded him, repudiated the treaty and refused to recognize Texan independence. In Mexico, Santa Anna was widely considered a traitor.

## Return to the Military

Santa Anna's reputation was rehabilitated in 1838, when France demanded monetary reparations from Mexico, resulting in war between the two countries. Santa Anna was considered the only man in Mexico who could successfully defend his country against this invasion, and Bustamante named him commander of the military forces at Veracruz. Initially surprised by the French invasion, Santa Anna rallied his troops, routed the French, and with characteristic vigor, pursued them to the harbor. There he led a dockside charge. But the French had anticipated such a move and were prepared. They fired a cannon loaded with shrapnel, killing Santa Anna's horse and shattering his lower left leg. In the confusion that followed, the French troops escaped. Santa Anna's leg was amputated below the knee.

Santa Anna's convalescence was interrupted by a call to the capital to serve as interim president while President Bustamante attended to ongoing revolts. When Bustamante's efforts faltered, Santa Anna himself returned to the battlefield, directing operations from a litter. In the victory that followed, Santa Anna's popularity eclipsed that of Bustamante, and in 1841, Santa Anna was once again elected president. The following three years comprised Santa Anna's longest presidential administration. According to Santa Anna's own account, it was a time marked by peace, reform, and progress. It is true that Mexico's first railroad was built during these years, the country's currency was revamped, and harmonious foreign relations were maintained. But Santa Anna's administration was a dictatorship. He developed a new constitution, known as Las Bases Organicas, which concentrated power in his own hands and insured the ascendancy of the wealthiest. He strengthened the army and the central bureaucracy, filled political positions with corrupt friends and financed it all through forced domestic loans and foreign borrowing. In keeping with his propensity for self-aggrandizement, he filled Mexico City with statues of himself.

In 1844, Santa Anna's wife, Ines-whom he had long neglected in favor of a succession of young mistresses-died of pneumonia. A few months later, the 50-year-old Santa Anna shocked the nation by announcing his intention to marry 15-year-old Maria Dolores de Tosta. Santa Anna's political position was already tenuous due to the country's deteriorating financial condition, and his unpopular marriage was the last straw. When his former ally, General Mariano Paredes, turned on him and led an army to the capital in December of 1844, Santa Anna was for once unable to raise troops adequate to his needs, and he fled. He was captured and imprisoned while his enemies pondered charges of treason. Ultimately, though, they decided not to put him on trial, and he was exiled to Havana, Cuba.

The year following Santa Anna's exile was a chaotic one in Mexico. Among other problems, the United States—having earned Mexico's enmity by annexing Texas—declared war. Armies of invasion challenged Mexican defenses. This military emergency brought Santa Anna to the forefront of Mexican political affairs once again. In order to accept command of Mexico's military forces, Santa Anna needed to cross the U.S. blockade of Veracruz. He engineered this by negotiating with emissaries sent to Havana by U.S. President James Knox Polk. He agreed to make every effort to conclude the war on terms favorable to the United States in return for his safe passage across the blockade. Once on Mexican soil, he forgot his promises.

With money lent by the church, Santa Anna raised and equipped an army of 20,000. In February of 1847, he marched north to meet General Zachary Taylor at the Battle of Buena Vista. Buena Vista, called Angostura by the Mexicans, was Santa Anna's finest hour. With an ingenious battle plan and inspiring leadership, he staved off the better equipped U.S. troops for two days, remaining at the front lines constantly to direct and encourage his men—even when his horse was shot from under him. Only when he realized that his exhausted men could not withstand a third day of battle did he withdraw from the field. Back in Mexico City, Santa Anna declared the battle a great victory and accepted a return to the presidency as his reward.

The war with the United States continued, with Santa Anna's army suffering defeat repeatedly at the hands of General Winfield Scott, as Scott advanced on Mexico City. Santa Anna attempted to negotiate for peace, but was blocked by his congress, which declared that treating with the enemy constituted treason. Scott captured Mexico City on September 14, 1847. The Mexican Congress stripped Santa Anna of his command and his presidency, and he fled the city. It fell to interim President Manuel de la Pena y Pena to negotiate the Treaty of Guadalupe Hidalgo, in which Mexico ceded to the United States Texas, California, and all the land between—amounting to the present-day states of New Mexico, Arizona, Nevada, Utah and part of Colorado. Mexico thus lost two thirds of her territory. In return, the United States agreed to pay $15 million and relieve Mexico of all outstanding U.S. claims. To escape an official inquiry into his conduct during the war, Santa Anna once again went into exile, this time in Jamaica, where he lived for the next two years. He then moved to Cartagena, Colombia, where he purchased a property near Turbaco. There he pursued a country life similar to that which he had enjoyed at Manga de Clavo. Santa Anna and his family lived in more or less comfortable exile in Colombia for several years.

In Mexico, political chaos continued. There were five liberal presidential administrations during Santa Anna's exile, with no appreciable improvement in conditions. By the time conservatives returned to power in 1853, ill feeling toward Santa Anna had dissipated. Conservative leader Lucas Alaman conceived a plan to create stability which included the appointment of Santa Anna as interim president for a period of one year, after which a monarch would be installed. Santa Anna accepted the proposal, returned to Mexico, and began his fifth and final term as president on April 20, 1853. Once again, he set about strenghthening the central government. Alaman had taken the precaution of personally choosing the members of Santa Anna's cabinet, and it was his intention to carefully monitor Santa Anna's activities. But when Alaman died the following June, the plan that might have protected the country from Santa Anna's despotic inclinations died with him. Santa Anna soon replaced Alaman's chosen cabinet with his own cronies, and his presidency descended into a dictatorship. In December of 1853, Santa Anna engineered an offer from the military to appoint him emperor, which he declined. Instead, he accepted the title of His Most Serene Highness, which carried with it an indefinite extension of his term and the right to name his successor.

To raise money to support the lavish spending that was always his hallmark, Santa Anna arranged to sell yet more Mexican territory. The Gadsden Purchase, completed in December, 1853, transferred there Mesilla Valley to the U.S. for the sum of $10 million. Santa Anna defended his action by pointing out that the United States would have taken the territory by force in any event, but his critics knew that the money from the purchase was needed to finance Santa Anna's extravagant spending and corrupt political practices. When Santa Anna instituted a huge tax increase the following year, dissent turned to revolt. Liberal rivals planned to oust Santa Anna and write a new constitution. Santa Anna managed to remain in power for several months, but in the face of his increasing inability to quell opposition, he appointed a triumvirate to take charge. He went, yet again, into exile.

### Waning Influence

This moment marked the end of Santa Anna's serious political influence in Mexico, but not the end of his ambitions. From his exile on the island of St. Thomas, he observed the installation of the European Maximilian as Emperor of Mexico in 1864, and made an abortive attempt to participate in the Maximilian government.

Later, when American Secretary of State William Seward paid a courtesy call on him while travelling in the Caribbean, Santa Anna mistakenly believed that the United States would support an attempt to overthrow Maximilian. Further misled by the activities of a swindler named Dario Mazuera, who claimed to be a go-between in fictitious negotiations with Seward, Santa Anna embarked on a misguided venture that ended in his financial ruin.

Disillusioned and impoverished, the old man made one last bid for power in an ill-advised foray against the United States-backed liberal government of **Benito Juarez**. Santa Anna was tried for treason and exiled to the Bahamas. There, he wrote his memoirs and corresponded with old friends. He was excluded from a general amnesty issued by Juarez in 1870, and it was only after Juarez's death of Juarez that he at last returned to his own country. He was eighty years old when he arrived in Mexico City in 1874, in poor health, nearly blind and deaf. His return was ignored by his countrymen, and he lived his remaining two years in obscurity, dying on June 21, 1876.

### SOURCES:

*Antonio López de Santa Anna,* by Steven O'Brien, New York, Chelsea, 1992.
*Autobiography of Santa Anna,* edited by Ann Fears Crawford, Austin TX, State House Press, 1988.
*The Men Who Made Mexico,* by Clarke Newlon, New York, Dodd, Mead, 1973.
*Mexico: A History,* by Robert Ryal Miller, Norman, OK, University of Oklahoma Press, 1985.

*—Sketch by Julie Henderson Jersyk*

# Andrés de Santa Cruz
## 1792-1865
**Bolivian statesman**

Andrés de Santa Cruz was a native Bolivian who served as one of **Simón Bolívar**'s generals, became president of Bolivia in 1829, and led the Peruvian-Bolivian Confederation from 1837 until it was defeated in 1839. Herbert Klein, in his book *Bolivia: The Evolution of a Multi-Ethnic Society,* called Santa Cruz "one of the most able administrators Bolivia would ever know." During his term as president of Bolivia he instituted a number of reforms, encouraging trade, industry, and public works. He was also instrumental in the expansion of education and founded Bolivia's first state universities. According to William Carter in *Bolivia,* "His efforts were lauded by Europeans—among them Hugo Wilson, then British consul in Bolivia, who wrote of Santa Cruz, 'I approach this Indian with more respect than I have for the King of England.'" Despite all these achievements, however, Santa Cruz was unsuccessful in his efforts to forge an Andean unity between Peru and Bolivia.

Little is known of Santa Cruz's life before his rise to power under Bolívar. A mestizo Indian, he was born in 1792 on the eastern shore of Lake Titicaca, in a small settlement near La Paz called Huarina. His father was a Spanish sub-delegate. His mother, Juana Basilia Calaumana, was an Indian noblewoman who claimed to be a descendant of Chief Calaumana of the Incan dynasty.

Santa Cruz served in the Spanish royalist army, rising to the rank of colonel, and fought for the Spanish during Peru's war of independence. In his book *Latin America: A Cultural History,* John Edwin Fagg observed that Santa Cruz "was an excellent officer, careful of his men and relying on sound strategy instead of brilliant tactical strokes to win battles." In 1817 he was captured by an Argentine expeditionary force to Upper Peru (now Bolivia). Santa Cruz was sent as a prisoner to Argentina, but he escaped and rejoined the Spanish army in Lima.

Klein asserted, however, that "his experiences among the Argentines and his frustrations with the changing and vacillating policies of the Crown ... led him to join forces with the rebels. Thus, in southern Peru in January 1821, he offered his services to General **[José de] San Martín** and his Chilean-Argentine army of invasion."

Now a colonel in the patriot army, Santa Cruz was involved in many battles in Peru. In 1822, San Martín sent an expeditionary force under Santa Cruz's command to aid General **Antonio José de Sucre**. Sucre and his troops, under Bolívar's command, were involved in a heated battle to wrest Quito (Ecuador) from royalist control. The combined forces were victorious in May. "The result," according to Klein, "was that Santa Cruz and his troops now became fully allied with Sucre and broke their allegiance to San Martín." That same year, Bolívar promoted Santa Cruz to general. By 1823 the Sucre-Santa Cruz alliance was in the region of northern Peru. Santa Cruz convincingly proposed that a large army could conquer the region, and proceeded to do so. In August Santa Cruz captured his native city of La Paz. In the famous battle of Zepita that followed, he also captured Oruro. He was forced to exit La Paz within a few months, however, as communication problems with Lower Peru developed and the royalist forces proved too powerful to resist. Upper Peru remained in royalist hands until early 1825.

### Became President of Bolivia

General Sucre was Bolivia's first president. In 1828 he was forced at gunpoint to resign from office and there began a rapid turnover in Bolivia's leadership. Sucre was able to turn command over to Santa Cruz, who convened the congress. The congress elected General Pedro Blanco president. He arrived in La Paz to take office on Christmas Day, 1828. His term lasted only five days before he was taken prisoner and murdered. He was succeeded by General **José Miguel Velasco**, who prudently suggested the presidency be offered to Santa Cruz, now a marshal. Santa Cruz accepted, and took up the reins of power in Bolivia in May 1829. He would serve for the next ten years.

The political climate throughout the newly formed Andean republics at the time was one of great instability. After Bolívar freed them from the yoke of Spanish rule, the Great Liberator imposed upon them his own constitution. As John Crow wrote in *The Epic of Latin America*, "Bolivia was the brainchild of Simón Bolívar; it bore his name; it was given life under his constitution." But practical application was not as easy as liberation had been, as Crow explained: "His refined [approach was] impractical in backward Bolivia. The Liberator attempted to organize and govern the country as if it were at least the semblance of a nation; what he actually had under him was only an aggregation of castes and tribes with no more feeling of unity than so many bands of wild Indians. Under these conditions, only two types of government were possible: regional or tribal rule, or absolute dictatorship."

It was thus that Santa Cruz inherited the mantle of leadership of Bolivia and became one of the *caudillos* (head; or, supervisor). Although Carter called him a "benevolent dictator," Fagg suggested that Santa Cruz "was cruel even for his times." Nonetheless, the Santa Cruz dictatorship was in many ways a notable exception among the military tyrannies of the time. As Crow explained, "Only through violence and tyranny was it possible to attain a modicum of peace." Klein added, "By the standards of his day, Santa Cruz was extraordinarily tolerant of his opponents and kept bloodshed to a minimum in political conflicts."

Although Crow argued that none of the *caudillo* governments were orderly or efficient, Klein stated that "The ten-year rule of Santa Cruz was to be a fundamental one in republican history, and the institutions which he founded were to provide the basic framework for the organization of civil life of the republic for the next two centuries." For example, Santa Cruz was credited with providing Bolivia economic stability, although in reality little positive change occurred. He did his best to establish a viable financial structure, enacting protective trade tariffs, reducing mining taxes, and constructing new roads. He also established new industries, including gunpowder production, weaving, and glassmaking. Lack of capital precluded expansion, however, and support of the military continued to be the primary drain on governmental resources. The only thing that kept income stable at all was rural population increases and the collection of their taxes. Santa Cruz was eventually forced to issue a new devalued silver currency.

Although Santa Cruz was unable to achieve significant economic reform, he did enact many progressive political and administrative reforms. He founded two state universities, established a medical college, and expanded the judicial court system. Ultimately, perhaps the greatest contribution of the Santa Cruz regime was the political stability engendered by his administration.

### Supported Peruvian-Bolivian Confederation

Throughout his term as president of Bolivia, Santa Cruz kept a wary eye on developments in Peru. In particular, he noted the rising turmoil brought on by the various military leaders there. In 1835, feeling he had the necessary support among the Peruvian ruling class as well as the Indian masses, he began negotiating to rule Peru in addition to Bolivia. By

1836 his detractors had been eliminated and he entered Lima as its new ruler. In 1837 he announced the unification of Bolivia and Upper and Lower Peru to form the Peruvian-Bolivian Confederation.

The Confederation, under a constitution based on the Napoleonic-Bolívarian model, lasted for two years. "For all the long-term uncertainties of the Confederation," Klein observed, "there is little question that it brought both peace to Peru and respect for its power along the entire Pacific region." He continued, "Unfortunately for Santa Cruz his potential to make Peru a major power was also recognized by the Chileans. They saw their own expansion as being one of northern movement along the disputed territory of the Pacific and were competing actively with Peru for the same European markets." To eliminate this new, vital competition, Chile began arming Peruvian dissidents and sent its own troops across the border in the guise of Peruvian rebels. These constant incursions weakened the Confederation. In 1838 the Chileans sent a regular army into Peru. In a major battle at Yungay in January 1839, both the Confederation and Santa Cruz were badly beaten.

In defeat, Santa Cruz had to abandon his Bolivian presidency and was forced into exile in Ecuador. Fagg noted, however, that he was given a chance to redeem his reputation: "In 1849 Bolivia gave him a liberal pension and allowed him to serve in diplomatic posts in Europe." Santa Cruz died in St. Nazaire, France, in 1865.

## SOURCES:

### Books

Arciniegas, Germán, *Latin America: A Cultural History,* translated by Joan MacLean, New York, Knopf, 1967.

*The Cambridge History of Latin America, Vol. 3,* edited by Leslie Bethell, Cambridge, England, Cambridge University Press, 1985.

Carter, William, *Bolivia,* New York, Praeger, 1971.

Crow, John, *The Epic of Latin America,* Garden City, NY, Doubleday, 1971.

*Encyclopedia of Latin American History,* edited by Michael Rheta Martin and Gabriel H. Lovett, Indianapolis, Bobbs-Merrill, 1968.

Fagg, John Edwin, *Latin America: A General History,* second edition, London, Collier-Macmillan, 1969.

Klein, Herbert S., *Bolivia: The Evolution of a Multi-Ethnic Society,* New York, Oxford University Press, 1982.

*The Spanish American Revolutions, 1808–1826,* New York, Norton, 1973.

—*Sketch by Ellen Dennis French*

# Irma Vidal Santaella
## 1924-
### Puerto Rican lawyer and jurist

Irma Vidal Santaella is the first Puerto Rican woman to become a lawyer in New York state and the first Puerto Rican from the Latino-rich county of Bronx to ascend to New York's Supreme Court. She is a "pioneer for the Puerto Rican-Hispanic community," according to New York State Senator Efraim Gonzalez, a longtime associate. Despite all Santaella's accomplishments, Gonzalez and other friends still affectionately refer to her as "mom." Senator Gonzalez noted in a telephone interview with Julia Edgar that the judge is a woman who arrived at the judicial pinnacle by "breaking down barriers. To us, she's great, because she has a sensitivity to people she presides over. She was like our mother. She still is." In a telephone interview, Carmen Pacheco, a Puerto Rican attorney and founding partner of New York City's first Hispanic women's law firm, likened Santaella to Spain's Queen Isabella, who made possible Christopher Columbus's first voyage to the Americas in the fifteenth century. "She has set our sails. She is somebody we should look at and try to model ourselves after."

Born in New York City October 4, 1924, and raised by her mother and aunts in Puerto Rico, Santaella has an extensive and diverse educational background. After graduating in 1942 from the Modern Business College in Ponce, Puerto Rico, she immediately undertook two years of pre-medical school classes at the Inter-American University in San German, Puerto Rico. She began her professional life as a licensed public accountant, graduating with a bachelor of arts degree from Hunter College in New York in 1957. While she worked, she put herself through law school and graduated from the Brooklyn Law School in New York in 1961. She then commenced a practice of civil law in the South Bronx until 1963.

Since then, Santaella has tirelessly championed the rights of minorities and women and children, serving on the New York City Commission on the Status of Women from 1975 to 1977 and heading the Children's Camp in South Bronx in 1967. Since 1982 she has been a member of the New York City Advisory Council on Minority Affairs. Santaella is also the founder of the National Federation of Puerto Rican Women, the National Caucus of Puerto Rican and Hispanic Women, the Hispanic Community Chest of America, Inc. and the National Association for Puerto Rican Civil Rights. As founder in 1962 and chairperson until 1968 of the Legion of Voters, Inc., Santaella played a significant role in advising the late New York Senator Robert F. Kennedy and Senator Jacob Javits on legislation involving Puerto Ricans in the provisions of the Voting Rights Act of 1965. The senators sought her counsel because she helped draft an amendment which ultimately eliminated English literacy tests for non-English speaking American citizens.

In 1968, Santaella launched her second campaign for a congressional seat while Senator Robert Kennedy, a friend, ran for the presidency. When Kennedy, who had served as U.S. attorney general under his brother, President John F. Kennedy, was assassinated during a speech, her campaign fizzled because Santaella was so dejected at her close friend's demise. "Something disappeared. We went through the exercise of the election, but our heart was no longer there," she said in an article printed in *Manhattan Lawyer* magazine in 1989.

Despite a personal and political setback, Santaella's idealism was still intact. She continued her work for the Legion of Voters, and in 1975, New York Governor Hugh L. Carey appointed her as chairperson of the state Human Rights Appeal Board, of which she had been a member since 1968. In 1976, Santaella helped found the National Association for Puerto Rican Civil Rights, the same year she served as a delegate to the Democratic National Convention for the third time.

### Became New York Supreme Court Justice

In 1983, Santaella won a seat on the New York Supreme Court, where her rulings have reflected her social activism, particularly for minority rights. In the summer of 1987, for example, she refused to allow the eviction of a doctor who practiced in a luxurious apartment building on Manhattan's Park Avenue. The landlord claimed Dr. Geoffrey Richstone had improperly made renovations to his office without permission. Santaella not only found that the doctor had openly added equipment and modified his office, but she learned that the building's tenants did not like the presence of Dr. Richstone's minority patients and had asked them to use the back door of the building to enter and leave. In refusing the eviction request, the judge said she could not understand why the landlord sought relief that would "deny black senior citizens access to their doctor's office—for no apparent reason

other than their age and race—in a state that is a citadel of freedom."

In early 1991, Santaella ordered the New York State Board of Elections (NYSBE) to implement a program to sign up more poor people and minorities as voters when they registered for a driver's license or applied for a government position. The program, initiated a year earlier, was stymied because of fighting between Democrats and Republicans on the NYSBE over whether state employees could answer questions from registrants. In her opinion, Santaella reasoned that the goal of the program was to give "New York City citizens, especially minorities, the opportunities to elect representatives of their choice" in an important City Council election the following September.

Santaella is also a strong advocate of First Amendment rights. While she is a practicing Catholic and has served as a board member of the Catholic Interracial Society, she refused to allow the church to stop the production of a play which it found blasphemous. In October, 1990, Santaella told the Roman Catholic Archdiocese of New York it could try to evict the RAPP Arts Center and its play, *The Cardinal Detoxes,* from a parochial school building, but could not stop the production in the meantime. "I am not a censor, and I'm not going to engage in any act of censorship," she wrote in her opinion, reprinted in part in the *New York Times* in October, 1990.

### Urged Settlement in Ross Perot-General Motors Case

Santaella "once again sided with the underdog," wrote Shaun Assael in *Manhattan Lawyer* magazine, when she refused to move a lawsuit against General Motors Corporation to Delaware. A company stockholder sued the corporation in New York State Supreme Court, contending General Motors (GM) breached its fiduciary duty by paying Texas billionaire and presidential candidate Ross Perot more than his stock was worth to surrender his seat on the company's board of directors. In a "remarkable scene" in her chambers, said an attorney who was present, Santaella "made a forceful, careful statement" urging settlement between the plaintiff, Perot and former GM Chairman Roger Smith. The Appellate Division of the New York Supreme Court, however, reversed Santaella's ruling in that case, deciding that GM, because it does business in every state, is subjected to the laws of each state.

Aside from numerous citations and awards she has received for her non-judicial work—including the National Puerto Rican Coalition Life Achievement award and Governor Mario M. Cuomo's Recognition Award—Santaella was cited by the New York State Assembly in 1989 for attaining the highest disposition rate of cases in Manhattan Supreme Court one year earlier. In fact, from 1983 to 1990, the judge heard and closed 21,000 cases, and from 1984 to 1989, she was reversed by higher courts only 24 times. Santaella, said Assembly members in their commendation of the judge, "so truly personifies that commitment to excellence which so distinguishes the Hispanic tradition of law, to that visible and honored predilection for the orderly disposition of concerns so essential to a just society."

In 1990, Santaella, a divorced mother of two, received an honorary law degree from Sacred Heart University in Connecticut. She is a board member of dozens of organizations, including the Community Service Society, Puerto Rican Crippled Children's Fund, Talbott Perkins Children's Services, the American Judicature Society, Planned Parenthood, Inc., and the New York City Steering Committee for Quality Education. Santaella's civic achievements were noted in citations from former New York Governors Nelson Rockefeller in 1972 and Carey in 1982. Other awards include the 1991 National Council of Hispanic Women's Life Achievement award and the 1992 National Latinas Excellence Award of Leadership.

*Carlos Santana*

**SOURCES:**

**Periodicals**

*Manhattan Lawyer,* February 21, 1989.
*New York Times,* October 12, 1990, p. B2; February 24, 1991, p. 32.
*Washington Post,* July 7, 1987, p. A15.

**Other**

Gonzalez, Efraim, telephone interview with Julia Edgar, August 12, 1992.
Pacheco, Carmen, telephone interview with Julia Edgar, August 6, 1992.
State Assembly of New York Legislative Resolution commending the Honorable Irma Vidal Santaella, June 1, 1989.

—*Sketch by Julia Edgar*

# Carlos Santana
## 1947-
### Mexican guitarist and bandleader

arlos Santana is an enduring name in popular music. Whether heading his self-named band or performing with other musicians, Santana has demonstrated his talent and sense of purpose for more than three decades. Under Santana's direction, the Santana band fused African American rock 'n' roll sounds with driving Latin rhythms and soaring, biting guitar lines to create a signature sound. Santana has gone on numerous international tours, performed for sell-out crowds, and has recorded dozens of best-selling albums. Though the band's makeup has changed repeatedly throughout the years, Santana has been its unifying and driving force. For Santana, music is not just a career, it is a vocation. He sees his music as a vehicle for his religious and political beliefs. "I play music because I know it can elevate the spirit, because it has the power to build the bridge of love between people," Santana told Dan Ouellette in a *Down Beat* interview.

The son of a mariachi, or violinist, Carlos Santana was born in Autlán de Navarro, Jalisco, Mexico on July 20, 1947. Santana's father encouraged his son to take up the guitar, and while in his teens, Santana cut his musical teeth playing in Tijuana nightclubs. "I learned a lot of my music in the streets, and I give the streets a lot of value," he told *Musician* writer Jim Macnie. "The street has a different story to tell; that's what I'm looking for, that substance. The clean thing's not for me; I need the dirt, the essence. . . . If it don't have that it will lose my ear." The Santana family moved to San Francisco in 1962, where five years later Santana formed the Santana Blues Band.

## Band Rocks Woodstock

For about three years, the Santana Blues Band, which soon was known simply as Santana, played in small clubs in the San Francisco Bay area, particularly the Hispanic Mission District. There, it gathered a following devoted to its hard-hitting guitar sound, Latin beat, and low-profile, bluesy vocals. Santana received several contract offers from record companies but turned them down. In 1969 the group, still unrecorded, entranced the crowd of 500,000 at the famous Woodstock Festival with "Soul Sacrifice," a piece especially written for the occasion. Recalling his Woodstock experience, Santana told *Rolling Stone,* "Some people called it a disaster area, but I didn't see nobody in a state of disaster. I saw a lot of people coming together, sharing and having a great time. If that was out of control, then America needs to lose control at least once a week." He added: "I saw a lot of positive, artistic, creative stimuli for America. In the 1960s, people didn't go to concerts to get drunk and pick up chicks; they went to get bombarded with music and be taken somewhere else. When you came out, you knew you were never gonna be the same. You didn't go to a concert to escape. You went to a concert to expand." The Woodstock performance brought the band important exposure and increased its following outside of the San Francisco Bay area.

Soon after the Santana band performed at the Woodstock Festival, it appeared on the *Ed Sullivan Show* and signed a contract with Columbia Records. When its first album, *Santana,* climbed to the top of record charts and went platinum, it presaged a future full of precious metal; of Santana's more than 30 albums with and without his band, at least nine have gone platinum and 16 gold. In the early 1970s, the group, made up of guitars, keyboards, drummers, and vocals, was a top rock 'n' roll attraction. Its albums *Abraxas* and *Santana Three* went gold, and the singles "Black Magic Woman" (written by Peter Green), "Evil Ways," and "Oye Como Va" (written by Tito Puente) leapt up the charts. In addition to performing with his own band, Santana teamed up with other popular instrumentalists for concerts and recordings.

## Explores Jazz Fusion

From an unlikely starting point—Santana once told a *Down Beat* reviewer that he thought jazz was "boring cocktail music"—he broadened his Latin rock 'n' roll sound to include elements of jazz, in what has become known since as jazz fusion. In 1972, Santana learned to improvise and teamed up with Buddy Miles, recording the album *Carlos Santana and Buddy Miles Live.* With his own group, he recorded the jazzy *Caravanserai.* "When I turned over a new musical leaf and recorded *Caravanserai,* I felt insecure," Santana recalled to Lee Underwood in *Down Beat.* "I was moving into the unknown. I didn't

read music. I was working with advanced musicians . . . who were well into jazz. I was trying to stretch myself beyond rock n' roll." Santana focused his efforts on jazz to the detriment of the rock 'n' roll that had made him famous, and his band broke up as a result. When Santana met the guru Sri Chinmoy, he became a follower and changed his name to the pseudo-Hindu moniker Devadip Carlos Santana. In 1972, Santana collaborated with guitarist Mahavishnu John McLaughlin to record the jazz-fusion *Love, Devotion, Surrender,* another album that went gold and was critically acclaimed as the first successful fusion of rock 'n' roll and jazz. With jazz pianist Alice Coltrane, Santana also recorded the album *Illuminations.*

## Returns to Rock 'n' Roll Roots

In the mid-1970s, long-time friend and manager Bill Graham urged Santana to return from the more esoteric jazz to his roots in Latin rock 'n' roll. Santana gathered a new band and recorded a handful of Latin rock 'n' roll albums, among them *Amigos,* a top 10 success, and *Moonflower,* which included the hit single "She's Not Here." To promote the group's albums, Santana toured with the band. In 1976, the band headed a concert simultaneously broadcast on television and radio by the British Broadcasting Corporation (BBC). The band closed the decade with its album *Marathon.*

During the 1980s, Santana continued his pattern of band tours and individual projects. In 1981 *Zebop!* came out of the studio. In 1986, Santana worked with the group Los Lobos on the music for the popular motion picture *La Bamba,* about Chicano rock 'n' roll star Ritchie Valens. Two years later, while Santana toured with jazz saxophonist Wayne Shorter, Columbia records marked the 20th anniversary of Santana's first album with *Viva Santana!,* a three album retrospective that mixed Santana standards with old studio tracks and live recordings. Despite the long-term success of his music, Santana's pieces were receiving less radio play than they did during the band's first decade on the air.

In 1992 Santana left Columbia Records for the Polydor label and cut his album *Milagro* (which means "miracle"), a tribute to friend and manager Bill Graham and jazz trumpeter Miles Davis, who both died in 1991. Santana's music had never been more eclectic. "Elements of salsa, pop, blues, jazz, R&B, rock, world music and reggae work their way in and out of the arrangements on *Milagro,*" commented Thom Jurek in *Rolling Stone.* "Santana is the most successful practitioner of fusion because he understands the style not as a souped-up rock-jazz hybrid but as an embrace of musical pantheism." For his own part, Santana explained his expansive tastes to *Musician*'s Macnie, "Music is like a huge garden, there's room for all the textures and aromas. As long as you play from your heart, your flower's not made out of plastic."

Santana believes in giving something back to the world; he has performed at a wide range of charity concerts over the years. In 1985 he played the "Live Aid" concert and in 1986 he headlined a show to benefit Amnesty International. Two years later, he helped organize the "Blues for Salvador" concert in Oakland, California, which raised $100,000 for children in El Salvador. In 1992, Santana and his wife Deborah opened their San Francisco home to host a benefit concert for the Marin County public schools, where the Santana children, Salvador and Stella go to school.

### Launches Own Label

In 1992 Santana created his own label, Guts and Grace, and released its first recording, *Live Forever,* which preserved the last performances of deceased artists Marvin Gaye, John Coltrane, Jimi Hendrix, and Stevie Ray Vaughan. "We wanted to create the atmosphere that they were all on the same stage doing it, at the same concert, and honor their music and spirit," Santana explained to *Down Beat* reviewer Robin Tolleson.

During his long career, Santana has won dozens of awards. To mention just a few, in 1991 he received the MVP Award for outstanding creative and artistic contribution from the San Francisco chapter of the National Academy of Recording Arts and Sciences. The following year he was presented with the Golden Eagle award to recognize the best Latino achievements in the entertainment industry. Despite his success, Santana is humble about his position in the music world. Instead of striving for commercial success, he focuses on expressing himself. "Our music continues to be tremendously appealing to all kinds of people—young, old, black, white, hip, square—and all cultures," Santana told Ouellette. "I don't deliberately try to make it appealing to lots of different audiences. . . . I just try to get to that next note, to get inside it so the listener can do the same."

### SELECTED DISCOGRAPHY:

### Collaborations

*Carlos Santana and Buddy Miles Live,* 1972.
*Love, Devotion, Surrender* (with John McLaughlin), 1973.
*Illuminations* (with Alice Coltrane), 1974.

### With the Santana Band

*Santana,* Columbia, 1969.
*Abraxas,* Columbia, 1970.
*Caravanserai,* Columbia, 1972.

*Santana Three,* Columbia, 1972.
*Lotus,* Columbia, 1973.
*Borboletta,* Columbia, 1976.
*Moonflower,* Columbia, 1977.
*Marathon,* Colubmia, 1979.
*Zebop!,* Columbia, 1981
*Blues for Salvador,* Columbia, 1987.
*Freedom,* Columbia, 1987.
*Viva Santana!,* Columbia, 1988.
*Spirits Dancing in the Flesh,* Columbia, 1990.
*The Swing of Delight,* Columbia, 1990.
*Milagro,* Polydor, 1992.
*Sacred Fire Live in South America,* Polydor, 1993.

### SOURCES:

### Books

*Baker's Biographical Dictionary of Musicians,* 8th edition, edited by Nicolas Slonimsky, New York, Macmillan, 1992.
*Contemporary Musicians,* volume 1, Detroit, Gale, 1989.
Morehead, Philip D. with Anne MacNeil, *New American Dictionary of Music,* New York, Dutton, 1991.
*New Grove Dictionary of American Music,* edited by H. Wiley Hitchcock and Stanley Sadie, London, Macmillan, 1986.
*New Grove Dictionary of Jazz,* edited by Barry Kernfeld, London, Macmillan, 1988.
Stambler, Irwin, *Encyclopedia of Pop, Rock & Soul,* revised edition, New York, St. Martin's Press, 1989.

### Periodicals

*Billboard,* November 17, 1984, p. 38; October 24, 1987, p. 80.
*Down Beat,* September, 1989, p. 90; July, 1991, p. 45; March, 1991, pp. 37, 39; July, 1991, p. 45; August, 1991, pp. 28–29; February, 1992, p. 36; May, 1992, p. 74; August, 1992, pp. 37–38; February, 1993, p. 49; February, 1994, p. 11.
*Guitar Player,* July, 1985, p. 26; January, 1987, p. 57; November, 1988, p. 12; March, 1989, p. 138.
*Hispanic,* October, 1992, pp. 80, 96.
*Life,* August, 1994, pp. 32–44.
*Musician,* September, 1988, pp. 92–106; December, 1990, pp. 76–78.
*New York Times,* November 11, 1990, section 1, p. 67.
*Rolling Stone,* September 22, 1988, p. 27; August 24, 1989, p. 65; November 28, 1991, p. 35; September 3, 1992, p. 68; November 28, 1991, p. 35; December 12, 1991, p. 76; October 28, 1993, p. 30; December 9, 1993, p. 24.

*Stereo Review*, August, 1983 pp. 67–8.
*Variety*, October 5, 1988, p. 143; October 22, 1990, p. 80.
*Village Voice*, August 14, 1990, p. 79.

—*Sketch by J.M. Lesinski*

# Francisco de Paula Santander
## 1792-1840
### Colombian patriot and statesman

Called "the man of laws" by his admirers and "the general of the quill pen" by his enemies, Francisco de Paula Santander was a distinguished veteran of **Simón Bolívar**'s war of independence who later served his country as a uncompromising liberal and democratic statesman. As vice president of Gran Colombia under Bolívar from 1821 to 1828, and as president of New Grenada (now Colombia) from 1832 to 1837, Santander exhibited leadership characterized by progressivism and strict adherence to the law. In *The Epic of Latin America*, John A. Crow wrote that Santander strove "through precept and example to instill in the hearts of all Colombians a respect for impersonal law. 'Our arms gave us independence,' he said. 'Laws will give us our liberty.' Santander placed on Colombia the stamp of civil government which even today so clearly distinguishes it from the other Latin American republics." In the 50 years following independence, the various South American republics were ruled by Bolívar's generals, a series of dictators who had little or no government experience and who continued to live by the sword. Crow observed that "Santander was the only exception in a generation of military tyrants." He also noted that although Santander kept a sword on his desk, he placed a copy of the constitution on top of it.

### Joins Patriot Military

Little is known of Santander's life before he rose to prominence as one of Bolívar's trusted generals. He was born in April, 1792, in Rosario de Cúcuta, Colombia, the son of a poor but respected Creole family. Jesús María Henao and Gerardo Arrubia noted in *History of Colombia* that Santander "was a student at the College of San Bartolomé at Santa Fe when the revolution broke out. There he received lessons in law and had barely reached eighteen when he took up arms." He began his military career in 1810 as a banner-bearer in the national guard and then served as adjutant to the commander at Mariquita. In January of 1813, Santander was captured along with about 1,000 other soldiers in the brief civil uprising between Cundinamarca's President Nariña and its congress. He was repatriated only a few days later.

Over the next six years Santander served the cause of liberation with distinction, eventually reaching the rank of general. In 1817 he joined Bolívar's army in the Venezuelan province of Barcelona, and participated in the Caracas campaign of 1818. In August of that year, Santander was promoted to brigadier general and then given command of the army at Casanare. He was 26. In January of 1819, Bolívar ordered Santander to recruit and train as large an infantry as possible. Within a few months Santander had succeeded in assembling and training a combined force of infantry and cavalry; the division was some 2,000-strong. This force was intended to serve as the advance guard, based at Santander's headquarters at Tame, in the Casanare province.

In May, Bolívar planned for the liberation of New Grenada. The various armies—including a rearguard British legion—began an arduous march on May 24. Crossing the flooded Casanare plains in order to join Santander's forces was only the first of many hardships the army faced. Reaching Tame in early June, the army journeyed to Pore, still battling floods caused by the rainy season. On June 22, they began the brutal ascent of the Andean Cordillera. The Andean crossing presented new adversities: cruelly rocky terrain, dangerous sickness brought on by the thin mountain air, and agonizing cold. Irene Nicholson wrote in *The Liberators:* "No horse survived. The reserve supply of arms and even some of those the soldiers carried had to be abandoned. It was a mere skeleton of an army that reached . . . the heart of the province of Tunja on July 6, 1819." Rested and resupplied in Socha, the army engaged the royalist forces in the area in several skirmishes.

Established in the area known as the Vargas Swamp, the patriots braced for battle. Santander's forces climbed the nearby hillsides to an advantageous position on the army's right flank. In a series of ferocious attacks, the patriots forced a Spanish retreat. Its numbers increased by local conscripts and its stores replenished with ammunition from Casanare, the patriot army occupied Tunja by August 5.

The most decisive battle in the war for the independence of New Grenada was fought two days later on August 7, 1819 at the Boyacá Bridge. The Spanish commander Barreiro and his veteran royalist army of 3000 were trapped there by Bolívar's forces. Santander's division forced a separation of Barriero's main army and his advance guard, with the bridge dividing them. As the patriot army of 2000 engaged the royalists, "Santander overcame the vigorous resistance of the Spanish vanguard and, crossing the bridge, completed the victory," according to Henao and Arrubla. In this famous battle—which lasted less than two hours—the Spanish were completely routed, and surrendered more than 1,600 men. Henao and Arrubla suggested: "Boyacá is in itself not a great battle, either because of its duration, or by virtue of the number of combatants and the amount of blood spilled. But it was decisive in its consequences." The core of Spanish resistance was defeated and Bolívar entered Bogotá three days later—unopposed.

### Named Vice President of Gran Colombia

In late 1819 the republic of Gran Colombia was formed, composed of the vice-royalty of New Grenada, the audiencia of Quito, and the captaincy-general of Venezuela. Although historians refer to this union as Gran Colombia, it was simply called Colombia at the time. A provisional government was established in September, 1819, and Santander was named vice president under Bolívar. It was not until 1821 that the congress at Cúcuta finally held elections. At that time, Bolívar was again named president. In a close contest, Santander emerged as vice president, defeating Antonio Nariño. *The Independence of Latin America* (1987) stated: "Santander's success was a tribute to his efficient work as head of the regional administration . . . entrusted to him by Bolívar in 1819. . . ."

As Bolívar continued his liberating campaigns, day-to-day administration of Gran Colombia fell to Santander. John Lynch wrote in *The Spanish American Revolutions*: "Santander . . . led his country in a moderate liberal revolution, in which he maintained government control against the forces of anarchy, preserved civil rights, supplied the armed forces, sustained the war effort, and attempted to apply a program of reform." One of his successes, the expansion of education, was noted by Germán Arciniegas in *Latin America: A Cultural History*: "Santander opened the campaign for elementary schools by decree, founded grade and high schools in Colombia, Venezuela, and Ecaudor, girls' schools and normal schools and universities in the provinces, established the national museum, (and) the library. . . ."

Despite Santander's best efforts, Colombia was a divided republic by 1826. Many factors contributed to the internal situation, fiscal instability chief among them. Lynch cited "an amalgam of economic recession induced by war, reluctance of the affluent . . . to pay income or property taxes, the poor quality of the fiscal bureaucracy, and above all military expenses, which accounted for 75 per cent of total expenditure. Rising deficits and failure to balance budgets sabotaged reforms, . . . and ultimately made the government vulnerable to criticism." Lynch called this "latent bankruptcy" the primary cause of the collapse of Santander's liberal administration.

Bolívar was critical of what he considered to be Santander's indiscriminate liberalism. The two men differed widely on ideology; Bolívar supported Páez and his Venezuelan administration, even though they openly defied the central government. In 1827 a complete break occurred when Bolívar deposed Santander and denounced him as a friend. Bolívar assumed dictatorial powers in 1828; opposition members attempted his assassination. Forewarned, Bolívar escaped.

Following the assassination attempt, the conspirators were tried and convicted. Many were sentenced to death. Santander was accused of involvement in the conspiracy, and was convicted and sentenced to death as well. But since the charges could not be proven, his sentence was commuted to exile for life. Santander was imprisoned for several months in Cartagena and was then permitted to go to Europe.

### Returns From Exile to Lead New Grenada

Bolívar's dictatorship did not last long. By the end of 1829 the Colombian union had disintegrated, and Bolívar resigned in March of the fopllowing year. Santander was in New York when he received word early in 1832 that he had been elected to the presidency of the Republic of New Grenada. He returned and took office in October, 1832. His administration was initially a popular one. In his book, *Latin America: A General History,* John Edwin Fagg detailed many of Santander's accomplishments, noting that he "re-established the National Academy, reopened the observatory, encouraged the institutions of higher learning, and increased elementary schools until there were five hundred of them."

Santander restored credit and settled the public debt. His financial policies were effective, but did not endear him to the constituency. During the course of his tenure, several plots to overthrow his administration were uncovered and put down. Fagg wrote: "Santander, like so many others of the time, found himself vilified by nationalists and localists, by conservatives and liberals. His prestige declined so precipitously that he was unable to persuade, and unwilling to try to force, the country to accept his choice for a successor when his term ended. . . ."

By the end of Santander's term in 1836, New Grenada was on the threshold of civil war. By 1840, the violence had erupted; the congress met to discuss an end to the rebellion. In response to attacks on his administration, Santander spoke in opposition to the current government and defended of his own record. It was his final public appearance. A liver ailment worsened and caused his death in early May, 1840. In later years Santander's contributions were more fully recognized; he has been honored with bronze statues in Bogotá and other cities.

## SOURCES:

*Encyclopedia Americana,* Vol. 24, Danbury, CT, Grolier, 1991.

*Encyclopedia of Latin American History,* edited by Michael Rheta Martin and Gabriel H. Lovett, Indianapolis, Bobbs-Marrill Company, 1968.

*History of Columbia,* by Jesús María Heano and Gerardo Arrubla, translated and edited by J. Fred Rippy, Chapel Hill, NC, University of North Carolina Press, 1938.

*Latin America: A Cultural History,* by Germán Arciniegas, translated Joan Mac Lean, New York, Alfred A. Knopf, 1967.

*Latin America: A General History,* by John Edwin Fagg, London, Macmillan, 1969.

*The Epic of Latin America,* by John A. Crow, Garden City, NY, Doubleday & Company, 1971.

*The Independence of Latin America,* edited by Leslie Bethell, Cambridge, Cambridge University Press, 1987.

*The Liberators,* by Irene Nicholson, New York, Frederick A. Praeger, 1969.

*The Spanish American Revolutions, 1–1826,* by John Lynch, New York, W.W. Norton & Co., 1973.

—*Sketch by Ellen Dennis French*

*George Santayana*

# George Santayana
## 1863-1952
### Spanish philosopher

George Santayana was an eminent philosopher and a man of letters. Santayana's unconventional genius as a philosopher was succinctly captured by a critic in the *London Times* in 1952: "Santayana—who described himself as a recalcitrant materialist—was not a philosopher's philosopher; he was never given to the pursuit of metaphysical abstractions, and was in closer sympathy with the artist than with the metaphysician. In substance his philosophy, though at once eclectic and intellectually inconsistent, is a restatement of the materialism of Democritus cast in a profoundly humanist mould." A poet of note, Santayana held a high place among the thinkers of his generation, and although his poetry has failed to garner the continued readership that works of his contemporaries have found, his influence as a humanist philosopher endures in academic circles.

Santayana was renowned for his solitude. He was born in Spain and retained his Spanish passport, but spent most of his life outside his native country. Richard Butler in his 1968 book, *The Mind of Santayana,* asserted, "he never lost the sense of being a stranger, always on the outside of everything looking in, always alone." Butler wrote in *The Life and World of George Santayana* (1960) that Santayana remarked, "Detachment leaves you content to be where you are, and what you are. Why should you hanker to be elsewhere or someone else? Yet in your physical particularity detachment makes you ideally impartial; and in enlightening your mind it is likely to render your action also more successful and generous." A master of English, Santayana never wrote in his native tongue, stating that "it is as an American writer that I must be counted if I am counted at all," according to Willard Arnett in *George Santayana,* 1968.

Jorge Agustín Nicolás Ruiz de Santayana y Borrás was born in Madrid on December 16, 1863 to Josefina Borrás y Carbonell de Santayana and Colonel Agustín Ruiz de Santayana. Santayana was named for his mother's late first husband. Shortly after Santayana's birth his family moved to Avila. When Santayana was five his mother moved to Boston with his half brother and two half sisters to observe her first husband's request that his children be educated in the United States. Santayana remained in Spain with his father until he was nine, when they moved to Boston.

## Travels to America

On his arrival in Boston on July 16, 1872 Santayana spoke no English. His father returned to Spain shortly after their arrival. In Boston Santayana's half sister, Susana, became his mentor; in his autobiography *Persons and Places* Santayana declared that she "was I think the greatest power, and certainly the strongest affection in my life." Susana taught him English and anglicized his name to George. Santayana's dislocation from his homeland and encounter with the U.S. profoundly influenced him. Of his childhood he recalled, "For by chance I was a foreigner where I was educated; and although the new language and customs interested me and gave me no serious trouble, yet speculatively and emotionally, especially in regard to religion, the world around me was utterly indigestible."

Santayana's first encounter with U.S. education was at Miss Welchman's kindergarten. Aged nine, he was twice the age of his classmates. The following year he briefly attended the Brimmer School, a public grammar school, where he was bullied. This torment encouraged his intoversion to a world of books. In 1874 Santayana enrolled at the Boston Latin School, where he established his academic prowess. He won first prize for his poem "Day and Night" in 1880 and his poetry was published in the school journal, *The Latin School Register,* between 1881 and 1882. During his final year he was Lieutenant Colonel and Major of the school regiment—despite his lack of athletic ability—in recognition of his academic achievements.

Santayana entered Harvard in 1882. Despite an avid interest in architecture and painting, he majored in philosophy. He was tutored by the philosophers William James and Josiah Royce; as an undergraduate he was influenced most deeply by the philosopher Benedict de Spinoza. In the summer of 1883 he visited Spain and realized that his feelings of alienation extended there. At Harvard, in contrast with the conspicuous solitude of his older years, Santayana was a socialite, renowned for his comic verses. He was an active member of numerous clubs and societies, including the Hasty Pudding Club, the O.K. Society, the Philosophical Club, and the Shakespeare Club. In the literary sphere he was a board member of *The Harvard Monthly,* an avant-garde literary magazine, founded in 1885, which served as a forum for his poetry. He also contributed 51 cartoons to the *Harvard Lampoon* between February 1883 and June 1886. Santayana graduated *summa cum laude* in 1886.

He embarked on graduate studies in philosophy in 1886 at the University of Berlin, sharing the Walker Traveling Fellowship fund with fellow Harvard graduate Charles Augustus Strong, who remained a lifelong friend. Rather than devote all his time to scholastic pursuits, Santayana enjoyed Germany's art galleries, museums and operas. Fortunately, his fellowship was renewed, enabling him to study at Cambridge in England before returning to Harvard in 1888. At Harvard, Santayana produced his dissertation on the philosophy of Hermann Lotze and was awarded his doctorate in 1889. Santayana toyed with the idea of studying architecture at the Massachusetts Institute of Technology until he was offered a teaching position at Harvard.

## Begins Teaching Career at Harvard

Santayana's approach to philosophy was poetic rather than scientific. During his early academic career he wrote a substantial volume of poetry; he harbored a deep yearning to be a successful poet. John McCormick in *George Santayana: A Biography* (1987), observed, "More than anything in life, Santayana wanted desperately to be a poet and to be recognized as one." Although his poetry was highly popular among his contemporaries, it was not considered great. Santayana's first book *Sonnets and Other Verses* was published in 1894. Its content was not appreciated by the Harvard administration; they wanted specialization in philosophy, not poetry.

Santayana was an unconventional lecturer who found the institutional side of academic life difficult. He avoided administrative affairs, which generated resentment from the bureaucratic quarters of the university. Conversely, he was popular with the undergraduates and joined the functions of various societies including the Signet, the Delphic Club, and the Zeta Psi Club. He organized poetry gatherings and recited Keats, Shakespeare, and Shelley. Santayana's Harvard students counted among them future famous figures such as Gertrude Stein, T. S. Eliot, Wallace Stevens, Walter Lipmann and Bronson Cutting.

Santayana developed close relationships with particular students. Around 1892 he was involved in a deep friendship with Warwick Potter, an undergraduate. When Potter died tragically in 1893 Santayana declared "the renunciation of the temporal and transitory for the timeless and eternal," according to William Holzberger in *The Complete Poems of George Santayana,* (1979). He dedicated his following sonnets, entitled "to W.P.," to Potter. 1893 was a sad year for Santayana, compounded by the death of his father and Susana's marriage. He became increasingly unhappy, with America and his sense of a lack of achievement, and through his disenchantment with religion. Santayana retreated into "a life of detatched contemplation" observed William Holzberger.

At Harvard Santayana created a philosophy course in aesthetics which incorporated his literary desires. He referred to it as his 'sham' course. His lectures on aesthetics, which defined and examined aesthetics in a philosophical context, were published in 1896 as *The Sense of Beauty.* His debut philosophical work was highly praised; a critic for *The Philosophical Review,* March 1897, wrote, "Mr. Santayana's theory is . . . consistent and one of the clearest and simplest, and most adequate that has ever been advanced on this subject." It was also approved by the Harvard administration, complying with their demand for a publication on philosophy. Santayana's enlarged edition of poetry, *Sonnets and Other Verses,* was well received by his publishers the same year.

He left for a sabbatical to King's College, Cambridge, in England and studied under Henry Jackson, the Plato scholar, from 1896 to 1897. At Cambridge he made the acquaintance of the renowned philosopher Bertrand Russell. When Santayana returned to the United States he went to live with his mother at Longwood. In 1898 he was named assistant professor of philosophy. The following year he published a collection of poetry entitled *Lucifer: A Theological Tragedy,* which was not critically acclaimed. His subsequent volume of poems, *A Hermit of Carmel and Other Poems,* (1901), signalled the peak of Santayana's poetic career according to William Holzberger. It also marked the close of his poetic endeavors; most critics attribute this change to Santayana's realization that he would never be a great poet. He turned his writing emphasis more solidly towards philosophy, producing *Interpretations of Poetry and Religion* in 1900. An avid traveler, Santayana spent the academic year of 1904–5 in Italy, Greece, and Egypt. He taught at the Sorbonne in Paris on an exchange program during the following academic year.

Santayana's reputation as a philosopher was solidly endorsed with the publication of *The Life of Reason* (five volumes, 1905–06), which contained the gems of his philosophy that he later refined. A major success, it resulted in a doubling of his salary and his promotion to professor in 1907. It also brought him prestige as a philosopher; George Howgate in *George Santayana,* 1971, wrote, "In 1900 Santayana was known to his reading public as a young poet who dabbled in philosophy; in 1910 he was a moral philosopher who had once been a poet." In 1911 he was conferred with a Doctor of Letters from the University of Wisconsin.

Santayana was never entirely satisfied with teaching or comfortable in the Harvard environment. Butler wrote in 1960 that Santayana described his Harvard career as "slow and insecure, made in an atmosphere of mingled favor and distrust." Indeed, Santayana had started planning his departure from Harvard in 1888. He wrote, "I began to prepare for my retirement from teaching before I had begun to teach." Santayana journeyed to England in January of 1912. In February he learned of his mother's death and his inheritance of a legacy; he resigned from Harvard on June 6, 1912.

## Achieves International Recognition in Europe

From 1912 until his death in 1952, Santayana lived in Europe, spending time in England, France, Spain, and Italy; he never returned to the United States. He devoted himself to his literary and philosophical métier, attaining international distinction as a philosopher and writer. Arnett wrote that, in Europe, free from institutional contraints, Santayana realized that, "all was now a voluntary study, a satirical survey, a free reconsideration: the point of view had become at once frankly personal and speculatively transcendental. A spirit, the spirit in a stray individual, was settling its accounts with the universe."

Sympathetic to the allies, he spent the war years of 1914 to 1918 at Oxford, occasionally lecturing, but declined an invitation to stay. After the war he stayed with his Harvard friend, Charles Strong, in Paris during the summers, while retreating to Rome and Florence in Italy, and the Riviera in France for the winters. Santayana contemplated retiring in Spain with his sister, Susana, but she died in 1928, and he never returned.

The 1920s were a profitable and productive literary period for Santayana, with the publication of *Character and Opinion in the United States* (1920), *Soliloquies in England* (1923), *Scepticism and Animal Faith* (1923) and *Platonism and the Spiritual Life* (1927). Santayana was accorded numerous accolades. In 1927 he was awarded the Gold Medal from the Royal Society of Literature in London. In 1929 he was offered the prestigious Norton Chair of Poetry, at Harvard, but he had already firmly renounced his teaching career.

Santayana wrote one novel, *The Last Puritan: A Memoir in the Form of a Novel,* published in 1935, which relates the life story of Anthony Aden, from his birth to his premature death. Biographer John McCormick wrote that Mr. O. Kyllmann of Constable & Co., Santayana's London publishers declared of *The Last Puritan,* "The writing is so clear and lucid that I read it very slowly for the delight of reading it, and at the back of my mind I was regretfully conscious that eventually I should come to the last page." The novel was highly popular and achieved widespread acclaim; it was nominanted for the Pulitzer Prize and chosen by the Book of the Month Club. Santayana continued producing philosophical works, notably *Realms of Being* (1942). By the 1940s he was the subject of other philosophers.

Santayana had a dark side, which is not well recorded. Biographer John McCormick acknowledges that Santayana was anti-Semitic, describing his politics as "occasionally chilling." Santayana was attacked for his views, particularly for his initial support for Mussolini.

In old age, believing that he was no longer capable of taking care of himself, Santayana retired to the Blue Sisters Nursing Home in Rome. He suffered during the Second World War because his money was tied up in the United States. He wrote his autobiography *Persons and Places* (1944). After reading The Bible he wrote *The Idea of Christ in the Gospels* (1946). On his 88th birthday he told reporters, "I find things are not so simple to explain as I has imagined, and so I am not reconciled." In June of 1952 he suffered a fall and subsequently, a rapid deterioration in his health; he also had problems with his eyesight and reading.

Santayana died from stomach cancer on September 26, 1952. In an essay published after his death he claimed: "I can identify myself heartily with nothing in me except with the flame of spirit itself. Therefore the truest picture of my inmost being would show none of the features of my person, and nothing of the background of my life. It would show only the light of the understanding that burned within me and, as far as it could, consumed and purified all the rest."

## SELECTED PUBLISHED WORKS:

*The Sense of Beauty,* New York, Charles Scribner's Sons, 1896.

*Lucifer, A Theological Tragedy,* Chicago, H.S. Stone & Co., 1899.

*Interpretations of Poetry and Religion,* New York, Charles Scribner's Sons, 1900.

*The Life of Reason,* New York, Charles Scribner's Sons; Volume 1, *Reason in Common Sense,* 1905; Volume 2, *Reason in Society,* 1905; Volume 3, *Reason in Religion,* 1905; Volume 4, *Reason in Art,* 1905; Volume 5, *Reason in Science,* 1906.

*Three Philosophical Poets,* Cambridge, MA, Harvard University Press, 1910.

*Winds of Doctrine,* London, J.M. Dent & Sons, Ltd., 1913.

*Character and Opinion in the United States,* London, Constable & Co., Ltd., 1920.

*Poems,* London, Constable & Co., Ltd., 1922.

*Scepticism and Animal Faith,* London, Constable & Co., Ltd., 1923.

*Platonism and the Spiritual Life,* New York, Charles Scribner's Sons, 1927.

*Some Turns of Thought in Modern Philosophy,* London, Cambridge University Press, 1930.

*The Genteel Tradition at Bay,* New York, Charles Scribner's Sons, 1931.

*The Last Puritan* (novel), London, Constable & Co., Ltd., 1935.

*Egotism in German Philosophy,* London, J.M. Dent & Sons, Ltd., 1940.

*Dialogues in Limbo,* New York, Charles Scribner's Sons, 1941.

*Realms of Being,* New York, Charles Scribner's Sons, 1942.

*Persons and Places,* London, Constable & Co., Ltd., 1944.

*The Idea of Christ in the Gospels,* New York, Charles Scribner's Sons, 1946.

*The Middle Span,* London, Constable & Co., Ltd., 1947.

*Dominations and Powers,* New York, Charles Scribner's Sons, 1951.

*My Host the World,* New York, Charles Scribner's Sons, 1953.

## SOURCES:

### Books

Arnett, Willard E., *George Santayana,* New York, Washington Square Press, Inc., 1968.

Butler, Richard, *The Life and World of George Santayana,* A Gateway Edition, Chicago, Henry Regnery Company, 1960.

Butler, Richard, *The Mind of Santayana,* New York, Greenwood Press, 1968.

Howgate, George W., *George Santayana,* New York, Russell & Russell, 1971.

Kirkwood, M.M., *Santayana: Saint of the Imagination,* Toronto, University of Toronto Press, 1961.

McCormick, John, *George Santayana: A Biography,* New York, Alfred A. Knopf, 1987.

Santayana, George, *The Complete Poems of George Santayana: A Critical Edition,* edited by William G. Holzberger, Lewisburg, PA, Bucknell University Press, 1979.

### Periodicals

*Times* (London) September 29, 1952.

*Times Literary Supplement,* April 17, 1969, pp. 401–3.

*—Sketch by Amanda Beresford*

# Cristina Saralegui
## 1948-

**Cuban American television talk show host and editor**

With her Spanish language talk show, Cristina Saralegui has become Hispanic television's answer to Oprah, Sally, and Donahue. The writer and talk show host is unafraid of controversy and insists

*Cristina Saralegui*

that she only has one objective: to inform Hispanics. Saralegui emphasized her concern for Hispanics during an interview with *Hispanic* magazine: "We do the show to help Hispanics here. Once you cross the border you are an immigrant, not a tourist. This is where our kids grow up, and we have to be concerned about our community."

Cristina Maria Saralegui was born January 29, 1946, in Havana, Cuba, to Francisco and Cristina Saralegui. Her grandfather, the publishing tycoon Don Francisco Saralegui, was the dominant influence in her early life. Recognized throughout Latin America as "the Paper Czar," or "Don Pancho," her grandfather introduced young Saralegui to his business. "I was four or five," Saralegui recalls in her official biography, "when I would stroll by the hand of my grandfather visiting the huge rotary presses and the editorial departments of our family owned and operated magazines, *Bohemia, Carteles,* and *Vanidades.* They were the three most successful magazines published out of the island."

In 1960, at the age of 12, Saralegui and her family left their comfortable life in Havana and started a new life in Miami's Cuban exile community. "I remember my last day in Havana," Saralegui relates in her biography. "Looking out of the balcony at the beautiful sea, and thinking as my vision became blurry with tears, that this was probably the last time I would see my friends and this magnificent view, which I loved so much."

In Miami, Saralegui prepared herself to enter the family's traditional business by studying mass communications and creative writing at the University of Miami. During her last year at the university, she began an internship with *Vanidades,* the number-one ladies' service magazine in Latin America. In her biography, Saralegui recalled that she worked hard at *Vanidades:* "At the time it was a huge challenge. I had to teach myself to write in Spanish. Having attended high school and college in the United States, and receiving all my formal training in English, I was more fluent in the English language."

Saralegui, however, was determined enough to earn a position as the features editor of *Vanidades Continental.* She maintained that position from 1970 to 1973, when she became the editor of *Cosmopolitan-en-Español.* In 1976 she took a position as the entertainment director for the *Miami Herald* newspaper. By 1977, Saralegui was the editor-in-chief of *Intimidades* magazine.

### Editor of *Cosmopolitan-en-Español*

In 1979, Saralegui was named editor-in-chief of the Spanish-language version of Hearst's *Cosmopolitan* magazine. The internationally distributed *Cosmopolitan-en-Español* circulated in all Latin American countries and all major cities in the United States. Saralegui held this position for ten years, until her resignation in 1969 to become executive producer and host of Univision Network's *El show de Cristina.*

Saralegui admits it was not an easy transition adapting to the demands of television. After 23 years as a journalist, where appearance is irrelevant, Saralegui could not understand the importance of looks for the visual medium. A size 18, she had never exercised, spending most of her time behind a desk. But good friends Emilio and **Gloria Estefan** sent her their personal fitness trainer. "They saved my life" she told the *Miami Herald.* Saralegui started jogging three miles a day, watched her weight, changed her hair, and shrank six dress sizes.

### Host of *El show de Cristina*

*El show de Cristina,* in the style of *Donahue* and *Oprah,* became known for discussing controversial topics, such as sex, previously considered "taboo" in Spanish language media. Soon Saralegui went from being dubbed "the Latin Helen Gurley Brown" to "Oprah con salsa." While Saralegui did not mind such comparisons, she was disturbed by those who voiced early objections to her blonde looks. "People would write me hate letters. How dare I try to represent Hispanics when I was so white? I tried to make them see it was racism," she told the *Chicago Tribune.* In an interview with the *Los Angeles Times,* Saralegui recalled, "At the beginning they said 'it won't work. You're a Cuban woman. You have a Cuban accent. How dare you represent us [the Hispanics] because you're so white?' I understand that brown is beautiful, but so is white, pink, or whatever you are. We're a cultural minority. We go from [the darker skin tones of] Celia Cruz to me, and everything in the middle."

Saralegui was also worried that she'd have a hard time finding Hispanic guests willing to talk about personal or controversial issues. "Everybody thought the Hispanics wouldn't talk about their problems, but they just needed a forum to discuss these things," Saralegui told the *Chicago Tribune*. "After the first show letters started coming in, and they told me stuff that I would not tell my pastor, my gynecologist or my husband."

### Emmy Award for *El show de Cristina*

It turned out that the objections regarding Saralegui's complexion and her worries about the show did not matter. *El show de Cristina* was a huge success. It has been rated the number one day-time television show and ranked among the top ten Spanish-language programs in the United States. Moreover, it won an Emmy Award in 1991.

Later in 1991 the outspoken Saralegui launched a three-minute daily radio show entitled *Cristina opina*. Prior to the debut of the nationally syndicated program, distributed through the Cadena Radio Centro Network, Saralegui said in her biography, "I am very excited about *Cristina opina* because it is going to give me an opportunity to share my thoughts, my feelings, my concerns, the experiences I have gathered working hands-on with Hispanics of every country in the past 29 years, and will be a great addition to the work we have accomplished on television."

When asked by *La opinion* if there have been changes in her personal life since she began to work on television, Saralegui replied "Yes, for good. The routine of my private life has remained almost the same. I've never been a pretentious person, since childhood I got used to leading a tranquil and healthy life. I've always dedicated myself to writing, I love to read a lot, especially biographies. I consider myself a very private person and my family respects this behavior from me. Even if it doesn't seem so, I am a person with time for herself. Be it at home, on the plane, in the hotel, at the studio, wherever I may be, I'll always find five or ten minutes to study, because I like to do so. This routine has remained the same with or without the programs."

In November 1991, Saralegui launched another project, *Cristina la revista* (*Cristina the Magazine*). She is executive director of this monthly lifestyle magazine, which is an off-shoot of her television program, distributed by Editorial America. "The magazine is more trouble than the two TV shows put together. Print is always harder to do than television," the former journalist confessed to the *Miami Herald*.

By 1992 Saralegui had achieved another of her professional goals by adding one more dimension to her career. She became the executive producer and host of *Cristina,* an English-language version of her Spanish talk show, making Saralegui the first Hispanic to host daily television programs in two languages. She is quick to point out that any *Cristina* show is unmistakably a Cristina production. She chooses the subjects. "I tell the producers what angles I want. I OK all the angles. I'm very hands on," she explained to the *Miami Herald.*

In addition to her own television series, Saralegui has been a guest on numerous national and local television programs. She has made frequent appearances on the Spanish-language program *Sabado gigante,* acted as creative consultant for *TV mujer* and appeared in the Univision soap opera *Amandote.* She also produced a series of television specials in the style of *This Is Your Life,* celebrating the lives of leading Latin entertainers. "The reason we do these programs," Saralegui told *Hollywood Latinews,* "is because celebrities many times are people who started off in life very poor and they don't have the opportunities that middle class people have, yet they reach such heights. And we want to see, motivationally speaking, how they have made it. They are super-achievers. So when I do these special programs what I stress is that aspect that if they could do it, we can do it too." As was noted in *New York Newsday,* she once shared with a friend the secret to her own success: "To be absolutely fearless and plow ahead, no matter what."

Saralegui told *La opinion* that future goals include to appear in a movie, learn to pilot a plane, and learn deep-sea diving. "I want to have fun while I work. Life is not only work and work, you also have to do what most appeals to you." She also admits two of her virtues are being much too honest and being consistent, but reveals her biggest flaws are being "intolerably perfectionistic, much too honest and not too patient."

Saralegui is managed by her second husband, Marcos Avila, 11 years her junior, a former bass player and part founder of the music group Miami Sound Machine. In an interview with the *Chicago Tribune* she recalled: "I got married the first time because I wanted to have a family. I thought romance was for foolish ladies. I met Marcos when I was 35, and I thought, God sent me this to show me how wrong I was before. I was eleven years older than him, I wore a suit, I was the editor-in-chief of a ladies' magazine and I had a big staff. He was a little musician with a ponytail and an earring. Imagine him at an editorial cocktail party! Everybody's family had a fit!"

They married in 1964 and Avila heads Cristina Saralegui Enterprises, Inc., the company that handles all of Saralegui's operations and business ventures. "That's the secret of our marriage" she told *Más* magazine. "Be together and talk about everything twenty-four hours a day." She also told *Hollywood Latinews*, "I think the most important thing I learned from my failure in my first marriage is that you have to have the same dreams and you have to go in the same direction. It's really important you work in the same kind of job."

The green-eyed blonde has more than 25 years of journalism experience and has received numerous distinctions. She was named one of the "Legendary Women of Miami," received the Corporate Leader Award from the National Network of Hispanic Women, and has addressed organizations ranging from Women in Communications to the Union of American Women of Puerto Rico. She has served on international juries of beauty pageants, has participated as Celebrity Grand Marshal at several national parades and has been awarded the keys to many cities in the United States and Latin America. As the Hispanic spokesperson for Crest Toothpaste, Saralegui has yet another reason to smile.

When Cristina Saralegui is not writing, taping, touring, consulting, or exercising, she can be found with her husband, her two daughters, Cristina Amalia and Stephanie Ann, and her son, Jon Marcos, in their Miami home.

### SOURCES:

#### Periodicals

*Chicago Tribune,* May 31, 1992.
*Hispanic,* November 1991, pp. 18–24.
*La opinion* (translated from Spanish by Elena Kellner), Panorama section, October 20, 1991.
*Los Angeles Times Calendar,* June 22, 1992; June 25, 1992.
*Más* (translated from Spanish by Elena Kellner) July/August 1991, pp. 43–50.
*Miami Herald,* June 21, 1992, pp. 11–31.
*New York Newsday,* April 2, 1992, June 22, 1992.

#### Other

*Hollywood Latinews* (television program), interview with Elena Kellner, October 16, 1991.
Saralegui, Cristina, official biography provided by Magikcity Communications.

*—Sketch by Elena Kellner*

# Elgio "Kid Chocolate" Sardinas
## 1910-
### Cuban boxer

One of the most celebrated Hispanics in boxing history, Eligio Sardiñas, or **"Kid Chocolate"** was the first Cuban world champion in boxing history. He enjoyed brief fame and wealth in the 1920s and 1930s in the United States, but then spiralled downward, as many boxers did, into poverty and alcoholism after his time in the limelight ended.

Born in Havana, Cuba on January 6, 1910, Sardiñas was known as a "picture boxer," having learned his technique from movies of famous fighters. His manager, Luis Guitierrez, elaborated on this method in the *The Encyclopedia of World Boxing Champions* in 1975: "When the Keed first came to me, neither he nor myself knew anything much about boxing. We figured the best thing to do was to study the methods of the masters." The first fight Kid Chocolate watched was Gans-Nelson. Chocolate and Guitierrez watched the movie of the fight every day of its run at one of the Havana movie houses. They studied how Gans used his left hand. Kid Chocolate practiced what he saw in the movie in the gym every day. The pair continued to study boxing films. They picked up the tricks and skills of boxing, such as tying up the opponent in a clinch and blocking and feinting with the right hand. Kid Chocolate studied and worked on boxing from films for eight years.

Chocolate's studies paid off. A featherweight as an amateur, he posted 100 straight wins in Cuban Leagues, including 86 knockouts. In 1928, he embarked on his professional career and accumulated another 21 knockouts in a row. In August of 1928, he moved to the United States.

In the United States, Kid Chocolate increased his run of consecutive victories by another 13 with eight knockouts, bringing his totals to 144 straight wins and 114 knockouts. Many boxing enthusiasts rank Kid Chocolate as one of the greatest featherweights ever, in the same category as Young Griffo and Willie Pep.

On July 15, 1931, Kid Chocolate knocked out Benny Bass in the seventh round of the fight to win the Junior Lightweight Title in Philadelphia. For that fight, he weighed in at 126 pounds and stood 5'6". Next he beat Lew Feldman in 12 rounds, after which he challenged Fidel LaBarba for the featherweight crown.

### Recognized as World Champion

Kid Chocolate fought LaBarba three times, winning two of the three fights. One of those occasions was in New York City on December 9, 1932, with the victory coming via a decision. Beating the standing champion, he was named the world boxing champion by the New York Boxing Commission. In that moment, he became the first Cuban to hold the world championship title in the history of boxing. He was 26 years old.

Although brief, Chocolate's time in the spotlight was long enough for him to enjoy it. He held the title for one year and 17 days, defeating seven challengers before losing to Frankie Klick. On December 26, 1933 (Boxing Day), Frankie Klick knocked him out in the seventh round in Philadelphia to capture the championship title. Klick remained dormant, never defending his own title, until 1949 when Sandy Saddler claimed the championship.

Undaunted, Kid Chocolate continued to fight but never regained the championship. He competed until his retirement in 1938. In his 10-year career in the United States, he posted 145 wins of 161 with 64 knockouts, one of the best records ever compiled in featherweight history. Out of those 161 bouts, he was counted out only twice.

Kid Chocolate was a true champion. He won the support of the New York Hispanic and the national boxing communities. He was revered by all-time boxing great Joe Louis, who stated, "Nights I hung out at the corner with the Catherine Street boys. Most all they ever talked about was how much the big fighters took home in their purses. I had just started to take violin lessons, and one of the gang showed me that Kid Chocolate and Jack Dempsey made more money in one fight than a good fiddler could make in a couple of lifetimes." Inspired, Louis left the violin behind and took up boxing gloves, becoming one of the greatest boxers of all time.

Though Kid Chocolate inspired many, this did not save him. He was immortalized on stage and screen. Like many boxers of his time, however, he was exploited and cheated by dishonest managers and has lived the rest of his life in poverty.

## SOURCES:

Fleischer, Nat and Andre, Sam, *A Pictorial History of Boxing,* 2nd edition, Secaucus, NJ, Citadel Press, 1987.

Grombach, John V., *The Saga of the Fist: The 9000 Year Story of Boxing in Text and Pictures,* 2nd edition, New York, A.S. Barnes & Co., 1977.

*Hispanic-American Almanac,* edited by Nicolás Kanellos, Detroit, Gale, 1993.

McCallum, John D., *The Encyclopedia of World Boxing Champions,* Radnor, PA, Chilton, 1975.

McCallum, John, *The World Heavyweight Boxing Championship: A History,* Radnor, PA, Chilton, 1974.

—*Sketch by Christopher B. Tower*

# Domingo Faustino Sarmiento
## 1811-1888
**Argentine journalist, writer, educator, and politician**

Domingo Faustino Sarmiento had the distinction of being one of the most accomplished Argentineans in the nineteenth century. Sarmiento was a successful journalist, writer, educator, and politician during Argentina's volatile political reconstruction. He is noted for founding and editing nine political and educational newspapers in both Chile, the United States, and Argentina. A prolific writer, Sarmiento's *Obras Completas* comprise 52 volumes of political and educational treatises, letters, essays, memoirs, travel sketches, and local color novellas. Further, he published several novels, with the most critically acclaimed being the romantic *Civilización y Barbarie* (*Civilization and Barbarism*), or otherwise known as *El Facundo.* Politically, Sarmiento held the offices of both governor of San Juan in 1862, and president of Argentina 1868 to 1874.

Domingo Faustino Sarmiento was born on February 11, 1811, in San Juan, to José Clemente Sarmiento and Paula Albarracín. Sarmiento was a self-educated man who learned by reading world literature. While working as a clerk for his aunt's general store in 1827, Sarmiento spent hours reading and educating himself. Sarmiento read and translated all of Sir Walter Scott's works in order to learn English, and read the French and Italian Romantics to gain a rudimentary knowledge of these two languages. Sarmiento was also greatly influenced by the *Autobiography of Benjamin Franklin.* This autobiography would serve Sarmiento as a model for both his character, as well as his democratic political philosophies.

In 1839 Sarmiento began his career as an educator and journalist. Believing that women should have more opportunities, Sarmiento founded the first high school for women in San Juan. While directing this school, he also founded a literary society with his friends Quiroga Rosas, Cortínez Rodríguez, and Dionisio Rodríguez. With the help of the individuals of the literary society, he founded his first politically opinionated paper entitled *El Zonda*. However, because of his democratic ideologies in the articles, which called for free press, charity, and free elections, the paper was shut down. Furthermore, the paper's anti-governmental stance against the gaucho politics of Argentina, enraged Governor Benavida, a supporter of the dictator Juan Manuel de Rosas. In 1840, because of these political opinions in his paper, Sarmiento was exiled to Chile and was ordered never to return.

During his exile in Chile, Sarmiento continued to write against the gaucho leaders of Argentina and became a famous political reporter for a newspaper entitled *El Mercurio* (1841). His most accomplished piece was written while in Chile, his book *El Facundo*. Originally, the book was introduced in installments in his paper *El Progresso* from May 2 to July 28, 1845. Though modern critics have classified *El Facundo* under the varied genres of Romantic literature, biography, and local color literature, to Sarmiento it was a political statement. *El Facundo* was the biography of a true-life gaucho leader who invaded the province of San Juan. Though not historically accurate, the book exposes the inherent negative aspects of Argentine gaucho politics after the disarray of Spanish Colonialism. Through *El Facundo*, Sarmiento attacks Juan Manuel de Rosa's dictatorship in Argentina. The theme and message that is presented in his novel is that such dictatorships should be removed from Argentine society. *El Facundo* served Sarmiento as a powerful piece of propaganda that helped destroy the image of the dictator in nineteenth-century Argentina. Today, *El Facundo* is considered to be one of the most important works in Latin American history. As renowned scholar, Allison Williams Bunkley, argues in her book, *Life of Sarmiento*, "*El Facundo* has come to be known as one of the masterpieces of Hispanic American literature."

After the publication of *El Facundo*, Sarmiento traveled throughout Europe, North America, and Africa for three years. Through his varied travels, he gained a vast universal knowledge that later served him in his political career. He returned to Chile in 1848 to Marry Benits Martinez Pastoriza, and adopted her son and named him Domingo Fidel. While in Chile, he wrote a book of his travels entitled *Viajes por Europa, Africa America* (*Travels Through Europe Africa and America*) and an educational treatise entitled *Educación Popular* (*Popular Education*). Sarmiento spent the next few years with his family and in various administrative positions in Chile. He also continued to publish and edit politically opinionated works against the gaucho leaders of Argentina, in the newspapers entitled *La Tribuna, La Cronica*, and the *People's Advisor*.

### Sarmiento's Return

After the demise of Sarmiento's political enemy, **Juan Manuel de Rosas** in 1852 at the Battle of Caseros, the political climate in Argentina was much different. The people and government of Argentina were more accepting of Sarmiento's political ideas when he returned to Buenos Aires in 1855. On August 27, Sarmiento became a professor at the University of Buenos Aires teaching constitutional law. That same year he was elected to the Senate and was appointed to the head of the Department of Schools in Buenos Aires. As the director of education, Sarmiento reorganized the public school system for the better in Buenos Aires. While in Buenos Aires, he also founded the newspaper entitled *Anales de la educación commun* (*Annals of Common Education*). As the first of its kind, the newspaper's mission was to keep the people of Buenos Aires informed of the organizational, as well as the new systems of education in their country.

Upon the election of Sarmiento's colleague **Bartolomé Mitre** as the president of Argentina, Mitre appointed Sarmiento as governor of San Juan in 1862. While governor in San Juan, Sarmiento sought to democratize the region by modeling the political structures after those in Europe and the United States. He created new offices, refined government, and retrained the military to the modern military standards of the world. He also built bridges, created an urban police, paved roads and sidewalks, built legislative buildings, and vastly improved the public educational system. As governor, he also waged wars against the gaucho political leaders of the regions who had remained after Juan Manuel de Rosa's regime fell. One such gaucho that Sarmiento waged war against and eventually ordered to death was El Chacho. This decision to kill El Chacho enraged the political leaders as well as the people of San Juan. Sarmiento failed to realize that by going against El Chacho, he was going against the archetype of the entire country, the gaucho. Because of his action, Sarmiento was forced to leave office and was appointed by Bartolomé Mitre as the ambassador to the United States in 1864.

Sarmiento's years as ambassador were spent traveling on diplomatic missions to Chile, Peru, and the United States. Sarmiento's years in the United States were fruitful both politically and socially. While there he met and studied with Ralph Waldo Emerson and Henry Wadsworth Longfellow. In the United States, he continued to publish extensively and wrote *Vida de Abrán Lincoln* (*Lincoln's Life*), and *Las escuelas base de la prospedad y de la republica en los Estados Unidos* (*The Schools, Foundation and Prosperity and the Republic in the United States*). This educational treatise was based on Sarmiento's close friend Horace Mann's philosophies and pedagogical approaches. During his stay in the United States he also founded a newspaper in New York entitled *Ambas Americas* (*Both Americas*). Sarmiento's articulate articles, which called for unity between Argentina and the United States in this paper, helped to bridge the political gap between the two countries.

In 1868, the term of Bartolomé Mitre was ending and the Argentine constitution forbade him to succeed himself. With the help of his colleague, Colonel Mansilla, Sarmiento's candidacy was announced. Sarmiento himself did not take this nomination seriously on the account of the El Chacho incident that destroyed his govenorship and political career in 1862. However, the respect that he gained as a diplomat in the United States and the support of his writings, lead to an overwhelming victory. Sarmiento was inaugurated into office October 12, 1868. Similar to his term as governor, Sarmiento's mission in his presidency was to democratize his country. His first act as president was to destroy the last of the gaucho leaders, Lopéz Jordán and Entre Ríos. He also forced his opponent in the elections, an old gaucho leader named General Urquiga, to resign from politics. However, Sarmiento's most successful accomplishments as president was in his works of education. To Sarmiento, education was a means of giving his people the knowledge that the gauchos, who had ruled and destroyed the country for generations, were unjust and should never regain control. Through his guidance, primary school enrollment jumped from 30,000 to more than 100,000. He also implemented compulsory school attendance and began a program that allowed teachers to travel to sparsely populated areas. He was also the first to found a school for the physically and mentally impaired.

Sarmiento's attempts to democratize his country eventually led him to lose his presidency. By attacking the gauchos, he was going against the powerful families and political leaders that continued to promulgate gaucho politics for generations. Furthermore, Sarmiento's controversial acts regarding immigration brought more than 34,000 foreigners to Argentina by 1874. Sarmiento's legislation allotted foreigners opportunities to acquire vital land that many Argentineans never had the opportunity to take advantage of. These two political decisions enraged many people of his country, and Sarmiento was forced to resign after a death threat in 1874. After his resignation, he was appointed as a senator of San Juan. In 1875, he continued to work as an educator and became director of schools in Buenos Aires. The following years were disheartening for Sarmiento. He unsuccessfully ran for president of Argentina in 1879, and in 1885 he was defeated as senator of San Juan. On September 11, 1888, Sarmiento died of heart failure in Paraguay and was buried in Buenos Aires.

The legacy of Sarmiento lives in both the Argentinean educational system and Latin American literature. Because of Sarmiento's educational acts in the nineteenth century, the Argentine educational system is considered to be one of the best in the world. Literally, Sarmiento's works will remain a model for writers of today and tomorrow. As Gwen Kirk Patrick and Francine Masiello argue in their book, *Sarmiento: Author of a Nation,* "Fiction writers as diverse as Alejo Carpentier, Gabriel García-Márquez, and Augusto Roa Bastos, in their novelistic portrayals of political power and dictatorship in Latin America, have depended on Sarmiento's portraits of dictators in Latin America, and on Sarmiento's own political role in the definition of national and regional power building." Sarmiento's work as journalist, educator, writer and politician, represent a pivotal aspect of Argentinean politics, culture, and philosophy.

## SELECTED PUBLISHED WORKS:

*Vida de Abrán Lincoln,* New York, Appleton, 1866.
*Las Escuelas, base de la prosperidad y de la república en los Estados Unidos,* [Buenos Aires], 1884.
*Obras Completas,* 52 volumes, [Buenos Aires], 1884.
*Educación Popular,* [Buenos Aires], 1915.
*El Facundo,* [Buenos Aires], 1938.
*Viajes por Europa, Africa y America,* [Buenos Aires], Hachette, 1955.

## SOURCES:

Bunkley, Allison Williams, *The Life of Sarmiento,* New Jersey, Princeton University Press, 1952.
Crowley, Frances G., *Domingo Faustino Sarmiento,* New York, Twayne Publishers, 1972.
Donghi, Tulio Halperin, Iván Jaksic', Gwen Kirkpatrick, and Francine Masiello, *Sarmiento: Author of a Nation,* Berkeley, University of California Press, 1994.
Patton, Elda Clayton, *Sarmiento in the United States,* Evansville, University of Evansville Press, 1976.
*Sarmiento and His Argentina,* edited by Joseph T. Criscenti, Lynne Rienner Publishers, 1993.
*A Sarmiento Anthology,* edited by Allison Williams Bunkley, New Jersey, Princeton University Press, 1948.

—*Sketch by John-Michael Rivera*

# Jon Secada
## 1961(?)-
### Cuban American singer-songwriter

After laboring as a songwriter and backup singer under the tutelage of Miami Sound Machine 's Emilio Estefan, Jr., Jon Secada went solo in 1992 to worldwide acclaim. His first two albums were released bilingually, so *Jon Secada* was released simultaneously as *Otro Dia Mas Sin Verte*, while *Heart, Soul & A Voice* was also released as *Si Te Vas* in 1994. Both incarnations of his first album appeared on the album and singles charts around the globe, and it eventually became certified multi-platinum in its English and Spanish versions alike. *Heart, Soul & A Voice* spawned a number-one hit, "If You Go," within months of its release.

Juan Secada was nine years old when he and his parents were allowed to leave their hometown of Havana, Cuba, during 1971. Jose and Victoria, who owned a coffee shop, were concerned about the prospects for their only child. Though he was sent to prison and a work camp for several years for his dissidence, Jose finally succeeded in relocating his family to Hialeah, Florida. The couple opened another coffee shop in the Miami neighborhood to help put their son through school.

## A Family Talent

An aunt named Moraima Secada had once been a bolero singer of great repute in Cuba, but nephew Juan did not discover any musical inclinations until he was well into high school. When his performances drew enthusiasm and encouragement from other students and teachers, Secada responded by specializing in music as an undergraduate in college. After earning his bachelor's degree from the University of Miami, he decided to stay on for a master's in jazz vocal performance. Secada's musical interests were eclectic, since he had grown up listening to dance and pop and was particularly influenced by such crossover rhythm-and-blues singer-songwriters as Stevie Wonder and Marvin Gaye.

However, his first job in the music business was less than glamorous: Secada was a voice teacher at Miami-Dade Community College for six years. During that time he married one of his students, Jo Pat Cafaro, in 1988. Meanwhile, two of his friends from college had joined the popular dance band Miami Sound Machine. They relayed a demo tape of Secada performing his own material to lead singer **Gloria Estefan** and her husband, producer Emilio Estefan, Jr. Jon, as he had been rechristened in 1990, then gained recognition as a songwriter and backup singer.

Secada worked for Pia Zadora and Don Johnson, as well as the Estefans, while preparing for his eventual pop stardom.

## Launched Solo Career

The next stage of Secada's career was launched when Gloria Estefan allowed him a four-minute solo turn during a performance on her world tour. As a result, Secada finally won the chance to record his own album, at Crescent Moon Studios in Miami. After his debut, *Jon Secada,* attained such wild success, the new star was on the road quite often. Secada traveled to South Africa, where he told the *New York Times* that it was a pleasant surprise to be accepted as an Afro-Cuban by the natives, and to hear his music on black-run radio stations. After so many periods of separation, however, Secada and his wife divorced in 1993.

Though Secada admitted in *Esquire* that he never really learned to dance very well, he proved instrumental in capturing a Latin audience for his record label, SBK Records, a division of EMI Records Group. *Otro Dia Mas Sin Verte* launched four successive number-one singles on the "Hot Latin Tracks" chart in *Billboard* magazine and became the number-one Latin album of 1992. After setting a record as the longest-running album on its chart, it finally garnered a Grammy Award for Best Latin Pop Album.

Yet Secada also reached a crossover market with "Just Another Day," the biggest single from the English-language version, which remained in the Top 10 for 11 weeks in a row. His second project was modeled more after his childhood heroes, like the band Earth, Wind, and Fire. *Heart, Soul & A Voice* contained more straightforward blues ballads, like Diane Warren's "Where Do I Go from You." Pop legend Frank Sinatra was so impressed with Secada's range and vocal skill that he featured the young singer on his album *Duets II.*

After producing back-to-back winners with his first two albums, Secada continued to tour in the United States and throughout Latin America. He helped his parents settle into retirement in the Miami area, and was considering a film debut in the near future.

## SELECTED DISCOGRAPHY

*Jon Secada,* SBK/EMI Latin, 1992.
*Otro Dia Mas Sin Verte,* SBK/EMI Latin, 1992.
*Heart, Soul and a Voice,* SBK/EMI Latin, 1994.
*Si Te Vas,* SBK/EMI Latin, 1994.

## SOURCES:

### Periodicals

*Entertainment Weekly,* June 17, 1994.

*Esquire,* November 1994, p. 150.
*Interview,* June 1994, p. 22.
*New York Times,* February 17, 1993, p. C14.
*People Weekly,* July 11, 1994.

### Other

"Jon Secada" (biography and promotional copy), SBK Records, 1995.

—*Sketch by Jennifer Kramer*

*Andrés Segovia*

# Andrés Segovia
## 1893-1987
### Spanish classical guitarist

Andrés Segovia was one of the most important musicians of the twentieth century. He established the guitar as an important concert instrument, made prolific recordings, and inspired generations of guitarists. Perhaps the greatest testament to what he accomplished for the guitar was the renaissance in music composed for it by important composers, including Manuel de Falla, Heitor Villa-Lobos, Manuel Ponce, Mario Castelnuovo-Tedesco, Joaquín Turina, and Joaquín Rodrigo. This astounding enrichment of the guitar's repertoire stands in stark contrast to the eighteenth and nineteenth centuries, when practically none of the major composers—like Mozart, Hayden, and Beethoven—wrote music for the guitar.

### Renaissance of the Guitar

In the first part of the nineteenth century, the guitar, which for centuries had been considered an accompanying instrument for singing and dancing, staked out its own territory as an appropriate instrument for music in the classical style. The Spaniard Fernando Sor and the Italian Mauro Giuliani were the two most important figures for the renaissance of this instrument, both of whom were virtuoso performers and prolific composers.

But by 1840 both Sor and Giuliani were dead, and the guitar seemed to be languishing along with them. In Segovia's own words, "the guitar was caught in kind of vicious circle: there were few guitarists because no music was being written for it, and no music was being written for it because there were so few guitarists."

Yet the tradition survived, thanks to at least one major figure in the succeeding generations who kept the spirit of Sor and Giuliani alive. In the 1840s and 1850s the Frenchman Napoleon Coste performed and composed for the guitar, and toward the end of the century the Spaniard Francisco Tárrega composed important works of a more national character for the instrument, in addition to transcribing the music of Bach, Mendelsohn, and Albéniz for the guitar.

In the first part of the twentieth century, though there were guitarists of renown, like Tárrega's disciple Miguel Llobet and the Paraguayan Augustín Barrios, Segovia was by far the predominant figure in the renaissance classical guitar enjoyed. Segovia added to the repertoire with important transcriptions—Bach's "Chaconne" being perhaps the most famous—and discoveries of forgotten composers—like the seventeenth-century lutenist Robert de Visée. In addition, he achieved a status for the guitar that it never was able to attain in the nineteenth century: that of an appropriate and even majestic concert instrument.

### "Don Quijote de la Guitarra"

Segovia's rise to success was remarkable considering the obstacles he was forced to overcome. Born into a very humble family in Linares in the South of Spain in 1893, he was brought up by his Uncle Eduardo and Aunt María, and spent most of his youth in Granada. His family opposed his interest in music, and as Segovia explained, "Since I had to fight against the stubborn opposition of my family, I had to forego teachers, conservatories, or any other accepted method of instruction." Segovia taught himself not only the rudiments of his instrument, but the ability to read music as well. "From that time I would be my own master and disciple," he commented.

He gave his first concert at the "Círculo Artístico" of Granada in 1910, at the age of 16. Concerts followed in Seville, and then the young Segovia departed for Madrid. In his autobiographical writings Segovia neglected to assign dates to many key events, but he must have been 17 or 18 years old when he made this trip to the Spanish capital. While on the train, Segovia told of a conversation he had with his traveling companions, during which he put forth an eloquent defense of the guitar. "First, no string instrument offers such complete harmonic potential; second, it is light and can be transported effortlessly from one place to another; and thirdly, its sound is naturally melancholic and beautiful." As they left the train, one of the passengers said, "So long, Don Quijote of the Guitar, may the world restore your sanity."

### Concerts in Spain and Abroad

After some difficulty in Madrid, Segovia enjoyed his first great stroke of luck: not the concert which had been arranged at the *ateneo* of Madrid, but rather his encounter with the guitar maker Manuel Ramírez. In what became a famous anecdote, Segovia offered to rent a guitar from Ramírez for his concert, much in the same way a piano would be rented locally for touring musicians. Yet when Ramírez heard the young Segovia play one of his guitars, he said, "Take it; it's yours."

The concert took place in 1913, and though it received mixed reviews, it attracted considerable attention to Segovia and his instrument. Concerts followed in Valencia, where one reviewer praised Segovia for "bypassing the guitar's hackneyed repertoire and playing instead works by Debussy, Tchaikovsky, and other 'strangers' to the instrument." Perhaps more significant than these concerts, Segovia met and befriended Miguel Llobet, the most important disciple of the great Francisco Tárrega. Llobet invited Segovia to follow him to his native Barcelona, where he helped arrange recitals for the 25-year-old Segovia, the most important being in Barcelona's famous *Palau* or "Palace." The large hall was filled to capacity. "In a night abounding in emotions," Segovia recalled, "the one that moved me most was the realization that I had broadened the scope of the guitar and proved it *could* be heard from any stage."

Until 1920, Segovia continued giving concerts all over Spain, played for the Queen, and met the impresario Quesada, who was to act as his agent until 1956. Quesada organized Segovia's first venture abroad, a South American tour which began in 1920. Yet before his departure, he had secured an important

landmark for his instrument. "For the first time, a composer who was not a guitarist wrote a piece for the guitar. It was Federico Moreno-Torroba [who] in a few weeks came up with the truly beautiful *Dance in E Major. . . .* That success prompted Manuel de Falla to compose his very beautiful *Homage,* and Joaquín Turina his splendid *Sevillana.*" Even before Segovia left Spain, these compositions had elevated the rank of the guitar to a level that it had not reached in a century.

Segovia's successful pattern of playing concerts while continually broadening his instrument's horizons continued in Latin America. Once again he showed the guitar to be an immensely appealing concert instrument, while inspiring composers who heard him to direct their efforts to the guitar. In Mexico he made the acquaintance of Manuel Ponce, who would go on to become one of the guitar's greatest composers. Segovia said of Ponce's *Folías de España* that "it is the most important work that has been written for the solo guitar."

But perhaps the event that sealed Segovia's success was his Paris debut. It took place on April 7, 1924, in the concert hall of the Conservatoire and was attended by a capacity audience. One of the pieces on the program was a newly composed virtuoso piece called "Segovia" by Roussel. Rarely had a performer enjoyed such a prestigious public. Present at the recital were Paul Dukas, Manuel de Falla, Albert Roussel, Joaquín Nin, and even the philosopher **Miguel de Unamuno,** who heard the recital from Madame Debussy's box. This recital came to be considered one of the most important musical events of the century, perhaps after Igor Stravinsky's debut of *The Rite of Spring* in the same city ten years earlier. After a European tour that led him through England, Italy, Germany, Hungary, and the Soviet Union, Segovia's next great success was in the New York Town Hall on January 8, 1928. This was followed by concert tours of Japan, the Philippines, China, and Indonesia.

The Spanish Civil War, and then World War II, interrupted Segovia's residence in Barcelona, and he spent those years in the Americas, especially in Mexico, Uruguay, and New York City. He resumed world touring afterwards, and began pursuing intensely a routine of university teaching, especially at the Academia Chigiana in Sienna, Italy. He also gave classes at the University of California at Berkeley, and held annual master classes at Santiago de Compostela in Spain. Thousands of guitarists received instruction from him, and the greatest of the following generation, including John Williams, Julian Bream, Alirio Diaz, Oscar Gighlia, and Christopher Parkening, were largely indebted to him for their stature.

Segovia continued playing, teaching, and recording—almost 30 records with Decca and several more with RCA—up the to end of his life in 1987. He received numerous awards and honors during his lifetime, including an honorary Doctor of Music degree from Oxford University in 1974, being made Marquis of Salobrena by a royal Spanish decree in 1981, and the Gold Medal of the Royal Philharmonic Society of London in 1985.

## SOURCES:

### Books

Clinton, George, *Andrés Segovia,* London, 1978.

Grunfeld, Frederic, *The Art and Times of the Guitar,* London, 1969.

Segovia, Andrés, *Andrés Segovia: An Autobiography of the Years 1893–1920.*

### Periodicals

*Guitar Review* ("La guitarra y yo"—a series of autobiographical articles by Segovia), Nos. 4 (1947), 6 (1948), 7 (1948), 10 (1949), 13 (1952).

*—Sketch by Paul Miller*

# Juan Nepomuceno Seguín
## 1806-1890
### Mexican American political leader and soldier

Juan Nepomuceno Seguín was proclaimed a hero in Texas for his service in the war to gain independence from Mexico. He served as a state senator and as mayor of San Antonio. Seguin was born to a wealthy, influential family in San Antonio de Bexar on October 29, 1806. His father, Erasmo Seguín, was a politician and served as a representative in Congress. Seguín was schooled in San Antonio and at the young age of 18, he was elected mayor. His family was supportive of the Anglo settlers that were moving into Texas.

### Joins the Texas Calvary

When he was 28 years old, Seguín was elected to the office of jefe político ("political chief"). At that time, **Antonio López de Santa Anna** was trying to set up a centralized Mexican government in Texas. Seguín was a leader against Santa Anna's centralized government. A convention was planned to discuss the problems with the Mexican government and Seguín implored citizens to send delegates to the convention. In the 1830s, with the influx of Anglos in Texas, the American immigrants greatly outnumbered the Mexican Americans. The Anglos and Mexican Americans joined together in a movement against Santa Anna. Seguín joined the militia October 13, 1835, when his friend, Stephen F. Austin, appointed him captain in the Texas cavalry. Austin introduced him to General Sam Houston. Seguín was given a brigade and fought in the Battle of San Antonio. The Mexican Army retreated and his brigade was put on patrol. After the acting governor, Henry Smith, approved his commission, Seguín was ordered to go to the Alamo. He then was sent to Goliad for reinforcements. While he was gone, Santa Anna attacked the Alamo with tremendous force for 13 days and massacred the Texas cavalry.

During this time, native Texans were leaving their homes to escape the Mexican army. This exodus was called the "runaway scrape." Seguín's family left, and at the Brazos crossing the family's sheep were lost. They lost their main source of income and never recovered their wealth. Seguín went to General Houston in Gonzales, who ordered him to recall his men to the San Jacinto River. At the Battle of San Jacinto, Seguín captured three Mexican colonels and he became the "Hero of San Jacinto." The capture proved fruitful for the Texas cavalry. One of the men was a chief of staff who told Seguín where they could find some 18,000 pesos. Seguín, promoted to lieutenant colonel, was ordered to Lavaca to recruit the Second Texas Cavalry at his own expense. In 1836, Seguín returned to San Antonio with the gruesome job of gathering the bodies of soldiers from the Alamo and giving them proper burials. He was commissioned as Commandant of the San Antonio garrison. When he received orders from General Felix Huston, chief military officer of the Republic of Texas, to move the citizens of San Antonio to the Brazos and destroy the city, he protested. Seguín went directly to the new President Sam Houston with the order. Houston canceled the order and General Huston became a hostile enemy to Seguín.

In 1838, Seguín resigned his command and resumed his political career. He was a hero and the town of Walnut Creek changed its name to Seguín in his honor. He became a Senator to Congress from Bexar. After serving his two years in the Senate, Seguín ran for mayor of San Antonio and won the election. He took office January 9, 1841. Anglo adventurers were inundating San Antonio at that time. The city was in chaos with cattle rustlers, smugglers, and bandits. The president of the republic, Mirabeau B. Lamar, went to Seguín and asked him to form a brigade to work with Mexican Federalist Antonio Canales. This endeavor failed and Seguín went further into debt. Some of the Anglos turned against Seguín, accusing him of cohorting with the Mexican Army. Fearing for his family, he moved them to his father's ranch. Because of the threat to his life and harm to his family, Seguín resigned his post as mayor and moved his family to Nuevo Laredo just across the Rio Grande in Mexico.

### Arrested in Mexico

Seguín was arrested in Nuevo Laredo, and under threats of life imprisonment from Santa Anna, he was coerced into joining the Mexican Army. He fought in the Mexican War from 1846–1847 while in the Mexican Army. Seguín commanded a brigade at a battle in San Antonio with General Adrian Woll. In 1858, he published his memoirs, the *Personal Memoirs of John N. Seguin,* using the English translation of his name. At the Battle of Buena Vista, Seguín was wounded. In 1862, he fought his last battle at Puebla. Seguín was promoted to full colonel and appointed governor of Texcoco. He remained in Texcoco until 1874, when he retired. He returned to his home at Villa Santiago, and in 1883, he moved back to Nuevo Laredo where his son, Santiago, was mayor. On August 27, 1890, almost 84 years old, Seguín died. He was buried in Nuevo Laredo. In 1974 his body was exhumed and returned to Seguín, Texas, where he was declared a hero and honored for his contribution in the fight for independence from Mexico.

### SOURCES:

Lindheim, Milton, *The Republic of the Rio Grande: Texans in Mexico, 1839–40*, Waco, TX, W.M. Morrison, 1964.

Meier, Matt S., *Mexican American Biographies: A Historical Dictionary, 1836–1987*, 1988.

Padilla, Genaro, *My History, Not Yours: An American Autobiography*, Madison, WI, University of Wisconsin Press, 1993.

—*Sketch by Phyllis Noah*

# Selena
## 1971-1995
### Mexican American pop singer

The undisputed "Queen of Tejano," Selena Quintanilla-Pérez rocketed meteorically into the spotlight in the late 1980s. Within a few years, the artist, known simply as Selena, won a Grammy Award for her album *Selena Live.* Selena sold six albums between 1987 and 1994. By the age of 19, she was a millionaire; by the age of 21, she could draw crowds of 20,000 at the fairgrounds at Pasadena, Texas. Music critics proclaimed she would be the next Madonna, i.e. a mega-star of music and movies. Tragically, however, Selena's career was cut short at the age of 23, when she was murdered by the president of her fan club.

Selena and her band performed Tejano music— Mexican *ranchera* style music mixed with German polka sounds owing influence to pop, country and western, and Caribbean music. Tejano traditionally meant music by Texans of Mexican descent. But Selena, among others, modernized the traditional accordion-based Tejano or Tex-Mex music with country twangs, techno-pop beats, dance mixes, and international influences. More than 70 radio stations playing the uniquely, Latino-styled tunes form a corridor from south Texas through California.

Selena Quintanilla was born April 16, 1971, in Lake Jackson, Texas, a small industrial town near Houston. Her father Abraham Quintanilla, Jr. worked as a shipping clerk at the Dow Chemical plant. Abraham and his wife Marcela had three children: Abraham III, Suzette, and Selena, the youngest.

In his own youth, Quintanilla had performed as a vocalist with Los Dinos ("the boys") a popular South Texas band. When Quintanilla heard his daughter sing at six years of age, he knew Selena was destined for a musical career and encouraged the musical talents that she revealed. In a 1995 *People* article, Quintanilla affirmed that Selena's "timing and pitch were perfect. I could see it from day one."

Selena practiced with the music she enjoyed, a wide range of music from the soul music of Little Anthony and the Imperials to country and western music and even the stylized R&B of Michael Jackson. Through her love of all different kinds of music and early jam sessions with her brother on bass and her sister on drums, Selena demonstrated her passion for the musical arts.

After years of working for others, Abraham Quintanilla opened his own Tex-Mex restaurant in Lake Jackson. There Selena first performed in public with her brother and sister as members of her band. But the economic recession of the early 1980s delivered a knockout blow that closed the family restaurant, forcing them to leave their home and sell all their belongings. Selena's talent would save them.

### Took Family Band on the Road

While the rest of the Quintanilla's relocated in Corpus Christi, Selena and her siblings hit the road, performing throughout southern Texas as Selena y Los Dinos ("Selena and the Boys"). They played at weddings and in cantinas and honky-tonks to very small audiences—oftentimes less than ten people. In a dilapidated van with one foldout bed in the back, the troupe traveled and performed. In 1979, eight-year-old Selena recorded her first tune—a country song sung in Spanish; her Tex-Mex band was in full swing by 1980.

Selena left school in the eighth grade to spend more time travelling with the band and earning money for her family, but she eventually completed her high school equivalency requirements through a correspondence course. The band started playing larger venues, including ballrooms. They also recorded nearly one dozen albums for a small regional label.

In 1987, Selena—then 15-years-old—won Tejano Music Awards for best female vocalist and performer of the year. This was the big break that Selena and the band had worked for years to achieve. Two years later, the Latin division of the EMI Records Group signed the band to a record deal.

Though Selena was the rising star of Latino pop, she was still very much a Texan. She could not speak Spanish and learned the Spanish lyrics for her lively songs and romantic ballads phonetically, coached by her brother, who wrote the songs. At the advice of her father, turned manager, she began taking Spanish lessons in the early 1990s, so that she could project a more genuine Latino image during interviews on Spanish-language radio.

In 1992 Selena Quintanilla married the band's guitarist Chris Pérez. The union did not hamper Selena's sexy image. Rather, Selena became known as the "Tex-Mex Madonna" because of her sexy bustiers and provocative smiles on-stage though off-stage she remained a wholesome, married woman who was devoted to her family.

### Hired Fan Club President

Selena had repeatedly refused offers for fan clubs, keeping her career a family project. But then came Yolanda Saldivar who expressed interest in founding and running Selena's fan club. She was an aunt of one of Selena's childhood friends, but beyond that she was a stranger. Saldivar lived near San Antonio, working as a registered nurse, and caring for three children abandoned by her brother. Despite Saldivar's remote connection to the Quintanillas, Selena and her family appointed Saldivar as the president of the Selena fan club, an unpaid position. In just four years, Selena's fan club attracted 9000 members.

When speaking of her desire to work for Selena, Saldivar told the *Dallas Morning News* in 1994 that she became a devoted Selena fan after seeing a San Antonio concert in 1989. "Selena just inspired me—with her talent, her motivation. She gives her whole to

you." The two developed a close friendship. Though Saldivar did not receive an official salary, Selena often bestowed the woman with gifts. Selena indulged Saldivar's penchant for spotted cows with cow-patterned rugs and phones; Saldivar reciprocated by transforming her apartment into a Selena shrine, laden with Selena photos and memorabilia, including a life-size cardboard pop-up of the singer.

In 1993 *Selena Live* received a Grammy Award for best Mexican American album. Selena's 1994 album, *Amor Prohibido* (*Forbidden Love*)—recipient of a Grammy nomination—sold 600,000 copies in the United States. The fourth single from the album, "Fotos y Recuerdos" ("Photographs and Memories"), reached the top ten on *Billboard* magazine's Latino charts.

By 1995, Selena's albums had sold a combined total of 3 million copies. Twice, she played to record crowds of 60,000 at Houston's annual Livestock Show and Rodeo. Selena's "Bidi Bidi Bom Bom" won the singer a song of the year award at the Tejano Music Awards in early 1995. She also won five more of the 15 awards presented at the 1995 Tejano Music Awards ceremonies, including best female entertainer; best female vocalist; album of the year; Tejano crossover song; and record of the year. An amazed Selena was quoted as saying in *Time* magazine, "Never in my dreams would I have thought I would become this big. I am still freaking out."

In 1994, Selena promoted Saldivar to a paid position as head of Selena Etc. Inc., a company devoted to overseeing two Selena boutiques/salons—one in Corpus Christi and one in San Antonio—and to marketing a line of Selena fashions to be sold in the boutiques as well as in other retail venues. But things began falling apart rapidly. First, fashion designer Martin Gomez quit, claiming that he could not work with Saldivar, who he accused of being "mean and manipulative." The problem escalated with reports of other lapses by Saldivar involving misuse of funds.

Meanwhile, fans were not receiving t-shirts and other Selena items for which they had paid, and money was disappearing from one of the salons. Selena and her father both confronted Saldivar about the reported abuses. Saldivar protested claiming that she had documentation to prove her innocence, and offered to show Selena the alleged papers.

Selena and Saldivar were supposed to meet alone at the Days Inn, where Saldivar was staying. Instead Selena brought her husband; Saldivar proved not to have the papers she'd claimed to possess. The next day Selena went to the Days Inn sometime before noon to talk with Saldivar again. At 11:50 a.m., the Corpus Christi police received a 911 emergency call of a shooting at the motel.

Police detailed that Saldivar met Selena at the door of her motel room with a .38-caliber revolver, shooting the singer in the back and shoulder. Selena staggered to the lobby before collapsing, though she remained conscious until paramedics arrived. Response teams rushed Selena to the hospital. Despite blood transfusions, Selena died a few hours after being shot, on March 31, 1995. Saldivar was charged with Selena's murder.

But the ordeal did not end with Selena's death. Saldivar holed up with the revolver in the cab of a pickup truck in the Days Inn parking lot. For hours she threatened to shoot herself while negotiating with police via a cellular car phone. As the news of Selena's murder spread, the singer's fans stood vigil at the Days Inn. Saldivar finally surrendered at 9:30 p.m.

In the wake of Selena's murder, grieving fans swamped the Quintanilla family with remembrances, including bouquets, rosaries, and votives. Condolences were sent to the Quintanillas by **Julio Iglesias, Gloria Estefan,** Madonna, and La Mafia, a well-known Latino group. Local radio stations devoted their programming to Selena's music, and more than 1,000 Selena tapes and compact discs were sold at a frenzied pace during the next couple of weeks.

1,500 mourners attended a vigil for the singing star at the Bayfront Plaza and Convention Center prior to her funeral held at Corpus Christi's Memorial Coliseum, the arena where she had recorded her smash hit *Selena Live.* 10,000 people flooded Corpus Christi to pass by Selena's coffin. In Los Angeles, 4,000 people gathered at the Sports Arena Memorial to honor the slain singer. Mourners also gathered in San Antonio, the capital of Tejano music, at two separate sites.

Selena was killed just as her career was about to skyrocket in new directions. She had recorded six songs for an English-language album, her first with EMI's SBK division, making her only the third Latino performer to ever cross from the Latin division to the more mainstream part of the record company. In addition, she had made her film debut as herself in *Dos Mujeres, Un Camino,* a Latino Television soap. In 1995, she continued to advance her film career as a mariachi singer in the film *Don Juan DeMarco,* and she had collaborated with former Talking Heads leader David Bryne on the song "God's Child" for the film *Blue in the Face.*

Cameron Randle, a recording industry executive specializing in Tex-Mex music, voiced his opinions of Selena in a retrospective of her career published in *Entertainment Weekly* in April of 1995. "Selena was not merely forging an exceptional career, she was defining a new genre as uniquely American as Delta blues or New Orleans jazz. There's every indication she would have been as enormously popular as [fellow Latinos] **Jon Secada** or Gloria Estefan. She was about to take center stage as the first Tejano performer to

attempt a full-scale crossover, and she was robbed of that opportunity."

Nevertheless, Selena's posthumous recording *Dreaming of You* entered *Billboard* magazine's pop album ratings chart, The Billboard 200, at no. one—the second-highest chart debut after Michael Jackson's *HIStory*—and was also a no. one album on The Billboard Latin 50. The jump into the top pop slot made Selena one of the fastest selling female artists of all time, second only to Janet Jackson. An amazing 175,000 copies of the compact disc were sold on the first day of release. In addition, Selena became the third contemporary Hispanic artist—following Carlos Santana and Los Lobos, as first and second respectively—to reach the top of the chart. Originally meant to be her all-English debut, *Dreaming of You* includes a mixture of English and Spanish tunes as well as a couple bilingual duets with former Talking Head's lead figure David Byrne and with the Barrio Boyzz. According to John Lannert in *Billboard,* the newest release "join[ed] five other titles by Selena that have remained entrenched in the top 10 of the [Latin] chart" since her death. As of August 1995, two songs—"Tú Sólo Tú" and "I Could Fall in Love"—were steadily displacing competition on the Hot Latin Tracks chart. Issued in Mexico, Europe, and Asia, as well as in the U.S., EMI Records president/CEO Davitt Sigerson described *Dreaming* in *Billboard* as a turning point in Latin music, noting, "This is a crossover dream that may be realized not just by Selena, but also for a whole new wave of artists." Selena left enough recorded material behind that another album of unreleased material may be forthcoming.

## SELECTED DISCOGRAPHY:

*Entre A Mi Mundo,* Capitol/EMI Latin, 1992.
*Mis Mejores Canciones,* Capitol/EMI Latin, 1993.
*Selena Live,* Capitol/EMI Latin, 1993.
*Amor Prohibido,* Capitol/EMI Latin, 1994.
*Dreaming of You,* Capitol/EMI Latin, 1995.

Contributor to *Don Juan De Marco* soundtrack, 1995.

## SOURCES:

*Billboard,* February 25, 1995; August 5, 1995, pp. 1, 99.
*Entertainment Weekly,* April 14, 1995, p. 30.
*Hispanic,* December 31, 1994, p. 36.
*Los Angeles Times,* April 1, 1995, pp. A1, A21-A22; April 2, 1995, pp. A1-A9; April 3, 1995, pp. B1-B3.
*La Prensa de San Antonio,* June 11, 1993, p. B1; November 19, 1993, p. B1; April 29, 1994, p. B2.

*Newsweek,* July 31, 1995, p. 16.
*New York Times,* April 2, 1995, p. A18; April 3, 1995, p. A15.
*People,* April 17, 1995, pp. 48–53; July 10, 1995, pp. 36–41.
*Time,* April 10, 1995, p. 91.
*USA Today,* July 27, 1995.

—*Sketch by Christopher B. Tower*

*Ramón José Sender*

# Ramón José Sender
## 1901(?)-1982
**Spanish American novelist, journalist, poet, short story writer, dramatist, and essayist**

Sender was "one of the most distinguished Spanish novelists of his generation," according to *The Times* in 1982. Internationally renowned as a novelist, Sender was also a journalist, poet, short story writer, dramatist, and essayist. A Spanish expatriate, he spent much of his life in the United States. His output was prolific; he authored more than 80 books. His early novels were mostly realistic accounts of the Spanish campaigns in Morocco, the portrayal of life and society in pre-Civil War Spain, and the effects of the Spanish Civil War, such as *Imán* ("Magnet," 1930) and *Siete domingos rojos* ("Seven Red Sundays," 1932). His later novels were more symbolic and philosophical, such as *Proverbio de la muerte* (1939, revised edition published as *La esfera,* "The Sphere," 1969) and *El verdugo afable* ("The Affable Hangman," 1952).

Ramón José Sender Garcés was born February 3, 1901 (some sources say 1902), in Chalamera de Cinca, in Aragon, Spain, to José and Andrea Garcés Sender. His father served as the local town clerk in Chalamera de Cinca and neighboring Alcolea de Cinca, where Sender's family moved in 1902. Sender was the oldest son of ten children. Around 1911 the family moved to Tauste, where Sender, considered an intelligent child, passed his entrance examination to the Institute of Zaragoza in 1912. A deep rift between father and son resulted in Sender's enrollment at boarding school, the Colegio de San Ildefonso in Reus, between 1913 and 1914. The much-recorded incompatibility between father and son has often been cited as a reason for Sender's rebellious, nonconformist nature.

### Begins Literary Career

Sender returned to the family home, now in Zaragoza, where his father managed an insurance business. During this period he started displaying his literary proclivities. He won a short story competition sponsored by the *Heraldo de Aragón* and was awarded first prize for his short novel entitled *Una hoguera en la noche* ("A Bonfire at Night"), which was published in the Barcelona journal *Lecturas.* He also launched *El Cinquito,* a student literary journal.

In 1917 Sender moved on his own to Alcañiz, where he supported himself as a pharmacy clerk. He completed his secondary education through the Institute of Teruel and the Colegio de los Padres Escolapios de Alcañiz, graduating in 1918. He then enrolled at the Law School of the Central University of Madrid. Shortly after his course began, however, Sender was summoned back to the family home, now in Huesca. He became the unofficial editor of *La Tierra,* the provincial newspaper, and remained there for the following three years. In 1921 Sender resumed his studies at the University of Madrid, supporting himself as an assistant pharmacist. In the university, his political activism led to his suspension and brief imprisonment for "subversion" against the monarchy. Charles C. King, writing in *Ramón J. Sender* (1974), contended that Sender never earned a degree, whereas other sources have indicated that Sender graduated with a *Licenciado en filosofía y letras* (degree in philosophy and literature) in 1924.

Sender was conscripted into the army in 1923, in the Regiment of Asturias, to serve in Spain's war with Morocco. He swiftly scaled the military ranks, eventually reaching the rank of *alférez* ("second lieutenant"). He was cited for bravery and conferred the Medal of Morocco, prior to his discharge in 1924. He would utilize his military experience in his successful novel *Imán,* published in English as *Earmarked for Hell* and *Pro Patria,* which he first published in 1930. In semi-journalistic style, Sender conveyed the futility of the military campaign.

In 1924 Sender joined the staff of *El Sol,* Madrid's prestigious liberal newspaper, as an editor and literary critic. He established a reputation as a radical journalist. In 1927 he was incarcerated without a trial in Madrid's Cárcel Modelo following publication of his articles on a rebellion at the artillery academy in Segovia. He was released three months later following pleas from the Press Association of Madrid.

Encouraged by his friends, Sender published his first book in 1928, a collection of articles on the Church and State in Mexico entitled *El problema religioso en Méjico* ("The Religious Problem in Mexico"). Following its publication Sender was appointed secretary of the Ibero-American section of the Ateneo, Madrid's renowned literary association. The enormous success of *Iman's* American edition, *Pro Patria,* prompted Sender to leave *El Sol* in 1930 and concentrate on his writing.

He entered a productive period as a freelance writer contributing articles to *La Libertad,* a newspaper, and *Solidarid Obrera,* the official voice of the National Labor Federation, of which Sender was a member. Sender visited Russia for five months in 1933 as a guest of the Unión Internacional de Escritores, and became increasingly sympathetic to the Communist cause.

Sender married Amparo Barayón, a concert pianist, on January 7, 1934. They had two children: Ramón and Andrea. By the onset of the civil war Sender had completed seven novels, five compilations of journalistic articles and one travel book. *Mister Witt en el cantón* ("Mister Witt Among the Rebels," 1936) won the Spanish National Prize for Literature in 1935.

The Spanish Civil War began on July 18, 1936. Sender's loyalty lay with the Republicans in opposition to **Generalissimo Francisco Franco** and the Nationalists. During the war he was a member of the Alliance of Intellectuals for the Defense of Democracy. He joined the Republican militia as a private, rising to serve briefly as Chief of Staff to General Lister. Sender received the Military Cross of Merit.

Sender's wife was executed without trial by rebel forces for her Republican connections on October 11, 1936. One of Sender's brothers, Manolo, and Amparo's two brothers, Saturnino and Antonio, were also executed by the Nationalists. The International Red Cross helped Sender move his children to southern France for the remainder of the war. He married Elizabeth de Altube in December 1936 in Barcelona. They had a son, Emmanuel, but Sender abandoned them in 1938.

### Exile Begins

In April 1938 Sender was commissioned by the Spanish government along with José Bergamín, a writer, Ojier Preteceille, press secretary of the Spanish General Union of Workers, and Carmen Meana, a Madrid social worker, to tour Europe and the United States to procure international support for the flagging Republicans. Shortly after his return from the United States, Sender was asked to establish *La Voz de Madrid,* a war propaganda magazine, in Paris. He soon returned to Madrid. However, with the onset of the Republican defeat, Sender slipped into exile across the French border in December, 1938.

Sender rejoined his children in France and traveled on to Paris, where he directed José Zorrilla y Moral 's play *Don Juan Tenorio* in aid of a Spanish refugee organization. In March 1939 he departed for New York. Sender proceeded to Mexico, leaving his children in the care of Jay Allen, an American war correspondent. When the Spanish Republic fell, Sender's Spanish passport was invalidated and he applied for Mexican citizenship. His children were placed with Julia Davis, who became their adoptive mother; they remained with her even after Sender returned to live in the United States. Sender's time in Mexico City was productive: he founded and managed Ediciones Quetzal, a publishing firm, published several of his own books, and lectured at the National University of Mexico.

In 1942 Sender was awarded a Guggenheim Fellowship and decided to emigrate to the United States. He moved to Santa Fe, New Mexico, where he collaborated on the Inter-American Spanish Research Project at New Highlands University in Las Vegas. The following year he was named a corresponding member of the Hispanic Society in America. In the academic year of 1943 to 1944 he lectured at several universities. Sender married Florence Hall on August 12, 1943. During the succeeding academic year he served as Professor of Spanish Literature at Amherst College in Massachusetts.

Sender moved to New York City and worked for Metro-Goldwyn-Mayer as a translator and adaptor. In 1946 he became a naturalized citizen of the United States. In 1947 Sender became Professor of Spanish Literature at the University of New Mexico, in Albuquerque, a post he held until 1963.

He returned to France in 1963 to join his relatives. Later that year he divorced Florence Hall and moved to California. He resided in Manhattan Beach and devoted his time to writing but found that he missed the academic environment. In 1965 he returned to the academic arena as a visiting professor of Spanish Literature at the University of Southern California, where he remained until 1971. In 1968 the University of New Mexico awarded Sender a D. Litt. He accepted further appointments as a visiting professor at the University of Washington in 1967 and at Michigan State University in 1968.

As the Spanish government began relaxing its attitude toward former Republicans, Sender's books gradually appeared on the shelves of Spanish bookstores. In 1966 he was conferred the Premio de la Literatura in Spain for his novel *Crónica del alba* (1942; published in English as *Chronicles of Dawn* in 1944), which tells the story of a dying refugee's nostalgic reminiscences of Spain. During the late 1960s Sender's work was highly popular in Spain. For example, *Mister Witt en el cantón,* first published in 1936, was a Spanish bestseller in 1969. In 1969 Sender was awarded the Premio Planeta, Spain's most lucrative literary prize, for his novel *En la vida de Ignacio Morel* ("*In the Life of Ignacio Morel,*" 1968).

Sender decided to return to Spain in 1968; initially granted a visa, it was revoked when Spanish officials learned that a group of workers planned to greet him on his arrival. He eventually returned to Spain in 1974, shortly before Franco's death in 1975. In 1971 Sender moved to San Diego, California where he devoted himself to his literary calling. Six days before his death he told his accountant, "I'm through with this business of writing books! Now I'm going to have a good time!" (cited in *A Death in Zamora* by Ramón Sender Barayón, 1989). He died of a heart attack in San Diego on January 15, 1982.

## SELECTED PUBLISHED WORKS:

(With Alicia Bay Laurel) *Being of the Sun* (nonfiction), Harper, 1973.
*The Morning Star Scrapbook,* Friends of Morning Star, 1976.
*Zero Weather* (novel), Family Publishing, 1980.
*A Death in Zamora* (nonfiction), University of New Mexico Press, 1989.

## SOURCES:

### Books

*Hispanic Writers: A Selection of Sketches from Contemporary Authors,* edited by Bryan Ryan, Detroit, Gale, 1991.
King, Charles C., *Ramón J. Sender,* Twayne's World Author Series, 1974.
Sender Barayón, Ramón, *A Death in Zamora,* Albuquerque, University of New Mexico Press, 1989.

### Periodicals

*The Times,* January 19, 1982.

—*Sketch by Amanda Beresford*

# Junipero Serra
## 1713-1784
### Spanish missionary

Born on the island of Majorca in the Mediterranean, Father Junipero Serra came to the New World and established Catholic missions which proved important in the settlement and development of the American West. Serra founded a total of nine missions in California from San Diego to San Francisco. The Catholic Church considers him one of their greatest missionaries, and since 1934 Serra has been eligible for canonization.

Born on November 24, 1713, Serra spent the first 35 years of his life on the Mediterranean island of Majorca. His father and mother, Antonio and Margarita Serre (the Majorquin spelling of Serra) worked as farmers in the small town of Petra and had five children, though only two of them, Junipero and an older sister, Juana, lived to adulthood. They baptized their son Miguel José Serra. Scholars know very little about Serra's boyhood. His earliest biographer and close friend, Francisco Palou, wrote his *Life of Serra* from his own recollections, leaving the reader to infer much of the story of his childhood.

In *Mission to Paradise,* Kenneth King says that despite the lack of information about Serra's youth, "in outlines it seems pretty clear." King asserts that as a "frail boy," Serra found himself excluded from the most strenuous play, causing him to study instead. His parents' piety channeled his studious nature toward religion. From his babyhood, They took him to the Franciscan church of San Bernadino near their home. Palou claims that Serra got his first years of education from the friars of that institution. Several years later Serra moved to the capital of the island, Palma, where he studied philosophy at the convent of St. Francis. After some effort, including an initial rejection because of his unhealthy appearance, Serra entered the Franciscan Order in 1730.

*Junipero Serra*

His entrance into the order taught him the discipline and devotion to his faith that one day would characterize his work. He spent about seven hours a day praying, the rest of his time occupied with the menial tasks of maintaining the monastery. In his time as an intitiate he also resolved to go to the New World and work as a missionary. In 1731 he gained the status of a Brother in the Franciscan Order, taking the name Junipero.

For the next 18 years Serra studied and preached on Majorca, developing quite a reputation as an orator and a scholar. Palou says that Serra was "as highly appreciated in university circles as by his colleagues." During recesses in the academic year, Serra spoke from the pulpit, becoming, as Omer Engelbert says in his book *The Last of the Conquistadors*, "the great orator of the island." Yet he became dissatisfied. Palou even wrote that Serra wept because "he had let himself be distracted by his academic studies" from his true goal of working as a missionary in America.

In 1748, Father Rafael Verger of Serra's university decided to travel with Father Mezquia, who had come to Spain recruiting for the missions in Mexico. He decided to take two younger friars with him, and when Palou and Serra told him how eager they were to go, Verger readily accepted them as his assistants. Three days after Easter in 1749, Serra and his friend began their journey. Vowing to "go there and never return," Serra spent 99 rough days at sea before arriving at Veracruz on the eastern coast of Mexico, where he began his career as a missionary.

## Travels Through New Spain

Serra set out from Veracruz on foot with few supplies, suffering hunger, insect bites, extreme heat, freezing cold, and the thin air of high altitudes. He arrived in Mexico City some time later. Though given up for dead, Serra made it to the college of San Fernando where the rector of the college, upon seeing the hardships Serra had overcome, greeted him with the words, "I would I had a forest of such junipers!"

Serra did not care for the opulence of Mexico City, and after five months he left for the Sierra Gorda, a place famous for its "most unhealthy" climate and the "least friendly" natives in the region. Serra welcomed this as an opportunity, eager even to be martyred. He did not die for his faith in Sierra Gorda, however. In fact, he succeeded in learning some of the local language, teaching the natives Spanish agriculture and weaving, and successfully converting many of them to Catholicism. He soon became the president of all the Sierra Gorda missions, which he found less enjoyable than the day-to-day work at the mission.

In 1758, Serra received an order to go to Texas to try to establish permanent missions there. Until then, no successful missions had taken hold, and as Serra prepared to go, the Tonkawa tribe attacked and destroyed the San Saba mission—near present-day Menard, Texas. The extremely dangerous conditions appealed to Serra, but the Church rescinded its order, and Serra's destiny changed.

## Is Sent to California

King Charles III came to power and vowed to remove the Jesuit order from his kingdom. The Jesuits organized themselves in a way that, according to King, "made it an international competitor of Bourbon despotism." In 1767 Serra left with 16 other Franciscan monks for California. The guardian of the San Fernando community had named Serra the president of all the lower-California missions, and he began his work in that capacity on April 1, 1768 in Loreto.

Discouraged by the *de facto* military rule of the lower-California missions, Serra longed to move on to upper-California, where he would be able to build his own missions. In 1769, Serra left with Galvez on a land-sea expedition which aimed to establish missions at San Diego, San Carlos (at Monterey) and San Buenaventura (in the Santa Barbara Channel).

In his first months in San Diego, Serra became frustrated with open and sometimes deadly conflict with the natives. Once tensions eased, Serra still had difficulty imparting his religion to the local inhabitants, but he persisted. Suffering then through chronic shortages, Serra's San Diego mission survived, prompting him to travel to Monterey in 1770 to establish the Mission San Carlos.

In the next two years, Serra's zeal for establishing a missionary presence did not wane. He established the San Antonio, San Carlos, and San Gabriel missions, although the mission at Monterey suffered under the tyrannical rule of the new commandant, Pedro Fages. Serra wrote to Palou in 1771, "In all fields, he strove to make trouble for us."

Fages obstructed the work of Serra's mission, but he could not prevent Serra from building new missions. 1772 saw the San Luis Obispo Mission built. It became one of the most prosperous outposts in California, but San Buenaventura, one of the original three Serra had envisioned, remained unbuilt. When Fages rejected his requests for additional supplies for the San Buenaventura Mission, Serra traveled to Mexico to make an appeal above the head of the young commandant. That year and in 1773, Serra convinced colonial authorities that the missions needed additional funding and supplies. Worried and nearly convinced that the colonization of California had failed, the Viceroy in Mexico listened to Serra. He accepted Serra's premise that stronger missions would make the colony stronger, and some credit Serra, therefore, with saving the New California.

Serra continued to work building missions, including San Buenaventura in 1782. Yet this last mission appeared at a time which saw Serra's health failing badly. His constitution had never been suited to great strain, and as he fought the Dominican Order for control of the missions he himself had founded, he could no longer remain active. He became more ill, and confined to his bed by 1784, he called his friend Palou to be with him for his last days. He also asked the mission carpenter to make him a simple coffin of redwood.

When he died that same year, Father Serra became a semi-legendary figure. King claims that "the clamour for relics [of Serra] was astonishing." Clergy and the laity scrambled to have some part of his possessions, and they gave him the most elaborate funeral possible in still-remote Monterey. Other legends have emerged about Serra since that day, including one in which he stumbled onto a small house, hungry and wet during his travels. There he received food and shelter from a young couple and an infant child. When he returned to tell the story, maps proved that no dwelling could possibly have stood where Serra said he found it. God, the legend's believers said, had provided for his servant.

## SOURCES:

DeNevi, Don and Moholy, Noel, *Junipero Sierra*, San Francisco, Harper and Row, 1985.

Engelbert, Omer, *The Last of the Conquistadors, Junipero Serra*, New York, Harcourt, Brazil, 1956.

King, Kenneth, *Mission to Paradise*, London, Burns and Oates, 1956.

*—Sketch by James McCarthy*

# Lupe Serrano
## 1930-
### Hispanic American ballerina

Affiliated for nearly two decades with the American Ballet Theatre (ABT), prima ballerina Lupe Serrano has enjoyed a long and rewarding career in the field of dance, first as a performer and most recently as a teacher. Indeed, dancing has been the focus of her life for almost as long as she can remember.

Serrano's father, Luis Martinez Serrano, was a musician and songwriter from Barcelona, Spain, who was raised in Buenos Aires. On a tour that took him to Mexico City, he met Luciana Desfassiaux, a Mexican native whose parents had come from France. The success of his tour detained Serrano in Mexico long enough for him to marry Luciana and start a family. But in 1930, Luis, eager to take his expectant wife home to meet his parents, agreed to conduct an orchestra that was traveling through South America. The group was in Santiago, Chile, when Lupe arrived on December 7. During Luciana's recovery from the birth, Luis fell ill. The tour moved on, but the Serranos remained in Chile for the next 13 years.

Even as a small child, Lupe was oblivious to anything other than dancing. Family legend has it that she danced constantly, and according to her parents, on her third birthday she made all her guests sit down while she performed for them. Luis and Luciana eventually decided their daughter should have formal lessons, and despite the rather limited educational choices they faced in Chile, they managed to find a suburban school that offered some training in modern dance, oriental, soft shoe, pointe work, and castanets.

### Received Formal Ballet Training in Mexico City

The Serranos returned to Mexico City when Lupe was 13, and it was then that her formal ballet training began. "I had terrible habits by then!" Serrano remembered in an interview with Peg McNichol. "But I had been in so many recitals that I had a

*Lupe Serrano*

sense of how to fill the stage." She studied seriously with a ballet company in Mexico City and soon earned a position in the Corps de Ballet—"the very last row of the corps," as she recalled. Her efforts paid off, however, and at the age of 14, she debuted in the company's production of Les Sylphides.

Serrano worked especially hard in high school, condensing the work of her last two years into one so she would be free to tour. Her devotion to ballet left no time for a college education, but she studied extensively on her own to prepare for the dances themselves and to learn about the places to which she traveled. At the Palacio de Bellas Artes, for example, Serrano broadened her knowledge of English and French and took courses in such subjects as drama, history, music, and folklore.

Around the time she was 18, Serrano went on a tour with Cuban prima ballerina **Alicia Alonso** that took her through Central America and Colombia. When she returned to Mexico City, she found that her teacher had formed a ballet company. The experience provided Serrano with a harsh lesson in the economic realities of being a dancer. "Ballet is not a self-supporting art anywhere in the world," she observed in her interview. "It has to be sponsored. A person like my ballet teacher, who was devoted to the art of ballet, of course would not have the ability to raise funds." The company folded after only 18 months, unable to bear the weight of expenses for toe shoes, costumes, and other needs.

## Moved to New York City

Serrano then joined the government-sponsored Ballet Folklorika of Mexico, but she soon felt the pull of New York City and the promise it held out to young dancers. Having saved a little money, she arrived there at the age of 20 and obtained a position with the Ballet Russe de Monte Carlo, where she was featured in her first solo performances and had the opportunity to travel throughout North and South America.

But that company went bankrupt, too, and Serrano returned to Mexico City and a starring role on a television program about the classical arts. It was 1952 and television was still fairly new, so Serrano had to make adjustments for the cameras. "We had to rearrange the way we covered space on the floor, because the cameras were not very mobile," she recalled in her interview. "And you had to be much more subtle in expression, because the camera brings you much closer to the audience. On the stage, you have to think of projecting yourself a block away. Television is much more intimate."

One day Serrano's phone rang with a long distance call from New York. On the other end of the line was the former road manager of the Ballet Russe de Monte Carlo. He was now with the ABT in New York, and he wanted to know if Serrano was interested in auditioning for the troupe.

## Auditioned for the American Ballet Theatre

Serrano wasted little time returning to the United States. She took classes and auditioned several times. When she was accepted in 1953, she joined as principal dancer, a position of great honor. "I remember having such respect for the company itself," she said to McNichol. The first time she led her fellow dancers in a big finale, Serrano thought to herself, "'Well, look at you now, leading this group of wonderful dancers.' I felt a great sense of pride." During the nearly two decades Serrano performed with the ABT, she appeared in more than 50 different roles ranging from classics such as *Swan Lake* and *Giselle* to a variety of contemporary works.

One of Serrano's most memorable experiences as a member of the ABT came in 1961, when the troupe visited the Soviet Union as part of a cultural exchange aimed at thawing the Cold War. They had to deal with many cultural and linguistic barriers (many eventually settled on French or German as a common language), but when they danced, everyone understood. During their 11-week tour, the ABT performed portions of Balanchine's *Theme and Variations* and excerpts from other American ballets such as *Rodeo, Fancy Free,* and *Combat* as well as classical pas de deux such as *La Fille Mal Gardee.* Serrano enchanted the audience in Leningrad so completely that they insisted she repeat her solo performance rather than just take a bow for it.

The tour also included dates in parts of Europe. Serrano remembers being in Athens and standing in the Acropolis under the full moon during a party hosted by the American Embassy. At one point, staff members invited the dancers to stroll around the ruins. For Serrano, it was a magical evening, "to be stepping on those stones that had been laid down so many years ago."

In 1963, Serrano and her husband since 1957, ABT conductor Kenneth Schermerhorn, welcomed their first child, Erica. The ballerina noted to McNichol that returning to dancing after having a baby was "not that difficult," but she did notice that she had "a completely different feeling, as though dancing was a wonderful self-indulgence. I had a much more relaxed approach to it then." By this time, Schermerhorn was affiliated with the New Jersey Symphony. The family lived in New Jersey, and a busy Serrano commuted to New York for classes and rehearsals.

In 1967, the ballerina experienced perhaps the most active year of her entire career. She danced excerpts from *Raiymonda* at a White House performance for President Lyndon Johnson, toured the Soviet Union for a second time and was met with a reception as enthusiastic as the first, and gave birth to her second daughter, Veronica.

Serrano then took a year off, returning to the ABT as a permanent guest artist and choosing her own performances. After Kenneth Schermerhorn accepted a position with the Milwaukee Orchestra, the family moved to Wisconsin. Serrano continued to make guest appearances with the ABT and also started teaching at the University of Milwaukee and the Conservatory of Milwaukee. She found teaching to be a superb way to communicate her love for ballet. She enjoyed watching young dancers blossom and professional dancers refine their skills under her tutelage.

### Retired from the Stage

In 1970, Serrano turned 40. The press began referring to her as a "veteran ballerina" and making references to her age before commenting on her performances with the ABT. Despite her desire and ability to perform, the remarks unsettled her, so in 1971 she decided to retire from the stage. At the same time, her marriage ended in divorce. Her family urged her to return to Mexico City, but she felt the United States was her home, especially since she had her two young daughters.

Serrano soon accepted her first full-time teaching position as assistant director at the National Academy of Arts in Illinois. Like many ballet companies, the school struggled with overwhelming financial demands before it was finally forced to close. In 1974, the Pennsylvania Ballet School named Serrano company teacher and director of the apprentice program. A year later she became school director, a position she held until 1983. Among her students during this period were her daughters; only Veronica, however, opted to continue her lessons and pursue a career in dance, eventually becoming a soloist with the ABT as her mother had before her.

In addition to her duties with the Pennsylvania Ballet School, Serrano taught master classes for professional dancers. She also judged dance events and was invited to guest teach at the San Francisco Ballet, Minnesota Dance Theatre, Cleveland Ballet, Washington Ballet, Cincinnati Ballet, Rome Opera Ballet and the American Ballet Theatre.

In 1988, Serrano left Philadelphia to become the artistic associate for the Washington (D.C.) Ballet. She continues to dance, but only within the confines of the classroom, where she concentrates on instructing advanced students aged 13 to 18 and professionals. "I have never lost my love for that," she declared in her interview. "It still gives me great pleasure."

Sometimes Serrano thinks she should try choreography, or perhaps develop a video or write a book about ballet technique. But most of her time is devoted to teaching. She says she has reached a point in her life where she no longer feels driven to be the best at everything she does. For now, insists Serrano, it is enough to do her best with three classes a day and individual coaching sessions.

### SOURCES:

Serrano, Lupe, interview with Peg McNichol, September 1992.

—*Sketch by Peg McNichol*

# Charlie Sheen
## 1965-
### Spanish American actor

Born Carlos Irwin Estevez in 1965, Charlie Sheen made his screen debut at age 14 in Martin Scorsese's *Apocalypse Now*. Although only an extra, Sheen knew that his day as an actor with spoken lines could not be far off. As the son of actor Martin Sheen, Charlie Sheen moved easily into celebrity status as a

*Charlie Sheen*

major movie star in the 1980s. Although his critical and commercial fortunes have fallen and risen, he has remained one of the most widely known actors of his generation.

## Family Influenced His Career Choice

Born on September 3, 1965, in New York City, Sheen grew up in a family filled with on-screen performers. His father, born Ramon Estevez, came to New York City from his birthplace of Ohio. Though he worked onstage with many actors who would eventually become movie greats, in the mid-1960s Ramon Estevez found his professional career hampered by his unmistakably Hispanic name. To avoid the typecasting that plagued Hispanic actors, Estevez created the name Martin Sheen. Charlie Sheen likewise took the new name, though perhaps more for the association with his father's fame than to avoid a negative stereotype. His brother Emilio, also an actor, retained the surname Estevez.

Martin Sheen's rise to celebrity made a move to Hollywood inevitable. From 1967, when the elder Sheen made his first movie, *The Incident,* Charlie Sheen came to be around the famous and the children of the famous on an everyday basis. He went to school with actors Rob Lowe and Sean Penn, and through his father's influence he got constant exposure to the business of movie making. At age nine, Sheen appeared in a TV movie called *The Execution of Private Slovik.* His father got critical acclaim for his role, but Sheen got a whole new career.

The following year, he traveled with his father and mother, Janet, his two older brothers, Emilio and Ramon, and his younger sister, Renee, to the Philippines to make *Apocalypse Now.* The experience had a strong impression on Sheen. His father suffered a near-fatal heart attack during filming, and shooting of the movie went on for nearly 300 days, during which the cast and crew endured typhoons, political turmoil, and money problems. All of these setbacks could not deter Sheen from pursuing a movie career, however, and although he only appeared as an extra in Scorcese's movie, he knew that he did not want to do anything else.

Discussing his father's influence in an interview with David Healy for the *Chicago Tribune,* Sheen called Martin Sheen "definitely the best guy I know, not just as a father but as an individual." In the days before Sheen had his own professional career, he tried to learn everything he could from his father's experiences and whatever project he happened to be working on. "I talked to him about what he was actually doing and how he got to certain points in a performance ... really picking his brain," Sheen told David Wallace in a *Los Angeles Times* interview. When asked by Healy what was the best advice his father had given him about acting, Sheen replied: "He said, 'Just don't tell any lies. Make the camera your best friend, but ignore it at the same time.' And he said that we are the commodity in this business and this town loves talent. He said, 'Always remember that, because they're going to try to suck you dry.'"

Although he participated in school drama clubs and made home movies with Penn and Lowe, Sheen had no significant experience when his performance in high school began to drop steadily. A few weeks before graduation, Santa Monica High School expelled Sheen because he had stopped attending virtually all of his classes and did not qualify for his diploma. A total amateur, Sheen was risking his future on a career for which he had very few credentials. Sheen's parents, though they supported his ambitions in movies, did not approve of his abandoning his education. Sheen placated his parents in the only way he could, as he explained to Wallace: "I made a deal with my parents that if I didn't get an acting job, I'd return and get my high school degree and go on to college."

Sheen said that his father began to give him Hollywood survival tips before Sheen had even established himself as an actor. Sheen described his reaction to this early advice in the interview with Healy: "I said, 'Dad, how do you know I'm going to work after this?' And he said: 'I just know. I see it in your eyes.'" Sheen later credited his father's certainty that he would succeed for his confidence in himself.

His first audition brought him his first work. The project, called *Grizzly II: The Predator,* never reached theaters, but Sheen made the most of this initial step into the business. As Sheen explained to Wallace, "It never came out, but it was a chance to get a Screen Actor's Guild card and experience." Perhaps more importantly, it gained him respect for his decision to leave school and focus on acting.

### Gained Respect with Early Films

Self-doubts continued to plague Sheen, though the movie roles came one after another. In 1984, he starred in *Red Dawn,* a hit movie about a group of teenagers fighting a guerilla war against the Soviet military, which had taken over the United States. Healy contrasted the confident, talkative movie star Charlie Sheen with his earlier persona as the "quiet kid who muttered through the group interviews for *Red Dawn.*" Sheen admitted that early in his career, "I didn't think people cared about what I had to say. I didn't think they were listening. It was just an insecurity thing."

After making a TV movie about teen suicide called *Silence of the Heart,* Sheen landed a short but memorable role in the big 1986 hit *Ferris Bueller's Day Off.* His portrayal of an offbeat, handsome rebel with wise words for a troubled girl got "all kinds of attention," as Sheen told Wallace. Director Oliver Stone also saw something special in the brief appearance, and he decided to cast Sheen in the role that would change his career and his life.

When *Platoon* won the Academy Award for best picture in 1987, Charlie Sheen, as its star, met with overwhelming critical and commercial approval. Sheen reacted with surprise and a certain amount of gratitude when discussing the movie that made him a major movie star. Sheen expressed his continuing amazement to Wallace that Stone cast him, a near-novice, in the lead: "For him to take that chance on me when nobody knew my work!" Sheen also experienced the fear that such success would be fleeting, though he believed very much in the quality of *Platoon.* Yet he confessed to Healy that "you still second-guess yourself, though. You think, 'maybe I was lucky on that one'. . . . I think I'm more confident because now I can trust that the compliments I get on *Platoon* are genuine."

Stone liked Sheen's work so much in his first movie that he decided to give him a second starring role, though Sheen admitted that for a time Stone could not decide whether or not make a sequel to his incredibly successful Vietnam War epic. Sheen was still working on *Platoon* in the Philippines when Stone offered him the lead in his next project. Sheen described the moment in the interview with Wallace of the *Los Angeles Times:* "He said it's either going to be 'Second Life,' a film which would bring the Chris

Taylor character [Sheen's in *Platoon*] back home, or he was going to do an epic fictional tale based on Wall Street. He pulled out a napkin and drew up a rough contract and I signed it right in the middle of the Luzon jungle!"

The success of *Wall Street* and Sheen's own outstanding performance made him the most acclaimed actor of his generation. At age 22, Sheen had a remarkable record of appearing in good roles as a part of quality films. *Wall Street* also gave him the opportunity to work with his father, and as the co-star with Michael Douglas, Sheen had actually moved above his father on the credits list.

Since *Wall Street,* however, Sheen has appeared in a mixed bag of failures and successes, and his critical fortunes have never reached the heights they attained after his two films with Stone. Some of his most memorable movies since then include: *Major League* and *Major League II,* baseball comedies in which Sheen plays a nearly blind pitcher who goes from prison to celebrity; *Men at Work,* another comedy, directed by, written by, and co-starring Sheen's brother Emilio Estevez; and *Hot Shots* and *Hot Shots Part Deux,* slapstick parodies of the hit movie *Top Gun.*

Sheen has also battled addictions to drugs and alcohol. Looking back over some of his film performances from this difficult period, Sheen told Wallace: "I was committing unconscious suicide . . . I think I was looking for a cushion, a buffer between the public and who I thought I was." It took an emotional confrontation arranged by his family and friends on the occasion of his father's fiftieth birthday to convince him to get help. But after undergoing a 32-day rehabilitation program in 1990, he told Wallace he has managed to avoid the "lifestyle I thought was part of being a celebrity." Sheen has a daughter named Cassandra, born in 1984 to his childhood sweetheart, and though he has been engaged, he has not married. He now lives at a house he built in the Malibu Hills of southern California.

## SELECTED DISCOGRAPHY

*Red Dawn,* 1984.
*Silence of the Heart,* 1984.
*The Boys Next Door,* 1985.
*Amazing Stories, Book 3,* 1986.
*Ferris Buller's Day Off,* 1986.
*Lucas,* 1986.
*Platoon,* 1986.
*No Man's Land,* 1987.
*Three for the Road,* 1987.
*Wall Street,* 1987.
*The Wraith,* 1987.
*Eight Men Out,* 1988.
*Never on Tuesday,* 1988.
*Young Guns,* 1988.

*Backtrack,* 1989.
*Cadence,* 1989.
*Courage Mountain,* 1989.
*Major League,* 1989.
*Tale of Two Sisters,* 1989.
*Men at Work,* 1990.
*Navy SEALS,* 1990.
*The Rookie,* 1990.
*Hot Shots!,* 1991.
*Hot Shots! Part Deux,* 1993.
*National Lampoon's Loaded Weapon,* 1993.

## SOURCES:

### Books

*The Hispanic-American Almanac,* edited by Nicolas Kanellos, Detroit, Gale Research, 1993.
*Who's Who in Hollywood,* edited by David Ragan, New York, Facts on File, 1992.

### Periodicals

*Chicago Trune,* November 11, 1987, Section 13, p. 24.
*Los Angeles Times,* July 31, 1991, p. F1.

—*Sketch by James McCarthy*

*Martin Sheen*

# Martin Sheen
## 1940-
### Spanish American actor

During a career that has spanned more than three decades, Martin Sheen has forged a reputation as a multi-talented actor. He has interpreted numerous roles on the stage, television, and silver screen. Though Sheen has long been known as one of the busiest actors in Hollywood, he commits himself seriously to peace and social justice issues as well. Sheen was born Ramón Estevez on August 3, 1940, in Dayton, Ohio. In the family of ten children born to Francesco, a drill-press operator, and Mary Ann Estevez, Ramón was the seventh of nine sons. When Mary Ann died in 1951, Francesco struggled to keep his family together, getting support from the local Catholic community. Like his siblings, Ramón attended Catholic school. He earned money to pay his tuition by caddying at the Dayton Country Club. Carrying heavy bags of golf clubs was a challenge for Estevez, whose left arm had been injured during his birth. Yet for nine years he persevered, learning a great deal about human nature and how to play golf in the process. Young Ramón's hero was Ed Furgol, a golfer who, despite his crippled left arm, won the U.S. Open golf tournament in 1954.

During his years at the Catholic Chaminade High School, Estevez discovered his vocation. By his junior year, he had appeared in more than a dozen theatrical productions. At age 17, Estevez won a talent show sponsored by a local television station. The prize was a trip to New York City and an audition with a casting director at CBS. The casting director encouraged Estevez to return to New York City after he graduated from high school.

### Strikes Out on Own

Francesco Estevez wanted his children to attend college and was dismayed by Ramón's career choice. But rather than hurt his father's feelings by refusing to continue his studies, Ramón intentionally failed the college entrance exam for Dayton University. A priest at Chaminade High School then loaned Estevez the money to go to New York City and convinced the young man's father that it was a good move. In New York, Estevez quickly found a night job as a clerk, so that he could go to casting calls during the day. Soon he decided that he should adopt a stage name because he believed that his Hispanic name was limiting his audition opportunities, though Estevez did not look especially Hispanic since his mother was Irish. At this time, few Hispanic roles were being written. Ramón Estevez renamed himself Martin Sheen, after Fulton J. Sheen, a Catholic bishop whom Estevez admired.

Martin Sheen's first years as an actor were both an apprenticeship and a challenge. Sheen could not afford acting lessons, so he helped organize the Actor's Co-op, a group that performed scenes from plays. Later he was hired as the general backstage handyman for The Living Theatre, an off-Broadway troupe. Soon he was developing his acting skills with the troupe. Because actors must perform at night, Sheen could no longer work nights as a clerk and lived precariously. During this period, Sheen met Janet Templeton, an art student at the New School for Social Research, only a few blocks from The Living Theatre. After living together for some time, the couple was married on December 23, 1961, shortly after the troupe returned from representing the United States at the Theater of Nations Festival in Paris.

Sheen gradually expanded his acting repertoire to include Broadway shows and television roles. In 1961, he made his television acting debut in an episode of the legal drama series *The Defenders*. Two years later, he made a guest appearance on the critically acclaimed *East Side, West Side*. He made his Broadway theatrical debut in 1964 with the short-lived play *Never Live Over a Pretzel Factory* and later co-starred in the Broadway drama *The Subject Was Roses*, in which he portrayed a young soldier home from war. After Sheen was nominated for—but did not win—a Tony Award for his interpretation of the role, he concluded that such awards were irrelevant. Since then, whenever he has been nominated for an award, he has asked that he be removed from consideration. During the play's long run on Broadway, Sheen arranged a very successful benefit performance for the civil rights movement.

As Sheen's reputation grew, he became a very busy actor. To provide for his family, which by 1967 included sons Emilio, Ramón, Carlos, and daughter Renee, Sheen accepted as many television guest spots as he could get, often in the role of an alienated loner. He appeared on such shows as *The Mod Squad, My Three Sons,* and *Medical Center,* and had a year-long stint on the daytime serial *As the World Turns*. In 1967 Sheen won his first role in a motion picture, *The Incident,* in which he played a New York City hoodlum. The following year he starred in the film version of *The Subject Was Roses*. Though the film garnered mixed reviews, it led to a role in the anti-war motion picture *Catch–22*. Because the film was shot on location in Mexico, California, and Italy, Sheen moved his family to Los Angeles, eventually settling in Malibu.

If the 1960s were busy years, the next decade was hectic. In 1969 and the early 1970s, Sheen appeared in several made-for-television movies, including *Catholics, Then Came Bronson, Goodby, Raggedy Ann, Mongo's Back in Town, Welcome Home, Johnny Bristol,* and *Pursuit*. His roles of the doomed private in the television movie *The Execution of Private Slovik* and President Kennedy's brother Robert in *The Missiles of October* were praised by critics. Sheen also had parts in the motion pictures *No Drums, No Bugles, Rage,* and *Badlands,* in which he portrayed a teenage boy who—with his lover (played by Sissy Spacek)—terrorized Nebraska in 1958 with their crime spree. Sheen believes that it is one of his best performances.

In the mid-1970s, Sheen's workaholic lifestyle began to take its toll. Admitting to Jim Hargrove, author of *Martin Sheen: Actor and Activist,* that at this time he was abusing alcohol and smoking heavily, Sheen recounted: "I was really fragmented. That was a term I used a lot. I was smoking and trying to work out. I was a contradiction. I was interested in spirituality, and I was interested in the flesh. I was drinking heavily. I was angry about a lot of things. I was disappointed in myself and my career, my personal life. I was fragmented. I was just not whole, not healthy on any level. I was miserable to live with."

### Becomes Acting Superstar

In the midst of this personal crisis, Sheen was offered one of the most important roles of his career—the lead in Francis Ford Coppola's Vietnam War picture *Apocalypse Now*. Sheen portrayed Captain Willard, a U.S. Special Services soldier whose job was to find and kill a renegade U.S. Army officer. In early 1976, the Sheen family moved to the Philippines, the site of the new film. The Philippine jungle was a difficult place to live and make a movie. Several months after shooting began, a typhoon destroyed the sets, and the cast returned to the United States while new ones were built. Sheen, who was in almost every scene, dreaded returning to finish the project. His children were unhappy and wanted to stay in California. Eating poorly and smoking incessantly, Sheen succumbed to both a nervous breakdown and a heart attack on March 5, 1977. After six weeks of physical and mental treatment, Sheen returned to the set and the film was quickly completed. Though *Apocalypse Now* received mixed reviews when it opened in 1979, it was a big draw at the box office. Sheen was nominated for an Academy Award for best actor but declined to be considered. Nevertheless, he had become an acting superstar.

For three years after the filming of *Apocalypse Now,* Sheen went on a personal spiritual journey. "It was a dark night for my soul," he recalled to Hargrove. "We all go through that, you know, that dark night of the soul, when we have to face ourselves and accept ourselves and learn to love ourselves." During this time, Sheen suffered marital problems, drank heavily, and went on working. He played the role of John Dean, the advisor to President Richard Nixon, in the made-for-televison movie *Blind Ambition*. In 1980 Sir Richard Attenborough asked Sheen to portray a reporter in the motion picture *Gandhi*, the story of an East Indian political leader who used non-violent means to combat injustice. The short time that Sheen spent in India was pivotal. Somehow, seeing the teeming masses of impoverished Indians sparked a religious revival in Sheen, who returned to the Catholic Church after a decade-long absence. Sheen soon put his renewed conviction into action, donating most of the $200,000 he earned from the *Gandhi* film to Mother Teresa.

While Sheen's convictions have narrowed his roles to ones that more closely mirror his religious and political beliefs—he declines roles in movies with gratuitous violence or explicit sex—he is a working actor, accepting roles for the money. "I'm just as much in love with luxury as the next one," Sheen confided to Reese Erlich of the *Christian Science Monitor*. "I love my house, my pool, my credit card, my power." During the 1980s, Sheen appeared in several dozen television films and motion pictures. For television, he played roles in *The Guardian, The Atlanta Child Murders, News at Eleven,* and others. Among his big screen credits are *The Believers, Firestarter, Walking After Midnight,* and *Wall Street*. Wanting to have greater control over the final product, with *Da* and *Judgement in Berlin*, Sheen also took on the responsibilities of executive producer.

Although Sheen never encouraged his children to pursue acting careers, all four of them did. Sheen worked with sons Ramón and Carlos, who goes by the stage name Charlie Sheen, on the motion picture *Cadence* which pits Martin Sheen in the role of U.S. Army stockade commander against Charlie Sheen in the role of an independent-minded private. The made-for-television film *Beverly Hills Brats* boasted the acting talents of Martin and son Ramón, the directing talent of Martin, and the producing talent of Janet Estevez. Both **Emilio Estevez** and **Charlie Sheen** have put their acting careers on the fast track with major motion pictures, much to the astonishment of their proud parents.

During the 1990s, Sheen appeared in the made-for-television movies *The Last P.O.W.?*, the story of a prisoner of war who collaborated with the enemy, and *Roswell*, about a UFO incident in 1947 and its cover-up by the U.S. government. His portrayal of General Robert E. Lee in the Civil War film *Gettysburg* garnered mixed reviews. On Broadway with the National Actors Theater, Sheen interpreted the role of John Proctor in Arthur Miller's classic *The Crucible*.

### Supports Religious and Political Causes

Sheen balances moviemaking and political activism, gaining a deep sense of satisfaction from both activities. Sheen admits that his activism has cost him acting jobs, but he has not suffered from a lack of work. "I don't stop being an actor when I attend a demonstration," Sheen told Erlich. "I don't stop being an activist when I go to work as an actor." Among the causes that Sheen has supported are improved conditions for migrant farm workers and the homeless. He has demonstrated against the development and use of nuclear weapons, getting arrested numerous times in the process. Sheen explained to *The News and Observer* staff writer Grant Parsons, "I'm doing this for myself, to make myself free. I knew that many of the causes were not popular. I do it to learn who I am, not to be an observer of my times, but a participant in them."

## SELECTED VIDEOGRAPHY

*The Incident,* 1967.
*The Subject Was Roses,* 1968.
*Then Came Bronson,* 1969.
*The Andersonville Trial,* 1970.
*Catch–22,* 1970.
*Goodbye, Raggedy Ann,* 1971.
*Mongo's Back in Town,* 1971.
*When the Line Goes Through,* 1971.
*No Drums, No Bugles,* 1972.
*Pickup on 10,* 1972.
*Pursuit,* 1972.
*Rage,* 1972.
*Welcome Home, Johnny Bristol,* 1972.
*That Certain Summer,* 1972.
*Pursuit,* 1972.
*Where the Eagle Flies,* 1972.
*Crime Club,* 1973.
*Letters from Three Lovers,* 1973.
*Catholics,* 1973.
*Message to My Daughter,* 1973.
*Badlands,* 1974.
*The Execution of Private Slovik,* 1974.
*Missles of October,* 1974.
*The Story of Pretty Boy Floyd,* 1974.
*The California Kid,* 1974.
*The Legend of Earl Durand,* 1975.
*The Last Survivors,* 1975.
*Sweet Hostage,* 1975.
*The Cassandra Crossing,* 1977.
*The Little Girl Who Lives Down the Lane,* 1977.
*Apocalypse Now,* 1979.
*The Final Countdown,* 1980.
*Eagle's Wing,* 1980.
*Loophole,* 1980.
*Blind Ambition,* 1982.
*Gandhi,* 1982.
*That Championship Season,* 1982.
*In the Custody of Strangers,* 1982.
*Enigma,* 1983.
*Man, Woman, and Child,* 1983.
*The Dead Zone,* 1983.

*No Place to Hide,* 1983.
*Choices of the heart,* 1983.
*Kennedy,* 1983.
*Firestarter,* 1984.
*The Guardian,* 1984.
*Out of the Darkness,* 1985.
*Consenting Adult,* 1985.
*In the Name of the People,* 1985.
*Broken Rainbow,* 1985.
*Fourth Wise Man,* 1985.
*From Blitzkrieg to the Bomb,* 1985.
*The Real Thing,* 1985.
*Shattered Spirits,* 1985.
*The Atlanta Child Murders,* 1985.
*News at Eleven,* 1986.
*Samaritan: The Mitch Synder Story,* 1986.
*State of Emergency,* 1986.
*Secrets of the Titanic,* 1987.
*Siesta,* 1987.
*Wall Street,* 1987.
*Conspiracy: The Trial of the Chicago 8,* 1987.
*The Believers,* 1987.
*Da,* 1988.
*Judgement in Berlin,* 1988.
*Walking After Midnight,* 1988.
*Beyond the Stars,* 1989.
*Beverly Hills Brats,* 1989.
*Cadence,* 1989.
*Pesonal Choice,* 1989.
*Cold Front,* 1989.
*Nightbreaker,* 1989.
*The Maid,* 1990.
*Original Intent,* 1990.
*Touch and Die,* 1990.
*Hearts of Darkness: A Filmmaker's Apocalypse,* 1991.
*Paper Hearts,* 1991.
*JFK,* 1991.
*Gettysburg,* 1993.
*Hear No Evil,* 1993.

## SOURCES:

### Books

*Contemporary Theatre, Film, and Television,* volume 6, Detroit, Gale, 1989.
*Current Biography Yearbook, 1977,* New York, Wilson, 1977.
Hargrove, Jim, *Martin Sheen: Actor and Activist,* Children's Press, 1991.
*Hispanic-American Almanac,* edited by Nicolás Kanellos, Detroit, Gale, 1993.
Shumacher, David, and Lee Riley, *The Sheens: Martin, Charlie, and Emilio Estevez,* New York, St. Martin's Press, 1989.

### Periodicals

*Atlanta Constitution,* June 7, 1989, p. A11; February 15, 1991, p. D6; October 4, 1993, p. B7.
*Chicago Tribune,* May 27, 1989, section 1, p. 10; December 27, 1990, section 5, p. 13G.
*Christian Science Monitor,* December 28, 1990, p. 14.
*Detroit News,* February 15, 1991, p. D3; October 8, 1993, p. D3.
*Guardian,* April 24, 1989, p. 37; May 22, 1989, p. 8; February 23, 1993, section 2, p. 7; September 22, 1994, section 2, p. 6; October 27, 1994, section 2, p. 8.
*Los Angeles Times,* May 18, 1989, section II, p. 2; May 26, 1989, section II, p. 3; October 10, 1989, section VI, p. 12; November 23, 1989, p. Bl; February 25, 1991, p. F3; March 17, 1991, p. CAL 29; January 28, 1993, p. F10; July 30, 1994, p. F16.
*News and Observer,* February 27, 1994, p. G1.
*New York Times,* May 26, 1989, p A10; March 15, 1991, p. C18; October 3, 1991, p. C23; December 11, 1991, p. C17; December 18, 1994, section 2, p. 45.
*People Weekly,* April 1, 1991, p. 12.
*San Francisco Chronicle,* April 10, 1993, p. A16.
*St. Louis Post-Dispatch,* February 15, 1991, p. F3.
*Times-Picayune,* December 1, 1989, LAG, p. 26; May 17, 1991, LAG, p. 22; October 15, 1993, LAG, p. 28; December 25, 1994, p. TV7.
*USA Today,* February 18, 1991, p. D2; December 12, 1991, p. D8.
*Washington Post,* May 16, 1989, p. C1; February 15, 1991, p. D 7, WW45; October 3, 1991, p. C7; May 15, 1992, p. A22; M1993, p. A2.
*Washington Times,* March 8, 1989, p. El; February 15, 1991, p. E6, F2.

—*Sketch by J.M. Lesinski*

# David Alfaro Siqueiros
## 1896-1974
**Mexican artist**

David Alfaro Siqueiros was a key figure, along with **Diego Rivera** and **José Clemente Orozco,** in the Mexican Renaissance—the "aggressively proletarian" art movement, as *New York Times* critic John Canaday has described it, that provided "visual propaganda" for the Mexican revolution. A painter, Siqueiros spent many years as a union organizer, soldier, and diplomat. He was twice imprisoned for his political activities. Siqueiros put his art at the service of socialist political change, and his work retained a forceful, controversial character throughout his career. He produced many easel paintings and published many essays on art and politics, but he remains best known as a muralist.

Siqueiros sought always to integrate the mural's design and the architectural conditions of the mural site. His murals acknowledge the viewer's movement past them, providing a series of shifting vanishing points which render the experience dynamic, architectonic, and participatory. Siqueiros saw the mural as "an integral work" and "a true collective art." Throughout his career Siqueiros worked towards what he called a "plastic integration" or synthesis of painting, architectural space, and sculpture in a "total aesthetic."

Siqueiros was born to Cipriano Alfaro Palomino, a lawyer, and Teresa Siqueiros Bárcenas on December 29, 1896 in Chihuahua, Mexico. He attended the Colegio Franco Inglés from 1907 to 1911, and studied at the San Carlos Academy of Fine Arts. In 1913 he joined the Constitutionalist Army

In Barcelona Siqueiros published his three-part "Manifesto to the Painters of America" (1921) which set forth a plan for an American art free of European constraints. The first part looked back to the Renaissance and beyond, drawing upon Cubism and Impressionism, but insisting that an American art should encompass the technological present, the modern, and a dynamic future. The second part argued for structure over decoration, insisting that American artists must "create volumes in space" and not just lines and colors. In the third part Siqueiros rejected academicism-even the open-air academies that he had helped found-in favor of a romantic directness.

In 1922 Siqueiros returned to Mexico and founded the National Union of Technical Workers, Painters, and Sculptors. Its "fundamental aesthetic goal," he said, was "to socialize artistic expression," to create an art "for the people . . . an art for all, of education, and of battle." (de Micheli, 1968). Siqueiros's first mural commission, along with Orozco and Rivera, was for the National Preparatory School in Mexico City. When that work was interrupted by conservative forces Siqueiros abandoned art for several years in favor of direct political activism. In 1930 he was imprisoned for organizing Communist demonstrations, and here he took up painting again in earnest, producing a large number of canvases in a two-year period. Exiled in 1932 to the United States, Siqueiros taught fresco techniques at the Chouinard School of Art in Los Angeles, producing a mural, *Meeting in the Street.* An *Art Digest* critic at the time described its "brutality and darkness" and its "brooding sense of tragedy." In New York Siqueiros established a workshop to teach mural techniques and

explore "pictorial accident" in painting. Among his students was Jackson Pollock, whose "action painting" technique was developed from this work with Siqueiros. Siqueiros served in the People's Army during the Spanish civil war, reaching the rank of brigade commander. He returned to Mexico in 1939 and continued his anti-fascist work in Latin America throughout World War II.

## Paints Mexican Epics

Acquitted of a 1940 assassination attempt on Leon Trotsky, Siqueiros left Mexico, securing a mural commission in the Mexican diplomatic mission in Chile. The mural, *Death to the Invader* (1941–42) was the first of many to feature **Cuauhtémoc,** the Aztec hero. In 1944 Siqueiros painted *Cuauhtémoc Against the Myth,* which depicted Cuauhtémoc's denial of the myth of invincibility of Cortez—an image considered allegorical of the exploded myth of Nazi power. Siqueiros returned to this figure with two more depictions of Mexican history and heroism, *The Torment of Cuauhtémoc* and *Cuauhtémoc Reborn* (1950–51). In 1945 he published *There Is No Other Road but Ours,* a collection of previously published controversial writings on art and politics. At this time, partly on the strength of his easel paintings, Siqueiros began to achieve a reputation as a major international artist, winning second prize, after Henri Matisse, in the foreign artists division of the 1950 Venice Biennale. Following this success Siqueiros published *How to Paint a Mural* (1951) and traveled widely in Europe, Asia, and Africa. During a visit to Poland and the USSR in 1955 he was openly critical of officially-sanctioned Soviet art.

## Technology and the Future

In the 1950s, with such works as *Man The Master, Not the Slave, of Technology* (1952), Siqueiros turned his attention to technology and the future. He continued to explore this theme throughout the decade with the exterior relief mural, *The People for the University, The University for the People* (1952–56) at the National Autonomous University in Mexico City, and *Apologia for the Future Victory of Medicine over Cancer* (1958) in Mexico City's Centro Medico. In these works, which feature dynamic futuristic imagery, Siqueiros tried to suggest links between scientific advance and radical political change.

In 1960, while working on the government-commissioned mural *From the Dictatorship of Porfirio Diaz to the Revolution* in Chapultepec Palace, Siqueiros was arrested. He spent two years in jail before being brought to trial, then two more years of an eight-year sentence for "social dissolution" as an anti-government agitator, before being released and pardoned in 1964 in recognition of his prior services to the state. His imprisonment brought further international attention and widespread protest. Over a million signatures came from Japan, and many artists, including **Picasso** and Henry Moore, petitioned for his release. *Time* magazine described the "martyrdom" of "Mexico's . . . No. 1 artist." In 1966, only two years after his release, Siqueiros received the National Art Prize from the Mexican government.

It was in the confined space of prison that Siqueiros conceived and planned his largest and most ambitious work yet, *The March of Humanity On Earth and Toward the Cosmos.* The preliminary painting was done in a vast workshop in Cuernavaca, and its realization required the collaboration of many artists whom Siqueiros had invited from around the world. He described the mural as depicting "immense crowds setting out from a distant past of misery and oppression and moving forward toward industrialization, emancipation, and progress. It is not only a Mexican theme; it is a theme that concerns all of Latin America." (de Micheli) This work combined mural painting with sculptural relief and architecture in a vast expression of some 50,000 square feet-the largest mural ever painted. Here the painting and the building, called the Polyforum Siqueiros, are inseparable, each designed in the context of the other. The installation of *The March of Humanity* as a tourist attraction also expressed the new realities, on the eve of the 1968 Olympic Games, of Mexico's position in the world tourist industry. The patronage of wealthy industrialist Manuel Suárez and Siqueiros's rapprochement with President Echeverria's government resulted in his expulsion from the Communist party in July of 1971.

At the end of his career Siqueiros was a wealthy man and a national institution, but he lived modestly and he remained devoted to socialism. He died of cancer, aged 77, on January 6, 1974. In an obituary essay for the *New York Times* John Canaday noted that while Siqueiros had "outlived his movement," he "must be given an important chapter in any history of Mexican art." Alden Whitman concurred, calling Siqueiros "one of Mexico's treasures."

## SOURCES:

### Books

Folgarait, Leonard, *So Far From Heaven: David Alfaro Siqueiros' "The March of Humanity" and Mexican Revolutionary Politics* Cambridge: Cambridge University Press, 1987.
Micheli, Mario de, *Siqueiros,* New York: Abrams, 1968.
Rochfort, Desmond, *Mexican Muralists,* New York: Universe, 1993.

*70 Obras Recientes de David Alfaro Siqueiros,* Mexico City: Museo Nacional de Artes Plasticas, 1947.

### Periodicals

*Art Digest,* August 1, 1932, p. 13.
*New York Times,* January 7, 1974.
*Time,* March 23, 1962. p. 35.

—*Sketch by Simon Dixon*

# Antonio Skámeta
## 1940-
### Chilean novelist and dramatist

Skámeta is one of Chile's most renowned novelists and playwrights. Exiled from his native country during the **Pinochet** regime, Skámeta's work often embodies his feelings and experiences as an expatriot and his search for identity amidst the social and political troubles of Latin America. His intense yearning to communicate has brought him into the field of academia, radio, film, journalism, translation and writing.

A writer who began composing stories and poems when he was 11 or 12, Skámeta explained the genesis of his writing to Ciro Bianchi Ross in *Spanish American Authors: The Twentieth Century:* "Since I was a child I have had deep feelings about the fragility of the human being and the permanence of nature, as well as a precocious certainty of death; I have meditated since then on the meaning of life. . . . I began to seek out the company of girls and books. I was lacking in the language to seduce them, but books offered me a glimpse of lives more interesting than mine. In that love for girls and books lies the root of my aesthetics, my desire to communicate, and my need to fantasize myself into the books I loved. There I place the origin of my vocation."

Antonio Skámeta was born on November 7, 1940, to Antonio and Magdalena (Vranicic) Skámeta, both of Yugoslavian descent, in Antofagasta, Chile. When Skámeta was nine his father went bankrupt and his family was forced to move to Argentina. They lived in poverty, sharing one room, in a boarding house with 60 other inhabitants. Skámeta later utilized this experience in his film *Reina la tranquilidad en el pais* and his novel *Soñé que la nieve ardía.*

Poverty compelled him to seek work when he was ten. He worked as a porter in a fruit market in the mornings, while he attended school in the afternoons. Skámeta's father smuggled contraband cloth into Chile, and the young Skámeta assisted his father by taking the parcels to the central Post Office in Buenos Aires before midnight. This acquainted him with Buenos Aires nightlife. Skámeta continued his education in Santiago, studying philosophy and literature at the University of Chile.

After graduating, Skámeta became a professor of literature and narrative yechnique at the School of Journalism of La Universidad Católica of Santiago; he also held writing workshops. He then went to the United States and earned a Master of Arts degree from Columbia University. While in New York he perfected his English, which enabled him to become a translator of works by Melville, Golding, Mailer, and Kerouac. Parallel to his career in journalism and academia, Skámeta held important posts in the **Allende** government, under which "exercise of free speech suffered no limits," he wrote in *Lives on the Line*. During this period he wrote his fist book *El entusiasmo* in 1967. It was followed by *Desnudo en el tejado,* published in 1969, a collection of short stories, which was awarded the Premio Casa de las Américas by the government of Cuba in 1969.

The overthrow of the Allende regime in a bloody military coup in 1973 instituted a new era for Skámeta. Bereft of freedom, suffering under the repression and insecurity of the new regime, Skámeta elected to abandon Chile for exile. He remained in West Berlin after attending the Program for Artists of the German Office for Academic Exchange. There he worked as a freelance writer, an academic and a filmmaker. Skámeta moved into radio and screenplays, fostered by a desire to be closer to public taste. In 1973 he wrote the script for *La Victoria*, which was directed by Peter Lilienthal. He collaborated with Lilienthal again on *Reina la tranquilidad en el Pais,* which was shown at the Paris Film Festival and later awarded the German Cinema Prize for best film of the year. Between 1978 and 1981 he was professor of screenwriting at the Film and Television Academy in West Berlin. He continued writing novels, such as, *No pasó nada,* 1980, and *La insurrección,* 1982. The latter novel tells the story of a humble family, during the popular rebellion led by the Sandinistas against Somoza dictatorship in the city of León, Nicaragua, in 1978. It was made into a prizewinning film, Skámeta collaborating again with the director Lilienthal. He received widespread acclaim for his next film, *Ardiente paciencia*—the chronicle of a friendship between Pablo Neruda, Chile's great poet and Nobel laureate, and a young postman, conveying Skámeta's homage to Neruda and the cultural development under Allende. Skámeta was awarded a Guggenheim fellowship in 1986.

In 1989 Skámeta returned to Chile with his Nora and their son (he divorced his first wife, Cecilia

Biosier in 1964), motivated by his love for Chile and a desire to participate in his country's new democracy. He told Georgiana Colville for *Latin American Literary Review* that he returned to Chile "as a simple man . . . [to] just enjoy my family, my friends, the landscape and my people. . . . My project when I came to Chile was to sit in my office and write." However, he has become absorbed in numerous projects, including filmscripts, television programs and magazines, stating, "I think that after so many years in exile I was hungering after participation in my people's culture."

## SELECTED PUBLISHED WORKS:

### Short Stories

*El entusiasmo* (title means "Enthusiasm"), ZigZag, 1967.

*Desnudo en el tejado* (title means "Nude on the Housetop"), Sudamericana, Buenos Aires, 1969.

*Tiro libre,* Siglo Veintiuno, Buenos Aires, 1973.

*No pasó nada y otros relatos* (title means "Nothing Happened and Other Stories), Pehuên, 1965.

*Mira donde va el lobo,* translated by D. L. Schmidt and F. Cordovez as *Watch Where the Wolf is Going,* Readers International, 1991.

### Novels

*El ciclista del San Cristóbal* (title means "The Cyclist of San Cristobal"), Quimantu, 1973.

*Soñê que la nieve ardía,* Planeta, Barcelona; translation by Malcolm Coad published as *I Dreamt the Snow Was Burning,* Readers International, 1985.

*Novios y solitarios,* Losada, Buenos Aires, 1975.

*Chileno!,* translated by Hortense Carpentier, Morrow, 1979.

*La insurrección,* Ediciones del Norte, Hanover, New Hampshire, 1982; translation by Paula Sharp published as *The Insurrection,* Ediciones del Norte, 1983.

*Ardiente paciencia,* Ediciones del Norte, 1985; translation by Katherine Silver published as *Burning Patience,* Pantheon, 1987.

*Matchball,* Sudaméricana, 1989.

## SOURCES:

### Books

*Hispanic Writers: A Selection of Sketches From Contemporary Authors,* edited by Bryan Ryan, Detroit, Gale Research, 1991, pp. 443–44.

*Lives on the Line: The Testimony of Contemporary Latin American Aurhors,* edited by Doris Meyer, University of California Press, 1988, pp. 248–64.

*Spanish American Authors: The Twentieth Century,* edited by Angel Flores, New York, H. W. Wilson, 1992, pp. 808–11.

### Periodicals

*Latin American Literary Review,* January/June 1992, pp. 27–35.

*Times Literary Supplement,* 1969, p. 1050.

*World Literature Today,* Volume 60, 1986, p. 450.

—*Sketch by Amanda Beresford*

# Jimmy Smits
## 1955-
### Puerto Rican American actor

Jimmy Smits has become one of the most prominent Hispanic actors in American television. Best known for his portrayal of angry young lawyer Victor Sifuentes on the long-running program *L.A. Law,* Smits has helped to increase the visibility of Hispanics in non-typecast roles for the small screen. He has also appeared in several movies and lends his support to groups concerning themselves with Hispanic issues.

### Early Love of Acting

Born on July 9, 1955, in Brooklyn, New York, Smits spent most of his early childhood in Puerto Rico. His father came from Dutch Guyana (now Surinam) and his mother from Puerto Rico. Smits eventually returned to Brooklyn, where he attended Thomas Jefferson High School. From a young age, Smits enjoyed acting in whatever form he could find it. One of his favorite stories involved the time he was six years old and imitated Soviet leader Nikita Khrushchev, hitting the table with his shoe, for the benefit of his family. Smits played football in high school, standing six-feet-two-inches tall, but he eventually decided that sports would have to take second place to acting. He quit football and joined every dramatic production he possibly could, even going to other schools to join theirs.

His father had been a merchant marine, and no one in his family had ever achieved post-secondary schooling. Smits changed that by going to Brooklyn College to study drama. He took his B.A. from Brooklyn before going on to Cornell to earn an M.A. in theater. In going from a "lower-middle class laborer" background to the Ivy League, Smits encountered a certain amount of misunderstanding, if not resistance, from his family. He described the difference between his ideas of acting and his family's to Merrill Shindler of the *Chicago Tribune:* "They're simple folks, and their knowledge of acting is limited to what they see on TV. They didn't understand why I wanted to do the classics, stuff like Shaw and Ibsen. They couldn't understand why I wasn't doing Pepsodent commercials."

As an ambitious young actor, Smits wanted to perfect his craft, working on high-quality projects with high-minded people. In reality, however, he spent his first years in the business playing roles that did not meet his artistic expectations. As Smits explained to Shindler, he paid his dues by portraying "everything from a Tibetan monk to some banana republic army captain." He also experienced some typecasting, which he one day would overcome. As Smits remarked in the interview with Shindler: "The good news is that there are lots of roles out there for Hispanics. The bad news is that they are often as unshaven thugs." He eventually appeared in the New York Shakespeare Festival productions of *Hamlet* and *The Ballad of Soapy Smith* as well as an off-Broadway production starring Linda Hunt called *Little Victories.* Though he recognized his good fortune at being able to make a living as an actor, he still felt frustration at not being able to land a major role.

### Victor Sifuentes and L.A. Law

Smits landed a role as Don Johnson's partner in the very popular *Miami Vice* television series, but his character was killed off only 15 minutes into the series pilot to make way for Philip Michael Thomas, Johnson's partner throughout the series' long run. From there Smits appeared in a major movie called *Running Scared* with Billy Crystal and Gregory Hines. Unfortunately, playing the role of a drug dealer made Smits feel that he had again been typecast. Though he was happy to make it to the big screen, he feared that too much of this kind of good fortune would limit him permanently to playing thugs and criminals.

In 1986, Smits auditioned for the role of lawyer Victor Sifuentes in the new NBC series *L.A. Law.* He went to the NBC offices in New York for his tryout, but as he told Shindler, he was "so bad, they didn't even bother to call me back." Rather than giving up on the role, Smits flew out to California, where NBC was holding simultaneous auditions for the part. This time he did a better job, and NBC gave him the role.

Smits explained to Shindler how strongly he felt about the Sifuentes character, and why he went to such great lengths for a second chance: "I saw it as a chance to establish an intelligent, alternative image [of Hispanics], someone who's neither a thug, nor a womanizer." In 1987, the Hispanic Media Image Task Force gave Smits the Imagen Award for his achievements in improving both the image of Hispanics on television and the prospects for Hispanic actors and actresses. In 1988 the National Hispanic Bar of Mexico honored him for improving the perception of Hispanic lawyers.

Smits accepted the acclaim, but he also expressed some ambivalence to Shindler about being viewed as a role model: "You have to ask yourself, 'Am I going to be this role model for a lot of people?', or 'Am I going to take this part as a villain because it's real juicy.' A lot of the best roles you'll ever get are as meanies. I'm really proud to be this role model on *L.A. Law;* that's one of my contributions to making the world a better place. But I also ask myself, 'Do I have to be a knight in shining armor every time I pick a role?' Man, I hope not."

Though Smits has received praise as a good role model, he has also had some problems in his personal life. At age 19, Smits fathered a daughter, Talna, with his then-girlfriend. He married his daughter's mother in 1981, and two years later his son Joaquin was born. In 1987, however, Smits and his wife were "very amicably" divorced, and his ex-wife and children returned to New York to live. During *L.A. Law,* Smits divided his time between Los Angeles and New York, frequently flying home to visit his children.

In 1987 the tabloid press descended on Smits, reacting to his *nolo contendere* plea to charges of assault and battery of his then-girlfriend, actress Wanda De Jesus. Smits received a sentence of community service and expressed regret about what happened.

Smits played Victor Sifuentes on *L.A. Law* until 1991. During his years with the television program, he also made the movies *The Believers,* with the very successful Hispanic actor **Martin Sheen,** and a production of the **Carlos Fuentes** novel *The Old Gringo,* with Hollywood superstars Jane Fonda and Gregory Peck. In *The Old Gringo,* Smits played a general in the Mexican Revolution, a role which provided him with another opportunity to play a strong and interesting Hispanic character.

In 1994, Smits returned to television. He appeared in the title role of a TV movie called *The Cisco Kid,* but compared to the original character, Smits's Cisco Kid was more assertive of his culture and less comical. In late 1994 Smits joined the cast of the popular ABC series *NYPD Blue,* replacing David Caruso, who left after salary disputes with the network. The role allowed Smits once again to reinterpret Hispanics for mainstream America, this time in the role of police detective Bobby Simone.

## A Mainstream Actor

Although some viewed Smits as a champion of minority actors trying to avoid being typecast, Smits said that he still struggles to assert himself as a total actor. Though he could appreciate the importance of projecting a positive image of Hispanics and portraying good role models for Hispanic youths, he did not reject the idea of playing villains. On playing Hispanic characters, he commented in the interview with Shindler that "Al Pacino doesn't worry about doing just Italian roles." Smits explained that his greatest wish is to be seen as "a mainstream actor": "I think that what's important here is to re-educate the powers that be, and the public, that a Hispanic isn't necessarily one type of a character or another. It's the same way as an actor's main job is to be versatile. I think I can be both versatile and Hispanic at the same time."

## SELECTED VIDEOGRAPHY

*L.A. Law,* 1986.
*Running Scared,* 1986.
*The Believers,* 1987.
*Stamp of a Killer,* 1987.
*Glitz,* 1988.
*Old Gringo,* 1989.
*Vital Signs,* 1990.
*Fires Within,* 1991.
*Switch,* 1991.
*Stephen King's The Tommyknockers,* 1993.
*The Cisco Kid,* 1994.

## SOURCES:

### Books

*The Complete Actors' Television Credits,*
   *1948–1988,* edited by James Robert Parish
   and Vincent Terrace, Metuchen, NJ, Scarecrow
   Press, 1989.
*The Hispanic-American Almanac,* edited by Nicolas Kanellos, Detroit, Gale, 1993.

### Periodicals

*Chicago Tribune,* October 16, 1988, Sec. 13, p. 4.
*TV Guide,* February 12, 1994, p. 28.

—*Sketch by James McCarthy*

# Carlos Solórzano
## 1922-
### Guatemalan playwright, novelist, director and educator

As playwright, editor, scholar and artistic director Carlos Solórzano has been a major force in Mexican theater for more than 40 years. Solórzano is responsible for introducing to Mexican theater-goers important dramatic works by Shakespeare, Kafka, Pirandello, Sophocles, and Ben Jonson among others, and for injecting into Mexican cultural life what Frank Dauster, in *Modern Drama* (1964), has called an "eclectic cosmopolitanism." Solórzano has brought to his audiences both classical and avant-garde drama and added breadth and depth to the Mexican theater arts.

Solórzano is a major dramatist in his own right. His work has successfully translated the absurdist and existentialist themes and the unsettling performance practices of avant-garde European drama-of Brecht, Beckett, Ionesco, Artaud, Sartre and Camus-into the Spanish American context, finding archetypes of the human condition in the everyday and lending them an epic weight. Solórzano's view of the human condition is, as he has said to Teresa Méndez-Faith, a pessimistic one; a dominant theme in his plays is rebellion against oppressive clerical authority and religious fanaticism, and the burdensome exercise of personal freedom in a secular universe. Solórzano is one of a group of contemporary Latin American dramatists whose works, according to George W. Woodyard in *Comparative Drama* (1969), "transcend national limitations and become significant commentaries on a universal scale." He avoids regionalism and takes on themes and forms which can address the dilemmas and struggles of 20th century existence. His work has been translated into many languages.

As a scholar Solórzano has published a number of works on the history of Latin American theater, including *Teatro latinoamericano del siglo XX* (1961) and *Testimonios teatrales de Mexico* (1973), and he has edited three anthologies of plays, *El Teatro Hispanoamericano Contemporáneo* (1964), *Teatro guatemalteco contemporáneo* (1964) and *Teatro breve hispanoamericano* (1971). Solórzano has represented Mexico at numerous international theater festivals, and has held visiting professorships at the University of Southern California, the University of Kansas, and Columbia University. He has worked as a correspondent and theater critic for such journals as *Rendezvous du théatre, Primer Acto,* and *Siempre,* and he has been a frequent contributor to journals in Latin America, Europe, and the United States.

Solórzano was born May 1, 1922, into wealthy and privileged family in Guatemala City, Guatemala. His great grandfather, Justo Rufino Barrios, was at one time President of Guatemala, and Solórzano's own father was an engineer and landowner. Life under the dictatorship of Jorge Ubico, between 1931 and 1944, was harsh for most Guatemalans, and while Solórzano's family background and his schooling at a strict religious school protected him from the immediate effects of political tyranny, he developed a critical attitude toward oppressive clerical institutions.

In 1938, at the age of 16, Solórzano went to Europe, and upon his return in 1939 he moved permanently to Mexico. His work as a dramatist and educator has been more closely identified ever since with his adopted country. Solórzano attended the National Autonomous University of Mexico (UNAM) in Mexico City and received a bachelor's degree in architecture. He remained at the university as a graduate student, but turned his attention to literature, earning his Master's degree in 1946. Following his marriage in 1946 to Beatrice Caso, Solórzano continued his studies, earning his doctorate in 1948. An early interest in and identification with Basque philosopher **Miguel de Unamuno y Jugo** led to Solorzano's early works *El sentimiento plástico en la obra de Unamuno* (1944) which he presented as his master's thesis, and *Espejo de novelas* (1945), his doctoral dissertation. Among the influences of Unamuno on Solórzano's drama, as Francesca Colecchia has said, is a desire to "make his audience think" and "a preoccupation with death, its rationale, its apparent finality, and its absurdity."

### Parisian Interlude

After receiving his doctorate Solórzano continued his studies in Paris on a Rockefeller Foundation scholarship, attending the Sorbonne from 1948 to 1951 and receiving a doctorate in drama. This Parisian interlude was a significant time in Solórzano's career. There he tasted the rich intellectual and cultural life of the city and discovered the exciting and innovative work of the existentialist movement. He met and was influenced by the Belgian playwright Michel de Ghelderode and the French existentialist novelist and dramatist Albert Camus, who recognized in Solórzano genuine dramatic talent. In a subsequent interview Solórzano acknowledged the personal importance of this time in France and his feeling of belonging to an entire generation which had, for the first time, voiced open rebellion against authority.

Upon his return to Mexico Solórzano began a ten-year appointment as artistic director of the *Teatro Universitario* of UNAM. He served as director of the *Museo Nacional de Teatro,* and founded the *Grupos Teatrales Estudiantiles.* At this time he began in earnest his career as a playwright. Solórzano's first play *Doña Beatriz* (1952) was influenced by Camus' *Caligula*. Set in 1541, it combines historical setting with modern dialogue. Nominally historical figures-conquistador Pedro de Alvarado and his wife Batriz de la Cueva—the characters become in Solórzano's hands generic and symbolic vehicles for philosophical problems. In his next three-act play, a reworking of the legend of the philosopher's stone, *El Hechicero* ("The Magician," 1954) Solórzano continues to embody philosophical ideas in major characters. Here, Merlin represents what Frank Dauster called "the ideal of peace and good," and the play has the sparse quality of Greek tragedy.

With his best-known play, *Las manos de Dios* ("The Hands of God," 1956) Solórzano developed further what Francesca Colecchia has called this "trend toward the abstract, toward characters representative of concepts" and expressed a "rebellious spirit" against the Church. Here Solórzano inverts the Christian drama, making the Devil an attractive character who stands, according to Dauster, for "individual liberty" and is "spiritually akin to Christ" while the authoritarian Priest is an evil force. Solórzano's next three plays, *Los fantoches* ("The Puppets," 1958), *Cruce de vías* ("Crossroads," 1959), and *El crucificado* ("The Crucified," 1958) are separate one-act pieces published together as *Three Acts,* but Solórzano employs a variety of styles and demonstrates his versatility as a playwright. The theme of anticlericalism is repeated in *El sueño del angel* ("The Angel's Dream," 1960). This bitter and pessimistic attack on the oppressive politics of religion takes the form of an exchange between a woman and an angel, in which the woman's capacity for rebellion against religious dogma is slowly but inexorably worn down.

### Son's Death Reaffirms Fatalism

In 1960 Solórzano was appointed professor at UNAM, a position he held until his emeritus appointment in 1985, combining teaching and directing with drama scholarship. Four years after this appointment, Solórzano's 22-year-old son, while working on his doctorate in the United States, was killed in a hunting accident. This tragic loss, Solórzano said in an interview with Teresa Méndez-Faith (*American Theater Review,* 1984), deepened his pessimism and confirmed his belief that human existence is governed more by chance than by logic. For two years Solórzano gave up writing altogether.

Solórzano's next work, originally conceived as a play, was his first published piece of prose fiction, *Los falsos demonios* (1966). Set in Guatemala, the novel explores the effect of political tyranny on the daily life of citizens. Solórzano continued his dramatic writing in 1966 with *El zapato* ("The Shoe") and in 1967 with *Mea culpa.* He wrote a second novel, *Las celdas* ("The

Jail Cells," 1971) based upon an historic event in Mexico. In 1977 Solórzano was appointed Director of Mexico's National Theatre, a position he held until 1982. Since 1985 Solórzano has been professor emeritus ("Profesor de Carrera") at UNAM and he teaches courses on Hispanic theater and on drama criticism. In 1989 he received the Premio Nacional de Literatura "Miguel Angel Asturias" in Guatemala, and the Premio Universidad in Mexico. Solórzano currently serves as editor for Latin America of the *Enciclopedia Mundial del Teatro Contemporáneo.*

### SELECTED PUBLISHED WORKS:

*El hechicero: Tragedia en tres actos,* Cuadernos Americanos, 1955.
*Tres actos,* El Unicornio, 1959.
*El Teatro Hispanoamericano Contemporáneo,* 2 vols. (anthology editor), Mexico, Fondo de Cultura Económica (includes *Las manos de Dios*), 1964.
*El Teatro Latinoamericano en el siglo XX,* Mexico, Editorial Promaca, 1964.
*Las celdas,* J. Moritz, 1971.
*Los falsos demonios,* J. Moritz, 1973.
*Testimonios teatrales de México,* Universidad Nacional Autónoma de México, 1973.
*Crossroads and Other Plays,* translated and edited by Francesca Colecchia. Rutherford, Fairleigh Dickinson University Press, 1993.

### SOURCES:

*Comparative Drama,* vol. VIII, Fall 1969, No. 3, pp.183–192.
*Latin American Theatre Review,* Spring 1984, pp. 39–48. Fall 198–110, Fall 1991, pp. 123–133.
*Modern Drama,* vol. VII, May 1964, No. 1, pp. 89–100.

—*Sketch by Simon Dixon*

# Anastasio Somoza Garcia
## 1896-1956
### Nicaraguan dictator

Anastasio Somoza established a military dynasty in Nicaragua through military coercion, canny support of American objectives, and harsh intolerance of dissent. In his 20 years as Nicaragua's actual and *de facto* head of state, from 1936 to 1956, he made many economic and political reforms—some which may have benefitted elements of the population, but others which simply reinforced his own authority and allowed for the transfer of power to his sons upon his death. One of the wealthiest men in Central America at the time, Somoza died at the hands of an assassin in 1956.

### Sandino and U.S. Marines

Known popularly as Tacho, Somoza was born in 1896 in San Marcos, Nicaragua. His father owned coffee plantations and, being a man of wealth, made certain his son pursued an education. The younger Somoza first attended the Instituto Nacional de Oriente of Granada and eventually went to the United States to study at the Pierce School of Business Administration in Philadelphia. He married a woman from a politically influential family shortly after he left school and returned to Nicaragua.

Through most of the twentieth century, two names dominated the landscape of Nicaraguan politics: Somoza and Sandino. Instability in the Nicaraguan government during the 1920s led the United States to help establish the Nicaraguan National Guard. Although the United States favored the governing Conservative party, elections held in 1928 and 1932 gave victories to the Liberals. Guerilla General Augusto Sandino rejected the continued presence of U.S. troops despite the Liberal victories. By refusing to lay down weapons, Sandino provided the perfect justification for the continued improvement and reinforcement of the National Guard. As a fast-rising general in the Guard, Somoza, along with the U.S. Marines, carried out a long and brutal campaign against Sandino. By the time the Marines left Nicaragua in 1932, Somoza had reached the top of the Guard's chain of command.

Political agreements reached between the Liberal and Conservative parties in 1932 put Juan Batista Sacasa in power, but without the true support of either Sandino or Somoza, Sacasa's government stood on a shaky foundation. The Guard had been established as a non-partisan constabulary in 1927, and the leaders of the Guard came from lists of equal numbers of Liberal and Conservative candidates. But Knut Walter explained the flaw in the system in his book *The Regime of Anastasio Somoza, 1936–1956*. Even though the top officers would be chosen from balanced partisan lists, "the commanding officer . . . would be chosen at will by the president elect," in effect assuring that "the national army . . . would continue in the tradition of the partisan armed forces that had characterized Nicaragua for so long."

Against his own desires, Liberal President-elect Sacasa bent to pressure from several sources and nominated Somoza. Somoza did not hesitate to assert his dominance over the Guard, and Sacasa gradually lost his authority, despite his democratic credentials as head of state. Conceived as the source of the government's legitimacy, the Guard slowly became a symbol of the Sacasa government's total lack of authority.

Once the U.S. Marines had gone, Sandino agreed to negotiate a peace, even though his forces had reached their height. In 1933, Somoza rode triumphantly through the streets of Managua with Sandino, praising him for his patriotism. The government had allowed Sandino to retain a small army and gave him some land in exchange for peace.

Tensions again grew, however, between the two generals, with the increasingly powerless President Sacasa in the middle. Sandino came to Managua in February 1934 for negotiations with Sacasa, but National Guard troops arrested Sandino and executed him.

### Somoza Rises to Power

This bold political move put Somoza only one step from control of the country. As the leader of the military, Somoza held the trump card—physical coercion—but only if he could be certain that the U.S. military would not intervene again on behalf of the duly elected president. Somoza did everything he could to assure U.S. diplomats that he would support American positions in every way. Sacasa could see where Somoza's ambitions led, and many in the Liberal party feared the emergence of a new military dictator.

Somoza used his power and influence to make Congress declare an amnesty for those involved in the "events of February," meaning the unlawful execution of Sandino. Above the objections of the president, the Congress voted 33 to 4 for the bill, despite the fact that Sandino himself had received a pledge of amnesty after the cessation of hostilities. Sacasa's inability to control his own party proved that his days in power were drawing closer to an end.

In his book *Dictators Never Die*, Eduardo Crawley described Somoza's method of extending his control: "Somoza's favorite tactic was to stage a riot in a town or city . . . then move in with the Guardia and, on the pretext of guaranteeing law and order, place the local government under military control." With most of Nicaragua under his command in this way, Somoza declared himself the only fit candidate for the nomination of both political parties in the 1936 elections. Frustrated with legal disputes with Sacasa over the general's eligibility for political office, Somoza used military force, attacking positions loyal to the president and the Presidential Palace. Sacasa surrendered and fled to El Salvador.

## Somoza Becomes Dictator

With no one in his way, Somoza engineered an election which would prove his legal claim to office. Fraud occurred on a ridiculous level: initial vote counts gave the opposition 1,200 votes, but later support dwindled to only 169 votes. The numbers mattered little, because the election served only to legitimize Somoza's authority.

Once in office, Somoza broadened the scope of the National Guard's duties. It took over the railroads, prisons, radio, and trade of almost all kinds. Personally Somoza put himself at the center of a vast web of kickbacks and bribery. Crawley explained, "It soon became the rule that the best, indeed often the only way of opening a business or even staying in business was to make a 'contribution' to the General's personal funds." His personal land holdings, augmented by his ability to "persuade" landowners to sell to him for rock-bottom prices, became incredibly profitable. His beef exports outsold every other producer in the country, thanks to the 1.5 cent per pound tax they all had to pay.

In 1939, Somoza called on the Congress to pass laws preventing political nepotism, establishing term limits, and instituting other measures designed to improve efficiency. Somoza was personally exempt from the laws, of course, and in the spirit of improved efficiency, Somoza canceled the 1940 election. The Congress, and Somoza as president, would be held over for another eight years. Thus he had dispensed with even the previous election's show of a popular mandate for his power.

Unassailable from within, Somoza needed allies abroad as well. Support for Allied nations in World War II gave Somoza the U.S. recognition he wanted so badly. A famous anecdote retold by Crawley depicted President Franklin D. Roosevelt looking at a list of guests invited to attend a White House reception. On seeing Somoza's name, the president said, "Isn't that man supposed to be a son of a bitch?" To which Secretary of State Cordell Hull replied, "Yes, but he is *our* son of a bitch."

Support for the Allies got Somoza arms and money during the war, but U.S. opposition to Somoza's potential re-election in 1947 grew. Somoza clearly wanted to stay in office, but even his National Guard buzzed with talk of mutiny. The General gave in, abandoning his re-election bid and temporarily loosening restrictions on dissent. Somoza backed a candidate whom he thought he could manipulate once in office, Dr. Leonardo Arguello, and the opposition nominated Dr. Enoc Aguado. Despite intimidation tactics like forcing voters to stand in the line of the candidate for whom they would vote, it became clear early in the election that Aguado, and not Somoza's candidate, would win. In *Guardians of the Dynasty,* Richard Millett described the voting conditions by the end of the day: "By nightfall, lines of voters for Arguello were nonexistent, but ... long lines of people were still waiting to vote for Aguado. At this point the Guardia dispersed the crowds and rushed the ballots, under heavy guard, to the National Palace to be counted." Predictably, Somoza's man became the new president, and although he did attempt to use the legitimacy of his office to weaken Somoza's influence, Arguello simply could not persuade the Guard to abandon Somoza in large enough numbers. Turning his guns directly on Arguello and his supporters, Somoza regained total control of power. He justified his actions to Congress by saying that Arguello had attempted to become a dictator, but under siege by Somoza's own men, Congress very likely agreed to Somoza's wishes for no reason other than fear.

The United States and other Allied governments refused to recognize the new regime, but when the Congress named Victor Ramon y Reyes, Somoza's uncle who was firmly under his control, as the new president, the diplomatic boycott broke down, leading in 1948 to U.S. recognition.

President Roman y Reyes died two weeks before the 1950 election, and Somoza became the provisional head of state. He won the election and once again ruled Nicaragua in title as well as in fact. Five years later, after a term marked by hostilities with Costa Rica, Somoza again desired and sought re-election. At a reception the night after Somoza's re-nomination, however, Rigoberto Lopez Perez evaded Somoza's tight security and shot the president four times. Somoza's bodyguards killed Perez on the spot. Somoza flew by helicopter to an American hospital in the Panama Canal Zone, but he never regained consciousness. Somoza died on September 29, 1965.

His two sons succeeded him as president of Nicaragua until 1979, when they were finally deposed by the Sandinistas—rebel forces named for Augusto Sandino, whose killing had first propelled Somoza into Nicaragua's political limelight.

## SOURCES:

Crawley, Eduardo, *Dictators Never Die: A Portrait of Nicaragua and the Somoza Dynasty,* London, C. Hurst and Company, 1979.

Millett, Richard, *Guardians of the Dynasty,* Maryknoll, New York, Orbis Books, 1977.

Walter, Knut, *The of Anastasio Somoza, 1936–1956,* Chapel Hill, University of North Carolina Press, 1993.

—*Sketch by James McCarthy*

# Fernando Sor
# 1778-1839
## Spanish composer and classical guitar virtuoso

Fernando Sor, perhaps the most distinguished figure amongst a group of early nineteenth century innovators of the classical or Spanish guitar, was born in Barcelona in February of 1778. His etudes, duets, and sonatas for the guitar have become an important foundation of the classical guitarist's repertoire, and in his own lifetime he was not only a successful composer of operas and ballets, but also a virtuoso concert performer.

Just as Sor's music cannot be characterized as typically "Spanish," but must be considered as more generically European or classical, so the circumstances of his life also carried him far beyond the geographical borders of Spain. His father, Joan Sor, was an amateur musician. He permitted his son to study at the famous monastery of Monserrat, where he first heard the music of Haydn. After completing his education, Sor was able to obtain a military sinecure which permitted him to compose and perform in Madrid, Barcelona, and Malaga. This pleasant existence was interrupted by the Napoleonic invasion of Spain in 1808. According to Brian Jeffrey's *Fernando Sor*, Sor was probably present in Madrid on the second of May, 1808, during the uprising and its horrifying conclusion the following day. Though Sor participated in the general resistance, he soon accepted the new regime. Like the great majority of Spanish artists and intellectuals, he hoped that the ideas of liberalism and progress represented by the French were Spain's best chance for much needed reform. When Napoleon lost his European campaigns and Fernando VII was restored to the Spanish throne, these artists and intellectuals-including Sor and Goya-were forced into exile.

In the years that followed, Sor lived in Paris and London composing operas, ballets, guitar and piano music, playing the guitar, and singing in concerts. He published the important *Method for the Guitar* in 1830 in which he expressed his views on the musical potential of the guitar, technique, guitar construction, and use of the fingernails (which Sor, unlike almost all modern guitarists, considered inferior to the fingertips).

Sor also spent approximately three years in Russia, after passing through Germany and Poland where he gave concerts. In Russia three of his ballets were produced, and he was commissioned to compose a funeral march for the death of Czar Alexander.

He spent the last decade of his life in Paris, and witnessed the decline of the classical guitar in favor of the pianoforte. Wishing to spend the remainder of his life in his native Catalonia, he wrote a letter to Fernando VII. declaring his patriotism and pointing out that he had been decorated by the pope. Sor received no answer, and died in Paris on July 10, 1839.

In addition to guitar music, Sor composed works for the piano, ballets, operas, symphonies, and many songs in a variety of styles. Most of these have been lost, while much of his guitar works are widely known and admired. While the guitar was traditionally considered an instrument of accompaniment, especially for singing, Sor was able to render the guitar more autonomous, exploiting its potential for carrying melody on the higher strings with independent accompanying voices in the lower strings. This required a much more specialized technique, one that was unheard of in London when Sor astounded audiences there in the 1820s. In fact, the dearth of guitarists who were proficient in this "classical style" made it difficult for Sor to publish very sophisticated or elaborate works, since publishers could only sell music that was simple enough for beginners. In Sor's *Method* he complains that the demand for simplicity has caused the musical quality of his published work to suffer.

The most famous of these works is undoubtedly his *Opus 9, "Variations on a Theme of Mozart."* Published by Messonier in Paris in 1817 it has not only remained in print but has been a perennial favorite among guitarists to this day. Julian Bream has called the work a "miniature masterpiece." Its slow introduction builds tension through a series of chromatic melodic movements not traditionally associated with the guitar. The theme, coming from Mozart's *The Magic Flute,* along with the accompanying variations, shows the extent to which Sor had reconceptualized the guitar's fretboard as an efficient vehicle for classical music.

Sor's other major works include Opus 7, "Fantasy with Theme and Variations", and Opus 30, another "Fantasy" followed by a "Theme and Variations" which reworks the theme suggested in the slow introduction. All three of these major works have been recorded by Julian Bream.

Some of Sor's most beautiful pieces for the guitar are his etudes. Though pedagogical in design, they contain great charm with a strong emphasis on melody, and are often performed in concert. Twenty of Sor's etudes were assembled by Andrés Segovia and published in 1945. This edition is still widely available today.

## SOURCES:

Bone, Philip J., *The Guitar and Mandolin,* Schott and Co. Ltd., 1954.

Jeffrey, Brian, *Fernando Sor,* Miami Beach: Hansen Publications, Inc., 1977.

*The Classical Guitar,* edited by Frederick Noad, New York: Amsco Publications, 1976.

*Studies for the Guitar by Fernando Sor,* edited by Andrés Segovia, New York: Edward B. Marks Music Company, 1945.

**Periodicals**

*Guitar Review,* Summer 1974, pp. 6–10; Spring 1982, pp. 1–10.

**Other**

Additional information for this profile was obtained from the video *Guitarra,* by Julian Bream.

—*Sketch by Paul B. Miller*

# Mercedes Sosa
## 1935-
**Argentine singer**

The life of Mercedes Sosa—"the doyenne of Latin American folk singers," as writer Larry Rohter called her in a *New York Times* profile—epitomizes the challenges faced by socially-engaged artists in modern culture. Born in 1935, Sosa is one of the chief architects of the *nueva canción,* or "new song" i.e. a musical form that emerged in Latin America during the 1960s, combining traditional folk rhythms with lyrics inspired by contemporary struggles. The music was interpreted as a form of political protest, as an artist's way of combating repression and brutality.

When she was named one of the *Esquire's* "Women We Love" in 1989, a tribute article explained that Sosa's youth was spent, "in Tucumán, Argentina, in a province as fantastic in her memory as a landscape created by **[Jorge Luis] Borges.** The place was called the Garden of the Republic, a wonderful name, for not only was it lush there, but Argentina had not yet been taken over by military dictators." Located in northwest Argentina, rural Tucumán exerted a strong influence on the singer's artistic development. As Sosa explained to *Esquire's* reporter: "In Tucumán, we were closer to Bolivia and the culture of the Incas than we were to Buenos Aires, and that was an advantage for someone who wanted to be a folk singer." Her early life also conditioned her social conscience. Her parents worked as a day laborer and as a washerwoman and the family's poverty, Sosa told Rohter, was "where my sympathy for the downtrodden was born."

Despite a folk tradition dominated by conservative, male voices in her country—and her own shyness and attacks of stage fright—Sosa became one of Argentina's most popular singers. Her career began at age 15, when she won a contest for amateurs at a local radio station. In 1962 she was one of the singers who issued the "nuevo canciónero," a manifesto that announced the movement to revitalize the old song forms. Her professional life coincided with the years of Argentina's military dictatorship, a government which was hardly receptive to *nueva canción* and its political implications. At one point in 1978, Sosa was performing at concert in La Plata. After she began "When They Have the Land," a song that calls for agrarian reforms, Sosa found herself interrupted by security troops, who subjected her to a humiliating search before arresting her. Sosa's band, her son, and her audience were also arrested.

Although she was soon released, Sosa found it impossible to continue her career in Argentina. Her songs were banned from Argentine radio and television; bomb threats forced the cancellation of sold-out concerts. Then Sosa was barred from holding concerts altogether. With the added difficulty of recent widowhood, Sosa left her country for Europe in January of 1979.

Sosa spent the next three years in exile, basing herself in France and Spain. For a time she was unable to sing. "It was a mental problem, a problem of morale," she told Rohter. "It wasn't my throat or anything physical. When you are in exile, you take your suitcase, but there are things that don't fit. There are things in your mind, like colors and smells and childhood attitudes, and there is also the pain and the death you saw. You shouldn't deny those things, because to do so can make you ill."

By the time she returned to Buenos Aires in 1982, Sosa had turned adversity to her artistic benefit. She declared to Rohter that her exile "opened new horizons. By distancing me from my homeland and ripping me out by my roots, it forced my repertory to become more international. Before, I was always tied to our [Argentine] rhythms and our songs. I wouldn't be able to do the things I am doing now if I had not made a path for myself outside Argentina."

During the 1980s Sosa's work became increasingly pan-American. *Nueva canción* has never been limited to Argentina—in fact, it has enjoyed far more popularity elsewhere in Latin America—but Sosa has been an important force propelling the careers of artists from other countries, such as the Brazilian singer-songwriters Milton Nascimento and Chico Buarque de Holanda. She was also a key participant in a series of concerts called "Without Borders," featuring women singers from Brazil, Colombia, Peru, and Mexico. In 1989 *Boston Globe* reporter Fernando Gonzalez praised Sosa's artistic growth and adaptability, stating that as the years advance Sosa "has kept pace, incorporating rock and pop songs into her repertoire, collaborating with young rock artists in Argentina and even informing the arrangements of her traditional material with jazz and pop influences."

Sosa has deeply impressed United States audiences. Scott Allan Stevens reviewed a 1992 concert at Boston's Symphony Hall for the *Christian Science Monitor;* in doing so, he declared that Sosa "has the presence and vocal power to work an audience into a roaring, fist-waving frenzy of the type usually reserved for rock stars." Stevens wrote that her voice "seems to contain the full power of the reawakening indigenous peoples of the Americas. And closing one's eyes, the electronic echo effect makes it possible to imagine hearing her voice reverberating around a mountainous Andean village." *Esquire* added: "Your Spanish may or may not be good, but Mercedes Sosa requires no translation. Hers is the song of all those who have overcome their fear of singing out." Hispanic American folk singer **Joan Baez,** after sharing a stage with Sosa, was so moved by the Argentine singer's music that she literally kissed Sosa's feet.

Despite her reputation and history, Sosa has rebelled against the description of herself as a "singer of protests" and shies from political labels. "Like everyone else," Rohter quoted her as saying, "the artist should be able to live and work in tranquillity. It's as simple as that."

## SELECTED DISCOGRAPHY

*De Mi,* 1992.
*Sino,* 1993.
*30 Años,* 1994.
*Gracias a La Vida,* 1994.
*Mercedes Sosa en Argentina,* 1994.
*Sera Posible Sur,* 1994.

## SOURCES:

### Books

*Contemporary Musicians,* vol. 3, edited by Michael L. LaBlanc, Detroit, Gale, 1990.
*The New Woman Poems: A Tribute to Mercedes Sosa,* by Néstor Rodríguez Lacorén, New York, Latin Culture Publishers, 1989.
*World Music: The Rough Guide,* edited by Simon Broughton et. al., London, Rough Guides, 1994.

### Periodicals

*Boston Globe,* November 3, 1989, p. 52.
*Christian Science Monitor,* November 17, 1992, p. 10.
*Esquire,* May 19–25.
*New York Times,* October 9, 1988, pp. H21, H29; November 17, 1992, p. C16.

—*Sketch by Erika Dreifus*

# Roberto Sosa
## 1930-
### Honduran poet and cultural leader

Noted Honduran writer Roberto Sosa is someone whose "striking achievement," as David Garrison wrote in *Hispania,* "is a poetry of social concern that is not political propaganda." Thom Tammaro elaborated in *Library Journal:* "Writing of the poor and oppressed, Sosa captures the mood and spirit of his people in clear and direct language.... [His] poems truly dignify humanity, affirming clearly and compassionately that 'The poor are many. That's why/we cannot forget them.'" His works have been translated into English, German, French, and Russian.

Sosa was born on April 18, 1930, in the Honduran village of Yoro, a community, he recalled for *Spanish American Authors,* that "was out of touch with the rest of Honduras from when it was founded until the first decade of the second half of the 20th century. No one was able to leave there, except on the back of a mule, on horseback, or on foot." Sosa and his family did leave Yoro in 1933, not to return for nine years. During that time Sosa traveled through Honduras and El Salvador. "My father taught me the letters of the alphabet, and my mother completed the learning process of reading and writing. I felt such astonishment during that time in the joy of being able to repeat aloud the letters printed on walls, doors, and windows."

Sosa's favorite poem is dedicated to his father. "The poem I most love is 'Mi padre.' My father, Acisclo Sosa, was a musician by trade; he knew how to read music and could wrench the most fascinating of harmonies from the brass. I have never known, to this day, a more human man than he." Another poem honors Sosa's mother. "'El llanto de las cosas,' a poem about parental love, provides the title for one of my unpublished collections . . . and is a tribute to my mother. I have gleaned much of my verse from her

*Roberto Sosa*

conversation. I have always admired the cultivated vocabulary used by the author of my days, knowing as I do, that her education did not go beyond the second grade; my mother was like the vast majority of country women in Honduras who are born, live, and die in medieval conditions."

## Early Literary Influences

As a teenager Sosa fell under the influence of poetry by **Rubén Darío,** Juan Ramon Molina, Amado Nervo, Victor Hugo, and Juan de Díos Peza. He commenced studies to become a secondary school teacher and eventually settled in the Honduran capital city of Tegucigalpa. He arrived at a time when the dictatorship of Tiburcio Carías Andino had at last ended, a new flexibility permeated the atmosphere. Sosa remembered in *Spanish American Authors:* "The perceptive poets, Claudio Barrera and Daniel Laínez, objects of my rustic admiration, filled the air of the capital. During those days I also met Pompeyo del Valle and David Moya Posas, future companions of my literary generation. . . . It was a time of indiscriminate reading: Papini, Nietzsche, Schopenhauer, Goethe, Socrates, Plato, Dante, Virgil, Oscar Wilde, Voltaire, Arthur Conan Doyle. . . . They were days and nights equally without bread and without alcohol."

## Writer, Observer, Editor

Around 1958 Sosa wrote *Caligramas,* published in the collection of the journal *Pegaso.* Sosa candidly admitted that this early work was motivated in large part by his desire to see his name in print. Critics, however, treated it seriously and Sosa listened to their comments, especially to those of playwright Andrés Morris. In 1966 Sosa published *Muros;* this was followed the next year by *Mar interior.* Subsequent books included *Los pobres* and *Un mondo para todos dividido,* as well as the essay collection entitled *Prosa armada,* which contains much of Sosa's philosophical ideas about literature.

A keen observer, Sosa has not shied away from expressing harsh opinions. He criticized his own generation of Hondurans, from whom, he wrote in *Spanish American Authors,* there "emanated a complete lack of brotherhood." He also lamented the rise to power of Roberto Suazo Córdova. This event, he believed, "resulted in the surrender of Honduran sovereignty to the United States, marked by formal military occupation of our land by the U.S. army. . . . Not even art is left free of total surveillance. My works have been classified by the police . . . as 'anti-militarist' and 'highly dangerous' and my name is inscribed on the screens of the computers of death factories." For Sosa, the 1980s marked a time of bitterness; he considered his country utterly humiliated and demoralized.

Sosa has also devoted himself to editorial engagements. In 1964 he began editing the magazine *Presente,* a publication notable for its exceptional longevity among Central American journals. He has served as editor for *Diario Tiempo* and director of the University of Honduras Press. The University of Honduras is also where Sosa has spent much of his professorial career, but his return to the classroom in 1986 was short-lived. Hostilities between Sosa and the institution's Rector resulted in the termination of Sosa's employment. Sosa left Honduras and accepted a teaching post in the United States. A *Publishers Weekly* article noted already in 1983 that "though Sosa's poems have been banned by his government, they are often recited in the popular cafes of Honduras-a situation that has sometimes led commentators to suggest that censorship has a certain beneficial effect on the dissemination of poetry."

Sosa is married to Lidia Ortíz Luna; they are the parents of two daughters. He is the recipient of numerous awards, including the Juan Ramón Molinas Award in 1967 for *Mar interior* and the Casa de las Américas Award four years later for *Un mundo para todos dividido.* In addition, as Sosa wrote in *Spanish American Authors,* "A primary school in the capital of my homeland, a small school for children located in San Pedro Sula, and a street in my hometown carry my name. Those tributes paid by the Honduran people involve me even more in its suffering and history.

## SELECTED PUBLISHED WORKS:

*Muros* (title means "Walls"), Tegucigalpa, Honduras, 1966.

*Mar interior* (title means "The Sea Inside"), Tegucigalpa, Escuela Superior del Profesorado Francisco Morazán, 1967.

(Editor and author of notes and prologue with Oscar Acosta) *Antología de la nueva poesía hondureña* (poetry anthology), Tegucigalpa, Editorial Ulúa, 1967.

(Editor and author of notes with Acosta) *Antología del cuento Hondureño* (story anthology), prologue by Arturo Quesado, Tegucigalpa, Departamento de Extensión Universitaria, 1968.

*Breve estudio sobre la poesía y su creación* (title means "A Brief Study of Poetry and Its Creation"), Escuela Superior del Profesorado Francisco Morazán, 1969.

*Los pobres* (also see below; poems; title means "The Poor"), Madrid, Ediciones Rialp, 1969; reprinted Tegucigalpa, Editorial Guaymuras, 1983.

*Un mundo para todos dividido* (also see below; poems; title means "A World for All divided"), Havana, Casa de las Américas, 1971.

*Prosa armada*, Editorial Guaymuras, 1981.

*The Difficult Days* (includes poems, in English and the original Spanish, from *Un mundo para todos dividos* and *Los pobres;* also includes interviews with Sosa from *Plural* and *Alcaraván*), translated by Jim Lindsey, Princeton University Press, 1983.

*Poems by Roberto Sosa: Bilingual Edition,* translated and introduced by Edward V. Coughlin, Spanish Literature Publications, 1984.

*Secreto militar* (poems), Editorial Guaymuras, 1985.

*13 poemas* (bilingual edition in Spanish and German), Ediciones Hormiga Roja, 1987.

*Hasta el sol de hoy: Antología poética* (poems), Instituto de Cooperación Iberoamericana, Ediciones Cultura Hispánica, 1987.

## SOURCES:

### Books

*Hispanic Writers,* edited by Bryan Ryan, Detroit, Gale, 1991.

*Spanish American Authors, The Twentieth Century,* by Ángel Flores, New York, H.W. Wilson, 1992.

### Periodicals

*Hispania,* March 1986, pp. 123 - 124.
*Library Journal,* Sept. 15, 1983.

*Publishers Weekly,* August 12, 1983, p. 62.

—*Sketch by Kathe A. Conti*

# Gary Soto
## 1952-
### Mexican American poet, author, and educator

Gary Soto was one of the first Chicano writers to be nominated for the Pulitzer Prize. He has won many awards for his numerous books of poetry, short fiction, and young adult fiction. Soto writes only in English, though he grew up among people who spoke primarily Spanish. Much of his writing depicts the poverty and misery that characterizes the lives of many Mexican Americans. Rooted in his own experience as a migrant laborer, Soto's work recreates the urban and rural communities of Spanish-speaking Americans with concrete imagery that makes it accessible to his readers.

Soto was born to American-born parents of Mexican heritage on April 12, 1952, in Fresno, California. When Soto was five years old, his father was killed in a work-related accident. Soto grew up in the San Joaquin Valley, working with his family and an entire community of Mexican Americans in the fields and factories of many companies, including Sun Maid Raisins.

These early years had a profound effect upon Soto and his writing. In autobiographical notes addressed to Juan Rodriguez in May 1977, Soto explained: "I write because there is pain in my life, our family, and those living in the San Joaquin Valley. My work may appear personal, but perhaps it should remain that way. . . . I write because those I work and live among can't write. I only have to think of the black factory worker I worked with in L.A. or the toothless farm laborer I hoed beside in the fields outside of Fresno. . . . They're everything."

### Finds Poetic Voice

Soto began his studies at Fresno City College after graduating from high school in 1970. He decided to study maps because he "liked seeing the world in print," he said in an unpublished interview in 1988. Soto gave up geography for poetry when he discovered a kinship of social alienation in "Unwanted," a poem by Edward Field. With this poem, Soto found a form of writing that powerfully addressed universal experience.

*Gary Soto*

Soto began studying writing at California State University under the poet Philip Levine. Soto graduated Magna Cum Laude from Cal State in 1974 and married Carolyn Oda on May 24, 1975. By 1977, with a master of fine arts degree in creative writing from the University of California at Irvine, he began teaching at the University of California at Berkeley, where he soon became an associate professor in both the English and Chicano Studies departments.

Even before he finished school, Soto won at least one award per year between 1975 and 1978. In 1975, he won the Academy of American Poets Prize, along with the *Discovery-Nation* Award. He won two major awards again in 1976: the United States Award of the International Poetry Forum, and the University of California at Irvine's Chicano Contest Literary Prize.

But the year 1977 marked his true literary breakthrough. He published his first book of poetry, *The Elements of San Joaquin,* and won *Poetry* magazine's Bess Hokin Prize. His first book was met with many positive reactions by critics. In *Library Journal,* Kathleen Purnell wrote that "Soto's poems are brief, revealing, complete glimpses of his reality." His next book earned him even more positive reviews and recognition. Soto's book *The Tale of Sunlight* was a finalist for the Lenore Marshall Poetry Award in 1978, in addition to being nominated for both the Pulitzer Prize for Literature and the National Book Award. Soto has also won Guggenheim and National Education Association fellowships. In 1985 he won

the American Book Award for *Living Up the Street: Narrative Recollections.*

## Diversity As a Writer

Though Soto has won most of his awards for poetry, he has written fiction for both adults and young adults. Soto recreated his childhood for readers in *Living Up The Street* (1985), *Small Faces* (1986), and *Lesser Evils: Ten Quartets* (1988). In these books, rife with optimism and nostalgia, Soto rendered people and places from his younger years. During the 1990s, he began publishing books specifically aimed at young adults, and as a result he received the American Library Association's "Best Book for Young Adults" award for *Baseball in April and Other Stories.* Soto's portrayal of the Americanization of Chicano teenagers thematically unifies his young adult work.

Though his inspirations have come largely from his Chicano roots, Soto felt that his work should not be placed in a separate category for Chicano writers. Instead, he wanted to be regarded as a writer, and not just as a Chicano writer. Soto managed to transcend his heritage and gain a universal appeal by creating vivid worlds and characters with whom readers could identify. In *Bloomsbury Review,* Alicia Fields noted that "Soto's remembrances are as sharply defined and appealing as bright new coins. His language is spare and simple yet vivid."

Others critics have been equally impressed. For example, Raymund Paredes stated in the *Rocky Mountain Review* that all of Soto's work "establishes his acute sense of ethnicity and, simultaneously, his belief that certain emotions, values, and experiences transcend ethnic boundaries and allegiances." Others have echoed these sentiments, suggesting that Soto portrayed his characters so convincingly, and with such clarity and veracity, that the Chicano condition about which he wrote became the human condition.

## SELECTED PUBLISHED WORKS:

### Poetry

*The Elements of San Joaquin,* University of Pittsburgh Press, 1977.
*The Tale of Sunlight,* University of Pittsburgh Press, 1978.
*Father Is a Pillow Tied to a Broom,* Slow Loris Press, 1980.
*Where Sparrows Work Hard,* University of Pittsburgh, 1981.
*Black Hair,* University of Pittsburgh Press, 1985.
*A Fire in my Hands,* Scholastic, 1990.
*Who Will Know Us?,* Chronicle, 1990.
*Home Course in Religion,* Chronicle, 1991.
*Neighborhood Odes,* Harcourt, 1992.

*New and Selected Poems,* 1995.

## Fiction

*Small Faces,* Arte Publico, 1986.
*The Cat's Meow,* Strawberry Hill Press, 1987.
*Baseball in April and Other Stories,* Harcourt, 1990.
*Taking Sides,* Harcourt, 1991.
*Pacific Crossing,* Harcourt, 1992.
*The Skirt,* Delacorte, 1992.
*Local News,* Harcourt, 1993.
*The Pool Party,* Delacorte, 1993.
*Too Many Tamales,* Putnam, 1993.
*Crazy Weekend,* Scholastic, 1994.
*Jesse,* Harcourt, 1994.
*Boys At Work,* 1995.
*The Mustache,* 1995.
*Chato's Kitchen,* 1995.

## Other

*Living up the Street: Narrative Recollections,* Strawberry Hill Press, 1985.
*Lesser Evils: Ten Quartets,* Arte Publico, 1988.
*A Summer Life,* University Press of New England, 1990.

## SOURCES:

### Books

*Chicano Literature: A Reference Guide,* edited by Julio A. Martinez and Francisco A. Lomeli, Westport, Connecticut, Greenwood Press, 1985.
*Contemporary Authors,* Volume 125, Detroit, Gale Research, 1989.
*Contemporary Literary Criticism,* Volume 32, Detroit, Gale Research, 1985.
*Dictionary of Literary Biography,* Volume 82, edited by Francisco A. Lomeli and Carl R. Shirley, Detroit, Gale Research, 1989.
*Hispanic Literature Criticism,* Volume 2, edited by Jelena Krstovic, Detroit, Gale Research, 1994.
*Hispanic Writers,* edited by Bryan Ryan, Detroit, Gale Research, 1991.
*Identification and Analysis of Chicano Literature,* edited by Francisco Jimenez, Binghmapton, New York, Bilingual/Editorial Bilingue, 1979.
Salidvar, Ramon, *Chicano Narrative,* Madison, University of Wisconsin Press, 1990.
*Twentieth Century Young Adult Writers,* edited by Laura Standley Berger, Detroit, St. James Press, 1994.

### Periodicals

*Bloomsbury Review,* January/February 1987, p. 10.
*Choice,* November 1977, p. 1217.
*Library Journal,* March 1, 1977, p. 612.
*Rocky Mountain Review of Language and Literature,* Volume 41, 1987, pp. 126–128.

—Sketch by Christopher B. Tower

# Marta Sotomayor
## 1939-
### Hispanic American gerontologist and educator

Marta Sotomayor has devoted her life to improving the quality of life for Latinos in the United States, particularly in the area of health care. An educator, author, and advocate of the Latino elderly, Sotomayor is president of the National Hispanic Council on Aging (NHCoA) in Washington, D.C., and first vice president of the National Council of La Raza.

Born in San Diego, California, on December 7, 1939, Sotomayor is one of four daughters of Venancio Sotomayor, a grocer, and Catalina Gonzalez, a schoolteacher. During the Great Depression, the Sotomayors moved to Mexico and did not return to California until the 1940s, at which time Venancio Sotomayor once again assumed ownership of the family's supermarket chain.

In an interview with Sandra Márquez, Sotomayor recalled that her parents placed a very strong emphasis on education. "I don't remember any other option but that I would attend college and do well," she said. Following in one of her older sister's footsteps, she enrolled at the University of California in Berkeley in 1955 to study economics and social welfare. Completing her education meant enduring cultural isolation, however; as Sotomayor told Márquez, she does not remember meeting any other Chicano students during her years at Berkeley or later while she pursued her master's degree in social sciences.

### Awakens to Need for Latino Empowerment

The realization that Latinos lacked political and economic power eventually spurred Sotomayor to action. "I had a sense that something had to give," she explained to Márquez. "Things had to change for us. Ever since then I've been an agent for change."

Sotomayor decided to combat powerlessness with knowledge. In 1970, for example, she went to Colombia as a Fulbright scholar to study that coun-

*Marta Sotomayor*

try's higher education system. And in 1973, she earned a doctorate in social policy and planning from the University of Denver with a dissertation entitled "Status and Tradition: A Study of Chicano Grandparents in an Urban Barrio." It was the first such work to address the issue of the Hispanic elderly.

Prior to becoming president of the National Hispanic Council on Aging in 1986, Sotomayor held a variety of academic positions. She taught in the school of social work and urban planning at San Jose State University in California and in the schools of social work at both California State University in San Diego and Howard University in Washington, D.C. She has also taught community psychiatry at Baylor School of Medicine in Houston and urban planning at Metropolitan State College in Denver. In addition, she is a former assistant dean and associate professor in the graduate school of social work at the University of Houston.

Sotomayor also has a long record of service in public health, including various positions with the Administration for Mental Health, Drug Abuse and Alcohol and the National Institute of Mental Health. In 1979, she was appointed to the U.S. Commission to UNESCO, and from 1984 until 1986 she served with the National Institutes of Health as the senior policy advisor on the secretary's task force on minority health.

In Sotomayor's view, Latino health care concerns have reached a critical point in the United States.

Factors such as poverty, inadequate outreach, language barriers, overcrowding in homes, and cultural insensitivity among health care providers discourage access to health care services and have resulted in what she terms a "prohibitive" system that ignores the needs of a growing segment of the population.

## Assumed Presidency of the National Hispanic Council on Aging

Since the mid-1980s, Sotomayor has tried to address some of those needs as president of the National Hispanic Council on Aging, or NHCoA. Founded in 1980, its stated mission is to eliminate the social, civic, and economic injustices that impact negatively on the quality of life for elderly Hispanics and their families. In an article Sotomayor wrote for *California Sociologist,* she describes NHCoA's philosophy: "The programs of the organization are to be based on self-help.... The long range goal of the organization is to make available to the elderly the necessary resources required to create changes and to enhance their capacity to make the process of self-help, self-sufficiency, and independent living a reality."

NHCoA relies on family support, community involvement, and intergenerational linkages to fashion its programs, which not only pass along information but provide opportunities for leadership development as well. And in keeping with Sotomayor's belief that the current U.S. health care system is too disease- and illness-oriented—a focus she would like to see changed—NHCoA health promotion campaigns all stress the benefits of preventive medicine.

Assisting Sotomayor with these tasks is a full-time staff of four in NHCoA's Washington, D.C., office plus six others who do grass roots work in various communities across the country. They operate with an average annual budget of $800,000.

## Examines Hispanic Health Care Needs

Sotomayor has edited several books that address the topic of health care for Latinos. In *Hispanic Elderly: A Cultural Signature*, for instance, she points out that the role of culture cannot be overlooked when considering the needs of elderly Latinos. The Hispanic population is not a homogeneous one; there are many sub-groups that share a common cultural and linguistic heritage. According to Sotomayor, these unique cultural traits are often ignored or misunderstood by most policy makers and health care providers.

Rapidly changing demographics will necessitate increased attention to the health care needs of Latinos, states Sotomayor in *Empowering Hispanic Families: A Critical Issue for the '90s.* "Because of their tremendous growth rate and the diminishing birth rate of the majority society," she declares, "the well-being of this society depends on the well-being of this one group, for Hispanics will constitute the bulk of the labor force in the next two decades." She goes on to explain that the challenge in helping professionals meet the needs of the Hispanic population is in finding tools that address the relationship between family and society, for the problems of one cannot be viewed separately from the other.

Poverty, a condition that often results from social factors and is later perpetuated by kinship ties, is often the root cause of Latino disenfranchisement, maintains Sotomayor. "At the emotional level, poverty leads to self-blame, which is usually followed by a sense of powerlessness. . . . Powerlessness and the subsequent inability to believe in the possibility of change preclude people's ability to mobilize local helping resources." This point underscores her fundamental belief that one cannot "empower others"; instead, individuals empower themselves in the process of improving their own lives. By linking elderly Latinos with an array of health care services meeting their self-identified needs, Marta Sotomayor is helping Latinos take a very critical step toward personal and communal empowerment.

Sotomayor's brings her commitment to improving the quality of life for all segments of society to her many different personal and community interests. Besides serving as a member and vice chair of the governor's commission on Hispanic affairs for the state of Maryland, she is also on the board of the YWCA of Washington, D.C. In addition, she continues to monitor the status of the mentally ill, explaining to Márquez that "it's an area I follow closely. I feel a lot of us don't want to look at that."

Sotomayor lives in the Washington, D.C., metropolitan area with her husband, Guillermo Chávez, director of the human and political rights division of the United Methodist Church. Her only child, Carlos Schatter, is a trained classical guitar player who now heads his own music center in Corpus Christi, Texas. A member of a family known for its long life spans, Sotomayor says she looks forward to the day when she can slow down her busy pace and relish the many years ahead.

## SELECTED PUBLISHED WORK:

(Editor with Herman Curiel) *Hispanic Elderly: A Cultural Signature,* Pan American University Press, 1988.

(Editor) *Empowering Hispanic Families: A Critical Issue for the '90s,* Family Service America, 1991.

## SOURCES:

### Books

*Empowering Hispanic Families: A Critical Issue for the '90s,* edited by Marta Sotomayor, Family Service America, 1991.

*Hispanic Elderly: A Cultural Signature,* edited by Herman Curiel and Marta Sotomayor, Pan American University Press, 1988.

### Periodicals

*California Sociologist,* winter 1989, pp–89.

### Other

Sotomayor, Marta, interview with Sandra Márquez, September 14, 1992.

—*Sketch by Sandra Márquez*

# Alfonsina Storni
## 1892-1938
### Argentine poet

Alfonsina Storni was acclaimed as one of the foremost women writers of Argentina. She wrote fiction, poetry, and drama, and gradually gained acceptance within her country's male-dominated literary circles. Her major themes included love and feminism, which led some reviewers to criticize her during her lifetime. In the years since her death, however, the continuing critical examination of her work has established her place in literary history. María A. Salgado summed up Storni's influence in an essay for *Spanish American Women Writers:* "There is no doubt that as one of Argentina's early feminists she worked hard to secure sexual equality, and her life and her accomplishments have served as living examples to other women. As a writer, and within Spanish literary canons, she wrote books of great value and originality. Thus, it may be asserted that her life and her works have been fundamental in establishing the foundations of contemporary feminist discourse in Hispanic letters."

Storni was born on May 29, 1892, either at sea en route to Switzerland or in Sala Caprisca, where her parents went to visit family and friends. Her parents, Alfonso and Paulina, lived in San Juan, Argentina, where her father owned a beer factory with his brothers. The family, which also included Storni's older brother and sister, did not leave Switzerland to return to their home in Argentina until Storni was four years old. Upon their return, the business began failing and her father began drinking heavily. When Storni was eight years old, the family moved to Rosario, Argentina, where her mother made money by sewing. Her father then opened a cafe that also failed, and at age 13 Storni began working in a hat factory to help support the family.

### Developed Interest in Theater

In 1907, Storni became interested in the theater and acted in a play with a touring company that came to Rosario. She was 16 when she got a job with Jose Tallavi's touring company. Storni toured with the company for one year, but she grew unhappy living on the road and returned to her home in Rosario, only to find that her mother had moved away with a new husband while she was on tour. Storni decided to go back to school and enrolled at the Normal Academy at Coronda, where she finished her schooling to become a teacher. She sang in a bar on weekends and worked at the school to support herself.

Storni's first teaching job was in an elementary school in Rosario, and her poetry was published for the first time in some of the local newspapers. During this time, Storni fell in love with a married man and got pregnant. She then decided to move to the large city of Buenos Aires, where she was not known. Her son, Alejandro Alfonso, was born in April of 1912, when Storni was not yet 20 years old.

### Continued to Write

Her first short story, "De la vida" ("About Life"), was published in 1912 by the journal *Fray Mocho*. Four years later she completed her first book of poetry, *La inquietud del rosal* (*Uneasiness of the Rosebush*). Although the book was not later considered one of her best, it reflected the major themes she wrote about in many of her works—love and feminist protest.

Many of her feminist writings were published in journals such as *La Nota* (*The Note*), *Nosotros* (*We*), and *La Nacion* (*The Nation*). Storni began teaching again in 1917. From 1918 to 1920 she published three books, *El dulce dano* (*Sweet Sorrow*), *Irremediablemente* (*Irremediably*), and *Languidez* (*Languor*), for which she gained recognition in the literary world. *El dulce dano* was written in two parts and told a love story. However, at the time the book was considered erotic and Storni was criticized for it. Storni expressed her bitterness about male attitudes of that time succinctly in one of her poems, "Tu me quieres blanca" ("You want me pure"). Her book *Languidez* received the Buenos Aires Municipal Prize and was runner-up for the National Prize for Literature. This was a busy and prolific period for Storni: she wrote

essays, short stories, and novels; she joined two literary groups, Nosotros and Anaconda; and in 1921 she began teaching and writing plays for the Teatro Infantil Labarden (Labarden Children's Theater) in Buenos Aires. Storni's next book, *Ochre*, was published in 1925.

Storni's first full-length play opened in 1927 and closed after three days. Her second play was never produced but, undaunted, she continued to write plays. She went to Europe in 1930, and the influence of the writers she met in Spain was evident in her works that followed the trip. She wrote two full-length plays, *Dos farsas pirotecnicas* (*Two Pyrotechnical Farces*), in 1932. Storni returned to Spain in 1934. The last two books she wrote were considered a drastic change in her writing style. *Mundo de siete pozos* (*World of Seven Wells*), published in 1934, seemed obsessed with death, hopelessness, and despair. In the introduction to *Mascarilla y trebol: Circulos imantados*(*Mask and Clover: Magnetic Circles*), published in 1938, Storni explained that she wrote parts of the book when she was "near loss of consciousness."

Soon after writing her last book, Storni became ill with cancer. She had a radical mastectomy in 1935, but by 1938 the cancer had spread throughout her body. Storni wrote her last poem, "Voy a dormir" ("I am going to sleep"), and sent it to *La Nacion*. The poem was published one day after she drowned herself in the Mar del Plata on October 25, 1938. Storni was a dramatic, controversial poet who was chastised for her feminist stances, but even after her death critics have studied her work and published numerous books about her.

## SELECTED PUBLISHED WORKS:

*La inquietud del rosal,* La Facultad, 1916.
*El dulce dano,* Sociedad Cooperativa Editorial Limitada, 1918.
*Irremediablemente,* Sociedad Cooperativa Editorial Limitada, 1919.
*Languidez,* Sociedad Cooperativa Editorial Limitada, 1920.
*Ocre,* Babel, 1925.
*Poemas de amor,* Nosotros, 1926.
*Mundo de siete pozos,* Tor, 1934.
*Mascarilla y trebol: Circulos imantados,* El Ateneo, 1938.

## SOURCES:

*Nine Latin American Poets,* translated by Rachel Benson, New York, Las Americas, 1968.
*Spanish American Women Writers: A Bio-Bibliographical Source Book,* edited by Diane E.

Marting, Westport, Connecticut, Greenwood Press, 1990, pp. 501–512.

—*Sketch by Phyllis Noah*

# Alfredo Stroessner
## 1912-
**Paraguayan dictator**

Stroessner was the dictator and President of Paraguay from 1954 until he was ousted in 1989. His regime was characterized by manipulation, institutionalized corruption, and brutal suppression. Mac Margolis of *The Times* (London) wrote in 1989, "He ruled by a combination of fear and favors which secured his hold over the four pillars of government, the bureaucracy, the police, the army, and the Colorado Party." Stroessner held the reigns of power longer than any other head of state in the non-communist world.

Alfredo Stroessner was born on November 3, 1912, in Encarnación, Paraguay. His father, Hugo, was a German immigrant who established a brewery, while his mother, Heriberta, was from a wealthy Paraguayan family. Stroessner received his early education in Encarnación, but received his secondary education in Rio de Janeiro, Brazil. At the age of sixteen he enlisted as a cadet at the military school in Asunción, where he rapidly ascended the ranks. Before finishing his studies, he was sent to fight in the Chaco War (1932–1935) with Bolivia, in 1932. Stroessner distinguished himself at the Battle of Boquerón, and rose to the rank of section commander. He received a citation for distinguished conduct at the Battle of El Carmen on December 5, 1934. By the end of the war Stroessner was an officer.

Stroessner received artillery training in Brazil and was then posted to the Superior War School. In 1945 he was promoted to the post of Commandant of the "General Bruguez" Artillery Regiment, which proved crucial to his involvement in the 1947 Paraguayan Civil War. Stroessner was one of the few military officers to remain loyal to President Higinio Moríngo during the civil war, although his reasons remain unclear. He played a decisive role in thwarting rebel troops from taking Asunción. However, Stroessner's support for Moríngo soon dissipated. His loyalty fluctuated according to his personal gains and the following years were characterized by Stroessner assisting and deposing a succession of leaders in coups d'état.

After Molas López promoted Stroessner to general, López was deposed by Stroessner who had switched his loyalty to Dr. Federico Chávez and the Colorado Party. In 1951 Chávez appointed Stroessner Commander in Chief of the Armed Forces. With the aid of Epifanio Méndez of the Colorado Party, Stroessner engineered the downfall of Chávez, ousting him in a coup d'état on May 5, 1954. Stroessner assumed the Colorado presidential candidacy and took office on August 15, 1954.

As president, Stroessner secured his position by outlawing and systematically eliminating the opposition and assuming absolute control of the government and the army. Cabinet posts and Colorado Executive posts were only conferred to loyal and trusted associates. Membership in the Colorado Party was a prerequisite to obtaining almost any form of employment in government service, the military, and even in nursing. Freedom of the press was denied. In addition to his repressive powers, Stroessner was able to maintain absolute control for so long because of his organizational skills and dedication to hard work.

Stroessner's was a brutal regime. Carlos Miranda, in *The Stroessner Era: Authoritarian Rule in Paraguay,* related that "He had laws tailored to conduct systematic harassment of the opposition, earning one of the worst human rights violation records in Latin America." Under the Stroessner regime, Paraguay was a notorious asylum for the infamous: **Juan Perón,** Anastasio Somoza, and Nazis, including Josef Mengele.

Stroessner was overthrown in a coup on February 3, 1989, led by General Andres Rodriguez. The coup was precipitated by increasing disaffection and the split of the Colorado Party in 1987. According to Carlos Miranda, "Stroessner was ousted because he could no longer make his political machine work. The duplicitousness, cunning, and repression that marked his reign were no longer enough to keep things going. And, finally, the corruption that had built the fiefdom brought it down."

Stroessner has been described as a private and uncharismatic man. He married Eligia Flora Delgado, a school teacher. They had three children: Gustavo Adolfo, Graciela Concepción, and Hugo Alfredo. Richard Bourne interviewed Stroessner for *Political Leaders in Latin America* and learned that the dictator enjoyed chess, fishing, and flying. Stroessner lives in exile in Brazil under threat of extradition.

## SOURCES:

### Books

*Biographical Dictionary of Latin American and Caribbean Political Leaders,* edited by Robert J. Alexander, Westport, CT, Greenwood Press, Inc., 1988, pp. 423–24.

Bourne, Richard, *Political Leaders of Latin America,* New York, Alfred A. Knopf, 1970, pp. 100–36.

Miranda, Carlos R., *The Stroessner Era: Authoritarian Rule in Paraguay,* Boulder, CO, Westview Press Inc., 1990.

**Periodicals**

*Newsweek,* February 13, 1989, pp. 26–29.

*The Sunday Times* (London), February 5, 1989, p. A14.

*Time,* February 13, 1989, p. 48.

*The Times* (London), February 4, 1989, p. 7; January 25, 1993, p. 15.

—*Sketch by Amanda Beresford*

# Roberto Suárez
## 1928-
**Cuban American newspaper publisher**

Since 1987 Roberto Suárez has been the publisher of *El Nuevo Herald,* the Spanish newspaper published by the *Miami Herald.* Suárez is a distinguished journalism executive who has won numerous awards from organizations such as Knight-Ridder Newspapers, the media consortium that publishes the *Miami Herald* and other dailies, the InterAmerican Businessmen's Association, and the Association of Latin American Advertisers. His achievements and hard work in newspaper publishing have earned him a well deserved position at the top of his profession.

Suárez was born in Havana, Cuba, on May 5, 1928, to Miguel A. Suárez and Esperanza de Cárdenas de Suárez. As a youth he demonstrated both academic and athletic talents. He attended Havana's Colegio de Belén and excelled at track and field, baseball, and basketball. Due to his athletic prowess, Suárez was awarded the first "Capi Campuzano" medal for best athlete his third year in school. Although Suárez would establish his career outside of the sporting world, his tenure at the Colegio had life-long repercussions. Suárez married his coach's daughter, Miriam ("Pitucha") Campuzano. Together, Pitucha and Roberto had seven sons and five daughters.

Suárez earned a bachelor's degree in economics from Pennsylvania's Villanova University in 1949. He returned to Cuba, however, and spent the next decade working in real estate, construction, and finance. he emigrated to the United States in 1961 and settled in Miami, Florida. His first post at the *Miami Herald* was a part-time mailroom position. Eventually he became controller of all the *Herald's* subsidiaries.

In 1972 Suárez left the *Herald* to work for the *Charlotte Observer,* another Knight-Ridder publication. He served as controller there until 1978 when he was promoted to the position of vice-president and general manager. Eight years later, Suárez was named president of the publication. During this time in North Carolina, he devoted considerable time to other organizations. Suárez served as treasurer for the School of Journalism, North Carolina Foundation, and the North Carolina Press Association. He was also the president of the Spirit Square Arts Center (1984–85) and the Arts and Science Council (1985–86) in North Carolina.

In 1987 Suárez returned to Miami, where he was appointed publisher of *El Nuevo Herald.* After just two years in that position, he was awarded the Knight-Ridder Gold Medal of Excellence Award, and the following year he received the Role Model of Journalism Award. Suárez also accepted the Hispanic Alliance Heritage Award for media and entertainment in 1990. He was appointed president of the *Miami Herald* the same year, and served in that capacity until 1994. In Miami, Suárez has continued to work with professional, cultural, and civic organizations, including service as a board member of the Greater Miami Convention and Visitor's Bureau and the United Way. His achievements and contributions have been recognized repeatedly with such awards as the InterAmerican Businessmen's Association 's Businessman of the Year (1993) and the "Mariano Guastella" publicity award from the Association of Latin American Advertisers (1993).

**SOURCES:**

Suárez, Roberto, letter to Conner C. Gorry, December 2, 1994.

—*Sketch by Conner C. Gorry*

# Antonio Jose de Sucre
## 1795-1830
**Venezuelan revolutionary and statesman**

Born in 1795 at the dawn of the independence movement in the western hemisphere, Antonio Jose de Sucre played a large role in the military and political liberation of several South American countries. He led Bolivia as its first president. Sucre achieved extraordinary military success and fought alongside **Simon Bolivar**, called by some the "George Washington of South America." Political enemies conspired to kill him for much of his career, and he died at their hands in 1830.

## A Military Tradition

Vincente de Sucre lived with his wife and six children in Cumana on the northwest coast of Venezuela. As a colonel in the colonial militia, the elder Sucre saw himself as an inheritor of a military tradition within his family. His father had risen to the rank of lieutenant colonel and his grandfather, Antonio Jose de Sucre's great-grandfather, had been the captain-general of the entire province. The Sucres had settled in the *New World* for several generations, but the mark of their aristocratic Spanish forbears remained strong. The ranks of military officers counted few who did not come from nobility. In some ways well-to-do young men expected a military commission as a birthright.

Vincente de Sucre's seventh child, Antonio Jose, joined the army under those circumstances, but by the end of his career, no one could accuse him of not earning his military credentials. The young boy suffered deeply at his mother's death in 1802, only seven years after his birth on February 3, 1795. His father remarried in 1803, and the boy could not abide this new mother figure. Vincente Sucre decided that his son should go and live instead with the boy's uncle, Jose Manner de Sucre. In his biography of Sucre entitled *Admirable Warrior: Marshal Sucre, Fighter for South American Independence,* John Hoover notes that the boy's personality became "introverted and reserved."

Sucre received an education befitting a young aristocrat. His private tutor supplemented the lessons he got in a local mathematics school. When he got old enough, his family sent him to Caracas to attend a military school, which, according to Hoover, was "run by an anti-monarchist Spanish colonel." Sucre spent so much time moving from school to home and back that his travels, Hoover noted, "reinforced a withdrawn and solitary nature."

In 1810, Sucre returned to Cumana. The province had declared independence, and Sucre's hometown had, therefore, become the capital of the Republic of Cumana. Many of the officials of the small new nation happened to be Sucre's relatives, and at the age of 15, Sucre had no trouble receiving a commission as a lieutenant in the armed forces.

With his father as his commander, Sucre saw combat almost immediately, fighting in civil conflicts in nearby Barcelona. He also trained under Francisco Miranda, who had gained some fame as a participant in the first successful revolution in the western hemisphere—the United States' campaign for independence from Britain. Sucre fought with Miranda against Royalists, who probably had the support of the majority. In 1912 an earthquake flattened most of the rebel strongholds and left the Royals town essentially intact. The independence-minded group could not endure long after the strangely selective catastrophe.

## Simon Bolivar and Ideas of Freedom

Sucre went home beaten but still convinced of the righteousness of his cause. Venezuela had gone almost totally into Royalist hands, but by 1813, the struggle had begun again. This time the rebels had more success. Under the leadership of Santiago Marino, the rebels retook Cumana, Maturin, and Barcelona. Sucre became the chief of staff of one of the army's divisions.

Simon Bolivar added his weight and prestige to the conflict by entering Venezuela from the west. Bolivar charged that the Royalists had violated the human rights of civilians during their reign, killing even non-combatants in the towns they captured and executing every prisoner of war. As Sucre and Marino capleting her education meantme from the east they met Bolivar in triumph. A triumph for his political cause, this most recent fighting also established Sucre's reputation as an excellent soldier. He even drew praise from Bolivar.

The victory could not hold. Under General Boves the Royalists regrouped, and on June 16 the king's men destroyed most of the rebel forces. Many of those who did not die in battle faced execution. Sucre's own brother and many other relatives perished as well. Spanish reinforcements from the sea ended all hope of a rebel comeback, and Sucre took to the mountains to save his own life. He eventually fled all the way to Haiti.

## Anarchy and Rivalries

Though public opinion had begun to turn in favor of independence, the leaders of that movement persistently damaged their own cause by failing to achieve solidarity. The rivalry between Bolivar and Marino infuriated Sucre, but in time Sucre developed his own strong dislike of Marino. The various leaders often employed tactics which would place them ahead of the others, at the expense of the whole cause. In the end Sucre sided with Bolivar and went with his brothers to serve the General.

Struggling to recruit willing soldiers, much less competent ones, and to bring crucial supplies to his camps, Sucre managed to contribute to the modest rebel gains in Guayana and Margarita. By 1818 the rebels had established control over these areas in a struggle that had no apparent end. In 1819 Bolivar established the Republic of Colombia, which consisted of Venezuela and, somewhat wishfully, New Granada (now Colombia), which still lay under royalist control.

Bolivar's struggle to liberate New Granada went well. Sucre's role in it substantial, earning him promotion to Brigadier General. Sucre had such respect for Bolivar, however, that a story emerged from the first meeting of the two men after Sucre's battlefield promotion. Hoover recounts that "when his boat neared Bolivar's, the Liberator [Bolivar] shouted a query as to his identity. The reply, 'General Sucre!' brought Bolivar's rejoinder that there was no such general. Sucre then explained that, though he had been promoted for merit, he wouldn't keep the rank unless Bolivar approved."

### Conflict and Government

Sucre became the Minister of War and Navy for the Colombian government. Then he moved up to Chief of the General Staff. Sucre's skill at negotiating gained the diplomatic recognition of some countries and a cessation of hostilities with several local foes. Sucre again turned to the sword, however, when Bolivar asked him to lead the campaign on Quito.

Sucre had his first opportunity to prove himself as a general capable of success on his own. He traveled to Guayanquil in present-day Ecuador and worked with the junta that had overthrown the Royalist forces but could not govern. He tried to convince them to join the Colombian republic. This would let him pay more attention to the conquest of Quito, which for logistical reasons became quite difficult. Various forces rose up to try and claim Guayanquil, and defending his own territory thwarted Sucre's ambitions for new ones. During this time he had an amorous affair with a local woman, who gave birth to his daughter. Sucre supported the woman and her baby, but would not marry her.

In late spring of 1821, Sucre finally occupied Quito. His victory demonstrated remarkable technical virtuosity as a general. He had used the Andes, traditionally thought to be a natural barrier, as a way to cause uncertainty in his enemies' minds as to where he would attack. Quito joined the Colombian Republic. Bolivar made Sucre a Major General, and the people of Cumana elected him to the senate.

### Governing Hero

Sucre at first resisted the role of Governor of Quito. He felt underqualified. He eventually accepted it, however, and tried to establish democratic institutions there. The struggle for independence in Peru began to emerge as a more precarious matter, however, and Sucre could not resist the struggle. Loss of

Peru to Royalist forces would leave Colombia vulnerable to recapture.

The battle to determine the fate of independence came in December, 1824. In an engagement totalling more than 15,000 men, Sucre crushed the Royalists, but spared the defeated. Bolivar could not have praised Sucre more lavishly: "He is the redeemer of the Children of the Sun [the Incas]; he has broken the chains with which Pizarro bound the empire of the Incas." Bolivar backed up his praise with a promotion to Grand Marshall.

Sucre's victory inspired great emotions around the world. In the United States, several towns changed their name to "Bolivar". In the conservative monarchies of Europe, many shuddered for the future. Bolivar had conceptualized a United States of South America, and Sucre began to believe that Bolivar wanted him to be a major political figure in it. According to Hoover, Sucre "cautioned his chief [Bolivar] against dragging him into a career he loathed." "He didn't know how to govern people," Hoover writes, "and he didn't want to learn."

He became the governor of the territory of Bolivia despite his wishes, and at age 30 began to try to establish a democracy where none had ever been. This tried him, and he began to complain frequently of sickness. In fact, he longed to leave Bolivia. Yet he managed to establish elections, secular education and a free press among his other democratic reforms. Elected Bolivia's first president, Sucre's success at democratizing the country had ensured that he would remain where he did not want to be.

Sucre lost touch with events in Bolivia, and his popularity began to wane. A failed rebellion depressed him even more. He became desperate to return to Quito, where, in 1928, he married his longtime sweetheart Mariana. Though he tried to convince all parties that he wanted to retire from public life, Sucre still found himself the target of a failed asssassination attempt.

From there things went badly for Sucre. Colombia itself began to show signs of weakness. His wife gave birth to a daughter, but his wife became sick. His financial situation had deteriorated as well. When Bolivar's defeat became total, and Colombia moved inevitably toward its end, Sucre became the target of assassins. On June 4, 1830, Sucre died of musket fire. Historians remain unconvinced of the person behind the plot, but an undistinguished army Colonel Apolinar Morillo was convicted of it in 1942.

**SOURCES:**

*Admirable Warrior: Marshal Sucre, Fighter for South American Independence,* John Hoover, Blaine-Ethridge Books, 1977.

*—Sketch by James McCarthy*

# T

## Paco Ignacio Taibo II
### 1949-
### Hispanic American novelist

Paco Ignacio Taibo II was born in Spain and emigrated to Mexico at age nine. His detective stories have earned him wide recognition in Mexico and the Spanish-speaking world although he has also written widely as an academic and an historical essayist. Many critics have said that Taibo's heroes have an erudition and self-awareness which makes them deeper and more substantial than the detectives which routinely appear in the genre. Besides his success as a novelist he has also taught periodically through his career at several Mexican universities.

Born on January 11, 1949, in Gijon, Spain, Taibo grew up in a literary household. His father, Paco Ignacio Taibo I, developed a substantial reputation in Spain as a novelist and biographer. In a foreword written for one of his father's books, the younger Taibo describes early memories of his father at work and the awe with which his father's profession filled him. He recalls hearing the sound of his father at the typewriter and feeling that "what he is doing is the most important thing anyone can do with his life: he is writing a novel."

When young Taibo was nine his family moved to Mexico; although he didn't become a naturalized citizen of Mexico until 1980, he became a Mexican author rather than a Spanish one in the eyes of critics and readers. His incorporation of Mexican history as a part of even his detective novels shows his personal involvement with Mexico as a nation grappling with its history. During the 1960s Taibo joined the Movement of 1968, while half-heartedly pursuing a college education. Student activism held more interest for him, and as the Movement ended in a bloodbath at the hands of government soldiers Taibo moved toward his true profession as a writer.

Although *Heroes convocados,* a novel in which Mexican peasants storm the National Palace, did not appear until 1982, the events of 1968 are unmistakably reflected in his writing. In the spirit of a student revolutionary, Taibo's own ideas about writing demand action and passion from the author and emotion from the reader. In common with his father, Taibo feels "blind passion, raging and amorous, for the written word." He sees the role of the good writer

*Paco Ignacio Taibo II*

as akin to an "artisan devoted to breaking down solitude." Not only must the author be a "mason of words" who "tells what others are not able to tell," but Taibo's author would be one who "[fights] with toothpicks against the systematic abuse of power."

Taibo began his freelance career as a journalist in 1969. He edited a few publications, including *Revista de la Semana, Bronca,* and *Enigma.* During the 1970s he began writing detective novels and the first to be published, *Dias de combate,* appeared in 1976 to some critical success. His first novel was adapted for the screen in the Alfredo Gurrola movie of the same name in 1982. The following year he published *Cosa facil,* which William Neuman translated into English in 1990 as *An Easy Thing.* In 1981 he published *No habra final feliz.*

In addition to his writing, Taibo taught for a time at the Escuela Nacional de Antropologia y Historia and the Universidad Nacional Autónoma de Mexico in Mexico City before taking a professorship at the Universidad Autónoma at Azcapotzalco from 1984 to 1989. He has won several awards, including the 1982 Premio Crijalbo Novela and the Premio Francisco Javier Clavijero for the best book of history in 1987 for *Los Bolsheviks.* He received the Premio Hammett for best crime fiction novel in Spanish in 1987 for *La vida misma*, and two years later claimed the Premio Novela Latinoamerica.

Taibo is a member of both PEN and the Mystery Writers of America, and has served as president of the International Association of Crime Writers. He has occasionally worked with comic books, and several of his books have been made into television and movie productions. Translations of his novels into English have garnered him an appreciative audience, and he has spoken in many countries on labor issues.

**SELECTED PUBLISHED WORKS:**

*Dias de combate,* 1976.
*Cosa facil,* 1977, translated by William Neuman as *An Easy Thing,* 1990.
*No habra final feliz,* 1981.
*Heroes convocados,* 1982.
*Los Bolsheviks,* 1987.
*La vida misma,* 1987.

**SOURCES:**

*Hispanic Writers,* edited by Bryan Ryan, Detroit Gale, 1991.
*Spanish American Authors,* edited by Angel Flores, New York, H. W. Wilson, 1992.

—*Sketch by Jim McCarthy*

# Rufino Tamayo
## 1899-1991
**Mexican artist**

Painter and printmaker Rufino Tamayo combined the mythic art of pre-Columbian Mexico with a personal aesthetic to produce pictures, as *Art News* critic Henry McBride wrote, "both Mayan and modern at the same time." Although deeply rooted in Indian tradition Tamayo's semi-abstract paintings address universal themes. "[Art is] a way of expression that has to be understood by everybody everywhere," he once commented in *Arts Magazine.* "It grows out of the earth, the texture of our lives and experiences." His bold and vivid palette owed much to the influence of indigenous Mexican folk art, but the humanist themes in his work and the plastic

*Rufino Tamayo*

problems he explored opened his vision to an international public.

A spokesman for individual artistic freedom, Tamayo felt constricted by the demands of the Mexican Revolution. Tamayo's closeness to the ancient Indian art of Mexico distinguished his work from that of important revolutionary muralists **Diego Rivera, David Alfaro Siqueiros,** and **José Clemente Orozco.** While describing himself as "totally sympathetic to the revolution," Tamayo rejected the claim that Mexican art must itself advance the revolutionary struggle. Rather, he wanted his art to express not the "surface nationalism" of the muralist movement, but "something beyond." Influenced by the School of Paris, Tamayo was committed to easel painting, considering it "a laboratory, a field of experimentation without limitations." McBride described Tamayo's human forms as "posed against the mystical and portentous skies" and the "masklike faces and statuesque figures" of his paintings.

A Zapotec Indian, Tamayo was born on August 26, 1899, in Oaxaca, Mexico, to Florentina and Manuello Arellanes Tamayo. His father was a businessman. In 1911, after the death of his parents, Tamayo went to live in Mexico City where he worked in his aunt's fruit business and studied commerce. Determined to become an artist, Tamayo secretly began art studies at night. From 1917 he took art classes at the San Carlos Art Academy in Mexico City; by 1921, having grown tired of the strict academic instruction, he began to paint on his own.

## Discovered Pre-Columbian Sources

A crucial moment in Tamayo's career was his 1921 appointment as head of the drawing section of the Ethnographic Department in Mexico City's National Museum of Archaeology. This position enabled him to draw and study pre-Columbian art objects, and from this point Indian art became an important and lasting influence on his own work. As he noted in an interview with *Art News*'s Geri Trotter, he was fascinated by these "fragments of ancient Indian sculpture with their diversified distortions of human proportion," and he frequently drew sketches of them.

Finding no galleries in Mexico City, Tamayo organized his first one-man show in 1926. That same year he made his first trip to New York City—a successful journey that resulted in a one-man show at the small but prestigious Weyhe Gallery. Sickness obliged Tamayo to return to Mexico City in 1928, and he taught at the National School of Fine Arts. However, uncomfortable with both the conservative and the Communist artistic camps, Tamayo yearned to return to New York's artistic milieu, which he did in 1931 for a one-man exhibition at the John Levy Galleries. In 1932 he was appointed head of Department of Plastic Arts in the Secretariat of Education, Mexico City, and the following year he finished his first mural commission, "Music," for the National Conservatory of Music. While working on this mural Tamayo met a student at the conservatory, Olga Flores Rivas. Like Tamayo, she was a native of Oaxaca; the two fell in love and were married in 1934. Two years later Tamayo was appointed one of the Mexican delegates—along with Orozco and Siqueiros—to the Congress of Artists in New York. Following this visit Tamayo decided to leave Mexico for a protracted period and test his work fully in the international art arena.

## Artistic Maturity

In 1938 Tamayo began teaching art at the Dalton School in Manhattan, a connection he was to maintain for nine years, spending the winters in New York and the summers in Mexico City while taking part in exhibitions at the Museum of Modern Art (1940) and exhibiting at the Valentine Gallery. In New York Tamayo saw **Pablo Picasso**'s "Guernica," which changed his artistic course by exerting a direct influence on his style and subject matter. As Tamayo's reputation grew he received commissions to paint murals, a form he was to explore for many years to come. But these works still resisted the rhetoric of the Mexican mural movement, avoiding the political stridency of Orozco and Siqueiros.

In 1946 a brief *Art News* review of Tamayo's Valentine Gallery show described the artist as "at the height of his powers" with such paintings as "The Troubadour" and "Women of Mexico." Tamayo's reputation was enhanced the following year when the National Institute of Fine Arts in Mexico City honored him with his first major retrospective, marking his 25 years as a painter. With success came more travel, and Tamayo's international status blossomed; his showing at the 1950 Venice Biennale was hailed as his "Venetian triumph." At the same time Tamayo continued to find his artistic inspiration in Mexico; he sought, he told *Art News*'s Geri Trotta, to "take elements from the country's great plastic past, to resort to Mexican shapes and colors and to fuse them in a contemporary and international way." Tamayo's murals illustrate this fusion of the national and the international. He executed the important commissions "Birth of Nationality" and "Modern Mexico" for the Palace of Fine Arts in Mexico City. These domestic successes brought Tamayo's work further international attention, resulting in the 1957 mural "Prometheus Bringing Fire to Man" at the UNESCO building in Paris. Another United Nations mural, "Brotherhood," was installed at the General Assembly Building in New York in 1968.

## Paris and the World

By the time Tamayo moved to Paris in 1957 his stature as an important international artist was secure; hardly a year passed without a new international honor. Tamayo was made a Companion, Officer, and finally a Commander of the French *Legion d'honneur*, and he received similar honors from Italy and the United States. At home, the President of Mexico presented him with the *Premio Nacional* in 1964, and in 1972 he was awarded the Juárez Medal by the government of Oaxaca. In addition, there were major exhibitions of Tamayo's work. In 1968 a major retrospective at the Palace of Fine Arts in Mexico City—featuring 103 oils and lithographs—honored Tamayo's 50th year as a painter. In the same year he was an honored guest, with a one-man exhibition, at Venice Biennale. In the 1970s such exhibitions became frequent, and the international scope of Tamayo's *oeuvre* was most fully realized. An important exhibition at the City of Paris Museum of Modern Art, featuring 100 oil paintings from the '60s and '70s, was matched by retrospective exhibitions at the Phillips Collection in Washington, D.C. and at New York's Guggenheim Museum. Tamayo repaid the honors with two especially generous personal gifts: In 1974 he donated to the people of Oaxaca 1,300 pieces of art and a museum to house them, the Museum of Pre-Hispanic Art; and in 1981 he donated a small number of his own works and his large collection of paintings, sculpture and drawings by such modern masters as Picasso, **Joán Miró,** Jean Dubuffet, Max Ernst, Fernand Léger, and **Salvador Dali** to the Rufino Tamayo International Museum of Contemporary Art in Mexico City. The greatest retrospective and celebration of Tamayo's life and work occurred in 1987, involving two Mexico City museums, the Museum of the Palace of Fine Arts and the Tamayo Museum.

Frequent public engagements did not interfere with Tamayo's work. Into the 1980s he continued to explore plastic problems and new print media, working extensively in sculpture and lithography. Increasingly aware of the perils of blind technological advancement, he had become, as he revealed to biographer Emily Genauer, "haunted by the fear that technology will reduce men and women to robots and calculating machines if it even lets them live at all." The cosmological view that had enabled Tamayo to see the importance of pre-Columbian art for a modern artist began to seem especially prescient in the age of manned space exploration. Tamayo died in Mexico City on June 24, 1991.

## SOURCES:

### Books

Corredor-Matheos, José, *Tamayo,* New York, Rizzoli, 1987.

Genauer, Emily, *Tamayo,* New York, Abrams, 1975.

Paz, Octavio, and Jacques Lassaigne, *Rufino Tamayo,* New York, Rizzoli, 1982.

*Rufino Tamayo: Myth and Magic,* New York, Solomon R. Guggenheim Foundation, 1979.

### Periodicals

*Architectural Digest,* September 1987, pp. 56–58.

*Art News,* January 1–14, 1946, p. 18; October 1951, pp. 28–30, 67; December 1951, p. 54; February 1987, pp. 27–28.

*Arts Magazine,* December 1971-January 1972, p. 68; December 1977, p. 134.

*New York Times,* June 25, 1991, p. D25.

—*Sketch by Simon Dixon*

# Luis Tapia
## 1950-

### Hispanic American sculptor

New Mexican artist Luis Tapia has won national acclaim as one of the leading sculptors of the late twentieth century. One of the best known modern artists of the American Southwest, he is known as a contemporary *santero,* combining the traditional and the non-traditional to create images of the saints of Hispanic religious culture.

Luis Eligio Tapia was born on July 6, 1950 in Santa Fe, New Mexico. He lived and went to school in Santa Fe, graduating from St. Michael's High School in 1958. Though he attended New Mexico State University at Las Cruces from 1958–59, he did not finish. In 1969 Tapia married Star Rodríguez; also an artist, Rodríguez took Tapia as her last name.

That same year, Tapia found work as a stock-boy at Cooper's Western Wear in Santa Fe. By the time he left in 1974, he had been promoted to store manager. With five years experience in retail, Tapia developed his own business, restoring old southwestern furniture and selling santos (saints, usually as statues). Fortunately, he managed to earn enough from his restoration work—which by then included work for museums—to support himself and a growing family. Tapia and his wife had two children—a son and a daughter; they divorced in 1980.

### Discovers his Medium with Saints

Tapia began studying *santos* in museums, out of a curiosity about his heritage. "In the late 1960s," he explained to Chuck and Jan Rosenak in their *Encyclopedia of Folk Art,* "the Brown Berets started shouting 'Viva La Raza' and I realized that I knew very little about my Hispanic origins. I started listening to music and looking at old *santos* in museums and churches." At the same time, Tapia began to explore his own artistic means of expression to address the issues of his time: the plight of Chicano farm workers in the '60s and the contentious land reform movement in the New Mexican villages near his home.

Tapia has become well-known as a contemporary *santero,* a sculptor of traditional Hispanic saints. Of his own work, Tapia told the Rosenaks: "I think that what I am doing is very traditional—in line with what my ancestors did 200 years ago. It is religious; it is made of wood; and it is covered with gesso and paint." He began making his own *santos* in 1971. "At first," he said, "I gave them away to older people. And then more and more people came to my house, so I started selling."

### Breaks with Tradition

Tapia first exhibited his work in the early '70s at the Spanish Market held each July in Santa Fe. But eventually he stopped showing there. The Spanish Colonial Arts Society insisted that he copy the designs of old *santos* in order to exhibit his work. Tapia, who wanted to "advance the tradition," declined and quit showing at the Spanish Market. At this stage, the artist began to work with both traditional and non-traditional representations of saints. Saint Veronica, one of his nontraditional subjects, is rarely found in New Mexico churches. Sometimes to alter the form, he places his figures in unusual groupings, such as "Christ Calming the Sea," a painted wood carving from 1988 in which Tapia reinterprets a traditional, biblical story. In this way, he modernized his vision and style. At times, his work appeared very angular or even cubist. Tapia often used the figure of *La Muerte* ("death") and his "death carts" in his sculptures; both are examples of the sculptor's efforts to modernize the form. In fact, Tapia's penitent image of death, Doña Sebastiana, in her *carreto de muerto* (death cart) has proved to be very popular. Tapia's work is more horrific than most Hispanic death carts—his part-skeleton, part-human figures have impressed many art critics and patrons. "People forget Doña Sebastiana is a woman," Tapia told Stephen Lewis in *American Craft.*

But not all of his work has been religious. Tapia has created non-religious images of guitar players, nudes, and abstracts as well. Carving his work almost exclusively from different kinds of wood, Tapia paints his hundreds of sculptures with acrylics and watercolors. Most sculptures range in size from eight inches to seven feet in height. He has carved *retablos* (depictions of saints on slabs of pine wood) and *reredos* (altar screens) for church altars that have been as large as 20 by 40 feet.

Tapia has won recognition for his work. In 1980 he received a National Endowment for the Arts grant to fund his work, and Santa Fe's Museum of International Folk Art has exhibited his sculpture many times. The Smithsonian Institution, the National Museum of American Art, and the Los Angeles Craft and Folk Art Museum each have included Tapia's work as part of their permanent collections.

### Joined Brotherhood of Artists

During the 1970s, in an effort to combat prejudices against work by minorities, particularly Hispanics, Tapia joined with other southwestern artists in a *cofradia* or brotherhood. Through this alliance, the artists aggressively fought to have their work recognized and organized their own exhibits. Though the group eventually dissolved, it achieved a strong impact on the Santa Fe arts community and also raised awareness throughout the nation, giving greater validity to themselves and their people as artists.

## SOURCES:

### Books

*Folk Arts Biographical Index,* edited by George H. Meyer, Detroit, Gale, 1987.

*Hispanic-American Almanac,* edited by Nicolás Kanellos, Detroit, Gale, 1993.

Rosenak, Chuck, and Jan Rosenak, *Museum of American Folk Art Encyclopedia of 20th-Century American Folk Art and Artists*, New York, Abbevill Press, 1990.

### Periodicals

*American Craft,* February/March 1991, pp. 38–47.

—*Sketch by Christopher B. Tower*

# Antoni Tàpies
## 1923-
### Spanish artist

Born Antoni Tàpies Puig on December 13, 1923, Tàpies has been hailed as Spain's "greatest living painter." The son of a lawyer who served in the Republican provincial government during the 1930s, Tàpies was profoundly affected by the rise of **Francisco Franco.** Under Franco's dictatorship, Tàpies told *ARTnews*'s Robin Cembalest, "My father was interrogated. My family and our friends were terrorized."

Although his father had hoped that Tàpies would follow in his own professional footsteps—he did attend law school for a time—Tàpies recognized early his passion for art. After suffering a heart attack and being diagnosed with tuberculosis, Tàpies spent much of 1942 and 1943 convalescing. During that time he began to draw, to listen to the music of Richard Wagner and to read philosophical books.

In 1946 Tàpies quit law school to devote himself to art. He and a group of friends began publishing an avant-garde magazine called *Dau al Set,* a title referring to the quest to achieve the impossible. Tàpies held his first exhibition along with several other artists in Barcelona in 1948. Religious leaders forced the show to close because of Tàpies's controversial painting, "Collage of the Crosses." The painting stirred Christian ire because of Tàpies's use of black crosses alongside white paper patches that resembled toilet paper. To protest Francisco Franco's repression of Barcelona's native Catalan language, the artists titled their show "Saló d'Octubre," a Catalan phrase. It was an early example of the passion and conviction that has characterized Tàpies's career. "From the time I was very young, I felt like a missionary," he told Cembalest. By engaging in art "I was convincing myself that with artistic expression I would liberate myself from my problems and could

*Antoni Tàpies*

also help to liberate people who were oppressed by the political situation."

During the early 1950s—Tàpies's "Magic Period"—the artist created heavenly scenes such as The Legerdemain of Wotan (1950) and "The Sorrow of Brunhilda" (1950). The works were named by his friend and collaborator, poet Joan Brossa. During this time, Tàpies also held his first one-man show. In 1951 a scholarship from the French Institute in Barcelona enabled Tàpies to study in Paris. Once ensconced in the French capital, Tàpies visited the Spanish painter **Pablo Picasso.** Picasso told him that a picture is a weapon of attack and a defense against enemies, perhaps the inspiration for "Homage to Picasso" (1983) which consists of broken furniture enclosed in a glass cube.

Tàpies vaulted to international prominence when he and the sculptor Eduardo Chillida represented Spain at the Venice Biennale in 1956. Around this time, Tàpies began to experiment with informalism, a style utilizing impasto mixed with discarded materials such as rags, sand, chalk dust, mirrors, cardboard, and cast iron. In his paintings "Swirling Sand" (1955) and "Two Blankets Filled with Straw" (1968), Tàpies used cloth, sand, straw, and paint. Many of his paintings contain graffiti-type scribbles, and his canvasses are often attacked with gouges and scratches. His dimensional creations have stirred considerable controversy within the art world.

A largely self-taught artist, Tàpies's work defies conventional classifications, although it displays some similarities to art povera, Surrealism,and Abstract Expressionism. Tàpies was strongly influenced by both Picasso and **Joán Miró,** and in due course was commissioned to design medals to commemorate the centennial celebrations of their birthdays.

After Franco's death in 1975, Spain evolved into a democracy. Catalan language and culture were revived. In 1990 Tàpies was commissioned by the Generalitat (the Catalan parliament) to paint a mural in one of the parliament halls. Also in 1990, the Tàpies Foundation opened in Barcelona. Tàpies donated 2,000 of his works to the foundation, including sculptures, paintings, assemblages, and prints. Other artists represented at the foundation include Louise Bourgeois, Brassaï, and **Diego Rivera.** In 1992 the new National Museum of Catalan Art in Barcelona commissioned Tàpies to create a sculpture. His design of a 60-foot white sock—with a hole in it—again provoked heated comments.

Tàpies married his wife, Teresa, in 1954. They are the parents of three children: Antoni, Miguel, and Clara. In his personal life, Tàpies has surrounded himself with books and art. Included in his art collection are paintings by Miró, Picasso, seventeenth century painter Francisco de Zurbarán, and the Western artists Wassily Kandinsky, **Wifredo Lam,** and Mark Tobey. Medieval and contemporary Catalan books and works on Asian philosophy are part of his book collection. Tàpies maintains a studio both in his Barcelona home and at his country house in Campins.

Asked in a 1994 *Unesco Courier* interview to describe himself, Tàpies responded that he was an "anxious" person, someone who has "the desire, or rather the intense need, to do something useful for society, and that is what stimulates me." Tàpies concluded in the same interview, "I am interested in study, reflection, philosophy—but always as a dilettante. I also consider myself a dilettante as a painter."

**SOURCES:**

*Architectural Digest,* January, 1992, pp. 128–31.
*ARTnews,* Summer, 1990, pp. 143–47.
*Town and Country,* July, 1992, pp. 94–5.
*Unesco Courier,* June, 1994, pp. 4–6.

—*Sketch by Phyllis Noah*

# Grace Martinez Tatum
## 1960-
### Hispanic American engineer

When the United States began its air war against Iraq in 1991, engineer Grace Martinez Tatum saw the fruits of her labor. As a supervisor in the Naval Air Warfare Center in Point Magu, California, she oversees a staff of 45 engineers and technicians that test many of the U.S. Navy and Air Force missiles. "Our primary concern was the safe carry and safe launch of a missile—safe in terms of protecting the pilot and the ground troops," Tatum explained in an interview with Anna Macias Aguayo. "We don't frame what we do in the context of whether we're destroying anything. We are asked to keep that perspective."

Born November 11, 1960, Tatum began her engineering training around her family's dinner table in San Antonio, Texas, where her father Jose C. Martinez, an engineering technician for the government, would explain the intricacies of a salt shaker. Tatum's mother, Alice Martinez, would never miss an opportunity to preach about going to college. "If we were in the car, waiting at a red light, and saw a construction crew, my mother would point out the sweaty, dirty guy with the jack hammer and the man in the business suit with a clip board," recalled Tatum in her interview. "She would ask us: 'Which one of those do you think has a college degree?'" Thus, Tatum's aspiration for an education in a subject she found fascinating was instilled.

### Becomes an Engineer

"I think we were brainwashed into going into engineering," continued Tatum in her interview with Aguayo. "My brothers also went into that. There wasn't a lot of thought that went into it. It was just assumed that I would do it too." After finishing her primary studies in Catholic schools, Tatum earned two academic scholarships that helped her obtain an engineering degree from Trinity University in San Antonio. She immediately went to work in what was formerly called the Pacific Missile Testing Center in Point Magu. She began as a journeyman engineer in 1983, but rose quickly through the ranks. "I went from handling individual projects to managing the entire branch," Tatum remarked in her interview. Later, she became head of a division, and Tatum and her employees were charged with redesigning and updating some of the missiles used by American forces during the Persian Gulf War, specifically the Mavericks and Sidewinders.

Tatum has earned commendations for her work almost annually. She attributes her career success to her attitude. She said she has never considered her status as a woman or a Hispanic to be a limitation. "I've only stayed in positions that I've felt good about, where I have had managers that have believed in me." Tatum tries never to let her life as a wife or mother interfere with work. "I have seen another woman trying to come up in the ranks, but she was having trouble with how people perceived her," related Tatum in her Aguayo interview. "She would say she couldn't attend a late meeting because she needed to be with her children. I've seen other women who abuse their leave, saying, 'Oh, my stomach hurts.' I don't make excuses." Tatum likes to project the image of a dedicated, serious-minded professional. When she speaks to youths about how she rose to the level of a general manager earning $60,000 a year, Tatum confidently tells them that they need to make a career plan and stick to it.

### SOURCES:

Tatum, Grace interview with Anna Macias Aguayo, October 6, 1992.

—*Sketch by Anna Macias Aguayo*

# Saint Teresa de Avila
## 1515-1582
### Spanish Carmelite nun and mystic

Teresa de Avila was founder of the Reformed Discalced (shoeless) Carmelite Convent of San Jose and she was known as a mystic. She was canonized in 1622 by Pope Gregory XV. Teresa de Alhumadawas born in Gotarrendura, Spain, March 28, 1515, on a farm near Avila. Her father was Alonso (Pina) de Cepeda, son of a wealthy Jewish businessman and her mother was Beatriz de Ahumada, a farmer's daughter. According to tradition, Teresa could choose either her mother's surname or her father's and she chose her mother's. She had nine brothers, one sister, one half-brother and one half-sister.

Honor was of utmost importance to the Castilian way of life. To maintain honor in the community, there were two very rigid codes of acceptance. One was the virtuosity of each woman, maintaining her virginity before marriage and maintaining her fidelity to her husband. The other important code of acceptance was lineage. To be accepted by the Castilian standards, a person could not be a descendant of Jews or other non-Christian societies. It was not always that way for the Jewish people in Spain. During the reign of St. Ferdinand(1217–1252), King of Castile, the Jews prospered. Castile was the only nation in Europe during the Middle Ages that accepted Jews. In 1480, the Spanish Inquisition, an anti-Semitic movement was founded by Torquemada. Jews were banned, tortured, imprisoned or killed. All male Jewish _conversos_ (New Christians) were fair game during the Inquisition. With money, titles of _Hidalgo_ could be bought and lineages could be changed. Many went to the Indies where titles were easily purchased.

Teresa's grandfather, Juan Sanchez, was a wealthy cloth trader in Toledo and a Jewish convert to the Christian church. Many of the converts practiced some of the Jewish traditions in secret. When the Inquisitors arrived in Toledo, they promised an Edict of Grace with leniency to any who came forward and confessed their sins. Sanchez and his sons went before the Inquisitors. Alonso, Teresa's father, was only ten years old and his brother was 12. His oldest brother, 14, fled to another city and changed his name. Boys over ten years old were considered old enough to make public confessions. Their mother, who had died, was from an impressive lineage, including Simon de Fonseca Pina, an international financier, and Archbishop Alonso de Fonseca, who was editor and chief translator of the Polyglot Bible. When they appeared before the Inquisitor, Juan Sanchez and his sons were sentenced to parade down the streets of Toledo. They were stripped half naked wearing a _sambenito,_ a robe painted with flames, devils, and black crosses, usually worn by those condemned to the stake. They carried green unlit candles as a symbol that the "light of salvation" was out in their souls. This procession took place every Friday for seven weeks. The Christian citizens were obligated to show their faith by throwing stones and spitting at the people in the procession.

After his "period of grace" ended, Sanchez took his new wife, Ines Lopez, and moved to Ciudad Real where he changed his name to Juan de Cepeda. He left his sons with a sister. He still maintained some of his wealth and prospered as a shopkeeper selling luxury fabrics. In 1492, Torquenada expelled the Jews from Spain and the country fell into financial turmoil. The Jews were the financiers and businessmen that kept Spain economically sound. The Spanish government ruled by Catholic monarchs, Queen Isabella and King Ferdinand, instituted a new tax structure. Sanchez saw a way to secure status and financial security for his family in the future by securing a knighthood. Knights were the tax-gathers for the church and state and the position had to be purchased. Sanchez had many friends in Avila and they made certain that a knighthood position became

available for him. He purchased a shop in Avila and sent a cousin to run it and his son, Alonso, to work for him. Alonso took the name of Pina. Six years later, in 1500, he became Don Juan de Cepeda and his second wife became Dona Ines. The family reunited and settled in Avila.

Teresa's father, Alonso, married Catalina del Peso who died of the plague after bearing two children, Maria and Juan. Teresa always considered them her brother and sister. Alonso's father, Juan, also died. After his father died, Alonso took over the tax-gathering business and became Don Alonso de Cepeda. Neither Teresa nor her mother ever knew him as Alonso Pina. He met Teresa's mother, Beatriz de Ahumada, when she was only 13 years old. She was described as "very beautiful." Beatriz became pregnant and Alonso declared their betrothal. He was 32, they married and had two sons within 15 months. They were both excommunicated from the church because she was a fourth cousin to his first wife. Beatriz had to hide until Alonso could save her honor through a costly dispensation by the church. They had a third son, Rodrigo, and shortly after Alonso was asked to fight in the conquest of Navarre. He returned home from the war after three years and Beatriz became pregnant with "his favorite child" Teresa.

When Teresa was eight years old, her half-brother, Juan de Cepeda, joined the infantry and was killed in a battle with the Moors in North Africa. He was considered a "martyr" as were all the men who died in battle. After his death, Teresa's mother became a recluse, wearing nothing but black and reading "books about knights" incessantly. When Teresa was 14, her mother died while giving birth to her sister, Juana. Teresa's mother taught her to be a devout Catholic at a young age. In Teresa's time, there were only two choices for girls—marriage or the convent.

Teresa wrote about her life as a child. She told of a time when she was 16 (1531) that she would sneak out of the house to meet with a man she loved. Teresa said her downfall was a "love for good conversation." When the gossip about the relationship reached her father, he took her to an enclosed Augustinian convent nearby. But he waited for an excuse to take her there so that "it wouldn't look strange." Her sister, Maria, who was 25 and described as drab and "ten years past the market age" married suddenly that year. It was not uncommon for husbands to be bought and later it was said that Alonso purchased Maria's husband, Martin de Guzman. Now, he had an excuse she wrote in her autobiography, "because with my sister married, it wasn't good for me to live without a mother."

## Decided to Become a Nun

Teresa wrote in her autobiography _Life_ (1611) that her "honor was very, very badly damaged." She stayed at Our Lady of Grace convent for 19 months until she became ill in 1532. She ran a high fever and had fainting spells. Teresa had a weak heart and suffered with rheumatoid arthritis for the rest of her life. After recuperating at her sister's farmhouse, she decided to become a nun. When she told her father, he was determined not to give her to the church. But when her brother, Rodrigo, left for Peru, Teresa ran away to the Carmelite's Convent of the Encarnacion (Incarnation). One of her greatest fears was going to hell when she died. She claims that she became a nun because of that fear. Teresa was almost 21 when she went to the convent. Two years later in 1537, she became a Carmelite nun. She took the name of Teresa de Jesus. The convent was an unenclosed convent with much freedom for the nuns. They wore perfume, jewelry and colorful sashes. Later, Teresa called it "an inn just off the road of hell." While she was there, she met a nobleman and fell in love, which was very disturbing to Teresa.

### Learned About "Mystical Theology"

About a year later, she became ill again and left the convent to recuperate at her sister's house. The doctors said that she was fatally ill with consumption. Her Uncle Pedro had become very religious and gave Teresa religious books to read the last time she was ill. This time, he discovered "mystical theology" and gave Teresa a book *The Third Spiritual Alphabet* by Francisco de Osuna, a Franciscan monk. This was the beginning of her "peace within herself" and she began collecting books on this new theology. Teresa learned the "prayer of quiet." When she became strong enough, Teresa decided to go to a healer in Becedas for a "cure." The treatment almost killed her. She became so ill from the "cure" that her father had to take her home to die. Teresa went into a coma for four days. She slowly recovered and insisted on going back to the Carmelite convent where she spent the next three years in the infirmary.

Teresa's father visited her frequently, bringing her more mystical books to read. She appealed to St. Joseph and gave him credit for the miracle of her recovery. Teresa named many of the convents she founded in his name. In the meantime, Alonso began reading the mystical books and became more devout. After her recovery, Teresa rejoined the Carmelites and spent the next three years "from pastime to pastime, from vanity to vanity, from occasion to occasion."

### Reached Major Turning Point in Life

In 1543, Teresa's father became very ill and she was with him when he died. She loved her father very much and after he died, she put off seeing a confessor for ten months. Teresa called it the "most sinful year of her life." She went to Father Barron, a Dominican who had been her father's confessor. He admonished Teresa and told her not to give up her "mental prayer." She went through a long struggle of inner conflict. Although she suffered internally the next ten years, the people around her saw her as a "distinguished lady" who was "gay and witty." She agonized over her feelings for men, especially Garcia de Toledo, nobleman and priest. In 1554, Teresa went through a conversion when she saw a statue of the wounded Christ. Then someone gave her a copy of *Confessions* of St. Augustine to read. She identified with him and realized that she was not damned. She then turned her attention to more important issues that threatened the church.

### Experienced First Rapture

In 1556, Teresa made her mystical betrothal and asked for permission to leave the convent. Her practices in penance and prayer was "extreme" to the casual lifestyle at the convent and the Carmelites allowed her to leave. For the next three years she lived with a friend, Dona Guiomar de Ulloa (Yomar). With the help of her Jesuit confessor, Juan de Pradanos who was vice-rector of the College of St. Gil, Teresa found more depth in her spiritual experience and following his instructions had her first rapture. She gave up some of her friendships with men, especially Garcia de Toledo. De Pradanos became very ill and he was moved into Yomar's home for Teresa and Yomar to nurse him. This caused a scandal in the community.

After they nursed de Pradanos back to health, the three of them left Avila. Teresa went to her sister's home in Alba for a while then visited her Uncle Lorenzo. Yomar went to visit her mother and de Pradanos was transferred to Valladolid. After two months, Teresa was ordered to return to the Carmelite convent in Avila. A young Jesuit priest became her new confessor but because of the scandal, he did not talk to her "about the things of God" which Teresa had always cherished with her confessors. She spent her time reading until 1557 when the Pope banned many of the "mystical" books and in 1559, Teresa's books were burned by the Inquisitors.

By 1562, Teresa finished her book *Life* and the Inquisitors ordered her to expand it, filling in where she had omitted events. They wanted to know more about her visions. Many times she fell into seizures or trance-like states and did not remember what had occurred. Witnesses described the events and gossip spread throughout the community. Teresa heard voices and saw visions both of the devil and of Christ. Many people thought she was possessed of the devil and should be exorcised. There were other accounts of Teresa's experiencing levitation. She ordered the other nuns not to tell anyone. At the time, the

Inquisitors were investigating anyone who were considered "heretics" and burned them at the stake.

One of her most famous visions was portrayed in Bernini's baroque painting the "Ecstasy of St. Teresa." It depicts her description of an angel piercing her heart with the burning tip of a lance. "The pain was so great that it made me moan over and over, and the sweet delight into which that pain threw me was so intense that one could not want it to stop, or the soul be contented with anything but God. It is not bodily pain, but spiritual, though the body does not cease to share in it somewhat—and even very much so," she wrote. The church described her experience as the miracle of "Transverberation." She finished her expanded version of *Life* in 1559.

By 1560, Teresa made a decision to reform the Carmelite Order. After much opposition and struggle, in 1562, Pope Pius IV granted her a brief for the founding of the San Jose convent for the Reformed Carmelite Order. She began writing *The Way of Perfection* and four nuns were transferred from the Convent of the Encarnacion to the reformed convent. Four novices joined the order with opposition from members of the church and the city. But Teresa continued in her quest and she continued to write. In 1566, she wrote *Meditations on the Song of Songs*. She traveled extensively founding more convents throughout Spain and in 1569 wrote *Exclamations* and in 1572, she wrote *Spiritual Challenge* after seeing a vision of the Virgin. Her books are considered classics in mystical literature. Teresa was considered instrumental in reforming not only the Carmelite convents but also the Carmelite monasteries. She spent the remainder of her life traveling for the Reformed Carmelite Order and writing her many books.

### Died With Joyful Attitude

There were several accounts of Teresa's last days before her death, October 4, 1582. One account said that she was kidnapped by Friar Antonio de Jesus Heredia to go to Alba to be present at the birth of an heir for the Duke and Duchess of Alba. Another account said that he ordered Teresa to go and even though she was ill, she went willingly. After arriving in Alba, Teresa went to the convent and became weaker. She suffered a hemorrhage and taken to the infirmary knowing that she was dying. But she was joyful at the end, saying, "Lord, I am a daughter of the church." There were accounts from those present that a sweet fragrance filled the room at her death. Teresa was buried at the convent chapel in Alba, although many friends protested, wanting her to be buried in Avila. The tomb emitted the mysterious sweet fragrance and miracles were reported.

Nine months later, Gracian, a Reformed Carmelite superior, had Teresa's body exhumed. Although her robes were rotting, her body was totally intact.

Gracian cut off her left hand and took it back to Avila. He cut off one finger to use as a talisman then reburied her in the tomb. Three years later, Gracian convinced the Chapter of the Discalced to exhume her body and take it to Avila. They agreed to leave one arm in Alba to console the nuns there. Teresa's body was still intact and preserved. They considered it supernatural since she had not been embalmed. The Duchess was outraged and the Duke convinced the Pope to order Teresa's body to be returned to Alba. Teresa's body was returned to Alba and by the eighteenth century, her body had been exhumed many times for examination and little by little body parts, bones and pieces of flesh began to be missing. Her heart was removed and "it was found to be seared as if by a knife ... the edges of the wound appearing charred."

## SELECTED PUBLISHED WORKS:

*Apuntaciones* (*Notes*).
*Avisos* (*Warnings*).
*Constituciones* (*Constitutions*).
*Cuentas de conciencia* (*Accounts of conscience*).
*Desafío espiritual* (*Spiritual Challenge*).
*Epistolario* (*Correspondence*).
*Exclamaciones* (*Exclamations*).
*Libro de la vida* (*The Book of Her Life*).
*Libro de las fundaciones* (*The Book of Foundations*).
*Camino de perfeccion* (*Way of Perfection*).
*Meditaciones sobre los Cantares* (*Meditations on the Song of Solomon*).
*Moradas del castillo interior* (*Mansions of the Inner Castle*).
*Obras completas,* edited by Efren de la Madre de Dios and Otger Steggink, [Madrid], 1962.
*Ordenanza de una cofradia* (*Rules for a Brotherhood*).
*Poesiasas* (*Poetry*).
*Vejamen* (*Rebuke*).
*Visita de Descalzas* (*The Visitation of Discalced Nuns*).

## SOURCES:

Clissold, Stephen, *St. Teresa of Avila,* Sheldon Press, London, 1982.
Lincoln, Victoria, *Teresa, a Woman: A Biography of Teresa of Avila,* edited by Elias Rivers and Antonio T. de Nicolas, Albany, State University of New York Press, 1984.

—*Sketch by Phyllis Noah*

# Piri Thomas
## 1928-
**Puerto Rican American author**

In his three well-known autobiographies—*Down These Mean Streets, Savior, Savior, Hold My Hand,* and *Seven Long Times*—Piri Thomas has chronicled his struggles to find his racial identity and to survive life on the streets, drug addiction, and imprisonment for armed robbery. In *The Nuyorican Experience: Literature of the Puerto Rican Minority,* Eugene V. Mohr called Thomas "the most serious and interesting spokesman for second-generation Puerto Ricans in New York."

Thomas was born on September 30, 1928, in New York City's Harlem Hospital, the first of seven children. His name was originally John Peter Thomas. As a youth, he drew inspiration from his mother, Dolores Montanez, a highly spiritual white woman raised in Puerto Rico. His father, Juan (James) Thomas, who moved to Puerto Rico from Cuba, was a dark-skinned laborer.

Thomas grew up during the Great Depression in El Barrio, New York's well-known poor district. At this time he became confused as to his racial identity, a theme that runs through his work. His family embraced its Puerto Rican heritage, yet society considered Thomas a Negro because of his skin color. Adding to this confusion was his father, who, ashamed of his own features, showed more favor to Thomas's lighter-skinned brothers and sisters.

Thomas had little interest in school, which ignored his community's language and values. As a teenager, petty theft and the gang life fed his desire to reach manhood. "I reached the 'age of the gang,'" he told Wolfgang Binder of *Minority Voices.* "It's an age in which you have to prove your [mettle], your *corazon* (courage)."

His parents, wishing their children to enter the mainstream, moved to the white middle-class enclave of Babylon, Long Island. But Thomas, because of his race, could not fit in. "I felt that I belonged in Harlem; it was my kind of kick," he wrote in *Down These Mean Streets.* At the age of 16, he moved back to Spanish Harlem on his own.

During these years, "The question of racial identity [grew] more and more pressing for Piri," Mohr explained. He traveled, but found segregation everywhere: in the Deep South while traveling with a black friend, and in Europe and South America as a merchant marine. He grew to hate everything white, save for his mother and Trina, a Puerto Rican immigrant he courted. After his mother died, Thomas fell into drug dealing and heroin addiction. He

*Piri Thomas*

managed to quit his habit "cold turkey," but took up armed robbery as a way to make money.

## Imprisonment Leads to Writing

In 1950, during an armed robbery of a Greenwich Village nightclub, Thomas got into a shootout that left both him and a policeman wounded. He was convicted of attempted armed robbery and served seven years in jail. There, he endured confinement and the ignominy of being stripped of his name, and he survived prison racism. Also while in prison, Thomas bucked the odds by earning a high-school equivalency diploma and becoming a voracious reader and writer. "I said, 'Man, where am I at? I got a mind; let's see if I can use it, so I jumped into books,'" Thomas told Christopher Lehmann-Haupt of the *New York Times.*

For a short time, Thomas adopted the Black Muslim faith, but he left prison a Christian. In church, he met Daniela, a recent Puerto Rican immigrant, whom he married. He had difficulty finding work because of his race and because he was an ex-convict. He began to counsel black, Italian, and Puerto Rican gang members in a church youth center, and later worked for a drug rehabilitation program in Puerto Rico.

In 1962, Thomas was placed in touch with Angus Cameron, an editor with the Alfred A. Knopf publishing company. He spent the next five years writing

*Down These Mean Streets,* supported by a grant. The book, written in a Spanish Harlem dialect spiced with prison language, was widely praised. For example, Elmer Bendiner stated in the *Nation* that Thomas "has done it all in Harlem's mean streets and gone on from machismo to manhood, acquiring during the journey an understanding of man."

Thomas followed this success in 1972 with *Savior, Savior, Hold My Hand,* which focused on his relationship with "John Clause," a Christian community leader who stole credit for Thomas's accomplishments and betrayed his trust. Critical response was lukewarm for this work, which was more mature and reflective than Thomas's previous book and far removed from the ghetto. Larry Garvin, writing in *Crisis,* blamed critics' tendency to categorize authors for the book's more limited success: "It represents a stylistic break from the peculiar niche into which Third World writers are consistently thrust: chroniclers of the ghetto street experience. So long as these writers remain in the ghetto, actually and figuratively, they are acceptable to the WASP-oriented critics; if they attempt to break out of the Third World mold, the critics will be waiting like ravenous hounds to keep them in their places." Thomas completed his autobiographies in 1974 with *Seven Long Times,* which detailed his prison survival and ended with suggested improvements to the penal system.

Several critics have warned of pitfalls in interpreting Thomas's work. As Bendiner wrote, "Middle-class Americans may smile contentedly when they finish [*Down These Mean Streets*'] horrors and say: 'You see, I knew it could be done. There is some good in them after all, and if they only try like Piri Thomas, they can all make it'. . . . It would have been good if Piri had a bit more anger and a bit less of the Puerto Rican's Christ-like tolerance."

Thomas has written plays, poetry, and a 1978 young adult book, *Stories from El Barrio.* He also paints and travels the world to lecture, particularly to young ethnic people in need of affirmation and pride. Thomas has been married three times and is the father of five children. He has lived in Brooklyn and the Bronx, Puerto Rico, and San Francisco.

## SELECTED PUBLISHED WORKS:

*Down These Mean Streets,* Knopf, 1967.
*Savior, Savior, Hold My Hand,* Doubleday, 1972.
*Seven Long Times,* Praeger, 1974.
(Author of introduction) Lefty Barretto, *Nobody's Hero: A Puerto Rican Story,* New American Library, 1977.
*Stories From El Barrio,* Knopf, 1978.

## SOURCES:

### Books

*Biographical Dictionary of Hispanic Literature in the United States: The Literature of Puerto Ricans, Cuban Americans, and Other Hispanic Writers,* edited by Nicolás Kanellos, Westport, Connecticut, Greenwood Press, 1989.
*Hispanic Writers,* edited by Bryan Ryan, Detroit, Gale Research, 1991.
Mohr, Eugene V., *The Nuyorican Experience: Literature of the Puerto Rican Minority,* Westport, Connecticut, Greenwood Press, 1982.

### Periodicals

*Crisis,* June/July 1975, pp. 196–203.
*Minority Voices,* spring 1980, pp. 63–78.
*Nation,* September 25, 1967, pp. 283–84.
*New York Times Book Review,* May 21, 1967, pp. 45–47.

—*Sketch by Eric Patterson*

---

# Jacobo Timerman
## 1923-
### Argentine newspaper publisher and writer

As publisher of the prominent Argentine newspaper *La Opinión,* Jacobo Timerman became known for his controversial stances on a number of heated political issues. He gained international attention in the late 1970s, when his vocal opposition to Argentine government practices led to his unlawful imprisonment and torture at the hands of his enemies. He authored a book about his experiences, *Prisoner without a Name, Cell without a Number,* as well as several other works that protested against human rights violations. His background and political views remained a subject of intense debate into the 1990s.

Born January 6, 1923, in Bar, Ukraine, U.S.S.R., Timerman immigrated to Argentina at age five. His parents were Natan, a clothing vendor, and Eva Berman Timerman. Timerman attended the National University of La Plata, and married pianist Risha Mindlin in 1950. The couple would have three children: Daniel, Hector, and Javier.

At the outset of his career, Timerman began to raise himself economically by gaining the support of a young financier, David Gravier, to help him start *La*

*Jacobo Timerman*

*Opinión.* Although active in various writing and publishing ventures, it was his role as publisher of *La Opinión* that launched Timerman as an outspoken crusader within a fierce political arena.

### Held as Political Prisoner

The newspaper publisher's ordeal began on the night of April 15, 1977, when he was kidnapped from his apartment by 20 armed men posing as militia. Already, several thousand Argentineans had disappeared in the midst of political and religious upheaval; in the end, 1,500 of them—ten percent—would be Jews. Timerman had provoked his own arrest by harshly criticizing the brutal human rights violations and anti-Semitism of the Argentine military government in *La Opinión,* and repeatedly demanding an explanation for illegal imprisonments by printing the names of missing citizens.

Although his kidnappers were unable to secure any legal charges against him, his accusers believed him to be a key figure in a Jewish conspiracy plot to overthrow Argentina; they feared that Jews intended to replace their country for Israel as the Jewish homeland. Timerman spent nearly two and one-half years either under surveillance or house arrest. During periods of physical detainment Timerman was beaten, given electrical shocks while strapped to a torture apparatus, and subjected to psychological abuse and deprivation. His ordeal, as well as the overall campaign of violence taking place in his country, attracted the attention of international human rights groups. When U.S. president Jimmy Carter and the Vatican came to his aid, his captors were hard pressed to release him.

Timerman was finally freed in September 1979, although the Argentine government immediately revoked his citizenship and forced him into exile in Israel. Within weeks, he received several awards for defending freedom of the press and championing human rights. While in Israel, he wrote a memoir of his experiences as a political prisoner. *Prisoner without a Name, Cell without a Number* recounts several early attempts to silence *La Opinión,* the circumstances surrounding his abduction, and the methods he used to survive his confinement and torture.

Timerman soon resumed his career as a journalist, writing numerous controversial articles about international affairs. When Israel invaded Lebanon in 1982, he published *The Longest War: Israel in Lebanon,* a protest against the official rationale for the military action and the resulting human rights infractions. When publication of *The Longest War* made him unpopular in Israel, he relocated to the United States. By 1984 the political scene in Argentina had changed sufficiently that Timerman was able to return to his homeland and recoup his citizenship. His firsthand experience with human rights violations continued to influence his writing, however. In 1987 he authored *Chile: Death in the South,* a vivid portrayal of Argentina's neighboring country as cruelly autocratic and inhumane. Timerman's *Cuba: A Journey,* published in 1990, covers the history, politics, and human rights concerns of twentieth-century Cuba.

### Outspokenness Provokes Detractors

While gaining renown for his ordeal, Timerman's political views and personal agendas became the subject of intense debate in Argentina, Israel, and the United States. He made enemies among both Argentine Jews—whom he chastised for their apathy and lack of vocal intervention during his imprisonment—and U.S. officials when, in *Prisoner Without a Name,* he compared Argentina's missing Jews to those killed in Europe by Nazi activity and Soviet pogroms. Attacks on Timerman eventually extended to his character and his activities prior to his imprisonment and exile, and included his relationship with Grazier, whose financial dealings had since come under scrutiny. Timerman's advocacy of the overthrow of Isabel Perón's government support of the junta was used as evidence that he was anti-democratic and interested in improving his own influence and prestige.

Despite such criticism, however, Timerman continued to enjoy international support for his work on behalf of human rights. In *Encounter,* James Neilson declared Timerman personally responsible for the "impressive achievement" of raising international awareness of the problems in Latin America.

## SELECTED PUBLISHED WORKS:

*Preso sin nombre, celda sin numero,* Israel, Ateneo, 1981, translated by Toby Talbot as *Prisoner without a Name, Cell without a Number,* New York, Knopf, 1981.
*The Longest War: Israel in Lebanon,* translated by Miguel Acoca, New York, Vintage, 1982.
*Chile: Death in the South,* translated by Robert Cox, New York, Knopf, 1987.
*Cuba: A Journey,* New York, Knopf, 1990.

## SOURCES:

### Books

*Fascismo y Experiencia Literaria: Reflexiones para una Recanonizacion,* edited by Hernan Vidal, Minneapolis, Institute for the Study of Ideologies and Literature, 1985.
*Hispanic Writers,* edited by Bryan Ryan, Detroit, Gale, 1991.

### Periodicals

*Advertising Age,* March 4, 1985, p. 60.
*Encounter,* November 1981, pp. 74–84
*New York Times Book Review,* May 10, 1981.

—*Sketch by Brett A. Lealand*

# Tirso de Molina
## 1583-1648
**Spanish playwright**

Tirso de Molina is the pseudonym for Fray Gabriel Téllez and the name by which he is most commonly known. He is considered the most important disciple of **Lope de Vega,** founder of the Spanish National Theater, and is best known for his creation of the character of Don Juan in *El burlador de Sevilla* (*The Trickster of Seville*). Tirso de Molina lived and wrote during the Spanish Golden Age, when the Spanish Empire was in its decline. He was a member of the Mercedarian order of monks, in whose shelter he spent a good part of his adult life. He is best known for his *comedias,* which are three act plays depicting romance, intrigue and the important theme of honor. Alongside of Lope Vega and **Calderón de la Barca** he is one of the most famous writers of Spanish Golden Age Theater.

## The Mysterious Monk

Very little is known of the life of Tirso de Molina and some data is of a speculative nature. His most famous biographer, Doña Blanca de los Rios, believed that he was born in Madrid in 1583; and based on a baptismal certificate dated March 9, 1584, she proposed that he was the illegitimate son of the Duke of Osuna. Her thesis has been disputed by those who claim it would have been impossible for an illegitimate person to succeed in the Mercedarian order without receiving special dispensation. There is no record that this occurred. It is also argued that any suspicion of illegitimacy would have been exploited mercilessly by his rivals, a very common practice in the literary circles of the time.

Tirso de Molina studied at the University of Alcalá de Henares and took his vows in Guadalajara in 1601. He lived almost exclusively in Toledo during the years 1605–1615 and it is likely that his first plays were written there. In 1621 he claimed to have written 300 *comedias* in the preceding 14 years. Many of his plays are set in Galicia, a province in north western Spain, and in Portugal, two areas to which he travelled. He also spent some time in Aragón in 1614 where he was probably exiled for satirizing the Castillian nobility and in 1616 he was in Hispaniola (now the Dominican Republic), where he stayed for two years. He emerged again in Madrid in 1620 and was threatened with excommunication by the Council of Castile in 1625 for his too vivid portrayal of vice on stage and was ordered never again to write plays of a secular nature. From this time on there are only three surviving *comedias, La huerta de Juan Fernández* (*The Garden of Juan Fernandez,* 1626), *Las quinas de Portugal* (1638), and a redrafting of *En Madrid y en la casa* (*In Madrid and at Home*)

He spent his last years in the service of the Mercedarian order and in 1637 was appointed chronicler of the order, at which time he wrote *Historia general de la Order de Nuestra Señora de las Mercedes* (*General History of the Order of Our Lady of Mercies*). Everything that he wrote from this time on was of a religious theme. Tirso died in Almazán, Soria, Spain on March 12, 1648.

## The Legend of Don Juan

Tirso's greatest contribution to Spanish drama and to Western literature in general was the creation of Don Juan. Don Juan is a young Spaniard of noble birth whose main purpose in life is to seduce young women, a cause he pursues more out of a desire to trick people than out of lust itself. Considering his victims to be silly creatures deserving of his cruel treatment, he has no regard for any of society's norms and is completely selfish in his pursuit of scandal. The most important thing to him is the actual hunt and the ingenious ways in which he snares his prey. Also of great importance is his personal honor, which he interprets to be his courage in the face of any challenge. During the three acts Don Juan seduces a total of four women, two from the peasantry and two from the upper class. Not only does he dishonor these women but on occasion he does so in such a way that other men are falsely accused of his deeds. A father of one of the women, the Commander of Calatrava, hears his daughter calling for help and attempts to rescue his daughter from the clutches of Don Juan, who kills the father with his sword while trying to escape. Later in the play Don Juan encounters the tomb of the murdered commander and mockingly invites his stone statue to dine with him. The statue presents itself at Don Juan's table and extends an invitation to Don Juan to a supper in the graveyard. Don Juan accepts this invitation in order to demonstrate his courage and is served a dinner of scorpions and serpents. After dinner the statue gives his hand to Don Juan and, upon contact, both descend into hell while the chorus chants, "No debt in life is left unpaid." This final damnation is foreshadowed throughout the play by Don Juan's servant, Catalinon, who is constantly admonishing him for his abominable behavior and warns him that the women he fools and seduces will make him pay by dying.

Tirso created in Don Juan one of the most powerful modern myths. Only Faust can rival him in his quest for breaking the boundaries of human limitations. Don Juan is nowadays seen as a seducer and his figure is sometimes confused with that of the historical Italian seducer Giacomo Casanova. But the character of Don Juan has a mythical side that is impossible to confine to the narrow limits of the figure of the seducer. Actually, Tirso's Don Juan does not seduce with his beauty or manners, rather, he tricks his victims by taking advantage of his social position or of a misunderstanding.

In modern times there have been many attempts to understand the strong magnetism of Don Juan. For instance, he has been considered an insecure character who tries to affirm his dubious virility by boasting of his conquests in front of other males. He has also been considered a latent homosexual trying to deny his homosexuality with his amorous exploits. But these approaches in many cases employ modern psychoanalytical methods that are of dubious utility for a literary character of the seventeenth century.

The mythical figure of the "trickster" that exists in many cultures covers several of the main features of Don Juan. The trickster is a character that plays cruel jokes on people. He breaks the boundaries of a taboo by not obeying established rules, both secular and sacred. In the highly hierarchical seventeenth-century Spanish society, Don Juan attacks the establishment in one of its most conventional points—the honor system. He mocks the institution of matrimony and the reputation of women, destabilizing all of society with his attack.

This irreverent side of Don Juan is what appealed so much to Romantic poets such as Byron and Zorrilla, who made him a hero of demoniac characteristics. Although Tirso's Don Juan possesses many of these attributes in a latent state, Tirso never devised his creation as a hero but as a negative example. However, any literary creation belongs to the reader and not exclusively to the original intention of the writer. Don Juan was created in the Baroque, a period of huge contradictions which were reflected in its literature. The fact that a religious man like Tirso created such a powerful representation of the chaotic and destructive forces within a human being is a typical example. After all, Tirso's depiction of the sin proved to be more vital than the moral lesson he was trying to exemplify with Don Juan's final damnation.

The legend of Don Juan has lent itself to many other works and never has a character or a theme been so exploited as that of Don Juan. Tirso gave western literature his creation and it has been reworked and analyzed by such writers as Zorrilla, Moliere, Pushkin, Browning, Byron, Shaw, Grabbe and Hoffman. Mozart's opera, *Don Giovanni* is based on the Don Juan story and Gluck and Strauss also dealt with the theme. The plot is approached in different ways. For example, Mozart treated it as a serious drama with some comic undertones whereas Byron made Don Juan a hero. Byron's version (1819–1824) is a satiric poem in which Don Juan is presented as an innocent, unsophisticated youth who has many romantic encounters and thrilling adventures as he travels throughout Europe. He is used as a means to measure and reflect the absurdities and injustices of the world. Byron died before finishing his Don Juan, leaving us with sixteen cantos.

There have been many other changes in the structure of the theme since the original version. Don Juan has been portrayed as a trickster, hero, romantic figure, and philosophical libertine. Today in Spain the most popular version is that of Zorrilla's (1844) which is traditionally performed on the Eve of All Soul's Day (November 1). Zorrilla's version borrows from French sources and presents a pious heroine who loves Don Juan and ultimately saves him from damnation.

## Appearance of Feminine Character Development

It is ironic that not until Tirso, who created the most notorious exploiter of women of all time, was the feminine character developed in Spanish drama.

The mother figure, noticeably absent in Golden Age Spanish Theater, does not emerge fully until Tirso and he seems to have possessed both insight and affection for women. This may be attributed to the inherent gentleness of a Mercedarian monk as well as his privileged position listening to confessions, which would have afforded him great insights into human nature in general. In Tirso's works, women play a much more meaningful part than we see in other Spanish works of this period, where women are presented in a more limited capacity such as an object of romantic love. Tirso gives us women of substance, women who think, who contribute and influence the world around them. However, Tirso's female characters are just as liable to succumb to human frailties as his male characters, as we see with the vengeful Laurencia in *La dama del Olivar* (*The Lady of the Olive Grove*) and Ninfa, the countess thief.

### Religious and Philosophical Subjects

Tirso de Molina is best known for his *comedias* and is considered a master of this genre. Amongst his religious *comedias* his most outstanding is *El condenado por desconfiado* (*Damned for Despair*). The plot deals with two people of opposite character, a pious hermit, Enrico and a bandit, Paulo. Instigated by a demon, the hermit learns that his death will be the same as the thief's and embarks on a life of sin. Upon dying he is condemned to hell in accordance with his sinful behavior. The thief, on the other hand, has many admirable characteristics hidden under his criminal facade and he repents prior to his death, saving himself at the last moment. This play deals with the issue of predestination and free will, an important theological controversy of the times discussed by Dominicans and Jesuits. This theme was also dealt with by Calderón in his *La vida es sueño* (*Life is a Dream*) which takes a different approach to the problem. *Don Gil de las calzas verdes* (*Gil of the Green Breeches*) is a comedy well known for its delightful intrigues and popular lyricism.

Taking into consideration the large number of works which Tirso wrote, it is amazing that this plays are as well written as they are. His characters have much more depth and realism than those of Lope de Vega and as in the case of Don Juan, have become universal figures.

Tirso also wrote *auto sacramentales* that were written for open air performance on the Feast of *Corpus Christi*. They were one-act religious plays that used poetry, allegory, and historical backgrounds to symbolize human life. The plays, rather than using personal characters, used allegorical characters such as Wisdom and Compassion to symbolically represent abstract ideas, making them more accessible to the populace. Every major city in Spain staged a new *auto sacramental* yearly and there was intense competition to present the finest one, so authors were commissioned to write them months in advance of their presentation. Only four *autos* can be attributed to Tirso with any certainty, of which *El colmenero divino* (*The Divine Beekeeper*) is probably his first work. It presents God as the beekeeper, the church as the beehives, the soul as the honey bee, the body as the drone and the devil as the bear which steals and eats the honey. *No le arriendo la ganancia* is best described as a sacramental farce which contrasts village life with life of the court, employing the allegorical characters of *Acuerdo* (Agreement) who is the legitimate son of Understanding and Experience, and Honor, the illegitimate son of Understanding and Fame. *Los hermanos parecidos* (*The Similar Brothers*) deals with Christ as a dualistic, God-human character by presenting the mystery of the Redemption as a ingenious trick in which Christ is substituted by an allegorical figure representing the sinner. In *El laberinto de Creta* (*The Labyrinth of Crete*) Tirso utilizes the classical Greek myth of the Minotaur, which was very popular in the period but his version is very symbolic and confusing and therefore little appreciated.

### SOURCES:

Agheana, Ion Tudor, *The Situational Drama of Tirso de Molina,* New York, Plaza Mayor Ediciones, 1972.

Bushee, Alice Huntington, *Three Centuries of Tirso de Molina,* Philadelphia, University of Pennsylvania Press, 1939.

Cotarelo y Mori, Emilio, *Tirso de Molina: Investigaciones bio-bibliográficas,* [Madrid], 1893.

Hesse, Everett W., "Catálogo bibliográfico de Tirso de Molina" in *Estudios,* [Madrid], 1949.

*Tirso de Molina: Ensayos sobre la biografía y la obra del Padre Maestro Fray Gabriel Téllez,* edited by Fray Manuel Penedo-Rey, Madrid, Padres Mercedarios, 1949.

*Tirso's Don Juan: The Metamorphosis of a Theme,* edited by Joseph Sola-Solé and George E. Gingras, Washington, D.C., Catholic University of America Press, 1988.

—*Sketch by Enrique Fernandez*

# Celia G. Torres
## 1936-

**Hispanic American businesswoman and community leader**

Highly respected both in her community and nationally in leadership circles, Celia G. Torres describes herself as an "agent of change." Cofounder of the National Network of Hispanic Women, Torres is among a few Latina women who have made a difference overcoming both personal and public challenges. "Since high school I have often found myself being the only one doing what I was doing," she explained to Oralia Michel during a telephone interview. "I seemed to be making a path for others; I was always ahead of my time."

An only child and the granddaughter of Mexican immigrants from a small community near Guadalajara, Torres was born on February 28, 1936, in Los Angeles to Angelina Gonzales and Francisco Estrada. She was raised in an all-female household at the end of the Depression. Her mother, a garment worker, became seriously ill and was hospitalized for three years, leaving her eight-year-old daughter to be raised by her invalid grandmother and married aunt. Torres says that some of her early influences for her social consciousness were from her aunt and uncle, who were foster parents, and from her uncle's involvement in unions.

### Uses Education to Leave Barrio Behind

At a young age, Torres saw one way out of the barrio—education. Her mother and her aunt, who was also her godmother, combined their resources to send Celia to Catholic schools. In addition to her family, Torres credits her teachers, the sisters of St. Joseph of Carondolet, for teaching her the values she lives by today. This investment in her future paid off in more ways than one. From St. Mary's Academy, where in the fifth grade she learned parliamentary procedure, Torres went on to St. Vincent's Parish school, where in the sixth grade she was asked to be sodality prefect (leader of a religious-oriented student organization). With this role, her skills as a leader began to develop.

From sixth grade through her college years at Mount St. Mary's College, Torres held at least one office per year. She worked her way through high school and college, paying for transportation, tuition, and books from the age of 15. Sometimes holding down three jobs at a time, she worked as a babysitter, sales clerk, waitress, and library assistant. When Torres's mother returned from the hospital, she developed a new reliance upon her daughter, believing that when she finished high school, she would help her raise her two children from a subsequent marriage, which did not last. Though Torres went against her mother's wishes and was determined to pursue a career, an understanding between mother and daughter soon developed. While pursuing her bachelor's degree in sociology at Mount St. Mary's, Torres represented her college at state and national conferences, which contributed to her "hands on" interest in community and civic affairs.

As a Catholic woman in the 1950s, Torres did what was expected of her. She became a social worker and got married. Marrying Julio Torres, she helped her husband start his medical practice, their business, and had five children. Drawing from her childhood and education, Torres enjoyed raising her children. "I used a lot of creativity," she related in the *Los Angeles Times.* "We had art shows in which the neighborhood children could sell their artwork." She was always active in parent-teacher groups and participated in her children's extracurricular activities, having no regrets about the years she spent mothering; she chose to re-direct her life to accommodate her family. In the midst of giving so much of herself to her husband and family, Torres promised herself that she would one day pursue her graduate education. Deriving strength from the spiritual and human values instilled by her family and the Carondolet Sisters, she never lost sense of where she was going. "I was determined to keep my identity and not be known as 'Mrs. Dr. Torres,' as someone from the hospital once called me," Torres related in her telephone interview.

Resolving to focus on herself, she became increasingly involved in civic and community work in her hometown of Rancho Palos Verdes, California, a conservative Anglo community. In 1974 she became the first Hispanic woman to serve as the President of the local Parent, Teachers Association (PTA), a high-profile position. "That was a difficult time because getting elected required being under so much scrutiny. But once I made it, I became known by Hispanics as 'the hand that can reach the Anglo community.' Through me, Hispanics now had access to the private sector," Torres remarked in her interview. The position marked a turning point in her career—attaining a position of power in an Anglo community gave her the determination and confidence to work for other changes. At age 42 Torres fulfilled her promise to herself by commencing work on a master's degree, and in 1980 she graduated from the University of Southern California with a master's in social work.

### Finds Success in Real Estate Business

Before and after her graduate studies, Torres joined her husband in developing a successful group of real estate holdings in the Southwest. "We didn't set out to be in business," Torres declared in her telephone interview. "We wanted to help people. We lived during a time when opportunities were available, and we managed to build on them." Torres's duties as executive vice president included financial reporting and portfolio development. She traveled around the country for site visits, conducting research and inspection of new properties.

In addition to being a businesswoman, Torres volunteers time working for the Hispanic community. Some of the issues Torres has advocated are fair housing, police utilization, various women's issues—including women in the church—and the prevention of substance abuse, teen pregnancy, and child abuse. She helped institutionalize Latino student support groups at several colleges and universities and has successfully raised funds for such projects as child abuse prevention, AIDS, the homeless, scholarship, and political candidates. She also helped establish and chaired the National Network of Hispanic Women (NNHW). Among what Torres considers her greatest contributions are her support of education through participation on educational boards, the scholarships she and her husband have given, funding of new projects, and her work with the NNHW. "We put many pieces of the puzzle together to empower Latinas; the work of NNHW has its place in history."

Along with her success, Torres has also experienced difficult lessons and has had to overcome several barriers. She pointed out in a *Latina* magazine interview that these barriers are invisible and sometimes so subtle that one might spend half a career without ever quite knowing they exist. "But they do," she said. "I think you can recognize them when you find yourself swimming upstream as hard as you can, knowing you're just as good as anyone else, and getting nowhere." These barriers she believes are cultural and structural. She explained in *Latina* that Hispanic women have "been raised with religious and family values that are a little tighter and stronger [than those of Anglo women]. The Latina is very much expected to fulfill a mothering female role in some way. There is tremendous pressure form both inside and outside. I'm not sure that the same pressure from family and religion exists for the Anglo woman."

According to *Latina,* Torres speaks from the collective experience of the many women she was in touch with as cofounder of NNHW, an organization that seeks to find and advance "outstanding Hispanic women for leadership positions in education, industry, business and government." What Hispanics need most, according to Torres, is a support system. "With the kind of bicultural lives we lead, we need to have a place to express both those parts. Otherwise there is a part of us that doesn't develop, that shuts down." She learned much from her own experience in college. "Our culture is a very warm culture," she said. "We relate people-to-people, person-to-person, face-to-face, and that's an important value to us. Institutions of higher learning are traditionally very cold, unfriendly places where the attitude is sink or swim. So, someone coming from a warm family environment, and particularly a female who has been protected by her family, many times finds the transition difficult."

In 1989 health problems led Torres to redirect her path when, as she says, cancer gave her a wake up call. "My husband and I are making a transition into the next phase of our lives," she stated in her telephone interview. Torres calls it the "research and development" phase and says she believes in second beginnings. "We are looking for the best way to use our talent and experiences but without being in the fast lane." Torres hopes to write a book and continue giving counseling and support to those seeking empowerment and transformation, particularly women.

## SOURCES:

### Periodicals

*Latina,* November 1985, pp. 51–52.
*Los Angeles Times,* November 3, 1986, Section 5, pp. 1,6.

### Other

Torres, Celia G., telephone interview with Oralia Michel, September 1, 1992.

—*Sketch by Oralia Michel*

# Esteban Edward Torres
## 1930-
### Hispanic American legislator

In 1982 Esteban Edward Torres was elected as a Democratic candidate for the U.S. House of Representatives from the San Gabriel Valley district of California. During his political career, he has earned a reputation as a skilled negotiator capable of achieving compromise among groups with vastly different interests. Some of his most visible work has involved water resource cleanup, free trade, illegal immigrant rights, and disaster relief.

Torres was born on January 27, 1930, in Miami, Arizona. From 1949 to 1953 Torres served in the U.S. Army, ending his military term as a sergeant first class. He married Arcy Sanchez on January 22, 1955, and they eventually had five children: Carmen, Rena, Camille, Selina, and Esteban Jr. He began his college education in Los Angeles, California, where he attended East Los Angeles Community College from 1959 to 1963, and California State University at Los Angeles from 1963 to 1964. In 1965 Torres attended the University of Maryland, and in 1966 he studied international labor at American University. In 1987 Congressman Torres was awarded an honorary doctorate from National University in San Diego, California.

Torres began his career as an assembly line worker in the automotive industry and worked his way up. He ascended to his first elected position in 1954, when his peers voted him chief shop steward at a Chrysler Corporation plant. His political career began during the years when he was employed with the United Auto Workers (UAW). There he directed the Inter-American Bureau for Caribbean and Latin American Affairs from 1964–1968. Torres co-founded and acted as chief executive officer of TELACU from 1968 to 1974, then returned to the UAW as assistant director for the International Affairs department from 1976 to 1979.

Torres entered government service in 1978, when he was appointed by President Jimmy Carter to the position of U.S. ambassador to the United Nations Educational, Scientific, and Cultural Organization (UNESCO) in Paris, France. He also worked with Carter as his advisor on Hispanic affairs. In 1982 Torres was elected a congressman in the U.S. House of Representatives for the 34th district of California. Through much of his political career he has focused on issues relevant to the Hispanic population, and he served as chair of the Congressional Hispanic Caucus from 1986 to 1987.

**Focuses on the Environment**

In October of 1992, the *Los Angeles Times* endorsed Democrat Torres, honoring his ten years of service for his San Gabriel Valley district. The *Times* lauded Torres for his ethics, diplomacy, and environmental efforts on Capitol Hill, specifically highlighting his efforts directed at water cleanup. Torres was considered progressive in dealing with the dilemma of water resource contamination, a long-standing problem that was often neglected due to bureaucratic obstacles. Since Torres's California district—which was located northeast of Los Angeles and encompassed 195 square miles—included one of the nation's larger potable ground water basins, his handling of the pollution problem could set precedents for other parts of the country.

The basin, which provides over one million people with drinking water, has been seriously polluted with hazardous waste for more than a decade.

Twenty-five percent of the basin's water wells have been contaminated, and over $30 million has been spent since the contamination was discovered. However, little cleanup has occurred due to litigation over who was responsible. In response to this situation, Torres introduced an innovative and goal-oriented bill based on commerce and teamwork to resolve the problem. Rather than waiting for the Environmental Protection Agency (EPA) to identify hazardous waste offenders and then applying punitive measures, Torres suggested an incentive-based approach for business and industry to voluntarily contract with the EPA. Those contractors that voluntarily helped to eliminate the problem of contamination would then become exempt from further liability. Congressman Torres's bill seemed likely to circumvent further obstacles to cleanup of one of the nation's most polluted ground water sources.

During his terms as a U.S. representative, Torres has also been active in disaster relief and immigration issues. However, his involvement and interest in minority and social issues began in the late 1960s and early 1970s, when he held important positions in several organizations which dealt with these areas. From 1969 to 1970, for example, he served as president of the Congress of Mexican American Unity, and from 1970 to 1972 he was the commissioner of the Mexican American Education Commission. In addition, Torres was involved with the Los Angeles County Commission on Economic Development from 1970 to 1972. In 1973 he was president of the Plaza de la Raza Cultural Center, and in 1974 Torres served as vice president of the National Congress on Community Development.

Holding administrative positions in labor and community groups helped Torres to garner the support he needed for his Congressional campaign as well as for the programs he introduced while in office. For example, his own experiences helped him to evaluate all the issues involved in the North American Free Trade Agreement (NAFTA), which would create a free-trade bloc among Canada, the United States, and Mexico. When he finally decided to vote in favor of NAFTA, he could be confident about organizational support for the initiative.

Torres explained his reasons for supporting NAFTA in a letter to the editor of the *Washington Post:* "I decided to support NAFTA because the Clinton administration agreed to include two important provisions to address the legitimate fears that some American workers will lose jobs in the short term because of NAFTA." Torres negotiated with the Clinton administration to develop social programs to provide employment and training for at-risk communities and individuals. Torres also introduced legislation which called for the creation of the North American Development Bank, and gained the support of 24 members of Congress for his plan.

## Negotiates on Social Issues

As an advocate of immigrants' rights, Torres has often been branded as a liberal. Though the political tide in California was turning against illegal immigrants in the mid–1990s—as evidenced by the controversial Proposition 187, which would deny tax-funded health care and other services to non-citizens—Torres voiced his support for immigrant rights in the *Los Angeles Times:* "Whenever there is a disaster in Mexico City, Bangladesh or elsewhere, Americans are the first ones there and we never say can't help these people. You can't deny people here what we so generously give away from our borders."

Social policy had become a matter of pressing economic importance for Californians. In 1994 Torres joined with six other House Democrats and proposed a balanced package of legislation on immigration. Group members put aside their differences and were able to develop four measures for alleviating specific concerns. One measure increased border patrols by nearly 50 percent, and another advocated federal reimbursement to the state for the $18,000 annual cost of imprisoning each illegal alien convicted of a crime. A third measure targeted discrimination, while a fourth sought to encourage those legally residing in the United States to become citizens. The constructive approach taken by Torres and his network provided a plausible solution to a sensitive social issue.

Also in the mid–1990s, Congressman Torres was applauded for his work to ensure swift passage of a bill providing relief for victims of a significant earthquake in Southern California. Despite differences of constituency make-up and party affiliation, Appropriations Committee member Torres "broke ranks" to form an alliance with Republican Representative Jerry Lewis and "help steer the $8.6-billion California earthquake aid bill through the House with uncharacteristic swiftness."

While many appreciated Torres's positions on disaster relief and illegal aliens, some also criticized him for compromising too much in the negotiations. In fact, Alan C. Miller of the *Los Angeles Times* predicted a "backlash" against Torres, and quoted another California Democrat as saying, "Some people look at this as betrayal. It was giving ground, whether symbolic or not."

In all his notable efforts to clean up water supplies in his district and provide viable solutions to difficult social policy issues, Torres has developed a reputation as a skilled negotiator and a team player. The congressman's later organizational affiliations have reflected an interest in global alliance and networking. He became a delegate to the International Monetary Fund Central Committee in Geneva, Switzerland, and chair of the Japan-Hispanic Institute. He also became Deputy Whip in the House, served on the United States Committee for UNICEF, and was a member of the board for the Pan-American Development Foundation.

## SOURCES:

### Periodicals

*Advertising Age,* August 20, 1990, p. S20.
*Elastomerics,* September 1990, p. 6.
*Los Angeles Times,* October 30, 1992, p. B6; August 9, 1993, p. B6; February 11, 1994, p. A3; March 16, 1994, p. B6.
*Washington Post,* November 1, 1993, p. A1; November 16, 1993, p. A20.

—*Sketch by Brett A. Lealand*

# Jaime Torres Bodet
## 1902-1974
### Mexican statesman and writer

Jaime Torres Bodet was a distinguished statesman and literary figure. Nationally renowned for his crusade against illiteracy, he served two terms as Mexico's Minister of Education. Internationally, Torres Bodet was a prominent and respected politician who was Director-General of the United Nations Educational, Scientific, and Cultural Organization (UNESCO), between 1948 and 1952. A staunch advocate of human rights and literacy, Torres Bodet placed the inherent value of education beyond simply reading and writing; he perceived it as a precondition for democracy and world peace. A man who strived tirelessly for the betterment of humankind, he once declared: "A man possesses nothing if he does not use what he has for the well-being of humanity," according to James Sewell in his *UNESCO and World Politics.*

Torres Bodet was also one of his country's—and Latin America's—most talented intellectuals and writers. His literary output was prodigious given his eminent political career; he was the author of over 30 books, including 15 volumes of poetry, seven collections of essays, and six novels. His exceptional literary accomplishments were formally recognized when Torres Bodet was awarded the National Prize for Literature by President Gustavo Díaz Ordaz in 1966.

Jaime Torres Bodet was born in Mexico City on April 17, 1902 to Alejandro Torres Girbent, a theatrical producer and businessman, and Emilia Bodet de Torres. His literary aspirations were kindled by his mother who, of French descent, recited works by Victor Hugo, José de Espronceda y Delgado, and Gustavo Adolfo Bécquer. He learned fluent French, which would be an asset in his future diplomatic career. Torres Bodet attended the National Preparatory School in Mexico City, where his classes in Spanish literature were taught by the poet Enrique Fernández Granados, who introduced young Torres Bodet to his literary circle and inspired him to become a writer. In 1918, at the age of 16, his verse was published in a volume entitled *Fervor*. Between 1918 and 1921, he studied law and philosophy at the National University, attending lectures by noted philosopher Antonio Caso.

### Torres Bodet: The Statesman

Torres Bodet embarked on his memorable career in government in 1921, when José Vasconcelos, Chancellor of the National University, appointed him as his private secretary. The following year, the centralized Ministry of Education was created and Vasconcelos was named Minister of Education; he appointed Torres Bodet as head of its Department of Libraries. In 1924 Torres Bodet returned to his alma mater as professor of French literature at the Faculty of Philosophy and Letters. His diplomatic career in Latin America and Europe was launched in 1929. In March, before leaving for Europe, he married Josefina Juárez. From 1929 to 1931 he served as third secretary to the Mexican legation in Madrid. In Spain he encountered poets and writers of the Generation of 1936, including Pedro Salinas y Serrano and Benjamín Jarnés. He spent the following nine years in various diplomatic positions in France, the Netherlands, Argentina, and Belgium, returning briefly to Mexico as the head of the diplomatic department in the Ministry of Foreign Affairs from 1936 to 1937.

In 1940 Torres Bodet returned to Mexico, following Adolf Hitler's invasion of Belgium, and was appointed under-secretary for foreign affairs by President Manuel Ávila Camacho. Three years later he was named Minister of Education, charged with formulating a strategy to eradicate Mexican illiteracy. On August 21, 1944, Congress ratified Torres Bodet's famous "Each One Teach One" literacy campaign; within two years 1,000,000 Mexicans had learned to read. As the Mexican Minister of Education, Torres Bodet attended the UNESCO Preparatory Commission, which convened in London in November of 1945. He played an instrumental role in drafting the UNESCO constitution; three years later he would become the organization's Director-General.

In 1946 President Miguel Alemán appointed Torres Bodet Minister of Foreign Affairs. One of his most noteworthy coups in this position was as the Mexican representative to the Ninth International Conference of American States in Bogotá, in 1948, which founded the Charter of the Organization of American States. According to Sonja Karsen in *Américas,* "There is probably no one more intimately connected with the creation of the Organization of American States in its present form than Torres Bodet."

In November of 1948 at the Beruit General Conferences, Torres Bodet was elected Director-General of UNESCO, succeeding Julian Huxley. An eloquent spokesman with diplomatic experience, he became a powerful voice for lesser developed countries, often antagonizing wealthier member states. Torres Bodet was particularly interested in educational, health, and agricultural issues. He attacked illiteracy as "the most unjust of all frontiers," continuing, "we sometimes forget that, without prisons or barbed wire, more than 1,200 million men and women live in the implacable, invisible, inner dungeon of ignorance." He rigorously promoted a world-wide educational plan under UNESCO's Fundamental Education Program, which advanced the development of educational materials tailored to a country's specific requirements. He equated peace with literacy; with half the world's population illiterate, the concept of world security would remain elusive. A staunch advocate of world human rights, according to Walter L. C. Laves and Charles A. Thomso in *UNESCO: Purpose, Progress, Prospects,* Torres Bodet "missed no chance by speech, message, draft resolution, or letter to governments to urge more effective recognition of the basic human rights that must form the foundation for any civilized and peaceful world community."

Torres Bodet's belief that UNESCO should concentrate its efforts and programs on world peace, and his attendant insistence on an increased budget, roused objections. At the General Conference in Florence in 1950, he threatened to resign unless he received a vote of confidence. The Conference supported him and he remained Director-General until 1952. On November 22 of that year Torres Bodet resigned when his budget was cut by $2.5 million, believing himself no longer equipped to pursue his duties effectively.

In 1954 Torres Bodet resumed his diplomatic career when President Ruiz Cortines appointed him Mexican Ambassador to France. Returning to Mexico in 1958, he accepted the post of Minister of Education for a second term under President Adolfo López Mateos. He instigated the 11-Year Plan, ratified by Congress on December 30 1959, which aimed to expand Mexico's educational system to more than 7,000,000 children by 1970. At the third Inter-American Conference of Ministers of Education, which convened in Bogotá in 1963, Torres Bodet's proposition that every child in Latin America receive six years of education by 1970 was unanimously approved. In 1964, after completing his second term as Minister of Education, he officially retired from the political scene and devoted himself to literature.

## Torres Bodet: The Writer

Writing was Torres Bodet's first chosen career; outside Mexico he was probably better known as a writer than as a statesman. In 1928 he founded the literary journal *Contemporáneos,* which inspired the formation of a group by the same name. As a prominent member of the "Contemporáneos" Torres Bodet was an influential force in his literary generation. The group instigated the revival of Mexican lyric poetry, influenced by the Mexican poets González Martínez and López and Velarde. The Contemporáneos also introduced new prose styles into Mexican literature, drawing from the techniques of such contemporary European writers as Marcel Proust, Franz Kafka, D. H. Lawrence, and James Joyce. The European influence is especially evident in his novels, written between 1927 and 1937. Torres Bodet's poetry and prose embraced a broad spectrum of themes: "the search for his identity and the attempt to establish an identity with his fellow man . . . loneliness, of being and not being . . . the constant awareness of fleeting time, which leads to the ever-present theme of death," explained Karsen in *Latin American Writers.*

In retirement, Torres Bodet penned four volumes of his autobiography, *Memorias,* published between 1969 and 1972. He was awarded the Belisario Domínguez Medal by the Mexican Senate in 1971 for service to his country. Karsen, writing in *Américas,* noted that Torres Bodet's fundamental beliefs altered very little. "Both in his work as a public servant and as an artist, his endeavor has been to realize *el hombre cabal,* the total man. For Torres Bodet the writer is not merely an artist, but a servant and defender of democracy." Suffering from an incurable form of cancer, Torres Bodet shot and killed himself on May 13, 1974, at his home in Mexico City. In his suicide letter he explained, "waiting for death on a day-to-day basis, . . . I prefer to call on death myself at the right time."

## SELECTED PUBLISHED WORKS:

### Poetry

*Fervor,* introduction by E. González Martínez, Mexico, Ballescá, 1918.
*Canciones,* Mexico, Cultura, 1922.
*El corazón delirante* ("The Impassioned Heart"), introduction by Arturo Torres Rioseco, Mexico, Porrúa, 1922.
*La casa* ("The House"), Herrero, 1923.
*Los días* ("The Days"), Herrero, 1923.

*Nuevas canciones* ("New Songs"), Madrid, Calleja, 1923.
*Poemas,* Herrero, 1924.
*Biombo* ("Folding Screen"), Herrero, 1925.
*Poesías,* Madrid, Espasa-Calpe, 1926.
*Destierro* ("Exile"), Madrid, Espasa-Calpe, 1930.
*Cripta* ("Crypt"), Mexico, R. Loera y Chávez, 1937.
*Sonetos,* Mexico, Gráfica Panamericana, 1949.
*Selección de poemas,* selected by Xavier Villaurrutia, Mexico, Nueva Voz, 1950.
*Fronteras,* Mexico, Fondo de Cultura Económica, 1954.
*Poesías escoqidas,* Buenos Aires, Espasa-Calpe, 1954.
*Sin trequa* ("No Truce"), Mexico, Fondo de Cultura Económica, 1957.
*Trébol de cuatro hojas* ("Four-leaf Clover"), Paris, privately printed, 1958, Universidad Veracruzana, 1960.
*Selected Poems of Jaime Tories Bidet,* edited and translated by Sonja Karsen, Indiana University Press, 1964.
*Poesía de Jaime Tories Bidet,* Mexico, Finistere, 1965.
*Obra poética* (collected poems, 1916–66), introduction by Rafael Solona, two volumes, Porrúa, 1967.
*Viente Poemas,* Monterrey, Mexico, Ediciones Sierra Madre, 1971.

### Fiction

*Margarita de niebla* ("Margaret's Fog"), Cultura, 1927.
*La educación sentimental* ("The Sentimental Education"), Madrid, Espasa-Calpe, 1929.
*Proserpina rescatada* ("Proserpina Rescued"), Madrid, Espasa-Calpe, 1931.
*Estrella de día* ("Movie Star"), Madrid, Espasa-Calpe, 1933.
*Primero de enero* ("First of January"), Madrid, Ediciones Literatura, 1935.
*Sombras* ("Shades"), Cultura, 1937.
*Nacimiento de Venus y otros relatos* ("Birth of Venus, and Other Stories"), Mexico, Nueva Cultura, 1941.

### Criticism

*Perspectiva de la literatura mexicana actual 1915–1928* ("View of Present-Day Mexican Literature 1915–1928"), Contemporáneos, 1928.
*Contemporáneos: Notas de crítica* ("Contemporaries: Notes on Literary Criticism"), Herrero, 1928.
*Tres inventores de realidad: Stendhal, Dostoyevski, Pérez Galdós* ("Three Inventors of Reality: Stendhal, Dostoyevski, Pérez Galdós"), Mexico, Imprenta Universitaria, 1955.

*Balzac,* Fondo de Cultura Económica, 1959.

*Maestros venecianos* ("Venetian Masters"), Porrúa, 1961.

*León Tolstoi: Su vida y su obra* ("Leo Tolstoy: His Life and Work"), Porrúa, 1965.

*Rubén Darío: Abismo y cima* ("Rubén Darío: Fame and Tragedy"), Universidad Nacional Autónoma de México/Fondo de Cultura Económica, 1966.

*Tiempo y memoria en la obra de Proust* ("Time and Memory in Proust's Work"), Porrúa, 1967.

### Speeches

*Educación mexicana: discursos, entrevistas, mensajes* ("Mexican Education"), Mexico, Secretaría de Educación Pública, 1944.

*La escuela mexicana; Exposición de la doctrine educativa,* Secretaría de Educación Pública, 1944.

*Educación y concordia internacional: Discursos y mensajes (1941–1947)* ("Education and International Concord"), El Colegio de México, 1948.

*Teachers Hold the Key to UNESCO's Objectives,* Naldrett Press, 1949.

*Doce mensajes educativos* ("Twelve Educational Messages"), Secretaría de Educación Pública, 1960.

*La voz de México en Bogotá y Los Angeles* ("The Voice of Mexico in Bogotá and Los Angeles"), Secretaría de Educación Pública, 1963.

*Patria y cultura,* Secretaría de Educación Pública, 1964.

*Discursos (1941–1964),* Porrúa, 1964.

### Other

*Memorias,* four volumes, Porrúa, 1969–1972.

### SOURCES:

#### Books

*Hispanic Writers,* edited by Bryan Ryan, Detroit, Gale, 1991.

*Latin American Writers,* edited by Carlos A. Solé, New York, Scribner's, 1989.

Laves, Walter H. C., and Charles A. Thomson, *UNESCO: Purpose, Progress, Prospects,* Bloomington, Indiana University Press, 1957.

Sewell, James P., *UNESCO and World Politics,* New Jersey, Princeton University Press, 1975.

#### Periodicals

*Américas,* August 1969, pp. 6–11.

*Antioch Review,* Vol. 28, 1968, pp. 477–90.

*New York Times,* May 14, 1974, p. 40.

*Times* (London), May 15, 1974, p. 21; May 31, 1974, p. 18.

—*Sketch by Amanda Beresford*

---

# Joaquín Torres García
## 1874-1949
### Uruguayan painter

Joaquín Torres García was considered one of the leading modernist artists in South America. He was born in Montevideo, Uruguay on July 28, 1874 to Joaquín Torres Fradera and María García Pérez. His father emigrated from Mataro, Spain, to Uruguay, where he set up a bazaar at the Plaza de las Carretas and had a lumber yard and carpenter's shop where Torres García worked as a young boy. His maternal grandfather was from the Canary Islands and his maternal grandmother was from the Amerindians and early Spanish settlers. Torres García had a brother, Gaspar, and a sister, Inés, who were also active in the many family businesses.

Torres García was ill as a child and his mother taught him reading, writing, and arithmetic at home. He was an avid reader and began sketching at an early age. Some of his sketches date back to 1886 when he was 12 years old. After they lost their savings due to a bank failure and the government restricted foreign imports, the family was in financial distress. Torres García's father packed up the whole family and boarded a ship for Spain in July of 1891. After they arrived in Spain, Torres García enrolled in the Arts and Crafts School in Mataro. In 1892, the family moved to Barcelona, where the fourth centennial of the discovery of America was being celebrated.

Torres García was captivated by the city. He enrolled in the Official School of Fine Arts of Barcelona, where he studied with Catalán artists who would later become highly recognized for their art: Joaquim Mi, Isidre Nonell and Joaquim Sunyer. While his artist friends rambled through the countryside, Torres García searched the library for books and took classes in the afternoon at Academia Baixas before taking night courses at the Llotja ("Exchange"). In 1897 the Barcelona newspaper, *La Vanguardia,* published a drawing he submitted for a special edition for the New Year. The drawing was titled "La compra de turrones" ("Buying the nougat") and depicted Christmas shoppers in a street scene. He signed the drawing "Quim Torras." The newspaper displayed many of his unpublished posters and drawings in their entrance hall a few days later. One of the journalists described Torres García as a brilliant talent.

Torres García was a member of an association of Catholic artists, the Cercle Artistic de Sant Lluc, which provided a library where he learned about the famous artists and writers of the time. But the association was inhibiting to Torres García. They did not allow live nude models and they were opposed to "frivolous" art. He would draw from live models at the studio of brothers Joan and Julio González Pellicer. In 1899 he published work in *La Vida Literaria* in Madrid and in 1901 in *Hispania* in Barcelona. Torres García went into a depression and his art was transformed. His greatest influence was Ramon Casas, a well-known Catalán artist at the turn of the century. In July 1901, an art review magazine in Barcelona, *Pel i Ploma,* published some of Torres García's art, including a full-color picture on the cover. An art critic, Eugeni d'Ors, saw his work at the Sala Pares in 1905 and in a review said that Torres García should be doing monumental work such as in a church or palace.

### Finds Freedom to Teach

Torres García illustrated books and magazines and taught art in schools and private homes. He became friends with the father of one of his students, Roberto J. Payro, who was a correspondent with a Buenos Aires newspaper, *La Nación.* Torres García began teaching at the Mont d'Or school in Barcelona in 1906. The founder of the school, Joan Palau i Vera, encouraged advanced teaching methods and Torres García was allowed more freedom to teach. Then, in 1908 he had his first opportunity to paint a mural; it was one of several commissions for large murals, but in each case the work was later either destroyed or disappeared. He was commissioned to paint six huge canvases for the Chapel of the Holy Sacrament at the Church of San Agustín in Barcelona; during the Civil War in Spain, they were all destroyed by fire. Torres García was commissioned to decorate another church, but the nuns were displeased with his work and covered it. Pere Corominas, chief of the finance department in the municipal government of Barcelona and an old friend of Torres García, asked the artist's advice on decorating his office. Torres García painted four large panels for the office, but after Corominas left office, the panels were removed and disappeared.

### Publishes First Book

Torres García fell in love with a student's younger sister, Manolita, and they were married in 1910. They traveled to Brussels, Belgium, where his work was on exhibit, and then settled in Vilasar de Mar, on the Mediterranean coast near Barcelona. It was here, in Vilasar de Mar, that they had their first child, a daughter, Olimpia. Later the couple had three more children: Ifigenia, Augusto, and Horacio. In 1913, Torres García published his first of many books, *Notes sobre art,* a collection of numerous articles he had written for periodicals. In 1915 he published a second book, *Dialegs,* and wrote articles about art for various magazines and publications throughout the years. His work was influenced by the Mediterranean while living in Vilasar de Mar. Torres García traveled to Italy with his wife and young daughter in 1912. He went to see all the masters but was more impressed with some of the small painting in the catacombs, especially a primitive painting in the Vatican library.

The Mont d'Or school had moved to a small town and at the end of 1912, when they returned from Italy, Torres García and his family moved to Tarrasa. When the founder left the school, Pere Moles took his place. Not only was Moles an old friend of Torres García's, he was married to Manolita's sister. The two couples worked in the school together, the sisters teaching music and working in the office. Torres-García began painting a mural in the Salon de San Jorge in 1913. He received much criticism about his rendering of the mural and in 1917, the Provincial Council told him to suspend his work. He offered to finish the work without pay and they refused. Torres García was very disappointed, but immediately set up several exhibitions.

Torres García went to Paris, where he drew pictures of everything he could in the city. He was fascinated with Paris but he had been thinking about going to the United States. He went to Picasso to ask his advice but Picasso would not see him. Finally, on July 5, 1920, he and his family boarded a ship to New York. This journey proved difficult for the artist, because he spoke no English and could not sell his work in New York. Instead, he took a job with a toy manufacturer, Artist Makers Toys, and was sent to Italy to find carpenters to make wooden toys for the company. In 1922 the family moved to Genoa, Italy, where he was so busy with the toy business that he could not find time to paint. Because of the Fascist regime that ruled Italy at the time, he moved his family to the coast of France in Villefrance-sur-Mer. He began painting again and in 1928 his art became more abstract. In 1930, Torres García developed what he called "Constructivism." He was one of the founders of the Cercle et Carre, a group of artists in Paris. Three of his children were also painting and an exhibition of their art was held at the Galerias Dalmau.

In 1934 Torres García and his family moved to Uruguay, where he taught and exhibited his work in numerous shows. He was very successful in Uruguay and set up a workshop where his influence changed the style of Latin American art. In 1939, he published his autobiography, *Historia de me vida*, in Montevideo. He founded the School of the South in 1942— also known as El Taller Torres García —which remained in operation for 20 years. In 1944 he was commissioned by the Martirene Hospital in the Colonia Saint Bois to paint seven murals; he published what is considered his best literary work, *Universalismo Constructivo*, and was awarded the Gran Premio Nacional de Pintura. His last show was held at the Amigos del Arte in Montevideo in July 1949. On August 8, 1949, Torres García died at the age of 75 in Montevideo, the town where he was born.

## SELECTED PUBLISHED WORKS:

*Notes sobre art*, 1913.
*Dialegs*, 1915.
*Historia de me vida*, Montevideo, 1939.
*Universalismo Constructivo*, Buenos Aires, Editorial Poseidon, 1944.

## SOURCES:

### Books

*Torres García*, translated by Kenneth Lyons, Barcelona, Ediciones Poligrafa, nd.

### Periodicals

*New York Times*, December 4, 1992, p. C20.

—*Sketch by Phyllis Noah*

# Jesus Salvador Treviño
## 1946-

### Hispanic American filmmaker

Born in 1946, Jesus Salvador Treviño has become a noted film writer, director, and producer. With a number of films to his credit, Treviño attacks issues that more commercial film makers do not have the freedom to address. His films focus on life in America's barrios, in which Treviño himself grew up. As an artist who sees himself as an inheritor of both Chicano tradition and mainstream American tradition, Treviño tries to bring human stories to the screen. While his personal background leads him to depict Hispanics in his work, Treviño emphasizes the primacy of the story rather than the race of the protagonist.

## Working-Class Background Inspires Art

On March 26, 1946, Evangelina Mercado Treviño gave birth to a son and named him for his father. Though Treviño was born in El Paso, Texas, he moved during his childhood to East Los Angeles, which has the largest concentration of Latinos in the United States. His adolescence and early adulthood found him among a generation of people just beginning to awaken to their ethnic identity as distinct from the rest of the country. As a person with artistic inclinations, Treviño found film to be an effective way to add his voice to this new chorus. In *Creative Differences*, Treviño called his entrance into film "a way of expressing the concerns, aspirations, and strategies of that [Latino] community."

Indeed Treviño's earliest works recall major events from the Chicano movement's early days. *Creative Differences'* authors Barbara Zheutlin and David Talbot asserted that his career "paralleled the rise of the Chicano movement," recalling events like the 1968 high school "walkouts" and the 1970 antiwar demonstration in which *Los Angeles Times* reporter Ruben Salazar died.

Treviño attended Occidental College on a scholarship and graduated in 1968 with a degree in philosophy. He learned the fundamentals of filmmaking the summer after graduation in a government program called New Communicators. With those skills, Treviño went to work the next year for southern California public television station KCET as a journalist and producer of features for the nightly Mexican American talk show *Ahora!* Treviño survived the show's cancellation the next year when the station asked him to continue producing, only now with more independence.

During the early 1970s he produced three notable documentaries: *Soledad*, which detailed the lives of Hispanic and black prisoners in the prison of the same name; *America Tropical*, about controversial Mexican mural artist **David Siqueiros;** and *Yo Soy Chicano*, a work that Zheutlin and Talbot called "an elegantly composed history of the Chicano people from the Spanish conquest . . . to the social struggle of the 1970s."

Treviño has worked primarily with public television but does not disdain mainstream film. To the contrary, he appreciates the "creative momentum" of Hollywood's artists. Zheutlin and Talbot have suggested that Treviño would like to keep the entertaining pace and style of mainstream American movies and rearrange the substantive elements to present a more balanced view of the world.

To that end, Treviño turned to fictional films in 1977 with *Raices de Sangre* ("Roots of Blood"). With funding from public television and Mexican film companies, Treviño's motion picture dramatized historical figures' lives as integral parts of the story of the Latino experience. "How to relate several hundred years of history that is so filled with injustice, manifest destiny, and other forms of aggression against Latinos by the U.S. government, and how to allow people to feel it, and not make it boring. This is my task," Treviño noted. "I think this is where I get to explore how to be subtle and artful."

*Raices* met with critical success, named in 1991 as one of the top 25 Latin American films of all time at the Valladolid Film Festival. Treviño's nationally broadcast children's series *Infinity Factory* received a Special Achievement in Children's Programs award from the Action for Children's Television group in 1977. *Soledad* won a gold medal at the Atlanta film festival in 1971.

In the 1980s Treviño continued to produce award-winning films, including *Gangs,* which won the 1988 Directors Guild of America award for best daytime drama and first place among one-hour dramas in the 1988 National Latino Film and Video Festival of New York. Since 1986 he has worked as a freelance writer and director. Treviño married Barbara Murray in 1989, and continues to work and live in southern California.

## SOURCES:

### Books

Zheutlin, Barbara, and David Talbot, *Creative Differences: Profiles of Hollywood Dissidents,* Boston, South End Press, 1978.

### Periodicals

*Hispanic,* August 1992, p. 76
*Los Angeles Times,* May 18, 1986, section B, p. 4; November 9, 1986, section B, p. 13; May 3, 1987; section B, p. 4; December 27, 1987, section B, p. 11; August 7, 1988; section B, p. 2; February 10, 1991, section BR, p. 11; June 15, 1992, sec 3; October 3, 1993, section M, p. 5.
*Variety,* September 21, 1988, p. 76.

—*Sketch by James McCarthy*

# Lee Trevino
## 1939-
### Hispanic American professional golfer

**B**orn in Texas in 1939, Lee Trevino overcame poverty and his own unorthodox golfing style to become one of the most successful golfers of his age. In their book *The Masters of Golf,* Dick Aultman and Ken Bowden describe Trevino's style as "five wrongs [that] add up to an immaculate right." Trevino has won many major tournaments, including the U.S. Open and the British Open. He also claimed the PGA Championship in 1974 and 1984. In addition to his success on the greens, Trevino established Lee Trevino Enterprises, based in Dallas, Texas. He also works for the National Broadcasting Corporation (NBC) as a golf commentator.

Joseph and Juanita Trevino welcomed their new son, Lee Buck Trevino, on December 1, 1939. Though they lived in relative poverty, Trevino overcame that disadvantage. After four years in the U.S. Marines, he began to play par-3 golf frequently, and worked at a driving range in the Dallas area. In *The Complete Book of Golf,* John Allan May recounts a story of Trevino's winning bet that he could defeat another player using a Dr. Pepper bottle rather than clubs.

When not performing such stunts, Trevino spent his time on the Dallas courses perfecting his most unusual swing. May describes it in detail: "He stands wide open, with his shoulders aiming about 30 degrees to the left of his line-of-aim. His left wrist is cupped at the address, his right palm well behind the shaft. His hip turn is restricted. At the top of his swing his left wrist is bowed-out to an exaggerated extent. The clubface is closed. He then drags the club down and along, hitting very late against a firm left side and fades the ball left-to-right."

Trevino joined the professional tour briefly in 1966, finishing 54th at the U.S. Open, but after his wife Claudia convinced him to try again, he finished fifth the following year. He became professional golf's Rookie of the Year in 1967, and in 1971, the PGA named him Player of the Year. *Sports Illustrated* named Trevino Sportsman of the Year in 1971, after he had won the U.S. Open for the second time in four years. His 1971 championship came in a playoff round against the formidable Jack Nicklaus. Trevino won the playoff 68–71.

Since then, Trevino has won tournaments all over the world. His back-to-back victories in the British Open in 1971 and 1972 supported his position as one of the foremost players in the world. He has also won the 1972 Hartford Open; the Canadian Open in 1971, 1977, and 1979; the Mexican Open, in 1973

*Lee Trevino*

and 1975; and both the 1969 and 1971 World Cup golf tournaments. Trevino also joined and captained several U.S. Ryder Cup teams from 1971 through 1985.

Trevino joined the senior tour in 1990 and quickly began to duplicate his earlier success. In that year, he became the first Senior PGA player to earn more prize money than the money leader of the regular tour. Still living in Dallas, where he has raised his six children, Trevino continues to play on the Senior tour and work for NBC. Saying, "you can't keep a good man down," May asserts that "one of his [Trevino's] greatest gifts to golf has been his buoyant attitude, even when losing."

**SOURCES:**

**Books**

Aultman, Dick, and Ken Bowden, *The Master Learning From Their Methods,* Galahad Books, 1994.

May, John Allan, *The Complete Book of Golf: A Guide to Equipment, Techniques, and Courses,* Smithmark Publishing, 1991.

*—Sketch by Jim McCarthy*

# Rafael Leónidas Trujillo
## 1891-1961
**Dominican dictator**

In an area notorious for its dictators, Rafael Leónidas Trujillo ranks among the most infamous. Extravagant, tyrannical, and vain, the self-proclaimed Benefactor of the Fatherland, Rebuilder of the Financial Independence of the Republic, First Journalist, Chief Protector of the Dominican Working Class, and Genius of the Peace, Generalissimo Doctor Trujillo was military dictator and ultimate ruler of the Dominican Republic from 1930 until his assassination in 1961. Trujillo's regime stands out as one of the longest in the history of Latin America. By the time of his death, "the Dominican Republic was not only ruled by Trujillo, it was his property," a *Newsweek* writer commented.

Despite Trujillo's personal crusade for wealth, power and self-aggrandizement, some observers have claimed that his regime did accrue material benefits to the Dominican people. To this extent his rule has been described as "enlightened"; certainly, the façade of the Dominican Republic was a striking contrast next to neighboring Haiti and Cuba. As Trujillo's obituary in the London *Times* rationalized, "It was above all an efficient dictatorship—efficient in its organization of widespread social services and efficient in maintaining itself in power for a long period." The price, however, was "a degradation of the human spirit such as has rarely been seen in the modern world."

The true facts surrounding Trujillo's background and adolescence are rather clouded. Rafael Leónidas Trujillo Molina was born on October 24, 1891, the third of 11 children, in San Cristóbal, a poor agricultural village on the Dominican Republic's south coast. Official eulogists erroneously claimed that Trujillo was of noble descent, his forebears including a French marquis and a Spanish army officer. Trujillo himself denied his partially Black heritage; during his rule it was an act of treason to make such a declaration. His father, José Trujillo Valdez, was a humble postal clerk who was rumored to supplement his income by rustling cattle. In San Cristóbal, Trujillo received a rudimentary education. At the age of 16, he worked as a telegraph operator and later as a guard on a sugar plantation. During this period he was allegedly a member of "The 44" gang, who indulged in theft, forgery, and blackmail; a fire in the Dominican Supreme Court Building in 1927 destroyed any evidence of Trujillo's holding a criminal record.

### Ascends to Power

Official Marine records show that Trujillo received his commission in the National Constabulary and took his oath on January 11, 1919, during the U.S. occupation of the Dominican Republic from 1916–1924. Described by Ian Bell in *The Dominican Republic* as "a man born to command," Trujillo's ascent through the military ranks was meteoric. Trained by U.S. Marines, he graduated from the Haina Military Academy in 1921 and assumed the rank of lieutenant colonel in 1924 (some sources say 1926). In 1927 he was promoted to brigadier general and assumed command of what would become the Dominican Army a year later.

Trujillo's chance to seize power arose in 1930 when President Horacio Vásquez was opposed by a small band of revolutionaries. As Chief-of-Police, Trujillo declared his "neutrality" and Vásquez was forced to resign. By May, Trujillo had maneuvered himself into the presidential seat. The sole candidate in the presidential election, he procured 95 percent of the vote, ensured by acts of intimidation and violence. Trujillo's hold on the presidency was consolidated after a hurricane devastated the capital, Santo Domingo, on September 3, 1930, and killed two thousand people. His indisputable organizational skills facilitated the rapid reconstruction of Santo Domingo and the imposition of a tightly controlled economy. *Time* acknowledged that Trujillo "had a natural talent for autocratic management."

### Terror and Development under Trujillo

Trujillo secured his supremacy through the systematic elimination of all his opponents. Benefitting from the confusion created in the aftermath of the 1930 hurricane, his political adversaries began to disappear; there were unexplained suicides, strange car crashes, summary arrests, and executions. Opposition parties were eradicated, the press censored, the right of assembly denied, and independent trade unions abolished. Trujillo founded and became chief of the Partido Dominicano, the sole political party in the Dominican Republic. He personally dominated every aspect of power and control, ensuring complete loyalty through bribery, terror, and blackmail.

One of Trujillo's most horrific outrages was the Haitian massacre of October 1937. Between 5,000 and 25,000 Haitian squatters on the Dominican border were slaughtered at Trujillo's behest in an onslaught that lasted for 36 hours. While the atrocity received comparatively little attention from the international media, it was enough to make Trujillo relinquish the presidential title in the 1938 "elections" and installed a puppet president, Jacinto Peynado, followed by Manuel de Jesús Troncoso de la Concha from 1940 to 1942.

While Trujillo resumed the presidency in 1943, there would be other nominal presidents during his dictatorship, including his brother Hector in 1953, and **Joaquín Balaguer** in 1960. When Trujillo was not

titular president he endowed himself other titles, such as Chief and Benefactor, or Commander of the Armed Forces. Trujillo was always absolute ruler; as a London *Times* reporter concluded, "his precise title did not matter. . . . Wherever it came from, the voice of command was the same."

"I wish there were a Trujillo in every country of South and Central America" stated Allen Ellender, a U.S. Democratic senator, in *Time* magazine. Under Trujillo's strong-arm management, the Dominican Republic was visibly modernized, particularly development of the sugar industry, grazing, manufacturing, and infrastructure: roads, schools and hospitals were built. Trujillo even managed to liquidate the Republic's debts within 17 years of assuming power. As a result of this achievement he declared that the Dominican Republic was "absolutely free, absolutely sovereign, absolutely independent," as Bell noted in *The Dominican Republic*. Literacy levels were raised from 30 percent to 96 percent. However, some observers contend that the Dominican people never really benefitted from Trujillo's schemes; the ambitious public works program was accompanied by his own private investment program where, by 1939, his income was $200,000 a month.

Corruption and blatant nepotism were features of Trujillo's dictatorship, and he and his family accumulated small fortunes. Selden Rodman noted in *Quisqueya* that in the 1950s Trujillo ranked among the world's two or three richest individuals. He personally owned 12 palaces and ranches and was the largest landowner, while family members were given outrageous titles and positions, monopolized the salt, tobacco and beer industries, and acquired approximately one third of the Republic's cultivated land. During Trujillo's silver jubilee year in 1954 the ruler decreed a "Fair of Peace and Fraternity of the Free World" at an estimated cost of $35 million, a third of the nation's annual budget. His daughter María de los Angeles de Corazón de Jesús was crowned Queen Angelita I at the opening of the fair in December 1955. His son Rafael was commissioned as a colonel in the Dominican Army when only four.

Trujillo's regime was characterized by an absurd level of sycophancy. Bernard Diederich wrote in *Trujillo: The Death of the Goat:* "The cult of adulation had no limits. The capital city bore Trujillo's name, as did the highest mountain peak and hundreds of streets, parks and sites. The tropical landscape was literally dotted with his likeness in statues and on bronze plaques. Every town, sports event, or billiard game had to be dedicated to the Benefactor of the Fatherland and Father of the New Fatherland. The humblest dirt-floor hut carried the sign: 'In this house Trujillo is Chief.' In the streets of the capital, neon signs blinked the message 'God and Trujillo.'"

Although Trujillo initially enjoyed a warm relationship with the United States, it soured toward the end of his regime. In 1956 Jesús de Galíndez, a Columbia University lecturer who criticized the Trujillo dictatorship in his doctoral dissertation, was kidnapped from New York and murdered in the Dominican Republic. Gerald Murphy, the U.S. pilot who claimed to have delivered Galíndez to the Dominican Republic, disappeared.

In 1960 Trujillo attempted the overthrow and assassination of president Rómulo Betancourt of Venezuela, who instigated an indictment against Trujillo for his human rights abuses. He also suspected Betancourt of being involved in a second invasion attempt to oust him. Trujillo found himself condemned and ostracized by the international community; the Organization of American States urged fellow members to break ties with the Dominican Republic. When he no longer found favor in the United States, Trujillo courted Moscow. However, the Trujillo edifice had begun to crumble and the Dominican Republic was heading for an economic crisis. In frustration, Trujillo turned his attack on the Roman Catholic Church. When six bishops proposed an amnesty for political prisoners, hundreds of people were rounded up by the police in an alleged conspiracy; Trujillo even entertained the idea of killing the Pope.

Trujillo was assassinated on May 30, 1961. Traveling to a midnight tryst with one of his numerous mistresses he was killed in an ambush headed by Brigadier General Juan Tomas Díaz. At the time of his death Trujillo was worth an estimated $800 million. He was married three times—to Aminta Ledesma, Bienvenida Ricardo, and María Martínez—and had four acknowledged children.

## SOURCES:

### Books

Bell, Ian, *The Dominican Republic,* Boulder, CO, Westview Press, 1981.
*Biographical Dictionary of Latin American and Caribbean Political Leaders,* edited by Robert J. Alexander, Westport, CT, Greenwood Press, 1988.
Diederich, Bernard, *Trujillo: The Death of the Goat,* London, Bodley Head, 1978.
Roberts, T. D., *Area Handbook for the Dominican Republic,* Washington, D.C., U.S. Government Printing Office, 1966.
Rodman, Selden, *Quisqueya: A History of the Dominican Republic,* Seattle, University of Washington Press, 1964.

Wiarda, Howard J., *The Dominican Republic: Nation in Transition,* London, Pall Mall Press, 1969.

### Periodicals

*Newsweek,* June 12, 1961, pp. 18–19.
*Time,* June 9, 1961, pp. 26–29.
*Times* (London), June 2, 1961, pp. 17, 23.

—*Sketch by Amanda Beresford*

# Roberto Trujillo
## 1951-
### Hispanic American curator and librarian

Roberto Trujillo has made significant contributions to the field of library sciences and has become a noted curator of Mexican American scholarship. He currently works at Stanford University in Palo Alto, California, where he has undertaken the task of expanding the university's collection of Latin Americana. He has compiled several significant bibliographical works, most notably *Literatura Chicana: Creative and Critical Writings through 1984.*

Born in Mora, New Mexico, on February 1, 1951, Roberto Gabriel Trujillo spent the early years of his youth in the state where his parents, Rudolfo and Caroline, had grown up. Trujillo told James McCarthy that his parents' roots in New Mexico extended back "pre-statehood." Trujillo, one of six children, moved with his parents to Cheyenne, Wyoming, where he spent his elementary school years. The family returned to New Mexico in time for Trujillo to go to high school in his hometown. After graduation, Trujillo went to the University of New Mexico at Albuquerque, where he earned his undergraduate degree in 1972.

Trujillo left New Mexico in 1973 for California State University at Fullerton, where he received his master's degree in library sciences in 1974. After completing his graduate work, he started his professional career in the Los Angeles Public Library, as a librarian for Young Adult Services. He later became the project director for an adult literacy program with the Los Angeles County Public Library, before leaving for the University of California at Santa Barbara in 1976.

While at Santa Barbara, Trujillo established a significant collection of scholarship on Mexican American issues. During his seven years there, he was

*Roberto Trujillo*

most proud of making what he called "a single room" of books into a "major research collection." He also taught at the University of California at Berkeley, in the School of Library and Information Studies. In 1982 he went to Stanford University.

Trujillo developed the Stanford library's collection of books and periodicals on Mexican American issues, and he went further by beginning to gather manuscripts and build archives. Trujillo feels that although Latin America has received scholarly attention for some time, Mexican Americana has largely been marginalized. Trujillo has said that "by recovering a literary and historical heritage, we are adding to the canon of the cultural production of Mexican Americans." Trujillo sees current scholars as pioneers and noted that "Twenty years ago, this kind of work was just not being done."

Married in 1988 to Tamara Frost, Trujillo has established himself as one of Stanford's chief librarians and senior curators. He recently became the head curator not only of the library's Mexican American collection program, but the entire Latin American and Iberian collection as well. He hopes to focus and expand them in the same way as the Mexican American collection.

A member of the American Library Association, the Association of College and Research Libraries, the Seminar on the Acquisition of Latin American Library Materials, and REFORMA, the National Association to Promote Library Services to the Spanish Speaking, Trujillo sees libraries as a key to the perpetuation of knowledge: "Libraries give permanence to historical records that otherwise might not be saved. Even at a private university like Stanford, a library is a public record."

## SOURCES:

Trujillo, Roberto, interview with James McCarthy, January 17, 1995.

*—Sketch by James McCarthy*

# Miguel de Unamuno
## 1864-1936
### Spanish philosopher and writer

Miguel de Unamuno became one of the most important Spanish authors and philosophers of his time. He wrote prolifically, publishing novels, dramas, poetry, and hundreds of essays. Throughout his academic career he distinguished himself as Spain's leading heretic, vocally opposed to the administration of the Catholic church, but quite religious himself. Though noted for his patriotism, he frequently dispensed harsh criticism of the things he loved. His political inclinations changed over time, sometimes seeming to contradict themselves, and in general Unamuno resisted ready classification. Nevertheless, many of his contemporaries saw him as a giant in the landscape of Spanish culture, and scholars continue to study him as such today.

### Basque Boyhood

Born on September 29, 1864, Miguel de Unamuno y Jugo grew up in Bilbao at the mouth of the Nervion. As a major port and the capital of one of the three Basque provinces of Spain, Bilbao connected the Basque world to the world outside Spain. His father, a merchant named Felix Unamuno, married his niece, Salome de Jugo, and they had four children, including Miguel. Although his father died before he reached six years old, Unamuno exhibited what his family called "*caracter* Unamuno," or the Unamuno nature. Whenever Unamuno or one of his relatives showed stubbornness or a frustrating willfulness, the family customarily attributed it to the "*caracter* Unamuno."

He attended the *colegio* as a boy, avoiding the free institutions for the less fortunate. He experienced the strict Catholic orthodoxy of the middle-class to which his family belonged. He entered secondary school in 1875, and while at the Instituto Vizcaíno Unamuno's health turned poor. Although he found his studies dull, he began to enjoy the prescribed treatment for his physical weakness—long walks in nature. He spent vacations at his grandmother's country home, walking through the mountains and trees of the countryside.

In addition to his curiosity about nature, the adolescent Unamuno started to find questions about spirituality fascinating. He occasionally opened the Bible at random to find a scripture that would inspire or puzzle him. His study of Catholic philosophy, though not intellectually satisfying because of its often dogmatic nature, sent him toward a wider range of thinkers such as Kant, Descartes, and Hegel.

In 1880 Unamuno went to study at the School of Philosophy and Letters at the University of Madrid. The capital had become increasingly cosmopolitan, and Unamuno gained exposure to influences and ideas that often stood in total contrast to the conventionality of his upbringing. The great novelist Benito Perez Galdos had challenged the notion that Spain's great strength lay in its peasant heart. He also advocated freedom of religion in a 100 percent Catholic country, and many Spanish intellectuals opposed such progressive ideas. Unamuno very likely came to Madrid predisposed against these new thinkers, but as Margaret Rudd stated in her book *The Lone Heretic,* "Thus they faced each other, the Church of San Luis and the [liberal social and artistic club] Ateneo, and between them Miguel was to be torn for the next four years in Madrid." His time in the capital helped eventually to make him the "arch-heretic" of Spanish thought, but Unamuno never clearly resolved the conflict between the church and the university hall.

Unamuno completed his doctorate in 1884, but he never cared for the noise and pace of the capital, so with his degree in hand, he returned to Bilbao. While in Madrid he missed the countryside, his family, and perhaps most of all he missed his childhood sweetheart, Concepción Lizárraga Ecénarro, whom he called Concha. For the first few years after leaving university, Unamuno taught private lessons and wrote various pieces for local newspapers, but his goal of a permanent position at a university eluded him. Partly because he had studied Basque but denied its validity as a political subject, Unamuno had trouble finding a university with a post he could enjoy.

### The Domesticated Bear

In 1891, however, he married Concha and took a position teaching at the University of Salamanca. As biographer Martin Nozick wrote in *Miguel de Unamuno,* "Unamuno looked upon his Concha as . . . a mate who would exercise a civilizing influence on his unsociability." She played a major role in his professional career, often navigating her mercurial husband through the waters of the university social world. She also gave Unamuno ten children. Unamuno came to call himself *oso casero* (domesticated bear) because of the stability of his new situation.

Although he once described Salamanca as a "clutter of farmhouses giving the impression of pasture ground," he settled into life there, writing and publishing widely. In 1895 he published the essays of *En torno al casticismo,* and two years later he published his famous novel *Paz en la guerra (Peace in War).* His fame increased, and he soon became Salamanca's premier citizen. Unamuno seemed to enjoy these years, although he suffered bouts of depression. Nozick claimed that after several years at Salamanca, Unamuno had achieved "a position in Spanish intellectual life matched only by that of Croce in Italy."

Unamuno became the rector of the university in 1900, and once installed in that position, began to decry the weaknesses of Spain's academic establishment and society at large. Nozick stated that Unamuno advocated government inspections of professors which, though unpleasant, might prevent the grave inadequacies he saw all around him. He emphasized educating students in a way that would make them good all-around thinkers rather than specialists, trapped in a purely academic environment. He even told students not to attend certain classes in the university which taught clearly obsolete material such as Ptolemaic astronomy. He strongly condemned the Jesuits for their emphasis of faith over reason. He called the Jesuit way of learning a producer of "holy ignorance," and their ideas "confused, useless erudition."

### Trouble with the Crown

Unamuno remained as rector until 1914, publishing massively, including the 1913 book *Del sentimiento trágico de la vida en los hombres y en los pueblos,* (*The Tragic Sense of Life in Men and Peoples*) and many poems, essays, and other nonfiction prose. On August 13, 1914, however, the Salamanca paper ran an oversized headline which read, "Dismissal of Senor Unamuno." No clear reason came down from university administration for his dismissal, but some, including Rudd, have suggested that his support of state-controlled education had made him some powerful enemies. University officials tried to suggest that Unamuno had illegally approved a degree for a foreign student, but Unamuno clearly refuted the charge in the newspapers.

His enemies, with the support of the Crown, even gave him a sixteen-year prison sentence, but Unamuno's popularity prevented any part of it from being served. Demoted and humiliated, Unamuno turned to meditation and his writing. He wrote a religious poem

entitled *El Cristo de Velázquez* (*The Christ of Velazquez*) in 1914, but did not publish it until 1920.

In that same year he returned to the University of Salamanca as the vice-rector, but when dictator Primo de Rivera came to power in 1923, Unamuno's anti-monarchical fury grew. Although Spanish newspapers could express no dirisive opinions about the King or Rivera, Unamuno turned to Latin American newspapers for his virulent, bitter attacks. The public conflict ended in February 1924, when the King ordered Unamuno into exile on the Canary Islands.

He escaped from his exile on the African islands the following year and went to Paris. He then moved into the French countryside and lived at Hendaye until 1930. In that year, Rivera's rule ended, and the Spanish Republic triumphantly returned Unamuno to his former post as rector.

In 1934 his wife and one daughter died, prompting him to retire from teaching, although he retained the title of lifetime rector. In 1936, however, he publicly supported **Francisco Franco**'s bid to topple the Republic and again faced removal. When Franco took power, he reinstated Unamuno, but Unamuno's support for Franco turned to public disapproval, and this time the dictator confined Unamuno to his home.

Unamuno died on December 31, 1936, in Salamanca, where he is buried and continues to be a part of local culture. Nearly 20 years after his death, when the University of Salamanca prepared to celebrate its 700th anniversary, eminent thinkers from around the country came to praise the university's greatest member and visit his grave, in plain defiance of Franco's decree that no one even speak Unamuno's name during the entire festivities.

### SELECTED PUBLISHED WORKS:

#### Essays

*En torno al casticismo,* F. Fe, 1902.

*Vida de Don Quijote y Sancho,* F. Fe, 1905; translation by Homer P. Earle published as *The Life of Don Quixote and Sancho,* Knopf, 1927.

*Del sentimiento trágico de la vida en los hombres y en los pueblos,* 1913, Renacimiento, 1928; translation by J. E. Crawford published as *The Tragic Sense of Life in Men and Peoples,* Macmillan, 1926.

*La agonía del cristianismo,* 1925, Renacimiento, 1931; translation by Pierre Loving published as *The Agony of Christianity,* Payson & Clark, 1928; translation by Kurt F. Reinhardt published as *The Agony of Christianity,* Ungar, 1960.

## Fiction

*Paz en la guerra,* F. Fe, 1897; translation by Allen Lacy and Martin Nozick with Anthony Kerrigan published as *Peace in War,* edited by Kerrigan, Princeton University Press, 1983.

*Niebla,* 1914, Renacimiento, 1928; translation by Warner Fite published as *Mist,* Knopf, 1928.

*Abel Sánchez: Una historia de pasión,* Renacimiento, 1917; translation published as *Abel Sanchez,* edited by Angel del Río and Amelia de del Río, Holt, 1947.

*San Manuel Bueno, mártir, y tres historias más,* Espasa-Calpe, 1933; translation by Francisco de Segovia and Jean Pérez published in bilingual edition as *San Manuel Bueno, mártir,* Harrap, 1957.

## Poetry

*El Cristo de Velázquez,* Calpe, 1920; translation by Eleanor L. Turnbull published as *The Christ of Velazquez,* Johns Hopkins Press, 1951.

## SOURCES:

### Books

*Hispanic Writers,* edited by Bryan Ryan, Detroit, Gale Research, 1991.

Nozick, Martin, *Miguel de Unamuno,* Boston, Twayne Publishing, 1971.

Rudd, Margaret Thomas, *The Lone Heretic,* Austin, University of Texas Press, 1963.

*—Sketch by James McCarthy*

# Joseph A. Unanue
## 1926-

### Hispanic American business executive

Joseph A. Unanue became prominent as the president and chief executive officer of Goya Foods Inc. In 1992, under Unanue's guidance, Goya Foods gained the distinction of being the largest Hispanic-owned company in the United States. Goya Foods has built its success upon selling and marketing Hispanic foods in the United States.

Goya Foods was founded by Unanue's father, Prudencio Unanue Ortiz, in 1936. The elder Unanue had immigrated from his native Spain to Puerto Rico in 1904, and then came to the United States in 1915. Upon his arrival, he worked in the food industry by importing olives and canned sardines to America from Spain. However, due to the Spanish Civil War, Unanue's original import business eventually failed. Nevertheless, he did not give up his struggle to supply Hispanic foods to the immigrants of the United States. Rhonda Richards explained the family's commitment to the business in *USA Today:* "Homesick for the foods of Spain and Puerto Rico, Unanue believed Puerto Ricans, Cubans, and other Caribbean immigrants were too. So in 1936, he and his wife, Carolina, also of Spanish descent, started Goya Foods, the name borrowed from the sardine label he imported."

After obtaining an engineering degree, Joseph A. Unanue took over the United States based chain in 1976, after the death of his father. Under the younger Unanue's guidance, the company grew to sell more than 800 products and its revenue rose about 12 percent annually to reach $453 million in 1992. Much of this revenue success was due to Unanue's innovative idea to expand the company's product lines to reach all individuals of Hispanic descent. Specifically, Unanue began marketing his new products to the growing Hispanic population that were of Mexican descent. As Richards explained, "Coping with these different tastes means an extensive expansion of Goya's product line, because Hispanics of Mexican and Central American descent enjoy many foods unfamiliar to Hispanics of Caribbean descent—and visa versa." Unanue accomplished this marketing feat with a relatively simple plan, as he told Laura Zinn in *Business Week:* "Follow the trend of migrating Hispanics who are coming in and market the products that they know from home."

Despite the innovative methods Unanue has used to increase revenue since his father passed away, the company remained conservative and loyal to its original customers. As Rick Mendoza noted in *Hispanic Business,* "A company that has been successful for so long often becomes conservative, and Goya Foods is no exception. In some ways it is so conservative it's almost radical. For example, Goya Foods gives the same price to the little mom and pop *bodegas* as to the giant supermarket chains." When asked about this unusual pricing policy, Unanue explained, "We've done that since the company started. . . . We found that it is good for us, so we kept it."

### Hispanic Foods Have Broad Appeal

During the 1980s Goya Foods began to target non-Hispanic, mainstream consumers with its ethnic foods. In particular, Unanue focused upon health-conscious, non-Hispanic consumers with Goya's popular beans and rice products, using commercials in various television markets. As Richards described the business philosophy: "Health-conscious consumers are replacing meat with beans to reduce cholesterol and increase fiber. So Goya is pumping up advertising. The old 'Goya, oh boya' slogan is gone. In its place are slick TV commercials and magazine adds for Goya pre-seasoned rice mixes and black bean soup. The commercials feature a light-skinned woman and her family, who could be Anglo or Hispanic, depending on one's point of view. They are as mainstream as a Rice-a-Roni commercial. The slogan: "For better meals, turn to Goya.'" Many business insiders believed that Goya had made a good start in the non-Hispanic market.

Goya Foods also attributed its success to the fact that the company is family owned and operated. As Kim Bergheim described it in *Hispanic,* "There are eight Unanues, who range in age . . . who work for Goya across the country, including in Puerto Rico, Miami, Chicago, and the Secaucus [New Jersey] headquarters." Unanue's son Joseph F. Unanue became head of marketing for Goya after receiving his bachelor's degree from Duke University and his master's in marketing from North Carolina University. He has also written articles about the marketing of Hispanic foods in the United States.

Under Unanue's direction, a small, family-owned business has developed into one of the largest wholesale food corporations in the United States. Unanue continued and built upon his father's legacy, and also gave other family members an opportunity to contribute to the company. His hard work and innovative business practices have benefitted not only the food industry, but also Hispanic American culture.

## SOURCES:

### Periodicals

*Business Week,* December, 7, 1987, pp. 137–138; June 20, 1994, pp. 70–71.
*Hispanic,* December 1993, p. 64.
*Hispanic Business,* August 191, p. 70–71.
*USA Today,* May 10, 1993, p. E2; June 14, 1993, p. B2.

—*Sketch by John Michael Rivera*

# Teresa Urrea
## 1873-1906
### Mexican mystic and *curandera*

A gifted, enigmatic, and highly complex young woman, Teresa Urrea achieved notoriety with her extraordinary psychic abilities and healing powers rarely heard of in her time. She lived and practiced her healing arts at the Cabora ranch in northern Mexico, which for a time became known as the Lourdes of Mexico. In her brief life she cured tens of thousands of people of real or imaginary ills, and became known as the Saint of Cabora, even though the title was not conferred on her by any church authority. She is as well known for the part she may have innocently played in the inception of the Mexican Revolution as she is for her extrasensory powers. Contemporary Mexican historians call her the Mexican Joan of Arc.

Urrea was born on October 15, 1873, on Rancho Santana, north of Ocoroni in the state of Sinaloa, Mexico. Her mother was 14-year-old Cayetana Chavez, a poor Yaqui Indian girl, and her father was Don Tomas Urrea, a Mexican patron of the ranch. Her parents were not married, and Teresita (the diminutive form of her name) was half-sister to all of her father's 18 children and her mother's four.

### Discovers Healing Powers

In 1888, Urrea moved to her father's ranch in Cabora, and it was here that the sensitive, fragile girl learned from one of her father's Indian servants, Maria Sonora, the use of herbs in caring for the sick and injured. Shortly after her arrival at Cabora, Urrea lapsed into an inexplicable catatonic state that lasted three months and 18 days. After three disoriented months of recovery, she began to experience trances and believed she had been charged by the Virgin Mary to cure people. She demonstrated her powers on a few nearby patients—many of her reported cures were spectacular—and a slow but steady stream of devotees began to make their way to the ranch.

The news of the beautiful girl of Cabora who could cure all illnesses spread quickly, and soon Teresita had a large following, especially among the Tarahumaras, Yaqui, and Mayo Indians, who regarded her with awe. Her reputation caused great concern among the Mexican government and the Catholic church. Mexican president (and later dictator) **Porfirio Diaz** in particular was troubled by the influence that one young woman could exercise over the tribes, although it was a power she apparently neither wanted nor encouraged. The Indians sought her blessing for a series of revolts over land boundaries, but Urrea would only remark, according to the *Southern California Quarterly,* "God intended for you to have the lands, or He would not have given them to you." Although no evidence has ever been uncovered that Urrea or her father inspired these rebellions, the Mexican government exiled both of them in 1892.

### Flees North with Followers

Political controversy followed Teresa to Nogales, Arizona, where the thousands of pilgrims flocking to see her became recruitment prospects for the revolutionists plotting to overthrow the government of Diaz. The household later relocated to Solomonville in eastern Arizona in 1895, and then to El Paso in 1896. Continued harassment from the Mexican government forced the family to move away from the border to Clifton, Arizona. Throughout the moves, Urrea, known by this time as the "santa de Cabora," continued to minister to the sick and the poor. The Indians who followed her became fanatical, attacking a customs house in Nogales, Mexico, with shouts of "Viva la Santa de Cabora," resulting in the deaths of 14 people.

Urrea publicly refused to have any part in the affairs of Mexico. According to *Voices: Readings from El Grito,* she issued a statement in 1896 printed in the *El Paso Herald,* one of only three documents in existence that contain direct quotations from her. It says, in part, "I have noticed with much pain that the persons who have taken up arms in Mexican territory have invoked my name in aid of the schemes they are carrying through. But I repeat I am not one who authorizes or at the same time interferes with these proceedings."

Urrea's life took an uncharacteristically commercial turn in 1900 when she joined forces with a medical company in New York that would tour the United States on a "curing crusade." She agreed to accept the $10,000 contract on the condition that none of her patients would be charged for her help. When she discovered that scheming promoters were indeed collecting hefty fees, Urrea found a lawyer to terminate her contract. In the meantime, she had a one-day marriage to mine worker Guadalupe Rodriguez, who was later tried for a crime, found insane, and sent to an asylum. She later married John Van Order of Arizona, and had two daughters, Laura in 1902 and Magdelena in 1904.

Urrea returned to Clifton, Arizona, where her health began to fail. On January 11, 1906, Urrea died peacefully of consumption (pulmonary tuberculosis) at the age of 33. Many of her followers insisted she had simply worn out her spirit in the service of her people. Hundreds of mourners followed her casket in a funeral procession to Shannon Hill Catholic cemetery, where she was buried beside her father, Don Tomas.

## SOURCES:

### Books

Holden, William Curry, *Teresita,* Stemmer House, 1978.
*Voices: Readings from El Grito, A Journal of Contemporary Mexican American Thought, 1967–1973,* Quinto Sol, 1973.

### Periodicals

*Historia Mexicana* (Durango, Mexico), April/June, 1957, pp. 627–644.
*New York Times,* August 13, 1896, p. 1; August 14, 1896, p. 1; August, 1896, p. 1; August 20, 1896, p. 1.
*Southern California Quarterly,* September 1963.

—*Sketch by Julie Catalano*

# Luis Valdez
## 1940-
### Mexican American playwright and director

Legitimately called the father of Chicano theater, playwright and director Luis Valdez has given this movement a voice since 1963, when his first play was staged by the drama department at San Jose State College. From there he went on to found El Teatro Campesino in 1965, a touring farm workers' theater troupe. El Teatro Campesino produced one-act plays, often without stage, script, or props, that dramatized the circumstances of migrant workers and ignited a national Chicano theater movement, or teatro chicano.Valdez has written, co-written, and directed many plays depicting the Hispanic experience, including *La Carpa de los Rasquachis* (1973), *El Fin del Mundo* (1976), *Zoot Suit* (1978), and *Tibercio Vasquez* (1980). He also directed the box-office smash movie *La Bamba* in 1987.

Valdez has received numerous honors and awards for his work. These include an Obie in 1968, as well as Los Angeles Drama Critics awards in 1969, 1972, and 1978, and an Emmy in 1973. In 1983 the San Francisco Bay Critics Circle awarded him Best Musical. He was also honored that same year by President Reagan's Committee on Arts and Humanities. He has received honorary doctorates from Columbia College, San Jose State University, and the California Institute of the Arts.

### Theater Career Begins in College

Luis Valdez was born June 26, 1940, in Delano, California, to Francisco and Armeda Valdez. He was the second of ten children in a migrant worker family that moved from harvest to harvest in the central valleys of California. Due to this peripatetic existence, he attended many different schools before the family finally settled in San Jose. Graduating from high school there, he then entered San Jose State College (now University) on a scholarship in 1960.

Valdez did more than just earn a bachelor's degree in English at San Jose State. In 1961 his one-act play *The Theft* won a writing contest, and his first full-length play, *The Shrunken Head of Pancho Villa*, was produced in 1963 by the school's drama department. After graduating in 1964, Valdez spent the next few months with the San Francisco Mime Troupe. Its lessons in agitprop (agitation and propaganda) theater

were valuable, for they laid the groundwork for his next venture.

In 1965 Valdez went to Delano, where he joined **César Chávez** in his effort to educate and organize migrants into a viable farm workers' union. It was in support of Chávez's movement that he put his theatrical talents to work to form El Teatro Campesino, a farm workers' theater troupe. The theater was used to educate and inform not only the farm workers, but the public as well. El Teatro Campesino toured the migrant camps with their *actos,* or (one-act plays) that explored political and cultural issues of concern to the movement. In 1967 Valdez left the union movement in an effort to broaden his theater's reach and to amplify its messages. The troupe toured the United States in 1967 and 1968, winning the Obie in 1968. The theater moved beyond agitprop and migrant concerns, delving into traditional Mexican theatrical forms. They staged musical *corridas*, or dramatized ballads, religious pageants, and *peladitos*, or vaudeville-type dramas featuring an underdog.

Valdez had established a Chicano cultural center in Del Ray, California, in 1967. In 1969 he moved both theater and cultural center to Fresno, where they remained for two years. While in Fresno, Valdez taught at Fresno State College, produced the film *I Am Joaquin,* and created TENAZ, the national Chicano theater organization with groups throughout the Southwest. Valdez moved the theater a final time in 1971, to San Juan Bautista, south of San Francisco. Combined now with the cultural center, it was called El Centro Campesino Cultural, and it became a fully professional production company. The company toured Mexico and Europe and staged productions in New York City.

### Theater Movement Expands Nationally

The 1970s saw Chicano theater in full flower, thanks to Valdez and El Teatro Campesino. What began as a farm workers' theater in the migrant camps of Delano now exploded into a national Chicano theater movement. Theater groups sprang up with surprising speed on college campuses and in communities throughout the United States. Stressing ethnic pride and the preservation of cultural traditions, the groups adhered to Valdez's dictate that the theaters remain true to *la raza*—the grassroots Mexican. In so doing, they were wildly successful, and the theater's popularity grew and built upon itself. The theater movement reached its zenith in 1976. In the summer of that year the national Bicentennial was celebrated with five different Mexican theater festivals.

By the 1980s many theater groups had disbanded. Other, more successful groups, such as Denver's Su Teatro and San Antonio's Guadalupe Theater, took root as local repertory companies. Although the Chicano theater movement largely dispersed during this decade, its artists and directors did not disappear. The popular surge of Chicano theater created opportunities where few had existed before. Actors and theater directors were absorbed into the mainstream of professional theater in the various communities and universities as well as in television and film.

In 1977 both Valdez and his brother Daniel had parts in the Richard Pryor film *Which Way Is Up?.* The following year, however, marked a more important milestone in Valdez's career. In 1978 he wrote, directed, and produced a play that would eventually serve as his springboard to film directing. The play was *Zoot Suit,* based on the 1942 Los Angeles Sleepy Lagoon case. Its production at the Mark Taper Forum in Los Angeles marked Valdez's breakthrough to mainstream theater. *Zoot Suit* ran successfully for two years in Los Angeles theaters, and it was produced at New York City's Winter Garden in 1979—the first play written and produced by a Mexican American ever to play on Broadway. It was made into a film in 1982, which Valdez also directed. This version, however, was not as successful as the play.

In 1980 Valdez directed his play *Tibercio Vasquez. Corridos* followed, with successful theater and television productions. In 1984 Valdez wrote and produced the play *I Don't Have to Show You No Stinking Badges,* which ran successfully at the Los Angeles Theater Center in 1986. His greatest success came in 1987, when he directed the hit film *La Bamba.* The film depicted the brief life of Chicano singer **Richie Valens,** who helped pioneer early rock and roll.

### Challenges Hollywood Stereotypes

In the wake of the tremendous success of *La Bamba,* Valdez has continued to direct productions illustrating the Hispanic condition. The *New York Times* observed in 1991 that "Valdez has a reputation as a cultural provocateur, thanks to his activism on behalf of the United Farm Workers of America, his authorship of works that challenge stereotypes of Hispanic Americans, and his fondness for bringing together performers of widely varying cultural backgrounds."

Two recent projects have demonstrated that cultural commitment. In 1991 Valdez directed a made-for-public-television version of the traditional folk tale *La Pastorela (The Shepherd's Play).* A version of the Nativity story, *La Pastorela* changes the focus from the Three Wise Men to a group of shepherds making their way to Bethlehem. "La Pastorela is part of a tradition that is at least 1,000 years old," Valdez told the *New York Times* in 1991. He has adapted the play in order to appeal to a wider television audience. The result, with actors like **Paul Rodriguez, Freddy Fender,** and **Linda Ronstadt,** is a very modern version. John Leonard, writing in *New York,* described it with good humor as "the Nativity . . . tricked up to look like a road-show amalgam of *The Wizard of Oz* and *Cats.*"

In 1994 Valdez directed a remake of the 1950s television series *The Cisco Kid.* Again Valdez modernized an old story, transforming Cisco (played by actor **Jimmy Smits**) from a bandit into a respectable Chicano adventurer. The *New York Times* stated, "*The Cisco Kid* is part of a larger effort to counter 90 years of omissions and distortions in the way Latino characters have been depicted in westerns." The article continued, "Film makers like . . . Valdez . . . say they are trying to provide a humanized alternative to the hot-blooded lovers, Frito banditos, drug dealers, gang leaders, and other two-dimensional characters that [have] traditionally represented Mexican Americans on television and films."

Although the 1980s and 1990s have produced several films with a Latino focus, including *La Bamba* (1987), *Stand and Deliver* (1988), and *Like Water for Chocolate* (1993), the *New York Times* noted in 1994 that Hispanics "remain underrepresented in the film and television industry." The paper quoted John Trevino, chairman of the Directors Guild Latino committee, as saying, "In any given year, less than one percent of the directors with films in production are Latinos."

In spite of these disappointing numbers, they would probably be even smaller if not for Luis Valdez. Many Hispanic actors and theater directors owed their careers, directly or indirectly, to the pioneering efforts of Luis Valdez's El Teatro Campesino. Actor-comedian Paul Rodriguez acknowledged his debt in an interview with the *New York Times* in 1991: "The first time I ever saw the Teatro Campesino, I was just a *chavalito* hanging on to my mamma's hand, with my daddy saying, 'This is important; you've got to watch this.' As a matter of fact, I'll credit the Teatro Campesino with first allowing myself to even dream of being in this business."

### SOURCES:

**Books**

*Hispanic-American Almanac,* edited by Nicolás Kanellos, Detroit, Gale, 1993.

*Mexican-American Biographies,* edited by Matt S. Meier, New York, Greenwood Press, 1988.
*Who's Who in the Theater,* 17th edition, edited by Ian Herbert, Detroit, Gale, 1981.

**Periodicals**

*New York,* February 7, 1994, pp. 60–61.
*New York Times,* July 28, 1991, pp. H25, H32; January 30, 1994, pp. H32, H40.

—*Sketch by Ellen Dennis French*

*Ritchie Valens*

# Ritchie Valens
## 1941-1959
**Mexican American singer and musician**

Ritchie Valens was the first successful Mexican American rock musician. Born in a Los Angeles barrio, he rose quickly to stardom that was cut prematurely short by a fatal plane crash. Although his musical career was tragically brief, he made a significant impact on rock and roll. His unique style, a combination of Latin and American rhythms, moved his ethnic sounds into the mainstream of popular music, leading the way for other Latin musicians.

Valens was born in Pacoima, California on May 13, 1941, to Joseph Steve and Concepcion Reyes Valenzuela. Richard Steve Valenzuela was the first child for the couple, although Concepcion had another son, Robert Morales, from a previous marriage. Valens eventually had three other siblings—two sisters, Connie and Irma and a brother, Mario. His parents separated when he was three. After the separation, Valens spent most of his time with his father who, along with other relatives, encouraged Valens's musical talents. They made toy guitars for him until he got his first real guitar when he was about nine years old.

Richard Cota, Valens's cousin, gave him guitar lessons when he was about 11 or 12 years old. Cota exposed Valens to Latin songs, including "La Bamba." As a young man, Valens played a lot of country-western music and his idols were singing cowboys like Roy Rogers and Gene Autry. Valens practiced for hours and by the time he entered Pacoima Junior High School at age 13, he and his second-hand, turquoise-and-white guitar were inseparable. He took it to school with him so that he could sing for the other students during lunch breaks and after school.

Valens was popular among his peers. His teachers and classmates remembered him as a quiet, shy, and likeable boy. He had a good sense of humor and a natural talent for music. Valens was able to take a song written by someone else and improvise on it until he had created something entirely original and often nonsensical. During his years in junior high school, he played for many private parties throughout the San Fernando Valley. By this time he was singing a lot of Little Richard tunes and he became known as the "Little Richard of the Valley."

On January 31, 1957, disaster struck Pacoima when a navy plane collided with a jet over Las Tuna Canyon, near the school. Burning debris from the explosion was scattered over the junior high's athletic field, injuring 90 people and killing three children and the jet's five crew members. Although Valens was not present at school that day because he was attending the funeral of his Grandfather Reyes, the incident left him with a fear of planes.

In October 1957, shortly after entering San Fernando High School, Valens joined a group called the Silhouettes. They played for private parties, social clubs, wedding receptions, and on occasion rented halls for dances, charging a cover of about 25 cents. The band played the popular music of the time including some rhythm and blues, rock and roll, and Latin music. Valens played with the Silhouettes until he made his first recording. After that time his schedule put more demands on him, making it difficult for him to continue with the group.

## Rises to Fame

In May 1958, Valens auditioned for a recording contract with Bob Keane of Del-Fi Records. Keane had a recording studio set up in his basement for auditions and demos. Valens's unique style caught Keane's attention, so the producer signed a contract with the young musician and shortened his name to Ritchie Valens. Del-Fi recorded Valens's first single, "Come On, Let's Go," which was a Top 50 hit in the United States by October 1958, and was also a hit in Britain. His reputation and popularity began to grow, not only in California but across the country and overseas.

Keane arranged promotional events through KFWB, a Los Angeles-based AM radio station. Valens, who was well-liked by the DJs, visited the radio talk shows and participated in events like the "Oh Boy, Pizza" contest, in which winners enjoyed pizza delivered by Valens and an evening with the teen idol. He also appeared at local hops and on television teen dance shows.

By September 1958, "Come on, Let's Go" was making the national charts. Keane decided to promote Valens nationally with a road tour to 11 cities along the East Coast. On his mother's birthday, October 6, Valens made his first appearance on *American Bandstand* in Philadelphia. While touring in the East he also appeared on Alan Freed's show in New York. Once back on the West Coast he traveled to San Francisco for an appearance on a local television show there.

Engagements in southern California increased and the demands forced Valens to drop out of school. He was asked to appear on more television shows including the *Dick Clark Show, American Bandstand,* and *The Music Shop.* He also had a cameo role in the Hal Wallis rock and roll movie entitled, *Go Johnny, Go,* in which he sang "Ooh, My Head."

His second recording for Del-Fi, released in October 1958, was a two-sided single featuring "Donna" and "La Bamba." Both songs climbed to the Top Ten by December. "Donna" is a song he wrote for his 16-year-old, high school sweetheart—Donna Ludwig Fox—and was his greatest hit. "La Bamba" is a Mexican folk song traditionally performed at weddings—a *huapango,* which is a song containing nonsense verses with hidden meanings. Valens's version of "La Bamba," sung with a rock twist, was the first successful recording of the song, popularizing it beyond its cultural boundaries. Although Valens's ethnic background was partly responsible for his distinguishing style, it was not a well-known fact that he was of Mexican American heritage. He didn't even speak Spanish well and had some trouble with his accent and the words when recording "La Bamba."

## Begins Fatal Tour

In January 1959, Valens signed a long-term contract with a booking agency that arranged packaged tours. The agency planned an extensive promotion of the star with the first of the tours to be the "Winter Dance Party." Traveling with Valens were four other acts including, Frankie Sardo, J. P. Richardson (known as the Big Bopper), Dion and the Belmonts, and Buddy Holly and the Crickets. The circuit, which began January 23, was scheduled to extend to the midwestern states of Minnesota, Wisconsin, and Iowa.

Valens had purchased a new home in Pacoima for his mother and family several months earlier. Before he left on tour, his family held a housewarming and farewell party in the home. Many of his friends and members of his family came to wish him well on his trip, unaware that they were bidding him farewell forever.

Once on the road, the shows were successful but the accommodations were less than desirable. During January in the Midwest, winters can be extreme and the weather took its toll on the travelers. Several of the buses broke down and most of them did not have adequate heating systems. The band members were not afforded the luxury of hotel stays more than a few nights and soon several of the touring members were sick with colds. After the performance in the Surf Ballroom in Clear Lake, Iowa, Holly made the decision to travel on to the next town—some 400 or more miles away in Minnesota—by air. He chartered a single-engine plane to take some of his band members ahead of the bus.

Valens was also ill and, although he was usually afraid to fly, he asked Tommy Allsup, one of the backup musicians, for his seat on the plane. They flipped a coin for the seat and Valens won the toss. On the flight that night were Valens, the Big Bopper, Holly, and the pilot. They took off at about 1:00 am from Mason City Airport with winds blowing and a light snow falling, unaware that a weather warning had been issued. The plane crashed eight miles northwest of the airport in a cornfield and was discovered the next morning with no survivors.

The Winter Dance Party continued on as a memorial to the late stars. Valens's funeral was held Saturday, February 7, at St. Ferdinand's Catholic Church in San Fernando. Over 1,000 people attended the services. Del-Fi released three albums of Valens's songs after his death; "Donna" went gold and Keane presented a gold record to Valens's mother. Many tribute songs have been written for Valens and the other stars who died in the tragic accident. Columbia pictures made a movie about Valens's life entitled, *La Bamba,* with Lou Diamond Phillips in the starring role. The movie's soundtrack features Latin rock musicians Los Lobos and **Carlos Santana.**

## SELECTED DISCOGRAPHY:

*Ritchie Valens,* London, 1979.
*Ritchie Valens,* Rhino, 1984.
*Ritchie,* Rhino, 1984.
*Ritchie Valens in Concert at Pacoima Jr. High,*
    Rhino, 1984.
*The History of Ritchie Valens,* Rhino, 1986.

## SOURCES:

### Books

Hardy, Phil, and others, *Encyclopedia of Rock,*
    New York, Schirmer Books, 1987.
Mendheim, Beverly, *Ritchie Valens: The First La-
    tino Rocker,* Tempe, AZ, Bilingual Press,
    1987.
Nite, Norm N., *Rock On, the Illustrated Encyclo-
    pedia of Rock n' Roll: The Solid Gold Years,*
    New York, Harper, 1982.
*Rolling Stone Encyclopedia of Rock and Roll,* edit-
    ed by Jon Pareles and Patricia Romanowski,
    New York, Rolling Stone Press/Summit Books,
    1983.
Stambler, Irwin, *Encyclopedia of Pop, Rock, and
    Soul,* New York, St. Martin's Press, 1989.

—*Sketch by Denise Marecki-Arriola*

# Luisa Valenzuela
## 1938-
### Argentine writer

Called "the heiress of Latin American literature"
by Mexican novelist **Carlos Fuentes** in *Interviews with Latin American Writers,* Luisa Valenzuela
is one of the most celebrated contemporary female
authors in Latin America. Nearly all her novels and
short stories have been translated into English and
some have been published as far afield as Holland and
Japan.

Critic Evelyn Picon Garfield has described Valenzuela's prose as "critical and revolutionary," identifying cyclical change within the pivotal search for
self-knowledge as recurrent themes. Set in a world of
both fantasy and reality, Valenzuela's work revolves
around central themes of politics and women's issues.
Also rooted within her work is the violence and
suffering experienced in many Latin American countries under authoritarian regimes. In her novel *Cola*

*Luisa Valenzuela*

*de lagartija* (*The Lizard's Tail*) for example, the
protagonist, a cruel sorcerer, was based on José López
Rega, Isabel Perón's Minister of Social Welfare.

Valenzuela was born November 26, 1938 in
Buenos Aires, Argentina. Her father, Pablo Francisco
Valenzuela, was a physician and her mother, Luisa
Mercedes Levinson, a noted writer. Valenzuela, a
voracious reader, was raised in an academic environ-
ment; during her childhood she met such famed
Argentine writers as **Jorge Luis Borges,** Sábato, and
Nalé Roxlóand Peyrou. She had early aspirations to
become a painter or a mathematician, but attributed
her literary vocation to her fervent imagination.
Valenzuela completed her formal education at the
University of Buenos Aires.

Valenzuela began her writing career contributing
articles to the magazines *Esto Es, Atlántida,* and *El
Hogar.* Shortly after, at 17, her first story "Cuidad
Ajena"—then titled "Ese Canto"—was published in
Juan Goyanarte's literary magazine *Ficción.* In 1958,
recently married, she moved to Paris, where her
daughter, Anna-Lisa was born. Intense feelings of
dislocation from her homeland inspired her to write
her first novel *Hay que sonreír* (translated as *Clara*).
She also worked for Radio Difusion Française as a
program writer for Latin America.

She returned to Buenos Aires in 1961 and
resumed her journalistic career. Notably she became
assistant editor of *La Nación*'s Sunday supplement,
where she remained until 1972. In 1963 Valenzuela

won honorable mention in the Premio Kraft for her journalism, and in 1965 won the Kraft Award. 1966 and 1967 saw the publication of *Hay que sonreír* and *Los heréticos*. In 1973 Valenzuela was conferred an award from Argentina's Instituto Nacional de Cinematografía for the script *Clara*,

Valenzuela received a Fulbright grant in 1969 to 1970 to participate in the International Writers Program at the University of Iowa. During this period she wrote her third book, *El gato eficaz* (translated as *Cat-O-Nine Deaths*), published in 1972. During the next two years she spent time in Barcelona, Paris, and Mexico, supported with a grant from the National Arts Foundation of Argentina. While in Barcelona, inspired by her alien environment, she also wrote 1977's *Como en la guerra*.

In 1974 Valenzuela returned to Buenos Aires, amidst an atmosphere of paramilitary violence and repression. She edited *Crisis*, a socio-political literary magazine, while working as a star reporter for the popular magazine *Gente*, which took her to boxing matches and world soccer championships. The alien nature of Argentina's political environment fired a new collection of stories, *Aquí pasan cosas raras*, which appeared in 1975. She also taught writing workshops. In 1976 she traveled to New York for the launch of *Clara*, and in October of that year she accepted an invitation to the Feria del Libro de Frankfurt, celebrating Latin American literature. In 1978 Valenzuela attended a Writing Conference in Ottawa, the first of many over the following 15 years that have taken her to Mexico, Costa Rica, Israel, Ireland, Australia, Ecuador, Chile, Uruguay and the United States.

Worried about the restrictions of self-censorship, Valenzuela decided to leave Argentina. In 1979 she was offered a position as writer-in-residence at Columbia University for one semester; she remained in the United States, a voluntary exile, returning only occasionally to Argentina.

Valenzuela has been the recipient of numerous grants and awards. In 1983 she received a Guggenheim fellowship and in 1985 was named writer-in-residence at New York University, where she remained until 1990. Since 1982 she has been a fellow at the New York Institute for the Humanities and a member of the Freedom to Write committee of PEN's American Center. Concerned about human rights, Valenzuela also joined Amnesty International. In the United States she conducted numerous writing workshops, while continuing with her journalistic vocation as a contributor to the *New York Times, Village Voice,* and *New York Review of Books*.

In April 1989, with Argentina returned to democracy, Valenzuela resettled in Buenos Aires, where she has divided her time with New York City. Her short story "Realidad nacional desde la cama" was inspired by the return to her native country. In 1990 she won second prize from Plaza y Janés publishers for her novel *Novela negra con argentinos*, translated as *Black Novel With Argentines*.

## SELECTED PUBLISHED WORKS:

*Hay que sonreír*, Buenos Aires, Americalee, 1966, translated, with *Los heréticos*, by Hortense Carpentier and Jorge Castello as *Clara: Thirteen Short Stories and a Novel*, New York, Harcourt, 1976.

*Los heréticos*, Buenos Aires, Paidós, 1967, translated as *The Heretics*, n.p. 1976.

*El gato eficaz*, Mexico City, J. Mortiz, 1972, translated as *Cat-O-Nine Deaths*, n.p.

*Aquí pasan cosas raras*, Buenos Aires, La Flor, 1976, translated by Helen Lane as *Strange Things Happen Here: Twenty-Six Short Stories and a Novel*, New York, Harcourt, 1979, translated as *He Who Searches*, Dalkey Archive Press, 1987.

*Como en la guerra*, Buenos Aires, Sudamericana, 1977.

*Libro que no muerde*, Mexico City, UNAM, 1980.

*Cambio de armas*, Hanover, NH, Norte, 1982, translated by Deborah Bonner as *Other Weapons: Novellas*, 1985.

*Cola de lagartija*, Buenos Aires, Bruguera, 1984, translated by Gregory Rabassa as *The Lizard's Tale*, New York, Farrar, Straus, 1983.

*Donde viven las águilas*, Buenos Aires, Celtia, 1983.

*Open Door* (short stories), translated by Hortense Carpentier and Jorge Castello, Berkeley, CA, North Point Press, 1988.

*Novela negra con argentinos*, Mexico City, Plaza y Janés, 1990, translated by T. Talbot as *Black Novel With Argentines*, New York, Simon & Schuster, 1992.

*Simetrías* (short stories), Buenos Aires, Sudamericana, 1993.

*Bedside Manners: Serpent's Tail, High Risk,* [United States], 1995.

## SOURCES:

### Books

Gazarian Gautier, Marie-Lise, *Interviews with Latin American Writers*, Dalkey Archive Press, 1989.

*Hispanic Writers*, edited by Bryan Ryan, Detroit, Gale, 1991.

*Latin American Writers*, Volume 3, edited by Carlos A. Solé, New York, Scribner's, 1989.

*Spanish American Authors: The Twentieth Century,*
edited by Angel Flores, New York, H. W.
Wilson, 1992.

*Spanish American Women Authors: A Bio-bibliographical Source Book,* edited by Diane E.
Marting, Westport, CT, Greenwood Press,
1990.

—*Sketch by Amanda Beresford*

# Ramón del Valle-Inclán
## 1866-1936
### Spanish writer

R amón del Valle-Inclán stands as one of the most
memorable Spanish writers of the early twentieth century. He achieved most of his popular success
in prose, but Valle-Inclán's drama remains most
highly regarded by critics. As one of the great voices
of the "1898 Generation," Valle-Inclán struggled to
find personal renewal amidst the feeling of national
self-doubt following the loss of the last vestiges of
empire in 1898. During his lifetime, Valle-Inclán
developed a flamboyant appearance and memorable
personality, known for his egotism and public
brashness. Although sometimes overshadowed by his
public persona, Valle-Inclán's works have garnered
increasing respect since his death.

Born on October 26, 1866, in Villanueva de
Arosa, Pontevedra, Galicia, as Ramón Jose Simon,
Valle-Inclán came from two distinguished families
whose fortunes had somewhat declined but who still
commanded respect. His father, Don Ramón Valle,
apparently squandered a considerable fortune inherited from his father, forcing the family to live modestly,
although socially quite separate from the commoners
of the village. His mother, Dona Dolores Pena, came
from a family of some standing, rumored even to be
of royal descent.

The young Valle-Inclán loved books and took
advantage of his father's library to study Latin,
literature, and other subjects. He finished high school
in 1885 at the Instituto de Pontevedra before going to
the University of Santiago de Compostela to study
law. He decided to attend law school partly because
he would not inherit enough money to be able to
support himself without a profession. He had already
worked as a part-time journalist, coastguardsman,
and writer, but these jobs could hardly sustain the
family estate. His interest in law waned before he
could finish his degree, however, and when his father

died in 1890, Valle-Inclán left law school to pursue
his true ambitions in the literary world.

### Developed New Identity

Having published several articles and short stories while in law school, Valle-Inclán had developed
some confidence in his abilities. When he arrived in
Madrid, he immediately set out to establish a literary
reputation. He succeeded in having several articles
and short stories published in a liberal newspaper
called *El Globo*. In this time he also developed the
character Pedro Pondal, who appears in later writings,
in two chapters of an unfinished novel called *El Gran
Obstaculo*.

In 1892 Valle-Inclán decided to travel to Mexico.
He landed in April of 1892, and after only a few days
in Mexico challenged the editor of the newspaper *El
Tiempo* to a duel over something the paper had
published which he considered offensive to Spaniards. Although no violence actually ensued, Valle-
Inclán demonstrated his lifelong tendency to make his
opinions known at all costs.

While in Mexico he supported himself as a
journalist for several newspapers, although he published only a few literary works in that time. "A una
mujer ausente por la muerte" appeared just after he
arrived in Mexico City in *El Correo Espanol*. In *El
Universal* he published several short stories and short
novels. He left Mexico after about one year and
returned to Galicia, stopping by Cuba for several days
on the return journey.

Perhaps because of his short visit to Cuba, Valle-
Inclán developed a strong sympathy for the Cuban
movement for independence led by **Jose Marti.** He
later wrote that "the Cuban War was won by the
Cubans on their soil and by me on the streets of
Madrid." His return to Galicia also saw him reject the
professional appearance he had maintained throughout his Mexican career as a journalist. He grew his
hair and beard, wore a wide-brimmed hat, large,
round glasses, and a serape. He also completed the
transformation, through several experimental stages,
to his pseudonym Don Ramón del Valle-Inclán.

Between 1893 and 1896 Valle-Inclán remained in
Pontevedra, publishing several pieces in local magazines and enjoying the impressive library of Don
Jesus Muruais. He also published *Femeninas* in 1894,
a book containing six short stories. Besides Valle-
Inclán's few publications in those years, however, he
apparently kept a low profile.

He returned to Madrid in winter of 1896,
ostensibly to accept a job in the government. He
promptly quit and began to establish himself as a
fixture among Madrid's *tertulias* (gatherings of artists
and thinkers), gaining respect among these intellectuals. His second book, *Epitalamio,* appeared in 1897,

and though it did not bring any financial relief to his relative poverty, it did establish him as one of the primary voices of his considerable circle. As critic and biographer Robert Lima explained: "To the painters, writers, and others who gathered around his table (among them Picasso, Lorca, Dario, Solana, Martinez Sierra, Zuloaga, Rivera, Matisse) Valle-Inclán was the standard bearer of the tenet 'Art for Art's Sake' and an instigator of their imaginations."

In July 1899, Valle-Inclán lost his arm when a heated discussion with Manuel Bueno prompted him to throw a jug of water at Bueno. Bueno responded by hitting Valle-Inclán with a cane, driving Valle-Inclán's cufflink into his left arm. A few days later the wound had become so infected that doctors had no choice but to amputate, ending Valle-Inclán's hopes of becoming an actor. Though he was unable to pursue an acting career, Valle-Inclán's dramas began to be performed over the next few years. His friends produced one of his works as a benefit to buy the author a prosthetic arm.

During this time, the Spanish nation was enduring the humiliation of military defeats at the hands of its colonies and the United States. Valle-Inclán and his compatriots saw this moment not as a defeat, but as a chance to redefine Spain as a nation through its cultural past, looking toward the twentieth century. Early critics saw this desire to use the past as the bridge to the future in a negative light. Lima noted that the critic Clarin "regretted that [Valle-Inclán's] work looked back to innovations of an earlier era," but acknowledged that "these critics had not realized that the past was merely a springboard for Valle-Inclán and not a rut."

## A Prolific Writer

Valle-Inclán published widely for several years, including his book *Jardin umbrio* in 1903. His financial situation had improved, enabling him to move to better accommodations and attend the theater. During the production of his play *El Marques de Bradomin*, Valle-Inclán met young actress Josefina Blanco, whom he married on August 24, 1907. He shaved his hair and started wearing normal-sized glasses. Though he and his wife began immediately to have children, his health also began to fail. For the rest of his life, he would do most of his writing in his bed.

He continued to publish prolifically, and his dramatic works often found their way to the stage. In 1909 he accompanied his wife as she toured with her old dramatic company in South America. There Valle-Inclán lectured widely to appreciative audiences in Argentina, Paraguay, Uruguay, Chile, and Bolivia. The tour continued until 1910, when he returned to Spain.

Back in Spain he ran unsuccessfully for Congress as a Traditionalist. The death of his mother in 1911 preceded the publication of the poem "A la luna," which several critics viewed as a transition in his writing. He moved back to Galicia in 1912, where his second son, Joaquin Maria, died in an accident.

Personal tragedies did not prevent the appearance of more work. For several years, he published books amidst ill health. During World War I, he worked for a time as a war correspondent. Some of his war sketches appeared in *La media noche: Vision estelar de un momento de guerra,* which was published in 1917.

He traveled to Mexico and Cuba again in 1921, making comments in favor of land reforms which lost him popularity among the Spanish land-owning class in Mexico. From around this point Valle-Inclán began to develop the idea that an artist's first duty was to seek justice. He often criticized the political and social nature of his own country, but his directness won him admirers as well as detractors.

In 1927 Valle-Inclán organized his own theatrical group, called El Cantaro Roto. Some of the works appearing in 1927's *Retablo de la avaricia, la lujuria y la muerte* made their way to the stage with Valle-Inclán's company. His theatrical productions gained acclaim and, with his other works, provided him a comfortable living, though his health remained shaky. According to biographers, his literary fame reached its greatest height during this time.

His last years saw new problems. His publisher went out of business, plunging him again into poverty. He divorced his wife in 1932, leaving the next year to run the Spanish Academy of Fine Arts in Rome. His health failed, and he soon returned to Galicia, where he entertained young thinkers as an "elder statesman" of scholarship and mysticism. His last published work, a commentary on a friend's book, appeared on October 2, 1935. He died on January 5, 1936, of cancer of the bladder. Hundreds of people from around the country came to his funeral, including a young man who—in removing a crucifix placed on the casket—inadvertently fell into the grave along with Valle-Inclán's remains. The scene reminded observers of the grotesque elements of Valle-Inclán's own works. As he had originally requested, Valle-Inclán went to his grave with no religious symbols attached.

## SELECTED PUBLISHED WORKS:

*Femeninas,* c. 1984.
*Epitalamio,* 1897.
*Jardin umbrio,* 1903.
*Sonata de otono: Memorias del Marques de Bradomin,* 1902.

*Sonata de estio: Memorias del Marques de Bradomin,* 1903.

*Sonata de primavera: Memorias del Marques de Bradomin,* 1904.

*Sonata de invierno: Memorias del Marques de Bradomin,* 1905.

*Aguila de blason: Comedia barbara,* 1907.

*Romance de lobos: Comedia barbara,* 1908.

*El resplandor de la hoguera,* 1909.

*Voces de gesta: Tragedia pastoril,* 1911.

*La Marquesa Rosalinda: Farsa sentimental y grotesca,* 1913.

*La lampara maravillosa: Ejercicios espirituales,* 1916.

*La media noche: Vision estelar de un momento de guerra,* 1917.

*La pipa de kif,* 1919.

*Divinas palabras: Tragicomedia de aldea,* 1920.

*Cara de Plata: Comedia barbara,* 1923.

*Luces de Bohemia,* 1924.

*Los cuernos de don Friolera: Esperpento,* 1925.

*Tirano Banderas: Novela de Tierra Caliente,* 1926.

*Retablo de la avaricia, la lujuria y la muerte,* 1927.

*Viva mi dueno,* 1928.

## SOURCES:

### Books

Lima, Robert, *Ramón del Valle-Inclán,* New York, Columbia University Press, 1972.

Lima, Robert, *Valle-Inclán: The Theatre of His Life,* Columbia, University of Missouri Press, 1988.

*Ramón del Valle-Inclánsal of His Life and Works,* edited by Anthony Zahareas, New York, Las Americas, 1968.

—*Sketch by James McCarthy*

# César Vallejo
## 1892-1938
**Peruvian poet and writer**

Poetry and politics often dovetail in Latin America and the career of Peruvian poet César Abraham Vallejo was no exception. He was born on March 16, 1892, in Santiago de Chuco, Peru to a large family of seven boys and four girls. His father, Francisco de Paula Vallejo, was the son of a Galician priest and a Chimu Indian, as was his mother, María de los Santos Mendoza. His mixed origins were often noted by biographers as significant in the poet's development.

Vallejo was raised as a Catholic and groomed to become a priest, a choice he soon rejected. He studied in the small schools of his northern Andes town and, at a very early age, showed an interest in books. He sporadically studied at Trujillo University, where he received a bachelor's degree in literature in 1915, followed by a law degree. He also briefly studied medicine at the University of San Marcos in Lima in 1911. In between periods of university studies, Vallejo held a variety of jobs. These included stints as a clerk in his father's notary office, working as a miner, and on a ranch as a tutor for the ranch-owner's children. Another job, which brought him in close contact with both the poor working class and Indian slaves, was as an assistant cashier on a sugar plantation.

When he returned to Trujillo University in 1913—having switched from the School of Letters to the School of Philosophy—Vallejo also got a job as a teacher. To keep his botany and anatomy students' attention, he wrote poems of scientific explanations. This first dalliance with poetry led him to join a prestigious literary group, where he was exposed to the writings of Walt Whitman, Paul Verlaine, Count Maeterlinck, and Soren Kierkegaard, the father of Existentialism. While this exposure fed his poetic soul, Vallejo experienced a personal loss that profoundly effected him. His favorite brother died and inspired the poem, "A mi hermano Miguel."

Vallejo studied law from 1916 to 1917 and continued to teach and write poems that would become part of his first book, *Los heraldos negros* ("The Black Messengers"), which was published in 1918. The poems in this first collection of his work show the author's perplexity over the rigors of urban life in Trujillo and Lima. During his studies, Vallejo was introduced to the ideas of Karl Marx, Charles Darwin, and Rationalist philosophers whose theories prompted him to reject the Catholic faith. He learned more about his pre-Columbian heritage and the condition of Peruvian Indians.

The year 1918 marked not only the publication of Vallejo's first collection of poems, but more tragic personal losses as well. His mother, with whom he had a close and supportive relationship, died that year, as did two of his mentors. By 1919 Vallejo had had enough. Although his book was well received and praised, he was unemployed and feeling the devastation of too many deaths in too short a time. He decided to move to Europe.

### The Difficult Move to Paris

Before he left Peru, Vallejo stopped at his hometown to say his farewells. In an ironic twist of fate, he somehow became caught up in an uprising in Santiago de Chuco in August 1920. It is unclear whether Vallejo was actually an instigator of the riot or whether he tried to restore order. The police decided it was the former and Vallejo served nearly four months in prison. It was, Flores noted, a traumatic experience for the young poet, which would be reflected in several poems that would appear in his next collection, *Trilce.* "The subject of a number of poems, that experience reinforced his belief in the world's arbitrary cruelty and his sense of inadequacy in the face of it," James Higgins observed in *A History of Peruvian Literature.*

After being released from prison on parole, Vallejo returned to Lima to teach. He won first prize for the short story "Entre Nous" in a national contest sponsored by the Sociedad Gemenina. With his winnings, the poet published *Trilce* in 1922. It was, to say the least, ahead of its time—so far ahead that critics and readers alike rejected the poems.

In a reprinted letter regarding his collection Vallejo wrote: "[The book] has fallen into a total void. I am responsible for the book. I assume complete responsibility for its aesthetics. Today, perhaps more than ever, I sense an until now unknown and sacred obligation gravitating over me as a man and as an artist: to be free!" Upon examination of the book's title some of what Vallejo was doing in his controversial work is revealed. "The word *Trilce* is both a combination of *triste* (sad) and *dulce* (sweet) and an evocation of three-ness, as in triple. (Numbers, odd and even, are one of Vallejo's obsessions as a poet)," Christopher Maurer wrote in *New Republic.* "What *Trilce* is 'about' is not easy to say. Like all great poetry, it was designed to survive paraphrase, and these poems range from the manageably mysterious to the truly hermetic."

Mauer called Vallejo one of the greatest and least-known poets of the century. The book of 77 poems is one of the masterpieces in the Spanish language. "The title itself is an untranslatable neologism, one of many in a book that pushes Spanish to its syntactical and lexical breaking point." It is in his manipulation of the language, in the creation of his own unique syntax, that Vallejo's brilliance shines through. However, this brilliance was not easily understood and, indeed, not studied or praised until decades later.

While critics in succeeding generations would find much to admire in Vallejo's poetry, he had little success in his lifetime. The poor reception of *Trilce* and the rumors that a trial was still pending over the riots, prompted Vallejo to leave for Paris; he arrived there in July, 1923. He struggled to find work and, at times, suffered heartbreaking poverty.

As he struggled to make ends meet in Paris, Vallejo's health started to fail. He spent a month in a charity hospital where he was operated on for an intestinal hemorrhage. His health was never the same again. After recovering, he traveled often to Madrid to collect a scholarship he had managed to receive. Although it was intended for Peruvian scholars studying in Spanish, Vallejo somehow became its recipient. He was involved with two women in Paris, one of whom, Georgette Philippart, he married in 1934. And he traveled, extensively and, significantly, to the Soviet Union several times.

While his political agenda became more pronounced in his activities and fiction, Vallejo's views did not permeate his poetry to the same extent. He helped found the Centro Latinoamericano de Estudios Marxistas ("Latin American Center for Marxist Studies"). Though his health and economic situation did not improve, he traveled to various cities such as Berlin, Leningrad, Prague, Vienna, Budapest, Rome, and Genoa in 1929. Around this same time he also finished a collection entitled *Poemas en prosa,* though it was not published during his life.

### Banished From France

In December of 1930, the French government banned Vallejo from the country for attending public protests, numerous arrests, participating in secret meetings, having connections with Bolsheviks, visiting the library of a Marxist newspaper, and traveling to the U.S.S.R. So, in 1931 Vallejo and Philippart moved to Madrid, where life was no easier than it had been in Paris. A commissioned short story for children was rejected by an editor and while his essay collection *Ruisa en 1931: reflexiones al pie de Kremlin* ("Russia in 1931: Reflections at the Foot of the Kremlin") was a number-two best seller, he could not get his author's rights and royalties. His second work on Russia was rejected, as was a collection of plays. Soon, the couple was back in Paris secretly—and then openly. Though told by the government to watch his step, Vallejo did participate in a demonstration. Despite this, he was allowed to remain in Paris until his death in 1938.

His last great political endeavor was being involved in the Spanish Civil War. At first Vallejo wanted to go the battlefront itself, but had to settle for writing propaganda from the safety of Paris. In 1938 his numerous illnesses at last caught up with him, and Vallejo died on the morning of April 15th. After his death, his widow selected some of his poems for publication in *Poemas humanos.* Though he earned little critical acclaim prior to his death, afterward Vallejo was "to be recognized as an artist of world stature, the greatest poet not only of Peru but of all Spanish America," Higgins claimed in *The History of Peruvian Literature.*

## SELECTED PUBLISHED WORKS:

*Trilce,* Lima, Penitenciaría, 1922, translated by David Smith, New York, Grossman, 1973.

*El tungsteno: La novela proletaria,* Madrid, Editorial Cenit, 1931, translated by Robert Mezey as *Tungsten: A Novel,* Syracuse, NY, Syracuse University Press, 1988.

*Poemas humanos,* Paris, Presses Modernes, 1939; translated by Clayton Eshleman as *Poemas humanos: Human Poems,* New York, Grove Press, 1969.

*Twenty Poems* (bilingual edition), selected and translated by Robert Bly, James Wright, and John Knoepfle, Sixties Press, 1962.

*César Vallejo: An Anthology of His Poetry,* edited by James Higgins, Elmsford, NY, Pergamon Press, 1970.

*César Vallejo: The Complete Posthumous Poetry,* translated by Clayton Eshleman and José Rubia Barcia, Berkeley, University of California Press, 1978.

*Battles in Spain,* translated by Clayton Eshleman and José Rubia Barcia, Black Sparrow Press, 1978.

*Autopsy on Surrealism,* translated by Richard Schaaf, Willimantic, CT, Curbstone Press, 1982.

## SOURCES:

### Books

*Borzoi Anthology of Latin American Literature,* Volume II, edited by Emir Rodriguez Monegal, New York, Knopf, 1977.

Flores, Angel, *Spanish American Authors,* New York, H. W. Wilson, 1992.

Higgins, James F., *A History of Peruvian Literature,* F. Cairns, 1987.

*Hispanic Writers,* edited by Bryan Ryan, Detroit, Gale, 1991.

### Periodicals

*New Republic,* July 12, 1993, pp. 34–39.

—*Sketch by Kathe A. Conti*

# Mario Vargas Llosa
## 1936-
**Peruvian writer and politician**

Mario Vargas Llosa has gained international recognition as a major figure in contemporary literature. Usually associated with the younger writers of "El Boom"—a remarkable period of achievement and world renown in Latin American letters initiated by writers such as **Gabriel Garcia Marquez** and **Julio Cortez** during the 1960s—Vargas Llosa is perhaps best known for his formal experimentation in novels and short stories that explore the complexity and contradiction of modern South American life. He has applied techniques such as nonlinear plot structure and multiple narrative perspective in an attempt to reflect the chaos within the social, political, economic, and cultural reality of Peru.

Vargas Llosa has published novels and short stories, as well as several critical essays. Among his many works, the following three have received perhaps the most favorable critical attention: *La ciudad y los perros* (*The Time of the Hero*), a satire based partly on his experience in a Peruvian military academy published in 1963; *La casa verde* (*The Green House*), a controversial mythic exploration of Peruvian culture published in 1966; and *La guerra del fin del mundo* (*The War of the End of the World*), an epic account of a series of late-nineteenth-century Brazilian battles, published in 1981. Vargas Llosa has received numerous international awards for his fiction, including the Premio de la Critica Española, the Romulo Gallegos Award, and the Ritz Paris Hemingway Award.

### Strict Upbringing and Rebellious Youth

Jorge Mario Pedro Vargas Llosa was born on March 28, 1936, the only son of a middle-class family living in Arequipa, Peru. His parents, Ernesto Vargas and Dora Llosa, separated the following year, and Mario went with his mother to live in Cochabama, Bolivia, where his grandfather was consul. His early childhood was filled with dreams of becoming a trapeze artist and a bullfighter, romantic aspirations developed by reading about characters like Tom Sawyer, Sinbad, and the Musketeers and adding his own chapters and endings to their stories. This idyllic childhood came to an end in 1945, when his family moved back to Peru, settling in the desert city of Piura. The following year, his parents reconciled and moved to Lima, where they enrolled Mario in a parochial secondary school. Later, after his father discovered that he had started to write poetry, Vargas Llosa was sent to the Peruvian military school Leoncio Prado, which he was forced to attend from

1950 to 1952 in an attempt to deter him from the "unmanly" pursuit of a literary career. "The Lima bourgeoisie thinks that being a writer or an artist is only a pretext for being either a pansy or a good-for-nothing," Vargas Llosa stated in Luis Harss and Barbara Dohmann's *Into the Mainstream.* "So my vocation grew and solidified a bit secretly. It was an outlet for my revolt against the Leoncio Prado. At that time literature became something very important for me."

After finishing high school—where he led a student strike, wrote articles for a local newspaper, and produced his first play—Vargas Llosa began studying law and literature at San Marcos University in Lima, rejecting his family's wish that he attend an elite Catholic University. As he explained in the *New York Times Magazine,* "I didn't want to be a 'good boy.' In the romantic way that children discover prejudice and social inequality, I had discovered, in my last year of high school, that the country had severe social problems. I wanted to be identified with the poor and to be part of a revolution that would bring justice to Peru." While studying the fiction of modernists such as James Joyce, Ernest Hemingway, **Jorge Luis Borges,** and William Faulkner, he also participated in various socialist causes at the university, but soon grew tired of the orthodox communist ideology in vogue at the time. In 1955, about midway through his undergraduate career, he married Julia Orquidi, a distant relative, and took on several odd jobs to cover their expenses.

As Vargas Llosa was completing his bachelor's degree, he began to publish his short stories in journals and newspapers. In 1958 one of his stories, "El desafio" ("The Challenge") was awarded first place—a trip to France—in a competition sponsored by *Revue francaise.* During this time, he also travelled extensively through the jungles of Peru, learning more about his country's various cultures and the complexity of its social problems. Upon his return, he won a scholarship to the University of Madrid and began writing his doctoral thesis, a thematic and stylistic study of Gabriel Garcia Marquez 's fiction. Vargas Llosa concentrated on his own fiction as well, winning the Spanish Leopoldo Alas award for *Los jefes* (translated as *The Cubs, and Other Stories*)—a collection of short stories written during his late teenage years, which a Barcelona press published in 1959.

After finishing his studies at Madrid, he began a 15-year period of self-imposed exile by moving to Paris. After he was denied a scholarship that would have funded his writing there, he again resorted to working various part-time jobs, including a position at a French radio network that enabled him to meet prominent Latin American writers such as **Julio Cortazar,** Borges, and **Carlos Fuentes.** Although the economic constraints of this phase of his life limited his writing output, he did find enough time to revise a rough draft of his first novel, *La ciudad y los perros* (translated as *The Time of the Hero*).

## Childhood Experiences Inspire Writing

First published in 1962, the novel—based on Vargas Llosa's adolescent experiences at the Leoncio Prado military academy—"established the author as one of the most promising writers of his generation," asserted Dick Gerdes in his biographical and critical study *Mario Vargas Llosa.* The plot of the novel centers around the theft of an exam at the school and the resulting suspension of weekend privileges for all cadets, a punishment which exacerbates various existing conflicts and leads eventually to the mysterious murder of a cadet who accused another of the theft. While the novel, on one level, provides a scathing critique of the machismo of the military culture—1,000 copies were burned in protest on the grounds of Leoncio Prado—it received widespread praise for its technical accomplishments. Noted for its experimentation with cinematic narrative techniques and its daring use of slang and taboo vocabulary, the novel was awarded the prestigious Biblioteca Breve Prize. "With that prize and a great deal of hoopla, his name," wrote Chilean novelist Jose Donoso in *The Boom in Spanish American Literature,* "suddenly became popular in the entire Spanish-speaking world. *The Time of the Hero* caused the whole continent to talk."

As Vargas Llosa prepared material for a second novel, he began to take a more recognizable role in the literary world: he judged literary competitions, served on the editorial committee of journals, and taught at Queen Mary College—endeavors which, as he became more famous in later decades, evolved into more prominent positions, such as the PEN presidency and a visiting professorship at Columbia University. The next two years also brought changes in his personal life: in 1964 he divorced his wife, and the following year married his cousin Patricia Llosa, with whom he would have two sons and a daughter.

Vargas Llosa rose to international prominence with the publication of his second novel, *La casa verde* (*The Green House*), the following year. Honored with the Premio de la Critic Española, the Premio National de la Novela, and the $22,000 Romulo Gallegos award for the best novel written in Spanish during the previous five years, the novel is "probably the most accomplished work of fiction ever to come out of Latin America," according to Harss and Dohmann, who found that "It has sweep, beauty, imaginative scope, and a sustained eruptive power that carries the reader from first page to last like a fish in a bloodstream." Vargas Llosa again relied upon his childhood experiences for his subject matter, drawing extensively from his memories of spying on the local brothel, commonly known as the Green House, as a ten-year-old growing up in Piura. In addition to serving as the focal point for the disparate stories loosely joined together in a nonlinear narrative pattern, the Green House takes on a larger significance. As Gregory Rabassa stated in *World Literature Today*, the novel's title "is the connective theme that links the primitive world of the jungle to the primal lusts of 'civilization' which are enclosed by the green walls of the whorehouse." Other critics commended the novel's intricate structure, finding that it richly underscored what Gerdes called a "fragmented, complex, confusing, and alienating" worldview, one offering a "significant comment on the nature of reality as perceived by contemporary humanity."

During the 1970s and 1980s, Vargas Llosa continued his prolific output, writing two novels that revealed a new dimension of the author: a sense of humor to balance the seriousness of his themes. *Pantaleon y las visitadoras* (*Captain Pantoja and the Special Services*), a satiric novel about a military officer ordered to find prostitutes for troops in the jungle, was praised by Gene Bell-Villad in *Commonweal* for its "humorous ribald tone," as well as for its ability to "sniff out corruption in high places." His next novel, *Aunt Julia and the Scriptwriter,* centers around a writer of a radio soap opera, affording Vargas Llosa the opportunity to raise timeless questions about the relationship between fiction and reality. As Ronald de Feo observed in *New Republic,* the novel is "a multilayered, high-spirited, and in the end a terribly affecting text about the interplay of fiction and reality, the transformation of life into art, and life seen and sometimes even lived as fiction."

*The War of the End of the World,* published in 1985, further solidified his reputation as a major writer. Richard Locke, writing in the *Washington Post Book World,* went so far as to suggest that the winner of the Ritz Paris Hemingway Award "makes most recent American fiction seem very small, very private, very gray, and very timid." Focusing on the Canudos wars of nineteenth-century Brazil, the massive novel has been read as a commentary of contemporary Latin American conflicts between right-wing dictatorships and communist guerrillas. Ending in a fight to the death between representative of opposing armies—an image which Salman Rushdie in *New Republic* found "to crystallize Vargas Llosa's political vision"—the highly ironic novel paints the author as "a humanist who reviles with equal vigor tyrannies of the right or left," according to Curt Supplee in the *Washington Post.*

## Gains Presidential Nomination

While continuing to write prolifically through the 1980s and into the 1990s—and adding the genre of erotic literature to his repertoire with *In Praise of the Stepmother*—Vargas Llosa also gained international prominence as a politician. In response to the 1987 attempt by the Peruvian government to nationalize the country's banks, he led a mass protest that forced the government to change their policy. Encouraged by this success, Vargas Llosa's supporters formed Fredemo, a grass-roots party devoted to democracy, a free market economy, and individual liberty. After forming the coalition Liberty Movement, supporters nominated Vargas Llosa as a presidential candidate. Although opinion polls as late as June of 1989 showed him to be leading his nearest competitor by as much as 44 percent, he lost the 1990 election. The outcome, however, was viewed as something of a blessing by many admirers of his work, who have argued that it is from his position as a writer—not a politician—that Vargas Llosa can best fulfill his long-held role as Peru's "national conscience."

## SELECTED PUBLISHED WORKS:

### Novels

*La ciudad y los perros,* Barcelona, Seix Barral, 1963, translation by Lysander Kemp as *The Time of the Hero,* New York, Grove Press, 1966.

*La casa verde,* Barcelona, Seix Barral, 1966, translated by Gregory Rabassa as *The Green House,* New York, Harper, 1968.

*Conversacion en la catedral,* Barcelona, Seix Barral, 1969, translated by Gregory Rabassa as *Conversation in the Cathedral,* New York, Harper, 1975.

*Pantaleon y las visitadoras,* Barcelona, Seix Barral, 1973, translated by Ronald Christ and Gregory Kolovakos as *Captain Pantojo and the Special Service,* New York, Harper, 1978.

*La guerra del fin del mundo,* Plaza y Janes, 1981, translated by Helen R. Lane as *The War of the End of the World,* New York, Farrar, Straus, 1984.

*Aunt Julia and the Scriptwriter,* New York, Farrar, Straus, 1982.

*Historia de Mayta,* Barcelona, Seix Barral, 1985, translated by Alfred MacAdam as *The Real Life of Alejandro Mayta,* New York, Farrar, Straus, 1986.

*Quien mato a Palomino Molero?,* Barcelona, Seix Barral, 1986, translated by Alfred MacAdam as *Who Killed Palomino Molero?,* New York, Farrar, Straus, 1987.

*El hablador,* Barcelona, Seix Barral, 1987, translated by Helen R. Lane as *The Storyteller,* New York, Farrar, Straus, 1989.

*Elogio de la madrastra,* Tusquets, 1988, translated by H. Lane as *In Praise of the Stepmother,* New York, Farrar, Straus, 1990.

## Other

*Los jefes,* Editorial Rocas, 1959.

*Los cachorros,* Editorial Lumen, 1967, translated by Ronald Christ and Gregory Kolovakos in *The Cubs, and Other Stories,* New York, Harper, 1979.

*Carta de batalla por "Tirant lo Blanc,"* Barcelona, Seix Barral, 1969.

*Antologia minima de M. Vargas Llosa,* Editorial Tiempo Contemporaneo, 1969.

(With Julio Cortazar and Oscar Collazos) *La litteratura en la revolucion y la revolucion en la litteratura,* Siglo Vientiuno Editores, 1970.

*Garcia Marquez: Historia de un deicidio,* Barcelona, Seix Barral, 1971.

*La historia secreta de una novela,* Tusquets, 1971.

*Obras escogidas,* Aguilar, 1973.

*La orgia perpetua: Flaubert y "Madame Bovary,"* Barcelona, Seix Barral, 1975, translation by Helen R. Lane published as *The Perpetual Orgy: Flaubert and "Madame Bovary,"* New York, Farrar, Straus, 1986.

*Art, Authenticity and Latin American Culture: A Dialogue with Mario Vargas Llosa and Ariel Dorfman,* Wilson Center, 1981.

*La senorita de Tacna,* Barcelona, Seix Barral, 1982.

*Kathie y el hipopotamo: Comedia en dos actos,* Barcelona, Seix Barral, 1983, translation by Kerry McKenny and Anthony Oliver-Smith produced as *Kathie and the Hippopotamus,* Edinburgh, Scotland, 1986.

*Contra viento y marea,* Barcelona, Seix Barral, 1983.

*La cultura de la libertad de la cultura,* Fundacion Eduardo Frei, 1985.

*La chunga,* Barcelona, Seix Barral, 1986.

*La verdad de las mentiras: ensayos sobre literatura,* Barcelona, Seix Barral, 1990.

*Contra viento y marea, III (1964–1988),* Barcelona, Seix Barral, 1990.

*A Writer's Reality,* edited by Myron I. Lichtblau, Syracuse University Press, 1991.

*En pez en el agua: Memorias del inca,* Barcelona, Seix Barral, 1993.

## SOURCES:

### Books

*Contemporary Authors New Revision Series,* Volume 32, edited by Susan M. Trosky, Detroit, Gale, 1994.

*Contemporary Literary Criticism,* Detroit, Gale, Volume 3, 1975, Volume 6, 1976, Volume 9, 1978, Volume 10, 1979, Volume 15, 1980, Volume 31, 1985, Volume 42, 1987.

Donoso, Jose, *The Boom in Spanish American Literature,* New York, Columbia University Press, 1977.

Gerdes, Dick, *Mario Vargas Llosa,* Boston, Twayne, 1985.

Harss, Luis, and Barbara Dohmann, *Into the Mainstream: Conversations with Latin-American Writers,* New York, Harper, 1967.

*Hispanic Writers,* edited by Bryan Ryan, Detroit, Gale, 1991.

*Mario Vargas Llosa: A Collection of Critical Essays,* edited by Charles Rossmann and Alan Warren Friedman, Austin, University of Texas Press, 1978.

Williams, Raymond Leslie, *Mario Vargas Llosa,* New York, Ungar, 1986.

### Periodicals

*Commonweal,* June 8, 1979, pp. 346–347.

*New Republic,* August 16–23, 1982, pp. 38–39.

*New York Times Book Review,* October 29, 1989.

*New York Times Magazine,* November 20, 1983.

*Washington Post,* August 26, 1984; February 9, 1986.

*Washington Post Book World,* August 26, 1984, pp. 1, 11.

*World Literature Today,* winter 1978.

*—Sketch by Jason Gallman*

---

# José Vasconcelos
## 1882-1959
### Mexican educational reformer, philosopher, and lawyer

One of the most formidable intellects of twentieth-century Mexico, José Vasconcelos taught, lectured, took part in the political life of his country, and wrote voluminously during the course of a long life. He is perhaps best remembered for the educational reforms he instituted during his years as Minister of Education and for his racial theories put forth in *La raza cósmica* and other writings. His intellectual range was vast, however, and the subject matter of his writing encompasses history, philosophy, law, international relations, and educational systems.

### Parents Stressed Education

He was born in the state of Oaxaca on February 28, 1882, the son of Ygnacio and Carmen Calderon

Vasconcelos. His mother came from a wealthy family; his father was an out-of-wedlock child from a poor background. Both were of predominantly Spanish descent. Ygnacio Vasconcelos earned his living as a customs official, and his work obliged him to move the family frequently. During José's adolescence they lived near the Texas border, where tensions between the two cultures ran high. Much of the uneasiness dated from earlier in the century, when Mexico had suffered military defeat at the hands of the United States, eventually losing more than half its territory to its northern neighbor. José attended a public school in Texas, where he encountered firsthand the racial hostility of U.S. citizens toward Mexicans. It is quite likely that these early experiences informed his later writings on the subject of race.

The Vasconcelos parents placed a high priority on the education of their children. In 1897 they took José to Mexico City and enrolled him in the National Preparatory School. Always an outstanding student, he went on to the Escuela Nacional de Jurisprudencia (National School of Jurisprudence), where he received his law degree with honors in 1905. Having distinguished himself in literature and philosophy as well, he embarked upon a literary career and soon established himself as one of the leading young thinkers of his day.

In 1909, he became a founding member of El Ateneo de la Juventud (Athenaeum of Youth), a society that devoted itself to philosophical and artistic inquiry and whose membership included the leading young intellectuals, writers, and artists. That same year, he married Serafina Miranda. At about the same time, he became involved in political activities with the anti-reelectionists, whose goal it was to prevent the reelection of the long-term dictator **Porfirio Diaz.** For a time, Vasconcelos edited an anti-reelectionist newspaper. With the coming of the Revolution of 1910, he duly allied himself with Francisco Madero against Porfirio Diaz. During the stormy political events of the next several years, as political power passed alternately between the warring factions, Vasconcelos was twice forced to seek political asylum outside of his country. He spent these periods in various Latin American countries and in the United States, where he continued to write and to involve himself in Mexican political affairs at long distance. In 1914, he briefly held a post in the Ministry of Education in the administration of President Eulalio Gutierrez before being forced into exile again when Venustiano Carranza succeeded Gutierrez. During the next three years, he resumed his travels in the United States and Latin America, returning to Mexico upon the death of Carranza in 1920.

### Instituted Reform as Minister of Education

Politically outspoken and intellectually formidable, Vasconcelos was arguably the best-educated man in Mexico when the interim president, Adolfo de la Huerta, appointed him rector of the National University in 1920. The following year, when Alvaro Obregon become president, Vasconcelos was given an unprecedented opportunity. Obregon was committed to education and had a profound respect for Vasconcelos's abilities. He reorganized the Ministry of Education, appointing Vasconcelos its director and providing him with money and autonomy to put his educational philosophy to work. His four years in that position were perhaps the most productive of his life.

With the goal of bringing educational opportunities to all, especially Indian children in rural areas, he expanded teacher training facilities, and his contagious enthusiasm inspired hundreds of young men and women to devote themselves to teaching, even at very low wages. He assigned them to remote areas, where he constructed more than one hundred new schools. He instituted "cultural missions," mobile units composed of teachers, public health workers, and agricultural specialists, and sent these into outlying areas as well.

He had a personal interest in promoting classical learning, an area in which he was deeply versed. Declaring that "what this country needs is to sit down and read the Iliad," he distributed inexpensive editions of Plato, Dante, Virgil, and Homer to Mexican schoolchildren, a practice that was considered eccentric by some. Vasconcelos, however, wished to promote a love of learning for its own sake, rather than as a means to power.

He did not neglect vocational and technical education. He preached the importance of training a specialized work force to combat national dependence on foreign technology and expertise, and toward that end he established technical institutions equipped with modern machinery and sent talented students to Europe with scholarships to study engineering and chemistry.

Support for the work of native artists and craftsmen was another cornerstone of Vasconcelos's program. He encouraged musicians such as **Carlos Chavez** and Manuel Ponce, who incorporated indigenous themes in their work; he urged architects to abandon designs imitative of Europe and to turn instead to their own environment for inspiration. A centerpiece of his efforts in the arts was the work of the great muralists such as **Diego Rivera** and others, who, under Vasconcelos's auspices, covered the walls of Mexico's public buildings with scenes commemorating and celebrating Mexico's history. The social and political messages of these works, which portrayed the spirit of the revolution, were an important national inspiration.

Vasconcelos resigned the post in 1924 and made an unsuccessful run for governor of Oaxaca, following which he embarked upon extensive travels in Europe and the Americas, lecturing and continuing to write. During the next several years he taught at the Universities of Puerto Rico, Chicago, California at Berkeley, and at Stanford University.

### The Cosmic Race

In 1925, Vasconcelos published *La raza cósmica* (*The Cosmic Race*), in which he introduced his vision of a strong multicultural Latin American people whose destiny it would be to dominate the future. The idea of the cosmic race was further developed in *Indologia,* which appeared the following year. Vasconcelos's theory of the cosmic race was actually a complex ideology that he continued to develop throughout his life and which has been subject to various interpretations. At its root, it stated that out of a mixture of the four racial types—the black, the Indian, the Mongol, and the white—a fifth, the cosmic race, a superior race made up of the strongest qualities of each, would emerge. The home of the cosmic race was to be the tropics of Latin America, as Vasconcelos believed that tropical climates provided a more nurturing environment for higher civilizations than temperate climates. He foresaw a great capital city, called Universopolis, arising on the banks of the Amazon.

For the purposes of his ideology, Vasconcelos divided human history into three periods: the first was a material or warrior stage; the second, his own time, the rational or intellectual; and the third, which would be the age of the cosmic race, a spiritual phase characterized by aesthetic appreciation and harmony.

Most analysts have seen the theory of the cosmic race as a response to social injustice and an attempt on Vasconcelos's part to exalt the Mestizo culture of Mexico and to instill hope and pride in the people for whose betterment he worked so hard as Minister of Education. It was influenced in part by the Indianismo movement, which, among other things, encouraged the appreciation of indigenous American culture and its incorporation into the national life. One critic, Nicandro Juarez, in an extended analysis of Vasconcelos's racial theory, viewed it in part as a reaction against biological racism, which makes claims for the superiority of racially pure, largely Aryan peoples. It was Vasconcelos's conviction that racially mixed peoples are superior to racially pure peoples. But Juarez, following the line of Vasconcelos's reasoning, saw a number of contradictions, and accused Vasconcelos of engaging in the type of thinking which leads to racial stereotyping. Finally, he believed, Vasconcelos's aim was to have the racial traits he considered inferior counteracted by superior characteristics.

### Politics and Philosophy

Following his extended travels in the late 1920s, Vasconcelos returned to Mexico in 1929. Disgusted by the caliber of the major candidate for president that year, Pascual Ortiz Rubio, a tool of the military alliance, Vasconcelos decided to run for the office himself. Although well received on his campaign travels throughout the country, Vasconcelos nevertheless lost the election by a large majority. He declared the election a fraud and called for the overthrow of the government, but when no revolution resulted, he retired to a self-imposed exile, and spent most of the following seven years in the United States. This marked the end of his active involvement in politics. From then on, he devoted himself to his interest in philosophy. He did not, however, refrain from political comment. He was a frequent critic of what he saw as the undue influence of the United States on the affairs of Mexico.

During the years of his exile, and following his permanent return to Mexico in 1939, he wrote and published prolifically. He held strong opinions, many of which changed radically during the course of his career. As a philosopher, he was an impassioned and original thinker. His philosophical system, "aesthetic monism," revolved around the belief that intuition is an important adjunct to scientific experience. His most important sources were Pythagorus, Plotinus, Schopenhauer, Niezsche, Whitehead, and Bergson.

The first volume of what would eventually grow into a five-volume autobiography appeared in 1936. Entitled *Ulises criollo* (*Creole Ulysses*), it set the style for later volumes, relating the events of his life in the context of the history and politics of his country. The last volume appeared the year of his death.

Vasconcelos remained active all his life. He served as director of the National Library and the Library of Mexico, and was a founding member of the Colegio de Mexico. In 1942, he was married a second time, to Esperanza Cruz, having previously become a widower. They added a son, Hector, to the family of two children, José Ygnacio and Carmen, from the first marriage. Vasconcelos was the recipient of numerous honors and awards from institutions including the Academy of Letters, the National Historical Society, and the National College. He died on June 30, 1959, and was buried at the National Cemetery of Illustrious Mexicans.

### SELECTED PUBLISHED WORKS:

### Autobiography

*Ulises criollo: la vida del autor escrita por el mismo,* [Mexico City], 1935.
*La tormenta: segunda parte de Ulises criollo,* [Mexico City], 1935.
*El desastre: tercera parte de Ulises criollo,* [Mexico City], 1938.

*El proconsulado: cuarta parte de Ulises criollo,*
[Mexico City], 1939.
*La flama: los de arriba en la revolución; historia y
tragedia,* [Mexico City], 1959.

### Education, History, and Philosophy

*La raza cósmica,* [Barcelona], 1925.
*Indologia: una interpretación de la cultura iber-
oamericana,* [Paris and Barcelona], 1926.
*Bolivarismo y monroismo: temas iberoamericanos,*
[Santiago, Chile], 1934.
*Breve historia de México,* [Mexico City], 1937.
*Hernán Cortés: creador de la nacionalidad,* [Mexi-
co City], 1941.
*Apuntes para la historia de Mexico: desde la con-
quista hasta la revolución de 1910,* [Mexico
City], 1943.

## SOURCES:

### Books

De Beer, Gabriella, "José Vasconcelos," *Latin
American Writers,* edited by Carlos A. Solé,
three volumes, New York, Scribners, 1989.
Johnson, Kenneth F., *Mexican Democracy: A Crit-
ical View,* Boston, Allyn and Bacon, 1971.
Johnson, William Weber, *Heroic Mexico: The Nar-
rative History of a Twentieth Century Revolu-
tion,* Garden City, New York, Doubleday,
1968.
Miller, Robert Ryal, *Mexico: A History,* Norman,
University of Oklahoma Press, 1985.
Newlon, Clarke, *The Men Who Made Mexico,*
New York, Dodd, Mead, 1973.
Romanell, Patrick, *Making of the Mexican Mind,*
Lincoln, University of Nebraska Press, 1952.

### Periodicals

*Aztlan,* Volume 3, 1972, p. 82; Volume 14, pp.
307–341.
*Hispanic Review,* Volume 50, 1982, pp. 143–157.

*—Sketch by Julie Henderson Jersyk*

# Catalina Vasquez Villalpando
## 1940-
### Mexican American politician

As a U.S. Republican Party organizer and Special
Assistant to the President during the Reagan
Administration, Catalina Villalpando opened the
ranks of government to Hispanic Americans. Later, as
one of the few Hispanic women to achieve such high
governmental office, Villalpando served as U.S. Treasurer to President Bush during his administration.
Her eventual conviction on tax evasion and obstruction charges threatens to overshadow her achievements. However, it must be noted that she was
honored with special achievement awards from various government agencies, and was also asked to serve
on the U.S. Commission on Civil Rights.

The father of Catalina Vasquez Villalpando was
born in Mexico, while her mother was a Texan of
Mexican descent. Agustin, who had six children with
his wife Guadalupe, was a hardware store salesman.
Catalina—or Cathi—was born April 1, 1940 in San
Marcos, a little town between Austin and San Antonio. Her father would often take the children on trips
to local fields in order to show them what it was like
to pick crops, always the most likely job for a new
immigrant. The family was religiously conservative
and not prosperous. Though the Villalpandos were
staunch Democrats, their eldest child was destined to
make a name for herself among the rival Republicans.

After attending local public schools and graduating from the high school in San Marcos, Villalpando
enrolled as a part-time student at Southwest Texas
State University. Meanwhile, a short-lived marriage
to a high school sweetheart produced no children.
While she never completed a degree, she did take
courses at various institutions including Southern
Methodist University and the Austin College of
Business. It was while taking a business course that
Villalpando stumbled across Republican Party recruiters. As she recalled in *Nuestro,* Republican
headquarters just happened to be in the same building, and coincidentally in need of part-time clerical
help. While she felt politically jaded at the time, she
confessed that she became slowly impressed by the
openness of the party. Villalpando formally became a
Republican Party member in 1969.

She began immediately to work in certain federal
positions that required her to work in Texas, especially in the Austin and Dallas regions. Her specialties
became economic development, particularly regarding minority businesses, and public relations. Villalpando worked for the Department of Commerce, the
Office of Economic Opportunity and the Minority
Business Development Administration during the
1970s. After two and a half years as Hispanic Liaison
for the Party, the Republicans trusted her with
campaign assignments during 1980. Villalpando coordinated the Hispanic outreach effort during George
Bush's primary bid, then later filled in as assistant
director at the state level during Reagan's presidential
run.

### From DC to Dallas and Back

After the Reagan victory, Villalpando was
brought to the White House as personnel staff assis-

tant for the Transition Team. When her work was done there, she returned to Texas and entered the private sector. Two businesses offered her high offices. First Mid-South Oil Company of Dallas made her vice-president. Then Communications International, Inc. of Atlanta, Georgia, elected her senior vice-president. In 1983, however, Senator John Tower of Texas recommended her for a post in the Reagan Administration. Villalpando worked from the Public Liaison Office as Special Assistant to the President regarding Hispanic affairs.

Villalpando was proud of her success in bringing together groups which may not have otherwise interacted on issues crucial to Hispanics. She was also instrumental in coordinating the efforts of the Department of Education and a congressman who had been working on a bill regarding bilingual education. A controversial immigration bill was studied by Villalpando and the Public Liaison Office, in order to help offer an alternative to deportation by fostering the reform of employment practices.

### Named U.S. Treasurer

While still involved with Communications International, Inc., Villalpando was appointed U.S. Treasurer by President Bush in the late 1980s. While Villalpando had apparently cleared the company's payment of a quarter-million-dollar bonus after she accepted the government post, she was still reprimanded during 1990 over how the payments had been handled. As the controversy over the CII fee and other suspected dealings increased, members of the National Council of La Raza and the Congressional Hispanic Caucus Institute came to her personal defense. However, the FBI increased their surveillance, eventually searching company offices and Villalpando's apartment.

While Villalpando herself was never accused directly of influence peddling, the charges brought against her after she was forced to take administrative leave included obstruction. She eventually admitted, while pleading guilty to three felonies, to obstructing an investigation of a housing scandal dating back to the Reagan Administration. Villalpando was also charged with evading income taxes and deliberately underreporting income to the government. While the maximum possible sentence for each of these charges might have been five years, Villalpando was instead sentenced in 1994 to a four-month term in federal prison. Following that term, she was additionally required by the court to be allowed only supervised release for another three years, and to perform 200 hours of community service.

### SOURCES:

*New York Times,* February 18, 1994, pp. A11, 17; September 14, 1994, p. A12.

*Nuestro,* January-February 1985, pp. 16–19.
*Time,* February 28, 1994, p. 19.
*Washington Post,* September 15, 1983; October 30, 1992, p. A1; October 31, 1992, p. A8; January 10, 1993, p. A1; September 14, 1994, p. A5.

—*Sketch by Jennifer Kramer*

# Lope de Vega y Carpio
## 1562-1635
### Spanish dramatist and poet

Lope de Vega is Spain's most popular dramatist and ranks as one of the country's most influential writers. Known as the developer of the literary genre known as the Spanish *comedia,* he was also the founder of the Spanish National Theater. Lope de Vega's myriad contributions to Spanish drama have even led some critics to draw parallels between his impact on Spanish drama and William Shakespeare's influence on the English stage.

Lope de Vega's writings are acknowledged to be a cornerstone of Spain's extensive and rich collection of dramatic works. **Miguel de Cervantes** referred to the playwright as *el monstruo de la naturaleza* ("the freak of nature") because of his astoundingly vast body of work. A tremendously prolific artist, historians believe he may have penned more than 1,000 works, of which some 400 have been preserved. Lope de Vega's *comedias*—which often featured themes of bravery, honor, and romantic intrigue—were immensely popular with the general public. They also mirrored their creator to a degree, for Lope de Vega was a romantic, passionate character who led a turbulent life.

Lope de Vega was born in Madrid on November 25, 1562. His father, an embroiderer named Félix de Lope de Vega, and mother, Francisca Fernández Flores, were of humble origin. Lope de Vega was the second son and the third child of the family. As a child he studied in the Colegio de los Teatinos. It is said that as a very young boy Lope de Vega dictated verse to the older boys who could write. He compensated them for this service by sharing his lunch with them. His first biographer, Montalbán, who wrote about Lope de Vega in 1636, exalted the playwright. He claimed that the dramatist wrote his first play, *El verdadero amante* (*The True Lover*) at the age of 12.

The school that Lope de Vega attended in Madrid was run by Vicente Espinel, author of the *Vida del escudero Marcos de Obregón* (*The Life of*

*Lope de Vega y Carpio*

*Squire Marcos de Obregón*), a well-known and influential picaresque novel. From this school he graduated to the Jesuits' School where, according the usual curriculum of the time, he received a rigorous education in grammar and rhetoric. Later he attended the Academia Real, where he most likely learned astronomy and mathematics.

### Prolific Poet, Promiscuous Lover

Lope de Vega spent the years 1577 to 1581 at the University of Alcalá, probably at the expense of Jerónimo Manrique, the Bishop of Avila, to whom he dedicated several poems. He left the university without finishing his studies to pursue a love affair. He studied briefly at the University of Salamanca before joining an expedition that sought to conquer Portuguese Terceira, the only Azore island not administered by Spain. Upon Lope de Vega's return to Madrid, he fell in love with Elena Osorio, the wife of the actor Cristóbal Calderón. Osorio became the basis for the character "Dorotea" in his play *La Dorotea.* Their love affair lasted for five years, but Osorio's mother finally forbade them from continuing the relationship.

Elena replaced Lope de Vega with a new lover, a development that enraged the poet. He retaliated, publishing scurrilous verse against the Osorio family. His attack was so harsh, however, that he was cast into prison. He was sentenced to eight years exile from Madrid and two years exile from Castile, and

was warned that he faced death if he defied the sentence. But even such a threat could not stop his secret return to Madrid in order to pursue Isabel de Urbina, an aristocrat whom he married by way of proxy due to his inability to appear publicly in Madrid.

Forbidden from appearing in Madrid, some historians have suggested that Lope de Vega may have sailed with the Spanish Armada on its ill-fated journey against England. In any event, the poet and his new wife eventually took up residence in Valencia in 1588. Here Lope de Vega wrote his early plays and established a reputation as a writer of ballads. This period spent in Valencia was decisive in the formation of his vocation as a playwright. He was greatly influenced by the Valencian dramatist Cristóbal de Virués. Lope de Vega wrote in *El laurel de Apolo* that Cristóbal laid the very foundation of the *comedia* in his "famous tragedies."

In 1591 Lope de Vega moved to Toledo and took office as the secretary to the Duke of Alba, one of the most important noblemen of the era. It was common practice for poets to seek positions with the gentry so they could write under their sponsorship. In 1594 Lope de Vega's wife died giving birth to their second daughter, who also died.

In 1596 Lope de Vega returned to Madrid. Not long after his return, he was accused of carrying on an illicit affair with a widow, Antonia Trillo. In 1598 he married Juana de Guardo, daughter of a wealthy meat wholesaler. It was widely believed that he married her only for her money, although they eventually had three children. Soon after the marriage, however, Lope de Vega set up residence with another woman, Micaela de Luján, who bore him five children. This scandalous situation was accentuated by the copious number of love poems composed by Lope de Vega that were dedicated to Micaela. But his tolerant wife remained with him until her death in 1613 shortly after the death of their seven-year-old son Carlos Félix.

### The Poet Turned Priest

After the death of his second wife and his son Carlos, Lope de Vega underwent a spiritual crisis that culminated in his decision to become a priest at the age of 52. His ordination as a priest did little to curb his amorous appetites, though. In 1616 he met Marta de Nevares, the model for *Amarílis* in his verses. The poet referred to de Nevares in his letters as "the physician for my wounds." She was a beautiful married woman in her mid-twenties who Lope de Vega, over 50 years old at this point, pursued with zeal. The woman's husband—who, according to Lope de Vega, was a brutish man—brought the poet and his wife before an ecclesiastical court. The ensuing weeks of the trial created a huge scandal. By this time de

Nevares was pregnant with Lope de Vega's child and was anxious to rid herself of the unwanted husband. Then, prior to resolution of the litigation, the husband died, leaving Lope de Vega so ecstatic that he celebrated the turn of events in verse. A daughter, Antonia Clara, was born, and she and her mother took up residence with Lope de Vega and two of his other children.

Lope de Vega and Marta de Nevares remained together for some 15 years. During his years with her he produced some of his better-known dramas, including *El caballero de Olmedo* (*The Gentleman of Olmedo*) and *El mejor alcalde, el Rey* (*The King, the Greatest Mayor*). But while his writing career thrived, Lope de Vega suffered several blows in his personal life. In 1628 Marta de Nevares went blind and began to lose her sanity, a development that Lope de Vega interpreted as a form of divine punishment for his past transgressions. In 1632 Marta de Nevares died. Two years later one of the poet's children drowned. The same year Antonia Clara, much loved daughter of Lope de Vega and Marta de Nevares, was abducted by a *hidalgo,* a member of the aristocracy. In his final years Lope de Vega was a sad and remorseful man who had lost touch with his audience. He died on August 27, 1635. Madrid went into mourning for nine days, an honor never before bestowed on a Spanish writer.

### The "Monster" of the Golden Age

Lope de Vega lived and worked in Spain during the reign of Philip II, at a time when the country was at the height of its cultural and political power. Madrid, which had been declared the capital of Spain by Philip II, quickly became the hub of the immense Spanish empire. The city was full of nobility and all the writers of the day congregated in Madrid in an attempt to gain their patronage. Plays were presented in *corrales* or open courtyards and there existed a large theater-going audience whose appetite for new works was insatiable.

For several decades Lope de Vega held sway as the city's most popular dramatist. He had the ability to divine what the public wanted and to deliver works with universal appeal. Particularly adept at lyrical improvisation, the dramatist was able to conjure up complex plots full of intrigue and emotion, albeit with little character development or intellectual content. In his famous *Arte nuevo de hacer comedias* (*New Art of Writing "Comedias"*)—a 1609 treatise in verse concerning his theories on writing *comedias*—Lope de Vega defended his style of writing, contending that the box office is the ultimate judge of the success of any play. Lope de Vega rejected the standards of classical and neoclassical play writing in favor of a blend of tragedy and comedy.

Lope de Vega is regarded as the creator of the *comedia* in three acts. The *comedia* was a social drama that reflected the norms and values of the day. Respect for the church and the throne was an integral element, as was the concept of human dignity as manifested by one's *pundonor* ("*point of honor*") or social reputation. Male honor was linked to courage and pride, while honor for women meant chastity for maidens and fidelity for wives. Duels to the death were a standard plot device used by Lope de Vega; fencing ability was thus an indispensable asset for actors of the day. Other features common to Lope de Vega's plays included servant characters who parodied the main action and a *gracioso* ("*clown*") character, who provided insight with his wit and powers of perception.

Lope de Vega's works encompassed a wide range of themes, but the two broad categories in which he specialized were the heroic historical play and the cloak and sword drama. Lope de Vega drew on medieval chronicles as well as popular legends and songs for his plots. The crown was often represented as the disperser of justice and champion of the humble, a representation that inspired some of his best work. In other dramas, however, common towns-folk are Lope de Vega's heroes.

*Fuente Ovejuna,* considered by many critics to be Lope de Vega's most important work, relates a tale about the peasants of the village of Fuente Ovejuna. After a revolt by the peasants wherein their cruel and arrogant governor is killed, the king and queen (Ferdinand and Isabella) send a judge to the village to conduct an investigation and punish the guilty parties. The practice of the time was to torture witnesses in order to extract the truth, but the peasants—women and children included—withstand the torture and remain unified. The judge's question, "Who killed the Comendador?" and the peasants' reply, "Fuente Ovejuna, señor," are among the most famous lines in Spanish drama. The drama ends with the exoneration of the entire village. A celebration of the honor and integrity of the common person, *Fuente Ovejuna* enjoyed success outside of Spain. It proved particularly popular in Russia, where the anti-Czarists manipulated the story to fit their fight against the Russian monarchy. Other revolutionary groups have adopted the same theme in their struggle against tyranny. Another of his most important works, *El Caballero de Olmedo* (*The Gentleman of Olmedo*) was a tragedy based in part on a haunting refrain from a popular folk song of that period.

Later in his life Lope de Vega voiced unhappiness with his plays. He complained that he was unable to dedicate enough time to their creation because his career was predicated on the volume of work he churned out. Although there may be some validity to this claim many scholars feel that the lyrical quality and sharp dramatic sense of his plays make them both memorable and highly entertaining. Lope de Vega's popular dramas were often pirated by others, while works by other playwrights were sometimes attributed to him in order to take advantage of his popularity.

But while Lope de Vega was popular with the public, he had many literary enemies. His greatest adversary was **Luis de Góngora** who, after reading Lope de Vega's *La Dragontea* exclaimed, "What a small streak of lightning for such a loud clap of thunder!" While most scholars agree that his work was flawed—character development, for instance, was not one of Lope de Vega's strengths—most contend that an understanding of his work is still of vital importance to anyone who wishes to become familiar with the world of drama during that period.

Lope de Vega himself defended his style at length in his *Nueva arte de hacer comedias* (*New Art of Writing "Comedias"*). He wrote that the person who tries to write in accordance with the classic Aristotelian rules will not succeed financially: "When I sit down to write a play, I lock up the rules with six keys and drive Plautus and Terence out of my study to stop their howling. I keep an eye on the box office, and because the common man pays the piper, I pipe the tune he likes." While French and Italian dramatists clung to the Aristotelian format, Spanish drama, led by Lope de Vega, broke away and explored new avenues of interpretation and expression.

### Poetic Works

Although Lope de Vega was most well-known as a playwright, he also produced a considerable amount of poetry, sonnets, ballads, and songs. Although he composed ballads throughout his lifetime, the bulk of them were produced in his younger days, when he wrote of his many love affairs. Many of these works were brought together in *Romancero general*. *Rimas sacras* and the *Romancero espiritual* contain his religious ballads.

Lope de Vega was also a talented creator of sonnets. He wrote more sonnets than any other Spanish writer; his epic work *Dragontea* is regarded as one of the finest examples of the Spaniard's faculty in this area. His remaining poetic work included songs, odes, eclogues, and epistles. Many of the epistles were published in *El jardín de Lope de Vega*, which was made available around 1621. *Amarilis*, written after the death of Marta de Nevares, is considered to be the best of his eclogues.

### SELECTED PUBLISHED WORKS:

*La Arcadia,* 1598.
*La hermosure de Angélica con otras diversas rimas,* 1602.
*El peregrino en su patria,* 1604.
*Lo fingido verdadero (From Make-believe to Reality),* 1608.
*La buena guarda (The Erring Nun),* 1610.
*Fuente Ovejuna,* 1612.
*El caballero de Olmedo (The Gentleman of Olmedo),* 1620.
*El mejor alcalde, el Rey (The King, the Greatest Mayor),* 1620.
*La Circe,* 1624.
*Poesías líricas,* 2 volumes, 1926–27.
*Rimas divinas y humanas del licenciado Tomé de Burguillos,* 1634.
*La Vega del Parnaso,* 1637.

### SOURCES:

#### Books

Astrana Marín, Luis, *Lope de Vega,* Barcelona, Editorial Juventud, 1963.
Castro, Américo, and Hugo A. Rennert, *Vida de Lope de Vega (1562–1635),* Salamanca, Anaya, 1969.
Vega, Lope de, *Fuente Ovejuna,* translated by Victor Dixon, Warminster, England: Aris & Phillips,
Zamora Vicente, Alonso, *Lope de Vega: su vida y su obra,* Madrid, Gredos, 1961.

—*Sketch by Enrique Fernández*

---

# José Maria Velasco
## 1840-1912
### Mexican landscape painter

José Maria Velasco was the most important Mexican painter of the nineteenth century and is considered by many authorities to be one of the greatest landscape painters of all time. His best known works are a series of large oil on canvas paintings of the Valley of Mexico. Velasco was born in Temascaltzingo, Mexico, on July 6, 1840. The early death of his father in 1846 resulted in the family's move to Mexico City where his mother worked to support the family. Velasco's father had followed the traditional family occupation of weaving, and his mother reportedly hoped her son would follow suit. However, he showed an early aptitude as a draftsman and at the age of 18 entered the Art Academy of San Carlos, where he studied drawing and painting.

Although his early painting shows the influence of his teachers at the academy, Velasco soon displayed the same independence in his art that he had showed in his decision to abandon the family craft of weaving. Artist Juan O'Gorman remarked in a 1943 article in the *Magazine of Art* that "as soon as he mastered the technical difficulties of the craft he shed that influence completely and painted directly from nature in a way so original, so sensitive, and so plastically exact, that it is impossible to classify his work as academic in any sense whatsoever." Nevertheless, the early influences can be detected in his work. From the family weaving tradition, he inherited his eye for detail and the dexterity to work in a demandingly intricate style. From his teachers, Eugenio Landesio and Santiago Rebull, he learned his lifelong dedication to the works of nature and the practice of careful draftsmanship respectively.

### Paints the Valley of Mexico

The natural setting that Velasco chose to paint with single-minded attention all his life was the Valley of Mexico, which Carlos Pellicer, writing in the catalog of a 1944 exhibition of Velasco's work, called "one of the major phenomena in the history of our planet." Situated a mile and a half above the tropics, the valley offers a panorama of volcanic rock, hills, lagoons, a diverse—if sparse—vegetation, and magnificent cloudscapes. The valley is surmounted by the great snow capped peaks of Popocatepetl and Ixacchuatl, which rise another 10,000 feet. The lighting, in Pellicer's words "runs all the way from the spherical and slightly misty to the prismatic and incomprehensibly luminous. . . ." Velasco captured all of this in his vast canvases, rendering it with faithful realism. In the same catalog, Henry Clifford notes that "as Renaissance painters achieved one Madonna and Child after another, as Cezanne persisted in his series of Still Lifes, so Velasco painted his mistress, the Valley of Mexico, innumerable times."

In order to better understand his subject, the painter studied geology, botany, natural history, meteorology, physics, and mathematics. According to O'Gorman, Velasco developed a complicated scale of tones of colors so as to locate in space the objects and forms of the paintings. This enabled him to express "the action of time on nature, and in this," says O'Gorman, "he was an original master." He worked mainly in oil on canvas, although he also produced many drawings and watercolors. As time went on, he experimented on his oil canvases with thinner paints, producing more transparent-looking colors, and managing often to express the thin, luminous atmosphere of the highlands.

During the 1860s, Velasco's achievement was publicly recognized when he was awarded prizes from the Academy, from President **Benito Juarez,** and from the Emperor Maximilian. In 1868 he was appointed professor of landscape perspective at the Academy of San Carlos, a position he retained for the next five years. Among the students he influenced was **Diego Rivera,** who became famous as a painter of murals.

Velasco married in 1859, one year after entering the Academy, and founded a family which eventually included 13 children. In 1874 he moved his family to La Villa de Guadalupe, where he remained until his death. Although he rarely travelled, he did visit the Philadelphia Centennial Exhibition in 1876, where his "Valley of Mexico" was exhibited and won a prize. In 1889 he travelled to Paris, exhibiting 68 of his paintings at the World's Fair and winning the Legion of Honor, which was presented to him by Jean Louis Ernest Meissonier, the leading official painter of France. During the same trip, he visited England, Germany, Italy, and Spain before returning to teach landscape painting in 1890.

In 1893, Velasco spent three months in Chicago at the World's Fair, where he exhibited his work and won a prize. In 1902 he was decorated by the Austrian Emperor. The same year, he suffered a heart attack which rendered him an invalid for the remaining years of his life. During this last period, he painted small pictures, some of postcard size and many of them from memory. He died on August 25, 1912, while working on a small landscape that remained unfinished.

By all accounts, Velasco was a simple-hearted man who loved his home, family and country; he was a deeply religious man who made a habit of reading the Psalms before beginning a major composition. He belonged to no school of painting, took no part in the Bohemian life common to many artists, and at all times pursued his own vision, seemingly uninfluenced by the work of other artists—although a few of his early paintings bear some resemblance to the work of the French landscape painter Corot, he had rejected impressionism, with its preoccupation with light.

In 1942, Velasco was honored by a large retrospective exhibition at the Palacio de Bellas Artes, and in 1944 in exhibitions of his landscapes were held at the Philadelphia Museum of Art and the Brooklyn Museum. Pellicer called Velasco "a man of genius, the greatest artist Mexico has produced," and Clifford declared that he "deserves to be known internationally as one of the great landscape painters of modern times." Nevertheless, Velasco's work has not received the attention it deserves either in Mexico or elsewhere.

SOURCES:

**Books**

*José Maria Velasco 1840–1912: Exhibition Organized by the Philadelphia Museum of Art and the Brooklyn Museum,* privately printed, 1944.

**Periodicals**

*Magazine of Art,* October 1943, pp. 202–06.

—Sketch by Julie Henderson Jersyk

# Jose Maria Velasco Ibarra
## 1893-1979
### Ecuadorean statesman

Jose Maria Velasco Ibarra was a charismatic political leader in Ecuador who served five terms as president in a 38-year span. Not much is known about his childhood. He went to Paris to study and earned a law degree at the University of Paris. When he returned to Ecuador, he was a professor of law at the Central University at Quito and the University of Guayaquil. He was a prolific writer. Velasco Ibarra was exiled several times when military coups took over the government. He was elected as leader of the conservatives when he became president the first time in 1934. One year later he was deposed by a military coup and was exiled to Colombia. A political movement in the 1930s that included a diverse cross-section of the Ecuadorean population joined together to support Velasco Ibarra. The movement was called Velasquismo.

Velasco Ibarra ran for president in 1940 but the liberal Arroyo del Rio won the election. He led a failed rebellion and was forced back into exile, this time to Chile. He had toured the country in his presidential campaign and had many followers. In 1941 there was a border conflict with Peru in which Ecuador lost a vast area—half of the national territory—the size of Scotland and England combined. The people were very unhappy with their radical liberal leader and Velasco Ibarra had become a champion for the people of Ecuador.

In 1943 a new party emerged that supported the exiled Velasco Ibarra as a candidate in the forthcoming elections, the Alianza Democratica Ecuatoriana (ADE; Democratic Ecuadorean Alliance). Every political party with the exception of the Liberals joined the ADE to support Velasco—the Socialist, Communist, Socialist Revolutionary Vanguard, and the Democratic parties. Velasco Ibarra ran his campaign near the border in Colombia. An uprising took place in Guayaquil and in other cities in Ecuador on May 28 and 29, 1944, when the citizens and the military fought to depose the radical liberal regime under President Carlos Alberto Arroyo del Rio. The May revolution was caused by several factors that occurred under the liberal regime. The *carabineros* (the regime's elite police force) had killed two people that month: one was a university student and the other was a 15-year-old girl. Mass demonstrations were held at the victims' funerals. Other factors in the revolution were the military loss against Peru in 1941, hostility against the regime's *carabineros*, poor economic conditions, and possible electoral fraud. There were only two candidates for president: liberal Miguel Angel Albornoz, supported by Arroyo del Rio, and Velasco Ibarra, supported by ADE. The liberals would not let Velasco Ibarra into the country to direct his campaign and when the people thought that the election was fraudulent, they revolted. Velasco Ibarra was once again placed in power as president by virtue of a decree in June, 1944.

### Savior of Ecuador

The effect that Velasco Ibarra had on the people of Ecuador throughout his career has puzzled both social and political scientists. The Velasquismo movement was the beginning of organized mass political activity in the country. The people shouted "Viva Velasco Ibarra!" and even though he was in exile, they continued to support him. Eventually, merely saying these words became a crime and people were sent to jail. The Ecuadorian people began using the "V" sign with both hands instead of speaking the words. Velasco Ibarra was called "El Gran Ausente" ("The Great Absentee") and was considered a savior to the people of Ecuador. Many analyses have been written about Velasco Ibarra and how he cultivated his image with the people of Ecuador. He never stayed in the country except when he was campaigning or in office. He was the first politician to go out to meet the people. Wherever he went, his supporters greeted him with parades and banners. He presented himself as a moral, religious leader who would save the people from the liberals.

When Velasco Ibarra returned to Guayaquil by plane, on June 4, 1944, he was greeted by 80,000 people and was taken in a parade to El Palacio de la Zona. The director of ADE of Guayas Province, Francisco Arizago Luque, gave a speech about him and then invited Velasco Ibarra to talk. The returning politician addressed the people as "the heroic people of Guayaquil." He spoke with great clarity and drama about the fight for higher moral values. He presented the liberals as evil and stated that he had returned to Ecuador to save his country. He was not affiliated with any political party. Velasco Ibarra's populist attitude was that moral values and ethics nullified the rights of others. He disregarded democratic procedures and became a dictator.

In 1947, Velasco Ibarra turned against some of his political supporters and was deposed by a military coup. He went into exile, this time to Argentina. When he returned in 1952, he was elected president and served until 1956, the only time he actually completed his full term in office. He returned to Argentina and in 1960 was again elected president. In 1961 he was again deposed by a military coup. Velasco Ibarra went into exile yet again in Argentina until 1966, when the military was ousted from power. He ran for president and was victorious even with opposition from all of the political parties. In February, 1972, Velasco Ibarra was deposed by the military for the last time. He wanted to return Ecuador to democratic rule and the military opposed this move. He returned to exile in Argentina where he died on March 30, 1979.

## SELECTED PUBLISHED WORKS:

*Un momento de transicion politica,* [Quito], 1935.
*Conciencia a barbarie,* [Buenos Aires], 1938.
*Experiencias juridicas hispanoamericanas,* [Buenos Aires], 1943.
*Mensaje presentado a la honorable asamblea nacional constituyente, . . . 10 de agosto de 1946,* [Quito], 1946.

## SOURCES:

### Books

Blanksten, George I., *Ecuador: Constitutions and Caudillos,* New York, Russell & Russell, 1964.
Moss, Joyce, and George Wilson, *Peoples of the World: Latin Americans,* Detroit, Gale, 1989.
*Biographical Dictionary of Latin American and Caribbean Political Leaders,* edited by Robert J. Alexander, Westport, CT, Greenwood Press, 1988.

### Periodicals

*Journal of Latin American Studies,* October 1994, pp. 683–711.

—*Sketch by Phyllis Noah*

# Diego Velázquez
## 1465-1524
**Spanish conqueror**

Diego Velázquez travelled to the New World with Christopher Columbus and eventually made his way to the island of Cuba. There he conquered in the name of the Spanish Crown and ruled as governor for more than a decade. His reign marked the beginning of Cuba's colonial history and the end of its native condition.

Scholars know so little about the early years of Diego Velázquez de Cuellar that even his place of birth remains an issue of discussion. While most historians believe he was born in Cuellar, some suppose he might have been born in a surrounding village, because no record of his christening can be found in the records of Cuellar between 1450 and 1480. Cuellar and its environs lie in the region of Segovia, or Old Castile. Describing his early career in their book *A History of the Cuban Nation,* Juan Cosculluela and Jose Cabrera stated only that "Velázquez took active part in the wars which Spain held against Italy. He was an infantry man in the 'tercios' or detachments commanded by the famous captain, Gonzalo Fernandez de Cordova." Other historians had little to add about the first two decades of Velázquez's life.

### The New World Calls

Columbus made his second voyage to the West Indies in 1493, and Velázquez accompanied him. Still very young, Velázquez had high hopes for his prospects in these unknown territories. Columbus landed at Hispaniola—the island of the modern countries of Haiti and the Dominican Republic—which was to become the site of the first permanent Spanish settlement. There Velázquez succeeded as an administrator, a soldier, and colonizer. Velázquez, described as very handsome, though increasingly overweight as he aged, carried himself with resolve and confidence. Even Father **Bartolome de las Casas,** the famous advocate of native rights, thought Velázquez to be personable and smart. The approval of Columbus and his own industriousness secured Velázquez royal favors, land, and even *encoer* and *miendas,* or grants of natives to be used as slaves.

By 1501, Christopher Columbus had been removed as the executive authority of Spanish power in the New World, but Velázquez, under new governor Nicolas de Ovando, had come to high office in Hispaniola. Partly because of Velázquez's record as a courageous and fierce subduer of native resistance and partly because of the King of Spain's growing desire to know if Cuba held any gold, Diego Columbus, son of Christopher, appointed Velázquez governor of Cuba in 1510. The sailor Ocampo had only two years previously completed the first Spanish circumnavigation of Cuba, putting to an end the uncertainty in Spanish minds as to whether Cuba lay at the eastern tip of the Asian continent or stood alone as an island. Ocampo also wrote in his journals that the natives of Cuba had hosted his sailors peacefully and graciously. For the Spanish government, Velázquez, as lieutenant governor and veteran of West Indian life, seemed the perfect man to bring this pleasant, large, and possibly rich new land under the power of the Crown.

### Conquering Cuba

Nearly 20 years of service in the new colonies had made Velázquez a rich man, and his blonde hair, fair skin, and charismatic demeanor had given him personal prestige that he would use to outfit himself for the biggest task of his career. He recruited men in Salvatierra de la Sabana in western Hispaniola. Although most sources say that Velázquez took about 300 men with him, some others, including the *Historical Dictionary of Cuba,* put the number at around 100. Historians also debate his date of departure. Las Casas, who accompanied Velázquez, recorded a departure in late 1511, and historian Genaro Artiles put the date as far back as November 1509. However, most agree that between late 1510 and early 1511, Velázquez left Hispaniola's southwestern peninsula and landed on the eastern end of Cuba at Maisí.

Velázquez's party had the task of taking eastern Cuba. This they did without apprehension and with great force. In *Cuba: Between Reform and Revolution,* Louis Perez asserted that "Indians of the east were neither unfamiliar with Spanish motives nor unprepared for Spanish methods. Many . . . had fled . . . to Cuba for safety and sanctuary. . . . Massacre became the means of conquest, terror the method of control."

Velázquez's march preceded the landing of a smaller force commanded by Panfilo de Narvaez, coming from Jamaica and landing on the southern coast near the Gulf of Guacanayabo. When these two forces met, they divided again into three: one would march west through the inland regions, one would sail along the north coast, and the other would sail along the south, meeting again in the west at Carenas (now Havana) Bay. Velázquez meant not only to defeat the native resistance but also to crush their will to fight. At the village of Caonao, his forces carried out what Perez called "an unprovoked massacre" of as many as 2,000 bewildered natives, who began to see that resistance brought only greater terror. Hostilities gradually came to an end, but not before Father Bartolome de las Casas began to doubt the morality of

Spanish conquest. Perez quoted Las Casas as saying, "I do not remember with how much spilling of blood he [Narvaez, under orders from Velázquez] marked that road." Las Casas also claimed that not one Spaniard suffered injury during the entire campaign.

### Velázquez in Power

Between the years 1512 and 1514 Velázquez established seven Spanish settlements: Baracoa, Bayamo, Trinidad, Sancti Spiritus, Havana, Puerto Principe, and Santiago de Cuba. Most of the settlements lay by navigable waters. Some served areas containing gold. The modern capital, Havana, actually started as a settlement on the Gulf of Batabano, but in 1519 Velázquez decided to relocate it to its present location on the north coast. Velázquez himself occupied the new capital at Baracoa, where he built large haciendas and eventually a fortress. Baracoa was the first Cuban settlement to be designated as a city and receive a coat of arms. In early 1513, Velázquez received Cristobal de Cuellar, treasurer of the Indies, and his daughter Dona Maria. Velázquez succeeded in securing her hand in marriage, but Dona Maria died less than a week later.

Gold began to flow from the highland streams of the island, and Velázquez's many subordinates began to desire reward for their service in subduing Cuba. Velázquez began to distribute land formerly belonging to the natives, and then distributed the natives themselves. Although new restrictions applied to the granting of *encomiendas,* Velázquez could still distribute them to four specific groups: royal officials; explorers and settlers; those who held warrants of concession; and whoever else Velázquez deemed worthy. Velázquez had, therefore, almost total freedom in giving away human life. King Ferdinand did request that Velázquez teach Catholicism to the natives and treat them in a way "which should best preserve their lives," according to *History of the Cuban Nation.*

But the lives of the natives certainly did not improve under Velázquez's administration. Velázquez responded to new laws regarding the treatment of natives—applicable first to Puerto Rico and Hispaniola, but in 1515 also to Cuba—by creating a system whereby *encomenderos* held native slaves not permanently, but for a specified, finite period. On the surface the law appeared relatively sympathetic to the plight of the natives, but Cosculluela and Cabrera claimed that "the transitory nature of *encomienda* spurred the greed of the possessors of these grants, who were then eager to get the most profit from this temporary ownership of slaves."

Besides cruel treatment at the hands of the Spaniards, natives suffered Old World diseases and the ravages of thousands of wild pigs that had been brought from Spain. The beasts ran wild with no New

World predators, eating crops cultivated by natives and destroying land to the point of uselessness. Suicide and infanticide among natives increased, including instances in which entire villages chose to die together rather than face life in Velázquez's Cuba. Before conquest, the native population stood at around 112,000, but eight years later, it had dropped to 19,000. By the middle of the century, it would fall to less than 3,000. Velázquez's governance, though consistent with most in European colonies, brought calamity and misery to the native population.

## Velázquez's Decline

In 1515, Velázquez made Santiago de Cuba his new capital. Located on the southeast coast, it made it easy for Velázquez to communicate and trade with both Jamaica and Hispaniola. Indeed, the flow of gold (which peaked at about 100,000 pesos per year between 1517 and 1519) and Cuba's position at the edge of the known world brought Santiago into some prominence. In 1517 Francisco Hernandez de Cordoba discovered the Yucatan Peninsula, and in 1518 Juan de Grijalva discovered Mexico for the Crown. The discovery of these vast new lands made Caribbean holdings far less compelling in the eyes of Spaniards in the home country. The advantage of Santiago's position became a distinct disadvantage as the focus of empire shifted west. Velázquez failed to consider the possibility of further discoveries in locating his capital, and Cuba came to suffer for his mistake. Ambitious men, like Velázquez in his youth, struck out for the mainland discoveries with dreams of riches. Some of them returned, but most either died abroad or stayed to make their fortunes.

Velázquez had sponsored Cordoba's mission that had discovered the Yucatan peninsula, and it had come to be a great bane to Cuba. Yet even more bitter irony lay in store for Velázquez in the discovery of Mexico. In 1919, Velázquez equipped **Hernando Cortez** to explore further the lands to the west. Cordoba had died shortly after returning from his voyage of discovery to the Yucatan Peninsula, but he brought with him two natives of that land who told stories of a land of gold and beauty. Spanish Cubans could not resist the appeal of their stories, although some doubted them.

Cortez found Mexico, and once he made contact with Aztec society he began to ignore the limitations of his authority as Velázquez had described them. He even destroyed most of the ships which had carried his men to Mexico so that there could be no turning back. In 1518 the King had given Velázquez not only permission to explore lands west of Cuba, but also the rank of governor over any further lands that he might discover. Therefore, Velázquez could not tolerate Cortez's ambition to rule the biggest and richest Spanish colony of all. Although he pleaded through higher channels for the government to bring Cortez back into line, Velázquez could not argue against the gold that Cortez managed to ship back to Spain. As smallpox and measles ravaged Cuba in 1519, Velázquez recruited Narvaez, his compatriot in the original conquest of Cuba, to take 13 ships to Mexico and bring Cortez to justice. Cortez in Mexico heard of Narvaez's mission and left the Aztec metropolis of Tenochtitlan to meet him at Veracruz, which Cortez himself had established. Cortez persuaded Narvaez's men to join him and then arrested their leader before returning to the great Aztec city, which he would eventually destroy. Velázquez suffered financially from the expense of two voyages, but more significantly his personal prestige also suffered. He had garnered the trust of the Crown, but his inability to control even his own sailors colored his political future.

*History of the Cuban Nation* stated that "disgrace soured the last years of his life," and no political development proved that more certainly than the arrival of Alonso Zuazo to replace Velázquez as provisional governor in early 1521. Zuazo came at the behest of Diego Columbus, who felt that Velázquez's management of the island had become unacceptable. Zuazo would not only be the provisional governor, but also judge of Velázquez's competence. Zuazo, however, forgot that part of his role, preferring to exercise his new power over the island, even distributing *encomiendas.*

King Charles eventually sided with Velázquez and removed Zuazo from Cuba, but the island continued to decline. By the time of his death in Santiago de Cuba on the June 11 or 12, 1524, Velázquez had destroyed a native people, only to see his prosperity fade and an empire pass him by.

## SOURCES:

### Books

*Hispanic-American Almanac,* edited by Nicolás Kanellos, Detroit, Gale Research, 1993.

*A History of the Cuban Nation,* Volume 1: *Primitive Culture, Discovery, Conquest, and Colonization,* edited by Juan Cosculluela and Jose Cabrera, Editorial Lex, 1958.

Las Casas, Bartolome de, *Devastation of the Indies: A Brief Account,* Baltimore, Johns Hopkins University Press, 1992.

Perez, Louis, *Cuba: Between Reform and Revolution,* Oxford University Press, 1988.

Suchlicki, Jaime, *Historical Dictionary of Cuba,* Methuen, New Jersey, Scarecrow Press, 1988.

Wright, Irene A., *The Early History of Cuba, 1492–1586,* New York, Octagon Books, 1970.

—*Sketch by James McCarthy*

# Diego Rodriguez Velázquez
## 1599-1660
### Spanish painter

During his 40-year career as royal painter at the court of the Spanish King Philip IV, Velázquez earned the reputation of a masterful painter of elegant portraits; became a knight of the order of Santiago; and rose to the important position of chamberlain of the palace. Velázquez's genius lay in his ability to capture as if frozen in time the essence behind the pictorial reality of his subjects during the tumultuous period in history that saw the Spanish empire decline dramatically. Of his portraits, Jon Manchip White wrote in *Diego Velázquez:* "They are more remarkable for what they conceal than what they reveal. On the whole he managed to represent a disturbed and foundering dynasty in a light which made it seem exceptionally urbane, dignified, and secure."

The eldest son of Juan Rodriguez de Silva and Gerónima Velázquez was born in the summer of 1599 in the Spanish city of Seville, then a flourishing commercial and artistic center. At age 11, the boy was apprenticed to Francesco Pacheco, a renowned Sevillian artist who quickly recognized Velázquez's innate talent. Spain of this era boasted a number of famous writers, many of them satirists, and Velázquez was exposed to literature as well as painting at the weekly gatherings Pacheco held in his home. Velázquez matured rapidly in his ability to draw and paint, and in 1617, he passed his examination as a Master Painter.

At age 19, Velázquez married Juana de Miranda, Pacheco's daughter. Little is known about their life together, other than that they had two daughters, Francisca, born in 1619, and Ignacia, born in 1621. Sadly, Ignacia did not live to adulthood.

### Arrives at Spanish Court

In 1622, Velázquez traveled to Madrid in hope of making connections at the royal court of King Philip IV. Velázquez struck up a friendship with poet **Luis de Góngora y Argote,** whose portrait he later painted. Because Velázquez was not received at court, he returned to Seville. The following year he tried again, this time painting the portrait of Don Juan de Fonseca, an admiral at the court. The painting garnered great attention and appreciation and won for Velázquez a commission to paint a portrait of King Philip IV as a young man.

The portrait was so successful that Count-Duke of Olivares, prime minister of the court, requested that Velázquez stay at the palace, known as the Escorial. From this day, Velázquez worked for the monarchs, not only as a painter but as an administrator. In the course of his duties, he designed stage sets, solved architectural problems, and made travel arrangements.

Velázquez's entire body of work numbers 120 paintings, including 80 portraits, mostly of the royal family—a meager output compared with many artists of his epoch. Velázquez worked at a leisurely pace, producing only three or four paintings a year, and perhaps because so many of his paintings hung in the royal palace, he retouched them in a way that suggests he had a perfectionist nature. In general, most of Velázquez's paintings were commissioned by Philip IV and used to decorate the interiors of buildings, including Buen Retiro Palace and the Torre de Ia Prada—the royal hunting lodge at the foot of the Guadarrama Mountains.

Throughout his career Velázquez placed his subjects in a pose that he learned from Pacheco: the subject standing with one leg slightly to the front of the other. The right hand is extended, gripping an object, such as a gun or the back of a chair, and the left hand loosely holds another object, such as a hat or handkerchief. The convention of the times dictated that people dress in clothing of somber colors and fewer adornments than had previously been in vogue. Therefore, Velázquez used crimson tablecloths or draperies to set off a figure from the background. Smaller details, like a pair of gloves, a handkerchief, a bunch of ribbons, or a gold chain might become the focal point of a painting.

In Velázquez's portraits, the light always falls from above and the left side. He frequently used the colors of the Spanish landscape: black, burnt browns, bitter yellows, olive green, and silvery greys. Velázquez primed the surface of his canvas, but then instead of sketching in detail the painting he envisioned, he went rapidly to painting. His brush-work varied from painting to painting. On some canvases he employed splashes or blotches of color that when viewed from an optimal distance created the effect he sought. This quality of his work would later attract the attention and elicit the admiration in the twentieth century of the French Impressionists, who used similar techniques.

In addition to portraits, Velázquez's work falls into several categories: *badegones* (kitchen scenes that had been popularized by Flemish painters), *bamboch-*

das (scenes of drinking parties or musicians), and *retablos* (scenes of holy figures or events intended for church use). Even in such an early work as his *The Old Cook,* it is easy to discern the sense of mystery Velázquez evoked about humble figures and objects. They are rendered without striving for dramatic effect as was characteristic of the Italian master Michelangelo Caravaggio, whose works were very influential.

Velázquez purposely rejected the dynamic structure and often gruesome subject matter that Caravaggio and his admirers embraced in favor of a more subtle and elegant style. However, there is a certain revolutionary flavor about Velázquez's paintings: he painted lowly beggars and subtly mocked the mythological gods by portraying them as Spaniards.

In 1627 Velázquez painted his first historical painting: *Expulsion of the Moriscoes.* Unfortunately this work was destroyed by fire in the eighteenth century, but as the winner of a contest of the royal painters at Philip IV's court, it gave Velázquez the primary position among his painter rivals. Velázquez had a studio in the east wing of the palace, which he shared with the other court painters, and another at his own home on Calle Concepción Jerónima. Many years later he lived at Casa del Tesoro near the palace itself.

### Journey to Italy Inspires Painter

After the famous Flemish painter Peter Paul Rubens visited the Royal Palace for nine months in 1628, Velázquez requested a leave of absence to tour Italy. In 1629 he traveled to Venice, Rome, and Naples, in a journey that lasted 18 months. While staying in the Villa Medici, he made sketches of many works, including statues and frescoes by Michelangelo. He also painted two canvases, *Joseph's Bloody Coat Brought to Jacob* and *The Forge of Vulcan,* which demonstrate Velázquez's mature style. Hallmarks of this style include a harmonious mathematical structure in the placement of figures and objects in the scene. He used Spaniards as models for figures and showed off his great ability to render the human form.

When Velázquez returned to Madrid in 1631, he learned that King Philip IV had let no one paint a portrait of him during his favorite painter's absence. Velázquez then became involved with the creation of the king's new palace, Buen Retiro. For the Buen Retiro, Velázquez rendered equestrian portraits of Philip IV and Count-Duke Olivares. For the Torre de La Prada, he painted a portrait of the young Prince Balthasar Carlos. These paintings are remarkable for Velázquez's compassionate depiction of his subjects.

Because Velázquez believed firmly in the divine right of kings, he viewed his royal subjects with empathy, often smoothing away their blemishes. He added dogs as accessories to his portraits, imbuing even these animals with personalities that reflected upon their owners. The brooding outdoor backgrounds of these canvases were unusual, for Spanish artists did not paint landscapes until a much later epoch.

In 1634 Velázquez painted for the new palace, Buen Retiro, one of his most celebrated canvases—*The Surrender of Breda* (later known as *The Lances*)—which celebrated the successful capture of Breda by the Spanish during the Thirty Years War. Compared with paintings by contemporaries, this very large canvas is unusual in that Velázquez did not portray any of the gore of warfare. He focused instead on the graciousness with which the conqueror treated the vanquished foe.

The decade of the 1940s was a difficult period for the Spanish monarchy as Portugal wrestled its independence from Spain, and King Louis XIII of France captured Catalonia. War broke out in the Spanish-ruled Netherlands. In effect, the empire disintegrated. King Philip IV joined his army to fight for the survival of his empire. During a campaign in Aragón during 1643, Velázquez accompanied the king and painted him in uniform in a matter of three days. The portrait, made as propaganda to inspire the Spaniards in their war effort, was displayed publicly in Madrid and elsewhere.

### Second Italian Trip Energizes Painter

In November of 1648, Velázquez made a second voyage to Italy, ostensibly to purchase art works to redecorate portions of the Escorial, and he procured a number of paintings and statues. His first trip had been as a provincial painter exploring the wonders of the Italian Renaissance and Post-Renaissance; this time Velázquez wanted to demonstrate that Spain could produce a virtuoso painter as well. Thus Velázquez was very productive during his two-year stay, though few of his works survived.

Among the extant paintings are portraits of Juan de Pareja, Velázquez's servant, and Pope Innocent X. The portrait of the pope caused an uproar because Velázquez painted the pontiff wearing scarlet robes and used a bright red drape to set him off from the background. Moreover, Velázquez did not depict him as the handsome man he was not. During this time, Velázquez also painted several remarkable landscapes that feature the Villa Medici: *Midday* and *Evening.* The brush-work on these paintings, in reality oil sketches, created a spontaneous atmosphere, which would be used later by the French Impressionists.

The Spanish Inquisition forbade the painting of female nudes, but while Velázquez was in Italy he accepted a private commission to paint a female nude in what became *The Toilet of Venus,* the first female nude in Spanish history and the only one for some 150 years. The lounging female figure has her back to the viewer as she gazes at her face in a mirror.

Since arriving at court, Velázquez had risen through the administrative ranks to the favored position of supervisor of the works of the palace. Seven months after his return from Italy, the king promoted Velázquez to the position of chamberlain of the palace, a post that included taking responsibility for cleaning and heating arrangements in addition to furnishing and decorating the palace, and organizing tournaments, masquerades, balls, and theatrical performances.

Despite his many responsibilities, Velázquez painted portraits of the king and the king's new wife Queen Mariana (his first wife had died) and her daughter Princess Margarita and half-sister Princess Maria Teresa. While all of these portraits provided the opportunity for Velázquez to use a wider range of colors than was characteristic, the five portraits of the pretty Maria Teresa are particularly noteworthy for Velázquez's treatment of the child's elaborate clothing. Again, his impressionistic technique flowered. During the time, Velázquez also painted several portraits of King Philip IV. In contrast to the happy feminine portraits, these canvases displayed the signs of the hardships the monarch had suffered in recent years as royal portraits were often copied by underling painters and sent to far-away relatives, much like photographs are shared in the twentieth century.

During the 1650s Velázquez painted four works for the Hall of Mirrors in the Escorial. Of these, *The Spinners* and *Las Meninas* (*The Royal Family*) are the most famous. In the foreground of the first canvas, Velázquez placed women at work, spinning a tapestry while in the background the gods of Greek mythology weaved the course of human destiny. Based on Ovid's *Metamorphoses, The Spinners* depicts the fable of Arachne, who was changed into a spider when she tried to outdo the god Athene. Accroding to some historians, this theme was, perhaps, Velázquez's reflection on the crumbling Spanish empire. At any rate, the painting demonstrates that the painter's technique was at its height in composition, brushwork, and mystery.

### Paints Celebrated Masterpiece

In 1656 Velázquez painted *Las Meninas*. Set in the artist's studio, the scene focuses on the Princess Margarita, who is surrounded by her maids-in-waiting, the palace dwarves, and a dog. Brush in hand, Velázquez stands before his easel. Because the easel faces the painter, the viewer cannot see what he is actually painting, which has led to much speculation by scholars. As in many of Velázquez's paintings, mysteries abound. The supreme quality of

Velázquez's painterly skill was not obscured, however. He was in complete command of his medium.

In November of 1659, after much lobbying by King Philip IV and Velázquez's colleagues, Velázquez was made a knight of the order of Santiago, a honor that accorded him status as a member of the nobility. It was a dream realized for Velázquez. Unfortunately he did not live long to enjoy the honor. In April 1660, an ailing Velázquez and several servants prepared the groundwork for the trip to France of the king's daughter Maria Teresa, who was to marry the France's young King Louis XIV. After his return from the elaborate wedding, Velázquez took to bed with a fever. He died on August 6, 1660.

### SOURCES:

#### Books

Brown, Jonathan, *Velszauez: Painter and Courtier,* New Haven, CT, Yale University Press, 1986.

Harris, Enriqueta, *Velázquez,* Oxford, Phaidon, 1982.

Kahr, Madlyn Millner, *Velázquez: The Art of Painting* New York, Harper & Row, 1976.

Lopez-Rey, Jose, *Velázquez's Work and World,* Greenwich, New York Graphic Society, 1968.

Muller, Joseph-Émile, *Velázquez,* London, Thames and Hudson, 1976.

Sutton, Denys, *Diego Velázquez,* New York, Barnes and Noble, 1967

White, Jon Manchip, *Diego Velazauez: Painter and Courtier,* New York, Rand McNally, 1969.

*—Sketch by J. M. Lesinski*

# Nydia Margarita Velázquez
## 1953-
**Puerto Rican American politician**

Nydia Margarita Velázquez, the daughter of a poor sugar-cane cutter, is the first Puerto Rican woman to be elected to the U.S. House of Representatives. Velázquez, a Democrat, won her seat in Congress in November 1992, after a grueling and controversial Democratic primary that pitted her against longtime incumbent Stephen J. Solarz and a crowded field of Hispanic challengers. Velázquez now represents the 12th Congressional District in New

*Nydia Margarita Velázquez*

York City, a heavily Democratic and Hispanic district that was created in 1992 to encourage the election of a Hispanic representative. The district of just over 500,000 people encompasses poor and working-class neighborhoods in Queens, Manhattan, and Brooklyn.

As a Puerto Rican woman raised in a hardworking rural household with few modern conveniences, Velázquez brings a unique perspective to national politics. She was born March 23, 1953, in Yabucoa, Puerto Rico. Once famous for its sugar-cane industry, Yabucoa is located in a lush valley on the island's southeast coast. Velázquez and her twin sister were among nine children raised by Benito and Carmen Luisa (Serrano) Velázquez, who lived at the edge of town in a small wooden house surrounded by sugar-cane fields and the Rio Limon River.

To support the family, Carmen sold *pasteles,* a traditional Puerto Rican food, to cane cutters in the fields. Benito, who had a third-grade education, cut sugar cane and later became a butcher and the owner of a legal cockfighting business. A local political leader, Benito founded a political party in his town and, significantly, passed on to his daughter Nydia a strong social conscience, according to the *New York Times.* During Nydia's childhood, dinner conversations often revolved around workers' rights and other political issues. "I always wanted to be like my father," she said in an interview with the *New York Times.*

Always eager to learn, Velázquez convinced her family to allow her to start school at the age of five.

She proved to be a bright student, skipping several grades to graduate early and become the first in her family to receive a high school diploma. At 16, Velázquez was already a freshman at the University of Puerto Rico in Rio Piedras. She graduated magna cum laude in 1974 with a bachelor's degree in political science. After teaching briefly in Puerto Rico, she won a scholarship to continue her studies in the United States. She left the island, with her family's reluctant support, to enter New York University. Velázquez earned a master's degree in political science in 1976, then returned to the University of Puerto Rico in Humacao to teach political science. Leaving Puerto Rico again in 1981, she became an adjunct professor of Puerto Rican studies at Hunter College at the City University of New York, where she taught for two years.

In a September 21, 1992, interview with *Newsday,* Velázquez revealed that she left Puerto Rico for more reasons than simply to advance her education and career. "I was harassed when I was a professor at the University of Puerto Rico, when the [conservative] New Progressive Party took power in Puerto Rico," she said. Velázquez said that she was accused of being a Communist and leftist. She eventually made her home in New York, but her career in politics and public service has subsequently included work in both the United States and Puerto Rico.

She received her first taste of New York City politics in the early 1980s. In 1983 she served as special assistant to former U.S. Representative Edolphus Towns, a Democrat from Brooklyn. As a special assistant, Velázquez was in charge of immigration issues, and part of her job included testifying before Congress on immigration legislation. In 1984, Velázquez was appointed to the New York City Council, filling the vacancy left when former councilman, Luis Olmedo, was convicted on charges of federal conspiracy and attempted extortion. At the age of 31, Velázquez became the first Latina to serve on the council.

After losing her council seat in the next election in 1986, Velázquez returned to Puerto Rico to serve as the national director of the Migration Division Office of the Department of Labor and Human Resources of Puerto Rico until 1989. In that year the governor of Puerto Rico appointed Velázquez secretary of the Department of Puerto Rican Community Affairs in the United States, a cabinet-level position that functions as a major link between Puerto Rico and the U.S. government. Responsible for the New York City headquarters and four regional offices, Velázquez advised the Puerto Rican government on Puerto Rico's public policy and its commitment to the Puerto Rican community in the United States. She exercised her political influence in 1989 when Hurricane Hugo devastated Puerto Rico. Velázquez personally called General Colin Powell, head of the joint chiefs of staff, and shortly after, the commonwealth received a promise of federal assistance. During her tenure as secretary, Velázquez also led successful voter registration drives that led to the registration of more than 200,000 voters in Puerto Rican communities in the Northeast and Midwest; and in 1991 she initiated *Unidos contra el sida* (United Against AIDS ), a project to fight the spread of AIDS among Puerto Ricans.

Velázquez's close ties with the Puerto Rican government came under scrutiny during her 1992 bid for Congress. Her critics charged she was more concerned with Puerto Rican politics than with the problems of her constituents—an accusation she repeatedly denied. During the campaign, it was disclosed that Velázquez, while working for the Puerto Rican Government, had personally supported the pro-commonwealth position in the fierce ongoing debate over the island's colonial status. During the race, she took a neutral stance on whether Puerto Rico should become a state or nation or continue as a commonwealth. "My responsibility as a member of Congress is to support whatever pledge Puerto Ricans make to resolve the situation," she told *Newsday.* Acknowledging that she is concerned about Puerto Rico, she related to a *Newsday* reporter during the campaign: "I say that, yes, we have been oppressed and disenfranchised for too long."

Velázquez's bid for Congress came at a time of national efforts to bring Hispanics and other minorities to the polls. The 12th Congressional District was one of nine new districts created in 1992 to increase minority voting power under the Voting Rights Act. The district includes a patchwork of Hispanic neighborhoods in three boroughs, including Corona, Elmhurst, and Jackson Heights in Queens, the Lower East Side in Manhattan, and Williamsburg, Bushwick, Sunset Park, and East New York in Brooklyn. According to the *New York Times,* the average income in the district is $22,500, more than $10,000 less than the state average. Some 22 percent of the people are on public assistance, and 27 percent are non-citizens. While a majority of the district's population is Hispanic—including Puerto Ricans, Dominicans, Colombians, and emigrants from other Spanish-speaking countries—the region also includes whites, blacks, and Asian Americans.

Former Representative Solarz's Brooklyn district, which was heavily Jewish, was dissolved by the redistricting process. As a non-Hispanic, Solarz was criticized for seeking to represent a district designed for minority leadership. But he insisted that he was the best person for the job. "I categorically reject that only a black can represent a black district, or a Hispanic an Hispanic district," he told the *New York Times.* Although Solarz was a respected foreign policy expert in Congress, he was one of many legislators caught in the House bank scandal in the early 1990s,

after it was revealed that he had written 743 overdrafts, according to the *New York Times.*

The 1992 Democratic primary in the 12th district was a bitter battle, pitting five Hispanic candidates against the popular Solarz, a nine-term Congressman. Velázquez ran an old-fashioned, grassroots campaign, pounding the pavement, making phone calls, and garnering support from family and friends. She could not afford much campaign literature or television advertisements. Although she raised just a fraction of Solarz's campaign fund of over $2 million, she had the endorsements of New York City Mayor David Dinkins, the Hispanic union leader Dennis Rivera, president of Local 1199 of the Drug, Hospital and Health Care Workers Union, and the Reverend Jesse Jackson. Dinkins's support was in part a political thank-you for Velázquez's 1989 voter registration efforts, which helped Mayor Dinkins win the Hispanic vote in the mayoral election.

Still, with four Hispanic opponents, one of her biggest challenges was to unite the district's diverse and politically fractured Hispanic community. Not only did Velázquez have to prove that she could represent all Hispanics in her district—not just the Puerto Ricans—she also had to fight the prejudice that often separates Puerto Ricans raised on the island from those with roots on the mainland. Even Velázquez's supporters describe her as controversial. "I think that Nydia just provokes very strong opinions of love and hate from people because she's so passionate herself," said Luis A. Miranda, Jr., president of the Hispanic Federation of New York City, in an interview with the *New York Times.*

Velázquez won the September 15 primary. Soon after, she returned to Puerto Rico and her hometown, where she was given a heroine's welcome. According to an account in the *New York Times,* she rode into Yabucoa in a pickup truck, accompanied by Mayor Angel Luis Ramos and a state senator. A loudspeaker proclaimed: "She's back! Our Nydia Velázquez, who will be the first Puerto Rican woman in Congress, is back in Sugartown!" Velázquez told the crowd that she dedicated her victory to her mother and the women of Puerto Rico. In an interview with *Newsday,* Ramos commented, "She represents a good example for the children. She came from a poor family and went to public school."

The low point of the 1992 campaign came in early October, when an anonymous source sent information to news organizations detailing Velázquez's attempted suicide and hospitalization the previous year. The incident was given much attention by the *New York Post,* which broke the story, and spread to the national media. Velázquez never denied the charges. Instead, she held a press conference where, surrounded by friends and family, she acknowledged that she had suffered serious depression as the result of personal problems, including her mother's illness and a brother's drug addiction. "In 1991, in a troublesome period of my life, I attempted to commit suicide," said Velázquez, as reported by the *New York Times*. "It was a sad and painful experience for me, and one I thought was now in the past." She noted that she was "appalled" and "outraged" that privileged medical information in the form of confidential hospital records had been released to the public, in violation of state law.

Velázquez's supporters must have recognized their candidate as a survivor who had overcome personal adversity and proven her potential to lead their communities. Velázquez, at the age of 39, defeated both Republican and independent challengers in the November election, taking more than three-quarters of the vote. At her election-night party in Williamsburg, Brooklyn, surrounded by "Fair Housing" signs, Velázquez said, in Spanish, that her victory was important for herself, her parents, and her people in the 12th District. "For you, I'm going to fight to gain better jobs, better lives, and better opportunities," she said.

As a non-traditional politician, Velázquez does not fit the standard conservative or liberal labels; instead, she often calls herself progressive. She hopes to concentrate her congressional career on the problems confronting her urban district, including jobs, the economy, child care, and housing. She supports federal construction projects to create jobs and government loans to help small businesses. Shortly before her election-day victory, Velázquez told the *New York Post* that she wanted to improve the educational system and stem the tide of crime and drugs. On the international front, she opposes Jewish settlements on the West Bank and favors increased economic aid to Latin America.

Velázquez also plans to prove that Hispanic women can serve proudly in the political arena. "We are the ones who go out and collect signatures, but when it came to the final process, we were not good enough to run for office," said Velázquez in *USA Today*. She is one of 47 female representatives in the 103rd Congress. "New blood is good," she told the *New York Times* on election day. Along with providing a new voice for Hispanics in Congress, she pledged to work with other minority and progressive members of Congress to improve the quality of life for all people in the nation's inner cities.

## SOURCES:

### Periodicals

*Newsday*, September 21, 1992, p. 37; September 26, 1992, p. 10; September 27, 1992, p. 18; October 10, 1992, p. 13.

*New York Post*, November 4, 1992, p. 4.
*New York Times*, July 9, 1992, p. B3; September 7, 1992, pp. 21–22; September 27, 1992, p. 33; October 10, 1992, p. 25; October 29, 1992, p. B7; November 2, 1992, p. B1, B4; November 4, 1992, p. B13.
*Noticias del Mundo*, November 4, 1992, pp. 1A, 4A *USA Today*, October 27, 1992, p. 2A.
*Washington Post*, October 9, 1992, p. A12.

—*Sketch by Ann Malaspina*

# Bob Vila
## 1946-
### Hispanic American home construction contractor and TV personality

Known as the "guru" of home remodeling, Bob Vila has hosted numerous television shows and has written many books on restoring, renovating, and rehabilitating homes. He was born Robert Joseph Vila in Miami, Florida, June 20, 1946. His father was Robert Vila, a U.S. Army intelligence officer, and his mother was Hope Robles Vila. He grew up in Miami and went to college at the Miami Dade Junior College where he received his A.A. degree in 1966. He received his B.A in communications science at the University of Florida in Gainesville in 1969. After college he entered the Peace Corps as a volunteer from 1969 to 1970 in Panama. Vila then went to West Germany where he worked as a translator of scientific papers and also as a stagehand in Stuttgart.

### Hosted Popular Television Series

When Vila moved to Boston after the Peace Corps job, in 1971, he was an independent home improvement contractor and in 1973, he became a project director for Barrett Associates. There were three investors involved in the project and Diane Barrett was one of them. She was a professor at the Harvard School of Public Health. He married Barrett October 3, 1975 and they had two children, Christopher Anthony Vila-Barrett and Monica Patricia Vila-Barrett. He had a real estate development firm, R. J. Vila, Inc., from 1975 to 1985, during which time the Vilas bought an old house in Boston and "rehabbed" it. They were special guests on a television program at WGBH-TV in Boston in January 1977 to discuss their "rehabbed" home. When the producer saw Vila, he hired him to host the show, which was a predecessor to the Public Broadcasting System (PBS) series that made Vila famous. Later in 1977, the Vilas bought another old house in the city to rehab and built a new house on Cape Cod. Vila remained on "This Old House" series from 1979 to 1989 when his contract was not renewed.

Vila became more and more popular on television and became known as the TV "guru" of home remodeling. He used a construction crew of specialists for plumbing, electric, carpentry and many other specialized skills in the home remodeling field. They would demonstrate how to modernize an old house, maintaining its character, while Vila discussed the renovation process to his vast audience. His approach was to preserve the home and yet make the home comfortable to live in. His half-hour show received an Emmy Award for the New England region in 1979 and another Emmy Award for the national region in 1985. In the meantime, Vila began authoring and co-authoring numerous books on remodeling old homes. He wrote the first book with Jane Davison, *This Old House: Restoring, Rehabilitating, and Renovating,* published in 1980. Since then he has written many books including guide books to old homes in New England, historic buildings, guide books to tools, building materials, and various subjects in the home remodeling field.

In 1984, Vila hosted a PBS series "The All New This Old House" featuring the building of a new house in Boston. The house was built by a Boston utility and it was a solar powered 4,500-square-foot showplace. By this time, Vila's show was viewed by about five million people across the country. The producer and director of the show was Russell Morash, who also produced and directed "Dinner at Julia's" and "The Victory Garden." Vila worked without any script, using only an outline of each show. In one show, Vila took the television viewer into Trump Towers, where the apartments sell for up to $5 million.

In March of 1989, Vila was fired as the host of "This Old House" for making outside endorsements. He began making plans for a new series and Sears hired him in 1990 for a national television campaign to promote the Craftsman Home & Yard Centers. He began his new syndicated television series on home improvement called "Home Again With Bob Vila" in September 1990. Vila also had his own production company, BVTV. A three-way agreement between Sears, BVTV and Ogilvy and Mather, sponsored Vila's new series. Vila canceled all his other commercial endorsements when he made the deal with Sears. Vila's show traveled to different regions of the country and in his 1991 to 1992 series, the show revolved around the remodeling of a raised ranch in Plymouth, Massachusetts, and an old home in Naples, Florida. Vila shared his knowledge of home remodeling and repair to millions of viewers throughout the years including tips on interior design, painting, tools

and numerous other subjects for the do-it-yourself remodeler. Norm Abram, a master carpenter, appeared with Vila in many of his shows. The fast-paced half-hour show was one of the most popular home-improvement shows on television.

## SELECTED PUBLISHED WORKS:

### Books

With Jane Davison, *This Old House: Restoring, Rehabilitating, and Renovating an Older House,* Boston, Little, Brown, 1980.
With Anne Henry, *Bob Vila's This Old House,* New York, Dutton, 1981.
*This Old House Guide to Building and Remodeling Materials,* New York, Warner Books, 1986.
With Carl Oglesby, *Bob Vila's Guide to Buying Your Dream House,* Boston, Little, Brown, 1990.
*Bob Vila's Guide to Historic Homes of New England,* New York, Lintel Press, Quill, 1993.
*Bob Vila's Guide to Historic Homes of the Mid-Atlantic,* New York, Lintel Press, Quill, 1993.
*Bob Vila's Guide to Historic Homes of the South,* New York, Lintel Press, Quill, 1993.
*Bob Vila's Tool Box,* New York, W. Morrow, 1993.

### Videos

"Creating a New Kitchen, Part 1: Plumbing and Electricity", WGBH Educational Foundation, produced and directed by Russell Morash, Beverly Hills, Calif., PBS Home Video, distributed by Pacific Arts Video, c. 1989.
"Creating a New Kitchen, Part 2: Cabinets, Appliances, Countertops and Flooring", WGBH Educational Foundation, produced and directed by Russell Morash, Beverly Hills, California, PBS Home Video, distributed by Pacific Arts Video, 1990.

## SOURCES:

### Books

*Contemporary Authors,* Volume 106, Detroit, Gale Research, 1982.

### Periodicals

*Advertising Age,* February 5, 1990.
*TV Guide,* March 17, 1984, pp. 44–45.

—*Sketch by Phyllis Noah*

# Pancho Villa
## 1878-1923
### Mexican revolutionary

Francisco "Pancho" Villa was a charismatic, controversial leader during the Mexican Revolution of 1910–1920. Born into the peon class and shaped by his early life experiences, he spent his life fighting the wealthy Mexican landowners and attempting to liberate the impoverished peasants. As a champion of the poor, he became a symbol of the revolution. He was a ruthless and brutal outlaw, a brilliant leader, and a generous hero dedicated to his cause. He was feared and hated by some, admired and respected by others. His legend has endured because of his colorful personal and public life and the impact he made on Mexican history.

Pancho Villa was born Doroteo Arango on June 5, 1878, in the village of San Juan del Rio, in the state of Durango, Mexico. He was the first of five children; his siblings were Hipolito, Antonio, Mariana, and Martinita. His parents, Augustin Arango and Maria Micaela Arambula, were farm laborers, working and living on an estate known as Hacienda del Rio Grande. During that period of Mexican history, the ruling upper class controlled much of the land and wealth of Mexico, while the peon class was kept in subservience, unable to rise above the societal position into which they were born. **Porfirio Diaz** was the country's president, ruling the Mexican people over a period of 34 years, from 1877 until the time of his defeat in 1911.

Doroteo became the head of the family as a young man, after the death of his father. He worked long hours to support his mother and four siblings. When the opportunity arose to make more money, he accepted a job without obtaining permission from his *patron* at the Hacienda del Rio Grande. When his moonlighting was uncovered, he was tied behind a horse and forced to run barefoot all the way back to the town square in San Juan del Rio, where he was publicly flogged for his crime. He made a second attempt to leave the estate at the age of 16 but was soon captured, tried, and convicted of cattle theft. He was released after serving several months in prison and moved to Chihuahua City, where he worked to continue to support his family. There he met, courted, and became engaged to Maria Luz Corral. They married in 1909.

### Became Pancho Villa the Bandit

In 1894, Doroteo committed yet another crime against the aristocracy. He murdered the son of the hacienda owner to avenge the rape of his youngest sister. To avoid execution—which was the punishment for murdering a member of the upper class—he fled to the rugged Sierra Madre, where he was successful at avoiding capture by the police. He knew the terrain well and survived by hunting and stealing. There he met and joined a band of outlaws lead by Ignacio Parra. Doroteo renamed himself Francisco "Pancho" Villa after a legendary early nineteenth-century outlaw, who was said to have robbed from the rich to give to the poor. During his 16 years with the bandit gang, Pancho Villa was involved in many bank robberies, train robberies, and hacienda raids. When he assumed the role of gang leader after Parra's death, he earned the reputation of being a Mexican Robin Hood, like his namesake. His exploits were widely known along the border from Sonora and Durango to Chihuahua.

### From Bandit to Revolutionary

While Pancho Villa used his anger to refine his skills as an outlaw leader, others in Mexico were busy organizing against President Diaz. Led by Francisco Indalecio Madero, anti-Diaz forces called for an honest and democratic election in 1910. They organized the antireelectionist party, with Madero as presidential candidate and Abran Gonzalez as his running mate. In 1910, Gonzalez met with Pancho Villa in Chihuahua City to outline the goals of the party and to recruit Villa to join in their cause. Villa was impressed with Gonzalez and with Madero's courage and idealism. He enthusiastically joined the revolutionary army with the rank of captain.

When Diaz realized that the antireelectionist campaign was gaining momentum and was indeed a threat to his presidency, he imprisoned Madero and thereby secured the election of 1910. Upon his release from prison after the election, Madero escaped to San Antonio, Texas. There, refusing to remain silent, he began to reorganize his revolutionary campaign. He declared himself the legitimate president of Mexico, and on November 20, 1910, called for the armed uprising that was the beginning of the Mexican Revolution.

By the time Villa received word that the insurrection was beginning, he had already enlisted 500 men to fight for the revolution. He led them in an attack that resulted in the capture of the town of San Andres, Chihuahua. In March of 1911, Madero's rebel army suffered a defeat at Casa Grandes, Chihuahua, which led Diaz and his men to conclude that the revolution had been effectively thwarted. Madero quickly regrouped with his remaining forces better organized and equipped for the next battle. By now, Villa was in charge of 800 men and had established himself as a daring and ingenious leader. Madero and Villa, together with other military leaders, planned their objective—the takeover of Ciudad Juarez.

On May 10, 1911, after a critical battle, the revolutionaries won a decisive victory over federal troops with the capture of this vital border city. Villa played an essential role in the planning and implementation of the attack on Ciudad Juarez and was promoted to the rank of colonel for his brilliant performance. Villa's military victory in the north, along with successful uprisings in the south led by **Emiliano Zapata,** caused the collapse of the Diaz regime. Diaz resigned on May 21, 1911, and went into exile. Madero marched into Mexico City, along with Villa and the other officers, to assume control of the government. In October of 1911, Madero was elected president of Mexico. Villa returned to his home and family in Chihuahua City, where he planned to settle down as a legitimate citizen.

Once back in Chihuahua, Villa opened a butcher shop to earn an honest living for his wife and two children. He and his family lived in a large house in town and for a short while enjoyed a peaceful life together. But this quiet interlude was not long-lived. By February of 1912, the new government was at risk, as Madero's former ally Pascual Orozco plotted to overthrow Madero. Once again Villa was recruited by Madero to defend his cause and his country. Quickly he responded, gathering his former followers, 500 in all, to help in the campaign against Orozco's troops. Madero appointed Victoriana Huerta to command the government troops, and Huerta took control of all the forces in Northern Mexico, including Villa's. Villa, proud and independent, did not like taking orders from anyone, but he reluctantly did so to preserve Madero's government. On May 23, Villa and Huerta defeated Orozco's army at the battle of Tellano.

Once the attempted coup was subdued, the relationship between Villa and Huerta deteriorated. Villa refused to follow Huerta's orders and accused him of disloyalty to Madero. Huerta ordered Villa arrested and condemned to death for insubordination. On October 26, 1912, Villa stood in front of the firing squad awaiting execution. Moments before his death he was saved by Raul Madero, the president's brother. Villa was transported to a Mexico City penitentiary, and his sentence was reduced to a two-year term of imprisonment.

While in prison, Villa became friends with Carlos Jauregi, a young clerk who helped the outlaw to improve his reading and writing. Villa used his new skills to study the strategies of Napoleon Bonaparte with the aim of polishing his military efficiency. He had perfected his riding and shooting skills long ago, as a young man living the life of a bandit. He knew how to inspire respect, fear, and loyalty in his men. He was daring, shrewd, and cunning by nature. But now he was learning to use all of his skills and natural instincts in a more organized and systematic way. In December of 1912, bored with life in the penitentiary,

he enlisted the help of his tutor to escape. Together they fled to El Paso, Texas.

In February of 1913, Huerta instigated a counter-revolutionary movement. Madero and his vice president were both assassinated on February 22. Several days later Abran Gonzalez, then governor of Chihuahua, was also murdered—shot and thrown under a train. Villa grieved the loss of his compatriots and once again took up his guns—to avenge their deaths as well as save of his country from the despotic government of Huerta.

Huerta's regime was challenged by many formidable opponents. Among them were Pancho Villa, Emiliano Zapata, and Venustiano Carranza. Villa used any means possible to realize his goal of defeating Huerta. He borrowed, bought, or stole the horses and supplies he needed and set out for Chihuahua City with only eight men. His army of eight grew to 500 followers within one month and to greater than 1,000 within six months. They were known as Villa's Division del Norte. Villa's army proved to be superior to any other in Mexico; they took Northern Mexico by storm, soon controlling many of the villages and important cities, such as San Andres, Torreon, Chihuahua City, Ciudad Juarez, and Tierra Blanca. The Division del Norte seized considerable amounts of military supplies, including guns, ammunition, and even whole trains. Villa, once a bandit and guerrilla fighter, had now become a rebel general, with the ability to effectively command his ever-growing army, which by October numbered 10,000 troops.

## At the Height of Power

Villa's continued success in battle increased his fame and prestige, not only in Mexico, but in the United States and Europe as well. Now he became a public figure and the center of many news stories. He was scrutinized for his controversial behavior, which could be ruthless and brutal as well as benevolent. He customarily executed all captured enemy officers and shot anyone who dared to challenge his authority. His prejudice against the Spanish, whom he believed were all supporters of Huerta, caused him to unremittingly mistreat them. Yet he was capable of noble deeds also. During the year that he occupied Juarez, he paved the streets, improved the water systems, and built new schools and hospitals.

Along with his newfound world renown, Villa began to develop his political savvy as well. On April 22, 1914, President Woodrow Wilson sent U.S. troops to occupy the port of Veracruz, Mexico, to pressure the Huerta regime. Their invasion and occupation of Veracruz was regarded with rancor throughout Mexico and nearly led to a war between the United States and Mexico. Huerta asked for the support of his enemies Carranza, Zapata, and Villa to drive the invading troops out of Mexico. Villa refused to support Huerta in anything, and was the only Mexican leader who refused to condemn Wilson's actions. His influence was such that the other leaders knew they could not succeed without his support.

On July 15, 1914, Huerta was finally forced to resign after Pancho Villa and his army captured Zacatecas, Huerta's last stronghold. Carranza became Mexico's provisional president. For a short while there seemed to be hope for peace in the country as Villa, Zapata, Carranza, and other Mexican officials met in a national convention to establish the new government. Villa and Carranza had been allies only out of necessity, to defeat Huerta. Now they were contending for political power. Neither Villa or Zapata would back Carranza as president and so the negotiations deteriorated again into civil war.

As Villa and his 40,000-man army began marching south, Carranza fled the capitol to retreat in Veracruz. On December 6, 1914, Villa with his troops from the north and Zapata with his troops from the south paraded 30,000 strong through the streets of Mexico City. They occupied the capitol for two months, until Villa left in February to return to Chihuahua. His aim was to match his military might with political power. He established a provisional government with himself as president and began his campaign against Carranza's military commander, General Alvaro Obregon, and the pro-Carranza forces.

### Fall from Power

On April 6, 1915, Villa disregarded the counsel of his advisors and attacked Obregon in Celaya. He suffered terrible defeats in two separate battles, losing half of his army. Still unwilling to surrender, he took the remainder of his army—some 10,000 men—to Aguacalientes. Again he was overcome by Obregon, whose victories allowed Carranza to resume control of the government.

The United States recognized Carranza as the official president of Mexico, offering him military backing and cutting off aid to Villa. In the eyes of the United States, Villa was reduced from a revolutionary general to an outlaw gang leader. Feeling angry and betrayed, Villa staged yet another attack against Obregon at Agua Prieta. With the United States aiding Carranza's army, he was catastrophically defeated once again at Agua Prieta and finally at Hermoso. Having suffered great losses, and with many of his men deserting, he no longer posed a threat to Carranza's government. Villa and his remaining followers retreated again to the Sierra Madre.

During this period of hiding, Villa was extremely resentful towards the United States, and historians theorize this may have motivated him to seek revenge. In the predawn hours of March 9, 1916, Villa's forces attacked Columbus, New Mexico. Their raid left the town in flames and eight Americans dead. The U.S. army retaliated, forcing Villa's men to retreat after one hour of fighting. President Wilson ordered General John Joseph Pershing to lead a 3,000 man Punitive Expedition into Mexico to find and destroy Villa and his band. They entered Mexico on March 15, without authorization from the Mexican government. They spent nearly a year in pursuit of Villa, but were unable to capture him. By February of 1917, with the United States facing involvement in World War I, President Wilson was forced to withdraw his troops from Mexico.

With the pressure of U.S. troops removed, Villa was free to regroup his forces and resume his attacks on Carranza's regiments. Between 1917–1918 he launched a number of successful raids. His army grew by the spring of 1919 to number 1,500 men, and Villa planned to take back Ciudad Juarez. He attacked just after midnight on June 15, 1919. At first he seemed to be victorious, but as the fighting escalated, it spilled over the border into the United States. Angry U.S. officials sent infantry and cavalry units to annihilate Villa's army. Villa himself escaped to the mountains of Chihuahua.

On May 21, 1920, Carranza's murder ended his regime. Obregon was elected as Carranza's successor. Obregon's political philosophy was one of social reform; the decade of civil war in Mexico at last ended. Villa finally agreed to retire from military life. Obregon offered him a general's pension and a 25,000-acre ranch—Rancho del Canutillo.

For three years, Pancho Villa lived the life of a rancher, enjoying his retirement with his wife and family. There were, however, those to whom Villa would always be a threat. His enemies were many and his life was never completely secure. On July 20, 1923, Pancho Villa and four of his bodyguards were ambushed and gunned down near Parral, Mexico. He was struck by seven bullets and died instantly. He was buried in the Parral cemetery.

To some people the name Pancho Villa evoked the image of a crude and ruthless villain, but to many he remained a glorious legend and a symbol of freedom. He lived on in Mexican folklore, songs, and history, and in the hearts of the Mexican people, to whom he was a liberator and a hero.

### SOURCES:

Guzman, Martin Luis, *Memoirs of Panco Villa,* University of Texas Press, 1965.

Knight, Alan, *The Mexican Revolution,* 2 Vols., Cambridge University Press, 1986.

Machado, Manuel A., Jr., *Centaur of the North: Francisco Villa, the Mexican Revolution and Northern Mexico,* Eakin Press, 1988.

Torres, Elias L., *Twenty Episodes in the Life of Panch Villa,* Encino Press, 1973.

*—Sketch by Denise Marecki*

# Carlos Raúl Villanueva
## 1900-1975
### Venezuelan architect

Carlos Raúl Villanueva made more valuable contributions to architecture and urban community design than any other architect in Latin America in the twentieth century. Villanueva practiced architecture in Venezuela for 40 years, creating concepts, designs, and plans that have served all those who have designed and planned in communities since his death.

Although Venezuelan—and though he lived his life in Venezuela—Villanueva was born in Croydon, Surrey, England on May 30, 1900. His mother was French; his father worked for the Venezuelan diplomatic service and wrote books on South American history. His diverse upbringing in Europe and Venezuela and his special ties to France would be reflected later in his work. Villanueva studied at the Lycée Condorcet in Paris and later received an architectural degree from the Ecole Nationale des Beaux-Arts in Paris.

### Designs First Contemporary Bullring

Villanueva returned to Caracas, Venezuela in 1928 and opened his own office. In 1933 he married Margot Arismendi, with whom he had four children: Francisco Raúl, Jose Carlos, Pavlona, and Carlos Raúl. From 1929–1939 he served as architect to the Ministry of Public Works. During these years, which are known as his eclectic period, Villanueva incorporated the beauty of the traditional Venezuelan/Spanish architecture into his own designs. He found ways to transform Spanish Andalusian designs to more modern forms. One example of these designs was the Bullring at Maracay. The first bullring of contemporary design, it incorporated new materials and historical continuity. In this design, Villanueva introduced the expressed skeleton—a French architect's concept of separating load-bearing piers with thin, recessed panels—for the first time to South American architecture. For his work in the first decade of his career, Villanueva won many awards and honors, including the first prize for the Venezuelan Pavilion at the International Exposition in Paris in 1937 as well as knighthood in the French Legion of Honor.

Villanueva continued to experiment, introducing new design concepts, materials, and ways to use materials to South America, especially Venezuela. In 1939 his design for the Escuela Gran Colombia in Caracas, an elementary school, broke new ground. It was not only as the first of Villanueva's buildings without historical influences, but also utilized reinforced concrete, which was still considered experimental by Venezuelan contractors and builders. This was the first of Villanueva's strictly modern buildings, influenced by Cubism yet still symmetrical in design; it was also the premiere public building project for Latin America, opening the door for other architects to follow.

### Works to Improve Public Housing

Villanueva turned his attention to solving the problems of the housing shortage and the abysmal living conditions in Venezuela. Before embarking on this project, he studied at the Institute d'Urbanism of the University of Paris. He returned to Venezuela in 1940 and took a position with the Worker's Bank as its chief architect and adviser. The Worker's Bank of Venezuela was a group created to solve the shelter problem and to improve living conditions for laborers. Villanueva worked on redeveloping El Silencio—one of the worst slum district of Caracas—for this purpose. No other Latin American government had yet undertaken such a project. Though some of the original project has been torn down, Villanueva's designs still provide the best housing in the tropics. Villanueva incorporated excellent cross-ventilation, glare protection, and noise insulation in the apartments. He added balconies to the buildings, enabling the residents to watch some of the most spectacular sunsets on earth. He achieved the same goals with the housing project of Maracaibo, which offered different challenges. On this project, Villanueva finally ended the attempt to create a miniature villa and instead began to develop a new style of architecture that fit the changing world. He emphasized the urban centers of gathering places, churches, and schools with the new dwellings in Maracaibo, adding walkways and yards to improve the neighborhood's character. In a development in Caracas, he integrated dwellings along a hillside in a visually pleasing pattern and situated the buildings so that the peasant tenants could enjoy the breezes of the hills blowing through their apartments.

Villanueva's 40-year career focused on buildings for public use. In the 1940s he designed the first phase of buildings for the Central University of Venezuela where he served as a founding professor of architecture starting in 1944. He continued to design different phases of the university's growth throughout his life. His university designs furthered his ideas for community design. The buildings and walkways are also accented at every major area by murals and sculptures that Villanueva designed as part of the structure, notably an Alexander Calder sculpture in the university's auditorium.

In 1957 Villanueva designed the university's School of Architecture for which the university named him Doctor honoris causa in 1961. The nine-story School of Architecture represents Villanueva's crowning achievement as an architect and as a teacher. An imposing structure, the building "imposes on the student the fearful decision to come to terms with the future he/she has chosen," according to Sibyl Moholy-Nagy in her book, *Carlos Raúl Villanueva and the Architecture of Venezuela.*

Throughout his career, Villanueva designed many great structures, such as the Olympic Stadium and the Medical Center for the university and later the Museo de Bellas Artes in Caracas, for which he won the Venezuelan National Architecture Prize in 1963. Throughout his life, however, he remained focused on community development and urban planning, serving as president of the National Board of Historic and Artistic Protection and Conservation and as founder/director of the National Planning Commission. He continued to work and design until his death in Caracas on August 16, 1975.

## SOURCES:

### Books

Bayon, Damian, and Paolo Gasparini, *The Changing Shape of Latin American Architecture: Conversations with Ten Leading Architects,* New York, Sussex, 1979.

*Contemporary Architects,* 3rd edition, edited by Muriel Emanuel, New York, St. James Press, 1994.

Moholy-Nagy, Sibyl, *Carlos Raúl Villanueva and the Architecture* New York, Praeger, 1964.

### Periodicals

*AIA Journal,* December 1975.

—*Sketch by Christopher Tower*

# Tino Villanueva
## 1941-
### Mexican American writer

During the of the 1960s and 1970s, Tino Villanueva emerged as a reasonable voice for elevated awareness of Chicano culture and its integral double sensitivity, both as Anglo-American and as Hispanic. Through his work, he advocates that his Chicano people gird themselves with education and self-awareness.

Tino Villanueva was born on December 11, 1941, in San Marcos, an arid barrio in south-central Texas. His parents, Lino B. and Leonor (Rios) Villanueva were migrant field workers. Villanueva's early years were marked by a struggle with his own culture. He was embarrassed about his parents job as migrant farmers. Like many other Chicano children, he lied about his summer plans at the end of each school year to the teachers who asked. He was ashamed of the work he did in the fields until the age of seventeen and how, like many of his Chicano friends, he was often not ready to go back to school until after the October harvests.

Villanueva graduated from high school even though the only lessons he learned were ones of racial prejudice and Texas history. After failing his college entrance exam, he took a job in a furniture factory and committed himself to a self-improvement regimen including studies of such things as the section of the *Reader's Digest* devoted to increasing one's word power. His self-refinement routine ended when he was drafted into the United States Army in 1963 and spent two years in the Panama Canal Zone. There he rediscovered his Hispanic roots in a new light and began reading the works of poets like **Ruben Dario** and revolutionary **Jose Marti.**

Upon returning to San Marcos, he began studies of English and Spanish at Southwest Texas University. He wrote his first poem—a sonnet—in a class for native Spanish-speakers. The poem, "Camino y Capricho eterno," was published in the *San Antonio Express and News* in 1968. Professors turned Villanueva to poets like T. S. Eliot, e. e. cummings, and especially Dylan Thomas, with whom he found a special kinship. After receiving his B.A. in 1968, Villanueva moved to Buffalo, New York and attended the State University of New York there on a fellowship. In Buffalo, he began to realize his literary and spiritual alliance with other Chicanos. This connection would inform and guide all of Villanueva's work.

He finished his Master's in 1971 and moved to Boston University, where he began his doctoral studies. In 1972, he published a collection of poems,

*Tino Villanueva*

his first, called *Hay Otra Voz: Poems* (*There Is Another Voice: Poems*) that included what many believe to be one of his best poems, one inspired by Dylan Thomas, called "My Certain Burn Toward Pale Ashes." That year he also wrote "Chicano Is an Act of Defiance," dedicated to **Ruben Salazar**, the journalist killed in racial turmoil that erupted in East L.A. that year. For Villanueva, the poem and the collection spoke to the injustices committed against him and his people. Since in 1972 virtually no journals published poems by Chicaers or reviews about their books, Villanueva's book received no reviews from the anglo-American literary circles.

### Creates Chicano Anthology

After publishing his collection, Villanueva traveled a great deal, giving readings throughout the United States and in Europe. He continued to write and publish poetry in addition to articles about Chicano and Spanish literature. Villanueva finished and published a general anthology of Chicano literature in 1980, *Chicanos, Antologia Historica y Literaria*, compiling literature from 1848 and the end of the United States-Mexican War through the end of the twentieth century. A year later, Villanueva completed his doctorate in Spanish from Boston University and accepted a full-time post at Wellesley College.

### Launches Chicano Poetry Journal

In 1984, he began publishing *Imagine: International Chicano Poetry Journal*. Though the emphasis

was on Chicano literature, Villanueva called for submissions of poems in any language accompanied by English translations. Villanueva had a variety of beliefs that guide his work and his actions. One was what he called "bisensibilidad" or double sensitivity; another was that Chicanos faced the world from two perspectives, a Hispanic one and an anglo-American one. He furthered this idea with a discussion of this bicultural perspective in both language and behavior. He suggested that this tandem relationship infused Chicano poetry with aesthetics and style that was not found in other poetry.

In an article in the *Denver Quarterly* in 1981, Villanueva wrote: "most of my compositions dealing with the American experience from a Chicano perspective grow out of a sense of being at odds with Anglo America and her national habit of racism, which I find incomprehensible and morally unjustifiable. . . . My poetry of political dimension is an assault against oppression and, at least ideally, a strategy to rescind the powers of unfairness; to obliterate the stench which racism creates in a liberal democracy."

He published several books of poetry since earning his Ph.D., including *Chronicle of My Worst Years* (1994), *Scene From the Movie Giant* (1993), *Autobiographical Disclosures* (1988), and *Shaking off the Dark*. Bruce-Novoa wrote of Villanueva's poetry that "confronted by a world of empty words, realizing that his people have been silently anonymous, Villanueva finds a voice between meaningless sounds and silence. . . . It becomes the language of ritual for his people; in it, they begin to transform themselves."

In Villanueva's 1994 collection, he furthered Bruce-Novoa's comments with in the last poem of the book: "We're substance now and time, because it's the transparent weight of ourselves, and not History by itself alone that marks a different direction of the air, different roads."

## SELECTED PUBLISHED WORKS:

### Poetry

*Hay Otra Voz: Poems,* Editorial Mensaje, 1972.
*Shaking off the Dark,* Arte Publico Press, 1984.
*Autobiographical Disclosures,* Americas Review, 1988.
*Scene From the Movie Giant,* Curbstone Press, 1993.
*Chronicle of My Worst Years,* Northwestern University Press, 1994.

### Other

*Chicanos, Antologia Historica y Literaria,* Fondo de Cultura Economica, 1980.

## SOURCES:

### Books

Bruce-Novoa, Juan, *Chicano Poetry: A Response to Chaos,* Austin, University of Texas Press, 1982.

*Chicano Literature: A Reference Guide,* edited by Julio A. Martinez and Francisco A. Lomeli, Westport, Connecticut, Greenwood Press, 1985.

*Cuentos Chicanos: A Short Story Anthology,* edited by Rudolfo A. Anaya and Antonio Marquez, Alburquerque, University of New Mexico, Press, 1984.

*Dictionary of Literary Biography,* Volume 82: *Chicano Writers,* First Series, edited by Francisco A. Lomeli and Carl R. Shirley, Detroit, Gale Research, 1989.

*Hispanic Writers,* edited by Bryan Ryan, Detroit, Gale Research, 1991.

*Identification and Analysis of Chicano Literature,* edited by Francisco Jimenez, Binghmapton, New York, Bilingual/Editorial Bilingue, 1979.

Villanueva, Tino, *Chronicle of My Worst Years,* translated by James Hoggard, Evanston, Northwestern University Press, 1994.

### Periodicals

*Denver Quarterly,* fall 1981, pp.101–6.

—*Sketch by Christopher B. Tower*

# José Antonio Villarreal
## 1924-
### Mexican American author

José Villarreal became the first Chicano writer to publish a novel with a major publishing company in the United States when Doubleday published his first novel, *Pocho,* in 1959. Since then Villarreal has published other novels, stories, poems, critical essays, and various magazine articles. *Pocho* has been widely recognized as an important work of literature and Chicano culture. Despite the controversy the novel stirred up in the Chicano community, many critics praised it, comparing it to James Joyce's *Portrait of the Artist as a Young Man* because of its themes of self-discovery and maturation.

Villarreal was born in Los Angeles on July 30, 1924, to Mexican parents, Jose Heladio Villarreal and Felicitaz Ramirez. Villarreal's father fought in **Pancho Villa**'s army during the Mexican Revolution, and then moved his family to California in 1921, where they found work as migrant farm workers. Until he was six years old, Villarreal's family wandered through California, finding work where they could and living among other Mexican immigrants in tents pitched in the fields. These years provided Villarreal with the underpinnings of his first novel, since his family lived in what he called a "Mexican enclave" in *Bilingual Review.*

### Discovers Storytelling

Before he truly entered urban American society, Villarreal recounted an idyllic existence of warmth and security. Since the poor migrant workers had no other means of entertainment, they told stories among themselves in the evenings. Villarreal recalled the effect this had on him in an interview with Francisco Jiménez for *Bilingual Review:* "And so they talked and told tales of their region, and I listened. Long into the night I listened until I dropped off to sleep and my father would pick me up onto his lap as he continued to talk about the Revolution. . . . And every camp was different, none existing for more than six or seven weeks, then off we would go to the next harvest, where new people would gather and there would be new tales to be told and heard. I knew when I was six years old that the one thing I most wanted from life was to be a storyteller."

Villarreal wasted no time pursuing his dreams He started first grade in 1930, once his father obtained year-round employment in Santa Clara, California. By the third grade, he was reading English so ardently that the principal promoted him to the fourth grade. Though Villarreal adapted well to urban American life, his early years were not without hardship. Villarreal was literally caught between two separate worlds. For many years, he was forbidden to speak English at home by his parents, who were reluctant to learn it. This reluctance was indicative of the cultural, social, psychological, and philosophical conflicts pre-World War II Mexican Americans faced in their struggle to adapt to life in the United States.

### Cultural Conflicts Enliven *Pocho*

Growing up, and later in interviews and his writing, Villarreal preferred English to Spanish, and his parents gradually accepted the language, too. For Villarreal, growing up *pocho* ("between cultures") in Santa Clara influenced his first novel as much as the stories from the migrant camps of his early years. He graduated from high school in 1942 and served three years in the navy, stationed in the South Pacific, during World War II. He returned from the war and earned a bachelor's degree in English from the University of California at Berkeley in 1950. Though he tried graduate study, he chose writing over scholarship before finishing his master's degree.

Villarreal married Barbara Gentles in 1953, and the couple had three children by 1958. During these years, Villarreal dedicated himself to his family first and his writing second. Though he was working on *Pocho,* he provided for his family by working in public relations, by driving a delivery truck, and by writing technical documents for the aerospace industry. During the 1950s, Villarreal moved back and forth between the United States and Mexico. In 1973, Villarreal became a Mexican citizen—more out of economic necessity than because of disenchantment with the United States—and living in Mexico provided him with themes that he explored in all his novels. He finished *Pocho* in 1956, but he did not find a publisher for the book until 1959, when Doubleday released it.

*Pocho* tells the story of Richard Rubio, whose parents, like Villarreal's, immigrated to the United States around the time of the Mexican Revolution. The family encounters problems adjusting to the American way of life. Richard's mother, Consuelo, becomes more and more jealous of her husband, Juan, rejecting the traditionally submissive role of the Mexican wife. Juan is unable to accept the changes in his wife and leaves her for a younger, more traditional Mexican woman. Richard refuses to assume the role of bread-winner for the family that his father deserted, instead obsessing about how to establish his own identity free of cultural and social norms. Rejecting his ethnic heritage and his responsibilities, Richard joins the navy at the end of the novel.

Though *Pocho* was the first novel by a Hispanic writer ever published by a major American publishing house, the novel did not receive much attention until it was re-released by Anchor Books in 1970. By then, members of the surging Chicano movement condemned Villarreal for understating the cultural differences between Anglo-Americans and Mexican Americans, and the ensuing intolerance. Others criticized his sympathetic portrayal of a Chicano character unwilling to embrace his heritage. These critics claimed that the novel, and the novelist, advocated assimilation.

Villarreal reacted strongly to the criticism of *Pocho.* He repeatedly claimed that he never viewed himself as a Chicano writer: "I think of myself as a writer, and if I should do something good, it will be for the world I live in, not merely for a select group," he explained to Jiménez. He also questioned the idea of "Chicano literature, " claiming that most Chicanos wrote in English, not Spanish, and drew heavily from American and European literary traditions.

### *Pocho* Gains Landmark Status

Regardless of the criticism, *Pocho* sold 160,000 copies and was often mentioned as the predecessor of modern Chicano literature. In *Aztlan,* Juan Bruce-Novoa considered the dichotomy of reactions to the novel: "it must be observed that the success of the book is directly attributable to the new Chicano cultural awareness. However, this interest, that has sold so many copies of *Pocho,* has had disadvantages. The novel has been treated usually as a sociological, anthropological, or historical document; or even as a psychological case study, and hardly ever as literature. It is no wonder that Villarreal has reacted against such treatment and has raised serious questions about the study and criticism of Chicano literature."

Villarreal felt that his second novel, *The Fifth Horseman,* was artistically superior to *Pocho.* Many critics agreed, finding the story of Heraclio Ines, a *jinete* ("horseman") in the cavalry of the Mexican Revolution, rich in language, characterization, and story line. But Chicano critics still dissented, taking Villarreal to task for distorting the historical reality of the time period.

Undaunted by the criticism, Villarreal persevered and wrote *Clemente Chacón,* his most complex and artistically sophisticated work. Villarreal claimed *Clemente Chacón* was also his best work, as evidenced by its selection in both the Madrid and the Frankfurt book fairs of 1984. The novel, which is not arranged chronologically, recounts a Chicano variation on the Horatio Alger story, a rags-to-riches story of Ramon/Clemente moving from the poverty-stricken streets of Juarez, Mexico, to the upwardly mobile world across the border in El Paso, Texas.

In a speech for the Modern Language Association in 1977, Villarreal spoke out both for and against the Chicano movement: "As artists we must, through our pride and arrogance, and perhaps even insolence, ignore the warnings from the gods and, although it be a grievous sin, transcend the codes of the Movement as we create. Then, and only then, will we have a literature. Then, we will truly contribute to the Cause. What we create may not be called Chicano Literature . . . but it will belong to us and it will express our singular experience and lay bare, for the world to see, the soul of our people."

### SELECTED PUBLISHED WORKS:

*Pocho,* Doubleday, 1959, Anchor Press, 1970.
*The Fifth Horseman,* Doubleday, 1974.
*Clemente Chacón,* Bilingual/Editorial Bilingue, 1984.

### SOURCES:

#### Books

*Chicano Literature: A Reference Guide,* edited by Julio A. Martinez and Francisco A. Lomeli, Westport, CT, Greenwood Press, 1985.

*Dictionary of Literary Biography, Volume 82: Chicano Writers,* First Series, edited by Francisco A. Lomeli and Carl R. Shirley, Detroit, Gale, 1989.

*Hispanic Literature Criticism,* edited by Jelena Krstovic, Detroit, Gale, 1994.

*Hispanic Writers,* edited by Bryan Ryan, Detroit, Gale, 1991.

*Identification and Analysis of Chicano Literature,* edited by Francisco Jiménez, Binghampton, NY, Bilingual/Editorial Bilingue, 1979.

*Iguana Dreams: New Latino Fiction,* edited by Delia Poey and Virgil Suarez, New York, Harper Perennial, 1992.

Salidvar, Ramon, *Chicano Narrative,* Madison, University of Wisconsin Press, 1990.

**Periodicals**

*Aztlan,* Spring 1976, pp. 65–77.
*Bilingual Review,* Spring 1976, pp. 66–72.
*Nation,* January 9, 1960, pp. 36–37.

—*Sketch by Christopher B. Tower*

# Nelly de Vuksic
## 1939-

**Argentine conductor and musician**

Argentina-born conductor and vocalist Nelly Vuksic unites classical and contemporary music from Latin America and the United States to create a musical experience that is both enjoyable and educational. Vuksic's eclecticism has taken her throughout the Western Hemisphere in search of new conducting experiences and new music. She proudly informed Tom Pendergast during a telephone interview that every performance of her musical group, Americas Vocal Ensemble, is a premiere performance, at least in the United States. In addition to her work with various choral groups, Vuksic also performs regularly with her husband, pianist Cesar Vuksic. Her journey from a small town in rural Argentina to New York City is as interesting as the music her groups have performed.

Nelly Perez Trevisan de Vuksic was born to Emilio and Lydia Perez on August 19, 1938, in Totoras, Argentina, a small town outside of the larger city of Rosario. Rosario, a port city on the Parana River upstream from the coastal city of Buenos Aires, is one of the largest cities in the Santa Fe province of Argentina. Vuksic's family enjoyed a great deal of prestige in Totoras where, Vucksic recalled in her interview, "everyone knew everyone else": her grandmother had been the first schoolteacher in town, and her grandfather had founded what was once the town's largest general store and grocery. Her parents were not rich, however, for the family store, which her father managed, no longer did a booming business. Her mother was a seamstress and taught sewing to a group of young neighborhood girls which included her daughter.

Vuksic's education was not very organized. She studied in her grandmother's private school until she was eight years old, when she began to attend the public schools. She finished her primary schooling, but it was years before she could attend secondary school. If her formal education was scattered, her musical education was more thorough, disciplined, and continuous. "My family was very musically oriented," Vuksic explained in her interview. "My dad played guitar and loved Argentinean tangos, and he and mom organized musical evenings, where everyone in the family would gather and sing popular songs." In addition to singing at home, she sang from a very early age at the Catholic church she attended, where she also learned to play the harmonium, an instrument similar to the organ. Revealed Vuksic, "I learned two important things about music under the supervision of the nuns: how to sing in a group and how to sing a Gregorian chant."

When she was eight, Vuksic began to take piano lessons under the supervision of a teacher she characterized as "mean but talented." Though the teacher often rapped Vuksic's knuckles when she made a mistake, Vuksic learned rapidly and was soon a talented pianist. The teacher had many students in the bigger town of Rosario and Vuksic would play at the concerts and challenges her teacher organized at the El Circulo Theatre. Vuksic remembered the theatre as being "very beautiful, very lavish, and very French, and I went there to play music by Schuman, Beethoven, Chopin, difficult pieces by the classical composers." After she had been playing for a time she got a piano of her own, which her family in Argentina still uses, and she practiced until late at night. "Piano was my job," she told her interviewer, "and it made my mother very proud."

Since her family could not afford to send her to the secondary school in a neighboring town, Vuksic worked as a seamstress and taught piano. Eventually she had earned enough money to pay her own way through school, though she did not finish secondary school until she was in her early twenties. "Luckily," she remembered, "I looked young enough to fit in with the teenagers." Even while she was in the American equivalent of high school, Vuksic began attending courses at nearby Rosario University, where she attracted attention with her musical talents. Urged to study the practical field of music education,

Vuksic began to learn to conduct and was invited to be a conductor with the Choral Establo de Rosario, the university's prestigious youth choir.

### Discovers Fulfillment in Conducting

Despite the fact that she had won numerous prizes for her piano playing and was building a reputation in Rosario as a fine pianist, Vuksic began to devote herself to conducting. "I discovered I could conduct, that I was a conductor," she stated in her interview. "It was a new way of expressing myself. A conductor can shape the music with her hands, where in teaching you don't get that fulfillment." She became very interested in choir, and also assisted the conductor of the university's adult chorus. But her progress as a conductor was interrupted briefly when, shortly after her graduation, Vuksic married a young pianist named Cesar Vuksic. The musical couple was married on February 14, 1969, in her hometown of Totoras, and they soon began a joint career of travel and music that has continued for over 20 years.

Cesar was supported in his musical career by his family, but he wanted to leave the country "to gain experience and to grow," explained Vuksic. In 1972, the renowned pianist Pia Sebastiani offered Cesar a scholarship to Ball State University in Muncie, Indiana. He accepted, and his wife followed a year later with their young son, Alejandro. Though she knew little English, Vuksic was also offered a scholarship in the School of Music where, she said, she "did everything that could be done—taught piano, sang, accompanied people and, most of all, learned English." Soon, however, she was offered the conductorship of the women's chorus and assisted with the concert choir as well. By 1978 she had received her Ph.D. in conducting from Ball State University, and was twice awarded the university's Music Concerto Night Award, in 1976 and 1977. In 1978 she followed Cesar to Western Michigan University, where he had received a visiting musicianship. There she conducted the choir and several chamber orchestras and taught piano.

In 1979, Vuksic accepted a position that would change her musical life forever: she left the United States to work at the Conservatorio del Tolima, in Colombia, South America. In her interview Vuksic declared: "In Colombia, I became Latin American. They played Latin American music, both contemporary and traditional, instead of European music and I discovered the charm of folk music." Vuksic was offered the conductorship of the well-known Los Chorus de Tolimo and with this group won the Concurso Polifomico Internacional Colombia, a prestigious international music award, in 1980. More important than the award, claimed Vuksic, was the widening of her musical horizons. After her experience in Colombia, she became committed to musical eclecticism, to understanding all the different varieties of music produced in all the Americas, North, Central, and South.

Despite their success in Colombia, Vuksic and her husband felt that it was "important to keep growing—musically, professionally, and spiritually"—and so they moved to New York City in 1982. Yet New York City was not, at first, all they had hoped it would be. "It was not easy finding work in New York," Vuksic told her interviewer. "I did all kinds of work, cleaning houses, menial jobs, just to keep busy. I would not have done this in my country, but in the United States doing these things was acceptable. I felt resentful, but at the same time I learned that I could do anything." Her first job in New York came almost by accident. She went to an Italian poetry reading—though she did not know Italian—and ran into an Italian tenor who was singing at the same place. She offered to accompany him on piano, he hired her, and soon they were working in restaurants and night clubs, playing Broadway music, Italian songs, and songs from operas.

Soon other jobs came Vuksic's way. When she first came to the city, she had visited the Americas Society and there had met "her angel," Lucille Duncan, the director of the performing department. Duncan mentioned her name to Hugh Ross, a well-known New York City choral conductor and, some time later, Ross contacted Vuksic and asked her to assist him in performing some works of a contemporary European musician. "I was thrilled at the thought of working with him," explained Vuksic, "but it turns out he wanted me as a singer, not a conductor." However, a friend who Vuksic met doing this job became very interested in Vuksic's desire to conduct performances of contemporary and traditional Latin American music and encouraged her to form the choral group that became Americas Vocal Ensemble.

### Founds Americas Vocal Ensemble

Vuksic founded the Ensemble in 1982 and soon the group recorded some choral works of Colombian composer Luis Antonio Escobar. Escobar was so thrilled by Las Cantatas Madrigales that, in a note he wrote for the album cover, he praised Vuksic for picking up ideas that he thought were not perceived by any other conductors. "I was very gratified to receive his admiration," noted Vuksic. The Ensemble has also recorded *Opus One: Americas Vocal Ensemble Performs the Music of Joel Wallach* and *Music of the Americas,* and it plans to release a compact disc titled *Hispanic Christmas Collection.* When the group was beginning, it relied on individual contributions for support but, as its reputation has grown, the group has received enough recognition to secure grants. The Ensemble has begun to perform throughout New York City and the east coast, including a performance at the American Music Festival in Washington, D.C. The growth of Vuksic's reputation in the 1980s and early–1990s has allowed her to conduct or direct numerous New York choral groups, including the Hudson Valley Singers, the Riverside Singers, the United Nation Singers, and numerous others.

During the time that she was struggling to establish the reputation of Americas Vocal Ensemble in New York, Vuksic also happened onto a teaching job. A friend encouraged her to introduce herself to a New York choral director, and she told the director that she was looking for work. It just so happened that he was looking for a bilingual music teacher, and he hired her on the spot for a position at the Blooming-dale House of Music in 1982. Later Vuksic worked for the Friends Seminary, where she taught voice, first on the high school level and later on all grade levels. She taught there from 1985 to 1990, when she took a job at Columbia University's program for teaching music to gifted children. Although teaching has always been Vuksic's second love, she admitted during her interview that "teaching people to sing fulfills my soul. One of my favorite lyrics in a song is "Keep my heart in tune, I want to teach the world to sing.'" Though she has often taught in organized schools, she prefers teaching voice to individuals.

Vuksic's greatest joy in conducting Americas Vocal Ensemble is that she is able to introduce people to a wide variety of music. She is as likely to present music by a contemporary Colombian composer as she is by a seventeenth-century U.S. composer. She is pleased that every performance she presents is a premiere for at least one of the pieces she plays. "Each piece of music has its moment," Vuksic claimed, "and I am interested in working in all kinds of music." Another consistent pleasure in her life has been the opportunity to often work alongside her husband. Together they perform a program of Argentine tangos and sambos, in both traditional and classical arrangements and often accompanied by their commentaries on the pieces. When she needs a pianist to accompany her Ensemble, she often hires Cesar; when Cesar needs an alto to accompany his piano, he hires her. She is always on the lookout for new opportunities, especially if they further her professed mission of "expanding and disseminating Latin American music." Asked to name her favorite music to perform, Vuksic said without hesitation: "My favorite music is the music that I am preparing for my next performance."

## SOURCES:

### Periodicals

*Imagen,* December 1990, p. 42.
*Más,* October 1990, p. 11.

### Other

Vuksic, Nelly, telephone interview with Tom Pendergast conducted on September 14, 1992.

—*Sketch by Tom Pendergast*

# Raquel Welch
**1940-**

**Hispanic American actress, singer, producer, and writer**

Since she first appeared in *Life* magazine in 1964, Raquel Welch has had little difficulty garnering attention. By 1966, the internationally known actress had become so popular that *Life* named her the most photographed woman of the year. The winner of various California beauty contests, Welch suddenly found herself on magazine covers, in movies, and in her own television specials. She later expanded her career as she maintained her company, Raquel Welch Productions, produced films, performed on stage, wrote a fitness book, and recorded a pop single. While Welch has been celebrated as a sex symbol, she has proven that she is a serious actress and has won the respect of critical audiences with her performances in the Broadway musical *Woman of the Year* and in the television movie *Right to Die.* Welch described her current status in *Hispanic:* "I've won my stripes. . . . I've gone from just being a sex symbol to being thought of as a legitimate actress."

Raquel Tejada was born to Armand Tejada, a Bolivian immigrant of Spanish heritage, and American Josephine Hall Tejada in Chicago, Illinois, on September 5, 1940. Two years later, her family relocated to La Jolla, a beach town in southern California, where Armand Tejada was employed as a structural engineer at a General Dynamics plant. At the public high school in La Jolla, Tejada, or "Rocky," as her friends called her, was a cheerleader, a member of the dramatic club, and the vice president of her senior class. She took ballet lessons and began to enter and win beauty contests; after her first victory at the age of 15, Welch became Miss La Jolla, Miss San Diego, and Maid of California. After her 1958 graduation she tried to pursue a career as an actress, with no success. So she took a job as a weather girl with a local television station in San Diego and spent a year studying acting at San Diego State College.

On May 8, 1959, Raquel Tejada became Raquel Welch when she married her high school sweetheart, James Westley Welch. The couple later separated and then divorced in 1964. Leaving her children, Damon and Tahnee, in California to live with her parents, Welch went to Texas, where she modeled for Neiman-

*Raquel Welch*

Marcus and worked as a cocktail hostess. Welch's dream was to move to New York City to better her chances of finding acting jobs, but she could not raise enough money for the trip. Welch returned to southern California, where she collected her children and found a home in Hollywood. Welch once again looked for work as an actress, and by the end of 1964, she had found minor parts in the film *A House Is Not a Home* and in the Elvis Presley movie *Roustabout.*

When publicist Patrick Curtis, a former child actor, met Welch, he left the public relations firm of Rogers & Cowan to head his own firm, Curtwel Productions. He devoted much of his time to managing Welch's career. His promotion of Welch gave her the opportunities she needed to rise to fame. She won a role in *A Swingin' Summer,* which brought her notice. In 1964, Welch appeared as a billboard girl in ABC-TV's *The Hollywood Palace,* and later that same year, Welch was featured in *Life* magazine. Twentieth Century-Fox contracted with Welch and designed a part especially for her in the memorable science fiction film, *Fantastic Voyage.* However, it was the image of Welch in a tight skin-diving suit, rather than her performance, which garnered the most media attention.

## Achieved International Stardom

Although Welch "had a very Puritan upbringing," she said in *Hispanic,* she was well on her way to becoming a sex symbol by 1967. Welch explained in the same article that she thought it fun "to strut my stuff," and didn't complain when Twentieth Century-Fox loaned her out to Hammer Film Productions for the making of *One Million Years B.C.* in 1967. Cast as Loana Shell, a cavewoman, Welch almost speechlessly romped around the set in a fur bikini, to the delight of European audiences. While Welch's role in this film was not very challenging, it won her fame, especially after Curtis advertised Welch as America's Ursula Andress. The actress appeared on some 92 European magazine covers, and Welch's popularity soon spread to the United States, where her image graced at least 16 American magazine covers. By the time Welch starred as a prostitute in the Italian comedy *Shoot Loud, Louder . . . I Don't Understand You* and as a spy in *Fathom,* she had definitely achieved international star status. When she and Curtis married on Valentine's Day in 1967, in Paris, the media had a field day trying to capture the romantic image of Welch in a tiny, white crocheted dress.

Welch's next assignments were to portray a gang member in *The Biggest Bundle of Them All* and to star in the British comedy *Bedazzled,* a Faustian film in which Welch played the role of a deadly sin, Lillian Lust. While the former film was not well-received by critics, it did not damage Welch's image, and the latter film enhanced her sex-symbol status. Welch created a stir with the daring costume she wore to the 1967 Academy Awards, and her tour of South Vietnam with Bob Hope brightened what had been a dreary Christmas for many American soldiers.

From 1968 to 1970, producers capitalized on Welch's fame and beauty to entice audiences to theaters, and she was cast in many films. In 1968, Welch starred in *The Queens: The Oldest Profession,* a film about prostitution, *Bandolero,* a western with James Stewart, and *Lady in Cement,* one of Frank Sinatra's Tony Rome movies. In 1969, the actress portrayed a go-go dancer in the suspense film *Flare Ups* and traveled to Spain to make *100 Rifles.* As Welch's character made love in a scene in *100 Rifles* with a black character, played by actor Jim Brown, the actress found herself enmeshed in controversy, and a great box office success.

A cameo role as a driver whipping her slaving oarswomen in *The Magic Christian* followed in 1970. Welch then chose another controversial role, that of Myra, the man-like female personality of the transsexual Myron, in the film *Myra Breckenridge,* which also featured Rex Reed, Mae West, and John Huston. Unfortunately, the movie, based on Gore Vidal's novel about homosexuality in Hollywood, failed to win the admiration of critics, and it was rumored that

Welch's disagreements with the director and Mae West had contributed to the disastrous product. Disputing the label of being a "difficult" actress, Welch explained in *Hispanic:* "All I ever fought for was quality in my films. I really felt I was being penalized for being the sex symbol they had created, and that made my Spanish blood boil." Despite the disappointing reception of *Myra Breckinridge,* and her unfair portrayal in the media, Welch met with some positive response in the same year with her CBS television special, *Raquel.*

## Decade of Professional Success

Although 1971 brought the actress personal turmoil as she divorced Patrick Curtis, 1972 was a productive year for Welch. She starred in *Fuzz Bluebeard, Hannie Caulder,* and *Kansas City Bomber.* In 1973 she made *The Last of Sheila,* and in 1974 she won a Golden Globe Award for best actress in *The Three Musketeers.* The movies she made in the mid-to-late 1970s included *Wild Party, The Four Musketeers, Mother, Jugs, and Speed, Crossed Swords, The Prince and the Pauper, Restless,* and *L'Animal.* In 1979, Welch made a guest appearance on the very popular television series, *The Muppet Show.*

It was during the filming of *L'Animal* in Paris in 1977 that Raquel Welch met her third husband, screenwriter-producer Andre Weinfeld. Welch and Weinfeld were married in a small ceremony in Mexico in 1980. In *People* magazine, Welch praised Weinfeld's "funny, generous, sensual spirit." Although, according to a *People* article, Welch had vowed never to mix business and marriage again, her new husband worked on her next television special, *From Raquel with Love,* that appeared on ABC-TV shortly after their wedding and was rated very highly. *Hispanic* reported that the couple had "a wonderful working relationship" managing Welch's production company; however, they separated in late 1989.

In 1981, Welch's professional career took a substantial and very public blow when she was replaced by Debra Winger after production had already begun on the film *Cannery Row.* While Metro-Goldwyn-Mayer (MGM) claimed that Welch had behaved unprofessionally on the set, Welch believed that she had been unfairly fired to cut the cost of the film's production. She filed a $20 million lawsuit against the company, and a lengthy legal battle ensued. In 1986, she finally was awarded $10.8 million by the court, an award which was later overturned. The experience traumatized Welch. She told people that she felt that she had been "blackballed" by Hollywood, and she explained in the *New York Times* that the episode had "stunned" her. "After that, I thought I was completely dead. . . . I never want to feel that way again—I'd rather die for real," she lamented.

As it turned out, Welch's experience surrounding *Cannery Row* led her to accept some serious and challenging acting roles. The actress acknowledged in *People* that the rough experience incited her to defend herself, "I operate on the premise that you always have to fight for what you want." She confided in the *New York Times* as well, "If it hadn't been for the 'Cannery Row' experience, I wouldn't have been predisposed to stick my neck out on 'Woman of the Year.'"

### Created Sensation with Broadway Role

Welch's performance in the hit musical *Woman of the Year* in 1981 marked a turning point in her career and a transformation of her reputation. When Lauren Bacall needed a vacation from the role she made famous on Broadway, Welch was asked to replace her for two weeks. Welch's years of presenting her nightclub act, "Live in Concert," in Atlantic City, Las Vegas, Rio de Janeiro, and other entertainment hot spots had given her the experience in singing and dancing that she needed to excel on stage. The popularity of her act suggested to the play's producers that Welch was capable of filling Bacall's shoes for two weeks. Her performance in *Woman of the Year* was lauded. After creating a sensation, Welch was asked to return later when Bacall took a six-month break. Welch was elated with this exciting revision of her acting career, and felt that she had finally won the respect she deserved. She declared in the *New York Times:* "When we got the reviews—the only way I can describe it is the phrase, 'The thrill of a lifetime.' I'm totally hooked. I can't wait to get back."

Before she returned to Broadway for her six-month stint in *Woman of the Year,* Welch starred in *The °Legend of Walks Far Woman* a movie made for television. Her "dramatic debut," as a *People* magazine critic dubbed the appearance, was to portray an independent, tough Native American woman who witnesses the battle of Little Big Horn and survives. Welch related her enthusiasm for the role to the *New York Times:* "I like the idea of heroines who survive and struggle. It's important to have your own principles, to have dignity and follow your own code, as Walks Far does. I like a woman character with backbone." A *People* magazine critic found the movie "solemn but worthwhile." Welch's reputation as a legitimate actress was beginning to solidify.

Despite these changes in her work and reputation, Welch's sex symbol image stubbornly maintained itself. Welch was well aware of this, and she was quoted in *People* as saying: "Why hate it? It doesn't do me any good. The sex symbol image is there. I don't dislike it. I don't love it. It's like Mount Rushmore. It's not going to go away." As perpetual as her image, Welch's beauty was intact, and she capitalized on her amazing vitality by writing a book about it in 1984. Entitled *The Raquel Welch Total Beauty and Fitness Program,* the book focused on retaining one's physical and mental health with yoga, specialized diets, and exercise, and was released with an accompanying videocassette. Welch's work was a best-seller. Despite a $1 million damage suit by Bikram Choudhury, Welch's former yoga instructor and good friend who charged that the actress had stolen his moves and format and claimed her instructions could lead to injuries, Welch continued to introduce fitness programs on video. She produced and starred in the home exercise video, *Raquel: Lose 10 Lbs. in 3 Weeks,* and *Body and Mind: Total Relaxation and Stress Relief Program.* In 1987, she released another video, *A Week with Raquel,* which also became a top seller.

1987 was a productive year for Welch. She starred in a made-for-television movie, *Right to Die,* which dramatized the trauma of decision-making in life and death situations. Welch's portrayal of a woman dying of amyotrophic lateral sclerosis, better known as Lou Gehrig's Disease, won her praise. Instead of playing a glamorous, sexy woman, she effectively characterized a pale, suffering woman in a state of rapid physical decay. Although a *People* magazine critic berated the movie and described it as "an inappropriate and exploitive exercise in emotional voyeurism," a reviewer for the *New York Times* wrote, "Ms. Welch gives an enormously affecting performance as Emily Bauer, not only uncompromising but also admirably sensitive to the intentions of the film."

Welch was pleased with her performance as well. She remarked to the *New York Times,* "I wasn't making a conscious search for something like this, but I had always known I had a whole part of my being and my professional ability that I'd never had a chance to use fully, and this satisfied that." She continued: "Everything that was the public Raquel Welch, I got rid of . . . in this role. . . . There was a great freedom in knowing for myself how much there was without all that, and what a range of things I can look forward to personally, as well as for myself as an actress. I'm very grateful I found that out." One of the things Welch was looking forward to was the European release of an energetic pop single—and the continental tour that would promote it—later in 1987. Entitled "This Girl Is Back in Town," Welch's song communicated her renewed confidence. A *Hispanic* writer quoted a portion of its lyrics: "Well, now I know right from wrong, and . . . the only place where I belong. No more fooling around / This girl's back in town."

In 1988, during the production of another critically acclaimed television movie, *Scandal in a Small Town,* Welch commented in *Hispanic,* "I've always thought the older I got the more people would see that I have more to me than just my good looks." Many would agree that, while Welch is finally receiving the recognition that she deserves, she hasn't lost her good looks. Although she is in her mid-fifties, she maintains the image that made her famous and intends to create her own acting opportunities. Welch's physical vitality, her determination to emerge as a serious actress, and her clever utilization of all of her talents have made her an inspirational figure. The Los Angeles Hispanic Women's Council confirmed her status by naming her Woman of the Year in 1990.

## SELECTED VIDEOGRAPHY

*A House Is Not a Home,* 1964.
*Roustabout,* 1964.
*Do Not Disturb,* 1965.
*A Swingin' Summer,* 1965.
*Fantastic Voyage,* 1966.
*Fathom,* 1966.
*Shoot Loud, Louder, I Don't Understand!,* 1966.
*Bedazzled,* 1967.
*The Queens: The Oldest Profession,* 1967.
*One Million Years B.C.,* 1967.
*Bandolero!,* 1968.
*The Biggest Bundle of Them All,* 1968.
*Lady in Cement,* 1968.
*Flare Ups,* 1969.
*100 Rifles,* 1969.
*The Magic Christian,* 1970.
*Myra Breckenridge,* 1970.
*Hannie Caulder,* 1971.
*Bluebeard,* 1972.
*Fuzz,* 1972.
*Kansas City Bomber,* 1972.
*The Last of Sheila,* 1973.
*The Three Musketeers,* 1974.
*Wild Party,* 1974.
*The Four Musketeers,* 1975.
*Mother, Jugs and Speed,* 1976.
*L' Animal,* 1977.
*Crossed Swords,* 1978.
*The Prince and the Pauper,* 1978.
*Restless,* 1978.
*You and Me Together,* 1979.
*Stuntwoman,* 1981.
*The Legend of Walks Far Woman,* 1982.
*Right to Die,* 1987.
*Scandal in Small Town,* 1988.
*Trouble in Paradise,* 1988.
*Hero for Hire,* 1990.

## SOURCES:

### Books

Haining, Peter, *Raquel Welch: Sex Symbol to Super Star,* St. Martin's Press, 1984.

### Periodicals

*Chicago Tribune,* June 25, 1986, p. 4.
*Cosmopolitan,* May 1983, pp. 250–56; May 1990, pp. 320–24.
*Good Housekeeping,* October 1984, pp. 116–20.
*Harper's Bazaar,* August 1982, p. 116; November 1984, pp. 244–48.
*Hispanic,* April 1988, pp. 20–24.
*Life,* August 26, 1966; July, 1982, pp. 74–78.
*Los Angeles Magazine,* January 1985, p. 18.
*Los Angeles Times,* March 23, 1985, p. V1; June 25, 1986, Section 2, p. 1.
*Mademoiselle,* March 1988, p. 86.
*New York Times,* May 30, 1982; October 7, 1987, p. C1; October 12, 1987, p. C18.
*People,* July 21, 1980, p. 51; December 7, 1981, pp. 127–28; February 11, 1985, p. 40; October 12, 1987, p. 9.
*Redbook,* May 1983, pp. 10–11; February, 1985, pp. 98–99.
*Time,* August 16, 1982, p. 62.
*TV Guide,* May 29, 1982, pp. 18–22; October 10, 1987, pp. 26–29.
*Woman's Day,* November 11, 1984, pp. 124–25.

*—Sketch by Ronie-Richele Garcia-Johnson*

# Mary Rose Wilcox
## 1949-
### Hispanic American politician

Mary Rose Wilcox's victory in the 1992 primary for the 5th District Maricopa County, Arizona, supervisor was typical of her political career. Since winning a spot on the Phoenix, Arizona, city council in 1982, Wilcox has had consistent success. In addition to becoming the first Hispanic woman to serve on the council, she won her seat five consecutive times. Wilcox has been a key figure in Phoenix housing and is known for her strong commitment to the improvement of her community.

Wilcox grew up in Superior, a rural mining town about 60 miles east of Phoenix. Her maternal grandparents cofounded Superior, which included a population of 5000 that was more than 80 percent Hispanic. Her father, John Garrido, was a copper miner involved in unionization. Her mother, Betty Nunez Garrido, was a homemaker active in the Roman Catholic church and the public school system. Family pride and a strong sense of community duty were stressed in the Garrido household. Wilcox was

*Mary Rose Wilcox*

deeply influenced by the political activism of her parents, who were part of the first Hispanic generation that began to reject racial discrimination.

Wilcox's father left for World War II service while she was still in elementary school. Having served the United States in war, he returned with a new perspective, and he no longer wanted to be treated like a second-class citizen. Wilcox watched her father and miners form a union in the 1950s. Changes in the adult world were mirrored in her own transition from a segregated to integrated school. Like her parents, Wilcox became an active participant in the community, especially at Superior High School. While attending the school, she played clarinet in the band and served on the student council. Through her parents' and her own activities, Wilcox felt a strong Hispanic influence in the community. "We were on the student council, in the band, on the football and basketball teams," Wilcox remembered in a telephone interview with Peg McNichol.

When Wilcox attended Arizona State University, however, she abruptly discovered her minority status. She expected to transfer the sense of community responsibility and interaction from Superior to Phoenix. Instead, she and the three other minority women in her dorm were relegated to a single room and otherwise ignored. Wilcox did not remain invisible for long. In 1967 the Chicano movement was sweeping the nation. She joined the on-campus activism and participated in a strike to improve working conditions for the university's laundry workers, the

majority of whom were Hispanic. Wilcox had witnessed how the unionization of the copper miners in Superior had provided her family with health insurance and education, and she was convinced solidarity would provide the laundry workers with similar benefits.

While working towards a degree in social work, Mary met Earl V. Wilcox. He came from the southeast section of Phoenix, a heavily Hispanic area mottled with poverty and crime. His sensibilities and commitment to the community were met and matched by hers—he was a youth project director. The couple married in 1971, and she left school to support his efforts toward a master's degree in education.

The Wilcoxes joined the Hispanic political movement and campaigned for Alfredo Guitierrez, an Arizona politician. Wilcox also worked in Scottsdale, Arizona, as a job developer for the Maricopa County Manpower program, helping create career ladders for people in the private sector. Much of Wilcox's work involved members of the Yaqui, a Native American tribe with Hispanic influences that had unhappily relocated to Scottsdale from northern Arizona due to a flood control project. Relocating the entire village meant finding more than jobs. Wilcox's attempts to identify new housing and support systems for the Yaqui caught the attention of U.S. Senator Dennis DeConcini. DeConcini invited her to become a caseworker with his office.

Wilcox joined DeConcini's staff in 1977, eventually attaining the status of special assistant and later serving as liaison to the Small Business Administration and the U.S. Immigration and Naturalization Service. In 1978, Wilcox's casework led to an association with Friendly House. Patterned after the old Settlement Houses of Chicago, Friendly House is a 75-year-old nonprofit organization devoted to helping immigrants. Wilcox helped develop an educational arm for Friendly House that extends to local school districts. Programs supported by Friendly House target at-risk children during after school hours. Some help youngsters improve their grade-point average by raising their level of literacy. Others work with adults to improve parenting skills. By 1992, Wilcox was a Friendly House Foundation board member and had watched the group expand from a $100,000 annual working budget to $4 million. It remains one of her favorite organizations.

### Cofounded Hispanic Woman's Corporation

In 1983, Wilcox and five other women cofounded the Hispanic Woman's Corporation, a group that offers annual seminars to help Hispanic women upgrade their careers and educations. In Arizona it is the largest conference of its kind, drawing up to 1,800 women. The conference is privately funded by corporations that use the event as a recruiting opportunity. Also in 1983, Wilcox helped create IMAGE, a coalition of Hispanic government employees at the federal, state, and local level. From 1983 to 1986, Wilcox served as the group's president. Though membership averaged 60, Wilcox saw the number of luncheon attendees mushroom due to speakers who discussed civil rights, politics, and social changes. One of the key issues was Arizona state politics.

Republicans have dominated the Arizona political scene since the mid–1950s, but strong pockets of Democrats remain, many of them in cities like Phoenix. Until 1982, Phoenix had been represented primarily by middle-aged caucasian men, many of them business owners from the city's central district. Wilcox's work for DeConcini put her at the heart of the community and resulted in her election to the Human Resources Commission. In that post she campaigned to restructure Phoenix's city council from at-large representation to districts (expanding the council from six to eight members), with the mayor elected at-large. By this time, Wilcox was a working mother feeling the effects of the women's movement. The success of her districting campaign inspired her to run for the 7th District position, which she won in 1982. It was a time she remembered in her interview as "the most satisfying in my life."

Wilcox took office with liberal reform Mayor Terry Goddard and Calvin Goode, a black colleague who was one of the few survivors of the reform campaign. Some of her key projects were chairing the city council's housing commission and working to pass a $37 million bond for affordable housing in 1988. The bond issue funded projects dedicated to safe, affordable single family housing and transitional housing for the impoverished and aged.

Wilcox gained a reputation as a housing advocate with the bond's passage and by teaming up with Goode in 1987 to establish a $1 million fund for an anticrime program called Neighborhood Fightback. The monies were granted to strong community associations willing to upgrade the community. The grants were as high as $250,000 and paid for repairs, house painting, and street lighting. Crime rates in neighborhoods with these programs dropped as much as 22 percent. After three years, the program was adopted on a state-wide level.

### Became Vice Mayor of Pheonix

In 1988, Wilcox was chosen vice mayor by other members of the city council. During that two year-term, which was concurrent with her seat on council, she became very visible. Wilcox credited Goddard for his confidence in her abilities to do more than the traditional vice mayor. It appeared that Wilcox would become a near institution in city politics. She won a four-year term of office in 1989 after an uncontested

campaign in which she called for a ban on semiautomatic weapons like the AK–47 assault rifle, a weapon commonly used by gang members on the city's south side. She also supported a proposition to build a baseball stadium in her district, on the premise that it would draw new jobs and more money into the area.

Wilcox's main thrust as a candidate, however, continued to be that she was the grassroots choice. She described herself as someone not glamorous or mysterious but more like a member of the voter's family. Her campaign speeches often included comparisons between herself and her constituency. "Look at me," she would ask. "Don't I look like your sister or your daughter or the woman next door?" Despite her appeal as an "average" woman, Wilcox has demonstrated her political savvy. After Goddard left his post to seek a state office, there were rumors that Wilcox planned to run for mayor. In May of 1991, however, Wilcox's name was on the short list as a possible replacement for the 5th District Maricopa County Supervisor Ed Pastor.

Her decision to seek another term on the city council was greeted with some speculation that she would not finish the four-year term. Wilcox vowed to do so, but in June 1992, she did resign. Among the factors cited by the press was her disappointment over not receiving the supervisory appointment in 1991 and her frustration with conservative Phoenix Mayor Paul Johnson. The move, which forced a $95,000 special election, created some negative feelings in the community, but Wilcox managed to assuage those with the explanation that her efforts toward neighborhood improvement and better health care services for low income families would have greater strength at the county level.

Wilcox faced a tough primary. She did not have the luxury of an unopposed campaign. This time, she faced four challengers: two Democrats and two Republicans. She won by targeting members of the Democratic community who knew her well: Hispanic women over age 35, telling them "our voice counts." Discussing her success, Wilcox noted in her interview, "If I'd been a male doing the stuff I'd done in the last nine years, there is no way another male would have run against me." Wilcox anticipated a significant win in November 1992, that would make her the first Hispanic woman to serve as a supervisor.

Though politics play a vital role in Wilcox's life, she has other priorities. The importance of family is a constant theme. She has remained supportive of her husband's career—he was a state representative before accepting the role of Maryvale justice of the peace in 1991. The couple started a joint venture, as publishers of the quarterly *Aqui Magazine* for the Hispanic community. They consciously limited their own family to one child, daughter Yvonne, due to busy schedules. Wilcox credits motherhood with making her a well-rounded person. Her experience as a child with many siblings and her large extended family (her husband comes from a family of 13) convinced her that, regardless of structure, strong family connections are important. She has transferred her feelings for strong family commitment to the Hispanic community in general. She is committed to being a role model not just for Hispanic women but for women in general. She sees it as a responsibility that never lets up, but she is gratified when she meets a woman who has entered politics citing Wilcox's career as inspiration.

When Wilcox has time to herself, after the board meetings and family commitments, she occasionally plays her clarinet, but she is more likely to read or do some light impact aerobics. She still harbors hopes of finishing her degree. Since her three-and-a-half years at Arizona State, she has returned to college periodically. Even without her degree, her accomplishments and contributions to the Phoenix area are significant.

## SOURCES:

### Periodicals

*Arizona Republic,* September 13, 1989; April 10, 1992; June 18, 1992; June 30, 1992; July 2, 1992.
*Arizona Republic/The Phoenix Gazette,* April 29, 1991.
*Arizona Republic Voter's Guide,* October 2, 1989.
*Phoenix Gazette,* May 25, 1992; June 17, 1992; June 19, 1992.

### Other

Wilcox, Mary Rose, telephone interview with Peg McNichol, September 1992.

—*Sketch by Peg McNichol*

# Agustin Yanez
## 1904-1980
### Mexican educator and writer

Agustin Yanez made one of the greatest contributions to Mexican Literature with novels that were poetic, stylized, and thoroughly modern. Compared to such novelists as Marcel Proust and Balzac, Yanez pioneered the modernist trend in Mexican fiction. Additionally, he was a teacher and a government administrator.

Agustin Yanez was born May 4, 1904 in Guadalajara, in Jalisco, Mexico to parents Elpidio Yanez and Maria Santos Delgadillo. He attended the University of Guadalajara and the National University of Mexico, where he earned degrees in law and philosophy. He married Olivia Ramirez Ramos with whom he had six children: four daughters and two sons.

As early as age 15, he held positions at educational institutions in Guadalajara. He began teaching in 1923 at the age of 19. He continued his teaching career as a professor at the National University. In 1942, he was made professor of literary theory. From 1946-1950, he served as a professor at the Universidad Femenina. And in 1952 he was awarded the highest honor in Mexico when he was named to the Mexican National College by the Republic of Mexico. He was a powerful intellectual and critical voice in the Mexican literary world. He wrote introductions to books published by the National University and lectured on the creative process. Through his career in education, he found a new career in the government. He represented Mexico at national and international meetings on education.

### Begins Work in Government

After almost 30 years as an educator, Yanez began to turn his attentions to government. He served as governor of his home state of Jalisco—one of the largest and most important states in Mexico—from 1953-1959. As governor, Yanez took action. He built numerous schools and many, many roads better uniting Jalisco and better linking it to the rest of Mexico. He continued his public service after his term as governor ended. He participated in UNESCO and functioned as Ambassador to Argentina. Later, he worked as an advisor to Mexican President Adolpho

*Agustin Yanez*

Lopez Mateos and as secretary of education under Gustavo Diaz Ordaz. In his work for national education, he launched a series of reforms hoping to improve the system for the common good.

### Life-long Career in Journalism

Yanez began writing at an early age and published as a journalist long before he published the novels for which he would be best known. Starting in 1929, he assumed the editorship of one of the three journals that he would edit during his lifetime. He worked as editor on Guadalajara's *Bandera de Provincias* from 1929-1930. Though he served on the editorial boards of many journals, he did only two other year stints as editor, one on *Occidente* in Mexico City from 1944-1945 and then with *Filosofia y Letras* from 1946-1947. It was just after this last editorship that Yanez published, *Al Filo del agua*. Though this was not his first novel, it was the first novel translated by Ethel Brinton into English in 1963 as *The Edge of the Storm*.

## Begins Career as Novelist

With *The Edge of the Storm,* Yanez wrote of the time in Mexican history preceding the Mexican Revolution of 1910. He set the novel in his home region of Guadalajara. He fashioned a group of villagers forever engrossed in a Lent that never ends. The church wields an iron fist over the villagers, suppressing any signs of happiness with guilt and discipline. "Village of black-robed women," the novel begins. "It is a barren village ... only the general cleanliness of everything reveals the hidden life.... The chief concern [of everyone] is with the next world.... The idea of comfort is foreign to the village. Life is not for enjoyment."

Through intense scrutiny, Yanez expresses a deep understanding of his Mexican people, exposing the struggles they faced between their own human desires and the oppressive fears of nature, of their God's wrath.

Yanez followed *The Edge of the Storm* with *Las tierras flacas* in 1962 that Brinton translated in 1968 as *The Lean Lands.* This novel deals with a village even farther removed from the world of greater Mexico. The farmers of this novel live far beyond the village (pueblo) of Yahualica, the setting for *The Edge of the Storm.* Here the people are so remote they are unaffected by doctors and priests and instead put their faith in a system of magic and superstition.

Yanez has been complimented for not being as didactic a writer as Cervantes, Orwell, or especially other novelists that were truly his contemporaries. His novels employed a deeply rooted psychological perspective to address the changes that occurred in Mexico since the revolution. He developed a modern style patterned after European and American writers of the time that employed dream sequences, multiple narratives, flashbacks, thematic counterpoints, and interior monologues as part of his aesthetic. The images he created transcend time and place, and thus historical context. With an infusion of the elements of poetry, such as an emphasis on the rhythm of language, Yanez developed a functional, highly stylized aesthetic admired by many, such as Robert Clements who wrote of *The Lean Lands* in the *Saturday Review,* calling it "lively reading" and "completely satisfying." Yanez wrote over 20 major works of fiction and nonfiction in over 30 years and is considered one of the greatest Mexican novelists of the twentieth century.

## SELECTED PUBLISHED WORKS:

*Al Filo del agua,* translation by Ethel Brinton published as *The Edge of the Storm,* Austin, University of Texas Press, 1963.
*Las tierras flaces,* translation by Ethel Brinton published as *The Lean Lands,* Austin, University of Texas Press, 1968.

## SOURCES:

### Books

*Dictionary of Mexican Literature,* edited by Eladio Cortes, Westport, Connecticut, Greenwood Press, 1992.
*Hispanic Writers,* edited by Bryan Ryan, Detroit, Gale Research, 1991.
*Identification and Analysis of Chicano Literature,* edited by Francisco Jimenez, Binghmapton, New York, Bilingual/Editorial Bilingue, 1979.

### Periodicals

*Saturday Review,* June 21, 1969, pp. 60–61.

# Bernice Zamora
## 1938-
### Mexican American poet

**B**ernice Zamora's most important contribution to the world of Chicano literature is *Restless Serpents,* a book of poems which also contains poetry by José Antonio Burciaga. The work expresses Zamora's anger at being a victim of a dual system of repression; as a Chicana Zamora feels oppressed both by the dominance of the male within the context of her own Latino culture and by the dominance of Anglos in society at large. "Zamora's poetry in *Restless Serpents,*" wrote Nancy Vogeley in *Dictionary of Literary Biography,* "explores such topics as Chicano cultural traditions, the experience of women in that culture, language, and the power of poetry." In her role as poet, Zamora finds the strength to resist Anglo and male domination.

### Early Years

Zamora was born Bernice Ortiz on January 20, 1938, in the rural environment of Aguilar, a small farming community in the sparsely populated southeastern portion of the state of Colorado. Her ancestors from both sides of the family had made their living in the area for generations. Her father was a coal miner, farmer, and automobile painter; her mother (whose maiden name was Valdez) spent some time employed by an optical company. When Zamora was seven, she moved with her family to the more urban setting of Pueblo, Colorado, but returned to Aguilar during summer vacations from school. Pueblo was to be the poet's home for most of the years she spent in Colorado, until her move to California in the mid–1970s.

As a child Zamora spoke Spanish with her family, but attended Catholic schools in Pueblo where English was the language of instruction. Although she excelled in art in high school, she left the traditional educational system to work at a bank and take classes at night. She married (Zamora was her husband's name) and had two daughters, Rhonda and Katherine. The poet didn't begin working toward her college degree until she was nearly 30, when she enrolled at Southern Colorado University. She earned a bachelor of arts degree in English and French, then began graduate studies at the Colorado State University in Fort Collins. She received her master of arts degree in 1972, writing her thesis on the poetry of Wallace Stevens and Francis Ponge, and spent the next year pursuing additional studies at Marquette University.

### Resumes Education

After her marriage ended in 1974, Zamora moved with her two daughters to California. She decided to continue work on her doctorate in English and American literature at Stanford University. During the seventies, she contributed poetry, short stories, and critical articles to various publications. In 1976, she published *Restless Serpents* and appeared at that year's national conference of the Modern Language Association. At the meeting Zamora delivered a paper entitled "Archetypes in Chicana Poetry" (later published in the journal *De colores*), focusing on work she was preparing for her doctoral dissertation. The following year, she was invited to be guest editor for the summer issue of the Chicano review *El fuego de Aztlán.* As she continued her studies she also taught at Stanford and at the University of San Francisco, and was an instructor in Chicano studies at the University of California at Berkeley.

As the 1980s began, Zamora moved to Albuquerque, New Mexico, to work on *De colores.* In 1980, she and José Armas coedited an anthology of works gleaned from the *Flor y Canto* festivals held in the late 1970s in Albuquerque and Tempe, Arizona. The publication, entitled *Flor y Canto IV and V: An Anthology of Chicano Literature,* was to be her last before she suffered a serious illness in Houston, Texas. In 1982, she returned to California where she has continued to write poetry, but has refrained from publishing. She was granted her Ph.D. from Stanford University in 1986.

Although her most important book, *Restless Serpents,* was issued in an edition of only two thousand copies, the poetry collection is considered a "seminal work" by *Dictionary of Literary Biography* contributor Vogeley, who quoted from several other critics to substantiate her claim. Vogeley noted, for example, that in *Caracol* Juan Bruce-Novoa wrote about *Restless Serpents:* "Like those serpents, Zamora's poetry fascinates: inscrutable signs of life and death in beautiful form, capable of demonic possession; gods of mysterious, lost worlds, only accessible to us in the surface of the images they themselves are." Vogeley also included a statement from poet Lorna Dee Cervantes's review of *Restless Serpents,* originally published in *Mango*. Cervantes claimed that with the book's "carefully crafted poems, [Zamora] proves herself to be one of the most (if not *the* most) outstanding Chicana poets today."

## SELECTED PUBLISHED WORK:

(With José Antonio Burciaga) *Restless Serpents* (poems), Diseños Literarios, 1976.
(Editor with José Armas) *Flor y Canto IV and V: An Anthology of Chicano Literature*, Pajarito, 1980.
*Releasing Serpents*, Biling Press, 1994.

## SOURCES:

### Books

Bruce-Novoa, Juan, *Chicano Authors: Inquiry by Interview*, University of Texas Press, 1980.
*Dictionary of Literary Biography*, Volume 82: *Chicano Writers*, First Series, Gale Research, 1989, pp. 289-94.
Sánchez, Marta Ester, *Contemporary Chicano Poetry: A Critical Approach to an Emerging Literature*, University of California Press, 1985.

### Periodicals

*De colores*, Volume 4, number 3, 1978, pp. 43–52.
*El fuego de Aztlán*, summer 1977, p. 4.

—*Sketch by Marian C. Gonsior*

# Carmen Zapata
## 1927-
### Hispanic American actress, producer, and community activist

Often referred to as "The First Lady of the Hispanic Theatre," Carmen Zapata has been the cofounder, president and managing producer of the non-profit Bilingual Foundation of the Arts (BFA). This Los Angeles-based performing arts organization is dedicated to bringing the Hispanic experience and culture, through the medium of bilingual theatre, to both English and Spanish-speaking audiences. Zapata has received much acclaim for these productions from the community as well as from critics and reviewers. She works closely with the Los Angeles Unified School District to introduce the works of great Hispanic authors to the students.

Carmen Margarita Zapata was born in New York City on July 15, 1947, to Julio Zapata, a Mexican immigrant, and Ramona Roca, a woman from Argentina. Zapata and Roca had met and married in New York; they lived with their three daughters in Spanish Harlem. As the family spoke Spanish exclusively in their home, Zapata's first day of school was so traumatic that even now she cannot remember her first years of schooling. Despite the language her family spoke, and the neighborhood in which they lived, Carmen Zapata was not well informed about Mexican culture as a child.

Zapata's talent manifested itself at an early age; the youngster played the piano and the violin at family gatherings, sang in the school choir, and appeared in school plays. Although, in the beginning, she did not approve of her daughter's desire to have a career in show business, Carmen Zapata's mother sacrificed much to give young Carmen dancing and music lessons. That sacrifice was not made in vain. After studies at the Actors Studio and with Uta Hagen, Zapata was on her way to success.

Zapata made her debut in the chorus of the hit 1946 Broadway musical *Oklahoma*. Zapata graduated to a lead role in *Oklahoma* when the play went on the road. When she finally returned to Broadway, she took over one of the principal roles in *Stop the World, I Want to Get Off*. She also appeared in *Bells Are Ringing* and *Guys and Dolls*.

Zapata performed in musicals for 20 years. Between plays, she worked at night clubs as "Marge Cameron" in a singing and comedy act she had created. At one point she emceed for strippers at a burlesque house in Toledo, Ohio. She explained this job to the *Los Angeles Times:* "At the time it was not 'in' to be Hispanic. I had a hard time getting club owners to hire me, unless I shook my fanny and played the maracas."

A brief marriage to comedy writer Roy Freedman ended in divorce after five years. In 1967, following her mother's death, Zapata moved to California and began what would become an extensive film and television career. Her first film role was as a prostitute in the 1968 movie *Sol Madrid*. When producers claimed that "Marge Cameron" didn't look "all-American," and that she looked "ethnic," Zapata began to use her real name once again. As a result, she now found herself stereotyped in the role of a maid or a mother. This displeased her, despite the fact that she made good money and received a great deal of visibility.

Recognizing the need for change within the Hollywood entertainment industry, Zapata helped form the initial minority committee of the Screen Actors Guild. She was also one of the original members of the Hispanic actors organization called, "Nosotros," which was begun by actor **Ricardo Montalban**.

While television and films kept her busy, Zapata was dissatisfied with the roles she was finding. She also missed the theatre. When a daring Cuban director, Margarita Galban, offered Zapata the opportunity to return to the theater, the frustrated actress was enthusiastic. At that time, Galban's company, "Seis Actores," was producing a Spanish-language play. Galban offered Zapata the opportunity to play the lead in *Cada quien su vida* (*To Each His Own*), but Zapata was hesitant. She recalled to the *Los Angeles Times*, "She invited me to do a piece in Spanish. I'd never acted in Spanish before; I was petrified." But Galban reassured her that the character was that of a drunkard, so mistakes in speech were permissible. "And after I did it, I became very interested in Spanish-language theater. Why? It's beautiful! There are some glorious pieces that non-Spanish speaking people are not aware of. When I realized that, I started doing my translations."

### Translates the Work of Federico Garcia Lorca

Zapata delved further into her Hispanic roots and co-translated some of the classics of Hispanic literature. Dissatisfied with the plays available in Spanish, the actress set out to create her own stage works. She accomplished the formidable task of bringing into English **Federico Garcia Lorca**'s trilogy: *Blood Wedding, Yerma,* and *The House of Bernarda Alba,* as well as Fernando de Rojas's *La celestina* and J. Humberto Robles Arenas 's *Uprooted*. Zapata and her partner, Michael Dewell, were appointed by the Lorca Estate as official translators. Their translation of the trilogy was published by Bantam Books in 1986.

In 1970 Zapata, Galban, and scenic designer Estela Scarlata joined forces. With $5,000 provided by Zapata, the trio rented a theater in downtown Los Angeles and borrowed sets, lights, and costumes from the studios. They then launched their theatre which, in 1973, became the Bilingual Foundation of the Arts.

Interviewed by the *Los Angeles Times,* Zapata pointed out there now exists a trend toward Hispanic theatre, something her BFA has been doing for years. "That was always the idea—to have everyone learn about, share and become part of our literature, our tradition." This is done at the BFA theatre where, on different nights, performances alternate between English-speaking and Spanish-speaking versions. "We decided in 1979 to go bilingual, because that would make us unique as a theater. We also thought it would be nice if we reached into the non-Hispanic community, and had them enjoy the beauty of our literature."

Zapata, who confesses that the theatre is her "baby" and that running it leaves her little time for acting, nonetheless has extensive credits, which include more than 300 appearances in television programs such as *Marcus Welby, Owen Marshall, Medical Center, Mod Squad, The Rookies, The Bold Ones, Bonanza, Treasury Agent, Streets of San Francisco, MacMillan and Wife, Switch, Charlie's Angels, Chico and the Man, Barreta, Fantasy Island, Archie Bunker's Place, Trapper John, M.D.,* and many others. She appeared regularly in the Anthony Quinn series for ABC *Man and the City* and had recurring roles on *The Dick Van Dyke Show* and the NBC soap-opera *Santa Barbara.* In 1976 she starred in her own ABC television series *Viva Valdez,* and from 1981 to 1982 she had a recurring role in the series *Flamingo Road.* Zapata admitted to *Hollywood Latinews* that she is most proud of the nine seasons in which she starred as the matronly "Doña Luz" in the PBS bilingual children's television show, *Villa Alegre.*

### Garners Emmy Nominations

Zapata's professional recognitions include the 1984 Best Actress Award for best dramatic performance in the play *Blood Wedding,* given by Dramalogue, a local Emmy for her 1973 documentary *Cinco Vidas,* and a 1971 Emmy nomination for the television series *The Lawyers.*

As a guest speaker, Zapata has addressed audiences at various California universities and at fundraising functions for charitable groups. Her community involvement includes service on the board of the National Conference of Christian and Jews, the United Way, the Boy Scouts of America, the National Repertory Theatre Foundation, and the Mexican American Opportunity Foundation. She is also a member of the Mayor's Committee on the Arts (Los Angeles), the California Arts Council's Ethnic Advisory Minority Panel and many other organizations. She has served as a panel member of the Expansion Arts Program of the National Endowment for the Arts, the Los Angeles Special Olympics Events Committee and other programs.

Zapata, a tireless activist, has received countless awards for her efforts. These awards include an Outstanding Woman in Business Award from Women in Film, the Boy Scouts of America Community Leadership Award, a Mexican-American Foundation award, and recognition from the Hispanic Women's Council. She was granted an Honorary Doctorate Degree in Human Services from Sierra University. In 1990 Carmen Zapata received what she admits is her favorite award—the Civil Order of Merit (*El Lazo de Dama de la Orden del Merito Civil*) by His Majesty Juan Carlos I, King of Spain. The Order recognizes Zapata's commitment to Hispanic concerns within the arts and in the realm of community service. Only a few have been honored with this Order of Knighthood from the Spanish Head of State, an honor which could be likened to the Knighthoods bestowed upon Dame Judith Anderson and Sir Laurence Olivier by the Queen of England. Finally, on November 22, 1991, in recognition of her outstanding contributions to the arts in the state of California, Carmen Zapata was among nine Californian artists, arts organizations and patrons to receive the prestigious 1991 Governor's award for the Arts presented by Governor and Mrs. Pete Wilson.

At the Bilingual Foundation, Zapata is involved with the newly developed Teen Theatre Project (*Teatro Para Los Jovenes*), an innovative theatre-in-education program designed by BFA to meet the needs of junior and high school students who have been identified as "at risk." Play productions are performed in the schools by professional, ethnically diverse actors chosen for their ability to relate to and communicate with students. Performances are followed by an open discussion of the issues affecting teenagers. This program is made possible through grants from the Seaver Institute and Kraft General Foods Foundation. Zapata feels it is one of the most important steps in addressing the needs of the student population of many urban schools. In a television interview with *Hollywood Latinews*, Zapata pointed out that a 1990 study of New York City schools showed arts programming to be the single most effective deterrent to drop-out rates. The Teen Theatre Project was modeled after BFA's highly successful theatre-in-education program for elementary students, which has served nearly one million children since its inception in 1985.

During an interview with *La opinion,* the busy actress/producer who makes her home in Van Nuys, California, admitted, "If I stop working I die. Work keeps me alive. I need to have something to do when I get up in the morning, to have a place to go, and that place is my theater."

## SOURCES:

### Periodicals

*Los Angeles Times,* Calendar section, February 5, 1989.
*La opinion* (translated from Spanish by Elena Kellner), Panorama section, December 29, 1991,

### Other

*Hollywood Latinews* (television program), interview with Elena Kellner, February 1992.

Zapata, Carmen, biography provided by the Bilingual Foundation of the Arts, 1992.

—*Sketch by Elena Kellner*

# Emiliano Zapata
## 1879(?)-1919
### Mexican revolutionary leader

Emiliano Zapata rose from a small landowner in southern Mexico to become a major figure in the Mexican Revolution of the 1910s and finally a legend. In his biography *Zapata,* Roger Parkinson stated that historians treat Zapata "with either romance or horror." At the pinnacle of his power, Zapata controlled nearly one-third of Mexico, with a peasant army of more than 20,000 soldiers. He fought fiercely for his ideas of a new Mexico, land reform being chief among these. Zapata died in an ambush at the hands of a rival general in 1919.

### From Ploughshare to Pistol

Historians differ on Zapata's date of birth. Some put it as early as 1873 or as late as 1883, but many have settled on August 1879. About 400 people lived in the thirteenth-century village of Anenecuilco, and Zapata's family, while not rich, was prestigious and commanded respect among other villagers. Parkinson described Zapata's father, Gabriel, as "hard-working, quiet and [having] a slight stutter." His mother, Cleofus, also came from a respectable family. She had two sons, including Emiliano, and two daughters.

The family lived in an adobe house rather than the straw huts of most of their neighbors. Neither Zapata nor his brother ever had to perform the manual labor by which most others lived, but nonetheless John Womack asserted in *Zapata and the Mexican Revolution* that "he was still one of them." In fact, Parkinson claimed that "despite his relative comfort and contentment Zapata remained surrounded by the poverty and frequent misery of Mexican village life." For most people, a long day of work led only to an evening meal and another night's sleep, preparing for more work the next day. Though Zapata avoided the worst of village life, his social identity lay with the peasants and in contrast to the moneyed haciendas.

Womack described the struggle of Zapata's followers as a story of "country people who did not want to move and therefore got into a revolution." By the

1880s, new technology in extracting sugar from the stalk created a wave of land acquisition among ambitious planters. Often influential plantation owners used dubious, and sometimes outright illegal, methods of obtaining village lands. This phenomenon took away most of the Zapata family's ancestral orchards, prompting them to learn the livestock trade, at which they prospered.

Though Zapata and his family survived their loss of land, he remembered his father's tears and their own helplessness under the law to stop the planters. Zapata also realized that his family had been fortunate; for many, loss of land meant loss of subsistence food. That in turn meant either starvation or allegiance to the haciendas who had caused the calamitous situation. If they could not find work as day laborers, the peasants resorted to becoming permanent resident workers on the plantations.

Like many villages, Anenecuilco organized resistance to its decline—electing delegations to make protests in the municipal seat of Villa de Ayala and consulting with lawyers and government officials. Beginning when he was about 17, Zapata took part in these delegations. He attracted admiration from his fellow villagers for his open opposition to district authorities in a land dispute. At one point he fled for Puebla to avoid being arrested, but when he returned he found himself increasingly involved in leading the legal defense of his hometown.

On December 15, 1908, Governor Manuel Alarcon of Zapata's Morelos died of gastroenteritis. During his administration, Alarcon managed to make the peasants believe that he was working for them, and in certain instances he even granted their petitions. He believed he could avoid stronger peasant resistance to his rule by at least occasionally taking their side. His death came at a time when Mexican president **Porfirio Diaz** had already announced his plans to retire in 1910. Diaz no longer insisted on nominating all gubernatorial candidates and instead said that he would submit to the will of the people of Morelos.

Yet when opposition mounted against Pablo Escandon—the candidate favored by the moneyed planters—supporters of General Leyta, who was popular among peasants and with Zapata himself, came under increasing persecution. Many even went to jail for the duration of the campaign. Predictably, Escandon won the election amid evidence of widespread fraud.

Although Escandon managed to give some tax relief to the peasants, he did nothing to stop the further encroachment of the haciendas on the property of peasants and small landowners. This prompted the men of Anenecuilco to look to the rising generation for a new leader. Parkinson called Zapata's

acceptance of this position "the most important step so far in his progress toward revolution."

## Zapata Becomes a Public Figure

Zapata began his term in office emulating those who had come before him. He protested through the law, petitioning the governor's office with little effect, hiring lawyers who either could not or would not produce any benefit for the village, and enduring the eventual, almost inevitably unfavorable results. Frustrated, Zapata decided to travel to Mexico City to visit some notable opponents of the Diaz regime. This journey caught the suspicious eye of the government in Mexico City, who notified the regional governments of the possible "dissidents" in their midst. Zapata, as the leader and from a family with a militant history, drew special notice. In February 1910, authorities informed him that he had been drafted into the army.

Conscription worked well as a means of quieting dissent. Desertion brought death, and in the service a soldier like Zapata could expect to face all kinds of adversity and deprivation. Parkinson stated that soldiers drafted for political reasons went without pay and had scant rations and inadequate uniforms. Zapata had the good fortune to be well-connected, however, and after a month and a half a former business associate secured his discharge. Parkinson noted that time spent in the military may have benefitted Zapata in his future struggles. Knowing his enemy's strengths and weaknesses probably aided him in later campaigns.

Zapata returned to Anenecuilco after working in a stable to pay back the man who had secured his release from the military. In his time away, Zapata's fellow villagers had not planted their spring crops, because their petition to the governor for permission to do so had been politely delayed until the planting season had long ended. This final injury coincided with Zapata's return to Anenecuilco and the presidential election, in which **Francisco Madero** was making a significant challenge to long-time president Diaz.

As Governor Escandon occupied himself with the interior decoration of a new hotel to be opened in Cuernavaca, Zapata recruited and armed 80 men to help him in the first stages of his revolutionary activity. Madero went to jail the night before the election, but Zapata organized his troops and took over lands which had been co-opted by Hospital hacienda. Unable to win an armed struggle, the Hospital leaders decided instead to demand rent from the peasants on the land which previously had belonged to them. The peasants refused to pay.

Meanwhile Madero escaped Mexico for Texas, conceding that Diaz would only leave office through force. From his San Antonio headquarters, he planned the revolution that Zapata's actions had already started. Zapata helped organize village after village for its own defense, with little resistance from the intimidated planters. Madero's manifesto for a Mexico controlled by "the forces of the public" appeared in the south. Madero had declared himself provisional president of the country, and the Mexican Revolution began shortly thereafter in a state bordering Morelos.

Zapata cautiously supported Madero, particularly pleased with Madero's pledge to "restore to the former owners the lands of which they were dispossessed so arbitrarily." Though he did not know Madero personally and could not judge his sincerity, Zapata recognized the need to coordinate the military and political faces of the movement. Fighting in the south became more and more frequent; planters began stockpiling weapons and arresting revolutionaries.

Zapata, too, expanded his network, growing into the role of leader not merely of his local group but of other revolutionary leaders as well. On March 11, 1911, Zapata and Torres Burgos led their men in a successful takeover of the police station at Villa de Ayala. Later that evening, the local peasants gathered to hear Burgos and Zapata expound the principles of revolution. Amid cries of *"Viva Madero!"* Zapata resolved to move his followers to open military confrontation with the government.

With 1,500 men Zapata began to move north, striking fear in the federal troops. With the support of most people in the areas they moved through, Zapata's men easily resupplied themselves with provisions. On April 8, federal reinforcements arrived with heavy artillery against which Zapata's rifles could not hope to triumph. Zapata used tactical retreat to avoid pitched battles, and preferred surprise attacks. Parkinson described an attack on a military guard house in Yautepec in which boys, not soldiers, played a key role. Lighting objects which looked like toys, the boys threw the crude bombs into the military post. The explosion caused a general panic, at which time Zapata began his assault on the city.

Zapata also struggled to sustain unity among revolutionary leaders. Southern General Figueroa had even formulated a plan to abandon Zapata at the very moment of an attack on a government installation in hopes of eliminating him. Although Zapata suspected treachery and requested a delay, he would continue to distrust his fellow revolutionary leaders, including **Pancho Villa** and Madero himself, all through his struggles.

Zapata fought on, and in May the Treaty of Ciudad Juarez called for Diaz to leave office. Madero, the likely eventual president, commanded Zapata to cease hostilities against the haciendas. Zapata realized that Madero had turned his back on the principles of

the revolution and he rejected the legitimacy of his authority. His struggle became one to overthrow Madero, who had taken office on November 6, 1911. Madero began calling Zapata a "bandit" and used all his legal powers to stop the Zapatista rebellion.

Hostility between the two sides continued; martial law brought misery and atrocities to the people and international condemnation to Madero. Zapata never halted his campaign against federal troops, vowing to remove Madero physically from the presidential palace. Revolution exploded in the northern state of Chihuahua, strengthening Zapata's ability to move on the overtaxed federal forces.

On August 5, 1912, Aniceto Villamar came to office as interim governor of Morelos, siding more with the Indian peasants than the haciendas. Revolution died down, though Zapata insisted it remained necessary. Few listened until Victoriano Huerta, leading an army mutiny against Madero, took power. Madero was killed February 22, 1913, by Huerta's men.

Zapata insisted even then that the revolution must continue, and Venustiano Carranza, leader of the revolution of the north, agreed. Huerta faced threats from all sides. Federal army discipline often broke down, and Zapata moved rapidly north toward the capital; Villa and Carranza marched on, and the United States for a time landed U.S. Marines on Mexican soil. On July 15, Huerta resigned, but the war continued.

Unity between the elements of the rebellion vanished, and Zapata began to withdraw south, as Carranza took the capital. Zapata saw the new leader as far too ambitious to be trusted, and he quickly moved to consolidate his own territorial control over Morelos. Villa too opposed Carranza, and together Zapata and Villa's forces prompted Carranza into retreat from the capital, where the two generals met for the first time as their troops occupied the city in late 1914.

Yet the feeling of solidarity they achieved in the days and nights of celebration in Mexico city faded quickly. Bickering, distrust, and disillusionment grew between the Villistas and Zapatistas. Zapata gradually lost interest in the question of Mexican politics and gained interest in Morelos. A brief military engagement of Zapata's forces in the capital could not stop Carranza's loyalists from retaking it. Carranza gained wide international recognition as the legitimate ruler of Mexico, and revolution on a national scale ended.

Zapata tried to hold onto his territories in Morelos, eager to protect land reforms he had implemented. In 1915 government forces reached Morelos, attacking the capital. Zapata's ability to resist gradually weakened; General Pablo Gonzalez, the leader of federal troops, used severe measures to punish any resistance. Zapata used his broad popular support to drive Gonzalez from Morelos, but this victory led ultimately to his undoing.

Spring of 1917 saw Morelos in ruins and only temporarily free. Without an outside enemy, Zapata could not maintain the unanimous support he had once enjoyed. Mutiny even broke out among his own troops. With Zapata so weakened, federal troops attacked Morelos again in 1918. Another military stalemate ensued.

On April 10, 1919, Zapata rode with his men to Chinameca, where a federal officer had claimed to wish to defect to his side. Entering the military installation, Zapata stood by to inspect federal soldiers. Seemingly saluting Zapata, the soldiers suddenly turned from a "present-arms" position to shoot him at point-blank range. He died on the spot.

Zapata continued to be a figure of legend and romance in Mexico, even making his way into contemporary politics. In 1994, a group opposed to the Mexican government caused a brief, but bloody uprising. They called themselves Zapatistas.

## SOURCES:

### Books

Parkinson, Roger, *Zapata,* New York, Stein and Day, 1975.

Womack, John, *Zapata and the Mexican Revolution,* New York, Alfred A. Knopf, Inc., 1969.

—*Sketch by James McCarthy*

# Ernesto Zedillo
## 1951-
### Mexican politician

Ernesto Zedillo took office as president of Mexico on December 1, 1994, following what many believed to be the fairest vote count in modern Mexican history. Having received the nomination of Mexico's longtime ruling party, the Institutional Revolutionary Party (PRI), only after the original nominee, Donaldo Colosio, was assassinated, Zedillo received just over half of the votes in an election in which a record 77 percent of registered voters went to the polls. A Yale-trained economist described by *Time*'s Bruce W. Nelan as "an unassuming technocrat plucked from obscurity," Zedillo—who served as budget and planning secretary and secretary of education under his predecessor, **Carlos Salinas**—has pledged to continue the modernization of the Mexican economy while opening up the semi-authoritarian government to a more democratic process. But his more urgent duty has been to stabilize the Mexican economy in the wake of a foreign-debt crisis.

Ernesto Zedillo Ponce de León was born on December 27, 1951, to a working-class family in Mexico City. Three years later his father, an electrician who installed movie screens, moved his wife and six children to the northern border city of Mexicalli, where Zedillo spent his formative years in a lower-middle-class neighborhood called Pueblo Nuevo. While an undergraduate economics major at the National Polytechnic Institute in Mexico City, Zedillo was awarded a position in the President's economic policy office, where he came under the influence of Leopoldo Solis, a respected government economist. At 20, a year after joining the PRI, he completed his degree early and met his future wife, Nilda Nuñez, with whom he would eventually have five children. A top student, Zedillo received a Mexican government-funded scholarship that enabled him to study economics at Yale University, where he earned his doctorate, writing a dissertation focusing on Mexico's external debt crisis. After completing his graduate studies, Zedillo returned to Mexico City to work under Solis at the Central Bank of Mexico. As the Deputy Manager of Finance and Economic Research, he was in charge of a trust fund designed to help the country's most prominent industrialists in restructuring their foreign debts. During his four years there he also served as an advisor to the Board of Directors.

With his appointment as Minister of Planning and Budget in 1987, Zedillo moved closer to the PRI inner circle of economists, serving three years before he was appointed Secretary of Education by Salinas in 1992. Although the promotion placed him in a position to seek the party's 1994 presidential nomination, a series of conflicts with the powerful teachers' union and controversy over his commissioning of a series of revisionist history textbooks forced him to withdraw. With the selection of Colosio as the party nominee, Zedillo was immediately appointed his campaign manager—a position which Colosio and Salinas had both held before gaining the nomination. After Colosio was assassinated in April, Zedillo became the party's nominee.

Cloaking himself in the mantle of the fallen hero, Zedillo stated in a speech reported in *Time* that he was "not starting a new campaign" but "continuing one." Against the chaotic backdrop of political assassination, an armed peasant rebellion in Chiapas, and kidnappings of wealthy businessmen, Zedillo "offered security and familiarity even to the multitudes who have yet to share the fruits of economic reform," Nelan commented. Although many doubted the political ability of the man often believed to be nothing more than an intelligent technocrat—or a "cold fish" as one Mexican put it—Zedillo ran an aggressive campaign and defeated the opposition candidates from the leftist Democratic Revolutionary Party (PRD) and the conservative National Action Party (PAN) handily, winning more than 50 percent of the vote. His victory margin was slim by PRI standards; but the elections were generally thought to be free from the systematic fraud that has traditionally marred Mexican elections.

Since taking office in November of 1994, Zedillo has been hampered by one of the more serious economic crises in recent Mexican history, forcing him to hold back on his plans to increase public spending aimed at helping the millions of Mexico's poor and delay taking substantive steps toward democracy. In an effort to stabilize an economy on the verge of collapse following the poor performance of foreign investments, Zedillo and his team of economists have made the controversial decision to let the peso trade freely against the American dollar, result-ing in a dramatic devaluation that has, in the short term, resulted in widespread unemployment and general economic stagnation. Nevertheless, many analysts have expressed confidence in Zedillo's economic expertise and leadership ability. As *The New York Times* editorial staff argued, he "could turn out to be the right man for these times."

## SOURCES:

*New York Times,* August 23, 1994, p. A1; August 24, 1994, p. A1; September 27, 1994, p. D1; December 23, 1994, p. A1; December 25, 1994; p. A1; December 29, 1994, p. A20.

*Time,* April 11, 1994, p. 56; September 5, 1994, pp. 48–49.

*U.S. News and World Report,* April 11, 1994, p. 10.

*Washington Post,* August 23, 1994.

—*Sketch by Jason Gallman*

# Occupation Index

**surgeon**
René Geronimo Favaloro, 323

**television newscaster**
Linda Alvarez, 35

**television talk show host**
Geraldo Rivera, 745
Cristina Saralegui, 825

**theater director**
José Quintero, 718

**translator**
Julio Cortázar, 245
Angel Flores, 341

**TV personality**
Bob Vila, 942

**U.S. Secretary of Education**
Lauro F. Cavazos, 204

**U.S. treasurer**
Romana Acosta Bañuelos, 97

**union activist**
Luisa Capetillo, 165

**union leader**
Ernesto Galarza, 357
Arturo S. Rodriguez, 753

**writer**
Fernando Alegría, 10
José María Arguedas, 51
Homero Aridjis, 58
Roberto Arlt, 60

Miguel Angel Asturias, 71
José Agustín Balseiro, 94
Mario Benedetti, 115
Luisa Capetillo, 165
Adolfo Bioy Casares, 118
María Luisa Bombal, 128
Juan Bosch, 134
Lydia Cabrera, 149
Guillermo Cabrera Infante, 150
Alejo Carpentier, 177
Lourdes Casal, 187
Rosario Castellanos, 191
Carlos Castaneda, 193
Jorge G. Castañeda, 194
Fray Angélico Chávez, 219
Linda Chávez, 221
Jesús Colón, 237
Julio Cortázar, 245
Salvador Dalí, 265
José Donoso, 292
Ariel Dorfman, 295
Clarissa Pinkola Estés, 318
Angel Flores, 341
Carlos Fuentes, 352
Ernesto Galarza, 357
Juan Goytisolo, 398
Ricardo Güiraldes, 408
Rolando Hinojosa, 430
Eugenio María de Hostos, 432
Jorge Icaza, 441
Nicolás Kanellos, 465
Bartolomé de las Casas, 471
John Leguizamo, 477
José López Portillo, 491
Leopoldo Lugones y Argüello, 500
Salvador de Madariaga, 506
René Marqués, 519
Nicholasa Mohr, 554

Cherríe Moraga, 577
Luis Muñoz Marín, 592
Alvaro Mutis, 594
Julian Nava, 599
Josephina Niggli, 603
Victoria Ocampo, 614
Américo Paredes, 654
Juan Domingo Perón, 678
Mary Helen Ponce, 694
Estela Portillo Trambley, 702
José Quintero, 718
Horacio Quiroga, 720
John Rechy, 726
Alfonso Reyes, 732
Julio Ramón Ribeyro, 734
Rita Ricardo-Campbell, 736
Tomás Rivera, 748
Augusto José Antonio Roa Bastos, 749
Luis Rodriguez, 759
Richard Rodriguez, 761
Juan Rulfo, 783
Gary Soto, 865
Piri Thomas, 885
Domingo Faustino Sarmiento, 829
Jacobo Timerman, 886
Jaime Torres Bodet, 894
Miguel de Unamuno, 905
Luisa Valenzuela, 915
Ramón del Valle-Inclán, 917
César Vallejo, 919
Mario Vargas Llosa, 921
Tino Villanueva, 948
José Antonio Villarreal, 950
Raquel Welch, 955
Agustin Yanez, 963

# Nationality/Ethnicity Index

Entries are listed by country of origin and/or citizenship.

# Subject Index

A **boldface** page number indicates the full entry.

A **boldface** page number refers to the full entry

Subject Index

A **boldface** page number refers to the full entry

Subject Index

A **boldface** page number refers to the full entry

A **boldface** page number refers to the full entry